Koren Talmud Bavli

THE NOÉ EDITION

YEVAMOT · PART ONE

Shefa

KOREN

תלמוד בבלי

KOREN TALMUD BAVLI

THE NOÉ EDITION

יבמות א

YEVAMOT · PART ONE

COMMENTARY BY

Rabbi Adin Even-Israel Steinsaltz

EDITOR-IN-CHIEF

Rabbi Dr Tzvi Hersh Weinreb

EXECUTIVE EDITOR

Rabbi Joshua Schreier

•

SHEFA FOUNDATION

KOREN PUBLISHERS JERUSALEM

Supported by the Matanel Foundation

Koren Talmud Bavli, The Noé Edition
Volume 14: Tractate Yevamot, Part One

Standard Size Color Edition, ISBN 978 965 301 575 3
Daf Yomi Size B&W Edition, ISBN 978 965 301 620 0

First Hebrew/English Edition, 2014

Koren Publishers Jerusalem Ltd.
PO Box 4044, Jerusalem 91040, ISRAEL
PO Box 8531, New Milford, CT 06776, USA
www.korenpub.com

Shefa Foundation

Shefa Foundation is the parent organization of institutions established by Rabbi Adin Even-Israel Steinsaltz

PO Box 45187, Jerusalem 91450 ISRAEL
Telephone: +972 2 646 0900, Fax +972 2 624 9454
www.hashefa.co.il

Cover images by Rabbi Eliahu Misgav

Hardcover design by Ben Gasner

הִנֵּה יָמִים בָּאִים, נְאֻם אֲדֹנָי יֱהֹוִה, וְהִשְׁלַחְתִּי רָעָב בָּאָרֶץ,
לֹא־רָעָב לַלֶּחֶם וְלֹא־צָמָא לַמַּיִם, כִּי אִם־לִשְׁמֹעַ אֵת דִּבְרֵי יהוה.

Behold, days are coming – says the Lord God –
I will send a hunger to the land, not a hunger for bread
nor a thirst for water, but to hear the words of the Lord.

(AMOS 8:11)

The Noé edition of the Koren Talmud Bavli
with the commentary of Rabbi Adin Even-Israel Steinsaltz
is dedicated to all those who open its cover
to quench their thirst for Jewish knowledge,
in our generation of Torah renaissance.

This beautiful edition is for the young, the aged,
the novice and the savant alike,
as it unites the depth of Torah knowledge
with the best of academic scholarship.

Within its exquisite and vibrant pages,
words become worlds.

It will claim its place in the library of classics,
in the bookcases of the Beit Midrash,
the classrooms of our schools,
and in the offices of professionals and businesspeople
who carve out precious time to grapple with its timeless wisdom.

For the Student and the Scholar

DEDICATED BY LEO AND SUE NOÉ

Shefa

Managing Editor
Rabbi Jason Rappoport

Senior Content Editor
Rabbi Dr. Shalom Z. Berger

Editors
Rabbi Joshua Amaru, *Coordinating Editor*
Amy Kaplan Benoff
Menucha Chwat
Rabbi Yoel Domb
Rabbi Yonatan Shai Freedman
Rabbi Alan Haber
Rabbi Tzvi Chaim Kaye
Catriel Lev
Elisha Loewenstern
Adina Luber
Rabbi Avishai Magence, *Content Curator*
Gavriel Reiss
Rabbi David Sedley
Shira Shmidman
Rabbi Michael Siev
Avi Steinhart
Rabbi Binyamin Zimmerman

Copy Editors
Aliza Israel, *Coordinator*
Bracha Hermon
Ita Olesker
Debbie Ismailoff
Shira Finson
Ilana Sobel
Deena Nataf
Eliana Kurlantzick Yorav
Nava Wieder

Language Consultants
Dr. Stephanie E. Binder, *Greek & Latin*
Yaakov Hoffman, *Arabic*
Dr. Shai Secunda, *Persian*

KOREN

Design & Typesetting
Raphaël Freeman, *Design & Typography*
Dena Landowne Bailey, *Typesetting*
Tani Bayer, *Jacket Design*

Images
Rabbi Eliahu Misgav, *Illustration & Image Acquisition*

Once upon a time, under pressure of censorship,
printers would inscribe in the flyleaves
of volumes of the Talmud:

Whatever may be written herein about gentiles
does not refer to the gentiles of today,
but to gentiles of times past.

Today, the flyleaves of our books bear a similar inscription,
albeit an invisible one:

Whatever may be written herein about Jews
does not refer to the Jews of today,
but to Jews who lived in other times.

So we are able to sit down and study Torah, Talmud,
books of ethics, or books of faith
without considering their relevance to our lives.

Whatever is written there
does not apply to us or to our generation,
but only to other people, other times.

We must expunge from those invisible prologues
the notion that the words are written about someone else,
about others, about anyone but us.

Whether the book is a volume of Torah,
a tractate of the Talmud, or a tract of faith,
the opposite must be inscribed:

Whatever is written herein refers only to me;
is written for me and obligates me.

First and foremost, the content is addressed to me.

– From a public address by Rabbi Adin Even-Israel Steinsaltz
as quoted in חיי עולם (*Talks on Parashat HaShavua*)
Maggid Books, 2011

Contents

For the vocalized Vilna Shas layout, please open as a Hebrew book.

Haskama

Rabbi Moshe Feinstein

RABBI MOSES FEINSTEIN
455 F. D. R. DRIVE
New York N. Y. 10002
OЯegon 7-1222

משה פיינשטיין
ר"מ תפארת ירושלים
בנוא יארק

בע"ה

בע"ה ראיתי הפירוש החשוב של הרב הגאון מוהר"ר עדין שטיינזלץ שליט"א מעיה"ק ירושלים, על מסכתות ביצה ור"ה. באמת כבר ידוע לי פירושו של הרה"ג הנ"ל על מסכתות מתלמוד בבלי, וכבר כתבתי מכתב הסכמה עליהם. ובאתי בזה רק להדגיש מחוש איך שהפירושים של הרה"ג הנ"ל, שכולל פירוש חדש על הגמרא עצמו וגם פירוש שיש בו סיכום להלכה מהנידונים שבגמרא, נוסף לעוד כמה חלקים, הם באמת עבודה גדולה, שיכולים להיות לתועלת לא רק לאלו שכבר מורגלים בלמוד הגמרא, ורוצים להעמק יותר, אלא גם לאלו שמתחילים ללמוד, להדריכם בדרכי התורה איך להבין ולהעמיק בים התלמוד.

והריני מברך להרה"ג הנ"ל שיצליחהו השי"ת בספריו אלו ושיזכה לחבר עוד ספרים, להגדיל תורה ולהאדירה, לתפארת השם ותורתו.

ועל זה באתי על החתום לכבוד התורה ביום ז' לחודש אייר תשמ"ג.

משה פיינשטיין

משה פיינשטיין

...These new commentaries – which include a new interpretation of the Talmud, a halakhic summary of the debated issues, and various other sections – are a truly outstanding work; they can be of great benefit not only to those familiar with talmudic study who seek to deepen their understanding, but also to those who are just beginning to learn, guiding them through the pathways of the Torah and teaching them how to delve into the sea of the Talmud.

I would like to offer my blessing to this learned scholar. May the Holy One grant him success with these volumes and may he merit to write many more, to enhance the greatness of Torah, and bring glory to God and His word...

Rabbi Moshe Feinstein
New York, 7 Adar 5743

ר' משה פיינשטיין שליט"א
הנה ראיתי את מסכת אחת מהש"ס שנקד אותה וגם צייר צורות הצמחים וכדומה מדברים שלא ידוע לכמה אנשים הרה"ג ר' עדין שטיינזלץ מירושלים שליט"א וגם הוסיף שם בגליון פירושים והידושים וניכר שהוא ת"ח וראויין לעיין בהם ת"ח ובני הישיבה וטוב גם לקנותם בבתי כנסיות ובבתי מדרשות שיש שיהיו להם לתועלת. — ועל זה באתי עה"ח ג' אדר ב' תש"ל.
נאם משה פיינשטיין
ר"מ תפארת ירושלים, ניו־יורק, ארה"ב

I have seen one tractate from the Talmud to which the great scholar Rabbi Adin Steinsaltz שליט״א has added *nikkud* (vowels) and illustrations to explain that which is unknown to many people; he has also added interpretations and innovations, and is evidently a *talmid ḥakham*. *Talmidei ḥakhamim* and yeshiva students ought to study these volumes, and synagogues and *batei midrash* would do well to purchase them, as they may find them useful.

Rabbi Moshe Feinstein
New York, Adar 5730

Haskama

Rabbi Menachem Mendel Schneerson

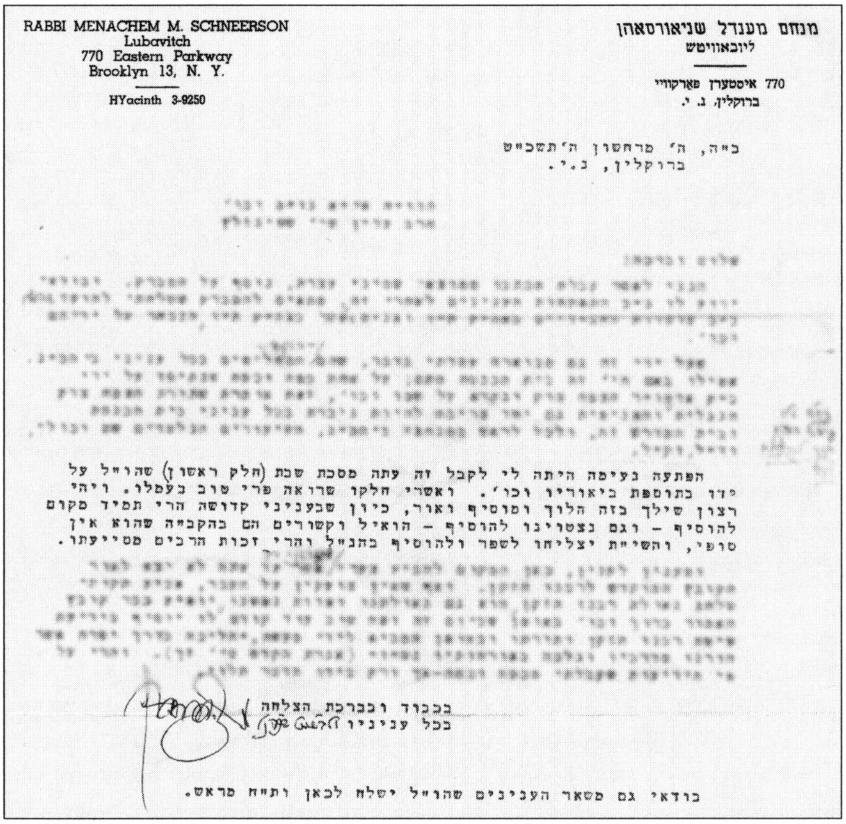
RABBI MENACHEM M. SCHNEERSON
Lubavitch
770 Eastern Parkway
Brooklyn 13, N. Y.

HYacinth 3-9250

מנחם מענדל שניאורסאהן
ליובאוויטש

770 איסטערן פארקוויי
ברוקלין, נ. י.

ב"ה, ה' מרחשון ה'תשכ"ט
ברוקלין, נ.י.

הפתעה נעימה היתה לי לקבל זה עתה מסכת שבת (חלק ראשון) שהו"ל על ידו בתוספת ביאוריו וכו'. ואשרי חלקו שרואה פרי טוב בעמלו. ויהי רצון שילך בזה הלוך ומוסיף ואור, כיון שבעניני קדושה הרי תמיד מקום להוסיף – וגם נצטוינו להוסיף – הואיל וקשורים הם בהקב"ה שהוא אין סופי, והשי"ת יצליחו לשפר ולהוסיף בהנ"ל והרי זכות הרבים מסייעתו.

בכבוד וברכת הצלחה
בכל עניניו

בודאי גם משאר העניגים שהו"ל ישלח לכאן ותח"ח מראש.

... I have just had the pleasant surprise of receiving tractate *Shabbat* (part one), which has been published by [Rabbi Steinsaltz] along with his explanations, etc. Happy is the man who sees good fruits from his labors. May he continue in this path and increase light, for in the matters of holiness there is always room to add – and we have been commanded to add – for they are linked to the Holy One, Blessed be He, Who is infinite. And may the Holy One grant him success to improve and enhance this work, since the greater good strengthens his hand ...

Rabbi Menachem Mendel Schneerson
The Lubavitcher Rebbe
Brooklyn, 5 Marḥeshvan 5729

Haskama

Rabbi Moshe Zvi Neria

מכתבו של הרב משה צבי נריה

ב"ה

"ושמעו ביום ההוא החרשים דברי ספר"
(ישעי' כט' יח')

תרגום ספרי קדמונים לשפת דורות אחרונים – היא משימתם של חכמי דור ודור. ובישראל שמצוות "ושננתם לבניך" מקיפה את כל חלקי האומה, ודאי שהיתה זאת המשימה בכל עידן ועידן.

בכל דור כך, ובדורנו אשר רבים בו הקרובים שנתרחקו וחוזרים ומתקרבים – לא כל שכן. כי רבים היום האומרים "מי ישקנו מים מבאר" התלמוד, ומועטים הם הדולים ומשקים.

ראוי אפוא להערכה מיוחדת נסיונו המבורך של הצעיר המופלא, הרב עדין שטיינזלץ, לפרש פרקי-תלמוד בהסברה מורחבת-תמציתית, אשר נוסף על הפרוש המלולי והעניני הוא מעלה גם את ההגיון של הדברים ומתרגמת אותם לשפת-המושגים של בן-דורנו.

דומה שכל הנגשים אל חומר למודי מתוך רצון להבינו – התלמיד החרוץ והמבוגר המשכיל – לא יתקלו בשום קושי בבואם ללמוד סוגיא תלמודית לפי פרוש זה. ולא עוד אלא שיש לקוות כי ההסברה הגיונית תעמידם מיד על טוב-הטעם של דף-הגמרא, והם ימשכו יותר ויותר אל הלמוד העיוני הזה אשר טובי המוחות בישראל לנו בעומקו, ואשר ממנו פינה, ממנו יתד לבנין חיינו.

נועם ד' על המפרש הנמרץ להמשיך במפעלו, וברוכים כל העוזרים להוצאתו לאור-עולם.

ביקר אורייתא

(חתימה)

The translation of the books of our past into the language of the present – this was the task of the sages of every generation. And in Israel, where the command to "teach them repeatedly to your children" applies to all parts of the nation, it was certainly the task of every era. This is true for every generation, and in our time – when many of those who have strayed far are once again drawing near – all the more so. For many today say, "Who will let us drink from the well" of Talmud, and few are those who offer up the waters to drink.

We must, therefore, particularly commend the blessed endeavor of Rabbi Adin Steinsaltz to explain the chapters of the Talmud in this extensive yet succinct commentary, which, in addition to its literal interpretation of the text, also explicates the latter's underlying logic and translates it into the language of our generation.

It appears that all those who seek to study Talmud – the diligent student and the learned adult – will have no difficulty understanding when using this commentary. Moreover, we may hope that the logical explanation will reveal to them the beauty of the talmudic page, and they will be drawn deeper and deeper into the intellectual pursuit which has engaged the best Jewish minds, and which serves as the cornerstone of our very lives…

Rabbi Moshe Zvi Neria

Haskama

Rabbi Mordechai Eliyahu

ב"ה

MORDECHAI ELIAHU | **מרדכי אליהו**

FORMER CHIEF RABBI OF ISRAEL & RICHON LEZION | ראשון לציון והרב הראשי לישראל לשעבר

ז' בתשרי תשנ"ד
5-137.נד

מכתב ברכה

הגמרא בעירובין כ"א: אומרת: דרש רבא מאי דכתיב ויותר שהיה קהלת חכם, עוד לימד דעת את העם - ואזן וחקר תקן משלים הרבה". לימד דעת את העם - קבע כיצד לקרוא פסוק וסימנים בין תיבות המקרא וממשיכה הגמרא ואומרת: אמר עולא אמר ר' אליעזר בתחילה היתה תורה דומה לכפיפה שאין לה אזנים עד שבא שלמה ועשה לה אזנים". וכדברי רש"י שם: "וע"י כך אוחזין ישראל במצוות שנתרחקו מן העבירה כדרך שנוח לאחוז בכלי שיש לו בית יד וכו' (ערובין כ"א, י').

דברים מעין אלו אפשר לאמר על האי גברא יקירא, על איש מורם מעם, משכמו ומעלה בתורה ובמידות. ויותר ממה שעשה בתורה שבע"פ עושה בתורה שבכתב - מלמד דעת את העם. ולא זו בלבד אלא גם עושה אזנים לתורה, היא תורת התלמוד שהוא חתום וסתום בפני רבים. ורק מעט מזער מבני עליה שהם מועטים ומי שלומד בישיבה יכל כיום ללמוד בש"ס ולהבין מה שלפניו, ואף שיש לנו פירוש רש"י, עדין לא הכל ממשמשין בו. עד שקם הרב הגדול מעוז ומגדול הרה"ג ר' **עדין שטיינזלץ** שליט"א ועשה אזנים לתורה, שאפשר לאחוז גמרא ביד וללמוד, ואפי' לפשוטי העם ועשה פרושים ושם אותם בצד הארון, פרושים נאים בשפה ברורה ונעימה דבר דבור על אופניו. ועם הסברים וציורים להבין ולהשכיל, כדי שמי שרוצה לקרבה אל מלאכת ה' ללמוד יכל לעשות זאת.

ועיני ראו ולא זר שבשיעורי תורה בגמרא הרבה באים עם גמרות בידם ואלה שבאים עם "פירוש הרב שטיינזלץ לתלמוד הבבלי" הם מוכנים ומבינים טוב יותר. כי כבר יש להם הקדמה מפרושיו ומבאוריו.
ואמינא לפועלו יישר ומן שמיא זכו ליה ללמד דעת את העם .

ויהי רצון שחפץ בידו יצלח, וכל אשר יפנה ישכיל ויצליח, ויזכה להגדיל תורה ולהאדירה, ויוסיף לנו עוד גמרות מבוארות כהנה וכהנה עד לסיומו , "וישראל עושה חיל".

ובזכות לימוד תורה ואני זאת בריתי וכו', ובא לציון גואל, בב"א.

מרדכי אליהו
ראשון לציון הרב הראשי לישראל לשעבר

The Talmud in *Eruvin* 21b states: Rava continued to interpret verses homiletically. What is the meaning of the verse: "And besides being wise, Kohelet also taught the people knowledge; and he weighed, and sought out, and set in order many proverbs" (Ecclesiastes 12:9)? He explains: He taught the people knowledge; he taught it with the accentuation marks in the Torah, and explained each matter by means of another matter similar to it. And he weighed [*izen*], and sought out, and set in order many proverbs; Ulla said that Rabbi Eliezer said: At first the Torah was like a basket without handles [*oznayim*] until Solomon came and made handles for it. And as Rashi there explains: And thus were Israel able to grasp the mitzvot and distance themselves from transgressions – just as a vessel with handles is easily held, etc.

Such things may be said of this beloved and eminent man, a great sage of Torah and of virtue. And far more than he has done with the Oral Torah, he does with the Written Torah – teaching the people knowledge. And beyond that, he also affixes handles to the Torah, i.e., to the Talmud, which is obscure and difficult for many. Only the intellectual elite, which are a precious few, and those who study in yeshiva, can today learn the Talmud and understand what it says – and even though we have Rashi, still not everyone uses him. But now the great scholar Rabbi Adin Steinsaltz שליט"א has come and affixed handles to the Torah, allowing the Talmud to be held and studied, even by simple men. And he has composed a commentary alongside the text, a fine commentary in clear, comprehensible language, "a word fitly spoken" with explanations and illustrations, so that all those who seek to study the work of God can do so.

Rabbi Mordechai Eliyahu
Former Chief Rabbi of Israel, 7 Tishrei 5754

Message from Rabbi Adin Even-Israel Steinsaltz

The Talmud is the cornerstone of Jewish culture. True, our culture originated in the Bible and has branched out in directions besides the Talmud, yet the latter's influence on Jewish culture is fundamental. Perhaps because it was composed not by a single individual, but rather by hundreds and thousands of Sages in *batei midrash* in an ongoing, millennium-long process, the Talmud expresses not only the deepest themes and values of the Jewish people, but also of the Jewish spirit. As the basic study text for young and old, laymen and learned, the Talmud may be said to embody the historical trajectory of the Jewish soul. It is, therefore, best studied interactively, its subject matter coming together with the student's questions, perplexities, and innovations to form a single intricate weave. In the entire scope of Jewish culture, there is not one area that does not draw from or converse with the Talmud. The study of Talmud is thus the gate through which a Jew enters his life's path.

The *Koren Talmud Bavli* seeks to render the Talmud accessible to the millions of Jews whose mother tongue is English, allowing them to study it, approach it, and perhaps even become one with it.

This project has been carried out and assisted by several people, all of whom have worked tirelessly to turn this vision into an actual set of books to be studied. It is a joyful duty to thank the many partners in this enterprise for their various contributions. Thanks to Koren Publishers Jerusalem, both for the publication of this set and for the design of its very complex graphic layout. Thanks of a different sort are owed to the Shefa Foundation and its director, Rabbi Menachem Even-Israel, for their determination and persistence in setting this goal and reaching it. Many thanks to the translators, editors, and proofreaders for their hard and meticulous work. Thanks to the individuals and organizations that supported this project, chief among them the Matanel Foundation and the Noé family of London. And thanks in advance to all those who will invest their time, hearts, and minds in studying these volumes – to learn, to teach, and to practice.

Rabbi Adin Even-Israel Steinsaltz
Jerusalem 5773

Acknowledgments

We are indeed privileged to dedicate this edition of the *Koren Talmud Bavli* in honor of the generous support of Leo and Sue Noé of London.

The name Noé is synonymous with philanthropy. The family's charitable endeavors span a vast range of educational projects, welfare institutions, and outreach organizations across the globe, with a particular emphasis on the "nurturing of each individual." Among so many other charitable activities, the Noés have been deeply involved with *Kisharon*, which provides the British Jewish community with vital support for hundreds of people with learning difficulties and their families; they provide steadfast support of SEED, which stands at the forefront of adult Jewish education in the UK, and *Kemach*, an organization in Israel that "helps Haredi students sustain themselves in dignity," providing both professional and vocational training for the Haredi community in Israel.

The Noés are not simply donors to institutions. They are partners. Donors think of a sum. Partners think of a cause, becoming rigorously and keenly involved, and giving of their time and energy. We are honored that they have chosen to partner with our two organizations, *Shefa* and *Koren Publishers Jerusalem*, enabling us to further and deepen learning among all Jews.

Leo and Sue are the proud parents and grandparents of five children and their families. The next generation has been taught by example that with life's gifts come the responsibilities to be active within and contribute to society – both Jewish and non-Jewish – as is consistent with the noblest of Jewish values.

Rabbi Adin Even-Israel Steinsaltz
Matthew Miller, Publisher
Jerusalem 5773

Introduction by the Editor-in-Chief

The vastly expanded audience of Talmud study in our generation is a phenomenon of historical proportions. The reasons for this phenomenon are many, and include the availability of a wide array of translations, commentaries, and study aids.

One outstanding example of such a work is the translation of the Talmud into modern Hebrew by Rabbi Adin Even-Israel Steinsaltz. The product of a lifetime of intense intellectual labor, this translation stands out in its uniqueness.

But what can the interested student do if he or she does not comprehend the Hebrew, even in its modern form? Where is the English speaker who wishes to access this instructive material to turn? The *Koren Talmud Bavli* that you hold in your hand is designed to be the answer to those questions.

This work is the joint effort of Rabbi Steinsaltz himself, his closest advisory staff, and Koren Publishers Jerusalem. It is my privilege to have been designated editor-in-chief of this important project, and to have worked in close collaboration with a team of translators and copy editors, artists and graphic designers, scholars and editors.

Together we are presenting to the English-speaking world a translation that possesses all the merits of the original Hebrew work by Rabbi Steinsaltz and provides assistance for the beginner of any age who seeks to obtain the necessary skills to become an adept talmudist.

To date we have published thirteen volumes completing the orders of *Zera'im* and *Moed*. Our work has been enthusiastically received by a broad and diverse audience. Particularly gratifying is the fact that many have chosen to use our text as the basis for the group study of Talmud. We appreciate the comments and suggestions from our readers the world over and are committed to improving future editions of the *Koren Talmud Bavli* on the basis of that input. Indeed, a second edition of our first volume, *Berakhot*, has already been released, incorporating much of the advice brought to our attention by our readers. We encourage you to continue to advise us of your experience with our work.

The order of *Nashim* begins with tractate *Yevamot*, which we are printing in two volumes. *Yevamot*, Part I, is the fourteenth volume of this project. It includes the entire original text, in the traditional configuration and pagination of the famed Vilna edition of the Talmud. This enables the student to follow the core text with the commentaries of Rashi, *Tosafot*, and the customary marginalia. It also provides a clear English translation in contemporary idiom, faithfully based upon the modern Hebrew edition.

At least equal to the linguistic virtues of this edition are the qualities of its graphic design. Rather than intimidate students by confronting them with a page-size block of text, we have divided the page into smaller thematic units. Thus, readers can focus their attention and absorb each discrete discussion before proceeding to the next unit. The design of each page allows for sufficient white space to ease the visual task of reading. The illustrations, one of the most innovative features of the Hebrew edition, have been substantially enhanced and reproduced in color.

The end result is a literary and artistic masterpiece. This has been achieved through the dedicated work of a large team of translators, headed by Rabbi Joshua Schreier, and through the unparalleled creative efforts of Raphaël Freeman and the gifted staff at Koren.

The group of individuals who surround Rabbi Steinsaltz and support his work deserve our thanks as well. I have come to appreciate their energy, initiative, and persistence. And I thank the indefatigable Rabbi Menachem Even-Israel, whom I cannot praise highly enough. The quality of his guidance and good counsel is surpassed only by his commitment to the dissemination and perpetuation of his father's precious teachings.

Finally, in humility, awe, and great respect, I acknowledge Rabbi Adin Even-Israel Steinsaltz. I thank him for the inspirational opportunity he has granted me to work with one of the outstanding sages of our time.

Rabbi Tzvi Hersh Weinreb
Jerusalem 5774

Preface by the Executive Editor

Toward the beginning of tractate *Pesaḥim* (3a), the Gemara questions the Mishna's use of the term *or* rather than the standard term *leil* when referring to the evening of the fourteenth of Nisan. The Gemara introduces a discussion of the value of euphemism and refraining from the use of crude language. It concludes that despite the importance of euphemism, if the euphemism comes at the expense of clarity and requires a less succinct formulation, it is preferable to speak concisely. Only when the choice is between equally concise phrases is the euphemism preferred.

In his *peirush*, Rabbi Steinsaltz's language is both concise and aesthetic. While explaining often difficult passages, he avoids the temptation to over-explain, inviting the reader to study the Talmud with him rather than doing all the thinking in the reader's place. We have attempted to follow his path in translating and editing the *Koren Talmud Bavli*.

My involvement in the production of the *Koren Talmud Bavli* has been both a privilege and a pleasure. The Shefa Foundation, headed by Rabbi Menachem Even-Israel and devoted to the dissemination of the wide-ranging, monumental works of Rabbi Adin Even-Israel Steinsaltz, constitutes the Steinsaltz side of this partnership; Koren Publishers Jerusalem, headed by Matthew Miller, with the day-to-day management of the project in the able hands of Dena Landowne Bailey, constitutes the publishing side of this partnership. The combination of the inspiration, which is the hallmark of Shefa, with the creativity and professionalism for which Koren is renowned and which I experience on a daily basis, has lent the *Koren Talmud Bavli* its outstanding quality in terms of both content and form.

I would like to express my appreciation for Rabbi Dr. Tzvi Hersh Weinreb, the Editor-in-Chief, whose insight and guidance have been invaluable. The contribution of my friend and colleague, Rabbi Dr. Shalom Z. Berger, the Senior Content Editor, cannot be overstated; his title does not begin to convey the excellent direction he has provided in all aspects of this project. In addition, I would like to thank Rabbi Jason Rappoport, Managing Editor; Rabbi Joshua Amaru, Coordinating Editor; and Rabbi Avishai Magence, Content Curator, whose tireless devotion to this project has been and continues to be crucial to the continued success of this project. The erudite and articulate men and women who serve as translators, editors, and copy editors have ensured that this project adheres to the highest standards.

There are several others whose contributions to this project cannot be overlooked. On the Steinsaltz side: Meir HaNegbi, Yacov Elbert, and Tsipora Ifrah. On the Koren side, my colleagues at Koren: Rabbi David Fuchs, Rabbi Hanan Benayahu, Efrat Gross, Rachel Hanstater Meghnagi, Rabbi Eliahu Misgav, and Rabbi Yinon Chen. Their assistance in all matters, large and small, is appreciated.

At the risk of being repetitious, I would like to thank Rabbi Dr. Berger for introducing me to the world of Steinsaltz. Finally, I would like to thank Rabbi Menachem Even-Israel, with whom it continues to be a pleasure to move forward in this great enterprise.

Rabbi Joshua Schreier
Jerusalem 5773

Introduction by the Publisher

The Talmud has sustained and inspired Jews for thousands of years. Throughout Jewish history, an elite cadre of scholars has absorbed its learning and passed it on to succeeding generations. The Talmud has been the fundamental text of our people.

Beginning in the 1960s, Rabbi Adin Even-Israel Steinsaltz שליט"א created a revolution in the history of Talmud study. His translation of the Talmud, first into modern Hebrew and then into other languages, as well the practical learning aids he added to the text, have enabled millions of people around the world to access and master the complexity and context of the world of Talmud.

It is thus a privilege to present the *Koren Talmud Bavli*, an English translation of the talmudic text with the brilliant elucidation of Rabbi Steinsaltz. The depth and breadth of his knowledge are unique in our time. His rootedness in the tradition and his reach into the world beyond it are inspirational.

Working with Rabbi Steinsaltz on this remarkable project has been not only an honor, but a great pleasure. Never shy to express an opinion, with wisdom and humor, Rabbi Steinsaltz sparkles in conversation, demonstrating his knowledge (both sacred and worldly), sharing his wide-ranging interests, and, above all, radiating his passion. I am grateful for the unique opportunity to work closely with him, and I wish him many more years of writing and teaching.

Our intentions in publishing this new edition of the Talmud are threefold. First, we seek to fully clarify the talmudic page to the reader – textually, intellectually, and graphically. Second, we seek to utilize today's most sophisticated technologies, both in print and electronic formats, to provide the reader with a comprehensive set of study tools. And third, we seek to help readers advance in their process of Talmud study.

To achieve these goals, the *Koren Talmud Bavli* is unique in a number of ways:

- The classic *tzurat hadaf* of Vilna, used by scholars since the 1800s, has been reset for greater clarity, and opens from the Hebrew "front" of the book. Full *nikkud* has been added to both the talmudic text and Rashi's commentary, allowing for a more fluent reading with the correct pronunciation; the commentaries of *Tosafot* have been punctuated. Upon the advice of many English-speaking teachers of Talmud, we have separated these core pages from the translation, thereby enabling the advanced student to approach the text without the distraction of the translation. This also reduces the number of volumes in the set. At the bottom of each *daf*, there is a reference to the corresponding English pages. In addition, the Vilna edition was read against other manuscripts and older print editions, so that texts which had been removed by non-Jewish censors have been restored to their rightful place.

- The English translation, which starts on the English "front" of the book, reproduces the *menukad* Talmud text alongside the English translation (in bold) and commentary and explanation (in a lighter font). The Hebrew and Aramaic text is presented in logical paragraphs. This allows for a fluent reading of the text for the non-Hebrew or non-Aramaic reader. It also allows for the Hebrew reader to refer easily to the text alongside. Where the original text features dialogue or poetry, the English text is laid out in a manner appropriate to the genre. Each page refers to the relevant *daf*.
- Critical contextual tools surround the text and translation: personality notes, providing short biographies of the Sages; language notes, explaining foreign terms borrowed from Greek, Latin, Persian, or Arabic; and background notes, giving information essential to the understanding of the text, including history, geography, botany, archeology, zoology, astronomy, and aspects of daily life in the talmudic era.
- Halakhic summaries provide references to the authoritative legal decisions made over the centuries by the rabbis. They explain the reasons behind each halakhic decision as well as the ruling's close connection to the Talmud and its various interpreters.
- Photographs, drawings, and other illustrations have been added throughout the text – in full color in the Standard and Electronic editions, and in black and white in the Daf Yomi edition – to visually elucidate the text.

This is not an exhaustive list of features of this edition; it merely presents an overview for the English-speaking reader who may not be familiar with the "total approach" to Talmud pioneered by Rabbi Steinsaltz.

Several professionals have helped bring this vast collaborative project to fruition. My many colleagues are noted on the Acknowledgments page, and the leadership of this project has been exceptional.

RABBI MENACHEM EVEN-ISRAEL, DIRECTOR OF THE SHEFA FOUNDATION, was the driving force behind this enterprise. With enthusiasm and energy, he formed the happy alliance with Koren and established close relationships among all involved in the work.

RABBI DR. TZVI HERSH WEINREB שליט״א, EDITOR-IN-CHIEF, brought to this project his profound knowledge of Torah, intellectual literacy of Talmud, and erudition of Western literature. It is to him that the text owes its very high standard, both in form and content, and the logical manner in which the beauty of the Talmud is presented.

RABBI JOSHUA SCHREIER, EXECUTIVE EDITOR, assembled an outstanding group of scholars, translators, editors, and copy editors, whose standards and discipline enabled this project to proceed in a timely and highly professional manner.

RABBI MEIR HANEGBI, EDITOR OF THE HEBREW EDITION OF THE STEINSALTZ TALMUD, lent his invaluable assistance throughout the work process, supervising the reproduction of the Vilna pages.

RAPHAËL FREEMAN created this Talmud's unique typographic design which, true to the Koren approach, is both elegant and user-friendly.

It has been an enriching experience for all of us at Koren Publishers Jerusalem to work with the Shefa Foundation and the Steinsaltz Center to develop and produce the *Koren Talmud Bavli*. We pray that this publication will be a source of great learning and, ultimately, greater *Avodat Hashem* for all Jews.

Matthew Miller, Publisher
Koren Publishers Jerusalem
Jerusalem 5773

Introduction to **Yevamot**

Yevamot is the first tractate in the order of *Nashim*. Admittedly, some commentaries place *Yevamot* after *Gittin* (Meiri), but this is not widely accepted. While the tractate focuses mainly on the *halakhot* of levirate marriage, the elucidation of these *halakhot* necessitates an in-depth clarification of the *halakhot* of marriage in general. These include forbidden and disqualified marriages, i.e., those women with whom relations are forbidden with a certain man, whether by Torah law or by rabbinic law, as well as the definition and severity of these prohibitions. Consequently, the comprehensive discussions of tractate *Yevamot* form the basis of the entire order of *Nashim*.

As stated above, in addition to the *halakhot* of levirate marriage, this tractate serves as an important and sometimes the only source for various aspects of forbidden sexual relations, as well as the *halakhot* of converts and conversion, and the definition of separation between man and wife, which concerns mainly the *halakhot* of refusal and the case of a deserted wife. Many of these discussions are complemented in *Kiddushin*, the last tractate in *Nashim*.

The issue of levirate marriage is explicitly stated in the Torah in only one short passage (Deuteronomy 25:5–10). In addition, there are two episodes in the Bible that are connected to the idea of levirate marriage: The incident involving Judah, his sons, and Tamar (Genesis, chapter 38), and the marriage of Ruth and Boaz (Ruth, chapters 3–4). Both early commentaries and later commentaries discuss the relationship between these stories and the *halakhot* of levirate marriage set out in Deuteronomy. In any case, levirate marriage, as well as being a far-from-rare occurrence, is such a fundamental concept that an entire tractate is devoted its many details, on both the theoretical and the practical levels.

Levirate marriage is a novel *halakha*; see the Gemara on 17b. In other words, it deviates from the norms of the legal system of the Torah. Generally, one who engages in relations with the wife of his brother violates a severe prohibition that makes him liable to *karet* (Leviticus 18:16, 20:21). However, if this woman's husband dies childless, not only is she permitted to the brother, it is actually a mitzva for him to marry her. Since forbidden sexual relationships are among the most severe of Torah prohibitions, indeed one of the three cardinal sins for which one must allow himself to be killed rather than transgress, the fact that one is permitted and even commanded to marry his brother's wife renders levirate marriage a highly exceptional case.

Several halakhic discussions in this tractate concern the basic question of whether the mitzva of levirate marriage merely overrides the prohibition with regard to a brother's wife to a limited extent, or whether, in these special circumstances, the prohibition does not apply at all. One of the ways the Sages express this dialectic tension is with the statement that the verses "You shall not uncover the nakedness of your brother's wife" (Leviticus 18:16) and "Her brother-in-law will have intercourse with her" (Deuteronomy 25:5) were pronounced together (Jerusalem Talmud, *Nedarim* 3:5).

According to this line of reasoning, it is incorrect to say that a forbidden sexual relationship is permitted in the case of levirate marriage. In fact, the opposite is the case: The mitzva of levirate marriage applies only when no prohibition is in effect. If a potential levirate marriage would violate any other forbidden sexual relationship apart from that of a brother's wife, not only is there no mitzva to marry the woman, the obligation of levirate marriage does not apply in this case at all and she is actually forbidden to the brother.

Levirate marriage is unique not only with regard to the performance of the mitzva itself, but also in the fact that the obligation can be released by the act of *ḥalitza*. Typically, the Torah imposes either absolute obligations that every Jew must fulfill at all times, e.g., the love of God; or mitzvot that are incumbent upon certain people part of the time, such as donning phylacteries; or commandments that apply if particular conditions are met, e.g., the *halakhot* of commerce or ritual slaughtering. In all these cases, once the mitzva is in force, one cannot release himself from the obligation.

By contrast, the option of *ḥalitza* effectively provides the brother-in-law with the choice of whether or not he wants to perform levirate marriage. Consequently, the Sages apparently viewed *ḥalitza* not as the negation of levirate marriage but as an alternative mitzva. Accordingly, the Torah allows the brother-in-law in this situation to select between two equivalent mitzvot. Some even maintain that *ḥalitza* is preferable to levirate marriage; see 39b. This issue is also possibly connected to the debate in the Jerusalem Talmud as to whether *ḥalitza* is itself a form of acquisition or simply an act that exempts the brother-in-law and releases the *yevama*.

With these points in mind, these mitzvot can be explained in the following terms. When a man dies childless, he leaves behind a void in a soul that was unable to come to full fruition in the world. Consequently, his surviving brother must replace him by marrying his widow. In this manner the surviving brother is considered to be continuing his late brother's life. For this reason, by Torah law there is no new ritual of betrothal or a wedding ceremony in the case of levirate marriage, as it carries on the previous bond. This consideration also affects the *halakhot* of inheritance and the marriage contract, among other matters. If the brother-in-law bears a child he is viewed as completing his brother's mission.

See the Ramban's Commentary on the Torah with regard to both the episode of Judah and Tamar and the chapter on levirate marriage itself, where he discusses the fundamental idea of levirate marriages in light of these passages. Indeed, the story of Judah and Tamar, among other things, teaches the great responsibility of this task and the punishment of those who refuse to fulfill it in the proper manner.

Conversely, *ḥalitza* is essentially a ritual of atonement and purification, through which the brother-in-law and his *yevama* are released from their mutual bond and from the weighty obligation placed on their shoulders. Moreover, this is the means by which the life cycle of the deceased brother is brought to a close.

Another feature of levirate marriage is that in contrast to a regular marriage, in which the man chooses the woman he wishes to wed, the *yevama* and brother-in-law are tied together by a decree of the Torah. This connection, called by the Sages the levirate bond, is one of the central topics of the tractate. Some Sages view this link as merely an obligation to marry a particular woman, which in practical terms simply means that she is not permitted to marry anyone else until the obligation has been released by means of *ḥalitza*. This opinion is expressed as: There is no bond. However, the *halakha* is that there is a bond, i.e., the link between a brother-in-law and a *yevama* is virtually akin to a marital bond, as she is considered betrothed to him to a certain extent. One of the ramifications of this ruling is that her close female relatives are forbidden to the brother-in-law.

In light of the above, to preserve the boundaries of modesty and to prevent any miscomprehension of the *halakhot* of marriage, the Sages enacted that a brother-in-law should perform an act of betrothal with his *yevama*. This is called a *ma'amar*, a levirate betrothal. Furthermore, if he gives her a bill of divorce while she is waiting for either levirate marriage or *ḥalitza*, his act is effective to a certain extent. On the one hand, these rabbinic enactments draw levirate marriage closer to a regular marriage, but on the other hand they can cause many problems for the marriage and for *ḥalitza*.

Likewise, other decrees of the Sages involving marriage, such as those concerning the marriage of a minor girl who is an orphan and the annulment of this tie by her refusal of her husband, as well as the marriage of deaf-mutes, also complicate the *halakhot* of levirate marriage, despite the fact that these enactments serve the public welfare. Some of these prohibitions stem from sanctity, i.e., they were enacted in order to preserve the sanctity of the Jewish people or the priesthood, and some of them apply to the entire people, such as having a sexual relationship with a *mamzer* or a man with crushed genitals or other genital wounds, or with converts from different nations. Other forbidden sexual relationships are secondary relationships forbidden by rabbinic law.

All these cases require not only a thorough analysis on their own account, but they must be properly defined before one can establish the relationship between these marriages and levirate marriage, which applies by Torah law. This matter concerns the validity of levirate marriage and *ḥalitza*, the whole range of monetary issues that arise with regard to inheritance and the marriage contract, and the concomitant prohibitions and rights, e.g., the permission to partake of *teruma* and the conditions of the marriage contract.

Furthermore, numerous other problems with levirate marriage can result from various causes, either due to complicated family relationships, e.g., if the *yevama* is permitted to only one of several brothers, or if a few deaths occur in succession, or because of factual or halakhic uncertainties. These might be doubts with regard to the halakhic and family status of a certain person, or unclear and possibly erroneous testimony concerning someone's death.

The debates and analysis of all these problems, both separately and in various combinations, is why tractate *Yevamot* is considered one of the hardest, most complex tractates in the entire Talmud.

Tractate *Yevamot* is comprised of sixteen chapters. Some deal with one clearly defined topic, while others discuss several issues spread over different chapters. The first seven chapters are included in the present volume:

Chapter One focuses on the *halakhot* of women to whom the duty of levirate marriage does not apply, either because they are among those with whom relations are forbidden or for some other reason. Additionally, the chapter discusses the basic halakhic principles of when one mitzva overrides another.

Chapter Two deals with the prohibition with regard to the wife of a brother with whom the *yavam* did not coexist. It also discusses the basic principles of the types of women who are obligated in levirate marriages, and those who have no option but to perform *ḥalitza* due to a prohibition that would be violated by a sexual relationship; whether it is a definite or an uncertain prohibition, and whether it applies by Torah law or by rabbinic law.

Chapter Three discusses those cases in which women who are relatives of each other are liable in levirate marriage, as well as a woman who is bound by an obligation of levirate marriage with two brothers.

Chapter Four contains many topics: The case of erroneous *ḥalitza* and levirate marriage, the *halakhot* of inheritance and the marriage contract of a brother-in-law and his *yevama*, the basic definitions of *mamzer* status, and the *halakhot* of conversion.

Chapter Five discusses a single issue: The validity of a levirate betrothal [*ma'amar*] and the bill of divorce of a brother-in-law to his *yevama*, including all various permutations and combinations of these actions.

Chapter Six deals with the definition and *halakhot* of the act of intercourse, particularly with regard to a *yevama*, but also as it concerns marital relations in general. A portion of the chapter also discusses the prohibitions that apply only to priests, specifically to the High Priest, and the mitzva to be fruitful and multiply.

Chapter Seven focuses on the *halakhot* of partaking of *teruma* as they apply to the daughter or the wife of a priest, and those actions that disqualify them from eating *teruma*.

Explanation of Diagrams in **Yevamot**

Man **Woman**

Married couple

Siblings are indicated by identical patterning:

Members of the same generation are usually on the same horizontal row:

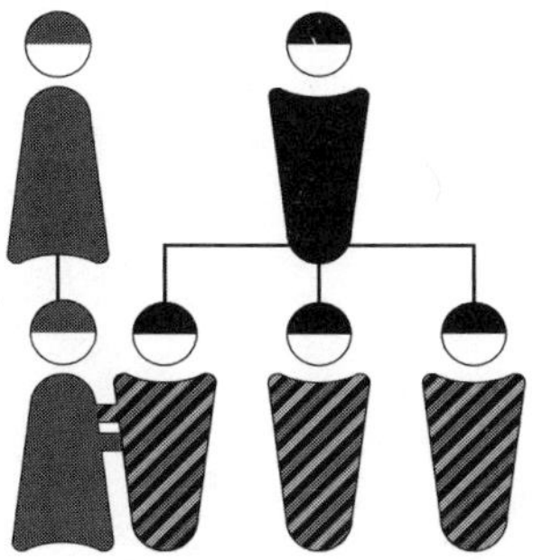

Parents and their offspring are either connected by a vertical line, indicated by identical shading on their heads, or both:

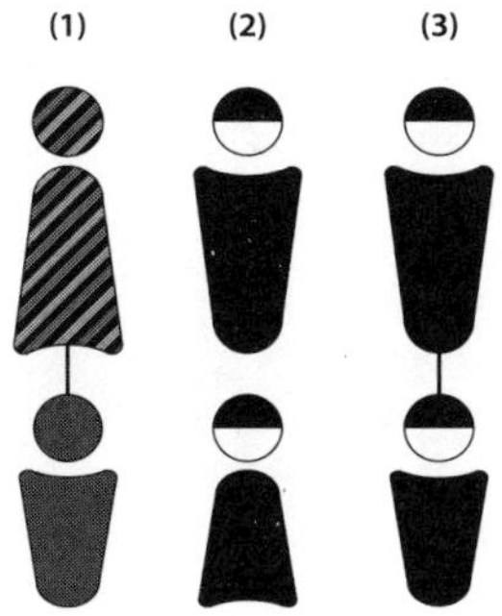

For the offspring of an unmarried couple, the shading on the head reflects that of both the father and the mother:

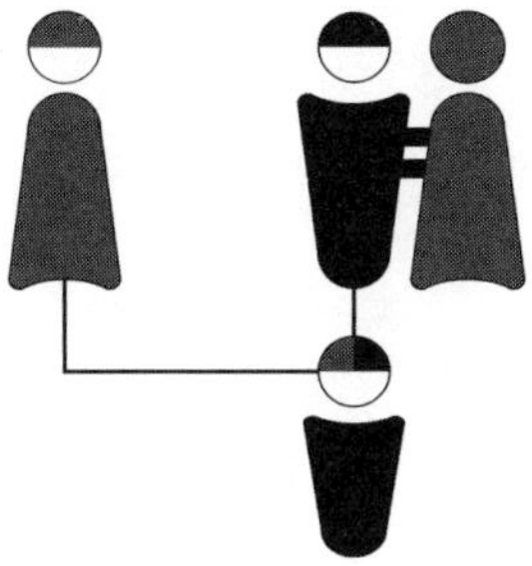

A deceased individual is indicated by an X on his head:

If more than one individual has died, each subsequent death is indicated by an additional X above the deceased's head. When more than one event is described in a single diagram, an arrow points to the later event.

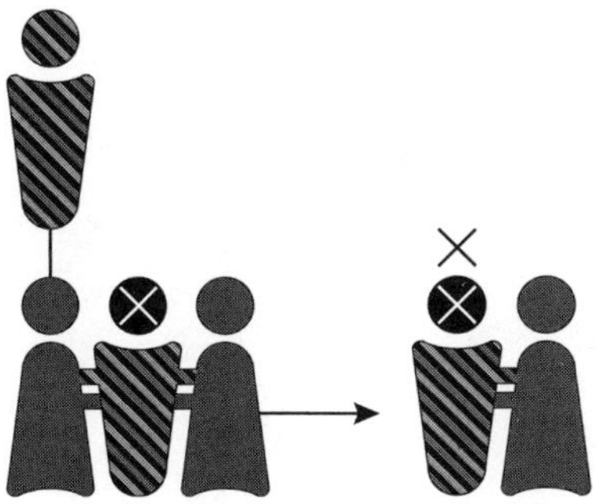

Introduction to **Perek I**

You shall not uncover the nakedness of your brother's wife; it is your brother's nakedness.

(Leviticus 18:16)

If brothers dwell together and one of them dies and he has no child, the wife of the dead man shall not be married outside of the family to one not of his kin; her brother-in-law will have intercourse with her and take her to him to be his wife and consummate the levirate marriage.

(Deuteronomy 25:5)

By definition, the commandment of levirate marriage refers to an unusual situation: Generally, it is prohibited to marry one's brother's wife even after their divorce or after his brother's death. However, if the deceased brother did not leave any children, it is a mitzva for the surviving brother to marry his former wife. In other words, the mitzva of levirate marriage overrides the severe prohibition proscribing a brother's wife.

One of the practical questions of levirate marriage is whether this mitzva overrides other sexual prohibitions between the brother-in-law, who is referred to as the *yavam*, and his potential *yevama*, his brother's widow. In this regard, the tradition of the Sages in unambiguous: The mitzva of levirate marriage overrides the prohibition with regard to a brother's wife alone, not those who are forbidden by another prohibition. However, the precise halakhic definition of this tradition must be clarified. Does this mean that the mitzva of levirate marriage does not apply at all in these cases, and the prohibition against marrying a brother's wife remains in force, as in the case of a deceased brother who did have children? Or is this a case in which the mitzva of levirate marriage applies, but due to other prohibitions it cannot be performed in practice, and the *yavam* must perform *ḥalitza* instead?

A related issue is whether in a case of this kind the mitzva of levirate marriage is entirely canceled with regard to this brother, or whether the prohibition affects only his relationship with that particular woman. If so, he would have the option, either practical or at least theoretical, of entering into levirate marriage with another wife of the deceased brother, a so-called rival wife.

To resolve these problems, it is necessary to arrive at a comprehensive understanding of the Torah's resolution of practical cases of conflict between two mitzvot, i.e., cases when the fulfillment of a certain positive commandment entails the violation of a prohibition.

The clarification of these issues and their practical ramifications form the main topics of this chapter.

The Torah law obligating a man whose brother died without children [*yavam*] to marry his deceased brother's widow [*yevama*] or to free her from her levirate bonds through the act of *ḥalitza* applies only when it is permitted for the widow to marry her surviving brother-in-law. However, in cases where the *yevama* is forbidden to her *yavam* due to her status as a close family relative, the mitzva of levirate marriage is not applicable, and she is exempt from both levirate marriage and *ḥalitza*.

The Sages further taught that the exemption of a *yevama* from levirate marriage also exempts her rival wife. In other words, if the deceased brother had two wives, each a so-called rival of the other, and only one wife is a relative of the surviving brother, then the rival wife is also exempt from both levirate marriage and *ḥalitza*. Moreover, if that same rival wife entered into levirate marriage with a different brother of the deceased, one to whom she is not forbidden, then were this third brother also to die childless, so that the obligation of levirate marriage would again be incurred by the second brother, not only is the forbidden rival wife exempt from levirate marriage and *ḥalitza*, her new rival wives from her second marriage are also exempt.

That is to say, any other wife of the third brother is exempt from the mitzva of levirate marriage, as she is the rival wife of that first rival wife, who was exempted from levirate marriage following her first husband's death due the exemption of her original rival wife. The same principle applies if that second rival wife subsequently enters into levirate marriage with another permitted brother, and so on. In summary, every widow who is exempt from marrying her brother-in-law due to her status as rival wife of a forbidden relative is treated as a forbidden relative herself and is therefore exempt from both *ḥalitza* and levirate marriage and causes exemption for future rival wives as well.

מתני׳ חֲמֵשׁ עֶשְׂרֵה נָשִׁים פּוֹטְרוֹת צָרוֹתֵיהֶן וְצָרוֹת צָרוֹתֵיהֶן מִן הַחֲלִיצָה וּמִן הַיִּיבּוּם, עַד סוֹף הָעוֹלָם.

MISHNA The mishna[N] describes various cases that invoke the principles above. **Fifteen** categories of **women**[H] constitute familial relations that are forbidden as incestuous, and consequently, these women **exempt their rival wives**[B] **and the rival wives of their rival wives**[B] **from *ḥalitza* and from levirate marriage**[N] **forever,**[N] i.e., they also exempt rival wives of rival wives of rival wives, and so on.

NOTES

The placement of this tractate in the order of *Nashim* – מְקוֹמָהּ שֶׁל הַמַּסֶּכֶת בְּסֵדֶר נָשִׁים: The early authorities ask why *Yevamot* is the first tractate in the order of *Nashim* when it would apparently be more logical to begin with the tractate dealing with marriage contracts, *Ketubot*, or the *halakhot* of betrothals, *Kiddushin*. One explanation is that in no other case is marriage fully obligatory for a man, especially not to a particular woman, whereas levirate marriage is a positive mitzva that is obligatory for a *yavam* (Rambam). Others explain that the discussion of the *halakhot* of levirate marriage serves to clarify the principles of forbidden incestuous or adulterous sexual relations, an explanation that necessarily must precede the *halakhot* of betrothals and marriage contracts (Rosh). Indeed, many tractates begin with complex and complicated *halakhot* rather than opting for a more logical order, to engage the attention of students. The Rosh adds another reason: This tractate immediately follows the last tractate of the order of *Moed*, which in some versions is *Moed Katan*. Since the end of that tractate discussed the *halakhot* of mourning following a misfortune, *Yevamot*, which deals with a man who dies childless, was placed immediately afterward. Alternatively, as the practice of levirate marriage incorporates both *halakhot* specific to levirate marriage as well as general *halakhot* of marriage, it precedes *Ketubot*, which for the most part discusses only the *halakhot* of marriage (*Tosefot Yom Tov*). However, according to the order of tractates accepted by some commentaries, *Yevamot* comes after tractate *Gittin*, which also deals with marriages that were terminated (Meiri).

From *ḥalitza* and from levirate marriage – מִן הַחֲלִיצָה וּמִן הַיִּיבּוּם: The Gemara explains that the apparent redundancy of mentioning both *ḥalitza* and levirate marriage, as well as the mention of *ḥalitza* before levirate marriage, serve to emphasize the opinion of this *tanna* that the performance of *ḥalitza* is preferable to the mitzva of levirate marriage.

Forever – עַד סוֹף הָעוֹלָם: *Tosafot* ask why this expression is necessary and it is not enough simply to state: The rival wives of the rival wives. The commentaries explain that in light of the fact that according to one of the opinions in the Gemara there is an interpretation that refers to a rival wife and a rival wife's rival wife, it might be thought that the *halakha* applies only to these two and no more (*Tosafot*; *Tosefot HaRosh*). Conversely, others claim that this form of expression is typical of the language in the Mishna, and it indicates a particular emphasis only in special circumstances (Ramban; Rashba).

HALAKHA

Fifteen women – חֲמֵשׁ עֶשְׂרֵה נָשִׁים: Each of the fifteen women listed in the mishna is exempt from levirate marriage and does not even require *ḥalitza* if her husband dies childless, as she is forbidden to her *yavam* by a prohibition that entails *karet*. Not only is she exempt, but her rival wives are also exempt from levirate marriage. If a rival wife entered into levirate marriage with another brother, to whom she was not forbidden, and this brother also died, which means that she once again comes for levirate marriage before one to whom she is forbidden, then not only is she exempt but so is her new rival wife, who is the rival wife of a rival wife of a woman forbidden in levirate marriage. These rival wives of rival wives are classified as forbidden relatives and in turn render their own rival wives forbidden in levirate marriage (Rambam *Sefer Nashim, Hilkhot Yibbum VaḤalitza* 6:14; *Shulḥan Arukh, Even HaEzer* 173:1).

BACKGROUND

A daughter's rival wife – צָרַת הַבַּת: Shimon married Ḥanna, daughter of his brother, Reuven. In addition he had another wife, Peninna, Ḥanna's rival wife. If Shimon dies childless his wives will come before Reuven for levirate marriage. In this case, not only is Ḥanna, Reuven's daughter, exempt from *ḥalitza* and levirate marriage, but her rival wife Peninna is as well.

The rival wife of a daughter's rival wife – צָרַת צָרַת הַבַּת: In the previous example, after Shimon's death, a third brother, Levi, entered into levirate marriage with his late brother's wife Peninna, as both she and Hanna are permitted to him. If Levi subsequently dies as well, both Peninna and Levi's other wife Miriam come before the surviving brother, Reuven, for levirate marriage. In this case, not only is Peninna, the rival wife of his daughter Ḥanna, exempt from both *ḥalitza* and levirate marriage, but Miriam, the rival wife of his daughter's rival wife, is as well.

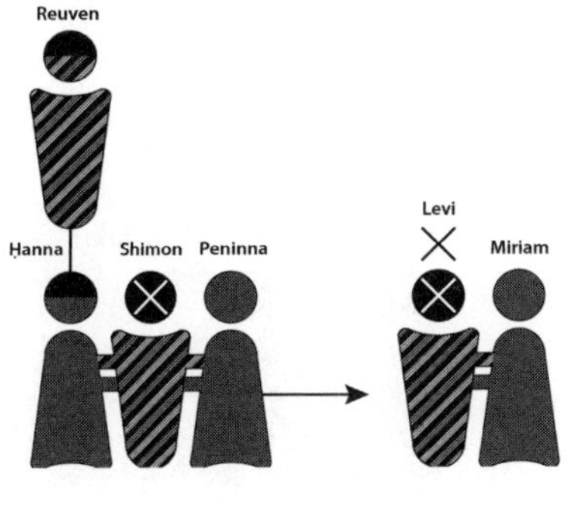

וְאֵלּוּ הֵן: בִּתּוֹ, וּבַת בִּתּוֹ, וּבַת בְּנוֹ. בַּת אִשְׁתּוֹ,

And these women **are: The daughter** of the *yavam*, i.e., the deceased brother had married a daughter of his brother, which means that when he died childless, his brother's own daughter came before her father for levirate marriage, and therefore she is exempt. **And** the same applies if the deceased brother's widow is **the daughter of** the **daughter of** the *yavam*,[B] **or** if she is **the daughter of his son,**[B] or **the daughter of** his **wife.**[B]

וּבַת בְּנָהּ, וּבַת בִּתָּהּ. חֲמוֹתוֹ, וְאֵם חֲמוֹתוֹ וְאֵם חָמִיו.

And similarly, if the *yevama* is **the daughter of** the **son** of the wife of her *yavam*[B] **or the daughter of** his wife's **daughter,**[B] **or** if she is the **mother-in-law** of her *yavam*,[B] **or his mother-in-law's mother,**[B] **or his father-in-law's mother,**[B] then she is exempt from *ḥalitza* and levirate marriage.

BACKGROUND

The daughter of the daughter of the *yavam* – בַּת בִּתּוֹ: Shimon married Adda, the daughter of Ḥanna, the daughter of Reuven, Shimon's brother. If Shimon dies childless, not only is Adda, his daughter's daughter, exempt both *ḥalitza* and from levirate marriage, but the same applies to her rival wife, Tzila.

The daughter of his son – בַּת בְּנוֹ: Shimon married Ḥanna, daughter of Ḥanokh, son of Reuven, Shimon's brother. If Shimon dies childless, both Ḥanna, Reuven's son's daughter, and her rival wife, Peninna, are exempt from both *ḥalitza* and levirate marriage.

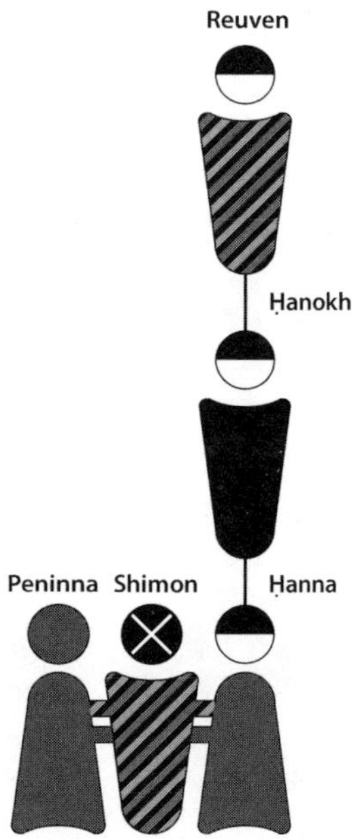

The daughter of his wife – בַּת אִשְׁתּוֹ: Shimon married Ḥanna, the daughter from a previous husband of Miriam, the current wife of Shimon's brother Reuven. If Shimon dies childless, Ḥanna is exempt from both *ḥalitza* and levirate marriage as the daughter of Reuven's wife, while Peninna is also exempt, because she is the rival wife of his wife's daughter.

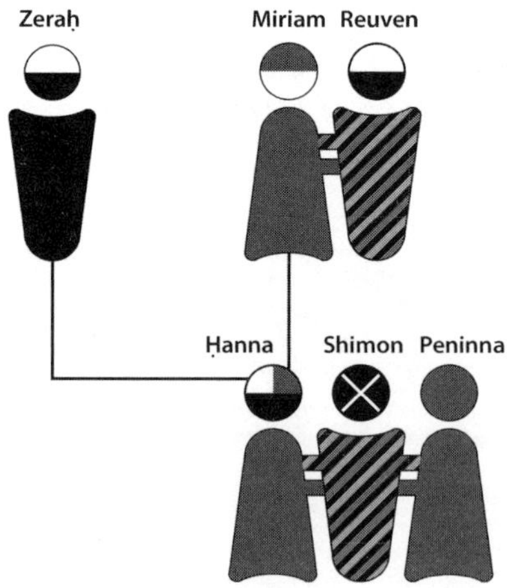

The daughter of the son of the wife of her *yavam* – בַּת בְּנָהּ: Reuven's wife Miriam had a son, Ḥur, from her previous husband, Zeraḥ. Shimon, Reuven's brother, married Ḥanna, daughter of Ḥur. If Shimon dies childless, both Ḥanna, the daughter of Reuven's wife's son, and her rival wife, Peninna, are exempt from both *ḥalitza* and levirate marriage.

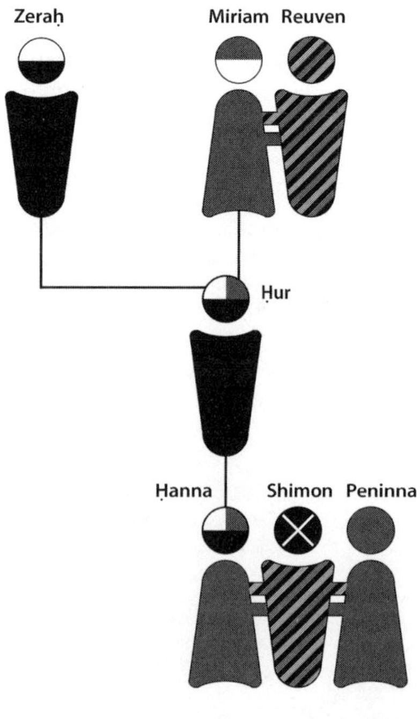

BACKGROUND

The daughter of his wife's daughter – בַּת בִּתָּהּ: Reuven's wife Miriam had a daughter, Adda, from her previous husband, Zeraḥ. Shimon, Reuven's brother, married Ḥanna, daughter of Adda. If Shimon dies childless, both Ḥanna, the daughter of Reuven's wife's daughter, and her rival wife, Peninna, are exempt from both *ḥalitza* and levirate marriage.

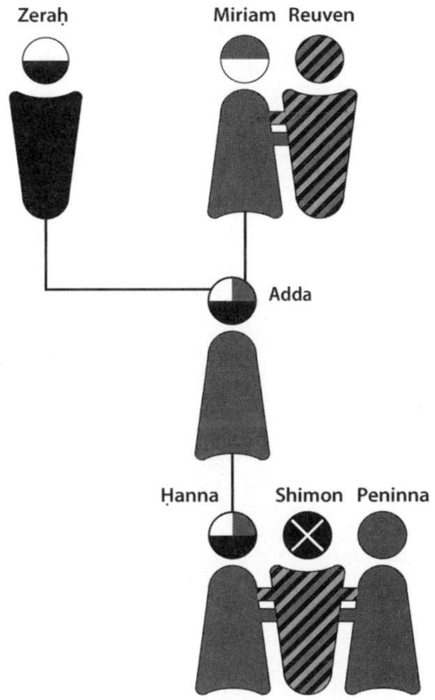

The mother-in-law of her *yavam* – חֲמוֹתוֹ: Reuven married Miriam, the daughter of Ḥanna, his brother Shimon's wife. If Shimon dies childless, both Ḥanna, Reuven's mother-in-law, and her rival wife, Peninna, are exempt from both *ḥalitza* and levirate marriage.

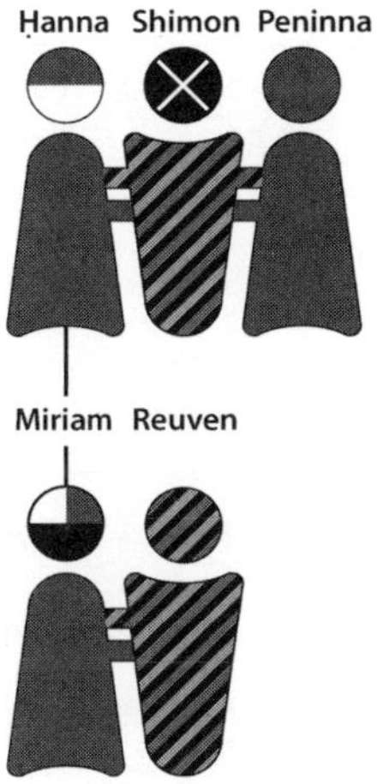

His mother-in-law's mother – אֵם חֲמוֹתוֹ: Reuven married Mikhal, daughter of Adda, daughter of Ḥanna, the wife of his brother Shimon. If Shimon dies childless, Ḥanna is exempt from *ḥalitza* and levirate marriage as Reuven's mother-in-law's mother, i.e., Adda's mother. Peninna is also exempt as Ḥanna's rival wife.

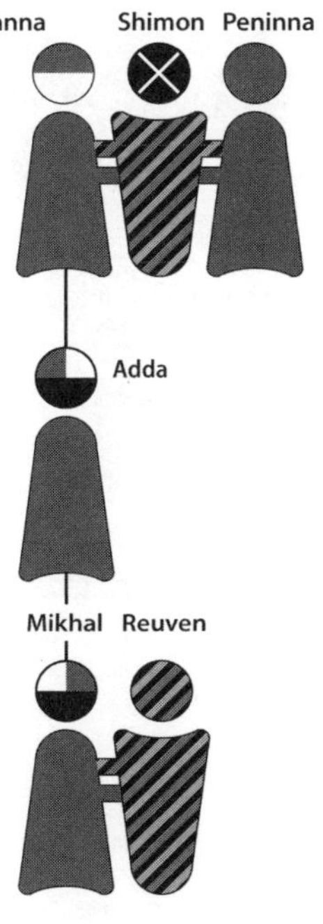

His father-in-law's mother – אֵם חָמִיו: Shimon married Ḥanna, while his brother Reuven married Mikhal, daughter of Zeraḥ, son of Ḥanna. If Shimon dies childless, Ḥanna is exempt from both *ḥalitza* and levirate marriage as she is the mother of Reuven's father-in-law, Zeraḥ. Peninna is also exempt from *ḥalitza* and levirate marriage as Ḥanna's rival wife.

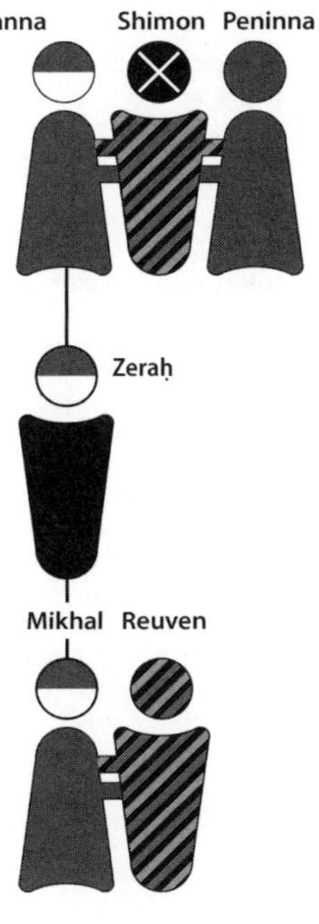

אֲחוֹתוֹ מֵאִמּוֹ, וַאֲחוֹת אִמּוֹ, וַאֲחוֹת אִשְׁתּוֹ, וְאֵשֶׁת אָחִיו מֵאִמּוֹ,

The mishna continues its list of close relatives. If the *yevama* is the **maternal** half **sister**[B] of the *yavam*, **or** if she is the **sister of his mother,**[B] **or his wife's sister,**[NB] then she is exempt from both *ḥalitza* and levirate marriage **Or** if she was **the wife of his maternal** half **brother,**[NB] and after this brother died or divorced his wife, she married another of his father's brothers, who was not her relative, and this brother died, she is exempt. In this case, the obligation to enter into levirate marriage should be incurred by the surviving brother, but since she was previously the wife of his maternal brother, she is exempt.

NOTES

His wife's sister – **אֲחוֹת אִשְׁתּוֹ:** If the mishna includes one's wife's sister, who is in some cases permitted, i.e., if one's wife has died, shouldn't a menstruating woman be listed as well, despite the fact that her prohibition is temporary and therefore differs in kind from the other relationships mentioned in the mishna? Admittedly, there is a difference between a menstruating woman, who will certainly and automatically be permitted later, and his wife's sister, who might remain forbidden to him forever (see *Ḥeshek Shlomo*). Nevertheless, it remains the case that a menstruating woman is also sometimes forbidden. Apparently, most commentaries hold that the principal reason for the exclusion of a menstruating woman is that she is prohibited to all men, even to her own husband, not only to her *yavam*.

The wife of his maternal half brother – **אֵשֶׁת אָחִיו מֵאִמּוֹ:** A maternal half brother is in certain respects considered a full brother, while in other cases he is not treated as a brother. With regard to the prohibition against marrying a brother's wife, as well as matters of testimony and the *halakhot* of mourning, a half brother is considered a brother. However, concerning matters of inheritance, and particularly levirate marriage, only a paternal half brother is classified as a brother, not a maternal half brother (Rambam).

BACKGROUND

His maternal half sister – **אֲחוֹתוֹ מֵאִמּוֹ:** Ya'akov and his wife Leah had a son, Shimon. Ya'akov also married Miriam, who had a daughter, Ḥanna, from her previous husband, Zeraḥ. Ya'akov and Miriam bore a son, Reuven. Shimon, Ya'akov's son, married Ḥanna, who is not forbidden to him, as she is the daughter of his father's wife. If Shimon dies childless and Ḥanna falls before Reuven for levirate marriage, she is exempt as Reuven's sister, because they are the children of the same woman, Miriam. Ḥanna's rival wife, Peninna, is also exempt from *ḥalitza* and levirate marriage.

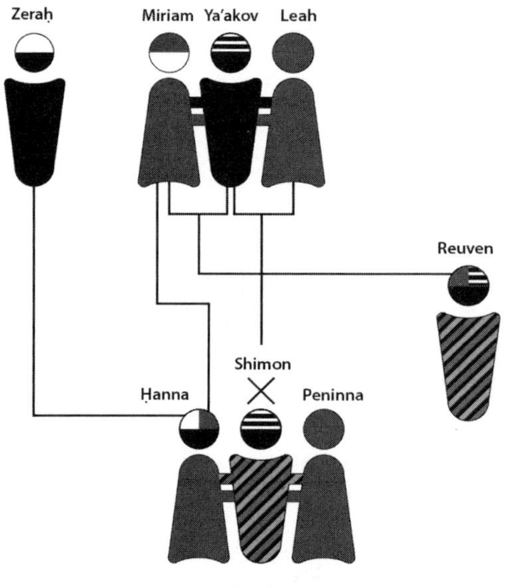

The sister of his mother – **אֲחוֹת אִמּוֹ:** Ya'akov and his wife Miriam had a son, Shimon. Ya'akov also married Ḥogla, with whom he had another son, Reuven. Shimon married Milka, his father's wife's sister, before dying childless. Milka is exempt from *ḥalitza* and levirate marriage, as she is the sister of Reuven's mother Ḥogla. Peninna, Milka's rival wife, is likewise exempt.

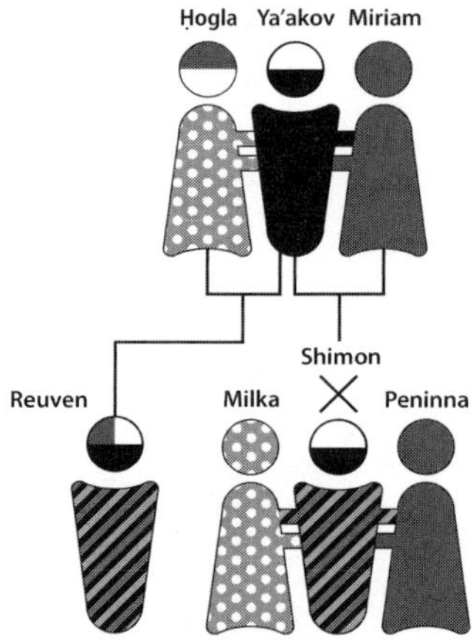

His wife's sister – **אֲחוֹת אִשְׁתּוֹ:** Two brothers, Reuven and Shimon, married two sisters, Ḥogla and Milka. If Shimon dies childless, Milka is exempt from *ḥalitza* and levirate marriage as the sister of Reuven's wife, Ḥogla. Her rival wife, Peninna, is also exempt.

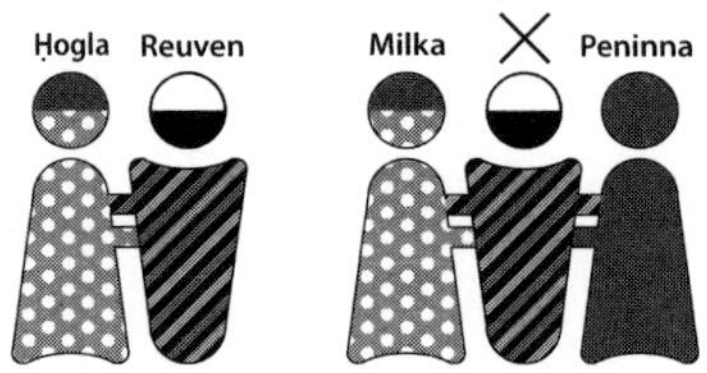

The wife of his maternal half brother – **אֵשֶׁת אָחִיו מֵאִמּוֹ:** Ya'akov married Miriam, who had a son, Levi, from her previous marriage with Zeraḥ. Ya'akov and Miriam had a son named Reuven. Ya'akov had another wife, Leah, with whom he also had a son, Shimon. Levi married Ḥanna and died. After his passing, Shimon married Ḥanna, who is permitted to him, as Levi is the son of his father's wife. If Shimon dies childless, Ḥanna is forbidden to Reuven because she was his maternal brother's wife, as Levi was the son of Miriam, Reuven's mother. Peninna, Ḥanna's rival wife, is likewise exempt from *ḥalitza* and levirate marriage.

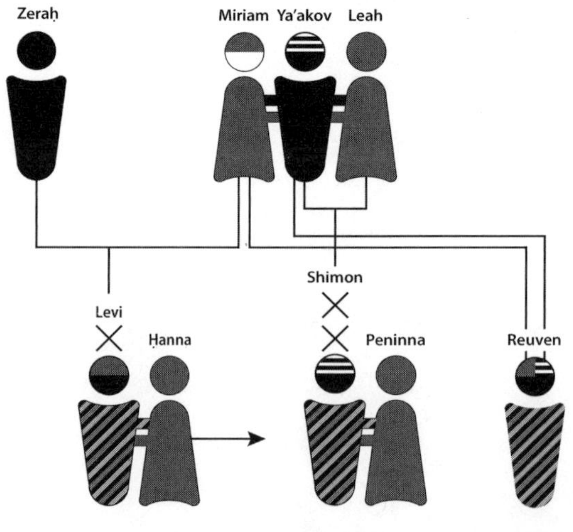

וְאֵשֶׁת אָחִיו שֶׁלֹּא הָיָה בְּעוֹלָמוֹ, וְכַלָּתוֹ. הֲרֵי אֵלּוּ פּוֹטְרוֹת צָרוֹתֵיהֶן וְצָרוֹת צָרוֹתֵיהֶן מִן הַחֲלִיצָה וּמִן הַיִּבּוּם עַד סוֹף הָעוֹלָם.

And the same applies to the **wife of a brother with whom he did not coexist,**[B] i.e., the wife of a man who died before his brother was born. As will be explained, the obligation of levirate marriage does not apply to the *yavam* in this case. Since levirate marriage does not apply to him, the *yevama* remains forbidden to him as his brother's wife. **And** the last case is if one's *yevama* had previously been **his daughter-in-law,**[B] and after his son had died one's brother married her, before he too passed away. **These** fifteen women **exempt their rival wives and the rival wives of their rival wives from *halitza* and levirate marriage forever.**

וְכוּלָּן, אִם מֵתוּ, אוֹ מֵיאֲנוּ,

§ **And** with regard to **all of these** women listed as prohibited relations, these *halakhot* apply only if they were married to the deceased brother until the time of his death. However, this is not the case **if they died**[HN] during the deceased brother's lifetime, **or** if **they refused**[N] their husbands when they were minors. This refusal is referring to the decree of the Sages that a girl under the age of twelve whose father is no longer alive may be married off by her mother or brothers. However, this marriage is not final, as she can terminate it by performing an act of refusal, i.e., by declaring, while still a minor, that she does not desire this marriage. In this case, the marriage is annulled retroactively and she is considered as though she were never married at all.

HALAKHA

And all of these, if they died, etc. – **וְכוּלָּן אִם מֵתוּ וכו׳**: If one's brother was married to two women, one of whom is a forbidden relative to the *yavam*, and the forbidden wife dies, is divorced, or performed refusal during her husband's lifetime, the other rival wife is permitted to enter into levirate marriage (*Shulḥan Arukh, Even HaEzer* 173:7).

NOTES

And all of these, if they died, etc. – **וְכוּלָּן אִם מֵתוּ וכו׳**: The sequence in the mishna is taught in the style of: Not only this but also that. In other words, it moves from the simpler to the more complex cases, beginning with a woman who is no longer alive, continuing to the case of refusal, which involves the retroactive nullification of a marriage, before proceeding to the *halakha* of a divorce, where the husband ends the marriage from a certain point in time. Finally, the mishna addresses the status of a woman who was discovered to be an *aylonit* (*Tosefot HaRosh*).

Refusal – **מֵיאוּן**: The *halakhot* of refusal are analyzed extensively in this tractate, mainly in the thirteenth chapter. The basic concept is that a minor girl orphaned of her father may be married off by her mother and brothers with her consent. However, since a minor is not legally competent and responsible for her actions, her marriage is valid only by decree of the Sages. Therefore, the Sages instituted an ordinance that if she declares that she does not desire the match she can nullify it retroactively, and it is as though she was never married at all. The early commentaries note that since her father is evidently alive in the cases mentioned in the mishna, it must be referring to a so-called orphan in her father's lifetime. If a minor who was married off by her father, who has the authority to do so by Torah law, is divorced from her husband while still a minor, she returns to her father's household, but her father loses the right to marry her off again. Consequently, for the purposes of marriage she is considered an orphan.

BACKGROUND

The wife of a brother with whom he did not coexist – **אֵשֶׁת אָחִיו שֶׁלֹּא הָיָה בְּעוֹלָמוֹ**: Reuven and Shimon are paternal brothers. Reuven married Peninna and then died. After his death, a third brother, Levi, was born. For Levi, Peninna is the wife of a brother with whom he did not coexist, as he was not alive while she was married to his brother. Consequently, if Shimon entered into levirate marriage with Peninna and subsequently died childless, Peninna remains forbidden to Levi due to the fact that for a period of time, i.e., between Levi's birth and Shimon's levirate marriage, she had been forbidden to Levi as the wife of a brother with whom he did not coexist. Peninna's rival wife Ḥanna is likewise exempt from *halitza* and levirate marriage.

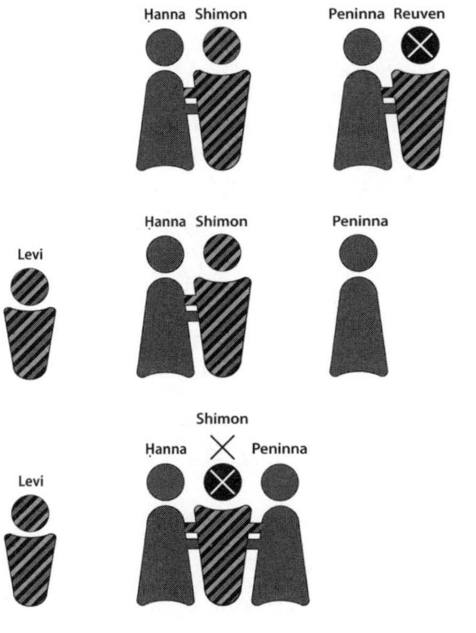

His daughter-in-law – **כַּלָּתוֹ**: Reuven's son Ḥanokh was married to Ḥanna. After Ḥanokh's death Reuven's brother, Shimon, married Ḥanna. If Shimon dies childless, his wives come before Reuven for levirate marriage. As Ḥanna was previously Reuven's daughter-in-law, she is permanently forbidden to him; she is therefore exempt from *halitza* and levirate marriage and exempts her rival wife as well.

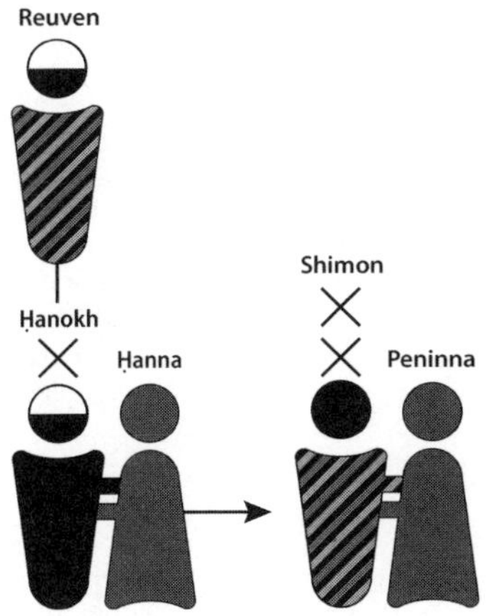

אוֹ נִתְגָּרְשׁוּ, אוֹ שֶׁנִּמְצְאוּ אַיְלוֹנִית צָרוֹתֵיהֶן מוּתָּרוֹת.

Or if those women **were divorced** by their husband, the deceased brother, **or were found to be a sexually underdeveloped woman [*aylonit*],**[HBN] i.e., a woman who is so underdeveloped that she is not considered a woman in the full sense, these *halakhot* do not apply. Her marriage is considered a mistaken marriage and is null and void. In all these cases **their rival wives are permitted,** as the exemption for rival wives of forbidden relatives applies only when the forbidden relative was the brother's wife at the time of his death, when the *halakhot* of levirate marriage came into effect.

וְאִי אַתָּה יָכוֹל לוֹמַר בַּחֲמוֹתוֹ וּבְאֵם חֲמוֹתוֹ וּבְאֵם חָמִיו שֶׁנִּמְצְאוּ אַיְלוֹנִית אוֹ שֶׁמֵּיאֲנוּ.

§ **And** the mishna comments that the language of this principle is imprecise, as **you cannot say**[N] **with regard to his mother-in-law and with regard to his mother-in-law's mother and with regard to his father-in-law's mother that they were found to be an *aylonit*,** as an *aylonit* is sterile and therefore cannot become a mother or a mother-in-law. **Nor** is the mishna precise when it states: **Or refused,** as refusal applies only to minors, who cannot give birth.

כֵּיצַד פּוֹטְרוֹת צָרוֹתֵיהֶן? הָיְתָה בִּתּוֹ אוֹ אַחַת מִכָּל הָעֲרָיוֹת הָאֵלּוּ נְשׂוּאוֹת לְאָחִיו, וְלוֹ אִשָּׁה אַחֶרֶת, וּמֵת – כְּשֵׁם שֶׁבִּתּוֹ פְּטוּרָה כָּךְ צָרָתָהּ פְּטוּרָה. הָלְכָה צָרַת בִּתּוֹ וְנִשֵּׂאת לְאָחִיו הַשֵּׁנִי וְלוֹ אִשָּׁה אַחֶרֶת, וּמֵת – כְּשֵׁם שֶׁצָּרַת בִּתּוֹ פְּטוּרָה כָּךְ צָרַת צָרָתָהּ פְּטוּרָה.

§ The mishna explains: **How do** these women **exempt their rival wives?** If, for example, **his daughter or any one of those** women **with whom relations are forbidden was married to his brother and** this brother **had another wife, and** the brother **died,** then **just as his daughter is exempt** from levirate marriage, **so too her rival wife is exempt. If his daughter's rival wife** subsequently **went and married his second brother,** to whom she is permitted, **and he had another wife, and he died** childless as well, which means that his wife comes before the first *yavam*, the daughter's father, for levirate marriage, then **just as his daughter's rival wife is exempt, so too the rival wife of her rival wife is exempt.**

אֲפִילּוּ הֵן מֵאָה.

The mishna adds: **Even if they are one hundred** brothers, the same logic applies. If a woman is exempt from levirate marriage because she is the rival wife of a forbidden relative or the rival wife of a rival wife of this kind, and she herself has an additional rival wife, this rival wife is also exempt and in turn exempts her own rival wives from levirate marriage.

כֵּיצַד אִם מֵתוּ צָרוֹתֵיהֶן מוּתָּרוֹת? הָיְתָה בִּתּוֹ אוֹ אַחַת מִכָּל הָעֲרָיוֹת הָאֵלּוּ נְשׂוּאוֹת לְאָחִיו, וְלוֹ אִשָּׁה אַחֶרֶת, מֵתָה בִּתּוֹ אוֹ נִתְגָּרְשָׁה, וְאַחַר כָּךְ מֵת אָחִיו – צָרָתָהּ מוּתֶּרֶת.

How so? What are the cases in which **if they died their rival wives are permitted?** If, for example, **one's daughter or any one of those** women **with whom relations are forbidden was married to his brother, and** this brother **had another wife,** and then **his daughter died or was divorced and afterward his brother died, her rival wife is permitted** to him.

וְכָל הַיְכוֹלָה לְמָאֵן וְלֹא מֵיאֲנָה – צָרָתָהּ חוֹלֶצֶת וְלֹא מִתְיַיבֶּמֶת.

§ The mishna states another principle: **And if any** of these forbidden relatives was a minor **who could refuse**[HN] her husband, then even if **she did not refuse, her rival wife performs *ḥalitza* and does not enter into levirate marriage.** The rival wife may not enter into levirate marriage, as she is the rival wife of a forbidden relative. However, she is not entirely exempt from levirate marriage and must be released by *ḥalitza* because the marriage of the forbidden relative was not a fully valid marriage, and therefore, by Torah law, the other woman is not considered a rival wife of a forbidden relative.

HALAKHA

The rival wife of a forbidden relative who is an *aylonit* – צָרַת עֶרְוָה שֶׁהִיא אַיְלוֹנִית: If one's *yevama* is a forbidden relative, and is therefore thought to be prohibited to him for levirate marriage, but she is later is discovered to be an *aylonit*, then even if her husband was aware of her condition and married her willingly, she does not exempt her rival wife from levirate marriage (*Shulḥan Arukh, Even HaEzer* 173:9).

And any who could refuse – וְכָל הַיְכוֹלָה לְמָאֵן: If one's *yevama* was a minor who could perform refusal, and she is a forbidden relative to her *yavam*, then because her marriage is valid by rabbinic law the Sages decreed that her rival wife must be released by *ḥalitza* and that she may not enter into levirate marriage (Rambam *Sefer Nashim, Hilkhot Yibbum VaḤalitza* 6:22).

BACKGROUND

***Aylonit* – אַיְלוֹנִית:** An *aylonit* is a woman who is so severely sexually underdeveloped that she is incapable of bearing children. This is a general term for women who have a basic flaw in their reproductive system. Sometimes the secondary reproductive signs of these women is not present at all or in other cases is barely developed. A comprehensive inquiry into the definition of an *aylonit*, from both a biological and halakhic perspective, can be found on 80a–b.

NOTES

Who were found to be an *aylonit* – שֶׁנִּמְצְאוּ אַיְלוֹנִית: Rashi, and many other commentaries in his wake, including *Tosafot* and the Rosh, explain that marriage to an *aylonit* is considered a mistaken transaction, as it is certain that one would not marry a woman who could never give birth. Consequently, this marriage is annulled the moment her condition becomes known to the husband. Some commentaries deliberate about whether this refers only to a woman who was discovered to be an *aylonit* during her husband's lifetime, or whether the *halakha* is the same even if her status came to light after his death, as stated explicitly in a *baraita* (*Tosafot*; Meiri). Others maintain that an *aylonit* is not eligible for levirate marriage at all, as she cannot fulfill the purpose of the mitzva of levirate marriage, which is to continue her deceased husband's family line. Therefore, she has no connection whatsoever with the mitzva of levirate marriage, no matter when her status was discovered, and her rival wife is not forbidden to her *yavam* (Rashba; *Nimmukei Yosef*; Meiri). This is in accordance with the opinion of Rava (12a), a ruling that is accepted as *halakha*. It is also explicitly stated in the Jerusalem Talmud that with regard to all matters involving levirate marriage an *aylonit* is viewed as though she had never been married to the deceased brother at all. Some claim that Rashi's explanation is based on a precise reading of the language of the mishna, which states: Found to be an *aylonit*. This indicates that the matter was revealed only at a later stage, as a result of which the marriage was annulled (Rabbi Akiva Eiger).

You cannot say – אִי אַתָּה יָכוֹל לוֹמַר: This paragraph serves to emphasize that it is never possible for a woman who has given birth to perform a refusal later (*Otzar HaShitot*).

And any who could refuse – וְכָל הַיְכוֹלָה לְמָאֵן: This *halakha* applies to any minor whose marriage is valid only by decree of the Sages, not necessarily one who performs refusal. The mishna does not simply state: A minor, because certain marriages of minors are valid by Torah law.

גמ׳ מִכְּדֵי, כּוּלְּהוּ מֵאֲחוֹת אִשָּׁה יָלְפִינַן, לִיתְנֵי אֲחוֹת אִשָּׁה בְּרֵישָׁא!

GEMARA The Gemara asks a question with regard to the order of the mishna's list: **Now, since** the *halakha* that **all these** women with whom relations are forbidden are exempt from levirate marriage and exempt their rival wives **is derived from** the case of **a wife's sister,** as demonstrated later, **let** the mishna **teach** the case of **a wife's sister first**[N] and only afterward mention the other instances, which are derived from that *halakha*.

וְכִי תֵּימָא תַּנָּא חוּמְרֵי חוּמְרֵי נָקַט, וְרַבִּי שִׁמְעוֹן הִיא, דְּאָמַר שְׂרֵיפָה חֲמוּרָה –

And if you would say that **the *tanna* cited** the cases in order of **severity,** then you must say that **it is in accordance with** the opinion of **Rabbi Shimon, who says** that execution by **burning is more severe** than stoning. For this reason, the *tanna* began with the cases of one's daughter and his daughter's daughter and his son's daughter and so forth, since one who has relations with these women is punished by burning, after which the *tanna* listed those cases that entail a lesser penalty.

אִי הָכִי, לִיתְנֵי חֲמוֹתוֹ בְּרֵישָׁא, דְּעִיקַּר שְׂרֵיפָה בַּחֲמוֹתוֹ כְּתִיבָא! וְעוֹד: בָּתַר חֲמוֹתוֹ לִיתְנֵי כַּלָּתוֹ, דְּבָתַר שְׂרֵיפָה סְקִילָה חֲמוּרָה!

However, the Gemara argues that even so, the order of the mishna remains problematic. **If so, let him teach** the case of **one's mother-in-law first, as the main** transgression that entails **burning is written with regard to his mother-in-law,** as it is stated: "And if a man take with his wife also her mother, it is wickedness; they shall be burnt with fire, both he and they" (Leviticus 20:14). **And furthermore, after his mother-in-law let him teach his daughter-in-law,**[N] **as after** execution by **burning, stoning is the most severe**[HBN] of the other capital punishments imposed by the courts.

אֶלָּא: בִּתּוֹ, כֵּיוָן דְּאָתְיָא מִדְּרָשָׁא – חֲבִיבָא לֵיהּ.

Rather, the Gemara retracts the previous explanation in favor of the following: With regard to **his daughter, since** this prohibition is actually **derived from a homiletical interpretation**[N] and is not explicitly stated in the Torah, **it is** therefore **dear** to the *tanna*. Consequently, he listed this novel case of a daughter first.

HALAKHA

Stoning and burning – סְקִילָה וּשְׂרֵיפָה: Rabbi Shimon and the Rabbis dispute whether stoning or burning is the more severe capital punishment. Rabbi Shimon maintains that burning is more severe, while the Rabbis maintain that stoning is more severe. The *halakha* is in accordance with the opinion of the Rabbis (Rambam *Sefer Shofetim, Hilkhot Sanhedrin* 14:4).

BACKGROUND

Stoning and burning – סְקִילָה וּשְׂרֵיפָה: The four capital punishments prescribed by the Torah and administered by a court of twenty-three members are stoning, burning, decapitation, and strangulation. Generally speaking, stoning is considered the most severe punishment, although, as noted in the Gemara, Rabbi Shimon holds that burning is more severe. The Sages maintain that an accused could be convicted only if he was properly warned beforehand and was fully cognizant of the consequences when performing the forbidden act. This is one reason why capital punishment was rarely carried out in practice.

NOTES

Let it teach a wife's sister first – לִיתְנֵי אֲחוֹת אִשָּׁה בְּרֵישָׁא: Although the Gemara elsewhere (*Sanhedrin* 49b) states that the Mishna does not typically arrange its subjects in logical order, it is nevertheless proper to seek a rationale for its order even if it has no halakhic implications (Meiri).

After his mother-in-law let him teach his daughter-in-law – בָּתַר חֲמוֹתוֹ לִיתְנֵי כַּלָּתוֹ: The commentaries ask why the Gemara states: And furthermore, as this is apparently a new question (*Otzar HaShitot*). Perhaps this phrase indicates that even if some reason is found for why the mishna begins with a daughter, e.g., due to the fact that they are blood relatives, as stated below, nevertheless, with regard to the severity of the prohibition involved, the case of a daughter-in-law should follow that of a mother-in-law.

After burning, stoning is the most severe – דְּבָתַר שְׂרֵיפָה סְקִילָה חֲמוּרָה: Some commentaries add that since the other forbidden incestuous relations, apart from a mother-in-law and daughter-in-law, are punishable by *karet* and not court-imposed capital punishment, the mishna should certainly have taught the case of the daughter-in-law before them (*Tosafot*). Others claim that according to the opinion of *Tosafot*, as well as that of many other authorities, relations with a mother-in-law after the death of one's wife are punishable by *karet*, and therefore the above distinction does not apply (*Ḥeshek Shlomo*).

His daughter…is derived from a homiletical interpretation – בִּתּוֹ...דְּאָתְיָא מִדְּרָשָׁא: This homiletical interpretation relates to the status of a man's daughter from a woman he raped. Since her mother was not his wife, the verse: "You shall not uncover the nakedness of a woman and her daughter" (Leviticus 18:17), which refers to a married woman, does not apply to this case. Some commentaries indicate that it is considered as though the prohibition against relations with one's own daughter is explicitly written in the Torah, as it is stated that one's daughter's daughter is forbidden, and this is due to his daughter's status as a forbidden relative. This is not considered an *a fortiori* inference, which would be problematic, as a prohibition cannot be derived by *a fortiori* inference. Rather, it is as though the case of a daughter is explicitly written. Other commentaries ask: How is the prohibition against relations with one's daughter from the woman to whom he is married derived from the *halakha* of a wife's daughter? After all, although the prohibitions of a paternal half sister and a maternal half sister are both explicitly stated, the Gemara elsewhere explains that it was nevertheless necessary to deduce that there is also a prohibition with regard to one's full sister (Rabbi Avraham *Av Beit Din*; *Tosafot*). Some explain that the general instruction: "The nakedness of a woman and her daughter," includes all cases. Others say that since the Torah did not explicitly differentiate between the cases here, as it did with regard to a sister, there is no reason to assume that there is a difference between them.

כּוּלְּהוּ נַמִּי מִדְּרָשָׁא אָתוּ! נְהִי דִּלְעִנְיַן יִיבּוּם אָתְיָין מִדְּרָשָׁא, עִיקַּר אִיסּוּרַיְיהוּ בְּהֶדְיָא כְּתִיב בְּהוּ, בִּתּוֹ – עִיקַּר אִיסּוּרָא מִדְּרָשָׁא.

The Gemara challenges this conclusion: **All** of the exemptions from levirate marriage for forbidden relatives listed in the mishna **are also derived from a homiletical interpretation.** The Gemara responds: **Although the matter of levirate marriage is derived from a homiletical interpretation, the main** aspect **of their prohibition is explicitly written.** By contrast, with regard to **his daughter** from a woman he raped but did not marry, **the main** aspect **of** this **prohibition is** derived **by homiletical interpretation,** as the prohibition itself is not written explicitly in the Torah.

דְּאָמַר רָבָא: אָמַר לִי רַב יִצְחָק בַּר אַבְדִּימִי: אָתְיָא ״הֵנָּה״ ״הֵנָּה״,

As Rava said: Rav Yitzḥak bar Avdimi[P] **said to me:** This prohibition is **derived** by means of a verbal analogy between the word ***hena,*** in the verse: "The nakedness of your son's daughter, or of your daughter's daughter, even their nakedness you shall not uncover; for theirs [*hena*] is your own nakedness" (Leviticus 18:10) and the word ***hena*** in a different verse: "You shall not uncover the nakedness of a woman and her daughter; you shall not take her son's daughter, or her daughter's daughter, to uncover her nakedness: they [*hena*] are near kinswomen; it is wickedness" (Leviticus 18:17), indicating that every daughter is prohibited, even one from rape, just like one's daughter through his wife.

אָתְיָא ״זִמָּה״ ״זִמָּה״.

Furthermore, it is **derived** from a verbal analogy between the word **"wickedness"** (Leviticus 18:17) and the word **"wickedness"** in the verse: "And if a man take with his wife also her mother, it is wickedness; they shall be burnt with fire, both he and they, that there be no wickedness among you" (Leviticus 20:14), that one who has sexual intercourse with a daughter from a rape is liable to burning.

הַשְׁתָּא דְּאָמְרַתְּ כׇּל מִלְּתָא דְּאָתְיָא מִדְּרָשָׁא חֲבִיבָא לֵיהּ, לִיתְנֵי לַאֲחוֹת אִשָּׁה לְבַסּוֹף! אַיְּידֵי דְּאַיְירֵי בְּאִיסּוּר אַחְווֹתָא תְּנָא אֲחוֹת אִשְׁתּוֹ.

§ The Gemara asks: **Now that you said** that **all matters that are derived from a homiletical interpretation are dear to** the *tanna*, and he therefore he gives them precedence, **let him teach** the case of **a wife's sister last,** as this is the source of the *halakha* and is therefore the most straightforward case. The Gemara responds: **Since** the *tanna* **was dealing with the prohibition** with regard **to** different types of **sisters, he** also **taught** together with them the prohibition with regard to **his wife's sister.**

וְלִיתְנְיֵיא לְהַאי בָּבָא לְבַסּוֹף! אֶלָּא: תְּנָא קוּרְבֵי קוּרְבֵי נָקֵט; תְּנָא בִּתּוֹ וּבַת בִּתּוֹ וּבַת בְּנוֹ דִּקְרוֹבֵי עַצְמוֹ,

The Gemara asks: **But** if so, **let him teach this** entire **section** involving sisters **at the end,** when he mentions a wife's sister. **Rather,** the Gemara rejects the above answer in favor of an alternative explanation: **The *tanna* cited** the cases in order of **closeness,**[N] i.e., the mishna is ordered in accordance with the relative closeness of the various incestuous relations. How so? The *tanna* **taught** the cases of **one's daughter, and the daughter of his daughter, and the daughter of his son, who are his own** blood **relatives.**

וְאַיְּידֵי דִּתְנָא שְׁלֹשָׁה דּוֹרוֹת לְמַטָּה דִּידֵיהּ, תְּנָא נַמִּי שְׁלֹשָׁה דּוֹרוֹת לְמַטָּה דִּידַהּ. וְאַיְּידֵי דִּתְנָא שְׁלֹשָׁה דּוֹרוֹת לְמַטָּה דִּידַהּ – תְּנָא שְׁלֹשָׁה דּוֹרוֹת לְמַעְלָה דִּידַהּ.

And since he taught three generations of one's offspring **below,** i.e., his daughter, his daughter's daughter, and his son's daughter, he **also taught three generations of** his wife's offspring **below,** i.e., his wife herself, her daughter, and her daughter's daughter. **And since he taught three generations of** his wife's offspring **below, he** also **taught three generations of her** family **above,** i.e., from previous generations, namely herself, her mother, i.e., his mother-in-law, and his mother-in-law's mother.

PERSONALITIES

Rav Yitzḥak bar Avdimi – רַב יִצְחָק בַּר אַבְדִּימִי: The Talmud mentions two Sages of this name (see *Tosafot*). The other Sage lived in the transitional generation between the *tanna'im* and the *amora'im*, whereas the Rav Yitzḥak bar Avdimi mentioned here was a Babylonian *amora* from the third and fourth generations. He was probably a disciple-colleague of Rav Ḥisda, and was famous for his breadth of knowledge of the Bible, as well as for his unique method of study, by which he would seek out and find evidence and allusion to all statements of the Sages in the Bible itself. Rava said of him that any verse that Rav Yitzḥak bar Avdimi did not explain cannot be elucidated (*Zevaḥim* 43b). Rav Yitzhak bar Avdimi's interpretations of verses appear in many places in the Talmud. Occasionally he disagrees with Rav Ḥisda with regard to the interpretation of a verse. Numerous *halakhot* are also stated in his name. Apparently, both Abaye and Rava were his disciples concerning matters of biblical explication, as they attribute various traditions to him.

NOTES

Rather, the *tanna* cited the cases in order of closeness – אֶלָּא תְּנָא קוּרְבֵי קוּרְבֵי נָקֵט: This answer could have been combined with the previous suggestion by saying that the *tanna* began with one's daughter because it was a novel case, after which he dealt with one's other blood relatives. However, the Gemara wanted to emphasize that the primary rationale for the sequence of this mishna is the closeness of the relationship, and therefore it rejected the first explanation entirely (*Tosefot HaRosh*).

וְתָנָא אֲחוֹתוֹ וַאֲחוֹת אִמּוֹ דִּקְרוֹבֵי עַצְמוֹ, וְאַיְּידֵי דְּאַיְּירֵי בְּאִיסּוּר אַחֲוָה – תָּנָא אֲחוֹת אִשְׁתּוֹ. וּבְדִין הוּא דְּלִיקַדְּמָהּ לְכַלָּתוֹ מִקַּמֵּי אֵשֶׁת אָחִיו שֶׁלֹּא הָיָה בְּעוֹלָמוֹ, דְּלָא מִשּׁוּם קוּרְבָא הוּא דַּאֲסִירָא, אֶלָּא אַיְּידֵי דְּאַיְּירֵי בְּאִיסּוּר אַחֲוָה – תָּנָא אֵשֶׁת אָחִיו שֶׁלֹּא הָיָה בְּעוֹלָמוֹ, וַהֲדַר תָּנָא כַּלָּתוֹ.

And afterward **he taught** the case of **his sister and his mother's sister, who are his own** blood **relatives** but less closely related to him than his daughter. **And since he was dealing with the prohibition** with regard **to sisters, he** also **taught** the case of **his wife's sister. And by right** the *tanna* should have **preceded** the case of **his daughter-in-law before** that of **a wife of a brother**[N] **with whom he did not coexist, as it is not due to their relationship that she is prohibited** but rather because she is excluded from the mitzva of levirate marriage. **However, since he was dealing with the prohibition** with regard **to siblings, he taught** the case of **a wife of a brother with whom he did not coexist,** as this also involves a sibling. **And then** the *tanna* **taught** the case of **his daughter-in-law.**

וּמַאי אִירְיָא דְּתָנָא "פּוֹטְרוֹת", לִיתְנֵי "אוֹסְרוֹת"! אִי תָּנָא אוֹסְרוֹת הֲוָה אָמִינָא: אָסוּר לְיַיבֵּם, אֲבָל מִיחֲלַץ חָלְצָה, קָא מַשְׁמַע לָן.

§ The Gemara continues to analyze the language of the mishna: **And why does** the *tanna* **specifically teach: They exempt** their rival wives? **Let him teach: They prohibit**[N] them, as ultimately the rival wives are not only exempt from levirate marriage but each is actually forbidden to her *yavam*. The Gemara explains that **if** he had **taught: They prohibit** them, **I would say** that this means **it is prohibited to enter into levirate marriage, but she must perform *ḥalitza*.** Therefore, **it teaches us** using the language of exemption to indicate that she is entirely exempt and does not even perform *ḥalitza*.

וְלִיתְנֵי אֲסוּרָה לַחֲלוֹץ! מַאי קָעָבֵיד? אַלְמָה לָא? אִם אַתָּה אוֹמֵר חוֹלֶצֶת – מִתְיַיבֶּמֶת!

The Gemara raises a difficulty: If so, **let him teach: She is prohibited from performing *ḥalitza*.** The Gemara rejects this suggestion: It is impossible to formulate the *halakha* in this manner, as even if they perform *ḥalitza*, **what has he** really **done?** What is wrong with a man allowing a woman to take off his shoe, which is the act of *ḥalitza*? Consequently, it is not possible to state: Prohibited from performing *ḥalitza*. The Gemara asks: **Why not?** There is in fact a prohibited element here: **If you say she performs *ḥalitza*,** it might be said that **she may** also **enter into levirate marriage** and that in this specific instance he performed *ḥalitza* merely because he did not wish to marry her. In that case, it might erroneously be claimed that if another wished to marry the rival wife of his *yevama* he is permitted to enter into levirate marriage.

כֵּיוָן דְּבִמְקוֹם מִצְוָה הוּא דַּאֲסִירָה צָרָה, וְשֶׁלֹּא בִּמְקוֹם מִצְוָה שַׁרְיָא, מִשּׁוּם הָכִי תָּנֵי "פּוֹטְרוֹת".

In light of the previous argument, the Gemara suggests another reason that the mishna does not use the expression: Prohibited. **Since** it is only **in cases where the mitzva** of levirate marriage **applies that the rival wife is forbidden** to him, **and where no mitzva applies she is permitted,** as it is permitted for the man to marry the widowed rival wife of a non-relative, **due to that** reason **he taught: They exempt** their rival wives, and not: **They prohibit** them. In other words, the *tanna* is teaching that they are not prohibited to him in their own right.

וּמַאי אִירְיָא דְּתָנֵי "מִן הַחֲלִיצָה וּמִן הַיִּיבּוּם", לִיתְנֵי "מִן הַיִּיבּוּם" לְחוּדֵיהּ! אִי תָּנָא מִן הַיִּיבּוּם הֲוָה אָמִינָא: מִיחֲלַץ חָלְצָה, יַבּוֹמֵי לָא מִיַּיבְּמָה, קָא מַשְׁמַע לָן: כָּל הָעוֹלָה לְיִיבּוּם עוֹלֶה לַחֲלִיצָה וְכָל שֶׁאֵינוֹ עוֹלֶה לְיִיבּוּם – אֵינוֹ עוֹלֶה לַחֲלִיצָה.

§ The Gemara continues its analysis of the wording of the mishna. **And why does** the *tanna* **specifically teach:** Exempt **from *ḥalitza* and from levirate marriage? Let him teach:** Exempt **from levirate marriage,**[N] **alone.** The Gemara answers: **If** he were to **teach: From levirate marriage, I would say** that **she must perform *ḥalitza*** and **she must not enter into levirate marriage.** The *tanna* therefore **teaches us** that **every** woman **who is eligible for levirate marriage is eligible for *ḥalitza*, and anyone who is ineligible for levirate marriage is** likewise **ineligible for *ḥalitza*,**[H] as no obligation of *ḥalitza* applies unless there is an obligation of a levirate marriage.

NOTES

Should have preceded the case of his daughter-in-law before that of a wife of a brother, etc. – **לִיקַדְּמָהּ לְכַלָּתוֹ מִקַּמֵּי אֵשֶׁת אָחִיו וכו׳**: Since none of these are blood relatives, a daughter-in-law should have been listed first, as this prohibition is more severe in that it is never permitted, unlike a brother's wife (Rashi). Alternatively, a daughter-in-law is considered a closer relation that a brother's wife due to the greater closeness of a son than a brother (*Tosafot*). They apparently had before them a version of the Gemara that supports this explanation. However, others explain simply that the prohibition proscribing the wife of a brother with whom one did not coexist is not due to a prohibited incestuous relation at all; rather, it is derived from the *halakhot* of levirate marriage themselves (Ramban; Meiri).

Let him teach: They prohibit – **לִיתְנֵי אוֹסְרוֹת**: Some commentaries note that the term: Exempt, is precise only when there is a single brother, as in that case the *yevama* is entirely exempt from *ḥalitza* and levirate marriage. However, in a case involving several brothers she may be forbidden only to a specific *yavam* but remain obligated to enter into levirate marriage with one of the other brothers to whom she is not considered a forbidden relative (*Meromei Sadeh*).

Let him teach: Exempt from levirate marriage – **לִיתְנֵי מִן הַיִּיבּוּם**: It can be claimed that the term: Levirate marriage, refers both to the specific act of levirate marriage itself as well as to the general obligations and bonds to the *yavam*, including *ḥalitza*. Therefore, the use of the phrase: Exempt from levirate marriage, can be explained as referring to the more general meaning, indicating that none of the *halakhot* of levirate marriage pertain to them at all (Rashash).

HALAKHA

Every woman who is eligible for levirate marriage is eligible for *ḥalitza*, and anyone who is ineligible for levirate marriage is ineligible for *ḥalitza* – **כָּל הָעוֹלָה לְיִיבּוּם עוֹלָה לַחֲלִיצָה וְכָל שֶׁאֵינוֹ עוֹלֶה לְיִיבּוּם אֵינוֹ עוֹלֶה לַחֲלִיצָה**: There are apparently many cases that do not follow this principle, e.g., those marriages that were a transgression of a prohibition, which are ineligible for levirate marriage but are eligible for *ḥalitza*; however, one is rendered ineligible from levirate marriage in these cases by rabbinic law, not Torah law. With regard to all matters that apply by Torah law, this principle is accurate (see Meiri; Rambam *Sefer Nashim*, *Hilkhot Yibbum VaḤalitza* 1:19).

וְלִיתְנֵי מִן הַיִּיבּוּם וּמִן הַחֲלִיצָה, אִי נַמִּי מִן הַחֲלִיצָה לְחוּדָהּ! אַבָּא שָׁאוּל הִיא, דְּאָמַר: מִצְוַת חֲלִיצָה קוֹדֶמֶת לְמִצְוַת יִיבּוּם.

§ The Gemara further inquires: **And let him teach: From levirate marriage and from *ḥalitza*,** as the Torah states the option of levirate marriage first. **Alternatively,** let him teach: **From *ḥalitza*, alone,** as this would indicate that she may not enter into levirate marriage either. The Gemara answers: **This** mishna **is** in accordance with the opinion of **Abba Shaul, who said: The mitzva of *ḥalitza* takes precedence over the mitzva of levirate marriage,** as he maintains that one who does not enter into levirate marriage for the sake of Heaven transgresses the prohibition against marrying one's brother's wife, and therefore it would be better in every case to perform *ḥalitza*. Consequently, the *tanna* mentions *ḥalitza* before levirate marriage.

מִנְיָנָא דְּרֵישָׁא לְמַעוּטֵי מַאי, וּמִנְיָנָא דְּסֵיפָא לְמַעוּטֵי מַאי?

§ The Gemara asks another question with regard to the language of the mishna: **The enumeration of the first clause** of the mishna: Fifteen women, which indicates that those women alone are included in this list, serves **to exclude what?** Which other cases might have been included? **And the enumeration of the latter clause,** which states: These exempt their rival wives, again meaning these and no others, serves **to exclude what?** Since the mishna specifies only these women and no others, the Gemara asks which other women might have been included in these lists.

Perek **I**
Daf **3** Amud **b**

לְמַעוּטֵי דְּרַב וּדְרַב אַסִי. לְרַב וּלְרַב אַסִי לְמַעוּטֵי מַאי?

The Gemara answers that these enumerations come **to exclude** those additions **of Rav and of Rav Asi.**[N] Rav added the rival wife of a woman suspected by her husband of adultery [*sota*], while Rav Asi added the rival wife of an *aylonit*. The Gemara asks: **And according to** the opinion of **Rav and according to** the opinion of **Rav Asi,** the enumeration of the mishna comes **to exclude what?**

אִי סְבִירָא לְהוּ דַּהֲדָדֵי – חֲדָא לְמַעוּטֵי צָרַת מְמָאֶנֶת, וַחֲדָא: לְמַעוּטֵי צָרַת מַחֲזִיר גְּרוּשָׁתוֹ.

The Gemara responds: **If each maintains** in accordance with the opinion **of the other,** then **one** enumeration of the mishna comes **to exclude the rival wife of a wife who performed refusal.**[N] If the deceased brother had two wives, one of whom was a minor, and she refused the *yavam*, her rival wife is prohibited from levirate marriage with him. However, the latter is not entirely exempt and must perform *ḥalitza*. **And the other one comes to exclude the rival wife** of the wife **of one who remarries his divorcée,**[B] i.e., a woman who was illicitly remarried by her former husband after she had been married to another man.

וְאִי לָא סְבִירָא לְהוּ דַּהֲדָדֵי – חֲדָא לְמַעוּטֵי דְּחַבְרֵיהּ, וַחֲדָא לְמַעוּטֵי אוֹ צָרַת מְמָאֶנֶת אוֹ צָרַת מַחֲזִיר גְּרוּשָׁתוֹ.

And if Rav and Rav Asi **do not** each **maintain** in accordance with the opinion **of the other,** then **one** enumeration comes **to exclude** the opinion **of the other,** as they do not agree that the *halakha* stated by the other should be included in the mishna, **and** the other **one** comes **to exclude** one of the above suggestions, **either the rival wife of** a wife **who performed refusal or the rival wife** of the wife **of one who remarries his divorcée.**

לְרַב וּלְרַב אַסִי לִיתְנִינְהוּ!

The Gemara asks: If so, **according to** the opinion of **Rav and according to** the opinion of **Rav Asi, let** the *tanna* **teach these** cases. Since in their opinions there are more than fifteen women to whom the principle of the mishna applies, why weren't they all stated by the *tanna* of the mishna? The Gemara answers: They were not taught because they do not completely fit all of the halakhic rulings here.

NOTES

To exclude those of Rav and of Rav Asi – לְמַעוּטֵי דְּרַב וּדְרַב אַסִי: Some commentaries ask: Since, as stated later in the Gemara, Rav and Rav Asi concede that the mishna could not have listed their extra cases because the case of a rival wife of a rival wife does not apply, why do they not simply state that the list is indeed coming to exclude their cases for that reason, despite the fact that the mishna agrees in principle with their halakhic ruling (Ramban)? The Ramban claims that the Gemara could indeed have answered in this manner, but it provided a better resolution. Others commentaries discuss whether Rav and Rav Asi in fact exempt these women from both *ḥalitza* and levirate marriage, or whether they obligate them to perform *ḥalitza*, in which case there is no reason to think that they disagree with the *tanna* of the mishna at all.

To exclude the rival wife of a wife who performed refusal – לְמַעוּטֵי צָרַת מְמָאֶנֶת: The Gemara does not state: To exclude the opinion of Shmuel, who is the author of this *halakha* (12a), as the mishna does not in fact dispute Shmuel's *halakha*. The reason is that although Shmuel maintains that the rival wife of a wife who performed refusal is forbidden to the *yavam*, he does not exempt her from *ḥalitza*, whereas the mishna enumerates those cases in which the *yavam* and *yevama* are exempt from both levirate marriage and *ḥalitza* (*Tosefot HaRosh*; see *Tosafot Yeshanim*).

BACKGROUND

One who remarries his divorcée – מַחֲזִיר גְּרוּשָׁתוֹ: The Torah states (Deuteronomy 24:1–4) that if a divorced woman marries another man, she may not remarry her first husband even after her second husband dies or divorces her. This prohibition is not in the category of adulterous or incestuous relationships for which one is liable to receive capital punishment. Rather, it is a regular prohibition.

לְפִי שֶׁאֵינָהּ בְּצָרַת צָרָה.

The Gemara elaborates: This is **because they do not** involve the case **of a rival wife of a rival wife.** With regard to the fifteen women listed, the discussion of the mishna concerning rival wives and rival wives of rival wives is appropriate. However, the two cases cited by Rav and Rav Asi do not leave room for such deliberations, as both a *sota* and an *aylonit* are exempt and forbidden equally to all of the brothers, because their prohibition does not result from a familial relation to one of the living brothers but from a personal issue relating to the women themselves. Since none of the brothers may marry her rival wife, there is no possibility of a rival wife of a rival wife, and consequently these cases were omitted from the mishna's list of fifteen women.

מְנָא הָנֵי מִילֵּי? דְּתָנוּ רַבָּנַן: ״אִשָּׁה אֶל אֲחוֹתָהּ לֹא תִקָּח לִצְרוֹר לְגַלּוֹת עֶרְוָתָהּ עָלֶיהָ בְּחַיֶּיהָ״. ״עָלֶיהָ״ מַה תַּלְמוּד לוֹמַר?

§ After analyzing the order and language of the mishna, the Gemara discusses the *halakhot* themselves. **From where are these matters,**[N] that if one's forbidden relative comes before him for levirate marriage he is prohibited from marrying her or her rival wife, derived? It is **as the Sages taught** with regard to the verse: **"And you shall not take a woman to her sister, to be a rival to her, to uncover her nakedness, with her in her lifetime"** (Leviticus 18:18). **What** is the meaning when **the verse states** the apparently superfluous phrase: **"With her"?**

לְפִי שֶׁנֶּאֱמַר ״יְבָמָהּ יָבֹא עָלֶיהָ״ שׁוֹמֵעַ אֲנִי אֲפִילּוּ בְּאַחַת מִכׇּל עֲרָיוֹת הָאֲמוּרוֹת בַּתּוֹרָה הַכָּתוּב מְדַבֵּר, נֶאֱמַר כָּאן ״עָלֶיהָ״ וְנֶאֱמַר לְהַלָּן ״עָלֶיהָ״,

The *baraita* explains: **Since it is stated** with regard to the wife of a deceased brother: **"Her brother-in-law will have intercourse with her"** (Deuteronomy 25:5), I would **derive** that when **the verse speaks of** the mitzva of levirate marriage, it includes **even any one of those with whom relations are forbidden,** as **mentioned in the Torah.** Therefore, one derives a verbal analogy: **It is stated here,** with regard to a wife's sister: **"With her," and it is stated there,** with regard to a levirate marriage: **"With her."**

מַה לְהַלָּן בִּמְקוֹם מִצְוָה – אַף כָּאן בִּמְקוֹם מִצְוָה, וְאָמַר רַחֲמָנָא ״לֹא תִקָּח״.

The *baraita* explains the verbal analogy. **Just as there,** a levirate marriage involves **the performance of a mitzva, so too, here,** the statement "uncover her nakedness with her" includes **the performance of a mitzva, and the Merciful One states** in the Torah: **"You shall not take."** The phrase "with her" teaches that even in a case where there is an obligation of levirate marriage, the Torah prohibition proscribing forbidden relatives remains in force.

וְאֵין לִי אֶלָּא הִיא, צָרָתָהּ מִנַּיִן? תַּלְמוּד לוֹמַר ״לִצְרוֹר״. וְאֵין לִי אֶלָּא צָרָתָהּ, צָרַת צָרָתָהּ מִנַּיִן? תַּלְמוּד לוֹמַר ״לִצְרוֹר״ וְלֹא ״לָצוֹר״.

The *baraita* continues: **And I have** derived **only** that **she,** his wife's sister, is exempt from levirate marriage; **from where** do I derive that **her rival wife** is also exempt? **The verse states: "To be a rival** to her" (Leviticus 18:18), which indicates that not only is she prohibited, but so too is her rival wife. **And I have** derived **only her rival wife; from where** is it derived that **the rival wife of her rival wife** is also exempt? **The verse states: "To be a rival [*litzror*],"** using the full spelling with a double *reish,* **and not *latzor*;**[N] this indicates that there are several rival wives, one after another.

NOTES

The source of the prohibition in levirate marriage of women with whom relations are forbidden – מְקוֹר אִיסּוּר עֶרְוָה בְּיִיבּוּם: Some commentaries cite an alternative source from the Torah for this *halakha* (Rambam). The verse states: "Take her to him to be his wife and consummate the levirate marriage" (Deuteronomy 25:5), which indicates that the *halakhot* of levirate marriage apply only when there is a possibility of taking, i.e., marriage. Marriage is inapplicable in the case of any relationship that is punishable by *karet,* and therefore there is no mitzva of levirate marriage in that case. The Rambam further derives the prohibition with regard to rival wives from the verse: "Build his brother's house" (Deuteronomy 25:9), from which it may be inferred that he must have the ability to build, i.e., he must be able to marry each of his brother's wives. If one of the wives is forbidden to him, he can build only a part of his brother's house.

It has been noted that when the Rambam suggests interpretations that are not found in the Gemara, his intention is not to dispute the statements of the Sages but to suggest an alternative reason that he feels is more straightforward (see *Or HaHayyim*). However, in this case it is possible that the Rambam bases his opinion on the discussion later in the Gemara (6a–8b), in which it is stated that the interpretation mentioned here is groundless because there is no need for a source in the Torah to teach that it is prohibited to marry forbidden relatives. This indicates that there is room to suggest alternative sources for this basic *halakha* (see *Yam shel Shlomo*).

The verse states: To be a rival [*litzror*] and not *latzor* – לִצְרוֹר וְלֹא לָצוֹר: An alternative version of the text reads: The verse states *tzeror,* i.e., it is a general expression that includes all types of rival wives (Meiri, citing Rif).

וְאֵין לִי אֶלָּא אֲחוֹת אִשָּׁה, שְׁאָר עֲרָיוֹת מִנַּיִין? אָמַרְתָּ: מָה אֲחוֹת אִשָּׁה מְיוּחֶדֶת – שֶׁהִיא עֶרְוָה, וְחַיָּיבִין עַל זְדוֹנָהּ כָּרֵת וְעַל שִׁגְגָתָהּ חַטָּאת, וַאֲסוּרָה לַיָּבָם, אַף כָּל שֶׁהִיא עֶרְוָה, וְחַיָּיבִין עַל זְדוֹנָהּ כָּרֵת וְעַל שִׁגְגָתָהּ חַטָּאת – אֲסוּרָה לַיָּבָם.

And I have derived from this verbal analogy **only** that the mitzva of levirate marriage does not apply to **a wife's sister. From where** is it derived that the same applies to **the other** women **with whom relations are forbidden? You** can **say** as follows: **Just as** the case of **a wife's sister is specific** in **that she is a forbidden relative, and** this is a prohibition **for whose intentional** violation, i.e., for intentional sexual relations with her, **one is liable to** receive ***karet*****, and for whose unwitting** violation one is liable to bring **a sin-offering, and she is prohibited to the** ***yavam*** in levirate marriage; **so too,** with regard to **all** women **with whom relations are forbidden** by a prohibition **for whose intentional** violation **one is liable to** receive ***karet*** **and for whose unwitting** violation one is liable to bring **a sin-offering,** they are **prohibited to the** ***yavam*** in levirate marriage.

וְאֵין לִי אֶלָּא הֵן, צָרוֹתֵיהֶן מִנַּיִין? אָמַרְתָּ: מָה אֲחוֹת אִשָּׁה מְיוּחֶדֶת – שֶׁהִיא עֶרְוָה וְחַיָּיבִין עַל זְדוֹנָהּ כָּרֵת וְעַל שִׁגְגָתָהּ חַטָּאת, וַאֲסוּרָה לַיָּבָם, וְצָרָתָהּ אֲסוּרָה – אַף כָּל שֶׁהִיא עֶרְוָה וְחַיָּיבִין עַל זְדוֹנָהּ כָּרֵת וְעַל שִׁגְגָתָהּ חַטָּאת וַאֲסוּרָה לַיָּבָם צָרָתָהּ אֲסוּרָה. מִכָּאן אָמְרוּ חֲכָמִים: חֲמֵשׁ עֶשְׂרֵה נָשִׁים פּוֹטְרוֹת צָרוֹתֵיהֶן וְצָרוֹת צָרוֹתֵיהֶן מִן הַחֲלִיצָה וּמִן הַיִּיבּוּם עַד סוֹף הָעוֹלָם.

The *baraita* continues: **And I have** derived **only** the cases of **those** women themselves with whom relations are forbidden; **from where** is it derived that **their rival wives** are also exempt from levirate marriage? **You** can **say** as follows: **Just as a wife's sister is specific** in **that she is a forbidden relative and** this is a prohibition **for whose intentional** violation **one is liable to** receive ***karet*****, and for whose unwitting** violation one is liable to bring **a sin-offering,** and she is **prohibited to the** ***yavam*** in levirate marriage, **and her rival wife is** likewise **prohibited; so too, any** woman **with whom relations are forbidden and** this is a prohibition **for whose intentional** violation **one is liable to** receive ***karet*****, and for whose unwitting** violation one is liable to bring **a sin-offering, and** this woman is one **who is forbidden to the** ***yavam*****, her rival wife is** likewise **forbidden.** The *baraita* concludes: **From here the Sages stated** that **fifteen women exempt their rival wives and the rival wives of their rival wives from** ***ḥalitza*** **and from levirate marriage forever.**

יָכוֹל שֶׁאֲנִי מְרַבֶּה אַף שֵׁשׁ עֲרָיוֹת חֲמוּרוֹת מֵאֵלּוּ שֶׁיְּהוּ צָרוֹתֵיהֶם אֲסוּרוֹת!

§ One **might** have thought **that I** should **include** in this principle **even the six** women **with whom relations are forbidden that are more severe than these,** i.e., one's mother, his father's sister, and so on, as stated in a later mishna (13b), since they too are forbidden by a prohibition entailing *karet*. This would mean **that their rival wives should** likewise **be prohibited** to enter into levirate marriage with this *yavam* as forbidden rival wives.

אָמַרְתָּ: מָה אֲחוֹת אִשְׁתּוֹ מְיוּחֶדֶת, שֶׁהִיא עֶרְוָה, וְחַיָּיבִין עַל זְדוֹנָהּ כָּרֵת וְעַל שִׁגְגָתָהּ חַטָּאת, וְאֶפְשָׁר לִינָּשֵׂא לָאַחִים וַאֲסוּרָה לַיָּבָם – וְצָרָתָהּ אֲסוּרָה, אַף כָּל שֶׁהִיא עֶרְוָה, וְחַיָּיבִין עַל זְדוֹנָהּ כָּרֵת וְעַל שִׁגְגָתָהּ חַטָּאת וְאֶפְשָׁר לִינָּשֵׂא לָאַחִים וַאֲסוּרָה לַיָּבָם – צָרָתָהּ אֲסוּרָה.

In response, **you can say: Just as a wife's sister is specific** in **that she is a forbidden relative and** this is a prohibition **for whose intentional** violation **one is liable to** receive ***karet*** **and for whose unwitting** violation one is liable to bring **a sin-offering, and** yet she is **permitted to marry** one of the **brothers but** she is **prohibited to the** ***yavam*** in levirate marriage, **and her rival wife is** likewise **prohibited** in levirate marriage; **so too,** with regard to **any** woman **with whom relations are forbidden and** this is a prohibition **for whose intentional** violation **one is liable to** receive ***karet*** **and for whose unwitting** violation one is liable to bring **a sin-offering, and** who is **permitted to marry** one of the **brothers but** she is **prohibited to the** ***yavam*** in levirate marriage, **her rival wife is** also **prohibited** in levirate marriage.

יָצְאוּ שֵׁשׁ עֲרָיוֹת חֲמוּרוֹת מֵאֵלּוּ, הוֹאִיל דְּאִי אֶפְשָׁר לִינָּשֵׂא לָאַחִים – צָרוֹתֵיהֶן מוּתָּרוֹת, שֶׁאֵין צָרָה אֶלָּא מֵאָח.

This excludes the **six** women **with whom relations are forbidden** by a **more severe** prohibition **than those, since they may not marry the brothers,** i.e., they are forbidden to all of the brothers. One's mother may never marry his brother, either because she is also that brother's mother, or because she is his father's wife. Consequently, **their rival wives are permitted,** as the *halakha* with regard to **a rival wife applies only** due **to the brother.**[N] In other words, the prohibition against marriage to the rival wife of a forbidden relative is applicable only in instances of levirate bonds. When the levirate bond does not take effect at all, the rival wife is not forbidden.

NOTES

The ***halakha*** **with regard to a rival wife applies only due to the brother – אֵין צָרָה אֶלָּא מֵאָח:** This expression explains the aforementioned *halakha*. It means that the Torah renders a rival wife forbidden not due to her status as the rival wife of a forbidden relative, but because she was exempted from levirate marriage along with her rival wife. In other words, she is forbidden to the *yavam* in her own right, as a brother's wife concerning whom there is no mitzva to marry. Consequently, if she were married to someone who does not render her forbidden to the *yavam*, she would not be forbidden at all (*Tosefot HaRosh*).

אַזְהָרָה שָׁמַעְנוּ, עוֹנֶשׁ מִנַּיִין? אָמַר קְרָא ״כִּי כָּל (אִישׁ) אֲשֶׁר יַעֲשֶׂה מִכֹּל הַתּוֹעֵבוֹת״ וגו׳.

The *baraita* adds: **We have learned the warning** concerning this prohibition that the *yavam* may not marry his forbidden relative from the verse: "And you shall not take a woman to her sister, to be a rival to her, to uncover her nakedness, with her in her lifetime" (Leviticus 18:18). **From where**[N] is **the punishment**[N] that he incurs if he transgresses and marries her derived? **The verse states: "For whoever shall do any** of these **abominations,** the souls that do them shall be cut off from among their people" (Leviticus 18:29).

טַעֲמָא דִּכְתַב רַחֲמָנָא ״עָלֶיהָ״, הָא לָאו הָכִי הֲוָה אָמִינָא אֲחוֹת אִשָּׁה מִיַּיבֶּמֶת, מַאי טַעְמָא? דְּאָמְרִינַן: אָתֵי עֲשֵׂה וְדָחֵי לֹא תַעֲשֶׂה,

§ Up until this point, the Gemara has cited the *baraita* that interprets the biblical basis for the *halakha* of the mishna. The Gemara further analyzes the foundational principles of this topic. **The reason** that these women are exempt from levirate marriage is **that the Merciful One writes "with her,"** from which it may be inferred that **if that was not so, I would say** that **a wife's sister enters into levirate marriage** with her sister's husband. **What is the reason** that one would have assumed that this is the case? It is **as we say,** in accordance with a principle, that **a positive** mitzva **comes and overrides a prohibition.**[HB] In this case, the positive mitzva to enter into levirate marriage overrides the prohibition against marrying one's wife's sister.

אֵימַר דְּאָמְרִינַן אָתֵי עֲשֵׂה וְדָחֵי לֹא תַעֲשֶׂה – לֹא תַעֲשֶׂה גְּרֵידָא, לֹא תַעֲשֶׂה שֶׁיֵּשׁ בּוֹ כָּרֵת מִי דָּחֵי? וְתוּ: לֹא תַעֲשֶׂה גְּרֵידָא מְנָלַן דְּדָחֵי?

The Gemara asks if that principle is applicable in this case. One can **say that we said** that **a positive** mitzva **comes and overrides a prohibition** only when there is **a prohibition** for which one is punished by lashes **alone.** However, with regard to **a prohibition that includes** the punishment of ***karet*, does** a positive mitzva **override** it?[N] This prohibition is more severe than a regular one, and therefore perhaps a positive mitzva does not override it. **And furthermore,** with regard to **a prohibition** for which one is punished by lashes **alone, from where do we** derive **that** a positive mitzva **overrides** it?

HALAKHA

A positive mitzva comes and overrides a prohibition – אָתֵי עֲשֵׂה וְדָחֵי לֹא תַעֲשֶׂה: Whenever both a positive mitzva and a prohibition are applicable, the positive mitzva overrides the prohibition (Rambam *Sefer Nashim, Hilkhot Yibbum VaḤalitza* 6:10 and *Sefer Tahara, Hilkhot Tumat Tzara'at* 10:5).

This principle refers to a conflict between a positive mitzva and a regular prohibition. However, some authorities maintain that in cases of a prohibition that entails the punishment of *karet*, the positive mitzva does not override the prohibition. In addition, a positive mitzva does not override both another positive mitzva and a prohibition together.

BACKGROUND

A positive mitzva comes and overrides a prohibition – אָתֵי עֲשֵׂה וְדָחֵי לֹא תַעֲשֶׂה: According to this halakhic principle, the obligation to perform a positive mitzva overrides the prohibition against performing a prohibited act when the two come into conflict. As noted by the Gemara, the source for this principle is the mitzva to wear ritual fringes even when it involves a prohibited mixture of wool and linen. However, the principle does not extend to the performance of a mitzva that conflicts with a severe prohibition, e.g., one that entails the punishment of *karet*.

NOTES

From where, etc. – מִנַּיִין וכו׳: Rashi explains that the Gemara is asking about the punishment both for one who has intercourse with women with whom relations are forbidden as well as one who has intercourse with the rival wives of those women. This is somewhat puzzling, as the punishment for engaging in intercourse with women with whom relations are forbidden is explicitly stated in the Torah. Others maintain that the question refers only to a rival wife (Meiri).

From where is the punishment – עוֹנֶשׁ מִנַּיִן: The early commentaries note that the *tanna* merely inquires as to the source of the punishment, and they ask: Why is he sure that this transgression entails a punishment at all? They explain that certain rulings of *halakha* are accepted by tradition, and therefore the question refers only to the source. Matters that are less clear are investigated in a more fundamental manner, by means of phrases such as: Does this commandment override that one, and the like (*Nimmukei Yosef*; Meiri).

A prohibition that includes *karet*, does it override it – לֹא תַעֲשֶׂה שֶׁיֵּשׁ בּוֹ כָּרֵת מִי דָּחֵי: Some commentaries ask: Doesn't the very concept of levirate marriage itself prove that the positive mitzva to marry one's brother's widow overrides the prohibition against marrying one's brother's wife, which is punishable by *karet* (*Tosafot*)? Their answer is that the mitzva of levirate marriage is applicable solely in the case of a brother's wife, and therefore it necessarily cancels out that prohibition (see Ramah in *Sanhedrin*). This idea is discussed further in the Jerusalem Talmud, where the principle is cited that certain mitzvot were stated simultaneously, i.e., two apparently conflicting mitzvot are actually interdependent. In other words, this is not a case of a positive mitzva overriding a prohibition at all. Rather, from the outset this prohibition was applicable only to a brother's wife who bore children. Consequently, in the case of levirate marriage there is no prohibition whatsoever (see *Kovetz He'arot*).

דִּכְתִיב ״לֹא תִלְבַּשׁ שַׁעַטְנֵז״, ״גְּדִלִים תַּעֲשֶׂה לָּךְ״.

As it is written: "You shall not wear diverse kinds of wool and linen together. **You shall make for yourself twisted fringes** on the four corners of your covering with which you cover yourself" (Deuteronomy 22:11–12). These verses teach that despite the prohibition against wearing diverse kinds of wool and linen, it is permitted to prepare ritual fringes of diverse kinds, e.g., sky-blue dyed threads of wool on linen garments. This shows that the positive mitzva of ritual fringes overrides the prohibition of diverse kinds.

וְאָמַר רַבִּי אֶלְעָזָר: סְמוּכִים מִן הַתּוֹרָה מִנַּיִן – שֶׁנֶּאֱמַר ״סְמוּכִים לָעַד לְעוֹלָם עֲשׂוּיִם בֶּאֱמֶת וְיָשָׁר״.

And Rabbi Elazar said: From where in the Torah is it derived that one may draw homiletical interpretations from the **juxtaposition**[N] of verses? In other words, from where is it derived that the fact that certain verses are adjacent one to the other is a reason to apply the *halakhot* from one verse to the other? **As it is stated:** "The works of His hands in truth and justice, all His commandments are sure. **Juxtaposed forever and ever, made in truth and uprightness**" (Psalms 111:7–8). This verse indicates that it is appropriate to draw inferences from the juxtaposition of God's commandments.

וְאָמַר רַב שֵׁשֶׁת אָמַר רַבִּי אֶלְעָזָר מִשּׁוּם רַבִּי אֶלְעָזָר בֶּן עֲזַרְיָה: מִנַּיִן לִיבָמָה שֶׁנָּפְלָה לִפְנֵי מוּכֵּה שְׁחִין שֶׁאֵין חוֹסְמִין אוֹתָהּ – שֶׁנֶּאֱמַר ״לֹא תַחְסוֹם שׁוֹר בְּדִישׁוֹ״ וּסְמִיךְ לֵיהּ ״כִּי יֵשְׁבוּ אַחִים יַחְדָּיו״.

And similarly, **Rav Sheshet said** that **Rabbi Elazar said in the name of Rabbi Elazar ben Azarya: From where** is it derived with regard **to a** *yevama* **who came before** a *yavam* **afflicted with boils**[H] **that one may not muzzle her,**[N] i.e., she cannot be forced to enter into levirate marriage, and he is compelled to release her by *ḥalitza*? **As it is stated: "You shall not muzzle an ox while it treads out the corn"** (Deuteronomy 25:4), **and, juxtaposed to it,** is the verse: **"If brothers dwell together"** (Deuteronomy 25:5), which begins the passage that deals with the *halakhot* of levirate marriage. This teaches that just as it is prohibited to muzzle the ox, so too, one may not muzzle and ignore the complaints of a *yevama* who does not wish to marry a *yavam* afflicted with boils.

וְאָמַר רַב יוֹסֵף: אֲפִילּוּ לְמַאן דְּלָא דָּרֵישׁ סְמוּכִים בְּעָלְמָא – בְּמִשְׁנֵה תוֹרָה דָּרֵישׁ, דְּהָא רַבִּי יְהוּדָה בְּעָלְמָא לָא דָּרֵישׁ, וּבְמִשְׁנֵה תוֹרָה דָּרֵישׁ.

And Rav Yosef said: Even according to the one who does not generally derive homiletic interpretations from juxtaposed verses, nevertheless, he does **derive** them **from Deuteronomy, as Rabbi Yehuda does not generally derive homiletic interpretations** from juxtaposed verses,[N] **and** yet **he does derive** them **from Deuteronomy.**[N]

וּבְעָלְמָא מְנָלַן דְּלָא דָּרֵישׁ? דְּתַנְיָא, בֶּן עַזַּאי אוֹמֵר: נֶאֱמַר ״מְכַשֵּׁפָה לֹא תְחַיֶּה״ וְנֶאֱמַר ״כָּל שׁוֹכֵב עִם בְּהֵמָה מוֹת יוּמָת״, סָמְכוּ עִנְיָן לוֹ, מַה שּׁוֹכֵב עִם בְּהֵמָה בִּסְקִילָה – אַף מְכַשֵּׁפָה בִּסְקִילָה.

§ The Gemara asks: **And from where do we** derive that Rabbi Yehuda **generally does not derive homiletic interpretations** from juxtaposed verses? **As it is taught** in a *baraita* with regard to the punishment of a sorceress that **ben Azzai says** that **it is stated: "You shall not allow a sorceress to live"** (Exodus 22:17), although the manner of her execution is not specified, **and it is stated: "Whoever lies with a beast shall surely be put to death"** (Exodus 22:18). The Torah **juxtaposed this matter to that** so as to say: **Just as one who lies with a beast** is executed **by stoning** (see Leviticus 20:16), **so too, a sorceress** is executed **by stoning.**[H]

אָמַר לוֹ רַבִּי יְהוּדָה: וְכִי מִפְּנֵי שֶׁסָּמְכוּ עִנְיָן לוֹ נוֹצִיא זֶה לִסְקִילָה?

With regard to this proof, **Rabbi Yehuda said to** ben Azzai: **And** simply **due to** the fact **that** the Torah **juxtaposed this matter to that** one, **shall we take this** person **out to be stoned?** Should he be sentenced to the most severe of the death penalties on the basis of a juxtaposition of passages?

אֶלָּא אוֹב וְיִדְּעוֹנִי בִּכְלַל מְכַשְּׁפִים הָיוּ, וְלָמָּה יָצְאוּ – לְהַקִּישׁ לָהֶם, וְלוֹמַר לָךְ: מָה אוֹב וְיִדְּעוֹנִי בִּסְקִילָה – אַף מְכַשֵּׁפָה בִּסְקִילָה.

Rather, Rabbi Yehuda claims that the source is the following statement: **Mediums and wizards**[B] **were included among all sorcerers. And why were they singled out** from the rest in the verse: "And a man or a woman who is a medium or a wizard shall surely be put to death; they shall stone them with stones, their blood is upon them" (Leviticus 20:27)? It is to **draw an analogy to them and say to you: Just as a medium and a wizard** are executed **by stoning, so too, a sorceress** is executed **by stoning.** This shows that Rabbi Yehuda does not derive homiletic interpretations from juxtaposed verses.

NOTES

Deriving from juxtaposed verses – דְּרִישַׁת סְמוּכִים: The dispute over deriving homiletic interpretations from juxtaposed verses arises when two verses are stated next to each other. The question is whether or not to draw conclusions based on the proximity of the verses. However, when two *halakhot* appear in the same verse, even if there is no essential connection between them, it is clear that they were brought together so that one would learn from the juxtaposition. This is called the exegetical principle of juxtaposition and is considered nearly as authoritative as an explicit statement in the Torah (Ra'avad).

That one may not muzzle her – שֶׁאֵין חוֹסְמִין אוֹתָהּ: In other words, one may not muzzle and ignore her claims. If the *yavam* has a defect that would have been grounds for divorce had she been his wife, he does not first enter into levirate marriage and then divorce her. Rather, her claim is accepted and he must perform *ḥalitza* (Rashba).

The dispute over inferring from juxtaposed verses – הַמַּחְלוֹקֶת בִּדְרִישַׁת סְמוּכִים: Some commentaries claim that this dispute with regard to deriving homiletic interpretations from juxtaposed verses is connected to the dispute as to whether the Torah was given at once or scroll by scroll, each at a different time (*Gittin* 60a). If the Torah was given on a single occasion, it stands to reason that conclusions may be drawn from the connections between passages. However, if the Torah was given scroll by scroll, each passage stands on its own, as it is unknown how the scrolls were originally divided (Rabbi Tzvi Hirsch Chajes).

He does derive in Deuteronomy – בְּמִשְׁנֵה תוֹרָה דָּרֵישׁ: Apparently, Rabbi Yehuda maintains that for a *halakha* to be derived by homiletic interpretation from juxtaposed verses, the matter must be evident, as discussed later in the Gemara. Some commentaries claim that the entire Torah, except for Deuteronomy, is considered one long passage. Consequently, nothing can be proven from juxtapositions, as it all constitutes one single subject (Ramban). Others write that since the rest of the Torah was composed directly by God, one cannot fully understand the reasoning behind its order, whereas Deuteronomy, which was arranged by Moses, was most certainly ordered by subject matter. Therefore, one can derive interpretations from juxtaposed verses in Deuteronomy.

HALAKHA

A *yevama* who came before a *yavam* afflicted with boils – יְבָמָה שֶׁנָּפְלָה לִפְנֵי מוּכֵּה שְׁחִין: With regard to a *yevama* who came for levirate marriage before a *yavam* who is afflicted with boils, or has any other defect on account of which a wife may demand a divorce, she cannot be forced to enter into levirate marriage. Instead he performs *ḥalitza* and she receives the payment of her original marriage contract from her first husband's estate (*Shulḥan Arukh, Even HaEzer* 165:4).

The punishment of a sorcerer – עוֹנֶשׁ מְכַשֵּׁף: A sorcerer or sorceress who performed sorcery is punished by stoning (Rambam *Sefer Shofetim, Hilkhot Sanhedrin* 15:10).

BACKGROUND

Mediums and wizards – אוֹב וְיִדְּעוֹנִי: The Torah prohibits all forms of witchcraft, and condemns to death those who practice these arts. Mediums and wizards were people who claimed to have the power to call upon the dead to learn about secrets unknown to ordinary men, including glimpses into the future. Although some of the early commentaries believed that the future could indeed be foretold by these people, the Rambam rejects these opinions and argues that turning to mediums is prohibited specifically because these powers do not exist at all.

וּבְמִשְׁנֵה תּוֹרָה מְנָלַן דְּדָרֵישׁ – דִּתְנַן: נוֹשֵׂא אָדָם אֲנוּסַת אָבִיו וּמְפוּתַּת אָבִיו, אֲנוּסַת בְּנוֹ וּמְפוּתַּת בְּנוֹ. רַבִּי יְהוּדָה אוֹסֵר בַּאֲנוּסַת אָבִיו וּמְפוּתַּת אָבִיו

§ **And from where do we** derive **that** Rabbi Yehuda **does derive** homiletic interpretations **in Deuteronomy? As we learned** in a mishna: **A person may wed** a woman **raped by his father**[H] **and** one **seduced by his father,** despite the fact that his father's wife is forbidden to him. Similarly, he may marry a woman **raped by his** son **and** one **seduced by his son.** Although one is prohibited by Torah law from marrying the wife of his father or the wife of his son, these prohibitions do not apply to a woman raped or seduced by them. **And Rabbi Yehuda prohibits** him from marrying **a woman raped by his father and a woman seduced by his father.**

וְאָמַר רַב גִּידֵּל אָמַר רַב: מַאי טַעְמָא דְּרַבִּי יְהוּדָה – דִּכְתִיב ״לֹא יִקַּח אִישׁ אֶת אֵשֶׁת אָבִיו וְלֹא יְגַלֶּה כְּנַף אָבִיו״ כָּנָף שֶׁרָאָה אָבִיו לֹא יְגַלֶּה.

And Rav Giddel said that Rav said: What is the reason for Rabbi Yehuda's** opinion? **As it is written: "A man shall not take his father's wife, and shall not uncover his father's skirt"** (Deuteronomy 23:1). The latter expression: "And shall not uncover his father's skirt," is referring to **a skirt that has been seen by his father,** i.e., any woman who has had relations with his father **may not be uncovered** by his son, meaning that his son may not marry her.

וּמִמַּאי דְּבַאֲנוּסָה כְּתִיב – מֵעִילָּוֵיהּ דִּקְרָא, דִּכְתִיב ״וְנָתַן הָאִישׁ הַשּׁוֹכֵב עִמָּהּ לַאֲבִי הַנַּעֲרָה חֲמִשִּׁים כָּסֶף״ וּסְמִיךְ לֵיהּ ״לֹא יִקַּח אִישׁ״ וגו׳.

And from where is it known **that** the verse **is written with regard to a woman raped by his father?** It is **from the previous** verse, which deals with the *halakhot* of rape, **as it is written: "And the man who lay with her must give the maiden's father fifty shekels of silver"** (Deuteronomy 22:29), **and juxtaposed to it** is the verse: **"A man shall not take his father's wife** and shall not uncover his father's skirt." This shows that Rabbi Yehuda does derive homiletic interpretations from juxtaposed verses in Deuteronomy.

וְרַבָּנַן: אִי הֲוָה סְמִיךְ לֵיהּ – כִּדְקָאָמְרַתְּ, הָשְׁתָּא דְּלָא סְמִיךְ לֵיהּ (דִּכְתִיב ״לֹא יִקַּח אִישׁ אֶת אֵשֶׁת אָבִיו״ בֵּינְתַיִם) –

§ The Gemara asks: **And** how do **the Rabbis,**[N] who disagree with the opinion of Rabbi Yehuda, respond to this argument? They say: **If** the two verses were fully **juxtaposed,** it would be interpreted **as you said.** However, **now** that **it is not** properly **juxtaposed, as it is written: "A man shall not take his father's wife," in between** the *halakhot* of rape and the pronouncement with regard to uncovering one's father's garment, this serves to break the juxtaposition.

בְּשׁוֹמֶרֶת יָבָם הַכָּתוּב מְדַבֵּר, וְלַעֲבוֹר עָלָיו בִּשְׁנֵי לָאוִין.

Consequently, this particular **verse** concerning the uncovering of one's father's garment **is speaking of a woman waiting for her *yavam*,** in this case one's father.[N] In other words, the *yevama* of a father who is waiting for levirate marriage to the father is already considered "his father's skirt," and she is therefore forbidden to the son. Although this woman who is awaiting levirate marriage is in fact his uncle's wife and explicitly prohibited to him in any case, this passage comes to teach that **he violates two prohibitions.** In other words, were he to engage in relations with her he would be penalized both for relations with his uncle's wife and relations with "his father's skirt."

וּבְמִשְׁנֵה תּוֹרָה מַאי טַעְמָא דְּדָרֵישׁ? אִיבָּעֵית אֵימָא מִשּׁוּם דְּמוּכָח, וְאִיבָּעֵית אֵימָא מִשּׁוּם דְּמוּפְנֵי.

§ The Gemara asks: **But** as Rabbi Yehuda does not generally derive homiletic interpretations from juxtaposed verses, **what is the reason that he derives** these interpretations **in Deuteronomy?**[N] The Gemara responds: **If you wish, say** that it is **because** it **is evident** from the context; **and if you wish, say** instead that it is **because** this verse is extraneous and is therefore **free** for this inference.

אִיבָּעֵית אֵימָא מִשּׁוּם דְּמוּכָח – דְּאִם כֵּן, לִכְתְּבֵיהּ רַחֲמָנָא גַּבֵּי עֲרָיוֹת. וְאִיבָּעֵית אֵימָא מִשּׁוּם דְּמוּפְנֵי, דְּאִם כֵּן, לִכְתּוֹב רַחֲמָנָא ״לֹא יִקַּח אִישׁ אֶת אֵשֶׁת אָבִיו״, ״לֹא יְגַלֶּה כְּנַף אָבִיו״ לָמָּה לִי?

The Gemara elaborates: **If you wish, say** it is **because** it **is evident; as, if** it is **so** that the verse did not intend to teach by juxtaposition, **let the Merciful One write** this *halakha* prohibiting marriage to a father's wife **alongside** the other women **with whom relations are forbidden,** in Leviticus. Since this verse is out of place, it is certainly coming to teach by way of juxtaposition. **And if you wish, say** instead that it is **because** this verse is **free, as, if** it is **so** that the verse is not coming to teach an additional *halakha,* **let the Merciful One write** only: **"A man shall not take his father's wife." Why do I** need the phrase: **"And shall not uncover his father's skirt"?** This phrase is superfluous, and therefore it teaches by juxtaposition.

HALAKHA

A woman raped by one's father – אֲנוּסַת אָבִיו: It is permitted for one to marry a woman raped or seduced by his father (Rambam *Sefer Kedusha, Hilkhot Issurei Bia* 2:13; *Shulḥan Arukh, Even HaEzer* 15:5; see *Beit Yosef* on *Tur, Even HaEzer* 15).

NOTES

The interpretation of the Rabbis with regard to: Shall not uncover – דְּרָשַׁת חֲכָמִים בְּעִנְיַן לֹא יְגַלֶּה: It is puzzling that the Rabbis, who derive homiletic interpretations from juxtaposed verses throughout the Torah, would not do so here, when even Rabbi Yehuda explains the verses in this manner. The answer is that in fact the Rabbis do interpret the juxtaposition here as well; however, they maintain that it teaches a different matter, namely the definition of a *mamzer*, which is a son born from an incestuous or adulterous relationship. They reject Rabbi Yehuda's explanation because the two matters to which he refers are not truly juxtaposed (Rashba; Ritva).

A woman waiting for her *yavam*, who is his father – שׁוֹמֶרֶת יָבָם שֶׁל אָבִיו: The Rabbis claim that it is evident from the context of the passage that the verse is speaking about a woman awaiting levirate marriage. The reason is that the first part of the verse refers to marriage, and therefore it stands to reason that the second part is referring to some form of marriage as well (Meiri). Others add that there is an allusion to this claim in the book of Ruth (3:9), where it is stated, with regard to a situation similar to a levirate marriage: "Spread your skirt over your handmaid" (Rashash).

When does Rabbi Yehuda derive interpretations from juxtaposed verses – מָתַי דּוֹרֵשׁ רַבִּי יְהוּדָה סְמוּכִים: The commentaries explain that Rabbi Yehuda derives homiletic interpretations from juxtaposed verses only when two conditions are met: It must be evident that the verse is coming for this purpose, as it is out of place, and the verse must be superfluous in the context (*Tosafot* on *Sukka* 31a).

NOTES

Ritual fringes as well, it is free and it is evident – צִיצִית נַמִי מוּפְנֶה וּמוּכָח: Some commentaries say that this statement is in accordance with the opinion of Rabbi Yehuda, who derives homiletical interpretations from a juxtaposed verse only if it is free in its context and the juxtaposition is evident. Others maintain that this opinion is unanimous, as it was necessary that this particular case of ritual fringes fulfill both parameters for it to serve as the source of the principle that one derives interpretations from juxtaposed verses in the entire Torah (Ramban).

And even sellers of coverings – וַאֲפִילּוּ מוֹכְרֵי כְסוּת: Rashi explains that as the sellers of coverings do not intend to derive benefit from their merchandise, they may wear a mixture of linen and wool. Several early commentaries remark that this is correct only according to those authorities who accept the opinion that an unintentional act is not prohibited. However, this opinion is a matter of dispute among the *tanna'im*. Consequently, the Gemara must be referring to sellers of garments during the summer months, when no benefit is derived from the coverings at all.

שְׁמַע מִינַּהּ לְאַפְנוּיֵי. וְגַבֵּי צִיצִית נַמִי, אִיבָּעֵית אֵימָא מִשּׁוּם דְּמוּכָח, וְאִיבָּעֵית אֵימָא מִשּׁוּם דְּמוּפְנֶה.

Learn from this that this phrase is **free** to teach an additional *halakha*. **And with regard to ritual fringes as well,** there is a particular reason to derive a homiletic interpretation from the juxtaposition of verses. **If you wish, say** that it is **because** it **is evident** from the context, **and if you wish, say** instead that it is **because** this verse is **free**[N] for this inference.

אִיבָּעֵית אֵימָא מִשּׁוּם דְּמוּכָח – דְּאִם כֵּן לִכְתְּבֵיהּ רַחֲמָנָא גַּבֵּי פָּרָשַׁת צִיצִית, לְמַאי הִלְכְתָא כְּתָבֵיהּ הָכָא. וְאִיבָּעֵית אֵימָא מִשּׁוּם דְּמוּפְנֶה, מִכְּדֵי כְּתַב ״וּבֶגֶד כִּלְאַיִם שַׁעַטְנֵז לֹא יַעֲלֶה עָלֶיךָ״, ״לֹא תִלְבַּשׁ שַׁעַטְנֵז״ לָמָּה לִי? שְׁמַע מִינַּהּ לְאַפְנוּיֵי.

The Gemara elaborates: **If you wish, say** it is **because** it **is evident; as, if** it is **so** that no inference should be drawn from the adjacent verses, **let the Merciful One write** this verse **by the portion of ritual fringes** (Numbers, chapter 15). With regard **to what *halakha*** did the Torah **write it here?** Clearly, the Torah is teaching a *halakha* from the adjacent verses. **And if you wish, say** it is **because** this verse is **free, since** the Torah has already **written: "Neither shall there come upon you a garment of diverse kinds mingled together"** (Leviticus 19:19). **Why,** then, **do I** need the verse: **"You shall not wear diverse kinds,** wool and linen together" (Deuteronomy 22:11)? **Learn from this that** the verse is **free** for the derivation of a homiletic interpretation from juxtaposed verses.

הָנֵי מִצְרָךְ צְרִיכִי; דְּאִי כְּתַב רַחֲמָנָא ״לֹא יַעֲלֶה עָלֶיךָ״ הֲוָה אָמֵינָא: כׇּל דֶּרֶךְ הַעֲלָאָה אָסַר רַחֲמָנָא, וַאֲפִילּוּ מוֹכְרֵי כְסוּת – כְּתַב רַחֲמָנָא ״לֹא תִלְבַּשׁ שַׁעַטְנֵז״ דּוּמְיָא דִּלְבִישָׁה דְּאִית בֵּיהּ הֲנָאָה,

The Gemara rejects this explanation: Both of **these** verses **are necessary, as, had the Merciful One written** only: **"Neither shall there come upon you," I would say** that **the Merciful One prohibits every manner by** which a garment of diverse kinds **comes upon** you,[H] **and** this applies **even** to **sellers of coverings,**[NH] who do not wear the garments but merely rest them on their shoulders. Therefore, **the Merciful One writes: "You shall not wear diverse kinds,"** to teach that the prohibition applies only in cases **similar to wearing, which provides benefit**[H] and does not simply involve placing the covering upon oneself.

וְאִי כְּתַב רַחֲמָנָא ״לֹא תִלְבַּשׁ״ הֲוָה אָמֵינָא: דַּוְקָא לְבִישָׁה דְּנָפֵישׁ הֲנָיָיתָהּ, אֲבָל הַעֲלָאָה לָא – כְּתַב רַחֲמָנָא ״לֹא יַעֲלֶה עָלֶיךָ״ –

And had the Merciful One written only: **"You shall not wear," I would say** that this means **specifically wearing, which** provides **significant benefit,** both warmth and adornment, **but** merely **placing** a garment of diverse kinds upon oneself is **not** prohibited, even if one is warmed by the clothing. Therefore, **the Merciful One writes: "Neither shall there come upon you."**

אִם כֵּן לִכְתּוֹב רַחֲמָנָא ״לֹא תִלְבַּשׁ שַׁעַטְנֵז״, ״צֶמֶר וּפִשְׁתִּים״ לָמָּה לִי?

The Gemara challenges: In any case part of the verse is superfluous, as, **if so, let the Merciful One write** only: **"You shall not wear diverse kinds." Why do I** need the addition of **"wool and linen"?** The definition of diverse kinds in clothing is already known from another source.

HALAKHA

The Merciful One prohibits every manner by which a garment of diverse kinds comes upon you – כׇּל דֶּרֶךְ הַעֲלָאָה אָסַר רַחֲמָנָא: By Torah law it is prohibited only to wear or place upon oneself coverings of diverse kinds of wool and linen, whereas it is permitted to sit or lie upon them. However, the Sages prohibited this practice as well (*Shulḥan Arukh, Yoreh De'a* 301:1).

Sellers of coverings – מוֹכְרֵי כְסוּת: Sellers of garments may place upon themselves mixtures of wool and linen as they do other garments. The reason for this leniency is that they do not intend to benefit from their protection from sun or the rain, and therefore they are not using the garments in the manner of a covering. Those who are careful in the performance of mitzvot hang them on a stick. It is prohibited to wear these garments even if one does not intend to derive benefit from the act of wearing itself, e.g., to check measurements (Rambam). However, some authorities permit this (Rema, citing Rosh and Rabbi Shimshon of Saens; *Shulḥan Arukh, Yoreh De'a* 301:6).

Wearing, which provides benefit – לְבִישָׁה דְּאִית בֵּיהּ הֲנָאָה: The prohibition of diverse kinds applies only to garments that provide warmth, e.g., a tunic, trousers, or a hat. However, objects that are not made for this purpose, such as a wallet for holding money, are not included in the prohibition against diverse kinds (*Shulḥan Arukh, Yoreh De'a* 301:14).

מִכְּדֵי כְּתַב ״וּבֶגֶד כִּלְאַיִם שַׁעַטְנֵז לֹא יַעֲלֶה עָלֶיךָ״ וְתָנָא דְּבֵי רַבִּי יִשְׁמָעֵאל: הוֹאִיל וְנֶאֶמְרוּ בַּתּוֹרָה סְתָם ״בְּגָדִים״ וּפָרַט לְךָ הַכָּתוּב בְּאֶחָד מֵהֶן ״צֶמֶר וּפִשְׁתִּים״ אַף כָּל צֶמֶר וּפִשְׁתִּים. צֶמֶר וּפִשְׁתִּים דִּכְתַב רַחֲמָנָא לָמָּה לִי? שְׁמַע מִינָּה לְאַפְנוּיֵי.

How so? **Since it is written: "Neither shall there come upon you a garment of diverse kinds mingled together"** (Leviticus 19:19), **and the school of Rabbi Yishmael taught: Since** the word **garments is stated in the Torah unmodified,** without stating from what materials those garments were made, **and the verse specified in one of** its references to garments, in the context of the *halakhot* of ritual impurity of leprosy: **"A woolen garment or a linen garment"** (Leviticus 13:47), the following conclusion can be drawn: Just as when the Torah mentions a garment in the case of leprosy it is referring to one made of wool or linen,[H] **so too, all** garments mentioned in the Torah are those made from **wool or linen.**[H] Other fabrics are not classified as those used for garments. If so, **why do I** need the phrase: **"Wool and linen" that the Merciful One wrote** with regard to diverse kinds? **Learn from this that** the superfluous passage is **free.**

וְאַכַּתִּי אִיצְטְרִיךְ, סָלְקָא דַּעְתָּךְ אָמִינָא: הַעֲלָאָה הִיא, דְּלָא נָפֵישׁ הֲנָאָתָהּ, אֲבָל לְבִישָׁה דִּנְפֵישׁ הֲנָיָיתָהּ – כָּל תְּרֵי מִינֵי אָסַר רַחֲמָנָא, כְּתַב רַחֲמָנָא ״צֶמֶר וּפִשְׁתִּים״.

The Gemara raises a difficulty: **But** the verse is **still necessary,** as it could **enter your mind to say** that it **is** referring only to **placing** a garment on oneself, **which does not** provide **great benefit; however,** with regard to the actual **wearing** of a garment, **which** entails **great benefit, the Merciful One prohibits** wearing **any two types** together. Therefore, **the Merciful One writes "wool and linen"** with regard to wearing garments of diverse kinds as well.

אִם כֵּן לִשְׁתּוֹק קְרָא מִינֵּיהּ, וְתֵיתֵי ״שַׁעַטְנֵז״ ״שַׁעַטְנֵז״ מֵהַעֲלָאָה.

The Gemara responds: **If so, let the verse be silent** and refrain **from** mentioning wool and linen at all, **and** the *halakha* that only wearing wool and linen together is prohibited can **be derived** by means of a verbal analogy between the terms **"diverse kinds"** (Deuteronomy 22:11), and **"diverse kinds"** from **placing**[N] a covering of diverse kinds upon oneself (Leviticus 19:19). The repetition of wool and linen must be coming to teach that one should derive a homiletic interpretation from these juxtaposed verses.

וְתָנָא דְּבֵי רַבִּי יִשְׁמָעֵאל, טַעְמָא דִּכְתַב רַחֲמָנָא צֶמֶר וּפִשְׁתִּים, הָא לָאו הָכִי – כִּלְאַיִם בְּצִיצִית הֲוָה אָמִינָא דְּאָסַר רַחֲמָנָא? וְהָכְתִיב ״וְעָשׂוּ לָהֶם צִיצִית עַל כַּנְפֵי בִגְדֵיהֶם״,

The Gemara asks: **And** according to that which **the school of Rabbi Yishmael taught,** that the mention of wool and linen is superfluous and teaches that they are not prohibited in the case of ritual fringes, **the reason** is **that the Merciful One** specifically **writes wool and linen.** From here it may be inferred **that if that were not so, I would say that the Merciful One prohibits** a mixture of **diverse kinds in ritual fringes.** Can it be considered that this is the case? **But isn't it written: "That they make themselves fringes on the corners of their garments"** (Numbers 15:38)?[N]

HALAKHA

When does the prohibition of diverse kinds apply – בְּמָה יֵשׁ אִיסּוּר שַׁעַטְנֵז: The prohibition of diverse kinds applies only to wool mixed together with linen by Torah law. The Sages, however, prohibited several other kinds, due to the appearance of prohibition (Rambam *Sefer Zera'im*, *Hilkhot Kilayim* 10:1).

The types of clothing that require ritual fringes – סוּגֵי בְגָדִים הַחַיָּבִים בְּצִיצִית: By Torah law, one is obligated to attach ritual fringes only to garments made of linen or lamb's wool (Rif; Rambam). This ruling is in accordance with the opinion of Rav Naḥman (*Menaḥot* 39b). However, some authorities claim that the biblical mitzva to place ritual fringes applies to every type of fabric (Rema, citing *Tosafot*; Rosh; *Sefer Mitzvot Gadol*). These commentaries accept the opinion of Rava in tractate *Menaḥot*.

It is preferable for a God-fearing person to wear a four-cornered garment made of wool, so as to fulfill his obligation according to all opinions *ab initio* (*Mishna Berura*, citing *Eliyahu Rabba*; *Shulḥan Arukh*, *Oraḥ Ḥayyim* 9:1).

NOTES

And it can be derived by means of…diverse kinds from placing – וְתֵיתֵי...שַׁעַטְנֵז מֵהַעֲלָאָה: It could be argued that the phrase "diverse kinds" is not free in one place. As a result, this is a verbal analogy that is not free on both sides, and verbal analogies of this kind can be refuted if there is a logical argument against them. This is certainly the case here, since there is a difference between the benefit of covering and that of wearing, as stated in the Gemara. Some commentaries answer that this passage is in accordance with the opinion of Rabbi Yishmael, who maintains that one can derive verbal analogies even if they are free on only one side (*Tosefot HaRosh*, citing Maharam of Rothenberg). Some explain that this is not a proper verbal analogy at all but rather an attempt to learn about an unclear case from a more explicit one.

On the corners of their garments, etc. – עַל כַּנְפֵי בִגְדֵיהֶם וכו׳: Some say that the plural form: "Their garments," alludes to two kinds of garments, both wool and linen (Meiri).

BACKGROUND

Sky-blue – תְּכֵלֶת: The color sky-blue is mentioned several times in the Torah. However, this is not the name of a hue, like red or black, but a certain type of dyed material, similar to wool dyed scarlet or purple.

Sky-blue dye was extracted from a type of snail called a *ḥilazon*. Already in the talmudic period, the use of sky-blue dye was very rare, and in later generations the identity of the *ḥilazon* became uncertain. Many contemporary researchers believe that this dye was extracted in a special process from the species *Murex trunculus* found in the Mediterranean Sea. Others have suggested the common cuttlefish, *Sepia officinalis*, and the raft snail, *Janthina*.

Although this is not explicitly stated in the Torah, apparently all of the dyed fabrics to which it refers, i.e., sky-blue, purple, and scarlet, were prepared from wool. It is possible that these dyes could not be absorbed in linen threads at all.

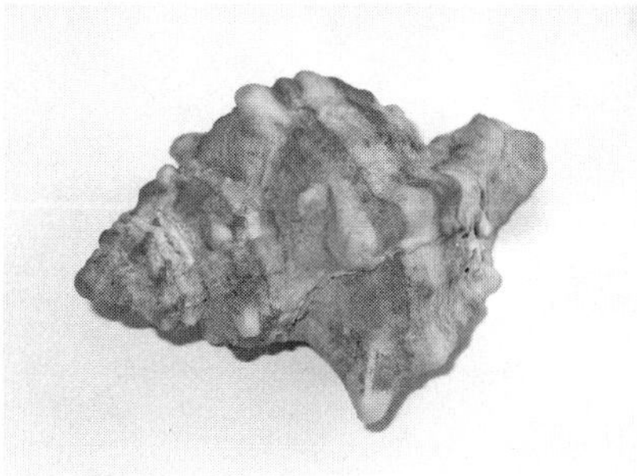

Murex trunculus

Common cuttlefish

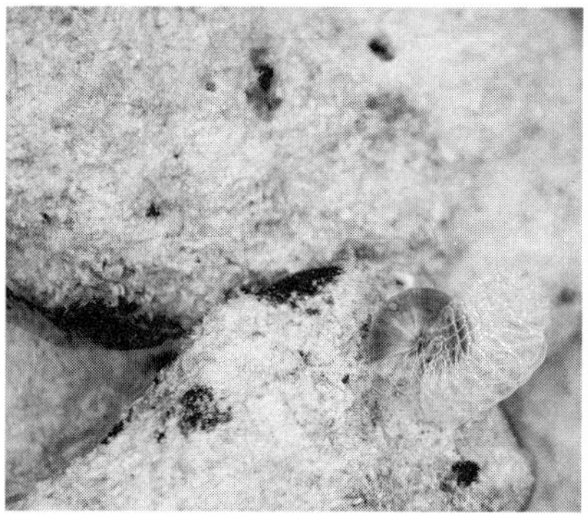

Raft snail

NOTES

From the fact that *shesh* means linen, other threads including sky-blue are wool – מִדְּשֵׁשׁ כִּיתָּנָא תְּכֵלֶת עַמְרָא הוּא: Some commentaries cite an additional allusion from the verse: "And no wool shall come upon them" (Ezekiel 44:17), from which it may be inferred that the other priestly clothes are prepared from wool alone.

וְתָנָא דְּבֵי רַבִּי יִשְׁמָעֵאל: כׇּל בְּגָדִים צֶמֶר וּפִשְׁתִּים הֵם, וְאָמַר רַחֲמָנָא: עֲבֵיד לֵיהּ תְּכֵלֶת, וּתְכֵלֶת עַמְרָא הוּא. וּמִמַּאי דִּתְכֵלֶת עַמְרָא הוּא? מִדְּשֵׁשׁ כִּיתָּנָא – תְּכֵלֶת עַמְרָא הוּא.

And the school of Rabbi Yishmael taught: All garments mentioned in the Torah **are of wool or linen, and the Merciful One says,** with regard to ritual fringes: **Prepare it**[H] with **a sky-blue**[B] dye,[H] **and a sky-blue** dyed **thread is** prepared from **wool.** The Torah explicitly commands that at least one woolen thread of sky-blue dye must be tied even to a linen cloth, which proves that diverse kinds are permitted in the context of ritual fringes. The Gemara establishes the previous claim: **And from where** is it derived **that the sky-blue** thread is made of **wool? From** the fact that the Torah specifies that one of the strands of the priestly garments was made **of *shesh*,** which means **linen,** this indicates that the other threads, including the **sky-blue** thread, **are** from **wool.**[N]

אִיצְטְרִיךְ, סָלְקָא דַּעְתָּךְ אָמִינָא כִּדְרָבָא. דְּרָבָא רָמֵי: כְּתִיב ״הַכָּנָף״ – מִין כָּנָף, וּכְתִיב ״צֶמֶר וּפִשְׁתִּים״!

§ Returning to the question, the Gemara explains that the mention of wool and linen **is necessary,** as it could **enter your mind to state** an argument **in accordance with** the opinion of **Rava. As Rava raised a contradiction** from the following verse: **It is written:** "That they make themselves fringes on the corners of their garments" (Numbers 15:38). The phrase **"the corners"** indicates that it must be from the same **type** of thread as the **corner,** i.e., the threads of the fringes must consist of the same kind of material as the corner of the garment. **And yet it is written: "Wool and linen"** (Deuteronomy 22:11), which indicates that ritual fringes may be prepared from only those materials and no others.

הָא כֵּיצַד? צֶמֶר וּפִשְׁתִּים פּוֹטְרִין בֵּין בְּמִינָן בֵּין שֶׁלֹּא בְּמִינָן, שְׁאָר מִינִין, בְּמִינָן פּוֹטְרִין, שֶׁלֹּא בְּמִינָן – אֵין פּוֹטְרִין.

How so? How can this contradiction be resolved? Fringes made of **wool and linen fulfill** the obligation of ritual fringes **whether** the clothing is of **the same type** of material, i.e., wool or linen, **or** whether it is **not of the same type**[H] of fabric. Conversely, with regard to all **other kinds** of material, if the ritual fringes are **of the same kind,** e.g., silk fringes on silk clothing, **they fulfill** the obligation, but if the cloth is **not of the same type, they do not fulfill** the obligation of ritual fringes. Consequently, were it not for the phrase "wool and linen," it would have been necessary to prepare ritual fringes from the same material as the garment itself, even when using wool or linen.

HALAKHA

Diverse kinds in ritual fringes – כִּלְאַיִם בְּצִיצִית: In principle, it is permitted to prepare ritual fringes from diverse kinds of wool and linen. However, as nowadays the sky-blue dye has not been identified with certainty, wool fringes may not be used for linen garments, and all the more so, linen fringes, which cannot be used for the sky-blue dye, may not be placed on woolen garments (*Shulḥan Arukh, Oraḥ Ḥayyim* 9:2).

Prepare it with a sky-blue dye – עֲבֵיד לֵיהּ תְּכֵלֶת: The Torah commands that one must place a wool thread dyed sky-blue on one's fringes. Nowadays there is uncertainty as to the identity of this sky-blue dye, and therefore this obligation is fulfilled with white threads alone, as stated in tractate *Menaḥot*. Some later commentaries maintain that it is possible to prepare the sky-blue dye nowadays as well, and that one is obligated to do so (*Sefunei Temunei Ḥol*). Some communities, such as the Hasidim of Radzin and others, do act in accordance with this practice; however, most of the Jewish people have not accepted this opinion (see Rambam *Sefer Ahava*, *Hilkhot Tzitzit* 1:5).

They fulfill the obligation whether of the same type or not of the same type – פּוֹטְרִין בֵּין בְּמִינָן בֵּין שֶׁלֹּא בְּמִינָן: One may fulfill his obligation of ritual fringes with wool or linen fringes on any garment, with the exception nowadays of wool fringes for linen garments. However, fringes of any other material fulfill the obligation only for a garment of that same material (*Shulḥan Arukh, Oraḥ Ḥayyim* 9:3).

וְהָא תַּנָּא דְּבֵי רַבִּי יִשְׁמָעֵאל לֵית לֵיהּ דְּרָבָא!

The Gemara asks: **But the *tanna* from the school of Rabbi Yishmael does not** maintain in accordance with this opinion **of Rava,** since that *tanna* holds that there is no obligation to place ritual fringes on clothing that is not made of wool or linen. The reason is that when the Torah speaks of garments it is referring exclusively to clothes made of wool or linen. Consequently, Rava's interpretation with regard to different types of material does not apply to the opinion of the *tanna* from the school of Rabbi Yishmael.

אִיצְטְרִיךְ, סָלְקָא דַּעְתָּךְ אָמִינָא כִּי דִּיוּקָא דְּרָבָא ״הַכָּנָף״ – מִין כָּנָף, וְהָכִי קָאָמַר רַחֲמָנָא: עֲבֵיד לֵיהּ צֶמֶר לְצֶמֶר וּפִשְׁתִּים לְפִשְׁתִּים, וְכִי עָבֵידַת צֶמֶר לְצֶמֶר – צְבָעֵיהּ, אֲבָל צֶמֶר לְפִשְׁתִּים וּפִשְׁתִּים לְצֶמֶר – לָא, כְּתַב רַחֲמָנָא ״צֶמֶר וּפִשְׁתִּים״ דַּאֲפִילּוּ צֶמֶר לְפִשְׁתִּים, וּפִשְׁתִּים לְצֶמֶר.

The Gemara responds: It **is** nevertheless **necessary** to state: "Wool and linen," as it could **enter your mind to say, in accordance with the inference of Rava,** that the phrase **"the corners"** indicates that it must be from the same **type** of thread as the **corner, but** in a different manner: **This is what the Merciful One is saying: Prepare for** it **wool** fringes **for a wool** garment **and linen** fringes **for a linen** garment, **and when you prepare wool** fringes **for wool** clothing, **dye it**[N] sky-blue. **However,** if you prepare **wool** fringes **for linen** garments **or linen for wool** clothing, you need **not** include a sky-blue thread. Therefore, **the Merciful One states: "Wool and linen,"** which teaches **that** one fulfills the obligation of fringes **even** with **wool** fringes **for a linen** garment[N] **or linen** fringes **for a woolen** one.

NOTES

And when you prepare wool for wool, dye it – וְכִי עָבֵידַת צֶמֶר לְצֶמֶר צְבָעֵיהּ: According to this interpretation, the phrase "the corners" means the same type as the corner, i.e., the fringes must be the same color as the corner, regardless of the type of woven material from which the threads are prepared. The Rambam accepts this opinion as *halakha* (Meiri; see *Einayim LaMishpat*).

Even with wool for a linen garment, etc. – אֲפִילּוּ צֶמֶר לְפִשְׁתִּים וכו׳: The early commentaries deliberate about whether or not the Gemara here disputes the accepted opinion of Reish Lakish that whenever it is possible to fulfill a positive mitzva without violating a prohibition, the positive mitzva does not override that prohibition. Some write that this is indeed a matter of dispute and that the statement of the Gemara here with regard to linen fringes on woolen clothing proves that even in a case of this kind, where it is not necessary to override the prohibition since the Torah has allowed mixtures of wool and linen in fringes, the prohibition is no longer in effect at all. Others maintain that the Gemara is referring to a specific case in which it is impossible in practice to fulfill the mitzva with woolen threads, as none are available. Consequently, the positive mitzva overrides the prohibition (Ramban; Rashba; see *Kovetz He'arot*).

Perek **I**
Daf **5** Amud **a**

תֵּינַח לְתַנָּא דְּבֵי רַבִּי יִשְׁמָעֵאל, לְרַבָּנַן מְנָא לְהוּ?

§ The Gemara comments: **This works out well** with regard to that **which the school of Rabbi Yishmael taught,** that all garments mentioned in the Torah are composed of linen or wool. However, **according to** the opinion of **the Rabbis,** who do not accept this opinion, **from where do they** derive[N] the principle that a positive mitzva overrides a prohibition? As stated previously, the conclusion that the positive mitzva to place fringes on a garment overrides the prohibition against mixing linen and wool is derived from a free expression in a biblical verse; however, the expression is free for interpretation only in the opinion of the *tanna* from the school of Rabbi Yishmael.

נָפְקָא לְהוּ מֵ״רֹאשׁוֹ״. דְּתַנְיָא: ״רֹאשׁוֹ״ מַה תַּלְמוּד לוֹמַר? לְפִי שֶׁנֶּאֱמַר ״לֹא תַקִּיפוּ (אֶת) פְּאַת רֹאשְׁכֶם״ שׁוֹמֵעַ אֲנִי אַף מְצוֹרָע כֵּן,

The Gemara responds: **They derive it from** the verse mentioned with regard to the *halakhot* of the purification of a leper from his leprosy [*tzara'at*]: "And it shall be on the seventh day, that he shall shave all his hair off **his head** and his beard and his eyebrows, even all his hair he shall shave off" (Leviticus 14:9).[N] **As it is taught** in a *baraita*: Since it states "all his hair," **what** is the meaning when **the verse states "his head"?** The *baraita* explains that **as it is stated: "You shall not round the corners of your heads"** (Leviticus 19:27), i.e., it is prohibited to shave the corners of the head, **I** would **derive** that **even a leper**[BH] **is** included in this prohibition.

NOTES

According to the Rabbis, from where do they derive – לְרַבָּנַן מְנָא לְהוּ: Some commentaries maintain that this question refers only to the opinion of Rabbi Yehuda, who does not derive *halakhot* from juxtaposed verses. Consequently, if he agrees with the opinion of the Rabbis, who disagree with Rabbi Yishmael, it is necessary to find an alternative source for the principle that a positive mitzva overrides a prohibition (see *Tosafot*). Others claim that the question applies even according to the opinion of the other Rabbis who disagree with Rabbi Yehuda. The reason is that the passage can be interpreted in accordance with the opinion of Rava that the adjacent verses come to teach a *halakha* concerning ritual fringes, and therefore the general halakhic principle cannot be learned from here (*Tosefot HaRosh*, citing Maharam of Rothenberg; see *Tosafot Yeshanim*). Yet others claim that this deliberation does in fact accord with the view of those Rabbis who dispute Rabbi Yehuda, as for a verse to teach a general principle that applies to the entire Torah, the juxtaposition must be both evident and free, and those who dispute Rabbi Yishmael do not consider this verse free in its context (Rashba; Meiri; see Ritva).

They derive it from: His head – נָפְקָא לְהוּ מֵרֹאשׁוֹ: According to the opinion of Rabbi Yishmael, this phrase teaches by the exegetical method of generalization and detail that the mitzva of shaving applies only to those places on the body where there is a concentration of hair. The Rabbis derive this *halakha* from the phrase "his eyebrows," which appears in the same verse (*Tosefot HaRosh*).

BACKGROUND

Leper – מְצוֹרָע: The *halakhot* of *tzara'at*, traditionally rendered as leprosy but not necessarily identified medically with that illness, are recorded in the Torah in the book of Leviticus in the portions of *Tazria* and *Metzora*. They are detailed in tractate *Nega'im*, which deals exclusively with the different types of leprosy. The *halakha* distinguishes between the impurity of a quarantined leper, i.e., a suspected leper who is isolated for a period of up to two weeks until his status is clarified, and that of a confirmed leper. A confirmed leper must grow his hair long, rend his garments, and cover his head in a particular way. Part of the purification process involves removing all of his body hair.

HALAKHA

The shaving of a leper – תִּגְלַחַת מְצוֹרָע: When purifying himself, a leper shaves by passing a razor over all his visible flesh, including the hair on his head and his entire beard (Rambam *Sefer Tahara, Hilkhot Tumat Tzara'at* 11:1).

תַּלְמוּד לוֹמַר "רֹאשׁוֹ", וְקָא סָבַר הַאי תַּנָּא: הַקָּפַת כָּל הָרֹאשׁ שְׁמָהּ הַקָּפָה.

Therefore, **the verse states** explicitly: **"His head,"** to teach that the mitzva that a leper must shave overrides the prohibition against rounding the corners of one's head by shaving. The Gemara adds: **And this *tanna* holds** that **the shaving of the entire head**[H] **is considered rounding.** Some Sages maintain that one violates the prohibition against rounding the corners of his head only when he leaves some hair intact and removes the corners alone. Conversely, this *tanna* holds that even when one removes all of the hair on the head, as a leper does when he performs his ritual shaving, as this act includes the corners, he thereby transgresses the prohibition against rounding the corners. This demonstrates that a positive mitzva overrides a prohibition.

אִיכָּא לְמִיפְרַךְ: מַה לְּלָאו דְּהַקָּפָה – שֶׁכֵּן לָאו שֶׁאֵין שָׁוֶה בַּכֹּל!

The Gemara raises an objection against that claim. This proof **can be refuted: What** about the fact **that the prohibition against rounding**[N] is specific **in that this prohibition is not equally applicable for all,**[H] as it does not apply to women, and therefore other cases cannot be derived from it? One cannot learn from this *halakha* that a positive mitzva that applies only to some people overrides even a prohibition that applies equally to all people.

אֶלָּא, אָתְיָא מִ"זְּקָנוֹ", דְּתַנְיָא: "זְקָנוֹ" מַה תַּלְמוּד לוֹמַר? לְפִי שֶׁנֶּאֱמַר "וּפְאַת זְקָנָם לֹא יְגַלֵּחוּ" שׁוֹמֵעַ אֲנִי אַף כֹּהֵן מְצוֹרָע כֵּן – תַּלְמוּד לוֹמַר "זְקָנוֹ".

Rather, the Gemara provides an alternative suggestion: The principle that a positive mitzva overrides a prohibition **is derived from** the superfluous phrase: **"His beard"** (Leviticus 14:9). **As it is taught** in a different *baraita*: **What** is the meaning when **the verse states: "His beard"?** After all, a beard is already included in the phrase: "All his hair." The *baraita* answers: **As it is stated** with regard to priests: **"Neither shall they shave off the corners of their beard"** (Leviticus 21:5),[N] I would **derive** that **even a leper who is a priest is included** in this prohibition against shaving his beard. Therefore, **the verse states "his beard"** in the case of a leper.

וְאִם אֵינוֹ עִנְיָן לְלָאו שֶׁאֵין שָׁוֶה בַּכֹּל – תְּנֵהוּ עִנְיָן לְלָאו הַשָּׁוֶה בַּכֹּל.

However, the shaving of one's beard is also a prohibition that is not equally applicable for all, as it does not apply to women. Therefore, it is necessary to develop this argument further. **And if** this derivation from the term "his beard" **is not** referring to **the matter of a prohibition that is not equally applicable for all,** as the principle that a positive mitzva overrides a prohibition that does not apply equally for all has already been derived from the phrase "his head," then the repetition of this specific scenario must serve to expand upon the teaching. Consequently, **refer it to the matter of a prohibition that is equally applicable for all,** i.e., that a positive mitzva that is not equally applicable for all overrides even prohibitions that apply equally to all people.

HALAKHA

Shaving of the entire head – הַקָּפַת כָּל הָרֹאשׁ: Whether one shaves only the corners of his head or his entire head including the corners, he has violated the prohibition against rounding his head, in accordance with the conclusion of the Gemara in tractate *Nazir*. Some authorities claim that according to the Rambam one is liable only if he shaves with a razor, whereas the Rosh rules that the violation includes shaving the corners with scissors (*Tur*; *Shulḥan Arukh*, *Yoreh De'a* 181:2).

Rounding…this prohibition is not equally applicable for all – הַקָּפָה...לָאו שֶׁאֵין שָׁוֶה בַּכֹּל: Since women are not included in the prohibition: "Neither shall you mar the corners of your beard" (Leviticus 19:27), they are not included in the prohibition against rounding the corners of the head either. Some authorities (Ra'avad) say that although a woman is not liable for rounding her own head, by rabbinic decree she may not round the corners of a man's head. Others (Rif; Rosh) hold that she is not prohibited from doing so, although the man may not permit her to proceed (*Shulḥan Arukh*, *Yoreh De'a* 181:6).

NOTES

The prohibition against rounding – לָאו דְּהַקָּפָה: This prohibition is stated in the Torah in the following terms: "You shall not round the corners of your heads, neither shall you mar the corners of your beard" (Leviticus 19:27). The primary point is that it is prohibited to cut one's hair in a manner that completely removes all hair from the corners of the head. In other words, the hair of the temples may not be cut so that it is even with the hair behind the ears. The reason for this prohibition may be so as not mimic the customs of the gentiles who shave in such a manner that the hair on their heads is entirely rounded, without any growing at the temples, in service of idolatry (Rambam). Alternatively, it is simply a statute of the Torah (see *Tur*). The Sages dispute whether this prohibition applies only if one shaves off just the corners while leaving hair elsewhere on the head, or whether rounding the entire head and cutting off the corners also constitutes a violation of the prohibition. The fact that this prohibition appears in the same verse as the prohibition against shaving the beard is an indication that it, too, applies only to men.

As it is stated: Neither shall they shave off the corners of their beard, etc. – לְפִי שֶׁנֶּאֱמַר וּפְאַת זְקָנָם לֹא יְגַלֵּחוּ: The early commentaries ask why the *baraita* states that the phrase "his beard" comes to exempt leprous priests from this prohibition. Why doesn't it release all Jews from the general prohibition against marring the beard (Leviticus 19:27), as ordinary Israelites and priests are equal in this regard? Some explain that the novelty is that even in the case of a priest, upon whom the Torah conferred additional prohibitions, the mitzva to shave overrides the prohibition (Meiri). Others say that as this precise wording was used only with regard to priests, one might have thought that this exemption includes only them, and not other Jews, for whom the prohibition is not called shaving. This is the case despite the fact that the *halakha* with regard to other Jews is itself derived from the passage dealing with priests (*Tosafot Yeshanim*).

וְאַכַּתִּי אִיצְטְרִיךְ, סָלְקָא דַּעְתָּךְ אָמִינָא: שָׁאנֵי כֹּהֲנִים, הוֹאִיל וְרִיבָּה בָּהֶן הַכָּתוּב מִצְוֹת יְתֵירוֹת, אֲפִילּוּ לָאו שֶׁאֵין שָׁוֶה בַּכֹּל לָא דָּחֵי – קָא מַשְׁמַע לַן דְּדָחֵי.

The Gemara rejects this proof: **Still, it is necessary** for the verse to state: "His beard." This phrase is not in fact superfluous at all, as it has a novelty: It could **enter your mind to say** that **priests are different; since the verse includes for them additional mitzvot**[N] it is appropriate to be more stringent with them, and therefore one might think that a positive mitzva should **not even override a prohibition that is not equally applicable for all.** Consequently, the verse states: "His beard," and it thereby **teaches us that** even with regard to priests a positive mitzva **overrides** a prohibition that is not equally applicable for all. This means that the principle that a positive mitzva overrides even a prohibition that is equally applicable for all cannot be derived from here.

אֶלָּא: אָתְיָא מֵ"רֹאשׁוֹ" דְּהַךְ תַּנָּא, דְּתַנְיָא: "רֹאשׁוֹ" מַה תַּלְמוּד לוֹמַר? לְפִי שֶׁנֶּאֱמַר "תַּעַר לֹא יַעֲבוֹר עַל רֹאשׁוֹ" שׁוֹמֵעַ אֲנִי אַף מְצוֹרָע וְנָזִיר כֵּן, תַּלְמוּד לוֹמַר "רֹאשׁוֹ"–

§ **Rather,** the Gemara rejects this line of reasoning in favor of an alternative answer. The principle that a positive mitzva overrides a prohibition **is derived** from a different interpretation of the phrase "**his head,**" cited **by this *tanna*. As it is taught** in a *baraita* with regard to the verse: "He shall shave all his hair off his head" (Leviticus 14:9); **what** is the meaning when **the verse states: "His head"?** The *baraita* explains: **As it is stated** with regard to a nazirite: **"No razor shall come upon his head"** (Numbers 6:5), **I** would **derive** that **even a leper who is a nazirite**[N] is prohibited from shaving his head upon purification. Therefore, **the verse states: "His head."** This teaches that the positive mitzva for a leper to shave overrides the prohibition of a nazirite.

אִיכָּא לְמִיפְרַךְ: מַה לְנָזִיר מְצוֹרָע – שֶׁכֵּן יֶשְׁנוֹ בִּשְׁאֵלָה. דְּאִי לָא תֵּימָא הָכִי, הָא דְּקַיְימָא לַן דְּאֵין עֲשֵׂה דּוֹחֶה לֹא תַעֲשֶׂה וַעֲשֵׂה.

The Gemara responds that this proof **can be refuted** as well: **What** about the fact that the prohibition of a nazirite is not especially severe, **as a leprous nazirite can request** to have his nazirite vow dissolved by a Sage? Since he can nullify the prohibition against shaving, this prohibition is evidently not very severe, and therefore one cannot prove anything with regard to all of the prohibitions of the Torah from this case. The Gemara adds: **As, if you do not say this,** that the prohibitions of a nazirite are not as severe as other prohibitions, **that** halakhic ruling **that we maintain** that **a positive mitzva does not override** both **a prohibition and a positive mitzva**[H] would be negated.

לִיגְמַר מִנָּזִיר! אֶלָּא, מִנָּזִיר מַאי טַעְמָא לָא גָּמְרִינַן, דְּאִיכָּא לְמִיפְרַךְ שֶׁכֵּן יֶשְׁנוֹ בִּשְׁאֵלָה – הָכִי נַמִי אִיכָּא לְמִיפְרַךְ שֶׁכֵּן יֶשְׁנוֹ בִּשְׁאֵלָה.

The Gemara explains the previous claim: **Let us derive** the opposite of this principle **from** the case of **a nazirite,**[N] as in this case the positive mitzva for a leper to shave apparently overrides both the positive mitzva for a nazirite to grow hair and the prohibition against shaving. **Rather, what is the reason** that **we do not derive** this principle **from** the case of **a nazirite?** The reason is **that there is room to refute** this proof in the aforementioned manner: One cannot learn from a nazirite, **as** a leprous nazirite **can request**[H] to have his nazirite vow dissolved. **So too, there is room to refute** the proof from the *halakha* of a nazirite that a positive mitzva overrides a prohibition, **as** he **can request** to have his vow dissolved.

אֶלָּא לְעוֹלָם

§ If so, no proof can be brought from the case of a nazirite. **Rather,** the Gemara offers a different explanation: **Actually,**

HALAKHA

A positive mitzva does not override both a prohibition and a positive mitzva – אֵין עֲשֵׂה דּוֹחֶה לֹא תַעֲשֶׂה וַעֲשֵׂה: Although a positive mitzva overrides a prohibition, it does not override both a prohibition and a positive mitzva together (Rambam *Sefer Zemanim, Hilkhot Yom Tov* 3:8, *Sefer Nashim, Hilkhot Yibbum VaḤalitza* 6:11, and *Sefer Hafla'a, Hilkhot Nezirut* 7:15).

A nazirite…can request – נָזִיר...יֶשְׁנוֹ בִּשְׁאֵלָה: One who takes a nazirite vow and regrets doing so may request from a Sage to dissolve it, like any other vow (Rambam *Sefer Hafla'a, Hilkhot Nezirut* 2:1).

NOTES

Since the verse includes for them additional mitzvot – הוֹאִיל וְרִיבָּה בָּהֶן הַכָּתוּב מִצְוֹת יְתֵירוֹת: If the *halakha* is stringent with priests due to the additional mitzvot imposed upon them, shouldn't this reasoning also apply to positive mitzvot, not only prohibitions? In other words, their positive mitzvot should be proportionally stronger as well, and therefore these mitzvot should override prohibitions in the same manner as regular mitzvot. One answer is that in the case of priests one can argue that the stringency of a prohibition that is not equally applicable for all is like that of a prohibition that is equally applicable for all, whereas this halakhic differentiation simply does not apply in the case of a positive mitzva (*Melo HaRo'im*).

The shaving of a leprous nazirite – תִּגְלַחַת נָזִיר מְצוֹרָע: The early commentaries dispute the reason why the positive mitzva for a leper to shave overrides both the positive mitzva and the prohibition of a nazirite. Some claim that as the nazirite has been rendered ritually impure by leprosy, the positive mitzva of his naziriteship is nullified, and therefore only the prohibition remains intact (Rambam). Conversely, others apply the reasoning of the Gemara here: Since a nazirite can request from a Sage to dissolve his vow, his prohibitions are relatively less severe (Ra'avad; Meiri; see *Kovetz He'arot* and Rambam *Sefer Hafla'a, Hilkhot Nezirut* 7:15, and *Kesef Mishne* there).

Let us derive from a nazirite – לִיגְמַר מִנָּזִיר: The early commentaries ask: Why can't one derive the principle that a positive mitzva overrides a prohibition from both the cases of a nazirite and a priest together, by the exegetical principle of the common factor? In other words, if a *halakha* appears in two cases but with regard to each case there is a particular reason why its *halakha* cannot be extended to other cases, one can derive a general halakhic principle from both cases together, as the unique circumstances of each individual case is not found in the other. That specific *halakha* is the common factor of the two. Some answer that this proof can be refuted, as in the case of a leper his shaving is possibly permitted due to the important mitzva to be fruitful and multiply, as while he is a leper he is separated from all people, including his wife. Likewise, his purification brings peace to his home. Consequently, it can be argued that only a positive mitzva of great importance, like this one, overrides a prohibition (Rashba; Ritva).

מִקְּרָא קַמָּא: אִם כֵּן לֵימָא קְרָא ״צִיצִית תַּעֲשֶׂה לְּךָ״, ״גְּדִילִים״ לָמָּה לִי? שְׁמַע מִינָּהּ לְאַפְנוֹיֵי.

they learn this **from the first verse,** which permits a mixture of diverse kinds of wool and linen in ritual fringes. As for the previous claim that in the opinion of the Rabbis the phrase "wool and linen" is not superfluous and therefore there is no cause to derive from the juxtaposed verses, the answer is as follows: **If so,** that no homiletical interpretation can be derived from this source, **let the verse say** only: **You shall make fringes for yourself. Why do I** need the expression **"twisted fringes"** (Deuteronomy 22:12)?[N] **Conclude from** this **that** this phrase **is free,** i.e., a homiletical interpretation can be derived by the juxtaposition of verses due to this superfluous phrase.

הַאי לְשִׁיעוּרָא הוּא דַּאֲתָא: ״גְּדִיל״ – שְׁנַיִם, ״גְּדִילִים״ – אַרְבָּעָה, עֲשֵׂה גְּדִיל וּפוֹתְלֵהוּ מִתּוֹכוֹ!

The Gemara raises a difficulty: **This** term, "twisted fringes," **comes to** teach **the measure** of ritual fringes, i.e., the requisite number of strings for the fringes, as it is taught: **Twisted fringe,** in the singular, indicates that it is entwined, which requires at least **two** strings. Consequently, when the verse says **"twisted fringes"** in the plural, it is referring to **four**[H] strings. This means that one must **prepare a twisted fringe and double it over**[NH] **from the middle,** so that there are eight strings. Consequently, the term "twisted fringes" is not superfluous at all.

אִם כֵּן לֵימָא קְרָא ״לֹא תִלְבַּשׁ שַׁעַטְנֵז״, ״צֶמֶר וּפִשְׁתִּים יַחְדָּו״ לָמָּה לִי? שְׁמַע מִינָּהּ לְאַפְנוֹיֵי.

The Gemara responds: **If so,** that this phrase is not extraneous at all, and therefore it cannot be used as a homiletical interpretation by the juxtaposition of verses, **let the verse say** merely: **You shall not wear diverse kinds** [*sha'atnez*].[N] **Why do I** need the verse to add the phrase **"wool and linen together"? Conclude from** this **that** this phrase **is free,** and a homiletical interpretation can be derived from the juxtaposition of verses.

וְאַכַּתִּי מִיבָּעֵי לֵיהּ: לְתוֹכֵף שְׁתֵּי תְכִיפוֹת – חִיבּוּר, וּתְכִיפָה אַחַת – אֵינוֹ חִיבּוּר! אִם כֵּן לִכְתּוֹב רַחֲמָנָא ״לֹא תִלְבַּשׁ צֶמֶר וּפִשְׁתִּים יַחְדָּו״, ״שַׁעַטְנֵז״ לָמָּה לִי? שְׁמַע מִינָּהּ לְאַפְנוֹיֵי.

The Gemara raises a further difficulty: **And still,** it is **necessary** for the verse to state "wool and linen together" **to** teach another *halakha* concerning diverse kinds: When **one** combines a woolen garment with a linen garment, if he **stitches two stitches** with a needle, this is considered **attachment,**[H] **but a single stitch is not attachment.**[N] This *halakha* is derived from the term "together," which indicates that they are attached as one. The Gemara answers: **If so, let the Merciful One write: You shall not wear wool and linen together. Why do I** need the verse to add the phrase **"diverse kinds"? Conclude from** this **that** this phrase **is free.**

NOTES

Why do I need: Twisted fringes – **גְּדִילִים לָמָּה לִי**: Some commentaries explain that the superfluity is based on the fact that the Hebrew term for twisted fringes, *gedilim*, has one more letter than the synonym *tzitzit*, ritual fringes (Meiri).

Prepare a twisted fringe and double it over – **עֲשֵׂה גְּדִיל וּפוֹתְלֵהוּ**: Some commentaries explain that one should prepare the fringes in such a manner that there is both a portion that is tied and a twisted portion with strings of its own (Rashi; Meiri). Apparently, others derive this from the term *tzitzit*, ritual fringes, which does not have the connotation of being twisted. Some cite support for Rashi's interpretation from the fact that the Gemara first states: Prepare a twisted fringe, before adding: Double it over. Had the Gemara merely been referring to doubling the fringes, it would simply have stated: Prepare a doubled-over fringe (*Otzar HaShitot*).

Diverse kinds [*sha'atnez*] – **שַׁעַטְנֵז**: This term is used in the Torah in reference to a mixture of wool and linen, and the Sages could not find a source for it in other languages. Even the interpretation by way of acronym stated here: *Shoa, tavui, noz*, is linguistically obscure. Most commentaries maintain that *shoa* is connected to the root *sh-a-a*, meaning smoothing or to be smooth, referring to the mixture being smoothed by the combing of its fibers. Various interpretations have been suggested for *noz*, from both halakhic and linguistic perspectives. Some suggest that this is a shortened version of *naloz*, which refers to the production of felt. Most commentaries are of the opinion that it is a term coined by the Sages to describe a certain stage in the preparation of fibers for weaving.

A single stitch is not attachment – **תְּכִיפָה אַחַת אֵינוֹ חִיבּוּר**: Why is this derivation necessary? It is obvious that an unstable connection is not considered proper attachment. One explanation is that since the Torah prohibited any mixture of wool and linen, it might be thought that any kind of attachment of the two materials is prohibited, even an unstable one (Ritva).

HALAKHA

Twisted fringes is referring to four – **גְּדִילִים אַרְבָּעָה**: Ritual fringes must be composed of four doubled strings, a total of eight. Any additional strings disqualify the mitzva. This is the opinion of most of the authorities, in accordance with the ruling of the Rambam. Some (Vilna Gaon, citing *Ba'al HaIttur*) maintain that any number of additional strings may be added, while others (*Tosafot*) limit the number to sixteen (Rambam *Sefer Ahava, Hilkhot Tzitzit* 1:6; *Shulḥan Arukh, Oraḥ Ḥayyim* 11:12).

Prepare a twisted fringe and double it over – **עֲשֵׂה גְּדִיל וּפוֹתְלֵהוּ**: Ritual fringes must be partly made of knots, with an addition of separated strings extending from the knots. According to Rashi, the Gemara here is the source for this *halakha* (*Shulḥan Arukh, Oraḥ Ḥayyim* 11:14).

Two stitches is attachment – **שְׁתֵּי תְכִיפוֹת חִיבּוּר**: If one stitches a single stitch of wool and linen with a needle and ties the ends of the thread together, or stitches two threads without tying, this is permanent attachment and has thereby violated the prohibition of diverse kinds. Some authorities (Rema, citing Rosh) maintain that a single stitch, even tied together, is not considered attachment; rather, one must stitch together the ends of two threads to be liable (Rambam *Sefer Zera'im, Hilkhot Kilayim* 10:3; *Shulḥan Arukh, Yoreh De'a* 300:2).

וְאַכַּתִּי מִיבָּעֵי לֵיהּ: עַד שֶׁיְּהֵא שׁוּעַ טָווּי וְנוּז! אֶלָּא כּוּלָּהּ מִ״שַּׁעַטְנֵז״ נָפְקָא.

The Gemara comments: **And still,** it is **necessary** for the verse to state "diverse kinds [*sha'atnez*]," as this is interpreted as an acronym that teaches that the *halakha* of diverse kinds applies only **when it is smooth combed [*shoa*], spun [*tavui*]** as a thread, **and attached [*noz*],**[HN] but without these characteristics the connection is not considered diverse kinds. **Rather,** the Gemara explains that **the entire** interpretation **is derived from** the term **"diverse kinds."**[N] Since the Torah uses the highly distinctive word "*sha'atnez*," in addition to functioning as the above acronym it serves as the source of the verbal analogy with the term in the verse: "Neither shall there come upon you a garment of diverse kinds [*sha'atnez*] mingled together" (Leviticus 19:19), from which it may be inferred that a positive mitzva overrides a prohibition.

אַשְׁכְּחַן דְּאָתֵי עֲשֵׂה וְדָחֵי לֹא תַעֲשֶׂה גְּרֵידָא, לֹא תַעֲשֶׂה שֶׁיֵּשׁ בּוֹ כָּרֵת הֵיכָא אַשְׁכְּחַן דְּדָחֵי דְּאִיצְטְרִיךְ ״עָלֶיהָ״ לְמֵיסְרָהּ?

§ The Gemara returns to the issue of a mitzva overriding a prohibition: **We have found that a positive mitzva overrides a regular prohibition.** However, **where do we find that** a positive mitzva **overrides**[N] **a prohibition that includes *karet*,** as the phrase **"with her" is necessary to prohibit her?** It was mentioned previously that the superfluous phrase "with her" teaches that the mitzva of levirate marriage does not override the prohibition against taking a wife's sister. However, why is this necessary? Why would it have been assumed that a positive mitzva is so powerful that it overrides even a prohibition that is punishable by *karet*?

וְכִי תֵּימָא נֵילַף מִמִּילָה – מָה לְמִילָה שֶׁכֵּן נִכְרְתוּ עָלֶיהָ שְׁלֹשׁ עֶשְׂרֵה בְּרִיתוֹת,

And if you suggest an answer and **say: Let us derive** this claim **from** the mitzva of **circumcision,** as there is a positive mitzva to perform circumcision on the eighth day of the boy's life even on Shabbat,[H] and this mitzva overrides the prohibition against performing labor on Shabbat, which is punishable by *karet*, one could respond: **What** about the fact **that circumcision**[N] is an extremely important and severe positive mitzva, **as thirteen covenants were established over it?** The term "covenant" is mentioned thirteen times in the chapter of circumcision (Genesis, chapter 17).

מִפֶּסַח – מָה לְפֶסַח שֶׁכֵּן כָּרֵת,

The Gemara adds: And if you say it is derived **from the** slaughter of **the Paschal lamb,** which overrides Shabbat[H] and is therefore a positive mitzva that overrides a prohibition punishable by *karet*, this too can be rejected: **What** about the fact **that the Paschal lamb** is different, as it is a positive mitzva that is so severe that its neglect entails ***karet***[H] for those who do not bring it, unlike all other positive mitzvot?

HALAKHA

Smooth combed [*shoa*], spun [*tavui*], and attached [*noz*] – שׁוּעַ טָווּי וְנוּז: The commentaries and authorities dispute both the meaning of these terms and the manner in which these parameters constitute a violation of the prohibition of diverse kinds. The consensus is that if one mixes wool and linen and smooth-combs them together, or spins them together to weave a garment, or sews together two garments, one containing thread of one kind and one containing thread of the other kind, he violates the prohibition of diverse kinds by Torah law. By rabbinic law it is prohibited to combine wool and linen even if they are not smooth-combed or spun together (*Shulḥan Arukh, Yoreh De'a* 300:2).

Circumcision on Shabbat – מִילָה בְּשַׁבָּת: Circumcision at the proper time, on the eighth day of life, overrides Shabbat, and the circumcision is performed just as on any other day of the week (*Shulḥan Arukh, Yoreh De'a* 266:2).

The Paschal offering on Shabbat – פֶּסַח בְּשַׁבָּת: If the fourteenth of Nisan occurs on Shabbat, the Paschal offering is sacrificed as on any other day of the week (Rambam *Sefer Korbanot, Hilkhot Korban Pesaḥ* 1:16).

***Karet* for neglecting the Paschal lamb – כָּרֵת עַל בִּיטּוּל פֶּסַח:** One who deliberately neglects the mitzva to bring the Paschal lamb, without being ritually impure or on a distant journey, is liable to receive *karet* (Rambam *Sefer Korbanot, Hilkhot Korban Pesaḥ* 1:2).

NOTES

Smooth combed [*shoa*], spun [*tavui*], and attached [*noz*] – שׁוּעַ טָווּי וְנוּז: The commentaries and authorities debate the meanings of these terms extensively. Some explain that *shoa* means sticking together by a type of felt. *Tavui* refers to the spinning of one thread composed of both wool and linen, or the weaving together of two threads. *Noz* means weaving or attaching by stitches (Rav Hai Gaon). Some claim that attaching by stitches is prohibited by rabbinic decree (Meiri, citing *ge'onim*). Others discuss the various opinions at length, whether all three parameters are necessary or each one alone suffices (*Tosafot*). Yet others maintain that *noz* means entwined (Rabbeinu Tam).

The entire interpretation is derived from diverse kinds [*sha'atnez*] – כּוּלָּהּ מִשַּׁעַטְנֵז נָפְקָא: The Torah's use of this unique term teaches that positive mitzvot override prohibitions throughout the entire Torah, in addition to the fact that diverse kinds must be smooth-combed, spun, and attached (Rashi). Other early commentaries reject this interpretation in favor of the claim that the general principle of the juxtaposition of verses in the entire Torah is derived from the superfluous term "together," while the *halakha* that a single stitch is not considered attachment is learned from the word "*sha'atnez*," which indicates that the material is attached together as one, as it does not state *sha'atnezim*, in the plural (Ramban; Rashba).

Where do we find that it overrides – הֵיכָא אַשְׁכְּחַן דְּדָחֵי: The early commentaries ask: Why doesn't the Gemara derive from the very fact that the phrase "with her" is necessary, that in the rest of the Torah a positive mitzva overrides a prohibition that entails *karet* (*Tosafot*)? One answer is that this indirect proof is not enough to establish a principle that applies throughout the entire Torah. Rather, it must be derived from a superfluity (Ramban).

What about the fact that circumcision, etc. – מָה לְמִילָה וכו׳: The reason that the Gemara does not answer here, as it does later, that failure to circumcise entails *karet*, is because lack of circumcision specifically on the eighth day does not incur *karet*, as this punishment applies only to one who has reached adulthood (*Tosafot Yeshanim*; Ramban). Later, when the Gemara rejects the possibility of drawing an inference by way of the common factor, it does mention the fact that failure to circumcise incurs *karet*. This is because there is a principle that a proof by way of the common factor between two cases can be rejected by any similar factor. Since the mitzva of circumcision itself does include an element of *karet*, this is considered a common factor with the Paschal lamb (Ritva).

BACKGROUND

Daily offering – תָּמִיד: The daily offering consisted of two lambs, one sacrificed in the morning and one in the afternoon of each day. These served to open and close the daily sacrificial service in the Temple. No offerings were brought either before the morning offering or following the afternoon offering. The single exception was the Paschal lamb, which was sacrificed after the daily afternoon offering on Passover eve.

HALAKHA

The daily offering on Shabbat – תָּמִיד בְּשַׁבָּת: The daily offering is brought even on Shabbat, and its limbs are burnt on the altar on the same day (Rambam *Sefer Avoda*, *Hilkhot Temidin UMusafin* 1:7).

Honoring one's parent and Shabbat – כִּבּוּד אָב וְשַׁבָּת: If one was instructed by his father or mother to transgress a mitzva of the Torah, whether it was a positive mitzva or a prohibition, or even a decree of the Sages, he must pay no heed (*Shulḥan Arukh*, *Yoreh De'a* 240:15).

מִתָּמִיד – מָה לְתָמִיד שֶׁכֵּן תָּדִיר.

The Gemara offers yet another suggestion: Perhaps it is derived **from the daily offering,**[B] which was slaughtered every day, even on Shabbat.[H] This is a positive mitzva that overrides the prohibition against performing labor on Shabbat, which is punishable by *karet*. The Gemara rejects this claim as well: **What** about the fact **that the daily offering** is special in **that it is frequent?** Since the mitzva of the daily offering is performed every day, it is perhaps especially important, whereas a positive mitzva that applies only at certain times might not be powerful enough to override a severe prohibition.

מֵחֲדָא לָא אָתְיָא תֵּיתֵי מִתַּרְתֵּי. מֵהֵי תֵּיתֵי? מִמִּילָה וּפֶסַח – שֶׁכֵּן כָּרֵת, מִפֶּסַח וְתָמִיד – שֶׁכֵּן צוֹרֶךְ גָּבוֹהַּ,

The Gemara says: Clearly, the principle **cannot be derived from** any single **one** of these cases. However, **let it be derived from two** of these cases combined together, by analyzing their common features. The Gemara asks: **From which** two cases can **it be derived?** If one would say that it can be derived **from circumcision and the Paschal lamb,** the factor common to both is their particular severity, **as** their neglect entails ***karet***. If one would seek to derive this **from the Paschal lamb and the daily offering,** these have a different common factor, **as** both are **a requirement of** the altar in **the Temple,** not for personal benefit.

מִמִּילָה וְתָמִיד – שֶׁכֵּן יֶשְׁנוֹ לִפְנֵי הַדִּבּוּר. וְאַלִּיבָּא דְּמַאן דְּאָמַר עוֹלָה שֶׁהִקְרִיבוּ יִשְׂרָאֵל בַּמִּדְבָּר עוֹלַת תָּמִיד הֲוָה. וּמִכּוּלְּהוּ נַמִי – שֶׁכֵּן יֶשְׁנָן לִפְנֵי הַדִּבּוּר.

Likewise, if one would suggest deriving the principle **from circumcision and the daily offering,** this too must be rejected, as both of these mitzvot **were** known by the Jewish people **before the word**[N] of God was revealed at Mount Sinai. **And** this is **according to** the opinion of **the one who said** that **the burnt-offering brought by the Jewish people in the desert was the daily offering. And** moreover, **from all of these** together, i.e., circumcision, the Paschal lamb, and the daily offering, it is **also** not possible to derive a conclusion, **as** all three of **these were** known **before the word** of God was revealed. If so, no principle can be derived from these three mitzvot.

אֶלָּא אִיצְטְרִיךְ, סָלְקָא דַּעְתָּךְ אָמִינָא תֵּיתֵי מִכִּבּוּד אָב וָאֵם,

§ **Rather,** the Gemara suggests an alternative explanation: The inference from "with her" **is necessary,** as were it not for this inference it might be assumed that the mitzva of levirate marriage overrides the prohibition against marrying one's wife's sister despite the fact that this prohibition incurs *karet*, since it could **enter your mind to say** that this *halakha* **is derived from** the mitzva of **honoring one's father and mother.**[N]

דְּתַנְיָא: יָכוֹל יְהֵא כִּבּוּד אָב וָאֵם דּוֹחֶה שַׁבָּת, תַּלְמוּד לוֹמַר ״אִישׁ אִמּוֹ וְאָבִיו תִּירָאוּ וְאֶת שַׁבְּתוֹתַי תִּשְׁמוֹרוּ״ – כּוּלְּכֶם חַיָּיבִין בִּכְבוֹדִי,

As it is taught in a *baraita*: One **might** have thought **that honoring one's father and mother overrides Shabbat;** therefore, **the verse states: "You shall fear every man his mother and his father and you shall keep My *Shabbatot*,** I am the Lord your God" (Leviticus 19:3). The *baraita* explains the derivation from the verse: **All of you,** both parent and child, **are obligated in My honor,**[HN] and therefore honoring one's parents does not override the honor of God, Who commanded the Jewish people to observe Shabbat.

מַאי לָאו דְּאָמַר לֵיהּ: ״שְׁחוֹט לִי״ ״בַּשֵּׁל לִי״, וְטַעְמָא – דִּכְתַב רַחֲמָנָא ״אֶת שַׁבְּתוֹתַי תִּשְׁמוֹרוּ״ הָא לָאו הָכִי – דָּחֵי! לָא

The Gemara analyzes this *baraita*: **What, is it not** referring to a situation **where** his father **said to him: Slaughter for me, cook for me,** or any other labor prohibited on Shabbat on pain of *karet*? **And the reason** that **the Merciful One** specifically **writes: "Keep My *Shabbatot*,"** is to warn against violating the prohibition against performing labor on Shabbat, a transgression which incurs *karet*, for the purpose of honoring one's parents. It may therefore be inferred that **if that was not so,** the positive mitzva would **override** Shabbat. It is therefore possible to deduce from here that in general, positive mitzvot override even prohibitions that entail *karet*. The Gemara rejects this proof: **No,**

NOTES

As they were before the word – שֶׁכֵּן יֶשְׁנוֹ לִפְנֵי הַדִּבּוּר: One problem with this claim is that it is indicated in the Jerusalem Talmud that a mitzva that existed prior to the revelation at Mount Sinai is less important than one given at Mount Sinai. Some explain that the Gemara here is stating that regardless of the importance of a mitzva, a later mitzva can nullify it only if this is explicitly stated, and provided that it existed previously. Some early commentaries ask: Isn't levirate marriage also a mitzva that pre-dated the revelation at Sinai, as Judah performed this mitzva (see Genesis, chapter 38)? Some explain that the Patriarchs entered into levirate marriage not as the fulfillment of a mitzva, but as a practical custom. Levirate marriage became an obligatory mitzva only after the giving of the Torah (Ritva; Meiri). Apparently, different *midrashim* dispute this matter (see *Bereshit Rabba* 85, *Vayikra Rabba* 2, and *Yalkut Mishlei*).

Rather…it is derived from honoring one's father and mother – אֶלָּא...תֵּיתֵי מִכִּבּוּד אָב וָאֵם: Although the mitzva to honor one's parents was also given at Mara, before the revelation at Sinai, the mitzva to observe Shabbat was likewise given at Mara (see Exodus, chapter 16; *Otzar HaShitot*). The commentaries note that the Gemara does not provide an exhaustive discussion of all relevant possibilities, as further questions and answers can be raised (*Tosafot*).

All of you are obligated in My honor – כּוּלְּכֶם חַיָּיבִין בִּכְבוֹדִי: Most of the commentaries maintain that this conclusion is derived from the end of the verse: "I am God" (see *Tosafot*). Some claim that this is learned from the term "keep," which indicates an additional level of stringency with regard to the observance of Shabbat.

לָאו דִּמְחַמֵּר, וַאֲפִילּוּ הָכִי לֹא דָּחֵי.

the reference is not to a situation where a father demanded that his child perform prohibited labor on Shabbat that entails *karet*. Rather, he instructed him to transgress the **prohibition against driving** a laden **animal.**[N] Although it is prohibited to cause animals to work on Shabbat, this does not entail the penalty of *karet*, as it has the status of a regular prohibition. **And** this shows that if one's father told him to desecrate Shabbat by driving a donkey, **even so,** the positive mitzva to honor one's parents does **not override** the prohibition against driving a laden animal.

אֶלָּא דְּקַיְימָא לָן דְּאָתֵי עֲשֵׂה וְדָחֵי לֹא תַעֲשֶׂה, לִיגְמַר מֵהָכָא דְּלָא לִידְחֵי!

§ The Gemara asks: If so, **rather** than that principle in **which we maintain that a positive mitzva comes and overrides a prohibition, let us derive from here that it does not override**[N] even a regular prohibition. Just as it was inferred above from the case of ritual fringes, in which the positive mitzva overrides the prohibition against diverse kinds, that all other positive mitzvot similarly override any prohibition, perhaps one should infer from the case of honoring one's parents that positive mitzvot do not override prohibitions at all.

וְכִי תֵּימָא: שָׁאנֵי לָאוֵי דְּשַׁבָּת דַּחֲמִירִי – וְהָא תַּנָּא בְּעָלְמָא קָאֵי וְלָא קָפְרִיךְ!

And if you say that one should not infer this from here, as the **prohibitions of Shabbat are different** in **that they are** more **serious,**[N] and for this reason the mitzva to honor one's parents does not override these prohibitions, this cannot be the case, **as the *tanna* speaks generally** of a father who instructs a son to perform a regular prohibition, not to desecrate Shabbat, **and he does not raise any difficulty** of this kind.

דְּתַנְיָא: יָכוֹל אָמַר לוֹ אָבִיו: הִיטָּמֵא! אוֹ שֶׁאָמַר לוֹ: אַל תַּחֲזִיר! יָכוֹל יִשְׁמַע לוֹ, תַּלְמוּד לוֹמַר ״אִישׁ אִמּוֹ וְאָבִיו תִּירָאוּ וְאֶת שַׁבְּתוֹתַי תִּשְׁמוֹרוּ״ – כּוּלְּכֶם חַיָּיבִין בִּכְבוֹדִי.

As it is taught in a different *baraita*: One **might** have thought **that if one's father said to** his son, who is a priest or nazirite: **Be rendered ritually impure**[N] with impurity imparted by a corpse, so as to bring me an item from a ritually impure place, **or if he said to him: Do not return** this lost item, it **might** have been supposed that his son **should obey him.** Therefore, **the verse states: "You shall fear every man his mother and his father and you shall keep My *Shabbatot*,** I am the Lord your God" (Leviticus 19:3). This verse teaches: **All of you are obligated in My honor.**[N] This proves that the *tanna* does not differentiate between desecrating Shabbat, which is a severe prohibition, and a priest becoming ritually impure with impurity imparted by a corpse, which is a lighter prohibition.

NOTES

The prohibition against driving a laden animal – לָאו דִּמְחַמֵּר: Although one who drives a laden animal on Shabbat has not performed a prohibited labor himself, his animal has performed work, and therefore he has transgressed the prohibition: "You shall not do any manner of work, neither you…nor your cattle" (Exodus 20:9). However, this transgression does not merit as serious a penalty as one who desecrates Shabbat directly. Some commentaries note that the Gemara could have cited other examples of actions that are prohibited on Shabbat by Torah law according to all opinions, e.g., leaving the Shabbat limit (*Arukh LaNer*).

Some commentaries ask why the Gemara initially thought that the *baraita* is referring to the overriding of a prohibition so severe that it entails *karet*, rather than one of the more minor Shabbat prohibitions. The answer given is that the term "keep" indicates the observance of the fundamental prohibitions of Shabbat, which are punishable by *karet* (*Tosafot Yeshanim*).

Let us derive…that it does not override – לִיגְמַר...דְּלָא לִידְחֵי: The early commentaries ask: Perhaps this case is different, as the use of animals for work on Shabbat violates both a prohibition and a positive mitzva, as derived from the verse: "On the seventh day you shall rest, that your ox and your donkey may have rest" (Exodus 23:12). One answer given is that as the honoring of one's parents is so important that it is juxtaposed to the honor of God, if it does not override Shabbat, regardless of the positive mitzva of Shabbat, one can indeed conclude from here that a regular positive mitzva does not override a regular prohibition (*Tosafot*). Others state that the positive mitzva to rest on Shabbat applies exclusively to people, whereas the driving of an animal involves only a prohibition, not a positive mitzva (Rashba, citing Rabbeinu Yona).

The prohibitions of Shabbat are…serious – לָאוֵי דְּשַׁבָּת דַּחֲמִירִי: Some commentaries explain that the severity of Shabbat prohibitions is due to the positive mitzva associated with them (Rambam; Meiri). Rashi, however, explains that the unique severity of Shabbat is due to the *halakha* that one who publicly desecrates Shabbat is likened to an idolater and is treated as though he was a gentile. In comparison with other prohibitions, those associated with Shabbat are also more serious in that their desecration entails the capital punishment of stoning, which is the most severe of the four types of court-imposed executions.

One's father said to him: Be rendered ritually impure – אָמַר לוֹ אָבִיו הִיטָּמֵא: Rashi explains that his father instructed him to become ritually impure so as to return a lost item to its owner, as indicated by the context of this statement in tractate *Bava Metzia*. Others, however, maintain that the father asked him to become ritually impure for his own requirements, e.g., to bring him an object from a cemetery (Rashba; Ritva). It can be inferred from Rashi's opinion that the *baraita* is teaching that not even two positive mitzvot override a prohibition (see *Arukh LaNer*).

All of you are obligated in My honor – כּוּלְּכֶם חַיָּיבִין בִּכְבוֹדִי: This explains why in this particular case the positive mitzva does not override even a minor prohibition, as the father himself has no right to demand an action of this kind. Some commentaries add that this *halakha* is necessary only in a case when the father requires the object in question, or if he needs it for the fulfillment of a mitzva (Rashi), since if he demands that his son transgress a prohibition for no reason he is considered a wicked person, to whom the mitzva to honor one's father does not apply (Meiri). Others argue the opposite: The very fact that there was room to deliberate about whether or not one should obey his father is an indication that the father is not considered wicked simply because he issued an instruction to violate a prohibition (*Haggahot Maimoniyyot*).

אֶלָּא מִשּׁוּם דְּאִיכָּא לְמִיפְרַךְ:

§ **Rather,** the Gemara rejects this line of reasoning and accepts the claim that the *baraita* does not speak of one whose father asked him to desecrate Shabbat by performing a prohibited labor that entails *karet,* but of a father who instructed his son to drive a laden animal. As for the difficulty that this apparently indicates that a positive mitzva does not override any type of prohibition, the reason that this is not the case is **because there is room to refute** this argument.

מַה לְּהָנָךְ – שֶׁכֵּן הֶכְשֵׁר מִצְוָה,

The Gemara explains how the previous claim can be countered: **What** about the fact **that these** instructions of a father are different, **as** when one drives an animal on Shabbat in honor of his parents this is merely **preparation for the mitzva**[N] of honoring one's parents, since the son is not actually feeding or clothing his father at the time. Consequently, this is not a proper fulfillment of a positive mitzva, and therefore the case of a father who instructs his son to drive an animal cannot be used as a source with regard to other instances.

אֶלָּא סָלְקָא דַּעְתָּךְ אָמִינָא: תֵּיתֵי מִבִּנְיַן בֵּית הַמִּקְדָּשׁ. דְּתַנְיָא יָכוֹל יְהֵא בִּנְיַן בֵּית הַמִּקְדָּשׁ דּוֹחֶה שַׁבָּת, תַּלְמוּד לוֹמַר ״אֶת שַׁבְּתוֹתַי תִּשְׁמוֹרוּ וּמִקְדָּשִׁי תִּירָאוּ״ – כּוּלְּכֶם חַיָּיבִין בִּכְבוֹדִי.

Rather, it could **enter your mind to say:** The principle that a positive mitzva overrides even a prohibition that entails *karet* is **derived from the building of the Temple. As it is taught** in a *baraita*: One **might** have thought that **the building of the Temple should override**[N] Shabbat; therefore, **the verse states: "You shall keep My *Shabbatot* and revere My Sanctuary,** I am the Lord" (Leviticus 19:30), which means that **all of you are obligated in My honor.**[H] God is honored when Shabbat is observed, and He demands the observance of Shabbat even when the Temple is being built.

מַאי לָאו בְּבוֹנֶה וְסוֹתֵר, וְטַעְמָא דִּכְתַב רַחֲמָנָא ״אֶת שַׁבְּתוֹתַי תִּשְׁמוֹרוּ״, הָא לָאו הָכִי – דָּחֵי!

The Gemara analyzes this *baraita*: **What, is it not** referring **to** building the Temple by performing prohibited labors on Shabbat whose violation entails *karet,* such as **building and demolishing? And the reason** the building of Temple does not override Shabbat is that **the Merciful One** specifically **writes: "Keep My *Shabbatot,*"** from which it may be inferred that **if that were not so,** the positive mitzva **would override** Shabbat. It is therefore possible to deduce from here that in general, positive mitzvot override even prohibitions that entail *karet.*

לָא, לָאו דְּמַחְמֵר, וַאֲפִילּוּ הָכִי לָא דָּחֵי. וְאֶלָּא דְּקַיְימָא לַן דְּאָתֵי עֲשֵׂה וְדָחֵי לֹא תַעֲשֶׂה, לִיגְמַר מֵהָכָא דְּלָא דָּחֵי!

The Gemara responds: **No,** here too the reference is to the **prohibition against driving** a laden **animal, and even so** the positive mitzva to build the Temple does **not override** the prohibition against driving a laden animal on Shabbat. The Gemara asks again, as before: If so, **rather** than that principle in **which we maintain that a positive mitzva comes and overrides a prohibition, let us derive from here that it does not override** even a regular prohibition.

וְכִי תֵּימָא: שָׁאנֵי לָאוֵי דְּשַׁבָּת דַּחֲמִירִי – וְהָא תַּנָּא בְּעָלְמָא קָאֵי וְלֹא קָא פָּרֵיךְ! דְּתַנְיָא: יָכוֹל אָמַר לוֹ אָבִיו: הִיטַּמֵּא! אוֹ שֶׁאָמַר לוֹ: אַל תַּחֲזִיר! יָכוֹל יִשְׁמַע לוֹ, תַּלְמוּד לוֹמַר ״אִישׁ אִמּוֹ וְאָבִיו תִּירָאוּ״ וגו׳ – כּוּלְּכֶם חַיָּיבִים בִּכְבוֹדִי.

And if you say that prohibitions of Shabbat are different in **that they are** more **severe,** this cannot be the case, **as the *tanna* speaks generally and he does not raise any difficulty** of this kind **as it is taught** in the aforementioned *baraita*: One **might** have thought **that if one's father said to** his son who is a priest or nazirite: **Be rendered ritually impure, or if he said to him: Do not return** this lost item, it **might** have been supposed that his son **should obey him.** Therefore, **the verse states: "You shall fear every man his mother and his father** and you shall keep My *Shabbatot,* I am the Lord your God" (Leviticus 19:3), which means: **All of you are obligated in My honor.**

אֶלָּא, מִשּׁוּם דְּאִיכָּא לְמִיפְרַךְ: מַה לְּהָנָךְ – שֶׁכֵּן הֶכְשֵׁר מִצְוָה. הֶכְשֵׁר מִצְוָה תֵּיפּוֹק לִי מֵהָתָם?

Rather, there is no proof from here with regard to all Torah prohibitions, **because there is room to refute** that argument as follows: **What** about the fact **that these** instances of driving an animal on Shabbat are merely **a preparation for the mitzva** of building the Temple, and is not a mitzva in itself? The Gemara raises a difficulty: **Let** the *halakha* that **preparation for a mitzva** does not override a prohibition **be derived from there,** the case of honoring one's parents, as stated previously. Why repeat this matter with regard to the building of the Temple?

NOTES

Preparation for the mitzva – הֶכְשֵׁר מִצְוָה: Rashi explains that preparation for the mitzva means that the performance of the mitzva, in this instance honoring one's father, cannot be accomplished without violating a prohibition at the very same moment. This is not the case in levirate marriage, as one can perform *ḥalitza*. The phrase: What about the fact that these, provides a measure of support for his interpretation, as this phrase typically refers back to the previous case, which is that of a father who instructs his son to commit a prohibition, not a son who drives an animal in his father's honor, as claimed by other commentaries.

However, most early commentaries raise difficulties against Rashi's explanation from both linguistic and substantive perspectives. They prefer the interpretation of Rabbeinu Ḥananel that the Gemara is referring to the prohibition against driving an animal on Shabbat, and the phrase: Preparation for the mitzva, means preparatory work that does not in itself fulfill the mitzva (*Tosafot*; Ramban; Rashba). Some add that as most of the actions one performs for his father do not constitute an actual fulfillment of the mitzva to honor him, as that is achieved only by providing him with food and clothing, it can be argued that even when one is providing his father with food and clothing this positive mitzva does not override a prohibition (*Tosafot*).

The building of the Temple should override, etc. – יְהֵא בִּנְיַן בֵּית הַמִּקְדָּשׁ דּוֹחֶה וכו׳: Although the observance of Shabbat involves both a positive mitzva and a prohibition, it might have been claimed that the positive mitzva to build the Temple, which involves the entire community, is important enough to override even Shabbat (*Arukh LaNer*). One problem that arises here is that the Gemara describes Shabbat as God's honor, and although the Temple is also built in the honor of Heaven, nevertheless, as it is constructed primarily so that the Divine Presence should dwell among the Jewish people and to atone for their sins, it is more to man's benefit than the mitzva of Shabbat.

HALAKHA

Building the Temple on Shabbat – בִּנְיַן הַמִּקְדָּשׁ בְּשַׁבָּת: The building of the Temple does not override the Festivals, which are termed Shabbat (Rashi), and all the more so does it not override Shabbat itself (Rambam *Sefer Avoda, Hilkhot Beit HaBeḥira* 1:12).

אין הכי נמי. "וְאֶת שַׁבְּתוֹתַי תִּשְׁמוֹרוּ וּמִקְדָּשִׁי תִּירָאוּ" לָמָּה לִי? מִיבְּעֵי לֵיהּ לְכִדְתַנְיָא: יָכוֹל יִתְיָירֵא אָדָם מִמִּקְדָּשׁ – תַּלְמוּד לוֹמַר "אֶת שַׁבְּתוֹתַי תִּשְׁמוֹרוּ וְאֶת מִקְדָּשִׁי תִּירָאוּ" – נֶאֶמְרָה שְׁמִירָה בְּשַׁבָּת וְנֶאֶמְרָה מוֹרָא בְּמִקְדָּשׁ, מַה שְּׁמִירָה הָאֲמוּרָה בְּשַׁבָּת,

The Gemara responds: **Yes, it is indeed so.** And **why do I** need the verse: **"You shall keep My *Shabbatot*, and revere My Sanctuary"** (Leviticus 19:30)? After all, the *halakha* that the building of the Temple does not override the prohibition against driving an animal on Shabbat is derived from the case of honoring one's parents. The Gemara answers: **It is necessary**[N] to derive **that which is taught** in a *baraita*: One **might** have thought that **a person should be in reverence of the Temple** and turn the Temple itself into an object of worship. Therefore, **the verse states: "You shall keep My *Shabbatot*, and revere My Sanctuary."** The term **keeping is stated** with regard **to Shabbat, and** the term **reverence is stated** with regard **to the Temple. Just as** in the case of **keeping stated** with regard **to Shabbat,**

NOTES

Revere My Sanctuary… it is necessary, etc. – מִקְדָּשִׁי תִּירָאוּ...מִיבְּעֵי לֵיהּ וכו׳: How can this verse serve as the source for this *halakha*? After all, the *tanna* already derived from this verse that the building of the Temple does not override Shabbat. The commentaries explain that the derivation brought by the *tanna* with regard to the reverence of the building of the Temple is cited merely in support, while the primary purpose of the verse is to teach a different matter (Ritva).

Perek **I**
Daf **6** Amud **b**

לֹא מִשַּׁבָּת אַתָּה מִתְיָירֵא, אֶלָּא מִמִּי שֶׁהִזְהִיר עַל הַשַּׁבָּת. אַף מוֹרָא הָאֲמוּרָה בְּמִקְדָּשׁ, לֹא מִמִּקְדָּשׁ אַתָּה מִתְיָירֵא אֶלָּא מִמִּי שֶׁהִזְהִיר עַל הַמִּקְדָּשׁ.

you do not revere Shabbat[N] itself, as reverence is not mentioned in this context, but **rather,** one reveres **He Who warned about** the observance of **Shabbat, so too,** the same applies to **the reverence stated** with regard **to the Temple: You do not revere the Temple**[NH] itself **but He Who warned about the Temple.**

וְאֵי זוֹ הִיא מוֹרָא מִקְדָּשׁ? לֹא יִכָּנֵס אָדָם בְּהַר הַבַּיִת בְּמַקְלוֹ, בְּמִנְעָלוֹ, בְּפוּנְדָּתוֹ, וּבְאָבָק שֶׁעַל גַּבֵּי רַגְלָיו, וְלֹא יַעֲשֶׂנּוּ קַפֶּנְדַּרְיָא, וּרְקִיקָה מִקַּל וָחוֹמֶר.

The *baraita* explains: **And what is the reverence of the Temple?**[NH] In deference to the Temple, **a person may not enter the Temple Mount with his staff, his shoes, his money belt** [*punda*],[L] **or** even **the dust on his feet. One may not make** the Temple **a shortcut** [*kappendarya*][L] to pass through it, **and through an *a fortiori*** inference,[B] all the more so **one may not spit** on the Temple Mount, as no disrespect is meant by the other actions, whereas spitting is repulsive even in one's own private home, and certainly on the Temple Mount.

וְאֵין לִי אֶלָּא בִּזְמַן שֶׁבֵּית הַמִּקְדָּשׁ קַיָּים, בִּזְמַן שֶׁאֵין בֵּית הַמִּקְדָּשׁ קַיָּים מִנַּיִן? תַּלְמוּד לוֹמַר "אֶת שַׁבְּתוֹתַי תִּשְׁמוֹרוּ וּמִקְדָּשִׁי תִּירָאוּ", מַה שְּׁמִירָה הָאֲמוּרָה בְּשַׁבָּת – לְעוֹלָם, אַף מוֹרָא הָאֲמוּרָה בְּמִקְדָּשׁ – לְעוֹלָם.

And I have derived **only** that one is obligated to act in this manner **when the Temple is standing. From where** do I derive that the mitzva to revere the Temple is in force **when the Temple is not standing,**[NH] i.e., that it is prohibited to be disrespectful toward the place where the Temple stood? **The verse states: "You shall keep My *Shabbatot*, and revere My Sanctuary"** (Leviticus 19:30). **Just as the keeping stated** with regard **to Shabbat** applies **forever, so too, the reverence stated** with regard **to the Temple is forever.**

NOTES

You do not revere Shabbat – לֹא מִשַּׁבָּת אַתָּה מִתְיָירֵא: This statement is cited in support of the claim of *Sefer Yere'im* that there is a special mitzva to revere Shabbat. In other words, one must be respectful and fearful lest he fail to fulfill all of its mitzvot in the proper manner. A similar idea is found in the *Tikkunei HaZohar* (*Gilyonei HaShas*).

You do not revere the Temple – לֹא מִמִּקְדָּשׁ אַתָּה מִתְיָירֵא: Why is it necessary to stress this point particularly with regard to the Temple rather than, say, in relation to honoring one's parents? One novel answer is that one need not be worried for the safety of the Temple and appoint guards to watch over it. Admittedly, there is a mitzva for priests and Levites to stand as guards over the Temple, but that is performed in honor of God, not to provide protection for the Temple itself. Accordingly, the comparison here is between guarding Shabbat and guarding the physical building of the Temple (*Iyyun Ya'akov*).

What is the reverence of the Temple – אֵי זוֹ הִיא מוֹרָא מִקְדָּשׁ: The commentaries note that although the term: Temple, in its most precise sense, refers only to the area from the courtyard inward, the mitzva to revere the Temple applies to its entrance as well (*Gilyonei HaShas*). Others claim that the mitzva to revere the Sanctuary applies by Torah law only up to the courtyards, and the Sages extended the mitzva to include the entire Temple Mount.

Reverence for the Temple in its destruction – מוֹרָא מִקְדָּשׁ בְּחֻרְבָּנוֹ: Some commentaries note that there is a dispute as to whether the sanctity of the Temple applies only when it is standing or whether it lasts forever. If its sanctity is permanent, why is it necessary to derive from a specific verse that there is an obligation to revere it even in its state of destruction? They answer that it is possible to claim that although the sanctity of the Temple Mount remains intact even in its desolation, nevertheless, with its destruction the mitzva of reverence is nullified. Therefore, this special derivation was necessary (*Arukh LaNer*).

HALAKHA

You do not revere the Temple – לֹא מִמִּקְדָּשׁ אַתָּה מִתְיָירֵא: There is a positive mitzva to revere the Temple, in accordance with the verse: "Revere My Sanctuary" (Leviticus 19:30). However, it is not the Temple itself that is the object of reverence but the One Who commanded that it must be revered (Rambam *Sefer Avoda, Hilkhot Beit HaBeḥira* 7:1).

What is the reverence of the Temple – אֵי זוֹ הִיא מוֹרָא מִקְדָּשׁ: Revering the Temple entails not entering even the Temple Mount with one's walking stick, pouch, shoes on one's feet, or dust on one's feet, coins bundled in one's clothing, and needless to say, it is prohibited to spit anywhere in the Temple Mount. Furthermore, one may not use the Temple Mount as a shortcut for his own needs, and one may enter only for the purpose of a mitzva (Rambam *Sefer Avoda, Hilkhot Beit HaBeḥira* 7:2).

Reverence of the Temple in its destruction – מוֹרָא מִקְדָּשׁ בְּחֻרְבָּנוֹ: Even after the Temple was destroyed, one must continue to revere it just as when it was standing. One may enter only those places where it was previously permitted, one may not sit in the courtyard, and one may not act with negligence or in a disrespectful manner in the vicinity of the eastern gate (Rambam *Sefer Avoda, Hilkhot Beit HaBeḥira* 7:7).

LANGUAGE

Money belt [*punda*] – פֻּנְדָּה: From the Greek φοῦνδα, *funda*, or the Latin funda, meaning belt or sling. A *punda*, which is occasionally rendered in the text as *apunda*, is a hollow belt that serves as both a belt and a wallet, with a pocket for money.

Shortcut [*kappendarya*] – קַפֶּנְדַּרְיָה: Apparently from the Latin compendiaria, which means a short way, i.e., a shortcut through a house or courtyard.

BACKGROUND

An *a fortiori* inference – קַל וָחוֹמֶר: One of the fundamental principles of rabbinic exegesis, the *a fortiori* inference appears in all of the standard lists of exegetical principles. In essence, it is a principle of logical argumentation in which a comparison is drawn between two cases, one more lenient and the other more stringent. The *a fortiori* assertion is that if the *halakha* is stringent in a case where the ruling is usually lenient, all the more so it will be stringent in a more serious case. Likewise, if the *halakha* is lenient in a case where the ruling is not usually lenient, it will certainly be lenient in a less stringent case. *A fortiori* reasoning appears in the Bible, and the Sages compiled lists of verses that employ the logic of *a fortiori*, e.g., "If you have run with the foot soldiers, and they have wearied you, how can you contend with horses?" (Jeremiah 12:5).

NOTES

What is the meaning when the verse states this, etc. – מה תלמוד לומר וכו׳: This section, from the reiteration of: What is the meaning when the verse states this, until: Why do I need the term "habitations" that the Merciful One writes with regard to Shabbat, does not belong to the *baraita* but rather is part of the Gemara's own analysis of the matter at hand. The *baraita* continues with the answer of Rabbi Yishmael's student (Rashba).

HALAKHA

Court-imposed capital punishment on Shabbat – מיתת בית דין בשבת: A court may not administer any bodily punishment on Shabbat or a Festival, neither capital punishment nor lashes. Accordingly, capital cases are not tried on the eve of a Shabbat or a Festival, lest the death penalty be pronounced. Since it is not permitted to carry out the sentence on Shabbat or Festivals, this would delay the execution of justice, which is prohibited (Rambam *Sefer Zemanim*, *Hilkhot Shabbat* 24:7 and *Sefer Shofetim*, *Hilkhot Sanhedrin* 11:2).

אלא סלקא דעתך אמינא: תיתי מהבערה, דתנא דבי רבי ישמעאל: ״לא תבערו אש בכל מושבותיכם״, מה תלמוד לומר?

§ With regard to the issue at hand, the Gemara has not yet found an explanation as to why a specific inference was required to teach that a positive mitzva overrides a prohibition that incurs *karet*. **Rather,** it might **enter your mind to say** that this claim might **be derived from** the *halakha* of **kindling, as the school of Rabbi Yishmael taught** with regard to the verse: **"You shall kindle no fire throughout your habitations** on Shabbat day" (Exodus 35:3). **What** is the meaning when **the verse states** this, as the general prohibition against performing labor on Shabbat appears elsewhere?

מה תלמוד לומר?! אי לרבי יוסי – ללאו, אי לרבי נתן – לחלק!

The Gemara expresses puzzlement at this question: **What** is the meaning when **the verse states** this?[N] What kind of question is this? **If** the *halakha* is in accordance with the opinion **of Rabbi Yosei,** the verse comes to teach **that** one who kindles fire on Shabbat merely violates a regular **prohibition,** which does not entail the penalty of stoning, unlike other prohibited labors. **If** the *halakha* is in accordance with the opinion **of Rabbi Natan,** kindling was singled out **to divide** the various prohibited labors of Shabbat and to establish liability for the separate performance of each of them.

דתניא: הבערה ללאו יצתה, דברי רבי יוסי. רבי נתן אומר: לחלק.

As it is taught in a *baraita*: The prohibition against **kindling was** singled **out** from the general category of prohibited labors and written explicitly to teach that it is unlike other prohibited labors, **as** it is a regular **prohibition,** which does not entail the punishment of stoning. This is **the statement of Rabbi Yosei. Rabbi Natan says:** Kindling is like any other labor prohibited on Shabbat, and **it was** singled out **to divide.** In other words, by stating one prohibited labor separately, the Torah teaches that each labor on Shabbat constitutes its own separate prohibition. Consequently, one who unwittingly violates several categories of labor is obligated to bring as many sin-offerings as the prohibited labors he violated.

ואמר רבא: תנא – מושבות קא קשיא ליה: ״מושבות״ מה תלמוד לומר?

And Rava said in explanation of the question asked by the school of Rabbi Yishmael: For this ***tanna,*** the term **"habitations"** poses **a difficulty with regard to** his opinion. The *baraita* should be understood as follows: **What** is the meaning when **the verse states "habitations"?** What additional inference is indicated by this term, which might lead to the erroneous conclusion that this Shabbat prohibition applies only in certain places of habitation?

מכדי שבת חובת הגוף היא, וחובת הגוף נוהגת בין בארץ בין בחוץ לארץ, מושבות דכתב רחמנא בשבת למה לי?

The Gemara explains why "habitations" cannot mean that Shabbat observance applies only in certain places. **Since Shabbat is an obligation** that applies **to the body,** i.e., to the individual himself and not to an external object, **and** there is a principle that **obligations of the body apply both in Eretz** Yisrael **and outside** of **Eretz** Yisrael, then **why do I** need the term **"habitations" that the Merciful One writes** with regard **to Shabbat?**

משום רבי ישמעאל אמר תלמיד אחד: לפי שנאמר ״וכי יהיה באיש חטא משפט מות והומת״ שומע אני בין בחול בין בשבת, ומה אני מקיים ״מחלליה מות יומת״ – בשאר מלאכות, חוץ ממיתת בית דין. או אינו אלא אפילו מיתת בית דין, ומה אני מקיים ״והומת״ – בחול, ולא בשבת,

A student said in the name of Rabbi Yishmael that **since it is stated: "And if a man has committed a sin worthy of death, and he is put to death"** (Deuteronomy 21:22), **I** would **derive** that the death penalty is administered **whether on a weekday** or **on a Shabbat. And how do I establish** the verse: "And you shall keep Shabbat, for it is sacred to you; **every one who profanes it shall surely be put to death"** (Exodus 31:14)? This verse applies **to other** prohibited **labors, except for court-imposed capital punishment,** which must be administered even on Shabbat. **Or** perhaps **it is only** the case that **even court-imposed capital punishment** is included in the list of prohibited labors on Shabbat. **How,** then, **do I establish** the verse: **"And he is put to death"?** This is referring **to a weekday and not to Shabbat.**[H]

או אינו אלא אפילו בשבת? תלמוד לומר: ״לא תבערו אש בכל מושבותיכם״ ולהלן הוא אומר ״והיו אלה לכם לחקת משפט לדורותיכם בכל מושבותיכם״.

Surprisingly, the *tanna* reverts back to his earlier claim: **Or** perhaps **it is only** the case that capital punishments may be administered **even on Shabbat?** Therefore, **the verse states** by way of a verbal analogy: **"You shall kindle no fire throughout your habitations** on Shabbat day" (Exodus 35:3) **and below it says,** at the end of the chapter dealing with murderers: **"And these things shall be for you a statute of judgment to you throughout your generations in all your habitations"** (Numbers 35:29).

מַה מוֹשָׁבוֹת הָאֲמוּרִים לְהַלָּן בְּבֵית דִּין – אַף מוֹשָׁבוֹת הָאֲמוּרִים כָּאן בְּבֵית דִּין, וְאָמַר רַחֲמָנָא "לֹא תְבַעֲרוּ".

Just as the term **"habitations" stated below,** in Numbers, means **in the court,** where judgment is performed, **so too,** the term **"habitations" stated here** means **in the court,** i.e., in the place where judges preside. **And the Merciful One states** in the Torah: **"You shall kindle no** fire." Since one of the court-imposed death penalties is burning, which is performed by kindling fire, then evidently, court-imposed death penalties do not override Shabbat.

מַאי לָאו רַבִּי נָתָן הִיא, דְּאָמַר לְחַלֵּק יָצְתָה, וְטַעְמָא דִּכְתַב רַחֲמָנָא "לֹא תְבַעֲרוּ", הָא לָאו הָכִי דָּחֵי!

With the above conclusion in mind, the Gemara comments: **What, is it not** the case that the opinion of the school of Rabbi Yishmael is in accordance with that of **Rabbi Natan, who said** that the prohibition against kindling fire **was** singled **out to divide,** and therefore lighting a fire is punishable by *karet* and stoning? **And** if so, **the reason** why capital punishments are not administered on Shabbat is **that the Merciful One writes: "You shall kindle no** fire," from which it may be inferred that **if it were not so,** then court-imposed capital punishment **would override** Shabbat. In other words, the positive mitzva of legal execution would override the prohibition against lighting a fire on Shabbat, which incurs *karet.*

לָא, רַבִּי יוֹסֵי. וְתֶיהֱוֵי נַמִי רַבִּי יוֹסֵי, אֵימַר דְּאָמַר רַבִּי יוֹסֵי הַבְעָרָה לְלָאו יָצְתָה – הַבְעָרָה גְּרֵידְתָּא,

The Gemara rejects this: **No,** there is no proof from here, as it can be claimed that the opinion of the *tanna* from the school of Rabbi Yishmael is in accordance with the opinion of **Rabbi Yosei** that kindling fire is an ordinary prohibition. The Gemara retorts: **And let it even be** according to the opinion of **Rabbi Yosei. You** can **say that** when **Rabbi Yosei said** that **kindling was** singled **out as a prohibition,** he was referring to **kindling alone,** i.e., that lighting a regular fire is only a regular prohibition.

הַבְעָרָה דְּבֵית דִּין בִּישּׁוּל פְּתִילָה הוּא,

Conversely, the **kindling by the court** for the execution of burning **is** actually the **cooking**[N] **of** a leaden **wick.**[B] Since execution by burning involves melting, or cooking, a piece of lead, called a wick, and pouring it into the mouth of the convict, it therefore constitutes the prohibited labor of cooking, which is a different prohibition than kindling fire.

וְאָמַר רַב שֵׁשֶׁת: מַה לִּי בִּישּׁוּל פְּתִילָה מַה לִּי בִּישּׁוּל סַמָּנִין!

And Rav Sheshet said in this regard: **What** difference **is** there **to me** between **cooking a wick,** which is performed for court-imposed capital punishments, and **what** difference **is** there **to me** between the **cooking of herbs**[N] used to dye curtains for the Tabernacle, from whose work the list of prohibited labors on Shabbat is derived? Since the court-imposed death penalty involves the prohibited labor of cooking, which according to all opinions incurs *karet,* this apparently indicates that without the special verse that renders this prohibited, one would have said that a positive mitzva overrides a prohibition for which one is liable to receive *karet.*

אֲמַר רַב שִׁימִי בַּר אָשֵׁי: הַאי תַּנָּא לָא מִשּׁוּם דְּאָתֵי עֲשֵׂה וְדָחֵי לֹא תַעֲשֶׂה, אֶלָּא מִשּׁוּם דְּמַיְיתֵי מִקַּל וָחוֹמֶר, וְהָכִי קָאָמַר: מָה אֲנִי מְקַיֵּים "מְחַלְלֶיהָ מוֹת יוּמָת" בִּשְׁאָר מְלָאכוֹת, חוּץ מִמִּיתַת בֵּית דִּין, אֲבָל מִיתַת בֵּית דִּין – דָּחְיָא שַׁבָּת מִקַּל וָחוֹמֶר.

The Gemara rejects this argument as well. **Rav Shimi bar Ashi said: This** *tanna* does **not** raise the possibility that a court-administered death penalty might override Shabbat **because a positive mitzva comes and overrides a prohibition. Rather,** he entertains this option **because he learns this by** means of an *a fortiori* inference, **and this is what** he **is saying: How do I establish** the verse **"Every one who profanes it shall surely be put to death"** (Exodus 31:14)? This applies **to other** prohibited **labors, except for court-imposed capital punishment. However,** it could be said that **court-imposed capital punishment overrides Shabbat, by an** *a fortiori* inference:

NOTES

The kindling by the court is cooking – הַבְעָרַת דְּבֵית דִּין בִּישּׁוּל...הוּא: Some commentaries ask why the Gemara does not respond by pointing out that the cooking of a wick is merely the preparation for a mitzva. One answer is that the cooking of the wick and the execution occur simultaneously (Ramban; Ritva). Others reject this claim, as the cooking of the wick necessarily occurs prior to the execution (Rashba). The Rashba himself prefers the resolution suggested by *Tosafot* in several places, that although there are several possible ways to refute this proof, the Gemara chose what it felt was the best of the different answers.

What difference is there to me between the cooking of herbs – מַה לִּי בִּישּׁוּל סַמָּנִין: This comparison was necessary to refute the claim that the prohibited labor of cooking applies only to foods. The Gemara therefore cites a statement to the effect that cooking herbs is also a prohibited labor, and the same applies to the cooking of a wick (Ritva; see *Tosafot* on *Shabbat* 106a).

BACKGROUND

Cooking of a wick [*petila*] – בִּישּׁוּל פְּתִילָה: The Sages learned by tradition that court-imposed capital punishment of burning was not performed by the actual burning of the skin, but by pouring burning lead down the throat of the sentenced convict. Although the term wick [*petila*] generally refers to strings tied together, it is also used in reference to objects that look like wicks, i.e., any small and elongated item. Here it is referring to a piece of lead that was melted, or cooked, for this purpose.

ומה עֲבוֹדָה שֶׁהִיא חֲמוּרָה וְדוֹחָה שַׁבָּת – רְצִיחָה דּוֹחָה אוֹתָהּ, שֶׁנֶּאֱמַר "מֵעִם מִזְבְּחִי תִּקָּחֶנּוּ לָמוּת", שַׁבָּת, שֶׁנִּדְחֵית מִפְּנֵי עֲבוֹדָה, אֵינוֹ דִּין שֶׁתְּהֵא רְצִיחָה דּוֹחָה אוֹתָהּ?

If the Temple **service,** which includes the sacrifice of offerings, **is** so **severe that it overrides Shabbat,** as offerings were brought on Shabbat, and yet the *halakha* of **murder**[N] **overrides it,**[N] i.e., the obligation to execute a sentenced convict overrides the Temple service, **as it is stated** with regard to one sentenced to death: **"You shall take him from My altar, that he may die"** (Exodus 21:14), then in the case of **Shabbat, which is overridden by** the Temple **service, is it not right that** the *halakhot* of **murder should** likewise override it?

וּמַאי "אוֹ אֵינוֹ" דְּקָאָמַר? הָכִי קָאָמַר: קְבוּרַת מֵת מִצְוָה תּוֹכִיחַ, שֶׁדּוֹחָה אֶת הָעֲבוֹדָה וְאֵין דּוֹחָה אֶת הַשַּׁבָּת. הֲדַר אֲמַר: קְבוּרַת מֵת מִצְוָה תִּדְחֶה שַׁבָּת מִקַּל וָחוֹמֶר; וּמָה עֲבוֹדָה שֶׁהִיא דּוֹחָה שַׁבָּת, קְבוּרַת מֵת מִצְוָה דּוֹחָה אוֹתָהּ,

§ The Gemara analyzes a puzzling statement in the above *baraita*. **And what** is the meaning of the claim: **Or** perhaps **it is only** the case that capital punishments may be administered even on Shabbat, **which** the *tanna* **stated** in an unexplained reversion to his previous suggestion? The Gemara explains that **this is what** he **is saying:** The *a fortiori* reasoning can be refuted, as the obligation **to bury a corpse with no one** available **to bury it** [*met mitzva*][B] **can prove** otherwise, as the obligation to bury a *met mitzva* **overrides** the Temple **service, and yet it does not override Shabbat.** The *tanna* **then** retracted his statement and **said** that one can claim that **the burial of a** ***met mitzva*** **overrides Shabbat by** means of the same ***a fortiori*** inference: **If** the Temple **service overrides Shabbat,** and **the burial of a** ***met mitzva*** **overrides** it.

מִ"וּלְאַחוֹתוֹ", שַׁבָּת, שֶׁנִּדְחָה מִפְּנֵי עֲבוֹדָה, אֵינוֹ דִּין שֶׁתְּהֵא קְבוּרַת מֵת מִצְוָה דּוֹחָה אוֹתָהּ? תַּלְמוּד לוֹמַר "לֹא תְבַעֲרוּ".

The Gemara pauses in the middle of the *a fortiori* inference to explain this last point. This is derived **from** the superfluous phrase **"or for his sister"** in the verse "He shall not make himself ritually impure for his father, or for his mother, for his brother, or for his sister, when they die" (Numbers 6:7), which is referring to a nazirite. This verse teaches that even a nazirite on his way to sacrifice the Paschal lamb must render himself ritually impure to bury a *met mitzva*. The Gemara resumes the *a fortiori* inference: If so, as **Shabbat is overridden by** the Temple **service, is it not right that the burial of a** ***met mitzva*** **should override it? Therefore, the verse states: "You shall kindle no** fire throughout your habitations on Shabbat day" (Exodus 35:3).

וּלְמַאי דִּסְלֵיק אַדַּעְתֵּיהּ מֵעִיקָּרָא דְּאָתֵי עֲשֵׂה וְדָחֵי לֹא תַעֲשֶׂה – מַאי "אוֹ אֵינוֹ" דְּקָאָמַר?

This concludes Rav Shimi bar Ashi's interpretation of the *baraita*, that the *tanna* suggested that a court-administered death penalty might override Shabbat not because of the principle that a positive mitzva overrides a prohibition, but due to a potential *a fortiori* inference. The Gemara asks: **And according to that which entered his mind at the outset, that** the assumption of the *tanna* was indeed based on the principle that **a positive mitzva comes and overrides a prohibition, what** is the meaning of the clause: **Or** perhaps **it is only** the case that capital punishments may be administered even on Shabbat, **that** the *tanna* **said?** How should the *baraita* be explained according to the initial interpretation?

NOTES

Murder – רְצִיחָה: It is clear from the context that the Gemara is referring to the punishment that is meted out to a murderer by the court. The term murder in the Torah does not exclusively mean criminal killings, as it is used with regard to an avenger of blood as well: "Whosoever kills any person, the murderer shall be murdered according to witnesses" (Numbers 35:30).

Murder overrides it – רְצִיחָה דּוֹחָה אוֹתָהּ: Some commentaries add that even if no other priest is available, and the Temple service would be entirely neglected, the obligation to execute a priest who is guilty of murder nevertheless overrides the Temple service. Rashi maintains that if the guilty priest is in the middle of the Temple service, he is allowed to complete it, whereas the Rambam rules that even if the priest merely began his service he is not given the chance to finish it. The commentaries point out that this opinion of the Rambam's brings the *halakha* of murder closer in line with the cases of levirate marriage and Shabbat in this regard (*Arukh LaNer* on *Mishne LaMelekh*).

BACKGROUND

A corpse with no one to bury it [*met mitzva*] – מֵת מִצְוָה: It is an important religious duty to attend to the burial of the dead. If the deceased has no acquaintances or relatives to bury him, all are obligated to assist in his burial. The *halakha* is that a corpse with no one available to bury it acquires its place, i.e., the body must be interred where it was found. This is the case provided that it is in a dignified location; otherwise, the body must be buried in the nearest cemetery. This obligation is so important that even priests and nazirites, who are ordinarily prohibited from coming into contact with a corpse, must bury an abandoned corpse if there is no one else available to do so. Likewise, the obligation to bury this corpse takes precedence over nearly all other religious duties.

הָכִי קָאָמַר: מָה אֲנִי מְקַיֵּים ״מְחַלְלֶיהָ מוֹת יוּמָת״ בִּשְׁאָר מְלָאכוֹת, חוּץ מִמִּיתַת בֵּית דִּין, אֲבָל מִיתַת בֵּית דִּין דָּחֵי שַׁבָּת, דְּאָתֵי עֲשֵׂה וְדָחֵי לֹא תַעֲשֶׂה.

The Gemara explains that **this is what** the *tanna* **is saying:** It would have been possible to say the following: **How do I establish** the verse **"Every one who profanes it shall surely be put to death"** (Exodus 31:14)? This applies **to other** prohibited **labors, except for court-imposed capital punishment. However, court-imposed capital punishment overrides Shabbat,**[N] **as a positive mitzva comes and overrides a prohibition.**

הֲדַר אֲמַר: אֵימַר דְּאָמְרִינַן דְּאָתֵי עֲשֵׂה וְדָחֵי לֹא תַעֲשֶׂה – לֹא תַעֲשֶׂה גְּרֵידָא, לֹא תַעֲשֶׂה שֶׁיֵּשׁ בּוֹ כָּרֵת – מִי שָׁמְעַתְּ לֵיהּ דְּדָחֵי? הֲדַר אֲמַר: אַטּוּ עֲשֵׂה דּוֹחֶה אֶת לֹא תַעֲשֶׂה, לָאו לֹא תַעֲשֶׂה חָמוּר מִינֵּיהּ, וְקָאָתֵי עֲשֵׂה וְדָחֵי לֵיהּ,

The *tanna* **then** retracted his statement and **said:** You can **say that we stated** the principle **that a positive mitzva comes and overrides a prohibition,** yet this is true for a regular **prohibition alone.** However, **did you hear that it overrides a prohibition that includes** ***karet*****?** The *tanna* **then said,** hinting at a counterclaim: **Is that not to say,** with regard to the principle that **a positive mitzva overrides a prohibition,** that **the prohibition is more stringent than** the positive mitzva?[N] After all, the court punishes one who violates a prohibition with lashes, which is not the case for a failure to uphold a positive mitzva. **And** yet by Torah law **the positive mitzva comes and overrides it.**

מַה לִּי חוּמְרָא זוּטָא, וּמַה לִּי חוּמְרָא רַבָּה? תַּלְמוּד לוֹמַר ״לֹא תְבַעֲרוּ״.

If so, **what difference** is it **to me** if it is a case of **a minor stringency**[N] **and what difference** is it **to me** if it is **a major stringency?** Once the Torah has stated that a positive mitzva supersedes a prohibition, there should be no difference between a relatively stringent prohibition and a lenient one. Therefore, **the verse states: "You shall not kindle."**[N] In sum, the Gemara has not found a clear proof for the opinion that a positive mitzva supersedes a prohibition that incurs *karet*.

אֶלָּא [אִיצְטְרִיךְ]: סָלְקָא דַּעְתָּךְ אָמִינָא, תֶּיהֱוֵי הַאי אֵשֶׁת אָח דָּבָר שֶׁהָיָה בִּכְלָל וְיָצָא מִן הַכְּלָל לְלַמֵּד, לֹא לְלַמֵּד עַל עַצְמוֹ יָצָא אֶלָּא לְלַמֵּד עַל הַכְּלָל כּוּלּוֹ יָצָא.

Consequently, the Gemara suggests a different interpretation. The superfluous phrase "with her" indeed teaches that the obligation of levirate marriage does not override the prohibition with regard to women with whom relations are forbidden. However, this derivation is required not because one might have thought that a positive mitzva supersedes a prohibition that incurs *karet*. **Rather,** this phrase **is necessary** because it could **enter your mind to say: Let this** case of **a brother's wife,** to whom the mitzva of levirate marriage applies, **be** treated in accordance with a well-established hermeneutical principle: **A matter that was included in a generalization,**[N] **but emerged to teach, emerged to teach not just about itself**[N] **but to teach about the entire generalization.**

NOTES

Court-imposed capital punishment overrides Shabbat – **מִיתַת בֵּית דִּין דָּחֵי שַׁבָּת:** Why is this even a consideration? After all, the court can simply postpone the capital punishment until after Shabbat. There is no reason to arrive at a situation where it is necessary for the positive mitzva to override the prohibition. One answer, as stated in tractate *Sanhedrin*, is that if the matter were postponed, the judges might forget the full depth of the reasoning that led to their decision, and consequently, if fresh exculpating evidence were found, they would be unable to study the issue properly. Therefore, this mitzva must be performed without delay (*Tosefot HaRosh*).

The prohibition is more stringent than the positive mitzva – **לֹא תַעֲשֶׂה חָמוּר מִינֵּיהּ:** According to Rashi, what makes a prohibition more stringent is that one receives lashes for its violation, which is not the case for a positive mitzva. Some commentaries challenge this explanation, as it is sometimes stated that a prohibition is so severe that one is not given lashes for it, because one cannot make amends for it in this manner. Some write that the various levels of atonement indicate that one who transgresses a positive mitzva can more readily achieve penitence. Others disagree and say that an analysis of this issue from the perspective of the ease of repentance does not constitute conclusive proof (*Iggeret HaTeshuva*). Yet others suggest that one who transgresses a positive mitzva does so merely by refraining from action, whereas one who violates a prohibition actively sins (*Arukh LaNer*). See Ramban's commentary on Exodus 20:8 and the question of the *Yad Malakhi* there (see *Meshekh Ḥokhma*).

What difference is it to me if it is a case of a minor stringency, etc. – **מַה לִּי חוּמְרָא זוּטָא וכו׳:** Since the entire discussion of the Gemara has been based on the assumption that there is a difference between ordinary prohibitions and those that incur *karet*, how is it possible for the Gemara suddenly to reverse this assumption without any proof (*Tosafot Yeshanim*)? The answer given is that if the phrase "with her" is not teaching that certain relatives remain forbidden, but rather it is indicating that the previously forbidden relation of a sister-in-law is permitted, this shows that there is no difference between an ordinary prohibition and one that incurs *karet*.

The verse states, You shall not kindle – **תַּלְמוּד לוֹמַר לֹא תְבַעֲרוּ:** One could argue that the reason kindling does not override Shabbat is that it is merely a preparation for the fulfillment of the mitzva to perform an execution by burning, whereas an execution by stoning or decapitation, in which the prohibition is violated at the very moment the mitzva is fulfilled, would indeed override Shabbat. The commentaries explain that once the Gemara has stated the argument: What difference is it to me if it is a case of a minor stringency, etc., this differentiation is no longer applicable (Rashba).

A matter that was included in a generalization, etc. – **דָּבָר שֶׁהָיָה בִּכְלָל וכו׳:** In essence, the principle: A matter that was included in a generalization, etc., is similar to inferences by analogy or the method of: What do we find with regard to, etc. In other words, it makes use of inductive reasoning, from the detail to the generalization, i.e., that which is correct for the specific case is true for the entire general category. Incidentally, an analogy differs in this regard, as it is not limited to a particular category, whereas here the novel *halakha* of the detail applies only to other cases within the same generalization. The difference between this principle and: A matter specified to discuss a new matter, is that when the detailed case is singled out here from the generalization, the novel *halakha* does not run counter to the generalization but instead adds to it. Conversely, in the case of: A matter specified to discuss a new matter, the additional detail contradicts the generalization to a greater or lesser extent. In these cases the special ruling is not considered part of the general category but a unique case of its own.

To teach not about itself, etc. – **לֹא לְלַמֵּד עַל עַצְמוֹ וכו׳:** Some commentaries note that this case is unlike the other instances of: A matter intended to teach not only about itself, as here the verse does not teach anything new with regard to peace-offerings at all, and therefore it cannot be classified as a matter that teaches about itself. Some explain that the generalization stated with regard to this subject refers exclusively to priests (Leviticus 7:20), and therefore the mention of peace-offerings does teach a novelty about itself, i.e., that this prohibition applies equally to all Jews (Ritva).

דְּתַנְיָא: דָּבָר שֶׁהָיָה בַּכְּלָל וְיָצָא מִן הַכְּלָל
וכו׳ כֵּיצַד?

The Gemara explains the application of this principle to the current case. Since the prohibition proscribing a brother's wife is included in the general prohibition with regard to women with whom relations are forbidden, it can be claimed that the *halakha* of levirate marriage renders not only a brother's childless wife permitted, but in this case it renders permitted all women with whom relations are usually forbidden. **As it is taught** in a *baraita* that clarifies this hermeneutical principle: **A matter that was included in a generalization, but emerged** to teach, emerged to teach not just about itself but to teach about the entire generalization. **How so?**

״וְהַנֶּפֶשׁ אֲשֶׁר תֹּאכַל בָּשָׂר מִזֶּבַח
הַשְּׁלָמִים וְטוּמְאָתוֹ עָלָיו״, וַהֲלֹא שְׁלָמִים
בִּכְלַל קָדָשִׁים הָיוּ, וְלָמָּה יָצְאוּ – לְהַקִּישׁ
אֲלֵיהֶן, וְלוֹמַר לְךָ: מַה שְּׁלָמִים מְיוּחָדִים
קָדְשֵׁי מִזְבֵּחַ – אַף כָּל קָדְשֵׁי מִזְבֵּחַ, יָצְאוּ
קָדְשֵׁי בֶּדֶק הַבַּיִת.

The *baraita* provides an example of this principle by citing a verse: **"But the soul that eats of the flesh of the sacrifice of peace-offerings** that belong to the Lord, **with his ritual impurity upon him,** that soul shall be cut off from his people" (Leviticus 7:20). **But aren't peace**-offerings **included in** the general category **of** all **consecrated offerings? And why were they** explicitly **singled out** from of the rest in the above verse? **To draw an analogy between them and to say to you: Just as peace**-offerings **are unique** in that they are **consecrated for the altar, so too,** this *halakha* that one who eats of them is liable to receive *karet* applies to **all** food that is **consecrated for the altar,** which **excludes** objects that are **consecrated for the Temple maintenance.**

הָכָא נַמִי: הָא אֵשֶׁת אָח בִּכְלַל כָּל
הָעֲרָיוֹת הָיְתָה, וְלָמָּה יָצְתָה – לְהַקִּישׁ
אֵלֶיהָ וְלוֹמַר לְךָ: מָה אֵשֶׁת אָח שַׁרְיָא –
אַף כָּל עֲרָיוֹת נַמִי שַׁרְיָין.

The above *baraita* provided an example of the principle that an item singled out from a general category teaches a *halakha* with regard to the entire category. **Here too,** one can argue: **This** case of **a brother's wife was included in** the general category of **all** women **with whom relations are forbidden, and why was she singled out? To compare to her and say to you: Just as** a childless **brother's wife is permitted, so too, all** women **with whom relations are forbidden are likewise permitted.**

מִי דָּמֵי? הָתָם כְּלָל בְּאִיסּוּר וּפְרָט
בְּאִיסּוּר. הָכָא – כְּלָל בְּאִיסּוּר וּפְרָט
בְּהֶיתֵּר!

The Gemara raises an objection: **Is it comparable? There,** in the case cited as an example of this hermeneutical principle, **the generalization,** i.e., all offerings, are included **in the prohibition** against eating offerings while ritually impure, **and the detailed** case of peace-offerings is also included **in the prohibition.** Consequently, it can be said that the specific case was singled out to teach about the entire category. By contrast, **here,** in the case of levirate marriage with forbidden relatives, **the generalization** is included **in the prohibition** against engaging in forbidden relations, **and** yet **the detailed case is permitted.** Therefore, it cannot be said that the detail has been singled out so as to clarify some aspect of the general category; rather, its *halakha* differs from the rest.

הָא לָא דָּמֵי אֶלָּא לְדָבָר שֶׁהָיָה בַּכְּלָל
וְיָצָא לִידּוֹן בְּדָבָר הֶחָדָשׁ, שֶׁאִי אַתָּה
יָכוֹל לְהַחֲזִירוֹ לִכְלָלוֹ עַד שֶׁיַּחֲזִירֶנּוּ לְךָ
הַכָּתוּב בְּפֵירוּשׁ. דְּתַנְיָא: דָּבָר שֶׁהָיָה
בַּכְּלָל וְיָצָא לִידּוֹן בְּדָבָר הֶחָדָשׁ אִי אַתָּה
רַשַּׁאי לְהַחֲזִירוֹ לִכְלָלוֹ עַד שֶׁיַּחֲזִירֶנּוּ לְךָ
הַכָּתוּב בְּפֵירוּשׁ.

Instead, this case **is comparable only to** those that fit a different hermeneutical principle, concerning **a matter that was included in a generalization but emerged to discuss a new matter.** If a novel aspect or special ruling is taught with regard to a specific case within a broader general category, **then you cannot return it to its generalization** even for other matters, to the extent that this case has been entirely removed from the general category **until the Torah explicitly returns it** to its generalization. **As it is taught** in a *baraita*: With regard to **a matter that was included in a generalization but emerged to discuss a new matter, you may not return it to its generalization until the Torah explicitly returns it**[N] to its generalization.

כֵּיצַד? ״וְשָׁחַט אֶת הַכֶּבֶשׂ בִּמְקוֹם אֲשֶׁר
יִשְׁחַט אֶת הַחַטָּאת וְאֶת הָעוֹלָה בִּמְקוֹם
הַקֹּדֶשׁ כִּי כַּחַטָּאת הָאָשָׁם הוּא לַכֹּהֵן״
שֶׁאֵין תַּלְמוּד לוֹמַר ״כַּחַטָּאת הָאָשָׁם״,
וּמַה תַּלְמוּד לוֹמַר ״כַּחַטָּאת הָאָשָׁם״ –

How so? The *baraita* provides an example of this principle. With regard to the guilt-offering of a leper, the verse states: **"And he shall slaughter the sheep in the place where they slaughter the sin-offering and the burnt-offering, in the place of the Sanctuary; for as the sin-offering is the priest's, so is the guilt-offering"** (Leviticus 14:13). **As** there is **no** need for **the verse to state: "As the sin-offering ... so is the guilt-offering,"** since apparently this comparison does not teach anything new because the *halakhot* of guilt-offerings are already stated elsewhere (Leviticus 7:1–10), then **what** is the meaning when **the verse states: "As the sin-offering ... so is the guilt-offering"?**

NOTES

Until the Torah restores it, etc. – עַד שֶׁיַּחֲזִירֶנּוּ הַכָּתוּב וכו׳: Since the Torah restored a leper's guilt-offering to its general category, why not learn from it that all guilt-offerings require the placement of blood on the thumb and toe (*Tosafot*)? One answer is that the limiting phrase "This is the law of the guilt-offering" (Leviticus 7:1) serves to exclude this possibility. Furthermore, there is a difference between offerings that provide atonement, e.g., other guilt-offerings, and those that enable their owner to return to his former state of ritual purity, such as the guilt-offering of a leper.

לְפִי שֶׁיָּצָא אֲשַׁם מְצוֹרָע לִידּוֹן בְּדָבָר הֶחָדָשׁ, בְּבֹהֶן יָד וּבֹהֶן רֶגֶל הַיְמָנִית, יָכוֹל לֹא יְהֵא טָעוּן מַתַּן דָּמִים וְאֵימוּרִים לְגַבֵּי מִזְבֵּחַ,

Since the guilt-offering of a leper was specified from the general category of all guilt-offerings **to discuss a new matter,** i.e., that the blood is placed on **the thumb** of the right hand **and the big toe of the right foot** of the leper, one **might** have thought that this guilt-offering **does not require placement of the blood**[H] **and sacrificial parts on the altar,** as for this guilt-offering the placement of blood on the leper is sufficient.

HALAKHA

Placement of the blood for the guilt-offering of a leper – מַתַּן דָּמִים שֶׁל אֲשַׁם מְצוֹרָע: Two priests receive the blood of a leper's guilt-offering. One accepts the blood in a vessel and throws it onto the altar, while the other takes the blood in his right hand and pours it into his left hand, and then sprinkles it with his right index finger. He places the blood in his palm on the leper's right earlobe, the thumb of his right hand, and the big toe of his right foot (Rambam *Sefer Korbanot, Hilkhot Meḥusrei Kappara* 4:2).

Perek **I**
Daf **7** Amud **b**

תַּלְמוּד לוֹמַר ״כִּי כַּחַטָּאת הָאָשָׁם הוּא״, מָה חַטָּאת טְעוּנָה מַתַּן דָּמִים וְאֵימוּרִים לְגַבֵּי מִזְבֵּחַ – אַף אָשָׁם טָעוּן מַתַּן דָּמִים וְאֵימוּרִים לְגַבֵּי מִזְבֵּחַ.

Therefore, **the verse states: "As the sin-offering… so is the guilt-offering"** (Leviticus 7:13), to teach that **just as the sin-offering requires placement of the blood and sacrificial parts on the altar, so too, the** leper's **guilt-offering requires placement of the blood and sacrificial parts on the altar.**

וְאִי לָא אַהַדְרֵיהּ קְרָא הֲוָה אָמֵינָא: לְמַאי דִּנְפַק נְפַק, וּלְמַאי דְּלָא נְפַק – לָא נְפַק. הָכָא נַמִי הֲוָה אָמֵינָא: אֵשֶׁת אָח דְּאִשְׁתְּרָא אִשְׁתְּרַאי, שְׁאָר עֲרָיוֹת – לָא.

The Gemara comments: **And had the verse not** explicitly **restored this** case of guilt-offering to its generalization, **I would say: With regard to that which was excluded** from the generalization as a novel ruling in this case, it was **excluded, and with regard to that** case **which was not excluded,** it was **not excluded, and** therefore the *halakha* would have been different in the various cases. **Here, too, I would say: A brother's wife who was permitted** is **permitted,** whereas the **other** women **with whom relations are forbidden** were **not** permitted at all. Consequently, there is no proof from here that one might have thought that women with whom relations are forbidden are in fact permitted in levirate marriage.

אֶלָּא סָלְקָא דַּעְתָּךְ אָמֵינָא: תֵּיתֵי בְּמָה מָצִינוּ מֵאֵשֶׁת אָח; מָה אֵשֶׁת אָח מִיַּיבְּמָה אַף אֲחוֹת אִשָּׁה תִּתְיַיבֵּם.

§ **Rather,** the suggestion that other women with whom relations are usually forbidden might be permitted for levirate marriage was based on a different argument: It might **enter your mind to say:** Let this claim **be derived by** the hermeneutical principle of: **What do we find**[N] with regard to, which is a principle of inductive reasoning involving a comparison between cases that include similar details. In other words, the *halakha* of all other women with whom relations are forbidden can be derived **from** that of **a brother's wife: Just as a brother's wife enters levirate marriage, so too, a wife's sister should enter into levirate marriage.**

מִי דָּמֵי? הָתָם חַד אִיסּוּרָא, הָכָא – תְּרֵי אִיסּוּרֵי! מַהוּ דְּתֵימָא: הוֹאִיל וְאִשְׁתְּרֵי – אִשְׁתְּרֵי.

The Gemara wonders about this: **Is it comparable?** How can one case be derived from the other? **There,** in the case of a brother's wife, only **one prohibition**[N] has been permitted, the prohibition with regard to a brother's wife, whereas **here,** we are dealing with **two prohibitions,** both a brother's wife and a wife's sister. The Gemara answers: It is nevertheless necessary to refute this suggestion, **lest you say: Since it is permitted, it is permitted.** In other words, as the Torah permitted a brother's wife in levirate marriage despite the fact that she is ordinarily forbidden, she remains permitted even if the additional prohibition with regard to a wife's sister applies to her.

NOTES

Let this be derived by: What do we find – תֵּיתֵי בְּמָה מָצִינוּ: Since the Gemara has already concluded that this case includes a novel aspect, how can it suggest that the case can serve as a source for the entire generalization (Rabbi Avraham *Av Beit Din*)? The answer given is that in fact the *halakha* of levirate marriage is not considered a case of: A matter that was included in a generalization but was specified to discuss a new matter, as this possibility was raised in the Gemara only by way of rejection. In other words, the Gemara was saying that this case certainly cannot be treated as: A matter that was included in a generalization. If anything, it is more similar to the other principle of: A matter that was included in a generalization but was specified to discuss a new matter. The early commentaries discuss why this is not in fact a case of: A new matter. See the Ramban's explanation and the Rashba's objection to his opinion. One opinion is that there is indeed nothing new here, as the entire *halakha* of levirate marriage concerns a brother's wife (Rashba, citing Rabbeinu Yona). Others explain that the principle: A matter that was included in a generalization, is stated only with regard to those subjects that appear in the Torah by way of generalization, after which a certain detail is singled out. With regard to women with whom relations are forbidden, however, although several generalizations can be drawn from them, each specific case is mentioned individually. Consequently, there is no proper generalization here at all (Ritva; Meiri).

There, one prohibition – הָתָם חַד אִיסּוּרָא: The commentaries question this point in light of the previously stated principle that in this regard there is no difference between a prohibition of major severity and one of minor severity. They answer that this idea was stated only concerning a single prohibition, but it does not apply to two independent prohibitions (Rashba).

ומנא תימרא דאמרינן הואיל ואישתרי אישתרי? דתניא: מצורע שחל שמיני שלו בערב הפסח וראה קרי בו ביום וטבל, אמרו חכמים: אף על פי שאין טבול יום אחר נכנס, זה – נכנס,

And from where do you say that we state this reasoning of: **Since it is permitted, it is permitted? As it is taught** in a *baraita*: With regard to a **leper whose eighth** day, on which he becomes ritually pure from his leprosy and brings his last offerings to the Temple,[N] **occurs on the eve of Passover,**[H] **and he experienced a seminal emission**[B] **on that** eighth **day and** then **immersed** in a ritual bath, **the Sages said: Although any other** individual **who immersed himself that day** for purification from his ritual impurity **may not enter** the Temple before sunset, **this** leper, who saw an emission of semen and immersed, **may enter** the Temple.

מוטב שיבא עשה שיש בו כרת וידחה עשה שאין בו כרת. ואמר רבי יוחנן: דבר תורה אפילו עשה לית ביה,

The *baraita* explains the reason for this exception. It is **better that a positive mitzva that includes** ***karet***, i.e., bringing the Paschal lamb at the right time, **comes and overrides a positive mitzva that does not include** ***karet***, i.e., not entering the Temple in a state of ritual impurity. If the leper does not become purified of his leprosy he may not sacrifice the Paschal lamb. **And Rabbi Yoḥanan said:**[N] **By Torah law there is not even** the overriding of **a positive mitzva in this** case of one who immersed himself during the day entering the Temple.

שנאמר "ויעמוד יהושפט בקהל יהודה לפני החצר החדשה". מאי חצר החדשה? אמר (רבי יוחנן): שחדשו בה דברים, ואמרו: טבול יום לא יכנס למחנה לויה.

Rabbi Yoḥanan explains his claim: **As it is stated: "And Jehoshaphat stood in the congregation of Judah** and Jerusalem, in the House of the Lord, **before the new courtyard"** (II Chronicles 20:5). **What is** the meaning of **"the new courtyard"? Rabbi Yoḥanan said:** This is referring to the place **where they issued new matters**[N] **and said** that **one who immersed himself that day**[B] **may not enter the camp of the Levites,** which in Jerusalem is the Temple Mount, despite the fact that by Torah law no such prohibition applies.

ואמר עולא: מה טעם – הואיל והותר לצרעתו הותר לקריו – מי דמי לדעולא?

And with regard to this *halakha* itself, that a leper who experienced a seminal emission may nevertheless sacrifice offerings in the Temple, **Ulla said: What is the reason**[N] that this is permitted to him? **Since it is permitted for his leprosy,** i.e., the Torah allowed him to enter the Temple Mount while still a leper to achieve full ritual purification, which requires that he sacrifice offerings, **it is permitted with regard to his seminal emission** as well. This shows that the *tanna* accepts the principle that as one prohibition is permitted, two prohibitions are likewise permitted. The Gemara rejects this argument: **Is this** assumption **comparable to** the case **of Ulla?**

HALAKHA

A leper whose eighth day occurs on the eve of Passover – מצורע שחל שמיני שלו בערב הפסח: With regard to a leper whose eighth day of his process of ritual purification occurs on the eve of Passover, if he experienced a seminal emission on that day, he immerses himself in a ritual bath, after which he may enter the Women's Courtyard to bring his offerings. Anyone else who immersed that day is prohibited from entering the courtyard. However, as this prohibition applies only by decree of the Sages, and since if the leper does not bring his offerings of purification he will be unable to sacrifice the Paschal lamb, the performance of this positive mitzva, whose neglect incurs *karet*, overrides a prohibition that applies by rabbinic law (Rambam, *Sefer Korbanot, Hilkhot Korban Pesaḥ* 6:5).

BACKGROUND

And he experienced a seminal emission – וראה קרי: Whether an emission of semen occurred involuntarily, intentionally, or during sexual relations, the individual who experienced it becomes ritually impure and cannot enter the Temple precincts. To purify himself, he must immerse in a ritual bath, and after nightfall on the day of his immersion he becomes ritually pure (Leviticus 15:16–18).

One who immersed himself that day – טבול יום: There are many instances of ritual impurity whose elimination involves the two-step process of immersion in a ritual bath, and waiting until nightfall of the day of his immersion. During the period between immersion and nightfall, a certain measure of impurity remains. Consequently, in most cases, it remains prohibited for one who immersed himself during that day to eat offerings or *teruma* if he is a priest; however, it is permitted for him to eat the second tithe.

NOTES

The ritual purification of a leper – טהרת מצורע: This final ritual of the purification of a leper is performed in the following manner: The leper enters the Women's Courtyard and inserts his thumb and big toe through the Gate of Nicanor into the Israelite courtyard, as one who lacks atonement may not enter the Temple. While he stands there, the priest places upon him the blood of the guilt-offering. The purified leper may enter the sacred area of the courtyard and inward only upon the completion of this entire process. See Meiri, who cites various opinions with regard to both the location of the Gate of Nicanor and whether the prohibition against his entry into the Israelite courtyard applies by Torah law or by rabbinic law.

And Rabbi Yoḥanan said, etc. – ואמר רבי יוחנן וכו׳: Rashi on *Zevaḥim* 32b explains that Rabbi Yoḥanan disputes the opinion of the *tanna* of the *baraita*. According to the *tanna*, the reason for this ruling is that a major positive mitzva overrides a minor positive mitzva, whereas Rabbi Yoḥanan holds that there is no positive mitzva here at all. Others disagree and maintain that Rabbi Yoḥanan is actually clarifying the statement of the *baraita* (*Tosafot*). One of their reasons is that since Rabbi Yoḥanan is an *amora*, it is not possible for him to dispute an explicit ruling of a *baraita*. This is also the opinion of the Ramban, the Rashba, and probably the Rambam. However, others agree with Rashi and explain that Rabbi Yoḥanan's opinion is supported by the mishna that, he claims, disputes this *baraita* (*Tosefot Rabbi Shimshon of Saens*). Yet others, who also contend that Rabbi Yoḥanan is explaining the *baraita*, state that although the Sages occasionally strengthened their decrees to the level of Torah law itself, which is why the *baraita* calls it a positive mitzva, in this case they did not do so in opposition to a positive mitzva that incurs *karet* (Ritva).

Where they issued new matters – שחידשו בה דברים: This is supported by the fact that the verse states: "In the congregation of Judah," as the Sages would gather the community together when they wanted to issue a new halakhic ruling, in an effort to publicize it (*Gilyonei HaShas*).

And Ulla said: What is the reason, etc. – ואמר עולא מה טעם וכו׳: Some commentaries maintain that Ulla disagrees with the opinion of Rabbi Yoḥanan and suggests an alternative reason for the leniency (Ritva). However, most commentaries hold that Ulla is simply elaborating further on the matter. Consequently, some ask why Ulla requires another explanation, as Rabbi Yoḥanan has already provided one (*Tosafot Yeshanim*). They answer that there are two aspects to the leniency granted here. First, the leper is allowed to enter the Women's Courtyard. Second, he may extend his thumb and big toe into the sanctified area. With regard to this issue, it cannot be suggested that the positive mitzva does not apply, as Ulla maintains that even partial entrance is classified as entering and is prohibited by Torah law on pain of *karet*. Accordingly, Ulla required the additional reason that once it is permitted with regard to one prohibition, the other prohibition is permitted as well. Some commentaries inquire as to why Rabbi Yoḥanan's statement is cited here at all, since the discussion focuses solely on the opinion of Ulla (*Otzar HaShitot*; see *Arukh LaNer*).

תֵּינַח הֵיכָא דְּנָשָׂא מֵת וְאַחַר כָּךְ נָשָׂא חַי, דְּמִגּוֹ דְּאִישְׁתְּרִי אִיסּוּר אֵשֶׁת אָח – אִישְׁתְּרֵי נַמִי אִיסּוּר אֲחוֹת אִשָּׁה.

This works out **well when the deceased** brother had first **married** one of the sisters, who was thereby rendered prohibited to the *yavam* as his brother's wife, **and** only **afterward** had **the living** brother **married** her sister, which renders his brother's wife forbidden to him on another count, this time as his wife's sister. **As** in that case one can say that **since** the first **prohibition** with regard to **a brother's wife was** subsequently nullified and thereby **permitted** by the mitzva of levirate marriage, **the prohibition** with regard to **a wife's sister was also** nullified and thereby **permitted.**

אֶלָּא, נָשָׂא חַי וְאַחַר כָּךְ נָשָׂא מֵת, אִיסּוּר אֲחוֹת אִשָּׁה קָדֵים!

However, if the reverse occurred, and first the **living** brother had **married** his wife **and** only **afterward the deceased** brother had **married** her sister, in this case **the prohibition** with regard to **a wife's sister precedes** the prohibition proscribing a brother's wife, i.e., she was initially forbidden to him as his wife's sister. Consequently, even when the second prohibition lapses upon the death of his childless brother, the first prohibition should remain intact.

וַאֲפִילּוּ נָשָׂא מֵת נַמִי, תֵּינַח הֵיכָא דְּנָשָׂא מֵת וּמֵת, וְאַחַר כָּךְ נָשָׂא חַי, דַּחֲזְיָא לֵיהּ דְּבֵינֵי בֵּינֵי. אֶלָּא, נָשָׂא מֵת וְלֹא מֵת, וְאַחַר כָּךְ נָשָׂא חַי – לָא אִיחַזְיָא לֵיהּ כְּלָל!

And furthermore, **even** in a case where **the deceased** brother had **married** first, **it** works out **well** only **when the deceased** brother had **married** the woman **and** then **died, and** only **afterward the surviving** brother **married** that brother's wife's sister. The reason is **that** in this case, the sister of the wife of the deceased brother **was fit for him in between,** i.e., during the period from when the deceased brother died until he married that brother's wife's sister. Therefore, it can be claimed that the second prohibition should not apply. **However,** if **the deceased** brother **married** first, **and did not die** yet, **and afterward,** during the deceased brother's lifetime, **the living** brother **married** the deceased brother's sister, **she was not fit for him at all,** as there was no period of time during which she was permitted to him.

מִי לָא מוֹדֵי עוּלָּא שֶׁאִם רָאָה קֶרִי בְּלֵיל שְׁמִינִי – שֶׁאֵין מַכְנִיס יָדָיו לְבְהוֹנוֹת?! שֶׁלֹּא יָצָא בְּשָׁעָה שֶׁהִיא רְאוּיָה לְהָבִיא בָּהּ קָרְבָּן!

The Gemara provides proof for this claim: **Doesn't Ulla agree**[N] **that** if a leper **experienced a seminal emission on the night of the eighth,** not on the eighth day but on the previous night, **that he may not insert his hands** and feet **to the thumb and big toe**[B] to receive the blood and oil for his purification? The reason is **that** in this case he is ritually impure due to the emission and **he** had **not** yet **emerged** from the impurity of leprosy **at a time that is fitting to bring an offering,** as he cannot sacrifice his offerings until the daylight hours of the eighth day. Since there was not a single moment when he was permitted to enter the Temple in his state of ritual impurity, in this case one cannot apply the principle: Since it is permitted, it is permitted.

אֶלָּא: כִּי אִיצְטְרִיךְ "עָלֶיהָ" הֵיכָא דְּנָשָׂא מֵת, וּמֵת, וְאַחַר כָּךְ נָשָׂא חַי.

§ **Rather,** the Gemara suggests that the phrase **"with her,"** which teaches the prohibition with regard to a wife's sister in levirate marriage, **is necessary** for a case **where the deceased** brother had first **married**[N] **and** then **died, and** only **afterward the living** brother **married** the sister of the deceased brother's wife, in which case his brother's wife was permitted to him for a period of time. Accordingly, one might have applied the principle: Since it is permitted, it is permitted. For this reason it was necessary to write "with her," to teach that this second woman is nevertheless forbidden as his wife's sister.

NOTES

Doesn't Ulla agree, etc. – מִי לָא מוֹדֵי עוּלָּא וכו׳: The commentaries ask how the Gemara knows that Ulla would agree on this matter (see *Tosafot* on Gemara here and on *Zevaḥim*). Others say that the Gemara's claim is not based on a derivation of Ulla's opinion in the case of one who experienced a seminal emission, as claimed by *Tosafot*; rather, it is a simple matter of logical reasoning. It was Ulla who stated the principle: Since it is permitted, it is permitted, and therefore where this rationale does not apply, Ulla would not disagree (Rashba).

With her is necessary where the deceased married, etc. – כִּי אִיצְטְרִיךְ עָלֶיהָ הֵיכָא דְּנָשָׂא מֵת וכו׳: Some commentaries note that in this case, where the *yavam* married the sister of his *yevama* only after the death of his brother, the *halakha* of a rival wife of a forbidden relation does not apply, as the rival wife in this case was never prohibited to him (*Tosafot Yeshanim*). In other words, although the sister of the surviving brother's wife is indeed forbidden to him, any other wives of the deceased brother remain permitted. *Tosafot Yeshanim* explain that the derivation from "with her" refers solely to the forbidden relation herself, whereas the prohibition proscribing a rival wife applies only when the deceased brother married first, after which the surviving brother married during his brother's lifetime (see *Sefer Aḥiezer*).

BACKGROUND

Insert his hands and feet to the thumb and big toe – מַכְנִיס יָדָיו לִבְהוֹנוֹת: The purification process for lepers is detailed in the Torah (Leviticus, chapter 14). This ritual includes the requirement that a priest apply oil that has been sanctified for this purpose, as well as blood from the guilt-offering, upon the leper's right earlobe, right big toe, and right thumb. For this reason, the leper had to extend his thumb, big toe, and head into the Temple courtyard.

וְאִי בָּעֵית אֵימָא: אָתְיָא בְּהֶיקֵּישָׁא מִדְּרַבִּי יוֹנָה. דְּאָמַר רַבִּי יוֹנָה, וְאִיתֵּימָא רַב הוּנָא בְּרֵיהּ דְּרַב יְהוֹשֻׁעַ: אָמַר קְרָא "כִּי כָּל אֲשֶׁר יַעֲשֶׂה מִכֹּל הַתּוֹעֵבוֹת הָאֵלֶּה וְנִכְרְתוּ" הוּקְשׁוּ כָּל הָעֲרָיוֹת כּוּלָּן לְאֵשֶׁת אָח; מָה אֵשֶׁת אָח שַׁרְיָא אַף כָּל עֲרָיוֹת נַמִּי שַׁרְיָין – כְּתַב רַחֲמָנָא "עָלֶיהָ".

And if you wish, **say** instead that the suggestion that other women with whom relations are forbidden are permitted in levirate marriage **is derived from the juxtaposition of Rabbi Yona.**[N] **As Rabbi Yona said, and some say** this was stated by **Rav Huna, son of Rav Yehoshua: The verse states: "For whoever shall do any of these abominations,** the souls that do them **shall be cut off** from among their people" (Leviticus 18:29). In this verse **all of the** women **with whom relations are forbidden are juxtaposed with** the case of **a brother's wife.** Consequently, one might say that **just as a brother's wife is permitted** in levirate marriage, **so too, all** women **with whom relations are forbidden are likewise permitted.** Therefore, **the Merciful One writes: "With her,"** which excludes the prohibition with regard to a wife's sister.

אֲמַר לֵיהּ רַב אַחָא מִדִּפְתִּי לְרָבִינָא: מִכְּדִי, כָּל עֲרָיוֹת אִיכָּא לְאַקּוּשִׁינְהוּ לְאֵשֶׁת אָח וְאִיכָּא לְאַקּוּשִׁינְהוּ לַאֲחוֹת אִשָּׁה, מַאי חָזֵית דְּאַקַּשְׁתְּ לַאֲחוֹת אִשָּׁה – אַקְשִׁינְהוּ לְאֵשֶׁת אָח!

Against this proof, **Rav Aḥa of Difti said to Ravina: Since** the *halakha* of **all** women **with whom relations are forbidden can be juxtaposed with** the case of **a brother's wife** and thereby rendered permitted in levirate marriage, **and** these cases **can** equally **be juxtaposed with** the *halakha* of **a wife's sister,** which would mean that they are forbidden, **what did you see that you juxtaposed them with a wife's sister? Juxtapose them** instead **with a brother's wife.** If so, the opposite could be derived from the phrase "with her," i.e., not that all women with whom relations are forbidden are prohibited like a wife's sister, but that all these women are permitted in levirate marriage, even a wife's sister.

אִיבָּעֵית אֵימָא: לְקוּלָּא וְחוּמְרָא – לְחוּמְרָא מַקְשִׁינַן, אִיבָּעֵית אֵימָא: הָכָא תְּרֵי אִיסּוּרֵי וְהָכָא תְּרֵי אִיסּוּרֵי, וּתְרֵי מִתְּרֵי יָלְפִינַן; אֲבָל הָכָא חֲדָא אִיסּוּרָא – וּתְרֵי מֵחֲדָא לָא יָלְפִינַן.

The Gemara answers: **If you wish, say** that if one must decide between two possible ways of understanding juxtaposed cases, one of which leads **to a lenient** ruling **and** the other to **a stringent** ruling,[N] **we juxtapose to** reach **the stringent ruling,** not the leniency. **If you wish, say** instead: **Here,** there are **two prohibitions,** a brother's wife and a wife's sister, **and there,** in the case of all other women with whom relations are forbidden, there are also **two prohibitions. And one** may **derive** a case involving **two** prohibitions **from** another case that involves **two** prohibitions. **However, here,** in the case of a regular levirate marriage that does not involve any other forbidden relation, there is only **one prohibition** proscribing a brother's wife, **and one may not derive** a case involving **two** prohibitions **from** a case that involves only **one.**

רָבָא אֲמַר: עֶרְוָה לָא צְרִיכָא קְרָא, דְּאֵין עֲשֵׂה דּוֹחֶה לֹא תַעֲשֶׂה שֶׁיֵּשׁ בּוֹ כָּרֵת. כִּי אִיצְטְרִיךְ קְרָא – לְמֵיסַר צָרָה.

§ **Rava said** that this entire *halakha* must be understood differently. With regard to **a forbidden relation** herself, it is **not necessary** for **a verse** to teach that she cannot enter into levirate marriage, **as a positive mitzva does not override a prohibition that includes** ***karet*****.**[N] Rather, **the verse** "with her" **is necessary to prohibit a rival wife,**[N] as a rival wife is not prohibited to the *yavam* as a forbidden relation.

וְעֶרְוָה לָא צְרִיכָא קְרָא?! וְהָא תַּנְיָא: אֵין לִי אֶלָּא הִיא!

The Gemara asks: **And** does the *tanna* in fact maintain with regard to **a forbidden relation** that it is **not necessary** for **a verse** to teach that she is prohibited in levirate marriage? **But isn't it taught** in that same *baraita*: **I have** derived **nothing other** than that **this** woman is exempt from levirate marriage. From where is it inferred that the same applies to her rival wife? This shows that the case of a forbidden relation does require a special inference from a verse.

מִשּׁוּם צָרָתָהּ.

The Gemara answers: It is **due to her rival wife,** i.e., the *baraita* does not mean that the *halakha* of women with whom relations are forbidden is derived from this verse; rather, this case is mentioned only to introduce the case of a rival wife.

וְהָא קָתָנֵי: אֵין לִי אֶלָּא הֵן! מִשּׁוּם צָרוֹתֵיהֶן.

The Gemara raises another difficulty: **But it is taught** in the *baraita*: **I have** derived **nothing other** than that **these** sisters are exempt from levirate marriage, which again suggests that the derivation from the verse applies to all of them. This is similarly rejected: This is also stated **due to their rival wives.**

NOTES

From the juxtaposition of Rabbi Yona – בְּהֶיקֵּישָׁא מִדְּרַבִּי יוֹנָה: Rabbi Yona did not establish this juxtaposition with the aim of rendering all women with whom relations are forbidden permitted in levirate marriage. Rather, he said it in relation to a different issue, the first stage of sexual intercourse with a forbidden relation. The juxtaposition teaches that all women with whom relations are forbidden are equivalent to each other in that regard. However, as there is no such thing as a partial juxtaposition, it can be claimed that this juxtaposition teaches additional comparisons between the cases of those with whom relations are forbidden (Rashi; see Ritva).

To a lenient ruling and a stringent ruling, etc. – לְקוּלָּא וְחוּמְרָא וכו׳: Some commentaries suggest that there is a fundamental distinction between levirate marriage in the case of a brother's wife and all other women with whom relations are forbidden, as the *halakha* itself refers specifically to a brother's wife. If so, one cannot learn from this case with regard to the other women with whom relations are forbidden (Rashba). The Rashba explains that it would indeed have been possible to refute the suggestion in this manner, but the other difficulties raised by the Gemara are preferable.

A positive mitzva does not override a prohibition that includes *karet* – אֵין עֲשֵׂה דּוֹחֶה לֹא תַעֲשֶׂה שֶׁיֵּשׁ בּוֹ כָּרֵת: This issue of whether or not a positive mitzva overrides a prohibition that incurs *karet* is not thoroughly clarified by the Gemara, nor is the matter clearly decided by the ruling of the Rambam (Rambam *Sefer Zemanim*, *Hilkhot Shabbat* 19:20). Some commentaries apparently accept Rava's opinion that a positive mitzva does not generally override a prohibition that incurs *karet* (*Tosafot*; Meiri). However, others hold that Rava's statement is not accepted, and a positive mitzva overrides even a prohibition that incurs *karet*, provided that the opposite conclusion is not explicitly stated in that particular case (*Sefer HaKeritut*; see *Yad Malakhi*).

The verse is necessary to prohibit a rival wife – כִּי אִיצְטְרִיךְ קְרָא לְמֵיסַר צָרָה: In fact, both here and in the continuation of the discussion, the Gemara indicates that no explicit verse was necessary to render a rival wife prohibited, and this verse renders a rival wife permitted in those cases when she is not a forbidden relation. However, as this is derived from a verse that uses an expression of a prohibition, the Gemara states that it serves to prohibit a rival wife in certain cases (Rashba; see Ritva).

תָּא שְׁמַע: רַבִּי אוֹמֵר, "וְלָקַח" "וְלָקְחָהּ" "וְיִבֵּם" "וְיִבְּמָהּ", לֶאֱסוֹר צָרוֹת וַעֲרָיוֹת!

The Gemara suggests: **Come** and **hear** a different *baraita* that contradicts Rava's statement: **Rabbi** Yehuda HaNasi **says** that there is a different proof that a forbidden relation and her rival wife are prohibited in levirate marriage. The Torah says: "He will have intercourse with her and take her to him to be his wife and consummate the levirate marriage with her" (Deuteronomy 25:5). Since the verse does not say simply: **Have intercourse,** but: **"Have intercourse with her,"** this indicates that he takes this woman specifically, not a different woman who is forbidden. Furthermore, the verse does not simply state: **And consummate the levirate marriage,** but: **"And consummate the levirate marriage with her."** These additions serve **to prohibit rival wives and** women **with whom relations are forbidden.**

אֵימָא: לֶאֱסוֹר צָרוֹת שֶׁל עֲרָיוֹת. וְהָא תְּרֵי קְרָאֵי קָנְסִיב לֵיהּ, מַאי לָאו: חַד לְעֶרְוָה וְחַד לְצָרָה!

This shows that even the prohibition with regard to women with whom relations are forbidden requires a special inference. The Gemara answers: Amend the language of the *baraita* and **say: To prohibit rival wives of** those **with whom relations are forbidden,**[N] not the women themselves with whom relations are forbidden. The Gemara raises a difficulty: **But he brought two** proofs from the **verse,** both "have intercourse with her" and "and consummate the levirate marriage with her." **What, is it not** because **one** phrase is required for the *halakha* **of** a woman **with whom relations are forbidden and** the other **one for a rival wife?**

לָא, אִידִי וְאִידִי לְצָרָה, חַד לְמֵיסַר צָרָה בִּמְקוֹם מִצְוָה, וְחַד לְמִישְׁרֵי צָרָה שֶׁלֹּא בִּמְקוֹם מִצְוָה.

The Gemara rejects this suggestion: **No, this** source **and that** source **are** necessary **for a rival wife,** and both phrases are required, for the following reason. **One** of them comes **to prohibit a rival wife in a place where the mitzva** of levirate marriage is applicable, **and one** serves **to permit a rival wife in a place where the mitzva** is **not** applicable. If a woman is the rival wife of one of those relatives forbidden to a given man, he is permitted to marry her following the death of her husband, as the prohibition proscribing rival wives of women with whom relations are forbidden pertains only to cases where the *halakhot* of levirate marriage are applicable, i.e., in the case of a brother's wife.

מַאי טַעְמָא – "וְיִבֵּם" "וְיִבְּמָהּ", בִּמְקוֹם יִיבּוּם הוּא דַּאֲסִירָא צָרָה, שֶׁלֹּא בִּמְקוֹם יִיבּוּם – שַׁרְיָא צָרָה.

The Gemara elaborates: **What is the reason** for this *halakha*? It is derived from the fact that the verse does not merely state: **And consummate the levirate marriage,** but instead emphasizes: **"And consummate the levirate marriage with her."** This comes to teach: **It is in a place where levirate marriage** applies **that a rival wife is prohibited;** however, **in a place where the levirate marriage** is **not** applicable, **a rival wife is permitted.**

אָמַר רַב אַשִׁי: מַתְנִיתִין נַמִּי דַּיְקָא: דְּקָתָנֵי, חֲמֵשׁ עֶשְׂרֵה נָשִׁים פּוֹטְרוֹת צָרוֹתֵיהֶן, וְאִילּוּ "פְּטוּרוֹת וּפוֹטְרוֹת" – לָא קָתָנֵי, שְׁמַע מִינַּהּ.

Rav Ashi said: The mishna is also precisely formulated[N] in accordance with the opinion of Rava, **as it teaches: Fifteen women exempt their rival wives, whereas** the phrase: **Are exempt and exempt** others, **is not taught.** This indicates that the exemption of these women who are themselves forbidden relations does not necessitate any special inference, as this is not a novel *halakha*, and therefore the mishna does not even state this point explicitly. The novelty is that they exempt their rival wives. The Gemara summarizes: **Conclude from this** that Rava's opinion is correct.

וּמַאי שְׁנָא עֶרְוָה דְּלָא צְרִיכָא קְרָא – דְּאֵין עֲשֵׂה דּוֹחֶה לֹא תַעֲשֶׂה שֶׁיֵּשׁ בּוֹ כָּרֵת – צָרָה נַמִּי לָא תִּיבְעֵי קְרָא מִשּׁוּם דְּאֵין עֲשֵׂה דּוֹחֶה לֹא תַעֲשֶׂה שֶׁיֵּשׁ בּוֹ כָּרֵת!

The Gemara asks: **And** if so, **what is different** about **a forbidden relation that** a special **verse is not necessary** to exclude it? The reason must be **that a positive mitzva does not override a prohibition that entails *karet*.** If so, **a rival wife** should **also not require an** additional **verse, due to** the fact that **a positive mitzva does not override a prohibition that entails *karet*.** The phrase "to be a rival to her" (Leviticus 18:18) teaches that the rival wife of a wife's sister is prohibited like the wife's sister herself.

אָמַר לֵיהּ רַב אַחָא בַּר בֵּיבַי מָר לְרָבִינָא: הָכִי קָאָמְרִינַן מִשְּׁמֵיהּ דְּרָבָא, צָרָה נַמִּי לָא אִיצְטְרִיךְ קְרָא, כִּי אִיצְטְרִיךְ קְרָא

Rav Aḥa, son of Beivai Mar, said to Ravina that **this is what we say in the name of Rava:** With regard to **a rival wife too, a verse is not necessary,**[N] as is the case with a forbidden relation herself, since the prohibition in her case as well incurs *karet*, and therefore one would not think that the positive mitzva of levirate marriage overrides that prohibition. **The verse is necessary**

NOTES

Say to prohibit rival wives of those with whom relations are forbidden – אֵימָא לֶאֱסוֹר צָרוֹת שֶׁל עֲרָיוֹת: This is not an arbitrary adjustment of the text, as the unusual order of the *baraita*, which mentions rival wives before those with whom relations are forbidden, alludes to this interpretation (*Arukh LaNer*).

The mishna is also precisely formulated – מַתְנִיתִין נַמִּי דַּיְקָא: In other words, the phrasing of the mishna indicates that the *tanna* maintains that there is no need for a special inference to render prohibited those with whom relations are forbidden. Since he did not emphasize the exemption of women with whom relations are forbidden, but assumed that it was understood, it stands to reason that he holds in accordance with the opinion of Rava that no verse is required in this case (Ramban).

With regard to a rival wife too, a verse is not necessary – צָרָה נַמִּי לָא אִיצְטְרִיךְ קְרָא: But if no verse is required even for a rival wife, Rav Ashi's earlier comment that the mishna is in accordance with Rava's opinion is no longer valid (*Tosafot*). *Tosafot* note that in any case it is necessary for the mishna to state explicitly that rival wives are prohibited, whereas the prohibition with regard to women with whom relations are forbidden is mentioned in other tractates. Others explain that this *halakha* is indeed unnecessary for the matter at hand, but it serves as an introduction to the next mishna, which deals with the six stringent cases of those with whom relations are forbidden. In those cases a rival wife is permitted, as no levirate marriage at all is involved.

לְמִישְׁרֵי צָרָה שֶׁלֹּא בִּמְקוֹם מִצְוָה. מַאי טַעְמָא? אָמַר קְרָא "עָלֶיהָ", בִּמְקוֹם "עָלֶיהָ" הוּא דַּאֲסִירָא, שֶׁלֹּא בִּמְקוֹם "עָלֶיהָ" – שַׁרְיָא.

to permit a rival wife in a place where the mitzva of levirate marriage is **not** applicable. **What is the reason,** i.e., how is this inferred? **The verse states: "With her."** In other words, **it is in a place** where the obligation "her brother-in-law will have intercourse **with her" is** applicable **that** a rival wife is **prohibited,** whereas **in a place** where the obligation "Her brother-in-law will have intercourse **with her" is not** applicable, a rival wife is **permitted.**

אָמַר לֵיהּ רָמִי בַּר חָמָא לְרָבָא: אֵימָא עֶרְוָה גּוּפַהּ שֶׁלֹּא בִּמְקוֹם מִצְוָה תִּישְׁתְּרֵי! וְלָאו קַל וָחוֹמֶר הוּא? בִּמְקוֹם מִצְוָה – אֲסִירָא, שֶׁלֹּא בִּמְקוֹם מִצְוָה – שַׁרְיָא?!

Rami bar Ḥama said to Rava: If the phrase "with her" is referring only to a case where levirate marriage is applicable, one can **say** that **a forbidden relative herself**[N] **should be permitted in a place** where the **mitzva** of levirate marriage is **not** applicable. According to this interpretation, the prohibitions with regard to all those with whom relations are forbidden are in effect only when levirate marriage applies. Rava answered: **And is it not an *a fortiori*** inference? If these relatives are **prohibited in a place** where there is **a mitzva,** could they be **permitted in a place** where there is **no mitzva?**

אֲמַר לֵיהּ: צָרָה תּוֹכִיחַ, דִּבִמְקוֹם מִצְוָה – אֲסִירָא, וְשֶׁלֹּא בִּמְקוֹם מִצְוָה – שַׁרְיָא! אֲמַר לֵיהּ: עָלֶיךָ אָמַר קְרָא "בְּחַיֶּיהָ" – כָּל שֶׁבְּחַיֶּיהָ.

Rami bar Ḥama **said to** Rava: That is no proof, as the case of **a rival wife** herself **can prove** that this *a fortiori* inference is incorrect, **as in a place** where there is **a mitzva she is prohibited and in a place** where there is **no mitzva she is permitted.** Rava **said to** Rami bar Ḥami: **With regard to your** claim, **the verse states:** "And you shall not take a woman to her sister… **in her lifetime"** (Leviticus 18:18). This indicates that **all** cases in which it **is in the lifetime** of her sister she is forbidden, even when no mitzva applies.

הַאי "בְּחַיֶּיהָ" מִיבָּעֵי לֵיהּ לְמַעוּטֵי לְאַחַר מִיתָהּ! הַהִיא מִ"וְאִשָּׁה אֶל אֲחוֹתָהּ" נָפְקָא.

The Gemara asks: **This** phrase **"in her lifetime" is necessary,** as indicated by the plain meaning of the phrase, **to exclude the time after death,** i.e., to teach that a wife's sister is forbidden only while the wife is still alive, whereas after her death the sister is permitted. The Gemara answers: **That** *halakha* that a woman is permitted after her sister's death **is derived from** "and you shall not take **a woman to her sister"** (Leviticus 18:18), as when one of them is dead it is no longer considered "a woman to her sister."

אִי מִ"וְאִשָּׁה אֶל אֲחוֹתָהּ" הֲוָה אָמִינָא: נִתְגָּרְשָׁה שַׁרְיָא, תַּלְמוּד לוֹמַר "בְּחַיֶּיהָ" – כָּל שֶׁבְּחַיֶּיהָ, דְּאַף עַל גַּב דְּנִתְגָּרְשָׁה – לָא.

The Gemara further asks: **If** this *halakha* is derived **from "a woman to her sister," I would say** that even **if she were divorced,** her sister **is permitted.** Therefore, **the verse states: "In her lifetime,"** which indicates that the prohibition is in effect in **all** cases **that** are **in her lifetime. This** teaches **that although she is divorced,** her sister is **not**[H] permitted.

אֶלָּא אֲמַר רַב הוּנָא בַּר תַּחֲלִיפָא מִשְּׁמֵיהּ דְּרָבָא: תְּרֵי קְרָאֵי כְּתִיבִי: כְּתִיב "אִשָּׁה אֶל אֲחוֹתָהּ לֹא תִקָּח לִצְרוֹר" וּכְתִיב "לְגַלּוֹת עֶרְוָתָהּ", דְּחֲדָא מַשְׁמַע, הָא כֵּיצַד? בִּמְקוֹם מִצְוָה – שְׁתֵּיהֶן אֲסוּרוֹת, שֶׁלֹּא בִּמְקוֹם מִצְוָה – הִיא אֲסוּרָה וְצָרָתָהּ מוּתֶּרֶת.

§ **Rather,** the Gemara suggests a different interpretation. **Rav Huna bar Taḥlifa said in the name of Rava: Two verses are written,** i.e., two separate issues are mentioned in the same verse. **It is written: "And you shall not take a woman to her sister, to be a rival [*litzror*],"** which indicates that two rival wives are prohibited. **And it is written: "To uncover her nakedness"** (Leviticus 18:18), in the singular, **which means one** and not both of them. **How is it** possible to reconcile this apparent contradiction? **In a place** where there is **a mitzva** of levirate marriage, **both** the forbidden relation and her rival wife **are prohibited. In a place** where there is **no mitzva** of levirate marriage, the forbidden relation **is prohibited but her rival wife is permitted.**

אֵיפּוֹךְ אֲנָא: בִּמְקוֹם מִצְוָה – הִיא אֲסוּרָה וְצָרָתָהּ מוּתֶּרֶת, וְשֶׁלֹּא בִּמְקוֹם מִצְוָה – שְׁתֵּיהֶן אֲסוּרוֹת! אִם כֵּן, לֹא יֹאמַר "עָלֶיהָ".

The Gemara raises a difficulty: I can **reverse this**[N] and suggest the opposite. **In a place** where there is **a mitzva,** the forbidden relation **is prohibited and her rival wife is permitted, and in a place** where there is **no mitzva, both of them are prohibited.** The Gemara answers: **If so, let** the verse **not say "with her,"** at all, as this superfluous phrase teaches that the prohibition with regard to a rival wife applies only when there is a mitzva of "her brother-in-law will have intercourse with her."

NOTES

Say that a forbidden relative herself, etc. – אֵימָא עֶרְוָה גּוּפַהּ וכו׳: Some commentaries maintain that this does not mean to suggest that all those with whom relations are forbidden should be permitted when no mitzva of levirate marriage applies, but merely that a wife's sister alone, to whom the phrase "with her" applies, should be permitted. In her case it is possible to suggest that the prohibition applies only when the mitzva of levirate marriage is in effect (*Arukh LaNer*).

I can reverse this, etc. – אֵיפּוֹךְ אֲנָא וכו׳: The commentaries explain that this reversal is based on the reasoning that a prohibition is more likely to be permitted in a situation where there is a mitzva involved, as opposed to when there is no mitzva of levirate marriage (*Tosafot Yeshanim*).

HALAKHA

A wife's sister – אֲחוֹת אִשָּׁה: One's wife's sister is forbidden by Torah law during one's wife's lifetime, even after they have divorced. However, after the death of one's wife, her sister is permitted to him (*Shulḥan Arukh, Even HaEzer* 15:26).

אָמַר לֵיהּ רַב אַשִׁי לְרַב כָּהֲנָא: מִמַּאי דְּהַאי "עָלֶיהָ" לְאִיסּוּרָא? דִּלְמָא לְהֶתֵּירָא, וְהָכִי קָאָמַר רַחֲמָנָא: "אִשָּׁה אֶל אֲחוֹתָהּ לֹא תִקָּח לִצְרוֹר" – לֹא הִיא וְלֹא צָרָתָהּ, שֶׁלֹּא בִּמְקוֹם "עָלֶיהָ", אֲבָל בִּמְקוֹם "עָלֶיהָ" שְׁתֵּיהֶן מוּתָּרוֹת!

Rav Ashi said to Rav Kahana: From where is it derived **that this** superfluous phrase **"with her,"** comes **to prohibit,** i.e., although there is an obligation that "her brother-in-law will have intercourse with her," a wife's sister remains prohibited? **Perhaps** it serves **to permit, and this is what the Merciful One is saying: "You shall not take a woman to her sister, to be a rival"** (Leviticus 18:18), i.e., **neither her nor her rival wife.** When is this the case? It is **in a place where** the obligation of "her brother-in-law will have intercourse **with her"** does **not** apply. **However, in a place where "with her" does apply** and there is an obligation of levirate marriage, **both of them are permitted.**

אִם כֵּן "לְגַלּוֹת עֶרְוָה" דַּחֲדָא הֵיכִי מַשְׁכַּחַתְּ לַהּ? אִי בִּמְקוֹם מִצְוָה – שְׁתֵּיהֶן מוּתָּרוֹת, אִי שֶׁלֹּא בִּמְקוֹם מִצְוָה – שְׁתֵּיהֶן אֲסוּרוֹת.

Rav Kahana replied to Rav Ashi: **If** the above statement is **so,** and **"to uncover her nakedness"** is referring **to one**[N] woman, under **what circumstances** can **you find** this case? When is only one of them prohibited? **If** it is **in a place** where there is **a mitzva, they are both permitted; if** it is **in a place** where there is **no mitzva, they are both forbidden.** Therefore, the earlier line of reasoning must be accepted: A rival wife is forbidden only in a case where the mitzva of levirate marriage is in effect.

גּוּפָא, רַבִּי אוֹמֵר: "וְלָקַח" "וּלְקָחָהּ" "וְיִבֵּם" "וְיִבְּמָהּ" – לֶאֱסוֹר צָרוֹת וַעֲרָיוֹת. מִידֵי צָרוֹת כְּתִיבָא הָכָא? וְעוֹד: צָרוֹת – מִ"לִּצְרוֹר" נָפְקָא!

§ While clarifying the exposition of the phrase "with her," an alternative interpretation attributed to Rabbi Yehuda HaNasi was mentioned. The Gemara discusses **the** matter **itself. Rabbi** Yehuda HaNasi **says:** The verse does not say **have intercourse,** but **"have intercourse with her."** And it does not say **and consummate the levirate marriage,** but **"and consummate the levirate marriage with her."** These phrases serve **to prohibit rival wives and** women **with whom relations are forbidden.** The Gemara asks: **Are rival wives written here?** In other words, what is the connection between the verse and the topic of rival wives, an issue that is not even mentioned in the verse? **And furthermore:** The prohibition with regard to **rival wives is derived** from the phrase **"To be a rival wife** [*litzror*]**,"** not from this source.

"לִצְרוֹר" מַפֵּיק לֵיהּ רַבִּי לְכִדְרַבִּי שִׁמְעוֹן.

The Gemara answers: **Rabbi** Yehuda HaNasi **derives** a different *halakha* **from** the phrase **"to be a rival wife," in accordance with that** statement **of Rabbi Shimon.** In Rabbi Shimon's opinion, the exemption of two sisters from levirate marriage applies not only when the *yavam* is married to one of the sisters, but also if two sisters who come before him for levirate marriage were previously married to two of his brothers. In that case, the levirate bond itself is sufficient for them to be considered rival wives of one another.

צָרָה הָכָא כְּתִיב? הָכִי קָאָמַר: אִם כֵּן לֵימָא קְרָא "וְלָקַח", מַאי "וּלְקָחָהּ" – כָּל הֵיכָא דְּאִיכָּא תְּרֵי לְקוּחִין, דְּאִי בָּעֵי נָסֵיב הַאי וְאִי בָּעֵי נָסֵיב הַאי – שַׁרְיָא, וְאִי לָא – תַּרְוַיְיהוּ אֲסִירִין.

And with regard to the previous question: **Are rival wives written here?** The answer is that **this is what he is saying: If so,** that the verse does not come to exempt rival wives, **let the verse state** only: **Have intercourse. What is** the meaning of **"have intercourse with her"?** It serves to limit the case to one woman and not two, in the following manner: **Anywhere that there are two** possibilities of **having intercourse,** i.e., there is a choice between marrying one of two women in levirate marriage, in such a way **that if he wants he may marry this one, and if he wants he may marry that one,** then each one is **permitted. And if** he does **not** have a choice and is obligated to marry one of them, e.g., if the other is a forbidden relation to him, **they are both prohibited,** including the rival wife.

"וְיִבְּמָהּ", בִּמְקוֹם יִיבּוּם – הוּא דַּאֲסִירָא צָרָה, שֶׁלֹּא בִּמְקוֹם יִיבּוּם – שַׁרְיָא צָרָה. וְרַבָּנַן, הַאי "וּלְקָחָהּ" מַאי עָבְדִי לֵיהּ?

When the verse states: **"And consummate the levirate marriage with her,"** it comes to teach the following. **It is in a place** where **levirate marriage** is applicable **that a rival wife is prohibited,** whereas **in a place** where **levirate marriage** is **not** applicable, a **rival wife is permitted.** The Gemara asks: **And** with regard to **the Rabbis,** who do not interpret the verse in this manner, **what do they do with this** emphasis on **"have intercourse with her"?** How do they interpret it?

NOTES

If so, and: To uncover her nakedness, is referring to one, etc. – **אִם כֵּן לְגַלּוֹת עֶרְוָה דַּחֲדָא וכו׳**: The difficulty raised by Rami bar Ḥama is evidently based on the assumption that a positive mitzva overrides even a prohibition that incurs *karet*. However, according to the opinion of Rava, the verse is necessary to render permitted a rival wife, and therefore this problem does not arise. Consequently, Rava's response to the difficulty is not in accordance with his own opinion, but in line with the reasoning of the question (*Tosefot HaRosh*).

מִיבָּעֵי לְהוּ לְכִדְרַבִּי יוֹסֵי בַּר חֲנִינָא. דְּאָמַר רַבִּי יוֹסֵי בַּר חֲנִינָא: ״וּלְקָחָהּ״, מְלַמֵּד שֶׁמְּגָרְשָׁהּ בְּגֵט וּמַחֲזִירָהּ. ״וְיִבְּמָהּ״ – עַל כׇּרְחָהּ.

The Gemara responds: **They need this for that which Rabbi Yosei bar Ḥanina** said, **as Rabbi Yosei bar Ḥanina said: "And have intercourse with her"** means marriage, i.e., she is fully his wife from that moment onward. This **teaches that he divorces her with a bill of divorce** after levirate marriage, and she can no longer be released by *ḥalitza*, **and he** may subsequently **remarry her**[HN] if he so wishes. And the verse **"and consummate the levirate marriage with her,"** this means **against her will.**[H] Although betrothal in general does not take effect without the woman's consent, levirate marriage can be effected against her will.

וְרַבִּי? דְּרַבִּי יוֹסֵי בַּר חֲנִינָא מִ״לְאִשָּׁה״ נָפְקָא. עַל כׇּרְחָהּ מִ״יְּבָמָהּ יָבֹא עָלֶיהָ״ נָפְקָא.

The Gemara asks: **And** from where does **Rabbi** Yehuda HaNasi derive these widely accepted *halakhot*? The Gemara responds: **That** *halakha* cited by **Rabbi Yosei bar Ḥanina,** that a woman taken in levirate marriage has the status of a regular wife who may be divorced and remarried, **is derived from** the verse "and take her to him **to be his wife"** (Deuteronomy 25:5),[N] which means that she will be his wife for all purposes, like any other wife. And the *halakha* that levirate marriage can be effected **against her will is derived from "her brother-in-law will have intercourse with her,"** which indicates that it can be achieved without her consent.

וְרַבִּי, הַאי ״עָלֶיהָ״ מַאי עָבֵיד לֵיהּ? מִיבָּעֵי לֵיהּ לְכִדְתַנְיָא: אֵין חַיָּיבִין בֵּית דִּין אֶלָּא עַל דָּבָר שֶׁזְּדוֹנוֹ כָּרֵת וְשִׁגְגָתוֹ חַטָּאת, וְכֵן הַמָּשִׁיחַ.

The Gemara asks: **And what does Rabbi** Yehuda HaNasi **do with this** superfluous phrase, **"with her"?** The Gemara responds: **He needs it for that which is taught** in a *baraita* with regard to a different matter. The Sages said: **The court is obligated** to bring a bull as a sin-offering for an unwittingly committed communal sin on account of an erroneous *halakha* they taught **only for a matter whose intentional** transgression incurs ***karet* and whose unwitting** violation necessitates the sacrifice of **a sin-offering.**[HN] **And similarly, the anointed**[H] High Priest, who also brings a bull for an unwittingly committed sin, is obligated to do so only if his mistake involved a matter whose intentional transgression incurs *karet* and whose unwitting transgression necessitates the sacrifice of a sin-offering.

HALAKHA

That he divorces her with a bill of divorce and he may remarry her – שֶׁמְּגָרְשָׁהּ בְּגֵט וּמַחֲזִירָהּ: After a *yavam* takes his *yevama* in levirate marriage she is considered to be his wife for all purposes. Consequently, if he wishes to divorce her he must do so by means of a bill of divorce, and he may subsequently remarry her (*Shulḥan Arukh, Even HaEzer* 168:1).

And consummate the levirate marriage with her, against her will – וְיִבְּמָהּ עַל כׇּרְחָהּ: If a *yavam* engages in sexual relations with his *yevama* in a case where the *halakha* of levirate marriage applies, he has taken her as a wife for all purposes, even if he rapes her (*Shulḥan Arukh, Even HaEzer* 166:7).

The obligation of a court that issued an erroneous ruling – חִיּוּב בֵּית דִּין בְּהוֹרָאַת טָעוּת: In a case where the Great Sanhedrin issued an erroneous ruling that rendered permitted a matter whose intentional transgression incurs *karet* and whose unwitting transgression entails bringing a fixed sin-offering, if most of the community acted in accordance with the ruling of the court, the court must sacrifice a bull for an unwitting communal sin (Rambam *Sefer Korbanot, Hilkhot Shegagot* 12:1).

And similarly, the anointed – וְכֵן הַמָּשִׁיחַ: If the High Priest issued an erroneous ruling that permitted a matter whose intentional transgression incurs *karet* and whose unwitting transgression entails bringing a sin-offering, if he himself acted according to his own instructions he must bring a bull sin-offering for his atonement. This offering is called the bull of the anointed priest (Rambam *Sefer Korbanot, Hilkhot Shegagot* 15:1).

NOTES

That he divorces her with a bill of divorce and he may remarry her – שֶׁמְּגָרְשָׁהּ בְּגֵט וּמַחֲזִירָהּ: The commentaries raise a difficulty here: It is apparently necessary to provide a source proving that the *yavam* is permitted to engage in additional sexual relations with his *yevama* after the levirate marriage, as although the first sexual relations are commanded by the Torah, any further relations are merely optional. As stated below, it is for this very reason that one may not take a forbidden relation in levirate marriage (*Tosafot*). *Tosafot* explain that it stands to reason that this is permitted, as the Torah would not say that one should engage in sexual relations with a woman and immediately divorce her. Others suggest that whenever a mitzva overrides a prohibition, provided that the individual continues to perform the mitzva, he is even permitted to add elements that are not essential to the obligation itself (*Meromei Sadeh*).

Derived from: To be his wife – מִלְאִשָּׁה נָפְקָא: The commentaries ask what those Rabbis who dispute the opinion of Rabbi Yehuda HaNasi derive from the phrase: "To be his wife." The answer given is that they require two verses, one for the *halakha* that he divorces her with a bill of divorce and not by *ḥalitza*, and another to teach that he is permitted to remarry her after their divorce (*Arukh LaNer*).

A matter whose intentional transgression incurs *karet* and whose unwitting violation necessitates a sin-offering – דָּבָר שֶׁזְּדוֹנוֹ כָּרֵת וְשִׁגְגָתוֹ חַטָּאת: When there is an obligation to bring a sin-offering for a particular unwittingly committed transgression, intentional performance of that transgression is almost always penalized by *karet*. Still, it is necessary to specify both of these characteristics because there are some exceptions to this principle. These include cases that are penalized by a court-imposed death penalty instead of *karet*, e.g., striking or cursing one's parents, and prohibitions that render one liable to bring a sin-offering but do not incur *karet*, such as taking an oath in vain. For this reason it is necessary to specify that the intentional violation of the prohibitions incurs *karet*. Furthermore, sacrifice of the Paschal lamb and circumcision are both positive mitzvot that incur *karet* for an intentional transgression, but do not obligate the unwitting violator to bring a sin-offering (see *Arukh LaNer*).

וְלֹא בַּעֲבוֹדָה זָרָה, אֶלָּא עַל דָּבָר שֶׁחַיָּיבִין עַל זְדוֹנוֹ כָּרֵת וְשִׁגְגָתוֹ חַטָּאת. וּתְנַן נַמִּי: כָּל מִצְוָה שֶׁבַּתּוֹרָה שֶׁחַיָּיבִין עַל זְדוֹנוֹ כָּרֵת וְעַל שִׁגְגָתוֹ חַטָּאת – יָחִיד מֵבִיא כִּשְׂבָּה אוֹ שְׂעִירָה, נָשִׂיא מֵבִיא שָׂעִיר, מָשִׁיחַ וּבֵית דִּין מְבִיאִין פַּר.

And a community brings a bull for an unwitting communal sin **for idolatrous worship only** if the act of idolatry involved **a matter that for its intentional** violation **one is liable to** receive ***karet* and for its unwitting** violation one is liable to bring **a sin-offering. And we also learned** in a mishna: With regard to **any mitzva in the Torah for whose intentional** violation **one is liable to** receive ***karet* and for its unwitting** violation one is liable to bring **a sin-offering,** if a private **individual** sinned unwittingly, he **brings a ewe or a she-goat.** If it was **a *Nasi*, he brings a goat** for a sin of this kind, and if the sinner was **an anointed** High Priest **or the court, they bring a bull.**

וּבַעֲבוֹדָה זָרָה – יָחִיד, נָשִׂיא וּמָשִׁיחַ מְבִיאִין שְׂעִירָה. צִבּוּר מְבִיאִים פַּר וְשָׂעִיר, פַּר לְעוֹלָה וְשָׂעִיר לְחַטָּאת. מְנָא הָנֵי מִילֵּי?

And if they unwittingly sinned in a matter **involving idolatrous worship,** a private **individual, a *Nasi*, and an anointed** High Priest **bring a she-goat,** whereas **a community brings a bull and a goat,**[H] the **bull as a burnt-offering and** the **goat as a sin-offering.**[H] The Gemara asks: **From where are these matters,** that one must bring a sin-offering for this transgression, derived?

דְּתָנוּ רַבָּנַן: ״וְנוֹדְעָה הַחַטָּאת אֲשֶׁר חָטְאוּ עָלֶיהָ״, רַבִּי אוֹמֵר: נֶאֱמַר כָּאן ״עָלֶיהָ״ וְנֶאֱמַר לְהַלָּן ״עָלֶיהָ״, מָה לְהַלָּן – דָּבָר שֶׁחַיָּיבִים עַל זְדוֹנוֹ כָּרֵת וְעַל שִׁגְגָתוֹ חַטָּאת, אַף כָּאן – דָּבָר שֶׁחַיָּיבִין עַל זְדוֹנוֹ כָּרֵת וְעַל שִׁגְגָתוֹ חַטָּאת.

The Gemara answers: **As the Sages taught** with regard to an unwitting communal sin offering: **"And the sin by which they have sinned is known"** (Leviticus 4:14). **Rabbi** Yehuda HaNasi **says: It is stated here,** with regard to a sin-offering: **"By which [*aleha*],"** and **it is stated there,** with regard to the prohibition with regard to a wife's sister: **"Unto [*aleha*]."** This teaches by verbal analogy: **Just as there,** in the case of a wife's sister, it is **a matter that for its intentional** violation **one is liable to** receive ***karet* and for its unwitting** violation one is liable to bring **a sin-offering,**[N] **so too here,** the offering is brought for **a matter that for its intentional** violation **one is liable to** receive ***karet* and for its unwitting** violation one is liable to bring **a sin-offering.**

אַשְׁכְּחַן צִבּוּר, מָשִׁיחַ מְנָלַן? דִּכְתִיב בְּמָשִׁיחַ ״לְאַשְׁמַת הָעָם״ – הֲרֵי מָשִׁיחַ כְּצִבּוּר.

The Gemara continues: **We found** a source for the *halakha* that the offering brought by the community is a sin-offering; **from where do we** derive that **an anointed** High Priest also brings a sin-offering for this transgression? **As it is written** with regard **to an anointed** High Priest: "If the anointed priest shall sin **so as to bring guilt on the people"** (Leviticus 4:3), which indicates that **an anointed** High Priest brings an offering **like the community.**

יָחִיד וְנָשִׂיא – אָתְיָא ״מִצְוֹת״ ״מִצְוֹת״.

From where is it derived that a private **individual and a *Nasi*** bring sin-offerings only for a severe transgression of this kind? **This is derived** by verbal analogy between the words **"mitzvot"** and **"mitzvot"** that are stated three times, with regard to the community's sin-offering, a private individual's sin-offering, and the sin-offering of a *Nasi*: "Any of the mitzvot of the Lord that He has commanded not to be done" (Leviticus 4:2, 13, 22).

וְלֹא בַּעֲבוֹדָה זָרָה אֶלָּא עַל דָּבָר שֶׁחַיָּיבִין עַל זְדוֹנוֹ כָּרֵת וְעַל שִׁגְגָתוֹ חַטָּאת. צִבּוּר בַּעֲבוֹדָה זָרָה יָלֵיף ״מֵעֵינֵי״ ״מֵעֵינֵי״.

And it was stated above that this *halakha* applies to **idolatrous worship only** if it involved **a matter that for its intentional** violation **one is liable to** receive ***karet* and for its unwitting** violation one is liable to bring **a sin-offering.**[H] The *halakha* of **a community** that was guilty **of idolatrous worship is derived** by a verbal analogy between the phrases **"from the eyes"** and **"from the eyes."** With regard to the bull for an unwitting communal sin, the verse states: "From the eyes of the assembly" (Leviticus 4:13), while concerning an unwitting sin of idol worship, it says: "From the eyes of the congregation" (Numbers 15:24). This verbal analogy teaches that a congregation brings a sin-offering for idolatrous worship only if it involved a transgression that incurs *karet* when performed intentionally.

HALAKHA

The offering of a community for an unwittingly committed sin of idolatrous worship – קׇרְבַּן צִיבּוּר בְּשִׁגְגַת עֲבוֹדָה זָרָה: A court that erroneously permitted an idolatrous practice is obligated to bring an offering. This *halakha* applies only if that which they permitted is a prohibition that incurs *karet* when performed intentionally (Rambam *Sefer Korbanot, Hilkhot Shegagot* 12:1).

Types of offerings for unwitting violation – סוּגֵי קׇרְבָּנוֹת שְׁגָגָה: With regard to all prohibitions that incur *karet* for their intentional violation and that involve the performance of some action, except for idolatry, an unwitting sinner must bring a sin-offering. However, the offerings differ in accordance with the status of the sinner. If the offender was an ordinary person, he must bring a she-goat or a ewe. If a *Nasi* unwittingly transgressed, he brings a goat. If an anointed High Priest issued an erroneous ruling and acted accordingly, he must bring a bull. Finally, a court that unwittingly transgressed brings a bull (Rambam *Sefer Korbanot, Hilkhot Shegagot* 15:1).

An unwitting sin of idol worship – שִׁגְגַת עֲבוֹדָה זָרָה: If an individual, whether he is an ordinary person, a *Nasi*, or an anointed High Priest, unwittingly engaged in idolatrous worship, he must bring a one-year-old she-goat as a sin-offering. The court brings a bull as a burnt-offering and a goat as a sin-offering for each tribe that transgressed (Rambam *Sefer Korbanot, Hilkhot Shegagot* 12:1, 15:3).

NOTES

Just as there…for its unwitting violation one is liable to bring a sin-offering – מָה לְהַלָּן...עַל שִׁגְגָתוֹ חַטָּאת: The commentaries point out that the fact that one is liable to bring a sin-offering for the unwitting violation of the prohibition with regard to a wife's sister is not actually established, and was mentioned only incidentally (*Tosafot*). Indeed, certain commentaries omit this clause (Rivan). Others explain that as it is explicitly stated that the intentional violation of the prohibition with regard to a wife's sister incurs *karet*, this indicates that its unwitting transgression causes one to be liable to bring a sin-offering (Ritva).

יָחִיד, נָשִׂיא וּמָשִׁיחַ – מִ״וְאִם נֶפֶשׁ אַחַת״, אֶחָד יָחִיד וְאֶחָד נָשִׂיא וְאֶחָד מָשִׁיחַ בְּמַשְׁמָע, וָי״ו מוֹסִיף עַל עִנְיָן רִאשׁוֹן,

The cases of a private **individual, a *Nasi*, and an anointed** High Priest are derived **from** a verse that deals with an unwitting sin of idolatry: **"And if one person** sin" (Numbers 15:27). **All** of these, a private **individual, a *Nasi*, and an anointed** High Priest, **are included** in this verse. In this case the principle: The letter ***vav* adds to the previous matter,** applies. When a phrase begins with the conjunction *vav*, meaning: And, it is a continuation of the previous matter rather than a new topic. Based on this principle, these two *halakhot* are connected with one another.

וְיִלְמַד תַּחְתּוֹן מִן הָעֶלְיוֹן.

And therefore **let the lower,** i.e., the second, subject, a private individual, **be derived from the upper** issue, the community. Just as a community brings this offering only for a transgression whose intentional violation incurs *karet*, the same is true of a private individual. The verbal analogy stated in this *baraita* is Rabbi Yehuda HaNasi's inference from the phrase "with her."

וְרַבָּנַן, הַאי סְבָרָא מְנָא לְהוּ? נָפְקָא לְהוּ מִדְּמַקְרֵי לֵיהּ רַבִּי יְהוֹשֻׁעַ לִבְרֵיהּ: ״תּוֹרָה אַחַת יִהְיֶה לָכֶם לָעוֹשֶׂה בִּשְׁגָגָה...וְהַנֶּפֶשׁ אֲשֶׁר תַּעֲשֶׂה בְּיָד רָמָה״.

§ The Gemara asks: **And** with regard to **the Rabbis,** who interpret "with her" with regard to rival wives, **from where do they derive this conclusion** that one is liable to bring the offering for idolatrous worship only for a transgression whose intentional violation incurs *karet*? The Gemara answers: **They derive it from that which Rabbi Yehoshua** ben Levi **read out to his son** to teach him the verses that summarize the case of unwitting idol worship: **"You shall have one law [*Torah*] for him that does unwittingly. But the soul that does with a high hand,** whether he be home born or a stranger, he blasphemes the Lord; and that soul shall be cut off from among his people" (Numbers 15:29–30).

הוּקְּשָׁה כָּל הַתּוֹרָה כּוּלָּהּ לַעֲבוֹדָה זָרָה, מָה עֲבוֹדָה זָרָה – דָּבָר שֶׁחַיָּיבִין עַל זְדוֹנוֹ כָּרֵת וְעַל שִׁגְגָתוֹ חַטָּאת, אַף כָּל דָּבָר שֶׁחַיָּיבִין עַל זְדוֹנוֹ כָּרֵת וְעַל שִׁגְגָתוֹ חַטָּאת.

In this manner, **the entire Torah is juxtaposed**[B] **with idolatrous worship. Just as** in the case of **idolatrous worship** there is no obligation to bring an offering unless it is **a matter that for its intentional** violation **one is liable to** receive ***karet* and for its unwitting** violation one is liable to bring **a sin-offering,** as indicated by the verse: "That soul shall be cut off from among his people," **so too,** the same applies to **any matter that for its intentional** violation **one is liable to** receive ***karet* and for its unwitting** violation one is liable to bring **a sin-offering.**

אַשְׁכַּחַן יָחִיד וְנָשִׂיא וּמָשִׁיחַ, בֵּין בַּעֲבוֹדָה זָרָה וּבֵין בִּשְׁאָר מִצְוֹת, צִבּוּר בַּעֲבוֹדָה זָרָה מִנַּיִן? אָמַר קְרָא ״וְאִם נֶפֶשׁ״, וְיִלְמַד עֶלְיוֹן מִתַּחְתּוֹן.

The Gemara comments: **We found** a source for a private **individual, a *Nasi*, and an anointed** High Priest, **whether** with regard **to idolatrous worship or** with regard **to the other mitzvot. From where** is it derived that **a community** is liable only for an unwitting transgression **of idolatrous worship** of this kind? **The verse states: "And if one person** sin" (Numbers 15:27). Once again, the letter *vav* teaches that these two cases are connected, **and let the upper,** the first, issue of a community, **be derived from the lower** case, that of a private individual.

אֶלָּא צִבּוּר בִּשְׁאָר מִצְוֹת מְנָלַן? יָלֵיף ״מֵעֵינֵי״ ״מֵעֵינֵי״. וְרַבִּי, הַאי ״תּוֹרָה אַחַת״ מַאי עָבֵיד לֵיהּ? מִיבָּעֵי לֵיהּ לִכְדְתַנְיָא: לְפִי שֶׁמָּצִינוּ שֶׁחִלֵּק הַכָּתוּב בֵּין יְחִידִים לִמְרוּבִּים,

However, from where do we derive that **a community** brings an offering **for other mitzvot** only if the intentional violation of the prohibition incurs *karet*? The Gemara responds: **He derives** it from the aforementioned verbal analogy between **"from the eyes"** and **"from the eyes."** The Gemara asks: **And what does Rabbi** Yehuda HaNasi **do with this** verse: **"One law"?** The Gemara answers: **He requires it for that which is taught** in a *baraita*: **Since we find that the Torah differentiates between** private **individuals** who sinned **and the many**[H] who sinned in idol worship.

יְחִידִים – בִּסְקִילָה, לְפִיכָךְ מָמוֹנָן פָּלֵט, מְרוּבִּין – בְּסַיִיף, לְפִיכָךְ מָמוֹנָן אָבֵד.

The *baraita* elaborates: Private **individuals** who worshipped idols are sentenced **to stoning,** and **therefore their money is spared**[N] from destruction. Although the sinner is put to death, his possessions are not destroyed. By contrast, the **many** are condemned to the lighter death penalty of decapitation **by sword,** the punishment for those who worshipped idols in an idolatrous city, and **therefore their money is forfeited,** as by Torah law all possessions belonging to the residents of an idolatrous city must be burned.

BACKGROUND

Juxtaposed – הוּקְּשָׁה: Derivations based on the juxtaposition of biblical texts is an important exegetical principle. When two cases are mentioned together in the same verse, or in adjacent verses, the Talmud usually assumes that they are analogous. Consequently, legal inferences may be drawn by comparing the two cases.

HALAKHA

Individuals and groups with regard to idol worship – יְחִידִים וְרַבִּים בַּעֲבוֹדָה זָרָה: Individuals who intentionally transgressed and practiced idolatry, even if they are only a minority of the city, are sentenced to stoning, but their possessions are spared. However, if an entire city, or most of its residents, engaged in idolatry and was classified as an idolatrous city, each transgressor is executed by the sword, and the entire city, including all of its possessions, is burned (Rambam *Sefer HaMadda*, *Hilkhot Avoda Zara* 4:6).

NOTES

Therefore their money is spared – לְפִיכָךְ מָמוֹנָן פָּלֵט: One explanation is that because the physical punishment of individuals is harsher than that of the many, the ruling is more lenient toward their possessions, whereas in the case of many offenders, the physical punishment is relatively light and therefore a more stringent ruling is stated with regard to their possessions (Rivan). Others claim that the term: Therefore, does not appear in the source of this *halakha* in tractate *Horayot*, and there is no connection between these matters, as these rulings are merely by decree of the Torah. Overall, there are lenient and stringent elements in both the cases of an individual and a community, and consequently it cannot be claimed that one is more lenient than the other (*Yosef Lekaḥ*).

יָכוֹל נַחֲלוֹק בְּקָרְבְּנוֹתֵיהֶן? תַּלְמוּד לוֹמַר ״תּוֹרָה אַחַת יִהְיֶה לָכֶם״.

Due to this difference, one **might** have thought that **we** should likewise **differentiate between their offerings,** i.e., if an individual and a community unwittingly practiced idolatrous worship, different offerings are brought in the two cases. Therefore, **the verse states: "One law for you."** The word: "you" is in the plural, which indicates that an individual and a community that worshipped idols are subject to the same *halakha*.

מַתְקִיף לָהּ רַב חִלְקִיָּה מֵהַגְרוֹנְיָא: טַעֲמָא דִּכְתַב רַחֲמָנָא ״תּוֹרָה אַחַת יִהְיֶה לָכֶם״, הָא לָאו הָכִי – הֲוָה אָמִינָא נַחֲלֹק, מַאי לַיְיתוּ? לַיְיתוּ פַּר – צִבּוּר בִּשְׁאָר מִצְוֹת הוּא דְּמַיְיתוּ,

Rav Ḥilkiya from the city of **Hagronya strongly objects to this: The reason** for this ruling is **that the Merciful One** specifically **writes: "One law for you,"** from which it may be inferred that **if that were not so, I would say** that we should **differentiate** between the offerings of an individual and a community. If so, it is appropriate to ask: **What** offering **would they bring**[N] if we were to differentiate? You cannot say **they would bring a bull,** as **it is a community** that sinned unwittingly **in** transgressing **other mitzvot who bring** a bull, and as this case is written separately, clearly its *halakha* is different.

כִּשְׂבָּה – יָחִיד בִּשְׁאָר מִצְוֹת הוּא דְּמַיְיתִי, שָׂעִיר – נָשִׂיא בִּשְׁאָר מִצְוֹת הוּא דְּמַיְיתִי, פַּר לְעוֹלָה וְשָׂעִיר לְחַטָּאת – צִבּוּר בַּעֲבוֹדָה זָרָה הוּא דְּמַיְיתוּ. וְאֶלָּא מַאי, שְׂעִירָה – יָחִיד נַמִי הַיְינוּ קָרְבָּנוֹ!

Likewise, you cannot say that they should bring **a ewe,** as **it is an individual** who sinned **in** transgressing **the other mitzvot who brings** a ewe. Nor can you say that they bring **a goat,** as **it is a** *Nasi* who sinned **in** transgressing **the other mitzvot who brings** a goat. And you cannot say that they would bring **a bull as a burnt-offering and a goat as a sin-offering,** as **it is the community,** i.e., the majority of Jews, who sinned **in** performing **idolatrous worship who bring** these. **Rather, what** might they bring? If one were to suggest **a she-goat,** that would not be appropriate, because **this is the offering** of a private **individual as well,** since an individual brings a ewe or a she-goat as a sin-offering. Apparently there is no need for a special inference in this case, as there are no other possibilities.

אִיצְטְרִיךְ, סָלְקָא דַּעְתָּךְ אָמִינָא: הוֹאִיל וְצִבּוּר בְּהוֹרָאָה מַיְיתוּ פַּר לְעוֹלָה וְשָׂעִיר לְחַטָּאת – אִינְהוּ נַמִי נַיְתוּ אִיפְּכָא.

The Gemara answers: It **is necessary** for a verse to teach that there is no difference between the offerings of an individual and a community, as it might **enter your mind to say: Since a community** that sinned **by** the erroneous **instruction** of the court that it is permitted to practice idolatry **brings a bull as a burnt-offering and a goat as a sin-offering,** then, when a community sins of its own accord **they too** should **bring** these animals, but **the opposite,** i.e., a bull as a sin-offering and a goat as a burnt-offering.

אִי נַמִי: צָרִיךְ וְאֵין לוֹ תַּקָּנָה, קָא מַשְׁמַע לַן.

Alternatively, it could be argued: Theoretically a community **must** bring a different form of atonement from that of an individual, yet **they have no remedy,**[N] as the Torah did not specify which offering is brought for a sin of the many. Therefore, the verse **teaches us** by means of the phrase "one law for you" that there is indeed an offering for the many who practiced idol worship.

אָמַר לֵיהּ לֵוִי לְרַבִּי: מַאי אִירְיָא דְּתָנֵי חֲמֵשׁ עֶשְׂרֵה? לִיתְנֵי שֵׁשׁ עֶשְׂרֵה! אָמַר לֵיהּ: כִּמְדוּמֶּה לִי שֶׁאֵין לוֹ מוֹחַ בְּקָדְקֳדוֹ.

§ After discussing different interpretations of the relevant verses, the Gemara addresses the details of the *halakhot* of the mishna. It first considers the numbers that comprise the structure of the mishna as a whole. The Sage **Levi**[P] **said to Rabbi** Yehuda HaNasi: **Why does** the *tanna* **specifically teach**[N] the cases of **fifteen women? Let him teach** the cases of **sixteen** women, including the case of a rival wife of a forbidden relation. Rabbi Yehuda HaNasi **said to him:** Judging by his question, **it seems to me that** this Sage **has no brain in his head.**

מַאי דַּעְתָּךְ – אִמּוֹ אֲנוּסַת אָבִיו?

Rabbi Yehuda HaNasi proceeded to explain the question and the answer himself: **What is your thinking?** Is it that the *tanna* should have included the case of **his mother** who had been **raped by his father?** In the opinion of the Rabbis, a woman raped by one's father is permitted in marriage to another of his sons. Consequently, it is possible that she might give birth to a son and later marry one of the other sons of the rapist. If her husband subsequently died childless, this woman would come before the brother of the deceased for levirate marriage, who is in this case her son. If so, there are in fact sixteen women with whom relations are forbidden.

NOTES

What would they bring – מַאי לַיְיתוּ: The commentaries explain that as a special *halakha* applies to the many who worship idols, in that their possessions are destroyed, this case is an exception to the general category of court-imposed death penalties. Therefore it is appropriate to suggest that the sin-offering in this case might also be unique (Ramban). Some commentaries ask why the Gemara does not propose that they bring a sheep or ram as a sin-offering (*Tosefot HaRosh*). The Rosh answers that one may not invent a new type of offering that is not mentioned in the Torah. Accordingly, the real question is: If their offering is like other offerings, then there is nothing different about their case; conversely, the alternative, that one should invent an entirely new offering, is wholly unacceptable. Certain commentaries accept this interpretation, but they ask why the Gemara did not formulate the question accordingly (*Tosafot Yeshanim*).

Alternatively a community must, yet they have no remedy – אִי נַמִי צָרִיךְ וְאֵין לוֹ תַּקָּנָה: Some commentaries explain that this does not mean that there is no remedy at all, but simply that the remedy is not stated in the Torah, and therefore one would not know what to do in this situation (*Yosef Lekaḥ*).

Why does the *tanna* specifically teach – מַאי אִירְיָא דְּתָנֵי: The fact that Levi posed this question to Rabbi Yehuda HaNasi indicates that this mishna was not formulated by Rabbi Yehuda HaNasi, the redactor of the Mishna; rather, it existed before his time (*Sefer Keritut*). In the Jerusalem Talmud it is likewise stated that *mishnayot* that contain structured enumerations of *halakhot* date back to a very early source, from the period of the First Temple (Maharatz Ḥayyut).

PERSONALITIES

Levi – לֵוִי: This is the Sage Levi, son of Sisi, who lived in the transitional generation between the *tanna'im* and the *amora'im*. Levi was the preeminent disciple of Rabbi Yehuda HaNasi and was close to both him and his son Rabbi Shimon. The phrase: It was taught before the Sages, is said to refer to Levi, who would debate halakhic issues with Rabbi Yehuda HaNasi. Although Rabbi Yehuda HaNasi occasionally issued harsh statements toward Levi, this was merely Rabbi Yehuda HaNasi's style of teaching, through which he would assert his authority over his disciples. In fact, Rabbi Yehuda HaNasi held Levi in very high esteem and even called him: A man like myself.

In his time, Levi was considered a Sage who achieved perfection in all areas. He was a master of *halakha* and *aggada*, knowledgeable in the Bible, and an important teacher. It is said of his public prayers that he would hurl his words up toward Heaven, and although his prayers were answered, he paid a price in terms of his health.

After Rabbi Yehuda HaNasi's death, Levi was left without a teacher, and he therefore traveled to Babylonia. He apparently spent most of his time there in the city of Neharde'a, where he befriended Shmuel's father and renewed his ties with Rav. Many sources in the Gemara depict these three, together with Shmuel, engaged in halakhic discussions concerning various issues. It is probable that Levi passed away in Babylonia.

Like Rabbi Yehuda HaNasi's other important disciples, Levi edited an important collection of *baraitot* called by the Gemara: The Mishna of Levi. Some commentaries say that the renowned *amora* Rabbi Yehoshua ben Levi was his son, but this seems unlikely in light of the order of the generations.

NOTES

Does not deal with disputed cases – בִּפְלוּגְתָּא לָא קָא מַיְירִי: Some commentaries point out that there is a dispute below with regard to refusal, as Rabbi Yishmael disputes the ruling of the first *tanna* of the mishna (Ritva). The Ritva explains that although there are disagreements with regard to details of these cases, the basic *halakhot* are not in dispute (see *Tosafot*).

Concerning which Rabbi Akiva and the Rabbis disagree – דִּפְלִיגִי רַבִּי עֲקִיבָא וְרַבָּנַן: How does the Gemara know that Rabbi Akiva invariably exempts women forbidden by a regular prohibition even from *ḥalitza*? Various solutions are suggested by the early commentaries (Ramban; Ritva) and the later commentaries (*Arukh LaNer*; *Gilyonei HaShas*). Some explain simply that the *amora'im* had a tradition to this effect, and there is no need to cite further proof (Rashba).

אִמּוֹ אֲנוּסַת אָבִיו פְּלוּגְתָּא דְּרַבִּי יְהוּדָה וְרַבָּנַן הִיא, וּבִפְלוּגְתָּא לָא קָא מַיְירִי.

However, continued Rabbi Yehuda HaNasi, this is incorrect, as the case of **his mother raped by his father is** a matter of **dispute between Rabbi Yehuda and the Rabbis.** According to Rabbi Yehuda, a woman raped by one's father could never come before him for levirate marriage, as it is prohibited for her to marry his brothers. **And** the *tanna* of this mishna **does not deal with disputed** cases.[N] The mishna enumerates only those cases that are accepted by all opinions, not those that are a matter of dispute.

וְלָא? וַהֲרֵי אִיסּוּר מִצְוָה וְאִיסּוּר קְדוּשָּׁה,

The Gemara asks: **And** does the *tanna* really **not** mention disputed cases? **But** there are the cases of **a prohibition** resulting from **a mitzva** of the Sages, **and a prohibition** stemming from **sanctity.** In other words, the *tanna* does refer to the cases of a woman who one is prohibited to marry by decree of the Sages, e.g., a distant secondary forbidden relation, and one who is prohibited due to a regular prohibition that preserves the sanctity of the Jewish people or the priesthood.

דִּפְלִיגִי רַבִּי עֲקִיבָא וְרַבָּנַן, וְקָתָנֵי!

These are cases concerning **which Rabbi Akiva and the Rabbis disagree**[N] whether these women are entirely exempt from both levirate marriage and *ḥalitza* like a forbidden relation, or whether the mitzva of levirate marriage does in fact apply but since the *yavam* may not marry her in practice, she must be released by *ḥalitza*. **And** yet these disputed cases **are taught** in the mishna.

בְּפִרְקִין קָא אָמְרִינַן, וְהָא בֵּית שַׁמַּאי מַתִּירִין אֶת הַצָּרוֹת לָאַחִין וּבֵית הִלֵּל אוֹסְרִין!

The Gemara responds: When **we say** that only accepted *halakhot* are included in the mishna, we are referring only to **our** present **chapter,** whereas the dispute between Rabbi Akiva and the Rabbis is stated in the second chapter. The Gemara raises a difficulty: **But** in this chapter it is stated that **Beit Shammai permit rival wives to the brothers,** as they hold that there is no prohibition against rival wives of those with whom relations are forbidden, **and Beit Hillel prohibit** this. Evidently, the first chapter does deal with disputed cases.

בֵּית שַׁמַּאי בִּמְקוֹם בֵּית הִלֵּל – אֵינָהּ מִשְׁנָה. וַהֲרֵי אֵשֶׁת אָחִיו שֶׁלֹּא הָיָה בְּעוֹלָמוֹ,

The Gemara answers: When **Beit Shammai** express an opinion **where Beit Hillel** disagree, their opinion is considered as if it were **not** in the **mishna,** i.e., it is completely disregarded, as it is commonly accepted that the opinion of Beit Shammai is rejected and not ruled as *halakha*. Therefore, this cannot be considered a true dispute. The Gemara raises a further difficulty: **But** there is the case of **a wife of a brother with whom he did not coexist,** i.e., the *yavam* was not alive at the time of his brother's death.

Perek **I**
Daf **9** Amud **b**

דִּפְלִיגִי רַבִּי שִׁמְעוֹן וְרַבָּנַן, וְקָתָנֵי! בְּנוֹלַד,

This is a case concerning **which Rabbi Shimon and the Rabbis disagree, and** yet it **is taught.** If this *halakha* is taught, evidently this mishna does deal with matters subject to dispute. The Gemara answers **that** Rabbi Shimon does not disagree with the Rabbis concerning all cases of a wife of a brother with whom he did not coexist. If this *yavam* was **born** after his brother's death, he concedes that the obligation of levirate marriage does not apply to the newborn *yavam*. Rather, the *yevama* is prohibited to him as his brother's wife.

וּלְבַסּוֹף יִיבֵּם לָא פָּלֵיג רַבִּי שִׁמְעוֹן.

Furthermore, in a case where he was born **and at the end,** i.e., afterward, a second older brother **entered into levirate marriage** with the *yevama* and subsequently died as well, and the same woman again came before that same younger brother, **Rabbi Shimon did not disagree** with the opinion of the Rabbis here either, as he admits that this woman is permanently forbidden to him because when he was born she was classified as the wife of a brother with whom he did not coexist.

In fact, Rabbi Shimon disagreed only with regard to a different case, when there were two brothers, one of whom died, and the second took the *yevama* in levirate marriage. If a third brother was subsequently born and afterward the second brother died, Rabbi Shimon maintains that the youngest brother may enter into levirate marriage with this woman because she was never forbidden to him, as what occurred prior to his birth is of no relevance. Since even in Rabbi Shimon's opinion it is possible to find a case in which the wife of a brother with whom he did not coexist is forbidden to him, it can be claimed that the mishna is taught in accordance with all opinions.

וְהָאָמַר רַבִּי אוֹשַׁעְיָא: חָלוּק הָיָה רַבִּי שִׁמְעוֹן אַף בָּרִאשׁוֹנָה!

The Gemara raises a difficulty: **But didn't Rabbi Oshaya say** that **Rabbi Shimon disagreed**[N] **even with regard to the first** case? In other words, Rabbi Shimon disagreed not only in the case of a woman who entered into levirate marriage before the young brother was born, but even if the young brother was born before the initial levirate marriage took place.

הָא אִיתּוֹתַב רַבִּי אוֹשַׁעְיָא.

The Gemara rejects this suggestion: This statement of **Rabbi Oshaya was conclusively refuted.** Consequently, it remains possible to say that the mishna does not deal with disputes.

The Gemara raises a difficulty from another angle. The third chapter discusses a case involving four brothers, two of whom passed away after they were married to two sisters. As a result, the two sisters simultaneously came before the surviving brothers for levirate marriage or *ḥalitza*. The Sages ruled that in this case the brothers may not enter into levirate marriage with the sisters, as it is as though the two sisters came before each brother individually, and due to the levirate bond each sister was, in a sense, considered married to each brother to a certain extent.

Consequently, for each brother the other sister is viewed as his wife's sister, as it were, and is forbidden to him. Since this occurs to both sisters simultaneously, it is prohibited for both of them to enter into levirate marriage. However, the Sages further said that if one of these sisters was a forbidden relation to one of the surviving brothers, e.g., if he had married her daughter or some other relative, the second sister, to whom he is not a close relative, is permitted to him. If the same applies to the other brother and the second sister, the two brothers could perform *ḥalitza* with the two sisters or even enter into levirate marriage with them.

וְהָאָמַר רַב יְהוּדָה אָמַר רַב, וְכֵן תָּנֵי רַבִּי חִיָּיא: בְּכוּלָּן אֲנִי קוֹרֵא בָּהֶן הָאֲסוּרָה לָזֶה מוּתֶּרֶת לָזֶה, וְהָאֲסוּרָה לָזֶה מוּתֶּרֶת לָזֶה, וַאֲחוֹתָהּ שֶׁהִיא יְבִמְתָּהּ חוֹלֶצֶת אוֹ מִתְיַיבֶּמֶת.

With this in mind, the Gemara states its objection: **And didn't Rav Yehuda say** that **Rav said, and likewise Rabbi Ḥiyya taught** in a *baraita*: With regard **to all of those** fifteen women enumerated in the mishna, it is possible to find a scenario in which **I** would **call them: The** woman **who is forbidden to this** brother **is permitted to that** brother, **and the one who is forbidden to this** brother **is permitted to that** brother. **And** consequently, **her sister who is her sister-in-law**[B] **performs *ḥalitza* or enters into levirate marriage.** This complex situation can be demonstrated with regard to each of the women enumerated in the mishna, e.g., if one sister is the mother-in-law of one brother, and the second sister is the mother-in-law of the second brother, and so on.

BACKGROUND

Her sister who is her sister-in-law – אֲחוֹתָהּ שֶׁהִיא יְבִמְתָּהּ: The brothers Yehuda and Levi married two sisters, Milka and Ḥogla, which means that these two sisters became sisters-in-law as well. Two other brothers married their daughters: Shimon married Ḥanna, daughter of Milka, while Reuven wed Miriam, daughter of Ḥogla.

Subsequently, both Yehuda and Levi died childless and their wives came before Shimon and Reuven for levirate marriage. Although Shimon may not enter into levirate marriage with Milka, his mother-in-law, he is permitted to enter into levirate marriage with her sister Ḥogla. Likewise, Reuven is forbidden to his mother-in-law, Ḥogla, but may enter into levirate marriage with her sister Milka. Consequently, this is a case of a sister who is a sister-in-law who either performs *ḥalitza* or levirate marriage.

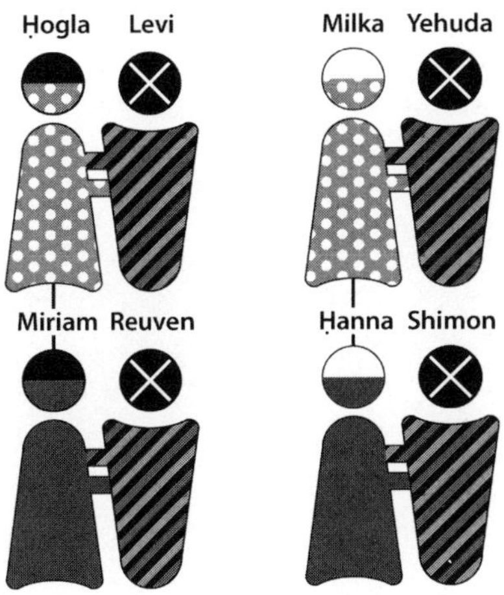

NOTES

Rabbi Shimon disagreed, etc. – חָלוּק הָיָה רַבִּי שִׁמְעוֹן וכו׳: The early commentaries ask: Even according to the opinion of Rabbi Oshaya, there is a case of a wife of a brother with whom he did not coexist that Rabbi Shimon would concede is prohibited, i.e., if at first there was only one brother who died childless and then later another brother was born, in which case the *yevama* would be forbidden to the newborn *yavam*. Some answer that as Rabbi Shimon did not mention a scenario of this kind in the mishna it is not taken into account (*Tosafot Yeshanim*). Others point out that this case does not allow for the possibility of a rival wife of the rival wife of a forbidden relation (*Tosefot HaRosh*).

וְרַב יְהוּדָה מְתַרְגֵּם מֵחֲמוֹתוֹ וְאֵילָךְ, אֲבָל שִׁיתָּא בָּבֵי דְּרֵישָׁא – לָא, מַאי טַעֲמָא?

And Rav Yehuda explains[N] that this is not true of all of the women listed in the mishna. Only **from** the case of **his mother-in-law and onward,** until the end of the list, is it possible for one sister to be a forbidden relation to one brother and the other sister not to be forbidden at all. **However, in the first six cases, no,** this option does not apply. **What is the reason** for this?

כֵּיוָן דְּבִתּוֹ,

Since, for example, in the case of **one's daughter,** although it is possible that one of the sisters is the daughter of one of the brothers, her mother is prohibited to all of the brothers as their brother's wife, and therefore she could not possibly have a daughter from another brother. This case is possible only if one brother raped a woman who subsequently gave birth to his daughter. Since the prohibition with regard to a brother's wife applies only in the case of marriage, this same woman is not forbidden to a different brother. If another brother came and raped her as well and she gave birth to his daughter too, and these two daughters later married two other brothers, each of these sisters who are sisters-in-law is forbidden to one of the brothers but permitted to the other.

בְּאוֹנָסִין מַשְׁכַּחַתְּ בְּנִשּׂוּאִין לָא מַשְׁכַּחַתְּ לַהּ, בְּנִשּׂוּאִין קָמַיְירֵי בְּאוֹנָסִין – לָא קָא מַיְירֵי.

Accordingly, **in** the case of **rape you** can **find** this scenario, but **in** the case of **marriage you cannot find** it. However, the mishna cannot be interpreted as referring to a case of this kind, as **it deals with marriage** and **it does not deal with rape.**[N]

וְאַבַּיֵי מְתַרְגֵּם אַף בִּתּוֹ מֵאֲנוּסָתוֹ, כֵּיוָן דְּאַשְׁכּוּחֵי מַשְׁכַּחַתְּ לַהּ, אִי בָּעֲיָא מִן הָאוֹנָסִין – תֶּהֱוֵי. [אִי בָּעֲיָא מִן הַנִּשּׂוּאִין – תֶּהֱוֵי], אֲבָל אֵשֶׁת אָחִיו שֶׁלֹּא הָיָה בְּעוֹלָמוֹ – לָא, מַאי טַעֲמָא?

And Abaye explains differently, as he would include in this scenario **even his daughter from the woman he raped.** Why would he include this case? **Since you can find** this possibility, **if you wish it can be by rape, and if you wish it can be by marriage,**[N] i.e., regardless of the details, this situation can occur. **However,** the last case, that of **a wife of a brother with whom he did not coexist,** he would **not** include. **What is the reason** for this?

כֵּיוָן דִּלְרַבִּי שִׁמְעוֹן הוּא דְּמַשְׁכַּחַתְּ לַהּ לְרַבָּנַן לָא מַשְׁכַּחַתְּ לַהּ – בִּפְלוּגְתָּא לָא קָא מַיְירֵי.

Since it is only **according to** the opinion of **Rabbi Shimon that you find this** potential scenario, as he permits a *yevama* to her *yavam* in a case where he was born after she first entered levirate marriage, it is therefore possible that one sister might be forbidden to one brother if he was born before his brother took her in levirate marriage. Likewise, another sister might be forbidden to another brother for the same reason, although the first woman would be permitted to him, as in his lifetime she was never the wife of a brother with whom he did not coexist. **According to** the opinion of **the Rabbis,** however, **you cannot find this** scenario, and the mishna **does not deal with disputes** but only with those cases that are accepted by all opinions.

וְרַב סָפְרָא מְתַרְגֵּם אַף אֵשֶׁת אָחִיו שֶׁלֹּא הָיָה בְּעוֹלָמוֹ, וּמַשְׁכַּחַתְּ לַהּ בְּשִׁיתָּא אַחִים, וְאַלִּיבָּא דְּרַבִּי שִׁמְעוֹן

But Rav Safra explains that the possibility of one brother permitted only to one woman and another brother likewise permitted to only one woman exists **even** in the case of **a wife of a brother with whom he did not coexist, and you can find this** scenario **in** a case involving **six brothers, and** this is **in accordance with** the opinion **of Rabbi Shimon.**

NOTES

And Rav Yehuda explains, etc. – וְרַב יְהוּדָה מְתַרְגֵּם וכו׳: That is to say, although he transmitted this *halakha* in the name of Rav or Rabbi Ḥiyya, he himself did not hold that one should interpret the entire mishna in this manner. Rabbi Ḥiyya, however, did maintain that it is possible to explain the entire mishna in this way.

It does not deal with rape – בְּאוֹנָסִין לָא קָא מַיְירֵי: Some commentaries explain that this is referring to the mishna that deals with her sister who is her sister-in-law, whereas the mishna here is discussing rape as well. They attempt to prove this by means of a close reading of Rashi's commentary (*Arukh LaNer*).

If you wish it can be by marriage, etc. – אִי בָּעֲיָא מִן הַנִּשּׂוּאִין תֶּהֱוֵי וכו׳: The wording here is imprecise, as this scenario can occur only by means of rape, as explained above. Abaye means to say that as she is his daughter, there is no difference between a daughter through marriage or through other means (Rivan; see Meiri).

וְסִימָנֵיךְ: מֵת נוֹלַד וְיִבֵּם, מֵת נוֹלַד וְיִבֵּם.

And your mnemonic to remember how this might occur is as follows: **Died, was born, entered into levirate marriage, died, was born, entered into levirate marriage.** In other words, there were several brothers, and one, Reuven, **died,** before another, Yissakhar, **was born, and** another brother, Shimon, **entered into levirate marriage** with the deceased's wife, and there was another brother, Levi, who **died** as well, and yet another brother, Zevulun, **was born, and** a sixth brother, Yehuda, **entered into levirate marriage** with the deceased's wife. In this case, if Shimon and Yehuda were to die childless, their wives would come before the surviving brothers, Yissakhar and Zevulun, for levirate marriage. To one of them, Yissakhar, the wife of the first brother, Reuven, is prohibited, and for the other brother, Zevulun, the wife of the second brother, Levi, is likewise prohibited.

This is an example of the type of case analyzed in the third chapter, in which the ruling is that the woman who is forbidden to this brother is permitted to that one, and she who is forbidden to this one is permitted to that one. In any case, Rabbi Ḥiyya incorporates the opinion of Rabbi Shimon into this principle, as he maintains that this scenario can apply to each case stated in the mishna. If so, the mishna evidently does deal with disputed legal rulings. How, then, can Rabbi Yehuda HaNasi claim that the cases of the mishna are unanimous?

אֶלָּא, לְרַבִּי – הָנֵי כְּלָלֵי לֵית לֵיהּ. רַב אַדָּא קַרְחִינָא קַמֵּיהּ דְּרַב כָּהֲנָא אָמַר מִשְּׁמֵיהּ דְּרָבָא: לְעוֹלָם אִית לֵיהּ לְרַבִּי הָנֵי כְּלָלֵי, וְהָכִי קָאָמַר לֵיהּ: אִמּוֹ אֲנוּסַת אָבִיו – בַּחֲדָא מַשְׁכַּחַתְּ לַהּ, בִּתְרָתֵי – לָא קָמַשְׁכַּחַתְּ לַהּ.

§ **Rather, Rabbi** Yehuda HaNasi **does not hold** in accordance with **these general statements** applied by Rabbi Ḥiyya, and therefore he maintains that no issue subject to dispute was taught in the mishna. **Rav Adda Karḥina,** who was sitting **before Rav Kahana, said in the name of Rava: Actually,** one can explain that **Rabbi does hold** in accordance with **these general statements** laid out by Rabbi Ḥiyya. **And this is what** he **said** to Levi: In the case of **his mother** who had been **raped by his father, you find this** case **with** only **one** of the women; however, **you cannot find it with two.** In other words, the terms mentioned by Rabbi Ḥiyya above: She who is forbidden to this one is permitted to that one, and: A sister who is a sister-in-law performs either *ḥalitza* or levirate marriage, apply only partly to this complex case.

אִי יַעֲקֹב שְׁתֵּי אֲחָיוֹת אָנַס, אֲחוֹתָהּ שֶׁהִיא יְבִמְתָּהּ – מַשְׁכַּחַתְּ לַהּ, הָאֲסוּרָה לָזֶה מוּתֶּרֶת לָזֶה – לָא מַשְׁכַּחַתְּ,

The Gemara elaborates: **If Ya'akov,** the father, **raped two sisters** who gave birth to two sons, and he had two other sons who married these raped sisters and died, in this scenario **you find** a case of **her sister who is her sister-in-law,** as there is a *yevama* who comes before one of the brothers who is a forbidden relative and also a sister and a sister-in-law of another *yevama*. However, **you cannot find** the principle of: **She who is forbidden to this one is permitted to that one.** Although it is possible that one's brother's wife who is one's mother might come before one for levirate marriage, just as he is forbidden to his mother, he is likewise forbidden to his mother's sister.

וְאִי שְׁתֵּי נָכְרִיּוֹת אָנַס – הָאֲסוּרָה לָזֶה מוּתֶּרֶת לָזֶה מַשְׁכַּחַתְּ לַהּ, אֲחוֹתָהּ שֶׁהִיא יְבִמְתָּהּ – לָא מַשְׁכַּחַתְּ לַהּ.

And if the father **raped two unrelated women,** who gave birth to two sons and then married two other sons of the same father who subsequently died, **you find** the case of: **She who is forbidden to this one is permitted to that one,** as each of the two raped women comes before one of the brothers for levirate marriage while she is forbidden to the other as his mother. However, **you do not find** a situation of: **Her sister who is her sister-in-law.** Therefore, the case of one's mother who was raped by one's father cannot be included in the list of the mishna, as the characteristics stated by Rabbi Ḥiyya do not apply to this case.

רַב אַשִׁי אָמַר: לְעוֹלָם לֵית לֵיהּ לְרַבִּי הָנֵי כְּלָלֵי, וּבִפְלוּגְתָּא קָמַיְירֵי. וּמַאי "כִּמְדוּמֶּה אֲנִי שֶׁאֵין לוֹ מוֹחַ בְּקָדְקֳדוֹ" דְּקָאָמַר לֵיהּ –

§ **Rav Ashi stated**[N] a different explanation: **Actually, Rabbi** Yehuda HaNasi **does not hold** in accordance with **these general statements** of Rabbi Ḥiyya, **and** the mishna **does deal with** *halakhot* that are in **dispute.**[N] According to his opinion, **what is** the meaning of the phrase: **It seems to me that he has no brain in his head, that** Rabbi Yehuda HaNasi **said to** Levi?

הָכִי קָאָמַר לֵיהּ: מַאי טַעְמָא לָא דָּיְיקַתְּ מַתְנִיתִין? דְּמַתְנִיתִין רַבִּי יְהוּדָה הִיא, [דְּאָסַר בַּאֲנוּסַת אָבִיו].

According to Rav Ashi, **this is what** Rabbi Yehuda HaNasi **said** to Levi: **What is the reason** that **you were not precise** in your interpretation of **the mishna? As the mishna is** in accordance with the opinion of **Rabbi Yehuda, who prohibited** the case **of a woman** who was **raped by one's father.** Accordingly, the rulings of the mishna cannot be attributed to any opinion that is not in line with that of Rabbi Yehuda. What is the proof that this mishna is indeed in accordance with the opinion of Rabbi Yehuda?

דְּקָתָנֵי: שֵׁשׁ עֲרָיוֹת חֲמוּרוֹת מֵאֵלּוּ מִפְּנֵי שֶׁהֵן נְשׂוּאוֹת לַאֲחֵרִים צָרוֹתֵיהֶן מוּתָּרוֹת: אִמּוֹ, וְאֵשֶׁת אָבִיו, וַאֲחוֹת אָבִיו. מַאי אִמּוֹ? אִילֵימָא נְשׂוּאַת אָבִיו – הַיְינוּ אֵשֶׁת אָבִיו!

As it teaches in the next mishna: **Six** women **with whom relations are forbidden**[N] **are more severe than these** enumerated in the previous mishna, **because they** may **marry** only **others** and can never be married to any of the brothers, and therefore **their rival wives are permitted.** These women include: **His mother, his father's wife, and his father's sister.** Rav Ashi infers: **What is** the meaning of: **His mother? If we say** that this mother is **married to his father,** then **this is the same** case as: **His father's wife,** which would mean that the mishna lists only five cases, not six.

אֶלָּא לָאו – אֲנוּסַת אָבִיו, וְקָתָנֵי: מִפְּנֵי שֶׁהֵן נְשׂוּאוֹת לַאֲחֵרִים, לַאֲחֵרִים – אִין, לָאַחִין – לָא. מַאן שָׁמְעַתְּ לֵיהּ דְּאִית לֵיהּ הַאי סְבָרָא – רַבִּי יְהוּדָה, דְּאָסַר בַּאֲנוּסַת אָבִיו, מִשּׁוּם הָכִי לָא תָּנֵי לֵיהּ.

Rather, is it not referring to **a woman raped by his father? And it is taught** in the mishna that the *halakhot* of levirate marriage do not apply to them **because they may marry** only **others,** which indicates: **Others, yes; the brothers, no.** Since each of the brothers are sons of the same father, each one is prohibited from marrying the mother of one of the other brothers, as although she is not his mother, she is nevertheless a woman raped by his father, whom one may not marry. **Who did you hear who holds** in accordance with **this conclusion** that a woman raped by one's father is prohibited to all his sons? It is **Rabbi Yehuda who prohibits a woman raped by his father. Due to that** reason the case of a woman raped by one's father **was not taught** in the first mishna.

אֲמַר לֵיהּ רָבִינָא לְרַב אַשִׁי: לְרַבִּי יְהוּדָה נָמֵי מַשְׁכַּחַתְּ לַהּ. דְּאִי עָבַר וְנָסֵיב! "דְּאִי" לָא קָתָנֵי.

Ravina said to Rav Ashi: Even according to the opinion of **Rabbi Yehuda you** can **find this** possibility that a woman raped by a father comes before the son for levirate marriage. **What if one** of the brothers **transgressed and married**[N] a woman raped by his father? Even Rabbi Yehuda concedes that this is a violation of a regular prohibition that does not incur *karet*, and therefore the marriage is valid. Consequently, if this brother died childless, this woman would come before her son for levirate marriage. The Gemara rejects this proof: The *tanna* **does not teach** cases of **what if,** i.e., the mishna does not cite an example that could result only from a transgression.

NOTES

Rav Ashi stated, etc. – רַב אַשִׁי אָמַר וכו׳: This discussion is found in the Jerusalem Talmud as well, although it follows a different logical order and is attributed to other Sages. There, the first explanation is that of Rav Ashi, which is challenged on several accounts and subsequently combined with the answer stated here by Rava.

The mishna does deal with *halakhot* in dispute – בִּפְלוּגְתָּא קָמַיְירֵי: The early commentaries ask: According to this opinion, Levi should have enumerated even more than sixteen cases (*Tosafot*). Several answers are suggested. The consensus opinion is that even Levi did not list all of the possibilities according to all of the various opinions, but only those rulings that the *tanna* of the mishna would accept (Rashba).

As it teaches, six women with whom relations are forbidden, etc. – דְּקָתָנֵי שֵׁשׁ עֲרָיוֹת וכו׳: Rav Ashi's inference is obvious; clearly none of the especially stringent six cases could be included in the first mishna. How, then, could Levi have thought that he should add the case of one's mother to the first mishna (*Tosafot*)? Some early commentaries suggest that Levi maintains that the case of a mother mentioned in that mishna could be referring to a mother who is married to his father, whereas a father's wife means the wife of his father who is not his mother (Rashba; Ritva).

What if one transgressed and married – דְּאִי עָבַר וְנָסֵיב: In the Jerusalem Talmud, *Tosafot*, and other early commentaries the point is raised that this can be explained according to the opinion of Rabbi Yehuda even without the hypothetical case cited in the Gemara, e.g., if the brother betrothed the woman raped by his father but did not actually marry her. In this case, no prohibition has been violated. Most early commentaries explain that as the purpose of the betrothal is marriage and ultimately sexual relations, the betrothal itself is prohibited, and therefore it is still considered a case involving a prohibition, which is not discussed by the mishna.

אָמַר לֵיהּ רַב אַשִׁי לְרַב כָּהֲנָא: בְּלָא "דְּאִי" נַמִּי מַשְׁכַּחַתְּ לַהּ: יַעֲקֹב אָנַס כַּלָּתוֹ וְהוֹלִיד מִמֶּנָּה בֵּן, וּמֵת [רְאוּבֵן] בְּלֹא בָּנִים, וְנָפְלָה לָהּ קַמֵּי בְּרַהּ, וּמִיגּוֹ דְּאִיהִי אֲסִירָה – צָרָתָהּ נַמִּי אֲסִירָה.

Rav Ashi said to Rav Kahana: Even without a hypothetical: **What if, you** can **find**[N] an example of a woman raped by a father who is not forbidden to the son in marriage. How so? **Ya'akov,** the father, **raped his daughter-in-law,**[NB] **from whom he fathered a son. And** the son, **Reuven,** the husband of the daughter-in-law, **died childless. And** as Ya'akov had two sons, the deceased Reuven and a son by Reuven's wife whom Ya'akov had raped, Reuven's wife **would** then **come before her son** for levirate marriage. **And since she is forbidden, her rival wife is also forbidden.** Consequently, a case of this kind is possible without the levirate marriage resulting from an illicit marriage.

אָמַר לֵיהּ: בְּאַחְוָותָא דְּהֶתֵּירָא – קָמַיְירִי, בְּאַחְוָותָא דְּאִיסּוּרָא – לָא קָמַיְירִי. וְאַף עַל פִּי כֵן בְּדַקָה לֵוִי בְּמַתְנִיתִין,

Rav Kahana **said to** Rav Ashi: The mishna **deals with** cases of **legitimate brothers,** whereas **it does not deal with cases of illegitimate brothers.** The offspring of a man who rapes his daughter-in-law is a *mamzer,* and cases of this kind are not discussed in the mishna. The Gemara comments: **Nevertheless,** despite Rabbi Yehuda HaNasi's criticism, **Levi established this** additional possibility of a woman raped by one's father **in his *mishnayot*.**

דְּתָנֵי לֵוִי: אִמּוֹ, פְּעָמִים פּוֹטֶרֶת צָרָתָהּ וּפְעָמִים אֵינָהּ פּוֹטֶרֶת צָרָתָהּ. כֵּיצַד? הָיְתָה אִמּוֹ נְשׂוּאַת אָבִיו, וְנִשֵּׂאת לְאָחִיו מֵאָבִיו וּמֵת – זוֹ הִיא אִמּוֹ שֶׁאֵין פּוֹטֶרֶת צָרָתָהּ,

As Levi taught in his *baraita*: With regard to the case of **his mother, at times she exempts her rival wife, and at** other **times she does not exempt her rival wife. How so?** If **his mother was married to his father and** after his father's death she illicitly **married** her son's **paternal brother, who then died, this is** a case of: **His mother who does not exempt her rival wife.** The reason is that her marriage to his brother does not take effect at all, as it was forbidden on pain of *karet.* Since this marriage never occurred, only the other wife, the so-called rival wife, is considered a wife of the brother, and she may enter into levirate marriage.

BACKGROUND

Ya'akov raped his daughter-in-law – יַעֲקֹב אָנַס כַּלָּתוֹ: Ya'akov had a son Reuven who had two wives, Peninna and Ḥanna. If Ya'akov raped his daughter-in-law Ḥanna, who bore him a son, Zeraḥ, this son would be Reuven's paternal brother. If Reuven dies childless, both his wives would come before his brother Zeraḥ for levirate marriage, and yet Ḥanna, one of these women, is Zeraḥ's mother. This is a case in which a mother comes before her son for levirate marriage.

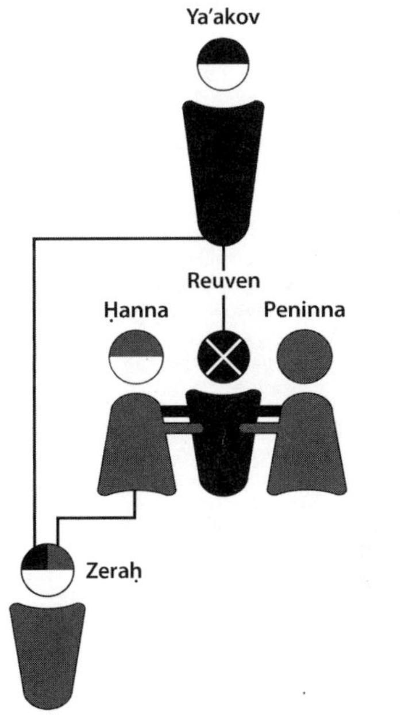

NOTES

Even without what if, you can find, etc. – בְּלָא דְּאִי נַמִּי מַשְׁכַּחַתְּ וכו׳: An obvious question arises here: If the mishna does not discuss cases that result from a transgression, the situation of a father who raped his daughter-in-law involves an even more serious transgression. How, then, can this scenario be suggested as part of the answer? Rashi's brief comment: That this deceased individual did not transgress when he married her, alludes to an answer: It is only if the marriage that caused the obligation of levirate marriage involved a transgression that the mishna will omit this case. Others explain that the issue is not merely the existence of a prohibition, as a marriage that involves a transgression in which both the husband and the wife are sinners is a rare occurrence. In contrast, in cases of rape, only one individual transgresses, and therefore the mishna does discuss examples of this kind (*Arukh LaNer*).

Raped his daughter-in-law – אָנַס כַּלָּתוֹ: The Gemara specifies that he raped her, because if the act was performed willingly, the woman would be a *sota*, which would mean that the mitzva of levirate marriage does not apply at all. Alternatively, as marriage with one's daughter-in-law is entirely invalid, even a marriage in this situation can be called a rape (Ritva).

Perek **I**
Daf **10** Amud **b**

הָיְתָה אִמּוֹ אֲנוּסַת אָבִיו, וְנִשֵּׂאת לְאָחִיו מֵאָבִיו וּמֵת – זוֹ הִיא אִמּוֹ שֶׁפּוֹטֶרֶת צָרָתָהּ.

If, however, **his mother was a woman** who was **raped by his father and** subsequently **married his paternal brother, and** the brother **died, this is** a case of **his mother who exempts her rival wife.** According to the opinion of the Rabbis this marriage is permitted, and even according to the opinion of Rabbi Yehuda the marriage is valid despite the transgression. Consequently, both the mother and her rival wife come before the son for levirate marriage. Since the mother is a forbidden relation to him, her rival wife is exempt as well.

וְאַף עַל פִּי שֶׁשָּׁנוּ חֲכָמִים בְּמִשְׁנָתֵנוּ "חֲמֵשׁ עֶשְׂרֵה", יֵשׁ לָנוּ לְהוֹסִיף שֵׁשׁ עֶשְׂרֵה, כְּגוֹן זוֹ. אָמַר לֵיהּ רֵישׁ לָקִישׁ לְרַבִּי יוֹחָנָן: לְלֵוִי דְּאָמַר "דְּאִי" נַמִּי קָתָנֵי, לִתְנֵי: הַחוֹלֵץ לִיבִמְתּוֹ וְחָזַר וְקִדְּשָׁהּ וּמֵת בְּלֹא בָּנִים, דְּמִגּוֹ דְּאִיהִי אֲסוּרָה – צָרָתָהּ נַמִּי אֲסִירָא!

And although[N] the Sages taught in the mishna: Fifteen women, **we must add a sixteenth** case, **for example,** the situation described above. **Reish Lakish said to Rabbi Yoḥanan: According to** the opinion of **Levi, who said** that the mishna **teaches even** cases of: **What if,** which involve a transgression, **let** the mishna also **teach** the case of **one who performs *ḥalitza* with his *yevama* and went back and betrothed her, and** then **died childless.** His betrothal is a transgression, as after *ḥalitza* the *yevama* is permanently forbidden to him. **As,** in this case, **since she is forbidden** to all the brothers, due to the *ḥalitza* performed by the deceased *yavam,* **her rival wife is also forbidden.** This is an additional case of a woman who exempts her rival wife.

אָמַר לֵיהּ: לְפִי שֶׁאֵינָהּ בְּצָרַת צָרָה.

Rabbi Yoḥanan **said to** Reish Lakish: This example is not cited **because** the case **does not** include the possibility **of a rival wife of a rival wife.**[N] All of the other cases listed in the mishna involve both rival wives and rival wives of rival wives. Here, however, this is impossible, as the same prohibition applies equally to all of the brothers, and therefore none of them may marry her.

וְלֵימָא לֵיהּ: חַיָּיבֵי לָאוִין הִיא, וְחַיָּיבֵי לָאוִין בְּנֵי חֲלִיצָה וְיִבּוּם נִינְהוּ?

The Gemara asks: **And let** Rabbi Yoḥanan **say** a different answer **to** Reish Lakish, as he could simply have pointed out that marriage to a woman who had performed *ḥalitza* is not a violation that incurs *karet*, neither for the one who performed the *ḥalitza* nor for his brothers if they marry her after he dies. Rather, **it is** an act for which they are **liable for** violating a regular **prohibition, and those liable for** violating **a prohibition are** obligated **in *ḥalitza* and levirate marriage.** In these cases the mitzva of levirate marriage still applies, and although the woman should be released by *ḥalitza*, she is not entirely exempt from levirate marriage, and therefore her rival wife is not exempt either.

לִדְבָרָיו קָאָמַר לֵיהּ: לְדִידִי חַיָּיבֵי לָאוִין הֵם, וְחַיָּיבֵי לָאוִין בְּנֵי חֲלִיצָה וְיִבּוּם נִינְהוּ, אֶלָּא לְדִידָךְ חַיָּיבֵי כָּרֵיתוֹת נִינְהוּ, לְפִי שֶׁאֵינָן בְּצָרַת צָרָה.

The Gemara responds that Rabbi Yoḥanan **is speaking in accordance with the statement of** Reish Lakish, as follows: According **to my** opinion your question is groundless, as **they are liable for** violating **a prohibition, and those liable for** violating **a prohibition are** obligated **in *ḥalitza* and levirate marriage. However,** according **to your** opinion, **those** brothers who marry a *yevama* who had performed *ḥalitza* **are liable to** receive ***karet***, and therefore you must resolve the difficulty by saying that the mishna did not teach this case **because** it **does not** include the possibility **of a rival wife of a rival wife.**

אִיתְּמַר, הַחוֹלֵץ לִיבִמְתּוֹ וְחָזַר וְקִדְּשָׁהּ. אָמַר רֵישׁ לָקִישׁ: הוּא אֵין חַיָּיב עַל הַחֲלוּצָה כָּרֵת,

The Gemara discusses the dispute alluded to in the previous paragraph. **It was stated:** With regard to **one who performs *ḥalitza* with his *yevama* and went back and betrothed her,**[N] **Reish Lakish said:** The brother who earlier performed *ḥalitza* **is not liable to** receive ***karet*** **for** returning to **the *yevama* who performed *ḥalitza* [*ḥalutza*].** She is no longer forbidden as a brother's wife, although she is forbidden by a regular prohibition.

וְהָאַחִין חַיָּיבִין עַל הַחֲלוּצָה כָּרֵת. עַל הַצָּרָה – בֵּין הוּא וּבֵין הָאַחִים חַיָּיבִין עַל הַצָּרָה כָּרֵת.

And the brothers who did not actually perform the *ḥalitza* **are liable to** receive ***karet*** **for** having relations with **a *ḥalutza*.**[N] In their case, the woman retains her status as a forbidden brother's wife even after the *ḥalitza*. **With regard to the rival wife** of the *ḥalutza*, although she too is released from the levirate bond, since the act of *ḥalitza* itself was not performed with her, **both** the brother who performed the *ḥalitza* **and the** other **brothers are liable to** receive ***karet*** **for** having relations with **the rival wife,** as she retains her forbidden status as a brother's wife.

וְרַבִּי יוֹחָנָן אָמַר: בֵּין הוּא וּבֵין הָאַחִין אֵינָן חַיָּיבִין לֹא עַל הַחֲלוּצָה כָּרֵת וְלֹא עַל הַצָּרָה כָּרֵת. מַאי טַעְמָא דְּרֵישׁ לָקִישׁ? אָמַר קְרָא "אֲשֶׁר לֹא יִבְנֶה" כֵּיוָן שֶׁלֹּא בָּנָה – שׁוּב לֹא יִבְנֶה.

And Rabbi Yoḥanan said: Neither he nor the other **brothers are liable to** receive ***karet***, **neither for the *ḥalutza* nor for** having relations with **the rival wife.** The Gemara explains: **What is the rationale of Reish Lakish? The verse states** with regard to one who performs *ḥalitza* with his *yevama*: **"Who does not build up** his brother's house" (Deuteronomy 25:9), which teaches that **since he did not build** his brother's house by entering into levirate marriage, opting instead for *ḥalitza*, **he shall never build** it **again.** This statement is understood not only as a negative description of events, but also as a prohibition against marrying this woman at any point in the future.

NOTES

And although, etc. – וְאַף עַל פִּי וכו׳: Levi included this sentence in his *mishnayot* as well, in explanation of why he changed his version from the one accepted by Rabbi Yehuda HaNasi (Rivan).

Because the case does not include the possibility of a rival wife of a rival wife – לְפִי שֶׁאֵינָהּ בְּצָרַת צָרָה: Apparently, the reason this case does not include the possibility of a rival wife of a rival wife is that she is equally forbidden to all of the brothers. But if so, she should have been listed alongside the six severe transgressions involving women with whom relations are forbidden, who are exempt from levirate marriage and with regard to whom a situation of a rival wife of a rival wife cannot occur, as they are likewise forbidden to all of the brothers. One answer is that this woman is indeed included in that list, under the heading of: The wife of his paternal brother (Rashba).

And went back and betrothed her – וְחָזַר וְקִדְּשָׁהּ: The *baraita* specifies that he betrothed her, not that he engaged in sexual intercourse with her, because this is the more common occurrence, especially as one might assume that after *ḥalitza* he may change his mind and betroth her (*Tosefot HaRosh*).

The liability of a *ḥalutza* and the brothers to receive *karet* – חִיּוּב חֲלוּצָה וְהָאַחִין בְּכָרֵת: This dispute between Rabbi Yoḥanan and Reish Lakish appears in the Jerusalem Talmud as well. However, the Gemara there cites several versions that include intermediate opinions and different halakhic rulings for the *ḥalutza* as opposed to her rival wife, as well as different rulings for the brother who performed *ḥalitza* as opposed to the other brothers.

Some commentaries explain that the fundamental argument according to the opinion of Reish Lakish is apparently that the prohibition proscribing a brother's wife remains intact, although the Torah allowed the *yavam* obligated by the duty of levirate marriage to defer this prohibition (Rashba). After the *ḥalitza*, a new prohibition of: Does not build up, goes into effect. In other words, once a brother has refused to build his deceased brother's house by means of *ḥalitza* he is now prohibited from doing so. According to this interpretation, the prohibition with regard to a brother's wife remains in force for all the brothers except for the one who performed *ḥalitza*. By contrast, Rabbi Yoḥanan holds that upon the death of the childless brother, the prohibition proscribing a brother's wife is entirely removed from the *yevama*. Although she must still undergo *ḥalitza* to be released from the levirate bond, the penalty of *karet* no longer applies to this situation at all.

It is possible to connect this idea to the opinion cited in the Jerusalem Talmud that the dispute stems from differing concepts of *ḥalitza*. While Rabbi Yoḥanan maintains that *ḥalitza* merely releases those involved from their obligation, Reish Lakish holds it to be a form of acquisition, in that the performance of *ḥalitza* enables a new prohibition to take effect (see *Mei Neftoaḥ*, *Kovetz He'arot*, and *Einayim LaMishpat*). According to this explanation, Rabbi Yoḥanan's statement here that the brother who performs *ḥalitza* acts as an agent of the others brothers does not represent his main reasoning. Rather, this statement serves only to clarify why *ḥalitza* by one brother exempts all of the others (see *Kovetz He'arot*).

איהו הוא דְּקָאֵי בְּ״לֹא יִבְנֶה״, אֲבָל אֶחָיו – כִּדְקַיְימִי קָיְימִי,

However, **it is** the man who performed the act of *ḥalitza* **who stands** liable **to** receive punishment for violating this prohibition of: **Does not build up,** i.e., the prohibition against marrying his *ḥalutza*. For him the prohibition involving *karet* has been replaced by the regular prohibition of: Who does not build up his brother's house. **However,** with regard to his **brothers, where they stood** before, **they stand** now. In other words, just as before the mitzva of levirate marriage applied to them this woman was forbidden to them as a brother's wife, once the obligation of levirate marriage has been removed they remain bound by the same prohibition. Consequently, she is forbidden to the brothers on pain of *karet*.

וַעֲלַהּ דִּידַהּ הוּא דְּקָאֵי בְּ״לֹא יִבְנֶה״, הָא צָרָה – כִּדְקַיְימִי קָיְימִי.

And furthermore, only **with regard to her,** the *ḥalutza*, **does he stand** liable **for: Does not build up,** but as for **the rival wife,** who did not perform *ḥalitza*, **where** all the brothers **stood** before, **they stand** now. Just as before her rival wife performed *ḥalitza* she was forbidden on pain of *karet*, the same applies after the *ḥalitza*, both for the man who performed *ḥalitza* and his brothers.

וְרַבִּי יוֹחָנָן: מִי אִיכָּא מִידֵּי דְּמֵעִיקָּרָא, אִי בָּעֵי הַאי חָלֵיץ וְאִי בָּעֵי הַאי חָלֵיץ, וְאִי בָּעֵי לְהַאי חָלֵיץ וְאִי בָּעֵי לְהַאי חָלֵיץ, וְהָשְׁתָּא קָאֵי עֲלַהּ בְּכָרֵת?

And Rabbi Yoḥanan claims: **Is there anything** of this kind in *halakha*? After all, **at the outset,** before the *ḥalitza*, **if this** brother **wanted** he could **perform *ḥalitza*, and if that** brother **wanted** he could **perform *ḥalitza*, and if he wanted** he could **perform *ḥalitza* with this** woman **and if he wanted** he could **perform *ḥalitza* with that** woman. All the deceased brother's wives were included in the levirate obligation of marriage or *ḥalitza*, and therefore the prohibition proscribing a brother's wife was negated for all of them at that time. **And now,** after the *ḥalitza*, **they stand to** incur ***karet*** **for** having relations with **her?** How can the prohibition proscribing a brother's wife return after it was nullified by the death of the childless brother?

אֶלָּא: אִיהוּ שְׁלִיחוּתָא דְּאַחִים קָעָבֵיד, אִיהִי שְׁלִיחוּתָא דְּצָרָה קָעָבְדָה.

Rather, he who performs *ḥalitza* **performs the agency of the** other **brothers,** and therefore he also releases her from the levirate bond of his brothers. Similarly, **she** who performs *ḥalitza* **performs the agency of the rival wife,** as the *ḥalitza* of one wife serves to release the other one as well. Consequently, it is as though all of the brothers released all of the wives, and there is no longer any prohibition that incurs *karet*.[H]

אֵיתִיבֵיהּ רַבִּי יוֹחָנָן לְרֵישׁ לָקִישׁ: הַחוֹלֵץ לִיבִמְתּוֹ וְחָזַר וְקִדְּשָׁהּ, וּמֵת – צְרִיכָה חֲלִיצָה מִן הָאַחִין. בִּשְׁלָמָא לְדִידִי דְּאָמֵינָא חַיָּיבֵי לָאוִין נִינְהוּ, הַיְינוּ דִּצְרִיכָה חֲלִיצָה מִן הָאַחִין.

§ The Gemara cites the ensuing discussion between the two disputing Sages. **Rabbi Yoḥanan raised an objection to** the opinion of **Reish Lakish** from a *baraita*: In the case of **one who performs *ḥalitza* with his *yevama* and went back and betrothed her, and** then **died, she requires *ḥalitza*** from one of **the brothers. Granted,** this makes sense according **to my** opinion, **as I say** that brothers who marry a *ḥalutza* **are liable** only **for** violating **a prohibition,** and **that is** why **she requires *ḥalitza* from the** other **brothers.** The principle is that a woman with whom relations are forbidden by a regular prohibition that does not incur *karet* may not enter into levirate marriage, but she must undergo *ḥalitza*.

אֶלָּא לְדִידָךְ, אַמַּאי צְרִיכָה חֲלִיצָה?

However, according **to your** opinion that the penalty of *karet* does apply here, **why does she require *ḥalitza*** at all? The penalty of *karet* indicates that the betrothal did not take effect at all, and therefore she is not bound to the brothers with regard to the requirement of *ḥalitza*.

וּלְטַעְמֵיךְ, אֵימָא סֵיפָא: עָמַד אֶחָד מִן הָאַחִין וְקִדְּשָׁהּ – אֵין לָהּ עָלָיו כְּלוּם. וְאִי חַיָּיבֵי לָאוִין נִינְהוּ – אַמַּאי אֵין לָהּ עָלָיו כְּלוּם?

Reish Lakish answered: **And according to your reasoning,** how would you **state** and explain **the latter clause** of the *baraita*: If **one of the brothers arose and betrothed her, she has no claims on him,** i.e., the marriage does not take effect at all and she does not require a bill of divorce from him? **But if** the brothers **are liable** only **for** violating **a prohibition, why does she have no claim on him?** After all, in cases of regular prohibitions a betrothal is valid. According to my opinion that these brothers are liable to receive *karet* the matter is clear, as the betrothal is invalid. This indicates that there is a contradiction between the first and latter clauses of the *baraita*. How, then, can Rabbi Yoḥanan cite a proof from an apparently flawed *baraita*?

HALAKHA

The prohibition proscribing a *ḥalutza* to the man who performed *ḥalitza* and to his brothers – אִיסּוּר חֲלוּצָה לְחוֹלֵץ וְאֶחָיו: If a *yavam* performs *ḥalitza* with his *yevama*, she and her rival wives are forbidden to him and the other brothers. However, this prohibition does not incur *karet* but is a regular prohibition. This ruling is in accordance with the opinion of Rabbi Yoḥanan, as the *halakha* follows his opinion against that of Reish Lakish (*Tur*). According to the Rambam, the prohibition is a decree of the Sages, and that is how he interprets the opinion of Rabbi Yoḥanan (see *Maggid Mishne*). However, others (*Tosafot*; Ramban) maintain that according to Rabbi Yoḥanan a marriage between one of the brothers and one of these women constitutes the violation of a prohibition (Rambam *Sefer Nashim, Hilkhot Yibbum VaḤalitza* 1:12; *Shulḥan Arukh, Even HaEzer* 162:2).

אֲמַר רַב שֵׁשֶׁת: סֵיפָא אֲתַאן לְרַבִּי עֲקִיבָא, דְּאָמַר: אֵין קִידּוּשִׁין תּוֹפְסִין בְּחַיָּיבֵי לָאוִין. וְלִיתְנֵי: לְדִבְרֵי רַבִּי עֲקִיבָא אֵין לוֹ עָלָיו כְּלוּם!

Rav Sheshet said in resolution of this contradiction: In the **latter clause** of the *baraita* **we have come to** a different opinion, that of **Rabbi Akiva,**[N] **who said: Betrothal with those** who are forbidden as they are **liable for** violating **a prohibition is not valid.** In Rabbi Akiva's opinion there is no difference between regular prohibitions and prohibitions that incur *karet* in this regard, as in both cases the betrothals are invalid. The Gemara raises a difficulty: **But** if the first clause of the *baraita* is in accordance with the opinion of the Rabbis, while the latter clause is in accordance with a different opinion, **let** the mishna **teach** explicitly: **According to the statement of Rabbi Akiva**[N] **she has no claims on him,** as this represents a different opinion.

NOTES

In the latter clause we have come to Rabbi Akiva – סֵיפָא אֲתַאן לְרַבִּי עֲקִיבָא: If this is indeed Rabbi Akiva's opinion, then even if the brother who performed *ḥalitza* subsequently betrothed the *ḥalutza*, she still would not require a bill of divorce. Consequently, Rabbi Akiva must interpret the phrase: One of the brothers, to refer to all the brothers of the deceased, including the one who performed *ḥalitza* (*Tosafot Yeshanim*; *Tosefot HaRosh*).

But let the mishna teach: According to the statement of Rabbi Akiva – וְלִיתְנֵי לְדִבְרֵי רַבִּי עֲקִיבָא: The early commentaries ask: There are many statements of this kind in the Gemara, where the mishna is explained as reflecting the opinions of two different *tanna'im*, and yet elsewhere the Gemara does not insist that the mishna should have mentioned the name of the specific *tanna* who authored the second opinion (*Tosafot*). The answer given is that the difficulty is not the mere omission of the phrase: According to the statement of Rabbi Akiva, but that if indeed this ruling is Rabbi Akiva's, he should have explicitly disagreed in the first case as well by stating that she does not require *ḥalitza* from the brothers (Ramban; Ritva).

Perek **I**
Daf **11** Amud **a**

קַשְׁיָא. רַב אַשִׁי סָבַר לָהּ כְּרֵישׁ לָקִישׁ, וּמְתָרֵץ לָהּ כְּרַבִּי שִׁמְעוֹן. רָבִינָא סָבַר לָהּ כְּרַבִּי יוֹחָנָן, וּמְתָרֵץ כְּרַבָּנַן.

§ The Gemara comments: Rav Sheshet's explanation of the contradiction between the first clause and latter clause of the *baraita* **is difficult.** Consequently, the Gemara cites different resolutions of this contradiction. **Rav Ashi holds in accordance with** the opinion of **Reish Lakish and resolves** the *baraita* **in accordance with** the opinion of **Rabbi Shimon. Ravina,** in contrast, **holds in accordance with** the opinion of **Rabbi Yoḥanan and resolves** the *baraita* **in accordance with** the opinion of **the Rabbis.**[N]

רַב אַשִׁי סָבַר לָהּ כְּרֵישׁ לָקִישׁ וּמְתָרֵץ לָהּ כְּרַבִּי שִׁמְעוֹן: הַחוֹלֵץ לִיבִמְתּוֹ וְחָזַר וְקִדְּשָׁהּ צְרִיכָה חֲלִיצָה מִן הָאַחִין. מַאן אַחִין –

The Gemara elaborates: **Rav Ashi holds in accordance with** the opinion of **Reish Lakish and resolves** the *baraita* **in accordance with** the opinion of **Rabbi Shimon.** This is his interpretation: In the case of **one who performs *ḥalitza* with his *yevama* and went back and betrothed her,** and then died, **she requires *ḥalitza* from** one of **the brothers.**[N] **Who are** the **brothers** referred to here?

אַחִין הַיְלוּדִים, כְּמַאן – כְּרַבִּי שִׁמְעוֹן.

Rav Ashi explains that they are the **newborn brothers,** i.e., those who were born only after the brother betrothed her. Consequently, although this woman was the wife of the first deceased brother before they were born, after their birth she was already the wife of a living brother. Therefore, the prohibition of a wife of a brother with whom he did not coexist never applied, and she requires *ḥalitza*. **In accordance with whose** opinion is this ruling? It is **in accordance with** the opinion of **Rabbi Shimon,** who maintains that in a case of this kind the brothers are not considered to be coexisting.

עָמַד אֶחָד מִן הַנּוֹלָדִים וְקִדְּשָׁהּ – אֵין לָהּ עָלָיו כְּלוּם, כְּמַאן – כְּרֵישׁ לָקִישׁ.

Meanwhile, the latter clause speaks of a case where **one of the** brothers who was **born** in the lifetime of the first brother **arose and betrothed her,** after another brother had performed *ḥalitza*. In this case, **she has no claims** of a bill of divorce **on him. In accordance with whose** opinion is this ruling? It is **in accordance with** the opinion of **Reish Lakish,** who maintains that the penalty of *karet* applies in this case, and therefore the betrothal is entirely invalid.

NOTES

The dispute concerning a *yevama* who performed *ḥalitza* – הַמַּחֲלוֹקֶת בִּיבָמָה שֶׁנֶּחְלְצָה: In the Jerusalem Talmud several other versions of the same basic dispute between Rabbi Yoḥanan and Reish Lakish are cited. These versions differ in both the opinions held by the two Sages and the details of their argument.

In accordance with Rabbi Shimon…she requires *ḥalitza* from the brothers – כְּרַבִּי שִׁמְעוֹן...צְרִיכָה חֲלִיצָה מִן הָאַחִין: The commentaries ask: If the brothers were born only after the betrothal of the widow of their already-deceased brother to their other brother, this woman should be permitted to them in levirate marriage; why, then, must they perform *ḥalitza* (*Tosafot*)? One suggestion is that since the second brother had performed *ḥalitza* with her, she retains a measure of the levirate bond from the first brother. Consequently, even Rabbi Shimon concedes that the newborn brothers are not permitted to marry her (*Keren Or*).

רָבִינָא סָבַר לַהּ כְּרַבִּי יוֹחָנָן וּמְתָרֵץ לַהּ אַלִּיבָּא דְּרַבָּנַן: הַחוֹלֵץ לִיבִמְתּוֹ וְחָזַר וְקִדְּשָׁהּ צְרִיכָה חֲלִיצָה מִן הָאַחִין, מַאן אַחִין – אַחִין הַנּוֹלָדִים, כְּמַאן – כְּרַבִּי יוֹחָנָן.

The Gemara continues its explanation of the opinions. **Ravina holds in accordance with** the opinion of **Rabbi Yoḥanan and resolves** the *baraita* **in accordance with** the opinion of **the Rabbis.**[N] How so? In the case of **one who performs *ḥalitza* with his *yevama* and went back and betrothed her** and then died, **she requires *ḥalitza*** from one of **the brothers. Who are** these **brothers?** This is referring to the **brothers** already **born** in the lifetime of the first brother. **In accordance with whose** opinion is this interpretation? It is **in accordance with** the opinion of **Rabbi Yoḥanan,** who held that this case constitutes a regular prohibition. Consequently, the *yevama* is not exempt from the obligation of *ḥalitza*.

עָמַד אֶחָד מִן הַיְלוּדִים וְקִדְּשָׁהּ – אֵין לָהּ עָלָיו כְּלוּם, כְּמַאן – כְּרַבָּנַן.

If **one of the newborn**[N] brothers, who were born after the death of the first brother, **arose and betrothed her, she has no claim on him.** Since he is considered a brother who did not coexist with his deceased brother, the *yevama* is prohibited to him as a brother's wife, and as this prohibition entails *karet*, the betrothal is invalid. This is the *halakha* even if he was born after the second deceased brother betrothed her. **In accordance with whose** opinion is this ruling? It is **in accordance with** the opinion of **the Rabbis,** who maintain that the prohibition of a wife of a brother with whom one did not coexist applies even to a brother's widow who entered into levirate marriage before the younger brother was born.

אִיתְּמַר, הַבָּא עַל יְבִמְתּוֹ, וּבָא אֶחָד מִן הָאַחִין עַל צָרָתָהּ. פְּלִיגִי בָּהּ רַב אַחָא וְרָבִינָא, חַד אָמַר: בְּכָרֵת; וְחַד אָמַר: בַּעֲשֵׂה.

It was stated that there is a similar dispute between *amora'im* with regard to **one** who **had relations with** his ***yevama*** and thereby performed the mitzva of levirate marriage as required, **and one of the** other **brothers had relations with her rival wife.**[NH] **Rav Aḥa and Ravina disagree** with regard to this matter. **One said:** The second brother is liable **to** receive ***karet*.** **And** the other **one said** that he is in violation **of** only **a positive mitzva.** The verse: "Who does not build up his brother's house" (Deuteronomy 25:9), is a positive mitzva, as it teaches that one house may be built up, but not two houses, i.e., no more than one wife of a deceased brother may be married by one of his brothers. Any mitzva formulated as a positive injunction has the status of a positive mitzva, even if it is violated by the performance of an action, in the manner of a prohibition.

מַאן דְּאָמַר בְּכָרֵת – כְּרֵישׁ לָקִישׁ, וּמַאן דְּאָמַר בַּעֲשֵׂה – כְּרַבִּי יוֹחָנָן.

The Gemara explains: **The one who said that he** is liable **to** receive *karet* holds **in accordance with** the opinion of **Reish Lakish,** who maintains that after the mitzva is performed with one *yevama* who required levirate marriage, the prohibition of a brother's wife is once again fully applicable to her rival wife. **And the one who said** that he is in violation **of** only **a positive mitzva** holds **in accordance with** the opinion of **Rabbi Yoḥanan.**

NOTES

Resolves it in accordance with the Rabbis – מְתָרֵץ לַהּ אַלִּיבָּא דְּרַבָּנַן: According to Rashi, this means only in accordance with the opinion of the Rabbis, and not in accordance with the opinion of Rabbi Shimon at all. Other commentaries explain that it means: Even according to the opinion of the Rabbis. The reason is that even if the brothers were born after the living brother with whom they coexisted had performed *ḥalitza* with the *yevama*, she would still be prohibited to them, as *ḥalitza* releases one from the obligation of levirate marriage but it is not considered an act of acquisition on the part of the brother with whom they coexisted, as explained in the Jerusalem Talmud (Ramban; Rashba).

Newborn [*yeludim*] and born [*noladim*] – יְלוּדִים וְנוֹלָדִים: According to the version of the text accepted by Rashi, the *yeludim* are those who were born at some time after the brother had performed *ḥalitza* or betrothal, whereas the *noladim* were born while the first deceased brother was still alive. The version of the Gemara and the explanation found in *Tosafot*, however, indicate the opposite. Support can be found for both versions from a linguistic perspective; however, as pointed out by *Tosafot*, the regular use of language indicates that their version is correct, as *yelud* generally refers to one already born, as in the verse: "Born [*yelud*] of woman" (Job 14:1). The word *nolad* typically denotes something born at a later point in time, as in the expression: He who anticipates the future [*et hanolad*], translated literally as: What will be born, and in several other places, e.g., with regard to objects that came into being [*nolad*], a concept in the *halakhot* of *muktze* in tractate *Beitza*. In all these cases the term refers to items or people that will be born in the future or were only recently born.

The prohibition of the rival wife of a *yevama* to the brothers – אִיסּוּר צָרַת יְבָמָה לָאַחִין: Some commentaries hold that instead of: A positive mitzva, the correct version of the text is: Transgresses a prohibition, i.e., that of the verse: "Does not build up." Since he released his *yevama* by *ḥalitza* and did not build his brother's house, he may never do so in the future (Rabbeinu Ḥananel; *Tosafot*). Conversely, others read: Violation of a positive mitzva, as they maintain that the verse: "Build up his brother's house" (Deuteronomy 25:9) is a positive mitzva to build only one house (*Ba'al Halakhot Gedolot*; Rashi; Rif). Although one could object that this prohibition apparently applies only to the brother who fulfills the duty of levirate marriage and not to the others, Rashi points out that this brother is considered the agent of the other brothers, meaning that it is as though they all performed the act (Ritva).

Some raise a difficulty against Rashi's opinion from the verse itself. Since the Torah states: "Does not build up" in the negative, how could this be viewed as a positive mitzva (Rabbeinu Tam)? One answer is that the verse must be read in its entirety: "So shall be done to the man who does not build up his brother's house." This shows that the negative formulation of the mitzva does not refer to the action in question, but to the failure to do so. Consequently, the mitzva is actually a positive one (Ritva). Others avoid any potential difficulty with this verse by finding an alternative source for the positive mitzva in the phrase (Deuteronomy 25:5): "Her brother-in-law will have intercourse with her" (Rambam). The Rambam adds that the phrase: "Will have intercourse with her" indicates: Not with another, i.e., the positive mitzva applies to one woman alone (see *Yam shel Shlomo*).

HALAKHA

The rival wife of a *yevama* to the brothers after levirate marriage – צָרַת יְבָמָה לָאַחִין לְאַחַר יִיבּוּם: After one of the brothers enters into levirate marriage with the *yevama*, neither he nor the other brothers may have relations with the rival wives. If he or one of the other brothers has relations with a rival wife, they have violated a positive mitzva. The *halakha* is in accordance with the opinion of Ravina, following the principle that in his disputes with Rav Aḥa the *halakha* is in accordance with the more lenient position. This is certainly the case here, as Ravina accepts the opinion of Rabbi Yoḥanan (*Beit Yosef*; *Shulḥan Arukh*, *Even HaEzer* 162:1).

HALAKHA

A *sota* and the rival wife of a *sota* – סוֹטָה וְצָרַת סוֹטָה: In the case of a woman who willingly commits adultery and there are witnesses who testify to that effect, if her husband dies before he can divorce her, she is exempt from *ḥalitza* and levirate marriage. Her rival wife is likewise entirely exempt. This is the ruling of the *Shulḥan Arukh*, in accordance with the opinion of the Rambam (*Sefer Nashim, Hilkhot Yibbum VaḤalitza* 6:19), and the discussion in the Gemara here indicates that there is no dispute in this regard. Some commentaries claim that even if it is clear that the woman was adulterous, she still requires *ḥalitza* (Ra'avad on *Sota* 5b). It is proper to act in accordance with this more stringent opinion (*Shulḥan Arukh, Even HaEzer* 173:11, and in the comment of Rema).

The prohibition of an uncertain *sota* to her husband – אִיסּוּר סָפֵק סוֹטָה לְבַעְלָהּ: In the case of a husband who in the presence of witnesses warns his wife against secluding herself with a specific man, if she disobeys her husband and is observed to be alone with that man long enough to engage in relations, she is forbidden to her husband. Some commentaries maintain that the husband must explicitly declare himself jealous (Rema, citing Rabbeinu Ya'akov Weil; *Shulḥan Arukh, Even HaEzer* 115:8).

אָמַר רַב יְהוּדָה אָמַר רַב: צָרַת סוֹטָה – אֲסוּרָה,

The Gemara further analyzes the list of women exempt from levirate marriage. **Rav Yehuda said** that **Rav said: The rival wife of a *sota* is forbidden.**[HN] In this context, *sota* refers to an unfaithful wife.[H] If the husband died, the unfaithful wife and her rival wife are exempt from both *ḥalitza* and levirate marriage.

טוּמְאָה כְּתִיב בָּהּ, כָּעֲרָיוֹת.

What is the reason for this? The term **defilement is written in that** passage dealing with an unfaithful wife: "She being defiled secretly" (Numbers 5:13), just **as** defilement is written with regard to **those with whom relations are forbidden**[N] in the verse: "Defile not yourselves in any of these things, for in all these the nations are defiled, which I cast out from before you" (Leviticus 18:24). This teaches that the *halakha* of an unfaithful wife is like that of a woman with whom relations are forbidden; both she and her rival wife are exempt from levirate marriage and *ḥalitza*.

מְתִיב רַב חִסְדָּא: רַבִּי שִׁמְעוֹן אוֹמֵר: בִּיאָתָהּ אוֹ חֲלִיצָתָהּ מֵאָחִיו שֶׁל רִאשׁוֹן פּוֹטֶרֶת צָרָתָהּ!

Rav Ḥisda raised an objection to this from the case of a woman who heard that her husband had died and remarried, only afterward to discover that he had still been alive at that time before dying later. What is the *halakha* in this case? **Rabbi Shimon says: Her relations** with **or *ḥalitza* from the brother of the first** husband **exempts her rival wife.** This shows that the obligation of levirate marriage applies to this woman. Although she lived as a married woman with someone else during her husband's lifetime, Rabbi Shimon nevertheless maintains that her sexual intercourse or *ḥalitza* fulfills the mitzva of levirate marriage and exempts her rival wife. This suggests that the rival wife of an unfaithful wife requires levirate marriage.

[אָמַר לָךְ רַב]: אָמֵינָא לָךְ אֲנָא סוֹטָה דְּאוֹרָיְיתָא, וְאַתְּ אָמְרַתְּ לִי סוֹטָה דְּרַבָּנַן?!

The Gemara answers that **Rav** could have **said to you** in response: **I spoke to you** about the *halakha* of **a *sota* by Torah** law, i.e., a wife who was intentionally unfaithful, **and you speak to me** of **a *sota* by rabbinic** law? The case you mentioned is an unavoidable accident, as the wife married another man only because she received testimony that her husband was deceased. When the Sages instituted that she was forbidden to both her first and second husbands, this was a penalty designed to ensure that women would examine testimony of this kind very thoroughly. However, this is not a case of a *sota* by Torah law, as she was not intentionally unfaithful, and therefore the mitzva of levirate marriage certainly applies to her.

וּדְקָאָרֵי לַהּ מַאי קָאָרֵי לַהּ! קָסָבַר: כָּל דְּתַקּוּן רַבָּנַן – כְּעֵין דְּאוֹרָיְיתָא תַּקּוּן.

Since this response is overwhelmingly obvious, the Gemara asks: **And he who asked it, why did he ask it?** There are apparently no grounds for this comparison at all. The Gemara explains: **He held that all** ordinances **that the Sages instituted, they instituted parallel to Torah** law. Consequently, if a *sota* by Torah law is exempt from levirate marriage and exempts her rival wife as though she were a forbidden relative, the same should apply to a *sota* by rabbinic law.

NOTES

The rival wife of a *sota* is forbidden – צָרַת סוֹטָה אֲסוּרָה: This is also the *halakha* with regard to a *sota* herself, which is assumed to be understood (Ramban). This statement is in accordance with the opinion that the rival wife of a *sota* is not only prohibited in levirate marriage but is also exempt from *ḥalitza*, which is the opinion of most commentaries and authorities. However, some authorities apparently maintain that even according to the opinion of Rav, the rival wife of a *sota* does perform *ḥalitza* despite the fact that she may not enter into levirate marriage (Ra'avad). According to this opinion, the Gemara is precise in its wording. Some commentaries demonstrate at length how several difficulties can be resolved by this opinion (*Arukh LaNer*; see Vilna Gaon on *Shulḥan Arukh, Even HaEzer* 173:11).

Defilement is written in that passage, just as it is with regard to those with whom relations are forbidden – טוּמְאָה כְּתִיב בָּהּ, כָּעֲרָיוֹת: The commentaries ask: Since the defilement in that context refers only to the woman's husband and the man with whom she was unfaithful, not to the *yavam*, why should she be forbidden to him (*Arukh LaNer*)? Some commentaries explain that this can be derived by an *a fortiori* inference: If she is forbidden to someone to whom she is generally permitted, i.e., her husband, she is certainly forbidden to one to whom she is usually forbidden, her brother-in-law (*Tevuot HaShor*; *Kovetz He'arot*). Others write, in accordance with the version cited in the Jerusalem Talmud, that the term defilement is actually written three times in connection to a *sota*: Once for the husband, once for the adulterer, and once for the *yavam* (*Kehillot Ya'akov*). Yet others maintain that the term defilement in the chapter of a *sota* refers specifically to the *yavam*, as it is only with regard to him that it is necessary for the verse to teach that she is a forbidden relative. She is not considered a forbidden relative for her husband, as their marriage is not annulled by her unfaithfulness (Ramban).

מְתִיב רַב אָשֵׁי: נִכְנְסָה עִמּוֹ לְסֵתֶר וְשָׁהֲתָה עִמּוֹ כְּדֵי טוּמְאָה – אֲסוּרָה לְבֵיתָהּ, וַאֲסוּרָה לֶאֱכוֹל בִּתְרוּמָה. וְאִם מֵת – חוֹלֶצֶת

Rav Ashi raised an objection to Rav's opinion from a different source: The *halakha* is that a wife who was warned by her husband not to be secluded with a specific man and yet **entered** alone **with him in private, and remained with him** long enough **to be defiled,** i.e., sufficient time to have sexual relations, she **is forbidden to her house,** i.e., her husband, from that moment until she undergoes the *sota* ritual. **And** likewise, if she was the wife of a priest **she is prohibited from partaking of *teruma*,**[H] as she was possibly disqualified by unfaithfulness. **And if he dies,**[H] **she performs *ḥalitza***

HALAKHA

Prohibited from partaking of *teruma* – אֲסוּרָה לֶאֱכוֹל בִּתְרוּמָה: In the case of the wife of a priest concerning whom witnesses testified both that her husband warned her against secluding herself with a certain man, and that she was alone with the man in question, she is prohibited from partaking of *teruma* until she undergoes the *sota* procedure (Rambam *Sefer Zera'im, Hilkhot Teruma* 8:15).

An uncertain *sota* and levirate marriage – סְפֵק סוֹטָה בְּיִיבּוּם: In the case of a wife who secluded herself with a man despite having been warned by her husband not to do so, if her husband dies before she performs the *sota* procedure, she neither undergoes *ḥalitza* nor is fit for levirate marriage (Rambam *Sefer Nashim, Hilkhot Yibbum VaḤalitza* 6:19).

Perek **I**
Daf **11** Amud **b**

וְלֹא מִתְיַיבֶּמֶת! [אָמַר לָךְ רַב]: אָמֵינָא לָךְ אֲנָא סוֹטָה וַדַּאי, וְאָמְרַתְּ לִי אַתְּ סוֹטָה סָפֵק! וּמַאי שְׁנָא סוֹטָה וַדַּאי (מַאי טַעְמָא), מִשּׁוּם דִּכְתִיב בָּהּ טוּמְאָה –

and may not enter into levirate marriage. This indicates that the levirate bond does apply to a *sota*, which contradicts Rav's statement. The Gemara retorts that **Rav** could have **said to you: I spoke to you** about **a *sota*** whose infidelity was **definite, and you speak to me** of **an uncertain *sota*.** There is no proof that this wife who secluded herself with another man was actually unfaithful, and due to the uncertainty she must still undergo *ḥalitza*. The Gemara raises a difficulty: **And what is different** about **a definite *sota*?** Is it different **because** the term **defilement is written** with regard **to her?**

סוֹטָה סָפֵק נַמִי טוּמְאָה כְּתִיבָא בָּהּ! דְּתַנְיָא: רַבִּי יוֹסֵי בֶּן כֵּיפַר אוֹמֵר מִשּׁוּם רַבִּי אֶלְעָזָר: הַמַּחֲזִיר גְּרוּשָׁתוֹ מִן הַנִּישּׂוּאִין – אֲסוּרָה, מִן הָאֵירוּסִין – מוּתֶּרֶת, מִשּׁוּם שֶׁנֶּאֱמַר ״אַחֲרֵי אֲשֶׁר הֻטַּמָּאָה״,

But with regard to **an uncertain *sota*,** who was alone with a specific man enough time to engage in relations, **defilement is written as well.**[N] **As it is taught** in a *baraita*: **Rabbi Yosei ben Keifar**[P] **said in the name of Rabbi Elazar:** With regard to **one who remarries his divorcée** after she had been married to another man, an act prohibited by Torah law, if he remarried her **following** actual **marriage** to another, **she is forbidden**[H] to her first husband. However, if he remarried her **following** mere **betrothal** to another man, **she is permitted, because it is stated:** "Her former husband, who sent her away, may not take her again to be his wife, **after she was defiled**" (Deuteronomy 24:4), and a woman who was merely betrothed was never defiled, as no sexual relations had taken place.

וַחֲכָמִים אוֹמְרִים: אַחַת זוֹ וְאַחַת זוֹ – אֲסוּרָה. אֶלָּא מָה אֲנִי מְקַיֵּים ״אַחֲרֵי הֻטַּמָּאָה״ – לְרַבּוֹת סוֹטָה שֶׁנִּסְתְּרָה.

And the Rabbis say: Both **this one and that one,** i.e., whether she had been fully married or merely betrothed to another, **she is forbidden** to her first husband. **Rather, how do I establish** the phrase: **"After she was defiled"?** This verse does not refer at all to the case of a woman who married another man lawfully, as she is not called "defiled." Rather, it comes **to include a *sota* who secluded herself**[NH] with another man, as she is forbidden to her husband due to the concern that she might have committed adultery. This *baraita* shows that a *sota* is termed "defiled," despite the fact that hers is an uncertain case.

HALAKHA

The prohibition of one's divorcée who married another – אִיסּוּר גְּרוּשָׁה שֶׁנִּישְּׂאָה לְאַחֵר: If one divorced his wife and she was subsequently betrothed to another, even if no sexual relations were involved, she is forbidden to her first husband. This ruling is in accordance with the opinion of the Rabbis, who disagree with Rabbi Yosei ben Keifar (Rambam *Sefer Nashim, Hilkhot Geirushin* 11:12 and *Maggid Mishne* there; *Shulḥan Arukh, Even HaEzer* 10:1).

The prohibition of a *sota* – אִיסּוּר סוֹטָה: A married woman who willingly had relations with another man is forbidden to her husband, and he receives lashes if he engages in sexual intercourse with her. In circumstances where she was secluded with the man against whom she was warned, but her adultery was not proven, some authorities apparently maintain that he does not receive lashes (Rambam). Others (*Maggid Mishne*; *Kesef Mishne*) rule that he has indeed violated the prohibition (Rambam *Sefer Nashim, Hilkhot Geirushin* 11:14).

PERSONALITIES

Rabbi Yosei ben Keifar – רַבִּי יוֹסֵי בֶּן כֵּיפַר: This Sage from the last generation of *tanna'im* is mentioned in the *Tosefta* and in *baraitot* but not in the Mishna.

He was apparently a primary disciple of Rabbi Elazar ben Shamua, and most of the statements he cites are in this teacher's name. It is related that he was one of the emissaries sent to Babylonia to raise funds for the scholars of Eretz Yisrael. He is grouped together with Rabbi Dostai, son of Rabbi Yehuda, and Rabbi Dostai, son of Rabbi Yannai, who were also among the last of the *tanna'im*.

A Rabbi Yosei ben Keifar is also mentioned in relation to an important mission of the Sages of Eretz Yisrael to quash the attempts of Ḥananya to determine the calendar outside Eretz Yisrael. However, based on the timeline of these events, this was apparently a different Sage with the same name.

NOTES

With regard to an uncertain *sota*, defilement is written as well – סוֹטָה סָפֵק נַמִי טוּמְאָה כְּתִיבָא בָּהּ: Several early commentaries deal with this issue, both from the perspective of the wording of the passage as well as its halakhic implications. Many authorities maintain that one who engages in sexual relations with his *sota* wife before she was tested by the *sota* procedure has violated a Torah prohibition. In addition, by secluding herself with the specified man, she is rendered forbidden both to her husband and to that other man, and may not partake of *teruma*. This indicates that her defilement is treated as definite even in an uncertain case, which apparently contradicts the analysis here.

The commentaries explain that although the Torah indeed considers her secret rendezvous as evidence of her certain defilement, this is only for the purposes of stringencies, not leniencies. Consequently, she still requires *ḥalitza* (Rosh; Rashba). Others maintain that the classification of defilement refers solely to definite adultery, whereas in uncertain circumstances she has transgressed a rabbinic decree (Meiri).

To include a *sota* who secluded herself – לְרַבּוֹת סוֹטָה שֶׁנִּסְתְּרָה: The commentaries ask how the Rabbis could uproot this phrase from its plain meaning in this manner (*Tosafot*). They explain that as the term "defiled" cannot possibly refer to a woman who was lawfully married to another man, it must certainly refer to a *sota*. Some suggest that even in the opinion of the Rabbis, the simple meaning of the verse is not entirely disregarded. Rather, they maintain that there is a prohibition involved both in remarrying one's former wife after she had been married to another man, and in taking a woman who had been defiled (Ritva). Yet others state that it stands to reason that a man would not divorce his wife in the first place unless he found in her some sort of infidelity, and therefore there is a double prohibition against him remarrying her after she had already been defiled by her actions while still married to him (*Arukh LaNer*).

וּמַאי נִסְתְּרָה – נִבְעֲלָה, וְאַמַּאי קָרֵי לֵיהּ נִסְתְּרָה – לִישָּׁנָא מַעַלְיָא נָקַט. נִבְעֲלָה, טוּמְאָה בְּהֶדְיָא כְּתִיב בָּהּ ״וְנִסְתְּרָה וְהִיא נִטְמָאָה״!

The Gemara rejects this argument: **And what does: Secluded herself,** mean in this context? It means that she had actually **engaged in relations. And why** does the *baraita* **call this: Secluded herself,** instead of the more straightforward: Engaged in sexual relations? The *baraita* **employed a euphemistic expression,** but it actually means that she engaged in intercourse. The Gemara asks: If this is referring to a woman who had **engaged in relations,** the term **defilement** is already **explicitly written** with regard **to her,** in the chapter that deals with a *sota*. Why is it necessary to derive that she is defiled from a different source, as in the context of a *sota* herself the verse states: **"She being defiled secretly"** (Numbers 5:13)?

לְמֵיקַם עֲלָהּ בְּלָאו. וְרַבִּי יוֹסֵי בֶּן כֵּיפַר לָאו בְּסוֹטָה לֵית לֵיהּ, וַאֲפִילּוּ זְנַאי נַמִּי.

The Gemara explains that "may not take her again to be his wife after she was defiled" does not teach that she is called "defiled," but rather that the *halakha* **establishes upon her a prohibition.** In other words, if the husband engages in relations with his wife after she had had intercourse with another, he transgresses a prohibition. **And** the Gemara comments that **Rabbi Yosei ben Keifar does not hold** the opinion that there is **a prohibition** in the case **of a** *sota*, as he maintains that a husband who has relations with his *sota* wife does not transgress any prohibition at all, **and the same** is true **even if she** definitely **fornicated**[N] with another man.

מַאי טַעֲמָא – הֲוָיָה וְאִישׁוּת כְּתִיב בָּהּ.

What is the rationale of Rabbi Yosei ben Keifar? In his opinion, "after she was defiled" does not refer to a *sota* but to a woman who had been legally divorced from her first husband and subsequently married another man. This is indicated by the fact that both **becoming,** i.e., betrothal, **and matrimony are written in this** context:[N] "Becomes another man's wife" (Deuteronomy 24:2) and: "Or if the latter husband die, who took her to be his wife" (Deuteronomy 24:3). Here it is clear that the reference is to halakhically valid marriage, whereas a *sota* had never been another man's wife, as she cannot marry another man while she is still married.

בְּעָא מִינֵּיהּ רַב יְהוּדָה מֵרַב שֵׁשֶׁת: הַמַּחֲזִיר גְּרוּשָׁתוֹ מִשֶּׁנִּיסֵּת, וּמֵת, צָרָתָהּ מַהוּ? אַלִּיבָּא דְּרַבִּי יוֹסֵי בֶּן כֵּיפַר לָא תִּיבָּעֵי לָךְ, כֵּיוָן דְּאָמַר רַבִּי יוֹסֵי בֶּן כֵּיפַר טוּמְאָה בְּמַחֲזִיר גְּרוּשָׁתוֹ הוּא דִּכְתִיבָא – צָרָתָהּ כְּמוֹתָהּ.

§ The Gemara discusses a similar case. **Rav Yehuda raised a dilemma before Rav Sheshet:** In the case of **one who remarries his divorcée after she had married** another, **and** then he **dies** childless, **what is** the *halakha* with regard to the levirate marriage of **her rival wife? According to** the opinion of **Rabbi Yosei ben Keifar, do not raise the dilemma, since Rabbi Yosei ben Keifar said** that **it is** with regard **to one who remarries his divorcée** that **defilement is written,** and therefore the status of **her rival wife is the same as hers.**

וְאִי מִשּׁוּם דִּכְתִיב בָּהּ ״תּוֹעֵבָה הִיא״, הִיא תּוֹעֵבָה וְאֵין בָּנֶיהָ תּוֹעֲבִין – הָא צָרָתָהּ תּוֹעֵבָה.

And if one would claim that the dilemma does in fact arise **because it is written: "That is an abomination"** (Deuteronomy 24:4), and the emphasis on "that" serves to limit the range of the prohibition and teaches that this *halakha* applies only to her and not her rival wife, still, the accepted interpretation of this verse is as follows: **She is an abomination, but her children are not abominations.**[NH] In other words, if he transgressed the prohibition and remarried this woman, their children are not disqualified from marrying priests. If so, the term "that" does not come to exclude her rival wife from this *halakha*, and therefore **her rival wife is an abomination** for the purposes of levirate marriage, just like the wife herself, and she too is exempt.

כִּי תִּיבָּעֵי לָךְ – אַלִּיבָּא דְּרַבָּנַן, אַף עַל גַּב דַּאֲמוּר רַבָּנַן טוּמְאָה בְּסוֹטָה הוּא דִּכְתִיב – אֵין מִקְרָא יוֹצֵא מִידֵי פְּשׁוּטוֹ,

Rather, **let the dilemma be raised according to** the opinion of **the Rabbis. Although the Rabbis said** that **it is** with regard **to a** *sota* **that defilement is written,** perhaps here they apply the principle that **a verse does not depart from its literal meaning.** In other words, notwithstanding the fact that the Rabbis derive from here a halakhic ruling concerning a *sota*, the straightforward meaning of the verse should not be entirely disregarded. Accordingly, as the context here is remarriage to one's divorced wife, this verse would teach that hers is a case of defilement.

NOTES

And the same is true even if she fornicated – וַאֲפִילּוּ זְנַאי נַמִּי: A version of the Gemara mentioned by the *ge'onim* and early and later commentaries is cited by the Vilna Gaon in the following form: But if someone engaged in relations with a divorcée, even though she fornicated with that man she is permitted to her husband. This version resolves several difficulties of the standard text (see Rabbi Yehuda bar Natan and Maharshal).

Becoming and matrimony are written in this context – הֲוָיָה וְאִישׁוּת כְּתִיב בָּהּ: Some commentaries explain that this refers to the phrase: "May not take her again to be his wife" (Deuteronomy 24:4), which teaches that one may not remarry his divorcée without a new act of betrothal (Ritva). In addition, the phrase: "Her husband…may not" (Deuteronomy 24:4), indicates that even the second husband may marry her only by means of an act of betrothal.

She is an abomination but her children are not abominations – הִיא תּוֹעֵבָה וְאֵין בָּנֶיהָ תּוֹעֲבִין: But why would one even consider that her children might be forbidden (Meiri)? After all, her husband violated only a regular prohibition, and the children of a prohibited union of this kind are not disqualified. Some explain that as the term "abomination," which usually appears only in reference to prohibitions entailing *karet*, is stated in this context, one might have thought that this child is also considered a *mamzer*. Alternatively, there is a principle that in every case of a marriage that involves a transgression the status of the child is generally determined by the parent with the more inferior lineage. Consequently, it is not unreasonable to think that the children themselves might be forbidden (Meiri; see *Tosafot* on 14b).

HALAKHA

The children of a remarried divorcée – בְּנֵי גְרוּשָׁה שֶׁהֶחֱזִירָהּ: If one remarries his divorced wife after she had been married to another, then although she is forbidden to him the children born of this union are not classified as *mamzerim* (Rambam *Sefer Kedusha, Hilkhot Issurei Bia* 15:2).

או: דִּלְמָא, כֵּיוָן דְּאִיעֲקַר – אִיעֲקַר? אִיכָּא דְּאָמְרִי: אַלִּיבָּא דְרַבָּנַן לָא תִּיבְּעֵי לָךְ, כֵּיוָן דְּאִיתְעֲקַר – אִיעֲקַר.

Or perhaps once a verse **is uprooted** from its context, **it is** entirely **uprooted** and no longer teaches anything about the subject matter of the chapter in which it is written. This would mean that the sole significance of this particular verse is in reference to a *sota*. **There are** those **who say** the opposite: **According to** the opinion of **the Rabbis, do not raise the dilemma,** as **once** a verse **is uprooted** from its context, **it is** entirely **uprooted.** Consequently, there is no defilement when a man remarries his divorcée, neither with regard to her nor concerning her rival wife.

כִּי תִּיבְּעֵי לָךְ – אַלִּיבָּא דְּרַבִּי יוֹסֵי בֶּן כֵּיפַר, מַאי? אַף עַל גַּב דְּאָמַר רַבִּי יוֹסֵי בֶּן כֵּיפַר טוּמְאָה בִּמַחֲזִיר גְּרוּשָׁתוֹ הוּא דִּכְתִיבָא – מִיעֵט רַחֲמָנָא "הִיא תּוֹעֵבָה" וְאֵין צָרָתָהּ תּוֹעֵבָה, אוֹ: דִּלְמָא, הִיא תּוֹעֵבָה וְאֵין בָּנֶיהָ תּוֹעֵבִין, הָא צָרָתָהּ – תּוֹעֵבָה!

Rather, **let the dilemma be raised according to** the opinion of **Rabbi Yosei ben Keifar. What is** the dilemma? **Although Rabbi Yosei ben Keifar said** that **it is** with regard **to one who remarries his divorcée** that **defilement is written,** one can ask: Does **the Merciful One limit** this *halakha* by the phrase **"that is an abomination,"** which indicates: **And her rival wife is not an abomination? Or perhaps** this verse teaches that **she is an abomination but her children are not abominations,** which indicates that **her rival wife is an abomination.**

אָמַר לֵיהּ, תְּנֵיתוּהָ: הָיְתָה אַחַת כְּשֵׁרָה וְאַחַת פְּסוּלָה, אִם הָיָה חוֹלֵץ – חוֹלֵץ לַפְּסוּלָה, וְאִם הָיָה מְיַיבֵּם – מְיַיבֵּם לַכְּשֵׁרָה.

Rav Sheshet **said to him: You learned it** in a *baraita* that deals with a case of two *yevamot* who came before a *yavam* for levirate marriage. In a situation where **one** of the women **was**[N] **fit and the other disqualified, if he would** like to **perform *ḥalitza* he performs *ḥalitza* with the disqualified** woman, **and if he would** like to **enter into levirate marriage he enters into levirate marriage with the fit** woman.[H]

מַאי כְּשֵׁרָה וּמַאי פְּסוּלָה? אִילֵימָא כְּשֵׁרָה – כְּשֵׁרָה לְעָלְמָא, פְּסוּלָה – פְּסוּלָה לְעָלְמָא, כֵּיוָן דִּלְדִידֵיהּ חַזְיָא מַאי נָפְקָא לֵיהּ מִינַּהּ?

Rav Sheshet analyzes this *baraita*: **What is** the meaning of **fit, and what is** the meaning of **disqualified? If we say** that **fit** means **fit for all** men, and **disqualified** means **disqualified in general,** e.g., a woman who had already been divorced is disqualified from marrying any priest, despite the fact that she is fit to marry this particular man himself, then **since for him she is suitable, what difference does it make for him** whether she is disqualified from or fit for marriage to others?

אֶלָּא לָאו: כְּשֵׁרָה – כְּשֵׁרָה לֵיהּ, פְּסוּלָה – פְּסוּלָה לֵיהּ. וּמַאי נִיהוּ – מַחֲזִיר גְּרוּשָׁתוֹ. וְקָתָנֵי: וְאִם הָיָה מְיַיבֵּם – מְיַיבֵּם לַכְּשֵׁרָה!

Rather, is it not the case that **fit** means **fit for him,** and **disqualified** means **disqualified for him? And what is that** case in which a woman is fit or disqualified only with regard to him but not any other man? This is evidently referring to the case of **one who remarries his divorcée.**[N] The deceased brother had remarried his divorced wife after she had married another man, and therefore she is disqualified from entering into levirate marriage with that particular man but she is permitted to other men. **And it is taught** there that **if he would** like to **enter into levirate marriage, he** may **enter into levirate marriage** even **with the fit** woman. This indicates that the rival wife of a remarried divorcée is fit for levirate marriage.

לָא, לְעוֹלָם כְּשֵׁרָה – כְּשֵׁרָה לְעָלְמָא, פְּסוּלָה – פְּסוּלָה לְעָלְמָא. וּדְקָאָמְרַתְּ כֵּיוָן דִּלְדִידֵיהּ חַזְיָא מַאי נָפְקָא לֵיהּ מִינַּהּ – מִשּׁוּם דְּרַב יוֹסֵף.

The Gemara rejects this argument: **No; actually, fit** means **fit to all** men, and **disqualified** means **disqualified in general,** e.g., a woman who had already been divorced is disqualified from marrying any priest. **And that which you said: Since for him she is suitable what difference does it make for him,** this is significant **because of** the statement **of Rav Yosef.**

דְּאָמַר רַב יוֹסֵף, כָּאן שָׁנָה רַבִּי: לֹא יִשְׁפּוֹךְ אָדָם מֵי בּוֹרוֹ וַאֲחֵרִים צְרִיכִים לָהֶם.

As Rav Yosef said: Here Rabbi Yehuda HaNasi **taught** a valuable moral lesson, that **a person should not pour the water from his well when others are in need of it.** That is, one should not cause loss in any situation, even when this relates to his own personal life, if he might thereby cause a future loss to others. The same reasoning applies here: If he intends to perform *ḥalitza* it does not matter to him which of the women he chooses, but if he does so with the one who is fit to others, he thereby disqualifies her from marrying a priest, as the legal status of a woman who underwent *ḥalitza* is like that of a divorcée. It is therefore preferable to perform *ḥalitza* with the one who in any case was disqualified from marrying a priest.

NOTES

You learned it, one was, etc. – **תְּנֵיתוּהָ, הָיְתָה אַחַת וכו׳**: Some commentaries maintain that this answers only the dilemma according to the first version of the discussion, not the second, as according to the second version the *baraita* can be attributed to the opinion of the Rabbis (*Tosafot*). However, the Rashba cites an explanation of the Gemara according to which Rav Sheshet sought to resolve both difficulties. Some maintain that Rashi interprets the Gemara in a similar manner (Maharsha).

And what is that, one who remarries his divorcée – **וּמַאי נִיהוּ מַחֲזִיר גְּרוּשָׁתוֹ**: Rashi and others explain that Rav Sheshet maintains that this must refer to one who remarries his divorcée and not to other transgressions, as otherwise there would be nothing novel in this ruling. This claim is somewhat problematic. Others suggest that the reasons this must be referring only to a remarried divorcée is because it states that one performs *ḥalitza* in the proper manner with the disqualified woman, which is not the case with regard to other transgressions (*Meromei Sadeh*; see *Tosafot*).

HALAKHA

He performs *ḥalitza* with the disqualified woman… he enters into levirate marriage with the fit woman – **חוֹלֵץ לַפְּסוּלָה...מְיַיבֵּם לַכְּשֵׁרָה**: If two *yevamot* came before a *yavam* for levirate marriage, one of whom was fit to marry a priest while the other was disqualified, if he opts for levirate marriage he may marry whichever he chooses, provided that he is not himself a priest. If he decides to perform *ḥalitza*, he must do so with the one who is already disqualified, so as not to disqualify the other woman from marriage to a priest (Rambam *Sefer Nashim, Hilkhot Yibbum VaḤalitza* 1:10; *Shulḥan Arukh, Even HaEzer* 161:2).

תא שמע: המחזיר גרושתו משנשאת – היא וצרתה חולצת. היא וצרתה סלקא דעתך?! [אלא] אימא: או היא או צרתה.

The Gemara suggests: **Come and hear** a different *baraita*: With regard to **one who remarries his divorcée after she had married another, she and her rival wife perform *ḥalitza*.**[H] The Gemara first analyzes the wording of the *baraita*: Can it **enter your mind** that both **she and her rival wife** must perform *ḥalitza*? After all, only one wife of a deceased brother undergoes *ḥalitza*, not two. **Rather, say: Either she or her rival wife.** This indicates that both women are unfit for levirate marriage.

ולאו תרוצי קמתרצת לה? תריץ הכי: היא חולצת, צרתה – או חולצת או מתייבמת.

The Gemara rejects this claim: **And did you not** already **resolve**[N] a difficulty **in the** *baraita* by adjusting its language and not interpreting it as it is? If so, you cannot cite a proof from here, as you can adjust it differently and **answer as follows: She performs *ḥalitza*,** while **her rival wife either performs *ḥalitza* or enters into levirate marriage.** If so, this *baraita* provides no conclusive proof that might resolve Rav Yehuda's dilemma.

אמר רבי חייא בר אבא, רבי יוחנן בעי: המחזיר גרושתו משניסת, צרתה מהו? אמר ליה רבי אמי: ותיבעי לך היא גופה! היא גופה לא קמיבעיא לי,

§ On the same issue, **Rabbi Ḥiyya bar Abba said** that **Rabbi Yoḥanan raised a dilemma:** With regard to **one who remarries his divorcée after she had been married to another, what is** the *halakha* concerning the levirate marriage of **her rival wife? Rabbi Ami said to him: And** you can **raise the dilemma** with regard to this woman **herself.** Why not ask if she requires levirate marriage when her husband dies? Rabbi Ḥiyya bar Abba replied: The *halakha* of the divorcée **herself is not a dilemma for me,** as she is certainly forbidden.

דאמרינן: קל וחומר: במותר לה אסורה, באסור לה – לא כל שכן?! כי קא מיבעיא לי – צרתה מאי? מי אלים קל וחומר למידחי צרה, או לא?

Rabbi Ḥiyya bar Abba elaborates: **As** in this case **we state an *a fortiori* inference:** If **she is** now **forbidden to one who** was previously **permitted to her,**[N] i.e., her first husband, with regard **to one who was forbidden to her,** the *yavam*, is it **not all the more so** the case that she remains forbidden to him? **Where I raise the dilemma** it is with regard to **her rival wife. What is** the *halakha* in this case? **Is** the aforementioned ***a fortiori*** inference **strong** enough **to invalidate her rival wife or not?** The divorcée herself is certainly exempt from levirate marriage, but the question is whether the *a fortiori* inference applies to the rival wife as well.

רב נחמן בר יצחק מתני הכי: אמר רבי חייא בר אבא, בעי רבי יוחנן: המחזיר גרושתו משניסת מהו? אמר ליה רבי אמי: ותיבעי לך צרתה? צרתה לא קמיבעיא לי, דלא אלים קל וחומר למידחי צרה. אלא, כי קמיבעיא לי – היא גופה מאי, מי אלים קל וחומר במקום מצוה, או לא?

Rav Naḥman bar Yitzḥak would **teach** a different version of this discussion, **as follows: Rabbi Ḥiyya bar Abba said** that **Rabbi Yoḥanan raised a dilemma:** With regard to **one who remarries his divorcée after she had been married to another, what is** the *halakha* concerning her levirate marriage? **Rabbi Ami said to him: And** you can **raise the dilemma** with regard to **her rival wife** as well. Rabbi Ḥiyya bar Abba replied: The *halakha* of **her rival wife is not a dilemma for me, as the *a fortiori*** inference **is not strong** enough **to invalidate a rival wife. Rather, where I raise the dilemma** it is with regard to the divorcée **herself. What is** the *halakha*? **Is the *a fortiori*** inference **strong**[N] enough that it can be accepted even **in place of a mitzva** to enter into levirate marriage, **or not?**

Perek **I**
Daf **12** Amud **a**

אמר ליה: תניתוה, היתה אחת כשרה ואחת פסולה, אם היה חולץ – חולץ לפסולה, ואם היה מייבם – מייבם לכשרה. מאי כשרה ומאי פסולה? אילימא כשרה – כשרה לעלמא, פסולה – פסולה לעלמא, כיון דלדידיה חזיא מאי נפקא ליה מינה?

Rabbi Ami **said to** Rabbi Ḥiyya bar Abba: **We learned it** in the same *baraita*: In a case where **one** of the women **was fit and the other disqualified, if he would** like to **perform *ḥalitza*** he performs ***ḥalitza* with the disqualified** woman, **and if he would** like to **enter into levirate marriage, he enters into levirate marriage with the fit woman. What is fit and what is disqualified? If we say that fit** means **fit to all men,** and **disqualified** means **disqualified to all men, since for him she is suitable, what difference does it make for him** whether she is disqualified from or fit for marriage to others?

HALAKHA

Levirate marriage for a remarried divorcée – יבום מחזיר גרושתו: If one remarries his divorced wife after she had been married to another man, and then dies childless, she must perform *ḥalitza*, not levirate marriage. Her rival wife performs either *ḥalitza* or engages levirate marriage. This ruling is in accordance with the discussion here and the opinion (12b) of Rabbi Yoḥanan cited later (Rambam *Sefer Nashim, Hilkhot Yibbum VaḤalitza* 6:13; *Shulḥan Arukh, Even HaEzer* 174:2).

NOTES

And did you not resolve, etc. – ולאו תירוצי וכו׳: The commentaries note that no actual change was made to the text of the *baraita*, as the letter *vav*, which generally means: And, can often mean: Or (*Tosafot*). *Tosefot HaRosh* explains that this interpretation of the letter *vav* is appropriate only when it is evidently necessary from the context. Here, however, as the matter is not clear, this is indeed considered an adjustment to the text.

She is forbidden to one who was permitted to her, etc. – במותר לה אסורה וכו׳: It could be argued that based on this *a fortiori* inference, in every situation where the woman is forbidden by a regular prohibition, her rival wife should be exempt. The commentaries answer that as this prohibition applies to the deceased brother, she has the status of a brother's wife to whom the mitzva of levirate marriage does not apply, and this is considered a prohibition that entails *karet* (*Yosef Lekaḥ*; see *Kovetz He'arot*).

Is the *a fortiori* inference strong, etc. – מי אלים קל וחומר וכו׳: The commentaries ask: In *Sota* 5b the Gemara states that a wife caught secluding herself with the man about whom she was warned must undergo *ḥalitza* and may not enter into levirate marriage, and the Gemara there proves that ruling by this very *a fortiori* inference. Why, then, is the Gemara here uncertain as to whether the *a fortiori* inference can be applied to the woman herself? The answer must be that in Rabbi Yoḥanan's opinion that *halakha* is actually derived from the alternative reason mentioned by the Gemara there, that it is by Torah law that a *sota* cannot enter into levirate marriage. If so, no proof can be brought from there with regard to this issue (*Tosefot HaRosh*).

אֶלָּא לָאו: כְּשֵׁרָה – כְּשֵׁרָה לֵיהּ, פְּסוּלָה – פְּסוּלָה לֵיהּ, וּמַאי נִיהוּ – מַחֲזִיר גְּרוּשָׁתוֹ, וְקָתָנֵי: אִם הָיָה מְיַיבֵּם – מְיַיבֵּם לַכְּשֵׁרָה!

Rather, is it not the case that fit means **fit for him,** and **disqualified** means **disqualified for him? And what is that** case in which a woman is fit or disqualified only with regard to him but not to any other man? This is referring to the case of **one who remarries his divorcée. And it is taught** that **if he would** like to **enter into levirate marriage, he enters into levirate marriage with the fit** woman. This answers Rabbi Yoḥanan's question.

לָא, כְּשֵׁרָה לְעָלְמָא, פְּסוּלָה לְעָלְמָא. וּדְקָאָמְרַתְּ: כֵּיוָן דִּלְדִידֵיהּ חֲזָיָא מַאי נָפְקָא לֵיהּ מִינָּהּ – מִשּׁוּם דְּרַב יוֹסֵף. דְּאָמַר רַב יוֹסֵף: כָּאן שָׁנָה רַבִּי לֹא יִשְׁפּוֹךְ אָדָם מֵי בּוֹרוֹ וַאֲחֵרִים צְרִיכִים לָהֶם.

The Gemara rejects this argument: **No; actually, fit** means **fit to all** men, and **disqualified** means **disqualified in general,** e.g., a woman who had already been divorced is disqualified from marrying any priest. **And that which you said: Since for him she is suitable, what difference does it make for him,** this is significant **because of** that statement **of Rav Yosef. As Rav Yosef said: Here Rabbi** Yehuda HaNasi **taught** a valuable moral lesson, that **a person should not pour the water from his well when others are in need of it.**

תָּא שְׁמַע: הַמַּחֲזִיר גְּרוּשָׁתוֹ מִשֶּׁנִּיסֵּת – הִיא וְצָרָתָהּ חוֹלֶצֶת. הִיא וְצָרָתָהּ סָלְקָא דַּעְתָּךְ? אֶלָּא אֵימָא: אוֹ הִיא אוֹ צָרָתָהּ. וְלָאו תֵּרוּצֵי קָא מְתָרְצַתְּ לַהּ? תְּרֵיץ הָכִי: הִיא חוֹלֶצֶת, צָרָתָהּ – אוֹ חוֹלֶצֶת אוֹ מִתְיַיבֶּמֶת.

Come and **hear** a different *baraita*: With regard to **one who remarries his divorcée**[N] **after she had married another, she and her rival wife must perform *ḥalitza*.** Can it **enter your mind** that both **she and her rival wife** must perform *ḥalitza*? **Rather, say: Either she or her rival wife.** This indicates that both women are unfit for levirate marriage. The Gemara rejects this claim: **And did you not** already **resolve** a difficulty **in the** *baraita*? If so, **answer as follows: She performs *ḥalitza*,** while **her rival wife either performs *ḥalitza* or enters into levirate marriage.** If so, this *baraita* provides no conclusive proof that might resolve Rabbi Yoḥanan's dilemma.

אָמַר רַב לִילִי בַּר מֶמֶל אָמַר מַר עוּקְבָא אָמַר שְׁמוּאֵל: צָרַת מְמָאֶנֶת אֲסוּרָה. לְמַאן? אִילֵימָא לָאַחִים – הַשְׁתָּא הִיא גּוּפָהּ שַׁרְיָא, דְּאָמַר שְׁמוּאֵל: מֵיאֲנָה בָּזֶה מוּתֶּרֶת בָּזֶה, צָרָתָהּ מִיבַּעְיָא?

§ The Gemara cites another discussion concerning women who are forbidden in levirate marriage. **Rav Lili**[N] **bar Memel said** that **Mar Ukva said** that **Shmuel said:** The **rival wife of** a girl **who performed refusal**[H] **is forbidden.**[N] If the deceased brother had two wives, one of whom was a minor who refused the brother who sought to be her *yavam*, not only is she forbidden in levirate marriage, but so too is her rival wife. The Gemara asks: **To whom** is she forbidden? **If we say** that she is forbidden **to the** other **brothers,** this cannot be the case, as **now** that **she herself,** the girl who actually performed refusal, **is permitted** to them, **as Shmuel said:** A minor *yevama* who **refused this** brother **is permitted to that**[H] other brother of the deceased husband, **is it necessary** to state that **her rival wife** is likewise permitted?

אֶלָּא לְדִידֵיהּ, וּמַאי שְׁנָא מְמָאֶנֶת דְּשַׁרְיָא לְאַחִין – דְּלָא עָבְדָא בְּהוּ מַעֲשֶׂה, צָרָה נַמִּי לָא עָבְדָא בְּהוּ מַעֲשֶׂה!

Rather, it means that she is forbidden **to him,** i.e., as she refused a specific brother, both she and her rival wife are forbidden to him. The Gemara clarifies: **And** in **what** way **is** this *halakha* of the rival wife **different from** that of **one who performed refusal, who is permitted to the** other **brothers?** If the reason is **that she did not perform any act** of refusal **with them** that might nullify the obligation of levirate marriage, **her rival wife did not perform any act with them either,** and therefore she should be permitted to all of the brothers.

HALAKHA

The rival wife of a girl who performed refusal – צָרַת מְמָאֶנֶת: If a man's minor wife was a forbidden relative of her *yavam*, and she performed refusal with regard to this *yavam* despite not having refused her husband, her rival wife performs *ḥalitza* but does not enter into levirate marriage. In other words, her refusal of the *yavam* is not considered a refusal of the deceased. However, the rival wife of a girl who is not a forbidden relative of her *yavam* and who performs refusal is permitted in levirate marriage, in accordance with the opinion of Rabbi Yoḥanan on *daf* 12b (Rambam *Sefer Nashim, Hilkhot Yibbum VaḤalitza* 6:22; *Shulḥan Arukh, Even HaEzer* 173:7).

She who refused this is permitted to that – מֵיאֲנָה בָּזֶה מוּתֶּרֶת בָּזֶה: The wife of a deceased man who refused one of his brothers is permitted to the other brothers, in accordance with the opinion of Shmuel. Although Rav and Rav Asi dispute this matter (107b), the *halakha* is ruled in accordance with the opinion of Shmuel, as Rabbi Yoḥanan holds accordingly (Rambam *Sefer Nashim, Hilkhot Geirushin* 11:17; *Shulḥan Arukh, Even HaEzer* 155:11; 173:14).

NOTES

Come and hear, one who remarries his divorcée, etc. – תָּא שְׁמַע הַמַּחֲזִיר גְּרוּשָׁתוֹ וכו׳: At first the Gemara attempted to resolve the dilemma posed by Rabbi Yoḥanan in accordance with both versions of his dilemma (see Rashi). This suggestion refers only to the first of the two versions, as the second does not deal with the case of a rival wife at all (*Tosefot HaRosh*; Maharsha).

Lili – לִילִי: Apparently, this is not a proper name but an epithet or a nickname. The full name is Hillel, a common name among the Sages. Lili might be a shortened form of the foreign equivalent of this name, Julianus or Lulianus.

The rival wife of a girl who performed refusal is forbidden – צָרַת מְמָאֶנֶת אֲסוּרָה: The commentaries ask why the girl who performed refusal is herself forbidden. Since her refusal retroactively annuls the marriage entirely, she should be considered like any other woman who was never married at all. Some answer in accordance with the reason stated later, that since she first came before the *yavam* for levirate marriage and only later performed refusal she has the appearance of a brother's wife, and therefore the Sages rendered her forbidden (Rabbi Yehuda bar Natan; *Tosafot Yeshanim*; Ritva). Some say that due to her refusal she is similar to a *yevama* who received a bill of divorce from her first husband and who is consequently forbidden to the *yavam* (*Tosefot Rid*).

גְּזֵירָה מִשּׁוּם צָרַת בִּתּוֹ מְמָאֶנֶת. וְצָרַת בִּתּוֹ מְמָאֶנֶת מִי אֲסִירָא? וְהָתְנַן: וְכוּלָּן, אִם מֵתוּ אוֹ מֵיאֲנוּ צָרוֹתֵיהֶן מוּתָּרוֹת!

The Gemara answers: This is a rabbinic **decree** imposed **due to** the case of **a rival wife of one's daughter**[N] **who performed refusal.** If the girl who refused was his daughter or any other forbidden relative, her rival wife would be forbidden as the rival wife of one's daughter. Therefore, the Sages rendered forbidden the rival wives of other women who performed refusal, not only his daughter. The Gemara asks: **And is the rival wife of a daughter who performed refusal**[N] actually **forbidden? But didn't we learn** in the mishna: **And** with regard to **all of these** women, **if they died or performed refusal** with their husbands, **their rival wives are permitted.**

דְּמֵיאֲנָה בְּמַאן? אִילֵימָא דְּמֵיאֲנָה בְּבַעַל – הַיְינוּ גְּרוּשָׁה, אֶלָּא לָאו בְּיָבָם!

The Gemara analyzes this statement: **Whom did** this girl **refuse? If we say that she refused the husband,** i.e., the deceased brother before he passed away, **this is** exactly the same as the case of **a divorcée,** and the mishna explicitly states that if one's relative who had been married to his deceased brother died, or refused her husband, or was divorced, no prohibition applies to her rival wife. What is the difference between refusal and divorce? **Rather, is it not** referring to a case where she refused **the** ***yavam*****?** If she refuses the *yavam*, her levirate bond is broken and her rival wife is no longer considered the rival wife of a forbidden relative. Consequently, the rival wife is fit for levirate marriage. This shows that no prohibition applies to the rival wife of a daughter who performed refusal.

לָא, לְעוֹלָם בְּבַעַל, וּתְרֵי גַּוְונֵי גֵּירוּשִׁין, וּמַאי שְׁנָא כִּי מֵיאֲנָה בְּבַעַל, דְּעָקְרִינְהוּ לְנִשּׂוּאִין,

The Gemara answers: **No; actually,** it means **that** she refused **the husband, and two types of divorce** are listed in the mishna: Divorce by Torah law and refusal, which is a form of divorce that applies by rabbinic law. The Gemara asks: **And what is different** between the two cases? Since refusal is not actually divorce but is a form of annulment that nullifies the matrimonial bond retroactively, **when she refuses her husband** it must be said **that she uproots the marriage,** and therefore the rival wife is rendered permitted.

כִּי מֵיאֲנָה בְּיָבָם נַמִי נִשּׂוּאִין קַמָּאֵי קָא עָקְרָא!

If so, **when she refuses the** ***yavam*****,** one should **also** say that **she uproots the first marriage.**[N] The reasoning is that she cannot actually refuse the *yavam*, as she was never married to him. Rather, it must be that she annuls her first marriage, and the bond with the *yavam* is canceled automatically. Consequently, it is as though she were not married at all, and there was never a rival wife.

מִשּׁוּם דְּתָנֵי רָמִי בַּר יְחֶזְקֵאל. דְּתָנֵי רָמִי בַּר יְחֶזְקֵאל: מֵיאֲנָה בְּבַעַל – מוּתֶּרֶת לְאָבִיו, בְּיָבָם – אֲסוּרָה לְאָבִיו.

The Gemara explains that Shmuel's reasoning is **due to** the statement **that Rami bar Yeḥezkel taught** in a *baraita* **as Rami bar Yeḥezkel taught:** If a minor **refused her husband, she is permitted** in marriage even **to his father,** as refusal completely nullifies the marriage, and it is as though there had never been any earlier marriage with the son. However, if she refused **the** ***yavam*****,** not her husband, **she is forbidden to his father.**[H]

אַלְמָא: מִשְּׁעַת נְפִילָה נִרְאֵית כְּכַלָּתוֹ,

Apparently, from the moment **when she came before** the *yavam* for levirate marriage **she appears to be** his father's **daughter-in-law.** Since at the time of the husband's death she had not yet performed refusal, to all appearances she was the father's daughter-in-law. Consequently, although the marriage of this minor was not valid by Torah law, any observer would have assumed it was a proper marriage. Therefore, the Sages rendered a girl who refused her *yavam* forbidden to his father, so that people not take lightly the prohibition of those with whom relations are forbidden.

NOTES

Due to the rival wife of one's daughter, etc. – מִשּׁוּם צָרַת בִּתּוֹ וכו׳: At first glance this seems to be a decree enacted in addition to another decree, as the rival wife of one's daughter who performed refusal is herself forbidden only by rabbinic decree, as she has the appearance of a fully married daughter's rival wife. Apparently, Shmuel holds that this is all one decree, and he maintains that if the Sages permitted the rival wife of any other girl who refused her husband they allow the rival wife of a daughter who refuses as well. In contrast, Rabbi Yoḥanan states (12b) that this rabbinic decree was never enacted (Rashba).

One's daughter who performed refusal – בִּתּוֹ מְמָאֶנֶת: Rashi addresses the question of how a girl could perform refusal during her father's lifetime, as only a fatherless girl married off by her mother and brothers can perform refusal. He explains that the Gemara is referring to a so-called orphan during her father's lifetime, i.e., a minor girl who was married off by her father only to be divorced or widowed. In these circumstances her father can no longer betroth her by Torah law, and she is therefore considered like an orphan. With regard to the refusal itself, Rashi indicates that the girl performs refusal with her own father. Several early commentaries are puzzled by this, as she could never come before him for levirate marriage, which means that there is no opportunity for refusal at all. In their opinion, she refuses one of the other brothers to whom she is permitted. Since there was an act of refusal after the mitzva of levirate marriage came into effect, she has the appearance of a married woman (Ritva).

She uproots the first marriage – נִשּׂוּאִין קַמָּאֵי קָא עָקְרָא: This discussion appears in full later in the Gemara (107b). See also the Jerusalem Talmud, in which the matter is explained similarly. The basic question concerns the possibility of refusal with regard to a *yavam*, in light of the fact that the act of refusal annuls the previous marriage retroactively. It is possible that her refusal of her *yavam* is not considered a proper refusal, as it might actually be her first marriage that she seeks to annul. The commentaries also discuss whether the rival wife of a forbidden relative who performed refusal is forbidden to the *yavam*, due to the fact that she was not fit when the mitzva of levirate marriage initially came into effect. They explain that the rival wife remains forbidden, as anyone examining the case at the time when the mitzva of levirate marriage came into effect would have concluded that she is forbidden (*Melo HaRo'im*). Several other later commentaries explain this in a similar manner.

HALAKHA

If she refused the ***yavam*** **she is forbidden to his father – מֵיאֲנָה...בְּיָבָם אֲסוּרָה לְאָבִיו:** Although refusal nullifies a marriage, and the relatives of the husband are therefore permitted to marry the girl who performed refusal, nevertheless, one who refused her *yavam* is forbidden to his father, as she came for levirate marriage when his son died, and therefore she appeared to be his daughter-in-law, as stated by Rami bar Yeḥezkel. With regard to the other relatives of the deceased brother, some commentaries say that she is permitted to them (Rambam), while others rule that she is forbidden (Ramban; Rashba). She is permitted to the relatives of the *yavam* (Rema, citing *Beit Yosef*; Rambam *Sefer Nashim*, *Hilkhot Geirushin* 11:17; *Shulḥan Arukh*, *Even HaEzer* 155:11).

הָכָא נַמִי – מִשְּׁעַת נְפִילָה נִרְאֵית כְּצָרַת בִּתּוֹ.

Here, too, the same reasoning applies: **From** the moment **when** the other wife **came before** the *yavam* for levirate marriage **she appears to be the rival wife of** his father's **daughter.** For this reason she is forbidden, despite the fact that she is permitted by Torah law. Shmuel's ruling that the rival wife of a girl who performed refusal is forbidden is therefore a decree due to the case of the rival wife of a daughter who performed refusal.

אָמַר רַב אַסִי: צָרַת אַיְלוֹנִית אֲסוּרָה, שֶׁנֶּאֱמַר "וְהָיָה הַבְּכוֹר אֲשֶׁר תֵּלֵד" – פְּרָט לְאַיְלוֹנִית שֶׁאֵינָהּ יוֹלֶדֶת.

§ The Gemara continues to discuss various cases of forbidden women. **Rav Asi said: The rival wife of a sexually underdeveloped woman [*aylonit*] is forbidden.**[N] In other words, if one of the wives of the deceased brother was an *aylonit*, who is incapable of giving birth, the mitzva of levirate marriage does not apply. **As it is stated** with regard to a woman who requires levirate marriage: **"The firstborn that she bears"** (Deuteronomy 25:6), which comes **to exclude an *aylonit*,**[H] **who cannot give birth.** Since the *halakhot* of levirate marriage do not apply to an *aylonit*, she retains her status as a brother's wife who is forbidden, and therefore her rival wife is also exempt from levirate marriage.

מְתִיב רַב שֵׁשֶׁת: שְׁלֹשָׁה אַחִין נְשׂוּאִין שָׁלֹשׁ נָשִׁים נָכְרִיּוֹת, וּמֵת אֶחָד מֵהֶם, וְעָשָׂה בָּהּ שֵׁנִי מַאֲמָר,

Rav Sheshet raised an objection to this from a mishna: **Three brothers are married to three unrelated women, and one of** the brothers **died, and a second** brother **performed levirate betrothal with** the *yevama*. A levirate betrothal does not have the legal status of a regular betrothal, as the levirate bond between *yavam* and *yevama* is not dependent upon betrothal; rather, it represents a kind of continuation of the previous marriage with her deceased husband. Full marriage with a *yevama* is effected by sexual intercourse alone. However, for reasons of modesty, the Sages instituted that the act of betrothal should apply to a *yevama* as well.

וּמֵת – הֲרֵי אֵלּוּ חוֹלְצוֹת וְלֹא מִתְיַבְּמוֹת, שֶׁנֶּאֱמַר "וּמֵת אַחַד מֵהֶם יְבָמָהּ יָבֹא עָלֶיהָ" – מִי שֶׁעָלֶיהָ זִיקַת יָבָם אֶחָד, וְלֹא זִיקַת שְׁנֵי יְבָמִין.

And this brother who performed the levirate betrothal **died** before consummation of the marriage. In this case, both of **these,** the wife of the first brother, who had already come before the second brother for levirate marriage, and the wife of the second brother, **perform *ḥalitza* and may not enter into levirate marriage. As it is stated: "And one of them dies** and he has no child, the wife of the dead man shall not be married outside of the family to one not of his kin; **her brother-in-law will have intercourse with her"** (Deuteronomy 25:5). This implies that the option of levirate marriage applies only to **one who is subject to** the levirate **bond of one *yavam*,** for only one deceased brother, **and not** the **bond of two *yevamin*.**[N] Since it is considered as though the first widow has two levirate duties to fulfill, neither she nor her rival wife may enter into levirate marriage.

וְקָתָנֵי עֲלָהּ, אָמַר רַב יוֹסֵף: זוֹ הִיא צָרַת אֵשֶׁת אָח מֵאָב, שֶׁאִיסּוּר נְפִילָה גָּרַם לָהּ, שֶׁלֹּא מָצִינוּ בְּכׇל הַתּוֹרָה כּוּלָּהּ כְּגוֹן זֹאת.

And it is taught with regard to this issue that **Rav Yosef said: This is** an example of **a rival wife of a paternal** half **brother's wife,** i.e., a fully fit *yevama,* **for whom coming before** the *yavam* for levirate marriage **caused her to be forbidden.** In other words, she was fully fit for levirate marriage by Torah law, as all conditions of the mitzva are present in her case. The reason for her prohibition has nothing to do with her particular status but is the result of her having come before a *yavam* for levirate marriage once already. **We have not found in the entire Torah an example** like **this,** where the fact that she was obligated in a mitzva she was unable to fulfill means that not only she, but her rival wife as well, are both rendered forbidden.

"זוֹ הִיא" לְמַעוּטֵי מַאי? לָאו לְמַעוּטֵי צָרַת אַיְלוֹנִית דְּשַׁרְיָא?

The Gemara analyzes Rav Yosef's statement: The emphasis of: **This is,** which indicates that it applies to this case and no other, comes **to exclude what? Doesn't** it come **to exclude the rival wife of an *aylonit*,** which would mean **that** she **is permitted?** Although an *aylonit* herself may marry any man, she is not suitable for levirate marriage. If so, Rav Yosef's comment indicates that only a woman subject to a double levirate bond, not any other case, renders her rival wife forbidden merely by coming before the *yavam* for levirate marriage.

NOTES

The rival wife of an *aylonit* is forbidden – צָרַת אַיְלוֹנִית אֲסוּרָה: Rav Asi maintains that an *aylonit* whose status was known at the time of her marriage is considered a forbidden relative, as she is unfit for levirate marriage. Accordingly, her rival wife is forbidden as well, as Rav Asi does not distinguish between the reasons for this prohibition. In the Jerusalem Talmud, it is stated that Rav Asi holds in accordance with the opinion of Rabbi Meir that a woman forbidden in levirate marriage exempts her rival wife in all circumstances.

And not the bond of two *yevamin* – וְלֹא זִיקַת שְׁנֵי יְבָמִין: The Gemara states later (31b) that despite the apparent proof from the Torah, this prohibition applies by rabbinic law. The reason for the decree is so that people not think that two *yevamot* from a single household could both enter levirate marriage.

HALAKHA

To exclude an *aylonit* – פְּרָט לְאַיְלוֹנִית: An *aylonit* is entirely exempt from levirate marriage and is forbidden to her *yavam* (Rambam *Sefer Nashim*, *Hilkhot Yibbum VaḤalitza* 6:8).

NOTES

No, it was meant to exclude the rival wife of an *aylonit* – לָא, לְמִיעוּטֵי צָרַת אַיְלוֹנִית: Why should this exclude the rival wife of an *aylonit* at all, rather than a *sota* or a remarried divorcée (*Tosafot*)? One answer is that these two cases each entail an additional prohibition, whereas in the case of a double levirate bond there is no additional prohibition beyond that of a brother's wife. The only analogous case is that of an *aylonit*, who is also forbidden only as a brother's wife (*Tosafot Yeshanim*; *Tosefot HaRosh*).

לָא, לְמַעוּטֵי צָרַת אַיְלוֹנִית דַּאֲסִירָא, וּמַאי ״זוֹ הִיא״ – זוֹ הִיא דְּאִיסּוּר נְפִילָה גָּרַם לָהּ – צָרָתָהּ בָּעֲיָא חֲלִיצָה, אַיְלוֹנִית – אֲפִילּוּ חֲלִיצָה לָא בָּעֲיָא. מַאי טַעְמָא? הָא – דְּאוֹרָיְיתָא, הָא – דְּרַבָּנַן.

The Gemara rejects this suggestion: **No,** Rav Yosef's statement was meant **to exclude the rival wife of an *aylonit*,**[N] that she **is forbidden. And what is** the meaning of: **This is?** It means that **this is the one for whom coming before** the *yavam* for levirate marriage **caused her to be forbidden,** and therefore **her rival wife requires *ḥalitza*** and is not entirely exempt. In contrast, in the case of the rival wife of an ***aylonit,*** she does **not even require *ḥalitza*. What is the reason** for this difference between the two cases? **This** one, an *aylonit*, is exempt from levirate marriage **by Torah** law, while **this one,** who was betrothed by levirate betrothal to the other brother, is forbidden **by rabbinic** law, and she therefore must perform *ḥalitza*.

תְּנַן: וְכוּלָּן, אִם מֵתוּ אוֹ מֵיאֲנוּ אוֹ נִתְגָּרְשׁוּ אוֹ שֶׁנִּמְצְאוּ אַיְלוֹנִית – צָרוֹתֵיהֶן מוּתָּרוֹת! לָא קַשְׁיָא: כָּאן שֶׁהִכִּיר בָּהּ,

§ The Gemara cites another relevant source. **We learned** in the mishna: **And** with regard to **all of these** women with whom relations are forbidden, **if they died, or they refused** their husbands, **or were divorced, or were found to be *aylonit,* their rival wives are permitted** in levirate marriage. This ruling apparently contradicts the statement of Rav Asi that the rival wife of an *aylonit* is forbidden. The Gemara responds: This is **not difficult. Here,** Rav Asi is referring to a situation in **which** her husband **knew** that **she** was an *aylonit* prior to marriage, and as he married her regardless of her condition their marriage is fully valid. Since the mitzva of levirate marriage does not apply to her because she cannot give birth, her rival wife is also exempt.

כָּאן – שֶׁלֹּא הִכִּיר בָּהּ.

There, in the mishna, it is referring to a case **where he did not know** that **she** was an *aylonit* at the time of marriage, but only at a later stage. Since in this case it can be said that he would not choose to marry an *aylonit*, hers was a mistaken betrothal, and it is therefore nullified. Consequently, her rival wife is permitted.

דַּיְקָא נָמֵי, דְּקָתָנֵי: שֶׁנִּמְצְאוּ, וְלָא קָתָנֵי שֶׁהָיוּ. שְׁמַע מִינַּהּ. אָמַר רָבָא:

The Gemara comments: The language of the mishna **is also precise, as it teaches: Were found to be** an *aylonit*, **and it does not teach: Were** an *aylonit*. This indicates that her condition was not known to the husband at the time of marriage but was discovered by him only later. The Gemara summarizes: **Conclude from this** that this is the correct interpretation of the mishna. Consequently, the mishna does not contradict the opinion of Rav Asi. **Rava said:**

Perek **I**
Daf **12** Amud **b**

HALAKHA

The rival wife of an *aylonit* – צָרַת אַיְלוֹנִית: If the deceased brother had two wives, one of whom was an *aylonit*, her rival wife is permitted and must either perform *ḥalitza* or enter into levirate marriage, in accordance with the opinion of Rava and Rabbi Yoḥanan (Rambam *Sefer Nashim*, *Hilkhot Yibbum VaḤalitza* 6:20; *Shulḥan Arukh*, *Even HaEzer* 172:1).

The rival wife of an *aylonit* who is a forbidden relative – צָרַת עֶרְוָה אַיְלוֹנִית: If the *yevama* is a forbidden relative of the *yavam* and she is also an *aylonit*, even if her husband knew of her condition and accepted her, only her rival wife performs *ḥalitza* or levirate marriage (Rambam *Sefer Nashim*, *Hilkhot Yibbum VaḤalitza* 6:21; *Shulḥan Arukh*, *Even HaEzer* 173:9).

הִלְכְתָא, צָרַת אַיְלוֹנִית מוּתֶּרֶת, וַאֲפִילּוּ הִכִּיר בָּהּ, וַאֲפִילּוּ צָרַת בִּתּוֹ אַיְלוֹנִית.

And the *halakha* is that the **rival wife of an *aylonit***[H] **is permitted,**[N] and this is the case **even if** her first husband **knew** of **her** status and her marriage was fully valid. The mitzva of levirate marriage does not apply to an *aylonit*, but her rival wife is not forbidden. **And even** in the case of **the rival wife of his *aylonit* daughter**[H] who was recognized as such, the other wife is not considered the rival wife of a forbidden relative.

NOTES

The rival wife of an *aylonit* is permitted – צָרַת אַיְלוֹנִית מוּתֶּרֶת: The differences between the opinions of Rav Asi and Rava are explained in greater detail in the Jerusalem Talmud. Rav Asi maintains that an *aylonit* remains included in the prohibition of a brother's wife, as she may not enter into levirate marriage. Accordingly, her rival wife, like all rival wives of those with whom relations are forbidden, is also forbidden. This is similar to the case of the rival wife of the wife of a brother with whom he did not coexist, as she too is forbidden.

Conversely, according to Rava and Rabbi Yoḥanan these cases are dissimilar, as there is no prohibition against an *aylonit* entering into levirate marriage. Rather, the mitzva of levirate marriage simply does not apply to her. This is expressed in the Jerusalem Talmud as: It is as though she is not there. That is, she is considered non-existent with regard to all matters of levirate marriage, and therefore her rival wife is not the rival wife of a forbidden relative. There are numerous other explanations, but the essential idea remains the same: The rival wife of a forbidden relative is forbidden herself only if the mitzva takes effect, whereas for an *aylonit* the mitzva of levirate marriage does not apply at all (Rashi and many others).

וְאֶלָּא הָא דְּקָתָנֵי שֶׁנִּמְצְאוּ? תְּנֵי שֶׁהָיוּ. כִּי אֲתָא רָבִין אֲמַר רַבִּי יוֹחָנָן: אַחַת צָרַת מְמָאֶנֶת וְאַחַת צָרַת אַיְלוֹנִית, וְאַחַת צָרַת מַחֲזִיר גְּרוּשָׁתוֹ – כּוּלָּן מוּתָּרוֹת.

The Gemara asks: **However,** with regard to **that which** the mishna **teaches: Were found to be,** from which it was inferred that there is a difference between an *aylonit* whose condition was known by the husband beforehand and one who was recognized by him only later, how is this to be explained? The Gemara answers that one should emend this and **teach** simply: **That were,**[N] and not: Were found to be. **When Ravin came** from Eretz Yisrael **he said** that **Rabbi Yoḥanan said:** There is **one** *halakha* with regard to the **rival wife of a girl who refused** her husband, and **the rival wife of an** ***aylonit*****, and also** the **rival wife of one who remarries his divorcée: They are all permitted.**

תָּנֵי רַב בֵּיבָי קַמֵּיהּ דְּרַב נַחְמָן: שָׁלֹשׁ נָשִׁים מְשַׁמְּשׁוֹת בְּמוֹךְ: קְטַנָּה, מְעוּבֶּרֶת, וּמֵנִיקָה. קְטַנָּה – שֶׁמָּא תִּתְעַבֵּר וְשֶׁמָּא תָּמוּת, מְעוּבֶּרֶת – שֶׁמָּא תַּעֲשֶׂה עוּבָּרָהּ סַנְדָּל, מֵנִיקָה – שֶׁמָּא תִּגְמוֹל בְּנָהּ וְיָמוּת.

§ Incidental to the case of refusal, the Gemara cites a related *halakha*. **Rav Beivai taught** a *baraita* **before Rav Naḥman: Three women** may **engage in relations with** a contraceptive **resorbent,**[NHB] a soft fabric placed at the entrance to their wombs to prevent conception, despite the fact that this practice is generally prohibited. They are as follows: **A minor,** a woman who is already **pregnant, and a nursing woman.** The *baraita* specifies the reason for each exception: **A minor** may do so **lest she become pregnant and perhaps die; a pregnant woman, lest** she be impregnated a second time and **her** previous **fetus becomes** deformed[B] into the shape of **a sandal** fish[B] by being squashed by the pressure of the second fetus. As for **a nursing woman,** she does so **lest** she become pregnant and her milk dry up, in which case **she will wean her son** too early, thereby endangering him, **and he will die.**

וְאֵיזוֹ הִיא קְטַנָּה – מִבַּת אַחַת עֶשְׂרֵה שָׁנָה וְיוֹם אֶחָד עַד שְׁתֵּים עֶשְׂרֵה שָׁנָה וְיוֹם אֶחָד, פָּחוֹת מִכָּאן וְיָתֵר עַל כֵּן מְשַׁמֶּשֶׁת כְּדַרְכָּהּ וְהוֹלֶכֶת, דִּבְרֵי רַבִּי מֵאִיר, וַחֲכָמִים אוֹמְרִים: אַחַת זוֹ וְאַחַת זוֹ מְשַׁמֶּשֶׁת כְּדַרְכָּהּ וְהוֹלֶכֶת, וּמִן הַשָּׁמַיִם יְרַחֲמוּ. מִשּׁוּם שֶׁנֶּאֱמַר ״שׁוֹמֵר פְּתָאִים ה׳״.

And the *baraita* continues: **Who is** considered **a minor?** It is a girl **from the age of eleven years and one day until** the age of **twelve years and one day.** If she was **younger than this or older than this,**[N] **she may go ahead and engage in relations in her usual manner.** This is **the statement of Rabbi Meir.** Since it is assumed that a minor who is less than eleven years old cannot become pregnant, she is considered to be in no danger. **And the Rabbis say: Both this** one **and that** one, i.e., in all these cases, she **may go ahead and engage in relations in her usual manner, and Heaven will have mercy**[N] upon her and prevent any mishap, **since it is stated: "The Lord preserves the simple"** (Psalms 116:2).

מִדְּקָאָמַר שֶׁמָּא תִּתְעַבֵּר וְשֶׁמָּא תָּמוּת, מִכְּלָל דְּאִיכָּא קְטַנָּה דְּמִיעַבְּרָא וְלָא מֵתָה, אִם כֵּן מָצִינוּ חֲמוֹתוֹ מְמָאֶנֶת,

The Gemara analyzes the *baraita*: **From** the fact that the *baraita* **states: Lest she become pregnant and perhaps die,** this indicates **by inference that there is a minor who can become pregnant and will not die,** although the conditions for this scenario of a minor giving birth and surviving are unclear. **If so,** that a minor might be impregnated and give birth, **we find** the case of **one's mother-in-law who refused** her husband. Since it is possible for a woman to give birth to a daughter while still a minor, if a man betroths this daughter while still an infant, the mother might be a mother-in-law who performed refusal.

HALAKHA

Engage in relations with a contraceptive resorbent – מְשַׁמְּשׁוֹת בְּמוֹךְ: The *halakha* is in accordance with the opinion of the Rabbis that these women may not use a contraceptive resorbent. In clearly dangerous situations some permit this in practice in various ways. Later commentaries deliberate with regard to other methods of birth control that do not entail the placement of an actual interposition before the sperm, and there are various halakhic rulings in this regard (*Shulḥan Arukh, Even HaEzer* 23; *Pitḥei Teshuva* 2).

BACKGROUND

Three women may engage in relations with a contraceptive resorbent – שָׁלֹשׁ נָשִׁים מְשַׁמְּשׁוֹת בְּמוֹךְ: The issue of women using a contraceptive resorbent, or any other contraceptive device, is discussed at length in the halakhic literature; see also 65b. Here the discussion concerns the use of mechanical means for preventing the penetration of sperm into the uterus. The method of placing a contraceptive resorbent after sexual relations, as described by Rabbeinu Tam in *Tosafot*, is of minimal to no effectiveness. The use of these contraceptive methods is permitted only in cases of danger to life, and the dispute between Rabbi Meir and the Rabbis apparently involves the question of how cautious one should be. Nowadays these cases are extremely rare.

Her fetus becomes deformed – תַּעֲשֶׂה עוּבָּרָהּ: In every case of twins or simultaneous pregnancies, which are possible albeit infrequent, one of the embryos occasionally develops more quickly and thereby severely reduces the blood supply to the other embryo. In these situations the undernourished fetus does not develop at all but remains a fleshy mass adjoined to the placenta, similar in shape to the sandal fish.

Sandal fish – סַנְדָּל: This fish is referred to today as the species sole, a group of flatfish, a name derived from the Latin solea, referring to both the fish and the sole of a shoe. The common sole, *Solea solea*, possesses an interesting feature: Both of its eyes are on the right side of its body.

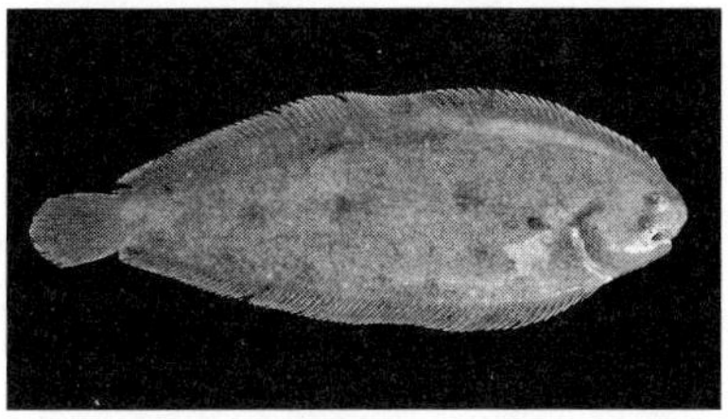

Common sole, referred to in talmudic times as the sandal fish

NOTES

Teach, that were – תְּנֵי שֶׁהָיוּ: Although the Gemara initially inferred from the wording of the mishna that it is referring to a situation where it was not known at first that the woman was an *aylonit*, Rava nevertheless held that this was not necessarily the case. The reason is that the phrase: They were found, might be referring to the court who determined that she was an *aylonit*, and if so there is no essential difference between this phrase and the simple: They were (Ritva).

Three women may engage in relations with a contraceptive resorbent – שָׁלֹשׁ נָשִׁים מְשַׁמְּשׁוֹת בְּמוֹךְ: There is a dispute among the early commentaries both with regard to the meaning of this statement as well as its halakhic implications. Rashi and others maintain that the woman inserts a contraceptive resorbent into the entrance to her uterus to prevent the entrance of sperm. Others hold that she inserts a contraceptive resorbent after sexual relations to prevent the semen from reaching the uterus (Rabbi Yehuda bar Natan; *Tosafot*). They base their opinion on the fact that sexual relations with a contraceptive resorbent in place would entail the unavoidable destruction of sperm, which is a transgression for the man. However, Rashi contends that provided that the sexual relations take place in the usual manner and there is no intention of destroying the sperm, this is not prohibited (see *Tosefot Rid*).

This dispute extends to the *halakha* as well. Rashi contends that these women are only permitted to use a contraceptive resorbent. Others rule that these women are obligated to do so, while others are merely permitted to engage in this practice (Rabbeinu Tam; Rabbi Yehuda bar Natan; Rashba). This is apparently the explanation of the *ge'onim* as well, who may have been even more lenient on this issue. For an attempt to reconcile all of these opinions, see *Yam shel Shlomo*.

Younger than this or older than this – פָּחוֹת מִכָּאן וְיָתֵר עַל כֵּן: Many early commentaries connect this discussion, including the opinions of Rav Safra and Rav Zevid cited later, to the related matter of signs of puberty that appear in a young woman during this period, between age eleven and twelve. If she develops the sign of pubic hairs before this time, everyone agrees that the hairs are only a mole and she has certainly not reached maturity, while after this period hair is definitely a sign of maturity. The dispute concerns whether this intermediate period is considered like the time before or after (see *Tosafot*, Rashba, Ritva, and Meiri).

And Heaven will have mercy – וּמִן הַשָּׁמַיִם יְרַחֲמוּ: Some commentaries explain that the Rabbis felt that the danger is highly unlikely, and therefore the women are not obligated, or permitted according to certain opinions, to use a contraceptive resorbent (Meiri). Several later commentaries explain similarly, as the phrase: Heaven will have mercy, indicates that one is acting in the usual fashion, without concern for some uncertain danger. If the danger is definitely present, however, this principle does not apply (see *Aḥiezer*).

וּתְנַן: אִי אַתָּה יָכוֹל לוֹמַר בַּחֲמוֹתוֹ וְאֵם חֲמוֹתוֹ וְאֵם חָמִיו שֶׁנִּמְצְאוּ אַיְלוֹנִית אוֹ שֶׁמֵּיאֲנוּ! אֵימָא: שֶׁמָּא תִּתְעַבֵּר וְתָמוּת.

And yet we learned in the mishna: **You cannot say,** i.e., the possibility does not exist, in the case **of his mother-in-law, his mother-in-law's mother, and his father-in-law's mother, that they were found to be an *aylonit* or performed refusal,** as refusal may be performed only by a minor, who cannot give birth. If so, there is apparently a contradiction between the mishna and the *baraita*. The Gemara answers: Do not say: Lest she become pregnant and perhaps die, which indicates that it is possible for her not to die from the impregnation. Rather, **say: Lest she become pregnant and die.** In other words, although it is uncertain whether she will be impregnated, if she does become pregnant she will certainly die, which means that there is no case in which a minor could give birth and live.

דְּאָמַר רַבָּה בַּר לִיוָאִי: גְּבוּל יֵשׁ לָהּ: קוֹדֶם הַזְּמַן הַזֶּה אֵינָהּ מִתְעַבֶּרֶת כָּל עִיקָּר, תּוֹךְ הַזְּמַן הַזֶּה הִיא מֵתָה וְעוּבָּרָהּ מֵת, לְאַחַר זְמַן הַזֶּה – הִיא חַיָּה וְעוּבָּרָהּ חַי.

As Rabba bar Livai said: There is a limit with regard to her pregnancy, i.e., that of a young girl. **Before this time,** the age of eleven, **she cannot be impregnated at all.**[B] **During this time,** from age eleven to twelve, **she dies and her fetus dies.**[N] **After this time,** from twelve onward, **she lives and her fetus lives.**

אִינִי? וְהָא תָּנֵי רַבָּה בַּר שְׁמוּאֵל: אִי אַתָּה יָכוֹל לוֹמַר בַּחֲמוֹתוֹ וְאֵם חֲמוֹתוֹ וְאֵם חָמִיו שֶׁנִּמְצְאוּ אַיְלוֹנִית אוֹ שֶׁמֵּיאֲנוּ, שֶׁכְּבָר יָלְדוּ! אֶלָּא, לְעוֹלָם – שֶׁמָּא תִּתְעַבֵּר וְשֶׁמָּא תָּמוּת. וְאֶלָּא קַשְׁיָא הָךְ!

The Gemara raises a difficulty: **Is that so? But didn't Rabba bar Shmuel teach: You cannot say** in the case **of his mother-in-law, and his mother-in-law's mother, and his father-in-law's mother that they were found to be an *aylonit* or performed refusal, as they already gave birth.** This indicates that a minor can give birth, as otherwise he should have stated: As they are already mature. **Rather, actually,** the original version of the *baraita* is correct: **Lest she become pregnant and perhaps die. But this is difficult**[N] with regard to the mishna, which indicates that this scenario is impossible.

אָמַר רַב סַפְרָא: בָּנִים הֲרֵי הֵם כְּסִימָנִים. וְאִית דְּאָמְרִי: בָּנִים עֲדִיפֵי מִסִּימָנִים. לְמַאי נָפְקָא מִינָּהּ? דַּאֲפִילּוּ לְרַבִּי יְהוּדָה, דְּאָמַר: עַד שֶׁיִּרְבֶּה הַשָּׁחוֹר, בְּבָנִים מוֹדֶה.

Rav Safra said: Children are equivalent to signs[NH] of puberty. In other words, a girl who gives birth does not retain the legal status of a minor, as the very fact that she bore children is equivalent to a physical sign of maturity, usually in the form of pubic hairs. **And some say: Children are preferable to signs** of puberty. The Gemara asks: **What is the practical difference** that arises from the question of whether bearing children is equivalent or preferable to signs of maturity? The Gemara answers: The difference is **that even according to** the opinion of **Rabbi Yehuda, who said** that a minor may perform refusal even after she develops two pubic hairs, **until the black** hairs of her genitals **are more plentiful**[N] than the hairless skin, in the case **of children he concedes** that she is considered mature and may not perform refusal.

NOTES

During this time she dies and her fetus dies – תּוֹךְ הַזְּמַן הַזֶּה הִיא מֵתָה וְעוּבָּרָהּ מֵת: In the Jerusalem Talmud a different version of this statement is cited, which includes a further distinction: If she was impregnated prior to showing signs of puberty and gave birth after showing these signs, she lives and her fetus dies.

But this is difficult – וְאֶלָּא קַשְׁיָא הָךְ: Some commentaries explain that this is difficult according to Rabba bar Livai, who said that a minor cannot give birth at all, whereas Rabba bar Shmuel indicates that a minor can give birth (*Tosafot*). However, most of the early commentaries accept Rashi's explanation that it is difficult according to the mishna, which clearly indicates that one's mother-in-law cannot perform refusal (Rashba; *Nimmukei Yosef*).

Children are equivalent to signs – בָּנִים הֲרֵי הֵם כְּסִימָנִים: The early commentaries dispute the precise meaning of this expression. Apparently, the Rif maintains that the term: Signs, does not necessarily mean hairs. Rather, children themselves are proof of maturity, even if they were born before the mother reached the age of twelve (see Ramban and Rashba). Others contend that the pregnancy itself, not the birth of children, is a sign of maturity, and therefore from the onset of pregnancy she is considered mature (*Tosafot*). According to this interpretation, children were mentioned to teach that a pregnancy is retroactively considered a sign of maturity from the onset of the pregnancy only if it results in a living child, not a stillborn.

Until the black are more plentiful – עַד שֶׁיִּרְבֶּה הַשָּׁחוֹר: The Gemara in *Nidda* 52a explains that there is no need for the black, hairy, area actually to be more plentiful than the hairless area. Rather, there must be two hairs lying down in such a manner that it appears as though the black area is greater.

HALAKHA

Children and signs – בָּנִים וְסִימָנִים: A girl who gives birth after the age of twelve is considered mature even if she has no signs of puberty, as children are equivalent to signs (Rambam). This *halakha* is in accordance with the opinion of Rav Safra, who apparently maintains that even if she gave birth as a minor she is not considered mature until the age of twelve years. This has implications for *ḥalitza* and other matters. Some commentaries (*Maggid Mishne*) claim that even the Rambam agrees that after a minor has given birth she can no longer perform refusal (*Beit Shmuel*). The *Shulḥan Arukh* writes that a minor may refuse her husband until she either develops signs or gives birth. Some rule that she is already considered mature at the time of pregnancy (Rema, citing *Or Zarua*). The Vilna Gaon contends that according to this opinion she might be considered mature even before the age of twelve, in accordance with the ruling of *Tosafot*.

Some commentaries write that she may not perform refusal even as a minor if she is pregnant, but this does not hold true if she miscarries (*Beit Shmuel*). Others dispute this ruling (see *Pitḥei Teshuva*). With regard to *ḥalitza*, however, she is not considered mature before the age of twelve (Rambam *Sefer Nashim*, *Hilkhot Ishut* 2:9; *Shulḥan Arukh*, *Even HaEzer* 155:12, 169:11, and in the comment of Rema).

BACKGROUND

A minor who gives birth – קְטַנָּה שֶׁיּוֹלֶדֶת: The question of whether a minor can give birth depends upon the definition of the relevant terms. The appearance of two pubic hairs is one stage in the process of sexual maturation. Apparently, the definition of adulthood as the stage when two hairs appear is based on the fact that this sign of maturity can be checked objectively by witnesses. Generally, the appearance of hairs occurs prior to the advent of ovulation and the menstrual cycle, which allow for the possibility of impregnation and childbirth. Consequently the claim stated later in the Gemara that children are preferable to signs of puberty is accurate, as childbearing occurs at a much later stage in the process of maturation, even if the hairs are not visible.

The Sages determined that the appearance of signs of puberty alone before the appropriate age, twelve for females and thirteen for males, is not sufficient for establishing adulthood. Nevertheless, despite the average age of puberty, physical maturity may be reached earlier depending on nutrition and hereditary factors. There have even been cases of extremely early maturation. It is clear, however, that complications in pregnancy and childbirth are more prevalent among girls than among mature women. Especially in the days of the Talmud, it was consequently assumed that childbirth before full physiological development would likely lead to an inability to give birth or severe tearing of the womb that could cause the death of the mother and baby at birth.

וְרַב זְבִיד אָמַר: אֵין בָּנִים בְּלֹא סִימָנִים. וְנִבְדּוֹק! חָיְישִׁינַן שֶׁמָּא נָשְׁרוּ. הָנִיחָא לְמַאן דַּאֲמַר חוֹשְׁשִׁין,

§ **And Rav Zevid said: There are no children without signs**[N] of puberty. In other words, if a girl gives birth, she definitely possesses the signs of puberty. The Gemara asks: **But** if so, **let us examine** to see whether these physical signs are present, so that there is no need to depend on a presumption. The Gemara answers: **We are concerned lest** the hairs that constitute the sign **have fallen off.** The Gemara comments: **This** works out **well according to the one who said** that in general **we are concerned** lest signs fall off, i.e., that there are cases in which she is in fact mature but the hairs have come off.

אֶלָּא לְמַאן דַּאֲמַר אֵין חוֹשְׁשִׁין מַאי אִיכָּא לְמֵימַר? אֲפִילּוּ לְמַאן דַּאֲמַר אֵין חוֹשְׁשִׁין, מִשּׁוּם צַעַר לֵידָה – חָיְישִׁינַן.

However, according to the one who said that if there are in fact hairs they will certainly be found, and **we are not concerned** that they may have fallen out, **what is there to say?** The Gemara answers: **Even according to the one who said** that in ordinary circumstances **we are not concerned** that the hairs may have fallen out, in this case, **due to the pain of childbirth we are concerned** that they might have fallen out, and therefore it is impossible to examine the matter conclusively.

"כֵּיצַד פּוֹטְרוֹת צָרוֹתֵיהֶן" וכו׳. מְנָהָנֵי מִילֵּי? אָמַר רַב יְהוּדָה: דְּאָמַר קְרָא "לִצְרוֹר", הַתּוֹרָה רִיבְּתָה צָרוֹת הַרְבֵּה.

§ The Gemara returns to the mishna: **How do they exempt their rival wives** and the rival wives of their rival wives? The Gemara asks: **From where are these matters,** that not only is a rival wife exempt but the rival wife of a rival wife is exempt as well, **derived? Rav Yehuda said** that this is **as the verse states:** "And you shall not take a woman to her sister, **to be a rival** [***litzror***][N] to her" (Leviticus 18:18). The term *litzror* is written, with the letter *reish* appearing twice, rather than *latzor*, with a single *reish*, which means that **the Torah amplified** and included **many rival wives.** In other words, this verse includes not only the rival wife of a forbidden relative, but also the rival wife of a rival wife.

רַב אַשִׁי אֲמַר: סְבָרָא הִיא, צָרָה מַאי טַעֲמָא אֲסִירָא – דְּבִמְקוֹם עֶרְוָה קַיְימָא, צָרַת צָרָה נַמִי – בִּמְקוֹם עֶרְוָה קַיְימָא.

Rav Ashi said: It is a logical inference, which does not require a source from the Torah. **What is the reason** that **a rival wife** of a forbidden relative **is prohibited?** The reason is **that she stands in place of a forbidden relative.** Since the forbidden relative caused her exemption from levirate marriage, she too is considered a forbidden relative who remains categorized as a brother's wife. Therefore, **the rival wife of a rival wife also stands in place of a forbidden relative,** as she is like the rival wife of a forbidden relative and is therefore forbidden herself.

"כֵּיצַד אִם מֵתוּ הֵן" כו׳. וַאֲפִילּוּ כָּנַס וּלְבַסּוֹף גֵּירֵשׁ?

§ The mishna taught: **How so? If** the forbidden relative **died,** performed refusal, or was divorced, from that moment onward their rival wives are no longer considered the rival wives of a forbidden relative and are permitted. The Gemara remarks: This legal ruling with regard to a divorce is presented as a general principle **and** is therefore correct **even** if at the time that the deceased brother **married** the rival wife he was married to the forbidden relative, **and ultimately divorced**[H] the relative, which means that for a period of time the women were rival wives. Even under these circumstances the prohibition of a rival wife of a forbidden relative does not apply, and she is permitted to enter into levirate marriage.

NOTES

There are no children without signs – אֵין בָּנִים בְּלֹא סִימָנִים: The early commentaries dispute the precise meaning of this statement. Rashi explains that in Rav Zevid's opinion, a minor who gives birth is assumed to have developed signs of puberty, and signs of puberty from eleven to twelve years of age are equivalent to signs after age twelve. Others agree, but for a different reason: Although Rav Zevid maintains that under ordinary circumstances the appearance of signs between the ages of eleven and twelve is equivalent to the earlier appearance of signs, childbirth is considered not a regular sign but an absolute sign of maturity (Rabbeinu Yitzḥak in *Tosafot*). Ramban and Rashba explain similarly, albeit with a slight variation.

Yet others contend that childbirth is not possible at any age without prior definite signs of puberty. When the Gemara suggests an examination, it does so not because a physical examination is necessary; rather, it is asking about the presumption itself. In other words, it is saying that if this presumption is correct, the matter could be confirmed by examination (Ramban; Rashba; Ritva). The answer, according to this opinion, is that there are in fact signs, but even if they are not found this would not constitute contradictory evidence, as it is possible that due to the pain of childbirth and the difficulty of performing an examination at the right time, the signs have fallen off (see Rashba).

A completely different opinion is that although there is no childbearing without signs, these signs are efficacious only after the age of twelve (Rabbi Yehuda bar Natan). This is apparently the opinion of Rabbi Avraham *Av Beit Din* as well (see Ramban).

As the verse states: To be a rival [*litzror*] – דְּאָמַר קְרָא לִצְרוֹר: Several commentaries omit this statement from the *baraita* cited earlier (3b), since if this opinion is explicitly stated in a *baraita* it does not stand to reason that Rav Ashi would take issue with it (*Tosafot*). Others maintain that this interpretation refers only to the rival wife of a rival wife (*Tosefot HaRosh*). Yet others contend that in the opinion of Rav Ashi the *baraita* does not cite this homiletic interpretation as the true source of the *halakha*, but merely as support, as the ruling that the rival wife of a rival wife is exempt is actually based on logical reasoning (Ritva).

HALAKHA

Even if he married and ultimately divorced – אֲפִילּוּ כָּנַס וּלְבַסּוֹף גֵּירֵשׁ: With regard to a man who was married both to a woman who was a forbidden relative of her potential *yavam* and to another woman, if during the lifetime of the husband the forbidden relative died or if he divorced her, or if she performed refusal, and he subsequently died childless, her rival wife is permitted in levirate marriage, as a forbidden relative renders her rival wife forbidden only at the moment when the mitzva of levirate marriage takes effect, in accordance with the opinion of Rava (Rambam *Sefer Nashim, Hilkhot Yibbum VaḤalitza* 6:21; *Shulḥan Arukh, Even HaEzer* 173:7).

וּרְמִינְהוּ: שְׁלֹשָׁה אַחִים, שְׁנַיִם מֵהֶן נְשׂוּאִים שְׁתֵּי אֲחָיוֹת וְאֶחָד נָשׂוּי נׇכְרִית, גֵּירֵשׁ אֶחָד מִבַּעֲלֵי אֲחָיוֹת אִשְׁתּוֹ וּמֵת הַנָּשׂוּי נׇכְרִית, וּכְנָסָהּ הַמְגָרֵשׁ וּמֵת – זוֹ הִיא שֶׁאָמְרוּ: שֶׁאִם מֵתוּ אוֹ נִתְגָּרְשׁוּ – צָרוֹתֵיהֶן מוּתָּרוֹת.

And the Gemara **raises a contradiction** from a different mishna (30a), which discusses **three brothers, two of whom are married to two sisters and one is married to an unrelated woman. One of the husbands of the sisters** subsequently **divorced his wife, and the one who was married to the unrelated woman died, and the one who divorced** his wife **married** the *yevama* by levirate marriage **and** afterward **died** as well, which means that this *yevama* once again came for levirate marriage before the remaining brother, who was married to one of the sisters. **It is with** regard to **this** case **that they said that if they died or were divorced their rival wives are permitted.** This concludes the mishna.

טַעְמָא דְּגֵירֵשׁ וְאַחַר כָּךְ כָּנַס, אֲבָל כָּנַס וְאַחַר כָּךְ גֵּירֵשׁ – לָא!

The Gemara infers from this mishna: **The reason** she is permitted is **that** the *yavam* first **divorced** the sister **and** only **afterward married** the unrelated woman. In this case, the unrelated woman was never actually the rival wife of a sister, despite the fact that they were, at different times, married to the same man. **However,** if the *yavam* first **married** the unrelated woman **and afterward divorced** the sister, she would **not** be permitted to enter into levirate marriage because for a period of time she had been the rival wife of a forbidden relative.

אָמַר רַבִּי יִרְמְיָה: תַּבְרָא, מִי שֶׁשָּׁנָה זוֹ לֹא שָׁנָה זוֹ. הַאי תַּנָּא סָבַר: מִיתָה מַפֶּלֶת,

These two *mishnayot* apparently contradict each other. **Rabbi Yirmeya said:** This mishna is **disjointed,**[N] i.e., the *mishnayot* are truly incompatible, and the *tanna* **who taught this** *halakha* **did not teach that** *halakha*. The reason for the difference in opinions is that **this** ***tanna***, of the mishna here, **maintains** that **death causes** her to **come before** him for levirate marriage. In other words, the decisive moment that determines the obligation in or exemption from levirate marriage is the moment of the childless brother's death. Since in the case of the mishna here she was not the rival wife of a forbidden relative at the time of his death, the prohibition does not apply to her.

וְהַאי תַּנָּא סָבַר: נִשּׂוּאִין הָרִאשׁוֹנִים מַפִּילִים.

And that ***tanna*** of the mishna dealing with three brothers **maintains** that **the first marriage causes** her to **come before** him for levirate marriage. In other words, the levirate bond is established at the time of the marriage, and since the second wife was the rival wife of a forbidden relative for at least a brief period, her exemption from levirate marriage was determined then.

רָבָא אֲמַר: לְעוֹלָם חַד תַּנָּא הוּא, ״וְזוֹ וְאֵין צָרִיךְ לוֹמַר זוֹ״ קָתָנֵי.

Rava said: Actually, both *mishnayot* represent the opinion of **a single** ***tanna***,[N] **but he teaches** the mishna employing the style: **This and it is unnecessary to say that.** In other words, the mishna here is referring to a case where he first married and later divorced, while the mishna that deals with three brothers is speaking of a simpler, more obvious case, in which he first divorced and later married the second wife. In that case she is certainly permitted. Accordingly, there is no real contradiction here between the *mishnayot*, as they utilize different styles of teaching.

״וְכׇל שֶׁיְּכוֹלָה לְמָאֵן״. וּתְמָאֵן הָשְׁתָּא וְתִתְיַיבֵּם! לֵימָא מְסַיְּיעָא לֵיהּ לְרַבִּי אוֹשַׁעְיָא,

§ The mishna taught: **And** if **any** of these forbidden relatives was a minor **who could refuse** her husband, then even if she did not refuse him, her rival wife performs *ḥalitza* and does not enter into levirate marriage. The Gemara asks: **And let** the minor **perform refusal now,**[N] thereby annulling the marriage retroactively after the death of her husband, **and let her** rival wife **enter into levirate marriage.** Since this option is not accepted, **let us say that it supports** the opinion **of Rabbi Oshaya.**

דְּאָמַר רַבִּי אוֹשַׁעְיָא: מְמָאֶנֶת לְמַאֲמָרוֹ וְאֵינָהּ מְמָאֶנֶת לְזִיקָתוֹ!

As Rabbi Oshaya said: A *yevama* who is a minor can **refuse the levirate betrothal of** the *yavam*. In other words, if he betrothed her she is free to say that she does not desire to marry him, a declaration that severs any connection between them. **But she cannot refuse his bond.**[N] Provided that he has not performed a levirate betrothal, this minor *yevama* cannot annul the ties between them by a refusal, as theirs is not a bond of marriage, and the institution of refusal was established only with regard to marriage. According to this opinion, it is evident that a minor *yevama* who is a forbidden relative cannot perform refusal so as to enable her rival wife to enter levirate marriage.

NOTES

Disjointed [*tavra*] – תַּבְרָא: This expression generally means that various sections of a single mishna or *baraita* reflect disputing opinions. Some commentaries claim that this phrase is used only when the dispute is not explicit (see *Yad Malakhi*). Rashi and others explain that the term *tavra* means broken. In other words, the mishna does not constitute a single unit but is composed of two or more separate sections. Others maintain that this term denotes the taking of an oath, or that it is an expression of special emphasis. In other words: It is clear and evident that such and such is the case. Accordingly, the Gemara should be read as follows: Certainly, he who taught this did not teach that (*Arukh*, citing Rabbeinu Ḥananel).

Actually, a single *tanna* – לְעוֹלָם חַד תַּנָּא: According to this interpretation, the phrase: It is with regard to this case that they said, does not come to exclude other examples but simply to include the present case (Rabbi Yehuda bar Natan).

And let her perform refusal now – וּתְמָאֵן הָשְׁתָּא: Some commentaries ask: In light of the statement that the mishna is in accordance with the opinion of Abba Shaul that the mitzva of *ḥalitza* is preferable to that of levirate marriage, this question is surprising. Why should she perform an act of refusal to enable levirate marriage rather than *ḥalitza*? They answer that the wording of the mishna: Performs *ḥalitza* and does not enter into levirate marriage, indicates that she must undergo *ḥalitza* and does not have the option of levirate marriage at all. *Tosafot* cite a similar interpretation; however, see Meiri.

This question was also raised in the Jerusalem Talmud, in a slightly different form. The Gemara there explains that the phrase: Who could refuse even if she did not, refers to a minor who died, which means that she can no longer perform refusal at all. The early commentaries write that the Gemara here could have explained likewise, but it preferred to interpret the mishna in a manner that suits all cases rather than limit it to a specific example (see Ramban and Rashba).

Can refuse the levirate betrothal…but she cannot refuse his bond – מְמָאֶנֶת לְמַאֲמָרוֹ וְאֵינָהּ מְמָאֶנֶת לְזִיקָתוֹ: The main discussion on this matter of the refusal of a *yevama* appears later in the Gemara (107a). According to one opinion, refusal nullifies only an extant connection. Rabbi Oshaya rules in accordance with this opinion when he states that refusal applies solely to marriage, as this is a relationship based on mutual consent. In contrast, refusal does not apply to a levirate bond, which is a duty mandated by Torah law. The dissenting opinion is that the refusal of a *yevama* is in fact the retroactive annulment of the first marriage, which dissolves the levirate bond automatically. In the Jerusalem Talmud other opinions are cited that differentiate between the ways in which a *yevama* can perform the act of refusal.

לָא, צָרַת עֶרְוָה שָׁאנֵי. דְּתָנֵי רָמִי בַּר יְחֶזְקֵאל: מֵיאֲנָה בְּבַעַל – מוּתֶּרֶת לְאָבִיו, מֵיאֲנָה בְּיָבָם – אֲסוּרָה לְאָבִיו,

The Gemara rejects this suggestion: **No;** it is possible that a minor *yevama* can indeed refuse a levirate bond, but **the rival wife of a forbidden relative is different,** as she is not permitted in levirate marriage even if the forbidden relative herself can perform refusal. Why? **As Rami bar Yeḥezkel taught** in a *baraita*: If **she refused the husband,** thereby annulling the marriage, **she is permitted to his father,** as the marriage bond was entirely nullified retroactively and she is not considered his daughter-in-law at all. If, however, **she refused** only **the** ***yavam*****, she is forbidden to his father.**

אַלְמָא: מִשְּׁעַת נְפִילָה נִרְאֵית כְּכַלָּתוֹ, הָכָא נַמִּי מִשְּׁעַת נְפִילָה נִרְאֵית כְּצָרַת בִּתּוֹ.

Apparently, the reason is that **at the moment** of her **coming before** him for levirate marriage **she had the appearance of his daughter-in-law.** Since people will think she is his daughter-in-law, she is forbidden to the father. **Here, too, at the moment** of her **coming before** him for levirate marriage **she had the appearance of his daughter's rival wife.**[N] Consequently, the Sages did not permit her to enter into levirate marriage even if the other wife refuses the husband.

מתני׳ שֵׁשׁ עֲרָיוֹת חֲמוּרוֹת מֵאֵלּוּ, מִפְּנֵי שֶׁנְּשׂוּאוֹת לַאֲחֵרִים, צָרוֹתֵיהֶן מוּתָּרוֹת:

MISHNA Six women **with whom relations are forbidden** who were not enumerated in the first mishna **are** forbidden by prohibitions that are **more severe**[H] **than those**[N] listed in that mishna **because they may be married** only **to others** and may never be married to any of the brothers, due to the closeness of their relationship. However, this stringency entails a corresponding leniency: Since the *halakha* of levirate marriage is entirely inapplicable in these cases, **their rival wives are permitted.** The rival wife of a forbidden relative is forbidden herself only if the mitzva of levirate marriage is applicable, but where it is not in effect she is permitted.

אִמּוֹ, וְאֵשֶׁת אָבִיו, וַאֲחוֹת אָבִיו, אֲחוֹתוֹ מֵאָבִיו, וְאֵשֶׁת אֲחִי אָבִיו, וְאֵשֶׁת אָחִיו מֵאָבִיו.

The six women with whom relations are forbidden are as follows: **His mother, and his father's wife, and his father's sister, and his paternal** half **sister, and the wife of his father's brother, and the wife of his paternal** half **brother.** Each of these women with whom relations are forbidden is forbidden equally to all of the brothers, and the mitzva of levirate marriage is inapplicable. Therefore, her rival wife is permitted.

בֵּית שַׁמַּאי מַתִּירִין הַצָּרוֹת לָאַחִים, וּבֵית הִלֵּל אוֹסְרִים.

§ Up to this point, the discussions were based on the assumption that not only may a forbidden relative not enter into levirate marriage, but her rival wife is also exempt. However, this issue is subject to a long-standing dispute. **Beit Shammai permit the rival wives to the brothers,** as they did not accept the interpretation of the verses that indicates that rival wives are prohibited. **And Beit Hillel forbid** them. The previous *mishnayot* are in accordance with the opinion of Beit Hillel.

HALAKHA

Six women with whom relations are forbidden are… severe – שֵׁשׁ עֲרָיוֹת חֲמוּרוֹת: In a case where a woman was apparently married to a relative with whom marriage is actually invalid, and this man died, the *yavam* is permitted to take her rival wife in marriage. If this woman who was forbidden to the deceased brother was permitted to the *yavam*, he may marry her and also enter into levirate marriage with the other woman, the proper wife of the deceased (Rambam *Sefer Nashim, Hilkhot Yibbum VaḤalitza* 6:12; *Shulḥan Arukh, Even HaEzer* 173:2).

NOTES

She had the appearance of his daughter's rival wife – נִרְאֵית כְּצָרַת בִּתּוֹ: Some commentaries maintain that according to the opinion of Rami bar Yeḥezkel, a refusal indeed annuls the marriage retroactively and cancels the levirate bond entirely. Consequently, if there is no rival wife of a forbidden relative, the levirate bond is nullified by the refusal. In this case, however, as the woman appears to be his daughter's rival wife, there is concern lest a rival wife of a forbidden relative might be mistakenly permitted in other cases, which is a transgression punishable by *karet*. In standard cases of refusal there is no such concern, as even if they mistakenly render the *yevama* permitted to all, this would entail only a regular prohibition (Rid).

Six women with whom relations are forbidden are more severe than those – שֵׁשׁ עֲרָיוֹת חֲמוּרוֹת מֵאֵלּוּ: Since these forbidden women may not marry the *yevamin* but only other men, their rival wives should be defined as rival wives of those with whom relations are forbidden where the mitzva does not apply. Yet they are not forbidden at all, but the reason is not because they are forbidden by prohibitions that are more severe than those of the first list. Some commentaries explain that the mishna is teaching that even if a *yavam* did marry one of these women, whether intentionally or unwittingly, the marriage is entirely invalid, and therefore her rival wives are permitted (Rambam's Commentary on the Mishna).

חָלְצוּ, בֵּית שַׁמַּאי פּוֹסְלִין מִן הַכְּהוּנָּה, וּבֵית הִלֵּל מַכְשִׁירִין. נִתְיַיבְּמוּ, בֵּית שַׁמַּאי מַכְשִׁירִין וּבֵית הִלֵּל פּוֹסְלִין.

If any of the rival wives of the brother **performed *ḥalitza*,**[H] **Beit Shammai disqualify** her **from** marrying into **the priesthood,** as in their opinion these rival wives were fit for levirate marriage, which means that the *ḥalitza* was fully valid. Consequently, they are disqualified from marrying a priest, like all other women who perform *ḥalitza*. **And Beit Hillel**[P] **deem** them **fit,** as they maintain that no legal act of *ḥalitza* was performed here at all. If **they entered into levirate marriage, Beit Shammai deem** them **fit**[N] for the priesthood, as in their opinion, this is a fully legal levirate marriage. **And Beit Hillel disqualify them,** because they engaged in licentious sexual relations as the rival wives of a forbidden relative.

אַף עַל פִּי שֶׁאֵלּוּ אוֹסְרִים וְאֵלּוּ מַתִּירִין, אֵלּוּ פּוֹסְלִין וְאֵלּוּ מַכְשִׁירִין – לֹא נִמְנְעוּ בֵּית שַׁמַּאי מִלִּישָּׂא נָשִׁים מִבֵּית הִלֵּל, וְלֹא בֵּית הִלֵּל מִבֵּית שַׁמַּאי. כָּל הַטְּהָרוֹת וְהַטְּמְאוֹת שֶׁהָיוּ אֵלּוּ מְטַהֲרִים וְאֵלּוּ מְטַמְּאִין – לֹא נִמְנְעוּ עוֹשִׂין טְהָרוֹת אֵלּוּ עַל גַּבֵּי אֵלּוּ.

§ The mishna comments: **Although** Beit Hillel **prohibit** the rival wives to the brothers **and** Beit Shammai **permit** them, and although **these disqualify** these women **and those deem** them **fit, Beit Shammai did not refrain**[N] **from marrying women from Beit Hillel, nor did Beit Hillel** refrain from marrying women **from Beit Shammai.** Furthermore, with regard to **all of the** disputes concerning the *halakhot* of **ritual purity and impurity, where these** rule that an article is **ritually pure and those** rule it **ritually impure, they did not refrain from handling ritually pure** objects **each with the other,** as Beit Shammai and Beit Hillel frequently used each other's vessels.

גמ׳ אָמַר רַבִּי שִׁמְעוֹן בֶּן פָּזִי: מַאי טַעֲמָא דְּבֵית שַׁמַּאי – דִּכְתִיב ״לֹא תִהְיֶה אֵשֶׁת הַמֵּת הַחוּצָה לְאִישׁ זָר״, ״חוּצָה״ מִכְּלָל דְּאִיכָּא פְּנִימִית. וְאָמַר רַחֲמָנָא: ״לֹא תִהְיֶה״.

GEMARA **Rabbi Shimon ben Pazi said: What is the reason** for the opinion **of Beit Shammai?**[N] **As it is written: "The wife of the dead man shall not be married outside of the family to one not of his kin"** (Deuteronomy 25:5). The term **"outside"** indicates **by inference that there is**[N] a woman who is considered **inside,** i.e., a close relative of the *yavam*, who is inside his family. **And the Merciful One states: "Shall not be** married" and also "to one not of his kin." In other words, even when one of the wives is a forbidden relative, the rival wife who is outside the family of the *yavam* is obligated in levirate marriage.

וּבֵית הִלֵּל: מִיבָּעֵי לְהוּ לְכִדְרַב יְהוּדָה אָמַר רַב. דְּאָמַר רַב יְהוּדָה אָמַר רַב מִנַּיִן שֶׁאֵין קִידּוּשִׁין תּוֹפְסִין בִּיבָמָה, שֶׁנֶּאֱמַר ״לֹא תִהְיֶה אֵשֶׁת הַמֵּת הַחוּצָה לְאִישׁ זָר״ – לֹא תִהְיֶה בָּהּ הֲוָיָה לְזָר.

And how do **Beit Hillel** respond to this argument of Beit Shammai? **They require these** passages **for that which Rav Yehuda said** that **Rav said,**[N] **as Rav Yehuda said** that **Rav said: From where** is it derived **that betrothal is not effective** in the case **of a *yevama*** who did not perform *ḥalitza*, if the betrothal is performed by an unrelated man and not a *yavam*? This betrothal is not valid at all, **as it is stated: The wife of the dead man shall not be married outside of the family to one not of his kin"** (Deuteronomy 25:5). This verse indicates that **there shall not be in her** case **the becoming** married **to one not of his kin.**

וּבֵית שַׁמַּאי: מִי כְּתִיב ״לַחוּץ״? ״חוּצָה״ כְּתִיב. וּבֵית הִלֵּל: כֵּיוָן דִּכְתִיב ״חוּצָה״ כְּמַאן דִּכְתִיב ״לַחוּץ״ דָּמֵי.

And how do **Beit Shammai** respond to this claim? They ask: **Is it written: To the outside** [*laḥutz*], which might indicate betrothal to an unrelated man? **It is** actually **written "outside** [*ḥutza*]," which is an adjective describing this woman as one who is from the outside. **And Beit Hillel,** what is their response? They maintain that **since it is written "outside," it is considered as though it is written: To the outside.**

HALAKHA

***Ḥalitza* for rival wives** – חֲלִיצָה לְצָרוֹת: If one performs the act of *ḥalitza* with a woman exempt from levirate marriage and *ḥalitza*, e.g., the rival wife of a forbidden relative, it is not considered *ḥalitza* and she is fit to marry a priest, in accordance with the opinion of Beit Hillel (Rambam *Sefer Nashim, Hilkhot Yibbum VaḤalitza* 4:16).

NOTES

If they entered into levirate marriage Beit Shammai deem them fit, etc. – נִתְיַיבְּמוּ, בֵּית שַׁמַּאי מַכְשִׁירִים וכו׳: Rashi and most commentaries explain that question is whether a rival wife who entered into levirate marriage and was subsequently widowed by the *yavam* is fit to marry a priest. Others claim that the dispute is with regard to the status of the children born to these rival wives. According to Beit Shammai they are legitimate, whereas Beit Hillel maintain that they are disqualified as *mamzerim*.

Beit Shammai did not refrain, etc. – לֹא נִמְנְעוּ בֵּית שַׁמַּאי וכו׳: This observation was stated specifically with regard to this dispute rather than one of the many other disagreements between Beit Shammai and Beit Hillel, because in other cases it is possible simply to act stringently in accordance with the conflicting opinion. Here, however, the adoption of the stringency of the other opinion would constitute a violation of a prohibition of their own ruling, and therefore the conflict could not be resolved in this manner (*Lekaḥ Yosef*; see Ritva).

What is the reason of Beit Shammai – מַאי טַעֲמָא דְּבֵית שַׁמַּאי: Why doesn't the Gemara simply state that Beit Shammai do not accept Beit Hillel's interpretation of the term *litzror* (*Tosafot*)? Some commentaries explain that the Gemara did not want to say that Beit Shammai merely negate the opinion of Beit Hillel, as it preferred to seek a positive reason for their ruling.

Outside, indicates by inference that there is, etc. – חוּצָה מִכְּלָל דְּאִיכָּא וכו׳: Some commentaries say that this statement serves to explain why the verse is superfluous. Since the simple meaning of the term: Outside, is not necessary to understand the verse, it is therefore available for interpretation (*Tosefot Rid*). In the Jerusalem Talmud (1:6) a problematic comparison is drawn between the opinion of Beit Shammai and that of the Samaritans, who similarly derived from here that only a woman betrothed, who is outside a proper marriage is fit for levirate marriage.

For that which Rav Yehuda said that Rav said – לְכִדְרַב יְהוּדָה אָמַר רַב: The commentaries point out that Rav's opinion is not accepted by everyone, as Shmuel disagrees with him (*Tosafot*). They explain that Shmuel requires this verse for a different *halakha*. Some explain that as the Gemara will conclude that a different ruling is derived from this verse, it did not deem it necessary to clarify all of the various opinions (Rashba).

PERSONALITIES

Beit Shammai and Beit Hillel – בֵּית שַׁמַּאי וּבֵית הִלֵּל: These refer to the groups of disciples of the Sages Hillel and Shammai. Although there are only three recorded matters of dispute between Hillel and Shammai themselves, their students were constant disputants who served together in the Sanhedrin at the end of the Second Temple period and after its destruction, and disagreed about many points of *halakha*. With regard to the disagreements of these two houses, a mishna (*Avot* 5:20) states: Any controversy waged for the sake of Heaven shall in the end be of lasting worth, but any that is not waged for the sake of Heaven shall in the end lead to no permanent result. Which controversy was an example of one waged in the service of Heaven? It is the controversy of Hillel and Shammai. And which was not for the sake Heaven? It is the controversy of Korah and his company.

Generally speaking, the disciples of Hillel and Shammai mirrored the positions of their teachers, the open, tolerant Hillel and the harsh, severe Shammai, although there are exceptions to this rule. All of the cases in which the disciples of Shammai were more lenient than the disciples of Hillel are listed in tractate *Eduyyot*. In most disputes between Beit Shammai and Beit Hillel, the *halakha* is in accordance with the opinion of Beit Hillel.

דְּתַנְיָא, רַבִּי נְחֶמְיָה אוֹמֵר: כׇּל תֵּיבָה שֶׁצְּרִיכָה לָמֶ״ד בִּתְחִלָּתָהּ – הִטִּיל לָהּ הַכָּתוּב הֵ״א בְּסוֹפָהּ. וְתַנָּא דְּבֵי רַבִּי יִשְׁמָעֵאל: כְּגוֹן ״אֵלִים״ ״אֵלִימָה״, ״מַחֲנַיִם״ ״מַחֲנַיְמָה״, ״מִצְרַיִם״ ״מִצְרַיְמָה״, ״דִּבְלָתָיְמָה״, ״יְרוּשָׁלַיְמָה״, ״מִדְבָּרָה״.

As it is taught in a *baraita*: **Rabbi Neḥemya says** that with regard to **any word that requires** the letter ***lamed* at its beginning,** meaning: To, **the verse** at times **placed** a letter ***heh* at its end,**[N] but the meaning is the same. **And the school of Rabbi Yishmael taught: For example,** the term: To **"Elim"** (Exodus 16:1) can be rendered as ***"Elima"*** (Exodus 15:27) instead of *le'Elim*; **"Maḥanaim"** (I Kings 2:8) becomes ***"Maḥanaima"*** (II Samuel 17:24); ***"Mitzraim"*** (e.g., Genesis 13:1) into ***"Mitzraima"*** (Genesis 12:10); Divlatayim is ***"Divlataima"*** (Numbers 33:46); to *Yerushalaim* is ***"Yerushalaima"*** (Ezekiel 8:3); and ***"midbara"*** (Joshua 18:12) means: To the wilderness [*midbar*]. All these words that contain the letter *heh* at the end mean the same as if there were a *lamed* at the beginning.

וּבֵית שַׁמַּאי, דְּרַב יְהוּדָה אֲמַר רַב מְנָא לְהוּ? מִ״לְּאִישׁ זָר״ נָפְקָא.

The Gemara asks: **And Beit Shammai, from where do they** derive that *halakha* **that Rav Yehuda** said that **Rav said?** The Gemara answers: They **derive it from** the phrase: **"To one not of his kin"** (Deuteronomy 25:5). This phrase indicates that marriage is invalid with an unrelated man. However, they learn another matter from the term "outside."

וּבֵית הִלֵּל נַמִי, תֵּיפּוֹק לְהוּ מִ״לְּאִישׁ זָר״! אִין הָכִי נַמִי ״חוּצָה״ לָמָּה לִי – לְרַבּוֹת הָאֲרוּסָה.

The Gemara asks: **But** if so, **let Beit Hillel, too, derive this** *halakha* **from: "To one not of his kin."** The Gemara answers: **Yes, it is indeed so.** They, too, infer it from this source. Then **why do I** need the term **"outside"?** This word was necessary **to include a betrothed woman.**[NH] With regard to a woman who was betrothed but not yet married to the deceased brother, although she is still technically outside his house, she is nevertheless obligated in levirate marriage.

וְאִידָךְ: מִ״חוּצָה״ ״הַחוּצָה״ – וְאִידָךְ: ״חוּצָה״ ״הַחוּצָה״ לָא מַשְׁמַע לְהוּ.

And the other one, Beit Shammai, infers this halakhic ruling **from** a single superfluous letter, as instead of "outside" being written as *ḥutza* it is written as ***haḥutza*.** **And** as for **the other** one, Beit Hillel, they **do not derive** a *halakha* from the linguistic difference between ***ḥutza* and *haḥutza*,** as they maintain that this is not a significant enough difference.

רָבָא אֲמַר: טַעֲמַיְיהוּ דְּבֵית שַׁמַּאי, דְּאֵין אִיסּוּר חָל עַל אִיסּוּר.

§ **Rava said: The rationale of Beit Shammai** for their opinion that rival wives are permitted in levirate marriage is not due to a specific verse. Rather, Beit Shammai apply the well-known halakhic principle **that a prohibition does not take effect** where **another prohibition** already exists.[NH] Since the first wife was already a prohibited relation to her brother-in-law during his brother's lifetime, the second prohibition of a wife's sister does not apply to her. Accordingly, her presence is entirely disregarded, as though there is no forbidden relative here to exempt the rival wife.

תֵּינַח הֵיכָא דְּנָשָׂא מֵת וְאַחַר כָּךְ נָשָׂא חַי – לָא אָתֵי אִיסּוּר אֲחוֹת אִשָּׁה וְחָיֵיל אַאִיסּוּר אֵשֶׁת אָח, אֶלָּא נָשָׂא חַי וְאַחַר כָּךְ נָשָׂא מֵת, אֲחוֹת אִשָּׁה קָדֵים!

The Gemara raises a difficulty: This works out **well where the deceased** brother had first **married** one sister **and afterward the surviving** brother had **married** another sister, as in this case it is possible to say that the **prohibition of a wife's sister does not come and apply** in addition **to the prohibition of a brother's wife. However,** if **the surviving** brother had **married** one sister **and afterward** the **deceased** brother had **married** another sister, in this case the prohibition of **a wife's sister precedes** that of a brother's wife. How can it be said in this situation that this prohibition of a forbidden relative does not take effect where another prohibition already exists, if actually it came first?

NOTES

Placed a *heh* at its end – הִטִּיל לָהּ...הֵ״א בְּסוֹפָהּ: In the Jerusalem Talmud the point is raised that the variation on the term netherworld [*she'ol*] in the verse: "The wicked shall return to the netherworld [*lishe'ola*]" (Psalms 9:18), apparently contradicts this principle, as it includes both a *lamed* at the beginning and a *heh* at the end. The Gemara there explains that this refers to an extra level of depth inside the netherworld, i.e., the lowest chamber in the netherworld (Ritva).

To include a betrothed woman – לְרַבּוֹת הָאֲרוּסָה: The commentaries ask why this is not simply derived from the phrase "wife of the dead man" (Deuteronomy 25:5), which includes both married and betrothed women. They answer that since the Torah later states: "His brother's house" (Deuteronomy 25:9), an expression that apparently refers only to a married woman, a special verse was necessary to include a betrothed woman. Others add that the assumption that a betrothed woman is unfit for levirate marriage is based on the reference to the deceased as having no child, which indicates that he was fully married and could have fathered a child (Rashba).

Beit Shammai apply that a prohibition does not take effect where another prohibition already exists – בֵּית שַׁמַּאי דְּאֵין אִיסּוּר חָל עַל אִיסּוּר: Despite the apparently straightforward logic of this explanation, it raises many difficulties, which are scrutinized by the early and later commentaries. One difficulty is that this principle, here applied by Beit Shammai, is in fact accepted as *halakha*; many *tanna'im* and *amora'im* hold that a prohibition does not take effect where another prohibition already exists, and it cannot be that they all follow the ruling of Beit Shammai. Evidently, Beit Hillel also accept that principle in most cases, but this instance is an exception, as the term *litzror* indicates a different ruling (*Tosafot Yeshanim*; Ritva).

Some claim that there is a difference between the opinions, as Beit Shammai maintain that a prohibition does not take effect at all where another prohibition already exists, and it is as though there were no prohibition, whereas Beit Hillel maintain that although the second prohibition does not entail any penalty, it is not entirely negated (*Aḥiezer*). An additional difficulty is that it does not stand to reason that Beit Shammai would reject the interpretation of *litzror* merely because of their application of the principle that a prohibition does not take effect where another prohibition already exists. Consequently, some commentaries explain that Beit Shammai do not entirely reject the interpretation of the verse, as they hold that this interpretation is valid in cases where the two prohibitions come into effect simultaneously. In these cases, Beit Shammai concede that the prohibition of a rival wife of a forbidden relative applies (*Tosafot Yeshanim*; see Meiri). According to this interpretation the ensuing deliberations of the Gemara with regard to which prohibition came first may be more readily understood (see Rashba).

Tosafot and most early commentaries explain that one further difficulty is that if in fact the principle that a prohibition does not take effect where another prohibition already exists applies to these cases, then even the forbidden relative herself should be permitted. Some commentaries explain that the prohibition of a forbidden relative is suspended until the death of the husband. When he dies, the prohibition of a brother's wife is nullified, and the other prohibition comes into effect. However, for the exemption of a rival wife the prohibition would have had to have been in effect during his lifetime.

HALAKHA

Levirate marriage with a betrothed woman – יִיבּוּם לַאֲרוּסָה: The mitzva of levirate marriage applies whether the *yevama* was married to the deceased brother or betrothed to him (Rambam *Sefer Nashim*, *Hilkhot Yibbum VaḤalitza* 1:1; *Shulḥan Arukh*, *Even HaEzer* 44:7).

A prohibition does not take effect where another prohibition already exists – אֵין אִיסּוּר חָל עַל אִיסּוּר: It is an important principle with regard to all prohibitions in the Torah that a prohibition does not take effect where another prohibition already exists, unless both prohibitions came into effect at once, or if one prohibition adds to the other prohibition, or if the second is a more inclusive prohibition (Rambam *Sefer Kedusha*, *Hilkhot Issurei Bia* 17:8).

HALAKHA

The time of reading of the Scroll of Esther – זְמַן קְרִיאַת מְגִילָּה: The Scroll of Esther is read on the fifteenth of Adar in cities that has been surrounded by a wall from the days of Joshua, and on the fourteenth in all other places. In earlier generations, it was read in the small villages only on Monday or Thursday, which meant that they would read even on the eleventh, twelfth, or thirteenth of Adar (Rambam *Sefer Zemanim*, *Hilkhot Megilla* 1:4, 7).

Cutting over the dead – חֲבוּרָה עַל מֵת: One who makes a single incision in his flesh in mourning for the dead is liable to receive lashes for violating the prohibition: "You shall not cut yourselves…for the dead" (Deuteronomy 14:1; Rambam *Sefer HaMadda*, *Hilkhot Avoda Zara* 12:12, 13).

NOTES

You shall not cut yourselves [*titgodedu*] – לֹא תִתְגּוֹדְדוּ: The root *g-d-d* bears several meanings, two of which can be found in the Torah: the creation of a wound or bruise, or a group or gathering. As a result of this double meaning, the statement in Deuteronomy is interpreted by the Sages as referring to two separate prohibitions.

Let the verse state: You shall not cut – לֵימָא קְרָא לֹא תְגוֹדְדוּ: If the verse were stated in this form, it would be evident that there is a prohibition against cutting one's flesh. The meaning of the reflexive form of the verb: "You shall not cut yourselves," further indicates the division of the people into separate and individual factions (Ritva).

But say that the entire verse comes for this – וְאֵימָא כּוּלֵּיהּ לְהָכִי הוּא דַּאֲתָא: According to Rashi, the Gemara is suggesting that the entire verse might come only to prohibit the formation of factions and is not related to the practices of mourning at all. The problem is that it is unlikely that a verse would not refer to its context at all. However, it is possible to explain that as the Torah had just stated: "You are children of the Lord" (Deuteronomy 14:1), it might have been thought that the verse follows this statement with two prohibitions that involve behavior unbecoming for children of God: Gathering into contentious factions and making a bald spot for the dead (Ritva; *Ramat Shmuel*). Other early commentaries cite the interpretation of the *ge'onim* that the question is actually whether the verse might be prohibiting only cutting for the dead.

כֵּיוָן דְּלָא אָתֵי אִיסּוּר אֵשֶׁת אָח וְחָיֵיל אַאִיסּוּר אֲחוֹת אִשָּׁה – הָוְיָא לָהּ צָרַת עֶרְוָה שֶׁלֹּא בִּמְקוֹם מִצְוָה, וְשַׁרְיָא.

The Gemara answers: **Since the prohibition of a brother's wife does not come and apply** in addition **to the prohibition of a wife's sister,** the status of a brother's wife does not pertain to her and she is not obligated in levirate marriage with him at all. This means that the other wife **is a rival wife of a forbidden relative where no mitzva applies, and she is** therefore **permitted.**

״חָלְצוּ, בֵּית שַׁמַּאי פּוֹסְלִים״ וכו׳. פְּשִׁיטָא!

§ The mishna taught: If any of the rival wives of the brother **performed *ḥalitza*, Beit Shammai disqualify** her from marrying into the priesthood, as they hold that the *ḥalitza* was fully valid. The Gemara asks: If the rival wives are obligated in the mitzva of levirate marriage and they performed *ḥalitza*, it **is obvious** that the status of a woman who had undergone *ḥalitza* applies to them.

לְאַפּוֹקֵי דְּרַבִּי יוֹחָנָן בֶּן נוּרִי, דַּאֲמַר: בּוֹאוּ וּנְתַקֵּן לָהֶם לַצָּרוֹת שֶׁיְּהוּ חוֹלְצוֹת וְלֹא מִתְיַיבְּמוֹת – קָא מַשְׁמַע לָן דְּבֵית הִלֵּל מַכְשִׁירִים.

The Gemara answers: This statement comes **to exclude** the opinion **of Rabbi Yoḥanan ben Nuri, who said: Come and let us institute for rival wives** of women with whom relations are forbidden **that they should perform *ḥalitza* and not enter into levirate marriage.** If this ordinance were accepted, these rival wives would be disqualified by rabbinic law, even according to the opinion of Beit Hillel. The mishna therefore **teaches us that Beit Hillel deem** the rival wives fully **fit** to marry into the priesthood, as no *ḥalitza* was instituted for rival wives and any *ḥalitza* performed with them is entirely meaningless.

״נִתְיַיבְּמוּ בֵּית הִלֵּל פּוֹסְלִין״ כו׳. הָא תּוּ לָמָּה לִי? אַיְּידֵי דְּתָנָא חָלְצוּ, תָּנָא נַמִי נִתְיַיבְּמוּ.

§ The mishna further taught: If **they entered into levirate marriage,** Beit Shammai deem them fit for the priesthood and **Beit Hillel disqualify them.** The Gemara asks: **Why do I need this as well,** as this *halakha* follows logically from the previous statement concerning *ḥalitza*? The Gemara answers that **since** the mishna **taught: Performed *ḥalitza*, it also taught** the case of: **Entered into levirate marriage,** despite the fact that this was not necessary, as even without this ruling the matter would have been understood.

תְּנַן הָתָם: מְגִילָּה נִקְרֵאת בְּאַחַד עָשָׂר וּבִשְׁנֵים עָשָׂר וּבִשְׁלֹשָׁה עָשָׂר וּבְאַרְבָּעָה עָשָׂר וּבַחֲמִשָּׁה עָשָׂר, לֹא פָּחוֹת וְלֹא יוֹתֵר.

§ Apropos the mishna's comments concerning the details of the relationship between Beit Shammai and Beit Hillel, the Gemara discusses the issue of disputes in general. **We learned** in a mishna **there,** in tractate *Megilla* (2a): **The Megilla,** the Scroll of Esther, **is read**[H] **on the eleventh** of Adar, **on the twelfth, on the thirteenth, on the fourteenth, or on the fifteenth,** in cities surrounded by a wall, **no earlier and no later** than this. The obligation to read the Megilla on the fourteenth or fifteenth of Adar is stated in the Megilla itself, while the additional days were instituted by the Sages to allow residents of villages, who would come to the cities on Mondays and Thursdays and supply water and rations to the residents of the cities, to hear the reading of the Megilla at that opportunity.

אֲמַר לֵיהּ רֵישׁ לָקִישׁ לְרַבִּי יוֹחָנָן: אִיקְּרֵי כָּאן ״לֹא תִתְגּוֹדְדוּ״ – לֹא תַּעֲשׂוּ אֲגוּדּוֹת אֲגוּדּוֹת! הַאי ״לֹא תִתְגּוֹדְדוּ״ מִיבְּעֵי לֵיהּ לְגוּפֵיהּ, דְּאָמַר רַחֲמָנָא: לֹא תַּעֲשׂוּ חַבּוּרָה עַל מֵת!

Reish Lakish said to Rabbi Yoḥanan: I should **read here** the verse: **"You shall not cut yourselves [*titgodedu*]"** (Deuteronomy 14:1),[N] which is interpreted as meaning: **Do not become numerous factions [*agudot*].** In other words, the Jewish people should be united, rather than divided into disparate groups that act in different ways. Before analyzing this issue, the Gemara asks: **This** verse: **"You shall not cut yourselves," is required for the matter itself, as the Merciful One is saying: Do not cut yourselves over the dead.**[H] How is the *halakha* concerning factions derived from this apparently straightforward verse?

אִם כֵּן לֵימָא קְרָא ״לֹא תְגוֹדְדוּ״, מַאי ״תִּתְגוֹדְדוּ״ – שְׁמַע מִינָּהּ לְהָכִי הוּא דַּאֲתָא. וְאֵימָא כּוּלֵּיהּ לְהָכִי הוּא דַּאֲתָא? אִם כֵּן לֵימָא קְרָא ״לֹא תָגוֹדוּ״ מַאי ״לֹא תִתְגּוֹדְדוּ״ – שְׁמַע מִינָּהּ תַּרְתֵּי.

The Gemara answers: **If so,** that the verse comes to teach only about the practices of mourning, **let the verse state** only: **You shall not cut.**[N] **What** is the meaning of: **"You shall not cut yourselves"? Learn from this** that **it comes for this** purpose as well, to teach the prohibition against splitting into factions. The Gemara asks: **But** in that case, one can **say** that **the entire** verse **comes for this**[N] purpose and does not refer to cutting for the dead at all. The Gemara answers: **If so, let the verse state: *Lo tagodu*,** rather than *lo titgodedu*, both of which mean: **You shall not cut. What** is the meaning of: ***"Lo titgodedu"*? Conclude two** conclusions **from it:** Both the simple prohibition against making cuts for the dead and the matter of dividing into factions.

אמר ליה: עד כאן לא שנית מקום שנהגו לעשות מלאכה בערבי פסחים עד חצות – עושין, מקום שנהגו שלא לעשות – אין עושין?

After this incidental discussion, the Gemara returns to the basic question raised by Reish Lakish: Why doesn't the reading of the Scroll of Esther in different places at different times violate the prohibition against breaking into factions? Rabbi Yoḥanan **said to him:** Have **you not taught until now:**[N] In **a place where** the people were **accustomed to perform labor on Passover eve**[H] **until midday, one may do** so on that day; in **a place where** the people were **accustomed not to perform** labor, **one may not do** so? This shows that different places can have different customs without violating the prohibition against dividing into factions.

אמר ליה: אמינא לך אנא איסורא, דאמר רב שמן בר אבא אמר רבי יוחנן: "לקיים את ימי הפורים בזמניהם", זמנים הרבה תיקנו להם חכמים, ואת אמרת לי מנהגא!

Reish Lakish **said to** Rabbi Yoḥanan: **I speak to you** of **a prohibition,** as residents of villages are prohibited from reading the Megilla with a blessing on the fifteenth of Adar, **as Rav Shemen bar Abba said** that **Rabbi Yoḥanan said:** The verse **"to confirm** these **days of Purim in their appointed times"** (Esther 9:31) teaches that **the Sages instituted many times for their** reading, and it is prohibited to deviate from these dates. **And you speak to me** about **a custom** that does not involve a prohibition. How can a prohibition be established in a manner that involves the formation of factions among the people?

והתם לאו איסורא הויא? והתנן: (בלילה) בית שמאי אוסרין ובית הלל מתירין!

Rabbi Yoḥanan replied: **And** in that case **there,** on Passover eve, is **there no prohibition** involved? **But didn't we learn** in a mishna: **On the night** before the fourteenth of Nisan, **Beit Shammai prohibit** the performance of work **and Beit Hillel permit it.** Evidently, there is indeed a prohibition involved, and yet some perform work while others do not, which splits the people into factions.

אמר ליה: התם הרואה אומר מלאכה הוא דלית ליה. והא בית שמאי מתירין הצרות לאחים, ובית הלל אוסרים!

Reish Lakish **said to him:** In that case **there,** the different factions are not noticeable, as **one who sees** another idle **says: It is** because **he has no labor** to perform. Therefore, refraining from work does not have the appearance of breaking off into factions. Rabbi Yoḥanan raises a difficulty: **But Beit Shammai permit rival wives to the brothers, and Beit Hillel prohibit** this practice. This is an example of a clear prohibition, and yet two different traditions were followed.

NOTES

Have you not taught until now – **עד כאן לא שנית**: This raises the question: Doesn't Reish Lakish's question apply to this *halakha* as well? If so, this is not an answer but an additional difficulty. Evidently, even Reish Lakish would agree that divergent behavior in different places does not constitute the formation of factions. Rabbi Yoḥanan is attempting to say that different legal rulings for villages, towns, and cities stem from the disparate customs in these places (Rosh).

HALAKHA

Performing labor on Passover eve – **עשיית מלאכה בערב פסח**: In a place where it is customary to perform labor on Passover eve, the residents may do so, and in a place where this is not the custom, they may not perform labor (Rambam *Sefer Zemanim, Hilkhot Yom Tov* 8:18; *Shulḥan Arukh, Oraḥ Ḥayyim* 468:3).

Perek **I**
Daf **14** Amud **a**

מי סברת עשו בית שמאי כדבריהם? לא עשו בית שמאי כדבריהם. ורבי יוחנן אמר: עשו ועשו, ובפלוגתא [דרב ושמואל], דרב אומר: לא עשו בית שמאי כדבריהם, ושמואל אמר: עשו ועשו.

Reish Lakish said to him: **Do you hold** that **Beit Shammai** actually **acted in accordance with their** own **statement? Beit Shammai did not** in fact **act in accordance with their** own **statement,**[N] as the dispute was merely theoretical. **And Rabbi Yoḥanan said:** Beit Shammai **certainly did act**[N] in accordance with their opinion. The Gemara comments: **And** this is also reflected **in the dispute between Rav and Shmuel, as Rav says: Beit Shammai did not act in accordance with their** own **statement, and Shmuel said: They certainly did act** in that manner.

אימת? אילימא קודם בת קול – מאי טעמא דמאן דאמר לא עשו? ואלא לאחר בת קול – מאי טעמא דמאן דאמר עשו?

The Gemara inquires: **When** does this question apply? **If we say** that it is referring to the period **prior to** the **Divine Voice** that declared that the *halakha* is in accordance with the opinion of Beit Hillel, then **what is the rationale of the one who said that** Beit Shammai **did not act** in accordance with their opinion? **But rather,** if one would say it is referring to **after** the **Divine Voice, what is the reason for the one who said** that **they did act** in accordance with their opinion? After all, the Divine Voice established that the *halakha* is in accordance with the opinion of Beit Hillel.

NOTES

Beit Shammai did not act in accordance with their statement – **לא עשו בית שמאי כדבריהם**: The suggestion is that Beit Shammai demanded that the rival wives perform *ḥalitza*, which prevented them from coming into conflict with the opinion of Beit Hillel (Ritva). Many early and later commentaries discuss the possibility that Beit Shammai followed their own opinion only with regard to stringent rulings, not leniencies. The same question applies in general to other disputes between Beit Shammai and Beit Hillel.

They certainly did act [*asu ve'asu*] – **עשו ועשו**: Although this kind of emphatic language by doubling the word is common, in this case some commentaries explain that the repetition of the word *asu* means: They themselves did so and also instructed others to do the same (Rashba).

HALAKHA

You shall not cut yourselves – לֹא תִתְגּוֹדְדוּ: It is prohibited to maintain two courts in one city if one follows one custom and the other a different custom (Rambam). This ruling is apparently in accordance with the opinion of Abaye. The commentaries on the Rambam question why he accepts the opinion of Abaye against that of Rava, which contradicts both the principle that the halakha is generally ruled in accordance with the opinion of Rava in his disputes with Abaye and the flow of the talmudic discussion here. Some suggest that the *halakha* is in accordance with the opinion of Rava against Abaye only when their dispute concerns their own statements, not when they are explaining other opinions, as is the case here (*Kesef Mishne*). Others resolve the difficulty by changing the wording of the Rambam's ruling so that he actually rules in accordance with the opinion of Rava. In other words, only if some members of the same court issued a different ruling than their colleagues would this be a violation of the prohibition: Do not become numerous factions. However, these commentaries are uncertain about this claim (see *Leḥem Mishne*).

Both the Rif and the Rosh rule in accordance with the opinion of Rava that the prohibition applies only when a single court is divided in its rulings. The Rema states that there should not be two different customs in the same city, which is apparently in accordance with the ruling of the Rambam (Rambam *Sefer HaMadda*, *Hilkhot Avoda Zara* 12:14; *Shulḥan Arukh*, *Oraḥ Ḥayyim* 493:3, and in the comment of Rema).

אִי בָּעֵית אֵימָא קוֹדֶם בַּת קוֹל, וְאִי בָּעֵית אֵימָא לְאַחַר בַּת קוֹל. אִי בָּעֵית אֵימָא קוֹדֶם בַּת קוֹל: וּכְגוֹן דְּבֵית הִלֵּל רוּבָּא, לְמַאן דַּאֲמַר לֹא עָשׂוּ דְּהָא בֵּית הִלֵּל רוּבָּא,

The Gemara answers: Neither of these options poses a difficulty. **If you wish, say** that it is referring to the period **prior to the Divine Voice, and if you wish, say** instead that it is **after** the **Divine Voice.** The Gemara elaborates: **If you wish, say** it is **prior to the Divine Voice, and** it is referring to the period **when Beit Hillel** formed **the majority** of the Sages. Therefore, **according to the one who said** that Beit Shammai **did not act** in accordance with their opinion, the reason is **that Beit Hillel** was **the majority,** and the *halakha* is in accordance with the majority.

וּמַאן דַּאֲמַר עָשׂוּ – כִּי אָזְלִינַן בָּתַר רוּבָּא הֵיכָא דִּכְי הֲדָדֵי נִינְהוּ, הָכָא – בֵּית שַׁמַּאי מְחַדְּדֵי טְפֵי.

And the one who said that **they did act** in accordance with their opinion maintains that **when do we follow the majority?** It is in a case **where** the disputing parties **are equal** in wisdom **to one another. Here,** however, **Beit Shammai are sharper** than Beit Hillel, and therefore they acted in accordance with their own opinion despite the fact that they were in the minority.

וְאִי בָּעֵית אֵימָא לְאַחַר בַּת קוֹל: מַאן דַּאֲמַר לֹא עָשׂוּ – דְּהָא נָפְקָא בַּת קוֹל, וּמַאן דַּאֲמַר עָשׂוּ – רַבִּי יְהוֹשֻׁעַ הִיא, דַּאֲמַר: אֵין מַשְׁגִּיחִין בְּבַת קוֹל.

And if you wish, say instead that it was **after** the **Divine Voice. The one who said** that Beit Shammai **did not act** in accordance with their opinion would say **that** this was due to the **pronouncement** of the **Divine Voice. And the one who said** that **they did do so, this is** in accordance with the opinion of **Rabbi Yehoshua, who said,** with regard to the Divine Voice that emerged and proclaimed that the *halakha* is in accordance with the opinion of Rabbi Eliezer in the case of the oven of *akhnai* (*Bava Metzia* 59b), that **one disregards a Heavenly Voice.** Just as he disregarded the Divine Voice in his dispute with Rabbi Eliezer, so too, one disregards the Divine Voice that proclaimed that the *halakha* is in accordance with the opinion of Beit Hillel.

וּמַאן דַּאֲמַר עָשׂוּ, קָרֵינַן כָּאן ״לֹא תִתְגּוֹדְדוּ״ – לֹא תַעֲשׂוּ אֲגוּדּוֹת אֲגוּדּוֹת! אֲמַר אַבַּיֵי: כִּי אָמְרִינַן ״לֹא תִתְגּוֹדְדוּ״ – כְּגוֹן שְׁתֵּי בָּתֵּי דִינִים בְּעִיר אַחַת, הַלָּלוּ מוֹרִים כְּדִבְרֵי בֵית שַׁמַּאי וְהַלָּלוּ מוֹרִים כְּדִבְרֵי בֵית הִלֵּל. אֲבָל שְׁתֵּי בָּתֵּי דִינִים בִּשְׁתֵּי עֲיָירוֹת – לֵית לָן בָּהּ.

And yet the question remains: According to **the one who said** that Beit Shammai **acted** in accordance with their opinion, **we** should **read here: "You shall not cut yourselves"** (Deuteronomy 14:1),[H] which is interpreted to mean: **Do not become numerous factions. Abaye said: When we say** that the prohibition: **"You shall not cut yourselves"** applies, we are referring to a case **where two courts** are located **in one city,** and **these rule in accordance with the statement of Beit Shammai and those rule in accordance with the statement of Beit Hillel. However,** with regard to **two courts**[N] located **in two** different **cities, we have no** problem **with it.**

אֲמַר לֵיהּ רָבָא: וְהָא בֵּית שַׁמַּאי וּבֵית הִלֵּל כִּשְׁתֵּי בָּתֵּי דִינִים בְּעִיר אַחַת דָּמֵי! אֶלָּא אֲמַר רָבָא: כִּי אָמְרִינַן ״לֹא תִתְגּוֹדְדוּ״ – כְּגוֹן בֵּית דִּין בְּעִיר אַחַת, פֶּלֶג מוֹרִין כְּדִבְרֵי בֵית שַׁמַּאי וּפֶלֶג מוֹרִין כְּדִבְרֵי בֵית הִלֵּל. אֲבָל שְׁתֵּי בָּתֵּי דִינִין בְּעִיר אַחַת – לֵית לָן בָּהּ.

Rava said to him: But the dispute between **Beit Shammai and Beit Hillel is considered like** a case of **two courts**[N] **in one city,** as these two schools of thought were found everywhere, not in any specific place. **Rather, Rava said: When we say** that the prohibition: **"You shall not cut yourselves"**[N] applies, we are referring to a case **where** there is **a court in one city, a section** of which **rules in accordance with the statement of Beit Shammai and** another **section rules in accordance with the statement of Beit Hillel. However,** with regard to **two courts** located **in one city, we have no** problem **with it.**

NOTES

However, two courts, etc. – אֲבָל שְׁתֵּי בָּתֵּי דִינִים וכו׳: The early commentaries discuss the apparent conflict between Abaye's statement and the custom of villagers to read the Scroll of Esther on various dates in Adar. The problem is that even when these villagers would go to the city they would read in accordance with the custom of their own place. Some answer that the villagers did not, in fact, read in the cities at all, but only in their own locales (*Tosafot*; Rav Avraham Av Bet Din).

Others suggest that the question refers to those who would read on the fourteenth or fifteenth of Adar, as in these cases the people who do not read in accordance with the tradition of a specific place are in violation of a prohibition, as stated in the Megilla itself. With regard to the villagers, however, all agree that they are simply following a custom, and therefore this does not present a difficulty to the opinion of Abaye (Rashba).

But the dispute between Beit Shammai…is…like two courts – וְהָא בֵּית שַׁמַּאי...כִּשְׁתֵּי בָּתֵּי דִינִים: Some commentaries are puzzled by this language, as Beit Shammai and Beit Hillel are in fact two courts in one city, not merely comparable to this model (Ritva). The answer given is that the question does not refer to the students of later generations but to the original Sages Shammai and Hillel themselves: How could they have allowed their schools to split up into two courts?

Rather, Rava said…you shall not cut yourselves – אֶלָּא אֲמַר רָבָא...לֹא תִתְגּוֹדְדוּ: Some commentaries explain that Rava does not disagree with Abaye's opinion concerning the prohibition: "You shall not cut yourselves." Rather, he differentiates between a case where one court holds that acting against their opinion entails the transgression of a prohibition, and a case where the dispute involves a custom alone. In his opinion, disputes over customs violate the prohibition against factions only if they occur within a single court, not between two different courts (*Meromei Sadeh*). This resolves the difficulty in the ruling of the Rambam.

תָּא שְׁמַע: בִּמְקוֹמוֹ שֶׁל רַבִּי אֱלִיעֶזֶר הָיוּ כּוֹרְתִים עֵצִים לַעֲשׂוֹת פֶּחָמִים בְּשַׁבָּת, לַעֲשׂוֹת בַּרְזֶל. בִּמְקוֹמוֹ שֶׁל רַבִּי יוֹסֵי הַגְּלִילִי הָיוּ אוֹכְלִים בְּשַׂר עוֹף בְּחָלָב.

§ The Gemara cites other relevant sources. **Come and hear: In the locale of Rabbi Eliezer,** where his ruling was followed, **they would cut down trees** on Shabbat **to prepare charcoal** from them **to fashion iron** tools with which to circumcise a child **on Shabbat.** In Rabbi Eliezer's opinion, not only does the mitzva of circumcision override Shabbat, but also any action required for the preparation of the tools necessary for the circumcision likewise overrides Shabbat. The *baraita* adds: **In the locale of Rabbi Yosei HaGelili they would eat poultry meat in milk,** as Rabbi Yosei HaGelili held that the prohibition of meat in milk does not include poultry.

בִּמְקוֹמוֹ שֶׁל רַבִּי אֱלִיעֶזֶר אִין, בִּמְקוֹמוֹ שֶׁל רַבִּי עֲקִיבָא – לָא. דְּתַנְיָא, כְּלָל אָמַר רַבִּי עֲקִיבָא: כׇּל מְלָאכָה שֶׁאֶפְשָׁר לַעֲשׂוֹתָהּ מֵעֶרֶב שַׁבָּת – אֵין דּוֹחָה אֶת הַשַּׁבָּת.

The Gemara infers: **In the locale of Rabbi Eliezer, yes,** they would act in this manner, whereas **in the locale of Rabbi Akiva,** for instance, **no,** they would not do so, **as it is taught** in a *baraita* that **a principle was stated by Rabbi Akiva: Any prohibited labor that can be performed on Shabbat eve**[H] **does not override Shabbat** even if it involves a mitzva. A mitzva whose proper time is on Shabbat overrides Shabbat only if its performance was impossible earlier, e.g., the act of circumcision itself, which cannot be performed earlier.

וְהַאי מַאי תְּיוּבְתָּא? מְקוֹמוֹת מְקוֹמוֹת שָׁאנֵי! וּדְקָאָרֵי לַהּ מַאי קָאָרֵי לַהּ?

The Gemara asks: **And what is this refutation?** As stated above, **it is different** when dealing **with numerous places,** and the *baraita* explicitly states that this practice was followed in Rabbi Eliezer's locale. Consequently, there is no violation of the prohibition against splitting into factions. The Gemara asks: **He who asked it, why did he ask it,** i.e., what is the basis for the question in the first place? It is obvious that the *baraita* is referring to a specific place.

סָלְקָא דַּעְתָּךְ אָמֵינָא: מִשּׁוּם חוּמְרָא דְּשַׁבָּת כְּמָקוֹם אֶחָד דָּמֵי – קָא מַשְׁמַע לַן.

The Gemara answers: It might **enter your mind to say** that **due to the severity of Shabbat,**[N] **it,** i.e., the world, **is considered like a single locale.** In other words, one might have thought that the permission to tolerate diverse customs in different places applies only to other prohibitions, whereas the prohibition of Shabbat is so severe that it is unacceptable to allow different customs, as this might lead people to disrespect Shabbat. Therefore, the *baraita* **teaches us** that even in the case of Shabbat there can be different customs in various locales.

תָּא שְׁמַע, דְּרַבִּי אַבָּהוּ, כִּי אִיקְּלַע לְאַתְרֵיהּ דְּרַבִּי יְהוֹשֻׁעַ בֶּן לֵוִי הֲוָה מְטַלְטֵל שְׁרָגָא, וְכִי אִיקְּלַע לְאַתְרֵיהּ דְּרַבִּי יוֹחָנָן – לָא הֲוָה מְטַלְטֵל שְׁרָגָא.

§ The Gemara cites another relevant case involving Shabbat: **Come and hear that Rabbi Abbahu, when he happened** to come **to the place of Rabbi Yehoshua ben Levi, would move** an oil **lamp** [*sheraga*][NL] after the flame that had been lit for that Shabbat had burned out, as Rabbi Yehoshua accepted the ruling that it is permitted to carry items of this sort that had been set aside. **But when he happened** to come **to the place of Rabbi Yoḥanan,** who prohibited carrying items of this kind that had been set aside on Shabbat, **he would not move** an oil **lamp.** This indicates that divergent customs are followed in different places.

וְהַאי, מַאי קוּשְׁיָא? וְלָא אָמְרִינַן מְקוֹמוֹת שָׁאנֵי? אֲנַן הָכִי קָאָמְרִינַן: רַבִּי אַבָּהוּ, הֵיכִי עָבֵיד הָכָא הָכִי וְהֵיכִי עָבֵיד הָכָא הָכִי?

Again, the Gemara asks: **And what is this difficulty? Didn't we say** that **it is different** when dealing **with numerous places?** The Gemara explains that **this is what we are saying:** With regard to **Rabbi Abbahu** himself, **how could he act**[N] **in this manner here and how could he act in that manner there?**

רַבִּי אַבָּהוּ כְּרַבִּי יְהוֹשֻׁעַ בֶּן לֵוִי סְבִירָא לֵיהּ, וְכִי מִקְּלַע לְאַתְרֵיהּ דְּרַבִּי יוֹחָנָן – לָא הֲוָה מְטַלְטֵל, מִשּׁוּם כְּבוֹדוֹ דְּרַבִּי יוֹחָנָן. וְהָאִיכָּא שַׁמָּעָא! דְּמוֹדַע לֵיהּ לְשַׁמָּעָא.

The Gemara answers: **Rabbi Abbahu holds in accordance with** the opinion of **Rabbi Yehoshua ben Levi** that it is permitted to carry this item. **And when he happened** to come **to the place of Rabbi Yoḥanan he would not carry it, in deference to Rabbi Yoḥanan,** so as not to act contrary to his ruling in the place where he was the authority. The Gemara asks: **But there was a servant**[N] accompanying Rabbi Abbahu who would see him carrying these types of articles that had been set aside. Wasn't Rabbi Abbahu concerned that the servant might carry them in Rabbi Yoḥanan's locale? The Gemara explains **that he would inform the servant** and explain to him the reason for his change in behavior.

HALAKHA

Prohibited labor that can be performed on Shabbat eve – מְלָאכָה שֶׁאֶפְשָׁר לַעֲשׂוֹתָהּ מֵעֶרֶב שַׁבָּת: Any prohibited labor in preparation for a mitzva that could have been performed on the eve of Shabbat may not be performed on Shabbat. This is true even if refraining from performing such labor on Shabbat leads to the neglect of a mitzva, in accordance with the opinion of Rabbi Akiva (Rambam *Sefer Ahava, Hilkhot Mila* 2:7; *Shulḥan Arukh, Oraḥ Ḥayyim* 331:6 and *Yoreh De'a* 266:2).

NOTES

Due to the severity of Shabbat – מִשּׁוּם חוּמְרָא דְּשַׁבָּת: Some commentaries explain that the reason for the prohibition against breaking into factions is due to the concern that people might come to disrespect prohibitions if they observe divergent customs in different places. Consequently, as Shabbat is so severe, it stands to reason that the *halakha* should be more stringent in this case, to prevent people from taking it lightly (see *Sukkat David*). The early commentaries discuss whether this difficulty was raised specifically with regard to the opinion of Abaye or whether it is a general question that applies to all opinions.

He would move an oil lamp – הֲוָה מְטַלְטֵל שְׁרָגָא: Some commentaries explain that this was an old oil lamp that had not been lit and was therefore *muktze* due to repugnance (Rabbi Yehuda bar Natan; *Tosafot*).

Rabbi Abbahu, how could he act – רַבִּי אַבָּהוּ הֵיכִי עָבֵיד: Some commentaries explain that if one person is permitted to adjust his custom from place to place, it should be likewise be permitted for many people to act in accordance with different customs in the same place (*Tosefot HaRosh*).

But there was a servant – וְהָאִיכָּא שַׁמָּעָא: Some commentaries note that if the servant were to carry the object in Rabbi Yoḥanan's locale, it would also be a mark of disrespect to him (*Otzar HaShitot*). Many early commentaries do not accept this explanation. Instead, they claim that the servant would infer from Rabbi Abbahu's behavior that it is permitted to act in accordance with different customs in different places, which would be an erroneous understanding of the prohibition against breaking into factions (Rabbi Yehuda bar Natan; *Tosafot Yeshanim*). Others maintain, based on Rashi's explanation, that the servant might think that Rabbi Abbahu was of the same opinion as Rabbi Yoḥanan and simply acted more leniently in the presence of Rabbi Yehoshua ben Levi (Rashba).

LANGUAGE

Lamp [*sheraga*] – שְׁרָגָא: This word was borrowed from Iranian into several Aramaic dialects. In Modern Persian, the form of the word is chirāgh, meaning lamp or candelabrum.

HALAKHA

Who is a *mamzer* – אֵיזֶהוּ מַמְזֵר: A child born of a forbidden union that entails either a court-imposed death penalty or *karet*, excluding a union with a menstruating woman, is a *mamzer*. This ruling is in accordance with the mishna in tractate *Kiddushin* and the conclusion of several discussions in the Gemara (*Shulḥan Arukh, Even HaEzer* 4:13).

BACKGROUND

***Mamzer* – מַמְזֵר:** A *mamzer* is a child born from an adulterous relationship, i.e., relations between a married woman and a man other than her husband, or an incestuous relationship, i.e., relations between relatives who are prohibited from marrying by Torah law where the participants in this relationship are subject to *karet*, apart from the offspring of a menstruating woman. The offspring of an unmarried couple who are permitted to marry is not a *mamzer*. A *mamzer* is halakhically considered his father's son in all respects. A male *mamzer* may marry only a *mamzeret*, i.e., a female *mamzer*, or a convert. The offspring of that union is a *mamzer* as well.

תָּא שְׁמַע: אַף עַל פִּי שֶׁאֵלּוּ אוֹסְרִים וְאֵלּוּ מַתִּירִים, לֹא נִמְנְעוּ בֵּית שַׁמַּאי מִלִּישָּׂא נָשִׁים מִבֵּית הִלֵּל, וְלֹא בֵּית הִלֵּל מִבֵּית שַׁמַּאי. אִי אָמְרַתְּ בִּשְׁלָמָא לֹא עָשׂוּ, מִשּׁוּם הָכִי לֹא נִמְנְעוּ. אֶלָּא אִי אָמְרַתְּ עָשׂוּ – אַמַּאי לֹא נִמְנְעוּ?

§ The Gemara continues to discuss the question of whether Beit Shammai followed their own rulings. **Come and hear** that which is taught in the mishna: **Although** Beit Hillel **prohibit and** Beit Shammai **permit,** and these disqualify the women and those deem them fit, **Beit Shammai did not refrain from marrying women from Beit Hillel, nor did Beit Hillel** refrain from marrying women **from Beit Shammai. Granted, if you say** that Beit Shammai **did not act** in accordance with their opinion, it is **due to that** reason that **they did not** have to **refrain** from marrying women from Beit Hillel. **However, if you say** that **they did act** in accordance with their opinion, **why didn't they refrain** from marrying one another?

בִּשְׁלָמָא בֵּית שַׁמַּאי מִבֵּית הִלֵּל לֹא נִמְנְעוּ – דִּבְנֵי חַיָּיבֵי לָאוִין נִינְהוּ.

The Gemara elaborates: **Granted, Beit Shammai did not refrain** from marrying into **Beit Hillel,** as even if Beit Shammai maintain in a certain case that a rival wife required levirate marriage or *ḥalitza*, if she went ahead and married another man their **children are** born to a union whose partners are **liable by** a regular **prohibition:** "The wife of the dead man shall not be married outside" (Deuteronomy 25:5). Since this transgression does not entail *karet*, the children of this relationship are not *mamzerim*.

אֶלָּא בֵּית הִלֵּל מִבֵּית שַׁמַּאי – אַמַּאי לֹא נִמְנְעוּ? בְּנֵי חַיָּיבֵי כָּרֵיתוֹת מַמְזֵרִים נִינְהוּ!

However, why did Beit Hillel not refrain from marrying into **Beit Shammai?** In the opinion of Beit Hillel the **children** of these rival wives who entered into levirate marriage are born of a union whose partners are **liable to** receive ***karet***, as the prohibition of a brother's wife was never nullified in this case, which means that the children **are *mamzerim*.**[H] If so, how could Beit Hillel allow these marriages?

וְכִי תֵּימָא קָסָבְרִי בֵּית הִלֵּל דְּאֵין מַמְזֵר מֵחַיָּיבֵי כָּרֵיתוֹת – וְהָאֲמַר רַבִּי אֶלְעָזָר: אַף עַל פִּי שֶׁנֶּחְלְקוּ בֵּית שַׁמַּאי וּבֵית הִלֵּל בְּצָרוֹת – מוֹדִים שֶׁאֵין מַמְזֵר אֶלָּא מִמִּי שֶׁאִיסּוּרוֹ אִיסּוּר עֶרְוָה, וְעָנוּשׁ כָּרֵת! אֶלָּא לָאו שְׁמַע מִינָּהּ – לֹא עָשׂוּ!

And if you would say that **Beit Hillel maintain that** the child of a union whose partners are **liable to** receive ***karet*** **is not a *mamzer*,**[B] as a *mamzer* is only one whose parents violated a prohibition that entails the death penalty, **didn't Rabbi Elazar say: Although Beit Shammai and Beit Hillel disagreed** with regard **to rival wives, they concede that a *mamzer* is only from** a union **whose prohibition** is **a prohibition of forbidden relations punishable by *karet*?** Consequently, the children of rival wives are *mamzerim* according to Beit Hillel. **Rather, isn't it** correct to **conclude from** here that Beit Shammai **did not act** in accordance with their own opinion?

לָא, לְעוֹלָם עָשׂוּ, דְּמוֹדְעֵי לְהוּ וּפָרְשִׁי.

The Gemara rejects this conclusion: **No; actually,** Beit Shammai **did act** in accordance with their opinion. As for the problem with these marriages, the answer is **that they would inform** Beit Hillel **and** Beit Hillel would **withdraw**[N] from the match. When those who acted in accordance with the opinion of Beit Hillel would come to marry women from those who followed the rulings of Beit Shammai, they would be notified that certain children were born of rival wives and that those people were considered *mamzerim* in the opinion of Beit Hillel, who therefore declared them forbidden in marriage.

וְהָכִי נַמִי מִסְתַּבְּרָא, דְּקָתָנֵי סֵיפָא: כָּל הַטְּהָרוֹת וְכָל הַטְּמָאוֹת שֶׁהָיוּ אֵלּוּ מְטַהֲרִין וְאֵלּוּ מְטַמְּאִין – לֹא נִמְנְעוּ עוֹשִׂים טְהָרוֹת אֵלּוּ עַל גַּבֵּי אֵלּוּ.

The Gemara comments: **And so too, it is reasonable** that this is the case, **as** the mishna **teaches** in **the latter clause:** With regard to **all of the** disputes concerning the *halakhot* of **ritual purity and impurity, where those,** Beit Hillel, rule an article **ritually pure and these,** Beit Shammai, rule it **ritually impure, they did not refrain from handling ritually pure** objects **each with the other.**

NOTES

They would inform them and they would withdraw – מוֹדְעֵי לְהוּ וּפָרְשִׁי: But if Beit Shammai actually notified Beit Hillel, what is novel about this statement? The commentaries explain that Beit Hillel trusted that Beit Shammai would notify them even in a case of a slight concern, and if they were not notified they took this to mean that the person was fully qualified according to all opinions (Ritva). The early commentaries prove from here that in instances of this kind there is no concern with regard to the testimony of those who have a personal stake in the matter, as provided that they remain faithful to their tradition they can be trusted to inform others who accept a different tradition (Meiri; *Yam shel Shlomo*).

אִי אָמְרַתְּ בִּשְׁלָמָא דְּמוֹדְעֵי לְהוּ – מִשּׁוּם הָכִי לֹא נִמְנְעוּ. אֶלָּא אִי אָמְרַתְּ דְּלָא מוֹדְעֵי לְהוּ, בִּשְׁלָמָא בֵּית שַׁמַּאי מִבֵּית הִלֵּל לֹא נִמְנְעוּ. דְּטָמְאוֹת דְּבֵית הִלֵּל – לְבֵית שַׁמַּאי טְהָרוֹת נִינְהוּ,

Granted, if you say that they notified them, it is **due to that** reason that **they did not** need to **refrain** from using their objects. **However, if you say that they did not notify them, granted,** it is logical that **Beit Shammai**[N] **did not refrain from** handling items belonging to **Beit Hillel, as ritually impure** objects **for Beit Hillel are ritually pure for Beit Shammai,** and therefore no special care is necessary.

אֶלָּא, בֵּית הִלֵּל מִבֵּית שַׁמַּאי לָמָּה לֹא נִמְנְעוּ? טְהָרוֹת דְּבֵית שַׁמַּאי לְבֵית הִלֵּל טְמֵאוֹת נִינְהוּ! אֶלָּא לָאו דְּמוֹדְעֵי לְהוּ – שְׁמַע מִינָּהּ.

However, why didn't Beit Hillel refrain from touching articles that belonged to **Beit Shammai?** After all, **ritually pure** objects **for Beit Shammai are ritually impure for Beit Hillel. Rather, is it not** the case that Beit Shammai **notified** Beit Hillel that these items were ritually pure only in their own opinion, and Beit Hillel separated themselves from them? The Gemara summarizes the discussion: **Conclude from** here that this is the correct interpretation.

וּמַאי אוּלְמֵיהּ דְּהָךְ מֵהָךְ? מַהוּ דְּתֵימָא: צָרָה – קָלָא אִית לָהּ, קָא מַשְׁמַע לַן.

The Gemara asks: **In what** way **is this** case **stronger than that** case? In other words, why is the statement with regard to ritual purity and impurity more conclusive than the one that deals with marriage? Since the practice of notification was not explicitly stated in the case of ritual purity but was merely inferred logically, the same reasoning applies equally to the case of marriage. The Gemara answers: **Lest you say** that since it is so unusual, a marriage to **a rival wife** generates **publicity** and is so widely known that no special notification is required, therefore, the Gemara **teaches us** that even in this case notification is required.

גּוּפָא, אָמַר רַבִּי אֶלְעָזָר: אַף עַל פִּי שֶׁנֶּחְלְקוּ בֵּית שַׁמַּאי וּבֵית הִלֵּל בְּצָרוֹת – מוֹדִים שֶׁאֵין מַמְזֵר אֶלָּא מִמִּי שֶׁאִיסּוּרוֹ אִיסּוּר עֶרְוָה וְעָנוּשׁ כָּרֵת. מַאן מוֹדִים? אִילֵימָא בֵּית שַׁמַּאי לְבֵית הִלֵּל – פְּשִׁיטָא, בְּנֵי חַיָּיבֵי לָאוִין כְּשֵׁרִים נִינְהוּ!

§ Since the statement of Rabbi Elazar was mentioned, the Gemara turns to discuss **the matter itself. Rabbi Elazar said: Although Beit Shammai and Beit Hillel disagreed** with regard **to rival wives, they concede that a** ***mamzer*** **is only from** a union **whose prohibition** is **a prohibition of forbidden relations punishable by** ***karet.*** The Gemara asks: **Who concedes** to whom? **If we say** that **Beit Shammai** concede **to Beit Hillel,** this is **obvious,** since if they acted in accordance with their own opinion that rival wives who married others without *ḥalitza* **are liable** only **for** violating a regular **prohibition,** their **children are** therefore **fit** and are not *mamzerim* at all.

אֶלָּא בֵּית הִלֵּל לְבֵית שַׁמַּאי – הִיא גּוּפָא חַיָּיבֵי כָּרֵיתוֹת הִיא!

Rather, one could say that **Beit Hillel** concede **to Beit Shammai.** But in that case **she herself,** the rival wife of a forbidden relative who married one of the *yevamin,* **is liable to** receive ***karet*** in the opinion of Beit Hillel, and the child is a *mamzer,* whereas Rabbi Elazar's statement indicates that they concede with regard to a different case.

לְעוֹלָם בֵּית שַׁמַּאי לְבֵית הִלֵּל, וּלְאַפּוֹקֵי מִדְּרַבִּי עֲקִיבָא, דְּאָמַר: יֵשׁ מַמְזֵר מֵחַיָּיבֵי לָאוִין, קָא מַשְׁמַע לַן דְּאֵין מַמְזֵר מֵחַיָּיבֵי לָאוִין.

The Gemara explains: **Actually, Beit Shammai** concede **to Beit Hillel,** and this is not a novelty with regard to their basic dispute. Instead, the statement comes **to exclude** the opinion **of Rabbi Akiva, who said:** The offspring **from** forbidden relations for which one is **liable for** violating **a prohibition is a** ***mamzer.*** Rabbi Elazar **teaches us** that Beit Shammai and Beit Hillel agree that the offspring **from** forbidden relations for which one is **liable for** violating **a prohibition is not a** ***mamzer***; rather, one is a *mamzer* only if he is born of a union punishable by *karet.*

תָּא שְׁמַע: אַף עַל פִּי שֶׁנֶּחְלְקוּ בֵּית שַׁמַּאי וּבֵית הִלֵּל בְּצָרוֹת, וּבַאֲחָיוֹת,

§ The Gemara returns to the initial question of whether or not Beit Shammai acted in accordance with their own opinion. The Gemara suggests: **Come** and **hear: Although Beit Shammai and Beit Hillel disagreed** with regard **to** several cases, nevertheless, they did not refrain from marrying women from each other's communities. The cases with regard to which they disagreed include **rival wives, and sisters,** i.e., if two sisters had been married to two brothers and simultaneously became obligated in levirate marriage, Beit Hillel prohibit both in levirate marriage, and if they violated the prohibition and married regardless, they require a divorce. By contrast, Beit Shammai permit them to remain married.

NOTES

Granted, Beit Shammai, etc. – **בִּשְׁלָמָא בֵּית שַׁמַּאי וכו׳**: This version of the text, which is accepted by Rashi, raises one serious difficulty. It indicates that in matters of ritual purity and impurity the opinion of Beit Hillel is invariably more stringent than that of Beit Shammai, yet it is known that this is not always the case. In fact, Beit Shammai are generally more stringent in these cases. Some commentaries explain that this comment refers to the *mishnayot* of tractate *Eduyyot,* where all of the stringencies of Beit Hillel are listed (Rivan). Similarly, others state that although Beit Shammai are usually more stringent, the mishna is referring to those cases where the opinion of Beit Hillel is the more stringent (Rashba). However, it is possible that in practice Beit Shammai were more stringent with regard to ritual purity than Beit Hillel, as stated in the Jerusalem Talmud. Due to this difficulty, many early commentaries (*Tosafot*; Ramban; Rashba) prefer the version of the Gemara cited by Rabbeinu Ḥananel, which states the exact opposite. In other words, the Gemara is saying that Beit Shammai did not act leniently in opposition to their opinion, and it is equally clear that Beit Hillel acted in accordance with their own opinion, as they were the majority, and yet each school did not refrain from handling the vessels belonging to the other, because they would notify one another.

Some point out that according to this version the Gemara's question: In what way is this case stronger than that case, is unclear, as one can reply that in the first case Beit Hillel did not refrain from marrying into Beit Shammai because Beit Shammai did not insist on acting in accordance with their own opinion, which cannot be said in the case of ritual impurity, where Beit Shammai's opinion is more stringent (see *Otzar HaShitot*). Indeed, some commentaries omit this question for this very reason. Some suggest that Beit Shammai acted stringently in accordance with their opinion, and yet they did not violate the prohibition against forming factions, as they did not require the vessels or items that were ritually pure in accordance with the opinion of Beit Hillel. The same reasoning applies to marriage: Since they did not necessarily have to marry these particular women, there is no proof from here with regard to forming a faction (*Tosefot HaRosh*). Accordingly, the question of why this proof is stronger than the other is appropriate according to Rabbeinu Ḥananel's version as well.

HALAKHA

An outdated bill of divorce – גֵּט יָשָׁן: If one wrote a bill of divorce for his wife and changed his mind and did not divorce her, and he secluded himself with her after it was written, he may not subsequently divorce her with that same bill of divorce, in accordance with the opinion of Beit Hillel (*Shulḥan Arukh, Even HaEzer* 148:1).

An uncertain married woman – סָפֵק אֵשֶׁת אִישׁ: An orphan girl married off by her mother and brothers can refuse either her betrothal or marriage, whether to a regular husband or a *yavam* in levirate marriage, and whether it is her first husband or her second, in accordance with the opinion of Beit Hillel (*Shulḥan Arukh, Even HaEzer* 155:4–6).

Who divorces his wife and she lodged with him – מְגָרֵשׁ אֶת אִשְׁתּוֹ וְלָנָה עִמּוֹ: In the case of a man who divorced his wife and later was found by witnesses to have secluded himself with her, there is a concern that he may have retracted and engaged in sexual relations with her for the purpose of marriage. Due to this doubt, she requires a second bill of divorce, in accordance with the opinion of Beit Hillel (*Shulḥan Arukh, Even HaEzer* 149:2).

Betrothal money – כֶּסֶף קִידּוּשִׁין: One who wishes to betroth a woman with money must give her either a *peruta* or its equivalent in the presence of witnesses, in accordance with the opinion of Beit Hillel (*Shulḥan Arukh, Even HaEzer* 27:1).

בְּגֵט יָשָׁן, וּבִסְפֵק אֵשֶׁת אִישׁ, וּבִמְגָרֵשׁ אֶת אִשְׁתּוֹ וְלָנָה עִמּוֹ בְּפוּנְדָּק,

Furthermore, Beit Shammai and Beit Hillel disagreed with regard **to an outdated bill of divorce**[H] that had been written but not delivered. Beit Shammai maintain that if the husband and wife continued to live together after the writing of the bill of divorce, the same bill of divorce can still be used later, whereas Beit Hillel dispute this. **And** they likewise **disagreed** with regard **to an uncertain married woman,**[HN] i.e., whether a minor who was actually married, and not merely betrothed, may perform refusal. **And** they also **disagreed** with regard **to one who divorces his wife and** later **she lodged** together **with him**[H] **at an inn,** as to whether or not this is sufficient grounds for assuming that they remarried.

בְּכֶסֶף וּבְשָׁוֶה כֶּסֶף, בִּפְרוּטָה וּבְשָׁוֶה פְרוּטָה –

Additionally, they disagreed with regard to the issue of betrothal **by money and with** the equivalent **value of money,** and **by a *peruta* or with** the equivalent **value of a *peruta*.**[H] According to Beit Shammai, the minimal amount of money effective for betrothal is a dinar or the equivalent of a dinar, whereas Beit Hillel maintain that even the less valuable *peruta* or its equivalent is sufficient.

לֹא נִמְנְעוּ בֵּית שַׁמַּאי מִלִּישָּׂא נָשִׁים מִבֵּית הִלֵּל, וְלֹא בֵּית הִלֵּל מִבֵּית שַׁמַּאי, לְלַמֶּדְךָ שֶׁחִיבָּה וְרֵיעוּת נוֹהֲגִים זֶה בָּזֶה, לְקַיֵּים מַה שֶּׁנֶּאֱמַר ״הָאֱמֶת וְהַשָּׁלוֹם אֱהָבוּ״. רַבִּי שִׁמְעוֹן אוֹמֵר: נִמְנְעוּ הֵן מִן הַוַּדַּאי, וְלֹא נִמְנְעוּ מִן הַסָּפֵק.

Despite the fact that these *halakhot* entail important ramifications depending on whether or not these women were married or fit for marriage, or whether their offspring are fit for marriage, **Beit Shammai did not refrain from marrying women from Beit Hillel, nor did Beit Hillel** refrain from marrying women **from Beit Shammai.** This serves **to teach you that** they **practiced affection and camaraderie between them, to fulfill that which is stated: "Love truth and peace"** (Zechariah 8:19). **Rabbi Shimon says: They did refrain in the certain** cases, **but they did not refrain in the uncertain**[N] cases. In other words, Beit Hillel were not worried that any ordinary woman from Beit Shammai might be one of those of uncertain status.

אִי אָמְרַתְּ בִּשְׁלָמָא עָשׂוּ – מִשּׁוּם הָכִי נִמְנְעוּ, אֶלָּא אִי אָמְרַתְּ לֹא עָשׂוּ – אַמַּאי נִמְנְעוּ? וְתִסְבְּרָא, נְהִי נַמִּי דְּעָשׂוּ, בִּשְׁלָמָא בֵּית הִלֵּל נִמְנְעוּ מִבֵּית שַׁמַּאי, דְּחַיָּיבֵי כָּרֵיתוֹת נִינְהוּ, וּמַמְזֵרִים הֵם לְבֵית הִלֵּל.

The Gemara infers from the opinion of Rabbi Shimon: **Granted, if you say** that Beit Shammai **did act** in accordance with their opinion, it is **due to that** reason that **they refrained** in the certain cases. **However, if you say** that **they did not act** in accordance with their opinion, **why did they refrain** from marriage? The Gemara replies: **And** how can **you understand** it that way, that Beit Shammai acted in accordance with their opinion? **Even if they acted** in accordance with their opinion, **granted** that **Beit Hillel refrained from** marrying into **Beit Shammai,** as **those** rival wives who entered into levirate marriage **are liable to** receive ***karet*** **and** their children **are *mamzerim* according to** the opinion of **Beit Hillel.**

אֶלָּא בֵּית שַׁמַּאי אַמַּאי נִמְנְעוּ מִבֵּית הִלֵּל? בְּנֵי חַיָּיבֵי לָאוִין נִינְהוּ, וּכְשֵׁרִים נִינְהוּ! כִּדְאָמַר רַב נַחְמָן בַּר יִצְחָק: לֹא נִצְרְכָה אֶלָּא לְצָרָה עַצְמָהּ – הָכָא נַמִּי לֹא נִצְרְכָה אֶלָּא לְצָרָה עַצְמָהּ.

However, why did Beit Shammai refrain from marrying the offspring of rival wives of **Beit Hillel?** The parents are **liable for** violating a regular **prohibition, and** therefore their children **are fit.** The Gemara answers **as Rav Naḥman bar Yitzḥak said** with regard to a different matter: **This** *halakha* **was necessary** not for the children of the rival wife, but **only for the rival wife herself.**[N] **Here too, it was necessary only for the rival wife herself.** The *halakha* was not taught with regard to the children of the rival wives; rather, it is referring only to the rival wives.

NOTES

An uncertain married woman – סָפֵק אֵשֶׁת אִישׁ: Rashi, in his first interpretation, and the Meiri explain that this is referring to a married minor who wishes to perform refusal. However, this explanation is linguistically problematic, as that case does not involve any uncertainty at all. Consequently, Rashi provides the alternative explanation that this is referring to a sick man who gave a bill of divorce to his wife and subsequently secluded himself with her. See *Tosafot*, who challenge this interpretation, and *Arukh LaNer*, who further explains Rashi's opinion. Several early commentaries explain, following Rabbeinu Ḥananel, that the phrase: An uncertain married woman, does not refer to a separate case at all. Rather, it is a heading for the ensuing cases of an outdated bill of divorce and one who divorced his wife and subsequently lodged with her at the same inn, i.e., it is indicating that both these cases involve uncertainty (see *Tosefot HaRosh* and Ritva).

Uncertain – סָפֵק: See Rashi and Ramban, cited by Rashba and Ritva, who interpret this as referring to a woman from a family whose status is in doubt. That is, it is unclear whether or not a forbidden rival wife was married into this family at some point in time.

Necessary only for the rival wife herself – לֹא נִצְרְכָה אֶלָּא לְצָרָה עַצְמָהּ: One can answer that Beit Shammai did need to avoid marrying women from Beit Hillel, as although the child of a woman requiring levirate marriage who married outside the family is not a *mamzer*, nevertheless, he is disqualified from the priesthood. The Gemara, however, preferred a more straightforward explanation (Rivan; see *Tosafot*).

וּמַאי שְׁנָא מִן הַוַּדַּאי – דְּאִיסּוּרָא הוּא, סָפֵק נַמִּי אִיסּוּרָא הוּא!

The Gemara asks further: **And in what** way are uncertain cases **different from the certain**[N] cases, such as forbidden rival wives? If you say **that** certain cases are undoubtedly **prohibited** in the opinion of Beit Hillel, the cases involving **uncertain** circumstances, e.g., one who divorced his wife and then stayed with her in the same inn, **are also prohibited.** Even if Beit Hillel render these cases prohibited only due to some uncertainty, the ruling is the same.

לָא תֵּימָא מִן הַסָּפֵק, אֶלָּא אֵימָא: מִן הַסְּתָם, דְּמוֹדְעִי לְהוּ וּפָרְשִׁי,

The Gemara answers: **Do not say: In the uncertain** cases, i.e., that the *halakha* involved doubtful circumstances. **Rather, say: From the unspecified** case. In other words, barring clear knowledge of an uncertain betrothal within a specific family, they would take women from that family in marriage. The reason is **that** Beit Shammai **would notify** Beit Hillel of the prohibition according to their opinion, **and** they would **refrain** from the marriage. If there was no notification, this was a clear sign that no doubt was involved in this case at all.

וּמַאי קָא מַשְׁמַע לָן – דְּאַהֲבָה וְרֵיעוּת נוֹהֲגִים זֶה בָּזֶה – הַיְינוּ רֵישָׁא! הָא קָא מַשְׁמַע לָן דְּכוּלָּהּ רַבִּי שִׁמְעוֹן הִיא.

The Gemara asks: **But** if so, **what** does **this** come to **teach us?** Is it **that** they had **relations of affection and camaraderie between them,** i.e., that each trusted that the other side would never cause them to err with regard to something they held to be prohibited? **This is** the same as the **first clause** of the *baraita*. What is Rabbi Shimon adding by his statement? The Gemara answers: This comes to **teach us that the entire** *baraita* **is** the opinion of **Rabbi Shimon.** This is not a dispute between two Sages. Rather, Rabbi Shimon's opinion elucidates the earlier statement.

תָּא שְׁמַע, דְּאָמַר רַבִּי יוֹחָנָן בֶּן נוּרִי: הֵיאַךְ הֲלָכָה זוֹ רוֹוַחַת בְּיִשְׂרָאֵל? נַעֲשֶׂה כְּדִבְרֵי בֵּית שַׁמַּאי – הַוָּלָד מַמְזֵר לְדִבְרֵי בֵּית הִלֵּל, נַעֲשֶׂה כְּדִבְרֵי בֵּית הִלֵּל – הַוָּלָד פָּגוּם לְדִבְרֵי בֵּית שַׁמַּאי, בּוֹאוּ וּנְתַקֵּן לָהֶן לַצָּרוֹת

§ The Gemara offers an alternative resolution: **Come** and **hear, as Rabbi Yoḥanan ben Nuri said: How should** one act with regard to **this *halakha*** of rival wives? In what form should it **become widespread among the Jewish people? If we act in accordance with the statement of Beit Shammai** and permit a rival wife in levirate marriage, **the offspring** will be a ***mamzer***[N] **according to the statement of Beit Hillel.** If **we act in accordance with the statement of Beit Hillel** and grant full exemption to the rival wives, **the offspring will** be of **flawed** lineage **according to** the opinion of **Beit Shammai,** as he is the child of a woman prohibited in marriage by a regular prohibition. Although he is not a *mamzer*, his lineage is nevertheless defective. Instead, **let us enact** a general decree **for rival wives**

NOTES

And in what way are uncertain cases different from the certain, etc. – **וּמַאי שְׁנָא מִן הַוַּדַּאי וכו׳**: Some commentaries maintain that this question does not concern the matter at hand, but since the *baraita* was cited, the Gemara clarified it (*Tosafot*). Conversely, others claim that this statement is the conclusion of the first proof. If it were not proven that the entire *baraita* reflects the opinion of Rabbi Shimon and that they did not refrain from marriage in unspecified cases, one might have thought that due to the affection between the two schools Beit Shammai did not act on their opinions at all, so as not to increase the dispute. However, the statement of Rabbi Shimon clearly indicates that they did in fact act in accordance with their opinion, and that they would notify the other school when a conflict arose (*Tosefot HaRosh*; see *Sukkat David*).

The offspring will be a *mamzer*, etc. – **הַוָּלָד מַמְזֵר וכו׳**: Why does the Gemara refer only to the status of the child and not the actual prohibition involving the rival wife herself? After all, it is the marriage to this woman that entails *karet*, in the opinion of Beit Hillel, or involves the violation of a prohibition if performed by a man outside the family, according to Beit Shammai. It is likely that the Gemara preferred this formulation because although the prohibition with regard to a rival wife is transgressed at the time, the disqualification of a child from marriage bears ramifications for generations (Rashash).

Perek **I**
Daf **15** Amud **a**

שֶׁיְּהוּ חוֹלְצוֹת וְלֹא מִתְיַיבְּמוֹת, לֹא הִסְפִּיקוּ לִגְמוֹר אֶת הַדָּבָר עַד שֶׁנִּטְרְפָה הַשָּׁעָה.

that they **should perform *ḥalitza* and not enter into levirate marriage.** If they act in this manner, they will be permitted to marry others and the problem will be solved according to all opinions. **They were unable to finalize the matter** according to the proposition raised by Rabbi Yoḥanan ben Nuri **before times of trouble** arrived. Due to the outbreak of war they were unable to gather together to vote and establish an accepted halakhic ruling.

אָמַר לֵיהּ רַבָּן שִׁמְעוֹן בֶּן גַּמְלִיאֵל: מַה נַּעֲשֶׂה לָהֶם לַצָּרוֹת הָרִאשׁוֹנוֹת מֵעַתָּה?

Sometime later, when they returned to discuss the issue, **Rabban Shimon ben Gamliel said to** the other Sages: **What shall we do with those earlier rival wives**[N] **from now** onward? Since in the meantime some rival wives had entered into levirate marriage, if we issue a collective ruling that rival wives may not do so, their children will be declared *mamzerim*. Therefore, it is better not to establish this *halakha* at all.

NOTES

What shall we do with those earlier rival wives – **מַה נַּעֲשֶׂה לָהֶם לַצָּרוֹת הָרִאשׁוֹנוֹת**: There is also a concern for the children of flawed lineage born from these unions (see Maharsha). Some commentaries explain that it is impossible that children born from relations permitted by the ruling of the Sages at the time, as is the case here, would later be deemed of flawed lineage (*Yosef Lekaḥ*). It is likewise stated in *Arza DeVei Rav* that provided that there is no conclusive halakhic ruling, these children cannot be considered definite *mamzerim*, as the status of a *mamzer* cannot be determined solely on the basis of a majority opinion. Rather, an established decision of the court is necessary.

אִי אָמְרַתְּ בִּשְׁלָמָא עָשׂוּ – הַיְינוּ דְּקָאָמַר ״מַה נַּעֲשֶׂה״, אֶלָּא אִי אָמְרַתְּ לֹא עָשׂוּ – מַאי ״מַה נַּעֲשֶׂה״?

The Gemara analyzes this episode in relation to the matter at hand. **Granted, if you say** that Beit Shammai **did act** in accordance with their own opinion, **this is** the meaning of **what** Rabban Shimon ben Gamliel **said: What shall we do?** Since these rival wives had already entered into levirate marriage, it was impossible to change the status of their children retroactively. **However, if you say** that **they did not act** in accordance with their opinion, **what is** the meaning of: **What shall we do?** If Beit Shammai did not act upon their ruling, they never actually permitted a *yavam* to take a rival wife in levirate marriage.

אָמַר רַב נַחְמָן בַּר יִצְחָק: לָא נִצְרְכָה אֶלָּא לַצָּרָה עַצְמָהּ, וּמַה נַּעֲשֶׂה – הָכִי קָאָמַר: הָנָךְ צָרוֹת דְּבֵית הִלֵּל לְבֵית שַׁמַּאי הֵיכִי נַעֲבֵיד לְהוּ?

Rav Naḥman bar Yitzḥak said: This amendment was **necessary,** not for the benefit of the children of rival wives, as Beit Shammai never in fact acted on their ruling; **rather,** it was necessary **only for the rival wife herself.** If these rival wives married others, in the opinion of Beit Shammai their marriages were flawed, as they did not perform *ḥalitza*. And as for the question: **What shall we do, this is what** Rabban Shimon ben Gamliel **is saying:** With regard to **those rival wives** who were entirely exempt according **to Beit Hillel, what** should **we do with them** according **to Beit Shammai,** as these rival wives had already married others without performing *ḥalitza*?

לִיחָלְצוּ – מִימָּאֲסִי אַגַּבְרַיְיהוּ, וְכִי תֵּימָא לִימָּאֲסָן – ״דְּרָכֶיהָ דַרְכֵי נוֹעַם וְכָל נְתִיבוֹתֶיהָ שָׁלוֹם״!

The Gemara elaborates: If you say **let them perform *ḥalitza*,**[N] **they will be repulsive to their husbands,** as it will seem to the husband that the woman he has been living with for some time suddenly requires a permit for marriage. **And if you would say, let them be repulsive** to their husbands, as that is not our concern, this is not the case, as the Torah says: **"Her ways are ways of pleasantness,**[N] **and all her paths are peace"** (Proverbs 3:17).

תָּא שְׁמַע, דְּאָמַר רַבִּי טַרְפוֹן: תְּאֵבָנִי, מָתַי תָּבֹא צָרַת הַבַּת לְיָדַי וְאֶשָּׂאֶנָּה! אֵימָא: וְאַשִּׂיאֶנָּה.

§ The Gemara suggests further: **Come and hear** another source, **as Rabbi Tarfon said: I yearn**[N] for the following scenario: **When shall my daughter's rival wife come before me and I will marry her?** In other words, in this hypothetical case I would act in accordance with the opinion of Beit Shammai and take her in levirate marriage. This statement indicates that those who held by the traditions of Beit Shammai did indeed act upon their opinion. The Gemara amends this statement. **Say: And I will marry her off,** i.e., I shall act in accordance with the opinion of Beit Hillel and marry her off to others.

וְהָא ״תְּאֵבָנִי״ קָאָמַר! לְאַפּוֹקֵי מִדְּרַבִּי יוֹחָנָן בֶּן נוּרִי.

The Gemara asks: **But he said: I yearn,**[N] and if he meant that he would follow the ruling of Beit Hillel, which is the common practice, what is the novelty of Rabbi Tarfon's statement? The Gemara responds: Rabbi Tarfon comes **to exclude** the statement of **Rabbi Yoḥanan ben Nuri,** who maintains that all rival wives perform *ḥalitza*. Rabbi Tarfon yearned for an opportunity to demonstrate that the *halakha* is not in accordance with the opinion of Rabbi Yoḥanan ben Nuri.

תָּא שְׁמַע: מַעֲשֶׂה בְּבִתּוֹ שֶׁל רַבָּן גַּמְלִיאֵל שֶׁהָיְתָה נְשׂוּאָה לְאַבָּא אָחִיו, וּמֵת בְּלֹא בָּנִים, וְיִיבֵּם רַבָּן גַּמְלִיאֵל אֶת צָרָתָהּ. וְתִסְבְּרָא, רַבָּן גַּמְלִיאֵל מִתַּלְמִידֵי בֵּית שַׁמַּאי הוּא?!

The Gemara suggests: **Come** and **hear an incident involving Rabban Gamliel's daughter, who was married to Abba, his brother, and** Abba **died childless, and Rabban Gamliel entered into levirate marriage with her rival wife.** This is apparently conclusive proof that the rival wife of a daughter may enter into levirate marriage. The Gemara asks: **And** how can **you understand it** that way? Was **Rabban Gamliel among the disciples of Beit Shammai?** In fact, Rabban Gamliel, who was a descendant of Hillel himself, certainly followed the opinion of Beit Hillel.

אֶלָּא: שָׁאנֵי בִּתּוֹ שֶׁל רַבָּן גַּמְלִיאֵל דְּאַיְלוֹנִית הֲוַאי. הָא מִדְּקָתָנֵי סֵיפָא: אֲחֵרִים אוֹמְרִים בִּתּוֹ שֶׁל רַבָּן גַּמְלִיאֵל אַיְלוֹנִית הָיְתָה, מִכְּלָל דְּתַנָּא קַמָּא סָבַר לָאו אַיְלוֹנִית הָיְתָה!

Rather, the case of **Rabban Gamliel's daughter is different, as she was a sexually underdeveloped woman** [*aylonit*], and therefore the prohibition against marrying her rival wife does not apply, as explicitly stated in the mishna. The Gemara asks: But **from** the fact **that it is taught** in **the latter clause** of the same *baraita*: **Others say** that **Rabban Gamliel's daughter was an *aylonit*,** it can be derived **by inference that the first *tanna* holds** that **she was not an *aylonit*.**

NOTES

Let them perform *ḥalitza* – לִיחָלְצוּ: Another reason can be suggested as to why they cannot perform *ḥalitza* at this late stage: This would mean that any of those women who were married to priests would be rendered forbidden to their husbands. The commentaries explain that the Gemara did not mention this reason because it preferred to cite an explanation that applies in all circumstances (*Sukkat David*).

Her ways are ways of pleasantness – דְּרָכֶיהָ דַרְכֵי נוֹעַם: This verse is cited with regard to several halakhic rulings. For example, in the case of a doubt over a *halakha*, if one option entails suffering or unpleasantness, the Gemara will say that "her ways are ways of pleasantness" and the Torah does not desire that its mitzvot be fulfilled through pain and suffering.

Rabbi Tarfon said, I yearn, etc. – אָמַר רַבִּי טַרְפוֹן תְּאֵבָנִי וכו׳: In *Tosafot Yeshanim* the following question is raised: If one assumes, as Rashi does, that Rabbi Tarfon was a disciple of Beit Shammai, then according to those who maintain that Beit Shammai acted on their opinion, there is in fact no novelty in his marrying a rival wife, as this is precisely in accordance with their ruling. Furthermore, according to this opinion, the solution that he wished to act in opposition to the statement of Rabbi Yoḥanan ben Nuri is also somewhat problematic, as this is not sufficient reason for him to disobey the ruling of Beit Shammai. Consequently, some commentaries reverse the text so that it first states: I yearn to marry her off, from which the Gemara sought to prove that the disciples of Beit Shammai did not act on their opinions, and the ensuing answer is that he actually said: I yearn to marry her. In other words, he desired to act according to the opinion of Beit Shammai, and although there is nothing novel in his desire to follow the ruling of his masters, his action would serve to exclude the statement of Rabbi Yoḥanan ben Nuri. Some commentaries raise a different question: How could Rabbi Tarfon yearn for his daughter's rival wife to come before him for levirate marriage, as this effectively means that he desires his brother's death (Rosh)? The Rosh therefore states in the name of his teacher that Rabbi Tarfon was not referring to his own daughter's rival wife, but rather the rival wife of someone else's daughter. Accordingly, he meant to say that he yearned to act against the opinion of Beit Shammai and marry a daughter's rival wife without levirate marriage or *ḥalitza* (see *Arukh LaNer*).

But he said, I yearn – וְהָא תְּאֵבָנִי קָאָמַר: Some commentaries explain that this expression is appropriate only with regard to something one performs in person and that provides him with benefit. If Rabbi Tarfon meant that he wished to marry her off to others, this is apparently not something he would do for himself. The Gemara therefore explains that by instructing that she be married off to another he would actually be doing something himself, as he would be actively negating the opinion of Rabbi Yoḥanan ben Nuri.

הִכִּיר בָּהּ וְלֹא הִכִּיר בָּהּ אִיכָּא בֵּינַיְיהוּ.

The Gemara answers: The dispute between the *tanna'im* was not about whether or not she was an *aylonit*, as she certainly was. Rather, the practical difference **between them** is whether **he knew** that **she** was an *aylonit* at the time of marriage and decided to marry her regardless. Some maintain in general that if the husband was aware of her condition prior to marriage, her rival wife is forbidden, **but** if **he did not know about her** status, the rival wife is permitted.

וְאִיבָּעֵית אֵימָא: כָּנַס וּלְבַסּוֹף גֵּירֵשׁ אִיכָּא בֵּינַיְיהוּ.

And if you wish, say that the practical difference **between them** concerns a different case, that of one who **married and ultimately divorced.** This is referring to an issue discussed above of whether a woman is considered the rival wife of a forbidden relation simply by virtue of her marriage to the specific man or whether she must be married to him at the time when the mitzva of levirate obligation takes effect, i.e., at the time of the brother's death.

אִיבָּעֵית אֵימָא: יֵשׁ תְּנַאי בְּבִיאָה אִיכָּא בֵּינַיְיהוּ.

And if you wish, say that the practical difference **between them** concerns a case where **there is a condition in sexual relations.**[N] In other words, the first *tanna* holds that Rabban Gamliel's daughter was married only conditionally, and since the condition was never fulfilled the marriage was nullified. Consequently, Rabban Gamliel could marry the other wife regardless of his daughter's status as an *aylonit*, as she was never married to his brother at all. However, according to the other *tanna*, even if the marriage was dependent upon a condition that was not fulfilled, because the man engaged in sexual relations with her the act of intercourse itself serves to nullify the condition. Accordingly, he maintains that the only reason Rabban Gamliel could enter into levirate marriage with his daughter's rival wife was not because of the condition, but due to the fact that his daughter was an *aylonit*. Whichever explanation is accepted, this case provides no proof with regard to the issue of whether or not Beit Shammai acted in accordance with their ruling.

מְתִיב רַב מְשַׁרְשִׁיָּא: מַעֲשֶׂה בְּרַבִּי עֲקִיבָא שֶׁלִּיקֵּט אֶתְרוֹג בְּאֶחָד בִּשְׁבָט, וְנָהַג בּוֹ שְׁנֵי עִשּׂוּרִין;

§ **Rav Mesharshiyya raised an objection** against those who claim that Beit Shammai did not act in accordance with their opinion. It is taught in a mishna: There was **an incident involving Rabbi Akiva, who collected an *etrog***[HN] **on the first of** the month **of Shevat and performed with it two tenths.**[N] In other words, he separated two tithes from the fruit, as though it belonged to two different tithing years. He removed both the second tithe and the poor man's tithe at the same time, two tithes that should not be separated in the same year.

HALAKHA

Collected an *etrog* – לִיקֵּט אֶתְרוֹג: The *etrog* differs from other fruits in that the decisive moment for the determination of its tithes is the removal of the fruit from the tree, as is the case with vegetables (*Shulḥan Arukh, Yoreh De'a* 331:126).

NOTES

There is a condition in sexual relations – יֵשׁ תְּנַאי בְּבִיאָה: According to some commentaries, this is referring to the dispute as to whether one who betroths a woman by sexual intercourse and not with money can do so conditionally, a dispute that appears in *Ketubot* 74a (Rashba; Ritva, citing Ra'avad).

Collected an *etrog* – לִיקֵּט אֶתְרוֹג: The commentaries in tractate *Rosh HaShana* and elsewhere explain that the term: Collected, is used with regard to an *etrog* because these fruits do not all ripen at the same time. Consequently, this is comparable to collecting vegetables in a garden. Others state that the tree itself is called an *etrog* and therefore it means that he took the tree's fruits (Rivan).

Performed with it two tenths – נָהַג בּוֹ שְׁנֵי עִשּׂוּרִין: In addition to the first tithe, which is given to the Levites and is separated every year, there is also a second tithe, which is removed and taken by the owner to be eaten in Jerusalem in the first, second, fourth, and fifth years of the Sabbatical cycle. In the third and sixth years of the cycle, the poor man's tithe is separated.

Since this incident occurred between the second and third years, it was unclear to Rabbi Akiva which of these additional tithes should be separated. *Tosafot* cite the explanation in the Jerusalem Talmud as to how Rabbi Akiva solved other difficulties arising from this double tithing.

אֶחָד כְּדִבְרֵי בֵית שַׁמַּאי וְאֶחָד כְּדִבְרֵי בֵית הִלֵּל, שְׁמַע מִינַּהּ: עָשׂוּ!

The mishna explains: **One** tithe he removed **in accordance with the statement of Beit Shammai,** who hold that the new year for trees occurs on the first of Shevat, which means that the *etrog* required tithing according to the regulations of the upcoming year. **And one** tithe was **in accordance with the statement of Beit Hillel,** who hold the new year for trees is on the fifteenth of Shevat, and therefore the *etrog* required tithing in accordance with the previous year. The Gemara infers: **Conclude from here** that Beit Shammai **did act** in accordance with their opinion, as Rabbi Akiva took care to act in accordance with the ruling of Beit Shammai.

רַבִּי עֲקִיבָא גְּמָרֵיהּ אִסְתַּפַּק לֵיהּ, וְלָא יָדַע אִי בֵּית הִלֵּל בְּאֶחָד בִּשְׁבָט אָמוּר אוֹ בַּחֲמִשָּׁה עָשָׂר בִּשְׁבָט אָמוּר.

The Gemara answers: **Rabbi Akiva was uncertain as to his tradition, and he did not know if Beit Hillel said** that the New Year for trees occurs **on the first of Shevat or if they said** it is **on the fifteenth of Shevat.**[H] He did not act in accordance with the opinion of Beit Shammai at all; rather, he sought to act in accordance with the ruling of Beit Hillel but was uncertain about their opinion on this matter.

מְתִיב מָר זוּטְרָא: מַעֲשֶׂה וְיָלְדָה כַּלָּתוֹ שֶׁל שַׁמַּאי הַזָּקֵן וּפִיחֵת אֶת הַמַּעֲזִיבָה, וְסִיכֵּךְ עַל גַּבֵּי מִטָּה בִּשְׁבִיל קָטָן. שְׁמַע מִינַּהּ: עָשׂוּ! הָתָם הָרוֹאֶה אוֹמֵר לְאַפּוּשֵׁי אֲוִיר קָעָבֵיד.

§ **Mar Zutra raised an objection** to this issue from a different source: There was **an incident in which the daughter-in-law of Shammai the Elder**[P] **gave birth** to a son. In Shammai's opinion this newborn baby is immediately obligated in the mitzva to sit in a *sukka*, **and he** therefore **removed the mortar** [*ma'aziva*][B] covering the ceiling **and he placed** ***sukka*** **covering over the bed for the minor. Conclude from here** that Beit Shammai **did act**[N] in accordance with their opinions. The Gemara answers: There is no proof from **there,** as anyone **watching** would **say** that **he did it** merely **to increase** the **air.** Since people would not necessarily think that he removed the mortar as a ruling of *halakha*, this behavior is not considered the formation of a faction.

מְתִיב מָר זוּטְרָא: מַעֲשֶׂה בְּשׁוֹקֶת יְהוּא שֶׁהָיְתָה בִּירוּשָׁלַיִם וְהָיְתָה נְקוּבָה לַמִּקְוֶה, וְכׇל טְהָרוֹת שֶׁהָיוּ בִּירוּשָׁלַיִם נַעֲשִׂים עַל גַּבָּהּ. וְשָׁלְחוּ בֵּית שַׁמַּאי וְהִרְחִיבוּהָ, שֶׁבֵּית שַׁמַּאי אוֹמְרִים: עַד שֶׁתִּיפָּחֵת בְּרוּבָּהּ.

Mar Zutra raised a further **objection:** There was **an incident involving the Yehu water trough**[HN] **in Jerusalem, which had a hole** that connected it **to a ritual bath, and all the ritual purifications in Jerusalem were performed in it,** i.e., people immersed their utensils in this trough. **And Beit Shammai sent** messengers **and they widened** the opening in the water trough, as in the opinion of Beit Shammai the hole was not large enough for the trough to be considered connected to the adjacent ritual bath **as Beit Shammai say:** The two areas are not connected **unless the majority of it is opened.** In other words, they require the major portion of the barrier between the ritual bath and the nearby trough to be open.

HALAKHA

The year of tithes for trees – שְׁנַת מַעֲשֵׂר לָאִילָנוֹת: The fifteenth of Shevat is the beginning of the New Year for the tithing of trees, in accordance with the opinion of Beit Hillel (Rambam *Sefer Zera'im, Hilkhot Teruma* 5:11; *Shulḥan Arukh, Yoreh De'a* 331:57, 125).

The Yehu water trough – שׁוֹקֶת יְהוּא: Any body of water mixed with a ritual bath has the status of the ritual bath itself and may be used for immersion in the same manner as the ritual bath (*Shulḥan Arukh, Yoreh De'a* 201:57).

BACKGROUND

Removed the mortar [*ma'aziva*] – פִּיחֵת אֶת הַמַּעֲזִיבָה: Houses in the mishnaic period were mainly built of stone, but their roofs sat on large wooden logs in between wooden planks fastened and sealed by mortar and pebbles. This covering was called a *ma'aziva*, apparently from the root *a-z-v*, which means to strengthen. When this covering was removed, only the planks remained, and these could easily be converted into the roofing of a *sukka*.

NOTES

Conclude from here that Beit Shammai did act – שְׁמַע מִינַּהּ עָשׂוּ: Since Beit Shammai's decision to act in accordance with their own ruling can be viewed as merely the adoption of a stringency, this does not provide conclusive proof with regard to the basic dilemma of a division into factions, as in a different case they might not have acted leniently in accordance with their own opinion against that of Beit Hillel. One explanation is that as these actions were performed publicly, the concern over breaking into factions is relevant, despite the fact that their ruling was a stringency (Ritva).

The Yehu water trough – שׁוֹקֶת יְהוּא: Rashi apparently maintains that this trough was connected to a spring. Others raise several difficulties with this interpretation, and most commentaries explain instead that the water trough was attached to a valid ritual bath (Ritva).

PERSONALITIES

Shammai the Elder – שַׁמַּאי הַזָּקֵן: Shammai, occasionally called the Elder, formed a pair with Hillel; he served as deputy *Nasi* while Hillel was the *Nasi* of the Sanhedrin. Hillel and Shammai, the last of the pairs of Sages, lived about one hundred years prior to the destruction of the Temple, at the beginning of the reign of Herod. Despite the fact that the pair founded two schools, Beit Hillel and Beit Shammai, which lasted for many years after their passing, they themselves disagreed about only three or four issues. The difference between Hillel and Shammai themselves was mainly one of personality. Hillel treated himself and others in an easygoing manner, avoiding conflict whenever possible. Shammai, in contrast, took a more severe approach, attempting to scrutinize people's motivations and habits. Nevertheless, it was Shammai who coined the phrase: One should receive every person with a pleasant countenance (*Avot* 1:15). Little is known about Shammai's personal life, but he was apparently an architect or builder by trade, as he is portrayed on several occasions standing with a builder's measuring rod in hand.

וּתְנַן: עֵירוּב מִקְוָאוֹת כִּשְׁפוֹפֶרֶת הַנּוֹד, בְּעוֹבְיָיהּ, וּבַחֲלָלָהּ כִּשְׁתֵּי אֶצְבָּעוֹת חוֹזְרוֹת לִמְקוֹמָן. שְׁמַע מִינָּהּ: עָשׂוּ! הָתָם

And we learned in a mishna: Beit Hillel hold that **a joining of ritual baths**[H] is effective if the hole has the **width of the tube** used to pour water in and out **of a wineskin,**[B] **and in its** open **space** there is enough room for **about two fingers that can return to their place.** In other words, if it is possible to insert into the hole two fingers that can move around on all sides, the cavity is sufficiently large to be considered a connection. According to Beit Shammai, however, the hole must open up the majority of the barrier between the two areas. If so, **conclude from this** that Beit Shammai **did act** in accordance with their opinions. The Gemara rejects this contention: **There,**

HALAKHA

Joining of ritual baths – עֵירוּב מִקְוָאוֹת: If one wishes to join an invalid ritual bath and an adjacent valid ritual bath so that both can be used, he must bore a hole between them the size of the tube of a wineskin. This is a size that enables the insertion and freedom of movement for the first two fingers of the hand (*Shulḥan Arukh*, *Yoreh De'a* 42, 50).

Wineskin made from an intact hide

BACKGROUND

The tube of a wineskin – שְׁפוֹפֶרֶת הַנֹּאד: Wineskin canteens were prepared from whole animal skins. These sacks served various purposes, primarily containing objects of different kinds, but also storing provisions. When these were used as canteens for liquids such as water, wine, or oil, precautions were usually taken to ensure that the skin of the animal remained whole and did not tear. Furthermore, the skin of the legs was left intact. A tube, usually fashioned from cane, would subsequently be inserted into one of the legs, through which the liquid was poured inside.

Perek **I**
Daf **15** Amud **b**

הָרוֹאֶה אוֹמֵר: לְאַפּוּשֵׁי מַיָּא הוּא דְּקָא עָבֵיד.

anyone **watching** would **say** that **he did** it **to increase the water** flow, and he did not intend to change the *halakha*. Rather, they would think that he widened the water trough only because there was not enough water flow.

תָּא שְׁמַע, דְּאָמַר רַבִּי אֶלְעָזָר בַּר צָדוֹק: כְּשֶׁהָיִיתִי לוֹמֵד תּוֹרָה אֵצֶל רַבִּי יוֹחָנָן הַחוֹרָנִי רָאִיתִי שֶׁהָיָה אוֹכֵל פַּת חֲרֵיבָה בְּמֶלַח בִּשְׁנֵי בַּצּוֹרֶת. בָּאתִי וְהוֹדַעְתִּי אֶת אַבָּא. אָמַר לִי: הוֹלֵךְ לוֹ זֵיתִים, וְהוֹלַכְתִּי לוֹ. רָאָה אוֹתָן שֶׁהֵן לַחִין, אָמַר לִי: אֵין אֲנִי אוֹכֵל זֵיתִים.

§ The Gemara cites another relevant source. **Come** and **hear, as Rabbi Elazar bar Tzadok said: When I studied Torah with Rabbi Yoḥanan the Ḥorani,**[P] who was a disciple of Beit Shammai, **I saw that he would eat dry bread in salt in years of drought. I went and informed** my **father** of his meager meal, and **he said to me: Take olives** for **him, and I took** for **him** some olives. Rabbi Yoḥanan **saw that they were moist** with the liquid that oozes from olives, which renders them susceptible to ritual impurity. Concerned that they had already become ritually impure, **he said to me: I do not eat olives.**[N] He spoke politely and stated that he did not eat olives because he did not wish to embarrass his benefactor by disclosing that he feared they had become ritually impure.

NOTES

I do not eat olives – אֵין אֲנִי אוֹכֵל זֵיתִים: If one receives a gift from an important individual but fears that it may be in some way prohibited, for reasons of courtesy it is not appropriate to say so explicitly. Rather, one should speak indirectly, so as not to insult the giver (Meiri). With regard to this particular matter, some commentaries claim that, according to Rashi, Rabbi Yoḥanan was concerned that Rabbi Tzadok might not be careful about the ritual impurity of an *am ha'aretz*, a common, uneducated individual (*Tosafot*). This is certainly the interpretation of Rivan, a disciple of Rashi. Since Rashi states that the concern was that the olives had contracted ritual impurity through their earthenware container, which had been touched by an *am ha'aretz*, some later commentaries inquire how that earthenware container itself became ritually impure, as an earthenware vessel cannot contract ritual impurity from the outside; it contracts impurity only if a ritually impure object is placed inside it. Some explain that there is a specific decree that an earthenware vessel can contract ritual impurity through contact with impure liquids. See *Arukh LaNer* and *Sukkat David*, who attempt to explain that Rabbi Tzadok acted in accordance with his own opinion in this regard.

Alternatively, the concern might refer to ritual impurity contracted by movement, which would render both the barrel and its contents impure (Rashash). Some state that since people are generally not careful to crush olives in a state of ritual purity, it is simply assumed that a ritually impure individual touched them (Ritva).

PERSONALITIES

Rabbi Yoḥanan the Ḥorani – רַבִּי יוֹחָנָן הַחוֹרָנִי: Rabbi Yoḥanan the Ḥorani, or Horonite, is mentioned in several places as one of the important Sages of the generation before the destruction of the Temple. He was highly regarded by both Beit Shammai, of which he was a member, and Beit Hillel. His opinion on the disputes between the schools was similar to that of other Sages from Beit Shammai, e.g., Baba ben Bota from the previous generation. In general, they sought to act in accordance with the opinion of Beit Hillel. This explains why Rabbi Tzadok of Beit Hillel would send his son to study with Rabbi Yoḥanan the Ḥorani. Nothing is known of Rabbi Yoḥanan the Ḥorani's life or activities, although certain sources indicate that he was destitute and lived in conditions of severe poverty.

HALAKHA

A barrel of preserved olives – חָבִית שֶׁל זֵיתִים מְגוּלְגָּלִים: If a barrel of preserved olives is not perforated to allow the juices to escape, the olives are rendered susceptible to ritual impurity. If the barrel was pierced and then the hole clogged with sediments, the olives are not rendered susceptible to ritual impurity (Rambam *Sefer Tahara, Hilkhot Tumat Okhalin* 11:7).

BACKGROUND

Clogged by sediments – סְתָמוּהָ שְׁמָרִים: The term sediments is imprecise in this context, as oil does not actually contain sediments. However, the oil that comes out of olives does thicken partially, due to contact with oxygen in the air, particularly when it is not refined. As a result, it can form masses that could clog up the hole in a barrel.

בָּאתִי וְהוֹדַעְתִּי אֶת אַבָּא. אָמַר לִי: לֵךְ וֶאֱמוֹר לוֹ: חָבִית נְקוּבָה הָיְתָה, אֶלָּא שֶׁסְּתָמוּהָ שְׁמָרִים. וּתְנַן: חָבִית שֶׁל זֵיתִים מְגוּלְגָּלִים, בֵּית שַׁמַּאי אוֹמְרִים אֵין צְרִיכָה לְנַקֵּב,

Rabbi Elazar bar Tzadok continued his account. **I went and informed** my **father. He said to me: Go and say to him** that the **barrel** containing the olives **was perforated, but it was clogged by sediments** in the oil and therefore some moisture remained inside. However, due to the presence of the hole, the olives were not rendered susceptible to ritual impurity. **And we learned** this in a mishna: With regard to **a barrel of preserved olives,**[NH] **Beit Shammai say it does not need to be perforated,** as the juice issuing from the olives does not render them susceptible to ritual impurity.

וּבֵית הִלֵּל אוֹמְרִים: צְרִיכָה לְנַקֵּב, וּמוֹדִים שֶׁאִם נִיקְּבָה וּסְתָמוּהָ שְׁמָרִים – שֶׁהִיא טְהוֹרָה.

And Beit Hillel say that **it does need to be perforated,** as they maintain that the juice of olives is considered oil and it therefore renders the olives susceptible to ritual impurity. **And** Beit Hillel **concede that if** the barrel **was perforated and** subsequently **clogged by sediments**[B] **it is ritually pure,** despite the moisture on the olives. Since liquids render food susceptible to ritual impurity only if they were placed on them intentionally, the hole in the barrel clearly shows that one did not intend for the juice to be there. By boring a hole in the barrel he has rendered it obvious that he did not desire the presence of the olive juices, and therefore it does not matter that the hole became blocked.

וְאַף עַל פִּי שֶׁתַּלְמִיד שַׁמַּאי הָיָה – כׇּל מַעֲשָׂיו לֹא עָשָׂה אֶלָּא כְּדִבְרֵי בֵית הִלֵּל. אִי אָמְרַתְּ בִּשְׁלָמָא עָשׂוּ – הַיְינוּ רְבוּתֵיהּ, אֶלָּא אִי אָמְרַתְּ לֹא עָשׂוּ – מַאי רְבוּתֵיהּ?

The *baraita* adds: **And although** Rabbi Yoḥanan the Ḥorani **was a disciple of Shammai, he always acted only in accordance with the statements of Beit Hillel.** The Gemara infers: **Granted, if you say** that Beit Shammai **acted** in accordance with their opinions, **this is** Rabbi Yoḥanan the Ḥorani's **greatness,** i.e., he is praised for acting in accordance with the opinion of Beit Hillel. **However, if you say** that Beit Shammai **did not act** in accordance with their own rulings, **what is the greatness** and uniqueness **of** Rabbi Yoḥanan the Ḥorani? From here it can be inferred that Beit Shammai generally did act in accordance with their opinions.

תָּא שְׁמַע: שָׁאֲלוּ אֶת רַבִּי יְהוֹשֻׁעַ: צָרַת הַבַּת מַהוּ? אָמַר לָהֶם: מַחְלוֹקֶת בֵּית שַׁמַּאי וּבֵית הִלֵּל. וַהֲלָכָה כְּדִבְרֵי מִי? אָמַר לָהֶם: מִפְּנֵי מָה אַתֶּם מַכְנִיסִין רֹאשִׁי בֵּין שְׁנֵי הָרִים גְּדוֹלִים, בֵּין שְׁתֵּי מַחְלוֹקוֹת גְּדוֹלוֹת, בֵּין בֵּית שַׁמַּאי וּבֵין בֵּית הִלֵּל, מִתְיָירֵא אֲנִי שֶׁמָּא יָרוֹצּוּ גֻּלְגׇּלְתִּי.

§ The Gemara adds: **Come** and **hear** a different proof. **They asked**[N] **Rabbi Yehoshua: What is** the *halakha* with regard to the **rival wife of a daughter? He said to them:** It is a matter of **dispute between Beit Shammai and Beit Hillel.** They continued to ask him: **And in accordance with whose statement is the** ***halakha*****? He said to them: Why are you inserting my head between two great mountains,** i.e., **between two great disputing** opinions, **between Beit Shammai and Beit Hillel? I fear lest** these two mountains **break my skull.**[N]

NOTES

A barrel of preserved olives – חָבִית שֶׁל זֵיתִים מְגוּלְגָּלִים: The commentaries discuss whether or not the juice that issues from olives is considered a form of liquid that renders foods susceptible to contract ritual impurity (*Tosafot*). Some write that olive juices do not render foods susceptible to ritual impurity at the time of harvest, but only from the moment they are prepared for pressing (Meiri). Since this barrel was filled with preserved olives, it is obvious that the owner wants the juice to be there, as it assists in the pressing of the olives. Others explain that although olive juice generally does render foods susceptible to ritual impurity, these olives were designated exclusively for consumption. Consequently, the juice was undesirable, and a liquid that is not desired by the owner does not render foods susceptible to impurity (Rivan).

Come and hear, they asked, etc. – תָּא שְׁמַע שָׁאֲלוּ וכו׳: Some commentaries inquire about the need for this additional source. After all, the Gemara already proved from the previous story involving Rabbi Yoḥanan the Ḥorani that Beit Shammai indeed acted in accordance with their rulings. Some explain that the previous proof can be refuted by saying that Rabbi Yoḥanan the Ḥorani was praised for acting in all cases in accordance with the rulings of Beit Hillel, not only in those cases in which the opinion of Beit Hillel was the more stringent (*Otzar HaShitot*).

I fear lest they break my skull – מִתְיָירֵא אֲנִי שֶׁמָּא יָרוֹצּוּ גֻּלְגׇּלְתִּי: The commentaries ask: By his very admission of fear, Rabbi Yehoshua is indicating that he holds in accordance with the opinion of Beit Hillel, which means the children of rival wives who entered into levirate marriage are *mamzerim*. If so, he did in fact reveal his opinion and harmed those affected by this ruling (Maharsha). The Maharsha suggests that perhaps Rabbi Yehoshua did not answer those who asked him in this manner. Rather, he said this privately to his disciples in explanation of why he did not provide a precise response. Some commentaries explain, in a homiletic vein, that since Rabbi Yehoshua was the Sage who declared that we pay no attention to a Divine Voice (see *Bava Metzia* 59b), if he were to say here that the *halakha* is in accordance with the opinion of Beit Hillel due to a Divine Voice he would be contradicting himself (*Iyyun Ya'akov*).

אֲבָל אֲנִי מֵעִיד לָכֶם עַל שְׁתֵּי מִשְׁפָּחוֹת גְּדוֹלוֹת שֶׁהָיוּ בִּירוּשָׁלַיִם: מִשְׁפַּחַת בֵּית צְבוֹעִים מִבֶּן עַכְמַאי, וּמִשְׁפַּחַת בֵּית קוּפַאי מִבֶּן מְקוֹשֵׁשׁ, שֶׁהֵם בְּנֵי צָרוֹת וּמֵהֶם כֹּהֲנִים גְּדוֹלִים, וְשִׁמְּשׁוּ עַל גַּבֵּי הַמִּזְבֵּחַ.

However, I shall testify to you[N] **about two great families that were in Jerusalem, the Beit Tzevo'im family** who came **from** the town of **Ben Akhmai, and the Beit Kofai family from** the town of **Ben Mekoshesh: They were the descendants of rival wives** who married others, in accordance with the opinion of Beit Hillel, **and from them** came **High Priests who served on the altar.** Accordingly, I can testify that this was the accepted halakhic practice throughout the generations.

אִי אָמְרַתְּ בִּשְׁלָמָא עָשׂוּ – הַיְינוּ דְּקָאָמַר מִתְיָירֵא אֲנִי, אֶלָּא אִי אָמְרַתְּ לֹא עָשׂוּ – אַמַּאי קָאָמַר מִתְיָירֵא אֲנִי? וְנְהִי נַמִי דְּעָשׂוּ, מַאי מִתְיָירֵא אֲנִי?

The Gemara infers from this statement: **Granted, if you say** that Beit Shammai **acted** in accordance with their opinions, **this is why** Rabbi Yehoshua **said: I fear,** since a conclusive halakhic ruling would mean that certain children are *mamzerim*, and the descendants of that family might take vengeance upon him. **However, if you say** that **they did not act** in accordance with their opinions, **why did he say: I fear?** The Gemara retorts: **And even** if Beit Shammai **did act** in accordance with their rulings, **what is** the reason that he said: **I fear?**

הָא אָמַר רַבִּי יְהוֹשֻׁעַ: אֵין מַמְזֵר אֶלָּא מֵחַיָּיבֵי מִיתוֹת בֵּית דִּין! נְהִי נַמִי דְּמַמְזֵר לָא הָוֵי, פָּגוּם מִיהוּ הָוֵי,

Didn't Rabbi Yehoshua say that in his opinion **a *mamzer* is only** someone born **from** a union **of those liable to** receive **the court-imposed capital punishments,**[H] not from those liable to receive *karet*. If so, in the opinion of Rabbi Yehoshua, the children of rival wives who entered into levirate marriage would not be *mamzerim* at all, and therefore he had no reason to fear reprisals. The Gemara answers: **Even if** this is the case, nevertheless, he had something to fear, as, although the child of a rival wife would **not be a *mamzer*,** he would **nevertheless be** of **flawed** lineage and disqualified from the priesthood.

מִקַּל וָחוֹמֶר מֵאַלְמָנָה: מָה אַלְמָנָה, שֶׁאֵין אִיסּוּרָהּ נוֹהֵג בַּכֹּל – בְּנָהּ פָּגוּם, זוֹ שֶׁאִיסּוּרָהּ שָׁוֶה בַּכֹּל כו׳.

The Gemara adds that this can be derived **by an *a fortiori*** inference **from** the case of **a widow: Just as** in the case of **a widow, whose prohibition does not apply to all,** as she is forbidden in marriage only to a High Priest and not to any other man, **and** yet the lineage of **her son is flawed,** as he is disqualified from the priesthood, the son of **this** rival wife should certainly be disqualified from the priesthood, as **her prohibition applies equally to all,** even regular Israelites.

קָבָעוּ מִינֵּיהּ צָרוֹת וְקָפָשֵׁיט לֵיהּ בְּנֵי צָרוֹת! תַּרְתֵּי קָא בָּעֵי מִינֵּיהּ: צָרוֹת מַאי, וְאִם תִּמְצֵי לוֹמַר צָרוֹת כְּבֵית הִלֵּל – בְּנֵי צָרוֹת דְּבֵית הִלֵּל לְבֵית שַׁמַּאי מַהוּ?

§ Incidentally, the Gemara notes a problem with the above discussion: **They asked** Rabbi Yehoshua about **rival wives, and he answered them** about **the children of rival wives.** He did not refer to the rival wives themselves. The Gemara explains: **They asked him** questions on **two** matters: First, **what is** the *halakha* with regard to **rival wives? And if you say** that the *halakha* in the case of **rival wives** is **in accordance with** the opinion of **Beit Hillel** and they are exempt, **what is** the *halakha* **according to Beit Shammai** in the case of **the children of rival wives** who, following **Beit Hillel,** married others without *ḥalitza*?

לְמַאי נָפְקָא מִינָּהּ? לְמִיפְשַׁט וְלָד מַחֲזִיר גְּרוּשָׁתוֹ לְבֵית הִלֵּל.

The Gemara asks: **What difference** does this question make? Since Rabbi Yehoshua maintains that the *halakha* is in accordance with the ruling of Beit Hillel, why even discuss Beit Shammai's opinion on this matter? The Gemara explains: His answer enables one **to resolve** a different issue, the case of a **child of one who remarries his divorcée according to** the opinion of **Beit Hillel.** Is the child of a divorcée who remarried her previous husband after she had been married to another man fit or disqualified from the priesthood?

מִי קָאָמְרִינַן קַל וָחוֹמֶר: וּמַה אַלְמָנָה לְכֹהֵן גָּדוֹל שֶׁאֵין אִיסּוּרָהּ שָׁוֶה בַּכֹּל – בְּנָהּ פָּגוּם, זוֹ שֶׁאִיסּוּרָהּ שָׁוֶה בַּכֹּל – אֵינוֹ דִּין שֶׁבְּנָהּ פָּגוּם?

The Gemara elaborates: **Do we say** the following **an *a fortiori*** inference: **And just as** with regard to **a widow** married **to a High Priest,**[H] **whose prohibition does not apply to all,** as she is prohibited in marriage only to a High Priest, **and** yet the lineage of **her son is flawed** as he is disqualified from the priesthood, so too, in the case of **this** rival wife, **whose prohibition applies equally to all** men, **is it not right that her son** should be of **flawed** lineage?

NOTES

However, I shall testify to you, etc. – אֲבָל אֲנִי מֵעִיד לָכֶם וכו׳: This indicates that rival wives who married other men are not disqualified from the priesthood. Clearly, this is not the opinion of Rabbi Yoḥanan ben Nuri (see 14b), who states that Beit Shammai maintain that the child is disqualified. It is possible that Rabbi Yehoshua witnessed that in practice Beit Shammai were not concerned about disqualification in this case, whereas Rabbi Yoḥanan ben Nuri was not aware of this fact. Alternatively, Beit Shammai did object to these High Priests, but the opinion of Beit Hillel prevailed. If so, this case provides no conclusive evidence with regard to the actual opinion of Beit Shammai (Ramban).

HALAKHA

Who is a *mamzer* – אֵיזֶהוּ מַמְזֵר: A child born from a forbidden union is a *mamzer*, whether that relationship entails court-imposed capital punishment or *karet*, with the exception of a union with a menstruating woman, in accordance with the opinion of Shimon the Temanite on 49a (*Shulḥan Arukh, Even HaEzer* 4:13).

A High Priest to a widow – כֹּהֵן גָּדוֹל בְּאַלְמָנָה: If a High Priest engages in sexual intercourse with a widow she is disqualified from marrying into the priesthood, and any child born to her, from him or any other man, is likewise disqualified (*Shulḥan Arukh, Even HaEzer* 7:12).

NOTES

What about the fact that a widow is different as she herself is disqualified – מַה לְאַלְמָנָה שֶׁהִיא עַצְמָהּ מִתְחַלֶּלֶת: The Meiri explains that even according to the opinion, which he himself accepts, that every woman who engages in sexual intercourse in violation of a prohibition is disqualified from marrying a priest, including a woman obligated in levirate marriage who marries without *ḥalitza*, she is nevertheless not rendered unfit to eat *teruma* if she is the daughter of a priest. This explains why the Gemara said that she becomes disqualified from marrying a priest, not that she is unfit for eating *teruma* (see *Keren Ora*).

אוֹ דִּלְמָא אִיכָּא לְמִיפְרַךְ: מַה לְאַלְמָנָה – שֶׁהִיא עַצְמָהּ מִתְחַלֶּלֶת! וְאָמַר לְהוּ: צָרוֹת – מִתְיָירֵא אֲנִי,

Or perhaps this comparison **can be refuted: What** about the fact **that a widow** is different, **as she herself is disqualified**[N] from marrying a priest, i.e., if a High Priest has intercourse with her she is disqualified from marrying any member of the entire priesthood, including common priests, whereas a remarried divorcée herself is not disqualified from marrying into the priesthood? **And** Rabbi Yehoshua **said to them: I fear** that if I issue a decisive ruling concerning **rival wives** this might lead to a conflict,

NOTES

With regard to the children of rival wives, I testify to you – בְּנֵי צָרוֹת אֲנִי מֵעִיד לָכֶם: The early commentaries discuss the meaning of this testimony from different perspectives. One interpretation is that as Rabbi Yehoshua testified that the children of rival wives are undoubtedly qualified, he thereby indicated that the *halakha* is entirely in accordance with the opinion of Beit Hillel, including the status of the rival wives themselves (*Tosefot HaRosh*).

LANGUAGE

Harkinas – הַרְכִּינָס: The form of this name is Greek, perhaps from the name Ἀρχῖνος, Archinos, which means great or head. In the Jerusalem Talmud the name appears as Arginas, perhaps from ἀργεννός, *argennos*, meaning white.

בְּנֵי צָרוֹת אֲנִי מֵעִיד לָכֶם.

whereas with regard to the **children of rival wives, I testify to you**[N] that they are not disqualified, since, as stated, their descendants served as High Priests.

תָּא שְׁמַע: בִּימֵי רַבִּי דּוֹסָא בֶּן הַרְכִּינַס הוּתְּרָה צָרַת הַבַּת לָאַחִין. שְׁמַע מִינַּהּ: עָשׂוּ, שְׁמַע מִינַּהּ.

§ The Gemara states: **Come** and **hear** another source that indicates Beit Shammai did act upon their opinions: **In the time of Rabbi Dosa ben Harkinas,**[LP] **the rival wife of a daughter was permitted to the brothers. Conclude from this** that Beit Shammai **did act** in accordance with their opinions. The Gemara summarizes these proofs: Indeed, **conclude from** these sources that Beit Shammai did put their rulings into practice.

גּוּפָא, בִּימֵי רַבִּי דּוֹסָא בֶּן הַרְכִּינַס הִתִּירוּ צָרַת הַבַּת לָאַחִין וְהָיָה הַדָּבָר קָשֶׁה לַחֲכָמִים, מִפְּנֵי שֶׁחָכָם גָּדוֹל הָיָה וְעֵינָיו קָמוּ מִלָּבֹא לְבֵית הַמִּדְרָשׁ.

§ Since the last source is only part of a larger incident, the Gemara cites **the** matter **itself. In the time of Rabbi Dosa ben Harkinas** the Sages **permitted the rival wife of a daughter to the brothers.** In other words, it became known that Rabbi Dosa ben Harkinas rendered permitted a daughter's rival wife. **And this matter was difficult** in the eyes of **the Rabbis because he was a great Sage** and his decision in favor of Beit Shammai carried great weight. They could not approach him immediately, as he was very old **and his eyes had dimmed** so much that he was incapable **of coming to the study hall.**

(אָמַר: וּמִי יֵלֵךְ) וְיוֹדִיעוֹ? אָמַר לָהֶן רַבִּי יְהוֹשֻׁעַ: אֲנִי אֵלֵךְ. וְאַחֲרָיו מִי? רַבִּי אֶלְעָזָר בֶּן עֲזַרְיָה, וְאַחֲרָיו מִי? רַבִּי עֲקִיבָא. הָלְכוּ וְעָמְדוּ עַל פֶּתַח בֵּיתוֹ, נִכְנְסָה שִׁפְחָתוֹ, אָמְרָה לוֹ: רַבִּי, חַכְמֵי יִשְׂרָאֵל בָּאִין אֶצְלְךָ. אָמַר לָהּ: יִכָּנְסוּ, וְנִכְנְסוּ.

They **said: And who will go and notify him** that this matter requires clarification? **Rabbi Yehoshua said to them: I will go.** They asked: **And who** shall go **after him?** They selected **Rabbi Elazar ben Azarya,** who was one of the great Sages of the generation, notwithstanding his youth. They further inquired: **And who after him? Rabbi Akiva.**[P] **They went and stood at the entrance of** Rabbi Dosa ben Harkinas's **house. His maidservant entered** and **said to him: Rabbi, the Sages of Israel have come to you. He said to her: Let them enter, and they entered.**

PERSONALITIES

Rabbi Dosa ben Harkinas – רַבִּי דּוֹסָא בֶּן הַרְכִּינָס: Rabbi Dosa ben Harkinas was one of the earliest *tanna'im*. He was already considered a Sage of great stature in the period of the Second Temple. He engaged in disputes with Akavya ben Mahalalel and Ḥananya the deputy High Priest, and he was apparently from the same generation as Rabbi Yoḥanan ben Zakkai, whom he outlived. As a result of his longevity, he is described as participating in various deliberations during the time of Rabban Gamliel in Yavne, although he would not come to the study hall due to his old age. If this is the case, he lived well over a hundred years. See the Rambam's introduction to the order of *Zera'im*, where his wondrously long life span is recounted. Rabbi Dosa ben Harkinas was universally respected due to his old age and wisdom, and Rabbi Yehoshua asked his advice on several issues. He was apparently an expert in the history of the Jewish people, and he could recall even small details of events. He possibly preserved for himself relics from earlier eras, such as the mortar of the prophet Haggai. The story recounted here indicates that he was also extremely wealthy, but there are no records of his profession or family, besides the younger brother he himself mentions. His statements, which are also cited in the Mishna, deal with both *aggada* and *halakha*. When the name Rabbi Dosa is mentioned without any qualifiers in the Mishna, the reference is to Rabbi Dosa ben Harkinas.

Rabbi Akiva – רַבִּי עֲקִיבָא: Rabbi Akiva, who lived just after the destruction of the Second Temple, was one of the greatest of the *tanna'im*. Unlettered until the age of forty, Akiva was encouraged by his wife, Rachel, to devote himself to the study of Torah. After years of study under the tutelage of Rabbi Eliezer ben Hyrcanus, Yehoshua ben Ḥananya, and others, he acquired thousands of students and established his own academy in Benei Berak. Rabbi Akiva systematized and arranged many oral traditions, and it was the tradition of Rabbi Akiva as received by his disciple, Rabbi Meir, that ultimately became the basis of the six orders of the Mishna. Rabbi Akiva was the spiritual leader of the bar Kokheva revolt. He even proclaimed bar Kokheva the Messiah early in the struggle, but he later retracted this opinion. Despite Roman decrees against disseminating Torah, the aged Rabbi Akiva continued to teach. Rabbi Akiva was arrested by the Romans, imprisoned, tried, and sentenced to death. He suffered a martyr's death at the hands of the Romans, and is listed as one of the ten martyrs executed by the Romans. As the Romans were torturing him to death, he explained to his students that he now had the opportunity to fulfill the true meaning of loving God with all of one's soul (*Berakhot* 61b).

תְּפָסוֹ לְרַבִּי יְהוֹשֻׁעַ וְהוֹשִׁיבָהוּ עַל מִטָּה שֶׁל זָהָב, אָמַר לוֹ: רַבִּי, אֱמוֹר לְתַלְמִידְךָ אַחֵר וְיֵשֵׁב. אָמַר לוֹ: מִי הוּא? רַבִּי אֶלְעָזָר בֶּן עֲזַרְיָה. אָמַר: וְיֵשׁ לוֹ בֵּן לַעֲזַרְיָה חֲבֵירֵנוּ?

Rabbi Dosa ben Harkinas **grabbed Rabbi Yehoshua,** with whom he was already acquainted, **and sat him on a bed of gold,** as Rabbi Dosa was extremely wealthy. Rabbi Yehoshua **said to him: Rabbi, call your other disciple** so **that he may sit.**[H] He asked him to call the other Sage as well, as it is a mark of respect when speaking to a great scholar to call every other Sage his disciple. **He said to him: Who is it?** Rabbi Yehoshua replied: **Rabbi Elazar ben Azarya.** Rabbi Dosa **said: And does our colleague Azarya have a son?** Due to his old age and prolonged absence from the study hall he had not heard of him.

קָרָא עָלָיו הַמִּקְרָא הַזֶּה: ״נַעַר הָיִיתִי גַּם זָקַנְתִּי וְלֹא רָאִיתִי צַדִּיק נֶעֱזָב וְזַרְעוֹ מְבַקֶּשׁ לָחֶם״. תְּפָסוֹ וְהוֹשִׁיבוֹ עַל מִטָּה שֶׁל זָהָב. אָמַר לוֹ: רַבִּי, אֱמוֹר לְתַלְמִידְךָ אַחֵר וְיֵשֵׁב. אָמַר לוֹ: וּמִי הוּא? עֲקִיבָא בֶּן יוֹסֵף. אָמַר לוֹ: אַתָּה הוּא עֲקִיבָא בֶּן יוֹסֵף, שֶׁשִּׁמְךָ הוֹלֵךְ מִסּוֹף הָעוֹלָם וְעַד סוֹפוֹ? שֵׁב בְּנִי, שֵׁב, כְּמוֹתְךָ יִרְבּוּ בְּיִשְׂרָאֵל!

Rabbi Dosa ben Harkinas **recited this verse about** Rabbi Elazar ben Azarya: **"I have been young, and now am old; yet I have not seen the righteous forsaken,[N] nor his seed begging bread"** (Psalms 37:25). He interpreted this verse to mean that the son of a Torah scholar also becomes a Torah scholar. **He grabbed him and sat him on a bed of gold.** Rabbi Yehoshua **said to him: Rabbi, call your other disciple** so **that he may sit. He said to him: Who is that?** He said to him: **Akiva ben Yosef.** Rabbi Dosa **said to him: You are Akiva[N] ben Yosef, whose name has spread from one end of the world to the other?** Even Rabbi Dosa had heard of Rabbi Akiva's reputation as a great man. **Sit, my son, sit. May the likes of you multiply in Israel.[N]**

הִתְחִילוּ מְסַבְּבִים אוֹתוֹ בַּהֲלָכוֹת, עַד שֶׁהִגִּיעוּ לְצָרַת הַבַּת. אָמְרוּ לֵיהּ: צָרַת הַבַּת מַהוּ? אָמַר לָהֶן: מַחֲלוֹקֶת בֵּית שַׁמַּאי וּבֵית הִלֵּל. הֲלָכָה כְּדִבְרֵי מִי? אָמַר לָהֶן: הֲלָכָה כְּבֵית הִלֵּל. אָמְרוּ לֵיהּ: וַהֲלֹא מִשְּׁמְךָ אָמְרוּ הֲלָכָה כְּבֵית שַׁמַּאי!

Out of courtesy, they did not wish to broach the subject immediately. Rather, **they began to encircle him with** deliberations on different ***halakhot*****, until they came to** the case of the **rival wife of a daughter. They said to him: What is** the *halakha* with regard to the **rival wife of a daughter? He said** that it is a matter of **dispute between Beit Shammai and Beit Hillel.** They asked him: **According to whose statement is the *halakha*? He said to them: The *halakha* is in accordance with** the opinion of **Beit Hillel. They said to him: But didn't they say in your name that the *halakha* is in accordance with** the opinion of **Beit Shammai?**

אָמַר לָהֶם: דּוֹסָא שְׁמַעְתֶּם, אוֹ בֶּן הַרְכִּינָס שְׁמַעְתֶּם? אָמְרוּ לֵיהּ: חַיֵּי רַבִּי, סְתָם שָׁמַעְנוּ. אָמַר לָהֶם: אָח קָטָן יֵשׁ לִי, בְּכוֹר שָׂטָן הוּא, וְיוֹנָתָן שְׁמוֹ, וְהוּא מִתַּלְמִידֵי שַׁמַּאי.

He said to them: Did you hear that **Dosa** ben Harkinas issued this ruling, **or did you hear** that it was stated by **ben Harkinas? They said to him: On your life, Rabbi, we heard simply** ben Harkinas. **He said to them:** If so, it is no wonder, as **I have a younger brother who is the firstborn of the Satan,[N]** i.e., he is extremely sharp and as brazen as a demon. **And his name is Yonatan, and he is among the disciples of Shammai.** It is he who issued this ruling.

HALAKHA

Call your other disciple that he may sit – אֱמוֹר לְתַלְמִידְךָ אַחֵר וְיֵשֵׁב: A disciple is not permitted to sit before his master until he is instructed to do so (*Shulḥan Arukh, Yoreh De'a* 242:16).

NOTES

I have not seen the righteous forsaken, etc. – לֹא רָאִיתִי צַדִּיק נֶעֱזָב וכו׳: Some commentaries note that this quotation also alludes to Rabbi Elazar ben Azarya's great wealth (Rivan).

You are Akiva, etc. – אַתָּה הוּא עֲקִיבָא וכו׳: In the Jerusalem Talmud the following is added: I am aware that he is a great man in Torah. In some versions an additional verse befitting Rabbi Akiva's personality is added: "A good name is better than precious oil" (Ecclesiastes 7:1). Rabbi Akiva came from a family of converts, and yet the name he made for himself spread far and wide like the fragrance of precious oil (*Ein Ya'akov*).

May the likes of you multiply in Israel – כְּמוֹתְךָ יִרְבּוּ בְּיִשְׂרָאֵל: Some commentaries suggest that this too is an allusion to Rabbi Akiva's background from a family of converts (Maharsha). Rabbi Dosa is saying: I wish that there were those like you from the Jewish people itself, not only from converts. Others explain that although the Sages were generally wary of accepting converts, this concern did not include personalities such as Rabbi Akiva, and that he wished for more converts of his kind (*Iyyun Ya'akov*).

Who is the firstborn [*bekhor*] of the Satan – בְּכוֹר שָׂטָן הוּא: Those commentaries who accept this version of the text interpret this statement as an expression of both affection and reproof. It is as though he said that his brother is intellectually very sharp but does not know how to arrive at the proper conclusions, or, as some put it: He too readily turns around his proofs (Rivan). Other commentaries cite the version of the text found in *Ein Ya'akov*: Witty firstborn, and some read: Witty youth (Maharatz Ḥayyut). The version of the text found in several manuscripts states that the number of proofs Yonatan ben Harkinas could provide was equivalent to the numerical value of the Hebrew word Satan: Three hundred and fifty-nine. An entirely different interpretation of the term *bekhor* in this context is that Khor Satan or Bor Satan is the name of the place where Yonatan ben Harkinas lived (*Tosafot Yeshanim*).

וְהִזָּהֲרוּ שֶׁלֹּא יְקַפֵּחַ אֶתְכֶם בַּהֲלָכוֹת. לְפִי שֶׁיֵּשׁ עִמּוֹ שְׁלֹשׁ מֵאוֹת תְּשׁוּבוֹת בְּצָרַת הַבַּת שֶׁהִיא מוּתֶּרֶת. אֲבָל מֵעִיד אֲנִי עָלַי שָׁמַיִם וָאָרֶץ שֶׁעַל מְדוֹכָה זוֹ יָשַׁב חַגַּי הַנָּבִיא וְאָמַר שְׁלֹשָׁה דְּבָרִים: צָרַת הַבַּת אֲסוּרָה,

Rabbi Dosa ben Harkinas added: **And beware that he not batter you with *halakhot*** in this matter, **as he has with him three hundred proofs with regard to** the **rival wife of a daughter that she is permitted. However,** you need not worry about the issue itself, as **I call as witnesses before me the heavens and the earth that on this** very **mortar,** which was preserved in my house due to its historical importance, **Haggai the prophet sat,**[N] **and** I have a tradition that **he said three matters**[N] of *halakha*: First, that the **rival wife of a daughter is forbidden.**

עַמּוֹן וּמוֹאָב מְעַשְּׂרִין מַעְשַׂר עָנִי בַּשְּׁבִיעִית, וּמְקַבְּלִים גֵּרִים מִן הַקַּרְדּוּיִין וּמִן הַתַּרְמוֹדִים.

Second, that the halakhic rulings for the territories of **Ammon and Moab** in Transjordan, although similar to those of Eretz Yisrael, are not exactly the same, as their residents **tithe the poor man's tithe**[B] **in the Sabbatical Year.**[HB] The total abandonment of fields in the seventh year does not apply in Ammon and Moab, as they are not part of Eretz Yisrael. Instead, in those areas one must bring the poor man's tithe to the paupers of Eretz Yisrael, as there are no tithes in Eretz Yisrael in the Sabbatical Year. Lastly, Haggai testified: **And one accepts converts from the Karduyin and the Tarmodim,** without concern that there might be Jews mingled among them, which could render them *mamzerim* and prohibited from entering the community.

תָּנָא: כְּשֶׁנִּכְנְסוּ נִכְנְסוּ בְּפֶתַח אֶחָד, כְּשֶׁיָּצְאוּ – יָצְאוּ בִּשְׁלֹשָׁה פְּתָחִים. פָּגַע בּוֹ בְּרַבִּי עֲקִיבָא, אַקְשֵׁי לֵיהּ וְאוֹקְמֵיהּ.

The Sage **taught: When they entered,** they all **entered through one entrance. When they left, they left through three entrances,** in an effort to try to find Rabbi Dosa's brother. **Rabbi Akiva encountered him.** Yonatan ben Harkinas **raised against him** all of his **objections** to the opinion of Beit Hillel, **and he withstood him,**[N] i.e., Rabbi Akiva was able to respond to all of them.

אָמַר לוֹ: אַתָּה הוּא עֲקִיבָא שֶׁשִּׁמְךָ הוֹלֵךְ מִסּוֹף הָעוֹלָם וְעַד סוֹפוֹ? אַשְׁרֶיךָ שֶׁזָּכִיתָ לְשֵׁם, וַעֲדַיִין לֹא הִגַּעְתָּ לְרוֹעֵי בָקָר. אָמַר לוֹ רַבִּי עֲקִיבָא: וַאֲפִילּוּ לְרוֹעֵי צֹאן.

Yonatan ben Harkinas grew angry and **said to him: You are Akiva ben Yosef, whose name has spread from one end of the world to the other? Be happy that you have merited a** great **name, and** yet **you have not yet reached** the level **of cattle herders.**[N] Cattle herders were generally simple individuals who were not familiar even with ordinary matters, and certainly not with *halakha*. **Rabbi Akiva said to him** with characteristic modesty: **And** I have not **even** reached the level **of shepherds,** who are considered even worse than cattle herders, as they are unfit for giving testimony.

NOTES

On this mortar Haggai the prophet sat – עַל מְדוֹכָה זוֹ יָשַׁב חַגַּי הַנָּבִיא: All of the sources indicate that Rabbi Dosa ben Harkinas was exceedingly old, and this is especially clear from the account in the Jerusalem Talmud. Nevertheless, it would be implausible to claim that he was alive at the beginning of the Second Temple period during the prophet Haggai's lifetime. Some explain that precise traditions that referred even to the slightest of details were often passed down in the academies, and therefore specifics of events dating back even hundreds of years were sometimes well-known (Rav Sherira Gaon). This might explain how Rabbi Dosa held such an ancient tradition.

He said three matters – אָמַר שְׁלֹשָׁה דְּבָרִים: The commentaries explain that although it was necessary to mention only the pertinent issue of a daughter's rival wife, and the three matters are not in fact connected to each other, Rabbi Dosa transmitted all three together. The reason is that the Gemara states elsewhere (98a) that if a scholar seeks to strengthen his opinion by citing a tradition, he might be viewed as having a personal stake in the testimony. Consequently, the testimony is better founded if, in addition to the specific *halakha* in question, he relates other rulings that were issued at the same time (*Beit Shlomo*).

He raised against him objections, and he withstood him – אַקְשֵׁי לֵיהּ וְאוֹקְמֵיהּ: This entire story is also related in the Jerusalem Talmud, but in a very different form. There, all three Sages met Rabbi Dosa's brother, who lectured them on matters so complex that they were unable to follow his reasoning, until they all eventually fell asleep.

You have not yet reached the level of cattle herders, etc. – עֲדַיִין לֹא הִגַּעְתָּ לְרוֹעֵי בָקָר וכו׳: See the Maharsha, who interprets this talmudic discussion homiletically. The *Arukh LaNer* writes that Yonatan ben Harkinas was alluding to the fact that Rabbi Akiva was once a mere cattle herder for Kalba Savua.

HALAKHA

Ammon and Moab…in the Sabbatical Year – עַמּוֹן וּמוֹאָב...בַּשְּׁבִיעִית: The Sages decreed that *terumot* and tithes must be separated in the Sabbatical Year in the territories adjacent to Eretz Yisrael. Consequently, in the lands of Egypt, Ammon, and Moab, the first tithe and poor man's tithe are set aside, in accordance with the testimony of Rabbi Dosa ben Harkinas (Rambam *Sefer Zera'im*, *Hilkhot Mattenot Aniyyim* 6:5; *Shulḥan Arukh*, *Yoreh De'a* 331:1).

BACKGROUND

The poor man's tithe – מַעְשַׂר עָנִי: This is a special tithe set aside from agricultural produce and distributed to the poor. During the third and sixth years of the Sabbatical cycle, after the priests' share of the produce and the first tithe have been set aside, one-tenth of the remaining produce is distributed to the poor. This tithe is called the poor man's tithe. During the other years of the Sabbatical cycle, the second tithe is set aside instead of poor man's tithe. The poor man's tithe is not sacred, but until it has been set aside the produce is deemed untithed produce [*tevel*] and may not be eaten. The poor man's tithe is separated from doubtfully tithed produce [*demai*] but it is not given to the poor, due to the principle that the burden of proof rests upon the claimant. In other words, a pauper who laid claim to the poor man's tithe in this case had to prove that the tithe had not already been separated from this produce.

Sabbatical Year – שְׁבִיעִית: The Sabbatical Year is the last year of the seven-year Sabbatical cycle. The first of these cycles began after the conquest of Canaan by Joshua. It is also known as *Shemitta*, which literally means abandonment, release. The *halakhot* of the Sabbatical Year are based on Torah law (Leviticus 25:1–7; Deuteronomy 15:1–6). However, most authorities maintain that the conditions for the mitzva of the Sabbatical Year by Torah law have lapsed, and its present-day observance is based on rabbinic decree. During the Sabbatical Year all agricultural land in Eretz Yisrael must lie fallow. It is prohibited to work the land except for what is necessary to maintain existing crops. All produce that does grow is ownerless and must be left unguarded in the fields so that any creature, including wild animals and birds, can have ready access to it. As long as produce can still be found in the fields, that type of produce may be eaten, although it may not be bought and sold in the normal manner or used for purposes other than food. After the last remnants of a crop have been removed from the field, that crop may no longer be eaten, unless a removal ceremony is promptly performed. It is prohibited by rabbinic decree to consume produce that grew from seeds during the Sabbatical Year, even if it grew by itself; according to some authorities, it is prohibited by Torah law.

״עַמּוֹן וּמוֹאָב מְעַשְּׂרִין מַעְשַׂר עָנִי בַּשְּׁבִיעִית״, דְּאָמַר מַר: הַרְבֵּה כְּרַכִּים כְּבָשׁוּ עוֹלֵי מִצְרַיִם וְלֹא כְּבָשׁוּם עוֹלֵי בָבֶל, וּקְדוּשָּׁה רִאשׁוֹנָה קִדְּשָׁה לְשַׁעְתָּהּ וְלֹא קִדְּשָׁה לֶעָתִיד לָבֹא,

§ Since the *halakhot* of the prophet Haggai were mentioned, the Gemara discusses them here. Haggai said that **Ammon and Moab tithe the poor man's tithe in the Sabbatical Year, as the Master said: Many cities were conquered by those who returned from Egypt, and were not conquered by those who returned from Babylonia** after the destruction of the First Temple. **And the initial consecration**[H] of Eretz Yisrael, by those who returned from Egypt, **sanctified it for its time and did not sanctify it forever,** as the future sanctification of Eretz Yisrael depended on the renewed conquest of the land by the Jewish people.

וְהִנִּיחוּם כְּדֵי שֶׁיִּסְמְכוּ עֲלֵיהֶן עֲנִיִּים בַּשְּׁבִיעִית.

And those who returned from Babylonia **left those** places aside and did not consider them part of Eretz Yisrael even after Jewish settlement was renewed there. They would plow and harvest in these places in the Sabbatical Year and tithe the poor man's tithe **so that the poor** of Eretz Yisrael who did not have sufficient income from the previous years **could rely upon them.** Consequently, **in the Sabbatical Year** the poor received help from this tithe.

וּמְקַבְּלִים גֵּרִים מִן הַקַּרְדּוּיִים וְהַתַּרְמוֹדִים. אִינִי? וְהָא תָּנֵי רָמִי בַּר יְחֶזְקֵאל: אֵין מְקַבְּלִים גֵּרִים מִן הַקַּרְדּוּיִים! אָמַר רַב אַשִׁי: קַרְתּוּיִים אִתְּמַר. כִּדְאָמְרִי אֱינָשֵׁי: קַרְתּוּיִים פְּסוּלִים.

§ Haggai also declared: **And one accepts converts**[HN] **from the Karduyim**[B] **and the Tarmodim.** The Gemara asks: **Is that so? But didn't Rami bar Yeḥezkel teach** in a *baraita*: **One does not accept converts from the Karduyim? Rav Ashi said: Kartuyim,** not Karduyim, **was stated** by Rami bar Yeḥezkel. **As people say** in common discourse: **The Kartuyim are unfit.**

וְאִיכָּא דְּאָמְרִי, תָּנֵי רָמִי בַּר יְחֶזְקֵאל: אֵין מְקַבְּלִים גֵּרִים מִן הַקַּרְתּוּיִים. מַאי לָאו – הַיְינוּ קַרְתּוּיִים הַיְינוּ קַרְדּוּיִים? אָמַר רַב אַשִׁי: לָא, קַרְתּוּיֵי לְחוּד וְקַרְדּוּיֵי לְחוּד. כִּדְאָמְרִי אֱינָשֵׁי: קַרְתּוּיֵי פְּסִילֵי.

And there are those **who say** a slightly different version of this discussion. **Rami bar Yeḥezkel taught: One does not accept converts from the Kartuyim. What, is it not** the case that **Kartuyim is** the same as **Karduyim?** If so there is a contradiction between the *baraita* of Rami bar Yeḥezkel and the statement of Rabbi Dosa ben Harkinas. **Rav Ashi said: No; the Kartuyim are** one **discrete** category **and the Karduyim are** another **discrete** category, **as people say: Kartuyim are unfit.**[N]

רַבִּי יוֹחָנָן וְסָבַיָּא דְּאָמְרִי תַּרְוַיְיהוּ: אֵין מְקַבְּלִים גֵּרִים מִן הַתַּרְמוֹדִים. וּמִי אֲמַר רַבִּי יוֹחָנָן הָכִי? וְהָתְנַן: כׇּל הַכְּתָמִים הַבָּאִים מִן הָרֶקֶם טְהוֹרִים,

Rabbi Yoḥanan and the Elders both say: One does not accept converts from the Tarmodim.[N] The Gemara asks: **And did Rabbi Yoḥanan** actually **say this,** that one does not accept converts from the Tarmodim due to a concern that Jews may have intermingled with them? **But didn't we learn** in a mishna: **All** clothing with **stains**[H] of blood that might be from a menstruating woman and **that come from the** city on the border of Eretz Yisrael called **Rekem are ritually pure,** as it can be assumed that they belong to gentiles, and the blood of a menstruating gentile woman is not ritually impure.

וְרַבִּי יְהוּדָה מְטַמֵּא, מִפְּנֵי שֶׁהֵם גֵּרִים וְטוֹעִים, מִבֵּין הַגּוֹיִם טְהוֹרִים. וְהָוֵינַן בָּהּ:

And Rabbi Yehuda deems it **ritually impure because those** residents of that place **are converts and are in error.** In other words, some of the inhabitants of Rekem assimilated and no longer observe the *halakhot* of the Torah, and therefore one must be wary lest the stains are in fact from a Jewish menstruating woman. Stains that came **from among the gentiles,** however, **are ritually pure. And we discussed** the following problem:

HALAKHA

The initial consecration – **קְדוּשָּׁה רִאשׁוֹנָה:** The initial consecration of Eretz Yisrael came into effect upon the conquest of Joshua. It lapsed after the destruction of the First Temple. In contrast, the second consecration, by those who returned from Babylonia, was permanent (Rambam *Sefer Zera'im, Hilkhot Terumot* 1:5).

One accepts converts, etc. – **מְקַבְּלִים גֵּרִים וכו׳:** Nowadays converts are accepted from all places without concern that Jews may have intermingled with them or that they might be unfit by Torah law, as all the nations have mixed with each other (Rambam *Sefer Kedusha, Hilkhot Issurei Bia* 12:25; *Shulḥan Arukh, Even HaEzer* 4:10).

Stains found – **כְּתָמִים הַנִּמְצָאִים:** Garments stained with blood that come from Jews are presumed to be ritually impure, whereas those of gentiles are considered pure, as the blood of gentiles does not have the status of ritual impurity. Those garments found in a public location are ritually pure, as Jews would hide away their stained garments and not discard them (Rambam *Sefer Tahara, Hilkhot Metamei Mishkav UMoshav* 4:10).

BACKGROUND

Karduyim – **קַרְדּוּיִים:** This apparently refers to the inhabitants of areas of northern Iraq, near the source of the Tigris River, the region known primarily as Kurdistan today. It is probable that the Kartuyim are from the same region, albeit from a different area.

NOTES

One accepts converts, etc. – **מְקַבְּלִים גֵּרִים וכו׳:** In the Jerusalem Talmud it is related that two Sages disputed this matter. One Sage rendered children born to a Jewish woman and a slave or a gentile entirely fit, and therefore he would accept converts from Tarmod. Another Sage would also accept converts from Tarmod, not because he rendered them fit as a general halakhic ruling, but because he held that there were in fact no mixed lineages in Tarmod at all.

Kartuyim are unfit – **קַרְתּוּיֵי פְּסִילֵי:** Some commentaries maintain that this quote was habitually cited as an example of those who are rendered unfit on account of their lineage. Others say that Kartuyim is a kind of unclean fowl, and this name was applied to those who came from places that can be described in terms of this kind (Rivan).

Rabbi Yoḥanan…one does not accept converts from the Tarmodim – **רַבִּי יוֹחָנָן...אֵין מְקַבְּלִים גֵּרִים מִן הַתַּרְמוֹדִים:** Some commentaries ask how Rabbi Yoḥanan could dispute a testimony cited by Rabbi Dosa in the name of Haggai the prophet (*Tosafot*). Some answer that Rabbi Yoḥanan doubted the validity of this tradition. The same applies to Yonatan ben Harkinas, and there are in fact other examples of this kind of objection (*Yosef Lekaḥ*). Others explain that Rabbi Yoḥanan maintained that the statement of Haggai the prophet has the status of a prophecy and is not a binding halakhic ruling (*Arza DeVei Rav*).

קָפָסֵיק וְתָנֵי: מִבֵּין הַגּוֹיִם – וַאֲפִילּוּ מִן תַּרְמוֹד. וְאָמַר רַבִּי יוֹחָנָן: זֹאת אוֹמֶרֶת: מְקַבְּלִין גֵּרִים מִתַּרְמוֹד.

The *tanna* **concluded and taught:** All stains from **among the gentiles** are pure, from which it may be inferred: **And even from Tarmod.**[B] This indicates that in all places inhabited by gentiles there is no need to be concerned about stains. **And Rabbi Yoḥanan said: That is to say, one accept converts from Tarmod** without concern that they might be Jewish, albeit *mamzerim*. This contradicts the previous opinion attributed to Rabbi Yoḥanan that converts from the Tarmodim are not accepted.

וְכִי תֵּימָא: זֹאת, וְלָא סְבִירָא לֵיהּ – וְהָא אָמַר רַבִּי יוֹחָנָן: הֲלָכָה כִּסְתַם מִשְׁנָה! אָמוֹרָאֵי נִינְהוּ, וְאַלִּיבָּא דְּרַבִּי יוֹחָנָן.

And if you would say that Rabbi Yoḥanan specifically emphasized: **That** is to say, i.e., he meant that this conclusion may be logically inferred from the mishna, **and** yet **he** himself **does not hold** by **this** opinion, **but didn't Rabbi Yoḥanan state** a principle that the ***halakha* is in accordance with** the ruling of **an unattributed mishna,** as is the case here? The Gemara answers: **They are *amora'im*,**[N] **and** they disagree **in accordance with** the opinion of **Rabbi Yoḥanan.** Some Sages said in Rabbi Yoḥanan's name that the Tarmodim are unfit, while others maintain that they are fit.

מִתַּרְמוֹד מַאי טַעְמָא לָא? פְּלִיגִי בָּהּ רַבִּי יוֹחָנָן וְסָבַיָּא: חַד אָמַר: מִשּׁוּם עַבְדֵי שְׁלֹמֹה, וְחַד אָמַר: מִשּׁוּם בְּנוֹת יְרוּשָׁלַיִם.

§ The Gemara asks: **And what is the reason** that the Sages do **not** accept converts **from Tarmod? Rabbi Yoḥanan and the Elders disagree** about **this** matter. Although they concur that converts from Tarmod are not accepted, they disagree with regard to the reason. **One** of them **said** that it is **due to the servants of** King **Solomon.**[N] Solomon built a city in Tarmod (see I Kings 9:18), and his gentile servants, taking advantage of their status and power, married Jewish women unlawfully. Therefore, it is possible that the inhabitants of Tarmod and their descendants are *mamzerim*. **And** the other **one said**[N] that it is **due to the daughters of Jerusalem,** who were taken captive and raped and gave birth to children among the gentiles.

NOTES

They are *amora'im* – אָמוֹרָאֵי נִינְהוּ: The Gemara could have answered that Rabbi Yoḥanan's opinion is based on a different unattributed mishna, as on 69b an unattributed mishna that is not accepted as *halakha* states that the child of a gentile or slave and a Jewish woman is a *mamzer*. However, since this would raise the question of why Rabbi Yoḥanan chose to base his opinion on one unattributed mishna rather than the other, this would in any case lead to the conclusion that there is a dispute with regard to his opinion (*Tosafot Yeshanim*; *Tosefot HaRosh*).

The servants of Solomon – עַבְדֵי שְׁלֹמֹה: The servants of Solomon are mentioned in the Bible: "All the people that were left of the Amorites, the Hittites, the Perizzites…even their children who were left after them in the land…from them Solomon raised a levy of bondservants, until this day" (I Kings 9:20–21). There is some evidence that these servants enjoyed a privileged status, as generations later, during the time of Ezra, they are listed as a special group unto themselves, separate from the other descendants of the Gibeonites (see Ezra 2:55–58). Since it is explicitly related that Solomon built the city of Tadmor in the desert, it stands to reason that he used primarily these servants for its construction.

One said…and the other one said – חַד אָמַר...וְחַד אָמַר: What is the difference between the two reasons? After all, both are based on the same idea that the offspring of a gentile or a slave and a Jewish woman is a *mamzer*. One answer is that they disagree about when the general disqualification came into effect. If the reason is because of the slaves of Solomon, this dates back to the beginning of the First Temple period, whereas if the cause is the daughters of Jerusalem, this occurred during the destruction of the Second Temple (*Iyyun Ya'akov*).

BACKGROUND

Tarmod – תַּרְמוֹד: The city of Tarmod, more commonly referred to as Tadmor, is located in an oasis in the Syrian desert. Tadmor is an ancient city and was called by this name beginning thousands of years ago. In the Bible, the city is also called Tamar, meaning palm. In other languages it is known as Palmyra, which is derived from the name for palm trees.

For many generations Tadmor was an important center of commerce and served as a crossroads for different trading routes across Syria, Arabia, and Babylonia. The Bible relates that King Solomon built and fortified this city (see I Kings 9:18–19 and II Chronicles 8:4). This is the source for the claim that Solomon's bondservants lived there, as well as the reason for the Jewish influence on the religion and culture of this city.

The kingdom of Tadmor grew powerful in the middle of the third century CE, as its ruler, Odaenathus, called Papa bar Nasser in the Gemara, established Tadmor as a great power under Roman patronage, along with his wife, Zenobia. Papa bar Nasser destroyed the city of Neharde'a, and his wife even reigned over Eretz Yisrael. Apparently, the Jews opposed these rulers and treated them with hostility and contempt. In the year 273 CE the Roman emperor Aurelian conquered Tadmor, and from that point onward its influence waned considerably. However, although it was conquered and partially destroyed several times, the city remains standing to this day.

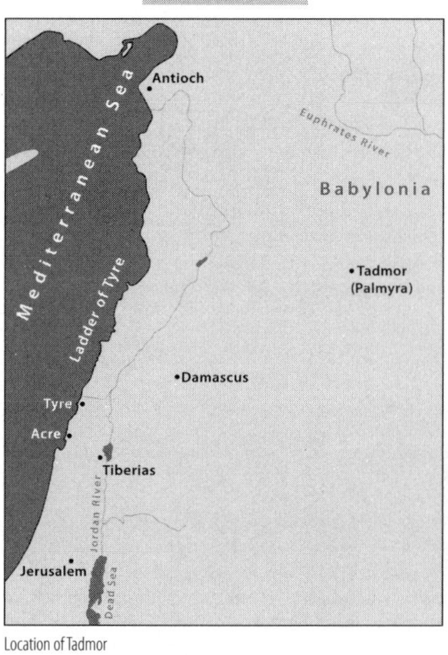

Location of Tadmor

Ruins of Tadmor

בִּשְׁלָמָא לְמַאן דְּאָמַר מִשּׁוּם עַבְדֵי שְׁלֹמֹה – קָסָבַר: גּוֹי וְעֶבֶד הַבָּא עַל בַּת יִשְׂרָאֵל הַוָּלָד מַמְזֵר. אֶלָּא לְמַאן דְּאָמַר מִשּׁוּם בְּנוֹת יְרוּשָׁלַיִם – מַאי הִיא? פְּלִיגִי בָּהּ רַב יוֹסֵף וְרַבָּנַן, וְתַרְוַיְיהוּ מִשְּׁמֵיהּ דְּרַבָּה בַּר בַּר חָנָה.

The Gemara comments: **Granted, according to the one who said** that it is **due to the servants of Solomon,** this is logical, as **he holds** that in the case of **a gentile or a slave who had intercourse with a Jewish woman,**[H] **the offspring is a *mamzer*.** Accordingly, as the servants of Solomon were slaves and they engaged in intercourse with Jewish women, their children are considered *mamzerim*. **However, according to the one who said** that it is **due to the daughters of Jerusalem, what is** the reason that the concern applied specifically to Tarmod and no other cities? **Rav Yosef and the Rabbis disagree** with regard to **this** question, **and both** stated their opinions **in the name of Rabba bar bar Ḥana.**

חַד אָמַר: תְּרֵיסַר אַלְפֵי גַּבְרֵי וְשִׁיתָּא אַלְפֵי קַשְׁתּוֹיֵי, וְחַד אָמַר תְּרֵיסַר אַלְפֵי גַּבְרֵי וּמִנַּיְיהוּ שִׁיתָּא אַלְפֵי קַשְׁתּוֹיֵי. בְּשָׁעָה שֶׁנִּכְנְסוּ גּוֹיִם לַהֵיכָל, הַכֹּל נִפְנוּ עַל כֶּסֶף וְזָהָב, וְהֵם נִפְנוּ עַל בְּנוֹת יְרוּשָׁלַיִם, שֶׁנֶּאֱמַר "נָשִׁים בְּצִיּוֹן עִנּוּ בְּתוּלוֹת בְּעָרֵי יְהוּדָה".

The Gemara elaborates: **One** of them **said** that **twelve thousand men and six thousand archers** came from Tarmod, **and** the other **one said** that there were **twelve thousand men, of whom six thousand** were **archers. When the gentiles entered the Sanctuary** during the conquest of Jerusalem, they **all turned to** plunder the **silver and the gold** they saw there, **but** the warriors of Tarmod **turned to the daughters of Jerusalem, as it is stated: "They have ravished the women in Zion, the maidens in the cities of Judah"** (Lamentations 5:11). According to the opinion that children born of relations between gentiles and Jewish women are *mamzerim*, all the children born to these women are *mamzerim*.

אָמַר רַבִּי שְׁמוּאֵל בַּר נַחְמָנִי אָמַר רַבִּי יוֹנָתָן, פָּסוּק זֶה שַׂר הָעוֹלָם אֲמָרוֹ: "נַעַר הָיִיתִי גַּם זָקַנְתִּי", מַאן אֲמָרֵיהּ? אִילֵימָא קוּדְשָׁא בְּרִיךְ הוּא – מִי אִיכָּא זִקְנָה קַמֵּיהּ? וְאֶלָּא דָּוִד אֲמָרֵיהּ – מִי קַשִּׁישׁ כּוּלֵּי הַאי? אֶלָּא שְׁמַע מִינַּהּ – שַׂר הָעוֹלָם אֲמָרוֹ.

§ In relation to a verse cited earlier, **Rabbi Shmuel bar Naḥmani said** that **Rabbi Yonatan said: This verse was stated by the ministering angel** appointed over **the world:**[N] **"I have been young, and now am old;** yet I have not seen the righteous forsaken, nor his seed begging bread" (Psalms 37:25). **Who said this? If we say** that it was **the Holy One, Blessed be He, is there old age before Him?** Could God possibly say: "I have been young, and now am old"? **And rather,** one could say that **David** himself **said it,** from his own experience; but **was he indeed so old?** After all, David died at the age of seventy. **Rather, conclude from this** that **the ministering angel** appointed over **the world said it,** as he can speak both of youth and old age, and it is he who reported his observations from around the world.

וַאֲמַר רַבִּי שְׁמוּאֵל בַּר נַחְמָנִי אָמַר רַבִּי יוֹנָתָן: מַאי דִּכְתִיב: "יָדוֹ פָּרַשׂ צָר עַל כָּל מַחֲמַדֶּיהָ" – זֶה עַמּוֹן וּמוֹאָב. בְּשָׁעָה שֶׁנִּכְנְסוּ גּוֹיִם לַהֵיכָל הַכֹּל נִפְנוּ עַל כֶּסֶף וְזָהָב, וְהֵם נִפְנוּ עַל סִפְרֵי תּוֹרָה. אָמְרוּ: זֶה שֶׁכָּתוּב בּוֹ "לֹא יָבֹא עַמּוֹנִי וּמוֹאָבִי בִּקְהַל ה'"?! יִשָּׂרֵף בָּאֵשׁ.

And Rabbi Shmuel bar Naḥmani further **said** that **Rabbi Yonatan said: What is** the meaning of that **which is written: "The adversary has spread out his hand upon all her treasures;** for she has seen that the heathens have entered into her Temple, concerning which You commanded that they should not enter into Your congregation" (Lamentations 1:10)? **This** is referring to **Ammon and Moab.** How so? **When the gentiles entered the Sanctuary, all turned to** plunder **the silver and the gold, and** the soldiers from Ammon and Moab **turned to the scrolls of Torah** to destroy them. **They said:** Is **this** the scroll **in which it is written: "An Ammonite and a Moabite shall not enter into the assembly of the Lord"** (Deuteronomy 23:4)? **Let it be burnt by fire.**

"צִוָּה ה' לְיַעֲקֹב סְבִיבָיו צָרָיו", אֲמַר רַב: כְּגוֹן הוּמָנְיָא לְפוּם נַהֲרָא.

With regard to the Ammonites, the Gemara cites another verse: **"The Lord has commanded against Jacob that they who are round about him should be his adversaries"** (Lamentations 1:17). **Rav said: For an example** of this, there is the city **Homanya**[B] in relation **to** the city **Pum Nahara,** as the descendants of the Ammonites live in Homanya, and they harass the Jews of Pum Nahara.

אֲמַר רַב יְהוּדָה אָמַר רַב אַסִּי: גּוֹי שֶׁקִּידֵּשׁ בַּזְּמַן הַזֶּה – חוֹשְׁשִׁין לְקִדּוּשִׁין, שֶׁמָּא מֵעֲשֶׂרֶת הַשְּׁבָטִים הוּא. וְהָא כָּל דְּפָרֵישׁ מֵרוּבָּא פָּרֵישׁ!

§ **Rav Yehuda said** that **Rav Asi said:** With regard to **a gentile who betrothed** a Jewish woman **nowadays,**[H] **we are concerned that the betrothal** might be valid, despite the fact that a betrothal of a gentile is meaningless, **lest he be from the ten tribes** of Israel who intermingled with the gentiles. The Gemara raises an objection: **But** there is an important principle in *halakha* that **any** item **separated,** i.e., not fixed in its place, is presumed to have been **separated from the majority.** In this case, it can be assumed that any individual singled out from the gentiles belongs to the majority of gentiles and has no Jewish roots at all.

HALAKHA

A gentile or slave who had intercourse with a Jewish woman – גּוֹי וְעֶבֶד הַבָּא עַל בַּת יִשְׂרָאֵל: If a gentile or slave had relations with a Jewish woman, whether she is married or single, their offspring is fit. If she gives birth to a girl, it is prohibited for this daughter to marry a priest, in accordance with the conclusion of the Gemara (Rambam *Sefer Kedusha, Hilkhot Issurei Bia* 15:3; *Shulḥan Arukh, Even HaEzer* 4:19).

A gentile who betrothed a Jewish woman nowadays – גּוֹי שֶׁקִּידֵּשׁ בַּזְּמַן הַזֶּה: If a gentile performs betrothal with a Jewish woman nowadays, his action is meaningless. If, however, a Samaritan performs betrothal with a Jewish woman, she requires a bill of divorce from him (Rambam *Sefer Nashim, Hilkhot Ishut* 4:15; *Shulḥan Arukh, Even HaEzer* 44:8, 10).

NOTES

Was stated by the ministering angel appointed over the world – שַׂר הָעוֹלָם אֲמָרוֹ: Although this chapter of Psalms was written by David, as stated in its opening verse, the Sages explained that in the writing of his book David adapted the hymns of ten Elders of previous generations. The Gemara here likewise teaches that this particular verse did not originate with David himself (*Iyyun Ya'akov*; see *Yosef Lekaḥ*).

BACKGROUND

Homanya – הוּמָנְיָא: This Babylonian city with a gentile population was located near Pum Nahara. According to an ancient tradition, the population of the city was of Ammonite origin (see *Kiddushin* 72a). It is mentioned among those cities situated adjacent to Jewish settlements that were known for their hostile relationship with the Jews.

בְּדוּכְתָּא דִּקְבִיעִי, דְּאָמַר רַבִּי אַבָּא בַּר כָּהֲנָא: ״וַיַּנְחֵם בַּחְלַח וּבְחָבוֹר נְהַר גּוֹזָן וְעָרֵי מָדָי״. חְלַח – זֶה חַלְזוֹן, וְחָבוֹר

The Gemara responds: Rav Yehuda means that there is a concern only with regard to those who came from **the permanent** dwelling **places** of the ten tribes. **As Rabbi Abba bar Kahana said** that the verse states about those exiled from Samaria: **"And he put them in Halah, and in Habor, on the river of Gozan, and in the cities of the Medes"** (I Kings 18:11). Rabbi Abba bar Kahana proceeded to identify these places. **Halah; this is** the place called **Ḥalzon. And Habor;**

זוֹ חַדְיַיב, נְהַר גּוֹזָן – זוֹ גִּינְזַק, וְעָרֵי מָדַי – זוֹ חַמַדָן וְחַבְרוֹתֶיהָ, וְאָמְרִי לָהּ: זוֹ נִיהַר וְחַבְרוֹתֶיהָ. חַבְרוֹתֶיהָ מַאן? אֲמַר שְׁמוּאֵל: כְּרַךְ, מוּשְׁכֵי, חִידְקֵי וְדוֹמַקְיָא. אָמַר רַבִּי יוֹחָנָן: וְכוּלָּן לִפְסוּל,

this is Ḥadyab. The river of Gozan; this is Ginzak. And the cities of the Medes; this is Ḥamadan and its surroundings.[B] **And some say: This is Nihar and its surroundings.** The Gemara asks: **Which are its surroundings? Shmuel said: Kerakh, Mushkhei, Ḥidkei, and Domakya** are the surroundings of Ḥamadan. **Rabbi Yoḥanan said: And all of them are for disqualification.**[N] In other words, if someone from one of these places wishes to convert, there is concern that he might be a descendant of a Jew and therefore a *mamzer*. Consequently, they all are disqualified.

כִּי אָמְרִיתָהּ קַמֵּיהּ דִּשְׁמוּאֵל: אָמַר לִי: בִּנְךָ הַבָּא מִן יִשְׂרְאֵלִית קָרוּי בִּנְךָ, וְאֵין בִּנְךָ הַבָּא מִן הַגּוֹיָה קָרוּי בִּנְךָ – אֶלָּא בְּנָהּ.

Rav Yehuda continued his recounting: **When I said this** *halakha*, that there is a concern about the betrothal of gentiles nowadays, **before Shmuel, he said to me:** One need not worry about this, as **your son from a Jewish woman**[N] **is called your son,** i.e., he inherits his lineage from you, **and your son from a gentile woman is not called your son,** but **rather her son.**[H] Consequently, all children born to Jews from gentile women are not considered Jews, as their lineage is determined by their gentile mothers.

וְהָאִיכָּא בָּנוֹת, וְאָמַר רָבִינָא: שְׁמַע מִינַּהּ בֶּן בִּתְּךָ הַבָּא מִן הַגּוֹי קָרוּי בִּנְךָ! גְּמִירִי דִּבְנָתָא דְּהַהוּא דָּרָא אִיעַקְרוּיֵי אִיעַקְרוּ.

The Gemara asks: **Aren't there** Jewish **girls** who were captured by gentiles, whose children are considered to be Jews? **And Ravina said: Learn from this** that **the son of your daughter from a gentile**[H] **is called your son.** If so, the descendants of Jewish women captured by gentiles would indeed be Jews. The Gemara answers: This is no concern, as it **is learned** as a tradition **that the girls** from the ten tribes **of that generation became barren**[N] and did not give birth to any offspring, whereas some of the exiled men of the ten tribes married gentile women. Consequently, all of the children born there were gentiles.

BACKGROUND

The exile of the ten tribes – גָּלוּת עֲשֶׂרֶת הַשְּׁבָטִים: The Sages identified the places to which the ten tribes were exiled, all of which were close to the sources of the Tigris and Euphrates Rivers, or in the land of Medes, northeast of the Jewish settlement in Babylonia. Some of the places listed have been identified with near certainty, while the exact names and locations of others remain doubtful.

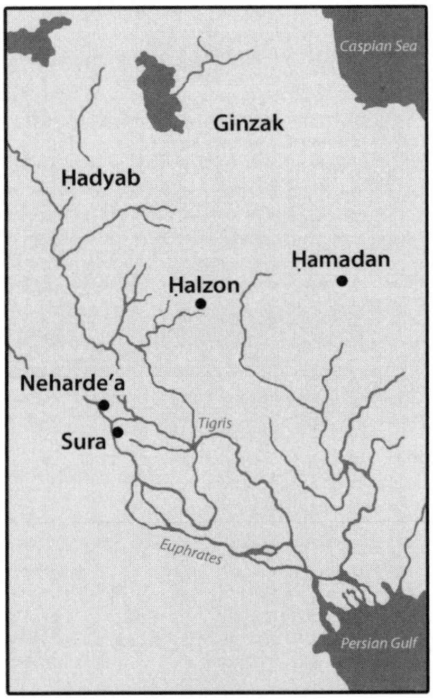

Places of exile of the ten tribes, relative to cities of Jewish settlement

HALAKHA

A son from a gentile woman – בֵּן מִן הַנָּכְרִית: The son of a Jew from a gentile woman or slave woman is not considered his son (Rambam *Sefer Kedusha*, *Hilkhot Issurei Bia* 12:7).

The son of your daughter from a gentile – בֶּן בִּתְּךָ הַבָּא מִן הַגּוֹי: The offspring of a gentile man and a Jewish woman is a fit Jew, as he is called: Your son. However, he is disqualified from the priesthood (*Shulḥan Arukh*, *Even HaEzer* 4:19).

NOTES

And all of them are for disqualification – וְכוּלָּן לִפְסוּל: Rashi explains that those born in these places were not careful about forbidden unions, and their offspring are therefore *mamzerim*. The other commentaries ask why Rashi interpreted the Gemara in this manner. After all, the offspring of a Jewish man and a gentile woman is himself a *mamzer*, as Rashi himself wrote, in accordance with the opinion of Rav Asi (Maharsha). If so, it is enough to state that these tribes intermingled, without having to stipulate that they engaged in sexual intercourse with forbidden relations. Some explain that Rabbi Yoḥanan issued his statement even in accordance with the opinion that the offspring of a Jewish man and a gentile woman is not a *mamzer*. Rabbi Yoḥanan is saying that even so, they would all be disqualified as *mamzerim*, due to marriage with women with whom relations are forbidden (*Yosef Lekaḥ*; see Maharsha and *Arza DeVei Rav*).

Your son from a Jewish woman, etc. – בִּנְךָ הַבָּא מִן הַיִּשְׂרְאֵלִית וכו׳: The statements of Shmuel and Ravina refer to a homiletical interpretation of the following verses: "Neither shall you make marriages with them: Your daughter you shall not give to his son, nor his daughter shall you take for your son. For he will turn away your son from following Me, that they may serve other gods" (Deuteronomy 7:3–4). Rashi explains that as the verse states: "For he will turn away your son," and not: She will turn away, it is evidently referring to the offspring of a gentile man and a Jewish woman. Since the verse does not deal with the fate of the son of a gentile woman, this indicates that he is not considered to be a Jew at all. Others add that it stands to reason that a son raised as a Jew would not turn astray to idol worship, and therefore the verse is certainly referring to the son of one's daughter who was raised among the gentiles (*Tosafot Yeshanim*). Others maintain that the phrase "He will turn away your son" is referring to the father of the gentile wife, who is in fact the subject of the verse. According to this interpretation, the turning away mentioned in the verse actually means that the son of this union will be removed from the continuation of Judaism, as his children will not be considered Jews. The Rambam explains likewise.

Became barren – אִיעַקְרוּיֵי אִיעַקְרוּ: Some commentaries explain that they purposely drank a tonic to make themselves barren (Rivan), or that they made themselves repulsive to those who wished to have intercourse with them (Meiri), or that their wombs were damaged from consecutive acts of rape (*Tosefot Rid*). Alternatively, some state that the pain from the long journey and slavery caused them to lose the ability to bear children (Meiri; see Rashi and Rif on *Kiddushin*).

איכא דאמרי: כי אמריתה קמיה דשמואל אמר לי: לא זזו משם עד שעשאום גוים גמורים, שנאמר ״בה׳ בגדו כי בנים זרים ילדו״.

There are those who say that Rav Yehuda actually related the following: **When I said this *halakha* before Shmuel, he said to me: They did not move from there,** the place where they deliberated on this matter, **until they rendered** all of **them,** including those who intermingled with the ten tribes in different locations, **full-fledged gentiles.**[N] Consequently, there is no concern that their betrothals might be of any effect, **as it is stated: "They have dealt treacherously against the Lord, for they have begotten strange children"** (Hosea 5:7).

יתיב רב יוסף אחוריה דרב כהנא, ויתיב רב כהנא קמיה דרב יהודה, ויתיב וקאמר: עתידין ישראל דעבדי יומא טבא כי חרבי תרמוד. והא חריב! ההיא תמוד הואי. רב אשי אמר: היינו תרמוד היינו תמוד, אכפולי הוא דמכפל. חריב מהאי גיסא – אותיב מהאי גיסא, ואי חריב מהאי גיסא – אותיב מהאי גיסא.

§ The Gemara relates: **Rav Yosef sat behind**[B] **Rav Kahana, and Rav Kahana sat before Rav Yehuda, and he sat and he said** this tradition: **In the future, the Jews will establish a Festival day when Tarmod is destroyed.**[N] The Gemara asks: **But it has** already **been destroyed.** The Gemara answers: **That** place that was destroyed **was Tamud,** not Tarmod. **Rav Ashi said: Tarmod is** the same as **Tamud.** However, the city **is doubled.** In other words, when it **is destroyed from this side it is settled on that side, and** when it **is destroyed from that side it is settled on this side.** Consequently, it has not yet been entirely destroyed.

יתיב רב המנונא קמיה דעולא וקא הוי בשמעתא. אמר: מה גברא ומה גברא, אי לאו דהרפניא מאתיה! אכסיף. אמר ליה: כסף גלגלתא להיכא יהבת? אמר ליה: לפום נהרא. אמר ליה: אם כן – מפום נהרא את.

The Gemara relates: **Rav Hamnuna**[P] **sat before Ulla and was engaged in** the study of ***halakha.*** Ulla **said** about him: **What a man; what a man.** In other words: What a great man this Rav Hamnuna is. **If only Harpanya were not his city,** as the inhabitants of that place are all of flawed lineage, which indicates that the lineage of Rav Hamnuna is likewise impaired. Rav Hamnuna **was ashamed.** Ulla **said to him: Where do you give the money for** payment of the **poll** tax? **He said to him:** I pay it **to** the city of **Pum Nahara,** as my city is subject to taxation by that city. **He said to him: If so, you are from Pum Nahara,** not Harpanya, and your lineage is evidently not flawed.

מאי הרפניא? אמר רבי זירא: הר שהכל פונין בו. במתניתא תנא: כל שאין מכיר משפחתו ושבטו נפנה לשם. אמר רבא: והיא עמוקה משאול, שנאמר ״מיד שאול אפדם ממות אגאלם״, ואילו פסול דידהו – לית להו תקנתא.

§ The Gemara asks: **What is** the meaning of the name **Harpanya? Rabbi Zeira said:** It means **the mountain to which all turn** [***har shehakol ponin bo***]. In other words, it is the destination for all those who could not find wives anywhere else, as most of its population is of flawed lineage. **It is taught in a *baraita*:**[N] **All those who do not know their family or tribe turn there. Rava said: This** type of flaw is appalling and **is deeper than the netherworld, as is stated: "Shall I ransom them from the power of the netherworld? Shall I redeem them from death?"** (Hosea 13:14). This verse indicates that it is possible to be ransomed and released from the netherworld, **whereas their disqualification cannot be rectified.**

BACKGROUND

Sat behind – יתיב...אחוריה: In the earlier generations, it was customary for Torah scholars to sit before their masters in a particular order, with the most prominent students in the first rows and the lesser students behind them. A significant portion of the time was dedicated to discussions between the rabbi and the more outstanding students seated in the front row, especially when there was no study hall where the lecture could be transmitted to everyone. Younger students would ask older students for explanations of the rabbi's statements or pose questions to them that they dared not pose directly to the rabbi.

PERSONALITIES

Rav Hamnuna – רב המנונא: Rav Hamnuna was a second-generation Babylonian, a disciple of Rav. There was another Rav Hamnuna in the following generation who was also associated with Rav, although he was primarily a student of Rav Ḥisda. This Rav Hamnuna perpetuated the tradition of the school of Rav. He was affiliated with Rav Huna, whose halakhic authority he accepted. Rav Hamnuna was also the head of an academy in his own right and taught many of the outstanding Sages of the next generation, including Rabbi Zeira and Rav Yosef.

NOTES

Until they rendered them full-fledged gentiles – עד שעשאום גוים גמורים: Some commentaries derive from here that the Sages decreed that someone who is fully assimilated among gentiles is considered a gentile for all intents and purposes, and neither he nor his descendants are Jews at all. This is the opinion of several early commentaries with regard to an apostate, that he is no longer considered a Jew with regard to levirate marriage or *ḥalitza*.

Establish a Festival day when Tarmod is destroyed – דעבדי יומא טבא כי חרבי תרמוד: Rashi says that this is due to the disqualification of *mamzerim*. Others suggest that the reason is that the inhabitants of Tarmod were sworn enemies of the Jews, and according to tradition they participated in the conquests of Jerusalem during the destruction of both the First and Second Temples (*Arukh LaNer*).

It is taught in a *baraita* – במתניתא תנא: Some commentaries ask what this *baraita* adds to the statement of Rabbi Zeira. A different version of the text reads: He should turn there. In other words, this is a recommendation, as they are not strict about lineage in Harpanya, and for this reason their lineage is considered flawed (Rivan). Others differentiate between the opinion of Rabbi Zeira, who maintains that everyone turns to Harpanya, even actual *mamzerim*, which indicates that its residents are definitely disqualified, and the statement of the *baraita*, from which it can be inferred that the inhabitants of Harpanya are merely of uncertain lineage (*Yosef Lekaḥ*).

פְּסוּלֵי דְּהַרְפַּנְיָא מִשּׁוּם פְּסוּלֵי דְּמֵישׁוֹן וּפְסוּלֵי דְּמֵישׁוֹן מִשּׁוּם פְּסוּלֵי דְּתַרְמוֹד. פְּסוּלֵי דְּתַרְמוֹד מִשּׁוּם עַבְדֵי שְׁלֹמֹה,

The Gemara comments: **Those** who are **disqualified from Harpanya** are unfit **due to the disqualification** of the inhabitants **of** nearby **Meishon,**[N] who were unfit and intermarried with the residents of Harpanya. **Those disqualified from Meishon** are unfit **due to those disqualified from Tarmod, and those disqualified from Tarmod** are disqualified **due to the servants of Solomon.**

וְהַיְינוּ דְּאָמְרִי אֵינָשֵׁי: קַבָּא רַבָּא וְקַבָּא זוּטָא, מִיגַּנְדַּר וְאָזֵיל לִשְׁאוֹל, וּמִשְּׁאוֹל לְתַרְמוֹד, וּמִתַּרְמוֹד לְמֵישָׁן, וּמִמֵּישָׁן לְהַרְפַּנְיָא.

The Gemara comments: **And this** explains the folk saying **that people say** in this regard: **A large ephah and a small ephah,**[N] which are both inaccurate utensils that may not be used for measuring, **roll onward to the netherworld, and from the netherworld to Tarmod, and from Tarmod to Meishon, and from Meishon to Harpanya.**[B] The same idea expressed by the Sages with regard to the disqualification of lineage was also incorporated into a well-known adage among commoners.

הדרן עלך חמש עשרה נשים

NOTES

Due to the disqualification of Meishon – מִשּׁוּם פְּסוּלֵי דְּמֵישׁוֹן: In the Jerusalem Talmud it is stated that the disqualified residents of Meishon were not *mamzerim* but were priestly families that assimilated and became disqualified from the priesthood [*ḥalalim*] by marrying unfit women. Consequently, they are uncertain *ḥalalim*.

A large ephah and a small ephah – קַבָּא רַבָּא וְקַבָּא זוּטָא: Some commentaries cite a different interpretation: Both great individuals of prestigious lineage, the so-called large ephah, and lesser ones of disqualified lineage, a small ephah, descended to Babylonia, which is a geographically low place and for this reason is dubbed the netherworld. There, these individuals intermarried. A similar expression appears later in the tractate (70a).

BACKGROUND

Meishon and Harpanya – מֵישָׁן וְהַרְפַּנְיָא: The region of Meishon was east-southeast of the central Jewish settlement in Babylonia and was considered a place bereft of Torah and populated by individuals of unfit lineage. In contrast, Pum Nahara, which was apparently considered within the primary Jewish settlement and was home to important Sages, was viewed as pure with regard to the lineage of its residents.

Tadmor, or Tarmod, is located hundreds of kilometers northwest of Meishon, and there is no geographical link between the two places. However, it is possible that there were ties of other kinds between these two cities.

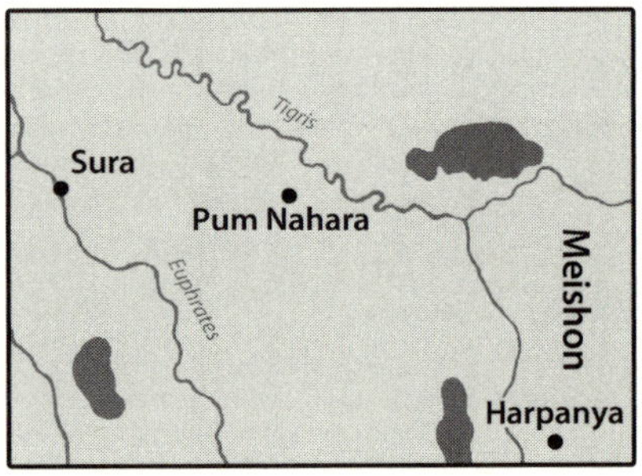

Meishon and Harpanya

Summary of **Perek I**

This chapter discussed three problems in detail, all of which pertain to the issue of *yevamot* and their rival wives but have broader ramifications.

It is a principle in *halakha* that a positive mitzva overrides a prohibition. One might think that the mitzva of levirate marriage is a perfect example of this principle, as this positive commandment overrides a prohibition that entails *karet*, i.e., a brother's wife. However, a closer analysis reveals that in fact a positive mitzva overrides a regular prohibition alone, and it does so only in situations when both commandments cannot be fulfilled. Furthermore, a positive mitzva does not override both a prohibition and a positive mitzva.

The discussion of the source for the exemption of the rival wife of a woman who may not enter into levirate marriage led the Gemara to touch upon the question of whether *ḥalitza* merely releases the couple from the obligation of levirate marriage or whether it is a different form of levirate marriage that changes the relationship between the brother-in-law and the *yevama*.

The exemption of rival wives itself is the subject of a dispute between Beit Shammai and Beit Hillel. This chapter discussed various aspects of this disagreement, e.g., whether Beit Shammai acted upon their own ruling or if the dispute was merely theoretical. The Gemara also debated several related issues, including when and to what extent the prohibition against splitting into factions, i.e., different practical implementations of the *halakha*, is in effect.

Introduction to **Perek II**

If brothers dwell together and one of them dies and he has no child, the wife of the dead man shall not be married outside of the family to one not of his kin; her brother-in-law will have intercourse with her and take her to him to be his wife and consummate the levirate marriage.

(Deuteronomy 25:5)

In the first chapter, the Gemara discussed women who are prohibited from entering into levirate marriage due to their being close relatives of, and therefore severely forbidden to, their *yavam*, together with the rival wives of such women. It was explained that these women are exempt from both levirate marriage and *ḥalitza*. However, there are other problems that can arise in cases of levirate marriage. Some women are not forbidden to their *yavam* with a prohibition of *karet* but are forbidden due to another prohibition or by rabbinic law. In these instances does the mitzva of levirate marriage override the prohibition?

Another issue discussed in this chapter is the definition of some fundamental concepts in levirate marriage. The Torah states that the brother must perform the levirate marriage, but the question of who exactly is considered a brother requires clarification. The first chapter mentioned the concept of: A brother with whom he did not coexist, to whom the *halakhot* of levirate marriage and *ḥalitza* do not apply. In such a case the exemption from levirate marriage is not due to a forbidden union but rather from the *halakhot* of levirate marriage themselves, as the verse states: "If brothers dwell together." This chapter defines this concept, and clarifies the details and application of the *halakha*.

Another issue discussed in this chapter is what the Torah means when it uses the term "brother." Does it refer to any brother or only the eldest, and does it apply equally to paternal and maternal half brothers? Must the brother performing levirate marriage be legitimate, or are illegitimate brothers included as well?

Another topic clarified in this chapter is the term "child" used in the verse. Since the Torah uses the masculine word for "child" does it also include a daughter? Does it include grandchildren and descendants? Does it refer only to legitimate children or also to illegitimate children? In cases of doubt as to whether or not there is a surviving child when the *yavam* dies is there an obligation to perform levirate marriage and *ḥalitza*?

These questions, along with several other corollary issues, constitute the primary substance of this chapter.

מתני׳ כֵּיצַד אֵשֶׁת אָחִיו שֶׁלֹּא הָיָה בְּעוֹלָמוֹ? שְׁנֵי אַחִים, וּמֵת אֶחָד מֵהֶן; וְנוֹלַד לָהֶן אָח, וְאַחַר כָּךְ יִיבֵּם הַשֵּׁנִי אֶת אֵשֶׁת אָחִיו וָמֵת. הָרִאשׁוֹנָה יוֹצְאָה מִשּׁוּם אֵשֶׁת אָחִיו שֶׁלֹּא הָיָה בְּעוֹלָמוֹ, וְהַשְּׁנִיָּה מִשּׁוּם צָרָתָהּ.

MISHNA Each of the women enumerated in the first chapter causes exemption from levirate marriage and *ḥalitza* for her rival wives. This is due to the close family relationship she has with her brother-in-law, making her forbidden to him. The single exception is the case explained in this mishna. **What is** the case of **the wife of a brother**[N] **with whom he did not coexist?**[H] For example: If there were **two brothers, and one of them died** childless, **and** subsequently **a brother of theirs was born, after which the second brother,** the elder, **took his** deceased **brother's wife in levirate marriage, and** then **died** as well. Consequently, two women require levirate marriage: The widow of the first brother who had been taken in levirate marriage by the second brother, and the widow of the second brother, the first widow's rival wife. **The first** widow, who had been the wife of the first brother to die, **goes out** without any obligation to be taken in levirate marriage by the youngest brother who was born later, **since** she is **the wife of a brother with whom he did not coexist.** The first deceased brother never lived at the same time as the newly born brother. **The second** widow, who had been married to the second brother, is exempt **due to her rival wife.**

עָשָׂה בָּהּ מַאֲמָר וָמֵת – שְׁנִיָּה חוֹלֶצֶת וְלֹא מִתְיַיבֶּמֶת.

The mishna discusses an additional situation: If the second brother had **performed** only **levirate betrothal**[B] **with her,** meaning that he had not yet consummated the marriage, **and then died,** both the wife betrothed by a levirate betrothal to the second brother and the wife of the second brother fall before the youngest brother born after the death of the first brother. In that case, the first wife certainly goes out and is exempt from both *ḥalitza* and levirate marriage, since she is to him the wife of a brother with whom he did not coexist. **The second,** however, was never effectively the rival wife of the first brother's wife, as the first brother's wife had only been betrothed by levirate betrothal and was not fully married to the second brother. Therefore, **she performs *ḥalitza* and may not enter into levirate marriage.**

גמ׳ אָמַר רַב נַחְמָן: מַאן דְּתָנֵי רִאשׁוֹנָה לָא מִשְׁתַּבֵּשׁ, מַאן דְּתָנֵי שְׁנִיָּה לָא מִשְׁתַּבֵּשׁ. מַאן דְּתָנֵי

GEMARA **Rav Naḥman said: He who taught** the version of the mishna which reads: **The first** widow goes out, **is not mistaken** in his version, and **he who taught** a variant version of the mishna which reads: **The second** widow goes out, **is not mistaken** either, since it is possible to understand the mishna both ways. Both versions of the text can refer to the same woman, i.e., the wife of the first brother, by different titles. The Gemara explains that **he who taught:**

NOTES

What is the case of the wife of a brother, etc. – כֵּיצַד אֵשֶׁת אָחִיו וכו׳: The mishna comes to clarify the fundamental principle concerning the *halakha* of the wife of his brother with whom he did not coexist, and not to discuss all of its details, since those were already discussed in the previous chapter (Rashba).

HALAKHA

The wife of a brother with whom he did not coexist – אֵשֶׁת אָחִיו שֶׁלֹּא הָיָה בְּעוֹלָמוֹ: The levirate bond does not apply at all to the wife of a brother with whom one did not coexist. Therefore, she is exempt from levirate marriage and consequently forbidden to the *yavam*, and also causes exemption for her rival wives. In fact, she causes exemption for the rival wives of her rival wives as well, as per the ruling concerning all forbidden relations (Rambam *Sefer Nashim, Hilkhot Yibbum VaḤalitza* 6:16–17; *Shulḥan Arukh, Even HaEzer* 173:12).

BACKGROUND

Levirate betrothal [*ma'amar*] – מַאֲמָר: The betrothal performed by a *yavam* based on his levirate bond with his *yevama* is called *ma'amar*. A levirate betrothal does not have the halakhic status of an ordinary betrothal, since the levirate bond between *yavam* and widow is not dependent upon betrothal. Rather, it is a sort of continuation of the previous marriage to her deceased husband. Full marriage with one's sister-in-law comes into effect by intercourse alone. However, the Sages instituted this type of betrothal with a *yevama* for reasons of modesty, so that the *yavam* would not have intercourse with her without betrothal.

רִאשׁוֹנָה לָא מִשְׁתַּבֵּשׁ. מַאי רִאשׁוֹנָה – רִאשׁוֹנָה לִנְפִילָה, וּמַאן דְּתָנֵי שְׁנִיָּה לָא מִשְׁתַּבֵּשׁ: מַאי שְׁנִיָּה – שְׁנִיָּה לְנִשּׂוּאִין. מִי לָא עָסְקִינַן דְּיִבֵּם וְאַחַר כָּךְ כָּנַס? אֶלָּא: מַאי שְׁנִיָּה – שְׁנִיָּה בְּנִשּׂוּאִין.

The first, is not mistaken, as **what is** the meaning of **first?** It means **the first to fall** before her *yavam* for levirate marriage. **And he who taught** referring to her as **the second is not mistaken** either, as **what is** the meaning of **second?** It means **the second to enter marriage.** Since the second deceased brother was already married to one woman, this *yevama* whom he took in levirate marriage was his second wife. The Gemara wonders: Is this the necessary order of events? **Are we not** also **dealing with** a scenario **in which** the second brother **took** the wife of the first brother **in levirate marriage and then later took** another wife? Would such a situation not merit the same ruling? **Rather, what is** the meaning of calling the wife of the first brother **the second?** It means **she who had been married for a second time.** She had already been married twice, whereas the wife of the second brother had been married only once.

אֵשֶׁת אָחִיו שֶׁלֹּא הָיָה בְּעוֹלָמוֹ הֵיכָא כְּתִיבָא? אָמַר רַב יְהוּדָה אָמַר רַב: אָמַר קְרָא ״כִּי יֵשְׁבוּ אַחִים יַחְדָּו״ – שֶׁהָיְתָה לָהֶם יְשִׁיבָה אַחַת בָּעוֹלָם, פְּרָט לְאֵשֶׁת אָחִיו שֶׁלֹּא הָיָה בְּעוֹלָמוֹ. ״יַחְדָּו״ – מְיוּחָדִים בְּנַחֲלָה, פְּרָט לְאָחִיו מִן הָאֵם.

§ The Gemara turns from a review of the language used in the mishna to a discussion of the *halakhot* of a wife of a brother with whom one did not coexist. **Where is it written** that the mitzva of levirate marriage does not apply in the case of **the wife of a brother with whom he did not coexist?**[N] **Rav Yehuda said** that **Rav said: The verse states "If brothers dwell together** and one of them dies" (Deuteronomy 25:5), meaning **that they had a common dwelling** together **in the world.** This **excludes the wife of a brother with whom he did not coexist.** Furthermore, it is derived: **"Together"** means that they were **united** together **in an inheritance;**[N] i.e., they are united in that they inherit together. In other words, since property is inherited by sons from their father, it can be inferred that the verse is speaking specifically of brothers from the same father. This **excludes his maternal** half **brother,**[H] with whom he is not united by inheritance, since only brothers who share the same father inherit from each other.

רַבָּה אָמַר: אַחִין מִן הָאָב – יָלֵיף ״אַחֲוָה״ ״אַחֲוָה״ מִבְּנֵי יַעֲקֹב, מָה לְהַלָּן מִן הָאָב וְלֹא מִן הָאֵם, אַף כָּאן מִן הָאָב וְלֹא מִן הָאֵם.

Rabba said: One learns the ruling that levirate marriage applies only to **brothers from the** same **father** by the verbal analogy between the term **brotherhood** used in the context of levirate marriage and the term **brotherhood from the children of Jacob. Just as there,** with regard to the children of Jacob, they are all brothers **from the father and not from the mother,** since they were from four different mothers, **so too, here,** in the case of levirate marriage, it is referring specifically to brothers **from the father and not from the mother.**

וְלֵילַף ״אַחֲוָה״ ״אַחֲוָה״ מֵעֲרָיוֹת! דָּנִין ״אַחִים״ מֵ״אַחִים״, וְאֵין דָּנִין אַחִים מֵ״אָחִיךָ״.

The Gemara raises an objection: Why should we learn from the children of Jacob? **Let it derive** the meaning of the term **brotherhood** by verbal analogy to the term **brotherhood from** the verses discussing **those with whom relations are forbidden.** In the *halakhot* of forbidden relations, both paternal and maternal half brothers are considered brothers, and are thereby subject to such prohibitions as those against relations with a brother's wife. The Gemara answers: The first analogy is preferable, as **we infer "brothers" from "brothers."** The word "brothers" is stated both with regard to the children of Jacob and with regard to the *halakhot* of levirate marriage, **whereas** with regard to forbidden relations it says "your brother," and **one cannot make an inference to "brothers" from "your brother."**

מַאי נָפְקָא מִינָּהּ? הָא תָּנָא דְּבֵי רַבִּי יִשְׁמָעֵאל: ״וְשָׁב הַכֹּהֵן״ ״וּבָא הַכֹּהֵן״ זוֹ הִיא שִׁיבָה זוֹ הִיא בִּיאָה! הָנֵי מִילֵּי הֵיכָא דְּלֵיכָּא מִידֵּי דְּדָמֵי לֵיהּ, אֲבָל הֵיכָא דְּאִיכָּא מִידֵּי דְּדָמֵי לֵיהּ – מִדְּדָמֵי לֵיהּ יָלְפִינַן.

The Gemara objects: **What difference does it make** if there is a minor difference between the words being compared? **As the school of Rabbi Yishmael taught** a verbal analogy with regard to leprosy of houses between the verse "**and the priest shall return** [*veshav*]" (Leviticus 14:39) and the verse "**and the priest shall come** [*uva*]" (Leviticus 14:44), from which it is derived that **this is** the *halakha* with regard to **returning,** i.e., it is after seven days, and **this is** the same *halakha* with regard to **coming,** that it is after seven days. Consequently, a less pronounced difference of one letter between the Hebrew words for "brothers" and "your brother" should certainly not prevent the teaching of a verbal analogy. The Gemara responds: **This applies when nothing** else **was** more **similar, but where there is something similar we infer from that which is more similar.** In such situations, it is preferable to learn from the word that bears greater similarity.

וְלֵילַף ״אַחֲוָה״ ״אַחֲוָה״ מִלּוֹט, דִּכְתִיב ״כִּי אֲנָשִׁים אַחִים אֲנַחְנוּ״! מִסְתַּבְּרָא, מִבְּנֵי יַעֲקֹב הֲוָה לֵיהּ לְמֵילַף, מִשּׁוּם דְּמִפְנֵי. מִדַּהֲוָה לֵיהּ לְמִכְתַּב ״שְׁנֵים עָשָׂר עֲבָדֶיךָ בְּנֵי אָבִינוּ״ וּכְתִיב ״אַחִים״ – שְׁמַע מִינָּהּ לְאַפְנוּיֵי.

The Gemara objects on another count: **Let** the *halakha* **derive** the meaning of the term **brotherhood** from the term **brotherhood from Lot, as it is written** that Abraham said to Lot: **"For we are brothers"** (Genesis 13:8). From here one could conclude that the word brothers means relatives and not necessarily brothers. The Gemara rejects this: **It is** more **reasonable to derive from the children of Jacob, due to** the fact that the word "brothers" **is free** in its context and is therefore available to be used in a verbal analogy: **Since it could have written: We your servants are twelve children of our father,** but instead it **writes:** "Twelve **brothers,** the children of one man" (Genesis 42:13), **learn from here** that this comes **to render** the word "brothers" **free** so that it may be allocated to another matter, i.e., the definition of brothers.

NOTES

Wife of a brother with whom he did not coexist – אֵשֶׁת אָחִיו שֶׁלֹּא הָיָה בְּעוֹלָמוֹ: *Tosafot* ask: Why doesn't the Gemara employ the principle that the Torah's ways are pleasant (see Proverbs 3:17), used in several other areas of *halakha*, and say that it would not be appropriate for a woman to wait her entire life for a brother to possibly be born to her late husband? In the Jerusalem Talmud the applicability of this concept is discussed. *Tosafot* answer that the verse comes to exclude even the case where the mother-in-law was pregnant at the time of the husband's death, so that the wait would be finite. The Rashba adds that the verse is necessary to teach the case when several *yevamin* were alive, in which case the principle of the Torah's ways of pleasantness would not apply, as well as to exclude any later born brother from the obligation of levirate marriage.

United in an inheritance – מְיוּחָדִים בְּנַחֲלָה: The Rashba challenges this explanation, as there are certain situations in which maternal half brothers inherit a common inheritance from their mother. He answers that since such a case occurs only infrequently, that cannot be the criterion used to determine brotherhood with regard to levirate marriage.

HALAKHA

Excludes his maternal half brother – פְּרָט לְאָחִיו מִן הָאֵם: Maternal half brothers are not considered brothers for purposes of levirate marriage. If a man dies and has brothers only by his mother, then his widow is permitted to marry anyone (Rambam *Sefer Nashim*, *Hilkhot Yibbum VaḤalitza* 1:7; *Shulḥan Arukh*, *Even HaEzer* 157:1).

וְאִיצְטְרִיךְ לְמִכְתַּב ״אַחִים״, וְאִיצְטְרִיךְ לְמִכְתַּב ״יַחְדָּו״. דְּאִי כָּתַב רַחֲמָנָא ״אַחִים״ הֲוָה אָמִינָא: לֵילַף ״אַחֲוָה״ ״אַחֲוָה״ מִלּוֹט. וְכִי תֵּימָא לָא מֻפְנֵי – לָאֵי, אַפְנוּיֵי מֻפְנֵי, מִדַּהֲוָה לֵיהּ לְמִכְתַּב ״רֵעִים״ וּכְתִיב ״אַחִים״, שְׁמַע מִינָּהּ לְאַפְנוּיֵי – כָּתַב רַחֲמָנָא ״יַחְדָּו״, הַמְיוּחָדִים בְּנַחֲלָה.

The Gemara comments: **And** although Rav Yehuda and Rabba learned the same ruling from two different passages, according to both **it was necessary to write "brothers"**[N] **and it was necessary to write "together"** in the verses discussing levirate marriage, **as, if the Merciful One had written** only **"brothers," I would say that one should infer** the meaning of the term **"brothers"** from the term **"brothers" from Lot. And if you would say it is not free**[N] there in the same way that the word "brothers" is free in the passage concerning the children of Jacob, this is **not so;** in fact, **it is free.** With regard to Lot **it could have written: Friends,** as they were not actual brothers but relatives, **and yet "brothers" is written.** One might **learn from** here **that this is free** to be allocated elsewhere and teach that such relatives are called brothers even for levirate marriage. Therefore, **the Torah wrote "together"** to teach that this applies specifically to **those** brothers who are **united in an inheritance.**

וְאִי כָּתַב רַחֲמָנָא ״יַחְדָּו״, הֲוָה אָמִינָא: דְּמִיַּיחֲדִי בְּאַבָּא וּבְאִמָּא, צְרִיכָא.

And if the Merciful One had written "together" alone and not added "brothers," **I would say that** they must **have** both **the same father and mother together,** and that otherwise the mitzva of levirate marriage would not apply. Therefore, "brothers" is written to compare this to the children of Jacob, who were brothers from the same father but not the same mother. It is for this reason, then, that **it is necessary** to write both.

וְהָא מֵהֵיכָא תֵּיתֵי? יִבּוּם בְּנַחֲלָה תְּלָא רַחֲמָנָא, וְנַחֲלָה מִן הָאָב וְלֹא מִן הָאֵם הִיא! אִיצְטְרִיךְ, סָלְקָא דַּעְתָּךְ אָמִינָא: הוֹאִיל וְחִידּוּשׁ הוּא, דְּקָמִשְׁתְּרֵי עֶרְוָה גַּבֵּיהּ – אֵימָא עַד דְּמִיַּיחֲדִי בְּאַבָּא וּבְאִמָּא, צְרִיכָא.

The Gemara asks about the last supposition: **But from where would it be derived** that perhaps levirate marriage would apply only if they are full brothers, sharing both a father and mother? Why should one assume that maternal brotherhood is also of import here? Doesn't **the Merciful One make levirate marriage dependent upon inheritance?** The Torah states that the *yavam* who performs the levirate marriage will establish the name of his deceased brother, meaning that he inherits from him, **and inheritance** comes **from the father and not from the mother.** Nevertheless, this **was necessary,** as **it could enter your mind to say that since this** *halakha* of levirate marriage **is a novelty** in **that** a woman who was a **forbidden relation to him** as a brother's wife **is** now **rendered permitted, say** that this permissibility will be limited **only to** cases of brothers **with the same father and same mother together.** It is due to this possibility that the verbal analogy to the brothers who were the children of Jacob is **necessary.**

אָמַר רַב הוּנָא אָמַר רַב: שׁוֹמֶרֶת יָבָם שֶׁמֵּתָה – מוּתָּר בְּאִמָּהּ. אַלְמָא קָסָבַר: אֵין זִיקָה. וְלֵימָא: הֲלָכָה כְּדִבְרֵי הָאוֹמֵר אֵין זִיקָה!

§ **Rav Huna said** that **Rav said:** In the case of **a widow** whose husband had died childless and who is **waiting for her** *yavam* to perform levirate marriage or set her free with *ḥalitza,* **who** then **died** before her *yavam* could take her in levirate marriage, the *yavam* **is permitted to** marry **her mother.** The levirate obligation does not create a familial relation between them. **Apparently,** Rav Huna says that Rav **holds** that **the** levirate **bond** [*zikka*][BL] **is not substantial.** In other words, the bond formed between the *yevama* and her *yavam* requiring levirate marriage does not create a halakhic connection between the two. The Gemara asks: **Then let him say** explicitly: The *halakha* **is in accordance with the statement of he who says** that **the** levirate **bond is not substantial,** as this issue is in fact a matter of dispute between *tanna'im.* Why did he not simply conclude that the *halakha* is in accordance with the opinion of the *tanna* who held that the levirate bond is not substantial?

אִי הֲוָה אָמַר הָכִי הֲוָה אָמִינָא: הָנֵי מִילֵּי בִּתְרֵי, אֲבָל בְּחַד יֵשׁ זִיקָה.

The Gemara answers: **If he had said that, I would say: This** statement that the levirate bond is not substantial **applies** only in reference **to two** brothers, each of whom has the possibility to take her in levirate marriage. In such cases the levirate bond between either one of the brothers and the *yevama* is not absolute, as it is always possible for the other brother to marry her instead. **But in** cases of **one** brother, then since the obligation to the *yevama* is exclusively his, I would say that **the** levirate **bond is substantial.**

NOTES

It was necessary to write brothers, etc. – **אִיצְטְרִיךְ לְמִכְתַּב אַחִים וכו׳**: *Tosafot Yeshanim* raise the question: Would it not have been possible to omit the word "brothers" in reference to Lot and to omit "together" in the verses that discuss levirate marriage? If so, they are both unnecessary. Ramban answers that if the word "brothers" had not been written, the word "brother" might have been interpreted in the widest sense as referring to fellow men and not necessarily to relatives, just as many times in the Torah the words "your brother" refer to any Jewish person. Consequently, it was necessary to write "brothers" in reference to Lot to teach that the "brothers" referred to in the context of levirate marriage are specifically relatives (see Ritva).

Free – **מֻפְנֵי**: There is a tannaitic dispute with regard to the authority of a verbal analogy [*gezera shava*] where the key words are not superfluous in their respective contexts. In the Jerusalem Talmud, even in the case of a verbal analogy where the key words are not at all superfluous, the analogy may be expounded, with the caveat that it is open to refutation. This type of verbal analogy is really an enhanced analogy [*binyan av*] and is essentially nothing more than a logical connection based on the idea that identical expressions in two *halakhot* indicate that the Torah intended to emphasize the connection between them. However, in the Babylonian Talmud, a verbal analogy may be expounded only if the key word is superfluous in at least one of the verses. According to Rabbi Yishmael, the superfluity of the key word in one verse is sufficient proof that the Torah intended that this verbal analogy should be derived, and it cannot be refuted. The Sages who disagree with him hold that even that type of verbal analogy can be logically refuted.

BACKGROUND

Levirate bond – **זִיקָה**: This refers to the relationship between a *yevama* and her deceased husband's brothers, from the time of the husband's death until one of the brothers performs levirate marriage or *ḥalitza* with the widow. The precise nature of the relationship between the *yevama* and her *yevamin* during this period is the subject of much talmudic debate. In certain respects they are already considered to be betrothed from the time of the husband's death. For this reason, for example, a *yavam* may not marry a close relative of his *yevama.* The bond is either transformed into marriage by levirate marriage or nullified and severed by *ḥalitza.*

LANGUAGE

Levirate bond [*zikka*] – **זִיקָה**: From the root *z-k-k,* meaning connected or tied. The modern Hebrew words *zikim* or *azikim,* meaning handcuffs, come from the same source. While this root is also used literally in certain contexts, most of its usage by the Sages is abstract or metaphorical and represents legal, psychological, or sometimes sexual bonds. The word *zikka* is an abstract noun meaning a tie or a connection, and it indicates that an element is lacking.

וְלֵימָא: הֲלָכָה כְּדִבְרֵי הָאוֹמֵר אֵין זִיקָה אֲפִילּוּ בְּחַד?! אִי אָמַר הָכִי הֲוָה אָמֵינָא אֲפִילּוּ מֵחַיִּים, קָמַשְׁמַע לָן: לְאַחַר מִיתָה – אִין, מֵחַיִּים – לָא, מִשּׁוּם דְּאָסוּר לְבַטֵּל מִצְוַת יְבָמִין.

The Gemara asks: **Then let him say:** The ***halakha* is in accordance with the statement of the one who says that the** levirate **bond is not substantial, even in** the case of **one** brother. The Gemara answers: **If he had said that, I would say: Even** if his *yevama* were **alive** and required levirate marriage with him, he would be allowed to take her mother in marriage. Therefore, **this comes to teach us** that **after death, yes, he is** permitted to marry her mother; but **while** she is **alive,** he is **not.** Why not? This is **because it is prohibited to nullify the mitzva of levirate marriage.** Were he to marry her mother, he would no longer be able to take the daughter in levirate marriage because his wife's daughter is forbidden to him. As a result of his marriage, he would cancel the mitzva of levirate marriage so that it could no longer apply to him.

תְּנַן: יְבִמְתּוֹ שֶׁמֵּתָה – מוּתָּר בַּאֲחוֹתָהּ. בַּאֲחוֹתָהּ אִין, בְּאִמָּהּ לָא!

The Gemara raises an objection to the statement of Rav Huna: **We learned** in a mishna (49a): If **his *yevama* dies, he is permitted to** marry **her sister.** A precise reading of this phrase leads to the implication that with regard to **her sister, yes,** it is permitted, as even if it had been his wife who had died he would be permitted to marry her sister. But with regard to **her mother, no,** it is not permitted.

הוּא הַדִּין דַּאֲפִילּוּ בְּאִמָּהּ, וְאַיְּידֵי דִּתְנָא רֵישָׁא אִשְׁתּוֹ שֶׁמֵּתָה מוּתָּר בַּאֲחוֹתָהּ, בַּאֲחוֹתָהּ – אִין, אֲבָל בְּאִמָּהּ – לָא, דְּהָוְיָא לַהּ אִיסּוּרָא דְּאוֹרָיְיתָא, תְּנָא נַמִי סֵיפָא מוּתָּר בַּאֲחוֹתָהּ.

The Gemara rejects this: No evidence can be derived from here, as it is possible to say that **the same is true even for her mother,** that she too is permitted. **But since it taught in the first clause** of this mishna: If **his wife dies he is permitted to take her sister,** and there the language is precise and implies: **Her sister, yes, but her mother, no, as she is forbidden by Torah** law because it is prohibited for a man to marry both a woman and her daughter even after one of them dies, therefore he used the same language when **he taught the latter clause** of the same mishna that **he is permitted to** take **her sister.** However, in the latter clause it is not an exact reading, and in actuality one is allowed to marry any of her relatives. This completes the Gemara's explanation of Rav Huna's opinion.

וְרַב יְהוּדָה אָמַר: שׁוֹמֶרֶת יָבָם שֶׁמֵּתָה – אָסוּר בְּאִמָּהּ. אַלְמָא קָסָבַר: יֵשׁ זִיקָה. וְלֵימָא: הֲלָכָה כְּדִבְרֵי הָאוֹמֵר יֵשׁ זִיקָה!

And Rav Yehuda said: In the case of **a widow who dies** while **waiting for her brother-in-law** to perform *ḥalitza* or levirate marriage, **he is prohibited from** marrying **her mother.**[H] The Gemara comments: **Apparently** Rav Yehuda **holds** that **the levirate bond is substantial;** this would mean that the attachment between the *yevama* and the *yavam* is like that of marriage and that the *yavam* is therefore prohibited from marrying her relatives. **But** it must be asked: Why does Rav Yehuda say it in such a way? **Let** him **say:** The ***halakha* is in accordance with the statement of the one who says that the** levirate **bond is substantial.**

אִי הֲוָה אָמַר הָכִי הֲוָה אָמֵינָא: הָנֵי מִילֵּי בְּחַד, אֲבָל בִּתְרֵי אֵין זִיקָה. וְהָא כִּי פְּלִיגִי – בִּתְרֵי פְּלִיגִי! אֶלָּא, אִי אָמַר הָכִי

The Gemara responds: **If he would have said that, I would say that** with regard to the levirate bond, **this applies in** the case of **one** brother, **but** if there were **two** brothers then **the** levirate **bond is not substantial.** The Gemara objects: **But when** the *tanna'im* **disagree,** they **disagree in** a case of **two** brothers, so how could one think that Rav Yehuda is speaking only in the case of a single brother? **Rather,** one must say: **If he were to say that** the conclusive halakhic ruling is that the bond is substantial,

HALAKHA

A widow who dies while waiting for her bother-in-law, he is prohibited from marrying her mother – שׁוֹמֶרֶת יָבָם שֶׁמֵּתָה אָסוּר בְּאִמָּהּ: If one's *yevama* dies before he performs *ḥalitza*, then her relatives are forbidden to him as though she had been his wife.

This *halakha* is ruled in accordance with the opinion of Rav Yehuda in the name of Shmuel (18b), because it seems from the talmudic discussion that the *amora'im* made great efforts to resolve the difficulties in accordance with his opinion, and this implies that the *halakha* is ruled in accordance with his opinion (*Beit Yosef*). Although this contradicts the principle that the *halakha* is ruled in accordance with the opinion of Rav in his disputes with Shmuel, some versions of the text show that Rav Yehuda's statement was in fact said in the name of Rav. In that case, there is an amoraic dispute with regard to his opinion, and the *halakha* is ruled in accordance with the more certain opinion (Rabbeinu Ḥananel; Rambam *Sefer Nashim*, *Hilkhot Yibbum VaḤalitza* 1:13; *Shulḥan Arukh*, *Even HaEzer* 159:5).

הוה אמינא: מחיים, אבל לאחר מיתה פקעה לה זיקה, קא משמע לן דזיקה בכדי לא פקעה. לימא מסייע ליה: יבמתו שמתה מותר באחותה, באחותה – אין, באמה – לא.

I would say that the levirate bond applies as long as the *yevama* requiring levirate marriage **is alive but** that **after** her **death the bond was terminated.** In other words, after the *yevama* died any relationship between the two dissolved. **This comes to teach us that the bond is not terminated without cause** but instead requires an actual act, such as *ḥalitza* or levirate marriage. Until one of these acts is performed, the bond remains in place. **Let us say that it supports** Rav Yehuda's opinion from that which was taught: If **his** *yevama* **dies, he is permitted to** marry **her sister.** From here the Gemara deduces: **Her sister, yes; her mother, no,** in accordance with the opinion of Rav Yehuda.

הוא הדין דאפילו באמה, ואיידי דתנא רישא אשתו שמתה מותר באחותה, דווקא באחותה אבל באמה לא, דהויא לה איסורא דאורייתא – תנא נמי סיפא מותר באחותה.

The Gemara rejects this: **The same is true, that even her mother** is permitted. **And** this language was used only **since he taught in the first clause** of the *baraita*: If **his wife dies he is permitted to** take **her sister; specifically her sister but not her mother, as she is forbidden by Torah law.** Therefore, **he also taught in the latter clause** that **he is permitted to** marry **her sister.**

מתיב רב הונא בר חייא: עשה בה מאמר ומת – שניה חולצת ולא מתייבמת. טעמא – דעבד בה מאמר, הא לא עבד בה מאמר – שניה נמי יבומי מייבמה. ואי אמרת יש זיקה, הויא לה צרת אשת אחיו שלא היה בעולמו בזיקה!

Rav Huna bar Ḥiyya raised an objection to this from the mishna: If **he performed levirate betrothal with her and** then **died,** the **second** woman **performs *ḥalitza* and may not enter into levirate marriage.** This implies that **the reason is** specifically **that he performed levirate betrothal with her. Had** the brother **not performed levirate betrothal with her, the second** woman **would also** be permitted to **enter into levirate marriage. And if you say that the** levirate **bond is substantial,** then she would be considered **a rival wife of the wife of a brother with whom** the third brother **did not coexist by that bond.**[H] Since the wife of a brother with whom he did not coexist is prohibited from entering into levirate marriage, her rival wife would likewise be forbidden from doing so.

אמר רבה: הוא הדין דאף על גב דלא עבד בה מאמר – שניה מחלץ חלצה, יבומי לא מייבמה,

Rabba said: This should not be read precisely, as **the same is true even if** the second brother **did not perform levirate betrothal;** the **second** woman **must perform *ḥalitza* but may not enter into levirate marriage,** as the levirate bond renders her a rival wife of the wife of a brother with whom the third brother did not coexist.

והא דקתני מאמר – לאפוקי מבית שמאי, דאמרי: מאמר קונה קנין גמור, קא משמע לן.

And the reason **that** it **teaches** the case of **levirate betrothal** specifically was **in order to exclude** the opinion of **Beit Shammai,**[N] **who said:** The legal status of **levirate betrothal** with a *yevama* eligible for levirate marriage **is** that of **a full-fledged acquisition,** and it is legally binding to the same degree as an actual betrothal. Therefore, even *ḥalitza* would be unnecessary, similar to the case of a rival wife of a forbidden relation. This is what **it comes to teach us:** Even if he performed levirate betrothal she is not truly considered the rival wife of a forbidden relation; the prohibition concerning her is by rabbinic law, and she is therefore required to perform *ḥalitza*.

איתיביה אביי: שני אחין בעולם אחד, ומת אחד מהן בלא ולד, ועמד השני הזה לעשות מאמר ביבמתו, ולא הספיק לעשות בה מאמר עד שנולד לו אח, ומת, הראשונה יוצאה משום אשת אחיו שלא היה בעולמו, ושניה – או חולצת או מתייבמת. ואי אמרת יש זיקה – הויא לה צרת אשת אחיו שלא היה בעולמו בזיקה!

Abaye raised an objection to this from that which was taught: In the case of **two brothers who coexisted, and one died childless and the second arose to perform levirate betrothal with his** *yevama* **but did not manage to perform levirate betrothal before** a third **brother was born, and** then the second brother, who also had a wife, **died,** whereby both women would fall before the newly born brother for levirate marriage, then **the first goes out** and is not obligated in levirate marriage **because** she is **the wife of his brother with whom he did not coexist, and the second** woman, who was the wife of the second brother, **either performs *ḥalitza* or enters into levirate marriage. But if you say that the** levirate **bond is substantial,** then the wife of the second brother **would be rendered a rival wife of the wife of a brother with whom he did not coexist** by that **bond.**

HALAKHA

A rival wife of the wife of a brother with whom he did not coexist by that bond – צרת אשת אחיו שלא היה בעולמו בזיקה: If there were two brothers and one died childless, and subsequently a third brother was born, then if the second brother dies, even if he had not yet performed levirate betrothal to the widow of the first brother, the third brother must nevertheless perform *ḥalitza* for the wife of the second brother, and she may not enter into levirate marriage with him, since they ruled that the levirate bond is substantial. Accordingly, the levirate bond rendered the wife of the second brother a rival wife of the wife of the first brother, with whom the third brother did not coexist, as per Shmuel's opinion.

Rambam explains that this *halakha* applies only if the second brother had performed levirate betrothal. The author of the *Maggid Mishne* challenges this, since Rambam himself concludes explicitly that there is a levirate bond even if there was no levirate betrothal (Rambam *Sefer Nashim, Hilkhot Yibbum VaḤalitza* 6:18; *Shulḥan Arukh, Even HaEzer* 173:12).

NOTES

In order to exclude the opinion of Beit Shammai – לאפוקי מבית שמאי: *Tosafot Yeshanim* raise the question: Isn't it already known that when Beit Shammai express an opinion and Beit Hillel disagree, the opinion of Beit Shammai is considered as though it were not in the mishna at all and is completely disregarded? If so, why would it be necessary to explicitly exclude the opinion of Beit Shammai? The answer given is that in fact, the opinion that levirate betrothal constitutes a fully effective acquisition is not exclusive to Beit Shammai but is actually the opinion of several other *tanna'im*, and so it was necessary to exclude that opinion.

HALAKHA

Two brothers married to two sisters – שְׁנֵי אַחִים נְשׂוּאִים לִשְׁתֵּי אֲחָיוֹת: If two brothers were married to two sisters and both died childless, since both women would require levirate marriage but cannot both be married to the same man because they are sisters, both perform *ḥalitza* and neither may enter into levirate marriage, as stated in the mishna (Rambam *Sefer Nashim, Hilkhot Yibbum VaḤalitza* 7:1; *Shulḥan Arukh, Even HaEzer* 175:3).

הָא מַנִּי – רַבִּי מֵאִיר הִיא, דְּאָמַר: אֵין זִיקָה. וּמִי סְבִירָא לֵיהּ לְרַבִּי מֵאִיר אֵין זִיקָה? וְהָתְנַן: אַרְבָּעָה אַחִים, שְׁנַיִם מֵהֶן נְשׂוּאִים שְׁתֵּי אֲחָיוֹת, וּמֵתוּ הַנְּשׂוּאִין הָאֲחָיוֹת – הֲרֵי אֵלּוּ חוֹלְצוֹת וְלֹא מִתְיַיבְּמוֹת.

The Gemara rejects that: In accordance with **whose** opinion **is this? It is** the opinion of **Rabbi Meir, who said: The** levirate **bond is not substantial.** The Gemara asks: **Does Rabbi Meir hold that the** levirate **bond is not substantial?** After all, unattributed *mishnayot* are in accordance with the opinion of Rabbi Meir, and **didn't we learn** in a mishna (26a): In the case of **four brothers, two of whom are married to two sisters,**[H] if **those married to the sisters died,** whereby both sisters fall before the surviving brothers for levirate marriage, **then those** two sisters **must perform *ḥalitza* and may not enter into levirate marriage.** It would seem that the reason for this is that each of the sisters has a levirate bond to both remaining brothers.

וְאִי סָלְקָא דַּעְתָּךְ סָבַר רַבִּי מֵאִיר אֵין זִיקָה – הָנֵי מִתְּרֵי בָּתֵּי קָאָתְיָין, הַאי לַיְיבֵּם חֲדָא וְהַאי לַיְיבֵּם חֲדָא!

And if it enters your mind to say that **Rabbi Meir held that the** levirate **bond is not substantial,** didn't **these** two sisters **come from two** different **houses,** as each was married to a different brother? If so, **one** brother **should take one in levirate marriage and the other should take one in levirate marriage.**

לְעוֹלָם אֵין זִיקָה, מִשּׁוּם דְּקָסָבַר: אָסוּר לְבַטֵּל מִצְוַת יְבָמִין, דְּדִלְמָא אַדְּמְיַיבֵּם חַד מָיֵית אִידַּךְ, וְקָא בָּטְלַתְּ מִצְוַת יְבָמִין.

The Gemara answers: **Actually,** in Rabbi Meir's opinion **the** levirate **bond is not substantial.** The mishna states that they perform *ḥalitza* and do not enter into levirate marriage **because he held that it is prohibited to nullify the mitzva of levirate marriage.** That is to say, it is prohibited to act in such a way that the mitzva of levirate marriage becomes obviated. Under these circumstances there is concern that **perhaps as one** brother **performs levirate marriage** to one of the sisters **the other** brother **dies** before he manages to perform levirate marriage to the other. If that were to happen, **you** would thereby **nullify the mitzva of levirate marriage** since the sister that would now fall before the remaining brother would be his wife's sister and therefore prohibited from entering into levirate marriage with him.

וְאִי אֵין זִיקָה – תִּיבָּטֵל, דְּהָא רַבָּן גַּמְלִיאֵל אָמַר אֵין זִיקָה, וּמוּתָּר לְבַטֵּל מִצְוַת יְבָמִין.

The Gemara objects: **But if the** levirate **bond is not substantial,** then **let** the mitzva of levirate marriage **be nullified.** That is, if the levirate bond does not carry any real obligation, then the mitzva itself never truly came into effect. **As Rabban Gamliel said: The** levirate **bond is not substantial, and it is permitted to nullify the mitzva of levirate marriage.**

דִּתְנַן: רַבָּן גַּמְלִיאֵל אוֹמֵר: אִם מֵאֲנָה – מֵאֲנָה, וְאִם לֹא מֵאֲנָה – תַּמְתִּין עַד שֶׁתַּגְדִּיל וְתֵצֵא הַלֵּזוּ מִשּׁוּם אֲחוֹת אִשָּׁה!

As we learned in a mishna (109a): That mishna discusses a case of two brothers who were married to two sisters. One sister is an adult and therefore her marriage was fully effectual, and one sister is still a minor, and she was orphaned from her father, and her marriage was valid only by rabbinic ordinance. If the brother who was married to the elder sister died, then that sister falls for levirate marriage before the brother married to the minor. Under these circumstances, the Sages suggested directing the minor to refuse her marriage to her husband so that he would be able to take his brother's wife in levirate marriage. If the minor does not do so, he would be unable to take her sister in marriage, as she would be the sister of his minor wife and thereby fully exempt from the levirate obligation. **Rabban Gamliel said: If** the minor **refused**[N] in the meantime of her own accord, **then she refused, but if she did not refuse, let her wait until she reaches** the age of **maturity,**[N] **and** then **that other** adult sister **will be exempt** from performing *ḥalitza* or levirate marriage **due to** the fact that she is his **wife's sister.** Here it is apparent that Rabban Gamliel is not concerned about nullifying the mitzva of levirate marriage from one of them.

NOTES

Refusal – מִיאוּן: A girl under the age of twelve can be married off by her father. However, if her father is no longer alive then by Torah law she cannot marry while still a minor. Nevertheless, the Sages ordained that her mother or brothers may marry her off with her consent. Since her consent is not legally valid until she reaches the age of maturity, the girl may terminate this marriage once she reaches twelve years of age by performing an act of refusal, i.e., declaring that she does not desire this marriage. In such cases, no bill of divorce is necessary. When a girl performs the act of refusal, the marriage is nullified retroactively, and it is considered as though she had never been married at all.

Let her wait until she reaches the age of maturity – תַּמְתִּין עַד שֶׁתַּגְדִּיל: Rashi understands this to mean that the adult sister must wait until her minor sister matures before she marries anyone else. *Tosafot* interpret this to mean that the minor must wait and not engage in intercourse until she becomes fully mature.

אֲמַר לֵיהּ: דְּרַבָּן גַּמְלִיאֵל אַדְּרַבִּי מֵאִיר קָרָמֵית? לָא, הָכִי קָאָמְרִינַן: רַבִּי מֵאִיר חָיֵישׁ אֲפִילּוּ לִסְפֵיקָא, רַבָּן גַּמְלִיאֵל – אֲפִילּוּ לְוַדַּאי לָא חָיֵישׁ?! דִּלְמָא, מַאן דְּלָא חָיֵישׁ אֲפִילּוּ לְוַדַּאי לָא חָיֵישׁ, וּמַאן דְּחָיֵישׁ – אֲפִילּוּ לִסְפֵיקָא חָיֵישׁ.

Rabba **said to** Abaye: Do you wish to **raise a contradiction between** the words of **Rabban Gamliel and Rabbi Meir?** This would imply that the contradiction needs to be resolved, but statements from two different *tanna'im* do not need to agree or to be resolved. Abaye responded: **No,** in fact **this is what we meant to say:** How could one possibly say that **Rabbi Meir is concerned** lest there be nullification of the mitzva of levirate marriage **even when it is uncertain** because perhaps the first brother will not die, whereas **Rabban Gamliel is not concerned** that the mitzva be nullified **even when it is certain?** It is surprising that there should be such a great difference between the tannaitic opinions. Rabba answered: **Perhaps the one who is not concerned** about nullification of the mitzva of levirate marriage **is not concerned even if** nullification **is certain, and the one who is concerned is concerned even if** nullification **is uncertain.**

אֲמַר לֵיהּ אַבָּיֵי לְרַב יוֹסֵף: הָא דְּרַב יְהוּדָה – דִּשְׁמוּאֵל הִיא, דִּתְנַן:

With regard to the actual dispute between Rav Huna and Rav Yehuda, **Abaye said to Rav Yosef: This** *halakha* stated **by Rav Yehuda,** that even if a woman waiting for levirate marriage dies her mother is still forbidden to the *yavam,* **is** from his teacher **Shmuel** and not from Rav, who was also one of his teachers. Evidence for this can be found in **that** which **we learned** in a mishna (41a):

Perek **II**
Daf **18** Amud **b**

שׁוֹמֶרֶת יָבָם שֶׁקִּדֵּשׁ אָחִיו אֶת אֲחוֹתָהּ, מִשּׁוּם רַבִּי יְהוּדָה בֶּן בְּתֵירָה אָמְרוּ: אוֹמְרִים לוֹ, הַמְתֵּן עַד שֶׁיַּעֲשֶׂה אָחִיךָ מַעֲשֶׂה. וְאָמַר שְׁמוּאֵל: הֲלָכָה כְּרַבִּי יְהוּדָה בֶּן בְּתֵירָה.

In the case of **a widow waiting for her** ***yavam*** to take her in levirate marriage or perform *ḥalitza,* if **his brother betrothed**[H] **her sister**[N] **they said in the name of Rabbi Yehuda ben Beteira: They say to** the brother who betrothed her: **Wait** and do not marry your betrothed **until your brother performs** the required **action,** either *ḥalitza* or levirate marriage. This is because until that time the levirate bond is still applicable and the woman betrothed to you is forbidden to you as the sister of a woman bonded to you. **And Shmuel said:** The ***halakha*** **is in accordance with** the opinion of **Rabbi Yehuda ben Beteira.** From here one may infer that Shmuel holds that the levirate bond is substantial.

אֲמַר לֵיהּ: דְּאִי דְּרַב מַאי? (אֲמַר לֵיהּ:) קַשְׁיָא דְּרַב אַדְּרַב! דִּלְמָא אָמוֹרָאֵי נִינְהוּ, וְאַלִּיבָּא דְּרַב? כֵּיוָן דְּאִיתְּמַר מִשְּׁמֵיהּ דִּשְׁמוּאֵל בְּהֶדְיָא, וּמִשְּׁמֵיהּ דְּרַב כְּאָמוֹרָאֵי – לָא שָׁבְקִינַן מִשְּׁמֵיהּ דִּשְׁמוּאֵל בְּהֶדְיָא וּמוֹקְמִינַן כְּאָמוֹרָאֵי וְאַלִּיבָּא דְּרַב.

Rav Yosef **said to him: And if** it were the opinion **of Rav, what** problem would there be? Abaye **said to him: It is difficult** because there would be a contradiction between the opinion **of Rav** and another statement **of Rav,** since Rav Huna cited Rav, and the conclusion from his statements was that the levirate bond is not substantial. He said to him: Rav Huna and Rav Yehuda each cited Rav. **Perhaps they are** ***amora'im*** **and** disagree **in accordance with** the opinion of **Rav,** i.e., with regard to his opinion? The Gemara answers: **Since that which was stated in the name of Shmuel was explicit, while that** said **in the name of Rav** must be explained **as an amoraic** dispute, **we will not leave** that statement said **explicitly in the name of Shmuel and explain it as an amoraic** dispute **according to** the opinion **of Rav.**

אָמַר רַב כָּהֲנָא, אָמְרִיתָהּ לִשְׁמַעְתָּא קַמֵּיהּ דְּרַב זְבִיד מִנְּהַרְדְּעָא, אֲמַר: אַתּוּן הָכִי מַתְנִיתוּ לַהּ, אֲנַן בְּהֶדְיָא מַתְנֵינַן: אָמַר רַב יְהוּדָה אָמַר שְׁמוּאֵל: שׁוֹמֶרֶת יָבָם שֶׁמֵּתָה – אָסוּר בְּאִמָּהּ. אַלְמָא קָסָבַר: יֵשׁ זִיקָה. וְאַזְדָּא שְׁמוּאֵל לְטַעְמֵיהּ, דַּאֲמַר שְׁמוּאֵל: הֲלָכָה כְּרַבִּי יְהוּדָה בֶּן בְּתֵירָה.

Rav Kahana said: I reported this discussion before Rav Zevid of Neharde'a. He said: That is how you teach this, without knowing for certain that Rav Yehuda was stating the *halakha* in the name of Shmuel. **We learn it explicitly: Rav Yehuda said** that **Shmuel said:** In the case of **a widow waiting for her** ***yavam*** who **died** before he could perform *ḥalitza* or levirate marriage, **he is prohibited from** marrying **her mother. Apparently** Shmuel **holds** that **the** levirate **bond is substantial.**[H] **And Shmuel** conforms **to his** standard line of **reasoning, as Shmuel** also **said:** The ***halakha*** **is in accordance with** the opinion of **Rabbi Yehuda ben Beteira.**

HALAKHA

A widow waiting for her ***yavam*****, if his brother betrothed, etc. – שׁוֹמֶרֶת יָבָם שֶׁקִּדֵּשׁ אָחִיו וכו׳:** If a woman happened before several brothers for levirate marriage, and one of the brothers betrothed the sister of this woman who was bound to him, he is prohibited from marrying his betrothed until one of the brothers takes the widow in levirate marriage or performs *ḥalitza* for her, in accordance with the opinion of Rabbi Yehuda ben Beteira and Shmuel. Some say that if he already married her he is permitted to engage in intercourse even before another brother releases the widow (*Tosafot*), whereas others disagree (*Nimmukei Yosef*). The later commentaries say that if there is another brother who can perform *ḥalitza,* the brother who is married to the widow's sister should wait to consummate the marriage until after *ḥalitza* has been performed (*Pitḥei Teshuva*; *Shulḥan Arukh, Even HaEzer* 159:5).

The levirate bond is substantial – יֵשׁ זִיקָה: Where the mitzva of levirate marriage applies, the relatives of the *yevama* are forbidden to the *yavam* whether there is a single *yavam* or there are many. Even if she dies, her close relatives are forbidden to him (*Shulḥan Arukh, Even HaEzer* 159:5).

NOTES

His brother betrothed her sister – קִדֵּשׁ אָחִיו אֶת אֲחוֹתָהּ: The early commentaries discuss the reasons for this *halakha*, as one might have thought that the brother's betrothal of the sister effectively terminated the levirate bond between him and his brother's widow. *Tosafot* explain that the reason that he must wait is as a penalty because it was prohibited for him to betroth the sister of a woman with whom he has a levirate bond. However, Ramban challenges this answer, and suggests that the levirate bond lessens the validity of the betrothal to her sister, as the existence of a levirate bond renders this case similar to that of one who betroths the sister of his betrothed.

Some authorities hold that even if he actually married his betrothed he is told to wait and not engage in intercourse with her (Ritva; Meiri; *Nimmukei Yosef*; see Halakha section).

HALAKHA

The wife of a brother with whom he did not coexist – אֵשֶׁת אָחִיו שֶׁלֹּא הָיָה בְּעוֹלָמוֹ: The wife of a brother with whom a newly born brother did not coexist is forbidden to him, whether this youngest brother was born before or after another brother took her in levirate marriage. This ruling is in accordance with the opinion of the first *tanna* in the mishna (Rambam *Sefer Nashim, Hilkhot Yibbum VaḤalitza* 6:17; *Shulḥan Arukh, Even HaEzer* 173:12).

וּצְרִיכִי, דְּאִי אַשְׁמְעִינַן יֵשׁ זִיקָה – הֲוָה אָמִינָא: הָנֵי מִילֵּי – בְּחַד, אֲבָל בִּתְרֵי – לָא, קָא מַשְׁמַע לַן. וְאִי אַשְׁמְעִינַן הֲלָכָה כְּרַבִּי יְהוּדָה בֶּן בְּתֵירָה – הֲוָה אָמִינָא הָנֵי מִילֵּי מֵחַיִּים, אֲבָל לְאַחַר מִיתָה – פָּקְעָה לָהּ זִיקָה, קָא מַשְׁמַע לַן: דְּזִיקָה בִּכְדִי לָא פָּקְעָה.

The Gemara comments: Both statements by Shmuel on the subject **are necessary** and there was no redundancy here, **as, if he were to teach us** only the principle that **the** levirate **bond is substantial, I would say** that **this applies** only **to** the case of **one** *yavam* **but not to** a case of **two** *yevamin*, where the levirate bond is not as strong. **This comes to teach us** that even in the case of two *yevamin* there is a bond, and that is the conclusive *halakha* put forth by Rabbi Yehuda ben Beteira. **And if he were to teach us** only that the ***halakha* is in accordance with** the opinion of **Rabbi Yehuda ben Beteira, I would say that this applies** only in the case **where** the woman awaiting levirate marriage **is living, but after her death the** levirate **bond is terminated** and he is permitted to marry her relatives. **This comes to teach us that the** levirate **bond is not terminated without cause** but rather it is necessary to perform some act in order to exempt her from it.

מתני׳ שְׁנֵי אַחִים וּמֵת אֶחָד מֵהֶן, וְיִבֵּם הַשֵּׁנִי אֶת אֵשֶׁת אָחִיו, וְאַחַר כָּךְ נוֹלַד לָהֶן אָח וָמֵת – הָרִאשׁוֹנָה יוֹצְאָה מִשּׁוּם אֵשֶׁת אָחִיו שֶׁלֹּא הָיָה בְּעוֹלָמוֹ, וְהַשְּׁנִיָּה מִשּׁוּם צָרָתָהּ. עָשָׂה בָּהּ מַאֲמָר, וָמֵת – הַשְּׁנִיָּה חוֹלֶצֶת וְלֹא מִתְיַיבֶּמֶת.

MISHNA If there were **two brothers, and one died, and the second entered into levirate marriage with his brother's wife** while he was already married to another woman, **and subsequently** a third **brother was born to them, and** the second brother then **died,** whereby both of his wives happened before the third brother for levirate marriage, then **the first woman,** who was the wife of the first brother, **is exempt due to** the fact that she is **the wife of a brother with whom** the third brother **did not coexist,**[H] **and the second** woman, who was the first wife of the second brother, is exempt **due to her rival wife.** If the second brother had **performed** only **levirate betrothal with her and** then **died** before fully marrying her, **the second** woman **performs *ḥalitza* and may not enter into levirate marriage,** as the levirate betrothal is not considered a sufficiently valid marriage so as to render her the rival wife of a relation forbidden to the third brother.

רַבִּי שִׁמְעוֹן אוֹמֵר: מְיַיבֵּם לְאֵיזוֹ מֵהֶן שֶׁיִּרְצֶה, אוֹ חוֹלֵץ לְאֵיזוֹ מֵהֶן שֶׁיִּרְצֶה.

Rabbi Shimon says with regard to the first clause of the mishna: The third brother either **enters into levirate marriage with whichever one he wishes, or he performs *ḥalitza* with whichever one he wishes.** Since he was born after his second brother had already entered into levirate marriage with the first brother's widow, she is considered the wife of a brother with whom he did coexist, not the wife of a brother with whom he did not coexist. Therefore, he may enter into levirate marriage with her.

גמ׳ אָמַר רַב אוֹשַׁעְיָא: חָלוּק הָיָה רַבִּי שִׁמְעוֹן אַף בָּרִאשׁוֹנָה. מִמַּאי – מִדְּקָתָנֵי מִשְׁנָה יְתֵירָה –

GEMARA **Rav Oshaya**[N] **said: Rabbi Shimon's opinion differed even on the first** mishna. That is, Rabbi Shimon disagreed not only in the case stated explicitly in this mishna, in which the newly born brother came into the world after the widow of his first brother had already married his second brother, but he also disagreed in the case of the first mishna in the chapter, where the third brother was born prior to his second brother entering into levirate marriage with the widow. **From where** is this derived? Rav Oshaya came to this conclusion **from** the fact **that it teaches a superfluous mishna.**

NOTES

Rav Oshaya – רַב אוֹשַׁעְיָא: *Masoret HaShas* emends the text here to read: Rabbi Oshaya. The reason for this is that later (19a) the Gemara cites a *baraita* which challenges this opinion, and states: This is a conclusive refutation of the opinion of Rabbi Oshaya. Rabbi Oshaya, also known as Rabbi Hoshaya, was a first generation *amora* who lived in Eretz Yisrael.

However, elsewhere in this discussion, Rav Oshaya is also mentioned. Rav Oshaya, also known as Rav Hoshaya, was a third generation *amora* who was born and lived in Babylonia. He was a student of Rav Yehuda and Rav Huna, and a friend of Rava. He eventually moved to Eretz Yisrael, where he received ordination.

בְּבָא דְּרֵישָׁא לְמַאן קָתָנֵי לָהּ? אִילֵימָא לְרַבָּנַן – הָשְׁתָּא יִבֵּם וּלְבַסּוֹף נוֹלַד, דְּכִי אַשְׁכַּחָהּ בְּהֶתֵּירָא אַשְׁכַּחָהּ, אָסְרִי רַבָּנַן – נוֹלַד וְאַחַר כָּךְ יִבֵּם מִיבַּעְיָא? אֶלָּא לָאו – לְרַבִּי שִׁמְעוֹן אִיצְטְרִיךְ,

How so? **In accordance with whose** opinion **is it teaching the section of the first clause,** i.e., the previous mishna? **If we say** it is the opinion of **the Rabbis,** who prohibit marriage to the wife of a brother with whom one did not coexist in all cases, then let us look at the second mishna. **Now** that even in the case where the second brother **entered into levirate marriage and afterward** the third brother **was born,**[B] such that **when he found her,** i.e., when he was born, she had a **permitted** status, as she was already married to the second brother, she was never in his lifetime the wife of a brother with whom he did not coexist but was in fact for him the wife of a living brother. Nevertheless, even under such circumstances, **the Rabbis prohibit** him from entering into levirate marriage with her. **Is** it **necessary,** then, to teach the case presented in the first mishna of a third brother who was **born and subsequently** the second brother **entered into levirate marriage** with the wife of the first brother?[B] According to the opinion of the Rabbis, this first mishna is redundant. **Rather, is it not** that it **was necessary** to state this first mishna **for** the opinion of **Rabbi Shimon?**

וְתָנָא רֵישָׁא לְהוֹדִיעֲךָ כֹּחוֹ דְּרַבִּי שִׁמְעוֹן, וְתָנָא סֵיפָא לְהוֹדִיעֲךָ כֹּחָן דְּרַבָּנַן. וּבְדִין הוּא דְּנִפְלוֹג רַבִּי שִׁמְעוֹן בְּרֵישָׁא, אֶלָּא נָטַר לְהוּ לְרַבָּנַן עַד דִּמְסַיְּימֵי לְמִילְּתַיְיהוּ, וַהֲדַר פָּלֵיג עֲלַיְיהוּ.

If so, this is how it must be understood: **The first** mishna **was taught in order to convey to you the far-reaching nature** of the opinion of **Rabbi Shimon,** which allows even the case specified in the first mishna, **and the latter clause,** i.e., the present mishna, **was taught to convey the far-reaching nature** of the opinion of **the Rabbis,** that even if the third brother was born after levirate marriage to the second brother she remains forbidden to the third brother. **And by right it** should have explained **that Rabbi Shimon disagrees** even **in the first** mishna, **but** the author of the mishna **waited until the Rabbis finished their words, and then he went back** and wrote that Rabbi Shimon **disagreed with them.**

אֶלָּא, אֵשֶׁת אָחִיו שֶׁלֹּא הָיָה בְּעוֹלָמוֹ, לְרַבִּי שִׁמְעוֹן הֵיכִי מַשְׁכַּחַתְּ לָהּ? בְּחַד אַחָא, וּמִית, וְנוֹלַד לוֹ אָח. אִי נַמִי: בִּתְרֵי, וְלֹא יִבֵּם וְלֹא מִית.

The Gemara asks: **But according to** the opinion of **Rabbi Shimon, how can you find**[N] this case of **the wife of a brother with whom he did not coexist?** The Gemara answers: It is in the case of a **single brother who died and** subsequently another **brother was born to him.** Here, the widow would be the wife of a brother with whom he did not coexist, and she would not be required to perform *ḥalitza* or enter into levirate marriage with him. **Alternatively,** it can be found in the case of **two** brothers, one of whom died, **and** the remaining brother **did not take** the deceased brother's wife **in levirate marriage, and did not die,**[N] and in the meantime a third brother was born. She still has the levirate bond due to the deceased brother, who was a brother with whom the newly born brother did not coexist.

BACKGROUND

Died, then taken in levirate marriage, then born – מֵת יִבֵּם וְנוֹלַד: Reuven and Shimon were brothers from the same father, and Reuven was married to Peninna. Reuven died childless and Shimon entered into levirate marriage with Peninna. Later, a third brother, Levi, was born. According to Rabbi Shimon, since at the time that Levi was born Peninna was already the wife of Shimon, a brother with whom he did coexist, when Shimon dies Peninna is permitted to Levi.

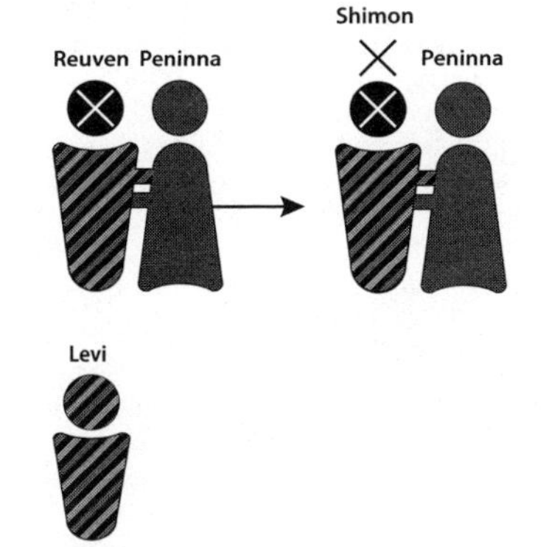

Died, then born, and then taken in levirate marriage – מֵת נוֹלַד וְיִבֵּם: Reuven and Shimon were brothers from the same father. Reuven was married to Peninna and subsequently died. After his death, a third brother, Levi, was born. To Levi, Peninna is a wife of a brother with whom he did not coexist. Therefore, even if Shimon later enters into levirate marriage with her and then dies childless, Peninna remains forbidden to Levi. According to most authorities, in the Gemara Rabbi Shimon agrees that in this case, Peninna is forbidden to Levi because for the period of time between Levi's birth and the levirate marriage to Shimon she was forbidden to Levi as the wife of a brother with whom he did not coexist.

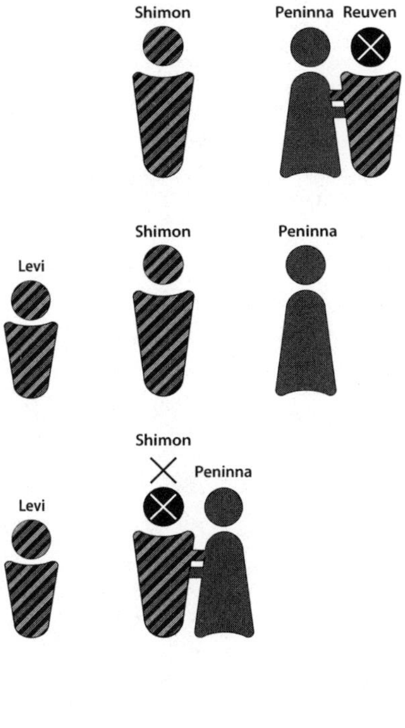

NOTES

According to the opinion of Rabbi Shimon how can you find – לְרַבִּי שִׁמְעוֹן הֵיכִי מַשְׁכַּחַתְּ לָהּ: One may ask how the Gemara knew that Rabbi Shimon holds that the wife of a brother with whom one did not coexist is in fact forbidden. It seems that it was clear to the Gemara that the fifteen women enumerated in the mishna (2a–2b) are agreed on by all opinions, and that even Rabbi Shimon agreed with this *halakha* in principle (Ritva).

Two brothers and the remaining brother…did not die – בִּתְרֵי...וְלֹא מִית: If the levirate bond is like marriage, then the widow of the first brother should be forbidden to any newly born brother, since she is the wife of the living brother, even if that brother has not yet performed levirate marriage. If so, then in Rabbi Shimon's opinion why was it necessary for the verse to state the word "together" specifically to render the *yevama* forbidden to a newly born brother? Perhaps his reasoning can be explained simply by saying that after another brother is born, the bond with the living brother was retroactively never absolute (see Ritva).

בִּשְׁלָמָא יִבֵּם וְאַחַר כָּךְ נוֹלַד – כִּי אַשְׁכְּחָהּ בְּהֶיתֵּירָא אַשְׁכְּחָהּ, אֶלָּא נוֹלַד וְאַחַר כָּךְ יִבֵּם – מַאי טַעְמָא? קָסָבַר: יֵשׁ זִיקָה, וְזִיקָה כִּכְנוּסָה דָּמְיָא.

The Gemara proceeds to clarify Rabbi Shimon's position: **Granted,** in the case when the second brother first **performed levirate marriage** and **subsequently** the third brother **was born,** it is possible to explain **that when** the third brother **found her,** i.e., when he was born, **he found her in a permitted** state because when he was born she was already the wife of a living brother with whom he coexisted. **But if he was born and subsequently** the second brother **performed levirate marriage, what is the reason** that Rabbi Shimon renders her permitted? The Gemara answers: One must say that Rabbi Shimon **holds that the** levirate **bond is substantial,** and that the bond itself created a tie of kinship. Moreover, a woman with a levirate **bond is considered like a married woman.** Since there is a bond between the *yevama* and the living brother it is as though she were already married to him. Accordingly, she is, for the new brother, like the wife of his brother with whom he coexisted.

מַתְקִיף לָהּ רַב יוֹסֵף: הָשְׁתָּא זִיקָה וּמַאֲמָר מְסַפְּקָא לֵיהּ לְרַבִּי שִׁמְעוֹן אִי כִּכְנוּסָה דָּמְיָא אִי לָאו כִּכְנוּסָה דָּמְיָא, זִיקָה לְחוּדָהּ מִיבַּעְיָא?

Rav Yosef strongly objects to this:[N] **Now** that in the case of a levirate **bond and a levirate betrothal** together **Rabbi Shimon is uncertain as to whether she is similar to a married woman or an unmarried woman, is it necessary** to say that by levirate **bond alone** she is not like a married woman? If so, how can the Gemara assume that for Rabbi Shimon, the levirate bond alone gives her the status of a married woman?

מַאי הִיא? דִּתְנַן: שְׁלֹשָׁה אַחִין נְשׂוּאִין שָׁלֹשׁ נָשִׁים נָכְרִיּוֹת, וּמֵת אֶחָד מֵהֶם וְעָשָׂה בָּהּ שֵׁנִי מַאֲמָר, וָמֵת – הֲרֵי אֵלּוּ חוֹלְצוֹת וְלֹא מִתְיַיבְּמוֹת,

What is the proof that this is Rabbi Shimon's opinion? **As we learned** in a mishna (31b): In the case of **three brothers** who were **married**[H] **to three unrelated women, and one of** the brothers **died, and the second** brother **performed levirate betrothal** with the widow **and** subsequently **died, then these** women, both the first wife of the second brother and the betrothed widow of the first brother, **must perform *ḥalitza* and may not enter into levirate marriage** with the third brother.

שֶׁנֶּאֱמַר "וּמֵת אֶחָד מֵהֶם יְבָמָהּ יָבֹא עָלֶיהָ" – מִי שֶׁעָלֶיהָ זִיקַת יָבָם אֶחָד, וְלֹא שֶׁעָלֶיהָ זִיקַת שְׁנֵי יְבָמִין.

What is the reason that the wife of the first brother is not eligible for levirate marriage? **As it is stated: "And one of them dies… her brother-in-law will have intercourse with her** and will take her to him to be his wife and consummate the levirate marriage" (Deuteronomy 25:5). From here it is derived: **She who is subject to** a levirate **bond with a single *yavam*** enters levirate marriage **and not she who is subject to** a levirate **bond with two *yevamin*.** This woman requires levirate marriage due to the death of the first brother, and also, due to the subsequent levirate betrothal, requires levirate marriage following the death of the second brother.

רַבִּי שִׁמְעוֹן אוֹמֵר: מְיַיבֵּם לְאֵיזֶה מֵהֶן שֶׁיִּרְצֶה, וְחוֹלֵץ לַשְּׁנִיָּה. יַבּוֹמֵי תַּרְוַיְיהוּ לָא – דְּדִלְמָא יֵשׁ זִיקָה, וְהָווּ שְׁנֵי יְבָמוֹת הַבָּאוֹת

However, **Rabbi Shimon says: Let him enter into levirate marriage** with **whichever he wishes and perform *ḥalitza* with the second.** Rabbi Shimon does not accept the homiletical interpretation forbidding a woman who is subject to two levirate bonds. The Gemara explains his opinion: Rabbi Shimon does **not** allow him to **take both in levirate marriage.** Why not? **Perhaps the** levirate **bond is substantial,** and combined with the levirate bond to the second brother the woman might be considered to be already married to the second brother, **and** then **these** two women **would be two *yevamot* who come**

NOTES

Rav Yosef strongly objects to this – מַתְקִיף לָהּ רַב יוֹסֵף: The early commentaries ask why the Gemara did not state that Rabbi Shimon held the levirate bond to be like marriage specifically in the case where she later entered into levirate marriage, and why it sufficed to mention only that he performed a levirate betrothal. The Ramban answers that the principle that a levirate bond renders her like a married woman fully applies only if she ultimately marries. But if he does not take her in levirate marriage, she is not considered like a married woman (see Meiri). The Ritva explains that the Sages relied here upon the common sense reasoning that a bond to two brothers cannot render her like a married woman, even in Rabbi Shimon's opinion. Additionally, from the continuation of the discussion it would seem that this difficulty was not pertinent to the matter of the levirate bond but rather related to the validity of the levirate betrothal (Meiri).

HALAKHA

Three brothers married, etc. – שְׁלֹשָׁה אַחִין נְשׂוּאִין וכו׳: If three brothers were married to three unrelated women and one died childless, and the second brother performed a levirate betrothal with his *yevama* and then died before he could consummate the marriage, whereby both his wife and the *yevama* fall before the third brother, those women must perform *ḥalitza* and may not enter into levirate marriage. This is because the wife of the first deceased brother is subject to two levirate bonds and therefore cannot enter into levirate marriage, and the second, as her rival wife, performs *ḥalitza* but may not enter into levirate marriage, as she is forbidden to the third brother by rabbinic law (Rambam *Sefer Nashim, Hilkhot Yibbum VaḤalitza* 6:27; *Shulḥan Arukh, Even HaEzer* 174:4).

מִבֵּית אֶחָד, יַבּוּמֵי חֲדָא וְאִיפְּטוֹר אִידָךְ – לָא, דְּדִלְמָא אֵין זִיקָה כִּכְנוּסָה וְהָווּ לְהוּ שְׁתֵּי יְבָמוֹת הַבָּאוֹת מִשְּׁנֵי בָּתִּים. אַלְמָא: מְסַפְּקָא לֵיהּ.

from a single household, i.e., husband, and everyone agrees that only one wife from each household may be taken in levirate marriage, as the verse states: "To build his brother's house," which is interpreted to mean that the remaining brother may perform levirate marriage with only one wife of his late brother and not with two. To **take one in levirate marriage and exempt the other** without any procedure, he may **not** do, **as perhaps** the levirate **bond is not substantial** enough to make the first brother's widow **like a married woman** to the second brother. In that case this woman whose husband died first remains the wife of the first brother, and the second woman is the wife of the second brother. Then there would be two separate levirate obligations, and one could not exempt the other; **they would be two *yevamot* who come from two households.** Therefore, **apparently** even when levirate betrothal was performed Rabbi Shimon **is uncertain** whether or not the levirate bond is substantial.

וְכִי תֵּימָא: מִדְּאוֹרָיְיתָא הָכִי נַמִי דְּמִייַּבְּמָא חֲדָא, וּמִפַּטְרָא חֲדָא, וּמִדְּרַבָּנַן הוּא דְּאָסוּר, גְּזֵירָה מִשּׁוּם שֶׁמָּא יֹאמְרוּ: שְׁתֵּי יְבָמוֹת הַבָּאוֹת מִשְּׁנֵי בָתִּים, חֲדָא מִייַּבְּמָא וְאִידָךְ מִיפַּטְרָא בְּלֹא כְלוּם,

And if you would say that **by Torah** law, **indeed, one** of them **may be taken in levirate marriage and** thereby **exempt the other,** and **this was prohibited** only **by rabbinic law,** this would be a rabbinic **decree due to** the concern **lest those** who were not aware of the details mistakenly **say** that in general if **two *yevamot*[N] come from two households** then **one is taken in levirate marriage and the other is exempt without anything.** One might have thought that the reason Rabbi Shimon required the other woman to perform *ḥalitza* is to avoid the possibility of such a mistake.

וְהָא טַעְמָא דְּרַבִּי שִׁמְעוֹן מִשּׁוּם מַאֲמָר וְלָאו מַאֲמָר הוּא! דְּתַנְיָא, אָמַר לָהֶם רַבִּי שִׁמְעוֹן לַחֲכָמִים: אִם מַאֲמָרוֹ שֶׁל שֵׁנִי מַאֲמָר – אֵשֶׁת שֵׁנִי הוּא בּוֹעֵל,

But this cannot be, **as Rabbi Shimon's reason** is mentioned explicitly in the *baraita*, and there he does not state that this is a decree of the Sages. Rather, his reason **is due to** the question with regard to the strength of levirate betrothal, specifically whether the status of marriage is achieved by **levirate betrothal or not** achieved by **levirate betrothal. As it is taught** in a *baraita*: **Rabbi Shimon said to the Rabbis** in explanation of his opinion that one of the women could enter into levirate marriage: **If the levirate betrothal of the second** brother **is indeed levirate betrothal and** is considered as a fully valid marriage, then the third brother **is engaging in relations with the wife of the second** brother when he takes her in levirate marriage. That is, if the levirate betrothal by the second brother has the same status as full marriage, then she becomes the wife of this second brother, and all previous connections are no longer relevant.

וְאִם מַאֲמָרוֹ שֶׁל שֵׁנִי אֵינוֹ מַאֲמָר – אֵשֶׁת רִאשׁוֹן הוּא בּוֹעֵל.

But if the levirate betrothal of the second brother **is not levirate betrothal,** i.e., it does not have the full status **of** marriage, then there was never in fact any connection between the two. If she is then taken by the third brother in levirate marriage, **he would be engaging in relations with the wife of the first** brother. From here one can conclude that the basis for Rabbi Shimon's uncertainty is related to the questions concerning the strength of the levirate betrothal.

אֲמַר לֵיהּ אַבָּיֵי: וְלָא שָׁנֵי לָךְ בֵּין זִיקַת יָבָם אֶחָד לְזִיקַת שְׁנֵי יְבָמִים? דִּלְמָא, כִּי אָמַר רַבִּי שִׁמְעוֹן זִיקָה כִּכְנוּסָה דָּמְיָא – בְּיָבָם אֶחָד, אֲבָל בִּשְׁנֵי יְבָמִין – לָא.

Abaye said to him: From here you cannot prove what Rabbi Shimon's opinion was. **Is there no difference to you between** a levirate **bond to a single *yavam* and a bond to two *yevamim*?[N] Perhaps when Rabbi Shimon said** that a levirate **bond** is substantial enough to render her **like a married woman,** this applies only **when** there is **a single *yavam*.** If these were the circumstances of the case discussed, that when one brother died there remained only one *yavam*, then because the obligation of levirate marriage would apply only to him, she would be considered his wife. **But** perhaps he held that if there were **two *yevamin*,** then **no,** she would not be considered a married woman, as here the bond would apply to both at once. Accordingly, Rabbi Shimon's uncertainty is with regard to the case of a levirate bond with two *yevamin*.

NOTES

Lest those say two *yevamot*, etc. – **שֶׁמָּא יֹאמְרוּ שְׁתֵּי יְבָמוֹת וכו׳**: Several early commentaries discuss a fundamental question that arises from this Gemara: Since Rabbi Shimon's opinion is that a woman subject to a levirate bond is considered like a married woman, then if two *yevamot* came from two households, it would have been appropriate for one to enter into levirate marriage and the second to be exempt. Rashi explains that the case involves two *yevamot* who fell simultaneously for levirate marriage. Some early commentaries consider this proposal far-fetched, since it is difficult to assume that a decree was made for such a rare occurrence (see Rashba).

A levirate bond to one or to two *yevamin* – **זִיקַת יָבָם אֶחָד וּשְׁנַיִם**: Certainly the opinion that a levirate bond to two *yevamin* is not substantial is more easily understood, as a woman cannot be married to two brothers simultaneously. However, it is possible to explain that the levirate bond to two *yevamin* is substantial by saying that provided neither has performed levirate betrothal, both brothers may potentially marry her and the levirate bond applies. If so, all prohibitions connected to marriage apply to both brothers at once (see Ramban).

ומי שני ליה לרבי שמעון? והתניא, כלל אמר רבי שמעון: כל שהלידה קודמת לנשואין – לא חולצת ולא מתייבמת, נשואין קודם ללידה – או חולצת או מתייבמת.

The Gemara challenges: **Does Rabbi Shimon differentiate** between the case of one *yavam* and the case of two *yevamin* in the matter of a wife of a brother with whom he did not coexist? **But it is taught** in a *baraita* with regard to the wife of a brother with whom he did not coexist: **Rabbi Shimon stated a principle: Whenever the birth** of the third brother **precedes the** levirate **marriage** of the second brother, if this second brother dies and the *yevama* falls before the third brother, **she does not perform *ḥalitza* and she does not enter into levirate marriage.** In such circumstances she is the wife of a brother with whom he did not coexist. But if **the** levirate **marriage preceded his birth, she either performs *ḥalitza* or enters into levirate marriage.**

מאי לאו ביבם אחד, וקתני: לא חולצת ולא מתייבמת! לא, בשני יבמים.

What, is it not referring to the case of **a single *yavam*, and it is taught** in a *baraita*: **She does not perform *ḥalitza* and she does not enter into levirate marriage.** Even if there is only a single *yavam* this is not considered full marriage, and she remains forbidden as the wife of a brother with whom he did not coexist. Consequently, she who is subject to a levirate bond is not like a married woman. The Gemara answers: **No.** it refers to a case of **two *yevamin*.**

אבל ביבם אחד מאי, הכי נמי או חולצת או מתייבמת? אי הכי, אדתני נשואין קודמין ללידה או חולצת או מתייבמת – ליפלוג וליתני בדידה: במה דברים אמורים – בשני יבמים, אבל ביבם אחד – או חולצת או מתייבמת!

The Gemara asks: **But what,** then, is the ruling for **a single *yavam*? So too,** one should say **she either performs *ḥalitza* or enters into levirate marriage,** as the woman who requires levirate marriage is like the wife of the second brother for all purposes. **If so, rather than teaching** the case when **the marriage** of the second brother **precedes the birth** of the third brother, that if this second brother dies and she falls before the third brother, **she either performs *ḥalitza* or enters into levirate marriage, let** Rabbi Shimon **distinguish and teach** the distinction **within** the situation **itself** and say: **In what** case **is this statement said? When** there are **two *yevamin*. But** if there is **one *yavam*, she either performs *ḥalitza* or enters into levirate marriage.**

כולה בשני יבמין קמיירי. ואלא מאי כללא?

The Gemara rejects this: No, **the entire *baraita* is in reference to two *yevamin*** and differentiates between various cases involving two *yevamin*, namely, the case where the birth of the third brother preceded the marriage of the second brother and the case where the marriage of the second brother preceded the birth of the third brother. The Gemara asks: **Rather, what is the principle** in this matter? If Rabbi Shimon is speaking of two *yevamin* and not a single *yavam*, then it makes no sense to speak of a principle, as the *halakha* is different in the case of a single *yavam*.

ועוד, מתיב רב אושעיא: שלשה אחין, שנים מהן נשואין שתי אחיות, או אשה ובתה, או אשה ובת בתה, או אשה ובת בנה – הרי אלו חולצות ולא מתייבמות, ורבי שמעון פוטר.

Moreover, Rav Oshaya raised an objection from that which was taught in a mishna (28b): If there were **three brothers, two of whom were married to two sisters,**[H] **or to a woman and her daughter, or a woman and her daughter's daughter, or a woman and her son's daughter,** who are, in each case, two women who may not be married to the same person simultaneously, and subsequently these brothers who were married to relatives died, **then those** two women **must perform *ḥalitza* and may not enter into levirate marriage.** Since they both have a levirate bond to the third brother at the same time and he is prohibited from marrying both, they cause one another to be unable to perform levirate marriage. **And Rabbi Shimon exempts** them even from *ḥalitza*.

ואי סלקא דעתך קסבר רבי שמעון זיקה ככנוסה דמיא – לייבם לקמייתא ותיפטר אידך!

And if it enters your mind that Rabbi Shimon held that a levirate **bond is substantial** enough to make her **like a married woman,** then **let** the third brother **consummate the levirate marriage to the** widow of the **first** husband to die, since as soon as her husband dies she has a levirate bond with the other brothers and should be considered to be like his wife, **and let the other be exempt** as a result, as her levirate bond began only with the death of the second husband.

אמר רב עמרם: מאי פוטר נמי – פוטר בשניה. והתניא: רבי שמעון פוטר בשתיהן!

Rav Amram said: What is **really** the meaning of the word **exempt** used by Rabbi Shimon? Only **the second is exempt.** The Gemara objects: **But it is taught** in a *baraita*: **Rabbi Shimon exempts both.** From here it is clear that in his opinion a woman subject to a levirate bond does not have the same status as a married woman.

HALAKHA

Three brothers, two of whom…married…sisters – שלשה אחין, שנים...נשואין...אחיות: If there were three brothers, two of whom married two sisters, and those brothers died consecutively, then both sisters are forbidden to the third brother, as due to the levirate bond they become rival wives to each other. They must perform *ḥalitza* and may not enter into levirate marriage, in accordance with the opinion of the unattributed mishna and contrary to the opinion of Rabbi Shimon (*Shulḥan Arukh, Even HaEzer* 175:6).

אֲמַר רָבָא: שְׁנִיָּה שֶׁבְּזוּג זֶה וְהַשְּׁנִיָּה שֶׁבְּזוּג זֶה.

Rava said: In the case mentioned in that *baraita*, there were three brothers, two of whom died. Each of the deceased brothers had four wives who were related to the wives of the other brother as described in the mishna. One wife of the first brother was the sister of a wife of the second brother. Another wife was the mother of a wife of the second brother. Another was the daughter of the daughter of a wife of the second brother. And another was the daughter of the son of a wife of the second brother. When these brothers died, all eight women happened before the remaining brother for levirate marriage. When Rabbi Shimon deemed both of them exempt, he was referring to **the second from this pair and the second from that pair.** That is, since one of them was bound to the third brother her relative became exempt as a forbidden relative, and the other of the pair was her rival wife in each of the cases.

קָא טָעֵי רָבָא בְּאַרְבָּעָה זוּגֵי, חֲדָא: דְּ״אוֹ״ ״אוֹ״ קָתָנֵי. וְעוֹד: ״רַבִּי שִׁמְעוֹן פּוֹטֵר בְּאַרְבַּעְתָּן״ מִיבְּעֵי לֵיהּ.

The Gemara comments: **Rava was mistaken about** there being **four pairs.**[B] He mistakenly understood that the mishna spoke of two brothers who married four pairs of relatives. Why does the Gemara assume that he was mistaken? **One** piece of evidence **is that** the mishna **teaches** the case using the expression: **Or, or.** The mishna teaches: Or to a woman and her daughter, or to a woman and her daughter's daughter, or a woman and her son's daughter, meaning that not all of the pairs happened before a single *yavam* for levirate marriage. **And further,** the *baraita* **should have said: Rabbi Shimon exempts all four of them,**[N] i.e., the four women married to the second brother.

וְעוֹד: תַּנְיָא, רַבִּי שִׁמְעוֹן פּוֹטֵר בִּשְׁתֵּיהֶן מִן הַחֲלִיצָה וּמִן הַיִּיבּוּם, שֶׁנֶּאֱמַר ״וְאִשָּׁה אֶל אֲחוֹתָהּ לֹא תִקָּח לִצְרוֹר״ בְּשָׁעָה שֶׁנַּעֲשׂוּ צָרוֹת זוֹ לָזוֹ לֹא יְהֵא לְךָ לִיקּוּחִין אֲפִילּוּ בְּאַחַת מֵהֶן.

And further, it is taught explicitly in a *baraita* that **Rabbi Shimon exempts both of them from** both ***ḥalitza* and levirate marriage, as it is stated: "And you shall not take a woman to her sister, to be a rival to her"** (Leviticus 18:18). From here it is derived that **when** two sisters are about to **become rival wives one to the other,** that is, at the moment they fall before one brother for levirate marriage, **you do not have** the option of **taking even one of them.** In other words, levirate marriage to either of them is not permitted, and therefore both are exempt and not only the second. Thus Rava's explanation is rejected.

אֶלָּא אֲמַר רַב אַשִׁי: אִי דִּנְפוּל בְּזֶה אַחַר זֶה – הָכִי נַמִּי. הָכָא בְּמַאי עָסְקִינַן – דִּנְפוּל בְּבַת אַחַת, וְרַבִּי שִׁמְעוֹן סָבַר לַהּ כְּרַבִּי יוֹסֵי הַגְּלִילִי, דְּאָמַר: אֶפְשָׁר לְצַמְצֵם.

Rather, Rav Ashi said an alternative answer to the Gemara's challenge: **If** these *yevamot* **happened** before him for levirate marriage **one after the other, indeed it is so** that the first woman bound is like a married woman, and she exempts the second, who is her close relative. However, **here we are dealing with** a case when both brothers died at once and so both women **happened** before him **at once. And Rabbi Shimon holds in accordance with** the opinion of **Rabbi Yosei HaGelili, who said: It is possible to be precise.**[N] He held, contrary to the opinion of the Rabbis, that it was possible to be exact about measurements of time. Therefore, it is possible for two things to truly occur at once, and it is possible that both brothers died simultaneously.

BACKGROUND

Mistaken about there being four pairs – טָעֵי...בְּאַרְבָּעָה זוּגֵי: There were nine brothers by the same father. Shimon and Levi married the sisters Ḥogla and Milka, respectively; Yehuda married Dina, and Yissakhar married her daughter Osnat; Gad married Miriam, and Asher married Miriam's daughter's daughter, Tzila; Dan married Ruth and Naftali married her son's daughter, Adda. If these eight brothers were to die and all of the women were to fall before Binyamin for levirate marriage, clearly for each pair there are two women who cannot be taken in marriage at once. According to *Tosafot Yeshanim*, this is the description of the case at hand. According to Rashi, however, the situation is that Shimon married Ḥogla, Dina, Miriam, and Ruth, while his brother Levi married Milka, Osnat, Tzila, and Adda, and all of these women happened before Binyamin for levirate marriage.

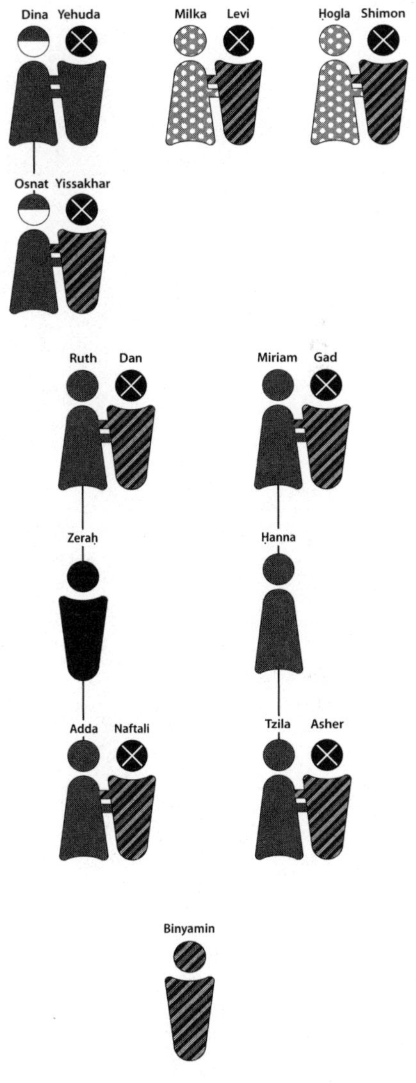

NOTES

Exempts all four of them – פּוֹטֵר בְּאַרְבַּעְתָּן: *Tosafot Yeshanim* raise the following objection: In actuality, it is not four wives who are exempt, but seven. He can perform levirate marriage on only one woman from each household, so that three women are exempt from the first household, and the four from the other household include a forbidden relation and her rival wives who are also forbidden. For this reason, an alternate explanation is suggested: The reference here is not to two brothers but to nine brothers, eight of whom were married in such a way that one was married to a woman and another to her daughter, and one was married to a woman and another to her sister, and so on. When they all happened before the ninth brother for levirate marriage, four were exempt (see *Tosefot HaRosh*).

It is possible to be precise – אֶפְשָׁר לְצַמְצֵם: This opinion, held by Rabbi Yosei HaGelili, relates to several areas in *halakha* and refers in essence to the question of whether or not in reality two entities can ever be absolutely equal, be it in questions of exact size or time of occurrence. According to the Rabbis, even if it appears that two things occurred simultaneously, this is only because humans are not able to measure precisely; in reality there must have been some gap between them.

רַב פַּפָּא אָמַר: בְּיִיבֵּם וְאַחַר כָּךְ נוֹלַד – פְּלִיג רַבִּי שִׁמְעוֹן, בְּנוֹלַד וְאַחַר כָּךְ יִיבֵּם – לָא פְּלִיג.

Until this point the Gemara dealt with Rav Oshaya's opinion stating that according to Rabbi Shimon's statement, even in the case of one who was born before his brother's levirate marriage the ruling of a wife of a brother with whom one did not coexist would not apply. However, **Rav Pappa said: Rabbi Shimon disagreed** in the case where the second brother **performed levirate marriage and after that** the third brother **was born;** however, **where** the third brother **was born** after the death of the first brother **and after that** the second brother **performed levirate marriage** Rabbi Shimon **did not disagree.** He agreed that in this case she would be forbidden to the newly born brother as the wife of a brother with whom he did not coexist.

וְתַרְוַויְיהוּ לְרַבָּנַן אִיצְטְרִיךְ, וְ״לֹא זוֹ אַף זוֹ״ קָתָנֵי.

As for the question that Rav Oshaya raised with regard to the apparent redundancy of the similar rulings in both the first mishna of the chapter and the mishna on 18b, it can be explained that **both were necessary for** the opinion of **the Rabbis** who prohibited marriage to the wife of a brother with whom one did not coexist in every case. The difficulty raised concerning the apparent redundancy of the first mishna, given the greater scope of the opinion revealed in the second mishna, can be explained by saying that the *tanna* **teaches** the mishna employing the style: **Not** only **this** but **also that.** That is, the mishna follows the stylistic principle of first teaching the obvious case and continues by saying that this principle applies not only in the obvious case but even in the less obvious case. If so, there is no need to assume that there is an additional dispute with Rabbi Shimon.

תַּנְיָא כְּווֹתֵיהּ דְּרַב פַּפָּא, וּתְיוּבְתָּא דְּרַבִּי אוֹשַׁעְיָא: שְׁנֵי אַחִים בָּעוֹלָם אֶחָד, וּמֵת אֶחָד מֵהֶם בְּלֹא וָלָד, וְעָמַד הַשֵּׁנִי הַזֶּה לַעֲשׂוֹת מַאֲמָר בִּיבִמְתּוֹ, וְלֹא הִסְפִּיק לַעֲשׂוֹת בָּהּ מַאֲמָר עַד שֶׁנּוֹלַד לוֹ אָח, וּמֵת. הָרִאשׁוֹנָה יוֹצְאָה מִשּׁוּם אֵשֶׁת אָחִיו שֶׁלֹּא הָיָה בְּעוֹלָמוֹ, וּשְׁנִיָּה אוֹ חוֹלֶצֶת אוֹ מִתְיַיבֶּמֶת.

The Gemara continues: **It is taught** in a *baraita* **in accordance with** the opinion **of Rav Pappa, and this is a conclusive refutation of** the opinion of **Rabbi Oshaya:** If there were **two coexisting brothers, and one died childless, and the second was about to perform levirate betrothal with his** *yevama* **but did not manage to perform levirate betrothal before his brother was born, and** then the second brother **died,** then **the first** woman **goes out** and is free to remarry without *ḥalitza* or levirate marriage **due to** the fact that **she was the wife of a brother with whom** the third brother **did not coexist, and the second either performs** *ḥalitza* **or enters into levirate marriage.** She was never the rival wife of the widow of the first brother.

עָשָׂה בָּהּ מַאֲמָר, וְאַחַר כָּךְ נוֹלַד אָח, אוֹ שֶׁנּוֹלַד לוֹ אָח וְאַחַר כָּךְ עָשָׂה בָּהּ מַאֲמָר, וּמֵת – הָרִאשׁוֹנָה יוֹצְאָה מִשּׁוּם אֵשֶׁת אָחִיו שֶׁלֹּא הָיָה בְּעוֹלָמוֹ, וּשְׁנִיָּה חוֹלֶצֶת וְלֹא מִתְיַיבֶּמֶת.

If the second brother **performed levirate betrothal with her and afterward his brother was born, or if his brother was born and then he performed the levirate betrothal, and then he died, the first goes out** and is free to remarry **as the wife of a brother with whom he did not coexist, and the second,** the wife of the second brother, **must perform** ***ḥalitza*** **and may not enter into levirate marriage.** This is because, due to the levirate betrothal, she is considered by the Rabbis to be the rival wife of a wife of a brother with whom he did not coexist.

Perek **II**
Daf **19** Amud **b**

רַבִּי שִׁמְעוֹן אוֹמֵר: בִּיאָתָהּ אוֹ חֲלִיצָתָהּ שֶׁל אַחַת מֵהֶם פּוֹטֶרֶת צָרָתָהּ, חָלַץ לְבַעֲלַת מַאֲמָר לֹא נִפְטְרָה צָרָה. כְּנָסָהּ וָמֵת, וְאַחַר כָּךְ נוֹלַד לוֹ אָח, אוֹ שֶׁנּוֹלַד לוֹ אָח וְאַחַר כָּךְ כְּנָסָהּ וָמֵת – שְׁתֵּיהֶן פְּטוּרוֹת מִן הַחֲלִיצָה וּמִן הַיִּיבּוּם.

Rabbi Shimon says: Intercourse or ***ḥalitza***[N] **with one of them,** i.e., the wife of the second brother, **exempts her rival wife,** but if **he performed** ***ḥalitza*** **with** the one **who received the levirate betrothal, then** her **rival wife,** i.e., the wife of the second brother, **is not** thereby **exempt,** since possibly levirate betrothal does not have the same strength as marriage. If the second brother **married** his deceased brother's wife **and** then **died** himself, **and afterward a brother was born, or if a brother was born and then he married her and died,** the two wives **are both exempt from** ***ḥalitza*** **and levirate marriage.** In this case, one was the wife of a brother with whom he did not coexist and the other her rival wife.

NOTES

Intercourse or ***ḥalitza***, **etc.** – בִּיאָתָהּ אוֹ חֲלִיצָתָהּ וכו׳: The early commentaries asked why the rival wife requires *ḥalitza*. If Rabbi Shimon holds that the levirate bond is significant, she would be considered the rival wife of a wife of a brother with whom he did not coexist through the bond, and therefore totally exempt. *Tosafot* claim that according to Rabbi Shimon's opinion there is no bond. The Meiri explains that the bond is not significant enough to completely exempt the rival wife. Ramban explains that Rabbi Shimon holds that a woman subject to a levirate bond is considered like a married woman retroactively only in cases where she later actually married. But if she did not eventually marry her *yavam*, the bond is not considered significant (see *Tosafot Yeshanim* and *Tosefot HaRosh*).

כְּנָסָהּ וְנוֹלַד לוֹ אָח, וְאַחַר כָּךְ מֵת – שְׁתֵּיהֶן פְּטוּרוֹת מִן הַחֲלִיצָה וּמִן הַיִּיבּוּם, דִּבְרֵי רַבִּי מֵאִיר. וְרַבִּי שִׁמְעוֹן אוֹמֵר: הוֹאִיל וּבָא וּמְצָאָהּ בְּהֶיתֵּר, וְלֹא עָמְדָה עָלָיו שָׁעָה אַחַת בְּאִיסּוּר – מְיַיבֵּם לְאֵיזוֹ מֵהֶן שֶׁיִּרְצֶה, אוֹ חוֹלֵץ לְאֵיזוֹ מֵהֶן שֶׁיִּרְצֶה.

The *baraita* continues: If he **married** his *yevama* **and** then **a brother was born, and then he died, both** the wife of the first deceased brother and the original wife of the *yavam* **are exempt from *ḥalitza* and levirate marriage;** this is **the statement of Rabbi Meir. And Rabbi Shimon says: Since** the third brother **came and found her in a permitted state, and she was never for a moment prohibited to him,** as when he was born she was already the wife of the second brother, who was still alive, **he** therefore **takes whichever he wishes in levirate marriage, or** performs ***ḥalitza* with whichever he wishes.**

הָא בָּבָא דְּסֵיפָא לְמַאן קָתָנֵי לָהּ? אִילֵימָא לְרַבִּי מֵאִיר קָתָנֵי לָהּ – מִכְּדִי, לָא שָׁנֵי לֵיהּ לְרַבִּי מֵאִיר בֵּין יִיבֵּם וְאַחַר כָּךְ נוֹלַד, בֵּין נוֹלַד וְאַחַר כָּךְ יִיבֵּם – לְעָרְבִינְהוּ וְלִיתְנִינְהוּ.

The Gemara clarifies: **The section of the latter clause** of the *baraita*, which refers to the case of a brother born after the levirate marriage, **according to whom is it taught? If we say it is taught for** the purpose of clarifying the opinion of **Rabbi Meir,** it does not make sense, **since it makes no difference to Rabbi Meir whether the levirate marriage preceded the birth or the birth preceded the levirate marriage.** In his opinion under both circumstances she is the wife of a brother with whom he did not coexist. And if this were in fact taught for the purpose of clarifying his opinion **it should have combined** the cases **and taught them**[N] together.

אֶלָּא, לָאו רַבִּי שִׁמְעוֹן, וּבְיִיבֵּם וְאַחַר כָּךְ נוֹלַד – פָּלֵיג, בְּנוֹלַד וְאַחַר כָּךְ יִיבֵּם – לָא פָּלֵיג, שְׁמַע מִינָּהּ.

Rather, is it not that the latter segment was meant to clarify the opinion of **Rabbi Shimon,** since the different parts of the *baraita* enumerate different possibilities? **And** Rabbi Shimon **disagrees in** the case when the brother first **performed levirate marriage and afterward** his brother **was born,** but he **does not disagree in** the case where the younger brother **was born and afterward** the second brother performed **levirate marriage.** The Gemara summarizes: **Conclude from this** that Rabbi Shimon disagrees only here, as Rav Pappa explained.

אֲמַר מָר: עָמַד הַשֵּׁנִי לַעֲשׂוֹת מַאֲמָר בִּיבִמְתּוֹ, וְלֹא הִסְפִּיק לַעֲשׂוֹת מַאֲמָר בִּיבִמְתּוֹ עַד שֶׁנּוֹלַד לוֹ אָח, וָמֵת – רִאשׁוֹנָה יוֹצְאָה מִשּׁוּם אֵשֶׁת אָחִיו שֶׁלֹּא הָיָה בְּעוֹלָמוֹ, וּשְׁנִיָּה – אוֹ חוֹלֶצֶת אוֹ מִתְיַיבֶּמֶת. מַאי עָמַד וּמַאי לֹא הִסְפִּיק? אִי עֲבַד – עֲבַד, וְאִי לֹא עֲבַד – לָא עֲבַד!

§ The Gemara proceeds to discuss the *baraita* itself. **The Master said: The second was about to perform levirate betrothal with his *yevama*, but did not manage to perform levirate betrothal with his *yevama* before his brother was born, and** then the second brother **died. The first** woman **goes out** and is free to remarry without *ḥalitza* or levirate marriage **due to** the fact that **she was the wife of a brother with whom** the third brother **did not coexist, and the second** woman **performs *ḥalitza* or enters into levirate marriage.** The Gemara asks: **What is** the meaning of the phrase: **Was about to, and what is** the meaning of: **Did not manage** to perform levirate betrothal? The important issue is not his intention but his actions. **If he did it, he did it; and if he did not do it, he did not do it.**

אֶלָּא: עָמַד – מִדַּעְתָּהּ, וְלֹא הִסְפִּיק מִדַּעְתָּהּ, אֶלָּא בְּעַל כָּרְחָהּ. וּדְלָא כְּרַבִּי דְּתַנְיָא: הָעוֹשֶׂה מַאֲמָר בִּיבִמְתּוֹ שֶׁלֹּא מִדַּעְתָּהּ, רַבִּי אוֹמֵר: קָנָה, וַחֲכָמִים אוֹמְרִים: לֹא קָנָה.

Rather, the correct interpretation is: **Was about to** means that he was about to perform levirate betrothal **with her consent. Did not manage** means that he did not manage to perform it **with her consent, but instead** did it **against her will.** Consequently, it is understood that this *baraita* **is not in accordance** with the opinion of **Rabbi** Yehuda HaNasi, **as it is taught** in a *baraita*: With regard to **one who performs levirate betrothal with his *yevama* without her consent, Rabbi** Yehuda HaNasi **says: He acquired** her and the betrothal is fully valid, like a consensual levirate betrothal with his *yevama*; **and the Rabbis say: He did not acquire** her.[H]

HALAKHA

A levirate betrothal performed against her will – מַאֲמָר בְּעַל כָּרְחָהּ: If one performs a non-consensual levirate betrothal, it is wholly ineffectual, The *halakha* is ruled in accordance with the opinion of the Rabbis, who are the majority, against the opinion of Rabbi Yehuda HaNasi (Rambam *Sefer Nashim, Hilkhot Yibbum VaḤalitza* 2:1; *Shulḥan Arukh, Even HaEzer* 166:3).

NOTES

It should have combined and taught them – לְעָרְבִינְהוּ וְלִיתְנִינְהוּ: This objection could not be derived from the mishna itself, because the mishna detailed each ruling separately, which is the linguistic style of the Mishna. The *baraita*, on the other hand, does combine some rulings, and so the question is based on the fact that not all the rulings were combined here (Rivan; *Tosafot*). Also, it could be said that the *baraita* is clearly teaching by employing the style of: Not only this but also that, unlike the mishna. Rav Oshaya was of the opinion that it was preferable to explain each phrase in the mishna and not resort to saying that it is employing the style of: Not only this but also that. However, once it is clear that the *baraita* uses that style, it is reasonable to assume that the mishna also employs that style (*Tosefot HaRosh*).

מַאי טַעֲמָא דְּרַבִּי? גָּמַר מִבִּיאָה דִּיבָמָה, מַה בִּיאָה דִּיבָמָה בְּעַל כָּרְחָהּ, אַף קִדּוּשִׁין דִּיבָמָה בְּעַל כָּרְחָהּ. וְרַבָּנַן גָּמְרִי מִקִּדּוּשִׁין דְּעָלְמָא, מַה קִדּוּשִׁין דְּעָלְמָא – מִדַּעְתָּהּ, אַף קִדּוּשִׁין דִּיבָמָה – מִדַּעְתָּהּ.

The Gemara explains: **What is the reason for Rabbi** Yehuda HaNasi's opinion? **He learned** this **from** the case of a *yavam* engaging in **intercourse with a *yevama*.**[N] **Just as** even **non-consensual intercourse with the *yevama*** renders her his wife, as the matter does not require her consent, **so too, betrothal of a *yevama*** can be **non-consensual. But the Rabbis learned from** the *halakhot* of **betrothal in general; just as betrothal in general requires consent**[N] by the woman, **so too, betrothal of a *yevama*** for purposes of levirate marriage **requires consent.**

בְּמַאי קָמִיפַּלְגִי? מָר סָבַר: מִילֵּי דִּיבָמָה מִמִּילֵּי דִּיבָמָה הֲוָה לֵיהּ לְמֵילַף, וּמָר סָבַר: מִילֵּי דְּקִדּוּשִׁין מִמִּילֵּי דְּקִדּוּשִׁין הֲוָה לֵיהּ לְמֵילַף.

The Gemara explains: **With regard to what** principle do Rabbi Yehuda HaNasi and the Rabbis **disagree? One Sage,** Rabbi Yehuda HaNasi, **holds** that halakhic **matters concerning *yevamot* must be inferred from matters concerning *yevamot*** and not from other areas of *halakha*. **And one Sage,** the Rabbis, **holds** that halakhic **matters concerning** levirate **betrothal must be inferred from matters concerning betrothal.**

עָשָׂה בָּהּ מַאֲמָר וְאַחַר כָּךְ נוֹלַד לוֹ אָח, אוֹ שֶׁנּוֹלַד לוֹ אָח וְאַחַר כָּךְ עָשָׂה בָּהּ מַאֲמָר, וּמֵת, רִאשׁוֹנָה יוֹצְאָה מִשּׁוּם אֵשֶׁת אָחִיו שֶׁלֹּא הָיָה בְּעוֹלָמוֹ, וּשְׁנִיָּה חוֹלֶצֶת וְלֹא מִתְיַבֶּמֶת. רַבִּי שִׁמְעוֹן אוֹמֵר: בִּיאָתָהּ אוֹ חֲלִיצָתָהּ שֶׁל אַחַת מֵהֶן פּוֹטֶרֶת צָרָתָהּ.

The Gemara clarifies another segment of the *baraita*. It is taught: If the second brother **performed levirate betrothal with her, and afterward his brother was born, or if his brother was born and then he performed levirate betrothal and died, the first** woman **goes out** and is free to remarry **because** she is **the wife of a brother with whom he did not coexist, and the second,** the wife of the second brother, **performs *ḥalitza* but does not enter into levirate marriage. Rabbi Shimon says: Intercourse or *ḥalitza* with one of them exempts her rival wife.**

רַבִּי שִׁמְעוֹן אַהַיָּיא קָאֵי? אִילֵימָא אַנּוֹלַד לוֹ אָח וְאַחַר כָּךְ עָשָׂה בָּהּ מַאֲמָר – הָא אָמְרַתְּ בְּנוֹלַד וּלְבַסּוֹף יִיבֵּם לָא פָּלֵיג רַבִּי שִׁמְעוֹן! אֶלָּא – אַעָשָׂה בָּהּ מַאֲמָר וְאַחַר כָּךְ נוֹלַד לוֹ אָח.

The Gemara asks: **To which** case is **Rabbi Shimon referring? If we say** that he is referring to the case when **his brother was born and then he performed levirate betrothal with her, didn't you** already **say** that **Rabbi Shimon did not dispute** the case where the brother **was born and then ultimately he performed a levirate marriage,** and she would be forbidden as the wife of a brother with whom he did not coexist. **Rather,** one must say that Rabbi Shimon disputed the case where **he performed levirate betrothal with her and afterward his brother was born.**

חָלַץ לְבַעֲלַת מַאֲמָר לֹא נִפְטְרָה צָרָה, מַאי טַעֲמָא? מִשּׁוּם דַּהֲוַאי צָרָה וַדַּאי וּבַעֲלַת מַאֲמָר סָפֵק, וְאֵין סָפֵק מוֹצִיא מִידֵי וַדַּאי.

Later in the *baraita* it is taught: If the third brother **performed *ḥalitza* with** the wife of the first brother, **to whom** the second brother **performed levirate betrothal, her rival wife is not exempt.** The Gemara clarifies: **What is the reason** for this? It is **because the rival wife,** the widow of the second brother, has a **definite** legal status that requires an act to free her to remarry, as she is the wife of a brother with whom he did coexist, **whereas** the widow of the first brother **with whom** the second brother **performed levirate betrothal** had only **an uncertain** legal status, as it is not clear if she is to be considered truly the wife of the second brother by means of the levirate betrothal or not. **And** the principle is that **an uncertainty does not override a certainty.** Therefore, even if the third brother performs *ḥalitza*, since the status of the first woman's obligation is uncertain, the status of the *ḥalitza* itself is uncertain, as it is possible that she did not require *ḥalitza* at all. Consequently, this *ḥalitza* is not sufficient to exempt her rival wife. This teaches that he must perform *ḥalitza* or levirate marriage with the woman who is definitely obligated, and then the other will be exempt.

יְתֵיב רַב מְנַשֶּׁה בַּר זְבִיד קַמֵּיהּ דְּרַב הוּנָא, וִיתֵיב וְקָאָמַר: מַאי טַעֲמָא דְּרַבִּי שִׁמְעוֹן? מַאי טַעֲמָא דְּרַבִּי שִׁמְעוֹן?! כְּדַאֲמַר טַעֲמָא: הוֹאִיל וּבָא וּמְצָאָהּ בְּהֶיתֵּר, וְלֹא עָמְדָה עָלָיו שָׁעָה אַחַת בְּאִיסּוּר!

Rav Menashe bar Zevid sat before Rav Huna. He sat and said: What is the reason that Rabbi Shimon allows the third brother to marry the wife of his brother with whom he did not coexist where she was taken in levirate marriage prior to his birth? The Gemara also wonders: **What is Rabbi Shimon's reason? The reason** is **as he stated** in that same *baraita*: **Since** the third brother **came and found her in a permitted state, and she was never for a moment prohibited to him** he may perform levirate marriage with her.

NOTES

He learned this from the case of intercourse with a *yevama* – גָּמַר מִבִּיאָה דִּיבָמָה: *Tosafot* ask how Rabbi Yehuda HaNasi can derive the *halakha* pertaining to levirate betrothal, which is by rabbinic law, from the laws of levirate marriage, which is by Torah law. They answer that rabbinic enactments were often established as though they were Torah law. In the Jerusalem Talmud there is an opinion that considers levirate betrothal to be a Torah law itself, and if so, the laws of a levirate betrothal can certainly be derived from the laws of levirate marriage (see *Keren Ora*).

Betrothal in general requires consent – קִדּוּשִׁין דְּעָלְמָא מִדַּעְתָּהּ: Some early commentaries point out that there is an exception to this rule: A minor may be married off against her will if her father accepts the betrothal. Nevertheless, even in that case the father must give consent, and so it still requires some form of consent (Rivan).

אֶלָּא: מַאי טַעְמָא דְּרַבָּנַן? אָמַר קְרָא "וּלְקָחָהּ לוֹ לְאִשָּׁה וְיִבְּמָהּ" – עֲדַיִין יִבּוּמִים הָרִאשׁוֹנִים עָלֶיהָ. אֶלָּא, הָא דִּתְנַן: כְּנָסָהּ – הֲרֵי הִיא כְּאִשְׁתּוֹ לְכׇל דָּבָר, וְאָמַר רַבִּי יוֹסֵי בַּר חֲנִינָא: מְלַמֵּד

Rather, the question was as follows: Rabbi Shimon gave such a persuasive explanation of his opinion that it raises the question: **What is the reason for the Rabbis**' opinion? The Gemara answers that **the verse states:** "Her brother-in-law will… **take her to him to be his wife and consummate the levirate marriage** [*veyibbema*]" (Deuteronomy 25:5). This means that **the first levirate bond is still upon her.**[N] Even after she is taken as a wife by the second brother, her earlier status as wife of her late first husband is still in effect. The Gemara challenges this: **But** what about **that which we learn** in a mishna (38a): If **he took** his *yevama* **in marriage** as his wife, **then** her legal status is **that of his wife in every sense; and Rabbi Yosei bar Ḥanina said:** This **teaches**

NOTES

The first levirate bond [*yibbumin*] is still upon her – עֲדַיִין יִבּוּמִים הָרִאשׁוֹנִים עָלֶיהָ: The early authorities ask: If the levirate bond remains, why is he allowed to continue to live with his *yevama*? Once he performs *yibbum*, she apparently remains his brother's wife, who is forbidden to him now that he has already performed the mitzva. They answer that the Torah did not intend to prohibit relations with the *yevama* after the act of consummation, as it states: "He will take her to him to be his wife." However, she remains a *yevama* even after she is married, in that if the couple were to divorce, they would not be permitted to remarry (Rashba).

Perek **II**
Daf **20** Amud **a**

שֶׁמְּגָרְשָׁהּ בְּגֵט וּמַחֲזִירָהּ, הָתָם נָמֵי לֵימָא: "וְיִבְּמָהּ" עֲדַיִין יִבּוּמִין הָרִאשׁוֹנִים עָלֶיהָ, וְתִיבְּעֵי חֲלִיצָה!

that he must divorce his *yevama* **with a bill of divorce** and she does not also require *ḥalitza*. **And he may remarry her,** if he wishes, after the divorce; as the *halakha* is not ruled in accordance with the opinion that after he performs the mitzva she is once more forbidden to him as his brother's wife. Why? **There, too, let** the *halakha* **say**[N] that the verse states: **"And consummate the levirate marriage** [*veyibbema*]," as explained above, meaning that **the first levirate bond is still upon her and she should** also **require *ḥalitza*.**

שָׁאנֵי הָתָם, דְּאָמַר קְרָא "וּלְקָחָהּ לוֹ לְאִשָּׁה", כֵּיוָן שֶׁלְּקָחָהּ נַעֲשֵׂית כְּאִשְׁתּוֹ לְכׇל דָּבָר. אִי הָכִי, הָכָא נָמֵי! הָא כְּתַב רַחֲמָנָא "וְיִבְּמָהּ".

The Gemara answers: **It is different there, as the verse states: "And take her to him to be his wife"** (Deuteronomy 25:5) to teach that **once he has taken her,** her legal status is **that of his wife in every sense.** The Gemara objects: **If so, here too,** in the case of a brother born after the levirate marriage, according to the opinion of the Rabbis this same principle should apply. The Gemara answers that **The Merciful One states: "And consummate the levirate marriage** [*veyibbema*]," that is, even after the marriage she is still considered to be the wife of the deceased brother [*yevama*] with respect to any brothers who are born later.

וּמָה רָאִיתָ? מִסְתַּבְּרָא: שְׁדִי הֶיתֵּירָא אַהֶיתֵּירָא, וּשְׁדִי אִיסּוּרָא אַאִיסּוּרָא.

The Gemara asks: **What did you see** to distinguish in this way and say that once she is married the levirate obligation is totally abrogated with regard to *ḥalitza*, but that she remains prohibited as the wife of a brother with whom one did not coexist with respect to any brothers born in the future? The Gemara answers: **It stands to reason** to say: **Toss that which is permitted on that which is permitted, and toss that which is prohibited on that which is prohibited.** In other words, in cases where the woman becomes permitted to her *yavam* through levirate marriage, it stands to reason that this permitted state is absolute, but with regard to the prohibition against taking the wife of a brother with whom one did not coexist, it stands to reason that the verse comes to teach that she retains her prohibited status with respect to any brothers born in the future.

וּלְרַבִּי שִׁמְעוֹן, דְּאָמַר: הוֹאִיל וּבָא וּמְצָאָהּ בְּהֶיתֵּר וְלֹא עָמְדָה עָלָיו שָׁעָה אַחַת בְּאִיסּוּר, אֶלָּא מֵעַתָּה, אֲחוֹתוֹ מֵאִמּוֹ שֶׁנִּשֵּׂאת אָחִיו מֵאָבִיו, וְאַחַר כָּךְ נוֹלַד אָח, וּמֵת – תִּתְיַיבֵּם, הוֹאִיל וּבָא וּמְצָאָהּ בְּהֶיתֵּר!

The Gemara suggests: **But according to Rabbi Shimon, who said** that **since he came and found her in a permitted state** a brother born subsequently may perform levirate marriage **since she was never for a single moment prohibited to him; however, if** that is **so,** consider the case of **one's maternal** half **sister,** who **married his paternal** half **brother;** their marriage was fully permissible since the husband and wife were in no way related to each other. **And then his brother was born and** the married brother **died;** in that case, **let** the sister **enter into levirate marriage** with her newly born half brother for the same reason, i.e., **since he came and found her in a permitted state,** as when he was born she was already his brother's wife.

NOTES

There, too, let the *halakha* say, etc. – הָתָם נָמֵי לֵימָא וכו׳: Rabbeinu Ḥananel had a different version of the text here, and many early commentaries preferred his version. According to his text, the Gemara is discussing two challenges to the concept of the first levirate bond still being upon her: First, if a *yavam* performs levirate marriage and subsequently divorces his *yevama*, he may remarry her afterward. Since he has already performed levirate marriage, she is no longer forbidden to him as his brother's wife, even if he divorces her. This indicates that the original levirate bond is completely removed. Second, if he divorces his *yevama* he does so only with a bill of divorce and does not perform *ḥalitza*. This also indicates that the levirate bond is removed. Although Rashi has a different version of the text, his explanation accords with that of Rabbeinu Ḥananel.

אִיסּוּר אֲחוֹתוֹ לְהֵיכָן אֲזַל?! הָכָא נַמִי, אִיסּוּר אָחִיו שֶׁלֹּא הָיָה בָּעוֹלָם לְהֵיכָן אֲזַל! הַאי, אִיסּוּרָא דְּלֵית לֵיהּ הֶיתֵּירָא, הַאי – אִיסּוּרָא דְּאִית לֵיהּ הֶיתֵּירָא.

The Gemara challenges this suggestion: How can you say that? What happened to **the prohibition against** marrying **his sister, to where did it go?** This widow is the maternal sister of the newly born brother and is therefore forbidden to him. The Gemara objects: If so, **here too,** one could have said: What happened to **the prohibition** against marrying the wife of **a brother with whom one did not coexist, to where did it go?** In this case as well, the prohibition against marrying the wife of a brother with whom he did not coexist already applied from the first brother, so why does Rabbi Shimon see this as abrogated by marriage? The Gemara answers that the comparison is unsound. **This prohibition** against marrying one's sister **has no** case where it is **permitted** and so in this case is also not canceled, whereas **that prohibition** against marrying a brother's wife **has** a case where it is **permitted,**[N] when the mitzva of levirate marriage applies to a second brother and is therefore removed completely before the third brother is born.

מתני׳ כְּלָל אָמְרוּ בַּיְבָמָה: כׇּל שֶׁהִיא אִיסּוּר עֶרְוָה, לֹא חוֹלֶצֶת וְלֹא מִתְיַיבֶּמֶת. אִיסּוּר מִצְוָה וְאִיסּוּר קְדוּשָּׁה – חוֹלֶצֶת וְלֹא מִתְיַיבֶּמֶת.

MISHNA The Sages **stated a principle about a** ***yevama*****: Whoever is** forbidden **by a prohibition of forbidden relations** to her *yavam* **neither performs** ***ḥalitza*** **nor enters into levirate marriage** and is completely exempt. If she is forbidden by **a prohibition** resulting from **a mitzva** or by **a prohibition** stemming from **sanctity,**[H] as will be explained later, then since in these cases the obligation of levirate marriage is not fundamentally nullified **she performs** ***ḥalitza*** in order to become free of the levirate bond, **and** due to her prohibition **she does not enter into levirate marriage.**

אֲחוֹתָהּ שֶׁהִיא יְבִמְתָּהּ – חוֹלֶצֶת אוֹ מִתְיַיבֶּמֶת.

The Sages stated another principle: If two sisters who had been married to two brothers who subsequently died happened before the third brother for levirate marriage, and one of those sisters is a close relation to this third brother and is therefore forbidden to him, she is exempt from levirate marriage. But the other, **her sister who is her** ***yevama*****,**[H] i.e., her sister-in-law, **performs** ***ḥalitza*** **or enters into levirate marriage.** In this case, they are not ruled to be two sisters who happened before him simultaneously for levirate marriage, since one of them is prohibited to him as a forbidden relation, and therefore she never actually happened before him at all.

אִיסּוּר מִצְוָה: שְׁנִיּוֹת מִדִּבְרֵי סוֹפְרִים. אִיסּוּר קְדוּשָּׁה: אַלְמָנָה לְכֹהֵן גָּדוֹל, גְּרוּשָׁה וַחֲלוּצָה לְכֹהֵן הֶדְיוֹט, מַמְזֶרֶת וּנְתִינָה לְיִשְׂרָאֵל, וּבַת יִשְׂרָאֵל לְנָתִין וּמַמְזֵר.

The mishna explains: **A prohibition** resulting from **a mitzva** is referring to **secondary** forbidden **relationships,** which are prohibited **by rabbinic law.** The Sages prohibited marriage to certain women who were not forbidden by the Torah but were nevertheless deemed forbidden incestuous relations. **A prohibition** stemming from **sanctity** is referring to marriage of **a widow to a High Priest, a divorcée or a woman who has performed** ***ḥalitza*** **[*****ḥalutza*****] to a common priest, a daughter born from an incestuous or adulterous relationship [*****mamzeret*****]** or **a Gibeonite woman to an Israelite, and also an Israelite woman to a Gibeonite or** to **a son born from an incestuous or adulterous relationship [*****mamzer*****].**

גמ׳ כְּלָל לְאֵתוֹיֵי מַאי? אָמַר רַפְרַם בַּר פַּפָּא: לְאֵתוֹיֵי צָרַת אַיְלוֹנִית, וְכִדְרַב אַסִי.

GEMARA The Gemara asks: This **principle** stated in the mishna about *yevamot*, **what** other cases does it **add?** Since the entire list of cases involving a forbidden relation was already detailed in the first chapter, what is this mishna adding? **Rafram bar Pappa said: It comes to include the** case of a **rival wife of a sexually underdeveloped woman [*****aylonit*****]**, who is incapable of bearing children. Not only does an *aylonit* herself not enter into levirate marriage, since she is unable to give birth, but her rival wife is exempt as well. **And** this is **like** the principle **of Rav Asi,** who said that the rival wife of an *aylonit* is forbidden because the *aylonit* herself remains prohibited to the *yavam* as the wife of his brother, as she was never rendered permitted by the obligation of levirate marriage. Therefore, her rival wife is the rival wife of someone prohibited as a forbidden relation.

NOTES

That prohibition has a case where it is permitted – אִיסּוּרָא דְּאִית לֵיהּ הֶיתֵּירָא: Rashi explains that the case where the prohibition is lifted is when the *yevama* is permitted to marry her *yavam*. According to *Tosafot*, however, the Gemara here is referring to the fact that the prohibition against marrying a brother's wife is totally nullified after levirate marriage, and the *yavam* may remarry her if he divorces her (see Ritva).

HALAKHA

A prohibition resulting from a mitzva or a prohibition stemming from sanctity – אִיסּוּר מִצְוָה וְאִיסּוּר קְדוּשָּׁה: A *yevama* who is forbidden to her *yavam* by a prohibition, or as a secondary forbidden relation, must perform *ḥalitza* and may not enter into levirate marriage, as explained in the mishna (Rambam *Sefer Nashim, Hilkhot Yibbum VaḤalitza* 6:7, 10; *Shulḥan Arukh, Even HaEzer* 174:1).

Her sister who is her *yevama* – אֲחוֹתָהּ שֶׁהִיא יְבִמְתָּהּ: If two sisters happened before their *yavam* for levirate marriage and one of them was prohibited to him as a forbidden relation, he may either perform *ḥalitza* with the other or take her in levirate marriage, as stated in the mishna and explained in the Gemara (Rambam *Sefer Nashim, Hilkhot Yibbum VaḤalitza* 7:1; 10; *Shulḥan Arukh, Even HaEzer* 175:2).

וְאִיכָּא דְּאָמְרִי: "כׇּל שֶׁאִיסּוּרָהּ אִיסּוּר עֶרְוָה" הוּא דַּאֲסִירָא צָרָתָהּ, הָא לָא אִיסּוּרָהּ אִיסּוּר עֶרְוָה – צָרָתָהּ לָא אֲסִירָא. לְמַעוּטֵי מַאי? אָמַר רָפְרָם: לְמַעוּטֵי צָרַת אַיְלוֹנִית, וּדְלָא כְּרַב אַסִי.

And there are those **who say** that Rafram bar Pappa's statement was made in a different context. It was taught in the mishna: **Whoever is forbidden** to her *yavam* **by a prohibition of forbidden relations** is completely exempt, which implies that **it is** specifically in such a case **that her rival wife is forbidden. But** any case when one wife **is not forbidden by a prohibition of forbidden relations** but is instead forbidden for some other reason, then **her rival wife is not forbidden.** This case comes **to exclude what? Rafram said: It excludes the rival wife of an *aylonit*,** who requires levirate marriage or *ḥalitza* because the *aylonit* is not prohibited as a forbidden relation.[H] **And this** statement is **not in accordance with** the opinion of **Rav Asi.**

"אֲחוֹתָהּ שֶׁהִיא יְבִמְתָּהּ". אֲחוֹתָהּ דְּמַאן? אִילֵימָא דְּאִיסּוּר מִצְוָה, כֵּיוָן דְּמִדְּאוֹרַיְיתָא רָמְיָא קַמֵּיהּ פָּגַע בַּאֲחוֹת זְקוּקָתוֹ! אֶלָּא: אֲחוֹתָהּ דְּאִיסּוּר עֶרְוָה.

The mishna states: **Her sister who is her *yevama*** performs *ḥalitza* or enters into levirate marriage. The Gemara clarifies this: **Whose sister? If we say** it is the sister of one **who is** forbidden due to **a prohibition** resulting from **a mitzva, since by Torah** law **she is cast before him** for levirate marriage, then this would in fact simply be a case of two sisters who fell simultaneously before him, both requiring levirate marriage, since according to Torah law there is no prohibition against entering into levirate marriage with such a woman. If so, it turns out that **he encounters the sister of the woman with whom he has** a levirate **bond; but** that case has already been taught. **Rather,** it must refer to **the sister of** a woman who is forbidden to him by a **prohibition of forbidden relations,** and since he may not enter into levirate marriage with a forbidden relation, her sister is not considered to be the sister of a woman with whom he has a levirate bond. Therefore, the sister may be taken in levirate marriage.

"אִיסּוּר מִצְוָה שְׁנִיּוֹת". אַמַּאי קָרֵי לֵיהּ אִיסּוּר מִצְוָה? אָמַר אַבָּיֵי: מִצְוָה לִשְׁמוֹעַ דִּבְרֵי חֲכָמִים.

The mishna states that **a prohibition** resulting from **a mitzva** is referring to **secondary** forbidden **relationships,** which are prohibited by rabbinic law. The Gemara asks: **Why is this called a prohibition** resulting from **a mitzva? Abaye said:** This is because **it is a mitzva to listen to** and obey **the words of the Sages.**[N]

"אִיסּוּר קְדוּשָּׁה אַלְמָנָה לְכֹהֵן גָּדוֹל גְּרוּשָׁה וַחֲלוּצָה לְכֹהֵן הֶדְיוֹט", וְאַמַּאי קָרֵי לְהוּ אִיסּוּר קְדוּשָּׁה? דִּכְתִיב "קְדֹשִׁים יִהְיוּ לֵאלֹהֵיהֶם".

The mishna states: **A prohibition** stemming from **sanctity** is referring to a marriage of **a widow to a High Priest, a divorcée or a *ḥalutza* to a common priest.** The Gemara asks: **Why are these called a prohibition** stemming from **sanctity? As it is written** with regard to the priests: **"They shall be sacred**[N] **to their God…** they shall not take a woman that is a harlot, or profaned; neither shall they take a woman divorced by her husband" (Leviticus 21:6–7).

תַּנְיָא, רַבִּי יְהוּדָה מַחְלִיף: אִיסּוּר מִצְוָה – אַלְמָנָה לְכֹהֵן גָּדוֹל, גְּרוּשָׁה וַחֲלוּצָה לְכֹהֵן הֶדְיוֹט. וְאַמַּאי קָרֵי לֵיהּ אִיסּוּר מִצְוָה? דִּכְתִיב "אֵלֶּה הַמִּצְוֹת".

It is taught in a *baraita*: **Rabbi Yehuda switches** the terms: **A prohibition** resulting from **a mitzva** is referring to **a widow to the High Priest,** or **a divorcée or a *ḥalutza* to a common priest. And why is this called a prohibition** resulting from **a mitzva? As it is written** in summarization at the end of Leviticus: **"These are the *mitzvot*** that the Lord commanded Moses for the children of Israel in Mount Sinai" (Leviticus 27:34).

HALAKHA

The rival wife of a sexually underdeveloped woman [*aylonit*], etc. – צָרַת אַיְלוֹנִית: If the two wives of one man fall before his brother for levirate marriage and one of them is an *aylonit*, then her rival wife may either perform *ḥalitza* or enter into levirate marriage. This is in accordance with the opinion cited in the Gemara as: And there are those who say, and contrary to the opinion of Rav Asi (Rambam *Sefer Nashim, Hilkhot Yibbum VaḤalitza* 6:20; *Shulḥan Arukh, Even HaEzer* 172:1).

NOTES

It is a mitzva to listen to the words of the Sages – מִצְוָה לִשְׁמוֹעַ דִּבְרֵי חֲכָמִים: The *Nimmukei Yosef* notes that this mitzva is explicit in the Torah: "And you shall come…to the judge that shall be in those days…and you shall act according to the tenor of the sentence, which they shall declare…do not turn aside from the sentence that they shall declare" (Deuteronomy 17:9–11).

A prohibition stemming from sanctity…they shall be sacred, etc. – אִיסּוּר קְדוּשָּׁה...קְדֹשִׁים יִהְיוּ וכו׳: The Rivan adds that although this verse refers specifically to priests, there is another verse that refers to Israelites: "Sanctify yourselves and be holy" (Leviticus 20:7). From here it is derived that there are prohibitions stemming from sanctity for Israelites as well, which are those forbidden sexual relations that are pertinent to them.

Some commentaries point out that included among those relationships enumerated as prohibitions due to sanctity is a woman who has performed *ḥalitza* [*ḥalutza*] marrying a priest, which is prohibited by rabbinic law, and a Gibeonite woman marrying an Israelite, which according to many opinions is also prohibited by rabbinic law and not by Torah law. Some commentaries explain that since these women are prohibited to all Jews these relationships can be called prohibitions due to sanctity, and the prohibition in these cases is unlike the safeguards established by the Sages, e.g., secondary forbidden relations (*Yosef Lekaḥ*).

איסור קְדוּשָּׁה – "שְׁנִיּוֹת מִדִּבְרֵי סוֹפְרִים", וְאַמַּאי קָרֵי לֵיהּ אִיסּוּר קְדוּשָּׁה? אֲמַר אַבַּיֵי: כָּל הַמְקַיֵּים דִּבְרֵי חֲכָמִים נִקְרָא קָדוֹשׁ. אֲמַר לֵיהּ רָבָא: וְכָל שֶׁאֵינוֹ מְקַיֵּים דִּבְרֵי חֲכָמִים, קָדוֹשׁ הוּא דְּלָא מִיקְרֵי, רָשָׁע נַמִי לָא מִיקְרֵי?! אֶלָּא אָמַר רָבָא: קַדֵּשׁ עַצְמְךָ בַּמּוּתָּר לָךְ.

A prohibition stemming from **sanctity** is referring to **secondary relationships** forbidden **by rabbinic law. And why is this called a prohibition** stemming from **sanctity? Abaye said: Whoever fulfills the words of the Sages**[N] **is called sacred. Rava said to him:** The language you use is not precise, since if so, **whoever does not fulfill the words of the Sages is not called sacred,** which implies that **he is also not called wicked.** However, anyone who transgresses the words of the Sages is in fact referred to as wicked. **Rather, Rava said** that the reason why this is called a prohibition stemming from sanctity is that the term sanctity indicates differentiation or separation, and there is a principle that **you must sanctify yourself** by refraining from that **which is permitted to you**[N] by Torah law. The Sages decreed against secondary forbidden relations so that one would not eventually come to transgress Torah law.

"אַלְמָנָה לְכֹהֵן גָּדוֹל". קָפְסֵיק וְתָנֵי, לָא שְׁנָא מִן הַנִּשּׂוּאִין וְלָא שְׁנָא מִן הָאֵירוּסִין.

The mishna states that the levirate bond of **a widow to a High Priest**[H] requires her to perform *ḥalitza,* and she may not enter into levirate marriage. The Gemara comments: The *halakha* that a widow does not enter into levirate marriage with a High Priest is **taught categorically,** merely in a general manner. **It is no different** whether she is a widow **from marriage or** she is a widow **from betrothal** alone.

בִּשְׁלָמָא מִן הַנִּשּׂוּאִין – עֲשֵׂה וְלֹא תַעֲשֶׂה, וְאֵין עֲשֵׂה דּוֹחֶה לֹא תַעֲשֶׂה וַעֲשֵׂה. אֶלָּא מִן הָאֵירוּסִין, לֹא תַעֲשֶׂה גְּרֵידָא הוּא, יָבֹא עֲשֵׂה וְיִדְחֶה לֹא תַעֲשֶׂה!

Granted, she certainly may not enter into levirate marriage if she is a widow **from marriage,** since she is forbidden to the High Priest by the **positive mitzva** stated in the verse: "And he shall take a wife in her virginity" (Leviticus 21:13), **and** by the **prohibition** stated in the verse: "A widow, or one divorced… these he shall not take" (Leviticus 21:14). **And a positive mitzva,** levirate marriage, **does not override** both **a prohibition,** not marrying a widow, **and a positive mitzva,** marrying a virgin, together. **However,** if she is a widow **from betrothal,** then **there is only a prohibition,** as she is still a virgin. In that case, why not say that **the positive mitzva** of levirate marriage should **come and override the prohibition** against marrying a widow from betrothal?

אֲמַר רַב גִּידֵּל אֲמַר רַב: אָמַר קְרָא "וְעָלְתָה יְבִמְתּוֹ הַשַּׁעְרָה" שֶׁאֵין תַּלְמוּד לוֹמַר "יְבִמְתּוֹ", מַה תַּלְמוּד לוֹמַר יְבִמְתּוֹ – יֵשׁ לְךָ יְבָמָה אַחַת שֶׁעוֹלָה לַחֲלִיצָה וְאֵינָהּ עוֹלָה לְיִיבּוּם. וְאֵיזוֹ – זוֹ חַיָּיבֵי לָאוִין.

Rav Giddel said that **Rav said** in response: **The verse states: "His *yevama* shall ascend to the gate** to the Elders and say: My brother-in-law refused to establish a name for his brother in Israel, he did not wish to consummate the levirate marriage" (Deuteronomy 25:7). **As** there is **no need** for **the verse to state: "His *yevama*,"** since it is clear to whom the verse refers and no new information is added by this word, **what** is the meaning when **the verse states: "His *yevama*"?** It comes to teach that **there is one *yevama* who ascends for *ḥalitza* but may not ascend for levirate marriage,** and her brother-in-law is not given a choice. **Who is this? This is** a woman with whom it is prohibited for her *yavam* to enter into levirate marriage, as he would be **liable** for the violation of **a prohibition,** and the positive mitzva of levirate marriage does not override the prohibition.

וְאֵימָא חַיָּיבֵי כָּרֵיתוֹת! אֲמַר קְרָא "וְאִם לֹא יַחְפּוֹץ הָאִישׁ לָקַחַת" הָא חָפֵץ – מְיַיבֵּם, כָּל הָעוֹלֶה לְיִיבּוּם עוֹלֶה לַחֲלִיצָה וְכָל שֶׁאֵין עוֹלֶה לְיִיבּוּם. – אֵינוֹ עוֹלֶה לַחֲלִיצָה.

The Gemara asks: **Say** that this is referring to **those** women who are forbidden and would be **liable** to receive the penalty of *karet* as well, i.e., that these too may not enter into levirate marriage but nevertheless require *ḥalitza.* The Gemara answers: **The verse states: "And if the man does not wish to take** his *yevama*" (Deuteronomy 25:7). This **implies** that if **he wishes, he takes her in levirate marriage;** it depends upon his wishes. However, **one who is eligible for levirate marriage is eligible for *ḥalitza.* And** conversely, **one who is ineligible for levirate marriage is ineligible for *ḥalitza*** and therefore does not require *ḥalitza* at all. Since those relations that carry a penalty of *karet* have no possibility of entering into levirate marriage, they do not require *ḥalitza* either.

אִי הָכִי, חַיָּיבֵי לָאוִין נַמִי! הָא רַבֵּי רַחֲמָנָא "יְבִמְתּוֹ". וּמָה רָאִיתָ?

The Gemara asks: **If so, those** relations who are forbidden as he would be **liable** for the violation of a standard **prohibition** also should not require *ḥalitza,* as they may not enter into levirate marriage. The Gemara answers: **But the Merciful One included** one category of *yevama* who is eligible for *ḥalitza* alone and not levirate marriage through the term: **"His *yevama*."** The Gemara asks: **And what did you see** to conclude that the additional term is referring to relations who are forbidden and with whom he would be liable for the violation of a prohibition and not those who are liable to receive *karet*?

NOTES

Whoever fulfills the words of the Sages – כָּל הַמְקַיֵּים דִּבְרֵי חֲכָמִים: The Rivan writes that this is alluded to in the verse: "And it shall come to pass that he that is left in Zion, and he that remains in Jerusalem, shall be called sacred" (Isaiah 4:3).

You must sanctify yourself by refraining from that which is permitted to you – קַדֵּשׁ עַצְמְךָ בַּמּוּתָּר לָךְ: The Ramban explains that this is the true meaning of the mitzva: "You shall be sacred" (Leviticus 19:2). Sanctity requires one to refrain from even that which the Torah permitted. The Ramban explains that it is possible for one to be vile without violating any other explicit Torah prohibitions. The Torah does not limit how much one may eat or how frequently one may engage in intercourse; a hedonist could spend all his time indulging in sensual pleasures. Therefore the Torah stressed: "You shall be sacred" (see Rashi on *Sanhedrin* 53a; Ritva).

HALAKHA

A widow to a High Priest – אַלְמָנָה לְכֹהֵן גָּדוֹל: If the brother of a High Priest dies childless and leaves a widow, even a widow from betrothal, then she must perform *ḥalitza* and not enter into levirate marriage. If he engages in intercourse with her, her rival wife is not exempt from *ḥalitza* (Rambam *Sefer Nashim, Hilkhot Yibbum VaḤalitza* 6:11 and *Sefer Kedusha, Hilkhot Issurei Bia* 17:12).

מִסְתַּבְּרָא, חַיָּיבֵי לָאוִין תָּפְסֵי בְּהוּ קִדּוּשִׁין, חַיָּיבֵי כָּרֵיתוֹת לָא תָּפְסֵי בְּהוּ קִדּוּשִׁין.

The Gemara answers: That **stands to reason,** since **betrothal takes effect** with those women who are forbidden and with whom he would be **liable** for the violation of **a prohibition.**[N] That is, if a man betroths a woman who is forbidden to him and with whom he would be liable for the violation of a prohibition, then although he violates a prohibition in doing so, the betrothal is valid and cannot be ended without a bill of divorce. Therefore, such a woman also requires *ḥalitza*. In contrast, **betrothal does not take effect** at all with **those** who are forbidden and would be **liable** to receive the punishment of ***karet***, and therefore in these cases the laws of levirate marriage and *ḥalitza* do not apply at all.

מְתִיב רָבָא: אִיסּוּר מִצְוָה וְאִיסּוּר קְדוּשָּׁה, בָּא עָלֶיהָ אוֹ חָלַץ לָהּ – נִפְטְרָה צָרָתָהּ. וְאִי סָלְקָא דַּעְתָּךְ חַיָּיבֵי לָאוִין מִדְּאוֹרָיְיתָא לַחֲלִיצָה רָמְיָא, לְיִיבּוּם לָא רָמְיָא – כִּי בָּא עָלֶיהָ אַמַּאי נִפְטְרָה צָרָתָהּ?

Rava raised an objection to the explanation of Rav: It is taught in a *baraita* with regard to **a prohibition** resulting from **a mitzva and a prohibition** stemming from **sanctity** that if **he engages in intercourse with** such a woman[H] **or performs *ḥalitza* with her,**[H] **her rival wife is exempt,** even though it was prohibited for him to have engaged in intercourse with her in the first place. **If it enters your mind** that women who are forbidden, as he would be **liable** for the violation of **a prohibition, require *ḥalitza*** by **Torah** law **but do not require levirate marriage,** then **when he engages in intercourse with** his *yevama* **why is her rival wife exempt?** If there is no biblical mitzva to engage in intercourse with her, his action would carry no halakhic validity and the rival wife should not be exempt.

הוּא מוֹתִיב לַהּ וְהוּא מְפָרֵק לַהּ: לִצְדָדִין קָתָנֵי, בָּא עָלֶיהָ – אַאִיסּוּר מִצְוָה, חָלַץ לָהּ – אַאִיסּוּר קְדוּשָּׁה.

Rava **raised the objection and he resolved it:** The *baraita* **teaches it disjunctively;** it did not all deal with the same case. When the *baraita* says: **Engages in intercourse with her,** it is referring **to a prohibition** resulting from **a mitzva.** If one engages in intercourse with a *yevama* prohibited to him by rabbinic law, since by Torah law levirate marriage with her is valid, then although his act involved the transgression of a rabbinic decree, he nevertheless fulfilled the Torah mitzva and the rival wife is thereby exempt. When the *baraita* says: **Performs *ḥalitza* with her, it is referring to a prohibition** stemming from **sanctity,** and by Torah law there is no option of levirate marriage because of the prohibited relation; therefore, only *ḥalitza* exempts her rival wife.

מְתִיב רָבָא: פְּצוּעַ דַּכָּא וּכְרוּת שָׁפְכָה, סְרִיס אָדָם וְהַזָּקֵן – אוֹ חוֹלְצִין אוֹ מְיַיבְּמִין. כֵּיצַד? מֵתוּ, וְלָהֶם אַחִים וְלָהֶם נָשִׁים, וְעָמְדוּ אַחִין וְעָשׂוּ מַאֲמָר בִּנְשׁוֹתֵיהֶן, וְנָתְנוּ גֵּט, וְחָלְצוּ, מַה שֶּׁעָשׂוּ עָשׂוּ, וְאִם בָּעֲלוּ קָנוּ.

Rava raised an objection from that which was taught in the *Tosefta* (*Yevamot* 11:3): **A man with crushed testicles**[H] or with other wounds to his genitals **or one whose penis has been severed, one who is a eunuch**[H] caused **by man** and not from birth or by disease, or **an elderly man,**[H] all of whom are incapable of fathering children, **one either performs *ḥalitza* or levirate marriage. How so?** If any of these infertile men **died, and they had brothers and they** also **had wives,** and they then died childless, **and the brothers proceeded to perform levirate betrothal with their wives, or gave them a bill of divorce, or performed *ḥalitza*, whatever they did is done;** i.e., their act was effective. **And if** any one of the brothers **engaged in intercourse** with the widow of one of those infertile men, he thereby **acquired** the woman as a wife according to the laws of levirate marriage.

NOTES

Betrothal takes effect with those women who are forbidden, and with whom he would be liable for the violation of a prohibition – חַיָּיבֵי לָאוִין תָּפְסֵי בְּהוּ קִדּוּשִׁין: Rashi explains that the inference connecting betrothal to levirate marriage is from the term "to take" in the verse: "And if the man does not wish to take his *yevama*" (Deuteronomy 25:7), which means taking in marriage. Marriage, even through intercourse, is not valid in cases where one would be liable to receive *karet* for marrying such a woman and is therefore not considered taking in marriage. However, in the case of relations forbidden by a standard prohibition, although one transgresses Torah law, the betrothal nevertheless comes into effect and they are considered married for all purposes (see Rashba and Ritva).

HALAKHA

Intercourse with one's *yevama* who is prohibited due to a mitzva or sanctity – הַבָּא עַל יְבִמְתּוֹ אִיסּוּר מִצְוָה וְאִיסּוּר קְדוּשָּׁה: In cases where a *yevama* is forbidden to her *yavam* due to a prohibition or a positive mitzva, or where she is a secondary relation forbidden by rabbinic law, if he transgressed and engaged in intercourse with her she is considered married to him for all purposes; he must divorce her with a bill of divorce, and her rival wife is exempt from levirate marriage and *ḥalitza* (Rambam *Sefer Nashim, Hilkhot Yibbum VaḤalitza* 6:10; *Arukh HaShulḥan, Even HaEzer* 174:8).

One who performs *ḥalitza* with a *yevama* who is prohibited due to a mitzva or sanctity – הַחוֹלֵץ לְאִיסּוּר מִצְוָה וּקְדוּשָּׁה: In a case where two women were married to a brother and one of them was forbidden to her *yavam* by a prohibition or positive mitzva or by being a secondary forbidden relation, if he performs *ḥalitza* with this forbidden woman, then her rival wife is not exempt from levirate marriage or *ḥalitza* (Rambam *Sefer Nashim, Hilkhot Yibbum VaḤalitza* 7:10). However, in the opinion of the *Halakhot Gedolot* and many others, if he wishes to perform levirate marriage he should do so with the woman who is permitted to him, and if he wishes to perform *ḥalitza* he should do so with the woman who is forbidden to him, and her rival wife is thereby exempt; *Shulḥan Arukh, Even HaEzer* 170:18, 174:1).

The wife of a man with crushed testicles – אֵשֶׁת פְּצוּעַ דַּכָּא: If a woman had been prohibited to marry her husband due to a positive mitzva or prohibition, e.g., if he had been castrated by a person, etc., but this prohibition does not apply to her *yavam*, then she is permitted to enter into levirate marriage (Rambam *Sefer Nashim, Hilkhot Yibbum VaḤalitza* 6:13; *Shulḥan Arukh, Even HaEzer* 174:2).

A *yavam* who is a eunuch – יָבָם סָרִיס: If a woman falls for levirate marriage before one who was castrated by a person but who had previously been fit to marry, then he must perform *ḥalitza* and may not take her in levirate marriage, as he is prohibited from entering into the congregation, i.e., marrying a Jew. If he transgressed and engaged in intercourse with her he acquires her as his wife, but he must divorce her with a bill of divorce (Rambam *Sefer Nashim, Hilkhot Yibbum VaḤalitza* 6:4; *Shulḥan Arukh, Even HaEzer* 172:3).

An elderly man – הַזָּקֵן: The Rambam states that if the *yavam* is elderly then he should not take the woman in levirate marriage but rather should perform *ḥalitza* (*Sefer Nashim, Hilkhot Yibbum VaḤalitza* 6:4). However, most authorities hold differently, and this ruling does not appear in the *Shulḥan Arukh*.

NOTES

However, if that is so, the wife of a paternal brother, etc. – אֶלָּא מֵעַתָּה, אֵשֶׁת אָחִיו מֵאָבִיו וכו׳: *Tosafot* explain this section as not referring to typical cases, as that would undermine the entire concept of levirate marriage. Rather, it is referring to particular examples, each of which is similar enough to the topic of the Gemara that it might deserve a rabbinic decree (see Ritva and *Tosafot Yeshanim*). The Ramban sees this explanation as far-fetched and objects on various grounds. He holds that the Gemara must be understood in a straightforward manner, and that the purpose of these challenges is to illustrate the absurdity of issuing a rabbinic decree to defer the mitzva of levirate marriage in favor of *ḥalitza*.

מֵתוּ אַחִים, וְעָמְדוּ הֵם וְעָשׂוּ מַאֲמָר בִּנְשׁוֹתֵיהֶן, וְנָתְנוּ גֵּט, אוֹ שֶׁחָלְצוּ – מַה שֶּׁעָשׂוּ עָשׂוּ. וְאִם בָּעֲלוּ – קָנוּ וְאָסוּר לְקַיְּימָן, מִשּׁוּם שֶׁנֶּאֱמַר ״לֹא יָבֹא פְצוּעַ דַּכָּא״. וְאִי סָלְקָא דַּעְתָּךְ חַיָּיבֵי לָאוִין מִדְּאוֹרַיְיתָא לַחֲלִיצָה רָמְיָא, לְיִיבּוּם לָא רָמְיָא, אִם בָּעֲלוּ – אַמַּאי קָנוּ?

The inverse is also true: If **the brothers died** childless, **and** the infertile men **proceeded to perform levirate betrothal with their wives,** or **gave a bill of divorce, or performed *ḥalitza*, whatever they did is done** and took effect. **And if they engaged in intercourse** with their *yevama*, **they** thereby **acquired** the *yevama* as their wife. However, **it is forbidden to maintain them,** i.e., allow them to continue to live as husband and wife, **because it is stated: "One with crushed testicles** or whose penis has been severed shall not enter into the assembly of the Lord" (Deuteronomy 23:2); they are prohibited from entering the congregation, i.e., marrying a Jew. **And if it enters your mind** that women who are forbidden, as he would be **liable** for the violation **a prohibition, require *ḥalitza* by Torah** law **but do not require levirate marriage, then** one could ask: **if they engaged in intercourse why are they acquired** as wives even though there would be no mitzva of levirate marriage because the men are prohibited from marrying them?

אֶלָּא אָמַר רָבָא: אַלְמָנָה מִן הָאֵירוּסִין נַמִי עֲשֵׂה וְלֹא תַעֲשֶׂה הוּא, דִּכְתִיב ״קְדוֹשִׁים יִהְיוּ לֵאלֹהֵיהֶם״.

Rather, Rav's opinion is rejected, and **Rava said** an alternative explanation: The reason why a High Priest does not take **a widow from betrothal** in levirate marriage is because that relationship is **also** a violation of both **a positive mitzva and a prohibition** and therefore a different positive mitzva does not override it. How so? **As it is written: "They shall be sacred to their God"** (Leviticus 21:6), which teaches that there is a positive mitzva of sanctity associated with all prohibitions applying to priests. Therefore, any such prohibition contains both a positive and a negative mitzva.

מַמְזֶרֶת וּנְתִינָה מַאי אִיכָּא לְמֵימַר? כְּתִיב ״וְהִתְקַדִּשְׁתֶּם״

The Gemara asks: This resolves the issue of priestly prohibitions, but **what is there to say** about **a daughter born from an incestuous or adulterous relationship [*mamzeret*] or a Gibeonite woman,** who are prohibited from entering the congregation due to considerations of sanctity? They too may not enter into levirate marriage despite the positive mitzva, which would ordinarily override a prohibition. The Gemara answers: **It is written** with regard to all of the mitzvot: **"Sanctify yourselves,"** therefore, and be sacred" (Leviticus 11:44). This teaches that in addition to the prohibition, there is the positive mitzva of sanctity.

אִי הָכִי, כָּל הַתּוֹרָה כּוּלָּהּ נַמִי עֲשֵׂה וְלֹא תַעֲשֶׂה הוּא, דִּכְתִיב ״וְהִתְקַדִּשְׁתֶּם״! אֶלָּא אָמַר רָבָא: גְּזֵירָה אַלְמָנָה מִן הָאֵירוּסִין אַטּוּ אַלְמָנָה מִן הַנִּשּׂוּאִין.

The Gemara raises an objection: **If so,** then every single prohibition in **the entire Torah** contains both **a positive mitzva and a prohibition, as it is written: "Sanctify yourselves"** (Leviticus 11:44). **Rather,** this reasoning must be rejected, and **Rava stated** a different reason: While in essence the mitzva of levirate marriage does apply here, nevertheless, **a widow from betrothal** is prohibited from entering into levirate marriage with the High Priest **by** rabbinic **decree, due to** the case of **a widow from marriage.**

מַמְזֶרֶת וּנְתִינָה מַאי אִיכָּא לְמֵימַר? גְּזֵירָה בִּמְקוֹם מִצְוָה אַטּוּ שֶׁלֹּא בִּמְקוֹם מִצְוָה.

The Gemara asks: **What is there to say** about the case of **a *mamzeret* or a Gibeonite woman?** There appears to be no reason for a rabbinic decree in such cases. The Gemara answers: There, one must say that intercourse with a *mamzeret* even **when the mitzva** of levirate marriage **applies** was prohibited by rabbinic **decree due to** cases **when the mitzva** of levirate marriage **does not apply.** The decree was issued lest one come to think that since in the case of levirate marriage a *mamzeret* is permitted, even in cases when there is no levirate marriage a *mamzeret* is similarly permitted.

אֶלָּא מֵעַתָּה, אֵשֶׁת אָחִיו מֵאָבִיו לֹא תִתְיַיבֵּם, גְּזֵירָה מִשּׁוּם אֵשֶׁת אָחִיו מֵאִמּוֹ! יִיבּוּם בְּנַחֲלָה תְּלָא רַחֲמָנָא, מֵידַע יְדִיעַ.

The Gemara asks: **However, if** that is **so,** and the levirate marriage is prohibited lest it become confused with another case, then **the wife of a paternal brother**[N] **should not enter into levirate marriage;** i.e., by the same logic, although the Torah allowed it, the Sages should have established a **rabbinic decree** requiring that she perform *ḥalitza* **due to** the case of **the wife of a maternal brother,** who always remains prohibited as a brother's wife. The Gemara answers: **The Merciful One made levirate marriage dependent upon inheritance,** and it **is well known** by everyone that only patrilineal relatives inherit, so there is no likelihood of confusion.

אִשָּׁה שֶׁאֵין לָהּ בָּנִים לֹא תִּתְיַיבֵּם, גְּזֵירָה מִשּׁוּם אִשָּׁה שֶׁיֵּשׁ לָהּ בָּנִים! בְּבָנִים תְּלָא רַחֲמָנָא, מֵידַע יְדִיעַ.

The Gemara objects further: Then **a childless woman should not enter into levirate marriage** even though the mitzva applies to her; there should be a rabbinic **decree due to** the case of **a woman who has children.** The Gemara answers: **The Merciful One made levirate marriage dependent upon children; it is well known** by everyone that the entire purpose of levirate marriage is to establish one's brother's name and that levirate marriage applies only when there are no children. Here, too, there is no likelihood of error.

אֵשֶׁת אָחִיו שֶׁהָיָה בְּעוֹלָמוֹ לֹא תִּתְיַיבֵּם, גְּזֵירָה מִשּׁוּם אֵשֶׁת אָחִיו שֶׁלֹּא הָיָה בְּעוֹלָמוֹ! בִּישִׁיבָה תְּלָא רַחֲמָנָא, מֵידַע יְדִיעַ.

The Gemara challenges further: **The wife of a brother with whom one did coexist should not enter into levirate marriage;** there should be a rabbinic **decree due to** the case of **the wife of a brother with whom he did not coexist.** The Gemara responds: **The Merciful One made levirate marriage dependent upon** a common **dwelling** together and coexistence of brothers, and this **is well known** by everyone since the matter is explicit in the Torah.

כָּל הַנָּשִׁים לֹא תִּתְיַיבֵּמְנָה, גְּזֵירָה מִשּׁוּם אַיְלוֹנִית! לָא שְׁכִיחָא. מַמְזֶרֶת וּנְתִינָה נַמִי לָא שְׁכִיחָא!

The Gemara continues to object: **No woman should enter into levirate marriage;** there should be a rabbinic **decree due to** the case of **an *aylonit*.** Since an *aylonit* may not enter into levirate marriage, all other women should be prohibited by rabbinic decree from doing so to avoid confusion. The Gemara answers: The case of an *aylonit* is **not commonplace,** and the Sages did not institute rabbinic decrees on matters that are not common. The Gemara asks: If so, **neither a *mamzeret* nor a Gibeonite woman is commonplace either.** Therefore, since the likelihood of taking a *mamzeret* in levirate marriage is so small, there is no danger that one might think it is permitted to marry a *mamzeret* even where the mitzva does not apply.

אֶלָּא אֲמַר רָבָא: גְּזֵירָה בִּיאָה רִאשׁוֹנָה אַטּוּ בִּיאָה שְׁנִיָּה.

Rather, Rava said that it is necessary to reject the previous suggestion and to offer a different reason: **The first** act of **intercourse** is prohibited by rabbinic **decree**[H] **due to** the likelihood of **a second** act of **intercourse.** Although intercourse the first time with the *yevama* is the fulfillment of a positive mitzva, which does override the prohibition, once the mitzva is fulfilled with that act there is no longer any positive mitzva involved. Afterward, this *yevama* becomes prohibited because there is no longer a positive mitzva to override the prohibition. Therefore, due to the possibility that one might engage in intercourse a second time with this woman, the Sages decreed that even the first act is prohibited.

תַּנְיָא נַמִי הָכִי: אִם בְּעָלוּ – קָנוּ בְּבִיאָה רִאשׁוֹנָה, וְאָסוּר לְקַיְּימָן בְּבִיאָה שְׁנִיָּה.

The Gemara comments: **This is also taught** in a *baraita*: **If** one of those *yevamin* who may not marry their *yevama* due to a prohibition **engaged in intercourse** with her, **he acquired** her **with the first** act **of intercourse; however, it is prohibited to retain** her **for a second act of intercourse.**

הֲדַר אֲמַר רָבָא, וְאִיתֵּימָא רַב אַשִׁי: לָאו מִילְּתָא הִיא דַּאֲמָרִי, דְּאָמַר רֵישׁ לָקִישׁ: כָּל מָקוֹם שֶׁאַתָּה מוֹצֵא עֲשֵׂה וְלֹא תַעֲשֶׂה, אִם אַתָּה יָכוֹל לְקַיֵּים שְׁנֵיהֶם מוּטָב, וְאִם לָאו יָבֹא עֲשֵׂה וְיִדְחֶה אֶת לֹא תַעֲשֶׂה, הָכָא נַמִי אֶפְשָׁר בַּחֲלִיצָה דִּמְקַיֵּים עֲשֵׂה וְלֹא תַעֲשֶׂה.

The Gemara continues with a retraction from Rava: **Rava then said, and some say** it was actually **Rav Ashi** who said: **That which I said,** that the reason for the rabbinic decree was to prevent a second act of intercourse, **is not correct,** as there is a simpler explanation. **As Reish Lakish said** about the same matter: **In every place that you find a positive mitzva and a prohibition**[H] applying to the same matter, **if you can fulfill both of them** together, **this is best,** and the positive mitzva does not override the prohibition. **And if** there is **not** any possibility of fulfilling both, then **let the positive mitzva come and override the prohibition. Here, too,** in the case of levirate marriage, **it is possible, by way of *ḥalitza*, to fulfill the positive mitzva and** not to transgress **the prohibition** prohibiting marriage to these women.

מֵיתִיבִי: וְאִם בְּעָלוּ קָנוּ! תְּיוּבְתָּא.

The Gemara **raises an objection** to this last statement by Rava from that which is taught in a *baraita*: **And if** one of those *yevamin* **engaged in intercourse,**[N] **he acquired** her as a wife. This shows that although it is possible to perform the mitzva by way of *ḥalitza*, if he nevertheless performs levirate marriage then the positive mitzva overrides the prohibition and the *yevama* is thereby acquired as his wife. The Gemara concludes: This is **a conclusive refutation,** and Rava's last explanation is rejected. The previous explanation is the correct one: The prohibition is due to rabbinic decree.

HALAKHA

The first act of intercourse is prohibited by rabbinic decree – גְּזֵירָה בִּיאָה רִאשׁוֹנָה וכו׳: Although the *halakhot* of levirate marriage apply to a woman whom one is prohibited from marrying due to a positive mitzva or a prohibition, the Sages decreed that she should not be taken in levirate marriage. They prohibited the first act of intercourse, which fulfills a mitzva, due to the second act, which involves a prohibition and no mitzva. Therefore, one who transgressed and engaged in intercourse with a *yevama* who was forbidden to him fully acquired her as his wife. However, he must divorce her with a bill of divorce, in accordance with the opinion of Rava (Rambam *Sefer Nashim, Hilkhot Yibbum VaḤalitza* 6:10; *Shulḥan Arukh, Even HaEzer* 174:1).

A positive mitzva and a prohibition – עֲשֵׂה וְלֹא תַעֲשֶׂה: In every case where a positive mitzva and a prohibition contradict one another, if it is possible to find a way to fulfill both, this is best. If not, the positive mitzva overrides the negative one, in accordance with the opinion of Reish Lakish (Rambam *Sefer Ahava, Hilkhot Tzitzit* 3:6).

NOTES

The Gemara raises an objection: And if one of those *yevamin* engaged in intercourse, etc. – מֵיתִיבִי וְאִם בְּעָלוּ וכו׳: *Tosafot* point out that Rava himself cited this *baraita* earlier and ask how it could be that he did not notice this difficulty with his own words. Some commentaries answer that for this reason the Gemara presented alternate versions attributing this *halakha* to different names, to either Rava or Rav Ashi, in order to explain that the Sage who cited the *baraita* is not the same as Rava to whom the objection was directed.

אִיתְּמַר: בִּיאַת כֹּהֵן גָּדוֹל בְּאַלְמָנָה, רַבִּי יוֹחָנָן וְרַבִּי אֶלְעָזָר: חַד אָמַר: אֵינָהּ פּוֹטֶרֶת צָרָתָהּ, וְחַד אָמַר פּוֹטֶרֶת צָרָתָהּ.

§ On the same subject, **it was stated** with regard to the case of **a High Priest who engaged in intercourse with a widow** who was his *yevama* requiring levirate marriage that the *amora'im* **Rabbi Yoḥanan and Rabbi Elazar** disputed the matter. **One said** that intercourse **does not exempt her rival wife** who had also been married to the High Priest's brother, since the act was prohibited, **and one said** that it does **exempt her rival wife**, because although intercourse was forbidden, it is nevertheless a valid enactment of levirate marriage, and so her rival wife is thereby exempt.

Perek **II**
Daf **21** Amud **a**

HALAKHA

A High Priest who engaged in intercourse with a widow from marriage – **בִּיאַת כֹּהֵן גָּדוֹל בִּיבִמְתּוֹ אַלְמָנָה**: If a High Priest engaged in intercourse with his *yevama* who had been widowed from marriage, her rival wife is not thereby exempt, as a positive mitzva does not override both a negative and a positive mitzva together, as the Gemara states here (Rambam *Sefer Nashim, Hilkhot Yibbum VaḤalitza* 6:11).

בְּאַלְמָנָה מִן הַנְּשׂוּאִין כּוּלֵּי עָלְמָא לָא פְּלִיגִי דְּלָא פָּטְרָה, דְּאֵין עֲשֵׂה דּוֹחֶה לֹא תַעֲשֶׂה וַעֲשֵׂה. כִּי פְּלִיגִי – בְּאַלְמָנָה מִן הָאֵרוּסִין. מַאן דְּאָמַר פּוֹטֶרֶת, אָתֵי עֲשֵׂה וְדָחֵי אֶת לֹא תַעֲשֶׂה, וּמַאן דְּאָמַר אֵינָהּ פּוֹטֶרֶת – לָא אָתֵי עֲשֵׂה וְדָחֵי אֶת לֹא תַעֲשֶׂה, כֵּיוָן דְּאֶפְשָׁר בַּחֲלִיצָה.

As for **a widow from marriage,**[H] **everyone agrees that this does not exempt** the rival wife, **as a positive mitzva does not override a prohibition and a positive mitzva** together. **When they disagree,** it is in the case of **a widow from betrothal. The one who said that it exempts** the rival wife holds that **the positive mitzva** of levirate marriage **comes and overrides** the **prohibition** against a High Priest marrying a widow. **And the one who said that it does not exempt** the rival wife held that **a positive mitzva does not come and override a prohibition, since it is possible** to perform ***ḥalitza.***

מֵיתִיבִי: וְאִם בָּעֲלוּ – קָנוּ! תְּיוּבְתָּא.

The Gemara **raises an objection** to the opinion that the rival wife would not be exempt, from the previously cited *baraita*: **If** one of those *yevamin* **engaged in intercourse, he acquired** her as a wife. This shows that the act of levirate marriage is valid, even when prohibited. If so, in the case of the High Priest and a widow as well, her rival wife should be exempt. **This is a conclusive refutation,** and that opinion is rejected.

לֵימָא תֶּיהֱוֵי נַמִי תְּיוּבְתָּא דְּרֵישׁ לָקִישׁ! אָמַר לָךְ רֵישׁ לָקִישׁ: כִּי אָמֵינָא אֲנָא – הֵיכָא דִּמְקַיְּימֵי מִצְוָה, אֲבָל הָכָא, חֲלִיצָה בִּמְקוֹם יִיבּוּם לָאו מִצְוָה הִיא.

The Gemara asks: **Shall we say that** this is **also a conclusive refutation** of the opinion of **Reish Lakish** and therefore reject his principle? The Gemara answers: **Reish Lakish** could have **said to you: When I say** that in every place that you find a positive mitzva and a prohibition applying to the same matter, if you can fulfill both of them together without transgressing the prohibition, this is best, and the positive mitzva does not override the prohibition, this is applicable only **when the mitzva is fulfilled** properly; **but here, *ḥalitza* in place of levirate marriage is not** considered a proper fulfillment of the **mitzva.**[N]

אָמַר רָבָא: רֶמֶז לִשְׁנִיּוֹת מִן הַתּוֹרָה מִנַּיִן? שֶׁנֶּאֱמַר ״כִּי אֶת כָּל הַתּוֹעֵבֹת הָאֵל עָשׂוּ אַנְשֵׁי הָאָרֶץ״. ״הָאֵל״ קָשׁוֹת, מִכְּלָל דְּאִיכָּא רַכּוֹת, וּמַאי נִינְהוּ – שְׁנִיּוֹת.

§ **Rava said: Where** is the prohibition against **secondary** forbidden **relationships hinted at in the Torah? As it is stated** at the end of the portion discussing forbidden incestuous relations: **"For all these abominations have the men of the land done"** (Leviticus 18:27). **"These"** must be understood to mean **the harsh ones,** i.e., the severe transgressions. This proves **by inference that there are** also lesser transgressions that are, as it were, **soft ones. And what are those** soft ones? They are **secondary** forbidden **relationships.**

וּמַאי מַשְׁמַע דְּ״הָאֵל״ לִישָּׁנָא דְּקָשֶׁה הוּא? דִּכְתִיב ״וְאֶת אֵילֵי הָאָרֶץ לָקָח״.

The Gemara asks: **From where** may it **be inferred** that the word **"these" [*ha'el*] is an expression** meaning **harsh? As it is written: "And the mighty [*eilei*] of the land he took away"** (Ezekiel 17:13). The similarity of these words implies that "these" also has connotations of mighty or harsh.

NOTES

***Ḥalitza* in place of levirate marriage is not a mitzva** – **חֲלִיצָה בִּמְקוֹם יִיבּוּם לָאו מִצְוָה**: In the *Yosef Lekaḥ* it is explained that *ḥalitza* is a less than ideal option; it is valid but not preferred. Therefore, the positive mitzva of *ḥalitza* is not considered perfect performance of the mitzva. The *Me'a Kesita* explains that the positive mitzva of levirate marriage is similar to a mitzva whose lack of fulfillment can be rectified by fulfillment of another mitzva, i.e., *ḥalitza*. This is similar to the idea that the positive mitzva of returning a lost item rectifies the prohibition against theft. Therefore, *ḥalitza* is equivalent in importance to levirate marriage, but only when levirate marriage is not possible. Consequently, it is not considered a mitzva when levirate marriage is possible.

לֵימָא פְּלִיגָא דְּרַבִּי לֵוִי, דְּאָמַר רַבִּי לֵוִי: קָשֶׁה עוֹנָשִׁין שֶׁל מִדּוֹת יוֹתֵר מֵעוֹנָשִׁין שֶׁל עֲרָיוֹת, שֶׁזֶּה נֶאֱמַר בָּהֶן "אֵל" וְזֶה נֶאֱמַר בָּהֶן "אֵלֶּה". "אֵל" – קָשֶׁה: "וְאֵלֶּה" – קָשֶׁה מֵ"אֵל".

The Gemara asks: **Shall we say** that this statement **contradicts** the opinion of **Rabbi Levi? As Rabbi Levi said: The harshness of the punishment for** using dishonest **measures**[H] **is more than the punishment for** transgressing the prohibition of **forbidden relationships, as** with regard to **this,** forbidden relations, it **is stated** only: **"These [*el*]," whereas** with regard to **that,** dishonest measures, it **is stated: "These [*eleh*]"** with an additional letter *heh* as a suffix: "For all that do these [*eleh*] things, even all that do unrighteously, are an abomination unto the Lord your God" (Deuteronomy 25:16). This implies that the word *eleh* indicates harshness and not the word *el*. The Gemara answers: This does not contradict his opinion. The word ***el*** has the connotation of **harsh, but *eleh*** has the connotation of even **harsher than *el*.**

גַּבֵּי עֲרָיוֹת נַמִי, הָא כְּתִיב "אֵלֶּה". הַהוּא לְמַעוּטֵי מִדּוֹת מִכָּרֵת.

The Gemara asks: **With regard to forbidden relationships** the word ***eleh* is also written:** "For whosoever shall do any of these [*eleh*] abominations, even the souls that do them shall be cut off from among their people" (Leviticus 18:29). If so, why is the punishment for using dishonest measures considered harsher? The Gemara answers: **That** expression meaning these [*eleh*] in the context of forbidden relations does not emphasize their severity; rather, it comes **to exclude** one who uses deception in **measures from** the penalty of ***karet*.**

אֶלָּא, מַאי חוּמְרַיְיהוּ? הָנֵי אֶפְשָׁר בִּתְשׁוּבָה, הָנֵי – לָא אֶפְשָׁר בִּתְשׁוּבָה.

The Gemara asks: **Rather,** in **what** way is deception in measurements more **severe** than forbidden relations? The Gemara answers: **Those** who engage in forbidden relations have the **possibility of repentance.**[N] If one engaged in relations with a forbidden relative he can rectify the sin through repentance. In the case of **those** who deceive the public with dishonest measures, **it is not possible to repent** fully because, having deceived the general public, they have no way of returning the money. Whereas generally a thief can return stolen property to its rightful owner, one who used dishonest measures with multiple customers has no way to track them all down in order to return the money.

רַב יְהוּדָה אָמַר מֵהָכָא: "וְאִזֵּן וְחִקֵּר תִּקֵּן מְשָׁלִים הַרְבֵּה" וְאָמַר עוּלָּא אָמַר רַבִּי אֶלְעָזָר: קוֹדֶם שֶׁבָּא שְׁלֹמֹה הָיְתָה תּוֹרָה דּוֹמָה לִכְפִיפָה שֶׁאֵין לָהּ אָזְנַיִם, עַד שֶׁבָּא שְׁלֹמֹה וְעָשָׂה לָהּ אָזְנַיִם.

Rav Yehuda said that the prohibition of secondary forbidden relationships is learned **from here:** As it says with regard to King Solomon: **"He weighed [*izzen*] and sought out,**[N] **and set in order many proverbs"** (Ecclesiastes 12:9), **and Ulla said** that **Rabbi Elazar said: Before Solomon came, the Torah was like a basket [*kefifa*]**[B] **without handles [*oznayim*], until Solomon came and made handles for it.** By means of his explanation and proverbs he enabled each person to understand and take hold of the Torah, fulfill its mitzvot, and distance himself from transgressions.

רַבִּי אוֹשַׁעְיָא אָמַר מֵהָכָא: "פְּרָעֵהוּ אַל תַּעֲבָר בּוֹ שְׂטֵה מֵעָלָיו וַעֲבוֹר".

Rabbi Oshaya said that the prohibition of secondary forbidden relationships is learned **from here: "Avoid it, pass not by it; turn from it, and pass on"** (Proverbs 4:15). One must distance oneself from any prohibited act and not pass near a place of forbidden objects or situations.

HALAKHA

The punishment for using dishonest measures – עוֹנָשִׁין שֶׁל מִדּוֹת: The punishment for deception in weights and measures is harsher than the punishment for transgressing the prohibition against forbidden relationships, based on the opinion of Rabbi Levi (Rambam *Sefer Nezikim, Hilkhot Geneiva* 7:12; *Shulḥan Arukh, Ḥoshen Mishpat* 231:19).

BACKGROUND

Basket [*kefifa*] – כְּפִיפָה: A *kefifa* was generally made from palm leaves and was used for carrying various items. It occasionally served to hold animal feed. These baskets would have handles attached to them after they were woven.

Basket with handles that were added after the initial weaving

NOTES

Those have the possibility of repentance – הָנֵי אֶפְשָׁר בִּתְשׁוּבָה: In the *Tosafot Yeshanim* it is written that full repentance for such people is possible only if their forbidden union has not produced a *mamzer*. However, if a *mamzer* has been born, this is considered a situation described by the verse: "That which is crooked cannot be made straight" (Ecclesiastes 1:15). However, the *Tosefot HaRosh* and the Meiri explain that even if a *mamzer* is born, repentance is still possible. If, on the other hand, one deceived others about measurements, full repentance is possible only if he returns that which was stolen. Since it is impossible to return the stolen money if he deceived the general public, because the sinner does not know from whom he stole, complete repentance is impossible.

He weighed and sought out – וְאִזֵּן וְחִקֵּר: The Rivan explains that the verses were interpreted as stating that King Solomon made safeguards around the Torah, as it says: "The words of the wise are as goads…and more than them, my son, beware" (Ecclesiastes 12:11–12). That is, one must be additionally cautious beyond the words of the Torah themselves.

It would seem from this Gemara that King Solomon instituted the decree against secondary forbidden relationships (see *Tosafot*; *Tosafot Yeshanim*). Alternatively, the author of *Ramat Shmuel* explains that the Gemara here does not propose that it was Solomon who instituted this decree, but that when they made a safeguard around the words of the Torah the Sages acted in accordance with the principle that Solomon laid down.

אֲמַר רַב אַשִׁי: מָשָׁל דְּרַבִּי אוֹשַׁעְיָא לְמָה הַדָּבָר דּוֹמֶה – לְאָדָם מְשַׁמֵּר פַּרְדֵּס, מְשַׁמְּרוֹ מִבַּחוּץ – כּוּלּוֹ מִשְׁתַּמֵּר, מְשַׁמְּרוֹ מִבִּפְנִים – שֶׁלְּפָנָיו מִשְׁתַּמֵּר, שֶׁלְּאַחֲרָיו – אֵינוֹ מִשְׁתַּמֵּר. וְהָא דְּרַב אַשִׁי בְּדוּתָא הִיא: הָתָם, שֶׁלְּפָנָיו מִיהָא מִשְׁתַּמֵּר, הָכָא, אִי לָאו שְׁנִיּוֹת – פָּגַע בְּעֶרְוָה גּוּפָהּ.

Rav Ashi said a parable: To what is this matter, the opinion **of Rabbi Oshaya, comparable?** It is comparable **to a man guarding an orchard;** if he **guards it from the outside, all of it is guarded.** But if **he guards it from the inside,** only **that which is in front of him** that he can see **is guarded,** while **that which is behind him is unguarded.** The Gemara comments: **And this** parable **of Rav Ashi is a mistake** [*beduta*][N] and is not accurate. **There,** in his metaphor, **that which is in front of him at least is guarded; here,** in the case of forbidden relationships, **were it not for** the rabbinic decree against **secondary** forbidden **relationships one would** eventually **encounter** and transgress **the** biblically **forbidden relationship itself.** Guarding from the outside is not only preferable, it is essential.

רַב כָּהֲנָא אָמַר מֵהָכָא: ״וּשְׁמַרְתֶּם אֶת מִשְׁמַרְתִּי״ – עֲשׂוּ מִשְׁמֶרֶת לְמִשְׁמַרְתִּי.

Rav Kahana said that the prohibition of secondary forbidden relationships is alluded to **from here,** in the verse stated at the conclusion of the verses discussing the *halakhot* of forbidden relationships: **"Therefore shall you protect** [*ushmartem*] **My prized possession** [*mishmarti*], that you do not any of these abominable customs" (Leviticus 18:30). This means: **Establish a safeguard** [*mishmeret*] **for My prized possession.**[N]

אֲמַר לֵיהּ אַבַּיֵי לְרַב יוֹסֵף: הָא – דְּאוֹרַיְיתָא, הִיא דְּאוֹרַיְיתָא וּפֵירְשׁוּ רַבָּנַן. כָּל הַתּוֹרָה נַמִי פֵּירְשׁוּ רַבָּנַן! אֶלָּא: מִדְּרַבָּנַן, וּקְרָא – אַסְמַכְתָּא בְּעָלְמָא.

Abaye said to Rav Yosef: If the prohibition against secondary forbidden relationships is learned from here **then it would be by Torah** law, yet the prohibition against secondary forbidden relationships is by rabbinic law. He answered him: The requirement to add an additional safeguard itself is in fact **by Torah** law, **and the Sages interpreted** and defined where and when to apply this law. Abaye objected: But isn't **all of the Torah also interpreted by the Sages** and yet has the force of Torah law? In that case, why are these laws considered to be rabbinic? **Rather,** the prohibition of secondary forbidden relationships was decreed **by rabbinic** law, **and the verse is a mere support**[B] but does not indicate a Torah law.

תָּנוּ רַבָּנַן: מָה הֵם שְׁנִיּוֹת? אֵם אִמּוֹ, וְאֵם אָבִיו, וְאֵשֶׁת אֲבִי אָבִיו, וְאֵשֶׁת אֲבִי אִמּוֹ, וְאֵשֶׁת אֲחִי הָאָב מִן הָאֵם, וְאֵשֶׁת אֲחִי הָאֵם מִן הָאָב, וְכַלַּת בְּנוֹ, וְכַלַּת בִּתּוֹ. וּמוּתָּר אָדָם בְּאֵשֶׁת חָמִיו וּבְאֵשֶׁת חוֹרְגוֹ, וְאָסוּר בְּבַת חוֹרְגוֹ. וְחוֹרְגוֹ מוּתָּר בְּאִשְׁתּוֹ וּבִתּוֹ.

§ **The Sages taught** in a *baraita*: **What are the secondary** forbidden **relationships**[B] that were prohibited? **His mother's mother, and his father's mother, and his father's father's wife,**[H] **and his mother's father's wife, and the wife of his father's maternal** half **brother, and the wife of his mother's paternal** half **brother,**[H] **and his son's daughter-in-law,**[H] **and his daughter's daughter-in-law.**[H] **A man is permitted to take his father-in-law's** former **wife,**[H] provided she is not the mother of his wife, **and his stepson's wife,**[H] if the stepson died or divorced her. **And he is prohibited** from marrying **the daughter of his stepson.**[H] **And it is permitted for one's stepson** to marry the stepfather's **wife or daughter.**[H]

NOTES

Mistake [*beduta*] – בְּדוּתָא: This term appears in several places in the Talmud, usually in the context of a complete rejection of statements attributed to later *amora'im*, e.g., Rav Ashi. There are two versions of the Gemara text. According to the first version, the statement is erroneous and unfounded. In other words, Rav Ashi could never have issued this statement, and it must have been attributed to him erroneously. According to a variant reading found in several sources the word is: External [*berota*]. According to this reading, when the Sages wanted to suggest that a certain opinion was without basis, they would do so in a respectful manner, saying: It is external, indicating that it is an outside opinion and should not be introduced into the study hall (*Arukh*).

Establish a safeguard for My prized possession – עֲשׂוּ מִשְׁמֶרֶת לְמִשְׁמַרְתִּי: The author of the *Sefer Halakhot Gedolot* explains that although the Sages learned from this verse that they should make safeguards around the entire Torah, the verse itself is referring to the *halakhot* of forbidden relations. For this reason they made more safeguards around the *halakhot* of forbidden relationships than any others. This is a fulfillment of the mitzva of: "You shall be sacred" (Leviticus 19:2), which the Sages interpreted to mean: Separate yourselves from forbidden relationships.

BACKGROUND

Mere support – אַסְמַכְתָּא בְּעָלְמָא: Sometimes the Gemara states that a verse cited as the basis for a *halakha* is merely an allusion to the *halakha* rather than its actual source. In such cases, the verse is called a support for the *halakha*. Since *halakhot* of this kind are not actually derived from the biblical text, which serves instead as a mnemonic device, they are generally rabbinic decrees. This is indicated in the Talmud by the phrase: The law is rabbinic, and the verse is a mere support.

Secondary forbidden relationships – שְׁנִיּוֹת: See diagram following this chapter, p. 160.

HALAKHA

His mother's mother, and his father's mother, and his father's father's wife – אֵם אִמּוֹ, וְאֵם אָבִיו, וְאֵשֶׁת אֲבִי אָבִיו: One's mother's mother and one's father's mother and their mothers going back all generations, as well as the wife of his father's father and the wives of his fathers going back all generations are forbidden as secondary forbidden relationships by rabbinic law (Rambam *Sefer Nashim, Hilkhot Ishut* 1:6; *Shulḥan Arukh, Even HaEzer* 15:2, 4–6).

His mother's father's wife and his uncles' wives – אֵשֶׁת אֲבִי אִמּוֹ וּנְשֵׁי דוֹדָיו: His mother's father's wife is prohibited as a secondary forbidden relationship, as are the wife of his father's maternal half brother and the wife of his mother's maternal or paternal half brother. This prohibition applies only to these women themselves and not to their progenitors or descendants in accordance with the opinion of Ze'eiri (Rambam *Sefer Nashim, Hilkhot Ishut* 1:6; *Shulḥan Arukh, Even HaEzer* 15:7–9, 18).

His son's daughter-in-law – כַּלַּת בְּנוֹ: The daughter-in-law of one's son is prohibited as a secondary forbidden relationship, as is his son's son's daughter-in-law, and daughters-in-law of all later generations (Rambam *Sefer Nashim, Hilkhot Ishut* 1:6; *Shulḥan Arukh, Even HaEzer* 15:19).

His daughter's daughter-in-law – כַּלַּת בִּתּוֹ: The daughter-in-law of one's daughter is prohibited as a forbidden secondary relationship, but this prohibition applies only to her alone and not to her descendants (Rambam *Sefer Nashim, Hilkhot Ishut* 1:6; *Shulḥan Arukh, Even HaEzer* 15:20).

His father-in-law's wife – אֵשֶׁת חָמִיו: One's father-in-law's wife who is not his wife's mother is permitted to him (Rif), based on the conclusion in the Gemara. Some hold that she is forbidden to him (*Sefer Halakhot Gedolot*; *Tosafot*) and follow the Jerusalem Talmud, which prohibits a relationship with her because it appears like a prohibition. Due to this dispute, marriage to her should not be allowed *ab initio*, but if he takes her in marriage he need not divorce her (*Be'er Heitev* on *Shulḥan Arukh, Even HaEzer* 15:24).

His stepson's wife – אֵשֶׁת חוֹרְגוֹ: One is permitted to marry the former wife of his stepson (*Shulḥan Arukh, Even HaEzer* 15:21).

The daughter of his stepson – בַּת חוֹרְגוֹ: It is prohibited by Torah law to marry one's stepson's daughter, i.e., the daughter of his wife's son (*Shulḥan Arukh, Even HaEzer* 15:13).

It is permitted for one's stepson to marry the stepfather's… daughter – חוֹרְגוֹ מוּתָּר...וּבִתּוֹ: A woman is permitted to marry her stepbrother, the son of her mother's husband by another woman. So too, a man is permitted to marry the daughter of his mother's husband by another woman, even if they grew up together in the same household, as is stated explicitly in *Sota* 43b (*Shulḥan Arukh, Even HaEzer* 15:11).

וְאֵשֶׁת חוֹרְגוֹ אוֹמֶרֶת לוֹ: אֲנִי מוּתֶּרֶת לָךְ, וּבִתִּי אֲסוּרָה לָךְ.

Due to these rabbinic decrees concerning stepsons, unusual situations might arise. For example: **And his stepson's wife says to** him, i.e., her husband's stepfather, **I am permitted to you, but my daughter is forbidden to you,** since she is your stepson's daughter.

בַּת חוֹרְגוֹ – דְּאוֹרַיְיתָא הִיא, דִּכְתִיב "אֶת בַּת בְּנָהּ וְאֶת בַּת בִּתָּהּ"! מִשּׁוּם דְּקָבָעֵי לְמִיתְנֵי סֵיפָא: אֵשֶׁת חוֹרְגוֹ אוֹמֶרֶת לוֹ: אֲנִי מוּתֶּרֶת לָךְ וּבִתִּי אֲסוּרָה לָךְ, וְאַף עַל גַּב דְּבִתִּי אֲסוּרָה לָךְ מִדְּאוֹרַיְיתָא – בְּדִידִי לָא גְּזוּר בֵּיהּ רַבָּנַן, תְּנָא רֵישָׁא נַמִי בַּת חוֹרְגוֹ.

The Gemara challenges that which is stated in the *baraita*: **His stepson's daughter** is not a secondary relation by rabbinic law. **She is** forbidden **by Torah** law, since the daughter of his stepson is the daughter of his wife's son, **as it is written:** "You shall not take **her son's daughter or her daughter's daughter**" (Leviticus 18:17). The Gemara answers: This case was included **because** the *baraita* **wanted to teach the latter clause,** which states: **His stepson's wife says to him: I am permitted to you, but my daughter is forbidden to you. And although my daughter is forbidden to you by Torah** law, nevertheless **the Sages did not issue a decree** forbidding **me.** Therefore, the case of **his stepson's daughter was also taught in the first clause,** even though she is forbidden by Torah law and is not a secondary relation.

אִי הָכִי, אֵשֶׁת חָמִיו נַמִי תֵּימָא: אֲנִי מוּתֶּרֶת לָךְ וּבִתִּי אֲסוּרָה לָךְ, דְּהָוְיָא אֲחוֹת אִשְׁתּוֹ! הָא – פְּסִיקָא לֵיהּ, הָא – לָא פְּסִיקָא לֵיהּ.

The Gemara raises an objection: **If so,** that the *baraita* wished to teach this peculiarity, then why did it not teach: **His father-in-law's wife also says: I am permitted to you and my daughter is forbidden to you, as she is his wife's sister.** The Gemara answers: **This** matter **is conclusive for him.** In other words, his stepson's wife is forever permitted and his stepson's daughter is always forbidden to him. But as for the matter of his father-in-law's wife's daughter, **this is not conclusive for him.** This ruling is not final and might change, since if his wife dies her sister is permitted to him.

אָמַר רַב: אַרְבַּע נָשִׁים יֵשׁ לָהֶן הֶפְסֵק. נָקֵיט רַב בִּידֵיהּ תְּלָת: אֵשֶׁת אֲחִי הָאֵם מִן הָאָב, וְאֵשֶׁת אֲחִי הָאָב מִן הָאֵם, וְכַלָּתוֹ. וּזְעֵירִי מוֹסִיף אַף אֵשֶׁת אֲבִי אִמּוֹ. אָמַר רַב נַחְמָן בַּר יִצְחָק, וְסִימָנֵיךְ: דְּעִילָּאֵי דְּרַב.

Rav said that he received a tradition with regard to secondary forbidden relationships that **four women have a conclusion;**[H] i.e., the prohibition does not continue to later generations but applies only to those women who were mentioned explicitly. **Rav held three** of them **in his hand;** he knew with certainty three of the four categories. They were: **The wife of his mother's paternal** half **brother, and the wife of his father's maternal** half **brother, and his daughter-in-law. And Ze'eiri adds: Also the wife of his mother's father. Rav Naḥman bar Yitzḥak said: And your mnemonic** for remembering who said what is as follows: Ze'eiri adds an extra generation **on top** of the prohibitions **of Rav,**[N] i.e., the wife of his mother's father, which Rav did not mention.

וְרַב, מַאי טַעְמָא לָא חָשֵׁיב לֵיהּ? מִיחַלְפָא לֵיהּ בְּאֵשֶׁת אֲבִי אָבִיו.

The Gemara asks: **And what is the reason** that **Rav did not reckon this** category mentioned by Ze'eiri to be among those who have a conclusion? The Gemara answers: In his opinion, this category might be mistakenly **switched with** the category of **the wife of his father's father,** which does not have a conclusion. With regard to the wife of his father, the prohibition applies equally to the wife of all ancestors in the father's line. Therefore, according to Rav, the Sages also included the ancestors of the mother's father's wife as secondary forbidden relationships.

וּזְעֵירִי: לְהָתָם שְׁכִיחַ וְאָזֵיל, לְהָכָא – לָא שְׁכִיחַ וְאָזֵיל.

The Gemara asks: **And** why is **Ze'eiri** not concerned that the two categories will become confused? The Gemara answers: **He** is often **found there,** in his father's father's home, **and goes** there frequently, but **here,** to his mother's household, **he is not commonly found to go.** Since he goes to his father's home frequently, he knows that his father's relatives are forbidden to him, and he will not confuse them with his mother's relatives.

כַּלָּתוֹ

Among the women enumerated by Rav is **his daughter-in-law.**

NOTES

On top of Rav – **עִילָּאֵי דְּרַב**: The mnemonic refers to the names of the Rabbis: The word *rav* means large and the word *ze'eir* means small. Normally a small item is placed on top of a larger one.

HALAKHA

Secondary forbidden relations that have a conclusion – **שְׁנִיּוֹת שֶׁיֵּשׁ לָהֶם הֶפְסֵק**: The four women listed by Rav and Ze'eiri: The wife of one's mother's paternal half brother, the wife of one's father's maternal half brother, the wife of one's mother's father, and one's daughter's daughter-in-law, while forbidden as secondary relations, see an end to their prohibition, as it applies to them alone and not to their descendants. There are other secondary forbidden relations that have a conclusion, but only those listed in the *baraita* were mentioned (*Yam shel Shlomo*; Rambam *Sefer Nashim, Hilkhot Ishut* 1:6; *Shulḥan Arukh, Even HaEzer* 15:18, 20).

דְּאוֹרַיְיתָא הִיא, דִּכְתִיב ״עֶרְוַת כַּלָּתְךָ לֹא תְגַלֵּה״! אֵימָא: כַּלַּת בְּנוֹ. וְכַלַּת בְּנוֹ יֵשׁ לָהּ הֶפְסֵק? וְהָא תַּנְיָא: כַּלָּתוֹ – עֶרְוָה, כַּלַּת בְּנוֹ – שְׁנִיָּה, וְכֵן אַתָּה אוֹמֵר בִּבְנוֹ, וּבֶן בְּנוֹ, עַד סוֹף כָּל הַדּוֹרוֹת! אֶלָּא אֵימָא: כַּלַּת בִּתּוֹ.

The Gemara asks: Is this relationship not forbidden **by Torah law? As it is written: "You shall not uncover the nakedness of your daughter-in-law"** (Leviticus 18:15). The Gemara emends: **Say** instead **his son's daughter-in-law.**[H] The Gemara asks: **And does the** prohibition against having a relationship with **his son's daughter-in-law indeed have a conclusion? Isn't it taught** in a *baraita*: **His daughter-in-law is a forbidden relation** by Torah law, **his son's daughter-in-law is a secondary** forbidden **relation, and similarly, you say** the daughter-in-law of **his son and** the daughter-in-law of **his son's son until the end of all generations** are secondary forbidden relationships. **Rather, say** instead that Rav was referring to **his daughter's daughter-in-law.**

דְּאָמַר רַב חִסְדָּא: הָא מִילְּתָא מִגַּבְרָא רַבָּה שְׁמִיעַ לִי, וּמַנּוּ – רַבִּי אַמִּי: לֹא אָסְרוּ כַּלָּה אֶלָּא מִפְּנֵי כַּלָּה. וְאָמְרוּ לִי כַּלְדָּאֵי: מַלְפְּנָא הָוֵית.

As Rav Ḥisda said: I heard this matter from a great man, and who was that great man? It was **Rabbi Ami,**[P] and he said: **They prohibited a daughter-in-law only due to** the **daughter-in-law.** Rav Ḥisda heard this in his youth but did not understand the meaning. **The Chaldean** astrologers[B] **said to me: You will be a teacher.**

אָמִינָא: אִי גַּבְרָא רַבָּה הָוֵינָא – אַסְבְּרָא מִדַּעְתִּי, אִי מַקְרֵי דַּרְדְּקֵי הָוֵינָא – אַשְׁיְילָהּ מֵרַבָּנַן דְּאָתוּ לְבֵי כְּנִישְׁתָּא. הַשְׁתָּא סְבַרְתָּהּ מִדַּעְתִּי: לֹא אָסְרוּ כַּלַּת בִּתּוֹ אֶלָּא מִשּׁוּם כַּלַּת בְּנוֹ.

Rav Ḥisda further said: **I said** to myself: **If** the astrologers meant that **I will become a great man** and one who teaches the public, **I will** certainly be able to **reason** and understand this matter **with my knowledge. If** the astrologers meant that **I will become the teacher of children, I will ask it of the Sages who come to the synagogue** and in that way I will learn the meaning of Rabbi Ami's teaching. **Now I understand** the matter **on my own.** Rabbi Ami meant: **They prohibited his daughter's daughter-in-law only due to his son's daughter-in-law,** to avoid confusion between these daughters-in-law. The rabbinic decree prohibited one's daughter's daughter-in-law but did not extend to subsequent generations.

אֲמַר לֵיהּ אַבַּיֵי לְרָבָא: אַסְבְּרָהּ לָךְ, כְּגוֹן כַּלָּתָהּ דְּבֵי בַּר צִיתַאי. רַב פַּפָּא אָמַר: כְּגוֹן כַּלָּתָהּ דְּבֵי רַב פַּפָּא בַּר אַבָּא. רַב אַשִׁי אָמַר: כְּגוֹן כַּלָּתָהּ דְּבֵי מָרִי בַּר אִיסַק.

Various Sages proceed to give contemporary examples of families where the halakhic status of the daughters-in-law of the sons and the daughters-in-law of the daughters could be confused with each other. **Abaye said to Rava: I will explain to you** with an example how one might become confused about these daughters-in-law. **For example,** this would be possible in the case of **the daughter-in-law of the house of bar Tzitai,**[N] as there the children of the sons and the daughters of the same family lived together, and it was possible to confuse the halakhic status of the sons' daughters-in-law and the daughters' daughters-in-law. **Rav Pappa said: For example, the daughter-in-law of the house of Rav Pappa bar Abba. Rav Ashi said: For example, the daughter-in-law of the house of Mari bar Isak.**

אִיבַּעְיָא לְהוּ: אֵשֶׁת אֲחִי הָאֵם מִן הָאֵם, מַהוּ? אֵשֶׁת אֲחִי הָאָב מִן הָאֵם, וְאֵשֶׁת אֲחִי הָאֵם מִן הָאָב, דְּאִיכָּא צַד אָב – הוּא דִּגְזַרוּ רַבָּנַן, אֲבָל הֵיכָא דְּלֵיכָּא צַד אָב לָא גְּזַרוּ בְּהוּ רַבָּנַן, אוֹ דִּלְמָא לֹא שְׁנָא?

§ **A dilemma was raised before** the Sages: **What is the** *halakha* with regard to **the wife of** one's **mother's maternal** half **brother?**[H] The Gemara presents the different sides of the question: Both **the wife of** one's **father's maternal** half **brother and the wife of** one's **mother's paternal** half **brother contain** some **aspect of a father, and** perhaps **this** is the reason that **the Sages enacted** a prohibition. That is, they were both forbidden rabbinically to avoid confusion with the case of the wife of one's father's paternal half brother, who is forbidden by Torah law. **But** in the case of the wife of one's mother's maternal half brother, **where there is no aspect of a father** whatsoever, perhaps **the Sages did not make a decree? Or perhaps** this case **is no different?**

HALAKHA

His daughter-in-law and his son's daughter-in-law – כַּלָּתוֹ וְכַלַּת בְּנוֹ: One's son's wife is forbidden to him by Torah law, and his son's son's wife is forbidden by rabbinic law. This prohibition has no conclusion (Rambam *Sefer Nashim*, *Hilkhot Ishut* 1:6; *Shulḥan Arukh*, *Even HaEzer* 15:19).

The wife of a mother's brother – אֵשֶׁת אֲחִי הָאֵם: The wife of one's mother's maternal or paternal brother is forbidden by rabbinic law, as per the conclusion of the Gemara's discussion according to the statement of Rav Yehuda bar Sheila (Rambam *Sefer Nashim*, *Hilkhot Ishut* 1:6; *Shulḥan Arukh*, *Even HaEzer* 15:9, 18).

BACKGROUND

Chaldean – כַּלְדָּאֵי: The term Chaldean is a synonym for Chasdean, one of the names for the Babylonian people. This term is used in the Bible as a synonym for stargazers or astrologers, as in the following verse: "Then the king commanded to call the magicians, and the enchanters, and the sorcerers, and the Chaldeans, to tell the king his dreams" (Daniel 2:2).

Some Sages prohibited consulting astrologers to discern the future, based on the Torah injunction: "You shall be wholehearted with the Lord your God" (Deuteronomy 18:13). Nevertheless, many people did consult with them. Although the Sages accepted the belief that astrologers had certain powers to foretell the future, they advised that astrologers should be neither consulted nor overly trusted.

NOTES

For example, the daughters-in-law of the house of bar Tzitai – כְּגוֹן כַּלָּתָהּ דְּבֵי בַּר צִיתַאי: The *Arukh* explains that Tzitai was an important man in his generation, and for this reason all his daughters-in-law would boast of their family connection to him, including his son's daughters-in-law and his daughter's daughters-in-law.

PERSONALITIES

A great man…Rabbi Ami – גַּבְרָא רַבָּה...רַבִּי אַמִּי: Rabbi Ami was a well-known third-generation *amora* who lived in Eretz Yisrael at the end of the third century CE. He headed the yeshiva in Tiberias together with his colleague Rabbi Asi after the deaths of Rabbi Yoḥanan and Rabbi Elazar. Rabbi Ami considered Rabbi Yoḥanan to be his primary teacher, although he also studied under Reish Lakish, Rabbi Elazar, Rabbi Oshaya, and Rabbi Yehoshua ben Levi. During Rav Huna's lifetime Rabbi Ami deferred to his halakhic decisions, but after his death Rabbi Ami was considered the foremost authority. It may have been for this reason that he was known as a great man. In answer to one of the questions he received, he wrote: From me, Ami bar Natan, Torah emanates to all of Israel (*Gittin* 44a). Among those who sent him their queries were Rabbi Abbahu, Rav Naḥman, and Rava.

אָמַר רַב סָפְרָא: הִיא גּוּפָהּ גְּזֵירָה, וַאֲנַן נֵיקוּם וְנִגְזוֹר גְּזֵירָה לִגְזֵירָה?! אָמַר רָבָא: אַטּוּ כּוּלְּהוּ לָאו גְּזֵירָה לִגְזֵירָה נִינְהוּ? אִמּוֹ – עֶרְוָה, אֵם אִמּוֹ – שְׁנִיָּה, וְגָזְרוּ עַל אֵם אָבִיו מִשּׁוּם אֵם אִמּוֹ. וְטַעְמָא מַאי? כּוּלְּהוּ "דְּבֵי אִימָּא רַבָּתִי" קָרוּ לֵיהּ.

Rav Safra said: She herself, the wife of the mother's paternal half brother, **is** forbidden **by rabbinic decree,** and **will we** then **proceed to issue a decree to** prevent violation of **a decree?**[B] **Rava said: Is that to say that all of these** rabbinic decrees with regard to secondary relations **are not decrees** to prevent violation of **a decree?** For example, **his mother** is **a forbidden relation** by Torah law, and the Sages decreed that **his mother's mother is a secondary** forbidden **relationship. And they decreed** that **his father's mother** is also a secondary forbidden relationship **due to his mother's mother.**[H] **And what is the reason? They are all called the house of the grandmother,** and therefore people may confuse their halakhic status.

אֵשֶׁת אָבִיו – עֶרְוָה, אֵשֶׁת אֲבִי אָבִיו – שְׁנִיָּה, וְגָזְרוּ עַל אֵשֶׁת אֲבִי אִמּוֹ מִשּׁוּם אֵשֶׁת אֲבִי אָבִיו, וְטַעְמָא מַאי? כּוּלְּהוּ "דְּבֵי אַבָּא רַבָּה" קָרוּ לֵיהּ.

Rava continues: Similarly, **his father's wife is a forbidden relation** by Torah law, and the Sages decreed that **his father's father's wife is a secondary** forbidden **relationship. And they decreed** that **his mother's father's wife** is also a secondary forbidden relationship **due to his father's father's wife.**[H] **And what is the reason? They are all called the house of the grandfather.**

אֵשֶׁת אֲחִי הָאָב מִן הָאָב – עֶרְוָה, אֵשֶׁת אֲחִי הָאָב מִן הָאֵם – שְׁנִיָּה, וְגָזְרוּ עַל אֵשֶׁת אֲחִי הָאֵם מִן הָאָב מִשּׁוּם אֵשֶׁת אֲחִי הָאָב מִן הָאֵם, וְטַעְמָא מַאי – מִשּׁוּם דְּכוּלְּהוּ "דְּבֵי דוֹדֵי" קָרֵי לְהוּ.

Also, **the wife of his father's paternal** half **brother,** his uncle, who is mentioned explicitly in the Torah (Leviticus 18:16), **is a forbidden relation** by Torah law, and the Sages decreed that **the wife of his father's maternal** half **brother**[H] **is a secondary** forbidden **relationship. And they decreed** that **the wife of his mother's paternal** half **brother** is also a secondary forbidden relationship **due to the wife of his father's maternal** half **brother. And what is the reason?** It is **because they are all called the house of the uncle;** it seems that in the realm of forbidden relations the Sages did issue decrees to prevent violation of a decree, and Rav Safra's claim is incorrect.

מַאי? תָּא שְׁמַע: דְּכִי אֲתָא רַב יְהוּדָה בַּר שֵׁילָא אָמַר: אָמְרִי בְּמַעְרְבָא: כׇּל שֶׁבִּנְקֵבָה עֶרְוָה – בְּזָכָר גָּזְרוּ עַל אִשְׁתּוֹ מִשּׁוּם שְׁנִיָּה.

If so, then **what is** the *halakha* in this case of the wife of his mother's maternal half brother? **Come and hear: As when Rav Yehuda bar Sheila came** from Eretz Yisrael to Babylonia, **he said: In the West,** Eretz Yisrael, **they say** this principle: For **every female** relative who is **a forbidden relation**[N] by Torah law, the Sages **decreed on the wife of** the equivalent **male** relative **due to** her similarity to **a secondary** forbidden **relationship.**

וְאָמַר רָבָא: וּכְלָלָא הוּא? חֲמוֹתוֹ – עֶרְוָה, אֵשֶׁת חָמִיו מוּתֶּרֶת. בַּת חֲמוֹתוֹ – עֶרְוָה, אֵשֶׁת בֶּן חֲמוֹתוֹ מוּתֶּרֶת. בַּת חָמִיו – עֶרְוָה, אֵשֶׁת בֶּן חָמִיו – מוּתֶּרֶת. חוֹרַגְתּוֹ – עֶרְוָה, אֵשֶׁת חוֹרְגוֹ – מוּתֶּרֶת! בַּת חוֹרַגְתּוֹ עֶרְוָה אֵשֶׁת בֶּן חוֹרְגוֹ מוּתֶּרֶת.

And Rava said: Is this really an established **principle?** Isn't **his mother-in-law a forbidden relation** by Torah law, while **his father-in-law's wife is permitted?** Also, **his mother-in-law's daughter is a forbidden relation** by Torah law, as she is his wife's sister, yet **his mother-in-law's son's wife is permitted. His father-in-law's daughter is a forbidden relation** by Torah law, yet **the wife of his father-in-law's son is permitted. His stepdaughter is a forbidden relation** by Torah law, yet **his stepson's wife**[H] **is permitted. His stepdaughter's daughter,** i.e., his wife's granddaughter, **is a forbidden relation,** yet **the wife of his stepson's son is permitted.**

וְהָא דְּרַב יְהוּדָה בַּר שֵׁילָא לְאֵיתוֹיֵי מַאי? לָאו לְאֵיתוֹיֵי אֵשֶׁת אֲחִי הָאֵם מִן הָאֵם, דְּכׇל שֶׁבִּנְקֵבָה עֶרְוָה – בְּזָכָר גָּזְרוּ אִשְׁתּוֹ מִשּׁוּם שְׁנִיָּה!

The Gemara continues: If so, **what did that** statement of **Rav Yehuda bar Sheila come to include?** Since his principle is not true in every case, it must be intended to include a specific *halakha*. **Does it not come to include** the case of **the wife of** one's **mother's maternal** half **brother, since** for **every female** relative **who is a forbidden relation** by Torah law, such as his mother's maternal half sister, the Sages **decreed on the wife of** the equivalent **male** relative, in this case his mother's maternal half brother's wife, **due to** her similarity to **a secondary relation.**

מַאי שְׁנָא הָנֵי וּמַאי שְׁנָא הָא? הָא – בְּחַד קִידּוּשִׁין מִקָּרְבָא לַהּ, הָנֵי – עַד דְּאִיכָּא תְּרֵי קִידּוּשִׁין לָא מִקָּרְבָא לְהוּ.

The Gemara asks: **What is different** with regard to **these** cases, the wife of his father-in-law or the wife of his mother-in-law's son, who are permitted, **and this** case of the wife of a mother's maternal half brother, who is prohibited? The Gemara answers: **This,** the wife of a mother's maternal half brother, **is related by a single act of betrothal.** One's mother's brother is a blood relative, and his wife is therefore a secondary relation. In contrast, **these** other cases with regard to which the Sages did not issue a decree **are related** only **when there are two acts of betrothal.** For example, one's father-in-law is related to one through one's marriage to his own wife, and his father in law's wife is related to him through his father-in-law's marriage.

BACKGROUND

Decree to prevent violation of a decree – גְּזֵירָה לִגְזֵירָה: The reason that the Sages did not issue decrees to prevent violation of a decree is because although the Torah says that they must establish a fence around the mitzvot, they were not instructed to make a fence around that fence because, if that were to be done, it could continue ad infinitum. In some cases, however, the Gemara discusses a decree to prevent violation of another decree, and in those cases the Gemara explains that all the decrees were part of one original decree.

HALAKHA

His mother's mother and his father's mother – אֵם אִמּוֹ וְאֵם אָבִיו: One's mother is forbidden by Torah law, and one's mother's mother is forbidden by rabbinic law. The Sages decreed that one's father's mother is forbidden as well (Rambam *Sefer Nashim, Hilkhot Ishut* 1:6; *Shulḥan Arukh, Even HaEzer* 15:2, 4).

The wife of one's father's father and of one's mother's father – אֵשֶׁת אֲבִי הָאָב וַאֲבִי הָאֵם: One's father's wife is forbidden by Torah law, and one's father's father's wife and one's mother's father's wife are forbidden as secondary relations by rabbinic law (*Shulḥan Arukh, Even HaEzer* 15:5–7).

The wife of one's father's brother – אֵשֶׁת אֲחִי הָאָב: The wife of one's father's paternal half brother is forbidden by Torah law, and the wife of one's father's maternal half brother is forbidden by rabbinic law (*Shulḥan Arukh, Even HaEzer* 15:18)

His stepdaughter and his stepson's wife – חוֹרַגְתּוֹ וְאֵשֶׁת חוֹרְגוֹ: One's stepdaughter is forbidden by Torah law, but one's stepson's wife is permitted (*Shulḥan Arukh, Even HaEzer* 15:13, 21).

NOTES

Every female relative who is a forbidden relation, etc. – כׇּל שֶׁבִּנְקֵבָה עֶרְוָה וכו׳: According to the Gemara's conclusion, this principle applies in only a few cases. The Gemara is not stating a principle with regard to all forbidden relations but only with regard to aunts. Since one's father's sisters and mother's sisters and the wife of one's father's paternal half brother are forbidden by Torah law, the Sages decreed that anyone who is called an aunt is also forbidden, to avoid confusion between them (Ritva).

NOTES

The wife of a father's father's brother, etc. – אֵשֶׁת אֲחִי אֲבִי הָאָב וכו׳: The early commentaries ask why the Gemara did not similarly inquire about the sister of one's mother's mother, as she is an equally close relative. They answered that the Gemara did not ask about every possible case, but took these two cases as examples. These specific cases were used because the Gemara's question is based on the fact that one generation below them is a forbidden relation by Torah law.

HALAKHA

The wife of one's father's father's brother, etc. – אֵשֶׁת אֲחִי אֲבִי אָבִיו וכו׳: The wife of one's father's father's paternal half brother is permitted as well as both the maternal and paternal half sisters of one's father's father, in accordance with the statement of Ameimar. This is the *halakha* according to *She'iltot deRav Aḥai Gaon* and Rabbeinu Ḥananel and is also the opinion of the Rambam and the Rif. There is an opinion that these relations are forbidden (*Tur*, citing Ri; Rosh on *Yevamot* 40b). The *halakha* is ruled in accordance with the first opinion (*Shulḥan Arukh, Even HaEzer* 15:18).

PERSONALITIES

Mar, son of Rabbana – מָר בְּרֵיהּ דְּרַבָּנָא: Mar, son of Rabbana, was also known as Mar, son of Ravina. He was one of the outstanding fourth-generation Babylonian *amora'im* and the son of Ravina I. He was renowned in the Talmud as an extremely God-fearing man, and others derived proper behavior for a God-fearing individual from his conduct. He was vigilant in avoiding excessive levity or any matter that lessened the appropriate deference to God. He was particularly careful in his choice of words in order to avoid any possibility of affronting his teachers. He studied primarily with Rav Naḥman bar Yitzḥak as a disciple-colleague. The Talmud relates that he left halakhic notes that served as the basis for discussion in subsequent generations.

שְׁלַח לֵיהּ רַב מְשַׁרְשְׁיָא מִתּוּסְנְיָיא לְרַב פַּפִּי: יְלַמְּדֵנוּ רַבֵּינוּ, אֵשֶׁת אֲחִי אֲבִי הָאָב, וַאֲחוֹת אֲבִי הָאָב, מַהוּ? מִדִּלְמַטָּה עֶרְוָה – לְמַעְלָה נַמִּי גָּזְרוּ בֵּיהּ, אוֹ דִּלְמָא, הָא אִיתְפְּלֵיג דָּרָתָא?

§ **Rav Mesharshiyya from Tusneya sent** a message **to Rav Pappi: Let our Master teach us: What is** the *halakha* with regard to **the wife of a father's father's brother**[N] **and the sister of a father's father?** Did the Sages prohibit these as secondary forbidden relations? The Gemara presents the different sides of the dilemma: Since one generation **below is a forbidden relation,** i.e., a father's sister and the wife of a father's paternal brother, who are both forbidden by Torah law, perhaps the Sages **also decreed** about the women one generation **above. Or, perhaps the generations are separate** and the women in the generation above are not considered to be forbidden relatives.

תָּא שְׁמַע: ״מַה הֵן שְׁנִיּוֹת״, וְלָא קָחָשֵׁיב לְהוּ בַּהֲדַיְיהוּ.

The Gemara attempts to answer: **Come and hear** from that *baraita* cited above, which taught: **What are** the **secondary** forbidden **relationships** that were prohibited? **And these** women, i.e., the wife of one's father's father's brother and the sister of his father's father **were not reckoned among them.** This implies that these women are permitted.

תָּנָא וְשַׁיֵּיר. מַאי שַׁיֵּיר דְּהַאי שַׁיֵּיר? שַׁיֵּיר שְׁנִיּוֹת דְּבֵי רַבִּי חִיָּיא.

The Gemara replies that this is not conclusive. Perhaps the *tanna* of the *baraita* **taught** some examples **and omitted** other examples of secondary forbidden relations; i.e., perhaps the list is not exhaustive. The Gemara asks: **What else did he omit that he omitted this?** It cannot be that the *tanna* had an exhaustive list except for one case. He either left out more than one case or he included all possible cases. The Gemara answers: **He omitted** the list of **secondary** forbidden **relationships** that were enumerated by **the school of Rabbi Ḥiyya,** which is listed later. Therefore, this *baraita* is not conclusive, as the *tanna* left out many cases.

אֲמֵימַר אַכְשַׁר בְּאֵשֶׁת אֲחִי אֲבִי אָבִיו, וּבַאֲחוֹת אֲבִי אָבִיו. אָמַר לֵיהּ רַב הִלֵּל לְרַב אַשִׁי: לְדִידִי חֲזְיָא לִי שְׁנִיּוֹת מָר בְּרֵיהּ דְּרַבָּנָא, וּכְתִיבָן שִׁיתְּסְרֵי לְאִיסּוּרָא. מַאי לָאו תְּמָנֵי דְּמַתְנִיתָא וְשִׁית דְּבֵי רַבִּי חִיָּיא, וְהָנָךְ תַּרְתֵּי – הָא שִׁיתְּסְרֵי!

The Gemara states that Ameimar permitted the wife of one's father's father's brother[H] **and the sister of one's father's father. Rav Hillel said to Rav Ashi,** challenging Ameimar's statement: **I myself saw** a list of **secondary** forbidden **relationships** written by **Mar, son of Rabbana,**[P] **and it was written** there that **sixteen** women **were forbidden. What, is it not** that these sixteen must be the **eight** cases listed **in the** ***baraita*****, and six from the school of Rabbi Ḥiyya, and these two** cases of the wife of one's father's father's brother and one's father's father's sister, and **this** totals **sixteen?**

וּלְטַעֲמִיךְ שִׁיבְסְרֵי הָוְיָין, דְּהָא אִיכָּא אֵשֶׁת אֲחִי הָאֵם מִן הָאֵם, דְּפָשְׁטִינַן לְאִיסּוּרָא! הָא לָא קַשְׁיָא,

Rav Ashi defended Ameimar's opinion: **And according to your reasoning,** Rav Hillel, that these cases should be included, **there are seventeen** cases, **as there is** the additional case of **the wife of a mother's maternal** half **brother, whose status was resolved** earlier, concluding **that she is forbidden.** If it is as you say, then there should be seventeen cases. The Gemara answers on behalf of Rav Hillel: **This is not difficult.**

Perek **II**
Daf **22** Amud **a**

הָנָךְ תַּרְתֵּי דְּדָמְיָין לַהֲדָדֵי – כַּחֲדָא חָשֵׁיב לְהוּ, וְהָא שִׁיתְּסְרֵי. וְהָא מִכָּל מָקוֹם לְדִידִי חֲזְיָין לָן דִּכְתִיבָן לְאִיסּוּרָא! אֲמַר לֵיהּ: וְלִיטַעֲמִיךְ, אִי הֲוָה כְּתִיב לְהֶיתֵּירָא – מִי הֲוָת סָמְכַתְּ עֲלַיְיהוּ? דְּמָר בְּרֵיהּ דְּרַבָּנָא – מִי חֲתִים עֲלַיְיהוּ? הַשְׁתָּא נַמִּי דִּכְתִיב לְאִיסּוּרָא – לָאו מָר בְּרֵיהּ דְּרַבָּנָא חֲתִים עֲלַיְיהוּ.

Those two, the wife of a father's father's brother and the sister of a father's father, **are similar to each other** and **are counted as a single** case, **and** so **there are sixteen.** The Gemara restates Rav Hillel's challenge to Ameimar's opinion: **But in any case I myself saw them written as prohibited.** Rav Ashi **said to** Rav Hillel: **And according to your reasoning, if** in the list **it was written that they were permitted, would you have relied on that?** Is the signature **of Mar, son of Rabbana, signed on it?** Although you saw the list, you don't know for certain who wrote it. **Now too, that it is written that they are prohibited,** the same holds true; the signature of **Mar, son of Rabbana, is not signed on it,** and so it cannot be relied upon to reject the opinion of Ameimar.

תָּנֵי דְּבֵי רַבִּי חִיָּיא: שְׁלִישִׁי שֶׁבִּבְנוֹ וְשֶׁבְּבִתּוֹ: וְשֶׁבְּבֶן אִשְׁתּוֹ וְשֶׁבְּבַת אִשְׁתּוֹ – שְׁנִיָּה, רְבִיעִי שֶׁבַּחֲמִיו וְשֶׁבַּחֲמוֹתוֹ – שְׁנִיָּה.

§ One of the Sages **of the school of Rabbi Ḥiyya taught: The third** generation **from one's son and one's daughter,**[H] i.e., one's great-grandchildren, **and** the third generation **from his wife's son and his wife's daughter,**[H] i.e., one's wife's great-grandchildren, are all forbidden as **secondary** forbidden **relationships.** So too, **the fourth** generation **from his father-in-law and from his mother-in-law,**[H] i.e., his wife's great-grandmothers, are prohibited as **secondary** forbidden **relationships.**

אָמַר לֵיהּ רָבִינָא לְרַב אַשִׁי: מַאי שְׁנָא לְמַעְלָה, דְּקָחָשֵׁיב לָהּ לְאִשְׁתּוֹ, וּמַאי שְׁנָא לְמַטָּה, דְּלָא קָחָשֵׁיב לָהּ לְאִשְׁתּוֹ? לְמַעְלָה, דְּאִיסּוּרָא מִכֹּחַ אִשְׁתּוֹ קָא אָתֵי, חָשֵׁיב לָהּ. לְמַטָּה, דְּאִיסּוּרָא לָאו מִכֹּחַ אִשְׁתּוֹ קָאָתֵי – לָא קָחָשֵׁיב לָהּ.

Ravina said to Rav Ashi: What is different between the generations **above,** referring to his wife's great-grandmothers, such **that** the Sage **counts his wife** as one of the generations and refers to them as the fourth generation, **and what is different** with regard to the generations **below,** referring to his great-granddaughters, such **that he did not count his wife** and referred to them as only the third generation? The Gemara answers: When counting **above, the prohibition stems from his wife,** as they are not his blood relatives but his wife's. Therefore, **she is counted.** When counting **below,** however, **the prohibition does not stem from his wife,** as they are his own blood relatives, **and so she was not counted.**

וְהָא בֶּן אִשְׁתּוֹ וּבַת אִשְׁתּוֹ, דְּאִיסּוּרָא מִכֹּחַ אִשְׁתּוֹ קָאָתֵי וְלָא חָשֵׁיב לָהּ! אַיְּידֵי דְּתָנָא שְׁלֹשָׁה דּוֹרוֹת לְמַטָּה דִּידֵיהּ, וְלָא חֲשָׁבָהּ, תָּנָא נַמִּי שְׁלֹשָׁה דּוֹרוֹת לְמַטָּה דִּידָהּ וְלָא חֲשָׁבָהּ.

The Gemara objects: **But** he includes the granddaughter of **his wife's son and his wife's daughter** in his list of those **forbidden due to his wife, yet he does not count her** and refer to this as the fourth generation. The Gemara answers: **Since he** already **taught three generations below himself,** i.e., his own great-granddaughter, **and** there **he did not count** from his wife because it is his own blood relative, **he taught three generations below** his wife **and did not count her.** Instead, he referred to her great-granddaughter also as three generations below to maintain the uniform style of his words.

אָמַר לֵיהּ רַב אַשִׁי לְרַב כָּהֲנָא: שְׁנִיּוֹת דְּבֵי רַבִּי חִיָּיא יֵשׁ לָהֶן הֶפְסֵק אוֹ אֵין לָהֶם הֶפְסֵק?

Rav Ashi said to Rav Kahana: Do those **secondary** forbidden **relationships** taught by one of the Sages **of the school of Rabbi Ḥiyya have a conclusion,**[H] **or do they not have a conclusion?** Are those specified cases alone forbidden, or are all generations above and below also forbidden?

תָּא שְׁמַע דְּאָמַר רַב: אַרְבַּע נָשִׁים יֵשׁ לָהֶם הֶפְסֵק. וְתוּ לָא. דִּלְמָא, כִּי קָאָמַר רַב – לְהַהִיא מַתְנִיתָא: תָּא שְׁמַע, שְׁלִישִׁי וּרְבִיעִי. שְׁלִישִׁי וּרְבִיעִי – אִין, טְפֵי – לָא! דִּלְמָא מִשְּׁלִישִׁי וְאֵילָךְ, מֵרְבִיעִי וְאֵילָךְ.

Come and **hear** that **which Rav said: Four women have a conclusion.** This implies that it is only these four **and no more.** The Gemara rejects this: **Perhaps when Rav said this he was referring** only **to** the relationships listed in **the *baraita*** and not to all cases of secondary relationships. The Gemara suggests: **Come** and **hear** from the *baraita* itself, which states: **The third** generation from his son and his daughter **and the fourth** generation from his father-in-law and mother-in-law. This implies that with regard to **the third and the fourth** generations, **yes,** they are forbidden; but **more** than that, **no.** The Gemara rejects this: **Perhaps** this means **from the third onward and from the fourth onward.** The Gemara does not resolve this issue.

אֲמַר לֵיהּ רָבָא לְרַב נַחְמָן: חֲזֵי מָר הַאי מֵרַבָּנַן דַּאֲתָא מִמַּעַרְבָא וַאֲמַר: בָּעוּ בְּמַעַרְבָא, גָּזְרוּ שְׁנִיּוֹת בְּגֵרִים אוֹ לֹא גָּזְרוּ שְׁנִיּוֹת בְּגֵרִים?

§ **Rava said to Rav Naḥman: Did the Master see this one of the Sages who came from the West,** Eretz Yisrael, **who said: In the West they asked** whether the Sages **issued a decree** prohibiting **secondary** forbidden **relationships for converts, or** whether **they did not issue a decree** prohibiting **secondary** forbidden **relationships for converts?**[N]

HALAKHA

The third generation from one's son and one's daughter – שְׁלִישִׁי שֶׁבִּבְנוֹ וְשֶׁבְּבִתּוֹ: One's great-granddaughter is forbidden as a secondary relation (Rambam *Sefer Nashim, Hilkhot Ishut* 1:6; *Shulḥan Arukh, Even HaEzer* 15:12).

The third generation from the son and daughter of his wife – שְׁלִישִׁי שֶׁבְּבֶן וְשֶׁבְּבַת אִשְׁתּוֹ: One's wife's great-granddaughter is forbidden as a secondary relation (*Shulḥan Arukh, Even HaEzer* 15:14; and see Rambam *Sefer Nashim, Hilkhot Ishut* 1:6 and *Kesef Mishne* there).

The fourth generation from his father-in-law and from his mother-in-law – רְבִיעִי שֶׁבַּחֲמִיו וְשֶׁבַּחֲמוֹתוֹ: One's wife's great-grandmother is forbidden as a secondary relation (Rambam *Sefer Nashim, Hilkhot Ishut* 1:6; *Shulḥan Arukh, Even HaEzer* 15:15).

A conclusion for the secondary forbidden relationships of Rabbi Ḥiyya – הֶפְסֵק בִּשְׁנִיּוֹת דְּרַבִּי חִיָּיא: The Rosh holds that the secondary relations enumerated by Rabbi Ḥiyya do not end but continue upward and downward for all generations (see Ramban). According to the Rambam they do end, since the Gemara does not give a definitive answer, and in cases of uncertainty with regard to rabbinic decrees, the *halakha* is ruled in accordance with the lenient opinion (Rambam *Sefer Nashim, Hilkhot Ishut* 1:6; *Shulḥan Arukh, Even HaEzer* 15:15).

NOTES

Secondary forbidden relationships for converts – שְׁנִיּוֹת בְּגֵרִים: The reason for the rabbinic prohibition against marriage of converts to their relatives is lest the converts say that they came from a more stringent sanctity as gentiles to a state of lesser sanctity as Jews, since previously forbidden relationships would then be permitted to them. The Ritva writes that by this rationale, in the case of one who converts to Judaism from a religion that is more stringent with regard to forbidden relationships, these relations should remain forbidden to the convert even after his conversion to Judaism.

אֲמַר לֵיהּ: הַשְׁתָּא, וּמָה עֶרְוָה גּוּפָהּ, אִי לָאו שֶׁלֹּא יֹאמְרוּ בָּאִין מִקְּדוּשָּׁה חֲמוּרָה לִקְדוּשָּׁה קַלָּה לֹא גָּזְרוּ בְּהוּ רַבָּנַן – שְׁנִיּוֹת מִיבַּעְיָא?!

Rav Naḥman did not answer whether he had seen this Sage, but **said to him: Now, with regard to** all the **forbidden relationships themselves, were it not** for the fact that if converts would find that as Jews they were permitted to enter into relationships that were forbidden to them as gentiles and **would say** that they went from **a state of more stringent sanctity** as gentiles **to a state of lesser sanctity** as Jews, **then the Sages would not have decreed** to prohibit these relationships.[H] Without the rabbinic decree it would have been permitted for a convert to marry even a close female relative, even his twin sister, who also converted. This is because a convert has the legal status of a newborn, with no family ties. **Is it necessary** to state that the Sages did not extend that decree to include **secondary** forbidden **relationships?**[H] The purpose of the rabbinic prohibitions is to protect the Torah prohibitions, but in the case of converts this particular Torah prohibition does not apply.

אֲמַר רַב נַחְמָן: גֵּרִים, הוֹאִיל וְאָתוּ לִידַן נֵימָא בְּהוּ מִלְּתָא: אַחִין מִן הָאֵם לֹא יָעִידוּ, וְאִם הֵעִידוּ – עֵדוּתָן עֵדוּת. אַחִין מִן הָאָב מְעִידִין לְכַתְּחִלָּה. אַמֵימָר אָמַר: אֲפִילּוּ אַחִין מִן הָאֵם נַמִי מְעִידִין לְכַתְּחִלָּה.

Rav Naḥman said: Since the issue of **converts** and their relatives **has come to hand** and is the topic of discussion, **let us say a matter** of *halakha*: **Maternal** half **brothers** who both convert **may not testify** together as a pair of witnesses before the court, **but if they did testify, their testimony is valid.** Although blood relatives are invalid as witnesses, converts are considered as though they have no relations. **Paternal** half **brothers** who both convert **may testify** together ***ab initio***, since the *halakha* does not consider paternal half brothers of gentiles to be true relatives. **Ameimar said: Even maternal** half **brothers may also testify** together ***ab initio***.[H]

וּמַאי שְׁנָא מֵעֲרָיוֹת? עֶרְוָה לַכֹּל מְסוּרָה, עֵדוּת – לְבֵית דִּין מְסוּרָה, וְגֵר שֶׁנִּתְגַּיֵּיר כְּקָטָן שֶׁנּוֹלַד דָּמֵי.

In **what** way **is** this case **different from forbidden relations,**[N] where a convert may not marry his maternal sister due to rabbinic decree? The *halakhot* of **forbidden relations are handed over to all,** and every individual chooses his own wife. Therefore, the Sages issued a decree to prevent confusion between the status of a convert and that of a born Jew. However, **testimony is handed over to the court,** and the court knows to distinguish between the status of a born Jew and that of a convert. **And** the legal status of **a convert who** just **converted is like** that of **a child** just **born,**[HB] and all previous family ties become irrelevant.

מתני׳ מִי שֶׁיֵּשׁ לוֹ אָח מִכָּל מָקוֹם – זוֹקֵק אֶת אֵשֶׁת אָחִיו לְיִבּוּם, וְאָחִיו הוּא לְכָל דָּבָר, חוּץ מִמִּי שֶׁיֵּשׁ לוֹ אָח מִן הַשִּׁפְחָה וּמִן הַגּוֹיָה. מִי שֶׁיֵּשׁ לוֹ בֵּן מִכָּל מָקוֹם – פּוֹטֵר אֵשֶׁת אָבִיו מִן הַיִּבּוּם, וְחַיָּיב עַל מַכָּתוֹ וְעַל קִלְלָתוֹ, וּבְנוֹ לְכָל דָּבָר – חוּץ מִמִּי שֶׁיֵּשׁ לוֹ בֵּן מִן הַשִּׁפְחָה וּמִן הַגּוֹיָה.

MISHNA In the case of **anyone who has a brother of any kind,**[HN] that brother **creates a levirate bond** causing his *yevama* **to** be required to **perform levirate marriage** if the first brother dies childless. **And he is his brother in all respects, except for one who has a brother** born **from** a Canaanite **maidservant or from a gentile woman,** as these do not have the legal status of brothers. Similarly, in the case of **anyone who has a child of any kind,**[H] that child **exempts his father's wife from levirate marriage,** since his father did not die childless. **And** that child **is liable** to receive capital punishment **if he strikes** his father **or curses him. And he is his child in all respects, except for whoever has a child** born **from** a Canaanite **maidservant or from a gentile woman,** as these do not have the halakhic status of children.

HALAKHA

Forbidden relations for a convert – **אִיסּוּר עֲרָיוֹת בְּגֵר**: By Torah law it is permitted for a convert to marry any of his relatives who converted, even his mother or sister. However, the Sages decreed it prohibited for converts to marry close relatives so that one who converted would not think that he came from a greater state of sanctity, before he was Jewish, into a state of lesser sanctity (Rambam *Sefer Kedusha, Hilkhot Issurei Bia* 14:12; *Shulḥan Arukh, Yoreh De'a* 269:1).

Secondary relationships for a convert – **שְׁנִיּוֹת בְּגֵר**: The Sages did not render prohibited secondary relationships of converts. Therefore, a convert may marry his maternal grandmother. Similarly, a born Jew is permitted to marry a converted woman and her maternal grandmother, though marrying a woman and her grandmother who were born Jewish is a rabbinic prohibition (*Shulḥan Arukh, Yoreh De'a* 269:8).

Testimony of related converts – **עֵדוּת גֵּרִים קְרוֹבִים**: Once a gentile converts, his biological relations no longer have the legal status of relations. Even if twin brothers convert, they may testify together as a pair of witnesses (Rambam *Sefer Shofetim, Hilkhot Edut* 13:2; *Shulḥan Arukh, Yoreh De'a* 269:10 and *Ḥoshen Mishpat* 33:11).

The legal status of a convert who just converted is like that of a child just born – **גֵּר שֶׁנִּתְגַּיֵּיר כְּקָטָן שֶׁנּוֹלַד דָּמֵי**: A gentile who converts and a freed gentile slave have the legal status of newly born children, and any previous familial relationships are considered nonexistent (Rambam *Sefer Kedusha, Hilkhot Issurei Bia* 14:11; *Shulḥan Arukh, Yoreh De'a* 269:10 and *Ḥoshen Mishpat* 33:11).

A brother of any kind – **אָח מִכָּל מָקוֹם**: Every paternal half brother, even if he is of flawed lineage or a *mamzer*, causes his *yevama* to require levirate marriage or *ḥalitza*. A half brother whose mother is a gentile or a Canaanite maidservant is not considered a brother in this regard (Rambam *Sefer Nashim, Hilkhot Yibbum VaḤalitza* 1:6; *Shulḥan Arukh, Even HaEzer* 157:1).

A child of any kind – **בֵּן מִכָּל מָקוֹם**: If one dies and leaves a child or any descendants, whether of unflawed or flawed lineage, even a *mamzer*, his widow is exempt from levirate marriage. This holds true in all cases except for children from Canaanite maidservants or gentile women (Rambam *Sefer Nashim, Hilkhot Yibbum VaḤalitza* 1:3–4; *Shulḥan Arukh, Even HaEzer* 156:2).

NOTES

In what way is this case different from forbidden relations – **וּמַאי שְׁנָא מֵעֲרָיוֹת**: *Tosafot* ask: The reason just given, i.e., lest it be said that the converts came from a more stringent level of sanctity to a more lenient level, should be sufficient to explain the difference between forbidden relations and testimony. With regard to the *halakhot* of testimony there is no disqualification for gentiles who are related. They explain that the primary reason for the rabbinic decree is to avoid confusion with regard to such relationships between Jews. This rationale fits with the opinion that maternal brothers may not testify together *ab initio*, as in such a case there is also a concern that it may lead to confusion (see Ritva; *Tosafot Yeshanim*).

A brother of any kind – **אָח מִכָּל מָקוֹם**: The Gemara explains that this expression was adopted in order to teach the additional case of a brother who is a *mamzer*. This discussion is also the basis for those early commentaries who rule that a brother who converts to another religion still causes his *yevama* to require levirate marriage. Some commentaries differentiated between a brother who had already converted to another religion at the time of his brother's marriage and one who converted after the marriage (see *Otzar HaGe'onim*; Ritva).

BACKGROUND

The legal status of a convert who just converted is like that of a child just born – **גֵּר שֶׁנִּתְגַּיֵּיר שֶׁנּוֹלַד דָּמֵי כְּקָטָן**: This is a fundamental principle in *halakha*, and it means that through the act of conversion a convert becomes like a new person and all ties that he had with his previous gentile world are severed. Since he is considered like a newly born child, all his biological relations are consequently not considered by *halakha* to be related to him. Despite this, the Sages decreed that a gentile may not marry one of his blood relatives if they also converted. There are two reasons for this: (1) A convert might think that he has descended from a greater sanctity to a lesser sanctity. The Sages did not want him to think that what was forbidden to him as a gentile is now permitted. A convert intends to ascend to a higher sanctity and does not seek leniencies. (2) Others may not realize that this individual is a convert, and therefore when they see him marrying a woman who appears to be forbidden to him, this might lead them to erroneous conclusions.

גמ׳ מִכָּל מָקוֹם לְאַתּוּיֵי מַאי? אָמַר רַב יְהוּדָה לְאַתּוּיֵי מַמְזֵר. פְּשִׁיטָא, אָחִיו הוּא! מַהוּ דְּתֵימָא: לֵילַף אַחֲוָה אַחֲוָה מִבְּנֵי יַעֲקֹב, מַה לְהַלָּן כְּשֵׁרִין וְלֹא פְּסוּלִין, אַף כָּאן כְּשֵׁרִין וְלֹא פְּסוּלִין – קָא מַשְׁמַע לָן.

GEMARA The Gemara asks: With regard to the statement that a brother **of any kind** causes his *yevama* to be required to perform levirate marriage, **what** additional case does this come **to add? Rav Yehuda said: This adds** the case of **a** ***mamzer***, who, notwithstanding his status, is considered a brother. The Gemara wonders: But **isn't** that **obvious? He is his brother.** The Gemara explains: This is necessary **lest you say: Let us derive** a verbal analogy between the word **"brother"** stated in the verse with regard to levirate marriage and **"brother"** stated with regard to **the children of Jacob. Just as there,** Jacob's children **are of unflawed** lineage **and not** of **flawed** lineage and are not *mamzerim*, **so too here,** one might think that only brothers of **unflawed** lineage **and not** brothers of **flawed** lineage, i.e., *mamzerim*, obligate the *yevama* in levirate marriage. Therefore, **this teaches us** that a *mamzer* is considered a brother for the purposes of levirate marriage.

וְאֵימָא הָכִי נַמִי! כֵּיוָן דִּלְעִנְיַן יִבּוּם מִיפְטַר נָפְטַר

The Gemara asks: **And say that** is **indeed** the *halakha*. Perhaps a brother who is a *mamzer* does not obligate his *yevama* in levirate marriage. The Gemara answers: **Since with regard to levirate marriage,** if the husband had a child who was a *mamzer* he would **exempt** the wife from levirate marriage,

מִיזְקַק נַמִי זָקֵיק.

the husband's brother **also causes a levirate bond** with his *yevama* even if he is a *mamzer*.

״וְאָחִיו הוּא לְכָל דָּבָר״. לְמַאי הִלְכְתָא? לְיוֹרְשׁוֹ וְלִיטַּמֵּא לוֹ.

§ The mishna stated that **he is his brother in all respects.** The Gemara asks: **With regard to what** ***halakha*** was this said? The Gemara answers: **To inherit** from **him,**[H] **and to become ritually impure for him**[H] if he is a priest, as a brother is one of the relations for whom a priest is permitted to become ritually impure by attending his funeral.

פְּשִׁיטָא, אָחִיו הוּא! סָלְקָא דַּעְתָּךְ אָמִינָא: הוֹאִיל וּכְתִיב ״כִּי אִם לִשְׁאֵרוֹ הַקָּרוֹב אֵלָיו״ וַאֲמַר מָר: שְׁאֵרוֹ – זוֹ אִשְׁתּוֹ, וּכְתִיב ״לֹא יִטַּמָּא בַּעַל בְּעַמָּיו לְהֵחַלּוֹ״, יֵשׁ בַּעַל שֶׁמִּטַּמֵּא וְיֵשׁ בַּעַל שֶׁאֵין מִטַּמֵּא, הָא כֵּיצַד? מִטַּמֵּא הוּא לְאִשְׁתּוֹ כְּשֵׁרָה, וְאֵין מִטַּמֵּא לְאִשְׁתּוֹ פְּסוּלָה,

The Gemara asks: **Isn't** this **obvious,** as **he is his brother?** The Gemara answers: It might **enter your mind to say** that a priest does not become impure for his brother of flawed lineage, **since it is written** with regard to priests: "None shall defile himself for the dead among his people **except for his kin, that is near unto him**" (Leviticus 21:1–2), **and the Master said "his kin"; this is his wife,** and a priest may defile himself for his wife. **But it is written: "He shall not defile himself, being a husband among his people, to profane himself"** (Leviticus 21:4), implying that he may not defile himself for his wife. This apparent contradiction is resolved as follows: **There is a husband who does become impure** for his wife, **and there is a husband who does not become impure. How so? He becomes impure for his wife if she was fit** and was permitted to a priest, **but he does not become impure for his wife** if she was **unfit**[H] to marry a priest.

הָכִי נַמִי מִטַּמֵּא הוּא לְאָח כָּשֵׁר וְאֵין מִטַּמֵּא לְאָח פָּסוּל, קָא מַשְׁמַע לָן. וְאֵימָא הָכִי נַמִי! הָתָם לְאַפּוּקֵי קַיְימָא, הָכָא – אָחִיו הוּא.

So too, one might have thought that a priest **becomes impure for a brother who is** of **unflawed** lineage and not a *mamzer*, **but he does not become impure for a brother** of **flawed** lineage. Therefore, **this comes to teach us** that he does become impure for a brother who is a *mamzer*. The Gemara asks: **Say this also,** that by the same reasoning by which a priest may not become impure for a wife who was unfit for him, he may not become impure for an unfit brother either. Just as he does not become impure for an unfit wife, he should not become impure for an unfit brother? The Gemara answers: The two cases are different, as **there,** with regard to the unfit wife, **she stands to be dismissed,**[N] since according to Torah law unfit women must be divorced. For this reason he does not become impure for her. **Here, he is his brother.**

HALAKHA

To inherit from him – לְיוֹרְשׁוֹ: All relatives, even those born through transgression, inherit just as those born in accordance with *halakha*. A *mamzer* brother or son inherits just like offspring of unflawed lineage (Rambam *Sefer Mishpatim, Hilkhot Naḥalot* 1:7; *Shulḥan Arukh, Ḥoshen Mishpat* 276:6).

To become ritually impure for him – לִיטַּמֵּא לוֹ: A priest becomes ritually impure for his father, his mother, his brother, his unmarried sister, his son, and his daughter, even if they are unfit or *mamzerim* (Rambam *Sefer Shofetim, Hilkhot Evel* 2:9; *Shulḥan Arukh, Yoreh De'a* 373:4).

His wife if she was unfit – אִשְׁתּוֹ פְּסוּלָה: A priest becomes ritually impure for his wife if she was permitted to marry him, but if it was prohibited for her to marry him he may not become impure for her (Rambam *Sefer Shofetim, Hilkhot Evel* 2:9; *Shulḥan Arukh, Yoreh De'a* 373:4).

NOTES

She stands to be dismissed – לְאַפּוּקֵי קַיְימָא: With regard to the exceptions when a priest may become ritually impure, the Torah states: "Except for his kin, that is near unto him" (Leviticus 21:2). The Gemara explains that "his kin" is referring to his wife. A wife who is prohibited to the priest is not considered to be "his kin."

"חוץ ממי שיש לו אח מן השפחה ומן הגויה", מאי טעמא? אמר קרא "האשה וילדיה תהיה לאדוניה".

§ The mishna says: **Except for whoever has a brother** born **from a** Canaanite **maidservant or from a gentile woman,** as in these cases he is not considered a brother. The Gemara asks: **What is the reason** for this *halakha*? The Gemara answers: **The verse states** with regard to a Jewish slave who has children with a Canaanite maidservant: **"The wife and her children shall be her master's"** (Exodus 21:4). This means that the children also have the status of Canaanite slaves, which implies that the lineage of a Canaanite maidservant's child comes from the mother and not from the father.

"מי שיש לו בן מכל מקום פוטר" וכו'. מכל מקום לאתויי מאי? אמר רב יהודה: לאיתויי ממזר. מאי טעמא? דאמר קרא "ובן אין לו" – עיין עליו.

The mishna states: With regard to **anyone who has a son of any kind,**[N] that son **exempts** his father's wife from any levirate bond. The Gemara asks: **What is added** by the phrase: **Of any kind? Rav Yehuda said: It adds** a child who is **a** ***mamzer*****. What is the reason** that a *mamzer* exempts a woman from any levirate bond? **As the verse states** with regard to levirate marriage: **"And he has no [*ain lo*] child"** (Deuteronomy 25:5). The phrase *ain lo* can be understood as *ayyen alav*, meaning **investigate him.**[N] That is to say, investigate whether he is indeed childless, because any child, even a *mamzer*, exempts the widow from a levirate bond.

"וחייב על מכתו", אמאי? קרי כאן "ונשיא בעמך לא תאור" – בעושה מעשה עמך!

It states in the mishna that a child who is a *mamzer* **is liable** to receive punishment **if he strikes** his father or curses him.[H] The Gemara asks: **Why** should he be liable? **Read here** the verse: **"You shall not curse a ruler of your people"** (Exodus 22:27), which is interpreted to imply that the prohibition against cursing applies only **to one who acts according to the deeds of your people.**[N] However, this father must have engaged in sexual relations with a woman who was forbidden to him in order to have a child who is a *mamzer*. Therefore, he did not act according to the deeds of the people. In that case, why should this son be liable to receive punishment for hitting him or cursing him?

כדאמר רב פנחס משמיה דרב פפא: בעושה תשובה – הכא נמי כשעשה תשובה.

The Gemara answers: **As Rav Pineḥas said in the name of Rav Pappa** with regard to a different matter: This is referring to **one who performs repentance. Here too,** it is referring to **one who performed repentance** after the *mamzer* was born. He is thereafter considered to be living in accordance with *halakha*, and so his *mamzer* son is liable to receive punishment for cursing him.

והאי בר תשובה הוא? והתנן: שמעון בן מנסיא אומר: איזהו "מעוות לא יוכל לתקון", זה הבא על הערוה והוליד ממנה ממזר! השתא מיהא עושה מעשה עמך הוא.

The Gemara objects: **Is he in fact able to repent** after fathering a *mamzer*? **Didn't we learn** in a mishna that **Shimon ben Menasya says: Which is: "That which is crooked cannot be made straight"** (Ecclesiastes 1:15)? **This is** referring to **one who engaged in intercourse with a relative** who is **forbidden** to him **and fathered a** ***mamzer*** **with her.** This implies that he has no possibility of achieving total repentance. The Gemara responds: **At least now,** after repenting, **he** is considered as one who **acts according to the deeds of your people.** Although he cannot totally rectify his transgression, his child is liable to receive punishment for cursing or hitting him.

תנו רבנן: הבא על אחותו והיא בת אשת אביו – חייב משום אחותו, ומשום בת אשת אביו. רבי יוסי בן יהודה אומר: אינו חייב אלא משום אחותו בלבד, ולא מפני בת אשת אביו.

§ **The Sages taught: He who** unwittingly **engages in sexual relations with his sister, who is the daughter of his father's** lawful **wife,**[H] **is liable** and must bring two sin-offerings. He must bring one sin-offering **because** she is **his sister**[H] and another **because** she is **the daughter of his father's wife,** which is mentioned in a separate verse in the Torah. **Rabbi Yosei ben Yehuda says: He is liable only because** she is **his sister alone, and not because** of the prohibition against engaging in sexual relations with **the daughter of his father's wife.**

מאי טעמייהו דרבנן? אמרי: מכדי כתיב "ערות אחותך בת אביך או בת אמך" "ערות בת אשת אביך מולדת אביך אחותך היא" למה לי? שמע מינה: לחייבו משום אחותו ומשום בת אשת אביו.

The Gemara asks: **What is the reason** for the opinion **of the Rabbis,** the first *tanna* of the *baraita*? **They said: Since it is written** in the Torah: **"The nakedness of your sister, the daughter of your father, or the daughter of your mother**…you shall not uncover" (Leviticus 18:9), then **why do I need** the verse: **"The nakedness of your father's wife's daughter, begotten of your father, she is your sister**…you shall not uncover" (Leviticus 18:11)? **Conclude from this** that the additional verse serves **to make him liable** separately **due to** the fact that she is **his sister and due to** the fact that she is **his father's wife's daughter.**

NOTES

A son of any kind – בן מכל מקום: In the Jerusalem Talmud the following point is added: Since he is considered his son in all regards, the father fulfills the mitzva to be fruitful and multiply through this son. Also, he is considered his son with regard to all matters of forbidden relations.

And he has no child, meaning investigate him – ובן אין לו, עיין עליו: Rashi explains that the word "no [*ain*]" could have been written without the letter *yod*. The homiletical interpretation is derived from the additional letter; the word spelled in this way bears similarity to the word for eye [*ayyen*], which implies investigation (see *Tosefot Yom Tov*). In the *Sma* this interpretation is explained differently: The Torah's stress on the phrase "has no" indicates that he has absolutely no children of any kind in any place.

One who acts according to the deeds of your people – עושה מעשה עמך: Rambam maintains that a *mamzer* son is still obligated to respect his father and to fear him even if he is exempt from punishment for cursing or striking him (*Sefer Shofetim, Hilkhot Mamrim* 6:11). However, other authorities disagree (*Tur, Yoreh De'a* 240).

HALAKHA

He is liable to receive punishment if he strikes his father or curses him – חייב על מכתו ועל קללתו: According to the opinion of the Rambam and the Rif, even if parents were totally wicked and transgressors, and even if they were sentenced to death, it is prohibited for the son to strike them or curse them. However, *Tosafot* hold that in such a case there is no prohibition. If he did strike them or curse them in that case, then he is exempt from punishment. If they repented, even if they were sentenced to death, he is liable to receive punishment for striking or cursing them, even if he is acting as the agent of the court carrying out their punishment (Rambam *Sefer Shofetim, Hilkhot Mamrim* 5:12; *Shulḥan Arukh, Yoreh De'a* 241:4).

His sister…the daughter of his father's wife – אחותו...בת אשת אביו: If one engages in sexual relations with his sister born of a woman married to his father, he is liable twice, once for his sister and once for the daughter of his father's wife, in accordance with the opinion of the first *tanna* and against the lone dissenting opinion (Rambam *Sefer Kedusha, Hilkhot Issurei Bia* 2:4).

Prohibition against relations with one's sister – איסור אחותו: One's sister is forbidden to him by Torah law, whether she is his maternal or paternal half-sister, and whether she is fit or unfit for marriage, and even if she is a *mamzeret*, except for a sister born to his father by a gentile woman or a Canaanite maidservant, as then she is not considered his sister at all (*Shulḥan Arukh, Even HaEzer* 15:10).

וְרַבִּי יוֹסֵי בְּרַבִּי יְהוּדָה: אָמַר קְרָא "אֲחוֹתְךָ הִיא", מִשּׁוּם אֲחוֹתוֹ אַתָּה מְחַיְּיבוֹ וְאִי אַתָּה מְחַיְּיבוֹ מִשּׁוּם בַּת אֵשֶׁת אָבִיו –

And Rabbi Yosei, son of Rabbi Yehuda, says: **The verse states: "She is your sister,"** which comes to limit and emphasize that **you hold him liable due to** the fact that she is **his sister but you do not hold him liable** a second time **due to** the fact that she is also **his father's wife's daughter.**

וְרַבָּנַן, הַאי "אֲחוֹתְךָ הִיא" מַאי עָבְדִי לֵיהּ? מִיבְּעֵי לְהוּ לְחַיְּיבוֹ עַל אֲחוֹתוֹ בַּת אָבִיו וּבַת אִמּוֹ, לוֹמַר שֶׁאֵין מַזְהִירִין מִן הַדִּין.

The Gemara asks: **And what do the Rabbis do with this** verse: **"She is your sister"? They require it in order to hold him liable** to receive punishment **for** having relations with **his sister** who is both **the daughter of his father and the daughter of his mother, to say that** the Sages **do not** derive an additional Torah **prohibition by way of a logical derivation,** i.e., an *a fortiori* inference.[N] In other words, although it would seem that since he is liable to receive punishment for having relations with his father's daughter and also for his mother's daughter, this must be all the more true in a case where she is the daughter of both his father and his mother, yet nevertheless, there is no new prohibition here. Therefore, the matter was taught explicitly in the Torah, to teach that the Sages may not derive additional prohibitions by way of *a fortiori* inferences.

וְרַבִּי יוֹסֵי בְּרַבִּי יְהוּדָה? אִם כֵּן לִכְתּוֹב רַחֲמָנָא "אֲחוֹתְךָ", "הִיא" לָמָּה לִי – מִשּׁוּם אֲחוֹתְךָ אַתָּה מְחַיְּיבוֹ וְאִי אַתָּה מְחַיְּיבוֹ מִשּׁוּם בַּת אֵשֶׁת אָבִיו.

And Rabbi Yosei, son of Rabbi Yehuda, says: **If so,** that the matter was written for this purpose, **then the Merciful One should have written only: Your sister. Why do I** need the phrase **"she is"?** This limits the *halakha* and teaches that for unintentional intercourse with his sister who is also his father's wife's daughter **you hold him liable because** she is **his sister; you do not** additionally **hold him liable because** she is **his father's wife's daughter.**

וְרַבָּנַן? אַף עַל גַּב דִּכְתִיב "אֲחוֹתְךָ" אִיצְטְרִיךְ לְמִכְתַּב "הִיא", שֶׁלֹּא תֹּאמַר: בְּעָלְמָא מַזְהִירִין מִן הַדִּין.

And how do **the Rabbis** interpret the additional phrase "she is"? **Although "your sister" is written, it was necessary to write "she is" so that you not say** that **generally** the Sages may derive additional **prohibitions by way of a logical derivation,** i.e., an *a fortiori* inference.

וְכִי תֵּימָא: "אֲחוֹתְךָ" דִּכְתַב רַחֲמָנָא לָמָּה לִי – מִילְּתָא דְּאָתְיָא בְּקַל וָחוֹמֶר טָרַח וְכָתַב לָהּ קְרָא – כְּתַב רַחֲמָנָא "הִיא".

The Gemara explains how this principle is derived from the text. **As, if you would say: Why do I** need the term **"your sister" that the Merciful One writes** in the Torah, since it is possible to derive this by *a fortiori* inference and it therefore appears redundant? The answer is that the Torah wrote this apparently redundant term to teach the principle that with regard to **a matter that** could **be derived by** means of an ***a fortiori* inference, the verse unnecessarily wrote it** explicitly. **The Merciful One writes** the term **"she is"** in order to teach that just as in this case the Sages may not derive additional prohibitions by way of an *a fortiori* inference, so too, in all other cases they may not derive additional prohibitions that are not stated in the text.

וְרַבִּי יוֹסֵי בְּרַבִּי יְהוּדָה: אִם כֵּן לִיכְתְּבֵיהּ רַחֲמָנָא לַ"אֲחוֹתְךָ הִיא" בְּאִידָּךְ קְרָא.

And Rabbi Yosei, son of Rabbi Yehuda, says: **If** this is the reason for the verse, **then let the Merciful One write: She is your sister, in the other verse,** which states: "The nakedness of your sister, the daughter of your father, or the daughter of your mother," and not in the verse that speaks of the daughter of one's father's wife.

וְרַבִּי יוֹסֵי בְּרַבִּי יְהוּדָה, הַאי "בַּת אֵשֶׁת אָבִיךָ" מַאי עָבֵיד לֵיהּ? מִיבְּעֵי לֵיהּ: מִי שֶׁיֵּשׁ לוֹ אִישׁוּת לְאָבִיךָ בָּהּ, פְּרָט לַאֲחוֹתוֹ מִשִּׁפְחָה וְגוֹיָה, שֶׁאֵין אִישׁוּת לְאָבִיךָ בָּהּ.

The Gemara asks: **And what does Rabbi Yosei, son of Rabbi Yehuda, do with this** verse, which states: **"The daughter of your father's wife"** (Leviticus 18:9)? **He requires it** to teach that one is liable only for relations with a half-sister whose mother is **someone with whom there is no** possibility of forging **marital** ties **with your father,** even if she was not in actuality his wife. This comes **to exclude his sister from** a Canaanite **maidservant or a gentile woman, with whom your father cannot have marital** ties, since betrothal does not take effect with these women.

וְאֵימָא: פְּרָט לַאֲחוֹתוֹ מֵאֲנוּסָה? הַהִיא לָא מָצֵית אָמְרַתְּ, מִדְּרָבָא.

The Gemara asks: **So say:** "Your father's wife's daughter" comes to teach specifically the case of a daughter from a woman married to his father, thereby **excluding from** the definition of: His sister, **his sister from a woman who had been raped.** Perhaps if she was born of a woman who was not married to his father she would not be considered his sister. The Gemara answers: **You cannot say that due to** the reason said by **Rava.**

NOTES

The Sages do not derive an additional prohibition by way of a logical derivation – אֵין מַזְהִירִין מִן הַדִּין: Some commentaries explain that according to all opinions, one is permitted in general to draw his own *a fortiori* inferences. Therefore, there is concern that one might err in his considerations on the matter, and consequently these inferences may not be relied upon in cases where it would lead to one being liable to receive lashes. On the other hand, the Maharsha in tractate *Sanhedrin* cites the *Sefer Mitzvot Gadol* and states that it is unknown whether the punishment derived by an *a fortiori* inference is severe enough to atone for the transgression performed. Others explain that this principle is a Torah decree, without reason (*Yosef Lekaḥ*).

HALAKHA

His sister by a woman his father raped – אֲחוֹתוֹ מֵאֲנוּסָתוֹ: If a daughter was born from a woman his father raped, rather than married, then as that daughter's paternal half brother he is liable to receive punishment for relations with her only because she is his sister but not as the daughter of his father's wife (Rambam *Sefer Kedusha, Hilkhot Issurei Bia* 2:4).

דְּרָבָא רָמֵי: כְּתִיב "עֶרְוַת בַּת בִּנְךָ אוֹ בַת בִּתְּךָ לֹא תְגַלֶּה", הָא בַּת בְּנָהּ דִּידָהּ וּבַת בִּתָּהּ דִּידָהּ – שָׁרֵי, וּכְתִיב "עֶרְוַת אִשָּׁה וּבִתָּהּ לֹא תְגַלֵּה אֶת בַּת בְּנָהּ וְאֶת בַּת בִּתָּהּ". הָא כֵּיצַד?

As Rava raised a contradiction: In one verse **it is written: "The nakedness of your son's daughter, or of your daughter's daughter, you shall not uncover"** (Leviticus 18:10), which implies, **consequently,** that her **son's daughter or her daughter's daughter is permitted. And it is written** elsewhere: **"You shall not uncover the nakedness of a woman and her daughter; you shall not take her son's daughter or her daughter's daughter"** (Leviticus 18:17), which states explicitly that her son's daughter and daughter's daughter are prohibited. **How can these** texts be reconciled?

כָּאן בְּאוֹנָסִין כָּאן בְּנִשּׂוּאִין.

Here, it is referring to a daughter by a woman whom one **raped,** in which case he is allowed to marry her daughter provided she is not also his daughter. **There,** it is referring to a woman whom one **married,** in which case it is forbidden to marry her daughter under any circumstances. However, even in a case where one's father raped a woman, one is still permitted to marry the woman's daughter by another man. If one's father had a daughter with this woman, one would be prohibited from having a relationship with that daughter, as she is his paternal half-sister.[H]

Perek **II**
Daf **23** Amud **a**

HALAKHA

Betrothal comes into effect with women who are forbidden and one would be liable for violating prohibitions – חַיָּיבֵי לָאוִין תָּפְסִי בְּהוּ קִדּוּשִׁין: If one betroths a woman forbidden to him by a prohibition, the betrothal is nevertheless fully effective (Rambam *Sefer Nashim, Hilkhot Ishut* 4:14; *Shulḥan Arukh, Even HaEzer* 44:7).

Prohibition against union with one's sister – אִיסּוּר אָחוֹת: One's sister is forbidden to him by Torah law, whether she is a paternal or maternal sister, whether she is a sister from her father's marriage or outside of marriage. Even a sister born from a forbidden union is considered a sister and one is liable to receive punishment for having relations with her (Rambam *Sefer Kedusha, Hilkhot Issurei Bia* 2:1; *Shulḥan Arukh, Even HaEzer* 15:10).

וְאֵימָא פְּרָט לְחַיָּיבֵי לָאוִין? אָמַר רַב פַּפָּא: חַיָּיבֵי לָאוִין תָּפְסִי בְּהוּ קִדּוּשִׁין,

The Gemara raises a challenge: **And say** that the verse: "The daughter of your father's wife" comes to **exclude** women who were forbidden, as they are **liable** for violating **prohibitions** but were nevertheless married to his father, such as a *mamzeret*. If so, his sister from such a union would not be considered his sister. **Rav Pappa said: Betrothal comes into effect with** women who are forbidden, and one would be **liable** for violating **prohibitions**[H] despite the fact that union with them is forbidden, and so she is called the wife of your father.

דִּכְתִיב "כִּי תִהְיֶיןָ לְאִישׁ שְׁתֵּי נָשִׁים הָאַחַת אֲהוּבָה וְהָאַחַת שְׂנוּאָה", וְכִי יֵשׁ אֲהוּבָה לִפְנֵי הַמָּקוֹם וְיֵשׁ שְׂנוּאָה לִפְנֵי הַמָּקוֹם? אֶלָּא: אֲהוּבָה – אֲהוּבָה בְּנִישּׂוּאֶיהָ, שְׂנוּאָה – שְׂנוּאָה בְּנִישּׂוּאֶיהָ, וְאָמַר רַחֲמָנָא: "כִּי תִהְיֶיןָ".

This is derived from the verse in **which it is written: "If a man has two wives, the one beloved, and the other hated"** (Deuteronomy 21:15). **Is there one** who is **loved by the Omnipresent and one** who is **hated by the Omnipresent? Rather, "beloved"** means **her marriage is beloved,** as it was permitted for her to be married, in accordance with *halakha*, and **"hated"** means **her marriage is hated** because it was not permitted for her to be married, according to *halakha*. **And the Merciful One states: "If** a man **has** two wives," meaning that both are considered to be married.

וְאֵימָא פְּרָט לְחַיָּיבֵי כְּרֵיתוֹת – אָמַר רָבָא: אָמַר קְרָא "עֶרְוַת אֲחוֹתְךָ בַת אָבִיךָ אוֹ בַת אִמֶּךָ מוֹלֶדֶת בַּיִת אוֹ מוֹלֶדֶת חוּץ", בֵּין שֶׁאוֹמְרִים לוֹ לְאָבִיךָ: "קַיֵּים", בֵּין שֶׁאוֹמְרִים לוֹ לְאָבִיךָ "הוֹצֵא", וְאָמַר רַחֲמָנָא: "אֲחוֹתְךָ הִיא" –

The Gemara asks: **Say** that this verse comes to **exclude** a union between one's father and a woman that is forbidden to him as they are **liable** to receive *karet*, and that since betrothal does not come into effect with her there is no marriage bond. Perhaps a sister born of such a woman would not be prohibited as the daughter of one's father's wife. **Rava said** that **the verse states: "The nakedness of your sister, the daughter of your father, or the daughter of your mother, whether born at home or born outside"** (Leviticus 18:9).[H] This includes all daughters, **whether** from a woman **for whom** the Sages **tell your father: Maintain** her within your home, or **whether** the Sages **tell your father** she is a woman who is forbidden to him and therefore: **Send her out** of your home. **And the Merciful One states** that nevertheless: **"She is your sister."** Even the daughter of a woman who was forbidden to your father such that both parties are liable to receive *karet* is called your sister.

אֵימָא: בֵּין שֶׁאוֹמֵר לוֹ אָבִיךָ ״קַיֵּים״ בֵּין שֶׁאוֹמֵר לוֹ אָבִיךָ ״הוֹצֵא״, וְאָמַר רַחֲמָנָא ״אֲחוֹתְךָ הִיא״ – לְרַבּוֹת אֲחוֹתוֹ מִשִּׁפְחָה וְגוֹיָה – אָמַר קְרָא ״בַּת אֵשֶׁת אָבִיךָ״, מִי שֶׁיֵּשׁ לוֹ אִישׁוּת לְאָבִיךָ בָּהּ, פְּרָט לַאֲחוֹתוֹ מִשִּׁפְחָה וְגוֹיָה.

The Gemara asks: **Say that whether** the Sages **say to** your **father: Maintain** her, **or whether** they say to your father: **Send her out, and the Merciful One states** that **"she is your sister,"** this comes **to include** the additional cases of **his sister from** a Canaanite **maidservant or a gentile woman.** The Gemara rejects this: **The verse states: "The daughter of your father's wife,"** and this means **whoever can enter a marriage bond with your father.** This **excludes his sister from** a Canaanite **maidservant or gentile woman,** with whom no marital bond is possible.

וּמָה רָאִית? מִסְתַּבְּרָא, חַיָּיבֵי כָּרֵיתוֹת הֲוָה לֵיהּ לְרַבּוֹת, שֶׁכֵּן תָּפְסִי בָּהֶן קִדּוּשִׁין לְעָלְמָא.

The Gemara asks: Since the verse rendering his sister forbidden both includes and excludes cases, **what did you see** as a reason to include a daughter from a woman who is forbidden and both parties are liable to receive *karet*, and to exclude the daughter of a Canaanite maidservant or gentile woman? The Gemara answers: **It stands to reason** that those relationships that are forbidden because they render both parties **liable** to receive ***karet* should be included, since in general betrothal can come into effect with them.** This is because although this woman is forbidden to his father, she is nevertheless permitted to other men.

אַדְּרַבָּה, שִׁפְחָה וְגוֹיָה הֲוָה לֵיהּ לְרַבּוֹת, דְּאִי מִגַּיְּירָה – לְדִידֵיהּ נַמִּי תָּפְסִי בָּהּ קִדּוּשִׁין! לְכִי מִגַּיְּירָה גּוּפָא אַחֲרִינָא הִיא.

The Gemara rejects this: **On the contrary, it should include** a Canaanite **maidservant or a gentile woman, as, if she converts, betrothal can come into effect with** the father **himself.** The Gemara answers: **When she converts, she is** considered like **a different body,** i.e., a new person, but when she was a gentile there was no possibility of marital relations with her. Therefore, the verse excludes her.

וְרַבָּנַן, לְמַעוֹטֵי שִׁפְחָה וְגוֹיָה מְנָא לְהוּ? נָפְקָא לְהוּ מֵ״הָאִשָּׁה וִילָדֶיהָ תִּהְיֶה לַאדוֹנֶיהָ״.

The Gemara asks: **And** with regard to **the Rabbis,** who infer a different matter from the verse "your father's wife's nakedness," **from where do they** derive the *halakha* **to exclude** one's sister from a Canaanite **maidservant or gentile woman?** The Gemara answers: **They derive it** from that which was said with regard to a Canaanite maidservant who was married to a Hebrew slave: **"The wife and her children**[N] **shall be her master's"** (Exodus 21:4). From here they learn that the lineage of the maidservant's children is connected only to their mother and not at all connected to their Jewish father.

וְרַבִּי יוֹסֵי בְּרַבִּי יְהוּדָה: חַד – בְּשִׁפְחָה, וְחַד – בְּגוֹיָה. וּצְרִיכִי, דְּאִי אַשְׁמְעִינַן שִׁפְחָה – מִשּׁוּם דְּאֵין לָהּ חַיִּיס, אֲבָל גּוֹיָה דְּאִית לָהּ חַיִּיס – אֵימָא לָא.

The Gemara asks: **And** why does **Rabbi Yosei, son of Rabbi Yehuda,** not learn this from here? The Gemara responds: **One** verse was necessary to teach the case of a Canaanite **maidservant, and one** verse was necessary to teach the case of **a gentile woman. And** both verses **are necessary,** as, **if** the Torah **taught us** only about a Canaanite **maidservant,** one could say she is excluded only **because she does not have a pedigree,** since the Torah ascribes no family relationships to maidservants, **but** with regard to **a gentile woman who does have a pedigree,**[N] **say no.** It was therefore necessary to say that one's daughter by a gentile woman does not have the legal status of a daughter.

וְאִי אַשְׁמְעִינַן גּוֹיָה – מִשּׁוּם דְּלָא שַׁיְיכָא בְּמִצְוֹת, אֲבָל שִׁפְחָה, דְּשַׁיְיכָא בְּמִצְוֹת, אֵימָא לָא – צְרִיכָא.

Conversely, **if it would teach us** only the case of **a gentile woman,** one might say that this is **because she does not have any connection with the mitzvot** and therefore her children are in no way Jewish. **But** since a Canaanite **maidservant** has a **connection with the mitzvot,** as she is obligated to observe the prohibitions in the same way as a Jewish woman, **say no,**[H] i.e., her children should be considered children of their Jewish father. Therefore, this additional proof **is necessary.**

וְרַבָּנַן, אַשְׁכְּחַן שִׁפְחָה, גּוֹיָה מְנָא לְהוּ? וְכִי תֵּימָא: נֵילַף מִשִּׁפְחָה – הָנָהוּ מִצְרָךְ צְרִיכִי!

The Gemara asks: **And** according to the opinion of **the Rabbis, we found** a source that the children of a Canaanite **maidservant** are not considered the children of their Jewish father, but **from where** do we derive that children born to a Jewish father by **a gentile woman** are not considered his children? **And if you say: Let us derive** it **from** the case of the Canaanite **maidservant,** it has already been shown that **these are** both **necessary,** and one cannot be derived from the other.

NOTES

The wife and her children, etc. – מֵהָאִשָּׁה וִילָדֶיהָ וכו׳: Some commentaries explain that the status of the children is derived from a close reading of the text. Instead of stating: The wife and the children, it states: "The wife and her children." This implies that the children have the legal status of her children alone.

Does have a pedigree – אִית לָהּ חַיִּיס: The question of a pedigree here relates to paternal lineage. A child's status does not necessarily follow his father's lineage; rather, it depends on the specific *halakha*. For some realms of *halakha*, lineage follows the mother's family. Consequently, even when it is certain who the biological father is, the *halakha* does not necessarily consider the child a part of that family. The conclusion of the talmudic discussion here that *halakha* takes paternal lineage into account is not agreed upon by all. In the Jerusalem Talmud there is a dispute over whether gentiles follow their father's family lineage or not.

HALAKHA

A son from a Canaanite maidservant or a gentile woman – בֵּן מִשִּׁפְחָה וְנָכְרִית: A son born to a Jewish man from a Canaanite maidservant or from a gentile woman is not considered his son, neither for purposes of levirate marriage, nor inheritance, nor any other matter (Rambam *Sefer Nashim*, *Hilkhot Yibbum VaḤalitza* 1:4 and *Sefer Mishpatim*, *Hilkhot Naḥalot* 1:7).

NOTES

A son from a gentile woman – בֵּן מִן הַנָּכְרִית: This *halakha* appears to be explicit in the verses: "We have broken faith with our God, and have married foreign women of the peoples of the land… Now therefore let us make a covenant with our God to put away all the wives, and such as are born of them…" (Ezra 10:2–3). Nevertheless, the Gemara sought to find a source for this *halakha* from the Torah (see Jerusalem Talmud).

She is called a Jew who is unfit – יִשְׂרָאֵל פָּסוּל מִיקְרֵי: According to most commentaries, being unfit refers to disqualification from the priesthood. A daughter of a gentile father and Jewish mother is unfit for marriage to a priest. Others hold that the disqualification mentioned here is not related to the priesthood but relates only to a defect in lineage (Ramban; *Yam shel Shlomo*).

HALAKHA

Offspring from a gentile or slave – הַנּוֹלָד מִנָּכְרִי וְעֶבֶד: If a gentile or slave had relations with a Jewish woman and she gave birth to a child, that child is a Jew and is eligible to enter the congregation. If that offspring is a daughter, then she is unfit to marry a priest (*Shulḥan Arukh, Even HaEzer* 4:19; Rambam *Sefer Kedusha, Hilkhot Issurei Bia* 15:3).

אָמַר רַבִּי יוֹחָנָן מִשּׁוּם רַבִּי שִׁמְעוֹן בֶּן יוֹחַי: אָמַר קְרָא ״כִּי יָסִיר אֶת בִּנְךָ מֵאַחֲרַי״, בִּנְךָ מִיִּשְׂרְאֵלִית קְרוּי בִּנְךָ, וְאֵין בִּנְךָ הַבָּא מִן הַגּוֹיָה קְרוּי בִּנְךָ, אֶלָּא בְּנָהּ.

The Gemara answers: **Rabbi Yoḥanan said in the name of Rabbi Shimon ben Yoḥai:** The **verse states:** "Neither shall you make marriages with them: Your daughter you shall not give unto his son, nor his daughter shall you take unto your son, **for he will turn away your son from following Me**" (Deuteronomy 7:3–4). This teaches that **your son** born **from a Jewish woman is called your son, but your son born from a gentile woman is not called your son, but her son.**[N] The verse teaches that since the son of a gentile woman is her son alone, he is not considered related at all to his Jewish father.

אָמַר רָבִינָא שְׁמַע מִינַּהּ: בֶּן בִּתְּךָ הַבָּא מִן הַגּוֹי – קְרוּי בִּנְךָ. לֵימָא קָסָבַר רָבִינָא גּוֹי וְעֶבֶד הַבָּא עַל בַּת יִשְׂרָאֵל הַוָּלָד כָּשֵׁר? נְהִי דְּמַמְזֵר לָא הָוֵי – כָּשֵׁר נַמִי לָא הָוֵי, יִשְׂרָאֵל פָּסוּל מִיקְרֵי.

Ravina said: Conclude from here that **the son of your daughter by a gentile** father is nevertheless **called your son,** i.e., grandson. The Gemara asks: **Shall we say that Ravina holds that** if **a gentile or slave engaged in intercourse with a Jewish woman, the offspring is** of **unflawed** lineage?[H] The Gemara answers: There is no conclusive proof from here, because **granted, she is not a *mamzer*,** but nevertheless **she is still not** of **unflawed** lineage; rather, **she is called a Jew who is unfit**[N] to marry into the priesthood.

הַאי בְּשִׁבְעָה אוּמּוֹת כְּתִיב! ״כִּי יָסִיר״ לְרַבּוֹת כָּל הַמְסִירִים.

The Gemara asks with regard to Rabbi Shimon's reasoning: Was **this** verse not **written in** relation to **the seven nations** who inhabited the land of Canaan when Joshua entered Eretz Yisrael but not with regard to other nations? The Gemara responds that the words **"He will turn away" comes to include all those who would turn** one's grandson **away** from God, i.e., any gentile.

הָנִיחָא לְרַבִּי שִׁמְעוֹן, דְּדָרֵישׁ טַעְמָא דִּקְרָא, אֶלָּא לְרַבָּנַן מְנָא לְהוּ? מַאן תַּנָּא דִּפְלִיג עֲלֵיהּ דְּרַבִּי יוֹסֵי בְּרַבִּי יְהוּדָה – רַבִּי שִׁמְעוֹן הִיא.

The Gemara asks: **This works out well for Rabbi Shimon, who interprets the rationale** behind the mitzva **in the verse** and draws halakhic conclusions based on that interpretation. Although the verse is stated with regard to the seven nations, the reason for the verse applies to all other gentile nations. **However, according to the** opinion of **the Rabbis,** who do not draw inferences from the rationale of the verse to apply this ruling to all other nations, **from where** do they derive **this** *halakha*? The Gemara answers: **Who is the *tanna* who disagrees with Rabbi Yosei, son of Rabbi Yehuda? It is Rabbi Shimon,** who applies the rationale of the verse to all other nations.

Perek **II**
Daf **23** Amud **b**

NOTES

Betrothed one of two sisters – קִידֵּשׁ אַחַת מִשְּׁתֵּי אֲחָיוֹת: There are several possible ways in which this could happen. He might have, e.g., betrothed one sister prior to some tumultuous event after which he did not remember which of them he betrothed and others offered conflicting opinions. Such an occurrence is recorded as having taken place and was brought before the *ge'onim* for a decision. If the [illegible] knew to which sister he was betrothed, it must be a case where the two sisters appointed an emissary to accept their betrothals for them, and though the man intended to betroth one of them he did not explicitly designate which of them he desired.

מתני׳ מִי שֶׁקִּידֵּשׁ אַחַת מִשְּׁתֵּי אֲחָיוֹת וְאֵין יוֹדֵעַ אֵי זֶה מֵהֶן קִידֵּשׁ – נוֹתֵן גֵּט לָזוֹ וְגֵט לָזוֹ. מֵת, וְלוֹ אָח אֶחָד – חוֹלֵץ לִשְׁתֵּיהֶן.

MISHNA In the case of **one who betrothed one of two sisters**[NH] **and does not know which of them he betrothed,** so that both are forbidden to him, he **gives a bill of divorce to this one and a bill of divorce to that one** due to the uncertainty. If the man who had betrothed one of these women **died**[H] before he could give a bill of divorce, **and he had one brother,** that brother **performs *ḥalitza* with both of them,** but he may not take either in levirate marriage. This is because he does not know which woman is his *yevama* and which is forbidden to him as the sister of a woman with whom he has a levirate bond.

HALAKHA

Betrothed one of two sisters – קִידֵּשׁ אַחַת מִשְּׁתֵּי אֲחָיוֹת: One who betrothed one of two sisters and is uncertain as to which he betrothed may not consummate the marriage with either one of them. Rather, he must give a bill of divorce to each (Rambam *Sefer Nashim, Hilkhot Ishut* 9:3; *Shulḥan Arukh, Even HaEzer* 41:2, 176:1).

One who betroths one of two sisters and subsequently dies – הַמְקַדֵּשׁ אַחַת הָאֲחָיוֹת וּמֵת: If one betrothed one of two sisters and does not know which he betrothed, and then dies, his brother must perform *ḥalitza* with both of them in order to permit them to remarry. If the deceased had two brothers, one must perform *ḥalitza* with one sister, and the second is permitted to enter a levirate marriage with the other. One must not take one of the women in levirate marriage *ab initio*, as he would thereby encounter the sister of a woman with whom he has a levirate bond, as explained in the Gemara. If the two brothers both entered levirate marriage with the two sisters before consulting the court, they are not required to divorce (Rambam *Sefer Nashim, Hilkhot Yibbum VaḤalitza* 8:1; *Shulḥan Arukh, Even HaEzer* 176:1).

הָיוּ לוֹ שְׁנַיִם – אֶחָד חוֹלֵץ וְאֶחָד מְיַיבֵּם. קָדְמוּ וְכָנְסוּ – אֵין מוֹצִיאִין מִיָּדָם.

If the man who betrothed one of these women **had two** brothers, **one of them performs *ḥalitza*** with one of the sisters, but he may not enter into levirate marriage with her due to the possibility that she is the sister of a woman with whom he has a levirate bond. **And one takes** the other **in levirate marriage** if he so desires. If the two brothers **married** the two sisters **before** consulting the court, the court does not **remove them** from their marriage and they are permitted to remain married. The couple who performed levirate marriage second was even permitted to do so, since there was no longer any doubt about the levirate bond.

שְׁנַיִם שֶׁקִּדְּשׁוּ שְׁתֵּי אֲחָיוֹת, זֶה אֵינוֹ יוֹדֵעַ אֵי זוֹ קִידֵּשׁ, וְזֶה אֵינוֹ יוֹדֵעַ אֵיזוֹ קִידֵּשׁ – זֶה נוֹתֵן שְׁנֵי גִיטִּין, וְזֶה נוֹתֵן שְׁנֵי גִיטִּין. מֵתוּ, לָזֶה אָח וְלָזֶה אָח – זֶה חוֹלֵץ לִשְׁתֵּיהֶן, וְזֶה חוֹלֵץ לִשְׁתֵּיהֶן.

Furthermore, in the case of **two** unrelated men **who betrothed two sisters: If this one does not know which** sister **he betrothed and that one does not know which** sister **he betrothed, this one gives two bills of divorce,** one to each of the women, **and that one gives two bills of divorce.** If the two men **died** before they divorced, and **this one had a brother and that one had a brother,** then **this** brother **performs *ḥalitza* with both of them, and that** brother **performs *ḥalitza* with both of them.**

לָזֶה אֶחָד וְלָזֶה שְׁנַיִם – הַיָּחִיד חוֹלֵץ לִשְׁתֵּיהֶן. וְהַשְּׁנַיִם – אֶחָד חוֹלֵץ וְאֶחָד מְיַיבֵּם. קָדְמוּ וְכָנְסוּ – אֵין מוֹצִיאִין מִיָּדָם. לָזֶה שְׁנַיִם וְלָזֶה שְׁנַיִם – אָחִיו שֶׁל זֶה חוֹלֵץ לְאַחַת וְאָחִיו שֶׁל זֶה חוֹלֵץ לְאַחַת, אָחִיו שֶׁל זֶה מְיַיבֵּם חֲלוּצָתוֹ שֶׁל זֶה וְאָחִיו שֶׁל זֶה מְיַיבֵּם חֲלוּצָתוֹ שֶׁל זֶה.

If **this one had one** brother **and that one had two** brothers, **the single** brother **performs *ḥalitza* with both of them, and** of **the two** brothers, **one performs *ḥalitza* and one performs levirate marriage** if he so desires. If **they married** the sisters **before** consulting the court, the court **does not remove them** from the marriage and they are not told to divorce them. If **this one had two** brothers **and that one had two** brothers, **the brother of this one performs *ḥalitza* with one** sister, **and the brother of that one performs *ḥalitza* with one** sister. **The brother of this** one who performed *ḥalitza* **may take the woman who performed *ḥalitza*** [*ḥalutza*] **of that** other's brother **in levirate marriage, and the brother of that** second one who performed *ḥalitza* **may take the *ḥalutza* of that** other's brother **in levirate marriage.**

קָדְמוּ שְׁנַיִם וְחָלְצוּ – לֹא יְיַבְּמוּ הַשְּׁנַיִם, אֶלָּא אֶחָד חוֹלֵץ וְאֶחָד מְיַיבֵּם. קָדְמוּ וְכָנְסוּ – אֵין מוֹצִיאִין מִיָּדָם.

If the two brothers **performed *ḥalitza*** with both wives **before** consulting the court, **the** two brothers of the second man **may not take** sisters **in levirate marriage** lest one marry the sister of a woman who with whom he had a levirate bond. **Rather, one performs *ḥalitza* and one performs levirate marriage** if he so desires. If **they married** their wives **before** consulting the court, the court **does not remove them** from the marriage.

גמ׳ שְׁמַע מִינָּהּ: קִידּוּשִׁין שֶׁאֵין מְסוּרִין לְבִיאָה – הָווּ קִידּוּשִׁין!

GEMARA **Learn from here** in the mishna that **betrothals that cannot** ultimately **lead to consummation**[N] **are nevertheless betrothals.** There is a dispute between Abaye and Rava in tractate *Kiddushin* with regard to a case of a betrothal that, due to some halakhic complication, can never be consummated. The cases in this mishna may not be consummated, since each of the two sisters is forbidden due to the uncertainty as to whether she is the woman he betrothed or the sister of the woman he betrothed. Therefore, both are forbidden to him. Nevertheless, the mishna instructs that he must give a bill of divorce to both of them. This implies that such betrothals are valid, in contrast to Rava's opinion that betrothals that cannot ultimately be consummated are not betrothals at all.

הָכָא בְּמַאי עָסְקִינַן – כְּשֶׁהוּכְּרוּ וּלְבַסּוֹף נִתְעָרְבוּ. דַּיְקָא נַמִי, דְּקָתָנֵי ״וְאֵינוֹ יוֹדֵעַ״, וְלֹא קָתָנֵי ״וְאֵינוֹ יָדוּעַ״, שְׁמַע מִינָּהּ.

The Gemara rejects this: **With what are we dealing here?** We are dealing with a case **when** at first both sisters **were recognized** and at the moment of betrothal he knew whom he betrothed; it was a betrothal destined for consummation. **But later** the two sisters **were mixed up** so that he was no longer certain which he betrothed. If so, there was not any flaw in the betrothal itself initially. The language of the mishna **is also precise, as it teaches: And he does not know** which of them he betrothed, **but it does not teach: It is unknown** completely. This implies that the matter was known at some time. The Gemara adds: **Conclude from** here that this is the case.

NOTES

Betrothals that cannot ultimately lead to consummation – קִידּוּשִׁין שֶׁאֵין מְסוּרִין לְבִיאָה: *Tosafot* clarify that this principle does not apply in cases where there is some halakhic obstacle preventing sexual relations, e.g., some prohibition. The Gemara here is referring only to cases where the act of betrothal itself prevents the consummation of the marriage.

מַאי קָא מַשְׁמַע לָן? סֵיפָא אִיצְטְרִיכָא לֵיהּ: מֵת וְלוֹ אָח אֶחָד – חוֹלֵץ לִשְׁתֵּיהֶן, הָיוּ לוֹ שְׁנַיִם – אֶחָד חוֹלֵץ וְאֶחָד מְיַיבֵּם. דַּוְקָא מִיחֲלָץ וַהֲדַר יַבּוּמֵי, אֲבָל יַבּוּמֵי בְּרֵישָׁא – לָא, דְּקָא פָּגַע בַּאֲחוֹת זְקוּקָתוֹ.

The Gemara asks: If so, **what is** the mishna **teaching us** in the segment of the mishna referring to the giving of two bills of divorce? That is obvious. The Gemara answers: **It was necessary** to teach **the last clause** of the mishna, as there it teaches: If **he died and he had one brother,** that brother **performs *ḥalitza* with both of them;** if **he had two** brothers, **one performs *ḥalitza* and** the other **one enters into levirate marriage** if he so desires. **Specifically,** one brother must perform ***ḥalitza*** first, **and only subsequently** the other brother may perform **levirate marriage. But** one brother **may not enter levirate marriage first,** before the other brother has performed *ḥalitza*, **as he** would thereby **encounter the sister of a woman with whom he has a levirate bond.**

״שְׁנַיִם שֶׁקִּדְּשׁוּ שְׁתֵּי אֲחָיוֹת״ וכו׳. שְׁמַע מִינָּהּ: קִדּוּשִׁין שֶׁאֵין מְסוּרִין לְבִיאָה הָווּ קִדּוּשִׁין! הָכָא נַמִי: כְּשֶׁהוּכְּרוּ וּלְבַסּוֹף נִתְעָרְבוּ. דַּיְקָא נַמִי, דְּקָתָנֵי ״וְאֵין יוֹדֵעַ״ וְלֹא קָתָנֵי ״וְאֵין יָדוּעַ״, שְׁמַע מִינָּהּ.

The mishna says: In the case of **two** unrelated men **who betrothed two sisters:**[H] If this one does not know which sister he betrothed and that one does not know which sister he betrothed, this one gives two bills of divorce, one to each of the women, and that one gives two bills of divorce. The Gemara asks: **Learn from here** that **betrothals that cannot** ultimately **lead to consummation**[H] **are** valid **betrothals.** The Gemara rejects this: **Here too,** this is referring to a case **where they were recognized and later mixed up.** The language **is also precise, as it teaches: And he does not know,** meaning that he does not know now whom he betrothed, **and it does not teach: It is unknown.** The Gemara summarizes: Indeed, **conclude this from here** that this is the case.

וּמַאי קָא מַשְׁמַע לָן? סֵיפָא אִיצְטְרִיכָא לֵיהּ: ״מֵתוּ, לָזֶה אֶחָד וְלָזֶה שְׁנַיִם – הַיָּחִיד, חוֹלֵץ לִשְׁתֵּיהֶן. וְהַשְּׁנַיִם, אֶחָד חוֹלֵץ וְאֶחָד מְיַיבֵּם״.

The Gemara asks: If so, **what does it come to teach us** in relating that both of them must give bills of divorce? The Gemara explains: **It was necessary** to teach **the last clause,** where it says: If **they died** and **this one had one** brother **and this one had two, the single** brother **performs *ḥalitza* with both of them. And** of **the two, one performs *ḥalitza* and one enters levirate marriage** if he so desires.

פְּשִׁיטָא, הַיְינוּ רֵישָׁא! מַהוּ דְּתֵימָא: לִיגְזוֹר תְּרֵי אַטּוּ חַד, קָא מַשְׁמַע לָן.

The Gemara asks: **That is obvious,** as **this is** identical to the *halakha* taught in **the first clause** of the mishna. Why should this case be different from the previous case of two brothers? The Gemara answers: It is necessary to teach this **lest you say** the Sages should **issue a decree** in the case of **two** brothers **due to** the case of **one** brother. In a case of one brother he may only perform *ḥalitza* but may not enter into levirate marriage. Without this mishna one may have thought the same should be true for two brothers. **This comes to teach us** that they did not issue such a decree, and in this case one of them is allowed to enter into levirate marriage.

וְדַוְקָא מִיחֲלָץ וַהֲדַר יַבּוּמֵי, אֲבָל יַבּוּמֵי בְּרֵישָׁא – לָא, דְּקָא פָּגַע בִּיבָמָה לַשּׁוּק.

And this is specifically if the brother of one man first **performs *ḥalitza* and subsequently** the brother of the other man **consummates the levirate marriage, but if he consummated the levirate marriage first, then no,** that is prohibited. And why is that? He might **be encountering** the prohibition of **a *yevama* to** a member of the **public.** Possibly the woman he married was not his *yevama* but someone else's *yevama*, and until the other man's brother performs *ḥalitza* with her she is still forbidden to other men.

HALAKHA

Two who betrothed two sisters – שְׁנַיִם שֶׁקִּדְּשׁוּ שְׁתֵּי אֲחָיוֹת: With regard to the case of two unrelated men who betrothed two sisters but do not know who betrothed whom and then both men died, if each had one brother, each brother performs *ḥalitza* with both of the women, and they may not enter levirate marriage.

If one of the deceased had one brother and the other had two brothers, then the single brother performs *ḥalitza* with both sisters, and with regard to the two brothers of the second man, one must first perform *ḥalitza* with one of the wives and then the other may enter levirate marriage with the other if he so desires. However, if these two brothers both entered into levirate marriage with the sisters before consulting the court but after the brother of the other man had performed *ḥalitza*, they need not divorce.

If each of the deceased men had two brothers, then one brother of the first performs *ḥalitza* for one of the women, and one brother of the second performs *ḥalitza* with the other woman. Then the second brother of the first is permitted to enter into levirate marriage with the woman who performed *ḥalitza* with the brother of the second. Similarly, the second brother of the second may marry the woman who performed *ḥalitza* with the brother of the first.

If both brothers of one man performed *ḥalitza* with both sisters, then *ab initio* one brother of the second should perform *ḥalitza* with one of the women and the second may then take the other in levirate marriage. If, however, both brothers of the second entered into levirate marriage with the sisters after the sisters performed *ḥalitza* with the brothers of the first, then the men are not made to divorce them (Rambam *Sefer Nashim, Hilkhot Yibbum VaḤalitza* 8:2–3; *Shulḥan Arukh, Even HaEzer* 176:3).

Betrothals that cannot ultimately lead to consummation – קִידּוּשִׁין שֶׁאֵין מְסוּרִין לְבִיאָה: A betrothal that cannot ultimately be consummated due to a halakhic impediment is nevertheless a valid betrothal, and the bond can be broken only by a bill of divorce. This ruling is against the Gemara here, which attempts to resolve the matter in accordance with Rava's opinion as well. Rather, this ruling is the conclusion of the talmudic discussion in tractate *Kiddushin* (51b) and is one of six cases where the *halakha* is ruled in accordance with the opinion of Abaye and not Rava (Rambam *Sefer Nashim, Hilkhot Ishut* 9:3; *Shulḥan Arukh, Even HaEzer* 176:1).

״לָזֶה שְׁנַיִם וְלָזֶה שְׁנַיִם״ וכו׳. הָא תּוּ לָמָּה לִי, הַיְינוּ הַךְ! מַהוּ דְּתֵימָא: לִיגְזוֹר דִּלְמָא מְיַיבֵּם בְּלֹא חֲלִיצָה, קָא מַשְׁמַע לַן.

The mishna taught: If **this one had two** brothers **and that one had two** brothers, the brother of this who performed *ḥalitza* may take the *ḥalutza* of that other's brother in levirate marriage, and the brother of that second one who performed *ḥalitza* may take the *ḥalutza* of that other's brother in levirate marriage. The Gemara asks: **Why do I need this as well? This** clause **is identical** to **that** previous *halakha*. The Gemara answers: It is necessary **lest you say: Let** the Sages **issue a decree lest he consummate the levirate marriage without** the other first **performing *ḥalitza*** at all. **This comes to teach us** that such a decree is not issued. Rather, one of each pair of brothers can enter a levirate marriage.

מַאי שְׁנָא מֵהָא דִּתְנַן: אַרְבָּעָה אַחִין, שְׁנַיִם מֵהֶן נְשׂוּאִין שְׁתֵּי אֲחָיוֹת, וּמֵתוּ הַנְּשׂוּאִין אֶת הָאֲחָיוֹת – הֲרֵי אֵלּוּ חוֹלְצוֹת וְלֹא מִתְיַיבְּמוֹת?

The Gemara asks: In **what** way **is** this case **different from that which we learned** in a mishna (26a): If there were **four brothers,** and **two of them were married to two sisters, and those married to the sisters died, then those** two sisters **perform *ḥalitza* but may not enter into levirate marriage** with the remaining brothers, since each woman is the sister of a woman with a levirate bond to each of the brothers. Why not say here as well that each is the sister of a woman with a levirate bond?

הָכִי הָשְׁתָּא?!

The Gemara rejects this: **How can** these cases **be compared?**

Perek **II**
Daf **24** Amud **a**

הָתָם אִי לְמַאן דְּאָמַר יֵשׁ זִיקָה – יֵשׁ זִיקָה. וְאִי לְמַאן דְּאָמַר אָסוּר לְבַטֵּל מִצְוַת יְבָמִין – אָסוּר לְבַטֵּל מִצְוַת יְבָמִין. הָכָא – כָּל חַד וְחַד, אֵימוּר דִּידֵיהּ קָא מִתְרַמְיָא לֵיהּ.

There, in that mishna, **if** it is **according to the one who said** that the levirate **bond is substantial,** then **there is a bond** in that case, as two sisters were certainly married to the brothers and require levirate marriage. **And if** it is **according to the one who said that it is prohibited to nullify the levirate mitzva** through marrying the sister of the *yevama*, then the explanation of that mishna is that **it is prohibited to nullify the levirate mitzva** and for this reason they must perform *ḥalitza* and may not enter into levirate marriage. However, **here,** in this mishna, there is uncertainty concerning the betrothal such that with regard to **each one** of the brothers, one could **say that** possibly he **encountered his own** *yevama*. Perhaps each brother took his own brother's wife in levirate marriage, and for this reason the Sages did not issue a decree.

״קָדְמוּ וְכָנְסוּ אֵין מוֹצִיאִין״ כו׳. תָּנֵי שֵׁילָא: וַאֲפִילּוּ שְׁנֵיהֶם כֹּהֲנִים. מַאי טַעֲמָא? חֲלוּצָה דְּרַבָּנַן הִיא, וּסְפֵק חֲלוּצָה – לָא גְּזַרוּ בְּהוּ רַבָּנַן.

§ The mishna states that if **they married** their wives **before** consulting the court, the **court does not remove them**[N] from the marriage. **Sheila teaches** a *baraita* that clarifies the mishna: **And** this is the case **even** if **both of** the brothers were **priests.**[H] A woman who performed *ḥalitza* is normally forbidden to a priest, yet in this case, although the brother of the other man performed *ḥalitza*, they are not required to divorce. **What is the reason** for this *halakha*? It is as follows: **A *ḥalutza* is** forbidden to a priest by **rabbinic law** because her status is similar to that of a divorcée, who is forbidden to a priest by Torah law. **And** in a case of **uncertainty** as to whether she is a ***ḥalutza,*** since it may not have been her *yavam* who performed the ceremony, **the Sages did not issue a decree.**[N]

וַחֲלוּצָה דְּרַבָּנַן הִיא? וְהָתַנְיָא: ״גְּרוּשָׁה״, אֵין לִי אֶלָּא גְּרוּשָׁה, חֲלוּצָה מִנַּיִן? תַּלְמוּד לוֹמַר ״וְאִשָּׁה״! מִדְּרַבָּנַן הוּא, וּקְרָא אַסְמַכְתָּא בְּעָלְמָא הוּא.

The Gemara asks: **And is** the prohibition against a ***ḥalutza*** marrying a priest[H] really **by rabbinic** law? **But isn't it taught** in a *baraita*: "They shall not take a woman that is a harlot, or profaned; neither shall they take a woman **divorced** from her husband; for he is holy unto his God" (Leviticus 21:7). **I have derived only a divorcée; from where** do I derive that a priest may not marry **a *ḥalutza*? The verse states:** "Neither shall they take **a woman.**" The repetition of the word "woman" extends the *halakha* to include a *ḥalutza*. The Gemara answers: **This** prohibition **is by rabbinic** law, **and the verse is a mere support.**

NOTES

The court does not remove them – אֵין מוֹצִיאִין: In this case they are not required to divorce, because it is uncertain whether each woman is the sister of a woman with whom he has a levirate bond or not. However, the early commentaries write that in a case where she is certainly the sister of a woman with whom one has a levirate bond, then although that prohibition is rabbinic, nevertheless, one who transgresses it and marries her is required to divorce her.

In a case of uncertainty whether she is a *ḥalutza* the Sages did not issue a decree – סְפֵק חֲלוּצָה לָא גְּזַרוּ: *Tosafot* challenge this because later (36b) the Gemara implies that the Sages did indeed render it prohibited for a priest to marry a woman whose *ḥalitza* was uncertain. Ramah, cited by *Tosefot HaRosh*, explains that there is a distinction between a case of *ḥalitza* performed out of uncertainty and a case where it is uncertain whether or not *ḥalitza* was performed. In cases where there was an actual *ḥalitza*, even if it is not certain that the *ḥalitza* was necessary, the Sages decreed that the *ḥalutza* is forbidden to a priest. In the case where it is not certain whether or not there was a *ḥalitza*, the Sages did not decree that she is forbidden to a priest.

HALAKHA

They married their wives before consulting the court… even if both…were priests – קָדְמוּ וְכָנְסוּ...אֲפִילּוּ שְׁנֵיהֶם כֹּהֲנִים: Once they are married they are not required to divorce, even if they are priests, as the *ḥalitza* performed by the single brother is an uncertain *ḥalitza*, and the Sages did not apply their decree to such a case (Rambam *Sefer Nashim, Hilkhot Yibbum VaḤalitza* 8:2 and *Sefer Kedusha, Hilkhot Issurei Bia* 17:7; *Shulḥan Arukh, Even HaEzer* 176:3).

A *ḥalutza* marrying a priest – חֲלוּצָה לְכֹהֵן: A *ḥalutza* is forbidden to a priest by rabbinic law since she is considered similar to a divorcée (Rambam *Sefer Nashim, Hilkhot Yibbum VaḤalitza* 8:2; *Sefer Kedusha, Hilkhot Ishut* 1:6 and *Hilkhot Issurei Bia* 17:7; *Shulḥan Arukh, Even HaEzer* 6:1).

מתני׳ מִצְוָה בַּגָּדוֹל לְיַיבֵּם וְאִם קָדַם הַקָּטָן – זָכָה.

MISHNA **It is a mitzva for the eldest to consummate the levirate marriage,**[H] i.e., the eldest takes precedence over the other brothers, though they too are obligated. **But if the younger** brother consummated the levirate marriage **first, he acquires** the *yevama* as his wife.[H]

גמ׳ תָּנוּ רַבָּנַן: ״וְהָיָה הַבְּכוֹר״ – מִיכָּן שֶׁמִּצְוָה בַּגָּדוֹל לְיַיבֵּם: ״אֲשֶׁר תֵּלֵד״ – פְּרָט לְאַיְלוֹנִית שֶׁאֵין יוֹלֶדֶת: ״יָקוּם עַל שֵׁם אָחִיו״ – לְנַחֲלָה.

GEMARA **The Sages taught** the following interpretation of the verse: **"And it shall be that the firstborn** that she bears shall be established in the name of his dead brother and his name will not be blotted out of Israel" (Deuteronomy 25:6). **From here** the Sages derive **that the mitzva to consummate the levirate marriage is upon the eldest.** The next phrase: **"That she bears,"** is interpreted **to exclude** levirate marriage in the case of a widow who is **an *aylonit*, who cannot bear children.** From the next phrase: **"Shall be established in the name of his dead brother,"** it is derived that the same brother who performs the mitzva of levirate marriage is established in his brother's name with regard **to inheritance,**[H] i.e., he inherits his brother's property.

אַתָּה אוֹמֵר לְנַחֲלָה, אוֹ אֵינוֹ אֶלָּא לְשֵׁם, יוֹסֵף – קוֹרִין אוֹתוֹ יוֹסֵף, יוֹחָנָן – קוֹרִין אוֹתוֹ יוֹחָנָן? נֶאֱמַר כָּאן ״יָקוּם עַל שֵׁם אָחִיו״ וְנֶאֱמַר לְהַלָּן ״עַל שֵׁם אֲחֵיהֶם יִקָּרְאוּ בְּנַחֲלָתָם״, מַה ״שֵׁם״ הָאָמוּר לְהַלָּן – נַחֲלָה, אַף ״שֵׁם״ הָאָמוּר כָּאן – לְנַחֲלָה.

The *baraita* continues and asks: Do **you say** that he succeeds in the name of his brother **for inheritance, or** perhaps **it is only to** inherit **his name?** If, e.g., the deceased brother was named **Yosef, they** must **call** the son born from levirate marriage **Yosef,** or if his name was **Yoḥanan,** then **they** must **call him Yoḥanan.** The *baraita* answers: **It is stated here: "He shall succeed in the name of his brother," and it is stated there: "They shall be called after the name of their brothers in their inheritance"** (Genesis 48:6). **Just as** the word **"name" stated there** in Genesis is referring explicitly to **inheritance, so too,** the word **"name" stated here** in Leviticus means with regard **to inheritance.**

״וְלֹא יִמָּחֶה שְׁמוֹ״ – פְּרָט לְסָרִיס, שֶׁשְּׁמוֹ מָחוּי.

The *baraita* continues to expound the next phrase of the verse: **"And his name will not be blotted out** of Israel" (Deuteronomy 25:6). This **excludes** the case where the deceased was **a eunuch,**[H] **as his name is** already **blotted out,** since it is impossible for him to have children.

אֲמַר רָבָא: אַף עַל גַּב דִּבְכָל הַתּוֹרָה כּוּלָּהּ אֵין מִקְרָא יוֹצֵא מִידֵי פְּשׁוּטוֹ, הָכָא אֲתַאי גְּזֵירָה שָׁוָה אַפִּיקְתֵּיהּ מִפְּשָׁטֵיהּ לְגַמְרֵי.

Rava said: Even though in the entire Torah a verse does not depart from its literal meaning,[B] and even if the Sages offer a homiletical interpretation of the verses, the literal meaning remains intact, **here the verbal analogy**[B] teaching that the word "name" is referring to inheritance **comes to remove** the verse **from its literal meaning altogether.**[N]

וְאִי לָאו גְּזֵירָה שָׁוָה הֲוָה אָמִינָא ״שֵׁם״ שֵׁם מַמָּשׁ?! לְמַאן קָמַזְהַר רַחֲמָנָא, לְיָבָם – ״יָקוּם עַל שֵׁם אָחִיךָ״ מִיבְּעֵי לֵיהּ! אִי לְבֵי דִּינָא – ״יָקוּם עַל שֵׁם אֲחִי אָבִיו״ מִיבְּעֵי לֵיהּ!

The Gemara asks: **Were it not for the verbal analogy, would I have said** that the meaning of the word **"name" is the actual name?** The verse would be incomprehensible according to the literal reading. **Whom is the Merciful One instructing** in this verse? To whom does the possessive pronoun in the phrase "his brother" apply? If He is speaking **to the *yavam*, He should have** stated: **Shall succeed in the name of your dead brother. And if** the verse is instructing **the court** about the *halakha* in general, **it should have** said: **Shall succeed in the name of his father's brother.**

וְדִלְמָא הָכִי קָאָמַר לְהוּ רַחֲמָנָא לְבֵית דִּין: אִמְרוּ לֵיהּ לְיָבָם ״יָקוּם עַל שֵׁם אָחִיו!״. אֶלָּא, אֲתַאי גְּזֵירָה שָׁוָה אַפִּיקְתֵּיהּ לְגַמְרֵי.

The Gemara rejects this question: **And perhaps this is what the Merciful One is saying to the court: Say to the *yavam*** that the child born to him **shall be established in the name of his brother.** Were it not for the verbal analogy, the verse could have been understood according to its literal meaning. **Rather, the verbal analogy comes to remove it** from its literal meaning **altogether.**

הַשְׁתָּא דְּאָמְרַתְּ קְרָא בְּגָדוֹל כְּתִיב, אֵימָא: בְּכוֹר – לְיַיבֵּם, פָּשׁוּט – לֹא לְיַיבֵּם.

The Gemara challenges the *baraita*: **Now that you say that the verse:** "And it shall be that the firstborn that she bears" **is written** in reference to **the eldest** brother, **say** that **the firstborn** brother **consummates the levirate marriage** but that **an ordinary** brother, i.e., not the firstborn, **may not consummate the levirate marriage,** and that if the firstborn son is unable to enter into levirate marriage or is no longer alive, no one else may perform the mitzva.

HALAKHA

It is a mitzva for the eldest to consummate the levirate marriage – מִצְוָה בַּגָּדוֹל לְיַיבֵּם: The primary obligation to consummate the levirate marriage or perform *ḥalitza* devolves upon the eldest of the brothers (Rambam *Sefer Nashim, Hilkhot Yibbum VaḤalitza* 2:6; *Shulḥan Arukh, Even HaEzer* 161:4).

If the younger consummated the levirate marriage first, he acquires her as his wife – וְאִם קָדַם הַקָּטָן זָכָה: Although the mitzva of levirate marriage devolves primarily upon the eldest of the brothers, if one of the others went ahead and entered into levirate marriage, then it is effective (Rambam *Sefer Nashim, Hilkhot Yibbum VaḤalitza* 2:6; *Shulḥan Arukh, Even HaEzer* 161:7).

Shall be established in the name of his dead brother, with regard to inheritance – יָקוּם עַל שֵׁם אָחִיו לְנַחֲלָה: The brother who consummates levirate marriage with his brother's widow inherits all of the property that is actually in his brother's possession (Rambam *Sefer Mishpatim, Hilkhot Naḥalot* 3:7; *Shulḥan Arukh, Even HaEzer* 163:1).

Excludes a eunuch – פְּרָט לְסָרִיס: A man who became sexually impotent through illness is not eligible for *ḥalitza* or levirate marriage. If he performed *ḥalitza* or if others performed *ḥalitza* with his wife, it has no halakhic significance (Rambam *Sefer Nashim, Hilkhot Yibbum VaḤalitza* 6:2, 4; *Shulḥan Arukh, Even HaEzer* 172:1).

BACKGROUND

A verse does not depart from its literal meaning – אֵין מִקְרָא יוֹצֵא מִידֵי פְשׁוּטוֹ: Even when the Bible is interpreted metaphorically, and even when halakhic conclusions are reached by means of a homiletic interpretation of a verse, these conclusions do not negate the literal meaning of the text (*Alfei Menashe*).

Verbal analogy – גְּזֵירָה שָׁוָה: This is a fundamental talmudic principle of biblical exegesis appearing in all the standard lists of hermeneutical principles. If the same word or phrase appears in two places in the Torah, and a certain *halakha* is explicitly stated in one of these places, then on the basis of verbal analogy it is inferred that the same *halakha* applies in the other case as well.

Certain restrictions were placed on the use of this principle to prevent unfounded conclusions from being drawn. Most significantly: One cannot infer a verbal analogy on one's own, i.e., only a verbal analogy based on ancient tradition is valid.

NOTES

Remove the verse from its literal meaning altogether – אַפִּיקְתֵּיהּ מִפְּשָׁטֵיהּ לְגַמְרֵי: It is a transmitted tradition that there is no requirement to name the firstborn son of a levirate marriage after the deceased. Therefore, the verse cannot be read in accordance with its literal meaning (see Rashi).

The reason the Torah writes that the son will take the name of the deceased brother, even though that is not the *halakha*, is explained by the commentaries based on esoteric teachings. Through levirate marriage the soul of the deceased brother is reincarnated in the newborn son. This idea is elaborated upon in Ramban's Commentary on the Torah (Genesis, chapter 38; see *Sefer HaBoneh*).

אִם כֵּן, אֵשֶׁת אָחִיו שֶׁלֹּא הָיָה בְּעוֹלָמוֹ דְּמִיעֵט רַחֲמָנָא – לָמָּה לִי?

The Gemara answers: **If so** that the mitzva of levirate marriage applies only to the firstborn, then in the case of **a wife of a brother with whom he did not coexist,** which **the Merciful One excluded** by the verse: "If brothers dwell together," **why do I need** such an exclusion? If only the firstborn is obligated to perform levirate marriage, then there is no need to separately exclude the case of a wife of one's brother with whom one did not coexist, because by definition one in that position cannot be the firstborn.

פָּרֵיךְ רַב אַחָא: וְאֵימָא לְמַעוּטֵי בּוּכְרָא דְּאִמָּא! הַהוּא לָא מָצֵית אָמְרַתְּ, דְּיִבּוּם בְּנַחֲלָה תָּלָה רַחֲמָנָא, וְנַחֲלָה מִן הָאָב וְלֹא מִן הָאֵם.

Rav Aḥa refutes the Gemara's answer: **But say that** the verse comes **to exclude** the case of a brother with whom one did not coexist when one is nevertheless **the firstborn of the mother,** e.g., if the father had two wives. The Gemara rejects this: **You cannot say that, as the Merciful One made levirate marriage dependent upon inheritance,**[N] **and inheritance** comes **from the father**[H] **and not from the mother.**

וְאֵימָא: כִּי אִיכָּא בְּכוֹר תִּתְקַיֵּים מִצְוַת יִבּוּם, כִּי לֵיכָּא בְּכוֹר לָא תִּתְקַיֵּים מִצְוַת יִבּוּם! אָמַר קְרָא: ״וּמֵת אֶחָד מֵהֶם״, מִי לָא עָסְקִינַן דְּמִית בְּכוֹר, וְאָמַר רַחֲמָנָא לְיַיבֵּם קָטָן.

The Gemara again challenges the *baraita*: **Then say** that **when there is a firstborn the mitzva of levirate marriage can be fulfilled** by any of the brothers, **but that when there is no firstborn,** e.g., if he had already died, **the mitzva of levirate marriage may not be fulfilled** by any of the younger brothers. The Gemara answers: **The verse states: "And one of them dies"** (Deuteronomy 25:5), without specifying which brother dies. **Are we not dealing** even **with** the case **where the firstborn died, and** yet **the Merciful One states** that **the younger** brother **should consummate the levirate marriage?**

וְאֵימָא דְּמִית קָטָן, וְאָמַר רַחֲמָנָא לְיַיבֵּם בְּכוֹר! הָא מִיעֵט רַחֲמָנָא אֵשֶׁת אָחִיו שֶׁלֹּא הָיָה בְּעוֹלָמוֹ.

The Gemara refutes this answer: **Say that** the case in the Torah is referring to when **the younger** brother **died, and** only then **the Merciful One states that the firstborn must consummate the levirate marriage.** The Gemara answers: **Didn't the Merciful One** explicitly **exclude the wife of a brother with whom he did not coexist,** which can apply only to a brother who was not the firstborn?

וְאֵימָא: כִּי לֵיכָּא בְּכוֹר – קָדַם קָטָן זָכָה, וְאִי אִיכָּא בְּכוֹר – קָדַם קָטָן לֹא זָכָה! אָמַר קְרָא: ״כִּי יֵשְׁבוּ אַחִים יַחְדָּו״ – הוּקְשָׁה יְשִׁיבַת אַחִים זֶה לָזֶה.

The Gemara challenges the *halakha*: **Say** that **when there is no firstborn** brother, if **a younger** brother **went ahead** and consummated the levirate marriage, then **he acquires** his *yevama* as a wife. **But if there is a firstborn,** and **the younger** brother **went ahead** and performed levirate marriage first, then **he does not acquire** his *yevama* as a wife, because the Torah specifies that the firstborn brother must perform the mitzva. The Gemara rejects this: **The verse states: "If brothers dwell together"** (Deuteronomy 25:5), implying that **the brothers' dwellings were equated one with the other,** and all the brothers are equally obligated in this mitzva.

וְאֵימָא: כִּי אִיכָּא בְּכוֹר – לִיהֲדַר אַגָּדוֹל, כִּי לֵיכָּא בְּכוֹר – אֵין חוֹזְרִין אֵצֶל גָּדוֹל! אַלְמָה תָּנֵי אַבַּיֵּי קַשִּׁישָׁא: מִצְוָה בַּגָּדוֹל לְיַיבֵּם. לֹא רָצָה – הוֹלְכִים אֵצֶל אָחִיו הַקָּטָן, לֹא רָצָה – חוֹזְרִין אֵצֶל גָּדוֹל!

The Gemara challenges the *halakha* again: **Then say: When there is a firstborn, let** the mitzva **return to the eldest** brother if the other brothers refuse to perform levirate marriage. But **when there is no firstborn,** the court **does not return to the eldest,** as the mitzva primarily applies specifically to the firstborn, and if there is no firstborn, none of the brothers take precedence. **Why did Abaye the Elder teach: It is a mitzva for the eldest** of the brothers **to consummate the levirate marriage? If** the eldest **did not wish** to do so, then the court **goes to his younger brother.** If **he** also **did not wish** to do so, the court **returns** again **to the eldest.** This implies that the eldest, even if he is not the firstborn, has a greater mitzva than the younger brothers.

כִּבְכוֹר, מָה בְּכוֹר – בְּכוֹרָתוֹ גָּרְמָה לוֹ, אַף גָּדוֹל – גְּדוּלָּתוֹ גָּרְמָה לוֹ.

The Gemara answers: Since it is derived that the eldest brother takes precedence from the verse about the firstborn, then **just as** with regard to the firstborn, **his status as firstborn causes him**[N] to take precedence, **so too,** with regard to **the eldest, his status as eldest causes him** to take precedence.[H]

NOTES

The Merciful One made levirate marriage dependent upon inheritance – יִבּוּם בְּנַחֲלָה תָּלָה רַחֲמָנָא: Rashi explains that this is referring only to the firstborn son, who inherits a double portion from his father. Therefore the firstborn of only the father has relevance, not the firstborn of the mother. See Rabbi Yehuda bar Natan, *Tosefot HaRosh*, and Rashba, who suggest an alternative explanation.

Just as with regard to the firstborn, his status as firstborn causes him, etc. – כִּבְכוֹר מָה בְּכוֹר בְּכוֹרָתוֹ גָּרְמָה לוֹ וכו׳: In other words, since the Gemara has explained that with regard to levirate marriage the firstborn status is irrelevant, it is clear that the key factor is that he is the eldest of the brothers. This implies that the eldest takes precedence in matters of levirate marriage (*Tosefot HaRosh*).

HALAKHA

Inheritance from the father – נַחֲלָה מִן הָאָב: One's mother's family is not called family with regard to inheritance, and inheritance is received only from one's father's family. Therefore, maternal half brothers do not inherit from one another (Rambam *Sefer Mishpatim, Hilkhot Naḥalot* 1:6; *Shulḥan Arukh, Ḥoshen Mishpat* 276:4).

Order of the obligation to enter levirate marriage – סֵדֶר הַמְּצֻוִּים בְּיִבּוּם: The obligation of levirate marriage falls upon the eldest of the surviving brothers. If he does not wish to fulfill his mitzva, it devolves upon the next eldest. According to the Rambam it devolves equally on all of the remaining brothers. If none of the younger brothers fulfills the obligation, the obligation to perform the mitzva remains with the eldest (Rambam *Sefer Nashim, Hilkhot Yibbum VaḤalitza* 2:6; *Shulḥan Arukh, Even HaEzer* 161:4).

וְאֵימָא: כִּי מְיַיבֵּם בְּכוֹר – לִישְׁקוֹל נַחֲלָה, כִּי מְיַיבֵּם פָּשׁוּט לָא לִישְׁקוֹל נַחֲלָה! אָמַר קְרָא: ״יָקוּם עַל שֵׁם אָחִיו״ – וַהֲרֵי קָם.

The Gemara challenges the *halakha* again: **Then say that if the firstborn consummates the levirate marriage he receives** his deceased brother's **inheritance,** but **if an ordinary brother consummates the levirate marriage he does not receive the inheritance.** The Gemara answers that **the verse states:** "The firstborn that she bears **shall be established in the name of his** dead **brother**" (Deuteronomy 25:6), **and** if the younger brother performs levirate marriage he has **established** his brother's name and thereby earns the inheritance.

וְאֶלָּא בְּכוֹר דְּקָרְיֵיהּ רַחֲמָנָא,

The Gemara asks: **But** if there is no difference between the firstborn and the eldest, why does **the Merciful One call** the brother who enters levirate marriage the **firstborn?**

לְמַאי הִלְכְתָא? לִגְרִיעוּתָא, מָה בְּכוֹר אֵינוֹ נוֹטֵל בְּרָאוּי כִּבְמוּחְזָק – אַף הַאי אֵינוֹ נוֹטֵל בְּרָאוּי כִּבְמוּחְזָק.

With regard to what ***halakha*** was that word written in the Torah? **This is in order to limit**[N] the inheritance. **Just as a firstborn does not take** in inheritance property **due as** he does property **possessed,** but instead receives a double inheritance only from that property already in actual possession of their father, **so too, this** one who enters levirate marriage, whether firstborn or younger, **does not take** in inheritance property **due as** he does property **possessed.**[H]

מתני׳ הַנִּטְעָן עַל הַשִּׁפְחָה וְנִשְׁתַּחְרְרָה, אוֹ עַל הַגּוֹיָה וְנִתְגַּיְּירָה, הֲרֵי זֶה לֹא יִכְנוֹס. וְאִם כָּנַס – אֵין מוֹצִיאִין מִיָּדוֹ. הַנִּטְעָן עַל אֵשֶׁת אִישׁ וְהוֹצִיאוּהָ מִתַּחַת יָדוֹ, אַף עַל פִּי שֶׁכָּנַס – יוֹצִיא.

MISHNA **One suspected** by others of engaging in sexual relations **with a Canaanite maidservant**[N] **and she was** later **set free, or** one suspected of relations **with a gentile woman**[H] **and she** subsequently **converted, may not marry** that woman, since this will strengthen the suspicions against him. **But if he did marry her, they,** the judges of the court, **do not remove** her **from him,** i.e., they do not require him to divorce her. With regard to **one who is suspected of** illicit relations with **a married woman and they,** the judges of the court, **removed her from** her husband, i.e., required them to divorce due to this, **even if** the man suspected of the illicit relations subsequently **married** her, **he must divorce** her.

NOTES

In order to limit – לִגְרִיעוּתָא: *Tosafot* point out that equating the inheritance of one who performs levirate marriage with the inheritance of a firstborn is not solely a limitation, but also gives a benefit, as this additional inherited portion of land is not divided with the other brothers in the Jubilee Year. However, it is described as a limitation because Rabbi Elazar disagrees with regard to the benefit and holds that land inherited through levirate marriage does revert to be shared with the other brothers in the Jubilee Year (*Tosafot* on *Bekhorot* 52b and *Tosefot HaRosh*; see *Mei Neftoaḥ*).

One suspected of relations with a Canaanite maidservant, etc. – הַנִּטְעָן עַל הַשִּׁפְחָה וכו׳: This mishna and those following are not directly related to the main topic of this chapter. They appear here because the earlier mishna mentioned the distinction between cases where the court removes a wife from her husband and those where it permits her to remain married to him (*Yosef Lekaḥ*).

HALAKHA

One who enters levirate marriage does not take in inheritance property due – הַמְיַיבֵּם אֵינוֹ נוֹטֵל בְּרָאוּי: One who performs levirate marriage receives the property of his deceased brother and also receives his brother's portion in the inheritance from their father. However, this applies only to property in the brother's possession, as is the case when the father predeceased the brother but the inheritance had yet to be divided when the brother died. However, if the brother died prior to the father, the one who performed levirate marriage does not receive his brother's portion of the inheritance (Rambam *Sefer Mishpatim, Hilkhot Naḥalot* 3:7; *Shulḥan Arukh, Even HaEzer* 163:1).

One suspected of relations with a Canaanite maidservant… or with a gentile woman – הַנִּטְעָן עַל הַשִּׁפְחָה...אוֹ עַל הַגּוֹיָה: One who is suspected of relations with a Canaanite maidservant or a gentile woman may not marry her *ab initio* if the maidservant was set free or if the gentile woman converted. However, if he did marry her, the court does not require him to divorce her (Rambam *Sefer Nashim, Hilkhot Geirushin* 10:14; *Shulḥan Arukh, Even HaEzer* 11:5).

גמ׳ הָא גִּיּוֹרֶת מִיהָא הָוְיָא, וּרְמִינְהִי: אֶחָד אִישׁ שֶׁנִּתְגַּיֵּיר לְשׁוּם אִשָּׁה, וְאֶחָד אִשָּׁה שֶׁנִּתְגַּיְּירָה לְשׁוּם אִישׁ, וְכֵן מִי שֶׁנִּתְגַּיֵּיר לְשׁוּם שׁוּלְחַן מְלָכִים, לְשׁוּם עַבְדֵי שְׁלֹמֹה – אֵינָן גֵּרִים, דִּבְרֵי רַבִּי נְחֶמְיָה.

GEMARA The mishna teaches that one who is suspected of relations with a gentile woman who later converted may never marry her. **This** implies that **she is, however, a convert,** although it appears that she converted only in order that he might marry her. The Gemara **raises a contradiction** from a *baraita*: **Both a man who converted for the sake of a woman**[N] **and a woman who converted for the sake of a man, and similarly, one who converted for the sake of the king's table,**[N] so that he could serve in a prestigious capacity, or **for the sake of Solomon's servants,** who were also considered prestigious, in all of these cases **they are not converts;** this is **the statement of Rabbi Neḥemya.**

שֶׁהָיָה רַבִּי נְחֶמְיָה אוֹמֵר: אֶחָד גֵּירֵי אֲרָיוֹת וְאֶחָד גֵּירֵי חֲלוֹמוֹת, וְאֶחָד גֵּירֵי מָרְדְּכַי וְאֶסְתֵּר – אֵינָן גֵּרִים עַד שֶׁיִּתְגַּיְּירוּ בַּזְּמַן הַזֶּה.

As Rabbi Neḥemya would say: With regard to **converts** by **lions,** i.e., forced converts such as the Samaritans [*Kutim*] described in II Kings (17:24–25); **and converts** who convert based on their **dreams; and converts of** the time of **Mordecai and Esther** described in the verse, "And many from among the peoples of the land became Jews; for the fear of the Jews was fallen upon them" (Esther 8:17); all of these **are not converts until they are converted at this** present **time.**

בַּזְּמַן הַזֶּה סָלְקָא דַּעְתָּךְ?! אֶלָּא, אֵימָא: כְּבַזְּמַן הַזֶּה.

The Gemara clarifies the meaning of the words: Could it **enter your mind** to say only **at this** present **time?** Since he mentioned the converts of Mordecai and Esther, who were deceased before Rabbi Neḥemya made this statement, he therefore cannot possibly mean this phrase literally. **Rather, say: Like at this** present **time,** when the Jewish people are in exile and there is no material benefit to conversion.

הָא אִיתְּמַר עֲלַהּ, אָמַר רַב יִצְחָק בַּר שְׁמוּאֵל בַּר מָרְתָא מִשְּׁמֵיהּ דְּרַב: הֲלָכָה כְּדִבְרֵי הָאוֹמֵר כּוּלָּם גֵּרִים הֵם.

Returning to the question above: How could a woman who converted for the sake of a man be considered a true convert? The Gemara answers: But **wasn't it stated with regard to** that *baraita* that **Rav Yitzḥak bar Shmuel bar Marta said in the name of Rav:** The ***halakha*** **is** in accordance with **the statement of the one who says that they are all converts.**[H]

אִי הָכִי לְכַתְּחִלָּה נָמֵי! מִשּׁוּם דְּרַב אַסִי, דְּאָמַר רַב אַסִי: ״הָסֵר מִמְּךָ עִקְּשׁוּת פֶּה וּלְזוּת שְׂפָתַיִם״ וגו׳.

The Gemara asks: **If so,** why is one suspected of relations with such a woman not permitted to enter into marriage with her ***ab initio*** **as well?** The Gemara answers: The reason for the prohibition is **due to** the following statement **of Rav Asi. As Rav Asi said** with regard to such cases: **"Put away from yourself**[N] **a twisted mouth, and perverse lips** put far from you" (Proverbs 4:24). If they were to marry, they would give substance to the prior suspicions.

תָּנוּ רַבָּנַן: אֵין מְקַבְּלִין גֵּרִים לִימוֹת הַמָּשִׁיחַ. כַּיּוֹצֵא בּוֹ לֹא קִבְּלוּ גֵּרִים לֹא בִּימֵי דָוִד וְלֹא בִּימֵי שְׁלֹמֹה. אָמַר רַבִּי אֱלִיעֶזֶר: מַאי קְרָא – ״הֵן גּוֹר יָגוּר אֶפֶס מֵאוֹתִי מִי גָר אִתָּךְ עָלַיִךְ יִפּוֹל״ אֲבָל אִידָךְ – לָא.

The Sages taught: Converts are not accepted in the days of the Messiah. Similarly, they did not accept converts in the days of King **David or in the days of** King **Solomon.**[NH] **Rabbi Eliezer said: What is the verse** that hints at this *halakha*? **"Behold, they may gather together** [*gor yagur*],[N] **but without Me; whosoever shall gather together** [*gar*] **with you shall fall on yours"** (Isaiah 54:15). The word *gor* implies that only a convert [*ger*] who becomes part of the Jewish people when the Jews are living in exile, at a time when God is not clearly revealed, i.e., "without Me," are considered part of the Jewish people. **But another** who wishes to convert in a time when God is clearly revealed shall **not** be accepted.

HALAKHA

They are all converts – כּוּלָּם גֵּרִים הֵם: The court must examine the motivation of a potential convert to ensure that he wishes to convert solely for the sake of Heaven. If the court did not examine his motivation before converting him, and even if it subsequently became known that he converted for some ulterior motive, since he has been circumcised and immersed in a ritual bath before a court of three, he no longer has the status of a gentile but his status remains in doubt until it becomes clear that he accepted Judaism completely. He does not have the status of a Jew such that he should be trusted, e.g., in declaring food to be permitted, but nevertheless he is not considered a gentile, and if he marries a Jewish woman the marriage is valid. Even if he reverted to idol worship he is considered an apostate Jew, based on the opinion of Rav and the conclusion of the Gemara's discussion (Rambam *Sefer Kedusha, Hilkhot Issurei Bia* 13:14–17; *Shulḥan Arukh, Yoreh De'a* 268:12).

They did not accept converts in the days of King David or in the days of King Solomon – לֹא קִבְּלוּ גֵּרִים לֹא בִּימֵי דָוִד וְלֹא בִּימֵי שְׁלֹמֹה: The court did not accept converts in the eras of David and Solomon, as they feared that gentiles might convert due to the strength and glory of the Jewish kingdom (Rambam *Sefer Kedusha, Hilkhot Issurei Bia* 13:15).

NOTES

Who converted for the sake of a woman – שֶׁנִּתְגַּיֵּיר לְשׁוּם אִשָּׁה: *Mishpetei Uziel* derives from this Gemara that one can accept a convert *ab initio*, even if he intends to marry a Jewish woman at the time of his conversion, if it becomes clear that he would have married her anyway while remaining a gentile and instead chose of his own accord to become a Jew. He explains that the concern of the Sages is that a gentile who converts for the sake of a woman may still remain attached to his previous religion, and as soon as his love fades he will once again revert to his former religion. However, if it is apparent that he sincerely wants to become a Jew, even if there were other motives involved it can be assumed that the purer motives will prevail and he will maintain his principles even afterward. Moreover, it may be preferable to convert him in such a case so that the Jewish woman will not marry a gentile, since she would have been willing to marry him even if he did not convert. He bases this on the halakhic principle: "It is time to work for the Lord; they have made void Your Torah" (Psalms 119:126; see *Berakhot* 54a), which implies that when one needs to perform God's will, it is occasionally permitted to negate even a biblical precept or, in this case, a rabbinical decree (*Mishpetei Uziel, Yoreh De'a* 2:53).

For the sake of the king's table – לְשׁוּם שׁוּלְחַן מְלָכִים: In the minor tractate that discusses the *halakhot* of converts, known as tractate *Gerim*, there is a list of four different categories of converts. One of them is a convert for the sake of sustenance, which means that he saw poor Jews receiving sustenance from their brethren and converted so that he too could receive sustenance. He is therefore compared to a pauper, as it is written: "You shall leave them for the poor and the stranger [*ger*]" (Leviticus 19:10). It is possible that the king's table is also referring to this sustenance, as the poor would eat from the king's table (see Meiri).

The so-called minor tractates, some of which are rather long, were also called external tractates by the *ge'onim*. They deal with many subjects, but what they have in common is that their subject matter was generally not discussed in one specific tractate or chapter in the Mishna and Talmud, although many of them do refer to Torah laws and major halakhic principles. These tractates could be an indication that another order of the Mishna once existed.

As Rav Asi said, Put away from yourself, etc. – דְּאָמַר רַב אַסִי: הָסֵר מִמְּךָ וכו׳: Since this is a biblical verse, why is it attributed to Rav Asi? *Tosafot* on *Ketubot* 22b explain that Rav Asi would frequently cite this verse, and it became associated with him. The Maharatz Ḥayyut writes that there are alternative interpretations of the verse; it is only due to Rav Asi's interpretation that actions are prohibited if they appear to give validity to prior rumors.

Not…in the days of King David or in the days of King Solomon – לֹא בִּימֵי דָוִד וְלֹא בִּימֵי שְׁלֹמֹה: Rambam explains that in each of these two eras there was a different reason for refusing converts: In the time of King David converts were not accepted lest their conversion stem from fear of King David; in the days of King Solomon the concern was that they may have converted due to his glory and wealth.

Behold, they may gather together – הֵן גּוֹר יָגוּר: The homiletical interpretation is based on the fact that the word gather [*gar*] is similar to the word convert [*ger*]. Rabbi Yehuda bar Natan gives an alternative explanation. He writes that the word *gur* also means terror, as in the verse: "For I have heard the whispering of many, terror [*magor*] on every side" (Psalms 31:14). Therefore, if one converted due to fear he is considered "without Me," i.e., not part of God's people.

״הַנִּטְעָן עַל אֵשֶׁת אִישׁ״ וכו׳. אָמַר רַב: וּבְעֵדִים.

§ The mishna states that **one who was suspected of** relations with **a married woman** may not marry her even after she divorces her husband. Even if they marry without permission, they must divorce. **Rav said: This is** only in a case when there were **witnesses** to her infidelity, and because of their testimony the court required her first husband divorce her. However, if her first husband divorced her due to suspicion and rumors but without witnesses, her second husband would not be obligated to divorce her.

אָמַר רַב שֵׁשֶׁת: אָמִינָא כִּי נָיֵים וְשָׁכֵיב רַב אֲמַר לְהַאי שְׁמַעְתָּא. דְּתַנְיָא: הַנִּטְעָן עַל אֵשֶׁת אִישׁ וְהוֹצִיאוּהָ עַל יָדוֹ, וְנִתְגָּרְשָׁה מִתַּחַת יְדֵי אַחֵר, אִם כָּנַס – לֹא יוֹצִיא.

Rav Sheshet said: I say that when Rav was dozing or sleeping[N] **he said that** ***halakha***, and it is mistaken. **As it is taught** in a *baraita*: With regard to **one who was suspected of** adultery with **a married woman and** as a result the court requires her husband to **divorce her,** and later she married someone else[H] **and was then divorced by this other, if** the one who had been suspected of illicit relations with her then **married** her, **he need not divorce** her.

הֵיכִי דָּמֵי, אִי דְּאִיכָּא עֵדִים – כִּי אֲתָא אַחֵר וְאַפְסְקֵיהּ לְקָלָא מַאי הָוֵי? אֶלָּא לָאו דְּלֵיכָּא עֵדִים, וְטַעְמָא, דַּאֲתָא אַחֵר וְאַפְסְקֵיהּ לְקָלָא, הָא לָאו הָכִי – מַפְּקִינַן!

The Gemara clarifies this: **What are the circumstances** of this case? **If** it is referring to a case where **there are witnesses** to their adultery, **when another came and put an end to the rumor** of her misconduct by marrying her, **what of it?** If there were witnesses, the adulterers may never marry each other. **Rather, is it not** referring to a case **where there were no witnesses** to the adultery, **and the reason** she does not have to be divorced from her third husband, with whom she committed adultery while married to her first husband, is specifically **because another came** and, by marrying her, **put an end to the rumor? This** implies that **were it not so,** i.e., had she not married someone else before marrying the man suspected of committing adultery with her, the court **would have removed** her from him and required them to divorce, even without witnesses to their adultery. This contradicts Rav's statement above that they must divorce only if there were witnesses to the infidelity.

אָמַר לְךָ רַב: הוּא הַדִּין דְּאַף עַל גַּב דְּלָא אֲתָא אַחֵר וְאַפְסְקֵיהּ לְקָלָא. אִי אִיכָּא עֵדִים – מַפְּקִינַן, אִי לֵיכָּא עֵדִים – לָא מַפְּקִינַן, וְהָכִי קָאָמַר: דְּאַף עַל גַּב דַּאֲתָא אַחֵר וְאַפְסְקֵיהּ לְקָלָא – לְכַתְּחִלָּה לֹא יִכְנוֹס.

The Gemara responds: **Rav** could have **said to you** that **the same is true even if another did not come and put an end to the rumor** by marrying her. The same principle applies: **If there were witnesses** to the adultery the court **removes her** and requires them to divorce, but **if there were no witnesses,** the court **does not remove her. And this is what** the *baraita* **is saying:** The novelty in this *baraita* is **that even though another came and put an end to the rumor** by marrying her, nevertheless, the suspected adulterer may **not marry her** ***ab initio*** due to the original suspicions.

מֵיתִיבֵי: בַּמֶּה דְּבָרִים אֲמוּרִים – כְּשֶׁאֵין לָהּ בָּנִים, אֲבָל יֵשׁ לָהּ בָּנִים – לֹא תֵּצֵא. וְאִם בָּאוּ עֵדֵי טוּמְאָה – אֲפִילּוּ יֵשׁ לָהּ כַּמָּה בָּנִים תֵּצֵא.

The Gemara **raises an objection** from a different *baraita* that qualifies the previous one: **In what** case **is this statement,** that the court removes her from the suspected adulterer, **said?** It is **when she has no children** from her first husband. **But if she has children** from him, **she is not** required to be **divorced**[H] from the suspected adulterer. On the contrary, if they were required to divorce, it could strengthen the original rumor and others might suspect that her children are *mamzerim*. **However, if witnesses to** her **impurity,** i.e., her adultery, **came** and testified[H] that she had relations with this man while she was married, then **even if she has several children** from the first husband, **she is** required to be **divorced.** This implies that a woman without children from her first husband must separate from a man suspected of illicit relations with her on strength of suspicion alone.

רַב מוֹקֵי לָהּ לְמַתְנִיתִין בְּיֵשׁ לָהּ בָּנִים וְיֵשׁ לָהּ עֵדִים. וּמַאי דּוּחְקֵיהּ דְּרַב לְאוֹקְמֵי לְמַתְנִיתִין בְּיֵשׁ לָהּ בָּנִים וְיֵשׁ לָהּ עֵדִים, וְטַעְמָא דְּאִיכָּא עֵדִים – מַפְּקִינַן, וְאִי לֵיכָּא עֵדִים – לָא מַפְּקִינַן, לוֹקְמַהּ בְּשֶׁאֵין לָהּ בָּנִים, אַף עַל גַּב דְּלֵיכָּא עֵדִים?

The Gemara answers and explains that **Rav establishes the mishna** as referring only to a case **where she has children** by her first husband **and there are witnesses** to her adultery. In such a situation, she and the adulterer must divorce, but without witnesses they are not required to divorce. The Gemara asks: **What forced Rav to establish the mishna** as referring to a case **where she has children and there are witnesses** and explain that **the reason that** the court **removes her** from the suspected adulterer **is because there were witnesses, but that if there were no witnesses they do not remove her?** Why does he not **establish** the mishna as referring to a case **where there were no children** and that they must divorce **even if there were no witnesses?**

NOTES

When Rav was dozing or sleeping – כִּי נָיֵים וְשָׁכֵיב רַב: Some commentaries suggest that this is merely a polite way of saying that Rav's statement is incorrect.

HALAKHA

One who was suspected of adultery with a married woman and later she married someone else – הַנִּטְעָן עַל אֵשֶׁת אִישׁ וְנִשָּׂאָה לְאַחֵר: If one was suspected of committing adultery with a married woman, and due to this her husband divorced her and she married someone else and was later divorced from him, it is nevertheless prohibited for her to marry the suspected adulterer. However, if she transgressed and married him he need not divorce her, even if she had no children. The ruling applies even if there were witnesses to circumstantial evidence, provided they were not witnesses to the adultery itself, in which case the adulterer would be forced to divorce the adulteress (Rambam *Sefer Nashim, Hilkhot Sota* 2:15; *Shulḥan Arukh, Even HaEzer* 11:2).

If she has children she is not required to be divorced – יֵשׁ לָהּ בָּנִים לֹא תֵּצֵא: In the case of a husband who had not made a declaration of jealousy with regard to his wife, yet witnesses came forward and testified that she had been secluded with a man, if the husband then sent her away due to circumstantial evidence, she may not marry the man with whom she is suspected of misconduct. If the divorcée transgressed this *halakha* and married the suspected adulterer, the following distinction applies: If she had no children from the first husband, the court requires him to divorce her; if she had children from him she is not required to be divorced, based on the Rif's interpretation of the Gemara. If the first husband had made a declaration of jealousy with regard to his wife, then she must be divorced from the suspected adulterer even if she had children from him (Rambam *Sefer Nashim, Hilkhot Sota* 2:13; *Shulḥan Arukh, Even HaEzer* 11:1).

Witnesses to her impurity came and testified – בָּאוּ עֵדֵי טוּמְאָה: If witnesses testify that a married woman committed adultery, and consequently her husband divorces her, she may not marry the adulterer. If she transgressed and married him, even if she had children from the first husband, she must be divorced from him (Rambam *Sefer Nashim, Hilkhot Sota* 2:16; *Shulḥan Arukh, Even HaEzer* 11:2 and 178:18).

אָמַר רָבָא: מַתְנִיתִין קָשִׁיתֵיהּ: מַאי אִירְיָא דְּתָנֵי "הוֹצִיאוּהָ", לִיתְנֵי הוֹצִיאָהּ, אֶלָּא, כׇּל "הוֹצִיאוּהָ" בְּבֵית דִּין, וּבֵית דִּין – בְּעֵדִים הוּא דְּמַפְּקִי.

Rava said: The language of **the mishna** was **difficult for him;** due to that he deemed it necessary to interpret it as he did. **Why does the** *tanna* **specifically teach: They remove her** from him [*hotziuha*]? **Let it teach: He divorces her** [*hotziah*] in the singular. **Rather, every time** the plural form: **They remove her,** is used, it is referring **to** the judges of the **court. And a court removes** a woman from her suspected adulterer only **if there were witnesses,** and not due to suspicion alone.

וְאִי בָּעֵית אֵימָא: הָנֵי מַתְנְיָיתָא – רַבִּי הִיא, דְּתַנְיָא: רוֹכֵל יוֹצֵא וְאִשָּׁה חוֹגֶרֶת בְּסִינָר, אָמַר רַבִּי: הוֹאִיל וּמְכוֹעָר הַדָּבָר – תֵּצֵא. רוֹק לְמַעְלָה מִן הַכִּילָּה, אָמַר רַבִּי: הוֹאִיל וּמְכוֹעָר הַדָּבָר – תֵּצֵא.

If you wish, say a different answer for Rav's explanation: **Those** *baraitot* that require the wife and the suspected adulterer to divorce even without witnesses to the adultery are taught in accordance with the opinion of **Rabbi** Yehuda HaNasi. **As it is taught** in a *baraita*: With regard to a case where a husband saw **a peddler leaving**[N] the house, **and** when he entered he found his **wife retying her smock** [*sinar*],[L] i.e., putting her clothes back on, **Rabbi** Yehuda HaNasi **said: Since this is a distasteful matter**[H] because it looks as though she committed adultery with the peddler, **she** must be **divorced** by her husband. Alternatively, if the husband entered after the peddler had left and found **saliva above**[N] **the netting of the bed,** implying that someone had lain on the bed and spit upward, although no actual act was witnessed, **Rabbi** Yehuda HaNasi **said: Since this is a distasteful matter, she** must be **divorced.**

NOTES

A peddler leaving – רוֹכֵל יוֹצֵא: The Gemara refers to peddlers because they would frequently spend time selling their wares to women. Therefore, their actions were commonly suspected.

Saliva above – רוֹק לְמַעְלָה: The Meiri holds that this phrase is a euphemism meaning that signs of semen were found in the bed.

LANGUAGE

Smock [*sinar*] – סִינָר: The source of this word is not entirely clear, but some suggest that the word was borrowed from the Greek ζωνάριον, *zonariyon*, which comes from the term for belt and means a strap or girdle worn by women as an undergarment. However, the *sinar* described by the Sages is some kind of trousers worn as an undergarment.

HALAKHA

A distasteful matter – דָּבָר מְכוֹעָר: What is considered a distasteful matter? It is a case where, e.g., one entered the house of a married woman after some other man had left and found her standing next to the bed in her undergarments, or one saw the couple exiting from a secluded place, or one saw them lock themselves in a room, or any similar circumstance. Each case is judged at the judges' discretion (Rambam *Sefer Nashim, Hilkhot Sota* 2:13 and *Sefer Kedusha, Hilkhot Ishut* 24:15; *Shulḥan Arukh, Even HaEzer* 11:1, 178:18).

Perek **II**
Daf **25** Amud **a**

מִנְעָלִים הֲפוּכִים תַּחַת הַמִּטָּה, אָמַר רַבִּי: הוֹאִיל וּמְכוֹעָר הַדָּבָר – תֵּצֵא. מִנְעָלִים הֲפוּכִים? לֵיחֲזֵי דְּמַאן נִינְהוּ! אֶלָּא: מְקוֹם מִנְעָלִים הֲפוּכִים (תַּחַת הַמִּטָּה. אָמַר רַבִּי: הוֹאִיל וּמְכוֹעָר הַדָּבָר – תֵּצֵא).

The same applies if the husband found **the shoes reversed under the bed,** so that the toe of the shoe faced the bed; this is a sign that a stranger came in and placed them like that. **Rabbi** Yehuda HaNasi **said: Since this is a distasteful matter, she** must be **divorced.** The Gemara questions this: **Shoes turned around? Let him see whose they are** and clarify who the stranger was and then find out what he was doing there. **Rather,** the case was that he found the **place of the shoes,** i.e., shoe prints, **reversed**[N] **under the bed** and cannot recognize whose shoe prints they are. **Rabbi** Yehuda HaNasi **said: Since this is a distasteful matter, she** must be **divorced.**

NOTES

The place of the shoes reversed – מְקוֹם מִנְעָלִים הֲפוּכִים: According to Rashi and Rabbi Yehuda bar Natan, this means that the husband found prints of shoes that had been turned upside down so that the sole of the shoe faced up. Rashi holds that they were overturned so as to hide the ownership of the shoes. On the other hand, Rabbi Yehuda bar Natan holds that they were upside down due to the peddler's great haste, so that he did not have time to place the shoes in the regular fashion. According to the Meiri, the shoe prints were not under the bed but at the foot of the bed, indicating that apparently the shoes fell off while they were engaged in adultery. The Meiri also gives a second explanation, that the husband found footprints of his wife's shoes next to his own bed, suggesting that she lay there with someone else. This opinion is similar to Rashi's second explanation.

וְהִלְכְתָא כְּוָותֵיהּ דְּרַב, וְהִלְכְתָא כְּוָותֵיהּ דְּרַבִּי. קַשְׁיָא הִלְכְתָא אַהִלְכְתָא! לָא קַשְׁיָא: הָא – בְּקָלָא דְּפָסֵיק, הָא – בְּקָלָא דְּלָא פָּסֵיק. קָלָא דְּלָא פָּסֵיק וְלֵיכָּא עֵדִים – כְּרַבִּי, קָלָא דְּפָסֵיק וְאִיכָּא עֵדִים – כְּרַב.

The Gemara concludes: **The *halakha* is in accordance with** the opinion **of Rav,** that they must divorce only if there were witnesses, **and the *halakha* is in accordance with** the opinion of **Rabbi** Yehuda HaNasi, that they must divorce if there is a matter that is distasteful.[HN] The Gemara challenges this: One ***halakha*** is **difficult,** as it contradicts **the** other ***halakha.*** The Gemara answers: This contradiction is **not difficult. This one** relates to a case **where the rumor ceases** and the woman is sent away only if there are witnesses, but **that one** relates to a case **where the rumor does not cease,** in which case he divorces her even if there are no witnesses. The Gemara elucidates the cases: In cases of **a rumor that does not cease,** even if **there are no witnesses** the *halakha* is **in accordance with** the opinion of **Rabbi** Yehuda HaNasi and he divorces her. If **the rumor ceases and there are witnesses,** the *halakha* is **in accordance with** the opinion of **Rav,** and he divorces her because there are witnesses.

וְקָלָא דְּלָא פָּסֵיק עַד כַּמָּה? אֲמַר אַבַּיֵי, אֲמַרָה לִי אֵם: דּוּמֵי דְּמָתָא יוֹמָא וּפַלְגָא. וְלָא אֲמַרַן אֶלָּא דְּלָא פָּסַק בֵּינֵי וּבֵינֵי, אֲבָל פָּסַק בֵּינֵי וּבֵינֵי – הָא פָּסַק. וְלָא אֲמַרַן אֶלָּא דְּלָא פָּסַק מֵחֲמַת יִרְאָה, אֲבָל פָּסַק מֵחֲמַת יִרְאָה – מֵחֲמַת יִרְאָה הוּא. וְלָא אֲמַרַן אֶלָּא דְּלֵיכָּא אוֹיְבִים, אֲבָל אִיכָּא אוֹיְבִים – אוֹיְבִים הוּא דְּאַפְּקוּ לֵיהּ לְקָלָא.

The Gemara clarifies this: **At what point** is it considered to be **a persistent rumor?**[H] **Abaye said:** My **mother told me:**[B] **A rumor in the city** lasts **a day and a half.** The Gemara comments: **We said** that this is the length of time **only** if the rumor **did not cease in the meantime. But** if the rumor **did cease in the meantime,** even it was later renewed, **this is** considered a rumor that **has ceased** and is disregarded. **And we said** that a rumor that ceased is not considered persistent **only** if the reason it **ceased** was **not due to fear** of the individual about whom it is said. **But if it ceased due to fear, it is** only **due to fear** and is still considered a persistent rumor. **And we said** that a persistent rumor has validity **only** if the subject of the rumor **does not have any** known **enemies, but** if **he has enemies** it may be assumed that **it is the enemies who put out the rumor** about him.

HALAKHA

When does the court require a woman to be divorced from her husband or from a man suspected of adultery – מָתַי מוֹצִיאִים אִשָּׁה מִבַּעְלָהּ וּמִנִּטְעָן: In a case where the husband did not make a declaration of jealousy, if witnesses came forward that his wife was secluded alone with a certain man, and based on that testimony the husband divorces her, she may not marry the suspected adulterer. If the suspected adulterer ignored the *halakha* and married her anyway, and she bore him children, he is not required to divorce her. They may remain married if they had children together even if there was a persistent rumor in town that she had committed adultery with the suspected individual. This is in accordance with the opinion of Rabbi Yehuda HaNasi. However, if there was no rumor, or if the rumor ran its course and ended, then if she married the suspected individual she need not be divorced, even if she did not bear him any children. Even if a single witness came forward and testified that she had committed adultery with him she need not be divorced, according to the opinion of Rav.

Some say that if there was a persistent rumor along with witnesses to some distasteful matter the court requires her husband to divorce her, even though there are no witnesses that she actually committed adultery (Rema, citing Rashi; *Shulḥan Arukh, Even HaEzer* 11:1).

At what point is it a persistent rumor – אֵיזֶהוּ קוֹל שֶׁאֵינוֹ פּוֹסֵק: A persistent rumor is a rumor about a married woman and a suspected adulterer that is discussed in town continually for a day and a half or longer. Even if the rumor ceased in the middle, if it ceased due to fear, this is not considered a rumor that ended. All of this applies only if neither the woman, nor the suspected individual, nor the husband had any enemies who may have started the rumor (Ran; *Shulḥan Arukh, Even HaEzer* 11:1).

BACKGROUND

Mother told me – אֲמַרָה לִי אֵם: Abaye's mother died when he was an infant, and he was raised by a foster mother whom he called mother (*Kiddushin* 31b). He usually quoted her on issues of health and remedies, as she had expertise in these fields.

NOTES

The opinions of Rabbi Yehuda HaNasi and Rav – שִׁיטוֹת רַבִּי וְרַב: There are many explanations in the commentaries as to the opinions of Rabbi Yehuda HaNasi and Rav. Two main issues remain unresolved in the Gemara: Is the discussion over whether the woman must divorce her husband, or the suspected adulterer if she later married him, or both? Does the matter that is distasteful require witnesses? The following chart summarizes the various opinions:

Commentary	In order to require her to be divorced from her husband		In order to require her to be divorced from the suspected adulterer if she later married him	
	Rav requires	Rabbi Yehuda HaNasi requires	Rav requires	Rabbi Yehuda HaNasi requires
Rashi; Responsa of the Rashba	Witnesses to adultery	A distasteful matter	Witnesses to adultery	A distasteful matter
Rif; Rambam according to the understanding of Rashba	Witnesses to adultery	Witnesses to adultery	Witnesses to adultery	Witnesses to a distasteful matter
Rabbeinu Tam's initial opinion	Witnesses to adultery	Witnesses to adultery	Witnesses to adultery	A distasteful matter
Rabbeinu Tam's revised opinion	Witnesses to a distasteful matter	Witnesses to a distasteful matter	Witnesses to a distasteful matter	Witnesses to a distasteful matter
Ramban; Rambam according to the understanding of *Darkhei Moshe*	Witnesses to adultery	Witnesses to a distasteful matter	Witnesses to adultery	A persistent rumor
Rosh	Witnesses to adultery	Witnesses to a distasteful matter	Witnesses to adultery	Witnesses to a distasteful matter

תְּנַן הָתָם: הַמּוֹצִיא אֶת אִשְׁתּוֹ מִשּׁוּם שֵׁם רַע – לֹא יַחֲזִיר. מִשּׁוּם נֶדֶר – לֹא יַחֲזִיר. שְׁלַח לֵיהּ רַבָּה בַּר הוּנָא לְרַבָּה בַּר רַב נַחְמָן: יְלַמְּדֵנוּ רַבֵּינוּ, כָּנַס מַהוּ שֶׁיּוֹצִיא?

§ **We learned** in a mishna **there** (*Gittin* 45b): A man **who divorces his wife due to** her **bad reputation may not take** her **back** again, even if it turns out that the rumor was untrue. Likewise, if he divorced his wife **due to a vow**[H] of hers that is unbearable to him **he may not take** her **back** even if she is released from that vow. **Rabba bar Rav Huna sent** a question **to Rabba bar Rav Naḥman: Our teacher, instruct us.** If one of those men listed in that mishna divorced his wife due to her bad reputation or vow and it was therefore prohibited for him to take her back, yet he nevertheless **remarried** her, **what is the** *halakha*? **Must** he **divorce** her?[H]

אָמַר לֵיהּ, תְּנֵינָא: הַנִּטְעָן עַל אֵשֶׁת אִישׁ וְהוֹצִיאָהּ מִתַּחַת יָדוֹ, אַף עַל פִּי שֶׁכָּנַס יוֹצִיא. אָמַר לֵיהּ: מִי דָּמֵי? הָתָם ״הוֹצִיאוּהָ״ וְהָכָא ״הוֹצִיאָהּ״! וְרַבָּה בַּר רַב נַחְמָן – מַתְנִיתִין נַמִי ״הוֹצִיאָהּ״ תְּנַן.

Rabba bar Rav Naḥman **said to him: We** already **learned** in the mishna (24b): With regard to **one who is suspected of** committing adultery with **a married woman, and he,** her husband, **divorced her, even if he** subsequently **remarried** her **he must divorce** her. Rabba bar Rav Huna **said to him: Is this comparable** to the case I asked about? **There,** in the mishna, it says: **They,** the court, **remove her** from him, **whereas here** (*Gittin* 45b), the mishna states: **He divorced her** of his own accord. Perhaps if the court requires them to divorce, the *halakha* is different. The Gemara explains: **And Rabba bar Rav Naḥman,** who held that the two *mishnayot* were comparable, had a text of **the mishna** that **also** read: **He divorced her,** instead of: They remove her.

וְאַכַּתִּי מִי דָּמֵי? הָכָא – בַּעַל, וְהָתָם – בּוֹעֵל! אָמַר לֵיהּ: שַׁפִּיר דָּמֵי אַהֲדָדֵי: הָכָא אֲמוּר רַבָּנַן לֹא יִכְנוֹס, וְאִם כָּנַס יוֹצִיא – הָכִי נַמִי אָמְרִי רַבָּנַן לֹא יַחֲזִיר, וְאִם כָּנַס – יוֹצִיא.

Rabba bar Rav Huna asks: **Still, is this comparable? Here,** the question was raised in a case where **the** first **husband** remarried her, which will not strengthen the rumors of her bad reputation, **but there,** the mishna refers to **the man** with whom she committed **adultery** remarrying her, which strengthens those rumors. **He said to him: They are certainly comparable to each other: Here,** in the mishna discussing one who is suspected of committing adultery, **the Sages said that he may not marry** her **and if he did marry** her **he must divorce** her. **So too, the Sages said** in the case of one who divorced his wife due to her reputation or vow **that he may not take** her **back, and if he does remarry** her **he must divorce** her.

וְלֹא הִיא, הָתָם – אַלּוּמֵי אַלְּמֵיהּ לְקָלָא, הָכָא אָמְרִינַן קָם בֵּיהּ בְּקָלָא וְלֵיתֵיהּ.

The Gemara rejects this: **That is not so,** as **there,** when the man suspected of committing adultery marries the woman, **he thereby strengthens the rumor** of adultery. For this reason he must divorce her. **Here, we say that he,** the husband, **established** the facts of **the rumor** and found that it **was not so** and the rumor was baseless. Therefore, there is no need for him to divorce her if he remarries her. Rabba bar Rav Huna's question remains unresolved.

מתני׳ הַמֵּבִיא גֵּט מִמְּדִינַת הַיָּם וְאָמַר ״בְּפָנַי נִכְתַּב וּבְפָנַי נֶחְתַּם״ לֹא יִשָּׂא אֶת אִשְׁתּוֹ. ״מֵת״, ״הֲרַגְתִּיו״, ״הֲרַגְנוּהוּ״ – לֹא יִשָּׂא אֶת אִשְׁתּוֹ. רַבִּי יְהוּדָה אוֹמֵר ״הֲרַגְתִּיו״ – לֹא תִּנָּשֵׂא אִשְׁתּוֹ: ״הֲרַגְנוּהוּ״ – תִּנָּשֵׂא אִשְׁתּוֹ.

MISHNA An agent **who brought a bill of divorce from a country overseas**[N] **and said: It was written in my presence and it was signed in my presence,** as required in order to establish the bill of divorce as valid, **may not marry the wife,**[H] i.e., the divorcée. Since the validity of the bill of divorce is based upon his testimony, marrying the divorcée creates the impression that he had an ulterior motive for his testimony. Similarly, a witness who testified that a certain man **died,**[H] or testified: **I killed him,** or: **We killed him,**[H] **may not marry** that man's **wife. Rabbi Yehuda says:** If he testified: **I killed him, his wife may not be married**[N] at all based on that evidence, as his testimony is unreliable, but if he said: **We killed him, his wife may be married** to anyone other than those witnesses.

גמ׳ טַעְמָא דְּמִמְּדִינַת הַיָּם – דַּעֲלֵיהּ קָסָמְכִינַן, אֲבָל מֵאֶרֶץ יִשְׂרָאֵל, דְּלָאו עֲלֵיהּ קָסָמְכִינַן, יִשָּׂא אֶת אִשְׁתּוֹ.

GEMARA The Gemara clarifies: **The reason that** the agent may not marry the divorcée applies specifically in a case where he brings the bill of divorce **from a country overseas, as** in this case **we,** the court, **rely upon his** testimony to validate the bill of divorce. **But** an agent who brings a bill of divorce **from Eretz Yisrael** need not make any verbal declaration, and **since we,** the court, **do not rely upon his** testimony but upon the written bill of divorce alone, **he may marry his wife,** i.e., the divorcée, since it does not arouse suspicion.

HALAKHA

One who divorces his wife due to her bad reputation or vows – הַמּוֹצִיא אִשְׁתּוֹ מִשּׁוּם שֵׁם רַע אוֹ נְדָרִים: One who divorced his wife because she made vows that were unbearable to him, or because she came to have a bad reputation may not remarry her. Some say that this applies only if he told her explicitly that this is the reason for the divorce and if he confirmed that were it not for the vows or the reputation he would not have divorced her (*Tur*, citing Rosh). Some say that even if he did not confirm this explicitly, he may not remarry her (*Tur*, citing Ramah). One opinion (Rambam) holds that even if he did not tell her why he divorced her he may not take her back (*Shulḥan Arukh*, *Even HaEzer* 10:3).

One who takes back a wife he divorced due to a bad reputation – הַמַּחֲזִיר אִשָּׁה שֶׁגֵּרֵשׁ מִשּׁוּם שֵׁם רַע: If one divorces his wife due to her bad reputation or a similar issue, he may not remarry her. However, if he transgressed this prohibition and remarried her, he need not divorce her again, in accordance with the conclusion of the Gemara here (*Shulḥan Arukh*, *Even HaEzer* 11:5).

One who brings a bill of divorce and wishes to marry the divorcée – הַמֵּבִיא גֵּט וְרוֹצֶה לָשֵׂאת הַגְּרוּשָׁה: An agent who brings a woman her bill of divorce from a place for which he must testify: It was written in my presence and signed in my presence, may not marry her because this may arouse suspicions. However, if he brought the bill of divorce from a place for which he need not say this, he is permitted to marry the divorcée, based on the mishna and the conclusion of the Gemara (Rambam *Sefer Nashim*, *Hilkhot Geirushin* 10:14; *Shulḥan Arukh*, *Even HaEzer* 12:1).

One who testifies that the husband died – הַמֵּעִיד עַל הַבַּעַל שֶׁמֵּת: If a single witness came and testified to a woman that her husband died, she is allowed to marry by virtue of that testimony. However, she may not marry the witness, as this appears suspicious (Rambam *Sefer Nashim*, *Hilkhot Geirushin* 10:14; *Shulḥan Arukh*, *Even HaEzer* 17:3).

I killed him, we killed him – הֲרַגְתִּיו, הֲרַגְנוּהוּ: The testimony of one who testified that he killed a man, or that he was with the murderers, is accepted, and that man's wife is permitted to marry by virtue of that testimony (Rambam *Sefer Nashim*, *Hilkhot Geirushin* 13:10; *Shulḥan Arukh*, *Even HaEzer* 17:7).

NOTES

An agent who brought a bill of divorce from a country overseas – הַמֵּבִיא גֵּט מִמְּדִינַת הַיָּם: Two reasons are given in the Talmud to explain why an agent bringing a bill of divorce from overseas must testify that it was written and signed in his presence (*Gittin* 2a): First, the witnesses who signed the bill of divorce are not present and cannot establish its validity. The agent's testimony consequently prevents the husband from claiming that it is a forgery. Second, there was concern that in the Diaspora the scribes were not experts and might not write the bill correctly. If it was written and signed in the presence of the agent, the court can ask him, and verify, that the document was written correctly.

A witness who…testified: I killed him…his wife may not be married – הֲרַגְתִּיו לֹא תִּנָּשֵׂא אִשְׁתּוֹ: In Rambam's Commentary on the Mishna it is explained that Rabbi Yehuda does not accept the principle that an individual does not make himself wicked.

HALAKHA

So-and-so sodomized me – פְּלוֹנִי רְבָעַנִי: One who testified that he was sodomized by another may combine his testimony with that of another witness in order to put the sodomizer to death. This is regardless of whether it was an act of rape or whether the witness participated willingly, in accordance with Rava's opinion in the dispute with Rav Yosef that we divide the statement. His statement includes both self-incriminating testimony and other information, so the court divides his assertion, accepting as evidence only information that is not self-incriminating. His report about being a willing partner is discarded, and the court accepts only that another sodomized him (Rambam *Sefer Shofetim*, *Hilkhot Edut* 12:2; *Shulḥan Arukh*, *Ḥoshen Mishpat* 34:26).

A wicked witness – עֵד רָשָׁע: Wicked individuals who willingly violate the words of the Torah are unfit for giving testimony by Torah law (Rambam *Sefer Shofetim*, *Hilkhot Edut* 10:1).

וְהָא מֵת, דְּלָאו עֲלֵיהּ קָסָמְכִינַן, דְּאָמַר מָר: אִשָּׁה דַּיְיקָא וּמִינַּסְבָא, וְקָתָנֵי: לֹא יִשָּׂא אֶת אִשְׁתּוֹ!

The Gemara challenges this: **But** also in the case of a witness who said that the husband **died, we,** the court, **do not rely** solely **upon** his testimony. **As the Master said: A woman is exacting** in her investigation of the truth of the testimony that her husband died before she **marries** again, and it is primarily on that basis that she is permitted to remarry. **Yet it is taught that he** still **may not marry his wife.**

הָתָם לֵיכָּא כְּתָבָא, הָכָא – אִיכָּא כְּתָבָא. דִּתְנַן: מַה בֵּין גֵּט לְמִיתָה – שֶׁהַכְּתָב מוֹכִיחַ.

The Gemara answers: The two cases are not comparable, as **there,** in the case when a witness testifies that the husband has died, **there is not anything written** as proof, and therefore he may not marry the widow. However, **here,** in a case where an agent brings a bill of divorce from Eretz Yisrael, **there is a written** document that is valid without any testimony. **As we learned** in a mishna (117a): **What is the difference between a bill of divorce and death?** Why does the court rely upon those men who are not trusted as witnesses to the death of a husband if they act as agents to bring a bill of divorce, even from overseas, such that they must give testimony that it was written and signed in their presence? The difference is **that** with regard to a bill of divorce **the writing proves** their testimony.

״מֵת״, ״הֲרַגְתִּיו״, ״הֲרַגְנוּהוּ״ – לֹא יִשָּׂא אֶת אִשְׁתּוֹ. הוּא נִיהוּ דְּלֹא יִשָּׂא אֶת אִשְׁתּוֹ, הָא לְאַחֵר – תִּנָּשֵׂא.

The mishna stated that if the witness said with regard to the husband that **he died,** or: **I killed him,** or: **We killed him,** then **he may not marry** the **wife** of the deceased. The Gemara infers that **he,** the witness **himself, may not marry** the **wife; this** implies that **to another she may be married** on the basis of his testimony.

וְהָאָמַר רַב יוֹסֵף: ״פְּלוֹנִי רְבָעַנִי לְאוֹנְסִי״ – הוּא וְאַחֵר מִצְטָרְפִין לְהׇרְגוֹ. ״לִרְצוֹנִי״ – רָשָׁע הוּא, וְהַתּוֹרָה אָמְרָה: ״אַל תָּשֶׁת יָדְךָ עִם רָשָׁע לִהְיוֹת עֵד חָמָס״.

The Gemara challenges this: **Didn't Rav Yosef say:** With regard to one who testified that **so-and-so sodomized me**[H] **against my will,** then **he** who testified to being the victim of the sexual assault **and another** bystander witness can **combine** as a pair of witnesses in order **to put** the assailant **to death** for homosexual intercourse. But if he testified: I was **willingly** sodomized by so-and-so, then **he is wicked**[H] by his own admission, since he willingly transgressed. **And the Torah said: "Put not your hand with the wicked to be a corrupt witness"** (Exodus 23:1). If one renders himself unfit as a witness by admitting to murder, how can his testimony be accepted to permit the wife to remarry?

וְכִי תֵּימָא שָׁאנֵי עֵדוּת אִשָּׁה דְּאַקִילוּ בָּהּ רַבָּנַן – וְהָאָמַר רַב מְנַשֶּׁה:

And if you would say that **testimony** that **a woman's** husband died **is different, as the Sages ruled leniently** in such matters and perhaps accepted testimony of a wicked witness in such cases, **didn't Rav Menashe say:**

Perek **II**
Daf **25** Amud **b**

NOTES

A robber according to the words of the Sages – גַּזְלָן דְּדִבְרֵיהֶם: In tractate *Sanhedrin* (24b), there is a list of those who are unfit by rabbinic decree for giving testimony. This list includes those who take money from others but are not categorized as robbers according to Torah law.

A robber according to Torah law is unfit – גַּזְלָן דְּדִבְרֵי תּוֹרָה פָּסוּל: According to the Rif, even though a wicked individual is unfit for testifying that a woman's husband has died, if he were to make an incidental remark about the matter, this evidence would be accepted by the court. In this respect he is no worse than a gentile, who is believed if he makes an incidental remark.

גַּזְלָן דְּדִבְרֵיהֶם – כָּשֵׁר לְעֵדוּת אִשָּׁה, גַּזְלָן דְּדִבְרֵי תּוֹרָה – פָּסוּל לְעֵדוּת אִשָּׁה. נֵימָא רַב מְנַשֶּׁה דְּאָמַר כְּרַבִּי יְהוּדָה?

Although one who is considered **a robber according to the words of the Sages**[N] is unfit for other forms of testimony, **he is fit** as a witness **for testimony** that **a woman's** husband died. **A robber according to Torah law is unfit**[N] as a witness even **for testimony** that **a woman's** husband has died.[H] **Should we say that** what **Rav Menashe said** is **in accordance with** the opinion of **Rabbi Yehuda?** Rabbi Yehuda said in the mishna that one who is considered absolutely wicked because he admitted that he is a murderer is unfit for testifying to the death of a husband, but one who was merely present among a gang of murderers is not.

HALAKHA

A robber with regard to testimony rendering it permitted for a woman to remarry – גַּזְלָן בְּעֵדוּת אִשָּׁה: One who is unfit for giving testimony by Torah law is not believed when testifying that a woman's husband died, but one who is unfit by rabbinic law is believed in such instances (Rambam *Sefer Nashim*, *Hilkhot Geirushin* 12:17; *Shulḥan Arukh*, *Even HaEzer* 17:3).

אֲמַר לָךְ רַב מְנַשֶּׁה: אֲנָא דַּאֲמַרִי אֲפִילּוּ לְרַבָּנַן, וְטַעֲמָא דְּרַבָּנַן הָכָא – כִּדְרָבָא, דְּאָמַר רָבָא: אָדָם קָרוֹב אֵצֶל עַצְמוֹ, וְאֵין אָדָם מֵשִׂים עַצְמוֹ רָשָׁע.

The Gemara rejects this: **Rav Menashe** could have **said to you: I am speaking even according to** the opinion of **the Rabbis.** Although the Rabbis did not allow one who was wicked by Torah law to testify for a woman, a witness who admitted: I killed him, is nevertheless believed. **And the rationale of the Rabbis here is in accordance with** the opinion of **Rava, as Rava** disputed Rav Yosef's opinion and **said:** Even if one said that he was willingly sodomized by this man, he is not believed concerning his own actions, because **a person is his own relative.**[N] Consequently, he may not testify about himself, just as the testimony of any relative is disqualified. **And** furthermore, **a person does not make himself wicked.**[H] His testimony with regard to his own actions is inadmissible because he is his own relative, but his testimony is accepted both to put a sodomizer to death or to render it permitted for a woman to remarry by saying that he killed her husband.

לֵימָא רַב יוֹסֵף דְּאָמַר כְּרַבִּי יְהוּדָה!? אֲמַר לָךְ רַב יוֹסֵף: אֲנָא דַּאֲמַרִי אֲפִילּוּ לְרַבָּנַן, וְשָׁאנֵי עֵדוּת אִשָּׁה דְּאַקִילוּ בָּהּ רַבָּנַן, וְרַב מְנַשֶּׁה דְּאָמַר כְּרַבִּי יְהוּדָה.

The Gemara asks: **Shall we say** according to this explanation that the opinion **that Rav Yosef spoke is in accordance with the** opinion of **Rabbi Yehuda?** The Gemara rejects this: **Rav Yosef** could have **said to you: I am speaking even according to** the opinion of **the Rabbis,** as in my opinion, **testimony** enabling **a woman** to remarry **is different in that the Rabbis ruled more leniently** and they even accept testimony from a completely wicked individual. However, **Rav Menashe, who** renders unfit one who is wicked by Torah law from testimony enabling a woman to remarry, **spoke in accordance with** the opinion of **Rabbi Yehuda,** who differentiates even in such testimony between one who is considered wicked according to Torah law and one who is considered wicked by rabbinic law.

״הֲרַגְתִּיו״ כּו׳ ״הֲרַגְנוּהוּ״ תִּנָּשֵׂא כּו׳. מַאי שְׁנָא הֲרַגְתִּיו וּמַאי שְׁנָא הֲרַגְנוּהוּ? אֲמַר רַב יְהוּדָה: בְּאוֹמֵר ״אֲנִי הָיִיתִי עִם הוֹרְגָיו״.

In the mishna it is taught that the court accepts testimony from one who said: **I killed him,** or: **We killed him,** while Rabbi Yehuda differentiates between one who said: I killed him, whose testimony is not accepted, and one who said: We killed him, whose testimony is accepted and the woman **may be married** to others. The Gemara asks: **What is different between: I killed him, and: We killed him?** Isn't he a murderer by his own admission as well when he testifies: We killed him? **Rav Yehuda said:** Do not understand that by saying: We killed him, he included himself among the murderers. Rather, it is referring to a case **where he said: I was with his murderers,** but he was not an active participant to the murder.

וְהָתַנְיָא: אָמְרוּ לוֹ לְרַבִּי יְהוּדָה, מַעֲשֶׂה בְּלִסְטִים אֶחָד שֶׁיָּצָא לֵיהָרֵג בִּמְגִיזַת קַפּוֹטְקִיָּא, וַאֲמַר לָהֶם ״לְכוּ אִמְרוּ לָהּ לְאֵשֶׁת שִׁמְעוֹן בֶּן כֹּהֵן: אֲנִי הֲרַגְתִּי אֶת בַּעֲלָהּ בִּכְנִיסָתִי לְלוֹד״ וְאָמְרִי לָהּ ״בִּכְנִיסָתוֹ לְלוֹד״ – וְהִשִּׂיאוּ אֶת אִשְׁתּוֹ. אֲמַר לָהֶם: מִשָּׁם רְאָיָה?! בְּאוֹמֵר: אֲנִי הָיִיתִי עִם הוֹרְגָיו –

And it is taught in a *baraita* that this is the basis for Rabbi Yehuda's distinction: **They told Rabbi Yehuda:** There was **an incident involving an armed bandit** [*listim*][L] **who was taken out to be executed in** the **passage** [*megizat*][L] **of Cappadocia,**[B] **and he said to** those present: **Go and tell the wife of Shimon the Priest** that **I killed her husband as I entered Lod. And some say** that he said: **As he entered Lod. And they married off his wife** on the basis of this testimony. This implies that the court accepts testimony from the murderer himself. Rabbi Yehuda **said to them:** You derive **proof from there?** The case was **that he said: I was with his murderers,** but not that he himself murdered the woman's husband.

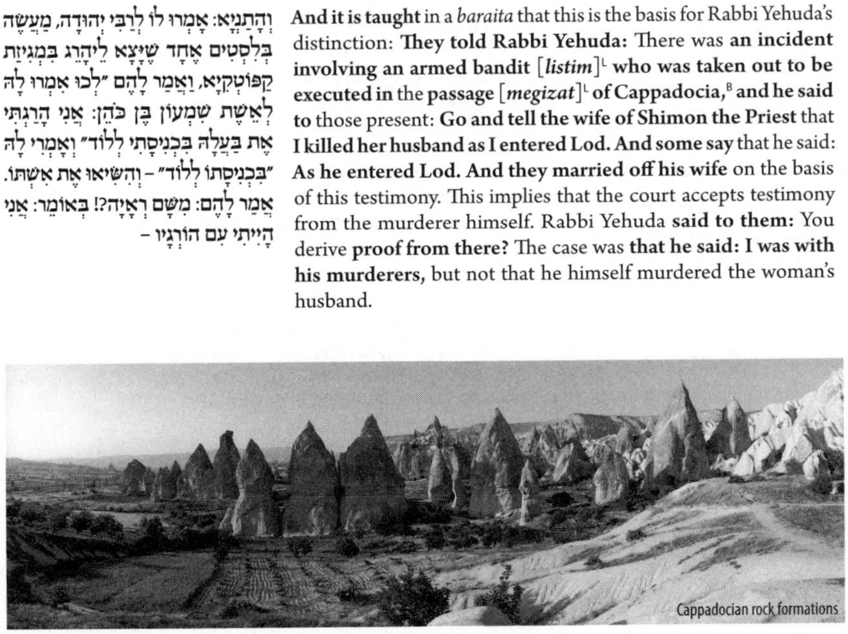
Cappadocian rock formations

NOTES

A person is his own relative – אָדָם קָרוֹב אֵצֶל עַצְמוֹ: This concept is connected to the halakhic principle that the court divides the statement of a witness, allowing them to reject the part of the testimony wherein the witness incriminates himself while accepting the rest of his testimony as valid. The court accepts the testimony that the individual he claimed to have murdered is dead, without accepting that this witness is a murderer. The halakhic principle applied is that just as one may not testify about a close relative, one may not testify about oneself.

There are differences of opinion concerning the rationale for the principle of dividing the statement of a witness. According to the Rashba, the court applies this principle only in cases where the witness's testimony could be interpreted in another way without negating its validity. If, e.g., a witness said: I killed him, it could be interpreted to mean that he was with the murderers or that he killed the victim unwittingly, etc. However, if there is no other possible interpretation of his testimony, his testimony is inadmissible. Many commentaries disagree with this and hold that even in such cases the court may divide the statement and accept the testimony (see *Noda Bihuda* and *Kovetz He'arot*).

HALAKHA

A person does not make himself wicked – אֵין אָדָם מֵשִׂים עַצְמוֹ רָשָׁע: One is not rendered unfit by admitting his own transgression, because an individual does not make himself wicked (Rambam *Sefer Nashim, Hilkhot Geirushin* 13:10 and *Sefer Shofetim, Hilkhot Edut* 12:2; *Shulḥan Arukh, Ḥoshen Mishpat* 34:26).

LANGUAGE

An armed bandit [*listim*] – לִיסְטִים: From the Greek ληστής, *lestès*. Several Aramaic and Hebrew forms were based upon this word in the language of the Sages. The written form was corrupted slightly to *listim* rather than *listis*.

Passage [*megizat*] – מְגִיזַת: This word apparently comes from the Arabic مجاز, *majāz*, meaning crossing or way.

BACKGROUND

Passage of Cappadocia – מְגִיזַת קַפּוֹטְקִיָא: Cappadocia is a country in Asia Minor west of the Euphrates River and north of the Taurus Mountains. The Hebrew name, Kappotkiyya, comes from the Greek Καππαδοκία, Kappadokia. At the time of the Talmud this was a Roman province with a large Jewish population, and there were Jewish scholars, mentioned in both the Jerusalem and Babylonian Talmuds, who came from Cappadocia to Eretz Yisrael. Today it is a popular tourist site famous for its unique rock formations, referred to as fairy chimneys.

Location of Cappadocia

HALAKHA

A Sage who rendered the wife forbidden to her husband by that vow – הֶחָכָם שֶׁאָסַר אֶת הָאִשָּׁה בְּנֶדֶר עַל בַּעְלָהּ: If a woman vowed not to receive any benefit from her husband and the husband did not nullify her vow, and she then came before a Sage but he did not find way to dissolve it, then that Sage may not subsequently marry her after she is divorced from her husband (Rambam *Sefer Nashim, Hilkhot Geirushin* 10:14; *Shulḥan Arukh, Even HaEzer* 12:2).

Before whom a woman performed refusal or… performed *ḥalitza* – מֵיאֲנָה אוֹ שֶׁחָלְצָה בְּפָנָיו: A woman who performed refusal or performed *ḥalitza* before a court may later marry one of the judges of the court (*Shulḥan Arukh, Even HaEzer* 12:2).

Dissolution of vows requires a court of three – הַתָּרַת נְדָרִים בִּשְׁלֹשָׁה: Dissolution of vows must be performed by an expert scholar or, if no expert can be found, by three ordinary men (Rambam *Sefer Hafla'a, Hilkhot Shevuot* 6:1; *Shulḥan Arukh, Yoreh De'a* 228:1).

וְהָא לִסְטִים קָתָנֵי! שֶׁנִּתְפַּס עַל יְדֵי לִסְטִיּוּת. וְהָא יָצָא לֵיהָרֵג קָתָנֵי! בֵּי דִינָא דְגוֹיִם דְּלָא דָּיְיקֵי וְקָטְלֵי.

The Gemara challenges: How could Rabbi Yehuda understand the incident in such a way? **But it is taught** in the *baraita* that the witness himself was **an armed bandit.** The Gemara answers: **He was captured** for a charge of **armed banditry.** The Gemara asks: **But it is taught that he was taken out to be executed,** implying that he was found guilty of murder. The Gemara answers: That was **a gentile court, and they execute without being precise.** One who is among a gang of bandits is executed by a gentile court regardless of whether or not he himself was a murderer. This *baraita* therefore provides evidence that Rabbi Yehuda admits the testimony of such a witness only if he says: I was with his murderers.

מתני׳ הֶחָכָם שֶׁאָסַר אֶת הָאִשָּׁה בְּנֶדֶר עַל בַּעְלָהּ – הֲרֵי זֶה לֹא יִשָּׂאֶנָּה, מֵיאֲנָה אוֹ שֶׁחָלְצָה בְּפָנָיו – יִשָּׂאֶנָּה, מִפְּנֵי שֶׁהוּא בֵּית דִּין.

MISHNA A **Sage who** refused to release a woman from a vow that **rendered the wife forbidden to her husband by** that **vow,**[H] resulting in her being divorced from her husband, **may not marry her,** so as to avoid suspicion that he rendered her forbidden to her husband in order to marry her himself. However, a judge before whom a woman **performed refusal** when she was a minor, declaring that she did not desire the husband chosen for her by her family, **or before whom** she **performed *ḥalitza*,**[H] **may marry her because** he was only one member of **the court,** thereby alleviating suspicion.

גמ׳ הָא הִתִּירָהּ יִשָּׂאֶנָּה, בְּמַאי עָסְקִינַן? אִילֵימָא בְּחַד – חַד מִי מָצֵי מַתִּיר? וְהָאֲמַר (רַב אֲמַר) רַבִּי חִיָּיא בַּר אָבִין אָמַר רַב עַמְרָם: תָּנָא, הַתָּרַת נְדָרִים בִּשְׁלֹשָׁה!

GEMARA The mishna taught that a Sage who rendered a woman forbidden to her husband may not then marry her. The Gemara deduces from here: **This** implies that if **he** rendered **her permitted** to her husband and she was later widowed or divorced, then **he may marry her.** The Gemara clarifies this: **With what are we dealing? If we say** that he was **a single** judge and not part of a court, **can a single** judge **dissolve** vows? **But didn't Rav** say that **Rabbi Ḥiyya bar Avin said** that **Rav Amram said: It is taught** in a *baraita*: **Dissolution of vows** requires a court of **three**[H] judges?

וְאֶלָּא בִּתְלָתָא – מִי חֲשִׁידִי? וְהָתְנַן: מֵיאֲנָה אוֹ שֶׁחָלְצָה בְּפָנָיו יִשָּׂאֶנָּה, מִפְּנֵי שֶׁהוּא בֵּית דִּין!

Rather, could it be a case **of three** judges rather than one? In such a case, **would they be suspect** of distorting judgment? **But didn't we learn** in the mishna: If **she performed refusal or performed *ḥalitza* before him, he may marry her because he** functioned as a member of **a court** of three? This teaches that there is no suspicion of a judge in a court of three.

לְעוֹלָם בְּחַד, וּכְדַאֲמַר רַב חִסְדָּא אֲמַר רַבִּי יוֹחָנָן: בְּיָחִיד מוּמְחֶה, הָכָא נַמִי – בְּיָחִיד מוּמְחֶה.

The Gemara answers: **Actually,** you should explain that this case is **that of a single** judge, **and** it is **as Rav Ḥisda said** that **Rabbi Yoḥanan said:** Vows may be dissolved even **by a single expert,**[B] and a three-member court is not always necessary. **Here too,** it is referring to **a single expert** refusing to nullify her vow.

״מֵיאֲנָה אוֹ שֶׁחָלְצָה״ וכו׳. טַעְמָא דְּבֵית דִּין, הָא בִּתְרֵי – לָא.

It is taught in the mishna that if a woman **performed refusal or performed *ḥalitza*** before a judge, he may still marry her, as he was part of a court. The Gemara deduces from here: **The reason is** specifically that he functioned on **the court** as one of three judges. The Gemara deduces: **Then, if there were** only **two** judges, **he would not** be permitted to marry her.

מַאי שְׁנָא מֵהָא דִּתְנַן: עֵדִים הַחֲתוּמִים עַל שְׂדֵה מִקָּח וְעַל גֵּט אִשָּׁה – לֹא חָשׁוּ חֲכָמִים לְדָבָר זֶה! הִיא גּוּפָהּ קָמַשְׁמַע לָן, לְאַפּוּקֵי מִמַּאן דְּאָמַר מֵיאוּן בִּפְנֵי שְׁנַיִם, קָמַשְׁמַע לָן: מֵיאוּן בִּשְׁלֹשָׁה.

If so, in **what** way **is** this case **different from that which we learned** in a *baraita*: If **witnesses signed on the** document of **sale of a field or on a woman's bill of divorce, the Sages were not concerned about this matter** if one of the witnesses subsequently purchased the field or married the divorcée. Since there are two witnesses, there is no suspicion that they collaborated for the benefit of one of them. The Gemara answers: If there were two judges there would also be no concern; however, **this** mishna **itself** comes **to teach us** that a refusal must be performed before a full court, **to exclude** the opinion of **the one who said that refusal may be performed before two. This teaches us** that **refusal** must be performed before **three** judges.

BACKGROUND

A single expert – יָחִיד מוּמְחֶה: In general a Jewish court comprises three judges for monetary matters and other cases, aside from cases of capital punishment. This ensures that there will be a majority, as at least two judges will agree on the verdict. In tractate *Avot* (4:10) it is written: Do not judge alone, as only God can judge alone. However, *Tosafot* explain that this is meant merely as advice, but if an individual judge is an expert in certain matters he may adjudicate on those matters by himself.

איבעיא להו: כנס, מהו שיוציא? רב כהנא אמר: כנס – מוציא, רב אשי אמר: כנס – אינו מוציא. תני להו רב זוטי דבי רב פפי כדברי האומר כנס אינו מוציא.

§ **A dilemma was raised before** the Sages with regard to one who was prohibited from marrying a certain woman: If he nevertheless **married** her despite the prohibition, **what is the** *halakha* with regard to whether **he must divorce** her? **Rav Kahana said:** If **he married** her, **he must divorce** her. **Rav Ashi said:** If **he married** her, **he need not divorce** her.[H] **Rav Zuti from the school of Rav Pappi taught** the Sages a *baraita* **in accordance with the statement of the** one who **said that** if **he married** her, **he need not divorce** her.

אמרו ליה רבנן לרב אשי: גמרא או סברא? אמר להו: מתניתין היא: הנטען משפחה ונשתחררה, מגויה ונתגיירה, הרי זה לא יכנוס, ואם כנס – אין מוציא. אלמא

The Rabbis said to Rav Ashi: With regard to the *halakha* that you said, that if he married her he need not divorce her, was it based upon **tradition or** is it your own **conclusion? He said to them: It is the mishna.** I reached this conclusion from the wording of the mishna, which taught that **one suspected** by others of engaging in sexual relations **with** a Canaanite **maidservant and she** was subsequently **set free, or with a gentile woman and she** subsequently **converted may not marry** that woman. **But if he did marry her, they,** the judges of the court, **do not remove** her from him. **Apparently,**

ברננה לא מפקינן, הכא נמי ברננה לא מפקינן.

we do not remove her from her husband owing to suspicion **due to rumor** alone. **Here too, we do not remove her** from her husband **due to a rumor.**

מתני׳ וכולם שהיו להם נשים ומתו – מותרות לינשא להם.

MISHNA And for **all of these**[N] who were involved in permitting the wife to remarry, i.e., the judge, the agent who brought a bill of divorce, and the one who testified for a woman that her husband died, if **they had wives**[NH] at the time of the ruling or the testimony **and** their wives **died** thereafter, then those women they had set free **are permitted to be married to them.** There is no concern that while their wives were still alive these individuals set their eyes upon another woman.

וכולן שנישאו לאחרים, ונתגרשו או שנתאלמנו – מותרות לינשא להם. וכולן מותרות לבניהם או לאחיהם.

And with regard to **all of these** women who were prohibited from marrying a certain man due to some suspicion, if **they were** subsequently **married to others**[H] **and** then **were divorced or widowed** from the second husband, **they are permitted to be married to them,** i.e., to the judge, messenger, or witness who permitted her to remarry. **And all of these** women who were prohibited from marrying due to some suspicion **are permitted to the sons or to the brothers**[NH] of those who set them free.

גמ׳ מתו – אין, נתגרשו – לא.

GEMARA The mishna taught that if any of the men had wives who subsequently died, they may marry those women freed by them. The Gemara deduces from here: **If** the wives of those who rendered the woman permitted **died, yes,** they are permitted to marry the woman that they freed for marriage; but if the wives **were divorced, no,** it is prohibited. In such a case, marrying the woman that one had rendered permitted would raise suspicions that he had in fact planned to marry her all along.

HALAKHA

If he married her, he need not divorce her – כנס אינו מוציא: If a Sage declared a wife forbidden to her husband due to her vow, that Sage is forbidden from marrying her *ab initio*. If he nevertheless married her he is not forced to divorce her, in accordance with the conclusion of the Gemara (Rambam *Sefer Nashim, Hilkhot Geirushin* 10:14; *Shulḥan Arukh, Even HaEzer* 12:2).

NOTES

And for all of these, etc. – וכולם וכו׳: Rashi explains that the term: All of these, is referring only to a Sage or a witness who testified for a woman (see Rid). Rambam, however, interprets this ruling as applying to one who was under suspicion of misconduct with a maidservant or other woman as well.

They had wives, etc. – היו להם נשים וכו׳: At the time of the mishna, bigamy was permitted, yet it was extremely rare, and so there was no concern that one would free a woman in order to marry her as a second wife.

Are permitted to the sons or to the brothers – מותרות לבניהם או לאחיהם: In the Jerusalem Talmud this is explained by the statement that it is not common for one to sin for the benefit of his relative or his teacher.

HALAKHA

They had wives – היו להם נשים: It is permitted for one who was married when he rendered a woman free to marry that woman if his wife subsequently died (Rambam *Sefer Nashim, Hilkhot Geirushin* 10:15; *Shulḥan Arukh, Even HaEzer* 12:4).

And all of these women, if they were subsequently married to others – וכולן שנישאו לאחרים: It is permitted for all of these women who subsequently married others and were then widowed or divorced to marry one of those men who permitted them to remarry (Rambam *Sefer Nashim, Hilkhot Ishut* 10:15; *Shulḥan Arukh, Even HaEzer* 12:3).

Are permitted to the sons or to the brothers – מותרות לבניהם או לאחיהם: All of these women are permitted to marry the close relatives of the witness or the Sage who freed them (Rambam *Sefer Nashim, Hilkhot Ishut* 10:16; *Shulḥan Arukh, Even HaEzer* 12:4).

אֲמַר לֵיהּ רַב הִלֵּל לְרַב אַשִׁי: וְהָתַנְיָא אֲפִילּוּ נִתְגָּרְשׁוּ! לָא קַשְׁיָא; הָא – דַּהֲוַאי קְטָטָה, הָא – דְּלָא הֲוַאי קְטָטָה.

Rav Hillel said to Rav Ashi: Yet it is taught in a *baraita*: **Even if they were divorced**[H] from their first wives they are permitted to marry the women they freed. The Gemara responds: **This is not difficult: This** mishna is referring to a case **when there was a quarrel** between the husband and the wife at the time that he freed the other woman, as then there is legitimate concern that he was already interested in her. **That** case of the *baraita* **was when there was no quarrel**[N] between them at the time, and therefore the divorce clearly resulted from some other reason.

וְאִיבָּעֵית אֵימָא: הָא וְהָא דְּלָא הֲוַאי קְטָטָה, וְלָא קַשְׁיָא; הָא – דְּאַרְגֵּיל הוּא, הָא – דְּאַרְגִּילָה הִיא.

And if you wish, say: Both this and that were said in cases **when there was no quarrel** between the one who freed the woman and his first wife, and only later did they quarrel and divorce. **And this is not difficult: This** case of the mishna **was when he started** the quarrel **himself,** as then there is legitimate concern that he had an interest in this other woman and therefore sought out a reason to divorce his wife. **And that** case of the *baraita* **was when** his wife **started** the quarrel, as then there would be no reason to suspect him of freeing the other woman in order to marry her.

״וְכוּלָּן שֶׁנִּישְּׂאוּ״ וכו׳. קָא סָלְקָא דַּעְתִּין מִיתָה אַמִּיתָה, וְגֵירוּשִׁין אַגֵּירוּשִׁין,

The mishna stated: **And** with regard to **all of these** women, **if they were married** to others and then were divorced or widowed, it is permitted for them to marry those who caused them to be free to marry in the first place. **It enters our mind to say** that the case referred to here was one of **death after death,** i.e., the case of a woman whose first husband's death had been substantiated by a single witness but whose second husband died as well, **and** also to the case of **divorce following** a bill of **divorce** that had been validated by a single witness.

נֵימָא מַתְנִיתִין דְּלָא כְּרַבִּי, דְּאִי כְּרַבִּי – הָאָמַר: בִּתְרֵי זִימְנֵי הָוְיָא חֲזָקָה!

Based on this, **should we say that the mishna,** which permits a woman to remarry even after her two previous husbands have died, **is not in accordance with** the opinion of **Rabbi** Yehuda HaNasi? **As, if it is in accordance with** the opinion of **Rabbi** Yehuda HaNasi, **didn't** Rabbi Yehuda HaNasi **say: After two times** a woman has the **presumptive status** to cause death to her husbands, and such a woman is considered murderous. Therefore, she may not remarry. Since there is no mention of such concern in the mishna, it appears that the mishna is not in accordance with the opinion of Rabbi Yehuda HaNasi.

לָא, מִיתָה אַגֵּירוּשִׁין וְגֵירוּשִׁין אַמִּיתָה.

The Gemara rejects this: **No** evidence can be derived from here, as the reference here may be to **death after divorce or divorce after death.** The mishna could be referring either to a woman who was at first divorced and then later widowed by her second husband's death, or to a woman whose first husband died and who was subsequently divorced, but not to a case where she was widowed by the death of two husbands.

״וְכוּלָּן מוּתָּרוֹת לִבְנֵיהֶם אוֹ לַאֲחֵיהֶם״. מַאי שְׁנָא מֵהָא דִּתְנַן: הַנִּטְעָן מִן הָאִשָּׁה – אָסוּר בְּאִמָּהּ וּבְבִתָּהּ וּבַאֲחוֹתָהּ!

§ The mishna taught: **And all of these** women who were prohibited from marrying the man who freed them due to some suspicion **are permitted to the sons or to the brothers** of those who set them free. The Gemara asks: In **what** way **is** this case **different from that which we learned** in the *Tosefta* (4:5) that **one suspected** of adultery **with** a specific **woman is prohibited** not only from marrying her, but also **from** marrying **her mother, and her daughter, and her sister.** Yet here we allow his sons and brothers to marry the woman despite the suspicion.

נָשֵׁי לְגַבֵּי נָשֵׁי – שְׁכִיחָן דְּאָזְלָן, גַּבְרֵי לְגַבֵּי – גַּבְרֵי לָא שְׁכִיחָן.

The Gemara answers: There is a distinction between the situations, for **it is common for women** to be **at** the house of other **women** and to stay overnight. Therefore, there is concern that a relative of the alleged adulterer's wife, with whom he was suspected of misconduct, might frequent his house and he might be tempted to repeat his transgression. On the other hand, **it is not common for men** to be **at** the house of other **men,** so that even if she was married to his relative, the one suspected of misconduct would not generally sleep at the house of the husband.

HALAKHA

They were divorced – נִתְגָּרְשׁוּ: If those who rendered these women permitted were married at the time and subsequently divorced because their wives started a quarrel, it is permitted for them to marry those women. If they themselves started the quarrel, they may not marry those women. There are those who render it prohibited for them to marry these women if their first wives were sick at the time they freed the women (Rema, citing *Nimmukei Yosef*; Rambam *Sefer Nashim*, *Hilkhot Ishut* 10:15; *Shulḥan Arukh*, *Even HaEzer* 12:4).

NOTES

That was when there was no quarrel – הָא דְּלָא הֲוַאי קְטָטָה: Rashi explains that if there was a quarrel between the Sage who permitted this woman and his wife before they divorced, it appears that the divorce resulted from the quarrel and not from interest in the other woman. However, in *Yam shel Shlomo* the opposite explanation is suggested: If there was a quarrel between them beforehand, there is suspicion that due to the quarrel he decided to divorce his wife and seek out another wife for himself. Meiri explains that if there was a quarrel, then the reason for the divorce is not clear, and so there is no room for suspicion. However, if he divorced his wife without another clear reason, there is concern that it appears that he did so due to his desire for the other woman.

אִי נַמִי: נָשֵׁי דְּלָא אָסְרָן שְׁכִיבְתָן אַהֲדָדֵי – לָא קָפְדֵי אַהֲדָדֵי, גַּבְרֵי דְּאָסְרָן שְׁכִיבְתָן אַהֲדָדֵי – קָפְדֵי אַהֲדָדֵי.

Alternatively, a different argument could be made: **Women are not so strict with one another, as lying with them** and having sexual relations with them **does not render them mutually forbidden.** In other words, if a man commits adultery with his wife's close relative, his wife does not become forbidden to him, so she may not pay attention to his behavior with the woman under suspicion. However, **men are strict with one another, as lying with them** and having sexual relations with the other man's wife **does render them,** the husband and wife, **mutually forbidden.** In other words, if another man has relations with a married woman, she is forbidden to her husband, and so men pay close attention to what the others are doing.

אִי הָכִי אָבִיו נַמִי! לָא מִיבָּעְיָא קָאָמַר, לָא מִיבָּעְיָא אָבִיו – דִּבְזִיז בְּנֵיהּ מִינֵּיהּ, אֲבָל בְּנוֹ דְּלָא בְּזִיז אָבִיו מִינֵּיהּ – אֵימָא לָא, קָא מַשְׁמַע לָן.

The Gemara asks: **If so, one's father** should be permitted to marry a woman set free by his son **as well.** So why does the mishna say: Their sons or their brothers, and not: Their fathers? The Gemara answers: Certainly his father is allowed as well, but the mishna **is speaking** utilizing the style of: **It is not necessary. It is not necessary** to mention the case of **his father** because he is most certainly permitted to marry a woman set free by his son, **as his son is embarrassed** [*baziz*][L] **before him** and so would not come to sleep with his father's wife. **But I might say that** since **the father is not embarrassed before his son,** she **may not** be married to the son of one for whom there is suspicion. Therefore, **this comes to teach us** that there is no such concern.

הדרן עלך כיצד אשת אחיו

LANGUAGE

Embarrassed [*keziz*] – כְּזִיז: Although this version of the text has *baziz*, the version of the text that reads *keziz* is more correct because it comes from the Aramaic root *k-u-z*, which means to be ashamed or fearful.

Rabbi Ḥiyya's Description of Forbidden Relationships According to Rambam

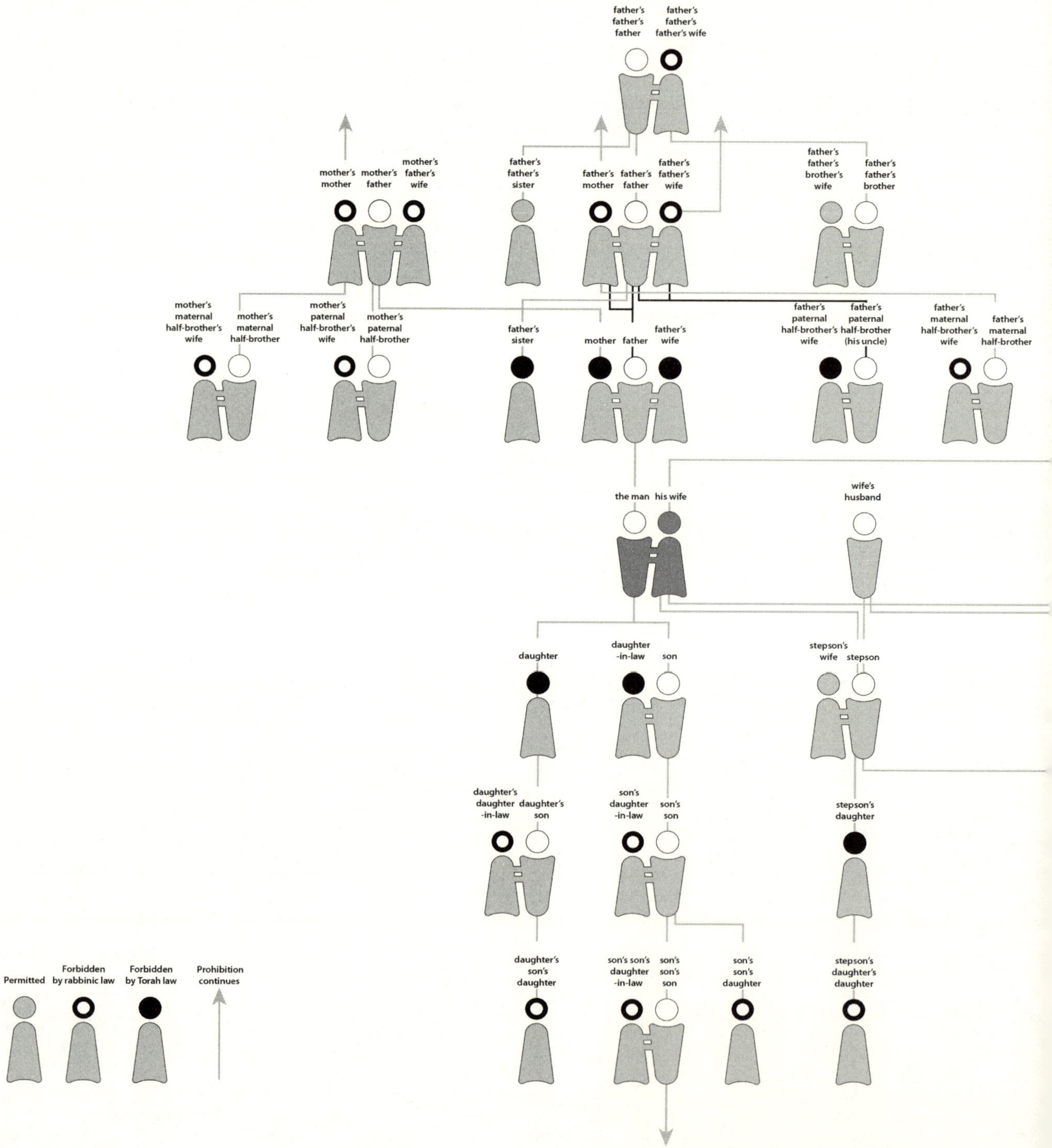

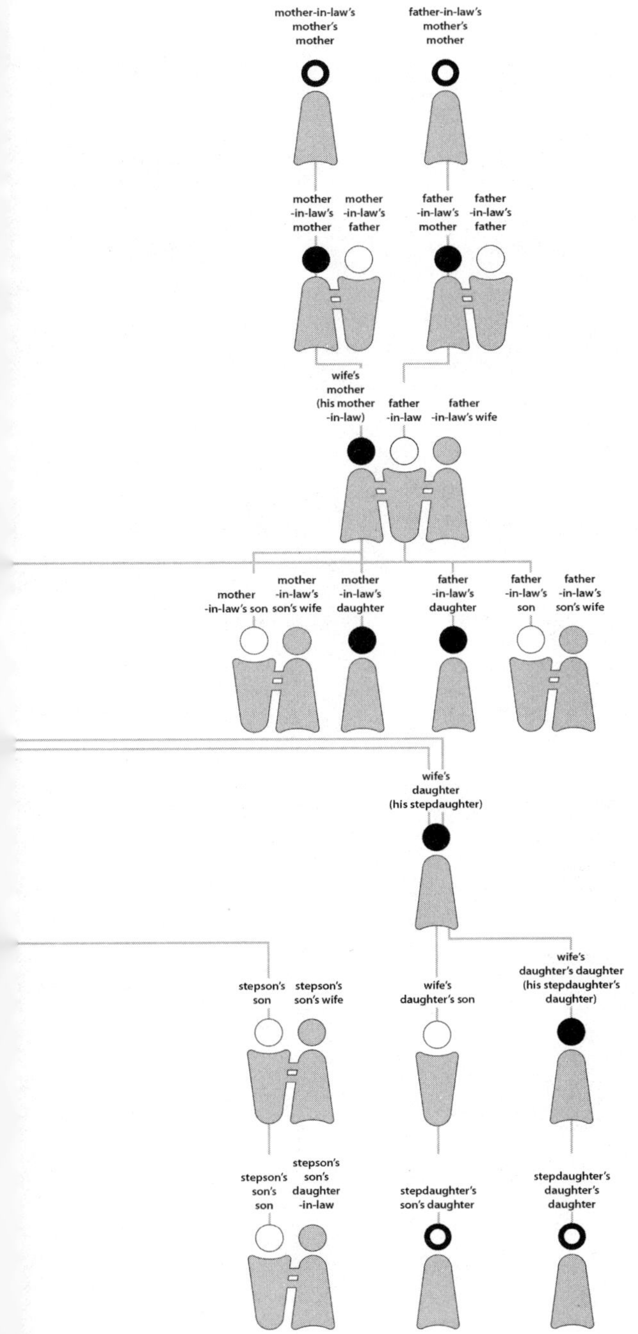

mother-in-law's mother's mother
father-in-law's mother's mother
mother -in-law's mother
mother -in-law's father
father -in-law's mother
father -in-law's father
wife's mother (his mother -in-law)
father -in-law
father -in-law's wife
mother -in-law's son
mother -in-law's son's wife
mother -in-law's daughter
father -in-law's daughter
father -in-law's son
father -in-law's son's wife
wife's daughter (his stepdaughter)
stepson's son
stepson's son's wife
wife's daughter's son
wife's daughter's daughter (his stepdaughter's daughter)
stepson's son's son
stepson's son's daughter -in-law
stepdaughter's son's daughter
stepdaughter's daughter's daughter

Summary of **Perek II**

This chapter, in addition to touching on a wide range of topics, primarily discusses several difficulties that arise in the *halakhot* of levirate marriage. It also deals with difficulties inherent in the general *halakhot* of marriage.

The *halakha* is that a brother is exempt from levirate marriage with the wife of a brother with whom he did not coexist. This means that if a brother was born after the death of the childless man whose wife requires levirate marriage, this newborn brother is exempt from performing levirate marriage. This applies even if the *yevama* had in the meantime been married to another brother who later died childless as well, whereby she would once again happen before a *yavam* for levirate marriage. She is exempt from both levirate marriage and *ḥalitza* and causes her rival wives to be exempt as well.

Although the eldest brother is specified by the Torah for the mitzva of levirate marriage, all of the brothers are eligible to perform the mitzva. The brother referred to by the Torah for the purposes of levirate marriage is specifically a paternal brother. Any paternal brother is included, even if he was born outside of marriage or is a *mamzer*. However, it does not include a brother whose mother was a gentile or a Canaanite maidservant.

The term "child" in the verse "If brothers dwell together and one of them dies and he has no child…" (Deuteronomy 25:5), is understood in the widest possible sense; it includes any descendants of the deceased brother. Whether it is a son, a daughter, or a grandchild, and whether that child is fit to enter the community or is disqualified, provided the descendant is not the child of a gentile woman or Canaanite maidservant, that child absolves the widow from the obligation of levirate marriage.

The Gemara concludes that in every case where the *yevama* is forbidden to the *yavam*, whether due to a prohibition resulting from a mitzva or a prohibition stemming from sanctity, including those prohibitions specific to the priestly class or those instituted by rabbinic law, even though she may not enter levirate marriage she must undergo *ḥalitza*. This is because the mitzva itself still applies to her by Torah law. If she had a rival wife who was not forbidden, then that rival wife is permitted to enter into levirate marriage. *Ḥalitza* rather than levirate marriage is also required in cases where it is uncertain whether the mitzva applies or to whom it applies.

As part of the deliberations over these issues, the matter of forbidden secondary relatives was also summarized in this chapter. These were defined as closely related women who did not fall under the category of forbidden relatives by Torah law, but were prohibited by rabbinic decree to create a safeguard, so that one not be confused between them and those women who are forbidden relatives by Torah law. The primary source for these *halakhot* is this chapter, and several issues were left unresolved, leading to disputes among halakhic authorities.

Another subject mentioned in this chapter is the general prohibition against marrying a woman if that marriage would raise suspicions of previous misconduct or cast doubt upon the veracity of testimony or the uprightness of judges.

Introduction to **Perek III**

If brothers dwell together and one of them dies and he has no child, the wife of the dead man shall not be married outside of the family to one not of his kin; her brother-in-law will have intercourse with her and take her to him to be his wife and consummate the levirate marriage.

(Deuteronomy 25:5)

The first two chapters of this tractate discussed the essential *halakhot* of levirate marriage in and of themselves. From Chapter Three onward, the Gemara's discussion concerns both how these *halakhot* apply to specific combinations of circumstances and the evaluation of different instructive examples. All of this is grounded in the principles that were clarified in the previous chapters. Based on these principles, the rulings are determined for situations where related women who were married to two or more brothers happen before their brothers-in-law, i.e., become candidates for levirate marriage with them, and the various possible relationships between these women and their brothers-in-law are evaluated as well. In the process it becomes clear that the relationship between brothers-in-law and *yevamot*, known in the Gemara as the levirate bond, requires further clarification.

From the verses, it is apparent that a sister-in-law requiring levirate marriage is bound to her brother-in-law and cannot marry another man until he releases her from the levirate bond via levirate marriage or *ḥalitza*. The Torah itself, however, does not provide any definition of this bond. Perhaps the bond can be understood simply as a one-sided obligation, whereby the sister-in-law is compelled to wait for her brother-in-law to perform some act. This opinion asserts that the levirate bond is not substantial. Alternatively, one could explain that the levirate bond is substantial, and the relationship between the parties obligated in levirate marriage is similar to that of those who are engaged, in that it would be prohibited for the *yavam* to marry the relatives of the *yevama*, in the same way that it would be prohibited for him to marry the relatives of his wife. Indeed, this perspective raises a certain difficulty, for there should apparently be some difference between the simple case of a *yevama* who is bonded to a single brother-in-law and the case where she is bonded to two brothers-in-law or more. However, by defining the levirate bond as a relationship that is substantial enough to create prohibitions for the parties involved, a fundamental contradiction arises in the case of a woman who is simultaneously bound to two different men.

Defining the parameters of the levirate relationship is also problematic when complex familial relations exist between the brothers-in-law and sisters-in-law. It must be determined precisely when the levirate bond is formed. Is it formed at the moment of the husband's death, following the opinion that a woman's status at the time of her husband's death determines her status with regard the levirate bond created between her and her brothers-in-law? Or, perhaps the original moment of marriage between the woman and her late husband created a levirate bond between her and her brothers-in-law, following the opinion that marriage determines a woman's status with regard to the levirate bond?

This chapter explores and clarifies these issues along with other questions that arise incidentally within the Gemara's discussions.

מתני׳ אַרְבָּעָה אַחִין, שְׁנַיִם מֵהֶם נְשׂוּאִים שְׁתֵּי אֲחָיוֹת, וּמֵתוּ הַנְּשׂוּאִים אֶת הָאֲחָיוֹת – הֲרֵי אֵלּוּ חוֹלְצוֹת וְלֹא מִתְיַיבְּמוֹת. וְאִם קָדְמוּ וְכָנְסוּ – יוֹצִיאוּ. רַבִּי אֱלִיעֶזֶר אוֹמֵר, בֵּית שַׁמַּאי אוֹמְרִים: יְקַיֵּים, וּבֵית הִלֵּל אוֹמְרִים: יוֹצִיאוּ.

MISHNA In the case of **four brothers,**[H] **two of whom were married to two sisters, and the ones married to the sisters died, then those** sisters must **perform *ḥalitza* and may not enter into levirate marriage.**[N] Since both sisters require levirate marriage with each of the surviving brothers, a levirate bond exists between each sister and the brothers. Each of them is considered the sister of a woman with whom each brother has a levirate bond and is therefore forbidden to him by rabbinic law. **And if they married** the sisters **before** consulting the court, **they should divorce** them, for the Sages decreed that in this situation they may not remain married. **Rabbi Eliezer says** that there is a dispute in this matter: **Beit Shammai**[N] **say: He may maintain** her as his wife, **while Beit Hillel say: They** must **divorce** them.

הָיְתָה אַחַת מֵהֶן אֲסוּרָה עַל הָאֶחָד אִיסּוּר עֶרְוָה – אָסוּר בָּהּ וּמוּתָּר בַּאֲחוֹתָהּ, וְהַשֵּׁנִי אָסוּר בִּשְׁתֵּיהֶן.

If **one of** the sisters **was forbidden**[H] **to one** of the brothers due to **a prohibition against forbidden relations** because she was a relative of his wife or a relative on his mother's side, then **he is forbidden to** marry **her but permitted to** marry **her sister.** Because she is his close relative, she is exempt from levirate marriage with him, and therefore she is not bound to him with a levirate bond. Consequently, her sister is not considered the sister of a woman with whom he has a levirate bond, and he is permitted to enter into levirate marriage with her. But **the second** brother, who is not a close relative of either sister, **is forbidden to** marry **both of them.** Indeed, for him each woman remains the sister of a woman with whom he has a levirate bond.

אִיסּוּר מִצְוָה וְאִיסּוּר קְדוּשָּׁה – חוֹלֶצֶת וְלֹא מִתְיַיבֶּמֶת.

If **a prohibition** resulting from **a mitzva**[N] or **a prohibition** stemming from **sanctity**[N] will be transgressed when one of the women marries one of the brothers, then her sister must **perform *ḥalitza* and may not enter into levirate marriage,** as she is considered the sister of a woman with whom he has a levirate bond. In this case, the sister who is forbidden to the brother due to a mitzva or due to sanctity is bound to the brother for the purpose of *ḥalitza*.

הָיְתָה אַחַת מֵהֶן אֲסוּרָה עַל זֶה אִיסּוּר עֶרְוָה, וְהַשְּׁנִיָּה אֲסוּרָה עַל זֶה אִיסּוּר עֶרְוָה – הָאֲסוּרָה לָזֶה מוּתֶּרֶת לָזֶה, וְהָאֲסוּרָה לָזֶה מוּתֶּרֶת לָזֶה.

If **one of those** women **was forbidden to this** one brother due to **a prohibition against forbidden relations and the second** woman **was forbidden to that** second brother due to **a prohibition against forbidden relations,** then **she who is forbidden to this** brother **is permitted to that** brother, **and she who is forbidden to that** brother **is permitted to this** one.

וְזוֹ הִיא שֶׁאָמְרוּ: אֲחוֹתָהּ כְּשֶׁהִיא יְבִמְתָּהּ – אוֹ חוֹלֶצֶת אוֹ מִתְיַיבֶּמֶת.

And this is the case that was referred to when **they said: When her sister is** also **her *yevama*,** i.e., in a case where two sisters are also *yevamot* and therefore happened for levirate marriage before two brothers, **she either performs *ḥalitza* or enters into levirate marriage.** This must be referring to a case where each sister is forbidden to one of the brothers due to a prohibition concerning forbidden relatives. In this case, each sister has a levirate bond only with the one brother to whom she is permitted, and the prohibition against marrying the sister of a woman with whom one has a levirate bond does not apply. Therefore, each brother can either perform the act of *ḥalitza* or consummate the levirate marriage with the sister to whom he is not related.

NOTES

Must perform *ḥalitza* and may not enter into levirate marriage – חוֹלְצוֹת וְלֹא מִתְיַיבְּמוֹת: One could suggest that one of the brothers performs *ḥalitza* with one sister and then afterward the second brother consummates the levirate marriage with the second sister, as she would then no longer be the sister of a woman with whom he has a levirate bond. This, however, is not allowed according to both explanations of the mishna. According to the opinion that it is prohibited to negate the mitzva of levirate marriage, there is a concern that they will confuse the order and perform the levirate marriage first. According to the opinion that the levirate bond is substantial, the second brother may not consummate the levirate marriage, as the woman was already forbidden to him once as the sister of a woman with whom he has a levirate bond, and she can no longer be rendered permitted (*Tosefot HaRosh*).

Rabbi Eliezer says, Beit Shammai, etc. – רַבִּי אֱלִיעֶזֶר אוֹמֵר, בֵּית שַׁמַּאי וכו׳: Although it is common for the Gemara to ask why a Sage saw fit to inform us of Beit Shammai's opinion when it does not accord with *halakha*, here there is an explanation. It seems that Rabbi Eliezer states this version of the dispute between Beit Shammai and Beit Hillel in order to exclude the opinion of Abba Shaul (*Yevamot* 28a), which sets forth an opposite tradition with regard to this dispute (*Tosefot HaRosh*).

A prohibition resulting from a mitzva – אִיסּוּר מִצְוָה: In addition to the sexual relationships prohibited on the basis of Torah prohibitions, there are additional relationships that are prohibited by rabbinic law. These are called prohibitions resulting from a mitzva, because the basis for the authority of rabbinic prohibitions is the Torah mitzva not to deviate from the words of the Sages, as it is stated: "According to the *halakha* that they shall teach you, and according to the judgment that they shall tell you, you shall do" (Deuteronomy 17:11).

A prohibition stemming from sanctity – אִיסּוּר קְדוּשָּׁה: This is referring to a marriage that is prohibited not because of the family relationship between the parties but because of the more elevated level of sanctity of one of the marriage partners. These include the prohibition against the marriage of a native-born Israelite to a *mamzer*, a priest to a divorcée, or a High Priest to a widow.

HALAKHA

Four brothers – אַרְבָּעָה אַחִין: In the case of four brothers, two of whom were married to two sisters and died childless, these sisters must perform *ḥalitza* and they may not enter into levirate marriage. If the brothers married the sisters before consulting with the court, they must divorce them (Rambam *Sefer Nashim, Hilkhot Yibbum* 7:1; *Shulḥan Arukh, Even HaEzer* 175:3).

If one was forbidden, etc. – הָיְתָה אַחַת אֲסוּרָה וכו׳: If one of the sisters was forbidden from marrying one of the brothers due to a prohibition against forbidden sexual relations, then he is permitted to marry her sister, and the other brother is prohibited from marrying both of them. If one of the sisters was forbidden to one brother and the second to another brother, each brother may marry the sister who is not forbidden to him (Rambam *Sefer Nashim, Hilkhot Yibbum* 7:1–2; *Shulḥan Arukh, Even HaEzer* 175:4–5).

NOTES

Levirate bond or negation of the mitzva of levirate marriage – זִיקָה אוֹ בִּטּוּל מִצְוַת יִבּוּם: *Yosef Lekaḥ* elaborates on both sides of this ancient dispute. It appears in the Jerusalem Talmud and in other places and is formulated as follows: Is *ḥalitza* a mitzva in and of itself or is its purpose only to release one from the levirate bond?

According to the opinion that *ḥalitza* is indeed the fulfillment of a mitzva, one can understand the rationale against negating the mitzva of levirate marriage. By consummating the levirate marriage with one sister, the *yavam* prevents the other sister from performing both the mitzva of *ḥalitza* and of levirate marriage.

If, however, *ḥalitza* merely releases the woman from the levirate bond, it should not matter if that exemption comes from the act of *ḥalitza* or from his marriage to her relative. According to the opinion that *ḥalitza* serves only to release the woman from the levirate bond, it is apparent that the reason for requiring *ḥalitza* here must be due to the levirate bond. Although there is no mitzva involved in performing *ḥalitza*, it is nevertheless necessary, as there is a prohibition against consummating the levirate marriage due to the levirate bond.

If so, three – אִי הָכִי תְּלָתָא: This question is based on the assumption of the Gemara that this case should involve three brothers, as all the cases in the continuation of the chapter involve three brothers. For this reason, the Gemara wonders why the number of brothers was increased to four in this mishna (Rashba; Ritva).

It is not necessary, etc. – לָא מִיבָּעֲיָא וכו׳: Many early commentaries ask: Why is this question raised specifically with regard to the opinion that the ruling is based on the prohibition against negating the mitzva of levirate marriage, but not with regard to the opinion that the levirate bond is substantial (see Rashi, Rivan, and *Tosafot*)?

The Ramban, in explanation of Rashi's comments, says: According to the opinion that the levirate bond is substantial, there is a novelty to be learned if the case involves specifically four brothers. This is because there is a dispute with regard to whether the levirate bond is substantial only if there is a single brother or even if there are two brothers. Accordingly, in order to teach that the levirate bond is significant even if there are multiple brothers, the case of four brothers is preferable to the case of three brothers.

However, according to the opinion that there is concern for the negation of the mitzva of levirate marriage, it stands to reason that the same concern should exist regardless of the number of brothers. Therefore, if the reasoning behind the ruling in the mishna is that the levirate bond is not substantial, it would have been appropriate to teach the case of three brothers, in order to indicate that although the levirate bond is not substantial, it is nevertheless prohibited to perform levirate marriage. It would then be clear that the rationale behind the ruling is based specifically on the idea that negating the mitzva of levirate marriage should be avoided. However, when the case involves four brothers the underlying rationale is not as clear (Ramban).

גמ׳ שְׁמַע מִינָּהּ: יֵשׁ זִיקָה. דְּאִי אֵין זִיקָה, מִכְּדִי הָנֵי מִתְּרֵי בָּתֵּי קָאָתְיָין, הַאי לֵייבַּם חֲדָא וְהַאי לֵייבַּם חֲדָא!

GEMARA The Gemara deduces from the *halakha* cited in the mishna: **Conclude from here** that the **levirate bond**[H] **is substantial.** That is, the very obligation of levirate marriage creates a bond that is similar to marriage. **For if the levirate bond were not substantial,** why would these two women not enter into levirate marriage? **After all, these** two women **come from two households,** as each had a different husband, and they both require levirate marriage. **Let this** brother **consummate the levirate marriage with one** sister **and let that** brother **consummate the levirate marriage with** the **other** sister. The fact that the mishna requires *ḥalitza* in this situation indicates that the levirate bond is substantial and resembles marriage to the extent that each sister is forbidden to each brother due to the prohibition against marrying the sister of a woman to whom one has a levirate bond.

לְעוֹלָם אֵימָא לָךְ: אֵין זִיקָה, וּמִשּׁוּם דְּקָסָבַר אָסוּר לְבַטֵּל מִצְוַת יְבָמִין; דִּלְמָא אַדְּמְיַיבֵּם חַד – מָיֵית אִידָךְ, וְקָמְבַטֵּל מִצְוַת יְבָמִין.

The Gemara rejects this: **Actually, I** could **say to you** that according to this *tanna* **the levirate bond is not substantial,** and yet they are prohibited from entering levirate marriage for a different reason. It is **because** the *tanna* **holds that it is prohibited to negate the mitzva of levirate marriage.**[N] It is prohibited to act in a way that would lead to a situation where the mitzva to perform levirate marriage is negated. How would this situation arise? **Perhaps before one** brother **consummates the levirate marriage, the other** brother **dies,** and only one brother remains. In that case, the second sister would also happen before him for levirate marriage, **and** by performing levirate marriage with one sister **he would** thereby **negate the mitzva of levirate marriage** with the other sister. When the remaining brother marries one of the sisters, the mitzva to enter into levirate marriage or perform *ḥalitza* is automatically negated from the second sister, as she is then forbidden to him as his wife's sister.

אִי הָכִי, תְּלָתָא נַמִי!

The Gemara asks: **If so,** if this is the rationale behind the ruling in the mishna, then the same concern would exist if there were **three**[N] brothers, **as well.** Why did the mishna specify four brothers? It could have cited the case of three brothers, two of whom were married to two sisters. In these circumstances, the concern for negating the mitzva of levirate marriage also exists.

לָא מִיבָּעֲיָא קָאָמְרִינַן; לָא מִיבָּעֲיָא תְּלָתָא, דְּוַדַּאי בָּטְלָה מִצְוַת יְבָמִין, אֲבָל אַרְבָּעָה, לְמִיתָה לָא חָיְישִׁינַן – קָא מַשְׁמַע לָן.

The Gemara answers: Indeed, the ruling would be the same in that case. However, the mishna **is speaking** utilizing the style of: **It is not necessary. It is not necessary**[N] to specify that the women must perform *ḥalitza* in a case involving **three** brothers, **as certainly the mitzva of levirate marriage is negated** with one of the sisters when the *yavam* marries the other sister. **But** in the case of **four** brothers, where there is concern only over the possibility that one of the brothers might die, we might have said that **we are not concerned over** the possibility of **the death** of a brother and therefore allow the brothers to consummate the levirate marriage. The mishna therefore **teaches us** that even in the case where there is concern only for the negation of the mitzva, they must perform *ḥalitza* and not consummate the levirate marriage.

אִי הָכִי,

The Gemara asks: **If so,** i.e., if we are concerned over the possibility that the remaining brother might die,

HALAKHA

The levirate bond – זִיקָה: In accordance with Shmuel's opinion here, the conclusive *halakha* is that the levirate bond is substantial. Although the halakha generally follows Rav's opinion in his disputes with Shmuel that pertain to prohibitions, the deliberation of the *amora'im* on Shmuel's opinion indicates that the *halakha* should be ruled according to him (Rosh; Rambam *Sefer Nashim, Hilkhot Yibbum* 1:13; *Shulḥan Arukh, Even HaEzer* 159:5).

חֲמִשָּׁה נַמִּי! לְמִיתָה דִּתְרֵי לָא חָיְישִׁינַן.

then this should **also** be true in a case of **five** brothers, two of whom were married to two sisters and died, and their wives happened before the three remaining brothers for levirate marriage. The Gemara answers: **We are not concerned over** the possibility of **the death of two**[N] brothers in such a short period of time.

אָמַר רָבָא בַּר רַב הוּנָא אָמַר רַב: שָׁלֹשׁ אֲחָיוֹת יְבָמוֹת שֶׁנָּפְלוּ לִפְנֵי שְׁנֵי אַחִין יְבָמִין, זֶה חוֹלֵץ לְאַחַת, וְזֶה חוֹלֵץ לְאַחַת, וְאֶמְצָעִית צְרִיכָה חֲלִיצָה מִשְּׁנֵיהֶם.

§ **Rava bar Rav Huna said** that **Rav said:** In a case where **three sisters** who were married to three brothers became *yevamot* and **happened before two** remaining **brothers** who were their *yevamin* for levirate marriage, then **this** one brother **performs *ḥalitza* with one** of the women, **and that** brother **performs *ḥalitza* with** another **one** of the women. **And the middle,** i.e., third, sister **requires *ḥalitza* with both of** the brothers.

אֲמַר לֵיהּ רַבָּה: מִדְּקָאָמְרַתְּ אֶמְצָעִית צְרִיכָה חֲלִיצָה מִשְּׁנֵיהֶם – קָסָבְרַתְּ יֵשׁ זִיקָה, וְהָוְיָא לַהּ חֲלִיצָה פְּסוּלָה, וַחֲלִיצָה פְּסוּלָה צָרִיךְ לַחֲזוֹר עַל כׇּל הָאַחִין.

Rabba said to them: From the fact **that you say** that **the middle one requires *ḥalitza* with both of** the brothers, it can be deduced that **you hold** that **the levirate bond is substantial** and creates a familial relationship, **and** similarly **this** *ḥalitza* performed by each of the brothers with the third sister **is invalid *ḥalitza*.**[NH] Since the third woman is the sister of a woman with whom he performed *ḥalitza*, it is not possible to consummate the levirate marriage with her. Therefore, the *ḥalitza* performed with her is not entirely valid and does not release her from the levirate bond between her and the two brothers. **And** there is a principle that **invalid *ḥalitza***[N] **must be repeated by all of the brothers;** each of them must perform an act of *ḥalitza* with this woman.

אִי הָכִי, קַמָּיְיתָא נַמִּי!

The Gemara asks: **If that is so, the first** two women should **also** require *ḥalitza* from each of the brothers because each act of *ḥalitza* was invalid, as each woman has the status of the sister of a woman with whom the man has a levirate bond, and it is therefore prohibited for the men to consummate the levirate marriage with them.

אִי דְּנָפוּל בְּבַת אַחַת – הָכִי נַמִּי, לָא צְרִיכָא דְּנָפוּל בְּזוֹ אַחַר זוֹ.

The Gemara responds: If the case is **that they,** i.e., the sisters, **happened** before the brothers **simultaneously,**[N] **it is indeed so** that the two brothers would each be obligated to perform *ḥalitza* with each of the three sisters. This *halakha* is **necessary only** in the case **where they happened** before the brothers, **one after the other.**

נָפְלָה חֲדָא – חָלַץ לַהּ רְאוּבֵן, נָפְלָה אִידַּךְ חָלַץ לַהּ שִׁמְעוֹן.

How so? **One** sister **happened** before the brothers for levirate marriage and then **Reuven,** one of the brothers, **performed** valid ***ḥalitza* with her. Another** sister **happened** before the brothers for levirate marriage, and the brother **Shimon performed *ḥalitza* with her.** In this case, Shimon was allowed to consummate the levirate marriage with her if he so desired, as she had no family relationship to him at all. When Reuven performed *ḥalitza* with the first sister, he removed the levirate bond between her and the other brothers, such that Shimon has no relationship with the first sister at all and is free to marry the second sister. Therefore, when he performed *ḥalitza*, the act was valid.

HALAKHA

Invalid *ḥalitza* – חֲלִיצָה פְּסוּלָה: The early authorities offer two definitions of invalid *ḥalitza*. The most common understanding is that in any case where the *yevama* is prohibited from consummating the levirate marriage but still requires *ḥalitza*, that *ḥalitza* is regarded as invalid and must be performed by all the brothers (Rashi; Rambam; see Vilna Gaon). The Rema, following *Tosafot*, writes that invalid *ḥalitza* occurs only when the relevant prohibition directly weakens the levirate bond, such as is the case when a *yavam* has a levirate bond with two sisters (Rambam *Sefer Nashim, Hilkhot Yibbum* 7:9; *Shulḥan Arukh, Even HaEzer* 170:5).

NOTES

We are not concerned over the possibility of the death of two – לְמִיתָה דִּתְרֵי לָא חָיְישִׁינַן: The Ritva writes that even according to those who hold that there might be legitimate concern over the possibility of two deaths, this is a case of a rabbinic decree that prohibits the negation of the mitzva of levirate marriage, where there need not be concerned for such a possibility.

Invalid *ḥalitza* – חֲלִיצָה פְּסוּלָה: The early commentaries dispute what constitutes invalid *ḥalitza*. According to one opinion, *ḥalitza* performed in a case where the *yavam* is prohibited from consummating the levirate marriage and the sister-in-law still requires *ḥalitza* is invalid *ḥalitza*. It must be performed by all the brothers before the *yevama* is permitted to remarry (Rashi; see Rambam).

According to *Tosafot*, however, invalid *ḥalitza* occurs only when the prohibition that precludes the possibility of performing levirate marriage directly weakens the levirate bond. The present case in the Gemara serves as an example: The woman requiring levirate marriage from the *yavam* is the sister of a woman who already underwent *ḥalitza* with him. If consummation of the levirate marriage is prohibited for a reason unrelated to her status as a *yevama*, such as when the initial marriage of the *yevama* was licentious due to her being her husband's remarried divorcée (see 11b), the proposed *ḥalitza* is not termed invalid and she needs to perform it only with one brother. The later commentaries discuss extensively how this dispute reflects a general question about the essence of *ḥalitza* (*Ḥiddushei Rav Shimon Shkop*; *Arza deVei Rav*).

The Ramban, following the Jerusalem Talmud, explains why invalid *ḥalitza* must be performed with all the brothers: Ordinary *ḥalitza* has two aspects. In one way it is similar to levirate marriage in that it a mitzva performed with one of the *yevamot* that concludes the levirate bond with both the *ḥalutza* and her rival wives. However, *ḥalitza* also bears resemblance to divorce in that it nullifies the connection between the *yavam* and the *yevama*. Invalid *ḥalitza* is limited in that it only operates in this second way and therefore the woman needs to sever her connection to each *yavam* separately.

The levirate bond is substantial…invalid *ḥalitza*, etc. – יֵשׁ זִיקָה...חֲלִיצָה פְּסוּלָה וכו׳: The Ritva and the Meiri explain that only if one maintains that the levirate bond is substantial is it possible to say that there was invalid *ḥalitza* and the *yevama* must repeat the *ḥalitza* with each of the *yevamin*. If, however, there is no levirate bond, then even invalid *ḥalitza* suffices to release the sister-in-law. However, from a discussion in the Jerusalem Talmud it would seem that these are two separate questions: First, is the *ḥalitza* an act of acquisition or release? Second, is the levirate bond an act of acquisition?

If the case is that they happened simultaneously – אִי דְּנָפוּל בְּבַת אַחַת: *Tosafot* comment that if the case is indeed referring to a situation where the two sisters became candidates for levirate marriage with the brothers simultaneously, then it would have been sufficient to state this ruling with regard to only two sisters. In this case, they would also need to repeat the *ḥalitza* with both brothers. Therefore, *Tosafot* raise the question as to why the Gemara specifically chose a case with three brothers. The Ramban writes that although, according to Rav's opinion, it would have sufficed to state this ruling with regard to two sisters, the case of three sisters was necessary according to Shmuel's statement later on. *Tosefot Ḥad MiKamma'ei* and the Meiri say that it was necessary to state the case of three sisters in order to inform us of a novel ruling: Even the third middle sister, whose levirate bond was weakened because she is the sister of a woman with whom he performed *ḥalitza*, requires *ḥalitza* from both of the brothers.

נָפְלָה אִידַךְ חָלַץ לָהּ הַאי מַפְקַע זִיקָתוֹ, חָלַץ לָהּ הַאי מַפְקַע זִיקָתוֹ.

Another third sister then **happened** before the brothers for levirate marriage. When **this** first brother **performs *ḥalitza* with her, he terminates his levirate bond, and** when **this** second brother **performs *ḥalitza* with her, he terminates his levirate bond.** However, neither brother can, by performing *ḥalitza*, terminate the other brother's levirate bond because each brother's *ḥalitza* is invalid, as each brother is unable to consummate the levirate marriage in this case. This is due to the woman's status as the sister of a woman with whom he performed *ḥalitza*.

וְהָאֲמַר רַב: אֵין זִיקָה! לְדִבְרֵי הָאוֹמֵר יֵשׁ זִיקָה קָאָמַר.

The Gemara asks: How can this statement be cited in the name of Rav? **But didn't Rav say: The levirate bond is not substantial.** This *halakha*, however, was explained based on the assumption that the levirate bond is substantial. The Gemara answers: Indeed, according to Rav himself it is unnecessary to perform *ḥalitza* with multiple brothers. He, however, **states** this *halakha* **in accordance with the statement of the one who says that the levirate bond is substantial,**[N] despite the fact that he does not hold this himself.

וּשְׁמוּאֵל אָמַר: אֶחָד חוֹלֵץ לְכוּלָּן. מִכְּדִי שָׁמְעִינַן לֵיהּ לִשְׁמוּאֵל דְּאָמַר: חֲלִיצָה מְעַלְּיָא בָּעֵינַן, דְּאָמַר שְׁמוּאֵל:

And with regard to the above case **Shmuel said** a different halakhic ruling: It is sufficient if **one** brother **performs *ḥalitza* with each** of the sisters. The Gemara raises a difficulty: **But since we have heard that Shmuel said: We require a full-fledged *ḥalitza*,** and invalid *ḥalitza* does not result in complete exemption, this ruling is difficult. It is not clear why the invalid *ḥalitza* in this case would be sufficient, **as Shmuel said:**

NOTES

In accordance with the statement of the one who says that the levirate bond is substantial – לְדִבְרֵי הָאוֹמֵר יֵשׁ זִיקָה: Most of the early commentaries hold that Rav presented an opinion that was not his own and that he does not accept. Rivan, however, says that there is an amoraic dispute as to whether or not Rav holds that the levirate bond is substantial, and the opinion presented here follows that of the *amora* who maintains that Rav is of the opinion that the levirate bond is substantial (see *Yevamot* 18b).

Perek **III**
Daf **27** Amud **a**

חָלַץ לָאֲחָיוֹת לֹא נִפְטְרוּ צָרוֹת. הֵיכָא דְּקַיְימָא חֲלִיצָה דְּשִׁמְעוֹן חֲלִיצָה כְּשֵׁרָה, חָלֵיץ לָהּ רְאוּבֵן חֲלִיצָה פְּסוּלָה.

In the case of three brothers, two of whom were married to several women, including two sisters, and the two married brothers later died, and their wives happened before the *yavam* for levirate marriage, if the *yavam* **performed *ḥalitza* with the sisters** who were among the wives, **the rival wives are not** thereby **exempt.**[H] One can deduce from here that since the *yavam* cannot consummate the levirate marriage with the sisters, as each is the sister of a woman with whom he has a levirate bond, then the act of *ḥalitza* is invalid, and invalid *ḥalitza* is ineffective in exempting their rival wives. It is concluded from here that even Shmuel requires valid *ḥalitza*, i.e., *ḥalitza* that occurs when there is a possibility of consummating the levirate marriage. According to this rationale, however, Shmuel's ruling in the above case is difficult: With regard to the second sister, **when there exists** the possibility for **Shimon's *ḥalitza*,** i.e., the *ḥalitza* of the second brother who did not yet perform *ḥalitza*, to be **a valid *ḥalitza*,**[N] would it be allowed for **Reuven,** the brother who already did *ḥalitza* with one sister, **to perform invalid *ḥalitza* with** her?

מַאי ״אֶחָד חוֹלֵץ לְכוּלָּן״ נַמִי דְּקָאָמַר – אַאֶמְצָעִית. וְהָא כּוּלָּן קָאָמַר! כֵּיוָן דְּרוּבָּה גַּבֵּיהּ קָרֵי לֵיהּ ״כּוּלָּן״. וְאִיבָּעֵית אֵימָא: כִּי קָאָמַר שְׁמוּאֵל חֲלִיצָה מְעַלְּיָא בָּעֵינַן – הָנֵי מִילֵּי לְמִיפְטַר צָרָתָהּ, אֲבָל מִפְּטְרָא נַפְשָׁהּ – פָּטְרָה.

The Gemara resolves this difficulty by reinterpreting Shmuel's statement. **What does it mean that it says: One performs *ḥalitza* with each of them, that** Shmuel **stated?** Shmuel **says that with regard to the middle one,** i.e., the third sister, one of the two brothers performs *ḥalitza* with her. The Gemara asks: **But didn't he say: Each of them,** indicating that one brother performs *ḥalitza* with all of the sisters? The Gemara answers: **Since** the brother who performed *ḥalitza* with one sister repeats the act with another, it turns out that **most** of the acts of *ḥalitza* **are** performed **with him,**[N] **and this is called:** With **each of them. And if you wish, say** a different answer: **When Shmuel said we require a full-fledged *ḥalitza*, this applies only to exempt her rival wife** by means of that *ḥalitza*. **But to exempt** the woman **herself,** even invalid *ḥalitza* would render her **exempt.**[H] In the case above, since no rival wives are involved, it would be sufficient for one brother to perform *ḥalitza* with each of the sisters.

HALAKHA

If he performed *ḥalitza* with the sisters the rival wives are not exempt – חָלַץ לָאֲחָיוֹת לֹא נִפְטְרוּ צָרוֹת: In the case of three brothers, two of whom were married to two sisters, where each had a rival wife, and the brothers died and their wives happened before the third brother for levirate marriage, if the *yavam* performs the act of *ḥalitza* with the rival wives then the sisters are thereby exempt as well. However, if he performs *ḥalitza* with the sisters, the rival wives do not become exempt, in accordance with the opinion of Shmuel as explained by Rav Ashi (Rambam *Sefer Nashim, Hilkhot Yibbum* 7:9; *Shulḥan Arukh, Even HaEzer* 170:17, 174:1).

To exempt the woman herself…exempt – מִפְּטְרָא נַפְשָׁהּ, פָּטְרָה: It would seem that even according to those authorities who rule that in the case of invalid *ḥalitza* the woman must repeat the *ḥalitza* with the other brothers, this is required in order to completely nullify the levirate bond and exempt the rival wives. The woman who performed the invalid *ḥalitza*, however, is free of her bond and is permitted to the general public without repeating the *ḥalitza*. At the very least, she is permitted after the fact (see *Beit Shmuel*; Rambam *Sefer Nashim, Hilkhot Yibbum* 5:12; *Shulḥan Arukh, Even HaEzer* 170:19).

NOTES

Shimon's *ḥalitza*, a valid *ḥalitza* – חֲלִיצָה דְּשִׁמְעוֹן חֲלִיצָה כְּשֵׁרָה: Some commentaries say that when Reuven performed *ḥalitza* with the first sister, Shimon's bond with her was completely nullified, and therefore when Shimon performs *ḥalitza* with the second sister it is a completely valid *ḥalitza* (see Rashba). Others explain that even if some aspect of Shimon's original bond with the first sister remains intact, his act of *ḥalitza* with the second sister is nevertheless more efficacious than the *ḥalitza* performed by Reuven (Rivan).

Since most are with him – כֵּיוָן דְּרוּבָּה גַּבֵּיהּ: This follows the principle that in any matter, the majority is equivalent to the entirety (Ritva).

גּוּפָא, אָמַר שְׁמוּאֵל: חָלַץ לָאֲחָיוֹת – לֹא נִפְטְרוּ צָרוֹת, לַצָּרוֹת – נִפְטְרוּ אֲחָיוֹת. חָלַץ לְבַעֲלַת הַגֵּט – לֹא נִפְטְרָה צָרָה, לַצָּרָה – נִפְטְרָה בַּעֲלַת הַגֵּט.

§ Apropos of Shmuel's statement, the Gemara examines **the** matter **itself. Shmuel said:** In the case of three brothers, two of whom were married to several women, including two sisters, and the two married brothers later died, and their wives happened before the *yavam* for levirate marriage, if the *yavam* **performed *ḥalitza* with the sisters,**[B] **the rival wives are not** thereby **exempt.** But if he performed *ḥalitza* **with the rival wives, the sisters are exempt.**[N] Similarly, if he gave a bill of divorce to one of these women, whereby he would no longer be permitted to consummate the levirate marriage with them due to a rabbinic decree, and he then **performed *ḥalitza* with the woman who received a bill of divorce, the rival wife is not** thereby **exempt.** Since he was unable to consummate the levirate marriage with her, the *ḥalitza* performed with her was invalid, and invalid *ḥalitza* does not exempt the rival wife. If he performed the act of *ḥalitza* **with the rival wife,** then **the woman who received a bill of divorce is exempt.**[N]

חָלַץ לְבַעֲלַת הַמַּאֲמָר – לֹא נִפְטְרָה צָרָה, לַצָּרָה – נִפְטְרָה בַּעֲלַת מַאֲמָר.

The ruling is similar with regard to the case where the *yavam* performed *ma'amar*, i.e., levirate betrothal,[N] to one of the wives. If **he** then **performed *ḥalitza* with** the woman **who received** his **levirate betrothal** then **the rival wife is not exempt.** Indeed, this *ḥalitza* is invalid as well, for once the *yavam* performed levirate betrothal, this act can be rescinded only by means of a bill of divorce. Because the woman needs to receive a bill of divorce in addition to the *ḥalitza* in order to exempt her from her bond, the *ḥalitza* is considered invalid and is not sufficient to exempt the rival wife. But if the *yavam* performed *ḥalitza* **with the rival wife,** then **she who received** his **levirate betrothal is exempt**[N] from *ḥalitza* and requires only a bill of divorce.[H]

מַאי שְׁנָא לָאֲחָיוֹת דְּלָא נִפְטְרוּ צָרוֹת – דְּהָוְיָא לוֹ אֲחוֹת אִשָּׁה בְּזִיקָה, חָלַץ לַצָּרוֹת נַמִּי לָא לִיפַּטְרוּ אֲחָיוֹת, דְּהָוְיָא לְהוּ צָרוֹת אֲחוֹת אִשָּׁה בְּזִיקָה! קָסָבַר שְׁמוּאֵל: אֵין זִיקָה.

The Gemara asks: **What is different** in the two cases? Why, if he performed *ḥalitza* **with the sisters, are the rival wives not exempt?** This is because the sister **is** related **to him** as **the sister of a woman with whom he has a levirate bond.** Since, under these circumstances he would not be permitted to consummate the levirate marriage with her, her *ḥalitza* is then considered invalid *ḥalitza*. However, if that is so, when **he performed *ḥalitza* with the rival wives, the sisters should not be exempt either, as the** rival wives **are** related **to him as rival wives of the sister of a woman with whom he has a levirate bond.** If the woman is forbidden to him due to a relationship created by the levirate bond, then her rival wife is forbidden to him in the same way, and her *ḥalitza* would be invalid as well. The Gemara answers: **Shmuel holds** that **the levirate bond is not substantial,** and therefore the levirate bond does not create a relationship between the *yavam* and the sisters such that the prohibition would be extended to the rival wives as well.

NOTES

With the rival wives, the sisters are exempt – לַצָּרוֹת נִפְטְרוּ אֲחָיוֹת: Even though there is some small deficiency in the performance of *ḥalitza* with the rival wives, this deficiency is, according to all opinions, negligible (*Tosefot Rid*).

The woman who received a bill of divorce is exempt – נִפְטְרָה בַּעֲלַת הַגֵּט: It is preferable to perform *ḥalitza* with the rival wife, although she is not eligible to enter into levirate marriage because the *yavam* did not perform any previous act with her, unlike with the woman who received a bill of divorce (*Tosefot Rid*).

Levirate betrothal – מַאֲמָר: The Sages instituted that even in cases of levirate marriage, which can be effected by conjugal relations alone according to Torah law, the *yavam* should first perform betrothal by means of a legal document or a transfer of money accompanied by a verbal declaration of betrothal. As opposed to standard betrothal, this levirate betrothal is not binding by Torah law.

She who received levirate betrothal is exempt – נִפְטְרָה בַּעֲלַת מַאֲמָר: Although the rival wife of one who received levirate betrothal is also forbidden to the *yavam*, as he is allowed to build one household and not two, it is still preferable to perform *ḥalitza* with the rival wife. This is because a woman who received levirate betrothal is not exempt from her connection with him by the act of *ḥalitza* alone but would require a bill of divorce as well (see *Tosefot Rid*).

With regard to the deficiency in the *ḥalitza* of a woman who had received levirate betrothal, some commentaries explain that the performance of levirate betrothal renders this woman ineligible for levirate marriage with the other brothers, and even a slight deficiency in the levirate bond renders the *ḥalitza* deficient (see Rivan and Ramban).

Tosafot explain that the woman who received levirate betrothal is somewhat similar to a woman who entered into marriage. Marriage completely nullifies the levirate bond; levirate betrothal weakens the levirate bond.

HALAKHA

Ḥalitza with a woman who received a bill of divorce or levirate betrothal – חֲלִיצָה לְבַעֲלַת הַגֵּט אוֹ מַאֲמָר: In the case of one who performed levirate betrothal with his *yevama* or gave her a bill of divorce, if she had a rival wife and he then came to perform *ḥalitza* with one of the women, *ḥalitza* with the woman who received the bill of divorce or levirate betrothal would not exempt her rival wife from performing *ḥalitza*. *Ḥalitza* with the rival wife, however, does render the woman who received a bill of divorce or levirate betrothal exempt from performing *ḥalitza*, in accordance with the statement of Shmuel (*Shulḥan Arukh, Even HaEzer* 170:17).

BACKGROUND

He performed *ḥalitza* with the sisters – חָלַץ לָאֲחָיוֹת: Reuven, Shimon, and Levi are paternal brothers. Shimon married Rachel and Ḥanna. Levi married Rachel's sister, Leah, and Miriam. When Shimon and Levi die childless, their wives happen before Reuven for levirate marriage. If Reuven first performs *ḥalitza* with Leah and then afterward with Rachel, Rachel's *ḥalitza* is considered invalid. Although Rachel herself is rendered exempt through this *ḥalitza*, her rival wife Ḥanna is not. However, Leah's *ḥalitza* is valid, and therefore her rival wife Miriam is rendered exempt by it.

וְהָא אֲמַר שְׁמוּאֵל: יֵשׁ זִיקָה! לְדִבְרֵי הָאוֹמֵר אֵין זִיקָה קָאָמַר.

The Gemara challenges: **But didn't Shmuel say** explicitly that **the levirate bond is substantial?** The Gemara responds: **He stated** this *halakha* **in accordance with the statement of those who say that the levirate bond is not substantial,**[N] although he himself maintains the opposite.

אִי הָכִי, חָלַץ לָאֲחָיוֹת אַמַּאי לֹא נִפְטְרוּ צָרוֹת? בִּשְׁלָמָא צָרָה דְּרָחֵל לָא תִּיפָּטֵר – דְּכֵיוָן דְּחָלַץ לָהּ לְלֵאָה וַהֲדַר חָלַץ לְרָחֵל – הָוְיָא לָהּ חֲלִיצָה דְּרָחֵל חֲלִיצָה פְּסוּלָה. אֶלָּא צָרָה דְּלֵאָה תִּיפָּטֵר!

The Gemara asks: **If that is** indeed **so,** that he stated this ruling in accordance with the opinion that the levirate bond is not substantial, then when the *yavam* **performed *ḥalitza* with the sisters, why were** their **rival wives not exempt? Granted, Rachel's rival wife,** i.e., the rival wife of the second sister, **would not be exempt, for once he performed *ḥalitza* with Leah,** the first sister, **and then** later **performed *ḥalitza* with Rachel,** it turns out that **Rachel's *ḥalitza* was invalid *ḥalitza*,**[H] as he could not consummate the levirate marriage with Rachel because she is the sister of a woman with whom he performed *ḥalitza*, and invalid *ḥalitza* does not exempt a rival wife. **However, the rival wife of Leah should be exempt** because if the levirate bond is not substantial, the *ḥalitza* with the first sister would have been completely valid.

מַאי "לֹא נִפְטְרוּ צָרוֹת" נַמִי דְּקָאָמַר – אַצָּרָה דְּרָחֵל, וְהָא "צָרוֹת" קָאָמַר! צָרוֹת דְּעָלְמָא.

The Gemara explains: **What** does it mean **that it says: The rival wives are not exempt, that** Shmuel **stated?** It is referring only **to the rival wife of Rachel,** the second sister, who is not exempt. The Gemara challenges: **But he said rival wives** in the plural, seeming to refer to both rival wives? The Gemara answers: He spoke of **rival wives in general.**[N] In other words, this is a general *halakha*, and for that reason it was stated in the plural. However, it does not mean that both the rival wife of the first sister and the rival wife of the second sister are not exempt.

אִי הָכִי, חָלַץ "לַצָּרוֹת נִפְטְרוּ אֲחָיוֹת", וְאַצָּרַת רָחֵל מִי מִיפַּטְרָא? וְהָא תְּנַן: אָסוּר אָדָם בְּצָרַת קְרוֹבַת חֲלוּצָתוֹ!

The Gemara challenges this: **If that is so,** that when Shmuel chose to speak in the plural he was referring only to the rival wife of Rachel, there arises a difficulty with the second half of the statement: If **he performed *ḥalitza* with the rival wives, the sisters are exempt. But would Rachel** become **exempt** by *ḥalitza* performed **with her rival wife? But didn't we learn** in a mishna: **A man is forbidden to** marry **the rival wife of a close relative of his *ḥalutza*?** Once the *yavam* performs *ḥalitza* with one sister, Leah, then her sister's rival wife, i.e., Rachel's rival wife, would be considered the rival wife of the sister of a woman with whom he performed *ḥalitza*. Being as she is forbidden to him, her *ḥalitza* is invalid and should not exempt Rachel.

שְׁמוּאֵל נַמִי, הִתְחִיל וְלֹא הִתְחִיל קָאָמַר: הִתְחִיל בָּאֲחָיוֹת – לֹא יִגְמוֹר בַּצָּרוֹת, דִּתְנַן: אָסוּר אָדָם בְּצָרַת קְרוֹבַת חֲלוּצָתוֹ, הִתְחִיל בַּצָּרוֹת – יִגְמוֹר אַף בָּאֲחָיוֹת, דִּתְנַן: מוּתָּר אָדָם בִּקְרוֹבַת צָרַת חֲלוּצָתוֹ.

The Gemara answers: **Shmuel also** meant to distinguish between a case where **he began**[N] **and** the case where **he did not begin.** This is how his statement should be understood: If **he began** by performing *ḥalitza* **with** one of **the sisters, he may not finish by** performing a second act of *ḥalitza* **with** any one of **the rival wives, as we learned** in a mishna (40b): **A man is forbidden** to marry **the rival wife of a close relative of his *ḥalutza*.**[H] Due to this prohibition, *ḥalitza* performed with the second rival wife is invalid *ḥalitza* and would not exempt the second sister. If, however, **he began with the rival wives** and performed the first *ḥalitza* with the rival wife of Leah, **he may finish with the sisters as well** and perform the second *ḥalitza* with Leah, **as we learned** in a mishna (40b): **A man is permitted to** marry **the close relative of the rival wife of his *ḥalutza*.**[H] Therefore, if he performed *ḥalitza* with Leah's rival wife, then Rachel, who is the sister of the rival wife of his *ḥalutza*, is permitted to him. He can therefore perform a completely valid *ḥalitza* with her and thereby exempt her rival wife.

NOTES

In accordance with the statement of those who say that the levirate bond is not substantial – לְדִבְרֵי הָאוֹמֵר אֵין זִיקָה: The early commentaries raise an objection: The Gemara maintains that the ruling that *ḥalitza* with a woman who received a bill of divorce does not exempt her rival wife was said only in accordance with the opinion that the levirate bond is substantial (*Yevamot* 51a). If so, how can the Gemara here explain that Shmuel stated this ruling in accordance with the opinion that the levirate bond is not substantial?

Tosafot, Ramban, and others hold that the present discussion is cited for the sake of the talmudic argumentation alone and does not represent a true summary of the issue. However, *Tosafot Yeshanim* say that the two *halakhot* mentioned follow two different opinions: The first *halakha*, which discusses *ḥalitza* with sisters, follows the opinion that the levirate bond is not substantial. The *halakha* that discusses *ḥalitza* with a woman who received a bill of divorce follows the opinion that the levirate bond is substantial.

Rival wives in general – צָרוֹת דְּעָלְמָא: This phrase indicates that this *halakha* applies to any case that is similar to this one. The Sages occasionally employ the plural forms in order to establish a general ruling (Rashi). The Rivan understands that this ruling extends to all instances of a rival wife of a woman who is forbidden to the *yavam* by rabbinic law. This includes not only women prohibited to the *yavam* due to the levirate bond, but also women who are secondary forbidden relationships by rabbinic law.

Shmuel…began, etc. – שְׁמוּאֵל...הִתְחִיל וכו׳: Some commentaries explain this passage specifically according to the opinion that the levirate bond is substantial, similar to the next answer suggested by the Gemara in the name of Rav Ashi. If so, the Gemara changes its assumption during the course of its discussion. Although this type of change would normally be noted by the word rather, as that word is generally employed to indicate the retraction of a previous explanation and the introduction of a new suggestion, this practice is not strictly adhered to if the first opinion is presented anonymously and not in the name of a specific *amora* (*Tosefot HaRosh*; Ramban).

HALAKHA

Invalid *ḥalitza* must be repeated – חֲלִיצָה פְּסוּלָה צְרִיכָה לַחֲזוֹר: There are a variety of opinions with regard to this *halakha*. Some authorities determined that in cases of invalid *ḥalitza*, if there are several *yevamin* the woman must repeat the *ḥalitza* with all of the *yevamin*. If, however, there are two sisters-in-law whose *ḥalitza* is considered invalid and only a single *yavam*, he can exempt them both through a single act of *ḥalitza*. Some say that if there are two sisters-in-law he must perform *ḥalitza* with each of them (Ramban). Other authorities hold that invalid *ḥalitza* does not necessitate that the woman repeat the *ḥalitza* with the other brothers, and even in the case of two *yevamin* and a single *yevama*, a single act of *ḥalitza* would suffice. It seems that most of the halakhic authorities hold in accordance with this opinion (Rambam *Sefer Nashim, Hilkhot Yibbum* 5:12; *Shulḥan Arukh, Even HaEzer* 170:5, 19).

Forbidden to marry the rival wife of a close relative of his *ḥalutza* – אָסוּר...בְּצָרַת קְרוֹבַת חֲלוּצָתוֹ: The Sages considered a woman with whom one performed *ḥalitza* to be like his wife, and therefore he is forbidden to marry her close relatives, including her sister, mother, etc. If a close relative of the woman with whom he performed *ḥalitza* is married to his brother, then her rival wife is likewise forbidden to him. If, however, she is married to another man, her rival wife is permitted to him, as per most halakhic authorities, but not in accordance with Rashi (Rambam *Sefer Nashim, Hilkhot Yibbum* 6:20; *Shulḥan Arukh, Even HaEzer* 162:5).

Permitted to marry the close relative of the rival wife of his *ḥalutza* – מוּתָּר...בִּקְרוֹבַת צָרַת חֲלוּצָתוֹ: A man is allowed to marry the sister, or any other relatives, of the rival wife of a woman with whom he performed *ḥalitza*, in accordance with the mishna cited here (Rambam *Sefer Nashim, Hilkhot Yibbum* 1:13; *Shulḥan Arukh, Even HaEzer* 162:4).

רַב אַשִׁי אָמַר: לְעוֹלָם כִּדְקָאָמְרַתְּ, וּמִשּׁוּם דְּלָא אַלִּימָא זִיקָה לְשַׁוּוֹיֵי לְצָרָה כְּעֶרְוָה.

Rav Ashi said: Actually, Shmuel's statement should be interpreted **as you** originally **said,** that Shmuel's rationale for these *halakhot* accords with his opinion that the levirate bond is substantial. As for the objection that was raised as to why the sisters would be exempted by *ḥalitza* performed with the rival wives if these rival wives were considered the rival wife of the sister of a woman with whom the *yavam* had a levirate bond, this can be resolved as follows: This **is because the levirate bond is not** so **strong**[N] **as to render the** status of **a rival wife like** an actual **forbidden relative.** The levirate bond is sufficient to prohibit levirate marriage with the sister of a woman with whom he has a levirate bond, but not sufficient to prohibit their rival wives to the *yavam*.

תַּנְיָא כְּווֹתֵיהּ דְּרַב אַשִׁי: חָלַץ לָאֲחָיוֹת – לֹא נִפְטְרוּ צָרוֹת, הָא לַצָּרוֹת נִפְטְרוּ אֲחָיוֹת – מַאי טַעְמָא, לָאו מִשּׁוּם דְּקָסָבַר יֵשׁ זִיקָה, וְלֹא אַלִּימָא זִיקָה לְשַׁוּוֹיֵי לְצָרָה כְּעֶרְוָה?!

The Gemara comments: It **is taught** in a *baraita* **in accordance with** the opinion **of Rav Ashi:**[N] **If he performed *ḥalitza* with the sisters, the rival wives are not exempt** from levirate marriage. From here one can deduce: **Consequently,** if he performed *ḥalitza* **with the rival wives, the sisters are exempt. What is the reason** for this? **Is it not because** this *tanna* **held** that **the levirate bond is substantial,** and therefore the rival wives were not rendered exempt by the *ḥalitza* of the sisters, **but** nevertheless **the levirate bond is not** so **strong as to render the rival wife equivalent to a forbidden relative** Therefore, the prohibition with regard to the rival wives in this case is less severe than the prohibition concerning the sisters themselves, and when they perform *ḥalitza*, the *ḥalitza* is valid and the sisters are exempt.

אָמַר רַבִּי אַבָּא בַּר מֶמֶל: הָא מַנִּי – בֵּית שַׁמַּאי הִיא, דִּתְנַן: בֵּית שַׁמַּאי מַתִּירִין הַצָּרוֹת לָאַחִין. אִי הָכִי, יַבּוּמֵי נַמִּי תִּתְיַיבֵּם!

Rabbi Abba bar Memel rejected this explanation and **said:** In accordance with **whose** opinion **is this** *baraita* taught? **It is** in accordance with the opinion of **Beit Shammai,**[N] **as we learned** in a mishna: **Beit Shammai permitted the rival wives to** marry **the brothers;** even if they are the rival wives of his actual relatives, they are permitted to enter into levirate marriage. In the case above, where they are merely rival wives of the sister with whom he has a levirate bond, all the more so they are permitted to enter into levirate marriage. The Gemara objects: **If that is so,** if this ruling is in accordance with the opinion of Beit Shammai, who say that the rival wives are permitted, then the rival wife **should enter into levirate marriage as well.** Why does it speak here only of *ḥalitza* but not of the possibility of entering levirate marriage?

כְּרַבִּי יוֹחָנָן בֶּן נוּרִי, דְּאָמַר: בּוֹאוּ וְנַתְקִין לָהֶם לַצָּרוֹת שֶׁיְּהוּ חוֹלְצוֹת וְלֹא מִתְיַיבְּמוֹת. וְהָאָמַר מָר לֹא הִסְפִּיקוּ לִגְמוֹר אֶת הַדָּבָר עַד שֶׁנִּטְרְפָה הַשָּׁעָה! אָמַר רַב נַחְמָן בַּר יִצְחָק: אַחֲרָיו חָזְרוּ וְתִקְּנוּ.

The Gemara answers: The ruling is **in accordance with** the opinion of **Rabbi Yoḥanan ben Nuri, who said: Come and let us establish** a ruling **that the rival wives must perform *ḥalitza* and may not enter into levirate marriage,** thereby circumventing the dispute between Beit Shammai and Beit Hillel. Although Beit Shammai permitted the rival wives to the perform levirate betrothal, they should perform *ḥalitza* instead in order to conform to Beit Hillel's opinion as well. The Gemara objects: **But didn't the Master say** that **they did not succeed in finalizing the matter** and establishing Rabbi Yoḥanan ben Nuri's amendment **before the times of trouble**[B] **came** in the form of the anti-Jewish decrees, and so this ruling was never actually established? **Rav Naḥman bar Yitzḥak said: After his** time, other Sages **returned** to this issue and **established** this amendment in accordance with his opinion.[N]

אִיבַּעְיָא לְהוּ:

§ Apropos of the statement of Shmuel with regard to a woman who received a bill of divorce and a woman who received levirate betrothal, **a dilemma was raised before** the Sages:

NOTES

The levirate bond is not so strong – לָא אַלִּימָא זִיקָה: This assertion does not mean that the bond does not affect the rival wives at all, as rival wives may not enter into levirate marriage, even according to Rav Ashi's opinion. Rather, this means that the levirate bond is not so strong as to disqualify the rival wives in the same way that it disqualifies the sisters.

It is taught in accordance with the opinion of Rav Ashi – תַּנְיָא כְּווֹתֵיהּ דְּרַב אַשִׁי: It is not possible to interpret this *baraita* as the words of Shmuel were interpreted, by adding: He began, and: He did not begin, since it would have been necessary for the *baraita* to add additional segments clarifying the matter (*Tosafot*; see Ritva).

Whose opinion is this? It is Beit Shammai – הָא מַנִּי, בֵּית שַׁמַּאי הִיא: This matter is also raised in the Jerusalem Talmud, and there, too, it was suggested that the *baraita* should be interpreted as the opinion of Rabbi Yoḥanan ben Nuri. There, however, the Gemara does not suggest the hard-pressed explanation that the Sages proceeded to established this amendment (see *Tosafot*). Instead, the Gemara establishes the *baraita* as one version of the opinion of Beit Shammai, which itself is the matter of a tannaitic dispute.

Summary of the talmudic discussion – סִיכּוּם הַסּוּגְיָה: In this complicated talmudic discussion, the Gemara assumes that Rav and Shmuel made statements opposing their own opinions and also suggests various interpretations of Shmuel's statements wherein it is unclear whether or not these interpretations concur with one another. This leads the commentaries and especially the halakhic authorities to arrive at vastly different conclusions. The Rema and the Ramban conclude that the *halakha* follows Rav with regard to invalid *ḥalitza*. Since Rav made his statement in accordance with the opinion that the levirate bond is substantial, as is the halakhic conclusion, we must follow the principle that the *halakha* is in accordance with the opinion of Rav in matters of prohibitions. Therefore, according to the Ramban and others, in cases of invalid *ḥalitza*, each sister must repeat the *ḥalitza* with all the other *yevamin*.

According to most authorities, the Rif concludes that the *halakha* is in accordance with the most straightforward explanation of Shmuel, which is the latter explanation of his words. Therefore, one *yavam* performs *ḥalitza* with each of the sisters. The Rif establishes the *halakha* in accordance with the opinion of Shmuel, in opposition to Rav, because the principle that the *halakha* follows Rav applies only if Rav employs his own opinion in the dispute but not when he offers an explanation of another opinion that is not his own (*Nimmukei Yosef*).

The early commentaries were divided over how to understand the Rambam's opinion here, for it would seem that his words support two different opinions. Most commentaries maintain that he establishes the *halakha* in accordance with Shmuel and the latter explanation in the Gemara (Ramban; Rashba; Meiri; *Tur*).

The Ra'avad, *Tosafot*, and the Rosh all establish the *halakha* in accordance with the opinion of Shmuel, but according to the first formulation. Accordingly, the middle woman does not require *ḥalitza* with all of the brothers but the second sister does require *ḥalitza* from the second brother. They reason that where it is possible to perform valid *ḥalitza*, invalid *ḥalitza* does not suffice to exempt the woman. There are, however, differences of opinion within these commentaries. It would seem that the Ra'avad holds that after the fact the latter explanation can be relied upon (see *Beit Shmuel*). However, *Tosafot* maintain that even after the fact the *halakha* is according to the first explanation.

BACKGROUND

Times of trouble – נִטְרְפָה הַשָּׁעָה: It would seem, according to the chronology of the generations, that this is referring to several times of distress that occurred successively over one period. This period extended from the polemic of Trajan and Kitos, also known as the Diaspora Revolt, which destroyed the Jewish settlement in several lands adjacent to Israel, through the bar Kokheva revolt, which caused total upheaval in Jewish life. These disturbances completely prevented the Sanhedrin's ability to take organized action, including instituting ordinances, e.g., obligatory *ḥalitza* for rival wives.

בַּעֲלַת הַגֵּט וּבַעֲלַת מַאֲמָר – אֵיזוֹ מֵהֶן קוֹדֶמֶת? בַּעֲלַת הַגֵּט עֲדִיפָא – מִשּׁוּם דְּאַתְחֵיל בָּהּ בַּחֲלִיצָה, אוֹ דִּלְמָא בַּעֲלַת מַאֲמָר עֲדִיפָא מִשּׁוּם דִּקְרוֹבָה לְבִיאָה?

If two women happened before a single *yavam* for levirate marriage, and one is **a woman who received a bill of divorce and** the other is **a woman who received levirate betrothal,**[H] **which has precedence** for *ḥalitza*? **Is the woman who received a bill of divorce preferred**[N] **because he began the** process of ***ḥalitza*** **with her,** as presenting a bill of divorce represents the first step separating the woman from him? **Or perhaps the woman who received levirate betrothal is preferred, because she is closest to** being able to enter into permitted **sexual intercourse.** The act of levirate betrothal is generally done just prior to levirate marriage and is equivalent to the act of betrothal in non-levirate contexts. As a result, levirate betrothal strengthens the connection between the woman and the *yavam*. For this reason, it may be preferable to perform *ḥalitza* with the woman who received levirate betrothal.

אָמַר רַב אַשִׁי, תָּא שְׁמַע: וּמוֹדֶה רַבָּן גַּמְלִיאֵל שֶׁיֵּשׁ גֵּט אַחַר מַאֲמָר, וּמַאֲמָר אַחַר גֵּט.

Rav Ashi said: Come and hear: The Sages disputed the ruling with regard to a *yavam* who performed levirate betrothal with one sister-in-law and then performed it with her rival wife as well, or conversely, gave both women a bill of divorce. In such cases, would the second levirate betrothal or bill of divorce be effective? It was taught: **And Rabban Gamliel concedes that a bill of divorce is effective after levirate betrothal.** Therefore, the bill of divorce that the *yavam* gave to one *yevama* after having performed levirate betrothal with the other *yevama* is effective to some degree. Similarly, Rabban Gamliel concedes that **levirate betrothal** performed **after a bill of divorce is effective.**

אִי גֵּט עָדִיף – לָא לִיהֱנֵי מַאֲמָר אַבַּתְרֵיהּ, וְאִי מַאֲמָר עָדִיף – לָא לִיהֱנֵי גֵּט אַבַּתְרֵיהּ! אֶלָּא לָאו שְׁמַע מִינָּהּ כִּי הֲדָדֵי נִינְהוּ, שְׁמַע מִינָּהּ.

If the bill of divorce is preferred to levirate betrothal, then **levirate betrothal** performed **afterward should not be effective.** The opposite would hold true as well: **And if levirate betrothal is preferred,** then **a bill of divorce** given **afterward should not be effective. Rather,** must one **not conclude from** this statement **that the two are equivalent to each other?**[N] The Gemara summarizes: Indeed, **conclude from** this statement that they are equivalent. Therefore, neither the woman who received a bill of divorce nor the woman who received levirate betrothal has precedence for *ḥalitza*.

אָמַר רַב הוּנָא אָמַר רַב: שְׁתֵּי אֲחָיוֹת יְבָמוֹת שֶׁנָּפְלוּ לִפְנֵי יָבָם אֶחָד, חָלַץ לָרִאשׁוֹנָה – הוּתְּרָה, חָלַץ לַשְּׁנִיָּיה – הוּתְּרָה.

§ **Rav Huna said** that **Rav said:** In a case of **two sisters** who became *yevamot*, i.e., the two sisters were married to two brothers who died, **who happened before one** ***yavam*** for levirate marriage,[H] if **he performed** ***ḥalitza*** **with the first** sister, then **she is permitted** to marry any man. If **he performed** ***ḥalitza*** **with the second** sister, then **she is permitted** to do so as well.

HALAKHA

A woman who received a bill of divorce and a woman who received levirate betrothal – בַּעֲלַת הַגֵּט וּבַעֲלַת מַאֲמָר: If two *yevamot* from a single household happened before a *yavam* for levirate marriage, and he delivered a bill of divorce to one and performed levirate betrothal with the other, then he can perform the act of *ḥalitza* with whichever of them he choose and thereby exempt the second (*Shulḥan Arukh, Even HaEzer* 170:17).

Two sisters, *yevamot*, who happened before one *yavam* for levirate marriage – שְׁתֵּי אֲחָיוֹת יְבָמוֹת שֶׁנָּפְלוּ לִפְנֵי יָבָם אֶחָד: In the case of two sisters who happened before a *yavam* for levirate marriage one after the other, if the second sister died before he had performed any act the first sister is permitted to him. If, however, the first sister died, the second is forbidden. This ruling is in accordance with the opinion of Rabbi Yoḥanan, as the *halakha* follows him in disputes with Rav (Rambam *Sefer Nashim, Hilkhot Yibbum* 7:4; *Shulḥan Arukh, Even HaEzer* 175:1).

NOTES

Is the woman who received a bill of divorce preferred, etc. – בַּעֲלַת הַגֵּט עֲדִיפָא וכו׳: The use of the word preferred does not accurately represent the meaning here, and therefore the early commentaries diverge in their interpretation of it. According to the first suggestion of *Tosafot*, the word preferred simply clarifies the question of which woman underwent an act of more importance, and therefore this clarification does not decide the ruling of precedence with regard to *ḥalitza*.

From the words of the Rivan, however, it seems that being preferred indicates precedence for the purposes of *ḥalitza*. According to this explanation, the question at hand is: Once the *yavam* began the process of nullification with the woman who received a bill of divorce, would it be more appropriate for him to continue the process and do ḥalitza with her, or would the woman who received levirate betrothal hold precedence because her levirate bond is more complete? Alternatively, *Tosafot Yeshanim* explain that the question is: Which woman is it preferable to release from the levirate bond by performing *ḥalitza* with her rival wife; the woman who received a bill of divorce, because her bond was already weakened and therefore *ḥalitza* with her would be less powerful, or the woman who received levirate betrothal, because her levirate bond was weakened by the performance of levirate betrothal?

The two are equivalent to each other – הֲדָדֵי נִינְהוּ: Some commentaries hold that since the act of *ḥalitza* with either one of the women is equally flawed, both acts are considered invalid *ḥalitza*. Accordingly, the *ḥalitza* would have to be repeated with both women in order to release them from their levirate bonds (*Tosefot HaRosh*; see *Tosafot* and Ramban). However, according to Rashi and most halakhic authorities, since each act of *ḥalitza* is equally flawed, *ḥalitza* with one woman is sufficient to exempt the other. The Meiri adds another reason for this ruling, and states that invalid *ḥalitza* requires repetition only if there was some form of levirate bond in place. In this case, a single act of *ḥalitza* suffices, as there is no levirate bond.

מֵתָה רִאשׁוֹנָה מוּתָּר בַּשְּׁנִיָּה, וְאֵין צָרִיךְ לוֹמַר מֵתָה שְׁנִיָּה שֶׁמּוּתָּר בָּרִאשׁוֹנָה, מִשּׁוּם דְּהָוְיָא יְבָמָה שֶׁהוּתְּרָה וְנֶאֶסְרָה וְחָזְרָה וְהוּתְּרָה – תַּחֲזוֹר לְהֶיתֵּירָהּ הָרִאשׁוֹן.

If **the first** sister **died** before the *yavam* was able to perform *ḥalitza* with her, then he **is permitted to** take **the second**[N] sister in levirate marriage, for even if had actually been married to the first sister, one is permitted to marry the sister of his wife after his wife dies. **And needless to say, if the second** sister **died, then he is permitted to** take **the first** sister in levirate marriage **because she would be** considered **a *yevama* who was permitted** at the time that she happened before the *yavam* for levirate marriage; **and** then later **forbidden** as the sister of a woman with whom he has a levirate bond when the second sister happened before him for levirate marriage; **and subsequently became permitted** by the death of the second sister. Therefore, **she can return** completely **to her original permitted status.**

וְרַבִּי יוֹחָנָן אָמַר: מֵתָה שְׁנִיָּה – מוּתָּר בָּרִאשׁוֹנָה. אֲבָל מֵתָה רִאשׁוֹנָה – אָסוּר בַּשְּׁנִיָּה. מַאי טַעֲמָא – שֶׁכָּל יְבָמָה שֶׁאֵין אֲנִי קוֹרֵא בָּהּ בִּשְׁעַת נְפִילָה ״יְבָמָהּ יָבֹא עָלֶיהָ״ הֲרֵי זוֹ כְּאֵשֶׁת אָח שֶׁיֵּשׁ לָהּ בָּנִים, וַאֲסוּרָה.

However, Rabbi Yoḥanan said: If **the second** sister **dies, he is permitted to** take **the first. But if the first** sister **dies, he is prohibited from** taking **the second** sister. **What is the reason** for this ruling? The reason is **that any *yevama* to whom the verse "her brother-in-law will have intercourse with her"** (Deuteronomy 25:5) **cannot be applied at the time that she happens** before him for levirate marriage because she was forbidden to him at that moment, **is then** forever considered to be **like the wife of a brother who has children, and she is forbidden** to him. Because the second sister was forbidden to the *yavam* at the time that she happened before him for levirate marriage, being the sister of a woman with whom he had a levirate bond, she can never again be permitted to him.

וְרַב לֵית לֵיהּ הַאי סְבָרָא? וְהָאָמַר רַב: כָּל אִשָּׁה שֶׁאֵין אֲנִי קוֹרֵא בָּהּ בִּשְׁעַת נְפִילָה ״יְבָמָהּ יָבֹא עָלֶיהָ״ הֲרֵי הִיא כְּאֵשֶׁת אָח שֶׁיֵּשׁ לוֹ בָּנִים וַאֲסוּרָה! הָנֵי מִילֵּי הֵיכָא דְּקָאֵי בְּאַפָּהּ אִיסּוּר אֲחוֹת אִשָּׁה דְּאוֹרַיְיתָא, אֲבָל הָכָא – זִיקָה דְּרַבָּנַן הִיא.

The Gemara asks: **And does Rav not accept that reason?**[N] **Didn't Rav** himself **say** the exact same words: **Any woman to whom the verse "her brother-in-law will have intercourse with her" cannot be applied at the time that she happens** before him for levirate marriage **is then** considered to be **like the wife of a brother who has children,**[N] **and she is forbidden** to him? The Gemara answers: **This applies only when** the prohibition **that stands before her** and prevents the levirate marriage **is the prohibition against marrying the sister of one's wife, which is prohibited by Torah** law. Therefore, if the woman who happens before the *yavam* for levirate marriage is his wife's sister, he is prohibited from performing levirate marriage even if his wife dies afterward. **But here** the prohibition to marry the sister stems from a relationship created by **a levirate bond.** This prohibition is **by rabbinic** law,[N] and therefore the bond does not render her forbidden to him forever.

NOTES

Rav said…the first died, he is permitted to take the second – אָמַר רַב...מֵתָה רִאשׁוֹנָה מוּתָּר בַּשְּׁנִיָּה: There are several different opinions as to how to explain Rav's ruling. Rabbeinu Ḥananel holds that Rav is consistent with his opinion that the levirate bond is not substantial, and he apparently thought that those who maintain that the levirate bond is substantial hold that the levirate bond has the force of Torah law (see Rashba). Therefore, the *yavam* is not permitted to consummate the levirate marriage with one of the sisters *ab initio* due to the prohibition against negating the mitzva of levirate marriage (see *Tosafot*).

The Meiri analyzes the issue in a similar way. He states that although Rav holds that the levirate bond is not substantial, the *yavam* is nevertheless unable to consummate the levirate marriage with any one of the sisters *ab initio*, since both of them happened before him for levirate marriage, and marrying one would negate the mitzva of levirate marriage with the other. Similarly, the *yavam* cannot perform the act of *ḥalitza* with one sister *ab initio* and then consummate the levirate marriage with the other since, she would be rendered forbidden to him as the sister of a woman with whom he performed *ḥalitza*.

Alternatively, the Ramban says that Rav's ruling is also consistent with the opinion that the levirate bond is substantial. Accordingly, the reason why the *yavam* is permitted to take the second sister is that a levirate bond has the force of rabbinic law and is therefore not sufficiently binding to cause the *yevama* to be forbidden to him forever.

And does Rav not accept that reason – וְרַב לֵית לֵיהּ הַאי סְבָרָא: The commentaries ask why the Gemara did not object to Rav based on an explicit mishna that states: She is now forbidden to him forever since she was forbidden to him at one time (*Yevamot* 32a; see *Tosafot*). The Ramban explains that had the Gemara objected based on that mishna, Rav could have resolved the objection by noting that the mishna explicitly refers to a case involving a relationship forbidden by Torah law. Alternatively, he could have said that the *halakha* in the mishna, as later becomes clear, is in accordance with the opinion of Rabbi Eliezer, but that the Rabbis disagree with him.

Like the wife of a brother who has children – כְּאֵשֶׁת אָח שֶׁיֵּשׁ לוֹ בָּנִים: One must say that this means that she is like the wife of a brother who has children at the time of his death, such that even if the children later died she would not again require *ḥalitza* (see *Meromei Sadeh*).

Here a levirate bond by rabbinic law – הָכָא זִיקָה דְּרַבָּנַן הִיא: According to those who maintain that this ruling of Rav is consistent with his opinion that the levirate bond is not substantial, this resolution proves difficult because, according to this opinion, there should be no bond at all.

The Rashba explains that Rav agrees that there is a prohibition in place. However, it does not stem from the levirate bond, but rather it is a rabbinic prohibition against negating the mitzva of levirate marriage. He would therefore interpret this phrase to mean that there is a rabbinic prohibition not to negate the levirate bond of the second woman.

Tosafot Yeshanim ask about a different aspect of this ruling: Why doesn't Rav prohibit the second woman, as she was forbidden to the *yavam* at the time of her husband's death due to the possibility of negating the mitzva of levirate marriage, as becomes clear later in the Gemara? He answers that one must differentiate between an actual prohibition with regard to a specific woman and a decree stemming from concern lest the mitzva of levirate marriage be negated, for such a concern indeed becomes irrelevant with the death of the other woman.

NOTES

Raised an objection to Rabbi Yoḥanan, etc. – אֵיתִיבֵיהּ...לְרַבִּי יוֹחָנָן וכו׳: Some commentaries suggest that Rabbi Yosei bar Ḥanina's objection poses a more significant difficulty to Rav's position, but it was not mentioned as an objection to Rav because Rav held that this mishna is in accordance with the opinion that the levirate bond is substantial, though Rav himself does not maintain that stance (*Tosafot*). The Meiri adds further that since there is a principle that Rav is considered like a *tanna*, in that he can disagree with a mishna, it is less compelling to challenge his ruling from a mishna. *Tosefot HaRosh* explains that in truth this objection applies to Rav as well, but since Rabbi Yosei bar Ḥanina was close to Rabbi Yoḥanan and from the same generation as him, he raised it against him specifically. Moreover, this issue is later resolved on its own in the process of the talmudic deliberations in accordance with Rav's opinion, as Rav is concerned lest the mitzva of levirate marriage be negated. Alternatively, the Rivan holds that there is no difficulty for Rav here at all because Rav holds that in cases of invalid *ḥalitza*, the woman must repeat the *ḥalitza* with all of the brothers. In that case, the second woman would be the sister of his *ḥalutza*, which would preclude the possibility of consummating the levirate marriage. The Rashba proves from the fact the Gemara did not resolve the issue in this way, according to Rabbi Yoḥanan's opinion, that Rabbi Yoḥanan agrees with Shmuel, both with regard to the question of whether the levirate bond is substantial as well as with regard to the issue of whether a woman who performed invalid *ḥalitza* must repeat it with all of the brothers.

אֵיתִיבֵיהּ רַבִּי יוֹסֵי בַּר חֲנִינָא לְרַבִּי יוֹחָנָן: אַרְבָּעָה אַחִין, שְׁנַיִם מֵהֶם נְשׂוּאִים שְׁתֵּי אֲחָיוֹת, וּמֵתוּ הַנְּשׂוּאִין אֶת הָאֲחָיוֹת – הֲרֵי אֵלּוּ חוֹלְצוֹת וְלֹא מִתְיַיבְּמוֹת. וְאַמַּאי? לֵיקוּ חַד מִינַּיְיהוּ לַחֲלוֹץ לָהּ לַשְּׁנִיָּה, וְתֶיהֱוֵי רִאשׁוֹנָה לְגַבֵּי אִידָּךְ כִּיבָמָה שֶׁהוּתְּרָה וְנֶאֶסְרָה וְחָזְרָה וְהוּתְּרָה – תַּחֲזוֹר לְהֶיתֵּירָהּ הָרִאשׁוֹן!

Rabbi Yosei bar Ḥanina raised an objection to the opinion of **Rabbi Yoḥanan**[N] from the mishna: In the case of **four brothers, two of whom were married to two sisters, and those married to the sisters died, then those** sisters **must perform *ḥalitza* and may not enter into levirate marriage. And why** does the mishna require *ḥalitza*? **Let one of** the brothers **rise and perform *ḥalitza* with the second** sister, i.e., the sister whose husband died later. As a result, **the first would be like a *yevama* who was permitted** at the time of her husband's death but later became **forbidden** due to the bond that was created with her sister, **and** she then **subsequently became permitted** by means of *ḥalitza* performed with her sister, **insofar as the other** brother, i.e., he who did not perform *ḥalitza*, **is concerned.** Therefore, **she should return to her original permitted status.**

אָמַר לֵיהּ: אֲחָיוֹת אֵינִי יוֹדֵעַ מִי שְׁנָאָן. וְלֵימָא לֵיהּ: מַאי ״חוֹלְצוֹת״ נַמִי דְּקָתָנֵי – חוֹלֶצֶת חֲדָא! ״חוֹלְצוֹת״ קָתָנֵי.

Rabbi Yoḥanan **said to him: I do not know who taught: Sisters.** Rabbi Yoḥanan was in doubt as to the correct version of this mishna, as he could not find any reasonable explanation of this mishna according to any known opinion. The Gemara asks: Why did Rabbi Yoḥanan respond in such an extreme manner. **Let him say to him,** to Rabbi Yosei bar Ḥanina, an alternate solution: **What is** the meaning of the ruling that the sisters **perform *ḥalitza*, which** the mishna **teaches?** The meaning is that **one** sister **performs *ḥalitza*.** The Gemara answers: Such a solution is untenable, as the mishna **teaches** the ruling using the words: **Perform *ḥalitza*,** in the plural.

וְלֵימָא לֵיהּ: מַאי ״חוֹלְצוֹת״ חוֹלְצוֹת דְּעָלְמָא! ״הֲרֵי אֵלּוּ״ קָתָנֵי. וְלֵימָא: דְּחָלֵיץ לֵיהּ לָרִאשׁוֹנָה בְּרֵישָׁא! ״חוֹלְצוֹת״

The Gemara suggests: **And let** Rabbi Yoḥanan **say to him: What is** the meaning of the ruling to **perform *ḥalitza*? They perform *ḥalitza* in general.** Accordingly, the mishna teaches that in such cases the second women performs *ḥalitza*. The Gemara responds: The mishna **teaches: Then those** women perform *ḥalitza*. The emphasis on the word: Those, indicates that it is specifically those two women who both perform *ḥalitza*. The Gemara asks further: **And let him say** that the mishna is referring only to the specific case **where** *the yavam* **performed ḥalitza with the first** sister **first.** As a result, there was no longer be any possibility of rendering the second sister permitted, as Rabbi Yoḥanan permitted levirate marriage only in the case where *ḥalitza* was performed with the second sister first. The Gemara answers: This cannot be suggested either, for the phrase: **Perform *ḥalitza*,**

Perek **III**
Daf **28** Amud **a**

NOTES

And let him say…lest he proceed, etc. – וְלֵימָא...דִּלְמָא קָדֵים וכו׳: One can ask with regard to this question: Doesn't Rabbi Yoḥanan himself hold that if the second sister dies the first is permitted? This indicates that he is not concerned that there might be confusion of this kind. This difficulty can be resolved by asserting that Rabbi Yoḥanan allows the first sister to enter into levirate marriage only in the case where one of the sisters died, as in such a situation there is no concern for confusion. However, in a case where both sisters are alive, perhaps there would be concern, and therefore this rabbinic decree would apply. The Gemara, however, did not assume this distinction when it raised the objection, but rather understood that the fear of confusing the women was a legitimate concern in all cases (Rashba).

It teaches they may not enter into levirate marriage – וְלֹא מִתְיַיבְּמוֹת קָתָנֵי: The Rivan explains that if the matter were prohibited by rabbinic decree, it would have sufficed to say: They perform *ḥalitza*. The fact that the mishna repeated the ruling and stressed that they may not enter into levirate marriage indicates that this matter was a conclusive halakhic ruling.

לְכַתְּחִלָּה קָתָנֵי. וְלֵימָא לֵיהּ גְּזֵירָה דִּלְמָא קָדֵים וְחָלֵיץ לָרִאשׁוֹנָה בְּרֵישָׁא! ״וְלֹא מִתְיַיבְּמוֹת״ קָתָנֵי, דְּלֵיכָּא דִּין יִבּוּם הָכָא כְּלָל.

implies that the mishna **teaches** a case in which *ḥalitza* is performed ***ab initio***. This indicates that this is the first course of action and the only way to resolve the situation. The Gemara asks further: And **let him say to him** the following: The mishna prohibits levirate marriage *ab initio* in this case, due to a rabbinic **decree lest he proceed**[N] **and perform the *ḥalitza* with the first**[H] sister **first,** whereby it would be prohibited to consummate the levirate marriage with the second. Perhaps for this reason the Sages decreed that it is prohibited to consummate the levirate marriage even if *ḥalitza* was performed with the second sister. The Gemara answers: **It teaches: They may not enter into levirate marriage.**[N] This indicates that **the *halakha* of levirate marriage does not apply here at all.** Accordingly, even after the fact, if he performed *ḥalitza* with the second sister, the *halakha* of levirate marriage would not apply to the first sister.

HALAKHA

Lest he proceed and perform the *ḥalitza* with the first, etc. – דִּלְמָא קָדֵים וְחָלֵיץ לָרִאשׁוֹנָה וכו׳: If there were four brothers, and two of them were married to two sisters, and the two married brothers died one after the other, and one of the surviving brothers proceeded to perform *ḥalitza* with the second sister, then the first sister is rendered permitted to the other brother. It seems that even Rabbi Yoḥanan is in agreement with this *halakha*, but he could not find a way to interpret the mishna to accord with this ruling (Rambam *Sefer Nashim, Hilkhot Yibbum* 7:1; *Shulḥan Arukh, Even HaEzer* 175:1).

וְלֵימָא לֵיהּ גְּזֵירָה שֶׁמָּא יָמוּת, וְאָסוּר לְבַטֵּל מִצְוַת יְבָמִין רַבִּי יוֹחָנָן לְמִיתָה לָא חָיֵישׁ.

The Gemara asks: **And let him say to him** a different reason for the ruling of the mishna: It is due to a rabbinic **decree lest** the second brother **die, and it is prohibited to negate the mitzva of levirate marriage.** Perhaps for this reason it would be forbidden to consummate the levirate marriage in the case where two sisters happened before him for levirate marriage, and not due to the prohibition proscribing the sister of a woman with whom he has a levirate bond. The Gemara answers: **Rabbi Yoḥanan was not concerned over** the possibility of the **death**[N] of a brother, and in his opinion there is no need to make a decree to address such cases.

וְלֵימָא לֵיהּ רַבִּי אֶלְעָזָר הִיא, דְּאָמַר: כֵּיוָן שֶׁעָמְדָה עָלָיו שָׁעָה אַחַת בְּאִיסּוּר נֶאֶסְרָה עָלָיו עוֹלָמִית! מִדְּסֵיפָא רַבִּי אֶלְעָזָר רֵישָׁא לָאו רַבִּי אֶלְעָזָר.

The Gemara asks: **And let** Rabbi Yoḥanan **say to him** that this mishna **is** in accordance with the opinion of **Rabbi Elazar, who said: Once** the *yevama* **stood before him at one time as forbidden,** even if it was not at the time that she happened before him, **she remains forbidden to him forever.** Perhaps the mishna could be explained according to Rabbi Elazar's opinion. The Gemara answers: **Since** the opinion of **Rabbi Elazar** is cited explicitly **in the latter clause** of the mishna, it can be deduced that **the first clause is not** according to the opinion of **Rabbi Elazar.** Therefore, this ruling cannot be attributed to Rabbi Elazar.

וְנֵימָא לְהוּ דִּנְפוּל בְּבַת אַחַת וְרַבִּי יוֹסֵי הַגְּלִילִי הִיא, דְּאָמַר: אֶפְשָׁר לְצַמְצֵם! לָא סָתַם לַן תַּנָּא כְּרַבִּי יוֹסֵי הַגְּלִילִי.

The Gemara asks: **And let him say to him** that here the reference is to a situation **where** the two brothers died at once, and consequently both of the women **happened before** the *yevamin* for levirate marriage **at the same time. And** this mishna **is** in accordance with the opinion of **Rabbi Yosei HaGelili, who says: It is possible to be precise.**[N] It is possible to determine that two events occurred at exactly the same moment, both sisters were forbidden at the time that they happened before the brothers-in-law. The Gemara answers: **The *tanna* did not teach an unattributed** mishna **in accordance with** the opinion of **Rabbi Yosei HaGelili.** Any time the mishna is cited in accordance with Rabbi Yosei HaGelili's opinion, it is always attributed to him explicitly.

וְלֵימָא לֵיהּ דְּלָא יָדְעִינַן הֵי נְפוּל בְּרֵישָׁא!

The Gemara asks: **And let him say to him** a different explanation for the ruling: This mishna is indeed addressing a case where the brothers died one after the other, yet **we do not know which** sister **happened** before the *yevamin* for levirate marriage **first.**[H] In that case, it would be impossible to determine which sister would be permitted.

אִי הָכִי, הַיְינוּ דְּקָתָנֵי "קָדְמוּ וְכָנְסוּ יוֹצִיאוּ"? בִּשְׁלָמָא רִאשׁוֹנָה אָמְרִינַן לֵיהּ: מַאן שַׁרְיָא לָךְ? אֶלָּא שְׁנִיָּה, אָמַר: חַבְרָאִי שְׁנִיָּה יִיבֵּם, אֲנָא רִאשׁוֹנָה מְיַיבֵּם!

The Gemara answers: **If so, that which** the mishna **teaches** in the latter clause: **And if they married** their wives **before** consulting the court **they should divorce them,** is difficult. Why must they divorce their wives in this situation? **Granted,** the brother who took **the first** sister in levirate marriage must divorce her, as **we say to him: Who permitted her to you?** Indeed, she was forbidden as the sister of a woman with whom he had a levirate bond, and so he must divorce her. **However,** the brother who took **the second** sister **could say: My fellow** brother **consummated the levirate marriage with the second**[N] sister, but **I am consummating the levirate marriage with the first** sister. It is possible that after the other brother consummated the levirate marriage with the second sister, the first sister would then be permitted to him after the fact, and he is not required to divorce her unless it is certain that he violated a prohibition.

הַיְינוּ דְּקָאָמַר לֵיהּ: אֲחָיוֹת אֵינִי יוֹדֵעַ מִי שְׁנָאָן.

The Gemara concludes: Indeed, **this is what** Rabbi Yoḥanan meant when he **said to** Rabbi Yosei bar Ḥanina: **I do not know who taught: Sisters,** for according to these considerations he cannot properly resolve the ruling of this mishna.

HALAKHA

We do not know which sister happened before the *yevamin* first – דְּלָא יָדְעִינַן הֵי נְפוּל בְּרֵישָׁא: If two brothers who were married to two sisters died, and it is unknown which died first, then both sisters must perform *ḥalitza* and may not enter into levirate marriage (Rambam *Sefer Nashim, Hilkhot Yibbum* 7:1; *Shulḥan Arukh, Even HaEzer* 175:2).

NOTES

He was not concerned over the possibility of the death – לְמִיתָה לָא חָיֵישׁ: The early commentaries object to this statement based on several sources, especially the discussion in the beginning of tractate *Yoma*, where the *tanna* Rabbi Yehuda is concerned that the wife of the High Priest might die. They point out that even if Rabbi Yoḥanan himself is not concerned over this eventuality, he could still interpret this mishna as following the opinion of those who are concerned for the possibility of death.

There are various suggestions as to how to resolve this difficulty. Some commentaries explain that Rabbi Yoḥanan held that although this opinion exists, it is the opinion of only a single Sage, and therefore it would not be presented in an unattributed manner in the mishna. This answer is similar to the one cited by the Gemara in the continuation of the discussion concerning the opinion of Rabbi Yosei HaGelili. The Gemara does not accept the suggestion that the mishna follows the opinion of Rabbi Yosei HaGelili, as his is the opinion of a single Sage.

Alternatively, since Rabbi Yoḥanan is not concerned about the possibility of death and because he always concludes the *halakha* follows the unattributed mishna, his opinion is that it is impossible for there to be an unattributed mishna that holds that there is no concern over the possibility of death (see Rashba and Ritva).

The Rashba explains that even if there is a concern over the possibility of death, such a concern would not be significant enough to negate the mitzva of levirate marriage, and this follows the opinion that *ḥalitza* is not considered a fulfillment of the mitzva of levirate marriage.

The Maharsha, in *Mahadura Batra*, states that there is concern about the possibility that the High Priest may die, despite the fact that it is an improbable scenario, only because all of Israel depend upon him for atonement on Yom Kippur. *Mitzpe Eitan* explains that there is concern over the possibility of death in cases where the death will cause the violation of a prohibition for which one is liable to receive the death penalty. This is not a concern in cases where death could prevent one from fulfilling a positive mitzva.

It is possible to be precise – אֶפְשָׁר לְצַמְצֵם: The Sages of the Mishna differ as to whether it is possible for two events to occur at precisely the same moment. The early commentaries differ in their understanding of this dispute. According to Rashi and the Rambam, it is physically impossible for two events to occur at the exact same moment. Therefore, the dispute between the *tanna'im* revolves around the question of how to relate to events that appear to occur simultaneously. According to the opinion that it is not possible to be precise, the assumption is that the events did not occur simultaneously. Because the order in which they took place cannot be ascertained, the instance is related to as a case of uncertainty. According to the opinion that it is possible to be precise, despite the fact that the events did not actually take place simultaneously, the *halakha* relates to them as if they had occurred at exactly the same time.

In contrast, *Tosafot* maintain that events can actually occur simultaneously. The dispute therefore relates to a situation where two events appear to occur simultaneously. In this case, is it assumed that the events indeed took place at the same time, or is it assumed that it is impossible to determine whether or not these events actually occurred simultaneously, and therefore this is a case of uncertainty?

My fellow brother consummated the levirate marriage with the second, etc. – חַבְרָאִי שְׁנִיָּה יִיבֵּם וכו׳: Some point out the following problem: According to this assertion, his brother transgressed and engaged in sexual relations with the sister of a woman with whom he had a levirate bond. However, according to the Gemara on 50b, licentious relations do not fully consummate levirate marriage, and the *yevama* under such circumstances still requires *ḥalitza*. Accordingly, in the case here, there is still a levirate bond connecting this sister to the second brother and the other sister remains forbidden as the sister of a woman with whom he has a levirate bond. This difficulty can be resolved by saying that the requirement for *ḥalitza* is a rabbinic decree, and even licentious relations between a *yavam* and *yevama* still uproot the levirate bond (*Ḥazon Ish*).

תְּנַן: הָיְתָה אַחַת מֵהֶן אֲסוּרָה עַל הָאֶחָד אִיסּוּר עֶרְוָה – אָסוּר בָּהּ וּמוּתָּר בַּאֲחוֹתָהּ, וְהַשֵּׁנִי אָסוּר בִּשְׁתֵּיהֶן. סָלְקָא דַּעְתָּךְ דְּנָפְלָה חֲמוֹתוֹ תְּחִלָּה.

We learned in the mishna: If **one of** the sisters **was forbidden**[H] **to one** of the brothers due to a **prohibition against forbidden relatives** because she was a relative of his wife or a relative from his mother's side, then **he is prohibited from** marrying **her but permitted to** marry **her sister.** But **the second** brother, who is not a close relative of either sister, **is prohibited from** marrying **both of them. It enters your mind** to say **that** a forbidden woman, such as **his mother-in-law, happened** before the *yavam* for levirate marriage **first.**[B]

וְאַמַּאי? לֵיקוּ חָתָן לְיַיבֵּם הַךְ דְּאֵינָהּ חֲמוֹתוֹ בְּרֵישָׁא, וְתֶהֱוֵי חֲמוֹתוֹ לְגַבֵּי אִידָךְ כִּיבָמָה שֶׁהוּתְּרָה וְנֶאֶסְרָה וְחָזְרָה וְהוּתְּרָה – תַּחֲזוֹר לְהֶיתֵּרָהּ הָרִאשׁוֹן.

Accordingly, the Gemara asks: **And why** would both women be forbidden to the second brother? **Let the son-in-law rise and consummate the levirate marriage with** the sister[N] **who is not his mother-in-law first. Consequently, with regard to the other** brother, **his mother-in-law would be** considered **a** *yevama* **who was permitted** to perform levirate marriage at the time that she happened before him, **and then forbidden** when her sister happened before him for levirate marriage as well, **and then subsequently became permitted** when his brother consummated the levirate marriage with her sister. If so, the mother-in-law **should return to her original permitted status** and may enter into levirate marriage with him.

אָמַר רַב פָּפָּא: כְּגוֹן דְּנָפְלָה הַךְ דְּאֵינָהּ חֲמוֹתוֹ בְּרֵישָׁא.

Rav Pappa said: The mishna is referring to a case **where** the woman **who was not his mother-in-law happened** before the brothers for levirate marriage **first,**[H] in which case she was permitted to both of them. When her sister, i.e., the mother-in-law, happened before them for levirate marriage as well, both women were rendered forbidden to the second brother, as each one is the sister of a woman with whom he has a levirate bond. Because the mother-in-law was forbidden from the time that she happened before the *yavam* for levirate marriage, she can never be permitted to him.

״רַבִּי אֱלִיעֶזֶר אוֹמֵר: בֵּית שַׁמַּאי אוֹמְרִים״ וכו׳. תַּנְיָא: רַבִּי אֱלִיעֶזֶר אוֹמֵר בֵּית שַׁמַּאי אוֹמְרִים: יְקַיְּימוּ, וּבֵית הִלֵּל אוֹמְרִים: יוֹצִיאוּ. רַבִּי שִׁמְעוֹן אוֹמֵר: יְקַיְּימוּ. אַבָּא שָׁאוּל אוֹמֵר: קַל הָיָה לָהֶם לְבֵית הִלֵּל בְּדָבָר זֶה, שֶׁבֵּית שַׁמַּאי אוֹמְרִים יוֹצִיאוּ וּבֵית הִלֵּל אוֹמְרִים יְקַיְּימוּ.

§ With regard to the case of two brothers who married their wives before consulting the court,[H] the mishna states that the women should be divorced. **Rabbi Eliezer** disagrees and **says** that this is a matter of dispute between Beit Shammai and Beit Hillel, as **Beit Shammai say:** They may maintain them as their wives, and Beit Hillel say: They should divorce them. An expanded version of this discussion **is taught** in the *Tosefta* (5:1): **Rabbi Eliezer says** that **Beit Shammai say: They may maintain them** as their wives, **and Beit Hillel say: They should divorce them. Rabbi Shimon says: They may maintain them** as their wives. **Abba Shaul** disagrees with Rabbi Eliezer and **says: This was a matter of leniency for Beit Hillel.**[N] They were the ones who put forth a lenient ruling, **as Beit Shammai say: They should divorce them, and Beit Hillel say: They may maintain** them as their wives.

HALAKHA

If one of them was forbidden, etc. – הָיְתָה אַחַת מֵהֶן אֲסוּרָה וכו׳: If one of the sisters was the forbidden relative of one brother, then that brother is permitted to marry the second woman, and the second brother is forbidden to both women. If each was forbidden to a different brother, then she who is forbidden to one is permitted to the other. This applies only in cases of forbidden relatives, but in cases of prohibitions stemming from sanctity or a mitzva, both women must perform *ḥalitza* (Rambam *Sefer Nashim, Hilkhot Yibbum* 7:5; *Shulḥan Arukh, Even HaEzer* 175:1).

A case where the woman who was not his mother-in-law happened before them first – כְּגוֹן דְּנָפְלָה הַךְ דְּאֵינָהּ חֲמוֹתוֹ בְּרֵישָׁא: If the first sister who happened before the *yevamin* for levirate marriage was a relative forbidden to the *yavam*, such as his mother-in-law, and he consummated the levirate marriage with the second sister, then the first sister is permitted to the other brother (Rambam *Sefer Nashim, Hilkhot Yibbum* 7:5; *Shulḥan Arukh, Even HaEzer* 175:1).

Two brothers who married their wives before consulting the court – קָדְמוּ וְכָנְסוּ: If two sisters happened before two brothers for levirate marriage, and the two brothers proceeded to marry them before consulting the court, they must divorce them, as is stated explicitly in the mishna. This ruling is not in accordance with the statement of Abba Shaul, which opposes both the unattributed mishna and the opinion of Rabbi Eliezer (Rif; Rambam; Rosh).

Some say that they are not required to divorce their wives (*Tur*). They explain that because Beit Hillel is generally the more lenient opinion, we follow the opinion of Rabbi Shimon and Abba Shaul (Rambam's Commentary on the Mishna). The *Baḥ*, however, holds that this is a scribal error in the *Tur* (Rambam *Sefer Nashim, Hilkhot Yibbum* 7:5; *Shulḥan Arukh, Even HaEzer* 175:3).

NOTES

Let the son-in-law rise and consummate the levirate marriage with the sister, etc. – לֵיקוּ חָתָן לְיַיבֵּם הַךְ וכו׳: This objection could apparently be resolved according to the suggestion that appeared previously in the Gemara, that there is a rabbinic decree in these cases to prevent his brother from consummating the levirate marriage with the wrong woman. This suggestion arose only in passing during the talmudic deliberations and was rejected outright because there is no concern for confusion between the women (Rashba).

This was a matter of leniency for Beit Hillel – קַל הָיָה לָהֶם לְבֵית הִלֵּל: In the Jerusalem Talmud, a question is raised about this formulation: Did Abba Shaul intend to speak disparagingly of Beit Hillel by suggesting that they acted leniently where there should have been a prohibition? It is explained there that he intended to say that, according to Beit Hillel, there was not an actual prohibition in place at all, and so it would be permitted to consummate the levirate marriage.

BACKGROUND

His mother-in-law happened before him first – נָפְלָה חֲמוֹתוֹ תְּחִלָּה: There were four brothers from the same father: Reuven, Shimon, Levi, and Yehuda. Reuven and Shimon married the sisters Milka and Ḥogla, while Yehuda married Adda, the daughter of Milka, Reuven's wife. If Reuven and Shimon die childless, the sisters Milka and Ḥogla happen before the two brothers, Yehuda and Levi, for levirate marriage. With regard to Levi, both Milka and Ḥogla are sisters who are *yevamot* but are otherwise unrelated to him. Consequently, they are both forbidden to him. With regard to Yehuda, however, Milka is his mother-in-law as well, and he is prohibited from marrying her. This renders her ineligible for levirate marriage with him. If Reuven died before Shimon, Milka was never eligible for levirate marriage with Yehuda because she was forbidden to him as his mother-in-law. His obligation of levirate marriage applies only to Ḥogla. Consequently, if Yehuda consummates the levirate marriage with Ḥogla, Milka is eligible to consummate the levirate marriage with Levi. She was initially permitted to him when Reuven died, as she was the only *yevama*; then forbidden to him when Shimon died, since two sisters happened before him for levirate marriage at that time; and subsequently became permitted by means of Yehuda's marriage to Ḥogla.

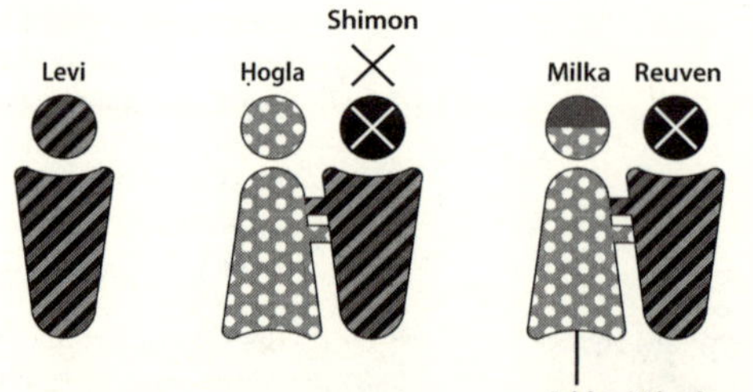

רַבִּי שִׁמְעוֹן כְּמַאן? אִי כְּבֵית שַׁמַּאי – הַיְינוּ רַבִּי אֱלִיעֶזֶר, אִי כְּבֵית הִלֵּל – הַיְינוּ אַבָּא שָׁאוּל! הָכִי קָאָמַר לֹא נֶחְלְקוּ בֵּית שַׁמַּאי וּבֵית הִלֵּל בְּדָבָר זֶה.

The Gemara asks about this *baraita*: **In accordance with whose** opinion **is** the statement of **Rabbi Shimon?**[N] This matter is a dispute between Beit Hillel and Beit Shammai, with different versions of their opinions, and therefore Rabbi Shimon should not have formulated the *halakha* in this manner. Indeed, **if** he holds **in accordance with** the opinion of **Beit Shammai,** then **that is** the same as the opinion of **Rabbi Eliezer.** He would thereby conclude that the *halakha* is in accordance with the opinion of Beit Shammai, as per Rabbi Eliezer's version. If so, he should have formulated his opinion in that way. **If,** however, he holds **in accordance with** the opinion of **Beit Hillel,** then **that is** the opinion of **Abba Shaul.** The Gemara responds: **This is what he is saying:** Rabbi Shimon actually maintains a third opinion: **Beit Shammai and Beit Hillel did not dispute this matter;** both agreed that the marriages may be maintained.

״הָיְתָה אַחַת מֵהֶם״ כּוּ׳. הָא תָּנֵינָא חֲדָא זִימְנָא: אֲחוֹתָהּ כְּשֶׁהִיא יְבִמְתָּהּ אוֹ חוֹלֶצֶת אוֹ מִתְיַיבֶּמֶת!

§ The mishna stated: If **one of** the sisters **was** forbidden to one of the brothers due to a prohibition against forbidden relations, then he is prohibited from marrying her but permitted to marry her sister. The Gemara asks: **We** already **learned** this **on one occasion: When her sister,** who is a forbidden relative to the *yavam*, **is her *yevama*** as well, **she either performs *ḥalitza* or enters into levirate marriage.**

צְרִיכָא, דְּאִי אַשְׁמוּעִינַן הָתָם מִשּׁוּם דְּלֵיכָּא לְמִיגְזַר מִשּׁוּם שֵׁנִי, אֲבָל הָכָא דְּאִיכָּא לְמִיגְזַר מִשּׁוּם שֵׁנִי – אֵימָא לָא.

The Gemara answers: It is **necessary** that this be said here as well, **for if it taught us** this *halakha* only **there** in its more general formulation (*Yevamot* 20a), then I might have said: The *yavam* is permitted to marry the sister **because there is no** reason **to issue** a rabbinic **decree due to a second** brother. There, there is only one *yavam*, to whom one sister is permitted and the other is forbidden. **Here, however,** in the case of two brothers, **where there is** reason **to issue** a rabbinic **decree due to the second** brother, lest he consummate the levirate marriage as well, **I would say** that we do **not** allow even the first brother to perform levirate marriage, and both sisters-in-law should be forbidden to both brothers.

וְאִי אַשְׁמוּעִינַן הָכָא – מִשּׁוּם דְּאִיכָּא שֵׁנִי דְּקָא מוֹכַח, אֲבָל הָתָם דְּלֵיכָּא שֵׁנִי – אֵימָא לָא, צְרִיכָא.

And if the mishna **had taught us** the *halakha* only **here,** it would have been possible to say that the permissibility of levirate marriage here is **because there is** a second brother who **indicates,** by refraining from performing levirate marriage, that the sister of a woman bound by a levirate bond is forbidden. **However, there,** where there **is not a second** brother, **I would say no,** this *halakha* would not apply, due to a concern that people might wrongly conclude that the sister of a woman bound by a levirate bond is permitted. Therefore, it is **necessary** to state this *halakha* in both places.

״אִיסּוּר מִצְוָה״ כּוּ׳. הָא נַמִּי תָּנֵינָא:

It was taught in the mishna: If one of the sisters was forbidden to one of the brothers due to **a prohibition** resulting from **a mitzva** or due to a prohibition stemming from sanctity, then her sister must perform *ḥalitza* and may not enter into levirate marriage. The Gemara wonders: **We** already **learned this as well:**

NOTES

In accordance with whose opinion is Rabbi Shimon – רַבִּי שִׁמְעוֹן כְּמַאן: It would be difficult to say that Rabbi Shimon stated his own opinion, as he lived long after the period of Beit Shammai and Beit Hillel and was therefore not in a position to dispute them (Rivan).

In the Jerusalem Talmud, Abba Shaul distinguishes between the opinions of Rabbi Shimon and Beit Hillel. There, it is explained that Rabbi Shimon allows the brothers to maintain their wives after the fact only when consummation had already taken place and specifically when both brothers had relations concurrently. However, according to Abba Shaul's version of Beit Hillel's opinion, the brothers would be allowed to consummate the levirate marriage even *ab initio* (see *Penei Moshe*).

NOTES

Here there is a prohibition resulting from a mitzva and her sister – **הָכָא אִיסּוּר מִצְוָה וַאֲחוֹתָהּ**: The question arises: The Gemara has explained the reason for this *halakha* in the current mishna, but the first mishna that states a ruling with regard to a prohibition resulting from a mitzva remains superfluous. Why does the mishna state this ruling earlier (20a)? It would have sufficed to state it here alone?

A similar question arises later on the Gemara, and it is resolved as follows: Were this *halakha* stated only here, one might have thought that the rabbinic decree not to enter into levirate marriage was issued only where there was an additional brother to whom the *yevama* is permitted, for in that case the levirate marriage could be fulfilled with him. If, however, there is no other brother, and the mitzva of levirate marriage will be negated, perhaps the Sages did not issue a decree, and the *yavam* is permitted to consummate the levirate marriage with this woman. Therefore, the *halakha* was necessary in the previous mishna as well (*Arukh LaNer*).

אִיסּוּר מִצְוָה וְאִיסּוּר קְדוּשָּׁה חוֹלֶצֶת וְלֹא מִתְיַיבֶּמֶת! הָתָם אִיסּוּר מִצְוָה לְחוּדָהּ. הָכָא אִיסּוּר מִצְוָה וַאֲחוֹתָהּ.

If a **prohibition** resulting from **a mitzva** or **a prohibition** stemming from **sanctity** will be transgressed through the levirate marriage, then the woman must **perform *ḥalitza* and she may not enter into levirate marriage.** The Gemara answers: There is a novelty here: **There,** where the *halakha* is reviewed in general terms, it speaks of **a prohibition due to a mitzva alone.** One woman happened before the *yavam* for levirate marriage and it is only as a result of this prohibition that she is prevented from entering levirate marriage. **Here,** there is **a prohibition** resulting from **a mitzva and,** in addition, **her sister**[N] happened before the *yevamin* for levirate marriage together with her.

סָלְקָא דַּעְתָּךְ אָמֵינָא: לֵיקוּם אִיסּוּר מִצְוָה בִּמְקוֹם אִיסּוּר עֶרְוָה, וְתִתְיַיבֵּם, קָא מַשְׁמַע לַן.

It might enter your mind to say: Let the prohibition resulting from **a mitzva stand in** the same **place,** i.e., level of severity, **as the prohibition against forbidden relatives.** Consequently, the woman who is forbidden to the *yavam* is considered a forbidden relative and her sister is permitted to him. Despite the fact that the prohibition resulting from a mitzva is not as severe, here is it is given equal status, **and** we might say: **Let** her sister **enter into levirate marriage.** Therefore, **this comes to teach us** that this is not the case.

וְתִתְיַיבֵּם! כֵּיוָן דְּמִדְּאוֹרַיְיתָא רָמְיָא קַמֵּיהּ קָא פָּגַע בַּאֲחוֹת זְקוּקָתוֹ, סָלְקָא דַּעְתָּךְ אָמֵינָא: מִשּׁוּם מִצְוָה עֲבוּד רַבָּנַן – קָא מַשְׁמַע לַן.

The Gemara asks: **And** why in fact **does** her sister not **enter into levirate marriage?** The Gemara answers: Her sister is forbidden to him **because by Torah** law the prohibited woman **is** still **set before** *the yavam* for levirate marriage. Were he to take the sister in levirate marriage **he would** essentially **be encountering the sister of the woman with whom he has** a levirate bond. **It might enter your mind to say** that **due to the mitzva** of levirate marriage, **the Sages did as they did** and nullified their decree prohibiting the sister of a woman with whom the *yavam* has a levirate bond from entering levirate marriage, when the original sister is forbidden only as the result of a mitzva. Therefore, it **teaches us** that they did not cancel their decree in this situation.

״הָיְתָה אַחַת מֵהֶן״ כו׳. הָא תּוּ לָמָּה לִי? הַיְינוּ הָךְ, מָה לִי לְחַד מָה לִי לִתְרֵי!

It was taught in the mishna: If **one of those** women was forbidden to this one brother due to a prohibition against forbidden relatives and the second was forbidden to that second brother due to a prohibition against forbidden relatives, then she who is forbidden to this brother is permitted to that brother, and she who is forbidden to that brother is permitted to this one. The Gemara asks: **Why do I need this** *halakha* **as well, for this is** identical to **that** which was taught earlier, when the mishna stated that if one of the sisters was forbidden to one of the brothers due to a prohibition against forbidden relatives, then he is forbidden to marry her but permitted to marry her sister. However, the second brother, who is not a close relative of either sister, is prohibited from marrying both of them. Once the mishna taught that the *yavam* is permitted to marry the woman to whom he is not related, **what is the** difference **to me** if there is **one** brother **or two** brothers? If this happened to both brothers, clearly both should be allowed.

צְרִיכָא, דְּאִי אַשְׁמוֹעִינַן הָתָם – מִשּׁוּם דְּאִיכָּא שֵׁנִי דְּמוֹכַח, אֲבָל הָכָא דְּלֵיכָּא שֵׁנִי דְּקָא מוֹכַח – אֵימָא לָא.

The Gemara answers: It is **necessary** to state this, **for if it taught us** the *halakha* only **there,** in the case where only one brother is permitted, one might have said: **This is because there is a second** brother **who indicates** that the sister of a woman bound by a levirate bond is forbidden to him by refraining from levirate marriage with her. **However, here,** where there **is not a second** brother **who indicates** this, as both brothers are performing levirate marriage, then **I would say no;** this *halakha* would not apply, due to the concern that people might wrongly conclude that the sister of a woman with whom the *yavam* has a levirate bond is permitted even in cases where the other woman is not a forbidden relative.

וְאִי אַשְׁמוּעִינַן הָכָא – אַדְּרַבָּה, תַּרְוַויְיהוּ מוֹכְחֵי אַהֲדָדֵי. אֲבָל אִידָּךְ לָא – צְרִיכָא.

And the opposite could also be said: **If it taught us** the ruling only **here,** in the case of two brothers, one might have said: **On the contrary, they both indicate** the nature of **each other's** status. Each of the brothers married a specific sister-in-law, i.e., the woman who was not his close relative, indicating he does not have a levirate bond with the other sister. **But in the other** case, where one brother is allowed to consummate the levirate marriage and the second brother is forbidden to both sisters, I might say that **no,** we would not allow marriage to the first brother either. Therefore, it is **necessary** to state the *halakha* in both instances.

״זוֹ הִיא שֶׁאָמְרוּ״ וכו׳. זוֹ הִיא לְמַעוּטֵי מַאי? לְמַעוּטֵי אִיסּוּר מִצְוָה לְזֶה וְאִיסּוּר מִצְוָה לְזֶה.

It was taught in the mishna: **And this is** the case that was referred to when **they said:** When her sister is also her *yevama*, she either performs *ḥalitza* or enters into levirate marriage. The Gemara asks: **What does** the expression: **This is,** come to **exclude?** The Gemara answers: **It excludes** the case where there is **a prohibition** resulting from **a mitzva for this** one **and a prohibition** resulting from **a mitzva for that** one. Although each woman is forbidden to a different brother due to a prohibition resulting from a mitzva, they may not both enter into levirate marriage.

הָא תּוּ לָמָּה לִי? הַיְינוּ הָךְ, מָה לִי לְחַד מָה לִי לְתְרֵי!

The Gemara asks: **Why do I need this as well? This is** identical to **that** which was taught previously, that if one of the sisters was forbidden to the *yavam* due to a prohibition resulting from a mitzva, then he is not permitted to consummate the levirate marriage with either of them. **What** difference **is there to me** if she happened before **one** brother **or two?**

מַהוּ דְּתֵימָא: כִּי לָא אָמְרִינַן אוֹקֵי אִיסּוּר מִצְוָה בִּמְקוֹם אִיסּוּר עֶרְוָה – הֵיכָא דְּאִיכָּא לְמִיגְזַר מִשּׁוּם שֵׁנִי, אֲבָל הֵיכָא דְּלֵיכָּא לְמִיגְזַר מִשּׁוּם שֵׁנִי – אֵימָא: לְהַאי אוֹקִימְנָא אִיסּוּר מִצְוָה בִּמְקוֹם אִיסּוּר עֶרְוָה וּלְהַאי [אוֹקִימְנָא] אִיסּוּר מִצְוָה בִּמְקוֹם אִיסּוּר עֶרְוָה, וְלִיַּיבְּמוּ. קָא מַשְׁמַע לַן.

The Gemara answers: **Lest you say:** There is only one instance **when we do not say: Let the prohibition** resulting from **a mitzva stand in** the same **place,** i.e., level of severity, **as a prohibition against forbidden relatives.** It occurs in a case **where it is** appropriate **to issue** a rabbinic **decree due to the second** brother, who is prohibited from marrying both sisters. **But** in a case **where it is not** appropriate **to issue** a rabbinic **decree due to the second** brother, as the second sister is permitted to the second brother as well, I might **say: For this** brother, **let us stand the prohibition** resulting from **a mitzva in** the same **place as a prohibition against forbidden relatives, and for this** brother **let us stand the prohibition** resulting from **a mitzva in** the same **place as a prohibition against forbidden relatives, and** as a result both brothers may **consummate the levirate marriage.** Therefore, **it teaches us** that this is not so.

אָמַר רַב יְהוּדָה אָמַר רַב. וְכֵן תָּנֵי רַבִּי חִיָּיא: בְּכוּלָּן אֲנִי קוֹרֵא בָּהֶן הָאֲסוּרָה לְזֶה מוּתֶּרֶת לְזֶה, וַאֲחוֹתָהּ כְּשֶׁהִיא יְבִמְתָּהּ – אוֹ חוֹלֶצֶת אוֹ מִתְיַיבֶּמֶת.

§ Incidental to this *halakha*, the Gemara cites the following statement: **Rav Yehuda said that Rav said, and similarly Rabbi Ḥiyya teaches** in a *baraita*: **With regard to all of those** women enumerated in the first mishna of the tractate, who are forbidden to the *yevamin* as forbidden relatives, the following situation could arise: These women could also be two sisters who were married to two brothers who happen before their *yevamin* for levirate marriage while each one is a forbidden relative to one of the *yevamin*. In these situations, **I could apply** the ruling that **she who is forbidden to this** brother **is permitted to that** brother, **as well as** the ruling that **when her sister is also her *yevama* she may either perform *ḥalitza* or enter into levirate marriage.**

וְרַב יְהוּדָה מְתַרְגֵּם מֵחֲמוֹתוֹ וְאֵילָךְ, אֲבָל שִׁיתָּא בָּבֵי דְּרֵישָׁא – לָא.

But Rav Yehuda interprets these principles as applying only to those cases found in the list **from** the **mother-in-law of** the *yavam* **and onward, but not to the six cases at the beginning,** which include his daughter, and his wife's daughter, and their descendants.

מַאי טַעֲמָא? כֵּיוָן דְּבִתּוֹ בְּאוֹנָסִין הוּא דְּמַשְׁכַּחַתְּ לָהּ, בְּנִשּׂוּאִין לָא מַשְׁכַּחַתְּ לָהּ,

What is the reason for Rav Yehuda's distinction? **This is because you find** the scenario where two women who are candidates for levirate marriage are both sisters as well as the daughters of the two *yevamin* only in a case where the women are the daughters of the *yevamin* **through rape, but you cannot find it** in a case where they are his daughters **through marriage.** If one brother married a woman and had a daughter with her, then this woman, the wife of a brother who has children, is forbidden to all of his brothers. Therefore, it would be impossible for another brother to have a daughter with that same woman, and therefore the two daughters could never be sisters. The scenario of daughters who are also sisters is possible only when the first brother raped a woman and gave birth to a daughter, such that the woman is not forbidden to his brothers. If one of the brothers then had a daughter with this woman and both daughters married other brothers who then died, it is possible that these daughters would happen before their fathers for levirate marriage.

בְּנִשּׂוּאִין – קָמַיְירֵי, בְּאוֹנָסִין – לָא קָא מַיְירֵי.

Rav Yehuda maintains that the current mishna **deals with** cases of **marriage but does not deal with** cases of **rape,**[N] and therefore he does not apply the principles governing sisters to those cases.

וְאַבַּיֵי מְתַרְגֵּם אַף בִּתּוֹ (בָּאָה) מֵאֲנוּסָתוֹ, כֵּיוָן דְּאַשְׁכּוּחֵי מַשְׁכַּחַתְּ לָהּ, אִי בָּעְיָא בְּאוֹנָסִין – תֶּיהֱוֵי, אִי בָּעְיָא בְּנִשּׂוּאִין – תֶּהֱוֵי. אֲבָל אֵשֶׁת אָחִיו שֶׁלֹּא הָיָה בְּעוֹלָמוֹ – לָא, כֵּיוָן דְּאַלִּיבָּא דְּרַבִּי שִׁמְעוֹן הוּא דְּמַשְׁכַּחַתְּ לָהּ – אַלִּיבָּא דְּרַבָּנַן לָא מַשְׁכַּחַתְּ לָהּ בִּפְלוּגְתָּא לָא קָמַיְירֵי.

And Abaye interprets these principles as applying **even to his daughter from a woman he raped. Since you can find this** scenario, **if** the statement **wants** to deal with cases of **rape, let it; if it wants** to deal with cases of **marriage, let it.** It is preferable to explain this matter with regard to cases of marriage, but if that is not possible, it can still be explained as dealing with cases of rape. **However, it cannot** be explained as referring to **the wife of a brother with whom he did not coexist.** Even according to the opinion of Abaye, this case cannot be included, **since you can find** a situation where two sisters happen before two brothers for levirate marriage while each woman is the wife of a brother with whom he did not coexist only **according to** the opinion of **Rabbi Shimon, while** such a case **cannot be found according to** the opinion of **the Rabbis.** And Rabbi Ḥiyya **does not deal with** cases that are subject to **dispute.**

וְרַב סָפְרָא מְתַרְגֵּם אַף אֵשֶׁת אָחִיו שֶׁלֹּא הָיָה בְּעוֹלָמוֹ, וּמַשְׁכַּחַתְּ לָהּ בְּשִׁיתָּא אָחֵי, וְאַלִּיבָּא דְּרַבִּי שִׁמְעוֹן. וְסִימָנִיךְ: מֵת נוֹלַד וְיִיבֵּם, מֵת נוֹלַד וְיִיבֵּם;

And Rav Safra interprets these principles as applying to the **wife of a brother with whom he did not coexist, and you can find this** scenario **in the case** of the **six brothers**[B] **and according to** the opinion of **Rabbi Shimon. And your mnemonic** to remember how this might come about **is** as follows: **Died, born, consummated the levirate marriage; died, born, consummated the levirate marriage.**[B]

NOTES

Does not deal with rape – בְּאוֹנָסִין לָא קָא מַיְירֵי: The reason why Rav Yehuda held that the mishna does not deal with cases of rape is not elaborated upon here at all. It is also unclear why he and Abaye do not assume that the mishna follows Rabbi Shimon's opinion. It seems that the opinions here relate to a question that was raised in Chapter One: Why was the case of his mother who was raped by his father not mentioned among the fifteen forbidden relatives? One of the answers is that the mishna there discusses only cases of marriage but not cases of rape. Alternatively, the mishna there does not list matters for which there are differing opinions. Therefore, these answers can be applied to the issue here. Rav Safra's opinion is that issues subject to dispute were cited in the mishna. The Gemara there (10a) raises objections to this opinion and proceeds to resolve the issues according to this opinion as well (*Arukh LaNer*).

BACKGROUND

Died, born, consummated the levirate marriage; died, born, consummated the levirate marriage – מֵת נוֹלַד וְיִיבֵּם, מֵת נוֹלַד וְיִיבֵּם: Originally, there were six brothers that were all the sons of one father: Reuven, Shimon, Levi, Yehuda, Gad, and Asher. Reuven and Shimon married two sisters, Ḥogla and Milka, and similarly Levi and Yehuda married two sisters, Rachel and Leah. Gad and Asher married women who were not related to each other or to any of the other wives. Gad married Adda and Asher married Miriam.

The order of events is as follows: Reuven dies without children, and his wife, Ḥogla, happens before the other brothers for levirate marriage. Before any of the brothers consummate the levirate marriage or perform *ḥalitza* with her, another brother, Yissakhar, is born. Yissakhar is prohibited from marrying Ḥogla, as she is considered the wife of a brother, Reuven, with whom he did not coexist. Consequently, Levi consummates the levirate marriage with Ḥogla, Reuven's wife. Afterward, Shimon dies without children and his wife, Milka, happens before all the brothers, including Yissakhar, for levirate marriage. Before any of the brothers act, another brother, Zevulun, is born, and he is prohibited from marrying Milka, as she is considered the wife of a brother to Shimon, with whom he did not coexist. Consequently, Yehuda consummates the levirate marriage with Milka. Afterward, both Levi and Yehuda die without children, and both sets of sisters, Ḥogla and Milka as well as Rachel and Leah, happen before the brothers for levirate marriage. At this point, Yissakhar is forbidden not only to Ḥogla, who is the wife of the brother Reuven, with whom he did not coexist, but also to Rachel, as she became the rival wife of Ḥogla and is therefore forbidden to Yissakhar as the rival wife of the wife of a brother with whom he did not coexist. These women, however, are not forbidden to Zevulun, according to the opinion of Rabbi Shimon, because at the time that he was born, they were both married to Levi, who is a brother with whom Zevulun did coexist. However, Zevulun is prohibited from marrying both Milka, who is the wife of the brother Shimon with whom he did not coexist, and her rival wife Leah.

If Gad and Asher consummate the levirate marriage with Rachel and Leah, thereby exempting Ḥogla and Milka from levirate marriage, and die afterward, it turns out that Adda, the wife of Gad, is the rival wife of Rachel, who is the rival wife of Ḥogla. Consequently, in relation to Yissakhar, Adda is considered the rival wife of the rival wife of the wife of a brother, Reuven, with whom he did not coexist. Similarly, Miriam is the rival wife of the rival wife of Milka, and she is forbidden to Zevulun because of Milka, who was the wife of a brother, Shimon, with whom he did not coexist. Therefore, the one who is permitted to this brother, i.e., Adda who is permitted to Zevulun, is forbidden to Yissakhar. Similarly, the one who is permitted to this brother, i.e., Miriam who is permitted to Yissakhar, is forbidden to Zevulun.

Additionally, with regard to Rachel and Leah, the ruling of: When her sister is also her *yevama* she can either perform *ḥalitza* or enter into the levirate marriage, applies as well. This is because Rachel and Leah are sisters who happen before the brothers for levirate marriage, and the one who is forbidden to one brother is permitted to the other. This ruling therefore applies in the case of a rival wife, as well in the case of the rival wife of a rival wife.

BACKGROUND

Six brothers – שִׁיתָּא אָחֵי:

רְאוּבֵן וְשִׁמְעוֹן נְשׂוּאִין שְׁתֵּי אֲחָיוֹת, לֵוִי וִיהוּדָה נְשׂוּאִין שְׁתֵּי נָכְרִיּוֹת. מֵת רְאוּבֵן נוֹלַד יִשָּׂשכָר וְיִיבֵּם לֵוִי, מֵת שִׁמְעוֹן נוֹלַד זְבוּלֻן וְיִיבֵּם יְהוּדָה. מֵתוּ לֵוִי וִיהוּדָה בְּלֹא בָּנִים, וְנָפְלוּ לְהוּ קַמֵּי יִשָּׂשכָר וּזְבוּלֻן,

How could this come about? There were two brothers, **Reuven and Shimon,** who were **married** to **two sisters.** And there were two other brothers, **Levi and Yehuda,** who were **married** to **two unrelated women. Reuven died, Yissakhar was born, and Levi consummated the levirate marriage** with Reuven's wife. Afterward, **Shimon died, Zevulun was born, and Yehuda consummated the levirate marriage** with Shimon's wife. Later, **Levi and Yehuda died childless and** these two sisters **happened before Yissakhar and Zevulun for levirate marriage.**

הָאֲסוּרָה לְזֶה מוּתֶּרֶת לְזֶה, וְהָאֲסוּרָה לְזֶה מוּתֶּרֶת לְזֶה, וַאֲחוֹתָהּ שֶׁהִיא יְבִמְתָּהּ.

In this scenario, the woman who had been Reuven's wife **is forbidden to this** brother, Yissakhar, as the wife of a brother with whom he did not coexist, because he was not alive at the same time as Reuven, and yet **she is** nevertheless **permitted to this** brother, Zevulun, because when Zevulun was born this woman was already the wife of Levi, a brother with whom he did coexist. According to Rabbi Shimon, the fact that she had previously been the wife of Reuven, a brother with whom he did not coexist, is not taken into account. Similarly, with regard to Shimon's wife, we find that **she who is forbidden to this** one **is permitted to that** one. Shimon's wife is forbidden to Zevulun as the wife of a brother with whom he did not coexist, but she is nevertheless permitted to Yissakhar. Accordingly, the situation of **her sister who is her *yevama*,** i.e., two sisters who are *yevamot* and yet are allowed to perform levirate marriage, can be applied to this case as well.

לָמָּה לִי יִיבֵּם יְהוּדָה? בְּלֹא יִיבֵּם יְהוּדָה נַמִּי מַשְׁכַּחַתְּ לָהּ!

The Gemara asks: **Why do I** need to assume that this is referring to a scenario where **Yehuda consummated the levirate marriage? You can find this** possibility **in** a case where **Yehuda did not consummate the levirate marriage as well.** This scenario can also take place with only five brothers and without Yehuda: Reuven and Shimon were married to two sisters, Reuven died, Yissakhar was born, and Levi consummated the levirate marriage with Reuven's wife. Then Shimon died and Zevulun was born. If Levi then dies, Levi's wife is forbidden to Yissakhar as the wife of his brother Reuven, with whom he did not coexist, but she would be permitted to Zevulun because she was already the wife of Levi when Zevulun was born. Shimon's wife would be forbidden to Zevulun but permitted to Yissakhar.

מִשּׁוּם צָרָה. הָא תֵּינַח צָרָה, צָרָה דְּצָרָה מַאי אִיכָּא לְמֵימַר?

The Gemara responds: This is **due to the rival wife.** It was taught in this way in order to make the principle applicable not only to the wives, but also to their rival wives. In this scenario, Levi and Yehuda were previously married to two sisters who then became the rival wives of a wife of a brother with whom one did not coexist. This allows the ruling to apply to the case of rival wives as well. The Gemara notes: **This works out well** if the mishna comes to include only **a rival wife** herself, but **what can be said** about **the rival wife of a rival wife?** How can this case explained? If one aims to include all of the details of the mishna in Rabbi Ḥiyya's principle, then the mishna must be referring not only to a case involving the brothers' rival wives, but also to the rival wives of those rival wives mentioned in the mishna.

כְּגוֹן דַּהֲדַר וְיַבְּמִינְהוּ נַמִּי גָּד וְאָשֵׁר.

The Gemara answers: Therefore, one must include a case **where Gad and Asher subsequently consummated the levirate marriage** with these women **as well.** That is, initially there were two other brothers, Gad and Asher, who consummated the levirate marriage with the previous wives of Levi and Yehuda, each of whom had taken one of the wives of Reuven and Shimon. Later, when Gad and Asher died, their previous wives, who are the rival wives of the rival wives of Reuven and Shimon's wives, happen before Yissakhar and Zevulun for levirate marriage.

מתני׳ שְׁלֹשָׁה אַחִין, שְׁנַיִם מֵהֶן נְשׂוּאִין שְׁתֵּי אֲחָיוֹת, אוֹ אִשָּׁה וּבִתָּהּ, אוֹ אִשָּׁה וּבַת בִּתָּהּ, אוֹ אִשָּׁה וּבַת בְּנָהּ – הֲרֵי אֵלּוּ חוֹלְצוֹת וְלֹא מִתְיַיבְּמוֹת, וְרַבִּי שִׁמְעוֹן פּוֹטֵר.

MISHNA In the case of **three brothers, two of whom were married to** close relatives, e.g., **two sisters; or a woman and her daughter; or a woman and her daughter's daughter; or a woman and her son's daughter,**[H] if the two brothers who were married to two close relatives died and their wives happened before a third brother for levirate marriage, **then these** two women must **perform *ḥalitza* and may not enter into levirate marriage,** as each of them is a relative of a woman with whom he has a levirate bond. **And Rabbi Shimon exempts**[N] them even from the obligation to perform *ḥalitza*.

הָיְתָה אַחַת מֵהֶן אֲסוּרָה עָלָיו אִיסּוּר עֶרְוָה – אָסוּר בָּהּ, וּמוּתָּר בַּאֲחוֹתָהּ. אִיסּוּר מִצְוָה אוֹ אִיסּוּר קְדוּשָּׁה – חוֹלְצוֹת וְלֹא מִתְיַיבְּמוֹת.

If **one of them was forbidden to him,** the third brother, due to a **prohibition against forbidden relatives,** then **he is prohibited from** marrying **her but is permitted to** marry **her sister.** Because the woman who is forbidden to him is not considered to be a woman who requires him for levirate marriage, there is only one woman who happens before him for levirate marriage. However, if one of the women was forbidden due to **a prohibition** resulting from **a mitzva or a prohibition** stemming from **sanctity,** then **they** must **perform *ḥalitza* and may not enter into levirate marriage.** This is because these prohibitions do not completely cancel the levirate bond.

גמ׳ תַּנְיָא: רַבִּי שִׁמְעוֹן פּוֹטֵר בִּשְׁתֵּיהֶן מִן הַחֲלִיצָה וּמִן הַיִּיבּוּם, שֶׁנֶּאֱמַר ״וְאִשָּׁה אֶל אֲחוֹתָהּ לֹא תִקָּח לִצְרוֹר״ – בְּשָׁעָה שֶׁנַּעֲשׂוּ צָרוֹת זוֹ לָזוֹ לֹא יְהֵא לְךָ לִיקּוּחִין אֲפִילּוּ בְּאַחַת מֵהֶן.

GEMARA **It is taught** in a *baraita*: **Rabbi Shimon exempts both of them from *ḥalitza* and from levirate marriage, as it is stated: "And you shall not take a woman to her sister, to be a rival to her"** (Leviticus 18:18). This indicates that **at the time that** a situation arises wherein **they are to become rival wives to each other,** e.g., two sisters happen before one *yavam* for levirate marriage, **you shall not have** the ability **to take even one of them** in marriage. In his opinion, both women are exempt from both levirate marriage and *ḥalitza* at the moment that they happen before the *yavam*, just as a forbidden relative is exempt from both levirate marriage and *ḥalitza*.

״הָיְתָה אַחַת מֵהֶן״ כּוּ׳. הָא תּוּ לָמָּה לִי? הַיְינוּ הָךְ!

It was taught in the mishna: If **one of them was** forbidden to him due to a prohibition against forbidden relatives, he is prohibited from marrying her but is permitted to marry her sister. The Gemara asks: **Why do I need this** statement **as well? This is** identical to **that** which was taught in the previous mishna.

לְרַבִּי שִׁמְעוֹן אִיצְטְרִיךְ: סָלְקָא דַּעְתָּךְ אָמֵינָא: הוֹאִיל וְאָמַר רַבִּי שִׁמְעוֹן שְׁתֵּי אֲחָיוֹת לֹא חוֹלְצוֹת וְלֹא מִתְיַיבְּמוֹת – לִגְזוֹר מִשּׁוּם שְׁתֵּי אֲחָיוֹת דְּעָלְמָא, קָמַשְׁמַע לַן.

The Gemara answers: **It was necessary** to state this again here **according to** the opinion of **Rabbi Shimon. It might enter your mind to say: Since Rabbi Shimon said** that **two sisters may not perform *ḥalitza* and may not enter into levirate marriage,** as the very fact that they require levirate marriage from the same man and stand to become rival wives to each other renders them forbidden, **we should issue** a rabbinic **decree** in this case as well. Although in this case only one of the sisters is eligible for levirate marriage, as the other is a forbidden relative, perhaps there should be a rabbinic decree prohibiting the *yavam* from marrying the permitted sister, **due to** the similarity to the case of **two sisters in general** who happen before him for levirate marriage. **This teaches us** that even Rabbi Shimon does not hold that there is a rabbinic decree in this case.

״אִיסּוּר מִצְוָה״ כּוּ׳.

It was taught in the mishna that if the wives are forbidden to the *yavam* due to **a prohibition** resulting from **a mitzva** or sanctity, they must perform *ḥalitza* and may not enter into levirate marriage.

NOTES

And Rabbi Shimon exempts – וְרַבִּי שִׁמְעוֹן פּוֹטֵר: The Gemara here explains the rationale behind Rabbi Shimon's opinion by way of a homiletical interpretation of the verse "And you shall not take a woman to her sister, to be a rival to her" (Leviticus 18:18). From here he learns that if two sisters happen before the *yavam* for levirate marriage, they are both rendered exempt.

In the Jerusalem Talmud, however, Rabbi Oshaya explains that Rabbi Shimon maintains that only the sister who happened before the *yavam* second is exempt from *ḥalitza* and levirate marriage. Accordingly, the rationale behind Rabbi Shimon's opinion is that a woman with a levirate bond is considered to be married to the *yavam*. Therefore, the second sister is exempt from levirate marriage, as she is equivalent to his wife's sister. If this is the rationale behind Rabbi Shimon's opinion, then when the Gemara here asserts that both women are exempt, it must be referring to a situation where both women happened before the *yavam* simultaneously, and it must be in accordance with the opinion that it is possible to determine that two events occur simultaneously (see *Ḥiddushei Anshei Shem*).

Tosafot explain that this ruling applies specifically in a case where the women happened before a single *yavam*. However, if they happened before two *yevamin*, Rabbi Shimon himself rules that the marriages may be maintained after the fact (*Yevamot* 28a). This must be due to a distinction in the strength of the levirate bond with two *yevamin* and the levirate bond with only one *yavam*. In the case of a levirate bond with only one *yavam*, Rabbi Shimon maintains that the woman is considered married to the *yavam*, while in the case of two *yevamin*, the levirate bond is not exclusive and therefore does not have the strength to render the woman married to the *yavam* (Rabbi Yehuda al-Madari).

HALAKHA

Two close relatives who happened for levirate marriage – שְׁתֵּי קְרוֹבוֹת שֶׁנָּפְלוּ לְיִיבּוּם: In the case of three brothers, two of whom were married to two sisters, if one of the brothers married to a sister dies, and later the second dies, and both sisters happen before the third brother for levirate marriage, then both women are forbidden to him. This is also the case for any other two women that he is prohibited from marrying simultaneously, e.g., a woman and her daughter, or a woman and her daughter's daughter. The two women are considered rival wives due to the levirate bond. Consequently, they must perform *ḥalitza* and may not enter into levirate marriage (Rambam *Sefer Nashim*, *Hilkhot Yibbum* 6:25; *Shulḥan Arukh*, *Even HaEzer* 175:6).

והא אמר רבי שמעון: שתי אחיות לא חולצות ולא מתייבמות!

This *halakha* was also taught in the previous mishna (26a), and it is cited in this mishna according to the opinion of Rabbi Shimon. The Gemara asks: **But didn't Rabbi Shimon say: Two sisters neither perform *ḥalitza* nor enter into levirate marriage?** Because these women are eligible for levirate marriage according to Torah law, they are considered the sisters of a woman with whom he has a levirate bond. In this case, Rabbi Shimon exempts them from both *ḥalitza* and levirate marriage. Why, then, does the mishna require them to perform *ḥalitza*?

גזירה משום איסור מצוה דעלמא.

The Gemara answers: It is **a rabbinic decree due to the general case of a prohibition** resulting from **a mitzva.** If they did not perform *ḥalitza* in this case, where they are sisters, there is a concern that people would assume that their exemption from *ḥalitza* stemmed not from their status as sisters but rather due to the prohibition. This would lead to the mistaken conclusion that women who are forbidden due to a mitzva do not require *ḥalitza*. Therefore, the Sages issued a rabbinic decree requiring *ḥalitza* in this case.

הא תינח איהי, אחותה מאי איכא למימר? גזירה אחותה משום לתא דידה.

The Gemara asks: **This works out well** for her, as **she** is forbidden due to the prohibition resulting from a mitzva. It is appropriate to require *ḥalitza* with her, to demonstrate that *ḥalitza* is generally applied in cases where there is a prohibition resulting from a mitzva. But with regard to **her sister, what is there to say?** Why must she perform *ḥalitza* as well? The Gemara answers: There is **a rabbinic decree** with regard to **her sister due to her.**[N]

והא גבי ערוה לא גזרינן! שאני ערוה דמגמר גמירי לה אינשי, וקלא אית לה.

The Gemara asks: If Rabbi Shimon issues a decree in this case requiring *ḥalitza* for the sister, out of concern for confusion, then there is a difficulty: **But, with regard to a forbidden relative we do not issue a decree**[N] requiring *ḥalitza* due to her sister; why does Rabbi Shimon issue a rabbinic decree requiring *ḥalitza* with a woman forbidden due to a prohibition resulting from a mitzva and not with a woman who is a forbidden relative? The Gemara answers: **Forbidden relatives are different, as people learn** the *halakhot* pertaining to **them** because they are stated explicitly in the Torah and are well known to all, **and** the ruling **has publicity.** Therefore, there is no concern lest people mistakenly confuse this case with cases of *yevamot* who are not sisters. Prohibitions resulting from mitzvot are not, however, explicit in the Torah, nor are they generally known.

מתני׳ שלשה אחין, שנים נשואים שתי אחיות, ואחד מופנה; מת אחד מבעלי אחיות ועשה בה מופנה מאמר, ואחר כך מת אחיו השני,

MISHNA In the case of **three brothers, two** of whom **were married to two sisters, and one who was single,**[N] the following occurred: **The husband of one of the sisters died** childless, leaving behind his wife, **and the single** brother **performed levirate betrothal [*ma'amar*]** to this wife.[H] The single brother performed an act of betrothal to the *yevama* but did not yet consummate the marriage by engaging in sexual intercourse. **Afterward, the second brother died,** and therefore the second brother's wife, the sister of the betrothed, happened before the single brother for levirate marriage as well.

NOTES

Due to her – משום לתא דידה: The Sages issued a decree requiring the sister of a woman forbidden as the result of a mitzva to perform *ḥalitza* in order to prevent people from permitting levirate marriage to the forbidden woman herself. This, however, would seem to be a decree to prevent the violation of another decree, which the Sages generally refrained from issuing. However, because this case is dealing with two sisters who are exempt primarily for the same reason, it is considered as if they are both included in one general decree (see Rivan and Rabbi Yehuda al-Madari).

But with regard to a forbidden relative we do not issue a decree – והא גבי ערוה לא גזרינן: Rashi interprets this question in a straightforward manner: Why is there not a similar decree in the cases of sisters of forbidden relatives (see Ritva)? There are, however, early commentaries who interpret the question as follows: If it turned out that the same woman was both a forbidden relative and forbidden as the result of a mitzva, why would the Sages not issue a decree in this case as well, so that others not come to allow cases where the woman is forbidden by a mitzva alone? They explain the Gemara's answer as asserting that everyone knows that she was exempt from levirate marriage as a forbidden relative. They would not come to think that there was also a prohibition resulting from a mitzva involved (Razah; Ramban; Rashba).

And one who was single – ואחד מופנה: As far as the *halakha* is concerned, it makes no difference if the third brother was single or married to a woman who was not related to his brothers' wives. It states that he was single due to the subsequent *mishnayot*, which also include the rulings pertaining to rival wives. In those cases, it is important to mention that the third brother was married to an unrelated woman, which is not the case in the present mishna (Rivan; Rabbi Yehuda al-Madari; *Nimmukei Yosef*). Others explain that this is stated due to the wording: Woe unto him. If he was single at first, he ends up without any wife at all and is therefore unfortunate. This would not be so if he was married (*Tosafot Yeshanim*; Meiri).

HALAKHA

Levirate betrothal and the levirate bond in the case of two sisters – מאמר וזיקה בשתי אחיות: There is a case of three brothers, two of whom were married to two sisters, and the husband of one of the sisters died. Afterward, the third brother performed levirate betrothal with the widowed sister, but before he could consummate the levirate marriage with her, the other sister's husband died as well, at which point this sister happened before the third brother for levirate marriage. In this case, the third brother must send both sisters away. She who received levirate betrothal is sent away with a bill of divorce and *ḥalitza*, and her sister must perform *ḥalitza*. This ruling is in accordance with the statement of Beit Hillel (Rambam *Sefer Nashim, Hilkhot Yibbum* 7:6; *Shulḥan Arukh, Even HaEzer* 175:6).

בֵּית שַׁמַּאי אוֹמְרִים: אִשְׁתּוֹ עִמּוֹ, וְהַלָּזוּ תֵּצֵא מִשּׁוּם אֲחוֹת אִשָּׁה. וּבֵית הִלֵּל אוֹמְרִים: מוֹצִיא אֶת אִשְׁתּוֹ בְּגֵט וּבַחֲלִיצָה, וְאֵשֶׁת אָחִיו בַּחֲלִיצָה. זוֹ הִיא שֶׁאָמְרוּ: אוֹי לוֹ עַל אִשְׁתּוֹ, וְאוֹי לוֹ עַל אֵשֶׁת אָחִיו.

In this case, **Beit Shammai say: His wife remains with him.** The woman he betrothed is considered like his wife, and he is not required to divorce her. **And this other** woman **leaves** the *yavam* and is exempt from levirate marriage **as the sister of a wife. Beit Hillel say:** Being as he had not yet entered into marriage with the first woman, he is required to perform levirate marriage with both women. Therefore, **he divorces his wife,** i.e., the woman to whom he performed levirate betrothal, **with a bill of divorce,** which nullifies levirate betrothal, **and by *ḥalitza,*** which nullifies the levirate bond. **And,** he sends away **the wife of his** second **brother with *ḥalitza*** as well. They comment: **This is** the case **that** was referred to when the Sages **said: Woe unto him**[N] **for his wife and woe unto him for the wife of his brother.** Due to the combination of circumstances, he loses them both.

גמ׳ ״זוֹ הִיא״ לְמַעוּטֵי מַאי? לְמַעוּטֵי הָךְ דְּרַבִּי יְהוֹשֻׁעַ, דְּלָא עָבְדִינַן כְּוָותֵיהּ, אֶלָּא אִי כְּרַבָּן גַּמְלִיאֵל אִי כְּרַבִּי אֶלְעָזָר.

GEMARA The Gemara asks: **What** does the mishna's formulation of the term: **This is,** which indicates limitation and exactitude, come **to exclude?** The Gemara answers: **It excludes that** statement **of Rabbi Yehoshua** (109a). There, Rabbi Yehoshua holds that if a man is married to a minor when her sister happens before him for levirate marriage, he must send both of the women away. He said there: Woe unto him for his wife and woe unto him for the wife of his brother. From the language in the mishna here, we learn **that we do not act in accordance with his** opinion. **Rather,** we act **either in accordance with** the opinion of **Rabban Gamliel**[N] **or in accordance with** the opinion of **Rabbi Elazar.** According to the opinion of both of these *tanna'im* in the mishna (109a), despite the conflict between the brother's marriage to the minor and the levirate bond with her sister, there is still a way for him to marry one of the women.

אָמַר רַבִּי אֶלְעָזָר: לָא תֵּימָא מַאֲמָר לְבֵית שַׁמַּאי קוֹנֶה קִנְיָן גָּמוּר, דְּאִי בָּעֵי לְאַפּוֹקֵי סַגִּי לַהּ בְּגִיטָּא, אֶלָּא: מַאֲמָר לְבֵית שַׁמַּאי אֵינוֹ קוֹנֶה אֶלָּא לִדְחוֹת בְּצָרָה בִּלְבַד.

§ With regard to the main issue of levirate betrothal, it would seem from this mishna that Beit Shammai hold that levirate betrothal has the legal force of levirate marriage. However, **Rabbi Elazar said: Do not say** that **levirate betrothal acquires** the woman **as a full-fledged acquisition according to** the opinion of **Beit Shammai,**[N] such that the first woman becomes his wife to the extent **that if he wants to divorce** her **a bill of divorce would suffice** without an act of *ḥalitza.* **Rather, for Beit Shammai, levirate betrothal acquires** the woman **only** insofar **as it precludes a rival wife** from entering levirate marriage.[N] The legal force of levirate betrothal is limited to preventing the rival wife[N] of the sister from performing levirate marriage; she is exempt from both levirate marriage and *ḥalitza.*

NOTES

This is the case when they said woe unto him – זוֹ הִיא שֶׁאָמְרוּ אוֹי לוֹ: *Nimmukei Yosef* explains that the phrase: Woe unto him, related to the fact this man acquired at the time of levirate betrothal the usufruct property of the woman as well as his brother's property, but now he must return it all.

Tosafot explain that the phrase: Woe unto him, apply only to a situation where one performed an act that should not have led to complications, but events outside of his control caused him to lose everything he had acquired. The *Mei Naftoaḥ* raises an objection: How did the third brother lose out? Had he not performed levirate betrothal he would have been unable to marry either woman, being as they were sisters who happened before him at the same time. He answers that in a case where the brothers were married to other rival wives, were it not for levirate betrothal, he would have been allowed to marry one of the rival wives. After levirate betrothal, however, he may no longer marry any of them.

Either in accordance with Rabban Gamliel – אִי כְּרַבָּן גַּמְלִיאֵל: Although it is later proven that the opinion of Beit Hillel does not accord with that of Rabban Gamliel, and the *halakha* does not accord with his opinion either, here the only deduction that can be made is that the mishna is not in accordance with the opinion of Rabbi Yehoshua. It is only from a different source that that it can be proven that the *halakha* accords with the opinion of Rabbi Eliezer specifically (Ramban; Rashba).

Do not say that levirate betrothal…according to the opinion of Beit Shammai, etc. – לָא תֵּימָא מַאֲמָר לְבֵית שַׁמַּאי וכו׳: The Jerusalem Talmud presents the opinion of Rabbi Elazar ben Arakh, who does assert that levirate betrothal completely acquires the *yevama*. According to his opinion, levirate betrothal completely establishes the relationship between the *yavam* and the *yevama*, just like sexual intercourse. In the course of the discussion in the Jerusalem Talmud, however, it is proven that Beit Shammai do not accord with this opinion.

In the Jerusalem Talmud, it is explained that Beit Shammai's opinion about the strength of levirate betrothal is the same as Rabbi Shimon's opinion concerning the levirate bond: These bonds are sufficiently effective to prevent the creation of a bond with another woman, e.g., the sister of the *yevama*, but are not sufficient to nullify the levirate bond completely. Therefore, if the *yavam* later wants to divorce the *yevama*, she requires *ḥalitza* (see Ramban and Rashba).

Only insofar as it precludes a rival wife from entering levirate marriage – אֶלָּא לִדְחוֹת בְּצָרָה בִּלְבַד: The question arises: If levirate betrothal cannot establish the union with the same legal force as sexual relations, how can it completely preclude the rival wife from performing levirate marriage? One commentary explains that levirate betrothal is equivalent to betrothal in the following matter: If the *yavam* betrothed one sister and then the other happened before him for levirate marriage, he need not divorce his betrothed. Rather, her sister is precluded from levirate marriage and is therefore exempt from it. Nevertheless, levirate betrothal does not terminate the levirate bond with the first sister, and she requires *ḥalitza* if the *yavam* later choses to divorce this woman (*Tosafot Yeshanim*).

Precluding a rival wife from performing levirate marriage – דְּחִיַּית צָרָה: Rashi explains here and throughout this talmudic discussion that the rival wife that the Gemara is referring to is in fact the sister who happened before the *yavam* for levirate marriage. Although these women are not actually rival wives, as each was married to a different brother, the sister is considered a rival wife in this context. However, *Tosafot* and the Meiri explain that the Gemara is referring to an actual rival wife. If the brother was married to two women and the *yavam* performed levirate betrothal with one of them, the levirate betrothal prevents the other wife from entering levirate marriage with the *yavam*.

אֲמַר רַבִּי אָבִין, אַף אֲנַן נַמִּי תָּנֵינָא: בֵּית שַׁמַּאי אוֹמְרִים: יְקַיְּימוּ, יְקַיְּימוּ – אִין, לְכַתְּחִלָּה – לָא,

Rabbi Avin said: We, too, learn in the mishna a proof that levirate betrothal is not a full-fledged act of acquisition, even according to Beit Shammai. The mishna at the beginning of this chapter (26a) teaches that when two sisters who are *yevamot* happen before two brothers for levirate marriage, if the brothers married their wives before consulting the court, then **Beit Shammai say: They may maintain them** as their wives. From here it can be deduced: If they already married them, **yes, they may maintain them.** However, marrying them ***ab initio*, no,** this is prohibited due to the prohibition against marrying the sister of a woman with whom one has a levirate bond.

Perek **III**
Daf **29** Amud **b**

וְאִי סָלְקָא דַּעְתָּךְ מַאֲמָר לְבֵית שַׁמַּאי קוֹנֶה קִנְיָן גָּמוּר – זֶה יַעֲשֶׂה מַאֲמָר וְיִקְנֶה, וְזֶה יַעֲשֶׂה מַאֲמָר וְיִקְנֶה!

And if it enters your mind that **according to Beit Shammai levirate betrothal acquires** the woman **as a full-fledged acquisition,** then this matter could potentially have been resolved *ab initio*: **This** brother **should perform levirate betrothal**[N] **and acquire** one sister, **and that** brother **should perform levirate betrothal and acquire** the other sister. As there is no prohibition whatsoever involved in performing levirate betrothal, the concern for violating a prohibition by consummating the levirate marriage with a sister of a woman with whom he has a levirate bond is avoided; he only betroths her, but does not engage in sexual intercourse with her. After the betrothal, the levirate bond of her sister is dissolved and he can freely consummate the levirate marriage with her.

אֶלָּא מַאי – דּוֹחֶה דְּחִיָּיה גְּמוּרָה? זֶה יַעֲשֶׂה מַאֲמָר וְיִדְחֶה, וְזֶה יַעֲשֶׂה מַאֲמָר וְיִדְחֶה.

The Gemara objects: **Rather, what** then? If levirate betrothal does not serve to fully acquire the woman, what is the alternative? It must be that according to Beit Shammai levirate betrothal **precludes** the rival wife from entering levirate marriage with **a complete preclusion.** If so, there is an additional potential scenario: **This one should perform levirate betrothal** with one sister **and preclude** the second sister from entering levirate marriage, **and that one should perform**[N] **levirate** betrothal with the second sister **and preclude** the first sister from entering levirate marriage. In this way, the *yevamin* can consummate the levirate marriage with the sisters *ab initio* as well. Yet the mishna does not allow for this possibility.

אֶלָּא מַאי אִית לָךְ לְמֵימַר: מַאֲמָר דְּהֶיתֵּירָא – דָּחֵי, דְּאִיסּוּרָא – לָא דָּחֵי – הָכִי נַמִּי: מַאֲמָר, אֲפִילּוּ לְמַאן דְּאָמַר מַאֲמָר קוֹנֶה קִנְיָן גָּמוּר, מַאֲמָר דְּהֶיתֵּירָא – קָנֵי דְּאִיסּוּרָא – לָא קָנֵי.

Rather, what have you to say? One must assert that **levirate betrothal** performed **in** circumstances where it is **permitted** to perform levirate marriage, i.e. where there is no prohibition with regard to the close relative of a woman with whom the *yavam* has a levirate bond, completely **precludes** the rival wife from entering levirate marriage. However, levirate betrothal performed **in** circumstances where it is **forbidden** to perform levirate marriage, **does not preclude** entering levirate marriage.[N] Therefore, in the case of two sisters who happen simultaneously before two brothers for levirate marriage, the sisters cannot be precluded from entering levirate marriage via levirate betrothal. **So too here,** with regard to **levirate betrothal** performed by the third brother, the same distinction can be made. **Even according to the one who said that levirate betrothal acquires** a woman **as a full-fledged acquisition,** just like marriage, there is the following difference: **Levirate betrothal under permitted** circumstances **acquires** the woman, but levirate betrothal **under forbidden circumstances does not acquire** the woman. Therefore, there is no proof as to the nature of levirate betrothal according to the opinion of Beit Shammai from the first mishna in the chapter.

NOTES

This brother should perform levirate betrothal – זֶה יַעֲשֶׂה מַאֲמָר: Rashi writes that performing levirate betrothal does not violate a prohibition, but engaging in sexual intercourse does. Similarly, the Rambam holds that there is no prohibition involved in betrothing a woman who is forbidden; the prohibition is only violated by engaging in sexual intercourse. The Rashba adds that only with regard to the special prohibitions relating to priests could an act of betrothal constitute violation of a prohibition. However, the *Smag* and *Sefer HaHinnukh* hold that one violates a Torah prohibition simply by performing betrothal with a forbidden woman. According to their opinion, one must explain that in situations where the mitzva of levirate marriage may be fulfilled, such betrothals are not prohibited (*Keren Ora*). Alternatively, one could explain that betrothals are prohibited only in cases where the sexual intercourse that would follow is forbidden. In this case, however, the sexual intercourse that follows the levirate betrothal would be permitted as the levirate betrothal served to cancel the prohibition (*Yosef Lekaḥ*).

This one should perform levirate betrothal…and that one should perform – זֶה יַעֲשֶׂה מַאֲמָר...וְזֶה יַעֲשֶׂה: Most of the early commentaries write that it is in fact sufficient for one of the brothers to perform levirate betrothal as this would eliminate the prohibition proscribing the second sister. In *Tosefot HaRosh*, however, it is explained that the Gemara here follows the opinion that we are concerned lest the mitzva of levirate marriage be negated. This concern can be allayed only by both brothers performing levirate betrothal at the same time via an agent. The later commentaries explain that although there is still concern that the levirate marriage may not be consummated, as the fulfillment of the mitzva primarily involves intercourse the levirate betrothal still represents the beginning of the performance of the mitzva, and that is sufficient to allay the concern (*Ḥiddushei Batra*).

In circumstances where it is forbidden to perform levirate marriage, it does not preclude levirate marriage – דְּאִיסּוּרָא לָא דָּחֵי: The question arises: If levirate betrothal is effective by Torah law, and there is no Torah prohibition against performing the levirate betrothal, why should it preclude the rival wife from levirate marriage? This can be resolved by stating that the Sages would not instruct one to perform levirate betrothal in order to preclude the possibility of levirate marriage in a case where rabbinic prohibitions are involved (*Tosefot HaRosh*).

רַב אַשִׁי מַתְנֵי הָכִי, אֲמַר רַבִּי אֶלְעָזָר: לָא תֵּימָא מַאֲמָר לְבֵית שַׁמַּאי דָּחֵי דְּחִיָּיה גְּמוּרָה, וְצָרָתָהּ חֲלִיצָה נַמִּי לָא בָּעֲיָא, אֶלָּא דּוֹחֶה וּמְשַׁיֵּיר הוּא.

Rav Ashi teaches this discourse in **this manner: Rabbi Elazar said: Do not say** that **according to Beit Shammai levirate betrothal precludes** entering levirate marriage as **a complete preclusion,** so that **the rival wife** of the woman who received levirate betrothal **does not require even *ḥalitza*. Rather, it precludes** entering levirate marriage **and** yet **leaves a remnant** of the levirate bond in place. Accordingly, levirate betrothal precludes the rival wife's entering levirate marriage to the degree that the *yavam* is not required to divorce the woman he betrothed, but the levirate bond with the rival wife remains to the extent that he must still perform *ḥalitza* with her.

אָמַר רַבִּי אָבִין: אַף אֲנַן נַמִּי תָּנֵינָא: בֵּית שַׁמַּאי אוֹמְרִים: יְקַיְּימוּ. יְקַיְּימוּ – אִין, לְכַתְּחִלָּה – לָא. וְאִי סָלְקָא דַּעְתָּךְ מַאֲמָר לְבֵית שַׁמַּאי דּוֹחֶה דְּחִיָּיה גְּמוּרָה – זֶה יַעֲשֶׂה מַאֲמָר וְיִדְחֶה, וְזֶה יַעֲשֶׂה מַאֲמָר וְיִדְחֶה! וְאֶלָּא הָא קָתָנֵי, בֵּית שַׁמַּאי אוֹמְרִים: אִשְׁתּוֹ עִמּוֹ, וְהַלֵּזוּ תֵּצֵא מִשּׁוּם אֲחוֹת אִשָּׁה!

Rabbi Avin said: We, too, **learn** this statement from the mishna, where it states: **Beit Shammai say: They may maintain them** as their wives. From here it can be deduced: **Yes, they may maintain them** as their wives after the fact; **no,** they are not allowed to marry them ***ab initio*. And if it enters your mind** to say that, **according to Beit Shammai, levirate betrothal precludes entering** levirate marriage as **a complete preclusion,** then **this** brother **should perform levirate betrothal and preclude** one sister from levirate marriage, **and that** brother **should perform levirate betrothal and preclude** the other sister from levirate marriage. The Gemara challenges this conclusion: **But didn't** the mishna **teach** that **Beit Shammai say: His wife remains with him, and this other is sent away due to** her status **as a sister of his wife?** This indicates that she is exempt from levirate marriage and does not even require *ḥalitza*.

אֶלָּא: יְבָמָה דְּחַזְיָא לְכוּלְּהוּ – חַזְיָא לְמִקְצָתָהּ. יְבָמָה דְּלָא חַזְיָא לְכוּלְּהוּ – לָא חַזְיָא לְמִקְצָתָהּ.

Rather, one must resolve this by asserting that **a *yevama* who is suitable for all of** the aspects of levirate marriage **is** also **suitable for part of it.** If a *yevama* is eligible for both levirate marriage and *ḥalitza* when she happens before the brothers, as in the case cited in the present mishna where the woman who happened before the third brother was permitted to enter into levirate marriage, she is eligible for part of it. This indicates that if the *yavam* does not take her in levirate marriage but performs only levirate betrothal, the levirate betrothal has sufficient legal force to preclude the rival wife completely. However, **a *yevama* who is not suitable for all of the** aspects of levirate marriage **is** also **not suitable for a part of it.** If the *yevama* is not eligible for levirate marriage, such as in the case referred to in the first mishna of this chapter, where both women happened simultaneously so that the *yavam* is not permitted to consummate the levirate marriage with either woman, she is not suitable for part of it. In that case, if the *yavam* performs levirate betrothal, it does not have the legal force to affect a total preclusion.

בָּעֵי רַבָּה: מַאֲמָר, לְבֵית שַׁמַּאי, נִישּׂוּאִין עוֹשֶׂה אוֹ אֵירוּסִין עוֹשֶׂה? אֲמַר לֵיהּ אַבָּיֵי: לְמַאי הִלְכְתָא?

§ With regard to Beit Shammai's opinion about levirate betrothal, **Rabba asks: Does levirate betrothal, according to** the opinion of **Beit Shammai, create** a full-fledged **marriage** bond? **Or, does** it merely **create betrothal,**[N] similar to all other acts of betrothal? **Abaye said to him: With regard to what *halakha*** do you ask this?

NOTES

Does it…create a marriage bond or does it create betrothal – **נִישּׂוּאִין עוֹשֶׂה אוֹ אֵירוּסִין עוֹשֶׂה**: The marriage process consists of two steps. The first is the act by which a woman becomes betrothed to a man. The bond created by betrothal is so strong that a betrothed woman requires a divorce before she can marry another man. Similarly, intercourse with other men is considered adulterous and is punishable by death. During the period of betrothal, a couple may not live together as man and wife, and most of the couple's mutual obligations do not yet apply.

The second step, marriage itself, is effected when the bride and groom enter the bridal canopy. This immediately confers upon the newlywed couple both the privileges and the responsibilities associated with marriage. In modern times, both betrothal and marriage take place during the wedding.

אִילֵימָא לְיוֹרְשָׁהּ וְלִיטַּמֵּא לָהּ וּלְהָפֵר נְדָרֶיהָ – הַשְׁתָּא אֲרוּסָה בְּעָלְמָא תָּנֵי רַבִּי חִיָּיא: אִשְׁתּוֹ אֲרוּסָה לֹא אוֹנֵן וְלֹא מִטַּמֵּא לָהּ, וְכֵן הִיא לֹא אוֹנֶנֶת וְלֹא מִטַּמְּאָה לוֹ, מֵתָה – אֵינוֹ יוֹרְשָׁהּ, מֵת הוּא – גּוֹבָה כְּתוּבָּתָהּ, עֲבַד בָּהּ מַאֲמָר מִיבַּעְיָא?

If we say it pertains **to inheriting** from **her** when she dies, **and to becoming ritually impure for her**[N] if he is a priest, **and to nullifying her vows,**[N] all of which are rights and obligations acquired by marriage, this is difficult. **Now,** with regard to **a betrothed woman in general,** i.e., a woman who was betrothed by Torah law, **Rabbi Ḥiyya teaches** in a *baraita*: **One does not enter acute mourning**[N] on the day of the death of **his betrothed wife, nor can he become ritually impure for her** if she dies if he is a priest. **Similarly, she does not enter acute mourning for him and** is **not** obligated **to become ritually impure for him.**[NH] **If she dies, he does not inherit from her;**[H] **if he dies, she collects** the payment of **her marriage contract;**[H] In a case where **he performed** only **levirate betrothal with her, is it necessary to say**[N] that he does not inherit from her, nor does he become ritually impure for her? Therefore, this *halakha* is obvious and Rabba's question seems superfluous.

וְאֶלָּא לְעִנְיַן מְסִירָה לְחוּפָּה, מַאי? נִישּׂוּאִין עוֹשֶׂה – וְלָא בָּעֲיָא מְסִירָה לְחוּפָּה, אוֹ דִּלְמָא אֵירוּסִין עוֹשֶׂה – וּבָעֲיָא מְסִירָה לְחוּפָּה!

Rather, the question must relate **to the matter of delivery** of the woman **to** the husband under **a wedding canopy.**[N] **What is** the ruling with regard to this? Is the *yavam* obligated to enter the wedding canopy in the manner that he would with any other betrothed woman, or not? This is the dilemma: Does levirate betrothal **create** a full-fledged **marriage** bond, whereby the *yevama* **would not require** further **delivery to a wedding canopy? Or, does** levirate betrothal **perhaps create** only **betrothal,** whereby **she would require delivery to a wedding canopy?**

HALAKHA

Mourning and impurity for a betrothed woman – אֲבֵלוּת וְטוּמְאָה בַּאֲרוּסָה: If a man's betrothed dies, he does not enter the state of acute mourning or regular mourning for her, nor does a woman enter acute or regular mourning over the death of her betrothed. If the man is a priest, he may not become ritually impure for her, and she is not obligated to become ritually impure for him (Rambam *Sefer Shofetim, Hilkhot Evel* 2:3; *Shulḥan Arukh, Yoreh De'a* 373:4, 374:4, *Even HaEzer* 55:5).

If she dies he does not inherit from her – מֵתָה אֵינוֹ יוֹרְשָׁהּ: If a man's betrothed dies, he does not inherit from her (Rambam *Sefer Nashim, Hilkhot Ishut* 22:2; *Shulḥan Arukh, Even HaEzer* 55:5).

If he dies she collects the payment of her marriage contract – מֵת הוּא, גּוֹבָה כְּתוּבָּתָהּ: If one betroths a woman, writes her a wedding contract, and then dies before he is able to bring her under the wedding canopy, then she may collect the primary dues that are a mandatory part of the contract from his available property, but not the voluntary additions that the husband added from his own accord.

Although some say that the Sages established that every betrothed woman should automatically receive a wedding contract, even if one was not actually written for her (Rosh; Ran), it is not the custom to act in accordance with this opinion, but rather according to the opinion that states that the automatic institution of a wedding contract only applies to married women (Rema; Rambam *Sefer Nashim, Hilkhot Ishut* 10:11; *Shulḥan Arukh, Even HaEzer* 55:6).

NOTES

To becoming ritually impure for her – לִיטַּמֵּא לָהּ: Priests are prohibited from contracting ritual impurity through proximity with a corpse. The exception to this principle is the funeral of certain relatives, including wives.

To nullifying her vows – לְהָפֵר נְדָרֶיהָ: The Torah authorizes a husband to nullify vows made by his wife (see Numbers, chapter 30). The vow must be nullified on the same day on which the husband hears of it. A husband is empowered to nullify only those vows which either directly or indirectly affect the personal relationship between him and his wife.

Enter into acute mourning – אוֹנֵן: The period of acute mourning begins on the day of the death of a close relative, i.e., a spouse, father, mother, son, daughter, brother, or sister. The mourner is exempt from all positive mitzvot from the time of the death of the close relative until after the burial. At that point, his status changes from that of an acute mourner to that of a mourner.

Not obligated to become ritually impure for him – לֹא מִיטַּמְּאָה לוֹ: There is a halakhic difficulty here, as there is no prohibition against a priestly woman becoming ritually impure for the dead. Why would she not become impure for her husband? Rashi maintains that this phrase is only cited in order to create a parallelism between the obligations of the man and the woman. Additionally he suggests perhaps this is referring to the period of the Festivals, where there is a general prohibition to become impure. The Ritva and other commentaries concur with the *Tosafot*, suggesting that this phrase indicates that the woman is not obligated to become impure for him.

He performed levirate betrothal with her, is it necessary to say – עֲבַד בָּהּ מַאֲמָר מִיבַּעְיָא: It would seem from Rashi that even according to Beit Shammai levirate betrothal only has the force of rabbinic law. Many commentaries challenge this opinion from several different sources. For example, it is stated in the Jerusalem Talmud that Beit Shammai derive the obligation to perform levirate betrothal from an explicit verse in the Torah: "And he shall take her" (Deuteronomy 25, 5). The Rashba, therefore, understands that Rashi did not intend to propose that Beit Shammai held levirate betrothal to have the force of rabbinic law, but rather that even according to their opinion that levirate betrothal has the force of Torah law, it is still not equivalent to actual betrothal. For example, a *yevama* who received levirate betrothal is not sentenced to stoning if she commits adultery.

To the matter of delivery to a wedding canopy – לְעִנְיַן מְסִירָה לְחוּפָּה: *Tosefot HaRosh* explains, in accordance with *Tosafot*, that this discussion does not refer to a case where the *yavam* performed levirate betrothal alone, but rather to a case where he performed levirate betrothal and also engaged in sexual intercourse. Since a woman is normally not considered to be married unless she willingly enters the wedding canopy, a question arises: When the *yavam* engages in intercourse with her against her will, is there no longer any need for her to willingly enter the wedding canopy, as levirate marriage is effective even without the woman's consent? Or perhaps, as Rabba asserts, once she received levirate betrothal consensually, she is now rendered like any other woman and cannot become his full wife without consenting to marriage?

אָמַר לֵיהּ: הַשְׁתָּא, לֹא עֲבַד בָּהּ מַאֲמָר כְּתִיב ״יְבָמָהּ יָבֹא עָלֶיהָ״, בְּעַל כָּרְחָהּ, עָבַד בָּהּ מַאֲמָר מִיבַּעְיָא?

Abaye **said to him** that this question is not necessary, as well: **Now,** if **he did not perform levirate betrothal with her** at all, **it is written: "Her brother-in-law will have intercourse with her"** (Deuteronomy 25:5). It is deduced from this verse that he can take her even **against her will. Is it necessary** to say **that** if **he performed levirate betrothal with her,** even without a wedding canopy, that he is allowed to engage in sexual intercourse with her?

אָמַר לֵיהּ: שֶׁאֲנִי אוֹמֵר כׇּל הָעוֹשֶׂה מַאֲמָר בִּיבִמְתּוֹ – פָּרְחָה מִמֶּנּוּ זִיקַת יְבָמִין, וְחָלָה עָלֶיהָ זִיקַת אֵירוּסִין. מַאי?

Rabba **said to him:** This question is relevant, as **I say** that **anyone who performs levirate betrothal with his** ***yevama*** **causes the levirate bond to be removed from him,** and he is no longer considered subject to the *halakhot* of levirate marriage. Instead, a standard **bond of betrothal applies to him.** Therefore, it is appropriate to ask if this act of levirate betrothal is similar to a standard betrothal insofar as the wedding canopy is concerned, and consequently the woman would be required to enter the wedding canopy. Alternatively, perhaps the *halakhot* of levirate marriage still apply somewhat, in which case the woman would not be required to enter a wedding canopy in order to become married, similar to a standard *yevama* to whom levirate betrothal was not performed. Does the performance of levirate betrothal weaken the capacity of intercourse to establish levirate marriage on its own? **What** is the halakhic ruling here?

תָּא שְׁמַע: שׁוֹמֶרֶת יָבָם, בֵּין יָבָם אֶחָד בֵּין שְׁנֵי יְבָמִין, רַבִּי אֱלִיעֶזֶר אוֹמֵר: יָפֵר, רַבִּי יְהוֹשֻׁעַ אוֹמֵר: לְאֶחָד וְלֹא לִשְׁנַיִם, רַבִּי עֲקִיבָא אוֹמֵר: לֹא לְאֶחָד וְלֹא לִשְׁנַיִם.

The Gemara suggests: **Come** and **hear** an answer from what is taught in a mishna (*Nedarim* 74a): What is the ruling with regard to the nullification of vows for **a widow** who is **waiting for her** ***yavam,***[H] **whether** she is waiting for **a single** ***yavam*** **or two** ***yevamin*****? Rabbi Eliezer says: Let him nullify** her vows. The *yavam* may nullify her vows as though he were her husband. **Rabbi Yehoshua says:** This holds true only if she is bonded to **a single** ***yavam,*** **but not** to **two. Rabbi Akiva says:** It does **not** hold true, neither **to one** *yavam* **nor to two** *yevamin*. They may not they nullify her vows.

וְהָוֵינַן בַּהּ: בִּשְׁלָמָא רַבִּי עֲקִיבָא סָבַר: אֵין זִיקָה אֲפִילּוּ לְחַד, לְרַבִּי יְהוֹשֻׁעַ: לְחַד – יֵשׁ זִיקָה, לִתְרֵי – אֵין זִיקָה. אֶלָּא לְרַבִּי אֱלִיעֶזֶר, נְהִי נָמֵי דְּקָסָבַר יֵשׁ זִיקָה. בִּשְׁלָמָא לְחַד – מֵיפַר, אֶלָּא לִתְרֵי – אַמַּאי?

And we discussed this issue, interpreting the various opinions: **Granted, Rabbi Akiva holds that the levirate bond is not substantial,**[N] **even in** the case of **one** *yavam*. In his opinion, the levirate obligation does not create a marriage bond at all, even if there is only a single *yavam*. And according **to Rabbi Yehoshua, the levirate bond with one** ***yavam*** **is substantial.** The *yevama* undoubtedly requires this *yavam* for levirate marriage, and therefore she is considered to be like his wife. **But with two** ***yevamin,*** **the levirate bond is not substantial,**[N] since it is not clear which brother will consummate the levirate marriage with her. **However, Rabbi Eliezer,** if he **indeed holds that the levirate bond is substantial,** his opinion is difficult. **Granted,** if there is **one** *yavam*, **he can nullify** her vows, **but** if there are **two,** why should only one of them suffice to nullify her vows, as it is not yet clear which of them will eventually marry her?

וְאָמַר רַבִּי אַמִי (בַּר אַהֲבָה): הָכָא בְּמַאי עָסְקִינַן – כְּגוֹן דַּעֲבַד בָּהּ מַאֲמָר, וּבֵית שַׁמַּאי הִיא, דְּאָמַר: מַאֲמָר קוֹנֶה קִנְיָן גָּמוּר.

And Rabbi Ami bar Ahava said: With what are we dealing here? This is a case **where** one of them **performed levirate betrothal with her, and this is** in accordance with **the opinion of Beit Shammai, who say: Levirate betrothal acquires** her **as a full-fledged acquisition.**

אִי אָמְרַתְּ בִּשְׁלָמָא נִשּׂוּאִין עוֹשֶׂה – מִשּׁוּם הָכִי מֵיפַר, אֶלָּא אִי אָמְרַתְּ אֵירוּסִין עוֹשֶׂה – הֵיכִי מָצֵי מֵיפַר? וְהָתְנַן: נַעֲרָה הַמְאוֹרָסָה אָבִיהָ וּבַעְלָהּ מְפִירִים נְדָרֶיהָ! אָמַר רַב נַחְמָן בַּר יִצְחָק: מַאי מֵיפֵר – מֵיפֵר בְּשׁוּתָּפוּת.

This interpretation can resolve Rabba's question. **Granted, if you say** levirate betrothal **creates** a full-fledged **marriage, it is due to that** reason that the *yavam* **can nullify** her vows just as a full-fledged husband does. **However, if you say** that levirate betrothal merely **creates betrothal,**[N] **how can he nullify** the vows? Even in standard cases of betrothal by Torah law the husband cannot nullify her vows, **for didn't we learn** in a mishna: With regard to **a betrothed young woman,** only **her father and her husband** together can **nullify her vows?**[H] How could a *yavam* nullify the vows without the father of the *yevama*, if he is not considered a full-fledged husband? **Rav Naḥman bar Yitzḥak said** that this proof can be rejected by interpreting the mishna as follows: **What is** the meaning of the phrase: He **nullifies? That he nullifies** her vows only **in conjunction** with her father.

HALAKHA

Nullification of vows for a widow waiting for her *yavam* – הֲפָרַת נִדְרֵי שׁוֹמֶרֶת יָבָם: With regard to a woman awaiting levirate marriage, the *yavam* may not nullify her vows, whether she is waiting for several *yevamin* or just one, in accordance with the statement of Rabbi Akiva (Rambam *Sefer Hafla'a, Hilkhot Nedarim* 11:23; *Shulḥan Arukh, Yoreh De'a* 234:7).

Nullification of vows for a betrothed young woman – הֲפָרַת נִדְרֵי נַעֲרָה מְאוֹרָסָה: With regard to a betrothed young woman, her father and betrothed nullify her vows together (Rambam *Sefer Hafla'a, Hilkhot Nedarim* 11:9; *Shulḥan Arukh, Yoreh De'a* 234:5).

NOTES

Rabbi Akiva holds that the levirate bond is not substantial – רַבִּי עֲקִיבָא סָבַר אֵין זִיקָה: According to Rashi, Rabbi Akiva holds that the levirate bond is not substantial on any level, and therefore this woman is not considered to be the wife of the *yavam*. Others explain that even Rabbi Akiva agrees that the levirate bond has the force of rabbinic law, but since the nullification of vows is a Torah law, the levirate bond is not effective with regard to these *halakhot* in this case (Rabbi Avraham min HaHar).

With two the levirate bond is not substantial – לִתְרֵי אֵין זִיקָה: Rashi states that in the case of multiple *yevamin*, the levirate bond is weakened. Other commentaries differ and explain that this ruling is due to the fact that nullification of vows entails a clear knowledge of the identity of the husband at the time of the nullification, as retroactive designation does not apply to the *halakhot* of vows. Even if the *yevama* is later married to the brother-in-law who nullified her vows, this clarification is not effectual after the fact.

However, if you say it creates betrothal, etc. – אֶלָּא אִי אָמְרַתְּ אֵירוּסִין עוֹשֶׂה וכו׳: Although Abaye and Rabba discussed only whether levirate betrothal is equivalent to a betrothal by Torah law, here the Gemara seems to entertain the notion that levirate betrothal might be more powerful than standard betrothal, in that the *yavam* would be able to nullify vows on his own (*Tosefot HaRosh*; see Rashba).

NOTES

Any woman who makes a vow, etc. – כָּל הַנּוֹדֶרֶת וכו׳: The commentaries ask: If providing a woman's sustenance is reason enough to justify the husband's ability to nullify his wife's vows, then why was it necessary for the Torah to write the passage on nullification of vows? It must be that this halakhic rationale was established after the Torah explicitly stated the primary ruling with regard to the nullification of vows (*Tosafot Yeshanim*). This idea can be found in a slightly different form in the Responsa of the Rosh, where he says that even though one does not generally interpret the *halakha* based on the underlying rationale of the verses, in the case of nullification of vows, one does utilize the underlying rationale in order to determine how to apply the *halakhot*.

וְלְרַבִּי אֶלְעָזָר, דְּאָמַר: מַאֲמָר לְבֵית שַׁמַּאי אֵינוֹ קוֹנֶה אֶלָּא לִדְחוֹת לַצָּרָה בִּלְבַד, אַמַּאי מֵיפֵר בְּשׁוּתָּפוּת? אָמַר לָךְ רַבִּי אֶלְעָזָר: אֵימַר דַּאֲמַרִי אֲנָא אֵינוֹ קוֹנֶה אֶלָּא לִדְחוֹת לַצָּרָה בִּלְבַד – דְּלָא סַגִּי לָהּ בְּגִיטָּא אֶלָּא בָּעֵי נַמִי חֲלִיצָה, לְהָפֵר נְדָרֶיהָ – מִי אָמְרִינַן?

The Gemara questions this reading of the mishna: **And according to** the opinion of **Rabbi Elazar, who said** that **for Beit Shammai levirate betrothal acquires** the woman **only** insofar **as it precludes a rival wife** from entering levirate marriage, and it is not a full-fledged acquisition, **why should** the *yavam* **nullify** her vows, even if he does so **in conjunction** with her father? The Gemara answers: **Rabbi Eliezer** could have **said to you:** One can **say that** when **I said** that levirate betrothal **acquires** the woman **only** insofar **as it precludes the rival wife** from entering levirate marriage, it was to emphasize **that a bill of divorce would not suffice for her, but rather she also requires *ḥalitza*.** However, with regard **to** the matter of **nullifying her vows, do we say** that levirate betrothal is not effective, and that he cannot nullify her vows alone?

וְאִיבָּעֵית אֵימָא, אָמַר לָךְ רַבִּי אֶלְעָזָר: וּלְרַב נַחְמָן בַּר יִצְחָק מִי נִיחָא? מִי קָתָנֵי ״יָפֵרוּ״? ״יָפֵר״ קָתָנֵי. אֶלָּא הָכָא בְּמַאי עָסְקִינַן – שֶׁעָמְדָה בְּדִין וּפָסְקוּ לָהּ מְזוֹנוֹת מִשֶּׁלּוֹ,

And if you wish, say an alternate explanation: **Rabbi Elazar** could have **said to you: And as for Rav Naḥman bar Yitzḥak, does this** resolution that the mishna is only referring to a case where the father and the *yavam* can nullify her vows together **work out well? Did the** mishna **teach** that **they** can **nullify** her vows? **It teaches** that **he** can **nullify** her vows in the singular, implying that he nullifies the vows alone and not in conjunction with anyone else. **Rather,** the mishna must be explained differently: **With what are we dealing here?** It is a case where the *yavam*, regardless of whether or not he performed levirate betrothal, did not want to consummate the levirate marriage or perform *ḥalitza*. Therefore, the *yevama* **stood in court** so as to compel him to consummate the levirate marriage or perform *ḥalitza*, **and it ruled that he** must supply **her sustenance.** Because she is bound to him and cannot marry another, the court ruled that he was responsible for her livelihood.

וְכִדְרַב פִּנְחָס מִשְּׁמֵיהּ דְּרָבָא, דְּאָמַר רַב פִּנְחָס מִשְּׁמֵיהּ דְּרָבָא: כָּל הַנּוֹדֶרֶת – עַל דַּעַת בַּעְלָהּ הִיא נוֹדֶרֶת.

And this is in accordance with the statement that **Rav Pineḥas** said **in the name of Rava, as Rav Pineḥas said in the name of Rava: Any woman who makes a vow,**[N] **makes her vow with the consent of her husband.** Because she is dependent upon her husband for her livelihood, she does not act without his consent. In this case, because the *yavam* is responsible to supply the *yevama* with sustenance, it is assumed that her vows are also made with his consent. It is for this reason that he can nullify her vows without her father. Consequently, no conclusive proof can be derived from here with regard to the strength of acquisition through levirate betrothal.

Perek **III**
Daf **30** Amud **a**

מתני׳ שְׁלֹשָׁה אַחִין, שְׁנַיִם מֵהֶם נְשׂוּאִים שְׁתֵּי אֲחָיוֹת וְאֶחָד נָשׂוּי נׇכְרִית. מֵת אֶחָד מִבַּעֲלֵי אֲחָיוֹת, וְכָנַס נְשׂוּי נׇכְרִית אֶת אִשְׁתּוֹ, וָמֵת – הָרִאשׁוֹנָה יוֹצְאָה מִשּׁוּם אֲחוֹת אִשָּׁה, וּשְׁנִיָּה מִשּׁוּם צָרָתָהּ. עָשָׂה בָּהּ מַאֲמָר וָמֵת – נׇכְרִית חוֹלֶצֶת וְלֹא מִתְיַיבֶּמֶת.

MISHNA In the case of **three brothers, two of whom were married to two sisters and one who was married to an unrelated woman,** the following occurred: **The husband of one of the sisters died** childless, **and** the brother **who was married to the unrelated woman married,** i.e., performed levirate marriage with, the deceased brother's **wife and** later **died** himself, childless. In this situation, both women happen for levirate marriage before the other, remaining, brother. **The first** woman **is dismissed due to** the prohibition proscribing **the sister of one's wife,** as she is the sister of this brother's wife, **and the second** woman is dismissed **due to** her status as the first woman's **rival wife.** Following the first levirate marriage, this second woman became the rival wife of the sister, and is therefore exempt from levirate marriage as well. If, however, the brother married to the unrelated woman **performed** only **levirate betrothal,** but had not yet consummated the levirate marriage with the sister, **and he died, the unrelated woman,** whose halakhic status with regard to *yibbum* is similar to that of a sister's rival wife, must **perform *ḥalitza* and may not enter into levirate marriage.**

גמ׳ טַעְמָא דַּעֲבַד בָּהּ מַאֲמָר, הָא לָא עֲבַד בָּהּ מַאֲמָר – נָכְרִית יַבּוּמֵי נַמִי מִיַּיבְּמָה. אָמַר רַב נַחְמָן: זֹאת אוֹמֶרֶת אֵין זִיקָה, וַאֲפִילּוּ בְּחַד אַחָא.

GEMARA The Gemara deduces the following *halakha* from the second clause of the mishna: **The reason** that the mishna requires *ḥalitza* is specifically **because he,** the brother who was married to the unrelated woman, **performed levirate betrothal with** the sister.[N] **Consequently, had he not performed levirate betrothal with her, the unrelated woman** would be permitted to **enter into levirate marriage as well.** This is true despite the fact that the levirate bond could potentially render her the rival wife of his wife's sister. **Rav Naḥman said: That is to say, the** levirate **bond is not substantial;**[N] the woman requiring levirate marriage is not considered married to the *yavam*. **And** this is true **even** if the levirate bond was **with a single brother,** as this widowed sister happened for levirate marriage only before the brother who was married to the unrelated woman; her levirate bond was with him alone.

מתני׳ שְׁלֹשָׁה אַחִים, שְׁנַיִם מֵהֶם נְשׂוּאִים שְׁתֵּי אֲחָיוֹת וְאֶחָד נָשׂוּי נָכְרִית. מֵת הַנָּשׂוּי נָכְרִית, וְכָנַס אֶחָד מִבַּעֲלֵי אֲחָיוֹת אֶת אִשְׁתּוֹ וָמֵת – הָרִאשׁוֹנָה יוֹצְאָה מִשּׁוּם אֲחוֹת אִשָּׁה, וּשְׁנִיָּה מִשּׁוּם צָרָתָהּ. עָשָׂה בָּהּ מַאֲמָר וָמֵת – נָכְרִית חוֹלֶצֶת וְלֹא מִתְיַיבֶּמֶת.

MISHNA In the case of **three brothers, two of whom were married to two sisters and one who was married to an unrelated woman,** the following occurred: **He who was married to the unrelated woman died, and one of the husbands of the sisters married his wife, and** then **died** childless as well. **The first** woman, i.e., the sister who was originally married to the brother who performed levirate marriage, **is dismissed** and is exempt from levirate marriage **due to** her status as **the sister of his wife. And the second** woman, i.e., the unrelated woman who had entered into levirate marriage, is dismissed **as her rival wife.**[H] If, however, **he performed levirate betrothal** with the unrelated woman, **and** then **died,** then this **unrelated woman** must **perform *ḥalitza* and may not enter into levirate marriage,** as levirate betrothal rendered her status with regard to *yibbum* as similar to the rival wife of his wife's sister.

גמ׳ הָא תּוּ לָמָּה לִי? הַיְינוּ הָךְ! הָשְׁתָּא, וּמָה הָתָם דַּאֲחוֹת אִשָּׁה הָוְיָא צָרָה לְנָכְרִית אָמְרַתְּ: נָכְרִית אֲסוּרָה, הָכָא, דְּנָכְרִית הָוְיָא צָרָה לַאֲחוֹת אִשָּׁה – לֹא כׇּל שֶׁכֵּן?

GEMARA The Gemara asks: **Why do I need this** mishna **as well? This** principle **is identical**[N] to the principle behind the ruling in the previous mishna, and therefore this ruling can easily be deduced from the previous ruling. **Now, just as there,**[N] **when** his **wife's sister became rival wife of the unrelated woman**[N] who was already the brother's wife, **you say that the unrelated woman is forbidden** despite the fact that the forbidden relative joined later, **here, where the unrelated woman became the rival wife of** his **wife's sister** afterward, is it **not all the more so** clear that she is exempt as a rival wife?

HALAKHA

Exemption for the rival wife of a forbidden relative – פְּטוֹר צָרַת עֶרְוָה: In the case where there were three brothers, two of whom were married to two sisters and one who was married to an unrelated woman, the following occurred: The brother who was married to the unrelated woman died, and the husband of the first sister married his wife, the unrelated woman, and then died childless as well. Two women now happen before the third brother, the husband of the second sister, for levirate marriage, and both are exempt from levirate marriage and *ḥalitza*, one as a sister of his wife and the other as the rival wife of that first sister. If the husband of a sister did not enter into marriage with the unrelated woman, whether or not he performed levirate betrothal with her, then the unrelated woman must perform *ḥalitza* and may not enter into levirate marriage, for she would be the rival wife of his wife's sister by levirate bond. This is the opinion of the Rif, the Rosh, and other halakhic authorities who conclude that the *halakha* is in accordance with the opinion of Rav Ashi, who states that the levirate bond is substantial, as appears later.

The Rambam, however, cites the language of the mishna, specifying that the husband performed levirate betrothal. According to the *Tur*, the Rambam holds that specifically if he performed levirate betrothal with the unrelated woman would she be required to perform *ḥalitza* (see *Or Same'aḥ*). The *Beit Yosef* holds, however, that the Rambam accepted the Rif's opinion but merely opted to copy the formulation found in the mishna rather than be precise (Rambam *Sefer Nashim, Hilkhot Yibbum* 7:7; *Shulḥan Arukh, Even HaEzer* 175:7).

NOTES

The reason is because he performed levirate betrothal with the sister – טַעְמָא דַּעֲבַד בָּהּ מַאֲמָר: In the Jerusalem Talmud as well, both this mishna and the following one are understood as referring specifically to cases where he performed levirate betrothal. They explain there that the ruling in the mishna conforms with both the opinion of Rabbi Shimon, who is in doubt as to whether levirate betrothal effects a full-fledged acquisition or does not bring about acquisition at all, as well as according to the opinion of the Rabbis, who hold that levirate betrothal effects a partial acquisition. According to both opinions, albeit for different reasons, the woman performs *ḥalitza* but may not enter into levirate marriage.

That is to say, the levirate bond is not substantial – זֹאת אוֹמֶרֶת אֵין זִיקָה: *Tosafot* wonder: Why did Rav Naḥman not deduce this from the first mishna of the second chapter of the tractate? One commentary explains that it could be said that the purpose of that earlier mishna was only to exclude the statement of Beit Shammai with regard to levirate betrothal, and therefore one could not deduce the status of the levirate bond from there. However, it was necessary to say this only once, such that when the mishna repeated this ruling it perforce indicated that the levirate bond is not substantial (Rabbi Akiva Eiger). Additionally, since the previous mishna in this chapter mentioned the dispute between the houses of Shammai and Hillel with regard to the issue of levirate betrothal, it would not be appropriate for the next mishna to categorically exclude the opinion of Beit Shammai (*Melo HaRo'im*).

This is identical, etc. – הַיְינוּ הָךְ וכו׳: *Tosafot* point out that in other cases the Gemara might have resolved this question by invoking the structural principle: This, and it is unnecessary to say that. There are times when the mishna states two *halakhot* and the second one seems to be unnecessary and obvious once the first one is stated. This redundancy is resolved by attributing the repetition to the style of: this, and it is unnecessary to say that. In this case, however, that explanation does not suffice, because the entire mishna is superfluous. Furthermore, if that were the case it would have been possible to unite the two *mishnayot* with a single opening (Ritva).

Now just as there, etc. – הָשְׁתָּא וּמָה הָתָם וכו׳: Rashi and most of the commentaries hold that the question and answer revolve primarily around the fact that he performed levirate betrothal. However, the Rashash holds that this could be referring to the principal *halakha* itself: Is the rival wife of a forbidden relative prohibited only if she was the second wife, married after the forbidden relative herself?

His wife's sister became rival wife of the unrelated woman – אֲחוֹת אִשָּׁה הָוְיָא צָרָה לְנָכְרִית: The later commentaries explain in various ways why there might be a difference between rulings in these cases. One commentary explains that if he married the forbidden relative first, the prohibition with regard to a wife's sister was already in place, and there was never any possibility for the rival wife to become eligible to enter into levirate marriage. If, however, he had married the rival wife first, it could be said that she was, by her very marriage, eligible to enter into levirate marriage, and that a forbidden relative cannot negate that original permitted status once it is in place (*Ḥiddushei Batra*; see *Or Same'aḥ*).

תַּנָּא הַךְ תָּנָא בְּרֵישָׁא, וְהַךְ חַזְיָא לְהֶיתֵּירָא, וְשַׁרְיָא. וַהֲדַר חַזְיָא לְאִיסּוּרָא.

The Gemara answers: This mishna was unnecessary, and this is how the duplication occurred: **The *tanna* taught this** mishna **at first, and** with regard to **that** previous case **saw it** fitting to render her **permitted, and he permitted** her to the brother, for he held that if the forbidden relative joined the man's household later, then she would not render the first wife prohibited as the rival wife of a forbidden relative. **And then** the *tanna* subsequently retracted and **saw it** fitting **to** render the woman **forbidden.** He decided that this woman should be considered the rival wife of a forbidden relative as well, and therefore rendered her forbidden to the brother.

וְאַיְּידֵי דַּחֲבִיבָה לֵיהּ – אַקְדְּמָהּ, וּמִשְׁנָה לֹא זָזָה מִמְּקוֹמָהּ.

And since that case was novel, **it was beloved to him and he taught it earlier.** In truth, it would have now been possible to eliminate the present mishna, for there was no longer any novelty in it; its ruling could be derived by an *a fortiori* argument from the previous ruling. **However, a mishna does not move from its place.**[B] Since this version of the mishna had already been fixed, it was deemed inappropriate to remove it completely, and it remained in place despite the fact that it was no longer necessary.

מתני׳ שְׁלֹשָׁה אַחִין, שְׁנַיִם מֵהֶם נְשׂוּאִים שְׁתֵּי אֲחָיוֹת וְאֶחָד נָשׂוּי נָכְרִית. מֵת אֶחָד מִבַּעֲלֵי אֲחָיוֹת, וְכָנַס נְשׂוּי נָכְרִית אֶת אִשְׁתּוֹ, וּמֵתָה אִשְׁתּוֹ שֶׁל שֵׁנִי, וְאַחַר כָּךְ מֵת נְשׂוּי נָכְרִית – הֲרֵי זוֹ אֲסוּרָה עָלָיו עוֹלָמִית, הוֹאִיל וְנֶאֶסְרָה עָלָיו שָׁעָה אַחַת.

MISHNA In the case of **three brothers, two of whom were married to two sisters and one who was married to an unrelated woman,** the following occurred: **One of the husbands of the sisters died, and he who was married to the unrelated woman married** the deceased husband's **wife, and** then **the wife of the second** brother, the other one of the sisters, **died. Afterward,** the brother **who was married to the unrelated woman died,** leaving two women for levirate marriage before the remaining brother: The unrelated woman and the woman who was previously prohibited as the sister of his deceased wife. In this case, the sister **is forbidden to him**[N] **forever.** She is not forbidden due to her status as his wife's sister, as his wife already died and one's wife's sister is permitted after the wife's death. However, **since she was** already **forbidden to him at one time,**[H] she is forbidden to him forever. When she first happened before the brothers for levirate marriage, before the third brother married her, she was forbidden to the second brother as his wife's sister. Therefore, she is forbidden to him forever. In addition, she exempts her rival wife, the unrelated woman, from levirate marriage.

גמ׳ אָמַר רַב יְהוּדָה אָמַר רַב: כָּל יְבָמָה שֶׁאֵין אֲנִי קוֹרֵא בָּהּ בִּשְׁעַת נְפִילָה ״יְבָמָהּ יָבֹא עָלֶיהָ״ הֲרֵי הִיא כְּאֵשֶׁת אָח שֶׁיֵּשׁ לָהּ בָּנִים, וַאֲסוּרָה. מַאי קָא מַשְׁמַע לָן? תְּנֵינָא: הֲרֵי זוֹ אֲסוּרָה עָלָיו עוֹלָמִית, הוֹאִיל וְנֶאֶסְרָה עָלָיו שָׁעָה אַחַת!

GEMARA **Rav Yehuda said** that **Rav said** a principle on this matter: **Any *yevama* to whom the verse "Her brother-in-law will have intercourse with her"** (Deuteronomy 25:5) **cannot be applied at the time that she happens** before him for levirate marriage because she was forbidden to him at that moment, **is then** forever considered to be **like the wife of a brother** with whom **she has children, and she is forbidden** to him. The Gemara asks: **What is** Rav **teaching us** with this statement? **We** already **learned** this in the mishna: **She is forbidden to him forever, since she was forbidden to him at one time.**

מַהוּ דְּתֵימָא: הָנֵי מִילֵּי – הֵיכָא דְּלָא אִיחַזְיָא לָהּ בִּנְפִילָה רִאשׁוֹנָה, אֲבָל הֵיכָא דְּאִיחַזְיָא לָהּ בִּנְפִילָה רִאשׁוֹנָה – אֵימָא תִּישְׁתְּרֵי, קָא מַשְׁמַע לָן.

The Gemara answers: This was necessary **lest you say that this** ruling **applies** only in cases **where she was not eligible** at all **during** the **first** time that she **happened** before the brothers for levirate marriage. Such is the case in the mishna, when she was forbidden to the *yavam* as his wife's sister the entire time that she was eligible for levirate marriage. Even though his wife died after the other *yavam* married this woman, because she was forbidden to him that entire time, she is forbidden to him forever. **But** in cases **where she was eligible** at some point **during** the **first** time she **happened** before the brothers for levirate marriage, such as in the scenario where the brother's wife died prior to the time when his other brother married her, one could **say** that **she would be permitted.** In that case, since the prohibition had in the meantime been canceled and she was indeed rendered eligible for levirate marriage with him during the period of the first time she happened before him, one might think that she would now be permitted. It is for this reason that Rav **teaches us** that even in this scenario she would be forbidden to him forever.

BACKGROUND

A mishna does not move from its place – מִשְׁנָה לֹא זָזָה מִמְּקוֹמָהּ: There is a dispute among the early commentaries, as well as among modern scholars, as to whether Rabbi Yehuda HaNasi actually wrote the Mishna or if he merely edited it into its final form for the purposes of oral study. In either case, even according to those who say that he fixed the Mishna in writing, it was not commonly available, and its study primarily continued orally. Since students learned the *mishnayot* orally in their proper order, omitting a particular mishna and replacing it with a similar one, or combining two *mishnayot* into one, could cause confusion in the students' learning. It is for this reason that Rabbi Yehuda HaNasi left the original mishna in place, even if it was unnecessary (see Ritva).

NOTES

The sister is forbidden to him – הֲרֵי זוֹ אֲסוּרָה עָלָיו: The Rambam in his Commentary on the Mishna writes that while the *halakha* with regard to a sister was explicit, the *halakha* with regard to the unrelated woman, her rival wife, was not, and in his opinion she must perform *ḥalitza* but may not enter into levirate marriage due to uncertainty. In contrast, the Rambam himself concludes in *Mishne Torah*, in accordance with the opinions of all the early commentaries, that this woman is released without *ḥalitza*. If we decide, as does Rav, that the sister is forbidden like the wife of a brother who has children, then her rival wife is the rival wife of a forbidden relative and is exempt. The later commentaries attempt to explain Rambam's uncertainty in this matter.

HALAKHA

She was forbidden to him at one time – נֶאֶסְרָה עָלָיו שָׁעָה אַחַת: In the case of three brothers, two of whom were married to two sisters and one who was married to an unrelated woman, the following occurred: One of the husbands of the sisters died, and the brother who was married to the unrelated woman married his wife. Later, the wife of the other brother, i.e., the sister of the woman who entered into levirate marriage, died. Afterward, the brother who was married to the unrelated woman died. In this case, the widowed brother is not permitted to take his deceased brother's wife in levirate marriage because she was forbidden to him the first time she happened before him for levirate marriage. As she was forbidden to him at one time, she is forbidden to him forever (Rambam *Sefer Nashim*, *Hilkhot Yibbum* 7:11; *Shulḥan Arukh*, *Even HaEzer* 175:1).

הָא נַמִּי תְּנֵינָא: שְׁנֵי אַחִין נְשׂוּאִין שְׁתֵּי אֲחָיוֹת, מֵת אֶחָד מֵהֶם וְאַחַר כָּךְ מֵתָה אִשְׁתּוֹ שֶׁל שֵׁנִי – הֲרֵי זוֹ אֲסוּרָה עָלָיו עוֹלָמִית, הוֹאִיל וְנֶאֶסְרָה עָלָיו שָׁעָה אַחַת!

The Gemara raises an objection: **We learned** this **as well,** as a later mishna (32a) states: In the case of **two brothers who were married to two sisters,** if **one of them,** i.e., one of the brothers, **died and afterward the wife of the second** brother **died, then she,** the surviving wife, **is forbidden to him,** the surviving brother, **forever, since she was forbidden to him** during the period she happened before him **at one time.**

מַהוּ דְּתֵימָא: הָתָם הוּא דְּאִידַּחִי לָהּ מֵהַאי בֵּיתָא לְגַמְרֵי. אֲבָל הָכָא, דְּלָא אִידַּחֵי לָהּ מֵהַאי בֵּיתָא לְגַמְרֵי, אֵימָא: מִיגּוֹ דַּחֲזְיָא לְהַאי נָשׂוּי נָכְרִית חַזְיָא נַמִּי לְהַאי, קָא מַשְׁמַע לָן.

The Gemara answers: One cannot learn the halakhic principle from that case. **Lest you say that there** she is forbidden forever because of the following argument: When she was forbidden to the brother, **she was precluded from** entering **this household completely,** i.e., from the entire obligation of levirate marriage. She received total exemption from the mitzva of levirate marriage because this obligation applied only to the one remaining brother, and she was forbidden to him at the time that she happened before him for levirate marriage. But **here, however,** in the case Rav is referring to, **where she was not completely precluded from** entering **this household** because she still required levirate marriage with another brother, one could **say: Since she is eligible** and permitted **to this** brother, **who was married to the unrelated woman, she is eligible for this** second brother following the death of his wife **as well,** in other words, she was not rendered completely exempt from the obligation of levirate marriage. Lest one make this argument, Rav **teaches us** that under any circumstances she who was forbidden at one time is forbidden forever.

מתני׳ שְׁלֹשָׁה אַחִים, שְׁנַיִם מֵהֶם נְשׂוּאִין שְׁתֵּי אֲחָיוֹת וְאֶחָד נָשׂוּי נָכְרִית. גֵּירֵשׁ אֶחָד מִבַּעֲלֵי אֲחָיוֹת אֶת אִשְׁתּוֹ, וּמֵת נָשׂוּי נָכְרִית, וּכְנָסָהּ הַמְגָרֵשׁ וָמֵת – זוֹ הִיא שֶׁאָמְרוּ: וְכוּלָּן שֶׁמֵּתוּ אוֹ נִתְגָּרְשׁוּ – צָרוֹתֵיהֶן מוּתָּרוֹת.

MISHNA In the case of **three brothers,**[B] **two of whom were married to two sisters and one who was married to an unrelated woman,** the following occurred: Shimon, **the husband of one of the sisters, divorced**[NH] **his wife, and** then Levi, **who was married to the unrelated woman, died, and** Shimon, **the man who divorced** his wife, **married,** i.e., performed levirate marriage with, **her,**[N] i.e., this unrelated woman. **And** then Shimon himself later **died,** so that the unrelated woman happened for levirate marriage before Reuven, the third brother, who is married to the second sister. In this scenario, Reuven is allowed to consummate the levirate marriage with the unrelated woman. **This is** the case that was referred to when **they said: And** with regard to **all those** fifteen forbidden relatives **who died or were divorced, their rival wives are permitted** to enter into levirate marriage. This is because at the time that they happened before the *yavam* for levirate marriage they were no longer the rival wives of a forbidden relative.

NOTES

Three brothers…divorced, etc. – שְׁלֹשָׁה אַחִים...גֵּירֵשׁ וכו׳: *Tosafot* ask why it was necessary to state that there were three brothers, for this *halakha* could have been taught in a case with only two brothers. They explain this according to several different opinions. The Rashba writes that according to Rava's opinion cited later it was indeed not necessary to describe a case with three brothers. However, as the entire chapter is referring to cases of three brothers, that number was used in this case as well despite the fact that it is not necessary.

The man who divorced his wife married her – כְּנָסָהּ הַמְגָרֵשׁ: *Tosafot* ask how the man who divorced his wife could possibly marry this woman, for is she not the rival wife of his wife's sister due to the levirate bond with the third brother? They explain that while the husband who divorced his wife is alive, it is not relevant to consider the unrelated woman as the rival wife of his wife's sister. The issue of the rival wife of his wife's sister by levirate bond is relevant only when the other brother dies and both women happen before the third brother for levirate marriage (see *Tosefot HaRosh*).

HALAKHA

He who divorces the close relative of his *yevama* – הַמְגָרֵשׁ אֶת קְרוֹבַת יְבִמְתּוֹ: In the case of three brothers, two of whom were married to two sisters and one of whom was married to an unrelated woman, the following occurred: The husband of one of the sisters divorced his wife, and the one married to an unrelated woman died, and the man who divorced his wife married this unrelated woman and then died. This woman would be permitted to the third brother, as she had never been the rival wife of his wife's sister.

If, however, the brother who was married to the unrelated woman died first, and then the husband of one of the sisters divorced his wife, even if he did not manage to marry the unrelated woman, she would nevertheless be forbidden to the remaining brother because she was the rival wife of his wife's sister by levirate bond, prior to the divorce.

And if the husband of one of the sisters entered into marriage with the unrelated woman and divorced the sister (whether the divorce took place before or after the marriage to the unrelated woman), if this brother dies as well then the unrelated woman is permitted to the husband of the other sister, for he takes her in levirate marriage as a consequence of the latest marriage, and at the time that she happened before him she was no longer the rival wife of his wife's sister (Rambam *Sefer Nashim, Hilkhot Yibbum* 7:12; *Shulḥan Arukh, Even HaEzer* 175:8).

BACKGROUND

Three brothers – שְׁלֹשָׁה אַחִים: There were three paternal brothers, Reuven, Shimon, and Levi. Reuven and Shimon married two sisters, Ḥogla and Milka, respectively, while Levi married Miriam, who was not related to either of them. Eventually, Milka died, after which Levi died childless, and Shimon took Miriam in levirate marriage. If Shimon then dies childless, Reuven is allowed to take Miriam in levirate marriage, since she was never the rival wife of his wife's sister.

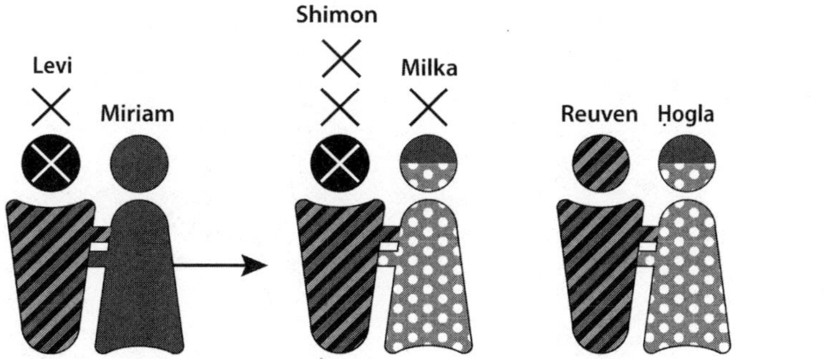

גמ׳ טַעְמָא דְּגֵירֵשׁ וְאַחַר כָּךְ מֵת, אֲבָל מֵת וְאַחַר כָּךְ גֵּירֵשׁ – אֲסוּרָה. אֲמַר רַב אַשִׁי; זֹאת אוֹמֶרֶת יֵשׁ זִיקָה, אֲפִילּוּ בִּתְרֵי אַחֵי.

GEMARA The Gemara deduces from here that **the reason** for this *halakha* is specifically **that** Shimon **divorced** his wife **and after that** Levi **died** and Shimon married the unrelated woman. **But** if Levi had **died** first, **and later** Shimon **divorced** his wife, then the unrelated woman would be **forbidden** to Reuven due to the levirate bond that existed between her and Shimon prior to the latter's divorce. She would be considered the rival wife of the divorced woman who is the sister of Reuven's wife. **Rav Ashi said: That is to say, the** levirate **bond is substantial, even with two brothers.** Although the unrelated woman required levirate marriage with two brothers, the levirate bond is substantial enough to create a relationship between the unrelated woman and Shimon such that the unrelated woman is considered the rival wife of the divorced woman, i.e., the sister of Reuven's wife.

וּלְרַב אַשִׁי קַשְׁיָא דְּרַב נַחְמָן! אֲמַר לָךְ רַב אַשִׁי: הוּא הַדִּין דְּאַף עַל גַּב דְּלָא עֲבַד בָּהּ מַאֲמָר נָכְרִית – מִיחֲלַץ חָלְצָה, יַבּוּמֵי לָא מְיַיבְּמָה. וְהָא דְּקָתָנֵי מַאֲמָר – לְאַפּוּקֵי בֵּית שַׁמַּאי, דְּאָמְרִי: מַאֲמָר קוֹנֶה

The Gemara asks: **And according to Rav Ashi,** that which **Rav Naḥman** said is **difficult,** as Rav Naḥman deduced from the earlier mishna that the levirate bond is not substantial even in the case of a single brother. The Gemara answers: **Rav Ashi** could have **said to you:** Rav Naḥman's deduction in the first mishna was not logically necessary. With regard to that mishna, one could have said that when the mishna requires *ḥalitza* in the case of levirate betrothal, **the same is true even** in the case **where he** who was married to the unrelated woman **did not perform levirate betrothal with her.** In that case as well, **the unrelated woman must perform *ḥalitza* and may not enter into levirate marriage** since she was the rival wife of his wife's sister by levirate bond. **And** the reason **that it teaches** the ruling in the case of **levirate betrothal** was not in order to inform us that she was forbidden due to levirate betrothal, but rather **to exclude** the statement of **Beit Shammai,**[N] **who say** that through the act of **levirate betrothal** one **acquires** the *yevama*

NOTES

To exclude the statement of Beit Shammai – לְאַפּוּקֵי בֵּית שַׁמַּאי: The question arises: If this mishna comes to exclude the statement of Beit Shammai, then why was it necessary to teach this twice, both here and in the second chapter? Alternatively, why was it necessary to teach in both places that the levirate bond is not substantial? Some commentaries explain that according to Rav Ashi, it is more reasonable to hold that the levirate bond is not substantial, and therefore it was necessary to repeat this in order to emphasize that the mishna is not teaching that the levirate bond is not substantial but rather that the mishna is excluding Beit Shammai's statement. Similarly, according to the opinion of Rav Naḥman, it is more reasonable to maintain that the levirate bond is substantial, and therefore the matter was taught twice in order to emphasize that it is not (*Tosefot HaRosh*; *Tosafot Yeshanim*).

קִנְיָן גָּמוּר, קָא מַשְׁמַע לָן דְּלָא כְּבֵית שַׁמַּאי.

as **a full-fledged acquisition.** According to that opinion, the unrelated woman does not even require *ḥalitza*, since she is considered to be a rival wife of a forbidden relative. This mishna **teaches us that** the *halakha* **is not in accordance with** the opinion of **Beit Shammai.**

וּלְרַב נַחְמָן קַשְׁיָא דְּרַב אַשִׁי! וְכִי תֵּימָא: הוּא הַדִּין דַּאֲפִילּוּ מֵת וְאַחַר כָּךְ גֵּירֵשׁ צָרָתָהּ מוּתֶּרֶת, אֶלָּא ״זוֹ הִיא״ לְמַעוּטֵי מַאי – לְמַעוּטֵי כָּנַס וְאַחַר כָּךְ גֵּירֵשׁ,

The Gemara raises a question from the opposite perspective: **And according to Rav Naḥman,** who deduced from the earlier mishna that the levirate bond is not substantial, the deduction **of Rav Ashi** that the levirate bond is substantial is **difficult. And if you would** try to resolve this in a similar manner and **say:** With regard to the ruling in the present mishna, which states that the sister's **rival wife,** i.e., the unrelated woman, **is permitted, the same is true even if** Levi had **died and** then **afterward** the brother married to the other sister **divorced** his wife, there is a difficulty. If that is the case, then **what does** the phrase **this is,** cited at the end of the mishna, come **to exclude?**[N] If we follow this explanation then the same ruling would hold true in all cases. The Gemara responds: **It excludes** the case where Shimon first **married** the unrelated woman **and** only **afterward divorced** the sister, as in such circumstances the unrelated woman is most certainly a rival wife of Reuven's wife's sister and is therefore not permitted.

הָנִיחָא אִי סָבַר לַהּ כְּרַבִּי יִרְמְיָה, דְּאָמַר: תַּבְרָא, מִי שֶׁשָּׁנָה זוֹ לֹא שָׁנָה זוֹ,

The Gemara states: **This works out well if he holds in accordance with** the opinion of **Rabbi Yirmeya, who said** with regard to a seeming contradiction between this mishna and an earlier mishna (13a): The *mishnayot* are **disjointed; he who taught this** mishna **did not teach that** mishna. The earlier mishna established the principle that if a man was married to two women, one of whom was a forbidden relative, and he divorced the forbidden relative before he died, then the rival wife is no longer prohibited to the brothers.

וְהַאי תַּנָּא סָבַר מִיתָה מַפֶּלֶת, וְהַאי תַּנָּא סָבַר נִישּׂוּאִין הָרִאשׁוֹנִים מַפִּילִים.

This dispute is based upon the following: **This *tanna*** from the earlier mishna **holds that death determines** her status when **she happens** before the brothers, i.e., the crucial moment for determining whether the prohibition relating to rival wives applies is the moment at which the brother dies. In other words, whether the *yevama* is permitted to the *yavam* is determined by the status of the *yevama* at that given moment. Therefore, in the case where he had married a forbidden relative and later divorced her, the rival wife would be permitted. **And this *tanna*** of our present mishna **holds that the original marriage determines** her status when **she happens** before the brothers. If, at the time the woman was married to the deceased brother she was forbidden as a close relative, and her rival wife was likewise forbidden as the rival wife of a forbidden relative, then even though the status of the relative had changed at the time of the death of the brother, both she and her rival wife remain forbidden.

״זוֹ הִיא״ לְמַעוּטֵי כָּנַס וּלְבַסּוֹף גֵּירֵשׁ. אֶלָּא אִי סָבַר לַהּ כְּרָבָא, דְּאָמַר לְעוֹלָם חַד תַּנָּא הוּא, וְ״זוֹ וְאֵין צָרִיךְ לוֹמַר זוֹ״ קָתָנֵי – ״זוֹ הִיא״ לְמַעוּטֵי מַאי? עַל כָּרְחָךְ כְּרַבִּי יִרְמְיָה סְבִירָא לֵיהּ.

According to this opinion, it is indeed possible to state that the phrase **this is** comes **to exclude** the case where **he married** one woman **and ultimately divorced** the other. According to this mishna, in that case, the rival wives would be prohibited. **However, if he holds in accordance with** the opinion of **Rava, who said: Actually,** understand **this** to be the opinion of **a single *tanna*, and he teaches** the mishna employing the style: **This, and it is unnecessary to say that,** a difficulty remains. According to Rava, both *mishnayot* maintain the position that in the case where the *yavam* married one woman and ultimately divorced the other, the rival wife would be permitted. If that is the case, **what** does the phrase **this is** come **to exclude?** In what case would the rival wife be prohibited to the *yavam*? The Gemara responds: **Perforce** Rav Naḥman **holds in accordance with** the opinion of **Rabbi Yirmeya** with regard to his interpretation of the *mishnayot*.

NOTES

What does the phrase: This is, come to exclude – זוֹ הִיא לְמַעוּטֵי מַאי: The commentaries held different opinions as to the meaning of this passage and its practical implications. According to Rashi, both Rav Naḥman and Rav Ashi hold in accordance with the opinion of Rabbi Yirmeya that this mishna follows the opinion that the original marriage determines the status of the woman when she happens before the brothers for levirate marriage. Therefore, according to Rav Ashi, the phrase: This is, comes to exclude the case where one of the husbands married to a sister divorces his wife after the brother married to the unrelated woman dies. If he subsequently marries the unrelated woman and dies, this woman is forbidden upon his death to his other brother because she became the rival wife of his wife's sister by levirate bond. This is all the more true in the case where he married her prior to divorcing his wife. For Rav Naḥman, the phrase: This is, comes to exclude specifically the case where he married and then later divorced. Rava, however, holds that: This is, comes to exclude the case where he dies without divorcing his wife at all.

The Rif's opinion on this matter is complicated. He rules in accordance with Rav Ashi's opinion that if Levi, the brother married to the unrelated woman, dies before Shimon divorces the sister to whom he is married, then when Shimon also dies the unrelated woman is forbidden to his brother Reuven as the rival wife of his wife's sister through the levirate bond. He also rules that the time of death of the husband determines the woman's status with regard to levirate marriage. It is unclear why it should matter whether the divorce took place before or after Levi died. As long as Shimon had already divorced the sister before he died, the unrelated woman should not be regarded as the rival wife of a forbidden relative.

The Rif offers two explanations as to why she is nevertheless forbidden to Reuven under such circumstances. According to the first explanation, this is a special stringency that is an extension of the rabbinic decree that the levirate bond creates substantial relationships. Since at the time of Levi's death she was the rival wife of Reuven's wife's sister due to the levirate bond, she is forbidden to Reuven after Shimon's death. This is despite the fact that in the parallel case, where Shimon was actually married to her and to Reuven's wife's sister, and then Shimon divorced the sister and subsequently died, she would be permitted to Reuven, because at the time of Shimon's death she was not the rival wife of a forbidden relative.

The Rif's second, preferred explanation is that in this case, at the moment of Levi's death, the unrelated woman becomes the rival wife of Reuven's wife's sister due to the levirate bond. She is therefore rendered forbidden to Reuven as such. Even though she loses this status after Shimon divorces his wife, once she was rendered forbidden to Reuven the first time she happened before him for levirate marriage, she can no longer be rendered permitted to him.

HALAKHA

Uncertainty with regard to the rival wife of a forbidden relative – סְפֵק צָרַת עֶרְוָה: If a woman underwent a betrothal whose status is uncertain or a divorce whose status is uncertain with the deceased brother, and she was a forbidden relative to her brother-in-law, and the deceased brother had another wife, then that rival wife must perform *ḥalitza* and may not enter into levirate marriage (Rambam *Sefer Nashim, Hilkhot Yibbum* 6:22; *Shulḥan Arukh, Even HaEzer* 173:3).

Uncertainty with regard to betrothal – סְפֵק קִדּוּשִׁין: If both the man and the woman were standing in the public domain, or in a domain that did not belong to either, and he threw her the betrothal item but it was lost before it reached her hand, if it fell in a place that was possibly closer to him and possibly closer to her in such a way that both could have guarded the object, or both could equally have not guarded the object, then this is a case of betrothal whose status is uncertain (Rambam *Sefer Nashim, Hilkhot Ishut* 4:22; *Shulḥan Arukh, Even HaEzer* 30:5).

וּלְרָבָא, הָנִיחָא אִי סָבַר לַהּ כְּרַב אַשִׁי – ״זוֹ הִיא״ לְמַעוּטֵי מֵת בְּלֹא גֵּירֵשׁ, אֶלָּא אִי סָבַר לַהּ כְּרַב נַחְמָן: ״זוֹ הִיא״ לְמַעוּטֵי מַאי? עַל כׇּרְחָךְ כְּרַב אַשִׁי סְבִירָא לֵיהּ.

The Gemara raises a question from a different perspective: **And according to Rava,** who maintains that in both cases the rival wife is permitted, **this works out well if he holds in accordance** with the opinion **of Rav Ashi** that the levirate bond is substantial. In that case the phrase **this is** comes **to exclude** the case where **he died without divorcing his wife.** In this case the rival wife is forbidden because the entire time she was the rival wife of a forbidden relative by levirate bond. **If, however, he holds in accordance** with the opinion of **Rav Naḥman** in this matter, **what** does the phrase **this is** come **to exclude?** The Gemara answers: **Perforce Rava holds in accordance with** the opinion of **Rav Ashi.** Accordingly, with regard to this *halakha* there is a connection between the various opinions as to how to interpret the *mishnayot* and the dispute.

מתני׳ וְכוּלָּן שֶׁהָיוּ בָּהֶן קִדּוּשִׁין אוֹ גֵּרוּשִׁין בְּסָפֵק – הֲרֵי אֵלּוּ הַצָּרוֹת חוֹלְצוֹת וְלֹא מִתְיַיבְּמוֹת. כֵּיצַד סְפֵק קִדּוּשִׁין? זָרַק לָהּ קִדּוּשִׁין, סָפֵק קָרוֹב לוֹ סָפֵק קָרוֹב לָהּ – זֶהוּ סְפֵק קִדּוּשִׁין.

MISHNA **And** if **any of these** fifteen women who are prohibited as forbidden relatives **had undergone a betrothal or divorce** whose status **is uncertain**[H] with the deceased brother, **then those** women who were their **rival wives** must **perform *ḥalitza* and may not enter into levirate marriage** since they are possibly the rival wives of forbidden relatives. The mishna elaborates: **How** could there be a situation of **uncertainty** with regard to **betrothal?**[H] If in the public domain **he threw her** an item for the purpose of **betrothal** and there were eight cubits between them, and the item **was possibly closer to him**[N] and did not enter into her domain, and **possibly closer to her,** i.e., within four cubits of her, whereby she could acquire the object, **this is** a case of **uncertainty** with regard to **betrothal.**

סְפֵק גֵּרוּשִׁין – כָּתַב בִּכְתַב יָדוֹ וְאֵין עָלָיו עֵדִים, יֵשׁ עָלָיו עֵדִים וְאֵין בּוֹ זְמַן, יֵשׁ בּוֹ זְמַן וְאֵין בּוֹ אֶלָּא עֵד אֶחָד – זֶהוּ סְפֵק גֵּרוּשִׁין.

Uncertainty with regard to **divorce** occurs when, for instance, **he wrote a** bill of divorce **in his handwriting**[N] **but there are no** signatures of **witnesses on** the document, or **there are** the signatures of **witnesses** on the document **but there is no date** written **in it,** or **the date is** written **in it but there is only** the signature of **a single witness.** Since there is doubt as to whether these three kinds of bills of divorce are valid, a woman who was divorced through them is only possibly divorced, and so **this** case **is** called **uncertainty** with regard to **divorce.**[N]

גמ׳ וְאִילּוּ בְּגֵרוּשִׁין סָפֵק קָרוֹב לוֹ סָפֵק קָרוֹב לָהּ – לָא קָתָנֵי,

GEMARA The Gemara remarks: **But yet when** discussing **divorce, it does not teach** the case where it is **uncertain** if the bill of divorce **is closer to him, and uncertain if it is closer to her.** It would have been appropriate to describe this case, as it parallels the case involving the object of betrothal. He could have tossed it in such a way that it was not clear to whom the bill was closer.

NOTES

Possibly closer to him – סָפֵק קָרוֹב לוֹ: Rashi interprets this *halakha* as pertaining to the specific instance where there were exactly eight cubits between the two (see *Gittin* 78a). The Rashba, however, maintains that those conditions were stated specifically in the case of a bill of divorce, as it is required that the bill of divorce be delivered either into the woman's hand or into her domain. In contrast, with regard to betrothal, this condition is not necessary. Therefore, it is possible to establish that in this case there were more than eight cubits between them but there was doubt as to whether the item of betrothal was close enough to her that she could successfully guard it.

He wrote a bill of divorce in his handwriting – כָּתַב בִּכְתַב יָדוֹ: Rashi derives proof that a handwritten document is considered authoritative from the *halakhot* of documents where a bill of debt handwritten by the debtor is effectual even without witnesses, allowing the collection of payment of the debt from his available property. *Nimmukei Yosef* claims that these are not similar cases, since in monetary law a bill serves merely as evidence as to what had transpired, whereas a bill of divorce in fact creates the divorce itself. Accordingly, he offers an alternative reason. Since the verse states: "And he writes her a bill of divorce," if the man divorcing his wife himself writes the bill, this sufficiently fulfills the primary requirements of the *halakha*. The opinion in the Jerusalem Talmud, however, accords with that of Rashi, as a comparison is drawn between a handwritten bill of divorce and the *halakhot* of monetary documents.

This is uncertainty with regard to divorce – זֶהוּ סְפֵק גֵּרוּשִׁין: In truth, there is no actual doubt with regard to the divorce itself, since by Torah law these bills of divorce are effective. If she were to remarry subsequent to such a bill she would not require a divorce from her second husband. Rather, the Sages rendered these bills of divorce disqualified for various reasons, some of which are elucidated later. In any case, since they are not to be used *ab initio*, the Sages judged a woman who was divorced through them to be a divorcée whose status is uncertain. This is how the mishna is explained in the Jerusalem Talmud (see *Penei Moshe* there).

מאי טעמא? אמר רבה: אשה זו בחזקת היתר לשוק עומדת, ומספק אתה בא לאוסרה – אל תאסרנה מספק.

The Gemara asks: **What is the reason** the mishna did not present this situation as well? **Rabba said:** When this type of uncertainty exists, the performance of *ḥalitza* is not mandatory, as **this woman,** the rival wife, **has the presumptive status of being permitted** to marry a man **from the** general **public.**[N] At the time of her marriage she was rendered a rival wife of a forbidden relative. **And due to an uncertainty** alone **would you render her forbidden** to the general public until she performs *ḥalitza*, simply because it is unclear to us whether or not the forbidden relative had indeed been divorced? **Do not render her forbidden due to an uncertainty.** This is not, however, the case with the various bills of divorce mentioned in the mishna, for they are all certainly considered effective bills of divorce, even if the circumstances involved raise some questions or doubts.

אמר ליה אביי: אי הכי בקדושין נמי, נימא: אשה זו בחזקת היתר ליבם עומדת, ומספק אתה בא לאוסרה – אל תאסרנה מספק!

Abaye said to him: If that is so, let us say in the case of **betrothal as well** that **this woman,** the rival wife, **has the presumptive status of being permitted to the *yavam***[N] before he betrothed the forbidden relative, **and due to the uncertainty** whether she is the rival wife of a forbidden relative **would you come and render her forbidden? Do not render her forbidden due to an uncertainty.** Consequently, you should permit her to enter into levirate marriage.

– התם לחומרא.

The Gemara explains: **There,** with regard to betrothal, the *halakha* follows **the stringent ruling,** because the rival wife is certainly his wife and requires levirate marriage. As there is uncertainty with regard to the betrothal with the forbidden relative, the ruling is stringent; she may not enter into levirate marriage and must only perform *ḥalitza*.

האי – חומרא דאתי לידי קולא הוא; זימנין דאזיל הוא ומקדש לה לאחותה קדושי ודאי,

The Gemara objects: Yet **this is a stringency that might bring about a leniency**[N] in another scenario. How so? **Sometimes** that same man who betrothed the forbidden relative might **go and betroth her sister** with **a betrothal** whose status is **certain.** If one says that due to a stringency the rival wife may not enter into levirate marriage due to her possible status as the rival wife of a forbidden relative, people might come to assume that the betrothal with the forbidden relative was a valid betrothal, and that the subsequent betrothal with her sister was not valid, since she is his wife's sister. This would be assumed because they would not know that the status of the first betrothal was itself uncertain and that only due to a stringent ruling is the rival wife not allowed to enter into levirate marriage. In fact, the status of the betrothal with the sister of the forbidden relative is also uncertain. As a result of this ruling, however, people might be led to think that a man's wife, i.e., the sister of the forbidden relative, is in fact permitted.

NOTES

Has the presumptive status of being permitted to a man from the general public – בחזקת היתר לשוק עומדת: *Tosafot* raise two issues with regard to this *halakha.* The first relates to the woman's presumed permitted status: If the forbidden relative was his first wife, and later he married this other woman, only after which he performed a divorce whose status is uncertain with the forbidden relative, then clearly the rival wife is presumed to be permitted to the general public. However, if he first divorced the forbidden relative with a divorce whose status is uncertain and later married the rival wife, what reason could there be for the rival wife to have the presumptive status of being permitted? *Tosafot* explain that even here it makes sense for her to have the presumptive status of being permitted, since the marriage to the forbidden relative was certain and the divorce was uncertain. Therefore, at the time of the rival wife's marriage, due to the marriage whose status was certain that had previously taken place, the rival wife was rendered a rival wife of a forbidden relative. The Ramban, on the other hand, explains that this passage was said only with regard to the case where he married the rival wife and then later divorced the forbidden relative, but in the opposite case there would be no presumption of permissibility.

The second issue is more fundamental. It says that this woman is presumed to be permitted to the general public. However, it would seem that she had not yet merited such a status, as she was formerly married and therefore should have the status of a married woman who is forbidden to the public; only when her husband dies is there doubt with regard to the obligation of levirate marriage, and the question arises as to whether she should be permitted to the general public or not. This question is strengthened in light of the point some commentaries add that in the context of other *halakhot*, such as when there is doubt as to whether an animal was slaughtered properly, we presume from prohibition to prohibition. In other words, the prohibition against eating the animal in its life was not nullified even after it was slaughtered before us. Similarly, the woman should remain prohibited to the general public as a man's wife until we are certain that this prohibition no longer applies. The Ramban resolves this by saying that it is possible for an animal to remain prohibited, for certain reasons, even after its death, and therefore the prohibition is not automatically terminated with its death. This is different from the case of a woman, whose prohibited status ceases upon the death of her husband. The Rashba explains that an animal does not lose its prohibited status until some act is done, i.e., the appropriate slaughtering rituals, in order to render it fit for consumption. For a woman, however, the death of her husband suffices without any additional action (see *Tosafot Yeshanim*).

Has the presumptive status of being permitted to the *yavam* – בחזקת היתר ליבם עומדת: Here too the commentaries ask: This *halakha* is understandable in circumstances where he was first married to the rival wife and then later performed a betrothal whose status is uncertain with the forbidden relative, as it is clear that betrothal whose status is uncertain is not strong enough to nullify the rival wife's status as being permitted to the *yavam*. If, however, the betrothal whose status is uncertain took place first, then why would one assume the rival wife was permitted to the *yavam*? They explain that because the forbidden relative was originally single, and there is a doubt whether she lost this status, she maintains her presumed status as unmarried, and her rival wife cannot be rendered forbidden due to a betrothal whose status is uncertain (*Tosafot Yeshanim*).

A stringency that might bring about a leniency – חומרא דאתי לידי קולא: Often the Sages are stringent in places of doubt in order to prevent individuals from transgressing, and this is generally the reason for the tendency toward stringency. Occasionally, however, such as here, it is possible that stringency in one place will lead to a leniency in another. In such cases, it is best to leave the matter alone.

וְאִי נַמִּי זִימְנִין דְּאָתָא אַחֵר וּמְקַדֵּשׁ לָהּ לְדִידָהּ קִדּוּשֵׁי וַדַּאי, וְכֵיוָן דְּאָסַר לָהּ מָר לַצָּרָה לְיַיבּוּמֵי, אָמְרִי: דְּקַמָּא – קִדּוּשִׁין וּדְבַתְרָא – לָאו קִדּוּשִׁין.

Alternatively, sometimes another man might come and betroth the forbidden relative **herself** with **a betrothal** whose status is **certain, and since the Master** rendered it **prohibited** for **the rival wife to enter into levirate marriage,** people would **say** that the betrothal **of the first** man, i.e., the deceased brother, was a fully effective **betrothal, and** that the betrothal **of the latter** man **was not** a valid **betrothal.** If she was married to the first man, then she is forbidden to the second as the man's wife, and betrothal cannot take effect with her. However, since the status of her betrothal to the first man was uncertain, then she is also considered possibly betrothed to the second man and would require a divorce from him as well. As a result, one can find a situation that would lead people to think that a man's wife is in fact permitted.

Perek **III**
Daf **31** Amud **a**

NOTES

All will know that this is merely a stringency – וּמֵידַע יָדְעִי דְּחוּמְרָא בְּעָלְמָא הוּא: The Rosh raises an objection: How would they know that this is a stringency? With regard to the case where there is a betrothal whose status is uncertain, if the rival wife is required to perform *ḥalitza* because she is not exempt from levirate marriage, it would be known that this is a stringent measure. With regard to divorce, however, they might think that the man is performing the *ḥalitza* simply because he does not wish to marry her for some other reason, and so there is no proof from here that there is a stringency involved. He resolves this by saying that Abaye is objecting to Rabba's line of reasoning, where it was suggested that requiring *ḥalitza* would constitute a stringency that could lead to a leniency. In that context it was clear that Rabba assumed that people were aware of why *ḥalitza* was being performed (*Tosefot HaRosh*).

If she performs *ḥalitza* she might also enter into levirate marriage – אִם חוֹלֶצֶת מִתְיַיבֶּמֶת: The following objection could be raised: Since in several places the Sages declared that a woman must perform *ḥalitza* due to some doubt, why did they not fear that she might mistakenly enter into levirate marriage in those cases as well? The commentaries resolve this by saying that if the concern and the doubt are general, then there is no reason to assume that they might make this mistake. Here, however, a new decree is being introduced by requiring *ḥalitza* for this woman, and therefore it is necessary to check that in fact all of the problems are solved thereby (*Yosef Lekaḥ*).

Let her enter into levirate marriage and there is no problem with that – וְתִתְיַיבֵּם וְאֵין בְּכָךְ כְּלוּם: The talmudic discussion is as follows: Initially, the Gemara assumed that the concern lest she enter into levirate marriage was that this would nullify the rabbinic decree requiring the woman to perform *ḥalitza* in this case. This response indicates that the concern is not for the rabbinic ordinance, but rather for the status of the woman, and since here she is presumed permissible, there is no reason to be concerned lest she enter into levirate marriage (Ritva; see *Melo HaRo'im*).

כֵּיוָן דְּקָא מַצְרְכַתְּ חֲלִיצָה – מֵידַע יָדְעִי דְּחוּמְרָא בְּעָלְמָא הוּא. אִי הָכִי גֵּירוּשִׁין נַמִי לִיתְנֵי, וְלִיצְרְכָהּ חֲלִיצָה, וּמֵידַע יָדְעִי דְּחוּמְרָא בְּעָלְמָא הוּא!

Rabba answered: **Since you require** ***ḥalitza*** and you do not exempt her completely, all will **know that this is merely a stringency**[N] and that the Sages did not decide with certitude that the first betrothal was fully valid. Consequently, they would not come to disregard the other betrothal. Abaye raised a challenge: **If so, let** the mishna **teach** the case where it is uncertain whether the item is closer to him or closer to her with regard to **divorce, and** stipulate **that she requires** ***ḥalitza*****. And they would know that this is merely a stringency** and not make a mistake.

אִם אַתָּה אוֹמֵר חוֹלֶצֶת – מִתְיַיבֶּמֶת. הָכָא נַמִי: אִם אַתָּה אוֹמֵר חוֹלֶצֶת – מִתְיַיבֶּמֶת! וְתִתְיַיבֵּם, וְאֵין בְּכָךְ כְּלוּם – אַחֲזָקָהּ קָא קַיְימָא.

He answered him: A mistake could in fact be made here, as, **if you say that** she must **perform** ***ḥalitza*** then **she** may also **enter into levirate marriage.** People might mistakenly think that if she is suitable for *ḥalitza* then she is also suitable for levirate marriage, and as a result the woman might enter into levirate marriage, despite the fact that it is forbidden for her to do so. Abaye objected: **Here too,** in the case of uncertain betrothal, the concern exists that **if you say that she performs** ***ḥalitza*** then **she** might also **enter into levirate marriage.**[N] Rabba answered: **So let her enter into levirate marriage, and** there is **no** problem **with that.**[N] In this instance **she remains with** her **presumptive status** as permitted because she was originally assumed to be permitted and was rendered forbidden only due to our concern. However, there would be no actual transgression involved even if she were to enter into levirate marriage.

אֵיתִיבֵיהּ אַבַּיֵי: נָפַל הַבַּיִת עָלָיו וְעַל בַּת אָחִיו, וְאֵין יָדוּעַ אֵיזֶה מֵהֶם מֵת רִאשׁוֹן – צָרָתָהּ חוֹלֶצֶת וְלֹא מִתְיַיבֶּמֶת.

Abaye raised an objection to Rabba by citing a case where even in places of doubt, the woman requires *ḥalitza*. As we learned in a mishna (67b): **A house fell on him,** on a certain man, **and on his brother's daughter** to whom this man was married, and he was childless, **and it is unknown which of them died first.** If the deceased wife had a rival wife, then **her rival wife** must **perform** ***ḥalitza*** **but may not enter into levirate marriage.** If the man had died first, then at the time of his death the rival wife was forbidden to the *yavam* as the rival wife of his daughter and exempt from levirate marriage. If, however, the daughter had died first, then at the time of the husband's death the second wife was not the rival wife of a forbidden relative, and requires levirate marriage. It is due to this doubt that she must perform *ḥalitza* and may not enter into levirate marriage.

אַמַּאי? הָכָא נַמִי נֵימָא: אִשָּׁה זוֹ בְּחֶזְקַת הֶיתֵּר לַשּׁוּק עוֹמֶדֶת, וּמִסָּפֵק אַתָּה בָּא לְאוֹסְרָהּ – אַל תַּאַסְרֶנָּה מִסָּפֵק!

And according to Rabba's opinion, **why is that so? Here too, let us say: This woman,** the rival wife, **has the presumptive status of** being **permitted** to marry a man **from the** general **public.** This is because she was exempt from levirate marriage for the entire period of her marriage as the rival wife of a forbidden relative. **And due to the uncertainty** whether her rival wife was the first to die **you come to render her forbidden** and require that she perform *ḥalitza*. **Do not render her forbidden due to an uncertainty.**

וְכִי תֵּימָא: הָכָא נַמִּי לְחוּמְרָא – חוּמְרָא דְּאָתֵי לִידֵי קוּלָּא הוּא, שֶׁאִם אַתָּה אוֹמֵר חוֹלֶצֶת – מִתְיַיבֶּמֶת! גֵּירוּשִׁין דִּשְׁכִיחִי גָּזְרוּ בְּהוּ רַבָּנַן, מַפּוֹלֶת דְּלָא שְׁכִיחִי – לָא גָּזְרוּ בְּהוּ רַבָּנַן.

And if you would say: Here too, we rule **more stringently** due to the uncertainty. Nevertheless, **this would be a stringency that brings about a leniency, for if you say that she** must **perform *ḥalitza*, she may** also **enter into levirate marriage.** However, it is forbidden for her to enter into levirate marriage, because she is possibly forbidden to the *yavam* as the rival wife of his daughter and therefore forbidden just like the daughter herself. Rabba replied: In cases of **divorce, which are common, the Sages issued a rabbinic decree** preventing her from performing *ḥalitza* due to a concern that if she were required to perform *ḥalitza* then she may enter into levirate marriage as well. In cases of **collapse, which are not common,**[N] **the Sages did not issue a rabbinic decree,** because they did not introduce decrees with regard to uncommon matters.

אִי נַמִּי: גֵּירוּשִׁין דְּקַיְימָא עֶרְוָה דְּקָא מוֹכַח, וְצָרָתָהּ קָמַצְרְכַתְּ לַהּ חֲלִיצָה – אָמְרִי: קָמוּ בֵּיהּ רַבָּנַן בְּגִיטָּא דְּגִיטָּא מַעַלְיָא הוּא, וְאָתוּ לְיַיבּוּמֵי לְצָרָה. מַפּוֹלֶת – מִי קָמוּ בְּהוּ רַבָּנַן בְּמַפּוֹלֶת?

Alternatively, there is another reason to differentiate between the cases. In the case of **divorce where there is a forbidden relative who indicates** that the rival wife is forbidden due to her status as the rival wife of a forbidden relative, **and you require that her rival wife perform *ḥalitza*,** people **will say: The Sages determined that this bill of divorce is a full-fledged bill of divorce.** Consequently, they required her rival wife to perform *ḥalitza*, **and** people **may come to consummate the levirate marriage with the rival wife** based on this mistaken assumption. In cases of **collapse,** however, **could the Sages have determined** who died first **in the collapse?** As it is known to all that there was a doubt that could not be clarified, it is clear that the Sages required the rival wife to perform *ḥalitza* only due to this uncertainty. Therefore, there is no concern that she would come to enter into levirate marriage because of this *ḥalitza*.

וְגַבֵּי גֵּירוּשִׁין מִי לָא תְּנַן? וְהָתְנַן: הָיְתָה עוֹמֶדֶת בִּרְשׁוּת הָרַבִּים וּזְרָקוֹ לָהּ, קָרוֹב לָהּ – מְגוֹרֶשֶׁת, קָרוֹב לוֹ – אֵינָהּ מְגוֹרֶשֶׁת. מֶחֱצָה עַל מֶחֱצָה – מְגוֹרֶשֶׁת וְאֵינָהּ מְגוֹרֶשֶׁת.

The Gemara asks: **But did we not learn** in a mishna about the case where it is uncertain whether the bill of divorce is closer to him or closer to her **with regard to** situations of **divorce** whose status is uncertain? **And didn't we learn** in a mishna: In a case where his wife **was standing in the public domain and he threw her** the bill of divorce, if the bill landed **closer to her, she is divorced.** If it was **closer to him, she is not divorced.** If it was **half and half,** i.e., if the bill of divorce landed midway between the man and the woman, there is uncertainty whether **she is divorced or** whether **she is not divorced.**[H]

וְאָמְרִינַן: לְמַאי הִלְכְתָא – דְּאִי כֹּהֵן הוּא אֲסוּרָה לֵיהּ, וְאִי עֶרְוָה הִיא – צָרָתָהּ בָּעֲיָא חֲלִיצָה. וְלָא אָמְרִינַן שֶׁאִם אַתָּה אוֹמֵר חוֹלֶצֶת מִתְיַיבֶּמֶת!

And we say: With regard to what *halakha*[N] was the ruling said that she is both divorced and not divorced? The Gemara explains that this affects two areas of *halakha*. The first is **that if** the man divorcing his wife **is a priest,** then his wife **is forbidden to him** due to the uncertainty that she may in fact be divorced through that bill of divorce. Consequently, he would then be unable to remarry her. The second ramification is that **if** the woman being divorced **was a forbidden relative** to her husband's brother, and her husband died childless, then **her rival wife would require *ḥalitza*.** The mishna indicates that in this type of divorce whose status is uncertain as well, the Sages require the rival wife to perform *ḥalitza*, and **we do not say that if you say** that **she** must **perform *ḥalitza*,** she may **enter into levirate marriage.** Here there is no concern.

HALAKHA

A bill of divorce about which it is uncertain if it was closer to her – גֵּט שֶׁסָּפֵק קָרוֹב לָהּ: If a man and his wife were standing in the public domain, or in a domain that did not belong to either of them, and the husband threw her a bill of divorce, the *halakha* is as follows: If it was closer to her, she is divorced. If it was closer to him, she is not divorced. If it was midway between them, she is both divorced and not divorced. In such a case, if her husband was a priest she would be forbidden to him, and if she herself was a forbidden relative with regard to her brother-in-law, then her rival wife must perform *ḥalitza* and may not enter into levirate marriage (Rambam *Sefer Nashim, Hilkhot Geirushin* 5:13; *Shulḥan Arukh, Even HaEzer* 139:13).

NOTES

Cases of collapse, which are not common – מַפּוֹלֶת דְּלָא שְׁכִיחִי: The Rashash raises an objection: If the Sages did not enact rabbinic decrees for matters that were not common, then why did they nevertheless issue a decree for the woman in this case, i.e., that she must perform *ḥalitza*? He responds that they decreed that she must perform *ḥalitza* for a different reason that is common: They were concerned that others might conclude that any time a forbidden relative dies, the rival wife does not require *ḥalitza*. In *Ḥiddushei Batra* this is resolved by the explanation that in cases where the woman's presumptive status cannot be conclusively determined, it cannot be relied upon with regard to Torah law. In this case, as there is no way to determine whether the rival wife was the rival wife of a forbidden relative at the time of death, her presumptive status cannot be relied upon and she must perform *ḥalitza*. However, the concern that others might mistakenly take her in levirate marriage is not commonplace, and therefore the Sages did not enact a decree on the basis of such a concern.

And we say: With regard to what *halakha* – וְאָמְרִינַן לְמַאי הִלְכְתָא: One could object to this interpretation of the mishna in light of the fact that it was asserted by the *amora'im*. How can the Gemara then object to Rabba, an *amora* himself, from their statement? In *Ḥiddushei Batra* the answer is given that perhaps this interpretation of the mishna was an authoritative tradition that had been passed down. *Arukh LaNer* writes that this interpretation could be deduced from the language of the mishna itself, since it does not state that she is a divorcée whose status is uncertain but rather that she is both divorced and not divorced, implying that the matter must be ruled stringently, as though she were both divorced and not divorced.

הָא אִיתְּמַר עֲלָהּ, רַבָּה וְרַב יוֹסֵף דְּאָמְרִי תַּרְוַויְיהוּ: הָכָא בִּשְׁתֵּי כִּיתֵּי עֵדִים עָסְקִינַן, אַחַת אוֹמֶרֶת: קָרוֹב לָהּ, וְאַחַת אוֹמֶרֶת: קָרוֹב לוֹ, דַּהֲוָה לֵיהּ סְפֵיקָא דְּאוֹרָיְיתָא. וּמַתְנִיתִין דְּהָכָא בְּכַת אַחַת, דַּהֲוָה לֵיהּ סְפֵיקָא דְּרַבָּנַן.

The Gemara responds: **But wasn't it stated with regard to** that mishna that this is referring to a very specific set of circumstances? It is **Rabba and Rav Yosef who both say:** The doubt here does not result from the facts of the case themselves, but from conflicting testimonies and an inability to decide between them. **Here, we are dealing with two sets of witnesses, one** of which **says** that the bill fell **closer to her, and one** of which **says** that it fell **closer to him. This,** then, **is an uncertainty** in matters **of Torah** law, for in this case there are two testimonies, each one complete by itself, yet they contradict one another. Such instances are deemed to have the status of an uncertainty with regard to Torah law, and therefore the ruling is stringent. **But the mishna here is referring to one set**[N] of witnesses who were divided in their testimony or who could not clarify exactly what had occurred. **This is** considered to be an **uncertainty** in matters **of rabbinic** law[N] alone, as there is only a single uncorroborated testimony, and in cases of uncertainty in matters of rabbinic law the ruling is lenient.

וּמִמַּאי דְּמַתְנִיתִין דְּהָכָא בְּכַת אַחַת? דּוּמְיָא דְּקִדּוּשִׁין, מַה קִּדּוּשִׁין בְּכַת אַחַת – אַף גֵּרוּשִׁין בְּכַת אַחַת. וְקִדּוּשִׁין גּוּפַיְיהוּ מִמַּאי דִּבְכַת אַחַת, דִּלְמָא בִּשְׁתֵּי כִּיתֵּי עֵדִים? אִי בִּשְׁתֵּי כִּיתֵּי עֵדִים – תִּתְיַיבֵּם, וְאֵין בְּכָךְ כְּלוּם.

The Gemara asks: **And from where** is it known **that the mishna here** is referring to a case of uncertainty **with one set** of witnesses? The Gemara responds: **It is similar to that of betrothal. Just as** with regard to **betrothal** it is referring to a case of uncertainty **with one set of witnesses, so too,** with regard to **divorce** it is referring to a case **of one set** of witnesses. The Gemara wonders: **And** with regard to **betrothal itself, from where** is it known that the mishna is referring to a case of uncertainty **that** involves **one set** of witnesses? **Perhaps** it is referring to a case **of two sets** of witnesses? The Gemara answers: **If** the mishna is referring to a case **of two sets of witnesses** who contradict one another, then **let her enter into levirate marriage, and** there is **no** problem **with that,** as there are two witnesses testifying that there was never a betrothal. Therefore, both the cases of betrothal and divorce must be referring to a situation where there is one set of witnesses.

קַיְימִי עֵדִים וְקָאָמְרִי "קָרוֹב לָהּ" וְאַתְּ אָמְרַתְּ תִּתְיַיבֵּם וְאֵין בְּכָךְ כְּלוּם?! וְתוּ: בִּשְׁתֵּי כִּיתֵּי עֵדִים נַמִי סְפֵיקָא דְּרַבָּנַן הִיא, דְּאָמְרִינַן: אוֹקֵי תְּרֵי לְבַהֲדֵי תְּרֵי, וְאִשָּׁה אוֹקְמָהּ אַחֲזָקָה.

The Gemara challenges: How can one say that? After all, **there are witnesses who are standing** before us **and saying** that the object of betrothal fell **closer to her.** Accordingly, she was betrothed and her rival wife is the rival wife of a forbidden relative. **And** yet **you say to let her enter into levirate marriage and** there is **no** problem **with that? And furthermore,** with regard to the fundamental difference between two pairs of witnesses and a single pair, the case **of two pairs of witnesses is also** considered an **uncertainty** in matters of **rabbinic** law. This is not considered to be uncertainty with regard to the reality of what actually happened, which would be a case of uncertainty in matters of Torah law, but rather a contradiction between two opposing testimonies. In these cases **we say: Place two** witnesses **against two**[N] witnesses, and let the two testimonies cancel each other out. Therefore, the *halakha* would be to **let the woman remain in her original presumptive status.** Accordingly, this type of uncertainty stems only from rabbinic law and not from Torah law.

מִידֵּי דַּהֲוָה אַנִּכְסֵי דְּבַר שַׁטְיָא. דְּבַר שַׁטְיָא זַבֵּין נִכְסֵי, אָתוּ בֵּי תְּרֵי וְאָמְרִי: כְּשֶׁהוּא חָלִים זַבֵּין, וַאֲתוּ בֵּי תְּרֵי וְאָמְרוּ כְּשֶׁהוּא שׁוֹטֶה זַבֵּין. וַאֲמַר רַב אַשִׁי: אוֹקֵי תְּרֵי לַהֲדֵי תְּרֵי

The Gemara cites a proof for this: This is **just as it is in** the case **concerning the property of** a man named **Bar Shatya,**[HB] who was referred to by this name because he would occasionally go insane. The case is as follows: **Bar Shatya sold property. Two** witnesses **came** forward **and said that he sold** it **when** he was **healthy** and therefore the sale was valid. **And two** others **came** forward **and said that he sold** it **when** he was **insane,** and so the sale was void. **Rav Ashi said** with regard to this matter: **Place two** witnesses **against two** witnesses and let the testimonies cancel each other out. As there is no valid testimony to rely on,

NOTES

The mishna…is referring to one set – מַתְנִיתִין...בְּכַת אַחַת: The commentaries have differing opinions as to what is meant by uncertainty with one set of witnesses. According to Rashi and those who follow his opinion, this is a case where one witness says that the bill of divorce was closer to him and one witness says that it was closer to her. According to Rabbeinu Ḥananel and the Rashba, the witnesses themselves are uncertain with regard to the facts (see *Beit Shmuel* and the later commentaries).

Uncertainty in matters of Torah law…uncertainty in matters of rabbinic law – סְפֵיקָא דְּאוֹרָיְיתָא...סְפֵיקָא דְּרַבָּנַן: In cases of uncertainties that arise either because the exact circumstances cannot be ascertained or because no clear halakhic decision has emerged, the principle is: In cases of Torah law, one adopts the stringent practice; in cases of rabbinic law, one adopts the lenient practice.

Place two against two – אוֹקֵי תְּרֵי לְבַהֲדֵי תְּרֵי: Although it seems here that the Gemara concludes that whenever two witnesses contradict another two witnesses it is considered an uncertainty in matters of rabbinic law, there are nevertheless those who disagree with this opinion and hold that this is considered a case of uncertainty in matters of Torah law. There are also those who differentiate between cases of prohibitions and monetary cases. The basis for this debate lies primarily in the question of whether both testimonies, despite the contradiction between them, nevertheless negate fully the previously existing presumptions altogether, or perhaps, since there is no definitive testimony on the matter, the original presumption remains in place (see *Derush VeḤiddush* on marriage contracts).

HALAKHA

The property of Bar Shatya – נִכְסֵי דְּבַר שַׁטְיָא: With regard to one who is sometimes sane and sometimes insane, when he is sane he is like a fully responsible agent for all matters, and all of his actions are binding. When he is insane, all of his actions are null and void.

If two witnesses come forth and say that he made a sale while insane, and two others testify that he made the sale while sane, any real estate remains in the possession of the seller, and movable property remains in the possession of the possessor (Rema, in accordance with *Tosafot* and Rosh; Rambam *Sefer Kinyan, Hilkhot Mekhira* 29:5; *Shulḥan Arukh, Ḥoshen Mishpat* 235:21).

BACKGROUND

Bar Shatya – בַּר שַׁטְיָא: Bar Shatya was a man who suffered from a psychological ailment that caused him to suffer periodic fits, but who nevertheless had his wits about him between bouts. In other words, he was sometimes sane and sometimes insane. With some of these ailments the fits occur with relative regularity, and with some they are caused by specific circumstances, but there can most certainly be periods when the individual is sane, lacking any abnormalities in his behavior whatsoever. It is for this reason that the *halakha* concludes that at times of sanity he is considered a normal individual, both with regard to his obligation to fulfill mitzvot and the legal validity of his actions. However, since the bouts of insanity occur at various times, and not always in a manner that is immediately recognizable to all, it is important to determine his mental state at the relevant times in order to ascertain the legal validity of specific actions.

וְאַרְעָא אוֹקְמָא בְּחֶזְקַת בַּר שַׁטְיָא.

let the land remain in the possession of Bar Shatya. Since no substantiated proof was brought forth, the land remains in the hands of its current possessor. As such, the same should be true with regard to cases of betrothal and divorce whose status is uncertain; the woman should remain in her former presumptive status.

אֶלָּא אָמַר אַבַּיֵי: ״יַגִּיד עָלָיו רֵיעוֹ״; תָּנָא בְּקִידּוּשִׁין – וְהוּא הַדִּין לְגֵירוּשִׁין, תָּנָא בְּגֵירוּשִׁין – וְהוּא הַדִּין לְקִידּוּשִׁין.

Rather, Rabba's understanding of the mishna must be rejected, and **Abaye said:** The mishna should be understood according to that which is written: **"His fellow speaks of him"** (Job 36:33). This principle teaches that a related case can be inferred from the single case cited. The mishna **teaches** the case where it is uncertain whether the item is closer to him or closer to her **with regard to betrothal, and the same is true with regard to divorce** if it is uncertain whether the bill of divorce fell closer to him or closer to her. Similarly, the mishna **teaches** the case of bills that were written in a questionable manner **with regard to divorce, and the same is true with regard to betrothal.**

אֲמַר לֵיהּ רָבָא: אִי יַגִּיד עָלָיו רֵיעוֹ – מַאי ״זֶהוּ״ דְּקָתָנֵי?

Rava said to him: If you understand that the legal ruling in all of these cases is the same, and the mishna was written in the style of: **His fellow speaks of him,**[N] then **what is** the meaning of the term: **This is, that** the mishna **teaches?** The mishna in fact emphasizes that this is a betrothal whose status is uncertain and this is a divorce whose status is uncertain, which indicates this case alone and no other.

אֶלָּא אָמַר רָבָא: כׇּל שֶׁיֵּשׁ בְּקִידּוּשִׁין – יֵשׁ בְּגֵירוּשִׁין, וְיֵשׁ בְּגֵירוּשִׁין מַה שֶּׁאֵין בְּקִידּוּשִׁין. וְ״זֶהוּ״ דְּגֵירוּשִׁין לָאו דַּוְקָא, אֶלָּא מִשּׁוּם דְּתָנָא ״זֶהוּ״ בְּקִידּוּשִׁין – תָּנָא נָמֵי ״זֶהוּ״ בְּגֵירוּשִׁין. וְ״זֶהוּ״ דְּקִידּוּשִׁין לְמַעוּטֵי מַאי? לְמַעוּטֵי זְמַן, דְּלֵיכָּא בְּקִידּוּשִׁין.

Rather, Rava said: All of the cases **that exist with regard to betrothal** whose status is uncertain **exist in** cases **of divorce** as well. However, **there are** some cases of uncertainty **with regard to divorce that do not exist with regard to betrothal,** as betrothal performed with a questionable bill is not disqualified. Accordingly, the term: **This is,** utilized in the mishna **with regard to divorce, is not specific** and does not imply exclusion of the case where it is possibly closer to him and possibly closer to her. **Rather, because** the mishna **teaches** the ruling of: **This is, with regard to betrothal,** where it is specific **it teaches** the phrase: **This is, with regard to divorce as well.** The Gemara asks: **And what does** the phrase: **This is,** mentioned **with regard to betrothal,** come **to exclude?** The Gemara answers: **It** comes **to exclude the** matter of the **date, which is not** essential **with regard to betrothal,** as when one betroths a woman by means of a document the date need not be written.

וּמִפְּנֵי מָה לֹא תִּקְנוּ זְמַן בְּקִידּוּשִׁין? הָנִיחָא לְמַאן דְּאָמַר מִשּׁוּם פֵּירֵי – אֲרוּסָה לֵית לַהּ פֵּירֵי.

The Gemara asks about this matter itself: **And for what** reason **did they not institute** that **the date** must be included **in the betrothal** document? This policy **works out well according to the one who says** that the reason the Sages instituted that the date must be written on a bill of divorce **is due to the profits.** As the husband receives the profits from the wife's properties during the period of their marriage, it was necessary to write a date on the bill of divorce in order to know at what point his right to receive or sell these items was terminated. However, it was not necessary to include a date on a deed of betrothal, as this document serves only to create a bond of betrothal, **and there are no profits from a betrothed woman.**[H] A husband does not have the right to receive profits from his betrothed's property until she is his full-fledged wife.

NOTES

If it was written in the style of his fellow speaks of him, etc. – אִי יַגִּיד עָלָיו רֵיעוֹ וכו׳: *Tosafot* suggest a different difficulty with this solution: If the Gemara was using this style, it could have listed all the examples in the context of the first betrothal, and only one in the context of divorce. Similarly, the Rivan points out that Abaye was not precise in his explanation of the mishna, because according to all opinions there is no requirement to include the date in betrothals, and therefore it is clear that not all matters stated with regard to divorce are relevant to cases of betrothal. These issues can be resolved by suggesting that the Gemara raised only a single difficulty among several possible difficulties that could have been raised.

HALAKHA

There are no profits from a betrothed woman – **אֲרוּסָה לֵית לַהּ פֵּירֵי:** The husband receives the profits from his wife's property following their marriage, but not the profits from the property of a woman to whom he was only betrothed (Rambam *Sefer Nashim, Hilkhot Ishut* 12:1, 3; *Shulḥan Arukh, Even HaEzer* 69:1, 3).

HALAKHA

Due to the daughter of his sister – מִשּׁוּם בַּת אֲחוֹתוֹ: The Sages instituted that one must include the date of the writing in the bill of divorce just as in other legal documents. This is in order that he not come to cover for his wife if she were licentious, giving her an undated bill so that she might claim that her misdeeds took place after she received the bill of divorce (Rambam *Sefer Nashim, Hilkhot Geirushin* 1:24; *Shulḥan Arukh, Even HaEzer* 127:1).

אֶלָּא לְמַאן דְּאָמַר מִשּׁוּם בַּת אֲחוֹתוֹ – לִיתְקֵין זְמַן!

However, according to the one who says that the Sages instituted the requirement of including the date in the bill of divorce **due to** a case where a man is married to **the daughter of his sister,**[HN] then **they should institute** that he must include **the date** in a deed of betrothal as well. Occasionally a man might marry the daughter of his sister, whom he loves all the more because she is his close relative in addition to being his wife. If he knows that she acted licentiously while she was married to him, he might grant her a bill of divorce without a date so as to save her from the death penalty. Were witnesses to come forth and testify to her behavior, she could claim that at the time of her licentious act she was already a divorced woman. If this was indeed the reason for the Sages' instituting the requirement of including the date in a bill of divorce, then the date should be included in a deed of betrothal as well, for an undated document of betrothal could be utilized equally well to prove the innocence of the daughter of his sister. If she acted licentiously in the period prior to her betrothal, she would not be penalized. Therefore, the date should be written on this document as well.

מִשּׁוּם דְּאִיכָּא דִּמְקַדֵּשׁ בְּכַסְפָּא וְאִיכָּא דִּמְקַדֵּשׁ בִּשְׁטָרָא – לָא תְּקוּן רַבָּנַן זְמַן.

The Gemara answers: **Because there are those who betroth by means of money and those who betroth by means of a deed,**[N] **the Sages did not institute** that **the date** must be written in the document. As the date of the betrothal has no place in the act of betrothal by means of money, the Sages did not distinguish between the various modes of betrothal.

אֲמַר לֵיהּ רַב אַחָא בְּרֵיהּ דְּרַב יוֹסֵף לְרַב אַשִׁי: וְהָא עַבְדָּא, דְּאִיכָּא דְּקָנֵי בְּכַסְפָּא וְאִיכָּא בִּשְׁטָרָא, וּתְקוּן רַבָּנַן זְמַן! הָתָם רוּבָּא בִּשְׁטָרָא, הָכָא – רוּבָּא בְּכַסְפָּא.

Rav Aḥa, son of Rav Yosef, said to Rav Ashi: But with regard to **a slave,**[N] **where there are** those **who acquire** them **with money and there are** those who acquire them **with a deed, the Sages** nevertheless **instituted** that **the date** must be written in a slave's deed of purchase. He responded: **There,** with regard to slaves, **the majority** of people purchase them **by means of a deed. Here,** with regard to betrothal, **the majority** of people perform betrothal **by means of money.**

אִיבָּעֵית אֵימָא: מִשּׁוּם דְּלָא אֶפְשָׁר. הֵיכִי לִיעֲבֵיד? לִינְחָה גַּבֵּי דִּידָהּ – מַחֲקָה לֵיהּ. לִינְחָה גַּבֵּי דִּידֵיהּ – זִמְנִין דְּבַת אֲחוֹתוֹ הִיא, וּמְחַפֶּה עֲלַהּ.

If you wish, say a different reason why the Sages did not institute that the date must be included in a deed of betrothal. This is **due to** the fact that **it is not possible** to institute this in a manner that will ensure that no problems will result. **How would we do** this? If **we leave** the deed of betrothal **with her, she will erase** the date, and so it would remain impossible to prove the juncture at which her licentious behavior took place. If **we leave** the deed **with him,** then **there are times when she is his sister's daughter and he might cover for her** by erasing the date himself.

NOTES

Due to the daughter of his sister – מִשּׁוּם בַּת אֲחוֹתוֹ: Marriage to any relative, and not only to the daughter of one's sister, is cause for concern in this regard, because a man is apt to show additional favor to her since she is part of his family. Moreover, since she is his relative, he may wish to save his family from disgrace and would therefore tend to cover for her misbehavior (see Rivan). The daughter of his sister was mentioned specifically because the Sages recommended marrying the daughter of one's sister, and therefore this phenomenon was relatively common.

There are those who betroth by means of money and those who betroth by means of a deed – אִיכָּא דִּמְקַדֵּשׁ בְּכַסְפָּא וְאִיכָּא דִּמְקַדֵּשׁ בִּשְׁטָרָא: There are three ways of betrothing a woman. The first is with money or its equivalent, such as a ring, which the bridegroom gives to the bride. The second is with a document in which he attests that he is betrothing the woman. The third is by engaging in sexual intercourse for the explicit purpose of betrothal. The third method, though legally valid, was banned by the Sages to prevent licentiousness.

But with regard to a slave – וְהָא עַבְדָּא: Rashi and those who follow his line of reasoning comment that the issue being discussed is the deed of purchase for a slave, and the date is required in order to know at what moment ownership of all of the slave's possessions was transferred to his master. According to this opinion, the reasoning applies not only to the case of a slave but also to all deeds of purchase. This interpretation is supported by the use of the term: Who acquire.

However, *Tosafot* and most other early commentaries object to this interpretation for various reasons. They explain that the issue at hand is a slave's bill of release, which requires a date in order to determine at what point he is allowed to marry a Jewish woman, or at what point a maidservant would be allowed to marry a Jew. Indeed, the master might have an interest in covering for children born to his slave so as to render them eligible for marriage. These commentaries interpret the word: Acquisition, as referring to the slave acquiring himself, i.e., acquiring his freedom, despite the linguistic difficulties with such a reading.

לִינְחָה גַּבֵּי עֵדִים, אִי דְּכִירִי – לֵיתוּ לִיסְהוּד, וְאִי לָא – זִמְנִין דְּחָזוּ מִכְּתָבָא, וְאָתוּ מַסְהֲדִי. וְרַחֲמָנָא אָמַר: ״מִפִּיהֶם״, וְלֹא מִפִּי כְּתָבָם.

If we leave it with the witnesses who signed the document, **if they remember** themselves the date when the deed was given to the woman, the date need not be written in the document itself, for **let them come forth and testify** from their memory. **And if** they do **not** remember by themselves, then **there are times when they see** the date **that is written and come forth to testify**[N] on that basis. **And the Merciful One states:** "By the mouth of two witnesses, or at the mouth of three witnesses, shall a matter be established" (Deuteronomy 19:15). From this verse it is derived: **From their mouths, and not from their writings,**[NH] indicating that testimony is proper only if the individual stated it of himself, and not on the basis of what is written.

אִי הָכִי בְּגֵירוּשִׁין נַמִי נֵימָא הָכִי! – הָתָם לְהַצָּלָה דִּידָהּ קָאָתֵי, הָכָא – לְחוֹבָה דִּידָהּ קָאָתֵי.

The Gemara asks: **If that is so, let us say that with regard to divorce as well.** In cases of divorce there should also be a concern lest the woman erase the date on the bill of divorce in her possession. The Gemara responds: **There,** in the case of a bill of divorce, the date **comes to save her,**[N] since the bill of divorce removes her status as a man's wife. She therefore would fear erasing anything lest she disqualify the bill altogether, thereby possibly rendering herself a married woman again (Ramban). **Here,** however, when dealing with a deed of betrothal, the date **comes to her disadvantage,** since until now she was presumed to be a single woman, and if there is no date on the document then she clearly cannot be punished.

מתני׳ שְׁלֹשָׁה אַחִין, נְשׂוּאִין שָׁלֹשׁ נָכְרִיּוֹת, וּמֵת אֶחָד מֵהֶן, וְעָשָׂה בָּהּ הַשֵּׁנִי מַאֲמָר וָמֵת – הֲרֵי אֵלּוּ חוֹלְצוֹת וְלֹא מִתְיַיבְּמוֹת.

MISHNA In the case of **three brothers** who **were married to three unrelated women,**[N] **and one of** the brothers **died,** the following occurred: **The second** brother **performed levirate betrothal with** the wife of the deceased brother **and** before he was able to consummate the levirate marriage **he died** as well, leaving behind two women who happen before the third brother for levirate marriage. **Then those** two women must **perform *ḥalitza* and may not enter into levirate marriage.**

שֶׁנֶּאֱמַר ״וּמֵת אַחַד מֵהֶן יְבָמָהּ יָבֹא עָלֶיהָ״ שֶׁעָלֶיהָ זִיקַת יָבָם אֶחָד וְלֹא שֶׁעָלֶיהָ זִיקַת שְׁנֵי יְבָמִין. רַבִּי שִׁמְעוֹן אוֹמֵר: מְיַיבֵּם לְאֵיזוֹ שֶׁיִּרְצֶה, וְחוֹלֵץ לַשְּׁנִיָּה.

As it is stated: "If brothers dwell together **and one of them dies** and he has no child, the wife of the dead man shall not be married outside of the family to one not of his kin; **her brother-in-law will have intercourse with her**" (Deuteronomy 25:5). This teaches that a woman eligible for levirate marriage is one **who has one levirate relationship and not one who has a double levirate relationship.**[NH] In this case, the wife of the first deceased brother requires levirate marriage due to both the marriage with her first husband as well as the levirate betrothal with the second brother. **Rabbi Shimon says: He** may **consummate the levirate marriage with whichever** woman **he wishes and** then **perform *ḥalitza* with the second.**

HALAKHA

From their mouths and not from their writings – מִפִּיהֶם וְלֹא מִפִּי כְּתָבָם: By Torah law, in monetary cases, and all the more so in capital cases, testimony is inadmissible unless it is received orally from the witnesses. It may not be handwritten. If their testimony is sent to the court in written form it is inadmissible.

The *Sma* states that it is customary to receive written testimony when the witnesses remember and are fit for oral testimony (see *Tosafot*, Rosh, *Tur*, and Mordekhai). In the opinion of the Rambam, in cases where the witnesses are signed on a document and they come to the court and confirm their signatures but state that they do not recall the event itself, the document is ruled invalid. *Tosafot* and others disagree and hold that their signatures are efficacious in this case. Even the later commentaries were divided over this matter: The Maharshal rules in accordance with *Tosafot*, while the *Shakh* rules in accordance with the Rambam (Rambam *Sefer Shofetim, Hilkhot Edut* 3:4, 8:5; *Shulḥan Arukh, Ḥoshen Mishpat* 28:11–12, 46:10).

A double levirate relationship – זִיקַת שְׁנֵי יְבָמִים: In the case of three brothers married to women who were not related to one another, if one brother died and his brother performed levirate betrothal with the deceased's wife but died prior to entering into marriage with her, then both the wife of the brother who died first as well as the wife of the brother who died second must perform *ḥalitza* and may not enter into levirate marriage. The Sages decreed that they may not enter into levirate marriage due to a concern lest others come to consummate the levirate marriage with two women from a single household (Rambam *Sefer Nashim, Hilkhot Yibbum* 7:27; *Shulḥan Arukh, Even HaEzer* 174:4).

NOTES

They see what is written and come forth to testify – חָזוּ מִכְּתָבָא וְאָתוּ מַסְהֲדִי: Some early commentaries ask: Why not leave the document with the witnesses who signed it and let its validity be established by the ratification of legal documents, just as would happen with any other bill? See *Tosefot HaRosh*, who explains why there is more reason for concern here than with other documents. The Rashba writes that since this document is not ratified in the usual manner and it merely serves as a form of reminder, the *halakhot* relevant to other bills do not apply to it. The Meiri explains that the ratification of a document is legally sufficient only in monetary cases; in cases involving prohibitions the Sages were reluctant to rely upon this.

From their mouths and not from their writings – מִפִּיהֶם וְלֹא מִפִּי כְּתָבָם: There are several different opinions among the early commentaries as to how to understand this ruling, as well as how to understand the principle that any document that has had the signatures of the witnesses confirmed is considered valid, regardless of whether the witnesses themselves remember the testimony.

The reason that written testimony is invalid depends on how one views its role. According to Rashi and the Razah, since a bill of debt is not written without the borrower's explicit knowledge, its validity does not rest upon what is written by the witnesses but rather upon the statement of obligation expressed by the one who wrote the document. According to the Ramban, however, testimony written as a deed falls under a legal category of its own, and is considered as though the testimony were checked and affirmed by the court. Therefore, the disqualification of written testimony expressed by the principle of: From their mouths, applies only in cases where there is no legal document.

In the opinion of Rabbeinu Tam, the disqualification of: From their mouths, applies only where the witnesses are incapable of testifying orally, but if they are capable of testifying, then their testimony is admissible in written form as well. The Rambam is of the opinion that according to Torah law there is no legal validity to written testimony, but the Sages nevertheless ordained that validity of documents could be legally established by the signatures of witnesses (see Rif and his commentaries; *Tosafot*; Ramban).

It comes to save her – לְהַצָּלָה דִּידָהּ קָאָתֵי: Most of the commentaries explain according to the opinion of *Tosafot*, who hold that since the bill of divorce renders her an unmarried woman, she is fearful that if she erases any part of it, it might be disqualified. This is not the case with a deed of betrothal, which renders her a married woman. The same explanation is mentioned by the Ramban, Rashba, and the Ritva. See also Rashi's interpretation.

Married to three unrelated women – נְשׂוּאִין שָׁלֹשׁ נָכְרִיּוֹת: The early commentaries, among them the Rivan, point out that the *tanna* could have taught here that one of the brothers was single, as the marital status of the third brother does not impact the *halakha*. The *Tiferet Yisrael* explains that because the status of the third brother has no legal implications, the *tanna* opted to teach this in the most concise fashion.

A double levirate relationship – זִיקַת שְׁנֵי יְבָמִין: The early commentaries remark that this really means that she requires two levirate marriages and not a levirate bond with two *yevamin*. The concern here is that she has two levirate obligations from two different husbands, which is referred to in other sources as: A wife of two deceased men.

גמ׳ וְאִי זִיקַּת שְׁנֵי יְבָמִין דְּאוֹרַיְיתָא, חֲלִיצָה נַמִּי לָא תִּיבָּעֵי! אֶלָּא מִדְּרַבָּנַן, וּגְזֵירָה שֶׁמָּא יֹאמְרוּ שְׁתֵּי יְבָמוֹת הַבָּאוֹת מִבַּיִת אֶחָד מִתְיַיבְּמוֹת.

GEMARA

The Gemara asks: **If** the *halakha* that a woman who has **a double levirate relationship** is exempt from levirate marriage is **by Torah** law, as indicated by the proof offered in the mishna, **she should not require *ḥalitza* as well,** but be completely exempt. **Rather,** it is **by rabbinic** law. The restriction on levirate marriage in this case is not by Torah law, as by Torah law the brother is allowed to consummate the levirate marriage with both of these women since each was the wife of a different brother. The requirement for *ḥalitza* in this case was instituted as a rabbinic **decree lest** people **say**[N] that **two *yevamot* who come from a single household can enter into levirate marriage.** Since the second brother had performed levirate betrothal, people might come to think that both were actually married to him. If the third brother consummates the levirate marriage with both women, it would lead people to think that it is permitted to take two of a brother's wives in levirate marriage, when in fact the Torah allows the *yavam* to marry only a single wife of the deceased.

וְנֵייבֵּם לַחֲדָא וְנִיחֲלוֹץ לַחֲדָא! גְּזֵירָה שֶׁמָּא יֹאמְרוּ: בַּיִת אֶחָד, מִקְצָתוֹ בָּנוּי

The Gemara asks: **So let him consummate the levirate marriage with one** woman **and perform *ḥalitza* with** the other **one,** and this would eliminate our concern. The Gemara responds: We do not do this due to a rabbinic **decree lest they say:** When there are two women from **a single household, part of it** must **be built**

Perek **III**
Daf **32** Amud **a**

וּמִקְצָתוֹ חָלוּץ.

and part of it must **be released by *ḥalitza*.** That is, if two women were married to a single man, one of these women must enter into levirate marriage and the other must perform *ḥalitza*.

וְיֹאמְרוּ! אִי דִּמְיַיבֵּם וַהֲדַר – חָלֵיץ הָכִי נַמִּי,

The Gemara wonders: **So let them say** it. Why would it be problematic if people thought that? Even were they to act upon this mistaken assumption it would cause no harm, as there is no transgression involved in performing *ḥalitza*. The Gemara answers: **If he were to consummate the levirate marriage** with one and then later **proceed to perform *ḥalitza***[N] with the other, then **indeed** there would be no reason for concern.

אֶלָּא גְּזֵירָה דִּילְמָא חָלֵיץ בְּרֵישָׁא וַהֲדַר מְיַיבֵּם, וְקָם לֵיהּ בְּ״אֲשֶׁר לֹא יִבְנֶה״, וְרַחֲמָנָא אָמַר: כֵּיוָן שֶׁלֹּא בָּנָה – שׁוּב לֹא יִבְנֶה.

Rather, the requirement to perform *ḥalitza* with both women is a rabbinic **decree** that was instituted **lest he first perform *ḥalitza***[N] with one of his brother's wives **and subsequently consummate the levirate marriage** with the other. Under such circumstances, he would in fact be violating a prohibition. Once he performs *ḥalitza* with the first woman **he is subject to** the prohibition indicated by the verse "So shall it be done to the man **who does not build** his brother's house" (Deuteronomy 25:9). In this verse **the Merciful One states** that **once he did not build** his brother's house but rather opted to perform *ḥalitza* with one of his brother's wives, **he may not proceed to build** it by consummating the levirate marriage with a different wife.

NOTES

A rabbinic decree lest people say – **גְּזֵירָה שֶׁמָּא יֹאמְרוּ**: This explanation of the ruling in the mishna is difficult, as the mishna explicitly states that the reason for this ruling is due to a double levirate bond and not due to a rabbinic decree. This can be resolved by explaining that the primary question of the Gemara is not about this woman, but rather about her rival wife. If the woman with a double levirate bond is not eligible for levirate marriage, then why is her rival wife not exempt from the obligation of *ḥalitza* as the rival wife of a forbidden relative?

The Gemara therefore answers that the prohibition proscribing the woman in the mishna is due to a rabbinic decree. Based on this assertion, the Gemara asks: If the woman is prohibited based on a rabbinic decree, why does the rival wife require *ḥalitza* as well, as the rival wife of a woman prohibited due to a mitzva is generally permitted to enter into levirate marriage? Consequently, they state that there is an additional decree requiring the rival wife to perform *ḥalitza*, and accordingly the suggestion: Let him enter into levirate marriage with one, in fact means that he should take the rival wife in levirate marriage and perform *ḥalitza* with the wife of the first brother (*Melo HaRo'im*).

NOTES

If he were to consummate the levirate marriage and proceed to perform *ḥalitza* – **אִי דִּמְיַיבֵּם וַהֲדַר חָלֵיץ**: From the commentaries it seems that this statement is referring to any case where two rival wives happen before a brother for levirate marriage, as there would be no harm were he to consummate the levirate marriage with one and then perform *ḥalitza* with the other. This is because there is no prohibition against performing *ḥalitza* that does not fulfill a mitzva. Rather, the rabbinic decree was ordained due to the possibility of reversing the order and performing the *ḥalitza* prior to consummating the levirate marriage. It is clear, however, from the words of the author of the *Halakhot Gedolot*, that he holds that the Gemara is referring specifically to a case involving both a wife of two deceased men and another woman, such that it would be permitted for him to consummate the levirate marriage with the rival wife first and then perform *ḥalitza* with the wife with whom levirate betrothal was performed. It is only in this case that the Sages issued a decree lest he first perform *ḥalitza* with the woman with whom levirate betrothal had been performed. It would seem that these two opinions are based on different textual versions of the Gemara.

A rabbinic decree lest he…perform *ḥalitza* – **גְּזֵירָה דִּילְמָא חָלֵיץ**: In the Jerusalem Talmud as well the question of why the rival wife should not enter into levirate marriage is raised, and there it states that the mishna follows Rabbi Meir's opinion, which establishes the principle: So long as you cannot take me in levirate marriage, you cannot take my rival wife in levirate marriage. Accordingly, in every case where one of the wives is forbidden to enter into levirate marriage, her rival wife is likewise forbidden.

אֲמַר רָבָא: נָתַן גֵּט לְמַאֲמָרוֹ – הוּתְּרָה צָרָתָהּ, אֲבָל הִיא אֲסוּרָה, דְּמִחַלְּפָה בְּבַעֲלַת גֵּט.

Rava said: If the brother who performed levirate betrothal in the case described in the mishna subsequently **gave a bill of divorce** to that wife in order to nullify **his levirate betrothal**[H] before he died, **her rival wife is rendered permitted**[N] to the third brother. The third brother is allowed to consummate the levirate marriage with the wife of the second brother because this wife is no longer considered to be the rival wife of a woman with a double levirate relationship. The bill of divorce serves to nullify the act of levirate betrothal completely. **However,** the woman with whom the brother performed levirate betrothal and then received the bill of divorce **is forbidden** to the third brother. Why is this? **She might be confused with** a woman **who receives a bill of divorce.** In general cases where levirate betrothal was not performed, if a man gives a *yevama* a bill of divorce, he is no longer allowed to consummate the levirate marriage with her. If it were permitted to consummate the levirate marriage in this case, people might mistakenly do so in other cases of divorce as well.

אִיכָּא דְּאָמְרִי, אֲמַר רָבָא: נָתַן גֵּט לְמַאֲמָרוֹ – הוּתְּרָה אֲפִילּוּ הִיא, מַאי טַעֲמָא? מַאי דַּעֲבַד בָּהּ – שַׁקְלֵיהּ.

There are those **who say** an alternative formulation of Rava's statement. **Rava said:** If the second brother **gave a bill of divorce** to the wife of the first deceased brother in order to nullify **his levirate betrothal** to her, then **even she** herself **is permitted**[N] to enter into levirate marriage with the third brother. **What is the reason** for this? **That which he performed with her, he removed.** The levirate betrothal was completely nullified by the bill of divorce, and it is as though he had done nothing at all. Therefore, as far as the third brother is concerned, she remains with her original, single levirate bond, as though her status had never been changed by the second brother.

מתני׳ שְׁנֵי אַחִין נְשׂוּאִין שְׁתֵּי אֲחָיוֹת, וּמֵת אֶחָד מֵהֶן, וְאַחַר כָּךְ מֵתָה אִשְׁתּוֹ שֶׁל שֵׁנִי – הֲרֵי זוֹ אֲסוּרָה עָלָיו עוֹלָמִית, הוֹאִיל וְנֶאֶסְרָה עָלָיו שָׁעָה אַחַת.

MISHNA In the case where **two brothers were married to two sisters,**[HB] **and one of** the brothers **died,** the widow at this point would be exempt from levirate marriage as the sister of his wife. **And afterward the wife of the second** brother **died.** Although the *yevama* is no longer the sister of his wife, **this** woman **is nevertheless forbidden to him forever, since she had** already **been forbidden to him at one time.**

BACKGROUND

Two brothers and two sisters – שְׁנֵי אַחִין וּשְׁתֵּי אֲחָיוֹת: The brothers Reuven and Shimon married two sisters, Milka and Ḥogla, respectively. When Shimon died childless, his wife Ḥogla happened before Reuven for levirate marriage, but was rendered exempt from both levirate marriage and *ḥalitza*, as she was the sister of his wife Milka. Even were Milka to later die, Ḥogla would never again be permitted to Reuven.

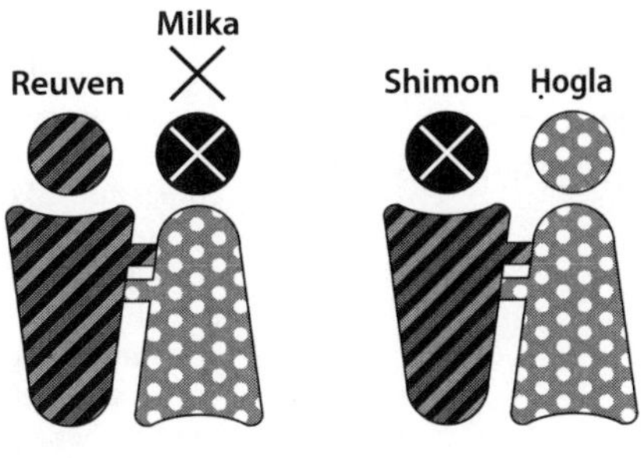

HALAKHA

Gave a bill of divorce in order to nullify his levirate betrothal – נָתַן גֵּט לְמַאֲמָרוֹ: In the case where a woman whose husband died childless happened before the *yavam* for levirate marriage and he performed levirate betrothal but later gave her a bill of divorce explicitly nullifying that levirate betrothal, the levirate betrothal is null and void, and it is permitted for her to enter into levirate marriage with his brothers. However, as per Rashi and Rambam, it is not permitted for her to enter into levirate marriage with him. If this *yavam* died and she happened before a different brother, she is allowed to enter into levirate marriage and is not considered a wife of two deceased men, in accordance with the latter formulation of Rava, which generally signifies the definitive legal ruling (Rambam *Sefer Nashim, Hilkhot Yibbum* 6:29; *Shulḥan Arukh, Even HaEzer* 174:5).

Two brothers were married to two sisters – שְׁנֵי אַחִין נְשׂוּאִין שְׁתֵּי אֲחָיוֹת: If two brothers were married to two sisters and one of the brothers died, even if the surviving brother's wife later died, the first wife remains exempt from levirate marriage, because she was forbidden to him at one time, i.e., during her sister's life (Rambam *Sefer Nashim, Hilkhot Yibbum* 7:12; *Shulḥan Arukh, Even HaEzer* 175:1).

NOTES

Her rival wife is rendered permitted – הוּתְּרָה צָרָתָהּ: Most of the commentaries follow Rashi in understanding the term rival wife to refer to the full wife of the second brother, who by virtue of levirate betrothal became a rival wife of sorts to the wife of two deceased men. However, the Rashba, along with *Nimmukei Yosef*, holds that the term rival wife refers to her actual rival wife. The case would therefore be one where the first brother had two wives, one of whom received levirate betrothal and later a bill of divorce from the second brother, and the other was her rival wife. Rava's statement permitting the rival wife is referring to her actual rival wife.

Even she is permitted – הוּתְּרָה אֲפִילּוּ הִיא: The commentaries and legal authorities were in dispute over to whom, in fact, such a woman would be permitted. Some said that in cases where a *yavam* both performed levirate betrothal and gave a bill of divorce to a woman, she is even permitted to marry that *yavam*. As the levirate betrothal was completely canceled by the bill of divorce, she reverts to her status as a woman with whom he has a levirate bond (Rivan). Others say that she is never again permitted to the man who gave her the bill of divorce but she is permitted to the other brothers (Ramban).

The Ritva explains the difference between the two formulations of Rava's statement. According to the latter version, the prohibition against consummating the levirate marriage with the woman who received the bill of divorce is by rabbinic law. Consequently, the Sages did not institute a decree in the case where the bill of divorce was issued in order to rescind the levirate marriage, which would prevent the violation of another decree due to the possibility of confusion with a woman who only received a bill of divorce. According to the first formulation, however, no special distinction was made for the woman who received a bill of divorce after levirate betrothal, so that there is in fact only one single decree for all *yevamot* who received bills of divorce under any circumstances.

גמ׳ פְּשִׁיטָא! הַשְׁתָּא, וּמַה הָתָם דְּלָא מִידַּחְיָא מֵהַאי בֵּיתָא לְגַמְרֵי – אָמְרַתְּ לָא, הָכָא דְּקָא מִידַּחְיָא מֵהַאי בֵּיתָא לְגַמְרֵי – לֹא כׇּל שֶׁכֵּן?! תָּנָא הָא תָּנָא בְּרֵישָׁא, וְהַדַר חֲזָא לְהֶיתֵּירָא וְשַׁרְיָא, וַהֲדַר חֲזָא לְאִיסּוּרָא. וְאַיְּידֵי דַּחֲבִיבָה לֵיהּ – אַקְדְּמַהּ, וּמִשְׁנָה לֹא זָזָה מִמְּקוֹמָהּ.

GEMARA The Gemara asks: **Isn't this obvious? Now, just as there,** in the earlier *mishnayot*, where there was a third brother and so the woman **was not disassociated from this household completely,** as the levirate obligation existed between her and the third brother to whom she was permitted, **you said** that **she may not** enter into levirate marriage because she was forbidden at one time, **here,** in the case of only two brothers, **where she is disassociated from this household**[N] **completely,** is it **not all the more so** clear that it should be prohibited for her to enter into levirate marriage? The Gemara answers: **The** ***tanna*** **taught this** mishna **at first,** at which time **he saw it** fitting to rule that **those** other cases are **permitted, and** therefore he **permitted them. And then he** subsequently **saw it** fitting to rule that **they are forbidden. And since** that case was novel, **it was beloved to him, he taught it earlier.** But despite the fact that this mishna was no longer necessary, **the mishna does not move from its place.**

תָּנוּ רַבָּנַן: בָּא עָלֶיהָ – חַיָּיב עָלֶיהָ מִשּׁוּם אֵשֶׁת אָח, וּמִשּׁוּם אֲחוֹת אִשָּׁה, דִּבְרֵי רַבִּי יוֹסֵי. רַבִּי שִׁמְעוֹן אוֹמֵר: אֵינוֹ חַיָּיב אֶלָּא מִשּׁוּם אֵשֶׁת אָח בִּלְבַד. וְהָא תַּנְיָא, רַבִּי שִׁמְעוֹן אוֹמֵר: אֵינוֹ חַיָּיב אֶלָּא מִשּׁוּם אֲחוֹת אִשָּׁה בִּלְבַד!

§ **The Sages taught:** If **he engaged in sexual intercourse** with this woman who was forbidden to him, **he is liable** to receive punishment **for** violating the prohibition against marrying **a brother's wife,** because she was never rendered permitted by the levirate mitzva, **and** he is liable to receive punishment **for** violating the prohibition against marrying **a wife's sister;**[N] this is **the statement of Rabbi Yosei. Rabbi Shimon says: He is liable** to receive punishment **only for** violating the prohibition proscribing **a brother's wife.** Rabbi Shimon holds that one prohibition does not take effect where another prohibition is already in place, and since she was already forbidden as his brother's wife, the additional prohibition cannot take effect. The Gemara asks: **But isn't it taught** in a *baraita*, **Rabbi Shimon says: He is liable only due to** the prohibition against marrying **a wife's sister?**

לָא קַשְׁיָא: כָּאן – שֶׁנָּשָׂא חַי וְאַחַר כָּךְ נָשָׂא מֵת, כָּאן – שֶׁנָּשָׂא מֵת וְאַחַר כָּךְ נָשָׂא חַי.

The Gemara answers: This is **not difficult. Here,** in the second *baraita*, it is referring to a case **where the living** brother **married** his wife first **and afterward the** brother who is now **deceased** married her sister. In that case, the first prohibition to take effect on the *yevama* was that of a wife's sister, and only later, when she was married to his now-deceased brother, did the additional prohibition proscribing a brother's wife take effect. **There,** in the first *baraita*, it is referring to a case **where the** brother who is now **deceased married** his wife first, whereby she became forbidden to the brother as a brother's wife, **and afterward the living** brother **married** her sister, rendering her forbidden as his wife's sister as well.

וְרַבִּי שִׁמְעוֹן, הֵיכָא דְּנָשָׂא מֵת וְאַחַר כָּךְ נָשָׂא חַי, כֵּיוָן דְּאִיסּוּר אֲחוֹת אִשָּׁה לָא חָיֵיל – תִּתְיַיבֵּם יַבּוּמֵי!

The Gemara asks: **And** according to the opinion of **Rabbi Shimon,** in a case **where the deceased** brother **married** one of the sisters first, in which case she was forbidden to his brother as a brother's wife, **and afterward the living** brother **married** her sister, the only prohibition in place is that of a brother's wife. Therefore, **since the prohibition** with regard to **a wife's sister never took effect,** then after her husband died **she should** now **enter into levirate marriage.** As the prohibition proscribing a brother's wife is canceled in the face of the levirate mitzva, she should indeed enter into levirate marriage.

אֲמַר רַב אַשִׁי: אִיסּוּר אֲחוֹת אִשָּׁה מִיתְלָא תָּלֵי וְקָאֵי, אִי פָּקַע אִיסּוּר אֵשֶׁת אָח – אָתֵי אִיסּוּר אֲחוֹת אִשָּׁה וְחָיֵיל, וְהִילְכָּךְ לָא פָּקַע.

Rav Ashi said: The prohibition with regard to **a wife's sister remains suspended. If the prohibition** proscribing **a brother's wife is terminated, the prohibition** proscribing **a wife's sister comes and takes effect. Therefore,** it is clear that the prohibition proscribing a wife's sister **is not** completely **terminated.** Accordingly, when a man dies and the prohibition proscribing a brother's wife is overridden by the levirate mitzva, the prohibition proscribing a wife's sister takes effect and she is forbidden to him due to that. The moment the first prohibition ceases to exist, the second immediately takes effect.

NOTES

Where she is disassociated from this household, etc. – **דְּקָא מִידַּחְיָא מֵהַאי בֵּיתָא וכו׳**: It would seem that the opposite conclusion could have been drawn as well. The Gemara could have suggested that in the case at hand, the sister reverted to being eligible for levirate marriage during the original period in which she happened before this brother for levirate marriage, whereas in the case of two *yevamin*, she was forbidden to the *yavam* for the entire period following the death of her first husband. Accordingly, it would be more likely to render her permitted in this case. One must conclude that once she was rendered disqualified to enter into levirate marriage with the brother at one time during the period when she happened before the brothers as a forbidden relative, she can never again revert to a permitted status (Ritva).

For violating the prohibition against marrying a brother's wife and…a wife's sister – **מִשּׁוּם אֵשֶׁת אָח וּמִשּׁוּם אֲחוֹת אִשָּׁה**: Rashi explains that this refers to a case where the relations took place during his wife's lifetime, for then he would be liable to receive punishment for marrying a wife's sister. Rabbeinu Ḥananel, however, holds that the case here is the same as that of the mishna, i.e., a situation where the wife died. The early commentaries (Rashba) were perplexed by this opinion, for even though the language in the *Tosefta* seems to support Rabbeinu Ḥananel's interpretation, it is difficult to understand how he might be held liable to receive punishment for marrying his wife's sister after his wife's death (see Meiri).

וְסָבַר רַבִּי יוֹסֵי אִיסּוּר חָל עַל אִיסּוּר? וְהָא תַּנְיָא: עָבַר עֲבֵירָה שֶׁיֵּשׁ בָּהּ שְׁתֵּי מִיתוֹת – נִידּוֹן בַּחֲמוּרָה, רַבִּי יוֹסֵי אוֹמֵר: נִידּוֹן בַּזִּיקָה הָרִאשׁוֹנָה הַבָּאָה עָלָיו.

The *baraita* indicates that Rabbi Yosei holds that if the brother consummated the levirate marriage with this woman he violated two prohibitions. The Gemara asks: **And does Rabbi Yosei hold** that **a prohibition takes effect** where another **prohibition** already exists?[N] **But isn't it taught** in a *baraita*: **One who committed a transgression deserving of two death penalties**[H] **is sentenced to the harsher** of the two deaths?[N] One would be guilty of such a transgression if he engaged in intercourse with a forbidden relative who was also a married woman, as he would incur one death penalty due to her being a forbidden relative and one death penalty due to her being a married woman. **Rabbi Yosei says: He is sentenced according to the first relationship that applied to him** with regard to this woman.

וְתַנְיָא: כֵּיצַד אָמַר רַבִּי יוֹסֵי נִידּוֹן בַּזִּיקָה הָרִאשׁוֹנָה הַבָּאָה עָלָיו? חֲמוֹתוֹ וְנַעֲשֵׂית אֵשֶׁת אִישׁ – נִידּוֹן בַּחֲמוֹתוֹ, אֵשֶׁת אִישׁ וְנַעֲשֵׂית חֲמוֹתוֹ – נִידּוֹן בְּאֵשֶׁת אִישׁ.

And it is taught in a *baraita*: **In what case did Rabbi Yosei say that he is sentenced according to the first relationship that applied to him?** If this woman was **his mother-in-law** who was widowed or divorced, and therefore forbidden to him only due to her status as his mother-in-law, and later she married **and became** forbidden as **a married woman** and he engaged in sexual relations with her, then **he is sentenced for** violating the prohibition proscribing **his mother-in-law,** since this was the first prohibition to apply. Alternatively, if she was **a married woman** and then he married her daughter so that she then **became his mother-in-law,** and then had sexual relations with her, **he is sentenced for** violating the prohibition proscribing **a married woman.**

NOTES

A prohibition takes effect where another prohibition already exists – אִיסּוּר חָל עַל אִיסּוּר: The Meiri comments that the question whether a prohibition takes effect where another prohibition exists is not a matter that relates to the essence of the prohibitions themselves but rather to the penalties that are incurred by them. Therefore, the principle that a prohibition does not take effect where another prohibition already exists expresses the idea that a transgressor is not doubly penalized for two violations, so that if he committed two transgressions requiring sin-offerings, he need bring only one sin-offering.

The later commentaries deliberated over how to understand the Gemara's question both with regard to the opinion of Rabbi Shimon and in light of Rav Ashi's novel idea. It would seem that the discussion revolves around the question of how to view the additional prohibition: Does it actually not take effect, or is there simply no practical possibility of applying it when another prohibition already exists?

Sentenced to the harsher of the two deaths – נִידּוֹן בַּחֲמוּרָה: There are four forms of capital punishment prescribed by the Torah and administered by a court of twenty-three members. They are, in diminishing order of harshness: Stoning, burning, decapitation by sword, and strangulation. The punishment for engaging in intercourse with one's mother-in-law is burning, whereas the punishment for engaging in intercourse with a married woman is strangulation. Therefore, according to this opinion in the *baraita*, one who engaged in intercourse with his mother-in-law who is also a married woman is sentenced to death by burning (Rashi).

HALAKHA

One who committed a transgression deserving of two death penalties – עָבַר עֲבֵירָה שֶׁיֵּשׁ בָּהּ שְׁתֵּי מִיתוֹת: One who committed a single transgression deserving of two death penalties, such as engaging in relations with his mother-in-law while she was a married woman, is sentenced to the harsher penalty (Rambam *Sefer Shofetim, Hilkhot Sanhedrin* 14:4).

Perek **III**
Daf **32** Amud **b**

אָמַר רַבִּי אַבָּהוּ: מוֹדֶה רַבִּי יוֹסֵי בְּאִיסּוּר מוֹסִיף.

Rabbi Abbahu said: Rabbi Yosei concedes that a prohibition takes effect where another prohibition already exists **when it is an expanded prohibition.**[N] An expanded prohibition is a prohibition that has a greater scope than the original prohibition, either because it applies with greater severity or because it applies to additional individuals. Rabbi Yosei holds that if the second prohibition incorporates additional individuals into the list of those for whom the original item is prohibited, then it takes effect in addition to the previous prohibition that had a more limited range.

NOTES

An expanded prohibition and a more inclusive prohibition – אִיסּוּר מוֹסִיף וְאִיסּוּר כּוֹלֵל: Even though both an expanded prohibition and a more inclusive prohibition are similar in that for both, the scope of the original prohibition is enlarged in some way, they nevertheless differ both in their fundamental natures as well as in their details. An expanded prohibition is defined as a prohibition that adds an additional element of prohibition to the item that is already prohibited. A more inclusive prohibition, on the other hand, occurs when the prohibition now includes other items, even if for the original item there is no actual addition to the prohibition itself.

An expanded prohibition comes about in two ways, either because it applies with greater severity or because it applies to additional individuals. The first might come about, for instance, when a prohibition against deriving benefit takes effect where a prohibition against consumption already exists, since here the second prohibition, against deriving benefit, is of greater severity. The second occurs when, as in the present talmudic discussion, the prohibition applies to a greater number of individuals, when it is not only prohibited for the original subject to perform an activity with a specific item, but it comes to be prohibited for others to perform that activity as well (Ritva), e.g., this woman was forbidden to one brother, and she is subsequently forbidden to all the brothers. A more inclusive prohibition occurs when the same prohibition applies to the same individual but with more items, e.g., it becomes prohibited for one brother to marry all the sisters of a woman instead of just the woman herself. The later commentaries examined these distinctions, since, e.g., with regard to the *halakhot* of forbidden relatives, the difference between a more inclusive prohibition and an expanded prohibition depends on the individual in question. That which is an expanded prohibition for a man is at the same time a more inclusive prohibition from the woman's perspective, and the opposite holds true as well (see *Yosef Lekaḥ*). According to the *Ḥazon Ish* it is clear that the ruling goes according to the perspective of the man and not according to the woman.

In addition to these fundamental differences, the details of these two categories differ as well. It would seem from *Tosafot* that a more inclusive prohibition does not take effect where another prohibition exists unless it is more severe, but never where it is more lenient (*Keren Ora*). Moreover, according to *Tosafot*, a more inclusive prohibition takes effect only where the prohibition is for a single category. In other words, those to whom the prohibition applies must all be included within a single category of the prohibition. This is not the case, for example, when a man marries a woman, for even though all of her relatives are rendered forbidden to him it is nevertheless for different reasons: One is her mother, the other her sister, etc. The Rashba, however, disagrees on this point.

The *Ḥazon Ish* writes that an expanded prohibition takes effect only when it actually causes additional prohibitions, i.e., there must in fact be additional people in the world who become subject to this prohibition. So, for example, where a man engages in relations with his wife's sister who became his brother's wife, the second prohibition would take effect only if there were in fact additional brothers who were incorporated into the prohibition by the marriage. Therefore, if there were only two brothers in the family, the prohibition of a brother's wife would not apply.

תֵּינַח – הֵיכָא דְּנָשָׂא חַי וְאַחַר כָּךְ נָשָׂא מֵת, מִגּוֹ דְּאִתּוֹסַף אִיסּוּר לְגַבֵּי אַחִים – אִתּוֹסַף אִיסּוּר לְגַבֵּי דִּידֵיהּ.

The Gemara asks: This **works out well** in cases **where the living** brother **married** his wife first, and her sister became forbidden to him as a wife's sister, **and then afterward the** brother who was subsequently **deceased married** his wife's sister. In that case it is possible to say: **Since a prohibition was added for** all **the brothers,**[N] **a prohibition was added for** the living brother as well, and he is liable due to both prohibitions, as this prohibition is more wide-ranging than the previous one. In other words, at first this sister was permitted to the other brothers, and when the second brother married her she was rendered a brother's wife and so she was additionally forbidden to the other brothers.

אֶלָּא, הֵיכָא דְּנָשָׂא מֵת וְאַחַר כָּךְ נָשָׂא חַי, מַאי אִיסּוּר מוֹסִיף אִיכָּא?

However, where the **deceased** brother **married** first and **afterward** the **living** brother **married** her sister, **in what way is there a prohibition that adds?** No additional individuals were incorporated into the prohibition as a result of the marriage of the living brother with the sister, since the prohibition here proscribing a wife's sister applies to him alone.

וְכִי תֵּימָא: מִגּוֹ דְּאִיתַּסַּר בְּכוּלְּהוּ אַחְוָותָא – הַאי אִיסּוּר כּוֹלֵל הוּא!

And if you would say: Since he himself now married a sister **he became prohibited to all of the other sisters,** as opposed to the prior state of affairs where only his brother was married to one of the sisters and all of the other sisters were permitted to him, and therefore an additional prohibition now applies to him, this is difficult. In this case the new prohibition is not considered an expanded prohibition, but rather **it is** considered **a more inclusive prohibition.**[N] It is more inclusive and more comprehensive in that it adds additional aspects to the prohibition for the same individual. This is not called an expanded prohibition, as it does not add prohibitions to additional individuals.

אֶלָּא אָמַר רָבָא: מַעֲלֶה אֲנִי עָלָיו כְּאִילּוּ עָשָׂה שְׁתַּיִם, וְאֵינוֹ חַיָּיב אֶלָּא אַחַת. וְכֵן כִּי אֲתָא רָבִין אָמַר רַבִּי יוֹחָנָן: מַעֲלֶה אֲנִי עָלָיו כְּאִילּוּ עָשָׂה שְׁתַּיִם, וְאֵינוֹ חַיָּיב אֶלָּא אַחַת. מַאי נָפְקָא מִינַּהּ? לְקׇבְרוֹ בֵּין רְשָׁעִים גְּמוּרִים.

Rather, Rava said[N] that when Rabbi Yosei stated in the *baraita* that the man is liable due to both prohibitions, for a brother's wife and for a wife's sister, he meant to say: **I ascribe to him** liability **as though he transgressed twice,** since indeed he violated two prohibitions, **yet he is liable** to receive punishment in human courts **on only one** count. **And likewise, when Ravin came** from Eretz Yisrael to Babylonia, he said that **Rabbi Yoḥanan said: I ascribe to him** liability **as though he transgressed twice, yet he is liable** to receive punishment **on only one** count. The Gemara asks: **What difference does it make** if we consider it as though he transgressed twice? The Gemara answers: It affects the decision whether or not **to bury him among the completely wicked.**[N] Just as a righteous individual is not buried among the wicked, so too, a wicked individual is not buried among those more wicked than himself. He who violated this prohibition is considered as though he committed two transgressions and not one, and so he would be buried accordingly.

NOTES

Since a prohibition was added for the brothers – **מִגּוֹ דְּאִתּוֹסַף אִיסּוּר לְגַבֵּי אַחִים**: The Gemara could have suggested that there is a different expanded prohibition; a prohibition was added to the entire populace since previously this woman was available for marriage but now she is a married woman. Nevertheless, the Gemara preferred to mention the prohibition proscribing a brother's wife, since it is not always nullified following the death of the husband (Ritva).

This is considered a more inclusive prohibition – **הַאי אִיסּוּר כּוֹלֵל הוּא**: The Rivan asks: Could not Rabbi Abbahu have said that Rabbi Yosei also concedes in cases of more inclusive prohibitions? He answers that since an expanded prohibition is more severe, it stands to reason that Rabbi Yosei concedes in that case specifically. Other commentaries point out that since Rabbi Yosei disagrees in the case of a married woman who became his mother-in-law, which is a more inclusive prohibition because he became forbidden to her and to her relatives, we can conclude that Rabbi Yosei does not in fact agree in these cases (see Ritva).

Rather Rava said – **אֶלָּא אָמַר רָבָא**: Some commentaries maintain that Rava's statement serves only to resolve Rabbi Yosei's opinion with regard to a wife's sister. However, most of the commentaries agree with the opinion of Rashi and assert that the word rather here indicates a fundamental dispute with Rabbi Abbahu, in that Rava holds that Rabbi Yosei does not concede that an additional prohibition can take effect where a prohibition already exists.

Among the completely wicked – **בֵּין רְשָׁעִים גְּמוּרִים**: Many early commentaries had a version of the text that read: Among the severely wicked, and therefore did not interpret this like Rashi, who explains this as meaning that he should be buried with those who had been stoned to death. They point out that he did not commit a crime so heinous as to deserve such a burial place. Rather, they state, he should be buried among those who were wicked like himself. *Tosefot HaRosh* explains that Rabbi Yosei holds that this man should be buried together with someone who committed sins with two different women, such as a brother's wife and a wife's sister, since he committed both of these transgressions as well. On the other hand, Rabbi Shimon holds that another prohibition cannot take effect where a prohibition already exists, so it is considered as though he committed a single transgression.

וּבִפְלוּגְתָּא, דְּאִיתְּמַר: זָר שֶׁשִּׁימֵּשׁ בְּשַׁבָּת, רַבִּי חִיָּיא אוֹמֵר: חַיָּיב שְׁתַּיִם, בַּר קַפָּרָא אוֹמֵר: אֵין חַיָּיב אֶלָּא אַחַת. קָפַץ רַבִּי חִיָּיא וְנִשְׁבַּע: הָעֲבוֹדָה! כָּךְ שָׁמַעְתִּי מֵרַבִּי: שְׁתַּיִם. קָפַץ בַּר קַפָּרָא וְנִשְׁבַּע: הָעֲבוֹדָה! כָּךְ שָׁמַעְתִּי מֵרַבִּי: אַחַת.

§ The Gemara comments that the issue of a prohibition taking effect where another prohibition already exists is taught **in the dispute** found in a *baraita*, **where it was stated:** With regard to **a non-priest who served** in some capacity in one of the Temple services, such as the burning of a burnt-offering on the altar **on Shabbat,**[H] **Rabbi Ḥiyya says: He is liable** to receive punishment on **two** counts,[N] both because he was a non-priest serving in the Temple and because he desecrated Shabbat. **Bar Kappara**[P] **says: He is liable** on **only one** count. **Rabbi Ḥiyya jumped up and swore:**[N] I swear **by the Temple service**[N] that **this I heard from Rabbi** Yehuda HaNasi: He is liable on **two** counts. **Bar Kappara jumped up and swore:** I swear **by the Temple service** that **this I heard from Rabbi** Yehuda HaNasi: He is liable on **one** count.

הִתְחִיל רַבִּי חִיָּיא לָדוּן: שַׁבָּת לַכֹּל נֶאֶסְרָה, כְּשֶׁהוּתְּרָה בַּמִּקְדָּשׁ – אֵצֶל כֹּהֲנִים הוּתְּרָה, לְכֹהֲנִים הוּתְּרָה וְלֹא לְזָרִים, יֵשׁ כָּאן מִשּׁוּם זָרוּת, וְיֵשׁ כָּאן מִשּׁוּם שַׁבָּת. הִתְחִיל בַּר קַפָּרָא לָדוּן: שַׁבָּת לַכֹּל נֶאֶסְרָה, כְּשֶׁהוּתְּרָה – בַּמִּקְדָּשׁ הוּתְּרָה, אֵין כָּאן אֶלָּא זָרוּת.

Since the matter could not be decided by tradition, **Rabbi Ḥiyya began to deliberate** and analyze the question logically. Prohibited labor on **Shabbat was prohibited to all. When** prohibited labor **was permitted in the Temple** for the purposes of the Temple service, **it was permitted** only **for priests.** This indicates that **it was permitted for priests and not for non-priests.** Therefore, when a non-priest serves in the Temple on Shabbat, **there is** a transgression **here due to** his serving as **a non-priest and there is** a transgression **here due to** his desecrating **Shabbat. Bar Kappara began to deliberate** in a different manner: **Shabbat was prohibited to all. When it was permitted it was permitted in the Temple,** so that if it was permitted for one to serve in the Temple, it was permitted for him to serve on Shabbat. Therefore, **there is** a transgression **here only** for his serving as **a non-priest,** since if this man were a priest his service would have been permitted. Therefore, he is not liable to receive punishment for desecrating Shabbat.

בַּעַל מוּם שֶׁשִּׁימֵּשׁ בְּטוּמְאָה, רַבִּי חִיָּיא אוֹמֵר: חַיָּיב שְׁתַּיִם, בַּר קַפָּרָא אוֹמֵר: אֵין חַיָּיב אֶלָּא אַחַת. קָפַץ רַבִּי חִיָּיא וְנִשְׁבַּע: הָעֲבוֹדָה! כָּךְ שָׁמַעְתִּי מֵרַבִּי: שְׁתַּיִם, קָפַץ בַּר קַפָּרָא וְנִשְׁבַּע: הָעֲבוֹדָה! כָּךְ שָׁמַעְתִּי מֵרַבִּי: אַחַת.

They disagreed over a similar issue as well, the case of a priest **with a blemish who served** in the Temple by sacrificing a public offering, which overrides ritual impurity, **while** he was **ritually impure.**[N] **Rabbi Ḥiyya says: He is liable on two** counts, both for serving with a blemish and for being ritually impure. **Bar Kappara says: He is liable on only one** count, for serving with a blemish. **Rabbi Ḥiyya jumped up and swore:** I swear **by the Temple service** that **this I heard from Rabbi** Yehuda HaNasi: He is liable on **two counts. Bar Kappara jumped up and swore:** I swear **by the Temple service** that **this I heard from Rabbi** Yehuda HaNasi: He is liable on **one** count.

הִתְחִיל רַבִּי חִיָּיא לָדוּן: טוּמְאָה לַכֹּל נֶאֶסְרָה, כְּשֶׁהוּתְּרָה בַּמִּקְדָּשׁ – אֵצֶל כֹּהֲנִים תְּמִימִים הוּתְּרָה, לְכֹהֲנִים תְּמִימִים הוּתְּרָה וְלֹא לְבַעֲלֵי מוּמִין, יֵשׁ כָּאן מִשּׁוּם בַּעֲלֵי מוּמִין, וְיֵשׁ כָּאן מִשּׁוּם טוּמְאָה. הִתְחִיל בַּר קַפָּרָא לָדוּן: טוּמְאָה לַכֹּל נֶאֶסְרָה, כְּשֶׁהוּתְּרָה בַּמִּקְדָּשׁ – הוּתְּרָה, אֵין כָּאן אֶלָּא מִשּׁוּם בַּעַל מוּם,

Rabbi Ḥiyya began to deliberate.[N] **Ritual impurity was prohibited to all,** as it was prohibited for all individuals who are ritually impure to enter into the Temple. **When it was permitted in the Temple** in circumstances where the entire public was impure, **it was permitted for unblemished priests.** Therefore, **it was permitted** only **for unblemished priests and not for** priests **with blemishes.** Consequently, if that priest with a blemish served while impure, **there is** a transgression **here due to** his status as **a blemished** priest **and there is** a transgression **here due to ritual impurity. Bar Kappara began to deliberate** in a different manner: **Ritual impurity was prohibited to all. When it was permitted in the Temple, it was permitted** for all. Therefore, the only problem was that this priest was blemished, and so **there is** a transgression **here only due to** his status as **a blemished** priest.

PERSONALITIES

Bar Kappara – בַּר קַפָּרָא: This Sage was among the last of the *tanna'im*, a leading pupil of Rabbi Yehuda HaNasi, and a colleague of Rabbi Shimon ben Rabbi Yehuda HaNasi and Rabbi Ḥiyya. His first name is unknown, although some say that he was the son of Rabbi Elazar HaKappar, and, being born after his father's death, was named Elazar as well.

Bar Kappara was among the greatest halakhic authorities of his generation, who even compiled a collection of *baraitot* called *Mishnat bar Kappara*. Excerpts from this compilation are cited several times throughout the Talmud. Bar Kappara was also famous for his sermons, and he was a master of language as well. Several proverbs, poetic phrases, and words of prayer are recorded in his name.

As he had a sense of humor and a sharp wit, he would often aim amusing criticism at the Sages, including the members of Rabbi Yehuda HaNasi's household. For this reason, and despite his closeness to his teacher, bar Kappara was never ordained. Bar Kappara was well versed in general wisdom and was therefore often sent to represent the Jewish community before the Roman authorities.

The majority of prominent *amora'im* of the first generation were among his students. The prominent *amora* Rabbi Yehuda ben Pedaya (bar Padda) was his nephew. He was among the Sages in the southern part of Eretz Yisrael, and active in the city of Parod, where he is buried.

HALAKHA

A non-priest who served on Shabbat, etc. – זָר שֶׁשִּׁימֵּשׁ בְּשַׁבָּת וכו׳: A non-priest who served in the Temple on Shabbat was liable to receive punishment both for violating Shabbat and for serving as a non-priest. Similarly, a blemished priest who served in the Temple service while ritually impure was liable both for serving while ritually impure as well as for serving as a blemished priest (Rambam *Sefer Avoda, Hilkhot Biat HaMikdash* 9:12).

NOTES

He is liable on two counts – חַיָּיב שְׁתַּיִם: According to Rashi and other commentaries, this means that he transgressed two prohibitions, the repercussions being that he is considered completely wicked. Ramban explains that this refers to the sets of lashes he would receive, according to the opinion that one receives lashes even for a prohibition for which one is punished with execution by the courts. One who violates such a prohibition is punished with lashes if certain factors prevent the court from administering the death penalty. One commentary explains that with regard to the three questions over which Rabbi Ḥiyya and Bar Kappara disagree, they differ from one another on precisely this point; the first is referring to a negative mitzva and court-administered capital punishment, the second to a negative mitzva and *karet*, and the third is referring to two negative mitzvot (Re'em Horowitz).

Rabbi Ḥiyya jumped up and swore, etc. – קָפַץ רַבִּי חִיָּיא וְנִשְׁבַּע וכו׳: It is possible that Rabbi Yehuda HaNasi changed his mind, and so both of them could indeed hear the words of Rabbi accurately, but at different times (*Ramat Shmuel*).

The Temple service – הָעֲבוֹדָה: According to the Maharsha, this form of oath, which is used on numerous occasions in the Babylonian Talmud, is not in fact referring to the Temple service, since at that time there was no Temple. The word service refers to divine service in accordance with the statement by the Rambam that an oath taken with the divine name is a form of service. The vowels of the word *avoda* are identical to the vowels of the four-letter divine name.

A non-priest on Shabbat, a blemished priest while ritually impure – זָר בְּשַׁבָּת, בַּעַל מוּם בְּטוּמְאָה: The Ramban writes that the Gemara could have asked many different questions, one of which was with regard to a blemished priest who served on Shabbat, yet it chose to use one example of many. However, it did not ask about a non-priest who served while ritually impure, because non-priests were never warned against performing the Temple service while ritually impure (Rivan; *Tosafot*). The Meiri contends that this question could have been asked as well.

Rabbi Ḥiyya began to deliberate – הִתְחִיל רַבִּי חִיָּיא לָדוּן: As later becomes clear, the essence of the dispute between these two Sages revolves around the question of whether a prohibition takes effect where another prohibition already exists. Nevertheless, it was important to clarify the opinion of Rabbi Yehuda HaNasi in these cases. Accordingly, the choice of the words: Began to deliberate, is precise, since this served only as a preliminary clarification of the opinions but did not constitute the heart of the discussion (Rashba).

HALAKHA

A non-priest who ate a bird killed by pinching – זָר שֶׁאָכַל מְלִיקָה: A non-priest who ate from a bird sin-offering is liable to receive punishment on two counts, one as a non-priest who ate consecrated animals, and one for eating an unslaughtered animal carcass (Rambam *Sefer Avoda, Hilkhot Ma'aseh HaKorbanot* 11:9).

NOTES

Pinching – מְלִיקָה: Turtledoves and young pigeons sacrificed as offerings in the Temple were killed not by ritually slaughtering them with a knife like other offerings, but rather by pinching their necks. This was considered an especially difficult activity to perform. The priest would hold the bird in his left hand with its legs and wings between his fingers, and the back of its neck stretched out and facing upward. With his right fingernail, which he grew especially long for this purpose, the priest would cut the bird's neck and spine from the back until he reached and severed its windpipe and gullet. If the bird was to be sacrificed as a burnt-offering, the priest would completely sever its head. If it was to be sacrificed as a sin-offering, he would leave the head partially attached. A bird killed by pinching and sacrificed as a sin-offering was permitted to be eaten by the priests, while a bird that was killed by pinching but not intended for sacrificial use was considered an unslaughtered carcass, and it was not permitted to eat it. The pinching could be performed only by a priest, whereas the slaughtering of animal offerings in the Temple could be performed by a non-priest.

זָר שֶׁאָכַל מְלִיקָה, רַבִּי חִיָּיא אוֹמֵר: חַיָּיב שְׁתַּיִם, בַּר קַפָּרָא אוֹמֵר: אֵין חַיָּיב אֶלָּא אַחַת. קָפַץ רַבִּי חִיָּיא וְנִשְׁבַּע: הָעֲבוֹדָה! כָּךְ שָׁמַעְתִּי מֵרַבִּי: שְׁתַּיִם. קָפַץ בַּר קַפָּרָא וְנִשְׁבַּע: הָעֲבוֹדָה! כָּךְ שָׁמַעְתִּי מֵרַבִּי: אַחַת.

They disagreed over a similar issue as well. This dispute is with regard to **a non-priest who ate a** bird sin-offering that was killed by **pinching**[H] the back of its neck. It is permitted for priests to consume such an offering, but it is prohibited to consume any other bird killed in such a manner, since it was not ritually slaughtered. **Rabbi Ḥiyya says: He is liable** to receive punishment **on two** counts, both for being a non-priest who ate a priestly offering and for eating something that was not properly slaughtered. **Bar Kappara says: He is liable on only one** count. **Rabbi Ḥiyya jumped up and swore:** I swear **by the Temple service** that **this I heard from Rabbi** Yehuda HaNasi: He is liable on **two** counts. **Bar Kappara jumped up and swore:** I swear **by the Temple service** that **this I heard from Rabbi** Yehuda HaNasi: He is liable on **one** count.

הִתְחִיל רַבִּי חִיָּיא לָדוּן: נְבֵלָה לַכֹּל נֶאֶסְרָה, כְּשֶׁהוּתְּרָה בַּמִּקְדָּשׁ – אֵצֶל כֹּהֲנִים הוּתְּרָה, לְכֹהֲנִים הוּתְּרָה וְלֹא לְזָרִים. יֵשׁ כָּאן מִשּׁוּם זָרוּת, וְיֵשׁ כָּאן מִשּׁוּם מְלִיקָה. הִתְחִיל בַּר קַפָּרָא לָדוּן: נְבֵלָה לַכֹּל נֶאֶסְרָה, כְּשֶׁהוּתְּרָה בַּמִּקְדָּשׁ – הוּתְּרָה, אֵין כָּאן אֶלָּא מִשּׁוּם זָרוּת.

Rabbi Ḥiyya began to deliberate. An unslaughtered animal carcass was prohibited to all. When it was permitted in the Temple, it was permitted to priests alone. Since **it was permitted to priests and not to non-priests, there is** a transgression **here due to** his **status as a non-priest** who ate of the sin-offering **and there is a** transgression **here due to** eating an animal killed by **pinching.**[N] **Bar Kappara began to deliberate: An unslaughtered animal carcass was prohibited to all. When it was permitted in the Temple, it was permitted** to all. Therefore **there is** a transgression **here only for being a non-priest,** since if he were a priest there would be no prohibition at all.

Perek **III**
Daf **33** Amud **a**

בְּמַאי קָמִיפַּלְגִי? בְּאִיסּוּר כּוֹלֵל, וְאַלִּיבָּא דְּרַבִּי יוֹסֵי: רַבִּי חִיָּיא סָבַר, רַבִּי יוֹסֵי בְּאִיסּוּר כּוֹלֵל מִיחַיֵּיב תַּרְתֵּי; בַּר קַפָּרָא סָבַר, לָא מִיחַיֵּיב אֶלָּא חֲדָא.

The Gemara asks: **With regard to what** principle **do they disagree?**[N] The Gemara suggests that they disagree with regard to the issue of **a more inclusive prohibition, and** this dispute pertains to the status of a more inclusive prohibition specifically **according to** the opinion of **Rabbi Yosei. Rabbi Ḥiyya holds that Rabbi Yosei** is of the opinion that **in** the case of **a more inclusive prohibition, one is liable on two** counts. **Bar Kappara holds** that Rabbi Yosei is of the opinion that **one is liable only on one** count.

וּמַאי אִיסּוּר כּוֹלֵל אִיכָּא הָכָא? בִּשְׁלָמָא זָר, מֵעִיקָּרָא שָׁרֵי בִּמְלָאכָה וְאָסוּר בַּעֲבוֹדָה, אָתְיָא לֵהּ שַׁבָּת – מִגּוֹ דְּקָא מִיתְּסַר בִּמְלָאכָה מִיתְּסַר נָמֵי בַּעֲבוֹדָה.

The Gemara asks: **And what more inclusive prohibition is there here** in these cases? **Granted,** in the case of **a non-priest** who served in the Temple on Shabbat, **initially he was permitted to perform labor** every day **and was prohibited from** engaging in **the** Temple **service.** When **Shabbat came, since he is** now **prohibited from** engaging in **prohibited labor** in all contexts due to Shabbat, **he is also prohibited from** engaging in labors related to the Temple **service** due to Shabbat. Indeed, the additional prohibition of Shabbat was added to the previously existing prohibition against performing service in the Temple. This is a more inclusive prohibition since it also includes prohibited labor outside of the Temple.

NOTES

With regard to what do they disagree – בְּמַאי קָמִיפַּלְגִי: Both the early and later commentaries ask: Why did the Gemara see fit to repeat this question when Rabbi Ḥiyya and bar Kappara explicitly stated the reasoning behind their positions? *Tosefot HaRosh* states that the Sages of the Talmud held a tradition that the root of the dispute was not based upon the previously suggested interpretation. The Rivan, however, states that this question is directed specifically toward bar Kappara, since his reasoning does not seem sufficient. Others say that because the two Sages demonstrated that each of these issues could be viewed from two different angles, they would not have depended solely upon their explicit explanations (*Tosafot Yeshanim*). The Rashba writes that there must be an alternate rationale behind this dispute, as otherwise one of the Sages would be telling a falsehood. Moreover, the words: Began to deliberate, indicate that this was not their primary reasoning, but that they intended to present further proofs of their statements (see *Tosafot*).

בַּעַל מוּם, מֵעִיקָּרָא שָׁרֵי בַּאֲכִילָה וְאָסוּר בַּעֲבוֹדָה, אִיטַּמֵּי לֵיהּ, מִגּוֹ דְּקָא מִיתְּסַר בַּאֲכִילָה מִיתְּסַר נַמִי בַּעֲבוֹדָה, אֶלָּא מְלִיקָה – בְּבַת אַחַת הִיא דְּמַשְׁכַּחַת לָהּ, בְּאִיסּוּר כּוֹלֵל לָא מַשְׁכַּחַת לָהּ!

The same is true with regard to **a blemished priest** who served in the Temple while ritually impure: **Initially,** prior to his becoming ritually impure, **he was allowed to eat** from the consecrated animals **but was prohibited from** performing **the** Temple **service,** like all blemished priests. When **he was rendered ritually impure, since he is** now **prohibited from eating** of the consecrated items, **he is also prohibited from** performing the Temple **service** due to that same ritual impurity. There is, then, a more inclusive prohibition here. **However,** with regard to the case of a bird that was killed by **pinching, you find** that the prohibition against the eating of consecrated items by a non-priest and the prohibition against eating an unslaughtered animal carcass take effect **simultaneously.**[N] **You do not,** however, **find a more inclusive prohibition** here as there was no original prohibition that took effect beforehand. Instead, this is a case of two prohibitions that take effect simultaneously.

אֶלָּא קָמִיפַּלְגִי בְּאִיסּוּר בְּבַת אַחַת וְאַלִּיבָּא דְּרַבִּי יוֹסֵי: רַבִּי חִיָּיא סָבַר, רַבִּי יוֹסֵי בְּאִיסּוּר בַּת אַחַת מִיחַיַּיב תַּרְתֵּי, וּבַר קַפָּרָא סָבַר, לָא מִיחַיַּיב אֶלָּא חֲדָא.

Rather, the previous explanation is rejected and the Gemara suggests instead that **they disagree with regard to** an additional **prohibition** that takes effect **simultaneously, and** this dispute pertains to the status of these prohibitions specifically **according to** the opinion of **Rabbi Yosei.**[N] **Rabbi Ḥiyya holds that Rabbi Yosei** is of the opinion that **one is liable on two** counts in cases of **prohibitions** that take effect **simultaneously. And bar Kappara holds** that Rabbi Yosei is of the opinion that **one is liable only on a single** count.

וְהָכָא – מַאי אִיסּוּר בַּת אַחַת אִיכָּא הָכָא? זָר שֶׁשִּׁימֵּשׁ בְּשַׁבָּת, כְּגוֹן דְּאַיְיתֵי שְׁתֵּי שְׂעָרוֹת בְּשַׁבָּת, דְּהָוְיָא לְהוּ זָרוּת וְשַׁבָּת בַּהֲדֵי הֲדָדֵי.

The Gemara challenges this explanation: **But here,** in the first two instances, **what** case of **simultaneous prohibitions is there here?** In the two previous cases the prohibitions took effect one after the other, and not simultaneously. The Gemara answers that these cases can also be interpreted as occurring simultaneously as follows: With regard to **the non-priest who served on Shabbat, this would be in a case where** a minor **grew two** pubic **hairs,**[N] signaling adulthood **on Shabbat.** Before that point he was considered a minor and therefore not liable for his actions. Therefore, **this is** a case where the prohibition against serving as **a non-priest and** the prohibition against violating **Shabbat** took effect **together.**

בַּעַל מוּם נַמִי – כְּגוֹן דְּאַיְיתֵי שְׁתֵּי שְׂעָרוֹת וְאִיטַּמֵּי לֵיהּ, דְּהָוְיָא לֵיהּ בַּעַל מוּם וְטוּמְאָה בַּהֲדֵי הֲדָדֵי. אִי נַמִי: שֶׁחָתַךְ אֶצְבָּעוֹ בְּסַכִּין טְמֵאָה.

With regard to the case of **one who was blemished,** this can be explained **as well:** This is referring to a case **where** a minor **grew two** pubic **hairs and was** immediately **rendered ritually impure. This is** a case where the prohibition with regard to **a blemished** priest **and** the prohibition with regard to **ritual impurity** took effect **together. Alternatively,** it could be a case **where he cut off his finger with a ritually impure knife.**[HN] Here, the cut and removal of his finger rendered him simultaneously blemished and ritually impure.

בִּשְׁלָמָא לְרַבִּי חִיָּיא, כִּי אַתְנְיֵיהּ לְדִידֵיהּ – אַלִּיבָּא דְּרַבִּי יוֹסֵי, כִּי אַתְנְיֵיהּ לְבַר קַפָּרָא – אַלִּיבָּא דְּרַבִּי שִׁמְעוֹן, אֶלָּא לְבַר קַפָּרָא – רַבִּי חִיָּיא שַׁקּוּרֵי קָא מְשַׁקֵּר?!

Following this clarification of the dispute, the matter is now considered from a different angle: **Granted, according to** the opinion of **Rabbi Ḥiyya,** the dispute between his version of Rabbi Yehuda HaNasi's ruling and that of bar Kappara can be explained as follows: **When Rabbi** Yehuda HaNasi **taught** Rabbi Ḥiyya, he taught him **according to** the opinion of **Rabbi Yosei,** and Rabbi Yosei holds that there are cases where two prohibitions can both take effect. And **when** Rabbi Yehuda HaNasi **taught bar Kappara,** he did so **according to** the opinion of **Rabbi Shimon** who holds that a new prohibition can never take effect where another prohibition already exists. Therefore, Rabbi Ḥiyya could understand why bar Kappara insisted on his opinion. Rabbi Ḥiyya thought that bar Kappara was in fact relating an accurate statement of Rabbi Yehuda HaNasi, as Rabbi Yehuda HaNasi was relating to the opinion of Rabbi Shimon. Rabbi Ḥiyya assumed that bar Kappara did not understand that Rabbi Yehuda HaNasi's statement was not in accordance with Rabbi Yosei's opinion. **According to bar Kappara, however, was Rabbi Ḥiyya then telling a falsehood?** How would bar Kappara relate to Rabbi Ḥiyya's oath? Did he think that Rabbi Ḥiyya would swear that he heard words from Rabbi Yehuda HaNasi that were never said?

NOTES

Pinching…takes effect simultaneously – מְלִיקָה בְּבַת אַחַת: *Tosafot* ask: Why is this case considered a case of prohibitions that take effect simultaneously, when the prohibition with regard to an unslaughtered animal carcass takes effect before the prohibition for a non-priest to eat consecrated food? Rabbi Avraham *Av Beit Din* explains that the case of eating a bird killed by pinching is also a case of a minor who grew two pubic hairs. He maintains that from that moment of maturity both prohibitions take effect at once. Indeed, the person in this case is both a non-priest and he is prohibited from eating from the pinched bird. This cannot, however, be said with regard to the case of ritual impurity, since the prohibition cannot apply unless one was actually rendered impure. The early commentaries discussed this opinion. Some rejected it (Rashba), while others showed how it could be supported (Ramban; Ritva).

A prohibition that takes effect simultaneously and according to Rabbi Yosei – אִיסּוּר בְּבַת אַחַת וְאַלִּיבָּא דְּרַבִּי יוֹסֵי: All agree that it is more reasonable for two prohibitions to take effect in cases where the prohibitions take effect simultaneously, as opposed to cases where an additional prohibition takes effect after the first has already taken effect. *Tosefot HaRosh* adds, however, that there is still a certain deficiency in cases where two prohibitions take effect at once. He maintains that in these cases the less severe prohibition would not take effect together with a more severe prohibition. However, in cases of additional prohibitions that take effect one after another, one could maintain that any additional prohibition would take effect, no matter how minor.

Where he grew two pubic hairs, etc. – דְּאַיְיתֵי שְׁתֵּי שְׂעָרוֹת וכו׳: The *Ḥazon Ish* says that one cannot explain the case of a brother's wife and a wife's sister as prohibitions that take effect simultaneously when one grows two pubic hairs. This is because there is a distinction between prohibitions that apply to a person himself, which apply immediately upon reaching adulthood, and prohibitions that apply to an object (see Ramban and Rashba).

Where he cut off his finger with a ritually impure knife – שֶׁחָתַךְ אֶצְבָּעוֹ בְּסַכִּין טְמֵאָה: *Tosafot* point out a difficulty with this explanation: While impurity is contracted immediately upon contact, the blemish appeared only afterward, and therefore this is not a case of simultaneous prohibitions. They resolve this by explaining that the situation is one where the finger was only loosely attached, so that by a single cut both the impurity was transferred and the blemish appeared at once. The Meiri adds that it must be that another individual cut one's finger off, for if one had himself wielded the knife, he would have been rendered impure already at the moment of contact with the knife. In contrast, *Tosafot Yeshanim* hold that since these two occurrences were so close in time, they are in fact considered a single act, and therefore both prohibitions took effect simultaneously.

HALAKHA

A prohibition that takes effect where another prohibition exists – אִיסּוּר חָל עַל אִיסּוּר: There is a general principle of prohibitions in the Torah that states that a prohibition cannot take effect where another prohibition exists unless both of the prohibitions take effect simultaneously or one prohibition makes additions to the previous prohibition or if it comes to include other matters that were not in the original prohibition (Rambam *Sefer Kedusha, Hilkhot Issurei Bia* 17:8, *Hilkhot Ma'akhalot Assurot* 8:6, and *Sefer Korbanot, Hilkhot Shegagot* 4:1).

אֶלָּא: קָמִיפַּלְגִי בְּאִיסּוּר בַּת אַחַת, וְאַלִּיבָּא דְּרַבִּי שִׁמְעוֹן. בִּשְׁלָמָא לְרַבִּי חִיָּיא, קָא מִישְׁתַּבַּע לְאַפּוֹקֵי לְרַבִּי שִׁמְעוֹן מֵחֶזְקֵיהּ, אֶלָּא לְבַר קַפָּרָא – לָמָּה לֵיהּ לְאִשְׁתַּבּוּעֵי? קַשְׁיָא.

Rather, this must be explained differently: Rabbi Ḥiyya and bar Kappara **disagree** with regard to cases where two **prohibitions** take effect **simultaneously, and** this dispute pertains to the status of these prohibition specifically **according to** the opinion of **Rabbi Shimon.** It could be suggested that when the two prohibitions take effect simultaneously, Rabbi Shimon would concede that they both take effect. However, this explanation raises a difficulty as well: **Granted, according to Rabbi Ḥiyya** it is clear why **he was swearing.** He did so in order **to exclude** the understanding of **Rabbi Shimon's** opinion that was based on **his presumed** opinion. As it was known that Rabbi Shimon holds that a new prohibition cannot take effect where another prohibition exists; this is the default understanding of his opinion. Therefore, it was incumbent upon Rabbi Ḥiyya to take an oath in order to emphasize that despite Rabbi Shimon's general opinion, in cases where the prohibitions take effect simultaneously, he would concede that both prohibitions can take effect. **However, according to bar Kappara, why was it necessary to swear?** It would have sufficed for him simply to make his statement, as it concurs with the default understanding of Rabbi Shimon's opinion. The Gemara comments: Indeed, this is **difficult.**

בִּשְׁלָמָא לְבַר קַפָּרָא, כִּי אַתְנְיֵיהּ רַבִּי לְדִידֵיהּ – אַלִּיבָּא דְּרַבִּי שִׁמְעוֹן, כִּי אַתְנְיֵיהּ לְרַבִּי חִיָּיא – אַלִּיבָּא דְּרַבִּי יוֹסֵי. אֶלָּא לְרַבִּי חִיָּיא, בַּר קַפָּרָא שַׁקּוּרֵי קָא מְשַׁקֵּר?

One can raise a difficulty with this explanation from a different angle as well: **Granted, according to bar Kappara, when Rabbi** Yehuda HaNasi **taught him,** he taught him **according to** the opinion of **Rabbi Shimon,** who holds that two prohibitions cannot take effect even in cases when they occur simultaneously, and **when he taught** the ruling **to Rabbi Ḥiyya** it was **according to** the opinion of **Rabbi Yosei.** Accordingly, Rabbi Ḥiyya did in fact swear that he heard that one is liable only on one count, but he wrongly understood that this was Rabbi Shimon's opinion. **However, according to Rabbi Ḥiyya,** who holds that Rabbi Shimon concedes that in cases where the prohibitions take effect simultaneously one is liable for both, was **bar Kappara lying?** His statement would accord neither with Rabbi Shimon nor with Rabbi Yosei.

אָמַר לָךְ רַבִּי חִיָּיא: כִּי אַתְנְיֵיהּ רַבִּי לְדִידֵיהּ – תַּרְתֵּי לִפְטוֹר אַתְנְיֵיהּ,

The Gemara answers: **Rabbi Ḥiyya** could have **said to you** that this is what transpired: **When Rabbi** Yehuda HaNasi **taught him,** bar Kappara, **he taught him two** cases involving **exemptions,** i.e., the cases of a non-priest who served in the Temple on Shabbat and that of the blemished priest who served while ritually impure. Both of these are cases of more inclusive prohibitions, and he was informing bar Kappara that Rabbi Shimon holds them liable on only one count, because Rabbi Shimon holds that a prohibition takes effect where another prohibition already exists only if the prohibitions take effect simultaneously, but not in cases of more inclusive prohibitions.

וְאִיסּוּר כּוֹלֵל אַתְנְיֵיהּ, וְאַלִּיבָּא דְּרַבִּי שִׁמְעוֹן, וְחַזְיָא לְבַר קַפָּרָא לְזָר שֶׁאָכַל מְלִיקָה, וְאַיְּידֵי דְּדָמְיָא לְהָ – עַרְבִּהּ בַּהֲדַיְיהוּ, וְעַיֵּין בַּהּ, וְלָא אַשְׁכַּח אֶלָּא בְּבַת אַחַת.

And he taught him the ruling with regard to **a more inclusive prohibition,** that in such cases there is an exemption, **and** this ruling is **in accordance with** the opinion of **Rabbi Shimon. And bar Kappara** then saw the case of **a non-priest who ate** a bird killed by **pinching, and since it was similar** to the previous cases, **he mixed them together.** Then, sometime later, it seemed to him as though he had in truth heard all of these cases together from Rabbi Yehuda HaNasi, **but** when **he examined this** last case, **he found** that it could exist **only** if the events occurred **simultaneously.**

וְסָבַר: מִדְּהָא בְּבַת אַחַת – הָא נַמִי בְּבַת אַחַת, וּמִדְּהָנָךְ לִפְטוֹר – הָנָךְ נַמִי לִפְטוֹר.

And he concluded that **since** the case of a non-priest eating a bird killed by pinching can occur only in a scenario where the prohibitions take effect **simultaneously,** the other cases are instances of **simultaneous** prohibitions **as well. And** similarly, **since** he was taught **to exempt** one individual from a second prohibition in **those cases, these cases** were taught **to exempt** one individual from a second prohibition **as well.** Therefore, according to Rabbi Ḥiyya, bar Kappara did not knowingly speak falsely. Rather, he heard certain matters from Rabbi Yehuda HaNasi and then mistakenly merged with them other matters. As a result, he confused the issue.

מֵיתִיבֵי: זָר שֶׁשִּׁימֵּשׁ בְּשַׁבָּת, וּבַעַל מוּם שֶׁשִּׁימֵּשׁ בְּטוּמְאָה – יֵשׁ כָּאן מִשּׁוּם זָרוּת, וּמִשּׁוּם שַׁבָּת, וּמִשּׁוּם בַּעַל מוּם, וּמִשּׁוּם טוּמְאָה, דִּבְרֵי רַבִּי יוֹסֵי. רַבִּי שִׁמְעוֹן אוֹמֵר: אֵין כָּאן אֶלָּא מִשּׁוּם זָרוּת וּבַעַל מוּם בִּלְבַד. וְאִילּוּ מְלִיקָה שַׁיְּירָהּ.

The Gemara **raises an objection** to the statement of bar Kappara from a *baraita*: In the case of **a non-priest who served on Shabbat and** the case of **a blemished priest who served while ritually impure, there is** liability **here, due to** the prohibition against serving as **a non-priest; and due to** the prohibition against desecrating **Shabbat; and due to** the prohibition against serving as **a blemished priest; and due to** the prohibition against serving after contracting **ritual impurity.** This is **the statement of Rabbi Yosei. Rabbi Shimon says: There is** liability **here only due to** the prohibition against serving as **a non-priest and due to** the prohibition against serving as **a blemished priest.** The Gemara notes: **And yet** the case of a non-priest who ate a bird killed by **pinching was left out**[N] and not mentioned among the cases subject to this dispute.

לְמַאן שַׁיְּירָהּ? אִילֵימָא לְרַבִּי יוֹסֵי – הַשְׁתָּא רַבִּי יוֹסֵי בְּאִיסּוּר כּוֹלֵל מִיחַיַּיב שְׁתַּיִם, בְּאִיסּוּר בַּת אַחַת מִיבַּעְיָא? אֶלָּא לָאו – לְרַבִּי שִׁמְעוֹן וּבְאִיסּוּר כּוֹלֵל הוּא דְּפָטַר – אֲבָל בְּאִיסּוּר בְּבַת אַחַת מִיחַיַּיב, תְּיוּבְתָּא דְּבַר קַפָּרָא! תְּיוּבְתָּא.

The Gemara asks: **According to whom was this left out?** That is, according to the opinion of which *tanna* would this question arise? **If we say** that this was left out **according to** the opinion of **Rabbi Yosei,** it is difficult. **Now** that **Rabbi Yosei** holds, even **in** cases of **a more inclusive prohibition, that one is liable on two** counts,[N] as was stated with regard to a non-priest who served on Shabbat, **is it necessary** to state that in the case **where the** additional **prohibition** takes effect **simultaneously** one would be liable on two counts? **Rather, is it not according to** the opinion of **Rabbi Shimon** that this case was left out, as Rabbi Shimon would concede that in this case one is liable on two counts? Therefore, Rabbi Shimon **exempts** one from liability for the second prohibition in cases of **more inclusive prohibitions, but in** cases of **simultaneous prohibitions** he would **deem** one **liable** on two counts. The Gemara summarizes: **The refutation** of the opinion **of bar Kappara** is indeed **a conclusive refutation,** and his statements are rejected.

״זָר שֶׁשִּׁימֵּשׁ בְּשַׁבָּת״, בְּמַאי? אִי בִּשְׁחִיטָה – שְׁחִיטָה בְּזָר כְּשֵׁרָה, וְאִי בְּקַבָּלָה וְהוֹלָכָה – טִלְטוּל בְּעָלְמָא הוּא.

The Gemara raises a question with regard to one of the laws mentioned above. The *baraita* mentioned the case of **a non-priest who served on Shabbat.** The Gemara wonders: **In what** form of service did he perform in the Temple? **If** this is referring to a case where a non-priest performed **the slaughtering** of the sacrificial animal, there would be no prohibition, as the **slaughtering by a non-priest is valid. And if** it is referring to **receiving** the blood **and carrying** the blood to the altar, while this is a case where he would be liable as a non-priest performing the service of a priest, insofar as Shabbat is concerned **this is a case only of moving,** and it does not entail a violation of any prohibited labor.

NOTES

And yet the case of a non-priest who ate a bird killed by pinching was left out – וְאִילּוּ מְלִיקָה שַׁיְּירָהּ: The question arises: How can evidence be derived from the fact that this *halakha* is absent? Must the *tanna* teach all of the cases? The commentaries answer that were the case of eating of a bird killed by pinching indeed included in this dispute, it would have been appropriate to state it here because it would teach the novel ruling that Rabbi Shimon dissents even in cases of simultaneous prohibitions. Moreover, if the dispute was indeed about simultaneous prohibitions, then in the case of a non-priest who served on Shabbat, Rabbi Shimon would hold that the more severe prohibition of Shabbat would apply, not the prohibition against being a non-priest. The fact that Rabbi Shimon states that one would be liable only for serving as a non-priest indicates that the case is one of two prohibitions that take effect one after another, where one is liable only for the first prohibition (*Arukh LaNer*).

One is liable on two counts – מִיחַיַּיב שְׁתַּיִם: According to all opinions, this does not refer to two sin-offerings but rather the transgression of two prohibitions, each according to its own ruling (Ramban; Rashba).

אִי בְּהַקְטָרָה – וְהָאָמַר רַבִּי יוֹסֵי: הַבְעָרָה לְלָאו יָצְאתָה!

If he served **by burning**[N] the sacrificial portions on the altar, then this discussion follows the opinion of Rabbi Yosei, **but didn't Rabbi Yosei say** that the prohibition against **kindling on Shabbat was** singled **out** to teach that one who lights a fire on Shabbat merely violates **a prohibition?** This is as opposed to the other prohibited labors, which incur death penalties when violated willfully and entail the bringing of a sin-offering when violated unintentionally. Why, then, would Rabbi Yosei deem one liable for two sin-offerings?

אָמַר רַב אַחָא בַּר יַעֲקֹב: בִּשְׁחִיטַת פָּרוֹ שֶׁל כֹּהֵן גָּדוֹל, וּכְדִבְרֵי הָאוֹמֵר: שְׁחִיטַת פָּרוֹ שֶׁל כֹּהֵן גָּדוֹל בְּזָר – פְּסוּלָה. אִי הָכִי מַאי אִירְיָא זָר, אֲפִילּוּ כֹּהֵן הֶדְיוֹט נַמִי! שֶׁזָּר אֶצְלוֹ קָאָמַר.

Rav Aḥa bar Yaakov said: The service referred to **in** this case is **the slaughtering of the High Priest's bull**[N] on Yom Kippur, **and this is in accordance with the statement of the one who says** that **the slaughtering of the High Priest's bull**[N] **is disqualified** if performed **by a non-priest,** for this service is designated specifically for the High Priest alone. The Gemara asks: **If so,** that this is referring to the slaughtering of the High Priest's bull, then **why specifically** state **a non-priest? The same would hold true even** for **a common priest as well.** The Gemara answers: **This is referring to one who is as a non-priest in relation to** the High Priest and not to an actual non-priest. The Hebrew word *zar* literally means foreigner, and this type of service is considered foreign to a common priest as well as a non-priest.

מַתְקִיף לָהּ רַב אַשִׁי: מִידֵי חַטָּאוֹת קָתָנֵי, אוֹ לָאוֵי קָתָנֵי? אֶלָּא: אִיסּוּרֵי בְּעָלְמָא קָא חָשֵׁיב. לְמַאי נָפְקָא מִינָּהּ – לְקוֹבְרוֹ בֵּין רְשָׁעִים גְּמוּרִים.

Rav Ashi strongly objects to this: The previous rejection that was based on the idea that the act of burning was not a full-fledged prohibited labor is in fact groundless. **Is the** *tanna* **teaching** how many **sin-offerings** would be incurred, **or is he teaching** how many **negative mitzvot** are being violated? **Rather, he merely** enumerates **the prohibitions**[N] violated by a certain action, without detailing their severities, and therefore the desecration of Shabbat involved in the Temple service can be any Shabbat violation. The Gemara asks: **What practical difference does it make** how many prohibitions are involved? The Gemara answers: It affects the decision whether or not **to bury him among the completely wicked.** If he violated two prohibitions, he is considered wicked on two counts and consequently must be buried accordingly.

מתני׳ שְׁנַיִם שֶׁקִּידְּשׁוּ שְׁתֵּי נָשִׁים, וּבִשְׁעַת כְּנִיסָתָן לְחוּפָּה הֶחֱלִיפוּ אֶת שֶׁל זֶה לָזֶה וְאֶת שֶׁל זֶה לָזֶה – הֲרֵי אֵלּוּ חַיָּיבִין מִשּׁוּם אֵשֶׁת אִישׁ. וְאִם הָיוּ אַחִין – מִשּׁוּם אֵשֶׁת אָח, וְאִם הָיוּ אֲחָיוֹת – מִשּׁוּם אִשָּׁה אֶל אֲחוֹתָהּ, וְאִם הָיוּ נִדּוֹת – מִשּׁוּם נִדָּה.

MISHNA In the case of **two** men **who betrothed two women, and at the time that they entered the wedding canopy,** after the betrothal, the men **switched**[H] **this** wife **with that** wife **and that** one **with this** one, **then these** two men **are liable for** engaging in forbidden sexual relations with **a married woman,** since each of them had intercourse with his fellow's wife. The act of betrothal is sufficient to prohibit a woman to all other men as a married woman. Therefore, when the women were switched, both men transgressed this violation. **And if they were brothers,**[N] then they are also liable **for** forbidden sexual relations with **a brother's wife. And if** these women **were sisters,** then they are liable **for** taking **a wife and her sister** as well. **And if they were menstruating women,** they would be liable **for** intercourse with **a menstruating woman** as well.

NOTES

If by burning – אִי בְּהַקְטָרָה: Rashi and others explain that this refers to the burning of the sacrificial portions on the altar. However, the Ritva seems to hold that this refers to the burning of incense. It is stated in the Jerusalem Talmud, in tractate *Shabbat*, that Rabbi Yosei does not deem one liable for kindling but rather for cooking. Although this seems to support Rashi's understanding, it can also be interpreted according to the Ritva's opinion.

The slaughtering of the High Priest's bull – שְׁחִיטַת פָּרוֹ שֶׁל כֹּהֵן גָּדוֹל: *Arukh LaNer* notes that this phrase in the Gemara indicates that the term Shabbat here is not referring to actual Shabbat but rather Yom Kippur, which is also called Shabbat. This is not a certain proof, however, since it could also be referring to a Yom Kippur that occurred on Shabbat. The Rivan writes that this suggested resolution of the Gemara is inexact, for even if the slaughtering of the High Priest's bull by a non-priest is prohibited, it is still not a prohibition that incurs *karet*, nor is it a negative mitzva. It would seem that the Gemara itself did not raise this objection because the suggestion is not sustained in the end.

The High Priest's bull – פָּרוֹ שֶׁל כֹּהֵן גָּדוֹל: On Yom Kippur, the High Priest sacrifices a bull as a sin-offering for himself, his family, and all the members of the priesthood (see Leviticus, chapter 16).

Rather he merely enumerates the prohibitions – אֶלָּא אִיסּוּרֵי בְּעָלְמָא קָא חָשֵׁיב: Rashi explains that according to this conclusion, Rabbi Yosei must be referring to receiving and carrying the blood. However, *Tosafot Yeshanim* explains that it is possible that he is even referring to burning. Although this does not entail the bringing of a sin-offering according to Rabbi Yosei, it is nevertheless prohibited by Torah law.

And if they were brothers, etc. – וְאִם הָיוּ אַחִין וכו׳: The commentaries note: If the mishna wanted to demonstrate cases where several prohibitions are violated by a single act, it could have enumerated more prohibitions. For example, it could have taught that these men were already married, and that the women that they inadvertently married were the daughters of their wives from a previous marriage. They therefore conclude that the mishna served to teach us only the different types of prohibitions that might be mutually applicable, each on the basis of the other's actions. Although according to this understanding it would have been unnecessary to mention the prohibition with regard to a menstruating woman, this case teaches a novelty in that it pertains to something that is presently prohibited but will eventually become permitted (*Tosefot HaRosh*).

HALAKHA

Switched women – נָשִׁים שֶׁהוּחְלְפוּ: If two men betrothed two women, who were then switched when they entered the wedding canopy, they are liable for having intercourse with a married woman. If they are brothers, they are also liable for intercourse with a brother's wife. If the women are sisters, they are also liable for intercourse with a wife's sister. If the women were menstruating, they are also liable for intercourse with a menstruating woman (Rambam *Sefer Korbanot*, *Hilkhot Shegagot* 4:1).

וּמַפְרִישִׁין אוֹתָן שְׁלֹשָׁה חֳדָשִׁים, שֶׁמָּא מְעוּבָּרוֹת הֵן, וְאִם הָיוּ קְטַנּוֹת שֶׁאֵינָן רְאוּיוֹת לֵילֵד – מַחֲזִירִים אוֹתָן מִיָּד, וְאִם הָיוּ כֹּהֲנוֹת – נִפְסְלוּ מִן הַתְּרוּמָה.

And following these forbidden sexual relations, **we separate** these women from their husbands **for three months,**[H] **lest they were impregnated** by that forbidden act of intercourse. Doing so makes it possible to distinguish a child born of these relations, so that he could be rendered a *mamzer*. **And if they were female minors and unable to bear children, then we immediately return them** to their original husbands. **And if they were daughters of priests, they are** thereby **disqualified from eating of** ***teruma*****.** By engaging in illicit sexual acts, they were rendered forbidden to priests and disqualified from eating *teruma*.

גמ׳ ״הֶחֱלִיפוּ״, מִידֵי בִּרְשִׁיעֵי עָסְקִינַן?! וְתוּ: הָא דְּתָנֵי רַבִּי חִיָּיא: הֲרֵי כָּאן שֵׁשׁ עֶשְׂרֵה חַטָּאוֹת. אִי בְּמֵזִיד – מִי אִיכָּא קָרְבָּן? אָמַר רַב יְהוּדָה, תְּנֵי: הוּחְלְפוּ.

GEMARA In the mishna it states: **They switched** this one with that one. **Are we dealing with** such **wicked individuals**[N] that they would intentionally switch their wives? **And furthermore,** consider **that which Rabbi Ḥiyya taught** on this subject: **There are sixteen sin-offerings here,** four sin-offerings for each of the men and four for each of the women. Yet, **if** they had acted **intentionally would there be an offering?**[N] Sacrifices are brought only for unintentional acts. **Rav Yehuda said: Teach** instead **they were switched,** which indicates that the switching was not done intentionally; rather, the women were accidentally mixed up.

הָכִי נַמִי מִסְתַּבְּרָא, דְּקָתָנֵי סֵיפָא: אִם הָיוּ קְטַנּוֹת שֶׁאֵינָן רְאוּיוֹת לֵילֵד – מַחֲזִירִין אוֹתָן מִיָּד. וְאִי בְּמֵזִיד – מִי שַׁרְיָא? הָא לָא קַשְׁיָא: פִּיתּוּי קְטַנָּה – אוֹנֶס נִינְהוּ, וְאוֹנֶס בְּיִשְׂרָאֵל מִישְׁרָא שָׁרֵי.

The Gemara comments: **This, too, stands to reason from the fact that the latter clause teaches: If they were female minors and unable to bear children, then we immediately return them. And if** this had been done **intentionally, would it be permitted** to return a woman who had engaged in illicit sexual acts to her husband? The Gemara comments: **This is not difficult** and does not disprove the notion that the act was intentional. Even if the act was intentional, these women would be permitted to return to their husbands. This is because the **seduction of a minor girl is** considered **rape, and** after **rape** a woman **is permitted** to return **to an Israelite**[H] husband.

אֶלָּא דְּקָתָנֵי: מַפְרִישִׁין אוֹתָן שְׁלֹשָׁה חֳדָשִׁים שֶׁמָּא מְעוּבָּרוֹת הֵן, הָא לָאו מְעוּבָּרוֹת – שַׁרְיָין, וְאִי בְּמֵזִיד – מִי שָׁרֵי? אֶלָּא לָאו שְׁמַע מִינָּהּ: הוּחְלְפוּ, שְׁמַע מִינָּהּ.

However, this can be derived from a different point **that** the mishna **teaches: We separate** these women from their husbands **for three months,** as **perhaps they** became **pregnant.** From here it can be deduced: **Were** it to become clear after three months that **they are not pregnant, they are permitted** to return to their husbands. **And if** they had acted **intentionally, would this be permitted? Rather,** must one **not conclude from here** that the mishna is referring to a case where **they were switched** inadvertently? The Gemara summarizes: Indeed, **conclude from here** that this is the case.

HALAKHA

We separate them for three months – מַפְרִישִׁין אוֹתָן שְׁלֹשָׁה חֳדָשִׁים: In cases where a woman was mistakenly married in a forbidden manner, if she engaged in sexual intercourse, she is then separated for three months to check if she became pregnant. This is in order to distinguish between an illegitimate child and one who was conceived lawfully. If she was a minor, she is not separated, since the Sages did not make decrees for impossible eventualities (Rambam *Sefer Nashim, Hilkhot Geirushin* 11:18; *Shulḥan Arukh, Even HaEzer* 13:8).

After rape a woman is permitted to return to an Israelite – אוֹנֶס בְּיִשְׂרָאֵל מִישְׁרָא שָׁרֵי: If the wife of an Israelite was raped, she is permitted to her husband but forbidden to priests, such that if she is widowed, she is prohibited from marrying a priest (Rambam *Sefer Kedusha, Hilkhot Issurei Bia* 18:7–8; *Shulḥan Arukh, Even HaEzer* 6:11).

NOTES

Are we dealing with wicked individuals, etc. – מִידֵי בִּרְשִׁיעֵי וכו׳: Although there are several *halakhot* in the Mishna that deal with cases of wicked individuals such as these, were the reference here to an intentional act, this particular mishna would not have taught anything especially novel. The only novel teaching would be the need to bury them among the completely wicked. If, however, the mishna is referring to a case where the men acted unintentionally, the novel element is the number of sin-offerings that they are obligated to bring (Rashash).

If intentionally, would there be an offering – אִי בְּמֵזִיד מִי אִיכָּא קָרְבָּן: Although it could be suggested that the husbands acted intentionally while the women were unaware and therefore acted unwittingly, such an explanation is not reasonable as the Mishna does not generally refer to two different types of behavior within a single case (Ramban).

Perek **III**
Daf **34** Amud **a**

וּמַאן הַאי תַּנָּא דְּאִית לֵיהּ אִיסּוּר כּוֹלֵל וְאִיסּוּר מוֹסִיף וְאִיסּוּר בַּת אַחַת?

The Gemara asks: According to Rabbi Ḥiyya, who teaches that this case incurs sixteen sin-offerings, **who is this** ***tanna*** **who holds** that a prohibition takes effect where another prohibition already exists[H] for **a more inclusive prohibition, an expanded prohibition, and a simultaneous prohibition?** If these men are brothers, the moment that one betrothed a woman, that woman was immediately rendered forbidden to the second brother both as a married woman and as his brother's wife. When the second brother betrothed her sister, this added the prohibition pertaining to his wife's sister. This is a more inclusive prohibition because, as a result of this betrothal, the second brother is prohibited from engaging in sexual intercourse not only with his wife's sister, who is his brother's wife, but also with all of her other sisters. When this woman becomes a menstruating woman, she is forbidden to her husband as well, which is an expanded prohibition. Consequently, the mishna includes examples of all three types of prohibitions and asserts that they all take effect in this case. Therefore, the Gemara wonders which *tanna* holds that in each of these cases the prohibition takes effect even where another prohibition exists.

HALAKHA

A prohibition takes effect where another prohibition already exists – אִיסּוּר חָל עַל אִיסּוּר: A prohibition takes effect where another prohibition already exists only if both prohibitions take effect simultaneously, or if the second prohibition is a more inclusive prohibition or an expanded prohibition (Rambam *Sefer Korbanot, Hilkhot Shegagot* 4:1).

HALAKHA

Obligation to bring four sin-offerings and one guilt-offering for a single eating – חִיּוּב אַרְבַּע חַטָּאוֹת וְאָשָׁם אֶחָד בַּאֲכִילָה אַחַת: One who was ritually impure and ate an olive-bulk of prohibited fats that were leftover from a consecrated animal on Yom Kippur is obligated to bring four sin-offerings: One for eating prohibited fat, one for eating *notar*, one for eating consecrated food while ritually impure, and one for eating on Yom Kippur. This ruling applies in a case where one had previously eaten other food, so that altogether he ate a total of a date-bulk. In addition, he is obligated to bring a guilt-offering for deriving benefit from consecrated property (Rambam *Sefer Korbanot*, *Hilkhot Shegagot* 6:4).

אָמַר רַב יְהוּדָה אָמַר רַב: רַבִּי מֵאִיר הִיא. דְּתַנְיָא: יֵשׁ אוֹכֵל אֲכִילָה אַחַת וְחַיָּיב עָלֶיהָ אַרְבַּע חַטָּאוֹת וְאָשָׁם אֶחָד.

Rav Yehuda said that Rav said: This is the opinion of **Rabbi Meir,**[N] **as it is taught** in a *baraita*: **There is** one who performs a single act of **eating**[N] an olive-bulk of food, **and he is liable to bring four sin-offerings and one guilt-offering.**[H]

טָמֵא שֶׁאָכַל חֵלֶב וְהוּא נוֹתָר מִן מוּקְדָּשִׁין בְּיוֹם הַכִּפּוּרִים.

How so? This *halakha* applies to one who is **ritually impure who ate** forbidden **fat**[N] that was ***notar* from a consecrated offering,** i.e., it remained after the time when it was permitted to eat it, and this occurred **on Yom Kippur.** One who did this is liable to bring one sin offering for eating consecrated food while impure, one for eating forbidden fat, one for eating *notar*,[N] and one for eating on Yom Kippur. He is also liable to bring a guilt-offering for misuse of consecrated items. In this case, it was prohibited to eat the fat from the moment the animal was born. When the animal was consecrated, the prohibition against deriving benefit from it took effect on the entire animal, rendering this an expanded prohibition. When the priest became ritually impure and thereby prohibited from partaking of all sanctified foods, a more inclusive prohibition took effect. The moment the fat was rendered *notar*, it became prohibited to offer it on the altar as well, so that that is another instance of an expanded prohibition. Lastly, on Yom Kippur, an additional, more inclusive prohibition took effect because on Yom Kippur it is prohibited to eat all food, even that which is not consecrated.

רַבִּי מֵאִיר אוֹמֵר: אִם הָיְתָה שַׁבָּת וְהוֹצִיאוֹ בְּפִיו – חַיָּיב. אָמְרוּ לוֹ: אֵינוֹ מִן הַשֵּׁם.

Rabbi Meir says: There is one more sin-offering for which he may be liable. **If it was Shabbat and he carried** this olive-bulk of food from one domain to another **in his mouth,**[N] **he is liable** for carrying out on Shabbat. The Rabbis **said to** Rabbi Meir: Liability for the sin-offering that you added **is not** incurred **from** violation **of the** same **type** of prohibition. He is liable for carrying out the food, not for eating it. In this example, the prohibitions of Shabbat and Yom Kippur take effect at the same moment, and therefore this last case would be an instance of simultaneous prohibitions, and Rabbi Meir holds that they take effect as well. Therefore, this *baraita* demonstrates that Rabbi Meir holds that prohibitions take effect where other prohibitions already exist in all of these instances: More inclusive prohibitions, expanded prohibitions, and simultaneous prohibitions.

NOTES

This is the opinion of Rabbi Meir – רַבִּי מֵאִיר הִיא: From the fact that the Gemara ascribes this opinion to Rabbi Meir, some infer that Rabbi Yosei does not hold that more inclusive prohibitions take effect where another prohibition already exists (see *Keren Or*). Many early commentaries, however, suggest that Rabbi Yosei maintains that more inclusive prohibitions take effect as well, and here the Gemara simply sought out a source where a *tanna* explicitly states that all three types of prohibitions do, in fact, take effect (*Tosafot Yeshanim*; Ritva; Meiri).

There is one who performs a single act of eating, etc. – יֵשׁ אוֹכֵל אֲכִילָה אַחַת וכו׳: Rabbeinu Ḥananel explains that the simultaneous prohibitions here involve one who was rendered ritually impure and then grew two pubic hairs, indicating that he reached maturity. Under such circumstances, both the prohibition against eating consecrated food while ritually impure and the prohibition against eating forbidden fats take effect at once. Accordingly, the first *tanna* also holds that these three types of prohibitions, i.e., expanded prohibitions, more inclusive prohibitions, and simultaneous prohibitions, all take effect where another prohibition already exists. The Gemara, however, preferred to attribute this opinion to Rabbi Meir because unattributed *mishnayot* are generally considered to follow Rabbi Meir's opinion (see Rivan).

The Rif quotes this opinion and disagrees on several counts. He explains that the instance of simultaneous prohibitions referred to here is specifically in the addition cited in the name of Rabbi Meir: Carrying on Yom Kippur and carrying on Shabbat. Because Yom Kippur occurred on Shabbat, these prohibitions took effect simultaneously. According to this opinion, it is clear why the mishna was attributed to Rabbi Meir and not to the first *tanna*, for even if the first *tanna* agrees in principle with the ruling of simultaneous prohibitions, the ruling was stated explicitly only by Rabbi Meir. Rashi also explains that the ruling with regard to simultaneous prohibitions is derived from Rabbi Meir's statement. However, according to Rashi's opinion, there is no prohibition against carrying from domain to domain on Yom Kippur. Therefore, he explains that the two simultaneous prohibitions are the prohibition against eating on Yom Kippur and the prohibition against carrying on Shabbat (see Ramban and Rashba).

Fat – חֵלֶב: This refers to the animal fats that are prohibited by Torah law. Intentionally eating these fats from kosher domesticated animals is incurs *karet* (see Leviticus 7:22–25), while one who does so unwittingly is liable to bring a sin-offering. The fats of non-domesticated kosher animals and of kosher birds may be eaten. Among the signs differentiating forbidden fats from permitted fats is that the forbidden fats lie above the meat and are not entwined with it. They are enclosed by a thin membrane and are easily peeled away from the meat. Most of the forbidden fats of a sacrificial animal were sacrificed on the altar.

***Notar* – נוֹתָר:** This refers to parts of an offering left over after the time permitted for it to be eaten. One who eats the leftover portion of an offering is liable for punishment by *karet*. The Sages decreed that the leftover portion should be considered ritually impure, so that the priests would be prompt and meticulous in its removal.

And he carried it in his mouth – וְהוֹצִיאוֹ בְּפִיו: Some early commentaries had a variant text that read only: And carried it out. This version raises a question: If there is no connection between this last activity and the eating previously mentioned, why did Rabbi Meir add this prohibited labor in particular when he could have cited any other prohibited labor performed at the same moment? His choice is understandable according to the version that reads: He took it out in his mouth, because eating can be considered a form of placing an item, which is a requisite element of the prohibition against carrying. Without it, there is no liability.

According to a different version, however, this choice would seem arbitrary. In truth, even according to the current version, there is difficulty, as the Sages debated the question of whether carrying in one's mouth would indeed be considered carrying, as this is not the normal way to carry food. Nonetheless, in this case, since one is doing so as part of the act of eating, it is considered normal to carry in one's mouth and he would be liable.

וְרַבִּי מֵאִיר אַלִּיבָּא דְּמַאן? אִי אַלִּיבָּא דְּרַבִּי יְהוֹשֻׁעַ – הָאָמַר: טָעָה בִּדְבַר מִצְוָה פָּטוּר. אֶלָּא אַלִּיבָּא דְּרַבִּי אֱלִיעֶזֶר.

The Gemara continues to clarify the opinion of Rabbi Meir: **And in accordance with whose opinion is** the statement of **Rabbi Meir?**[N] **If** you say that **it is in accordance** with the opinion of **Rabbi Yehoshua,** this is difficult. **Didn't** Rabbi Yehoshua **say that one who erred with regard to a mitzva is exempt** from bringing a sin-offering, i.e., one who unwittingly performed a transgression while intending to perform a mitzva is exempt from punishment?[H] In the case in the mishna as well, the men intended to perform the mitzva of marriage but unwittingly violated a transgression because the wives were switched. Therefore, according to the opinion of Rabbi Yehoshua, they should be exempt from a sin-offering. **Rather,** this must be **in accordance with** the opinion of **Rabbi Eliezer,** who holds that even if one mistakenly transgressed while attempting to perform a mitzva, he is still obligated to bring a sin-offering.

אִיבָּעֵית אֵימָא: לְעוֹלָם אַלִּיבָּא דְּרַבִּי יְהוֹשֻׁעַ, כִּי קָאָמַר רַבִּי יְהוֹשֻׁעַ: טָעָה בִּדְבַר מִצְוָה פָּטוּר – הָנֵי מִילֵּי גַּבֵּי תִּינוֹקוֹת, דִּזְמַנּוֹ בָּהוּל. אֲבָל הַאי, כֵּיוָן דְּאֵין זְמַנּוֹ בָּהוּל – לָא.

If you wish, resolve this differently and **say: Actually,** this can be explained even **according to** the opinion of **Rabbi Yehoshua. When Rabbi Yehoshua says that one who erred with regard to a mitzva is exempt, this applies** only **to** the case of **babies** who were mixed up in such a way that on Shabbat the *mohel* mistakenly circumcised a baby whose time had not yet come for circumcision. Since the *mohel* did not fulfill the mitzva of circumcision, he should be liable for performing prohibited labor on Shabbat. However, Rabbi Yehoshua exempts him from a sin-offering **since** he is **pressed for time.** Because circumcision must be performed only on the day specified, he was rushed and anxious to perform the circumcision, and due to this sense of urgency he erred and thought that the proper time was on Shabbat. **In this** case in the mishna, **however,** where the mistake involved marriage, **since** the brothers were **not pressed for time** Rabbi Yehoshua does **not** deem the brothers exempt.

וַהֲרֵי תְּרוּמָה דְּאֵין זְמַנּוֹ בָּהוּל, וְקָפָטַר! דִּתְנַן: הָיָה אוֹכֵל בִּתְרוּמָה, וְנוֹדַע שֶׁהוּא בֶּן גְּרוּשָׁה אוֹ בֶּן חֲלוּצָה – רַבִּי אֱלִיעֶזֶר מְחַיֵּיב קֶרֶן וָחוֹמֶשׁ, וְרַבִּי יְהוֹשֻׁעַ פּוֹטֵר.

The Gemara objects: **And yet** in the case of eating ***teruma,*** **where one is not pressed for time and** nevertheless Rabbi Yehoshua **exempts** him if the act involved a mitzva, **as we learned** in a mishna (*Pesaḥim* 72b): If a priest **was partaking of *teruma* and it became known that he was the son of a divorced woman**[N] **or the son of a *ḥalutza*** and thereby disqualified from the priesthood and prohibited from eating *teruma,*[H] **Rabbi Eliezer deems** him **liable** to pay **the** value of the **principal and** an additional **fifth,** like any non-priest who unwittingly ate *teruma.* However, **Rabbi Yehoshua exempts** him because at the time of consumption he intended to perform a mitzva, for he thought that he was a priest eating of the *teruma.*

הָא אִיתְּמַר עֲלַהּ, אָמַר רַב בֵּיבָי בַּר אַבַּיֵּי: הָכָא בִּתְרוּמָה בְּעֶרֶב הַפֶּסַח עָסְקִינַן, דִּזְמַנָּהּ בָּהוּל.

The Gemara responds: **But wasn't it stated with regard to** that mishna: **Rav Beivai bar Abaye said: Here we are dealing with** leavened ***teruma*** that was being eaten by the priest **on the eve of Passover, for he is pressed for time.** In this case, he would rush to eat it so that it would not have to be burned.

וְאִי בָּעֵית אֵימָא: בְּאִיסּוּר בַּת אַחַת, וְאַלִּיבָּא דְּרַבִּי שִׁמְעוֹן.

The Gemara offers a different attribution of the mishna: **And if you wish, say** a different explanation: The mishna is not according to the opinion of Rabbi Meir, who deems one liable in cases of more inclusive prohibitions and expanded prohibitions. Rather, the mishna is referring only to cases **of simultaneous prohibitions, and in accordance with** the opinion of **Rabbi Shimon.**

בִּשְׁלָמָא כּוּלְּהוּ – מַשְׁכַּחַת לְהוּ, דְּשַׁוְּינְהוּ שָׁלִיחַ, וְשַׁוּוּ אִינְהוּ שָׁלִיחַ, וּפָגַע שָׁלִיחַ בְּשָׁלִיחַ. אֶלָּא נִדּוֹת – הֵיכִי מַשְׁכַּחַתְּ לַהּ?

The Gemara asks: **Granted,** with regard to **all of** the prohibitions in the mishna, **you can find that they** take effect simultaneously in the case **where** the men **appointed** a single **agent** to betroth the women for them, **and** the women **appointed an agent** to accept the betrothals for them, **and** one **agent encounters** the other **agent.** In this scenario, all the men become betrothed to all the women the moment that the agents meet, and the prohibitions all take effect simultaneously. **However,** with regard to the prohibition pertaining to **menstruating women, how can you find** the case where both women become menstruating women at the exact time of betrothal?

NOTES

And in accordance with whose opinion is the statement of Rabbi Meir – וְרַבִּי מֵאִיר אַלִּיבָּא דְּמַאן: Most commentaries explain, like Rashi, that this question relates to the present mishna, which was attributed to Rabbi Meir. However, Rabbeinu Ḥananel explains that this question relates to the mishna pertaining to the eating of prohibited fats. Because the latter mishna is dealing the prohibition of *notar*, it could be said that one was attempting to perform a mitzva, for he intended to remove the leftover foods to be burnt. The Rif and early commentaries disagree with this ruling.

And it became known that he was the son of a divorced woman – וְנוֹדַע שֶׁהוּא בֶּן גְּרוּשָׁה: Some later commentaries wonder: Why should this priest be held liable? Since it was impossible for him to know beforehand that he would be disqualified, this should be considered a circumstance beyond his control, and he should therefore be exempt. The Ritva explains that the mishna is referring to a situation where a public rumor had been spread that this priest was disqualified, and so he should have acted with more caution.

HALAKHA

An unwitting violation in a matter that involved a mitzva – שָׁגַג בִּדְבַר מִצְוָה: One who performs a transgression that requires the bringing of a sin-offering in the course of performing a mitzva is exempt from the obligation to bring an offering. This ruling applies only when one was both obligated to perform the mitzva and pressed for time (Rambam *Sefer Korbanot, Hilkhot Shegagot* 2:8).

A priest who was partaking of *teruma* and it became known that he was disqualified – כֹּהֵן אוֹכֵל תְּרוּמָה וְנוֹדַע שֶׁהוּא פָּסוּל: If a priest was eating *teruma* and was informed that he was the son of a divorced woman or the son of a *ḥalutza*, he must pay the principal alone but does not need to add a fifth of the sum that is the usually a penalty for unintentionally eating *teruma*. If at the time of eating he was pressed for time, such as is the case of eating leavened *teruma* on the eve of Passover, then he is exempt from payment, in accordance with the opinion of Rabbi Yehoshua and the conclusion in the Gemara (Rambam *Sefer Zera'im, Hilkhot Terumot* 10:12).

אמר רב עמרם אמר רב: בשופעות מתוך שלשה עשר לאחר שלשה עשר לאחיובי אינהו, מתוך שנים עשר לאחר שנים עשר – לחיובי אינהי.

Rav Amram said that Rav said: This is referring to a situation **where** the women **continuously discharge** menstrual blood[B] **from within the thirteenth**[N] year of the brothers **until after** they reached the age of **thirteen,** in order **to deem** the men **liable** for the prohibition pertaining to a menstruating woman. At the moment that the boys reached maturity and the betrothals went into effect, the sisters were forbidden as menstruating women. And the women were continuously discharging blood **from within the twelfth** year of the women **until after** the age of **twelve, in order to deem** the women **liable** for engaging in relations as a menstruating woman. Therefore, if this took place in such a way that on the exact day when the men reached maturity, i.e., their thirteenth birthday, the women reached maturity, i.e., their twelfth birthday, and at that moment they were menstruating, then all of the prohibitions would take effect simultaneously and they would be liable on all counts, according to Rabbi Shimon as well.

״מפרישים אותן״. והא אין אשה מתעברת בביאה ראשונה! אמר רב נחמן אמר רבה בר אבוה: שבעלו ושנו. ואלא הא דתנא רבי חייא: הרי כאן שש עשרה חטאות, תלתין ותרתין הויין!

§ The mishna taught that **we separate** these women from their husbands for three months, as perhaps they became pregnant. The Gemara asks: **But isn't** it known that a virgin **woman does not become pregnant**[N] **from her first sexual act? Rav Naḥman said that Rabba bar Avuh said:** This is referring to a situation **where they engaged in intercourse and then repeated** the act, so that it is possible that the women were impregnated during the second act of intercourse. The Gemara asks: **But** if this is so, how can one explain **that which Rabbi Ḥiyya teaches:**[N] **Here, then, are sixteen sin-offerings?** If there were indeed two acts of intercourse, then **there** should **be thirty-two** sin-offerings, since each prohibition was violated twice.

וליטעמיך, לרבי אליעזר, דמחייב על כל כח וכח, טובא הויין! אלא, דבכח ראשון קחשיב – הכי נמי דביאה ראשונה קחשיב.

The Gemara answers: **And according to your reasoning, that** Rabbi Ḥiyya's enumeration of sin-offerings applies to all acts of intercourse, then **according to** the opinion of **Rabbi Eliezer, who deems one liable** to bring a sin-offering **for each and every thrusting** movement during a single act of intercourse, there would **be many** prohibitions that were violated. This would greatly multiply the number of sin-offerings required. **Rather,** it must be that Rabbi Ḥiyya, with regard to Rabbi Eliezer's opinion, **is enumerating** only **the first thrusting** movement **in the intercourse. And so too,** with regard to the Rabbis' opinion, **he is enumerating** only **the first act of intercourse.** If there were two acts of intercourse, however, the number of sin-offerings would be doubled.

אמר ליה רבא לרב נחמן:

Rava said to Rav Naḥman:

BACKGROUND

Continually discharge blood – שופעות: Generally, the flow of blood during a menstrual cycle continues several days. Although there are differences between the days insofar as the amount of blood is concerned, a woman is considered to be continually discharging blood during the entirety of her menstruation, generally five to seven days.

NOTES

Where they continuously discharge blood from within the thirteenth, etc. – בשופעות מתוך שלשה עשר וכו׳: Rashi posits that this is a case where male minors betrothed female minors prior to maturity, so that the betrothals and the prohibition with regard to a menstruating woman took effect simultaneously. *Tosafot*, the Ramban, and the Rashba question this explanation: Since there is no legal efficacy to an act performed by minors, how could these betrothals later take effect? Even if one were to suggest that this explanation follows Rabbi Meir's opinion, that it is possible to perform betrothal to effect acquisition with an item that has not yet come into being, it is still unclear whether this principle would apply to this a case, where the one performing the betrothal is in fact a minor himself. Rivan and *Tosefot HaRosh* explain that if the betrothal was conditional and previously agreed upon, it could take effect upon their arrival at maturity (see *Mishne LaMelekh*).

Due to this difficulty, many early commentaries preferred Rabbeinu Ḥananel's version of the text which reads: They were continuously discharging blood from within three until after three. This indicates that the situation is one of female minors betrothed by their fathers to adult males. Before the age of three, any intercourse that takes place has no legal status, so that none of the prohibitions mentioned could apply. When they reached the age of three all of the prohibitions took effect simultaneously. This would create a situation where the males would be liable for all of the prohibitions. However, when the Gemara states: Continuously discharging blood from within twelve, this is a separate scenario. It is a case where the women reached maturity and would therefore be liable for these prohibitions. According to this opinion, all of the prohibitions did not affect both the men and women at the same time. Rather there are two different scenarios: One in which all the prohibitions affected the men at the same time, and one where all the prohibitions affected the women at the same time. As a result, there is no need to adopt Rashi's unlikely description that this refers to two twin brothers who betrothed two twin sisters who were exactly one year younger than them.

But isn't it known that a virgin woman does not become pregnant, etc. – והא אין אשה מתעברת וכו׳: The early commentaries ask: Why does the Gemara assume that this case refers to virgins? Perhaps it refers to women who had previously engaged in permissible intercourse, such as widows, or even women who had engaged in illicit intercourse. According to Rabbeinu Ḥananel's reading, which states that this is a case of three-year-old girls, this question is irrelevant. However, according to Rashi's version of the text, this is difficult. *Tosefot HaRosh*, citing the name Maharam MiRotenburg, states that these women were necessarily virgins because the mishna was particular in stating that these prohibitions took effect only following entrance into the wedding canopy. Had these women been previously married, they would have already been subject to the prohibition pertaining to a married woman. Additionally, the Ritva explains the following: Given that neither the men nor the women were aware that the mix-up took place, it stands to reason that the women were modest virgins who would not be suspected of illicit sexual acts.

But if this is so, how can one explain that which Rabbi Ḥiyya teaches, etc. – ואלא הא דתנא רבי חייא וכו׳: Rashi explains that since the Gemara, in its previous discussion of Rabbi Meir's opinion, already established that the mishna is in accordance with Rabbi Eliezer's opinion, it was necessary to explain the *baraita* about the number of potential sin-offerings in the mishna in accordance with Rabbi Eliezer's opinion as well. Moreover, only according to Rabbi Eliezer is one obligated to bring more than one sin-offering for acts of intercourse performed in one lapse of awareness (see 92a and *Karetot* 15a). Rashi argues that the notion that each thrusting movement obligates one in a separate sin-offering is an extension of this idea.

According to the Vilna Gaon, the attempt to resolve Rabbi Ḥiyya's *baraita* in this context is a textual corruption, and both the question and the answer should be omitted (*Haggahot HaGra*). Once the Gemara explained that the mishna could be understood in accordance with Rabbi Shimon's opinion, in a case where all the prohibitions took effect simultaneously, it was unnecessary to further posit that it follows Rabbi Eliezer.

וְהָא תָּמָר בְּבִיאָה רִאשׁוֹנָה אִיעַבְּרָא! אָמַר לֵיהּ: תָּמָר בְּאֶצְבַּע מְעָכָהּ. דְּאָמַר רַבִּי יִצְחָק: כׇּל מוֹעֲכוֹת שֶׁל בֵּית רַבִּי תָּמָר שְׁמָן, וְלָמָּה נִקְרָא שְׁמָן תָּמָר? עַל שֵׁם תָּמָר שֶׁמְּעָכָהּ בְּאֶצְבָּעָהּ. וְהָא הָווּ עֵר וְאוֹנָן! עֵר וְאוֹנָן שִׁמְּשׁוּ שֶׁלֹּא כְּדַרְכָּן.

But didn't Tamar become pregnant from the first act of intercourse,[NB] despite the fact that she was a virgin at the time of her sexual act with Judah? Rav Naḥman **said: Tamar broke** her hymen **with her finger** prior to intercourse, and it is due to this that she became pregnant from the first act of intercourse, **as Rabbi Yitzḥak said: All of those** women **from the household of Rabbi** Yehuda HaNasi **who break** their hymens[N] **are named Tamar** by nickname. **And why are they named Tamar?** They are called this **on account of Tamar, who broke** her hymen **with her finger.** The Gemara wonders about the proof from Tamar itself: **But weren't there Er and Onan,** her previous husbands, who presumably engaged in sexual intercourse with her? The Gemara responds: **Er and Onan engaged in sexual intercourse in an atypical manner,** i.e., anal intercourse, and therefore she was still a virgin.

מֵיתִיבֵי: כׇּל עֶשְׂרִים וְאַרְבָּעָה חֹדֶשׁ דָּשׁ מִבִּפְנִים וְזוֹרֶה מִבַּחוּץ, דִּבְרֵי רַבִּי אֱלִיעֶזֶר. אָמְרוּ לוֹ: הַלָּלוּ אֵינוֹ אֶלָּא כְּמַעֲשֵׂה עֵר וְאוֹנָן!

The Gemara **raises an objection** from the *Tosefta* (*Nidda* 5:6): After a woman gives birth, her husband **penetrates inside and spills** his semen **outside**[H] for **the entire twenty-four months** during which the baby is breastfeeding, so that his wife not become pregnant, as that would terminate her milk production and the child might die. This is **the statement of Rabbi Eliezer. They said to him: These** acts **are nothing other** than acts **similar to those of Er and Onan,** which are prohibited. Regardless, it can be deduced from here that Er and Onan engaged in normative sexual intercourse with Tamar, only they did not fully complete the sexual act.

כְּמַעֲשֵׂה עֵר וְאוֹנָן, וְלֹא כְּמַעֲשֵׂה עֵר וְאוֹנָן. כְּמַעֲשֵׂה עֵר וְאוֹנָן – דִּכְתִיב "וְהָיָה אִם בָּא אֶל אֵשֶׁת אָחִיו וְשִׁחֵת אַרְצָה", וְלֹא כְּמַעֲשֵׂה עֵר וְאוֹנָן, דְּאִילּוּ הָתָם – שֶׁלֹּא כְּדַרְכָּהּ, וְהָכָא – כְּדַרְכָּהּ.

The Gemara answers: The *Tosefta* actually means that what they did was **similar to the act of Er and Onan** in some ways, but **not similar to the act of Er and Onan** in other ways. The Gemara elaborates: **It was similar to the act of Er and Onan** in that there was a spilling of semen, **as it is written: "And it came to pass when he had intercourse with his brother's wife, that he spilled it on the ground"** (Genesis 38:9). Yet it was **not similar to the act of Er and Onan, as there** Er and Onan engaged in sexual intercourse in **an atypical manner,** i.e., anal intercourse, **while here** the *Tosefta* is referring to sexual intercourse **in a typical manner.**

בִּשְׁלָמָא אוֹנָן – דִּכְתִיב בֵּיהּ "וְשִׁחֵת אַרְצָה", אֶלָּא עֵר מְנָלַן? אָמַר רַב נַחְמָן בַּר יִצְחָק: דִּכְתִיב "וַיָּמֶת גַּם אוֹתוֹ", אַף הוּא בְּאוֹתוֹ מִיתָה מֵת. בִּשְׁלָמָא אוֹנָן – מִשּׁוּם "לֹּא לוֹ יִהְיֶה הַזָּרַע", אֶלָּא עֵר מַאי טַעְמָא עֲבַד הָכִי? כְּדֵי שֶׁלֹּא תִּתְעַבֵּר וְיִכְחִישׁ יׇפְיָהּ.

The Gemara continues to clarify what took place: **Granted, Onan** engaged in unnatural sexual intercourse with her, **as it is written with regard to his** act: **"That he spilled it on the ground"** (Genesis 38:9). **However, from where do we** derive that **Er** engaged in unnatural sexual intercourse with her? **Rav Naḥman bar Yitzḥak said: As it is written** with regard to Onan: **"And He slew him also"** (Genesis 38:10). This indicates that **he, too, died the same death** for performing the same transgression as his brother. The Gemara asks: **Granted, Onan** engaged in anal intercourse because he did not want Tamar to give birth **as** "he knew that **the seed would not be his"** (Genesis 38:9). **However,** with regard to **Er, what is the reason he acted** in **this** way? The Gemara responds: He did so in order **that she not become pregnant and become less beautiful** as a result of her pregnancy.

NOTES

But didn't Tamar become pregnant from the first act of intercourse – וְהָא תָּמָר בְּבִיאָה רִאשׁוֹנָה אִיעַבְּרָא: The Maharsha raises a challenge: Why did the Gemara assume that Tamar was impregnated by her first act of intercourse, so that it was necessary to entertain far-fetched ideas in order to explain how she became pregnant? Indeed, according to the simple understanding of the biblical narrative, Tamar's first husbands had typical sexual intercourse with her (see Genesis, chapter 38, and Rashi's commentary there; see *Midrash Rabba*).

The Maharsha suggests that perhaps support for the idea that Er and Onan did not engage in typical intercourse can be found in an interpretation of the verses in the Torah. Indeed, the Rashash presents evidence from Ibn Ezra's commentary, which cites the interpretation that the phrase "and he spilled it on the ground" is referring to unnatural intercourse. Ibn Ezra ultimately rejects this interpretation.

The various commentaries challenge this suggestion based on the fact that this verse is stated only with regard to Onan, not Er. *Ramat Shmuel* tries to resolve this problem by invoking the opinion that Judah, after the entire ordeal became known to him, did not cease his relations with her. It interprets the verse that reads: "And he knew her again no more" (Genesis 38:26) to mean: He did not cease to know her, i.e., to engage with her sexually. This was permitted because Tamar had engaged only in unnatural intercourse with her previous husbands, and according to the Noahide laws she was never considered to be married to his sons. Accordingly, this opinion serves as a support for the idea that Er and Onan did not engage in natural intercourse.

All of those from the household of Rabbi Yehuda HaNasi who break their hymens – כׇּל מוֹעֲכוֹת שֶׁל בֵּית רַבִּי: Some early commentaries cite a version of the text that reads: The household of David. The commentaries explain the rationale behind the women's behavior according to both readings. The Ritva states these women were so upright that they did not want any act of intercourse to be in vain, and therefore they wished to become pregnant even from the first act. The Meiri points out that the disciples of the household of Rabbi Yehuda HaNasi were exceedingly pious in their separation from women and the soldiers of David's household were often off in battle. Therefore, their wives wanted to ensure that they would become pregnant from the first act of intercourse.

HALAKHA

Penetrates inside and spills outside – דָּשׁ מִבִּפְנִים וְזוֹרֶה מִבַּחוּץ: A man is prohibited from engaging in intercourse with his wife in a way that entails the spilling of his seed outside her body. One who does so has emitted semen in vain, which is a great sin (Rambam *Sefer Kedusha*, *Hilkhot Issurei Bia* 21:18; *Shulḥan Arukh*, *Even HaEzer* 23:1).

BACKGROUND

Become pregnant from the first act of intercourse – בְּבִיאָה רִאשׁוֹנָה אִיעַבְּרָא: According to contemporary medical knowledge, the fact that a woman is a virgin does not prevent her, in purely physiological terms, from becoming pregnant. However, it may be presumed that the pain that accompanies her first act of intercourse along with the accompanying psychological factors can cause tension and other effects. These could render the possibility of impregnation minimal. The women of Rabbi Yehuda HaNasi's house prepared themselves both physically and emotionally for intercourse and were therefore able to become pregnant.

תָּנוּ רַבָּנַן: ״אוֹתָהּ״ פְּרָט לְכַלָּה, דִּבְרֵי רַבִּי יְהוּדָה. וַחֲכָמִים אוֹמְרִים: פְּרָט לְשֶׁלֹּא כְּדַרְכָּהּ. אֲמַר לֵיהּ הוֹן בְּרֵיהּ דְּרַב נַחְמָן לְרַב נַחְמָן: לֵימָא קָא סָבַר רַבִּי יְהוּדָה הַתּוֹרָה חָסָה עַל תַּכְשִׁיטֵי כַלָּה? אֲמַר לֵיהּ: לְפִי שֶׁאֵין אִשָּׁה מִתְעַבֶּרֶת מִבִּיאָה רִאשׁוֹנָה.

The Sages taught: The verse states: "And the woman, **with whom** a man shall lie giving seed, they shall both bathe themselves in water, and be unclean until the evening" (Leviticus 15:18). The extra term **"with whom"** comes **to exclude a bride** who does not become ritually impure; this is **the statement of Rabbi Yehuda. And the Rabbis say: It excludes** the case of sexual intercourse performed **in an atypical manner.**[H] **Hon,**[P] **son of Rav Naḥman, said to Rav Naḥman: Shall we say that Rabbi Yehuda holds: The Torah spared a bride's adornments,** including her make-up, and therefore exempted her from submersion in water, as that might cause them ruin? Rav Naḥman **said to him:** That is not the reason. Rather, **it is because a woman does not become pregnant from the first act of intercourse.** Therefore, that act of intercourse would not cause ritual impurity, as it is not considered intercourse that can result in the implanting of seed.

בְּמַאי קָמִיפַּלְגִי? רַבָּנַן סָבְרִי ״שִׁכְבַת זֶרַע״ פְּרָט לְהַעֲרָאָה: ״אוֹתָהּ״ פְּרָט לְשֶׁלֹּא כְּדַרְכָּהּ. וְרַבִּי יְהוּדָה סָבַר: שֶׁלֹּא כְּדַרְכָּהּ וְהַעֲרָאָה – מִ״שִּׁכְבַת זֶרַע״ נָפְקָא: ״אוֹתָהּ״ פְּרָט לְכַלָּה.

The Gemara asks: **With regard to what do** Rabbi Yehuda and the Rabbis **disagree? The Rabbis hold** that the phrase **"giving seed" excludes the initial stage of intercourse,**[N] during which there is no emission of semen.[H] And the extra phrase **"with whom" excludes intercourse that is performed in an atypical way. Rabbi Yehuda,** on the other hand, **holds that** the exclusion of both **atypical** sexual intercourse **and the initial stage of intercourse were derived from** the phrase **"giving seed,"** as neither of these are sexual acts that might bring about the birth of a seed, i.e., a child. The phrase **"with whom"** then **excludes a bride.**[N]

כִּי אֲתָא רָבִין אָמַר רַבִּי יוֹחָנָן: כׇּל שֶׁשָּׁהֲתָה אַחַר בַּעְלָהּ עֶשֶׂר שָׁנִים וְנִשֵּׂאת – שׁוּב אֵינָהּ יוֹלֶדֶת. אָמַר רַב נַחְמָן: לֹא שָׁנוּ אֶלָּא שֶׁאֵין דַּעְתָּהּ לְהִנָּשֵׂא, אֲבָל דַּעְתָּהּ לְהִנָּשֵׂא – מִתְעַבֶּרֶת. אֲמַר לֵיהּ רָבָא לְבַת רַב חִסְדָּא: קָא מְרַנְּנֵי רַבָּנַן אֲבַתְרִיךְ. אֲמַרָה לֵיהּ: אֲנָא דַּעְתַּאי עֲלָךְ הֲוַאי.

On the topic of intercourse that cannot result in conception, the Gemara relates the following: **When Ravin came** from Eretz Yisrael to Babylonia, he said that **Rabbi Yoḥanan said: Any** woman who **waits after her husband** has died or divorced her for **ten years** without intercourse **and is then married can no longer bear children. Rav Naḥman said: They taught** this principle **only** with regard to cases **where she did not intend to get married** at a later time, **but** if **she intended to get married** at some point, **she can become pregnant** later on. **Rava said to** his wife, the **daughter of Rav Ḥisda:**[N] **The Sages are gossiping about you.** From the time she was widowed from her first husband until the time that she was married to Rava, more than ten years passed, yet she bore him children. It seemed as though she had engaged in intercourse in the meantime. **She said to him: My mind was on you.** Indeed, it is told that already as a young girl she prophesized that she would marry Rava.

הַהִיא דַּאֲתְיָא לְקַמֵּיהּ דְּרַב יוֹסֵף, אָמְרָה לוֹ: רַבִּי, אֲנָא שֶׁהִיתִי אַחַר בַּעְלִי עֶשֶׂר שָׁנִים וְיָלַדְתִּי. אֲמַר לָהּ: בִּתִּי, אַל תּוֹצִיאִי לַעַז עַל דִּבְרֵי חֲכָמִים. אָמְרָה לֵיהּ: לְגוֹי נִבְעַלְתִּי.

The Gemara relates: **A certain** woman **who came before Rav Yosef said to him: My teacher, I waited after my husband's** death for **ten years, and** nevertheless **I gave birth. He said to her: My daughter, do not cast aspersions on the statement of the Sages. She said to him** in confession: **I had sexual intercourse with a gentile** during those ten years.

HALAKHA

Ritual impurity from atypical intercourse – טוּמְאַת בִּיאָה שֶׁלֹּא כְּדַרְכָּהּ: If one engages in anal intercourse with his wife, she remains ritually pure because the Torah ruled there to be ritual impurity in the concealed parts of the body only from typical intercourse (Rambam *Sefer Tahara*, *Hilkhot Avot HaTumot* 5:9).

Ritual impurity in the initial stage of sexual intercourse – טוּמְאַת הַעֲרָאָה: If one engages in the initial stage of sexual intercourse with a woman, or even full intercourse but did not emit semen, then both the man and woman are ritually pure (Rambam *Sefer Tahara*, *Hilkhot Avot HaTumot* 5:10).

PERSONALITIES

Hon – הוֹן: This Sage, one of Rav Naḥman's sons, is rarely mentioned. It may be assumed that he is identical with Huna, son of Rav Naḥman, and that Hon is a nickname or a Hebrew form of the same name.

NOTES

Initial stage of intercourse – הַעֲרָאָה: The Gemara presents a dispute as to the definition of the initial stage of intercourse (55b). One opinion maintains that the initial stage of intercourse occurs at the moment of external contact of the sexual organs. The other holds that the initial stage of intercourse is defined by the penetration of the corona. With regard to forbidden relations, one is liable for violating a prohibition if one engaged in this initial stage of intercourse, even if one did not complete the act of intercourse.

With whom excludes a bride – אוֹתָהּ פְּרָט לְכַלָּה: This Torah law, which requires both the man and the woman to immerse following intercourse, is understood to be a special decree stated by the verses, as it does not follow the usual laws of ritual impurity. It overrides the principle that an emission of semen causes ritual impurity only upon touch, which does not include contact with concealed parts of the body. This decree of ritual impurity is imparted even though intercourse applies only to acts of full-fledged intercourse that can lead to childbirth.

The daughter of Rav Ḥisda – בַּת רַב חִסְדָּא: The daughter of Rav Ḥisda was married to Rami bar Ḥama. Over ten years after he died, she married Rava. The Gemara relates an incident that took place when she was a young girl (*Bava Batra* 12b). She was sitting in her father's lap when Rava and Rami bar Ḥama, both students of Rav Ḥisda, were sitting before him. Rav Ḥisda asked his daughter which of the two she desired, and she answered: Both. Rava responded: I will be the last.

אָמַר שְׁמוּאֵל: וְכוּלָּן צְרִיכוֹת לְהַמְתִּין שְׁלֹשָׁה חֳדָשִׁים, חוּץ מִגִּיּוֹרֶת וּמְשׁוּחְרֶרֶת קְטַנָּה. אֲבָל קְטַנָּה בַּת יִשְׂרָאֵל – צְרִיכָה לְהַמְתִּין שְׁלֹשָׁה חֳדָשִׁים.

§ **Shmuel said: And all of those** women who had sexual intercourse, and there is therefore a concern that they might be pregnant, **must wait three months** before marrying so as to differentiate between a child born from the previous intercourse and a child born from this marriage, **except for a female convert** who is a minor **and a female released slave who is a minor.** Although it is possible that they had sexual intercourse, they cannot become pregnant in any case. **However, a female Israelite who was a minor** and had intercourse **must wait three months** like all other women.

וּבְמַאי? אִי בְּמֵיאוּן – וְהָאָמַר שְׁמוּאֵל דְּלָא בָּעְיָא. וְאִי בְּגֵט – הָאָמְרָהּ שְׁמוּאֵל חֲדָא זִימְנָא. דְּאָמַר שְׁמוּאֵל: מֵיאֲנָה בּוֹ – אֵינָהּ צְרִיכָה לְהַמְתִּין שְׁלֹשָׁה חֳדָשִׁים, נָתַן לָהּ גֵּט – צְרִיכָה לְהַמְתִּין שְׁלֹשָׁה חֳדָשִׁים! אֶלָּא בִּזְנוּת.

The Gemara asks: **And with regard to what** situation is this statement referring? **If it is** referring to a minor who was released from her marriage **by refusal,** as a minor girl who was married to a man by her mother or brothers may refuse to remain married to her husband until reaching majority, **but didn't Shmuel say that she is not required** to wait three months? **And if** it is referring to a woman who received **a bill of divorce** as a minor, **didn't Shmuel** already **state** this *halakha* **one time?** Why would he repeat this ruling, **as Shmuel said: A female minor who refused** her husband **need not wait three months** before her second marriage,[H] but if **he gave her a bill of divorce, she must wait three months,**[H] so as not to make a distinction between an adult divorcée and a minor divorcée. **Rather,** it must be that this is referring to a female minor who was involved in **licentious sexual intercourse.**

HALAKHA

Waiting period for a female minor who performed refusal – הַמְתָּנָה בִּמְמָאֶנֶת: A female minor who refused her husband is not required to wait three months before marrying another man, as the rabbinic decree did not include her (Rambam *Sefer Nashim, Hilkhot Geirushin* 11:22; *Shulḥan Arukh, Even HaEzer* 13:6).

Waiting period for a divorced woman – הַמְתָּנָה בִּגְרוּשָׁה: Every woman who was divorced must wait three months before marrying another man. The Sages did not distinguish between divorced women, so that even a minor divorced woman who cannot bear children must still wait three months (Rambam *Sefer Nashim, Hilkhot Geirushin* 11:20; *Shulḥan Arukh, Even HaEzer* 23:1).

Perek **III**
Daf **35** Amud **a**

וְגָזְרוּ רַבָּנַן קְטַנָּה מִשּׁוּם גְּדוֹלָה.

And, although there is no possibility for her to become pregnant, **the Sages issued** a rabbinic **decree** requiring the three month waiting period **for a female minor due to** this requirement for **a female adult** who engaged in promiscuous sexual acts.

וּמִי גָּזְרִינַן קְטַנָּה מִשּׁוּם גְּדוֹלָה? וְהָתְנַן: אִם הָיוּ קְטַנּוֹת שֶׁאֵינָן רְאוּיוֹת לֵילֵד – מַחֲזִירִין אוֹתָן מִיָּד! אָמַר רַב גִּידֵּל אָמַר רַב: הוֹרָאַת שָׁעָה הָיְתָה. מִכְּלָל דַּהֲוַאי?! אֶלָּא כְּהוֹרָאַת שָׁעָה הָיְתָה, וְחִילּוּף לָא שְׁכִיחַ.

The Gemara asks: **And do we issue a decree** with regard to **a female minor due to** the ruling for **a female adult? But didn't we learn** in the mishna: **If they were female minors who could not bear children, we return them**[H] **immediately** to their husbands? This indicates that there is no concern for pregnancy, and the Sages did not issue a decree in this case. **Rav Giddel said** that **Rav said: This was a provisional edict** issued in exigent circumstances, and therefore one cannot extrapolate from the case in the mishna to other situations. The Gemara wonders: Can one assume **by inference that there was** such an occurrence? It would seem from the mishna that this was merely a possibility and not an actual occurrence, for if it actually happened it would have been appropriate for the mishna to relate the actual case. **Rather,** the ruling in the mishna is **like a provisional edict in that switching** of wives, such as described in the mishna, **is uncommon,** and in cases that are not common, the Sages do not issue a decree. Therefore, in the case of the mishna, the female minors were not required to wait.

HALAKHA

If they were female minors…we return them – אִם הָיוּ קְטַנּוֹת...מַחֲזִירִין אוֹתָן: In situations where a woman was mistakenly married and then removed from her husband by a court, if she was a minor at the time, she is allowed to marry another man. She need not wait because this is an uncommon occurrence and was not included in the rabbinic decree (Rambam *Sefer Nashim, Hilkhot Geirushin* 11:23; *Shulḥan Arukh, Even HaEzer* 13:8).

לִישָּׁנָא אַחֲרִינָא אָמְרִי לַהּ, אָמַר שְׁמוּאֵל: כּוּלָּן צְרִיכוֹת לְהַמְתִּין שְׁלֹשָׁה חֳדָשִׁים, חוּץ מִגִּיּוֹרֶת וּמְשׁוּחְרֶרֶת גְּדוֹלָה. [אֲבָל] קְטַנָּה בַּת יִשְׂרָאֵל – אֵינָהּ צְרִיכָה לְהַמְתִּין שְׁלֹשָׁה חֳדָשִׁים. בְּמַאי? אִי בְּמֵיאוּן – הָאַמְרָהּ שְׁמוּאֵל חֲדָא זִימְנָא, אִי בְּגֵט – הָא קָאָמַר שְׁמוּאֵל דְּבָעֲיָא, דְּאָמַר שְׁמוּאֵל: מֵיאֲנָה בּוֹ – אֵינָהּ צְרִיכָה לְהַמְתִּין שְׁלֹשָׁה חֳדָשִׁים, נָתַן לָהּ גֵּט – צְרִיכָה לְהַמְתִּין שְׁלֹשָׁה חֳדָשִׁים! אֶלָּא בִּזְנוּת, וּזְנוּת בִּקְטַנָּה לָא שְׁכִיחַ.

Some say another version of what was taught: **Shmuel said:**[N] **All** women **must wait three months, except for a female convert** who is an adult **and a freed maidservant**[H] **who is an adult;** these women need not wait. **However, an Israelite female minor need not wait three months** in any case. The Gemara clarifies: **With regard to what** situation is this statement referring? **If** it is referring to a female minor released from her marriage **by refusal,** it would be superfluous, **as didn't Shmuel** already **state this** ***halakha*** **one time?** If it is referring to a woman released **by a bill of divorce,** but **didn't Shmuel say that** in that case **she is required** to wait, **as Shmuel said: If she refused him she need not wait three months,** but **if he gave her a bill of divorce, she must wait three months? Rather,** this is referring to cases of **promiscuous sexual intercourse, and** an occurrence of **promiscuous sexual intercourse with female minors is uncommon,** and the Sages did not issue rabbinic decrees in uncommon instances.

גִּיּוֹרֶת וּמְשׁוּחְרֶרֶת, דִּשְׁכִיחַ בְּהוּ זְנוּת, לִיגְזוֹר! הוּא דְּאָמַר כְּרַבִּי יוֹסֵי. דְּתַנְיָא: הַגִּיּוֹרֶת וְהַשְּׁבוּיָה וְהַשִּׁפְחָה שֶׁנִּפְדּוּ וְשֶׁנִּתְגַּיְּירוּ וְשֶׁנִּשְׁתַּחְרְרוּ – צְרִיכוֹת לְהַמְתִּין שְׁלֹשָׁה חֳדָשִׁים, דִּבְרֵי רַבִּי יְהוּדָה. רַבִּי יוֹסֵי מַתִּיר לֵיאָרֵס וְלִינָּשֵׂא מִיָּד. אָמַר רַבָּה: מַאי טַעְמָא דְּרַבִּי יוֹסֵי – קָסָבַר: אִשָּׁה מְזַנָּה מְשַׁמֶּשֶׁת בְּמוֹךְ כְּדֵי שֶׁלֹּא תִּתְעַבֵּר.

The Gemara suggests: **Let** the Sages **issue a decree** requiring **a female convert and a released maidservant** to wait three months, **as** at the time that one was a gentile and the other a maidservant, **promiscuous sexual intercourse was common for them.** The Gemara responds: Shmuel **stated** his *halakhic* ruling **in accordance with the** opinion of **Rabbi Yosei, as it is taught** in a *baraita*: In the case of **the female convert; and the captured woman,** who is suspected of having been raped during her imprisonment; **and the maidservant, who were redeemed or who were converted or who were released, must wait three months** prior to marriage. This is **the statement of Rabbi Yehuda. Rabbi Yosei allows** them **to be betrothed and married immediately. Rabba said: What is the reasoning of Rabbi Yosei? He holds that a woman who engages in promiscuous sexual intercourse uses** a contraceptive **resorbent** that she places at the opening of her womb **so as not to become impregnated.** Therefore, there is no concern that she might be pregnant.

אָמַר לֵיהּ אַבָּיֵי: בִּשְׁלָמָא גִּיּוֹרֶת, כֵּיוָן דְּדַעְתָּהּ לְאִיגַּיּוֹרֵי – מְנַטְּרָה נַפְשָׁהּ. כְּדֵי לְהַבְחִין בֵּין זֶרַע שֶׁנִּזְרַע בִּקְדוּשָּׁה וּבֵין זֶרַע שֶׁנִּזְרַע שֶׁלֹּא בִּקְדוּשָּׁה. שְׁבוּיָה וְשִׁפְחָה נַמִי, דְּשָׁמְעִי מִמָּרַיְיהוּ וּמְנַטְּרֵי נַפְשַׁיְיהוּ. אֶלָּא יוֹצֵאת בְּשֵׁן וָעַיִן – הֵיכִי מִשְׁכַּחַתְּ לַהּ?

Abaye said to him: Granted, a female convert does this. **Since she is determined to convert, she guards herself** so as not to be impregnated while still a gentile **in order to distinguish between children conceived in sanctity,** i.e., after her conversion, **and children conceived out of sanctity.**[N] **A captured woman and a maidservant** would **also** be cautious because **they hear from their masters** that they are about to be redeemed or that they are about to be released, **and they guard themselves** so as not to be impregnated. **However,** with regard to a maidservant who **is released due to** damage caused her by her masters, i.e., loss of one of her extremities such as **a tooth or an eye, how can you find** a case where there is no concern for her becoming impregnated? Since she could not have known in advance that she would be released, she would have had no reason to be careful not to become pregnant.

וְכִי תֵּימָא: כָּל דְּמִמֵּילָא מוֹדֶה רַבִּי יוֹסֵי – וְהָתְנַן: אֲנוּסָה וּמְפוּתָּה צְרִיכָה לְהַמְתִּין שְׁלֹשָׁה חֳדָשִׁים, דִּבְרֵי רַבִּי יְהוּדָה. רַבִּי יוֹסֵי מַתִּיר לֵיאָרֵס וְלִינָּשֵׂא מִיָּד!

And if you would say that in **any** case **where** the situation occurs **by itself,** as in the case where a woman was unaware of her pending release, **Rabbi Yosei concedes** that she must indeed wait, this is difficult. **But didn't we learn** in a mishna: **A woman who was raped and a woman who was seduced**[NH] **must wait three months** as perhaps she became pregnant; this is **the statement of Rabbi Yehuda. Rabbi Yosei permits her to be betrothed and to be married immediately.** Clearly, a woman who was raped could not have prepared herself ahead of time so as not to become pregnant.

NOTES

Shmuel's opinion – שִׁיטַת שְׁמוּאֵל: Clarification of Shmuel's opinion, according to both formulations, and the relationship between his statement and the various tannaitic opinions on this issue is crucial to the understanding of the progression of the discussion here as well as the final halakhic conclusions (see 40a and onward).

According to Rabbeinu Ḥananel, Rashi, and other commentaries, Shmuel does not rule in accordance with Rabbi Yosei's opinion in all cases. Rather, in some situations he rules in accordance with the opinion of Rabbi Yehuda and holds that a woman who was raped or seduced requires a waiting period. Because Shmuel maintains that the primary reason for allowing a woman to marry immediately is the use of a contraceptive resorbent, in cases of rape and seduction he is concerned that the post-intercourse contraceptive will not be sufficient. Converts and released maidservants, however, would certainly protect themselves prior to intercourse (*Tosefot Rid*; see Responsa of the Radbaz 1:196).

Alternatively, Shmuel ruled that it is appropriate to issue a rabbinic decree in cases of rape and seduction, but not for converts, since occurrences of conversion are uncommon (Ramban; Rashba; see Razah).

However, according to the Rif, the Rambam, and other commentaries, Shmuel rules in accordance with the opinion of Rabbi Yosei on all issues. When he said: Except for female converts and released maidservants who were adults, he did not intend to imply that raped and seduced women require a waiting period for the purpose of distinction. On the contrary, he meant to say that even those who were not so cautious, since they nevertheless intended to convert, take steps to prevent pregnancy. If so, this is all the more true for women who were raped or seduced (Ramban).

The Ra'avad explains a different rationale for Shmuel's distinction with regard to converts and released maidservants. In these cases, there are two uncertainties: First, there is uncertainty as to whether the woman engaged in intercourse at all. Second, even if you say that she did engage in sexual intercourse, she might not have become pregnant. This is not the case for a raped or seduced woman. Since she certainly had intercourse, the only uncertainty that remains is whether or not she became pregnant. Therefore, she should be required to observe the waiting period.

In order to distinguish between children conceived in sanctity and children conceived out of sanctity – לְהַבְחִין בֵּין זֶרַע שֶׁנִּזְרַע בִּקְדוּשָּׁה וּבֵין זֶרַע שֶׁנִּזְרַע שֶׁלֹּא בִּקְדוּשָּׁה: Although when a pregnant woman converts, her fetus is converted along with her and does not need to immerse after birth, it is necessary to know the child's status at the time of his conception. As a child who converts no longer maintains the familial connections that he had before his conversion, it is important to know at what point he converted in order to establish his family status vis-à-vis children in that family who are conceived later.

A woman who was raped and a woman who was seduced – אֲנוּסָה וּמְפוּתָּה: With regard to this issue, in the Jerusalem Talmud there is also a ruling that women who were raped or seduced need not wait. There the question is raised as to why the mishna requires the women who were mistakenly switched, which is a type of rape, to nevertheless have a waiting period. This question is sharpened by the assertion that it is inappropriate to issue a rabbinic decree in cases of switched wives since this is an uncommon occurrence. The Gemara there answers that the ruling in the mishna comes to rectify the child's status. The Vilna Gaon explains that there is a distinction between the purposes of the separation period in different cases. In cases of rape and the like, the decree was made in order to know with certainty who was the father of the child. In this case, the rabbinic decree was not applied. However, in the case of the mishna, the separation is necessary in order to determine whether or not the child is a *mamzer*, and therefore the rabbinic decree was issued.

HALAKHA

A female convert and a freed maidservant – גִּיּוֹרֶת וּמְשׁוּחְרֶרֶת: Female converts and maidservants who were married before they became Jewish are required to wait three months before marrying. If the husbands converted they must separate from them for three months in order to distinguish between children conceived before and after the conversion. This ruling is in accordance with the opinion of Rabbi Yehuda, as explained by Abaye (*Maggid Mishne*; Rambam *Sefer Nashim, Hilkhot Geirushin* 11:21; *Shulḥan Arukh, Even HaEzer* 13:5).

A woman who was raped and a woman who was seduced, etc. – אֲנוּסָה וּמְפוּתָּה וכו׳: Women who were raped or seduced, and indeed any woman who engaged in promiscuous sexual acts, as well as a woman who was captured, need not wait three months. This ruling is in accordance with the opinion of Rabbi Yosei (Rambam). Some say that if the females are adult women and fit to become pregnant they must wait, in accordance with the opinions of Rabbi Yehuda and Shmuel (Rema; Rambam *Hilkhot Geirushin* 11:22; *Shulḥan Arukh, Even HaEzer* 13:6).

אֶלָּא אָמַר אַבַּיֵי: אִשָּׁה מְזַנָּה מִתְהַפֶּכֶת, שֶׁלֹּא תִּתְעַבֵּר. וְאִידָךְ: חָיְישִׁינַן שֶׁמָּא לֹא נִתְהַפְּכָה יָפֶה יָפֶה.

Rather, Abaye said: A woman who engages in promiscuous sexual intercourse turns over[NB] following intercourse, trying to prevent the absorption of the semen, so as **not to become pregnant.** Maidservants act in a similar manner. The Gemara asks: If indeed she tries not to become pregnant, how then would **the other** opinion, that of Rabbi Yehuda, explain why she must wait three months? The Gemara responds: **We are concerned** that **perhaps she did not turn over well enough** and therefore became pregnant.

"וְאִם הָיוּ כֹּהֲנוֹת" כו׳. כֹּהֲנוֹת – אִין, יִשְׂרְאֵלִית – לָא?! אֵימָא: אִם הָיוּ נְשֵׁי כֹּהֲנִים. נְשֵׁי כֹּהֲנִים – אִין, נְשֵׁי יִשְׂרְאֵלִים – לָא?

§ With regard to the case of two betrothed women who were switched at the time they entered the wedding canopy, the mishna states: **And if they were daughters of priests,** they are disqualified from partaking in *teruma*. The Gemara asks: Does this indicate that with regard to the **daughters of priests, yes,** they are disqualified from partaking in *teruma*, but with regard to **the daughter of an Israelite, no,** she would not be disqualified? It would seem that an Israelite woman married to a priest should most certainly be disqualified from eating of her husband's *teruma*. The Gemara answers: Rather, **say: If they were the wives of priests** then they are disqualified. The Gemara questions this formulation: Does this indicate that with regard to the **wives of priests, yes,** they are disqualified, but with regard to the **wives of Israelites, no,** they are not disqualified, and if their husbands died, they would be suitable for marriage to the priests?

וְהָאָמַר רַב עַמְרָם: הָא מִילְּתָא אֲמַר לָן רַב שֵׁשֶׁת, וְאַנְהֲרִינְהוּ לְעַיְינִין מִמַּתְנִיתִין: אֵשֶׁת יִשְׂרָאֵל שֶׁנֶּאֶנְסָה, אַף עַל פִּי שֶׁמּוּתֶּרֶת לְבַעְלָהּ – פְּסוּלָה לִכְהוּנָּה!

The Gemara objects to this: **But didn't Rav Amram say: Rav Sheshet said this matter to us, and he lit our eyes** by showing us that this ruling is indicated **from what was stated in the mishna** (*Yevamot* 53b). He said: **The wife of an Israelite who was raped, even though she is permitted to** return to **her husband, she** is nevertheless **disqualified from the priesthood.**[NH] If her husband later dies, she may not marry a priest, for although she is permitted to her husband the rape disqualified her for matters of priesthood.

אָמַר רָבָא, הָכִי קָאָמַר: אִם הָיוּ כֹּהֲנוֹת נְשׂוּאוֹת לְיִשְׂרָאֵל – נִפְסְלוּ מִן הַתְּרוּמָה דְּבֵי נָשַׁיְיהוּ.

Rava resolved this and **said: This is what** the *tanna* **is saying** in the mishna: **If they were daughters of priests** who **were married to an Israelite, they are disqualified from the *teruma***[H] **that is from the household of their fathers,** so that if their husbands die while they are childless, they may not go back to eat of the *teruma* in the house of their fathers. While other childless daughters of priests are again qualified to eat of the *teruma* the moment they leave their Israelite husbands, these women were disqualified by their act of forbidden sexual intercourse.

הדרן עלך ארבעה אחין

NOTES

Turns over – **מִתְהַפֶּכֶת**: According to *Tosafot Yeshanim*, there is room to differentiate between a maidservant who is released due to the loss of a tooth or an eye and a woman who was raped or seduced because an ordinary maidservant is not concerned with becoming pregnant. In fact, she might even desire it. According to this explanation, even Rabbi Yosei would agree that she requires a waiting period. On the other hand, the *Ḥazon Ish* holds that the primary dispute between Rabba and Abaye is not over the type of preventive measure chosen, i.e., the resorbent and turning over, respectively, as it might seem, but rather over the following question: Does a woman who is not married desire to become pregnant? In Abaye's opinion, she never desires this.

Disqualified from the priesthood – **פְּסוּלָה לִכְהוּנָּה**: The primary reason for this ruling is that any woman who engaged in intercourse, willingly or unwillingly, with a man for whom she incurs *karet* is considered a *zona*. Although a *zona* is not forbidden to an Israelite, except for in some special cases, she is nevertheless disqualified from marrying into the priesthood or partaking of *teruma* (see Rashi and *Tosafot*).

BACKGROUND

Turns over – **מִתְהַפֶּכֶת**: Medically speaking, turning over after intercourse is not an effective method of pregnancy prevention. However, it would seem that the Gemara is not referring specifically to the act of turning over, but rather to the fact that a woman who does not desire to become pregnant will take any measures necessary in addition to turning over, including taking drugs and the like. The Gemara's concern that she might not have turned over sufficiently therefore seems justified, since no measure taken following intercourse can fully ensure that a woman will not conceive.

HALAKHA

A married woman who was raped – **אֵשֶׁת אִישׁ שֶׁנֶּאֶנְסָה**: While a woman who was married to an Israelite and raped is permitted to her husband, she nevertheless may not marry a priest if her husband dies, as the act of prohibited intercourse disqualified her from marrying into the priesthood. This ruling is in accordance with the statement of Rav Sheshet (Rambam *Sefer Kedusha, Hilkhot Issurei Bia* 18:7; *Shulḥan Arukh, Even HaEzer* 13:6, 11).

Daughters of priests disqualified from partaking of *teruma* – **כֹּהֲנוֹת נִפְסָלוֹת לִתְרוּמָה**: If the daughter of a priest was married to an Israelite and was raped by another man, she is permitted to her husband. If she is divorced or widowed, she is prohibited from partaking of the *teruma* from her father's household, even if she has no children from her Israelite husband. This ruling is in accordance with the statement of Rava (Rambam *Sefer Zera'im, Hilkhot Teruma* 6:10).

Summary of **Perek III**

The nature of the levirate bond is not conclusively defined in this chapter. It is clear that the issue, which is disputed among the *amora'im*, is in fact a matter of dispute among the *tanna'im* as well. The various opinions and their conclusions on this matter are found within the many *mishnayot* of this chapter and in disputes pertaining to related fields that touch upon the status of women requiring levirate marriage.

The general halakhic conclusion is that the levirate bond is substantial, and it begins at the moment of the husband's death. The bond created is of a unique nature, at once similar in effect to the bond of betrothal yet with clear differences. Due to its unique status, the levirate bond can exist between a single woman and several *yevamin* at once, and need not be limited to a single *yavam*.

The problems that arise from combinations of possible situations involving different relatives led to discussion of a wider question in this chapter: To what extent might a prohibition take effect where another prohibition already exists? All of the different opinions were clarified, from those that maintain that prohibitions do take effect where others already exist to those that propose that they can take effect only under special circumstances, e.g., when there are more inclusive prohibitions, expanded prohibitions, or simultaneous prohibitions.

This chapter also discussed halakhic rulings in cases involving uncertainties. For example, the status of a woman who happens before a *yavam* is unclear because her betrothal or divorce is in doubt. In such cases, it was determined that the woman, and sometimes it is two women, require the act of *ḥalitza* in order to resolve the situation.

Introduction to **Perek IV**

The chapter begins with a consideration of cases in which there was no requirement to perform levirate marriage or *ḥalitza* but nevertheless they were mistakenly performed, e.g., if they were performed with a pregnant woman who later gave birth to a viable offspring. When *ḥalitza* is performed in such cases, the question arises of how to relate to it. Does such an act of *ḥalitza* have any significance? Does it effect any change in the woman's status? Does it render the woman unfit to marry a priest, and will it impact the levirate bond of her rival wife?

If the *yavam* and *yevama* engaged in relations together under the assumption that doing so would achieve the consummation of a levirate marriage, the situation is far more serious. This is because in cases where there is no requirement of levirate marriage, the two are prohibited from engaging in relations with each other by an explicit Torah prohibition. The Gemara discusses their liability for doing so and then further considers the status of a child born from such relations. Is it considered a *mamzer*? Will it be permitted to marry into the priesthood?

In many cases, if a child is born several months after the relations, there could be an uncertainty whether the child is actually the offspring of the original husband or of the *yavam*. If so, the child's status will be subject to uncertainty that will possibly render him a *mamzer*. Moreover, this uncertainty raises issues with regard to the legal status of the child vis-à-vis inheritance. The Gemara considers these issues in depth and discusses what the *halakha* is in various cases that might arise. Following this, the Gemara discusses the steps that should be taken to ensure such uncertainties never arise.

Another central issue discussed in the chapter is the relationship between a *yavam* and his *yevama* before any action has been taken, when there is only a levirate bond between them. In such cases, what rights does the *yavam* have over the property of the *yevama*? Is there a distinction between different categories of property, e.g., property that was bequeathed to her or her previous husband's property? This leads into a discussion of the legal obligations of a *yavam* to a *yevama* following the levirate marriage, especially with regard to the marriage contact.

The chapter concludes with a discussion of the *halakhot* of slaves and of conversion. Upon purchase, a slave must immerse in a ritual bath for the sake of becoming a slave. This is a process similar to conversion, and the Gemara discusses the similarities and the distinctions between the two.

מתני׳ הַחוֹלֵץ לִיבִמְתּוֹ וְנִמְצֵאת מְעוּבֶּרֶת. וְיָלְדָה. בִּזְמַן שֶׁהַוָּלָד שֶׁל קַיְימָא – הוּא מוּתָּר בִּקְרוֹבוֹתֶיהָ וְהִיא מוּתֶּרֶת בִּקְרוֹבָיו, וְלֹא פְּסָלָהּ מִן הַכְּהוּנָּה.

MISHNA When a man who has a brother dies childless, his widow [*yevama*] and one of his brothers [*yavam*] may perform a ritual through which she is freed of her levirate bonds [*ḥalitza*]. It is then considered, with regard to forbidden relationships, as though they had been married and divorced. Therefore, he is forbidden to her relatives, and she to his. However, with regard to **one who performs *ḥalitza* with his *yevama*** and then **she is found** to have been **pregnant**[H] at the time of the *ḥalitza* **and she gave birth, in the event that the offspring is viable,** the deceased husband has been survived by offspring and so there was never any levirate bond; consequently, the *ḥalitza* that was performed was entirely unnecessary and a meaningless act. As such, **he** remains **permitted to her relatives and she** remains **permitted to his relatives.** Furthermore, since the *ḥalitza* was meaningless, she is not afforded the status of a *ḥalutza*, i.e., a *yevama* who performed *ḥalitza*, a status akin to that of a divorcée. Therefore, the *ḥalitza* **does not disqualify her from** marrying into **the priesthood.**

אֵין הַוָּלָד שֶׁל קַיְימָא – הוּא אָסוּר בִּקְרוֹבוֹתֶיהָ וְהִיא אֲסוּרָה בִּקְרוֹבָיו, וּפְסָלָהּ מִן הַכְּהוּנָּה.

If **the offspring is not viable,** then it emerges that the *ḥalitza* was indeed necessary. Therefore, **he is forbidden** to engage in relations **with her relatives and she is forbidden** to engage in relations **with his relatives,** as though they had been married and divorced, **and** the *ḥalitza* **disqualifies her from** marrying into **the priesthood,** as she is afforded the status of a *ḥalutza*.

הַכּוֹנֵס אֶת יְבִמְתּוֹ וְנִמְצֵאת מְעוּבֶּרֶת וְיָלְדָה, בִּזְמַן שֶׁהַוָּלָד שֶׁל קַיְימָא – יוֹצִיא, וְחַיָּיבִין בְּקָרְבָּן.

With regard to **one who consummates** the levirate marriage with **his *yevama*,** i.e., he had intercourse with her under the assumption that there is a levirate bond and so there is a mitzva to do so, **and** then **she is found to** have been **pregnant** at the time of the intercourse **and she gave birth, in the event that the offspring is viable**[H] the deceased brother has been survived by offspring and it is evident that there was never any levirate bond. In that case, the relations they had, rather than being a mitzva, were a violation of the prohibition against engaging in relations with one's brother's wife. Therefore, the *yavam* **must send** her **out,** i.e., they must separate, as she is forbidden to him as his brother's wife, **and** to atone for the forbidden relations that they had, **they are** each **obligated** to bring a sin-**offering,** as is the *halakha* for all who inadvertently transgress a prohibition that, when performed intentionally, is punishable by *karet*.

וְאִם אֵין וָלָד שֶׁל קַיָּימָא – יְקַיֵּים.

And if the offspring is not viable,[H] and therefore there was in fact a levirate bond, **he may maintain** her as his wife since his intercourse with her was a valid consummation of levirate marriage.

HALAKHA

One who performs *ḥalitza* with his *yevama* and then she is found to have been pregnant – הַחוֹלֵץ לִיבִמְתּוֹ וְנִמְצֵאת מְעוּבֶּרֶת: With regard to one who performs *ḥalitza* with his *yevama* and then she is found to have been pregnant at the time, if she later gives birth to viable offspring, the *ḥalitza* is considered of no significance. Therefore, he is permitted to her relatives and she is permitted to his relatives, and the *ḥalitza* does not disqualify her from marrying into the priesthood. If the pregnancy did not result in viable offspring, either because she miscarried or because the child died within thirty days of birth, then the *ḥalitza* is valid. Therefore, he is forbidden to her relatives and she to his, and the *ḥalitza* disqualifies her from the priesthood (Rambam *Sefer Nashim, Hilkhot Yibbum VaḤalitza* 1:20; *Shulḥan Arukh, Even HaEzer* 164:2).

One who consummates a levirate marriage with his *yevama* and then she is found to have been pregnant with viable offspring – הַכּוֹנֵס יְבִמְתּוֹ וְנִמְצָאָה מְעוּבֶּרֶת בְּבֶן קַיְימָא: If one had intercourse with his *yevama* and then she was found to have been pregnant at the time, she must separate from him, although there is no need for a bill of divorce, and they are both obligated to bring a sin-offering (Rambam *Sefer Nashim, Hilkhot Yibbum VaḤalitza* 1:22 and *Sefer Korbanot, Hilkhot Shegagot* 1:1; *Shulḥan Arukh, Even HaEzer* 164:5).

One who consummates a levirate marriage with his *yevama* and she miscarries – הַכּוֹנֵס יְבִמְתּוֹ וְהִפִּילָה: In the case of one who consummates a levirate marriage with his *yevama* and then she is found to have been pregnant at the time, if she later miscarries then he is permitted to retain her as his wife. Some say that he is permitted to remain with her only if he married her before her pregnancy was recognizable, but if the pregnancy was already recognizable when he married her, then he is obligated to divorce her (Rema, citing *Tosafot*). In cases where he is permitted to maintain her as his wife, he must repeat the act of intercourse in order to consummate the marriage. This is in accordance with the conclusion of the Gemara that intercourse with a pregnant woman is not considered a valid consummation of levirate marriage (*Nimmukei Yosef*, citing Rabbeinu Yeruḥam). However, if he wishes to separate from her, he must both give her a bill of divorce and perform *ḥalitza* (Rambam *Sefer Nashim, Hilkhot Yibbum VaḤalitza* 1:22; *Shulḥan Arukh, Even HaEzer* 164:5).

סָפֵק בֶּן תִּשְׁעָה לָרִאשׁוֹן, סָפֵק בֶּן שִׁבְעָה לָאַחֲרוֹן – יוֹצִיא, וְהַוָּלָד כָּשֵׁר, וְחַיָּיבִין בְּאָשָׁם תָּלוּי.

If they consummated the levirate marriage and seven months later she gave birth, there is **uncertainty whether** the child **is nine** months **old,** i.e., counting from conception, and is the offspring **of the first** husband,[H] and as such there was no levirate bond, or **whether** the child is only **seven** months **old** and is the offspring **of the latter** husband, i.e., the *yavam*, and not of the deceased, in which case there was a levirate bond. In that case, due to the possibility that she is forbidden to him as his brother's wife, **he must send** her **out.** However, the lineage of **the child is unflawed,** since regardless of whether it was born of the first or second husband, there was no transgression involved in its conception. Furthermore, to atone for the possibility that they had forbidden relations **they are** both **obligated to bring a guilt-**offering for **uncertainty,**[HB] as is the *halakha* for anyone who is uncertain whether they inadvertently transgressed a prohibition that would require one to bring a sin-offering.

גמ׳ אִיתְּמַר, הַחוֹלֵץ לִמְעוּבֶּרֶת וְהִפִּילָה. רַבִּי יוֹחָנָן אָמַר: אֵינָהּ צְרִיכָה חֲלִיצָה מִן הָאַחִין, רֵישׁ לָקִישׁ אָמַר: צְרִיכָה חֲלִיצָה מִן הָאַחִין.

GEMARA An amoraic dispute **was stated** with regard to **one who performs *ḥalitza* with a pregnant woman**[H] **and she** later **miscarried.** Since she miscarried, she was certainly bound to the *yavam* by a levirate bond and may not marry anyone else; rather, she is obligated to consummate the levirate marriage or perform *ḥalitza*. The question is whether the *ḥalitza* that was performed while she was still pregnant is effective in releasing her from the levirate bond. **Rabbi Yoḥanan**[P] **said: She does not require** another ***ḥalitza* from the brothers. Reish Lakish**[P] **said: She requires** another ***ḥalitza* from the brothers.**[N]

HALAKHA

There is uncertainty whether the child is nine months old and is the offspring of the first husband – סָפֵק בֶּן תִּשְׁעָה לָרִאשׁוֹן: If one consummates a levirate marriage with his *yevama* and seven months later she gives birth, then there is an uncertainty whether the child is nine months old, counting from conception, and is the offspring of the first husband, or whether the child is only seven months old and is the offspring of the *yavam*. Therefore, the *yavam* must separate from her and give her a bill of divorce. The lineage of the child is certainly unflawed; however, any future children that he has with her will have the status of an uncertain *mamzer* (Rambam *Sefer Nashim*, *Hilkhot Yibbum VaḤalitza* 1:23; *Shulḥan Arukh*, *Even HaEzer* 164:6).

A guilt-offering for uncertainty – אָשָׁם תָּלוּי: If one consummates a levirate marriage with his *yevama* and she gives birth, and there is an uncertainty whether the child was born after nine months of gestation and is the offspring of the first husband, or after seven months of gestation and is the offspring of the latter husband, the *yavam* is not required to bring a guilt-offering for uncertainty. The *halakha* on this issue is not as ruled in the mishna because the mishna is in accordance with the opinion of Rabbi Eliezer, who holds that a guilt-offering for uncertainty may be brought whenever there exists the possibility that a transgression was performed. However, the Gemara in tractate *Karetot* rejects his opinion and rules that a guilt-offering for uncertainty is brought only in specific cases involving an uncertainty (Rambam *Sefer Korbanot*, *Hilkhot Shegagot* 8:1–2 and *Leḥem Mishne* and *Mishne LaMelekh* there).

***Ḥalitza* with a pregnant woman – חֲלִיצַת מְעוּבֶּרֶת:** In the case of one who performs *ḥalitza* with his *yevama* and then she is found to have been pregnant at the time, even if the offspring is not viable the *ḥalitza* is considered ineffective and another *ḥalitza* must be performed. Some say it may be performed either with the brother who originally performed *ḥalitza* with her or with any of the brothers. Others argue that this *ḥalitza* may be performed only with one of the other brothers (Rambam *Sefer Nashim*, *Hilkhot Yibbum VaḤalitza* 1:20; *Shulḥan Arukh*, *Even HaEzer* 164:2, and in the comment of Rema).

NOTES

She requires *ḥalitza* from the brothers – צְרִיכָה חֲלִיצָה מִן הָאַחִים: The commentaries debate who should perform the additional *ḥalitza* following the miscarriage. Some suggest, in accordance with the plain reading of Reish Lakish's words, that the additional *ḥalitza* cannot be performed by the brother who originally performed it; rather, one of the other brothers should do so. Others suggest the intention is only that she requires an additional *ḥalitza*, but this may be performed by any of the brothers, even the one who originally performed it (see *Tosafot*). The Ramban holds that the original *ḥalitza* is classified as an invalid *ḥalitza* that is partially effective to the extent that the *ḥalitza* of one of the brothers will no longer release her from the levirate bond she has with the other brothers. Consequently, she must now perform a separate *ḥalitza* with each and every one of the brothers.

BACKGROUND

A guilt-offering for uncertainty – אָשָׁם תָּלוּי: The guilt-offering for uncertainty is mentioned in the Torah (Leviticus 5:17–19) and its various *halakhot* are delineated in tractate *Karetot*. The standard case of a guilt-offering for uncertainty is where there is uncertainty whether or not a transgression warranting a sin-offering was committed. For example, if a piece of forbidden fat and a piece of permitted fat were mixed together and one thought that they were both permitted and ate one of them, he must bring a guilt-offering for uncertainty. The offering protects him from punishment until he determines whether or not he actually sinned, and if he did, he must bring a sin-offering.

PERSONALITIES

Rabbi Yoḥanan – רַבִּי יוֹחָנָן: This is Rabbi Yoḥanan bar Nappaḥa, one of the greatest *amora'im*, whose teachings are fundamental components of both the Babylonian Talmud and the Jerusalem Talmud. He resided in Tiberias and lived to an advanced age. Rabbi Yoḥanan was orphaned at a young age, and although his family apparently owned considerable property, he spent virtually all of his resources in his devotion to the study of Torah and eventually became impoverished. In his youth, he had the privilege of studying under Rabbi Yehuda HaNasi, the redactor of the Mishna, but most of his Torah study was accomplished under Rabbi Yehuda HaNasi's students: Ḥizkiya ben Ḥiyya, Rabbi Oshaya, Rabbi Ḥanina, and Rabbi Yannai, who lavished praise upon him. In time, he became the head of the yeshiva in Tiberias, at which point his fame and influence increased greatly.

For many years Rabbi Yoḥanan was the leading rabbinic scholar of the entire Jewish world, not only in Eretz Yisrael but in Babylonia as well, where he was respected by the Babylonian Sages. Many of them immigrated to Eretz Yisrael to become his students. A master of both *halakha* and *aggada*, Rabbi Yoḥanan's teachings in both disciplines are found throughout the Babylonian and Jerusalem Talmuds. As a testament to his intellectual and spiritual stature, the *halakha* is in accordance with his opinion in almost every case, even when Rav or Shmuel, the preeminent *amora'im* of Babylonia, whom he treated deferentially, disagree with him. Only in disputes with his teachers in Eretz Yisrael, such as Rabbi Yannai and Rabbi Yehoshua ben Levi, is the *halakha* not in accordance with his opinion.

Rabbi Yoḥanan was renowned for being handsome, and much was said in praise of his good looks. However, his life was full of suffering; ten of his sons died in his lifetime. There is a geonic tradition that one of his sons was the Babylonian *amora* Rabbi Mattana, who did not predecease him. The death of Rabbi Yoḥanan's disciple-colleague and brother-in-law, Reish Lakish, for which he considered himself responsible, hastened his own death. Rabbi Yoḥanan had many students. In fact, all the *amora'im* of Eretz Yisrael in succeeding generations were his students and benefited from his teachings, to the extent that he is often referred to as the author of the Jerusalem Talmud. His greatest students were his brother-in-law Reish Lakish, Rabbi Elazar, Rabbi Ḥiyya bar Abba, Rabbi Abbahu, Rabbi Yosei bar Ḥanina, Rabbi Ami, and Rabbi Asi.

Reish Lakish – רַבִּי שִׁמְעוֹן בֶּן לָקִישׁ: The name Reish Lakish is actually a contraction of Rabbi Shimon ben Lakish. Reish Lakish was among the greatest *amora'im* in Eretz Yisrael. He was the friend and brother-in-law of Rabbi Yoḥanan.

Reish Lakish lived an extraordinary life. He studied Torah from a young age, but, perhaps due to dire financial straits, he sold himself to a Roman circus as a gladiator. There are many stories in the Talmud that attest to his great strength. Some time later, in the wake of a meeting with Rabbi Yoḥanan, he resumed his Torah study, first as a student of Rabbi Yoḥanan, then as a friend and colleague. He ultimately married Rabbi Yoḥanan's sister.

Many halakhic disagreements between Reish Lakish and Rabbi Yoḥanan concerning central issues of *halakha* are recorded in the Talmud. His objective was not to disagree with Rabbi Yoḥanan but rather to help him hone his opinion through debate. Rabbi Yoḥanan related to him with great respect, often saying: My peer disagrees with me. He was well known for his strict piety, to the extent that one with whom Reish Lakish was seen conversing in public was said to be able to borrow money without guarantors, as Reish Lakish associated only with people beyond reproach. When he died he was survived by his wife and son, who was a child prodigy.

רַבִּי יוֹחָנָן אָמַר: אֵינָהּ צְרִיכָה חֲלִיצָה מִן הָאַחִין – חֲלִיצַת מְעוּבֶּרֶת שְׁמָהּ חֲלִיצָה, וּבִיאַת מְעוּבֶּרֶת שְׁמָהּ בִּיאָה. וְרֵישׁ לָקִישׁ אָמַר: צְרִיכָה חֲלִיצָה מִן הָאַחִין – חֲלִיצַת מְעוּבֶּרֶת לָא שְׁמָהּ חֲלִיצָה, וּבִיאַת מְעוּבֶּרֶת לָא שְׁמָהּ בִּיאָה.

The Gemara elaborates: **Rabbi Yoḥanan said** that **she does not require** another *ḥalitza* **from the brothers** because he holds: *Ḥalitza* performed **with a pregnant woman** who later miscarries **is considered** effective ***ḥalitza*** in order to release her from the levirate bond. **And** similarly, **intercourse with a pregnant woman** who later miscarries **is considered** a valid consummation of levirate marriage through **intercourse,** such that she and the *yavam* are considered to be married. **And Reish Lakish said she requires** another ***ḥalitza*** **from the brothers** because he holds: ***Ḥalitza*** performed **with a pregnant woman is not considered** effective ***ḥalitza***,[N] **and intercourse with a pregnant woman is not considered** a valid consummation of levirate marriage through **intercourse.** Therefore, after she miscarries, another *ḥalitza* must be performed in order to release her from the levirate bond.

בְּמַאי קָמִיפַּלְגִי? אִיבָּעֵית אֵימָא קְרָא, וְאִיבָּעֵית אֵימָא סְבָרָא.

With regard to what principle **do they disagree? If you wish, say** that they disagree over the interpretation of **a verse.**[N] **And if you wish, say** that they disagree on a point of **logical reasoning.**

אִיבָּעֵית אֵימָא סְבָרָא, רַבִּי יוֹחָנָן סָבַר: אִם יָבֹא אֵלִיָּהוּ וְיֹאמַר דְּהָא דְּאִיעַבְּרָא מַפּוֹלֵי מַפְּלָה – מִי לָאו בַּת חֲלִיצָה וְיִבּוּם הִיא? הָשְׁתָּא נַמִי, תִּגְלֵי מִילְּתָא לְמַפְרֵעַ.

If you wish, say that that they disagree over a point of **logical reasoning** in that **Rabbi Yoḥanan holds: If Elijah** the prophet **were to come** at the moment of the *ḥalitza* **and say**[N] **that this** woman **who is pregnant will miscarry, is she not eligible for *ḥalitza* or levirate marriage,** even though she is currently pregnant, since her husband died and will not be survived by offspring? **Now, too,** even though when the *ḥalitza* or levirate marriage is performed it is not known whether or not she will miscarry, **the matter will be revealed retroactively,** i.e., if she ultimately miscarries then it is apparent the *ḥalitza* or levirate marriage was always necessary and is therefore valid.

וְרֵישׁ לָקִישׁ אָמַר: תִּגְלֵי מִילְּתָא לְמַפְרֵעַ לָא אָמְרִינַן.

And Reish Lakish said: We do not say that **the matter will be revealed retroactively**[N] in order to validate the levirate marriage or *ḥalitza*. Since at the time of the levirate marriage or *ḥalitza* it was still unknown whether she would miscarry, the act is considered premature and ineffective.

וְאִיבָּעֵית אֵימָא קְרָא; רַבִּי יוֹחָנָן סָבַר "וּבֵן אֵין לוֹ" אָמַר רַחֲמָנָא, וְהָא לֵית לֵיהּ. וְרֵישׁ לָקִישׁ סָבַר: "וּבֵן אֵין לוֹ" עַיֵּין עָלָיו.

And if you wish, say that they disagree over the interpretation of **a verse** in that **Rabbi Yoḥanan holds: The Merciful One states** in the Torah: "If brothers dwell together, and one of them dies, **and he has no child**" (Deuteronomy 25:5), i.e., the obligation to consummate a levirate marriage or perform *ḥalitza* applies whenever a husband dies and is not survived by offspring. **And this** man, whose wife is currently pregnant, **does not have** any children who will survive him. Therefore, there is an obligation to consummate a levirate marriage or perform *ḥalitza*, and if done, they will be effective. **And Reish Lakish holds:** The phrase **"and he has no [*ein*] child"** is expounded by the Sages to teach that one should **inspect [*ayein*] him** carefully to determine if he is survived by offspring of any form, and currently he is in fact survived by the fetus. Therefore, there is currently no obligation to consummate a levirate marriage or perform *ḥalitza*, and consequently, even if done, they are ineffective.

אֵיתִיבֵיהּ רַבִּי יוֹחָנָן לְרֵישׁ לָקִישׁ: אֵין הַוָּלָד שֶׁל קַיָּימָא – הוּא אָסוּר בִּקְרוֹבוֹתֶיהָ, וְהִיא אֲסוּרָה בִּקְרוֹבָיו. וּפְסָלָהּ מִן הַכְּהוּנָּה. בִּשְׁלָמָא לְדִידִי, דְּאָמִינָא חֲלִיצַת מְעוּבֶּרֶת שְׁמָהּ חֲלִיצָה – מִשּׁוּם הָכִי פְּסָלָהּ. אֶלָּא לְדִידָךְ, דְּאָמְרַתְּ חֲלִיצַת מְעוּבֶּרֶת לָא שְׁמָהּ חֲלִיצָה – אַמַּאי פְּסָלָהּ מִן הַכְּהוּנָּה?

Rabbi Yoḥanan raised an objection to the opinion of **Reish Lakish** from the mishna: If *ḥalitza* was performed with a pregnant woman, and **the offspring is not viable,** then **he is forbidden to her relatives and she is forbidden to his relatives, and** the *ḥalitza* **disqualifies her from the priesthood.** Rabbi Yoḥanan explains the challenge: **Granted, according to my** opinion, **as I say** that ***ḥalitza*** performed **with a pregnant woman** who later miscarries **is considered** effective ***ḥalitza***, **it is due to that** reason that the *ḥalitza* **disqualifies her** from the priesthood. **However, according to your** opinion, **as you say that *ḥalitza*** performed **with a pregnant woman is not considered** effective ***ḥalitza***, **why** should the *ḥalitza* **disqualify her from the priesthood?** According to your opinion, shouldn't the *ḥalitza* be entirely disregarded?

NOTES

Ḥalitza performed with a pregnant woman is not considered effective *ḥalitza* – חֲלִיצַת מְעוּבֶּרֶת לָא שְׁמָהּ חֲלִיצָה: The commentaries debate whether according to Reish Lakish the *ḥalitza* performed with a pregnant woman has any significance. Some suggest that while the *ḥalitza* does not release her from being bound to her *yevamin*, it does preclude her from performing levirate marriage, either specifically with the brother who originally performed *ḥalitza* with her or with any of the brothers. Therefore, her only recourse is to perform another *ḥalitza* following the miscarriage (see Ritva).

If you wish, say a verse, etc. – אִיבָּעֵית אֵימָא קְרָא וכו׳: Normally, in cases where the Gemara suggest that a *halakha* could be based on logical reasoning, if a verse also exists that can teach that same *halakha* the Gemara will ask why the biblical source is necessary at all; does the force of logical reasoning not suffice? Often the justification for the biblical source is based on the fact that if the *halakha* is based on the verse, then some of the details of the *halakha* will be different than if it were solely based on logical reasoning. In this case, as well, there is such a distinction: Were the *halakha* to be purely based on logical reasoning, then Reish Lakish would agree that were Elijah the prophet to actually reveal beforehand that the woman will ultimately miscarry, then the *ḥalitza* would be effective. However, according to his biblical source, the possibility of performing *ḥalitza* with a pregnant woman is entirely precluded, even if it were already known that she will miscarry (*Keren Ora*).

If Elijah were to come and say – אִם יָבֹא אֵלִיָּהוּ וְיֹאמַר: The mishna in tractate *Eduyyot* rules that when Elijah the prophet appears, he will neither inform the people as to what is prohibited or permitted nor introduce new *halakhot*. This is based on the principle that a prophet is neither permitted to legislate *halakha* nor even to resolve halakhic dilemmas. Despite this principle, the Gemara here and elsewhere appears to state that halakhic dilemmas will be resolved by Elijah. Apparently a distinction should be made between deciding halakhic principles, which cannot be done through prophecy, and clarifying questions of fact utilizing his prophetic powers, which is permitted (*Mishne LaMelekh*).

We do not say that the matter will be revealed retroactively – תִּגְלֵי מִילְּתָא לְמַפְרֵעַ לָא אָמְרִינַן: Despite Reish Lakish's claim here, the principle that the facts of a matter can be revealed retroactively is used throughout the Talmud, and it would appear that even Reish Lakish agrees in those instances. What, then, is different about this case? The Ritva suggests that in this case, it is unsound to deduce from the ultimate miscarriage that the pregnancy had always been unviable. It is possible that at the time of the levirate marriage or *ḥalitza* the pregnancy had in fact been viable, and therefore the *yevama* had not been obligated to perform levirate marriage or *ḥalitza* at the time, and it was only afterward that some additional event occurred that caused the miscarriage.

Tosafot suggest that a distinction should be made between cases in which the future is undeterminable based on the current situation and cases where the outcome could be reasonably calculated from the outset. In the former, the facts of the future are considered halakhically meaningless to the extent that even were a prophet to reveal the future, such information would have no relevance to the *halakha* as it is practiced in the present. So too, in the case of *ḥalitza*, since the ultimate miscarriage is not something that could be known in the present, one cannot say the matter is revealed retroactively (see *Gilyonei HaShas*). Rabbi Avraham min HaHar suggests that the principle is applied only in cases of rabbinic law, but not where it would affect a Torah law, as in this case.

Another explanation is cited by the Ritva: According to the verse cited by Reish Lakish, the reason that levirate marriage and *ḥalitza* cannot be performed during pregnancy is because the very existence of the fetus itself is sufficient to exclude this case from the obligation to perform levirate marriage or *ḥalitza*, since it does not fulfill the basic condition that the *yavam* "has no child." If so, the ultimate demise of the fetus is of no relevance.

אָמַר לֵיהּ: מִדְּרַבָּנַן, וּלְחוּמְרָא בְּעָלְמָא.

Reish Lakish **said to** Rabbi Yoḥanan: Indeed, by Torah law the *ḥalitza* is to be entirely disregarded. The mishna's ruling that she is disqualified from the priesthood is **by rabbinic** decree **and is merely a stringency**[N] lest people not realize that she was pregnant and think that a *ḥalutza* is permitted to marry a priest.

אִיכָּא דְּאָמְרִי, אֵיתִיבֵיהּ רֵישׁ לָקִישׁ לְרַבִּי יוֹחָנָן: אֵין הַוָּלָד שֶׁל קַיָּימָא – הוּא אָסוּר בִּקְרוֹבוֹתֶיהָ, וְהִיא אֲסוּרָה בִּקְרוֹבָיו, וּפְסָלָהּ מִן הַכְּהוּנָּה. בִּשְׁלָמָא לְדִידִי, דְּאָמִינָא חֲלִיצַת מְעוּבֶּרֶת לָא שְׁמָהּ חֲלִיצָה – הַיְינוּ דְּקָתָנֵי פְּסָלָהּ מִן הַכְּהוּנָּה לְחוּמְרָא, וְלֹא קָתָנֵי: אֵינָהּ צְרִיכָה חֲלִיצָה מִן הָאַחִין.

There are those **who say** an alternate version of the dispute: **Reish Lakish raised an objection to** the opinion of **Rabbi Yoḥanan** from the mishna: If *ḥalitza* was performed with a pregnant woman and **the offspring is not viable,** then **he is forbidden to her relatives and she is forbidden to his relatives, and** the *ḥalitza* **disqualifies her from the priesthood.** Reish Lakish explains the challenge: **Granted, according to my** opinion, **as I say that** *ḥalitza* performed **with a pregnant woman is not considered** effective ***ḥalitza,*** **this is** consistent with **that which is taught** in the mishna: The *ḥalitza* **disqualifies her from the priesthood,** which should be understood **as** a rabbinic **stringency, and** it is understandable that the mishna **does not teach: She does not require** another ***ḥalitza* from the brothers,** because according to my opinion, once she miscarries, she does indeed require another *ḥalitza* from the brothers.

אֶלָּא לְדִידָךְ, אֵינָהּ צְרִיכָה חֲלִיצָה מִן הָאַחִין מִיבָּעֵי לֵיהּ! – אָמַר לֵיהּ: אִין הָכִי נַמִי, וְאַיְּידֵי דִּתְנָא רֵישָׁא לֹא פְּסָלָהּ – תְּנָא סֵיפָא פְּסָלָהּ.

However, according to your opinion that *ḥalitza* performed with a pregnant woman is an effective *ḥalitza,* the mishna **should have** taught the full extent of her permissible status, i.e., that **she does not** even **require** another ***ḥalitza* from the brothers** after she miscarries because the original *ḥalitza* was effective. Rabbi Yoḥanan **said to** Reish Lakish: **Yes, it is indeed so** that she does not require another *ḥalitza* from the brothers, **but since the first clause taught:** The *ḥalitza* **does not disqualify her** from the priesthood, therefore **the latter clause taught:** The *ḥalitza* **disqualifies her** from the priesthood, in order to directly contrast with the first clause rather than teach the greater novelty.

אֵיתִיבֵיהּ רַבִּי יוֹחָנָן לְרֵישׁ לָקִישׁ: אֵין הַוָּלָד שֶׁל קַיָּימָא – יְקַיֵּים. בִּשְׁלָמָא לְדִידִי דְּאָמִינָא חֲלִיצַת מְעוּבֶּרֶת שְׁמָהּ חֲלִיצָה וּבִיאַת מְעוּבֶּרֶת שְׁמָהּ בִּיאָה – מִשּׁוּם הָכִי קָתָנֵי יְקַיֵּים.

Rabbi Yoḥanan raised an objection to the opinion of **Reish Lakish** from the mishna: If a *yavam* had intercourse with his *yevama,* who was pregnant, and **the offspring is not viable,** and therefore she was bound by a levirate bond, **he may maintain** her as his wife. Rabbi Yoḥanan explains the challenge: **Granted, according to my** opinion, **as I say *ḥalitza*** performed **with a pregnant woman is considered** effective ***ḥalitza,*** **and** similarly, **intercourse with a pregnant woman is considered** a valid consummation of levirate marriage through **intercourse,** it is **due to that** reason that the mishna **teaches: He may maintain** her as his wife, because the levirate marriage was indeed valid.

אֶלָּא לְדִידָךְ, דְּאָמְרַתְּ חֲלִיצַת מְעוּבֶּרֶת לָא שְׁמָהּ חֲלִיצָה, וּבִיאַת מְעוּבֶּרֶת לָא שְׁמָהּ בִּיאָה – יַחֲזוֹר וְיִבְעוֹל וִיקַיֵּים מִיבָּעֵי לֵיהּ! – מַאי יְקַיֵּים – יַחֲזוֹר וְיִבְעוֹל וִיקַיֵּים, דְּלָא סַגִּי.

However, according to your opinion, **as you said** that ***ḥalitza*** performed **with a pregnant woman is not considered** effective ***ḥalitza,*** **and intercourse with a pregnant woman is not considered** a valid consummation of levirate marriage through **intercourse,** the mishna **should have** taught that **he should proceed to engage in intercourse** with her again in order to consummate the levirate marriage **and** only then **may he maintain** her as his wife. Reish Lakish responded: **What is** the intention of the mishna when it teaches: **He may maintain** her as his wife? Perforce it means that **he should proceed to engage in intercourse** again with her **and** then **he may maintain** her as his wife, **as** any other way **is insufficient** to release her from the levirate bond. Therefore, it is unnecessary for the mishna to teach this explicitly.

אִיכָּא דְּאָמְרִי, אֵיתִיבֵיהּ רֵישׁ לָקִישׁ לְרַבִּי יוֹחָנָן: אֵין הַוָּלָד שֶׁל קַיָּימָא – יְקַיֵּים. בִּשְׁלָמָא לְדִידִי, דְּאָמִינָא חֲלִיצַת מְעוּבֶּרֶת לָא שְׁמָהּ חֲלִיצָה וּבִיאַת מְעוּבֶּרֶת לָא שְׁמָהּ בִּיאָה, הַיְינוּ דְּקָתָנֵי יְקַיֵּים – יַחֲזוֹר וְיִבְעוֹל וִיקַיֵּים, דְּלָא סַגִּי בְּלָאו הָכִי.

There are those **who say** an alternate version of the dispute: **Reish Lakish raised an objection to** the opinion of **Rabbi Yoḥanan** from the mishna: If a *yavam* had intercourse with his *yevama,* who was pregnant, and **the offspring is not viable,** and therefore she was bound by a levirate bond, **he may maintain** her as his wife. Reish Lakish explains how the mishna poses a challenge to Rabbi Yoḥanan's opinion: **Granted, according to my** opinion, **as I say** that ***ḥalitza*** performed **with a pregnant woman is not considered** effective ***ḥalitza,*** **and intercourse with a pregnant woman is not considered** a valid consummation of levirate marriage through **intercourse, this is** consistent with **that which is taught** in the mishna: **He may maintain** her as a wife, which perforce means **he should proceed to engage in intercourse** with her again **and** then **he may maintain** her as his wife, **as** any other way **is insufficient** to release her from the levirate bond **without this** additional intercourse.

NOTES

By rabbinic decree and is merely a stringency – מִדְּרַבָּנַן וּלְחוּמְרָא בְּעָלְמָא: The Rashba notes that ostensibly, a similar decree should have been introduced in a case where the offspring was viable. Had an observer only witnessed the *ḥalitza* and been unaware that the offspring ultimately proved to be viable, then if he later saw that the *yavam* and *yevama* were permitted to marry each other's relatives, he might mistakenly conclude that relatives are permitted even in a case where the offspring was not viable and the *ḥalitza* was genuinely required. The Rashba explains that in truth, there is no need to be concerned for such a misunderstanding. The Gemara later explains that in cases where *ḥalitza* was unnecessarily performed, a public announcement is made. This, coupled with the continuing living presence of the offspring, should be sufficient to prevent any misunderstanding.

The Meiri suggests an entirely different approach to this statement of the Gemara and a correspondingly different understanding of the entire talmudic discussion: When the Gemara claims that, according to Reish Lakish, the *halakha* in the mishna is true only by force of a rabbinic decree, it is referring not to the disqualification from the priesthood, but rather to the actual requirement to repeat the *ḥalitza.* According to the Meiri, even Reish Lakish holds that the original *ḥalitza* is valid by Torah law, and consequently he also assumes that it is by Torah law that she is disqualified from the priesthood.

אֶלָּא לְדִידָךְ, רָצָה – יוֹצִיא, רָצָה – יְקַיֵּים, מִיבָּעֵי לֵיהּ! – אִין הָכִי נַמִּי, אַיְּידֵי דִּתְנָא רֵישָׁא יוֹצִיא – תְּנָא נַמִּי סֵיפָא יְקַיֵּים.

However, **according to your** opinion that intercourse with a pregnant woman is considered a valid consummation of levirate marriage and therefore she is certainly considered to be his wife, the mishna **should have** taught: **If he wishes he may send** her **out,** through divorce, or **if he wishes he may maintain** her as a wife. Rabbi Yoḥanan replied: **Yes, it is indeed so, but since the first clause taught: He should send** her **out,** therefore **the latter clause taught: He may maintain** her as a wife, in order to directly contrast the first clause, rather than teach the full *halakha* with all its details.

מֵיתִיבִי: הַכּוֹנֵס אֶת יְבִמְתּוֹ וְנִמְצֵאת מְעוּבֶּרֶת – הֲרֵי זוֹ לֹא תִּנָּשֵׂא צָרָתָהּ, שֶׁמָּא יְהֵא וָלָד בֶּן קַיָּימָא. אַדְּרַבָּה, כִּי הָוֵי הַוָּלָד בֶּן קַיָּימָא מִיפַּטְרָה צָרָתָהּ! אֶלָּא אֵימָא: שֶׁמָּא לֹא יְהֵא הַוָּלָד בֶּן קַיָּימָא.

The Gemara **raises an objection** to the opinion of Rabbi Yoḥanan from a *baraita*: In the case of **one who consummates** the levirate marriage with **his *yevama*,** and he does so under the assumption that there is a levirate bond and he is obligated to consummate a levirate marriage with her, **and** then **she is found to** have been **pregnant** at the time of the intercourse, **a rival wife of this** *yevama* **may not marry, lest the offspring be viable.** Before explaining the challenge, the Gemara notes that the reasoning of the *baraita* appears flawed: **On the contrary, when the offspring is viable,** that is a reason for **her rival wife to be released** from the levirate bond, and she should be able to marry any man. **Rather,** emend the *baraita* and **say: Lest the offspring not be viable.**

וְאִי סָלְקָא דַעְתָּךְ בִּיאַת מְעוּבֶּרֶת שְׁמָהּ בִּיאָה – אַמַּאי לֹא תִּנָּשֵׂא צָרָתָהּ? תִּיפָּטֵר בְּבִיאָה שֶׁל חֲבֵירְתָּהּ!

The Gemara now explains how the *baraita* poses a challenge to Rabbi Yoḥanan's opinion: **And if it enters your mind** to say that **intercourse with a pregnant woman is considered** a valid consummation of levirate marriage through **intercourse, why should her rival wife not** be permitted to **marry?** Indeed, her rival wife **should be released** from the levirate bond **by** virtue **of the intercourse of her fellow** wife. If the deceased had several rival wives, all of them become bound by the levirate bond. However, it is sufficient for one of them to either consummate a levirate marriage or perform *ḥalitza* in order to release the rest of them from their bond and thereby permit them to marry any man.

אָמַר אַבָּיֵי: בְּבִיאָה – כּוּלֵּי עָלְמָא לָא פְּלִיגִי דְּלָא פָּטְרָה, כִּי פְּלִיגִי – בַּחֲלִיצָה.

The Gemara defends Rabbi Yoḥanan's opinion: **Abaye said** that the opinion ascribed to Rabbi Yoḥanan above is not an accurate portrayal of his opinion. Rather, **with regard to intercourse** with a *yevama* who is pregnant at the time, **everyone agrees**[N] **that it does not release** her and her rival wives from the levirate bond; **when they disagree** it is only **with regard to** whether ***ḥalitza***[N] performed with a *yevama* who is pregnant at the time is effective in releasing her and her rival wives from the levirate bond.

רַבִּי יוֹחָנָן סָבַר: חֲלִיצַת מְעוּבֶּרֶת שְׁמָהּ חֲלִיצָה, בִּיאַת מְעוּבֶּרֶת לָא שְׁמָהּ בִּיאָה. רֵישׁ לָקִישׁ סָבַר: בִּיאַת מְעוּבֶּרֶת – לָא שְׁמָהּ בִּיאָה, וַחֲלִיצַת מְעוּבֶּרֶת – לָא שְׁמָהּ חֲלִיצָה.

Abaye continues to explain his opinion: **Rabbi Yoḥanan holds** that ***ḥalitza*** **with a pregnant woman is considered** effective ***ḥalitza***, but **intercourse with a pregnant woman is not considered** a valid consummation of levirate marriage through **intercourse** and therefore does not release her and her rival wives from the levirate bond. And **Reish Lakish holds** that **intercourse with a pregnant woman is not considered** a valid consummation of levirate marriage through **intercourse, and *ḥalitza* with a pregnant woman is not considered** effective ***ḥalitza*.** Therefore, the *baraita* cited above does not pose a challenge, since all agree that intercourse with a pregnant woman will not free her or her rival wives from the levirate bond.

אֲמַר לֵיהּ רָבָא: מַה נַּפְשָׁךְ: אִי בִּיאַת מְעוּבֶּרֶת שְׁמָהּ בִּיאָה – חֲלִיצַת מְעוּבֶּרֶת שְׁמָהּ חֲלִיצָה, וְאִי בִּיאַת מְעוּבֶּרֶת לָא שְׁמָהּ בִּיאָה – חֲלִיצַת מְעוּבֶּרֶת נַמִּי לָא שְׁמָהּ חֲלִיצָה. דְּהָא קַיְימָא לַן

Rava said to him: Whichever way you look at it, one cannot differentiate between the validity of consummating the levirate marriage through intercourse and the validity of *ḥalitza*. **If intercourse with a pregnant woman is considered** a valid consummation of levirate marriage through **intercourse** because if she miscarries it is apparent that there was always an obligation to perform levirate marriage or *ḥalitza*, then perforce ***ḥalitza*** **with a pregnant woman** should also **be considered** effective ***ḥalitza*.** **And if intercourse with a pregnant woman is not considered** a valid consummation of levirate marriage through **intercourse** because in her currently pregnant state there is no obligation to perform levirate marriage or *ḥalitza*, then perforce ***ḥalitza*** **with a pregnant woman** should also **not be considered** effective ***ḥalitza*.** **As we maintain**

NOTES

With regard to intercourse everyone agrees – בְּבִיאָה כּוּלֵּי עָלְמָא לָא פְּלִיגִי: The commentaries explain that Abaye assumes that the opinion initially ascribed to Rabbi Yoḥanan was never actually said by him. Rather, it was mistakenly assumed to be his opinion by some of his disciples, and it was the disciples of Rabbi Yoḥanan and Reish Lakish, not Rabbi Yoḥanan and Reish Lakish themselves, who then proceeded to debate the viability of that opinion.

When they disagree it is with regard to *ḥalitza* – כִּי פְּלִיגִי בַּחֲלִיצָה: *Tosafot* explain the logic of differentiating between the efficacy of performing a levirate marriage with a pregnant woman and performing *ḥalitza* with a pregnant woman: Rabbi Yoḥanan agrees that the levirate marriage cannot be consummated through intercourse while the *yevama* is still pregnant because there still exists the possibility that the offspring will be viable. Were that to be true, the standard prohibition against engaging in relations with one's brother's wife would remain in force. Consequently, it is certainly forbidden to attempt to consummate the levirate marriage, and therefore doing so is ineffective. In contrast, the act of *ḥalitza* itself is never forbidden, even were it to be unnecessary. Therefore, if it is ultimately revealed that it was necessary, it should certainly be effective. The Rivan suggests that with regard to intercourse, even if it is ultimately revealed that there was an obligation to perform levirate marriage, it is possible for the Sages to retroactively declare the intercourse to have been an illicit act and therefore ineffective in consummating the levirate marriage. However, similar logic could not be applied to invalidate an act of *ḥalitza*.

דְּכָל הָעוֹלֶה לְיִבּוּם עוֹלֶה לַחֲלִיצָה, וְכָל שֶׁאֵין עוֹלֶה לְיִבּוּם – אֵינוֹ עוֹלֶה לַחֲלִיצָה!

that anyone who is eligible for levirate marriage[H] **is eligible for *ḥalitza* and anyone who is not eligible for levirate marriage is not eligible for *ḥalitza*.**[N] Therefore, the original understanding of Rabbi Yoḥanan's opinion, that both the intercourse and the *ḥalitza* of a pregnant woman are valid, was accurate.

אֶלָּא אֲמַר רָבָא, הָכִי קָאָמַר: הַכּוֹנֵס יְבִמְתּוֹ וְנִמְצֵאת מְעוּבֶּרֶת – הֲרֵי זוֹ לֹא תִּנָּשֵׂא צָרָתָהּ, שֶׁמָּא יְהֵא וָלָד בֶּן קַיָּימָא, וּבִיאַת מְעוּבֶּרֶת לָא שְׁמָהּ בִּיאָה, וַחֲלִיצַת מְעוּבֶּרֶת לָא שְׁמָהּ חֲלִיצָה, וְהַוָּלָד אֵינוֹ פּוֹטֵר עַד שֶׁיֵּצֵא לַאֲוִיר הָעוֹלָם.

Rava therefore provides a different defense of Rabbi Yoḥanan's opinion: **Rather, Rava said** that **this is what** the *baraita* **is saying:** In the case of **one who consummates** the levirate marriage **with his *yevama*** under the assumption that there is a mitzva to do so, **and** then **she is found to** have been **pregnant** at the time of the intercourse, **a rival wife**[H] **of this *yevama* may not marry lest the offspring be viable, and intercourse with a woman pregnant** with viable offspring **is not considered** a valid consummation of levirate marriage through **intercourse, and *ḥalitza* of a woman pregnant** with viable offspring **is not considered** effective ***ḥalitza*. And** furthermore, even if **the offspring** is viable, it **does not release** her and her rival wives from the levirate bond **until it comes into the air of the world,** i.e., until it is actually born.

תַּנְיָא כְּוָותֵיהּ דְּרָבָא: הַכּוֹנֵס יְבִמְתּוֹ וְנִמְצֵאת מְעוּבֶּרֶת – הֲרֵי זוֹ לֹא תִּנָּשֵׂא צָרָתָהּ, שֶׁמָּא יְהֵא וָלָד בֶּן קַיָּימָא, וְאֵין בִּיאָה וַחֲלִיצָה פּוֹטֶרֶת, אֶלָּא וָלָד פּוֹטֵר, וְהַוָּלָד אֵין פּוֹטְרָהּ עַד שֶׁיֵּצֵא לַאֲוִיר הָעוֹלָם.

It is taught in a *baraita* **in accordance with** the opinion of **Rava:** In the case of **one who consummates** a levirate marriage with **his *yevama*, and** then **she is found to** have been **pregnant** at the time of the intercourse, **a rival wife of this *yevama* may not marry lest the offspring be viable.** This is because **intercourse or *ḥalitza*** with a woman pregnant with viable offspring **does not release** a *yevama* from the levirate bond; **rather,** the **offspring releases** her. **And** furthermore, even if **the offspring** is viable, it **does not release her** and her rival wives from the levirate marriage bond **until it comes into the air of the world.**

טַעְמָא – דְּשֶׁמָּא יְהֵא וָלָד בֶּן קַיָּימָא הוּא, הָא לָא הָוֵי וָלָד בֶּן קַיָּימָא – מִיפְּטַר צָרָתָהּ. לֵימָא תֶּיהֱוֵי תְּיוּבְתָּא דְּרֵישׁ לָקִישׁ!

The Gemara explains that the *baraita* appears to contradict Reish Lakish's opinion: According to the *baraita*, **the** only **reason** that levirate marriage with the pregnant *yevama* does not permit the rival wife to marry **is as** the *baraita* stated: **Lest the offspring be viable.** By inference, **were the offspring not viable, her rival wife would be released** from the levirate bond. If so, **let us say that** this *baraita* **is a conclusive refutation** of the opinion of **Reish Lakish.**

אֲמַר לָךְ רֵישׁ לָקִישׁ, הָכִי קָתָנֵי: הַכּוֹנֵס יְבִמְתּוֹ וְנִמְצֵאת מְעוּבֶּרֶת – הֲרֵי זוֹ לֹא תִּנָּשֵׂא צָרָתָהּ, שֶׁמָּא לֹא יְהֵא הַוָּלָד בֶּן קַיָּימָא, וַחֲלִיצַת מְעוּבֶּרֶת לֹא שְׁמָהּ חֲלִיצָה, וּבִיאַת מְעוּבֶּרֶת לֹא שְׁמָהּ בִּיאָה.

The Gemara defends Reish Lakish's opinion: **Reish Lakish** could have **said to you: This is what** the *baraita* **is teaching:** In the case of **one who consummates** a levirate marriage with **his *yevama*, and** then **she was found to** have been **pregnant** at the time of the intercourse, **a rival wife of this *yevama* may not marry lest the offspring not be viable,** which would mean that all the rival wives are bound by the levirate bond. **And** even if one of those wives has intercourse or preforms *ḥalitza* with the *yavam*, it would be ineffective in releasing them from the levirate bond because ***ḥalitza* with a pregnant woman is not be considered** effective ***ḥalitza*, and intercourse with a pregnant woman is not considered** a valid consummation of levirate marriage through **intercourse.**

וְאִם תֹּאמַר: הַלֵּךְ אַחַר רוֹב נָשִׁים, וְרוֹב נָשִׁים וָלָד מַעַלְיָא יָלְדָן? – וָלָד אֵין פּוֹטֵר עַד שֶׁיֵּצֵא לַאֲוִיר הָעוֹלָם.

Reish Lakish explains the need for the final clause of the *baraita*: **And** even **if you say:** Let the wives marry without the need for any levirate marriage or *ḥalitza* because one should **follow** the **majority of women, and the majority of women give birth to a full-fledged,** i.e., viable, **offspring,** and therefore one should presume no levirate bond exists, to counter this claim the *baraita* concludes: Even if the offspring will be viable, an **offspring does not release** a *yevama* and her rival wives from the levirate bond **until it comes into the air of the world.**

HALAKHA

Anyone who is eligible for levirate marriage, etc. – כָּל הָעוֹלָה לְיִבּוּם וכו׳: Whenever a woman is ineligible to consummate a levirate marriage, she is also ineligible to perform *ḥalitza* (Rambam *Sefer Nashim*, *Hilkhot Yibbum VaḤalitza* 1:19).

The rival wife of a pregnant *yevama* – צָרַת יְבָמָה מְעוּבֶּרֶת: If a *yevama* who is pregnant with a child from her deceased husband consummates a levirate marriage or performs *ḥalitza*, her rival wife is prohibited from remarrying until the child is born (Rambam *Sefer Nashim*, *Hilkhot Yibbum VaḤalitza* 1:22; *Shulḥan Arukh*, *Even HaEzer* 164:3).

NOTES

Anyone who is not eligible for levirate marriage is not eligible for *ḥalitza* – כָּל שֶׁאֵין עוֹלָה לְיִבּוּם אֵינוֹ עוֹלָה לַחֲלִיצָה: This principle is generally taken to mean that anyone who is precluded from consummating levirate marriage is not bound by a levirate bond and therefore does not need to perform *ḥalitza*. However, this poses a difficulty, as there are some cases where although it is forbidden to consummate levirate marriage, *ḥalitza* is nevertheless still required in order to release the *yevama* from the levirate bond. This is the case, for example, when the *yavam* is prohibited from engaging in relations with the *yevama* by force of a negative mitzva that does not carry the punishment of *karet*. The Meiri suggests that the principle is indeed sound because, by Torah law, when the levirate marriage is prohibited only by force of a negative mitzva that does not carry the punishment of *karet*, the mitzva to consummate levirate marriage overrides the prohibition. As such, by Torah law, she is in fact eligible to consummate a levirate marriage and therefore is also eligible to perform *ḥalitza*. Therefore, although the Sages decreed that one should not consummate the levirate marriage in such a case, there is still a need to perform *ḥalitza*.

The Ritva suggests a different approach. He explains that even when levirate marriage in such cases is forbidden by Torah law, *ḥalitza* is nevertheless required. He cites the Gemara elsewhere that provides a biblical source that teaches that in cases where the relationship between the *yavam* and the *yevama* is forbidden only by force of a negative mitzva, *ḥalitza* is required. The Gemara's principle here, however, relates exclusively to cases in which the relationship is forbidden by force of a negative mitzva that does carry the punishment of *karet*. In contrast to the above opinions, the Rambam appears to understand the principle in a more limited fashion. According to him, the principle states only that if at any point in time the option to consummate the levirate marriage is proscribed, then at that time, one cannot perform *ḥalitza* either. However, that does not necessarily mean that the *yevama* will be released from the levirate bond. Rather, she will have to wait until, if ever, it is possible to consummate the levirate marriage, at which point she may perform *ḥalitza* if she wishes.

This principle is unanimously accepted. However, in the Gemara, Rava adduces it as support for his understanding of Rabbi Yoḥanan's opinion. How does Abaye justify his understanding in light of the principle? The Ritva explains: Abaye assumes that if it emerges that the offspring is not viable, then it emerges in retrospect that in fact the woman was always eligible for levirate marriage. As such, it is incorrect to automatically consider a pregnant woman as ineligible. Therefore, if she performs *ḥalitza* it will be valid. However, according to Rava, while she is actually pregnant, even should the fetus not survive, she is deemed ineligible to consummate a levirate marriage at that time. Therefore, there is no possibility of performing *ḥalitza* either.

אָמַר רַבִּי אֶלְעָזָר: אֶפְשָׁר, אִיתָא לְהָא דְּרֵישׁ לָקִישׁ וְלָא תְּנַן לַהּ בְּמַתְנִיתִין?! – נְפַק, דַּק וְאַשְׁכַּח, דִּתְנַן: הָאִשָּׁה שֶׁהָלַךְ בַּעְלָהּ וְצָרָתָהּ לִמְדִינַת הַיָּם, וּבָאוּ וְאָמְרוּ לָהּ: "מֵת בַּעְלֵךְ" – הֲרֵי זוֹ לֹא תִּנָּשֵׂא וְלֹא תִּתְיַיבֵּם, עַד שֶׁתֵּדַע שֶׁמָּא מְעוּבֶּרֶת הִיא צָרָתָהּ.

Rabbi Elazar said: Is it **possible** that **there is** halakhic acceptance **of this**[N] opinion **of Reish Lakish and it was not** hinted to by something **taught in the Mishna? He went out** of the study hall, carefully **checked** the *mishnayot*, **and found** one that supported Reish Lakish's opinion, **as we learned** in a mishna: In the case of **a woman whose husband and rival wife went overseas,**[H] and then witnesses **came and said to her: Your husband died,** and her husband had a brother, **this** woman **may neither marry** someone other than his brother, **nor may she enter into levirate marriage** with that brother, **until she knows** whether **perhaps her rival wife is pregnant.** If she discovers that her rival wife is not pregnant, she would then be able to perform levirate marriage or *ḥalitza*. If she discovers her rival wife is pregnant, she would have to wait to see if the pregnancy is viable. If it is found to be viable, only at that point would she be permitted to marry someone else.

בִּשְׁלָמָא יִבּוּמֵי לָא – שֶׁמָּא יְהֵא וָלָד בֶּן קְיָימָא, וְיִפְגַּע בְּאִיסּוּר אֵשֶׁת אָח דְּאוֹרָיְיתָא. אֶלָּא לֹא תַּחֲלוֹץ, אַמַּאי? בִּשְׁלָמָא תַּחֲלוֹץ בְּתוֹךְ תִּשְׁעָה וְתִנָּשֵׂא בְּתוֹךְ תִּשְׁעָה – לָא, הַיְינוּ סָפֵק.

Rabbi Elazar explains how this mishna supports Reish Lakish's opinion: **Granted, she may not enter levirate marriage** as **perhaps** her rival wife is pregnant and the **offspring will be viable, and** therefore by consummating the levirate marriage the *yavam* would **encounter the Torah prohibition against** engaging in relations with one's **brother's wife. But why may she not perform *ḥalitza*? Granted, she may not perform *ḥalitza* during the** first **nine** months following her husband's death **and** then proceed to also **marry during** those **nine** months; **this is** prohibited due to the fact that there is the **uncertainty** whether her rival wife is pregnant with viable offspring, in which case she would be released from the levirate bond.

אֶלָּא תַּחֲלוֹץ בְּתוֹךְ תִּשְׁעָה, וְתִנָּשֵׂא לְאַחַר תִּשְׁעָה!

But let her perform *ḥalitza* during the first **nine** months following her husband's death **and** then wait to **marry** until **after** those **nine** months. By that point in time, even if the rival wife was pregnant she would have already given birth. If the offspring was viable, then it emerges that there was never a levirate bond, and if it is not viable, then she was released from her levirate bond through the *ḥalitza* she performed. Either way, she would now be permitted to remarry. Why, then, does the mishna not consider this possibility? Rabbi Elazar claims that the only explanation for this is if the mishna assumes that *ḥalitza* performed while one of the wives of the deceased is pregnant is not effective. As such, the mishna is a proof for Reish Lakish's opinion.

וּלְטַעְמִיךְ: תַּחֲלוֹץ וְתִנָּשֵׂא לְאַחַר תִּשְׁעָה!

The Gemara rejects Rabbi Elazar's proof: **But** even **according to your reasoning** that *ḥalitza* with a pregnant woman is not effective, the mishna should have considered an additional possibility: **Let her perform *ḥalitza* and marry,** doing both **after nine** months have passed since the death of her husband.Doing so should be effective according to both Reish Lakish and Rabbi Yoḥanan.

אֶלָּא: בַּר מִינַּהּ דְּהַהִיא, דְּאַבָּיֵי בַּר אַבָּא וְרַב חִינָּנָא בַּר אַבָּיֵי דְּאָמְרִי תַּרְוַיְיהוּ: שֶׁמָּא יְהֵא וָלָד בֶּן קְיָימָא, וְנִמְצָא אַתָּה מַצְרִיכָהּ כָּרוֹז לִכְהוּנָּה.

Rather, the discussion of this topic should be held **apart from that** mishna, as the true reason for that mishna's ruling is **as** it is **Abaye bar Abba and Rav Ḥinnana bar Abaye who both say** that she is prohibited from performing *ḥalitza* while one of the wives of the deceased is pregnant because **perhaps** the **offspring will be viable,** in which case any *ḥalitza* performed would be entirely unnecessary and therefore meaningless, and she would remain permitted to marry into the priesthood, as the opening mishna of the chapter rules. However, in this situation people might not realize that the *ḥalitza* she performed was meaningless, and they would think she is a *ḥalutza*, who is prohibited from marrying a priest. **And it would** therefore **emerge** that if she were allowed to perform *ḥalitza* while pregnant, it is possible that **you will** ultimately **require a public announcement** to be made **for her**[N] to attest to the fact that she is in fact still permitted **to** marry into the **priesthood.**

NOTES

Is it possible that there is halakhic acceptance of this – אֶפְשָׁר אִיתָא לְהָא: The Rivan notes that since ultimately the *halakha* is ruled in accordance with Reish Lakish's opinion, it would be peculiar if his opinion was not hinted to somewhere in the Mishna.

It would emerge that you will require a public announcement for her – וְנִמְצָא אַתָּה מַצְרִיכָהּ כָּרוֹז: *Tosafot* and other early commentaries note that a public announcement is made only if the woman is otherwise suitable for the priesthood, in order to indicate that despite the fact that she performed *ḥalitza*, it does not disqualify her, since it was meaningless. Therefore, had she been divorced or had some other disqualification, since no public announcement is made, it should follow that she should not need to wait for nine months before performing *ḥalitza*. The Meiri notes that this is stated explicitly in the Jerusalem Talmud, and the Ramban suggests that this is indicated by the precise formulation of the mishna, which chooses to refer to her simply as: A woman, as opposed to: The *yevama*, which suggests that the mishna relates to a standard woman who had not been previously divorced.

HALAKHA

A woman whose husband and rival wife went overseas – הָאִשָּׁה שֶׁהָלַךְ בַּעְלָהּ וְצָרָתָהּ לִמְדִינַת הַיָּם: In the case of a woman whose husband and rival wife went to a country overseas, and then witnesses came and said to her: Your husband died, the woman may neither perform *ḥalitza* nor consummate levirate marriage until it is established whether the rival wife has given birth (Rambam *Sefer Nashim, Hilkhot Yibbum VaḤalitza* 3:16; *Shulḥan Arukh, Even HaEzer* 156:13).

וְלַצְרְכָהּ! דִּלְמָא אִיכָּא אִינִישׁ דְּהָוֵי בַּחֲלִיצָה וְלָא הָוֵי בְּהַכְרָזָה, וְאָתֵי לְמֵימַר: קָשְׁרֵי חֲלוּצָה לְכֹהֵן.

The Gemara wonders why this poses a problem: **But** why not let her perform *ḥalitza* while still pregnant, and then if it becomes necessary, **require** a public announcement to be made **for her?** The Gemara explains why one should avoid having to rely on a public announcement: **Perhaps there were** some **people who were** present **at the *ḥalitza* and were not** present at the **public announcement, and** when that the courts permit her to marry a priest **they might come to say** that **they are permitting a *ḥalutza*** to marry **a priest.**

אָמַר לֵיהּ אַבַּיֵי: מִידֵי לֹא תַּחֲלוֹץ וְלֹא תִּתְיַיבֵּם קָתָנֵי? לֹא תִּנָּשֵׂא וְלֹא תִּתְיַיבֵּם קָתָנֵי, בְּלֹא חֲלִיצָה, אֲבָל אִי חָלֵיץ לָהּ – הָכִי נַמִי דְּשַׁרְיָא.

Abaye suggests another rejection of Rabbi Elazar's proof from that mishna: **Abaye said to** Rabbi Elazar: The very formulation of the mishna refutes Reish Lakish's opinion, as **does** the mishna **teach** that **she may neither perform *ḥalitza* nor enter into levirate marriage?** No, the mishna **teaches** only that **she may neither be married nor enter into levirate marriage,** which implies only that she may not marry **without** first performing ***ḥalitza*, but if** the *yavam* **performs *ḥalitza* with her, she would indeed be permitted** to marry after nine months have passed since her husband's death. This understanding of the mishna undermines the basis of Rabbi Elazar's proof from the mishna.

תַּנְיָא כְּוָותֵיהּ דְּרֵישׁ לָקִישׁ: הַחוֹלֵץ לִמְעוּבֶּרֶת וְהִפִּילָה – צְרִיכָה חֲלִיצָה מִן הָאַחִין.

Even if that mishna does not support Reish Lakish's opinion, nevertheless **it is taught** in a *baraita* **in accordance with** the opinion **of Reish Lakish:** In the case of **one who performs *ḥalitza* with a pregnant woman and she miscarries, she requires** another ***ḥalitza* with the brothers** in order to release her from the levirate bond. The *baraita* assumes that the original *ḥalitza* is ineffective because it was done while she was still pregnant, which is accordance with the opinion of Reish Lakish.

אָמַר רָבָא: הִלְכְתָא כְּוָותֵיהּ דְּרֵישׁ לָקִישׁ בְּהָנֵי תְּלָת: חֲדָא – הָא דַּאֲמָרַן. אִידָךְ – דִּתְנַן: הַמְחַלֵּק נְכָסָיו עַל פִּיו, רִיבָּה לְאֶחָד וּמִיעֵט לְאֶחָד, וְהִשְׁוָה לָהֶם אֶת הַבְּכוֹר – דְּבָרָיו קַיָּימִין.

Rava said: The *halakha* is in accordance with the opinion **of Reish Lakish**[N] **in these three**[N] disputes: **One, this** dispute **that we** already **stated** with regard to the *ḥalitza* of a pregnant woman. **The other** dispute concerns that **which we learned** in a mishna: In the case of **one who verbally divides up his possessions**[H] among his descendants, stating how he wishes his estate to be divided after his death, if **he increases** the proportion of his estate that should go **to one** of his children **or decreases** the proportion of his estate that should go **to** another **one** of his children, **or** if **he equally** distributes **between them** the double portion of **the firstborn,** then **his words are binding.**

וְאִם אָמַר מִשּׁוּם יְרוּשָּׁה – לֹא אָמַר כְּלוּם. כָּתַב, בֵּין בַּתְּחִלָּה בֵּין בַּסּוֹף בֵּין בָּאֶמְצַע, מִשּׁוּם מַתָּנָה – דְּבָרָיו קַיָּימִין.

But if he said explicitly that the receipt of those portions should be considered **as an inheritance,** then it as though the verbal division of his property that **he said is nothing,** i.e., it is non-binding, since his words directly contradict the *halakhot* of inheritance as they are written in the Torah.[B] However, if he wrote a will and somewhere therein **he wrote, whether at the beginning, whether at the end, or whether in the middle,** that the receipt of the portions should be considered **as a gift,** as opposed to an inheritance, then **his words are binding.**

NOTES

The *halakha* is in accordance with the opinion of Reish Lakish – הִלְכְתָא כְּוָותֵיהּ דְּרֵישׁ לָקִישׁ: According to Reish Lakish, if a woman is pregnant at the time of her husband's death, then at that moment she is ineligible to consummate a levirate marriage. The early commentaries raise the following question: If so, she should be entirely released from any levirate bond based on the principle, developed in the Gemara elsewhere, that the levirate bond is formed at the moment of the husband's death; therefore, if she is not subject to the requirement to consummate a levirate marriage at that point, then no bond is formed at all. Why, then, is she obligated to perform levirate marriage or *ḥalitza* if the offspring proves not to be viable? The early commentaries explain that even according to Reish Lakish, the requirement to consummate a levirate marriage does apply to a pregnant woman from the moment of her husband's death, and therefore a levirate bond is formed. However, since she is pregnant, she must first wait until the viability of the offspring is determined before she is able to act upon it (Rashba).

In these three – בְּהָנֵי תְּלָת: Generally, in disputes between Rabbi Yoḥanan and Reish Lakish the *halakha* is ruled in accordance with the opinion of Rabbi Yoḥanan. Therefore, it was necessary to delineate those cases in which the *halakha* is atypically decided in accordance with the opinion of Reish Lakish.

Many of the early commentaries note that there are many other cases in which the *halakha* is ruled in accordance with the opinion of Reish Lakish. Why, then, did Rava list only three cases? The Meiri suggests that Rava meant only to clarify the *halakha* in those three cases but never to suggest that these are the only cases in which the *halakha* is ruled in accordance with the opinion of Reish Lakish. Others suggest that Rava considered only those disputes about actions whose actual performance is never prohibited, e.g., *ḥalitza* (*Tosefot Ḥad MiKamma'ei*; Rabbi Avraham min HaHar; see *Arukh LaNer*).

HALAKHA

One who verbally divides up his possessions – הַמְחַלֵּק נְכָסָיו עַל פִּיו: In the case of one who is mortally ill who divides up his possessions, if he increases or decreases the proportion of his estate that should go to each child, or if he equally distributes the double portion of the firstborn between them, then his words are binding. However, if he states explicitly that the receipt of those portions should be considered an inheritance, then it as though he did not say anything and the inheritance is allotted according to the standard conventions. If he wrote a will and somewhere therein he wrote, whether at the beginning, middle, or end, that the receipt of the portions should be considered a gift, then even if he also referred to the portions as an inheritance, his words are binding (Rambam *Sefer Mishpatim, Hilkhot Naḥalot* 6:5; *Shulḥan Arukh, Ḥoshen Mishpat* 281:7).

BACKGROUND

The laws of inheritance – דִּינֵי יְרוּשָּׁה: The basic *halakhot* of inheritance are stated in Numbers 27:8–11 in the following manner: If one dies without sons, the inheritance is given to his daughter. If he has no daughters, the inheritance passes to his father. If the father is no longer alive, then it passes to the father's heirs. In addition, the firstborn son receives a double portion of the inheritance (Deuteronomy 21:17). The *halakhot* of inheritance apply only to property that the deceased had not already given away. During his lifetime he is entitled to divide up his possessions in whatever way he wishes, and he may even write a will just prior to his death dividing them up in whatever way he desires.

וְאָמַר רֵישׁ לָקִישׁ: לְעוֹלָם לֹא קָנָה עַד שֶׁיֹּאמַר ״פְּלוֹנִי וּפְלוֹנִי יִרְשׁוּ שָׂדֶה פְּלוֹנִית וּפְלוֹנִית שֶׁנְּתַתִּים לָהֶם בְּמַתָּנָה וִירָשׁוּם״.

Reish Lakish and Rabbi Yoḥanan dispute whether one must state that the receipt of the portions should be considered as a gift with regard to each recipient, or whether stating it with regard to one of them is enough to indicate that it is true for all. **And Reish Lakish said:** The inheritors **will only ever acquire** the portions as defined by the owner of the possessions **once he says: So-and-so and so-and-so shall inherit such and such a field and such and such** a field **that I have given to them as a gift, and they shall inherit them,** i.e., he must state explicitly for each recipient that their receipt of the portions should be considered a gift.[H] Rava ruled that in this dispute as well, the *halakha* is in accordance with Reish Lakish.

וְאִידָךְ – דִּתְנַן: הַכּוֹתֵב כָּל נְכָסָיו לִבְנוֹ לְאַחַר מוֹתוֹ, הָאָב אֵינוֹ יָכוֹל לִמְכּוֹר – מִפְּנֵי שֶׁנְּתָנָן לַבֵּן, וְהַבֵּן אֵינוֹ יָכוֹל לִמְכּוֹר – מִפְּנֵי שֶׁהֵן בִּרְשׁוּת הָאָב – מָכַר הָאָב מְכוּרִין עַד שֶׁיָּמוּת הוּא. מָכַר הַבֵּן – אֵין לַלּוֹקֵחַ כְּלוּם עַד שֶׁיָּמוּת הָאָב.

And the other dispute concerns that **which we learned** in a mishna: In the case of **one who writes** a bill transferring ownership of **all of his possessions to his son** stating that the transfer should take effect immediately so that the son should gain the rights to use the possessions **after his death,**[H] then although **the father** retained for himself the right to use the possessions until his death, he **is unable to sell** the possessions **due to** the fact **that he gave them to the son, and the son is unable to sell** the possessions **due to** the fact **that they are** still **in the father's possession.** If **the father sold**[H] the possessions, then **they are sold** to the extent that the purchaser may use them **until** the father **dies.** If **the son sold**[H] the possessions during his father's lifetime, **the purchaser does not** receive **any** rights to use the possessions **until the father dies.**

וְאִיתְּמַר, מָכַר הַבֵּן בְּחַיֵּי הָאָב, וּמֵת הַבֵּן בְּחַיֵּי הָאָב, רַבִּי יוֹחָנָן אָמַר: לֹא קָנָה לוֹקֵחַ, וְרֵישׁ לָקִישׁ אָמַר: קָנָה לוֹקֵחַ.

And an amoraic dispute **was stated** in the case in which **the son sold** the possessions **during the father's lifetime, and** then **the son died during the father's lifetime,**[H] following which the father died as well. **Rabbi Yoḥanan said: The purchaser does not acquire** anything, **and Reish Lakish said: The purchaser does acquire** the possessions.

רַבִּי יוֹחָנָן אָמַר: לֹא קָנָה לוֹקֵחַ, קִנְיַן פֵּירוֹת כְּקִנְיַן הַגּוּף דָּמֵי.

The Gemara explains their reasoning: **Rabbi Yoḥanan said** that **the purchaser does not acquire** anything, because he holds that the **ownership of** the rights to an item and its **produce is tantamount to** the **ownership of the item itself,**[B] i.e., the actual title to it. Since the father retained the rights to use the possessions until his death, as long as he lives he is considered to hold the title to them. Therefore, the son's sale can be effective only after the father's death, at which point the son becomes the title owner. However, if the son dies first, then since he never gained the title to the items, his sale can never come to fruition.

וְרֵישׁ לָקִישׁ אָמַר: קָנָה לוֹקֵחַ, קִנְיַן פֵּירוֹת לָאו כְּקִנְיַן הַגּוּף דָּמֵי.

And Reish Lakish said: The purchaser does acquire the possessions, as Reish Lakish holds that the **ownership of** the rights to an item and its **produce is not tantamount to** the **ownership of the item itself,** i.e., the actual title to it. Therefore, although the father is still alive, the son immediately gains the full title to the possessions, which he may sell to someone else. Nevertheless, since the father retains the rights to use the possessions, the purchaser may use the possessions he acquired only when the father dies.

BACKGROUND

Ownership of the rights to an item and its produce is tantamount to the ownership of the item itself – קִנְיַן פֵּירוֹת כְּקִנְיַן הַגּוּף דָּמֵי: If an item was acquired for its produce, one may derive benefit from it, but according to some authorities one cannot perform actions that require actual ownership of the item, e.g., bringing first fruits or selling the item to others. However, other authorities maintain that even if an item is acquired for its produce, this is akin to the purchase of the item itself, and it may be used for these activities.

HALAKHA

Inheritance and gift – יְרוּשָּׁה וּמַתָּנָה: With regard to one who is mortally ill, who divides up his possessions in a manner that departs from the standard conventions: If he expresses his wishes in a single unbroken statement, then as long as he refers to the receipt of those portions as a gift, even if he also refers to them as an inheritance, his words are binding. This is true even if he mentions that the portions should be considered a gift with respect to only one of the recipients or one of the possessions; provided he mentioned at some point in the statement that it should be considered a gift, it is all considered a gift. However, if he made two or more separate statements, then he must make it explicitly clear that his intention is that each part of the division should be considered a gift. This is in accordance with the opinion of Reish Lakish (Rambam *Sefer Mishpatim, Hilkhot Naḥalot*, 6:6; *Shulḥan Arukh, Ḥoshen Mishpat* 281:7).

One who writes a bill of all of his possessions to his son after his death – הַכּוֹתֵב כָּל נְכָסָיו לִבְנוֹ לְאַחַר מוֹתוֹ: If a father wrote a bill stating that the son should be able to use his possessions following the father's death, it is prohibited for both the father and the son to sell those possessions (Rambam *Sefer Kinyan, Hilkhot Zekhiya* 12:13; *Shulḥan Arukh, Ḥoshen Mishpat* 257:1).

The father sold – מָכַר הָאָב: If the father transgressed and sold the possessions that he had promised to his son, then the sale takes effect to the extent that the purchaser has the rights to the use and produce of those possessions until the death of the father. However, upon the father's death, the son becomes the owner of those rights. If at the time of the father's death there was produce that was still attached to the possessions, e.g., produce that grew on the land and was not yet harvested, the son must pay the purchaser its value. Any produce that was already detached belongs to the purchaser. Some (Rema; see *Tur* and *Beit Yosef*, citing Rashbam) argue with this and claim that upon the father's death, the son becomes the owner even of the produce that has already been detached (Rambam *Sefer Kinyan, Hilkhot Zekhiya* 12:13; *Shulḥan Arukh, Ḥoshen Mishpat* 257:3).

The son sold – מָכַר הַבֵּן: If the son transgressed and sold the possessions promised to him by his father, then the purchaser has no rights to them until the death of the father (Rambam *Sefer Kinyan, Hilkhot Zekhiya* 12:13; *Shulḥan Arukh, Ḥoshen Mishpat* 257:4).

The son sold the possessions and then died during the father's lifetime – מָכַר הַבֵּן וּמֵת בְּחַיֵּי אָבִיו: If the son sold the possessions promised to him by his father and then died during the father's lifetime, following which the father died, the purchaser acquires the possessions upon the death of the father. This is because the father retained only the rights to the use and produce of the possessions, and the ownership of the rights to an item and its produce is not tantamount to the ownership of the item itself. This is in accordance with the opinion of Reish Lakish (Rambam *Sefer Kinyan, Hilkhot Zekhiya* 12:13; *Shulḥan Arukh, Ḥoshen Mishpat* 257:5).

"אֵין הַוָּלָד שֶׁל קַיְּימָא" כו׳. תָּנָא: מִשּׁוּם רַבִּי אֱלִיעֶזֶר אָמְרוּ: יוֹצִיא בְּגֵט.

§ The mishna states that if a *yavam* consummates a levirate marriage with his *yevama* while she is pregnant, if it emerges that **the offspring is not viable** then he may maintain her as his wife because his intercourse with her was a valid consummation of levirate marriage. An opposing opinion **is taught** in a *baraita*: **In the name of Rabbi Eliezer they said: He must send her out with a bill of divorce.**[N] Although it emerged that the levirate marriage took effect, since at the time he consummated the levirate marriage it was prohibited to do so because the *yevama* was pregnant, he is therefore penalized and required to separate from her.

אָמַר רָבָא: רַבִּי מֵאִיר וְרַבִּי אֱלִיעֶזֶר אָמְרוּ דָּבָר אֶחָד. רַבִּי אֱלִיעֶזֶר – הָא דַּאֲמַרַן,

Rava said: Rabbi Meir and Rabbi Eliezer said the same thing, i.e., they both expressed the same opinion that if one marries a woman whom he is prohibited from marrying, he is penalized and required to divorce her, even if the reason for the prohibition no longer applies. **Rabbi Eliezer's** opinion was expressed in **this** ruling **we have** just **stated.**

רַבִּי מֵאִיר – דְּתַנְיָא: לֹא יִשָּׂא אָדָם מְעוּבֶּרֶת חֲבֵירוֹ וּמֵינֶקֶת חֲבֵירוֹ, וְאִם נָשָׂא – יוֹצִיא, וְלֹא יַחֲזִיר עוֹלָמִית, דִּבְרֵי רַבִּי מֵאִיר. וַחֲכָמִים אוֹמְרִים: יוֹצִיא, וְלִכְשֶׁיַּגִּיעַ זְמַנּוֹ לִכְנוֹס – יִכְנוֹס.

Where was **Rabbi Meir's** opinion expressed? **As it is taught** in a *baraita*: **A man may not marry a woman who is pregnant** with the child **of another** man, **nor a woman who is nursing** the child **of another** man.[H] **And if he** transgressed and **married** her, he is penalized for violating the prohibition, and **he must divorce** her with a bill of divorce, **and he may never take** her **back;**[H] this is **the statement of Rabbi Meir. And the Rabbis say: He must send** her **out, and when the time comes** in which it is permitted **to marry** her, i.e., after the child is weaned, **he may** then **marry** her again.

אָמַר לֵיהּ אַבָּיֵי: מִמַּאי? דִּלְמָא לָא הִיא, עַד כָּאן לָא קָאָמַר רַבִּי אֱלִיעֶזֶר הָכָא – אֶלָּא מִשּׁוּם דְּקָפָגַע בְּאִיסּוּר אֵשֶׁת אָח דְּאוֹרָיְיתָא, אֲבָל הָתָם דְּרַבָּנַן – כְּרַבָּנַן סְבִירָא לֵיהּ.

Abaye said to him: From where do you deduce that they are of one opinion? **Perhaps that is not so,** as it is possible that **Rabbi Eliezer states** his ruling **only here,** in the case of a *yavam* who consummated a levirate marriage with his *yevama* while she was still pregnant, **due to** the fact that by doing so he risks the possibility that the offspring will be viable, in **which** case **he encounters the Torah prohibition against** engaging in relations with one's **brother's wife. However, there,** in the case where one married a woman who is pregnant with the child of another man, **which is a rabbinic** prohibition, it is possible that **he holds in accordance with** the opinion of the **Rabbis** who argue with Rabbi Meir.

אִי נָמֵי: עַד כָּאן לָא קָאָמַר רַבִּי מֵאִיר הָתָם – אֶלָּא מִשּׁוּם דְּרַבָּנַן, וַחֲכָמִים עָשׂוּ חִיזּוּק לְדִבְרֵיהֶם יוֹתֵר מִשֶּׁל תּוֹרָה. אֲבָל הָכָא – מִדְּאוֹרָיְיתָא, מִפְרָשׁ פָּרְשִׁי מִינֵּהּ.

Alternatively, it is also possible that **Rabbi Meir states** his ruling **only there,** in the case where one married a woman who is pregnant with the child of another man, **due to** the fact **that** doing so is a violation of a **rabbinic** prohibition, and therefore it is possible that this is one of the cases in which **the Sages reinforced their pronouncements**[N] **with greater** severity **than** prohibitions of **Torah law** so that people would not treat them lightly. **However, here,** in the case of a *yavam* who consummated a levirate marriage with his *yevama* while she was still pregnant, where there was a risk of transgressing a prohibition written **in the Torah,** since people are generally careful to **distance themselves from** a Torah prohibition, there is no need to further penalize someone who nevertheless transgressed.

NOTES

He must send her out with a bill of divorce – יוֹצִיא בְּגֵט: Although Rabbi Eliezer's statement is not accepted as the *halakha*, the early commentaries discussed the meaning and rationale of his claim and thereby clarified important principles that lie at the heart of the Gemara's discussion.

Rashi's version of the Gemara text is the same as that which appears in the standard Vilna edition: He must send her out with a bill of divorce. This suggests that nothing more than a bill of divorce is necessary in order to permit her to remarry. The early commentaries note that, ostensibly, this is true only according to the opinion of Rabbi Yoḥanan that the consummation of a levirate marriage with a pregnant woman who later miscarries is valid. Since the marriage is valid, only a divorce is needed to dissolve it. However, according to the opinion of Reish Lakish, the consummation of the levirate marriage performed while the woman was pregnant was invalid, and therefore the couple was never actually married. As such, the levirate bond still exists, and it should be necessary to either repeat the consummation or perform *ḥalitza*. Some commentaries suggest that Rashi's version of the text may be resolved according to the conclusion of the Gemara that the mishna is referring to a case in which, following the miscarriage, the *yavam* indeed repeated the consummation. As such, all would agree that the couple was actually married and that only a bill of divorce is necessary (*Tosafot Yeshanim*; *Tosefot HaRosh*). Other commentaries explain that Rabbi Eliezer's intention was not to suggest that a bill of divorce is sufficient, as certainly according to Reish Lakish it is necessary to perform *ḥalitza*, since the levirate bond remains. Rather, the intention is that in addition to the *ḥalitza*, a bill of divorce is also required (Rambam; Rid; Maharam MiRotenburg).

The Rashba had a different version of the Gemara's text that merely states: He must send her out. According to this version, the Rashba explains, *ḥalitza* alone is sufficient and there is no need for a bill of divorce. The Ritva suggests further that the ambiguity provided by this version of the text means that it can be interpreted as meaning through a bill of divorce, according to the opinion of Rabbi Yoḥanan, or as referring to *ḥalitza*, according to the opinion of Reish Lakish.

The Rivan claims that Rabbi Eliezer's statement was never meant to explain how she should be permitted to remarry; rather, the intention was to teach that a penalty is imposed upon the *yavam* for unlawfully consummating the levirate marriage. He is therefore required to hand her a bill of divorce; by doing so it becomes prohibited for him to repeat the consummation, and therefore his only recourse is to perform *ḥalitza* (see *Baḥ*).

Reinforced their pronouncements – עָשׂוּ חִיזּוּק לְדִבְרֵיהֶם: *Tosafot* note that in many cases throughout the Gemara, Rabbi Meir is of the opinion that the Sages reinforced their pronouncements to be equally as severe as Torah law, but not to have greater severity. They raise various distinctions between the case here and those cases. Most commentaries suggest a simple distinction should be drawn between cases involving rabbinic prohibitions and those involving rabbinic enactments in monetary matters. In the former, Rabbi Meir is very strict and holds that in order to prevent laxity it was necessary for the rabbinic prohibitions to be more severe than Torah law. This is also the reason that in many cases, Rabbi Meir rules that when the Sages provided specific formulations to be used in the fulfillment of mitzvot or in creating a bill of divorce, if one deviates from those formulations, the entire matter is null and void even if the change does not affect the essential meaning. However, in monetary matters, the Sages deemed it sufficient if the rabbinic law was applied with equal severity to that of Torah law (Ramban).

HALAKHA

A woman who is pregnant with the child of another man nor a woman who is nursing the child of another man – מְעוּבֶּרֶת חֲבֵירוֹ וּמֵינֶקֶת חֲבֵירוֹ: It is prohibited to marry a woman who is pregnant with the child of another man or a woman who is nursing the child of another man, until the child reaches twenty-four months of age. It makes no difference whether the woman is a widow, divorced, or became pregnant out of wedlock. Some are more lenient in the latter case (Rema, citing Maharai Mintz). If the child died within that time, or if the child had already been weaned while the mother was still married to the child's father, or if the mother had never been able to nurse, it is permitted to marry her (Rambam *Sefer Nashim, Hilkhot Geirushin* 11:25; *Shulḥan Arukh, Even HaEzer* 13:11).

One who married a woman who is pregnant with the child of another man or a woman who is nursing the child of another man – הַנּוֹשֵׂא מְעוּבֶּרֶת וּמֵינֶקֶת חֲבֵירוֹ: If one transgressed and married a woman who is pregnant with the child of another man or a woman who is nursing the child of another man, he is ostracized until he divorces her with a bill of divorce, even if he is a priest and would thereby be prohibited from remarrying her. If he is an Israelite, then he is allowed to later remarry her once the child reaches twenty-four months of age. This is in accordance with the opinion of the Rabbis (Rambam *Sefer Nashim, Hilkhot Geirushin* 11:28 and in the comment of Ra'avad; *Shulḥan Arukh, Even HaEzer* 13:12).

אָמַר רָבָא: וּלְדִבְרֵי חֲכָמִים יוֹצִיאָהּ בְּגֵט. אָמַר מָר זוּטְרָא: דַּיְקָא נַמִי, דְּקָתָנֵי יוֹצִיא, וְלָא קָתָנֵי יַפְרִישׁ, שְׁמַע מִינַּהּ.

Rava said: According to the statement of the Rabbis who dispute Rabbi Meir and require one who married a pregnant woman to send her out, the intention is that **he must send her out with a bill of divorce** and not merely separate from her. **Mar Zutra said:** The language the Rabbis used **is also precise, as** they **teach: He must send** her **out, and** they **do not teach: He must separate** himself from her. **Conclude from here** that Rava's claim is correct.

אָמַר לֵיהּ רַב אַשִׁי לְרַב הוֹשַׁעְיָא בְּרֵיהּ דְּרַב אִידִי: הָתָם תְּנַן, רַבָּן שִׁמְעוֹן בֶּן גַּמְלִיאֵל אוֹמֵר: כׇּל שֶׁשָּׁהָא בָּאָדָם שְׁלֹשִׁים יוֹם – אֵינוֹ נֵפֶל. הָא לָא שָׁהָא – סְפֵיקָא הָוֵי.

Rav Ashi said to Rav Hoshaya, son of Rav Idi: We learned in a *baraita* **there** that **Rabban Shimon ben Gamliel says: Any human** baby **that survives for thirty days**[H] after its birth **is not** to be considered **a stillbirth.** Rather, the baby is considered to be viable, and so the wife of the baby's father is never subject to any obligation of levirate marriage. **But,** by inference, **were it not to survive** for thirty days, **there would be uncertainty** whether the baby was viable or not.

וְאִיתְּמַר, מֵת בְּתוֹךְ שְׁלֹשִׁים יוֹם, וְעָמְדָה וְנִתְקַדְּשָׁה.

And an amoraic dispute **was stated** in the case in which the only offspring of a man **died during** the first **thirty days** of its life, **and** the widow, under the misconception that she was exempt from any obligation of levirate marriage, **arose and was betrothed.**[H]

רָבִינָא מִשְּׁמֵיהּ דְּרָבָא אָמַר: אִם אֵשֶׁת יִשְׂרָאֵל הִיא – חוֹלֶצֶת, וְאִם אֵשֶׁת כֹּהֵן הִיא – אֵינָהּ חוֹלֶצֶת.

Ravina said in the name of Rava: If she became the **wife of an Israelite,** i.e., the man who betrothed her was not a priest, then **she performs *ḥalitza*** with the *yavam* due to the uncertainty whether or not the offspring was viable, and then they may remain married. **But if she** became the **wife of a priest, she does not perform *ḥalitza***[N] with him because if she were to do so, she would become a *ḥalutza* and would therefore be prohibited from remaining married to her husband, who is a priest. Therefore, in this case, in order to allow her to remain married to her husband, the Sages did not require her to be concerned for the possibility that the offspring was not viable.

רַב מְשַׁרְשִׁיָּא מִשְּׁמֵיהּ דְּרָבָא אָמַר: אַחַת זוֹ וְאַחַת זוֹ חוֹלֶצֶת.

The Gemara cites a different version of Rav's opinion: **Rav Mesharshiyya said in the name of Rava: Both this** woman **and that** woman **perform *ḥalitza*,** even though by doing so, if she was betrothed to a priest, she would become forbidden to him.

אֲמַר לֵיהּ רָבִינָא לְרַב מְשַׁרְשִׁיָּא:

Ravina said to Rav Mesharshiyya:

NOTES

If she became the wife of a priest she does not perform *ḥalitza* – אִם אֵשֶׁת כֹּהֵן הִיא אֵינָהּ חוֹלֶצֶת: The Gemara will explain that since her performance of *ḥalitza* would prohibit her from remaining married to her husband, the Sages were willing to rely on the opinion of the Rabbis who disagree with Rabban Shimon ben Gamliel and hold that even if the child does not survive for thirty days it is considered viable. This is especially reasonable because both opinions agree that by Torah law the child is considered viable; the dispute is only whether, by rabbinic law, the case should be treated as one of doubt.

Some question why the *ḥalitza* should not be performed in this case. The *halakha* is that if a *ḥalitza* is performed and it is uncertain whether it was valid, it does not disqualify the *yevama* from marrying a priest. In the case here, too, the *ḥalitza* is performed only to satisfy the possibility that the child was not viable. If so, why does Rava rule that she should not perform *ḥalitza*? To resolve this difficulty, a distinction must be drawn between two cases of uncertainty. The *halakha* that an uncertain *ḥalitza* does not disqualify a woman from marrying a priest applies only to cases where there is clearly a levirate bond, but it is uncertain whether the man who performed the *ḥalitza* was actually the *yavam*. However, in this case, the *ḥalitza* was certainly performed by the *yavam*, and the only question is whether it was necessary. Therefore it is treated like any other case of uncertainty in Torah law, in which one must be stringent, and so if *ḥalitza* was performed, the couple would have to divorce (Rid).

HALAKHA

Any human baby that survives for thirty days – כׇּל שֶׁשָּׁהָה בָּאָדָם שְׁלֹשִׁים יוֹם: Any child of whom it is known that he completed nine months in the womb is considered viable from the moment of birth. If it is not known whether he completed a full nine months, then once he lives for thirty days he is considered viable, and only then will the child's existence free his father's wives from the obligation to perform levirate marriage or *ḥalitza*. Some say that this is true only when his fingernails and hair have grown, as this is proof that the he has reached his ninth month (Rema, citing *Tur*). If the child survived thirty days and then died, and no one checked whether his fingernails and hair had grown, one may rely upon the first opinion (*Beit Shmuel*; *Taz*; Rambam *Sefer Nashim*, *Hilkhot Yibbum* 1:5; *Shulḥan Arukh*, *Even HaEzer* 156:4).

Died during the first thirty days and she arose and was betrothed – מֵת בְּתוֹךְ שְׁלֹשִׁים וְעָמְדָה וְנִתְקַדְּשָׁה: In the case of a *yevama* who gave birth to a child and it was not known whether he reached his ninth month, and then he died within thirty days of his birth, including on the thirtieth day, the *yevama* must perform *ḥalitza* since it is uncertain whether the child was viable. This is in accordance with the opinion of the Rabbis. Even if she was betrothed or married, she must still perform *ḥalitza*, and only then is she permitted to her husband. In the event that the *yavam* was not available to perform the *ḥalitza*, she may remain with her husband until the *yavam* becomes available (Rema, citing Mahari Mintz). However, if she was betrothed to a priest, she is not required to perform *ḥalitza* because if she were to do so she would become prohibited to her husband. In the event that the priest divorced her or died, ideally she should then perform *ḥalitza* in order to become permitted to non-priests. This is in accordance with the opinion of Ravina (Rambam *Sefer Nashim*, *Hilkhot Yibbum* 2:21; *Shulḥan Arukh*, *Even HaEzer* 164:7).

באורתא אמר רבא הכי, ובצפרא הדר ביה. אמר ליה: שריתו? יהא רעוא דתשתרו אף תרבא.

In the evening Rava stated this ruling in accordance with the way you cited him, **but in the morning he retracted** his opinion and ruled as I cited him. Rav Mesharshiyya **said to him: Do you** really **permit** her to marry without *ḥalitza*? He added sarcastically: **May it be** God's **will that you will even permit** forbidden fats [*tarba*][N] as well. In Rav Mesharshiyya's opinion, the prohibition against the widow remarrying without *ḥalitza* was as obvious as the prohibition of forbidden fats.

הכא גבי מעוברת חבירו ומינקת חבירו הנשואה לכהן, מאי? מי עבוד רבנן תקנתא לכהן, או לא?

After citing this dispute, Rav Ashi said to Rav Hoshaya, son of Rav Idi: According to Rava's citation of Rav, when a woman is married to a priest, the Sages were more lenient in order to allow the couple to remain married. **Here, with regard to a woman who is pregnant** with the child **of another** man **or a woman who is nursing** the child **of another** man, **who is married to a priest, what** is the *halakha*? **Did the Sages enact an ordinance for** the benefit of **a priest** and say that it is sufficient for him to separate from his wife and he does not need to divorce her, **or not?**

אמר ליה: הכי השתא! בשלמא התם, כיון דאיכא רבנן דפליגי עליה דרבן שמעון בן גמליאל, דאמרי: אף על גב דלא שהא ולד מעליא הוי, גבי אשת כהן, כיון דלא אפשר, עבדינן כרבנן.

He said to him: How can these cases **be compared? Granted, there,** in the case where the offspring died during its first thirty days of life, **since there are the Rabbis who disagree with Rabban Shimon ben Gamliel concerning it, as they say** that **although** the offspring **did not survive** for thirty days **it is** nevertheless considered **a full-fledged,** i.e., viable, **offspring,** therefore, **with regard to** the **wife of a priest, since it is not possible** for her to perform *ḥalitza* and remain permitted to her husband, **we** will be lenient and **act in accordance with** the opinion **of the Rabbis.**

אבל הכא, כמאן נעביד? אי כרבי מאיר – הא אמר יוציא ולא יחזיר עולמית, ואי כרבנן – האמרי בגט.

However, here, in the case of a woman who is pregnant with or nursing the child of another man, **in accordance with whose** opinion **should we act? If** we act **in accordance with** the opinion of **Rabbi Meir,** it will be of no benefit to the priest because Rabbi Meir **said** even with regard to the wife of an Israelite that **he must divorce** her **and may never take** her **back. And if** we act **in accordance with** the opinion of **the Rabbis,** it will also be of no benefit to the priest because **they say** he must send her out **with a bill of divorce** and only remarry her at a later point. Since there is no opinion that does not require a bill of divorce to be given, there is no possibility to be lenient in this case by not requiring a bill of divorce to be given.

איתמר, קדשה בתוך שלשה וברח פליגי בה רב אחא ורפרם, חד אמר: משמתינן ליה, וחד אמר: עירוקיה מסתייה. הוה עובדא, ואמר להו רפרם: עירוקיה מסתייה.

A pregnancy is generally noticeable only after three months have passed. Therefore, during the first three months after a woman is divorced or widowed, she may not remarry due to the possibility that she is pregnant. The Sages decreed that even betrothing her during that time is prohibited, lest one also marry her (see 41a). Concerning this, an amoraic dispute **was stated:** In a case in which a man **betrothed** a woman **during** the **three months** following her divorce or her husband's death, **and then he fled,**[H] **Rav Aḥa and Rafram disagree over** what should be done. **One said: We excommunicate him** for violating the prohibition. **And the other one said: His flight is sufficient for him,**[N] since it proves that he does not intend to marry her until it is determined that she is not pregnant. Therefore, there is no need to penalize him further. The Gemara relates: **There was an incident** like that, **and Rafram said to those** who asked what to do: **His flight is sufficient for him.**

NOTES

That you will even permit fats [*tarba*] – דתשתרו אף תרבא: Why did Rav Mesharshiyya specifically refer to the prohibition of forbidden fats? The *Arukh LaNer* suggests that Rav Mesharshiyya was hinting at the practice of the priests in the Temple to rely upon the opinions that it is permitted to eat the fats lining the stomach of an animal (see *Ḥullin* 49a). Accordingly, Rav Mesharshiyya was suggesting that since Rava's intention was to issue a ruling that would assist the priesthood, he should continue on that path and also rule that the fats lining the stomach are permitted.

Some early commentaries had a different version of the Gemara's text. In place of the word *tarba*, meaning fats, their text had *tarka*, meaning a divorcée. Accordingly, Rav Mesharshiyya was saying that if one permits a *yevama* to marry without *ḥalitza* then one will eventually also permit other types of forbidden marriages, even a divorcée to a priest (*Tosefot HaRosh*; Ritva on *Shabbat* 136b).

His flight is sufficient for him – עירוקיה מסתייה: The early commentaries discussed why the fact that he fled should save him from being excommunicated. The discussion surrounds the question of why he is excommunicated if he does not flee. Rashi, Ra'avad, and others explain that he is excommunicated in order to compel him to divorce his wife, so that he will not engage in intercourse before the appropriate time. Therefore, if he flees and it is clear that he has no intention of doing so in the immediate future, there is no need to excommunicate him. Accordingly, it is even appropriate to advise the husband in such a situation to flee rather than divorce his wife or suffer excommunication (Rosh). According to other opinions, the reason he is excommunicated is as a punishment for violating the pronouncements of the Sages (Rambam; see Ritva and *Maggid Mishne*). If so, it would seem that when he flees from his wife, he is not excommunicated because the very fact that he is unable to return to her until the appropriate time is itself considered a sufficient punishment.

HALAKHA

He betrothed her during the three months, and then he fled – קידשה בתוך שלשה וברח: One who betroths a woman during the three months following her divorce or her husband's death is excommunicated. Some say that he must divorce her, and then, if he is an Israelite and she is not pregnant, he may remarry her after three months. However, if he is a priest, he will be prohibited from remarrying her (*Tur*). Some say that if he betrothed her and was unaware of the fact that this was prohibited, he need not divorce her, and it is sufficient for the couple to separate (Mahari Weil). Others argue that even such a case requires a divorce (*Terumat HaDeshen*). In a case where the man is a priest, one may rely on the lenient opinion (Rema).

If he betrothed her and then fled, he is not excommunicated. This is in accordance with the opinion of Rafram in the Gemara. Furthermore, he even may be advised to flee *ab initio* (*Tur*). In a case in which not only did he betroth her, but he also married her, the Rambam rules that it is still sufficient for him to flee, whereas others (*Beit Shmuel*) rule that in such a case he must divorce her (Rambam *Sefer Nashim*, *Hilkhot Geirushin* 11:28; *Shulḥan Arukh*, *Even HaEzer* 13:10).

"סָפֵק בֶּן תֵּשַׁע" וכו׳. אֲמַר לֵיהּ רָבָא לְרַב נַחְמָן: לֵימָא הַלֵּךְ אַחַר רוֹב נָשִׁים, וְרוֹב נָשִׁים לְתִשְׁעָה יָלְדָן!

§ The mishna states that if a *yevama* consummated the levirate marriage and gave birth seven months later, there is **an uncertainty whether** the child **is nine** months **old,** counting from conception, and is the offspring of the first husband, i.e., the deceased brother, or whether the child is only seven months old and is the offspring of the second husband. If it is the child of the first husband, then there was never any obligation of levirate marriage, and the supposed consummation was in fact forbidden by penalty of *karet*. Due to that possibility, both the man and the woman are obligated to bring a guilt-offering for uncertainty. **Rava said to Rav Naḥman:** How can they bring a guilt-offering for uncertainty? **Let us say: Follow** the **majority of women, and** since the **majority of women give birth after nine** months, it should be presumed that the child is the offspring of the deceased brother. Accordingly, the couple would be obligated to bring a certain sin-offering, not a guilt-offering for uncertainty.

אֲמַר לֵיהּ: נָשֵׁי דִּידַן – לְשִׁבְעָה יָלְדָן. אֲמַר לֵיהּ: נָשֵׁי דִּידְכוּ הָווּ רוּבָּא דְּעָלְמָא?

Rav Naḥman **said to him:** The **women of our** family regularly **give birth after seven** months. Therefore, how can you presume that this woman gave birth after nine months? Rava **said to him: Do** the **women of your** family **constitute the majority of** the women of **the world?** Ultimately, the majority of women give birth after nine months, and one should therefore presume accordingly in a case of uncertainty.

אֲמַר לֵיהּ: הָכִי קָאָמִינָא, רוֹב נָשִׁים יָלְדָן לְתִשְׁעָה וּמִיעוּט לְשִׁבְעָה, וְכָל הַיּוֹלֶדֶת לְתִשְׁעָה – עוּבָּרָהּ נִיכָּר לִשְׁלִישׁ יָמֶיהָ. וְזוֹ, הוֹאִיל וְלֹא הוּכַּר עוּבָּרָהּ לִשְׁלִישׁ יָמֶיהָ – אִיתְרַע לֵיהּ רוּבָּא.

Rav Naḥman **said to him: This is what I am saying:** Although it is true that the **majority of women give birth after nine** months **and** only **a minority** give birth **after seven,** still, in the case of **every** woman **who gives birth after nine** months, **her fetus is** already **recognizable after a third of her days,** i.e., in the third month of her pregnancy. Accordingly, in the case of **this** woman, **since her fetus was not recognizable after a third of her days,** as were it already recognizable at that point then it would be obvious that the child was the offspring of the first husband, therefore, the ability to presume she is like the **majority** of women **is compromised,** and the uncertainty as to who the father of the child is remains. Consequently, the *yavam* and *yevama* should each bring a guilt-offering for uncertainty.

אִי כׇּל הַיּוֹלֶדֶת לְתִשְׁעָה עוּבָּרָהּ נִיכָּר לִשְׁלִישׁ יָמֶיהָ, הָא מִדְּלָא הוּכַּר לִשְׁלִישׁ יָמֶיהָ – עוּבָּרָהּ וַדַּאי בַּר שִׁבְעָה לְבַתְרָאָה הוּא! אֶלָּא אֵימָא: רוֹב הַיּוֹלֶדֶת לְתִשְׁעָה עוּבָּרָהּ נִיכָּר לִשְׁלִישׁ יָמֶיהָ, וְהַאי מִדְּלָא הוּכַּר לִשְׁלִישׁ יָמֶיהָ – אִיתְרַע לֵיהּ רוּבָּא.

The Gemara asks: **If** it is true that in the case of **every** woman **who gives birth after nine** months, **her fetus is** already **recognizable after a third of her days,** then with regard to **this** woman, **from** the fact that her fetus **was not recognized after a third** of her days, it follows that **her fetus was certainly** only **seven** months **old** and is the offspring **of the latter** husband, i.e., the *yavam*. If so, it is clear the *yavam* is father of the child and there should be no need to bring an offering at all. **Rather,** one must emend Rav Naḥman's words and **say:** In the **majority** of cases, with regard to a woman **who gives birth after nine** months, **her fetus is** already **recognizable after a third of her days, and** with regard to **this** woman, **from** the fact that her fetus **was not recognized after the a third** of her days, the ability to presume she is like the **majority** of women **is compromised.**

תָּנוּ רַבָּנַן: רִאשׁוֹן רָאוּי לִהְיוֹת כֹּהֵן גָּדוֹל, וְשֵׁנִי מַמְזֵר מִסָּפֵק. רַבִּי אֱלִיעֶזֶר בֶּן יַעֲקֹב אוֹמֵר: אֵין מַמְזֵר מִסָּפֵק.

§ The mishna states that the child of the *yevama* has unflawed lineage since regardless of whether it is the offspring of the deceased husband or the *yavam*, there was no transgression involved in its conception. With regard to this case, **the Sages taught** in a *baraita*: The **first** child **is** even **fit to become a High Priest.** However, since it is possible that the child is the offspring of the deceased husband, in which case the widow remains forbidden to the *yavam* as his brother's wife, if she has a **second** child with her *yavam* then that child is a ***mamzer* due to an uncertainty** with regard to his status. **Rabbi Eliezer ben Ya'akov says: One is not** rendered **a *mamzer* due to uncertainty.**

מַאי קָאָמַר? אֲמַר אַבַּיֵי: הָכִי קָאָמַר, רִאשׁוֹן רָאוּי לִהְיוֹת כֹּהֵן גָּדוֹל, וְשֵׁנִי – סְפֵק מַמְזֵר, וְאָסוּר בְּמַמְזֶרֶת. רַבִּי אֱלִיעֶזֶר אוֹמֵר: אֵינוֹ סְפֵק מַמְזֵר אֶלָּא וַדַּאי מַמְזֵר, וּמוּתָּר בְּמַמְזֶרֶת.

The meaning of Rabbi Eliezer ben Ya'akov's statement and how he differs from the first *tanna* is unclear. The Gemara clarifies: **What is the** *baraita* **saying? Abaye said: This is what it is saying:** The **first** child is even **fit to become a High Priest. And** if she has a **second** child, his status as a ***mamzer*** **is uncertain and** therefore he is both prohibited from marrying an Israelite woman of unflawed lineage, since he might actually be a *mamzer*, **and he is** also **prohibited from** marrying **a** ***mamzeret***, since he might not be a *mamzer*. **Rabbi Eliezer** ben Ya'akov **says: He is not** treated like one whose status as **a** ***mamzer*** is **uncertain; rather,** due to the uncertainty concerning his status **he is** treated like one who is **definitely a** ***mamzer***, **and he is permitted to** marry a ***mamzeret***. In other words, Rabbi Eliezer ben Ya'akov holds that even one whose status as a *mamzer* is uncertain is permitted to marry one who is definitely a *mamzeret*.

רָבָא אֲמַר, הָכִי קָאָמַר: רִאשׁוֹן – רָאוּי לִהְיוֹת כֹּהֵן גָּדוֹל, וְשֵׁנִי – מַמְזֵר וַדַּאי מִסָּפֵק, וּמוּתָּר בְּמַמְזֶרֶת. וְרַבִּי אֱלִיעֶזֶר בֶּן יַעֲקֹב אוֹמֵר: אֵין וַדַּאי מַמְזֵר מִסָּפֵק, אֶלָּא סְפֵק מַמְזֵר, וְאָסוּר בְּמַמְזֶרֶת.

Rava said: This is what the *baraita* **is saying:** The **first** child **is** even **fit to become a High Priest. And** if she has a **second** child, he is treated as though he **is definitely a** ***mamzer*** **due to** the **uncertainty** concerning his status,[N] **and** therefore **he is permitted to** marry a ***mamzeret***, i.e., this *tanna* holds that even one whose status as a *mamzer* is uncertain is permitted to marry one who is definitely a *mamzeret*. **And Rabbi Eliezer ben Ya'akov says: He** is **not** treated as though he is **definitely a** ***mamzer*** **due to an uncertainty** concerning his status; **rather,** his status as a ***mamzer*** is **uncertain**[H] and he is treated accordingly, **and** therefore he is both prohibited from marrying an Israelite woman of unflawed lineage since he might be a *mamzer*, **and he** is also **prohibited from** marrying **a** ***mamzeret*** since he might not be a *mamzer*.

וְקָמִיפַּלְגִי בִּדְרַבִּי אֶלְעָזָר. דִּתְנַן, רַבִּי אֶלְעָזָר אוֹמֵר: וַדָּאָן בְּוַדָּאָן – מוּתָּר. וַדָּאָן בִּסְפֵקָן, וּסְפֵקָן בְּוַדָּאָן, וּסְפֵקָן בִּסְפֵקָן – אָסוּר.

The Gemara explains: **And** Abaye and Rava **disagree with regard to** whether the *halakha* is decided in accordance with the opinion **of Rabbi Elazar. As we learned** in a mishna (*Kiddushin* 74a): With regard to the prohibition against marrying people with certain types of flawed lineage, **Rabbi Elazar said:** The marriage of **those** people whose flawed lineage status is **certain to those** whose status is **certain is permitted,** but the marriage of **those** whose status is **certain to those** whose status is **uncertain, and** the marriage of **those** whose status is **uncertain to those** whose status is **certain, and** even the marriage of **those** whose status is **uncertain to those** whose status is **uncertain, is prohibited.**[H]

וְאֵלּוּ הֵן סְפֵקָן: שְׁתוּקִי וַאֲסוּפִי וְכוּתִי,

The mishna concludes: **And these are those** who are considered to have an **uncertain** status:[H] **A child of unknown paternity** [***shetuki***], although his mother's identity is known; **and a foundling** who was found abandoned in the streets; **and a Samaritan** [***Kuti***],[B] who is possibly a *mamzer* since the Samaritans do not accept and abide by the *halakhot* of marriage.

וַאֲמַר רַב יְהוּדָה אֲמַר רַב: הֲלָכָה כְּרַבִּי אֶלְעָזָר. כִּי אָמְרִיתָהּ קַמֵּיהּ דִּשְׁמוּאֵל אֲמַר לִי: הִלֵּל שָׁנָה עֲשָׂרָה יוּחֲסִין עָלוּ מִבָּבֶל: כָּהֲנֵי, לְוָיֵי, וְיִשְׂרְאֵלֵי, חֲלָלֵי, גֵּירֵי, חֲרוּרֵי, מַמְזֵרֵי, נְתִינֵי, שְׁתוּקֵי, וַאֲסוּפֵי. וְכוּלָּן מוּתָּרִין לָבֹא זֶה בָּזֶה,

And with regard to this mishna **Rav Yehuda said** that **Rav said:** The ***halakha*** **is in accordance with** the opinion of **Rabbi Elazar.** But **when I said this** *halakha* of Rav's **in** the **presence of Shmuel, he said to me: Hillel taught** in a *baraita* that **ten** categories of **lineage came up from Babylon** to Eretz Yisrael: **Priests; Levites; and Israelites; priests disqualified due to flawed lineage** [***ḥalallim***]; **converts; freed slaves;** ***mamzerim***; **Gibeonites;** ***shetukei***; **and foundlings. And it is permitted** for **all** men and women in these categories **to marry one another,** i.e., the list is arranged such that the marriage between people in any two categories that are adjacent to one another is permitted. This is possible only if one assumes that it is permitted for one whose flawed lineage status is uncertain to marry one whose flawed lineage status is certain.

NOTES

He is definitely a *mamzer* due to the uncertainty concerning his status – מַמְזֵר וַדַּאי מִסָּפֵק: In tractate *Kiddushin*, Rava is cited as saying that one whose status as a *mamzer* is uncertain is permitted to marry an Israelite woman of unflawed lineage. However, this would appear to conform to neither opinion in the *baraita*, according to the way Rava explains it. Some have suggested that a distinction should be drawn between different cases of uncertainty. The *baraita* here concerns a case where there is a specific reason to be concerned that the child is a *mamzer*; if the first child is the son of the previous husband then the second one will be a *mamzer*. Therefore, Rava rules stringently. However, in tractate *Kiddushin*, Rava is considering the cases of a child whose father is entirely unknown and that of a foundling. In those cases, there are no specific indications that the child might be a *mamzer*; rather, there is simply a total lack of knowledge about the child's lineage. Rava therefore rules leniently that there is no need to open a Pandora's box of possibilities, and therefore in such a case there is no prohibition preventing him from marrying an Israelite woman of unflawed lineage (*Mei Naftoaḥ*). Alternatively, one could suggest a resolution based on the opinion of the Rambam that according to Torah law, one whose status as *mamzer* is uncertain is actually permitted to marry an Israelite woman of unflawed lineage. Accordingly, it can be explained that Rava in tractate *Kiddushin* was referring to Torah law, whereas here he is referring to the fact that according to rabbinic law it is prohibited.

HALAKHA

He is not definitely a *mamzer* due to an uncertainty, rather his status as a *mamzer* is uncertain – אֵין וַדַּאי מַמְזֵר מִסָּפֵק אֶלָּא סְפֵק מַמְזֵר: If a *yevama* and her *yavam* consummate the levirate marriage within three months of her husband's death, and then she gives birth to a viable child and there is an uncertainty whether the child was born after nine months of gestation and is the offspring of the first husband, or whether it was born after only seven months of gestation and is the offspring of the *yavam*, that child has unflawed lineage. If the *yavam* does not divorce her, and they have another child together, the second child's status as a *mamzer* is uncertain. He is therefore prohibited from marrying an Israelite woman of unflawed lineage, since he might be a *mamzer*; and he is also prohibited from marrying a *mamzeret*, as he might not be a *mamzer*. This is in accordance with the opinion of Rabbi Eliezer ben Ya'akov, as explained by Rava (Rambam *Sefer Nashim, Hilkhot Yibbum* 1:23; *Shulḥan Arukh, Even HaEzer* 4:25; 164:6).

Certain and uncertain disqualifications from marriage – פְּסוּלֵי חִיתּוּן וַדַּאי וְסָפֵק: By Torah law one whose status as a *mamzer* is uncertain is permitted to marry an Israelite of unflawed lineage. However, by rabbinic law it is prohibited. Only one who is definitely a *mamzer* is permitted to marry a *mamzeret*; if the status of the man, the woman, or both is uncertain, then they are prohibited from marrying one another (Rambam *Sefer Kedusha, Hilkhot Issurei Bia* 15:21; *Shulḥan Arukh, Even HaEzer* 4:24).

Uncertainties with regard to one's status as a *mamzer* – סְפֵקֵי מַמְזֵר: An uncertainty whether one is a *mamzer* can be created in various ways, e.g., whenever a child is born to a woman from a man who is not her husband in a case where her marital status is uncertain. This can occur either when there is uncertainty concerning the validity of the original betrothal or when there is uncertainty concerning the divorce from, or death of, her husband. A child whose father's identity is not known is also considered to be one whose status as a *mamzer* is uncertain (Rambam *Sefer Kedusha, Hilkhot Issurei Bia* 15:21; *Shulḥan Arukh, Even HaEzer* 4:24, 31, 36).

BACKGROUND

Samaritan [*Kuti*] – כּוּתִי: This term is used to describe the non-Jews who settled in Samaria and the surrounding territory after the exile of the ten tribes. Though they converted to Judaism, they had ulterior motives for doing so (see II Kings, chapter 17), and were not scrupulous in their observance of the mitzvot. Accordingly, it was a matter of debate among the Sages whether or not they were to be considered as Jews. In later generations, they abandoned Jewish practices entirely, and the Sages decreed that they should be treated as non-Jews.

וְאַתְּ אָמְרַתְּ הֲלָכָה כְּרַבִּי אֶלְעָזָר?!

After citing the baraita taught by Hillel, which assumes that it is permitted for one whose flawed lineage status is uncertain to marry one whose flawed lineage status is certain, Shmuel concluded: The *halakha* is certainly decided in accordance with the opinion of Hillel, **and** yet **you,** Rabbi Yehuda, **said** the ***halakha*** **is in accordance with** the opinion of **Rabbi Elazar,** which states that a marriage between two people whose flawed lineage status is uncertain is prohibited; your ruling is incorrect.

אַבַּיֵי סָבַר לָהּ כִּשְׁמוּאֵל דְּאָמַר הֲלָכָה כְּהִלֵּל, וּמוֹקֵי לָהּ רַבִּי אֱלִיעֶזֶר בֶּן יַעֲקֹב אַלִּיבָּא דְּהִלְכְתָא כִּי הֵיכִי דְּלָא תִּקְשֵׁי הִלְכְתָא אַהִלְכְתָא.

The Gemara proceeds to explain the dispute between Abaye and Rava: **Abaye holds in accordance with** the opinion of **Shmuel, who said** that the ***halakha*** **is** decided **in accordance with** the opinion of **Hillel** that it is permitted for one whose flawed lineage status is uncertain to marry one whose flawed lineage status is certain. Therefore, Abaye **establishes that** opinion of **Rabbi Eliezer ben Ya'akov** to be **in accordance with** this ***halakha,*** **in order that there should not be a contradiction between** one ***halakha,*** i.e., that the *halakha* is always decided in accordance with the opinion of Hillel, **and** another ***halakha,*** i.e., that the *halakha* is always decided in accordance with the opinion of Rabbi Eliezer ben Ya'akov.

רָבָא סָבַר לָהּ כְּרַב, דְּאָמַר הֲלָכָה כְּרַבִּי אֶלְעָזָר, וּמוֹקֵי לָהּ לְדְרַבִּי אֱלִיעֶזֶר בֶּן יַעֲקֹב אַלִּיבָּא דְּהִלְכְתָא, כִּי הֵיכִי דְּלָא תִּקְשֵׁי

Rava, however, **holds in accordance with** the opinion of **Rav, who said:** The ***halakha*** **is** decided **in accordance with** the opinion of **Rabbi Elazar** that the marriage of those whose status is certain to those whose status is uncertain is prohibited. Therefore, Rava **establishes that** opinion **of Rabbi Eliezer ben Ya'akov** to be **in accordance with** this ***halakha,*** **so that there should not be a contradiction** between

Perek **IV**
Daf **37** Amud **b**

הִלְכְתָא אַהִלְכְתָא.

one ***halakha,*** i.e., that the *halakha* in this case is in accordance with the opinion of Rav, **and** another ***halakha,*** i.e., that the *halakha* is always decided in accordance with the opinion of Rabbi Eliezer ben Ya'akov.

אָמַר אַבַּיֵי: מְנָא אָמִינָא לָהּ דְּכָל סְפֵיקָא לְרַבִּי אֱלִיעֶזֶר בֶּן יַעֲקֹב כְּוַדַּאי מְשַׁוֵּי לֵיהּ –

Abaye said: From where do I say that concerning **anyone** whose status as a *mamzer* is **uncertain, according to** the opinion of **Rabbi Eliezer ben Ya'akov** they **are treated equivalently to** one who is **definitely** a *mamzer*?

דְּתַנְיָא, רַבִּי אֱלִיעֶזֶר בֶּן יַעֲקֹב אוֹמֵר: הֲרֵי שֶׁבָּא עַל נָשִׁים הַרְבֵּה וְאֵין יוֹדֵעַ עַל אֵיזֶהוּ מֵהֶן בָּא. וְכֵן הִיא, שֶׁבָּאוּ עָלֶיהָ אֲנָשִׁים הַרְבֵּה וְאֵינָהּ יוֹדַעַת מֵאֵיזֶה מֵהֶן קִבְּלָה, נִמְצָא אָב נוֹשֵׂא אֶת בִּתּוֹ וְאָח נוֹשֵׂא אֶת אֲחוֹתוֹ, וְנִתְמַלֵּא כָּל הָעוֹלָם כּוּלּוֹ מַמְזֵרִין, וְעַל זֶה נֶאֱמַר "וּמָלְאָה הָאָרֶץ זִמָּה".

As it is taught in a *baraita* that **Rabbi Eliezer ben Ya'akov says:** With regard to one **who engaged in intercourse with** and impregnated **many women, but he does not know with which** women **he had intercourse, and similarly,** with regard to a woman, if **many men had intercourse with her** and she became pregnant, **but she does not know from which** man **she received** the seed that caused her to become pregnant, since the identities of the parents of those children are not known, **it could emerge** that **a father marries his daughter, and a brother marries his sister. And** in this way, **the entire world could become filled with** ***mamzerim.*** **And concerning this, it is stated: "And lest the land become full of lewdness"** (Leviticus 19:29). Abaye demonstrates his claim from the fact that even though it is not certain that the children in this situation are *mamzerim,* nevertheless, Rabbi Eliezer ben Ya'akov labels them as *mamzerim* and not as those whose status as a *mamzer* is uncertain.[N]

וְרָבָא אָמַר לָךְ: הָכִי קָאָמַר: "זוֹ מַה הִיא".

And Rava could have **said to you: This is what** the verse **is saying:** The word "lewdness [*zima*]" can be understood as an acronym of the words: *Zo ma hi,* meaning: **What is this.**[N] It is plausible to say that Rabbi Eliezer ben Ya'akov's citation of this verse indicates that he regards their status to be uncertain.

NOTES

One whose status as a *mamzer* is uncertain is treated the same way as one who is definitely a *mamzer* – סְפֵיקָא כְּוַדַּאי: Rashi explains that Abaye derives his proof from the fact that Rabbi Eliezer ben Ya'akov relates to the children whose *mamzer* status is uncertain as though they were definitely *mamzerim*. Another possible interpretation is that Abaye's proof is derived from Rabbi Eliezer ben Ya'akov's extended formulation. It would have been sufficient if he had highlighted the possibility that a father might marry his daughter and a brother his sister; why did he continue to emphasize: The entire world will become filled with *mamzerim*? Apparently, Rabbi Eliezer ben Ya'akov was also concerned that the children in these cases, whose status as a *mamzer* would be uncertain, would later marry people who are definitely *mamzerim* and in that way the number of *mamzerim* in the world would be greatly increased. The only reason to be concerned for that possibility is if one holds that one whose status as a *mamzer* is uncertain is permitted to marry one who is definitely a *mamzer*. From here Abaye derives his proof (*Yosef Lekaḥ*).

What is this – זוֹ מַה הִיא: According to Rava, the verse should not be understood as labeling the children in such cases as *mamzerim*; rather, that if one is not careful the world could become filled with people whose lineage status is not known (Rivan).

יָתֵר עַל כֵּן אָמַר רַבִּי אֱלִיעֶזֶר בֶּן יַעֲקֹב: לֹא יִשָּׂא אָדָם אִשָּׁה בִּמְדִינָה זוֹ, וְיֵלֵךְ וְיִשָּׂא אִשָּׁה בִּמְדִינָה אַחֶרֶת, שֶׁמָּא יִזְדַּוְּוגוּ זֶה לָזֶה וְנִמְצָא אָח נוֹשֵׂא אֶת אֲחוֹתוֹ.

The Gemara cites the continuation of the *baraita*: **Furthermore, Rabbi Eliezer ben Ya'akov said** that even in marriage, one should be careful not to create a situation that could lead to the birth of *mamzerim*. Therefore, **a man should not marry a woman in this country and** then **go and marry** another **woman in a different country,**[H] **lest** a son from one marriage and a daughter from the other, unaware that they are both children of the same father, **unite with one another, and it could emerge** that **a brother marries his sister,** the children of whom would be *mamzerim*.

אִינִי? וְהָא רַב, כִּי אִיקְּלַע לְדַרְדְּשִׁיר [מַכְרִיז] וְאָמַר: מַאן הָוְיָא לְיוֹמָא. וְרַב נַחְמָן, כִּי אִיקְּלַע לְשַׁכְנְצִיב [מַכְרִיז] וְאָמַר: מַאן הָוְיָא לְיוֹמָא!

The Gemara asks: **Is that so;** is there really such a prohibition? **But didn't Rav, when he happened** to come **to Dardeshir, make a public announcement saying: Which** woman **will be** my wife **for the day,** i.e., for the duration of his visit? Since his wife did not accompany him to Dardeshir, he wished to be married to another woman while he was there, in order to avoid a situation that could lead him to having forbidden thoughts. **And** also **Rav Naḥman, when he happened** to come **to Shakhnetziv, made a public announcement saying: Which** woman **will be** my wife **for the day?**[N] It would appear, from the fact that both Sages married wives in two different places, that there is no prohibition in doing so.

שָׁאנֵי רַבָּנַן דְּפָקִיעַ שְׁמַיְיהוּ.

The Gemara rejects the proof: **Sages are different, as their names are renowned,** and therefore their children are always identified by their connection to their father. Therefore, Rabbi Eliezer ben Ya'akov's concern does not apply to them.

וְהָאָמַר רָבָא: תְּבָעוּהָ לִינָּשֵׂא וְנִתְפַּיְּיסָה – צְרִיכָה לֵישֵׁב שִׁבְעָה נְקִיִּים!

The Gemara examines Rav and Rav Naḥman's actions: **But didn't Rava say:** With regard to a woman **who had an offer of marriage and accepted,** the emotional excitement may have caused her to have a flow of menstrual blood, which would making her ritually impure and prohibit her from engaging in intercourse. Even if she was unaware of any flow, she must consider the possibility that it occurred. To purify herself, **she needs to wait seven** consecutive days that are **clean**[B] from any flow of menstrual blood[H] and then immerse in a ritual bath. Only then may she marry. If so, how could Rav and Rav Naḥman marry women on the day they arrived?

NOTES

Which will be for the day – מַאן הָוְיָא לְיוֹמָא: The commentaries discuss why Rav and Rav Naḥman required a wife for one day, as there are many instances recounted in the Talmud where the same Sages went to different places, and they did not take a wife on those occasions. Moreover, if they intended to divorce these wives, they would be in violation of the dictum that one may not marry a woman with the intention of divorcing her. Indeed, the Rif and the Rosh do not quote this practice, and it appears that they do not consider it to be *halakha*.

Some later authorities suggest that Rav and Rav Naḥman were traveling to meet with the non-Jewish ruler, and it was the custom of the ruler to provide a mistress for those who visited him (see *Avoda Zara* 76b). Therefore, Rav and Rav Naḥman asked to marry a wife so that they would not be offered a mistress by the ruler, since the custom was to offer a mistress only to one who came without his wife (*Imrei David*).

HALAKHA

One should not marry women in different countries – לֹא יִשָּׂא נָשִׁים בְּכַמָּה מְדִינוֹת: A man should not marry a woman in one country and then go and marry another woman in a different country, lest a son from one marriage and a daughter from the other unite with one another and have children, who would be *mamzerim*. This is in accordance with the ruling of Rabbi Eliezer ben Ya'akov. However, if the man is renowned such that any children he has will be identified by their connection to their father, then it is permissible. This is in accordance with the Gemara's initial explanation of the actions of Rav and Rav Naḥman. The *Beit Shmuel* notes that the Rif and Rosh do not refer to this exception, and it would seem that they hold that the Gemara retracted this explanation in its conclusion. This is possible if one assumes that according to the conclusion of the Gemara, Rav and Rav Naḥman never actually married the women in the towns they visited (Rambam *Sefer Kedusha, Hilkhot Issurei Bia* 21:29; *Shulḥan Arukh, Even HaEzer* 2:11).

A woman who has an offer of marriage must wait seven clean days – תְּבָעוּהָ לִינָּשֵׂא יוֹשֶׁבֶת שִׁבְעָה נְקִיִּים: A woman who had an offer of marriage and accepted may not marry immediately; rather, she must count seven clean days since she may have experienced a flow of blood without being aware of it. She must check herself during those seven days to ensure she has not experienced any additional flow. Ideally, this should be done each day (Rema, based on the *Beit Yosef*). The Rambam rules that if the husband is a Torah scholar then she may marry him immediately, since he can be trusted to be careful not to engage in sexual relations with her. This ruling is based on the Gemara here. The Ra'avad disagrees and rules that the prohibition applies to a Torah scholar as well. It would appear that the majority of halakhic authorities concur with the opinion of the Ra'avad (Rambam *Sefer Kedusha, Hilkhot Issurei Bia* 11:9; *Shulḥan Arukh, Yoreh De'a* 192:1).

BACKGROUND

Seven clean days – שִׁבְעָה נְקִיִּים: When a woman accepts an offer of marriage, the emotional excitement can bring on early menstruation. This is especially true for a woman whose cycle is not totally regular. Furthermore, it is possible that out of her desire for her future husband, she may have experienced other vaginal secretions that masked the sensation of the flow of blood; therefore, even if she did not see or feel the release of blood, she must consider the possibility that there was blood. Consequently, she must observe the purification process for a menstruating woman and wait seven clean days before immersing in a ritual bath.

רַבָּנַן שְׁלוּחַיְיהוּ הֲווּ מְשַׁדְּרִי, וּמוֹדְעִי לְהוּ, וְאִיבָּעֵית אֵימָא: לְרַבָּנַן יִחוּדֵי בְּעָלְמָא הוּא דְּמִייחֲדִי לְהוּ, דַּאֲמַר מָר: אֵינוֹ דּוֹמֶה מִי שֶׁיֵּשׁ לוֹ פַּת בְּסַלּוֹ לְמִי שֶׁאֵין לוֹ פַּת בְּסַלּוֹ.

The Gemara explains: These **Sages would send messengers** seven days ahead of their arrival and **they would inform** the women of the Sage's arrival. In this way, the woman who agreed to marry the Sage would have time to count the seven clean days. **And if you wish, say** that **the Sages'** intentions **were merely to be in seclusion** [*meyaḥadi*] **with** the woman[N] but not to engage in intercourse with her. Therefore, it was permitted to marry her even if she became ritually impure. Being in seclusion with a woman was sufficient to help the Sages avoid any forbidden thoughts, **as the Master said: One who has bread in his basket**[N] **is incomparable to one who does not have bread in his basket,** i.e., just as the knowledge that food is readily available is sufficient to psychologically alleviate one's feelings of hunger, so too, the knowledge that one's sexual desires could be met lessens the strength of the desire itself.

תַּנְיָא, רַבִּי אֱלִיעֶזֶר בֶּן יַעֲקֹב אוֹמֵר: לֹא יִשָּׂא אָדָם אִשָּׁתוֹ וְדַעְתּוֹ לְגָרְשָׁהּ, מִשּׁוּם שֶׁנֶּאֱמַר ״אַל תַּחֲרֹשׁ עַל רֵעֲךָ רָעָה וְהוּא יוֹשֵׁב לָבֶטַח אִתָּךְ״.

The Gemara cites an additional statement of Rabbi Eliezer ben Ya'akov: It is **taught** in a *baraita* that **Rabbi Eliezer ben Ya'akov says: A man should not marry his wife** when at the same time **his intention is to divorce her,**[NH] **because it is stated: "Do not devise evil against your neighbor, as he dwells securely with you"** (Proverbs 3:29). It is wrong for one to intend to undermine the feelings of security that another has with him.

סָפֵק וְיָבָם שֶׁבָּאוּ לַחֲלוֹק בְּנִכְסֵי מִיתְנָא.

§ The mishna raises a case in which a *yavam* consummated the levirate marriage with his *yevama* and seven months later she gave birth. With respect to that child, there is an uncertainty whether he is the child of the deceased brother or whether he is the child of the *yavam*. The Gemara discusses the ramifications of this uncertainty in a dispute concerning inheritance. The case concerns one whose identity as the son of the deceased is **uncertain, and a** ***yavam*** who consummated the levirate marriage with the *yevama*, **who** both **came to divide up**[N] the **possessions of the deceased** brother[H] and each one claims to be the sole heir.

HALAKHA

A man should not marry his wife when at the same time his intention is to divorce her – לֹא יִשָּׂא אָדָם אִשְׁתּוֹ וְדַעְתּוֹ לְגָרְשָׁהּ: It is prohibited for a man to marry a woman if at the same time his intention is to divorce her, because it is stated: "Do not devise evil against your neighbor, as he dwells securely with you" (Proverbs 3:29). This is in accordance with the ruling of Rabbi Eliezer ben Ya'akov. The Rambam and *Shulḥan Arukh* rule that if he informs her in advance that his intention is only to be married for a short time, then it is permissible. It would appear that this ruling is based on the Gemara here (*Beit Yosef*; see *Derisha*; Rambam *Sefer Kedusha, Hilkhot Issurei Bia* 21:28 and *Sefer Nashim, Hilkhot Geirushin* 10:21; *Shulḥan Arukh, Even HaEzer* 2:10; 119:1).

The son of uncertain descent and the *yavam* who came to divide up the possessions of the deceased brother – סָפֵק וְיָבָם שֶׁבָּאוּ לַחֲלוֹק בְּנִכְסֵי הַמֵּת: If a *yavam* consummated the levirate marriage within three months of his brother's death and seven months later the *yevama* gave birth, then there is an uncertainty whether that child is the offspring of the deceased brother or of the *yavam*. If that child and the *yavam* come to divide up the possessions of the deceased, the possessions are to be divided up equally between them (Rambam *Sefer Mishpatim, Hilkhot Naḥalot* 5:4; *Shulḥan Arukh, Even HaEzer* 163:3).

NOTES

Their intentions were merely to be in seclusion [*meyaḥadi*] with the woman – יִחוּדֵי בְּעָלְמָא הוּא דְּמִייחֲדִי לְהוּ: This statement of the Gemara raises numerous difficulties: If a newlywed bride became impure from experiencing a menstrual flow before the couple had managed to consummate their marriage, it is prohibited for them to be in seclusion together, even if they do not engage in relations. Why, then, was it permitted for these Sages? Furthermore, since it was actually prohibited to engage in relations with these women, how was the Sages' seclusion with them considered like the case of one who has bread in his basket? Rabbi Avraham min HaHar raises an additional question: According to the opinion of the Rambam, one may not marry a woman who is ritually impure following her menstruation since there is no immediate possibility of engaging in relations with her. Why, then, was it permitted for these Sages to marry in such a manner?

With regard to the prohibition against being secluded with a bride who experienced a menstrual flow, numerous resolutions have been offered: *Tosafot* on *Yoma* 18b suggest that the prohibition does not actually apply to a newlywed couple but only to an unmarried man and his future bride. However, once they are married, there is no prohibition. The Rambam suggests that the prohibition is only due to the concern that the couple will not be able to withstand their desires and will engage in relations. This concern does not apply to a Torah scholar, and therefore he may be secluded with his newlywed wife in all circumstances.

The Rid interprets the prohibition as being limited to being in the same room; however, it is permitted for the couple to be in the same house. *Tosafot* here explain that from the outset the Sages would inform the women that their intention was only to be secluded with them, but not to engage in relations. Therefore, the excitement of marriage was not so great that it would lead to the women experiencing a flow. Accordingly, it was actually perfectly permissible for them to marry these women, and therefore the Sages could certainly be considered like one who has bread in his basket.

Other commentaries read the Gemara in a way that avoids the questions altogether. The Ra'avad and Meiri claim that these Sages never actually married these women. When the Gemara says *meyaḥadi*, the intention is not that the Sages were in seclusion with them; rather, they would merely designate them to be available to marry. Therefore, there was no question of any prohibition involved. Alternatively, the Ramban explains that the statement that they would merely be in seclusion with the women is not an alternative answer but a continuation of the first answer: They would inform the women of their arrival ahead of time, and even so, due to Rabbi Eliezer ben Ya'akov's concerns, they would not actually engage in relations with them. This answer also resolves a further difficulty raised by some of the early commentaries: If the Gemara's original suggestion that the Sages' names are renowned was rejected, then what would happen if these new wives did become pregnant and give birth to a child? Couldn't this lead to the eventual creation of *mamzerim*? However, according to the Ramban's explanation there was never any possibility of actually having children.

One who has bread in his basket – מִי שֶׁיֵּשׁ לוֹ פַּת בְּסַלּוֹ: The term: Bread in one's basket, is used literally to explain why the manna caused suffering to the Jews in the desert, as they did not have bread in their basket for the next day (*Yoma* 74b). However, bread is also a euphemism for a wife, as the Torah says with regard to Potiphar that he did not deny Yosef anything "save the bread that he did eat" (Genesis 39:6), and the Sages understand this to be a reference to his wife (*Bereshit Rabba* 86:6). Rashi also uses the same euphemism to explain Jethro's words with regard to Moses: "Call him, that he may eat bread" (Exodus 2:20) as a reference to the possibility that Moses will marry one of his daughters (*Menuḥat Aharon*).

A man should not marry his wife when at the same time his intention is to divorce her – לֹא יִשָּׂא אָדָם אִשְׁתּוֹ וְדַעְתּוֹ לְגָרְשָׁהּ: The reason for the prohibition is that doing so undermines the woman's trust, as indicated by the biblical source of the prohibition. Therefore, if the man would first inform the woman of his intentions to divorce her, it would be permitted (see HALAKHA). Therefore, it must be that in the cases of Rav and Rav Naḥman cited in the Gemara, they would make their intentions clear before marrying the women for the duration of their visits, as is already hinted to by the concluding phrase of their requests: Which woman will be my wife for the day (Rid; see Meiri).

One whose identity is uncertain and a *yavam* who came to divide up – סָפֵק וְיָבָם שֶׁבָּאוּ לַחֲלוֹק: The Rashba asks: Since the *yavam* consummated the levirate marriage, the possessions are considered to be under his control. Therefore, even if an uncertainty arises concerning who has a right to those possessions, that uncertainty should not be significant enough to allow the possessions to be removed from his control and divided up between the two sides. In resolution of this difficulty, the Rashba explains that the fact that in the majority of cases a woman gives birth after nine months supports the claim of the son of uncertain descent that he is in fact the son of the deceased, since he was born less than nine months after his mother remarried. The Gemara later explains that the force of this majority is not sufficient to award the inheritance to him; since her pregnancy was not noticeable after three months, the ability to presume that she is like the majority of women is compromised. Nevertheless, the force of the majority is still sufficient to allow the possessions to be removed from the control of the *yavam* and then, due to the uncertainty, to be divided up between them.

ספק אמר: אנא בר מיתנא הוא, ונכסי דידי הוא. ויבם אמר: את בראי דידי את, ולית לך ולא מידי בנכסי. הוי ממון המוטל בספק, וממון המוטל בספק – חולקין.

The one of **uncertain** descent **said: I am the son of the deceased, and** therefore, as the only heir, his **possessions are mine. And the *yavam* said** to him: **You are my son, and you have absolutely no** rights **to the possessions;** rather, by virtue of the fact that I consummated the levirate marriage with the widow of the deceased, I should inherit him. The Gemara rules on this case: This **is** a case of **property of uncertain ownership,**[N] as there is no way to determine who is the rightful heir, and the *halakha* is that **property of uncertain ownership** the claimants **divide up** between them.

ספק ובני יבם שבאו לחלוק בנכסי מיתנא, ספק אמר: ההוא גברא בר מיתנא הוא, ונכסי דידי הוא. בני יבם אמרי: את אחינו את, ומנתא הוא דאית לך בהדן.

The Gemara brings another case, that of one concerning whom there is **uncertainty** whether he is the son of the deceased or of the *yavam* **and the sons of** the ***yavam*,**[H] who consummated the levirate marriage with the *yevama* and has since died, **who came to divide up** the **possessions of the deceased,** and each one makes claim to the inheritance. The one of **uncertain** descent **said: That man,** referring to himself, **is the son of the deceased, and** therefore, as his sole heir, his **possessions are mine.** And the **sons of the *yavam* said** to him: **You are our brother, and** our uncle, the deceased, was not survived by any offspring and so by virtue of our father's levirate marriage he inherited our uncle's possessions, and now that our father has died and we are dividing up his possessions **you have** a right to inherit only **a portion** of the inheritance **together with us.**

סבור רבנן קמיה דרב משרשיא למימר: מתניתין היא, דתנן: הוא אינו יורש אותם, והם יורשין אותו.

The Rabbis who studied **before Rav Mesharshiyya thought to say:** This case **is** analogous to a case in **a mishna, as we learned** a similar case in a mishna (100a) in which a woman gave birth shortly after remarrying and there is uncertainty whether the child's father is the first or second husband. The mishna considers a case in which the husbands died and were each survived by a set of sons: If a son from either set died, the other sons of that set will inherit from him because as brothers they have an uncontested claim to the inheritance. However, **he,** the son of uncertain descent, **does not inherit** from **them** because his claim as a brother is uncertain and is therefore not powerful enough to allow him to take part of the inheritance from the other sons. **However,** if the son of uncertain descent died, **they,** the sons of both husbands, **will** jointly **inherit** from **him.** The claims of each set of sons to be his brothers are equally uncertain; therefore, since there is no one who has a definite claim to his inheritance, his possessions are split between them.

והכא איפכא, התם אמרי ליה: אייתי ראיה ושקול.

The Rabbis qualify their comparison of the cases: **But here,** the positions are **in reverse,** as follows: **There,** in the case of the mishna, when one of the sons dies, **they,** the other sons of that set, can **say to him,** the son of uncertain descent: **Bring proof** that you are actually a son of our father **and** only then can you **take** a portion. Since he cannot prove this, he will not receive any of the inheritance.

הכא אמר להו: אייתו ראיה ושקולו.

However, **here,** in the case where the son of uncertain descent is in dispute with the sons of the *yavam*, **he,** the son of uncertain descent, can **say to them: Bring proof** that I am not the son of the deceased, **and** only then can you **take** a portion together with me. The Rabbis claim that the principle in both cases is identical: When one party has an uncontested claim to the inheritance, and another party advances a claim to receive part of the inheritance that is based on an uncertainty, the uncertain claim is not accepted. In the mishna's case, it is the son of uncertain descent who has an uncertain claim. The Rabbis suggest that the reverse is true in the Gemara's case: The son of uncertain decent has an uncontested claim to the inheritance because whether he is the son of the first or second husband, he certainly has a right to some inheritance. It is the sons of the *yavam* who have an uncertain claim because they have a right to the inheritance only if the son of uncertain decent is actually their brother.

NOTES

This is property of uncertain ownership – הוי ממון המוטל בספק: Normally, in cases of property of uncertain ownership the *halakha* is that the property is left with the one who currently has control of it, based on the principle: The burden of proof rests upon the claimant. However, since in this case neither litigant has stronger control over the possessions, they are divided equally between the two sides (*Tosafot*; see the comments of Rashba cited on the previous page). The Ritva adds that since the case is one of inheritance, each side is considered to be equally in control of the possessions. He explains that this is why it is not appropriate in this case to remove the possessions from the parties and then award them based upon the discretion of the court, or alternatively to allow the parties to settle their differences by themselves and award the possessions according to their resolution. Furthermore, the court only ever resorts to using these methods when there is a possibility that the uncertainty will be resolved; however, in this case, the uncertainty is intractable.

HALAKHA

The son of uncertain descent and the sons of the *yavam* – ספק ובני יבם: If the son of uncertain descent and the sons of the *yavam* come to divide up the possessions of the deceased, then since the sons of the *yavam* concede that at the very least the son of uncertain descent has a right to a portion as one of the brothers, he takes that portion. The rest of the possessions are then divided into two, half going to the son of uncertain descent and the other half being split between the sons of the *yavam* (Rosh; *Tur*, citing Rashi). The Rambam rules that all of the deceased's possessions are to be split equally between the son of uncertain descent and the sons of the *yavam* (Rambam *Sefer Mishpatim*, *Hilkhot Naḥalot* 5:4; *Shulḥan Arukh*, *Even HaEzer* 163:4).

אֲמַר לְהוּ רַב מְשַׁרְשִׁיָּא: מִי דָּמֵי? הָתָם – אִינְהוּ וַדַּאי, וְאִיהוּ סָפֵק. הָכָא – אִידִי וְאִידִי סָפֵק.

Rav Mesharshiyya said to them: Is the case in the mishna really **comparable? There,** in the mishna's case, when one of the sons dies, **they,** the other sons in that set, have a **definite** claim to the inheritance, since their claim is based on the fact that they are the dead son's brothers, which is certainly true, **and he,** the son of uncertain descent, only has an **uncertain** claim. However, **here, each** party has only an **uncertain** claim.[N] Although the son of uncertain descent claims that ultimately, whatever the nature of his relationship with the deceased is, he should have the right to inherit, nevertheless, since it is not actually known what that relationship is, his claim in reality is merely a composite of uncertain claims.

אֶלָּא, אִי דָּמְיָא לְמַתְנִיתִין – [לְהָא] דָּמְיָא: לְסָפֵק וּבְנֵי יָבָם שֶׁבָּאוּ לַחֲלוֹק בְּנִכְסֵי יָבָם גּוּפֵיהּ, דְּהָתָם אָמְרִי לֵיהּ: אַיְיתֵי רְאָיָה דְּאָחוּנָא אַתְּ וּשְׁקוֹל.

Having rejected the analogy offered by the Rabbis, Rav Mesharshiyya offers his own analogy to the case in the mishna that the Rabbis cited: **Rather, if** there is a case that **is analogous to** the case in **the mishna,** then it is **to this** following case that it is **analogous:** It is comparable **to** a case in which following the levirate marriage a son was born, and there is uncertainty whether he is the son of the deceased or of the *yavam*, and that son of **uncertain** descent **and** the **sons of the** ***yavam*** **come to divide up** the **possessions of the** ***yavam*** **himself. As there,** those who are unquestionably the sons of the *yavam* have a definite claim; therefore, **they** can **say to him,** the son of uncertain descent: **Bring proof that you are** actually **our brother and** only then can you **take** a portion. Since he cannot prove this, he will not receive any of the inheritance.

סָפֵק וּבְנֵי יָבָם שֶׁבָּאוּ לַחֲלוֹק בְּנִכְסֵי יָבָם, לְבָתַר דִּפְלַג יָבָם בְּנִכְסֵי מִיתְנָא.

The Gemara brings yet another case, that of one concerning whom there is an **uncertainty** whether he is the son of the deceased or of the *yavam* **and the sons of the** ***yavam,*** i.e., the sons of the man who consummated the levirate marriage with the *yevama* and has since died, **who came to divide up** the **possessions of the** ***yavam***[H] **after the** ***yavam*** had already **divided up**[N] the **possessions of the deceased** brother between himself and the son of uncertain descent, as per the Gemara's ruling in the first case above.

בְּנֵי יָבָם אָמְרִי: אַיְיתֵי רְאָיָה דְּאָחוּנָא אַתְּ וּשְׁקוֹל. אָמַר לְהוּ סָפֵק: מַה נַּפְשַׁיְיכוּ, אִי אֲחוּכוֹן אֲנָא – הֲבוּ לִי מְנָתָא בַּהֲדַיְיכוּ, וְאִי בַּר מִיתְנָא אֲנָא – הֲבוּ לִי פַּלְגָא דִּפְלַג אֲבוּכוֹן בַּהֲדַאי.

The *yavam* then died and his sons and the son of uncertain descent each made a claim to the inheritance: **The sons of the** ***yavam*** **say** to the son of uncertain descent: **Bring proof that you are our brother, and** only then can you **take** a portion. The son of **uncertain** descent **said to them: Whichever way you** look at it, I should receive a portion of the inheritance. **If** you assume that **I am your brother,** then **give me a portion** of the inheritance **together with** all of **you, and if** you assume that **I am the son of the deceased,** then **give me the half** of the possessions **that your father** took when he **divided up** the possessions **with me** upon the deceased's death, because if you assume I am his son, then I am his sole heir and your father never had any rights to his possessions.

NOTES

Each party has only an uncertain claim – אִידִי וְאִידִי סָפֵק: Ostensibly, Rav Mesharshiyya's claim that in the Gemara's case each party has only an uncertain claim is difficult, because, as the Rabbis explained, whether the son of uncertain descent is the son of the first or second husband, he has a claim to the possessions. Why then does Rav Mesharshiyya's state that his claim is considered uncertain? Rashi explains that the key issue in defining a claim as certain is whether the potential heir can substantiate the nature of his relationship with the deceased. Since in this case he cannot, his claim is defined as uncertain. The later commentaries explain that this is uniquely true of inheritance rights. In regular monetary disputes, it is indeed sufficient to demonstrate that whatever the situation is, one has a right to the possessions. This is because the basis of one's rights to the possessions is one's acquisition of them, which exists even if unverified. However, in the *halakhot* of inheritance, one's rights to the possessions are merely a function of having the status of an heir, which is based on one's relationship to the deceased. That status can be established only once the relationship is verified. Therefore, as long as one cannot substantiate the precise nature of one's relationship with the deceased, one's claim is always defined as uncertain.

Had already divided up – פְּלַג: The Gemara does not consider what the *halakha* would be had the possessions of the deceased not yet been divided between the son of uncertain descent and the *yavam*. The Rashba, *Tosafot*, and others assume that in such a case, the claim of the son of uncertain descent would certainly be accepted.

The Rashba notes that since the *yavam* consummated the levirate marriage, it would seem that at that time he had an undisputed claim to the possessions. If so, this case should be dependent on the dispute between Admon and the Rabbis cited later in the Gemara, yet the Gemara does not connect the two. Therefore, it would seem that a distinction should be drawn between the two cases. The dispute between Admon and the Rabbis concerns a case where one's rights to the possessions were achieved through an act of acquisition. Only in this case is it possible to say that his act of acquisition strengthens his claim to the extent that it can withstand certain future developments that would have otherwise undermined his rights. However, in a case of inheritance, the fact that someone claimed to have a right to the inheritance and took control of those possessions does not strengthen his claim in any way.

HALAKHA

The son of uncertain descent and the sons of the ***yavam*****, with regard to the possessions of the** ***yavam*** **– סָפֵק וּבְנֵי יָבָם בְּנִכְסֵי יָבָם:** If the son of uncertain descent and the sons of the *yavam* come to divide up the possessions of the *yavam* after the *yavam* had previously divided up the possessions of his deceased brother between himself and the son of uncertain descent: If the son of uncertain descent claims that he is either willing to return the portion of the possessions of the deceased that he originally received and instead receive an portion equal to the sons of the *yavam*, or he will insist on receiving all of the possessions of the deceased, his claim is not heeded. This is in accordance with the opinion of Rav, who holds that the original verdict stands. However, the *Taz* and others rule that the original verdict is reconsidered (based on the *Tur*, citing Rosh). According to the *Beit Shmuel*, if the possessions of the deceased had not yet been divided up between the *yavam* and the son of uncertain descent, then the claim would be successful. Furthermore, if the son of uncertain descent had already obtained control of the possessions, they would not be removed from him (Rambam *Sefer Mishpatim, Hilkhot Naḥalot* 5:4; *Shulḥan Arukh, Even HaEzer* 163:5).

רַבִּי אַבָּא אֲמַר רַב: קָם דִּינָא. רַבִּי יִרְמְיָה אֲמַר: הֲדַר דִּינָא.

The son of uncertain descent's claim assumes that the original verdict to divide up the possessions of the deceased between the two sides may be reexamined in light of later developments. This assumption, however, is subject to a dispute: **Rabbi Abba said** that **Rav said: The** original **verdict stands,**[N] i.e., the original division of the deceased's possessions is considered a closed matter, and the new dispute concerning the possessions of the *yavam* is considered independently of it. Accordingly, the son of uncertain descent's claim cannot succeed, and so he receives no portion of the inheritance of the *yavam*. **Rabbi Yirmeya said: The** original **verdict is reconsidered** in light of the new circumstances, and therefore in this case the son of uncertain descent can put forward his undeniable claim to some of the possessions of the *yavam* based on the original uncertainties that existed with regard to the division of the deceased's possessions.

לֵימָא בִּפְלוּגְתָּא דְּאַדְמוֹן וְרַבָּנַן קָמִיפַּלְגִי, דִּתְנַן: מִי שֶׁהָלַךְ לִמְדִינַת הַיָּם וְאָבְדָה לוֹ דֶּרֶךְ שָׂדֵהוּ, אַדְמוֹן אָמַר: יֵלֵךְ בַּקְּצָרָה. וַחֲכָמִים אוֹמְרִים: יִקַּח לוֹ דֶּרֶךְ בְּמֵאָה מָנֶה, אוֹ יִפְרַח בָּאֲוִיר.

Let us say that Rabbi Abba and Rabbi Yirmeya **disagree over the dispute between Admon**[P] **and the Rabbis. As we learned** in a mishna (*Ketubot* 109b): With regard to **one** who owns a field and has the rights to a path that passes through land belonging to another, and **he traveled to a country overseas, and** when he returned the **path to his field was lost,**[H] i.e., he forgot where the path was located, **Admon says: He may go** only **on the shortest** path to his field, as although it is not known where the path is, he definitely did have a path, and therefore at the very least he has a right to the shortest path. **The Rabbis say: He must** either **purchase for himself** a new **path for** whatever price is asked, even if it is **one hundred dinars, or he will** have to **fly through the air** to reach his field, i.e., as long as he cannot prove where the original path was, he has no rights to any other path.

וְהָוֵינַן בָּהּ: לְרַבָּנַן; שַׁפִּיר קָאָמַר אַדְמוֹן! וְאָמַר רַב יְהוּדָה אֲמַר רַב: הָכָא בְּמַאי עָסְקִינַן – כְּגוֹן שֶׁהִקִּיפוּהָ אַרְבָּעָה בְּנֵי אָדָם מֵאַרְבַּע רוּחוֹת.

And we discussed the mishna and thereby established the parameters of the dispute as follows: It is difficult **for the Rabbis** because **Admon is saying well,** i.e., the logic of his opinion would seem to be compelling. **And** in defense of the Rabbis' opinion, **Rav Yehuda said** that **Rav said: With what are we dealing here?** It is with a case **where** his field was **surrounded by four individuals** who owned the land **on** each of its **four sides.** Therefore, he cannot demand a path from any one of the surrounding owners, since each one can deflect his claim by suggesting that the path might have passed through one of the other owners' land.

אִי הָכִי, מַאי טַעְמָא דְּאַדְמוֹן? וְאָמַר רָבָא: בְּאַרְבָּעָה דְּאָתוּ מִכֹּחַ אַרְבָּעָה, וְאַרְבָּעָה דְּאָתוּ מִכֹּחַ חַד – כּוּלֵּי עָלְמָא לָא פְּלִיגִי, דְּמָצוּ מַדְחֵי לֵיהּ.

However, this creates a further difficulty: **If so,** that the surrounding land is owned by different people, **what is Admon's rationale** for ruling that the owner of the field has a claim to the shortest path? **And** in order to justify Admon's opinion, **Rava said: With regard to** a case in which there are **four** current owners **who came** to own their land **on the basis of** purchase from **four** previous owners, i.e., each of the current owners acquired their land from a different previous owner, **and** also in a case in which there are **four** current owners **who came** to own their land **on the basis of** purchase from **one** previous owner who originally owned all four pieces of land, **everyone agrees that** the current owners **are able to deflect him** and his claim to a path.

כִּי פְּלִיגִי – בְּחַד דְּאָתֵי מִכֹּחַ אַרְבָּעָה. אַדְמוֹן סָבַר: מָצֵי אָמַר לֵיהּ: מִכֹּל מָקוֹם דַּרְכִּי גַּבָּךְ הוּא. וְרַבָּנַן סָבְרִי, דְּאָמַר לֵיהּ: אִי שָׁתְקַתְּ – שָׁתְקַתְּ, וְאִי לָא – מַהֲדַרְנָא שְׁטָרָא לְמָרַיְיהוּ, וְלָא מָצֵית לְאִשְׁתַּעוּיֵי דִּינָא בַּהֲדַיְיהוּ.

When they disagree, it is **in** a case in **which** there is only **one** current owner of all four pieces of land, **who came** to own his land **on the basis of** purchase from **four** previous owners. **Admon holds** that the owner of the field **can say to** the current owner of the surrounding land: **Whichever way** you construe the case, **my path** to my field is somewhere **with you** in the surrounding land. **And the Rabbis hold** that the owner of the surrounding land can deflect this claim because **he can say to him: If you** do not press your claim and **are silent,** then **be silent,** and I will sell you a path at a reasonable price. **But if not,** and you insist on pressing your claim, then **I will return the bills** of purchase of the land **to their** previous **owners,**[N] **and** then **you will not be able to** successfully **engage in a legal dispute with them,** as each one could claim that the path went through one of the other pieces of land not owned by them.

NOTES

The verdict stands – קָם דִּינָא: The *Terumat HaDeshen* suggests a rationale for this opinion: At the time of the original verdict to split up the possessions, it is assumed that the parties accepted the verdict and gave up any rights to those possessions awarded to the other party. This is true even though they believe the verdict to have been in error. Therefore, it is obvious that they cannot come later and try to regain those rights. See the Jerusalem Talmud for further discussion of this topic. From the discussion there it would appear that in the case of the sons of *yavam*, they would be able to offer a claim based on a reconsideration of the original verdict.

I will return the bills of purchase of the land to their previous owners – מַהֲדַרְנָא שְׁטָרָא לְמָרַיְיהוּ: *Tosafot* ask: Why doesn't the field owner respond: True, if you actually return the surrounding land to the previous owners then I would not able to make a claim to my path; however, until you actually do so, my claim is valid and you should provide me with a path? The early commentaries answer that the statement of the owner of the surrounding land is not to be taken as a threat. Indeed, it is possible that the previous owners will not be interested in repurchasing the land. Rather, his statement is simply his way of highlighting the fact that the land was originally in the possession of four previous owners who could have easily deflected the field owner's claim to a path. He therefore claims that since they could have done so, and he purchased the land from them, he also has the right to do so (Ritva; *Nimmukei Yosef*).

PERSONALITIES

Admon – אַדְמוֹן: The Admon cited here is Admon ben Gaddai, one of the Sages of Jerusalem in the generation before the destruction of the Temple. Admon was one of two edict judges in Jerusalem who stood at the head of the city judges. It was their responsibility, and part of their authority, to establish amendments and pass permanent public edicts in matters of robbery or damages. Several halakhic rulings are presented in Admon's name in tractate *Ketubot* (108b–110a).

HALAKHA

One whose path to his field was lost – מִי שֶׁאָבְדָה דֶּרֶךְ שָׂדֵהוּ: With regard to one who owns a field and has the rights to a path leading to his field that passes through land belonging to another, and he traveled to a country overseas and when he returned the path to his field was lost, if the surrounding land currently belongs to a single owner and had always belonged to a single owner, then the field owner may demand that the owner of the surrounding land provide him with at least the shortest path to his field. This is in accordance with the conclusion of the Gemara that in such a case everyone agrees with the ruling of Admon. However, if the surrounding land is currently owned by numerous individuals, even if they purchased their pieces of land from a single previous owner, then the owner of the field has no right to claim a path, and if he wants one, he much purchase it. This is also the ruling if the land is currently owned by a single individual who purchased it from numerous previous owners. This is in accordance with the opinion of the Rabbis (Rambam *Sefer Mishpatim*, *Hilkhot To'en VeNitan* 15:11; *Shulḥan Arukh*, *Ḥoshen Mishpat* 178:1–2).

לימא רבי אבא דאמר כרבנן,

Having established the parameters of the dispute, the Gemara suggests: **Let us say** that the statement of **Rabbi Abba, who said** that the original verdict stands, **is in accordance with** the opinion of **the Rabbis.** When the owner of the field forgot where his path was located, the surrounding land was owned by four different owners, and therefore at that time the verdict was that he had no ability to successfully claim his path. The Rabbis apparently assume that that verdict stands, and therefore the field owner is considered to have lost any rights to the path. Consequently, even if the surrounding pieces of land are later purchased by a single person, the owner of the field cannot make a claim for his path.

ורבי ירמיה דאמר כאדמון?

The Gemara continues: **And** the statement of **Rabbi Yirmeya, who said** that the original verdict is repealed, **is in accordance with** the opinion of **Admon.** Admon apparently assumes that although the original verdict was that the field owner has no ability to successfully claim his path, nevertheless, that does not mean he loses his rights to the path. Rather, once the situation changes and the surrounding pieces of land are purchased by a single person, the original uncertainty is revived to allow him to make a claim for at least the shortest path to his field.

אמר לך רבי אבא: אנא דאמרי אפילו כאדמון. עד כאן לא קאמר אדמון התם – אלא משום דאמר ליה: ממה נפשך,

The Gemara rejects the comparison: **Rabbi Abba** could have **said to you: When I stated** my ruling, it was **even in accordance with** the opinion of **Admon. Admon states** his ruling **only there,** in the case of the lost path, **because** the field owner **said to** the owner of the surrounding land: **Whichever way you** look at it,

Perek **IV**
Daf **38** Amud **a**

דרכי חד גבך הוא, אבל הכא – מי איכא למימר הכי?

my one path is with you[N] in one of your pieces of land. Since his claim is based on facts that are clear and certain, his claim is successful. **However, here,** in the dispute over the inheritance, **is** the son of uncertain descent **able to state** a claim like **this?** Although the son of uncertain descent claims that ultimately, whatever the nature of his relationship with the deceased is, he should have the right to inherit, nevertheless, since it is not actually known what that relationship is, his claim in reality is merely a composite of uncertain claims.

ורבי ירמיה אמר לך: אנא דאמרי אפילו לרבנן, עד כאן לא קאמרי רבנן התם אלא משום דאמר ליה: אי שתקת – שתקת, ואי לא – מהדרנא שטרא למרייהו, ולא מצית לאשתעויי דינא בהדייהו. אבל הכא – מי איכא למימר הכי?

And Rabbi Yirmeya could have **said to you: I stated** my ruling **even in accordance with** the opinion of **the Rabbis,** since perhaps **the Rabbis state** their ruling **only there,** in the case of the lost path, **because** the owner of the surrounding land **said to** the field owner: **If you** do not press your claim and **are silent,** then **be silent** and I will sell you the path at a reasonable price; **but if not,** then **I will return the bills** of purchase of the pieces of land **to their** previous **owners and** then **you will not be able to** successfully **engage in a legal dispute with them.** He is successful with this claim because it is within his power to return the fields and thereby recreate the original circumstances in which the owner of the field would forfeit the path. **However, here, are** the sons of the *yavam* **able to state** a claim like **this?** The original circumstance, in which the inheritance of the deceased had still not been divided, cannot be recreated. Therefore, a claim based on that circumstance will be unsuccessful.

NOTES

My one path is with you – דרכי גבך היא: The commentary here is in accordance with the explanation of Rashi that the distinction between the two cases is whether or not the claim is definite or uncertain. Other commentaries suggest a different interpretation: The distinction lies in whether it is possible to offer a claim based on the current situation. In the case of the path, the field owner's claim is tendered irrespective of any dealings he had with the previous owners of the surrounding pieces of land; it is made against the current owner of the surrounding land based on his ownership of it. However, in the dispute over the inheritance, the claim relates to the original situation, before the inheritance was divided; a situation that no longer exists (Rid; Rabbi Avraham min HaHar).

סָפֵק וְיָבָם שֶׁבָּאוּ לַחֲלוֹק בְּנִכְסֵי סָבָא, סָפֵק אָמַר: הַאי גַּבְרָא בַּר מִיתְנָא הוּא, וּפַלְגָא דִּידִי הוּא. יָבָם אָמַר: אַתְּ בְּרַאי דִּידִי אַתְּ, וְלֵית לָךְ וְלָא מִידֵּי,

The Gemara brings another case, that of one of **uncertain** descent, who is either the son of the deceased or the son of the *yavam*, **and the *yavam* who came to divide up** the **possessions of the grandfather**,[H] i.e., the father of the *yavam* and the deceased, and each one made a claim to the inheritance. The son of **uncertain** descent **said: That man,** referring to himself, **is the son of the deceased, and** therefore **half** of the possessions **are mine** because the inheritance should be split between the two sons, i.e., the deceased and the *yavam*, and since I am the sole heir of the deceased, I should receive his portion. **The *yavam* said** to him: **You are my son, and** therefore **you have absolutely no** rights to the possessions; rather, I should receive all the inheritance. One half is mine because I am the grandfather's son, and the other half, which would have gone to my deceased brother, I should receive by virtue of the fact that I consummated the levirate marriage with his widow.

הָוֵי יָבָם וַדַּאי, וְסָפֵק סָפֵק – וְאֵין סָפֵק מוֹצִיא מִידֵי וַדַּאי.

The Gemara rules on this case: This is a case in which **the *yavam* has a definite** claim[N] because he is the grandfather's son, **and** the son of **uncertain** descent has only **an uncertain** claim, and the *halakha* is that one with **an uncertain claim cannot extract** property **from** one who has **a definite** claim to it. Therefore, the *yavam* receives all the inheritance.

סָפֵק וּבְנֵי יָבָם שֶׁבָּאוּ לַחֲלוֹק בְּנִכְסֵי סָבָא, סָפֵק אָמַר: הַהוּא גַּבְרָא בַּר מִיתְנָא הוּא, וּפַלְגָא דִּידִי הוּא. וּבְנֵי יָבָם אָמְרִי: אָחוּנָא אַתְּ, וּמְנָתָא אִית לָךְ בַּהֲדַן.

The Gemara raises yet another case, that of one of **uncertain** descent, who is either the son of the deceased or the son of the *yavam*, **and the sons of the *yavam* who came to divide up** the **possessions of the grandfather**,[H] and each one made a claim to the inheritance. The son of **uncertain** descent **said: That man,** referring to himself, **is the son of the deceased, and** therefore **half** of the possessions **are mine** because the inheritance should be split between the two sons, i.e., the deceased and the *yavam*, and since I am the lone heir of the deceased I should receive his portion. **And the sons of the *yavam* said: You are our brother, and** therefore **you** should **receive** only **a portion together with us.**

פַּלְגָא דְּקָמוֹדֵי לְהוּ – שָׁקְלִי, תִּילְתָּא דְּקָא מוֹדוּ לֵיהּ – שָׁקַל. פַּשׁ לְהוּ דַּנְקָא, הָוֵי מָמוֹן הַמּוּטָּל בְּסָפֵק – וְחוֹלְקִין.

The Gemara rules on this case: **The half** of the grandfather's possessions **that** the son of uncertain descent **concedes** belongs **to them,** the sons of the *yavam*, **they take** for themselves. By claiming to be the son of the brother who died first, he forfeits any rights to the other brother's portion. **The third** of the grandfather's possessions **that** the sons of the *yavam* **concede** belong **to him,** the son of uncertain descent, **he takes** for himself. By claiming he is their brother, they admit that he should at least receive an equal portion to them, which would mean one-third if they are three. This **leaves them** with **one-sixth** [***danka***][L] of the possessions that **is property of uncertain ownership, and** so **they** should **divide it up** between them.

HALAKHA

One of uncertain descent and the *yavam* with regard to the possessions of the grandfather – סָפֵק וְיָבָם בְּנִכְסֵי סָבָא: In a case where the *yavam* and one of uncertain descent, who is either the son of the deceased or the son of the *yavam*, came to divide up the possessions of the grandfather, i.e., the father of the *yavam*, and the son of uncertain descent claims that he is the son of the deceased and therefore a portion of the possessions should be awarded to him, his claim is not accepted and all of the property is awarded to the *yavam* (Rambam *Sefer Mishpatim, Hilkhot Naḥalot* 5:5; *Shulḥan Arukh, Even HaEzer* 163:6).

One of uncertain descent and the sons of the *yavam* with regard to the possessions of the grandfather – סָפֵק וּבְנֵי יָבָם בְּנִכְסֵי סָבָא: In a case in which the sons of the *yavam* and one of uncertain descent, who is either the son of the deceased or the son of the *yavam*, came to divide up the possessions of the grandfather, i.e., the father of the *yavam*, the portion that each party concedes to the other side is awarded to that side, and then the remaining possessions are divided up between them, half given to the son of uncertain descent and the other half divided between those who are definitely sons of the *yavam* (Rambam *Sefer Mishpatim, Hilkhot Naḥalot* 5:5; *Shulḥan Arukh, Even HaEzer* 163:7).

LANGUAGE

One-sixth [*danka*] – דַּנְקָא: *Danka* is a Persian monetary unit that appears in Middle Persian sources as dāng. This unit was equal to one-sixth of a dinar. The term was then borrowed to refer to one-sixth of anything, as in this passage.

NOTES

The *yavam* has a definite claim – הָוֵי יָבָם וַדַּאי: Rashi and Rivan explain that his claim is deemed to be definite because he will definitely receive at least some portion of the inheritance. Therefore, he is considered to have control over the property, and the son of uncertain descent, whose claim is uncertain, is not able to extract any of that property from him. *Tosafot* question Rashi's opinion: Why should the fact that he definitely has a right to a portion of the inheritance grant him control over all of it? *Tosafot* therefore reject Rashi's explanation and suggest that the *yavam* is considered to have a definite claim because he indisputably has the status of an heir of the deceased; the only question is how much of the inheritance he should receive. However, the son of uncertain descent may not be an heir at all. Therefore, since the very basis of his right to inherit is uncertain, it is inappropriate that he should receive anything in the presence of one who is certainly an heir. The *Arukh LaNer* defends Rashi's explanation. He suggests that with regard to inheritance, the fact that one has a definite right to part of an inheritance proves that ultimately he has the basis for a claim to all the inheritance. Therefore, his claim is considered to be definite.

סָבָא וְיָבָם בְּנִכְסֵי סָפֵק, אוֹ סָבָא וְסָפֵק בְּנִכְסֵי יָבָם –

The Gemara presents two additional cases. One is a case where a son of uncertain descent, who is either the son of the deceased or the son of the *yavam*, died, and **the grandfather and the *yavam*** come to divide up the **possessions of the** son of **uncertain** descent. In the absence of any children, a father inherits from his son. The grandfather claims that the son of uncertain descent was actually the son of the deceased, and since the deceased has already died, the grandfather should be next in line to inherit from him. The *yavam* claims that the son of uncertain descent was his own son, and therefore he should inherit from him. **Or,** the second case is one in which the *yavam* died and **the grandfather and the** son of **uncertain** descent[N] come to divide up the **possessions of the *yavam*.** The son of uncertain descent claims to be the lone son of the *yavam* and therefore he should inherit, whereas the grandfather claims that the son of uncertain descent was the son of the deceased and that the *yavam* died childless, and therefore the grandfather, who is the father of the *yavam*, should inherit from him.

הֲוֵי מָמוֹן הַמּוּטָּל בְּסָפֵק, וְחוֹלְקִין.

The Gemara rules in these cases: This **is** a case of **property of uncertain ownership, and** so **they** should **divide up** the possessions between them.[H]

מתני׳ שׁוֹמֶרֶת יָבָם שֶׁנָּפְלוּ לָהּ נְכָסִים, מוֹדִים בֵּית שַׁמַּאי וּבֵית הִלֵּל שֶׁמּוֹכֶרֶת וְנוֹתֶנֶת וְקַיָּים.

MISHNA With regard to **a widow waiting for her *yavam***[N] to either consummate a levirate marriage or perform *ḥalitza* with her, i.e., a *yevama*, **to whom property was bequeathed:**[H] **Beit Shammai and Beit Hillel** both **agree that she may sell or give** away that property *ab initio*, **and** that if she did, the transfer **is valid.** Since she has only a levirate bond with the *yavam*, she retains total control of the property. This is in contrast to a betrothed woman, concerning whom Beit Hillel rule that she may not sell such property because her betrothed also has rights to it (*Ketubot* 78a).

מֵתָה – מָה יֵעָשֶׂה בִּכְתוּבָּתָהּ וּבִנְכָסִים הַנִּכְנָסִים וְיוֹצְאִין עִמָּהּ? בֵּית שַׁמַּאי אוֹמְרִים: יַחֲלוֹקוּ יוֹרְשֵׁי הַבַּעַל עִם יוֹרְשֵׁי הָאָב, וּבֵית הִלֵּל אוֹמְרִים: נְכָסִים בְּחֶזְקָתָן: כְּתוּבָּה בְּחֶזְקַת יוֹרְשֵׁי הַבַּעַל, נְכָסִים הַנִּכְנָסִים וְיוֹצְאִין עִמָּהּ בְּחֶזְקַת יוֹרְשֵׁי הָאָב.

If she **died, what should be done with** the money assured to her in **her marriage contract** by her deceased husband **and with** her **property that enters and leaves** the marriage **with her,** in which a husband only ever has a usufructuary interest?[H] **Beit Shammai say: The husband's heirs,** i.e., the *yavam*, who stands to inherit from the husband when he consummates the levirate marriage, **should divide up** the property **together with** her **father's heirs,** i.e., the woman's family. **And Beit Hillel say:** The **property** retains **its** previous ownership **status.**[N] Therefore, money assured to her in her **marriage contract** remains **in the possession of the husband's heirs.** Since it was to be paid from the husband's own property, the money is retained by his estate and passes to his heirs. And her **property that enters and leaves** the marriage **with her** remains **in the possession of the father's heirs.** Since those properties belonged to her, upon her death they are inherited by her father or his heirs.

NOTES

The grandfather and the son of uncertain descent – סָבָא וְסָפֵק: The grandfather in this case is unquestionably the father of the *yavam*; it is only the son whose identity is uncertain. If so, ostensibly, this is an additional case in which one party, in this case the grandfather, has a definite claim to the inheritance, whereas the other party, in this case the son of uncertain descent, has only an uncertain claim. Why, then, does the Gemara not adduce the *halakha* it cited above that in such cases the inheritance is awarded to the party with the definite claim? The early commentaries explain that whenever one is survived by a son, the other relatives are not considered to have the status of heirs at all. Therefore, although the grandfather's identity is unquestioned, his status as an heir is uncertain. Since both parties have equally uncertain claims, the possessions are divided between them (see Rid and Ramban).

A widow waiting for her *yavam* – שׁוֹמֶרֶת יָבָם: The Hebrew term for this woman is a *shomeret yavam*. The root *sh-m-r* usually denotes the concept of guarding. However, Rashi here and elsewhere notes that in this context the word denotes waiting, in this case for her *yavam*. Rashi cites proof for this from other instances in the Gemara (*Ketubot* 62b) and the Bible (Genesis 37:11; see *Tosefot Yom Tov*).

The property retains its previous ownership status – נְכָסִים בְּחֶזְקָתָן: According to this version of the mishna's text, which is the version cited by the *ge'onim*, it would appear that Beit Hillel first present a principle: The property retains its previous ownership status, and then proceed to demonstrate its application to the marriage contract and to the property that enters and leaves the marriage with her. This version does not mention explicitly what should be done with guaranteed property, i.e., property that the wife brings with her into the marriage that is explicitly recorded in the marriage contract and whose value the husband guarantees will be returned to her in the event of payment of the marriage contract. However, since such property is written as part of the marriage contract, it is assumed that it is treated in the same way as the marriage contract itself. This is how Rabbeinu Tam, the Rashba, and many other early commentaries rule.

Other early commentaries have a different version of the mishna's text that states: The property retains its previous ownership status and the marriage contract remains in the possession of the husband's heirs. The addition of the conjunctive: And, before: The marriage contract, indicates that the *halakha* cited concerning the marriage contract is not an elaboration of a previous principle but a new case. Accordingly, the opening clause: The property retains its previous ownership status, should not be taken as a principle but as an independent case. Therefore, according to this version the mishna actually presents three different cases: First it states what should be done with: The property, which is a reference to her guaranteed property; then it states what should be done with her marriage contract, which refers to both its principal value and any additional sums the husband may have promised; and finally it states what should be done with her property that enters and leaves the marriage with her. Although this version does explicitly make reference to her guaranteed property, it does not state what precisely should be done with it. However, the Gemara elsewhere (see *Bava Batra* 158a) elaborates on this point and rules that the property should be split between the parties. This is how Rashi on *Ketubot* 80a explains the mishna, and the Rambam rules accordingly.

HALAKHA

The grandfather and the *yavam*, the grandfather and the son of uncertain descent – סָבָא וְיָבָם, סָבָא וְסָפֵק: If a son of uncertain descent, who is either the son of the deceased or the son of the *yavam*, died, and the grandfather claims that the son of uncertain descent was actually the son of the deceased, and so the grandfather should inherit from him, and the *yavam* claims that the son of uncertain descent was his own son, and so he should inherit from him, then they should divide up the possessions equally between them. The same *halakha* would apply if the *yavam* died and the grandfather and the son of uncertain descent both claimed the possessions of the *yavam* (Rambam *Sefer Mishpatim, Hilkhot Naḥalot* 5:5; *Shulḥan Arukh, Even HaEzer* 163:8).

A widow waiting for her *yavam* to whom property was bequeathed – שׁוֹמֶרֶת יָבָם שֶׁנָּפְלוּ לָהּ נְכָסִים: If a widow waiting for her *yavam* is bequeathed property after she already happened before the *yavam* for levirate marriage, she is in full possession of that property; she may sell or give away the property *ab initio*. The Ran rules that this is the *halakha* even if the *yavam* had performed levirate betrothal with her (Rambam *Sefer Mishpatim, Hilkhot Naḥalot* 3:10 and *Sefer Nashim, Hilkhot Ishut* 22:10; *Shulḥan Arukh, Even HaEzer* 160:5).

Inheritance of a widow waiting for her *yavam* – יְרוּשַּׁת שׁוֹמֶרֶת יָבָם: If a widow waiting for her *yavam* dies, her heirs inherit the property that enters and leaves the marriage with her, and the husband's heirs inherit the money assured to her in the marriage contract. With regard to her guaranteed property, some say it is divided up equally between her heirs and her husband's heirs (Rashi; Rambam). Others say that the guaranteed property is awarded to the husband's heirs (Rabbeinu Tam; Rosh). Even according to the first opinion, if the husband's heirs had already taken control of the property, it is not to be removed from their possession (Ran). Some rule that in places where the custom is always to perform *ḥalitza* and never to allow levirate marriage, the husband's heirs gain no entitlement to the property (Rema, citing Maharik; Rambam *Sefer Nashim, Hilkhot Ishut* 22:10; *Shulḥan Arukh, Even HaEzer* 160:7).

כְּנָסָהּ – הֲרֵי הִיא כְּאִשְׁתּוֹ לְכׇל דָּבָר, וּבִלְבַד שֶׁתְּהֵא כְּתוּבָּה עַל נִכְסֵי בַעְלָהּ הָרִאשׁוֹן.

If the *yavam* **consummated the levirate marriage with her, then** her legal status is **that of his wife**[H] **in every sense,** and therefore the *yavam* has the same rights to her property as in a regular marriage. **And** the **only** exception to this is **that** her **marriage contract will** still **be** payable **from the property of her first husband**[H] and not from the property of the *yavam*.

גמ׳ מַאי שְׁנָא רֵישָׁא דְּלָא פְּלִיגִי, וּמַאי שְׁנָא סֵיפָא דִּפְלִיגִי?

GEMARA The Gemara asks: **What is different** about **the first clause,** concerning a *yevama* who is still alive, **that** Beit Shammai **do not disagree** with Beit Hillel that the woman has full possession of the property since there is only a levirate bond but no marriage, **and what is different** about **the latter clause that** Beit Shammai **disagree** with Beit Hillel and rule that the *yavam* does take a share of the property, which would imply that the levirate bond alone is sufficient to afford the *yavam* rights over her property?[N]

אָמַר עוּלָּא: רֵישָׁא – דְּנָפְלָה כְּשֶׁהִיא אֲרוּסָה, וְסֵיפָא – דְּנָפְלָה כְּשֶׁהִיא נְשׂוּאָה.

Ulla said: The two clauses concern different cases: **The first clause** concerns a case **where she happened** before her *yavam* for levirate marriage at a time **when she was a betrothed woman**[N] and only then did she come into the possession of property. Since when she was betrothed her husband did not have any rights to the property, neither does the *yavam*. **And the latter clause** concerns a case **where she happened** before her *yavam* at a time **when she was a married woman.** In such a case, were her husband still alive, he would have full rights to the property; therefore, so does the *yavam*.

וְקָסָבַר עוּלָּא: זִיקַת אֲרוּסָה – עוֹשָׂה סָפֵק אֲרוּסָה,

The Gemara explains: **And Ulla holds** that a levirate **bond** formed **with a betrothed woman affords** her a status equivalent to **a woman** about whom there is an **uncertainty** whether she is **betrothed,**[N]

HALAKHA

If the *yavam* consummated the levirate marriage with her then her legal status is that of his wife – כְּנָסָהּ הֲרֵי הִיא כְּאִשְׁתּוֹ: If a *yavam* consummated a levirate marriage with his *yevama*, then her legal status is that of his wife in every sense and he is able to separate from her only by means of a bill of divorce; afterward, if he wishes, he may remarry her (Rambam *Sefer Nashim*, *Hilkhot Ishut* 22:10; *Shulḥan Arukh*, *Even HaEzer* 168:1).

Her marriage contract is payable from the property of her first husband – כְּתוּבָּה עַל נִכְסֵי בַעְלָהּ הָרִאשׁוֹן: The marriage contract that a *yavam* gives to his *yevama* has to be paid only from the possessions he inherits from her first husband (Rambam *Sefer Nashim*, *Hilkhot Ishut* 22:10 and *Hilkhot Yibbum* 1:1; *Shulḥan Arukh*, *Even HaEzer* 166:4, 168:3).

NOTES

Interpretations of the mishna – פֵּירוּשֵׁי הַמִּשְׁנָה: The Gemara presents four different interpretations of the mishna in the name of Ulla, Rabba, Abaye, and Rava. The commentaries discuss the principal differences between the various opinions, as well as the question of which opinion was accepted as the *halakha*. In a responsum, Rav Hai Gaon claims that all of the opinions here are only explications of Beit Shammai's opinion. Accordingly, the entire talmudic discussion is irrelevant to the *halakha* since the *halakha* is in accordance with the opinion of Beit Hillel recorded in the mishna (see Ramban).

Where she happened before her *yavam* when she was a betrothed woman – דְּנָפְלָה כְּשֶׁהִיא אֲרוּסָה: This version of the Gemara text, which is also the version cited by Rashi, states: Where she happened. Accordingly, the mishna concerns a case where the property fell to her only after her husband had already died and she was awaiting levirate marriage. The distinction between the clauses lies in the strength of the levirate bond, which is dependent upon her status when her husband died. The *ge'onim*, however, had an alternate version that states: Where they fell to her, with the word they being a reference to the property. According to this version, the property fell to her when she was still married to her previous husband, and the distinction between the cases is due to whether her husband gained ownership of that property. If she was already married at the time, then when the property fell to her, her husband instantly gained rights to it, and those rights will pass over to the *yavam*. However, if she was still only betrothed to her husband at the time, the property would remain fully in her possession (see Rashba and Ritva).

Affords her a status equivalent to a woman about whom there is an uncertainty whether she is betrothed – עוֹשָׂה סָפֵק אֲרוּסָה: Rashi questions why it is necessary to afford her such a status; in truth, the *yavam* has no rights to property that is bequeathed to his *yevama* while she is still awaiting levirate marriage. Accordingly, the Gemara could have simply stated: A levirate bond formed with a betrothed woman is nothing. Rashi explains that the Gemara avoided describing her levirate bond in this way because doing so could have given the incorrect impression that there is no levirate bond at all and that she does not even require *ḥalitza*. By describing the bond in the way it did, the Gemara clarifies that although the bond indeed exists, nevertheless it does not afford the *yavam* with any rights.

The Rashba takes issue with Rashi's assertion that the *yavam* has no rights to her property. See his commentary for a resolution of Rashi's opinion He notes that in the mishna in *Ketubot* 78a, Beit Hillel rule that a betrothed woman may not sell property that was bequeathed to her *ab initio* because her husband also has rights to it. As such, it is clear why the Gemara could not have stated: The levirate bond is nothing, because were she to have already come into the possession of the property while betrothed to her previous husband, the levirate bond formed with the *yavam* would also prevent her from selling that property *ab initio*.

זִיקַת נְשׂוּאָה עוֹשָׂה סָפֵק נְשׂוּאָה.

and a levirate **bond** formed **with a married woman affords** her a status equivalent to that of **a woman** for whom there is an **uncertainty** whether she is **married,** i.e., when her husband dies, the same level of relationship that existed with the first husband is created with the *yavam*. However, since the new relationship exists only by virtue of a levirate bond, it exists to a lower degree, and so the rights afforded to the *yavam* are more limited than those the first husband would have enjoyed; the rights granted to the *yavam* are equivalent to the rights of husband in a case where there is uncertainty whether that level of relationship exists at all.

זִיקַת אֲרוּסָה עוֹשָׂה סָפֵק אֲרוּסָה, דְּאִי סָלְקָא דַעְתָּךְ וַדַּאי אֲרוּסָה – מוֹדִים בֵּית הִלֵּל שֶׁמּוֹכֶרֶת וְנוֹתֶנֶת וְקַיָּים?!

The Gemara proceeds to demonstrate this: It must be that a levirate **bond** formed **with a betrothed woman affords** her a status equivalent to that of **a woman** for whom there is an **uncertainty** whether she is **betrothed, because if it enters your mind** to suggest that her status is equivalent to that of **a definitely betrothed woman, would Beit Hillel concede that she may sell or give** away her property *ab initio*, **and that** if she does the transfer **is valid?**

וְהָתְנַן: נָפְלוּ לָהּ נְכָסִים מִשֶּׁנִּתְאָרְסָה, בֵּית שַׁמַּאי אוֹמְרִים: תִּמְכּוֹר, וּבֵית הִלֵּל אוֹמְרִים: לֹא תִּמְכּוֹר. אֵלּוּ וְאֵלּוּ מוֹדִים שֶׁאִם מָכְרָה וְנָתְנָה – קַיָּים. אֶלָּא שְׁמַע מִינָּהּ: זִיקַת אֲרוּסָה – עוֹשָׂה סָפֵק אֲרוּסָה.

But didn't we learn in a mishna (*Ketubot* 78a): If **property was bequeathed to** a woman **after she was betrothed,**[H] **Beit Shammai say: She may sell** that property, **and Beit Hillel say: She may not sell** that property. However, **both agree that if she sold** it **or gave** it away, the transfer **is valid.** The mishna clearly states that according to Beit Hillel, a woman who is definitely betrothed may not sell the property *ab initio*. **Rather, conclude from here,** from the fact that here Beit Hillel permit the *yevama* to sell her property *ab initio*, that a levirate **bond** formed **with a betrothed woman affords** her a status equivalent to that of **a woman** for whom there is an **uncertainty** whether she is **betrothed.**

זִיקַת נְשׂוּאָה עוֹשָׂה סָפֵק נְשׂוּאָה, דְּאִי סָלְקָא דַעְתָּךְ וַדַּאי נְשׂוּאָה בֵּית שַׁמַּאי אוֹמְרִים יַחֲלוֹקוּ יוֹרְשֵׁי הַבַּעַל עִם יוֹרְשֵׁי הָאָב?!

Similarly, it must be that a levirate **bond** formed **with a married woman affords** her a status equivalent to that of **a woman** for whom there is an **uncertainty** whether she is **married, because if it enters your mind** to suggest that her status is equivalent to that of **a definitely married woman,** would **Beit Shammai say** that **the husband's heirs should divide up** the property **together with the father's heirs?**

וְהָתְנַן: נָפְלוּ לָהּ נְכָסִים מִשֶּׁנִּשֵּׂאת – אֵלּוּ וְאֵלּוּ מוֹדִים שֶׁאִם מָכְרָה וְנָתְנָה שֶׁהַבַּעַל מוֹצִיא מִיַּד הַלָּקוֹחוֹת. אֶלָּא שְׁמַע מִינָּהּ: זִיקַת נְשׂוּאָה עוֹשָׂה סָפֵק נְשׂוּאָה.

But didn't we learn in a mishna (*Ketubot* 78a): If **property was bequeathed to** a woman **after she was married,**[H] **both** Beit Hillel and Beit Shammai **agree that if she sold** the property **or gave** it away, then **the husband repossesses** it **from the purchasers. Rather, conclude from here,** from the fact that here Beit Shammai assume the rights of the *yavam* are limited, that a levirate **bond** formed **with a married woman affords** her a status equivalent to **a woman** for whom there is an **uncertainty** whether she is **married.**

אֲמַר לֵיהּ רַבָּה: אַדְּמִפַּלְגִי בְּגוּפָהּ וּלְאַחַר מִיתָה, לִפְלְגוּ בְּחַיֶּיהָ וּלְפֵירוֹת!

Rabba challenges Ulla's understanding of the mishna: **Rabba said to him:** If your explanation is correct, then in the latter clause, **instead of disagreeing** with regard to who has the rights to the property **itself,** which necessitates considering the case **after** her **death, let** Beit Hillel and Beit Shammai **disagree with regard to** the more immediate case **when she is** still **alive and** dispute who has the rights **to** the use and **produce**[N] of the property.

HALAKHA

A betrothed woman's property – נִכְסֵי אֲרוּסָה: A betrothed woman may not sell property belonging to her *ab initio*, but if she does so, the sale is valid (Rambam *Sefer Nashim, Hilkhot Ishut* 22:8; *Shulḥan Arukh, Even HaEzer* 90:11, 160:5).

A married woman's property – נִכְסֵי נְשׂוּאָה: If a married woman sold her property of which the husband has a usufructuary interest, even if that property fell to her as an inheritance prior to her betrothal, then her husband continues to have rights to the use of that property as long as they are married. If she dies, he may also repossess the property from the buyer and need not compensate the buyer monetarily. Some (*Tur*; Rosh) say that he may repossess the property even while she is still alive (Rambam *Sefer Nashim, Hilkhot Ishut* 22:7; *Shulḥan Arukh, Even HaEzer* 90:9).

NOTES

Let them disagree with regard to the case when she is alive and dispute the rights to the produce – לִפְלְגוּ בְּחַיֶּיהָ וּלְפֵירוֹת: The early commentaries already note that this is certainly not the halakhic conclusion, as it is undisputed that the *halakha* is that before he consummates the levirate marriage the *yavam* has no rights to the use and produce of the property of the *yevama* (see Rashba). Rather, this statement of Rabba is only in accordance with the opinion of Ulla (see *Yosef Lekaḥ*).

אֶלָּא אֲמַר רַבָּה: אִידִי וְאִידִי דְּנָפְלָה כְּשֶׁהִיא נְשׂוּאָה, וְזִיקַת נְשׂוּאָה – עוֹשָׂה סָפֵק נְשׂוּאָה. רֵישָׁא דְּאִיהִי קַיְּימָא – הָוְה לָהּ אִיהִי וַדַּאי וְאִינְהוּ סָפֵק וְאֵין סָפֵק מוֹצִיא מִידֵי וַדַּאי.

Rather, Rabba said a different resolution to the apparent inconsistency in Beit Shammai's rulings: Both **this** first clause **and that** latter clause of the mishna concern a case in **which she happened** before her *yavam* for levirate marriage **once she was** already **a married woman, and** a levirate **bond** formed **with a married woman affords** her a status equivalent to that of **a woman** about whom there is an **uncertainty** whether she is **married.** The distinction between the two clauses is as follows: In the **first clause, where she is alive, she has a certain** claim to the property, **while they,** i.e., the *yavam,* are considered to have only **an uncertain claim** to the property, as she has the status of a woman for whom there is an uncertainty whether she is married. **And** since one who has **an uncertain claim cannot extract** property **from** one who has **a definite** claim to it,[N] she therefore retains full possession of the property.

סֵיפָא דְּמֵתָה – הַלָּלוּ בָּאִין לִירַשׁ וְהַלָּלוּ בָּאִין לִירַשׁ, וְיַחֲלוֹקוּ.

In **the latter clause,** however, **where she died,** neither party has a definite claim; rather, **these** heirs of the father **come to inherit, and those** heirs of the husband **come to inherit, and** therefore **they should divide up** the property.

אֵיתִיבֵיהּ אַבַּיֵי: וּלְבֵית שַׁמַּאי אֵין סָפֵק מוֹצִיא מִידֵי וַדַּאי?! וְהָתְנַן: נָפַל הַבַּיִת עָלָיו וְעַל אָבִיו, עָלָיו וְעַל מוֹרִישָׁיו, וְהָיוּ עָלָיו כְּתוּבַּת אִשָּׁה וּבַעַל חוֹב,

Abaye raised an objection to Rabba's opinion: **But** is it true that **according to Beit Shammai,** one with **an uncertain claim cannot extract** property **from** one who has **a definite** claim to it? **Didn't we learn** in a mishna (*Bava Batra* 157a): In a case where **a house collapsed upon** a person **and upon his father,**[H] or **upon him and upon those** from **whom he stood to inherit, and there were** outstanding debts **against** that person from his **wife's marriage contract and** to **a creditor,** but he had no money with which to pay those debts, and it is not known who died first, the following situation arises: If the father died first, then before the son died he had already inherited the father's property and therefore the son's creditors gained a lien over that property and have the rights to collect their debts from that property even after the son's death.

יוֹרְשֵׁי הָאָב אוֹמְרִים: הַבֵּן מֵת רִאשׁוֹן וְאַחַר כָּךְ מֵת הָאָב. וּבַעַל חוֹב אוֹמֵר: הָאָב מֵת רִאשׁוֹן וְאַחַר כָּךְ מֵת הַבֵּן,

Accordingly, the father's heirs and the creditor offer opposing claims: **The father's heirs say: The son died first and** only **afterward the father died.** Therefore, the creditor never gained any rights to collect from the property. **And the creditor says: The father died first and** only **afterward the son died.** Therefore, the father's property was liened to the son's debts, and the creditor has a right to collect.

בֵּית שַׁמַּאי אוֹמְרִים: יַחֲלוֹקוּ, וּבֵית הִלֵּל אוֹמְרִים: נְכָסִים בְּחֶזְקָתָן.

The mishna continues: **Beit Shammai say: They should divide up** the property between them. **And Beit Hillel say:** The **property** retains **its** previous ownership **status,** which in this case means that since the last known possessor was the father, so the father's heirs gain full rights to it.

וְהָא הָכָא, יוֹרְשֵׁי הָאָב – וַדַּאי, וּבַעַל חוֹב – סָפֵק, וְקָאָתֵי סָפֵק וּמוֹצִיא מִידֵי וַדַּאי!

Abaye explains his proof: **Isn't** it the case **here** that **the father's heirs** have a **definite** claim **and the creditor** has only **an uncertain** claim? Therefore, since Beit Shammai rule that the property should be divided up, it is apparent that they hold that one with **an uncertain claim can extract** property **from** one who has **a definite** claim to it.

NOTES

One who has an uncertain claim cannot extract property from one who has a definite claim to it – אֵין סָפֵק מוֹצִיא מִידֵי וַדַּאי: The Gemara discusses this principle in tractate *Pesaḥim* (9a) and suggests based on various sources that an uncertainty can override even a certainty. One example given is that of one who leaned over a pit, and it is known that at some point a corpse lay at the bottom of the pit. If the corpse was still there when he leaned over the pit, then he would be rendered ritually impure. However, there is uncertainty whether the corpse is in fact still there, since an animal may have dragged it away. The existence of that uncertainty is sufficient to undermine the certainty that there was a corpse there, and accordingly the person who leaned over the pit may be deemed ritually pure (see the Gemara there).

Why, then, does the Gemara here state unequivocally that an uncertainty cannot override a certainty? It would seem that with regard to monetary claims the *halakha* is different, due to the principle that the burden of proof rests upon the claimant. The later authorities explain that in the case in the Gemara here, although the woman presents a definite claim, since her status is uncertain that impacts her claim and prevents her from being able to lay claim to the property.

HALAKHA

A house collapsed upon a person and upon his father – נָפַל הַבַּיִת עָלָיו וְעַל אָבִיו: If a house collapsed upon a person and his father or anyone else from whom he stood to inherit, and it was unknown whether that person or his father died first, and there were outstanding debts against that person from his wife's marriage contract and to a creditor, this gives rise to the following situation: The father's heirs can claim that the son died first and since he had no properties of his own any debts against him became void, and the wife and the creditors can claim that the father died first, and so the son inherited from him before dying, and they therefore have a right to collect their debts from that money. The *halakha* in this case is that the property remains in the possession of the father's heirs, and the burden of proof rests upon the wife and the creditors. This ruling is in accordance with the opinion of Beit Hillel (Rambam *Sefer Mishpatim, Hilkhot Naḥalot* 5:8; *Shulḥan Arukh, Ḥoshen Mishpat* 280:12).

קָסָבְרִי בֵּית שַׁמַּאי: שְׁטָר הָעוֹמֵד לִגְבּוֹת כִּגְבוּי דָּמֵי.

Rabba rejects the proof: Beit Shammai's ruling in this case cannot be adduced as a proof because **Beit Shammai hold:** A debt recorded in **a bill of** debt **that is awaiting collection**[N] **is as though it was already collected** to the extent that the creditor is considered to be in possession of the debt. Therefore, the creditor is considered to be in possession of the property to the same extent as the father's heirs; consequently, the property is divided between them.

וּמְנָא תֵּימְרָא – דִּתְנַן: מֵתוּ בַּעֲלֵיהֶן עַד שֶׁלֹּא שָׁתוּ, בֵּית שַׁמַּאי אוֹמְרִים: נוֹטְלוֹת כְּתוּבָּתָן וְאֵינָן שׁוֹתוֹת, וּבֵית הִלֵּל אוֹמְרִים: אוֹ שׁוֹתוֹת אוֹ לֹא נוֹטְלוֹת כְּתוּבָּתָן.

And from where do you say that Beit Shammai hold this opinion? **As we learned** in a mishna (*Sota* 24a): A married woman who secluded herself with another man after her husband had warned her not to do so is suspected of having committed adultery. To establish her guilt or innocence she is brought to the Temple, where she drinks the bitter waters. With regard to such women, if **their husbands died before they drank**[H] the bitter waters, **Beit Shammai say: They collect** the money assured to them in **their marriage contracts and do not drink** the waters. **And Beit Hillel say: Either they drink,** and if they survive they collect their marriage contracts, **or** they do not drink and **they cannot collect their marriage contracts,** and all the husband's property passes to his heirs.

אוֹ שׁוֹתוֹת?! "וְהֵבִיא הָאִישׁ אֶת אִשְׁתּוֹ" אָמַר רַחֲמָנָא, וְלֵיכָּא! אֶלָּא: מִתּוֹךְ שֶׁלֹּא שׁוֹתוֹת לֹא נוֹטְלוֹת כְּתוּבָּתָן.

The Gemara clarifies the statement of Beit Hillel: Did Beit Hillel really mean: **Either they drink,** which implies they may actually choose to drink? But doesn't **the Merciful One state: "And the man shall bring his wife"** (Numbers 5:15), which indicates that the ritual of drinking the bitter waters applies only when the husband is still alive, **and** in this case **there is no** husband to do so; consequently, she should not be able to drink. **Rather,** Beit Hillel's intent is as follows: The only means by which a suspected adulteress is able to collect her marriage contract is by drinking the bitter waters and proving her innocence. Therefore, where this is not possible due to the death of the husband, **since** the wives **do not drink, they cannot collect their marriage contracts.**

וְהָא הָכָא, דִּסְפֵק הוּא, סָפֵק זַנַּאי סָפֵק לֹא זַנַּאי, וְקָאָתֵי סָפֵק וּמוֹצִיא מִידֵי וַדַּאי! אֶלָּא שְׁמַע מִינָּהּ: שְׁטָר הָעוֹמֵד לִגְבּוֹת כִּגְבוּי דָּמֵי.

Rabba explains his proof from this mishna: **Isn't** it the case **here that** the wife's claim to her marriage contract **is uncertain** because there is **uncertainty whether she was unfaithful or whether she was not unfaithful, and** so it would appear that one with **an uncertain** claim **is coming and undermining** the **definite** claim of the husband's heirs? This is untenable, as even were one to hold that someone with an uncertain claim can extract property from someone who has a definite claim to it, that would only allow for the money to be divided between the two sides, whereas in this case Beit Shammai rule that the creditor collects the entire debt. **Rather, conclude from** that mishna that Beit Shammai hold that a debt recorded in **a bill of** debt **that is awaiting collection is** considered **as though it were already collected** to the extent that the one who is owed the money is considered to be in possession of the debt. It is due to this reason that she is empowered to be able to collect her marriage contract.

וְאַבַּיֵי, לוֹתְבֵיהּ מֵהָא! דִּלְמָא כְּתוּבַּת אִשָּׁה שָׁאנֵי, מִשּׁוּם חִינָּא.

The Gemara asks: **And** why did **Abaye** object to Rabba's opinion based on the mishna in tractate *Bava Batra*? **Let him object to** Rabba's opinion **based on this**[N] mishna in tractate *Sota* since based on Abaye's assumption that a bill of debt is not considered as though it were already collected, this mishna perforce demonstrates that Beit Shammai hold that one with an uncertain claim can extract property from one who has a definite claim to it. The Gemara answers: Abaye did not object based on this mishna because he reasoned that **perhaps a woman's marriage contract is different** from a regular bill of debt in that the Sages uniquely reinforced a woman's hold over the debt in her marriage contract **due to** the increased **desirability**[N] that this would bring her when trying to remarry. This would ensure that she would bring some money with her into a new marriage.

NOTES

A bill of debt that is awaiting collection, etc. – שְׁטָר הָעוֹמֵד לִגְבּוֹת וכו׳: Rav Hai Gaon raises a difficulty with Rabba's claim. Even if one concedes that in general a bill of debt that is awaiting collection is considered as though it was already collected, it is unreasonable to apply that principle in a case such as this, where the son did not have any property. Therefore, he claims that the Gemara's question was not resolved by the Gemara.

And Abaye, let him object to Rabba's opinion based on this – וְאַבַּיֵי לוֹתְבֵיהּ מֵהָא: Rashi explains that the Gemara's difficulty is with the fact that Abaye raised his objection from a mishna in tractate *Bava Batra*, a tractate in the order of *Nezikin*, when he could have raised his objection from a mishna in tractate *Sota*, which, like tractate *Yevamot*, is in the order of *Nashim*. *Tosafot Yeshanim* explain differently: Since the Gemara had not yet demonstrated that according to Beit Shammai a document awaiting collection is considered as though it is already collected, the mishna in tractate *Sota* presents a more immediate difficulty: Why indeed should those women receive their marriage contracts, since isn't it the *halakha* that one with an uncertain claim cannot extract property from one who has a definite claim to it?

Tosafot note further that in any case the mishna proves difficult for Abaye's opinion because it states that she receives the entire marriage contract, whereas according to Abaye, Beit Shammai should hold that she should receive only half (see *Tosefot HaRosh*). *Tosafot* suggest that since the woman is able to present a definite claim that she was not unfaithful, whereas her relatives' claims are only uncertain, she is therefore in a stronger position and so she is awarded her entire marriage contract. Ramban offers an additional answer: Since Beit Shammai hold that one with an uncertain claim can extract property from one who has a definite claim to it, it would appear that they regard an uncertain claim to be like a definite claim. Therefore, it is possible that one follows the principle that unless proven otherwise, one presumes the original status remains unchanged and therefore one should presume the woman was not unfaithful. Consequently, she should receive the entire value of her marriage contract. It is also possible that Abaye holds that the mishna in tractate *Sota* does not actually mean that she collects the entire marriage contract but only that she collects from it; she would never actually receive more than half.

Due to desirability – מִשּׁוּם חִינָּא: *Tosafot* on *Ketubot* 84a cite the explanation of Rabbeinu Ḥananel that reinforcing the marriage contract makes women more attractive to men since it ensures that a woman will bring some money with her into a new marriage. Rashi on *Ketubot* 84a and *Arakhin* 22a suggests a different explanation: Reinforcing the marriage contract is not designed to make women more desirable to men but to make the institution of marriage more desirable to women. The existence of a strong marriage contract reduces the likelihood that the husband will divorce the wife without careful consideration, as the divorce would create a financial burden upon him.

This explanation would appear to assume that a woman is reluctant to marry and the Sages therefore needed to take steps to encourage her. However, this would seem to contradict another statement of the Sages that a woman wishes to marry as she cannot bear to be alone (*Kiddushin* 41a), and based on this concept the Sages ruled that a marriage contract is collected from the husband's lowest-quality possessions in order to make the institution of marriage more appealing to men. *Tosafot* raise this difficulty to Rashi's opinion but claim that it does not pose a full refutation because one cannot draw comparisons between different rabbinic decrees. The reason for this is that often, in one instance the Sages will favor one party while in another instance they may favor the other party.

HALAKHA

Their husbands died before they drank – מֵתוּ בַּעֲלֵיהֶן עַד שֶׁלֹּא שָׁתוּ: If a woman secluded herself with another man after her husband had warned her not to do so and her husband then died, she may not drink the bitter waters and does not receive her marriage contract. This is in accordance with the opinion of Beit Hillel, according to the conclusion of the Gemara (Rambam *Sefer Nashim*, *Hilkhot Sota* 2:7).

וְלוֹתְבֵיהּ כְּתוּבָּה דְּמַתְנִיתִין!

The Gemara asks again concerning Abaye's decision to object to Rabba's opinion based on the mishna in *Bava Batra*: **Let him object to** Rabba's opinion **based on** the case of the **marriage contract in the mishna** here (38a). In its latter clause, the mishna states that if a widow waiting for her *yavam* dies, Beit Shammai rule that her marriage contract and other property are divided between her father's heirs and the *yavam*. In that case, the *yavam* has certain possession of that property, and the father's heirs come with an uncertain claim to collect the value of the marriage contract. The fact that Beit Shammai rule that they should divide up the value of the marriage contract between them demonstrates that they hold that one with an uncertain claim can extract property from one who has a definite claim to it.

לָא פְּלִיגִי. וְלָא? וְהָא קָתָנֵי: מֵתָה, מַה יַּעֲשֶׂה בִּכְתוּבָּתָהּ וּבִנְכָסִים הַנִּכְנָסִים וְיוֹצְאִין עִמָּהּ? בֵּית שַׁמַּאי אוֹמְרִים: יַחֲלוֹקוּ יוֹרְשֵׁי הַבַּעַל עִם יוֹרְשֵׁי הָאָב, וּבֵית הִלֵּל אוֹמְרִים: נְכָסִים בְּחֶזְקָתָן!

The Gemara responds: In truth, Beit Shammai **do not disagree** on that point. The Gemara challenges this claim: Do they **not** disagree? **But it is** explicitly **taught** in the mishna that they disagree in that case: If the widow waiting for her *yavam* **died, what should be done with** the money assured to her in **her marriage contract, and with** her **property that enters and leaves** the marriage **with her? Beit Shammai say: The husband's heirs should divide up** the property **together with the father's heirs. And Beit Hillel say:** The **property** retains **its** previous ownership **status.**

הָכִי קָאָמַר: מֵתָה, מַה יַּעֲשֶׂה בִּכְתוּבָּתָהּ, וּשְׁבָקָהּ. נְכָסִים הַנִּכְנָסִים וְהַיּוֹצְאִים עִמָּהּ, בֵּית שַׁמַּאי אוֹמְרִים: יַחֲלוֹקוּ יוֹרְשֵׁי הַבַּעַל עִם יוֹרְשֵׁי הָאָב וּבֵית הִלֵּל אוֹמְרִים נְכָסִים בְּחֶזְקָתָן.

The Gemara answers: **This is what** that mishna **is saying:** If she **died, what should be done with** the money assured to her in **her marriage contract? And** the *tanna* then **left** this question unanswered, and addressed an additional case: What should be done with her **property that enters and leaves** the marriage **with her? Beit Shammai say: The husband's heirs should divide up** the property **together with the father's heirs. And Beit Hillel say:** The **property** retains **its** previous ownership **status.**

אָמַר רַב אַשִׁי: מַתְנִיתִין נַמִי דַּיְקָא, דְּקָתָנֵי: יַחֲלוֹקוּ יוֹרְשֵׁי הַבַּעַל עִם יוֹרְשֵׁי הָאָב, וְלָא קָתָנֵי יוֹרְשֵׁי הָאָב עִם יוֹרְשֵׁי הַבַּעַל – שְׁמַע מִינָּהּ.

Rav Ashi said: The language of **the mishna is also precise** according to this interpretation, **as it teaches:** Beit Shammai say that **the husband's heirs should divide up** the property **together with the father's heirs,** which implies that the father's heirs had de facto possession of the property and the husband's heirs then came and divided that property with them. This is true with regard to her property that enters and leaves the marriage with her. **And** the mishna **does not teach** using the reverse formulation: Beit Shammai say that **the father's heirs should divide up** the property **together with the husband's heirs,** which would imply that the husband's heirs had *de facto* possession of the property; this is true with regard to the payment of the marriage contract. **Conclude from here** that Beit Shammai did not rule what should be done with the payment of the marriage contract, as the Gemara claimed.

אַבָּיֵי אָמַר: רֵישָׁא דְּנָפְלוּ לָהּ כְּשֶׁהִיא שׁוֹמֶרֶת יָבָם, סֵיפָא דְּנָפְלוּ לָהּ כְּשֶׁהִיא תַּחְתָּיו דְּבַעַל.

The Gemara presents a third resolution to the apparent inconsistency in Beit Shammai's rulings in the mishna: **Abaye said: The first clause** concerns a case in **which** property **was bequeathed to her when she was** still **a widow waiting for her** *yavam* to perform levirate marriage or *ḥalitza*, and **the latter clause** concerns a case in **which** property **was bequeathed to her when she was** still **under,** i.e., married to, **her** first **husband,**[N] before he died.

NOTES

The latter clause concerns a case in which property was bequeathed to her when she was under her husband – סֵיפָא דְּנָפְלוּ לָהּ כְּשֶׁהִיא תַּחְתָּיו דְּבַעַל: Most commentaries claim that the present version of the Gemara's text is the correct version: When she was under her husband. Rav Hai Gaon had another version that states: When she was under him. This allows for Rav Hai Gaon's unique explanation that the reference is not to being married to her husband, but to being under the *yavam*, i.e., being bound to him through a levirate bond. Accordingly, the dispute between Beit Hillel and Beit Shammai is, in Abaye's opinion, whether the *yavam* is entitled to at least a portion of the property that enters and leaves the marriage with the woman, of which the husband has a usufructuary interest. Do the rights of the *yavam* fully parallel those of her husband, in which case he would have rights, or does he have weaker rights, in which case he should not be entitled to them at all?

וְקָסָבַר אַבַּיֵי יָדוֹ כְּיָדָהּ.

And Abaye holds that according to Beit Hillel, with regard to the husband's rights to his wife's property, **his hand is like her hand,** but not any stronger. Accordingly, the *yavam* has a weaker hand in her property than she does, because the rights of a *yavam* are always weaker than those of the husband himself. Therefore, she is considered to be in possession of the property, and when she dies, her heirs, i.e., her father and his heirs, inherit it. However, Beit Shammai assume that the husband's hand is stronger than his wife's hand. Therefore, the hand of the *yavam*, which is weaker than the husband's hand, is nevertheless equally as strong as the hand of the *yevama,* and therefore they rule that if she dies, the *yavam* and her heirs divide up the property.

אָמַר לֵיהּ רָבָא: אִי דְּנָפְלֵי לָהּ כְּשֶׁהִיא תַּחְתָּיו דְּבַעַל – דְּכוּלֵּי עָלְמָא לָא פְּלִיגִי דְּיָדוֹ עֲדִיפָא מִיָּדָהּ.

Rava[N] **said to him:** I hold that **if** the property **was bequeathed to her when she was** still **under the** first **husband, everyone,** i.e., both Beit Hillel and Beit Shammai, **agrees that his hand is stronger than her hand,** and therefore the hand of the *yavam* will be equally as strong as that of the *yevama,* and if she dies the property will be divided between the two sides.

אֶלָּא: אִידֵי וְאִידֵי דְּנָפְלוּ לָהּ כְּשֶׁהִיא שׁוֹמֶרֶת יָבָם, רֵישָׁא – דְּלָא עֲבַד בָּהּ מַאֲמָר, סֵיפָא – דַּעֲבַד בָּהּ מַאֲמָר.

Therefore, Rava presents his own resolution to the apparent inconsistency in Beit Shammai's rulings in the mishna: **Rather, both this** first clause **and that** latter clause concern cases in **which** property **was bequeathed to her when she was a widow waiting for her** ***yavam*****. The first clause** concerns a case in **which** the *yavam* **had not performed a levirate betrothal with her,**[N] and **the latter clause** concerns a case in **which he had performed a levirate betrothal with her.**

וְקָסָבַר רָבָא: מַאֲמָר לְבֵית שַׁמַּאי עוֹשֶׂה וַדַּאי אֲרוּסָה וּסְפֵק נְשׂוּאָה, וַדַּאי אֲרוּסָה – לִדְחוֹת בְּצָרָה, וּסְפֵק נְשׂוּאָה – לַחֲלוֹק בִּנְכָסִים.

The Gemara explains the rationale behind Rava's explanation: **And Rava holds** that **according to Beit Shammai a levirate betrothal** with a *yevama* **affords** her a status equivalent in some aspects to a woman who is **definitely betrothed and** in other aspects to a woman about whom there is **uncertainty** whether she is **married.** The Gemara elucidates: She is similar to a woman who is **definitely betrothed** with regard **to nullifying** the levirate bond of **her rival wife,** so that the rival wife need not perform levirate marriage or *ḥalitza.* **And** she is similar to a woman about whom there is **uncertainty** whether she is **married** with regard to empowering the *yavam* **to divide up the property** that she attained while she was waiting for her *yavam.*

NOTES

The opinions of Abaye and Rava – שִׁיטוֹת אַבַּיֵי וְרָבָא: The commentaries offer various interpretations of the dispute between Abaye and Rava (see Ramban and Rashba, who elucidate them). According to Rashi, Abaye assumes that Beit Hillel hold that a husband's hand over the possessions is equally as strong as his wife's, while in a case where a *yevama* is still awaiting levirate marriage, the hand of the *yavam* is weaker than that of the *yevama*. Therefore, in the latter case, if she dies, any property that fell to her will remain in her and her heirs' possession. Beit Shammai, however, hold that a husband's hand is stronger than the hand of his wife, and therefore the hand of a *yavam* is equally as strong as that of the *yevama*. Accordingly, in the latter case, if she dies, any property that fell to her should be divided up between the heirs of the *yevama* and the *yavam*. According to Rava, all agree that the husband's hand is stronger than that of his wife, and that if property fell to a woman awaiting levirate marriage then the hand of the *yavam* and that of the *yevama* are equally strong, and therefore they divide up the property between them. The dispute between Beit Hillel and Beit Shammai lies in the case where the *yavam* performed levirate betrothal. In that case, Beit Shammai hold that the betrothal affords her a status of a fully betrothed woman.

The Rif holds that according to Abaye, all agree that a husband's hand and his wife's are equally strong. Beit Shammai hold that when a woman happens before her *yavam* for levirate marriage, all of the husband's rights are transferred to the *yavam*, and so upon her death her heirs and the *yavam* or his heirs divide up the property equally between them. Beit Hillel hold that the husband's rights are not transferred to the *yavam*, and therefore the woman's property is awarded to her heirs. Rava claims that all agree that the hand of the *yavam* is actually stronger than that of the woman, and therefore upon her death her property that was bequeathed to her while she was married to her husband will go to his heirs. However, the Gemara here is discussing only property that she received once she was already awaiting levirate marriage.

The Rambam, Razah, and Ramban assume that the dispute between Abaye and Rava relates only to the opinion of Beit Shammai, but according to Beit Hillel the levirate bond does not render her equivalent even to a betrothed woman, and therefore the property is certainly fully in her possession and will pass to her heirs.

The first clause concerns a case in which he had not performed a levirate betrothal with her – רֵישָׁא דְּלָא עֲבַד בָּהּ מַאֲמָר: The Ritva explains that the distinction between the cases applies in cases in which property was bequeathed to her before the levirate betrothal was performed. Other commentaries differ, suggesting that in that case, even Beit Shammai would hold that the husband's heirs would have rights to the property. Instead, they explain that the dispute lies only in cases where she died, as then there would indeed be a difference if the levirate betrothal had taken place (*Keren Ora*).

אִיתְּמַר מִשְּׁמֵיהּ דְּרַבִּי אֶלְעָזָר כְּווֹתֵיהּ דְּרָבָא וְאִיתְּמַר מִשְּׁמֵיהּ דְּרַבִּי יוֹסֵי בְּרַבִּי חֲנִינָא כְּווֹתֵיהּ דְּאַבַּיֵי.

The Gemara notes: An interpretation of the mishna **was stated in the name of Rabbi Elazar** that is **in accordance with** the opinion **of Rava. And** an interpretation of the mishna **was stated in the name of Rabbi Yosei, son of Rabbi Ḥanina**[N] that is **in accordance with** the opinion **of Abaye.**

וּמִי אָמַר רַבִּי אֶלְעָזָר הָכִי? וְהָא אָמַר רַבִּי אֶלְעָזָר: מַאֲמָר לְבֵית שַׁמַּאי אֵינָהּ קוֹנָה אֶלָּא לִדְחוֹת בְּצָרָה בִּלְבָד!

The Gemara objects: **And did Rabbi Elazar** actually **state this** interpretation that is in accordance with the opinion of Rava? **But didn't Rabbi Elazar say: According to Beit Shammai a levirate betrothal acquires** the *yevama* **only** with regard **to nullifying** the levirate bond of **a rival wife** so that she need not perform levirate marriage or *ḥalitza*? This implies that it does not acquire her with regard to enabling the *yavam* to inherit from her. This, then, stands in contrast to Rava's interpretation.

אֵיפוֹךְ. וְאִי בָּעֵית אֵימָא: לְעוֹלָם לָא תֵּיפוֹךְ, אֲמַר לָךְ רַבִּי אֶלְעָזָר: כִּי אֲמַרִי אֲנָא – דְּלָא סַגִּי לָהּ בְּגֵט, אֶלָּא דְּבָעֵי נַמִי חֲלִיצָה, לַחֲלוֹק בִּנְכָסִים דְּלָא קָנֵי – מִי אֲמַרִי?

The Gemara offers two possible solutions: **Reverse** the opinions, so that Rabbi Elazar is in accordance with Abaye, and Rabbi Yosei, son of Rabbi Ḥanina, is in accordance with Rava. **And if you wish, say** instead: **Actually, do not reverse** the opinions, since Rabbi Elazar can be understood to be in accordance with the opinion of Rava, as **Rabbi Elazar** could have **said to you: When I said** the statement that implies that a levirate betrothal acquires in a very limited sense, the intention was only that its acquisition is limited in **that** giving her **a bill of divorce** is still **insufficient for her** in order to release her from the levirate bond; **rather, she also needs** to perform ***ḥalitza*.** But to suggest **that he does not acquire** her with regard **to dividing up** the **property** she attained, **did I say that?** Certainly not, as in fact a levirate betrothal acquires her to that extent as well, as Rava assumes.

אֲמַר רַב פַּפָּא: דִּיּוּקָא דְּמַתְנִיתִין כְּווֹתֵיהּ דְּאַבַּיֵי. וְאַף עַל גַּב דְּקַשְׁיָא "מֵתָה",

Rav Pappa said: The precise formulation of the mishna is in accordance with the opinion of **Abaye, even though** according to his opinion **it is difficult** that the mishna discusses the case in which **she died.**

דְּקָתָנֵי: "נְכָסִים הַנִּכְנָסִים וְיוֹצְאִים עִמָּהּ", מַאי נִכְנָסִין וּמַאי יוֹצְאִין? לָאו נִכְנָסִין: לִרְשׁוּת הַבַּעַל, וְיוֹצְאִים: מֵרְשׁוּת הַבַּעַל לִרְשׁוּת הָאָב,

The Gemara explains Rav Pappa's statement: The precise formulation of the mishna is in accordance with the opinion of Abaye, **as it teaches:** Her **property that enters and leaves** the marriage **with her. What** is the meaning of: **That enters, and what** is the meaning of: **That leaves? Is it not: That enters into the domain of the husband and leaves the domain of the husband** when she dies, and then enters **into the domain of the father?** Interpreted in this way, the mishna explicitly considers the period in which she was still married to her first husband, and likewise, the case in which she came into the possession of property should be understood as referring to a case in which she did so while still married. This is consonant with Abaye's interpretation, but not with Rava's.

וְאַף עַל גַּב דְּקַשְׁיָא מֵתָה, אַדְּמִפַּלְגִי בְּגוּפָהּ וּלְאַחַר מִיתָה לִפְלְגוּ בְּחַיֶּיהָ וּלְפֵירוֹת.

And when Rav Pappa said: **Even though** according to his opinion **it is difficult** that the mishna discusses the case in which **she died,** he meant as follows: **Instead of disputing** who has the rights to the property **itself,** which necessitates considering the case **after** her **death, let** Beit Hillel and Beit Shammai **dispute** the more immediate case **when she is** still **alive and** dispute who has the rights to the use and **produce** of the property.

וְתוּ לָא מִידֵּי.

The Gemara concludes: **And there is nothing more**[N] to say concerning this matter, i.e., as Rav Pappa noted, while it is undeniable that the mishna's formulation supports Abaye's interpretation, it is equally true that the case discussed by the mishna would appear to challenge his interpretation.

"כְּנָסָהּ הֲרֵי הִיא" כו'. לְמַאי הִלְכְתָא? אָמַר רַבִּי יוֹסֵי בַּר חֲנִינָא: לוֹמַר שֶׁמְּגָרְשָׁהּ בְּגֵט וּמַחֲזִירָהּ.

§ The mishna states: If the *yavam* **consummated the levirate marriage with her, then** her legal status is that of his wife in every sense.[H] The Gemara asks: **With regard to what *halakha*** is this said? **Rabbi Yosei bar Ḥanina said:** It is **to say that** once they have consummated the levirate marriage, the only way to legally dissolve the marriage is if **he divorces her with a bill of divorce,** but *ḥalitza* is of no avail, **and** after divorcing her, he is permitted to **take her back** to be his wife, as the prohibition against engaging in relations with one's brother's wife does not apply to her.

NOTES

And it was stated in the name of Rabbi Yosei, son of Rabbi Ḥanina – **וְאִיתְּמַר מִשְּׁמֵיהּ דְּרַבִּי יוֹסֵי בְּרַבִּי חֲנִינָא**: The Jerusalem Talmud also records an analysis of the distinction between the first and latter clauses of the mishna. There, Rabbi Yosei explains that the first clause concerns a case where the woman inherited property prior to her happening before her *yavam* for levirate marriage, and the latter clause concerns a case where the property was bequeathed to her after she was already awaiting levirate marriage. However, the *Penei Moshe* suggests modifying the text in a way that renders Rabbi Yosei bar Ḥanina's explanation consistent with Abaye's explanation in the Gemara here. Rabbi Zeira explains there that according to Beit Shammai, the *yavam* is afforded a status similar to that of a man concerning whom it is uncertain whether he is the husband. The *halakha* in such a case is that the property is divided equally between the parties. According to Beit Hillel, the status of the *yavam* vis-à-vis the inheritance is the same as that of any husband. Even so, since even a regular husband does not have full ownership of his wife's property but only a usufructuary interest in it, the *yavam* cannot lay claim to her property either. According to this opinion, Beit Shammai and Beit Hillel dispute what should be done with the value of the marriage contract as well, as is implied by the straightforward reading of the mishna, as opposed to Abaye's interpretation on 38b.

And there is nothing more – **וְתוּ לָא מִידֵּי**: Other commentaries explain that the Gemara's intention is to say that the inference from the formulation of the mishna is very convincing and no objection can be raised against it (Rabbi Avraham min HaHar).

HALAKHA

If he consummated the levirate marriage with her then her legal status is that of his wife in every sense – **כְּנָסָהּ הֲרֵי הִיא כְּאִשְׁתּוֹ לְכָל דָּבָר**: Once the *yavam* consummates the levirate marriage with his *yevama*, she is considered to be his wife in every sense. Therefore, the only way to divorce her is to by means of a bill of divorce, and following the divorce he is permitted to remarry her (Rambam *Sefer Nashim*, *Hilkhot Yibbum* 1:15; *Shulḥan Arukh*, *Even HaEzer* 168:1).

מגרשה בגט פשיטא! סלקא דעתך אמינא: הואיל וכתיב "ולקחה לו לאשה ויבמה" אמר רחמנא, ועדיין יבומי הראשון עליה. בחליצה – אין, בגט – לא, קא משמע לן.

The Gemara examines the first clause of Rabbi Yosei bar Ḥanina's statement: **Isn't it obvious** that to sever his relationship with her, **he divorces her with a bill of divorce?** The Gemara explains: It is necessary to teach this because **it could enter your mind to say** that **since it is written: "And take her to him to be his wife and consummate the levirate marriage with her"** (Deuteronomy 25:5), continuing to refer to the marriage as a levirate marriage even after the verse has stated that he took her as a wife, one might claim **the Merciful One is saying** that the **original levirate** bond **continues to be upon her,** and therefore, **with *ḥalitza*, yes,** they can sever the relationship, but **with a bill of divorce, no,** the relationship would not be severed. Therefore, the mishna **teaches us** that she is considered to be his wife to the extent that the relationship can be severed with a bill of divorce alone.

"מחזירה". פשיטא! סלקא דעתך אמינא: מצוה דרמיא רחמנא עליה עבדה. השתא תיקום עליה באיסור אשת אח – קא משמע לן.

The Gemara examines the second clause: **Isn't** it **obvious** that after divorcing her, he is permitted to **take her back** to be his wife? The Gemara explains: It is necessary to teach this because **it could enter your mind to say** that the **mitzva that the Merciful One imposes upon him, he has performed,** and therefore **now** that there is no longer any mitzva to marry her, **she should** once again **be established** as forbidden **to him by the prohibition** against engaging in relations with one's **brother's wife.** To dispel this notion, the mishna **teaches us** that she is considered to be his wife to the extent that there is no longer any prohibition against remarrying her.

ואימא הכי נמי! אמר קרא: "ולקחה לו לאשה", כיון שלקחה – הרי היא כאשתו לכל דבר.

The Gemara challenges this ruling: **But** why not **say** that this **is indeed so,** that she should be forbidden to him? The Gemara explains: **The verse states: "And take her to him to be his wife"** (Deuteronomy 25:5), indicating that **once he has taken her,** her legal status is **that of his wife in every sense.**

"ובלבד שתהא כתובתה" כו׳. מאי טעמא? אשה הקנו לו מן השמים.

§ The mishna states: The **only** exception to this is **that** her **marriage contract will** still **be** payable from the property of her first husband and not from the property of the *yavam*. The Gemara asks: **What is the reason** for this? The Gemara explains: **A wife was acquired to him by Heaven,** and since he did not choose her as a wife, he did not obligate himself to pay her marriage contract.

ואי לית לה מן הראשון – תקינו לה משני, כדי שלא תהא קלה בעיניו להוציאה.

The Gemara qualifies the mishna's ruling: **And if she has no** ability to collect her marriage contract **from the first** husband,[H] since he died without leaving any property with which to pay it, the Sages **instituted an ordinance for her** benefit that she must receive a new marriage contract **from** her **second** husband, i.e., the *yavam*. This was instituted **so that she will not be demeaned in his eyes such that** he will easily **divorce her,** since doing so would incur a financial burden on his part.

מתני׳ מצוה בגדול לייבם, לא רצה – מהלכין על כל האחין, לא רצו – חוזרין אצל גדול, ואומרים לו: עליך מצוה, או חלוץ או ייבם.

MISHNA The **mitzva** of levirate marriage **is for the eldest** of the brothers **to consummate the levirate marriage.**[H] If the eldest **does not want** to do so,[H] the court **goes to each of the** other **brothers** and requires them to do so. **If they do not want** to do so, the court **returns to** the **eldest** brother **and says to him:** The **mitzva** is incumbent **upon you; either perform *ḥalitza* or consummate the levirate marriage.**

תלה בקטן עד שיגדיל. או בגדול עד שיבא ממדינת הים, או חרש או שוטה – אין שומעין לו, אלא אומרים לו: עליך מצוה, או חלוץ או ייבם.

If a brother **made** his decision **dependent** upon the possibility that one of his other brothers will eventually consummate the levirate marriage, saying that he will do so only if they do not, then whether he makes it dependent **upon** a brother who is currently **a minor,**[H] meaning that the *yevama* should wait **until he matures, or upon** his **eldest brother,** who is not currently present, meaning the *yevama* should wait **until he comes from overseas, or** upon a brother who is **a deaf-mute or an imbecile,**[N] as perhaps they will recover from their disability, the court **does not listen to him; rather,** the judges of the court **say to him:** The **mitzva is** incumbent **upon you; either perform *ḥalitza* or consummate the levirate marriage.**

HALAKHA

And if she has no ability to collect her marriage contract from the first husband – ואי לית לה מן הראשון: If the deceased brother had no property, the *yavam* must give the *yevama* a marriage contract for one hundred dinars payable from his property, so that she will not be demeaned in his eyes such that he will easily divorce her (Rambam *Sefer Nashim, Hilkhot Ishut* 22:14; *Shulḥan Arukh, Even HaEzer* 168:9, and in the comment of Rema).

The mitzva is for the eldest to consummate the levirate marriage – מצוה בגדול לייבם: The mitzva of levirate marriage is for the eldest of the brothers to consummate the levirate marriage or perform *ḥalitza*. If he does not wish to do so or is incapable of doing so (Rivash), then the other brothers, starting with the next oldest and proceeding in descending order of age, are required to do so. If they refuse, the eldest brother is again required to either consummate the levirate marriage or perform *ḥalitza* (Rambam *Sefer Nashim, Hilkhot Yibbum* 2:6, 7; *Shulḥan Arukh, Even HaEzer* 161:4).

The eldest does not want to consummate the levirate marriage – לא רצה לייבם: If the eldest brother refuses to either consummate the levirate marriage or perform *ḥalitza*, he is forced to perform *ḥalitza*. This is true even though there is a younger brother who could do so, and even if the eldest brother had taken an oath not to do so, because since there is a mitzva incumbent upon him, the oath does not take effect (Rema). Nevertheless, to avoid a situation where it would appear as though he is violating his oath, he is first to be released from his oath (Rivash; Rambam *Sefer Nashim, Hilkhot Yibbum* 2:7; *Shulḥan Arukh, Even HaEzer* 161:4).

He made it dependent upon a minor – תלה בקטן: If a brother does not wish to consummate the levirate marriage or perform *ḥalitza* immediately, but instead says that he wishes to wait for a brother who is a minor to mature, or for a brother who is a deaf-mute to heal, or for an older brother to return from overseas, this is not accepted, and he must consummate the levirate marriage with her or perform *ḥalitza* immediately (Rambam *Sefer Nashim, Hilkhot Yibbum* 2:8–9; *Shulḥan Arukh, Even HaEzer* 161:5).

NOTES

A deaf-mute or an imbecile – או חרש או שוטה: Rambam, in his Commentary on the Mishna, along with most of the other commentaries, explains that the intention here is that the eldest brother wished to wait for the possibility that a brother who is a deaf-mute or imbecile will be healed. It would appear, however, that *Tosafot* understand that his request is that the deaf-mute or imbecile should consummate the levirate marriage in their current disabled state. Accordingly, *Tosafot* assume that a levirate marriage with such an individual is valid. Nevertheless, a *yevama* is never compelled to enter into levirate marriage in such a case.

NOTES

The consummation of a younger brother [*katan*] – בִּיאַת קָטָן: The Gemara here uses the term *katan*, which normally refers to a minor. However, Rashi explains that in this case the reference is not to a minor but to a younger brother who is already an adult and therefore fully capable of consummating the marriage according to all opinions. Others explain that the reference here is to an actual minor, but one who is above nine years of age, from which point his act of sexual intercourse has legal significance (Rivan; Meiri; see Rashba and Ritva).

Why should they return to the eldest brother – אַמַּאי חוֹזְרִין אֵצֶל הַגָּדוֹל: Ostensibly, it would seem that the very fact that the younger brothers are considered demonstrates that the consummation of a younger brother is preferable to the *ḥalitza* of the eldest, as if that were not the case, why wouldn't the eldest brother immediately be forced to perform *ḥalitza*? The reason that a proof cannot be drawn from here is because compulsion is always considered a last resort. Therefore, even if the *ḥalitza* of the eldest brother is preferable to the consummation of a younger brother, the consummation of a younger brother is nevertheless preferable to the forced *ḥalitza* of the eldest brother (*Yosef Lekah*).

Perhaps he will come and perform *ḥalitza* – דִּלְמָא אָתֵי וְחָלֵיץ: The Gemara mentions the possibility that the eldest brother might perform *ḥalitza* to emphasize that the eldest brother is preferred even if he does not intend to consummate the marriage (Rashba; Meiri; see *Haggahot Rav Yeshaya Pick-Berlin*).

We do not delay the performance of any mitzva – כָּל שֶׁהוּיֵי מִצְוָה לָא מַשְׁהִינַן: The *Ḥayyei Adam* cites the *Terumat HaDeshen*, who infers from the mishna here that one may delay the performance of a mitzva if doing so will enable one to perform it in its optimal manner later. This is derived from the fact that the mishna states only that one does not wait for the older brother to return from overseas in order to perform levirate marriage. By implication, if he were in the same country but merely not available immediately, then one should wait. Apparently, this is because the short delay is acceptable in order to perform a mitzva in its optimal manner. However, the *Sefer Ḥasidim* cites the verse: "I made haste and did not delay to observe Your commandments" (Psalms 119:60), and interprets it to mean that one should not delay performing a mitzva even if it could be performed in a more complete manner later. The *Ḥayyei Adam* notes that this is also implied by the straightforward reading of the Gemara, which states without qualifications that one should not delay the performance of a mitzva.

גמ׳ אִיתְּמַר, בִּיאַת קָטָן וַחֲלִיצַת גָּדוֹל, פְּלִיגִי בָּהּ רַבִּי יוֹחָנָן וְרַבִּי יְהוֹשֻׁעַ בֶּן לֵוִי, חַד אָמַר: בִּיאַת קָטָן עֲדִיפָא, וְחַד אָמַר: חֲלִיצַת גָּדוֹל עֲדִיפָא.

GEMARA An amoraic dispute **was stated: Rabbi Yoḥanan and Rabbi Yehoshua ben Levi disagree with regard to** a case in which there is the choice between **consummation of** the levirate marriage by **a younger** brother [***katan***][N] **or *ḥalitza*** performed **by the eldest** brother. **One said:** The **consummation of** the levirate marriage by **a younger** brother **is preferable and** the other **one said: *Ḥalitza*** performed by the **eldest** brother **is preferable.**[H]

מַאן דְּאָמַר בִּיאַת קָטָן עֲדִיפָא – דְּהָא מִצְוָה בְּיִיבּוּם, וּמַאן דְּאָמַר חֲלִיצַת גָּדוֹל עֲדִיפָא – בִּמְקוֹם גָּדוֹל – בִּיאַת קָטָן לָאו כְּלוּם הִיא.

The Gemara explains: With regard to **the one who said** that **consummation of** the levirate marriage by **a younger** brother **is preferable** this is due to the fact **that** the **mitzva** of levirate marriage **is through** the actual **consummation of the levirate marriage,** and therefore preference is always given to consummation over the performance of *ḥalitza*. **And the one who said *ḥalitza*** performed **by** the **eldest** brother **is preferable,** this is because **in the presence of** the **eldest** brother the **consummation of** the levirate marriage by **a younger** brother **is** considered **nothing.**

תְּנַן: לֹא רָצָה – מַחֲזִירִין עַל כָּל הָאַחִין. מַאי לָאו: לֹא רָצָה לְיַיבֵּם אֶלָּא לַחֲלוֹץ, וְקָתָנֵי: מְהַלְּכִין אֵצֶל הָאַחִין, שְׁמַע מִינָּהּ בִּיאַת קָטָן עֲדִיפָא –

The Gemara suggests proof for the first opinion: **We learned** in the mishna: If the eldest **does not want** to consummate the levirate marriage, the court **goes to each of the** other **brothers** and requires them to do so. The Gemara suggests: **What, is it not** that **he does not want to consummate the levirate marriage but** is willing **to perform *ḥalitza*? And** yet the mishna **teaches:** The court **goes to each of the** other **brothers** and requires them to consummate the levirate marriage. If so, **conclude from here** that the **consummation of** the levirate marriage by **a younger** brother **is preferable.**

לָא, לֹא רָצָה לַחֲלוֹץ וְלֹא לְיַיבֵּם, דִּכְוָותָהּ גַּבֵּי הָאַחִין לֹא רָצוּ – לֹא לַחֲלוֹץ וְלֹא לְיַיבֵּם, אַמַּאי חוֹזְרִים אֵצֶל הַגָּדוֹל, לְמִיכְפְּיֵיהּ – לְכַפְיֵיהּ לְדִידְהוּ! כֵּיוָן דְּמִצְוָה עֲלֵיהּ דִּידֵיהּ רַמְיָא – לְדִידֵיהּ כָּיְיפִינַן.

The Gemara rejects the proof: **No,** the mishna might concern a case where the eldest **does not want** either **to perform *ḥalitza* or to consummate the levirate marriage,** and it is only because he is unwilling to do either that the other brothers are considered. The Gemara asks: If this is so, then **in the corresponding situation** in the mishna in which **the brothers do not want** to do so, the case must be that they do not want either **to perform *ḥalitza* or to consummate the levirate marriage.** But if so, **why should** the court invest the extra effort to **return to the eldest** brother[N] **to force him** to fulfill his duty? **Let** the court **force** the other brothers to fulfill their duty. The Gemara responds: **Since** the **mitzva is incumbent upon** the eldest brother *ab initio*, **it is he who is forced.**

תְּנַן: תָּלָה בְּקָטָן עַד שֶׁיַּגְדִּיל – אֵין שׁוֹמְעִין לוֹ. וְאִי בִּיאַת קָטָן עֲדִיפָא, אַמַּאי אֵין שׁוֹמְעִין לוֹ? נִינְטַר דִּלְמָא גָּדֵיל וּמְיַיבֵּם!

The Gemara suggests another proof: **We learned** in the mishna: If a brother makes his decision **dependent upon** a brother who is currently **a minor,** the court **does not listen to him.** The Gemara suggests: **And if** the **consummation of** the levirate marriage by a **minor is preferable, why shouldn't** the court **listen to him? Let** the court **wait,** as **perhaps he will mature and consummate the levirate marriage.** Rather, it would appear that the mishna assumes that consummation by a younger brother is not preferable.

וְלִיטַעֲמִיךְ, וּבְגָדוֹל עַד שֶׁיָּבֹא מִמְּדִינַת הַיָּם אֵין שׁוֹמְעִין לוֹ, אַמַּאי? נִינְטַר, דִּלְמָא אָתֵי וְחָלֵיץ! אֶלָּא: כָּל שֶׁהוּיֵי מִצְוָה לָא מַשְׁהִינַן.

The Gemara responds: **But** even **according to your reasoning** that *ḥalitza* performed by an elder brother is preferable, what about the next case in the mishna, where a brother asks to wait **until the eldest brother comes from overseas?** In that case, as well, the mishna rules: **They do not listen to him;** but **why shouldn't** they listen to him? **Let** the court **wait,** as **perhaps he will come and** at the very least **perform *ḥalitza*.**[N] **Rather,** it is clear that the reason for the mishna's ruling is that **we do not delay the performance of any mitzva;**[N] therefore, if one of the brothers is currently unable to perform the mitzva, he is not considered at all. Consequently, no proof can be derived from the mishna.

HALAKHA

The consummation of a younger brother and the *ḥalitza* of the eldest brother – בִּיאַת קָטָן וַחֲלִיצַת גָּדוֹל: If the eldest brother does not wish to consummate the levirate marriage but only to perform *ḥalitza*, and a younger brother is willing to consummate the levirate marriage, then the consummation of the younger brother is preferable. Whenever *ḥalitza* is performed, preference is given to the eldest brother. This is the case today, as according to many opinions levirate marriage is never performed nowadays. Even those authorities who hold that levirate marriage is still performed agree that if the *yevama* does not wish to enter into levirate marriage then *ḥalitza* is performed, giving preference to the eldest brother (Rema, citing *Terumat HaDeshen*; *Shulḥan Arukh*, *Even HaEzer* 161:6).

אִית דְּאָמְרִי: בְּבִיאָה – כּוּלֵּי עָלְמָא לָא פְּלִיגִי דְּבִיאַת קָטָן עֲדִיפָא. כִּי פְּלִיגִי – בַּחֲלִיצַת קָטָן,

There are those **who say** that the dispute is more limited: **When** there is the possibility of **consummating** the levirate marriage, **everyone agrees that** the **consummation of** the levirate marriage by **a younger** brother **is preferable** to the *ḥalitza* of the eldest brother. **When they disagree** it is **with regard to the** significance of the *ḥalitza* **of a younger** brother.

וְהָכִי אִיתְּמַר: חֲלִיצַת קָטָן וַחֲלִיצַת גָּדוֹל – פְּלִיגִי בָּהּ רַבִּי יוֹחָנָן וְרַבִּי יְהוֹשֻׁעַ בֶּן לֵוִי. חַד אֲמַר: חֲלִיצַת גָּדוֹל עֲדִיפָא, וְחַד אֲמַר: כִּי הֲדָדֵי נִינְהוּ.

And this is how the dispute **was stated: Rabbi Yoḥanan and Rabbi Yehoshua ben Levi disagree with regard to** a case in which there is choice between the *ḥalitza* **of a younger** brother **or** the *ḥalitza* of the **eldest** brother. **One said:** The *ḥalitza* of the **eldest** brother **is preferable.**[H] **And** the other **one said:** The two options **are equivalent.**

מַאן דְּאָמַר חֲלִיצַת גָּדוֹל עֲדִיפָא – דְּהָא מִצְוָה בְּגָדוֹל. וְאִידָּךְ: כִּי אָמְרִינַן מִצְוָה בְּגָדוֹל – לְעִנְיַן יִבּוּם, אֲבָל לְעִנְיַן חֲלִיצָה – כַּהֲדָדֵי נִינְהוּ.

The Gemara explains: With regard to **the one who said** that the *ḥalitza* of the **eldest** brother **is preferable,** this is due to the fact **that** the **mitzva** of levirate marriage and *ḥalitza* **is** incumbent **upon** the **eldest** brother. **And the other** Sage would respond to this claim by saying that **when we say** that the **mitzva is** incumbent **upon** the **eldest** brother, that is only **with regard to** the consummation of the **levirate marriage; however, with regard to** performing *ḥalitza,* all the brothers **are equivalent.**

תְּנַן: לֹא רָצוּ – חוֹזְרִין אֵצֶל גָּדוֹל, מַאי לָאו: לֹא רָצוּ לְיַיבֵּם אֶלָּא לַחֲלוֹץ, וְקָתָנֵי חוֹזְרִין אֵצֶל גָּדוֹל, וּשְׁמַע מִינָּהּ: חֲלִיצַת גָּדוֹל עֲדִיפָא!

The Gemara suggests a proof for the first opinion: **We learned** in the mishna: If the younger brothers **do not want** to consummate the levirate marriage, the court **returns to** the **eldest** brother and demands that he at least perform *ḥalitza*. The Gemara suggests: **What, is it not** that the other brothers **did not want to consummate the levirate marriage but** are willing **to perform *ḥalitza*? And** yet the mishna **teaches:** The court **returns to** the **eldest** brother so that he can perform *ḥalitza*. If so, **conclude from here** that the ***ḥalitza* of** the **eldest** brother **is preferable.**

לָא, לֹא רָצוּ – לֹא לַחֲלוֹץ וְלֹא לְיַיבֵּם. דִּכְוָותֵיהּ גַּבֵּי גָּדוֹל – לֹא רָצָה לֹא לַחֲלוֹץ וְלֹא לְיַיבֵּם, אֶלָּא אַמַּאי חוֹזְרִין אֵצֶל גָּדוֹל, לְמִכְפְּיֵיהּ? לִכְפַּיְיהוּ לְדִידְהוּ! כֵּיוָן דְּמִצְוָה עֲלֵיהּ דִּידֵיהּ רַמְיָא – לְדִידֵיהּ כָּיְיפִינַן.

The Gemara rejects the proof: **No,** the mishna might concern a case where the other brothers **did not want** either **to perform *ḥalitza* or to consummate the levirate marriage,** and it is only because they are unwilling to do either that the court returns to the eldest brother. The Gemara asks: If this is so, then **in the corresponding** situation in which the mishna states: The **eldest** brother **does not want** to do so, the case must be that he does not want either **to perform *ḥalitza* or to consummate the levirate marriage. But** if so, when the younger brothers also refuse, **why should** the court invest the extra effort to **return to** the **eldest** brother **to force him** to fulfill his duty? **Let** the court **force them,** i.e., the younger brothers, to fulfill their duty. The Gemara responds: **Since the mitzva is incumbent upon** the eldest brother *ab initio,* **it is he who is forced.**

תָּא שְׁמַע: תָּלָה בְּגָדוֹל עַד שֶׁיָּבֹא מִמְּדִינַת הַיָּם – אֵין שׁוֹמְעִין לוֹ. וְאִי סָלְקָא דַּעְתָּךְ חֲלִיצַת גָּדוֹל עֲדִיפָא, אַמַּאי אֵין שׁוֹמְעִין לוֹ? נִינְטַר דִּלְמָא אָתֵי וְחָלֵיץ!

Come and **hear** another proof from the mishna: If a younger brother makes his decision **dependent upon** the **eldest brother,** who is currently unavailable, suggesting that the *yevama* wait **until he comes from overseas,** the court **does not listen to him. And if it enters your mind** to suggest that the ***ḥalitza* of** the **eldest** brother **is preferable, why doesn't** the court **listen to him? Let** the court **wait,** as **perhaps he will come and perform *ḥalitza*.** Rather, it would appear that the mishna assumes that the with regard to performing *ḥalitza,* all the brothers are equivalent.

HALAKHA

Ḥalitza of a younger brother and the eldest brother – חֲלִיצַת קָטָן וְגָדוֹל: If the brothers are willing only to perform *ḥalitza* but not to consummate the levirate marriage, then it is preferable for the *ḥalitza* to be performed by the eldest brother. This is especially true nowadays, when *ḥalitza* takes precedence over consummating the levirate marriage. Even according to the opinions that the consummation of the levirate marriage takes precedence, if the *yevama* wishes to perform *ḥalitza* then *ḥalitza* is preferred (Rema, citing *Terumat HaDeshen*; *Shulḥan Arukh, Even HaEzer* 161:6).

וְלְטַעֲמִיךְ, בְּקָטָן עַד שֶׁיַּגְדִּיל אֵין שׁוֹמְעִין לוֹ, אַמַּאי? נִינְטַר דִּלְמָא גָּדֵיל וּמְיַיבֵּם, (אִי נַמִּי אָתֵי אִיהוּ וּמְיַיבְּמָה). אֶלָּא כׇּל שֶׁהוּיֵי מִצְוָה לָא מְשַׁהֵינַן.

The Gemara challenges this: **But** even **according to your reasoning,** you certainly agree that the possibility of consummating the levirate marriage is always preferable. If so, what about the previous case in the mishna, where the eldest brother asks to wait **until** his brother who is **a minor will mature?** In that case as well the mishna rules: The court **does not listen to him;** but **why shouldn't** the court **listen to him? Let** the court **wait,** as **perhaps he will come and consummate the levirate marriage. Alternatively,** in the case where the eldest brother is overseas, let the court wait, as perhaps **he will come and consummate the levirate marriage with her. Rather,** it is clear that the reason for the mishna's ruling is that **we do not delay the performance of a mitzva.** Therefore, if one of the brothers is currently unable to perform the mitzva, he is not considered at all. Consequently, no proof can be derived from the mishna.

תְּנַן הָתָם: מִצְוַת יִבּוּם קוֹדֶמֶת לְמִצְוַת חֲלִיצָה – בָּרִאשׁוֹנָה שֶׁהָיוּ מִתְכַּוְּונִין לְשֵׁם מִצְוָה, עַכְשָׁו שֶׁאֵין מִתְכַּוְּונִין לְשֵׁם מִצְוָה – אָמְרוּ: מִצְוַת חֲלִיצָה קוֹדֶמֶת לְמִצְוַת יִבּוּם.

§ **We learned** in a mishna **there** (*Bekhorot* 13a): **The mitzva of** consummating the **levirate marriage takes precedence over** the **mitzva of** performing ***halitza*;**[H] this applied **initially, when** ***yevamin*** **would have intent for the sake of** fulfilling **the mitzva. Now, that they do not have intent for the sake of** fulfilling **the** mitzva, the Sages **say:** The **mitzva of** performing ***halitza*** **takes precedence over** the **mitzva of** consummating the **levirate marriage.**

אָמַר רַב: אֵין כּוֹפִין. כִּי אָתוּ לְקַמֵּיהּ דְּרַב אֲמַר לְהוּ: אִי בָּעֵית – חֲלוֹץ, אִי בָּעֵית – יַיבֵּם, בִּדִידָךְ תְּלָא רַחֲמָנָא, ״וְאִם לֹא יַחְפֹּץ הָאִישׁ״, הָא אִם חָפֵץ – אִי בָּעֵי חָלֵיץ, אִי בָּעֵי יַיבֵּם.

Rav said: Nevertheless, the court **does not force**[N] a *yavam* to perform *halitza*, and if he wishes it is still permitted to consummate the levirate marriage. The Gemara relates: **When a** ***yavam*** and a ***yevama*** **would come before Rav, he would say to them: If you want, perform** ***halitza,*** and **if you want, consummate the levirate marriage, as the Merciful One makes** the matter **dependent upon your** will, as it is stated: **"And if the man does not wish** to take his *yevama*" (Deuteronomy 25:7) then he should perform *halitza*. This implies that the Torah requires him to perform *halitza* only if he does not wish to consummate the levirate marriage, **but if he wishes** to do so, then the matter is dependent upon him, and **if he wants, he performs** ***halitza,*** or **if he wants, he consummates the levirate marriage.**

וְאַף רַב יְהוּדָה סָבַר אֵין כּוֹפִין. מִדְּאַתְקֵין רַב יְהוּדָה בְּגִיטָּא דַּחֲלִיצָה: אֵיךְ פְּלוֹנִית בַּת פְּלוֹנִי אַקְרִיבַת יָת פְּלוֹנִי יְבָמָהּ קֳדָמָנָא לְבֵי דִּינָא, וְאִשְׁתְּמוֹדְעִינְהוּ דַּאֲחוּהּ דְּמִיתְנָא מֵאַבָּא נִיהוּ, וְאָמְרִי לֵיהּ: אִי צָבֵית לְיַבֵּם – יַבֵּם, וְאִי לָא – אִיטְלַע לַהּ רַגְלָיךְ דִּימִינָא.

The Gemara notes: **And even Rav Yehuda holds** that the court **does not force** a *yavam* to perform *halitza* if he wishes to consummate the levirate marriage. This is apparent from the fact **that Rav Yehuda enacted** in his court that the following formulation should be used **in the bill of** ***halitza*****:**[H] **That so-and-so, daughter of so-and-so, brought so-and-so, her** ***yavam,*** **before the court; and we identified him, that he was** indeed **the paternal brother of the deceased, and we said to him: If you desire to consummate the levirate marriage,** then **consummate the levirate marriage, and if not, extend your right foot toward** your *yevama* so that she may perform *halitza* by removing your shoe.[B]

HALAKHA

Levirate marriage and *halitza* – יִבּוּם וַחֲלִיצָה: The mitzva to consummate levirate marriage takes precedence over the mitzva of performing *halitza* (Rif; Rambam). This is in accordance with the opinion of the Rabbis and the statement of Rami bar Hama. Others say that the mitzva of performing *halitza* takes precedence (Rashi). This is in accordance with the opinion of Abba Shaul and the assumption of Rav Nahman bar Yitzhak. According to the first opinion, in a case where the *yavam* wishes to consummate the levirate marriage and the *yevama* does not, if she does not have a sufficiently valid reason to refuse, then she is categorized as rebellious and does not receive the money allotted to her in her marriage contract. According to the second opinion, she is not categorized as rebellious for refusing to consummate the levirate marriage, and so when she performs *halitza* she receives the payment of her marriage contract. According to this opinion, although the *yavam* is not forced to perform *halitza*, he can be tricked into doing so (*Tur*, citing Rabbeinu Tam and Rosh). If the *yavam* falls into the category of one who, were he to be married, would be forced to divorce his wife, then he is also forced to perform *halitza* (*Tur*, citing *Smag*).

Some say that even if both the *yavam* and the *yevama* wish to consummate the levirate marriage, they are not permitted to do so unless it is clear that they are doing so for the sake of the fulfilling the mitzva (*Tur*, citing Rabbeinu Tam; see *Yam shel Shlomo*). The custom is not to force *halitza* unless the *yavam* refuses both to consummate the levirate marriage and to perform *halitza* (Maharam Padua). In recent generations, especially in Ashkenazic communities, the custom is not to allow levirate marriage under any circumstances, although there have been some questionable exceptions to this principle. This has also become the accepted practice in Eretz Yisrael (Rambam *Sefer Nashim, Hilkhot Yibbum VaHalitza* 1:2, 3:7; *Shulhan Arukh, Even HaEzer* 165:1).

Bill of *halitza* – גֵּט חֲלִיצָה: Although there is no requirement for the *halitza* to be documented in writing, it was nevertheless customary for the court to grant the *yevama* a document as proof that she performed *halitza* and that she is now permitted to marry a man from the general public. There was a standard formulation for this document, as is clear from the statements of Rav Yehuda and Rabbi Hiyya bar Avya. In some places it is not customary to write a bill of *halitza*; however the better custom is to write one (*Be'er Heitev*; Rambam *Sefer Nashim, Hilkhot Yibbum* 4:30; *Tur, Even HaEzer* 169; *Shulhan Arukh, Even HaEzer* 169:56).

BACKGROUND

The order of *halitza* – סֵדֶר חֲלִיצָה: A mishna in Chapter Twelve describes the order of the *halitza* ceremony and stresses that the ceremony was performed in Hebrew. The bill of *halitza* mentioned here is a later addition, written in Aramaic and designed to enable the woman to later prove that she has performed the mitzva of *halitza* and is therefore allowed to remarry. The Rif formulated a complete version of the bill of *halitza*, including the details mentioned, e.g., the requirement that the witnesses see the woman's saliva and that they recognize both the woman as the wife of the deceased and the man as his brother. The Rif also adds which phrases from the Torah must be said by the man and which by the woman and by the court, as well as describing the type of shoe required for the performance of *halitza*.

NOTES

The court does not force – אֵין כּוֹפִין: This statement of Rav can be understood in different ways. Rashi and most of the other commentaries understand it to mean that a *yavam* is not to be forced to perform *halitza* if he wishes to consummate the levirate marriage, and that this is true even if one asserts that the mitzva of *halitza* takes precedence. Rabbeinu Hananel and Rabbeinu Tam explain Rav's statement in the opposite manner: The *yavam* will not be forced to consummate the levirate marriage, even in cases where one assumes his motives will be pure.

It is similarly unclear to whom Rav's statement applies; who is not to be forced? Rashi explains that where both the *yavam* and the *yevama* are willing to consummate the levirate marriage, they cannot be forced to perform *halitza* even if *halitza* is considered preferable. Others explain that Rav was referring only to the *yavam*, meaning that he cannot be forced to consummate the levirate marriage; alternatively he was referring only to the *yevama*, meaning that she is never forced to consummate the levirate marriage.

The *Gilyonei HaShas* cites a geonic responsum that explains that the dispute with regard to compulsion is dependent upon the broader issue as to whether or not *halitza* is valid if not agreed to by both parties. If the *halitza* requires mutual consent, then there can be no forced *halitza*. According to that opinion, the opinions that do allow for a forced *halitza* must be explained as one of the cases in which the Sages retroactively annulled the original marriage, consequently obviating any need for a valid *halitza*. Nevertheless, an act of *halitza* is still required because otherwise it would be appear as though the *yevama* had been released from her levirate bonds without performing an act that would release her.

וְאִיטְלַע לָהּ רַגְלָא דִּימִינָא, וּשְׁרַת סֵינֵיהּ מֵעַל רַגְלוֹהִי, וְיָרְקַת בְּאַנְפּוֹהִי רוּקָא דְּמִתְחֲזְיָא לְבֵי דִינָא עַל אַרְעָא.

The bill of *ḥalitza* would continue with the account of what transpired: **And he extended [*itla*] his right foot**[N] **toward her and she removed his shoe from upon his foot and she spat toward his face spittle, which was visible to the court,** and which landed **upon the ground.**

וְרַבִּי חִיָּיא בַּר אָוְיָא מְסַיֵּים בָּהּ מִשְּׁמֵיהּ דְּרַב יְהוּדָה: וְאַקְרֵינְהוּ מַה דִּכְתִיב בְּסִפַר אוֹרַיְיתָא דְמֹשֶׁה.

And Rabbi Ḥiyya bar Avya in the name of Rav Yehuda would conclude the formulation of the bill of *ḥalitza* with an additional sentence: **And we dictated to** the *yavam* **that which is written in the book of the Torah of Moses,** i.e., those declarations that the *yavam* and the *yevama* are required to make.

אִשְׁתְּמוֹדְעִינְהוּ, פְּלִיגִי בָּהּ רַב אַחָא וְרָבִינָא. חַד אָמַר: בְּעֵדִים, וְחַד אָמַר: אֲפִילּוּ קָרוֹב, אֲפִילּוּ אִשָּׁה. וְהִלְכְתָא: גַּלּוֹיֵי מִילְּתָא בְּעָלְמָא הוּא, וַאֲפִילּוּ קָרוֹב וַאֲפִילּוּ אִשָּׁה.

The Gemara clarifies the intention of the phrase: **And we identified him**[H] as the brother of the deceased. **Rav Aḥa and Ravina disagree concerning** this phrase: **One said** that this identification must be made **through** legally valid **witnesses, and** the other **one said** that **even** the testimony of **a relative**[N] and **even** the testimony **a woman** is accepted in this case. The Gemara concludes: **And the *halakha* is** that the identification of the brother is considered to be **merely revealing** the facts of **the matter,** and therefore, **even a relative and even a woman** may tender this information.

בָּרִאשׁוֹנָה שֶׁהָיוּ מִתְכַּוְּונִין לְשֵׁם מִצְוָה – מִצְוַת יִבּוּם קוֹדֶמֶת לְמִצְוַת חֲלִיצָה, וְעַכְשָׁיו שֶׁאֵין מִתְכַּוְּונִין לְשֵׁם מִצְוָה – אָמְרוּ: מִצְוַת חֲלִיצָה קוֹדֶמֶת לְמִצְוַת יִבּוּם.

The Gemara paraphrases the mishna from tractate *Bekhorot*: **Initially, when** *yevamin* **would have intent for the sake of** fulfilling **the mitzva** of consummating the levirate marriage, **the mitzva of** consummating the **levirate marriage took precedence over the mitzva of** performing ***ḥalitza*. And now that they do not have intent for the sake of** fulfilling **the mitzva,** the Sages **say: The mitzva of** performing ***ḥalitza* takes precedence over the mitzva of** consummating the **levirate marriage.**

אָמַר רָמִי בַּר חָמָא אָמַר רַבִּי יִצְחָק: חָזְרוּ לוֹמַר מִצְוַת יִבּוּם קוֹדֶמֶת לְמִצְוַת חֲלִיצָה. אָמַר לֵיהּ רַב נַחְמָן בַּר יִצְחָק: אַכְשׁוּר דָּרֵי?!

Rami bar Ḥama said that **Rabbi Yitzḥak said:** In later generations **they went back to** once again **saying** that **the mitzva of** consummating the **levirate marriage takes precedence over the mitzva of** performing ***ḥalitza*. Rav Naḥman bar Yitzḥak said to him** in wonderment: Could it be that **the** later **generations improved** their spiritual level and now intend to consummate the levirate marriage solely for sake of fulfilling the mitzva?

מֵעִיקָּרָא סָבְרִי לָהּ כְּאַבָּא שָׁאוּל, וּלְבַסּוֹף סָבְרִי לָהּ כְּרַבָּנַן.

The Gemara explains that this does not mean that the later generations improved themselves; rather, **initially they held in accordance with** the opinion of **Abba Shaul,** and so the mitzva of performing *ḥalitza* took precedence, **and in the end they held in accordance with** the opinion of **the Rabbis,**[N] and so the mitzva of consummating the levirate marriage took precedence.

HALAKHA

Identification of the *yavam* and the *yevama* – הַכָּרַת הַיָּבָם וְהַיְּבָמָה: The court must substantiate that the man coming to perform *ḥalitza* is the paternal brother of the deceased, that the two brothers coexisted, and that this woman was the wife of the deceased. There is no need for two qualified witnesses to testify in this matter; rather, any testimony suffices, even that of a close relative, a woman, or anyone else generally disqualified from giving testimony. Even written testimony is acceptable if the parties can be recognized thereby (*Be'er Heitev*, citing Maharshdam). Some (*Be'er Heitev*, citing Rivash) say that a disqualified witness may not testify at the time of the *ḥalitza* itself; rather, the court must first confirm the identities of the *yavam* and the *yevama* and only then may the *ḥalitza* be performed (Rambam *Sefer Nashim, Hilkhot Yibbum VaḤalitza* 4:31; *Shulḥan Arukh, Even HaEzer* 169:8; 157:2; *Seder Ḥalitza* 38).

NOTES

He extended [*itla*] his right foot – אִיטְלַע...רַגְלָא דִּימִינָא: Rashi interprets the word *itla* as meaning incline. Accordingly, the phrase means that the *yavam* presented his foot to his *yevama* by extending it toward her. The commentaries explain that Rashi understood that the Aramaic word is related to the Hebrew word *tzela*, which can mean a side; Rashi similarly translates the phrase: "*Tzela hamishkan*" (Exodus 26:26) as being the side of the Tabernacle (Rabbi Yehuda al-Madari; *Noda BiHuda*). Rabbi Avraham min HaHar cites Rashi as explaining *itla* to mean prepare. The *Arukh* writes that the word means remove. Clearly the intention is not that he should remove his shoe; rather, it must mean that he should allow his shoe to be removed by her. Later commentaries note that it appears that the *Arukh* had a variant text of the Gemara that could support such a meaning. Other commentaries explain that the word means limp, and the intention is that the *yavam* should forcefully plant his foot on the ground to the point that he appears like one with a limp, who distributes his weight unequally by supporting himself on one leg (Meiri; Rabbi Avraham min HaHar; *Noda BiHuda*).

Even the testimony of a relative, etc. – אֲפִילּוּ קָרוֹב וכו׳: The early commentaries, based on the comments of the Rif, explain that this is certainly not to say that the court actually relied entirely on the testimony of a close relative or woman. Rather, in all cases the court would allow for the performance of *ḥalitza* only if they were certain of the identities of the parties involved. The novelty of the ruling is that it allows the court not to follow the standard protocol by which facts are established only through formal testimony supplied by independent valid witnesses (Meiri; *Tosafot*; see HALAKHA).

The dispute between Abba Shaul and the Rabbis – מַחְלוֹקֶת אַבָּא שָׁאוּל וַחֲכָמִים: The Gemara never explicitly rules on the dispute between the Rabbis and Abba Shaul as to whether nowadays one may consummate a levirate marriage even though there are reservations concerning one's purity of motives. The Gemara here appears to be inclined toward the opinion of the Rabbis; however, in other places the Gemara appears to accept the opinion of Abba Shaul. Already during the period of the *ge'onim* different communities followed different opinions. In Neharde'a the practice was to act in accordance with Abba Shaul, and in Sura the opinion of the Rabbis was followed. In later generations, the Sephardic commentaries generally permitted the consummation of the levirate marriage, while Ashkenazic commentaries permitted only *ḥalitza*.

דְּתַנְיָא, אַבָּא שָׁאוּל אוֹמֵר: הַכּוֹנֵס אֶת יְבִמְתּוֹ לְשֵׁם נוֹי, וּלְשׁוּם אִישׁוּת, וּלְשׁוּם דָּבָר אַחֵר – כְּאִילּוּ פּוֹגֵעַ בְּעֶרְוָה, וְקָרוֹב אֲנִי בְּעֵינַי לִהְיוֹת הַוָּלָד מַמְזֵר. וַחֲכָמִים אוֹמְרִים: ״יְבָמָהּ יָבֹא עָלֶיהָ״ – מִכׇּל מָקוֹם.

As it is taught in a *baraita*: **Abba Shaul says** that **one who consummates** a levirate marriage **with his *yevama* for the sake of** her **beauty, or for the sake of marital relations,**[N] **or for the sake of another matter,**[N] e.g., he wishes to inherit her husband's estate, **it** is considered **as though he encountered a forbidden relation, and I am inclined to view the offspring** born from such a union **as a *mamzer*.** Since the prohibition against engaging in relations with one's brother's wife is overridden only for the sake of fulfilling the mitzva of consummating the levirate marriage, when one does not have the intention to fulfill that mitzva, the baseline prohibition applies, and so any offspring from the union will be *mamzerim*. **The Rabbis say:** The Torah states: **"Her brother-in-law will have intercourse with her"** (Deuteronomy 25:5), which indicates that he should do so **in any case,** even if his intentions are not solely for the sake of fulfilling the mitzva.[N]

מַאן תָּנָא לְהָא דְּתָנוּ רַבָּנַן: ״יְבָמָהּ יָבֹא עָלֶיהָ״ מִצְוָה. שֶׁבַּתְּחִלָּה הָיְתָה עָלָיו בִּכְלַל הֶיתֵּר, נֶאֶסְרָה, וְחָזְרָה וְהוּתְּרָה, יָכוֹל תַּחְזוֹר לְהֶיתֵּירָהּ הָרִאשׁוֹן – תַּלְמוּד לוֹמַר ״יְבָמָהּ יָבֹא עָלֶיהָ״ מִצְוָה.

The Gemara asks: **Who is the *tanna*** who **taught** the following *baraita* **that the Sages taught:** The Torah states: **"Her brother-in-law will have intercourse with her"** (Deuteronomy 25:5); this is to be considered **a mitzva, as initially,** before she was married to his brother, **she was among** all other women who are **permitted to him,** and then when she married his brother **she became forbidden** to him, **and** when his brother died without offspring **she reverted** from her forbidden status **and became permitted to him.** One **might** have thought that **she would revert to her original permitted status;** therefore, **the verse states: "Her brother-in-law will have intercourse with her"** to teach that it is in fact **a mitzva** to do so.[H]

HALAKHA

The mitzva of levirate marriage – מִצְוַת יִיבּוּם: If one's paternal brother died childless, one is commanded to take his brother's widow in levirate marriage, whether she was married or only betrothed to his brother (Rambam *Sefer Nashim, Hilkhot Yibbum* 1:1; *Shulḥan Arukh, Even HaEzer* 156:1).

NOTES

For the sake of marital relations – לְשׁוּם אִישׁוּת: *Tosafot* explain that the use of the term: For the sake of marital relations, as it is used here differs from its use later in the Gemara. In the present context, such motivation is presented as being contemptible. Accordingly, the phrase means either that he desires to gain the status of a married man (*Tosafot*), that he desires the woman (Rivan), or that he wishes for her to serve him (*Otzar HaShitot*). However, later in the Gemara the phrase is used in contrast to the phrase: For the sake of her beauty. This implies that the phrase: For the sake of marital relations, indicates a more noble intention, i.e., that he wishes to have children with her. Nevertheless, even such motivation is still deficient in a case of a levirate marriage, where one must have intention for the specific goals of the levirate marriage (see *Otzar HaShitot*).

For the sake of another matter – לְשׁוּם דָּבָר אַחֵר: Rivan and others offer that the reference is to a case where the *yavam* is motivated by financial gain, either that he had his eye on her possessions or that he wants to inherit from his brother. Others interpret this to mean illicit sexual relations (*Hokhmat Manoaḥ*). Both positions find support in earlier sources.

The opinions of Abba Shaul and the Rabbis – שִׁיטוֹת אַבָּא שָׁאוּל וַחֲכָמִים: The early commentaries are divided as to what extent Abba Shaul intended to say that lack of appropriate motives would actually result in the violation of a prohibition, the offspring of which would be *mamzerim*. The Ramban understands Abba Shaul's opinion in the most extreme sense, i.e., when the *yavam* lacks the appropriate motives he does not acquire the *yevama* at all, and the children of such a union would actually be *mamzerim*. Others suggest that under all circumstances the *yavam* certainly acquires the *yevama*; Abba Shaul's point is that if the *yavam* lacks pure motives, then he transgresses a Torah prohibition by engaging in intercourse with her (*Keren Ora*). Still others hold that even Abba Shaul agrees that since the *yavam* is obligated to consummate the levirate marriage, there can be no Torah prohibition involved in doing so, even if he has impure motives. Nevertheless, the Sages prohibited the consummation of the levirate marriage unless his motives were pure. This interpretation explains why Abba Shaul specifically stated: As though he encountered a forbidden relation, and: I am inclined to view the offspring as a *mamzer*, instead of simply stating that the *yavam* encountered a forbidden relation and the offspring is a *mamzer* (*Nimmukei Yosef*).

Some commentaries explain that the dispute between Abba Shaul and the Rabbis hinges on the question of why it is permitted to consummate a levirate marriage in the first place, given that generally one is prohibited from engaging in relations with his brother's wife. They explain that Abba Shaul understood that in every case of levirate marriage there is a clash between two factors: The mitzva to consummate the levirate marriage and the prohibition against engaging in relations with one's brother's wife. The principle in such a case is that by performing the mitzva, one is permitted to disregard the prohibition. Accordingly, if one does not intend to fulfill the mitzva, one necessarily encounters the prohibition without permission to do so. This is readily understandable based on the comments of the Ramban that a mitzva overrides a prohibition because the former is an expression of one's love for God and the latter of one's awe, and when there is a choice between them, one should express one's love. As such, when one performs the mitzva not out of love but for some ulterior motive, the basis for permitting the prohibition is undermined. The Rabbis disagreed with the entire basis of this argument. They understood that it is not that the mitzva of levirate marriage overrides the prohibition against engaging in relations with one's brother's wife; rather, the scope of the prohibition itself is limited and does not apply to any case in which there is the possibility of consummating a levirate marriage. As such, the permission to consummate the levirate marriage is entirely unrelated to the intentions of the *yavam*, since there is simply no prohibition to speak of (*Kovetz He'arot*).

מַאן תַּנָּא? אָמַר רַבִּי יִצְחָק בַּר אַבְדִּימִי: אַבָּא שָׁאוּל הִיא, וְהָכִי קָאָמַר: "יְבָמָהּ יָבֹא עָלֶיהָ" מִצְוָה, שֶׁבִּתְחִלָּה הָיְתָה עָלָיו בִּכְלַל הֶיתֵּר, רָצָה לְשֵׁם נוֹי – כּוֹנְסָהּ, רָצָה לְשׁוּם אִישׁוּת – כּוֹנְסָהּ.

Who is the *tanna* who taught this *baraita*? Rav Yitzḥak bar Avdimi said: It is Abba Shaul, and this is what the *baraita* **is saying: "Her brother-in-law will have intercourse with her"** teaches that it is permitted to engage in intercourse with her only when his intention is to fulfill **a mitzva, as initially,** before she was married to his brother, **she** was **among** all other women who are **permitted to him,** and so, if **he wished,** then even **for the sake of** her **beauty he** was permitted to **marry her, or** similarly, if **he wished,** then even **for the sake of marital relations he** was permitted to **marry her.**

נֶאֶסְרָה, חָזְרָה וְהוּתְּרָה, יָכוֹל תַּחֲזוֹר לְהֶיתֵּירָהּ הָרִאשׁוֹן – תַּלְמוּד לוֹמַר "יְבָמָהּ יָבֹא עָלֶיהָ", לְמִצְוָה.

When she married his brother **she became forbidden** to him, and when his brother died without offspring **she reverted** from her forbidden status **and became permitted to him.** One **might** have thought that **she would** fully **revert to her original permitted** status; therefore, **the verse states: "Her brother-in-law will have intercourse with her"** to teach that he is permitted to marry her only when his intention is **for the mitzva.**

רָבָא אָמַר: אֲפִילּוּ תֵּימָא רַבָּנַן, וְהָכִי קָאָמַר: "יְבָמָהּ יָבֹא עָלֶיהָ" – מִצְוָה. שֶׁבִּתְחִלָּה הָיְתָה בִּכְלַל הֶיתֵּר. רָצָה – כּוֹנְסָהּ, רָצָה – אֵינוֹ כּוֹנְסָהּ.

Rava said: You can **even say** that the *baraita* is in accordance with **the Rabbis, and this is what** the *baraita* **is saying: "Her brother-in-law will have intercourse with her"** indicates that it is **a mitzva** to consummate the levirate marriage, **as initially,** before she was married to his brother, **she was among** all other women who are **permitted to him,** and so if **he wished, he** was permitted to **marry her, or** if **he wished, he** was permitted to choose **not to marry her.**

נֶאֶסְרָה, חָזְרָה וְהוּתְּרָה, יָכוֹל תַּחֲזוֹר לְהֶיתֵּירָהּ הָרִאשׁוֹן; רָצָה – כּוֹנְסָהּ, רָצָה – אֵינוֹ כּוֹנְסָהּ. רָצָה אֵינוֹ כּוֹנְסָהּ?

When she married his brother **she became forbidden** to him, and when his brother died without offspring **she reverted** from her forbidden status **and became permitted to him.** One **might** have thought that **she would** fully **revert to her original permitted status,** so that if **he wishes, he may marry her, or** if **he wishes, he** may choose **not to marry her.**

הָא אֲגִידָה בֵּיהּ, בִּכְדִי תֵּיפּוֹק?! אֶלָּא אֵימָא: רָצָה – כּוֹנְסָהּ, רָצָה – חוֹלֵץ לָהּ. תַּלְמוּד לוֹמַר: "יְבָמָהּ יָבֹא עָלֶיהָ" – מִצְוָה.

The Gemara interjects that the logic of this last statement seems implausible: Does he really have the option to do as he wishes? **Isn't she bound to him** with a levirate bond? Could it be that **she will be released** from that bond **without** doing **anything? Rather,** emend the previous argument and instead **say:** One might think that if **he wishes, he may marry her, or** if **he wishes** not to do so, **he performs *ḥalitza* with her.** Therefore, **the verse states: "Her brother-in-law will have intercourse with her,"** to teach that it is now **a mitzva** to consummate the marriage, and doing so is preferable to performing *ḥalitza*.

אֵימָא רֵישָׁא: "מַצּוֹת תֵּאָכֵל בְּמָקוֹם קָדוֹשׁ" – מִצְוָה,

The *baraita* under discussion also presents another case that follows a similar model of initially being permitted, then prohibited, and then once again permitted. The Gemara analyzes the explanations of Rav Yitzḥak and Rava based on that clause of the *baraita*: **Say the first clause** and try to explain it in a way consistent with the various explanations of the latter clause: The Torah states concerning the meal-offerings eaten by the priests: **"It shall be eaten unleavened in a sacred place"** (Leviticus 6:9); this indicates that doing so is **a mitzva,**

Perek **IV**
Daf **40** Amud **a**

שֶׁבִּתְחִלָּה הָיְתָה עָלָיו בִּכְלַל הֶיתֵּר, נֶאֶסְרָה, וְחָזְרָה וְהוּתְּרָה, יָכוֹל תַּחֲזוֹר לְהֶיתֵּירָהּ הָרִאשׁוֹן – תַּלְמוּד לוֹמַר "מַצּוֹת תֵּאָכֵל בְּמָקוֹם קָדוֹשׁ" מִצְוָה.

as initially, before the flour was consecrated, **it was among** all other foods that are **permitted to him,** and then when the flour was consecrated as a meal-offering, **it became forbidden** to him, **and** then once a handful of the offering was brought on the altar, **it reverted** from its forbidden status **and became permitted to him.** One **might** have thought that **it would revert to its original permitted status;** therefore, **the verse states: "It shall be eaten unleavened in a sacred place"** (Leviticus 6:9), which indicates that it is **a mitzva**[H] to eat it.

HALAKHA

It shall be eaten unleavened…indicates that it is a mitzva – מַצּוֹת תֵּאָכֵל...מִצְוָה: After the handful has been taken from the meal-offering and burned on the altar, it is a positive mitzva for the priests to eat the remainder of the offering (Rambam *Sefer Avoda*, *Hilkhot Ma'aseh HaKorbanot* 10:2).

בִּשְׁלָמָא לְרָבָא, דְּאָמַר הָא מַנִּי רַבָּנַן הִיא – הָכָא הָכִי קָאָמַר: ״מַצּוֹת תֵּאָכֵל בְּמָקוֹם קָדוֹשׁ״ מִצְוָה. שֶׁבַּתְּחִלָּה הָיְתָה עָלָיו בִּכְלַל הֶיתֵּר, רָצָה – אוֹכְלָהּ, רָצָה – אֵינוֹ אוֹכְלָהּ. (נֶאֶסְרָה, חָזְרָה וְהוּתְּרָה, יָכוֹל תַּחֲזוֹר לְהֶיתֵּירָהּ הָרִאשׁוֹן) – רָצָה אוֹכְלָהּ, רָצָה אֵינוֹ אוֹכְלָהּ.

The Gemara asks: **Granted, according to Rava, who said:** In accordance with **whose** opinion **is this** *baraita*? **It is** in accordance with the opinion of **the Rabbis;** according to him, **here,** in the first clause, **this is what** the *baraita* **is saying: "It shall be eaten unleavened in a sacred place"** indicates that it is **a mitzva** for the priest who prepares the offering to eat it himself. **As, initially,** before the flour was consecrated, **it was among** all other foods that are **permitted to him:** If **he wishes, he may eat it, and if he wishes, he may** choose **not to eat it.** When the flour was consecrated, **it became forbidden** to him, **and** then once a handful was brought on the altar, **it reverted** from its forbidden status **and became permitted to him.** One **might** have thought that **it would revert to its original permitted status,** so that if **he wishes, he may eat it, and if he wishes, he may** choose **not** to **eat it.**

רָצָה אֵינוֹ אוֹכְלָהּ?! וְהָכְתִיב ״וְאָכְלוּ אֹתָם אֲשֶׁר כֻּפַּר בָּהֶם״ מְלַמֵּד שֶׁהַכֹּהֲנִים אוֹכְלִים וּבְעָלִים מִתְכַּפְּרִין!

The Gemara interjects that the logic of this last statement seems implausible: Could it be that if **he wishes, he may** choose **not** to **eat it? But isn't it written: "And they shall eat those things through which atonement is attained"** (Exodus 29:33), which **teaches that the priests eat** portions of the offering **and** by their doing so **the owners** who brought the offering **attain atonement?**[H] Clearly, then, the eating of the offerings is not volitional.

אֶלָּא: רָצָה – הוּא אוֹכְלָהּ, רָצָה – כֹּהֵן אַחֵר אוֹכְלָהּ, תַּלְמוּד לוֹמַר ״מַצּוֹת תֵּאָכֵל בְּמָקוֹם קָדוֹשׁ״ – מִצְוָה.

Rather, the *baraita* should be understood as saying: One might have thought that if **he wishes, he may eat it, and if he wishes, another priest may eat it;** therefore, **the verse states: "It shall be eaten unleavened in a sacred place"** (Leviticus 6:9), to teach that it is a **mitzva** for the priest who prepares the offering to eat it himself. This explanation of the first clause of the *baraita* is entirely consistent with Rava's explanation of the latter clause concerning the mitzvot of levirate marriage. In his opinion, both clauses demonstrate that there is a mitzva to perform an action in a case where one might have thought there was none.

אֶלָּא לְרַב יִצְחָק בַּר אַבְדִּימִי, דְּאָמַר אַבָּא שָׁאוּל הִיא – הָכָא מַאי תְּרֵי גַּוְונֵי אִיכָּא?

However, according to Rav Yitzḥak bar Avdimi, who said that the *baraita* **is** in accordance with the opinion of **Abba Shaul** and explained the *baraita* accordingly as teaching the correct manner in which the mitzva is to be performed, **here,** in the first clause concerning the meal-offering, **what two manners** of eating **are there**[N] of which one would be prohibited?

וְכִי תֵּימָא: רָצָה – לְתֵאָבוֹן אוֹכְלָהּ, רָצָה – אֲכִילָה גַּסָּה אוֹכְלָהּ, אֲכִילָה גַּסָּה מִי שְׁמָהּ אֲכִילָה? וְהָאָמַר רֵישׁ לָקִישׁ: הָאוֹכֵל אֲכִילָה גַּסָּה בְּיוֹם הַכִּפּוּרִים – פָּטוּר מִ״לֹּא תְעֻנֶּה״!

And if you would say that the *baraita* might refer to two types of eating and is saying: One might have thought that if **he wishes he may eat it with an appetite, and if he wishes he may eat it** though an act of **excessive eating,** forcing himself to eat despite already being fully satiated; perforce this is not correct, as does **excessive eating have the** legal **status of** an act of **eating? Didn't Reish Lakish say: One who eats** through an act of **excessive eating on Yom Kippur**[NH] **is exempt from** the punishment of *karet* indicated in the verse: "For whatever soul it be that **shall not be afflicted** in that same day shall be cut off from his people" (Leviticus 23:29)? From this it is apparent that excessive eating does not have the legal status of an act of eating.

NOTES

What two manners are there – מַאי תְּרֵי גַּוְונֵי אִיכָּא: One could suggest that according to the opinion that in general the fulfillment of mitzvot is achieved only when one has intention to fulfill them, there is a very simple way of explaining the clause concerning the meal-offering: If it is eaten with intention to fulfill the mitzva, then it is permitted; otherwise it would be prohibited due to the general prohibition against benefiting from consecrated items. The *Keren Ora* suggests that the Gemara did not raise this option because even if in general one requires intention for the fulfillment of mitzvot, this might not apply to the consumption of sacred foods. The reason for this would be that their consumption by the priesthood is referred to as being given "for anointment" (Numbers 18:8), which the Gemara in *Zevaḥim* interprets elsewhere as meaning that it is to be eaten in grandeur, as kings eat. As such, it is possible that when eating it the priests are not required to focus on the fact that doing so is a mitzva but instead may eat it for their own purposes; provided they eat it with appetite, they fulfill what is required of them. Another resolution can be offered based on the opinion of *Tosafot* and Ran in tractate *Pesaḥim*. They explain that mitzvot that require one to eat never require specific intent to fulfill the mitzva, since the benefit of eating perforce defines the act as one of intention.

One who eats through an act of excessive eating on Yom Kippur – הָאוֹכֵל אֲכִילָה גַּסָּה בְּיוֹם הַכִּפּוּרִים: From the statement of Reish Lakish alone it would appear that the reason for the exemption is because the prohibition against eating on Yom Kippur is expressed by the Torah as one of affliction, which suggests that only acts that alleviate one's affliction are prohibited. Therefore, excessive eating, which causes one discomfort, should not be prohibited. This is the interpretation of Rabbi Avraham min HaHar. Accordingly, although excessive eating might be considered an unusual act of eating, it certainly has the legal status of an act of eating, and therefore one who eats forbidden foods in such a manner would be liable for doing so. The Meiri disagrees and claims that Reish Lakish's teaching is not unique to Yom Kippur; rather, it is a principle that an excessive act of eating does not have the legal status of an act of eating. Therefore, it applies to all cases in which an act of eating is necessary. This is also the opinion of the *Maggid Mishne* and the Ran. Accordingly, even if one were to eat forbidden foods through an act of excessive eating, one would be exempt.

Tosafot note that the Gemara states elsewhere that one who eats the Paschal lamb through an act of excessive eating does fulfill one's obligation, even though doing so is not the proper way to fulfill the mitzva. This would appear to imply, contrary to the Gemara here, that an act of excessive eating does have the legal status of an act of eating. To resolve this difficulty, *Tosafot* differentiate between two levels of excessiveness. The Gemara here discusses the case of one who has eaten to the point at which eating anything else would be repulsive to him. At that point, any further eating does not have the legal status of an act of eating; one in that state would not fulfill his obligation to eat the Paschal lamb. The Gemara that states that one does fulfill one's obligation of eating the Paschal lamb concerns an earlier stage, where one has already eaten to satiation, but further eating is still not repulsive. Eating in this manner, while inappropriate for the Paschal lamb, is certainly considered an act of eating.

The Ramban suggests a different distinction. The Gemara concerning the Paschal lamb does not actually discuss a case of excessive eating at all; rather, it concerns the motivation for eating the offering and discusses the case of one who, although he has still not achieved satiation, eats the Paschal lamb as part of an attempt to gorge himself. This is apparent from the precise formulation of the Gemara there, which states that he ate the Paschal lamb: For the stage of gorging. The Ramban offers an additional resolution that since the mitzva of the Paschal lamb is primarily fulfilled through its sacrifice and not through its consumption, the requirement to eat does not demand the same strict standards for an act of eating that apply elsewhere, and therefore even an act of excessive eating is sufficient. A similar approach is also suggested by *Tosafot Yeshanim*.

HALAKHA

The priests eat and the owners attain atonement – הַכֹּהֲנִים אוֹכְלִים וּבְעָלִים מִתְכַּפְּרִין: There is a positive mitzva for the priests to eat the meat of sin-offerings and guilt-offerings, and through their doing so the owners of those offerings attain atonement. Similarly, the consumption of other offerings by the priests is also a positive mitzva (Rambam *Sefer Avoda, Hilkhot Ma'aseh HaKorbanot* 10:1).

Excessive eating on Yom Kippur – אֲכִילָה גַּסָּה בְּיוֹם הַכִּפּוּרִים: If one eats excessively on Yom Kippur, e.g., if one continues to eat in addition to that which he ate prior to the onset of Yom Kippur to the point that he is repulsed by his food, he is exempt. Some rule that he would still be liable for eating sweet foods, since one continues to have an appetite for such foods even after one is fully satiated (Rema, citing *Kol Bo*). However, even for such foods, if one reached a point where he found even them to be repulsive, he would be exempt (*Baḥ*; Rambam *Sefer Zemanim, Hilkhot Shevitat Asor* 2:7; *Shulḥan Arukh, Oraḥ Ḥayyim* 612:6).

אֶלָּא: רָצָה – מַצָּה אוֹכְלָהּ, רָצָה – חָמֵץ אוֹכְלָהּ,

The Gemara therefore suggests a different interpretation of the *baraita* that is consistent with Rav Yitzḥak's opinion: **Rather,** say the *baraita* is referring to two different manners in which the meal-offering was prepared: If **he wishes he may eat it unleavened,** and if **he wishes he may eat it leavened.**

וְהָכְתִיב ״לֹא תֵאָפֶה חָמֵץ חֶלְקָם״, וְאָמַר רֵישׁ לָקִישׁ: וַאֲפִילּוּ חֶלְקָם לֹא תֵאָפֶה חָמֵץ! אֶלָּא: רָצָה – מַצָּה אוֹכְלָהּ, רָצָה – חָלוּט אוֹכְלָהּ.

The Gemara interjects that the logic of this last statement seems implausible: Could it be that if he wishes, the offering could be leavened? **But isn't it written: "Their portion shall not be baked leavened"** (Leviticus 6:10),[H] **and Reish Lakish said** that both the handful brought on the altar **and even the** priest's **portion shall not be baked leavened? Rather,** the *baraita* should be understood as saying: One might have thought that if **he wishes he may eat it unleavened,** and if **he wishes he may eat it** even if it was prepared by being **boiled.**[H] Therefore, the verse taught that one must eat it unleavened. Understood in this way, this clause of the *baraita* is also consistent with Rav Yitzḥak's opinion.

הַאי חָלוּט הֵיכִי דָּמֵי? אִי מַצָּה הִיא – הָא מַצָּה הִיא, וְאִי לָא מַצָּה הִיא – ״מַצּוֹת״ אָמַר רַחֲמָנָא!

The Gemara asks: With regard to **this** possibility of eating the meal-offering **boiled, what are the circumstances,** i.e., how is it classified? **If it is** considered to be **unleavened** because it is presumed that the flour never managed to rise before it was cooked, **then it is unleavened** and there is no reason to prohibit its use; **and if it is not** considered to be **unleavened** because it is presumed that the flour managed to rise before it was cooked, then it is certainly disqualified from use because **the Merciful One states** that the offering must be **"unleavened"** (Leviticus 10:12).[N] How, then, could one ever have questioned whether it is permitted to eat the meal-offering if it was boiled?

לָא, לְעוֹלָם אֵימָא לָךְ מַצָּה הִיא, וּלְהָכִי תְּנָא בֵּיהּ קְרָא – לְעַכֵּב.

The Gemara explains: **No; actually, I** could **say to you** that the boiled meal-offering **is** considered to be **unleavened, and** nevertheless it is disqualified because it is **for this** very reason that **the verse repeated** the requirement that it be unleavened, in order **to invalidate** a meal-offering that was boiled.

אֶלָּא חָלוּט מַצָּה הִיא דְּקָאָמְרִינַן, לְמַאי הִלְכְתָא? לוֹמַר שֶׁאָדָם יוֹצֵא בָּהּ יְדֵי חוֹבָתוֹ בְּפֶסַח, אַף עַל פִּי דְּחָלְטֵיהּ מֵעִיקָּרָא, כֵּיוָן דַּהֲדַר אֲפָיֵיהּ בְּתַנּוּר – ״לֶחֶם עוֹנִי״ קָרֵינָא בֵּיהּ, וְאָדָם יוֹצֵא בָּהּ יְדֵי חוֹבָתוֹ בְּפֶסַח.

The Gemara asks: **But** if boiled flour is invalid as a meal offering, then with regard to this statement **that we said** that **boiled** flour **is unleavened, for what *halakha* is it** relevant? The Gemara answers: It is **to say that a person fulfills his obligation with it on Passover.** This is because **even though he initially boiled it, since he subsequently baked it in an oven, it is called "bread of affliction"** (Deuteronomy 16:3),[N] **and** therefore **a person fulfills his obligation with it on Passover.**

מתני׳ הַחוֹלֵץ לִיבִמְתּוֹ – הֲרֵי הוּא כְּאֶחָד מִן הָאַחִין לְנַחֲלָה, וְאִם יֵשׁ שָׁם אָב – נְכָסִים שֶׁל אָב. הַכּוֹנֵס אֶת יְבִמְתּוֹ זָכָה בִּנְכָסִים שֶׁל אָחִיו. רַבִּי יְהוּדָה אוֹמֵר: בֵּין כָּךְ וּבֵין כָּךְ, אִם יֵשׁ שָׁם אָב – נְכָסִים שֶׁל אָב.

MISHNA **One who performs *ḥalitza* with his *yevama* is like** any **one of the** other **brothers with respect to the inheritance**[H] of the deceased brother's estate, i.e., each of the brothers takes an equal share of the inheritance. **And if there is a father** of the deceased, who is still alive, **the property** of the deceased **belongs to the father. One who consummates** levirate marriage with **his *yevama***[H] thereby **acquires his** deceased **brother's property** solely for himself. **Rabbi Yehuda says: In either** case, whether he consummated the levirate marriage or performed *ḥalitza*, **if there is a father** who is still alive, **the property belongs to the father.**

גמ׳ פְּשִׁיטָא! סָלְקָא דַּעְתָּךְ אָמִינָא: חֲלִיצָה בִּמְקוֹם יִבּוּם קָיְימָא, וְנִשְׁקוֹל כּוּלְּהוּ נִכְסֵי, קָא מַשְׁמַע לַן.

GEMARA The Gemara asks with regard to the opening clause of the mishna: The fact that one who performs *ḥalitza* does not gain any special rights to the inheritance of the deceased brother **is obvious;** why did the mishna teach it? The Gemara answers: **It could enter your mind to say** that the ***ḥalitza* takes the place of the levirate marriage and** therefore the brother who performs *ḥalitza* **should take all the property** in the same way as one who consummates the levirate marriage. Therefore, the mishna **teaches us** that this is not the case.

HALAKHA

Their portion shall not be baked leavened – לֹא תֵאָפֶה חָמֵץ חֶלְקָם: Although the priests are permitted to eat the remainders of the meal-offerings together with other foods prepared in any manner, it is nevertheless prohibited to eat them leavened. If the remainders of the meal-offerings became leavened, the priests responsible for doing so would transgress a negative mitzva and receive lashes. This is in accordance with the opinion of Reish Lakish (Rambam *Sefer Avoda, Hilkhot Ma'aseh HaKorbanot* 12:14).

Boiled unleavened bread – מַצָּה חֲלוּטָה: Flour scalded in boiling water and then baked is regarded as unleavened, and consequently one could fulfill one's obligation to eat *matza* on Passover by eating it. However, nowadays, no one knows how to scald the flour with enough speed and care to ensure it does not rise and become leavened. Therefore, flour boiled in water is considered to be leavened and is forbidden (*Tur*, citing the *ge'onim*; Rambam *Sefer Zemanim, Hilkhot Ḥametz UMatza* 6:6; *Shulḥan Arukh, Oraḥ Ḥayyim* 454:3).

The status of one who performs *ḥalitza* is like any one of the brothers with respect to the inheritance – הַחוֹלֵץ דִּינוֹ כְּאֶחָד הָאַחִים לְנַחֲלָה: One who performs *ḥalitza* with his *yevama* is like any one of the other brothers with respect to the inheritance of the deceased brother's estate. Each of the brothers takes an equal share of the inheritance. If the father is still alive, then he alone inherits from his son. The Rema notes that even if the *yavam* wishes to consummate the levirate marriage but the *yevama* refuses him, he still does not attain any rights to the deceased brother's estate. In some communities the custom has developed that the one who performs *ḥalitza* receives half of the brother's estate (*Shulḥan Arukh, Even HaEzer* 163:2).

One who consummates levirate marriage with his *yevama* – הַכּוֹנֵס אֶת יְבִמְתּוֹ: One who consummates levirate marriage with his *yevama* thereby acquires his deceased brother's property and any property that the brother was already due to inherit at the time of his death. However, he does not gain the rights to inherit the property that his brother would have inherited, were he still alive, if it only becomes available after his brother's death. This is in accordance with the opinion of the Rabbis (Rambam *Sefer Mishpatim, Hilkhot Naḥalot* 3:7; *Shulḥan Arukh, Even HaEzer* 163:1).

NOTES

The Merciful One states "unleavened" – מַצּוֹת אָמַר רַחֲמָנָא: Rashi claims the Gemara is citing the verse: "And eat it unleavened beside the altar" (Leviticus 10:12), which, although it concerns only one specific type of meal-offering, is understood to be true for all meal-offerings (see *Tosafot*). Other commentaries suggest that the Gemara is not citing a verse but is referring to the *halakha* that is established from the verse previously cited by the Gemara: "Their portion shall not be baked with leaven" (Leviticus 6:10), which teaches the requirement that all meal-offerings must be unleavened (*Tosafot Yeshanim*). The Rashba questions why, according to Rashi's understanding, there is a need for a verse to teach the requirement that the meal-offering be unleavened, given that there is already another verse prohibiting one from baking a leavened meal-offering. He explains that the additional verse is required to emphasize that it is not sufficient if the meal-offering is not leavened; rather, it must be baked such that it is clearly unleavened.

Bread of affliction – לֶחֶם עוֹנִי: Some commentaries explain that by describing the *matza* that one is required to eat on Passover as bread of affliction, the Torah indicates that it should be of an inferior quality, similar to the bread eaten by the poor. When *matza* is boiled its texture is enhanced, and it is no longer similar to the bread eaten by the poor (Razah and Ra'avad; see Rashi on *Pesaḥim* 36b). Others explain that dough boiled in water cannot be classified as bread (Rabbeinu Yehonatan of Lunel on *Pesaḥim* 36b). However, if it is baked again in an oven its original texture is restored, and in that case it may be used for the mitzva.

אִי הָכִי ״הֲרֵי הוּא כְּאֶחָד מִן הָאַחִים״? אֵינוֹ אֶלָּא כְּאֶחָד מִן הָאַחִים מִיבְּעֵי לֵיהּ!

The Gemara asks: **If so,** that the mishna's point is to teach that by performing *ḥalitza* one is not afforded any additional rights to the inheritance, why is the mishna formulated as: **He is like** any **one of the** other **brothers,** placing the emphasis on what he gains? **It should have** instead taught: **He is** still **only like one of the** other **brothers,** which would emphasize the mishna's point that by performing *ḥalitza* he does not gain any additional rights.

אֶלָּא, סָלְקָא דַּעְתָּךְ אָמִינָא: הוֹאִיל וְאַפְסְדָהּ מִיבּוּם לִקְנְסֵיהּ, קָא מַשְׁמַע לָן.

Rather, the mishna needs to teach the opening clause in this manner because **it could enter your mind to say** that **since** by performing *ḥalitza* with his *yevama* **he caused her to forfeit** the possibility of consummating the **levirate marriage,**[N] **he should be penalized** and should forfeit any entitlement to his brother's property. Therefore the mishna **teaches us** that this is not so.

״אִם יֵשׁ שָׁם אָב״. דַּאֲמַר מָר: אָב קוֹדֵם לְכָל יוֹצְאֵי יְרֵכוֹ.

§ The mishna states: **If there is a father** of the deceased, who is still alive, the property of the deceased belongs to the father. The Gemara explains: **As the Master said** with regard to the laws of inheritance (*Bava Batra* 115a): **A father** of the deceased **takes precedence over all** the father's **descendants.**[H] Therefore, since the father is still alive, the brothers do not inherit at all.

״הַכּוֹנֵס אֶת יְבִמְתּוֹ״ וכו׳. מַאי טַעֲמָא? ״יָקוּם עַל שֵׁם אָחִיו״ אָמַר רַחֲמָנָא, וַהֲרֵי קָם.

The mishna states: **One who consummates** levirate marriage with his *yevama* thereby acquires his deceased brother's property. The Gemara asks: **What is the reason** for this? **The Merciful One states** in the Torah: **"He shall succeed in the name of his** dead **brother"** (Deuteronomy 25:6), **and he has succeeded** him by marrying his wife; consequently, he succeeds him by acquiring his property as well.

״רַבִּי יְהוּדָה אוֹמֵר״ וכו׳. אָמַר עוּלָּא: הֲלָכָה כְּרַבִּי יְהוּדָה. וְכֵן אָמַר רַבִּי יִצְחָק נַפָּחָא: הֲלָכָה כְּרַבִּי יְהוּדָה.

§ The mishna continues by citing an opposing opinion. **Rabbi Yehuda says:** In either case, whether he consummated levirate marriage or performed *ḥalitza*, if there is a father who is still alive, the property belongs to the father. The Gemara cites a ruling on this dispute: **Ulla said:** The ***halakha* is in accordance with** the opinion of **Rabbi Yehuda. And similarly, Rabbi Yitzḥak Nappaḥa said: The *halakha* is in accordance with** the opinion **of Rabbi Yehuda.**

וַאֲמַר עוּלָּא וְאִיתֵימָא רַבִּי יִצְחָק נַפָּחָא: מַאי טַעֲמָא דְּרַבִּי יְהוּדָה – דִּכְתִיב ״וְהָיָה הַבְּכוֹר אֲשֶׁר תֵּלֵד״, כִּבְכוֹר: מַה בְּכוֹר אֵין לוֹ בְּחַיֵּי הָאָב – אַף הַאי נַמִי אֵין לוֹ בְּחַיֵּי הָאָב.

And Ulla said, and some say that it was **Rabbi Yitzḥak Nappaḥa** who said: **What is the reason** for the opinion **of Rabbi Yehuda? As it is written: "And it shall be that the firstborn that she bears** shall succeed in the name of his dead brother" (Deuteronomy 25:6). The term "firstborn" is understood to be a reference to the *yavam*. By referring to him in this way the Torah indicates that his rights to his brother's estate are **like** those of **a firstborn** child's rights to his father's estate: **Just as a firstborn has no** rights to any of his father's estate **during the lifetime of the father,** and he may take his double portion only upon the father's death, **so too, this** *yavam* **as well has no** rights to any of his brother's estate **during the lifetime of the father.**

אִי מַה בְּכוֹר נוֹטֵל פִּי שְׁנַיִם לְאַחַר מִיתַת הָאָב – אַף הַאי נוֹטֵל פִּי שְׁנַיִם לְאַחַר מִיתַת הָאָב!

The Gemara asks: **If** there is truly a comparison between the *yavam* who consummated the levirate marriage and a firstborn, then one should also say that **just as the firstborn takes a double portion** of his father's estate **after the death of the father, so too, this** *yavam* **should** become entitled to **take a double portion** of the father's estate **after the father's death,** i.e., the portion due to him as a son, and that portion that would have been awarded to his brother. However, this is not the case; if the *yavam* is not actually the father's firstborn then he receives only an equal portion of the inheritance together with the other brothers.

מִידֵי ״יָקוּם עַל שֵׁם אָבִיו״ כְּתִיב? ״יָקוּם עַל שֵׁם אָחִיו״ כְּתִיב, וְלֹא ״עַל שֵׁם אָבִיו״!

The Gemara explains: **Is it written** in the Torah: **He shall succeed in the name of his father?** No, **it is written: "He shall succeed in the name of his dead brother,"** which indicates that he succeeds his brother **but not in the name of his father,**[N] i.e., the Torah never granted him any special entitlement to his father's estate, and so he should not receive a double portion of it.

NOTES

Since he caused her to forfeit the possibility of levirate marriage – הוֹאִיל וְאַפְסְדָהּ מִיבּוּם: Some commentaries question why one who performs *ḥalitza* should be penalized. They note that *ḥalitza* is performed only after it is clarified that none of the brothers are willing to consummate the levirate marriage. If so, the one who ultimately performs *ḥalitza* is not preventing her from consummating the levirate marriage, as that possibility had already been ruled out. They explain that the case here must be one in which a younger brother performed *ḥalitza* before his older brothers had been given the opportunity to consummate the levirate marriage. As such, his *ḥalitza* actually precluded the possibility of her consummating the levirate marriage with the brothers he preempted, and therefore there is reason to assume that he should be penalized (see *Arukh LaNer* and *Yosef Lekaḥ*).

It is written: He shall succeed in the name of his dead brother, but not in the name of his father – יָקוּם עַל שֵׁם אָחִיו כְּתִיב וְלֹא עַל שֵׁם אָבִיו: The underlying principle indicated by this inference is that despite the fact that he consummated the levirate marriage, the *yavam* does not become entitled to the portion of his father's estate that would have been awarded to his deceased brother were he still alive. Therefore, according to Rabbi Yehuda, if the father is still alive at the time of the brother's death then the father takes full ownership of his estate, and when the father subsequently dies, the *yavam* who consummated the levirate marriage has no more claim to the estate than any of the other brothers. Many commentaries assume that this principle is similarly true according to the Rabbis. They explain that the Rabbis dispute Rabbi Yehuda's opinion only in their claim that even if the father is still alive when the brother dies, the *yavam* inherits the brother's estate at that time. However, even the Rabbis agree that when the father subsequently dies, the *yavam* does not become entitled to the portion of his father's estate that would have been awarded to his deceased brother (Rambam; Ramban). Other commentaries claim that the Rabbis do in fact dispute this principle and that according to them, when a *yavam* consummates the levirate marriage he becomes entitled not only to the estate of his deceased brother as it exists at that time, but also to his brother's inheritance rights, which will became germane only at a later date. Therefore, when the father subsequently dies, the *yavam* does receive both the portion that is due to him as a son, and the portion that would have been awarded to his brother (see *Yam shel Shlomo*).

HALAKHA

The father of the deceased take precedence over all the father's descendants – הָאָב קוֹדֵם לְכָל יוֹצְאֵי חֲלָצָיו: If one dies without descendants, then his father is entitled to his inheritance. If the father is not alive, the inheritance passes on to the father's descendants, e.g., the deceased's brothers; if they are not alive, the inheritance passes on to their descendants (Rambam *Sefer Mishpatim*, *Hilkhot Naḥalot* 1:2; *Shulḥan Arukh*, *Ḥoshen Mishpat* 276:1).

אֵימָא: הֵיכָא דְּלֵיכָּא אָב דְּלִשְׁקוֹל נַחֲלָה – תִּתְקַיֵּים מִצְוַת יִבּוּם, הֵיכָא דְּאִיכָּא אָב, [דְּלָא] שָׁקֵיל נַחֲלָה – לָא תִּתְקַיֵּים מִצְוַת יִבּוּם!

The Gemara asks: Since Rabbi Yehuda holds that the *halakha* that the *yavam* inherits from his brother, which is stated in the verses describing levirate marriage, applies only when the father is no longer alive, perhaps the other *halakhot* in those verses also apply only when the father is no longer alive, and accordingly one should **say: When there is no father** who is still alive, which means **that** the *yavam* **takes the inheritance,** only then **should the mitzva of levirate marriage apply,** but **when there is a father** who is still alive, which means **that** the *yavam* **does not take the inheritance,** in that case **the mitzva of levirate marriage should not apply.**

מִידֵּי יִבּוּם בְּנַחֲלָה תָּלָה רַחֲמָנָא? יְבוּמֵי מְיַבְּמִי, וְאִי אִיכָּא נַחֲלָה – שָׁקְלִי, וְאִי לָא – לָא שָׁקֵיל.

The Gemara rejects the possibility of saying this: **Does the Merciful One make** the mitzva of **levirate marriage dependent upon inheritance?**[N] Certainly not; rather, in all cases the *yavam* **should consummate the levirate marriage, and** then **if there is an inheritance** to which he is entitled, **he takes** it, **and if not, he does not take** it.

יָתֵיב רַבִּי חֲנִינָא קָרָא קַמֵּיהּ דְּרַבִּי יַנַּאי, וְיָתֵיב וְקָאָמַר: הֲלָכָה כְּרַבִּי יְהוּדָה. אָמַר לֵיהּ: פּוּק קְרִי קְרָיָיךְ לְבָרָא, אֵין הֲלָכָה כְּרַבִּי יְהוּדָה.

Rabbi Ḥanina Kara, the Bible expert,[P] **was sitting before Rabbi Yannai, and he was sitting and saying:** The *halakha* **is in accordance with** the opinion of **Rabbi Yehuda.** Rabbi Yannai **said to him: Leave** the study hall **and recite your verses outside,** as you are incorrect in your ruling; in fact, the ***halakha* is not in accordance with** the opinion of **Rabbi Yehuda.**

תָּנֵי תַּנָּא קַמֵּיהּ דְּרַב נַחְמָן: אֵין הֲלָכָה כְּרַבִּי יְהוּדָה. אָמַר לֵיהּ: אֶלָּא כְּמַאן, כְּרַבָּנַן? פְּשִׁיטָא, יָחִיד וְרַבִּים הֲלָכָה כְּרַבִּים!

In another incident, **a** ***tanna***[N] who would recite *baraitot* in the study hall **taught** a *baraita* **before Rav Naḥman:** The ***halakha* is not in accordance with** the opinion of **Rabbi Yehuda. Rav Naḥman said to him: But** then it follows that **in accordance with whose** opinion is the *halakha*? It is the opinion of **the Rabbis.** The Gemara asks: But this fact **is obvious,** as in a dispute between **one** individual Sage **and many**[N] other Sages, the ***halakha*** is always decided in accordance with the opinion of **the many.**

אָמַר לֵיהּ: אַסְמְיֵיהּ?! אָמַר לֵיהּ: לָא, אַתְּ "הֲלָכָה" אַתְנְיָיךְ, וּמוּקְשָׁה הוּא דְּאַקְשִׁי לָךְ, וְאַפְּכַתְּ, וּלְמַאי דְּאַפְּכַתְּ – שַׁפִּיר אַפְּכַתְּ.

The *tanna* **said to him:** Are you saying that this statement in the *baraita* is unnecessary and so **I should remove that** ruling from the *baraita* when I recite it in the future? Rav Naḥman **said to him: No,** do not remove it, as although the statement is unnecessary, it is correct. Rav Naḥman explained further: It must be that originally the *baraita* that **you were taught** stated: The ***halakha*** is in accordance with the opinion of Rabbi Yehuda, and **that** ruling **was difficult for you** because you knew that the *halakha* is always decided in accordance with many, **and so you reversed** the statement of the *baraita* to say, as you presently recited it, that the *halakha* is not in accordance with the opinion of Rabbi Yehuda. **And** with regard to the manner in **which you reversed it, you reversed it well,** and therefore you should leave it in its current form.

מַתְנִי׳ הַחוֹלֵץ לִיבִמְתּוֹ – הוּא אָסוּר בִּקְרוֹבוֹתֶיהָ, וְהִיא אֲסוּרָה בִּקְרוֹבָיו.

MISHNA In the case of **one who performs *ḥalitza* with his *yevama*,** by rabbinic decree it is as though she had been married to him and then he divorced her. Consequently, **he is forbidden** to engage in relations **with her relatives**[H] **and she is forbidden** to engage in relations **with his relatives.**

NOTES

Does the Merciful One make levirate marriage dependent upon inheritance – מִידֵּי יִבּוּם בְּנַחֲלָה תָּלָה רַחֲמָנָא: The Gemara elsewhere (see 17b) does appear to link the mitzva of levirate marriage with the ability to inherit the deceased brother's property. However, in truth, there is a clear distinction between the two discussions. The Gemara that links the two concerns the question of which fraternal relationships qualify for the mitzva to apply and establishes that only brothers who can inherit from one another are obligated in the mitzva of levirate marriage toward each other's wives. The Gemara here that states that the mitzva is not dependent on whether the *yavam* can inherit the deceased brother's property is discussing a case where the *yavam* has the appropriate fraternal relationship, but in the present circumstances he will not actually inherit from the deceased brother because the father is still alive. In summary, the relationship which creates the possibility of inheritance must exist in order for the mitzva to apply, but there is no need for the *yavam* to actually inherit from his brother (*Tosefot HaRosh*; *Tosafot Yeshanim*).

***Tanna* – תַּנָּא:** The *tanna* referred to here is not a Sage from the tannaitic period. Rather, the term refers to those who memorized large numbers of *mishnayot* and *baraitot* to be able to quote them for the Sages who were engaged in analysis. Occasionally, the Sage had to emend the versions of these sources that had become corrupted or that represented minority opinions that had been rejected.

It is obvious, as in a dispute between one and many, etc. – פְּשִׁיטָא, יָחִיד וְרַבִּים וכו׳: The early commentaries point out that apparently it is not so obvious that the *halakha* should be decided in accordance with the opinion of the Rabbis because the Gemara itself cites many Sages who in fact ruled in accordance with the opinion of Rabbi Yehuda, and many more rulings to this effect are cited in the Jerusalem Talmud. They explain that what truly troubled Rav Naḥman was not the actual ruling in accordance with the opinion of the Rabbis but the roundabout formulation of the *baraita*: If the *halakha* is indeed in accordance with the opinion of the Rabbis, why didn't it simply say so explicitly, since the reason to rule in accordance with their opinion is not because of some issue with Rabbi Yehuda's opinion but simply because they represent the majority (Rashba; Ritva).

PERSONALITIES

Rabbi Ḥanina Kara, the Bible expert – רַבִּי חֲנִינָא קָרָא: A second-generation *amora* in Eretz Yisrael, Rabbi Ḥanina was a disciple of Rabbi Ḥanina bar Ḥama, Rabbi Ḥanina the Great, and Rabbi Yannai. Apparently, Rabbi Ḥanina not only taught young children but was also a Bible expert, which is why he was called *Kara*, meaning: The reader. He is mentioned in the Talmud and the midrash in discussions with his two teachers, both on matters relating to his work and on other halakhic matters.

HALAKHA

One who performs *ḥalitza* with his *yevama* is forbidden to engage in relations with her relatives – הַחוֹלֵץ לִיבִמְתּוֹ אָסוּר בִּקְרוֹבוֹתֶיהָ: One who performs *ḥalitza* with his *yevama* is forbidden to her relatives, i.e., her mother, her mother's mother, etc., since by rabbinic decree it is considered as though she was actually married to him and then he divorced her. Similarly, she is forbidden to his relatives (Rambam *Sefer Nashim*, *Hilkhot Yibbum VaḤalitza* 1:13; *Shulḥan Arukh*, *Even HaEzer* 162:3).

HALAKHA

He is permitted to a relative of a rival wife of his *ḥalutza* – מוּתָּר בִּקְרוֹבַת צָרַת חֲלוּצָתוֹ: It is permitted to marry a sister or any other relatives of a rival wife of one's *ḥalutza* (Rambam *Sefer Nashim, Hilkhot Yibbum VaḤalitza* 1:13; *Shulḥan Arukh, Even HaEzer* 162:4).

He is forbidden to engage in relations with a rival wife of a relative of his *ḥalutza* – אָסוּר בְּצָרַת קְרוֹבַת חֲלוּצָתוֹ: If one performed *ḥalitza* with his *yevama*, and her sister or other relative was married to another brother, who also died, such that the relative and her rival wife happened before him for levirate marriage, then just as the relative of the *ḥalutza* is forbidden to him, so too, her rival wife is forbidden to him, and they must perform *ḥalitza* but may not consummate the levirate marriage. This is in accordance with the ruling of the Rambam and most of the commentaries (Rambam *Sefer Nashim, Hilkhot Yibbum VaḤalitza* 6:20; *Shulḥan Arukh, Even HaEzer* 162:5, 174:3).

הוּא אָסוּר בְּאִמָּהּ, וּבְאֵם אִמָּהּ, וּבְאֵם אָבִיהָ, וּבְבִתָּהּ, וּבְבַת בִּתָּהּ, וּבְבַת בְּנָהּ, וּבַאֲחוֹתָהּ בִּזְמַן שֶׁהִיא קַיֶּימֶת, וְהָאַחִין מוּתָּרִין.

Accordingly, **he is forbidden** to engage in relations **with her mother,**[N] **and with her mother's mother, and with her father's mother, and with her daughter, and with her daughter's daughter, and with her son's daughter, and with her sister while** his *yevama* **is** still **alive.** However, **the** other **brothers** who did not perform *ḥalitza* **are permitted** to her relatives.

וְהִיא אֲסוּרָה בְּאָבִיו, וּבַאֲבִי אָבִיו, וּבִבְנוֹ, וּבְבֶן בְּנוֹ, בְּאָחִיו, וּבְבֶן אָחִיו.

And she is forbidden to engage in relations **with his father,**[N] **and with his father's father, and with his son, and with his son's son, and with his brother, and with his brother's son.**

מוּתָּר אָדָם בִּקְרוֹבַת צָרַת חֲלוּצָתוֹ, וְאָסוּר בְּצָרַת קְרוֹבַת חֲלוּצָתוֹ.

The mishna states an additional principle: **A man is permitted** to engage in relations **with a relative of a rival wife of his *ḥalutza*,**[H] i.e., his *yevama* with whom he performed *ḥalitza*. Since he did not perform *ḥalitza* with her, she is not regarded as though she had actually been married to him. However, **he is forbidden** to engage in relations **with a rival wife of a relative of his *ḥalutza*,**[HN] i.e., in addition to being forbidden to the relatives of his *ḥalutza*, he is also forbidden to their rival wives.

גמ׳ אִיבַּעְיָא לְהוּ: גָּזְרוּ שְׁנִיּוֹת בַּחֲלוּצָה אוֹ לָא?

GEMARA A dilemma was raised before the Sages: In addition to the Torah prohibition against engaging in relations with one's wife's close relatives, the Sages decreed that it is also prohibited to engage in relations with one's wife's secondary relatives, i.e., those who are less closely related and so are permitted by Torah law. Since the Sages decreed that a *ḥalutza* is to be regarded as though she had actually been married to the one who performed *ḥalitza*, such that her close relatives are forbidden to him, did **they** also **decree** that the prohibition of **secondary** forbidden **relationships** should also apply **in** the case of **a *ḥalutza*, or not?**

NOTES

He is forbidden to engage in relations with her mother, etc. – הוּא אָסוּר בְּאִמָּהּ וכו׳: The prohibition against engaging in relations with the relatives of one's wife continues to remain in force even should the couple divorce. By Torah law this prohibition applies only in a case of a true marriage. However, by rabbinic law the prohibition is also applied to a *yavam* and *yevama* by virtue of the levirate bond between them, which, in certain respects, is akin to a marriage. It is explained in the Jerusalem Talmud that although the levirate bond is sufficient to generate a prohibition while the bond exists, nevertheless, unlike a true marriage, that prohibition does not continue once the bond is dissolved. Therefore, if the *yevama* dies, the prohibition ends immediately and the relatives of the *yevama* are again permitted to all of the brothers; this is also true in a case in which one of the brothers performs *ḥalitza*, since *ḥalitza* dissolves the levirate bond. However, in that case, the Sages decreed that with respect to the brother who actually performed *ḥalitza*, the prohibition continues. This is due to the fact that *ḥalitza* is viewed as equivalent to a divorce, and therefore the Sages decreed that with respect to the brother who actually performed *ḥalitza* the prohibition continues as though he had actually been married to the *yevama* and then divorced her.

And she is forbidden to engage in relations with his father, etc. – וְהִיא אֲסוּרָה בְּאָבִיו וכו׳: The commentaries note that some of the relatives listed in the mishna are forbidden irrespective of the fact that the *yavam* performed *ḥalitza*. For example, the *yevama* is forbidden to the father of the one who performed *ḥalitza* by virtue of the fact that he is also the father of her deceased husband, and therefore she is forbidden to him as his daughter-in-law. Therefore, while conceding that in fact it was not necessary to list all of the relatives in the mishna, the commentaries explain that for the sake of completeness the mishna chose to list them all (*Gilyon Maharsha*, citing Responsa of Rabbi Shmuel Abuhav).

He is forbidden to engage in relations with a rival wife of a relative of his *ḥalutza* – אָסוּר בְּצָרַת קְרוֹבַת חֲלוּצָתוֹ: Rashi describes the case very simply: If the *ḥalutza* had a relative, e.g., a sister, and that relative was married to a man who had another wife, then that wife would also be forbidden. However, the Ramban, the Rashba, and many others question Rashi's explanation (see *Tosafot* on 41a): If Rashi is correct, it emerges that the *halakha* is stricter with regard to the relatives of a *ḥalutza*, who are forbidden by rabbinic decree, than with the relatives who are forbidden by Torah law, since the *halakha* permits one to engage in relations with the rival wives of relatives forbidden by Torah law. Therefore, many of the early commentaries (see the *Halakhot Gedolot*, Rambam, and Rid) explain that the mishna's prohibition applies only in a case in which both the relative and her rival wife are also bound by a levirate bond to the same brother. This could occur if a brother performed *ḥalitza* with his *yevama* and then his brother married a female relative of the first brother's *ḥalutza* and an additional wife, and then he died. The relative and her rival wife would then be bound by a levirate bond to the first brother. Since it is prohibited for the first brother to consummate the levirate marriage with the relative, since she is the relative of his *ḥalutza*, it is also prohibited for him to consummate the levirate marriage with her rival wife.

The *Yam shel Shlomo* defends Rashi's opinion and notes that it would appear that both the Rif and Rabbeinu Ḥananel also understood this in the same manner. He explains that it is true that according to this opinion a unique stringency exists in the case of a *ḥalutza* but suggests that this is the meaning of the Gemara's question at the end of this *amud*: What is different about this woman, the relative of the rival wife, who is permitted, and what is different about that woman, the rival wife of a relative, who is forbidden? The Gemara explains there that this stringency is necessary because since the case is very complex, people might not appreciate all of the nuances of the case and draw incorrect conclusions from it. To prevent any misunderstanding, the Sages decreed that the rival wife should be forbidden as well, similar to the standard case of a levirate bond with a forbidden relative and a rival wife (see *Arukh LaNer*).

בָּעֲרָוָה דְּאוֹרַיְיתָא גָּזְרוּ בְּהוּ רַבָּנַן שְׁנִיּוֹת, בַּחֲלוּצָה לָא גָּזְרוּ רַבָּנַן שְׁנִיּוֹת, אוֹ דִּלְמָא לָא שְׁנָא?

The Gemara presents the sides of the dilemma: Did **the Sages decree** that the prohibition of **secondary** forbidden **relationships** applies only **in** a case where there is a relative with whom **relations** are **forbidden by Torah** law, but **in** the case of a ***ḥalutza*,** whose relatives are forbidden only by rabbinic decree, **they did not decree** that there should be a prohibition of **secondary** forbidden **relationships? Or perhaps** the case of a ***ḥalutza* is no different,**[H] and since the basis of the rabbinic prohibition applying to her relatives is that it is considered as though she had actually been married to her *yavam*, the prohibition should extend to her secondary relatives as well?

תָּא שְׁמַע: ״הוּא אָסוּר בְּאִמָּהּ וּבְאֵם אִמָּהּ״, וְאִילּוּ ״אֵם אֵם אִמָּהּ״ – לָא קָתָנֵי.

The Gemara suggests: **Come and hear** a proof from the mishna: A *yavam* **is prohibited** from engaging in relations **with the mother of** his *ḥalutza* **and with her mother's mother. However,** the mishna **does not teach** that it is prohibited to engage in relations with **her mother's mother's mother,** which is one of the secondary relationships. This would suggest that the prohibition of secondary relationships does not apply in this case.

דִּלְמָא הַיְינוּ טַעֲמָא דְּלָא תָּנֵי – מִשּׁוּם דְּקָבָעֵי לְמִיתְנֵי סֵיפָא ״וְהָאַחִין מוּתָּרִין״, וְאִי תָּנָא ״אֵם אֵם אִמָּהּ״ הֲוָה אָמֵינָא: הָאַחִין מוּתָּרִין דַּוְקָא בְּאֵם אֵם אִמָּהּ, אֲבָל בְּאֵם אִמָּהּ וּבְאִמָּהּ לָא.

The Gemara rejects the proof: **Perhaps this is the reason that** the mishna **does not teach** that case, **because it needs to teach in the latter clause:** However, **the** other **brothers** who did not perform *ḥalitza* **are permitted** to her relatives. **And if it** had **taught** the prohibition of **her mother's mother's mother** in the first clause, **I would** mistakenly **say** that **the brothers are permitted specifically to her mother's mother's mother, but not to her mother's mother.** Therefore, no proof can be adduced from that case of the mishna.

וְלִיתְנֵי ״אֵם אֵם אִמָּהּ״ וְלִיתְנֵי ״הָאַחִין מוּתָּרִין בְּכוּלָּן״! קַשְׁיָא.

The Gemara objects: **But** if he is forbidden to the great-grandmother, then **let it teach: Her mother's mother's mother** in the first clause, **and** then **let it teach: The brothers are permitted to all of them,** in the latter clause. This would avoid the concern stated above. The fact that the mishna did not do so would suggest that he is not forbidden to the great-grandmother, or any other secondary relatives. The Gemara concludes: Indeed, this is **difficult,** but still inconclusive.

תָּא שְׁמַע: הִיא אֲסוּרָה בְּאָבִיו וּבַאֲבִי אָבִיו. קָתָנֵי מִיהָא אֲבִי אָבִיו, מַאי לָאו – מִשּׁוּם חוֹלֵץ, דְּהָוְיָא לָהּ כַּלַּת בְּנוֹ!

The Gemara suggests: **Come** and **hear** another proof from the mishna: **She is prohibited** from engaging in relations **with his father, and with his father's father.** The Gemara explains the proof: **In any case,** the mishna **teaches** that she is forbidden to **his father's father. What, is it not** that she is forbidden to him **due to** the rabbinic decree that it is considered as though she had actually been married to **the one who performed *ḥalitza*** with her, and therefore she is forbidden to the grandfather because **she is considered to be** the grandfather's **son's daughter-in-law,** i.e., the wife of one of the grandfather's grandsons, which is a secondary relationship? If so, the mishna explicitly demonstrates that the prohibition of secondary relationships also applies in the case of a *ḥalutza*.

לָא, מִשּׁוּם מִיתְנָא, דְּהָוְיָא לָהּ כַּלַּת בְּנוֹ.

The Gemara rejects the proof: **No,** she is forbidden to his grandfather **due to** her previous marriage with **the deceased,** whose relatives are forbidden to her by Torah law, and it is due to that relationship **that she is considered** the grandfather's **son's daughter-in-law.** Therefore, no proof can be adduced from that case of the mishna.

תָּא שְׁמַע: וּבְבֶן בְּנוֹ. מַאי לָאו – מִשּׁוּם חוֹלֵץ, דְּהָוְיָא לָהּ (מִשּׁוּם) אֵשֶׁת אֲבִי אָבִיו!

The Gemara suggests: **Come** and **hear** another proof from the mishna: **And** she is prohibited from engaging in relations **with his son's son.** The Gemara explains the proof: **What, is it not** that she is forbidden to him **due to** the rabbinic decree that it is considered as though she had actually been married to **the one who performed *ḥalitza*** with her, and **she is** therefore forbidden to his grandson because **she is considered to be the wife** of that grandson's **father's father,** which is a secondary relationship? If so, the mishna explicitly demonstrates that the prohibition of secondary relationships also applies in the case of a *ḥalutza*.

HALAKHA

Secondary forbidden relationships of a *ḥalutza* – שְׁנִיּוֹת בַּחֲלוּצָה: Just as the Sages prohibited relations with secondary relatives in the case of relatives who are forbidden by Torah law, they also prohibited relations with secondary relatives in the case of a *ḥalutza*. This is in accordance with the conclusion of the Gemara (Rambam *Sefer Nashim, Hilkhot Yibbum VaḤalitza* 1:12; *Shulḥan Arukh, Even HaEzer* 162:3).

לָא, מִשּׁוּם מֵיתְנָא, וְהָוְיָא לַהּ אֵשֶׁת אֲחִי אֲבִי אָבִיו.

The Gemara rejects the proof: **No,** she is forbidden to his grandson **due to** her previous marriage with **the deceased,** whose relatives are forbidden to her by Torah law, and it is due to that relationship that **she is considered to be the wife of a brother of** that grandson's **father's father,** which is also a forbidden secondary relationship. Therefore, no proof can be adduced from that case of the mishna.

הָא אֲמֵימָר מַכְשַׁר בְּאֵשֶׁת אֲחִי אֲבִי אָבִיו!

The Gemara asks: **But Ameimar rules permissible** the marriage of a man **to the wife of a brother of** that man's **father's father.** Accordingly, the prohibition in the mishna cannot be due to that relationship.

אֲמֵימָר מוֹקֵי לַהּ בְּבַר בְּרָא דְּסָבָא.

The Gemara explains: **Ameimar** would **establish** the mishna's case of: His son's son, as referring to engaging in relations **with a son of a son of the grandfather.** The mishna states that she is forbidden to his father, to his father's father, to his son, and to his son's son. The Gemara assumed that antecedent of the pronoun: His, in the phrase: To his son and to his son's son, is the one who performed *ḥalitza*. As such, the mishna teaches that she is forbidden to the son and grandson of the one who performed *ḥalitza* with her, which are secondary relationships. Ameimar, however, would claim the antecedent of this pronoun is the father's father, which immediately precedes it in the mishna. As such, the mishna is teaching that she is forbidden to the grandfather of the one who performed *ḥalitza* with her, to that grandfather's sons, i.e., the brothers of the deceased, and to the grandfather's sons' sons, i.e., the nephews of the deceased. The *yevama* is forbidden to these relatives by Torah law. Therefore, no proof can be derived from that case of the mishna.

אִי הָכִי, הַיְינוּ אָחִיו וּבֶן אָחִיו! תָּנָא אָחִיו מִן הָאָב, וְקָתָנֵי אָחִיו מִן הָאֵם

The Gemara challenges this understanding of: His son and his son's son: But **if so, these** relatives **are** none other than **his brother and the son of his brother,** who are already explicitly mentioned in the mishna. The Gemara explains: This is not a case of unnecessary repetition because the mishna first **teaches** that she is forbidden to **his paternal** half **brother and** then **teaches** that she is forbidden to **his maternal** half **brother** as well.

תָּא שְׁמַע, דְּתָנֵי רַבִּי חִיָּיא: אַרְבַּע מִדִּבְרֵי תוֹרָה, וְאַרְבַּע מִדִּבְרֵי סוֹפְרִים. אָב וּבְנוֹ, אָחִיו וּבֶן אָחִיו – מִדִּבְרֵי תוֹרָה, אֲבִי אָבִיו וַאֲבִי אִמּוֹ, בֶּן בְּנוֹ, וּבֶן בִּתּוֹ – מִדִּבְרֵי סוֹפְרִים.

The Gemara suggests: **Come** and **hear** a proof from a *baraita* **that Rabbi Ḥiyya taught:** Of the relatives who are forbidden to a *ḥalutza*, **four** are forbidden **by Torah law and four by rabbinic law,** as follows: **The father** of the deceased husband, **and his son,**[N] **his brother, and his brother's son** are forbidden **by Torah law; his father's father, and his mother's father, his son's son,**[B] **and his daughter's son** are forbidden **by rabbinic law.**

קָתָנֵי מִיהָא אֲבִי אָבִיו, מַאי לָאו מִשּׁוּם חוֹלֵץ, וְהָוְיָא לַהּ כַּלַּת בְּנוֹ!

In any case, the *baraita* **teaches** that she is forbidden to **his father's father. What, is it not** that she is forbidden to him **due to** the rabbinic decree that it is considered as though she had actually been married to **the one who performed *ḥalitza*** with her, and therefore she is forbidden to the grandfather because **she is considered to be** the grandfather's **son's daughter-in-law,** which is a secondary forbidden relationship? This would prove that the prohibition of secondary relationships applies in the case of a *ḥalutza*.

BACKGROUND

She is forbidden to his son's son – אֲסוּרָה בְּבֶן בְּנוֹ: For example, Reuven and Shimon are the sons of Ya'akov and Leah. Shimon married Miriam and died childless, so that Miriam happened before Reuven for levirate marriage. Reuven performed *ḥalitza* with Miriam. Accordingly, Miriam is forbidden to Reuven's relatives as follows: She is forbidden to Reuven's paternal grandfather, Yitzḥak, since she is the daughter-in-law of his son, and she is forbidden to Reuven's maternal grandfather, Lavan, since she is the daughter-in-law of his daughter. She is also forbidden to Yoel and Mikha, the sons of Reuven's son and daughter, respectively. The reason she is forbidden to Yoel is both because it is considered as though she had actually been married to Reuven and therefore she is considered to be the wife of Yoel's paternal grandfather, and also because she was married to Shimon and therefore she was the wife of Yoel's paternal grandfather's brother. She is forbidden to Mikha due to the fact that it is considered as though she had actually been married to Reuven and therefore she is considered to be the wife of Mikha's maternal grandfather, which is a secondary forbidden relationship. However she would not be forbidden due to the fact that she was married to Shimon, because that renders her the wife of the brother of Mikha's maternal grandfather, which is a permitted relationship.

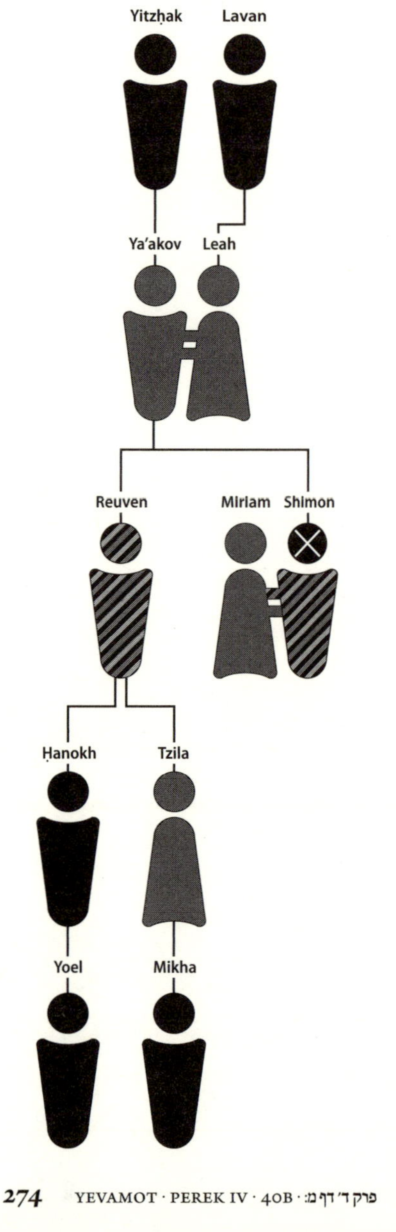

NOTES

The father and his son, etc. – אָב וּבְנוֹ וכו׳: Most commentaries explain that the phrase: The father and his son, in the *baraita* is referring to the father and son of the one who performed *ḥalitza*. The difficulty with this understanding is that the *baraita* continues to mention the prohibition of the brother of the one who performed *ḥalitza* and the brother's son, even though both the son of the one who performed *ḥalitza* and the son of his brother are forbidden to the *ḥalutza* for the identical reason that they are the sons of her deceased husband's brother. The commentaries concede this point and explain that the mishna wished to organize those forbidden to the *ḥalutza* by their relationship to the one who performed *ḥalitza*. The Maharam MiRotenburg suggests an explanation that avoids this difficulty. He interprets the reference: His son, not as a reference to the son of the one who performed *ḥalitza* but to the son of the father of the one who performed *ḥalitza*, who is mentioned immediately before. As such, it refers to the paternal half brother of the one who performed *ḥalitza*. He then proceeds to explain that when the *baraita* continues to refer to the brother of the one who performed *ḥalitza*, the reference is to his maternal half brother (*Tosefot HaRosh*).

לָא, מִשּׁוּם מֵיתְנָא, דְּהָוְיָא לָהּ כַּלַּת בְּנוֹ.

The Gemara rejects the proof: **No,** she is forbidden **due to** her previous marriage with **the deceased,** whose relatives are forbidden to her by Torah law, and it is due to that relationship that **she is considered** the grandfather's **son's daughter-in-law.** Therefore, no proof can be adduced from that case of the *baraita.*

תָּא שְׁמַע: אֲבִי אִמּוֹ – מַאי לָאו מִשּׁוּם חוֹלֵץ, דְּהָוְיָא לָהּ כַּלַּת בִּתּוֹ!

The Gemara proceeds to consider whether proof may be adduced from each of the other secondary relationships listed in the *baraita*: **Come** and **hear** a proof from that which the *baraita* teaches: She is forbidden to **his mother's father.** The Gemara explains the proof: **What, is it not** that she is forbidden to him **due to** the rabbinic decree that it is considered as though she had actually been married to **the one who performed *ḥalitza*** with her, and therefore she is forbidden to the grandfather because **she is considered to be** the grandfather's **daughter's daughter-in-law,** which is a secondary relationship? This would prove that the prohibition of secondary relationships applies in the case of a *ḥalutza.*

לָא, מִשּׁוּם מֵיתְנָא, דְּהָוְיָא לָהּ כַּלַּת בִּתּוֹ.

The Gemara rejects the proof: **No,** she is forbidden **due to** her previous marriage with **the deceased,** whose relatives are forbidden to her by Torah law, and it is due to that relationship that **she is considered** the grandfather's **daughter's daughter-in-law.** Therefore, no proof can be adduced from that case of the *baraita.*

תָּא שְׁמַע: וּבֶן בְּנוֹ, מַאי לָאו מִשּׁוּם חוֹלֵץ, דְּהָוְיָא לָהּ אֵשֶׁת אֲבִי אָבִיו!

Come and **hear** a proof from that which the *baraita* teaches: **And** she is forbidden to **his son's son.** The Gemara explains the proof: **What, is it not** that she is forbidden to him **due to** the rabbinic decree that it is considered as though she had actually been married to **the one who performed *ḥalitza*** with her, and so she is forbidden to his grandson because **she is considered to be the wife** of that grandson's **father's father,** which is a secondary relationship? If so, the *baraita* explicitly demonstrates that the prohibition of secondary relationships applies in the case of a *ḥalutza.*

לָא, מִשּׁוּם מֵיתְנָא, וְהָוְיָא לָהּ אֵשֶׁת אֲחִי אֲבִי אָבִיו.

The Gemara rejects the proof: **No,** she is forbidden to his grandson **due to** her previous marriage with **the deceased,** whose relatives are forbidden to her by Torah law, and due to that relationship **she is considered to be the wife of a brother of** that grandson's **father's father,** which is also a forbidden secondary relationship. Therefore, no proof can be adduced from that case of the *baraita.*

וְהָא אֲמֵימַר מַכְשִׁיר בְּאֵשֶׁת אֲחִי אֲבִי אָבִיו! אֲמֵימַר מוֹקֵים לַהּ מִשּׁוּם חוֹלֵץ, וְקָסָבַר גָּזְרוּ שְׁנִיּוֹת בַּחֲלוּצָה.

The Gemara asks: **But didn't Ameimar rule permissible** the marriage of a man **with the wife of a brother of his father's father?** Accordingly, the prohibition in the mishna cannot be due to that relationship. The Gemara concedes: **Ameimar** would **establish** the mishna's case of: His son's son, **as being due to** the rabbinic decree that it is considered as though she had actually been married to **the one who performed *ḥalitza*** with her, **and** as such it is evident that **he holds** that the Sages **decreed** that the prohibition of **secondary** forbidden **relationships** should apply **in** the case of **a *ḥalutza.***

תָּא שְׁמַע: וּבְבֶן בִּתּוֹ, מַאי לָאו מִשּׁוּם חוֹלֵץ, דְּהָוְיָא לָהּ אֵשֶׁת אֲבִי אִמּוֹ!

The Gemara continues to seek proof for those who disagree with Ameimar: **Come** and **hear** a proof from that which the *baraita* teaches: **And** she is forbidden to **his daughter's son.** The Gemara explains the proof: **What, is it not** that she is forbidden to him **due to** the rabbinic decree that it is considered as though she had actually been married to the **one who performed *ḥalitza*** with her, and so **she is** forbidden to his grandson because **she is considered to be the wife** of that grandson's **mother's father,** which is a secondary relationship? If so, the *baraita* explicitly demonstrates that the prohibition of secondary relationships applies in the case of a *ḥalutza.*

לָא, מִשּׁוּם מֵיתְנָא דְּהָוְיָא לָהּ אֵשֶׁת אֲחִי אֲבִי אִמּוֹ. וְהָא גַּבֵּי שְׁנִיּוֹת דְּעֶרְוָה לָא גָּזְרוּ!

The Gemara rejects the proof: **No,** she is forbidden to his grandson **due to** her previous marriage with **the deceased,** whose relatives are forbidden to her by Torah law, and due to that relationship **she is considered to be the wife of a brother of** the grandson's **mother's father.** The Gemara challenges this: **But** the Sages did **not decree** that such a person is included **among** those relatives who are forbidden as **secondary** forbidden **relationships.**

PERSONALITIES

Rav Tovi bar Kisna – רַב טוֹבִי בַּר קִיסְנָא: A second-generation *amora* who lived in Babylonia, Rav Tovi was a disciple of Shmuel, and most of his statements cite his teacher as their source. He is also known as Rav Tavi bar Kisna (*Eiruvin* 104b) and Rav Tavyomi bar Kisna (*Menaḥot* 70a).

אֶלָּא לָאו מִשּׁוּם חוֹלֵץ, וּשְׁמַע מִינַּהּ: גָּזְרוּ שְׁנִיּוֹת בַּחֲלוּצָה, שְׁמַע מִינַּהּ.

Rather, is it not, as the Gemara initially assumed, that she is forbidden to him **due to** the rabbinic decree that it is considered as though she had actually been married to **the one who performed *ḥalitza*** with her, **and** therefore must one not **conclude from** this case that the Sages **decreed** that the prohibition of **secondary** forbidden **relationships** should apply **in** the case of **a *ḥalutza*?** The Gemara confirms: One should indeed **conclude from it** that this is so.

״מוּתָּר אָדָם״ וכו׳. אָמַר רַב טוֹבִי בַּר קִיסְנָא אָמַר שְׁמוּאֵל: הַבָּא עַל צָרַת חֲלוּצָה – הַוָּלָד מַמְזֵר. מַאי טַעְמָא – בְּאִיסּוּרָהּ קַיְימָא.

§ The mishna states: **A man is permitted** to engage in relations with a relative of a rival wife of his *ḥalutza*; however, he is prohibited from engaging in relations with a rival wife of a relative of his *ḥalutza*. The Gemara cites a ruling: **Rav Tovi bar Kisna**[P] **said** that **Shmuel said:** With regard to **one who engages in intercourse with a rival wife of** his ***ḥalutza*, the offspring** of that union **is a *mamzer*. What is the reason** for this ruling? It is that **she remains in her** original **prohibition.**

Normally, it is prohibited to engage in relations with one's brother's wife. However, when there is a mitzva to consummate levirate marriage, that prohibition does not apply, due to the levirate bond between the *yavam* and *yevama*. Although following *ḥalitza* the levirate bond is dissolved, the woman's status as a *ḥalutza* means that only the lesser prohibition against marrying a *ḥalutza* applies to her, and she does not return to her original forbidden status. Shmuel claims that the rival wives of the *ḥalutza* are not considered to be represented in her act of *ḥalitza*; consequently, they are not afforded a status similar to that of the *ḥalutza* herself. Therefore, he assumes that following *ḥalitza* the rival wives once again become subject to the original prohibition against marrying a brother's wife. Since that prohibition entails *karet*, any offspring born from such a union is a *mamzer*.

אָמַר רַב יוֹסֵף: אַף אֲנַן נָמֵי תְּנֵינָא: מוּתָּר אָדָם בִּקְרוֹבַת צָרַת חֲלוּצָתוֹ. אִי אָמְרַתְּ בִּשְׁלָמָא צָרָה אַבָּרַאי – מִשּׁוּם הָכִי מוּתָּר בַּאֲחוֹתָהּ.

Rav Yosef said: We, too, learned this though an inference from the mishna: **A man is permitted** to engage in relations **with a relative of a rival wife of his *ḥalutza*.** Rav Yosef explains the inference: **Granted, if you say** that **a rival wife is outside,** i.e., she is not represented in the *ḥalitza* of the *ḥalutza* and so she is not afforded a status similar to that of the *ḥalutza* herself, then it is **due to that** reason that **he is permitted** to engage in relations **with her sister** and other relatives, because since they are not the relatives of his *ḥalutza*, there is no reason for them to be forbidden.

אֶלָּא אִי אָמְרַתְּ צָרָה כַּחֲלוּצָה דָּמְיָא – אַמַּאי מוּתָּר?

However, if you say that **a rival wife is** afforded a status **similar to** that of **the *ḥalutza*** herself, **why is he permitted** to her relatives? Rather, from the fact that the relatives of the rival wives are permitted, it is apparent that the rival wives are not represented in the *ḥalitza*. As such, it follows that they should return to their original forbidden status of a brother's wives, as Shmuel claims.

לֵימָא תֶּיהֱוֵי תְּיוּבְתָּא דְּרַבִּי יוֹחָנָן, דְּאָמַר: בֵּין הוּא בֵּין אָחִיו אֵין חַיָּיבִין לֹא עַל הַחֲלוּצָה כָּרֵת, וְלֹא עַל צָרָתָהּ כָּרֵת!

The Gemara suggests: **Shall we say,** then, that this mishna **is a conclusive refutation of** the opinion of **Rabbi Yoḥanan?**[N] **As** Rabbi Yoḥanan **said: Neither he** who performed the *ḥalitza* **nor his brothers are liable to** receive ***karet***; they are **neither** liable to receive ***karet* on account of** engaging in relations with **the *ḥalutza*, nor** are they liable to receive ***karet* on account of** engaging in relations with **her rival wife.**

NOTES

Shall we say that this is a conclusive refutation of the opinion of Rabbi Yoḥanan – לֵימָא תֶּיהֱוֵי תְּיוּבְתָּא דְּרַבִּי יוֹחָנָן: An objection to Rabbi Yoḥanan's opinion could be raised on different grounds: According to his opinion a rival wife is considered as though she herself had performed *ḥalitza*, since the *ḥalutza* is considered to have represented her in the act of *ḥalitza*, and furthermore, all of the brothers are considered as though they had themselves performed the *ḥalitza* since they were all represented by the brother who actually performed the act of *ḥalitza*. In that case, why aren't all of the brothers forbidden to the relatives of all of the rival wives? The commentaries explain that clearly the suggested explanation for the prohibition with regard to the rival wives of the relatives of the *ḥalutza*, i.e., that the relatives accompany her to court, does not exist when it comes to the brothers, who do not accompany each other to court (see Ritva). Moreover, since the prohibition is only rabbinic in nature, the Sages were not so stringent as to render the relative of a rival wife like the *ḥalutza* herself (*Tosafot*; Meiri).

אָמַר לָךְ רַבִּי יוֹחָנָן: וְתִסְבְּרָא אֲחוֹת חֲלוּצָה דְּאוֹרָיְיתָא? וְהָאָמַר רֵישׁ לָקִישׁ: כָּאן שָׁנָה רַבִּי: אֲחוֹת גְּרוּשָׁה – מִדִּבְרֵי תוֹרָה, אֲחוֹת חֲלוּצָה – מִדִּבְרֵי סוֹפְרִים.

The Gemara responds: **Rabbi Yoḥanan** could have **said to you: But** how can **you understand** it that way? Why do you assume that if the rival wives are considered to be represented in the *ḥalitza* that perforce means that their relatives should be forbidden to the *yavam*? Is **a sister of** one's ***ḥalutza*** forbidden **by Torah** law? **Didn't Reish Lakish say** with regard to another mishna (41a): **Here, Rabbi** Yehuda HaNasi **taught:** Engaging in relations with **a sister of** one's **divorcée** is forbidden **by Torah law,** whereas engaging in relations with **a sister of** one's ***ḥalutza*** **is** forbidden **by rabbinic law.** Since the prohibition with regard to the relatives of one's *ḥalutza* is rabbinic, it is reasonable to assume that it was applied to only the wife who actually performed *ḥalitza* and not extended to her rival wives, even if they are considered to be represented in her *ḥalitza* to the extent that they do not return to their original forbidden status.

מַאי שְׁנָא הַאי, וּמַאי שְׁנָא הַאי?

§ The Gemara questions the distinction indicated by the mishna: **What is different** about **this** woman, the relative of a rival wife of one's *ḥalutza*, that she is permitted, **and what is different** about **that** woman, the rival wife of a relative of one's *ḥalutza*, that she is forbidden?

הַךְ דְּאָזְלָא בַּהֲדָהּ לְבֵי דִינָא – גְּזַרוּ בְּהוּ רַבָּנַן, הַאי דְּלָא אָזְלָא בַּהֲדָהּ לְבֵי דִינָא – לָא גְּזַרוּ בְּהוּ רַבָּנַן.

The Gemara explains: With regard to **that** woman, the relative of the *ḥalutza*, **who** often **goes together with** the *ḥalutza*[N] **to court,** since she is present in the court during the *ḥalitza*, people might mistakenly assume that it was she who actually performed *ḥalitza*. Were the *yavam* permitted to marry her rival wife, people might incorrectly conclude that it is permitted to marry the rival wife of one's *ḥalutza*. To preclude this possibility, **the Sages decreed with regard to her** that her rival wife should be forbidden. However, with regard to **this** woman, the rival wife of the *ḥalutza*, **who does not go together with** the *ḥalutza* **to court,** since she is never present in the court during the *ḥalitza*, there is no concern that people will mistake her for the *ḥalutza* herself. Consequently, **the Sages did not** see any reason to **decree with regard to her** that her relatives should be forbidden.

מתני׳ הַחוֹלֵץ לִיבִמְתּוֹ, וְנָשָׂא אָחִיו אֶת אֲחוֹתָהּ, וָמֵת – חוֹלֶצֶת וְלֹא מִתְיַבֶּמֶת. וְכֵן הַמְגָרֵשׁ אֶת אִשְׁתּוֹ, וְנָשָׂא אָחִיו אֶת אֲחוֹתָהּ וָמֵת – הֲרֵי זוֹ פְּטוּרָה.

MISHNA In the case of a *yavam* **who performed** ***ḥalitza*** **with his** ***yevama*** **and** then **his brother married her sister**[H] **and died,** the sister **performs** ***ḥalitza*** with the *yavam*, **but she may not enter into levirate marriage** with him, since as a sister of his *ḥalutza* she is forbidden to him. **And similarly,** in the case of **one who divorced his wife and his brother married her sister and died,**[H] **then that** woman **is exempt** both from *ḥalitza* and from consummating levirate marriage, since as the sister of his former wife she is forbidden to him.

HALAKHA

One who performed *ḥalitza* with his *yevama* and then his brother married her sister – הַחוֹלֵץ לִיבִמְתּוֹ וְנָשָׂא אָחִיו אֶת אֲחוֹתָהּ: If a *yavam* performed *ḥalitza* with his *yevama* and then his brother married her sister or one of her other relatives, and then the brother died, the sister or other relative happens for levirate marriage before the *yavam* who originally performed the *ḥalitza*. However, as a relative of his *ḥalutza*, she is forbidden to him. Therefore, she performs *ḥalitza* but may not consummate the levirate marriage. Similarly, her rival wife performs *ḥalitza* but may not enter into levirate marriage (Rambam *Sefer Nashim, Hilkhot Yibbum VaḤalitza* 6:20; *Shulḥan Arukh, Even HaEzer* 174:3).

The sister of his divorcée – אֲחוֹת גְּרוּשָׁתוֹ: If one divorces his wife and then her sister falls before him for levirate marriage, she is exempt from both *ḥalitza* and from levirate marriage because, as long as his former wife is alive, her sister is prohibited by Torah law from engaging in relations with him (Rambam *Sefer Nashim, Hilkhot Yibbum VaḤalitza* 6:9; *Shulḥan Arukh, Even HaEzer* 173:1).

NOTES

That woman who goes together with the *ḥalutza* – הַךְ דְּאָזְלָא בַּהֲדָהּ: The version of the Gemara cited here has: That woman who goes together with her. Based on this version, Rashi, Rabbeinu Ḥananel, and the Rif explain that: Goes with her, is referring to people that accompany the *ḥalutza* to court. Based on this, they explain that since the relative of the *ḥalutza* accompanies her to court, some people might mistakenly think that it was the relative who performed *ḥalitza*. Therefore, it is necessary to render the rival wife of the relative of the *ḥalutza* forbidden, just as the rival wife of the *ḥalutza* herself is forbidden. However, since the rival wife never accompanies the *ḥalutza*, there is no concern that people might mistakenly think she performed the *ḥalitza*, and so there is no need to render her relatives forbidden.

Tosafot and other early commentaries challenge this explanation; *Yam shel Shlomo* suggests a defense of Rashi's opinion. *Tosafot* themselves suggest that a different version of the Gemara is preferable, which states: That woman who goes with him, where him refers to the *yavam* who performed the *ḥalitza*. Accordingly, the Gemara's distinction is simply between the *ḥalutza*, who actually underwent the *ḥalitza*, and her rival wives, who did not. The Sages expanded the prohibition only to the relatives of the former. The Ramban writes that this version is to be preferred but he questions the authenticity of this version of the text.

Based on the present version of the Gemara, the Maharam MiRotenburg suggests a third interpretation. He understands that the Gemara is referring to a point in time after the *ḥalitza* has already been performed, when the relatives of the *ḥalutza* go to court to inquire as to their status. At that point, the relatives of the *ḥalutza* are instructed that they may not marry the *yavam*. The Gemara states that since the relatives are accompanied by their rival wives, and there is a possibility that people will confuse them, the Sages also rendered the rivals wives of the relatives forbidden (*Tosefot HaRosh*).

שׁוֹמֶרֶת יָבָם שֶׁקִּידֵּשׁ אָחִיו אֶת אֲחוֹתָהּ, מִשּׁוּם רַבִּי יְהוּדָה בֶּן בְּתֵירָא אָמְרוּ: אוֹמְרִים לוֹ: הַמְתֵּן עַד שֶׁיַּעֲשֶׂה אָחִיךָ מַעֲשֶׂה.

In the case of **a widow waiting for her *yavam*** to consummate levirate marriage or perform *ḥalitza* with her, and the **brother of** the *yavam* **betrothed her sister,**[H] **they said in the name of Rabbi Yehuda ben Beteira: They say to** the brother: **Wait** and do not marry[N] the woman you betrothed **until your brother performs an act,**[N] either of *ḥalitza* or of consummating the levirate marriage, as until he does there remains a levirate bond between the *yevama* and each of the brothers, and it is prohibited to marry the sister of a woman to whom one is bound by a levirate bond.

חָלַץ לָהּ אָחִיו אוֹ כְּנָסָהּ – יִכְנוֹס אֶת אִשְׁתּוֹ. מֵתָה הַיְבָמָה – יִכְנוֹס אֶת אִשְׁתּוֹ. מֵת יָבָם – יוֹצִיא אֶת אִשְׁתּוֹ בְּגֵט, וְאֵשֶׁת אָחִיו בַּחֲלִיצָה.

If **a brother of** the one who betrothed the sister of the *yevama* **performed *ḥalitza* with** the *yevama* **or consummated a levirate marriage with her,** since by doing so the levirate bond between the *yevama* and the one who betrothed her sister is dissolved, **he may** then **enter into marriage** with **his wife,** who until that point was only betrothed to him, as she is no longer the sister of a woman to whom he is bound by a levirate bond. Similarly, if **the *yevama* died,** since his levirate bond to her is dissolved upon her death, **he may** proceed to **enter into marriage** with **his** betrothed **wife.** However, if the ***yavam* died**[H] without performing an act that would have dissolved the levirate bond, **he must divorce his wife with a bill of divorce,**[N] as she is forbidden to him as the sister of a woman to whom he is bound by a levirate bond, **and his brother's wife** he must send out **with *ḥalitza*,**[N] as she is forbidden to him as the sister of his divorcée.

גמ׳ מַאי ״וְכֵן״? אֵימָא: אֲבָל הַמְגָרֵשׁ.

GEMARA The mishna considers two cases in which there is no possibility of consummating levirate marriage with a *yevama*. In the first case the reason is that she is the sister of one's *ḥalutza*, and in the second it is that she is the sister of one's divorcée. The mishna appears to compare the two cases by introducing the second case with: And similarly. The Gemara questions this: **What is** the meaning of: **And similarly?** The two cases are not similar; in the first case the *yevama* must perform *ḥalitza*, and in the second she is entirely exempt from the need to do anything. The Gemara answers: Emend the mishna and **say: However, one who divorces.**[N]

HALAKHA

A widow waiting for her *yavam* and the brother of the *yavam* betrothed her sister – שׁוֹמֶרֶת יָבָם שֶׁקִּידֵּשׁ אָחִיו אֶת אֲחוֹתָהּ: It is prohibited for one to marry a relative of a woman to whom one is bound by a levirate bond. Therefore, if a woman happens for levirate marriage before a number of brothers, and one of them betroths her sister, it is prohibited for him to proceed to marry the relative he betrothed until after one of the other brothers either consummates the levirate marriage with the *yevama* or performs *ḥalitza* with her, thereby dissolving the levirate bond between her and the other brothers. Some say that if the brother who betrothed the sister transgressed and proceeded to marry her, then the levirate bond to him is thereby dissolved, and so he is allowed to engage in relations with his wife even before his brother performs levirate marriage or *ḥalitza* (*Tosafot*; Rosh). Rabbeinu Gershom Meor HaGola issued a ban prohibiting a man from being married to two women. Some say that included in the ban is the case of a *yavam* who is bound by a levirate bond to a *yevama*, such that it is prohibited for the *yavam* to marry any other woman until he has first performed *ḥalitza* with the *yevama* (Mahari Mintz). However, if the woman he wishes to marry had committed herself to marry him before the *yevama* happened before him for levirate marriage, then he is permitted to marry her even before he performs *ḥalitza* (*Haggahot Mordekhai*; Rambam *Sefer Nashim, Hilkhot Yibbum VaḤalitza* 1:14; *Shulḥan Arukh, Even HaEzer* 159:5).

The *yavam* died, etc. – מֵת יָבָם וכו׳: With regard to a *yavam* who is bound to his *yevama* through a levirate bond, who transgressed and betrothed the sister of his *yevama*, if his other brothers die, since the woman is then bound to him alone, he must divorce the betrothed sister with a bill of divorce and release his *yevama* by performing *ḥalitza* (Rambam *Sefer Nashim, Hilkhot Yibbum VaḤalitza* 1:14; *Shulḥan Arukh, Even HaEzer* 159:7).

NOTES

Wait and do not marry – הַמְתֵּן: The marriage process consists of two distinct stages. In the first stage, termed *kiddushin* or *eirusin*, a legal bond is formed between the couple that defines the woman as a wife to the extent that the dissolution of that bond requires a divorce, and sexual relations with other men are considered adulterous and are punishable by death. However, the couple may still not yet live together as man and wife, and most of the couple's mutual obligations do no yet apply. This stage is usually translated as "betrothal," even though that term fails to convey the fact that this stage is not a precursor to a marriage, but actually the first stage of the marriage.

The second stage of marriage, termed *nissuin*, and translated simply as "marriage," is usually effected by having the couple stand under a marriage canopy together or being secluded together. At this stage, the couple may live together as man and wife and all of the various mutual obligations apply.

The mishna discusses various situations in which one of a number of brothers, who were all bound through a levirate bond to a *yevama*, proceeded to betroth her sister. Due to the bond he has with the *yevama* he is forbidden to engage in relations with the sister. As such, he may not continue to complete the second stage of his marriage with her since the purpose of that stage is for them to live together as man and wife. Nevertheless, should another one of his brothers either consummate levirate marriage with the *yevama*, or perform *ḥalitza* with her, since that will dissolve the levirate bond between her and the other brothers, there will no longer be any impediment to completing the marriage with her sister.

Wait until your brother performs an act – הַמְתֵּן עַד שֶׁיַּעֲשֶׂה אָחִיךָ מַעֲשֶׂה: The commentaries explain that Rabbi Yehuda ben Beteira holds that the levirate bond is substantial, meaning that to a certain extent it is as though he is already married to her. Accordingly, the woman he betrothed is regarded as though she is his wife's sister, and therefore it is forbidden for him to now proceed to marry her. However, the commentaries explain that despite this, Rabbi Yehuda ben Beteira does not demand that he divorce the woman he betrothed; there is no need to take such drastic action because there is a possibility that she will be rendered entirely permissible through an action of his brother (*Tosefot HaRosh*).

Some commentaries raise the following question: Even if one holds that the levirate bond is substantial, shouldn't the brother's levirate bond to the *yevama* be entirely dissolved by virtue of his betrothal of her sister, since by doing so he renders the *yevama* forbidden to him by Torah law? They explain that since the levirate bond was in place before the betrothal, the strength of betrothal itself is deficient, and so it is not sufficiently efficacious to negate the bond (Rid; see Rashba).

He must divorce his wife with a bill of divorce, etc. – יוֹצִיא אֶת אִשְׁתּוֹ בְּגֵט וכו׳: The mishna on 29a discusses a similar case in which ultimately, he is prohibited from living with either his wife or his *yevama*, and expresses the lament: Woe is him on account of his wife, and woe is him on account of his brother's wife. *Tosafot* question why that expression of lament does not appear in this case as well. They suggest that the expression is used only where no prohibition was involved in the man's marriage to his wife, as in the case on 29a. However, in this case the situation was created due to the *yavam* marrying a woman whom he was forbidden to marry. Therefore, it is inappropriate to lament the situation. The Rivan explains that the lament is appropriate only in a case in which he had already lived together with his wife. However, in this case, the woman was only betrothed to him; therefore, since the couple is not as closely bound as was the couple in the first case, the pain of the ruling is less pronounced.

And his brother's wife with *ḥalitza* – וְאֵשֶׁת אָחִיו בַּחֲלִיצָה: This act of *ḥalitza* is required only by rabbinic decree, since as his wife's sister, the *yevama* is forbidden to her *yavam* by Torah law, and therefore by Torah law the *ḥalitza* is unnecessary. Alternatively, since he betrothed the sister of the *yevama* after the levirate bond to the *yevama* was already in place, the strength of betrothal itself is deficient, and so the bond is compromised, but only partially. As such, it is no longer possible to consummate the levirate marriage, but *ḥalitza* is necessary to fully dissolve the bond (Rashba; Ritva).

Say: However, one who divorces – אֵימָא אֲבָל הַמְגָרֵשׁ: One later commentary explains that the use of the phrase: And similarly, suggests only that there is some connection between the prohibitions with regard to the sister of one's divorcée and the sister of one's *ḥalutza*. When the Gemara suggests the emendation to: However, it is not rejecting that assumption and suggesting that the mishna should be emended; rather, it is simply explaining the correct interpretation of the phrase: And similarly, used in the mishna. The phrase should not be understood as implying that the *halakha* in both cases is the same; rather, it indicates only that the reason for the rabbinic prohibition with regard to the sister of one's *ḥalutza* is on account of the Torah prohibition with regard to the sister of one's divorcée (*Mei Naftoaḥ*).

אָמַר רֵישׁ לָקִישׁ: כָּאן שָׁנָה רַבִּי: אֲחוֹת גְּרוּשָׁה – מִדִּבְרֵי תוֹרָה, אֲחוֹת חֲלוּצָה – מִדִּבְרֵי סוֹפְרִים.

The Gemara explains the reason for the difference between the two cases: **Reish Lakish said: Here,** through this mishna, **Rabbi** Yehuda HaNasi **taught** that **a sister of** one's **divorcée**[H] is forbidden to him **by Torah law,** and that is why she is entirely exempt, whereas **a sister of a *ḥalutza***[H] is forbidden to him only **by rabbinic law,** and therefore, since there is still a levirate bond between her and the *yavam*, she requires *ḥalitza* to release her from it.

"שׁוֹמֶרֶת יָבָם שֶׁקִּידֵּשׁ" וכו׳. אָמַר שְׁמוּאֵל: הֲלָכָה כְּדִבְרֵי רַבִּי יְהוּדָה בֶּן בְּתֵירָא.

§ The mishna states that in the case of **a widow waiting for her *yavam*** where the brother of the *yavam* **betrothed** her sister, Rabbi Yehuda ben Beteira said that the brother may not proceed to marry his betrothed. The Gemara cites a ruling on this matter: **Shmuel said:** The ***halakha* is in accordance with the statement of Rabbi Yehuda ben Beteira.**

אִיבַּעְיָא לְהוּ: מֵתָה אִשְׁתּוֹ, מַהוּ בִּיבִמְתּוֹ? רַב וְרַבִּי חֲנִינָא דְּאָמְרִי תַּרְוַיְיהוּ: מֵתָה אִשְׁתּוֹ מוּתָּר בִּיבִמְתּוֹ, שְׁמוּאֵל וְרַב אַסִּי דְּאָמְרִי תַּרְוַיְיהוּ: מֵתָה אִשְׁתּוֹ אָסוּר בִּיבִמְתּוֹ.

A dilemma was raised before the Sages: If a *yavam* is betrothed to the sister of his *yevama*, then since the *yevama* is his betrothed wife's sister, it is forbidden for him to consummate a levirate marriage with her. However, if **his** betrothed **wife died, what is** the ***halakha* with regard to his *yevama***; is he then permitted to consummate a levirate marriage with her? It is **Rav and Rabbi Ḥanina who both say:** If **his wife died, he is permitted to** consummate a levirate marriage with **his *yevama*.**[H] Their opinion is disputed by **Shmuel and Rav Asi, who both say:** If **his wife died, he is forbidden to his *yevama*.**

אָמַר רָבָא: מַאי טַעְמָא דְּרַב? מִשּׁוּם דַּהֲוַאי יְבָמָה שֶׁהוּתְּרָה, וְנֶאֶסְרָה, וְחָזְרָה וְהוּתְּרָה – תַּחֲזוֹר לְהֶיתֵּירָהּ הָרִאשׁוֹן.

Rava said: What is Rav's reasoning?[N] She is permitted **due to** the fact that **she is a *yevama* who,** when her husband died, **was permitted** to the *yavam*, **and** then when the *yavam* betrothed her sister **she became forbidden** to him as his wife's sister, **and then** when his wife died the *yevama* **reverted** to her original status **and was permitted** to him. As such, **she should** also **revert to her original permitted status** with regard to levirate marriage and be permitted to consummate a levirate marriage with the *yavam*.

מְתִיב רַב הַמְנוּנָא: שְׁלֹשָׁה אַחִין, שְׁנַיִם נְשׂוּאִין שְׁתֵּי אֲחָיוֹת וְאֶחָד מוּפְנֶה, מֵת אֶחָד מִבַּעֲלֵי אֲחָיוֹת וְעָשָׂה בָּהּ מוּפְנֶה מַאֲמָר, וְאַחַר כָּךְ מֵת אָחִיו הַשֵּׁנִי,

Rav Hamnuna raised an objection from that which was taught in a *baraita*: With regard to a case of **three brothers, two** of whom **are married to two sisters and one** of whom **is a bachelor,** if **one of the sisters' husbands died and the bachelor performed levirate betrothal** with that sister, **and afterward the second brother** who was married to the other sister **died,** and so his wife also happened before the bachelor for levirate marriage, the bachelor is then bound to each of the sisters through a levirate bond. In such a case it is prohibited for the bachelor to consummate a levirate marriage with either one, as it is prohibited to marry the sister of a woman to whom one is bound through a levirate bond.

וְאַחַר כָּךְ מֵתָה אִשְׁתּוֹ אַחֲרָיו – אוֹתָהּ יְבָמָה חוֹלֶצֶת וְלֹא מִתְיַבֶּמֶת.

And if **afterward the wife** of the second brother **died after him,** i.e., after her husband had already died, which restored the original situation in which the bachelor was bound by a levirate bond only to the widow of the first brother, then in such a case **that *yevama*,** the widow of the first brother, **performs *ḥalitza* but may not enter into levirate marriage.**

HALAKHA

A sister of one's divorcée – אֲחוֹת גְּרוּשָׁה: If one divorces his wife, then her sister is forbidden to him by Torah law as long as the divorcée remains alive, irrespective of whether the sister is only a paternal or maternal half sister and irrespective of whether she was born in or out of wedlock (Rambam *Sefer Nashim, Hilkhot Issurei Bia* 2:7; *Shulḥan Arukh, Even HaEzer* 15:26).

A sister of a *ḥalutza* – אֲחוֹת חֲלוּצָה: The sister of one's *ḥalutza* is forbidden to him by rabbinic law (Rambam *Sefer Nashim, Hilkhot Yibbum VaḤalitza* 1:13; *Shulḥan Arukh, Even HaEzer* 162:3).

If His wife died he is permitted to his *yevama* – מֵתָה אִשְׁתּוֹ, מוּתָּר בִּיבִמְתּוֹ: With regard to one who betrothed the sister of his *yevama*, if the woman betrothed to him died, then he is permitted to consummate a levirate marriage with his *yevama*, or if he wishes he may perform *ḥalitza*. This is in accordance with the opinion of Rabbi Ḥanina (Rambam *Sefer Nashim, Hilkhot Yibbum VaḤalitza* 7:8; *Shulḥan Arukh, Even HaEzer* 159:7).

NOTES

What is Rav's reasoning – מַאי טַעְמָא דְּרַב: The later commentaries explains that the dispute between Rav and Shmuel here is not limited to the specific principle of whether a woman who is permitted, then forbidden, and then permitted again may consummate a levirate marriage. Rather, it is a fundamental dispute concerning the very nature of the allowance to marry one's brother's wife in a case of levirate marriage. Normally, one is prohibited from engaging in relations with the wife of one's brother. However, in the case of a levirate marriage it is permitted and a mitzva to do so. Rav assumes that in the case of a *yevama* who is permitted, then forbidden, and then permitted again, one may proceed to consummate the levirate marriage; he understands that the prohibition against engaging in relations with one's brother's wife is itself limited in that it does not apply in a situation where there is a mitzva of levirate marriage. Therefore, once any additional reason to prevent the levirate marriage is removed, the *yavam* may proceed to consummate the levirate marriage with the *yevama* without any concern about that prohibition. Shmuel, however, assumes that the prohibition against engaging in relations with one's brother's wife does fundamentally apply even in a situation where there is a mitzva of levirate marriage, but that in order to enable the fulfillment of the mitzva, the prohibition is waived. Therefore, should an additional prohibition be applied to his brother's wife that will inhibit the fulfillment of the mitzva, then since there is no longer a mitzva of levirate marriage, the original prohibition against engaging in relations with one's brother's wife is reinstated. Consequently, even should the additional prohibition be removed, the prohibition with regard to one's brother's wife will remain in force and the couple may not consummate the levirate marriage (*Mei Naftoaḥ*; *Yosef Lekaḥ*).

וְאַמַּאי? תֶּיהֱוֵי כִּיבָמָה שֶׁהוּתְּרָה, וְנֶאֶסְרָה, וְחָזְרָה וְהוּתְּרָה – תַּחֲזוֹר לְהֶיתֵּירָהּ הָרִאשׁוֹן!

Rav Hamnuna explains the challenge from the *baraita*: **But why** may she not consummate the levirate marriage? **She should be like a** ***yevama*** **who was** initially **permitted** to her *yavam*, **and** then **became forbidden** to him, **and then reverted** to her original status **and was permitted, and so** in this case **she should** also **revert to her original permitted status** with regard to levirate marriage and be permitted to consummate a levirate marriage with him. The fact that the *baraita* rules that she is prohibited from consummating the marriage demonstrates that she does not revert to her original permitted status.

אִישְׁתִּיק. לְבָתַר דִּנְפַק אֲמַר: אַמַּאי לָא אָמְרַתְּ לֵיהּ רַבִּי אֱלִיעֶזֶר הִיא, דַּאֲמַר: כֵּיוָן שֶׁעָמְדָה עָלָיו שָׁעָה אַחַת בְּאִסּוּר נֶאֶסְרָה עָלָיו עוֹלָמִית?

Rava **was silent,** as he had no immediate answer. **After** Rav Hamnuna **left** the study hall, Rava **said** to himself: **Why did you not say to him** that the *baraita* does not pose a challenge because **it is** in accordance with the opinion of **Rabbi Elazar,**[N] **who said** in a mishna (108b) with regard to the case of a man who divorced his wife, remarried her, and then died childless, that the *yevama* may not consummate levirate marriage with her *yavam* because **once** a *yevama* **has stood** before her *yavam* **in a forbidden state,** even **for a single moment, she** remains **forbidden to him forever,** and in that case, during the period she was divorced from her husband she was forbidden to her *yavam*? The Rabbis, however, disagree with his opinion, and the *halakha* is ruled in accordance with their opinion.

הֲדַר אֲמַר: אֵימוּר דַּאֲמַר רַבִּי אֱלִיעֶזֶר – הֵיכָא דְּלָא חַזְיָא בִּשְׁעַת נְפִילָה, אֲבָל הֵיכָא דְּחַזְיָא בִּשְׁעַת נְפִילָה – מִי אֲמַר?

He then said to himself: It is not certain that the *baraita* is in accordance with the opinion of Rabbi Elazar because one could **say**[N] **that Rabbi Elazar said** his opinion only **where she was not suitable** for the *yavam*, i.e., she was forbidden to him, already from **the time** of her **happening** before her *yavam* for levirate marriage at the moment of her husband's death. **However, where she was suitable** for her *yavam* **at the time of** her **happening** before him and became forbidden to him only at some later point, as in the case of a *yavam* who betrothed the sister of his *yevama*, **did he** actually **say** that if the reason for the prohibition is removed then she does not return to her permissible state? If the *baraita* does not represent the opinion of Rabbi Elazar, then it must be unanimously agreed upon, and therefore it indeed poses a challenge.

הֲדַר אֲמַר: אִין, וְהָתַנְיָא: רַבִּי אֱלִיעֶזֶר אוֹמֵר: מֵתָה יְבִמְתּוֹ – מוּתָּר בְּאִשְׁתּוֹ, מֵתָה אִשְׁתּוֹ אוֹתָהּ יְבָמָה חוֹלֶצֶת וְלֹא מִתְיַבֶּמֶת.

He then said: Yes, actually, Rabbi Elazar did state his opinion even in such a case, **and** so **it is taught** in a *baraita*: With regard to a *yavam* who betrothed the sister of his *yevama*, **Rabbi Elazar says:** If **his** ***yevama*** **dies, he is permitted to his wife.** If **his wife dies, that** ***yevama*** **performs** ***ḥalitza*** **but may not enter into levirate marriage** with him. Therefore, the challenge from the *baraita* can be dismissed since it represents only Rabbi Elazar's opinion.

לֵימָא שְׁמוּאֵל וְרַב אַסִי דְּאָמְרִי כְּרַבִּי אֱלִיעֶזֶר!

The Gemara suggests: **Shall we say** that **Shmuel and Rav Asi, who say** that she may not consummate the levirate marriage, hold **in accordance with** the opinion of **Rabbi Elazar?**

NOTES

It is in accordance with the opinion of Rabbi Elazar, etc. – רַבִּי אֱלִיעֶזֶר הִיא וכו׳: In the Jerusalem Talmud, this suggestion of Rav to link the *baraita* cited by Rav Hamnuna to the opinion of Rabbi Elazar is cited as an explicit statement of Rabbi Yoḥanan.

He then said, say, etc. – הֲדַר אֲמַר אֵימוּר וכו׳: The advantage of this suggestion is that if the *baraita* is not in accordance with the opinion of Rabbi Elazar, as taught in the mishna on 108b, then it is not subject to his dispute with the Rabbis and perforce it must be based upon an additional, unanimously agreed-upon principle. If so, it can provide a halakhic basis for the opinion of Shmuel and Rav Asi, since otherwise this *baraita*, which is the only support for their opinion, is in accordance only with an opinion that is not accepted as the *halakha*. In fact, Shmuel and Rav Asi themselves would have to explain the *baraita* in this way. However, Rava concludes that the *baraita* is in accordance only with the opinion of Rabbi Elazar, and therefore the *baraita* is not to be accepted as the *halakha* (*Tosefot HaRosh*; Rashba).

אפילו תימא כרבנן, עד כאן לא קמיפלגי רבנן עליה דרבי אלעזר – אלא משום דמנפילה ואילך לא מיתסר עלייהו, אבל הכא דאיתסר – אפילו רבנן מודו.

The Gemara rejects this: **You can even say** that they hold **in accordance with** the opinion of **the Rabbis,** as perhaps **the Rabbis disagree with Rabbi Elazar** in the case of a man who divorced and remarried his wife and then died childless **only due to** the fact **that** in that case, **from** the time of her **happening** for levirate marriage **and onward she was not forbidden to them,** i.e., her *yevamin*. The fact that the prohibition between her and her *yevamin* ended before she ever happened before them for levirate marriage means it has no bearing on her current eligibility for levirate marriage. **However, here,** in the case where the *yavam* betrothed the sister of his *yevama*, since **she became forbidden** after she had already happened before him for levirate marriage, **even the Rabbis** would **agree** that she remains permanently ineligible to consummate levirate marriage with him.

מתני׳ היבמה לא תחלוץ ולא תתייבם עד שיש לה שלשה חדשים. וכן כל שאר הנשים לא יתארסו ולא ינשאו עד שיהו להן שלשה חדשים אחד בתולות ואחד בעולות, אחד גרושות ואחד אלמנות, אחד נשואות ואחד ארוסות.

MISHNA **A *yevama* may neither perform *ḥalitza* nor enter into levirate marriage until** she has waited **three months**[H] from the time of her husband's death. **And similarly, all other women may not be betrothed**[H] **and may not marry until they have waited three months** since their previous marriage ended. This waiting period is necessary so that, should a woman give birth shortly after remarrying, it will be obvious who the father of the child is. This applies **both to virgins and non-virgins, both to divorcées and widows,** and **both to women** who were **married** to their previous husbands **and women** who were only **betrothed.** All of these women must wait three months before remarrying even though for some of them the reason for doing so does not apply.

רבי יהודה אומר: הנשואות יתארסו, והארוסות ינשאו, חוץ מן הארוסות שביהודה, מפני שלבו גס בה.

Rabbi Yehuda says: The women who were **married** to their previous husbands **may be betrothed, and the women** who were only **betrothed** to their previous husbands **may marry** without waiting three months. This is true **except for the betrothed women that are in** the area of **Judea,**[B] **due to** the fact **that** the groom **is familiar with her.** The custom in Judea was for the couple to be secluded together before the marriage so that they would become familiar with each other. This led to the possibility that they might cohabit even during their betrothal period. Rabbi Yehuda holds that one does not need to wait three months whenever the reason for doing so does not apply.

רבי יוסי אומר: כל הנשים יתארסו, חוץ מן האלמנה,

Rabbi Yosei says: All of the women[N] **may be betrothed** within three months even if they were previously married, **except for a widow,**

HALAKHA

A *yevama* may not perform *ḥalitza* until she has waited three months – היבמה לא תחלוץ עד שלשה חדשים: A woman who happened before her *yavam* for levirate marriage may neither perform *ḥalitza* nor enter into levirate marriage before first waiting ninety days, excluding the day of her husband's death and the day of her levirate marriage or *ḥalitza* (Rambam *Sefer Nashim*, *Hilkhot Yibbum VaḤalitza* 1:19; *Shulḥan Arukh*, *Even HaEzer* 164:1).

All other women may not be betrothed, etc. – כל שאר הנשים לא יתארסו וכו׳: Any woman who was divorced or widowed is forbidden to be betrothed or enter into levirate marriage with her *yavam* until she first waits ninety days, excluding the day of her husband's death or her divorce and the day of the betrothal. This is in accordance with the opinion of the first *tanna*, who is Rabbi Meir, and Rabbi Meir's opinion concerning decrees is also accepted as the *halakha*. However, it is permitted during this ninety-day period for the woman to commit herself to marry another man without actual betrothal (*Beit Yosef*, citing Rosh and *Terumat HaDeshen*; Rambam *Sefer Nashim*, *Hilkhot Geirushin* 11:18; *Shulḥan Arukh*, *Even HaEzer* 13:1).

BACKGROUND

The betrothed women that are in Judea – הארוסות שביהודה: Tractate *Ketubot* (12a) recounts that it was the custom in Judea for a couple to be secluded together before the marriage so that they would become familiar with each other. This was done despite the fact that this involved a certain compromise on the standards of modesty, as doing so could result in the couple engaging in sexual relations. The reason for the custom was that, at the time, the local gentile ruler would often force brides-to-be to first engage in sexual relations with him before entering their marriage. Although the communities would do everything in their power to prevent this, it was not always possible to avoid it. When it did occur, it could often lead to disharmony between the couple. Therefore, it was decided that before a couple would married, they should first be secluded together and thereby develop a close relationship between them that could help them withstand an assault from the local ruler.

NOTES

Rabbi Yosei says: All of the women, etc. – רבי יוסי אומר: כל הנשים וכו׳: Rashi explains that Rabbi Yosei fundamentally accepts the opinion of Rabbi Yehuda that the need for a waiting period applies only when there is both the possibility that the woman might already be pregnant from the previous husband and the possibility that she could become pregnant from the new husband. He disagrees only in the case of a widow. He would agree that a woman who was only betrothed to her previous husband is permitted to marry a new husband without waiting. However, other early commentaries argue that from the Gemara there is no indication that Rabbi Yosei agrees with Rabbi Yehuda on this point. Furthermore, the simple import of his words: All of the women may be betrothed, implies that he permits women to be betrothed without waiting, but never to marry during that three-month period. Therefore, they suggest that Rabbi Yosei actually represents a third opinion, and that his ruling concerning a widow is an additional, but independent, stringency (Rashba; Ritva; *Nimmukei Yosef*).

מִפְּנֵי הָאִיבּוּל.

due to the mourning period she must observe for her deceased husband.

גמ׳ בִּשְׁלָמָא לֹא תִּתְיַיבֵּם – שֶׁמָּא יְהֵא הַוָּלָד בֶּן קַיָּימָא, וְקָא פָּגַע בְּאִיסּוּר אֵשֶׁת אָח דְּאוֹרָיְיתָא. אֶלָּא לֹא תַּחֲלוֹץ – אַמַּאי?

GEMARA The Gemara questions the mishna's opening clause: **Granted, she should not enter into levirate marriage,**[N] as she might already be pregnant, which would still not be noticeable during the first three months, and **perhaps the baby will be viable.** In that case it would emerge that she was never subject to the mitzva of levirate marriage, **and** therefore, if the *yavam* consummates a levirate marriage **he will have encountered the Torah prohibition against** engaging in relations with one's **brother's wife. However, why should she not perform *ḥalitza*?**

לֵימָא תֶּיהֱוֵי תְּיוּבְתָּא דְּרַבִּי יוֹחָנָן דְּאָמַר: חֲלִיצַת מְעוּבֶּרֶת שְׁמָהּ חֲלִיצָה! וְלָאו מִי אוֹתְבִינֵיהּ לְרַבִּי יוֹחָנָן חֲדָא זִימְנָא? לֵימָא מֵהָא נַמִי תֶּיהֱוֵי תְּיוּבְתָּא!

The Gemara suggests: **Let us say** that this mishna, which states that a pregnant woman should not perform *ḥalitza,* **is a conclusive refutation of** the opinion of **Rabbi Yoḥanan, who said** that a ***ḥalitza*** performed **with a pregnant woman** who later miscarries **is considered** a valid ***ḥalitza.*** The Gemara asks: **But didn't they** already **conclusively refute** the opinion of **Rabbi Yoḥanan one time** previously from other sources? The Gemara rephrases the suggestion: **Let us say** that **from this** mishna **as well there is a conclusive refutation** of the opinion of Rabbi Yoḥanan.

לָא, הָכָא הַיְינוּ טַעְמָא שֶׁמָּא יְהֵא וָלָד בֶּן קַיָּימָא, וְנִמְצֵאת אַתָּה מַצְרִיכָהּ כָּרוֹז לִכְהוּנָּה.

The Gemara deflects this suggestion: **No,** it is possible that in the mishna **here, this is the reason** that she may not perform *ḥalitza*: **Perhaps** the **offspring will be viable,** in which case although she performed the act of *ḥalitza,* it is entirely meaningless since it was completely unnecessary, and she would remain permitted to marry into the priesthood. However, this could lead to a problem: People might not realize that the *ḥalitza* she performed was meaningless, and they would think she is a *ḥalutza* who is prohibited from marrying a priest. **It would** therefore **emerge** that if you permit her to perform *ḥalitza* even though it is possible that she is pregnant, it could be that **you will** ultimately **require a public announcement** to be made **for her** to attest to the fact that the *ḥalitza* she performed was meaningless and she is in fact still permitted to marry **into the priesthood.**

וְנִצְרְכַהּ! דִּלְמָא אִיכָּא דַּהֲוַאי בַּחֲלִיצָה וְלָא הֲוֵי בַּהַכְרָזָה, וּמַפְסְלוּהָ מִן הַכְּהוּנָּה.

The Gemara wonders why this poses a problem: **But** why not let her perform *ḥalitza* even though it is possible she is pregnant, and then, if it becomes necessary, **require** a public announcement to be made **for her?** The Gemara explains why one should avoid having to rely on a public announcement: **Perhaps there will be some** people **who are** present **at the *ḥalitza* but were not** present **at the public announcement, and** those people **will** incorrectly **disqualify her from** marrying into **the priesthood.** To avoid this situation, the mishna rules that she should wait three months before performing *ḥalitza.*

NOTES

Granted, she should not enter into levirate marriage – בִּשְׁלָמָא לֹא תִּתְיַיבֵּם: The waiting period is required only due to the possibility that the *yevama* might be pregnant from her previous husband. Therefore there should be no requirement to wait for a *yevama* who was only betrothed to her previous husband, as it can be assumed she is not pregnant since it is forbidden to engage in relations during the betrothal period. Nevertheless, the Sages required the waiting period in all cases. Were they not to have required it a case in which the *yevama* had only been betrothed, people could have made a mistaken comparison and incorrectly concluded that even where the *yevama* was in fact pregnant from her deceased husband, it is permitted for her to consummate a levirate marriage immediately, which would be violation of a prohibition that entails *karet.* Therefore, to avoid any confusion, the Sages required the waiting period in all cases (Ritva).

HALAKHA

One who is eligible for levirate marriage, etc. – כָּל הָעוֹלָה לְיִבּוּם וכו׳: A *yevama* may not consummate levirate marriage until she has waited ninety days from the day of her husband's death. Since she is ineligible for levirate marriage, she is also ineligible for *ḥalitza* (Rambam *Sefer Nashim, Hilkhot Yibbum VaḤalitza* 1:19).

A woman whose betrothal is uncertain with regard to levirate marriage – סָפֵק מְקוּדֶּשֶׁת לְעִנְיַן יִבּוּם: If a woman's betrothal to her husband was uncertain and her husband died, and the woman happened before her *yavam* for levirate marriage, he may consummate the levirate marriage with her since there is no reason to prohibit it (Rambam *Sefer Nashim, Hilkhot Yibbum VaḤalitza* 6:7; *Shulḥan Arukh, Even HaEzer* 173:15).

תֵּינַח אַלְמָנָה, גְּרוּשָׁה מַאי אִיכָּא לְמֵימַר? מִשּׁוּם דְּמַפְסִיד לָהּ מְזוֹנוֹת.

The Gemara asks: This answer **works out well** with regard to **a widow** because as a widow she is currently still permitted to marry into the priesthood, but with regard to **a divorcée,** who is already prohibited from marrying into the priesthood, **what is there to say;** why shouldn't she perform *ḥalitza* immediately? The Gemara provides an alternative reason to delay the *ḥalitza*: The reason is **because** by performing *ḥalitza* immediately **she will forfeit the sustenance payments** from her deceased husband's estate, which she otherwise would have been entitled to for the first three months. Since she is not permitted to remarry during those three months, she will have no means of support. Therefore, she should wait until after three months have passed before performing *ḥalitza*.

תֵּינַח נְשׂוּאָה, אֲרוּסָה גְּרוּשָׁה מַאי אִיכָּא לְמֵימַר?

The Gemara asks: This answer **works out well** with regard to a **woman** who was **married** to her previous husband and who is therefore entitled to sustenance payments, but with regard to **a divorcée who** was only **betrothed** to her previous husband, **what is there to say?** She is neither entitled to receive sustenance payments nor is she permitted to marry into the priesthood. Why, then, shouldn't she perform *ḥalitza* immediately?

אֶלָּא מִשּׁוּם דְּרַבִּי יוֹסֵי. דְּתַנְיָא: מַעֲשֶׂה בְּאָדָם אֶחָד שֶׁבָּא לִפְנֵי רַבִּי יוֹסֵי, אָמַר לוֹ: מַהוּ לַחֲלוֹץ בְּתוֹךְ שְׁלֹשָׁה? אָמַר לוֹ: לֹא תַּחֲלוֹץ. וְתַחֲלוֹץ וּמָה בְּכָךְ?

The Gemara therefore provides an alternative reason to delay the *ḥalitza*: **Rather,** it is **due to that** which **Rabbi Yosei** stated, **as it is taught** in a *baraita*: There was **an incident involving a certain man who came before Rabbi Yosei.** The man **said to him: What is** the *halakha* with regard **to performing *ḥalitza* within three** months of the husband's death? **He said to him: She may not perform *ḥalitza*.** He asked him: **Let her perform *ḥalitza*; what** would be the problem **with that?** Even if she is pregnant, no prohibition will have been transgressed.

קָרָא עָלָיו מִקְרָא זֶה: ״וְאִם לֹא יַחְפֹּץ״ הָא אִם חָפֵץ – יַבֵּם, כָּל הָעוֹלָה לְיִבּוּם – עוֹלָה לַחֲלִיצָה כו׳.

To explain his ruling, Rabbi Yosei **recited this verse about him: "And if the man does not wish** to take his *yevama*" (Deuteronomy 25:7) in levirate marriage, then he must perform *ḥalitza*. By inference, the possibility of performing *ḥalitza* exists only in a case in which **if he wishes he may consummate the levirate marriage.** This teaches the principle that **one who is eligible for levirate marriage**[H] **is eligible for *ḥalitza*,** and one who is ineligible for levirate marriage is ineligible for *ḥalitza*. This includes even a woman who is temporarily prohibited from marrying, e.g., a woman in the first three months following a previous marriage.

מְתִיב רַב חִינָּנָא: הַסְּפֵקוֹת חוֹלְצוֹת וְלֹא מִתְיַבְּמוֹת.

Rav Ḥinnana raised an objection from the following *baraita*: **Those women** whose status as a *yevama* **is uncertain perform *ḥalitza* but may not enter into levirate marriage.** According to this *baraita*, there are in fact cases in which a woman is eligible for *ḥalitza* but may not enter into levirate marriage.

מַאי סְפֵקוֹת? אִילֵימָא סְפֵק קִדּוּשִׁין אַמַּאי לֹא מִתְיַבְּמוֹת? תִּתְיַיבֵּם וְאֵין בְּכָךְ כְּלוּם!

The Gemara clarifies the case: **What is** the case of **women** whose status as a *yevama* **is uncertain? If we say** it is referring to a woman whose **betrothal** to her previous husband **is uncertain,** then **why does she not enter into levirate marriage? Let her enter into levirate marriage, and** there is **no** problem **with that,** because if the betrothal was never valid, then she is permitted to the *yavam* as she is not his brother's wife; and if it was valid, then she is now obligated to enter into levirate marriage with him.[H]

אֶלָּא לָאו – סָפֵק שֶׁקִּידֵּשׁ אַחַת מִשְּׁתֵּי אֲחָיוֹת וְאֵינוֹ יוֹדֵעַ אֵיזוֹ מֵהֶן קִידֵּשׁ, וְקָתָנֵי: חוֹלֶצֶת!

Rather, is it not referring to a case of **uncertainty** in **which** a man **betrothed one of two sisters and he does not know which** one **of them he betrothed?** If that man then died childless, the *yavam* may not consummate the levirate marriage with either sister because it is possible that he will do so with the sister who was not betrothed to his brother, who is therefore forbidden to him as the sister of a woman who is bound to him by a levirate bond. This is in fact the case of the *baraita*, **and** the *baraita* **teaches** that **she performs *ḥalitza*,** even though she is not permitted to enter into levirate marriage.

NOTES

For three months she receives sustenance payments from the husband's estate – שְׁלֹשָׁה חֳדָשִׁים נִזּוֹנֶת מִשֶּׁל בַּעַל: One of the conditions of the marriage contract is that in the event of the husband's death, the widow may remain in her husband's home and be sustained from his estate. This right continues to exist as long as the woman maintains her connection to her deceased husband and refrains from attempts to remarry. However, this is not true of a *yevama*. Since there is a mitzva to either consummate the levirate marriage or perform *ḥalitza*, she is automatically considered as though she is in the process of remarrying and therefore loses the right to be sustained from her husband's estate. However, during the first three months following her husband's death she is not permitted to proceed due to the rabbinic decree. Therefore, during that period she is not considered to be in the process of remarrying, and consequently she retains the rights to be sustained from her husband's estate.

He was brought to judgment and he ran away – עָמַד בַּדִּין וּבָרַח: Rashi explains that the *yavam* ran away to avoid complying with the court's ruling, and his obligation to provide subsistence for her is a penalty for neglecting his duty. However, most of the other early commentaries explain that the *baraita* is referring to a man who was forced to run away due to circumstances beyond his control. Nevertheless, since when he was brought to court, the court fixed a date by which he was expected to consummate the levirate marriage, when that date arrives he automatically takes on the financial responsibilities of a husband to support his wife. The *halakha* is the same in any case of a man who betrothed a woman and a date is set for them to be married; when the date arrives he takes on financial responsibility for her irrespective of whether he actually marries her (Ramban).

She was penalized by Heaven – מִשְּׁמַיָּא קְנָסוּהָ: Despite the Gemara's conclusion, several *ge'onim* ruled that in cases such as this, especially where the woman is unable to sustain herself through her own efforts, she should receive sustenance payments from the dowry that she brought with her to her previous marriage. Later, when the *yavam* matures, if he consummates the levirate marriage with her, he will take whatever is left of the dowry, and if he performs *ḥalitza* then she receives the remainder of the marriage contract.

הָכִי הָשְׁתָּא?! הָתָם, אִם יָבֹא אֵלִיָּהוּ וְיֹאמַר דְּהָא קִידֵּשׁ – בַּת חֲלִיצָה וְיִיבּוּם הִיא,

The Gemara rejects the proof: **How can these cases be compared? There,** in the case of uncertainty, **if Elijah were to come and say that** the man **betrothed this one** of the sisters, then **she would be eligible for *ḥalitza* and levirate marriage.** It is clear, then, that fundamentally the sister who was betrothed is actually eligible for levirate marriage, and it is merely a lack of knowledge that prevents her from entering into it.

הָכָא אִם יָבֹא אֵלִיָּהוּ וְיֹאמַר דְּהָא לָא אִיעַבְּרָה – מִי מַשְׁגַּח בֵּיהּ וְיַבְּמִינַן לַהּ? הָא קְטַנָּה דְּלָאו בַּת אִיעַבּוּרֵי הִיא, וַאֲפִילּוּ הָכִי צְרִיכָה לְהַמְתִּין שְׁלֹשָׁה חֳדָשִׁים,

However, **here,** with regard to a woman during the first three months following her previous marriage, **if Elijah were to come and say that this** woman **is not pregnant, would one pay heed to him and would we allow** the *yavam* **to consummate levirate marriage?** Certainly not, as is evident from the fact that **a minor girl, who cannot become pregnant, must** also **wait three months.**[H] Evidently, the requirement to wait three months applies in all situations, even those in which the reason for the requirement is irrelevant. Therefore, by virtue of that decree the *yevama* is considered to be fundamentally ineligible for levirate marriage and similarly is ineligible for *ḥalitza*.

תָּנוּ רַבָּנַן: יְבָמָה, שְׁלֹשָׁה חֳדָשִׁים הָרִאשׁוֹנִים – נִזּוֹנֶת מִשֶּׁל בַּעַל, מִכָּאן וְאֵילָךְ – אֵינָהּ נִזּוֹנֶת לֹא מִשֶּׁל בַּעַל וְלֹא מִשֶּׁל יָבָם.

§ The Gemara mentioned that a *yevama* is supported from her deceased husband's estate. It now proceeds to cite a *baraita* that teaches this *halakha*: **The Sages taught: A *yevama*** during **the first three months** following her husband's death **receives sustenance** payments[H] **from the husband's** estate.[N] This is because her previous marriage to him is the cause of her current unmarried state, since is it due to that marriage that she must first wait three months before remarrying. **From this** point **forward, she does not receive sustenance** payments, **neither from the husband's** estate **nor from the *yavam*,** as he has not yet consummated a levirate marriage with her.

עָמַד בַּדִּין וּבָרַח – נִזּוֹנֶת מִשֶּׁל יָבָם.

The *baraita* continues: If the *yavam* **was brought to judgment** and it was decided that he was obligated to either consummate the levirate marriage with her or perform *ḥalitza*, **and he ran away**[N] to avoid doing so, **she receives sustenance** payments **from** the estate **of the *yavam*,** which is his penalty for neglecting his duty.

נָפְלָה לִפְנֵי יָבָם קָטָן (מַאי)? מִיָּבָם – לֵית לַהּ, מִבַּעַל – מַאי?

The Gemara asks: If **she happened before** her ***yavam*** who is **a minor**[H] for levirate marriage, **what is** the *halakha*? **From the *yavam* she does not have** any right to sustenance payments because, as a minor, he is unable to consummate a levirate marriage, but as to payments **from** her **husband's** estate, **what** is the *halakha*? Since his death placed her in a situation that forces her to remain in an unmarried state, does his estate have to take the responsibility of supporting her?

פְּלִיגִי בַּהּ רַב אַחָא וְרָבִינָא; חַד אָמַר: אִית לַהּ, וְחַד אָמַר: לֵית לַהּ, וְהִלְכְתָא: לֵית לַהּ, מִשְּׁמַיָּא קְנָסוּהָ.

Rav Aḥa and Ravina disagree with regard to this matter: **One said she does have** rights to sustenance payments, **and** the other **one said she does not have** any rights. **And the *halakha*** is that **she does not have** any rights to sustenance payments. This is because the husband is not considered to be responsible for her situation; rather, it is thought that **she was penalized by Heaven.**[N]

תָּנוּ רַבָּנַן: יְבָמָה שֶׁחָלְצוּ לַהּ אַחִים בְּתוֹךְ שְׁלֹשָׁה – צְרִיכָה לְהַמְתִּין שְׁלֹשָׁה חֳדָשִׁים,

§ **The Sages taught:** In the case of **a *yevama* with whom the brothers** of her deceased husband **performed *ḥalitza* within three** months of her husband's death, she still **needs to wait three months** before remarrying.

HALAKHA

A minor girl must wait – קְטַנָּה צְרִיכָה לְהַמְתִּין: When the Sages decreed that no woman may marry until she has first waited three months since the end of her previous marriage, they did not distinguish between cases, and therefore even a woman who is unfit for childbirth, e.g., a minor, is included in the decree (Rambam *Sefer Nashim, Hilkhot Geirushin* 11:20; *Shulḥan Arukh, Even HaEzer* 13:1).

Sustenance payments for a *yevama* – מְזוֹנוֹת יְבָמָה: A *yevama* receives sustenance payments from her husband's estate, like any other widow, for the first three months following his death. From this point onward, she does not receive sustenance payments either from the husband or from the *yavam*. If, after three months, she demanded that the *yavam* consummate levirate marriage and he agreed to do so, or even if he did not agree (Rambam), then even if he was ultimately prevented from doing so due to circumstances beyond his control he becomes obligated to provide her with sustenance payments. If he ran away to avoid doing so, it would seem that he is obligated to provide for her according to all opinions (*Beit Shmuel*; Rambam *Sefer Nashim, Hilkhot Ishut* 18:15; *Shulḥan Arukh, Even HaEzer* 160:1).

She happened before her *yavam* who is a minor – נָפְלָה לִפְנֵי יָבָם קָטָן: In the case of a *yevama* who happened before a *yavam* who is a minor, after three months she no longer receives sustenance payments from the estate of the husband or that of the *yavam* until the *yavam* reaches maturity (*Beit Shmuel*; Rambam *Sefer Nashim, Hilkhot Ishut* 18:17; *Shulḥan Arukh, Even HaEzer* 160:3).

לְאַחַר שְׁלֹשָׁה – אֵין צְרִיכָה לְהַמְתִּין שְׁלֹשָׁה חֳדָשִׁים.

If they performed the *ḥalitza* **after three** months, **she does not need to wait three months** and may marry immediately.

הֲוֵי הַשְּׁלֹשָׁה חֳדָשִׁים שֶׁאָמְרוּ – מִשְּׁעַת מִיתַת הַבַּעַל, וְלֹא מִשְּׁעַת חֲלִיצַת הַיָּבָם.

The Gemara infers from the latter clause of the *baraita*: It **must be** that **the three months that are stated** throughout the *baraita* are counted **from the time of the husband's death and not from the time of the *ḥalitza* of the *yavam*.**[H]

מַאי שְׁנָא מִגֵּט, דְּרַב אָמַר מִשְּׁעַת נְתִינָה וּשְׁמוּאֵל אָמַר מִשְּׁעַת כְּתִיבָה?

The Gemara asks: In **what** way **is** this case **different from** the case of **a bill of divorce,**[H] **where Rav said** that the three months are counted **from the time of the giving** of the bill of divorce, **and Shmuel said** that the count is **from the time of the writing** of the bill. If a couple is secluded together after the bill of divorce is written, the bill of divorce is invalid. Therefore, there is no concern that they were secluded from that time. This is why Shmuel holds that the three months are counted from the writing. Rav apparently assumes that even so, the count always begins from the formal end of the marriage and not from the point from which there was no possibility of her becoming pregnant. Why, then, does the *baraita* not rule also in the case when a woman happens for levirate marriage, that the count should begin from the point of *ḥalitza*, since the marriage is only fully severed at that point?

אָמַר רָבָא: קַל וָחוֹמֶר: אִיסּוּר כָּרֵת הִתַּרְתָּ, אִיסּוּר לָאו לֹא כׇּל שֶׁכֵּן?

Rava said: With regard to a *yevama*, all agree that the count begins from the time of her husband's death. This can be derived through an ***a fortiori*** inference, as follows: If **a prohibition** that entails ***karet***, i.e., the prohibition against engaging in relations with one's brother's wife in the event she is pregnant and not subject to levirate marriage, **you have permitted** after three months from the husband's death, then in the case of a standard **negative prohibition,** such as the prohibition against engaging in relations with a woman within three months of the death of her previous husband, is it **not all the more so**[N] clear that she should be permitted to remarry after three months from her husband's death? Therefore, even Rav agrees that in this case, the count begins from the husband's death.

״וְכֵן שְׁאָר כׇּל הַנָּשִׁים״. בִּשְׁלָמָא יְבָמָה – כִּדְאָמְרַן. אֶלָּא שְׁאָר כׇּל הַנָּשִׁים אַמַּאי?

§ The mishna states: **And similarly, all other women may** not be betrothed or marry until they have waited three months. The Gemara asks: **Granted, a *yevama*** has to wait, **in accordance with** the reason **that we said,** that if she is pregnant with viable offspring, consummating the levirate marriage would violate the prohibition against engaging in relations with one's brother's wife. **But** with regard to **all other women, why** shouldn't they remarry immediately even if they are pregnant?

אָמַר רַב נַחְמָן אָמַר שְׁמוּאֵל: מִשּׁוּם דְּאָמַר קְרָא ״לִהְיוֹת לְךָ לֵאלֹהִים וּלְזַרְעֲךָ אַחֲרֶיךָ״ לְהַבְחִין בֵּין זַרְעוֹ שֶׁל רִאשׁוֹן לְזַרְעוֹ שֶׁל שֵׁנִי.

Rav Naḥman said that **Shmuel said:** It is **due to** the fact **that the verse states** with regard to Abraham: **"To be a God to you and your seed after you"** (Genesis 17:7), which indicates that the Divine Presence rests with someone only when his seed can be identified as being descended from him, i.e., there are no uncertainties with regard to their lineage. Therefore, to prevent any uncertainties concerning the lineage of her child, the woman must wait so that it will be possible **to distinguish**[N] **between the seed of the first** husband **and the seed of the second** husband. After three months, if she has conceived from her previous husband, the pregnancy will already be noticeable.

מְתִיב רָבָא: לְפִיכָךְ גֵּר וְגִיּוֹרֶת צְרִיכִין לְהַמְתִּין שְׁלֹשָׁה חֳדָשִׁים, הָכָא מַאי לְהַבְחִין אִיכָּא?

Rava raised an objection from a *baraita*: **Therefore,** on account of the requirement to wait three months, **a male convert and a female convert** who were originally married to each other and converted **need to wait three months**[H] before they may remarry following their conversion. Rava asks: **Here,** in this case, **what** reason **is there to distinguish?** Even if they do not wait and she is found to be pregnant, it is clear who the child's parents are.

HALAKHA

From when does a *yevama* wait – מֵמָתַי מַמְתִּינָה הַיְבָמָה: A *yevama* who performed *ḥalitza* within three months of her husband's death must still complete the three-month wait after her husband's death before remarrying. If she performed *ḥalitza* after three months had already passed, she need not wait any longer (Rambam *Sefer Nashim, Hilkhot Yibbum VaḤalitza* 1:19; *Shulḥan Arukh, Even HaEzer* 164:1).

From when does a divorcée wait – מֵמָתַי מַמְתִּינָה גְּרוּשָׁה: A divorcée must wait three months from the writing of her bill of divorce before remarrying. This applies even if the bill was made conditional or was given only some time later. This is in accordance with the opinion of Shmuel. Most halakhic authorities rule in accordance with his opinion because in tractate *Ketubot* Rav Ashi, one of the latest of the *amora'im*, rules in accordance with his opinion (*Kesef Mishne*). This is also the final ruling in the Jerusalem Talmud. However, the Rema (citing *Tur* and Rosh) rules that it is correct to be stringent and count from the time that the bill of divorce was given (Rambam *Sefer Nashim, Hilkhot Geirushin* 11:19; *Shulḥan Arukh, Even HaEzer* 13:1).

Separation of male and female converts – הַפְרָשַׁת גֵּר וְגִיּוֹרֶת: A maidservant or female convert who was married prior to conversion must wait ninety days before remarrying. This applies even to a husband and wife who converted together; they must separate from each other for that period. This is required so that it will be possible to distinguish between seed that was sown in sanctity and seed that was not sown in sanctity (Rambam *Sefer Nashim, Hilkhot Geirushin* 11:21; *Shulḥan Arukh, Even HaEzer* 13:5).

NOTES

A standard negative prohibition, all the more so – אִיסּוּר לָאו לֹא כׇּל שֶׁכֵּן: This reasoning cannot be applied in the case of a divorcée since she is still considered fully married until she has actually received a bill of divorce (Rivan).

To distinguish – לְהַבְחִין: The later commentaries deliberate whether the fact that a biblical source is cited renders this a true exegetical inference, which would mean that the need to distinguish is by Torah law, or whether the requirement is a rabbinic decree and the verse is cited merely as support for it. The *Keren Ora* states that the need to distinguish is a rabbinic decree, while *Arukh LaNer* cites the *Targum Yerushalmi* and certain formulations of the Rambam that suggest that the requirement is by Torah law.

Yosef Lekaḥ writes that although the concern of being unable to distinguish between the seed of the first and second husbands might seem unlikely, nevertheless, since remarriage for women is so common it is reasonable to assume that even this unusual situation will eventually arise.

הָכָא נַמִי: אִיכָּא לְהַבְחִין בֵּין זֶרַע שֶׁנִּזְרַע בִּקְדוּשָּׁה לְזֶרַע שֶׁלֹּא נִזְרַע בִּקְדוּשָּׁה.

The Gemara explains: **Here, too, there is** a need **to distinguish between seed that was sown in sanctity,**[N] i.e., a child conceived by a Jewish parents, **and seed that was not sown in sanctity,** i.e., a child conceived by gentile parents.

רָבָא אָמַר: גְּזֵירָה שֶׁמָּא יִשָּׂא אֶת אֲחוֹתוֹ מֵאָבִיו, וְיִיַבֵּם אֵשֶׁת אָחִיו מֵאִמּוֹ,

Rava stated a different reason for the need to wait: It is a rabbinic **decree**[N] **lest** a child be born and be incorrectly identified as the son of his mother's second husband when he is fact the son of her first husband. This could result in him **marrying his paternal sister,** unaware of the true relationship between them, **or consummating a levirate marriage with the wife of his maternal brother** under the misconception that his maternal brother was also his paternal brother. This would be prohibited because the prohibition to engage in relations with one's brother's wife is waived only in the case where there is a mitzva of levirate marriage, which applies only to paternal brothers.

וְיוֹצִיא אֶת אִמּוֹ לַשּׁוּק, וְיִפְטוֹר אֶת יְבִמְתּוֹ לַשּׁוּק.

Or in the event that his mother's second husband died and he was assumed to be his only offspring, **he would cause his mother to go out** and be permitted **to the** general **public** because, under the misconception that he was the offspring of the deceased, he assumed that there was no mitzva of levirate marriage. **Or,** in the event that his maternal brother died childless and the brother's widow became subject to levirate marriage, under the misconception that he was the paternal brother of the deceased he might perform *ḥalitza* and **permit** his supposed ***yevama*** **to** marry a man from **the** general **public.** To avoid these problems, the Sages decreed that a woman must wait before remarrying.

מְתִיב רַב חֲנַנְיָה: בְּכוּלָּן אֲנִי קוֹרֵא בָּהֶן מִשּׁוּם תַּקָּנַת עֶרְוָה, וְכָאן מִשּׁוּם תַּקָּנַת וָלָד. וְאִם אִיתָא – כּוּלְּהוּ מִשּׁוּם תַּקָּנַת עֶרְוָה!

Rav Ḥananya raised an objection from a *baraita*: **In all of those** cases where the Sages prohibit a woman from marrying or consummating a levirate marriage, **I identify**[N] that the prohibition is **due to an ordinance** instituted to prevent a violation of **forbidden relations, and here,** with regard to the prohibition against marrying within three months, it is **due to an ordinance for** the benefit of **the offspring.** Rav Ḥananya explains the challenge: **And if it is so** that Rava's understanding of the prohibition against marrying within three months is correct, then **all of the** cases of forbidden marriages are **due to an ordinance** to prevent violation of **forbidden relations.** However, the *baraita* indicates otherwise.

הַאי מִשּׁוּם תַּקָּנַת וָלָד דְּלָא לִפְגַּע בְּהוּ עֶרְוָה.

The Gemara defends Rava's opinion and explains that the *baraita* can be interpreted in a way that is consistent with his understanding: When the *baraita* says that **this** prohibition is **due to an ordinance for** the benefit of **the offspring,** it means **that** due to the prohibition the offspring **will not encounter** a prohibition of **forbidden relations.**

בִּשְׁלָמָא תַּמְתִּין שְׁנֵי חֳדָשִׁים וְתִנָּשֵׂא, לָא – דְּהַיְינוּ סְפֵיקָא, אִי בַּר תִּשְׁעָה לְקַמָּא אִי בַּר שִׁבְעָה לְבַתְרָא.

§ The Gemara analyzes the prohibition against marrying before three months have passed: **Granted, she should not wait** for only **two months and** then **marry, as this is** still a case that could give rise to **an uncertainty whether** the child born to her seven months after remarrying **is nine** months **old,** i.e., counting from conception, and it is the offspring **of the first** husband, or **whether** the child is only **seven** months **old** and is the offspring **of the latter** husband.

אֶלָּא, תַּמְתִּין חֹדֶשׁ אֶחָד וְתִנָּשֵׂא: וְאִי לְשִׁבְעָה יָלְדָה – הַאי בַּר שִׁבְעָה לְבַתְרָא הוּא, וְאִי לְתַמְנְיָא יָלְדָה – הַאי בַּר תִּשְׁעָה לְקַמָּא הוּא.

However, let her wait only **one month and** then **marry, and** then, since it is presumed that a baby born during its eighth month since conception is not viable[B] but a baby born during its seventh or nine month is viable, **if after seven** months since remarrying **she gives birth,** then the child **is** clearly **seven** months **old** and **is** the offspring **of the latter** husband, **and if after eight** months since remarrying **she gives birth,** then **this** child **is** clearly **nine** months **old and is** the offspring **of the first** husband. Why, then, is there a need to wait three months?

NOTES

Between seed that was sown in sanctity – בֵּין זֶרַע שֶׁנִּזְרַע בִּקְדוּשָּׁה: If the child was conceived before his parents' conversions, the child would also have the status of a convert. As such, if the child was a female she would be prohibited from marrying into the priesthood (Rivan). Furthermore, as a convert, the child would not inherit from his convert father. Some assume that halakhically, the child would be considered as though he were not descended from his father for all other matters as well.

Rava stated, it is a rabbinic decree, etc. – רָבָא אָמַר גְּזֵירָה וכו׳: An additional reason for the decree is cited in the *She'iltot deRav Aḥai Gaon*, and it is possible that this reason actually appeared in the author's version of the Gemara: Lest he set slaves free. The *Gilyonei HaShas* explains the concern: When one owns slaves and dies, his mastery over his slaves is inherited by his children. If the child in this case incorrectly identified who his father was, and then upon that father's death the son frees the father's slaves, his release of the slaves would be entirely ineffectual since he is not truly that father's son and does not actually inherit from him. This would create a situation where those slaves, assuming that they had been lawfully freed, might proceed to marry Jewish women, when in fact they would be prohibited from doing so because they remained slaves. A similar explanation can be offered for the requirement to distinguish between seed in the case of a maidservant, which requires her to wait three months after her release. Since her offspring conceived before her release would have the status of slaves, whereas those conceived after her release would be fully Jewish, there is a concern that her offspring might actually be slaves but will act as though they are free.

The Rivash notes that based on all the reasons that the Gemara provides, it would appear that when a man remarries his divorcée without her having since remarried in the interim, there is no reason to require her to wait three months.

In all of those cases I identify – בְּכוּלָּן אֲנִי קוֹרֵא בָּהֶן: According to *Tosafot*, the phrase: All of those cases, refers to all *yevamot* who are prohibited from marrying. However, Rashi and the Meiri explain that it refers to all cases of women who are prohibited from remarrying. This includes even cases such as those in which the evidence of a husband's death is not sufficient to allow a woman to remarry; even in such cases, the ultimate reason for the prohibitions is to prevent people from engaging in forbidden relations.

BACKGROUND

Born after eight months of pregnancy – אִי נַמִי לְתַמְנְיָא יָלְדָה: During talmudic times conventional wisdom held that a child born during the eighth month of pregnancy had no chance of survival, while a child born during the seventh month, and even one born during the sixth month, was more likely to survive. Nowadays, a baby born in the eighth month is considered to have greater chances of survival than one born earlier. Accordingly, despite the fact that the Gemara says that one may not desecrate the Shabbat to save a child born during the eighth month (*Shabbat* 135a), nowadays, since the child is likely to survive, the later authorities maintain that one may desecrate Shabbat to save him or her (*Minḥat Yitzḥak* 4:123; *Ḥazon Ish*, *Yoreh De'a* 155:3).

אִי נַמִּי לְתַמְנְיָא יָלְדָה – אִיכָּא לְמֵימַר דְּבַתְרָא הוּא, דִּלְמָא אִישְׁתַּהוּיֵי אִישְׁתַּהָא חֹדֶשׁ אֶחָד וְאִיעַבַּר.

The Gemara explains: **Even if she gave birth after eight** months since remarrying **one could say that** the child is the offspring **of the latter** husband,[N] as **perhaps she waited one month** after remarrying **and conceived** only then. As such, the baby would be only seven months old, and that would explain its viability.

וְתַמְתִּין שְׁנֵי חֳדָשִׁים וּמֶחֱצָה וְתִנָּשֵׂא, דְּאִי לְשִׁבְעָה יָלְדָה – הַאי בַּר שִׁבְעָה לְבַתְרָא הוּא. וְאִי לְשִׁיתָּא וּפַלְגָּא יָלְדָה – הַאי בַּר תִּשְׁעָה לְקַמָּא הוּא, דְּאִי בַּר בַּתְרָא הוּא – בַּר שִׁיתָּא וּפַלְגָּא לָא חַיֵּי!

The Gemara asks further: **But let her wait for two and a half months and** then **marry, as, if after seven** months since remarrying **she gives birth,** then **this** child **is** clearly **seven** months **old and is** the offspring **of the latter** husband. **And if after six and a half** months since remarrying **she gives birth,** then **this** child **is** clearly **nine** months **old** and **is** the offspring **of the first** husband, because **if** one would suggest **it is** the offspring **of the latter** husband, in that case it would be **six and a half** months **old,** at **which** age it **cannot survive.**

אִי נַמִּי לְשִׁיתָּא וּפַלְגָּא יָלְדָה – אִיכָּא לְמֵימַר דְּבַתְרָא הוּא, דְּאָמַר מָר זוּטְרָא: אֲפִילּוּ לְמַאן דְּאָמַר יוֹלֶדֶת לְתִשְׁעָה אֵינָהּ יוֹלֶדֶת לְמִקּוּטָּעִין – יָלְדָה לְשִׁבְעָה יוֹלֶדֶת לְמִקּוּטָּעִין,

The Gemara objects: **Even if after six and a half** months since remarrying **she gave birth, one could say that** the child is the offspring **of the latter** husband, **as Mar Zutra said: Even according to the one who says** that **a woman who gives birth after nine** months **does not give birth after an incomplete** number of months, i.e., she carries for a full nine months, nevertheless, **a woman who gives birth after seven months can give birth after an incomplete** number of months, and therefore it is possible that the baby was actually born after six and a half months.

שֶׁנֶּאֱמַר ״וַיְהִי לִתְקֻפוֹת הַיָּמִים״, מִיעוּט ״תְּקוּפוֹת״ – שְׁתַּיִם, מִיעוּט ״יָמִים״ – שְׁנַיִם.

This fact is derived from the verse concerning the birth of Samuel the prophet, **as it is stated: "And it came to pass, when the seasons of the days had come,** that Hannah conceived, and bore a son" (I Samuel 1:20). How much time is indicated by the phrase "the seasons of the days"? **The minimal sense of** the word **"seasons" is two,** and since each season of the year is three months, that indicates six months. **The minimal sense of** the word **"days" is two.** Accordingly, one may conclude that Samuel the prophet was born after six months and two days.

וְתַמְתִּין מַשֶּׁהוּ וְתִנָּשֵׂא, וְכִי מָלוּ שְׁלֹשָׁה חֳדָשִׁים לִבְדְקַהּ!

The Gemara suggests further: **But let her wait any** minimal **amount** of time, less than a month, **and** then **marry, and** then **when three months** after the end of her first marriage **are complete, examine her** body to see if she is noticeably pregnant. If she is, then perforce the baby is the offspring of her previous husband because a pregnancy is not noticeable until three months.

אָמַר רַב סַפְרָא: אֵין בּוֹדְקִין אֶת הַנְּשׂוּאוֹת, שֶׁלֹּא יִתְגַּנּוּ עַל בַּעֲלֵיהֶן. וְנִבְדְּקָהּ בַּהֲלוּכָהּ?

Rav Safra said: This solution is not possible because **one does not examine** the bodies of **married women so as not to shame them before their husbands.** The Gemara suggests: **But let her be examined through the way she walks,**[NB] since after three months a pregnant woman walks differently than a woman who is not pregnant.

אָמַר רָמִי בַּר חָמָא: אִשָּׁה מְחַפָּה עַצְמָהּ, כְּדֵי שֶׁיִּירַשׁ בְּנָהּ בְּנִכְסֵי בַעְלָהּ.

Rami bar Ḥama said: A woman who conceived from her previous husband would **mask herself** by purposefully walking in a manner in which her pregnancy will not be discerned, so that her child will be identified as the son of her new husband **in order that her child will** ultimately **inherit her** new **husband's property.** Therefore, it is impossible to rely upon a test of this kind. In summary, the Gemara has demonstrated that it would be ineffective to wait any less than three months.

הֵיכָא דְּקִים לַן דִּמְעוּבֶּרֶת הִיא תִּנָּשֵׂא, אַלְמָה תַּנְיָא: לֹא יִשָּׂא אָדָם מְעוּבֶּרֶת חֲבֵירוֹ וּמֵינֶקֶת חֲבֵירוֹ, וְאִם נָשָׂא יוֹצִיא וְלֹא יַחֲזִיר עוֹלָמִית.

§ The Gemara asks: In cases **where we are convinced that she is pregnant, let her marry** immediately, as the reason to wait three months does not apply. **Why,** then, **is it taught** in a *baraita*: **A man may not marry a woman who is pregnant** with the child **of another** man, **nor a woman who is nursing** the child **of another** man;[H] **and if he** transgressed and **married** her, he is penalized for violating the prohibition, and **he must divorce** her **and may never take** her **back?**

NOTES

One could say that the child is the offspring of the latter husband, etc. – **אִיכָּא לְמֵימַר דְּבַתְרָא הוּא וכו׳**: Why didn't the Gemara reject the possibility of waiting one month also due to the possibility that she had become pregnant from her previous husband one month before the end of the marriage? In that case, if a baby boy was born after eight months that child would actually be nine months old and the offspring of the first husband. Rashi suggests that Gemara could have considered this possibility; however, since in any case the Gemara rejects the possibility of waiting one month for the reasons it mentions, it was not necessary to state another reason. Others suggest that the Gemara considered it preferable to provide reasons that pertain to all cases, even to a case where she had been married to her previous husband for only a single day (Ramban; *Tosefot HaRosh*).

But let her be examined through the way she walks – **וְנִבְדְּקָהּ בַּהֲלוּכָהּ**: Rashi and Rivan cite the *ge'onim*, who explain that the fetus of a pregnant woman rests on one side of the womb and causes her steps to be uneven.

BACKGROUND

Let her be examined through the way she walks – **וְנִבְדְּקָהּ בַּהֲלוּכָהּ**: Rashi cites the explanation of the *ge'onim* that the woman's footprints are examined. There is also an additional change in pregnant women: Their posture becomes less stable in that the upper body begins to arch back more and more as the pregnancy progresses. This small change is discernible already in the first months of pregnancy. A woman who wishes to hide her state can do so by purposefully altering her posture. If she does so, her pregnancy will not be evident for some time.

HALAKHA

Pregnant and nursing women – **מְעוּבֶּרֶת וּמֵינֶקֶת**: A man may not marry a woman who is pregnant with the child of another man. He may also not marry a woman who is nursing the child of another man within twenty-four months of its birth. If he transgressed and married such a woman, he must divorce her with a bill of divorce. This applies even if he is a priest. If he is a non-priest he is permitted to remarry her after the nursing period has ended (Rambam *Sefer Nashim, Hilkhot Geirushin* 11:25; *Shulḥan Arukh, Even HaEzer* 13:11).

NOTES

Heaven will have mercy upon her – מִן הַשָּׁמַיִם יְרַחֲמוּ: This concept, based on the verse: "The Lord preserves the simple" (Psalms 116:6), applies only when one acts normally and does not take unusual risks. When there is definite danger involved, one is not permitted to take the risk and rely on God's protection. In the case here, there is only a very slight risk involved, and therefore this concept can be applied (Meiri; Ridvaz 3:596; *Aḥiezer* 1:23).

Due to the pressure – מִשּׁוּם דְּחָסָה: Usually when the Gemara challenges the logic of a given answer and proceeds by saying: Rather, it indicates that the given answer is rejected. Accordingly, it would appear that the Gemara here rejects the suggestion that the concern that the man might damage the fetus by applying too much pressure could be the reason for the prohibition. However, the Rambam does cite this reason when he codifies the *halakha*. Some suggest that the Rambam understood that the Gemara never meant to reject the reasons it raised; it merely held that they were insufficient. It is also possible that the Rambam had a different version of the Gemara text and that in his version the Gemara never stated: Rather. Alternatively, it is possible that the Rambam drew a distinction between the case of a pregnant woman and that of a nursing woman, and different reasons apply to each case (see *Kesef Mishne* and *Ha'amek She'ala*).

גְּזֵירָה שֶׁמָּא תַּעֲשֶׂה עוּבָּרָהּ סַנְדָּל, אִי הָכִי – דִּידֵיהּ נַמִּי,

The Gemara explains: This prohibition is a rabbinic **decree lest** she become pregnant a second time and **her** original **fetus will be deformed** into the shape of **a sandal fish.** The Gemara asks: **If so, even** if his wife is pregnant with **his own** child, the same concern applies.

אִי לְמַאן דַּאֲמַר בְּמוֹךְ – בְּמוֹךְ, וְאִי לְמַאן דַּאֲמַר מִן הַשָּׁמַיִם יְרַחֲמוּ – מִן הַשָּׁמַיִם יְרַחֲמוּ,

The Gemara responds: She is permitted to engage in relations, both **if** one holds **in accordance with the one who said** that a young girl, for whom it is dangerous to become pregnant, is permitted to engage in relations **using a** contraceptive **resorbent** placed at the entrance to her womb, then also a woman pregnant with her husband's child may engage in relations **using a resorbent, and** similarly **if** one holds **in accordance with the one who said** a young girl is permitted to engage in relations in her usual manner and **Heaven will have mercy** upon her[N] and prevent any mishap, then in this case as well a pregnant woman should continue to engage in relations and **Heaven will have mercy** upon her.

הָכָא נַמִּי: אִי לְמַאן דְּאָמַר בְּמוֹךְ – בְּמוֹךְ, אִי לְמַאן דְּאָמַר מִן הַשָּׁמַיִם יְרַחֲמוּ – מִן הַשָּׁמַיִם יְרַחֲמוּ!

The Gemara objects: But **here, too,** in the case of a woman who is pregnant with the child of another man, these solutions could be employed: Both **if** one holds **in accordance with the one who says** that a young girl may engage in relations **using a resorbent,** in this case as well she may do so **using a resorbent, and** similarly **if** one holds **in accordance with the one who says** that **Heaven will have mercy** upon her, in this case as well **Heaven will have mercy** upon her.

אֶלָּא מִשּׁוּם דְּחָסָה. אִי הָכִי דִּידֵיהּ נַמִּי! דִּידֵיהּ חָיֵיס עִילָּוֵיהּ. הָכָא נַמִּי חָיֵיס עִילָּוֵיהּ!

The Gemara suggests a different reason for the prohibition against marrying a woman who is pregnant with the child of another man: **Rather,** it is **due to the** damage that could be caused to the fetus by the **pressure**[N] applied to it at the time of intercourse. The Gemara asks: **If so, even** if his wife his pregnant with **his own** child, the same concern applies. The Gemara explains: When it is **his own** child, **he has mercy upon it** and tries not to apply too much pressure. The Gemara asks: But **here, too,** when it is the child of another man, **he will have mercy upon it,** as certainly one is careful not to cause harm to any human life and will be careful not to press down too hard.

אֶלָּא: סְתָם מְעוּבֶּרֶת לְמֵינְקָה קַיְימָא,

The Gemara suggests a different reason: **Rather,** the reason for the prohibition is that **a typical pregnant woman is poised to nurse** her child once it is born;

Perek **IV**
Daf **42** Amud **b**

BACKGROUND

She will become pregnant and her milk will dry up – אִיעַבְּרָה וּמְעַכַּר חֲלָבָהּ: The hormone responsible for producing milk in the mother's body also substantially hinders ovulation. As such, women generally do not become pregnant while nursing. However, if a nursing woman does become pregnant, the hormones that are then released into her body can affect the mother's milk and produce a change in the quality of the milk.

LANGUAGE

She will feed [*memasmesa*] – מְמַסְמְסָא: This verb apparently has two meanings: It can mean to soften or mash, which fits well with the current version of the Gemara, as the verb is applied to eggs. It can also mean to calm or give encouragement. Accordingly, in the Gemara here it would mean to calm the hungry infant by providing him with these foods. Indeed, Rashi translates the word here to mean that she feeds her child.

דִּלְמָא אִיעַבְּרָה, וּמְעַכַּר חֲלָבָהּ, וְקָטְלָה לֵיהּ. אִי הָכִי דִּידֵיהּ נַמִּי! דִּידֵיהּ מְמַסְמְסָא לֵיהּ בְּבֵיצִים וְחָלָב. דִּידָהּ נַמִּי מְמַסְמְסָא לֵיהּ בְּבֵיצִים וְחָלָב! לָא יָהֵב לָהּ בַּעַל. וְלִיתְבָּעֵינֵיהּ לְיוֹרְשִׁים! אָמַר אַבַּיֵי: אִשָּׁה בּוֹשָׁה לָבֹא לְבֵית דִּין, וְהוֹרֶגֶת אֶת בְּנָהּ.

therefore, one should be concerned that **perhaps she will become pregnant and her milk will dry up**[B] during pregnancy, **and** the lack of milk will **kill** her newborn child. The Gemara asks: **If so, even** if his wife is pregnant with **his own** child, the same concern applies. The Gemara explains: For **his own** child, **she will feed** [*memasmesa*][L] **him**[N] **with eggs and milk** as a substitute for the mother's milk. The Gemara asks: Even if the child is not his, it is still the mother's child, and for **her** child **she will also feed him with eggs and milk.** The Gemara answers: **The husband will not give her** money to procure food for a child that is not his. The Gemara asks: **But she could sue** her first husband's **heirs** to provide subsistence for the child. **Abaye said: A woman is embarrassed to come to court, and** therefore she will not obtain enough sustenance for him. Consequently, **she** effectively **kills her son** as a result.

NOTES

She will feed him – מְמַסְמְסָא לֵיהּ: Rashi explains the word as a reference to feeding. The Rivan explains it refers to preparing the food. Both of them assume that the food is for the baby. However, the *Ha'amek She'ala* cites the Rambam's version of the text, which implies that the eggs were not for the child but for the mother. He explains that sexual relations can affect a woman's milk, causing it to dry up, but consuming eggs can help restore the flow.

"אַחַת בְּתוּלוֹת וְאַחַת בְּעוּלוֹת". הֵי נִיהוּ בְּתוּלוֹת וְהֵי נִיהוּ אֲרוּסוֹת, הֵי נִיהוּ בְּעוּלוֹת וְהֵי נִיהוּ נְשׂוּאוֹת?

§ The mishna states: The requirement to wait three months before remarrying applies **both to virgins and non-virgins,** both to divorcées and to widows, and both to women who were married to their previous husbands and to women who were only betrothed. The Gemara asks: **Which** women **are** referred to as **virgins**[N] **and which are** referred to as those who were **betrothed?** Although the two terms appear to be synonymous, since a virgin will be subject to levirate marriage only if she was betrothed, they must certainly refer to two different categories of women. Similarly, **which** women **are** referred to as **non-virgins and which are** referred to as **married,** as a married woman is always considered to be a non-virgin?

אָמַר רַבִּי יְהוּדָה הָכִי קָאָמַר: אַחַת בְּתוּלוֹת וְאַחַת בְּעוּלוֹת שֶׁנִּתְאַרְמְלוּ אוֹ שֶׁנִּתְגָּרְשׁוּ, בֵּין מִן הָאֵירוּסִין בֵּין מִן הַנִּשּׂוּאִין.

Rabbi Yehuda said this is what the mishna **is saying:** The requirement to wait applies **to both virgins and non-virgins who were widowed or divorced, whether from betrothal or from marriage,** i.e., the mishna does not list different categories of women but instead establishes a general principle.

רַבִּי אֶלְעָזָר לָא עַל לְבֵי מִדְרְשָׁא, אַשְׁכְּחֵיהּ לְרַבִּי אַסִּי, אֲמַר לֵיהּ: מַאי אֲמוּר רַבָּנַן בְּבֵי מִדְרְשָׁא? אֲמַר לֵיהּ, הָכִי אָמַר רַבִּי יוֹחָנָן: הֲלָכָה כְּרַבִּי יוֹסֵי.

The Gemara relates: **Rabbi Elazar did not enter the study hall** one day. **He found Rabbi Asi** and **said to him: What was said by the Sages in the study hall** today? **He said to him: This** is what **Rabbi Yoḥanan said:** The *halakha* **is in accordance with** the opinion of **Rabbi Yosei** that a woman is permitted to be betrothed even before three months have passed, since the reason for waiting does not apply in that case.

מִכְּלָל דִּיחִידָאָה פָּלֵיג עֲלֵיהּ? אִין, וְהָתַנְיָא: הֲרֵי שֶׁהָיְתָה רְדוּפָה לֵילֵךְ לְבֵית אָבִיהָ, אוֹ שֶׁהָיָה לָהּ כַּעַס בְּבֵית בַּעְלָהּ, אוֹ שֶׁהָיָה בַּעְלָהּ חָבוּשׁ בְּבֵית הָאֲסוּרִין, אוֹ שֶׁהָיָה בַּעְלָהּ זָקֵן אוֹ חוֹלֶה, אוֹ שֶׁהָיְתָה הִיא חוֹלָה,

Rabbi Elazar said: **From the fact** that Rabbi Yoḥanan needed to state this, it would seem **that** there is **an individual** opinion that **disagrees with him,**[N] even though no such opinion is mentioned in the mishna. Rabbi Asi answered: **Yes,** that is correct, **and so it is taught** in a *baraita* in the *Tosefta* (*Yevamot* 6:6): With regard to a woman who is certainly not pregnant, for example, a woman who, at the time of her husband's death, had not lived with her husband for some time because she always eagerly hurried, like **one pursued, to go to her father's house, or because she had** been subject to **anger in her husband's house, or because her husband had been incarcerated in prison, or because her husband was elderly or infirm, or because she was infirm.**

אוֹ שֶׁהִפִּילָה אַחַר מִיתַת בַּעְלָהּ, אוֹ שֶׁהָיְתָה עֲקָרָה, אוֹ זְקֵנָה, אוֹ קְטַנָּה, אוֹ אַיְלוֹנִית, אוֹ שֶׁאֵינָהּ רְאוּיָה לֵילֵד – צְרִיכָה לְהַמְתִּין שְׁלֹשָׁה חֳדָשִׁים, דִּבְרֵי רַבִּי מֵאִיר. רַבִּי יְהוּדָה מַתִּיר לֵיאָרֵס וְלִינָּשֵׂא מִיָּד.

Or a woman who could not be pregnant **because she miscarried after her husband's death, or because she was barren,**[N] **or elderly, or a minor, or a sexually underdeveloped woman [*aylonit*], or** if for some other reason **she was unsuited to give birth;**[N] even though the reason for the decree to wait three months does not apply to such a woman, nevertheless, **she must wait three months.** This is **the statement of Rabbi Meir. Rabbi Yehuda permits** such women **to be betrothed or to marry immediately.** It is apparent from the *baraita* that the question of whether a woman is required to wait the three months when the reason to do so does not apply is subject to a dispute.

אָמַר רַבִּי חִיָּיא בַּר אַבָּא: חָזַר בּוֹ רַבִּי יוֹחָנָן. אָמַר רַב יוֹסֵף: אִי הֲדַר בֵּיהּ – מִמַּתְנִיתִין דִּכְרַמָא הֲדַר בֵּיהּ. דְּתַנְיָא, אָמַר רַבִּי יִשְׁמָעֵאל בְּנוֹ שֶׁל רַבִּי יוֹחָנָן בֶּן בְּרוֹקָה: שָׁמַעְתִּי מִפִּי חֲכָמִים בְּכֶרֶם בְּיַבְנֶה: כּוּלָּן צְרִיכוֹת לְהַמְתִּין שְׁלֹשָׁה חֳדָשִׁים.

Rabbi Ḥiyya bar Abba said: Rabbi Yoḥanan retracted his statement that the *halakha* is in accordance with the opinion of Rabbi Yosei. **Rav Yosef said:** Even **if he** wanted to **retract** his statement, would **he retract from the *baraita*** that records the opinions of the Sages **of the vineyard** of Yavne? **As it is taught** in a *baraita*: **Rabbi Yishmael, son of Rabbi Yoḥanan ben Beroka, said: I heard from the mouth of the Sages in the vineyard of Yavne**[B] that **all** those women enumerated in the *baraita* above **need to wait three months.**[H] If the great Sages of Yavne held in accordance with the opinion Rabbi Yosei, then the *halakha* is certainly in accordance with his opinion.

NOTES

Which are virgins – הֵי נִיהוּ בְּתוּלוֹת: Rashi assumes that the case of a virgin *yevama* is one in which she was widowed from betrothal. Accordingly the Gemara's question is that the cases of virgins and women who were betrothed are synonymous; why then are they listed as though they are two distinct cases? However, other early commentaries highlight that it is also possible that a married woman might be a virgin if she had not yet had the opportunity to consummate her marriage. Therefore, the *Arukh LaNer* explains the Gemara's question differently: A betrothed woman is certainly a virgin, and as such the additional reference to a virgin is superfluous.

That an individual opinion disagrees with him – דִּיחִידָאָה פָּלֵיג עֲלֵיהּ: In his Commentary on the Mishna, the Rambam explains that even in those places where the Mishna mentions the opinion of a single Sage, it does not necessarily mean that it was only that Sage who held that opinion. Rather, many other Sages held that opinion; the Sage mentioned was merely the leading exponent of it. However, when the Mishna cites an unattributed opinion or states: The Rabbis said, this is an indication that Rabbi Yehuda HaNasi maintained that the majority of the Sages held in accordance with that opinion.

Barren – עֲקָרָה: The Rivan and other commentaries explain that this refers to a woman whose womb had been removed. They explain that although the term barren is typically used in a more general sense, since the list here concludes with reference to a woman who is unsuited to give birth, which is a general statement, the earlier reference to a barren woman must be understood as referring to a specific case.

She was unsuited to give birth – שֶׁאֵינָהּ רְאוּיָה לֵילֵד: Rashi explains that this is referring to a woman who took a drug that rendered her barren. The Rif writes that this is referring to a woman above the age of forty, or to a woman who had been married for ten years without children, since in such cases the Gemara states elsewhere that such women are no longer suitable for childbirth.

BACKGROUND

The vineyard of Yavne – כֶּרֶם בְּיַבְנֶה: According to an ancient tradition, the Sanhedrin in Yavne was called a vineyard because when it was in session, the Sages themselves, along with their students, would sit in rows, like the rows of a vineyard (Jerusalem Talmud). It is also possible that the Sanhedrin may have been situated near vineyards, lending the name a double meaning.

HALAKHA

Which women require a waiting period for the purposes of distinguishing – אֵיזוֹ נָשִׁים צְרִיכוֹת הַבְחָנָה: The rabbinic decree that any woman who had been married must wait three months until she remarries is applied irrespective of whether the reason to wait is relevant. Therefore, a woman must wait even if it is clear that she is not pregnant, e.g., if she did not have the opportunity to engage in sexual relations with her husband, or if she is elderly, or a minor, or an *aylonit*, or if for some other reason she is unsuited to give birth. This is in accordance with the opinion of Rabbi Meir, as the *halakha* is ruled in accordance with his opinion in all cases of rabbinic decrees (Rambam *Sefer Nashim*, *Hilkhot Geirushin* 11:20; *Shulḥan Arukh*, *Even HaEzer* 13:1).

אֲמַר לֵיהּ רַבִּי יִרְמְיָה לְרַבִּי זְרִיקָא: כִּי עָיְילַתְּ לְקַמֵּיהּ דְּרַבִּי אַבָּהוּ רְמִי לֵיהּ: מִי אֲמַר רַבִּי יוֹחָנָן הֲלָכָה כְּרַבִּי יוֹסֵי? וְהָאָמַר רַבִּי יוֹחָנָן: הֲלָכָה כִּסְתָם מִשְׁנָה, וּתְנַן: כָּל הַנָּשִׁים לֹא יִנָּשְׂאוּ וְלֹא יִתְאָרְסוּ עַד שֶׁיְּהוּ לָהֶם שְׁלֹשָׁה חֳדָשִׁים, אַחַת בְּתוּלוֹת וְאַחַת בְּעוּלוֹת!

Rabbi Yirmeya said to Rabbi Zerika: When you come before Rabbi Abbahu, raise the following contradiction: Did Rabbi Yoḥanan actually say that the *halakha* is in accordance with the opinion of Rabbi Yosei? Didn't Rabbi Yoḥanan say that the *halakha* is always established in accordance with the ruling of an unattributed mishna? And we learned in the mishna an unattributed ruling: All women may not marry and may not be betrothed until they have waited three months since their previous marriage ended; this applies to both virgins and non-virgins.

אֲמַר לֵיהּ: דִּרְמָא לָךְ הָא – לָא חָשׁ לְקִמְחֵיהּ; סְתָם וְאַחַר כָּךְ מַחֲלוֹקֶת הִיא, וְאֵין הֲלָכָה כִּסְתָם. דְּאָמַר רַב פַּפָּא וְאִיתֵּימָא רַבִּי יוֹחָנָן: מַחֲלוֹקֶת וְאַחַר כָּךְ סְתָם – הֲלָכָה כִּסְתָם, סְתָם וְאַחַר כָּךְ מַחֲלוֹקֶת – אֵין הֲלָכָה כִּסְתָם

When Rabbi Zerika went and asked, Rabbi Abbahu said to him: The one who raised this contradiction to you is clearly not concerned for his flour;[N] this is a case of an unattributed ruling followed by a dispute[N] on that ruling, and in such cases the *halakha* is not necessarily in accordance with the unattributed opinion. As Rav Pappa said, and some say it was Rabbi Yoḥanan who said the following principle: When the Mishna first records a dispute, and afterward it records only one side of that dispute as an unattributed opinion, then the *halakha* is in accordance with the unattributed opinion. However, when the Mishna first records an unattributed opinion and afterward records that the ruling is subject to a dispute, the *halakha* is not necessarily in accordance with the unattributed opinion. In each case, the later reference is considered to be a summary of the matter.

מִסְתַּמֵּיךְ וְאָזֵיל רַבִּי אַבָּהוּ אַכַּתְפֵּיהּ דְּרַבִּי נַחוּם שַׁמָּעֵיהּ, מְנַקֵּיט וְאָזֵיל הִלְכְתָא מִינֵּיהּ. בְּעָא מִינֵּיהּ: מַחֲלוֹקֶת וְאַחַר כָּךְ סְתָם מַאי? אֲמַר לֵיהּ: הֲלָכָה כִּסְתָם. סְתָם וְאַחַר כָּךְ מַחֲלוֹקֶת מַאי? אֲמַר לֵיהּ: אֵין הֲלָכָה כִּסְתָם.

§ The Gemara relates: **Rabbi Abbahu would walk while leaning upon the shoulder of Rabbi Naḥum, his attendant,** and along the way Rabbi Naḥum would **walk and gather halakhic rulings from him.** Once, Rabbi Naḥum **asked him:** When the Mishna first records **a dispute, and afterward** it records only one side of that dispute as **an unattributed opinion, what** is the *halakha*? Rabbi Abbahu **said to him:** The ***halakha*** **is in accordance with the unattributed opinion.** Rabbi Naḥum then asked: When the Mishna first records **an unattributed opinion and afterward** records that the ruling is subject to **a dispute, what** is the *halakha*? Rabbi Abbahu **said to him:** The ***halakha*** **is not** necessarily **in accordance with the unattributed opinion.**[N]

סְתָמָא דְּמַתְנִיתִין וּמַחֲלוֹקֶת בְּבָרַיְיתָא מַאי? אֲמַר לֵיהּ: הֲלָכָה כִּסְתָם. מַחֲלוֹקֶת בְּמַתְנִיתִין וּסְתָמָא בְּבָרַיְיתָא מַאי? אֲמַר לֵיהּ:

Rabbi Naḥum asked: When a ruling is recorded in **the Mishna as unattributed and** it is subject to **a dispute in a *baraita*, what** is the *halakha*?[N] Rabbi Abbahu **said to him:** The ***halakha*** **is in accordance with** the **unattributed opinion** in the Mishna. Rabbi Naḥum then asked: When **the Mishna** records that a matter is subject to **a dispute, and** only one side is recorded as **an unattributed opinion in a *baraita*, what** is the *halakha*? Rabbi Abbahu **said to him:**

NOTES

He is not concerned for his flour – **לָא חָשׁ לְקִמְחֵיהּ**: Rashi explains the analogy as referring to one who does not show care and concern for the items that he himself produces. *Arukh* interprets it as a reference to one who is not wary of wasting his flour; here, he wasted the energy he gained from the bread he had eaten because he did not study thoroughly enough. Rabbi Avraham min HaHar explains the reference is to one who is not sufficiently aware of his own flour, i.e., one who does not taste his own food, which in this case is referring to one not paying attention to the words he says. The *ge'onim* had a different version of the text, which states: He does not fear that which is before him, meaning that he does not perceive that which is found directly before him.

An unattributed ruling followed by a dispute – **סְתָם וְאַחַר כָּךְ מַחֲלוֹקֶת**: The early commentaries engaged in a detailed clarification of this principle. For example, does it apply only to cases where named Sages are in dispute, or also to cases where an individual Sage disagrees with an unattributed opinion? The Meiri cites an opinion, also mentioned in *Sefer HaKeritut*, that whenever the Mishna cites a dispute between a named Sage and an unattributed opinion, the *halakha* is not necessarily in accordance with the unattributed opinion, irrespective of whether the unattributed opinion is cited first or last in the mishna. The commentaries also discuss whether this principle applies only when the opinions appear together within a single mishna or even when they appear in different *mishnayot* within the same tractate. The Gemara states in one place that the tractates of the Mishna are not ordered sequentially, so that if in one tractate a dispute is cited and in another tractate one of the opinions is cited as unattributed, one cannot claim that the opinions in one tractate were recorded before the other in order to determine what the *halakha* should be. However, some claim that there is a specific sequencing of the orders of the Mishna, and therefore if the two *mishnayot* appear in different orders, the principle can be applied (see *Tosefot Yom Tov* on *Sota*, chapter 9, *Sha'ar HaMelekh*, and *Arukh LaNer*).

The *halakha* is not in accordance with the unattributed opinion – **אֵין הֲלָכָה כִּסְתָם**: Ramban, Rashba, Ritva, and *Nimmukei Yosef* all note that the only intent of this statement is that in such a case Rabbi Yoḥanan's principle that the *halakha* is always established in accordance with the ruling of an unattributed mishna does not apply. It does not mean to state positively that the *halakha* is never in accordance with the unattributed opinion, but only that it is not necessarily so. Therefore, in such cases, the dispute must be analyzed based on the standard principles of halakhic decision-making.

A ruling recorded in the Mishna as unattributed and subject to a dispute in a *baraita* – **סְתָם בְּמִשְׁנָה וּמַחֲלוֹקֶת בְּבָרַיְיתָא**: The essence of this question lies in the fact that it was the disciples of Rabbi Yehuda HaNasi, the redactor of the Mishna, who taught the *baraitot*. It is therefore possible that they received Rabbi Yehuda HaNasi's final opinion on a matter and that he may have retracted his ruling recorded in the Mishna. The Rashba writes (*Bava Kama* 102a) that although the Gemara here states that one disregards the *baraita* in such a case, there are other *amora'im* who hold that the *baraita* does indeed carry greater authority than an unattributed mishna.

וְכִי רַבִּי לֹא שְׁנָאָהּ רַבִּי חִיָּיא מִנַּיִן לוֹ?

If Rabbi Yehuda HaNasi **had not taught** that ruling in the Mishna,[N] **from where would Rabbi Ḥiyya,** his disciple and redactor of the *baraitot,* **have** known **it?** Since the source of the unattributed ruling in the *baraita* is certainly the dispute recorded in the mishna, its lack of attribution in the *baraita* only reflects the fact that Rabbi Ḥiyya ruled in accordance with that opinion, but that cannot be used to indicate that it is the accepted *halakha*.

אֲמַר לֵיהּ: וְהָא תְּנַן: מַסְרֵק שֶׁל פִּשְׁתָּן שֶׁנִּיטְּלוּ שִׁינָּיו, וְנִשְׁתַּיְּירוּ בּוֹ שְׁתַּיִם – טְמֵאוֹת, וְאַחַת – טְהוֹרָה. וְכוּלָּן שֶׁנִּיטְּלוּ אַחַת אַחַת בִּפְנֵי עַצְמָן – טְמֵאוֹת.

Rabbi Naḥum questioned the principle that the *halakha* is always in accordance with an unattributed ruling in a mishna and **said to** Rabbi Ḥiyya: **Didn't we learn** in a mishna (*Kelim* 13:8): **A comb** made **for** combing beaten **flax**[H] in preparation for spinning, from **which its teeth were removed**[N] **and** only **two** of its teeth **remained in it,** is still suitable for combing. It is therefore considered a utensil and will become **ritually impure** if it comes in contact with ritual impurity. However, if only **one** tooth remained, so that the comb was no longer suitable for combing, it is no longer considered a utensil and so will remain **ritually pure** even if it comes in contact with ritual impurity. **And** with regard to **any** of the teeth **that were individually removed on their own,** since they do serve a purpose, e.g., they may be embedded and used as hooks, they are considered utensils and can become **ritually impure.**

שֶׁל צֶמֶר שֶׁנִּיטְּלוּ שִׁינָּיו אַחַת מִבֵּינְתַיִם – טָהוֹר, נִשְׁתַּיְּירוּ בּוֹ שָׁלֹשׁ בְּמָקוֹם אֶחָד – טָמֵא, הָיְתָה הַחִיצוֹנָה אַחַת מֵהֶן – טָהוֹר. נִיטְּלוּ שְׁנַיִם וַעֲשָׂאָן לְמַלְקֵט – טְמֵאוֹת, אַחַת וְהִתְקִינָהּ לְנֵר אוֹ לְמִיתּוּחַ – טְמֵאָה.

A comb made **for** combing **wool**[BHN] **from which every other one of its teeth were removed,** so that no two consecutive teeth remained in place, is no longer suitable for combing and so will remain **ritually pure. If three** teeth **remained in it in a single place** so that it could still be used for combing, then it could become **ritually impure.** However, if **one of those** teeth **was the external** frame of the comb itself, then it could not function as a comb, and so it will remain **ritually pure.** If **two** of the teeth **were removed and made into** small **pincers,** then they could become **ritually impure.** Alternatively, if **one** of the teeth was removed, **and it was prepared** in a manner that made it suitable **for** use in cleaning **an oil lamp**[N] **or for stretching**[N] ropes, then it would be considered a utensil and could become **ritually impure.**[H]

BACKGROUND

Combs for wool and flax – **מַסְרְקֵי צֶמֶר וּפִשְׁתָּן**: From the various descriptions in the Mishna and Talmud, it would appear that the comb made for flax was a large instrument with which the stalks of flax were combed in order to prepare them for spinning. The body of the comb and its external teeth were constructed from wood, while the internal teeth were metal nails. It is for this reason that no combs of this kind remain from that period, because wood generally decomposes, at which point any nails fall out.

There are differing opinions concerning the structure of the comb made for wool. Some explain that it was made in a similar fashion to the one for flax, the only difference being its thickness and the proximity of the teeth. Others, however, explain that the comb made for wool was an entirely different tool. It was constructed from a wooden board, or a pair of wooden boards, also known as cards, upon which several rows of metal nails were fastened. The combing was achieved by dragging the wool over the boards. According to this description, the Gemara's distinction between internal teeth and external teeth refers to the different rows of teeth.

Dried flax with threshing comb

Pair of wool cards

HALAKHA

A comb made for flax – **מַסְרֵק שֶׁל פִּשְׁתָּן**: With regard to a comb made for combing flax, from which the teeth were removed: If two teeth remain, the comb remains susceptible to ritual impurity, but if only a single tooth remains it is no longer susceptible to ritual impurity (Rambam *Sefer Tahara, Hilkhot Kelim* 11:4).

A comb made for wool – **מַסְרֵק שֶׁל צֶמֶר**: With regard to a comb made for combing wool, from which the teeth were removed, if three teeth remain in a single place, the comb remains susceptible to ritual impurity. However, if one of the three was the external frame, it would not be susceptible to ritual impurity. The *Kesef Mishne* questions why the Rambam rules in accordance with this mishna even though the Gemara states that it is not ruled as *halakha* (see NOTES; Rambam *Sefer Tahara, Hilkhot Kelim* 11:3).

The teeth of the comb – **שִׁינֵּי הַמַּסְרֵק**: If two teeth of a comb were removed and made into pincers, or if a single tooth was removed and prepared for an oil lamp or for stretching, then they are susceptible to ritually impurity. If that tooth was large and thick, then even if it was not specially prepared, it is susceptible to ritual impurity. This is in accordance with the resolution suggested by Rav Pappa (Rambam *Sefer Tahara, Hilkhot Kelim* 11:3).

NOTES

If Rabbi Yehuda HaNasi had not taught it, etc. – **וְכִי רַבִּי לֹא שְׁנָאָהּ וכו׳**: The Gemara assumes that since Rabbi Ḥiyya was Rabbi Yehuda HaNasi's disciple, it does not stand to reason that he would formulate an opinion as though it were the conclusive *halakha* when Rabbi Yehuda HaNasi clearly decided not to teach that opinion in such a way (Rav Sherira Gaon). The Maharik adds that Rabbi Yehuda HaNasi had a far greater breadth of knowledge than Rabbi Ḥiyya, and so it is improbable that Rabbi Ḥiyya would be aware that a certain opinion had been accepted as the *halakha* if Rabbi Yehuda HaNasi was not.

A comb whose teeth were removed, etc. – **מַסְרֵק שֶׁנִּיטְּלוּ שִׁינָּיו וכו׳**: Utensils are susceptible to ritual impurity only when they serve a useful purpose. Even if they break and no longer serve their original purpose, if they serve some other useful purpose they can still become impure. The import of this mishna is to define at which point a comb is considered broken to the extent that it no longer serves any useful purpose and therefore is no longer susceptible to ritual impurity.

Combs made for wool and flax – **מַסְרְקֵי צֶמֶר וּפִשְׁתָּן**: The early commentaries describe the differences between the two types of combs: The Rivan explains that the teeth of a flax comb are narrower than those of a wool comb. However, the Meiri claims the opposite to be true and adds that they are also distinct in their form and structure.

It was prepared for an oil lamp – **הִתְקִינָהּ לְנֵר**: Rashi suggests that this means that the tooth of the comb can be used to clean out the lamp. The Rivan suggests that a wax candle could be attached to it.

For stretching – **לְמִיתּוּחַ**: The Rambam, in his commentary on the Mishna on *Kelim* 13:6, explains that this term refers to wrapping a thread around a stick to make the thread easier to use.

NOTES

But we maintain that the *halakha* is not in accordance with that mishna – וְקַיְימָא לַן דְּאֵין הֲלָכָה כְּאוֹתָהּ מִשְׁנָה: Despite the Gemara's claim, the Rambam rules in accordance with this mishna. In addition, it appears that Rabbeinu Shimshon also rules in this manner. The *Yam shel Shlomo* explains that although the Gemara identifies the various difficulties inherent in the mishna, the mishna is nevertheless ruled as *halakha*, and ultimately the Rabbis disagree with Rabbi Shimon only on a single point, i.e., the question of ritual impurity for the teeth removed from the comb. Rabbi Shimon holds that these do not require preparation in order to be susceptible to ritual impurity, while the Rabbis hold that they do require preparation (see *Keren Ora* and *Arukh LaNer*).

BACKGROUND

Those who are exact – דַּוּוקְנֵי: Apparently, there were a number of Sages who were relied upon to establish the precise formulation of the mishna. Rav Sherira Gaon explains in his famous letter concerning the composition of the Mishna that this is why the Gemara is often willing to delete parts of a mishna or even an entire mishna on occasion, as sometimes the current version is erroneous or was not transmitted reliably.

וְקַיְימָא לַן דְּאֵין הֲלָכָה כְּאוֹתָהּ מִשְׁנָה! אֲמַר לֵיהּ: בַּר מִינַּהּ דְּהַהִיא, דְּרַבִּי יוֹחָנָן וְרֵישׁ לָקִישׁ דְּאָמְרִי תַּרְוַיְיהוּ: זוֹ אֵינָהּ מִשְׁנָה.

Rabbi Naḥum posed his question: **But we maintain that** the ***halakha* is not in accordance with that mishna.**[N] This would seem to contradict the principle that the *halakha* is always in accordance with an unattributed opinion. Rabbi Ḥiyya **said to** Rabbi Naḥum that the principle applies to all cases **apart from this** mishna, **as** with regard to this particular mishna there are **Rabbi Yoḥanan and Reish Lakish who both say: This is not** an authoritative **mishna,** and so it cannot be relied upon for a halakhic ruling.

מַאי טַעְמָא? אָמַר רַב הוּנָא בַּר מָנוֹחַ מִשְּׁמֵיהּ דְּרַב אִידִי בְּרֵיהּ דְּרַב אִיקָא: מִשּׁוּם דְּקַשְׁיָא רֵישָׁא לְסֵיפָא. דְּקָתָנֵי: שֶׁל צֶמֶר שֶׁנִּיטְּלוּ שִׁינָּיו אַחַת מִבֵּינְתַיִם – טָהוֹר, הָא נִשְׁתַּיְּירוּ בּוֹ שְׁתַּיִם בְּמָקוֹם אֶחָד – טָמֵא, וְהָדַר תָּנֵי: נִשְׁתַּיְּירוּ בּוֹ שָׁלֹשׁ – טָמֵא, שָׁלֹשׁ – אִין, שְׁתַּיִם – לָא!

The Gemara asks: **What is the reason** to say that the mishna is not authoritative? **Rav Huna bar Manoaḥ said in the name of Rav Idi, son of Rav Ika:** It is **because the first clause** of that mishna **contradicts the latter clause, as it teaches:** A comb used **for wool from which every other one of its teeth were removed** is no longer considered a utensil, and so it will remain **ritually pure. This** implies that **were two teeth to remain in it in one place,** it could become **ritually impure. And then** the mishna **continues and teaches:** If **three** teeth **remained in it in a single place** it is still considered a utensil and so it could become **ritually impure.** This indicates that if there are **three, yes,** it could become ritually impure, but if there are **two, no,** it would not become ritually impure.

וּמַאי קוּשְׁיָא? דִּלְמָא הָא בְּגַוָּויְיתָא הָא בְּבָרַיְיתָא!

The Gemara asks: **But what** is the **difficulty? Perhaps this** ruling that if two teeth remain it is considered a utensil is referring to **the internal** teeth, found in the middle of the frame, while **that** ruling that it is not considered a utensil is referring to **the outer** teeth, which are adjacent to the frame of the comb, which makes them unsuitable for use.

אֶלָּא מֵהָכָא, דְּקָתָנֵי: וְכוּלָּן שֶׁנִּיטְּלוּ אַחַת אַחַת בִּפְנֵי עַצְמָן טְמֵאוֹת, וְאַף עַל גַּב דְּלָא הִתְקִינָהּ. אֵימָא סֵיפָא: אַחַת וְהִתְקִינָהּ לְנֵר אוֹ לְמִיתּוּחַ – טְמֵאָה. הִתְקִינָהּ – אִין, לֹא הִתְקִינָהּ – לָא!

Rather, the difficulty with the mishna is **from here, as it teaches: And any** of the teeth **that were individually removed on their own,** since they can serve a useful purpose they are considered utensils and can become **ritually impure. And** the implication is that this is true **even though** the tooth **was not prepared** for that purpose. But **say the latter clause** as follows: If **one** of the teeth was removed, **and it was prepared** in a manner that rendered it suitable **for** use in cleaning **an oil lamp or for stretching** ropes, then it would be considered a utensil and could become **ritually impure.** The implication is that if **it was prepared** for use, then **yes,** it would be considered a utensil, but if **it was not prepared** for use, then **no,** it would not be considered a utensil.

אָמַר אַבָּיֵי: וּמַאי קוּשְׁיָא? דִּלְמָא הָא בְּקַתַּיְיהוּ, הָא בְּלָא קַתַּיְיהוּ.

Abaye said: But what is the **difficulty? Perhaps this** ruling, that further preparation is not required before it is considered a utensil, is referring to a case where the teeth were removed **with their base,** which allows them to be used immediately for various functions, whereas **that** ruling, that it is considered a utensil only once it is prepared for use, is referring to a case where the teeth were removed **without their base** and therefore require further preparation before they can be used.

אָמַר רַב פָּפָּא: וּמַאי קוּשְׁיָא? וְדִלְמָא הָא – בְּקַטִינָתָא, הָא – בְּאַלִּימָתָא.

Rav Pappa stated an alternative resolution: **But what** is the **difficulty? Perhaps this** ruling that further preparation is not required is referring to a case where the teeth **were narrow,** whereas **that** ruling that it is considered a utensil only once it is prepared for use is referring to a case where the teeth **were thick.**

אֶלָּא: מִשּׁוּם דִּמְסַיְּימִי בָּהּ דַּוּוקְנֵי: זוֹ רַבִּי שִׁמְעוֹן.

Rather, the reason that the mishna is not accepted as authoritative is not due to some difficulty in the formulation of the mishna, but **because those who are exact**[B] in their rendition of the tradition **conclude** this mishna with: **This is** the statement of **Rabbi Shimon.** In other words, this mishna is not unattributed but presents the minority opinion of a single Sage, and it is for this reason that it is not accepted as authoritative.

שְׁלַח רַבִּי חִיָּיא בַּר אָבִין: מְאָרְסִין תּוֹךְ שְׁלֹשָׁה, וְכֵן עוֹשִׂים מַעֲשֶׂה.

§ **Rabbi Ḥiyya bar Avin sent** a message from Eretz Yisrael with regard to the *halakha* cited in the mishna: **One may betroth** a woman, but not marry her, **within three** months of her previous marriage; **and so one acts in practice.**

וְכֵן הָיָה רַבִּי אֶלְעָזָר מְלַמְּדֵנוּ מִשּׁוּם רַבִּי חֲנִינָא הַגָּדוֹל: רוּבּוֹ שֶׁל רִאשׁוֹן, וְרוּבּוֹ שֶׁל שְׁלִישִׁי, וְאֶמְצָעִי שָׁלֵם.

And so Rabbi Elazar would teach us in the name of Rabbi Ḥanina the Great[P] that the three months are counted as follows: One counts **the majority of** the days of **the first** month,[N] **and the majority of the third** month, **and the entire middle** month.

אֲמֵימַר שְׁרָא לְיָאֵרֵס בְּיוֹם תִּשְׁעִים. אֲמַר לֵיהּ רַב אַשִׁי לַאֲמֵימַר: וְהָא רַב וּשְׁמוּאֵל דְּאָמְרִי תַּרְוַיְיהוּ: צְרִיכָה לְהַמְתִּין שְׁלֹשָׁה חֳדָשִׁים, חוּץ מִיּוֹם שֶׁמֵּת בּוֹ וְחוּץ מִיּוֹם שֶׁנִּתְאָרְסָה בּוֹ! הַהוּא לְעִנְיַן מֵינֶקֶת אִיתְּמַר. דְּרַב וּשְׁמוּאֵל דְּאָמְרִי תַּרְוַיְיהוּ: צְרִיכָה לְהַמְתִּין עֶשְׂרִים וְאַרְבָּעָה חֹדֶשׁ, חוּץ מִיּוֹם שֶׁנּוֹלַד בּוֹ וְחוּץ מִיּוֹם שֶׁנִּתְאָרְסָה בּוֹ.

Ameimar permitted one to betroth a woman **on the ninetieth day**[N] itself. **Rav Ashi said to Ameimar: Didn't Rav and Shmuel both say** that **she needs to wait three** full **months, excluding the day on which** the husband **died and excluding the day on which she is betrothed?** It is apparent that it is still prohibited to betroth a woman on the ninetieth day itself. Ameimar said to him: **That** which you heard, that the days of the husband's death and of the betrothal are not included, **was stated** only **with regard to a nursing woman,** as it was **Rav and Shmuel who both said:** A nursing woman **needs to wait twenty-four months** before being betrothed, **excluding the day on which** the baby **was born and excluding the day on which she is betrothed.**

וְהָא הַהוּא דַּעֲבַד סְעוּדַת אֵירוּסִין בְּיוֹם תִּשְׁעִים, וְאַפְסְדֵיהּ רָבָא לִסְעוּדָתֵיהּ! הַהִיא סְעוּדַת נִשּׂוּאִין הֲוַאי.

The Gemara asks: **Wasn't** there an incident concerning **a certain** person **who prepared a betrothal feast on the ninetieth day** following the death of the woman's first husband, **and Rava caused him to forfeit his feast** by prohibiting the betrothal on that day? The Gemara answers: **That** feast **was** actually **a marriage feast,** but had it been a betrothal feast it would have been permitted.

וְהִלְכְתָא: צְרִיכָה לְהַמְתִּין עֶשְׂרִים וְאַרְבָּעָה חוֹדֶשׁ, חוּץ מִיּוֹם שֶׁנּוֹלַד בּוֹ וְחוּץ מִיּוֹם שֶׁנִּתְאָרְסָה בּוֹ. וּצְרִיכָה לְהַמְתִּין שְׁלֹשָׁה חֳדָשִׁים, חוּץ מִיּוֹם שֶׁמֵּת בּוֹ וְחוּץ מִיּוֹם שֶׁנִּתְאָרְסָה בּוֹ.

The Gemara summarizes: **The *halakha* is** that a nursing mother **needs to wait twenty-four months,**[N] **excluding the day on which** the baby **was born and excluding the day on which she is betrothed. And** if she was widowed but was not nursing, then **she needs to wait** only **three months, excluding the day on which** her previous husband **died and excluding the day on which she is betrothed.**[H]

״חוּץ מִן הָאַלְמָנָה״ וכו׳. אָמַר רַב חִסְדָּא: קַל וָחוֹמֶר, וּמַה בְּמָקוֹם שֶׁאָסוּר לְכַבֵּס – מוּתָּר לְיָאֵרֵס, מָקוֹם שֶׁמּוּתָּר לְכַבֵּס – אֵינוֹ דִּין שֶׁמּוּתָּר לְיָאֵרֵס!

§ The mishna states that Rabbi Yosei says: All women may be betrothed within three months **except for a widow,** due to the mourning period she must observe for her deceased husband. **Rav Ḥisda** questioned the mishna's ruling and **said:** Based on an ***a fortiori*** inference, it should be permitted for a woman to be betrothed during the thirty-day mourning period for her husband: If during another period of mourning, which the Gemara will specify, **when it is prohibited to launder** clothes, **it is permitted to be betrothed,** then during the thirty-day morning period for a husband, **when it is permitted to launder** clothes, **isn't it logical that it** should also be **permitted to be betrothed?**

PERSONALITIES

Rabbi Ḥanina the Great – רַבִּי חֲנִינָא הַגָּדוֹל: This is Rabbi Ḥanina bar Ḥama, who is labeled this way because he was one of the outstanding Sages of his generation. In the Jerusalem Talmud he is known as Rabbi Ḥanina Rabba, which bears the same meaning. This epithet is generally used when Rabbi Ḥanina is mentioned alongside another Sage of that name, in this case Rabbi Ḥanina Kara, to differentiate between them.

NOTES

The majority of the first month – רוּבּוֹ שֶׁל רִאשׁוֹן: The Rivan claims that this novel ruling is limited and applies only to a woman who was merely betrothed to her previous husband. However, even Rabbi Ḥanina would concede that a woman who was married would have to wait three complete months.

Some commentaries suggest the basis for Rabbi Ḥanina's ruling is to be found in the narrative of Tamar, where it states that her pregnancy was discernible "about three months after" (Genesis 38:24), which they interpret to mean that there was not three full months but some part of them.

On the ninetieth day – בְּיוֹם תִּשְׁעִים: In the *She'iltot deRav Aḥai Gaon* it is written that the reason that the woman is permitted to marry on the ninetieth day itself is based on the principle that in many cases, once a portion of the day has passed it is considered as though the entire day had passed.

Twenty-four months, etc. – עֶשְׂרִים וְאַרְבָּעָה חוֹדֶשׁ וכו׳: The geonic responsa and several *midrashim* see an allusion to this *halakha* in the verse: "You shall not cook [*tevashel*] a kid in its mother's milk" (Exodus 23:19). The numerical value of the Hebrew word *tevashel* is 732, which is exactly the number of days in two solar years plus two additional days. However, the later commentaries discuss whether the twenty-four months referred to here are based on the solar or the lunar calendar, as well as what the *halakha* would be if one of the years were a leap year.

HALAKHA

The time of betrothal following the waiting period – זְמַן הָאֵירוּסִין אַחַר הַמְּתָנָה: Pregnant women and nursing mothers may not be betrothed, and certainly not married, until the period of nursing has ended. The time established by the Sages for this period is twenty-four months, excluding the day of the child's birth and the day of the betrothal. A woman who is widowed or divorced and is not pregnant or nursing must wait ninety days, excluding the day of the husband's death or the divorce and the day of the betrothal (Rambam *Sefer Nashim*, *Hilkhot Geirushin* 11:26; *Shulḥan Arukh*, *Even HaEzer* 13:1, 11).

מַאי הִיא? דִּתְנַן: שַׁבָּת שֶׁחָל תִּשְׁעָה בְּאָב בְּתוֹכָהּ – אָסוּר לְסַפֵּר וּלְכַבֵּס, וּבַחֲמִישִׁי מוּתָּר מִפְּנֵי כְּבוֹד הַשַּׁבָּת. וְתַנְיָא: קוֹדֶם הַזְּמַן הַזֶּה הָעָם מְמַעֲטִין בְּעִסְקֵיהֶם מִלִּישָּׂא וּמִלִּיתֵּן, מִלִּבְנוֹת וְלִנְטוֹעַ, וּמְאָרְסִין אֲבָל לֹא כּוֹנְסִין, וְאֵין עוֹשִׂין סְעוּדַת אֵירוּסִין.

The Gemara explains the cases involved: **What is** the period of mourning to which Rav Ḥisda is referring? **As we learned** in a mishna (*Ta'anit* 26b): During **the week in which the Ninth of Av occurs,**[H] **it is prohibited to cut hair and to launder** clothes, **but on Thursday it is permitted**[N] **in deference to Shabbat. And it is taught** in a *baraita*: **Prior to this time**[H] **the public reduce their activities,** refraining **from business transactions,**[N] **from building and planting, and they may betroth** women **but may not marry** them,[H] **and they may not make a betrothal feast.** The Gemara assumes that the *baraita* is referring to the days immediately preceding the Ninth of Av. Accordingly, during the days prior to the Ninth of Av it is prohibited to launder clothes, but it is permitted to be betrothed. It was upon this period of time that Rav Ḥisda based his *a fortiori* inference.

כִּי תַּנְיָא הַהִיא – קוֹדֶם דְּקוֹדֶם (תַּנְיָא).

To defend Rav Yosei's ruling in the mishna, the Gemara explains: **When that** *baraita* **is taught, it is taught** with regard to the period **prior to** the period that is **prior** to the Ninth of Av, i.e., the days prior to the week in which the Ninth of Av occurs. It is only then that it is permitted to be betrothed, but during the week in which the Ninth of Av occurs it is prohibited. Therefore, the basis of Rav Ḥisda's *a fortiori* inference is undermined.

אֲמַר רָבָא: וְקוֹדֶם דְּקוֹדֶם נַמִי, קַל וָחוֹמֶר: וּמַה בְּמָקוֹם שֶׁאָסוּר לִישָּׂא וְלִיתֵּן – מוּתָּר לְאָרֵס, מָקוֹם שֶׁמּוּתָּר לִישָּׂא וְלִיתֵּן – אֵינוֹ דִּין שֶׁמּוּתָּר לְאָרֵס?!

Rava said: From the period **prior to** the period that is **prior** to the Ninth of Av, a challenge to Rabbi Yosei's ruling can **also** be advanced based on an *a fortiori* inference, as follows: If in a period of mourning **when it is prohibited to conduct business transactions, it is permitted to be betrothed,** then during the thirty-day morning period for a husband, **when it is permitted to conduct business transactions, isn't it logical that it** should also be **permitted to be betrothed?**

לָא תֵּימָא דְּרַבִּי יוֹסֵי אוֹמֵר כָּל הַנָּשִׁים יִתְאָרְסוּ, אֶלָּא אֵימָא: כָּל הַנָּשִׁים יִנָּשְׂאוּ.

The Gemara accepts the conclusion of this *a fortiori* inference and therefore concludes: **Do not say** that **Rabbi Yosei says: All women may be betrothed** within three months; **rather,** emend his statement to **say: All women may be married** within three months except for a widow. However, even Rabbi Yosei agrees that it is permitted for a widow to be betrothed during this period.

Perek **IV**
Daf **43** Amud **b**

וְלֵית לֵיהּ לְרַבִּי יוֹסֵי לְהַבְחִין?

The Gemara asks: **But does Rabbi Yosei not accept** that there is a decree to wait three months in order **to distinguish** between the seed of the first and second husbands? According to the Gemara's emendation of his statement, it would appear there is no case in which Rabbi Yosei applies the decree.

לֵית לֵיהּ. וְאִיבָּעֵית אֵימָא: לְעוֹלָם אִית לֵיהּ, וְאֵימָא, רַבִּי יוֹסֵי אוֹמֵר: כָּל אֲרוּסוֹת גְּרוּשׁוֹת יִנָּשְׂאוּ.

The Gemara answers: Indeed, **he does not accept** the decree. **And if you wish, say** that **actually, he does accept** the decree and applies it in the case of a married woman who was divorced. **And** with regard to the challenge to his opinion from the *a fortiori* inference, emend the mishna and **say: Rabbi Yosei says** that **all** women **who were** only **betrothed** to their previous husbands and then **divorced may be married** within three months, since the reason to wait does not apply in this case.

HALAKHA

The week in which the Ninth of Av occurs – שַׁבָּת שֶׁחָל תִּשְׁעָה בְּאָב בְּתוֹכָהּ: It is prohibited to cut hair and to launder clothing during the week in which the Ninth of Av occurs. Laundered clothes may be worn only on Shabbat. There are several opinions with regard to which activities are classified as laundering and are therefore prohibited. This is the Sephardic custom. The Rema explains that it was customary to be more stringent and to adopt all of these restrictions from the first day of the month of Av. This is the Ashkenazic custom (Rambam *Sefer Zemanim, Hilkhot Ta'anit* 5:6; *Shulḥan Arukh, Oraḥ Ḥayyim* 551:3).

Prior to this time – קוֹדֶם הַזְּמַן הַזֶּה: Business transactions are reduced from the first day of the month of Av, and joyful building or planting is not performed unless it is done for the sake of a mitzva (Ran). This is in accordance with the Gemara in tractate *Ta'anit* (Rambam *Sefer Zemanim, Hilkhot Ta'anit* 5:6; *Shulḥan Arukh, Oraḥ Ḥayyim* 551:2).

Betrothal and marriage in the month of Av – אֵירוּסִין וְנִשּׂוּאִין בְּחוֹדֶשׁ אָב: It is prohibited to marry from the first day of Av until after the fast of the Ninth of Av, and betrothal feasts are also not permitted. However, it is permitted to perform a betrothal without a feast even on the Ninth of Av itself. This is in accordance with the Gemara in tractate *Ta'anit* (Rambam *Sefer Nashim, Hilkhot Ishut* 10:14; *Shulḥan Arukh, Oraḥ Ḥayyim* 551:2).

NOTES

On Thursday it is permitted – וּבַחֲמִישִׁי מוּתָּר: This ruling is not cited in the various codifications of *halakha*. The commentaries explain that this is because this *halakha* applies only when the Ninth of Av occurs on a Friday, in which case it is necessary to prepare for Shabbat on Thursday. However, once the calendar was fixed so that the Ninth of Av never occurs on a Friday, this *halakha* became obsolete (*Maggid Mishne*).

From business transactions – מִלִּישָּׂא וּמִלִּיתֵּן: This *halakha* is not cited by many of the early halakhic authorities. The commentaries explain that those authorities hold that refraining from business transactions was only a custom of the especially pious, or a regional custom limited to some places. The *Yam shel Shlomo* explains that there is an established ruling that since it was often very difficult for Jews in exile to earn a livelihood in any way other than business, it is improper to prohibit it (see *Tosafot* and *Tosafot Yeshanim*).

אִי הָכִי הַיְינוּ רַבִּי יְהוּדָה! אִיכָּא בֵּינַיְיהוּ נְשׂוּאָה לֵיאָרֵס; רַבִּי יְהוּדָה סָבַר: נְשׂוּאָה מוּתֶּרֶת לֵיאָרֵס, וְרַבִּי יוֹסֵי סָבַר: נְשׂוּאָה אֲסוּרָה לֵיאָרֵס.

The Gemara asks: **If so,** then **this** opinion of Rabbi Yosei **is** identical to the opinion of **Rabbi Yehuda.** What difference is there between them? The Gemara answers: **There is** a practical difference **between them** in the case of a woman who was **married** to her previous husband and seeks **to be betrothed. Rabbi Yehuda holds** that **it is permitted to betroth** a woman who was **married** to her previous husband without first waiting three months. **And Rabbi Yosei holds** that **it is prohibited to betroth** a woman who was **married** to her previous husband without first waiting three months.

וְסָבַר רַבִּי יוֹסֵי נְשׂוּאָה אֲסוּרָה לֵיאָרֵס? וְהָתַנְיָא, רַבִּי יוֹסֵי אוֹמֵר: כׇּל הַנָּשִׁים יִתְאָרְסוּ, חוּץ מִן הָאַלְמָנָה מִפְּנֵי הָאִיבּוּל, וְכַמָּה אִיבּוּל שֶׁלָּהּ – שְׁלֹשִׁים יוֹם. וְכוּלָּן לֹא יִנָּשְׂאוּ עַד שֶׁיְּהוּ לָהֶן שְׁלֹשָׁה חֳדָשִׁים!

The Gemara asks: **But does Rabbi Yosei** really **hold** that **it is prohibited to betroth** a woman who was **married** to her previous husband without first waiting three months? **Isn't it taught** in a *baraita*: **Rabbi Yosei says** that **all women may be betrothed** without waiting **except for a widow, due to the mourning period** she must observe for her deceased husband; **and how long is her mourning period?** It is **thirty days. And none of them may be married until they have** waited **three months.**

הַאי מַאי קוּשְׁיָא? אִילֵימָא דְּקָתָנֵי, רַבִּי יוֹסֵי אוֹמֵר: כׇּל הַנָּשִׁים יִתְאָרְסוּ – מִי אַלִּימָא מִמַּתְנִיתִין דְּאוֹקֵימְנָא בַּאֲרוּסוֹת גְּרוּשׁוֹת יִנָּשְׂאוּ – הָכָא נָמֵי כׇּל אֲרוּסוֹת גְּרוּשׁוֹת יִנָּשְׂאוּ.

The Gemara clarifies the question: **What difficulty does this** *baraita* pose? **If we say that** the *baraita* **teaches: Rabbi Yosei says** that **all women may be betrothed** without waiting, **is** the *baraita* **stronger than the mishna**[N] **that was established** as teaching that women who were only **betrothed** to their previous husbands and then **divorced may be married** within three months? **Here, too,** the *baraita* could be established as teaching that **all** women who were only **betrothed** to their previous husbands and then **divorced may be married** within three months.

אֶלָּא מִסֵּיפָא, דְּקָתָנֵי: וְכוּלָּן לֹא יִנָּשְׂאוּ עַד שֶׁיְּהוּ לָהֶן שְׁלֹשָׁה חֳדָשִׁים. אִינְסוּבֵי הוּא – דְּלָא, הָא אִיתְרוּסֵי – שַׁפִּיר דָּמֵי.

Rather, the difficulty arises **from the latter clause that teaches: And none of them may marry until they have** waited **three months.** This implies that Rabbi Yosei holds that it is specifically **marrying that** is **not** permitted, **but betrothing seems well** and is permitted. This challenges the Gemara's original claim that Rabbi Yosei disagrees with Rabbi Yehuda on this point.

אֲמַר רָבָא, תְּרֵיץ וְאֵימָא הָכִי: רַבִּי יוֹסֵי אוֹמֵר כׇּל אֲרוּסוֹת גְּרוּשׁוֹת יִנָּשְׂאוּ, חוּץ מִן הָאַלְמָנָה מִפְּנֵי הָאִיבּוּל, וְכַמָּה אִיבּוּל שֶׁלָּהּ – שְׁלֹשִׁים יוֹם. וּנְשׂוּאוֹת לֹא יִתְאָרְסוּ עַד שֶׁיְּהֵא לָהֶן שְׁלֹשָׁה חֳדָשִׁים.

Rava said: Resolve the difficulty **and** emend Rabbi Yosei's statement to **say this: Rabbi Yosei says** that **all** women who were only **betrothed** to their previous husbands and then **divorced may marry** within three months **except for a widow, due to the mourning period** she must observe for her deceased husband. **And how long is her mourning period?** It is **thirty days. And** women who were **married** to their previous husbands **may not be betrothed until they have** waited **three months.**

וְאַלְמָנָה מִן הָאֵירוּסִין מִי אִית לַהּ אִיבּוּל? וְהָתָנֵי רַבִּי חִיָּיא בַּר אַמִי: אִשְׁתּוֹ אֲרוּסָה – לֹא אוֹנֵן וְלֹא מִיטַּמֵּא לָהּ, וְכֵן הִיא לֹא אוֹנֶנֶת וְלֹא מִיטַּמְּאָה לוֹ. מֵתָה – אֵינוֹ יוֹרְשָׁהּ, מֵת הוּא – גּוֹבָה כְּתוּבָּתָהּ.

The Gemara asks: **But does** a woman who became **a widow from betrothal have** to observe **a mourning period** for her husband? **Didn't Rabbi Ḥiyya bar Ami teach** in a *baraita*: If one's **wife** to whom he was **betrothed** died, **he does not observe** a period of **acute mourning** for her, **and** if he is a priest **he is not** permitted **to become ritually impure for her. And similarly,** if he dies, **she does not observe** a period of **acute mourning** for him and **she does not become ritually impure for him.**[N] If **she dies, he does not inherit from her.** If **he dies, she collects** payment of **her marriage contract.** The *baraita* demonstrates that a widow is required to mourn her husband only if she was married to him and not merely betrothed. If so, clearly Rabbi Yosei's ruling in the mishna is referring to married women. Accordingly, all of the Gemara's emendations of Rabbi Yosei's statement, in order to defend his statement from Rav Ḥisda's *a fortiori* inference, are refuted.

NOTES

Is the *baraita* stronger than the mishna – מִי אַלִּימָא מִמַּתְנִיתִין: Since the language of the Mishna is assumed to be more exact than that of the *baraitot*, being that the latter were not proofread and examined to the same extent, it often happens that the Gemara revises the language found in a *baraita* or assumes that its formulation is not exact. Consequently, if the same expression is found in both a mishna and in a *baraita*, and it is revised or understood to be imprecise in the mishna, then it stands to reason that the same expression must be revised in the *baraita* as well.

She does not become ritually impure for him – לֹא מִיטַּמְּאָה לוֹ: The early commentaries note that this clause of the *baraita* is strange because a woman is never prohibited from becoming ritually impure, even if she is the daughter or wife of a priest. Rashi apparently avoided this difficulty by explaining that the intention of the *baraita* is just that a betrothed woman is not obliged to involve herself with his burial, which will usually result in her becoming ritually impure.

אֶלָּא תַּנָּאֵי הִיא. דְּתַנְיָא: מֵרֹאשׁ חֹדֶשׁ וְעַד הַתַּעֲנִית הָעָם מְמַעֲטִין מֵעִסְקֵיהֶן, מִלִּישָּׂא וּמִלִּיתֵּן, מִלִּבְנוֹת וְלִנְטוֹעַ, וּמִלֵּיאָרֵס וּמִלִּישָּׂא. שַׁבָּת שֶׁחָל תִּשְׁעָה בְּאָב בְּתוֹכָהּ – אָסוּר לְסַפֵּר וּלְכַבֵּס (וְאָסוּר לֵיאָרֵס). וְיֵשׁ אוֹמְרִים: כָּל הַחֹדֶשׁ אָסוּר.

Rather, it must be that the question of whether it is permitted to betroth a woman during the period prior to the week of the Ninth of Av **is** subject to a dispute between ***tanna'im*. As it is taught** in a *baraita*: **From the New Moon** of Av **and until the fast** on the ninth, **the public reduces its activities,** refraining **from business transactions, from building and planting, and from betrothing and marrying.** During **the week in which the Ninth of Av occurs, it is prohibited to cut** hair **and to launder** clothes, **and it is prohibited to be betrothed. And some say: It is prohibited for the entire month.** The Gemara's challenge to Rabbi Yosei's opinion that it is prohibited for a widow to be betrothed during her mourning period was based on an *a fortiori* inference that assumes that it is permitted to be betrothed during the mourning period preceding the week of the Ninth of Av. However, since this ruling is subject to a dispute, Rabbi Yosei could reject the *a fortiori* inference by stating that he holds in accordance with the opinion that it is in fact prohibited to be betrothed during that period.

מַתְקִיף לָהּ רַב אַשִׁי: מִמַּאי דְּלֵיאָרֵס – לֵיאָרֵס מַמָּשׁ? דִּלְמָא לְמִיעֲבַד סְעוּדַת אֵירוּסִין הוּא דְּאָסוּר, הָא לֵיאָרֵס – שַׁפִּיר דָּמֵי.

Rav Ashi strongly objects to this: From where is it known **that** when the *baraita* prohibits one **to be betrothed,** it is referring **to actually betrothing? Perhaps it is** only **to make a betrothal feast that is prohibited, but** merely **to be betrothed seems well** and is permitted.

אִי הָכִי, מִלִּישָּׂא? לִינְסֵא נַמִי לְמִיעֲבַד סְעוּדַת נִשּׂוּאִין הוּא דְּאָסוּר, הָא לִישָּׂא – שַׁפִּיר דָּמֵי! הָכִי הַשְׁתָּא! בִּשְׁלָמָא נִשּׂוּאִין בְּלֹא סְעוּדָה – אִיכָּא שִׂמְחָה, אֶלָּא אֵירוּסִין בְּלֹא סְעוּדָה – מִי אִיכָּא שִׂמְחָה?

The Gemara questions Rav Ashi's objection: **If so,** then with regard to the prohibition **against marrying** as well one could make the same claim: With regard to the prohibition **to marry, too, it is only to make a marriage feast that is prohibited, but** merely **to marry seems well** and is permitted. The Gemara rejects its question: **How can** these cases **be compared? Granted,** from **a marriage,** even **without a feast, there is joy, but** from **a betrothal without a feast,**[N] **is there** any **joy?** It is merely a legal ceremony.

אֶלָּא אֲמַר רַב אַשִׁי: שָׁאנֵי אֲבֵילוּת חֲדָשָׁה מֵאֲבֵילוּת יְשָׁנָה, וְשָׁאנֵי אֲבֵילוּת דְּרַבִּים מֵאֲבֵילוּת דְּיָחִיד.

Rather, Rav Ashi stated a different resolution of Rav Yosei's opinion: **New mourning,** i.e., the mourning for a relative who has just passed away, **is different**[N] **from old mourning,** i.e., the mourning over historic events such as the destruction of the Temple, and it is appropriate to be more lenient in the latter. **And the mourning of the public**[N] **is different from the** private **mourning of the individual,** and it is appropriate to be more stringent in the latter. As such, it is not possible to form an *a fortiori* inference from the *halakhot* of mourning for the Temple to those of a wife mourning for her husband.

מתני׳ אַרְבָּעָה אַחִין נְשׂוּאִין אַרְבַּע נָשִׁים, וָמֵתוּ. אִם רָצָה הַגָּדוֹל שֶׁבָּהֶם לְיַיבֵּם אֶת כּוּלָּן – הָרְשׁוּת בְּיָדוֹ.

MISHNA In a case of **four brothers**[H] **married to four women and** some of the brothers **died** childless, their wives thereby become *yevamot*. **If the eldest of** the brothers who survived **wished to consummate the levirate marriage with all of** his *yevamot*, **he has permission** to do so.

מִי שֶׁהָיָה נָשׂוּי לִשְׁתֵּי נָשִׁים וָמֵת – בִּיאָתָהּ אוֹ חֲלִיצָתָהּ שֶׁל אַחַת מֵהֶן פּוֹטֶרֶת צָרָתָהּ.

In the case of **one who was married to two women**[H] **and died** childless, the **intercourse or *ḥalitza*** of either **one of** the wives with the *yavam* **releases her rival wife** from the levirate bond, and the rival wife need not enter into levirate marriage or perform *ḥalitza*.

NOTES

Betrothal without a feast – אירוסין בלא סעודה: In the time of the Talmud formal betrothal would take place long in advance of marriage, often a year beforehand. Following the betrothal, the bride and groom are still not permitted to live together. Consequently, betrothal alone does not lead to a sense of joy unless a celebratory feast to mark the event is prepared, in which fine foods, meat, and wine are available. In contrast, the marriage represents the beginning of the couple's life together, and therefore it is a joyous occasion even if it is not celebrated with a feast.

New mourning is different, etc. – שָׁאנֵי אֲבֵילוּת חֲדָשָׁה וכו׳: Rashi explains that the mourning for the Ninth of Av is less severe than the mourning of a private individual on two counts, both because it is public and because it is old. Rabbeinu Tam raises a challenge to this in *Tosafot*: If this is so, then the *a fortiori* objection raised earlier by Rav Ḥisda is indeed valid. Ramban suggests a further objection, pointing out the repetitive language utilized in the Gemara, which states: New mourning is different from old mourning and the mourning of the public is different from the private mourning of the individual. This seems to imply that there is not a single difference, but rather two differences. The commentaries suggest that the aspects of some rulings on the Ninth of Av may be more lenient, while others must be more stringent, and therefore it is not possible to draw inferences from these *halakhot* to matters concerning private individuals.

Rabbeinu Tam holds that the *halakha* must be ruled stringently with regard to actions performed in the public sphere in matters of public mourning, as were it not so, it would appear that there is no need to be concerned over displays of mourning at all. However, in private matters such as betrothals, there is no reason to be stringent. The Ramban explains differently: Since the mourning on the Ninth of Av is old, people might tend to treat it lightly. Therefore, a stringent ruling was put in place with regard to laundering clothes, a restriction that does not exist in cases of new mourning. On the other hand, were the Sages to permit betrothal in cases of private mourning, people might end up preparing feasts to celebrate the event, and no one would stop them, whereas in cases of public mourning others would certainly prevent the one performing the betrothal from performing any prohibited actions.

The Meiri explains that public mourning is less intense, and so to emphasize the period, the Sages were more stringent in the matter of laundering clothes. However, they were concerned that if they were to impose a rabbinic decree against betrothals during periods of public mourning, people might not obey, and so they did not do so.

Mourning of the public – אֲבֵילוּת דְּרַבִּים: Rivan explains that public mourning is less intense because in such cases people comfort one another. Similarly, the Meiri explains that this type of mourning is in itself a partial consolation.

HALAKHA

Four brothers, etc. – אַרְבָּעָה אַחִין וכו׳: In a case where one had a number of brothers who died childless, so that their wives happened before him for levirate marriage, then if he has the means to do so, he must consummate levirate marriage with all of them, or he may perform *ḥalitza* with all of them, or he may consummate levirate marriage with some and perform *ḥalitza* with the others. However, he may do so with only one wife from each brother (Rambam *Sefer Nashim, Hilkhot Yibbum VaḤalitza* 1:11; *Shulḥan Arukh, Even HaEzer* 161:8).

One who was married to several women – מִי שֶׁהָיָה נָשׂוּי לְכַמָּה נָשִׁים: If a man married to several women died childless and was survived by his brother, then once that brother either consummates levirate marriage or performs *ḥalitza* with one of the wives, all of her rival wives are thereby released from their levirate bond (Rambam *Sefer Nashim, Hilkhot Yibbum VaḤalitza* 1:9; *Shulḥan Arukh, Even HaEzer* 161:1).

הָיְתָה אַחַת כְּשֵׁרָה וְאַחַת פְּסוּלָה, אִם הָיָה חוֹלֵץ – חוֹלֵץ לִפְסוּלָה, וְאִם הָיָה מְיַיבֵּם – מְיַיבֵּם לִכְשֵׁרָה.

If **one** of these women **was fit** to marry into the priesthood **and one was unfit,**[H] then **if he performs *ḥalitza*, he should perform *ḥalitza* with the unfit** woman rather than with the one who is fit for the priesthood, since doing so with the woman who is fit would needlessly disqualify her from marrying into the priesthood. **But if he consummates the levirate marriage, he may consummate the levirate marriage with** the one who is **fit.**

גמ׳ אַרְבָּעָה אַחִין סָלְקָא דַּעְתָּךְ? אֶלָּא אֵימָא: אַרְבָּעָה מֵאַחִין.

GEMARA The simple reading of the mishna's first clause implies that all four brothers died. The Gemara questions this: Can it **enter your mind** to say that all **four brothers** died? If they all died, then who remains to consummate the levirate marriage? **Rather,** emend the mishna and **say** instead: **Four** married men **of** a set of more than four **brothers** died.

״הָרְשׁוּת בְּיָדוֹ״. וְשָׁבְקִי לֵיהּ? וְהָתַנְיָא: ״וְקָרְאוּ לוֹ זִקְנֵי עִירוֹ״ – הֵן וְלֹא שְׁלוּחָן, ״וְדִבְּרוּ אֵלָיו״ – מְלַמֵּד שֶׁמַּשִּׂיאִין לוֹ עֵצָה הוֹגֶנֶת לוֹ,

The mishna continues: If the eldest of them wished to consummate the levirate marriage with all of his *yevamot*, **he has permission** to do so. The Gemara asks: **Do they** actually **leave him**[N] to do so? **Isn't it taught** in a *baraita*: The verse states: **"And the Elders of his city shall call him"** (Deuteronomy 25:8), which indicates that **they,** the Elders, **and not their agent,** should call him. The verse continues: **"And they speak to him";**[H] this phrase **teaches that they offer him advice that is appropriate for him.**

שֶׁאִם הָיָה הוּא יֶלֶד וְהִיא זְקֵנָה, הוּא זָקֵן וְהִיא יַלְדָּה – אוֹמְרִין לוֹ: מָה לְךָ אֵצֶל יַלְדָּה, מָה לְךָ אֵצֶל זְקֵנָה? כְּלָךְ אֵצֶל שֶׁכְּמוֹתְךָ, וְאַל תָּשִׂים קְטָטָה בְּבֵיתְךָ.

The *baraita* explains: Appropriate advice means **that if he was a young man and she an elderly woman** or if **he was an elderly man and she a young woman, they say to him: What do you** want **with a young woman** when you are elderly? Or: **What do you** want **with an elderly woman** when you are young? **Go after your own kind,** i.e., a woman of a similar age, **and do not place discord in your household** that could be caused by marrying a woman of a significantly different age. From the *baraita* it is apparent that if consummating the levirate marriage will ultimately lead to contention between the couple, it is preferable to perform *ḥalitza*. Similarly, in the case of the mishna, marrying four women will likely lead to contention since it is difficult to support so many people, and poverty will lead to strife. Therefore, the *yavam* should not be allowed to consummate levirate marriages with all of them.

לָא צְרִיכָא, דְּאֶפְשָׁר לֵיהּ. אִי הָכִי, אֲפִילּוּ טוּבָא נָמֵי! עֵצָה טוֹבָה קָא מַשְׁמַע לַן: אַרְבַּע – אִין, טְפֵי – לָא, כִּי הֵיכִי דְּנִמְטְיֵיהּ עוֹנָה בְּחֹדֶשׁ.

The Gemara qualifies the mishna's case: **No,** it is **necessary** to teach that he has permission to consummate the levirate marriage with all of his *yevamot* in the case **where it is possible for him** to provide for all four women. The Gemara asks: **If so,** then the same should be true **even** if there are **many** more women **as well;** why does the mishna specifically discuss a case of four women? The Gemara explains: The mishna **teaches us good advice;** in a case of up to **four** women, **yes,** if he can provide for them then it is acceptable to marry all of them. But if there are any **more** than that, **no,**[H] he should not, **in order that he will** be able to **meet the conjugal rights** of each woman at least once **in** each **month.**[N] A Torah scholar is expected to provide conjugal relations once a week. If he marries no more than four women, then that will ensure that each of his wives will receive their conjugal rights at least once a month.

HALAKHA

One was fit and one was unfit – הָיְתָה אַחַת כְּשֵׁרָה וְאַחַת פְּסוּלָה: In a case of several widows of the same man who happen before their *yavam* for levirate marriage, and some of them are fit to marry into the priesthood and some are not, if the *yavam* wishes to consummate the levirate marriage, he may do so with whichever one he chooses. However, if he wishes to perform *ḥalitza*, he should do so with one of the ones who are unfit. Some (*Beit Shmuel*, citing *Beit Yosef*) say that if he willingly violated this *halakha* after having been warned not to do so, then he is excommunicated or receives lashes (Rambam *Sefer Nashim, Hilkhot Yibbum VaḤalitza* 1:10; *Shulḥan Arukh, Even HaEzer* 161:2).

And they shall call him…and they speak to him – וְקָרְאוּ לוֹ...וְדִבְּרוּ אֵלָיו: When *ḥalitza* is to be performed, the norm is for the *yavam* and *yevama* to go to the court in the town of the *yavam*, at which point that court advises them whether it is more appropriate for them to consummate the levirate marriage or to perform *ḥalitza* (Rambam *Sefer Nashim, Hilkhot Yibbum VaḤalitza* 4:1; *Shulḥan Arukh, Even HaEzer* 166:1).

Four wives – אַרְבַּע נָשִׁים: By Torah law a man is permitted to marry as many women as he is able to provide for, i.e., to fulfill his legal obligation to provide them with food, clothing, and conjugal relations. However, the Sages said that one should not marry more than four women, so that he will be able to provide each of them with their conjugal rights at least once in each month. Some (*Beit Shmuel* and *Ḥelkat Meḥokek*) rule that if one belongs to a category of people who are obligated to provide conjugal relations more than once a week, then it would be permitted to marry even more than four women (Rambam *Sefer Nashim, Hilkhot Ishut* 14:1; *Shulḥan Arukh, Even HaEzer* 76:7).

NOTES

Do they leave him – וְשָׁבְקִי לֵיהּ: The early commentaries explain that the mishna's formulation: He has permission to do so, suggests that not only is he not forced to perform *ḥalitza*, but in fact it is entirely acceptable for him to consummate the levirate marriage with all of the *yevamot* and he would not be advised otherwise. The Gemara therefore challenges this understanding because the Gemara considers such a course of action to be inappropriate (Ritva).

Conjugal rights in each month – עוֹנָה בְּחוֹדֶשׁ: The obligation of a husband to provide his wife with conjugal relations varies based on the husband's occupation. Torah scholars are obligated to provide relations once a week, while men in other professions have a more or less frequent obligation dependent on their availability. The commentaries question why the number of women one marries should be based upon the expectations placed on a Torah scholar, when the mishna is certainly not referring only to Torah scholars. Some explain that the limitation of four women is true only in a case of levirate marriage; since the situation was brought about by Heaven and not by the free choice of the *yavam*, he is not expected to provide any more than the more minimal frequency of conjugal relations expected of a Torah scholar (Ritva; *Nimmukei Yosef*). This opinion was not accepted as the *halakha*. One commentary suggests that this number in fact applies only to a Torah scholar and is merely an example of the principle (*Tosefot Yom Tov*). Others suggest that the *halakha* is not based upon the Torah scholars' requirement to provide relations once a week but upon the fact that a Torah scholar is permitted to be absent from the house for up to thirty days without his wife's permission. From that *halakha* it is apparent that it is not considered overly distressing for a woman if she is provided with relations once a month (Rivan). Another commentary explains that the *halakha* is based on the fact that the average woman completes a cycle of menstruation and subsequent ritual purification once a month. At that point she has rights to conjugal relations (*Beit Shmuel*; see *Tosefot Yom Tov*).

״מִי שֶׁהָיָה נָשׂוּי״ וכו׳. וּנְיַיבֵּם לְתַרְוַיְיהוּ! אָמַר רַבִּי חִיָּיא בַּר אַבָּא אָמַר רַבִּי יוֹחָנָן: אָמַר קְרָא ״אֲשֶׁר לֹא יִבְנֶה אֶת בֵּית אָחִיו״ – בַּיִת אֶחָד הוּא בּוֹנֶה, וְאֵין בּוֹנֶה שְׁנֵי בָתִּים.

§ The mishna states: In the case of **one who was married** to two women[H] and died childless, the intercourse or *ḥalitza* of either one of them with the *yavam* releases her rival wife from the levirate bond. The Gemara questions why the mishna considers only the possibility that he would do so with only one of the women: **But let him** instead **consummate levirate marriages with both of them. Rabbi Ḥiyya bar Abba said** that **Rabbi Yoḥanan said: The verse states** that a *yavam* who performs *ḥalitza* is referred to as: "The man **who does not build his brother's house**" (Deuteronomy 25:9). The fact that the word "house" appears in the singular indicates that even had he instead chosen to consummate a levirate marriage, only **one house may he build,** by consummating a levirate marriage with one of his brother's wives, **but he may not build two houses.**

וְנַחֲלוֹץ לְתַרְוַיְיהוּ! אֲמַר מָר זוּטְרָא בַּר טוֹבִיָּה: אָמַר קְרָא ״בֵּית חֲלוּץ הַנָּעַל״ – בַּיִת אֶחָד הוּא חוֹלֵץ, וְאֵין חוֹלֵץ שְׁנֵי בָתִּים.

The Gemara suggests: **But let him perform *ḥalitza* with both of them;** why does the mishna state that he does so with only one woman? **Mar Zutra bar Toviya said: The verse states** that following the *ḥalitza* the man is called: **"The house of him who had his shoe removed"** (Deuteronomy 25:10). The fact that the word "house" appears in the singular indicates that **he performs *ḥalitza* with** only **one house,** i.e., only one of his brother's wives, **and he does not perform *ḥalitza* with two houses.**

וּנְיַיבֵּם לַחֲדָא וְנַחֲלוֹץ לַחֲדָא! – אֲמַר קְרָא ״אִם לֹא יַחְפּוֹץ״ הָא חָפֵץ – יַיבֵּם, כָּל הָעוֹלָה לְיִבּוּם – עוֹלָה לַחֲלִיצָה, כָּל שֶׁאֵין עוֹלָה לְיִיבּוּם – אֵין עוֹלָה לַחֲלִיצָה.

The Gemara suggests: **But let him consummate the levirate marriage with one and perform *ḥalitza* with the other.** The Gemara explains that **the verse states: "If** the man **does not wish** to take his *yevama*" (Deuteronomy 25:7), which implies that with regard to anyone who performs *ḥalitza,* **were he to wish** to, **he could consummate the levirate marriage.** This teaches the principle that only **one who is eligible for levirate marriage is eligible for *ḥalitza,*** but **one who is ineligible for levirate marriage is ineligible for *ḥalitza.*** And since, in the case of the mishna, if the *yavam* consummated the levirate marriage with one of his brother's wives he may not do so with the second, consequently he may not perform *ḥalitza* with her either.

וְעוֹד: שֶׁלֹּא יֹאמְרוּ בַּיִת מִקְצָתוֹ בָּנוּי וּמִקְצָתוֹ חָלוּץ. וְיֹאמְרוּ! אִי דִּמְיַיבֵּם וַהֲדַר חָלֵיץ – הָכִי נַמִי, אֶלָּא [דִּלְמָא] חָלֵיץ וַהֲדַר מְיַיבֵּם, וְקָם לֵיהּ בְּ״לֹא יִבְנֶה״.

And furthermore, an additional reason that one may not do so is so **that** people **should not say**[N] that the brother's **house was partially built** through levirate marriage **and partially released through *ḥalitza*.** The Gemara asks: **And** even if **they will say** that, what of it? The Gemara explains: **If he** first **consummated the levirate marriage** with one wife **and subsequently performed *ḥalitza*** with the other, **indeed,** there is no reason not to do this. **However, perhaps he** might first **perform *ḥalitza*** with one wife **and subsequently consummate levirate marriage** with the other, **and** by doing so **he is liable for** a violation of the prohibition **of: "He does not build** his brother's house" (Deuteronomy 25:9). The verse indicates that one who performs *ḥalitza* has not built his brother's house and is therefore subsequently prohibited from attempting to do so by consummating a levirate marriage with either the *ḥalutza* or any of her rival wives.

וְאֵימָא: כִּי אִיכָּא חֲדָא – תִּתְקַיֵּים מִצְוַת יִבּוּם, כִּי אִיכָּא תַּרְתֵּי – לֹא תִּתְקַיֵּים מִצְוַת יִבּוּם!

The Gemara asks. **But** since the Torah's description of levirate marriage mentions only a case in which the deceased brother had only one wife, **say: When there is only one** wife, **the mitzva of levirate marriage exists,** but **when there are two** wives, **the mitzva of levirate marriage does not exist.**[N]

אִם כֵּן, צָרַת עֶרְוָה דְּאָסַר רַחֲמָנָא לָמָּה לִי? הָשְׁתָּא, תַּרְתֵּי בְּעָלְמָא אָמְרַתְּ לָאו בְּנֵי חֲלִיצָה וְיִבּוּם נִינְהוּ, צָרַת עֶרְוָה מִיבַּעְיָא?

The Gemara suggests a proof: **If** that were **so, why do I** need the *halakha* concerning **a rival wife of a forbidden relation, which is forbidden by the Merciful One** in the Torah? **Now** that even in the case of **two** women in **general,** where neither woman is a forbidden relation, **you say** that **they are not eligible for *ḥalitza* and levirate marriage, is it necessary** to say **a rival wife of a forbidden relation** is also forbidden? The fact that the Torah does prohibit a rival wife of a forbidden relation indicates that the mitzva of levirate marriage does exist in a general case of two wives in which neither are a forbidden relation.

HALAKHA

Two wives from a single house – **שְׁתֵּי נָשִׁים מִבֵּית אֶחָד**: A man is not permitted to consummate levirate marriage with two women who were both married to his brother, as the verse states: "His brother's house," which indicates he may build one house for his brother, but not two (Rambam *Sefer Nashim, Hilkhot Yibbum VaḤalitza* 1:9).

NOTES

And furthermore that people should not say – **וְעוֹד שֶׁלֹּא יֹאמְרוּ**: *Tosafot* challenge the validity of this section of the Gemara. They assert that if it were indeed permitted by Torah law to consummate levirate marriage with one *yevama* and perform *ḥalitza* with the other, then the Sages would not have issued a decree prohibiting it. The Rivan adds further that since the Torah explicitly prohibits such a practice, it is superfluous for the Gemara to suggest additional reasons that it is prohibited. Therefore, they advocate removing this section entirely from the text of the Gemara.

The Ramban, however, presents a defense of this section. He explains that although by Torah law a *yevama* is released through the levirate marriage of her rival wife, one might have thought that it would be appropriate for the Sages to require that *yevama* to perform *ḥalitza* to avoid the appearance of a *yevama* being permitted without taking any action. The reason suggested here by the Gemara explains why the Sages did not do so. A different defense is offered by Rabbi Avraham min HaHar, who suggests that one might have assumed that the principle derived from the verse refers only to women who are forbidden by prohibitions entailing *karet*; however, if the *yevama* was forbidden by a prohibition punishable by lashes, one might have thought she would require *ḥalitza*. Therefore, the Gemara provides an additional reason to cover this case as well.

When there are two wives the mitzva of levirate marriage does not exist – **כִּי אִיכָּא תַּרְתֵּי לֹא תִּתְקַיֵּים מִצְוַת יִבּוּם**: The Gemara above derived from the verse "The man who does not build his brother's house" (Deuteronomy 25:9) that a *yavam* may build only one house by consummating a levirate marriage with one of his brother's wives, but he may not build two houses. Some commentaries note that the underlying assumption of this derivation is that the mitzva of consummating levirate marriage does exist even in a case where there are two wives. Why, then, does the Gemara question that fact here? They explain that were it not for the derivation mentioned later, which proves that the mitzva applies even in a case where the deceased had two wives, the verse "The man who does not build his brother's house" would have been expounded in a different manner, possibly to teach that the mitzva applies only where there is one "house," i.e., wife, but not where there are two (*Tosefot HaRosh*; *Tosafot Yeshanim*).

אַלְמָה לָא? אִצְטְרִיךְ, סָלְקָא דַּעְתָּךְ אָמִינָא עֶרְוָה אַבָּרַאי קַיְּימָא, וְתִתְיַיבֵּם צָרָתָהּ – קָא מַשְׁמַע לָן דַּאֲסִירָא,

The Gemara objects: **Why not?** Even if one assumes that there is no mitzva of levirate marriage when the deceased brother had two wives, **it is** still **necessary** to teach the *halakha* concerning a rival wife of a forbidden relation because it could **enter your mind to say** that since there is no possibility of consummating the levirate marriage with her, **the forbidden relation stands outside** the calculation such that her presence is disregarded, **and her rival wife should enter into levirate marriage** as though she were the only wife. Therefore, the verse needs to **teach us that** the rival wife **is forbidden.**

אֶלָּא: ״יְבִמְתּוֹ... יְבִמְתּוֹ״ – רִיבָּה.

Rather, the repeated use of the phrase **"his *yevama*," "his *yevama*"** in the verses concerning levirate marriage **amplifies** the mitzva of levirate marriage so that it applies even when the deceased brother had more than one wife.

״הָיְתָה אַחַת כְּשֵׁרָה״. אָמַר רַב יוֹסֵף: כָּאן שָׁנָה רַבִּי: לֹא יִשְׁפּוֹךְ אָדָם מֵי בּוֹרוֹ וַאֲחֵרִים צְרִיכִים לָהֶם.

§ The mishna states: If **one** of these wives of the deceased brother **was fit** for the priesthood and one was unfit, *ḥalitza* should not be performed with the fit woman since doing so would needlessly disqualify her from the priesthood. **Rav Yosef said** that **here,** through this mishna, **Rabbi** Yehuda HaNasi **taught** the principle that one should not perform an action that will needlessly disadvantage others, and so **a person should not spill out water** collected in **his pit**[N] that he does not need **when others are in need of it.**

מתני׳ הַמַּחְזִיר גְּרוּשָׁתוֹ, וְהַנּוֹשֵׂא חֲלוּצָתוֹ, וְהַנּוֹשֵׂא קְרוֹבַת חֲלוּצָתוֹ – יוֹצִיא, וְהַוָּלָד מַמְזֵר, דִּבְרֵי רַבִּי עֲקִיבָא.

MISHNA With regard to **one who remarries his divorcée** after she had been married to another man from whom she was then widowed or divorced, **or one who marries the woman with whom he performed *ḥalitza* [*ḥalutza*], or one who marries a relative of his *ḥalutza*,** since all such marriages are forbidden he **must divorce** her, **and the offspring** born from such unions **is a *mamzer*;** this is **the statement of Rabbi Akiva.** He holds that even the offspring from relations forbidden by a prohibition punishable by lashes is a *mamzer*.

וַחֲכָמִים אוֹמְרִים: אֵין הַוָּלָד מַמְזֵר. וּמוֹדִים בְּנוֹשֵׂא קְרוֹבַת גְּרוּשָׁתוֹ, שֶׁהַוָּלָד מַמְזֵר.

The Rabbis say: The offspring in those cases **is not a *mamzer*, but they concede with regard to one who marries a relative of his divorcée,** a union forbidden by a prohibition entailing *karet*, **that the offspring is a *mamzer*.** They hold that only the offspring from relations forbidden by a prohibition entailing *karet* is a *mamzer*.

גמ׳ וְסָבַר רַבִּי עֲקִיבָא הַנּוֹשֵׂא קְרוֹבַת חֲלוּצָתוֹ הַוָּלָד מַמְזֵר? וְהָאָמַר רֵישׁ לָקִישׁ, כָּאן שָׁנָה רַבִּי: אֲחוֹת גְּרוּשָׁה – מִדִּבְרֵי תוֹרָה, אֲחוֹת חֲלוּצָה – מִדִּבְרֵי סוֹפְרִים! תְּנֵי: קְרוֹבַת גְּרוּשָׁתוֹ.

GEMARA The Gemara asks: **But does Rabbi Akiva** actually **hold** that with regard to **one who marries a relative of his *ḥalutza*, the offspring is a *mamzer*? Didn't Reish Lakish say** that through the mishna **here, Rabbi** Yehuda HaNasi **taught** that **a sister of** one's **divorcée** is forbidden **by Torah law** whereas **a sister of** one's ***ḥalutza*** is forbidden **by rabbinic law?** If a relative of one's *ḥalutza* is forbidden by rabbinic law, how can the offspring of that union be a *mamzer*? The Gemara concedes: Emend the mishna and **teach** instead: **A relative of his divorcée.**[N]

NOTES

A person should not spill out water collected in his pit – לֹא יִשְׁפּוֹךְ אָדָם מֵי בּוֹרוֹ: The Rid writes that this imperative should not be confused with the principle that one compels another to refrain from behavior characteristic of Sodom. That principle teaches that if one denies another the use of his possessions even though doing so would incur no loss or damage to himself, then he should be forced to waive his rights to those possessions. The Rid explains that that principle is limited to cases where there is a specific individual who wishes to use the possessions. The imperative here goes much further in demanding that one not perform an action that could theoretically disadvantage an unidentified person in the future. Accordingly, it would appear that one would not be forcibly compelled to act in this manner. This is also how the *Keneset HaGedola* rules; he explains the Gemara to be indicating the proper course of behavior for ethical living but not a strict requirement. In contrast, Rabbeinu Yeruḥam (cited in *Beit Yosef*) understands the Gemara to actually require such behavior, and he therefore rules that one who refuses to a way that will avoid needlessly causing disadvantage to others should be excommunicated and flogged.

Teach: A relative of his divorcée – תְּנֵי קְרוֹבַת גְּרוּשָׁתוֹ: According to this emended version of the mishna, Rabbi Akiva states that the offspring resulting from one's union with a relative of his divorcée is a *mamzer*. While Rabbi Akiva certainly holds that this is true, one could question why he would choose to mention such a case. The novelty of Rabbi Akiva's opinion is that he holds that even the offspring from relations forbidden by a prohibition punishable by lashes is a *mamzer*, even though that prohibition is not punishable by *karet*. The prohibition against engaging in relations with a relative of one's divorcée, however, is punishable by *karet*. Therefore, even the Rabbis would agree that the offspring would be a *mamzer*. As such, what advantage is there for Rabbi Akiva to mention this case? One could suggest that Rabbi Akiva's entire statement is directed toward the Rabbis. He mentions the case of a relative of one's divorcée because he knows that the Rabbis agree with him in that case, and then he says that just as they agree in that case, they should agree in the other cases he goes on to enumerate.

הָכִי נַמִּי מִסְתַּבְּרָא, דְּקָתָנֵי סֵיפָא: וּמוֹדִים בְּנוֹשֵׂא קְרוֹבַת גְּרוּשָׁתוֹ שֶׁהַוָּלָד מַמְזֵר. אִי אָמְרַתְּ בִּשְׁלָמָא אַיְּירִי בָּהּ – הַיְינוּ דְּקָתָנֵי ״וּמוֹדִים״, אֶלָּא אִי אָמְרַתְּ לָא אַיְּירִי בָּהּ – מַאי ״וּמוֹדִים״?

The Gemara notes: **So, too, it is reasonable** that this is the correct version of the mishna, as **the latter clause teaches: But they concede** in the case of **one who marries a relative of his divorcée that the offspring is a** ***mamzer*****. Granted, if you say** that Rabbi Akiva **was talking about that** case, **this is** consistent with **that which** the mishna **teaches: They concede,** which implies that they agree to a case already mentioned. **However, if you say** that he **was not talking about that** case, **what** could the phrase: **They concede,** possibly be referring to?

וְדִלְמָא הָא קָא מַשְׁמַע לָן: דְּיֵשׁ מַמְזֵר מֵחַיָּיבֵי כָּרֵיתוֹת. הָא קָתָנֵי לָהּ לְקַמָּן: אֵיזֶהוּ מַמְזֵר – כׇּל שְׁאֵר בָּשָׂר שֶׁהוּא בְּ״לֹא יָבֹא״ דִּבְרֵי רַבִּי עֲקִיבָא, רַבִּי שִׁמְעוֹן הַתִּימְנִי אוֹמֵר: כׇּל שֶׁחַיָּיבִין עָלָיו כָּרֵת בִּידֵי שָׁמַיִם, וַהֲלָכָה כִּדְבָרָיו.

The Gemara objects: **But perhaps this** phrase **teaches us that** the Rabbis concede **that** the offspring **from** forbidden relations for which one **is liable to** receive ***karet*** **is a** ***mamzer*****.** The Gemara rejects this option: **This is already taught later on** in a mishna (49a): **Which** offspring of forbidden relations has the status of **a** ***mamzer*****?** It is the offspring of a union with **any next of kin that is subject to** a Torah prohibition that one **should not engage in sexual relations** with them; this is **the statement of Rabbi Akiva. Rabbi Shimon HaTimni says:** It is the offspring of a union with **any** forbidden relative **for which one is liable to** receive ***karet*** **at the hand of Heaven. And the** ***halakha*** **is in accordance with his statement.** Since the mishna explicitly rules in accordance with Rabbi Shimon HaTimni, it would be unnecessary for the mishna here to teach that fact.

וְדִלְמָא קְסָתֵים לָן תַּנָּא כְּרַבִּי שִׁמְעוֹן הַתִּימְנִי. אִם כֵּן לִיתְנֵי שְׁאָר חַיָּיבֵי כָּרֵיתוֹת, קְרוֹבַת גְּרוּשָׁתוֹ לָמָּה לִי? אֶלָּא שְׁמַע מִינָּהּ אַיְּירִי בָּהּ.

The Gemara persists: **But perhaps the** ***tanna*** **taught us as unattributed** a mishna that is **in accordance with** the opinion of **Rabbi Shimon HaTimni**[N] to indicate that this is indeed the accepted *halakha*. The Gemara rejects this: **If so, then let him teach other** cases of forbidden relations **for which one is liable to** receive ***karet*****; why do I** need the mishna to specifically consider the case of **a relative of** one's **divorcée? Rather, conclude from this** that Rabbi Akiva indeed **was talking about that** case.

[וְדִלְמָא] לְעוֹלָם לָא אַיְּירִי בָּהּ, וְאַיְּידֵי דְּתָנָא מַחֲזִיר גְּרוּשָׁתוֹ וְנוֹשֵׂא חֲלוּצָתוֹ וּקְרוֹבַת חֲלוּצָתוֹ – תָּנֵי נַמִּי קְרוֹבַת גְּרוּשָׁתוֹ.

The Gemara persists: **But perhaps he was not actually talking about that** case, **but since** Rabbi Akiva **taught** the cases of **one who remarries his divorcée, or one who marries his** ***ḥalutza*** **or a relative of his** ***ḥalutza*****,** the mishna **also taught** in the name of the Rabbis the case of one who marries **a relative of his divorcée** because it is a similar case. The Gemara concedes that this would be an acceptable reading of the mishna.

אֶלָּא קְרוֹבַת חֲלוּצָתוֹ לְרַבִּי עֲקִיבָא הָוֵי מַמְזֵר. אֲמַר רַבִּי חִיָּיא בַּר אַבָּא אָמַר רַבִּי יוֹחָנָן: הַיְינוּ טַעֲמָא דְּרַבִּי עֲקִיבָא, דְּאָמַר קְרָא ״בֵּית חֲלוּץ הַנָּעַל״ – הַכָּתוּב קְרָאוֹ בֵּיתוֹ.

Rather, the mishna should not be emended, and with regard to the Gemara's original question as to how Rabbi Akiva could claim that the offspring from one's union with a relative of his *ḥalutza* is a *mamzer* if that union is forbidden only by rabbinic law, one must conclude that **a relative of one's** ***ḥalutza*** is forbidden by Torah law **according to Rabbi Akiva** and therefore the offspring **is a** ***mamzer*****. Rabbi Ḥiyya bar Abba said** that **Rabbi Yoḥanan said** that **this is Rabbi Akiva's reasoning: As the verse states: "The house of he who had his shoe removed"** (Deuteronomy 25:10). **The verse called** his relationship with the *ḥalutza* **his house,** indicating that the *ḥalutza* is considered as though she had been married to the *yavam*, and therefore her relative is forbidden to him by Torah law.

אֲמַר רַב יוֹסֵף אֲמַר רַבִּי שִׁמְעוֹן בַּר רַבִּי: הַכֹּל מוֹדִים בְּמַחֲזִיר גְּרוּשָׁתוֹ

Rav Yosef said that **Rabbi Shimon bar Rabbi** Yehuda HaNasi **said: All agree in** the case of **one who remarries his divorcée**

NOTES

The ***tanna*** **taught us as unattributed a mishna in accordance with the opinion of Rabbi Shimon HaTimni, etc. – קְסָתֵים לָן תַּנָּא כְּרַבִּי שִׁמְעוֹן הַתִּימְנִי וכו׳:** What advantage is there in having an unattributed mishna in accordance with the opinion of Rabbi Shimon HaTimni when the mishna on 49a already explicitly states: The *halakha* is in accordance with his statement? The advantage is in that there is an accepted principle that the *halakha* may not be derived from the Mishna. Therefore, even when a mishna explicitly states what the *halakha* should be, that statement is not necessarily relied upon as the final *halakha*. This is because that statement might well have been only the opinion of an individual Sage that Rabbi Yehuda HaNasi preserved in his redaction of the Mishna. However, when there is an unattributed mishna in accordance with one opinion, that clearly indicates that the opinion was held by the majority of Sages, and therefore the *halakha* is to be fixed in accordance with that opinion (Ritva).

שֶׁהַוָּלָד פָּגוּם לִכְהוּנָּה. מַאן ״הַכֹּל מוֹדִים״ – שִׁמְעוֹן הַתִּימְנִי. דְּאַף עַל גַּב דְּאָמַר שִׁמְעוֹן הַתִּימְנִי: אֵין מַמְזֵר מֵחַיָּיבֵי לָאוִין – נְהִי דְּמַמְזֵר לָא הָוֵי, פָּגוּם – מִיהָא הָוֵי,

that the offspring, even if not a *mamzer*, **has flawed** lineage and, if the offspring is a girl, is unfit **to** marry into the **priesthood.** The Gemara clarifies: **Who is included by saying: All agree?**[N] It is **Shimon HaTimni, as although Shimon HaTimni said** that the offspring of relations **for which one is liable for** violating a **prohibition is not a** *mamzer*, nevertheless, **granted** that Shimon HaTimni holds that **he is not a** *mamzer*; he would agree, **however,** that **he is of flawed** lineage.

מִקַּל וָחוֹמֶר מֵאַלְמָנָה. וּמָה אַלְמָנָה לְכֹהֵן גָּדוֹל, שֶׁאֵין אִיסּוּרָהּ שָׁוֶה בַּכֹּל – בְּנָהּ פָּגוּם, זוֹ שֶׁאִיסּוּרָהּ שָׁוֶה בַּכֹּל – אֵינוֹ דִּין שֶׁבְּנָהּ פָּגוּם?

This is derived **through an** ***a fortiori*** inference **from the** *halakha* pertaining to **a widow,** as follows: **Just as** in the case of **a widow** who is married **to a High Priest, where the prohibition** that pertains **to her is not equally applicable to all,** i.e., only a High Priest is prohibited from marrying a widow, and nevertheless **her child** from that union will **have flawed** lineage, then so too with regard to **this** divorcée, who married another man and is therefore prohibited from marrying her original husband, **where the prohibition** that pertains **to her is equally applicable to all** Jews, as the prohibition to remarry one's divorcée after she was married to another man applies to all Jews, **isn't it logical that her child** from that union will have **flawed** lineage?

אִיכָּא לְמִיפְרַךְ: מָה לְאַלְמָנָה – שֶׁכֵּן הִיא עַצְמָהּ מִתְחַלֶּלֶת,

The Gemara raises a number of objections: The logic of this *a fortiori* inference **can be refuted: What** is true with regard **to a widow, where** her union with a High Priest is what makes **her herself disqualified** from subsequently marrying any priest and, if she is the daughter of a priest, from eating *teruma*, is not true with regard to a remarried divorcée, where her remarriage to another man is permitted and is not the cause of any further disqualification. Therefore, one case cannot be deduced from the other.

וְעוֹד: ״הִיא תּוֹעֵבָה״ כְּתִיב, וְאֵין בָּנֶיהָ תּוֹעֲבִין.

And furthermore,[N] **"She is an abomination"** (Deuteronomy 24:4) **is written** with regard to remarrying with one's divorcée, and the emphasis on the word "she" teaches that only she is considered so, **but her children are not abominations** and they have unflawed lineage.

וְעוֹד, תַּנְיָא: הַמַּחֲזִיר גְּרוּשָׁתוֹ, וְהַנּוֹשֵׂא חֲלוּצָתוֹ, וְהַנּוֹשֵׂא קְרוֹבַת חֲלוּצָתוֹ. רַבִּי עֲקִיבָא אוֹמֵר: אֵין לוֹ בָּהּ קִדּוּשִׁין, וְאֵינָהּ צְרִיכָה הֵימֶנּוּ גֵּט, וְהִיא פְּסוּלָה וּוְלָדָהּ פָּסוּל, וְכוֹפִין אוֹתוֹ לְהוֹצִיא. וַחֲכָמִים אוֹמְרִים: יֵשׁ לוֹ בָּהּ קִדּוּשִׁין, וּצְרִיכָה הֵימֶנּוּ גֵּט, וְהִיא כְּשֵׁרָה וּוְלָדָהּ כָּשֵׁר.

And furthermore, it is taught in a *baraita*: With regard to **one who remarries his divorcée,**[H] **and one who marries his** ***ḥalutza*****, and one who marries a relative of his** ***ḥalutza*****, Rabbi Akiva says** that **one's** betrothal of such women **is not** effective. **And** therefore, even if he attempts to do so, it is meaningless and **she does not require a bill of divorce from him** in order to separate from him. **And** if she has relations with him **she is** rendered **unfit and her child is unfit, and we force him to send** her away. **The Rabbis say** that **one's betrothal of** such women **is** effective, **and** therefore if he betrothed her **she requires a bill of divorce from him, and** if she has relations with him **she** remains **fit and her child is fit.**[N]

לְמַאן – לָאו לִכְהוּנָּה? לָא, לַקָּהָל. אִי הָכִי, הִיא כְּשֵׁרָה – לְמַאן? אִילֵימָא לַקָּהָל – פְּשִׁיטָא, מִשּׁוּם דְּזַנְיָא אִפַּסְלָה לַקָּהָל? אֶלָּא לָאו – לִכְהוּנָּה,

The Gemara clarifies: When the *baraita* states she and her child are rendered unfit, **to whom** are they unfit to be married? **Is it not to the priesthood? No,** it is **to the congregation** of Israel. **If so,** when the *baraita* states **she is fit, to whom** is she fit to be married? **If we say** it is **to the congregation** of Israel, **this is obvious;** could it be that **because she engaged in forbidden sexual relations that she is rendered unfit from** marrying into **the congregation** of Israel? Although by doing so she is rendered a *zona*, that can disqualify her only from marrying a priest. **Rather, is it not** that the intention is that she is fit **to** marry into **the priesthood?**

NOTES

Who is included by saying: All agree – מַאן הַכֹּל מוֹדִים: The Gemara does not need to mention that Rabbi Yehoshua agrees with this, because that was already made explicit on 15b. There, Rabbi Yehoshua testifies to the fact that such children are fit even to marry into the priesthood (Ritva).

This can be refuted…and furthermore – אִיכָּא לְמִיפְרַךְ...וְעוֹד: The Maharsha notes that it would appear that these two objections stand in direct contradiction to one another. If the objection derived from the *halakha* of a widow were truly compelling, then it would be unnecessary to have a scriptural derivation from the phrase "she is an abomination" to teach that her children have unflawed lineage; that derivation is necessary only to counter the import of the *a fortiori* inference. The Maharsha suggests that it is possible that the one who raised these objections did in fact believe that the objection derived from the *halakha* of a widow is conclusive. He understood that the objection is not contradicted by the subsequent derivation from the phrase: "She is an abomination" because, as the Gemara later suggests, there are other ways to expound the verse. Nevertheless, he cites the derivation from the verse because he reasoned that even if the derivation from the *halakha* of a widow were flawed, then it is still possible to raise the objection from the verse. The *Keren Ora* suggests that the *a fortiori* inference teaches in general about all cases for which one is liable for violating a prohibition, not only the case of one who remarries his divorcée. With regard to one who remarries his divorcée there is an independent reason to assume that the offspring would have flawed lineage because the verse describes the union as "impure" (Deuteronomy 24:4). Therefore, it was necessary to refute both reasons in order to prove that the offspring's lineage would be unflawed.

She remains fit and her child is fit – הִיא כְּשֵׁרָה וּוְלָדָהּ כָּשֵׁר: Some of the early commentaries claim that in all these cases, the woman and her daughter from the forbidden union would even be fit to eat *teruma* if they were to marry a priest or are the daughters of a priest. This is because the verse describing the qualification to eat *teruma* excludes only a woman who had relations with a "common man" (Leviticus 22:12), meaning one who was always forbidden to her, whereas in these cases the man was not initially forbidden to her (*Tosafot*; Rid). However, Rabbeinu Ḥananel claims that in the case of one who remarries his divorcée, the woman and her daughter are rendered unfit to eat *teruma*. This opinion is also found explicitly in the Jerusalem Talmud. The Maharam MiRotenburg explains that this is because the verse describes that union as "impure" (Deuteronomy 24:4).

HALAKHA

One who remarries his divorcée – הַמַּחֲזִיר גְּרוּשָׁתוֹ: It is prohibited to remarry one's divorcée after she had been married or betrothed to another man. This applies even if she had not engaged in intercourse with the other man. If one violates the prohibition, he is flogged and forced to divorce his wife. Nevertheless, she remains fit and her children are fit. This is in accordance with the opinion of the Rabbis (Rambam *Sefer Nashim*, *Hilkhot Geirushin* 11:12).

NOTES

She is an abomination but her rival wife is not an abomination – הִיא תּוֹעֵבָה וְאֵין צָרָתָהּ תּוֹעֵבָה: The commentaries ask: How would Rabbi Akiva interpret the restrictive implication of the word "she" in the verse: "She is an abomination" (Deuteronomy 24:4)? He is unable to interpret it in either manner suggested by the Gemara: It cannot be teaching about a rival wife because according to Rabbi Akiva, betrothal of a woman forbidden by a standard prohibition does not take effect. Therefore, she cannot have the status of a wife herself, and consequently she cannot have a rival wife. Furthermore, it cannot come to teach that the lineage of the offspring is unflawed, because according to Rabbi Akiva they are *mamzerim*. Some suggest that since the Gemara uses this verse to derive the *halakhot* of a *sota* as well, Rabbi Akiva could claim that the verse comes to exclude the case of a rival wife of a *sota* (*Tosafot Yeshanim*) or to exclude the offspring of a *sota* from having flawed lineage (*Tosefot HaRosh*).

וּמִדְּהִיא לִכְהוּנָּה – וְלָדָהּ נַמִי לִכְהוּנָּה. מִידֵי אִירְיָא? הָא כִּדְאִיתָא וְהָא כִּדְאִיתָא.

The Gemara suggests: **And since** in reference **to her** the word fit in the *baraita* means fit **for the priesthood,** it follows that for **the child as well,** the word fit means fit **for the priesthood.** The Gemara objects: **Are these cases comparable? This** case is **as it is, and that** case is **as it is,** and although the two cases are juxtaposed in the *baraita* they need not be relating to the same issue. Rather, when referring to the mother the *baraita* mentions fitness for the priesthood, and when referring to the child it mentions fitness for the congregation of Israel.

הָכִי נַמִי מִסְתַּבְּרָא, דְּקָתָנֵי רֵישָׁא: הִיא פְּסוּלָה וּוְלָדָהּ פָּסוּל. הִיא פְּסוּלָה לְמַאן? אִילֵימָא לַקָּהָל – מִשּׁוּם דִּזְנַיָּא אִפַּסְלָה לֵיהּ לַקָּהָל? אֶלָּא לָאו – לִכְהוּנָּה,

The Gemara notes: **So, too, it is reasonable** to assume that the two clauses concern different issues, **as the first clause teaches** in the name of Rabbi Akiva: **She is unfit and her child is unfit.** When that first clause states: **She is unfit, to whom** is she unfit to be married? **If we say** it is **to the congregation** of Israel, could it be that **because she engaged in forbidden sexual relations she is rendered unfit to** marry into **the congregation** of Israel? **Rather, is it not** that the intention that she is rendered unfit **to** marry into **the priesthood?**

וּוְלָדָהּ פָּסוּל, לְמַאן? אִילֵימָא לִכְהוּנָּה – הָא לַקָּהָל כָּשֵׁר? הָאֲמַר רַבִּי עֲקִיבָא הַוָּלָד מַמְזֵר! אֶלָּא פְּשִׁיטָא – לַקָּהָל,

And then when the first clause continues and states: **And her child is unfit, to whom** is she unfit to be married? **If we say** that it is **to** the **priesthood, that** would imply that the child **is fit to** marry into **the congregation** of Israel. However, this is untenable because **didn't Rabbi Akiva** himself **say** in the mishna here that **the offspring is a** ***mamzer*** and is unfit from entering the congregation of Israel? **Rather, it is obvious** that the intention of the *baraita* is that the child is unfit even **to** marry into **the congregation** of Israel.

וּמִדְּרֵישָׁא הָא כִּדְאִיתָא וְהָא כִּדְאִיתָא – סֵיפָא נַמִי הָא כִּדְאִיתָא וְהָא כִּדְאִיתָא.

And since in **the first clause** of the *baraita* it is apparent that, although two cases are juxtaposed, **this** case is **as it is and that** case is **as it is,** in **the latter clause as well** one should assume that **this** case is **as it is and that** case is **as it is.**

וְ״הִיא תוֹעֵבָה״ נַמִי, הִיא תוֹעֵבָה – וְאֵין צָרָתָהּ תּוֹעֵבָה, אֲבָל בָּנֶיהָ – תּוֹעֲבִין.

Having resolved the objection raised from the *baraita,* the Gemara returns to its preceding objection: **And** the objection raised from the verse: **"She is an abomination,"** in which the Gemara suggested that the emphasis on "she" teaches that only she is an abomination but her children are not, can **also** be resolved, as the emphasis on "she" could be interpreted differently to teach: **"She is an abomination" but her rival wife is not an abomination,**[N] and if they both fell together for levirate marriage, the *yavam* may consummate the levirate marriage with her rival wife. **However,** it is possible that **her children are** in fact **abominations** and are unfit to marry into the priesthood.

אֶלָּא אַלְמָנָה קַשְׁיָא: מַה לְאַלְמָנָה שֶׁכֵּן הִיא עַצְמָהּ מִתְחַלֶּלֶת!

The Gemara concludes: **However,** although two of the objections were resolved, the objection to the logic of the *a fortiori* inference from the case of **a widow** remains **difficult,** as the Gemara noted earlier: **What** is true with regard **to a widow, where** her union with a High Priest is what makes **her herself disqualified** from subsequently marrying any priest and, if she is the daughter of a priest, from eating *teruma*, is not true with regard to a remarried divorcée, where her remarriage to another man is permitted and is not the cause of any further disqualification. Therefore, there is no basis for assuming that the child of one who remarries his divorcée after she had been married to another man will have flawed lineage.

אֶלָּא אִי אִתְּמַר הָכִי אִתְּמַר: אָמַר רַב יוֹסֵף אָמַר רַבִּי שִׁמְעוֹן בְּרַבִּי: הַכֹּל מוֹדִים בְּבָא עַל חַיָּיבֵי כְּרֵיתוֹת שֶׁהַוָּלָד פָּגוּם. מַאן ״הַכֹּל מוֹדִים״ – רַבִּי יְהוֹשֻׁעַ, דְּאַף עַל גַּב דְּאָמַר רַבִּי יְהוֹשֻׁעַ אֵין מַמְזֵר מֵחַיָּיבֵי כְּרֵיתוֹת, נְהִי דְּמַמְזֵר לָא הָוֵי – פָּגוּם מִיהָא הָוֵי,

Rather, if this **was stated,** it **was stated as follows: Rav Yosef said** that **Rabbi Shimon, son of Rabbi** Yehuda HaNasi, **said: All agree with regard to one who engages in intercourse with** a forbidden relation **for which one is liable to** receive ***karet*** **that the offspring has flawed** lineage. The Gemara clarifies: **Who** is included by saying: **All agree?** It is **Rabbi Yehoshua, as although Rabbi Yehoshua said** in the mishna (49b) **that** the offspring born **from** a union **for which one is liable to** receive ***karet*** **is not a** ***mamzer,*** nevertheless, **granted** that Rabbi Yehoshua holds that **he is not a** ***mamzer;*** he would agree, **however,** that **he is of flawed** lineage.

מִקַּל וָחוֹמֶר מֵאַלְמָנָה. וּמָה אַלְמָנָה לְכֹהֵן גָּדוֹל, שֶׁאֵין אִיסּוּרָהּ שָׁוֶה בַּכֹּל – בְּנָהּ פָּגוּם, זוֹ שֶׁאִיסּוּרָהּ שָׁוֶה בַּכֹּל – אֵינוֹ דִּין שֶׁבְּנָהּ פָּגוּם?

This is derived **through an *a fortiori* inference from** the *halakha* of a **widow,** as follows: **Just as** in the case of **a widow** who is married **to High Priest, where the prohibition** that pertains **to her is not equally applicable to all,** i.e., only a High Priest is prohibited from marrying a widow, and nevertheless **her child** from that union will **have flawed** lineage, then so too with regard to **this** woman, **where the prohibition** that pertains **to her is equally applicable to all** Jews, **isn't it logical that her child** from that union should **have flawed** lineage?

וְכִי תֵּימָא: מָה לְאַלְמָנָה שֶׁכֵּן הִיא עַצְמָהּ מִתְחַלֶּלֶת – הָכָא נַמִי, כֵּיוָן שֶׁבְּעָלָהּ – עֲשָׂאָהּ זוֹנָה.

And if you would say that the logic of this *a fortiori* inference could be refuted in a manner similar to the suggestion above that **what** is true with regard **to a widow, who is herself disqualified** from marrying a priest, is not true with regard to a woman who is forbidden by a prohibition for which one is liable to *karet*, that is not correct because **here, too, once he has engaged in intercourse with her he renders her a *zona*,** and as such she is disqualified from marrying into the priesthood.

אָמַר רַבָּה בַּר בַּר חָנָה אָמַר רַבִּי יוֹחָנָן: הַכֹּל מוֹדִים בְּעֶבֶד וְגוֹי הַבָּא עַל בַּת יִשְׂרָאֵל שֶׁהַוָּלָד מַמְזֵר.

§ The Gemara considers the status of other children born from forbidden unions: **Rabba bar bar Ḥana said** that **Rabbi Yoḥanan said: All agree with regard to a slave**[N] **or a gentile who engaged in intercourse with a Jewish woman that the offspring** born from such a union **is a *mamzer*.**

מַאן "הַכֹּל מוֹדִים" שִׁמְעוֹן הַתִּימְנִי. דְּאַף עַל גַּב דְּאָמַר שִׁמְעוֹן הַתִּימְנִי אֵין מַמְזֵר מֵחַיָּיבֵי לָאוִין – הָנֵי מִילֵּי

The Gemara clarifies: **Who** is included by saying: **All agree?** It is **Shimon HaTimni, as although Shimon HaTimni said** that the offspring of relations for **which one is liable for** violating **a prohibition is not a *mamzer*, this applies** only

NOTES

All agree with regard to a slave, etc. – **הַכֹּל מוֹדִים בְּעֶבֶד וכו׳**: The early commentaries point out that the inclusive phrase: All agree, should not be understood as including Rabbi Yehoshua. This is because even if it could be proven that Rabbi Yehoshua holds that betrothal is ineffective when performed with relatives who are forbidden by a prohibition for which one is liable to *karet*, nevertheless, he would still hold that the offspring of such unions are not *mamzerim*. Accordingly, in the case of a union with a gentile or a slave, who are entirely excluded from the possibility of betrothal, he would certainly hold that the offspring would not be *mamzerim* (see *Tosafot*, *Tosafot Yeshanim*, and Ramban).

Perek **IV**
Daf **45** Amud **a**

מֵחַיָּיבֵי לָאוִין דְּתָפְסִי בְּהוּ קִדּוּשִׁין, אֲבָל הָכָא – גּוֹי וְעֶבֶד, כֵּיוָן דְּלָא תָּפְסִי בְּהוּ קִדּוּשִׁין – כְּחַיָּיבֵי כְּרֵיתוֹת דָּמֵי.

to forbidden relations **for which one is liable for** violation of **a prohibition** concerning **which a betrothal** between the couple **would take effect. However, here,** with regard to **a gentile and a slave, since their betrothal** of a Jewish woman **would not take effect,**[NH] a union with them **is comparable to** forbidden relations **for which one is liable to** receive ***karet,*** and therefore the offspring of such a union will be a *mamzer*.

מֵיתִיבֵי: גּוֹי וְעֶבֶד הַבָּא עַל בַּת יִשְׂרָאֵל – הַוָּלָד מַמְזֵר, רַבִּי שִׁמְעוֹן בֶּן יְהוּדָה אוֹמֵר: אֵין מַמְזֵר אֶלָּא מִמִּי שֶׁאִיסּוּרוֹ אִיסּוּר עֶרְוָה, וְעָנוּשׁ כָּרֵת.

The Gemara **raises an objection** from a *baraita*: In the case of **a gentile or a slave who engaged in intercourse with a Jewish woman, the offspring** born from such a union **is a *mamzer*. Rabbi Shimon ben Yehuda says:** The offspring is **a *mamzer* only** if born **from** relations with **one who is forbidden by a prohibition of forbidden relations** that are **punishable by *karet*.** It is apparent from the *baraita* that one who holds, as does Shimon HaTimni, that only the offspring from forbidden relations for which one is liable to receive *karet* is a *mamzer*, nevertheless holds that the offspring of a slave or gentile and a Jewish woman is not a *mamzer*.

אֶלָּא אָמַר רַב יוֹסֵף: מַאן "הַכֹּל מוֹדִים" – רַבִּי. אַף עַל גַּב דְּרַבִּי אוֹמֵר: אֵין הַדְּבָרִים הַלָּלוּ אֲמוּרִים אֶלָּא לְדִבְרֵי רַבִּי עֲקִיבָא, שֶׁהָיָה עוֹשֶׂה חֲלוּצָה כְּעֶרְוָה, וְלֵיהּ לָא סְבִירָא לֵיהּ – בְּגוֹי וְעֶבֶד מוֹדֶה. דְּכִי אֲתָא רַב דִּימִי אָמַר רַב יִצְחָק בַּר אֲבוּדִימִי מִשּׁוּם רַבֵּינוּ: גּוֹי וְעֶבֶד הַבָּא עַל בַּת יִשְׂרָאֵל – הַוָּלָד מַמְזֵר.

Rather, Rav Yosef said: Who is included by saying: **All agree?** It is **Rabbi** Yehuda HaNasi, as **although Rabbi** Yehuda HaNasi **says** in a *baraita* (52b) concerning the mishna (50a–51b) that states that a levirate betrothal between a *yavam* and a *yevama* with whom he had already performed *ḥalitza* is ineffective: **This statement was said only according to the statement of Rabbi Akiva, as he would consider a *ḥalutza* like a forbidden relative** such that if the *yavam* betrothed her it would not take effect. **And** although Rabbi Yehuda HaNasi **himself does not hold accordingly** with regard to that issue, **with regard to** the offspring of a union with **a gentile or a slave he concedes** that the offspring is a *mamzer*. **As, when Rav Dimi came** from Eretz Yisrael, he said that **Rav Yitzḥak bar Avudimi said in the name of our Master,** i.e., Rabbi Yehuda HaNasi: With regard to **a gentile or a slave who engaged in intercourse with a Jewish woman, the offspring is a *mamzer*.**

NOTES

The betrothal of a gentile or a slave with a Jewish woman does not take effect – **נָכְרִי וְעֶבֶד לָא תָּפְסִי בְּהוּ קִדּוּשִׁין**: The early commentaries offer various proofs that the betrothal of a gentile or a slave with a Jewish woman is ineffective. With regard to a slave, Rashi cites the homiletic derivation of the verse in which Abraham instructs his slave attendants to "remain here with [*im*] the ass" (Genesis 22:5), to indicate that slaves are considered to be a people [*am*] that is comparable to an ass in that their betrothal is entirely ineffective. With regard to a gentile, he cites the case of the gentile female prisoner of war (see Deuteronomy 21:10–14), from which it is clear that there is no possibility of betrothing her prior to her conversion. See Rashi for additional proofs that he cites in the name of the *She'iltot deRav Aḥai Gaon*. The Ramban also cites an additional proof from the *Mekhilta*: A gentile maidservant may be given to a Hebrew slave in order for them to bear children for their master. When eventually the Hebrew slave goes free, he does not take the gentile maidservant with him; rather, she remains as a slave. The *Mekhilta* demonstrates from here that no marital bond could have existed between them. Through a verbal analogy, the *Mekhilta* derives that the same is true of a gentile.

HALAKHA

Betrothal does not apply to a gentile or a slave – **אֵין קִדּוּשִׁין בְּנָכְרִי וְעֶבֶד**: If a gentile or a slave betroths a Jewish woman, the betrothal does not take effect at all. Similarly, if a Jew betroths a gentile woman or a maidservant, the betrothal does not take effect (Rambam *Sefer Nashim*, *Hilkhot Ishut* 4:15; *Shulḥan Arukh*, *Even HaEzer* 44:8).

רַבִּי אַחָא שַׂר הַבִּירָה וְרַבִּי תַּנְחוּם בְּרֵיהּ דְּרַבִּי חִיָּיא אִישׁ כְּפַר עַכּוֹ פְּרוּק הָנְהוּ שְׁבוּיָיתָא דְּאָתוּ מֵאַרְמוֹן לְטִבֶרְיָא. הֲוָה חֲדָא דְּאִיעַבְּרָא מִגּוֹי, וַאֲתוּ לְקַמֵּיהּ דְּרַבִּי אַמִי. אֲמַר לְהוּ: רַבִּי יוֹחָנָן וְרַבִּי אֶלְעָזָר וְרַבִּי חֲנִינָא דְּאָמְרִי, גּוֹי וְעֶבֶד הַבָּא עַל בַּת יִשְׂרָאֵל הַוָּלָד מַמְזֵר.

The Gemara cites a related incident: **Rabbi Aḥa, lord of the capital,**[P] **and Rabbi Tanḥum, son of Rabbi Ḥiyya, the man of Akko village, redeemed those captives who came from Armon**[B] **to Tiberias. One of them had been impregnated by a gentile, and they came before Rabbi Ami** to ask what the offspring's status would be when born. **He said to them that Rabbi Yoḥanan and Rabbi Elazar and Rabbi Ḥanina** all **say:** With regard to **a gentile or a slave who engaged in intercourse with a Jewish woman, the offspring is a** ***mamzer*****.**

אֲמַר רַב יוֹסֵף: רְבוּתָא לְמִחֲשַׁב גַּבְרֵי?! הָא רַב וּשְׁמוּאֵל בְּבָבֶל, וְרַבִּי יְהוֹשֻׁעַ בֶּן לֵוִי וּבַר קַפָּרָא בְּאֶרֶץ יִשְׂרָאֵל, וְאָמְרִי לָהּ: חִלּוּפֵי בַּר קַפָּרָא וְעַיְּילֵי זִקְנֵי דָּרוֹם, דְּאָמְרִי: גּוֹי וְעֶבֶד הַבָּא עַל בַּת יִשְׂרָאֵל – הַוָּלָד כָּשֵׁר.

Upon hearing this, **Rav Yosef said: Is it so great to enumerate men?** The fact that several great Sages held this opinion does not prove that their opinion is the accepted *halakha*. **But** there are **Rav and Shmuel in Babylonia, and Rabbi Yehoshua ben Levi and bar Kappara in Eretz Yisrael, and some say to remove bar Kappara** from this list **and insert** instead **the Elders of the South, who** all **say:** With regard to **a gentile or a slave who engaged in intercourse with a Jewish woman,** the lineage of **the offspring is unflawed,** and he or she may marry into the congregation of Israel.

אֶלָּא אֲמַר רַב יוֹסֵף: רַבִּי הִיא. דְּכִי אֲתָא רַב דִּימִי אֲמַר רַבִּי יִצְחָק בַּר אֲבוּדִימִי מִשּׁוּם רַבֵּינוּ אָמְרוּ: גּוֹי וְעֶבֶד הַבָּא עַל בַּת יִשְׂרָאֵל – הַוָּלָד מַמְזֵר.

Rather, Rav Yosef said the *halakha* is in fact that the offspring is a *mamzer* because this **is Rabbi** Yehuda HaNasi's opinion, **as when Rav Dimi came** from Eretz Yisrael he said that **Rav Yitzḥak bar Avudimi said in the name of our Master,** i.e., Rabbi Yehuda HaNasi, that **they say:** With regard to **a gentile or a slave who engaged in intercourse with a Jewish woman, the offspring is a** ***mamzer*****.**

רַבִּי יְהוֹשֻׁעַ בֶּן לֵוִי אוֹמֵר: הַוָּלָד מְקוּלְקָל. לְמַאן? אִילֵימָא לַקָּהָל – הָא אֲמַר רַבִּי יְהוֹשֻׁעַ הַוָּלָד כָּשֵׁר, אֶלָּא לִכְהוּנָּה – דְּכוּלְּהוּ אֲמוֹרָאֵי דְּמַכְשְׁרֵי מוֹדוּ שֶׁהַוָּלָד פָּגוּם לִכְהוּנָּה.

Rabbi Yehoshua ben Levi says: The lineage of **the offspring is sullied,** and if the child is a girl she is restricted in whom she may marry. The Gemara asks: **To whom** is she prohibited from marrying? **If we say** it is **to the congregation** of Israel, but **didn't Rabbi Yehoshua** himself **say** that the lineage of **the offspring is unflawed** and he or she may marry into the congregation of Israel? **Rather,** the offspring is prohibited **to** marry into **the priesthood, as all of the** ***amora'im*** **who render** the offspring **fit** to enter the congregation of Israel **agree that the offspring has flawed** lineage and is forbidden **to** marry into **the priesthood.**[NH]

מִקַּל וָחוֹמֶר מֵאַלְמָנָה: מָה אַלְמָנָה לְכֹהֵן גָּדוֹל, שֶׁאֵין אִיסּוּרָהּ שָׁוֶה בַּכֹּל – בְּנָהּ פָּגוּם, זוֹ שֶׁאִיסּוּרָהּ שָׁוֶה בַּכֹּל – אֵינוֹ דִּין שֶׁבְּנָהּ פָּגוּם.

This is derived **from an** ***a fortiori*** inference **from** the *halakha* of **a widow,** as follows: **Just as** in the case of **a widow** who is married **to a High Priest, where the prohibition** that pertains **to her is not equally applicable to all** Jews, i.e., only a High Priest is prohibited from marrying a widow, and nevertheless **her child** from that union will **have flawed** lineage, then so too with regard to **this** woman who engaged in relations with a gentile or slave, **where the prohibition** that pertains **to her is equally applicable to all** Jews, **isn't it logical that her child** from that union will **have flawed** lineage?[N]

מַה לְּאַלְמָנָה לְכֹהֵן גָּדוֹל שֶׁכֵּן הִיא עַצְמָהּ מִתְחַלֶּלֶת! הָכָא נַמִי, כֵּיוָן שֶׁנִּבְעֲלָה פְּסָלָהּ.

And if one would say that the logic of this *a fortiori* inference could be refuted by claiming that **what** is true with regard **to a widow** who is married **to a High Priest, where** her union with him is what makes **her herself disqualified** from subsequently marrying any priest and, if she is the daughter of a priest, from eating *teruma*, is not true with regard to the prohibition against a Jewish woman engaging in relations with a gentile or a slave. This is not correct, because **here, too, once he has engaged in intercourse with her,**[H] **he** thereby **renders her unfit** to marry into the priesthood.

PERSONALITIES

Rabbi Aḥa, lord of the capital – רַבִּי אַחָא שַׂר הַבִּירָה: This Rabbi Aḥa was a third-generation *amora* of Eretz Yisrael, and very little is known about his teachers. Apparently there was also a fifth-generation *tanna* in Eretz Yisrael of the same name; they may have been related.

Some explain that the title: Lord of the capital, was based on a family legacy, and that one of his ancestors had been the minister appointed over the capital, i.e., the Temple Mount in Jerusalem.

BACKGROUND

Armon – אַרְמוֹן: Some say that Armon is the name of a place in Eretz Yisrael, possibly Kadesh Naftali. Others suggest that Armon is the Hebraic rendition of the country Armenia. It is reasonable to assume that these captives came from a distant place because it is known that captors would bring Jewish captives from remote locations to Tiberias, at that point the main city of Eretz Yisrael, since the Jewish community there would take great efforts to redeem them.

NOTES

The offspring has flawed lineage and is prohibited from marrying into the priesthood – הַוָּלָד פָּגוּם לִכְהוּנָּה: The early commentaries debate whether this ruling is accepted as *halakha*. Most commentaries hold, based on the Gemara's *a fortiori* inference from the *halakha* of a widow, that a daughter of a gentile or slave with a Jewish woman would certainly be unfit to marry into the priesthood. This also appears to be the conclusion in the Jerusalem Talmud. However, a son from such a union would not be rendered unfit in any way, such that even if he were to father a daughter with a Jewish woman, that daughter would be fit to marry into the priesthood.

Other commentaries disagree and claim that even the daughter of the gentile or slave would be considered fit to marry into the priesthood. They bring support for their opinion from the conclusion of the Gemara's discussion, which states simply that the offspring of a gentile or slave and a Jewish woman is considered fit, without making any further distinctions. They reject the implication of the *a fortiori* inference because according to it, the woman should be rendered a *ḥalala*, who is unfit to marry a priest, and they hold that ultimately the *halakha* is that a woman can be rendered a *ḥalala* only in cases where there is a violation of one of the prohibitions that are unique to the priesthood (see *Yam shel Shlomo*). Some explain that even if the woman who engaged in intercourse with the gentile or slave is disqualified by doing so, the offspring will not be, because the offspring of a gentile with a Jewish woman is never halakhically recognized as relating to him. Since the offspring is not considered to be descended from him it cannot be disqualified on his account (Ritva).

Isn't it logical that her child [*benah*] from that union will have flawed lineage – אֵינוֹ דִּין שֶׁבְּנָהּ פָּגוּם: Rashi and Rivan both note that although the Gemara says *benah*, which literally means: Her son, it should be taken as meaning her child, and the intention is actually a daughter who will be rendered unfit to marry into the priesthood. However, others suggest that the Gemara can be understood as referring to a son. Although normally the status of *ḥalal*, one whose flawed lineage disqualifies him from the priesthood, is applied only to a descendant of a priest, in this case the son would be rendered unfit to the same extent as a *ḥalal* such that if he were to father a daughter with another Jewish woman, that daughter would be unfit to marry into the priesthood.

HALAKHA

The offspring has flawed lineage and is prohibited from marrying into the priesthood – הַוָּלָד פָּגוּם לִכְהוּנָּה: Although the offspring of a gentile or slave who engaged in intercourse with a Jewish woman is fit to marry into the congregation of Israel, if the offspring is a daughter then she is prohibited from marrying a priest. This is in accordance with the Gemara here and several other places where it is stated that this fact is unanimously accepted. Some (Rif; Ramban; Rambam, as explained by *Maggid Mishne*) rule that she is not unfit to marry into the priesthood. Therefore, later commentaries (*Beit Shmuel*; *Ḥelkat Meḥokek*) rule that if the daughter went and married a priest then this lenient opinion may be relied upon, and they need not divorce (Rambam *Sefer Kedusha, Hilkhot Issurei Bia* 15:4; *Shulḥan Arukh, Even HaEzer* 4:4–5, 19; 7:17).

A gentile who engaged in intercourse with a Jewish woman – נָכְרִי הַבָּא עַל בַּת יִשְׂרָאֵל: If a gentile or slave engaged in intercourse with a Jewish woman, she becomes a *zona* and is therefore prohibited from marrying into the priesthood (Rambam *Sefer Kedusha, Hilkhot Issurei Bia* 18:2; *Shulḥan Arukh, Even HaEzer* 6:8).

דְּאָמַר רַבִּי יוֹחָנָן מִשּׁוּם רַבִּי שִׁמְעוֹן: מִנַּיִן לְגוֹי וְעֶבֶד הַבָּא עַל הַכֹּהֶנֶת וְעַל הַלְוִיָּה וְעַל הַיִּשְׂרְאֵלִית שֶׁפְּסָלוּהָ – שֶׁנֶּאֱמַר "וּבַת כֹּהֵן כִּי תִהְיֶה אַלְמָנָה וּגְרוּשָׁה", מִי שֶׁיֵּשׁ לוֹ אַלְמָנוּת וְגֵירוּשִׁין בָּהּ, יָצְאוּ גּוֹי וְעֶבֶד שֶׁאֵין לָהֶם אַלְמָנוּת וְגֵירוּשִׁין בָּהּ.

As Rabbi Yoḥanan said in the name of Rabbi Shimon: From where is it derived with regard **to a gentile or a slave who engaged in intercourse with a daughter of a priest or with a female Levite or with a female Israelite that they** thereby **render her unfit** to marry into the priesthood? **As it is stated: "But a priest's daughter when she will become a widow, or a divorcée,** and have no child, she returns to her father's house as in her youth" (Leviticus 22:13). The verse indicates that she returns to her father's house and enjoys the rights of the priesthood only in a case where she engaged in intercourse with **one to whom widowhood and divorce can apply,** i.e., one with whom her marriage would be valid and would be broken only through death or divorce. **Excluded** from this is a union with **a gentile or a slave, to whom neither widowhood nor divorce can apply,** as no marriage bond can be formed with them.

אֲמַר לֵיהּ אַבָּיֵי: מַאי חָזֵית דְּסָמְכַתְּ אַדְּרַב דִּימִי? סְמוֹךְ אַדְּרָבִין! דְּכִי אֲתָא רָבִין אָמַר: רַבִּי נָתָן וְרַבִּי יְהוּדָה הַנָּשִׂיא מוֹרִים בָּהּ לְהֶיתֵּירָא, וּמַאן רַבִּי יְהוּדָה הַנָּשִׂיא – רַבִּי.

Abaye said to Rav Yosef: **What did you see that you rely upon Rav Dimi** and his tradition that Rabbi Yehuda HaNasi holds that the offspring of a gentile or a slave and a Jewish woman is a *mamzer*? **Rely** instead **upon Ravin, as when Ravin came** from Eretz Yisrael **he said** that **Rabbi Natan and Rabbi Yehuda HaNasi** both **rule** that the offspring is **permitted** to marry into the congregation of Israel. **And who is** the **Rabbi Yehuda HaNasi** referred to in Ravin's report? It is the one who is simply referred to as **Rabbi,** the redactor of the Mishna, whose opinion is accepted as the *halakha*.

וְאַף רַב מוֹרֶה בָּהּ לְהֶיתֵּירָא, דְּהַהוּא דַּאֲתָא לְקַמֵּיהּ דְּרַב, אֲמַר לֵיהּ: גּוֹי וְעֶבֶד הַבָּא עַל בַּת יִשְׂרָאֵל מַהוּ?

The Gemara notes: **And even Rav rules** that the offspring is **permitted, as** is evident from an incident involving **a certain** individual **who came before Rav** and **said to him:** With regard to the offspring of **a gentile or a slave who engaged in intercourse with a Jewish woman,**[H] **what is** its halakhic status?

אֲמַר לוֹ: הַוָּלָד כָּשֵׁר. אֲמַר לֵיהּ: הַב לִי בְּרַתָּךְ! לָא יָהֵיבְנָא לָךְ.

Rav **said to him:** The lineage of **the offspring is unflawed.** The individual who asked the question was himself such a child, and **he said to** Rav: If so, **give me your daughter** in marriage. He said to him: **I will not give** her **to you.**

אֲמַר שִׁימִי בַּר חִיָּיא לְרַב: אָמְרִי אֱינָשֵׁי: גַּמְלָא בְּמָדַי אַקַּבָּא רָקְדָא, הָא קַבָּא וְהָא גַּמְלָא וְהָא מָדַי – וְלָא רָקְדָא!

Shimi bar Ḥiyya,[P] Rav's grandson, **said to Rav: People** often **say** that **a camel in Medes**[NB] can **dance upon** a small space that holds only a single *kav* of produce. However, clearly that is an exaggeration, since if one would go to Medes one could demonstrate that **this is** a space that holds a ***kav*, and this is a camel, and this is Medes, and** yet the camel **is not dancing,**[N] i.e., the truth of a statement becomes apparent when it is put to the test. So too, it would appear that you do not truly believe in your ruling because when put to the test, you are unwilling to rely on it.

אֲמַר לֵיהּ: אִי נֶיהֱוֵי כִּיהוֹשֻׁעַ בִּן נוּן לָא יָהֵיבְנָא לֵיהּ בְּרַתִּי. אֲמַר לֵיהּ: אִי הֲוָה כִּיהוֹשֻׁעַ בִּן נוּן, אִי מָר לָא יָהֵיב לֵיהּ – אַחֲרִינֵי יָהֲבֵי לֵיהּ. הַאי, אִי מָר לָא יָהֵיב לֵיהּ – אַחֲרִינֵי לָא יָהֲבֵי לֵיהּ.

He said to him: Even **if he were as** great as **Joshua, son of Nun, I would not give him**[N] **my daughter** in marriage. My refusal to give her to him in marriage is not that I do not stand by my ruling; it is for other reasons. **He said to him: If he were as** great as **Joshua, son of Nun,** then even **if the Master would not give him** his daughter, **others would** still **give him** their daughters. However, with regard to **this** man, **if the Master does not give him** his daughter, **others will not give him** their daughters either out of fear of damaging the family lineage. Nevertheless, Rav remained unwilling to give his daughter to that individual.

HALAKHA

A gentile or slave who engaged in intercourse with a Jewish woman – גּוֹי וְעֶבֶד הַבָּא עַל בַּת יִשְׂרָאֵל: With regard to a gentile or slave who engaged in intercourse with a Jewish woman, the offspring of such a union is fit to enter into the congregation of Israel, irrespective of whether the woman was married or unmarried and whether the intercourse was consensual or forced (Rambam *Sefer Kedusha, Hilkhot Issurei Bia* 15:3; *Shulḥan Arukh, Even HaEzer* 4:5, 19).

NOTES

A camel in Medes, etc. – גַּמְלָא בְּמָדַי וכו׳: The Rivan interprets this to mean that the camels there are so well trained that they can stand with all four legs on a space that holds one *kav*. The Meiri explains that it means that the camels there are so small that they can stand inside of a space that holds one *kav*. See the *Arukh LaNer*, who explains how this imagery alludes to a deeper meaning.

This is a *kav*…and it is not dancing – הָא קַבָּא...וְלָא רָקְדָא: One commentary explains that the man who asked the question was himself a Torah scholar and that is why Rav Shimi bar Ḥiyya wanted to intervene on his behalf. He brings support for his claim from the fact that Rav compared the man to the biblical Joshua, which, at the very least, suggests that he was an important figure in his own right (Ya'avetz).

I would not give him – לָא יָהֵיבְנָא לֵיהּ: Some explain that Rav's hesitance was because he did not want to introduce anyone with flawed lineage into his family. Possibly he believed that the son of a gentile is unfit for the priesthood; alternatively, Rav considered the very fact that one is descended from a gentile to be a flaw, even if there are no associated prohibitions with that flaw (see Rivan). Others explain that his concerns had nothing to do with the man's lineage but were due to an entirely unrelated issue.

BACKGROUND

A camel in Medes – גַּמְלָא בְּמָדַי: In talmudic literature, Medes is often used as an example of a distant, unknown land. This example was first used in the period of the Mishna, when Medes was far from the Jewish center of life in Eretz Yisrael. Later, when the Jewish community was centered in Babylonia, the example continued to be used despite the fact that Medes is actually near Babylonia.

PERSONALITIES

Shimi bar Ḥiyya – שִׁימִי בַּר חִיָּיא: Rav Shimi bar Ḥiyya was among the second-generation *amora'im* of Babylonia. He was a grandson of Rav and apparently his preeminent disciple and much beloved by him. Even during his grandfather's lifetime, Rav Shimi was recognized as a significant Torah scholar. The Talmud records numerous halakhic teachings of his, both those he transmitted in the name of his grandfather and those of his own. In certain cases he even disagreed with the rulings of his grandfather. Given their close familial relationship, it is clear why here he allowed himself to address Rav in such an informal manner.

BACKGROUND

He placed his eyes upon him and he died – יָהֵיב בֵּיהּ עֵינֵיהּ וּשְׁכִיב: This concept is mentioned in the Talmud on a number of occasions. The *Or HaḤayyim* on Exodus 11:5 and 23:23 explains that when a righteous person looks at others he can draw out the sparks of holiness that each individual has, and if that individual does not have any other merits to stay alive, he might die as a result. This explanation might be challenged from the fact that the Talmud cites a similar event with Rav Sheshet (*Berakhot* 58b), despite the fact that he was blind. In the *Iggeret HaKodesh* (attributed to the Ramban) it is explained that the word eyes does not literally refer to eyes but rather to the thought process of a righteous person, which can affect other people for good or bad.

לָא הֲוָה קָאָזֵיל מִקַּמֵּיהּ, יָהֵיב בֵּיהּ עֵינֵיהּ וּשְׁכִיב.

That individual **would not go from** standing **before** Rav and continued to plead with him. Rav **placed his eyes upon him and he died.**[B]

וְאַף רַב מַתָּנָה מוֹרֶה בָּהּ לְהֶיתֵּירָא, וְאַף רַב יְהוּדָה מוֹרֶה בָּהּ לְהֶיתֵּירָא. דְּכִי אֲתָא לְקַמֵּיהּ דְּרַב יְהוּדָה אָמַר לֵיהּ: זִיל אִיטְמַר, אוֹ נְסֵיב בַּת מִינָךְ. וְכִי אֲתָא לְקַמֵּיהּ דְּרָבָא אָמַר לֵיהּ: אוֹ גְּלֵי, אוֹ נְסֵיב בַּת מִינָךְ.

The Gemara adds: **And even Rav Mattana rules** that the offspring is **permitted, and even Rav Yehuda rules** that the offspring is **permitted, as** is evident from the fact that **when** a child of a gentile or slave and a Jewish woman **came before Rav Yehuda, he said to him: Go** and **conceal** your paternal lineage[N] so that people will not refrain from giving you their daughters in marriage, as it is permitted for you to marry into the congregation of Israel, **or** otherwise, **marry** a woman **of your own kind,** i.e., a woman of similar lineage. **And** similarly, **when** such a person **came before Rava, he said to him: Either go into exile**[N] to a place where your lineage is unknown, so that others will give you their daughters in marriage, **or marry a woman of your own kind.**

שְׁלַחוּ לֵיהּ בְּנֵי בֵּי מִיכְסֵי לְרַבָּה: מִי שֶׁחֶצְיוֹ עֶבֶד וְחֶצְיוֹ בֶּן חוֹרִין הַבָּא עַל בַּת יִשְׂרָאֵל מַהוּ? אָמַר לְהוּ: הַשְׁתָּא עֶבֶד כּוּלּוֹ אָמְרִינַן כָּשֵׁר – חֶצְיוֹ מִיבַּעְיָא?

The residents of Bei Mikhsei sent the following question **to Rabba:** With regard to the offspring of **one who is a half-slave half-freeman, who engaged in intercourse with a Jewish woman, what is** its halakhic status? **He said to them: Now** that with regard to the offspring of **a full slave we say** that his lineage is **unflawed, is it necessary** to ask about **a half**-slave?

אָמַר רַב יוֹסֵף: מָרָא דִשְׁמַעְתָּא

Rav Yosef said: The Master who is responsible for dissemination **of this *halakha*** that the offspring of a slave and a Jewish woman is not a *mamzer*,

NOTES

Go and conceal your paternal lineage – זִיל אִיטְמַר: Evidently, Rav Yehuda maintains that the child of a gentile and a Jewish woman is fit to marry even a priest, as if this were not the case his advice might lead to a prohibited marriage, since the daughter of this man might mistakenly think that she is eligible to marry a priest as her father did not disclose his lineage (Rashba). However since the *halakha* is that such a child is considered to be of flawed lineage and may not marry a priest (see *Even HaEzer* 4:5 and 4:19), a father would not be allowed to conceal his lineage.

Another issue that arises from Rav Yehuda's advice is the propriety and ramifications of deceptive behavior between potential marriage partners, which Rav Yehuda appears to be encouraging. Apart from the ethical issues involved, doing so might render the betrothal as mistaken, thereby undermining its validity. The *Tzitz Eliezer* (17:48) suggests that Rav Yehuda's suggestion was permitted only at that time, as it was not universally accepted that the offspring of a gentile and a Jewish woman was of unflawed lineage, and there was a need to establish this *halakha* so that such people would be able to marry and would not be rejected even though they are permitted. However, the *Kehillot Ya'akov* (*Yevamot* 44) maintains that not revealing one's flawed lineage is not considered deceptive whenever the marriage itself is permitted. He rationalizes that even if one would respond unfavorably to certain information concerning lineage before the couple is married, it is obvious that once they are happily married they would not divorce over such an issue. Therefore, it cannot be considered a mistaken betrothal, and so the deception should be permitted for the sake of the mitzva to marry. Alternatively, it is possible that Rav Yehuda was merely advising him to go to a place where people do not examine lineage so closely, where he would have a better chance of marrying (see *Tosafot* on 47a).

Go and conceal your lineage…go into exile – זִיל אִיטְמַר...גְּלֵי: The later commentaries attempted to explain why these Sages differed in their choice of language. One explains that the man who asked this question of Rava was famous in his locale and therefore could not conceal his lineage (*Melo HaRo'im*).

מַנּוּ – רַב יְהוּדָה, וְהָא אָמַר רַב יְהוּדָה: מִי שֶׁחֶצְיוֹ עֶבֶד וְחֶצְיוֹ בֶּן חוֹרִין הַבָּא עַל בַּת יִשְׂרָאֵל – אוֹתוֹ וָלָד אֵין לוֹ תַּקָּנָה.

who is he? He is **Rav Yehuda,** as the Gemara cited above. **But didn't Rav Yehuda** himself **say:** With regard to **one who is a half-slave half-freeman**[H] **who engaged in intercourse with a Jewish woman, that offspring** of that union **has no recourse**[N] to be able to marry? It is apparent, then, that even one who permits the offspring of a slave to marry into the congregation of Israel does not permit the offspring of a half-slave to do so, contrary to Rava's assertion.

כִּי אִיתְּמַר דְּרַב יְהוּדָה כְּגוֹן דְּקַדֵּישׁ בַּת יִשְׂרָאֵל, דְּנִמְצָא צַד עַבְדוּת שֶׁבּוֹ מִשְׁתַּמֵּשׁ בְּאֵשֶׁת אִישׁ.

The Gemara resolves the difficulty: **When** this ruling **of Rav Yehuda was stated,** it was referring to a case **where** the half-slave **betrothed a Jewish woman.**[N] Since a slave's betrothal does not take effect, the result of that betrothal is that the woman is married to only the free half of the half-slave half-freeman, such **that it emerges** that when he has relations with her, the **slave side of him is engaging in relations with a married woman** to whom that side of him is not married, and so the offspring of that union is a *mamzer*.

וְהָאָמְרִי נְהַרְדָּעֵי מִשְּׁמֵיהּ דְּרַבִּי יַעֲקֹב: לְדִבְרֵי הַפּוֹסֵל – פּוֹסֵל אֲפִילּוּ בִּפְנוּיָה, לְדִבְרֵי הַמַּכְשִׁיר – מַכְשִׁיר אֲפִילּוּ בְּאֵשֶׁת אִישׁ.

The Gemara raises an objection: **But didn't** the Sages **of Neharde'a say in the name of Rabbi Ya'akov: According to the statement of the one who renders** the child of a gentile or slave and a Jewish woman **unfit** to marry into the congregation of Israel, **he renders** the child **unfit even when** the mother is **an unmarried woman.** And **according to the statement of the one who renders** the child **fit, he renders** the child **fit even when** the mother **is a married woman.**

וּשְׁנֵיהֶם לֹא לְמֵדוּהָ אֶלָּא מֵאֵשֶׁת אָב – מַאן דְּפָסֵיל סָבַר: מָה אֵשֶׁת אָב דְּלָא תָּפְסִי בָּהּ קִדּוּשִׁין [הַוָּלָד מַמְזֵר] – אַף כָּל דְּלָא תָּפְסִי בָּהּ קִדּוּשִׁין הַוָּלָד מַמְזֵר.

And both of them derived their opinions **only from** the *halakha* of one's **father's wife,**[N] as follows: **The one who renders** the child **unfit holds** that **just as** with regard to one's **father's wife,** one's **betrothal of her does not take effect** even after she is widowed or divorced, and so **the offspring** of such a union **is a** ***mamzer*****, so too,** with regard to **any** one for whom **betrothal of her does not take effect,** including a gentile or a slave, **the offspring is a** ***mamzer*****.**

HALAKHA

A half-slave half-freeman – חֶצְיוֹ עֶבֶד וְחֶצְיוֹ בֶּן חוֹרִין: If a half-slave half-freeman engaged in intercourse with a married woman, then the offspring is forbidden both to a Jewish woman and to a maidservant. If the offspring marries a convert, his children will share his status (Rambam *Sefer Kedusha, Hilkhot Issurei Bia* 15:5; *Shulḥan Arukh, Even HaEzer* 4:17).

NOTES

He has no recourse – אֵין לוֹ תַּקָּנָה: Most of the early commentaries explain that there is no one whom this offspring is permitted to marry because his status is half-*mamzer* and half-fit. He is therefore prohibited from marrying a Jewish woman on account of his *mamzer* status but he may also not marry a *mamzeret* due to his fit status. Furthermore, since he is not a gentile or a slave he is forbidden to a maidservant. However, Rashi appears to explain that the offspring will have full *mamzer* status, and therefore he would be permitted to marry a *mamzeret* or a maidservant. Some explain that Rashi's opinion is based on the *halakha* that the status of a *mamzer* status is transferred to his son, even when there is no transgression involved in his conception, e.g., where a *mamzer* married a female convert. It is apparent from that *halakha* that the *mamzer* status is considered dominant and therefore always defines the offspring. So too, in the case here, if the factors necessary to define the offspring as a *mamzer* exist, even if they exist only with regard to one side of his father, that is sufficient to render the offspring a full *mamzer* (*Mei Naftoaḥ*).

A case where he betrothed a Jewish woman – כְּגוֹן דְּקַדֵּישׁ בַּת יִשְׂרָאֵל: The Gemara in *Gittin* (43a) considers the status of a betrothal performed by a half-slave and remains in doubt as to whether it is at all effective (see *Tosafot* here). From the fact that the Gemara here establishes the case as one where the half-slave betrothed a Jewish woman, apparently the Gemara here assumes that such a betrothal is effective. Nevertheless, it would appear that even if it is effective, the bond between the couple is still incomparable to the bond formed by a standard betrothal. Rather, the betrothal will be effective only to render the woman partially betrothed, a state that is similar to the marital status of a designated maidservant, i.e., a half-free half-slave maidservant who was betrothed to a Hebrew slave (see Leviticus 19:20–22; *Keren Ora*).

They derived their opinions…from a father's wife – לְמֵדוּהָ...מֵאֵשֶׁת אָב: In the Torah, the prohibition against engaging in relations with one's father's wife is juxtaposed to the prohibition against allowing a *mamzer* to enter the congregation of God (Deuteronomy 23:1–3). Based on that juxtaposition, the Gemara derives that only unions that are similar to that of a man with his father's wife will result in the offspring having the status of a *mamzer*. The various opinions concerning who is a *mamzer* are all based on the issue of how to define whether a case is considered to be similar or dissimilar to the case of one's father's wife.

וּמַאן דְּמַכְשַׁר סָבַר: מָה אֵשֶׁת אָב, דִּלְדִידֵיהּ לָא תָּפְסֵי בָּהּ קִדּוּשִׁין לְאַחֲרִינֵי תָּפְסֵי בָּהּ קִדּוּשִׁין – לְאַפּוֹקֵי גּוֹי וְעֶבֶד דְּלָא תָּפְסֵי בְּהוּ קִדּוּשִׁין כְּלָל.

And the one who renders the child **fit holds** that the derivation from the *halakha* of one's father's wife is more limited, and it is derived that the offspring is a *mamzer* only in a case **just like** one's **father's wife,** in **that** although his **betrothal of her does not take effect, with someone else** his **betrothal** of her **does take effect. This is to the exclusion of a gentile and a slave, for whom betrothal** of any Jewish woman **does not take effect**[N] **at all,** and so the offspring of such a union will not be a *mamzer*. It is apparent from this statement of the Sages of Neharde'a that according to the lenient opinion, the offspring of a slave is never a *mamzer*, irrespective of the marital status of the Jewish woman. Therefore, the Gemara's resolution is undermined.

אֶלָּא, כִּי אִיתְּמַר דְּרַב יְהוּדָה – כְּגוֹן שֶׁבָּא עַל אֵשֶׁת אִישׁ וְנִמְצָא צַד חֵירוּת שֶׁבּוֹ מִשְׁתַּמֵּשׁ בְּאֵשֶׁת אִישׁ.

The Gemara offers a different resolution: **Rather, when** this statement **of Rav Yehuda was stated,** it was referring to a case **where** the half-slave half-freeman **engaged in intercourse with a married woman** who was married to someone else, **and it** therefore **emerges** that although the woman's union with the slave side of him will not render the offspring a *mamzer*, the **free side of him is engaging in relations with a married woman** to whom he is not married, and due to that side of him the offspring is a *mamzer*.

אֲמַר רָבִינָא אֲמַר לִי רַב גַּזָּא: אִיקְלַע רַבִּי יוֹסֵי בַּר אָבִין לְאַתְרִין, וַהֲוָה עוּבְדָּא בִּפְנוּיָה – וְאַכְשַׁר, בְּאֵשֶׁת אִישׁ – וּפְסִיל. אָמַר רַב שֵׁשֶׁת: לְדִידִי אֲמַר לִי רַב גַּזָּא: לָא רַבִּי יוֹסֵי בַּר אָבִין הֲוָה, אֶלָּא רַבִּי יוֹסֵי בְּרַבִּי זְבִידָא הֲוָה, וְאַכְשַׁר בֵּין בִּפְנוּיָה בֵּין בְּאֵשֶׁת אִישׁ. אָמַר לֵיהּ רַב אַחָא בְּרֵיהּ דְּרַבָּה לְרָבִינָא: אִיקְלַע אֲמֵימַר לְאַתְרִין. וְאַכְשַׁר בֵּין בִּפְנוּיָה בֵּין בְּאֵשֶׁת אִישׁ.

Ravina said: Rav Gazza said to me that **Rabbi Yosei bar Avin**[P] once **happened** to come **to our place, and there was an incident involving an unmarried woman** who had engaged in intercourse with a slave, **and** Rabbi Yosei bar Avin **rendered** her offspring **fit** to marry into the congregation of Israel. And there was another incident **involving a married woman** who had engaged in intercourse with a slave, **and he rendered** her offspring **unfit** to marry into the congregation of Israel by ruling the offspring was a *mamzeret*. **Rav Sheshet said: Rav Gazza told me** that it was **not Rabbi Yosei bar Avin; rather, it was Rabbi Yosei, son of Rabbi Zevida, and he rendered** the offspring **fit both in** the case of **an unmarried woman and in** the case of **a married woman. Rav Aḥa, son of Rabba, said to Ravina: Ameimar** once **happened** to come **to our place and rendered** the offspring **fit both in** the case of **an unmarried woman and in** the case of **a married woman.**

וְהִלְכְתָא: גּוֹי וְעֶבֶד הַבָּא עַל בַּת יִשְׂרָאֵל – הַוָּלָד כָּשֵׁר, בֵּין בִּפְנוּיָה בֵּין בְּאֵשֶׁת אִישׁ.

The Gemara concludes: **And the *halakha*** is that with regard to **a gentile or slave who engaged in intercourse with a Jewish woman,** the lineage of **the offspring is unflawed, whether** she was **an unmarried or a married woman.**

רָבָא אַכְשְׁרֵיהּ לְרַב מָרִי בַּר רָחֵל וּמַנְיֵיהּ בְּפוּרְסֵי דְּבָבֶל. וְאַף עַל גַּב דְּאָמַר מָר "שׂוֹם תָּשִׂים עָלֶיךָ מֶלֶךְ", כָּל מְשִׂימוֹת שֶׁאַתָּה מֵשִׂים אַל יְהוּ אֶלָּא מִקֶּרֶב אַחֶיךָ, הַאי כֵּיוָן דְּאִמּוֹ מִיִּשְׂרָאֵל – "מִקֶּרֶב אַחֶיךָ" קָרֵינַן בֵּיהּ.

The Gemara cites a related *halakha*: **Rava ruled** that **Rav Mari bar Raḥel,**[P] who was the son of a gentile father and a Jewish mother, was **fit** to marry into the congregation of Israel, **and** furthermore **he appointed him as one of the officials [*pursei*]**[L] **of Babylonia. And although the Master said** that from the verse, **"You shall place a king over you** whom the Lord your God shall chose; from among your brethren shall you place a king over you" (Deuteronomy 17:15) it is derived that not only with regard to the kingship but also with regard to **all positions** of authority **that you appoint,** the incumbents **may be** selected **only from among your brethren**[N] who share your Jewish lineage. Nevertheless, with regard to **this one,** i.e., Rav Mari bar Raḥel, **since his mother is of Jewish** lineage, **we call him "from among your brethren,"**[H] and so he is eligible.

NOTES

To the exclusion of a gentile and a slave, for whom betrothal does not take effect – לְאַפּוֹקֵי גּוֹי וְעֶבֶד דְּלָא תָּפְסֵי בְּהוּ קִדּוּשִׁין: The commentaries question the logic of this opinion that when the father of the offspring is a gentile or slave, the marital status of the woman is irrelevant. Ultimately the relations were adulterous and forbidden both for the Jewish woman herself and for the gentile, since adultery is included as one of the Noahide laws; why doesn't that automatically render the offspring a *mamzer*? Because of this difficulty, the Ramban and others prefer an alternative version of the text held by Rav Hai Gaon and the other *ge'onim*. According to that version, the reason that the offspring is not a *mamzer* is not solely dependent on the forbidden status of the union. Rather, it is based on the offspring being descended from a father and mother between whom betrothal is ineffective. The uniqueness of this case, then, is due to the fact that the offspring of a gentile father is never halakhically recognized as relating to him. Consequently, with regard to issues of lineage, the offspring is halakhically considered as having no father, and therefore it cannot be rendered a *mamzer*.

All positions…from among your brethren – כָּל מְשִׂימוֹת...מִקֶּרֶב אַחֶיךָ: The Gemara states that for this *halakha* it is sufficient even if only one's mother is of Jewish lineage. However, *Tosafot* and the other early commentaries note that the Gemara in tractate *Sota* appears to contradict this when it states that although Agrippas's mother was Jewish, since his father was not, he was not halakhically qualified to be king. See *Tosafot* for one resolution of this question. The Ramban suggests that a distinction be made between appointing one to be the king and appointing him to other positions of authority. To be a king one must indeed have both a Jewish mother and father; however, for other positions of authority it is sufficient if only the mother is Jewish. Some suggest that this distinction can be identified in the verse that provides the source of this *halakha*, by splitting it up into two clauses, as follows: "From among your brethren shall you place a king over you" (Deuteronomy 17:15) refers specifically to a king, and the phrase "among your brethren" implies that both parents must be Jewish. However, the continuation of the verse: "You may not put a foreigner over you, who is not your brother," refers to any position of authority where one individual is placed in charge of others, and for that position only someone who is "not your brother" is excluded. One is defined as "not your brother" only if he does not have a Jewish mother (see *Yam shel Shlomo*).

LANGUAGE

Officials [*pursei*] – פּוּרְסֵי: From the Greek ἔφορος, *eforos*, meaning a governor or appointee. In certain locations this became the title of city governors or officials appointed over large populations.

HALAKHA

From among your brethren – מִקֶּרֶב אַחֶיךָ: It is prohibited to appoint a king over the Jewish people if he descends from a line of converts. It is likewise prohibited to appoint such a man to any position of authority over the Jewish people. If, however, either his father or mother are not from a line of converts, he is eligible (Rambam *Sefer Shofetim*, *Hilkhot Melakhim* 1:4).

PERSONALITIES

Rabbi Yosei bar Avin – רַבִּי יוֹסֵי בַּר אָבִין: An *amora* from Eretz Yisrael, Rabbi Yosei appears frequently in the Jerusalem Talmud as Rabbi Yosei bar Bun. In the Jerusalem Talmud he is usually the final *amora* mentioned on each topic, and some see his role as similar to that of Rav Ashi in the Babylonian Talmud, who edited and organized the subject matter. In a number of places his name appears with that of Rabbi Yosei bar Zevida, who was apparently his colleague but who does not appear in the Jerusalem Talmud, even though he, too, lived in Eretz Yisrael.

Rav Mari bar Raḥel – רַב מָרִי בַּר רָחֵל: It would seem that Rav Mari bar Raḥel is the same person referred to various times in the Gemara as Rav Mari, son of Issur the convert. During the wars that took place in Neharde'a, the daughters of the great *amora* Shmuel, the leading Sage of that city, were captured. One of them, Raḥel, was taken by a gentile named Issur, who later became a righteous convert. Nevertheless, since Mari was conceived while his father was not yet Jewish, he was referred to by his matrilineal descent.

Rav Mari grew to become a Torah scholar and was considered one of the leading scholars in his generation. He even debated the great Sages Abaye and Rava, who also lived in his generation. The Gemara often refers to his virtues and to the fact that he was careful to act beyond the requirements of the *halakha*. He was also very wealthy and influential. Two of his sons, Mar Zutra and Rav Ada Saba, were also considered to be among the great scholars of their generation and were contemporaries of Rav Ashi.

§ A gentile slave purchased by a Jew must be circumcised and then immersed in a ritual bath. By being immersed for the sake of slavery, he takes on the status of a full slave, which, among other things, obligates him to keep certain mitzvot. However, if the slave, or any gentile, is immersed for the sake of conversion, he then becomes a full Jew and fully obligated in mitzvot like any other Jew.

עַבְדֵּיהּ דְּרַבִּי חִיָּיא בַּר אַמִּי אַטְבְּלָהּ לְהַהִיא גּוֹיָה לְשֵׁם אִנְתְּתָא. אֲמַר רַב יוֹסֵף: יָכֵילְנָא לְאַכְשׁוּרֵי בָּהּ וּבִבְרַתָּהּ.

The Gemara considers the result of different intentions accompanying an immersion: **Rabbi Ḥiyya bar Ami's slave immersed a certain gentile woman for the sake of** having **intimate relations,**[N] i.e., to purify her from her menstrual impurity. **Rav Yosef said: I am able to render** both **her and her daughter fit** to marry into the congregation of Israel.

בָּהּ – כִּדְרַב אַסִּי, דַּאֲמַר רַב אַסִּי: מִי לֹא טָבְלָה לְנִדּוּתָהּ?

With regard to her, I can render her fit **in accordance with** the opinion **of Rav Asi, as Rav Asi said** concerning a woman whose status as a convert was unclear but who lived as a part of the Jewish people and acted like all other Jewish women: **Didn't she immerse**[H] **for the sake of** purifying herself from **her menstruation?**[N] Therefore, even if the original immersion was invalid, her intention in subsequent immersions was sufficient to be considered for the sake of conversion, since ultimately she immersed as an expression of her commitment to Judaism. She is therefore fully Jewish.

בִּבְרַתָּהּ – גּוֹי וְעֶבֶד הַבָּא עַל בַּת יִשְׂרָאֵל הַוָּלָד כָּשֵׁר.

And **with regard to her daughter,** she is the daughter of **a gentile or slave who engaged in intercourse with a Jewish woman,** and the *halakha* is that the lineage of **the offspring is unflawed.**

הַהוּא דְּהָווּ קָרוּ לֵיהּ בַּר אֲרָמִיְּיתָא. אֲמַר רַב אַסִּי: מִי לֹא טָבְלָה לְנִדּוּתָהּ? הַהוּא דְּהָווּ קָרוּ לֵיהּ בַּר אַרְמָאָה, אֲמַר רַבִּי יְהוֹשֻׁעַ בֶּן לֵוִי: מִי לָא טָבַל לְקִרְיוֹ?

The Gemara details the circumstances of Rav Asi's ruling: There was **a certain** man **whom** people **would call: Son of the Aramean woman,** as they cast aspersions on the validity of his mother's conversion. With regard to that case, **Rav Asi said: Didn't she immerse for the sake of** purifying herself from **her menstruation?** A similar incident is recounted: There was **a certain** man **whom** people **would call: Son of an Aramean man,**[N] as they cast aspersions on the validity of his father's conversion. **Rabbi Yehoshua ben Levi said: Didn't he immerse for the sake of** purifying himself from **his seminal emission?** That intention is sufficient to consider the immersion an immersion for the sake of conversion.

אָמַר רַב חָמָא בַּר גּוּרְיָא אָמַר רַב: הַלּוֹקֵחַ עֶבֶד מִן הַגּוֹי, וְקָדַם וְטָבַל לְשֵׁם בֶּן חוֹרִין – קָנָה עַצְמוֹ בֶּן חוֹרִין. מַאי טַעְמָא?

Rav Ḥama bar Gurya said that **Rav said:** In the case of a Jew **who purchased a slave from a gentile, and** before he managed to immerse him for the sake of slavery the slave **preempted** him[N] **and immersed for the sake of** conversion to render himself **a freeman,**[H] **he** thereby **acquired himself** and becomes **a freeman,** i.e., his immersion effects a full conversion and he is no longer a slave. **What is the reason** for this *halakha*?

NOTES

He immersed her for the sake of intimate relations – אַטְבְּלָהּ לְשֵׁם אִנְתְּתָא: *Tosefot Ḥad MiKamma'ei* and many other early commentaries explain that the woman had already completed all of the various stages of conversion; however, her original immersion was invalid because it had not been done under the direction of a court, and therefore it was not clear that it had been done with the necessary intention. When she later immersed for the sake of purifying herself, in accordance with the *halakha*, that intention itself was sufficient to deem the later immersion as one for the sake of conversion. This is because she performed the immersion as an expression of her commitment to Judaism, and therefore that immersion completed her conversion process (see *Nimmukei Yosef*). However, many other commentaries explain that it was not the actual immersion for the sake of purifying herself that completed her conversion; rather, it merely served as proof that when she had originally immersed as part of her conversion, she had the necessary intentions.

Didn't she immerse for the sake of her menstruation – מִי לֹא טָבְלָה לְנִדּוּתָהּ: *Tosafot* and the other early commentaries question how this immersion, which was presumably done in private, could possibly be valid, since the Gemara states later (46b) that the conversion process must be done in the presence of a court of three. Some suggest that in fact, a court of three is necessary only when the potential convert formally accepts upon himself to observe the mitzvot, since that is the primary act of conversion. However, the immersion itself may be performed in private. Others suggest that provided it is known to the court that she immersed, that is sufficient, even if they do not actually see the immersion. The Rif rules that a court of three is only ever necessary *ab initio*. Accordingly, the difficulty does not arise, since the Gemara's case here is clearly after the fact.

Whom people would call: Son of an Aramean man – קָרוּ לֵיהּ בַּר אַרְמָאָה: Some commentaries ask: If his mother was Jewish, then he would be a full Jew. Furthermore, according to the Gemara's conclusion, with which Rabbi Yehoshua himself concurs, the offspring of a gentile and a Jewish woman is not a *mamzer*. If so, of what significance is it whether his father was a gentile? Some suggest that it is still significant according to the opinions that although he would not be a *mamzer*, he would be unfit for the priesthood (Maharsha). Others suggest that the case was not of the son of a questionable convert, but of a Jew who took a gentile woman in marriage, and it was the conversion of the son himself that was questionable. In support of this suggestion they cite an alternative version of the text that has: Son of an Aramean woman (*Arukh LaNer*; see Meiri).

One who purchased a slave…and the slave preempted him, etc. – הַלּוֹקֵחַ עֶבֶד...וְקָדַם וכו׳: The commentaries explain the connection between this section of the Gemara and the previous one: From the previous Gemara it is apparent that even if a convert immersed in private, not in the presence of the court, the immersion can still be valid because his intention was clear. The main issue in the following section of the Gemara is the very issue of the significance of one's intentions at the time of immersion (*Yosef Lekaḥ*).

HALAKHA

Didn't she immerse, etc. – מִי לֹא טָבְלָה וכו׳: In order to become Jewish, a convert is required to declare that he accepts upon himself to observe the mitzvot, and he must then be circumcised and immersed, all in the presence of a court of three. If a convert did not declare his acceptance of the mitzvot or was not immersed in the presence of a court of three, then the conversion can still be valid if it is apparent that he had continued to observe the mitzvot and Jewish customs and had immersed for the sake of purifying himself from a discharge of semen, or, in the case of a female convert, that she had immersed to purify herself from menstruation. In any case, if the convert married a Jewish woman, a child born from that union is not rendered unfit (Rambam *Sefer Kedusha, Hilkhot Issurei Bia* 13:9; *Shulḥan Arukh, Yoreh De'a* 268:3).

One who purchased a slave…and he immersed for the sake of rendering him a freeman – הַלּוֹקֵחַ עֶבֶד...וְטָבַל לְשֵׁם בֶּן חוֹרִין: If a Jew purchased a slave from a gentile, and the slave immersed for the sake of conversion, then that immersion effects a full conversion and he becomes a freeman. He must then compensate his previous master with the monetary value of himself when he was a slave (Rema, citing *Nimmukei Yosef*; Rambam *Sefer Kedusha, Hilkhot Issurei Bia* 13:11 and *Sefer Kinyan, Hilkhot Avadim* 8:19; *Shulḥan Arukh, Yoreh De'a* 267:9).

גּוֹי גּוּפָא לָא קָנֵי לֵיהּ, מַאי דְּקָנֵי לֵיהּ – הוּא דְּמַקְנֵי לֵיהּ לְיִשְׂרָאֵל, וְכֵיוָן דְּקָדַם וְטָבַל לְשֵׁם בֶּן חוֹרִין – אַפְקְעֵיהּ לְשִׁעְבּוּדֵיהּ.

His previous **gentile** owner **did not have ownership of the** slave's **body,** since a gentile is unable to have ownership of another's body; rather, he had rights to only the slave's labor. And only **that which he owned in him was he** able to **sell to the Jew.** Therefore, before immersion, the Jew had rights to only the slave's labor, but not ownership of his body, **and** therefore, **once** the slave **preempted** his owner **and immersed for the sake of** conversion to make him **a freeman, he abrogates** his master's **lien** upon him.

כִּדְרָבָא. דְּאָמַר רָבָא: הֶקְדֵּשׁ, חָמֵץ, וְשִׁחְרוּר – מַפְקִיעִין מִידֵי שִׁעְבּוּד.

The Gemara notes: This explanation is **in accordance with** the opinion **of Rava, as Rava said: Consecration** of an item to the Temple, the prohibition of **leavened bread**[H] taking effect upon a leavened food, **and the emancipation**[N] of a slave **abrogate** any **lien**[H] that exists upon them.

מְתִיב רַב חִסְדָּא: מַעֲשֶׂה בְּבְלוֹרְיָא הַגִּיּוֹרֶת שֶׁקָּדְמוּ עֲבָדֶיהָ וְטָבְלוּ לְפָנֶיהָ. וּבָא מַעֲשֶׂה לִפְנֵי חֲכָמִים וְאָמְרוּ: קָנוּ עַצְמָן בְּנֵי חוֹרִין. לְפָנֶיהָ – אִין, לְאַחֲרֶיהָ – לָא!

Rav Ḥisda raised an objection from a *baraita*: There was **an incident involving Beloreya the female convert**[P] **in which her slaves preempted** her **and immersed before her**[N] own immersion for her own conversion. **And** the details of the **incident came before the Sages, and they said:** The slaves **acquired themselves** and became **freemen.** Rav Ḥisda explains how the *baraita* poses a challenge: The *baraita* implies that only because the slaves immersed **before her,** while she was still a gentile, that **yes,** they became freemen; however, had they immersed **after her,**[H] i.e., after she had already converted, then **no,** they would not have become freemen. The reason for this is presumably that upon her conversion she attains the rights to her slaves' bodies, and therefore their immersion for the sake of becoming freemen would be ineffective. However, this contradicts the Gemara's explanation above that when a Jew gains ownership of a slave from a gentile, he has a right to only the slave's labor.

אָמַר רָבָא: לְפָנֶיהָ – בֵּין בִּסְתָם בֵּין בִּמְפוֹרָשׁ. לְאַחֲרֶיהָ, בִּמְפוֹרָשׁ – אִין, בִּסְתָם – לָא.

To resolve the challenge **Rava said:** When the *baraita* says that because they immersed **before her** they acquired themselves, that is **whether** they immersed **without a specified** intention **or whether** they immersed **with explicit** intention to convert and become freemen. However, had they immersed **after her,** if they did so **with explicit** intention to convert, then **yes,** the immersion would achieve that end, but if they did so **without a specified** intention, then **no,** their immersion would, by default, be considered for the sake of slavery and they would not become free.

אָמַר רַב אַוְיָא: לֹא שָׁנוּ אֶלָּא בְּלוֹקֵחַ מִן הַגּוֹי, אֲבָל גּוֹי גּוּפֵיהּ – קָנֵי,

Rav Avya[P] **said: They taught** that one acquires only the rights to the slave's labor **only with regard to** a Jew **who purchased** a slave **from a gentile** slave owner, **but if a gentile** sold **his own body** as a slave directly to a Jew, then the Jew **acquires**[H] his body.

HALAKHA

Consecration, leavened bread abrogate a lien – הֶקְדֵּשׁ, חָמֵץ מַפְקִיעִים מִידֵי שִׁעְבּוּד: With regard to consecration, Rabbeinu Tam and the Rambam hold that even consecrating an item with sanctity that inheres only in its value is effective to abrogate a lien upon it, whereas Rashi and the Ra'avad hold this applies only when one consecrates an item to the extent that the item is endowed with inherent sanctity. The abrogation caused by the onset of the prohibition of leavened bread is also true of the onset of any prohibition that prohibits one from gaining any benefit from the item. Even in a case where the lien is abrogated, the debt supported by the lien still exists, and the creditor may still attempt to collect it (Rambam *Sefer Hafla'a, Hilkhot Arakhin* 7:14, and *Sefer Mishpatim, Hilkhot Malve VeLoveh* 18:6–7; *Shulḥan Arukh, Ḥoshen Mishpat* 117:7).

Emancipation abrogates a lien – שִׁחְרוּר מַפְקִיעִין מִידֵי שִׁעְבּוּד: If one designated his slaves to be the sole property from which repayment of his debt may be collected and he then emancipated the slave, then the emancipation is effective and the lien is thereby abrogated. The debtor must still repay the creditor. Although the slave is no longer bound to the debt, the creditor is forced to write a bill of emancipation for him so that he will not later try to claim that the slave should be considered his own due to the lien that once existed upon him (Rambam *Sefer Kinyan, Hilkhot Avadim* 8:16; *Shulḥan Arukh, Yoreh De'a* 267:68).

Before her and after her – לְפָנֶיהָ וְאַחֲרֶיהָ: In a case where a Jew purchases a slave from a gentile and the slave preempts the owner and immerses on his own accord, if he immersed in the presence of his owner then he becomes a freeman, and if the immersion was not in the presence of his owner then he becomes free only if it was explicitly stated that the immersion was for the sake of becoming a freeman. This is according to the opinion of Rambam, based on the version of the text by which the Rif held. The *Shulḥan Arukh*, following the version of the text by which Rashi held, rules: In a case where a convert has owned a slave since before his conversion, if the slave immersed prior to the owner's conversion, the slave would thereby become a freeman, but if he immersed only after the owner's conversion, then he becomes free only if it was explicitly stated that the immersion was for the sake of becoming a freeman (*Tur*, citing Rosh; Rambam *Sefer Kinyan, Hilkhot Avadim* 8:19; *Shulḥan Arukh, Yoreh De'a* 267:9).

A gentile's body is acquired – נָכְרִי גּוּפוֹ קוֹנֶה: If a gentile sells himself as a slave, of his own volition, to a Jew, then the Jew acquires his body, and if the slave immerses, he cannot unilaterally define that immersion as one for the sake of becoming a freeman (*Shulḥan Arukh, Yoreh De'a* 267:9).

PERSONALITIES

Beloreya the female convert – בְּלוֹרְיָא הַגִּיּוֹרֶת: The name Beloreya is probably a variant of the name Valeria, a name used in Rome for women of the gens Valeria, which was one of the most celebrated and wealthy families in Rome. Beloreya converted during the Second Temple period, and the Talmud relates several questions that she posed to Rabban Gamliel concerning the meanings of various verses in the Bible.

Rav Avya – רַב אַוְיָא: A fourth-generation Babylonian *amora*, Rav Avya was a prominent disciple of Rav Huna but also studied in Eretz Yisrael with Rabbi Ami and Rabbi Yoḥanan. Rav Huna respected him greatly and valued his comments and questions. He married the sister of Rami bar Pappa, and some of his children became *amora'im* themselves. The most famous of these children, Rav Aḥa, son of Rav Avya, is quoted many times in the Talmud as a disciple of Rav Ashi.

NOTES

Consecration, leavened bread, and emancipation, etc. – הֶקְדֵּשׁ, חָמֵץ, וְשִׁחְרוּר וכו׳: In the present case, the slave's owner never actually emancipated him. Nevertheless, the slave's immersion rendered him a freeman, and in that way he effectively emancipated himself (*Tosafot Yeshanim*).

And immersed before her – וְטָבְלוּ לְפָנֶיהָ: The early commentaries record two different versions of the Gemara's text here that lead to two fundamentally different conclusions.

The text of the *Halakhot Gedolot*, Rif, and Rambam reads: Immersed in her presence. According to this version, when slaves immerse in the presence of their owner, unless the owner explicitly states otherwise, it is assumed that the owner consents to the fact that their immersion should be for the sake of conversion, and so they become freemen. However, if slaves immerse not in the presence of their owner, they cannot unilaterally define their immersion to be for conversion, and therefore they remain slaves. Essentially, only the owner has the ability to define the nature of her slaves' immersion.

The present text, which is the version by which Rashi and the Razah held, reads: Immersed before her, meaning their immersion preceded her own. According to this version, the ability for the slaves' immersion to effect their conversion is dependent on whether it took place while their owner was a Jew or a gentile. As a gentile, she would have rights to only their labor, and so their immersion could abrogate her lien upon them. However, if she immersed first and was already Jewish, then she would have already attained ownership of their bodies, and therefore they would not be able to immerse for the sake of conversion without her consent.

An underlying assumption of both explanations is that in some cases an immersion whose purpose was unspecified is considered, by default, to be for the sake of conversion. The *Yosef Lekaḥ* explains the rationale for this. In truth, the very act of immersion demonstrates an acceptance of the system of mitzvot; why else would the slaves be immersing? Therefore, unless it is made explicit that the immersion is for the sake of slavery, it is considered for the sake of conversion.

דכתיב "וגם מבני התושבים הגרים עמכם מהם תקנו" – אתם קונים מהם, ולא הם קונים מכם, ולא הם קונים זה מזה.

As it is written: "Moreover, of the children of the strangers that sojourn among you, of them you may acquire" (Leviticus 25:45). The verse states only that **you,** i.e., Jews, **can acquire** a slave **from them,** i.e., a gentile slave, **but they cannot acquire** a slave **from you,** i.e., a Jewish slave, **and they cannot acquire** a slave **from one another.**

ולא הם קונים מכם, למאי? אילימא למעשה ידיו – אטו גוי לא קני ליה לישראל למעשה ידיו? והכתיב "או לעקר משפחת גר" ואמר מר: "משפחת גר" – זה הגוי! אלא לאו – לגופיה, וקאמר רחמנא "אתם קונין מהם" – אפילו גופיה.

When it is derived that: **But they cannot acquire** slaves **from you, to what** type of acquisition is it referring? **If we say** it is **for his labor, is that to say** that **a gentile cannot acquire a Jew for his labor?**[H] **Isn't it written:** "And if a stranger who is a settler with you becomes rich, and your brother becomes poor beside him, and he sells himself to the stranger who is a settler with you, **or to the offshoot of a stranger's family"** (Leviticus 25:47), **and the Master said** in explanation of the phrase **"a stranger's family"** that **this** is referring to **a gentile.** If so, the verse explicitly states that a Jew can sell himself as a slave to a gentile. **Rather, is it not** that the reference is **to** selling **his body, and the Merciful One states** that **you,** i.e., Jews, **can acquire** a slave **from them,** which means **even his body.** Accordingly the verse indicates that a Jew can acquire a gentile slave's body, but a gentile is unable to acquire ownership of another's body, even that of another gentile.

פריך רב אחא: אימא בכספא ובטבילה! קשיא.

Rav Aḥa refutes Rav Avya's explanation: **Say** that the verse is referring to acquiring a gentile slave by both purchasing him **with money and** then **by immersing** him for the purpose of slavery, and only in that case does it teach that a Jew acquires the gentile slave's body. However, until he has been immersed the acquisition is not fully complete, and therefore if the slave immerses himself with the intention to become free, then his immersion would achieve that end. The Gemara concedes: This is **difficult.**

אמר שמואל: וצריך לתקפו במים.

Shmuel said: And if one wishes to ensure that one's slave does not declare the immersion to be for the sake of conversion, then **one needs to hold him tightly**[NH] **in the water** in a way that demonstrates the owner's dominance over the slave at that time, thereby defining the immersion as one for the sake of slavery.

כי האי דמנימין, עבדיה דרב אשי, בעא לאטבולי, מסריה ניהלייהו לרבינא ולרב אחא בריה דרבא, אמר להו: חזו דמינייכו קבעית ליה. רמו ליה ארויסא בצואריה, ארפו ליה. וצמצמו ליה.

That is as demonstrated **in this** incident **involving Minyamin, Rav Ashi's slave:** When **he wished to immerse** him, **he passed him to**[N] **Ravina and Rav Aḥa, son of Rava,** to perform the immersion on his behalf, and **he said to them: Be aware that I will claim** compensation **for him from you** if you do not prevent my slave from immersing for the sake of conversion. **They placed a bridle** [***arvisa***][L] **upon his neck,** and at the moment of immersion **they loosened it and** then immediately **tightened it** again while he was still immersed.

ארפו ליה – כי היכי דלא להוי חציצה, צמצמו ליה – כי היכי דלא לקדים ולימא להו: לשם בן חורין אני טובל. בהדי דדלי רישיה ממיא, אנחו ליה זולטא דטינא ארישיה. ואמרו ליה: זיל אמטי לבי מרך.

The Gemara explains their actions: **They** initially **loosened it in order that there should not be any interposition** between the slave and the water during the immersion, which would invalidate it. **They** immediately **tightened it** again **in order that** the slave **should not preempt** them **and say to them: I am immersing for the sake of** becoming **a freeman. When he lifted his head from the water they placed a bucket of clay**[N] **upon his head and said to him: Go** and **bring** this **to the house of your master.** They did this in order to demonstrate that the immersion had been successful and that he was still a slave.

NOTES

Then one needs to hold him tightly – וצריך לתוקפו: Rashi explains that this is necessary to demonstrate the owner's dominance over the slave. However, Rabbeinu Ḥananel and the Rif simply write that the slave must be held tightly in order to ensure the validity of the immersion. Simply read, it would appear that they mean only that the owner should ensure the slave is fully immersed in the water. Based on this understanding of their statements, the Razah rejects their explanation, seemingly because he assumes that it is such an obvious point that is should be unnecessary to state it. However, the Ramban in *Milḥamot HaShem* claims that the Rif's intention is similar to that of Rashi; if the owner is in physical control of the slave's immersion, it is clear that it is the owner who is in charge of the immersion, and therefore the nature of the immersion is defined by his intentions.

He passed him to them – מסריה ניהלייהו: Some commentaries suggest that from the fact that the Gemara mentions the involvement of only two Sages in this incident, it would appear that it is sufficient to have two judges preside over the immersion. The Ramban rejects this possibility outright, insisting that three judges are always required. He explains that even in this incident, there was certainly an additional judge present at the time. Presumably, the third judge was not of equal stature as Ravina and Rav Aḥa, and so he was not mentioned out of deference to them.

They placed a bucket of clay – אנחו ליה זולטא דטינא: This act was not halakhically significant. It was done only in order to demonstrate and publicize the fact that the man was still a slave so that no one could later suggest that the immersion might have been for the sake of making him a freeman (Rashba; *Nimmukei Yosef*).

LANGUAGE

Bridle [*arvisa*] **– ארויסא:** From the Middle Persian arwēs, meaning a rope or bridle.

HALAKHA

A Hebrew slave sold to a gentile – עבד עברי הנמכר לנכרי: A Jew may be sold as a slave only to either a born Jew or to a convert, but it is not permitted to sell him to a gentile. This applies both in the case where the court sold the Jew or where the Jew sold himself. Nevertheless, if a Jew sold himself to a gentile, the transaction is valid, even if he sold himself directly into the services of idolatry (Rambam *Sefer Kinyan, Hilkhot Avadim* 1:3).

One needs to hold him tightly – צריך לתקפו: One who immerses his slave needs to perform some act of enslavement at the same time. For example, he could hold him tightly in the water. By doing so he prevents the slave from immersing for the sake of becoming a freeman and thereby acquiring himself (Rambam *Sefer Kinyan, Hilkhot Avadim* 8:19 and *Sefer Kedusha, Hilkhot Issurei Bia* 13:11; *Shulḥan Arukh, Yoreh De'a* 267:9).

אָמַר לֵיהּ רַב פַּפָּא לְרָבָא: חָזֵי מָר הָנֵי דְּבֵי פַּפָּא בַּר אַבָּא דְּיָהֲבִי זוּזֵי לְאֶינָשֵׁי לְכַרְגַּיְיהוּ, וּמְשַׁעְבְּדִי בְּהוּ. כִּי נָפְקִי, צְרִיכִי גִּיטָּא דְּחֵירוּתָא אוֹ לָא?

Rav Pappa said to Rava: Has the Master seen those of the house of Pappa bar Abba[P] **who give money** to the tax-collectors **on behalf of** poor **people**[N] **to pay for their poll tax** [***karga***],[L] **and** as a result **they would enslave them.** Anyone who did not pay the tax would be taken as a slave for the king. By paying for such people's taxes, the members of the house of Pappa bar Abba essentially purchased those people, who had become the king's slaves, for themselves. Rav Pappa asked: **When** those slaves **go free, do they require a bill of emancipation,**[N] because the members of the house of Pappa bar Abba actually attained ownership of the slaves' bodies, **or not,** as they were owned only for the sake of their labor?

אָמַר לֵיהּ: אִיכּוּ שְׁכִיבִי לָא אָמְרִי לְכוּ הָא מִילְּתָא, הָכִי אָמַר רַב שֵׁשֶׁת: מוֹהַרְקַיְיהוּ דְּהָנֵי בְּטַפְסָא דְּמַלְכָּא מַנַּח, וּמַלְכָּא אֲמַר: מַאן דְּלָא יָהֵיב כַּרְגָּא – מִשְׁתַּעְבַּד לְמַאן דְּיָהֵיב כַּרְגָּא.

He said to him: Were I dead[N] **I could not say this matter to you,** so it is good that you have asked me while I am still alive, as I know that **this** is what **Rav Sheshet said** with regard to the matter: **The writ of slavery** [***moharkayehu***][L] **of these**[H] residents of the kingdom **rests in the treasury** [***tafsa***][L] **of the king,** and in fact all the residents of the kingdom are considered to be full slaves of the king, i.e., he owns their bodies, irrespective of whether they pay their taxes. **And** so when **the king says: One who does not give the poll tax is to be enslaved to the one who** does **give the poll tax** on his behalf, the king's decree is fully effective in making those residents full slaves of those who paid for them. As such, they will require a bill of emancipation when they are freed.

PERSONALITIES

Pappa bar Abba – פַּפָּא בַּר אַבָּא: Also known as Rav Pappa bar Abba, he was a well-respected and wealthy man who lived during the same time as Rav Pappa (see 21b). It seems that there were close relations between Rav Pappa and the house of Rav Pappa bar Abba; apparently the members of that household related to Rav Pappa as their rabbi and master, asking him various questions in *halakha*. The sons of Rav Pappa bar Abba were Torah scholars and are found participating in talmudic discussions concerning matters of *halakha* together with Rav Pappa and Ravina.

LANGUAGE

Poll tax [*karga*] – כַּרְגָּא: Related to the Middle Persian word harg, meaning tribute.

Writ of slavery [*moharka*] – מוֹהַרְקָא: From the Middle Persian muhrak, which means a document.

Treasury [*tafsa*] – טַפְסָא: The correct reading of this word, preserved in some manuscripts and commentaries, is *sefata*. It apparently is related to the New Persian term safad, meaning basket.

HALAKHA

The writ of slavery of these, etc. – מוֹהַרְקַיְיהוּ דְּהָנֵי וכו׳: If a gentile king declares that all of those who do not pay their taxes shall be sold to those who do, that law is halakhically binding, and a slave acquired in this matter is considered a Canaanite slave in every respect (Rambam *Sefer Kinyan, Hilkhot Avadim* 1:8; *Shulḥan Arukh, Yoreh De'a* 267:18).

NOTES

Give money on behalf of people, etc. – יָהֲבִי זוּזֵי לְאֶינָשֵׁי וכו׳: The Gemara does not state who these people were. Most commentaries assume that they were gentiles. Accordingly, Rav Pappa's question is whether they were enslaved only for the sake of their labor or even to the extent that their bodies were owned. However, Rabbeinu Ḥananel explains that these people were *gerei toshav*, i.e., gentiles who reside in Eretz Yisrael and observe certain mitzvot. In many regards, the status of a *ger toshav* is not similar to that of other gentiles. Rav Pappa therefore inquired whether or not their bodies can be fully owned as slaves in the same way as a gentile slave. Others explain that these people were Jews. According to this opinion, the question is whether it is possible to become a Hebrew slave in this manner; normally the status of a Hebrew slave is attained only if the Jew either sells himself or is sold as a slave by the court. Although Rav Pappa lived in a generation in which the status of a Hebrew slave could no longer be attained in the standard manner, it is possible that they might still be considered Hebrew slaves since the law of the land defined them as such (Ritva).

Do they require a bill of emancipation – צְרִיכִי גִּיטָּא דְּחֵירוּתָא: According to the opinions that these people were gentiles, various questions are raised: Why did Rav Pappa ask only about the need for a bill of emancipation? Would such slaves also require immersion for the sake of slavery? Why didn't Rav Pappa ask about that as well? The Ramban explains that the issue of immersion is directly dependent on whether there is a need for a bill of emancipation; therefore, there was no need to ask about it. If a bill of emancipation is required, that is because even the slaves' bodies were owned. Therefore, it would also be necessary to immerse them. If there is no need for a bill of emancipation, then it is apparent that they were acquired only for the sake of their labor, and so no immersion would be necessary.

The Gemara above explains that one gentile cannot acquire the body of another. If so, since these slaves were acquired from the gentile king, how is it possible for their new owners to have gained ownership of their bodies, a state which consequently requires a bill of emancipation? The commentaries explain that although it is true that under normal circumstances one gentile cannot acquire the body of another, in the present case the law of the land afforded the king such rights, and such rights are recognized as halakhically binding. This is because the king's ownership is not based on a mutual agreement but on the power of the king over his subjects.

Based on this discussion, some suggest that there may be a further example where one gentile can own the body of another in a case where one gentile takes another as a prisoner of war. In such a case it is possible that since the ownership of the captive is similarly not based on mutual agreement but due to the power of the captor over his captive, in that case as well the captor would acquire ownership of his captive's body (see *Tosefot HaRosh* and Rashba).

Were I dead – אִיכּוּ שְׁכִיבִי: This strange expression was also used once by Rava's teacher Rav Naḥman with regard to his own teacher Shmuel (*Shabbat* 152b), as well as by Rav Yehuda with regard to his teacher Rav (*Avoda Zara* 55a). *Ben Yehoyada* on *Shabbat* 152b suggests that the teachers of these *amoraim* had whispered various teachings to them, and they therefore assumed that no one else had heard them and that if they died, the statements would have been lost forever.

רַבִּי חִיָּיא בַּר אַבָּא אִיקְּלַע לְגַבְלָא. חֲזָא בְּנוֹת יִשְׂרָאֵל דִּמְעַבְּרָן מִגֵּרִים שֶׁמָּלוּ וְלֹא טָבְלוּ, וַחֲזָא חַמְרָא דְּיִשְׂרָאֵל דְּמָזְגִי גּוֹיִם וְשָׁתוּ יִשְׂרָאֵל, וַחֲזָא תּוּרְמוּסִין דְּשָׁלְקֵי גּוֹיִם וְאָכְלִי יִשְׂרָאֵל, וְלָא אֲמַר לְהוּ וְלָא מִידֵּי.

§ The Gemara relates: **Rabbi Ḥiyya bar Abba** once **happened** to come **to Gavla.**[B] **He saw Jewish women** there **who had become pregnant from converts who were circumcised but** had still **not immersed** to complete their conversion process; **and he saw wine of Jews that gentiles were pouring,**[N] **and Jews were drinking** it; **and he saw lupines** [*turmusin*][LB] **that gentiles were cooking, and Jews were eating** them; **but he did not say anything to them.**

אֲתָא לְקַמֵּיהּ דְּרַבִּי יוֹחָנָן. אֲמַר לֵיהּ: צֵא וְהַכְרֵז עַל בְּנֵיהֶם שֶׁהֵם מַמְזֵרִים, וְעַל יֵינָם מִשּׁוּם יֵין נֶסֶךְ, וְעַל תּוּרְמוּסָן מִשּׁוּם בִּישּׁוּלֵי גּוֹיִם, לְפִי שֶׁאֵינָן בְּנֵי תוֹרָה.

Later, **he came before Rabbi Yoḥanan** and told him what he had witnessed. **Rabbi Yoḥanan said to him: Go and make** a public **declaration concerning their children that they are *mamzerim*, and concerning their wine** that it is forbidden **because** it is like **wine poured as an** idolatrous **libation, and concerning their lupines** that they are forbidden **because** they are **food cooked by gentiles.** One should be stringent and make such a declaration **because they are not** well-versed **in Torah,** and if they are left to be lax in this regard they will eventually transgress Torah prohibitions.

עַל בְּנֵיהֶן שֶׁהֵם מַמְזֵרִים – רַבִּי יוֹחָנָן לְטַעְמֵיהּ, דְּאָמַר רַבִּי חִיָּיא בַּר אַבָּא אָמַר רַבִּי יוֹחָנָן: לְעוֹלָם אֵין גֵּר עַד שֶׁיִּמּוֹל וְיִטְבּוֹל, וְכֵיוָן דְּלָא טָבֵיל – גּוֹי הוּא. וְאָמַר רַבָּה בַּר בַּר חָנָה אָמַר רַבִּי יוֹחָנָן: גּוֹי וְעֶבֶד הַבָּא עַל בַּת יִשְׂרָאֵל – הַוָּלָד מַמְזֵר.

The Gemara explains: With regard to the declaration **concerning their children that they are *mamzerim*, Rabbi Yoḥanan** conforms **to his** standard line of **reasoning** in two *halakhot*: The first is **as Rabbi Ḥiyya bar Abba said** that **Rabbi Yoḥanan said:** One **is never** considered to be **a convert until he has been circumcised and has immersed.**[H] **And since** the convert in the case in Gavla **had not immersed, he is** still considered **a gentile. And** the second *halakha* is as **Rabba bar bar Ḥana said** that **Rabbi Yoḥanan said:** With regard to **a gentile or a slave who engaged in intercourse with a Jewish woman, the offspring** of that union **is a *mamzer*.**

וְעַל יֵינָם מִשּׁוּם יֵין נֶסֶךְ – מִשּׁוּם "לֵךְ לֵךְ", אָמְרִין נְזִירָא, "סְחוֹר סְחוֹר, לְכַרְמָא לָא תִּקְרַב".

And the reason to declare **concerning their wine** that it is forbidden **because** it is like **wine poured as an** idolatrous **libation**[H] is that although their wine was not actually poured as an idolatrous libation, it was prohibited by rabbinic decree **due to** the maxim that: **Go, go, we say to a nazirite, go around and go around,** but **do not come near to the vineyard.** Although a nazirite is prohibited only from eating produce of the vine, he is warned not even to come into close proximity of a vineyard as a protective measure to ensure that he will not transgress this prohibition. So too, in many cases, the Sages decreed certain items and actions to be prohibited because they understood that if people would partake of them, they would eventually transgress Torah prohibitions.

NOTES

That gentiles were pouring – דְּמָזְגִי גּוֹיִם: Rashi explains that the gentiles did not actually touch the wine itself but merely poured it; nevertheless, that was sufficient to render it forbidden. Apparently, according to Rashi it was this point that provided the novelty of the case, which Rabbi Ḥiyya bar Abba was initially unaware of. Rabbi Avraham min HaHar argues that it was unanimously understood that if a gentile actually pours wine, the wine is thereby rendered forbidden. The novelty in this case was that although the gentiles in fact merely diluted the wine by pouring water into it, the wine was nevertheless forbidden because by pouring the water, they caused the wine to be moved. This is sufficient to render the wine forbidden because the rabbinic prohibition is on account of the fact that idolaters sometimes worship their deity by simply swirling the wine around, and so it applies in any case where a gentile causes the wine to move.

HALAKHA

When is one considered a convert – מָתַי נֶחְשָׁב גֵּר: One is considered to be a convert only once he has both been circumcised and immersed in a ritual bath. This is in accordance with the opinion of Rabbi Yoḥanan (Rambam *Sefer Kedusha, Hilkhot Issurei Bia* 13:6).

Their wine because of wine poured as a libation – יֵינָם מִשּׁוּם יֵין נֶסֶךְ: It is forbidden to derive benefit from wine touched by gentiles. This is due to a rabbinic decree that was issued on account of wine poured as a libation offering to idols. The Rema cites opinions that nowadays, since idolaters do not pour libation offerings of wine to their idols, it is permitted to derive benefit from their wine, and so it is permissible to take wine from them in exchange for repayment of a debt or in other cases of possible loss (*Tur*, citing Rashbam and Rosh). Nevertheless, one may not trade in it *ab initio* (*Haggahot Maimoniyyot*). There are those who are lenient even in this regard, but it is proper to be stringent (*Smag*; Rambam *Sefer Kedusha, Hilkhot Ma'akhalot Assurot* 11:3; *Shulḥan Arukh, Yoreh De'a* 123:1).

BACKGROUND

Gavla – גַּבְלָא: Gavla is apparently a reference to the area of the Golan in the northern part of Eretz Yisrael. Despite the fact that it was relatively close to the centers of the Jewish settlement in Tiberias and its environs, it was nevertheless not considered a place of Torah scholars, and it was populated by both Jews and gentiles.

Lupines – תּוּרְמוּסִין: Lupine is the name of several plants from the legume family, of the *Faboideae* subfamily. White lupine, *Lupinus albus*, and yellow lupine, *Lupinus luteus*, are the most commonly grown kinds. The seeds of lupines, which can grow to a diameter of up to fifteen centimeters, are edible. However, due the presence of alkaloids, the natural taste of the seeds is extremely bitter. In order to prepare them for consumption one must cook them repeatedly in water. To this day the cooked seeds of lupines are sold as a delicacy.

White lupine

European yellow lupine

Lupine seeds

LANGUAGE

Lupine [*turmus*] – תּוּרְמוּס: From the Greek θέρμος, *thermos*, meaning lupine, the lupine plant from the legume family.

וְעַל תּוּרְמוּסָן מִשּׁוּם בִּשּׁוּלֵי גוֹיִם – לְפִי שֶׁאֵינָן בְּנֵי תוֹרָה, הָא בְּנֵי תוֹרָה שָׁרֵי? וְהָאָמַר רַב שְׁמוּאֵל בַּר רַב יִצְחָק מִשְּׁמֵיהּ דְּרַב: כׇּל הַנֶּאֱכָל כְּמוֹת שֶׁהוּא חַי – אֵין בּוֹ מִשּׁוּם בִּשּׁוּלֵי גוֹיִם, וְהָא תּוּרְמוּס אֵינוֹ נֶאֱכָל כְּמוֹת שֶׁהוּא חַי, וְיֵשׁ בּוֹ מִשּׁוּם בִּשּׁוּלֵי גוֹיִם!

And the final declaration **concerning their lupines** that they are forbidden **because** they are **food cooked by gentiles**[NH] is issued **because they are not** well versed **in Torah.**[N] The Gemara expresses astonishment: Does this imply that **were they students of the Torah** their lupines would **be permitted? Didn't Rav Shmuel bar Rav Yitzḥak say in the name of Rav: Any** food item **that is eaten as it is, raw, is not** subject **to** the prohibition of **food cooked by gentiles,** even when cooked by them? **But a lupine is not eaten as it is, raw, and** therefore **it is subject to** the prohibition of **food cooked by gentiles.**

רַבִּי יוֹחָנָן כְּאִידָךְ לִישָּׁנָא סְבִירָא לֵיהּ דְּאָמַר רַב שְׁמוּאֵל בַּר רַב יִצְחָק מִשְּׁמֵיהּ דְּרַב: כׇּל שֶׁאֵין עוֹלֶה עַל שׁוּלְחַן מְלָכִים לֶאֱכוֹל בּוֹ אֶת הַפַּת – אֵין בּוֹ מִשּׁוּם בִּשּׁוּלֵי גוֹיִם. וְטַעֲמָא דְּאֵינָן בְּנֵי תוֹרָה, הָא בְּנֵי תוֹרָה – שָׁרֵי.

The Gemara explains that **Rabbi Yoḥanan holds** in this matter **in accordance with** the opinion of **the other version** of what **Rav Shmuel bar Rav Yitzḥak said in the name of Rav: Any** food item that lacks sufficient importance such that it **does not appear on the table of kings** in order **to eat bread with it is not** subject **to** the prohibition of **food cooked by gentiles.** Lupines lack importance and are therefore permitted even if cooked by gentiles. **And** consequently, **the** only **reason** to make a declaration prohibiting the residents of Gavla from eating them is **because they are not** well versed **in Torah,** and if they are left to be lax in this regard they will eventually become lax in actual Torah prohibitions; by inference, to those well versed **in Torah, it is permitted.**

§ During their sojourn in Egypt, the children of Israel had the halakhic status of gentiles. At the revelation at Sinai they entered into a national covenant with God in which they attained their status of the Jewish people. This transformation was essentially the mass conversion of the people, and so their preparation for the revelation provides a paradigm of the process required for conversion for all generations. The *tanna'im* disagree as to which aspects of that original conversion are to be derived for all generations.

תָּנוּ רַבָּנַן: גֵּר שֶׁמָּל וְלֹא טָבַל, רַבִּי אֱלִיעֶזֶר אוֹמֵר הֲרֵי זֶה גֵּר, שֶׁכֵּן מָצִינוּ בַּאֲבוֹתֵינוּ שֶׁמָּלוּ וְלֹא טָבְלוּ. טָבַל וְלֹא מָל, רַבִּי יְהוֹשֻׁעַ אוֹמֵר: הֲרֵי זֶה גֵּר, שֶׁכֵּן מָצִינוּ בָּאִמָּהוֹת שֶׁטָּבְלוּ וְלֹא מָלוּ. וַחֲכָמִים אוֹמְרִים: טָבַל וְלֹא מָל, מָל וְלֹא טָבַל – אֵין גֵּר עַד שֶׁיָּמוֹל וְיִטְבּוֹל.

The Sages taught in a *baraita*: With regard to **a convert who was circumcised but did not immerse, Rabbi Eliezer says** that **this is a convert, as so we found with our forefathers** following the exodus from Egypt **that they were circumcised**[N] **but were not immersed.** With regard to one who **immersed but was not circumcised, Rabbi Yehoshua says** that **this is a convert, as so we found with our foremothers that they immersed but were not circumcised. And the Rabbis say:** Whether **he immersed but was not circumcised** or whether **he was circumcised but did not immerse, he is not a convert until he is circumcised and he immerses.**

וְרַבִּי יְהוֹשֻׁעַ נַמִּי – נֵילַף מֵאָבוֹת, וְרַבִּי אֱלִיעֶזֶר נַמִּי – נֵילַף מֵאִמָּהוֹת! וְכִי תֵּימָא: אֵין דָּנִין אֶפְשָׁר מִשֶּׁאִי אֶפְשָׁר –

The Gemara questions the opinions in the *baraita*: **But let Rabbi Yehoshua also derive** what is required for conversion **from** our **forefathers;** why didn't he do so? **And let Rabbi Eliezer also derive** the *halakha* **from** our **foremothers;** why didn't he do so? **And if you would say** that Rabbi Eliezer did not derive the *halakha* from our foremothers because he holds **one cannot derive** the **possible from** the **impossible,** i.e., one cannot derive that men do not require circumcision from the *halakha* that women do not require it, because for women it is a physical impossibility, that claim may be refuted.

וְהָתַנְיָא, רַבִּי אֱלִיעֶזֶר אוֹמֵר: מִנַּיִן לְפֶסַח דּוֹרוֹת שֶׁאֵין בָּא אֶלָּא מִן הַחוּלִּין – נֶאֱמַר פֶּסַח בְּמִצְרַיִם וְנֶאֱמַר פֶּסַח בְּדוֹרוֹת, מַה פֶּסַח הָאָמוּר בְּמִצְרַיִם – אֵין בָּא אֶלָּא מִן הַחוּלִּין, אַף פֶּסַח הָאָמוּר לְדוֹרוֹת – אֵין בָּא אֶלָּא מִן הַחוּלִּין.

It would appear that Rabbi Eliezer does not accept that principle, as **isn't it taught** in a *baraita* that **Rabbi Eliezer says: From where** is it derived with regard **to the Paschal lamb** brought throughout the **generations that it may be brought only from non-sacred** animals?[H] **A Paschal lamb is stated** in the Torah **in** reference to the lamb that the Jewish people brought prior to the exodus from **Egypt, and a Paschal lamb is stated in** reference to the yearly obligation throughout the **generations.** The association between them teaches that **just as the Paschal lamb stated in** reference to **Egypt was only brought from non-sacred** animals, since prior to the giving of the Torah there was no possibility to consecrate property, **so too,** with regard to **the Paschal lamb stated** in reference **to** the obligation throughout the **generations, it may be brought only from non-sacred** animals.

NOTES

Food cooked by gentiles – בִּישּׁוּלֵי גוֹיִם: The prohibition against eating foods cooked by gentiles does not stem from concern that some forbidden foods might have been mixed in. Rather, it is an independent rabbinic decree, issued by the Sages, to prevent Jews from intermingling with gentiles. It is for this reason that the prohibition is limited to items of significance, i.e., those that would appear on a king's table, and for which the act of cooking was significant, i.e., the food would not be eaten raw. In such cases, the fact that the gentile provided such foods to the Jews demonstrates a level of devotion and honor that could lead to an undesirable closeness between them.

Because they were not well versed in Torah – שֶׁאֵינָן בְּנֵי תּוֹרָה: This justification for a stringent ruling is offered in several places in the Talmud. It is used in places in which the correct practice requires a nuanced understanding of the *halakha* and the ability to distinguish between permitted practices and similar prohibited ones. In places in which Torah scholars lived, the Sages were lenient based on the assumption that they would know how to maintain the appropriate halakhic distinctions.

Circumcision of our forefathers – מִילָה בַּאֲבוֹתֵינוּ: Although the Torah does not explicitly record the fact that the children of Israel were circumcised prior to the revelation at Sinai, this may be inferred in several ways. The simplest way, suggested by the Rambam, is that they must have circumcised themselves before leaving Egypt in preparation for the Paschal lamb that they brought there, since there is an explicit Torah prohibition prohibiting an uncircumcised male from partaking of the Paschal lamb. Since that circumcision was performed for the sake of observing a mitzva, it was also valid as a preparation for the national conversion that was effected by the revelation at Sinai (see also Ramban).

HALAKHA

Food cooked by gentiles – בִּישּׁוּלֵי גוֹיִם: Any food item that is not eaten raw and appears on the table of kings in order to eat bread with it is subject to the rabbinic prohibition of food cooked by gentiles. This prohibition applies even to food cooked by a gentile in a Jew's house with his utensils. Most commentaries rule that a food is subject to the prohibition only if both the above stated conditions are fulfilled (Rambam *Sefer Kedusha, Hilkhot Ma'akhalot Assurot* 17:14; *Shulḥan Arukh, Yoreh De'a* 113:1).

The Paschal lamb…is brought…from non-sacred animals – פֶּסַח...בָּא...מִן הַחוּלִּין: All offerings brought by an individual, including the Paschal lamb, may be brought only from non-sacred animals (Rambam *Sefer Kedusha, Hilkhot Ma'aseh HaKorbanot* 16:15).

אָמַר לֵיהּ רַבִּי עֲקִיבָא: וְכִי דָּנִין אֶפְשָׁר מִשֶּׁאִי אֶפְשָׁר? אָמַר לֵיהּ: אַף עַל פִּי שֶׁאִי אֶפְשָׁר – רְאָיָה גְּדוֹלָה הִיא, וְנִלְמַד הֵימֶנָּה.

Rabbi Akiva said to him: But can one derive the **possible,** i.e., the *halakha* for the Paschal lamb throughout the generations, where a possibility exists to bring it from consecrated animals, **from the impossible,**[N] i.e., from the Paschal lamb in Egypt, where it was not a possibility? Rabbi Eliezer **said to him: Although it was impossible** to bring the Paschal lamb in Egypt from consecrated animals, nevertheless, **it is** still **a great proof, and we may learn from it.** It is apparent, then, that Rabbi Eliezer holds that one can derive the possible from the impossible. Therefore the original question stands: Why didn't Rabbi Eliezer derive from the foremothers that circumcision is not essential for conversion?

אֶלָּא

The Gemara concedes: **Rather,** the *baraita* must be reinterpreted as follows:

NOTES

The possible from the impossible – אֶפְשָׁר מִשֶּׁאִי אֶפְשָׁר: This issue is present in every system of logical thought with regard to logical constructs that are based on inductive reasoning. In fact, in certain areas of mathematics there are proofs based on inducing the possible from the impossible.

Perek **IV**
Daf **46** Amud **b**

בְּטָבַל וְלֹא מָל – כּוּלֵּי עָלְמָא לָא פְּלִיגִי דְּמַהֲנֵי. כִּי פְּלִיגִי – בְּמָל וְלֹא טָבַל. רַבִּי אֱלִיעֶזֶר יָלֵיף מֵאָבוֹת, וְרַבִּי יְהוֹשֻׁעַ: בְּאָבוֹת נַמִי טְבִילָה הֲוָה.

With regard to one who immersed but was not circumcised, everyone, i.e., both Rabbi Yehoshua and Rabbi Eliezer, **agrees that** the *halakha* is derived from the foremothers that immersion alone **is effective. Where they disagree** is **with regard to one who was circumcised but had not immersed; Rabbi Eliezer derives** that it is effective **from the forefathers, and Rabbi Yehoshua** disagrees because he maintains that **in** the conversion of the **forefathers there was also an immersion.**

מְנָא לֵיהּ? אִילֵימָא מִדִּכְתִיב ״לֵךְ אֶל הָעָם וְקִדַּשְׁתָּם הַיּוֹם וּמָחָר וְכִבְּסוּ שִׂמְלֹתָם״, וּמָה בְּמָקוֹם שֶׁאֵין טָעוּן כִּבּוּס – טָעוּן טְבִילָה, מָקוֹם שֶׁטָּעוּן כִּבּוּס – אֵינוֹ דִּין שֶׁטָּעוּן טְבִילָה?

The Gemara asks: **From where did he** derive this? **If we say** that he derived it **from** the fact **that it is written** that in preparation for the revelation at Sinai, God commanded Moses: **"Go unto the people and sanctify them today and tomorrow, and let them wash their garments"** (Exodus 19:10), as Rabbi Yehoshua understands that the washing mentioned in this verse is the ritual immersion of clothes, this leads to the following *a fortiori* inference: **Just as in a case where** one became impure through contact with some source of impurity, **washing,** i.e., immersion, of clothes **is not required** but **immersion** of one's body **is required,** then **in a case where washing** of clothes **is required,** as in the preparation for the revelation at Sinai, **isn't it logical that immersion** of one's body **should** also **be required?**

וְדִלְמָא נְקִיּוּת בְּעָלְמָא?

The Gemara rejects the proof: **But perhaps** when the verse states that they had to wash their clothes, it was **merely for cleanliness** and not for the sake of ritual purity. If so, no *a fortiori* inference can be drawn from it to the case of immersion for ritual purity.

אֶלָּא מֵהָכָא: ״וַיִּקַּח מֹשֶׁה אֶת הַדָּם וַיִּזְרֹק עַל הָעָם״ וּגְמִירִי דְּאֵין הַזָּאָה בְּלֹא טְבִילָה.

Rather, Rabbi Yehoshua derived it **from here,** where the verse states with regard to the formation of the covenant at Sinai: **"And Moses took the blood**[N] **and sprinkled it upon the people"** (Exodus 24:8), **and it is learned** as a tradition **that there is no** ritual **sprinkling without immersion.** Therefore, our forefathers also must have immersed at Sinai, and consequently that is also an essential requirement for all conversions.

NOTES

And Moses took the blood, etc. – וַיִּקַּח מֹשֶׁה אֶת הַדָּם וגו׳: The commentaries note that Onkelos translates this verse as: Moses took the blood and sprinkled it upon the altar to atone for the people, which explicitly assumes that the sprinkling of the blood was not upon the people but upon the altar. Rabbi Eliezer of Metz explains that the Gemara here differs with Onkelos on this matter. However, *Tosafot Yeshanim* suggests that Onkelos's translation might be in accordance with the opinion of Rabbi Eliezer, who does not accept the opinion of Rabbi Yehoshua and could therefore interpret the verse differently. Indeed, Maharatz Ḥayyut notes that elsewhere the Gemara explicitly states that Onkelos's translation is always in accordance with the opinions of Rabbi Eliezer and Rabbi Yehoshua, and if so, it makes sense that it renders the verse here according to one of them. If Rabbi Eliezer does not interpret the verse as Onkelos does, he could explain that it is referring to an act of sprinkling that took place after the giving of the Ten Commandments, as is suggested by the sequence of the verses in the Torah.

וְרַבִּי יְהוֹשֻׁעַ, טְבִילָה בְּאִמָּהוֹת מְנָלַן? סְבָרָא הוּא, דְּאִם כֵּן – בַּמֶּה נִכְנְסוּ תַּחַת כַּנְפֵי הַשְּׁכִינָה?

The Gemara asks: **And** with regard to the opinion of **Rabbi Yehoshua, from where do we** derive that also **in** the case of our **foremothers** there was **immersion?**[N] The Gemara answers: **It is** based on **logical reasoning, as, if so,** that they did not immerse, then **with what were they brought**[N] **under the wings of the Divine Presence?** Therefore, they also must have immersed.

אָמַר רַבִּי חִיָּיא בַּר אַבָּא אָמַר רַבִּי יוֹחָנָן: לְעוֹלָם אֵינוֹ גֵּר עַד שֶׁיִּמּוֹל וְיִטְבּוֹל. פְּשִׁיטָא, יָחִיד וְרַבִּים הֲלָכָה כְּרַבִּים!

Rabbi Ḥiyya bar Abba said that **Rabbi Yoḥanan said:** A man is **never** considered **a convert until he is** both **circumcised and has immersed.** The Gemara asks: **Isn't this obvious?** In all disputes between **an individual** Sage **and many** Sages the ***halakha* is in accordance with** the opinion of **the many** Sages; it is therefore obvious that the *halakha* is in accordance with the Rabbis.

מַאן חֲכָמִים – רַבִּי יוֹסֵי.

The Gemara explains: **Who are the Rabbis** referred to in the *baraita*? It is **Rabbi Yosei.** Since Rabbi Yosei is merely an individual Sage, it was necessarily for Rabbi Yoḥanan to state explicitly that the *halakha* is ruled in accordance with his opinion.

דְּתַנְיָא: הֲרֵי שֶׁבָּא וְאָמַר מַלְתִּי וְלֹא טָבַלְתִּי – מַטְבִּילִין אוֹתוֹ, וּמַה בְּכָךְ, דִּבְרֵי רַבִּי יְהוּדָה. רַבִּי יוֹסֵי אוֹמֵר: אֵין מַטְבִּילִין.

Rabbi Yosei's opinion is **as it is taught** in a *baraita*: With regard to a convert **who came and said: I was circumcised** for the sake of conversion **but I did not immerse,** the court **should immerse him,** as **what** would be the problem **with that;** this is **the statement of Rabbi Yehuda.** Since in any case the court immerses him, Rabbi Yehuda does not require proof of the convert's claim that he was circumcised for the sake of conversion because he holds that it is sufficient to be either circumcised or immersed for the sake of conversion. **Rabbi Yosei says:** The court **does not immerse** him. He holds that both circumcision and immersion must be performed specifically for the sake of conversion and are indispensable parts of the conversion process. Therefore, since it is impossible to verify the convert's claim with regard to his circumcision, there is no benefit to having him immerse.

לְפִיכָךְ מַטְבִּילִין גֵּר בְּשַׁבָּת, דִּבְרֵי רַבִּי יְהוּדָה. וְרַבִּי יוֹסֵי אוֹמֵר: אֵין מַטְבִּילִין.

The *baraita* states a ramification of their dispute: **Therefore,** the court **may immerse a convert** who was already circumcised **on Shabbat;** this is **the statement of Rabbi Yehuda.** Since he holds that circumcision alone effected conversion, the immersion will not effect any further change in his status, and so it is permitted on Shabbat. **And Rabbi Yosei says:** The court **may not immerse** him.[NH] Since he holds that both circumcision and immersion are necessary to effect a conversion, the immersion will effect a change in his status by making him Jewish. Therefore it is prohibited to do so on Shabbat by rabbinic decree, because it appears similar to preparing a vessel for use.

אָמַר מָר: לְפִיכָךְ מַטְבִּילִין גֵּר בְּשַׁבָּת, פְּשִׁיטָא, כֵּיוָן דְּאָמַר רַבִּי יְהוּדָה בַּחֲדָא סַגְיָא, הֵיכָא דְּמָל לְפָנֵינוּ – מַטְבִּילִין, מַאי לְפִיכָךְ?

The Gemara analyzes the latter clause: **The Master said** in the *baraita*: **Therefore,** the court **may immerse a convert** who was already circumcised **on Shabbat.** The Gemara asks: **Isn't** this an **obvious** extension of his opinion; **since Rabbi Yehuda said that** either **one** of circumcision or immersion **is sufficient, where** a convert **was circumcised in our presence** the court may certainly **immerse** him, even on Shabbat. **What,** then, is the need for the *baraita* to include the clause that begins with: **Therefore?**

מַהוּ דְּתֵימָא: לְרַבִּי יְהוּדָה טְבִילָה עִיקָּר, וּטְבִילָה בְּשַׁבָּת – לָא, דְּקָא מְתַקֵּן גַּבְרָא, קָא מַשְׁמַע לָן דְּרַבִּי יְהוּדָה אוֹ הָא אוֹ הָא בָּעֵי.

The Gemara explains: It is necessary to explicitly teach this ramification **lest you say** that **according to Rabbi Yehuda the immersion is** in fact **the principal** act that effects conversion, and when he said in the first clause that a convert who claims to have been circumcised should be immersed since there is no problem with that, his reasoning was that he holds it is only immersion that effects the conversion. **And** therefore performing the **immersion on Shabbat** would **not** be permitted, **as it establishes the person** with a new status and so would be prohibited by a rabbinic decree because it appears similar to preparing a vessel for use. The latter clause is therefore necessary to **teach us that Rabbi Yehuda requires either this or that,** i.e., either immersion or circumcision alone is sufficient to effect a conversion.

NOTES

Immersion of the foremothers – טְבִילָה בְּאִמָּהוֹת: The Gemara here is clearly referring to the women who were present at the revelation at Sinai as our foremothers. The Ritva questions the propriety of referring to them as such when the Gemara elsewhere states decisively that only four women are privileged with this title: Sarah, Rebecca, Rachel, and Leah. To resolve this difficulty, the Ritva suggests that the restrictions on the title foremother are limited to its use in prayer. Another resolution is suggested by the *Ahavat Eitan*, who suggests that since the Gemara here is referring to the entire generation and not to any specific individuals, it is acceptable to refer to them as foremothers. The Meiri cites a novel interpretation that the Gemara here is actually referring to the original four Matriarchs. This interpretation assumes that the three Patriarchs and four Matriarchs all required some act of conversion to become the forebearers of the Jewish people. The Patriarchs underwent circumcision, whereas the Matriarchs immersed.

As, if so, with what were they brought – דְּאִם כֵּן בַּמֶּה נִכְנְסוּ: The Rashba asks why the Gemara does not consider the possibility that the sprinkling of blood upon them is what effected their conversion. He answers that even if one were to claim that the sprinkling of the blood was part of the process, one cannot escape the conclusion that there was an immersion, since there is no ritual sprinkling without immersion, and therefore it is reasonable to assume that the immersion itself is part of the process of conversion. Furthermore, it is not certain that the blood was actually sprinkled upon the women; perhaps it was only sprinkled upon the men (see *Tosafot*). In fact, *Tosafot Yeshanim* explain the phrase "upon the people" as excluding the women.

Ultimately, the *halakha* is ruled in accordance with the understanding that the sprinkling was upon both men and women. There is therefore general agreement that full conversion actually involves four requirements: Acceptance of the mitzvot, circumcision, immersion, and sacrifice of a bird as a burnt-offering. The requirement to sacrifice an offering parallels the sprinkling of the blood at Sinai. Nowadays, when it is no longer possible to bring offerings, the conversion is considered valid even without it, as is explained in *Karetot* (9a) and elsewhere.

The court may not immerse a convert on Shabbat – אֵין מַטְבִּילִין גֵּר בְּשַׁבָּת: This ruling stands in contradistinction to the *halakha* that one may immerse on Shabbat in order to purify himself from a state of ritual impurity. Various distinctions have been offered between the two cases: *Tosafot* explain that immersing in order to purify oneself from a state of ritual impurity is a private matter. However, a conversion is performed in the presence of three judges and is therefore considered a public event. Since it is performed in public, the Sages prohibited it since it might appear in the eyes of the public to be similar to preparing a vessel for use. *Tosafot Yeshanim* suggest that immersing in order to purify oneself from a state of ritual impurity is permitted because the change in status is considered minor and is therefore not considered similar to preparing a vessel for use. However, the change effected by conversion is significant and is therefore prohibited. According to the Rambam, the question does not even arise. The Rambam explains that the reason to prohibit the immersion is not because it might resemble preparing a vessel for use but because presiding over conversion is considered to be an act of judgment and it is prohibited for a court to issue judgments on Shabbat.

HALAKHA

Immersion of a convert on Shabbat – טְבִילַת גֵּר בְּשַׁבָּת: Since the immersion of a convert is an act of judgment performed by the court, a convert may not be immersed on Shabbat or on a Festival. Nevertheless, if he does immerse, he is thereby rendered a convert (Rambam *Sefer Kedusha*, *Hilkhot Issurei Bia* 13:6; *Shulḥan Arukh*, *Yoreh De'a* 268:4).

רַבִּי יוֹסֵי אוֹמֵר אֵין מַטְבִּילִין. פְּשִׁיטָא, דְּכֵיוָן דְּאָמַר רַבִּי יוֹסֵי תַּרְתֵּי בָּעֵינַן – תַּקּוּנֵי גַּבְרָא בְּשַׁבָּת לָא מְתַקְּנִינַן!

The Gemara analyzes the next statement in the *baraita*: **Rabbi Yosei says:** The court **may not immerse** him. The Gemara asks: **Isn't** this an **obvious** extension of his opinion? **As, since Rabbi Yosei requires two** acts, both circumcision and immersion, to effect conversion, **we may** certainly **not establish** that **person** with a new status **on Shabbat** by completing his conversion by immersing him.

מַהוּ דְּתֵימָא: לְרַבִּי יוֹסֵי מִילָה עִיקָּר, וְהָתָם הוּא דְּלָא הֲוַאי מִילָה בְּפָנֵינוּ, אֲבָל הֵיכָא דַּהֲוְיָא מִילָה בְּפָנֵינוּ – אֵימָא לִיטְבֹּל זֶה בְּשַׁבְּתָא, קָא מַשְׁמַע לָן דְּרַבִּי יוֹסֵי תַּרְתֵּי בָּעֵי.

The Gemara explains: It is necessary to explicitly teach this ramification **lest you say** that **according to Rabbi Yosei circumcision is** in fact **the principal** act that effects conversion, **and** it is only **there,** in the first clause of the *baraita*, **where the circumcision was not performed in our presence** and so there is no way to verify whether it was done for the sake of conversion, that Rabbi Yosei states that the court should not proceed to immerse him; **however, where the circumcision was performed in our presence,** one might **say** that the conversion was already effected by the circumcision, and therefore **let us immerse this** convert **on Shabbat.** The latter clause is therefore necessary to **teach us that Rabbi Yosei requires two** acts, both circumcision and immersion, to effect conversion.

אֲמַר רַבָּה: עוּבְדָא הֲוָה בֵּי רַבִּי חִיָּיא בַּר רַבִּי, וְרַב יוֹסֵף מַתְנֵי רַבִּי אוֹשַׁעְיָא בַּר רַבִּי, וְרַב סָפְרָא מַתְנֵי רַבִּי אוֹשַׁעְיָא בְּרַבִּי חִיָּיא, דַּאֲתָא לְקַמֵּיהּ גֵּר שֶׁמָּל וְלֹא טָבַל. אֲמַר לֵיהּ שְׁהֵי כָּאן עַד לְמָחָר וְנַטְבְּלִינָךְ.

Rabba said: There was an incident in the house of Rabbi Ḥiyya bar Rabbi, and as **Rav Yosef teaches** it, **Rabbi Oshaya bar Rabbi** was also present, **and** as **Rav Safra teaches** it, a third Sage, **Rabbi Oshaya, son of Rabbi Ḥiyya,** was also present, in **which a convert came before him who was circumcised but had not immersed. He said to** the convert: **Remain here** with us **until tomorrow, and** then **we will immerse you.**

שְׁמַע מִינָּהּ תְּלָת: שְׁמַע מִינָּהּ גֵּר צָרִיךְ שְׁלֹשָׁה, וּשְׁמַע מִינָּהּ: אֵינוֹ גֵּר עַד שֶׁיִּמּוֹל וְיִטְבּוֹל, וּשְׁמַע מִינָּהּ: אֵין מַטְבִּילִין גֵּר בַּלַּיְלָה. וְנֵימָא: שְׁמַע מִינָּהּ נַמִּי בָּעֵינַן מוּמְחִין! דִּלְמָא דְּאִיקְלְעוּ.

Rabba said: **Learn from** this incident **three** principles: **Learn from it** that **a convert requires** a court of **three**[N] people to preside over the conversion, as Rav Safra taught that the case involved three Sages. **And learn from it** that **one is not** considered to be **a convert until he has been** both **circumcised and immersed. And learn from it** that the court **may not immerse a convert at night,** as they instructed him to remain there until the following day. The Gemara suggests: **And let us say** that one should **also learn from it** that **we require** a court of **experts** to preside over the conversion, as Rav Safra identified that three expert Sages were present. The Gemara rejects this: **Perhaps they** simply **happened to be** there, but in fact three laymen would suffice.

אֲמַר רַבִּי חִיָּיא בַּר אַבָּא אָמַר רַבִּי יוֹחָנָן: גֵּר צָרִיךְ שְׁלֹשָׁה "מִשְׁפָּט" כְּתִיב בֵּיהּ.

Rabbi Ḥiyya bar Abba said that **Rabbi Yoḥanan said: A convert requires** a court of **three** to preside over conversion, because **"judgment," is written with regard to him,** as the verse states: "And one judgment shall be both for you and for the convert that sojourns with you" (Numbers 15:16), and legal judgments require a court of three judges.[H]

תָּנוּ רַבָּנַן: מִי שֶׁבָּא וְאָמַר: "גֵּר אֲנִי", יָכוֹל נְקַבְּלֶנּוּ – תַּלְמוּד לוֹמַר "אִתְּךָ" – בְּמוּחְזָק לְךָ. בָּא וְעֵדָיו עִמּוֹ מִנַּיִן – תַּלְמוּד לוֹמַר "וְכִי יָגוּר אִתְּךָ גֵּר בְּאַרְצְכֶם".

The Sages taught in a *baraita*: With regard to **someone who came and said: I am a convert,**[N] one **might** have thought that **we should accept him;** therefore, **the verse states:** "And if a convert sojourns **with you** in your land, you shall not oppress him" (Leviticus 19:33). The emphasis on "with you" suggests that only someone who was already **presumed by you** to be a valid convert should be accepted as a convert. If **he came and** brought **witnesses** to his conversion **with him, from where** is it derived that he is to be accepted? It is from **the** beginning of that **verse,** which **states: "And if a convert sojourns with you in your land."**

NOTES

A convert requires three – גֵּר צָרִיךְ שְׁלֹשָׁה: The commentaries explain that this is derived from the fact that Rav Safra taught that the case involved three Sages. *Tosafot* explain that this must certainly have been Rav Safra's intention because the third scholar mentioned was not of the same caliber as the first two, and therefore it does not stand to reason that he would name him together with them unless his intention was to teach the need for a court of three. Furthermore, some note that Rav Yosef and Rav Safra would not have been particular to mention the names of the additional Sages who were present just so that the record of events would be more accurate. Rather, they clearly sought to teach a ruling by doing so. This is also suggested by the Gemara's formulation: And Rav Yosef taught, which indicates that he was adding to the statement of Rabba and was not in dispute with him (*Ramat Shmuel*).

Someone who came and said: I am a convert – מִי שֶׁבָּא וְאָמַר: גֵּר אֲנִי: This discussion applies only to one who is known to have been a gentile. If he had not been known originally as a gentile he would be accepted even without proof that he had converted, because he could just as easily have passed himself off as a Jew (Rabbeinu Tam; Ramban; Rashba), or because it is a fact that could easily be verified later and therefore it can be assumed he would not lie about it (Ritva). However, the Rambam writes that this applies only in Eretz Yisrael, whereas elsewhere a convert should never be accepted based on his own testimony without witnesses (Rambam *Sefer Kedusha, Hilkhot Issurei Bia* 13:10).

HALAKHA

Conversion in a court – גִּיּוּר בְּבֵית דִּין: One is considered to be a convert only after he accepts upon himself the yoke of mitzvot, undergoes circumcision, and immerses in a ritual bath. These acts must be performed before three individuals suitable for sitting in judgment and must be done during the day. After the fact, if one immersed at night, the conversion is still valid (Rambam *Sefer Kedusha, Hilkhot Issurei Bia* 13:6; *Shulḥan Arukh, Yoreh De'a* 268:3).

NOTES

I have derived only that a convert is accepted in Eretz Yisrael – אֵין לִי אֶלָּא בָּאָרֶץ: *Tosafot* explain that the Gemara here considers the possibility that conversion would be possible only in Eretz Yisrael. *Tosefot HaRosh* suggests a rationale for such an opinion. In Eretz Yisrael a convert stands to gain from the bounty of the land and the other benefits of living there. Therefore, it is less likely that a convert would revert back to his previous ways if he lives in Eretz Yisrael than if he lives elsewhere. Due to the concern that exists with a convert outside Eretz Yisrael, it is conceivable that the possibility of converting there is entirely precluded.

HALAKHA

One who comes and says: I converted – מִי שֶׁבָּא וְאָמַר נִתְגַּיַּירְתִּי: If one presumed to be a gentile comes and claims to have converted in accordance with the *halakhot* of conversion, whether in Eretz Yisrael or outside Eretz Yisrael, he is not accepted as a convert and may not marry in the congregation of Israel until he brings witnesses to his conversion. This ruling is in accordance with the opinion of the Rabbis (Rambam *Sefer Kedusha*, *Hilkhot Issurei Bia* 13:7; *Shulḥan Arukh*, *Yoreh De'a* 268:10).

אֵין לִי אֶלָּא בָּאָרֶץ, בְּחוּץ לָאָרֶץ מִנַּיִן? תַּלְמוּד לוֹמַר ״אִתְּךָ״ – בְּכׇל מָקוֹם שֶׁאִתָּךְ. אִם כֵּן מָה תַּלְמוּד לוֹמַר ״בְּאַרְצְכֶם״ – בָּאָרֶץ צָרִיךְ לְהָבִיא רְאָיָה, בְּחוּץ לָאָרֶץ – אֵין צָרִיךְ לְהָבִיא רְאָיָה. דִּבְרֵי רַבִּי יְהוּדָה. וַחֲכָמִים אוֹמְרִים: בֵּין בָּאָרֶץ בֵּין בְּחוּצָה לָאָרֶץ – צָרִיךְ לְהָבִיא רְאָיָה.

I have derived **only** that a convert is accepted **in Eretz** Yisrael;[N] **from where** do I derive that also **outside** of **Eretz** Yisrael he is to be accepted? **The verse states "with you,"** which indicates that **in any place that he is with you,** you should accept him. **If so, what** is the meaning when **the verse states: In the land?** This indicates that **in Eretz** Yisrael **he needs to bring evidence** that he is a convert, **but outside** of **Eretz** Yisrael **he does not need to bring evidence** that he is a convert; rather, his claim is accepted. This is **the statement of Rabbi Yehuda. And the Rabbis say: Whether** he is **in Eretz** Yisrael **or whether** he is **outside** of **Eretz** Yisrael, **he needs to bring evidence.**

בָּא הוּא וְעֵדָיו עִמּוֹ – קְרָא לָמָּה לִי? אָמַר רַב שֵׁשֶׁת, דְּאָמְרִי: שָׁמַעְנוּ שֶׁנִּתְגַּיֵּיר בְּבֵית דִּין שֶׁל פְּלוֹנִי. סָלְקָא דַּעְתָּךְ אָמֵינָא: לָא לֵיהֵמְנִינְהוּ, קָא מַשְׁמַע לַן.

The Gemara analyzes the *baraita*: In the case when **he came and** brought **witnesses** to his conversion **with him, why do I** need a **verse** to teach that he is accepted? In all cases, the testimony of witnesses is fully relied upon. **Rav Sheshet said:** The case is **where they say: We heard that he converted in** the **court** of **so-and-so,** but they did not witness the actual conversion. And it is necessary to teach this because it could **enter your mind to say** that **they should not be relied upon;** therefore, the verse **teaches us** that they are relied upon.

״בְּאַרְצְכֶם״, אֵין לִי אֶלָּא בָּאָרֶץ, בְּחוּצָה לָאָרֶץ מִנַּיִן? תַּלְמוּד לוֹמַר ״אִתְּךָ״ – בְּכׇל מָקוֹם שֶׁאִתָּךְ. וְהָא אַפִּיקְתֵּיהּ! חֲדָא מֵ״אִתְּךָ״ וַחֲדָא מֵ״עִמָּךְ״.

As cited above, the latter clause of the *baraita* states: "With you **in** your **land**" (Leviticus 19:33). **I have** derived **only** that a convert is accepted **in Eretz** Yisrael; **from where** do I derive that also **outside** of **Eretz** Yisrael he is to be accepted? **The verse states: "With you,"** which indicates that **in any place that he is with you,** you should accept him. The Gemara asks: **But didn't you** already **expound that** phrase in the first clause of the *baraita* to teach that one doesn't accept the claims of an individual that he is a valid convert? The Gemara explains: **One** of these *halakhot* is derived from the phrase **"with you"** in the verse cited, **and** the other **one** is derived from the phrase **"with you"** in a subsequent verse (Leviticus 25:35).

וַחֲכָמִים אוֹמְרִים: בֵּין בָּאָרֶץ בֵּין בְּחוּצָה לָאָרֶץ צָרִיךְ לְהָבִיא רְאָיָה. וְאֶלָּא, הָא כְּתִיב ״בְּאַרְצְכֶם״!

The *baraita* states: **And the Rabbis say: Whether** he is **in Eretz** Yisrael **or whether** he is **outside** of **Eretz** Yisrael, **he needs to bring evidence.** The Gemara asks: **But isn't "in your land" written** in the verse? How can the Rabbis deny any distinction between the *halakha* inside and outside of Eretz Yisrael?

הָהוּא מִיבְּעֵי לֵיהּ דַּאֲפִילּוּ בָּאָרֶץ מְקַבְּלִים גֵּרִים. דְּסָלְקָא דַּעְתָּךְ אָמֵינָא: מִשּׁוּם טִיבוּתָא דְּאֶרֶץ יִשְׂרָאֵל קָמִגַּיְירִי, וְהָשְׁתָּא נָמֵי דְּלֵיכָּא טִיבוּתָא – אִיכָּא לֶקֶט שִׁכְחָה וּפֵאָה וּמַעְשַׂר עָנִי, קָא מַשְׁמַע לַן.

The Gemara explains: **That** phrase **is necessary** to teach **that even in Eretz** Yisrael, the Jewish people should **accept converts, as it could enter your mind to say** that it is only **for the sake of** benefiting from **the goodness of Eretz Yisrael,** and not for the sake of Heaven, that **they are converting,** and therefore they should not be accepted. **And** it could also enter your mind to say that even **nowadays, when** God's blessing has ceased and **there is no** longer **the** original **goodness** from which to benefit, one should still suspect their purity of motives because **there are** the **gleanings,** the **forgotten sheaves, and** the **corners** of fields, **and the poor man's tithe** from which they would benefit by converting. Therefore, the verse **teaches us** that they are accepted even in Eretz Yisrael.

אָמַר רַבִּי חִיָּיא בַּר אַבָּא אָמַר רַבִּי יוֹחָנָן: הֲלָכָה, בֵּין בָּאָרֶץ בֵּין בְּחוּץ לָאָרֶץ – צָרִיךְ לְהָבִיא רְאָיָה. פְּשִׁיטָא, יָחִיד וְרַבִּים הֲלָכָה כְּרַבִּים! מַהוּ דְּתֵימָא: מִסְתַּבֵּר טַעְמָא דְּרַבִּי יְהוּדָה, דְּקָמְסַיְּיעֵי לֵיהּ קְרָאֵי, קָא מַשְׁמַע לַן.

Rabbi Ḥiyya bar Abba said that **Rabbi Yoḥanan said:** The *halakha* is that **whether** a convert is **in Eretz** Yisrael **or whether** he is **outside of Eretz** Yisrael, **he needs to bring evidence.**[H] The Gemara asks: **Isn't** this **obvious;** in all disputes between **an individual** Sage **and many** Sages the ***halakha* is in accordance with** the opinion of the **many** Sages. The Gemara explains: It is necessary to state this **lest you say** that **Rabbi Yehuda's reason** is more **logical, being that the verse supports him** when it states: "In your land." Therefore, it is necessary for Rabbi Yoḥanan to **teach us** that the *halakha* is not in accordance with his opinion.

תנו רבנן: "ושפטתם צדק בין איש ובין אחיו ובין גרו" מכאן אמר רבי יהודה: גר שנתגייר בבית דין – הרי זה גר, בינו לבין עצמו – אינו גר.

The Sages taught: The verse states that Moses charged the judges of a court: **"And judge righteously between a man and his brother, and the convert with him"** (Deuteronomy 1:16). **From here,** based on the mention of a convert in the context of judgment in a court, **Rabbi Yehuda said:** A potential **convert who converts in a court is a valid convert.** However, if he converts **in private, he is not a convert.**

מעשה באחד שבא לפני רבי יהודה, ואמר לו: נתגיירתי ביני לבין עצמי. אמר לו רבי יהודה: יש לך עדים? אמר ליה: לאו. יש לך בנים? אמר ליה: הן. אמר לו: נאמן אתה לפסול את עצמך, ואי אתה נאמן לפסול את בניך.

The Gemara relates: There was **an incident involving one** who was presumed to be Jewish **who came before Rabbi Yehuda and said to him: I converted in private,** and therefore I am not actually Jewish. **Rabbi Yehuda said to him:** Do **you have witnesses**[N] to support your claim? **He said to him: No.** Rabbi Yehuda asked: Do **you have children? He said to him: Yes.** Rabbi Yehuda **said to him: You are deemed credible** in order **to render yourself unfit**[NH] to marry a Jewish woman by claiming that you are a gentile, **but you are not deemed credible** in order **to render your children unfit.**[N]

[ומי] אמר רבי יהודה אבנים לא מהימן? והתניא: "יכיר" – יכירנו לאחרים. מכאן אמר רבי יהודה: נאמן אדם לומר: זה בני בכור. וכשם שנאמן לומר זה בני בכור כך נאמן לומר: בני זה בן גרושה הוא, או בן חלוצה הוא. וחכמים אומרים: אינו נאמן.

The Gemara asks: **But did Rabbi Yehuda** actually **say** that **with** regard to his **children he is not deemed credible? But isn't it taught** in a *baraita*: The verse states: **"He shall acknowledge** [*yakir*] the firstborn, the son of the hated, by giving him a double portion of all that he has" (Deuteronomy 21:17). The phrase "he shall acknowledge" is apparently superfluous. It is therefore expounded to teach that the father is deemed credible so that **he can identify him** [*yakirenu*] **to others. From here Rabbi Yehuda said: A man is deemed credible to say: This is my firstborn son,**[H] **and just as he is deemed credible to say: This is my firstborn son, so too,** a priest **is deemed credible to say: This son of mine is a son of a divorced woman** and myself, **or** to say: He is **a son of a *ḥalutza*** and myself, and therefore he is disqualified due to flawed lineage [*halal*]. **And the Rabbis say: He is not deemed credible.**[H] If Rabbi Yehuda holds that a father is deemed credible to render his children unfit, why did he rule otherwise in the case of the convert?

אמר רב נחמן בר יצחק, הכי קאמר ליה: לדבריך גוי אתה, ואין עדות לגוי. רבינא אמר: הכי קאמר ליה: יש לך בנים? הן, יש לך בני בנים? הן. אמר ליה: נאמן אתה לפסול בניך, ואי אתה נאמן לפסול בני בניך.

Rav Naḥman bar Yitzḥak said that **this is what** Rabbi Yehuda **said to him: According to your statement you are a gentile, and there is no testimony for a gentile,** as a gentile is a disqualified witness. Consequently, you cannot testify about the status of your children and render them unfit. **Ravina said** that **this is what** Rabbi Yehuda **said to him:**[N] **Do you have children? He said: Yes. He said to him:** Do **you have grandchildren?** He said: **Yes. He said to him: You are deemed credible** in order **to render your children unfit,** based on the phrase "he shall acknowledge," **but you are not deemed credible** in order **to render your grandchildren unfit,**[N] as the verse affords a father credibility only with respect to his children.

HALAKHA

Deemed credible in order to render himself unfit, etc. – נאמן לפסול עצמו וכו׳: With regard to one who was presumed to be Jewish who comes and says that he converted in private, he is deemed credible in order to render himself unfit and is therefore prohibited from marrying a Jewish woman until he converts in the presence of a court. If he has children, he is not deemed credible in order to render his children unfit. This is in accordance with the opinion of Rabbi Yehuda as explained by Rav Naḥman bar Yitzḥak (Rambam *Sefer Kedusha, Hilkhot Issurei Bia* 13:8; *Shulḥan Arukh, Yoreh De'a* 268:11).

He is deemed credible to say: This is my firstborn son – נאמן אדם לומר: זה בני בכור: A father is deemed credible to say concerning one of his sons, or even concerning someone who was presumed not to be his son at all, that he is in fact his firstborn son. He is likewise deemed credible to say that someone who was presumed to be his firstborn son is not actually his firstborn. The Rema writes that once a father has claimed that a certain person is his firstborn, he can no longer claim that someone else is (*Tur*, citing Ramban; *Beit Yosef*, citing Ran; Rambam *Sefer Mishpatim, Hilkhot Naḥalot* 2:14; *Shulḥan Arukh, Ḥoshen Mishpat* 277:12).

Credibility to render a son unfit – נאמנות לפסול בן: A father is deemed credible to render his son unfit, e.g., if he were to say that the son of his wife is not actually his own son and is therefore a *mamzer*. This is true only if that son does not have any children. If the son does have children, then the father is not believed even with regard to his own son. This is in accordance with the opinion of Ravina. The Rema, citing the Ramah, writes that if the son was presumed to be legitimate based on the testimony of his father, then the father is no longer able to render him unfit. In addition, a man is deemed credible to render unfit only someone who was always presumed to be his son, e.g., the child born to his wife. Therefore, if a single woman announces that her son is actually the child of so-and-so, that man is not deemed credible to claim that the child is a *mamzer* (*Terumat HaDeshen*; Rambam *Sefer Kedusha, Hilkhot Issurei Bia* 15:16; *Shulḥan Arukh, Even HaEzer* 4:29).

NOTES

Do you have witnesses – יש לך עדים: *Tosafot* ask how the convert could possibly have had witnesses if he had converted in private. *Tosefot HaRosh* explains that from here it is apparent that the need for a court of three to be present at the conversion is essential, and if three are not present, the conversion is invalid even after the fact. Accordingly, even if two witnesses were present, the conversion would still be defined as being in private. Other commentaries assume that a conversion can be valid even if performed in the presence of a single judge. If so, the question raised by *Tosafot* remains. One commentary suggests that Rav Yehuda's question was whether the individual had witnesses that he converted before he had children (*Yam shel Shlomo*). Alternatively, the Ra'avad suggests that it had previously been assumed that the individual here had always been a Jew. Rav Yehuda therefore asked him to provide witnesses that he was once a gentile (see Ramban and Rabbi Avraham min HaHar).

You are deemed credible in order to render yourself unfit – נאמן אתה לפסול את עצמך: The commentaries explain that since the testimony about his children was inadmissible, none of it could be accepted. Rav Yehuda's ruling that the convert was able to render himself unfit is based on the principle that if one claims that an item or action is prohibited to him, he is thereafter obligated to relate to that item or action as though it were indeed prohibited, irrespective of whether that claim could have been accepted as testimony in court (see *Tosafot* and *Nimmukei Yosef*).

You are not deemed credible in order to render your children unfit – אין אתה נאמן לפסול את בניך: The early commentaries ask: Even if that man was deemed credible with regard to his children, why would that render them unfit, since the *halakha* is that the offspring of a gentile and a Jewish woman is a Jew of unflawed lineage? The commentaries note that it is insufficient to resolve this question by assuming that this statement in accordance with the opinions that the offspring of a gentile and a Jewish woman is unfit for the priesthood, because according to Rabbi Yehuda, even the daughter of a valid convert is unfit to marry into the priesthood (see *Tosafot*, Ra'avad as cited by Ramban, and Rashba). Some explain that Rabbi Yehuda holds in accordance with the opinion of Rabbi Akiva, which is not accepted as *halakha*, that the offspring of a gentile father is actually a *mamzer* (see *Tosafot* and Ramban). Others explain that the case here was that both parents were converts who testified that they had not converted properly, and therefore according to their claim the children were not actually Jewish (Ramban; see *Yam shel Shlomo*). One commentary suggests that the disqualification referred to here is not a halakhic one; rather, it refers to the harm caused to the children's name by virtue of the fact they would be considered to be the children of gentiles (Rabbi Avraham min HaHar).

Ravina said that this is what he said to him, etc. – רבינא אמר: הכי קאמר ליה וכו׳: Rav Naḥman bar Yitzhak and Ravina appear to disagree over whether or not a gentile is deemed credible to testify about his son. One commentary explains that their dispute concerns the essential nature of the unique credibility that is afforded to a father with respect to his son. Rav Naḥman bar Yitzhak holds that this credibility is an extension of the standard *halakhot* of testimony. Therefore, just as a gentile is disqualified from providing testimony in a standard case, he is also not deemed credible with respect to his son. Ravina holds that the credibility that is afforded to a father is a unique *halakha* that is not based on the standard *halakhot* of testimony. Accordingly, there is no reason that a gentile should be excluded (*Ḥiddushei Batra*).

You are not deemed credible in order to render your grandchildren unfit – ואי אתה נאמן לפסול בני בניך: Most commentaries follow the understanding of this statement suggested by *Tosafot*: Since he is not deemed credible with regard to his grandchildren, then if he has any grandchildren from the children he is testifying about he is not deemed credible with regard to those children either, because rendering his children unfit will perforce have an effect on the status of his grandchildren. In contrast, the *She'iltot deRav Aḥai Gaon* does differentiate between children and grandchildren. He explains that a father is given the unique ability to render his children unfit; however, his power is limited so that no ramifications of his claims will be passed down to affect his grandchildren.

תַּנְיָא נַמִּי הָכִי, רַבִּי יְהוּדָה אוֹמֵר: נֶאֱמָן אָדָם לוֹמַר עַל בְּנוֹ קָטָן, וְאֵין נֶאֱמָן עַל בְּנוֹ גָּדוֹל. וְאָמַר רַבִּי חִיָּיא בַּר אַבָּא אָמַר רַבִּי יוֹחָנָן: לֹא קָטָן קָטָן מַמָּשׁ, וְלֹא גָּדוֹל גָּדוֹל מַמָּשׁ, אֶלָּא, קָטָן וְיֵשׁ לוֹ בָּנִים – זֶהוּ גָּדוֹל, גָּדוֹל וְאֵין לוֹ בָּנִים – זֶהוּ קָטָן.

This opinion of Ravina **is also taught** in a *baraita*: **Rabbi Yehuda says: A man is deemed credible to say about his minor son** that he is unfit, **but he is not deemed credible to say about his adult son** that he is unfit. **And** in explanation of the *baraita*, **Rabbi Ḥiyya bar Abba said** that **Rabbi Yoḥanan said:** The reference to **a minor** son does **not** mean one who is **literally a minor,** who has not yet reached majority, **and** the reference to **an adult** son does **not** mean one who is **literally an adult,** who has reached majority; **rather, a minor who has children, this is** what the *baraita* is referring to as **an adult,** and **an adult who does not have children, this is** what the *baraita* is referring to as **a minor.**

וְהִלְכְתָא כְּוָותֵיהּ דְּרַב נַחְמָן בַּר יִצְחָק. וְהָתַנְיָא כְּוָותֵיהּ דְּרָבִינָא! הַהוּא לְעִנְיַן ״יַכִּיר״ אִיתְּמַר.

The Gemara concludes: **And the *halakha* is in accordance with** the opinion of **Rav Naḥman bar Yitzḥak.** The Gemara asks: **But isn't it taught** in the *baraita* **in accordance with** the opinion **of Ravina?** If there is a *baraita* that supports his opinion, the *halakha* should be in accordance with his opinion. The Gemara explains: **That** *baraita* **was stated concerning the matter of "he shall acknowledge,"** that a father is deemed credible to render his son unfit; however, if one claims he is a gentile, he is not deemed credible to say the same about his son.

תָּנוּ רַבָּנַן: גֵּר שֶׁבָּא לְהִתְגַּיֵּיר בַּזְּמַן הַזֶּה אוֹמְרִים לוֹ: מָה רָאִיתָ שֶׁבָּאתָ לְהִתְגַּיֵּיר? אִי אַתָּה יוֹדֵעַ שֶׁיִּשְׂרָאֵל בַּזְּמַן הַזֶּה דְּווּיִים, דְּחוּפִים, סְחוּפִים וּמְטוֹרָפִין, וְיִסּוּרִין בָּאִין עֲלֵיהֶם? אִם אוֹמֵר: יוֹדֵעַ אֲנִי וְאֵינִי כְּדַאי – מְקַבְּלִין אוֹתוֹ מִיָּד.

§ **The Sages taught** in a *baraita*: With regard to a potential **convert who comes to** a court in order to **convert, at the present time,** when the Jews are in exile, the judges of the court **say to him:**[H] **What did you see that** motivated **you to come to convert? Don't you know that the Jewish people at the present time are anguished, suppressed, despised, and harassed, and hardships are** frequently **visited upon them? If he says: I know, and** although **I am unworthy** of joining the Jewish people and sharing in their sorrow, I nevertheless desire to do so, then the court **accepts him immediately** to begin the conversion process.

וּמוֹדִיעִין אוֹתוֹ מִקְצָת מִצְוֹת קַלּוֹת, וּמִקְצָת מִצְוֹת חֲמוּרוֹת, וּמוֹדִיעִין אוֹתוֹ עֲוֹן לֶקֶט שִׁכְחָה וּפֵאָה וּמַעְשַׂר עָנִי, וּמוֹדִיעִין אוֹתוֹ עָנְשָׁן שֶׁל מִצְוֹת, אוֹמְרִים לוֹ: הֱוֵי יוֹדֵעַ שֶׁעַד שֶׁלֹּא בָּאתָ לְמִדָּה זוֹ, אָכַלְתָּ חֵלֶב – אִי אַתָּה עָנוּשׁ כָּרֵת, חִלַּלְתָּ שַׁבָּת -אִי אַתָּה עָנוּשׁ סְקִילָה. וְעַכְשָׁיו, אָכַלְתָּ חֵלֶב – עָנוּשׁ כָּרֵת, חִלַּלְתָּ שַׁבָּת – עָנוּשׁ סְקִילָה.

And the judges of the court **inform him of some of the lenient mitzvot**[N] **and some of the stringent mitzvot, and they inform him of the sin** of neglecting the mitzva to allow the poor to take **gleanings, forgotten sheaves, and** produce in the **corner** of one's field, **and** about the **poor man's tithe. And they inform him of the punishment for** transgressing **the mitzvot,** as follows: **They say to him: Be aware that before you came to this status** and converted, **had you eaten forbidden fat, you would not be punished by *karet*,** and **had you profaned Shabbat, you would not be punished by stoning,** since these prohibitions do not apply to gentiles. **But now,** once converted, if **you have eaten forbidden fat you are punished by *karet*,** and if **you have profaned Shabbat, you are punished by stoning.**

וּכְשֵׁם שֶׁמּוֹדִיעִין אוֹתוֹ עָנְשָׁן שֶׁל מִצְוֹת, כָּךְ מוֹדִיעִין אוֹתוֹ מַתַּן שְׂכָרָן. אוֹמְרִים לוֹ: הֱוֵי יוֹדֵעַ שֶׁהָעוֹלָם הַבָּא אֵינוֹ עָשׂוּי אֶלָּא לַצַּדִּיקִים, וְיִשְׂרָאֵל בַּזְּמַן הַזֶּה אֵינָם יְכוֹלִים לְקַבֵּל

And just as they inform him about the **punishment for** transgressing the **mitzvot, so too, they inform him** about the **reward granted for** fulfilling **them. They say to him: Be aware that the World-to-Come is made only for the righteous,** and if you observe the mitzvot you will merit it, **and** be aware that **the Jewish people, at the present time, are unable to receive** their full reward in this world;

HALAKHA

What is said to one who comes to convert – מָה אוֹמְרִים לַבָּא לְהִתְגַּיֵּיר: When a gentile comes to convert, the judges of the court say to him: For what reason do you seek to convert? Don't you know that the Jewish people are oppressed and suffer nowadays? If he accepts this upon himself, the court informs him of some of the lenient mitzvot and some of the stringent mitzvot, and informs him of the punishment for not observing the mitzvot. The judges should not overwhelm him, nor are they exacting with him, and they inform him of the reward given for performance of the mitzvot in the World-to-Come (Rambam *Sefer Kedusha, Hilkhot Issurei Bia* 13:14; *Shulḥan Arukh, Yoreh De'a* 268:2).

NOTES

Some of the lenient mitzvot – מִקְצָת מִצְוֹת קַלּוֹת: The Meiri explains that since the gentile system of law does not relate to less serious issues and does not demand a commitment to minutiae, it is necessary to teach him some of the more lenient mitzvot and thereby demonstrate that the halakhic system is all-encompassing and relates to every detail of life. If he is unable to commit to this, he is given the opportunity to withdraw.

לֹא רוֹב טוֹבָה וְלֹא רוֹב פּוּרְעָנוּת. וְאֵין מַרְבִּין עָלָיו, וְאֵין מְדַקְדְּקִין עָלָיו.

they are **not** able to receive either **an abundance of good nor an abundance of calamities**,[N] since the primary place for reward and punishment is in the World-to-Come. **And they do not overwhelm him** with threats, **and they are not exacting with him** about the details of the mitzvot.

קִיבֵּל – מָלִין אוֹתוֹ מִיָּד. נִשְׁתַּיְּירוּ בּוֹ צִיצִין הַמְעַכְּבִין אֶת הַמִּילָה – חוֹזְרִים וּמָלִין אוֹתוֹ שְׁנִיָּה. נִתְרַפֵּא – מַטְבִּילִין אוֹתוֹ מִיָּד. וּשְׁנֵי תַּלְמִידֵי חֲכָמִים עוֹמְדִים עַל גַּבָּיו, וּמוֹדִיעִין אוֹתוֹ מִקְצָת מִצְוֹת קַלּוֹת וּמִקְצָת מִצְוֹת חֲמוּרוֹת. טָבַל וְעָלָה – הֲרֵי הוּא כְּיִשְׂרָאֵל לְכָל דְּבָרָיו.

If **he accepts** upon himself all of these ramifications, then **they circumcise him immediately.** If **there** still **remain on him shreds** of flesh from the foreskin **that invalidate the circumcision, they circumcise him again a second** time to remove them. When **he is healed** from the circumcision, **they immerse him**[N] **immediately,**[H] **and two Torah scholars stand over him** at the time of his immersion **and inform him of some of the lenient mitzvot and some of the stringent mitzvot.** Once **he has immersed and emerged, he is like** a born **Jew in every sense.**

אִשָּׁה – נָשִׁים מוֹשִׁיבוֹת אוֹתָהּ בַּמַּיִם עַד צַוָּארָהּ, וּשְׁנֵי תַּלְמִידֵי חֲכָמִים עוֹמְדִים לָהּ מִבַּחוּץ, וּמוֹדִיעִין אוֹתָהּ מִקְצָת מִצְוֹת קַלּוֹת וּמִקְצָת מִצְוֹת חֲמוּרוֹת.

For the immersion of **a woman: Women** appointed by the court **seat her in the water** of the ritual bath **up to her neck, and two Torah scholars stand outside** the bath house so as not to compromise her modesty, **and** from there **they inform her of some of the lenient mitzvot and some of the stringent mitzvot.**

אֶחָד גֵּר וְאֶחָד עֶבֶד מְשׁוּחְרָר. וּבְמָקוֹם שֶׁנִּדָּה טוֹבֶלֶת – שָׁם גֵּר וְעֶבֶד מְשׁוּחְרָר טוֹבְלִין. וְכָל דָּבָר שֶׁחוֹצֵץ בִּטְבִילָה – חוֹצֵץ בְּגֵר וּבְעֶבֶד מְשׁוּחְרָר וּבְנִדָּה.

The procedure applies for **both a convert and an emancipated slave**[HN] who, upon immersion at the time of his emancipation, becomes a Jew in every sense. **And in the same place that a menstruating woman immerses,** i.e., in a ritual bath of forty *se'a* of water, **there a convert and an emancipated slave also immerse. And anything that interposes** between one's body and the water of the ritual bath **with regard to immersion**[N] of a ritually impure person, in a manner that would invalidate the immersion, also **interposes** and invalidates the immersion **for a convert, and for an emancipated slave, and for a menstruating woman.**

HALAKHA

Circumcision and immersion – מִילָה וּטְבִילָה: Once a convert has been made aware of the ramifications of conversion and he nevertheless commits to undergo the process, he is circumcised immediately. As soon as his wound heals, he is immersed to complete the process (Rambam *Sefer Kedusha, Hilkhot Issurei Bia* 14:5; *Shulḥan Arukh, Yoreh De'a* 268:2).

Immersion of a convert and an emancipated slave – טְבִילַת גֵּר וְעֶבֶד מְשׁוּחְרָר: A convert or an emancipated slave requires immersion in a ritual bath that is valid for the immersion of a menstruating woman. Any substance that is considered an interposition and would invalidate the immersion of a menstruating woman also invalidates the immersion of a convert or slave (Rambam *Sefer Kedusha, Hilkhot Issurei Bia* 13:13 and *Sefer Tahara, Hilkhot Mikvaot* 2:22; *Shulḥan Arukh, Yoreh De'a* 268:2).

NOTES

Nor an abundance of calamities – וְלֹא רוֹב פּוּרְעָנוּת: This is a continuation of the explanation with regard to the reception of reward for the performance of the mitzvot. Although the Jewish people suffer in exile, the calamities will never dominate to such an extent that the nation might cease to exist completely, as has occurred with other nations (Rabbi Avraham min HaHar).

When he is healed, they immerse him – נִתְרַפֵּא מַטְבִּילִין אוֹתוֹ: The Ramban asks why the convert does not first immerse and only then undergo circumcision; doing so would avoid the delay in the conversion process while the convert waits for his wound to heal. The Ramban suggests that since the circumcision is difficult and painful, the insistence that he perform it first provides another opportunity for him to withdraw from the process.

The basic assumption of the Ramban is that even if the immersion would precede the circumcision, the conversion would be valid. The Ramban adduces proof for this assumption that the order of the two rituals is not essential from the case of a pregnant convert. The Gemara elsewhere states that the immersion of a pregnant woman counts for her fetus as well. However, if the fetus is a male, it will require circumcision once it is born. It would appear, then, that even if the immersion precedes the circumcision the conversion is still valid.

The Rashba and the Ritva reject the Ramban's claim and dismiss his proof. They claim that the immersion must always be the final stage of the process. They bring an analogy to support their claim from the *halakha* of immersing vessels purchased from gentiles, which requires that the vessels first be purged of any non-kosher substances and only then may they be immersed.

With regard to the Ramban's proof, the commentaries suggest various alternative ways to interpret that Gemara. Some claim that the immersion can count for the fetus despite the fact it has not yet been circumcised only because at the time of the immersion the fetus was still unfit for circumcision (*Tosafot*). Others explain that the immersion is effective only according to the opinions that a fetus is halakhically considered to be an extension of the mother's body. Consequently, the immersion alone effects the fetus's conversion (Rid). Other commentaries claim that the immersion is valid for the fetus only if it emerges that the fetus was female, but if the fetus turns out to be male, once it is born it will require first circumcision and then immersion in the correct order (see Rashba).

Immersion of an emancipated slave – טְבִילַת עֶבֶד מְשׁוּחְרָר: The early commentaries debate whether the immersion of a slave upon his emancipation is required by Torah law and effects the full conversion of the slave, rendering him a Jew, or whether it is only a rabbinic requirement and in actual fact the conversion process was completed when he was initially immersed upon becoming a slave, and the emancipation is only to remove his slave status (see *Tosafot*, *Tosefot HaRosh*, and Meiri).

And anything that interposes with regard to immersion – וְכָל דָּבָר שֶׁחוֹצֵץ בִּטְבִילָה: Rashi explains that the Gemara compares the case of a ritually impure person immersing to purify himself to the case of conversion. The present version of the Gemara text supports this. However, other commentaries had a variant text in which the comparison is to the immersion of a woman who is ritually impure due to menstruation, who immerses in order to be permitted to her husband (see Ramban and Ritva).

אָמַר מָר: גֵּר שֶׁבָּא לְהִתְגַּיֵּיר אוֹמְרִים לוֹ: מָה רָאִיתָ שֶׁבָּאתָ לְהִתְגַּיֵּיר? וּמוֹדִיעִים אוֹתוֹ מִקְצָת מִצְוֹת קַלּוֹת וּמִקְצָת מִצְוֹת חֲמוּרוֹת. מַאי טַעְמָא? דְּאִי פָּרֵישׁ – נִפְרוֹשׁ. דְּאָמַר רַבִּי חֶלְבּוֹ: קָשִׁים גֵּרִים לְיִשְׂרָאֵל כְּסַפַּחַת, דִּכְתִיב ״וְנִלְוָה הַגֵּר עֲלֵיהֶם וְנִסְפְּחוּ עַל בֵּית יַעֲקֹב״.

The Gemara analyzes the *baraita*. **The Master said** in the *baraita*: With regard to a potential **convert who comes to** a court in order **to convert,** the judges of the court **say to him: What did you see that** motivated **you to come to convert? And they inform him** of **some of the lenient mitzvot and some of the stringent mitzvot.** The Gemara asks: **What is the reason** to say this to him? It is so **that if he** is going to **withdraw** from the conversion process, **let him withdraw** already at this stage. He should not be convinced to continue, **as Rabbi Ḥelbo said: Converts are as harmful to the Jewish people as a** leprous **scab** [*sappaḥat*][N] on the skin, **as it is written: "And the convert shall join himself with them, and they shall cleave** [*venispeḥu*] **to the house of Jacob"** (Isaiah 14:1). This alludes to the fact that the cleaving of the convert to the Jewish people is like a scab.

״וּמוֹדִיעִים אוֹתוֹ עֲוֹן לֶקֶט שִׁכְחָה וּפֵאָה וּמַעְשַׂר עָנִי״. מַאי טַעֲמָא? אָמַר רַבִּי חִיָּיא בַּר אַבָּא אָמַר רַבִּי יוֹחָנָן: בֶּן נֹחַ נֶהֱרָג עַל פָּחוֹת מִשָּׁוֶה פְּרוּטָה, וְלֹא נִיתָּן לְהִשָּׁבוֹן.

The *baraita* continues: **And they inform him of the sin** of neglecting the mitzva to allow the poor to take **gleanings, forgotten sheaves,**[N] **and** produce in the **corner** of one's field, **and** about the **poor man's tithe.** The Gemara asks: **What is the reason** to specifically mention these mitzvot? **Rabbi Ḥiyya bar Abba said** that **Rabbi Yoḥanan said:** Because **a gentile is executed** even **on account of** stealing **less than the value of a *peruta*,**[H] since gentiles are particular about even such a small loss, **and** an item that a gentile steals **is not subject to being returned,** i.e., he is not obligated to return it to its owner. Since gentiles are unwilling to separate even from items of little value, a potential convert must be made aware that he if converts, he will be required to relinquish some of his property to others.

(וּמוֹדִיעִים אוֹתוֹ עֲוֹן שִׁכְחָה וּפֵאָה). ״וְאֵין מַרְבִּים עָלָיו וְאֵין מְדַקְדְּקִים עָלָיו״. אָמַר רַבִּי אֶלְעָזָר: מַאי קְרָאָה – דִּכְתִיב ״וַתֵּרֶא כִּי מִתְאַמֶּצֶת הִיא לָלֶכֶת אִתָּהּ וַתֶּחְדַּל לְדַבֵּר אֵלֶיהָ״,

The *baraita* continues: **And they inform him of the sin** of neglecting the mitzva to allow the poor to take **gleanings, forgotten sheaves, and** produce in the **corner** of one's field. **And they do not overwhelm him** with threats, **and they are not exacting with him** about the details of the mitzvot, i.e., the court should not overly dissuade the convert from converting. **Rabbi Elazar said: What is the verse** from which this ruling is derived? **As it is written: "And when she saw that she was steadfastly minded to go with her, she left off speaking with her"** (Ruth 1:18). When Naomi set out to return to Eretz Yisrael, Ruth insisted on joining her. The Gemara understands this to mean that Ruth wished to convert. Naomi attempted to dissuade her, but Ruth persisted. The verse states that once Naomi saw Ruth's resolve to convert, she desisted from her attempts to dissuade her. The Gemara infers from here that the same approach should be taken by a court in all cases of conversion.

אָמְרָה לָהּ: אֲסִיר לָן תְּחוּם שַׁבָּת – ״בַּאֲשֶׁר תֵּלְכִי אֵלֵךְ״, אֲסִיר לָן יִחוּד – ״בַּאֲשֶׁר תָּלִינִי אָלִין״,

The Gemara reconstructs the original dialogue in which Naomi attempted to dissuade Ruth from converting: Naomi **said to her:** On Shabbat, **it is prohibited for us** to go beyond **the Shabbat limit.**[NB] Ruth responded: **"Where you go, I shall go"** (Ruth 1:16), and no further. Naomi said to her: **It is forbidden for us to be alone together**[B] with a man with whom it is forbidden to engage in relations. Ruth responded: **"Where you lodge, I shall lodge"** (Ruth 1:16), and in the same manner.

NOTES

Converts are as harmful to the Jewish people as a leprous scab – קָשִׁים גֵּרִים לְיִשְׂרָאֵל כְּסַפַּחַת: Many different interpretations have been suggested in explanation of this statement. *Tosafot* suggest four different explanations. One explanation, also suggested by the Rambam, is that it is common for converts to revert to their old ways and beliefs, and when they do they exert a corrupting influence on other Jews. This is similar to the mixed multitude of peoples who accompanied the Jewish people in the exodus from Egypt and caused the sin of the Golden Calf. *Tosafot* on *Kiddushin* 70b cite the Gemara elsewhere that the continuing exile and dispersion of the Jewish people occurs in order to provide an opportunity for converts to join them. Consequently, it emerges that converts are actually part of the cause of the exile. *Tosafot* there also cite the opinion of Rabbi Avraham the convert. He claims that converts are generally punctilious and strict with regard to the mitzvot, and therefore their behavior casts aspersions on the practice of those born Jews who are not as vigilant.

And they inform him of the sin of gleanings, forgotten sheaves, etc. – וּמוֹדִיעִין אוֹתוֹ עֲוֹן לֶקֶט: Some commentaries connect this statement to the Gemara above (47a), where it is stated that a gentile might seek to convert in order to benefit from gleanings and forgotten sheaves. Consequently, he must be informed that there is a sin involved in denying these items to poor people, and it is not merely a right that the poor have (*Arukh LaNer*).

It is prohibited for us to go beyond the Shabbat limit – אֲסִיר לָן תְּחוּם שַׁבָּת: The Maharsha explains that Naomi informed Ruth of this *halakha* in fulfillment of the requirement to inform a potential convert of some of the lenient mitzvot, of which the Shabbat limit is one.

HALAKHA

A gentile is executed on account of stealing less than the value of a *peruta* – בֶּן נֹחַ נֶהֱרָג עַל פָּחוֹת מִשָּׁוֶה פְּרוּטָה: A gentile is liable for theft and is punished with execution, even for stealing an item whose value is less than a *peruta* (Rambam *Sefer Shofetim*, *Hilkhot Melakhim* 9:9).

BACKGROUND

Shabbat limit – תְּחוּם שַׁבָּת: By rabbinic decree, and some say by Torah law, on Shabbat one is not permitted to travel more than a certain distance away from the place where he established his residence at the onset of Shabbat. That distance is known as the Shabbat limit. Even animals and inanimate objects have a limit, determined by the limit of the person to whose care they are entrusted, beyond which they may not be taken. Generally, the Shabbat limit is defined as two thousand cubits outside of one's city in every direction.

Being alone together – יִחוּד: A man and a woman between whom sexual relations are forbidden are forbidden to be alone together in a manner in which it would be possible for them to engage in intercourse. Typically this means that they may not be secluded in a closed room together. According to tradition, in the era of King David this prohibition was extended to prohibit a man from being alone with an unmarried woman. Exceptions to these rules include a father and daughter and a mother and son. A man is also forbidden to be alone with two women.

מְפַקְּדִינַן שֵׁשׁ מֵאוֹת וּשְׁלֹשׁ עֶשְׂרֵה מִצְוֹת – "עַמֵּךְ עַמִּי", אֲסִיר לַן עֲבוֹדָה זָרָה – "וֵאלֹהַיִךְ אֱלֹהָי", אַרְבַּע מִיתוֹת נִמְסְרוּ לְבֵית דִּין – "בַּאֲשֶׁר תָּמוּתִי אָמוּת", שְׁנֵי קְבָרִים נִמְסְרוּ לְבֵית דִּין – "וְשָׁם אֶקָּבֵר".

Naomi said to her: **We are commanded** to observe **six hundred and thirteen mitzvot.**[N] Ruth responded: **"Your people are my people"** (Ruth 1:16). Naomi said to her: **Idolatrous worship is forbidden to us.**[N] Ruth responded: **"Your God is my God"** (Ruth 1:16). Naomi said to her: **Four types of capital punishment**[B] **were handed over to a court** with which to punish those who transgress the mitzvot. Ruth responded: **"Where you die, I shall die"** (Ruth 1:17). Naomi said to her: **Two burial grounds**[B] **were handed over to the court,** one for those executed for more severe crimes and another for those executed for less severe crimes. Ruth responded: **"And there I shall be buried"** (Ruth 1:17).

מִיָּד – "וַתֵּרֶא כִּי מִתְאַמֶּצֶת הִיא וגו'".

Immediately following this dialogue, the verse states: **"And when she saw that she was steadfastly minded** she left off speaking with her" (Ruth 1:18). Once Naomi saw Ruth's resolve to convert, she desisted from her attempts to dissuade her.

"קִיבֵּל – מָלִין אוֹתוֹ מִיָּד". מַאי טַעְמָא? שֶׁהוּיֵי מִצְוָה לָא מְשַׁהִינַן.

The *baraita* continues: If **he accepts** upon himself all of these ramifications, then **they circumcise him immediately.** The Gemara asks: **What is the reason** to act immediately? It is that **we do not delay** the performance of **a mitzva.**[N]

"נִשְׁתַּיְּירוּ בּוֹ צִיצִין הַמְעַכְּבִין הַמִּילָה" וכו'. כִּדְתְנַן: אֵלּוּ הֵן צִיצִין הַמְעַכְּבִין הַמִּילָה: בָּשָׂר הַחוֹפֶה אֶת רוֹב הָעֲטָרָה, וְאֵינוֹ אוֹכֵל בִּתְרוּמָה. וְאָמַר רַב יִרְמְיָה בַּר אַבָּא אָמַר רַב: בָּשָׂר הַחוֹפֶה רוֹב גּוֹבְהָהּ שֶׁל עֲטָרָה.

The *baraita* continues: If **there** still **remain on him shreds**[B] of flesh from the foreskin **that invalidate the circumcision,**[H] he is circumcised a second time to remove them. The Gemara explains: This is **as we learned** in a mishna (*Shabbat* 137a): **These are the shreds** of flesh **that invalidate the circumcision** if they are not cut: Any fragments of **the flesh that cover the greater part of the corona.** If such shreds remain, the child is considered uncircumcised, **and he may not partake of *teruma*. And** in explanation of this mishna, **Rav Yirmeya bar Abba said that Rav said:** This also includes **the flesh that covers the greater part of the height of the corona.**

"נִתְרַפֵּא מַטְבִּילִין אוֹתוֹ מִיָּד", נִתְרַפֵּא – אִין, לֹא נִתְרַפֵּא – לָא. מַאי טַעְמָא? מִשּׁוּם דְּמַיָּא מַרְזוּ מַכָּה.

The *baraita* continues: When **he is healed** from the circumcision, **they immerse him immediately.** The Gemara infers from the precise formulation of the *baraita* that when **he has healed,** then **yes,** he is immersed, but as long as **he has not healed,** then **no,** he is not. **What is the reason** for this? It is **because water agitates a wound.**[B]

"וּשְׁנֵי תַּלְמִידֵי חֲכָמִים עוֹמְדִים עַל גַּבָּיו". וְהָא אָמַר רַבִּי חִיָּיא אָמַר רַבִּי יוֹחָנָן: גֵּר צָרִיךְ שְׁלֹשָׁה! הָא אָמַר רַבִּי יוֹחָנָן לְתַנָּא: תְּנֵי שְׁלֹשָׁה.

The *baraita* continues: **And two Torah scholars stand over him** at the time of his immersion. The Gemara asks: **But didn't Rabbi Ḥiyya say** that **Rabbi Yoḥanan said** that **a convert requires** a court of **three** to be present at his conversion? The Gemara answers: In fact, **Rabbi Yoḥanan said to the *tanna*** reciting the mishna: Do not teach that there are two Torah scholars; rather, **teach** that there are **three.**

"טָבַל וְעָלָה הֲרֵי הוּא כְּיִשְׂרָאֵל לְכָל דְּבָרָיו". לְמַאי הִלְכְתָא? דְּאִי הָדַר בֵּיהּ, וּמְקַדֵּשׁ בַּת יִשְׂרָאֵל – יִשְׂרָאֵל מוּמָר קָרֵינָא בֵּיהּ, וְקִידּוּשָׁיו קִידּוּשִׁין.

The *baraita* continues: Once **he has immersed and emerged he is a Jew**[H] **in every sense.** The Gemara asks: **With regard to what *halakha*** is this said? It is **that if he reverts back** to behaving as a gentile, he nevertheless remains Jewish, **and** so if **he betroths a Jewish woman,** although **he is considered to be an apostate Jew, his betrothal** is a valid **betrothal.**

NOTES

We are commanded to observe six hundred and thirteen mitzvot, etc. – **מְפַקְּדִינַן שֵׁשׁ מֵאוֹת וּשְׁלֹשׁ עֶשְׂרֵה מִצְוֹת וכו'**: Some commentaries explain Naomi's statement and Ruth's response in the following manner: There are many mitzvot that apply only to certain segments of the community, e.g., only to men, priests, etc. Therefore, it is not possible for a single individual to fulfill all six hundred and thirteen mitzvot on his own; rather, their fulfillment is only fully achieved by the collective efforts of the entire people. This is the meaning of Ruth's response: "Your people are my people" (*Iyyun Ya'akov*; *Arukh LaNer*).

Idolatrous worship is forbidden to us – **אֲסִיר לַן עֲבוֹדָה זָרָה**: The commentaries question why Naomi had to inform Ruth of the prohibition against idolatrous worship when it was already prohibited to Ruth as one of the seven Noahide laws. One commentary suggests that it was necessary because the punishment for a Jew is more severe than the punishment for a gentile (*Shevut Ya'akov*). Others suggest that it was necessary because the prohibition for a Jew is more encompassing: It includes any expression of veneration toward a deity, such as embracing or kissing (Maharsha); it prohibits a Jew from even possessing an object of idolatrous worship in his home (Riaf); a Jew is punished for having idolatrous beliefs even if he never expresses them in action (*Iyyun Ya'akov*); and a Jew is prohibited from associating a deity together with God (*Arukh LaNer*).

We do not delay the performance of a mitzva – **שֶׁהוּיֵי מִצְוָה לָא מְשַׁהִינַן**: Although the Gemara states immediately that converts are as harmful as a leprous scab, and on 109b it is stated: Evil after evil will befall those who accept converts, *Tosafot* explain that this refers only to converts who were not initiated according to the process described in the Gemara or were encouraged to convert even though they were unwilling. However, if a gentile sincerely wishes to convert then there is a mitzva to accept him immediately, and one must not delay the performance of this mitzva. This may be seen from the midrash's comment that Abraham was punished for not accepting Timna when she wished to convert and join his family, and she eventually married Esau's son and gave birth to Amalek. Some early authorities write that the mitzva of converting gentiles is derived from the verse: "And you shall love the convert" (Deuteronomy 10:19), implying that one who desires to convert should be loved and encouraged (Rabbi Yehuda of Barcelona). Others derive the mitzva from the general mitzva to love God, which the *Sifrei* interprets to include Abraham's actions in encouraging people to worship God. In the same way, accepting converts enables them to enter a deeper relationship with God (Rabbi Yeruḥam Fishel Perla).

BACKGROUND

Four types of capital punishment – **אַרְבַּע מִיתוֹת...בֵּית דִּין**: These capital punishments are prescribed by the Torah and administered by a court of twenty-three members. They are, in diminishing order of severity: Stoning, burning, decapitation, and strangulation.

Two burial grounds – **שְׁנֵי קְבָרִים**: According to *halakha* one may not bury a wicked person adjacent to a righteous person (*Sanhedrin* 47a). Even one who transgressed a severe prohibition must be buried separately from one who transgressed a less severe prohibition. For this reason, the court maintained two separate burial grounds, one for those executed for more serious crimes and one for those executed for less serious crimes.

Shreds – **צִיצִין**: Circumcision involves two stages: First, the foreskin covering the corona is removed, and then the underlying membrane is ripped and folded back. Occasionally, and especially if this second stage is not performed in the proper manner, part of the membrane remains in its place, covering the corona. These are the shreds the Gemara refers to here.

Water agitates a wound – **מַיָּא מַרְזוּ מַכָּה**: Submerging a wound in water for an extended period can occasionally result in a light renewal of bleeding. In the Gemara here, however, the reference seems to be to a different phenomenon related specifically to ritual baths. In the Talmudic period, ritual baths were formed from collections of rain water that had been gathered, often in caves and the like. Such water can be presumed to contain different micro-organisms such as bacteria and algae. These could certainly cause the wound to become infected, even severely so.

HALAKHA

Shreds that invalidate the circumcision – **צִיצִין הַמְעַכְּבִין הַמִּילָה**: If following circumcision, some of the flesh of the foreskin remains upon the greater part of the height of the corona, even in a single spot, and certainly if it surrounds the entire circumference (*Shakh*), then the circumcision is invalid and the extra flesh must be removed (Rambam *Sefer Ahava, Hilkhot Mila* 2:3; *Shulḥan Arukh, Yoreh De'a* 264:5).

He has immersed and emerged, he is a Jew – **טָבַל וְעָלָה הֲרֵי הוּא כְּיִשְׂרָאֵל**: Once the conversion process has been completed as required the convert is considered to be a Jew in every sense. Therefore, even if he reverts back to his old ways and engages in idolatrous worship, he is still considered to be a Jew, albeit an apostate Jew, and so if he betroths a Jewish woman, the betrothal takes effect (Rambam *Sefer Kedusha, Hilkhot Issurei Bia* 13:17; *Shulḥan Arukh, Yoreh De'a* 268:2).

”אֶחָד גֵּר וְאֶחָד עֶבֶד מְשׁוּחְרָר“. קָסָלְקָא דַּעְתָּךְ לְקַבֵּל עָלָיו עוֹל מִצְוֹת, וּרְמִינְהוּ: בַּמֶּה דְּבָרִים אֲמוּרִים – בְּגֵר, אֲבָל בְּעֶבֶד מְשׁוּחְרָר – אֵין צָרִיךְ לְקַבֵּל!

The *baraita* continues: This applies **both for a convert and for an emancipated slave.** The Gemara considers the meaning of this clause: If **it enters your mind** to interpret the *baraita* to mean that a convert and an emancipated slave are the same **with regard to accepting upon oneself the yoke of mitzvot,** then one could **raise a contradiction** from that which is taught in another *baraita*: **In what** case **is this statement** that there is a need to accept the yoke of mitzvot **said?** It is **with respect to a convert; however, an emancipated slave does not need to accept** upon himself[H] the yoke of mitzvot when he immerses for the sake of emancipation. Rather, the immersion alone is sufficient to emancipate him and thereby render him a Jew.

אָמַר רַב שֵׁשֶׁת: לָא קַשְׁיָא, הָא – רַבִּי שִׁמְעוֹן בֶּן אֶלְעָזָר, הָא – רַבָּנַן.

Rav Sheshet said: This is **not difficult,** as **this** *baraita* that states that an emancipated slave is not required to accept the yoke of mitzvot **is** in accordance with the opinion of **Rabbi Shimon ben Elazar,** whereas **that** *baraita* that implies he is required to do so **is** in accordance with the opinion of **the Rabbis,** the first *tanna* of the following *baraita*.

דְּתַנְיָא, ”וּבָכְתָה אֶת אָבִיהָ וְאֶת אִמָּהּ“ וגו׳ בַּמֶּה דְּבָרִים אֲמוּרִים – שֶׁלֹּא קִבְּלָה עָלֶיהָ, אֲבָל קִבְּלָה עָלֶיהָ – מַטְבִּילָהּ, וּמוּתָּר בָּהּ מִיָּד.

As it is taught in a *baraita*: The Torah permits a Jewish soldier to take a beautiful female prisoner of war out of her captivity in order to marry her. Before he may do so, she must first undergo the process that the Torah describes: "And she shall shave her head, and do her nails; and she shall remove the raiment of her captivity from upon her, and she shall remain in your house **and bewail her father and her mother** a month of days" (Deuteronomy 21:12–13). She may then be immersed for the sake of conversion, even though she does not accept upon herself the yoke of mitzvot. At that point it is permitted to marry her. The *baraita* asks: **Under what** circumstance **are these matters stated?** It is **when she did not accept upon herself** the yoke of mitzvot; **however,** if **she** willingly **accepted upon herself**[H] the yoke of mitzvot, **he may immerse her** for the sake of conversion, **and he is permitted to** marry **her immediately** without the need for her to undergo the process described in the Torah.

רַבִּי שִׁמְעוֹן בֶּן אֶלְעָזָר אוֹמֵר: אַף עַל פִּי שֶׁלֹּא קִבְּלָה עָלֶיהָ – כּוֹפֶה, וּמַטְבִּילָהּ לְשֵׁם שִׁפְחוּת, וְחוֹזֵר וּמַטְבִּילָהּ לְשֵׁם שִׁחְרוּר, וּמְשַׁחְרְרָהּ,

Rabbi Shimon ben Elazar says: Even if she did not accept upon herself the yoke of mitzvot, the need for the process can still be circumvented if **he forces** her **and immerses her for the sake of slavery, and then he again immerses her for the sake of emancipation and** thereby **emancipates her,** rendering her a Jewess. Rabbi Shimon ben Elazar holds that the immersion of a slave for the sake of emancipation is effective even if the slave does not accept upon himself the yoke of mitzvot.

HALAKHA

An emancipated slave does not need to accept upon himself – עֶבֶד מְשׁוּחְרָר אֵין צָרִיךְ לְקַבֵּל: At the time of his emancipation, a slave must immerse in the presence of three judges. However, he need not be informed of the basic beliefs and mitzvot and he need not accept these upon himself, since he was already informed of them and accepted them at the time that he was immersed for the sake of becoming a slave (Rambam *Sefer Kedusha, Hilkhot Issurei Bia* 13:12; *Shulḥan Arukh, Yoreh De'a* 267:7).

A beautiful female prisoner of war who accepted the mitzvot upon herself – יְפַת תּוֹאַר שֶׁקִּבְּלָה עָלֶיהָ מִצְוֹת: A beautiful female prisoner of war who accepts the mitzvot upon herself may be immersed for the sake of conversion, upon which she becomes a Jew. In such a case, the procedures described by the Torah do not apply. If she does not initially accept the mitzvot upon herself, then the procedures described by the Torah must be fulfilled. Her captor then resides with her until she agrees to accept the mitzvot upon herself, at which point she may be immersed for the sake of conversion (Rambam *Sefer Shofetim, Hilkhot Melakhim* 8:5).

Perek **IV**
Daf **48** Amud **a**

וּמוּתָּר בָּהּ מִיָּד.

And he is permitted to marry **her immediately** afterward, without the need for her to undergo the process described in the Torah. The fact that the Rabbis do not suggest this course of action is evidently because they hold that even if she were to be rendered a slave and then immersed for the sake of emancipation, she would become Jewish only if she also accepted upon herself the yoke of mitzvot. Rav Sheshet assumes that the Rabbis would similarly rule that a regular slave who was immersed for the sake of emancipation becomes Jewish only if he also accepts upon himself the yoke of mitzvot.[N]

NOTES

The dispute between Rabbi Shimon ben Elazar and the Rabbis – מַחֲלוֹקֶת רַבִּי שִׁמְעוֹן בֶּן אֶלְעָזָר וַחֲכָמִים: Rabbi Shimon ben Elazar and the Rabbis dispute whether or not a slave who immersed upon his emancipation must accept the yoke of mitzvot in order to become Jewish. The Ramban discusses this dispute at length and suggests three possible interpretations of its parameters (see Rashba).

According to Rashi, all agree that the initial immersion of the slave for the sake of entering into slavery, after he is first purchased from a gentile, may be performed against his will. The dispute here concerns the immersion upon a slave's emancipation: Must that immersion be accompanied by the slave's acceptance of the yoke of mitzvot? The Ramban cites passages in the Jerusalem Talmud and *Pirkei deRabbi Eliezer* that support this interpretation.

A different interpretation, which appears consistent with the rulings of the Rif and Rambam, also assumes that the dispute concerns only the immersion upon a slave's emancipation. However, this interpretation assumes with regard to the initial immersion for the sake of slavery that everyone agrees that it requires the slave's consent.

A third interpretation, suggested by *Tosafot*, is that the dispute concerns both the original immersion for the sake of slavery and the immersion upon emancipation. The Rabbis assume that in both cases the immersion must be performed with the consent of the slave.

אֲמַר רָבָא: מַאי טַעֲמָא דְּרַבִּי שִׁמְעוֹן בֶּן אֶלְעָזָר – דִּכְתִיב ״כָּל עֶבֶד אִישׁ מִקְנַת כָּסֶף״, עֶבֶד אִישׁ וְלֹא עֶבֶד אִשָּׁה?! אֶלָּא: עֶבֶד אִישׁ אַתָּה מָל בְּעַל כָּרְחוֹ, וְאִי אַתָּה מָל בֶּן אִישׁ בְּעַל כָּרְחוֹ.

Rava said: What is the rationale for Rabbi Shimon ben Elazar's opinion? **As it is written** with regard to the Paschal lamb: **"Every slave of a man that is bought for money,** when you have circumcised him, then he may eat of it" (Exodus 12:44). Could the use of the phrase "slave of a man," rather than just: Slave, possibly indicate that the verse applies only to **a man's slave but not a woman's slave?** Certainly not; **rather,** the phrase "slave of a man" means that the slave himself is a man, i.e., an adult, and teaches that **a slave who is a man you may circumcise against his will,** and there is no need for him to accept upon himself the yoke of mitzvot, **but you may not circumcise** a gentile's **son who is a man,** i.e., an adult who is not a slave, **against his will.**

וְרַבָּנַן? אֲמַר עוּלָּא: כְּשֵׁם שֶׁאִי אַתָּה מָל בֶּן אִישׁ בְּעַל כָּרְחוֹ כָּךְ אִי אַתָּה מָל עֶבֶד אִישׁ בְּעַל כָּרְחוֹ. וְאֶלָּא, הָכְתִיב ״כָּל עֶבֶד אִישׁ״! הַהוּא מִיבָּעֵי לֵיהּ לִכְדִשְׁמוּאֵל.

The Gemara asks: **And** how would **the Rabbis** counter this argument? **Ulla said** that the Rabbis reason that **just as you may not circumcise a son who is a man against his will, so** too, **you may not circumcise a slave who is a man against his will.** The Gemara asks: **But isn't it written: "Every slave of a man"?** The Gemara explains: The Rabbis **require that** verse **for that which Shmuel** said.

דְּאָמַר שְׁמוּאֵל: הַמַּפְקִיר עַבְדּוֹ יָצָא לְחֵירוּת, וְאֵין צָרִיךְ גֵּט שִׁחְרוּר, שֶׁנֶּאֱמַר ״כָּל עֶבֶד אִישׁ מִקְנַת כָּסֶף״, עֶבֶד אִישׁ וְלֹא עֶבֶד אִשָּׁה? אֶלָּא: עֶבֶד שֶׁיֵּשׁ לוֹ רְשׁוּת לְרַבּוֹ עָלָיו – קָרוּי עֶבֶד, וְשֶׁאֵין רְשׁוּת לְרַבּוֹ עָלָיו – אֵין קָרוּי עֶבֶד.

As Shmuel said: With regard to one **who renounces ownership of his slave,**[H] the slave **is emancipated, and he does not** even **require a bill of emancipation,**[N] **as it is stated: "But every slave of a man that is bought for money."** Could the use of the phrase "slave of a man," rather than just: Slave, possibly indicate that the verse applies only to **a man's slave but not a woman's slave?** Certainly not; **rather,** the use of the phrase indicates that only **a slave whose master has possession of him,** and can rightfully be described as: a slave of a man, **is called a slave, but** a slave **whose master does not have possession of him** is not **called a slave,** and therefore he is considered a freeman and does not require a bill of emancipation.

מַתְקִיף לַהּ רַב פַּפָּא: אֵימוּר דְּשָׁמְעַתְּ לְהוּ לְרַבָּנַן בִּיפַת תּוֹאַר, דְּלָא שַׁיְיכָא בְּמִצְוֹת. אֲבָל עֶבֶד דְּשַׁיֵּיךְ בְּמִצְוֹת – הָכִי נַמִי דַּאֲפִילּוּ רַבָּנַן מוֹדוּ.

Rav Pappa strongly objects to Rav Sheshet's claim that the Rabbis of the *baraita* would hold that a regular slave who was immersed for the sake of emancipation becomes Jewish only if he also accepts upon himself the yoke of mitzvot: **Say that you heard** that **the Rabbis** insist on the acceptance of the yoke of mitzvot **with regard to** the case of **a beautiful female** prisoner of war, **who was not involved in** any **mitzvot** before being emancipated; **however,** with regard to **a slave,** who **was** initially **involved in mitzvot** before his emancipation, since as a slave he was obligated to observe certain mitzvot, perhaps **even the Rabbis would agree** that there is no need for the slave to accept upon himself the yoke of mitzvot.

דְּתַנְיָא: אֶחָד גֵּר וְאֶחָד לוֹקֵחַ עֶבֶד מִן הַגּוֹי צָרִיךְ לְקַבֵּל. הָא לוֹקֵחַ מִיִּשְׂרָאֵל – אֵין צָרִיךְ לְקַבֵּל,

As it is taught in a *baraita*: **Both** in the case of **a convert and** in the case of **one who purchases a slave from a gentile** whom he is now emancipating, the convert and the slave **need to accept** upon themselves the yoke of mitzvot in order to become Jewish. The Gemara infers: The *baraita* states the need to accept the yoke of mitzvot only in the case where one purchases a slave from a gentile, **but** if **one purchases** a slave **from a Jew,** then the slave **does not need to accept** upon himself the yoke of mitzvot, since he was involved in mitzvot before his emancipation.

מַנִּי? אִי רַבִּי שִׁמְעוֹן בֶּן אֶלְעָזָר – הָאֲמַר לוֹקֵחַ מִן הַגּוֹי נַמִי אֵין צָרִיךְ לְקַבֵּל. אֶלָּא לָאו – רַבָּנַן, וּשְׁמַע מִינָּהּ: דְּלוֹקֵחַ מִן הַגּוֹי צָרִיךְ לְקַבֵּל, אֲבָל לוֹקֵחַ מִיִּשְׂרָאֵל – אֵין צָרִיךְ לְקַבֵּל.

In accordance with **whose** opinion is this taught? **If** one suggests that it is in accordance with the opinion of **Rabbi Shimon ben Elazar,** that is incorrect because **didn't he say** that **also** in the case of **one who purchases a slave from a gentile,** the slave **does not need to accept** upon himself the yoke of mitzvot? **Rather, must it not** be in accordance with the opinion of **the Rabbis? And** so, **conclude from** this *baraita* **that** in the case of **one** who **purchases a slave from a gentile,** the slave **needs to accept** upon himself the yoke of mitzvot, **but** in the case of **one who purchases** a slave **from a Jew,**[H] the slave **does not need to accept** upon himself the yoke of mitzvot.

HALAKHA

One who renounces ownership of his slave – הַמַּפְקִיר עַבְדּוֹ: If one renounces ownership of his slave, the slave is set free but still requires a bill of emancipation. This is in accordance with the conclusion of the Gemara in tractate *Gittin* (Rambam *Sefer Kinyan, Hilkhot Avadim* 8:13; *Shulḥan Arukh, Yoreh De'a* 267:64).

One who purchases a slave from a gentile or a Jew – הַלּוֹקֵחַ מִנָּכְרִי וּמִיִּשְׂרָאֵל: If a slave is purchased from a gentile, before the slave is immersed for the sake of slavery, he must willingly accept the yoke of mitzvot upon himself. However, if he was purchased from a Jew, he need not do so (Rambam *Sefer Kedusha, Hilkhot Issurei Bia* 14:9; *Shulḥan Arukh, Yoreh De'a* 267:3).

NOTES

And he does not require a bill of emancipation – וְאֵין צָרִיךְ גֵּט שִׁחְרוּר: This opinion of Shmuel is subject to a debate on *Gittin* 38b. The Gemara there cites the opinion of Rav that although when one renounces ownership of his slave, the slave is no longer subjugated to his master, he still requires a bill of emancipation in order to fully modify his status from a slave to a freeman in order to permit him to marry a Jewish woman.

וְאֶלָּא קַשְׁיָא אֶחָד גֵּר וְאֶחָד עֶבֶד מְשׁוּחְרָר! כִּי תַּנְיָא הַהִיא – לְעִנְיַן טְבִילָה תַּנְיָא.

The Gemara asks: **But** if so, it is **difficult** to understand the meaning of the *baraita* cited above: This applies **both for a convert and for an emancipated slave.** That phrase appears to refer to the need for both a convert and an emancipated slave to accept the yoke of mitzvot, which is mentioned in the *baraita* beforehand. The Gemara explains: **When that** clause **is taught, it is taught** only **with regard to the matter of immersion,**[H] which is mentioned immediately beforehand, but not with regard to the need to accept the yoke of mitzvot that is mentioned prior to that.

תָּנוּ רַבָּנַן: "וְגִלְּחָה אֶת רֹאשָׁהּ וְעָשְׂתָה אֶת צִפָּרְנֶיהָ" רַבִּי אֱלִיעֶזֶר אוֹמֵר: תָּקוֹץ, רַבִּי עֲקִיבָא אוֹמֵר: תַּגְדִּיל.

§ Having cited it above, the Gemara focuses on the case of the beautiful female prisoner of war: **The Sages taught:** The verse states: **"And she shall shave her head and do her nails"** (Deuteronomy 21:12).[HN] The phrase "do her nails" is ambiguous. **Rabbi Eliezer says:** It means **she cuts** her nails. **Rabbi Akiva says:** It means **she grows** them.

אָמַר רַבִּי אֱלִיעֶזֶר: נֶאֶמְרָה עֲשִׂיָּה בָּרֹאשׁ וְנֶאֶמְרָה עֲשִׂיָּה בַּצִּפָּרְנַיִם, מַה לְּהַלָּן הַעֲבָרָה – אַף כָּאן הַעֲבָרָה. רַבִּי עֲקִיבָא אוֹמֵר: נֶאֱמַר עֲשִׂיָּה בָּרֹאשׁ, וְנֶאֱמַר עֲשִׂיָּה בַּצִּפָּרְנַיִם. מַה לְּהַלָּן נִיווּל – אַף כָּאן נִיווּל.

Each *tanna* explains the basis of his opinion: **Rabbi Eliezer said:** An act of **doing is stated with regard to the head,** that she should shave it, **and** an act of **doing is stated with regard to the nails; just as there,** with regard to the hair on her head, the Torah requires its **removal, so too, here,** with regard to her nails, the Torah requires their **removal. Rabbi Akiva says:** An act of **doing is stated with regard to the head,** that she should shave it, **and** an act of **doing is stated with regard to the nails; just as there,** with regard to the hair on her head, the Torah requires that she do something that makes her **repulsive, so too, here,** with regard to her nails, the Torah requires she do something that makes her **repulsive,** i.e., allowing them to grow.

וּרְאָיָה לְדִבְרֵי רַבִּי אֱלִיעֶזֶר "וּמְפִבֹשֶׁת בֶּן שָׁאוּל יָרַד לִקְרַאת הַמֶּלֶךְ לֹא עָשָׂה רַגְלָיו וְלֹא עָשָׂה שְׂפָמוֹ". מַאי עֲשִׂיָּה – הַעֲבָרָה.

And a proof for the statement of Rabbi Eliezer may be adduced from the verse that states: **"And Mephibosheth, the son of Saul, came down to meet the king; and he had neither done his feet nor done his mustache"** (II Samuel 19:25). **What** is the meaning of **doing** in that context? Clearly it means the **removal** of his toenails and his mustache.

תָּנוּ רַבָּנַן: "וּבָכְתָה אֶת אָבִיהָ וְאֶת אִמָּהּ",

The Sages taught in a *baraita*: The verse states: **"And she shall bewail her father and her mother** a month of days and after that you may come to her" (Deuteronomy 21:13).

HALAKHA

Immersion of an emancipated slave – **טְבִילַת עֶבֶד מְשׁוּחְרָר**: An emancipated slave must be immersed in the presence of three people in order to become Jewish and be allowed to marry a Jewish woman (Rambam *Sefer Kedusha, Hilkhot Issurei Bia* 13:13; *Shulḥan Arukh, Yoreh De'a* 267:3).

And do her nails – **וְעָשְׂתָה אֶת צִפָּרְנֶיהָ**: A beautiful female prisoner of war must grow her fingernails during the month she remains in her captor's home. This is in accordance with the opinion of Rabbi Akiva (Rambam *Sefer Shofetim, Hilkhot Melakhim* 8:5).

NOTES

And do her nails – **וְעָשְׂתָה אֶת צִפָּרְנֶיהָ**: One commentary explains that the dispute between Rabbi Eliezer and Rabbi Akiva is based upon two different understandings of the purpose of the procedures delineated by the Torah: Rabbi Eliezer views the procedures as a process of purification in anticipation of her conversion, which is performed at the conclusion of the process. The shaving of her head is also part of this process and is similar to the preparations of the Levites, who shaved their heads as part of their consecration, and the leper, who shaved as part of his purification process. Apparently, the idea is that in preparation for becoming pure, one should remove extraneous parts of the body. Therefore, he interprets the phrase "do her nails" as referring to removing them. This is paralleled in the custom that an apostate Jew, as part of his process of repentance, would shave his head and cut his nails. According to some opinions, a convert must do so as well.

Rabbi Akiva, however, views the procedures as part of the Torah's attempt to make the woman less appealing in the eyes of her captor in the hope that ultimately he will refrain from taking her as a wife. Accordingly, the purpose of shaving her head is to negatively affect her appearance, and likewise, the phrase "do her nails" refers to letting them grow (Malbim).

It should be noted that Rabbi Akiva certainly was aware of the verse relating to Mephibosheth that supports Rabbi Eliezer's opinion; nevertheless, he understood that the context of the phrase here indicates a meaning other than its standard meaning (*Gilyonei HaShas*).

Perek **IV**
Daf **48** Amud **b**

רַבִּי אֱלִיעֶזֶר אוֹמֵר: "אָבִיהָ" – אָבִיהָ מַמָּשׁ, "אִמָּהּ" – אִמָּהּ מַמָּשׁ. רַבִּי עֲקִיבָא אוֹמֵר: "אָבִיהָ וְאִמָּהּ" – זוֹ עֲבוֹדָה זָרָה, וְכֵן הוּא אוֹמֵר "אוֹמְרִים לָעֵץ אָבִי אַתָּה" וגו׳.

Rabbi Eliezer says: "Her father" means **her actual father** and **"her mother"** means **her actual mother. Rabbi Akiva says: Her father and her mother; this** is referring to the **idolatrous deity** that she had worshiped but will no longer be able to worship, **and so it says: "They say to a tree: You are my father,** and to a stone: You have given birth to us" (Jeremiah 2:27).[H]

"יֶרַח יָמִים" – יֶרַח שְׁלֹשִׁים יוֹם. רַבִּי שִׁמְעוֹן בֶּן אֶלְעָזָר אוֹמֵר: תִּשְׁעִים יוֹם, "יֶרַח" – שְׁלֹשִׁים, "יָמִים" – שְׁלֹשִׁים, "וְאַחַר כֵּן" – שְׁלֹשִׁים.

The verses states: **"A month of days**[H] and after that you may come to her" (Deuteronomy 21:13). This means **a thirty-day month. Rabbi Shimon ben Elazar says:** She must wait **ninety days.** This is derived as follows: The phrase **"a month"** connotes **thirty** days; the word **"days"** adds another **thirty** days; **and** the words **"after that"** indicate another period equal to one previously mentioned, i.e., a further **thirty** days.

מַתְקִיף לָהּ רָבִינָא: אֵימָא "יֶרַח" – שְׁלֹשִׁים, "יָמִים" – שְׁלֹשִׁים, "וְאַחַר כֵּן" – כִּי הָנֵי! – קַשְׁיָא.

Ravina strongly objects to this: If the words "after that" indicate another period equal to one previously mentioned, then one should **say:** The phrase **"a month"** connotes **thirty** days; the word **"days"** adds another **thirty** days; **and** then the words **"after that"** add another period which is **equal to** the total sum of all **those** days she has already waited, i.e., an additional sixty days. The Gemara concedes: Indeed, this is **difficult.**

HALAKHA

She shall bewail her father and her mother – **וּבָכְתָה אֶת אָבִיהָ וְאֶת אִמָּהּ**: A beautiful female prisoner of war, during her month-long stay in her captor's home, cries over her separation from her previous religion and her captor may not prevent her from doing so. This is in accordance with the opinion of Rabbi Akiva (Rambam *Sefer Shofetim, Hilkhot Melakhim* 8:5).

A month of days – **יֶרַח יָמִים**: The time designated for a female prisoner of war to perform the procedures delineated by the Torah is thirty days. This is in accordance with the opinion of the first *tanna*. Nevertheless, her captor must wait an additional two months before taking her in marriage, so that if it later emerges that she is pregnant, it will be clear whether the captor is the father (Rambam *Sefer Shofetim, Hilkhot Melakhim* 8:5 and *Leḥem Mishne* there).

תָּנוּ רַבָּנַן: מְקַיְּימִין עֲבָדִים שֶׁאֵינָם מָלִין, דִּבְרֵי רַבִּי יִשְׁמָעֵאל. רַבִּי עֲקִיבָא אוֹמֵר: אֵין מְקַיְּימִין. אָמַר לֵיהּ רַבִּי יִשְׁמָעֵאל: הֲרֵי הוּא אוֹמֵר "וְיִנָּפֵשׁ בֶּן אֲמָתְךָ"! אָמַר לֵיהּ: בְּלוֹקֵחַ עֶבֶד בֵּין הַשְּׁמָשׁוֹת וְלֹא הִסְפִּיק לְמוּלוֹ הַכָּתוּב מְדַבֵּר.

§ **The Sages taught** in a *baraita*: **One may maintain**[N] **slaves that are not circumcised** under one's control; this is **the statement of Rabbi Yishmael. Rabbi Akiva says: One may not maintain** such slaves, even for a moment. **Rabbi Yishmael said to him: But it says** with regard to Shabbat: **"And the son of your maidservant will be refreshed"** (Exodus 23:12). The verse prohibits a Jewish master from allowing his slave to perform labor on Shabbat. The Gemara will explain that this is referring to an uncircumcised slave. It is therefore apparent that it is permitted to keep such a slave. Rabbi Akiva **said to him: The verse speaks of one who purchases a slave at twilight**[N] on the eve of Shabbat **and** therefore **does not have the opportunity to circumcise him** before the onset of Shabbat.

דְּכוּלֵּי עָלְמָא מִיהַת "וְיִנָּפֵשׁ בֶּן אֲמָתְךָ" בְּעֶבֶד עָרֵל כְּתִיב, מַאי מַשְׁמַע? דְּתַנְיָא: "וְיִנָּפֵשׁ בֶּן אֲמָתְךָ" – בְּעֶבֶד עָרֵל הַכָּתוּב מְדַבֵּר. אַתָּה אוֹמֵר בְּעֶבֶד עָרֵל, אוֹ אֵינוֹ אֶלָּא בְּעֶבֶד מָהוּל? כְּשֶׁהוּא אוֹמֵר: "לְמַעַן יָנוּחַ עַבְדְּךָ וַאֲמָתְךָ כָּמוֹךָ" – הֲרֵי עֶבֶד מָהוּל אָמוּר, הָא מָה אֲנִי מְקַיֵּים "וְיִנָּפֵשׁ בֶּן אֲמָתְךָ"! – בְּעֶבֶד עָרֵל.

The Gemara notes: **In any event,** in the opinion **of everyone** the verse: **"And the son of your maidservant will be refreshed," is written with regard to an uncircumcised slave. From where** is this **inferred? As it is taught** in a *baraita*: **"And the son of your maidservant will be refreshed"; the verse speaks of an uncircumcised slave.** Do **you say** it speaks **of an uncircumcised slave, or** perhaps **it is** speaking **only of a circumcised slave? When it says** elsewhere: "And the seventh day is a Shabbat to the Lord your God, you shall not do any labor, you, and your son, and your daughter, and your slave, and your maidservant… **so that your slave and your maidservant may rest like you"** (Deuteronomy 5:13), **a circumcised slave is** already **mentioned; how,** then, **do I uphold** the verse **"And the son of your maidservant will be refreshed"?** It must refer **to an uncircumcised slave.**

"וְהַגֵּר" – זֶה גֵּר תּוֹשָׁב, אַתָּה אוֹמֵר זֶה גֵּר תּוֹשָׁב. אוֹ אֵינוֹ אֶלָּא גֵּר צֶדֶק? כְּשֶׁהוּא אוֹמֵר "וְגֵרְךָ אֲשֶׁר בִּשְׁעָרֶיךָ" – הֲרֵי גֵּר צֶדֶק אָמוּר, הָא מָה אֲנִי מְקַיֵּים "וְהַגֵּר" – זֶה גֵּר תּוֹשָׁב.

The verse continues: **"And the stranger** [*ger*]**"** (Exodus 23:12). **This** is referring to **a gentile who observes certain mitzvot** [***ger toshav***].[N] **Do you say** that **this is a** ***ger toshav,*** **or** perhaps **it is only a righteous convert** [***ger tzedek***], who is a Jew in every sense? **When it says** elsewhere: **"And your stranger** [*ger*] **that is within your gates"** (Deuteronomy 5:13), **a righteous convert is** already **mentioned. How,** then, **do I uphold** the verse **"And the stranger** [*ger*]**"?** It must be that **this is a** ***ger toshav.***

אָמַר רַבִּי יְהוֹשֻׁעַ בֶּן לֵוִי: הַלּוֹקֵחַ עֶבֶד מִן הַגּוֹי וְלֹא רָצָה לָמוּל, מְגַלְגֵּל עִמּוֹ עַד שְׁנֵים עָשָׂר חֹדֶשׁ. לֹא מָל – חוֹזֵר וּמוֹכְרוֹ לְגוֹיִם.

Rabbi Yehoshua ben Levi said: In the case of **one who purchases a slave from a gentile and** the slave **does not wish to be circumcised,**[H] **he abides with him up to twelve months.** If, after this period, **he** will still **not be circumcised, he then sells him** on **to gentiles.**

אַמְרוּהָ רַבָּנַן קַמֵּיהּ דְּרַב פָּפָּא: כְּמַאן – דְּלָא כְּרַבִּי עֲקִיבָא, דְּאִי רַבִּי עֲקִיבָא – הָאָמַר אֵין מְקַיְּימִין! אָמַר לְהוּ רַב פָּפָּא: אֲפִילּוּ תֵּימָא רַבִּי עֲקִיבָא, הָנֵי מִילֵּי – הֵיכָא דְּלָא פְּסָקָא לְמִילְּתֵיהּ, אֲבָל הֵיכָא דִּפְסָקָא לְמִילְּתֵיהּ – פְּסָקָא.

The Sages said this ***halakha*** **before Rav Pappa** and asked: **In accordance with whose** opinion is it? It seems **that it is not in accordance with** the opinion of **Rabbi Akiva, as,** if it were in accordance with the opinion of **Rabbi Akiva, didn't he say: One may not maintain** an uncircumcised slave even for a moment? Rav Pappa **said to them: You** can **even say** that it is in accordance with the opinion of **Rabbi Akiva,** since perhaps **that** ***halakha*** of Rabbi Yehoshua ben Levi **applies** only **where** the slave **did not make his** refusal to be circumcised **explicit;**[N] **however, where he did make his** refusal to be circumcised **explicit,** since **he has made it explicit,** it is prohibited to maintain him, as Rabbi Akiva rules.

אָמַר רַב כָּהֲנָא: אֲמַרִיתָא לִשְׁמַעְתָּא קַמֵּיהּ דְּרַב זְבִיד מִנְּהַרְדְּעָא, אָמַר לִי: אִי הָכִי, כִּי אָמַר לֵיהּ רַבִּי עֲקִיבָא בְּלוֹקֵחַ עֶבֶד בֵּין הַשְּׁמָשׁוֹת – לִישְׁנֵי לֵיהּ הָא! חֲדָא מִתְּרֵי טַעֲמֵי קָאָמַר.

Rav Kahana said: I said this ***halakha*** **before Rav Zevid from Neharde'a. He said to me: If so,** that Rabbi Akiva agrees that one may temporarily maintain a slave who has not explicitly refused to be circumcised, then **when Rabbi Akiva said to** Rabbi Yishmael that the verse with regard to an uncircumcised slave **is referring to one who purchases a slave at twilight** on the eve of Shabbat, **let him** instead **answer him** that the verse is referring to **this** case of a slave who has not explicitly refused to be circumcised. The Gemara explains: Rabbi Akiva **said** only **one out of two** possible **reasons** why it would be permitted to be in possession of such a slave.

NOTES

One may maintain, etc. – מְקַיְּימִין עֲבָדִים וכו׳: *Tosafot* explain that Rabbi Akiva's opinion is based on the fact that Abraham was commanded to circumcise everyone in his household including his slaves; if so, clearly one is not allowed to leave them uncircumcised. *Tosafot* conclude, therefore, that it is apparent that Rabbi Akiva's prohibition to maintain a slave without circumcision is by Torah law. This also explains why Rabbi Yishmael had to adduce biblical support for his claim that it is permitted to do so (see *Tosefot HaRosh* and *Mekhilta*).

One who purchases a slave at twilight – בְּלוֹקֵחַ עֶבֶד בֵּין הַשְּׁמָשׁוֹת: The Ritva explains that one should not conclude that the verse is referring only to this specific case. Rather, it refers to all cases where, due to some unavoidable circumstances, the master was unable to circumcise his slave before the onset of Shabbat, e.g., if no one who could perform the circumcision was available.

This is a *ger toshav* – זֶה גֵּר תּוֹשָׁב: The status of a *ger toshav*, and which mitzvot he is required to observe, is subject to significant debate both in the Gemara and the early commentaries. In order to explain the Gemara here, Rashi cites the opinion that a *ger toshav* must observe the prohibitions of Shabbat in the same manner as a Jew. *Tosafot* and the Ramban object to this explanation and explain that even if he is not obligated to observe Shabbat, it is prohibited by Torah law for him to perform any labor on behalf of a Jew. This is in contrast to the general prohibition against benefiting from labor that a gentile performed for a Jew, which is a rabbinic prohibition. The Ramban also cites an opinion that a *ger toshav* is prohibited from performing labor on Shabbat to the same extent that a Jew is prohibited from performing labor on a Festival. Accordingly, certain labors that are necessary for the preparation of food are permitted.

He did not make his refusal explicit – לָא פְּסָקָה לְמִילְּתֵיהּ: Rashi suggests two interpretations. According to the first, the phrase refers to the slave: As long as the slave does not explicitly state that he will not consent to be circumcised, the master is permitted to maintain him. According to the second interpretation, the phrase refers to the slave owner and should be translated as: He did not fix a time for the matter. Accordingly, it means that it is permitted for an owner to maintain his uncircumcised slave only if he set a time by which he will circumcise him. This time would have to be set at the moment of purchase. *Tosafot* cite the interpretation of Rabbeinu Yitzḥak, which is also the explanation of Rav Hai Gaon, that, on the contrary, once the slave has agreed to be circumcised it is then prohibited to maintain him in an uncircumcised state; rather, he must be circumcised and immersed immediately. However, if the slave refuses to be circumcised, then one is allowed to maintain him as such.

HALAKHA

One who purchases a slave from a gentile and he does not wish to be circumcised – הַלּוֹקֵחַ עֶבֶד מִן הַגּוֹי וְלֹא רָצָה לָמוּל: If one purchases a slave from a gentile and the slave does not wish to be circumcised, then he abides with him up to twelve months. If, after this period, the slave still refuses to be circumcised, the master then sells him on to gentiles. This is in accordance with the opinion of Rabbi Yehoshua ben Levi (Rambam *Sefer Ahava, Hilkhot Mila* 1:6 and *Sefer Kedusha, Hilkhot Issurei Bia* 14:9; *Shulḥan Arukh, Yoreh De'a* 267:4).

שָׁלַח רָבִין מִשְּׁמֵיהּ דְּרַבִּי אִילְעַאי, וְכָל רַבּוֹתַי אָמְרוּ לִי מִשְּׁמוֹ: אֵיזֶהוּ עֶבֶד עָרֵל שֶׁמּוּתָּר לְקַיְּימוֹ – זֶה שֶׁלְּקָחוֹ רַבּוֹ עַל מְנָת שֶׁלֹּא לְמוֹלוֹ. אֲמַרוּהָ רַבָּנַן קַמֵּיהּ דְּרַב פָּפָּא: כְּמַאן – דְּלָא כְּרַבִּי עֲקִיבָא, דְּאִי רַבִּי עֲקִיבָא – הָאֲמַר: אֵין מְקַיְּימִין! אֲמַר לְהוּ רַב פָּפָּא: אֲפִילּוּ תֵּימָא רַבִּי עֲקִיבָא, הָנֵי מִילֵּי – הֵיכָא דְּלָא אַתְנֵי בַּהֲדֵיהּ, אֲבָל הֵיכָא דְּאַתְנֵי – אַתְנֵי.

Ravin[P] **sent** a message citing a *halakha* **in the name of Rabbi Ilai: And all of my teachers said to me in his name: What is** the case of **an uncircumcised slave whom it is permitted to maintain? This is one whose master purchased him on condition not to circumcise him.**[H] **The Sages said this** *halakha* **before Rav Pappa** and asked: **In accordance with whose** opinion is it? It seems **that it is not in accordance with** the opinion of **Rabbi Akiva, as, if** it were in accordance with the opinion of **Rabbi Akiva, didn't he say: One may not maintain** an uncircumcised slave even for a moment? Rav Pappa **said to them: You can even say** it is in accordance with the opinion of **Rabbi Akiva,** since perhaps **that** ruling of Rabbi Akiva **applies** only **where** the master **did not make a condition with regard to** the slave that he would not be circumcised; **however, where he did make** such a **condition,** since **he made a condition,** even Rabbi Akiva would concede it is permitted to maintain him.

אֲמַר רַב כָּהֲנָא: אֲמַרִיתָא לִשְׁמַעְתָּא קַמֵּיהּ דְּרַב זְבִיד מִנְּהַרְדְּעָא, וַאֲמַר לִי: אִי הָכִי, כִּי קָאָמַר לֵיהּ רַבִּי עֲקִיבָא בְּלוֹקֵחַ עֶבֶד בֵּין הַשְּׁמָשׁוֹת וְלֹא הִסְפִּיק לְמוֹלוֹ – לִישְׁנֵי לֵיהּ הָא!

Rav Kahana said: I said this *halakha* **before Rav Zevid from Neharde'a and he said to me: If so,** that Rabbi Akiva agrees that one may maintain a slave who was purchased on condition that he would not be circumcised, then **when Rabbi Akiva said to** Rabbi Yishmael that the verse with regard to an uncircumcised slave **is referring to one who purchases a slave at twilight** on the eve of Shabbat **and** therefore **does not have the opportunity to circumcise him** before the onset of Shabbat, **let him** instead **answer him** that the verse is referring to **this** case of a slave who was purchased on condition that he would not be circumcised.

וְלִיטַעְמִיךְ – לִישְׁנֵי לֵיהּ הָךְ! אֶלָּא: חַד מִתְּרֵי וּתְלָת טַעֲמֵי קָאָמַר.

The Gemara responds: **But** even **according to your reasoning** that Rabbi Akiva disagrees, since you do agree with Rav Pappa's resolution of Rabbi Akiva's opinion with the *halakha* of Rabbi Yehoshua ben Levi, **let** Rabbi Akiva **answer him** that the verse is referring to **that** case of a slave who has not explicitly refused to be circumcised. The Gemara answers: Rabbi Akiva **said** only **one out of two or three** possible **reasons** that it would be permitted to be in possession of such a slave.

יְתֵיב רַבִּי חֲנִינָא בַּר פַּפִּי וְרַבִּי אַמִי וְרַבִּי יִצְחָק נַפָּחָא אַקִּילְעָא דְּרַבִּי יִצְחָק נַפָּחָא, וְיָתְבִי וְקָאָמְרִי: עִיר אַחַת הָיְתָה בְּאֶרֶץ יִשְׂרָאֵל וְלֹא רָצוּ עַבְדֶיהָ לָמוּל, וְגַלְגְּלוּ עִמָּהֶם עַד שְׁנֵים עָשָׂר חֹדֶשׁ, וְחָזְרוּ וּמְכָרוּם לְגוֹיִם. כְּמַאן –

Rabbi Ḥanina bar Pappi, and Rabbi Ami, and Rabbi Yitzḥak Nappaḥa were sitting in the courtyard of Rabbi Yitzḥak Nappaḥa. They were sitting and saying: There was one city in Eretz Yisrael whose slaves did not wish to be circumcised. Their masters **abided with them until twelve months** had passed **and then sold them to gentiles. In accordance with whose** opinion did they act?

PERSONALITIES

Ravin – רָבִין: Ravin was a fourth-generation *amora* who studied in Eretz Yisrael under Rabbi Abbahu, Rabbi Zeira, and Rabbi Ilai. He is known in the Jerusalem Talmud as Rabbi Avin or Rabbi Bun. He is best known for all of the traditions that he brought with him from Eretz Yisrael to Babylonia, which are frequently quoted in the Talmud with the introductory phrase: When Ravin came. The source of many of the traditions that Ravin brought with him was Rabbi Yoḥanan, and they were considered to be very precise. Apparently, Ravin also returned to visit his teachers in Eretz Yisrael and sent messages, possibly by letter, back to Babylonia, containing the traditions he learned from them (see *Ketubot* 49b and *Bava Metzia* 114a).

HALAKHA

He stipulated not to be circumcised – הִתְנָה שֶׁלֹּא לָמוּל: If a slave stipulated from the outset that he does not wish to be circumcised, and similarly, in times and places when the government prohibited conversion (*Mordekhai*), it is permitted to maintain the slave in one's house for as he long as he wishes. This is in accordance with the opinion of Rabbi Yehoshua ben Levi and Rav Pappa (Rambam *Sefer Ahava, Hilkhot Mila* 1:6; *Shulḥan Arukh, Yoreh De'a* 267:4 and in the comment of Rema).

כִּי הַאי תַּנָּא. דְּתַנְיָא: הַלּוֹקֵחַ עֶבֶד מִן הַגּוֹי וְלֹא רָצָה לָמוּל – מְגַלְגֵּל עִמּוֹ עַד שְׁנֵים עָשָׂר חֹדֶשׁ, לֹא מָל – חוֹזֵר וּמוֹכְרוֹ לְגוֹיִם. רַבִּי שִׁמְעוֹן בֶּן אֶלְעָזָר אוֹמֵר: אֵין מַשְׁהִין אוֹתוֹ בְּאֶרֶץ יִשְׂרָאֵל, מִפְּנֵי הֶפְסֵד טְהָרוֹת. וּבְעִיר הַסְּמוּכָה לַסְּפָר – אֵין מַשְׁהִין אוֹתוֹ כָּל עִיקָּר, שֶׁמָּא יִשְׁמַע דָּבָר, וְיֵלֵךְ וְיֹאמַר לַחֲבֵרוֹ גּוֹי.

It is in accordance with the opinion of **this *tanna*, as it is taught** in a *baraita*: In the case of **one who purchases a slave from a gentile and** the slave **does not wish to be circumcised,** the master **abides with him** for **up to twelve months. If,** after this period, the slave **will** still **not be circumcised,** the master **then sells him to gentiles. Rabbi Shimon ben Elazar says: One may not allow him to remain in Eretz Yisrael due to the loss of ritually pure items** he could cause. As long as the slave remains uncircumcised, he is considered to be a gentile; therefore, by rabbinic decree, ritually pure items that he touches are considered to be impure. **And in a city that is near to the border**[N] **he may not be allowed to remain at all, lest he hear some** secret **matter** concerning security **and go and say** it over **to his fellow gentile** in an enemy country. However, once he has been circumcised and accepted the yoke of mitzvot, this concern no longer exists.

תַּנְיָא, רַבִּי חֲנַנְיָא בְּנוֹ שֶׁל רַבָּן גַּמְלִיאֵל אוֹמֵר: מִפְּנֵי מָה גֵּרִים בַּזְּמַן הַזֶּה מְעוּנִּין, וְיִסּוּרִין בָּאִין עֲלֵיהֶן – מִפְּנֵי שֶׁלֹּא קִיְּימוּ שֶׁבַע מִצְוֹת בְּנֵי נֹחַ. רַבִּי יוֹסֵי אוֹמֵר: גֵּר – שֶׁנִּתְגַּיֵּיר כְּקָטָן שֶׁנּוֹלַד דָּמֵי. אֶלָּא מִפְּנֵי מָה מְעוּנִּין – לְפִי שֶׁאֵין בְּקִיאִין בְּדִקְדּוּקֵי מִצְוֹת כְּיִשְׂרָאֵל, אַבָּא חָנָן אוֹמֵר מִשּׁוּם רַבִּי אֶלְעָזָר: לְפִי שֶׁאֵין עוֹשִׂין מֵאַהֲבָה אֶלָּא מִיִּרְאָה.

§ **It is taught** in a *baraita*: **Rabbi Ḥananya, son of Rabban Gamliel, says: For what** reason **are converts at the present time**[N] **tormented and hardships come upon them?**[N] It is **because** when they were gentiles **they did not observe the seven Noahide mitzvot. Rabbi Yosei says:** They would not be punished for their deeds prior to their conversion because **a convert who** just **converted is like a child** just **born**[N] in that he retains no connection to his past life. **Rather, for what** reason **are they tormented?** It is **because they are not** as **well-versed in the intricacies of the mitzvot as** a born **Jew,** and consequently they often inadvertently transgress mitzvot. **Abba Ḥanan says in the name of Rabbi Elazar:** It is **because they observe** mitzvot **not out of love** of God, **but only out of fear** of the punishments for failing to observe them.

אֲחֵרִים אוֹמְרִים: מִפְּנֵי שֶׁשִּׁהוּ עַצְמָם לְהִכָּנֵס תַּחַת כַּנְפֵי הַשְּׁכִינָה. אֲמַר רַבִּי אַבָּהוּ וְאִיתֵימָא רַבִּי חֲנִינָא: מַאי קְרָאָה – ״יְשַׁלֵּם ה׳ פָּעֳלֵךְ וּתְהִי מַשְׂכֻּרְתֵּךְ שְׁלֵמָה מֵעִם ה׳ אֱלֹהֵי יִשְׂרָאֵל אֲשֶׁר בָּאת לַחֲסוֹת״ וְגוֹמֵר.

Others say: It is **because they waited**[N] **before entering under the wings of the Divine Presence,** i.e., they are punished for not converting sooner than they did. **Rabbi Abbahu said, and some say** it was **Rabbi Ḥanina** who said: **What is the verse**[N] from which it is derived that one should convert at the earliest opportunity? Boaz said to Ruth: **"The Lord shall recompense your work, and your reward shall be complete from the Lord, the God of Israel,** under whose wings **you have come to take refuge"** (Ruth 2:12).

NOTES

A city that is near to the border – עִיר הַסְּמוּכָה לַסְּפָר: The Gemara in tractate *Eiruvin* maintains that if marauders attack a border city, one may desecrate the Sabbath to confront them even if their sole intention is to steal produce. The early commentaries explain that that reason for this is because if they would succeed in entering into a border city, that would pose a significant security risk as it would allow them to penetrate further into the country. Similarly, the requirement to decimate an idolatrous city in Eretz Yisrael does not apply if that city is on the border, as doing so might encourage the enemy to attack other cities nearby. In the Gemara here, the concern is that the slave might know the language of the enemies, and since he lives adjacent to the border he would be able to direct them as to how to conquer the border cities (*Meshekh Ḥokhma*).

It remains unclear why, when discussing the fact the slave could disqualify ritually pure items, the *baraita* states: One may not allow him to remain, but when discussing the danger of leaving him near a border city, it states more emphatically: He may not be allowed to remain at all.

Rabbi Moshe Feinstein suggests that it is easier to protect ritually pure items in the short term until one finds a buyer for the slave, and therefore one may delay before selling the slave. However, in a border city, where there is imminent danger that the slave will undermine the security of the city, he must be sold to gentiles immediately.

Converts at the present time – גֵּרִים בַּזְּמַן הַזֶּה: The commentaries note that the Gemara emphasizes that this question applies specifically to the present time because those who convert at times when the Jews are of superior status are suspected of having chosen to convert not for the sake of Heaven. At the present time, however, when the Jews are downtrodden, it is certain that the conversion is for the sake of Heaven and so the question of why they suffer so much arises (*Iyyun Ya'akov*).

Tormented and hardships come upon them – מְעוּנִּין, וְיִסּוּרִין בָּאִין עֲלֵיהֶן: The Ritva explains that the question is asked specifically about converts. Born Jews might naturally conclude that they suffer due to the sins of their fathers. Converts, on the other hand, have no apparent reason to be suffering.

Like a child just born – כְּקָטָן שֶׁנּוֹלַד דָּמֵי: A convert is absolved of sins he committed while he was still a gentile only in cases where the punishment is in the hands of Heaven. However, if he was liable to be punished by the courts, converting will not exempt him from his liability (*Tosafot Yeshanim*).

Because they waited – מִפְּנֵי שֶׁשִּׁהוּ עַצְמָן: One commentary explains that this cannot refer to the fact that they did not decide to convert earlier, as gentiles are not commanded to convert. Rather, it refers to the time between the decision to convert and the actual act of conversion itself; once a convert has decided to convert he should act quickly to complete the process (Ya'avetz).

What is the verse, etc. – מַאי קְרָאָה וכו׳: Rashi and *Tosafot* explain that this verse is cited in support of the opinion attributed to: Others. The Maharsha explains that the proof is derived from the fact that Boaz gave Ruth a double blessing. The blessing: "God shall recompense your work," is for the act of conversion itself, and "Your reward shall be complete" is for the promptness involved. Re'em Horowitz, however, suggests that this verse is cited only to provide a source for the phrase: To enter under the wings of the Divine Presence. The Ritva holds that the verse is adduced to prove the statement of Rabbi Yosei that a convert is like a child just born. See *Arukh LaNer*, who explains how the verse provides proof for all of these positions.

מתני׳ אֵיזֶהוּ מַמְזֵר? כׇּל שְׁאֵר בָּשָׂר שֶׁהוּא בְּ״לֹא יָבֹא״, דִּבְרֵי רַבִּי עֲקִיבָא. שִׁמְעוֹן הַתִּימְנִי אוֹמֵר: כׇּל שֶׁחַיָּיבִים עָלָיו כָּרֵת בִּידֵי שָׁמַיִם. וַהֲלָכָה כִּדְבָרָיו. וְרַבִּי יְהוֹשֻׁעַ אוֹמֵר: כׇּל שֶׁחַיָּיבִין עָלָיו מִיתַת בֵּית דִּין.

MISHNA Which offspring of forbidden relations have the status of a ***mamzer*****?**[NH] It is the offspring of a union with **any next of kin**[N] **that is subject to** a Torah prohibition that **he should not engage in sexual relations** with them; this is **the statement of Rabbi Akiva. Shimon HaTimni**[P] **says:** It is the offspring of a union with **any** forbidden relation **for which one is liable to** receive ***karet*** **at the hand of Heaven. And the** ***halakha*** **is in accordance with his statement.**[N] **Rabbi Yehoshua says:** It is the offspring of a union with **any** forbidden relation **for which one is liable to** receive **court**-imposed **capital punishment.**

אָמַר רַבִּי שִׁמְעוֹן בֶּן עַזַּאי: מָצָאתִי מְגִלַּת יוֹחֲסִין בִּירוּשָׁלַיִם וְכָתוּב בָּהּ: אִישׁ פְּלוֹנִי מַמְזֵר מֵאֵשֶׁת אִישׁ, לְקַיֵּים דִּבְרֵי רַבִּי יְהוֹשֻׁעַ.

Rabbi Shimon ben Azzai said: I found a scroll recording people's **lineages in Jerusalem, and it was written in it** that **so-and-so is a** ***mamzer***[N] **from** an adulterous union with **a married woman,** a sin punishable by court-imposed capital punishment. The only reason for the scroll to state the reason that this individual is a *mamzer* is in order **to support the statement of Rabbi Yehoshua.**

אִשְׁתּוֹ שֶׁמֵּתָה – מוּתָּר בַּאֲחוֹתָהּ, גֵּרְשָׁהּ וּמֵתָה – מוּתָּר בַּאֲחוֹתָהּ. נִשֵּׂאת לְאַחֵר וּמֵתָה – מוּתָּר בַּאֲחוֹתָהּ. יְבִמְתּוֹ שֶׁמֵּתָה – מוּתָּר בַּאֲחוֹתָהּ, חָלַץ לָהּ וּמֵתָה – מוּתָּר בַּאֲחוֹתָהּ, נִשֵּׂאת לְאַחֵר וּמֵתָה – מוּתָּר בַּאֲחוֹתָהּ.

The mishna delineates the circumstances in which it is prohibited to engage in relations with the sister of one's wife and the sister of one's *yevama*: If a man's **wife died, he is permitted to her sister.**[H] **If he divorced her and** then **she died, he is permitted to her sister.** If he divorced his wife and then **she was married to another and** then **died, he is permitted to her sister.** If his ***yevama*** **died, he is permitted to her sister. If he performed** ***ḥalitza*** **with her and** then **she died, he is permitted to her sister.** If after *ḥalitza* **she was married to another and** then **died, he is permitted to her sister.** The principle underlying all these cases is that the prohibition against engaging in relations with her sister only applies while the wife or *yevama* remain alive, irrespective of their current relationship to the man.

גמ׳ מַאי טַעְמָא דְּרַבִּי עֲקִיבָא? דִּכְתִיב ״לֹא יִקַּח אִישׁ אֶת אֵשֶׁת אָבִיו וְלֹא יְגַלֶּה כְּנַף אָבִיו״ – כְּנַף שֶׁרָאָה אָבִיו לֹא יְגַלֶּה,

GEMARA **What is Rabbi Akiva's reasoning? As it is written: "A man shall not take his father's wife, and he shall not uncover his father's cloak"** (Deuteronomy 23:1). This teaches that a **cloak that his father saw,**[N] i.e., a woman with whom his father engaged in sexual relations, the son **may not uncover.**

HALAKHA

Which offspring have the status of a ***mamzer*** **– אֵיזֶהוּ מַמְזֵר:** The offspring born of a forbidden union for which one is liable to *karet* or a court-imposed death penalty is a *mamzer*, irrespective of whether the sexual relations were engaged in willfully or otherwise. This is true with the exception of the offspring of a union with a menstruating woman, which is not a *mamzer*. This is in accordance with the opinion of Shimon HaTimni, since the Gemara rules in accordance with his opinion (Rambam *Sefer Kedusha, Hilkhot Issurei Bia* 15:1; *Shulḥan Arukh, Even HaEzer* 4:13).

If a man's wife died he is permitted to her sister – אִשְׁתּוֹ שֶׁמֵּתָה מוּתָּר בַּאֲחוֹתָהּ: A man's wife's sister is forbidden to him throughout his wife's lifetime, even if they are divorced. After his wife's death, however, he is permitted to marry her sister. It is all the more true that the sister of a *yevama* is permitted to the *yavam* after the death of the *yevama* (Rambam *Sefer Kedusha, Hilkhot Issurei Bia* 2:9; *Shulḥan Arukh, Even HaEzer* 15:26).

PERSONALITIES

Shimon HaTimni – שִׁמְעוֹן הַתִּימְנִי: Shimon HaTimni was a *tanna* during the generation of Rabbi Akiva whose title was derived from his home city of Timna in Judea. He was one of the important Sages of the Sanhedrin in Yavne. He numbers among those few Sages who understood seventy languages. However, due to his young age, he was never ordained, and so he is instead referred to as one who deliberated before the Sages. Despite his young age, and even though he was connected to the disciples of Rabbi Akiva, he was nevertheless not his preeminent disciple. In fact, he occasionally disputed Rabbi Akiva's opinions.

Most statements cited in his name in the Mishna and *baraitot* involve matters of *halakha*, and he seldom comments on issues of *aggada*.

NOTES

Which offspring have the status of a ***mamzer*** **– אֵיזֶהוּ מַמְזֵר:** This mishna is not directly related to the general subject matter of this chapter. However, since the previous mishna cites the dispute between Rabbi Akiva and the Rabbis as to whether or not the offspring from various forbidden unions are *mamzerim*, this mishna cites the basic principles behind that dispute (Meiri).

Any next of kin – כׇּל שְׁאֵר בָּשָׂר: The mishna here appears to state that Rabbi Akiva regards only the offspring of forbidden unions between next of kin as *mamzerim*; however, the offspring of other forbidden unions would not be *mamzerim*. This would seem to contradict the mishna on 44a that states that Rabbi Akiva holds that with regard to one who remarries his divorcée after she had been married to another man, the offspring from that union is also a *mamzer*. Rashi suggests that the two *mishnayot* reflect the two different opinions with regard to Rabbi Akiva's position, and the mishna on 44a is in accordance with the understanding of Rabbi Simai. Others reject this suggestion because it would be highly unseemly for the Mishna to cite two statements in the name of a single Sage based on two opposing opinions of what his position is, especially when the two statements are cited in close proximity to each other. The Rashba therefore explains that one must conclude that one's divorcée who remarried is also considered next of kin because the prohibition is based on his close relationship to her.

From the Rambam's Commentary on the Mishna it would appear that he read Rabbi Akiva's statement in this mishna as comprising two clauses: The offspring of a union with any next of kin, or of a union that is subject to a Torah prohibition, is a *mamzer*. His interpretation is supported by the discussion of this mishna in the Jerusalem Talmud. According to this reading, there is no contradiction at all to the previous mishna.

And the ***halakha*** **is in accordance with his statement – וַהֲלָכָה כִּדְבָרָיו:** Some early commentaries, including the Rif and Rabbeinu Ḥananel, note that there is a principle, cited in the Jerusalem Talmud on tractate *Pe'a*, that the *halakha* is not decided based on rulings in a mishna. Therefore, despite the fact that this mishna explicitly states that the *halakha* is in accordance with the opinion of Shimon HaTimni, that itself has no force in deciding the ultimate ruling. Some explain that the reason for this is that when Rabbi Yehuda HaNasi redacted the Mishna, he collected and arranged many tannaitic statements that already existed. He would sometimes cite those statements without modification, even if they included claims about what the *halakha* should be. Accordingly, when a mishna includes a statement about the ruling of a *halakha*, it cannot be assumed that it reflects Rabbi Yehuda HaNasi's own opinion, and therefore it does not carry any halakhic weight.

And it was written in it that so-and-so is a ***mamzer*****, etc. – וְכָתוּב בָּהּ: אִישׁ פְּלוֹנִי מַמְזֵר וכו׳:** The purpose of keeping a record of lineages is so that people are aware of whom they may marry and whom they may not. Therefore, it is unnecessary for the scroll to detail the circumstances that led to one gaining a certain status. Accordingly, the fact that this scroll explicitly stated why a certain individual was a *mamzer* suggests that it meant to teach something about who is to be regarded as a *mamzer* (*Yosef Lekaḥ*; see *Tosafot*).

A cloak that his father saw, etc. – כְּנַף שֶׁרָאָה אָבִיו וכו׳: The Gemara explains that this refers to a woman raped by his father. However, it is difficult to understand why the offspring from a union with her would be a *mamzer*, since Rabbi Akiva states in the mishna that only the offspring of a union with a next of kin is a *mamzer*. Some resolve this question by saying that the essence of the condition that the union be with a next of kin is that the prohibition is a function of one's relationship to her. If so, even though a woman his father rapes is not actually a next of kin, since ultimately the prohibition against engaging in relations with her is due to the father's relationship to her, Rabbi Akiva will agree that the offspring of a union with her will be a *mamzer* (Rashash).

וְסָבַר לַהּ כְּרַבִּי יְהוּדָה, דְּאָמַר: בַּאֲנוּסַת אָבִיו הַכָּתוּב מְדַבֵּר, דְּהָוְיָא לַהּ חַיָּיבֵי לָאוִין.

And in this interpretation of the verse, Rabbi Akiva **holds in accordance with** the opinion of **Rabbi Yehuda, who said:** The verse states only that such relations are forbidden, but they would not render him liable to receive *karet*; perforce **the verse speaks of a woman raped by one's father,** since **she is** one of the women with whom relations render one **liable for** violating **a prohibition.** The verse could not refer to one's father's wife since relations with her render one liable to receive *karet*.

וּסְמִיךְ לֵיהּ "לֹא יָבֹא מַמְזֵר בִּקְהַל ה'". אַלְמָא: מֵהָנֵי הָוֵי מַמְזֵר.

The Gemara completes its explanation of Rabbi Akiva's opinion: **And in close proximity to that** verse is the verse: **"A *mamzer* shall not enter**[N] **into the congregation of the Lord"** (Deuteronomy 23:3). **Apparently,** even **from these** forbidden relations, which render one liable for the violation of a prohibition, the offspring **is a *mamzer*.**

וּלְרַבִּי סִימַאי דִּמְרַבֶּה שְׁאָר חַיָּיבֵי לָאוִין דְּלָאו דִּ"שְׁאֵר", וּלְרַבִּי יְשֵׁבָב דִּמְרַבֶּה אֲפִילּוּ חַיָּיבֵי עֲשֵׂה –

The Gemara asks: **But according to Rabbi Simai, who** holds that Rabbi Akiva **includes** as a *mamzer* the offspring of all **other** forbidden relations **for which one is liable** for violation of **a prohibition,** even those **that are not** with his **next of kin; and** also **according to Rabbi Yeshevav,**[P] **who** holds that Rabbi Akiva **includes even** the offspring of relations **for which one is liable** for the violation of a **positive mitzva;** since according to them, Rabbi Akiva includes cases that are not similar to the case a woman raped by his father, what is his source?

נָפְקָא לְהוּ מִ"וְּלֹא".

The Gemara answers: **They derive** it **from** the verse that states: **"And he shall not** uncover his father's cloak" (Deuteronomy 23:1). The word "and" is superfluous and serves to include additional cases.

וְשִׁמְעוֹן הַתִּימְנִי סָבַר לַהּ כְּרַבָּנַן, דְּאָמְרִי: בְּשׁוֹמֶרֶת יָבָם שֶׁל אָבִיו הַכָּתוּב מְדַבֵּר, דְּהָוְיָא לַהּ חַיָּיבֵי כְּרֵיתוֹת, וּסְמִיךְ לֵיהּ "לֹא יָבֹא מַמְזֵר", אַלְמָא: מֵחַיָּיבֵי כְּרֵיתוֹת הָוֵי מַמְזֵר.

And Shimon HaTimni[N] **holds in accordance with** the opinion of **the Rabbis, who say:** It is **with regard to the widow waiting for his father** to perform **levirate marriage that the verse is speaking,** and it indicates **that she is** one of the women with whom relations **render one liable** to receive ***karet*****. And in close proximity to that** verse is the verse: **"A *mamzer* shall not enter** into the congregation of the Lord" (Deuteronomy 23:3). **Apparently,** only the offspring of a union **for which one is liable** to receive ***karet*** **is a *mamzer*.**

וְרַבִּי יְהוֹשֻׁעַ: לִכְתּוֹב רַחֲמָנָא "לֹא יְגַלֶּה", "לֹא יִקַּח" ("וְלֹא יְגַלֶּה") לָמָּה לִי? אֶלָּא לָאו הָכִי קָאָמַר: מִ"לֹּא יִקַּח" עַד "לֹא יְגַלֶּה" – הָוֵי מַמְזֵר, טְפֵי – לָא הָוֵי מַמְזֵר.

And how does **Rabbi Yehoshua**[N] derive his opinion? If the verses should be derived as Rabbi Akiva and Shimon HaTimni suggest, **let the Merciful One write** only: **"He shall not uncover** his father's cloak." It is unnecessary for the verse to mention the prohibition with regard to one's father's wife, as the fact that the offspring of that union is a *mamzer* would be known through an *a fortiori* inference, since that prohibition is more stringent than the one derived from the verse: "And shall not uncover his father's cloak." **Why do I** need both the clause **"a man shall not take** his father's wife" and the clause **"and shall not uncover** his father's cloak"? **Rather, is it not** that **this is what** the Torah **is saying:** Only the offspring of relations with the woman mentioned in the verse **after** the words **"a man shall not take" until** the words **"he shall not uncover,"** i.e., his father's wife, **is a *mamzer*, but** the offspring of relations with the woman mentioned **beyond** that point, i.e., the woman referred to as "his father's cloak," **is not a *mamzer*.**

אָמַר אַבָּיֵי: הַכֹּל מוֹדִים בְּבָא עַל הַנִּדָּה

§ **Abaye said: All** *tanna'im* in the mishna **agree with regard to one who engages in sexual relations with a menstruating woman,**[N]

PERSONALITIES

Rabbi Yeshevav – רַבִּי יְשֵׁבָב: Rabbi Yeshevav was a third-generation *tanna* and scribe who was a disciple of Rabbi Yehoshua and a contemporary of Rabbi Akiva. He was exceedingly generous, and Rabbi Akiva criticized him for giving too much of his money to charity. Rabbi Yeshevav was one of the ten martyrs who were killed by the Romans during the bar Kokheva rebellion, and according to tradition (*Midrash Eleh Ezkera*), the ninety-year-old Sage told his disciples to support each other and uphold justice and peace. He was then thrown to the dogs and did not merit to be buried.

NOTES

And in close proximity to that verse is: "A *mamzer* shall not enter" – וּסְמִיךְ לֵיהּ לֹא יָבֹא מַמְזֵר: Generally, when a derivation is based on the fact that two verses are in close proximity to each other, the two verses are actually juxtaposed with nothing between them. However, in this case, the two verses are separated by a verse that states that a man whose sexual organs have been damaged is prohibited from marrying into the congregation. *Tosafot* note this difficulty and explain that since a man whose sexual organs have been damaged is unable to father any children, that verse can certainly not be utilized to identify which kinds of forbidden unions result in the offspring being a *mamzer*. Therefore, in this case it is acceptable to base the derivation on the proximity of the verse about a *mamzer* to the verse about a woman with whom one's father engaged in relations (see Ritva and *Nimmukei Yosef*).

The opinion of Shimon HaTimni – שִׁיטַת שִׁמְעוֹן הַתִּימְנִי: From an opinion in the Jerusalem Talmud, as well as from many early commentaries (see Ramban and Rashba), it would appear that Shimon HaTimni arrived at his opinion based on the hermeneutical principle that if a case was included as part of a general category but was singled out to teach something, what it teaches is to be applied not only to that case but to all of the cases in that general category. As applied to this case, it indicates that since the prohibition with regard to one's father's wife appears in Leviticus as part of the general category of incestuous relationships for which one is liable to receive *karet*, and then it is mentioned alone in Deuteronomy in order to teach that the offspring of a union with one's father's wife is a *mamzer*, it therefore teaches that this is true of all the cases in Leviticus, i.e., that the offspring from any one of those relationships is a *mamzer*.

Rabbi Yehoshua's proof – הוֹכָחַת רַבִּי יְהוֹשֻׁעַ: The commentaries suggest different interpretations of Rabbi Yehoshua's proof here. Rashi explains that since it is unnecessary to state both: "he shall not take" and "he shall not uncover," it is apparent that only the offspring of relations with the woman mentioned in between those phrases, i.e., one's father's wife, is a *mamzer*, as well as all similar cases where one would be liable for a court-imposed death penalty. The *ge'onim*, based on a different version of the text also cited by *Tosafot*, explain that since it is repetitious to state both "he shall not take" and "he shall not uncover," it must be that one should derive the *halakha* of a *mamzer* from the more stringent of the two.

Rabbeinu Ḥananel appears to have had a version of the Gemara in which the continuation: Rather is it not, etc., does not appear at all. Based on that version, he explains that since the expressions "he shall not take" and "he shall not uncover" are repetitious, their use must come to teach that only those prohibitions that are formulated in these ways are included.

All agree with regard to one who engages in sexual relations with a menstruating woman, etc. – הַכֹּל מוֹדִים בְּבָא עַל הַנִּדָּה וכו׳: In the Jerusalem Talmud it is explained that the offspring from relations with a menstruating woman is not a *mamzer* because the woman is not forbidden on account of being a next of kin, which the mishna here states is one of the conditions for the offspring to be a *mamzer*. This fits well with the explanation found in the Jerusalem Talmud that the specific case of one's father's wife teaches about the entire category of forbidden relations recorded in Leviticus. The prohibition against engaging in relations with a menstruating woman is not included in that category. Furthermore, that category of cases is introduced by the statement: "None of you shall approach to any that is next of kin to him, to uncover their nakedness" (Leviticus 18:6), which serves to emphasize that only the offspring from relations with those who are next of kin is a *mamzer*.

Rabbi Yehuda al-Madari notes that in addition to the Gemara's reasoning that betrothal with a menstruating woman takes effect, further proof can be derived from the fact that when a woman menstruates, the betrothal bond is not dissolved. This point, already mentioned by *Tosafot*, serves to prove that a menstruating woman is not to be fully classified in the same manner as other forbidden relations.

וְעַל הַסּוֹטָה שֶׁאֵין הַוָּלָד מַמְזֵר.

or with a *sota*,[N] **that the offspring is not a *mamzer*.**[H]

נִדָּה – דְּהָא תָּפְסִי בָּהּ קִידּוּשִׁין, שֶׁנֶּאֱמַר "וּתְהִי נִדָּתָהּ עָלָיו" – אֲפִילּוּ בִּשְׁעַת נִדָּתָהּ – תָּפְסֵי בָּהּ קִידּוּשִׁין.

With regard to **a menstruating woman** the offspring is not a *mamzer* **because** one's **betrothal of her takes effect,**[H] **as it is stated: "And her impurity shall be upon him"** (Leviticus 15:24). The phrase "shall be" alludes to the fact that a betrothal with her takes effect. The verse teaches that **even at the time of her** menstrual **impurity, betrothal with her takes effect.**

סוֹטָה נַמִי – דְּהָא תָּפְסֵי בָּהּ קִידּוּשִׁין.

With regard to **a *sota*, too,** the offspring is not a *mamzer* **because** one's **betrothal of her takes effect.**

תַּנְיָא נַמִי הָכִי: הַכֹּל מוֹדִים בְּבָא עַל הַנִּדָּה, וְעַל הַסּוֹטָה, וְעַל שׁוֹמֶרֶת יָבָם – שֶׁאֵין הַוָּלָד מַמְזֵר.

The Gemara notes: **This** teaching of Abaye **is also taught** in a *baraita*: **All agree with regard to one who engages in sexual relations with a menstruating woman, or with a *sota*, or with a widow waiting for her *yavam*** to perform levirate marriage, **that the offspring is not a *mamzer*.**

וְאַבָּיֵי: שׁוֹמֶרֶת יָבָם מְסַפְּקָא לֵיהּ, אִי כְּרַב אִי כִּשְׁמוּאֵל.

The Gemara explains: **And Abaye** did not mention the case of a **widow waiting for her *yavam*** because **he is uncertain**[N] **whether,** if someone other than the *yavam* betrothed her, the *halakha* is **in accordance with** the opinion of **Rav** that it does not take effect or **in accordance with** the opinion of **Shmuel** that it might take effect.

"אָמַר רַבִּי שִׁמְעוֹן בֶּן עַזַּאי" כו׳. תַּנְיָא, שִׁמְעוֹן בֶּן עַזַּאי אוֹמֵר: מָצָאתִי מְגִלַּת יוֹחֲסִין בִּירוּשָׁלַיִם, וְכָתוּב בָּהּ: אִישׁ פְּלוֹנִי מַמְזֵר מֵאֵשֶׁת אִישׁ. וְכָתוּב בָּהּ: מִשְׁנַת רַבִּי אֱלִיעֶזֶר בֶּן יַעֲקֹב קַב וְנָקִי. וְכָתוּב בָּהּ: מְנַשֶּׁה הָרַג אֶת יְשַׁעְיָה.

§ The mishna states: **Rabbi Shimon ben Azzai said:** I found a scroll recording people's lineages. The Gemara cites an expanded version of the contents of the scroll. **It is taught** in a *baraita* that **Rabbi Shimon ben Azzai said: I found a scroll** recording people's **lineages, in Jerusalem, and it was written in it**[N] that **so-and-so is a *mamzer* from** an adulterous union with **a married woman. And it was** also **written in it: The teachings of Rabbi Eliezer ben Ya'akov** measure only **a *kav* but are clean** and accurate, and so the *halakha* is decided in accordance with his opinions. **And it was written in it: Manasseh,** king of Israel, **killed Isaiah** the prophet.

HALAKHA

The offspring of a menstruating woman – וְלַד הַנִּדָּה: All agree that a child born from a menstruating woman is not a *mamzer* and is even permitted to marry into the priesthood (*Beit Shmuel*). However, he is considered to be of a sullied status and his family is not held to be of distinguished lineage (Rambam *Sefer Kedusha, Hilkhot Issurei Bia* 15:1; *Shulḥan Arukh, Even HaEzer* 4:3).

Betrothal of a menstruating woman – קִידּוּשֵׁי נִדָּה: If one betroths one of the forbidden relations whom, were he to engage in relations with them, he would be liable to receive *karet* or a court-imposed death penalty, then the betrothal does not take effect. The exception to this principle is a menstruating woman, in whose case the betrothal does take effect. Nevertheless, it is not appropriate to betroth a menstruating woman. The *Taz* writes that nowadays, due to the significant monetary loss involved in rescheduling a wedding if the bride is menstruating, people are not particular about avoiding this situation, but nevertheless one should try to prevent the situation *ab initio* (Rambam *Sefer Nashim, Hilkhot Ishut* 4:12; *Shulḥan Arukh, Even HaEzer* 44:6).

NOTES

Sota – סוֹטָה: The term *sota* is used to describe both a wife who was suspected by her husband of having been unfaithful and a wife who is known to have been unfaithful. In both cases, she is prohibited from engaging in relations with her husband.

Rashi explains that the Gemara here is referring to a case where it is known that she was unfaithful and nevertheless she remained married to her husband. Rashi explains that in this case the reason that everyone agrees that the offspring is not a *mamzer* is because the marriage bond is not abrogated despite the fact that the marriage is prohibited. *Tosafot* argue that the fact that the marriage bond is not abrogated is itself insufficient to explain why the offspring is not a *mamzer*. Therefore, they explain that the case here is where the husband divorced his adulterous wife and then remarried her. It is therefore apparent that his betrothal of her takes effect, and it is this fact that explains why the offspring is not a *mamzer*. Apparently, *Tosafot* assume that the key factor in defining whether the offspring will be a *mamzer* is whether or not the prohibition is a function of the familial relationship between them, i.e., only the offspring of forbidden relations between next of kin is a *mamzer*, and it is this factor that expresses itself in the fact that one cannot effect a betrothal between these relatives.

Rabbeinu Ḥananel writes that although the Gemara here states clearly that the offspring is not a *mamzer*, that is true only according to Torah law. However, by rabbinic law, the offspring is rendered a *mamzer*. He draws proof for his claim from the case of a woman who remarries after a single witness testified that her husband had died. In such a case, if it later emerges that in fact her original husband is still alive, she is prohibited by rabbinic decree from returning to him. If she does return to him and has a child by him, the Sages decreed that it is considered a *mamzer*. Rabbeinu Ḥananel understands that this provides a paradigm for other cases where the marriage is forbidden by rabbinic decree, and that in those cases as well the offspring is rendered a *mamzer* by the Sages. *Tosafot* cite the opinion of Rabbeinu Ḥananel and explain that this decree is a penalty on the couple for ignoring the rabbinic prohibition against their marrying.

Other authorities disagree with Rabbeinu Ḥananel's opinion and claim that the case of a woman who remarried based on the testimony of a single witness is unique because in that case she married her new husband under the assumption that it was a valid course of action. Since the new marriage has the appearance of a valid one, the Sages prohibited her from returning to her original husband. However, in the case of adultery, no such concern exists, and therefore there is no need to render the offspring a *mamzer* (*Tosefot Ḥad MiKamma'ei*; Meiri; see Rashi, *Tosafot*, and Ramban).

He is uncertain, etc. – מְסַפְּקָא לֵיהּ וכו׳: The connection made by the Gemara between whether to rule in accordance with Rav or Shmuel and the status of the offspring as a *mamzer* is far from simple because the prohibition against a *yevama* engaging in relations with someone other than her *yavam* is of an entirely different nature than other forbidden relations (see *Tosafot*). Some explain that even according to the opinion of Rav the betrothal does not take effect; there is no actual negative mitzva against the *yevama* engaging in relations with someone other than her *yavam*. Rather, the reason that betrothal does not take effect is because she is already bound to the *yavam* through a levirate bond, and that bond prevents any other marital bond from taking effect upon her. The offspring of such a union is a *mamzer* for the same reason that some opinions hold that the offspring of a gentile and a Jewish woman is a *mamzer*: Whenever it is not possible to effect a betrothal between two people, the offspring from a union between them is a *mamzer* irrespective of the nature of the prohibition that applies to them.

One commentary suggests that neither Rav nor Shmuel themselves would hold that the offspring is a *mamzer*, since they hold that only the offspring of forbidden relations for which one is liable to receive *karet* is a *mamzer*. Abaye's uncertainty was in accordance with the opinion of Rabbi Akiva that even the offspring of less stringent forbidden relations is a *mamzer* (see Ramban and Rabbi Avraham min HaHar).

A scroll recording people's lineages…and it was written in it, etc. – מְגִלַּת יוֹחֲסִין...וְכָתוּב בָּהּ וכו׳: Ostensibly, the other matters that were written in the scroll were of no relevance to the scroll's main purpose of recording people's lineages. However, some suggest that a connection may be drawn: The statement that the *halakha* is in accordance with Rabbi Eliezer ben Ya'akov could be understood to refer specifically to the fact that the *halakha* is decided in accordance with his opinion with regard to the *halakhot* of lineages. In fact, the Gemara in *Kiddushin* 77a cites a case of lineages where his opinion was followed. With regard to the statement about Manasseh, the relevance may have been related to the fact that Manasseh was the grandson of Isaiah. The scroll wished to proclaim that although lineage may be of some importance, good lineage it is not necessarily a guarantee for success (*Arukh LaNer*).

אֲמַר רָבָא: מֵידַן דַּיְינֵיהּ וּקְטַלֵיהּ. אֲמַר לֵיהּ: מֹשֶׁה רַבָּךְ אֲמַר ״כִּי לֹא יִרְאַנִי הָאָדָם וָחָי״ וְאַתְּ אָמְרַתְּ ״וָאֶרְאֶה אֶת ה׳ יוֹשֵׁב עַל כִּסֵּא רָם וְנִשָּׂא״, מֹשֶׁה רַבָּךְ אֲמַר ״מִי כַּה׳ אֱלֹהֵינוּ בְּכָל קָרְאֵנוּ אֵלָיו״ וְאַתְּ אָמְרַתְּ ״דִּרְשׁוּ ה׳ בְּהִמָּצְאוֹ״. מֹשֶׁה רַבָּךְ אֲמַר ״אֶת מִסְפַּר יָמֶיךָ אֲמַלֵּא״ וְאַתְּ אָמְרַתְּ ״וְהוֹסַפְתִּי עַל יָמֶיךָ חֲמֵשׁ עֶשְׂרֵה שָׁנָה״!

The Gemara expands on the events surrounding Isaiah's death: **Rava said:** Manasseh **judged him** as a false witness for issuing statements contradicting the Torah **and** only then **killed him.** Manasseh **said to** Isaiah: **Moses your master said** in the Torah: "And He said: You cannot see My face, **for man cannot see Me and live**" (Exodus 33:20), **and** yet **you said: "I saw the Lord sitting upon a high and lofty throne"** (Isaiah 6:1). **Moses your master said:** "For **which** great nation is there, that has God so near to it, **as the Lord our God is, whenever we call upon Him?"** (Deuteronomy 4:7), **and** yet **you said: "Seek the Lord while He may be found, call upon Him while He is near"** (Isaiah 55:6), which implies that God is not always near. **Moses your master said: "I will fulfill the number of your days"** (Exodus 23:26), which implies that each individual has a preordained allotted lifespan that he cannot outlive, **and** yet **you said** in a prophecy to King Hezekiah: **"And I will add to your days, fifteen years"** (II Kings 20:6).

אֲמַר יְשַׁעְיָה: יָדַעְנָא בֵּיהּ דְּלָא מְקַבֵּל מַה דְּאֵימָא לֵיהּ, וְאִי אֵימָא לֵיהּ – אִישַׁוְּיֵיהּ מֵזִיד. אֲמַר שֵׁם, אִיבְלַע בְּאַרְזָא. אַתְיוּהָ לְאַרְזָא וּנְסַרוּהָ. כִּי מְטָא לַהֲדֵי פּוּמָא – נָח נַפְשֵׁיהּ, מִשּׁוּם דַּאֲמַר ״וּבְתוֹךְ עַם טְמֵא שְׂפָתַיִם אָנֹכִי יוֹשֵׁב״.

Isaiah said to himself: **I know him,** i.e., Manasseh, **that he will not accept whatever** explanation **that I will say to him** to resolve my prophecies with the words of the Torah. **And** even **if I say it to him,**[N] **I will make him into an intentional transgressor** since he will kill me anyway. Therefore, in order to escape, **he uttered a** divine **name and was swallowed within a cedar** tree. Manasseh's servants **brought the cedar** tree **and sawed through it** in order to kill him. **When** the saw **reached to where his mouth was,** Isaiah **died.** He died specifically as this point **due to that which he said: "In the midst of a people of unclean lips,**[N] **I dwell"** (Isaiah 6:5). He was punished for referring to the Jewish people in a derogatory manner.

מִכָּל מָקוֹם קָשׁוּ קְרָאֵי אַהֲדָדֵי!

The Gemara asks: **In any case,** as Manasseh pointed out, these **verses contradict each other;** how are these contradictions to be resolved?

״וָאֶרְאֶה אֶת ה׳״ – כִּדְתַנְיָא: כָּל הַנְּבִיאִים נִסְתַּכְּלוּ בְּאַסְפַּקְלַרְיָא שֶׁאֵינָהּ מְאִירָה, מֹשֶׁה רַבֵּינוּ נִסְתַּכֵּל בְּאַסְפַּקְלַרְיָא הַמְּאִירָה.

The Gemara resolves the first contradiction: **"I saw the Lord"** is to be understood **as it is taught** in a *baraita*: **All of the prophets observed** their prophecies **through an obscure looking glass** [***aspaklaria***],[LN] i.e., their prophecies were given as metaphoric visions but were not a direct perception of the matter. However, **Moses our master observed** his prophecies **through a clear looking glass,** i.e., he gained a direct and accurate perception of the matter.

LANGUAGE

Looking glass [*aspaklaria*] – **אַסְפַּקְלַרְיָא:** Either from the Latin speculum, which is a mirror made of metal, or from the Latin specularis, meaning transparent, i.e., a transparent window. The word apparently entered Hebrew through the Greek σπεκλάριον, *speclarion*, meaning a small mirror.

In the Gemara, the word has two connotations: It can mean either a mirror made of metal, or a glass window or looking glass. In the context here, the reference is to the latter.

Ancient optical lens possibly used as a magnifying glass

Ancient Greek mirror

NOTES

If I say it to him, etc. – **אִי אֵימָא לֵיהּ וכו׳:** *Tosafot* cite the interpretation of Rabbeinu Ḥananel that Isaiah could have easily responded that the Torah itself states with regard to the Elders at the revelation at Sinai: "And they saw the God of Israel" (Exodus 24:10), which justifies the use of the verb: See, with regard to God. The *Otzar HaShitot* explains that the Gemara chose not to raise this issue because ultimately the root of the issue is, as the Gemara explains, due to the difference in the level of prophecy between Moses and others. This, then, also explains the verse: "And they saw the God of Israel," which also describes the prophetic vision of the Elders, whose prophecy was not at the level of Moses'. Isaiah could not explain this matter to Manasseh because it would have been damaging to his mission to state that his level of prophecy was comparable to looking through an obscure looking glass, which Manasseh would have taken to mean that his prophecy was unreliable and inaccurate.

Due to that which he said: In the midst of a people of unclean lips – **מִשּׁוּם דַּאֲמַר וּבְתוֹךְ עַם טְמֵא שְׂפָתַיִם:** Although Isaiah issued prophetic warnings to the Jewish people that contained much harsher statements, the commentaries explain that there was no claim against him for that because those statements were simply relaying what God had told him to say. He was punished only for expressing his own opinion about the nature of the Jewish people. See the Meiri and *Yam shel Shlomo* who discuss the halakhic conclusions that can be drawn from this Gemara.

The Ritva points out that in that same chapter in Isaiah, God's angels said to Isaiah: "Your iniquity is taken away and your sin shall be expiated" (Isaiah 7:6). This would seem to imply he was forgiven for his sin; why, then, was he later punished? The Ritva explains that Isaiah was forgiven only for expressing his sentiments before God, but he still had no right to later publicly recount what he had said, and he was punished for that. He also suggests another explanation: The phrase "and your sin shall be expiated" is stated in the future tense; it is not saying that he was already forgiven but that ultimately his sin would be expiated though his unseemly death.

Obscure looking glass – **בְּאַסְפַּקְלַרְיָא שֶׁאֵינָהּ מְאִירָה:** The commentaries (*ge'onim*; Rabbeinu Ḥananel; Rambam) wrote at length to explain this matter. Primarily they cite passages from *Vayikra Rabba* that include different tannaitic explanations of the subject. The essential idea is that one who does not see with sufficient clarity mistakenly sees things that do not exist or sees distorted forms. The Rambam, in *Sefer HaMadda* and in his Commentary on the Mishna, explains that only Moses could see God "face to face" (Deuteronomy 34:10) without any intervening imagery. The Ramban hints at a different understanding, according to which the other prophets experienced their prophecies as a mental image, whereas the prophecy of Moses was at such a high level that he gained an intimate understanding of the prophecy without the need for it to be diluted and encapsulated in a prophetic vision.

NOTES

This is with regard to the individual and this is with regard to a community – **הָא בְּיָחִיד הָא בְּצִבּוּר**: This distinction is evident in the verses themselves as well. The verse: "Whenever we call upon Him" clearly refers to a group of people, i.e., the community of the Jewish people, and the verse: "Seek the Lord while He may be found" continues "and let the wicked one forsake His way" (Isaiah 55:7), which clearly refers to an individual (Maharsha).

HALAKHA

Ten days of repentance – **עֲשֶׂרֶת יְמֵי תְשׁוּבָה**: While repentance is always effective, repentance of the individual is especially well received during the ten days between Rosh HaShana and Yom Kippur (Rambam *Sefer HaMadda, Hilkhot Teshuva* 2:6).

"דִּרְשׁוּ ה' בְּהִמָּצְאוֹ" – הָא בְּיָחִיד הָא בְּצִבּוּר. וְיָחִיד אֵימַת? אָמַר רַב נַחְמָן אָמַר רַבָּה בַּר אֲבוּהּ: אֵלּוּ עֲשָׂרָה יָמִים שֶׁבֵּין רֹאשׁ הַשָּׁנָה לְיוֹם הַכִּפּוּרִים,

The Gemara resolves the second contradiction: Isaiah's prophecy: **"Seek the Lord while He may be found,"** does not contradict the verse in the Torah that God is near to His nation "whenever we call upon Him," because **this** prophecy of Isaiah was made **with regard to the individual** and **this** verse in the Torah is stated **with regard to a community,**[N] as the prayer of the community is always accepted. The Gemara asks: **And when** is the time that God is to be found near **the individual? Rav Naḥman said Rabba bar Avuh said: These are the ten days between Rosh HaShana and Yom Kippur.**[H]

"אֶת מִסְפַּר יָמֶיךָ אֲמַלֵּא" – תַּנָּאֵי הִיא. דְּתַנְיָא "אֶת מִסְפַּר יָמֶיךָ אֲמַלֵּא"

The resolution of the third contradiction from the verse: **"I will fulfill the number of your days," is** subject to a dispute between *tanna'im*, **as it is taught** in a *baraita*: The verse states: **"I will fulfill the number of your days"**;

Perek **IV**
Daf **50** Amud **a**

אֵלּוּ שְׁנֵי דוֹרוֹת, זָכָה – מַשְׁלִימִין לוֹ, לֹא זָכָה – פּוֹחֲתִין לוֹ. דִּבְרֵי רַבִּי עֲקִיבָא. וַחֲכָמִים אוֹמְרִים: זָכָה – מוֹסִיפִים לוֹ, לֹא זָכָה – פּוֹחֲתִין לוֹ.

these are the **years of** the **generations,**[N] i.e., the allotted lifespan that is preordained for each individual before birth. If **he is deserving,** God **completes his** allotted lifespan. If **he is not deserving,** God **reduces his** lifespan; this is **the statement of Rabbi Akiva.** Rabbi Akiva assumes one cannot outlive one's preordained allotted lifespan. **The Rabbis say:** If **he is deserving,** God **adds** years **to his** lifespan.[N] If **he is not deserving,** God **reduces his** lifespan. According to the Rabbis, Isaiah's prophecy is referring to one who deserved to have extra years added to his allotted lifespan, and the verse in the Torah is referring to one who deserved to merely complete his lifespan.

אָמְרוּ לוֹ לְרַבִּי עֲקִיבָא: הֲרֵי הוּא אוֹמֵר "וְהֹסַפְתִּי עַל יָמֶיךָ חֲמֵשׁ עֶשְׂרֵה שָׁנָה"! אָמַר לָהֶם: מִשֶּׁלּוֹ הוֹסִיפוּ לוֹ. תֵּדַע, שֶׁהֲרֵי נָבִיא עוֹמֵד וּמִתְנַבֵּא "הִנֵּה בֵן נוֹלָד לְבֵית דָּוִד יֹאשִׁיָּהוּ שְׁמוֹ" וַעֲדַיִין לֹא נוֹלַד מְנַשֶּׁה.

The Rabbis **said to Rabbi Akiva:** How can you claim that one cannot outlive one's allotted lifespan when **there is** a verse that **states** that Isaiah prophesied to Hezekiah as Hezekiah lay on his deathbed: **"And I will add unto your days fifteen years"**? Rabbi Akiva **said to them:** Those additional years that God **added to his** lifespan are **from his own** allotted lifespan. When Hezekiah sinned God decreed that his lifespan be shortened, but when he repented God allowed him to live out those years. **Know** that this is so, **as a prophet** during the reign of King Jeroboam **stood and prophesied:**[N] **"Behold, a son shall be born unto the House of David, Josiah is his name"** (I Kings 13:2). Josiah was the grandson of Manasseh, Hezekiah's son, and at the time Hezekiah lay on his deathbed, **Manasseh had not yet been born.** Evidently, Hezekiah's preordained allotted lifespan had still not been completed.

NOTES

The years of the generations – **שְׁנֵי דוֹרוֹת**: Rashi and others interpret this as a reference to the years of life allotted to each generation, which are then divided and are allotted to each individual in that generation. *Tosefot HaRosh* explains that when God makes an accounting of people's lifespans He does so as part of a general decree relating to the lifespans of the entire generation. This is alluded to by the verse: "He that calls the generations from the beginning" (Isaiah 41:4). The *ge'onim* explain that the reference is to the number of years one should live based on his physical structure and health (see Meiri and Rabbi Avraham min HaHar). The Rambam wrote an important treatise in Arabic in which he summarized the various opinions on this subject, from both the philosophical and the medical perspectives.

If he is deserving, God adds years to his lifespan – **זָכָה מוֹסִיפִים לוֹ**: What is the significance of being given a preordained lifespan if one can merit additional years or lose years based on one's actions? The *Tzlaḥ* on *Yoma* 86b suggests that each day has its own unique goals to be fulfilled, and if one did not utilize each day correctly he will be called to account in the World-to-Come. However, if he merits it, he will receive additional days and consequently he will be able to complete the goals that he did not achieve during the amount of time that had been allotted to him.

As a prophet stood and prophesied, etc. – **שֶׁהֲרֵי נָבִיא עוֹמֵד וּמִתְנַבֵּא וכו'**: In a responsum written by Rav Hai Gaon on this matter he proves from here, as well as from Isaiah's prophecy concerning King Hezekiah's impending demise, that such prophecies are always conditional on one's actions and so one can change his fate by amending his ways and through prayer. See the Rambam, who discusses this subject at length when dealing with prophecy in *Mishne Torah* and elsewhere (see also in *Tosafot*).

וְרַבָּנַן: מִי כְּתִיב מֵחִזְקִיָּה? ״לְבֵית דָּוִד״ כְּתִיב, אִי מֵחִזְקִיָּה נוֹלַד, אִי מֵאֱינָשׁ אַחֲרִינָא.

And what would **the Rabbis** respond to Rabbi Akiva's proof? They could counter: **Is it written** that Josiah was to be born specifically **from** the descendants of **Hezekiah? It is written** only that he would be born **"unto the House of David,"** so **he could be born either from** the descendants of **Hezekiah or from a different person** of the House of David. Accordingly, no proof concerning Hezekiah's allotted lifespan can be deduced from that verse.

״אִשְׁתּוֹ שֶׁמֵּתָה וכו׳ יְבִמְתּוֹ שֶׁמֵּתָה וכו׳״. אָמַר רַב יוֹסֵף: כָּאן שָׁנָה רַבִּי מִשְׁנָה שֶׁאֵינָהּ צְרִיכָה.

§ The mishna details the prohibition with regard to one's wife's sister in various cases: If a man's **wife died,** he is permitted to her sister; if **his *yevama* died,** he is permitted to her sister. **Rav Yosef said: Here Rabbi** Yehuda HaNasi **taught an unnecessary mishna,**[N] since the prohibition with regard to one's wife's sister and the fact that the prohibition exists only in the lifetime of one's wife is stated explicitly in the Torah, and there is no additional novelty in this mishna's ruling.

הדרן עלך החולץ

NOTES

An unnecessary mishna – מִשְׁנָה שֶׁאֵינָהּ צְרִיכָה: From Rashi's commentary it is clear that he holds that at the very least, the clause referring to the permissibility of one's wife's sister after the wife's death is superfluous, since the matter is stated explicitly in the Torah. However, *Tosafot Yeshanim* suggest that even that clause of the mishna hints at a novelty that is not explicit in the Torah. They explain the novelty is in the case where one's previous wife married another man: Unless she dies, the prohibition with regard to her sister still remains in effect. One might have claimed that since, by marrying another man, the woman was rendered forbidden to her first husband, therefore her sister would become permitted to him. To dispel this notion the mishna teaches that the prohibition remains in force until the wife actually dies. Therefore, *Tosafot Yeshanim* suggest that it is the latter clause, which states that if one's *yevama* died one is permitted to her sister, which is entirely superfluous. Once the mishna has stated the *halakha* in the case of one's wife's sister, it is obviously true in the case of one's *yevama* through an *a fortiori* inference.

However, from an opinion in the Jerusalem Talmud it would appear that the primary novelty in the mishna is to be found specifically in the clause concerning the sister of one's *yevama*. The novelty does not lie in the case itself but in the fact that it implies that even after one's *yevama* dies, the levirate bond continues to exist to the extent that relatives of one's *yevama* will remain forbidden to him. The mishna states that the sister of one's *yevama* is an exception to this principle, but by inference the prohibition to other relatives, e.g., her mother or daughter, continue to apply. *Tosafot Yeshanim* and *Tosefot HaRosh* reject this suggestion.

The Ramban claims that only the clause that relates to the basic case of the sister of one's wife or *yevama* being permitted upon the death of one's wife or *yevama* are considered unnecessary because those cases are explicit in the Torah. However, although the principle is the same in the other cases, since they are not stated explicitly there is value in mentioning them here.

In contrast, the Ritva claims that the entire mishna is unnecessary and rejects the suggestion that the cases were taught to indicate some subtle novelty that may be inferred from them. Rather, the mishna was written to reëmphasize matters that are already known; doing so is considered "making the Torah great and glorious" (Isaiah 42:21).

Summary of **Perek IV**

The chapter began with a discussion of a case in which a woman performed *ḥalitza* or entered into levirate marriage under the assumption that she was required to do so, but it eventually emerged that she was pregnant at the time. The Gemara concludes that the validity of the *ḥalitza* or levirate marriage depends on whether she ultimately required them or not. Therefore, if she ultimately miscarries, in which case it is apparent that she did require them, they are valid. However, if she ultimately gave birth to viable offspring, then the levirate marriage or *ḥalitza* is of no significance.

As part of that discussion, the Gemara considered cases in which a child is born to the *yevama* following levirate marriage and it is unclear whether the child is the offspring of her first husband or the *yavam*. The Gemara then considered the steps that must be taken in all marriages to prevent such uncertainties from arising and to ensure that the lineage of the Jewish people is clear and apparent. The Gemara explained that for this purpose the Sages decreed that no woman should remarry until three months have passed since the end of her previous marriage and it is clear whether or not she is pregnant. With regard to a pregnant or nursing woman the Sages likewise decreed that she should wait a certain period before remarrying.

The Gemara proceeded to examine which cases of forbidden relations produce offspring with *mamzer* status. Although many views on the issue were presented, the accepted opinion is that only offspring from forbidden relations for which one is liable to receive *karet* are *mamzerim*, with the exception of a child born from a union with a menstruating woman, for which the punishment is not *karet*.

The chapter also considered the issues relating to the property of the *yevama* and of her deceased husband. As long as the *yevama* is still awaiting levirate marriage, her property remains her own and under her control. If she dies during that period then that property is bequeathed to her heirs, while the money promised to her in her marriage contract is inherited by her husband's heirs. However, after the levirate marriage the *yevama* is considered to be the wife of the *yavam* in every sense, and therefore the *yavam* has the same level of control over her property as any other husband has over his wife's property. The only exception to this principle is that her marriage contract remains payable from her first husband's estate.

The Gemara also discussed the *halakhot* of conversion and concluded that in order to convert it is necessary to be both circumcised and immersed for the sake of conversion before a court of three judges. A similar process is required for a slave; however, the Gemara examined whether there might be a distinction between the case of a convert and that of a slave with regard to whether it is necessary to willingly accept upon oneself the yoke of the mitzvot.

Introduction to **Perek V**

This chapter deals exclusively with one issue: The relationship between the various acts that a *yavam* might perform with a *yevama*. In total, there are four options: Intercourse or *ḥalitza*, which are effective by Torah law, and levirate betrothal [*ma'amar*] or a bill of divorce [*get*] by rabbinic law. This chapter clarifies the nature of the relationship between these options by discussing the relative efficacy of the modes of acquisition, i.e., intercourse or levirate betrothal, on the one hand, and the modes of release, i.e., *ḥalitza* or a bill of divorce, on the other. These issues come to the fore when two or more of these acts are performed successively, whether they are performed by a single *yavam* with a single *yevama*, a single *yavam* with two *yevamot* who are co-wives, several *yevamin* with one *yevama*, or several *yevamin* with several *yevamot*.

Examination of these various combinations helps clarify the relative legal validity of each of these acts. Does a given act conclusively determine the relationship between the *yavam* and the *yevama*, or does it leave room for a further act that might, if performed, alter matters?

This clarification proves especially important with regard to the two acts that are of rabbinic ordinance: The levirate betrothal and the bill of divorce for a *yevama*. Indeed, the Sages were in dispute with regard to the exact nature of levirate betrothal and its power of acquisition: Does it constitute a fully valid act of acquisition like regular betrothal, does it grant only partial acquisition, or is it merely symbolic and bereft of any legal validity whatsoever? Similarly, with regard to a bill of divorce given to a woman requiring levirate marriage, in what way is this bill similar to an ordinary bill of divorce? To what extent does it serve only as a symbol and merely resemble standard bills of divorce?

The clarification of these relationships and the various rabbinic ordinances involved constitute the subject matter for this chapter.

מתני׳ רַבָּן גַּמְלִיאֵל אוֹמֵר: אֵין גֵּט אַחַר גֵּט, וְלֹא מַאֲמָר אַחַר מַאֲמָר, וְלֹא בְּעִילָה אַחַר בְּעִילָה, וְלֹא חֲלִיצָה אַחַר חֲלִיצָה. וַחֲכָמִים אוֹמְרִים: יֵשׁ גֵּט אַחַר גֵּט, וְיֵשׁ מַאֲמָר אַחַר מַאֲמָר, אֲבָל לֹא אַחַר בְּעִילָה וְלֹא אַחַר חֲלִיצָה כְּלוּם.

MISHNA **Rabban Gamliel says:**[N] **A bill of divorce** *[get]*[B] **is not** effective when given **after a bill of divorce** was previously given to a *yevama*. Once a *yevama* receives a bill of divorce from a *yavam*, no bill of divorce given by that *yavam* to her rival wife or a bill of divorce given to her by a different *yavam* is of any effect. **And levirate betrothal**[B] **is not** effective **after** a previous **levirate betrothal** was performed, **and intercourse** with a second *yevama* **is not** effective **after intercourse** with the first one, **and *ḥalitza***[B] **is not** effective **after *ḥalitza*** was previously performed. **But the Rabbis say: A bill of divorce** is effective when given **after a bill of divorce,**[N] **and levirate betrothal is** effective **after levirate betrothal,**[H] **but nothing is** effective **after intercourse**[N] **or after *ḥalitza*.**[H] If a *yavam* has relations with the *yevama* or performs *ḥalitza* with her, no other action performed afterward is effective, whether performed by that *yavam* toward a different *yevama* or by any *yavam* with the original *yevama*.

כֵּיצַד? עָשָׂה מַאֲמָר בִּיבִמְתּוֹ, וְנָתַן לָהּ גֵּט – צְרִיכָה הֵימֶנּוּ חֲלִיצָה. עָשָׂה מַאֲמָר וַחֲלִיצָה – צְרִיכָה הֵימֶנּוּ גֵּט. עָשָׂה מַאֲמָר וּבָעַל – הֲרֵי זוֹ כְּמִצְוָתָהּ.

The mishna elaborates: **How**[N] do these laws work in practice? If a *yavam* **performed levirate betrothal**[N] **with his *yevama*, and he** later **gave her a bill of divorce,**[H] she nevertheless **requires *ḥalitza* from him.** The bill of divorce does not fully exempt her from levirate marriage, as the levirate bond remains intact. If **he performed levirate betrothal and** then ***ḥalitza*, she requires a bill of divorce from him** in order to cancel the levirate betrothal. If the *yavam* **performed levirate betrothal and** then engaged in **intercourse** with the *yevama*, **this is** the way to perform levirate marriage **in accordance with its mitzva,** as the Sages instituted this as the proper procedure for a *yavam* to perform levirate marriage.

NOTES

Rabban Gamliel's opinion – **שִׁיטַת רַבָּן גַּמְלִיאֵל:** Some early commentaries maintain that Rabban Gamliel's statement with regard to levirate betrothal follows Rabbi Akiva's opinion that betrothal does not take effect on a woman who is forbidden due to a regular prohibition. Accordingly, after the *yavam* performs levirate betrothal with the first *yevama*, the second *yevama* would be forbidden due to the prohibition indicated by the verse: "So shall it be done to the man who does not build his brother's house" (Deuteronomy 25:9); he may build one house, in the singular, but he may not build two houses. Therefore, a second levirate betrothal would not be effective. The Ramban explains that if this is true in cases where the *yavam* consummated the levirate marriage with the first *yevama*, it is true in cases where he merely performed levirate betrothal. *Tosafot*, however, explain that Rabban Gamliel's statement accords with the opinion of the Rabbis, who disagree with Rabbi Akiva and state that betrothal does take effect on a woman forbidden due to a regular prohibition. If the *yavam* had consummated the levirate marriage with the first *yevama*, then betrothal would indeed be effective with the second *yevama*. However, in this case only levirate betrothal was performed, and the Sages did not institute a ruling allowing levirate betrothal to be effective in cases where it was already performed with one *yevama*.

A bill of divorce is effective after a bill of divorce, etc. – **יֵשׁ גֵּט אַחַר גֵּט וכו׳:** The latter act of giving a bill of divorce or performing levirate betrothal is of legal consequence. Admittedly, such actions do not acquire the *yevama* or nullify the levirate bond completely, but they do serve to connect the *yavam* to the *yevama* and render him forbidden to her relatives (see the *Melekhet Shlomo*).

But nothing is effective after intercourse, etc. – **אֲבָל לֹא אַחַר בְּעִילָה וכו׳:** As the Gemara will explain, this broad statement is imprecise, for most Sages agree that in certain situations his actions are effective even after intercourse or *ḥalitza*. It is possible that this principle is only according to the opinion of Rabbi Akiva, or that it is stated in a comprehensive manner because it will later be qualified and elucidated.

How – **כֵּיצַד:** Rashi and *Tosafot* state that this question does not refer particularly to the dispute at the beginning of the mishna. Rather, the mishna details all the various combinations of a bill of divorce, *ḥalitza*, levirate betrothal, and intercourse. This explains why several cases mentioned by the mishna teach us nothing new, or something we easily could have deduced from the other cases, as the *tanna* lists all possibilities.

How…performed levirate betrothal, etc. – **כֵּיצַד עָשָׂה מַאֲמָר וכו׳:** The mishna first mentions a *yavam* who performed levirate betrothal or gave a bill of divorce because the levirate betrothal and bill of divorce of a *yevama* are rabbinical decrees. Afterward it turns to actions prescribed by the Torah – intercourse and *ḥalitza* (*Nimmukei Yosef*).

BACKGROUND

Bill of divorce *[get]* – **גֵּט:** Although the term *get* is sometimes applied to all legal documents, it is commonly used to refer specifically to a bill of divorce. The basic text of a bill of divorce includes the declaration of the husband that he divorces his wife and that she is permitted to marry any other man. He is identified by his name and his father's name, and his wife is identified by her name and her father's name. The document must contain the date it was written and the signatures of two witnesses. In talmudic times a bill of divorce could be written privately by a scribe at the request of the husband. In later generations it became customary for a bill of divorce to be written in a rabbinical court that had expertise in this field, so that no halakhic difficulties would arise that might lead to the invalidation of the document.

Levirate betrothal – **מַאֲמָר:** In the context of the *halakhot* of levirate marriage, levirate betrothal refers to an ordinary act of betrothal that is performed prior to the actual levirate marriage. According to the mishna (*Kiddushin* 1:1), betrothal can be performed with money or its equivalent, e.g., a ring, a legal document, or sexual intercourse. According to Torah law levirate marriage can be consummated only by means of sexual intercourse. The Sages ruled that when the *yavam* gives the *yevama* money and states that he is betrothing her and fulfilling the mitzva of levirate marriage by means of this money, they are betrothed by rabbinic law.

Ḥalitza – **חֲלִיצָה:** When a man dies without children, the Torah obligates his brother to perform levirate marriage with the deceased man's wife. The woman is not permitted to marry out of the family until this obligation is performed. If the brother does not wish to marry the woman he may perform the *ḥalitza* ceremony and thereby release the widow from her bond and allow her to remarry (see Deuteronomy 25:7–10). The term *ḥalitza* is derived from the central element of this ceremony, which involves the widow removing a special sandal from the foot of one of her deceased husband's brothers. *Ḥalitza* must be performed before a rabbinical court.

HALAKHA

A bill of divorce after a bill of divorce, etc. – **גֵּט אַחַר גֵּט וכו׳:** Levirate betrothal does not serve to completely acquire the *yevama*, nor does a bill of divorce serve to nullify the levirate bond entirely. Therefore any action performed with the *yevama* after levirate betrothal or a bill of divorce is effective, whether it is a bill of divorce, levirate betrothal, intercourse, or *ḥalitza*. This *halakha* applies both to situations of one *yavam* and two *yevamot*, one *yevama* and two *yevamin*, as well as two *yevamot* and two *yevamin*, in accordance with the opinion of the Rabbis (Rambam *Sefer Nashim*, *Hilkhot Yibbum* 5:14; *Shulḥan Arukh*, *Even HaEzer* 170:3).

Nothing is effective after intercourse and *ḥalitza* – **לֹא אַחַר בְּעִילָה וַחֲלִיצָה:** A *yavam* who has intercourse with a *yevama* has acquired her fully, and similarly *ḥalitza* serves to completely nullify the levirate bond. Consequently, any act performed after intercourse or *ḥalitza* is of no halakhic consequence (Rambam *Sefer Nashim*, *Hilkhot Yibbum* 5:14; *Shulḥan Arukh*, *Even HaEzer* 170:12).

If he performed levirate betrothal and gave a bill of divorce – **עָשָׂה מַאֲמָר וְנָתַן גֵּט:** If a *yavam* performed levirate betrothal with his *yevama* and gave her a bill of divorce, she still requires *ḥalitza*. If he performed levirate betrothal and *ḥalitza*, she requires a bill of divorce to cancel his levirate betrothal (Rambam *Sefer Nashim*, *Hilkhot Yibbum* 5:4; *Shulḥan Arukh*, *Even HaEzer* 170:2).

נָתַן גֵּט וְעָשָׂה מַאֲמָר – צְרִיכָה גֵּט וַחֲלִיצָה. נָתַן גֵּט וּבָעַל – צְרִיכָה גֵּט וַחֲלִיצָה. נָתַן גֵּט וְחָלַץ – אֵין אַחַר חֲלִיצָה כְּלוּם.

If the *yavam* **gave** the *yevama* **a bill of divorce and** afterward **performed levirate betrothal**[H] with her, **she requires** another **bill of divorce** to cancel the levirate betrothal, as well as ***ḥalitza*** to nullify the levirate bond. If **he gave** her **a bill of divorce and** then **engaged in intercourse** with her, **she requires a bill of divorce** to cancel the betrothal that took place via intercourse, **and *ḥalitza*** to nullify the levirate bond; the intercourse did not affect the levirate bond because once he gave her a bill of divorce she was forbidden to him. If **he gave** her **a bill of divorce and performed *ḥalitza*, nothing is** effective **after *ḥalitza*,** as the levirate bond was completely nullified.

חָלַץ וְעָשָׂה מַאֲמָר, נָתַן גֵּט וּבָעַל, אוֹ בָּעַל וְעָשָׂה מַאֲמָר, נָתַן גֵּט וְחָלַץ – אֵין אַחַר חֲלִיצָה כְּלוּם.

Similarly, if he **performed *ḥalitza*** with her **and** then either **performed levirate betrothal,** or **gave a bill of divorce, or engaged in intercourse** with her; **alternatively,** if he **engaged in intercourse** with her **and** then either **performed levirate betrothal,** or **gave a bill of divorce, or performed *ḥalitza*** after they engaged in relations, **nothing is** effective **after *ḥalitza*** or intercourse. Any action performed afterward is unrelated to the levirate bond.

HALAKHA

If he gave a bill of divorce and performed levirate betrothal – נָתַן גֵּט וְעָשָׂה מַאֲמָר: If a *yavam* gave a bill of divorce to his *yevama*, and he or his brother subsequently performed levirate betrothal with her, she requires a bill of divorce to cancel the levirate betrothal, and *ḥalitza* to nullify the levirate bond. Similarly, if he gave her a bill of divorce and afterward engaged in intercourse with her, she needs a bill of divorce to cancel the betrothal accomplished by intercourse, and *ḥalitza* to nullify the levirate bond (Rambam *Sefer Nashim*, *Hilkhot Yibbum* 5:7; *Shulḥan Arukh*, *Even HaEzer* 170:9).

Perek **V**
Daf **50** Amud **b**

אַחַת יְבָמָה אַחַת לְיָבָם אֶחָד, וְאַחַת שְׁתֵּי יְבָמוֹת לְיָבָם אֶחָד. כֵּיצַד? עָשָׂה מַאֲמָר בָּזוֹ וּמַאֲמָר בָּזוֹ – צְרִיכוֹת שְׁנֵי גִּיטִּין וַחֲלִיצָה. מַאֲמָר בָּזוֹ וְגֵט לָזוֹ – צְרִיכָה גֵּט וַחֲלִיצָה. מַאֲמָר בָּזוֹ וּבָעַל אֶת זוֹ – צְרִיכוֹת שְׁנֵי גִּיטִּין וַחֲלִיצָה. מַאֲמָר בָּזוֹ וְחָלַץ לָזוֹ – הָרִאשׁוֹנָה צְרִיכָה גֵּט.

The above principles apply **both** in cases of **one *yevama* to one *yavam*,** as well as in cases of **two *yevamot* to one *yavam*. How so?** If **he performed levirate betrothal with this** *yevama* **and levirate betrothal with that** one,[NH] i.e., her rival wife, **they require two bills of divorce,** each for her own levirate betrothal, **and *ḥalitza*** with one of them, to release them both from the levirate bond. If he performed **levirate betrothal with this** one **and** gave **a bill of divorce to that** one,[H] the first woman **requires a bill of divorce** to cancel the levirate betrothal, **and** one of them must receive ***ḥalitza***.[N] If he performed **levirate betrothal with this** one **and engaged in intercourse with that** one,[H] **they require two bills of divorce and** he must perform ***ḥalitza*** with one of them. If the *yavam* performed **levirate betrothal with this one and performed *ḥalitza* with that** one,[H] **the first** woman **requires a bill of divorce.**

NOTES

Levirate betrothal with this one and levirate betrothal with that one – מַאֲמָר בָּזוֹ וּמַאֲמָר בָּזוֹ: *Tosafot* ask: Why can't the *yavam* give a bill of divorce for his levirate betrothal and thereby permit the second woman to perform levirate marriage, as this is an effective way of revoking the levirate betrothal according to the Gemara in the third chapter (32a). The Rivan answers that the ruling in the third chapter only applies after the fact; it is forbidden to do so *ab initio*. The *Tosefot HaRosh* holds that there the Gemara is referring only to a case where the brother who performed the levirate betrothal and gave the bill of divorce subsequently died, and therefore that ruling cannot be applied to the case in this mishna. The Ramban cites an explanation of this mishna that maintains that it is speaking only of a man who does not want to perform levirate marriage, but the Ramban rejects this answer. He himself explains that the *tanna* here is stating the basic *halakha*, without mentioning the option instituted by the Sages. Alternatively, this mishna follows the more stringent opinion found in the Gemara there, whereby a bill of divorce given by one of the brothers to the *yevama* disqualifies the levirate betrothal of the other women involved.

She requires a bill of divorce and *ḥalitza* – צְרִיכָה גֵּט וַחֲלִיצָה: *Tosafot* point out that this is correct only according to the opinion that invalid *ḥalitza* serves to exempt the rival wife. According to the opinion that invalid *ḥalitza* must be repeated for both rival wives, one must say that the mishna used the more common singular form, but it actually means that he must perform *ḥalitza* twice. This principle of the singular form of *ḥalitza* used in place of the plural applies here and in similar cases.

HALAKHA

Levirate betrothal with this one and levirate betrothal with that one – מַאֲמָר בָּזוֹ וּמַאֲמָר בָּזוֹ: If a *yavam* performed levirate betrothal with one *yevama* and then he, or one of his brothers, performed levirate betrothal with her rival wife, each of the women requires a bill of divorce for the levirate betrothal, and the *yavam* must also perform *ḥalitza* with one of them in order to exempt them both from levirate marriage (Rambam *Sefer Nashim*, *Hilkhot Yibbum* 5:14; *Shulḥan Arukh*, *Even HaEzer* 170:6).

Levirate betrothal with this one and a bill of divorce to that one – מַאֲמָר בָּזוֹ וְגֵט לָזוֹ: If a *yavam* performed levirate betrothal with one *yevama*, and subsequently he, or one of his brothers, gave a bill of divorce to her rival wife, he must give a bill of divorce for his levirate betrothal, and he or one of his brothers must perform *ḥalitza* with one of them. Some authorities (*Tur*, citing *Tosafot*) rule that both require *ḥalitza* (Rambam *Sefer Nashim*, *Hilkhot Yibbum* 5:6; *Shulḥan Arukh*, *Even HaEzer* 170:7).

Levirate betrothal with this one and engaged in intercourse with that one – מַאֲמָר בָּזוֹ וּבָעַל אֶת זוֹ: If a *yavam* performed levirate betrothal with one *yevama* and he, or one of his brothers, engaged in intercourse with her rival wife, they both require a bill of divorce, and the *yavam* must perform *ḥalitza* with one of them (Rambam *Sefer Nashim*, *Hilkhot Yibbum* 5:6; *Shulḥan Arukh*, *Even HaEzer* 170:8).

Levirate betrothal with this one and performed *ḥalitza* with that one – מַאֲמָר בָּזוֹ וְחָלַץ לָזוֹ: If a *yavam* performed levirate betrothal with one *yevama* and he, or one of his brothers, performed *ḥalitza* with the other one, the first woman requires a bill of divorce (Rambam *Sefer Nashim*, *Hilkhot Yibbum* 5:6; *Shulḥan Arukh*, *Even HaEzer* 170:7).

גֵּט לָזוֹ וְגֵט לָזוֹ – צְרִיכוֹת הֵימֶנּוּ חֲלִיצָה. גֵּט לָזוֹ וּבָעַל אֶת זוֹ – צְרִיכָה גֵּט וַחֲלִיצָה. גֵּט לָזוֹ וּמַאֲמָר בָּזוֹ – צְרִיכָה גֵּט וַחֲלִיצָה. גֵּט לָזוֹ וְחָלַץ לָזוֹ – אֵין אַחַר חֲלִיצָה כְּלוּם.

If the *yavam* gave **a bill of divorce to this** *yevama* **and a bill of divorce to that one,**[H] **they require** ***ḥalitza*** **from him. If** he gave **a bill of divorce to this one and engaged in intercourse with that** one,[H] the latter **requires a bill of divorce and** ***ḥalitza.*** If he gave **a bill of divorce to this one and** performed **levirate betrothal with that** one,[H] the latter **requires a bill of divorce and** he must perform ***ḥalitza*** with one of them. If the *yavam* gave **a bill of divorce to** this woman **and performed** ***ḥalitza*** **with that** one,[H] **nothing is** effective **after** ***ḥalitza,*** and he cannot betroth the rival wife.

חָלַץ וְחָלַץ, אוֹ חָלַץ וְעָשָׂה מַאֲמָר, נָתַן גֵּט וּבָעַל, אוֹ בָּעַל וּבָעַל, אוֹ בָּעַל וְעָשָׂה מַאֲמָר, נָתַן גֵּט וְחָלַץ – אֵין אַחַר חֲלִיצָה כְּלוּם, בֵּין יָבָם אֶחָד לִשְׁתֵּי יְבָמוֹת. בֵּין שְׁנֵי יְבָמִין לִיבָמָה אַחַת.

If **he performed** ***ḥalitza*** with one *yevama* **and** then **performed** ***ḥalitza*** with a second *yevama,* **or he performed** ***ḥalitza*** with one *yevama* **and** then proceeded to either **perform levirate betrothal,**[N] **give a bill of divorce, or engage in intercourse** with a second; **alternatively, he engaged in intercourse** with one *yevama* and **engaged in intercourse** with the second *yevama,* **or he engaged in intercourse** with one *yevama* **and** proceeded to either **perform levirate betrothal, give a bill of divorce, or perform** ***ḥalitza*** with the second, **nothing is** effective **after** ***ḥalitza*** or intercourse. These *halakhot* apply **both** in cases of **one** ***yavam*** **to two** ***yevamot,*** **as well as two** ***yevamin*** **to one** ***yevama.***

חָלַץ וְעָשָׂה מַאֲמָר, נָתַן גֵּט וּבָעַל, אוֹ בָּעַל וְעָשָׂה מַאֲמָר, וְנָתַן גֵּט וְחָלַץ – אֵין אַחַר חֲלִיצָה כְּלוּם, בֵּין בַּתְּחִלָּה בֵּין בָּאֶמְצַע בֵּין בַּסּוֹף.

If **he performed** ***ḥalitza*** with one *yevama* **and** then proceeded to either **perform levirate betrothal, give a bill of divorce, or engage in intercourse** with a second *yevama*; **alternatively, he engaged in intercourse** with one *yevama* **and** then proceeded to **perform levirate betrothal, or give a bill of divorce, or perform** ***ḥalitza*** with a second *yevama,* **nothing is** effective **after** ***ḥalitza,*** **whether** the *ḥalitza* took place **at the beginning, in the middle,**[N] **or at the end.** All of these *halakhot* accord with the opinion of Rabbi Akiva, who maintains betrothal does not take effect on a woman who is forbidden due to the prohibition against betrothing a *yevama* after *ḥalitza*.[H]

וְהַבְּעִילָה, בִּזְמַן שֶׁהִיא בַּתְּחִלָּה – אֵין אַחֲרֶיהָ כְּלוּם. בָּאֶמְצַע וּבַסּוֹף – יֵשׁ אַחֲרֶיהָ כְּלוּם. רַבִּי נְחֶמְיָה אוֹמֵר: אַחַת בְּעִילָה וְאַחַת חֲלִיצָה, בֵּין בַּתְּחִלָּה בֵּין בָּאֶמְצַע בֵּין בַּסּוֹף – אֵין אַחֲרֶיהָ כְּלוּם.

But with regard to **intercourse, when it is at the beginning,** i.e., the first act the *yavam* performed with his *yevama,* **nothing is** effective **after it** and any subsequent action is void. However, if it was performed **in the middle, and** similarly if it was performed **at the end,** i.e., after some other action that impairs the validity of his intercourse, **something is** effective **after it.**[H] **Rabbi Neḥemya says: Both** with regard to **intercourse and** ***ḥalitza,*** **whether** performed **at the beginning, in the middle, or at the end, nothing is** effective **after it.**[N] If the *yavam* performed a valid action according to Torah law, any subsequent action is of no consequence according to *halakha.*

NOTES

Performed *ḥalitza* and then proceeded to perform levirate betrothal – חָלַץ וְעָשָׂה מַאֲמָר: According to Rashi, the mishna here returns to discuss the case of a single *yavam* and *yevama*, and it repeats this case in order to introduce the dispute between Rabbi Neḥemya and the Rabbis. The Rashba and other commentaries claim that it is not necessary to define the case in this way, as this statement can apply to the cases of multiple *yevamin* and *yevamot* as well.

***Ḥalitza* in the middle – חֲלִיצָה בָּאֶמְצַע:** Rashi explains that this refers to a *yavam* who gave a bill of divorce to one *yevama* and performed *ḥalitza* with another *yevama*. If he afterward performs levirate betrothal to either of the women, it is not effective. *Tosefot HaRosh* takes issue with this example, as this *ḥalitza* should not be considered in the middle, for there is nothing that must take place afterward. Instead, this is referring to a case where a *yavam* performed levirate betrothal followed by *ḥalitza*. In that case he must afterward give a bill of divorce to cancel his levirate betrothal. Despite the fact that the *ḥalitza* is considered to be in the middle as further action is demanded on his part, no other actions are effective after the *ḥalitza*.

Nothing is effective after it – אֵין אַחֲרֶיהָ כְּלוּם: According to Rashi's comments on the mishna, in cases where the *yavam* engaged in intercourse at some stage, nothing is required after it, and she can be released with a bill of divorce without the need for *ḥalitza* (see Maharsha). Other commentaries disagree and maintain that even according to Rabbi Neḥemya, she needs *ḥalitza* to release her from the levirate bond after invalid intercourse. The statement: There is nothing after it, only means that subsequent actions do not create a bond that would forbid him to marry her relatives. Rashi, in his commentary on the Gemara, concurs with this alternate explanation (Ramban).

HALAKHA

A bill of divorce to this one and a bill of divorce to that one – גֵּט לָזוֹ וְגֵט לָזוֹ: If a *yavam* gave a bill of divorce to one *yevama* and he, or one of his brothers, gave a bill of divorce to her rival wife, he must perform *ḥalitza* with one of them, and each *yavam* is forbidden to the relatives of the women to whom he gave a bill of divorce (Rambam *Sefer Nashim, Hilkhot Yibbum* 5:15; *Shulḥan Arukh, Even HaEzer* 170:1, 5).

A bill of divorce to this one and engaged in intercourse with that one – גֵּט לָזוֹ וּבָעַל אֶת זוֹ: If a *yavam* gave a bill of divorce to one *yevama* and he, or one of his brothers, engaged in intercourse with her rival wife, the latter requires a bill of divorce, and he must perform *ḥalitza* with one of them (Rambam *Sefer Nashim, Hilkhot Yibbum* 5:7; *Shulḥan Arukh, Even HaEzer* 170:14).

A bill of divorce to this one and levirate betrothal with that one – גֵּט לָזוֹ וּמַאֲמָר בָּזוֹ: If a *yavam* gave a bill of divorce to one *yevama* and he, or one of his brothers, performed levirate betrothal with her rival wife, the latter requires a bill of divorce, and he must perform *ḥalitza* with one of them (Rambam *Sefer Nashim, Hilkhot Yibbum* 5:9; *Shulḥan Arukh, Even HaEzer* 170:11).

A bill of divorce to this one and performed *ḥalitza* with that one – גֵּט לָזוֹ וְחָלַץ לָזוֹ: If a *yavam* gave a bill of divorce to one *yevama* and he, or one of his brothers, performed *ḥalitza* with her rival wife, nothing is necessary after *ḥalitza* (Rambam *Sefer Nashim, Hilkhot Yibbum* 5:14; *Shulḥan Arukh, Even HaEzer* 170:14).

Actions after *ḥalitza* – מַעֲשֶׂה לְאַחַר חֲלִיצָה: If a *yavam* performed *ḥalitza* with his *yevama* and afterward he, or one of his brothers, performed *ḥalitza* with her rival wife or gave her a bill of divorce, this last action is of no consequence; the second *ḥalitza* or bill of divorce does not render her relatives forbidden to him. However, if he or one of his brothers performed levirate betrothal with her rival wife or engaged in intercourse with her, she requires a bill of divorce. The *halakha* does not follow the mishna, which is in accordance with the opinion of Rabbi Akiva (*Shulḥan Arukh, Even HaEzer* 170:13).

Actions after intercourse with a *yevama* – מַעֲשֶׂה לְאַחַר בִּיאָה בִּיבָמָה: If one of the brothers has relations with the *yevama*, any further nullifying action he or one of his brothers performs with her rival wife is of no effect; it does not render her relatives forbidden to him. However, if any disqualifying action preceded the intercourse, for example if he performed levirate betrothal with the rival wife or gave her a bill of divorce, the act of intercourse does not fully acquire the *yevama*, and she requires a bill of divorce. If at this stage a *yavam* performs levirate betrothal with another rival wife, it serves to forbid him to her relatives. The *halakha* is not in accordance with Rabbi Neḥemya (Rambam *Sefer Nashim, Hilkhot Yibbum* 5:9; *Shulḥan Arukh, Even HaEzer* 170:12, 14).

גמ׳ עד כאן לא פליגי אלא בגט אחר גט ומאמר אחר מאמר, אבל גט אחד ביבמה [ומאמר אחד ביבמה] – מהני,

GEMARA Rabban Gamliel and the Rabbis **disagree only with regard to** the efficacy of **a bill of divorce** performed **after a bill of divorce and levirate betrothal** performed **after levirate betrothal, but one bill of divorce** given **to a single** ***yevama*****, or one levirate betrothal** performed **with a single** ***yevama*****,**[H] **is effective.** The bill of divorce prevents him from performing levirate marriage, and the levirate betrothal requires a bill of divorce to cancel it, in addition to *ḥalitza*.

מאי טעמא אמור רבנן גט ביבמה מהני – משום דמהני בעלמא. דאי אמרת לא מהני, אמרי: גט להוציאה וחליצה להוציאה ומדגט לא מהני – חליצה נמי לא מהני, ואתי למיבעל אחר חליצה.

The Gemara elaborates: **What is the reason that the Sages said** that **a bill of divorce is effective for a** ***yevama*****,** despite the fact that she is not his wife? This is **because it is effective in general** in cases of married women. **For if you say** that **it is not effective** in the case of a *yevama*, there are some who might mistakenly **say** the following: **A bill of divorce** is given to a woman in order **to remove her** from her husband, **and** ***ḥalitza*** likewise serves **to remove her** from the *yavam*; **since a bill of divorce is ineffective** for this *yevama*, ***ḥalitza*** **is also ineffective**[N] and does not sever their relationship completely. **And** perhaps the *yavam* **will come to engage in intercourse after** ***ḥalitza*****,** which is forbidden by the Torah prohibition derived from the verse: "So shall it be done to the man who does not build his brother's house" (Deuteronomy 25:9).

ומאי טעמא אמור רבנן מאמר ביבמה מהני – משום דמהני בעלמא. דאי אמרת לא מהני, אמרי: מאמר לקנות וביאה לקנות, ומדמאמר לא מהני – ביאה נמי לא מהניא ואתי למיבעל אחר ביאה.

And what is the reason the Sages said that **levirate betrothal is effective for a** ***yevama*****? Because it is effective in general,**[N] as levirate betrothal is essentially an act of betrothal. **For if you say** that **it is not effective,** there are some who might mistakenly **say: Levirate betrothal serves to acquire** a woman **and intercourse** serves **to acquire** a woman in general, as women can be betrothed by intercourse; **since levirate betrothal is ineffective** in the case of a *yevama*, **intercourse is also ineffective,** i.e., it does not acquire a *yevama* completely. **And** he will therefore **come to engage in intercourse** with a rival wife **after intercourse** with the first *yevama*.

ומאי טעמא אמור רבנן ביאה פסולה יש אחריה כלום?

And what is the reason the Sages who disagree with Rabbi Neḥemya **said** that **invalid intercourse,** i.e., intercourse that follows any disqualifying action with the rival wife of a *yevama*, does not fully acquire the *yevama*, such that **something is** effective **after it?** In this case the invalid intercourse does not cancel the levirate bond, and therefore further action with the *yevama* is effective.

אמרי: אי ביאה אחר הגט היא – גזירה ביאה אחר הגט משום ביאה אחר חליצה, ואי ביאה אחר מאמר היא – גזירה ביאה אחר מאמר משום ביאה אחר ביאה.

The Sages **say: If this is intercourse** performed **after a bill of divorce,** then it is considered invalid due to a rabbinic **decree** with regard to **intercourse after a bill of divorce**[N] **because** of its potential confusion with a case of **intercourse after** ***ḥalitza*****.** The Sages established that invalid intercourse of this kind should not cancel the levirate bond completely, for if it did, then people might come to engage in intercourse after *ḥalitza*, which would violate a Torah prohibition. **And if this is intercourse** performed **after levirate betrothal,** then it is considered invalid due to **a** rabbinic **decree** with regard to **intercourse after levirate betrothal because** of its potential confusion with a case of **intercourse** with the second *yevama* **after intercourse** with the first. If intercourse after levirate betrothal is effective, people might come to engage in intercourse with a second *yevama* after intercourse with a first, and this is forbidden as the woman is considered his brother's wife who is not eligible for levirate marriage.

ומאי טעמא אמור רבנן האי חליצה פסולה אין אחריה כלום – אמרי: מאי לגזור? נגזור חליצה אחר הגט משום חליצה אחר חליצה – כל כי הני תחלוץ ותיזיל!

And what is the reason the Sages said with regard to **this invalid** ***ḥalitza*** that **nothing is** effective **after it?** For **they say: What** is the reason that **we should we issue a decree** in that case? **Should we issue a decree** with regard to ***ḥalitza*** performed **after a bill of divorce due to** a concern for ***ḥalitza*** performed **after** ***ḥalitza*****?** In this case there is no concern, as there is no prohibition involved in repeating *ḥalitza*. In **any situation like these, let her continue performing** ***ḥalitza*****,**[N] for no harm is done if *ḥalitza* is performed unnecessarily.

HALAKHA

One bill of divorce or one levirate betrothal – גט אחד ומאמר אחד: Everyone agrees that a bill of divorce given to one *yevama* or levirate betrothal performed with one *yevama* serves to forbid the *yavam* to her rival wife and to render the relatives of the *yevama* prohibited to the one who gave the bill of divorce (Rambam *Sefer Nashim, Hilkhot Yibbum* 5:7; *Shulḥan Arukh, Even HaEzer* 170:1).

NOTES

Ḥalitza **is also ineffective – חליצה נמי לא מהני:** *Tosafot* point out that the Sages did not decree that women in general should require *ḥalitza* when being divorced from their husbands out of a concern that people will confuse the cases, as everyone knows that *ḥalitza* is not relevant for most women. In the Jerusalem Talmud the *halakha* that only a bill of divorce is effective for a married woman, and not *ḥalitza*, is derived from specific verses.

Because it is effective in general – משום דמהני בעלמא: The Gemara does not suggest that people will mistakenly conclude that if levirate betrothal is not effective, regular betrothal is also not effective. Even according to the opinion that betrothal by money is not from the Torah, people betroth in this manner all the time and will not doubt its efficacy (Ritva).

A decree with regard to intercourse after a bill of divorce, etc. – גזירה ביאה אחר הגט וכו׳: Even though the Sages already prohibited intercourse after a bill of divorce and required the *yavam* to perform *ḥalitza*, they also saw fit to decree that invalid intercourse should not be completely effective, for otherwise the initial prohibition would not be upheld (Rashba; see Ritva).

In any situation like these let her continue performing ***ḥalitza*** **– כל כי הני תחלוץ ותיזיל:** Rashi explains this as a straightforward statement: It is of no concern to us if she performs *ḥalitza* several times. The Rashba and the Ritva explain this as a question: Would a woman really perform *ḥalitza* multiple times? With regard to intercourse it makes sense to institute a decree, lest he engage in intercourse after performing *ḥalitza* with her rival wife, but with regard to *ḥalitza* there is no reason to suppose one will want to perform *ḥalitza* again; the *Nimmukei Yosef* offers a slightly different version of the same approach. These different interpretations have halakhic ramifications with regard to the issue of whether it is permitted to perform *ḥalitza* with two *yevamot* (see *Beit Shmuel* and *Arukh LaNer*).

לִיגְזוֹר חֲלִיצָה אַחַר מַאֲמָר מִשּׁוּם חֲלִיצָה אַחַר בִּיאָה – אַטּוּ חֲלִיצָה אַחַר מַאֲמָר מִי לָא בָּעֲיָא גֵּט לְמַאֲמָרוֹ? חֲלִיצָה אַחַר בִּיאָה נַמִּי – בָּעֲיָא גֵּט לְבִיאָתוֹ.

Alternatively, **should we issue a decree** stating that other actions are effective after *ḥalitza* is performed **after levirate betrothal due to** the concern for confusion with the case of *ḥalitza* performed **after intercourse?** In this case there is a concern that people will assume that no bill of divorce is required after intercourse so long as the *yavam* performed *ḥalitza*. The Gemara challenges this concern: **Is that to say** that in the case of ***ḥalitza*** **after levirate betrothal she does not require a bill of divorce for his levirate betrothal,** such that one would conclude the same for *ḥalitza* after intercourse? In the case of *ḥalitza* after levirate betrothal, the woman requires a bill of divorce, and similarly in the case of ***ḥalitza*** **after intercourse she likewise requires a bill of divorce for his intercourse.** Thus, the same action performed following *ḥalitza* after levirate betrothal is also performed following *ḥalitza* after intercourse, and therefore there is no need to issue a further decree.

אֲמַר רָבָא:

§ **Rava said:**

Perek **V**
Daf **51** Amud **a**

מַאי טַעְמָא דְּרַבָּן גַּמְלִיאֵל – דִּמְסַפְּקָא לֵיהּ: גֵּט, אִי דָּחֵי אִי לָא דָּחֵי, מַאֲמָר, אִי קָנֵי אִי לָא קָנֵי. גֵּט אִי דָּחֵי אִי לָא דָּחֵי, אִי קַמָּא דָּחֵי – בַּתְרָא מַאי קָעָבֵיד? אִי קַמָּא לָא דָּחֵי – בַּתְרָא נַמִּי לָא דָּחֵי.

What is the reason for the ruling of **Rabban Gamliel** that a bill of divorce is not effective after a bill of divorce? It is **because he is uncertain** with regard to **a bill of divorce whether** it effectively **precludes** levirate marriage or **whether** it **does not preclude** levirate marriage. Similarly, he is uncertain with regard to **levirate betrothal, whether it** effectively **acquires** the *yevama* **or does not acquire** her at all. The Gemara clarifies: With regard to **a bill of divorce,** he is uncertain as to **whether it precludes** levirate marriage **or does not preclude** it. **If the first** bill of divorce **precludes** levirate marriage, **what did he do** by giving **the latter** bill of divorce, as it has no substance? Alternatively, **if the first** bill of divorce **does not preclude** levirate marriage, **neither does the latter preclude** levirate marriage.

מַאֲמָר אִי קָנֵי אִי לָא קָנֵי, אִי קַמָּא קָנֵי – בַּתְרָא מַאי קָעָבֵיד? וְאִי קַמָּא לָא קָנֵי – בַּתְרָא נַמִּי לָא קָנֵי.

Likewise, with regard to **levirate betrothal,** he is uncertain as to **whether it acquires** the *yevama* **or does not acquire** her. **If the first** levirate betrothal effectively **acquires** the *yevama*, **what does the last one accomplish? And if the first one does not acquire** her, **the last one also does not acquire** her. For this reason Rabban Gamliel maintains that a bill of divorce is not effective after a bill of divorce was given, and similarly levirate betrothal is not effective after levirate betrothal was performed.[N]

NOTES

The opinions of Rabban Gamliel and the Rabbis – **שִׁיטוֹת רַבָּן גַּמְלִיאֵל וַחֲכָמִים**: The Jerusalem Talmud provides an analysis of Rabban Gamliel's opinion that is similar to the one found here. There it compares Rabban Gamliel's opinion to that of Rabbi Shimon, who maintains that levirate betrothal either acquires the *yevama* completely or it does not acquire her at all. The Jerusalem Talmud goes on to demonstrate, as Abaye argues here, that Rabban Gamliel must be of the opinion that levirate betrothal and a bill of divorce acquire her to a certain extent. The Rashba and others note that the Gemara here does not inquire into the reason behind the opinion of the Rabbis. Despite the fact that the Gemara briefly states subsequently that the effects of levirate betrothal and a bill of divorce were instituted by the Sages, this sentence does not appear in all versions of the text and is mentioned only incidentally rather than as a full explanation. These commentaries explain that this is because the reasoning of the Rabbis is clear; it is Rabban Gamliel's opinion that requires elucidation. The Rabbis' opinion is that since levirate betrothal is a rabbinic institution, its effect is not complete, and thus both levirate betrothal and a bill of divorce can be effective even after levirate betrothal.

אֵיתִיבֵיהּ אַבַּיֵי: וּמוֹדֶה רַבָּן גַּמְלִיאֵל שֶׁיֵּשׁ גֵּט אַחַר מַאֲמָר, וּמַאֲמָר אַחַר הַגֵּט, וְגֵט אַחַר בִּיאָה וּמַאֲמָר, וּמַאֲמָר אַחַר בִּיאָה וְגֵט.

Abaye raised an objection to his opinion from a *baraita*: **And Rabban Gamliel concedes that a bill of divorce is** effective **after levirate betrothal and levirate betrothal is** effective **after a bill of divorce.** If a *yavam* gave a bill of divorce to one *yevama* and then performed levirate betrothal with the other, or the reverse, both actions would be effective. **And** he also concedes that **a bill of divorce is** effective **after intercourse and levirate betrothal** such that if the *yavam* engaged in levirate betrothal with one *yevama,* engaged in intercourse with a second, and gave a bill of divorce to a third, the bill of divorce is effective and he is prohibited from marrying the relatives of the third *yevama.* **And** he concedes **that levirate betrothal is** effective **after intercourse and a bill of divorce,** such that if he gave a bill of divorce to one woman, engaged in intercourse with a second, and performed levirate betrothal with a third, the levirate betrothal is effective and the third woman requires a bill of divorce.

וְאִי מְסַפְּקָא לֵיהּ לְרַבָּן גַּמְלִיאֵל – תֶּהֱוֵי כְּבִיאָה דִּלְכַתְּחִלָּה, וְתִקְנֵי! דְּהָא תְּנַן: הַבְּעִילָה, בִּזְמַן שֶׁהִיא בַּתְּחִלָּה – אֵין אַחֲרֶיהָ כְּלוּם.

And if Rabban Gamliel is uncertain[N] with regard to the efficacy of levirate betrothal or a bill of divorce, then the third action should never be effective. Either the initial levirate betrothal or bill of divorce was completely effective, in which case any subsequent action is not effective, or these actions are not effective at all and the intercourse that followed them **should be like intercourse** performed **at the beginning, and** it should serve to **acquire** the *yevama* completely, and any actions performed afterward with the rival wife should be of no account. **For we learned** in the mishna: With regard to **intercourse, when it is at the beginning, nothing is** effective **after it.** Consequently, Rabban Gamliel's ruling is difficult.

אֶלָּא אֲמַר אַבַּיֵי: לְעוֹלָם פְּשִׁיטָא לֵיהּ לְרַבָּן גַּמְלִיאֵל בְּגֵט דְּדָחֵי, וּמַאֲמָר דְּקָנֵי. מִיהוּ, אֲמוּר רַבָּנַן: הָא יְבָמָה, בְּחַד צַד מְהַנֵּי בָּהּ גֵּט, וּבְחַד צַד מְהַנֵּי בָּהּ מַאֲמָר. גֵּט אַחַר גֵּט – לָא דָּחֵי, דְּהָא דָּחָה לֵיהּ קַמָּא, וּמַאֲמָר אַחַר מַאֲמָר – לָא קָנֵי, דְּהָא קָנֵי לֵיהּ קַמָּא. גֵּט אַחַר מַאֲמָר, וּמַאֲמָר אַחַר הַגֵּט – הַאי מִילְּתָא קָא דָּחֵי, וְהַאי מִילְּתָא קָא קָנֵי.

Rather, Abaye said: Actually, it is obvious to Rabban Gamliel that a bill of divorce precludes levirate marriage, **and that levirate betrothal acquires** the *yevama.* **Nevertheless, the Sages said** that with regard to **this *yevama,* in one respect a bill of divorce is effective for her, and in another respect levirate betrothal is effective for her,** but they are not effective in the same manner. Therefore, **a bill of divorce** given **after a bill of divorce does not preclude** levirate marriage, **as the first** bill of divorce **has** already **precluded** it **for him** as much as he can preclude it by means of a bill of divorce. **And levirate betrothal** performed **after levirate betrothal does not acquire** her, **as the first** levirate betrothal **has acquired** her **for him** as much as possible. However, with regard to **a bill of divorce after levirate betrothal, and levirate betrothal after a bill of divorce, this action precludes** levirate marriage **and that action acquires** the *yevama.* Since the acquisition of levirate betrothal and the nullification of a bill of divorce work in different ways, there can be both an acquisition and a nullification, and therefore one can be effective after the other.

וְרַבָּנַן: כׇּל חַד וְחַד תַּקִּינוּ לֵיהּ רַבָּנַן גֵּט וּמַאֲמָר בִּיבָמָה.

However, the Rabbis maintain that **the Sages instituted for each and every one** of the brothers-in-law both the nullification of **a bill of divorce and** the acquisition of **levirate betrothal for a *yevama,*** and they decreed that these should be effective for each of the *yevamot.* Therefore the strength of the first bill of divorce or levirate betrothal is equal to that of the second one, and both are effective.

NOTES

And if Rabban Gamliel is uncertain, etc. – וְאִי מְסַפְּקָא לֵיהּ לְרַבָּן גַּמְלִיאֵל וכו׳: Rashi explains this proof in the following manner: If Rabban Gamliel maintains that levirate betrothal either acquires the *yevama* fully or not at all, either way he should not concede in the case of a bill of divorce after intercourse and levirate betrothal. If levirate betrothal acquires her completely the subsequent intercourse and bill of divorce are of no consequence, and if levirate betrothal does not acquire her at all then the intercourse should acquire her fully, and any further action should be ineffective. The early commentaries note that according to Rashi's explanation, Abaye's statement is truncated, as he only mentions one side of the issue (Rashba; Ritva). They therefore prefer the following interpretation of Rabbeinu Ḥananel: If Rabban Gamliel is uncertain as to whether levirate betrothal acquires the *yevama,* how can something that only uncertainly acquires her nullify an act, i.e., intercourse, that definitely acquires her according to Torah law? Therefore, when the intercourse takes place after the levirate betrothal it should acquire her completely and the subsequent bill of divorce should not be effective. However, it has been pointed out that this argument is explained in the Jerusalem Talmud in precisely the manner suggested by Rashi.

וְהַאי בִּיאָה פְּסוּלָה עֲדִיפָא מִמַּאֲמָר, וּגְרִיעָא מִמַּאֲמָר. עֲדִיפָא מִמַּאֲמָר, דְּאִילּוּ מַאֲמָר אַחַר מַאֲמָר לָא מְהַנֵּי, וְאִילּוּ בִּיאָה אַחַר מַאֲמָר – מְהַנֵּי. וּגְרִיעָא מִמַּאֲמָר, דְּאִילּוּ מַאֲמָר אַחַר הַגֵּט קָנֵי לְכוּלֵּיהּ שִׁיּוּרָא דְּגֵט, וְאִילּוּ בִּיאָה אַחַר הַגֵּט – לָא קָנְיָא לֵיהּ לְכוּלֵּיהּ שִׁיּוּרָא דְּגֵט.

Abaye proceeds to explain the rest of Rabban Gamliel's teaching in the *baraita*: **And this invalid intercourse,** i.e., intercourse that was performed after a disqualifying action, such as levirate betrothal or a bill of divorce, **is superior to levirate betrothal**[N] **and** also **inferior to levirate betrothal: It is preferable to levirate betrothal** in the following respect: **whereas levirate betrothal after levirate betrothal is not effective** at all, **intercourse after levirate betrothal is effective,** because intercourse acquires a *yevama* according to Torah law. **And it is inferior to levirate betrothal, for whereas levirate betrothal after a bill of divorce** according to Rabban Gamliel **acquires the entire remainder** of the woman left **by the bill of divorce,**[N] such that any further levirate betrothal would be ineffective, **intercourse after a bill of divorce does not acquire the entire remainder** of the woman left **by the bill of divorce,** as it is not considered valid intercourse, and a subsequent levirate betrothal is effective.

תָּנוּ רַבָּנַן: כֵּיצַד אָמַר רַבָּן גַּמְלִיאֵל אֵין גֵּט אַחַר גֵּט? שְׁתֵּי יְבָמוֹת שֶׁנָּפְלוּ לִפְנֵי יָבָם אֶחָד, וְנָתַן גֵּט לָזוֹ וְגֵט לָזוֹ – רַבָּן גַּמְלִיאֵל אוֹמֵר: חוֹלֵץ לָרִאשׁוֹנָה וְאָסוּר בִּקְרוֹבוֹתֶיהָ, וּמוּתָּר בִּקְרוֹבוֹת שְׁנִיָּה.

§ **The Sages taught: How,** i.e., in what case, **did Rabban Gamliel say** that **a bill of divorce is not** effective **after a bill of divorce?** In **the case of two *yevamot* who happened before one *yavam* and he gave a bill of divorce to this one and a bill of divorce to that one. Rabban Gamliel says: He performs *ḥalitza* with the first one and is forbidden to** marry **her relatives,** as she is his *ḥalutza*, **and he is permitted to** marry **the relatives of the second one.** Because the bill of divorce he gave the second woman is of no consequence at all, she is merely the rival wife of his *ḥalutza*, and he is therefore permitted to marry her relatives.

וַחֲכָמִים אוֹמְרִים: נָתַן גֵּט לָזוֹ וְגֵט לָזוֹ – אָסוּר בִּקְרוֹבוֹת שְׁתֵּיהֶן, וַחֲלִיצָה לְאַחַת מֵהֶן. וְכֵן אַתָּה אוֹמֵר בִּשְׁנֵי יְבָמִים וִיבָמָה אַחַת,

But the Rabbis say: If he gave a bill of divorce to this one and a bill of divorce to that one,[H] **he is forbidden** to marry **the relatives of both of them, and** he must perform ***ḥalitza*** **with one of them. And you would say the same with regard to two *yevamim* and one *yevama*.** If the two *yevamin* gave one *yevama* a bill of divorce, one after the other, Rabban Gamliel maintains that the bill of divorce of the second *yavam* is of no account, and he is therefore permitted to marry her relatives, whereas the Rabbis hold that it is effective in that it renders him forbidden to her relatives.

כֵּיצַד אָמַר רַבָּן גַּמְלִיאֵל אֵין מַאֲמָר אַחַר מַאֲמָר? שְׁתֵּי יְבָמוֹת שֶׁנָּפְלוּ לִפְנֵי יָבָם אֶחָד וְעָשָׂה מַאֲמָר בָּזוֹ וּמַאֲמָר בָּזוֹ, רַבָּן גַּמְלִיאֵל אוֹמֵר: נוֹתֵן גֵּט לָרִאשׁוֹנָה, וְחוֹלֵץ לָהּ, וְאָסוּר בִּקְרוֹבוֹתֶיהָ, וּמוּתָּר בִּקְרוֹבוֹת שְׁנִיָּה. וַחֲכָמִים אוֹמְרִים: נוֹתֵן גֵּט לִשְׁתֵּיהֶן, וְאָסוּר בִּקְרוֹבוֹת שְׁתֵּיהֶן, וַחֲלִיצָה לְאַחַת מֵהֶן. וְכֵן אַתָּה אוֹמֵר בִּשְׁנֵי יְבָמִים וִיבָמָה אַחַת.

How, with regard to what circumstance, **did Rabban Gamliel say** that **there is no levirate betrothal after levirate betrothal?** In a case of **two *yevamot* who happened before one *yavam*, and he performed levirate betrothal with this one and levirate betrothal with that one,**[H] **Rabban Gamliel says: He gives a bill of divorce to the first one and performs *ḥalitza* with her, and is forbidden to her relatives, but** he **is permitted to the relatives of** the **second one,** as the levirate betrothal performed with the rival wife is ineffective. **But the Rabbis say: He gives a bill of divorce to both of them,** as the levirate betrothal is effective for both women, **and he is forbidden to the relatives of both of them;** and as for ***ḥalitza***, he must perform it **with one of them. And you would say the same with regard to two *yevamim* and one *yevama*.** If the first *yavam* performed levirate betrothal with the *yevama*, and the second *yavam* consequently performed levirate betrothal with her, they are both required to give her a bill of divorce and both are forbidden to marry her relatives.

אָמַר מָר: נוֹתֵן גֵּט לָזוֹ וְגֵט לָזוֹ, רַבָּן גַּמְלִיאֵל אוֹמֵר: חוֹלֵץ לָרִאשׁוֹנָה וְאָסוּר בִּקְרוֹבוֹתֶיהָ, וּמוּתָּר בִּקְרוֹבוֹת שְׁנִיָּה. לֵימָא תֶּיהֱוֵי תְּיוּבְתָּא דִּשְׁמוּאֵל, דְּאָמַר שְׁמוּאֵל: חָלַץ לְבַעֲלַת הַגֵּט – לֹא נִפְטְרָה צָרָה!

The Master said above in the *baraita*: **He gives a bill of divorce to this one and a bill of divorce to that one. Rabban Gamliel says: He performs *ḥalitza* with the first one and is forbidden to** marry **her relatives, and he is permitted to** marry **the relatives of the second one.** The Gemara asks: **Shall we say that** this **is a conclusive refutation of** the statement of **Shmuel?**[N] **For Shmuel said: If he performed *ḥalitza* with the woman who received a bill of divorce, the rival wife is not exempted** by this invalid *ḥalitza*. The *yavam* must therefore repeat the *ḥalitza* with the rival wife as well. This appears to contradict the *baraita*, where Rabban Gamliel rules that he has to perform *ḥalitza* with only one of the *yevamot*.

NOTES

This invalid intercourse is superior to levirate betrothal – הַאי בִּיאָה פְּסוּלָה עֲדִיפָא מִמַּאֲמָר: It would appear that one could similarly argue that a bill of divorce is also preferable to levirate betrothal, as it too is effective after levirate betrothal. However, the only reason a bill of divorce takes effect after levirate betrothal is that a bill of divorce works on a different plane than levirate betrothal, i.e., its effectiveness is not related to that of the levirate betrothal. In contrast, the power of acquisition of intercourse is certainly of the same type as levirate betrothal (*Tosafot Yeshanim*).

Acquires the entire remainder left by the bill of divorce – קָנֵי לְכוּלֵּיהּ שִׁיּוּרָא דְּגֵט: No further levirate betrothal is possible after levirate betrothal and a bill of divorce, as even Rabban Gamliel agrees that in the case of levirate betrothal after levirate betrothal and a bill of divorce, the second levirate betrothal is not effective (Ritva).

Shall we say that this is a conclusive refutation of Shmuel – לֵימָא תֶּיהֱוֵי תְּיוּבְתָּא דִּשְׁמוּאֵל: Most early commentaries follow Rashi's explanation that the difficulty only stems from Rabban Gamliel's opinion, as Rabban Gamliel maintains that even though the *yavam* can perform a superior *ḥalitza* with the rival wife, he can nevertheless exempt the rival wife by means of this invalid *ḥalitza*. The opinion of the Rabbis, however, presents no difficulty, for they maintain that the *ḥalitza* of the two rival wives is equally invalid. *Tosafot Yeshanim*, however, claim that the Gemara could have raised the difficulty according to the opinion of the Rabbis, but it preferred to cite Rabban Gamliel, who states this *halakha* explicitly.

HALAKHA

A bill of divorce to this one and a bill of divorce to that one – גֵּט לָזוֹ וְגֵט לָזוֹ: If two rival wives required levirate marriage, and the *yavam* gave a bill of divorce to each of them, he is forbidden to the relatives of both. Similarly, if two *yevamin* gave a bill of divorce to one *yevama*, they are both forbidden to her relatives, and likewise two *yevamin* who gave bills of divorce to two different rival wives, each is prohibited to the relatives of the woman to whom he gave the bill of divorce, in accordance with the opinion of the Rabbis (Rambam *Sefer Nashim, Hilkhot Yibbum* 5:15; *Shulḥan Arukh, Even HaEzer* 170:4).

Levirate betrothal with this one and levirate betrothal with that one – מַאֲמָר בָּזוֹ וּמַאֲמָר בָּזוֹ: If two rival wives happened before one *yavam*, and he performed levirate betrothal with both of them, he is forbidden to marry the relatives of both. Likewise, if two *yevamin* performed levirate betrothal with one *yevama*, they are both forbidden to marry her relatives, and if the two *yevamin* performed levirate betrothal with two different rival wives, each is forbidden to the relatives of the woman with whom he performed the levirate betrothal, as stated by the Rabbis (Rambam *Sefer Nashim, Hilkhot Yibbum* 5:15; *Shulḥan Arukh, Even HaEzer* 170:6).

אָמַר לָךְ שְׁמוּאֵל: כִּי אָמְרִי אֲנָא – אַלִּיבָּא דְּמַאן דְּאָמַר יֵשׁ זִיקָה, וְרַבָּן גַּמְלִיאֵל סָבַר אֵין זִיקָה.

The Gemara answers: **Shmuel** could have **said to you: When I said** my above teaching, it was **in accordance with** the opinion **of the one who said that the levirate bond is substantial,** and he must therefore perform a valid *ḥalitza* in order to cancel this bond. A *ḥalitza* performed with a woman who received a bill of divorce is not powerful enough to completely cancel the bond of the rival wife who did not performed *ḥalitza*. **But Rabban Gamliel holds** that **the levirate bond is not substantial,**[N] and therefore any *ḥalitza* that releases one of the women also serves to release the other.

וּמִדְּרַבָּן גַּמְלִיאֵל סָבַר אֵין זִיקָה

The Gemara asks: **But** if so, **from** the fact that **Rabban Gamliel holds** that **the levirate bond is not substantial,**

NOTES

The levirate bond is substantial…the levirate bond is not substantial – יֵשׁ זִיקָה...אֵין זִיקָה: Although the Torah (Deuteronomy 25:5) forbids a widow requiring levirate marriage from remarrying until *ḥalitza* has been performed, the nature of the connection between her and her *yavam* is not clear. Is this connection seen as a form of betrothal, i.e., the levirate bond is substantial, or is it seen as a unilateral obligation upon the widow to wait for her brother-in-law's action, i.e., the levirate bond is not substantial.

רַבָּנַן סָבְרִי יֵשׁ זִיקָה. וְקָתָנֵי סֵיפָא: וְכֵן אַתָּה אוֹמֵר בִּשְׁנֵי יְבָמִין וִיבָמָה אַחַת. לֵימָא תֶּיהֱוֵי תְּיוּבְתָּא דְּרַבָּה בַּר רַב הוּנָא אָמַר רַב. דְּאָמַר רַבָּה בַּר רַב הוּנָא אָמַר רַב: חֲלִיצָה פְּסוּלָה – צְרִיכָה לַחֲזוֹר עַל כׇּל הָאַחִין!

it can be inferred that **the Rabbis hold that the levirate bond is substantial,**[N] as it is assumed that they disagree with Rabban Gamliel in this regard as well. **And the latter clause** of that *baraita* **teaches: And you** would **say the same**[N] **with regard to two *yevamin* and one *yevama*** such that if the two *yevamin* gave one *yevama* a bill of divorce, she is exempted by the *ḥalitza* of one of them. If so, **let us say that it is a conclusive refutation of** the statement that **Rabba bar Rav Huna** said that **Rav said. For Rabba bar Rav Huna said** that **Rav said:** In cases of **invalid *ḥalitza*,** the *yevama* **is required to repeat** the *ḥalitza* **with all the brothers.** If the *ḥalitza* was invalid for some reason, all the brothers must perform *ḥalitza* with the *yevama*, as her bond with them is not canceled by an invalid *ḥalitza*.

אָמַר לָךְ רַבָּה בַּר רַב הוּנָא: בֵּין לְרַבָּן גַּמְלִיאֵל בֵּין לְרַבָּנַן סָבְרִי אֵין זִיקָה, וְהָכָא בְּגֵט אַחַר גֵּט וּמַאֲמָר אַחַר מַאֲמָר קָמִיפַּלְגִי.

The Gemara responds: **Rabba bar Rav Huna** could have **said to you: Both Rabban Gamliel and the Rabbis hold** that **the levirate bond is not substantial,** whereas my statement is in accordance with the opinion that the levirate bond is substantial. **And here** the dispute does not concern the topic of the levirate bond at all, but rather it only involves the explicitly mentioned issue: They **disagree with regard to** the efficacy of **a bill of divorce after a bill of divorce and levirate betrothal after levirate betrothal.**

אָמַר מָר: עָשָׂה מַאֲמָר בָּזוֹ וּמַאֲמָר בָּזוֹ, רַבָּן גַּמְלִיאֵל אוֹמֵר: נוֹתֵן גֵּט לָרִאשׁוֹנָה וְחוֹלֵץ לָהּ, וְאָסוּר בִּקְרוֹבוֹתֶיהָ, וּמוּתָּר בִּקְרוֹבוֹת שְׁנִיָּה. מִכְּדֵי קָסָבַר רַבָּן גַּמְלִיאֵל אֵין מַאֲמָר אַחַר מַאֲמָר – רִאשׁוֹנָה נַמִי תִּתְיַיבֵּם! גְּזֵירָה דִּלְמָא אָתֵי לְיַיבּוּמֵי לִשְׁנִיָּה.

The Master said above in the *baraita*: If **he performed levirate betrothal with this one and levirate betrothal with that one, Rabban Gamliel says: He gives a bill of divorce to the first one and performs *ḥalitza* with her and is forbidden to her relatives, but he is permitted to the relatives of the second one.** The Gemara poses a question: **Since Rabban Gamliel holds** that **levirate betrothal is not** effective **after levirate betrothal,** and the second levirate betrothal is of no consequence, the **first** woman **should also be permitted to enter into levirate marriage.** Why must he perform *ḥalitza* with her? The Gemara answers: It is prohibited due to a rabbinic **decree lest he perform levirate marriage with the second** woman. The Sages were concerned that in cases where the *yavam* performed levirate betrothal with both women, if he were permitted to consummate the levirate marriage with the first woman, he might do so with the second woman as well.

אָמַר רַבִּי יוֹחָנָן: רַבָּן גַּמְלִיאֵל, וּבֵית שַׁמַּאי, וְרַבִּי שִׁמְעוֹן, וּבֶן עַזַּאי וְרַבִּי נְחֶמְיָה – כּוּלְּהוּ סְבִירָא לְהוּ: מַאֲמָר קוֹנֶה קִנְיָן גָּמוּר. רַבָּן גַּמְלִיאֵל – הָא דַּאֲמָרַן.

§ **Rabbi Yoḥanan said: Rabban Gamliel, and Beit Shammai, and Rabbi Shimon, and ben Azzai, and Rabbi Neḥemya, they all hold** that **levirate betrothal acquires** the *yevama* **as a full-fledged acquisition,**[N] like a regular betrothal. The source for **Rabban Gamliel's** opinion is **that which we said** above, that levirate betrothal is not effective after levirate betrothal. Rabbi Yoḥanan maintains that the second levirate betrothal is not effective because she was already fully acquired by the first one.

NOTES

The Rabbis hold that the levirate bond is substantial – רַבָּנַן סָבְרִי יֵשׁ זִיקָה: Rashi explains that this inference cannot be proven from the mishna, but rather it is logical to assume that just as Rabban Gamliel and the Rabbis disagree with regard to the strength of levirate betrothal, they similarly disagree about the nature of the levirate bond itself. The Ramban and the Rashba, on the other hand, maintain that there is an inherent connection between the nature of the levirate bond and the strength of levirate betrothal. Rabban Gamliel maintains that the levirate bond is not substantial, and therefore levirate betrothal or a bill of divorce performed by one *yavam* is sufficient to nullify the levirate bond between this yevama and the other *yevamin* and between him and the other *yevamot* entirely. The Rabbis, however, maintain that the levirate bond is substantial, and therefore no one act of levirate betrothal or bill of divorce can completely cancel this bond. Therefore, all of the actions performed by all the *yevamin* and *yevamot* are effective.

And the latter clause teaches: And you would say the same, etc. – וְקָתָנֵי סֵיפָא וְכֵן אַתָּה אוֹמֵר וכו׳: The early commentaries ask: Why does the Gemara cite the latter clause in the *baraita* when it could have equally questioned the statement of Rabba bar Rav Huna by citing a proof from the first part of the *baraita*? With regard to one *yavam* and two *yevamot* the Rabbis rule that a single *ḥalitza* is enough. One could deduce that if a woman requires *ḥalitza* from all the brothers when her *ḥalitza* was invalid, then similarly in a case of one *yavam* and two *yevamot*, he should have to perform *ḥalitza* with all the *yevamot*. They answer that the Gemara could indeed have asked in this manner, but it preferred to raise a difficulty from a source that explicitly states that she does not require *ḥalitza* from all the brothers (*Tosefot HaRosh*; *Tosafot Yeshanim*). However, some authorities learn from the fact that the Gemara specifically cites the latter clause that in the case of invalid *ḥalitza*, it is not necessary to perform *ḥalitza* with all the *yevamot* (*Tosefot Ḥad MiKamma'ei*; Meiri).

Levirate betrothal acquires her as a full-fledged acquisition – מַאֲמָר קוֹנֶה קִנְיָן גָּמוּר: *Tosafot* point out that these *tanna'im* are not in complete agreement, as they disagree over the particulars of the acquisition. The common denominator is that they consider levirate betrothal to be very powerful. Rashi also notes that this does not mean that all these Sages maintain that levirate betrothal is a full-fledged acquisition, but rather it is at least a significant acquisition. The *Keren Ora* suggests that the shared feature of all these opinions might be that they all view levirate betrothal as having a certain validity from the Torah, not merely as a rabbinical institution.

בֵּית שַׁמַּאי – דִּתְנַן: שְׁלֹשָׁה אַחִין, שְׁנַיִם מֵהֶם נְשׂוּאִין לִשְׁתֵּי אֲחָיוֹת וְאֶחָד מוּפְנֶה, מֵת אֶחָד מִבַּעֲלֵי אֲחָיוֹת וְעָשָׂה בָּהּ מוּפְנֶה מַאֲמָר, וְאַחַר כָּךְ מֵת אָחִיו הַשֵּׁנִי, בֵּית שַׁמַּאי אוֹמְרִים: אִשְׁתּוֹ עִמּוֹ, וְהַלָּזוּ תֵּצֵא מִשּׁוּם אֲחוֹת אִשָּׁה.

The source for the opinion of **Beit Shammai** is **as we learned** in a mishna: In the case of **three brothers, two** of whom **were married to two sisters, and one who was single,** the following occurred: **The husband of one of the sisters died** childless, leaving behind his wife, **and the single** brother **performed levirate betrothal** with this wife. **Afterward, the second brother died,** whereby the second brother's wife, the sister of the betrothed, happened before him for levirate marriage as well. In this case, **Beit Shammai say: His wife remains with him,** i.e., the woman he betrothed is considered like his wife, and he is not required to divorce her. **And this other leaves** the *yavam* and is exempt from levirate marriage **due to** the fact that she is **the sister of a wife.** This indicates that Beit Shammai hold that the levirate betrothal performed with the first woman makes her fully betrothed, thereby nullifying the levirate bond with her sister.

רַבִּי שִׁמְעוֹן – דְּתַנְיָא, אָמַר לָהוּ רַבִּי שִׁמְעוֹן לַחֲכָמִים: אִם בִּיאַת רִאשׁוֹן בִּיאָה – בִּיאַת שֵׁנִי אֵינָהּ בִּיאָה, אִם בִּיאַת רִאשׁוֹן אֵינָהּ בִּיאָה – בִּיאַת שֵׁנִי נַמִי אֵינָהּ בִּיאָה. וְהָא בִּיאַת בֶּן תֵּשַׁע, דִּכְמַאֲמָר שַׁוְיוּהָ רַבָּנַן, וְקָאָמַר רַבִּי שִׁמְעוֹן אֵינָהּ בִּיאָה.

The source for the opinion of **Rabbi Shimon** is based on the following case cited in a mishna (96b): In the case of a boy aged nine years and one day old who had relations with his *yevama*, and afterward his brother, who is also nine years and one day old, had relations with her, the second brother disqualifies her from performing levirate marriage with the first one. Rabbi Shimon says he does not disqualify her. **As it is taught** in a *baraita* that **Rabbi Shimon said to the Rabbis: If the intercourse**[N] **of the first** brother is considered effective **intercourse, the intercourse of** the **second** brother **is not** considered effective **intercourse** such that it would disqualify her from performing levirate marriage with the first brother, as the first brother has already acquired her through his intercourse. **If the intercourse of** the **first** brother **is not** considered effective **intercourse, the intercourse of** the **second** brother **is also not** effective **intercourse. And the Sages considered the intercourse of a nine-year-old** boy[B] to be **like levirate betrothal,**[N] **and Rabbi Shimon says** that the intercourse of the second boy **is not** considered **intercourse.** This proves that in his opinion the intercourse of a nine-year-old fully acquires the *yevama*, and similarly, so does levirate betrothal.

בֶּן עַזַּאי – דְּתַנְיָא, בֶּן עַזַּאי אוֹמֵר: יֵשׁ מַאֲמָר אַחַר מַאֲמָר בִּשְׁנֵי יְבָמִין וִיבָמָה אַחַת, וְאֵין מַאֲמָר אַחַר מַאֲמָר בִּשְׁתֵּי יְבָמוֹת וְיָבָם אֶחָד. רַבִּי נְחֶמְיָה – דִּתְנַן, רַבִּי נְחֶמְיָה אוֹמֵר: אַחַת בְּעִילָה וְאַחַת חֲלִיצָה, בֵּין בַּתְּחִלָּה בֵּין בָּאֶמְצַע בֵּין בַּסּוֹף – אֵין אַחֲרֶיהָ כְּלוּם. וְהָא בִּיאָה פְּסוּלָה, דִּכְמַאֲמָר שַׁוְיוּהָ רַבָּנַן, וְקָתָנֵי: אֵין אַחֲרֶיהָ כְּלוּם.

This source for **ben Azzai's** opinion is **as it is taught** in a *baraita* that **ben Azzai says: Levirate betrothal is** effective **after levirate betrothal** in the case of **two** ***yevamin*** **and one** ***yevama*****, but levirate betrothal is not** effective **after levirate betrothal** in the case of **two** ***yevamot*** **and one** ***yavam*****.** Because the latter case involves only one *yavam*, his levirate betrothal fully acquires the *yevama*, and therefore the levirate betrothal he performs with the second woman is of no account, as he is already betrothed to the first *yevama*. The source for **Rabbi Neḥemya's** opinion is **as we learned** in a mishna that **Rabbi Neḥemya says:** With regard to **both intercourse and** ***ḥalitza*****, whether at the beginning, in the middle, or at the end, nothing is** effective **after it. And the Sages considered invalid intercourse** to be **like levirate betrothal,**[N] **and** Rabbi Neḥemya **teaches** that **nothing is** effective **after it.** This indicates that he maintains that no form of acquisition is effective after levirate betrothal, as levirate betrothal completely acquires the *yevama*.

"כֵּיצַד עָשָׂה מַאֲמָר" כו׳.

§ The mishna states: **How so?** If he **performed levirate betrothal** with his *yevama* and gave her a bill of divorce, **etc.**

NOTES

Rabbi Shimon, as it is taught…if the intercourse, etc. – **רַבִּי שִׁמְעוֹן דְּתַנְיָא...אִם בִּיאַת וכו׳**: The Ramban asks: Why is it necessary for the Gemara to derive a proof from invalid intercourse, by comparing it to levirate betrothal, when Rabbi Shimon explicitly makes the same claim with regard to levirate betrothal itself (see 19a). He answers, and the Rashba explains similarly, that it is possible that when Rabbi Shimon stated his argument there, he was speaking in accordance with the opinion of the Rabbis only in order to argue against their opinion, whereas he himself does not maintain that opinion (see *Arukh LaNer* and *Yosef Lekaḥ* for a different resolution).

The intercourse of a nine-year-old boy is like levirate betrothal – **בִּיאַת בֶּן תֵּשַׁע כְּמַאֲמָר**: Some commentaries are puzzled by this *halakha*: Since any type of intercourse acquires a *yevama*, whether it is performed intentionally or unwittingly, why should the intercourse of a nine-year-old not acquire her as well, being that the Sages considered this intercourse to be full-fledged intercourse with regard to forbidden relations? They answer that it is an established *halakha* that the wife of a minor is not fully acquired by him. Although his cohabitation has the status of intercourse, it is not considered an act of acquisition (*Tosefot HaRosh*; see Ramban, who attributes this response to Rabbi Avraham *Av Beit Din* and questions it).

The Sages considered invalid intercourse to be like levirate betrothal – **בִּיאָה פְּסוּלָה דִּכְמַאֲמָר שַׁוְיוּהָ רַבָּנַן**: The early commentaries raise a serious difficulty: Surely Rabbi Neḥemya distinguishes between invalid intercourse, after which no action is effective, and levirate betrothal, where subsequent action is effective. But if so, how can he prove that invalid intercourse is like levirate betrothal? Rabbeinu Ḥananel cites a proof from a *Tosefta* that states the following: When did they say that nothing is effective after intercourse? When it is at the beginning; but if it is not at the beginning it is like levirate betrothal. He adds that the principle is that an unattributed *Tosefta* follows the opinion of Rabbi Neḥemya, but the Ramban retorts that it is clear from the context that this particular *Tosefta* is not in accordance with Rabbi Neḥemya.

Rabbi Avraham *Av Beit Din* writes that invalid intercourse is like levirate betrothal in that neither of them enables the wife of a priest to eat *teruma*. However, the Ramban and the Rashba question this answer as well. They are similarly dissatisfied with the resolutions offered by *Tosafot*, as they do not fit the wording of the Gemara. The Ramban himself answers that Rabbi Neḥemya maintains that invalid intercourse is like levirate betrothal in that this type of intercourse does not exempt a *yevama* with whom an action had previously been performed. However, Rabbi Neḥemya disagrees with the Rabbis with regard to a different issue, as he maintains that no action is effective after invalid intercourse. His reasoning is that the decrees of the Sages are unnecessary in the case of intercourse, as intercourse is an effective method of acquisition from the Torah, and people will therefore not be confused with regard to its efficacy. The Rashba and the Ritva accept the basic premise of this opinion.

BACKGROUND

The intercourse of a nine-year-old boy – **בִּיאַת בֶּן תֵּשַׁע**: According to the Sages, sexual intercourse cannot be performed by a boy who is less than nine years old, and therefore it has no halakhic significance. From that age and onward such an act of intercourse is recognized as significant, even prior to the advent of physical maturity.

הַאי גֵּט אַחַר גֵּט הוּא! אָמַר רַב יְהוּדָה, הָכִי קָאָמַר: גֵּט אַחַר הַגֵּט וּמַאֲמָר אַחַר מַאֲמָר כְּדַאֲמָרַן, יָבָם אֶחָד וִיבָמָה אַחַת כֵּיצַד הַתָּרָתָן? עָשָׂה מַאֲמָר בִּיבִמְתּוֹ וְנָתַן לָהּ גֵּט – צְרִיכָה הֵימֶנּוּ חֲלִיצָה.

The Gemara is puzzled: Is **this case** upon which the mishna elaborates the case of **a bill of divorce after a bill of divorce** that is mentioned first in the mishna? The mishna first is referring to a bill of divorce after a bill of divorce, but when it comes to the specifics, it mentions a bill of divorce after levirate betrothal. **Rav Yehuda said: This is what** the *tanna* **is saying:** With regard to **a bill of divorce after a bill of divorce, and levirate betrothal after levirate betrothal,** it is **as we said** and these cases were explained in the *baraita*, but with regard to **one *yavam* and one *yevama*, how is their** complex bond **released?** He then proceeds to delineate: **If he performed levirate betrothal with his *yevama* and gave her a bill of divorce, she requires *ḥalitza* from him.**

״עָשָׂה מַאֲמָר וּבָעַל הֲרֵי זוֹ כְּמִצְוָתָהּ״. לֵימָא מְסַיַּיע לֵיהּ לְרַב הוּנָא, דְּאָמַר רַב הוּנָא: מִצְוַת יְבָמָה – מְקַדֵּשׁ וְאַחַר כָּךְ בּוֹעֵל. אֵימָא: אַף זֶה כְּמִצְוָתָהּ.

§ The mishna teaches: If the *yavam* **performed levirate betrothal and engaged in intercourse, this is** done **in accordance with its mitzva.**[H] The Gemara suggests: **Let us say that** this mishna **supports** the statement of **Rav Huna. As Rav Huna said: The mitzva of a *yevama*** is properly performed when the *yavam* **betroths** the *yevama* **and** only **afterward engages in intercourse.** This statement indicates that the levirate betrothal is a necessary component of the mitzva, and the mishna seems to imply the same. The Gemara refutes this claim: This is not necessarily the case, as you can read the mishna as stating that **this also is in accordance with its mitzva.** If he performed levirate betrothal and then engaged in intercourse, this too is a proper manner to proceed, but we do not have to interpret the mishna as indicating that this is the only way to fulfill the mitzva.

פְּשִׁיטָא! סָלְקָא דַּעְתָּךְ אָמִינָא: כֵּיוָן דְּאָמַר מָר: הָעוֹשֶׂה מַאֲמָר בִּיבִמְתּוֹ – פָּרְחָה הֵימֶנּוּ זִיקַת יְבָמִין, וְחָלָה עָלָיו זִיקַת אֵרוּסִין וְנִשּׂוּאִין, אֵימָא לָאו מִצְוָה קָעָבֵיד – קָא מַשְׁמַע לָן.

The Gemara asks: **Isn't** this **obvious?** If one can fulfill the mitzva without performing levirate betrothal, why would one think that levirate betrothal is detrimental? The Gemara answers: It was indeed necessary for the mishna to teach us this, for it might **enter your mind to say** that **since the Master said** above (29b): **One who performs levirate betrothal with his *yevama* causes the levirate bond to dissipate from himself, and a** standard **bond of betrothal and marriage takes effect on him,** you might **say** that he **no** longer **performs a mitzva** when he carries out levirate marriage, as the levirate bond is no longer in place. The *tanna* therefore **teaches us** that we consider the levirate betrothal and the subsequent intercourse as part of the same process, which constitutes a mitzva.

גּוּפָא אָמַר רַב הוּנָא: מִצְוַת יְבָמִין מְקַדֵּשׁ וְאַחַר כָּךְ בּוֹעֵל, וְאִם בָּעַל וְעָשָׂה מַאֲמָר – קָנָה. אִם בָּעַל וְעָשָׂה מַאֲמָר – פְּשִׁיטָא, דְּהָא קָנְיָהּ בְּבִיאָה! אֶלָּא אֵימָא: אִם בָּעַל בְּלֹא מַאֲמָר – קָנָה.

The Gemara continues: With regard to **the** matter **itself, Rav Huna said: The mitzva of levirate marriage** is properly performed when the *yavam* **betroths** the *yevama* **and afterward engages in intercourse, and if he engaged in intercourse and** later **performed levirate betrothal, he has acquired** the *yevama*. The Gemara is puzzled: **If he engaged in intercourse and** then **performed levirate betrothal it is obvious** that he has acquired her, **as he has** already **acquired her by intercourse.** The levirate betrothal does not affect the issue one way or another. **Rather, say** as follows: **If he engaged in intercourse without** prior **levirate betrothal,** even in that case **he has acquired** her.

HALAKHA

The levirate betrothal of a *yevama* – מַאֲמָר יְבָמָה: With regard to regular women, the process of marriage involved two stages. The first was betrothal, in which a man would give a woman money or a document or engage in consensual relations with her. This last method was abolished by the *amora* Rav. Through this act of betrothal the man acquired the woman and she was forbidden to all other men. At a later stage, usually a year later, the man would bring the woman into his home as his full-fledged wife. This was done through conjugal relations and was symbolized by the marriage canopy. With regard to a *yevama*, however, the Torah states that a *yavam* can acquire his *yevama* by intercourse alone. Nevertheless, the Sages instituted that he should betroth her with money or a document and that she requires a marriage canopy like all other women (Rema, citing the Rivash). Only afterward should they engage in intercourse (Rambam *Sefer Nashim*, *Hilkhot Yibbum* 2:1–2; *Shulḥan Arukh*, *Even HaEzer* 166:2).

וְהָתַנְיָא: לוֹקֶה! מַכַּת מַרְדּוּת מִדְּרַבָּנַן.

The Gemara challenges this: **But isn't it taught** in a *baraita* that a *yavam* who has intercourse without levirate betrothal **is flogged?**[NH] The Gemara answers: The lashes are not because he transgressed by not performing levirate betrothal, but rather they are **lashes for rebelliousness** given for transgressing a **rabbinic** law, namely for acting in an immodest manner.

דְּרַב מְנַגֵּיד מַאן דִּמְקַדֵּשׁ בְּבִיאָה, וּמַאן דִּמְקַדֵּשׁ בְּשׁוּקָא, וּמַאן דִּמְקַדֵּשׁ בְּלֹא שִׁדּוּכֵי,

The Gemara cites other instances where the Sages administered lashes for immodest behavior. **As Rav** would **flog one who betroths** a woman **by intercourse,**[H] despite the fact that betrothal is effective by this method, because he acted in a promiscuous manner. **And** he would likewise **flog one who betroths** a woman **in the marketplace,**[N] rather than at home, as this too is loose behavior, **and** he would also administer lashes **to one who betroths** a woman **without** a prior **marriage agreement** [*shiddukhei*],[N] as this too is an act of permissiveness.

וּמַאן דִּמְבַטֵּל גִּיטָּא, וּמַאן דְּמָסַר מוֹדָעָא אַגִּיטָּא,

And he would further lash **one who nullifies a bill of divorce**[H] he had earlier sent by declaring in the presence of witnesses that the bill of divorce is nullified. This action is effective, but by doing so he transgresses the rabbinic ordinance of the Sages that bans such an action as it might lead his wife to unlawfully wed another. **And** he would also flog **one who delivers a declaration** preemptively invalidating **a bill of divorce,** by informing three people before giving a bill of divorce that he is not doing so of his own free will and he wants to cancel it ahead of time. Here too he will mislead his wife, who will assume it is a valid bill of divorce.

וּמַאן דְּפָקֵיר שְׁלִיחָא דְּרַבָּנַן, וּמַאן דְּשָׁהֵי שַׁמְתָּא דְּרַבָּנַן עֲלֵיהּ תְּלָתִין יוֹמִין וְלָא אָתֵי לְבֵי דִינָא וְתָבַע לְשַׁמְתֵיהּ,

And he would lash **one who behaves irreverently** toward **a messenger of the Sages,**[H] even if the messenger is not a scholar, as he thereby shows disrespect to the Sages themselves. **And** he would administer lashes to **one who remained under an excommunication**[H] **of the Sages** for **thirty days and did not go to the court and petition for** the removal of **his excommunication after** correcting the sin that led to the excommunication in the first place. This behavior demonstrates that he does not care about the excommunication, and is therefore deserving of lashes.

NOTES

But isn't it taught that he is flogged – וְהָתַנְיָא לוֹקֶה: According to Rashi, the assumption of the Gemara at this stage is that he is lashed for transgressing a Torah law. The Rashba and other commentaries support this idea by citing the following homiletic interpretation of the verse that is cited in the Jerusalem Talmud. The Gemara there expounds the verse: "And he shall take her to him to be his wife and consummate the levirate marriage" (Deuteronomy 25:5), in the following manner: "And he shall take her to him to be his wife" by means of betrothal, and afterward he shall "consummate the levirate marriage" through intercourse. It is further explained in the Jerusalem Talmud that this line of reasoning follows the opinion that the action of one who transgresses a Torah law is not effective (see *Arukh LaNer*).

However, the Ritva points out that even according to this opinion the *yavam* should not be liable to lashes, as he has only transgressed a positive mitzva. Furthermore, it is Beit Shammai, not Beit Hillel, who maintain that levirate betrothal acquires the *yevama* by Torah law, and therefore, as the halakha does not accord with Beit Shammai's opinion, it is an established *halakha* that levirate betrothal is only effective by rabbinic decree. *Tosafot* suggest that the Gemara never considered that levirate betrothal is effective by Torah law, but merely that he should be lashed for transgressing a rabbinic ordinance. By not performing levirate betrothal, it is considered as though he had relations with his brother's wife without performing a mitzva. The Ramban explains that the question of the Gemara is not how he can acquire the *yevama* in this way if he receives lashes for his actions, but rather the Gemara is suggesting that he perhaps should be obligated to perform levirate betrothal before he has intercourse with the *yevama* again.

One who betroths a woman in the marketplace, etc. – מַאן דִּמְקַדֵּשׁ בְּשׁוּקָא וכו׳: The objection to this behavior is because the man acted in a disrespectful manner by betrothing in a marketplace or without prior preparation or appeasement of the woman and her family. Betrothing in the market gives the impression of an impromptu decision and is therefore considered licentious, as it is not dissimilar to soliciting a prostitute.

Marriage agreement [*shiddukhei*] – שִׁדּוּכֵי: The Aramaic root *sh-d-kh*, which is apparently the source of the Hebrew word, bears a variety of meanings. It seems that its chief meaning is to silence, from which several other meanings developed, such as to appease or to persuade. This is the likely etymology of the word as an appeasement and agreement between a woman and a man, or two families, as a preparation for marriage.

HALAKHA

If he engaged in intercourse without levirate betrothal he has acquired her and is flogged – בָּעַל בְּלֹא מַאֲמָר קָנָה וְלוֹקֶה: One who has relations with his *yevama* without performing levirate betrothal acquires her, but he receives lashes for rebelliousness from the Sages for acting in an immodest manner (Rambam *Sefer Nashim, Hilkhot Yibbum* 2:2; *Shulḥan Arukh, Even HaEzer* 166:2).

One who betroths a woman by intercourse – מַאן דִּמְקַדֵּשׁ בְּבִיאָה: One who betroths a woman by intercourse, or betroths her in the marketplace, or without a prior marriage agreement, receives lashes for rebelliousness but she is nevertheless betrothed. The Rema (based on *Tur* citing Rosh) writes that the custom is not to lash one who betrothed in the marketplace or without a marriage agreement (Rambam *Sefer Nashim, Hilkhot Ishut* 3:21–22 and *Sefer Kedusha, Hilkhot Issurei Bia* 21:14; *Shulḥan Arukh, Even HaEzer* 26:4).

One who nullifies a bill of divorce, etc. – מַאן דִּמְבַטֵּל גִּיטָּא וכו׳: One who sends a bill of divorce to his wife and subsequently retracts and nullifies it in the presence of witnesses, and similarly one who delivers a declaration preemptively invalidating a bill of divorce, receives lashes for rebelliousness, as stated by Rav (Rambam *Sefer Nashim, Hilkhot Geirushin* 6:26; *Shulḥan Arukh, Even HaEzer* 141:67).

One who behaves irreverently toward a messenger of the Sages – מַאן דְּפָקֵיר שְׁלִיחָא דְּרַבָּנַן: With regard to one who harasses or derides a messenger of the court who is carrying out his duty, if the messenger reports that he was belittled, the messenger is believed like two witnesses, and we place the offender under an excommunication. If there were witnesses to the event, the offender receives lashes for rebelliousness (Rambam *Sefer Shofetim, Hilkhot Sanhedrin* 25:5; *Shulḥan Arukh, Ḥoshen Mishpat* 8:5).

One who remained under an excommunication of the Sages – מַאן דְּשָׁהֵי שַׁמְתָּא דְּרַבָּנַן עֲלֵיהּ: If one was obligated to take an oath by the Sages but he refused to swear, the court places him under an excommunication for thirty days. If he does not come to the court to have the excommunication annulled, the court administers lashes for rebelliousness (Rambam *Sefer Mishpatim, Hilkhot To'en VeNitan* 1:5; *Shulḥan Arukh, Ḥoshen Mishpat* 87:9).

וְעַל חַתְנָא דְּדָאֵיר בְּבֵי חֲמוֹהִי. דְּדָאֵיר – אִין, דְּחָלֵיף – לָא. וְהָא הַהוּא דַּחֲלֵיף אַבָּבָא דְּבֵי חֲמוֹהִי, וְנַגְּדֵיהּ רַב שֵׁשֶׁת! הַהוּא – מֵידָם הֲוָה דָּיְים מֵחֲמָתֵיהּ.

And he would also lash **a son-in-law who lives in his father-in-law's house,**[NH] as this is likely to lead to temptation between the younger couple and older couple who share the same house. The Gemara asks: With regard to **one who lives** in his father-in-law's house, **yes,** he would lash him, but with regard to **one who** only **passed** through his father-in-law's house at regular intervals, **no,** he would not lash him? **But** an incident occurred involving **a certain** man **who passed by the entrance to his father-in-law's house and Rav Sheshet lashed him.** The Gemara explains: There was a special set of circumstances in that case, as **that** man **was suspected**[H] **with regard to his mother-in-law,** and therefore he was lashed merely for passing near her house, as he thereby gave credence to the rumors.

נְהַרְדְּעֵי אָמְרִי: בְּכוּלְּהוּ לָא מַנְגֵּיד רַב אֶלָּא לִמְקַדֵּשׁ בְּבִיאָה וּבְלֹא שִׁדּוּכֵי. וְאִיכָּא דְּאָמְרִי: אֲפִילּוּ בְּשִׁדּוּכֵי נַמִי, מִשּׁוּם פְּרִיצוּתָא.

The Sages **of Nehardea**[P] would **say: In all** these cases **Rav would not flog, apart from** the case of one who **betrothed by intercourse and without** a prior **marriage agreement. And there are** those **who say** he would flog a man who betrothed by intercourse **even** if he did so **with** a prior **marriage agreement, due to the immorality** involved, as he must invite witnesses to observe the act.

תָּנוּ רַבָּנַן: כֵּיצַד מַאֲמָר – נָתַן לָהּ כֶּסֶף אוֹ שָׁוֶה כֶּסֶף, וּבִשְׁטָר כֵּיצַד? בִּשְׁטָר כֵּיצַד?! כִּדְאָמְרַן: כָּתַב לָהּ עַל הַנְּיָיר אוֹ עַל הַחֶרֶס, אַף עַל פִּי שֶׁאֵין בּוֹ שָׁוֶה פְּרוּטָה: ״הֲרֵי אַתְּ מְקוּדֶּשֶׁת לִי״! אֲמַר אַבָּיֵי, הָכִי קָאָמַר: שְׁטַר כְּתוּבַּת יְבָמִין כֵּיצַד –

§ **The Sages taught: How** is **levirate betrothal** performed? **He gives her money or the equivalent** value of **money** and declares: You are hereby betrothed to me. The Gemara asks: **And with a document,**[N] **how** does he betroth her? The Gemara is puzzled by this question: **With a document, how** does he betroth her? It is **as we have said** by the *halakhot* of a regular document of betrothal: **If he wrote to her on paper or on earthenware, even though it is not worth a** ***peruta,*** the words: **You are hereby betrothed to me,**[H] it is effective. As a document is not effective as a means of betrothal due to its monetary value but rather due to the words it contains, there is no requirement that it be of a minimum value. However, because the *halakhot* of betrothal by a document were already taught, the Gemara is puzzled as to the nature of this question. **Abaye said** that **this is what** the *baraita* **is saying:** With regard to **the document of a marriage contract for levirate marriage, how** is it written? Abaye understands that the question did not refer to the document of betrothal but rather to the marriage contract of a levirate marriage.

כָּתַב לָהּ: אֲנָא פְּלוֹנִי בַּר פְּלוֹנִי קַבֵּילִית יַת פְּלוֹנִית יְבִמְתִּי עֲלַי לָזוּן וּלְפַרְנְסָהּ כָּרָאוּי, וּבִלְבַד שֶׁתְּהֵא כְּתוּבָּתָהּ עַל נִכְסֵי בַּעֲלָהּ הָרִאשׁוֹן. וְאִי לֵית לָהּ מֵרִאשׁוֹן – תִּקִּינוּ לָהּ רַבָּנַן מִשֵּׁנִי, כְּדֵי שֶׁלֹּא תְּהֵא קַלָּה בְּעֵינָיו לְהוֹצִיאָהּ.

The Gemara explains that **he writes to her: I, so-and-so, son of so-and-so, have accepted so-and-so, my *yevama* upon me, to feed and maintain her in a fitting manner, provided that her marriage contract will** still **be** payable **from the property of her first husband** and not from the property of the *yavam*.[H] The Gemara adds: **But if the first** husband **does not have** property, **the Sages instituted for her** that she should receive her marriage contract **from the second** husband, i.e., the *yavam*, for the same reason that they instituted the marriage contract in the first place: **So that she will not be demeaned in his eyes such that** he will easily **divorce her.** If he will suffer no financial penalty, he is likely to divorce over the smallest argument.

בְּעָא מִינֵּיהּ אַבָּיֵי מֵרַבָּה: נָתַן לָהּ גֵּט, וְאָמַר: הֲרֵי אַתְּ מְגוֹרֶשֶׁת הֵימֶנִּי, וְאִי אַתְּ מוּתֶּרֶת לְכָל אָדָם, מַהוּ? גֵּט יְבָמָה דְּרַבָּנַן הוּא, גֵּט דְּמַהֲנֵי בְּאֵשֶׁת אִישׁ מַהֲנֵי בִּיבָמָה. גֵּט דְּלָא מַהֲנֵי בְּאֵשֶׁת אִישׁ – לָא מַהֲנֵי בִּיבָמָה. אוֹ דִּלְמָא אָתֵי לְאַחְלוּפֵי בְּגִיטָּא?

§ **Abaye inquired of Rabba:** If a *yavam* **gave** his *yevama* **a bill of divorce, and said** the following formula: **You are hereby divorced from me but you are not permitted to** any other **man, what is** the status of such a bill of divorce? **Is the bill of divorce of a** ***yevama***[H] a bill of divorce **based on rabbinic** law and therefore subject to the *halakhot* of a regular bill of divorce; and consequently, **a bill of divorce that is effective for a married woman is also effective for a** ***yevama,*** and **a bill of divorce that is not effective for a married woman is not effective for a** ***yevama?*** Since this type of a divorce is invalid in the case of a married woman, it is similarly ineffective in the case of a *yevama*. **Or perhaps** the Sages were concerned that **perhaps** people **will come to confuse** this bill of divorce **with** an unqualified **bill of divorce** given by a *yavam* and they therefore decreed that it should affect the levirate bond, preventing the *yavam* from marrying the *yevama*.

NOTES

A son-in-law who lives in his father-in-law's house – חַתְנָא דְּדָאֵיר בְּבֵי חֲמוֹהִי: The *ge'onim* state that there is a concern that the mother-in-law might develop an attraction to her first son-in-law. In addition to the concern with regard to forbidden relations, there is also a concern with regard to the monetary aspects of the arrangement (Rabbi Avraham min HaHar). In this context the Rif cites a saying from *Sefer Ben Sira* quoted in tractate *Bava Batra* (89b): I have found no substance lighter than bran; yet, lighter than bran is a son-in-law who lives in the house of his father-in-law.

A document of betrothal – שְׁטָר קִידּוּשִׁין: The early commentaries explain that an act of using a document to perform levirate betrothal is also called a *ma'amar*, a saying. Admittedly, one who gives a woman a document of betrothal does not have to say anything, but since most betrothals were performed with money, when the man is required to speak, it was called *ma'amar*.

HALAKHA

A son-in-law who lives in his father-in-law's house – חַתְנָא דְּדָאֵיר בְּבֵי חֲמוֹהִי: The Sages forbade a son-in-law to live in his father-in-law's house. The Ra'avad writes that if a special area is set aside for him and his wife, it is permitted. It appears that we rely on this opinion in order to be lenient in this area (*Maggid Mishne*; see *Tosafot*). In addition, the early commentaries state in tractate *Kiddushin* that nowadays we are less concerned with regard to this issue (Rambam *Sefer Kedusha, Hilkhot Issurei Bia* 21:15).

He was suspected, etc. – מֵידָם הֲוָה דָּיְים וכו׳: If one is suspected of involvement with a forbidden relation, or if there are rumors circulating with regard to them, he may not live in the same alleyway as her, nor may he be seen in the same neighborhood, in accordance with Rav Sheshet. The Ra'avad claims that this *halakha* only applies to one's mother-in-law, as she is particularly close to him due to her daughter (Rambam *Sefer Kedusha, Hilkhot Issurei Bia* 2:12).

A document of betrothal – שְׁטָר קִידּוּשִׁין: If one writes a document on paper or any other material, even on something worth less than a *peruta*, that states: You are hereby betrothed to me, and gives it to a woman in the presence of witnesses, she is betrothed. The document must, however, be written in the name of that particular woman (Rambam *Sefer Nashim, Hilkhot Ishut* 3:3; *Shulḥan Arukh, Even HaEzer* 32:1).

The marriage contract of levirate marriage – כְּתוּבַּת יְבָמִין: A *yavam* is also required to write a marriage contract for his *yevama*, but the wording of his contract differs from that of a regular marriage contract. The main difference is that the fiscal responsibility for the marriage contract is upon the property of the deceased brother (Rambam *Sefer Nashim, Hilkhot Yibbum* 4:32).

The bill of divorce of a *yevama* – גֵּט יְבָמָה: If the *yavam* gives a bill of divorce to the *yevama* he disqualifies her and her rival wives from levirate marriage, both to himself and his brothers. Any bill of divorce that disqualifies a woman for marrying into the priesthood also disqualifies her from levirate marriage (Rambam *Sefer Nashim, Hilkhot Yibbum* 5:1; *Shulḥan Arukh, Even HaEzer* 170:1).

PERSONALITIES

The Sages of Nehardea – נְהַרְדְּעֵי: The Gemara states elsewhere that anonymous statements attributed to the Sages of Nehardea refer to Rav Ḥama from Nehardea, who served as the head of the yeshiva of Nehardea for several years following the passing of Rav Naḥman bar Yitzhak. Apparently, Rav Ḥama was related to the house of the Exilarch, and for a time was its official scholar. It is also possible that he was the same Rav Ḥama who met with the king of Persia and discussed Torah matters with him.

[אָמַר לֵיהּ: חָיְישִׁינַן דִּלְמָא אָתֵי לְאַחְלוּפֵי בְּגִיטָּא]. מַתְקִיף לָהּ רַבָּה בַּר חָנָן: אֶלָּא מֵעַתָּה, יָהֵיב לָהּ נְיָירָא בְּעָלְמָא הָכִי נַמִי דְּפָסְלָהּ? אָמַר לֵיהּ: הָתָם לָא פְּסֵיל בִּכְהוּנָּה, הָכָא – קָפָסֵיל בִּכְהוּנָּה.

Rabba **said to him: We are concerned** that **perhaps** they will come to **confuse** this bill of divorce **with a** regular **bill of divorce,** and it therefore disqualifies a *yevama*. **Rabba bar Ḥanan strongly objects to this: However, if that is so,** that we are stringent with the bill of divorce of a *yevama* out of concern that people might confuse the two types of bills of divorce, if **he gives her a mere** piece of **paper,** which does not mention divorce, **so too will it disqualify her? He said to him: There** it is different, as a mere piece of paper has no effect on any other woman, for **it does not disqualify** her **for** marrying into **the priesthood.** If a husband gives his wife a piece of paper that contains nothing about divorce, even if he says: This is a bill of divorce, his action is of no consequence, not even to forbid her to a priest. **Here,** however, a bill of divorce of this kind at least **disqualifies** a woman from marrying **into the priesthood.**[H]

דְּתַנְיָא: "וְאִשָּׁה גְּרוּשָׁה מֵאִישָׁהּ לֹא יִקָּחוּ" אֲפִילּוּ לֹא נִתְגָּרְשָׁה אֶלָּא מֵאִישָׁהּ – לֹא יִקָּחוּ, וְהַיְינוּ רֵיחַ הַגֵּט שֶׁפּוֹסֵל בִּכְהוּנָּה.

As it is taught in a *baraita*: "They shall not take a woman that is a harlot, or profaned; **and a woman divorced from her husband they shall not take,** as he is holy to his God" (Leviticus 21:7). This verse lists the women whom a priest is prohibited from marrying. From this verse it can be inferred: **Even if she was only divorced from her husband** who said when giving her a bill of divorce: You are divorced from me, but did not permit her to other men, even such a woman **they may not take** in marriage. Although a bill of divorce of this kind does not permit the woman to others, it does suffice to prohibit her from marrying a priest. **And this is** what is referred to as **the trace of a bill of divorce, which disqualifies** a woman from marrying **into the priesthood.**[N] Since this bill of divorce is valid to a certain extent, it also disqualifies a *yevama*.

אָמַר רָמִי בַּר חָמָא: הֲרֵי אָמְרוּ, אָמַר אֶחָד לְלַבְלָר "כְּתוֹב גֵּט לַאֲרוּסָתִי, לִכְשֶׁאֶכְנָסֶנָּה אֲגָרְשֶׁנָּה" הֲרֵי זֶה גֵּט, מִפְּנֵי שֶׁבְּיָדוֹ לְגָרְשָׁהּ.

Rami bar Ḥama said: They said that **if one said to a scribe** [*lavlar*]:[L] **Write a bill of divorce for my betrothed** now, **such that when I marry her I will divorce her** with the bill of divorce, if he indeed gave her this bill of divorce after their marriage **it is** a valid **bill of divorce.**[H] Why? **Because it is** already **in his power to divorce her** while she is betrothed to him, and therefore the bill of divorce written during their betrothal is valid.

LANGUAGE

Scribe [*lavlar*] – לַבְלָר: The root of the word is from the Latin librarius, a writer, especially of contracts. *Lavlar* was another name for a scribe or an expert in writing. His field of expertise was not only the writing itself but also the wording of various kinds of contracts.

HALAKHA

A bill of divorce that disqualifies her from marrying into the priesthood – גֵּט הַפּוֹסֵל בִּכְהוּנָּה: A woman who receives a bill of divorce is disqualified from marrying into the priesthood, even if the bill of divorce is invalid because it is an uncertain bill of divorce or if the bill of divorce stated: You are hereby divorced from me, but you are not permitted to any man (Rambam *Sefer Nashim, Hilkhot Geirushin* 10:1; *Shulḥan Arukh, Even HaEzer* 6:1).

If he wrote a bill of divorce to his betrothed, etc. – כָּתַב גֵּט לַאֲרוּסָתוֹ וכו׳: If one wrote a bill of divorce to his betrothed in order to divorce her with it after he marries her, it is a valid bill of divorce. This applies only if the bill of divorce includes the date on which it was given, but if he wrote the date on which it was written, it is invalid (Ra'avad; Rabbeinu Tam; Rambam *Sefer Nashim, Hilkhot Geirushin* 3:6; *Shulḥan Arukh, Even HaEzer* 132:1).

NOTES

The trace of a bill of divorce, which disqualifies for the priesthood – רֵיחַ הַגֵּט שֶׁפּוֹסֵל בִּכְהוּנָּה: The trace of a bill of divorce refers to a divorce which is lacking in some way and therefore does not effect a full divorce. Despite the fact that the woman is not divorced, in some cases the trace of a bill of divorce is enough to consider her a divorcée for the purposes of disqualifying her from marrying into the priesthood. In these cases, should her husband subsequently die, she would be considered a divorcée and not a widow who would be permitted to the priesthood. The question of which bills of divorce disqualify a woman for marrying into the priesthood is a matter of dispute among the authorities. The Rambam maintains that any bill of divorce about which the Sages said: It is not a bill of divorce, does not even disqualify a woman for marrying into the priesthood. Only this particular bill of divorce, expressed with the formula: You are divorced from me but you are not permitted to any man, disqualifies her due to its status as the trace of a bill of divorce. The Ra'avad disagrees and claims there are other invalid bills of divorce that prevent her from marrying a priest, depending on their similarity to a proper bill of divorce. The *Migdal Oz* writes that this dispute dates back to Rashi and *Tosafot* as well.

וְלְאִשָּׁה בְּעָלְמָא – אֵין גֵּט, מִפְּנֵי שֶׁאֵין בְּיָדוֹ לְגָרְשָׁהּ. בָּעֵי רָמִי בַּר חָמָא: לִיבִמְתּוֹ מַהוּ? כֵּיוָן דַּאֲגִידָא בֵּיהּ – כַּאֲרוּסָתוֹ דָּמְיָא, אוֹ דִּלְמָא: כֵּיוָן דְּלָא עֲבַד בָּהּ מַאֲמָר – לָא? תֵּיקוּ.

But if he wrote a bill of divorce **for a regular woman** who has no connection to him, even if he later married her, it is **not a** valid **bill of divorce.**[HN] This is **because** at the time of the writing of the bill of divorce, **it is not in his power to divorce her,** and therefore the bill of divorce is of no consequence. All this is evident, but in light of the above *halakhot* **Rami bar Ḥama inquires:** If he wrote a bill of divorce **for his *yevama*** and did not give it to her immediately, but only after they were married, **what is the *halakha*?**[N] Is it a valid bill of divorce or not? The Gemara clarifies the options: On the one hand, **since she is tied to him** she is **considered like his betrothed; or perhaps, since he has not** yet **performed levirate betrothal with her,** she is **not** even considered the equivalent of his betrothed, and the bill of divorce is not effective? The Gemara does not have a resolution for this and states that the question **shall stand** unresolved.

בָּעֵי רַב חֲנַנְיָה: כָּתַב גֵּט לְזִיקָתוֹ וְלֹא לְמַאֲמָרוֹ, לְמַאֲמָרוֹ וְלֹא לְזִיקָתוֹ, מַהוּ? מַאֲמָר עִילָּוֵי זִיקָה קָא רָמֵי, וַהֲוָה לֵיהּ כִּמְגָרֵשׁ חֲצִי אִשָּׁה, וְהַמְגָרֵשׁ חֲצִי אִשָּׁה לֹא עָשָׂה וְלֹא כְּלוּם, אוֹ דִּלְמָא: הַאי לְחוּדֵיהּ קָאֵי וְהַאי לְחוּדֵיהּ קָאֵי?

Rav Ḥananya inquires: If **he wrote a bill of divorce for his levirate bond,** by specifying in the bill of divorce that he is thereby severing the levirate bond between them, **but not for his levirate betrothal,** or if he wrote a bill of divorce **for his levirate betrothal and** stated that it is **not for his levirate bond, what is the *halakha*?**[H] Is the **levirate betrothal superimposed upon the levirate bond,** so that they are considered a single, continuous link, **and he is like one who divorces half a woman, and one who divorces half a woman has done nothing; or perhaps this stands on its own and that stands on its own,** and he can therefore cancel either the levirate bond or the levirate betrothal separately.

וְתִפְשׁוֹט לֵיהּ מִדְּרָבָא, דְּאָמַר רָבָא: נָתַן גֵּט לְמַאֲמָרוֹ – הוּתְּרָה צָרָתָהּ! לְרָבָא – פְּשִׁיטָא לֵיהּ, לְרַב חֲנַנְיָה – מִיבַּעְיָא לֵיהּ, מַאי? תֵּיקוּ.

The Gemara asks: **And** why do you not **resolve** the dilemma **from** a teaching of **Rava? For Rava said:** If a *yavam* **gave a bill of divorce for his levirate betrothal, her rival wife is permitted.** The levirate betrothal he had previously performed is thereby canceled, which leaves the bond intact, and the rival wife of this *yevama* remains available for levirate marriage. This indicates that levirate betrothal and the levirate bond are not connected. The Gemara answers: **To Rava it is obvious, but to Rav Ḥananya it is a dilemma. What,** then, is the *halakha*? Since no other proof is forthcoming, and Rav **Ḥananya** does not accept the teaching of Rava, the question remains undecided. The Gemara states that the dilemma **shall stand** unresolved.

HALAKHA

If he wrote a bill of divorce to one who is not his wife – כָּתַב גֵּט לְמִי שֶׁאֵינָהּ אִשְׁתּוֹ: If a man wrote a bill of divorce to a woman who is not his wife, with the intention of divorcing her with it after their marriage, the bill of divorce is ineffective. However, if he wrote it to his *yevama* before he married her, it is an uncertain bill of divorce (Rambam *Sefer Nashim, Hilkhot Geirushin* 3:6; *Shulḥan Arukh, Even HaEzer* 132:2).

A bill of divorce for levirate betrothal and a bill of divorce for a levirate bond – גֵּט לְמַאֲמָר וְגֵט לְזִיקָה: If a *yavam* performed levirate betrothal with his *yevama* and afterward gave her a bill of divorce for her levirate bond, he has thereby disqualified her for levirate marriage, both with himself and with the other brothers. If he does not specify the nature of the bill of divorce it is considered to have been written for her levirate bond. In order to permit her to marry any other man she requires another bill of divorce for her levirate betrothal, and *ḥalitza* to release the levirate bond. If he gave her a bill of divorce for her levirate betrothal and not for her levirate bond, she is permitted to the brothers, but not to him. Some say (*Tosafot*; Ra'avad; Rosh) that she is even permitted to him (Rambam *Sefer Nashim, Hilkhot Yibbum* 5:4; *Shulḥan Arukh, Even HaEzer* 170:15).

NOTES

But for a regular woman it is not a bill of divorce – וּלְאִשָּׁה בְּעָלְמָא אֵין גֵּט: Most early commentaries (see *Tosafot*) explain that since he appointed an agent to write the bill of divorce on his behalf, the agent cannot perform something the husband does not have the power to do, and at the time of the appointment he could not have written the bill of divorce himself. Rabbi Avraham min HaHar raises several difficulties with this explanation. He explains that the Rambam has a different opinion: As the woman could not be divorced at that time, the bill of divorce is considered like one that was not written for the sake of a particular woman, and such a bill of divorce is invalid.

For his *yevama* what is the *halakha* – לִיבִמְתּוֹ מַהוּ: Rashi understands this question in a straightforward manner: Is this bill of divorce that she receives when still a *yevama* effective for their divorce after they are married? The Rambam understands the question in a similar vein. *Tosafot*, however, claim that it is obvious that such a bill of divorce cannot be used for divorce after their marriage. Consequently, they explain that the question is whether a bill of divorce written before levirate betrothal can cancel that levirate betrothal. Alternatively, the reference is to the trace of a bill of divorce, i.e., does a bill of divorce of this kind disqualify her for marrying into the priesthood? *Tosafot Yeshanim* note that one might have thought it is evident that this bill of divorce disqualifies her for marrying into the priesthood, as a bill of divorce is effective for a *yevama* even before he has performed levirate betrothal. Nevertheless, there is a difference between the cases, as he does not give her the bill of divorce immediately, but only after their marriage. It is therefore possible that the decree of the Sages with regard to the bill of divorce of a *yevama* no longer applies to a married woman.

Tosefot HaRosh explains that the dilemma is whether his *yevama* is considered like his betrothed, since he can have intercourse with her, even against her will, and then divorce her; or perhaps there is no relationship between them as of yet, since they have yet to engage in relations. A different point is raised by the Ramban: If the question concerns the validity of the bill of divorce according to Torah law, including its ability to effect a regular divorce, why is the rabbinical levirate betrothal mentioned in this connection at all? He concludes that the question concerns the efficacy of this bill of divorce on a rabbinic level, such that if he divorced her with it after their marriage, would she be considered divorced by rabbinic law. Do we say that the fact that he can give her a bill of divorce when she is a *yevama* and thereby disqualify her indicates that there is a connection between them, or perhaps this bill of divorce is completely ineffective after their marriage, as stated by *Tosafot Yeshanim*? All this refers to the stage before levirate betrothal, for once he has performed levirate betrothal with her she is certainly considered his betrothed according to rabbinic law.

The Rashba continues the line of reasoning suggested by the Ramban, but he explains somewhat differently. In his opinion the Gemara is asking a pair of questions that involve two distinct possibilities. First, does the fact that he can perform *ḥalitza* with his *yevama* mean that it is as though he can give her a bill of divorce, and she is considered his betrothed with regard to the validity of this bill of divorce? Second, if we say that *ḥalitza* is dissimilar to a bill of divorce, perhaps this bill of divorce is strong enough to disqualify her from marrying into the priesthood before he performs levirate betrothal.

"חלץ ועשה מאמר". אמר רב יהודה אמר רב: זו דברי רבי עקיבא, דאמר: אין קדושין תופסין בחייבי לאוין. אבל חכמים אומרים: יש אחר חליצה כלום.

§ It was taught in the mishna: If the *yavam* **performed *ḥalitza* and** then **performed levirate betrothal,** nothing is effective after *ḥalitza* and this levirate betrothal is not valid. **Rav Yehuda said** that **Rav said: This is the statement of Rabbi Akiva,**[N] **who says** that **betrothal does not take effect on** those who are forbidden as they are **liable for** violating **a prohibition.** Once he has performed *ḥalitza*, the woman is forbidden to him due to the prohibition derived from the verse "So shall it be done to the man who does not build his brother's house" (Deuteronomy 25:9), and betrothal is ineffective. **But the Rabbis say something is** effective **after *ḥalitza*.** Although the woman who performed *ḥalitza* is forbidden to him, if he does betroth her, his betrothal is effective, as with any regular prohibition.

ומי מצית מוקמת לה כרבי עקיבא? והא קתני רישא: נתן גט ועשה מאמר – צריכה גט וחליצה, ואי רבי עקיבא – כיון דיהב לה גט מי מהני בה מאמר?

The Gemara asks: **And can you establish** that the mishna is **in accordance with** the opinion of **Rabbi Akiva? But doesn't the first clause** of the mishna **teach:** If he **gave a bill of divorce and performed levirate betrothal, she requires a bill of divorce and *ḥalitza*. Now if** this is in accordance with **Rabbi Akiva's** opinion, **once he gave her a bill of divorce, is levirate betrothal effective for her?**

והתניא, רבי עקיבא אומר: מנין לנותן גט ליבמתו שנאסרה עליו עולמית – שנאמר "לא יוכל בעלה הראשון אשר שלחה" אחר שילוח.

But isn't it taught in a *baraita* that **Rabbi Akiva says: From where** is it derived **that if one gives a bill of divorce to his *yevama*, she is forbidden to him forever** and he no longer has the option of marrying her? As it **is stated** with regard to a woman who was divorced and married another man who subsequently died or divorced her: **"Her former husband, who sent her away, may not** take her again to be his wife" (Deuteronomy 24:4). Rabbi Akiva emphasizes the words "who sent her away," implying that he may not remarry her **after sending** her **away.**[N] This indicates that there is an instance where a husband may not remarry his wife even if she has not married another, merely because he has given her a bill of divorce. This applies to the case of a *yevama* where the bill of divorce she receives renders her permanently prohibited to him. According to Rabbi Akiva, once she is rendered prohibited to him, no further action performed by the *yavam* is effective, so why does the levirate betrothal performed require a bill of divorce?

אמר רב אשי: גט יבמין מדרבנן. וקרא – אסמכתא בעלמא.

Rav Ashi said: This is not difficult because **the bill of divorce for levirate marriage** was established by the Sages and only has the force of **rabbinic law,**[H] **and the** aforementioned **verse** is not a Torah prohibition, but rather **a mere support.** Therefore there is no Torah prohibition against marrying a *yevama* who received a bill of divorce, and the levirate betrothal performed afterward is effective according to Rabbi Akiva as well.

תניא נמי הכי, אמר רבי: אין הדברים הללו אמורים אלא לדברי רבי עקיבא, שהיה עושה חלוצה כערוה. אבל חכמים אומרים: יש אחר חליצה כלום. ואני אומר: אימתי – בזמן שקדשה לשום אישות, אבל קדשה לשום יבמות – אין אחר חליצה כלום.

With regard to the *halakha* of betrothal after *ḥalitza*, the Gemara notes: **This *halakha* is also taught** in a *baraita* as **Rabbi** Yehuda HaNasi **said: These matters were only stated in accordance with the statement of Rabbi Akiva, who considers a *yevama* who underwent *ḥalitza* to be** prohibited **like a forbidden relation.** Therefore, any further betrothal is not effective with her, as is the case with forbidden relations. **But the Rabbis say something is** effective **after *ḥalitza*. And I say: When** is betrothal effective after *ḥalitza*? It is effective **when he betrothed for the purpose of marriage,** like the regular betrothal of any ordinary woman. **But if he betrothed her** after *ḥalitza* and specified that he is doing so **for the purpose of levirate marriage,** in that case **nothing is** effective **after *ḥalitza*.**

תניא אידך: החולץ ליבמתו, וחזר וקדשה. רבי אומר: אם קדשה לשום אישות – צריכה הימנו גט, לשום יבמות – אין צריכה הימנו גט וחכמים אומרים: בין שקדשה לשום אישות, בין שקדשה לשום יבמות – צריכה הימנו גט.

It is taught in **another** *baraita*: With regard to **one who performs *ḥalitza* with his *yevama* and then betroths her,**[H] **Rabbi** Yehuda HaNasi **says: If he betrothed her for the purpose of** regular **marriage she requires a bill of divorce from him;** if he betrothed her **for the purpose of levirate marriage she does not require a bill of divorce from him. And the Rabbis say: Whether he betrothed her for the purpose of** regular **marriage, or whether he betrothed her for the purpose of levirate marriage, she requires a bill of divorce from him,** as this betrothal is effective.

NOTES

This is the statement of Rabbi Akiva – זו דברי רבי עקיבא: In the Jerusalem Talmud, this conclusion is not accepted by all, as there are alternate ways to explain the mishna. For example, Reish Lakish maintains that a woman who performed *ḥalitza* is forbidden to the brothers due to a prohibition for which they are liable to *karet*, as are her rival wives, and therefore betrothal is not effective even according to the Rabbis. Another possibility is that the mishna is in accordance with Rabbi Yehuda HaNasi, and it is discussing a situation where the *yavam* betrothed the *yevama* for the purpose of levirate marriage.

After sending her away – אחר שילוח: Rabbi Akiva maintains that the words "who sent her away" are superfluous, and therefore he reads the verse as speaking of two separate mitzvot. One would therefore read the verse as having two subjects, as follows: "Her former husband" and similarly he "who sent her away," i.e., the *yavam*, "may not return to take her as a wife."

HALAKHA

The validity of a bill of divorce for levirate marriage – תקף גט יבמין: The Sages decreed that the bill of divorce of a *yavam* to his *yevama* is effective, and it disqualifies her and her rival wives from levirate marriage, both with him and his brothers (Rambam *Sefer Nashim*, *Hilkhot Yibbum* 5:1; *Shulḥan Arukh*, *Even HaEzer* 170:1).

One who performs *ḥalitza* with his *yevama* and then betroths her – החולץ ליבמתו וחזר וקדשה: If one performed *ḥalitza* with his *yevama* and then betrothed her, whether he did so for the purpose of regular marriage or levirate marriage, he is forbidden to marry her; but the betrothal is effective to the extent that she requires a bill of divorce from him (Rambam *Sefer Nashim*, *Hilkhot Yibbum* 5:15; *Shulḥan Arukh*, *Even HaEzer* 170:13).

אֲמַר רַב יוֹסֵף: מַאי טַעֲמָא דְּרַבִּי – עֲשָׂאוּהָ כְּעוֹדֵר בְּנִכְסֵי הַגֵּר וּכְסָבוּר שֶׁלּוֹ הֵן דְּלָא קָנֵי.

Rav Yosef said: What is the reason for Rabbi Yehuda HaNasi's distinction between one who betroths his *ḥalutza* for the purpose of levirate marriage and one who does so for the purpose of regular marriage? It is because the Sages **considered him like** one who **hoes the property of a convert**[H] who died without leaving heirs. The property of such a convert is ownerless, and whoever takes possession of it acquires its title. As one of the methods of taking possession of land is hoeing, if one hoed the property of this convert with the intention of acquiring it, it belongs to him. However, if he hoed the convert's property **while** mistakenly **thinking** that the land **was his own,** even though he performed an act of acquisition, since he lacked the requisite intention **he has not acquired** the land. Here too, since the *yavam* intended to betroth her for the purpose of levirate marriage, and the levirate bond no longer exists, his action is not effective.

אָמַר לֵיהּ אַבַּיֵי: מִי דָּמֵי? הָתָם – לָא קָא מְכַוֵּין לְמִיקְנֵי, הָכָא – קָא מְכַוֵּין לְמִיקְנֵי. הָא לָא דָּמְיָא אֶלָּא לְעוֹדֵר בְּנִכְסֵי גֵּר זֶה, וּכְסָבוּר שֶׁל גֵּר אַחֵר הוּא, דְּקָנֵי.

Abaye said to him: Are the two situations **comparable?**[N] **There,** in the case of hoeing, **he does not intend to acquire** the land as he works, as he thinks that it is already his, whereas **here he does intend to acquire** the woman. **This** case **is similar only to the one who hoes the property of this** deceased **convert while thinking it is that of a different convert.** The *halakha* in that case is **that he acquires** the land, despite his imprecise knowledge of what he is acquiring. Here too the betrothal should take effect regardless of his error.

אֶלָּא אֲמַר אַבַּיֵי: הָכָא בְּמַאי עָסְקִינַן – כְּגוֹן דְּאָמַר לָהּ "הִתְקַדְּשִׁי לִי בְּמַאֲמַר יְבָמִין". רַבִּי סָבַר: מַאֲמָר עִילָּוֵי זִיקָה קָא רָמֵי, וַאֲתַאי חֲלִיצָה אַפְקַעְתָּה לְזִיקָה. וְרַבָּנַן סָבְרִי: הַאי לְחוּדֵיהּ קָאֵי וְהַאי לְחוּדֵיהּ קָאֵי. מֵעִיקָּרָא, אִילּוּ אֲמַר לָהּ "הִתְקַדְּשִׁי לִי בְּמַאֲמַר יְבָמִין" מִי לָא מְהַנֵּי? הָשְׁתָּא נַמִי מְהַנֵּי.

Rather, Abaye said that the dispute between Rabbi Yehuda HaNasi and the Rabbis cannot be explained in the above manner. Instead, he suggests: **With what are we dealing here?** It is a case **where he said to** his *ḥalutza*: **Be betrothed to me with levirate betrothal. Rabbi** Yehuda HaNasi **holds** that **levirate betrothal is superimposed upon** the **levirate bond,** and is therefore only possible when the bond exists, **and** since ***ḥalitza* comes** and **releases the levirate bond,** levirate betrothal is not effective for her. **And the Rabbis hold: This,** the levirate bond, **stands on its own, and that,** levirate betrothal, **stands on its own.** Although the bond has been canceled, the formula of: Be betrothed to me with levirate betrothal, is effective. **At the outset,** before *ḥalitza,* **if he had said to her: Be betrothed to me with levirate betrothal,**[N] **would** this **not be** an **effective** betrothal despite the lack of connection between the levirate betrothal and the levirate bond? **Now too** it should be **effective,** even though she performed *ḥalitza.*

רָבָא אֲמַר: אִי דְּאָמַר לָהּ "בְּמַאֲמַר יְבָמִין" כּוּלֵּי עָלְמָא לָא פְּלִיגִי דִּמְהַנְּיָא, וְהָכָא בְּמַאי עָסְקִינַן – כְּגוֹן דְּאָמַר לָהּ "הִתְקַדְּשִׁי לִי בְּזִיקַת יְבָמִין". רַבִּי סָבַר:

Rava said: If he said to her: Be betrothed to me **with levirate betrothal, everyone agrees that it is effective,** and she is acquired. **And with what are we dealing here?** It is a case **where he said to her: Be betrothed to me with the levirate bond,**[H] and the dispute is as follows: **Rabbi** Yehuda HaNasi **holds**

HALAKHA

One who hoes in the property of a convert – הָעוֹדֵר בְּנִכְסֵי הַגֵּר: If one hoes the property of a convert who died without leaving heirs, under the mistaken impression that the land belonged to him, he has not acquired it. However, if he thought it belonged to a particular convert and it actually belonged to a different one, and he intended to acquire the ownerless property, the acquisition is effective (Rambam *Sefer Kinyan, Hilkhot Zekhiya UMattana* 2:13; *Shulḥan Arukh, Ḥoshen Mishpat* 275:25–26).

Levirate betrothal and a levirate bond – מַאֲמַר יְבָמִין וְזִיקַת יְבָמִין: If a *yavam* performed *ḥalitza* with his *yevama* and then betrothed her, whether he said he was doing so with levirate betrothal or with the levirate bond, his betrothal is effective. The *Beit Shmuel* claims that it is only valid by rabbinic law. She then requires a bill of divorce, in accordance with the opinion of the Rabbis (*Shulḥan Arukh, Even HaEzer* 170:14).

NOTES

Abaye said to him, Are they comparable – אָמַר לֵיהּ אַבַּיֵי מִי דָּמֵי: The early commentaries are puzzled by Abaye's opinion: After questioning Rav Yosef's comparison to one who hoes a field by asserting that a *yavam* acquires his *yevama* when he betroths her for the purpose of levirate marriage, he himself proceeds to claim that he cannot acquire her by levirate betrothal.

Tosafot offer two explanations, also cited, with slight variations, by *Tosafot Yeshanim*. The Ra'avad explains that Rav Yosef explains Rabbi Yehuda HaNasi's case as one where the *yavam* says he is betrothing so-and-so, his *yevama*. Abaye responds that there is no proof from the wording that he is acquiring her with levirate marriage in mind, as he might merely be mentioning that she was previously his *yevama*. Abaye therefore explains that Rabbi Yehuda HaNasi was referring specifically to one who said that he is acquiring her with levirate betrothal.

If he had said to her, Be betrothed to me with levirate betrothal – אִילּוּ אֲמַר לָהּ הִתְקַדְּשִׁי לִי בְּמַאֲמַר יְבָמִין: The Ritva indicates that a statement of this kind would be effective even with regard to a regular woman, despite the fact that it is not a precise expression of betrothal. Levirate betrothal is in essence an act of betrothal, and there is no reason to distinguish between them. For example, the Gemara in tractate *Kiddushin* 6a states that if one says to a woman: You are hereby tied to me by a bond, she is betrothed.

יֵשׁ זִיקָה, וַאֲתַאי חֲלִיצָה אַפְקַעְתֵּיהּ לְזִיקָה. וְרַבָּנַן סָבְרִי, אֵין זִיקָה. מֵעִיקָּרָא אִילּוּ אֲמַר לָהּ ״הִתְקַדְּשִׁי לִי בְּזִיקַת יְבָמִין״ מִי לָא מְהַנֵּי? הָשְׁתָּא נַמִי מְהַנֵּי.

that **the levirate bond is substantial,** and this betrothal is based on the levirate bond. **And** in this case, the *ḥalitza* **comes** and **releases the levirate bond.** Therefore this type of betrothal does not acquire the *ḥalutza*. **But the Rabbis hold** that **the levirate bond is not substantial,**[N] that is, the bond itself does not create a connection between the *yavam* and *yevama*, and that in general, levirate betrothal acquires a *yevama* as a form of betrothal unrelated to the levirate bond.[N] **And** consequently, **at the outset, if he had said to her: Be betrothed to me by the levirate bond, would** this **not be effective? Now too,** after *ḥalitza*, even without the bond, it should likewise be **effective.**

רַב שֵׁרֶבְיָא אֲמַר: בַּחֲלִיצָה כְּשֵׁירָה, אִי דַּאֲמַר לָהּ ״הִתְקַדְּשִׁי לִי בְּזִיקַת יְבָמִין״ כּוּלֵּי עָלְמָא לָא פְּלִיגִי דְּלָא מְהַנֵּי. וְהָכָא בַּחֲלִיצָה פְּסוּלָה קָמִיפַּלְגִי. מָר סָבַר: חֲלִיצָה פְּסוּלָה פּוֹטֶרֶת, וּמָר סָבַר: חֲלִיצָה פְּסוּלָה אֵינָהּ פּוֹטֶרֶת.

Rav Sherevya suggested a different point of dispute and **said:** In a case when the woman performed **valid *ḥalitza*, if he** later **said to her: Be betrothed to me by the levirate bond, everyone agrees**[N] **that it is not effective,** as there is no longer any bond. **And here,** they **disagree** with regard to one who performed **invalid *ḥalitza*.** One **Sage,** Rabbi Yehuda HaNasi, **holds** that **invalid *ḥalitza* exempts** her from the levirate bond and disqualifies her from betrothal as a *yevama*. **And** one **Sage,** i.e., the Rabbis, **holds** that **invalid *ḥalitza* does not** fully **exempt** her,[N] and some element of the levirate bond remains intact and she can therefore be betrothed with the levirate bond.

רַב אַשִׁי אֲמַר: דְּכוּלֵּי עָלְמָא חֲלִיצָה פְּסוּלָה אֵינָהּ פּוֹטֶרֶת. וְהָכָא בְּיֵשׁ תְּנַאי בַּחֲלִיצָה קָמִיפַּלְגִי. מָר סָבַר: יֵשׁ תְּנַאי בַּחֲלִיצָה, וּמָר סָבַר: אֵין תְּנַאי בַּחֲלִיצָה.

Rav Ashi said: Everyone agrees that **invalid *ḥalitza* does not exempt** her and does not entirely nullify the bond. **And here** they **disagree** as to whether **a condition is** effective **with regard to *ḥalitza*.** When the *yavam* states he is performing *ḥalitza* on the condition that the *yevama* give him one hundred dinars, for example, is this condition effective and therefore the *ḥalitza* is nullified if the condition is not fulfilled? One **Sage,** i.e., the Rabbis, **holds** that **a condition is** effective **with regard to *ḥalitza*.** If the *yevama* fails to comply with the condition, the *ḥalitza* is ineffective and she can still be betrothed with the levirate bond. **And** one **Sage,** Rabbi Yehuda HaNasi, **holds** that **a condition is not** effective **with regard to *ḥalitza*,**[H] and therefore the *ḥalitza* is always effective as is the subsequent levirate betrothal.

רָבִינָא אֲמַר: דְּכוּלֵּי עָלְמָא יֵשׁ תְּנַאי בַּחֲלִיצָה. וְהָכָא בִּתְנַאי כָּפוּל קָמִיפַּלְגִי; מָר סָבַר: בָּעֵינַן תְּנַאי כָּפוּל, וּמָר סָבַר: לָא בָּעֵינַן תְּנַאי כָּפוּל.

Ravina said: Everyone agrees that **a condition is** effective **with regard to *ḥalitza*, and here** they **disagree with regard to a compound condition.**[HB] One **Sage,** Rabbi Yehuda HaNasi, **holds** that **we require a compound condition.** The man must explicitly stipulate that the *ḥalitza* should be effective if the condition is upheld, and that it should not be effective if she does not fulfill the condition. If he did not state both the positive and negative sides of the condition it does not take effect, and the *ḥalitza* is effective and the levirate bond is canceled. Consequently, betrothal by the levirate bond is ineffective. **And** one **Sage,** i.e., the Rabbis, **holds that we do not require a compound condition.** Therefore, the condition applies and cancels the *ḥalitza*, which leaves the levirate bond intact.

NOTES

But the Rabbis hold that the levirate bond is not substantial – **וְרַבָּנַן סָבְרִי אֵין זִיקָה:** It is not that the Rabbis maintain that the levirate bond is not significant at all, as the *yevama* certainly requires levirate marriage. Rather, it means the bond does not have the halakhic force with regard to creating prohibitions, as it is does not create a family connection that would forbid the *yavam* from marrying the relatives of the *yevama* (*Tosefot HaRosh*). Rabbi Avraham min HaHar explains that this opinion holds the levirate bond is not substantial by Torah law but rather by rabbinic law.

The explanations of the dispute between Rabbi Yehuda HaNasi and the Rabbis – **פֵּירוּשֵׁי מַחְלוֹקֶת רַבִּי וְרַבָּנַן:** The early commentaries were puzzled by the variety of interpretations of this dispute, as they are based on assumptions that are not accepted as *halakha*. The Rif states, and the Rid writes similarly, that all these explanations of the Gemara are merely hypothetical exercises to sharpen the mind, and it is a mistake to analyze them too closely, as they are not meant as rulings for *halakha*.

Be betrothed to me by the levirate bond, everyone agrees, etc. – **הִתְקַדְּשִׁי לִי בְּזִיקַת יְבָמִין כּוּלֵּי עָלְמָא לָא פְּלִיגִי וכו׳:** The *Milḥamot HaShem* had an alternate version of the text that reads: If he said: Be betrothed to me by the levirate bond, everyone agrees that it is effective, as they did not disagree with regard to the levirate bond at all. According to this opinion, which is implied somewhat by Rashi as well, all the suggested interpretations of the dispute are in logical order, in the manner usually signaled by the words: And if you say, etc.

Invalid *ḥalitza* does not exempt her – **חֲלִיצָה פְּסוּלָה אֵינָהּ פּוֹטֶרֶת:** This suggestion is problematic, as the accepted principle throughout our chapter is that invalid *ḥalitza* exempts the woman and that anything afterward is ineffective. How, then, can the Gemara propose that such a *ḥalitza* does not exempt her? For this reason the Rif claims that this statement refers to the requirement to repeat the *ḥalitza* with the other brothers; and therefore, according to the opinion that invalid *ḥalitza* does not exempt her, she must perform *ḥalitza* with all the brothers. A different interpretation is cited by Rabbi Avraham min HaHar. He contends that invalid *ḥalitza* does not refer to *ḥalitza* performed after another action. Instead, it means *ḥalitza* performed with a pregnant woman, which is ineffective according to Reish Lakish.

HALAKHA

A condition with regard to *ḥalitza* – **תְּנַאי בַּחֲלִיצָה:** No conditions are effective with regard to *ḥalitza*, and therefore a mistaken *ḥalitza* is valid. For example, if the *yavam* was told to perform *ḥalitza* on condition that the *yevama* should give him a large sum of money, even if it was stated as a compound condition, the *ḥalitza* is valid whether or not she paid him the stipulated amount (Rambam *Sefer Nashim, Hilkhot Yibbum* 4:24; *Shulḥan Arukh, Even HaEzer* 169:50).

A compound condition – **תְּנַאי כָּפוּל:** Every condition must include the following four features: It must be double in the sense that he must specify what will happen both if the condition is fulfilled and if it is not fulfilled; the formulation of its positive aspect, i.e., its fulfillment, must precede the negative formulation of the condition; the condition must be stated before the action itself; and the fulfillment of the condition must be feasible. Any condition that lacks one of these elements is discounted (Rambam *Sefer Nashim, Hilkhot Ishut* 6:2; *Shulḥan Arukh, Even HaEzer* 38:2).

BACKGROUND

A compound condition – **תְּנַאי כָּפוּל:** This refers to conditions set out when creating contractual obligations. A simple condition merely states the positive side of a commitment: If X, then Y. A compound condition states its negative side, as well: If X, then Y, and if not X, then not Y. Some authorities, basing themselves on the agreement made between Moses and the tribes of Gad and Reuben (see Numbers 32:20–24), maintain that compound conditions are required so that violation of a simple condition, where the negative side of the case is not stated, does not nullify the agreement.

HALAKHA

Nothing is effective after intercourse – אֵין אַחַר בִּיאָה כְּלוּם: If a *yavam* engaged in valid intercourse with the *yevama*, i.e., the intercourse was not preceded by any action that would invalidate it, no action performed afterward is of any effect, whether performed by any other *yavam* with her, or by the *yavam* or one of his brothers with her rival wife, as stated by Abaye and Rava (Rambam *Sefer Nashim*, *Hilkhot Yibbum* 5:14; *Shulḥan Arukh*, *Even HaEzer* 170:12).

״חָלַץ וְעָשָׂה מַאֲמָר וְנָתַן גֵּט וּבָעַל״ וכו׳. וְנִיתְנֵי נַמִּי אֵין אַחַר בִּיאָה כְּלוּם! אַבַּיֵּי וְרָבָא דְּאָמְרִי תַּרְוַיְיהוּ, תְּנֵי: אֵין אַחַר בִּיאָה כְּלוּם. וְתַנָּא דִּידַן – הַתָּרַת יְבָמָה לַשּׁוּק עֲדִיפָא לֵיהּ.

§ The mishna teaches: If the *yavam* **performed *ḥalitza* and** then either **performed levirate betrothal, or gave a bill of divorce, or engaged in intercourse,** nothing is effective after *ḥalitza*. The Gemara asks: **And let the** *tanna* **likewise teach** that **nothing is** effective **after intercourse,**[H] for he also mentioned the case of one who engaged in intercourse and then proceeded to perform other actions such as levirate betrothal, divorce and *ḥalitza*. Indeed, **Abaye and Rava both say** that the mishna should **teach: Nothing is** effective **after intercourse,** as this clause is fit to be inserted into the mishna. The Gemara asks: **And the *tanna* of our** mishna;[N] why did he not state this? The Gemara explains: **The permission for a *yevama* to** marry a member of the **public is preferable to him.** He preferred to teach cases in which the *yevama* is permitted to marry any man from the general public as opposed to a situation where she is married to the *yavam*.

״אֶחָד יְבָמָה אַחַת אֶחָד שְׁתֵּי יְבָמוֹת״. מַתְנִיתִין דְּלָא כְּבֶן עַזַּאי. דְּתַנְיָא, בֶּן עַזַּאי אוֹמֵר: יֵשׁ מַאֲמָר אַחַר מַאֲמָר בִּשְׁנֵי יְבָמִין וִיבָמָה אַחַת, וְאֵין מַאֲמָר אַחַר מַאֲמָר בִּשְׁתֵּי יְבָמוֹת וְיָבָם אֶחָד.

The mishna teaches that all the *halakhot* with regard to levirate betrothal after levirate betrothal and the like apply **both** in cases of **one *yevama*** to one *yavam*, **as well as** in cases of **two *yevamot*** to one *yavam*. The Gemara comments: **The mishna is not in accordance with** the opinion of **ben Azzai. As it is taught** in a *baraita*: **Ben Azzai says: Levirate betrothal is** effective **after levirate betrothal in** the case of **two *yevamin* and one *yevama*, but levirate betrothal is not** effective **after levirate betrothal in** the case of **two *yevamot* and one *yavam*.** The *tanna* of the mishna, in contrast, does not differentiate between the cases.

״כֵּיצַד מַאֲמָר לָזוֹ״ וכו׳. לֵימָא מְסַיַּיע לֵיהּ לִשְׁמוּאֵל, דְּאָמַר שְׁמוּאֵל: חָלַץ לְבַעֲלַת מַאֲמָר לֹא נִפְטְרָה צָרָתָהּ,

The mishna further teaches: **How so?** If he performed **levirate betrothal with this** one and performed *ḥalitza* with that one, the first woman requires a bill of divorce to cancel the levirate betrothal. The Gemara suggests: **Let us say** that this teaching **supports** the opinion of **Shmuel.**[N] **As Shmuel said:** If a *yavam* **performed *ḥalitza* with** the woman **who received levirate betrothal,** then the **rival wife is not exempt** as this *ḥalitza* is invalid. The fact that the Gemara does not state that the *ḥalitza* be performed with the woman who received levirate betrothal indicates that this *ḥalitza* is not a valid *ḥalitza* and would not be sufficient to exempt the rival wife.

NOTES

And the *tanna* of our mishna, etc. – וְתַנָּא דִּידַן וכו׳: The wording here is confusing, for Abaye and Rava just stated that mishna should be adjusted, which means that in their opinion our *tanna* did in fact include this teaching in the mishna. *Tosafot Yeshanim* suggest that Abaye and Rava were pointing out a *baraita* that explicitly says that nothing is effective after intercourse, as indeed, such a *baraita* is found in the *Tosefta*. After noting that source, the Gemara inquires about the *tanna* of our mishna.

Let us say that this supports Shmuel, etc. – לֵימָא מְסַיַּיע לֵיהּ לִשְׁמוּאֵל וכו׳: *Tosafot* are puzzled by the assertion that this statement is both a support for the opinion of Shmuel and a refutation of the statement of Rav Yosef, for the opposite would appear to be the case; accepting Shmuel's opinion should remove any difficulty with the statement of Rav Yosef. Once it is established that *ḥalitza* with the woman who received levirate betrothal does not exempt the rival wife, it is clear that Rav Yosef's insistence on not performing *ḥalitza* when unnecessary is not relevant to this case, as here it is necessary. They answer that this line should be read as support for Shmuel or a refutation of Rav Yosef. However, the early commentaries point out that the letter *vav* usually means "and" and only rarely means "or" in the Gemara. Some commentaries therefore explain that the Gemara is saying that even according to Shmuel's opinion, if Rav Yosef's opinion is accepted the *yavam* should be obliged to perform *ḥalitza* with the first woman, such that when he later performs *ḥalitza* with the second one he should at least not disqualify her by Torah law (*Tosefot HaRosh*).

Rabbeinu Ḥananel has a very different opinion. He claims that the Gemara is not referring to Rav Yosef's opinion with regard to: He should not pour out the water of his pit, when others require them (12a), indicating that one should not needlessly disqualify a woman, but rather his opinion that: One who hoes the property of a convert…has not acquired it (52b). According to this interpretation, if the *yavam* performed levirate betrothal under the mistaken impression that it fully acquires her as a wife, the acquisition is considered an error, and it should therefore be entirely discounted.

The Ramban objects to this interpretation, as it would mean that the difficulty does not refer to this particular section of the mishna, but to multiple clauses of the mishna, and there was no reason to raise it at this juncture. The Ramban himself suggests that the Sages of the Gemara had a tradition that Rav Yosef disagrees with Shmuel. The *Tosefot HaRosh* similarly explains that the reference here is to Rav Yosef's assertion in tractate *Megilla* (18b) that Shmuel's opinion with regard to the levirate bond is a minority opinion. Therefore, if this mishna supports Shmuel it automatically presents a difficulty to that statement of Rav Yosef.

וּתְיוּבְתָּא דְּרַב יוֹסֵף! מִי קָתָנֵי "חוֹלֵץ"? "חָלַץ" קָתָנֵי, דִּיעֲבַד.

And this would constitute **a conclusive refutation of Rav Yosef's** opinion, for he holds that it is preferable to perform *ḥalitza* with the woman who received levirate betrothal and thereby exempt the second woman. As the first woman requires a bill of divorce and therefore is necessarily disqualified from marrying into the priesthood, it is preferable to perform *ḥalitza* with her as well and consequently leave the second woman eligible to marry a priest. The Gemara refutes this claim: **Does** the mishna **teach: He should perform *ḥalitza*,** which would imply that the *yavam* should do so *ab initio*? It **teaches** that **he performed *ḥalitza*,** implying that the ruling in the mishna is **after the fact.** Therefore, there is no indication in the mishna that the *yavam* should perform *ḥalitza* with the second woman, and it is possible that if he were to perform *ḥalitza* with the first woman he would thereby exempt the second one. It is simply that the particular case discussed by the mishna here concerns a man who performed levirate betrothal with this woman and *ḥalitza* with that one.

"גֵּט לָזוֹ וְגֵט לָזוֹ" כו׳. לֵימָא מְסַיַּיע לֵיהּ לְרַבָּה בַּר רַב הוּנָא, דְּאָמַר רַבָּה בַּר רַב הוּנָא: חֲלִיצָה פְּסוּלָה – צְרִיכָה לַחֲזוֹר עַל כׇּל הָאַחִין. מַאי "צְרִיכוֹת" צְרִיכוֹת דְּעָלְמָא.

It is further taught in the mishna: If he gave **a bill of divorce to this one and a bill of divorce to that one,** they require *ḥalitza* from him. The Gemara suggests: **Let us say** that **it supports** the statement of **Rabba bar Rav Huna.**[N] **As Rabba bar Rav Huna said:** In cases of **invalid *ḥalitza*,** the *yevama* **is required to repeat** the *ḥalitza*[H] **with all of the brothers,** as that single invalid *ḥalitza* is insufficient. Similarly, in this case of invalid *ḥalitza*, it would be necessary to perform *ḥalitza* with all of the *yevamot*. The Gemara rejects this suggestion: **What is** the meaning of **require** in this context? It means that such women **require in general.** The plural form does not refer to all the *yevamot* mentioned in the mishna, but rather it means that all *yevamot* in similar situations require *ḥalitza*.

"גֵּט לָזוֹ וְחָלַץ לָזוֹ". לֵימָא מְסַיַּיע לֵיהּ לִשְׁמוּאֵל וְתֶהֱוֵי תְּיוּבְתָּא דְּרַב יוֹסֵף! מִי קָתָנֵי "חוֹלֵץ"? "חָלַץ" קָתָנֵי, דִּיעֲבַד.

It was taught in the mishna: If he gave **a bill of divorce to this one and performed *ḥalitza* with that one,** nothing is effective after *ḥalitza*. The Gemara suggests: **Let us say that this supports** the opinion of **Shmuel,** as it indicates that the *yavam* should perform *ḥalitza* with the rival wife rather than the woman who received a bill of divorce. **And** it would likewise be **a conclusive refutation of** the opinion of **Rav Yosef,** who prefers performing *ḥalitza* with the disqualified woman. The Gemara again rejects this proof: **Does it teach: He should perform *ḥalitza*,** a ruling *ab initio*? **It teaches: He performed *ḥalitza*,** which is only **after the fact,** meaning he acted in that manner in this particular case.

"חָלַץ וְחָלַץ אוֹ חָלַץ" וכו׳. וְלִיתְנֵי נַמִי אֵין אַחַר בִּיאָה כְּלוּם! אַבָּיֵי וְרָבָא דְּאָמְרִי תַּרְוַיְיהוּ, תְּנִי: אֵין אַחַר בִּיאָה כְּלוּם. וְתַנָּא דִּידַן – הֶתֵּרַת יְבָמָה לַשּׁוּק עֲדִיפָא לֵיהּ.

The mishna taught that if **he performed *ḥalitza*** with one woman **and** then **performed *ḥalitza*** with another one, **or he performed *ḥalitza*** and then proceeded to perform levirate betrothal, nothing is effective after *ḥalitza*. The Gemara suggests: **And let** the *tanna* **also teach: Nothing is** effective **after intercourse,** as this is indicated in the mishna as well. The Gemara answers: Indeed, **Abaye and Rava both say** that it should **teach: Nothing is** effective **after intercourse.** The Gemara comments: **And the *tanna* of our** mishna did not state this because **the permission for a *yevama*** to marry a member of the **public is preferable to him,** and he therefore specified a case that involves *ḥalitza*.

"בֵּין יָבָם אֶחָד לִשְׁתֵּי יְבָמוֹת" כו׳. בִּשְׁלָמָא לְרַבִּי יוֹחָנָן, דְּאָמַר: כּוּלָּהּ בֵּיתָא בְּלָאו קָאֵי, אִיצְטְרִיךְ לְאַשְׁמוֹעִינַן דְּאֵין קִדּוּשִׁין תּוֹפְסִין בְּחַיָּיבֵי לָאוִין.

§ It was taught in the mishna: Nothing is effective after *ḥalitza*, **both** in cases of **one *yavam*** to **two *yevamot*,** as well as cases of two *yevamin* to one *yevama*. The Gemara comments: **Granted, according to** the opinion of **Rabbi Yoḥanan, who said** that once a *yavam* has performed *ḥalitza* with his *yevama*, **the entire household,** the woman who performed *ḥalitza* as well as her rival wives, **is liable due to a prohibition**[N] derived from the verse "So shall it be done to the man who does not build his brother's house" (Deuteronomy 25:9), but the women are not liable to *karet* due to the prohibition with regard to a brother's wife. In light of Rabbi Yoḥanan's ruling, **it was necessary to teach us that betrothal does not take effect on** the rival wife of the woman who performed *ḥalitza*, despite the fact that she is only **liable for** violating **a prohibition,** in accordance with the opinion of Rabbi Akiva.

NOTES

Let us say that it supports Rabba bar Rav Huna, etc. – לֵימָא מְסַיַּיע לֵיהּ לְרַבָּה בַּר רַב הוּנָא וכו׳: Rashi and other commentaries maintain that the proof is not from this precise section of the mishna that states that both *yevamot* must perform *ḥalitza*, but rather from the continuation: And similarly two *yevamin*, etc., from which we learn that another *ḥalitza* is required even when there are two *yevamin*. The Ritva claims that it is not necessary to explain in this manner, for if invalid *ḥalitza* must be repeated with all the women, it must certainly be repeated with multiple brothers.

The entire household is liable due to a prohibition – כּוּלָּהּ בֵּיתָא בְּלָאו: The Ramban notes that according to Rabbeinu Ḥananel's version of the text (11a), which states that Rabbi Yoḥanan maintains that if one of the brothers has relations with one of the rival wives after *yibbum* has been performed, he violates a prohibition, the Gemara can be read in a straightforward manner. But according to our reading of the text there, which states that in that situation the entire house is liable due to a positive mitzva, the Gemara here is difficult. It must be interpreted as saying that Rabbi Yoḥanan holds that this prohibition is certainly no more than a regular prohibition, and there is a novel ruling being taught if there is a prohibition and all the more so if there is merely a positive mitzva. The novelty in that case would be that betrothal is ineffective for those liable for violating a positive mitzva, as claimed by Rabbi Yesheivav (49a).

HALAKHA

Invalid *ḥalitza*, she is required to repeat it – חֲלִיצָה פְּסוּלָה צְרִיכָה לַחֲזוֹר: The dispute as to whether a woman who performed invalid *ḥalitza* must repeat the ḥalitza with all the brothers is left unresolved by the Gemara here. Indeed, some commentaries claim that according to the opinion that one who performed invalid *ḥalitza* is required to repeat it with all the brothers, the same *halakha* applies to all her rival wives, as they all require *ḥalitza* as well. According to the opinion that she does not require *ḥalitza* from all the brothers, however, a single *ḥalitza* is sufficient, whether we are dealing with two *yevamot* or two *yevamin* (Rambam *Sefer Nashim*, *Hilkhot Yibbum* 5:11; *Shulḥan Arukh*, *Even HaEzer* 170:5).

אֶלָּא לְרֵישׁ לָקִישׁ, דְּאָמַר: כּוּלָּהּ בֵּיתָא בְּכָרֵת קָאֵי – אִיצְטְרִיךְ לְאַשְׁמוֹעִינַן דְּאֵין קִדּוּשִׁין תּוֹפְסִין בְּחַיָּיבֵי כָּרֵיתוֹת?!

However, according to Reish Lakish, who said that the **entire household,** apart from the woman who received *ḥalitza,* **is liable** to receive ***karet*****, was it necessary to teach us that betrothal does not take effect on** forbidden relations for which one **is liable** to receive ***karet*****?** According to Reish Lakish, after the *yavam* performs *ḥalitza,* the mitzva of levirate marriage is canceled and the *karet* prohibition against marrying a brother's wife is once again in force. As all agree that betrothal does not take effect on those liable to receive *karet,* it is unnecessary for the mishna to teach this ruling.

אָמַר לָךְ רֵישׁ לָקִישׁ: וְלִיטַעֲמִיךְ, סֵיפָא דְּקָתָנֵי: בָּעַל וְעָשָׂה מַאֲמָר, אִיצְטְרִיךְ לְאַשְׁמוֹעִינַן דְּאֵין קִדּוּשִׁין תּוֹפְסִין בְּאֵשֶׁת אִישׁ?

The Gemara answers: **Reish Lakish** could have **said to you: And according to your reasoning,** that the mishna would not be teaching us an apparently obvious *halakha,* consider the **latter clause** of the mishna, **which teaches** that if a *yavam* **engaged in intercourse and** another *yavam* **performed levirate betrothal** with the same woman, the levirate betrothal is not effective. Now **was it necessary to teach us that betrothal is not effective for a married woman?** Once a *yavam* has engaged in relations with a *yevama* she is his full-fledged wife, and certainly no other betrothal is effective.

אֶלָּא: אַיְּידֵי דְּתָנָא הַתָּרַת יָבָם אֶחָד וִיבָמָה אַחַת – תָּנָא נַמִי שְׁתֵּי יְבָמוֹת וְיָבָם אֶחָד, וְאַיְּידֵי דְּתָנָא שְׁתֵּי יְבָמוֹת וְיָבָם אֶחָד – תָּנָא נַמִי שְׁתֵּי יְבָמִין וִיבָמָה אַחַת.

Rather, it must be that not every clause in the mishna teaches a novel *halakha,* and the reasoning of the *tanna* is as follows: **Since he teaches the release of** the bond between **one** ***yavam*** **and one** ***yevama*****, he also teaches** the case of **two** ***yevamot*** **and one** ***yavam*****,** **and since he teaches** the case of **two** ***yevamot*** **and one** ***yavam*****, he also teaches** the case of **two** ***yevamin*** **and one** ***yevama*****.** The *tanna* therefore listed all possible cases even though we do not learn a novel *halakha* from each and every one.

Perek **V**
Daf **53** Amud **b**

NOTES

It was necessary to teach the case of one who performed ***ḥalitza*** **and then performed levirate betrothal, etc. – חָלַץ וְעָשָׂה מַאֲמָר אִיצְטְרִיךְ וכו׳:** The Rosh asks why this justification is necessary as the Gemara could simply have explained as it did on the previous *amud,* that the mishna is emphasizing Rabbi Akiva's opinion that betrothal is ineffective for those liable due to regular prohibitions. He answers that the Gemara preferred to state an alternative explanation than to say that several sections of the mishna teach us the same thing.

We should issue a decree with regard to a bill of divorce that is given after intercourse, etc. – נִגְזוֹר גֵּט דְּבָתַר בְּעִילָה וכו׳: The Rashba and the Ritva explain this statement differently from Rashi. Rashi explains that the decree would require the woman who received a bill of divorce after *ḥalitza* to perform *ḥalitza* again so that it not be confused with a bill of divorce given initially. The others explain that one might have thought that since a bill of divorce given to a *yevama* before intercourse permanently disqualifies her from levirate marriage, we should therefore decree that the bill of divorce she receives after intercourse likewise disqualifies her, and she should once again be considered forbidden to the *yavam* as his brother's wife. The *tanna* therefore teaches that in this case they left the Torah law as it is and did not decree further. The *ge'onim* read: Since a bill of divorce before intercourse is effective, a bill of divorce after intercourse is also effective, a version of the text that supports the Rashba's interpretation.

״חָלַץ וְעָשָׂה מַאֲמָר וְנָתַן״ וכו׳. בִּשְׁלָמָא חָלַץ וְעָשָׂה מַאֲמָר אִיצְטְרִיךְ, סָלְקָא דַּעְתָּךְ אָמִינָא: נִגְזוֹר מַאֲמָר דְּבָתַר חֲלִיצָה אַטּוּ מַאֲמָר דְּקַמֵּי חֲלִיצָה – קָא מַשְׁמַע לָן דְּלָא גָּזְרִינַן. אֶלָּא חָלַץ וְנָתַן גֵּט לָמָּה לִי?

§ It was taught in the mishna: If **he performed** ***ḥalitza*** **and** then proceeded to either **perform levirate betrothal, or give** a bill of divorce, or engage in intercourse with a second woman, nothing is effective after *ḥalitza.* The Gemara asks: **Granted, it was necessary** to teach that in the case of one who **performed** ***ḥalitza*** **and then performed levirate betrothal**[N] the levirate betrothal is not effective. For **it might enter your mind to say** that **we should issue a decree** with regard to **levirate betrothal that** takes place **after** ***ḥalitza*** **due to levirate betrothal that** takes place **before** ***ḥalitza*****,** and rule that all levirate betrothal is effective. The mishna therefore **teaches us that we do not issue a decree** in this case. **However,** the case of one who **performed** ***ḥalitza*** **and gave a bill of divorce, why do I** need this case? What novelty is there in the teaching that a bill of divorce after *ḥalitza* is not effective?

וּלְטַעֲמִיךְ אֵימָא סֵיפָא: בָּעַל וְעָשָׂה מַאֲמָר, בָּעַל וְנָתַן גֵּט – בִּשְׁלָמָא בָּעַל וְנָתַן גֵּט אִיצְטְרִיךְ, סָלְקָא דַּעְתָּךְ אָמִינָא: נִגְזוֹר גֵּט דְּבָתַר בְּעִילָה אַטּוּ גֵּט דְּקַמֵּי בְּעִילָה, קָא מַשְׁמַע לָן דְּלָא גָּזְרִינַן. אֲבָל בָּעַל וְעָשָׂה מַאֲמָר לָמָּה לִי?

The Gemara answers: **And according to your reasoning,** that each new case must teach something new, **say the latter clause** of the mishna: If **he engaged in intercourse and** then proceeded to **perform levirate betrothal, or give a bill of divorce, or perform** ***ḥalitza*** with a second woman, nothing is effective. In this case the same question can be asked: **Granted, it was necessary** to teach the case of one who **engaged in intercourse and gave a bill of divorce.** This is because **it might enter your mind to say** that **we should issue a decree** with regard to **a bill of divorce that** is given **after intercourse,**[N] **due to a bill of divorce that** is given **before intercourse,** and decree that this bill of divorce alone is insufficient and she requires *ḥalitza* as well. The mishna therefore **teaches us that we do not issue** such **a decree. But** the case of a *yavam* who **engaged in intercourse and performed levirate betrothal, why do I** need to state it? Once he has engaged in intercourse with her she is his wife in all regards; what difference does levirate betrothal make?

אֶלָּא: אַיְּידֵי דְּתָנָא חָלַץ וְעָשָׂה מַאֲמָר – תָּנָא נַמִי בָּעַל וְעָשָׂה מַאֲמָר, וְאַיְּידֵי דְּבָעֵי לְמִיתְנֵי בָּעַל וְנָתַן גֵּט – תָּנָא נַמִי חָלַץ וְנָתַן גֵּט.

Rather, one must say that **since** the *tanna* **taught** the case of one who **performed *ḥalitza* and** then **performed levirate betrothal, he also taught** the case of one who **engaged in intercourse and** then **performed levirate betrothal,** due to the similarity between them. **And since he wished to teach** the case of one who **engaged in intercourse and** then **gave a bill of divorce, he also taught** the case of one who **performed *ḥalitza* and** then **gave a bill of divorce.** We should therefore not infer anything from these superfluous cases, as they are merely stated for stylistic reasons.

״בִּזְמַן שֶׁהִיא״ וכו׳. מַתְנִיתִין דְּלָא כִּי הַאי תַּנָּא. דְּתַנְיָא, אַבָּא יוֹסֵי בֶּן יוֹחָנָן אִישׁ יְרוּשָׁלַיִם אוֹמֵר מִשּׁוּם רַבִּי מֵאִיר: אַחַת בְּעִילָה וְאַחַת חֲלִיצָה, בַּתְּחִלָּה – אֵין אַחֲרֶיהָ כְּלוּם, בָּאֶמְצַע וּבַסּוֹף – יֵשׁ אַחֲרֶיהָ כְּלוּם.

§ The mishna taught: With regard to intercourse, **when it is** at the beginning nothing is effective after it, but if it was in the middle or at the end, something is effective after it. The Gemara comments: **The mishna is not in accordance with** the opinion of **this *tanna*. As it is taught** in a *baraita*: **Abba Yosei ben Yoḥanan, a man of Jerusalem, says in the name of Rabbi Meir:** With regard to **both intercourse and *ḥalitza*,** if one of them were performed **at the beginning, nothing is effective after it,** but if they were done **in the middle or at the end,** i.e., they were preceded by some other action, **something is** effective **after it.** According to the mishna, however, nothing is effective after *ḥalitza* regardless of when it was performed.

וְשָׁלֹשׁ מַחֲלוֹקֹת בַּדָּבָר, תַּנָּא קַמָּא סָבַר: בִּיאָה דְּאִיכָּא לְמִיגְזַר – גָּזְרִינַן, חֲלִיצָה דְּלֵיכָּא לְמִיגְזַר – לָא גָּזְרִינַן.

And therefore it can be concluded that there are **three disputes with regard to** this **matter,** i.e., three opinions on this issue. **The first *tanna* holds:** In the case of **intercourse** that is preceded by a disqualifying action, **where there is** a reason **to issue a decree,** lest one violate a prohibition by engaging in intercourse after *ḥalitza* or intercourse was performed, **we issue a decree** establishing that invalid intercourse should not be as effective as valid intercourse. With regard to ***ḥalitza*,** however, **where there is no** reason **to issue a decree** as there is no concern of a prohibition even if an action is performed after *ḥalitza*, **we do not issue a decree.**

וְרַבִּי נְחֶמְיָה סָבַר: בִּיאָה נַמִי לֵיכָּא לְמִיגְזַר. וּדְקָאָמְרַתְּ: לִיגְזוֹר בִּיאָה אַחַר הַגֵּט מִשּׁוּם בִּיאָה אַחַר חֲלִיצָה – כֵּיוָן דַּחֲלִיצָה דְּאוֹרַיְיתָא, מֵידַע יָדְעִי. וּדְקָאָמְרַתְּ לִיגְזוֹר בִּיאָה אַחַר מַאֲמָר מִשּׁוּם בִּיאָה אַחַר בִּיאָה – כֵּיוָן דְּבִיאָה דְּאוֹרַיְיתָא, הָא מֵידַע יְדִיעִי. וְאַבָּא יוֹסֵי בֶּן חָנָן סָבַר לָהּ כְּרַבָּנַן דְּגָזְרִי בְּבִיאָה, וְגָזַר חֲלִיצָה מִשּׁוּם בִּיאָה.

And Rabbi Neḥemya holds that with regard to **intercourse there is also no** reason **to issue a decree. And as** for what **you said** in justification of your ruling, **that we should issue a decree** in a case of **intercourse after a bill of divorce due to intercourse after *ḥalitza*,** there is no cause for such a concern. **Since *ḥalitza*** is effective **by Torah** law, people **know** that it is fully effective and cannot be followed by anything, and they will not confuse it with laws instituted by the Sages. **And as** for what **you said that we should issue a decree** with regard to **intercourse after levirate betrothal due to intercourse after intercourse, since** the acquisition of **intercourse** is **by Torah** law, **this** matter **is known** by people, and they will not err in this regard. **And Abba Yosei ben Ḥanan holds in accordance with** the opinion of **the Rabbis, who issue a decree with regard to intercourse,** but he adds **and issues a decree** with regard to ***ḥalitza* due to intercourse.** He therefore does not differentiate between *ḥalitza* and intercourse at all.

הדרן עלך רבן גמליאל

Summary of **Perek V**

From the discussion in this chapter it became clear that neither performing levirate betrothal nor giving a bill of divorce is a completely efficacious act for a woman requiring levirate marriage. While levirate betrothal effects some degree of acquisition and a bill of divorce effects some degree of release, there is room for subsequent acts to be applied, and if performed they are legally binding. This is true regardless of whether the act was performed by the original *yavam* with a different *yevama* or by a different *yavam* with the original *yevama*.

Insofar as intercourse and *ḥalitza* are concerned, we find that their *halakhot* are not identical. On the one hand, intercourse with a *yevama* is completely efficacious, and so long as the intercourse occurred first, i.e., before any other act that might invalidate it, any subsequent act is halakhically insignificant. However, if the act of intercourse followed a different previous act, the intercourse is considered invalid and other subsequent acts have legal implications. On the other hand, with regard to *ḥalitza*, it makes no difference whether it was performed first or after another act; after *ḥalitza* no other act of nullification, neither *ḥalitza* nor a bill of divorce, holds any legal validity. However, acts of acquisition, i.e., intercourse or levirate betrothal, are still efficacious.

In practice, it makes no difference whether any one of these combinations was performed by a single *yavam* with a single *yevama* or two *yevamot*, or by two *yevamin* with a single *yevama* or two *yevamot*. However, if a single *yavam* performed levirate betrothal and engaged in sexual relations with a single *yevama*, this is the proper way to perform the mitzva of levirate marriage. If he engaged in intercourse and then gave her a bill of divorce, then he performed the mitzva of levirate marriage and subsequently divorced the woman.

Halakhic conclusions of this chapter:

First act	Second act	Validity of subsequent acts	What must be done next
Levirate betrothal	Levirate betrothal	All acts are valid	Two bills of divorce and *ḥalitza*
	Bill of divorce	All acts are valid	Bill of divorce for the levirate betrothal and *ḥalitza*
	Intercourse	All acts are valid	Two bills of divorce and *ḥalitza*
	Ḥalitza	Intercourse and levirate betrothal are valid	Bill of divorce
Bill of divorce	Levirate betrothal	All acts are valid	Bill of divorce and *ḥalitza*
	Bill of divorce	All acts are valid	*Ḥalitza*
	Intercourse	All acts are valid	Bill of divorce and *ḥalitza*
	Ḥalitza	Intercourse and levirate betrothal are valid	
Intercourse	Levirate betrothal	All acts are invalid	
	Bill of divorce	All acts are invalid	
	Intercourse	All acts are invalid	
	Ḥalitza	All acts are invalid	
Ḥalitza	Levirate betrothal	Levirate betrothal and intercourse are valid	Bill of divorce
	Bill of divorce	All acts are invalid	
	Intercourse	Levirate betrothal and intercourse are valid	Bill of divorce
	Ḥalitza	All acts are invalid	

Introduction to **Perek VI**

If brothers dwell together and one of them dies and he has no child, the wife of the dead man shall not be married outside of the family to one not of his kin; her brother-in-law will have intercourse with her and take her to him to be his wife and consummate the levirate marriage.

(Deuteronomy 25:5)

By Torah law it is the act of intercourse itself by which the *yevama* is acquired by the *yavam* in fulfillment of the mitzva of levirate marriage. Therefore, it is necessary to determine the exact parameters of the act defined as intercourse for this purpose; both the objective definition of the act as well as the required intentions of the parties involved. Must they intend that the act be for the sake of performing a mitzva, or for the sake of validating the legal transaction? Or are their intentions irrelevant?

The clarification of what is considered a sexual act is useful for other areas of *halakha* as well. With regard to forbidden sexual relations, which acts constitute full-fledged violation of a prohibition? What is the severity of the punishment for a given act? Furthermore, when does a forbidden act of intercourse disqualify a woman from marrying a priest? In the case of marriage, when is a marriage considered to be consummated? These issues are discussed at the beginning of this chapter.

The chapter then turns to address the details governing women disqualified from marrying priests, especially the High Priest. How do these disqualifications come about? Who is included in these categories? Finally, the institution of marriage is addressed, with a particular emphasis on the mitzva to be fruitful and multiply. What is necessary in order to fulfill this mitzva? Who is included in the obligation to have children?

These matters form the bulk of this chapter, but, as is the way of the Talmud, several secondary matters stemming from these primary questions are also discussed.

מתני׳ הַבָּא עַל יְבִמְתּוֹ, בֵּין בְּשׁוֹגֵג בֵּין בְּמֵזִיד בֵּין בְּאוֹנֶס בֵּין בְּרָצוֹן, אֲפִילּוּ הוּא שׁוֹגֵג וְהִיא מְזִידָה, הוּא מֵזִיד וְהִיא שׁוֹגֶגֶת, הוּא אָנוּס וְהִיא לֹא אֲנוּסָה, הִיא אֲנוּסָה וְהוּא לֹא אָנוּס. אֶחָד הַמְעָרֶה וְאֶחָד הַגּוֹמֵר – קָנָה, וְלֹא חִילֵּק בֵּין בִּיאָה לְבִיאָה.

MISHNA **One who had intercourse with his** ***yevama*****, whether unwittingly,** i.e., he thought he was having intercourse with someone else, **or intentionally,**[N] i.e., he knew she was his *yevama* and nevertheless had intercourse with her without intent to perform levirate marriage; **whether** due to **coercion or willingly; even if he** was **unwitting and her** participation was **intentional, his** participation was **intentional and she** was **unwitting, he was coerced and she was not coerced,** or **she was coerced and he was not coerced; both one who** merely **engages in the initial stage of intercourse**[N] **and one who completes** the act of intercourse **has** thereby **acquired** his *yevama*.[H] **And** similarly, the Torah **did not distinguish between** an act of **intercourse** in an atypical manner, i.e., anal intercourse, **and intercourse** in a typical manner.

וְכֵן הַבָּא עַל אַחַת מִכָּל הָעֲרָיוֹת שֶׁבַּתּוֹרָה, אוֹ פְּסוּלוֹת, כְּגוֹן: אַלְמָנָה לְכֹהֵן גָּדוֹל, גְּרוּשָׁה וַחֲלוּצָה לְכֹהֵן הֶדְיוֹט, מַמְזֶרֶת וּנְתִינָה לְיִשְׂרָאֵל, בַּת יִשְׂרָאֵל לְמַמְזֵר וּלְנָתִין – פְּסָלָהּ, וְלֹא חִילֵּק בֵּין בִּיאָה לְבִיאָה.

And so too, with regard to a man **who had intercourse with any one of those with whom relations are forbidden** [***arayot***] **by the Torah or** with those who are **unfit for him** even though they are not in the category of *arayot*, **for example, a widow with a High Priest; a divorcée and a** ***yevama*** **who performed** ***ḥalitza*** [***ḥalutza***] **with a common priest;** **a** ***mamzeret***, i.e., a woman born from an incestuous or adulterous relationship, **or a Gibeonite woman with an Israelite; the daughter of an Israelite with a** ***mamzer*** **or a Gibeonite; he has disqualified her** from marrying into the priesthood through this act no matter how it was performed, **and** the Torah **did not distinguish between** the act of **intercourse** in an atypical manner, i.e., anal intercourse, **and intercourse** in a typical manner.[H]

גמ׳ מַאי אֲפִילּוּ?

GEMARA The Gemara asks: **What is** the significance of the word **even** in the statement that begins with: Even if he was unwitting and her participation was intentional? Since the mishna has already said that there is no halakhic difference whether the act of intercourse was performed intentionally, what is added by that statement?

לָא מִיבָּעֲיָא קָאָמַר: לָא מִיבָּעֲיָא הוּא שׁוֹגֵג וְהִיא קָמְכַוְּונָה לְמִצְוָה, אִי נַמִּי הוּא מֵזִיד וְהִיא קָמְכַוְּונָה לְמִצְוָה, אֶלָּא אֲפִילּוּ הוּא שׁוֹגֵג וְהִיא מְזִידָה, דְּתַרְוַיְיהוּ לֹא קָמְכַוְּונֵי לְשֵׁם מִצְוָה – אֲפִילּוּ הָכִי קָנָה. תָּנֵי רַבִּי חִיָּיא: אֲפִילּוּ שְׁנֵיהֶם שׁוֹגְגִים, שְׁנֵיהֶם מְזִידִים, שְׁנֵיהֶם אֲנוּסִים.

The Gemara answers: The mishna is stated in the style of: **Needless to say.** It is **needless to say** that if **he** was **unwitting and she intended** to fulfill the **mitzva,** or **alternatively, he** acted **intentionally** without intent to fulfill the mitzva **and she intended** to fulfill the **mitzva,** he has acquired her. **However, even if he** was **unwitting and she** acted **intentionally, where both of them did not intend** to act **for the sake of the mitzva, he nevertheless acquires** her. Similarly, **Rabbi Ḥiyya taught: Even if both of them** acted **unwittingly, intentionally,** or **were coerced,** he acquires the *yevama* through the act of intercourse.

אָנוּס דְּמַתְנִיתִין הֵיכִי דָּמֵי? אִילֵּימָא כְּשֶׁאֲנָסוּהוּ גּוֹיִם וּבָא עָלֶיהָ – וְהָאָמַר רָבָא: אֵין אוֹנֶס לְעֶרְוָה, לְפִי שֶׁאֵין קִישּׁוּי אֶלָּא לְדַעַת.

§ The Gemara asks: **What are the circumstances the mishna** is referring to when it mentions a man who **was coerced? If we say** that it is **when gentiles coerced him** by threatening to kill him if he did not have intercourse with her **and** he therefore **had intercourse with her, didn't Rava say** that **there is no** such thing as **coercion** of a man to have intercourse with a woman **with whom relations are forbidden,**[NH] **because there is no erection** of the male organ **without intent?**[B] Consequently, even if he acted due to the threat, his action is considered intentional.

אֶלָּא בְּיָשֵׁן – וְהָאָמַר רַב יְהוּדָה

Rather, the mishna must be referring to **one who was sleeping** and became erect, and his *yevama* drew him onto herself. However, **didn't Rav Yehuda say** that

NOTES

Whether unwittingly or intentionally, etc. – **בֵּין בְּשׁוֹגֵג בֵּין בְּמֵזִיד וכו׳**: *Tosafot* inquired why the mishna specified both the case of one who had intercourse intentionally and the case of one who had intercourse willingly. What is the difference between these cases? They explain that the term willingly indicates that one does so with intention to fulfill the mitzva, whereas the term intentionally means that one acts purposefully but without intent to fulfill the mitzva.

One who engages in the initial stage of intercourse – **הַמְעָרֶה**: This term is subsequently explained in the Gemara on 55b.

There is no coercion of a man to have intercourse with a woman with whom relations are forbidden – **אֵין אוֹנֶס לְעֶרְוָה**: The Ramban cites a dispute with regard to this principle. Some explain that if a man is threatened with death unless he engages in an act of forbidden relations, and he commits the act, he is punishable in court for the forbidden relations due to Rava's principle that there is no coercion of a man with regard to intercourse. Others say that the man is not punishable in court because he is considered to be coerced, despite the fact that, *ab initio*, he is obligated to give up his life rather than engage in forbidden relations. Rather, Rava's principle applies to a case in which a woman or a third person coerced him to engage in intercourse, but not under pain of death. In this case, Rava's principle determines that it is as though he intentionally committed the act and he is not considered coerced. Nevertheless, the Gemara did not explain that the case of coercion in the mishna is one where the man's life has been threatened, as, since he engages in the act of intercourse willingly but for a purpose other than the mitzva, it is no different from the case the mishna refers to as having intercourse intentionally. See also *Tosafot*.

HALAKHA

Any act of intercourse acquires a ***yevama*** – **כָּל בִּיאָה קוֹנָה בִּיבָמָה**: If one has intercourse with his *yevama*, whether intentionally or unwittingly, regardless of whether either party was coerced or willing, he has thereby acquired her and they are married. Furthermore, it makes no difference whether it was a typical act of intercourse or anal intercourse, nor whether he completed the act or merely began it (Rambam *Sefer Nashim*, *Hilkhot Yibbum* 2:3; *Shulḥan Arukh*, *Even HaEzer* 166:7).

Prohibited and disqualifying intercourse – **בִּיאָה אֲסוּרָה וּפוֹסֶלֶת**: A prohibited act of intercourse is considered to have occurred as soon as the act has begun, regardless of whether the act was completed or whether it was a typical act of intercourse or anal intercourse. Furthermore, the woman is disqualified from marrying a priest regardless of whether she or the man engaged in the act intentionally or willingly, as long as she is at least three years old and he is at least nine years old (Rambam *Sefer Kedusha*, *Hilkhot Issurei Bia* 18:6; *Shulḥan Arukh*, *Even HaEzer* 6:9; 20:1, and in the comment of Rema).

There is no coercion of a man to have intercourse with a woman with whom relations are forbidden – **אֵין אוֹנֶס לְעֶרְוָה**: A woman who was coerced to engage in forbidden relations is exempt from all penalties. However, a man who is coerced is liable to receive punishment. Since Rava ruled that erection occurs willingly, he is not considered to have been coerced at all. The Ra'avad adds that even a man can be coerced and therefore exempt from punishment if he became erect while intending to have intercourse with his wife, and then someone forcibly coerced him to engage in a prohibited act of intercourse. The *Maggid Mishne* writes that even the Rambam would agree that in this rare case, the man would be considered coerced and would be exempt from punishment (Rambam *Sefer Nashim*, *Hilkhot Issurei Bia* 1:9).

BACKGROUND

Intentional erection – **קִישּׁוּי לְדַעַת**: The nerves that cause erection are usually activated voluntarily. Although it is possible that an erection could be caused by a kind of mechanical stimulation, the assumption here is that a man's desire is largely in control of these nerves, and emotional causes are the decisive factor in the arousal of erection. The conclusion implied by the Gemara that erections are necessarily intentional is to be understood in the sense that there has to be some cooperation on the part of the man for it to occur.

יָשֵׁן לֹא קָנָה בִּיבִמְתּוֹ! אֶלָּא – בְּנִתְקָע? וְהָא אָמַר רַבָּה: נָפַל מִן הַגַּג וְנִתְקַע – חַיָּיב בְּאַרְבָּעָה דְּבָרִים, וּבִיבִמְתּוֹ לֹא קָנָה!

a sleeping man **has not acquired his** ***yevama*****,**[H] as he did not intend to perform the act of intercourse at all? **Rather,** the mishna was referring **to one who was inserted** into his *yevama* by accident. But **didn't Rabba say:** One who **fell from a roof and was inserted** into a woman due to the force of his fall **is liable** to pay **four** of the five **types of indemnity**[H] that must be paid by one who damaged another: Injury, pain, medical costs, and loss of livelihood. However, he is not liable to pay for the shame he caused her, as he did not intend to perform the act, **and if** she is **his** ***yevama*****, he has not acquired** her[H] in this manner.

אֶלָּא: כְּגוֹן שֶׁנִּתְכַּוֵּון לְאִשְׁתּוֹ, וּתְקָפַתּוּ יְבִמְתּוֹ, וּבָא עָלֶיהָ, שְׁנֵיהֶם אֲנוּסִים דְּבֵי רַבִּי חִיָּיא הֵיכִי דָמֵי? כְּגוֹן שֶׁנִּתְכַּוֵּון לְאִשְׁתּוֹ, וּתְקָפוּהוּ גוֹיִם וְדִבְּקוּם זֶה בָּזֶה, וּבָא עָלֶיהָ.

Rather, it is a case **where he intended** to have intercourse with **his wife** and became erect, **and his** ***yevama*** forcefully **grabbed hold of him and he had intercourse with her.** The Gemara further asks: If so, **what are the circumstances** of the case when **both of them were coerced** that was mentioned by **the school of Rabbi Ḥiyya?** The Gemara answers: It is a case **where he intended** to have intercourse with **his wife, and gentiles grabbed hold of him and pressed** him and his *yevama* **against each other, and he** thereby **had intercourse with her.**

מְנָא הָנֵי מִילֵּי? דְּתָנוּ רַבָּנַן: ״יְבָמָהּ יָבֹא עָלֶיהָ״ מִצְוָה. דָּבָר אַחֵר: ״יְבָמָהּ יָבֹא עָלֶיהָ״ בֵּין בְּשׁוֹגֵג בֵּין בְּמֵזִיד, בֵּין בְּאוֹנֶס בֵּין בְּרָצוֹן.

§ The Gemara inquires as to the source of these *halakhot*: **From where are these matters** derived? **As the Sages taught** with regard to the verse **"Her brother-in-law will have intercourse with her"** (Deuteronomy 25:5),[N] that this indicates that the act of intercourse in this circumstance is **a mitzva**, i.e., it is preferable to the alternative, which is *ḥalitza*. **Alternatively,** the verse **"Her brother-in-law will have intercourse with her,"** indicates that it does not matter how he had intercourse with her, **whether unwittingly or intentionally, whether** due to **coercion or willingly.**

וְהָא אַפֵּיקְתֵּיהּ לְמִצְוָה! לְמִצְוָה מ״וְאִם לֹא יַחְפֹּץ הָאִישׁ״ נָפְקָא, הָא חָפֵץ – יַבֵּם, וְכִי אֲתָא קְרָא – בֵּין בְּשׁוֹגֵג בֵּין בְּמֵזִיד בֵּין בְּאוֹנֶס בֵּין בְּרָצוֹן.

The Gemara asks: **Didn't you derive** from this phrase that the act of intercourse in this case is **a mitzva?** How can the same phrase also indicate that it does not matter what the intentions of the two parties were during the act of intercourse? The Gemara answers: The fact that it is **a mitzva is derived from** the verse: **"And if the man does not wish** to take his *yevama*" (Deuteronomy 25:7), which indicates that if he **wishes, he performs levirate marriage,** which is preferable to *ḥalitza*. Therefore, **when** the **verse** cited above **came,** it indicated that levirate marriage has occurred **whether** the parties acted **unwittingly or intentionally, whether** due to **coercion or willingly.**

תַּנְיָא אִידַּךְ: ״יְבָמָהּ יָבֹא עָלֶיהָ״ כְּדַרְכָּהּ, ״וּלְקָחָהּ״ שֶׁלֹּא כְּדַרְכָּהּ. ״וְיִבְּמָהּ״ בִּיאָה גּוֹמֶרֶת בָּהּ וְאֵין כֶּסֶף וּשְׁטָר גּוֹמְרִין בָּהּ. ״וְיִבְּמָהּ״ בְּעַל כָּרְחָהּ. דָּבָר אַחֵר: ״יְבָמָהּ יָבֹא עָלֶיהָ״ בֵּין בְּשׁוֹגֵג כו׳.

It is taught in **another** *baraita* that the phrase: **"Her brother-in-law will have intercourse with her"** indicates that levirate marriage has been performed if they engage in **typical** sexual intercourse. The next phrase, **"and take her,"** includes even **atypical,** i.e., anal, sexual intercourse. The concluding phrase of the verse, **"and consummate the levirate marriage,"** indicates that **sexual intercourse completes her** acquisition, **but money and a** marriage **document do not**[H] **complete her** acquisition to him as his fully betrothed wife, in contrast to the regular *halakhot* of marriage. By emphasizing **"and consummate the levirate marriage with her,"** the verse teaches that he acquires her even if he acted **against her will. Alternatively: "Her brother-in-law will have intercourse with her"** indicates that levirate marriage has occurred **whether** the parties acted **unwittingly** or intentionally, whether due to coercion or willingly.

וְהָא אַפֵּיקְתֵּיהּ לְכְדַרְכָּהּ! הַהוּא מ״לְהָקִים לְאָחִיו שֵׁם״ נָפְקָא, בְּמָקוֹם שֶׁמְּקִים שֵׁם. וְכִי אֲתָא קְרָא – בֵּין בְּשׁוֹגֵג בֵּין בְּמֵזִיד בֵּין בְּאוֹנֶס בֵּין בְּרָצוֹן.

The Gemara asks: **Didn't you derive** from this phrase that levirate marriage has been performed if they engage in **typical** sexual intercourse? How can it also indicate that it does not matter what the intentions of the two parties were during the act of intercourse? The Gemara answers: **That** *halakha* **is derived from** a different verse: **"To establish a name for his brother"** (Deuteronomy 25:7), which indicates that intercourse must occur **in the place where he establishes a name,** i.e., where it can lead to childbirth. Therefore, **when** the **verse** cited above **came,** it indicated that levirate marriage has occurred **whether** the parties acted **unwittingly or intentionally, whether** due to **coercion or willingly.**

HALAKHA

A sleeping man has not acquired his ***yevama*** **– יָשֵׁן לֹא קָנָה בִּיבִמְתּוֹ:** One who did not intend to perform an act of sexual intercourse, e.g., one who was asleep, drunk, or completely unaware of his actions, does not acquire his *yevama* even if they did engage in sexual intercourse (Rambam *Sefer Nashim, Hilkhot Yibbum* 2:4; *Shulḥan Arukh, Even HaEzer* 166:8).

One who fell from a roof and was inserted into a woman is liable to pay four types of indemnity – נָפַל מִן הַגַּג וְנִתְקַע חַיָּיב בְּאַרְבָּעָה דְּבָרִים: One who fell from a roof due to the force of a normal wind and hurt someone is liable to pay four types of indemnity: Indemnity due to injury, pain, medical costs, and loss of livelihood. However, he is exempt from paying for the victim's shame (Rambam *Sefer Nezikin, Hilkhot Ḥovel* 1:12; *Shulḥan Arukh, Ḥoshen Mishpat* 421:11).

And if she is his ***yevama*****, he has not acquired her – וּבִיבִמְתּוֹ לֹא קָנָה:** One who became erect while intending to have intercourse with his wife and then fell onto his *yevama* has not acquired her (Rambam *Sefer Nashim, Hilkhot Yibbum* 2:4; *Shulḥan Arukh, Even HaEzer* 166:8).

Sexual intercourse completes…but money or a marriage document do not – בִּיאָה גּוֹמֶרֶת...וְאֵין כֶּסֶף וּשְׁטָר: A *yevama* can be fully acquired by her *yavam* only through sexual intercourse, but not by other means that generally effect betrothal, i.e., money or a marriage document. However, the Sages decreed that one should not have intercourse with his *yevama* without betrothing her first (Rambam *Sefer Nashim, Hilkhot Yibbum* 5:9; *Shulḥan Arukh, Even HaEzer* 166:2, 170:2).

NOTES

Her brother-in-law will have intercourse with her, etc. – יְבָמָהּ יָבוֹא עָלֶיהָ וכו׳: The Gemara here cites several expositions of this verse and attempts to demonstrate that only one *halakha* is derived from each expression in the verse. Some of these expositions, as well as additional ones, are also cited in the Jerusalem Talmud, but there the Gemara sees no reason to avoid using a single phrase as the source of multiple expositions.

גּוּפָא, אָמַר רַב יְהוּדָה: יָשֵׁן לֹא קָנָה בִּיבִמְתּוֹ, דְּאָמַר קְרָא ״יְבָמָהּ יָבֹא עָלֶיהָ״ עַד דְּמִכַּוֵּין לָהּ לְשֵׁם בִּיאָה. וְהָתַנְיָא: בֵּין עֵר [בֵּין יָשֵׁן! אֵימָא: בֵּין עֵרָה בֵּין יְשֵׁנָה.

§ The Gemara addresses **the** matter **itself** cited in the previous discussion. **Rav Yehuda said: A sleeping** man **has not acquired his** ***yevama*****, as the verse states: "Her brother-in-law will have intercourse with her"** (Deuteronomy 25:5), which indicates that he does not acquire her **unless he intends** to act **for the sake of sexual intercourse.** Since a sleeping man does not intend to engage in sexual intercourse, he does not acquire his *yevama*. The Gemara asks: **Isn't it taught** in a *baraita* that one acquires his *yevama* through sexual intercourse regardless of **whether he** was **awake or asleep?** The Gemara answers: **Say** the *baraita* in the following emended form: **Whether she** was **awake or asleep.**[H] The woman's awareness is not a necessary component in order to perform levirate marriage.

וְהָתַנְיָא: בֵּין עֵר] הוּא בֵּין יָשֵׁן הוּא. בֵּין עֵרָה הִיא בֵּין יְשֵׁנָה הִיא! הָכָא בְּמַאי עָסְקִינַן – בְּמִתְנַמְנֵם. הֵיכִי דָּמֵי מִתְנַמְנֵם? אֲמַר רַב אַשִׁי: נִים וְלָא נִים, תִּיר וְלָא תִּיר, כְּגוֹן דְּקָרוּ לֵיהּ וְעָנֵי, וְלָא יָדַע לְאַהֲדוּרֵי סְבָרָא, וְכִי מַדְכְּרוּ לֵיהּ מִדְכַּר.

The Gemara asks further: **Wasn't it taught** in another *baraita* that one acquires his *yevama* through sexual intercourse regardless **of whether he was awake or he was asleep** and regardless of **whether she was awake or she was asleep?** The Gemara answers: **With what are we dealing here** when the *baraita* says that a sleeping man acquires his *yevama*? It is referring to a man **who is dozing.** The Gemara asks: **What are the circumstances** of **dozing? Rav Ashi said:** One is **asleep but not asleep, awake but not awake, when,** if **they call him, he** will **answer, but he is unable to provide a reasonable** answer. **And when they** later **inform him** of what happened, **he remembers** it.

גּוּפָא, אָמַר רַבָּה: נָפַל מִן הַגַּג וְנִתְקַע חַיָּיב בְּאַרְבָּעָה דְּבָרִים, וּבִיבִמְתּוֹ לֹא קָנָה: בְּנֶזֶק, בְּצַעַר, בְּשֶׁבֶת, בְּרִפּוּי, אֲבָל בּוֹשֶׁת לָא מִיחַיַּיב, דְּאָמַר מָר: אֵין חַיָּיב עַל הַבּוֹשֶׁת עַד שֶׁיִּתְכַּוֵּין.

The Gemara returns to the statement of Rabba cited earlier in order to discuss **the** matter **itself** that Rabba addressed. **Rabba said:** One who **fell from a roof and was inserted** into a woman due to the force of his fall **is liable** to pay **four** of the five **types of indemnity** that must be paid by one who damaged another, **and if** she is **his** ***yevama*** **he has not acquired** her in this manner. He is liable to pay for **injury, pain, loss of livelihood,** and **medical costs. However, he is not liable** to pay for the **shame** he caused her, **as the Master said: One is not liable** to pay **for shame unless he intends** to humiliate his victim.[H] Consequently, one who fell from a roof accidentally is not liable to pay for the shame he caused the woman.

אָמַר רָבָא: נִתְכַּוֵּון לְהַטִּיחַ בְּכוֹתֶל וְהִטִּיחַ בִּיבִמְתּוֹ – לֹא קָנָה. לְהַטִּיחַ בִּבְהֵמָה וְהִטִּיחַ בִּיבָמָה – קָנָה, דְּהָא קָמְכַּוֵּין לְשֵׁם בִּיאָה בָּעוֹלָם.

Rava said: If **he intended to press** his sexual organ **into a wall, and he** accidentally **pressed** it **into his** ***yevama*****, he has not acquired** her, as he did not intend to engage in an act of sexual intercourse. However, if he intended **to press** his sexual organ **into an animal, and he pressed** it **into his** ***yevama*****, he has acquired** her, **as he** at least **intended** to act **for the purpose of sexual intercourse in general,**[H] i.e., for some form of sexual intercourse.

״אֶחָד הַמְעָרֶה״. אָמַר עוּלָּא: מִנַּיִן לְהַעֲרָאָה מִן הַתּוֹרָה? שֶׁנֶּאֱמַר ״וְאִישׁ אֲשֶׁר יִשְׁכַּב אֶת אִשָּׁה דָּוָה וְגִלָּה אֶת עֶרְוָתָהּ אֶת מְקֹרָהּ הֶעֱרָה״ מִכָּאן לְהַעֲרָאָה מִן הַתּוֹרָה.

§ We learned in the mishna that **both one who** merely **begins the act of intercourse** and one who completes it has acquired the *yevama* through this act. **Ulla said: From where** is it derived that **the initial stage of intercourse** is considered an act of sexual intercourse **by Torah law? As it is stated: "And if a man shall lie with a woman having her sickness and shall uncover her nakedness, he has made naked** [***he'era***] **her fountain"** (Leviticus 20:18). The verse is referring to the first stage of intercourse, and **from here** it is derived that **the initial stage of intercourse** [***ha'ara'a***] is considered sexual intercourse **by Torah law.**

אַשְׁכַּחַן נִדָּה, שְׁאָר עֲרָיוֹת מִנַּיִן? וְכִי תֵּימָא: נֵילַף מִנִּדָּה – מַה לְנִדָּה שֶׁכֵּן מְטַמְּאָה אֶת בּוֹעֲלָהּ!

The Gemara asks: **We have found** a source for this *halakha* in the case of **a menstruating woman,** the subject of the verse cited above. **From where** is it derived that the initial stage of intercourse is considered sexual intercourse with regard to **the rest of those with whom relations are forbidden? And if you say we should derive it from** the *halakha* with regard to **a menstruating woman, what** comparison can be made **to a menstruating woman,** concerning whom the *halakha* is more stringent than others with whom relations are forbidden, **in that she causes one who has intercourse with her to become ritually impure?**[H]

HALAKHA

Whether she was awake or asleep – בֵּין עֵרָה בֵּין יְשֵׁנָה: One who had intercourse with his *yevama* has acquired her regardless of whether she was awake or asleep (Rambam *Sefer Nashim*, *Hilkhot Yibbum* 2:3; *Shulḥan Arukh*, *Even HaEzer* 166:7).

One is not liable to pay for shame unless he intends to humiliate his victim – אֵין חַיָּיב עַל הַבּוֹשֶׁת עַד שֶׁיִּתְכַּוֵּין: One is not liable to pay for shaming another individual unless he intended to do so. One who unintentionally shames another individual is exempt from monetary liability (Rambam *Sefer Nezikin*, *Hilkhot Ḥovel* 1:10; *Shulḥan Arukh*, *Ḥoshen Mishpat* 421:1).

As he at least intended to act for the purpose of sexual intercourse in general – דְּהָא קָמְכַּוֵּין לְשֵׁם בִּיאָה בָּעוֹלָם: If one intended to perform an act of sexual intercourse, and he happened to have intercourse with his *yevama*, he has acquired her. However, if he did not mean to engage in sexual intercourse at all and nevertheless had intercourse with his *yevama*, he has not acquired her, as stated by Rava (Rambam *Sefer Nashim*, *Hilkhot Yibbum* 2:4; *Shulḥan Arukh*, *Even HaEzer* 166:8).

A menstruating woman…causes one who has intercourse with her to become ritually impure – נִדָּה...מְטַמְּאָה אֶת בּוֹעֲלָהּ: One who had intercourse with a menstruating woman becomes a primary source of ritual impurity with the same *halakhot* as the menstruating woman herself. He transmits impurity to vessels or individuals that come in contact with him or carry him as well as to items that he causes to move. Additionally, if he sits or lies upon an item that is designated for this purpose, it becomes impure even if he did not have direct contact with it or cause it to move (Rambam *Sefer Tahara*, *Hilkhot Metamei Mishkav UMoshav* 3:1).

NOTES

It is within his power to increase – שֶׁכֵּן בְּיָדוֹ לְרַבּוֹת: The argument is that since this prohibition is stringent in that the number of individuals to whom it applies can be increased, perhaps it is also stringent with regard to the manner in which it can be violated. Therefore, it cannot be derived that if the initial stage of intercourse is considered an act of sexual intercourse in this case, it is always considered sexual intercourse (Ritva).

Let it come by deriving the *halakha* in any one case from two of the sources mentioned above – תֵּיתֵי חֲדָא מִתַּרְתֵּי: Rashi and *Tosafot* understood that the *halakha* is derived from the common denominator between two of the sources mentioned above. However, the *Tosefot HaRosh* apparently understood that the *halakha* with regard to some forbidden relations would be derived from one source, and that other *halakhot* would be derived from the other source. The *Arukh LaNer* notes that the *Tosefot HaRosh* must have had a slightly different version of the Gemara text, as the phrase: Let it come by deriving the *halakha* in any one case from two of the sources mentioned above, implies that both sources are needed to derive a single prohibition.

אֶלָּא: אָתְיָא מֵאֵשֶׁת אָח, דִּכְתִיב ״וְאִישׁ אֲשֶׁר יִקַּח אֶת אֵשֶׁת אָחִיו נִדָּה הִיא״, וְכִי אֵשֶׁת אָחִיו [לְעוֹלָם] נִדָּה הִיא? אֶלָּא: כְּנִדָּה, מַה נִּדָּה בְּהַעֲרָאָה – אַף אֵשֶׁת אָח בְּהַעֲרָאָה.

Rather, the *halakha* in other cases **comes from** a verse about **a brother's wife, as it is written: "And if a man shall take his brother's wife, it is impurity [*nidda*]"** (Leviticus 20:21). The word *nidda* generally refers to a menstruating woman, and so the Gemara asks: **Is his brother's wife always menstruating? Rather,** it means that the *halakha* with regard to her is **like** that of **a menstruating woman: Just as** one is liable to receive punishment for violating the prohibition against engaging in sexual intercourse with **a menstruating woman through the initial stage of intercourse, so too,** one is liable to receive punishment for violating the prohibition against engaging in sexual intercourse with **a brother's wife through the initial stage of intercourse.**

מַה לְּאֵשֶׁת אָח שֶׁכֵּן בְּיָדוֹ לְרַבּוֹת, דְּאִי בָּעֵי מְקַדֵּשׁ וְאָזֵיל כִּי אַלְפָּא!

The Gemara asks: **What** comparison can be made between **a brother's wife** and other women with whom relations are forbidden? The prohibition with regard to a brother's **wife is** more stringent in that **it is within his power to increase**[N] the number of women forbidden by this prohibition, **as, if he wishes, he can go on betrothing a thousand** women, all of whom would be forbidden to his brother. Consequently, the prohibition with regard to a brother's wife cannot serve as a model for other prohibitions.

אֶלָּא אָתְיָא מֵאֲחוֹת אָב וַאֲחוֹת אֵם, דִּכְתִיב ״וְעֶרְוַת אֲחוֹת אִמְּךָ וַאֲחוֹת אָבִיךָ לֹא תְגַלֶּה כִּי אֶת שְׁאֵרוֹ הֶעֱרָה״. אִיכָּא לְמִיפְרַךְ: מַה לַּאֲחוֹת אָב וַאֲחוֹת אֵם – שֶׁכֵּן אִיסּוּר הַבָּא מֵאֵלָיו!

Rather, the *halakha* in other cases **comes from** a verse with regard to **a father's sister and a mother's sister, as it is written: "And you shall not uncover the nakedness of your mother's sister nor of your father's sister; for he has made naked [*he'era*] his kin"** (Leviticus 20:19). The Gemara asks: **It is** possible **to refute** this source as follows: **What** comparison can be made between other women with whom relations are forbidden and **a father's sister and a mother's sister, which are** unique in that they are prohibited due to **a prohibition that comes on its own?** The prohibition with regard to a father's sister and a mother's sister does not stem from marriage, but from the biological fact that she is his father's or mother's sister. It is therefore dissimilar to prohibitions that result from marriage.

מֵחֲדָא לָא אָתְיָא, תֵּיתֵי [חֲדָא] מִתַּרְתֵּי. מְהֵי תֵּיתֵי? תֵּיתֵי מֵאֵשֶׁת אָח וַאֲחוֹת אָב וַאֲחוֹת אֵם – מַה לְּהָנָךְ, שֶׁכֵּן אֲסוּרִין מִשּׁוּם שְׁאֵר!

The Gemara states: The principle that the initial stage of intercourse is considered sexual intercourse **does not come from** any **one** of the sources cited above. **Let it come** by deriving the *halakha* in any **one** other case **from** the common denominator of **two** of the sources mentioned above.[N] The Gemara asks: **From which** two sources could this principle **come** to be derived? If you say it can **comes** to be derived **from** the combination of the source with regard to **a brother's wife and** the source with regard to **a father's sister and a mother's sister, what** comparison may be drawn from these cases, **which are** unique in that they are **prohibited because** they are **kin?**

אֶלָּא תֵּיתֵי מִנִּדָּה וַאֲחוֹת אָב וַאֲחוֹת אֵם – מַה לְּהָנָךְ, שֶׁכֵּן אִיסּוּר הַבָּא מֵאֵלָיו! אֶלָּא תֵּיתֵי מִנִּדָּה וְאֵשֶׁת אָח, דְּמַאי פָּרְכַתְּ?

Rather, let it come from the prohibition proscribing **a menstruating woman and** the prohibition with regard to **a father's sister and a mother's sister,** as a menstruating woman is not prohibited as a family relative. The Gemara raises a difficulty: **What** comparison may be drawn from these cases, **which are** each a **prohibition that comes of its own** accord, as neither one is created through marriage? **Rather, let it come from** the prohibition proscribing **a menstruating woman and** the prohibition proscribing **a brother's wife. As, what** can you say to **refute** this teaching? These two cases do not share any unique features that might be cause for stringency.

מַתְקִיף לַהּ רַב אַחָא בְּרֵיהּ דְּרַב אִיקָא: מַה לְּנִדָּה וְאֵשֶׁת אָח – שֶׁכֵּן אֵין לָהֶם הֶיתֵּר בְּחַיֵּי אוֹסְרָן, תֹּאמַר בְּאֵשֶׁת אִישׁ שֶׁכֵּן יֵשׁ לָהּ הֶיתֵּר בְּחַיֵּי אוֹסְרָהּ!

Rav Aḥa, son of Rav Ika, strongly objects to this: What comparison may be drawn based upon the precedent of **a menstruating woman and a brother's wife, which are** stringent in that **they cannot be permitted** to others for the duration of **the existence of the** factor **that renders them prohibited?** A menstruating woman is forbidden as long as she experiences a flow of menstrual blood, while a brother's wife is forbidden for the duration of the brother's lifetime. Can **you say** the same **with regard to a married woman, who can become permitted during the lifetime of the one who renders her prohibited,** i.e., if her husband divorces her?

אֲמַר לֵיהּ רַב אַחָא מִדִּפְתִּי לְרָבִינָא: אַטּוּ נִדָּה וְאֵשֶׁת אָח בְּחַיֵּי אוֹסְרָן הוּא דְּאֵין לָהֶם הֶיתֵּר, אֲבָל לְאַחַר מִכָּאן יֵשׁ לָהֶם הֶיתֵּר? נִדָּה

Rav Aḥa of Difti said to Ravina: Is that to say that it is only during **the existence of the** factor **that renders them prohibited that a menstruating woman and a brother's wife cannot be permitted** to others, **but afterward,** when the prohibiting factor has been resolved, **they can be permitted?** In the case of **a menstruating woman,**

Perek **VI**
Daf **54** Amud **b**

בְּיוֹמֵי תַּלְיָא מִילְּתָא. אֵשֶׁת אָח – בְּבָנִים תַּלְיָא רַחֲמָנָא.

the matter depends upon days, not blood. Although the flow of blood causes her to become impure, she remains impure for a full seven days regardless of whether she continues to experience menstrual bleeding for the duration of that time period. Similarly, in the case of **a brother's wife, the Merciful One makes** her forbidden status **dependent upon children,** as, if she has children she remains forbidden to her husband's brother even after her husband dies.

אֶלָּא פָּרֵיךְ הָכִי: מַה לְּנִדָּה וְאֵשֶׁת אָח – שֶׁכֵּן אֵין אוֹסְרָן מַתִּירָן, תֹּאמַר בְּאֵשֶׁת אִישׁ – שֶׁאוֹסְרָהּ מַתִּירָהּ!

Rather, the Gemara **refutes** the derivation in the following manner: **What** comparison can be drawn from **a menstruating woman and a brother's wife, which** are unique in **that** what **renders them prohibited does not render them permitted?** Each becomes permitted due to an external factor, i.e., the passing of seven days or the death of her childless husband. **Can you say** that the *halakhot* of these cases apply **to a married woman,** whose prohibited status is different **in that the one who renders her prohibited** to the rest of the world, i.e., her husband, has the capacity to **render her permitted** through divorce?

אֶלָּא אָמַר רַבִּי יוֹנָה וְאִיתֵּימָא רַב הוּנָא בְּרֵיהּ דְּרַב יְהוֹשֻׁעַ: אָמַר קְרָא "כִּי כָּל אֲשֶׁר יַעֲשֶׂה מִכֹּל הַתּוֹעֵבֹת הָאֵלֶּה וְנִכְרְתוּ הַנְּפָשׁוֹת הָעֹשֹׂת" הוּקְּשׁוּ כָּל הָעֲרָיוֹת כּוּלָּן לְנִדָּה, מַה נִּדָּה בְּהַעֲרָאָה – אַף כָּל בְּהַעֲרָאָה.

Rather, the Gemara offers another source for the *halakha* that the initial stage of intercourse is considered sexual intercourse. **Rabbi Yona said, and some say** it was **Rav Huna, son of Rav Yehoshua: The verse states** at the end of the chapter on forbidden relations: **"For whoever shall do any of these abominations, the souls that do them shall be cut off"** (Leviticus 18:29). **All those with whom relations are forbidden are compared** to each other in this verse, and therefore also **to a menstruating woman,** who is mentioned in that chapter. Consequently, **just as** one is liable to receive punishment for having sexual intercourse with **a menstruating woman** from the time of **the initial stage of intercourse, so too,** one violates **all** prohibitions against engaging in forbidden relations from the time of **the initial stage of intercourse.**

וְאֶלָּא נִדָּה דִּכְתִיבָא גַּבֵּי אֵשֶׁת אָח לָמָּה לִי? לְכִדְרַב הוּנָא. דְּאָמַר רַב הוּנָא: רֶמֶז לִיבָמָה מִן הַתּוֹרָה מִנַּיִן? מִנַּיִן?! הָא כְּתִיב "יְבָמָהּ יָבֹא עָלֶיהָ"! אֶלָּא: רֶמֶז לִיבָמָה שֶׁאֲסוּרָה בְּחַיֵּי בַּעֲלָהּ מִנַּיִן?

The Gemara further asks: **But** if that is the source of this *halakha*, **why do I need** the term ***nidda* that is written with regard to a brother's wife?** The Gemara answers that it is needed **for that which Rav Huna** taught, **as Rav Huna said: From where in the Torah** is there **a hint to** the *halakha* of **a *yevama*?** The Gemara expresses surprise: **From where? Isn't it written** explicitly in the verse **"Her brother-in-law will have intercourse with her"** (Deuteronomy 25:5)? **Rather,** Rav Huna meant to say: **From where** is there **a hint that a *yevama* is forbidden**[N] to her brother-in-law **in her husband's lifetime,** even after she is divorced from her husband?

הַאי – סְבָרָא הִיא, מִדַּאֲמַר רַחֲמָנָא: לְאַחַר מִיתַת בַּעֲלָהּ שַׁרְיָא – מִכְּלָל דִּבְחַיֵּי בַּעֲלָהּ אֲסוּרָה!

The Gemara remains puzzled: No proof is needed for this *halakha* either, as **this is** based upon **logical reasoning:**[N] **From** the fact **that the Merciful One says** the woman **is permitted** to her brother-in-law **after her husband's death it may be inferred that in her husband's lifetime she is forbidden** to him.

NOTES

From where is there a hint that a *yevama* is forbidden – רֶמֶז לִיבָמָה שֶׁאֲסוּרָה: The Ramban poses a basic question: Since it is explicitly prohibited by the Torah for one to marry his brother's wife, and the Torah explicitly permits her to him in only one particular circumstance, i.e., levirate marriage, why would one think that the prohibition does not apply in any other case? He explains that one might have thought that it is permitted for one to marry her in a case of levirate marriage not because the mitzva overrides the general prohibition, but because the prohibition never applied at all as long as his brother did not have children. If so, the prohibition would not apply even while his brother was alive (see *Tosafot*).

This is based upon logical reasoning – הַאי סְבָרָא הִיא: This is not merely intuitive logic, as it cannot be determined that one is liable to receive capital punishment or *karet* on the basis of abstract logic alone. It refers to logical reasoning based upon a verse (Ritva).

HALAKHA

One who has intercourse with a menstruating woman is liable to *karet* – נִדָּה בְּכָרֵת: One who intentionally had intercourse with a menstruating woman is liable to receive *karet*, as is similarly the case with any other forbidden relation, even if they merely perform the initial stage of intercourse (Rambam *Sefer Kedusha, Hilkhot Issurei Bia* 4:1).

A brother's wife…during her husband's lifetime – אֵשֶׁת אָח...בְּחַיֵּי בַעְלָהּ: One who has intercourse with his brother's wife while his brother is alive is liable to receive *karet*, even if his brother has already divorced her (Rambam *Sefer Kedusha, Hilkhot Issurei Bia* 1:1, 2:1).

One who performs the initial stage of intercourse with another male – הַמְעָרֶה בְּזָכוּר: One who performs the initial stage of intercourse with another male is liable to receive the punishment of stoning (Rambam *Sefer Kedusha, Hilkhot Issurei Bia* 1:14).

One who performs the initial stage of intercourse with an animal – הַמְעָרֶה בִּבְהֵמָה: A man or woman who performs the initial stage of intercourse with an animal is liable to receive the punishment of stoning. The animal is likewise stoned (Rambam *Sefer Kedusha, Hilkhot Issurei Bia* 1:16).

וְדִלְמָא: לְאַחַר מִיתַת בַּעֲלָהּ – מִצְוָה, בְּחַיֵּי בַעֲלָהּ – רְשׁוּת? אִי נַמִי: לְאַחַר מִיתַת בַּעֲלָהּ – אִין, בְּחַיֵּי בַעֲלָהּ – לָא, וְלָאו הַבָּא מִכְּלַל עֲשֵׂה – עֲשֵׂה!

The Gemara refutes this argument: **Perhaps after her husband's death** it is **a mitzva** for her brother-in-law to marry her, whereas **during her husband's lifetime** their marriage is **optional. Alternatively,** perhaps **after her husband's death, yes,** she is permitted to him, while **during her husband's lifetime, no,** they are not permitted to marry, but there is no punishment of *karet* if they do. This is because the source of the prohibition is the mitzva for them to marry after the husband's death, **and a prohibition that stems from a positive mitzva** has the status of **a positive mitzva,** but nothing more.

אָמַר קְרָא: ״וְאִישׁ אֲשֶׁר יִקַּח אֶת אֵשֶׁת אָחִיו נִדָּה הִיא״, וְכִי אֵשֶׁת אָחִיו נִדָּה הִיא? אֶלָּא כְּנִדָּה, מַה נִּדָּה, אַף עַל פִּי שֶׁיֵּשׁ לָהּ הֶיתֵּר לְאַחַר מִכָּאן – בִּשְׁעַת אִיסּוּרָא בְּכָרֵת, אַף אֵשֶׁת אָח [נַמִי], אַף עַל פִּי שֶׁיֵּשׁ לָהּ הֶיתֵּר לְאַחַר מִכָּאן – בְּחַיֵּי בַעֲלָהּ בְּכָרֵת.

Therefore, **the verse states: "And if a man shall take his brother's wife, it is impurity** [*nidda*]" (Leviticus 20:21). **Is his brother's wife** necessarily **a menstruating woman** [*nidda*]? **Rather,** she is **like a menstruating woman** in the following manner: **Just as** with regard to **a menstruating woman, although she has a permitted** stage **afterward, at the time** that she is **forbidden,** one who has intercourse with her is liable **to** receive the punishment of ***karet***,[H] **so too,** with regard to **a brother's wife, although she has a permitted** stage **afterward, during her husband's lifetime**[H] marriage to her brother-in-law is punishable **by *karet*.**

אֶלָּא הַעֲרָאָה דִּכְתִיבָא גַּבֵּי אֲחוֹת אָב וַאֲחוֹת אֵם לָמָּה לִי?

The Gemara asks: **But** if the source of the *halakha* that the initial stage of intercourse is considered sexual intercourse is as stated above, **why do I need** this *halakha* to be indicated by the word *he'era* (Leviticus 20:19) in the case of **a father's sister and a mother's sister?**

לְכִדְבָעָא מִינֵּיהּ רָבִינָא מֵרָבָא: הַמְעָרֶה בְּזָכוּר, מַהוּ? בְּזָכוּר – ״מִשְׁכְּבֵי אִשָּׁה״ כְּתִיבָא!

The Gemara answers that it is needed **for the dilemma that Ravina raised before Rava:** With regard to **one who performs the initial stage of intercourse with** another **male,**[H] **what is the** *halakha*? Is it considered to be a forbidden act of homosexual intercourse? The Gemara is puzzled by this dilemma: **With regard to a male, it is written** explicitly: "You shall not lie with a man **as with a woman**" (Leviticus 18:22), which indicates that anything considered an act of sexual intercourse with a woman is also considered an act of sexual intercourse with a man.

אֶלָּא: הַמְעָרֶה בִּבְהֵמָה מַהוּ? אֲמַר לֵיהּ: אִם אֵינוֹ עִנְיָן לְהַעֲרָאָה, דִּכְתִיבָא גַּבֵּי אֲחוֹת אָב וַאֲחוֹת אֵם, דְּאָתְיָא בְּהֶקֵּישָׁא מִדְּרַבִּי יוֹנָה – תְּנֵהוּ עִנְיָן לְהַעֲרָאָה דִּבְהֵמָה.

Rather, the word *he'era* in the case of a father's sister and a mother's sister is needed to resolve the following dilemma: With regard to **one** who **performs the initial stage of intercourse with an animal,**[H] **what is** the *halakha*? Rava **said to** Ravina: **If** the word *he'era* **does not** refer **to the matter of the initial stage of intercourse** in the context **where it is written,** i.e., the prohibition with regard to **a father's sister and a mother's sister, as** this *halakha* **is derived from a comparison based upon** the statement of **Rabbi Yona, refer it to the matter of the initial stage of intercourse** with **an animal.** The superfluous expression written in the case of a father's sister and a mother's sister teaches that the initial stage of intercourse is considered sexual intercourse even with an animal.

מִכְּדִי בְּהֵמָה חַיָּיבֵי מִיתוֹת בֵּית דִּין הִיא, מַאי טַעֲמָא כְּתִיב לְהַעֲרָאָה דִּידָהּ גַּבֵּי חַיָּיבֵי כְּרֵיתוֹת? לִכְתּוֹב גַּבֵּי מִיתַת בֵּית דִּין, וְנֵילַף מִיתַת בֵּית דִּין מִמִּיתַת בֵּית דִּין!

The Gemara asks: **Since** intercourse with **an animal is** a prohibition for which one is **liable to** receive **capital punishment from the court, what is the reason** that the *halakha* of **the initial stage of intercourse** that applies to **it is written with regard to** the prohibitions proscribing a father's sister and a mother's sister, for which one is **liable to** receive ***karet*? Let** the word *he'era* **be written with regard to** prohibitions for which one is liable to receive **capital punishment from the court, and let us derive** the *halakha* with regard to a prohibition punishable by **capital punishment from the court,** i.e., the case of bestiality, **from** another prohibition punishable by **capital punishment from the court.**

אַיְּידֵי דְּכוּלֵּיהּ קְרָא לִדְרָשָׁא אָתֵי – כְּתִיב בֵּיהּ נַמִי הָא מִילְּתָא לִדְרָשָׁא.

The Gemara answers: **Since the entire verse** of a father's sister and a mother's sister **comes for** the purpose of **an exposition,** as the Gemara is about to explain, **this matter,** i.e., that the initial stage of intercourse is considered intercourse, **is also written for** the purpose of **an exposition,** i.e., to indicate that this principle holds true in a different context, i.e., that of bestiality.

מַאי דְּרָשָׁא – דְּתַנְיָא: ״עֶרְוַת אֲחוֹת אָבִיךָ לֹא תְגַלֵּה״ בֵּין מִן הָאָב בֵּין מִן הָאֵם. אַתָּה אוֹמֵר בֵּין מִן הָאָב בֵּין מִן הָאֵם, אוֹ אֵינוֹ אֶלָּא מִן הָאָב וְלֹא מִן הָאֵם?

The Gemara asks: **What is the exposition** that the rest of the verse introduces? **As it is taught in a** *baraita*, the verse **"You shall not uncover the nakedness of your father's sister"** (Leviticus 18:12) indicates that the prohibition applies **whether** she is your father's sister **from** his **father, or from** his **mother.**[H] **Do you say** that she is forbidden **whether** she is your father's sister **from** his **father or from** his **mother, or** perhaps **it is only** a sister **from** his **father** who is forbidden, **but not from** his **mother?**

וְדִין הוּא: חַיָּיב כָּאן – וְחַיָּיב בַּאֲחוֹתוֹ. מָה אֲחוֹתוֹ – בֵּין מִן הָאָב בֵּין מִן הָאֵם, אַף כָּאן – בֵּין מִן הָאָב בֵּין מִן הָאֵם.

It may be inferred **logically** from the fact that the Torah **rendered him liable here and rendered him liable with his sister: Just as** with regard to **his sister**[H] he is liable to receive punishment **whether** she is his sister **from** his **father or from** his **mother, so too here,** he is liable **whether** she is his father's sister **from** his **father or from** his **mother.**

אוֹ כְּלָךְ לְדֶרֶךְ זוֹ: חַיָּיב כָּאן וְחַיָּיב בְּדוֹדָתוֹ, מָה דּוֹדָתוֹ – מִן הָאָב וְלֹא מִן הָאֵם, אַף כָּאן – מִן הָאָב וְלֹא מִן הָאֵם.

Or perhaps **go this way** and compare a father's sister and a mother's sister to a different *halakha*: The Torah **rendered him liable here and rendered him liable with his aunt,**[H] i.e., the wife of his father's brother: **Just as** concerning **his aunt,** he is liable to receive punishment only with regard to the wife of his father's brother **from** his **father,** i.e., the wife of his father's paternal brother, **and not** for the wife of his father's brother **from** his **mother,** i.e., the wife of his father's maternal brother, **so too here,** he is liable only with regard to a father's sister or a mother's sister **from** their **father,** i.e., a paternal sister, **and not from** their **mother,** a maternal sister.

נִרְאֶה לְמִי דּוֹמֶה: דָּנִין אִיסּוּר הַבָּא מֵאֵלָיו מֵאִיסּוּר הַבָּא מֵאֵלָיו, וְאַל תּוֹכִיחַ דּוֹדָתוֹ – שֶׁאֵין אִיסּוּר הַבָּא מֵאֵלָיו.

The Gemara analyzes these two possibilities: **Let us see to which** case **it is** more **similar,** i.e., which is a better comparison. **We** should **derive** the *halakha* with regard to **a prohibition that comes on its own,** i.e., a father's sister and a mother's sister, **from a prohibition that** also **comes on its own,** i.e., a sister, **and** the *halakha* with regard to **his aunt cannot** be used to **prove** otherwise, **as** it is **not a prohibition that comes on its own,** but through marriage.

אוֹ כְּלָךְ לְדֶרֶךְ זֶה: דָּנִין קְרוֹבֵי הָאָב מִקְּרוֹבֵי הָאָב, וְאַל תּוֹכִיחַ אֲחוֹתוֹ שֶׁקְּרוֹבֵי עַצְמוֹ?

The Gemara counters this argument: **Or** perhaps **go this way** and claim that **we** should **derive** the *halakha* with regard to **the relatives of** his **father,** i.e., his father's sister, **from the** *halakha* with regard to **the relatives of** his **father,** i.e., his father's brother's wife, **and** the case of **his sister cannot** be used to **prove** otherwise, **as** she is **his own relative.** Consequently, there is no conclusive proof based on reasoning alone.

תַּלְמוּד לוֹמַר ״עֶרְוַת אֲחוֹת אָבִיךָ לֹא תְגַלֵּה״ בֵּין מִן הָאָב בֵּין מִן הָאֵם. ״עֶרְוַת אֲחוֹת אִמְּךָ לֹא תְגַלֵּה״ בֵּין מִן הָאָב בֵּין מִן הָאֵם.

Therefore **the verse states: "You shall not uncover the nakedness of your father's sister,"** which teaches that this prohibition applies **whether** she is your father's sister **from** his **father or from** his **mother.** Similarly, the verse **"You shall not uncover the nakedness of your mother's sister"** indicates that the prohibition applies **whether** she is your mother's sister **from** her **father or from** her **mother.** These prohibitions are stated twice (Leviticus 18:12–13 and 20:19), and the superfluous verse indicates that the prohibition applies even to the maternal sister of one's father or mother.

לָמָּה לִי לְמִכְתְּבָא בַּאֲחוֹת אָב, לָמָּה לִי לְמִכְתְּבָא בַּאֲחוֹת אֵם? אָמַר רַבִּי אַבָּהוּ: צְרִיכִי, דְּאִי כְּתַב רַחֲמָנָא בַּאֲחוֹת אָב – שֶׁכֵּן יֵשׁ לָהּ חַיִּיס, אֲבָל אֲחוֹת אֵם – אֵימָא לָא.

The Gemara asks: **Why do I** need the Torah **to write** this *halakha* **with regard to a father's sister,** and **why do I** need the Torah **to write** it again **with regard to a mother's sister? Rabbi Abbahu said:** Both verses **are necessary. If the Merciful One had written** this *halakha* only **with regard to** one's **father's sister,** one might say that it is limited to that case, **as she has** common **lineage** with her nephew, since lineage goes through one's father. **However,** with regard to one's **mother's sister** you might **say** that she is **not** prohibited, as she is not considered to share common lineage with him.

וְאִי כְּתַב רַחֲמָנָא בַּאֲחוֹת אֵם – שֶׁכֵּן וַדָּאִית, אֲבָל אֲחוֹת אָב – אֵימָא לָא, צְרִיכָא.

And conversely, **if the Merciful One had written** this *halakha* only **with regard to** one's **mother's sister,** one might say that it is limited to that case, **as she is certainly** his relative, since one's biological relationship with his mother is absolutely certain. **However,** with regard to one's **father's sister,** one might **say no,** that she is not forbidden, as paternity can never be established beyond doubt. It is therefore **necessary** for this *halakha* to be stated in both cases.

HALAKHA

A father's sister – אֲחוֹת הָאָב: One's father's sister is a forbidden relative and he is liable to receive *karet* for having intercourse with her, regardless of whether she is his father's paternal sister or maternal sister (Rambam *Sefer Kedusha, Hilkhot Issurei Bia* 2:5; *Shulḥan Arukh, Even HaEzer* 15:16).

His sister – אֲחוֹתוֹ: One's sister is forbidden to him by Torah law, regardless of whether she is his paternal sister or maternal sister, or whether she was born in or out of wedlock. He is liable to receive punishment for engaging in intercourse with her even if she is a *mamzeret* (Rambam *Sefer Kedusha, Hilkhot Issurei Bia* 2:2; *Shulḥan Arukh, Even HaEzer* 15:10).

His aunt – דּוֹדָתוֹ: The wife of one's father's paternal brother is forbidden by Torah law. However, the wife of one's father's maternal brother is forbidden only by rabbinic law (Rambam *Sefer Kedusha, Hilkhot Issurei Bia* 2:2; *Shulḥan Arukh, Even HaEzer* 15:8).

וְדוֹדָתוֹ, דִּפְשִׁיטָא לֵיהּ לְתַנָּא דְּמִן הָאָב וְלֹא מִן הָאֵם, מְנָא לֵיהּ?

The Gemara asks: **And** with regard to **his aunt, where it is obvious to the *tanna*** that the prohibition includes only the wife of his father's brother **from** his **father and not from** his **mother, from where does he** derive this *halakha*?

אֲמַר רָבָא: אָתְיָא ״דּוֹדוֹ״ ״דּוֹדוֹ״, כְּתִיב הָכָא ״עֶרְוַת דֹּדוֹ גִּלָּה״ וּכְתִיב הָתָם ״אוֹ דֹדוֹ אוֹ בֶן דֹּדוֹ יִגְאָלֶנּוּ״ מַה לְּהַלָּן מִן הָאָב וְלֹא מִן הָאֵם – אַף כָּאן מִן הָאָב וְלֹא מִן הָאֵם.

Rava said: It is **derived** through a verbal analogy between the terms **"his uncle"** and **"his uncle." It is written here: "He has uncovered his uncle's nakedness"** (Leviticus 20:20), **and it is written there,** with regard to the redemption of a Jew who has been sold to a gentile: **"Either his uncle or his uncle's son shall redeem him"** (Leviticus 25:49). **Just as there,** in the case of redemption, it must be a relative **from the** side of his **father and not from the** side of his **mother, so too here,** with regard to forbidden relations, the prohibition applies to the wife of his father's brother **from** his **father,** i.e., the wife of his father's paternal brother, **and not from** his **mother.**

וְהָתָם מְנָלַן? אָמַר קְרָא ״מִמִּשְׁפַּחְתּוֹ יִגְאָלֶנּוּ״, מִשְׁפַּחַת אָב – קְרוּיָה מִשְׁפָּחָה, מִשְׁפַּחַת אֵם – אֵינָהּ קְרוּיָה מִשְׁפָּחָה.

The Gemara asks: **And there,** with regard to the *halakhot* of redemption, **from where do we** derive that a maternal relative is not included? **The verse states:** "Or any that is near of kin to him **of his family shall redeem him**" (Leviticus 25:49), and it is an established principle that only **the family of** one's **father is called family,** while **the family of** one's **mother is not called family,**[H] as lineage is determined based upon one's father.

וְהָדִתְנַן: אָמְרוּ לוֹ: מֵתָה אִשְׁתְּךָ, וְנָשָׂא אֲחוֹתָהּ מֵאָבִיהָ. מֵתָה, וְנָשָׂא אֲחוֹתָהּ מֵאִמָּהּ. מֵתָה, וְנָשָׂא אֲחוֹתָהּ מֵאָבִיהָ. מֵתָה, וְנָשָׂא אֲחוֹתָהּ מֵאִמָּהּ –

And with regard to **that which we learned** in a mishna: If **they said to him: Your wife is dead, and he** then **married her sister from her father.** He was subsequently informed that his second wife **died, and he married her sister from her mother,** i.e., his second wife's maternal sister. He was then informed that his third wife **died, and he married her sister from her father,** i.e., his third wife's paternal sister. He was then informed that his fourth wife **died, and he married her sister from her mother,** i.e., his fourth wife's maternal sister. It later became apparent that all these rumors were unfounded and all the women were still alive. Consequently, since one cannot marry his wife's sister during his wife's lifetime, some of the marriages are void.

מוּתָּר בָּרִאשׁוֹנָה וּבַשְּׁלִישִׁית וּבַחֲמִישִׁית, וּפוֹטְרוֹת צָרוֹתֵיהֶן. וְאָסוּר בַּשְּׁנִיָּה וּבָרְבִיעִית, וְאֵין בִּיאַת אַחַת מֵהֶן פּוֹטֶרֶת צָרָתָהּ.

The *halakha* in this case is that it is **permitted** for him to marry his **first, third, and fifth** wives, as they are not related to each other. Consequently, these marriages are valid, **and** these women **exempt their rival wives** from levirate marriage if they all became subject to levirate marriage and one of them performed levirate marriage or *ḥalitza*. However, it is **prohibited** for him to marry his **second and fourth** wives, as they are both sisters of one of his previous wives, and their marriages are therefore void. Consequently, **sexual intercourse** between **one of them** and his brother, if he has died childless, **does not exempt her rival wife,** i.e., the real wives of the deceased, from levirate marriage.

וְאִם בָּא עַל הַשְּׁנִיָּה לְאַחַר מִיתַת הָרִאשׁוֹנָה – מוּתָּר בַּשְּׁנִיָּה וּבָרְבִיעִית, וּפוֹטְרוֹת צָרוֹתֵיהֶן, וְאָסוּר בַּשְּׁלִישִׁית וּבַחֲמִישִׁית.

And if the first wife indeed died, **and he had intercourse with the second** woman **after the death of the first** one, it is **permitted** for him to marry **the second and fourth** women, who are not related to each other, **and they exempt their rival wives** from levirate marriage if they perform levirate marriage or *ḥalitza*, **and** it is **prohibited** for him to marry **the third and fifth** women, as they are sisters of his previous wives, who are still alive, and consequently these marriages are void.

HALAKHA

The family of one's mother is not called family – **מִשְׁפַּחַת אֵם אֵינָהּ קְרוּיָה מִשְׁפָּחָה**: The family of one's mother is not considered family with regard to inheritance. Therefore, maternal brothers are not considered heirs; each one is an heir of his paternal relatives only. Even if the identity of one's father is unknown, his maternal relatives are still not considered his heirs (*Terumat HaDeshen*; Rambam *Sefer Mishpatim, Hilkhot Naḥalot* 1:6; *Shulḥan Arukh, Ḥoshen Mishpat* 276:4).

אַלְמָא אֲחוֹת אִשְׁתּוֹ בֵּין מִן הָאָב בֵּין מִן הָאֵם אֲסוּרוֹת. מְנָלַן? יָלֵיף מֵאֲחוֹתוֹ, מָה אֲחוֹתוֹ – בֵּין מִן הָאָב בֵּין מִן הָאֵם, אַף כָּאן בֵּין מִן הָאָב בֵּין מִן הָאֵם.

Apparently, this mishna indicates that **his wife's sister,**[NH] **whether from the father,** i.e., a paternal sister, **or from the mother,** i.e., a maternal sister, **is forbidden. From where do we** derive this *halakha* that the prohibition applies even to his wife's maternal sister? The Gemara responds: **It is derived from** the prohibition proscribing **his sister. Just as his sister** is forbidden **whether** she is his sister **from** his **father** or **from** his **mother, so too here,** a wife's sister is forbidden **whether from the father or from the mother.**

וְלֵילַף מִדּוֹדָתוֹ, מָה דּוֹדָתוֹ – מִן הָאָב וְלֹא מִן הָאֵם, אַף כָּאן – מִן הָאָב וְלֹא מִן הָאֵם! מִסְתַּבְּרָא, מֵאֲחוֹתוֹ הֲוָה לֵיהּ לְמֵילַף, שֶׁכֵּן קְרוֹבֵי עַצְמוֹ מִקְּרוֹבֵי עַצְמוֹ.

The Gemara challenges the validity of this source: **And let it be derived from** the *halakha* with regard to **his aunt: Just as** the prohibition with regard to **his aunt** applies only to the wife of his father's brother **from** his **father but not from** his **mother,** i.e., the wife of his father's paternal brother but not the wife of his father's maternal brother, **so too here,** the prohibition with regard to his wife's sister should apply only to her sister **from** her **father but not** to her sister **from** her **mother.** The Gemara answers: **It is reasonable** that **he should derive** the *halakha* in this case **from** the case of **his sister, as** the *tanna* thereby derives the *halakha* of **one's own relatives from** another case of **his own relatives,** whereas his aunt is forbidden as his father's relative.

אַדְּרַבָּה, מִדּוֹדָתוֹ הֲוָה לֵיהּ לְמֵילַף שֶׁכֵּן דָּבָר עַל יְדֵי קִדּוּשִׁין מִדָּבָר שֶׁעַל יְדֵי קִדּוּשִׁין! אֶלָּא: מֵאֵשֶׁת אָח יָלְפִינַן, דְּשֶׁכֵּן דָּבָר עַל יְדֵי קִדּוּשִׁין, וּקְרוֹבֵי עַצְמוֹ.

The Gemara counters: **On the contrary, he should derive** the *halakha* in this instance **from** the case of **his aunt, as** he thereby derives the *halakha* in **a matter** prohibited **through betrothal from** another **matter** prohibited **through betrothal.** The Gemara concludes: **Rather,** the *halakha* of a wife's sister **is derived from** that of **a brother's wife,**[NH] as they are both **something** forbidden **by means of betrothal and** they are **his own relatives.**

וְאֵשֶׁת אָח גּוּפַהּ מְנָא לַן? דְּתַנְיָא: "עֶרְוַת אֵשֶׁת אָחִיךָ לֹא תְגַלֵּה" בֵּין מִן הָאָב בֵּין מִן הָאֵם.

The Gemara asks: **And** in the case of **a brother's wife itself, from where do we** derive that the prohibition applies to the wife of both a paternal and a maternal brother? **As it is taught in a** *baraita*: **"You shall not uncover the nakedness of your brother's wife"** (Leviticus 18:16), which indicates: **Whether from the father or from the mother.**

אַתָּה אוֹמֵר בֵּין מִן הָאָב בֵּין מִן הָאֵם, אוֹ אֵינוֹ אֶלָּא מִן הָאָב וְלֹא מִן הָאֵם? וְדִין הוּא: חַיָּיב כָּאן, וְחַיָּיב בַּאֲחוֹתוֹ. מָה אֲחוֹתוֹ – בֵּין מִן הָאָב בֵּין מִן הָאֵם, אַף כָּאן – בֵּין מִן הָאָב בֵּין מִן הָאֵם.

The *baraita* elaborates: **Do you say** the prohibition applies **whether** she is the wife of one's brother **from** his **father or from** his **mother,** i.e., whether she is the wife of one's paternal brother or maternal brother? **Or** perhaps **it is only** the wife of one's brother **from** his **father and not from** his **mother? It** may be inferred **logically** from the fact that the Torah **rendered him liable here and rendered him liable with** regard to **his sister: Just as** with regard to **his sister** he is liable to receive punishment **whether** she is his sister **from** his **father or from** his **mother, so too here,** he is liable to receive punishment **whether** she is the wife of his brother **from** his **father or from** his **mother.**

אוֹ כְּלָךְ לְדֶרֶךְ זוֹ: חַיָּיב כָּאן וְחַיָּיב בְּדוֹדָתוֹ. מָה דּוֹדָתוֹ – מִן הָאָב וְלֹא מִן הָאֵם, אַף כָּאן – מִן הָאָב וְלֹא מִן הָאֵם?

Or perhaps **go this way** and compare this case to the case of an aunt. The Torah **rendered him liable here and rendered him liable with** regard to **his aunt,** i.e., the wife of his father's brother: **Just as** with regard to **his aunt,** he is liable to receive punishment only for the wife of his father's brother **from** his **father and not** for the wife of his father's brother **from** his **mother, so too here,** he is liable to receive punishment only for the wife of his brother **from** his **father and not from** his **mother.**

נִרְאֶה לְמִי דּוֹמֶה; דָּנִין קְרוֹבֵי עַצְמוֹ מִקְּרוֹבֵי עַצְמוֹ, וְאַל תּוֹכִיחַ דּוֹדָתוֹ שֶׁקְּרוֹבֵי הָאָב. אוֹ כְּלָךְ לְדֶרֶךְ זוֹ: דָּנִין דָּבָר שֶׁעַל יְדֵי קִדּוּשִׁין מִדָּבָר שֶׁעַל יְדֵי קִדּוּשִׁין, וְאַל תּוֹכִיחַ אֲחוֹתוֹ שֶׁאִיסּוּר הַבָּא מֵאֵלָיו?

The Gemara analyzes these two possibilities: **Let us see to which** case **it is more similar. We** should **derive** the *halakha* with regard to **his own relatives,** i.e., his brother's wife, **from** another case of **his own relatives,** i.e., his sister, **and** the *halakha* with regard to **his aunt cannot** be used to **prove** otherwise, **as** she is his **father's relative. Or** perhaps **go this way: We** should **derive** the *halakha* of **a matter** prohibited **through betrothal,** i.e., a brother's wife, **from** another **matter** prohibited **through betrothal,** i.e., his father's brother's wife, **and** the *halakha* with regard to **his sister cannot** be used to **prove** otherwise, **as** it is **a prohibition that comes on its own.**

NOTES

Apparently, his wife's sister, etc. – אַלְמָא אֲחוֹת אִשְׁתּוֹ וכו׳: The proof that his wife's maternal sister is forbidden is from the ruling that the third woman is permitted to him. The implication is that she is permitted only because the marriage of the second woman was void. However, if that marriage had been valid, the woman would be forbidden because she is the maternal sister of the second woman (Rashi; see *Tosefot HaRosh*).

The *halakha* of a wife's sister is derived from that of a brother's wife – מֵאֵשֶׁת אָח יָלְפִינַן: The Ramban, who perhaps had a slightly different version of the text, explains as follows: The definition of brotherhood can be derived from the case of a brother's wife, as it is clear from the verses that the relationship is the same whether they are paternal or maternal brothers (see *Tosafot*). By extension, a maternal sister is also considered a sister. Furthermore, although one cannot administer corporal punishment for prohibitions derived from logical analysis, in this case the prohibition itself is written explicitly in the Torah, and it is the definition of the term sister that is derived on the basis of the comparison to a brother's wife.

HALAKHA

The prohibition proscribing a wife's sister – אִיסּוּר אֲחוֹת אִשְׁתּוֹ: The sister of one's wife is forbidden to him as long as his wife is alive. This applies both to paternal and maternal sisters, including those born out of wedlock (Rambam *Sefer Kedusha, Hilkhot Issurei Bia* 2:9; *Shulḥan Arukh, Even HaEzer* 15:26).

A brother's wife – אֵשֶׁת אָח: The wife of one's brother is forbidden to him. This applies to both paternal and maternal brothers, including brothers born out of wedlock (Rambam *Sefer Kedusha, Hilkhot Issurei Bia* 2:2; *Shulḥan Arukh, Even HaEzer* 15:22).

תַּלְמוּד לוֹמַר ״עֶרְוַת אָחִיךָ הִיא״ בֵּין מִן הָאָב בֵּין מִן הָאֵם.

Since it is impossible to prove which *halakha* should serve as the model for the case of a brother's wife, **the verse states** a second time in the same verse: **"It is your brother's nakedness"** (Leviticus 18:16), in order to emphasize that she is forbidden **whether** she is the wife of his brother **from** his **father or from** his **mother.**

וְאֵימָא: אִידִי וְאִידִי בְּאֵשֶׁת אָח מִן הָאָב, חֲדָא – דְּיֵשׁ לָהּ בָּנִים בְּחַיֵּי בַעְלָהּ, וַחֲדָא – דְּאֵין לָהּ בָּנִים בְּחַיֵּי בַעְלָהּ. אֵין לָהּ בָּנִים בְּחַיֵּי בַעְלָהּ – מִדְּרַב הוּנָא נָפְקָא!

The Gemara challenges this interpretation of the extra phrase in the verse: Say that both **this** first part of the verse **and that** latter part refer **to the wife of a brother from the father,** i.e., the wife of one's paternal brother. As for the repetition, **one** part of the verse renders prohibited a woman **who has children,** who is prohibited from marrying her husband's brother **during her husband's lifetime** even after they are divorced, **and** the other **one** renders prohibited a woman **who does not have children,** who is also prohibited from marrying her husband's brother **during her husband's lifetime,** even after she is divorced. The Gemara responds: The prohibition proscribing a woman who **does not have children** for the duration of **her husband's lifetime is derived from** the statement of **Rav Huna** (54b), and it requires no further source.

וְאֵימָא: אִידִי וְאִידִי בְּאֵשֶׁת אָח מִן הָאָב, חֲדָא – דְּיֵשׁ לָהּ בָּנִים בְּחַיֵּי בַעְלָהּ, וַחֲדָא – דְּיֵשׁ לָהּ בָּנִים לְאַחַר מִיתַת בַּעְלָהּ!

The Gemara presents another challenge: **Say** that both **this** first part of the verse **and that** latter part refer **to the wife of a brother from the father,** i.e., the wife of one's paternal brother. As for the repetition, **one** part of the verse renders a woman **who has children** prohibited from marrying her husband's brother for the duration of **her husband's lifetime,** even after she is divorced, **and** the other **one** renders prohibited a woman **who has children** and indicates that it is prohibited for her to marry her husband's brother even **after her husband's death.**

יֵשׁ לָהּ בָּנִים לְאַחַר מִיתַת בַּעְלָהּ לָא צְרִיכָא קְרָא, מִדְּאָמַר רַחֲמָנָא שֶׁאֵין לָהּ בָּנִים מוּתֶּרֶת – הָא יֵשׁ לָהּ בָּנִים אֲסוּרָה.

The Gemara responds: The *halakha* that it is prohibited for a woman **who has children** to marry her husband's brother even **after her husband's death does not require a verse. From** the fact **that the Merciful One says that** one **who has no children is permitted** to marry the brother after her husband's death, it can be inferred **that** if **she has children,** it is **prohibited** for her to marry her husband's brother.

וְדִלְמָא: אֵין לָהּ בָּנִים – אֲסוּרָה לְעָלְמָא וְשַׁרְיָא לְיָבָם. יֵשׁ לָהּ בָּנִים – שַׁרְיָא לְעָלְמָא וְשַׁרְיָא לְיָבָם! אִי נַמִי: אֵין לָהּ בָּנִים – מִצְוָה, יֵשׁ לָהּ בָּנִים – רְשׁוּת,

The Gemara raises another challenge: **But perhaps** if **she does not have children** it is **prohibited** for her to marry **everyone** else **and permitted** for her to marry her *yavam*, as specified by the Torah. However, if **she does have children** it **is permitted** for her to marry **everyone and** it **is permitted** for her to marry her ***yavam*** as well. **Alternatively,** perhaps **if she does not have children** it is **a mitzva** for her husband's brother to marry her, and **if she does have children** it is **optional.** Consequently, the extra phrase in the verse should be necessary in order to indicate that the prohibition against marriage applies in all of these cases.

אִי נַמִי: אֵין לָהּ בָּנִים – אִין, יֵשׁ לָהּ בָּנִים – לָא, וְלָאו הַבָּא מִכְּלַל עֲשֵׂה – עֲשֵׂה!

Alternatively, if **she does not have children, yes,** she is permitted to her husband's brother, and if **she does have children, no,** she is not permitted to him, but the punishment of *karet* does not apply to this prohibition. This is because the source of the prohibition is the mitzva for them to marry after the husband's death, **and a prohibition that stems from a positive mitzva** has the status of **a positive mitzva,** but nothing more. Consequently, the extra phrase in the verse should be necessary in order to indicate that the punishment of *karet* is still applicable.

כְּתַב קְרָא אַחֲרִינָא: ״עֶרְוַת אָחִיו גִּלָּה״.

The Gemara responds: The Torah **wrote a different verse** to teach that the prohibition against marrying one's brother's wife is in full force, including the punishment of *karet*, in these cases: **"He has uncovered his brother's nakedness;** they shall be childless" (Leviticus 20:21). Therefore, the extra phrase mentioned in the *baraita* can indicate that the prohibition against marrying one's brother's wife applies both to the wife of a paternal brother and to the wife of a maternal brother.

וְאֵימָא אֵשֶׁת אָח מִן הָאֵם כְּאֵשֶׁת אָח מִן הָאָב: מָה אֵשֶׁת אָח מִן הָאָב – לְאַחַר מִיתַת בַּעֲלָהּ שַׁרְיָא, אַף אֵשֶׁת אָח מִן הָאֵם – לְאַחַר מִיתַת בַּעֲלָהּ שַׁרְיָא! אָמַר קְרָא "הִיא" בַּהֲוָיָתָהּ תְּהֵא.

The Gemara suggests: **Say that the** *halakha* **of the wife of a brother from** one's **mother** should be just **like** that of **the wife of a brother from** his **father: Just as the wife of a brother from** one's **father is permitted,** i.e., one can marry her, **after her husband's death, so too, the wife of a brother from** his **mother should be permitted after her husband's death.** The Gemara responds: **The verse states:** "She is your brother's nakedness," thereby emphasizing that **she shall** remain after her husband's death **as she is** during his life.[H]

אֲחוֹתוֹ דִּכְתַב בָּהּ כָּרֵת לָמָּה לִי?

§ The Gemara above stated that all of the instances of forbidden intercourse are compared to one another. Therefore, since there is already a verse that states: "For whoever shall do any of these abominations, the souls that do them shall be cut off from among their people" (Leviticus 18:29), the Gemara asks: **Why do I need** the phrase **written with regard to one's sister** that states that intercourse is punishable by ***karet*?**

לְכִדְרַבִּי יוֹחָנָן. דְּאָמַר רַבִּי יוֹחָנָן: שֶׁאִם עֲשָׂאָן כּוּלָּם בְּהֶעְלֵם אַחַת – חַיָּיב עַל כָּל אַחַת וְאַחַת.

The Gemara answers that it is necessary **for that** which **Rabbi Yoḥanan** said, **as Rabbi Yoḥanan said that if he performed all of them,** i.e., he violated every prohibition against engaging in forbidden intercourse **in a single lapse of awareness, he is liable** to receive punishment **for each and every one.** One might have thought that there is one prohibition against engaging in forbidden intercourse, and many different ways to violate the prohibition. Therefore, if one violated the prohibition in different ways during one lapse of awareness, one is liable to bring only one sin-offering. This verse therefore indicates that each act of intercourse with a relative with whom intercourse is forbidden is a violation of an independent prohibition.

וּלְרַבִּי יִצְחָק, דְּאָמַר: כָּל חַיָּיבֵי כְּרֵיתוֹת בִּכְלָל הָיוּ, וְלָמָּה יָצְתָה כָּרֵת בַּאֲחוֹתוֹ – לְדוּנוֹ בְּכָרֵת וְלֹא בְּמַלְקוֹת, לְחַלֵּק מְנָלַן?

The Gemara asks: **And according to Rabbi Yitzḥak, who said** that **all** forbidden relations for which one is **liable to** receive ***karet* were included** in the verse: "The souls that do them shall be cut off from among their people," **why was** the punishment of ***karet* with regard to one's sister singled out?** In order **to sentence him to *karet* and not to flogging.** Although he has violated a prohibition, which generally carries a punishment of flogging, he is not flogged due to the fact that he is liable to receive the more severe punishment of *karet*. Since he has used the verse to teach this *halakha*, **from where do we** know **to divide** the prohibitions against engaging in forbidden intercourse and consider each an independent prohibition?

נָפְקָא לֵיהּ: מִ"וְאֶל אִשָּׁה בְּנִדַּת טוּמְאָתָהּ" לְחַיֵּיב עַל כָּל אִשָּׁה וְאִשָּׁה.

The Gemara answers: **He derives it from** the verse **"And** you shall not approach **a woman** to uncover her nakedness **as long as she is impure by her uncleanness"** (Leviticus 18:19), which serves **to render** him **liable** to receive punishment **for each and every woman.**

דּוֹדָתוֹ דִּכְתַב בָּהּ רַחֲמָנָא "עֲרִירִים יִהְיוּ" לָמָּה לִי? לְכִדְרַבָּה. דְּרַבָּה רָמֵי: כְּתִיב "עֲרִירִים יִהְיוּ" וּכְתִיב "עֲרִירִים יָמֻתוּ"! הָא כֵּיצַד? יֵשׁ לוֹ בָּנִים – קוֹבְרָן, אֵין לוֹ בָּנִים – הוֹלֵךְ עֲרִירִי.

The Gemara poses another question: **Why do I need** the phrase that **the Merciful One writes with regard to one's aunt,**[N] which states: **They shall be childless?**[N] The death of one's children is included in the punishment of *karet*, and it has already been established that all of the forbidden intercourse is punishable by *karet*. The Gemara answers that it is necessary **for that** which **Rabba** said, **as Rabba raised a contradiction: It is written** with regard to one who had intercourse with his brother's wife: **"They shall be childless"** (Leviticus 20:22), **and it** also **states** with regard to one who had intercourse with his aunt: **"They shall die childless"** (Leviticus 20:21). **How so?** If **he** already **has children, he will** eventually **bury them;** if **he does not have children, he will go childless.**

HALAKHA

She shall remain after her husband's death as she is during his life – הִיא בַּהֲוָיָיתָהּ תְּהֵא: The mitzva of levirate marriage applies only to the wife of one's paternal brother. The wife of a maternal brother remains forbidden forever (Rambam *Sefer Kedusha, Hilkhot Yibbum* 2:2; *Shulḥan Arukh, Even HaEzer* 157:1).

NOTES

The phrase the Merciful One writes with regard to one's aunt, etc. – דּוֹדָתוֹ דִּכְתַב בָּהּ רַחֲמָנָא וכו׳: Many commentaries have noted that the phrase "They shall be childless" (Leviticus 20:21) does not appear in the context of an aunt, but rather in the context of a brother's wife. In the context of an aunt, the Torah states: "They shall die childless" (Leviticus 20:20). In fact, there were medieval commentaries whose texts of the Gemara stated: Why do I need the phrase the Merciful One writes with regard to one's aunt that states: "They shall die childless."

Why do I need the phrase…They shall be childless – עֲרִירִים יִהְיוּ לָמָּה לִי: The commentaries note that this supports Rashi's opinion that being childless is included in the punishment of *karet*, whereas it is difficult to explain this according to the opinion of the Riva, who maintains that being childless is a special punishment in addition to *karet*, which simply consists of the offender's life being cut short (see *Tosafot* on 2a and *Yam shel Shlomo*).

NOTES

A designated maidservant – שִׁפְחָה חֲרוּפָה: Rashi explains that a designated maidservant is a Canaanite maidservant betrothed to a Hebrew servant. A Hebrew servant is permitted to marry such a woman, but she is forbidden to all other Jews.

HALAKHA

The initial stage of intercourse with regard to those liable for violating prohibitions and positive mitzvot – הַעֲרָאָה בְּחַיָּיבֵי לָאוִין וַעֲשִׂין: The initial stage of intercourse is considered sexual intercourse with regard to all forbidden relations, including those prohibited due to both negative and positive mitzvot. The one exception is the case of a designated maidservant (Rambam *Sefer Kedusha*, *Hilkhot Issurei Bia* 1:10).

וְאִיצְטְרִיךְ לְמִכְתַּב "עֲרִירִים יִהְיוּ" וְאִיצְטְרִיךְ לְמִכְתַּב "עֲרִירִים יָמֻתוּ". דְּאִי כְּתַב רַחֲמָנָא "עֲרִירִים יִהְיוּ" הֲוָה אָמֵינָא: עַד חֶטְאֵיהּ, אֲבָל מֵחֶטְאֵיהּ וְאֵילָךְ – לָא, כְּתַב רַחֲמָנָא "עֲרִירִים יָמֻתוּ". וְאִי כְּתַב רַחֲמָנָא "עֲרִירִים יָמֻתוּ" הֲוָה אָמֵינָא: מֵחֶטְאֵיהּ וְאֵילָךְ, אֲבָל מֵעִיקָּרָא – לָא, צְרִיכָא.

The Gemara comments: **And it is necessary to state: They shall be childless, and it is** also **necessary to state: They shall die childless. As, if the Merciful One had written** only: **They shall be childless, I would have said** that only those children he had **before his sin** will die, **but** those born to him **from** the time of **his sin and on, no,** they will not die. **The Torah** therefore **states: They shall die childless,** indicating that even if he has children afterward they will die and he will remain childless. **And** similarly, **if the Merciful One had written** only: **They shall die childless, I would have said** that this is referring to children born **from** the time of **his sin and on, but** those born **from the beginning,** before he sinned, **no,** they will not die. It is therefore **necessary** to mention both expressions.

הַעֲרָאָה דְּחַיָּיבֵי לָאוִין מְנָלַן?

§ The Gemara above (54a–54b) derived that the initial stage of intercourse is considered an act of sexual intercourse with regard to prohibitions that are punishable by capital punishment or *karet*. The Gemara asks: **From where do we** derive that **the initial stage of intercourse** is considered an act of sexual intercourse **with regard to those liable** to receive punishment **for** violating ordinary Torah **prohibitions?**

מִדִּגְלֵי רַחֲמָנָא "שִׁכְבַת זֶרַע" גַּבֵּי שִׁפְחָה חֲרוּפָה – מִכְּלָל דְּחַיָּיבֵי לָאוִין בְּהַעֲרָאָה.

The Gemara answers: **From** the fact that **the Merciful One reveals with regard to a designated maidservant**[N] that the prohibition has been violated only through an act of **cohabitation with seed,** i.e., a complete act of sexual intercourse, in the verse "And whoever lies with a woman in cohabitation with seed, and she is a bondmaid designated to a man" (Leviticus 19:20), **by inference, those liable** to receive punishment **for** violating ordinary **prohibitions** are liable even **through the initial stage of intercourse.**

אַדְּרַבָּה, מִדִּגְלֵי רַחֲמָנָא הַעֲרָאָה בְּחַיָּיבֵי כְּרֵיתוֹת – מִכְּלָל דְּחַיָּיבֵי לָאוִין בִּגְמַר בִּיאָה! אָמַר רַב אַשִׁי: אִם כֵּן לִשְׁתּוֹק קְרָא מִשִּׁפְחָה חֲרוּפָה.

The Gemara responds: **On the contrary, from** the fact **that the Merciful One reveals** that **the initial stage of intercourse** is considered sexual intercourse **with regard to** forbidden relationships for which one is **liable to** receive *karet*, then, **by inference, those liable for** violating ordinary **prohibitions** are liable only **through the completion of** the act of **sexual intercourse** and not merely for the initial stage of intercourse. **Rav Ashi said: If so, let the verse remain silent** in the case of a **designated maidservant,** and it would be assumed that one is liable to receive punishment only for completing the act of sexual intercourse. The fact that the Torah specified that in this case one is liable to receive punishment only for completing the act of sexual intercourse indicates that with regard to other ordinary prohibitions one is liable even for the initial stage of intercourse.

הַעֲרָאָה דְּחַיָּיבֵי לָאוִין דִּכְהוּנָּה מְנָלַן? אָתְיָא "קִיחָה" "קִיחָה".

The Gemara asks: **From where do we** derive that **the initial stage of intercourse** is considered an act of sexual intercourse **with regard to those liable** to receive punishment **for** violating **prohibitions** specific to **the priesthood?** Since these prohibitions are unique in that they apply only to priests, their parameters cannot be derived from prohibitions that apply to the entire population. The Gemara answers: It **is derived** from a verbal analogy between the words **taking** and **taking.** This verb appears in prohibitions punishable by *karet*, e.g., "And if a man shall take his sister" (Leviticus 20:17), and in prohibitions of the priesthood, where it states: "They shall not take a woman that is a harlot" (Leviticus 21:7).

דְּחַיָּיבֵי עֲשֵׂה מְנָלַן?

The Gemara asks further: **From where do we** derive that the initial stage of intercourse is considered an act of sexual intercourse with regard to **those liable** to receive punishment for violating **a positive mitzva,**[H] e.g., one who has intercourse with an Egyptian or Edomite convert? The verse states: "The children that are born to them of the third generation may enter into the assembly of the Lord" (Deuteronomy 23:9). It is therefore a positive mitzva that only the grandchildren of these converts may have intercourse with a Jew.

אתיא "ביאה" "ביאה".

It is derived from a verbal analogy between the terms **entering** and **entering.** The verse states in the context of a prohibition: "A *mamzer* shall not enter into the assembly of the Lord" (Deuteronomy 23:3), and in the context of a prohibition derived from a positive mitzva: "The children that are born to them of the third generation may enter into the assembly of the Lord" (Deuteronomy 23:9). Consequently, these types of prohibitions are equated.

יבמה לשוק מנלן? אי למאן דאמר לאו – לאו, אי למאן דאמר עשה – עשה.

The Gemara poses another question: **From where do we** derive that the initial stage of intercourse is considered sexual intercourse with regard to the prohibition against a ***yevama*** having intercourse with a man from **the general public?** The Gemara answers that there is no need for an independent source in this case: **If** you are asking **according to the one who said** that this is an ordinary **prohibition,** it is a **prohibition** like any other. **If** you are asking **according to the one who said** that this is **a positive mitzva,**[N] it is **a positive mitzva** like any other.

אלא יבמה ליבם מנלן? אתיא "ביאה" "ביאה".

Rather, the question is as follows: **From where do we** derive that a ***yevama*** is acquired by her ***yavam*** via the initial stage of intercourse? The Gemara answers: **It is derived** from a verbal analogy between the **words entering** and **entering.** This verb is used with regard to ordinary Torah prohibitions, as mentioned above, and also with regard to levirate marriage, in the verse "Her brother-in-law will have intercourse with her" (Deuteronomy 25:5).

אשה לבעלה מנלן? אתיא "קיחה" "קיחה".

The Gemara asks further: **From where do we** derive that **a woman** is betrothed **to her husband** through the initial stage of intercourse?[N] The Gemara answers: **It is derived** from a verbal analogy between the words **taking** and **taking.** With regard to betrothal, the verse states: "When a man takes a wife and marries her" (Deuteronomy 24:1). This verb is also used with regard to forbidden intercourse, as in the verse: "And if a man shall take his sister" (Leviticus 20:17).

אמר רבא: למה לי דכתב רחמנא "שכבת זרע" בשפחה חרופה, "שכבת זרע" באשת איש, "שכבת זרע" בסוטה.

§ **Rava said:** Now that it has been established that the initial stage of intercourse is considered an act of sexual intercourse, **why do I** need the expression **"cohabitation with seed"** (Leviticus 19:20) **that the Merciful One writes with regard to a designated maidservant;** the expression **"cohabitation with seed"** (Leviticus 18:20) written **with regard to a married woman;** and the expression **"cohabitation with seed"** (Numbers 5:13) written with regard to **a *sota*?**[B]

דשפחה חרופה – כדאמרן. דאשת איש – פרט למשמש מת.

The Gemara explains that the expression is necessary with regard to **a designated maidservant as we said** above (55a), because it indicates that one is liable to receive punishment only for a complete act of intercourse with a designated maidservant[H] but not for the initial stage of intercourse. With regard to **a married woman,** the word seed **excludes one who has intercourse** with a **dead** organ,[H] i.e., one that is not erect, as this cannot lead to childbirth.

הניחא למאן דאמר משמש מת בעריות פטור, אלא למאן דאמר חייב – מאי איכא למימר? אלא פרט למשמש מתה. דסלקא דעתך אמינא: [הואיל] לאחר מיתה נמי איקרי שארו, אימא ליחייב עלה באשת איש – קא משמע לן.

The Gemara questions this resolution: **This** works out **well according to the one who said** that one who **has intercourse** while his organ is **dead** with **those with whom relations are forbidden, is exempt,** as this is not considered an act of intercourse. **However, according to the one who said** that **he is liable, what is there to say? Rather,** according to this opinion, the verse **excludes one who has intercourse with a dead** woman.[H] **As** it might **enter your mind to say: Since after death** she **is also called** her husband's **kin, say that** one who had intercourse with her **should be liable** to receive punishment for committing adultery **with a married woman.** It therefore **teaches us** that intercourse with a dead woman is not considered intercourse at all.

NOTES

If you are asking according to the one who said that this is a positive mitzva, etc. – **אי למאן דאמר עשה וכו׳**: *Tosafot* omit this sentence, as they maintain that everyone agrees that a *yevama* who has intercourse with another man has transgressed a prohibition. Rabbeinu Ḥananel and most medieval commentaries concur. See the Ramban for an attempt to explain Rashi's opinion, which maintains this sentence.

From where do we derive that a woman is betrothed to her husband through the initial stage of intercourse – **אשה לבעלה מנלן**: The commentaries point out an apparent contradiction between this passage and the Gemara in tractate *Kiddushin* (10a), which states that in the case of betrothal via intercourse, since the man is focused on the completion of the act, betrothal takes effect only at completion and not after the initial stage of intercourse (see Rif and *Tosafot*).

BACKGROUND

Sota – **סוטה**: The Torah describes the procedure governing such a woman (Numbers 5:11–31). First, her husband warns her in the presence of witnesses against being alone together with a specific man about whom he is suspicious. If she disobeys this warning and is observed alone with that man, even though there is no concrete evidence that she actually committed adultery, she and her husband may no longer live together as man and wife until she has undergone the following ordeal to determine whether she has committed adultery. The woman, accompanied by her husband and two Torah scholars, is taken to the Temple in Jerusalem and forced by the priests to stand in a public place while holding the special meal-offering that she is required to bring. There she is again questioned about her behavior. If she continues to protest her fidelity and takes an oath to that effect, a scroll is brought and the curses of the *sota* mentioned in the Torah passage cited above are written on it. The scroll is submerged in a clay vessel filled with water taken from the Temple basin and some earth from the Temple floor, and the scroll's writing is dissolved in the water. She is then forced to drink that water. If she has committed adultery, in the words of the Torah, "her belly shall swell and her thigh shall fall away" (Numbers 5:27), until ultimately she dies from the water's curse. If she is innocent, the water will bring her blessing and she is permitted to resume normal marital relations with her husband.

HALAKHA

Intercourse with a designated maidservant – **ביאה בשפחה חרופה**: The unique *halakha* of a designated maidservant is that one is liable to receive punishment only for a complete act of intercourse and only if it is performed in a typical manner (Rambam *Sefer Kedusha*, *Hilkhot Issurei Bia* 3:15; *Tur*, *Even HaEzer* 20).

One who has intercourse with a dead organ – **משמש מת**: If one engages in a prohibited act of intercourse without an erection, but rather with a completely limp organ that he inserts manually, he is not liable to receive *karet* or lashes and he is certainly exempt from capital punishment. However, in accordance with the opinion of Rava in tractate *Shevuot* (18a), he is flogged by rabbinic decree (Rambam *Sefer Kedusha*, *Hilkhot Issurei Bia* 1:11; *Tur*, *Even HaEzer* 20).

One who has intercourse with a dead woman – **משמש מתה**: One who has intercourse with the corpse of a woman with whom relations are forbidden is exempt (Rambam *Sefer Kedusha*, *Hilkhot Issurei Bia* 1:12; *Tur*, *Even HaEzer* 20).

דְּסוֹטָה לָמָּה לִי? לְכִדְתַנְיָא: ״שִׁכְבַת זֶרַע״ פְּרָט לְדָבָר אַחֵר. מַאי דָּבָר אַחֵר? אָמַר רַב שֵׁשֶׁת: פְּרָט לְשֶׁקִּינֵּא לָהּ שֶׁלֹּא כְּדַרְכָּהּ. אָמַר לֵיהּ רָבָא: ״מִשְׁכְּבֵי אִשָּׁה״ כְּתִיב!

The Gemara addresses the third case: **Why do I need** the expression cohabitation with seed in the context of a ***sota*****?** It is needed **for that which is taught** in a *baraita*, that the expression **a cohabitation with seed excludes something else.** The Gemara asks: **What is this something else? Rav Sheshet said: It excludes** a case **where** the husband **was jealous with regard to her** and warned her not to seclude herself and have **atypical,** i.e., anal, sexual intercourse with another man. **Rava** objected to this explanation and **said to him: It is written: "The cohabitations of a woman"** (Leviticus 18:22), indicating that there are two types of intercourse with a woman, and the same *halakha* applies to both.

אֶלָּא אָמַר רָבָא: פְּרָט לְשֶׁקִּינֵּא לָהּ דֶּרֶךְ אֵבָרִים. אָמַר לֵיהּ אַבָּיֵי: פְּרִיצוּתָא אָסַר רַחֲמָנָא?

Rather, Rava said: It **excludes** a situation **where** the husband **was jealous with regard to her** and warned her not to seclude herself with another man and engage in intimate contact **by way of** other **limbs.** The verse indicates that the wife does not become prohibited to her husband if she secludes herself with the man after this warning. **Abaye said to him:** Does **the Merciful One prohibit** a woman to her husband due merely to **licentious** behavior without sexual intercourse? Since this behavior would not render a woman prohibited to her husband, it is obvious that a warning that explicitly mentions this behavior is insufficient to cause the woman to become a *sota* if she then secludes herself with the man.

אֶלָּא אָמַר אַבָּיֵי: פְּרָט לְשֶׁקִּינֵּא לָהּ בִּנְשִׁיקָה. הָנִיחָא לְמַאן דְּאָמַר הַעֲרָאָה זוֹ הַכְנָסַת עֲטָרָה, אֶלָּא לְמַאן דְּאָמַר זוֹ נְשִׁיקָה – מַאי אִיכָּא לְמֵימַר?

Rather, Abaye said: It excludes a case **where** he **was jealous with regard to her** and warned her not to seclude herself with another man and **kiss,** i.e., have external contact of the sexual organs. The Gemara asks: **This** works out **well according to the one who said** that the definition of **the initial stage of intercourse is the insertion of the corona;** therefore, mere external contact is not considered sexual intercourse. **However, according to the one who said** that the definition of the initial stage of intercourse is a **kiss, what is there to say?**

אֶלָּא, לְעוֹלָם לְשֶׁקִּינֵּא לָהּ דֶּרֶךְ אֵבָרִים, וְאִיצְטְרִיךְ: סָלְקָא דַּעְתָּךְ אָמִינָא: בְּקְפִידָא דְּבַעַל תָּלָה רַחֲמָנָא, וְהָא קָא קָפֵיד, קָא מַשְׁמַע לַן.

Rather, the expression: Something else, in the *baraita*, is **actually** referring to a case **where** the husband **was jealous with regard to her** and warned her not to seclude herself with another man and engage in intimate contact **by way of** other **limbs. And it is necessary** to state that the woman does not become prohibited to her husband as a *sota* in this case, as **it might enter your mind to say that the Merciful One made** this *halakha* **dependent on the husband's objection,** as it is his decision to warn his wife, **and** since **he objects** to contact of this nature, she becomes a *sota* if she secludes herself after this warning. The Torah therefore **teaches us** that this is not considered a warning.

אָמַר שְׁמוּאֵל: הַעֲרָאָה זוֹ נְשִׁיקָה, מָשָׁל לְאָדָם שֶׁמַּנִּיחַ אֶצְבָּעוֹ עַל פִּיו – אִי אֶפְשָׁר שֶׁלֹּא יִדְחוֹק הַבָּשָׂר.

§ The Gemara returns to the precise definition of the initial stage of intercourse. **Shmuel said:** The definition of **the initial stage of intercourse**[B] **is a kiss,** i.e., external contact of the sexual organs.[N] Shmuel explains: This is **comparable to a person who places his finger on his mouth;** it is **impossible that he not press the flesh** of his lips. Similarly, when there is contact of the sexual organs, there will certainly be at least a small amount of penetration, and this is considered an act of sexual intercourse.

כִּי אֲתָא רַבָּה בַּר בַּר חָנָה אָמַר רַבִּי יוֹחָנָן: גְּמַר בִּיאָה בְּשִׁפְחָה חֲרוּפָה – זוֹ הַכְנָסַת עֲטָרָה. מְתִיב רַב שֵׁשֶׁת: ״שִׁכְבַת זֶרַע״ אֵינוֹ חַיָּיב אֶלָּא עַל בִּיאַת הַמֵּירוּק. מַאי לָאו – מֵירוּק גִּיד? לָא, מֵירוּק עֲטָרָה.

When Rabba bar bar Ḥana came from Eretz Yisrael, **he said** that **Rabbi Yoḥanan said: The completion of intercourse** stated **with regard to a designated maidservant is the insertion of the corona,** and no more. **Rav Sheshet raised an objection** based upon the following *baraita*: The phrase **cohabitation with seed** indicates that **one is liable** to receive punishment **only for a complete** act of **sexual intercourse. What, does** this **not** refer to the **complete** insertion of the **member?** The Gemara responds: **No,** it is possible that it is referring to the **complete** insertion of the **corona.**

BACKGROUND

The initial stage of intercourse – הַעֲרָאָה: The definition of the term intercourse is problematic in virtually all legal systems. One of the missing features in this discussion with regard to the initial stage of intercourse, discussed by later halakhic commentaries, is the exact definition of the female sexual organ. Regardless, it seems that the halakhic conclusion concerning the first stage of sexual contact is, to a great extent, a minimal degree of penetration of the penis into the vagina.

NOTES

A kiss, i.e., external contact of the sexual organs – נְשִׁיקָה: It is noted in the Jerusalem Talmud that even according to Shmuel the contact must include a slight insertion of the organ.

כִּי אֲתָא רַב דִּימִי אָמַר רַבִּי יוֹחָנָן: הַעֲרָאָה – זוֹ הַכְנָסַת עֲטָרָה. אָמְרוּ לֵיהּ: וְהָא רַבָּה בַּר בַּר חָנָה לָא אָמַר הָכִי? אֲמַר לְהוּ: אוֹ אִיהוּ שַׁקְרַאי אוֹ אֲנָא שַׁקְרִי.

When Rav Dimi came[B] from Eretz Yisrael **he said** that **Rabbi Yoḥanan** said: The definition of **the initial stage of intercourse is the insertion of the corona. They said to him: But Rabba bar bar Ḥana did not say so,** as he taught that Rabbi Yoḥanan said that the insertion of the corona constitutes a complete act of sexual intercourse and is not considered merely the initial stage of intercourse. **He said to them: Either he lied or I am lying.** There is clearly a contradiction, and one of us cited Rabbi Yoḥanan's opinion incorrectly.

כִּי אֲתָא רָבִין אָמַר רַבִּי יוֹחָנָן: הַעֲרָאָה זוֹ הַכְנָסַת עֲטָרָה. אַדְּרַבָּה בַּר בַּר חָנָה – וַדַּאי פָּלֵיג, אַדִּשְׁמוּאֵל מִי לֵימָא פָּלֵיג?!

When Ravin came from Eretz Yisrael **he said** that **Rabbi Yoḥanan** said: The definition of **the initial stage of intercourse is the insertion of the corona.** The Gemara comments: He **certainly disagrees with Rabba bar bar Ḥana,** who cited Rabbi Yoḥanan as stating that insertion of the corona constitutes a complete act of sexual intercourse. **Shall we say that he** also **disagrees with Shmuel,** who defined the initial stage of intercourse as external contact of the sexual organs?

לָא, מִנְּשִׁיקָה וְעַד הַכְנָסַת עֲטָרָה – הַעֲרָאָה קָרֵי לַהּ.

The Gemara responds: **No;** it is possible that there is no dispute between them, and Ravin said that Rabbi Yoḥanan **calls** the entire process **from a kiss until the insertion of the corona the initial stage of intercourse,** while anything beyond that point is a complete act of sexual intercourse.

כִּי אֲתָא רַב שְׁמוּאֵל בַּר יְהוּדָה אָמַר רַבִּי יוֹחָנָן הַעֲרָאָה – זוֹ הַכְנָסַת עֲטָרָה, גְּמַר בִּיאָה – גְּמַר בִּיאָה מַמָּשׁ.

When Rav Shmuel bar Yehuda came from Eretz Yisrael he reported that **Rabbi Yoḥanan said:** The definition of **the initial stage of intercourse is the insertion of the corona,**[H] whereas a **complete** act of **sexual intercourse is literally a complete** act of **sexual intercourse,** i.e., insertion of the male organ beyond the corona.

BACKGROUND

When Rav Dimi came – כִּי אֲתָא רַב דִּימִי: Rav Dimi was one of the Sages who would often travel from Eretz Yisrael to Babylonia, primarily to transmit the Torah of Eretz Yisrael to the Torah centers of the Diaspora, although occasionally he traveled on business as well. Consequently, many questions, particularly those concerning the Torah of Eretz Yisrael, remained unresolved until the messenger from Zion, Rav Dimi, would arrive and elucidate the *halakha*, the novel expression, or the unique circumstances pertaining to a particular statement that required clarification.

HALAKHA

What is the initial stage of intercourse – מַה הִיא הַעֲרָאָה: The initial stage of intercourse is the insertion of the corona. Anything less than this is called mere external contact, for which one is exempt. The *halakha* is in accordance with the opinion of Ravin and Rav Shmuel bar Yehuda in the name of Rabbi Yoḥanan (Rambam *Sefer Kedusha, Hilkhot Issurei Bia* 1:10; *Shulḥan Arukh, Even HaEzer* 20:1, and in the comment of Rema; see *Beit Shmuel*).

Perek **VI**
Daf **56** Amud **a**

מִכָּאן וְאֵילָךְ אֵינוֹ אֶלָּא נְשִׁיקָה, וּפָטוּר עָלֶיהָ. וּפְלִיג אַדִּשְׁמוּאֵל.

From this point **forward,** insertion of anything less than the corona **is only** considered **a kiss, for which he is exempt. And** this statement **disagrees with** that of **Shmuel,** who maintains that one is liable to receive punishment for external contact of the sexual organs.

"אֶחָד הַמְעָרֶה וְאֶחָד הַגּוֹמֵר קָנָה". מַאי קָנָה? רַב אָמַר: קָנָה לַכֹּל. וּשְׁמוּאֵל אָמַר: לֹא קָנָה אֶלָּא לִדְבָרִים הָאֲמוּרִים בַּפָּרָשָׁה: לִירַשׁ בְּנִכְסֵי אָחִיו, וְלִפְטוֹרָהּ מִן הַיִּיבּוּם.

§ It was taught in the mishna that **both one who** merely **engages in the initial stage of intercourse and one who completes** the act of intercourse **have** thereby **acquired** the *yevama*. The Gemara asks: **What** does it mean that he has **acquired** his *yevama*?[NH] **Rav said:** He has **acquired** her **for everything.** In other words, she is considered his wife in all regards. Therefore, if he is a priest, she may partake of *teruma*. **And Shmuel said he has only acquired her with regard to the matters stated in the chapter** of levirate marriage, i.e., **to inherit his brother's property and to exempt her from levirate marriage** if he then dies and leaves behind children from another wife.

HALAKHA

What does it mean that he has acquired his *yevama* – מַאי קָנָה: If a priest performed a deficient act of intercourse with his *yevama*, meaning that he did not intend to thereby perform levirate marriage, and she had merely been betrothed to the deceased brother, she may not partake of *teruma* and they are not considered fully married. Some say that the same applies if he intended to perform levirate marriage, but performed only the initial stage of intercourse. However, if she had been not only betrothed but also married to the deceased brother, even a deficient act of intercourse effects levirate marriage, and she may partake of *teruma*, as she had in the past. The *halakha* is in accordance with the opinion of Rav as presented in the second interpretation of the dispute between Rav and Shmuel (Rambam *Sefer Zera'im, Hilkhot Terumot* 8:6; *Shulḥan Arukh, Even HaEzer* 166:9).

NOTES

What does it mean that he has acquired his *yevama* – מַאי קָנָה: The commentaries disagree over the meaning of this passage. According to *Tosafot*, the Ramban, and the Rashba, the discussion concerns a case in which his intercourse was deficient because he did not intend thereby to perform levirate marriage. However, if he intended to perform levirate marriage and engaged only in the initial stage of intercourse, all agree that they are fully married, as this is considered a complete act of intercourse.

Conversely, the Rif apparently understood that the discussion also applies to anyone who performs only the initial stage of intercourse. The Rambam explicitly endorses this opinion as well. According to this opinion, when the Gemara mentions unwitting and intentional intercourse, it is merely citing examples, but does not mean to exclude the case of one who performs only the initial stage of intercourse (Rabbi Avraham min HaHar). The *Arukh LaNer* claims that the Rif is consistent with his opinion above (see NOTES to 55b) that the initial stage of intercourse consummates a marriage only if the woman had previously been betrothed to the man. Consequently, the *amora'im* here dispute whether the levirate bond is sufficiently strong to allow the levirate marriage to be consummated via the initial stage of intercourse.

NOTES

Say as follows: If he did not have a chance, etc. – אֵימָא הָכִי: וְלֹא הִסְפִּיק וכו׳: Shmuel does not mean to say that the *baraita* is incomplete. Rather, he understands that when the *baraita* states that the woman may partake of *teruma* if her first husband died and the woman happens before her *yavam* for levirate marriage, it means that if she had already been married to her first husband before he died, she may partake of *teruma* after performing levirate marriage with her deaf-mute *yavam*. The case is not comparable to one where she had merely been betrothed to her first husband (Ritva).

מִן הַנְּשׂוּאִין לְדִבְרֵי הַכֹּל אָכְלָה, דְּהָא הֲוָת קָאָכְלָה מֵעִיקָּרָא. כִּי פְּלִיגִי – מִן הָאֵירוּסִין. רַב אָמַר: אוֹכֶלֶת, דְּהָא רַבֵּי רַחֲמָנָא בִּיאַת שׁוֹגֵג כְּמֵזִיד.

The Gemara adds: If she was a *yevama* **from marriage, everyone agrees** that she may **partake** of *teruma* after the initial stage of intercourse, **as she was** already **partaking at the outset,** when she was married to the deceased brother. Therefore, even a minimal act of intercourse is enough to allow her to continue to partake of *teruma*. **When they disagree** it is with regard to a *yevama* **from betrothal. Rav said:** She **may partake, as the Merciful One includes unwitting intercourse** and the other forms of intercourse listed in the mishna, and considers them **like intentional** intercourse.

וּשְׁמוּאֵל אָמַר: כִּי רַבֵּי רַחֲמָנָא – לְאוֹקְמֵיהּ בִּמְקוֹם בַּעַל, לְאַלּוּמֵי מִבַּעַל – לָא.

And Shmuel said: When the Merciful One includes these forms of intercourse, He does so only **to establish** the *yavam* **in place of** the **husband,** but **to strengthen** him more **than the husband, no.** Since she was merely betrothed to the deceased brother, she was not permitted to partake of *teruma*, and therefore she may not partake of *teruma* at this point either.

וְאַזְדָּא שְׁמוּאֵל לְטַעְמֵיהּ, דְּאָמַר רַב נַחְמָן אָמַר שְׁמוּאֵל: כָּל שֶׁהַבַּעַל מַאֲכִיל – יָבָם מַאֲכִיל, וְכָל שֶׁאֵין הַבַּעַל מַאֲכִיל – יָבָם אֵינוֹ מַאֲכִיל.

The Gemara comments: **And Shmuel follows his** regular line of **reasoning,** as **Rav Naḥman said** that **Shmuel said:** In **any** case **where the** woman's marriage to her original **husband entitles** her **to partake** of *teruma*, intercourse with the ***yavam*** in any of the manners described in the mishna also **entitles** her **to partake** of *teruma*, **and any** case **where** her relationship with her original **husband does not entitle** her **to partake** of *teruma*, i.e., if she had been betrothed but not married, intercourse with the ***yavam*** in the manners described in the mishna also **does not entitle** her **to partake** of *teruma*.

מֵיתִיבִי: בַּת יִשְׂרָאֵל פִּקַּחַת שֶׁנִּתְאָרְסָה לְכֹהֵן פִּקֵּחַ, וְלֹא הִסְפִּיק לְכוֹנְסָהּ עַד שֶׁנִּתְחָרֵשׁ – אֵינָהּ אוֹכֶלֶת. מֵת, וְנָפְלָה לִפְנֵי יָבָם חֵרֵשׁ – אוֹכֶלֶת. וּבְזוֹ יָפֶה כֹּחַ הַיָּבָם מִכֹּחַ הַבַּעַל.

The Gemara **raises an objection** from the following *baraita*: In the case of a mentally **competent daughter of an Israelite who was betrothed to a competent priest, and he did not have a chance to marry her before he became a deaf-mute** and was no longer mentally competent, **she may not partake** of *teruma*, as marriage to a deaf-mute does not enable a woman to partake of *teruma*. If the deaf-mute husband subsequently **died and** the *yevama* **happened before a deaf-mute *yavam*** for levirate marriage, **she** may **partake** of *teruma*. **And in this** regard **the strength of the *yavam* is greater than the strength of the husband.**

בִּשְׁלָמָא לְרַב – נִיחָא, אֶלָּא לִשְׁמוּאֵל – קַשְׁיָא!

Granted, according Rav, this **works out well,** as intercourse with the deaf-mute *yavam*, which is comparable to the unwitting intercourse mentioned in the mishna because the deaf-mute is not mentally competent, effects the levirate marriage and allows her to partake of *teruma* despite the fact that she could not do so during the lifetime of her first husband. **However, according to Shmuel,** this is **difficult,** as he maintains that a *yavam* cannot have more rights than the deceased husband due to intercourse undertaken without intent to perform levirate marriage.

אָמַר לָךְ שְׁמוּאֵל: אֵימָא הָכִי: וְלֹא הִסְפִּיק לְכוֹנְסָהּ עַד שֶׁנִּתְחָרֵשׁ – אֵינָהּ אוֹכֶלֶת בִּתְרוּמָה. כָּנַס וְאַחַר כָּךְ נִתְחָרֵשׁ – אוֹכֶלֶת, מֵת וְנָפְלָה לִפְנֵי יָבָם חֵרֵשׁ – אוֹכֶלֶת.

The Gemara answers: **Shmuel** could have **said to you:** Amend the *baraita* and **say as follows:** If **he did not have a chance**[N] **to marry her before he became a deaf-mute, she may not partake of *teruma*.** If **he married her and afterward became a deaf-mute, she** may **partake** of *teruma*. If he then **died, and** she **happened before a deaf-mute *yavam*** for levirate marriage, **she** may **partake** of *teruma*.

וּמַאי "בְּזוֹ" דְּאִילּוּ בַּעַל חֵרֵשׁ מֵעִיקָּרָא – לֹא אוֹכֶלֶת, וְאִילּוּ יָבָם חֵרֵשׁ מֵעִיקָּרָא – אָכְלָה.

And what is the meaning of the phrase: **In this** regard the strength of the *yavam* is greater than the strength of the husband? It means to say **that if** the original **husband** was a **deaf-mute from the outset,** i.e., before consummating the marriage, **she would not** have been allowed to **partake** of *teruma*, **whereas if the *yavam*** was a **deaf-mute from the outset** she may **partake** of *teruma* once they perform levirate marriage, because she had been fully married to the deceased brother.

וְאִיכָּא דְּאָמְרִי: מִן הָאֵירוּסִין – דִּבְרֵי הַכֹּל לֹא אָכְלָה, דְּהָא לָא אָכְלָה בְּחַיֵּי בַּעַל.

And some say a different version of the dispute between Rav and Shmuel: If she was a *yevama* **from betrothal,** i.e., her marriage with the deceased brother had never been completed, and she and the brother-in-law engaged in an inferior form of intercourse as described in the mishna, **everyone agrees** that she may **not partake** of *teruma*, **as she did not partake** of *teruma* **in her husband's lifetime.**

כִּי פְּלִיגִי – מִן הַנִּשּׂוּאִין. רַב אָמַר: אוֹכֶלֶת, דְּהָא הֲוַת אָכְלָה מֵעִיקָּרָא. וּשְׁמוּאֵל אָמַר: אֵינָהּ אוֹכֶלֶת, כִּי רַבֵּי רַחֲמָנָא בִּיאַת שׁוֹגֵג כְּמֵזִיד – לַדְּבָרִים הָאֲמוּרִים בַּפָּרָשָׁה, אֲבָל לְכָל מִילֵּי – לָא.

When they disagree, it is with regard to a *yevama* **from marriage. Rav says: She** may **partake** of *teruma* **as she was** permitted to partake of *teruma* **initially,** while married to the deceased brother. **And Shmuel says** she **may not partake** of *teruma*, because **when the Merciful One includes unwitting intercourse** and considers it **like intentional** intercourse, it was only with regard to **the matters stated in the chapter** of levirate marriage, **but for every** other **issue, no.**

וְהָאָמַר רַב נַחְמָן אָמַר שְׁמוּאֵל: כָּל שֶׁהַבַּעַל מַאֲכִיל – יָבָם מַאֲכִיל! אֵימָא: כָּל בִּיאָה שֶׁהַבַּעַל מַאֲכִיל בָּהּ – יָבָם מַאֲכִיל בָּהּ – וְכָל בִּיאָה שֶׁאֵין הַבַּעַל מַאֲכִיל בָּהּ – אֵין הַיָּבָם מַאֲכִיל בָּהּ.

The Gemara raises a difficulty: **Didn't Rav Naḥman say** that **Shmuel** himself **said:** In **any** case **where the** woman's marriage to her original **husband entitles** her to **partake** of *teruma*, intercourse with the *yavam* in one of the manners listed in the mishna also **entitles** her to **partake** of *teruma*? The Gemara answers: Emend the wording and **say** as follows: With regard to **any** act of **intercourse through which the husband entitles** her to **partake** of *teruma*, **a *yavam*** also **entitles** her to **partake** of *teruma*; **and** with regard to **any** act of **intercourse through which the husband does not entitle** her to **partake** of *teruma*, **a *yavam*** also **does not entitle** her to **partake** of *teruma*. Just as betrothal cannot be performed via an unwitting act of intercourse, this act does not entitle a *yevama* to partake of *teruma*.

מֵיתִיבֵי בַּת יִשְׂרָאֵל פִּקַּחַת שֶׁנִּתְאָרְסָה לְכֹהֵן פִּקֵּחַ, וְלֹא הִסְפִּיק לְכוֹנְסָהּ עַד שֶׁנִּתְחָרֵשׁ – אֵינָהּ אוֹכֶלֶת. מֵת וְנָפְלָה לִפְנֵי יָבָם חֵרֵשׁ – אוֹכֶלֶת, וּבְזוֹ יָפֶה כֹּחַ יָבָם מִכֹּחַ בַּעַל. בִּשְׁלָמָא לְרַב – מְתָרֵץ כְּדְתָרֵיץ מֵעִיקָּרָא. אֶלָּא לִשְׁמוּאֵל קַשְׁיָא! קַשְׁיָא.

The Gemara **raises an objection** from the following *baraita*: In the case of a mentally **competent daughter of an Israelite who was betrothed to a competent priest, and he did not have a chance to marry her before he became a deaf-mute** and was no longer mentally competent, **she may not partake** of *teruma*. If the deaf-mute husband subsequently **died, and the** *yevama* **happened before a deaf-mute *yavam*** for levirate marriage, **she** may **partake** of *teruma*.[H] **And in this** regard **the strength of the *yavam* is greater than the strength of the husband. Granted, according to Rav, he** can **answer as** Shmuel **answered initially,** i.e., according to the first version of the dispute between Rav and Shmuel. **However, according to Shmuel,** it is **difficult.**[N] The Gemara concludes: Indeed, it is **difficult.**

תָּנוּ רַבָּנַן: בַּת יִשְׂרָאֵל פִּקַּחַת שֶׁנִּתְאָרְסָה לְכֹהֵן פִּקֵּחַ, וְלֹא הִסְפִּיק לְכוֹנְסָהּ עַד שֶׁנִּתְחָרֵשׁ – אֵינָהּ אוֹכֶלֶת, נוֹלַד לָהּ בֵּן – אוֹכֶלֶת. מֵת הַבֵּן, רַבִּי נָתָן אוֹמֵר: אוֹכֶלֶת, וַחֲכָמִים אוֹמְרִים: אֵינָהּ אוֹכֶלֶת.

§ **The Sages taught:** In the case of a mentally **competent daughter of an Israelite who was betrothed to a** mentally **competent priest, and he did not have a chance to marry her before he became a deaf-mute** and was no longer mentally competent, **she may not partake** of *teruma*. **If a son was born to her**[H] from this priest, **she** may **partake** of *teruma* on account of her son. If **the son died, Rabbi Natan says she** may continue to **partake** of *teruma*, **and the Rabbis say she may not** continue to **partake** of *teruma*.

מַאי טַעְמָא דְּרַבִּי נָתָן? אָמַר רַבָּה: הוֹאִיל שֶׁכְּבָר אָכְלָה. אָמַר לֵיהּ אַבַּיֵי: אֶלָּא מֵעַתָּה בַּת יִשְׂרָאֵל שֶׁנִּיסֵּת לְכֹהֵן וּמִית לֵיהּ – תֵּיכוּל, שֶׁכְּבָר אָכְלָה! אֶלָּא, כֵּיוָן דְּמִית לֵיהּ פָּקַע לֵיהּ קְדוּשָּׁתֵיהּ מִינָּהּ – הָכָא נַמִי, כֵּיוָן דְּמִית לֵיהּ פָּקַע קְדוּשָּׁתֵיהּ מִינָּהּ!

The Gemara asks: **What is the reasoning of Rabbi Natan? Rabba said: Since she has** already **partaken of** *teruma* in a permitted manner, she may continue. **Abaye said to him: However, if** that is so, in the case of the **daughter of an Israelite who was married to a priest, and he died** childless, she **should** be allowed to **partake** of *teruma*, **as she has** already **partaken of** it in the past. **Rather,** it must be that **since he has passed away,** his priestly **sanctity has left her,** and she is considered a regular Israelite in all regards. **Here too, since** the son **has passed away,** his priestly **sanctity has left her,** and therefore she should not be entitled to partake of *teruma*. Rabba's explanation should consequently be rejected.

אֶלָּא אָמַר רַב יוֹסֵף: קָסָבַר רַבִּי נָתָן נִשּׂוּאֵי חֵרֵשׁ מַאֲכִילִין בִּתְרוּמָה, וְלָא גָּזְרִינַן נִשּׂוּאֵי חֵרֵשׁ אַטּוּ קִדּוּשֵׁי חֵרֵשׁ. אָמַר לֵיהּ אַבַּיֵי: אִי הָכִי, נוֹלַד לָהּ בֵּן לָמָּה לִי! מִשּׁוּם רַבָּנַן.

Rather, Rav Yosef said: Rabbi Natan holds that **the marriage of a deaf-mute** who was competent when he betrothed his wife **entitles her to partake of *teruma*, and we do not** issue a **decree** against the wife partaking of *teruma* through **marriage** to **a deaf-mute due to** the case of **betrothal** to **a deaf-mute.** Although the betrothal of a deaf-mute does not take effect, his consummation of a marriage does take effect and entitles his wife to partake of *teruma*. **Abaye said to him: If so, why do I** need the *baraita* to specify that **a son was born to her?** She should be entitled to eat *teruma* even if she did not have a son. Rav Yosef responded: That case is mentioned **due to** the opinion of **the Rabbis,** who hold that she is entitled to partake of *teruma* only if she has a child.

HALAKHA

A mentally competent woman who married a priest and he became a deaf-mute, etc. – **פִּקַּחַת שֶׁנִּשֵּׂאת לְכֹהֵן וְנִתְחָרֵשׁ וכו׳:** If a woman from a non-priestly family was betrothed to a priest, and before they were fully married he became a deaf-mute and was no longer mentally competent, she may not partake of *teruma*. If he died and she performed levirate marriage with her deaf-mute *yavam*, she still may not partake of *teruma*. However, if her first husband married her and only then became a deaf-mute, she may partake of *teruma*. If he then died and she performed levirate marriage with her deaf-mute *yavam*, she may partake of *teruma* (Rambam *Sefer Zera'im, Hilkhot Terumot* 8:10).

If a son was born to her – **נוֹלַד לָהּ בֵּן:** If a priest was a deaf-mute when he married, his wife may not partake of *teruma*. Nevertheless, if she has a child, she may partake of *teruma* on his account (Rambam *Sefer Zera'im, Hilkhot Terumot* 8:10).

NOTES

However, according to Shmuel it is difficult – **אֶלָּא לִשְׁמוּאֵל קַשְׁיָא:** Even so, Shmuel's opinion is not entirely refuted, as even according to Rav, the text of the *baraita* must be adjusted or interpreted in a manner that is not immediately obvious. Therefore, Shmuel's opinion cannot be rejected by dint of a *baraita* of questionable reliability (Ritva; see *Keren Ora*).

וְלִיפְלוֹג רַבִּי נָתָן עֲלַיְיהוּ בְּרֵישָׁא – שָׁבֵיק לְהוּ לְרַבָּנַן עַד דִּמְסַיְּימִי מִילְּתַיְיהוּ, וַהֲדַר פָּלֵיג עֲלַיְיהוּ. אִי הָכִי לִיתְנֵי: מֵת הַבֵּן אֵינָהּ אוֹכֶלֶת, רַבִּי נָתָן אוֹמֵר: אוֹכֶלֶת! קַשְׁיָא.

Abaye asks further: **And let Rabbi Natan disagree with them in the first clause** of the *baraita* as well. Rav Yosef responds: Rabbi Natan **left the Rabbis until they finished their statement, and then disagreed with them** with regard to their entire statement. The Gemara asks: **If so, let** the *baraita* first **teach** that if **the son died** she **may not partake** of *teruma*, and subsequently state: **Rabbi Natan said** she **may eat.** Why is Rabbi Natan's opinion mentioned before the Rabbis finished stating their opinion? The Gemara concludes: Indeed, this **is difficult** according to Rav Yosef.

"וְכֵן הַבָּא עַל אַחַת מִכׇּל הָעֲרָיוֹת". אָמַר רַב עַמְרָם: הָא מִילְּתָא אֲמַר לַן רַב שֵׁשֶׁת,

§ It was taught in the mishna: **And so too, one who had intercourse with any one of those with whom relations are forbidden** by **the Torah** in any form is liable to receive punishment. **Rav Amram said: This matter was said** to us by **Rav Sheshet,**

Perek **VI**
Daf **56** Amud **b**

וְאַנְהֲרִינְהוּ לְעַיְינִין מִמַּתְנִיתִין: אֵשֶׁת יִשְׂרָאֵל שֶׁנֶּאֶנְסָה, אַף עַל פִּי שֶׁמּוּתֶּרֶת לְבַעְלָהּ – פְּסוּלָה לִכְהוּנָּה. וְתָנָא תּוּנָא: וְכֵן הַבָּא עַל אַחַת מִכׇּל הָעֲרָיוֹת הָאֲמוּרוֹת בַּתּוֹרָה, אוֹ פְּסוּלוֹת.

and he illuminated our eyes from the mishna, i.e., he demonstrated that the mishna serves as the basis for his opinion: With regard to **the wife of an Israelite who was raped,**[NH] **although she is permitted to her husband, she is disqualified for the priesthood.** Therefore, if her husband dies, she may not marry a priest. **And the** ***tanna*** of our mishna also **taught: And so too,** in the case of **one who had intercourse with any one of those with whom relations are forbidden** [***arayot***] by **the Torah or** with those who are **unfit** to marry **him** even though they are not in the category of *arayot*, the woman is disqualified from marrying a priest.

מַאי "וְכֵן"? מַאי לָאו: לָא שְׁנָא בְּשׁוֹגֵג וְלָא שְׁנָא בְּמֵזִיד וְלָא שְׁנָא בְּאוֹנֶס וְלָא שְׁנָא בְּרָצוֹן. וְקָתָנֵי "פְּסָלָהּ".

What is the meaning of the phrase: **And so too? What, is it not** that **it is no different** whether they have intercourse **unwittingly or intentionally, and it is no different** whether they have intercourse **due to coercion or willingly? And it is taught** that **he has rendered her disqualified** from marrying a priest.

לָא, מַאי "וְכֵן" – אַהַעֲרָאָה. הַעֲרָאָה דְּמַאן? אִילֵּימָא דַּעֲרָיוֹת – לְמֵימְרָא דַּעֲרָיוֹת יָלְפִינַן מִיְּבָמָה? אַדְּרַבָּה, יְבָמָה יָלְפִינַן מֵעֲרָיוֹת, דְּעִיקַּר הַעֲרָאָה בַּעֲרָיוֹת כְּתִיב!

The Gemara refutes this proof: **No, what** is the meaning of the phrase: **And so too?** It is referring **to the initial stage of intercourse,** as this too invalidates her. The Gemara asks: **The initial stage of intercourse of whom? If we say** it is referring to **those with whom relations are prohibited** and carry a punishment of *karet* or death [***arayot***], **is this to say that** the *halakha* **with regard to those with whom relations are prohibited is derived from** the *halakha* with regard to **a** ***yevama***, as implied by the phrase: And so too? **On the contrary, we derive** the *halakha* **of a** ***yevama*** **from** the *halakha* **with regard to those with whom relations are prohibited, as the main** source that indicates that **the initial stage of intercourse** is considered intercourse **is stated in** the context of **those with whom relations are prohibited** and not in the context of a *yevama*.

אֶלָּא מַאי "וְכֵן" – אַשֶּׁלֹּא כְּדַרְכָּהּ דַּעֲרָיוֹת – אַדְּרַבָּה, עִיקַּר "מִשְׁכְּבֵי אִשָּׁה" בַּעֲרָיוֹת כְּתִיב?

Rather, what is the meaning of the phrase: **And so too?** It is referring **to atypical,** i.e., anal, **sexual intercourse with those with whom relations are prohibited** [***arayot***]. The Gemara rejects this suggestion: **On the contrary, the main** source that atypical intercourse is considered intercourse, which is based upon the verse **"The cohabitations of a woman"** (Leviticus 18:22) **is written with regard to those with whom relations are prohibited** [***arayot***].

אֶלָּא מַאי "וְכֵן" אַשֶּׁלֹּא כְּדַרְכָּהּ דְּחַיָּיבֵי לָאוִין.

Rather, what is the meaning of the phrase: **And so too?** It is referring **to atypical** intercourse **by those liable for** violating an ordinary **prohibition** not punishable by *karet*, with regard to whom the expression: The cohabitations of a woman, does not appear. In any event, Rav Sheshet's proof from the mishna is not conclusive.

NOTES

The wife of an Israelite who was raped – אֵשֶׁת יִשְׂרָאֵל שֶׁנֶּאֶנְסָה: Several of the dilemmas raised in this passage are related to defining who is considered a *zona* and is therefore forbidden to a priest. It was clear to the Sages that the halakhic category of *zona* does not refer to a prostitute, as it does in both biblical and modern Hebrew. It refers instead to a woman who had intercourse with a man whom it is prohibited for her to marry, and with whom an act of betrothal would be ineffective. There is room to suggest a difference in this regard between a married woman and other forbidden relationships. In the case of other forbidden relationships, the woman is prohibited to the man due to her personal status, either because she is his close relative or because she is Jewish and he is not. In the case of a married woman, the prohibition stems from the marital bond, which is itself initially dependent upon her consent. Furthermore, this tie can be broken through the death of the husband or their divorce. Consequently, adultery is an act of infidelity on the part of a woman toward her husband, and a married woman who was raped is not prohibited to her husband, as she was not unfaithful to him. One might therefore have assumed that just as the woman is permitted to her husband, she is not considered a *zona*, and it is permitted for her to marry a priest if she becomes a widow (see *Tosafot* and *Tosafot Yeshanim*).

HALAKHA

The wife of an Israelite who was raped – אֵשֶׁת יִשְׂרָאֵל שֶׁנֶּאֶנְסָה: If the wife of an Israelite was raped, she is permitted to her husband. However, if her husband dies, she is forbidden to a priest, in accordance with the ruling of Rav Sheshet (Rambam *Sefer Kedusha, Hilkhot Issurei Bia* 18:8; *Shulḥan Arukh, Even HaEzer* 6:11).

אָמַר רָבָא: אֵשֶׁת כֹּהֵן שֶׁנֶּאֶנְסָה – בַּעְלָהּ לוֹקֶה עָלֶיהָ מִשּׁוּם זוֹנָה. מִשּׁוּם זוֹנָה – אִין, מִשּׁוּם טוּמְאָה – לָא? אֵימָא: אַף מִשּׁוּם זוֹנָה.

§ **Rava said:**[N] With regard to **the wife of a priest who was raped,**[H] **her husband is flogged** if he later has intercourse with **her, due to** the fact that it is prohibited for a priest to have intercourse with a ***zona***.[B] The Gemara expresses surprise: **Due to** the prohibition proscribing a ***zona*****, yes; due to ritual impurity,**[N] **no?** The Torah refers to a married woman who has had intercourse with another man as ritually impure, and she is forbidden to her husband. The Gemara emends Rava's statement: **Say** that he is **also** flogged **due to** the prohibition with regard to a ***zona***.

מְתִיב רַבִּי זֵירָא: "וְהִיא לֹא נִתְפָּשָׂה" – אֲסוּרָה, הָא נִתְפְּשָׂה – מוּתֶּרֶת. וְיֵשׁ לְךָ אַחֶרֶת שֶׁאַף עַל פִּי שֶׁנִּתְפְּשָׂה – אֲסוּרָה, וְאֵי זוֹ – זוֹ אֵשֶׁת כֹּהֵן,

Rabbi Zeira raised an objection based upon a verse with regard to a *sota*: **"And neither was she taken"** (Numbers 5:13) indicates that **she is forbidden** to her husband because she willingly committed adultery, **but** if **she was** forcibly **taken**, i.e., raped, **she is permitted** to her husband. The term "And…she" indicates that although these principles apply in this case, **you have another** case of a woman **who is prohibited even though she was** forcibly **taken. And which is this? This is the wife of a priest.**

וְלָאו הַבָּא מִכְּלַל עֲשֵׂה – עֲשֵׂה!

And a prohibition that stems from a positive mitzva, e.g., the prohibition proscribing a priest's wife to her husband if she has been raped, which is derived from the fact that the Torah indicates that the wife of an Israelite remains permitted, has the status of **a positive mitzva,** not a prohibition. Consequently, one should not be flogged for this offense, as one is flogged only for violating a prohibition.

אָמַר רַבָּה: הַכֹּל הָיוּ בִּכְלַל זוֹנָה, כְּשֶׁפָּרַט לְךָ הַכָּתוּב גַּבֵּי אֵשֶׁת יִשְׂרָאֵל "וְהִיא לֹא נִתְפָּשָׂה" אֲסוּרָה, הָא נִתְפְּשָׂה – מוּתֶּרֶת, מִכְּלַל דְּאֵשֶׁת כֹּהֵן – כִּדְקַיְימָא קַיְימָא.

Rabba said in response: **All** married women who engaged in extramarital intercourse **were included** in the category of ***zona***.[N] **When the verse specified with regard to the wife of an Israelite: "And neither was she taken,"** as it is only in that case that she is **forbidden,** it thereby indicates that if in fact **she was** forcibly **taken,** she is **permitted. By inference,** unlike the wife of an Israelite, **the wife of a priest remains as she was.** Since the Torah does not limit the category of *zona* with regard to the wife of a priest, she is considered a *zona* even if she was raped.

וְאִיכָּא דְּאָמְרִי, אָמַר רַבָּה: אֵשֶׁת כֹּהֵן שֶׁנֶּאֶנְסָה – בַּעְלָהּ לוֹקֶה עָלֶיהָ מִשּׁוּם טוּמְאָה. מִשּׁוּם טוּמְאָה – אִין, מִשּׁוּם זוֹנָה – לָא, אַלְמָא: בְּאוֹנֶס לָא קָרֵינָא בֵּיהּ זוֹנָה.

And some say a different version of this discussion. **Rabba said:** With regard to **the wife of a priest who was raped, her husband is flogged for** having intercourse with **her due to** her **ritual impurity.** The Gemara asks: **Due to ritual impurity, yes; due to** the prohibition proscribing a ***zona*****, no? Apparently, in** a case of **rape,** the victim **is not called a *zona*.**

מְתִיב רַבִּי זֵירָא: "וְהִיא לֹא נִתְפָּשָׂה" – אֲסוּרָה, הָא נִתְפְּשָׂה – מוּתֶּרֶת, וְיֵשׁ לְךָ אַחֶרֶת שֶׁאַף עַל פִּי שֶׁנִּתְפְּשָׂה אֲסוּרָה, וְאֵיזוֹ זוֹ – אֵשֶׁת כֹּהֵן, וְלָאו הַבָּא מִכְּלַל עֲשֵׂה – עֲשֵׂה!

Rabbi Zeira raised an objection from the verse: **"And neither was she taken"** indicates that **she is forbidden** to her husband because she willingly committed adultery, **but** if **she was** forcibly **taken, she is permitted** to her husband. The term: "And…she," indicates that although these principles apply in this case, **you have another** case of a woman **who is forbidden even though she was** forcibly **taken. And which is this? This is the wife of a priest. And a prohibition that stems from a positive mitzva** has the status of **a positive mitzva,** not a prohibition. Consequently, one should not be flogged for this offense, as one is flogged only for violating a prohibition.

אָמַר רָבָא: הַכֹּל הָיוּ בִּכְלַל "אַחֲרֵי אֲשֶׁר הֻטַּמָּאָה", כְּשֶׁפָּרַט לְךָ הַכָּתוּב גַּבֵּי אֵשֶׁת יִשְׂרָאֵל "וְהִיא לֹא נִתְפָּשָׂה" אֲסוּרָה" הָא נִתְפְּשָׂה – מוּתֶּרֶת, מִכְּלַל דְּאֵשֶׁת כֹּהֵן כִּדְקַיְימָא קַיְימָא.

Rava said: All were included in the verse "Her former husband, who sent her away, may not take her again to be his wife **after she was made ritually impure"** (Deuteronomy 24:4). **When the verse specified with regard to the wife of an Israelite: "And neither was she taken,"** as it is only in that case that she is **forbidden,** it thereby indicates that if **she was** forcibly **taken** she is **permitted. By inference, the wife of a priest remains as she was,** and she is forbidden.

NOTES

Rava said – אָמַר רָבָא: Other versions of the text attribute this statement to Rabba, which seems to be more consistent with the Gemara's ensuing discussion.

Due to ritual impurity – מִשּׁוּם טוּמְאָה: This prohibition is derived from two sources. The first is a verse with regard to a *sota*: "And she was made ritually impure" (Numbers 5:13). Second, the Torah states with regard to a divorced woman who was remarried and then divorced from her second husband: "Her former husband, who sent her away, may not return to take her to be his wife after she was made ritually impure" (Deuteronomy 24:4). The Sages explain (see *Nidda* 11b) that this verse also renders prohibited a married woman who had intercourse with another man (see *Tosefot HaRosh*).

All married women who engaged in extramarital intercourse were included in the category of *zona* – הַכֹּל הָיוּ בִּכְלַל זוֹנָה: The commentaries are puzzled by this statement. Since a *zona* is forbidden only to a priest, what does it mean that initially the wife of an Israelite who was raped would also have been considered a *zona*, implying that she would have been prohibited to her husband, had the verse not excluded her from this prohibition? The *Tosefot HaRosh* explains that initially the wife of an Israelite was considered a *zona*, and was also prohibited to her husband due to becoming ritually impure. The Torah indicates that she is not prohibited to him if she was raped, but she remains classified as a *zona* and is prohibited to a priest. Consequently, the wife of a priest is also classified as a *zona* if she was raped, and therefore she is forbidden to her husband (see Rashba).

HALAKHA

The wife of a priest who was raped – אֵשֶׁת כֹּהֵן שֶׁנֶּאֶנְסָה: The wife of a priest who was raped is forbidden to her husband. If he engages in intercourse with her, he is flogged for violating the prohibition against having intercourse with a *zona* (*Mishne LaMelekh*), in accordance with the first version of Rabba's statement (Rambam *Sefer Kedusha*, *Hilkhot Issurei Bia* 18:7; *Shulḥan Arukh*, *Even HaEzer* 6:10).

BACKGROUND

Zona – זוֹנָה: In halakhic terms, the category of *zona* refers to a woman who has had sexual relations with a man forbidden to her by the Torah, with whom she cannot establish a marriage bond. Furthermore, it is prohibited for a woman who is categorized as a *zona* to thereafter marry a priest or remain married to one (Leviticus 21:7). There is no connection between the halakhic definition of this term and its everyday usage in modern Hebrew.

HALAKHA

A widow to a High Priest, etc. – **אַלְמָנָה לְכֹהֵן גָּדוֹל וכו׳**: If a widow is betrothed to a High Priest, or a divorcée is betrothed to a priest, even if they are daughters of priests, they may not partake of *teruma*. This is in accordance with the opinion of Rabbi Meir. If they were then widowed or divorced before completing the marriage, they may once again partake of *teruma*. However, if their marriage to the priest was consummated, they are *ḥalalot* and are permanently disqualified from partaking of *teruma* (Rambam *Sefer Zera'im, Hilkhot Terumot* 7:21).

A priest with crushed testicles who betrothed a valid woman – **פְּצוּעַ דַּכָּא כֹּהֵן שֶׁקִּדֵּשׁ כְּשֵׁרָה**: If a priest with crushed testicles betrothed a woman, even if she is the daughter of a priest, she may not partake of *teruma* (Rambam *Sefer Zera'im, Hilkhot Terumot* 7:14).

NOTES

Ḥalala – **חֲלָלָה**: If it is forbidden for a woman to marry a regular priest or a High Priest and she engages in sexual intercourse with him, she is rendered a *ḥalala*. A woman is also considered a *ḥalala* if she is born from the union of a priest and a woman who is forbidden from marrying a priest; or if she is the wife or daughter of a *ḥalal*, which is a son born from the union of a priest and a woman who is forbidden from marrying a priest. It is prohibited for a *ḥalala* to marry a priest or partake of *teruma*.

A priest with crushed testicles who betrothed the daughter of an Israelite – **פְּצוּעַ דַּכָּא כֹּהֵן שֶׁקִּדֵּשׁ בַּת יִשְׂרָאֵל**: Virtually all the commentaries prefer Rabbeinu Ḥananel's reading: A priest with crushed testicles who betrothed the daughter of a priest (see *Tosafot*).

מתני׳ אַלְמָנָה לְכֹהֵן גָּדוֹל, גְּרוּשָׁה וַחֲלוּצָה לְכֹהֵן הֶדְיוֹט מִן הָאֵירוּסִין – לֹא יֹאכְלוּ בִּתְרוּמָה, רַבִּי אֶלְעָזָר וְרַבִּי שִׁמְעוֹן מַכְשִׁירִין.

MISHNA **A widow to a High Priest,**[H] **a divorcée, or a *ḥalutza* to a common priest,** even if they had only engaged in **betrothal** and had not yet had intercourse, **may not partake of *teruma*.** Since they are forbidden to the men who betrothed them, the betrothal itself disqualifies them from the privileges of priesthood even if they are the daughters of priests. **Rabbi Elazar and Rabbi Shimon declare them fit** to partake of *teruma*. Since the prohibition is violated through the act of intercourse and not betrothal, the women are disqualified only once they have intercourse.

נִתְאַרְמְלוּ אוֹ נִתְגָּרְשׁוּ, מִן הַנְּשׂוּאִין – פְּסוּלוֹת, מִן הָאֵירוּסִין – כְּשֵׁרוֹת.

In a case where these women **were widowed or divorced,** if it was **from marriage, they are disqualified** from the priesthood and may not partake of *teruma*. This is because a woman prohibited from marrying a priest who has intercourse with a priest becomes a *ḥalala*,[N] and is thereby disqualified from partaking of *teruma*. However, if they were widowed or divorced **from** their state of **betrothal,** they are once again **fit** to partake of *teruma* according to all opinions.

גמ׳ תַּנְיָא, אָמַר רַבִּי מֵאִיר: קַל וָחוֹמֶר, וּמָה קִדּוּשֵׁי רְשׁוּת – אֵין מַאֲכִילִין, קִדּוּשֵׁי עֲבֵירָה – לֹא כׇּל שֶׁכֵּן?!

GEMARA **It is taught in a *baraita* that Rabbi Meir said:** This is **an *a fortiori* inference: Just as optional betrothal,** e.g., in the case of an Israelite who betroths the daughter of a priest, **does not entitle her to partake of** *teruma*, as her betrothal to a non-priest disqualifies her from partaking of her father's *teruma*, **is it not all the more so** true in a case of **betrothal** that constitutes **a transgression,** as in the cases in the mishna?

אָמְרוּ לוֹ: לֹא, אִם אָמַרְתָּ בְּקִידּוּשֵׁי רְשׁוּת – שֶׁכֵּן אֵין לוֹ לְהַאֲכִיל בְּמָקוֹם אַחֵר, תֹּאמַר בְּקִדּוּשֵׁי עֲבֵירָה – שֶׁכֵּן יֵשׁ לוֹ לְהַאֲכִיל בְּמָקוֹם אַחֵר.

They said to him: No, if you say that this is true with regard to an Israelite, **whose** status **cannot entitle her to partake** of *teruma* **in another case,** as one betrothed to an Israelite may never partake of *teruma*, **shall you** also **say** that this is the case with regard to **betrothal** to a priest that constitutes **a transgression, where his** status **does entitle her to partake** of *teruma* **in a different case,** as marriage to a priest entitles a woman to partake of *teruma* in a case where it is permitted for them to marry?

אָמַר רַבִּי אֶלְעָזָר אָמַר רַבִּי אוֹשַׁעְיָא: פְּצוּעַ דַּכָּא כֹּהֵן שֶׁקִּדֵּשׁ בַּת יִשְׂרָאֵל – בָּאנוּ לְמַחְלוֹקֶת רַבִּי מֵאִיר וְרַבִּי אֶלְעָזָר וְרַבִּי שִׁמְעוֹן.

Rabbi Elazar said that **Rabbi Oshaya said:** In the case of **a priest with crushed testicles** or with other wounds to his genitals **who betrothed the daughter of an Israelite,**[HN] which is prohibited by the verse "He that is crushed or maimed shall not enter into the congregation of the Lord" (Deuteronomy 23:2), **we have arrived at the dispute** between **Rabbi Meir** on the one hand **and Rabbi Elazar and Rabbi Shimon** on the other.

לְרַבִּי מֵאִיר דְּאָמַר מִשְׁתַּמֶּרֶת לְבִיאָה פְּסוּלָה דְּאוֹרָיְיתָא לָא אָכְלָה – הָא נָמֵי לָא אָכְלָה, לְרַבִּי אֶלְעָזָר וְרַבִּי שִׁמְעוֹן דְּאָמְרִי מִשְׁתַּמֶּרֶת לְבִיאָה פְּסוּלָה דְּאוֹרָיְיתָא אָכְלָה

According to Rabbi Meir, who said that a woman who is **reserved for intercourse that is invalid,** i.e., prohibited, **by Torah law may not partake** of *teruma*, **this one may also not partake** of *teruma*, as it is prohibited by Torah law for her to have intercourse with a man with crushed testicles. **According to Rabbi Elazar and Rabbi Shimon, who say** that a woman who is **reserved for intercourse that is invalid by Torah** law **may partake** of *teruma* until she actually engages in the prohibited act of intercourse,

Perek **VI**
Daf **57** Amud **a**

הָא נָמֵי אָכְלָה. מִמַּאי? דִּלְמָא עַד כָּאן לָא קָאָמְרִי רַבִּי אֶלְעָזָר וְרַבִּי שִׁמְעוֹן הָתָם אֶלָּא דְּיֵשׁ לוֹ לְהַאֲכִיל בְּמָקוֹם אַחֵר, אֲבָל הָכָא, דְּאֵין לוֹ לְהַאֲכִיל בְּמָקוֹם אַחֵר – לָא.

this one may also partake of *teruma* until that time. The Gemara refutes this argument: **From where** do we know that this is correct? **Perhaps Rabbi Elazar and Rabbi Shimon stated** their opinion **there only** with regard to a priest **whose** status **can entitle her to partake** of *teruma* **in another case, but here,** in the case of a priest with crushed testicles, **whose** status **cannot entitle her to partake** of *teruma* **in another case,** as it is forbidden for him to marry a woman who was born Jewish, **no,** they did not state their opinion.

וְכִי תֵּימָא: הָכָא נַמִּי יֵשׁ לוֹ לְהַאֲכִיל בְּבַת גֵּרִים – וְהָא מִיבַּעְיָא בָּעֵי לָהּ רַבִּי יוֹחָנָן מֵרַבִּי אוֹשַׁעְיָא, וְלָא פְּשֵׁיט לֵיהּ.

And if you say that **here too, his** status **can** at least **entitle** his wife **to partake** of *teruma* if he marries **the daughter of converts, wasn't it** already **raised as a dilemma** by **Rabbi Yoḥanan before Rabbi Oshaya**[P] whether the daughter of converts who married a priest with crushed testicles may partake of *teruma*, **and he was unable to resolve it** for **him?** Therefore, there is a difference between a priest with crushed testicles and other priests who betroth women who are disqualified by their intercourse.

אִיתְּמַר, אַבַּיֵי אָמַר: הוֹאִיל וּמַאֲכִילָהּ בְּלֹא יְדָעָהּ,

It was stated that **Abaye said:** Women betrothed to a priest with crushed testicles may eat *teruma* **since his** status **entitles** his wife **to partake** of *teruma* **in** a case where **he has not known her.** If a priest was properly married and then his testicles became crushed, as long as he has not known his wife, i.e., engaged in intercourse with her, after that point in time, she may continue partaking of *teruma* as his wife.

רָבָא אָמַר: הוֹאִיל וּמַאֲכִילָהּ בַּעֲבָדָיו וְשִׁפְחוֹתָיו הַכְּנַעֲנִים.

Rava said she may continue to partake of *teruma* for a different reason: She may eat *teruma* **since** the status of this priest **entitles his Canaanite slaves and maidservants to partake** of *teruma*. Because he has the power to enable others to partake of *teruma*, the case of a woman betrothed to a priest with crushed testicles is comparable to the cases in the mishna, and Rabbi Elazar and Rabbi Shimon would permit the woman to partake of *teruma*.

אַבַּיֵי לָא אָמַר כְּרָבָא, קִנְיָן דְּאִישׁוּת מִקִּנְיָן דְּאִישׁוּת – יָלְפִינַן, וְלָא יָלְפִינַן קִנְיָן דְּאִישׁוּת מִקִּנְיָן דַּעֲבָדִים.

The Gemara clarifies the two opinions. **Abaye did not say in accordance with** the opinion of **Rava** because he claims that **we derive** the *halakhot* related to **the acquisition of marriage from the acquisition of marriage, and we do not derive** the *halakhot* related to **the acquisition of marriage from the acquisition of slaves.**

וְרָבָא לָא אָמַר כְּאַבַּיֵי – שָׁאנֵי הָתָם שֶׁכְּבָר אָכְלָה. וְאַבַּיֵי: שֶׁכְּבָר אָכְלָה לָא אָמְרִינַן, דְּאִי לָא תֵּימָא הָכִי – בַּת יִשְׂרָאֵל שֶׁנִּיסֵּת לְכֹהֵן וּמֵת – תֵּיכוּל, שֶׁכְּבָר אָכְלָה. וְרָבָא: הָתָם – פָּקַע קִנְיָנֵיהּ, הָכָא – לָא פָּקַע קִנְיָנֵיהּ.

And Rava did not state his opinion **in accordance with** the opinion of **Abaye,** as he maintains that **it is different there, as she had already partaken of** *teruma*[N] before her husband's testicles were crushed and therefore she may continue to partake of it. **And Abaye** would respond that **we do not say** that the case is different because **she had already partaken of** *teruma*, **as, if you do not say so,** the **daughter of an Israelite who was married to a priest who died** childless **should** be allowed to **partake** of *teruma*, **as she had already partaken of** *teruma* while her husband was alive. **And Rava** replies that there is no comparison between the two cases: **There, his acquisition lapses** upon his death; **here, his acquisition does not lapse,** as she is still his wife.

גּוּפָא, בְּעָא מִינֵּיהּ רַבִּי יוֹחָנָן מֵרַבִּי אוֹשַׁעְיָא: פְּצוּעַ דַּכָּא כֹּהֵן שֶׁנָּשָׂא בַּת גֵּרִים, מַהוּ שֶׁיַּאֲכִילֶנָּה בִּתְרוּמָה? אִישְׁתִּיק וְלָא אֲמַר לֵיהּ וְלָא מִידֵּי. לַסּוֹף אֲתָא גַּבְרָא רַבָּה אַחֲרִינָא, וּבְעָא מִינֵּיהּ מִילְּתָא [אַחֲרִיתָא], וּפָשַׁט לֵיהּ. וּמַנּוּ – רֵישׁ לָקִישׁ. אָמַר לֵיהּ רַבִּי יְהוּדָה נְשִׂיאָה לְרַבִּי אוֹשַׁעְיָא: אַטּוּ רַבִּי יוֹחָנָן לָאו גַּבְרָא רַבָּה הוּא? אֲמַר לֵיהּ: דְּקָבָעֵי מִינָּאִי מִילְּתָא דְּלֵית לָהּ פִּתְרֵי.

§ The Gemara earlier mentioned a question that Rabbi Yoḥanan posed to Rabbi Oshaya, and it now turns its attention to that matter **itself. Rabbi Yoḥanan raised a dilemma before Rabbi Oshaya:** With regard to **a priest** with **crushed testicles** or with other wounds to his genitals **who married the daughter of converts, what is** the *halakha* concerning whether **his** status **entitles her to partake of** *teruma*? Rabbi Oshaya **was silent and said nothing to him. Eventually another great man came and raised a different dilemma before** Rabbi Oshaya, **and he resolved his** question. **And who was** this great man? **Reish Lakish. Rabbi Yehuda Nesia said to Rabbi Oshaya: Is Rabbi Yoḥanan not a great man?** Why didn't you address his dilemma? Rabbi Oshaya **said to him:** I did not respond **because he raised a dilemma before me that has no resolution.**

PERSONALITIES

Rabbi Oshaya – רַבִּי אוֹשַׁעְיָא: Rabbi Oshaya was one of the greatest of the first generation of *amora'im* in Eretz Yisrael. Due to his prominence and influence, he was known as Rabbi Oshaya the Great, and was also given the honorific title Father of the Mishna.

His family came from the south, where he was apparently born and raised. At some point he moved to the Galilee and settled in Tzippori and Caesarea. The verse "A threefold cord is not quickly broken" (Ecclesiastes 4:12) was used to describe him, as his father, Rabbi Ḥama, and his grandfather, Rabbi Bisa, were also renowned Sages.

Rabbi Oshaya was originally a disciple of bar Kappara, and later, probably after his move to the Galilee, he became a disciple of Rabbi Ḥiyya. Like Rabbi Ḥiyya, Rabbi Oshaya authored a collection of *baraitot* that is considered highly authoritative and reliable, to the extent that the Sages stated a principle that any collection of *baraitot* other than that of Rabbi Ḥiyya and Rabbi Oshaya is of questionable validity.

It seems that as a young man Rabbi Oshaya was a member of the rabbinical court of Rabbi Yehuda HaNasi. However, his most active years came during the time of Rabbi Yehuda HaNasi's students, and especially during the time of Rabbi Yehuda HaNasi's grandson, Rabbi Yehuda Nesia, when Rabbi Oshaya was considered the outstanding scholar of the generation. Rabbi Oshaya's family maintained close ties with the house of the *Nasi*.

All the important *amora'im* in Eretz Yisrael viewed themselves as Rabbi Oshaya's students, including the illustrious Rabbi Yoḥanan. Together with his greatness in Torah, Rabbi Oshaya was also known for his exemplary behavior and for his consideration in tending to the physical and emotional needs of those in distress. It seems that he was also well versed in worldly wisdom, as his masters occasionally sent him to explain issues to various individuals from other nations.

It is not known what Rabbi Oshaya's occupation was, but it is clear that he barely made a living. He lived a long life, as his students' students were prominent scholars in Eretz Yisrael during his own lifetime. His son, Rabbi Marinos, is mentioned in the Jerusalem Talmud.

NOTES

It is different there, as she had already partaken of ***teruma*** **– שָׁאנֵי הָתָם שֶׁכְּבָר אָכְלָה:** According to the text of Rabbeinu Ḥananel and many others, the case under discussion is about a priest with crushed testicles who betrothed the daughter of a priest. In that case, the woman has already partaken of *teruma* due to the fact that she is the daughter of a priest. Consequently, why should there be a distinction between that case and the case of the priest whose wife was entitled to partake of *teruma* before his testicles were crushed? The Ritva explains that by getting married she has left her father's household, and therefore her earlier consumption of *teruma* is no longer relevant.

למאן? אי לרבי יהודה – בין בקדושתיה קאי בין לאו בקדושתיה קאי – לא אכלה. אי בקדושתיה קאי לא אכלה, דהא אמר מר: בת גר זכר כבת חלל זכר.

The Gemara explains: **According to whom** did he raise his dilemma? If it was **in accordance with** the opinion of **Rabbi Yehuda,** then, **whether** the priest with crushed testicles **retains his** priestly **sanctity or whether he does not retain his** priestly **sanctity** and may marry women forbidden to priests, she **may not partake** of *teruma*. The reasoning is as follows: **If he retains his** priestly **sanctity she may not partake** of *teruma*, **as the Master said:** The status of the **daughter of a male convert is like** that of the **daughter of a male *ḥalal*.** They are both prohibited from marrying a priest, and therefore even if they marry a priest, it is prohibited for them to eat *teruma*.

אי לאו בקדושתיה קאי – לא אכלה, דהא אמרינן: קהל גרים איקרי קהל.

Even **if he does not retain his** priestly **sanctity she may not eat, as we say** that according to Rabbi Yehuda, **the congregation of converts is called** the **congregation** of the Lord. Therefore, when the Torah renders it prohibited for a man with crushed testicles to marry into the congregation of the Lord (see Deuteronomy 23:2), it renders it prohibited for him to marry converts.

ואי לרבי יוסי, בין בקדושתיה קאי בין לאו בקדושתיה קאי – אכלה. בקדושתיה קאי אכלה – דהא אמר: אף גר שנשא גיורת בתו כשרה לכהונה. אי לאו בקדושתיה קאי אכלה – דהא אמר: קהל גרים לא איקרי קהל.

And if he raised his dilemma **in accordance with** the opinion of **Rabbi Yosei,** then, **whether he retains his** priestly **sanctity** or **whether he does not retain his** priestly **sanctity, she** may **partake** of *teruma*. If **he retains his sanctity** she **may partake,** as Rabbi Yosei **said: Even** if a **convert married a convert, his daughter is fit for** marrying into **the priesthood. If he does not retain his sanctity** she **may partake, as** Rabbi Yosei **said:** The **congregation of converts is not called** the **congregation** of the Lord,[H] and therefore even those forbidden from entering the congregation may marry converts. Consequently, it is certainly permitted for the priest with crushed testicles to marry the daughter of converts.

אלא אליבא דהאי תנא. דתנן, רבי אליעזר בן יעקב אומר: אשה בת גרים לא תנשא לכהונה עד שתהא אמה מישראל.

Rather, Rabbi Yoḥanan raised his dilemma **in accordance with** the opinion of **this *tanna*, as we learned** in a mishna (*Bikkurim* 1:5) that **Rabbi Eliezer ben Ya'akov says: A woman** who is **the daughter of converts may not marry into the priesthood**[NH] **unless her mother was Jewish** from birth.

והכי קמיבעיא ליה: כשרות מיתוספא בה ואכלה, או דלמא קדושה מיתוספא בה ולא אכלה?

And his dilemma was as follows: Is the reason she may marry a priest if her mother was Jewish from birth that **fitness** to marry a priest **has been added to her,** but she is not considered a member of the congregation of the Lord and may therefore marry a man with crushed testicles? If so, since she may marry a priest, **she** may **partake** of *teruma* once she does so. **Or perhaps sanctity has been added to her** and she is considered a member of the congregation of the Lord. Consequently, she may not marry a man with crushed testicles, and if she does, **she may not partake** of *teruma* even if he is a priest.

תא שמע: כי אתא רבי אחא בר חיננא מדרומא, אתא ואייתי מתניתא בידיה: מנין לפצוע דכא כהן שנשא בת גרים שמאכילה בתרומה – שנאמר "וכהן כי יקנה נפש קנין כספו וגו' יאכל בו".

The Gemara suggests an answer to this dilemma. **Come and hear: When Rabbi Aḥa bar Ḥinnana came from the south,**[B] **he came and brought** this ***baraita*** **in hand: From where** is it derived that **a priest with crushed testicles** or with other wounds to his genitals[H] **who married the daughter of converts entitles her to partake of *teruma*? As it is stated: "But if a priest buys any soul, the purchase of his money,** he **may eat of it"** (Leviticus 22:11). In this context, a wife is also considered his monetary acquisition, and therefore she may partake of *teruma*.

HALAKHA

The congregation of converts is not called the congregation of the Lord – קהל גרים לא איקרי קהל: It is permitted for a convert to marry a *mamzeret*, and it is permitted for a female convert to marry a *mamzer* or a man with crushed testicles. The children of converts may also marry these individuals, even if they were conceived and born after their parents' conversion. This is true even after the passage of several generations, as long as they are still known as converts and neither of their parents is a natural-born Jew. The *halakha* is in accordance with the opinion of Rabbi Yosei (Rambam *Sefer Kedusha, Hilkhot Issurei Bia* 15:7–8; *Shulḥan Arukh, Even HaEzer* 4:22).

A woman who is the daughter of converts…into the priesthood – אשה בת גרים...לכהונה: A woman who is the daughter of two converts may not marry a priest. If she nevertheless married a priest, they are not forced to divorce if she was conceived after her parents converted. This is based upon the conclusion of the Gemara in tractate *Kiddushin* (78b) that, after the fact, the *halakha* is in accordance with the opinion of Rabbi Yosei. If one of her parents was a natural-born Jew, she may marry a priest even *ab initio*, as stated by Rabbi Eliezer ben Ya'akov (Rambam *Sefer Kedusha, Hilkhot Issurei Bia* 19:12; *Shulḥan Arukh, Even HaEzer* 7:21).

A priest with crushed testicles or with other wounds to his genitals – פצוע דכא כהן: If a priest with crushed testicles married a daughter of converts she may partake of *teruma* on his account, in accordance with the opinions of Rabbi Yosei and Rabbi Eliezer ben Ya'akov (*Kesef Mishne*; Rambam *Sefer Zera'im, Hilkhot Terumot* 7:13).

NOTES

A woman who is the daughter of converts may not marry into the priesthood – בת גרים לא תנשא לכהונה: As explained in tractate *Kiddushin* (78a), this *halakha* is based on the verse "Neither shall they take for their wives a widow…but they shall take virgins from the seed of the house of Israel" (Ezekiel 44:22). See the Gemara there for other reasons that apply to a female convert herself.

BACKGROUND

From the south – מדרומא: From the time of the bar Kokheva revolt, the center of Jewish life in Eretz Yisrael was in the Galilee. Judea was mostly desolate, as the majority of the population, and the Sanhedrin, were in the Galilee. However, some important centers of Jewish life in Judea remained, including Lod and other cities. There were some Sages who lived south of the Galilee and preserved ancient traditions. At times, these Sages would travel north to the Galilee and report halakhic traditions, *baraitot*, or statements of earlier Sages that were not known to the Sages in the Galilee.

לְמַאן? אִילֵימָא לְרַבִּי יְהוּדָה – הָאָמַר: בֵּין בִּקְדוּשָּׁתֵיהּ קָאֵי בֵּין לָאו בִּקְדוּשָּׁתֵיהּ קָאֵי – לָא אָכְלָה. וְאִי לְרַבִּי יוֹסֵי – לָמָּה לִי קְרָא? הָאָמַר: בֵּין בִּקְדוּשָּׁתֵיהּ קָאֵי, בֵּין לָאו בִּקְדוּשָּׁתֵיהּ קָאֵי – אָכְלָה. אֶלָּא לָאו – לְרַבִּי אֱלִיעֶזֶר בֶּן יַעֲקֹב, וּשְׁמַע מִינַּהּ: כַּשְׁרוּת אִיתּוֹסְפָא בָהּ, וְאָכְלָה. שְׁמַע מִינַּהּ.

The Gemara analyzes this source: **According to whom** is this *baraita* stated? **If we say** it is **in accordance with** the opinion of **Rabbi Yehuda, didn't he say** that **whether** this priest **retains his sanctity** or **whether he does not retain his sanctity,** she **may not partake** of *teruma*? **And if** it is **in accordance with** the opinion of **Rabbi Yosei, why do I** need a special **verse** to teach this *halakha*? **Didn't he say** that **whether** he **retains his sanctity** or **whether he does not retain his sanctity, she** may **partake** of *teruma*? **Rather, is it not in accordance with** the opinion of **Rabbi Eliezer ben Ya'akov? And** you can **learn from this** *baraita* that **fitness was added to her, and** therefore **she** may **partake** of *teruma*. The Gemara concludes: Indeed, **learn from this** that it is so.

אִיתְּמַר, רַב אָמַר

§ The Gemara cites a dispute with regard to an issue related to the previous discussion. **It was stated** that the *amora'im* disagreed about the following question. **Rav said:**

Perek **VI**
Daf **57** Amud **b**

יֵשׁ חוּפָּה לִפְסוּלוֹת, וּשְׁמוּאֵל אָמַר: אֵין חוּפָּה לִפְסוּלוֹת.

There is significance **to** a priest entering **a wedding canopy**[NB] with women who are **unfit** to marry a priest.[NH] If a priest's daughter who is unfit to marry a priest enters the wedding canopy with a priest, she becomes disqualified from partaking of *teruma* from her father's household. This is the case even if the priest did not betroth her and they did not engage in sexual intercourse. **And Shmuel said: There is no** significance **to** a priest entering the **wedding canopy** with women who are **unfit** to marry a priest. Only sexual intercourse disqualifies her from the privileges of priesthood.

אָמַר שְׁמוּאֵל: וּמוֹדֶה לִי אַבָּא בְּתִינוֹקֶת פְּחוּתָה מִבַּת שָׁלֹשׁ שָׁנִים וְיוֹם אֶחָד, הוֹאִיל וְאֵין לָהּ בִּיאָה – אֵין לָהּ חוּפָּה.

Shmuel said: And Abba, i.e., Rav, whose first name was Abba, **concedes to me,**[N] **with regard to a girl less than three years and one day old,** that she is not disqualified by merely entering the wedding canopy. **Since there is no** legal significance to an act of **intercourse** with **her, there is no** legal significance to entering the **wedding canopy** with **her.**

BACKGROUND

Wedding canopy – חוּפָּה: In the talmudic era, the wedding canopy was a kind of small, decorated room, sometimes constructed from braided myrtle branches, where the bride and groom would be left alone together. It was a closed space that afforded enough privacy for the couple to engage in intimate relations. In later generations, when the wedding canopy took on a more symbolic function, the Sages debated whether entering the wedding canopy still fulfills the halakhic requirements of marriage, as mentioned in the Talmud.

HALAKHA

A wedding canopy with women who are unfit to marry a priest – חוּפָּה לִפְסוּלוֹת: If the widowed daughter of a priest enters the wedding canopy in order to marry a High Priest, or if a divorcée enters the wedding canopy in order to marry a common priest, she becomes disqualified from partaking of *teruma*. With regard to ritual *halakha*, the *halakha* is in accordance with Rav in his disputes with Shmuel (Rambam *Sefer Zera'im, Hilkhot Terumot* 7:21).

NOTES

Wedding canopy [*ḥuppa*] – חוּפָּה: There are differences of opinion as to what constitutes a wedding canopy. Some maintain that it refers to the ceremony where a shawl is spread over the heads of the bride and groom. Others say that *ḥuppa* requires them to be secluded for the amount of time necessary to engage in intercourse. Still others contend that *ḥuppa* occurs when the groom brings his bride into his home as his wife (see *Shulḥan Arukh, Even HaEzer* 55).

A wedding canopy with women who are unfit to marry a priest – חוּפָּה לִפְסוּלוֹת: Among the commentaries, there are many opinions with regard to the meaning of this passage. According to Rashi, the reference is to entering the wedding canopy without betrothal. Rav and Shmuel agree that the couple is not considered married. Nevertheless, Rav holds that the woman becomes disqualified from partaking of *teruma* because entering the wedding canopy is a preparatory stage for sexual intercourse.

Most medieval commentaries, however, maintain that this is a case where they entered the wedding canopy after betrothal. Rabbeinu Tam, cited in *Tosafot*, claims that Rav and Shmuel disagree about whether a priest and a woman unfit to marry him are considered married once they enter the wedding canopy, so that she would be disqualified from partaking of *teruma* from her father's house, or if they are not considered married in this regard until they engage in intercourse (see *Tosafot*; *Tosefot Ḥad MiKamma'ei*; Ramban; Ritva; *Yam shel Shlomo*).

Abba concedes to me – מוֹדֶה לִי אַבָּא: Rashi and Rabbi Avraham min HaHar explain that Abba was an honorific title. However, *Tosafot* provide proofs that it was Rav's first name. It is possible that both explanations are correct, and Rashi is explaining why it was not disrespectful to call Rav by his first name. Halakhic commentaries address the question of whether it is permitted to call one's father by his first name if that name is also an honorific title, such as *Abba*, which means father, or *Morenu*, which means our master.

אָמַר רָבָא: אַף אֲנַן נָמֵי תָּנֵינָא, בַּת שָׁלֹשׁ שָׁנִים וְיוֹם אֶחָד מִתְקַדֶּשֶׁת בְּבִיאָה וְאִם בָּא עָלֶיהָ יָבָם קְנָאָהּ, וְחַיָּיבִין עָלֶיהָ מִשּׁוּם אֵשֶׁת אִישׁ, וּמְטַמְּאָה אֶת בּוֹעֲלָהּ לְטַמֵּא מִשְׁכָּב תַּחְתּוֹן כְּעֶלְיוֹן.

Rava said: We, too, learn in the following *baraita* that there is no legal significance to an act of intercourse with a girl less than three years old: **A girl three years and one day old can be betrothed via sexual intercourse;**[H] **and if** she was a *yevama* and her *yavam* **had intercourse with her, he has acquired her;**[H] **and** a man who has intercourse with her while she is married to someone else **is liable on her account because** of the prohibition of intercourse with **a married woman;**[H] **and** if she experiences a menstrual discharge **she renders ritually impure a man who has intercourse with her,**[H] **so that he renders impure the object upon which he lies like the upper one.**[N]

נִשֵּׂאת לְכֹהֵן – אוֹכֶלֶת בִּתְרוּמָה, בָּא עָלֶיהָ אֶחָד מִכָּל הַפְּסוּלִין – פְּסָלָהּ.

If **she is married to a priest she may partake of** ***teruma.***[H] If **one of those** who render women **unfit** for marrying a priest **had intercourse with her, he has disqualified her**[H] from being able to partake of *teruma*.

בַּת שָׁלֹשׁ שָׁנִים וְיוֹם אֶחָד הוּא דְּמִפַּסְלָה בְּבִיאָה – מִפַּסְלָה בְּחוּפָּה, הָא פְּחוּתָה מִבַּת שָׁלֹשׁ שָׁנִים וְיוֹם אֶחָד, דְּלָא מִפַּסְלָה בְּבִיאָה – לָא מִפַּסְלָה נָמֵי בְּחוּפָּה, שְׁמַע מִינָּהּ.

Rava infers from this *baraita* that **it is a girl three years and one day old who is disqualified via intercourse,** and consequently **she is** also **disqualified via the wedding canopy.** However, a girl who is **less than three years and one day old, who is not disqualified via intercourse, is also not disqualified via the wedding canopy.** The Gemara concludes: Indeed, **learn from this** that it is so.

אָמַר רָמִי בַּר חָמָא: יֵשׁ חוּפָּה לִפְסוּלוֹת – בָּאנוּ לְמַחְלוֹקֶת רַבִּי מֵאִיר וְרַבִּי אֶלְעָזָר וְרַבִּי שִׁמְעוֹן,

Rami bar Ḥama said: With regard to the question of whether **there is** legal significance **to** a priest entering the **wedding canopy** with women who are **unfit** to marry a priest, **we have arrived at the dispute** cited in the mishna between **Rabbi Meir** on the one hand **and Rabbi Elazar and Rabbi Shimon** on the other.

NOTES

So that he renders impure the object upon which he lies like the upper one – לְטַמֵּא מִשְׁכָּב תַּחְתּוֹן כְּעֶלְיוֹן: The Torah states that if a man has intercourse with a menstruating woman, "her impurity shall be upon him" (Leviticus 15:24). This indicates that he is not merely impure with a first-degree level of impurity, as one who touches a menstruating woman; rather, he becomes a primary source of impurity, similar to the woman herself. Nevertheless, there is a difference between the impurity of a menstruating woman and that of a man who has intercourse with her. If a menstruating woman or a *zav* sits or lies upon objects that are designated for that purpose, even if she does not make direct contact with those objects because there is something else covering them, the objects are rendered a primary source of impurity.

A man who has intercourse with a menstruating woman also renders these items impure, but only at the level of first-degree impurity, similar to the upper cover, i.e., the blanket on top of him, which is impure due to contact. Consequently, these items can render only food and drink impure, but not people or vessels.

HALAKHA

A girl three years and one day old can be betrothed via sexual intercourse – בַּת שָׁלֹשׁ שָׁנִים וְיוֹם אֶחָד מִתְקַדֶּשֶׁת בְּבִיאָה: An act of intercourse with a girl younger than three years and one day is not considered an act of intercourse and therefore, even if it is performed with her father's consent, betrothal cannot be accomplished. However, technically, in the case of a girl who is three years and one day old, betrothal can be accomplished by means of intercourse (Rambam *Sefer Nashim, Hilkhot Ishut* 3:11; *Shulḥan Arukh, Even HaEzer* 37:1).

If her *yavam* had intercourse with her he has acquired her – בָּא עָלֶיהָ יָבָם קְנָאָהּ: Intercourse with a *yevama* aged less than three years and one day does not accomplish levirate marriage (*Shulḥan Arukh, Even HaEzer* 167:4).

Liable on her account because of the prohibition of intercourse with a married woman – חַיָּיבִין עָלֶיהָ מִשּׁוּם אֵשֶׁת אִישׁ: An adult male who engaged in intercourse with a married minor less than three years and one day old is exempt from punishment for adultery with a married woman (Rambam *Sefer Kedusha, Hilkhot Issurei Bia* 3:2).

She renders ritually impure a man who has intercourse with her – מְטַמְּאָה אֶת בּוֹעֲלָהּ: One who has intercourse with a menstruating woman attains the status of a primary source of impurity, even if she is a minor, provided she is at least three years and one day old. If he sits or lies on an object that is designated for this purpose, the object attains first-degree impurity, even if he did not touch it directly. Therefore, it can render food and drink impure, but not people or vessels (Rambam *Sefer Tahara, Hilkhot Metamei Mishkav UMoshav* 3:1–3).

She may partake of *teruma* – אוֹכֶלֶת בִּתְרוּמָה: If a girl at least three years and one day old is married to a priest, she is permitted to partake of *teruma* (Rambam *Sefer Zera'im, Hilkhot Terumot* 6:3).

If one of those who render women unfit had intercourse with her, he has disqualified her – בָּא עָלֶיהָ אֶחָד מִכָּל הַפְּסוּלִין פְּסָלָהּ: If a man who renders a woman unfit for the priesthood, such as a *ḥalal*, a gentile, a Canaanite slave, or one of her relatives, has intercourse with her when she is at least three years and one day old, she is thereby disqualified from the priesthood (Rambam *Sefer Kedusha, Hilkhot Issurei Bia* 19:1–2; *Shulḥan Arukh, Even HaEzer* 6:9; 7:12).

לְרַבִּי מֵאִיר דְּאָמַר קִדּוּשִׁין פָּסְלִי – חוּפָּה נַמִי פָּסְלָה, לְרַבִּי אֶלְעָזָר וְרַבִּי שִׁמְעוֹן דְּאָמְרִי קִדּוּשִׁין לָא פָּסְלִי – חוּפָּה נַמִי לָא פָּסְלָה.

According to Rabbi Meir, who says that betrothal to a priest **disqualifies** a woman who is unfit to marry him from partaking of *teruma* even if she is the daughter of a priest, entering the **wedding canopy** with a priest **also disqualifies** her. Conversely, **according to Rabbi Elazar and Rabbi Shimon, who say** that **betrothal does not disqualify** her, entering the **wedding canopy also does not disqualify** her.

וּמִמַּאי? דִּלְמָא עַד כָּאן לָא קָאָמַר רַבִּי מֵאִיר הָתָם אֶלָּא בְּקִדּוּשִׁין דְּקָנֵי לַהּ. אֲבָל חוּפָּה דְּלָא קָנָה לַהּ – לָא.

The Gemara refutes this claim: **And from where** do we know that these *tanna'im* would apply their opinions with regard to betrothal to entering the wedding canopy? **Perhaps Rabbi Meir only stated** his opinion **there, with regard to betrothal, which acquires her. However,** in the case of **a wedding canopy, which does not acquire her, no,** she is not disqualified.

אִי נַמִי, עַד כָּאן לָא קָאָמְרִי רַבִּי אֶלְעָזָר וְרַבִּי שִׁמְעוֹן הָתָם – אֶלָּא בְּקִדּוּשִׁין, דְּלָא קְרִיבִי לְבִיאָה, אֲבָל חוּפָּה דִּקְרִיבָא לְבִיאָה – הָכִי נַמִי דְּפָסְלָה.

Alternatively, perhaps **Rabbi Elazar and Rabbi Shimon stated** their opinion **only there, with regard to betrothal, as it is not close to** an act of **sexual intercourse. However,** with regard to entering the **wedding canopy, which is close to** an act of **sexual intercourse,** as it is the place where the bride and groom are secluded together and symbolizes the woman's entrance into her husband's home, it is possible **that it also disqualifies** her from partaking of *teruma*.

אֶלָּא אִי אִיכָּא לְמֵימַר – בִּפְלוּגְתָּא דְּהָנֵי תַּנָּאֵי, דְּתַנְיָא: נִישְּׂאוּ זוֹ וָזוֹ, כְּשֵׁרוֹת וּפְסוּלוֹת, אוֹ שֶׁנִּכְנְסוּ לְחוּפָּה וְלֹא נִבְעֲלוּ – אוֹכְלוֹת מִשֶּׁלּוֹ וְאוֹכְלוֹת בִּתְרוּמָה.

Rather, if it can be said that this issue was already discussed by earlier Sages, it was **in the dispute** between **these** other ***tanna'im*, as it is taught in** a *baraita*: If **they married one another,** i.e., either a woman who is **fit or** a woman who is **unfit** married a priest, **or they entered the wedding canopy and did not** yet **have intercourse** with him, **they** are entitled to **eat of his** food **and** to **partake of *teruma*.**

נִכְנְסוּ, מִכְּלָל דְּנִישְּׂאוּ – נִישְּׂאוּ מַמָּשׁ?

The Gemara interrupts its presentation of the *baraita* to examine its wording. The fact that the *baraita* mentions a case where **they entered** the wedding canopy but did not yet have intercourse proves **by inference that** the earlier case, where **they married,** is referring to **actual marriage.** However, this is difficult because if they were actually married and had engaged in intercourse, the woman who was unfit to marry a priest is certainly disqualified from partaking of *teruma* due to the prohibited act of intercourse.

אֶלָּא לָאו – כְּגוֹן שֶׁנִּכְנְסוּ לְחוּפָּה וְלֹא נִבְעֲלוּ. וְקָתָנֵי: אוֹכְלוֹת מִשֶּׁלּוֹ וְאוֹכְלוֹת בִּתְרוּמָה.

Rather, is it not that the *baraita* is referring to a single case: **Where** they were married, and **they entered the canopy, and had not had intercourse? And it is taught** in the *baraita* that **they** are entitled to **partake of his** food **and** to **partake of *teruma*.** This indicates that entrance into the wedding canopy does not disqualify a woman who is unfit to marry a priest from eating *teruma*, although the act of intercourse does.

רַבִּי יִשְׁמָעֵאל בְּנוֹ שֶׁל רַבִּי יוֹחָנָן בֶּן בְּרוֹקָה אוֹמֵר: כׇּל שֶׁבִּיאָתָהּ מַאֲכִילָתָהּ – חוּפָּתָהּ מַאֲכִילָתָהּ, וְכׇל שֶׁאֵין בִּיאָתָהּ מַאֲכִילָתָהּ – אֵין חוּפָּתָהּ מַאֲכִילָתָהּ.

The *baraita* continues: Conversely, **Rabbi Yishmael, son of Rabbi Yoḥanan ben Beroka, says: Any** woman **whose** act of **intercourse entitles her to partake of *teruma*, her wedding canopy** also **entitles her to partake of *teruma*; and any** woman **whose** act of **intercourse does not entitle her to partake of *teruma*, her wedding canopy** also **does not entitle her to partake of *teruma*.** Consequently, it appears that the *tanna'im* cited in this *baraita* disagree over the very question of whether the entry of a priest and a woman unfit to marry him into the wedding canopy has legal significance.

מִמַּאי? דִּלְמָא רַבִּי יִשְׁמָעֵאל בְּנוֹ שֶׁל רַבִּי יוֹחָנָן בֶּן בְּרוֹקָה כְּרַבִּי מֵאִיר סְבִירָא לֵיהּ, דְּאָמַר: קִדּוּשִׁין לָא אָכְלָה.

The Gemara refutes this claim: **From where** do we know that this is correct? **Perhaps Rabbi Yishmael, son of Rabbi Yoḥanan ben Beroka, holds in accordance with** the opinion of **Rabbi Meir, who said** that in the case of the **betrothal** of a woman unfit for a priest **she may not partake of** *teruma*?

NOTES

Amen that I did not go astray while betrothed – אָמֵן שֶׁלֹּא שָׂטִיתִי אֲרוּסָה: These *halakhot* are apparently derived from the repetitive usage of the term amen in the phrase (Numbers 5:22): "And the woman shall say: Amen, amen" (see Rashi, Rivan, and *Tosafot*).

הַאי כָּל שֶׁאֵין בִּיאָתָהּ מַאֲכִילָתָהּ אֵין חוּפָּתָהּ מַאֲכִילָתָהּ? כָּל שֶׁאֵין בִּיאָתָהּ מַאֲכִילָתָהּ אֵין כַּסְפָּהּ מַאֲכִילָתָהּ מִיבְּעֵי לֵיהּ! דִּלְמָא, אַיְּידֵי דְּאָמַר תַּנָּא קַמָּא חוּפָּה – אֲמַר אִיהוּ נַמִי חוּפָּה.

The Gemara expresses surprise: According to this suggestion, **this** expression in the *baraita* is difficult: **Any** woman **whose** act of **intercourse does not entitle her to partake of** *teruma*, **her wedding canopy** also **does not entitle her to partake of** *teruma*. **It should have** said: **Any** woman **whose** act of **intercourse does not entitle her to partake of** *teruma*, **her** betrothal **money** also **does not entitle her to partake** of *teruma*, as it was the betrothal that disqualified her. The Gemara counters this argument: **Perhaps** it can be suggested that **since the first** *tanna* **said** his ruling with regard to **a wedding canopy,** Rabbi Yishmael, son of Rabbi Yoḥanan ben Beroka, **also said** his ruling with regard to **a wedding canopy,** even though he holds that she was already disqualified from the time of her betrothal.

אָמַר רַב עַמְרָם: הָא מִילְּתָא אֲמַר לַן רַב שֵׁשֶׁת, וְאַנְהַרִינְהוּ לְעַיְינִין מִמַּתְנִיתִין: יֵשׁ חוּפָּה לִפְסוּלוֹת, וְתַנָּא תּוּנָא: ״אָמֵן שֶׁלֹּא שָׂטִיתִי אֲרוּסָה, וּנְשׂוּאָה, שׁוֹמֶרֶת יָבָם, וּכְנוּסָה״.

§ **Rav Amram said: This matter was said** to us by **Rav Sheshet, and he illuminated our eyes from the mishna,** i.e., he demonstrated that the mishna serves as the basis for his opinion. Rav Sheshet's statement was as follows: **There is** significance **to** a priest entering the **wedding canopy** with women who are **unfit** to marry a priest. **And the** *tanna* of the mishna also **taught** this *halakha* with regard to a *sota* (*Sota* 18a–b): When a *sota* is brought to the Temple to drink the bitter waters, she affirms the oath imposed on her by a priest that she has not committed adultery. The mishna explains that when she says **amen,** it is as though she herself states **that: I did not go astray** while **betrothed,**[NH] **or married,** or as **a widow waiting for her** *yavam,* **or** as a fully **married** woman.

הַאי אֲרוּסָה הֵיכִי דָּמֵי? אִילֵימָא דְּקַנֵּי לַהּ כְּשֶׁהִיא אֲרוּסָה, וְקָא מַשְׁקֵה לַהּ כְּשֶׁהִיא אֲרוּסָה – אֲרוּסָה בַּת מִשְׁתְּיָא הִיא? וְהָא תְּנַן: אֲרוּסָה וְשׁוֹמֶרֶת יָבָם לֹא שׁוֹתוֹת וְלֹא נוֹטְלוֹת כְּתוּבָּה!

The Gemara inquires: **This** case of **a betrothed** woman, **what are the circumstances? If we say that he was jealous of her** and warned her not to seclude herself with a particular man **when she was betrothed, and he** also **causes her to drink** the waters **when she is betrothed,** is **a betrothed** woman **fit to drink** the waters of a *sota*? **Didn't we learn** in a mishna (*Sota* 23b): **A betrothed** woman **and a widow waiting for her** *yavam* **do not drink,**[H] as the *halakha* of the *sota* waters applies only to married women; **and they do not collect their marriage contract** if they secluded themselves after being warned, as they have acted in a licentious fashion?

אֶלָּא דְּקַנֵּי לַהּ כְּשֶׁהִיא אֲרוּסָה, וְאִיסְתַּתְּרָה, וְקָמַשְׁקֵה לַהּ כְּשֶׁהִיא נְשׂוּאָה – מִי בָּדְקִי לַהּ מַיָּא? וְהָתַנְיָא: ״וְנִקָּה הָאִישׁ מֵעָוֹן״ בִּזְמַן שֶׁהָאִישׁ מְנוּקֶּה מֵעָוֹן הַמַּיִם בּוֹדְקִין אֶת אִשְׁתּוֹ, אֵין הָאִישׁ מְנוּקֶּה מֵעָוֹן – אֵין הַמַּיִם בּוֹדְקִין אֶת אִשְׁתּוֹ!

Rather, the case in the first mishna cited above is **that he was jealous of her** and warned her not to seclude herself with a particular man **when she was betrothed, and she secluded herself** with that man, **and** her husband **causes her to drink when she is** already **married.** However, in that case **do the waters examine her? Isn't it taught** in a *baraita* with regard to the verse: **"And the man shall be clear from iniquity,** and that woman shall bear her iniquity" (Numbers 5:31), that **when the man is clear of iniquity**[H] **the waters examine his wife,** but if **the man is not clear of iniquity the waters do not examine his wife?** By secluding herself with the other man when she was betrothed, the woman rendered herself forbidden to her husband. If he then married her, he cannot be described as clear of iniquity, and therefore the *sota* waters are ineffective.

HALAKHA

Amen that I did not go astray while betrothed, etc. – אָמֵן שֶׁלֹּא שָׂטִיתִי אֲרוּסָה וכו׳: When a husband makes his wife drink the waters of a *sota*, he can extend her oath beyond the man he originally specified in his warning. Therefore, she must swear that she did not have intercourse with anyone other than her husband, including during the period of her betrothal. However, she may not be forced to swear that she was faithful while waiting for her *yavam* (Rambam *Sefer Nashim, Hilkhot Sota* 4:17).

A betrothed woman and a widow waiting for her ***yavam*** **do not drink, etc. – אֲרוּסָה וְשׁוֹמֶרֶת יָבָם לֹא שׁוֹתוֹת וכו׳:** A betrothed woman and a woman awaiting levirate marriage do not drink the bitter waters, even if they were warned about a particular man and they secluded themselves with him. Even if they want to drink the waters and their husbands also want them to, they may not do so. Rather, their husbands must divorce them, and they do not collect their marriage contract (Rambam *Sefer Nashim, Hilkhot Sota* 2:2).

When the man is clear of iniquity – בִּזְמַן שֶׁהָאִישׁ מְנוּקֶּה מֵעָוֹן: The waters examine the woman only if her husband is clear of iniquity. If he has engaged in relations prohibited by rabbinic law, the waters are ineffective (Rambam *Sefer Nashim, Hilkhot Sota* 2:8, 3:17).

אֶלָּא דְקַנֵּי לַהּ כְּשֶׁהִיא אֲרוּסָה, וְאִיסְתַּתְּרָה וְנִכְנְסָה לְחוּפָּה וְלֹא נִבְעֲלָה, וּשְׁמַע מִינַּהּ: יֵשׁ חוּפָּה לִפְסוּלוֹת.

Rather, it must be **that he was jealous of her when she was betrothed, and she secluded herself** with the other man anyway, **and she had entered the wedding canopy but did not** yet **have intercourse** with her husband when he brought her to the priest. Consequently, she is made to drink the *sota* waters as a married woman, and her husband has not committed a transgression, as he has not had intercourse with her. **Learn from this** that **there is** significance **to** a priest entering the **wedding canopy** with women who are **unfit** to marry a priest, as demonstrated by the fact that the *sota* waters will examine her in these circumstances.

אֲמַר רָבָא: וְתִסְבְּרָא דְּהָא מִתְרַצְתָּא הִיא? וְהָא כִּי אֲתָא רַבִּי אַחָא בַּר חֲנִינָא מִדָּרוֹמָא, אֲתָא וְאַיְיתֵי מַתְנִיתָא בִּידֵיהּ: ״מִבַּלְעֲדֵי אִישֵׁךְ״ מִי שֶׁקָּדְמָה שְׁכִיבַת בַּעַל לְבוֹעֵל, וְלֹא שֶׁקָּדְמָה שְׁכִיבַת בּוֹעֵל לְבַעַל.

Rava said: Do you hold that this *baraita* **is** sufficiently **accurate** to rely upon? **But when Rabbi Aḥa bar Ḥanina came from the South, he came with** this *baraita* **in hand:** The verse states with regard to the oath of the *sota*: "And some man has lain with you **besides your husband"** (Numbers 5:20), which indicates that it applies only **when the cohabitation of the husband preceded that of the adulterer, but not when the cohabitation of the adulterer preceded**[H] **that of the husband.** Consequently, in the case under discussion, drinking the *sota* waters would not be effective.

אֲמַר רָמִי בַּר חָמָא: מַשְׁכַּחַתְּ לַהּ כְּגוֹן שֶׁבָּא עָלֶיהָ אֲרוּסָהּ בְּבֵית אָבִיהָ.

Rami bar Ḥama said: You find it in a case **such as** where **her betrothed had intercourse with her** licentiously when she was a betrothed woman **in her father's house.** Since the act of intercourse was committed licentiously rather than for the purpose of consummating the marriage, the woman is still considered betrothed. Subsequently, her betrothed warned her not to seclude herself with a particular man, and she disobeyed. Then, they entered the wedding canopy together, despite the fact that they are forbidden to one another. Once they entered the wedding canopy, the woman can be made to drink the bitter waters. This proves that there is significance to entering the wedding canopy with a woman that is unfit for one to marry.

דִּכְווֹתַהּ גַּבֵּי שׁוֹמֶרֶת יָבָם – שֶׁבָּא עָלֶיהָ יָבָם בְּבֵית חָמִיהָ,

The Gemara asks: If so, in **the corresponding** case **with regard to a widow waiting for** her *yavam*, in **which** the *yavam* **had** licentious **intercourse with her in her father-in-law's house,**

HALAKHA

The cohabitation of the adulterer preceded – שֶׁקָּדְמָה שְׁכִיבַת בּוֹעֵל: If a woman who was warned by her husband secluded herself with the man in question before she had intercourse with her husband, she does not drink the *sota* waters. Her husband divorces her and she does not collect her marriage contract, as stated in the *baraita* cited by Rav Aḥa bar Ḥanina (Rambam *Sefer Nashim*, *Hilkhot Sota* 2:5).

Perek **VI**
Daf **58** Amud **b**

שׁוֹמֶרֶת יָבָם קָרֵית לַהּ?! אִשְׁתּוֹ מַעַלְיָא הִיא! דְּהָא אָמַר רַב: קָנָה לַכֹּל. כִּשְׁמוּאֵל דְּאָמַר: לֹא קָנָה אֶלָּא לַדְּבָרִים הָאֲמוּרִים בַּפָּרָשָׁה.

do you call her a widow waiting for her *yavam*? Once they have engaged in intercourse, **she is his proper wife, as Rav said** that one who has intercourse with his *yevama*, even without intending to thereby perform levirate marriage, **has acquired her for all** matters. The Gemara responds: This is in accordance **with** the opinion of **Shmuel, who said** that he **has acquired her only with regard to the matters stated in the chapter** of levirate marriage, but not with regard to other matters, and therefore she is not considered his wife with regard to the *halakhot* of *sota*.

מִידֵּי הוּא טַעְמָא – אֶלָּא לְרַב, הָא אָמַר רַב קָנָה לַכֹּל! הָכָא בְּמַאי עָסְקִינַן, כְּגוֹן דַּעֲבַד בַּהּ מַאֲמָר, וּבֵית שַׁמַּאי הִיא, דְּאָמְרִי: מַאֲמָר קוֹנֶה קִנְיָן גָּמוּר.

The Gemara responds: **The only reason** this proof was presented is to support the opinion of **Rav,** who is the one who holds that there is legal significance to a priest entering the wedding canopy with a woman who is unfit to marry him. **Didn't Rav say he has acquired her for all** matters? The Gemara answers: **With what are we dealing here? For example,** a case where the *yavam* **performed levirate betrothal with her** and afterward had intercourse with her for the sake of promiscuity. **And this is** in accordance with the opinion of **Beit Shammai, who say: Levirate betrothal acquires** a *yevama* in a **full-fledged** manner and removes the levirate bond. Therefore, when they have intercourse, they do not become fully married.

אִי הָכִי, הַיְינוּ אֲרוּסָה! וּלְטַעְמִיךְ, נְשׂוּאָה וּכְנוּסָה לָאו חֲדָא מִילְּתָא הִיא? אֶלָּא: נְשׂוּאָה – דִּידֵיהּ, וּכְנוּסָה – דְּחַבְרֵיהּ. הָכָא נַמִי: אֲרוּסָה – דִּידֵיהּ, וְשׁוֹמֶרֶת יָבָם – דְּחַבְרֵיהּ.

The Gemara raises a difficulty: **If so,** the case of the *yevama* who was betrothed **is** the same as the case of **a betrothed** woman. What is the difference between the two cases? The Gemara responds: **And according to your reasoning,** are the examples in the mishna of a **married** woman **and a fully married** woman **not a single matter? Rather,** the mishna must be referring to two very similar cases, with the following difference: **A married** woman means **his own** wife **and** a fully **married** woman is referring **to that of his fellow,** i.e., his brother's wife who became his wife through levirate marriage. **Here too,** the case of **a betrothed** woman is referring to **his own** wife **and** the case of **a widow waiting for her *yavam*** is **that of his fellow,** i.e., his *yevama*, who is now betrothed to him.

רַב פַּפָּא אֲמַר: הַאי תַּנָּא הוּא, דְּתַנְיָא: אֵין מְקַנִּין לָהּ לַאֲרוּסָה לְהַשְׁקוֹתָהּ כְּשֶׁהִיא אֲרוּסָה, אֲבָל מְקַנִּין אוֹתָהּ לְהַשְׁקוֹתָהּ כְּשֶׁהִיא נְשׂוּאָה.

Rav Pappa said: Rava's question can be resolved in a manner unrelated to the question about a priest entering the wedding canopy with a woman unfit for him. The *baraita* he cited **is** in accordance with **this *tanna*,** who does not require the man to be clear of iniquity, **as it is taught in a *baraita*: One cannot be jealous over a betrothed** woman and warn her not to seclude herself with a particular man in order **to cause her to drink** the *sota* waters **when she is betrothed, but one can be jealous over her to cause her to drink** the *sota* waters **when she is married,** even if she secluded herself with the man when she was still betrothed.

רַב נַחְמָן בַּר יִצְחָק אֲמַר: עַל יְדֵי גִלְגּוּל.

Rav Naḥman bar Yitzḥak said: The question never arises at all, as the oath is formulated **by means of extension.**[NH] The woman cannot be forced to drink the *sota* waters for events that took place while she was betrothed. However, if she is obligated to drink due to events that took place when she was married, the oath may be extended to include any possible acts of infidelity when she was betrothed.

שָׁלַח רַב חֲנִינָא מִשְּׁמֵיהּ דְּרַבִּי יוֹחָנָן: הָעוֹשֶׂה מַאֲמָר בִּיבִמְתּוֹ, [וְיֵשׁ לוֹ אָח], אֲפִילּוּ הוּא כֹּהֵן וְהִיא כֹּהֶנֶת – פְּסָלָהּ מִן הַתְּרוּמָה.

§ **Rav Ḥanina sent in the name of Rabbi Yoḥanan: One who performs levirate betrothal with his *yevama* and he has a brother, even if he is a priest and she is** the daughter of **a priest, he has disqualified her from** partaking of ***teruma*.** By Torah law, the other brother may still have intercourse with her and thereby perform levirate marriage, but by rabbinic law only the brother who betrothed her may perform levirate marriage. Due to the fact that she is considered to be waiting for levirate marriage even vis-à-vis the brother who is rabbinically prohibited from marrying her, she is classified as a woman who is waiting for an invalid act of intercourse. Consequently, she may not partake of *teruma* until the consummation of the levirate marriage.

לְמַאן? אִילֵימָא לְרַבִּי מֵאִיר, אֵימַר דַּאֲמַר רַבִּי מֵאִיר מִשְׁתַּמֶּרֶת לְבִיאָה פְּסוּלָה לָא אָכְלָה – מִדְּאוֹרַיְיתָא, דְּרַבָּנַן מִי אֲמַר? וְאֶלָּא לְרַבִּי אֶלְעָזָר וְרַבִּי שִׁמְעוֹן, הָשְׁתָּא מִשְׁתַּמֶּרֶת לְבִיאָה פְּסוּלָה דְּאוֹרַיְיתָא אָכְלָה, דְּרַבָּנַן מִיבַּעְיָא?

The Gemara asks: **According to whom** did Rabbi Yoḥanan make this statement? **If we say** it is **in accordance with** the opinion of **Rabbi Meir, say that Rabbi Meir said** that a woman who is **reserved for an invalid** act of **intercourse may not eat** *teruma* when the act of intercourse is prohibited **by Torah** law. However, if the act of intercourse is prohibited **by rabbinic** law, **did** Rabbi Meir actually **say** that the woman is disqualified from eating *teruma*? **Rather,** if we say it is **in accordance with** the opinions of **Rabbi Elazar and Rabbi Shimon, now** that they hold that even a woman who is **reserved for intercourse prohibited by Torah** law **may partake of** *teruma*, **is it necessary** to state that she may partake of *teruma* if she is reserved for intercourse prohibited **by rabbinic** law?

אֶלָּא כִּי אֲתָא רָבִין אֲמַר: עָשָׂה בָּהּ מַאֲמָר בִּיבִמְתּוֹ – דִּבְרֵי הַכֹּל אָכְלָה, יֵשׁ לוֹ אָח חָלָל – דִּבְרֵי הַכֹּל אֵינָהּ אוֹכֶלֶת. לֹא נֶחְלְקוּ אֶלָּא שֶׁנָּתַן לָהּ גֵּט, רַבִּי יוֹחָנָן אָמַר: אוֹכֶלֶת, רֵישׁ לָקִישׁ אָמַר: אֵינָהּ אוֹכֶלֶת.

Rather, when Ravin came from Eretz Yisrael **he said** an accurate version of Rabbi Yoḥanan's statement: If a *yavam* who **performed levirate betrothal with his *yevama*** has a brother, **all agree** that the *yevama* **may partake** of *teruma*. If **he has a brother** who is **a *ḥalal*,**[NH] e.g., his mother was a divorcée and therefore unfit to marry his father, who was a priest, **all agree** that the *yevama* **may not partake** of *teruma*, as she is considered reserved for an invalid act of intercourse. **They disagreed only** in a case when **he gave her a bill of divorce.**[NH] **Rabbi Yoḥanan said she may partake of** *teruma*, as she is considered to have returned to her father's house, while **Reish Lakish said** that **she may not partake of** *teruma*.

NOTES

By means of extension – עַל יְדֵי גִלְגּוּל: Rashi notes that this *halakha* is the source of the Torah law of the extension of oaths. This means that if an individual is required to take an oath in court due to a claim made by the opposing party, the latter can force him to extend his oath to include cases for which he would not otherwise have been liable to take an oath.

If he has a brother who is a *ḥalal* – יֵשׁ לוֹ אָח חָלָל וכו׳: The relationship between the woman and the *ḥalal* is not invalid in the normal sense of the term, as it is entirely permitted for them to marry. Nevertheless, since a *ḥalal* is considered like a regular Israelite, if she marries him she is disqualified from partaking of her father's *teruma* (Ritva).

He gave her a bill of divorce – שֶׁנָּתַן לָהּ גֵּט: Rashi explains that the *yavam* gave the *yevama* a bill of divorce, which makes her unfit to marry him by rabbinic law. Nevertheless, since by Torah law the levirate bond still exists, she is considered reserved for a prohibited act of intercourse. Rabbeinu Ḥananel explains differently, that he gave her a bill of divorce and subsequently performed levirate betrothal with her. In that case, he is prohibited from having intercourse with her, and yet she is considered to be reserved for him. This fits in well with the continuation of the discussion, as a priest who divorced his wife and betrothed her once again certainly does not entitle her to partake of *teruma* (see Rashba).

HALAKHA

By means of extension – עַל יְדֵי גִלְגּוּל: Although a betrothed woman who secluded herself with another man does not drink the *sota* waters or take an oath, if she becomes liable to do so for having secluded herself after marriage, she must extend her oath and confirm that she did not commit adultery while she was betrothed, as stated by Rav Naḥman bar Yitzḥak (Rambam *Sefer Nashim*, *Hilkhot Sota* 4:17).

One of the *yevamin* was a *ḥalal* – אֶחָד הַיְּבָמִים שֶׁהָיָה חָלָל: If the daughter of a priest was married to a priest who died without children, and one of his brothers was a *ḥalal*, she may not eat *teruma* due to the levirate bond she has with the *ḥalal*. Even if one of the other brothers performed levirate betrothal with her, she may not partake of *teruma* until after she is married to him (Rambam *Sefer Zera'im*, *Hilkhot Terumot* 7:22).

He gave her a bill of divorce – נָתַן לָהּ גֵּט: If a priest gave a bill of divorce to his *yevama* who is the daughter of a priest, although she is forbidden to him and yet bound to him by the levirate bond, as she has not undergone *ḥalitza*, she is nevertheless permitted to partake of *teruma*. This is because relations between them are prohibited by rabbinic law but not Torah law. The *halakha* is in accordance with the opinion of Rabbi Yoḥanan as opposed to that of Reish Lakish (Rambam *Sefer Zera'im*, *Hilkhot Terumot* 7:23).

רַבִּי יוֹחָנָן אָמַר: אוֹכֶלֶת, אֲפִילּוּ לְרַבִּי מֵאִיר דְּאָמַר אֵינָהּ אוֹכֶלֶת – הָנֵי מִילֵּי מִשְׁתַּמֶּרֶת לְבִיאָה פְּסוּלָה דְּאוֹרַיְיתָא, אֲבָל דְּרַבָּנַן – אָכְלָה.

The Gemara analyzes the two opinions: **Rabbi Yoḥanan said she may eat** *teruma* because **even according to Rabbi Meir, who said** in the mishna that **she may not partake** of *teruma*, **this applies only** when she is **waiting for intercourse** that is **invalid by Torah** law, **but** if the intercourse is prohibited **by rabbinic** law, **she may partake** of *teruma*. In this case, since they have not yet performed *ḥalitza*, the levirate bond still applies by Torah law, but they are prohibited by rabbinic law from consummating the levirate marriage.

וְרֵישׁ לָקִישׁ אָמַר: אֵינָהּ אוֹכֶלֶת, אֲפִילּוּ לְרַבִּי אֶלְעָזָר וְרַבִּי שִׁמְעוֹן דְּאָמְרִי אוֹכֶלֶת – הָנֵי מִילֵּי דְּיֵשׁ לוֹ לְהַאֲכִיל בְּמָקוֹם אַחֵר, אֲבָל הָכָא, כֵּיוָן דְּאֵין לוֹ לְהַאֲכִיל בְּמָקוֹם אַחֵר – לָא.

And Reish Lakish said: She may not partake of *teruma* **because even according to Rabbi Elazar and Rabbi Shimon, who say** in the mishna that **she may partake** of *teruma*, **this applies only** to a case of betrothal, as a priest **can entitle** a woman **to partake** of *teruma* **in another case** via betrothal. **But here,** where he gave her a bill of divorce, **since he cannot entitle** a woman **to partake** of *teruma* **in** any **other case** by giving her a bill of divorce, **no.**

וְכִי תֵּימָא: הָכָא נַמִי יֵשׁ לוֹ לְהַאֲכִילָהּ בְּחוֹזֶרֶת – חוֹזֶרֶת פְּסָקָה מִינֵּיהּ, וּקְרוֹבָה לְבֵי נָשָׁא, אֲבָל הָא אֲגִידָא בֵּיהּ.

And lest you say here too, in the case of a bill of divorce, **he can entitle her to partake of** *teruma* **when she returns** to her father's house, this case is different for the following reason: A woman **who returns** to her father's house **has been severed from** her husband **and she is close to her** father's **house** [***bei nasha***],[N] and therefore she may once again partake of *teruma* on her father's account. **However, this** *yevama* who has received a bill of divorce **is** still **bound to** her *yavam* until they perform *ḥalitza*, and she is therefore disqualified from eating *teruma*.

"נִתְאַרְמְלוּ אוֹ נִתְגָּרְשׁוּ" וכו׳. בְּעָא מִינֵּיהּ רַבִּי חִיָּיא בַּר יוֹסֵף מִשְּׁמוּאֵל: כֹּהֵן גָּדוֹל שֶׁקִּידֵּשׁ אֶת הַקְּטַנָּה וּבָגְרָה תַּחְתָּיו,

§ It was taught in the mishna that in the case of women who married priests despite the fact that they were unfit to do so, if **they were widowed or divorced** from that marriage, they are disqualified from eating *teruma*, but if they were widowed or divorced while they were only betrothed, they are fit to partake of *teruma*. **Rabbi Ḥiyya bar Yosef raised a dilemma before Shmuel:** In the case of **a High Priest who betrothed a minor and she matured under him,** i.e., while betrothed to him,

NOTES

Her father's house [*bei nasha*] – **בֵּי נָשָׁא**: Meaning literally a woman's house, this term is used in the general sense of a woman's family's house. Some explained, apparently in a homiletical sense, that the term comes from the from the root *n-sh-h*, meaning forget, as a woman forgets her father's house upon marriage.

Perek **VI**
Daf **59** Amud **a**

מַהוּ? בָּתַר נִישּׂוּאִין אָזְלִינַן, אוֹ בָּתַר אֵירוּסִין אָזְלִינַן?

what is the *halakha*? The Gemara clarifies the dilemma: **Do we follow** the time of **marriage,**[N] at which point she was unfit for him according to most *tanna'im*, who hold that a High Priest may not marry a grown woman, as she is no longer called "a wife in her virginity" (Leviticus 21:13)? **Or do we follow** the time of **betrothal,**[B] at which point she was of suitable age?

אָמַר לֵיהּ: תְּנֵיתוּהָ, נִתְאַרְמְלוּ אוֹ נִתְגָּרְשׁוּ, מִן הַנִּשּׂוּאִין – פְּסוּלוֹת, מִן הָאֵירוּסִין – כְּשֵׁרוֹת.

Shmuel **said to him: You learned it** in the mishna: If **they were widowed or divorced from marriage, they are disqualified** from partaking of *teruma*, but if they were widowed or divorced **from betrothal, they are fit** to partake of *teruma*. This indicates that disqualifications from the privileges of priesthood are determined based upon marriage rather than betrothal.

NOTES

What is the ***halakha*****? Do we follow the time of marriage, etc.** – **מַהוּ? בָּתַר נִשּׂוּאִין וכו׳**: According to Rashi and others, Shmuel's initial understanding of Rabbi Ḥiyya bar Yosef's question was the same as the Gemara's final interpretation: Is a High Priest permitted to marry a young woman who matured while she was betrothed to him? Others question this opinion based upon the continuation of the discussion recorded in the Gemara (see *Tosafot*). They explain that Shmuel initially thought that the question was whether the woman is considered to be designated for an invalid act of relations, in which case she would be prohibited from partaking of her father's *teruma* if she is the daughter of a priest (Ritva). The Rashba explains that the question was whether she should be permanently disqualified from the priesthood as a *ḥalala* if this High Priest died (Rashba).

BACKGROUND

Betrothal and marriage – **אֵירוּסִין וְנִשּׂוּאִין**: A Jewish wedding is divided into two distinct parts. Betrothal is the first stage of the marriage process. The bond created by betrothal is so strong that, after betrothal, a woman requires a divorce before she can marry another man. Similarly, sexual relations with other men are considered adulterous and are punishable by death. At this stage, the betrothed couple may not yet live together as husband and wife, and most of the couple's mutual obligations do not yet apply.

The second stage of the marriage occurs when the bride and groom come under the bridal canopy, and it immediately confers both the privileges and the responsibilities associated with marriage upon the newlywed couple. After marriage, if one spouse dies, all the *halakhot* of mourning for a close blood relation apply to the surviving spouse. If the wife of a priest dies, he is permitted to make himself ritually impure to bury her. All the monetary rights and obligations applying to married couples take effect after marriage. Today, betrothal and marriage are both performed in a single ceremony, but in talmudic times there was usually a year-long gap between the two.

אָמַר לֵיהּ: לְשַׁוּוּיָהּ חֲלָלָה – לָא קָמִיבַּעְיָא לִי דְּבִיאָה הִיא דִּמְשַׁוְּויָא חֲלָלָה. כִּי קָמִיבַּעְיָא לִי ״וְהוּא אִשָּׁה בִבְתוּלֶיהָ יִקָּח״ מַאי? קִיחָה דְּקִדּוּשִׁין בָּעֵינַן, אוֹ קִיחָה דְּנִישּׂוּאִין בָּעֵינַן?

Rabbi Ḥiyya bar Yosef **said to** Shmuel: With regard to **causing her** to become a ***ḥalala* I did not raise a dilemma, as** it is clear **that it is intercourse that causes her** to become a ***ḥalala*. When I raised a dilemma,** it was with regard to the verse pertaining to a High Priest: **"And he shall take a wife in her virginity"** (Leviticus 21:13). **What** does "take" mean in this verse? **Do we require** that only **the taking of betrothal** must occur when she is in her virginity, i.e., when she is a minor or a young woman, **or** perhaps **we require** even **the taking of marriage** to be performed when she is a minor or young woman?

אָמַר לֵיהּ, הָא נַמִי תְּנֵיתוּהָ: אֵירֵס אֶת הָאַלְמָנָה וְנִתְמַנָּה לִהְיוֹת כֹּהֵן גָּדוֹל – יִכְנוֹס. שָׁאנֵי הָתָם, דִּכְתִיב ״יִקַּח אִשָּׁה״.

Shmuel **said to him: This, too, you learned** in a mishna (61a): If **he betrothed a widow and was** subsequently **appointed to be High Priest,**[H] **he may marry** her, despite the fact that a High Priest is prohibited from marrying a widow. This indicates that her permissibility to him is determined according to the time of the betrothal rather than the time of marriage. The Gemara refutes this proof: **There it is different, as it is written: "He shall take for a wife"** (Leviticus 21:14). The superfluous expression "for a wife" indicates that he is permitted to marry the widow in this case.

הָכָא נַמִי כְּתִיב ״אִשָּׁה״. אַחַת וְלֹא שְׁתַּיִם.

The Gemara objects: **Here, too,** with regard to a woman who matured after betrothal, **it is written:** "And he shall take **a wife** in her virginity," and this should indicate that he may marry the grown woman in this case. The Gemara answers that the term "wife" allows for the inclusion of **one** case **but not two.**[N] Consequently, since a High Priest may marry a widow he had betrothed before he was appointed High Priest, it cannot also be derived that he may marry a grown woman that he had betrothed before she matured.

וּמָה רָאִיתָ? הָא אִישְׁתַּנֵּי גּוּפָהּ, וְהָא לָא אִישְׁתַּנֵּי גּוּפָהּ.

The Gemara asks: **And what did you see**[N] that led you to include the case of a widow and exclude that of a grown woman? The Gemara answers: In **this** case, of the grown woman, **her body has changed,**[NH] and therefore she is forbidden to him even though she was betrothed before she matured. In **that** case, of the widow, **her body has not changed.** It is the priest's personal status that has changed, and therefore she remains permitted.

מתני׳ כֹּהֵן גָּדוֹל לֹא יִשָּׂא אַלְמָנָה, בֵּין אַלְמָנָה מִן הָאֵירוּסִין בֵּין אַלְמָנָה מִן הַנִּישּׂוּאִין. וְלֹא יִשָּׂא אֶת הַבּוֹגֶרֶת, רַבִּי אֶלְעָזָר וְרַבִּי שִׁמְעוֹן מַכְשִׁירִין בְּבוֹגֶרֶת. [וְלֹא יִשָּׂא אֶת מוּכַּת עֵץ].

MISHNA **A High Priest may not marry a widow,**[H] **whether** she is **a widow from betrothal or a widow from marriage. And he may not marry a grown woman.**[H] He may marry only a minor or a young woman. **Rabbi Elazar and Rabbi Shimon declare a grown woman fit** to marry a High Priest. **And he may not marry a woman whose hymen was torn accidentally.**[H]

גמ׳ תָּנוּ רַבָּנַן: ״אַלְמָנָה לֹא יִקָּח״, בֵּין אַלְמָנָה מִן הָאֵירוּסִין, בֵּין אַלְמָנָה מִן הַנִּישּׂוּאִין. פְּשִׁיטָא! מַהוּ דְּתֵימָא: לֵילַף אַלְמָנָה אַלְמָנָה מִתָּמָר, מָה לְהַלָּן – מִן הַנִּישּׂוּאִין, אַף כָּאן – מִן הַנִּישּׂוּאִין, קָא מַשְׁמַע לַן.

GEMARA **The Sages taught:** The verse states with regard to a High Priest: **"A widow…he shall not take"** (Leviticus 21:14), which prohibits him from marrying any widow, **whether** she is **a widow from betrothal or a widow from marriage.** The Gemara is surprised by this statement: This is **obvious,** as the verse is referring to a widow without further specification. The Gemara answers: It is necessary; **lest you say that one should derive** a verbal analogy between the words **"widow"** and **"widow,"** based upon the usage of that term in a verse with regard to **Tamar,** Judah's daughter-in-law (Genesis 38:11), as follows: **Just as there,** Tamar was a widow **from marriage, so too here** the verse is referring only to a widow **from marriage.** The *tanna* therefore **teaches us** that this is not the case.

וְאֵימָא הָכִי נַמִי! דּוּמְיָא דִּגְרוּשָׁה, מָה גְּרוּשָׁה בֵּין מִן הַנִּישּׂוּאִין בֵּין מִן הָאֵירוּסִין, אַף אַלְמָנָה בֵּין מִן הָאֵירוּסִין בֵּין מִן הַנִּישּׂוּאִין.

The Gemara asks: **And say** that **it is indeed so,** that the suggested verbal analogy is correct. The Gemara answers: It is **similar to** the case of **a divorcée:**[N] **Just as a divorcée** is forbidden to a priest **whether** she was divorced **from marriage or from betrothal, so too a widow** is forbidden to a High Priest **whether** she is a widow **from marriage or from betrothal.**

HALAKHA

He betrothed a widow and was subsequently appointed to be High Priest – אֵירֵס אֶת הָאַלְמָנָה וְנִתְמַנָּה לִהְיוֹת כֹּהֵן גָּדוֹל: If a priest was appointed High Priest after he had betrothed a widow he is permitted to marry her (Rambam *Sefer Kedusha, Hilkhot Issurei Bia* 17:12).

Her body has changed – אִישְׁתַּנֵּי גּוּפָהּ: If a High Priest betrothed a minor and she matured before their marriage he may not marry her *ab initio*. However, if he did marry her, he is not forced to divorce her. This is because a High Priest is not forced to divorce his wife even if she was a grown woman when he betrothed her (Rambam *Sefer Kedusha, Hilkhot Issurei Bia* 17:17 and *Maggid Mishne* there).

A High Priest may not marry a widow – כֹּהֵן גָּדוֹל לֹא יִשָּׂא אַלְמָנָה: A High Priest may not marry a widow, whether she was widowed from betrothal or marriage (Rambam *Sefer Kedusha, Hilkhot Issurei Bia* 17:1, 11).

He may not marry a grown woman – לֹא יִשָּׂא אֶת הַבּוֹגֶרֶת: It is a mitzva for a High Priest to marry a young woman who is a virgin. He is prohibited from marrying a grown woman (Rambam *Sefer Kedusha, Hilkhot Issurei Bia* 17:13).

He may not marry a woman whose hymen was torn accidentally – לֹא יִשָּׂא אֶת מוּכַּת עֵץ: A High Priest may not marry a woman whose hymen was torn accidentally (Rambam *Sefer Kedusha, Hilkhot Issurei Bia* 17:14).

NOTES

A wife in one case but not two – אִשָּׁה אַחַת וְלֹא שְׁתַּיִם: In context, the simple meaning of this statement, as explained by Rashi and other commentaries, is that since there is only one superfluous usage of the word "wife" only one case can be permitted on the basis of this derivation. The Rambam however, understands the Gemara's statement literally, as reading: One wife and not two, and consequently rules that it is prohibited for a High Priest to marry two women (see *Maggid Mishne* and *Yam shel Shlomo*). The Ra'avad disagrees and offers proofs to the contrary, including the fact that Jehoiada the High Priest was righteous and had two wives (see II Chronicles 24:3).

And what did you see – וּמָה רָאִיתָ: It would seem to have been equally possible to arrive at the opposite conclusion, that it is permitted for the High Priest to marry the woman who matured while betrothed and prohibited for him to marry a widow he had betrothed before being appointed High Priest. This is especially reasonable given that the prohibition for a High Priest to marry a widow is more severe than the prohibition for him to marry a grown woman (Ritva).

In this case of the grown woman her body has changed – הָאי אִישְׁתַּנֵּי גּוּפָהּ: Apparently, since her body has changed, she is no longer viewed as the same person but as a different being, and therefore she is now forbidden to him (see *Keren Ora*).

Similar to the case of a divorcée – דּוּמְיָא דִּגְרוּשָׁה: *Tosafot* ask why the opposite cannot be stated: Just as the prohibition for a High Priest to marry a widow applies only to a woman who has been married, as indicated by the precedent of Tamar, so too a divorcée is prohibited only if she had been married. See the answers of *Tosafot*. *Tosefot HaRosh* and the Meiri explain that since a common priest is prohibited from marrying a divorcée but is permitted to marry a non-virgin, it must be the divorce itself that causes the prohibition regardless of whether her marriage had been consummated. The Ritva presents an alternative explanation, accepted by many later commentaries. He claims that although the case of Tamar is a biblical precedent, it is not a full-fledged verbal analogy and consequently cannot serve as a model for other *halakhot*.

"וְלֹא יִשָּׂא אֶת הַבּוֹגֶרֶת". תָּנוּ רַבָּנַן: "וְהוּא אִשָּׁה בִבְתוּלֶיהָ יִקָּח", פְּרָט לְבוֹגֶרֶת שֶׁכָּלוּ לָהּ בְּתוּלֶיהָ, דִּבְרֵי רַבִּי מֵאִיר. רַבִּי אֶלְעָזָר וְרַבִּי שִׁמְעוֹן מַכְשִׁירִין בְּבוֹגֶרֶת.

§ It was taught in the mishna: **And a High Priest may not marry a grown woman. The Sages taught** that the verse: **"And he shall take a wife in her virginity"** (Leviticus 21:13) **excludes a grown woman, whose hymen has worn away,**[B] i.e., it is no longer as complete as that of a minor or a young woman; this is **the statement of Rabbi Meir. Rabbi Elazar and Rabbi Shimon declare a grown woman fit** to marry a High Priest.

בְּמַאי קָא מִיפַּלְגִי? רַבִּי מֵאִיר סָבַר: "בְּתוּלָה" אֲפִילּוּ מִקְצָת בְּתוּלִים מַשְׁמַע, "בְּתוּלֶיהָ" עַד דְּאִיכָּא כָּל הַבְּתוּלִים, "בִּבְתוּלֶיהָ" בִּכְדַרְכָּהּ אִין, שֶׁלֹּא כְּדַרְכָּהּ לָא.

The Gemara asks: **With regard to what do they disagree?** The Gemara explains: **Rabbi Meir holds** that were the verse referring simply to **a virgin** it would have **indicated** that **even** a woman with **partial** signs of **virginity**, i.e., a grown woman, is permitted. Since the verse states **"her virginity,"** it means that she is fit to marry a High Priest only **if all of** the signs of **her virginity are** intact, which excludes a grown woman. The full expression **"in her virginity"**[N] indicates that if she has experienced sexual intercourse in **a typical** manner, which takes place in the area of her virginity, i.e., her hymen, **yes,** she is disqualified from marrying a High Priest; but if she has experienced sexual intercourse in **an atypical** manner i.e., anal intercourse, **no,** she is not disqualified.

וְרַבִּי אֶלְעָזָר וְרַבִּי שִׁמְעוֹן סָבְרִי: "בְּתוּלָה" בְּתוּלָה שְׁלֵימָה מַשְׁמַע, "בְּתוּלֶיהָ" וַאֲפִילּוּ מִקְצָת בְּתוּלִים, "בִּבְתוּלֶיהָ" עַד שֶׁיִּהְיוּ כׇּל בְּתוּלֶיהָ קַיָּימִין, בֵּין בִּכְדַרְכָּהּ בֵּין שֶׁלֹּא כְּדַרְכָּהּ.

And Rabbi Elazar and Rabbi Shimon hold that were the verse referring simply to **a virgin,** it would have **indicated** that only **a complete virgin** is fit to marry a High Priest, but not a grown woman. When it states **"her virginity,"** it indicates that **even** a woman with **partial** signs of **virginity,** i.e., a grown woman, is fit to marry the High Priest. The full expression **"in her virginity"** indicates that she is not fit to marry to marry a High Priest **unless all of her virginity is intact,** i.e., she has not engaged in intercourse of any kind, **whether typical** sexual intercourse **or atypical** sexual intercourse.

אָמַר רַב יְהוּדָה אָמַר רַב: נִבְעֲלָה שֶׁלֹּא כְּדַרְכָּהּ – פְּסוּלָה לִכְהוּנָּה. מְתִיב רָבָא: "וְלוֹ תִהְיֶה לְאִשָּׁה" בְּאִשָּׁה הָרְאוּיָה לוֹ, פְּרָט לְאַלְמָנָה לְכֹהֵן גָּדוֹל, גְּרוּשָׁה וַחֲלוּצָה לְכֹהֵן הֶדְיוֹט.

Rav Yehuda said that **Rav said:** If **she had atypical sexual intercourse,**[H] **she is disqualified from** the High **Priesthood,** i.e., from marrying the High Priest. **Rava raised an objection** based upon a *baraita*: The verse states with regard to rape: **"And she shall be his wife"** (Deuteronomy 22:19), and the Sages explained that this is referring only **to a woman suitable for him, excluding a widow for a High Priest**[H] and **a divorcée or a *ḥalutza* for a common priest.** In these cases, the rapist is not permitted to marry his victim.

הֵיכִי דָּמֵי? אִילֵימָא בִּכְדַרְכָּהּ – מַאי אִירְיָא מִשּׁוּם אַלְמָנָה? תֵּיפוֹק לֵיהּ מִשּׁוּם דַּהֲוָיָא לַהּ בְּעוּלָה. אֶלָּא לָאו שֶׁלֹּא כְּדַרְכָּהּ. וּמִשּׁוּם אַלְמָנָה – אִין, מִשּׁוּם בְּעוּלָה – לָא.

The Gemara clarifies: **What are the circumstances** of this *halakha*? **If we say** that the High Priest raped her by engaging **in typical** intercourse, **why** does the *baraita* **specifically** state that she is forbidden to him **because** she is **a widow? Let him derive** this *halakha* **from** the fact **that she is** now **a non-virgin.**[N] **Rather,** is it **not** that he had **atypical** intercourse with her, **and due to** the fact that she is **a widow, yes,** that is the reason she is forbidden, but **due to** the fact that she is **a non-virgin, no,** that is not the reason she is forbidden? This indicates that a woman who had intercourse in an atypical manner is not considered a non-virgin and is not disqualified from marrying a High Priest.

Perek **VI**
Daf **59** Amud **b**

הָא מַנִּי – רַבִּי מֵאִיר הִיא, וְרַב דְּאָמַר כְּרַבִּי אֶלְעָזָר.

The Gemara refutes this proof: In accordance with **whose** opinion **is this *baraita*? It is** in accordance with the opinion of **Rabbi Meir,** who maintains that a woman who engaged in atypical intercourse is permitted to a High Priest, **and when Rav said** his statement, it was **in accordance with** the opinion of **Rabbi Elazar,** who holds that such a woman is disqualified from marrying a High Priest.

BACKGROUND

A grown woman, whose hymen has worn away – בּוֹגֶרֶת שֶׁכָּלוּ לָהּ בְּתוּלֶיהָ: As *Tosafot* point out, this does not mean that the hymen has worn away completely, as it usually remains intact as long as it has not been forcibly broken. However, before the onset of adolescence the hymen is more prominent and relatively larger. As a girl matures, the size of the hymen decreases in relation to the vagina.

NOTES

A virgin, her virginity, in her virginity – בְּתוּלָה, בְּתוּלֶיהָ, בִּבְתוּלֶיהָ: It appears that the dispute concerns the meanings of the terms virgin and virginity. Do these words refer to the physical sign of virginity, i.e., a fully intact hymen, or are they abstract terms that refer to the status of a woman who has never experienced any form of sexual intercourse? In *Arukh LaNer*, it is explained how these *halakhot* are derived based upon the hermeneutical principle that one restrictive expression after another amplifies the *halakha* in regard to which the verse employs these expressions.

Let him derive this *halakha* from the fact that she is now a non-virgin – תֵּיפוֹק לֵיהּ מִשּׁוּם דַּהֲוָיָא בְּעוּלָה: One might argue that since mitzvot that are limited to specific individuals are generally considered less stringent than those that apply equally to all, the requirement that a rapist marry his victim should override the requirement that a High Priest marry a virgin. The Rashba explains, based upon tractate *Ketubot* (40a), that since the obligation for a rapist to marry his victim is not absolute, as the victim or her father have the right of refusal, it does not override the positive mitzva for a High Priest to marry a virgin.

HALAKHA

If she had atypical sexual intercourse – נִבְעֲלָה שֶׁלֹּא כְּדַרְכָּהּ: A High Priest may not marry a woman who has had atypical, i.e., anal, sexual intercourse (Rambam *Sefer Kedusha, Hilkhot Issurei Bia* 17:14).

Excluding a widow for a High Priest – פְּרָט לְאַלְמָנָה לְכֹהֵן גָּדוֹל וכו׳: One who raped a woman who is forbidden to him, even if she was forbidden to him by rabbinic decree, may not marry her despite the general requirement that a rapist marry his victim if she consents. Consequently, if a priest raped a divorcée or a *ḥalutza*, or if a High Priest raped a widow, he may not marry his victim (Rambam *Sefer Nashim, Hilkhot Na'ara Betula* 1:5; *Shulḥan Arukh, Even HaEzer* 177:4).

HALAKHA

One who refused – מְמָאֶנֶת: If a young girl was married off by her mother or brother and then refused to remain with her husband, she is permitted to a priest. This is the *halakha* even if he wrote her a bill of divorce, they subsequently married again, and she again refused to remain married to him (Rambam *Sefer Kedusha, Hilkhot Issurei Bia* 17:18).

A woman who had intercourse with an animal – נִבְעֲלָה לִבְהֵמָה: A woman who had intercourse with an animal is liable for capital punishment. However, she is not considered a *zona* and is not disqualified from marrying a priest. If she had only atypical intercourse with an animal, she is permitted even to a High Priest (Rambam *Sefer Kedusha, Hilkhot Issurei Bia* 18:1, 17:14; *Shulḥan Arukh, Even HaEzer* 6:8).

אִי כְּרַבִּי אֶלְעָזָר, מַאי אִירְיָא מִשּׁוּם בְּעוּלָה? תֵּיפוֹק לֵיהּ דְּהָוְיָא לַהּ זוֹנָה, דְּהָא אָמַר רַבִּי אֶלְעָזָר: פָּנוּי הַבָּא עַל הַפְּנוּיָה שֶׁלֹּא לְשֵׁם אִישׁוּת עֲשָׂאָהּ זוֹנָה!

The Gemara asks: **If** Rav's statement is **in accordance with** the opinion **of Rabbi Elazar,**[N] **why** did he **specifically** state that she is forbidden to him **because** she is **a non-virgin? Let him derive** it **from** the fact **that she is a *zona*,**[N] **as Rabbi Elazar said:** Even in the case of **an unmarried man who had intercourse with an unmarried woman not for the purpose of marriage, he has** thereby **caused her to become a *zona*.**

אָמַר רַב יוֹסֵף: כְּגוֹן שֶׁנִּבְעֲלָה לִבְהֵמָה, דְּהָתָם, מִשּׁוּם בְּעוּלָה – אִיכָּא, מִשּׁוּם זוֹנָה – לֵיכָּא.

Rav Yosef said: When Rav said that a woman who had anal intercourse is disqualified from marrying a High Priest, he was referring **to** a woman **who had intercourse with an animal, as there** she is disqualified **because** she is **a non-virgin,**[N] but she **is not** disqualified **because** of the prohibition of **a *zona*.**

אֲמַר לֵיהּ אַבַּיֵי: מִמַּה נַּפְשָׁךְ, אִי בְּעוּלָה הָוְיָא – זוֹנָה נַמִי הָוְיָא, וְאִי זוֹנָה לָא הָוְיָא – בְּעוּלָה נַמִי לָא הָוְיָא. וְכִי תֵּימָא: מִידֵּי דְּהָוְיָא אַמּוּכַּת עֵץ שֶׁלֹּא כְּדַרְכָּהּ – אִם כֵּן אֵין לְךָ אִשָּׁה שֶׁכְּשֵׁרָה לִכְהוּנָּה שֶׁלֹּא נַעֲשֵׂית מוּכַּת עֵץ עַל יְדֵי צְרוֹר.

Abaye said to him: Whichever way you look at it, there is a difficulty with this answer: **If she is** considered **a non-virgin, she is** also **a *zona*, and if she is not a *zona*** she is also **not a non-virgin. And lest you say** that it is **analogous to** a case of **a woman who lost her virginity via penetration by a foreign object atypically,** i.e., anally, whose hymen was therefore not damaged and she is not forbidden as a *zona*, yet she is no longer considered a virgin, that is not correct: **If so,** if such a woman is considered a non-virgin and forbidden to a High Priest, **you** would **have no woman who is fit for the** High **Priesthood, who has not lost her virginity via penetration by a foreign object** atypically, i.e., **by a pebble** used to clean herself in the lavatory.

אֶלָּא אֲמַר רַבִּי זֵירָא: בִּמְמָאֶנֶת.

Rather, Rabbi Zeira said that Rav was referring **to one who refused**[HN] her husband after having only atypical intercourse with him. Although the act of intercourse was not licentious, as she was married at the time, she is nevertheless disqualified from marrying into the priesthood because she is not a virgin.

אָמַר רַב שִׁימִי בַּר חִיָּיא: נִבְעֲלָה לִבְהֵמָה – כְּשֵׁרָה לִכְהוּנָּה. תַּנְיָא נַמִי הָכִי: נִבְעֲלָה לְמִי שֶׁאֵינוֹ אִישׁ, אַף עַל פִּי שֶׁבִּסְקִילָה – כְּשֵׁרָה לִכְהוּנָּה.

§ **Rabbi Shimi bar Ḥiyya said:** A woman who **had intercourse with an animal**[H] is like one whose hymen was torn accidentally. Consequently, she is not a *zona* and is **fit for the priesthood. This is also taught** in a *baraita*: If a woman **had intercourse with one who is not a man,**[N] i.e., an animal, **although** she is liable to **stoning** if she did so intentionally and in the presence of witnesses who forewarned her of her punishment, she is nevertheless **fit for the priesthood.**

NOTES

If Rav's statement is in accordance with the opinion of Rabbi Elazar, etc. – אִי כְּרַבִּי אֶלְעָזָר וכו׳: The commentaries raise the following difficulty with this question: Even if Rav agrees with Rabbi Elazar with regard to atypical intercourse, how does the Gemara know that Rav accepts his opinion with regard to the effect of intercourse between an unmarried man and an unmarried woman? In fact, there is a *tanna*, Rabbi Shimon, who agrees with Rabbi Elazar only with regard to atypical intercourse, and it is possible that Rav agrees with Rabbi Shimon. Some commentaries explain that the Gemara could have answered its question by making this point but chose instead to give a better answer (see Ramban and Rashba). Alternatively, as *Tosafot* explain, the Gemara's primary concern is not with the opinion of Rav himself but with the opinion of Rabbi Elazar (see Ritva).

Let him derive it from the fact that she is a *zona* – תֵּיפוֹק לֵיהּ דְּהָוְיָא לַהּ זוֹנָה: The commentaries wonder why the Gemara assumes that Rav does not hold that the woman is a *zona*. Perhaps Rav actually holds that she is prohibited for two reasons, because she is a non-virgin and also because she is a *zona*. The Rashba and Ritva answer that since there would be significant ramifications to such an opinion, as a *zona* is forbidden to all priests and not just the High Priest, Rav would have mentioned that she is considered a *zona*. The fact that he does not mention this point indicates clearly that he does not consider it to be correct.

The Maharsha explains that it was known that Rav made his statement with regard to the mishna, and therefore his *halakha* was stated only with regard to the High Priest, the subject of the mishna. Alternatively, if Rav were of the opinion that an unmarried man who had intercourse with an unmarried woman has caused her to become a *zona*, his *halakha* with regard to atypical intercourse would be obvious and unnecessary, as the mishna states at the beginning of the chapter that there is no difference between typical and atypical intercourse with regard to causing a woman to become disqualified from marrying into the priesthood (*Arukh LaNer*).

She is disqualified because she is a non-virgin – מִשּׁוּם בְּעוּלָה, אִיכָּא: The Rashba and others note that this issue appears to involve two separate factors: The prohibition against a High Priest marrying a non-virgin and his obligation to marry a woman "in her virginity." They explain that it is possible for a woman to have an intact hymen and yet not meet the criteria of a woman in her virginity.

One who refused – מְמָאֶנֶת: This refers to a girl under the age of twelve whose father is no longer alive. The Sages instituted that the girl's mother or brother may marry her off, but she may terminate the marriage by a process called refusal, whereby she announces that she is not interested in the marriage. The Ritva points out that, upon refusal, the girl is considered retroactively never to have been married. Therefore, this should be a case of intercourse between an unmarried man and woman, and according to Rabbi Elazar she should be considered a *zona*. He explains that Rabbi Elazar considers the woman to be a *zona* only if the act of intercourse was performed outside of the context of marriage, but in this case, at the time when the act was performed, they were considered married.

If a woman had intercourse with one who is not a man – נִבְעֲלָה לְמִי שֶׁאֵינוֹ אִישׁ: The *baraita* is precise in its wording, which includes any form of living being. Rashi notes that a woman who had intercourse with an animal is not any more fit to marry a High Priest than a woman who hymen was accidentally torn. Consequently, according to the opinions that hold that a woman whose hymen was accidentally torn in prohibited from marrying a High Priest, this statement about a woman who had intercourse with an animal must refer to one who had anal intercourse. Alternatively, if the woman had typical intercourse that broke her hymen, it means to say that she is permitted to an ordinary priest but not to a High Priest (see Meiri and *Yam shel Shlomo*).

כִּי אֲתָא רַב דִּימִי אֲמַר: מַעֲשֶׂה בְּרִיבָה אַחַת בְּהִיתְלוּ שֶׁהָיְתָה מְכַבֶּדֶת אֶת הַבַּיִת, וּרְבָעָהּ כֶּלֶב כּוּפְרִי מֵאַחֲרֶיהָ, וְהִכְשִׁירָהּ רַבִּי לִכְהוּנָּה. אֲמַר שְׁמוּאֵל: וּלְכֹהֵן גָּדוֹל. בִּימֵי רַבִּי כֹּהֵן גָּדוֹל מִי הֲוָה? אֶלָּא: רְאוּיָה לְכֹהֵן גָּדוֹל.

When Rav Dimi came from Eretz Yisrael **he said:** There was **an incident** involving **a certain girl** [*riva*][N] **in** the village of **Hitlu**[B] **who was sweeping the house, and a village** [*kufri*] **dog**[B] used for hunting **sodomized her from behind. And Rabbi** Yehuda HaNasi **permitted her to the priesthood,** as she was not considered a *zona*. **Shmuel said: And** Rabbi Yehuda HaNasi permitted her even **to a High Priest,** as she was still considered a virgin. The Gemara is puzzled by this comment: **Was there a High Priest in the days of Rabbi** Yehuda HaNasi?[N] **Rather,** Shmuel meant that **she is fit for a High Priest.**

אָמַר לֵיהּ רָבָא מִפַּרְקִין לְרַב אַשִׁי: מְנָא הָא מִילְּתָא דַּאֲמוּר רַבָּנַן אֵין זְנוּת לִבְהֵמָה – דִּכְתִיב ״לֹא תָבִיא אֶתְנַן זוֹנָה וּמְחִיר כֶּלֶב״,

Rava of Pirkin said to Rav Ashi: From where is this matter derived that the Sages stated that **there is no harlotry with regard to an animal?** Rav Ashi responded that it is **as it is written: "You shall not bring the hire of a harlot or the price of a dog** into the House of the Lord your God for any vow; for both of them are an abomination to the Lord your God" (Deuteronomy 23:19). This verse prohibits one from sacrificing an animal as an offering if that animal was ever used to pay a harlot for her services, or if it was ever used as payment in the purchase of a dog.

וּתְנַן: אֶתְנַן כֶּלֶב וּמְחִיר זוֹנָה מוּתָּרִין, (מִשּׁוּם) שֶׁנֶּאֱמַר ״גַּם שְׁנֵיהֶם״ שְׁנַיִם וְלֹא אַרְבָּעָה.

And we learned in a mishna (*Temura* 30a): **The hire of a dog,**[N] i.e., a kosher animal that a man or woman gave as payment to the owner of a dog in order to have sexual intercourse with it, **and** similarly **the price of a prostitute,**[H] a kosher animal used to purchase a prostitute as a maidservant, **are permitted** to be sacrificed as offerings. This is **because it is stated** that **both of them,** the specific items listed in the verse, are abominations. Consequently, only **two** items are prohibited, i.e., the payment given to a prostitute for her services, and the payment used in the purchase of a dog, **and not four,** as the reverse cases are excluded from this *halakha*.

תָּנוּ רַבָּנַן: אֲנוּסַת עַצְמוֹ וּמְפוּתַּת עַצְמוֹ – לֹא יִשָּׂא, וְאִם נָשָׂא – נָשׂוּי. אֲנוּסַת חֲבֵירוֹ וּמְפוּתַּת חֲבֵירוֹ – לֹא יִשָּׂא, וְאִם נָשָׂא, רַבִּי אֱלִיעֶזֶר בֶּן יַעֲקֹב אוֹמֵר: הַוָּלָד חָלָל, וַחֲכָמִים אוֹמְרִים: הַוָּלָד כָּשֵׁר.

§ **The Sages taught:** A High Priest **may not marry** a woman that **he himself raped and** a woman that **he himself seduced,**[H] as he is commanded to marry a virgin. **And if he married** her, **he is married.** With regard to a woman who was **raped by another** man **and** a woman **seduced by another** man,[H] **he may not marry** her. **And if he married** her, **Rabbi Eliezer ben Ya'akov says** that **the child** born from this union **is a** ***ḥalal*****,**[B] **and the Rabbis say** the lineage of **the offspring is unflawed.**

NOTES

Girl [*riva*] – **רִיבָה:** This word is usually understood as parallel to *roveh*, a child, young man. According to this interpretation, the word was influenced by or borrowed from the Aramaic word for child, *ravya*.

Others explain that *riva* is the diminutive of *rava*, in the sense of a lady, with *riva* meaning a young lady. Similar terms are found in other languages.

Was there a High Priest in the days of Rabbi Yehuda HaNasi – **בִּימֵי רַבִּי כֹּהֵן גָּדוֹל מִי הֲוָה:** The same question can be asked with regard to Rav, who stated that a woman who had intercourse with an animal is still fit to marry a High Priest. It is explained in *Arukh LaNer* that the Gemara does not refrain from discussing *halakhot* that do not apply in practice. However, Rabbi Yehuda HaNasi issued a halakhic ruling for an incident that actually occurred, and therefore there was no reason for him to say something of no relevance to the case at hand.

The hire of a dog – **אֶתְנַן כֶּלֶב:** Some commentaries point out that it is prohibited to sacrifice the kosher animal as an offering, even if the animal was used to pay for an act of intercourse that causes one to be liable to capital punishment. The principle that multiple punishments are not meted out for one transgression does not apply here. Nevertheless, some say that it is due to the aforementioned principle that Rashi interprets the case as one where a man said to a woman: Take this lamb and have intercourse with my dog.

In that case, the individual who gave the present did not personally violate a prohibition for which he is liable for capital punishment (Meiri).

HALAKHA

The hire of a dog and the price of a prostitute – **אֶתְנַן כֶּלֶב וּמְחִיר זוֹנָה:** Kosher animals given as payment for the services of a prostitute or as payment for the purchase of a dog are unfit to be sacrificed as offerings in the Temple. However, kosher animals given as payment for the purchase of a prostitute as a maidservant, or as payment to a dog's owner for permission to have intercourse with the dog remain fit for use as an offering (Rambam *Sefer Avoda, Hilkhot Issurei Mizbe'aḥ* 4:18).

A woman that he himself raped and a woman that he himself seduced – **אֲנוּסַת עַצְמוֹ וּמְפוּתַּת עַצְמוֹ:** A High Priest who raped or seduced a young woman who was a virgin is not permitted to marry her, even if the incident occurred before he was appointed High Priest. If he did marry her, he is forced to divorce her, in accordance with Rav Huna's explanation of the *baraita* (Rambam *Sefer Nashim, Hilkhot Na'ara Betula* 1:6 and *Sefer Kedusha, Hilkhot Issurei Bia* 17:16).

The child of a woman raped or seduced by another man – **וְלַד אֲנוּסַת וּמְפוּתַּת חֲבֵרוֹ:** If a High Priest had intercourse with a woman who had previously been raped or seduced by another man, he has rendered her a *ḥalala*. Furthermore, any child born from the relationship is a *ḥalal* (Rambam *Sefer Kedusha, Hilkhot Issurei Bia* 19:3).

BACKGROUND

Hitlu – **הִיתְלוּ:** According to versions found in manuscripts and different sources, it seems that Hitlu is Ayatlu, a village known from other sources as the home of a group of priests. Ayatlu was a town in the Galilee, which is referred to today as Illut. It is about 4 km west of Nazareth. The fact that most if not all of its inhabitants were priests explains the need to determine whether this girl was halakhically permitted to marry a priest.

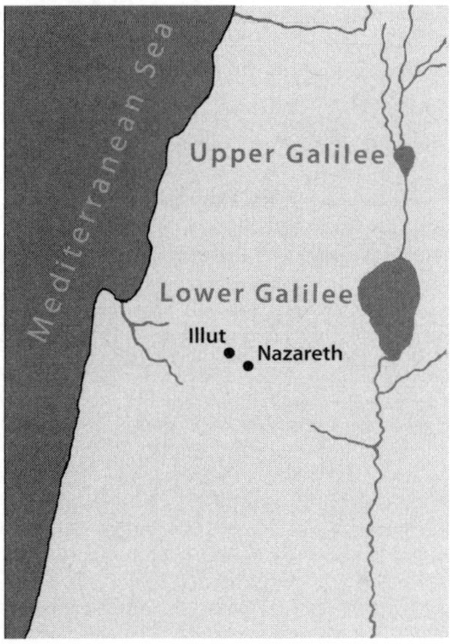

Location of Illut

Village [*kufri*] **dog** – **כֶּלֶב כּוּפְרִי:** The *kufri* is a special breed of dogs whose name is derived from the word *kefar*, village, that is to say, a dog raised in villages.

The mishna in tractate *Kilayim* (1:6) indicates that this kind of dog is similar to a fox, and it is therefore likely, in accordance with the explanation of the *Arukh* and others, that it was a small dog, similar in form to a jackal or a fox. These kinds of dogs were used to hunt mice, cats, and the like, and perhaps they also served as pets. The Rambam, in his commentary on that mishna, refers to a breed identified by some scholars today as the Saluki, a hound whose ancestors date back thousands of years. Some versions of the Talmud read monkey instead of dog.

Male Saluki

Ḥalal – **חָלָל:** A *ḥalal* refers to one disqualified from priesthood, usually the offspring of a priest and a woman forbidden to the priest, e.g., a divorcée or a *zona*. Even though the priest is considered the father of the *ḥalal*, the son does not have the legal status of a priest but a status similar to that of an Israelite. A daughter born of such a forbidden relationship may not marry a priest.

״אִם נָשָׂא – נָשׂוּי״. אָמַר רַב הוּנָא אָמַר רַב: וּמוֹצִיא בְּגֵט. וְאֶלָּא הָא דְּקָתָנֵי: ״אִם נָשָׂא – נָשׂוּי״! אָמַר רַב אַחָא בַּר יַעֲקֹב: לוֹמַר

The Gemara analyzes this *baraita*. It states that **if he married** the woman that he himself raped or seduced, **he is married. Rav Huna said** that **Rav said: And he must divorce** her **with a bill of divorce.** The Gemara asks: **But** consider **that which** the *baraita* **teaches: If he married** her, **he is married.** Since it is obvious that the marriage is technically valid, it must be saying that they are permitted to remain married. **Rav Aḥa bar Ya'akov said:** No, it means **to say**

Perek **VI**
Daf **60** Amud **a**

שֶׁאֵין מְשַׁלֵּם קְנָס בִּמְפוּתָּה.

that he does not pay the fine of a seduced woman.[N] One who seduced a woman and does not wish to marry her must pay a fine (see Exodus 22:14–15). Since in this case he did marry her, he is not liable to pay the fine even though he is required to divorce her.

אֲזַל רַב גְּבִיהָה מִבֵּי כְּתִיל, אַמְרַהּ לִשְׁמַעְתָּא קַמֵּיהּ דְּרַב אָשֵׁי. אָמַר לֵיהּ: וְהָא רַב וְרַבִּי יוֹחָנָן דְּאָמְרִי תַּרְוַיְיהוּ: בּוֹגֶרֶת וּמוּכַּת עֵץ – לֹא יִשָּׂא, וְאִם נָשָׂא – נָשׂוּי.

The Gemara relates that when **Rav Geviha went from Bei Ketil he stated this** ***halakha*** **before Rav Ashi,** who **said to him: Isn't it Rav and Rabbi Yoḥanan who both say:** A High Priest **may not marry a grown woman and a woman whose hymen was torn accidentally,**[H] **but if he married** one of them **he is married?**[N]

אַלְמָא: סוֹפָהּ לִהְיוֹת בּוֹגֶרֶת תַּחְתָּיו, סוֹפָהּ לִהְיוֹת מוּכַּת עֵץ תַּחְתָּיו, הָכָא נַמִי – סוֹפָהּ לִהְיוֹת בְּעוּלָה תַּחְתָּיו! קַשְׁיָא.

Apparently, the reason for this *halakha* is that since **she will eventually be a grown woman under him,** i.e., while married to him, and **she will eventually be a woman whose hymen was torn under him,** as she will not remain a virgin, they are permitted to remain married after the fact. **Here too,** in the case of a High Priest who married a woman he raped or seduced, since **she will eventually be a non-virgin**[N] **under him,** the *baraita* should be understood as stating that they may remain married. The Gemara concludes: Indeed, this is **difficult** for Rav Huna.

״אֲנוּסַת חֲבֵירוֹ וּמְפוּתַּת חֲבֵירוֹ – לֹא יִשָּׂא, וְאִם נָשָׂא, רַבִּי אֱלִיעֶזֶר בֶּן יַעֲקֹב אוֹמֵר: הַוָּלָד חָלָל, וַחֲכָמִים אוֹמְרִים: הַוָּלָד כָּשֵׁר״. אָמַר רַב הוּנָא אָמַר רַב: הֲלָכָה כְּרַבִּי אֱלִיעֶזֶר בֶּן יַעֲקֹב. וְכֵן אָמַר רַב גִּידֵּל אָמַר רַב: הֲלָכָה כְּרַבִּי אֱלִיעֶזֶר בֶּן יַעֲקֹב.

§ The *baraita* cited above taught: With regard to a woman who was **raped by another** man **and** a woman **seduced by another** man, the High Priest **may not marry** her. **And if he married** her, **Rabbi Eliezer ben Ya'akov says** that **the child** born from this union **is a** ***ḥalal*****, and the Rabbis say** the lineage of **the offspring is unflawed. Rav Huna said** that **Rav said: The** ***halakha*** **is in accordance with** the opinion of **Rabbi Eliezer ben Ya'akov. And, so too, Rav Giddel said** that **Rav said: The** ***halakha*** **is in accordance with** the opinion of **Rabbi Eliezer ben Ya'akov.**

HALAKHA

A grown woman and a woman whose hymen was torn accidentally, etc. – **בּוֹגֶרֶת וּמוּכַּת עֵץ וכו׳**: A High Priest may not marry a grown woman or a woman whose hymen was torn accidentally. Still, if he married one of these women, he is not forced to divorce her (Rambam *Sefer Kedusha, Hilkhot Issurei Bia* 17:13–15).

NOTES

That he does not pay the fine of a seduced woman – **שֶׁאֵין מְשַׁלֵּם קְנָס בִּמְפוּתָּה**: *Tosafot* ask: Since he is obligated to divorce her he must in any case pay her marriage contract. If so, what difference does it make whether he pays the sum as a fine or for the marriage contract? *Tosafot* offer several answers, one of which is that the Gemara is addressing Torah law, whereas the requirement that he divorce her and pay her marriage contract is by rabbinic law.

A grown woman and a woman whose hymen was torn accidentally, but if he married one of them he is married – **בּוֹגֶרֶת וּמוּכַּת עֵץ...וְאִם נָשָׂא, נָשׂוּי**: The Rashba asks what the source is for this ruling, as the mishna indicates simply that it is prohibited for a priest to be married to one of these women. He answers that Rav and Rabbi Yoḥanan rely on the *baraita* that states that a woman who had intercourse with an animal remains fit to marry a High Priest. This indicates that the definition of a virgin is one who has not had intercourse with a man. Consequently, a grown woman and a woman whose hymen was torn accidentally are also considered virgins.

It should also be noted that there is an alternate version of the mishna which is cited in the Jerusalem Talmud. According to that version, there are *tanna'im* who disagree with the ruling that a High Priest may not marry a woman whose hymen was accidentally torn.

Rav Huna explained the phrase: If he married one of them he is married, to mean that he is exempt from the fine but must divorce his wife. However, that interpretation is not applicable to the ruling of Rav and Rabbi Yoḥanan, as it does not address a case of rape or seduction, and therefore there is no fine involved. Consequently, the statement must be understood to mean that it is permitted for them to remain married (Rivan).

She will eventually be a non-virgin, etc. – **סוֹפָהּ לִהְיוֹת בְּעוּלָה וכו׳**: According to this reasoning, why should there be a distinction between a woman that he himself raped or seduced and a woman who was raped or seduced by another man? The argument that she would eventually have become a non-virgin while married to him is equally relevant to both cases. The Ritva answers that there is a difference between the cases due to the greater level of disgrace when the woman has been raped or seduced by another man. He adds that perhaps the reason that some halakhic authorities ruled in accordance with the statement of Rav Huna, despite Rav Ashi's question, is because they hold that there is disgrace even in the case of a woman that the priest himself raped or seduced.

אִיכָּא דְּאָמְרִי, אָמַר רַב הוּנָא אָמַר רַב: מַאי טַעֲמָא דְּרַבִּי אֱלִיעֶזֶר בֶּן יַעֲקֹב – סָבַר לָהּ כְּרַבִּי אֶלְעָזָר.

Some say a different version of this statement. **Rav Huna said that Rav said: What is the reason of Rabbi Eliezer ben Ya'akov? He holds in accordance with** the opinion of **Rabbi Elazar,** that an unmarried man who has intercourse with an unmarried woman has thereby caused her to become a *zona*. Consequently, since the other man had intercourse with this woman outside of the context of marriage, she is a *zona*.

וּמִי סָבַר לָהּ כְּוָתֵיהּ? וְהָא קַיְימָא לַן: מִשְׁנַת רַבִּי אֱלִיעֶזֶר בֶּן יַעֲקֹב קַב וְנָקִי, וְאִילּוּ בְּהָא אָמַר רַב עַמְרָם אָמַר רַב: אֵין הֲלָכָה כְּרַבִּי אֶלְעָזָר! קַשְׁיָא.

The Gemara asks: **Does** he really **hold in accordance with** the opinion of Rabbi Elazar? **Don't we maintain** that **the teaching of Rabbi Eliezer ben Ya'akov** measures **a *kav* but is clean,**[N] i.e., not many of his rulings have been recorded, but those that have been recorded are considered authoritative, and the *halakha* is always in accordance with his opinion? **However, with regard to this** ruling of Rabbi Elazar, **Rav Amram said that Rav said** that **the *halakha* is not in accordance with Rabbi Elazar.** The Gemara comments: This is indeed **difficult.**

רַב אַשִׁי אָמַר: בְּיֵשׁ חָלָל מֵחַיָּיבֵי עֲשֵׂה קָמִיפַּלְגִי. רַבִּי אֱלִיעֶזֶר בֶּן יַעֲקֹב סָבַר: יֵשׁ חָלָל מֵחַיָּיבֵי עֲשֵׂה, וְרַבָּנַן סָבְרִי: אֵין חָלָל מֵחַיָּיבֵי עֲשֵׂה.

Rav Ashi said: This is not the reason for the dispute. Rather, they **disagree with regard to whether there is a *ḥalal* from** a relationship for which the man and woman are **liable for** transgressing **a positive mitzva.** The marriage of a High Priest to a non-virgin is a violation of the mitzva that a High Priest marry a virgin, but it is not expressed in the Torah as a prohibition against a High Priest marrying a non-virgin. **Rabbi Eliezer ben Ya'akov holds** that **there is a *ḥalal* from** a relationship for which the man and woman are **liable for** violating **a positive mitzva,**[N] **and the Rabbis hold** that **there is no *ḥalal* from** a relationship for which the man and woman are **liable for** violating **a positive mitzva.**

מַאי טַעֲמָא דְּרַבִּי אֱלִיעֶזֶר בֶּן יַעֲקֹב – דִּכְתִיב ״אַלְמָנָה וּגְרוּשָׁה וַחֲלָלָה זוֹנָה אֶת אֵלֶּה לֹא יִקָּח כִּי אִם בְּתוּלָה״ וגו׳, וּכְתִיב ״וְלֹא יְחַלֵּל זַרְעוֹ בְּעַמָּיו״ אַכּוּלְּהוּ.

What is the reason of Rabbi Eliezer ben Ya'akov? As it is written: "A widow, or one divorced, or a *ḥalala*, or a *zona*, these shall he not take; but a virgin of his own people shall he take for a wife" (Leviticus 21:14), **and it states** subsequently: **"And he shall not profane his seed among his people"** (Leviticus 21:15). Rabbi Eliezer ben Ya'akov maintains that this profanation is referring **to all of them,** i.e., he profanes his seed by marrying any woman unfit for him, including a non-virgin.

וְרַבָּנַן ״אֵלֶּה״ הִפְסִיק הָעִנְיָן. וְרַבִּי אֱלִיעֶזֶר בֶּן יַעֲקֹב – אָמַר ״אֵלֶּה״ לְמַעוּטֵי נִדָּה.

And what do **the Sages** hold? The word **"these" concluded** discussion of **that matter.** Consequently, only the prohibitions listed before the phrase "these shall he not take" result in the offspring being a *ḥalal*. **And Rabbi Eliezer ben Ya'akov said:** The word **"these"** comes **to exclude a menstruating woman.** If a priest has relations with a menstruating woman, the offspring is not a *ḥalal*, as this is not a prohibition specific to priests.

כְּמַאן אָזְלָא הָא דְּתַנְיָא: מֵ״אֵלֶּה״ אַתָּה עוֹשֶׂה חָלָל, וְאִי אַתָּה עוֹשֶׂה חָלָל מִנִּדָּה, כְּמַאן – כְּרַבִּי אֱלִיעֶזֶר בֶּן יַעֲקֹב. וְרַבִּי אֱלִיעֶזֶר בֶּן יַעֲקֹב, נִכְתְּבֵיהּ לְ״אֵלֶּה״ לְבַסּוֹף! קַשְׁיָא.

The Gemara asks: **In accordance with whose** opinion **is that which is taught** in the following *baraita*: **From** the prohibitions preceding the phrase **"these** shall he not take" **you cause** your offspring to be **a *ḥalal*, but you do not cause** your offspring to be **a *ḥalal*** by having a child **with a menstruating woman.**[NH] **In accordance with whose** opinion is it? **It is in accordance with** the opinion of **Rabbi Eliezer ben Ya'akov.** The Gemara asks: **And** according to **Rabbi Eliezer ben Ya'akov, let** the verse **write** the word **these at the end,** after stating that a High Priest must marry a virgin, in order to make it clear that if he marries a non-virgin their child is a *ḥalal*. The Gemara responds: Indeed, this is **difficult.**

תָּנוּ רַבָּנַן: אֲחוֹתוֹ אֲרוּסָה, רַבִּי מֵאִיר וְרַבִּי יְהוּדָה אוֹמְרִים: מִטַּמֵּא לָהּ, רַבִּי יוֹסֵי וְרַבִּי שִׁמְעוֹן אוֹמְרִים: אֵין מִטַּמֵּא לָהּ. אֲנוּסָה וּמְפוּתָּה – דִּבְרֵי הַכֹּל אֵין מִטַּמֵּא לָהּ, וּמוּכַּת עֵץ – אֵין מִטַּמֵּא לָהּ, דִּבְרֵי רַבִּי שִׁמְעוֹן. שֶׁהָיָה רַבִּי שִׁמְעוֹן אוֹמֵר: רְאוּיָה לְכֹהֵן גָּדוֹל מִטַּמֵּא לָהּ, שֶׁאֵין רְאוּיָה לְכֹהֵן גָּדוֹל – אֵין מִטַּמֵּא לָהּ.

§ **The Sages taught:** With regard to a priest's **betrothed sister, Rabbi Meir and Rabbi Yehuda say: He** must **become impure for her** upon her death. **Rabbi Yosei and Rabbi Shimon say: He** may **not become impure for her.** With regard to his sister who has been **raped or seduced, all agree** that **he may not become impure for her** upon her death. With regard to his sister **whose hymen was torn accidentally, he may not become impure for her;** this is **the statement of Rabbi Shimon, as Rabbi Shimon would say** the following principle: If his sister was **fit for a High Priest, he** must **become impure for her,** but if she was **not fit for a High Priest, he may not become impure for her.**

NOTES

Measures a *kav*, but is clean – קַב וְנָקִי: This statement appears in several places in the Talmud. The commentaries discuss whether this principle is applied in every instance or if certain distinctions should be specified. Should one apply this principle only in the case of a mishna, or can it be applied to a *baraita* as well? Is Rabbi Eliezer ben Ya'akov's opinion accepted only in disputes with a single authority, or even when it is contrary to the majority opinion? The consensus is that the opinion of Rabbi Eliezer ben Ya'akov is accepted in all instances, even in a *baraita* and even contrary to the majority opinion, except where the Gemara explicitly rules otherwise. There is an ancient tradition that statements ascribed to Rabbi Eliezer ben Ya'akov are mentioned in 102 places, the numerical value of the word *kav*, and that his opinion is accepted in all of these cases. Consequently, the Sages have an aphorism that his teaching measures a *kav*, a common unit of measurement, but is clean (see *Yad Malakhi*; *Seder HaDorot*).

There is a *ḥalal* from a relationship for which the man and woman are liable for violating a positive mitzva – יֵשׁ חָלָל מֵחַיָּיבֵי עֲשֵׂה: Since there appears to be only one relationship included in this category, i.e., a High Priest who marries a non-virgin, why does the Gemara use the plural form: Those? One answer is that the woman herself becomes a *ḥalala* and her children also become *ḥalalim*. Furthermore, this ruling may impact other cases as well. If a woman has relations with a second-generation Egyptian convert, which constitutes the violation of a positive mitzva, she becomes a *zona*. If she then marries a priest, their children are *ḥalalim*, based upon the violation of that original positive mitzva (*Arukh LaNer*).

But you do not cause your offspring to be a *ḥalal* by having a child with a menstruating woman – וְאִי אַתָּה עוֹשֶׂה חָלָל מִנִּדָּה: The Ramban and Rashba point out that everyone agrees that the child of a menstruating woman is not a *ḥalal*, as only prohibitions specific to priests cause this status. They explain that the question here is merely related to the source of this *halakha*, as Rabbi Eliezer ben Ya'akov derives it from the word "these," while the Rabbis have a different source for the *halakha* (see *Tosafot*).

HALAKHA

But you do not cause a *ḥalal* by having a child with a menstruating woman – וְאִי אַתָּה עוֹשֶׂה חָלָל מִנִּדָּה: One who has intercourse with a menstruating woman does not thereby cause her to become a *zona*. A child conceived by this act is not considered a *ḥalal* (Rambam *Sefer Kedusha*, *Hilkhot Issurei Bia* 19:6; *Shulḥan Arukh*, *Even HaEzer* 6:8).

וּבוֹגֶרֶת מְטַמֵּא לָהּ – דִּבְרֵי כָּל אָדָם.

And if his sister was **a grown woman, he** must **become impure for her according to everyone.** Even those who hold that a High Priest may not marry a grown woman because her hymen is no longer whole agree that with regard to a priest becoming impure, she is considered a virgin and he must therefore become impure for her upon her death.

מַאי טַעֲמָא דְּרַבִּי מֵאִיר וְרַבִּי יְהוּדָה? דְּדָרְשִׁי הָכִי: ״וְלַאֲחוֹתוֹ הַבְּתוּלָה״ פְּרָט לַאֲנוּסָה וּמְפוּתָּה.

The Gemara analyzes this *baraita*: **What is the reason of Rabbi Meir and Rabbi Yehuda? They expound** the verse **as follows:** "And for his virgin sister, who is near to him, who has had no man, for her must he defile himself" (Leviticus 21:3). **"And for his virgin sister" excludes** one who has been **raped or seduced,** as they are not virgins.

יָכוֹל שֶׁאֲנִי מוֹצִיא אַף מוּכַּת עֵץ – תַּלְמוּד לוֹמַר ״אֲשֶׁר לֹא הָיְתָה לְאִישׁ״, מִי שֶׁהֲוָיָיתָהּ עַל יְדֵי אִישׁ, יָצְאָה זוֹ שֶׁאֵין הֲוָיָיתָהּ עַל יְדֵי אִישׁ. ״הַקְּרוֹבָה״ לְרַבּוֹת הָאֲרוּסָה. ״אֵלָיו״ לְרַבּוֹת הַבּוֹגֶרֶת.

One **might** have thought **that I should exclude even a woman whose hymen was torn accidentally** via a foreign object. **The verse** therefore **states: "Who has had no man,"** to include only **one whose becoming** a non-virgin was caused **by a man,** i.e., through intercourse. **This** case of a woman **whose becoming** a non-virgin **was not** caused **by a man** but rather by an object is thereby **excluded** from the category of a non-virgin, and her brother does become impure for her. **"Who is near"**; this is **to include a betrothed** sister.[N] **"To him"**; this is **to include a grown woman.**[H]

הָא לָמָּה לִי קְרָא? וְהָאָמַר רַבִּי מֵאִיר: ״בְּתוּלָה״ אֲפִילּוּ מִקְצָת בְּתוּלָה מַשְׁמַע! אִיצְטְרִיךְ, סָלְקָא דַּעְתָּךְ אָמִינָא: נֵילַף ״בְּתוּלָה״ ״בְּתוּלָה״ מֵהָתָם, מָה לְהַלָּן נַעֲרָה – אַף כָּאן נַמִי נַעֲרָה, קָא מַשְׁמַע לַן.

The Gemara asks: **Why do I need a verse** to include a grown woman? **Didn't Rabbi Meir say** that the word **"virgin" indicates even** a woman who is **partly a virgin,** i.e., a grown woman, whose hymen is partially intact? Consequently, when the verse states that the priest becomes impure for his virgin sister, a grown woman is included. The Gemara answers: The derivation from the verse is **necessary,** as it might **enter your mind to say** that **we should derive** a verbal analogy from the word **"virgin"** in this context and the word **"virgin" from there,** the context of a High Priest: In the analogy, **just as there** the virgin referred to is **a young woman and not a grown woman, so too here** she must be **a young woman.** The verse therefore **teaches us** that a priest becomes impure for his sister even if she is a grown woman.

וְרַבִּי יוֹסֵי וְרַבִּי שִׁמְעוֹן, מַאי טַעֲמַיְיהוּ? דָּרְשִׁי הָכִי: ״וְלַאֲחוֹתוֹ הַבְּתוּלָה״ פְּרָט לַאֲנוּסָה וּמְפוּתָּה וּמוּכַּת עֵץ, ״אֲשֶׁר לֹא הָיְתָה״ פְּרָט לַאֲרוּסָה, ״הַקְּרוֹבָה״ לְרַבּוֹת אֲרוּסָה שֶׁנִּתְגָּרְשָׁה, ״אֵלָיו״ לְרַבּוֹת אֶת הַבּוֹגֶרֶת. ״הַקְּרוֹבָה״ לְרַבּוֹת אֲרוּסָה שֶׁנִּתְגָּרְשָׁה?

And Rabbi Yosei and Rabbi Shimon, what is their reason? They expound as follows: "And for his virgin sister" excludes a woman who was **raped or seduced**[H] **and a woman whose hymen was torn accidentally,** who is also not considered a virgin. **"Who has had no man" excludes a betrothed** sister,[H] although she is not yet fully married. **"Who is near"**; this is **to include a betrothed** woman **who was** then **divorced,**[N] as she is once again near to her brother. **"To him"**; this is **to include a grown woman.** The Gemara asks: Can the term **"who is near"** come **to include a betrothed** woman **who was divorced?**

וְהָא אָמַר רַבִּי שִׁמְעוֹן: רְאוּיָה לְכֹהֵן גָּדוֹל – מְטַמֵּא לָהּ, שֶׁאֵין רְאוּיָה לְכֹהֵן גָּדוֹל – אֵין מְטַמֵּא לָהּ! שָׁאנֵי הָתָם דְּרַבֵּי רַחֲמָנָא ״קְרוֹבָה״.

Didn't Rabbi Shimon say: If she was **fit for a High Priest,** her brother must **become impure for her,** and if she was **not fit for a High Priest,** her brother **may not become impure for her?** A divorced woman is not fit for a High Priest even if she had been only betrothed before her divorce. The Gemara answers: **It is different there, as the Merciful One includes** her by the term: Who is **near,** which includes any sister who is close to him, even if she is unfit for a High Priest.

NOTES

Who is near, this is to include a betrothed sister – לְרַבּוֹת הָאֲרוּסָה הַקְּרוֹבָה: Both the *tanna'im* who hold that a priest must become impure for his sister even if she was betrothed, and those who hold that he may not, agree that the phrase: Who has had no man, would naturally be understood to mean that a priest becomes impure only for a sister who was never even betrothed. The dispute is whether there is another part of the verse that specifically includes any woman who had been betrothed, because she remains near to her brother. It should be noted that there are Sages cited in the Jerusalem Talmud who held that a sister is presumed to remain a part of one's family unit until proven otherwise, whereas a betrothed woman is presumed not to be included in her husband's family unit until proven otherwise.

To include a betrothed woman who was then divorced – לְרַבּוֹת אֲרוּסָה שֶׁנִּתְגָּרְשָׁה: The commentaries disagree about the status of a woman who was married but had not yet had intercourse with her husband: Is her status comparable to that of a betrothed woman with regard to whether her brother becomes impure for her if he is a priest, or is her status comparable to that of a fully married woman? The Ramban rules that she has the status of a betrothed woman and that consequently, Rabbi Meir and Rabbi Yehuda hold that her brother must become impure for her. He explains further that if she is divorced without having intercourse, even Rabbi Yosei and Rabbi Shimon would agree that her brother must become impure. The Rashba holds that as long as she is married, all would agree that her brother does not become impure for her. However, if she is divorced without having intercourse, her brother must become impure for her (see Ritva and *Arukh LaNer*).

HALAKHA

A woman whose hymen was torn accidentally and a grown woman – בּוֹגֶרֶת וּמוּכַּת עֵץ: A priest becomes impure for his sister who never had intercourse with a man, whether she was a minor or an adult. Similarly, he becomes impure for his sister if her hymen was accidentally torn. The *halakha* is not in accordance with Rabbi Shimon, as his is a lone opinion opposed by the majority (Rambam *Sefer Shofetim, Hilkhot Evel* 2:10–11; *Shulḥan Arukh, Yoreh De'a* 373:4).

Raped or seduced – אֲנוּסָה וּמְפוּתָּה: If the sister of a priest was raped or seduced, he does not become impure for her upon her death (Rambam *Sefer Shofetim, Hilkhot Evel* 2:10–11; *Shulḥan Arukh, Yoreh De'a* 373:4).

Betrothed sister – אֲחוֹת אֲרוּסָה: A priest may not become impure for his betrothed sister, even if she was betrothed to a priest. If she was betrothed and then divorced, he does become impure for her. The *halakha* is in accordance with the opinion of Rabbi Yosei and Rabbi Shimon, as the *halakha* generally follows the opinions of Rabbi Yosei over those of a colleague (Rambam *Sefer Shofetim, Hilkhot Evel* 2:10–11; *Shulḥan Arukh, Yoreh De'a* 373:4).

אִי הָכִי מוּכַּת עֵץ נַמִּי [רַבִּי]! "קְרוֹבָה" אַחַת וְלֹא שְׁתַּיִם. וּמָה רָאִיתָ? הָא אִתְעֲבִיד בָּהּ מַעֲשֶׂה, הָא לָא אִתְעֲבִיד בָּהּ מַעֲשֶׂה.

The Gemara asks: **If so, a woman whose hymen was torn accidentally** should **also** be **included.** The Gemara responds that the term: Who is **near,** which is written in the singular, includes only **one** additional case **and not two.** The Gemara asks: **And what did you see**[N] to render forbidden a woman whose hymen was accidentally torn and permit a divorcée who had previously been only betrothed, and not the opposite? The Gemara answers: In **this** case of the women whose hymen was torn, **an action has been performed** on her body, whereas in **that** case of the divorcée, **no action has been performed** on her body.

וְרַבִּי יוֹסֵי, מִדְּשָׁבְקֵיהּ לְבַר זוּגֵיהּ – מִכְּלָל דִּבְמוּכַּת עֵץ כְּרַבִּי מֵאִיר סְבִירָא לֵיהּ, מְנָא לֵיהּ? מִ"לֹא הָיְתָה לְאִישׁ".

The *baraita* cites Rabbi Yosei and Rabbi Shimon as holding that a priest may not become impure for his sister who was betrothed and then divorced, and it cites only Rabbi Shimon as holding that he may not become impure for his sister who was a grown woman. Based on this, the Gemara asks: **From** the fact **that Rabbi Yosei left his partner,** Rabbi Shimon, **it may be inferred that with regard to a woman whose hymen was torn accidentally he holds in accordance with** the opinion of **Rabbi Meir,** that a priest does become impure. **From where** does **he** derive this *halakha*? The Gemara explains that he derives it **from** the phrase: "Who **has had no man,**" as a woman whose hymen was torn accidentally has not been with a man.

וְהָא אַפִּיקְתֵּיהּ! חַד מִ"לֹּא הָיְתָה" וְחַד מִ"לְּאִישׁ".

The Gemara asks: **Haven't you** already **derived** the *halakha* of a betrothed woman from that phrase? The Gemara answers: Rabbi Yosei learns **one** *halakha* **from** the phrase **"has had no,"** which indicates that she has not even been betrothed, **and** he derives **one** *halakha* **from** the term **"man,"** which indicates that only a woman who was with a man is no longer considered a virgin with regard to this *halakha*, but not one whose hymen was torn accidentally.

"אֵלָיו" לְרַבּוֹת הַבּוֹגֶרֶת. וְהָא אָמַר רַבִּי שִׁמְעוֹן: "בְּתוּלָה" בְּתוּלָה שְׁלֵימָה מַשְׁמַע! טַעֲמָא דִּידֵיהּ נַמִּי הָתָם מֵהָכָא, דְּדָרֵישׁ הָכִי: מִדְּ"אֵלָיו" לְרַבּוֹת הַבּוֹגֶרֶת, מִכְּלָל דִּ"בְתוּלָה" בְּתוּלָה שְׁלֵימָה מַשְׁמַע.

It was stated previously that according to Rabbi Shimon, the term **"to him,"** comes **to include a grown woman.** The Gemara asks: **Didn't Rabbi Shimon say** with regard to a High Priest that the term **virgin indicates a complete virgin,** which does not include a grown woman? The Gemara answers: **His reason there is also** derived **from here, as he expounds as follows: From** the fact **that** the expression **"to him"** is needed **to include a grown woman,** it may be **inferred that** the term **virgin** by itself **indicates a complete virgin.**

תַּנְיָא, רַבִּי שִׁמְעוֹן בֶּן יוֹחַי אוֹמֵר: גִּיּוֹרֶת פְּחוּתָה מִבַּת שָׁלֹשׁ שָׁנִים וְיוֹם אֶחָד כְּשֵׁירָה לִכְהוּנָּה, שֶׁנֶּאֱמַר "וְכֹל הַטַּף בַּנָּשִׁים אֲשֶׁר לֹא יָדְעוּ מִשְׁכַּב זָכָר הַחֲיוּ לָכֶם" וַהֲרֵי פִּנְחָס עִמָּהֶם.

§ The Gemara cites another ruling of Rabbi Shimon ben Yoḥai, also related to the discussion of defining who is considered a virgin. **It is taught** in a *baraita* that **Rabbi Shimon ben Yoḥai says: A female convert**[N] who converted when she was **less than three years and one day old**[H] **is permitted to** marry into **the priesthood,**[N] **as it is stated: "But all the women children that have not known man by lying with him, keep alive for yourselves"** (Numbers 31:18). This verse indicates that these women were fit for all of the warriors, **and** since **Pinehas** the priest **was with them** (see Numbers 31:6), it is clear that young converts are permitted to priests.

וְרַבָּנַן: לַעֲבָדִים וְלִשְׁפָחוֹת. אִי הָכִי – בַּת שָׁלֹשׁ שָׁנִים וְיוֹם אֶחָד נַמִּי!

The Gemara asks: **And** how do **the Rabbis,** who disagree with Rabbi Shimon, interpret this verse? The Gemara responds: They understand the phrase "keep alive for yourselves" to mean that they could keep them **as slaves and as maidservants,** but they could not necessarily marry them. The Gemara asks: **If so,** if the source for Rabbi Shimon's ruling is this verse, a girl who converted at the **age of three years and one day old** should **also** be permitted to a priest, as long as she has never had intercourse, as stated by the verse.

NOTES

And what did you see – וּמָה רָאִיתָ: Since the verses are not conclusive, it would seem logical that one who was betrothed and divorced is more distant from her brother and the rest of her father's household than a woman whose hymen was torn accidentally (Ritva).

Female convert – גִּיּוֹרֶת: The primary discussion of a female convert's eligibility to marry a priest is in the final chapter of tractate *Kiddushin*. Some commentaries maintain that female converts are forbidden to priests because they have the status of a *zona*, as implied later in the Gemara here. This appears to be the opinion of Rashi and the Rambam.

Others commentaries question this explanation: If the definition of a *zona* is one who has had forbidden intercourse, how can any *tanna* disagree with Rabbi Shimon and hold that one who converted when she was less than three years old is prohibited from marrying a priest? Even if someone would have had intercourse with her before she converted, intercourse with a girl less than three years old is not halakhically recognized as intercourse. Furthermore, even if she converted as an adult it is not clear that she would still be considered a *zona* afterward, as one who converts is considered to be starting a new life.

Consequently, these commentaries explain that the prohibition is based upon a command of the prophet Ezekiel: "Neither shall they take for their wives a widow… but they shall take virgins of the seed of the house of Israel" (Ezekiel 44:22), as explained in tractate *Kiddushin* (78a).

The dispute among the *tanna'im* is over which type of convert is included in this verse. According to this opinion, despite the fact that this mitzva does not appear in the Torah, it is not a mere injunction of a prophet. Rather, the prophet only indicated that a Torah law was in existence (Ra'avad; Rashba). The Ritva combines these opinions and explains that the verse in Ezekiel indicates that the category of *zona* includes not only one who has engaged in forbidden relations but also anyone who is not from the seed of the house of Israel (see *Tosafot Yam shel Shlomo* and *Beit Shmuel*). Later commentaries attempt to prove from here that the prohibition for a priest to marry a convert is from Torah law, even if she converted when she was less than three years old.

A female convert less than…is permitted to the priesthood – גִּיּוֹרֶת פְּחוּתָה...כְּשֵׁירָה לִכְהוּנָּה: The fact that this is cited here, in the context of a discussion of whom the High Priest may marry, indicates that according to Rabbi Shimon, this convert is permitted to marry even a High Priest. The Gemara's proof from the story of Pinehas is consistent with this conclusion, as he was the priest anointed for war, and this priest has the same *halakhot* as a High Priest with regard to the prohibition against marrying a non-virgin (*Keren Ora*).

HALAKHA

A female convert less than three years and one day old – גִּיּוֹרֶת פְּחוּתָה מִבַּת שָׁלֹשׁ שָׁנִים: A priest may not marry a convert, even if she converted when she was less than three years old, as the *halakha* does not follow the opinion of Rabbi Shimon ben Yoḥai. If he married her, he is forced to divorce her (Rambam *Sefer Kedusha*, *Hilkhot Issurei Bia* 18:3; *Shulḥan Arukh*, *Even HaEzer* 6:8).

LANGUAGE

Hidrokan – הִדְרוֹקָן: From the Greek ὑδρωπικός, *hydropikos*, meaning one who suffers from ascites.

BACKGROUND

Hidrokan – הִדְרוֹקָן: The illness *hidrokan*, identified as ascites, has several causes, the most common being a dysfunction of the liver or the heart. Its symptoms are caused by a large accumulation of water under the skin, which causes significant swelling. Due to this accretion of water, and, occasionally, due to the effects of the illness itself, the faces of individuals suffering from this disease turn a pale yellow.

כִּדְרַב הוּנָא. דְּרַב הוּנָא רָמֵי: כְּתִיב ״כׇּל אִשָּׁה יֹדַעַת אִישׁ לְמִשְׁכַּב זָכָר הֲרֹגוּ״. הָא אֵינָהּ יוֹדַעַת – קַיְּימוּ, מִכְּלָל דְּהַטַּף בֵּין יָדְעוּ בֵּין לֹא יָדְעוּ – קַיְּימוּ, וּכְתִיב ״וְכֹל הַטַּף בַּנָּשִׁים אֲשֶׁר לֹא יָדְעוּ מִשְׁכַּב זָכָר הַחֲיוּ לָכֶם״, הָא יָדְעִי – הֲרוֹגוּ.

The Gemara replies: His reasoning is **as** stated by **Rav Huna, as Rav Huna raised a contradiction: It is written** in one verse: **"Kill every woman that has known man by lying with him"** (Numbers 31:17), which indicates that a woman who **has not known** a man in this way **you may keep** alive. This proves **by inference that the** female **children,** who are not classified as women, **you may keep** alive regardless of **whether they knew** a man **or they did not know** a man. **And it is written** in a different verse: **"But all the women children that have not known man by lying with him, keep alive for yourselves"** (Numbers 31:18), which indicates that **if they have known** men, **you must kill** them. This is an apparent contradiction.

הֱוֵי אוֹמֵר: בִּרְאוּיָה לִיבָּעֵל הַכָּתוּב מְדַבֵּר.

Rav Huna explains: **You must say that the verse is speaking of** a woman who is **fit for intercourse.** The verse does not mean to distinguish between women who have actually engaged in sexual intercourse and those who have not. Rather, it distinguishes between a girl over the age of three, with whom an act of intercourse is recognized as such, and a girl below the age of three.

תַּנְיָא נַמִי הָכִי: ״וְכׇל אִשָּׁה יוֹדַעַת אִישׁ״ בִּרְאוּיָה לִיבָּעֵל הַכָּתוּב מְדַבֵּר. אַתָּה אוֹמֵר בִּרְאוּיָה לִיבָּעֵל, אוֹ אֵינוֹ אֶלָּא נִבְעֲלָה מַמָּשׁ? כְּשֶׁהוּא אוֹמֵר ״וְכֹל הַטַּף בַּנָּשִׁים אֲשֶׁר לֹא יָדְעוּ מִשְׁכַּב זָכָר״ הֱוֵי אוֹמֵר בִּרְאוּיָה לִיבָּעֵל הַכָּתוּב מְדַבֵּר.

This is also taught in a *baraita*: **"Every woman that has known man"; the verse is speaking of** a woman **who is fit for intercourse.** The *baraita* proceeds to discuss this *halakha*: Do **you say** it is referring **to** one who is **fit for intercourse,** or perhaps **it is** referring **only to one who has actually had intercourse? When** the verse **states: "But all the women children that have not known man by lying with him,** keep alive for yourselves," which indicates that grown women must be killed even if they have not had intercourse with a man, **you must say that the verse is speaking of** a woman **who is fit for intercourse.**

מְנָא יָדְעִי? אָמַר רַב הוּנָא בַּר בִּיזְנָא אָמַר רַבִּי שִׁמְעוֹן חֲסִידָא: הֶעֱבִירוּם לִפְנֵי הַצִּיץ, כׇּל שֶׁפָּנֶיהָ מוֹרִיקוֹת – בְּיָדוּעַ שֶׁהִיא רְאוּיָה לִיבָּעֵל, כׇּל שֶׁאֵין פָּנֶיהָ מוֹרִיקוֹת – בְּיָדוּעַ שֶׁאֵינָהּ רְאוּיָה לִיבָּעֵל. אָמַר רַב נַחְמָן: סִימָן לַעֲבֵירָה הִדְרוֹקָן.

The Gemara asks a practical question with regard to the events described by the Torah: **From where did they know** whether a particular girl was already three years old and fit for intercourse? **Rav Huna bar Bizna said that Rabbi Shimon Ḥasida said: They passed them before the frontplate** of the High Priest. **Any** girl **whose face** miraculously **turned sallow, it was known that she was fit for intercourse,** and **any** girl **whose face did not turn sallow, it** was thereby **known that she was not fit for intercourse.** Similarly, **Rav Naḥman said: A sign of transgression** in the area of sexual morality **is** the disease ***hidrokan,***[LB] which causes one's face to turn sallow.

כַּיּוֹצֵא בַּדָּבָר אַתָּה אוֹמֵר: ״וַיִּמְצְאוּ מִיּוֹשְׁבֵי יָבֵישׁ גִּלְעָד אַרְבַּע מֵאוֹת נַעֲרָה בְתוּלָה אֲשֶׁר לֹא יָדְעוּ אִישׁ לְמִשְׁכַּב זָכָר״. מְנָא יָדְעִי? אָמַר רַב כָּהֲנָא: הוֹשִׁיבוּם עַל פִּי חָבִית שֶׁל יַיִן, בְּעוּלָה – רֵיחָהּ נוֹדֵף, בְּתוּלָה – אֵין רֵיחָהּ נוֹדֵף.

Similarly, you can **say** with regard to the verse: **"And they found among the inhabitants of Jabesh-gilead four hundred young virgins that had not known man by lying with him"** (Judges 21:12). **From where did they know** that they were virgins? **Rav Kahana said: They sat them on the opening of a barrel of wine.** If she was **a non-virgin, her breath** would **smell** like wine; if she was **a virgin, her breath did not smell** like wine.

וְנַעַבְרִינְהוּ לִפְנֵי צִיץ! אָמַר רַב כָּהֲנָא בְּרֵיהּ דְּרַב נָתָן: ״לְרָצוֹן לָהֶם״ כְּתִיב, לְרָצוֹן וְלֹא לְפוּרְעָנוּת. אִי הָכִי בְּמִדְיָן נַמִי! אֲמַר רַב אַשִׁי: ״לָהֶם״ כְּתִיב, לָהֶם לְרָצוֹן וְלֹא לְפוּרְעָנוּת, וּלְגוֹיִם – אֲפִילּוּ לְפוּרְעָנוּת.

The Gemara suggests: **They should** have **passed them before the frontplate,** as described previously with regard to the daughters of Midian. **Rav Kahana, son of Rav Natan, said:** The verse states with regard to the frontplate: "And it shall be upon Aaron's forehead… **that they may be accepted** before the Lord" (Exodus 28:38), which indicates that the frontplate is worn **for acceptance but not for calamity.** The Gemara raises a difficulty: **If so,** the frontplate should **also** not have been used **with regard to** the women of **Midian. Rav Ashi said:** The word **"they" is written** in the verse, indicating that **for them,** the Jewish people, the frontplate is **for acceptance but not for calamity; but for gentiles** it can be used **even for calamity.**

אָמַר רַבִּי יַעֲקֹב בַּר אִידִי אָמַר רַבִּי יְהוֹשֻׁעַ בֶּן לֵוִי: הֲלָכָה כְּרַבִּי שִׁמְעוֹן בֶּן יוֹחַאי. אֲמַר לֵיהּ רַבִּי זֵירָא לְרַבִּי יַעֲקֹב בַּר אִידִי: בְּפֵירוּשׁ שְׁמִיעַ לָךְ, אוֹ מִכְּלָלָא שְׁמִיעַ לָךְ?

Rabbi Ya'akov bar Idi said that **Rabbi Yehoshua ben Levi said: The** ***halakha*** **is in accordance with** the opinion of **Rabbi Shimon ben Yoḥai. Rabbi Zeira said to Rabbi Ya'akov bar Idi:** Did you **hear** Rabbi Yehoshua ben Levi say this **explicitly or** did **you learn** it **by inference?**

מַאי כְּלָלָא? דַּאֲמַר רַבִּי יְהוֹשֻׁעַ בֶּן לֵוִי: עִיר אַחַת הָיְתָה בְּאֶרֶץ יִשְׂרָאֵל שֶׁקָּרְאוּ עָלֶיהָ עַרְעָר, וְשִׁגֵּר רַבִּי אֶת רַבִּי רוֹמָנוּס וּבְדָקָהּ, וּמָצָא בָּהּ בַּת גִּיּוֹרֶת פְּחוּתָה מִבַּת שָׁלֹשׁ שָׁנִים וְיוֹם אֶחָד – וְהִכְשִׁירָהּ רַבִּי לִכְהוּנָּה. אֲמַר לֵיהּ: בְּפֵירוּשׁ שְׁמִיעַ לִי.

The Gemara asks: **What inference** was Rabbi Zeira hinting at? The Gemara explains: **As Rabbi Yehoshua ben Levi said: There was a certain city in Eretz Yisrael where they contested** the lineage[N] of a particular family. **And Rabbi** Yehuda HaNasi **sent Rabbi Romanus, and he examined** the family's lineage **and found** that **it** included **the daughter** of **a convert** who had converted when she was **less than three years and one day old,** and she had married a priest. **And Rabbi** Yehuda HaNasi **permitted her to the priesthood.** This indicates that Rabbi Yehoshua ben Levi ruled in accordance with Rabbi Shimon. Rabbi Ya'akov bar Idi **said to him: I heard explicitly** that Rabbi Yehoshua ben Levi ruled in this manner.

וְאִי מִכְּלָלָא מַאי? דִּלְמָא שָׁאנֵי הָתָם, הוֹאִיל וְאִנְּסִיב – אִנְּסִיב. דְּהָא רַב וְרַבִּי יוֹחָנָן דְּאָמְרִי תַּרְוַיְיהוּ: בּוֹגֶרֶת וּמוּכַּת עֵץ – לֹא יִשָּׂא, וְאִם נָשָׂא – נָשׂוּי.

The Gemara asks: **And if** Rabbi Yehoshua ben Levi's opinion had been derived **by inference, what** of it? The Gemara answers: **Perhaps it was different there,** because **since she** had already **married** a priest, **she** could remain **married** after the fact, but it would not be permitted for her to marry a priest *ab initio*, **as** it is **Rav and Rabbi Yoḥanan who both say:** A High Priest **may not marry a grown woman and a woman whose hymen was torn accidentally, but if he married** one of them **he is married** and not required to divorce her.

הָכִי הָשְׁתָּא?! בִּשְׁלָמָא הָתָם – סוֹפָהּ לִהְיוֹת בּוֹגֶרֶת תַּחְתָּיו, סוֹפָהּ לִהְיוֹת בְּעוּלָה תַּחְתָּיו. הָכָא – סוֹפָהּ לִהְיוֹת זוֹנָה תַּחְתָּיו?!

The Gemara refutes this claim: **How can** these cases **be compared? Granted, there,** in the case of a grown woman, it is reasonable for her to be permitted after the fact, as a young woman **will eventually be a grown woman under him,** i.e., while married to him, and **she will eventually be a non-virgin under him.** However, **here,** in the case of a convert, **will she eventually be a** ***zona*** **under him?** If she is forbidden to a priest *ab initio* it is because she has the status of a *zona*, in which case she should be prohibited after the fact as well. Consequently, it can be proven from the incident cited previously that Rabbi Yehoshua ben Levi rules in accordance with the opinion of Rabbi Shimon.

רַב סָפְרָא מַתְנֵי לָהּ מִכְּלָלָא, וְקַשְׁיָא לֵיהּ, וּמְשַׁנֵּי לֵיהּ הָכִי.

The Gemara comments: **Rav Safra taught this** *halakha* after deriving Rabbi Yehoshua ben Levi's ruling **by inference,** although he had never heard this ruling explicitly. **And** the question mentioned above was **difficult for him, and he resolved it in this** same manner.

הַהוּא כָּהֲנָא דְּאִנְּסִיב גִּיּוֹרֶת פְּחוּתָה מִבַּת שָׁלֹשׁ שָׁנִים וְיוֹם אֶחָד. אֲמַר לֵיהּ רַב נַחְמָן בַּר יִצְחָק: מַאי הַאי? אֲמַר לֵיהּ: דַּאֲמַר רַבִּי יַעֲקֹב בַּר אִידִי אֲמַר רַבִּי יְהוֹשֻׁעַ בֶּן לֵוִי: הֲלָכָה כְּרַבִּי שִׁמְעוֹן בֶּן יוֹחַאי. אֲמַר לֵיהּ: זִיל אַפֵּיק, וְאִי לָא – מַפֵּיקְנָא לְךָ רַבִּי יַעֲקֹב בַּר אִידִי מֵאוּנֵךְ.

The Gemara relates another incident related to this *halakha*: **A certain priest married a convert,** who had converted when she was **less than three years and one day old. Rav Naḥman bar Yitzḥak said to him: What is this?** Why are you violating the *halakha*? **He said to him:** It is permitted for me to marry her, **as Rabbi Ya'akov bar Idi said that Rabbi Yehoshua ben Levi said** that **the** ***halakha*** **is in accordance with** the opinion of **Rabbi Shimon ben Yoḥai. He said to him: Go remove** her, i.e., divorce her. **And if not, I will remove Rabbi Ya'akov bar Idi from your ear** [***me'unekh***][N] **for you.** In other words, I will take the necessary action to ensure that you obey and divorce her, so that you can no longer follow Rabbi Ya'akov bar Idi's opinion.

תַּנְיָא וְכֵן הָיָה רַבִּי שִׁמְעוֹן בֶּן יוֹחַאי אוֹמֵר

§ **It is taught** in a *baraita*: **And similarly, Rabbi Shimon ben Yoḥai would say:**[N]

NOTES

Where they contested the lineage, etc. – שֶׁקָּרְאוּ עָלֶיהָ עַרְעָר וכו׳: The Gemara indicates that a priest from that town married a woman who had converted when she was less than three years old. The Jerusalem Talmud offers an alternative account, in which the ruling follows the opinion of the Rabbis as well as that of Rabbi Shimon. According to that account, it was a regular Israelite who married the convert, and Rabbi Yehuda HaNasi permitted their descendants to marry priests.

From your ear [*me'unekh*] – מֵאוּנֵךְ: *Unekh* comes from the word *una*, a shortened form of *udna*, meaning ear. Some explain that he meant he would punish him until he removed the words of Rabbi Ya'akov bar Idi, so that his ears would no longer listen to him. Others maintain that he claimed he would make him forget Rabbi Ya'akov bar Idi until he would no longer mention his name (*Arukh*).

And similarly, Rabbi Shimon ben Yoḥai would say, etc. – וְכֵן הָיָה רַבִּי שִׁמְעוֹן בֶּן יוֹחַאי אוֹמֵר וכו׳: What is the connection between the following statement and the previous discussion? Rabbi Shimon must have taught many other *halakhot* that are not cited here. The Rivan explains that the *tanna* wanted to quote another case in which Rabbi Shimon ruled more leniently than the Rabbis. It is suggested in the *Yam shel Shlomo* that this statement is cited here in order to emphasize that just as the *halakha* does not follow the opinion of Rabbi Shimon with regard to the previous discussion, it does not follow his opinion with regard to the upcoming discussion, although this is subject to a dispute between the early commentaries. The *Keren Ora* and the *Arukh LaNer* explain simply that these two *halakhot* are cited together because Rabbi Shimon derived both of them from verses with regard to the war against Midian.

קִבְרֵי גוֹיִם אֵינָן מְטַמְּאִין בְּאֹהֶל, שֶׁנֶּאֱמַר "וְאַתֵּן צֹאנִי צֹאן מַרְעִיתִי אָדָם אַתֶּם" אַתֶּם קְרוּיִין "אָדָם", וְאֵין הַגּוֹיִם קְרוּיִין "אָדָם".

The graves of gentiles do not render items **impure though a tent,**[B] **as it is stated: "And you My sheep, the sheep of My pasture, are men** [***adam***]**"** (Ezekiel 34:31), from which it is derived that **you,** the Jewish people, **are called men** [***adam***][N] **but gentiles are not called men** [***adam***]**.** Since the Torah introduces the *halakha* of ritual impurity of a tent with the words: "When a man [*adam*] dies in a tent" (Numbers 19:14), this *halakha* applies only to corpses of Jews but not those of gentiles.[H]

מֵיתִיבִי: "וְנֶפֶשׁ אָדָם שִׁשָּׁה עָשָׂר אָלֶף"! מִשּׁוּם בְּהֵמָה.

The Gemara **raises an objection** based upon the verse with regard to captives taken during the war against Midian: **"And the persons** [***nefesh adam***] **were sixteen thousand"** (Numbers 31:40), which indicates that gentiles are also referred to as *adam*. The Gemara answers: They are given this title **due to** the need to distinguish the people taken captive from the **animals** that were taken as spoils of war.

"אֲשֶׁר יֶשׁ בָּהּ הַרְבֵּה מִשְׁתֵּים עֶשְׂרֵה רִבּוֹא אָדָם אֲשֶׁר לֹא יָדַע בֵּין יְמִינוֹ לִשְׂמֹאלוֹ (וּבְהֵמָה רַבָּה)". מִשּׁוּם בְּהֵמָה.

The Gemara raises another difficulty based upon a verse with regard to the city of Nineveh: **"Wherein are more than one hundred and twenty thousand men** [***adam***] **that cannot discern between their right hand and their left hand, and also much cattle"** (Jonah 4:11). The Gemara answers: There, too, the gentiles are given this title **due to** the need to distinguish them from the **animals** mentioned in the verse.

"כֹּל הֹרֵג נֶפֶשׁ וְכֹל נֹגֵעַ בֶּחָלָל תִּתְחַטְּאוּ"! דִּלְמָא אִיקְּטִיל חַד מִיִּשְׂרָאֵל. וְרַבָּנַן: "לֹא נִפְקַד מִמֶּנּוּ אִישׁ". וְרַבִּי שִׁמְעוֹן בֶּן יוֹחַי: "לֹא נִפְקַד מִמֶּנּוּ אִישׁ" לַעֲבֵירָה.

The Gemara continues to question Rabbi Shimon's ruling based upon a verse pertaining to the war against Midian: **"Whoever has killed anyone, and whoever has touched any slain, purify yourselves"** (Numbers 31:19). This indicates that gentile corpses convey ritual impurity. The Gemara answers: **Perhaps a Jew was killed,** and the concern was for impurity caused by his corpse. **And the Rabbis** reply that the verse attests: **"Not one man of us is missing"** (Numbers 31:49). No Jewish soldiers fell in battle, and therefore the concern for impurity must have been due to the corpses of gentiles. **And Rabbi Shimon ben Yoḥai** responds: The intent of that verse is that **not one man of us is missing** due to **transgression,** i.e., none of them sinned.

רָבִינָא אָמַר: נְהִי דְּמַעֲטִינְהוּ קְרָא מֵאִטַּמּוּיֵי בְּאֹהֶל, דִּכְתִיב "אָדָם כִּי יָמוּת בְּאֹהֶל", מִמַּגָּע וּמַשָּׂא מִי מַעֲטִינְהוּ קְרָא?

Ravina said that the explanation above is unnecessary: **Granted, the verse excluded** gentiles **from rendering** items **impure through a tent, as it is written: "When a man** [***adam***] **dies in a tent"** (Numbers 19:14); but **did the verse exclude them from** rendering items impure via **touching and carrying?**[N] Since gentile corpses convey impurity in these ways, they could have rendered impure the Jews involved in the war with Midian, even according to Rabbi Shimon ben Yoḥai.

BACKGROUND

The tent of a corpse – אֹהֶל הַמֵּת: The *halakhot* of the impurity imparted by a corpse, including the *halakhot* of a tent covering a corpse, are cited in great detail in tractate *Oholot*. The essential *halakhot* of the tent over a corpse are detailed in the Torah (Numbers, chapter 19). The Sages derived that any structure that has a cavity that is at least one cubic handbreadth in volume and contains a corpse or part of a corpse, e.g., its flesh, bones, or limbs, becomes a tent over a corpse. Not only do all articles subject to ritual impurity contained within it become ritually impure themselves, but they also become a primary source of ritual impurity, capable of imparting ritual impurity to people and objects.

HALAKHA

The impurity of a corpse of gentiles – טוּמְאַת הַמֵּת שֶׁל נָכְרִים: Some commentaries maintain that the corpses of gentiles do not convey impurity via a tent, in accordance with the opinion of Rabbi Shimon ben Yoḥai. Others disagree (*Tosafot*; Rosh). It is proper for a priest to act stringently in this regard. The corpse of a gentile certainly conveys impurity to one who touches or carries it (Rambam *Sefer Tahara, Hilkhot Tumat Met* 1:13 and *Sefer Shofetim, Hilkhot Evel* 3:3; *Shulḥan Arukh, Yoreh De'a* 372:2).

NOTES

You are called men [*adam*] – אַתֶּם קְרוּיִים אָדָם: Since the Torah was given to the Jewish people, it is assumed that whenever it refers to men [*adam*], it is referring to its primary audience, the Jewish people. If a wider meaning is intended the verse so specifies (see Maharatz Ḥayyut).

The commentaries analyze many instances where the Torah uses the term *adam*. Their conclusion is that the word *adam* is sometimes stated with regard to gentiles, but only when the verse must use this word, e.g., a verse that distinguishes between man and animal or between a commoner and a man of social standing.

Tosafot cite the opinion of Rabbeinu Meshullam that the Torah uses the term *adam* instead of referring directly to the Jewish people in the context of punishment or tragedy, while it refers directly to the Jewish people in more positive contexts. Rabbeinu Tam contends that the term: Man [*adam*], always refers to the Jewish people, whereas the term: The man [*ha'adam*], refers to the entire human race. Some commentaries note that the numerical value of: The man [*ha'adam*], is the same as the numerical value of the word impure [*tamei*]. See Rabbi Avraham min HaHar's response to this exposition. Later commentaries suggest other homiletic explanations of this idea (see *Iyyun Ya'akov*).

Did the verse exclude them from rendering items impure via touching and carrying – מִמַּגָּע וּמַשָּׂא מִי מַעֲטִינְהוּ קְרָא: Ezekiel prophesies that in the future any place that contains the bones of the corpses of Gog and Magog will be marked off (Ezekiel 39:15), which seemingly indicates that gentile corpses also convey impurity through a tent. The Ramban offers two answers: First, it is always possible that any corpse found is that of a Jew. Moreover, purity will be so widespread in the future that any source of impurity will be marked, even if it does not convey impurity through a tent (see Meiri).

מתני׳ אֵירַס אֶת הָאַלְמָנָה וְנִתְמַנָּה לִהְיוֹת כֹּהֵן גָּדוֹל – יִכְנוֹס. וּמַעֲשֶׂה בִּיהוֹשֻׁעַ בֶּן גַּמְלָא שֶׁקִּידֵּשׁ אֶת מָרְתָא בַּת בַּיְתוֹס, וּמִנָּהוּ הַמֶּלֶךְ לִהְיוֹת כֹּהֵן גָּדוֹל, וּכְנָסָהּ. שׁוֹמֶרֶת יָבָם שֶׁנָּפְלָה לִפְנֵי כֹּהֵן הֶדְיוֹט, וְנִתְמַנָּה לִהְיוֹת כֹּהֵן גָּדוֹל, אַף עַל פִּי שֶׁעָשָׂה בָּהּ מַאֲמָר – הֲרֵי זֶה לֹא יִכְנוֹס.

MISHNA If a priest **betrothed a widow**[N] **and was** subsequently **appointed to be High Priest,**[H] **he may marry** her. **And** there was **an incident with Yehoshua ben Gamla,**[P] **who betrothed Marta bat Baitos,**[P] a widow, **and the king** subsequently **appointed him to be High Priest, and** he nevertheless **married her.** Conversely, in the case of **a widow waiting for her** ***yavam*** **who happened before a common priest,** i.e., the priest was her *yavam*, **and he was** subsequently **appointed to be High Priest,** then **even if he** had already **performed levirate betrothal with her, he may not marry her,** because she is a widow.

גמ׳ תָּנוּ רַבָּנַן: מִנַּיִן שֶׁאִם אֵירַס אֶת הָאַלְמָנָה וְנִתְמַנָּה לִהְיוֹת כֹּהֵן גָּדוֹל שֶׁיִּכְנוֹס – תַּלְמוּד לוֹמַר ״יִקַּח אִשָּׁה״. אִי הָכִי שׁוֹמֶרֶת יָבָם נַמִי! ״אִשָּׁה״ וְלֹא יְבָמָה.

GEMARA The Sages taught: From where is it derived **that if** a priest **betrothed a widow and was** subsequently **appointed to be High Priest, that he may marry** her? **The verse states: "Shall he take for a wife"**[N] (Leviticus 21:14), an inclusive phrase that indicates that he may marry her in this situation despite the general prohibition for a High Priest to marry a widow. The Gemara asks: **If so, a widow waiting for her** ***yavam*** should **also** be permitted to a High Priest.[H] The Gemara answers: The word **"wife"** indicates that this does **not** include **a** ***yevama,***[N] who was not initially his wife but his brother's.

״מַעֲשֶׂה בִּיהוֹשֻׁעַ״ וכו׳. מִנָּהוּ – אִין, נִתְמַנָּה – לָא. אָמַר רַב יוֹסֵף: קְטִיר קְחָזֵינָא הָכָא. דְּאָמַר רַב אַסִּי: תַּרְקַבָּא דְּדִינָרֵי עַיְּילָה לֵיהּ מָרְתָא בַּת בַּיְתוֹס לְיַנַּאי מַלְכָּא, עַד דְּמוֹקֵי לֵיהּ לִיהוֹשֻׁעַ בֶּן גַּמְלָא בְּכָהֲנֵי רַבְרְבֵי.

The mishna related **an incident with Yehoshua** ben Gamla. The Gemara notes that the mishna states that the king **appointed him, yes,** but **not** that he **was** worthy of being **appointed. Rav Yosef said: I see a conspiracy here,**[N] as this was clearly not a proper appointment by the priests and the Sanhedrin but rather a political appointment, **as Rav Asi said: Marta bat Baitos brought** a vessel the size of a **half-*se'a* [*tarkav*]** full **of dinars to King Yannai**[P] **until he appointed Yehoshua ben Gamla High Priest.**

מתני׳ כֹּהֵן גָּדוֹל שֶׁמֵּת אָחִיו – חוֹלֵץ וְלֹא מְיַיבֵּם.

MISHNA A High Priest whose brother died without children **performs** ***halitza*** **and he does not perform levirate marriage,** as he may not marry a widow.

גמ׳ קָא פָּסֵיק וְתָנֵי, לָא שְׁנָא מִן הָאֵירוּסִין וְלָא שְׁנָא מִן הַנִּשּׂוּאִין. בִּשְׁלָמָא מִן הַנִּשּׂוּאִין – עֲשֵׂה וְלֹא תַעֲשֶׂה הוּא, וְאֵין עֲשֵׂה דּוֹחֶה לֹא תַעֲשֶׂה וַעֲשֵׂה. אֶלָּא מִן הָאֵירוּסִין, יָבֹא עֲשֵׂה וְיִדְחֶה אֶת לֹא תַעֲשֶׂה!

GEMARA The Gemara comments: The mishna **teaches** this *halakha* **categorically,** indicating that **it is no different** if she is his brother's widow **from betrothal, and it is no different** if she is his widow **from marriage.**[H] The Gemara analyzes this *halakha*: **Granted,** she is forbidden to him if she was widowed **from marriage, as,** if he were to marry her, **it** would be a violation of both the **positive mitzva** that the High Priest marry a virgin **and the prohibition** for him to marry a widow. **And a positive mitzva,** i.e., levirate marriage, **does not override a prohibition and a positive** mitzva together. **However,** if she was a widow **from betrothal** and is therefore still a virgin, **the positive mitzva** of levirate marriage **should come and override the prohibition** for a High Priest to marry a widow.

HALAKHA

Betrothed a widow and was appointed to be High Priest – אֵירַס אֶת הָאַלְמָנָה וְנִתְמַנָּה לִהְיוֹת כֹּהֵן גָּדוֹל: If a priest is appointed High Priest after betrothing a widow, he is permitted to marry her (Rambam *Sefer Kedusha, Hilkhot Issurei Bia* 19:12).

A widow waiting for her *yavam* should also be permitted to a High Priest – שׁוֹמֶרֶת יָבָם נַמִי: A High Priest must perform *ḥalitza* and not enter into levirate marriage. This applies even if the obligation to perform *ḥalitza* or levirate marriage took effect before he was appointed High Priest (Rambam *Sefer Kedusha, Hilkhot Issurei Bia* 19:12 and *Sefer Avoda, Hilkhot Kelei HaMikdash* 5:10).

A widow from marriage – אַלְמָנָה מִן הַנִּשּׂוּאִין: If a *yevama* was widowed from marriage and her *yavam*, the High Priest, had intercourse with her, they have not fulfilled the mitzva of levirate marriage because a positive mitzva does not override both a positive mitzva and a prohibition. Therefore, the rival wives of a *yevama* are not permitted to marry anyone else until they have performed *ḥalitza* (Rambam *Sefer Nashim, Hilkhot Yibbum* 6:11).

PERSONALITIES

Yehoshua ben Gamla – יְהוֹשֻׁעַ בֶּן גַּמְלָא: Yehoshua ben Gamla, referred to by Josephus as Yehoshua ben Gamliel, was apparently one of the last High Priests in the Second Temple. He was appointed by King Agrippa II and was killed during the destruction of the Second Temple. Although the Sages criticized the way he became High Priest, they also noted his good deeds. He was praised for donating golden lots for the Yom Kippur service and was especially commended for expanding the circle of Jewish education by establishing an extensive network of schools in every town in Eretz Yisrael. It is even said that were it not for him, the Torah would have been forgotten from the Jewish people. However, some claim that there were two men with the same name, and the Yehoshua ben Gamla mentioned here is not the one who established the network of schools (see *Tosafot Yeshanim*).

Marta bat Baitos – מָרְתָא בַּת בַּיְתוֹס: Marta bat Baitos is mentioned in several places in the Talmud. Due to her great wealth, she has served throughout the ages as the archetype of a very wealthy woman. The house of Baitos was one of the most powerful and wealthy families of priests in Jerusalem, and many members of this household served as High Priest or in other important positions in the Temple. According to the Jerusalem Talmud, Marta married Yehoshua ben Gamla as a result of trickery on his part, yet after becoming betrothed to him, she sought to secure him the most elevated position possible.

The Talmud relates that during the siege of Jerusalem all her wealth was to no avail and she died of starvation.

King Yannai – יַנַּאי מַלְכָּא: As *Tosafot* note, it is inconceivable that this could have been Yannai the Hasmonean king, as he himself was High Priest and would not have given up the position to someone else. The Sages referred to several kings from the second Temple era as Yannai, to indicate their disapproval of these kings' actions.

NOTES

If a priest betrothed a widow, etc. – אֵירַס אֶת הָאַלְמָנָה וכו׳: This policy does not extend to a case where a man betrothed a woman and then his testicles became crushed. The reason for the distinction is that the Torah expresses the prohibition to marry a man with crushed testicles by stating that he "shall not enter into the congregation of the Lord" (Deuteronomy 23:2). Conversely, with regard to a High Priest, the verse states that "he shall not take" a widow (Leviticus 21:14), which indicates that it is only the taking, i.e., the betrothal, that is prohibited (*Yosef Lekaḥ*).

Shall he take for a wife – יִקַּח אִשָּׁה: Since the word wife is entirely superfluous in this verse, the Sages derived that despite the requirement that the High Priest marry a virgin, there are instances where he may take even a woman who is not a virgin as a wife (Rivan).

The word wife indicates that this does not include a *yevama* – אִשָּׁה וְלֹא יְבָמָה: The Gemara does not employ the exposition cited earlier, that "wife" is written in singular and includes only one case but not two, because there is no legal difference between a woman waiting for her *yavam* and any other widow (Ritva).

I see a conspiracy here – קְטִיר קְחָזֵינָא הָכָא: In tractate *Bava Batra* (21a), the Gemara praises Yehoshua ben Gamla for strengthening Torah observance among the Jewish people; how does that fit in with the account here? In the *Tosafot Yeshanim*, it is suggested that the two passages are actually referring to two different individuals who had the same name. However, *Tosafot* on *Bava Batra* 21a and the *Tosefot HaRosh* explain that he was indeed great, but there were others who were more righteous and worthy of being appointed High Priest. Furthermore, he should not have accepted a royal appointment without the approval of the Sanhedrin. In the Jerusalem Talmud, it is stated that Yehoshua ben Gamla craftily spread a rumor that he had betrothed Marta bat Baitos. Once the rumor took hold, no one else would have agreed to marry her unless she obtained a bill of divorce from him. She therefore agreed to marry him and used her influence to have him appointed High Priest, as befitting her honor.

גְּזֵירָה בִּיאָה רִאשׁוֹנָה אַטּוּ בִּיאָה שְׁנִיָּה.

The Gemara answers: By Torah law, levirate marriage is permitted in this case. However, there is a rabbinic **decree** prohibiting their **first** act of **intercourse due to** their **second** act of **intercourse.**[H] After they have engaged in intercourse once, they have fulfilled the mitzva of levirate marriage, and any subsequent act of intercourse would constitute a violation of the prohibition without the fulfillment of a mitzva.

מתני׳ כֹּהֵן הֶדְיוֹט לֹא יִשָּׂא אַיְלוֹנִית, אֶלָּא אִם כֵּן יֵשׁ לוֹ אִשָּׁה וּבָנִים. רַבִּי יְהוּדָה אוֹמֵר: אַף עַל פִּי שֶׁיֵּשׁ לוֹ אִשָּׁה וּבָנִים – לֹא יִשָּׂא אַיְלוֹנִית, שֶׁהִיא זוֹנָה הָאֲמוּרָה בַּתּוֹרָה. וַחֲכָמִים אוֹמְרִים: אֵין זוֹנָה אֶלָּא גִּיּוֹרֶת, וּמְשׁוּחְרֶרֶת, וְשֶׁנִּבְעֲלָה בְּעִילַת זְנוּת.

MISHNA **A common priest may not marry a sexually underdeveloped woman** [*aylonit*],[H] who is incapable of bearing children, **unless he** already **has a wife and children. Rabbi Yehuda says: Even if he has a wife and children, he may not marry a sexually underdeveloped woman, as she is the** ***zona*** about whom it is **stated in the Torah** that a priest may not marry her. Intercourse with her is considered a licentious act because she is incapable of bearing children. **And the Rabbis say: The only** women in the category of ***zona***,[H] who are therefore forbidden to a priest, are **a female convert, a freed** maidservant, **and** any woman **who engaged in licentious sexual intercourse** with a man she is prohibited from marrying.

גמ׳ אָמַר לֵיהּ רֵישׁ גָּלוּתָא לְרַב הוּנָא: מַאי טַעְמָא – מִשּׁוּם פְּרִיָּה וּרְבִיָּה, אַפְּרִיָּה וּרְבִיָּה כֹּהֲנִים הוּא דְּמִפַּקְּדִי, וְיִשְׂרָאֵל לָא מִפַּקְּדִי?! אֲמַר לֵיהּ: מִשּׁוּם דְּקָא בָּעֵי לְמִיתְנֵי סֵיפָא, רַבִּי יְהוּדָה אוֹמֵר: אַף עַל פִּי שֶׁיֵּשׁ לוֹ אִשָּׁה

GEMARA **The Exilarch said to Rav Huna: What is the reason** for the *halakha* that a priest may not marry a sexually underdeveloped woman? It is **because** he is obligated to fulfill the mitzva to **be fruitful and multiply.**[N] **Is it** only **priests who were commanded to be fruitful and multiply, but Israelites were not commanded?** Why does the mishna specify that a priest may not marry a sexually underdeveloped woman? Rav Huna **said to him:** This *halakha* does in fact apply even to Israelites, and the *tanna* mentions priests **because he wants to teach** it in a way that would parallel **the latter clause** of the mishna, which states that **Rabbi Yehuda says: Even if he has a wife**

NOTES

It is because he is obligated to fulfill the mitzva to be fruitful and multiply, etc. – מִשּׁוּם פְּרִיָּה וּרְבִיָּה וכו׳: The Gemara could also have pointed out that if the reason was due to the mitzva to have children, the mishna should also have mentioned that it is prohibited for him to marry any barren or elderly woman. In any case, Rav Huna's answer resolves these difficulties as well (*Arukh LaNer*).

HALAKHA

There is a rabbinic decree prohibiting their first act of intercourse due to their second act of intercourse – גְּזֵירָה בִּיאָה רִאשׁוֹנָה אַטּוּ בִּיאָה שְׁנִיָּה: If a *yevama* was forbidden to her *yavam* due to an ordinary Torah prohibition, i.e., one that does not carry with it a punishment of *karet* or the death penalty; due to a positive mitzva; or due to a rabbinic decree, they must perform *ḥalitza* and not enter into levirate marriage. Although the mitzva of levirate marriage should override the prohibition, the Sages prohibited the first act of intercourse due to the possibility that they would engage in a further act of intercourse, in which case they would violate the prohibition without fulfilling the mitzva. If they entered into levirate marriage nevertheless, they are considered fully married, and the woman's rival wives are exempt from *ḥalitza*. However, the *yavam* is required to divorce her (Rambam *Sefer Nashim, Hilkhot Yibbum* 6:10).

He may not marry a sexually underdeveloped woman [*aylonit*] **– לֹא יִשָּׂא אַיְלוֹנִית:** A man may not marry a sexually underdeveloped woman or any other woman incapable of bearing children, unless he has already fulfilled the mitzva of procreation or unless he has another wife who can bear children (Rambam *Sefer Nashim, Hilkhot Ishut* 15:7; *Shulḥan Arukh, Even HaEzer* 1:8).

Who is considered a ***zona*** **– אֵיזוֹהִי זוֹנָה:** A woman who had intercourse with a man she is prohibited from marrying, a gentile, or a slave is classified as a *zona* and is forbidden to a priest. However, if she was prohibited from marrying only a priest but permitted to marry other Jewish men, and she had intercourse with a priest, she is not classified as a *zona*. The category of *zona* also includes a female convert and a freed maidservant (Rambam *Sefer Kedusha, Hilkhot Issurei Bia* 18:2; *Shulḥan Arukh, Even HaEzer* 6:8).

וְיֵשׁ לוֹ בָּנִים לֹא יִשָּׂא אַיְלוֹנִית, שֶׁהִיא זוֹנָה הָאֲמוּרָה בַּתּוֹרָה. דְּאַזּוֹנָה כֹּהֲנִים הוּא דְּמִפַּקְדִי, וְיִשְׂרָאֵל לָא מִפַּקְדִי, מִשּׁוּם הָכִי קָתָנֵי כֹּהֵן.

and he has children, he may not marry a sexually underdeveloped woman, as she is the ***zona*** about whom it is **stated in the Torah** that a priest may not marry her. **It is priests who were commanded** not to marry **a** ***zona*****, but Israelites were not commanded** this. It is **due to that** reason that **he taught** the first clause of the mishna about **a priest,** even though that *halakha* applies equally to Israelites.

אָמַר רַב הוּנָא: מַאי טַעְמָא דְּרַבִּי יְהוּדָה – דִּכְתִיב ״אָכְלוּ וְלֹא יִשְׂבָּעוּ הִזְנוּ וְלֹא יִפְרֹצוּ״, כׇּל בִּיאָה שֶׁאֵין בָּהּ פִּירְצָה – אֵינָהּ אֶלָּא בְּעִילַת זְנוּת.

Rav Huna said: What is the reason for the opinion **of Rabbi Yehuda? As it is written: "And they shall eat, and not have enough, they shall commit harlotry, and shall not increase"** (Hosea 4:10). He expounds the verse as follows: **Any intercourse that does not** have the possibility to **increase** the population because the woman is incapable of having children, **is nothing other** than **licentious sexual intercourse.**

תַּנְיָא, רַבִּי אֱלִיעֶזֶר אוֹמֵר: כֹּהֵן לֹא יִשָּׂא אֶת הַקְּטַנָּה. אֲמַר לֵיהּ רַב חִסְדָּא לְרַבָּה: פּוּק עַיֵּין בַּהּ, דִּלְאוּרְתָּא בָּעֵי לָהּ רַב הוּנָא מִינָּךְ. נְפַק עַיֵּין בַּהּ: רַבִּי אֱלִיעֶזֶר סָבַר לַהּ כְּרַבִּי מֵאִיר, וְסָבַר לַהּ כְּרַבִּי יְהוּדָה.

§ **It is taught** in a *baraita* that **Rabbi Eliezer says: A priest may not marry a minor. Rav Ḥisda said to Rabba: Go and investigate** this *halakha*, **as in the evening Rav Huna** will **ask you** the reason for Rabbi Eliezer's ruling. **He went** and **investigated it,** and arrived at the following conclusion: **Rabbi Eliezer holds in accordance with** the opinion of **Rabbi Meir, and he** also **holds in accordance with** the opinion of **Rabbi Yehuda.**

סָבַר לַהּ כְּרַבִּי מֵאִיר – דְּחָיֵישׁ לְמִיעוּטָא, וְסָבַר לַהּ כְּרַבִּי יְהוּדָה – דְּאָמַר: אַיְלוֹנִית זוֹנָה הָוְיָא.

Rabba explains: **He holds in accordance with** the opinion of **Rabbi Meir, who** says that **one must be concerned for the minority.** Rabbi Meir does not allow one to assume that an unknown case is similar to the majority of cases. Consequently, one must take into account the possibility that a minor will turn out to be sexually underdeveloped, although this will not be true of most individuals. **And** he also **holds in accordance with** the opinion of **Rabbi Yehuda, who said** that **a sexually underdeveloped woman is a** ***zona*** and therefore forbidden to a priest.

וּכְרַבִּי מֵאִיר מִי סְבִירָא לֵיהּ? וְהָתַנְיָא: קָטָן וּקְטַנָּה – לֹא חוֹלְצִין וְלֹא מְיַבְּמִין, דִּבְרֵי רַבִּי מֵאִיר. אָמְרוּ לוֹ לְרַבִּי מֵאִיר: יָפֶה אָמַרְתָּ שֶׁאֵין חוֹלְצִין ״אִישׁ״ כְּתִיב בַּפָּרָשָׁה, וּמַקְשִׁינַן אִשָּׁה לְאִישׁ. אֶלָּא מַאי טַעְמָא אֵין מְיַבְּמִין?

The Gemara challenges Rabba's explanation: **And does** Rabbi Eliezer **hold in accordance with** the opinion of **Rabbi Meir? Isn't it taught** in a *baraita*: **A boy minor and a girl minor may not perform** ***ḥalitza***[H] **or levirate marriage;** this is **the statement of Rabbi Meir.** The Rabbis **said to Rabbi Meir: You spoke well** when you said **that they may not perform** ***ḥalitza***, as the term **"man" is written in the passage** of *ḥalitza* (Deuteronomy 25:7–10), which limits the *halakha* to an adult male, **and we compare a woman to a man**[N] and therefore limit *ḥalitza* to an adult woman. **However, what is the reason that they may not perform levirate marriage?**

HALAKHA

The ***ḥalitza*** **of a minor** – **חֲלִיצַת קָטָן**: A minor boy cannot perform *ḥalitza*. If he was nine years and one day old and had intercourse with his *yevama*, he has partially acquired her and she must wait until he matures, at which point he must either marry her fully or perform *ḥalitza* and also write her a bill of divorce. Similarly, a girl may not perform *ḥalitza* until she is twelve years old and develops two pubic hairs, at which point she is considered an adult (Rambam *Sefer Nashim*, *Hilkhot Yibbum* 1:16–18; *Shulḥan Arukh*, *Even HaEzer* 167:3–4).

NOTES

And we compare a woman to a man – **וּמַקְשִׁינַן אִשָּׁה לְאִישׁ**: Rashi explains that the reason a minor girl may not perform *ḥalitza* is because the actions of a minor have no legal standing. Later commentaries question the need for Rashi to mention this: Since this has been derived from a verse, why would further explanation be necessary? It seems that according to the opinion of Rashi, this *halakha* is derived from the verse only according to Rabbi Meir. However, the Rabbis, who hold that a minor may perform levirate marriage, do not exclude minors based upon the verse, and therefore they must have another reason to exclude them from *ḥalitza* (see *Arukh LaNer*).

[אָמַר לָהֶם]: קָטָן – שֶׁמָּא יִמָּצֵא סָרִיס, קְטַנָּה – שֶׁמָּא תִּמָּצֵא אַיְלוֹנִית, וְנִמְצְאוּ פּוֹגְעִין בְּעֶרְוָה, וְתַנְיָא: קְטַנָּה – מִתְיַיבֶּמֶת וְאֵינָהּ חוֹלֶצֶת, דִּבְרֵי רַבִּי אֱלִיעֶזֶר.

Rabbi Meir **said to them: A boy minor** may not perform levirate marriage **lest he be found** to be **a eunuch,** i.e., one who is incapable of fathering children for his late brother. Similarly, **a girl minor** may not perform levirate marriage **lest she be found** to be **sexually underdeveloped** when she grows up. In either case, the mitzva of levirate marriage does not apply, **and they turn out** to have **encountered a forbidden relative. And it was taught** in a different *baraita*: **A girl minor enters into levirate marriage but does not perform *ḥalitza*;** this is **the statement of Rabbi Eliezer.** This proves that Rabbi Eliezer disagrees with Rabbi Meir and is not concerned that a girl may turn out to be sexually underdeveloped.

וּכְרַבִּי יְהוּדָה מִי סָבַר לַהּ? וְהָתַנְיָא: ״זוֹנָה״ זוֹנָה כִּשְׁמָהּ, דִּבְרֵי רַבִּי אֱלִיעֶזֶר. רַבִּי עֲקִיבָא אוֹמֵר: ״זוֹנָה״ זוֹ מוּפְקֶרֶת. רַבִּי מַתְיָא בֶּן חָרָשׁ אוֹמֵר: אֲפִילּוּ הָלַךְ בַּעְלָהּ לְהַשְׁקוֹתָהּ, וּבָא עָלֶיהָ בַּדֶּרֶךְ – עֲשָׂאָהּ זוֹנָה.

The Gemara continues to challenge Rabba's explanation of Rabbi Eliezer's ruling. **And does** Rabbi Eliezer **hold in accordance with** the opinion of **Rabbi Yehuda? Wasn't it is taught in** a *baraita*: The ***zona***[N] forbidden to a priest is as **the name *zona* implies,**[N] i.e., a married woman who committed adultery; this is **the statement of Rabbi Eliezer. Rabbi Akiva says: A *zona* is** a woman, even an unmarried woman, **who is available** to all, i.e., she has intercourse with whoever is interested. **Rabbi Matya ben Ḥarash says: Even if her husband went to make her drink**[N] the bitter waters after she disregarded his warning not to seclude herself with a certain man, and **he had intercourse with her on the way, he has** thereby **caused her** to become **a *zona*** because she was forbidden to him at the time, despite the fact that she is his wife.

רַבִּי יְהוּדָה אוֹמֵר: ״זוֹנָה״ זוֹ אַיְלוֹנִית. וַחֲכָמִים אוֹמְרִים: אֵין זוֹנָה אֶלָּא גִּיּוֹרֶת וּמְשׁוּחְרֶרֶת וְשֶׁנִּבְעֲלָה בְּעִילַת זְנוּת. רַבִּי אֶלְעָזָר אוֹמֵר: פָּנוּי הַבָּא עַל הַפְּנוּיָה שֶׁלֹּא לְשֵׁם אִישׁוּת – עֲשָׂאָהּ זוֹנָה.

Rabbi Yehuda says: A *zona* is a sexually underdeveloped woman. And the Rabbis say: The term ***zona*** applies **only to a female convert, a freed** maidservant, **and one who engaged in licentious sexual intercourse. Rabbi Elazar says:** Even in the case of **an unmarried man who had intercourse with an unmarried woman**[H] **not for the purpose of marriage, he has** thereby **caused her** to become **a *zona*.** This *baraita* proves that Rabbi Eliezer does not agree with Rabbi Yehuda.

אֶלָּא אָמַר רַב אַדָּא בַּר אַהֲבָה: הָכָא בְּכֹהֵן גָּדוֹל עָסְקִינַן, לְאֵימַת קָנֵי לַהּ – לְכִי גָּדְלָה, בְּעוּלָה הִיא.

Rather, Rav Adda bar Ahava said that Rabbi Eliezer's ruling that a priest may not marry a minor must be explained differently: **Here we are dealing with a High Priest,** and the problem is as follows: **When can he acquire her** as his wife? Only **when she is grown up.** However, if they had started living together as husband and wife when she was a minor, then when she is grown up and the marriage can legally take effect, **she is** already **a non-virgin,** and a High Priest is commanded to marry a virgin.

אָמַר רָבָא: מִכְּלֵי לֵב! אִי דְּקִדְּשָׁהּ אָבוּהָ – מֵהַהִיא שַׁעְתָּא הוּא דְּקָנֵי לַהּ, וְאִי דְּקִדְּשָׁה נַפְשַׁהּ – הָא רַבִּי אֱלִיעֶזֶר הִיא וְלָא רַבָּנַן!

Rava said: This explanation is **without reason.**[N] **If her father betrothed her** to her husband, her husband **acquired her from that time,** as betrothal that a father carries out on his daughter's behalf when she is a minor is effective by Torah law. **And if** the minor **betrothed herself,** is **this Rabbi Eliezer**'s opinion **and not** that of **the Rabbis?**[N] The Rabbis would certainly agree that a High Priest may not marry a minor under these circumstances.

אֶלָּא אָמַר רָבָא: לְעוֹלָם בְּכֹהֵן הֶדְיוֹט, וְחָיְישִׁינַן שֶׁמָּא תִּתְפַּתֶּה עָלָיו. אִי הָכִי יִשְׂרָאֵל נָמֵי! פִּתּוּיֵי קְטַנָּה אוֹנֶס הוּא, וְאוֹנֶס בְּיִשְׂרָאֵל מִישְׁרָא שְׁרֵי.

Rather, Rava said: Actually, Rabbi Eliezer's ruling includes **a common priest,** and the reason he cannot marry a minor is that **we are concerned lest she be seduced** by another man, due to her tender age and naïveté, while married **to him.** The Gemara asks: **If so,** the same concern should apply to **an Israelite also.** The Gemara answers: **The seduction of a minor is** considered **rape, and a rape** victim remains **permitted** to her husband **in** a case where she is married to **an Israelite,** but not if she is married to a priest.

NOTES

Who is considered a *zona* – אֵיזוֹהִי זוֹנָה: This dispute between the *tanna'im* relates to the meaning of this term with regard to the prohibition for a priest to marry a *zona* and with regard to the prohibition against sacrificing as an offering an animal used as payment for a *zona*. The word *zona* appears many times in the Bible, usually in reference to a prostitute. However, since these verses do not refer to halakhic topics, they cannot serve as proof of the halakhic meaning of the term, as it is possible that the term is borrowed from its precise legal meaning and used in other contexts. Therefore, it was necessary to clarify the precise legal definition of this term.

As the name *zona* implies – זוֹנָה כִּשְׁמָהּ: The commentaries explain that according to Rabbi Eliezer a *zona* is a married woman who committed adultery. The Meiri states that the word is understood as in the verse: "And they shall go astray [*vezanu*] after foreign gods" (Deuteronomy 31:16). In other words, she strays from her husband to another man.

Even if her husband went to make her drink, etc. – אֲפִילּוּ הָלַךְ בַּעְלָהּ לְהַשְׁקוֹתָהּ וכו׳: Her status as a *zona* would be significant only if her husband died and she then wanted to marry a priest. However, even if she did not engage in intercourse with her husband once she became a *sota*, if he died before she drank the waters, she no longer drinks the waters and therefore has no way to prove her innocence. Consequently, she would be forbidden to a priest in any event, due to the possibility that she is a *zona* because she committed adultery. Rabbi Akiva Eiger explains that intercourse between the husband and wife on her way to drink the *sota* waters is still significant, as it would cause the woman to be a definite *zona*, not merely an uncertain one. Consequently, if a priest marries her he is liable by Torah law to receive lashes.

Without reason [*mekhalei lev*] – מִכְּלֵי לֵב: According to the versions of the Gemara text recorded by the *ge'onim* and many of the early commentaries, this expression should read *mibeli lev*, i.e., something said without understanding or knowledge. The version of the text printed in the Vilna edition of the Talmud, which was also Rashi's version, is difficult to understand, but is interpreted in the same manner, in accordance with one of the connotations of the root *k-l-a*.

Is this Rabbi Eliezer's opinion and not that of the Rabbis – רַבִּי אֱלִיעֶזֶר הִיא וְלָא רַבָּנַן: The Rashba asks how Rava can be certain that the Rabbis would agree with Rabbi Eliezer. Perhaps, according to the Rabbis, if the High Priest marries her he is not required to divorce her, in accordance with the reasoning mentioned earlier in the Gemara, that she would have become a non-virgin while married to him anyway. Rabbi Eliezer, on the other hand, holds that he would have to divorce her. The Rashba answers that since all agree that the High Priest may not marry her *ab initio*, the ruling prohibiting their marriage would not have been stated in the name of Rabbi Eliezer alone.

HALAKHA

An unmarried man who had intercourse with an unmarried woman – פָּנוּי הַבָּא עַל הַפְּנוּיָה: If an unmarried man had intercourse with an unmarried woman not for the purpose of marriage, she does not thereby become a *zona*, even if she has made herself available to all for licentious purposes. The *halakha* is in accordance with the opinion of the Rabbis, that only the following women have the status of a *zona*: A female convert, a freed maidservant, and a woman who has had intercourse with a man she is not permitted to marry (Rambam *Sefer Kedusha*, *Hilkhot Issurei Bia* 18:2).

רַב פַּפָּא אָמַר: בְּכֹהֵן גָּדוֹל, וְהַאי תַּנָּא הוּא, דְּתַנְיָא: "בְּתוּלָה" יָכוֹל קְטַנָּה – תַּלְמוּד לוֹמַר "אִשָּׁה". אִי "אִשָּׁה" יָכוֹל בּוֹגֶרֶת – תַּלְמוּד לוֹמַר "בְּתוּלָה". הָא כֵּיצַד? יָצְתָה מִכְּלַל קְטַנּוּת, וְלִכְלַל בַּגְרוּת לֹא בָּאתָה.

Rav Pappa said: Rabbi Eliezer's ruling applies specifically **to a High Priest, and it is** the opinion of **this *tanna*, as it is taught** in a *baraita* that when the verse states: **"A virgin** of his own people shall he take for a wife [*isha*]" (Leviticus 21:14), one **might** have thought a High Priest may marry **a minor; the verse** therefore **states** that he must marry **a woman** [*isha*], i.e., an adult. **If** he must marry a **woman,** one **might** have thought it means **a grown woman. The verse** therefore **states** that he must marry **a virgin,** which excludes a grown woman, who is considered only a partial virgin because her hymen is not fully intact. **How so?** He must marry a woman who **has left the class of minority but** who **has not** yet **reached the class of grown womanhood,** i.e., he must marry a maiden.[H]

רַב נַחְמָן בַּר יִצְחָק אָמַר: הַאי תַּנָּא הוּא, דְּתַנְיָא "בְּתוּלָה" אֵין בְּתוּלָה אֶלָּא נַעֲרָה, וְכֵן הוּא אוֹמֵר "וְהַנַּעֲרָה טֹבַת מַרְאֶה מְאֹד בְּתוּלָה".

Rav Naḥman bar Yitzḥak said: It is the opinion of **this *tanna*, as it is taught** in a *baraita*: The High Priest must marry **a virgin, and** the term **virgin** refers **only** to **a maiden. And** a verse **similarly states: "And the maiden was very fair to look upon, a virgin,** and no man had known her" (Genesis 24:16).

רַבִּי אֶלְעָזָר אוֹמֵר: פְּנוּי הַבָּא עַל הַפְּנוּיָה שֶׁלֹּא לְשֵׁם אִישׁוּת – עֲשָׂאָהּ זוֹנָה. אָמַר רַב עַמְרָם: אֵין הֲלָכָה כְּרַבִּי אֶלְעָזָר.

The *baraita* cited above mentioned that **Rabbi Elazar says:** In the case of **an unmarried man who had intercourse with an unmarried woman not for the purpose of marriage, he has caused her** to become **a *zona*. Rav Amram said: The *halakha* is not in accordance with** the opinion of **Rabbi Elazar.**

מַתְנִי׳ לֹא יִבָּטֵל אָדָם מִפְּרִיָּה וּרְבִיָּה אֶלָּא אִם כֵּן יֵשׁ לוֹ בָּנִים. בֵּית שַׁמַּאי אוֹמְרִים: שְׁנֵי זְכָרִים, וּבֵית הִלֵּל אוֹמְרִים: זָכָר וּנְקֵבָה, שֶׁנֶּאֱמַר "זָכָר וּנְקֵבָה בְּרָאָם".

MISHNA **A man may not neglect** the mitzva to **be fruitful and multiply**[H] **unless he** already **has children.**[N] **Beit Shammai say:**[N] One fulfills this mitzva with **two males, and Beit Hillel say: A male and a female,**[H] **as it is stated: "Male and female He created them"** (Genesis 5:2).

גְּמ׳ הָא יֵשׁ לוֹ בָּנִים, מִפְּרִיָּה וּרְבִיָּה – בָּטֵיל, מֵאִשָּׁה – לָא בָּטֵיל. מְסַיְּיעָא לֵיהּ לְרַב נַחְמָן אָמַר שְׁמוּאֵל, דְּאָמַר: אַף עַל פִּי שֶׁיֵּשׁ לוֹ לְאָדָם כַּמָּה בָּנִים – אָסוּר לַעֲמוֹד בְּלֹא אִשָּׁה, שֶׁנֶּאֱמַר "לֹא טוֹב הֱיוֹת הָאָדָם לְבַדּוֹ".

GEMARA The Gemara infers from the mishna's wording that if **he** already **has children he may neglect** the mitzva to **be fruitful and multiply,** but **he may not neglect** the mitzva to have **a wife.** This **supports** what **Rav Naḥman said** in the name of **Shmuel, who said: Even if a man has several children, it is prohibited to remain without a wife,**[HN] **as it is stated: "It is not good that the man should be alone"** (Genesis 2:18).

וְאִיכָּא דְּאָמְרִי: הָא יֵשׁ לוֹ בָּנִים – בָּטֵיל מִפְּרִיָּה וּרְבִיָּה, וּבָטֵיל נַמִי מֵאִשָּׁה. נֵימָא תֶּיהֱוֵי תְּיוּבְתָּא דְּרַב נַחְמָן אָמַר שְׁמוּאֵל! לָא, אֵין לוֹ בָּנִים – נוֹשֵׂא אִשָּׁה בַּת בָּנִים, יֵשׁ לוֹ בָּנִים – נוֹשֵׂא אִשָּׁה דְּלָאו בַּת בָּנִים. נָפְקָא מִינַּהּ – לְמִכּוֹר סֵפֶר תּוֹרָה בִּשְׁבִיל בָּנִים.

And some say a different version of the inference from the mishna: If **he** already **has children, he may neglect** the mitzva to **be fruitful and multiply and** he **may also neglect** the mitzva to have **a wife. Shall we say this is a conclusive refutation of** what **Rav Naḥman said** that **Shmuel** said? The Gemara responds: **No,** it means that **if he does not have children he must marry a woman** capable **of** bearing **children,** whereas if **he has children he may marry a woman who is not** capable of bearing **children. A practical difference** between a man who has children and one who does not is whether he is permitted **to sell a Torah scroll in order to** marry a woman capable of having **children.** This is permitted only for one who does not yet have children.

"בֵּית שַׁמַּאי אוֹמְרִים שְׁנֵי זְכָרִים". מַאי טַעְמַיְיהוּ דְּבֵית שַׁמַּאי – יָלְפִינַן מִמֹּשֶׁה, דִּכְתִיב "בְּנֵי מֹשֶׁה גֵּרְשׁוֹם וֶאֱלִיעֶזֶר", וּבֵית הִלֵּל – יָלְפִינַן מִבְּרִיָּיתוֹ שֶׁל עוֹלָם. וּבֵית שַׁמַּאי, לֵילְפֵי מִבְּרִיָּיתוֹ שֶׁל עוֹלָם! אֵין דָּנִין אֶפְשָׁר

§ The mishna states that **Beit Shammai say** that one fulfills the mitzva to be fruitful and multiply when he has **two males.** The Gemara asks: **What is the reason of Beit Shammai?** The Gemara answers: **We learn** this **from Moses as it is written: "The sons of Moses, Gershom and Eliezer"** (I Chronicles 23:15). Since Moses did not have any other children, two sons must be sufficient to fulfill the mitzva. **And the reason of Beit Hillel** is that **we learn from the creation of the world,** as mankind was created male and female. The Gemara asks: **And Beit Shammai, let them learn from the creation of the world** as well. The Gemara answers that Beit Shammai could say to you: **We do not derive** a case where it is **possible**

HALAKHA

A High Priest must marry a maiden – נַעֲרָה לְכֹהֵן גָּדוֹל: A High Priest may not marry a minor or a grown woman. He must marry a maiden, i.e., a young woman in the first six months of adulthood (Rambam *Sefer Kedusha, Hilkhot Issurei Bia* 17:13).

A man may not neglect the mitzva to be fruitful and multiply – לֹא יִבָּטֵל אָדָם מִפְּרִיָּה וּרְבִיָּה: A man may not neglect the mitzva to be fruitful and multiply. Rather, he must marry and have children. Even if his wife foregoes her conjugal rights, he may desist from fulfilling them only if he has already fathered children (Rambam *Sefer Nashim, Hilkhot Ishut* 15:1; *Shulḥan Arukh, Even HaEzer* 1:1).

And Beit Hillel say, a male and a female – וּבֵית הִלֵּל אוֹמְרִים, זָכָר וּנְקֵבָה: A man who has a daughter and son who are capable of bearing children has fulfilled the mitzva to be fruitful and multiply, in accordance with the opinion of Beit Hillel (Rambam *Sefer Nashim, Hilkhot Ishut* 15:4; *Shulḥan Arukh, Even HaEzer* 1:5).

It is prohibited to remain without a wife – אָסוּר לַעֲמוֹד בְּלֹא אִשָּׁה: Even if a man has fulfilled the mitzva to be fruitful and multiply, the Sages nevertheless said that he should not remain without a wife. If he can, he should marry a woman who can bear children. If he has not fathered children and is in need of money in order to marry a wife, he may even sell a Torah scroll for this purpose. If he already has children he may not sell a Torah scroll in order to marry, although some authorities permit him to do so even in this case (Rambam *Sefer Nashim, Hilkhot Ishut* 15:16; *Shulḥan Arukh, Even HaEzer* 1:8).

NOTES

Unless he has children – אֶלָּא אִם כֵּן יֵשׁ לוֹ בָּנִים: *Tosafot* ask: why is it necessary to state this point if it was already made clear in the previous mishna? The *Arukh LaNer* contends that the precise formulation of this mishna adds a new element to what was stated earlier. The previous mishna said that one may not marry a sexually underdeveloped woman unless he has a wife and children. In this mishna, it states that one may not neglect the mitzva to procreate unless he has children. This emphasizes that unless one already has children, it is not sufficient to be married; one must actively try to have children.

Beit Shammai say, etc. – בֵּית שַׁמַּאי אוֹמְרִים וכו׳: The commentaries dispute whether Beit Shammai and Beit Hillel insist on these combinations of children. Many early commentaries cite Rashi as holding that Beit Shammai agree that one fulfills the mitzva if he has a son and daughter, and merely add that one can also fulfill the mitzva by fathering two sons. Conversely, some hold that it is Beit Hillel who are lenient and hold that one fulfills the mitzva with a son and daughter or with two sons (Rid; *Tosefot Ḥad MiKamma'ei*). This latter view is stated explicitly in the Jerusalem Talmud. However, most commentaries assume that according to Beit Hillel one must father a son and a daughter in order to fulfill the mitzva, and according to Beit Shammai one must father two sons.

It is prohibited to remain without a wife – אָסוּר לַעֲמוֹד בְּלֹא אִשָּׁה: On a basic level, the reason for this is so that one will not fall prey to sinful thoughts (*Nimmukei Yosef*). Alternatively, the verse indicates that mankind is complete only through marriage (see Maharsha).

מִשָּׁאִי אֶפְשָׁר. וּבֵית הִלֵּל נַמִי, לֵילְפוּ מִמֹּשֶׁה! אָמְרִי לָךְ: מֹשֶׁה מִדַּעְתֵּיהּ הוּא דַּעֲבַד. דְּתַנְיָא: שְׁלֹשָׁה דְּבָרִים עָשָׂה מֹשֶׁה מִדַּעְתּוֹ, וְהִסְכִּימָה דַּעְתּוֹ לְדַעַת הַמָּקוֹם: פֵּירַשׁ מִן הָאִשָּׁה, וְשִׁיבֵּר הַלּוּחוֹת, וְהוֹסִיף יוֹם אֶחָד.

from one that is **not possible.** Mankind was initially created with a male and female because otherwise reproduction would not have been possible. However, this fact cannot serve as a source that the mitzva to be fruitful and multiply is fulfilled only once one has a son and a daughter. The Gemara asks: **And Beit Hillel, let them also learn from Moses.** Beit Hillel could **say to you: Moses acted** based **on his own perception**[N] when he separated from his wife, but this does not mean that a man is permitted to neglect the mitzva to be fruitful and multiply after fathering two males, **as it is taught in** a *baraita*: **Moses did three things** based **on his own perception, and his perception agreed with the perception of the Omnipresent: He separated from** his **wife,**[N] **he broke the tablets, and he added one day** to the days of separation before the revelation at Sinai.

פֵּירַשׁ מִן הָאִשָּׁה, מַאי דָּרַשׁ? אָמַר: וּמָה יִשְׂרָאֵל שֶׁלֹּא דִּבְּרָה עִמָּהֶם שְׁכִינָה אֶלָּא לְפִי שָׁעָה, וְקָבַע לָהֶם זְמַן – אָמְרָה תּוֹרָה "אַל תִּגְּשׁוּ אֶל אִשָּׁה", אֲנִי שֶׁמְּיוּחָד לְדִבּוּר בְּכָל שָׁעָה וְשָׁעָה, וְלֹא קָבַע לִי זְמַן – עַל אַחַת כַּמָּה וְכַמָּה. וְהִסְכִּימָה דַּעְתּוֹ לְדַעַת הַמָּקוֹם, שֶׁנֶּאֱמַר "לֵךְ אֱמוֹר לָהֶם שׁוּבוּ לָכֶם לְאׇהֳלֵיכֶם וְאַתָּה פֹּה עֲמוֹד עִמָּדִי".

The Gemara clarifies: When Moses **separated from** his **wife** after the revelation at Sinai, **what did he interpret** that led him to do so? **He said:** If in the case of **Israel, with whom the Divine Presence spoke only temporarily and for whom** God **set** a specific **time for** revelation, **the Torah stated: "Do not approach a woman"** (Exodus 19:15), **I,** Moses, **who am set aside for** divine **speech all the time and for whom** God **did not set** a specific **time, all the more so** I must separate from my wife. **And his perception agreed with the perception of the Omnipresent, as it is stated** after the revelation at Sinai: **"Go say to them: Return to your tents; and you, stand here with Me"** (Deuteronomy 5:26–27). This indicates that whereas others could return to their homes and normal married life after the revelation at Sinai, Moses was to stay with God and not return to his wife.

שִׁיבֵּר אֶת הַלּוּחוֹת, מַאי דָּרַשׁ? אָמַר: וּמָה פֶּסַח, שֶׁהוּא אֶחָד מִשֵּׁשׁ מֵאוֹת וּשְׁלֹשׁ עֶשְׂרֵה מִצְוֹת, אָמְרָה תּוֹרָה "כׇּל בֶּן נֵכָר לֹא יֹאכַל בּוֹ", הַתּוֹרָה כּוּלָּהּ וְיִשְׂרָאֵל מְשׁוּמָּדִים – עַל אַחַת כַּמָּה וְכַמָּה.

Moses **broke the tablets** following the sin of the Golden Calf. **What did he interpret** that led him to do so? Moses **said:** If in the case of the **Paschal lamb, which is** only **one of 613 mitzvot, the Torah states: "No alien shall eat of it"** (Exodus 12:43), excluding not only gentiles but apostate Jews as well, then here, in the case of the Golden Calf, where the tablets represent **the entire Torah and** where **the Jewish people** are **apostates,** as they are worshipping the calf, **all the more so** must they be excluded from receiving them.

וְהִסְכִּימָה דַּעְתּוֹ לְדַעַת הַמָּקוֹם, דִּכְתִיב "אֲשֶׁר שִׁבַּרְתָּ", וְאָמַר רֵישׁ לָקִישׁ: אֲמַר לֵיהּ הַקָּדוֹשׁ בָּרוּךְ הוּא לְמֹשֶׁה: יִישַׁר כֹּחֲךָ שֶׁשִּׁבַּרְתָּ.

And his perception agreed with the perception of the Omnipresent, as it is written: "The first tablets **that you broke** [*asher shibbarta*]"[N] (Exodus 34:1), **and Reish Lakish said:** The word *asher* is an allusion to the fact that **the Holy One, Blessed be He, said to Moses: May your strength be true** [*yishar koḥakha*] **that you broke** the tablets.

הוֹסִיף יוֹם אֶחָד מִדַּעְתּוֹ, מַאי דָּרַשׁ? דִּכְתִיב "וְקִדַּשְׁתָּם הַיּוֹם וּמָחָר" הַיּוֹם כְּמָחָר, מַה מָּחָר לֵילוֹ עִמּוֹ – אַף הַיּוֹם לֵילוֹ עִמּוֹ. וְלַיְלָה דְּהָאִידָּנָא נָפַק לֵיהּ. שְׁמַע מִינָּהּ: תְּרֵי יוֹמֵי, לְבַר מֵהָאִידָּנָא. וְהִסְכִּימָה דַּעְתּוֹ לְדַעַת הַמָּקוֹם – דְּלָא שָׁרְיָא שְׁכִינָה עַד שַׁבְּתָא.

When Moses **added one day** to the days of separation before the revelation at Sinai based **on his** own **perception, what did he interpret** that led him to do so? He reasoned **that** since **it is written: "And sanctify them today and tomorrow"** (Exodus 19:10), the juxtaposition of the words "today" and "tomorrow" teaches that **today is like tomorrow: Just as tomorrow** the men and women will separate for that day **and** the **night** preceding **it, so too, today** requires separation for the day **and the night** preceding **it.** Since God spoke to him in the morning, **and the night of that day** already **passed,** Moses said: **Conclude from** this that separation must be in effect for **two days aside from now,** i.e., not including the day of the command. Therefore, he extended the mitzva of separation by one day. **And his perception agreed with the perception of the Omnipresent,** as the **Divine Presence did not rest** upon Mount Sinai **until Shabbat** morning, as Moses had determined.

NOTES

Moses acted based on his own perception – מֹשֶׁה מִדַּעְתֵּיהּ הוּא דַּעֲבַד: *Tosafot*, *Tosefot HaRosh*, and other commentaries attempt to prove that Moses' *a fortiori* inference with regard to separating from his wife is not irrefutable. Had it been a perfectly valid argument, the Gemara would not have said that he acted based on his own perception, as *a fortiori* inferences are a valid method of deriving *halakha*, and *halakhot* derived in this manner have the same status as those written explicitly in the Torah itself. The Gemara's point here is that the reason it was permitted for Moses to separate from his wife was not because he had already fulfilled the mitzva to be fruitful and multiply. His case was exceptional, and therefore it cannot serve as halakhic precedent with regard to the definition of the mitzva to be fruitful and multiply (Meiri; Rabbi Avraham min HaHar).

He separated from his wife – פֵּירַשׁ מִן הָאִשָּׁה: *Tosafot* ask how the Sages knew that Moses separated from his wife on his own accord; perhaps he did so only once God commanded him: "And you, stand here with Me" (Deuteronomy 5:27). The Ramban (*Shabbat* 87a) explains that this verse is stated after the revelation at Sinai. If God had wanted Moses to separate from his wife but Moses did not do so on his own, God would not have waited until after the revelation at Sinai to issue His command; He would have issued the command when He began to communicate regularly with Moses.

As it is written, The first tablets that you broke [*asher shibbarta*] – דִּכְתִיב, אֲשֶׁר שִׁבַּרְתָּ: The commentaries are puzzled by this proof, as the word *asher* appears many times in the Torah, and it is not generally understood to indicate approval of an action that a particular individual performed. The Maharsha explains that the phrase "that you broke" is entirely superfluous, as it had already been stated that Moses broke the tablets. Therefore, it must be taken to mean that God affirmed Moses' decision. The Ramban and the Ritva maintain (*Shabbat* 87a) that the proof that God approved of Moses' actions is from the verse in Deuteronomy (10:2) that states *asher shibbarta*, and continues: "And you shall place them in the Ark," which is understood to mean that the broken tablets were placed in the Ark together with the second, whole tablets. The fact that God commanded Moses to preserve the broken tablets demonstrates that He approved of his actions.

תַּנְיָא, רַבִּי נָתָן אוֹמֵר, בֵּית שַׁמַּאי אוֹמְרִים: שְׁנֵי זְכָרִים וּשְׁתֵּי נְקֵבוֹת, וּבֵית הִלֵּל אוֹמְרִים: זָכָר וּנְקֵבָה.

§ **It is taught in** a *baraita* that **Rabbi Natan says** that **Beit Shammai say:** The mitzva to be fruitful and multiply is fulfilled with **two males and two females. And Beit Hillel say: A male and a female.**

אָמַר רַב הוּנָא: מַאי טַעֲמָא דְּרַבִּי נָתָן אַלִּיבָּא דְּבֵית שַׁמַּאי – דִּכְתִיב ״וַתֹּסֶף לָלֶדֶת אֶת אָחִיו אֶת הָבֶל״ הֶבֶל וַאֲחוֹתוֹ, קַיִן וַאֲחוֹתוֹ. וּכְתִיב ״כִּי שָׁת לִי אֱלֹהִים זֶרַע אַחֵר תַּחַת הֶבֶל כִּי הֲרָגוֹ קָיִן״. וְרַבָּנַן אוֹדוּיֵי הוּא דְּקָא מוֹדֵית.

Rav Huna said: What is the reason of Rabbi Natan, in accordance with the opinion of **Beit Shammai?** It is **as it is written: "And again she bore his brother** [*et aḥiv*] **Abel** [*et Hevel*]**"** (Genesis 4:2). The use of the superfluous word "et" indicates that she gave birth to **Abel and his sister,** in addition to **Cain and his sister. And it states: "For God has appointed me another seed**[N] **instead of Abel; for Cain slew him"** (Genesis 4:25). This indicates that one must have at least four children. **And the Rabbis,** how do they understand this verse? In their opinion, Eve **was thanking God** for granting her another child, but one is not obligated to have four children.

תַּנְיָא אִידָךְ, רַבִּי נָתָן אוֹמֵר: בֵּית שַׁמַּאי אוֹמְרִים: זָכָר וּנְקֵבָה, וּבֵית הִלֵּל אוֹמְרִים: אוֹ זָכָר אוֹ נְקֵבָה. אָמַר רָבָא מַאי טַעֲמָא דְּרַבִּי נָתָן אַלִּיבָּא דְּבֵית הִלֵּל – שֶׁנֶּאֱמַר ״לֹא תֹהוּ בְרָאָהּ לָשֶׁבֶת יְצָרָהּ״ וְהָא עֲבַד לָהּ שֶׁבֶת.

It is taught in another *baraita* that **Rabbi Natan says** that **Beit Shammai say:** The mitzva to be fruitful and multiply is fulfilled with **a male and a female. And Beit Hillel say: Either a male or a female. Rava said: What is the reason of Rabbi Natan in accordance with the opinion of Beit Hillel?** It is **as it is stated: "He did not create it a waste; He formed it to be inhabited"** (Isaiah 45:18), **and** one **has made** the earth **inhabited** to a greater degree by adding even one child to the world.

אִיתְּמַר, הָיוּ לוֹ בָּנִים בְּגוֹיוּתוֹ וְנִתְגַּיֵּיר, רַבִּי יוֹחָנָן אָמַר: קִיֵּים פְּרִיָּה וּרְבִיָּה, וְרֵישׁ לָקִישׁ אָמַר: לֹא קִיֵּים פְּרִיָּה וּרְבִיָּה. רַבִּי יוֹחָנָן אָמַר: קִיֵּים פְּרִיָּה וּרְבִיָּה, דְּהָא הָווּ לֵיהּ. וְרֵישׁ לָקִישׁ אָמַר: לֹא קִיֵּים פְּרִיָּה וּרְבִיָּה – גֵּר שֶׁנִּתְגַּיֵּיר כְּקָטָן שֶׁנּוֹלַד דָּמֵי.

§ **It was stated** that *amora'im* disagreed over the following issue: If a man **had children when he** was **a gentile**[NH] **and he** subsequently **converted, Rabbi Yoḥanan said:** He has already **fulfilled** the mitzva to **be fruitful and multiply, and Reish Lakish said:** He has **not fulfilled** the mitzva to **be fruitful and multiply. Rabbi Yoḥanan said he has fulfilled** the mitzva **to be fruitful and multiply, as he** already **had** children. **And Reish Lakish said he has not fulfilled** the mitzva to **be fruitful and multiply,** as the legal status of **a convert who** just **converted is like** that of **a child** just **born,** and it is considered as though he did not have children.

וְאָזְדוּ לְטַעֲמַיְיהוּ, דְּאִיתְּמַר, הָיוּ לוֹ בָּנִים בְּגוֹיוּתוֹ וְנִתְגַּיֵּיר, רַבִּי יוֹחָנָן אָמַר: אֵין לוֹ בְּכוֹר לְנַחֲלָה, דְּהָא הֲוָה לֵיהּ ״רֵאשִׁית אוֹנוֹ״. וְרֵישׁ לָקִישׁ אָמַר: יֵשׁ לוֹ בְּכוֹר לְנַחֲלָה, גֵּר שֶׁנִּתְגַּיֵּיר כְּקָטָן שֶׁנּוֹלַד דָּמֵי.

The Gemara comments: **And they follow their** regular line of reasoning, **as it was stated: If one had children when he** was **a gentile and he** subsequently **converted, Rabbi Yoḥanan said: He does not have a firstborn with regard to inheritance,**[HB] i.e., the first son born to him after his conversion does not inherit a double portion, **as** this man already **had "the first of his strength"** (Deuteronomy 21:17), the Torah's description of the firstborn in this context, before he converted. **And Reish Lakish said: He does have a firstborn with regard to inheritance,** as the legal status of **a convert who** just **converted is like** that of **a child** just **born.**

וּצְרִיכָא, דְּאִי אַשְׁמְעִינַן בְּהַהִיא קַמַּיְיתָא – בְּהַהִיא קָאָמַר רַבִּי יוֹחָנָן, מִשּׁוּם דְּמֵעִיקָּרָא נַמִי בְּנֵי פְּרִיָּה וּרְבִיָּה נִינְהוּ, אֲבָל לְעִנְיַן נַחֲלָה, דְּלָאו בְּנֵי נַחֲלָה נִינְהוּ, אֵימָא מוֹדֵי לֵיהּ לְרֵישׁ לָקִישׁ.

The Gemara adds: **And** it is **necessary** to state their opinions in both cases. **As,** had it only been **taught to us with regard to that first** case of the mitzva to be fruitful and multiply, one might have said that it is only **in that** case that **Rabbi Yoḥanan said** his opinion, **because from the outset,** gentiles **are also subject to** the mitzva to be **fruitful and multiply.**[N] **However, with regard to inheritance,** since **they are not subject** to the *halakhot* of **inheritance,** one might **say** that Rabbi Yoḥanan **concedes to Reish Lakish.**

וְאִי אִיתְּמַר בְּהָא – בְּהָא קָאָמַר רֵישׁ לָקִישׁ, אֲבָל בְּהַהִיא – אֵימָא מוֹדֶה לֵיהּ לְרַבִּי יוֹחָנָן, צְרִיכָא.

And conversely, **if** their dispute **was stated** only **with regard to this** issue of inheritance, I would have said that it is only **in this** case that **Reish Lakish said** his opinion, as the *halakhot* of inheritance do not apply to gentiles. **But with regard to that** case, the mitzva to be fruitful and multiply, one might **say** that **he concedes to Rabbi Yoḥanan.** Consequently, it is **necessary** for both disputes to be recorded.

NOTES

For God has appointed me another seed – כִּי שָׁת לִי אֱלֹהִים זֶרַע אַחֵר: In order to prove that one must have two sons and two daughters this verse is also necessary. If only the first verse had been written, one might have thought that the Torah was merely relating how many children Adam and Eve had. This verse, however, indicates that it was necessary for them to have Seth as a replacement for Abel. Furthermore, one might have thought that one must father two daughters but that one son is sufficient, as a single male can father children through multiple females. The Gemara therefore cites a verse indicating that Adam required an additional son (*Ḥokhmat Shlomo*; see Maharsha).

If a man had children when he was a gentile – הָיוּ לוֹ בָּנִים בְּגוֹיוּתוֹ: According to the Rambam and other commentaries, Rabbi Yoḥanan stated his opinion only in a case where the children also converted, so that the father has Jewish offspring. Others, however, maintain that he has fulfilled the mitzva even if his children do not convert (Maharil; see *Tosafot*). This dispute depends upon the meaning of the Gemara's statement that gentiles are subject to the mitzva to be fruitful and multiply.

Gentiles are also subject to the mitzva to be fruitful and multiply – בְּנֵי פְּרִיָּה וּרְבִיָּה נִינְהוּ: Some commentaries cite this statement as proof that gentiles are commanded to be fruitful and multiply. This is indicated by the Torah as well, as the command to be fruitful and multiply was issued to Adam (Genesis 1:28) and Noah (Genesis 9:1). Others disagree, pointing to the fact that the mitzva to be fruitful and multiply is not listed as one of the seven Noahide mitzvot. This is consistent with the general principle that any mitzva mentioned in the Torah that is not repeated in Deuteronomy was given only to the Jewish people. They interpret the Gemara here as stating that gentiles fulfill the will of God by having children, although they do not fulfill an actual mitzva, as God created the world for it to be inhabited, and therefore it is praiseworthy for them to have children (see Meiri).

HALAKHA

If a man had children when he was a gentile – הָיוּ לוֹ בָּנִים בְּגוֹיוּתוֹ: If a gentile had children and subsequently converted to Judaism, he has fulfilled the mitzva to be fruitful and multiply through them if his children converted as well, in accordance with the opinion of Rabbi Yoḥanan. According to many authorities, he has fulfilled the mitzva even if his children did not convert (Rambam *Sefer Nashim, Hilkhot Ishut* 15:6; *Shulḥan Arukh, Even HaEzer* 1:7; Vilna Gaon).

A firstborn with regard to inheritance – בְּכוֹר לְנַחֲלָה: If a gentile who already had children converted and then fathered another son, the latter is not considered a firstborn with regard to the *halakhot* of inheritance, in accordance with the opinion of Rabbi Yoḥanan (Rambam *Sefer Mishpatim, Hilkhot Naḥalot* 2:12; *Shulḥan Arukh, Ḥoshen Mishpat* 277:9).

BACKGROUND

A firstborn with regard to inheritance – בְּכוֹר לְנַחֲלָה: A father's firstborn son receives an extra share in the inheritance (Deuteronomy 21:17). This privilege is granted even if he is not the mother's firstborn son and even if he is illegitimate. The firstborn son receives a share twice as great as that received by each of the other sons. This double share is, however, given only from property actually possessed by the estate at the time of the father's death, not from property accruing to the estate later. The latter property is divided equally among the heirs.

HALAKHA

A Canaanite slave, that he does not have family lineage – עֶבֶד שֶׁאֵין לוֹ חָיִיס: If a Canaanite slave and his children were freed and thereby become Jewish, the father has not fulfilled the mitzva to be fruitful and multiply because his children are not halakhically recognized as his offspring. Similarly, if a Jew fathers a son from a Canaanite maidservant, the boy is not considered his son, and therefore the first son born to him from a Jewish mother is considered his firstborn with regard to inheritance (Rambam *Sefer Nashim*, *Hilkhot Ishut* 15:6 and *Sefer Mishpatim*, *Hilkhot Naḥalot* 2:12; *Shulḥan Arukh*, *Even HaEzer* 1:7 and *Ḥoshen Mishpat* 277:9).

If a man had children and they died – הָיוּ לוֹ בָּנִים וּמֵתוּ: If a man's children died without leaving descendants, he has not fulfilled the mitzva to be fruitful and multiply, in accordance with the opinion of Rabbi Yoḥanan (Rambam *Sefer Nashim*, *Hilkhot Ishut* 15:5; *Shulḥan Arukh*, *Even HaEzer* 1:6).

אֵיתִיבֵיהּ רַבִּי יוֹחָנָן לְרֵישׁ לָקִישׁ: ״בָּעֵת הַהִיא שָׁלַח בְּרֹאדַךְ בַּלְאֲדָן בֶּן בַּלְאֲדָן מֶלֶךְ בָּבֶל״ וגו׳! אָמַר לֵיהּ: בְּגוֹיוּתָן – אִית לְהוּ חָיֵיס, נִתְגַּיְּירוּ – לֵית לְהוּ חָיֵיס.

Rabbi Yoḥanan raises an objection to Reish Lakish based upon the verse: **"At that time Berodach-baladan, son of Baladan, king of Babylon, sent** a letter" (II Kings 20:12), which indicates that gentiles are considered to be the children of their parents. Therefore, when they convert, they should already have fulfilled the mitzva to be fruitful and multiply. Reish Lakish **said to** Rabbi Yoḥanan: **When they are gentiles they do have** family **lineage,** but when **they convert they do not have lineage,** as they now belong to the family of the Jewish people and their previous lineage is disregarded.

אָמַר רַב: הַכֹּל מוֹדִין בְּעֶבֶד שֶׁאֵין לוֹ חָיֵיס, דִּכְתִיב ״שְׁבוּ לָכֶם פֹּה עִם הַחֲמוֹר״, עַם הַדּוֹמֶה לַחֲמוֹר. מֵיתִיבֵי: ״וּלְצִיבָא חֲמִשָּׁה עָשָׂר בָּנִים וְעֶשְׂרִים עֲבָדִים״! אֲמַר רַב אַחָא בַּר יַעֲקֹב: כְּ״פָר בֶּן בָּקָר״.

Rav said: Everyone agrees with regard to a Canaanite **slave, that he does not have lineage,**[H] **as it is written** that Abraham said to his slaves: **"Remain here with the donkey"** (Genesis 22:5). This verse is interpreted to mean that they are **a nation comparable to a donkey,**[N] which has no lineage. The Gemara **raises an objection** based upon a verse pertaining to Jonathan's Canaanite slave: **"And Ziba had fifteen sons and twenty servants"** (II Samuel 9:10), which indicates that a slave's sons are in fact considered his sons. **Rav Aḥa bar Ya'akov said:** This is **like** the expression: **A bullock, son of a bull.** The word son in this context merely denotes progeny, not lineage.

אִי הָכִי, הָכָא נַמִי! שָׁאנֵי הָתָם דְּיַחֲסִינְהוּ בִּשְׁמַיְיהוּ וּבִשְׁמָא דַּאֲבוּהוֹן, וְהָכָא לָא מְפָרֵשׁ. וְאִיבָּעֵית אֵימָא: יַחְסִינְהוּ בְּדוּכְתָּא אַחֲרִיתֵי בַּאֲבוּהוֹן וּבְאַבָּא דַּאֲבוּהוֹן, דִּכְתִיב ״וַיִּשְׁלָחֵם הַמֶּלֶךְ אָסָא אֶל בֶּן הֲדַד בֶּן טַבְרִימֹן בֶּן חֶזְיוֹן מֶלֶךְ אֲרָם הַיּוֹשֵׁב בְּדַמֶּשֶׂק לֵאמֹר״.

The Gemara asks: **If so, here too,** with regard to gentiles, there is no proof from the verse about Berodach-baladan that they have family lineage. The Gemara answers: **There it is different,** as the Bible **identified him by his name and by his father's name,**[N] thereby emphasizing the family connection. **But here,** it does **not specify** the names of Ziba's children. **And if you wish, say** instead that the Bible **identified** gentiles **elsewhere by their father and their father's father, as it is written: "And King Asa sent them to Ben-hadad, son of Tabrimmon, son of Hezion, king of Aram, who dwelled in Damascus, saying"** (I Kings 15:18). This indicates that there is lineage for gentiles.

אִיתְּמַר, הָיוּ לוֹ בָּנִים וּמֵתוּ, רַב הוּנָא אָמַר: קִיֵּים פְּרִיָּה וּרְבִיָּה, רַבִּי יוֹחָנָן אָמַר: לֹא קִיֵּים.

§ **It was stated** that *amora'im* disagreed over the following issue: If a man **had children and they died,**[H] **Rav Huna said:** He has **fulfilled** the mitzva to be **fruitful and multiply** through these children. **Rabbi Yoḥanan said:** He has **not fulfilled** the mitzva.

רַב הוּנָא אָמַר: קִיֵּים – מִשּׁוּם דְּרַב אַסִּי, דְּאָמַר רַב אַסִּי: אֵין בֶּן דָּוִד בָּא עַד שֶׁיִּכְלוּ כׇּל נְשָׁמוֹת שֶׁבַּגּוּף, שֶׁנֶּאֱמַר ״כִּי רוּחַ מִלְּפָנַי יַעֲטוֹף״ וגו׳. וְרַבִּי יוֹחָנָן אָמַר: לֹא קִיֵּים פְּרִיָּה וּרְבִיָּה, ״לָשֶׁבֶת יְצָרָהּ״ בָּעֵינַן – וְהָא לֵיכָּא.

The Gemara clarifies the reasons for their opinions: **Rav Huna said** he has **fulfilled** the mitzva **due to** a statement **of Rav Asi, as Rav Asi said** that the reason for this mitzva is that the Messiah, **son of David, will not come until all the souls of the body**[N] **have been finished,** i.e., until all souls that are destined to inhabit physical bodies will do so, **as it is stated: "For the spirit that enwraps itself is from Me,** and the souls that I have made" (Isaiah 57:16). Consequently, once a child has been born and his soul has entered a body the mitzva has been fulfilled, even if the child subsequently dies. **And Rabbi Yoḥanan said** he has **not fulfilled** the mitzva, as **we require "He formed it to be inhabited"** (Isaiah 45:18), **and this is not** fulfilled when the children have passed away and no longer inhabit the earth.

מֵיתִיבֵי

The Gemara **raises an objection** with regard to the opinion of Rav Huna based upon the following *baraita*:

NOTES

A nation [*am*] comparable to a donkey – עַם הַדּוֹמֶה לַחֲמוֹר: This interpretation is based on reading the word "with [*im*]" as though it were vocalized *am*, meaning nation. Furthermore, the Sages often interpret the word *im* in the Bible as indicating that a comparison can be drawn between two items (*Gilyonei HaShas*; see *Kiddushin* 76b).

By his name and by his father's name – בִּשְׁמַיְיהוּ וּבִשְׁמָא דַּאֲבוּהוֹן: The *Keren Ora* asks: Why does the Gemara choose the particular example of Berodach-baladan when there are many other instances where the Torah mentions the name of a gentile and his father, e.g., the list of Edomite kings in Genesis, chapter 37? The Ritva notes that this verse does not merely mention the name of Berodach-baladan's father, it demonstrates that his father's name was incorporated into his own name. It may be explained that this fact emphasizes the significance of the father-son relationship.

The souls of the body – נְשָׁמוֹת שֶׁבַּגּוּף: See NOTES on 63b for an explanation of this term.

בְּנֵי בָנִים הֲרֵי הֵן כְּבָנִים! כִּי תַּנְיָא הַהִיא – לְהַשְׁלִים.

Grandchildren are considered **like children.**[H] This indicates that if one's children have passed away, he has fulfilled the mitzva to be fruitful and multiply only if they had children of their own, as they are considered like his own children. The Gemara responds: **When that** *baraita* **is taught** it is with regard **to completing** the required number of children, e.g., if he had only a son, but his son had a daughter, he has fulfilled the mitzva to be fruitful and multiply.

מֵיתִיבֵי: בְּנֵי בָנִים הֲרֵי הֵם כְּבָנִים, מֵת אֶחָד מֵהֶם, אוֹ שֶׁנִּמְצָא סָרִיס, לֹא קִיֵּים פְּרִיָּה וּרְבִיָּה. תְּיוּבְתָּא דְּרַב הוּנָא! תְּיוּבְתָּא.

The Gemara **raises an objection** to the opinion of Rav Huna from another *baraita*: **Grandchildren are** considered **like children. If one** of a man's children **died or was discovered** to be **a eunuch,**[H] the father has **not fulfilled** the mitzva to be **fruitful and multiply.** This directly contradicts Rav Huna's statement that one fulfills the mitzva even if his children die. The Gemara concludes: **The refutation** of the opinion **of Rav Huna is** indeed **a conclusive refutation.**

״בְּנֵי בָנִים הֲרֵי הֵם כְּבָנִים״. סָבַר אַבַּיֵּי לְמֵימַר: בְּרָא לִבְרָא וּבְרַתָּא לִבְרַתָּא, וְכָל שֶׁכֵּן בְּרָא לִבְרַתָּא, אֲבָל בְּרַתָּא לִבְרָא – לָא. אָמַר לֵיהּ רָבָא: ״לָשֶׁבֶת יְצָרָהּ״ בָּעֵינָא, וְהָא אִיכָּא.

§ It was taught in the *baraita* that **grandchildren are** considered **like children. Abaye thought to say**[N] that if one's children die, he fulfills the mitzva to be fruitful and multiply through grandchildren, provided **a son** was born **to** his **son and a daughter to** his **daughter, and all the more so** if **a son** was born **to** his **daughter,** as his grandchildren take the place of his children in these cases. **However,** if **a daughter** was born **to** his **son, no,** she cannot take the place of her father. **Rava said to him:** We **require** merely fulfillment of the verse: **"He formed it to be inhabited," and there is** fulfillment in this case, as the earth is inhabited by his descendants.

דְּכוּלֵּי עָלְמָא מִיהַת תְּרֵי מֵחַד לָא. וְלָא?! וְהָא אָמְרִי לֵיהּ רַבָּנַן לְרַב שֵׁשֶׁת: נְסֵיב אִיתְּתָא וְאוֹלֵיד בְּנֵי! וַאֲמַר לְהוּ: בְּנֵי בְּרַתִּי בָּנַי נִינְהוּ.

The Gemara comments: **In any event, everyone** agrees that if one has **two** grandchildren **from one** child, **no,** he has not fulfilled the mitzva to be fruitful and multiply, even if he has both a grandson and a granddaughter. The Gemara asks: **And** has he **not? Didn't the Rabbis say to Rav Sheshet:**[P] **Marry a woman**[N] **and have sons,** as you have not yet fathered any sons, **and** Rav Sheshet **said to them: The sons of my daughter are my sons?** This indicates that one can fulfill the mitzva through grandchildren even if he did not have a son and daughter of his own.

הָתָם דַּחוּיֵי קָמַדְחֵי לְהוּ, דְּרַב שֵׁשֶׁת אִיעֲקַר מִפִּירְקֵיהּ דְּרַב הוּנָא.

The Gemara answers: **There,** Rav Sheshet **was** merely **putting them off.** The real reason he did not want to get remarried was **because Rav Sheshet became impotent from Rav Huna's**[P] **discourse.** Rav Huna's discourses were so lengthy that Rav Sheshet became impotent after waiting for so long without relieving himself.

אֲמַר לֵיהּ רַבָּה לְרָבָא בַּר מָארִי: מְנָא הָא מִילְּתָא דַּאֲמוּר רַבָּנַן בְּנֵי בָנִים הֲרֵי הֵן כְּבָנִים? אִילֵימָא מִדִּכְתִיב ״הַבָּנוֹת בְּנוֹתַי וְהַבָּנִים בָּנַי״ אֶלָּא מֵעַתָּה, ״וְהַצֹּאן צֹאנִי״ הָכִי נַמִי? אֶלָּא – דְּקָנֵית מִינַּאי, הָכָא נַמִי – דְּקָנֵית מִינַּאי!

Rabba said to Rava bar Mari: From where is this matter that the Sages stated derived, that **grandchildren are** considered **like children? If we say** it is derived **from** the fact **that it is written** in Laban's speech to Jacob: **"The daughters are my daughters and the children are my children"** (Genesis 31:43), which indicates that Jacob's children were also considered to be the children of their grandfather Laban, **if** that is **so,** does the continuation of Laban's statement: **"And the flocks are my flocks"** (Genesis 31:43), indicate that **so too,** Jacob's flocks were considered as belonging to Laban? **Rather,** Laban was saying **that you,** Jacob, **acquired** them **from me. Here too,** with regard to the children, Laban was saying: **You acquired** them **from me,** i.e., it is only due to me that you have children.

HALAKHA

Grandchildren are considered like children – בְּנֵי בָנִים הֲרֵי הֵן כְּבָנִים: If a man had a son and a daughter and both died, but one of them had a son and one of them had a daughter, since his surviving descendants include a male and a female, he has fulfilled the mitzva to be fruitful and multiply. However, if they were both the offspring of only one of his children, he has not fulfilled the mitzva (Rambam *Sefer Nashim, Hilkhot Ishut* 15:5; *Shulḥan Arukh, Even HaEzer* 1:6).

Or was discovered to be a eunuch – אוֹ שֶׁנִּמְצָא סָרִיס: If a man had a son who turned out to be a eunuch, or a daughter who grew up to be a sexually underdeveloped woman, he has not fulfilled the mitzva to be fruitful and multiply through them (Rambam *Sefer Nashim, Hilkhot Ishut* 15:4; *Shulḥan Arukh, Even HaEzer* 1:5).

PERSONALITIES

Rav Sheshet – רַב שֵׁשֶׁת: A prominent third-generation Babylonian *amora*, Rav Sheshet was the primary student of Rav Huna, even though he also served and studied under the rest of the Sages of Rav Huna's generation. Rav Sheshet was famous for his unsurpassed expertise in Mishna and *baraita*. Many of the Sages of his generation came to study under him, as they knew that his teachings were always based on early sources. In his later years Rav Sheshet became blind, but remained involved in all aspects of life and was a frequent visitor to the house of the Exilarch. He was characteristically extremely forceful, hard as steel, and did not defer even to eminent political leaders. Apparently, He supported himself as a garment merchant and earned enough to live comfortably.

Rav Huna – רַב הוּנָא: One of the great second-generation Babylonian *amora'im*, Rav Huna was most closely associated with his teacher, Rav. Rav Huna was of aristocratic descent, from the house of the Exilarchs, but despite that lineage, he lived in abject poverty for many years. Later in life he became wealthy and lived comfortably, and distributed his resources for the public good. Rav Huna was the greatest of Rav's students, to the extent that Shmuel, Rav's colleague, used to treat him deferentially and direct questions to him. After Rav's death Rav Huna became the head of the yeshiva of Sura and filled that position for forty years. His prominence in Torah and his loftiness of character helped make the yeshiva of Sura the preeminent center of Torah for many centuries. Because of Rav Huna's extensive Torah knowledge, the *halakha* is almost invariably ruled in accordance with his opinion in disputes with his colleagues and contemporaries. The only exception is in civil *halakha*, where the rulings are in accordance with the opinion of Rav Naḥman.

Rav Huna had many students, some of whom studied exclusively with him. Moreover, Rav's younger students remained to study with Rav Huna, his disciple, after Rav's death. Rav Huna's son, Rabba bar Rav Huna, was one of the greatest Sages of the following generation.

NOTES

Abaye thought to say, etc. – סָבַר אַבַּיֵי לְמֵימַר וכו׳: An opinion is cited in the Jerusalem Talmud that limits the possibility of fulfilling the mitzva to be fruitful and multiply through grandchildren to an even greater degree than Abaye had thought to say. According to this opinion, only the daughter of a daughter and the son of a son are counted as one's own children, but not a son of a daughter or a daughter of a son.

Marry a woman, etc. – נְסֵיב אִיתְּתָא וכו׳: Rav Sheshet's response does not appear to be sufficient, as Rabbi Yehoshua, cited below, holds that even if one has fulfilled the mitzva to be fruitful and multiply he should still have more children. Even according to the Gemara's statement that Rav Sheshet became impotent, he still should have gotten married, in accordance with the opinion of Shmuel that it is always preferable for a man to be married. It is possible that since he was constantly involved in Torah study it was permissible for him to remain unmarried, similar to the case of ben Azzai (see 63b; Ramban).

אֶלָּא מֵהָכָא: ״וְאַחַר בָּא חֶצְרוֹן אֶל בַּת מָכִיר אֲבִי גִלְעָד...וַתֵּלֶד לוֹ אֶת שְׂגוּב״, וּכְתִיב: ״מִנִּי מָכִיר יָרְדוּ מְחוֹקְקִים״ וּכְתִיב ״יְהוּדָה מְחוֹקְקִי״.

Rather, the proof is **from here: "And afterward Hezron went in to the daughter of Machir, the father of Gilead… and she bore him Segub"** (I Chronicles 2:21), **and it is written: "Out of Machir came down governors"** (Judges 5:14), **and it is written: "Judah is my governor"** (Psalms 60:9). Consequently, the governors, who were from the tribe of Judah, were also called the sons of Machir, who was from the tribe of Manasseh. This must be because they were the children of Machir's daughter and Hezron, indicating that grandchildren are considered like children.

מַתְנִיתִין דְּלָאו כְּרַבִּי יְהוֹשֻׁעַ. דְּתַנְיָא, רַבִּי יְהוֹשֻׁעַ אוֹמֵר: נָשָׂא אָדָם אִשָּׁה בְּיַלְדוּתוֹ – יִשָּׂא אִשָּׁה בְּזִקְנוּתוֹ, הָיוּ לוֹ בָּנִים בְּיַלְדוּתוֹ – יִהְיוּ לוֹ בָּנִים בְּזִקְנוּתוֹ, שֶׁנֶּאֱמַר ״בַּבֹּקֶר זְרַע אֶת זַרְעֶךָ וְלָעֶרֶב אַל תַּנַּח יָדֶךָ כִּי אֵינְךָ יוֹדֵעַ אֵי זֶה יִכְשַׁר הֲזֶה אוֹ זֶה וְאִם שְׁנֵיהֶם כְּאֶחָד טוֹבִים״.

§ The Gemara comments: **The mishna is not in accordance with** the opinion of **Rabbi Yehoshua. As it is taught in a** *baraita* that **Rabbi Yehoshua says: If a man married a woman in his youth,** and she passed away, **he should marry** another **woman in his old age. If he had children in his youth, he should have** more **children in his old age, as it is stated: "In the morning sow your seed, and in the evening do not withhold your hand; for you do not know which shall prosper, whether this or that, or whether they both alike shall be good"** (Ecclesiastes 11:6). This verse indicates that a man should continue having children even after he has fulfilled the mitzva to be fruitful and multiply.

רַבִּי עֲקִיבָא אוֹמֵר: לָמַד תּוֹרָה בְּיַלְדוּתוֹ – יִלְמוֹד תּוֹרָה בְּזִקְנוּתוֹ, הָיוּ לוֹ תַּלְמִידִים בְּיַלְדוּתוֹ – יִהְיוּ לוֹ תַּלְמִידִים בְּזִקְנוּתוֹ, שֶׁנֶּאֱמַר ״בַּבֹּקֶר זְרַע אֶת זַרְעֶךָ״ וגו׳. אָמְרוּ: שְׁנֵים עָשָׂר אֶלֶף זוּגִים תַּלְמִידִים הָיוּ לוֹ לְרַבִּי עֲקִיבָא מִגְּבָת עַד אַנְטִיפְּרָס, וְכוּלָּן מֵתוּ בְּפֶרֶק אֶחָד, מִפְּנֵי שֶׁלֹּא נָהֲגוּ כָּבוֹד זֶה לָזֶה.

Rabbi Akiva says that the verse should be understood as follows: If one **studied Torah in his youth**[N] **he should study** more **Torah in his old age; if he had students in his youth he should have** additional **students in his old age, as it is stated: "In the morning sow your seed, etc." They said** by way of example that **Rabbi Akiva had twelve thousand pairs**[N] **of students**[B] in an area of land that stretched **from Gevat to Antipatris**[B] in Judea, **and they all died in one period** of time, **because they did not treat each other with respect.**

וְהָיָה הָעוֹלָם שָׁמֵם, עַד שֶׁבָּא רַבִּי עֲקִיבָא אֵצֶל רַבּוֹתֵינוּ שֶׁבַּדָּרוֹם וּשְׁנָאָהּ לָהֶם: רַבִּי מֵאִיר, וְרַבִּי יְהוּדָה, וְרַבִּי יוֹסֵי, וְרַבִּי שִׁמְעוֹן וְרַבִּי אֶלְעָזָר בֶּן שַׁמּוּעַ. וְהֵם הֵם הֶעֱמִידוּ תּוֹרָה אוֹתָהּ שָׁעָה.

And the world was desolate of Torah **until Rabbi Akiva came to our Rabbis in the South and taught** his Torah **to them.** This second group of disciples consisted of **Rabbi Meir, Rabbi Yehuda, Rabbi Yosei, Rabbi Shimon, and Rabbi Elazar ben Shamua. And these are the very ones** who **upheld** the study of **Torah at that time.** Although Rabbi Akiva's earlier students did not survive, his later disciples were able to transmit the Torah to future generations.

תָּנָא: כּוּלָּם מֵתוּ מִפֶּסַח וְעַד עֲצֶרֶת. אָמַר רַב חָמָא בַּר אַבָּא וְאִיתֵּימָא רַבִּי חִיָּיא בַּר אָבִין: כּוּלָּם מֵתוּ מִיתָה רָעָה. מַאי הִיא? אָמַר רַב נַחְמָן: אַסְכָּרָה.

With regard to the twelve thousand pairs of Rabbi Akiva's students, the Gemara adds: It is **taught** that **all of them died** in the period **from Passover until** ***Shavuot.*** **Rav Ḥama bar Abba said, and some say** it was **Rabbi Ḥiyya bar Avin: They all died a bad death.** The Gemara inquires: **What is it** that is called a bad death? **Rav Naḥman said: Diphtheria.**

אָמַר רַב מַתָּנָא: הֲלָכָה כְּרַבִּי יְהוֹשֻׁעַ.

Rav Mattana said: The ***halakha*** **is in accordance with** the opinion of **Rabbi Yehoshua,** who said that one must attempt to have more children even if he has already fulfilled the mitzva to be fruitful and multiply.

BACKGROUND

The students of Rabbi Akiva – תַּלְמִידֵי רַבִּי עֲקִיבָא: It appears from the Gemara that most of Rabbi Akiva's disciples died in a plague. However, Rav Sherira Gaon explains in his letter that this was a *shemada*, meaning their death was due either to governmental persecution or to war. If so, this would appear to be related to the bar Kokheva revolt, of which Rabbi Akiva was an ardent supporter. It is reasonable to surmise that Rabbi Akiva's students served as soldiers under bar Kokheva and when the Romans suppressed the revolt with great brutality, these students were killed.

The image depicts an engraving that was prepared by the Roman senate in honor of Hadrian after he succeeded in suppressing the bar Kokheva revolt. It is currently at the Israel Museum in Jerusalem.

Engraving in honor of Hadrian after he suppressed the bar Kokheva revolt

From Gevat to Antipatris – מִגְּבָת עַד אַנְטִיפְּרָס: The location of Gevat is not entirely clear. Some identify it with a hill just north of Beersheba. According to some sources, Gevat is located on the border of the desert. Antipatris is the city of Ἀντιπατρίς, built by Herod in northern Judea. The city was located close to the source of the Yarkon River and near modern-day Rosh HaAyin. It served as a landmark, as it was the northernmost point in Judea, with Samaria continuing to the north.

The expression from Gevat to Antipatris means that the area stretched along the entire length of the land of Judea, from its southernmost edge to its northernmost edge.

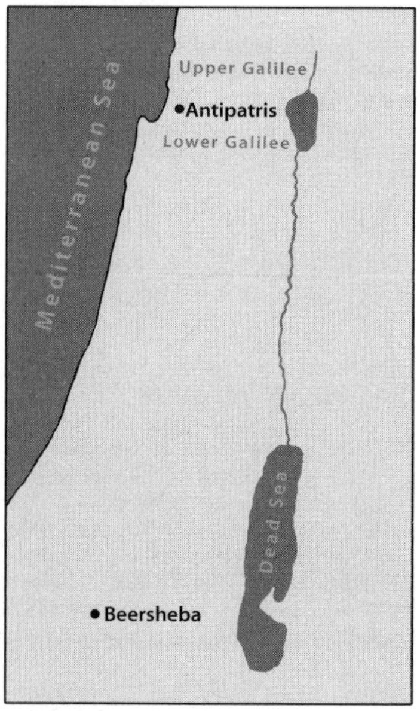

Location of Antipatris

Antipatris

NOTES

Studied Torah in his youth, etc. – לָמַד תּוֹרָה בְּיַלְדוּתוֹ וכו׳: The commentaries questioned the necessity of this exposition. Since Torah study is a mitzva that applies at all times, why is it necessary to derive from this verse that even if one studied in his youth he should study more in his old age? The *Keren Ora* suggests that this is referring to the additional toil in Torah that one must undertake in order to weaken his sinful inclinations. It might have been thought that since the evil inclination is not as strong in old age, he does not have to follow such a regimen. The *Iyyun Ya'akov* explains that even if one studied and fully clarified a particular issue in depth when he was young, he should not rely on this but should review the matter when the matter arises in his later years. He might change his mind or add new insights in his maturity.

Twelve thousand pairs, etc. – שְׁנֵים עָשָׂר אֶלֶף זוּגִים וכו׳: Most commentaries read this passage in a straightforward manner, offering various reasons for the fate that befell Rabbi Akiva's students. Rav Sherira Gaon, however, writes in a letter that the disciples perished in a time of persecution by the government. According to this opinion, the events are connected to the contemporaneous bar Kokheva rebellion. The Meiri writes that it is customary to observe certain customs of mourning during the period between Passover and *Shavuot* due to the fact that Rabbi Akiva's students died during this time. Following the tradition of the *ge'onim* that the students ceased dying on *Lag BaOmer*, the thirty-third day of that time period, mourning customs are not observed on that day.

אָמַר רַבִּי תַּנְחוּם אָמַר רַבִּי חֲנִילַאי: כׇּל אָדָם שֶׁאֵין לוֹ אִשָּׁה שָׁרוּי בְּלֹא שִׂמְחָה, בְּלֹא בְרָכָה, בְּלֹא טוֹבָה. בְּלֹא שִׂמְחָה – דִּכְתִיב ״וְשָׂמַחְתָּ אַתָּה וּבֵיתֶךָ״, בְּלֹא בְרָכָה – דִּכְתִיב ״לְהָנִיחַ בְּרָכָה אֶל בֵּיתֶךָ״, בְּלֹא טוֹבָה – דִּכְתִיב ״לֹא טוֹב הֱיוֹת הָאָדָם לְבַדּוֹ״.

§ Apropos the discussion with regard to the mitzva to have children, the Gemara cites statements about marriage in general. **Rabbi Tanḥum said** that **Rabbi Ḥanilai said: Any man who does not have a wife is** left **without joy, without blessing,**[N] **without goodness.** He proceeds to quote verses to support each part of his statement. He is **without joy, as it is written: "And you shall rejoice, you and your household"** (Deuteronomy 14:26), which indicates that the a man is in a joyful state only when he is with his household, i.e., his wife. He is **without blessing, as it is written: "To cause a blessing to rest in your house"** (Ezekiel 44:30), which indicates that blessing comes through one's house, i.e., one's wife. He is **without goodness, as it is written: "It is not good that man should be alone"** (Genesis 2:18), i.e., without a wife.

בְּמַעְרְבָא אָמְרִי: בְּלֹא תּוֹרָה, בְּלֹא חוֹמָה. בְּלֹא תּוֹרָה – דִּכְתִיב ״הַאִם אֵין עֶזְרָתִי בִי וְתֻשִׁיָּה נִדְּחָה מִמֶּנִּי״, בְּלֹא חוֹמָה – דִּכְתִיב ״נְקֵבָה תְּסוֹבֵב גָּבֶר״.

In the West, Eretz Yisrael, they **say:** One who lives without a wife is left **without Torah,** and **without a wall** of protection. He is **without Torah, as it is written: "Is it that I have no help in me, and that sound wisdom is driven from me?"** (Job 6:13), indicating that one who does not have a wife lacks sound wisdom, i.e., Torah. He is **without a wall, as it is written: "A woman shall go round a man"** (Jeremiah 31:21), similar to a protective wall.

רָבָא בַּר עוּלָּא אָמַר: בְּלֹא שָׁלוֹם, דִּכְתִיב ״וְיָדַעְתָּ כִּי שָׁלוֹם אׇהֳלֶךָ וּפָקַדְתָּ נָוְךָ וְלֹא תֶחֱטָא״.

Rava bar Ulla said: One who does not have a wife is left **without peace, as it is written: "And you shall know that your tent is in peace; and you shall visit your habitation and shall miss nothing"** (Job 5:24). This indicates that a man has peace only when he has a tent, i.e., a wife.

אָמַר רַבִּי יְהוֹשֻׁעַ בֶּן לֵוִי: כׇּל הַיּוֹדֵעַ בְּאִשְׁתּוֹ שֶׁהִיא יִרְאַת שָׁמַיִם, וְאֵינוֹ פּוֹקְדָהּ – נִקְרָא חוֹטֵא, שֶׁנֶּאֱמַר ״וְיָדַעְתָּ כִּי שָׁלוֹם אׇהֳלֶךָ״ וגו׳. וְאָמַר רַבִּי יְהוֹשֻׁעַ בֶּן לֵוִי: חַיָּיב אָדָם לִפְקוֹד אֶת אִשְׁתּוֹ בְּשָׁעָה שֶׁהוּא יוֹצֵא לַדֶּרֶךְ, שֶׁנֶּאֱמַר ״וְיָדַעְתָּ כִּי שָׁלוֹם אׇהֳלֶךָ״ וגו׳.

On the same verse, **Rabbi Yehoshua ben Levi said: Whoever knows that his wife fears Heaven**[N] and she desires him, **and he does not visit her,** i.e., have intercourse with her, **is called a sinner, as it is stated: And you shall know that your tent is in peace;** and you shall visit your habitation. **And Rabbi Yehoshua ben Levi said: A man is obligated to visit his wife** for the purpose of having intercourse **when he** is about to **depart on a journey,**[H] **as it is stated: "And you shall know that your tent is in peace, etc."**

הָא מֵהָכָא נָפְקָא? מֵהָתָם נָפְקָא: ״וְאֶל אִישֵׁךְ תְּשׁוּקָתֵךְ״ מְלַמֵּד שֶׁהָאִשָּׁה מִשְׁתּוֹקֶקֶת עַל בַּעְלָהּ בְּשָׁעָה שֶׁהוּא יוֹצֵא לַדֶּרֶךְ! אָמַר רַב יוֹסֵף: לֹא נִצְרְכָה אֶלָּא סָמוּךְ לְוֶוסְתָּהּ.

The Gemara asks: Is **this** last statement **derived from here?**[N] It is **derived from there: "And your desire shall be to your husband"** (Genesis 3:16), which **teaches that a wife desires her husband when he is about to depart on a journey. Rav Yosef said:** The additional derivation cited by Rabbi Yehoshua ben Levi **is necessary only near** the time of **her set pattern,**[N] i.e., when she expects to begin experiencing menstrual bleeding. Although the Sages generally prohibited intercourse at this time due to a concern that the couple might have intercourse after she begins bleeding, if he is about to depart on a journey he must have intercourse with her.

HALAKHA

A man is obligated to visit his wife when he is about to depart on a journey – חַיָּיב אָדָם לִפְקוֹד אֶת אִשְׁתּוֹ בְּשָׁעָה שֶׁהוּא יוֹצֵא: One who is about to depart on a journey that does not involve a mitzva must have intercourse with his wife, if she so desires, before he departs. This is permitted even if it is the time when she expects the onset of menstrual bleeding. However, some say that if he can accommodate her in some other manner instead, he is praiseworthy. Some say that if his wife is forbidden to him but will become permitted if he postpones his journey by a day or night, he must delay his departure (*Shulḥan Arukh*, *Oraḥ Ḥayyim* 240:1 and *Yoreh De'a* 184:10, and in the comment of Rema).

NOTES

Without blessing – בְּלֹא בְרָכָה: The *Beit Yosef* cites this statement as a source for the custom that an unmarried priest does not recite the Priestly Benediction, as one who is without a blessing cannot bless others. The *Zohar* states a similar opinion. Nevertheless, the common practice is that unmarried priests do recite the Priestly Benediction.

Whoever knows that his wife fears Heaven – כׇּל הַיּוֹדֵעַ בְּאִשְׁתּוֹ שֶׁהִיא יִרְאַת שָׁמַיִם: The meaning here is that since she is God-fearing she is reluctant to express her desire openly. If he realizes from her behavior that she desires him, it is a mitzva for him to have intercourse with her.

Is this derived from here – הָא מֵהָכָא נָפְקָא: Although the verse "And your desire shall be to your husband" does not refer specifically to a woman whose husband is about to depart on a journey, once it has been established that a woman desires her husband, and it is well known that this desire increases before a departure, no additional verse is necessary to teach that a man must satisfy his wife when she desires him (see *Tosafot*).

Near the time of her set pattern – סָמוּךְ לְוֶוסְתָּהּ: According to Rashi and others, this Gemara indicates that although it is generally forbidden to have intercourse at a time when a woman expects the onset of menstrual bleeding, in this case it is permitted. This is based upon the assumption that the general prohibition is by rabbinic decree, and the Sages did not apply this decree in cases where it would cause the woman suffering. However, other commentaries assert that intercourse at this time is forbidden even under these circumstances. *Tosafot* explain that the term visit referred to in the Gemara does not refer to intercourse, but to spending time together.

A different explanation is cited by the Ritva and the *Nimmukei Yosef*. They claim that this passage does not address the case of a woman who expects the onset of menstrual bleeding. Rather, the case is where the woman has already experienced menstrual bleeding, and the time for her to immerse herself in the ritual bath, and thereby become permitted to her husband, has almost arrived. In this case, the traveler must wait to leave home until it is permitted for him to have intercourse with his wife. It is with regard to this *halakha* that the Gemara states that the period of waiting is a night or a day, meaning that he must delay his trip if all he will have to wait is this amount of time. The next statement of the Gemara would then be understood as saying that if he is departing to fulfill a mitzva he should not delay his journey.

וְכַמָּה? אָמַר רָבָא: עוֹנָה. וְהָנֵי מִילֵּי – לִדְבַר הָרְשׁוּת, אֲבָל לִדְבַר מִצְוָה – מִיטְרִידִי.

The Gemara asks: **And how much** before the expected onset of menstrual bleeding is considered near the time of her set pattern? **Rava said: An interval** of time,[H] i.e., half a daily cycle, either a day or a night. The Gemara comments: **And this** statement that a man must have intercourse with his wife before he departs on a journey **applies** only if he is traveling **for an optional matter, but** if he is traveling in order to attend **to a matter** pertaining to a **mitzva,** he is not required to have intercourse with his wife so that he not become **preoccupied** and neglect the mitzva.

תָּנוּ רַבָּנַן: הָאוֹהֵב אֶת אִשְׁתּוֹ כְּגוּפוֹ, וְהַמְכַבְּדָהּ יוֹתֵר מִגּוּפוֹ, וְהַמַּדְרִיךְ בָּנָיו וּבְנוֹתָיו בְּדֶרֶךְ יְשָׁרָה, וְהַמַּשִּׂיאָן סָמוּךְ לְפִירְקָן – עָלָיו הַכָּתוּב אוֹמֵר ״וְיָדַעְתָּ כִּי שָׁלוֹם אׇהֳלֶךָ״. הָאוֹהֵב אֶת שְׁכֵינָיו, וְהַמְקָרֵב אֶת קְרוֹבָיו, וְהַנּוֹשֵׂא אֶת בַּת אֲחוֹתוֹ,

§ **The Sages taught:** One **who loves his wife as** he loves **himself,**[H] **and who honors her more than himself,**[N] **and who instructs his sons and daughters in an upright path, and who marries them off near the time** when **they** reach maturity,[HN] **about him the verse states: And you shall know that your tent is in peace.** As a result of his actions, there will be peace in his home, as it will be devoid of quarrel and sin. One **who loves his neighbors, and who draws his relatives close, and who marries the daughter of his sister,**[NH] a woman he knows and is fond of as a family relative and not only as a wife,

HALAKHA

Separating from one's wife for an interval of time – פְּרִישַׁת עוֹנָה: It is prohibited for a husband and wife to have intercourse at the time when the onset of menstrual bleeding is expected to occur. If this is expected to occur during the night they are forbidden to each other from the beginning of the night, and if it is expected to occur during the day they are forbidden to each other from the beginning of the day (Rambam *Sefer Kedusha, Hilkhot Issurei Bia* 4:12; *Shulḥan Arukh, Yoreh De'a* 184:2).

One who loves his wife as he loves himself – הָאוֹהֵב אֶת אִשְׁתּוֹ כְּגוּפוֹ: The Sages said that a man should love his wife as he loves himself and honor her more than himself. If he is a wealthy man, he should provide for her in accordance with his means (Rambam *Sefer Nashim, Hilkhot Ishut* 15:19).

Marries them off near the time when they reach maturity – מַשִּׂיאָן סָמוּךְ לְפִירְקָן: The Sages advised a man to marry off his sons and daughters near the time when they reach maturity so that they not be tempted by sinful thoughts (Rambam *Sefer Kedusha, Hilkhot Issurei Bia* 21:25; *Tur, Even HaEzer* 1).

The daughter of his sister – בַּת אֲחוֹתוֹ: The Sages counseled that a man should marry his sister's or his brother's daughter (Rambam *Sefer Kedusha, Hilkhot Issurei Bia* 2:14; see *Mishne LaMelekh*).

NOTES

And who honors her more than himself – וְהַמְכַבְּדָהּ יוֹתֵר מִגּוּפוֹ: With regard to all matters of honor a man must put his wife before himself. An example is with regard to clothing; a husband must make sure that his wife is dressed in a more respectable manner than himself (*Nimmukei Yosef*). Rabbi Yehuda al-Madari explains that the shame felt by a woman when her dignity is not upheld is greater than that of a man, and therefore upholding her dignity takes precedence.

Who marries them off near the time when they reach maturity – הַמַּשִּׂיאָן סָמוּךְ לְפִירְקָן: Most commentaries explain that this means that he marries them off before they reach adulthood. See *Tosafot*, who discuss how it is possible for a boy to get married at this age. Some say that the *baraita* is referring to a father who makes sure his son gets married as soon as he reaches the age of thirteen (see *Yam shel Shlomo*). The Meiri cites a different interpretation according to which the *baraita* is referring to a father who ensures that his son gets married near the usual age of marriage, eighteen.

And who marries the daughter of his sister – וְהַנּוֹשֵׂא אֶת בַּת אֲחוֹתוֹ: Some commentaries claim that this does not refer only to his sister's daughter but includes a brother's daughter as well (Rambam; *Tosafot*, citing Rashbam). The *Mishne LaMelekh* explains that family affection is a more natural feeling than the contingent, albeit stronger, love for a woman, and therefore a combination of these two emotions will ensure the success of the marriage.

Rabbeinu Tam and the Meiri maintain that this statement applies only to the daughter of a sister, because she is likely to be more compatible with him than the daughter of his brother. Rashi states that a man has stronger feelings for a sister than for a brother, and therefore he is closer to her daughter. Others contend that he should not marry his brother's daughter, as she would be unable to fulfill the mitzva of levirate marriage (*Tosafot Yeshanim*; Rivan). Yet others suggest that this is referring to a case of a sister's daughter who is fatherless, and it is a particular mitzva to marry her as an act of kindness, in order to provide for her (Rid). The *Yad Rama* explains in a similar fashion.

וְהַמַּלְוֶה סֶלַע לְעָנִי בִּשְׁעַת דָּחְקוֹ – עָלָיו הַכָּתוּב אוֹמֵר ״אָז תִּקְרָא וַה׳ יַעֲנֶה תְּשַׁוַּע וְיֹאמַר הִנֵּנִי״.

and who lends a *sela* to a pauper[N] **at his time of need, about him the verse states:**[N] **"Then shall you call, and the Lord will answer; you shall cry, and He will say: Here I am"** (Isaiah 58:9).

סִימָן אִשָּׁ״ה וְקַרְקַ״ע עֵזֶ״ר זֹא״ת שְׁתֵּ״י הַבְּרָכוֹ״ת תַּגָּרֵ״י פָּחְתֵ״י. אָמַר רַבִּי אֶלְעָזָר: כָּל אָדָם שֶׁאֵין לוֹ אִשָּׁה – אֵינוֹ אָדָם, שֶׁנֶּאֱמַר ״זָכָר וּנְקֵבָה בְּרָאָם וַיִּקְרָא אֶת שְׁמָם אָדָם״. וְאָמַר רַבִּי אֶלְעָזָר: כָּל אָדָם שֶׁאֵין לוֹ קַרְקַע – אֵינוֹ אָדָם, שֶׁנֶּאֱמַר ״הַשָּׁמַיִם שָׁמַיִם לַה׳ וְהָאָרֶץ נָתַן לִבְנֵי אָדָם״.

§ The Gemara provides **a mnemonic** device[B] for a series of statements cited in the name of Rabbi Elazar: **Woman; and land; helper; this; two; the blessings; merchants; lowly.** The Gemara presents these statements: **Rabbi Elazar said: Any man who does not have a wife is not a man,**[H] **as it is stated: "Male and female He created them…and called their name Adam"** (Genesis 5:2). **And Rabbi Elazar said: Any man who does not have** his own **land is not a man,**[N] **as it is stated: "The heavens are the heavens of the Lord; but the earth He has given to the children of men"** (Psalms 115:16).

וְאָמַר רַבִּי אֶלְעָזָר: מַאי דִּכְתִיב ״אֶעֱשֶׂה לּוֹ עֵזֶר כְּנֶגְדּוֹ״, זָכָה – עוֹזַרְתּוֹ, לֹא זָכָה – כְּנֶגְדּוֹ. וְאִיכָּא דְּאָמְרִי: רַבִּי אֶלְעָזָר רָמֵי, כְּתִיב ״כְּנַגְדּוֹ״ וְקָרֵינַן ״כְּנֶיגְדּוֹ״, זָכָה – כְּנֶגְדּוֹ, לֹא זָכָה – מְנַגַּדְתּוֹ.

And Rabbi Elazar said: What is the meaning of **that** which **is written: "I will make him a helpmate for him [*kenegdo*]"** (Genesis 2:18)? If one is **worthy** his wife **helps him;** if he is **not worthy** she is **against him.**[N] **And some say** a slightly different version: **Rabbi Elazar raised a contradiction: It is written** in the Torah with a spelling that allows it to be read: **Striking him [*kenagdo*], and we read** it as though it said: **For him [*kenegdo*].** If he is **worthy** she is **for him** as his helpmate; if he is **not worthy** she **strikes him.**

אַשְׁכְּחֵיהּ רַבִּי יוֹסֵי לְאֵלִיָּהוּ, אָמַר לֵיהּ: כְּתִיב ״אֶעֱשֶׂה לּוֹ עֵזֶר״, בַּמֶּה אִשָּׁה עוֹזַרְתּוֹ לְאָדָם? אָמַר לֵיהּ: אָדָם מֵבִיא חִיטִּין – חִיטִּין כּוֹסֵס? פִּשְׁתָּן – פִּשְׁתָּן לוֹבֵשׁ? לֹא נִמְצֵאת מְאִירָה עֵינָיו וּמַעֲמִידָתוֹ עַל רַגְלָיו?!

The Gemara relates that **Rabbi Yosei encountered Elijah** the prophet and **said to him: It is written: I will make him a helpmate. In what** manner **does a woman help a man?**[N] Elijah **said to him:** When **a man brings wheat** from the field, does he **chew** raw **wheat?** When he brings home **flax,** does he **wear** unprocessed **flax?** His wife turns the raw products into bread and clothing. Is his wife **not found** to be the one who **lights up his eyes and stands him on his feet?**

BACKGROUND

Mnemonic device – סִימָן: Because the Talmud was studied orally for many generations, mnemonic devices were necessary to remember a series of *halakhot* and the order in which they were taught.

HALAKHA

Is not a man – אֵינוֹ אָדָם: The Rema cites this teaching in the name of the *Tur*, in order to emphasize the importance of marriage (*Shulḥan Arukh*, *Even HaEzer* 1:1).

NOTES

Who lends a *sela* to a pauper, etc. – הַמַּלְוֶה סֶלַע לְעָנִי וכו׳: *Tosafot* raise an apparent contradiction between this statement and the statement in tractate *Ḥagiga* (5a) that providing money to a pauper at his time of need brings trouble for the pauper. The Ritva explains that he is praised if he lends the pauper money for food. However, if the pauper's creditors force him to sell his belongings in order to pay his debt, which is not to his benefit, it is improper to provide the pauper with money by purchasing those belongings at reduced rates. Others explain that one is criticized if he covets the pauper's property and lends him money with the aim of taking something for himself when the loan is due. The *Iyyun Ya'akov* explains homiletically that the expression: His time of need, is referring to the lender. A lender who himself has fallen on troubled times and yet does not refrain from giving the pauper a loan is praiseworthy.

About him the verse states – עָלָיו הַכָּתוּב אוֹמֵר: According to many commentaries, an earlier verse: "When you see the naked and you cover him, and you do not hide yourself from your own flesh" (Isaiah 58:7), is an important part of this proof, as it demonstrates that the context of the verse cited in the Gemara is helping the poor and taking responsibility to help one's relatives and neighbors (see *Yad Rama* and Maharsha).

Is not a man, etc. – אֵינוֹ אָדָם וכו׳: The Maharsha explains that in order to be complete, a man must participate in creation, either by raising children or by growing crops from the land.

Against him – כְּנֶגְדּוֹ: This is derived from the fact that the term *kenegdo* is superfluous, as the verse could simply have said: I will make him a helpmate. Alternatively, the Meiri explains that the word *kenegdo* itself can be interpreted to mean: Against him, i.e., opposed to him.

In what manner does a woman help a man – בַּמֶּה אִשָּׁה עוֹזַרְתּוֹ לְאָדָם: The commentaries express surprise at both this question and its answer. Was Rabbi Yosei unaware of the assistance a wife provides her husband? And what is the point of such a simple response? The Riaf explains that the question was based upon the fact that although the main purpose of marriage is in order to have children, a woman is not merely man's helpmate in this regard, and therefore the verse does not refer to this aspect of their relationship. The Meiri explains that the main thrust of the answer is that the help a man receives from his wife provides him with his basic needs so that he has time for Torah study. Consequently, her assistance is not merely practical but enables him to achieve the ultimate goal of a Jewish man.

ואמר רבי אלעזר: מאי דכתיב ״זאת הפעם עצם מעצמי ובשר מבשרי״ מלמד שבא אדם על כל בהמה וחיה ולא נתקררה דעתו עד שבא על חוה.

And Rabbi Elazar said: What is the meaning of that which is written: "This is now bone of my bones and flesh of my flesh" (Genesis 2:23)? This **teaches that Adam had intercourse**[N] **with each animal and beast** in his search for his mate, **and his mind was not at ease,** in accordance with the verse: "And for Adam, there was not found a helpmate for him" (Genesis 2:20), **until he had intercourse with Eve.**

ואמר רבי אלעזר: מאי דכתיב ״ונברכו בך כל משפחת האדמה״ אמר ליה הקדוש ברוך הוא לאברהם: שתי ברכות טובות יש לי להבריך בך: רות המואביה ונעמה העמונית. ״כל משפחות האדמה״ אפילו משפחות הדרות באדמה אין מתברכות אלא בשביל ישראל. ״כל גויי הארץ״ – אפילו ספינות הבאות מגליא לאספמיא אינן מתברכות אלא בשביל ישראל.

And Rabbi Elazar said: What is the meaning of **that which is written: "And in you shall all the families of the earth be blessed** [*nivrekhu*]" (Genesis 12:3)? **The Holy One, Blessed be He, said to Abraham: I have two good shoots**[N] **to graft** [*lehavrikh*] **onto you: Ruth the Moabite,** the ancestress of the house of David, **and Naamah the Ammonite,** whose marriage with Solomon led to the ensuing dynasty of the kings of Judea. **"All the families of the earth"** means: **Even families that live in the earth,** i.e., who have land of their own, **are blessed only due to the Jewish people.** Similarly, when the verse states: **"All the nations of the earth** shall be blessed in him" (Genesis 18:18), it indicates that **even ships that come from Galia to Hispania**[B] **are blessed only due to the Jewish people.**

ואמר רבי אלעזר: עתידים כל בעלי אומניות שיעמדו על הקרקע, שנאמר ״וירדו מאניותיהם כל תפשי משוט מלחים כל חבלי הים על הארץ יעמדו״. ואמר רבי אלעזר: אין לך אומנות פחותה מן הקרקע, שנאמר ״וירדו״. רבי אלעזר חזיא להההיא ארעא דשדי ביה כרבא לפותיא, אמר ליה: אי תשדייה לאורכיך – הפוכי בעיסקא טב מינך.

And Rabbi Elazar said: All craftsmen are destined[N] **to stand upon** and work **the land, as it is stated: "And all that handle the oar, the mariners, and all the pilots of the sea, shall come down from their ships, they shall stand upon the land"** (Ezekiel 27:29). **And Rabbi Elazar said: There is no occupation lowlier**[N] than working **the land, as it is stated: "And they shall come down,"** implying that one who works the land is of lower stature than even a sailor. The Gemara similarly relates: **Rabbi Elazar saw land that was plowed** across **its width.**[N] **He said to it:** Even **if they plow you** once more **lengthwise,** for further improvement, **conducting business**[B] **is better than** farming with **you,** as the potential profits gained by selling merchandise are far greater than those from working the land.

רב על לביני שיבלי, חזנהו דקא נייפן. אמר להו: אי נייפת איתנופי, הפוכי בעיסקא טב מינך. אמר רבא: מאה זוזי בעיסקא – כל יומא בשרא וחמרא, מאה זוזי בארעא – מילחא וחפורה. ולא עוד אלא מגניא ליה אארעא ומרמיא ליה תיגרי.

The Gemara relates a similar incident: **Rav entered between the sheaves** in a field **and saw them waving** in the wind. **He said to them: If you** want to **wave** go ahead and **wave,** but **conducting business is better than** farming with **you. Rava** similarly **said:** One who has **a hundred dinars** that are invested **in a business** is able to eat **meat and wine every day,** whereas he who has **a hundred dinars** worth **of land** eats only **salt and vegetables. And what is more,** working the land **causes him to lie on the ground**[N] at night in order to guard it, **and** it **draws quarrels upon him** with other people.

BACKGROUND

From Galia to Hispania – מגליא לאספמיא: Galia, or Gaul, is essentially modern-day France, while Hispania is Spain. Ships sailed back and forth frequently between the ports of France and Spain, especially when these two lands were Roman colonies. Commerce in the western Mediterranean serves here as an example of a matter that would seem to have no direct relevance to the Jewish people.

Conducting business – הפוכי בעיסקא: In the talmudic era most Jews still worked in agriculture, although this occupation was becoming harder, as farmers were laden with heavy tax burdens. In addition, the potential profit margin of commercial transactions was higher than anything that could be garnered from farming land in which one had invested a comparable sum of money.

NOTES

This teaches that Adam had intercourse, etc. – מלמד שבא אדם וכו׳: According to an interpretation cited by the Maharsha, this does not mean that he literally engaged in sexual intercourse with the animals but rather that he conducted an investigation in order to find a suitable creature to be his mate, without success. *Akedat Yitzḥak* explains this statement along the same lines, in greater detail.

Two good shoots, etc. – שתי ברכות טובות וכו׳: This exposition is based on the fact that the Torah uses the unusual expression *venivrekhu* to mean: They shall be blessed, as opposed to the more proper term *vehitbarkhu*. The Sages associated the word used in the Gemara with grafting [*havrakha*], as these women were grafted onto Abraham's family, i.e., they joined the Jewish people (Riaf; see Maharsha).

All craftsmen are destined, etc. – עתידים כל בעלי אומניות וכו׳: Rabbi Elazar's opinion toward working the land appears to be contradictory; previously he stated that one who does not own land is not a man, whereas here he stated that working the land is a lowly occupation. *Tosafot* explain that according to Rabbi Elazar, everyone should own land in order to grow food and build a house, but this does not mean that farming is a profitable occupation. The Maharsha interprets his comments about the future in this vein: Nowadays people seek a profession through which they can make money, but in the future they will be satisfied with little and will return to the land.

There is no occupation lowlier, etc. – אין לך אומנות פחותה וכו׳: The proof is from the phrase "They shall come down," as it is more common to describe those who go to sea as descending to the sea. Consequently, it is clear that the unusual use of descent in this verse to refer to returning to land is referring not a physical descent on the part of the sailors but rather to their social status (*Arukh LaNer*).

Land that was plowed across its width – ארעא דשדי ביה כרבא לפותיא: The Meiri cites a different version of the text, according to which a large pile of produce covered the entire width of the field. In this version Rabbi Eliezer said that even if the pile were large enough to cover the entire field lengthwise as well, farming the field would still not be a profitable enterprise.

Causes him to lie on the ground, etc. – מגניא ליה אארעא וכו׳: The Meiri explains that these are descriptions of poverty, as he lies on the ground because he cannot afford a bed, a sorry financial state that then causes constant arguments in his home (see Rashi).

אמר רב פפא: זרע ולא תזבין. אף על גב דכי הדדי נינהו – הני מברכן. זבין ולא תיזול, הני מילי – ביסתרקי. אבל גלימא – לא מיתרמיא ליה.

Rav Pappa[P] **said: Sow** your own produce **and do not buy** it. **Even though they are equal to each other** in value, **these** that you sow **will be blessed.** Conversely, **buy** your clothes **rather than weave** [*teizul*][L] them yourself. The Gemara comments: **This applies** only to **mats** [*bistarkei*],[L] **but** with regard to the **cloak** one wears, perhaps **he will not find it** precisely to his liking, and therefore he should make his own cloak, which fits his measurements.

טום ולא תשפיץ, שפוץ ולא תיבני, שכל העוסק בבנין מתמסכן. קפוץ זבין ארעא, מתון נסיב איתתא, נחית דרגא נסיב איתתא, סק דרגא בחר שושבינא.

Rav Pappa further advised: If there is a hole in your house, **close** it **up and do not** enlarge it and then **plaster** it,[N] or at least **plaster** it **and do not** knock it down and **build** it again. **As, whoever engages in construction becomes poor. Hurry** to **buy land** so that you do not lose the opportunity. Be **patient and marry a woman** who is suitable for you. **Descend a level** to **marry a woman** of lower social status, and **ascend a level** to **choose a friend** [*shushevina*].[L]

אמר רבי אלעזר בר אבינא: אין פורענות באה לעולם אלא בשביל ישראל, שנאמר "הכרתי גוים נשמו פנותם החרבתי חוצותם" וכתיב "אמרתי אך תיראי אותי תקחי מוסר".

Rabbi Elazar bar Avina said: Calamity befalls the world only[N] **due to** the sins of **the Jewish people, as it is stated: "I have cut off nations, their corners are desolate; I have made their streets waste"** (Zephaniah 3:6), **and it is written: "I said: Surely you will fear Me, you will receive correction"** (Zephaniah 3:7). This indicates that other nations were punished so that the Jewish people would mend their ways.

רב הוה מיפטר מרבי חייא, אמר ליה: רחמנא ליצלך ממידי דקשה ממותא. ומי איכא מידי דקשה ממותא? נפק, דק ואשכח "ומוצא אני מר ממות את האשה" וגו'. רב הוה קא מצערא ליה דביתהו, כי אמר לה "עבידי לי טלופחי" עבדא ליה חימצי, "חימצי" – עבדא ליה טלופחי.

The Gemara cites more statements with regard to wives. When **Rav**[P] **was taking leave of** his uncle and teacher, **Rabbi Ḥiyya,** upon his return from Eretz Yisrael to Babylonia, Rabbi Ḥiyya **said to him: May the Merciful One save you from something that is worse than death.** Rav was perplexed: **Is there anything that is worse than death?**[N] **He went, examined** the sources, **and found** the following verse: **"And I find more bitter than death the woman, etc."** (Ecclesiastes 7:26). Rabbi Ḥiyya was hinting at this verse, and indeed, **Rav's wife would** constantly **aggravate him. When he would say to her: Prepare me lentils, she would prepare him peas;** if he asked her for **peas, she would prepare him lentils.**

כי גדל חייא בריה, אפיך לה. אמר ליה: איעליא לך אמך! אמר ליה: אנא הוא דקא אפיכנא לה. אמר ליה: היינו דקא אמרי אינשי: דנפיק מינך – טעמא מלפך. את לא תעביד הכי, שנאמר "למדו לשונם דבר שקר העוה" וגו'.

When Ḥiyya, his son, grew up, he would reverse the requests Rav asked him to convey **to her,** so that Rav would get what he wanted. Rav **said to** his son Ḥiyya: **Your mother has improved** now that **you** convey my requests. **He said to** Rav: **It is I who reverse** your request **to her.** Rav **said to him: This is** an example of the well-known adage **that people say:** He **who comes from you shall teach you wisdom;** I should have thought of that idea myself. **You,** however, **should not do so,**[N] i.e., reverse my request, **as it is stated: "They have taught their tongue to speak lies, they** weary themselves to **commit iniquity, etc."** (Jeremiah 9:4). If you attribute such a request to me, you will have uttered a falsehood.

LANGUAGE

Weave [*teizul*] – **תיזול**: The versions of Gemara cited by the *ge'onim* and Rabbeinu Ḥananel read *teidul* or *teidvil*. In Syriac this word means weaving, which ties in well with the idea that one should buy an item ready-made.

Mats [*bistarkei*] – **ביסתרקי**: Apparently a loanword from the Middle Iranian bistarak, meaning bedding, mattress, or cover.

Friend [*shushevina*] – **שושבינא**: This word is originally Akkadian, from where it was adapted into both Aramaic and Hebrew. Its primary meaning is the one who accompanies the groom to the wedding canopy and helps with some of the technical arrangements of the wedding, and so forth. Its meaning was broadened to a general term for a close friend.

NOTES

Close it up and do not enlarge it and plaster it – **טום ולא תשפיץ**: According to the Meiri this is an injunction to fix things quickly before they get worse, as it is easier to close up a hole than to plaster an entire wall. Similarly, he should replaster the wall in order to ensure that he will not have to build it again from scratch.

Calamity befalls…only, etc. – **אין פורענות באה...אלא וכו'**: This complements the previous teaching: Just as the fate of the world depends on the Jewish people with regard to blessing, the same applies with regard to misfortune. Consequently, the Jewish people should know that their own fate as well as that of other nations lies in their hands (see Meiri and *Iyyun Ya'akov*).

Is there anything that is worse than death – **ומי איכא מידי דקשה ממותא**: Elsewhere the Sages list numerous problems that are worse than death, including captivity and famine. The *Iyyun Ya'akov* explains that it was due to these different possibilities that Rav sought to discover the precise nature of his mentor's blessing. Since he realized that Rabbi Ḥiyya had presumably also been giving him advice along with his blessing, he concluded that Rabbi Ḥiyya was referring to a bad wife. Furthermore, knowing that Rabbi Ḥiyya's own wife caused him to suffer, Rav realized that this must have been what he meant.

You should not do so – **את לא תעביד הכי**: Admittedly, it is permitted to depart from the truth for the sake of peace, but since in this case there is another way of achieving the same result, it is better not to grow accustomed to telling lies (Meiri; Rabbi Avraham min HaHar).

PERSONALITIES

Rav Pappa – **רב פפא**: Rav Pappa, from the fifth generation of Babylonian *amora'im*, was a student of both Abaye and Rava in Pumbedita. After Rava's death Rav Pappa established an academy in Neresh, where he was joined by his close friend, Rav Huna, son of Rav Yehoshua, who was appointed chief lecturer. Many of Rava's students came to study under Rav Pappa, who had more than two hundred students attending his lectures.

Rav Pappa's father was a wealthy merchant and supported him throughout many years of Talmud study. Rav Pappa became a wealthy businessman in his own right and a successful brewer of date beer. He also prospered in other business ventures. The Talmud records that he engaged in trade with both Jews and gentiles and had a reputation for fairness and generosity in his business dealings. Rav Huna became his partner in many such undertakings and became wealthy as well.

Rav Pappa had great respect for the Sages, and upon entering a city he would immediately call upon the rabbinic head of the community. Once, Rav Pappa felt that he had spoken inappropriately about one of the Sages, and he took upon himself a personal fast as penance for his act. He was reluctant to offer final rulings in various areas of *halakha*, and he often chose to be stringent in accordance with both opinions in the Talmud rather than rule in accordance with a single opinion.

Rav Pappa was blessed with ten sons, all of whom were Torah scholars. Traditionally, the names of the ten sons of Rav Pappa are recited as part of the ceremony at the completion of the study of a tractate. While the source of this tradition is unclear and the identities of the sons are uncertain as well, the Rema suggests that it commemorates the celebrations made by Rav Pappa with his sons upon completing a course of study.

Rav – **רב**: Rav, whose full name was Rabbi Abba ben Ayvu, was the first, and perhaps the greatest, of the Babylonian *amora'im*. Known as Abba Arikha because of his great height, Rav established the academy in Sura which lasted eight hundred years, through the period of the *ge'onim*. In addition to the visiting students who attended the academy only during the *kalla* months of Adar and Elul, the Gemara reports that twelve hundred full-time students studied in the academy throughout the year.

In his youth, Rav traveled to Eretz Yisrael with his uncle, Rabbi Ḥiyya, where he studied under Rabbi Yehuda HaNasi, the editor of the Mishna. He traveled back and forth between Israel and Babylonia until he settled in Babylonia in the year 219 CE. Rav's greatness is apparent not only in the large number of *amora'im* who were his students and who quote him throughout the Talmud, but also by the fact that in addition to his status as the first *amora*, he is recognized as the last of the *tanna'im* and consequently was permitted to disagree with tannaitic rulings.

Rav's teachings are found throughout both the Jerusalem and the Babylonian Talmuds. Among his many rulings are several that concern issues of marriage, such as his ruling that a man should not marry a woman without first meeting her, and that underage girls should not be married until they are old enough to state whom they want to marry. His rulings in the area of ritual *halakha* were invariably accepted, although the rulings of his colleague Shmuel were accepted in criminal and financial matters. Rav's son, Rabbi Ḥiyya, followed in his father's footsteps and became a great scholar; his other son, Ayvu, was a merchant.

רַבִּי חִיָּיא הֲוָה קָא מְצַעֲרָא לֵיהּ דְּבֵיתְהוּ. כִּי הֲוָה מַשְׁכַּח מִידֵּי – צָיֵיר לֵיהּ בְּסוּדָרֵיהּ, וּמַיְיתֵי נִיהֲלָהּ. אֲמַר לֵיהּ רַב: וְהָא קָא מְצַעֲרָא לֵיהּ לְמָר! אָמַר לֵיהּ: דַּיֵּינוּ שֶׁמְּגַדְּלוֹת בָּנֵינוּ, וּמַצִּילוֹת אוֹתָנוּ

The Gemara relates a similar story. **Rabbi Ḥiyya's wife would** constantly **aggravate him.** Nevertheless, **when he would find something** she would appreciate, **he would wrap it in his shawl and bring it to her. Rav said to him: Doesn't she** constantly **aggravate you?** Why do you bring her things? Rabbi Ḥiyya **said to him: It is enough for us** that our wives **raise our children and save us**

Perek **VI**
Daf **63** Amud **b**

NOTES

His iniquities crumble [*mitpakekin*] – עֲוֹנוֹתָיו מִתְפַּקְקִין: According to Rashi, *mitpakekin* means sealed. Riaf explains that Rashi means not that his sins are entirely forgiven, but that they are sealed up, pending his behavior after marriage. The *Arukh*, however, understands *mitpakekin* as meaning to become loosened.

Matza or *motze* – מָצָא אוֹ מוֹצֵא: Some commentaries explain that in addition to alluding to the two verses this phrase is a question on its own: *Matza* means a good find, while *motze* refers not to someone who finds an item, but to the author of the book of Ecclesiastes, King Solomon, who found, i.e., realized and publicized, that a bad wife is more bitter than death. The *Arukh LaNer* explains the fact that the word *matza* is in past tense indicates an unusual occurrence, whereas *motze* is the more common usage.

Her rival is at her side – צָרְתָהּ בְּצִדָּהּ: The Meiri explains that he should threaten to marry another woman.

A day of heavy rain – יוֹם סַגְרִיר: Just as one cannot escape the continual dripping in a leaky house by escaping outside on a rainy day, this husband suffers from a continuous downpour of abuse from which he cannot escape (Maharsha).

מִן הַחֵטְא. מַקְרֵי לֵיהּ רַב יְהוּדָה לְרַב יִצְחָק בְּרֵיהּ: "וּמוֹצֶא אֲנִי מַר מִמָּוֶת אֶת הָאִשָּׁה". אָמַר לֵיהּ: כְּגוֹן מַאן? כְּגוֹן אִמְּךָ.

from sin. We should therefore show our gratitude to them. The Gemara cites a related incident: **Rav Yehuda** was **teaching** Torah **to Rav Yitzḥak, his son,** and they encountered the verse: **"And I find more bitter than death the woman"** (Ecclesiastes 7:26). His son **said to him: For example, whom?** His father replied: **For example, your mother.**

וְהָא מַתְנֵי לֵיהּ רַב יְהוּדָה לְרַב יִצְחָק בְּרֵיהּ: אֵין אָדָם מוֹצֵא קוֹרַת רוּחַ אֶלָּא מֵאִשְׁתּוֹ רִאשׁוֹנָה, שֶׁנֶּאֱמַר "יְהִי מְקוֹרְךָ בָרוּךְ וּשְׂמַח מֵאֵשֶׁת נְעוּרֶיךָ". וְאָמַר לֵיהּ: כְּגוֹן מַאן? כְּגוֹן אִמְּךָ. מַתְקִיף תְּקִיפָא, וְעַבּוּרֵי מִיעַבְּרָא בְּמִלָּה.

The Gemara asks: **Didn't Rav Yehuda teach Rav Yitzḥak, his son,** the following *baraita*: **A man finds peace of mind only with his first wife, as it is stated: "Let your fountain be blessed, and have joy from the wife of your youth"** (Proverbs 5:18), **and** his son **said to him: For example, whom,** and his father responded in this case as well: **For example, your mother.** This indicates that Rav Yehuda did find peace of mind with his wife. The Gemara answers: She was aggressive and **forceful, but** she was **easily appeased.**

הֵיכִי דָּמֵי אִשָּׁה רָעָה? אֲמַר אַבַּיֵּי: מְקַשְּׁטָא לֵיהּ תַּכָּא, וּמְקַשְּׁטָא לֵיהּ פּוּמָא. רָבָא אֲמַר: מְקַשְּׁטָא לֵיהּ תַּכָּא, וּמְהַדְרָא לֵיהּ גַּבָּא.

The Gemara asks: **What are the circumstances** when a woman is considered **a bad wife? Abaye said: She arranges a table for him and arranges** her **mouth for him** at the same time. In other words, although she prepares food for him, she verbally abuses him while he eats. **Rava said: She arranges a table for him and** then **turns** her **back to him,** displaying her lack of interest in his company.

אָמַר רַבִּי חָמָא בַּר חֲנִינָא: כֵּיוָן שֶׁנָּשָׂא אָדָם אִשָּׁה – עֲוֹנוֹתָיו מִתְפַּקְקִין, שֶׁנֶּאֱמַר "מָצָא אִשָּׁה מָצָא טוֹב וַיָּפֶק רָצוֹן מֵה'". בְּמַעַרְבָא, כִּי נָסֵיב אֱינָשׁ אִיתְּתָא אָמְרִי לֵיהּ הָכִי: מָצָא אוֹ מוֹצֵא? מָצָא – דִּכְתִיב "מָצָא אִשָּׁה מָצָא טוֹב", "מוֹצֵא" – דִּכְתִיב "וּמוֹצֶא אֲנִי מַר מִמָּוֶת אֶת הָאִשָּׁה".

Rabbi Ḥama bar Ḥanina said: Once a man marries a woman his iniquities crumble [*mitpakekin*],[N] **as it is stated: "Whoever finds a wife finds good, and obtains** [*veyafek*] **favor of the Lord"** (Proverbs 18:22). **In the West,** i.e., Eretz Yisrael, **when a man married a woman they would say to him as follows: *Matza* or *motze*?**[N] In other words, they would ask the groom if the appropriate passage for his wife is that verse, which begins with the word ***matza*****, as it is written: Whoever finds** [*matza*] **a wife finds good,** or whether the more appropriate verse is the one beginning with the word ***motze*****, as it is written: "And I find** [*motze*] **more bitter than death the woman"** (Ecclesiastes 7:26).

אָמַר רָבָא: אִשָּׁה רָעָה מִצְוָה לְגָרְשָׁהּ, דִּכְתִיב "גָּרֵשׁ לֵץ וְיֵצֵא מָדוֹן וְיִשְׁבֹּת דִּין וְקָלוֹן". וְאָמַר רָבָא: אִשָּׁה רָעָה וּכְתוּבָּתָהּ מְרוּבָּה – צָרָתָהּ בְּצִדָּהּ, דְּאָמְרִי אֱינָשֵׁי: בַּחֲבֶרְתָּהּ וְלֹא בְּסִילְתָּא. וְאָמַר רָבָא: קָשָׁה אִשָּׁה רָעָה כְּיוֹם סַגְרִיר, שֶׁנֶּאֱמַר "דֶּלֶף טוֹרֵד בְּיוֹם סַגְרִיר וְאֵשֶׁת מִדְיָנִים נִשְׁתָּוָה".

Rava said: It is a mitzva to divorce a bad wife, as it is written: "Cast out the scorner and contention will depart; strife and shame will cease" (Proverbs 22:10). **And Rava said: A bad wife whose marriage contract** settlement **is** too **large** for her husband to pay in the event of a divorce, **her rival** wife **is at her side.**[N] In other words, the only way for him to improve matters is to take another wife. **As people say** in the well-known adage: The way to trouble a woman is **with her peer and not with a thorn. And Rava said: A bad wife is as troublesome as a day of heavy rain,**[N] **as it is stated: "A continual dropping on a very rainy day and a contentious woman are alike"** (Proverbs 27:15).

וְאָמַר רָבָא: בֹּא וּרְאֵה כַּמָּה טוֹבָה אִשָּׁה טוֹבָה – וְכַמָּה רָעָה אִשָּׁה רָעָה. כַּמָּה טוֹבָה אִשָּׁה טוֹבָה – דִּכְתִיב ״מָצָא אִשָּׁה מָצָא טוֹב״. אִי בְּגַוָּהּ מִשְׁתָּעֵי קְרָא – כַּמָּה טוֹבָה אִשָּׁה טוֹבָה שֶׁהַכָּתוּב מְשַׁבְּחָהּ, אִי בַּתּוֹרָה מִשְׁתָּעֵי קְרָא – כַּמָּה טוֹבָה אִשָּׁה טוֹבָה שֶׁהַתּוֹרָה נִמְשְׁלָה בָּהּ. כַּמָּה רָעָה אִשָּׁה רָעָה – דִּכְתִיב ״וּמוֹצֶא אֲנִי מַר מִמָּוֶת אֶת הָאִשָּׁה״. אִי בְּגַוָּהּ מִשְׁתָּעֵי קְרָא – כַּמָּה רָעָה אִשָּׁה רָעָה שֶׁהַכָּתוּב מְגַנָּהּ, אִי בְּגֵיהִנָּם מִשְׁתָּעֵי קְרָא – כַּמָּה רָעָה אִשָּׁה רָעָה, שֶׁגֵּיהִנָּם נִמְשְׁלָה בָּהּ.

And Rava said: Come and see how good a good wife is and how bad a bad wife is. How good is a good wife? As it is written: Whoever finds a wife finds good. If the verse speaks of her, a wife, this demonstrates **how good a good wife is, as the Bible praises her. If the verse speaks** metaphorically **of the Torah,** it nevertheless indicates **how good a good wife is, as the Torah is compared to her.** Conversely, **how bad is a bad wife? As it is written: "And I find more bitter than death the woman." If the verse speaks of her,** this demonstrates **how bad a bad wife is, as the Bible condemns her. If the verse speaks** metaphorically **of Gehenna,** it still demonstrates **how bad a bad wife is, as Gehenna is compared to her.**

״הִנְנִי מֵבִיא רָעָה אֲשֶׁר לֹא יוּכְלוּ לָצֵאת מִמֶּנָּה״. אָמַר רַב נַחְמָן אָמַר רַבָּה בַּר אֲבוּהּ: זוֹ אִשָּׁה רָעָה וּכְתוּבָּתָהּ מְרוּבָּה. ״נְתָנַנִי ה׳ בִּידֵי לֹא אוּכַל קוּם״ אָמַר רַב חִסְדָּא אָמַר מַר עוּקְבָא בַּר חִיָּיא: זוֹ אִשָּׁה רָעָה וּכְתוּבָּתָהּ מְרוּבָּה. בְּמַעְרְבָא אָמְרוּ: זֶה שֶׁמְּזוֹנוֹתָיו תְּלוּיִן בְּכַסְפּוֹ.

The Gemara cites further statements on the same issue. The verse states: **"Behold, I will bring evil upon them, which they shall not be able to escape"** (Jeremiah 11:11). **Rav Naḥman said** that **Rabba bar Avuh said: This is a bad wife whose marriage contract is large.** Similarly, with regard to the verse: **"The Lord has given me into the hands of those against whom I cannot stand"** (Lamentations 1:14), **Rav Ḥisda said** that **Mar Ukva bar Ḥiyya said: This is a bad wife whose marriage contract is large. In the West,** Eretz Yisrael, **they said this** verse is referring to one **whose food is dependent on his money.**[N] He is forced to purchase his food with cash, as he does not possess land of his own.

״בָּנֶיךָ וּבְנוֹתֶיךָ נְתוּנִים לְעַם אַחֵר״ אָמַר רַב חָנָן בַּר רָבָא אָמַר רַב: זוֹ אֵשֶׁת הָאָב. ״בְּגוֹי נָבָל אַכְעִיסֵם״ אָמַר רַב חָנָן בַּר רָבָא אָמַר רַב: זוֹ אִשָּׁה רָעָה וּכְתוּבָּתָהּ מְרוּבָּה. רַבִּי אֱלִיעֶזֶר אוֹמֵר: אֵלּוּ הַמִּינִים. וְכֵן הוּא אוֹמֵר ״אָמַר נָבָל בְּלִבּוֹ אֵין אֱלֹהִים״ וגו׳.

With regard to the verse: **"Your sons and your daughters shall be given to another people"** (Deuteronomy 28:32), **Rav Ḥanan bar Rava said** that **Rav said: This is** a reference to the children's **father's wife,** their stepmother. With regard to the verse: **"I will provoke them with a vile nation"** (Deuteronomy 32:21), **Rav Ḥanan bar Rava said** that **Rav said: This is a bad wife whose marriage contract is large. Rabbi Eliezer says** that **these are apostates, and so too** the verse **states: "The vile man has said in his heart: There is no God,** they have dealt corruptly" (Psalms 14:1), which proves that an apostate is called vile.

בְּמַתְנִיתָא תָּנָא: אֵלּוּ אַנְשֵׁי בַּרְבַּרְיָא וְאַנְשֵׁי מָרְטְנַאי, שֶׁמְּהַלְּכִין עֲרוּמִים בַּשּׁוּק. שֶׁאֵין לְךָ מְשׁוּקָּץ וּמְתוֹעָב לִפְנֵי הַמָּקוֹם יוֹתֵר מִמִּי שֶׁמְּהַלֵּךְ בַּשּׁוּק עָרוֹם. רַבִּי יוֹחָנָן אָמַר: אֵלּוּ חַבָּרִים. אָמְרוּ לֵיהּ לְרַ׳ יוֹחָנָן: אָתוּ חַבָּרֵי לְבָבֶל, שְׁגָא נָפַל. אָמְרוּ לֵיהּ: מְקַבְּלֵי שׁוּחֲדָא. תָּרֵיץ יָתֵיב.

It was taught in a *baraita* with regard to the verse: "I will provoke them with a vile nation," that **these are the inhabitants of Barbarya and the inhabitants of Martenai,**[B] **who walk naked in the marketplace, as none is more despised and abominable before the Omnipresent than one who walks naked in the marketplace. Rabbi Yoḥanan said: These are the *Ḥabbarim*,**[L] a sect of Persian priests. The Gemara relates: When **they said to Rabbi Yoḥanan:** The ***Ḥabbarim* have come to Babylonia,**[B] **he shuddered and fell** of his chair, out of concern for the Jews living there. **They said to him:** There is a way to deal with their persecution, as **they accept bribes.** Upon hearing that not all was lost, **he straightened himself** and **sat** in his place once again.

NOTES

Whose food is dependent on his money [*kaspo*] – שֶׁמְּזוֹנוֹתָיו תְּלוּיִן בְּכַסְפּוֹ: The version of the text cited by the Meiri reads: Whose food is dependent on his palm [*kappo*]. In other words, although manual labor is laudable, if it is one's only source of income, he will not earn a comfortable living.

LANGUAGE

Ḥabbarim – חַבָּרִים: This designation for Zoroastrian priests comes from the term "*ḥover ḥaver*" (Deuteronomy 18:11), referring to acts of sorcery. It implies that these priests were seen as involved in various magic rituals.

BACKGROUND

Barbarya and Martenai – בַּרְבַּרְיָא וּמָרְטְנַאי: Barbarya is a land in northern Africa, called Βαρβαρία in Greek, meaning foreign place. Their language sounded to the Greeks as though they were saying *barbarbar*, and consequently, the Greeks considered them to be uncivilized and primitive. The term has been used in various forms through the generations and in different languages, and it is still used today as the name for the local tribe, the Berbers as well as in the term barbarian, referring to uncivilized people.

Martenai is a version of the Roman province Mauritania, also in northern Africa, roughly corresponding to modern-day Morocco.

The Gemara is apparently referring to members of tribes from those two areas who were unaccustomed to wearing clothing, or who wore merely loincloths.

The *Ḥabbarim* have come to Babylonia – אָתוּ חַבָּרֵי לְבָבֶל: The *Ḥabbarim*, also called the *Amgoshim* in the Talmud, were priests of the Persian religion, Zoroastrianism. While the Parthians controlled Persia and Babylonia the *Ḥabbarim* did not enjoy important status, but at the beginning of the period of the *amora'im* the Sassanid dynasty rose to power, and as devout adherents to their religion they gave the *Ḥabbarim* great control. Apparently, it was the *Ḥabbarim* who initiated harsh decrees against the Jews. Rabbi Yoḥanan was therefore shocked and dismayed when he heard that they had reached Babylonia, then the largest Jewish center in the Persian Empire, with the new rulers. Nevertheless, it seems that this tribe of priests was corrupt and foolish, and through bribery and negotiations the Jews were able to withstand their decrees.

גָּזְרוּ עַל שְׁלֹשָׁה מִפְּנֵי שְׁלֹשָׁה; גָּזְרוּ עַל הַבָּשָׂר – מִפְּנֵי הַמַּתָּנוֹת, גָּזְרוּ עַל הַמֶּרְחֲצָאוֹת – מִפְּנֵי הַטְּבִילָה,

Apropos the *Ḥabbarim*, the Gemara cites the following statement of the Sages: The *Ḥabbarim* were able to **issue decrees against** the Jewish people with regard to **three** matters,[NB] **due to three** transgressions on the part of the Jewish people. **They decreed against meat,** i.e., they banned ritual slaughter, **due to** the failure of the Jewish people to give the priests **the gifts** of the foreleg, the jaw, and the maw. **They decreed against** Jews bathing in **bathhouses, due to** their neglect of ritual **immersion.**

קָא מְחַטְּטֵי שָׁכְבֵי – מִפְּנֵי שֶׁשְּׂמֵחִים בְּיוֹם אֵידָם, שֶׁנֶּאֱמַר ״וְהָיְתָה יַד ה׳ בָּכֶם וּבַאֲבוֹתֵיכֶם״, אֲמַר רַבָּה בַּר שְׁמוּאֵל: זוֹ חֲטוּטֵי שָׁכְבֵי, דְּאָמַר מָר: בַּעֲוֹן חַיִּים – מֵתִים מִתְחַטְּטִין.

Third, **they exhumed the dead** from their graves **because** the Jews **rejoice on** the **holidays** of the gentiles,[N] **as it is stated: "Then shall the hand of the Lord be against you and against your fathers"** (I Samuel 12:15). **Rabba bar Shmuel said: This** verse is referring to **exhuming the dead,** which upsets both the living and the dead, **as the Master said:** Due **to the iniquity of the living, the dead are exhumed.**

אֲמַר לֵיהּ רָבָא לְרַבָּה בַּר מָארִי: כְּתִיב ״לֹא יֵאָסְפוּ וְלֹא יִקָּבֵרוּ לְדוֹמֶן עַל פְּנֵי הָאֲדָמָה יִהְיוּ״ וּכְתִיב ״וְנִבְחַר מָוֶת מֵחַיִּים״. אֲמַר לֵיהּ: נִבְחַר מָוֶת לָרְשָׁעִים, שֶׁלֹּא יִחְיוּ בָּעוֹלָם הַזֶּה וְיֶחֶטְאוּ וְיִפְּלוּ בַּגֵּיהִנָּם.

Rava said to Rabba bar Mari: It is written: "They shall not be gathered nor buried; they shall be for dung upon the face of the earth" (Jeremiah 8:2), **and it is written: "And death shall be chosen rather than life"** (Jeremiah 8:3). If death will be so indecent that their bodies will not even be buried, why would people choose death over life? Rabba bar Mari **said to him:** The latter verse does not refer to the previously described state of affairs, but rather it means: **Death is preferable for the wicked,** as it is better **that they not live in this world and sin and** consequently **descend into Gehenna.**

כָּתוּב בְּסֵפֶר בֶּן סִירָא: ״אִשָּׁה טוֹבָה – מַתָּנָה טוֹבָה לְבַעְלָהּ״. וּכְתִיב ״טוֹבָה בְּחֵיק יְרֵא אֱלֹהִים תִּנָּתֵן. אִשָּׁה רָעָה – צָרַעַת לְבַעְלָהּ״. מַאי תַּקַּנְתֵּיהּ – יְגָרְשֶׁנָּה וְיִתְרַפֵּא מִצָּרַעְתּוֹ. ״אִשָּׁה יָפָה אַשְׁרֵי בַּעְלָהּ, מִסְפַּר יָמָיו כִּפְלַיִם״.

The Gemara cites more statements concerning women. **It is written in the book of Ben Sira:[B] A good wife is a good gift for her husband. And it is written: A good one will be placed in the bosom of a God-fearing man; a bad wife is a plague to her husband.[N] What is his remedy? He should divorce her and he will be cured of his plague. A beautiful wife, happy is her husband; the number of his days are doubled.** His pleasure in her beauty makes him feel as though he has lived twice as long.

״הַעְלֵם עֵינֶיךָ מֵאֵשֶׁת חֵן פֶּן תִּלָּכֵד בִּמְצוּדָתָהּ. אַל תֵּט אֵצֶל בַּעְלָהּ לִמְסוֹךְ עִמּוֹ יַיִן וְשֵׁכָר, כִּי בְּתוֹאַר אִשָּׁה יָפָה רַבִּים הוּשְׁחֲתוּ, וַעֲצוּמִים כָּל הֲרוּגֶיהָ״. ״רַבִּים הָיוּ פִּצְעֵי רוֹכֵל הַמַּרְגִּילִים לִדְבַר עֶרְוָה, כְּנִיצוֹץ מַבְעִיר גַּחֶלֶת, כִּכְלוּב מָלֵא עוֹף כֵּן בָּתֵּיהֶם מְלֵאִים מִרְמָה״,

Turn your eyes from a graceful woman who is married to another man, **lest you be caught in her trap. Do not turn to her husband to mix wine and strong drink with him,** which can lead to temptation. **For on** account of **the countenance of a beautiful woman many have been destroyed, and her slain is a mighty host.** Furthermore, **many have been the wounded peddlers.** This is referring to men who travel from place to place to sell women's jewelry. Their frequent dealings with women lead their husbands to harm the peddlers. **Those who accustom** themselves **to licentious matters are like a spark that ignites a coal. As a cage is full of birds, so are their houses full of deceit.**

NOTES

Issue decrees against the Jewish people with regard to three matters – **גָּזְרוּ עַל שְׁלֹשָׁה**: Some commentaries maintain that information about the decrees was included in the report delivered to Rabbi Yoḥanan, who proceeded to explain the reason for each decree. The Maharsha asks how it was possible that Babylonian Jews committed these transgressions. He explains that in the case of the priestly gifts, they would take on a gentile partner in order to be exempt, as one is exempt from giving the gifts to a priest if the animal was owned jointly by a Jew and a gentile. Furthermore, they actually performed ritual immersion, just not in precise accordance with halakhic requirements. Finally, they rejoiced on the gentiles' holidays on the pretext that the gentiles in their vicinity were not really idol worshippers.

Because the Jews rejoice on the holidays of the gentiles – **מִפְּנֵי שֶׁשְּׂמֵחִים בְּיוֹם אֵידָם**: The Maharsha, the Maharshal, and other commentaries attempt to explain how this punishment fits the crime. The Meiri explains that idols are considered dead, and therefore the Jews were punished for celebrating a festival of the dead by having their own deceased relatives mistreated.

A plague to her husband – **צָרַעַת לְבַעְלָהּ**: The Maharsha explains that as a man's wife is considered like his own flesh, a bad wife is like a plague on his own body. The *Arukh LaNer* suggests that this is a hint that just as a plague is a personal affliction that distances one from others, the same is true of a bad wife.

BACKGROUND

Issue decrees against the Jewish people with regard to three matters – **גָּזְרוּ עַל שְׁלֹשָׁה**: It is possible that the decrees mentioned here are linked to the beliefs of the *Ḥabbarim*, which included a complex set of laws concerning ritual purity. According to this cult, land possesses special sanctity; therefore, in addition to not burying their dead, they made every effort to remove corpses from their places of burial. Perhaps the decree barring Jews from bathhouses was due to the fact that the *Ḥabbarim* considered the Jews impure. Furthermore, it is reasonable to suggest that the ban against ritual slaughter was also related to these laws.

However, it is also possible that these decrees were promulgated in Eretz Yisrael as well, which would indicate that they were not promulgated by the *Ḥabbarim*, but were rather part of a general campaign to suppress Judaism.

The book of Ben Sira – **סֵפֶר בֶּן סִירָא**: The book of *Ben Sira*, also called the Wisdom of Sira and Ecclesiasticus, was one of the first works composed after the closing of the biblical canon. It was written before the Hasmonean period by Shimon ben Yehoshua ben Sira, a resident of Jerusalem and a younger contemporary of Shimon HaTzaddik. The book was widely available and very popular. The author's grandson, who lived in Alexandria, translated it into Greek in 132 BCE, making it available to those who could not read the original Hebrew.

In the Septuagint, and consequently in many other translations, Ecclesiasticus is one of the books of the Bible. The Sages considered it apocryphal and even criticized those who read it, both because its council is uneven in value and due to the fact that people confused it with the *Alphabet of Sira*, a book of folk wisdom of dubious worth. In any case, the Sages quotes the book of Ben Sira on many occasions, and sometimes even treated it as one of the sacred writings. They certainly did not refrain from citing its good advice in their sermons, or from making use of its wisdom.

For centuries, the book was known only through translations, but recent discoveries on Masada, among other places, have unearthed large portions of the work in Hebrew. As it was not a sacred book, copyists apparently allowed themselves certain liberties, which accounts for the different versions of the text. Moreover, it seems that the Sages of the Talmud were able to cite it from memory.

״אַל תֵּצַר צָרַת מָחָר כִּי לֹא תֵדַע מַה יֵּלֶד יוֹם, שֶׁמָּא מָחָר בָּא וְאֵינֶנּוּ, נִמְצָא מִצְטַעֵר עַל הָעוֹלָם שֶׁאֵין שֶׁלּוֹ״. ״מְנַע רַבִּים מִתּוֹךְ בֵּיתְךָ, וְלֹא הַכֹּל תָּבִיא בֵּיתֶךָ. רַבִּים יִהְיוּ דּוֹרְשֵׁי שְׁלוֹמֶךָ, גַּלֵּה סוֹד לְאֶחָד מֵאֶלֶף״.

The Gemara quotes additional statements from the book of Ben Sira: **Do not suffer from tomorrow's trouble,** that is, do not worry about problems that might arise in the future, **as you do not know what a day will bring. Perhaps** when **tomorrow comes,** the individual who was so worried will **not** be among the living, and **he was consequently upset over a world that is not his. Prevent a crowd from inside your house,** do not let many people enter, **and do not** even **bring all** your friends into **your house.** Make sure, however, that a **crowd seeks your welfare,** and that you have many allies. **Reveal a secret to** only **one in a thousand,** since most people are unable to keep a secret.

אָמַר רַבִּי אַסִי: אֵין בֶּן דָּוִד בָּא עַד שֶׁיִּכְלוּ כָּל הַנְּשָׁמוֹת שֶׁבַּגּוּף שֶׁנֶּאֱמַר ״כִּי רוּחַ מִלְּפָנַי יַעֲטוֹף וּנְשָׁמוֹת אֲנִי עָשִׂיתִי״. תַּנְיָא, רַבִּי אֱלִיעֶזֶר אוֹמֵר: כָּל מִי שֶׁאֵין עוֹסֵק בִּפְרִיָּה וּרְבִיָּה – כְּאִילּוּ שׁוֹפֵךְ דָּמִים שֶׁנֶּאֱמַר ״שׁוֹפֵךְ דַּם הָאָדָם בָּאָדָם דָּמוֹ יִשָּׁפֵךְ״ וּכְתִיב בַּתְרֵיהּ ״וְאַתֶּם פְּרוּ וּרְבוּ״.

Rabbi Asi said: The Messiah, **son of David, will not come until all the souls of the body**[N] **have been finished,** i.e., until all souls that are destined to inhabit physical bodies will do so. **As it is stated: "For the spirit that enwraps itself is from Me, and the souls that I have made"** (Isaiah 57:16). **It is taught** in a *baraita* that **Rabbi Eliezer says: Anyone who does not engage in** the mitzva to be **fruitful and multiply** is considered **as though he sheds blood, as it is stated: "Whoever sheds the blood of man, by man shall his blood be shed"** (Genesis 9:6), **and it is written** immediately **afterward: "And you, be fruitful and multiply"** (Genesis 9:7).

רַבִּי יַעֲקֹב אוֹמֵר: כְּאִילּוּ מְמַעֵט הַדְּמוּת, שֶׁנֶּאֱמַר ״כִּי בְּצֶלֶם אֱלֹהִים עָשָׂה אֶת הָאָדָם״ וּכְתִיב בַּתְרֵיהּ ״וְאַתֶּם פְּרוּ״ וגו׳. בֶּן עַזַּאי אוֹמֵר: כְּאִילּוּ שׁוֹפֵךְ דָּמִים, וּמְמַעֵט הַדְּמוּת, שֶׁנֶּאֱמַר ״וְאַתֶּם פְּרוּ וּרְבוּ״.

Rabbi Ya'akov says: It is as though he diminishes the Divine **Image, as it is stated: "For in the image of God He made man"** (Genesis 9:6), **and it is written** immediately **afterward: "And you, be fruitful** and multiply" (Genesis 9:7). **Ben Azzai says:** It is as **though he sheds blood and** also **diminishes the Divine Image,**[H] **as it is stated: "And you, be fruitful and multiply,"** after the verse that alludes to both shedding blood and the Divine Image.

אָמְרוּ לוֹ לְבֶן עַזַּאי: יֵשׁ נָאֶה דּוֹרֵשׁ וְנָאֶה מְקַיֵּים, נָאֶה מְקַיֵּים וְאֵין נָאֶה דּוֹרֵשׁ. וְאַתָּה – נָאֶה דּוֹרֵשׁ וְאֵין נָאֶה מְקַיֵּים! אָמַר לָהֶן בֶּן עַזַּאי: וּמָה אֶעֱשֶׂה שֶׁנַּפְשִׁי חָשְׁקָה בַּתּוֹרָה, אֶפְשָׁר לָעוֹלָם שֶׁיִּתְקַיֵּים עַל יְדֵי אֲחֵרִים.

They said to ben Azzai: There is a type of scholar who **expounds well and fulfills** his own teachings **well,** and another who **fulfills well and does not expound well. But you,** who have never married, **expound well** on the importance of procreation, **and** yet **you do not fulfill well** your own teachings. **Ben Azzai**[P] **said to them: What shall I do, as my soul yearns for Torah,**[NH] and I do not wish to deal with anything else. **It is possible for the world to be maintained by others,** who are engaged in the mitzva to be fruitful and multiply.

תַּנְיָא אִידָךְ, רַבִּי אֱלִיעֶזֶר אוֹמֵר: כָּל מִי שֶׁאֵין עוֹסֵק בִּפְרִיָּה וּרְבִיָּה – כְּאִילּוּ שׁוֹפֵךְ דָּמִים, שֶׁנֶּאֱמַר ״שׁוֹפֵךְ דַּם הָאָדָם״ וּסְמִיךְ לֵיהּ ״וְאַתֶּם פְּרוּ״ וגו׳. רַבִּי אֶלְעָזָר בֶּן עֲזַרְיָה אוֹמֵר: כְּאִילּוּ מְמַעֵט הַדְּמוּת, בֶּן עַזַּאי אוֹמֵר: וכו׳. אָמְרוּ לוֹ לְבֶן עַזַּאי יֵשׁ נָאֶה דּוֹרֵשׁ וכו׳.

It is similarly **taught** in **another** *baraita* that **Rabbi Eliezer says: Anyone who does not engage in** the mitzva to be **fruitful and multiply** is considered **as though he sheds blood, as it is stated: "Whoever sheds the blood of man," and** it is stated **near it: "And you, be fruitful** and multiply." **Rabbi Elazar ben Azarya says:** It is **as though he diminishes the** Divine **Image. Ben Azzai says:** It is as though he both sheds blood and diminishes the Divine Image. **They said to ben Azzai: There is** a type of scholar who **expounds well, etc.**

תָּנוּ רַבָּנַן: ״וּבְנֻחֹה יֹאמַר שׁוּבָה ה׳ רִבְבוֹת אַלְפֵי יִשְׂרָאֵל״

The Sages taught with regard to the mitzva to be fruitful and multiply: **"And when it rested, he would say: Return, Lord, to the ten thousands of the thousands of Israel"** (Numbers 10:36).

NOTES

The souls of the body – הַנְּשָׁמוֹת שֶׁבַּגּוּף: Many early commentaries explain that the body is referring to the place where the souls are kept. The *Arukh* states that it is a curtain before the Divine Presence with the images of all people destined to be born. Rabbi Avraham min HaHar cites a homiletic explanation that the final redemption will not arrive until all mankind's physical powers are worn out, and he is ready to become a receptacle for the spiritual.

As my soul yearns for Torah – שֶׁנַּפְשִׁי חָשְׁקָה בַּתּוֹרָה: Rabbi Avraham min HaHar explains that ben Azzai claimed he had such desire and fervor for Torah that he had no room left for other passions. He adds that this is why the Rambam says that this claim can be made only by one who is not troubled by his evil inclination.

HALAKHA

The mitzva of marriage – מִצְוַת נִשּׂוּאִין: A man who does not marry is considered like one who sheds blood, diminishes the Divine Image, and causes the Divine Presence to depart from the Jewish people. Upon his marriage, his transgressions vanish, as per the Gemara (*Shulḥan Arukh, Even HaEzer* 1:1).

My soul yearns for Torah – נַפְשִׁי חָשְׁקָה בַּתּוֹרָה: One whose soul yearns for Torah like ben Azzai, to the extent that his constant attachment to Torah study prevents him from getting married, is not considered a sinner, provided that he is not tempted by his evil inclination. Even so, he should not proceed in this manner *ab initio* (*Taz*; Rambam *Sefer Nashim, Hilkhot Ishut* 15:3; *Shulḥan Arukh, Even HaEzer* 1:4).

PERSONALITIES

Ben Azzai – בֶּן עַזַּאי: This is Shimon ben Azzai, one of the *tanna'im* of Yavne. Despite the fact that he was never ordained, which is why he is known by name alone, and usually simply as ben Azzai, he was considered among the greatest of the Sages and was renowned for his wisdom.

It appears that he did not study Torah in his youth, but only after he met Rabbi Akiva's daughter, who promised to marry him if he would become a scholar. Ben Azzai indeed went and studied under Rabbi Yehoshua, Rabbi Yishmael, and principally Rabbi Akiva. He was one of Rabbi Akiva's outstanding students and was eventually considered a disciple-colleague of Rabbi Akiva's, whom he considered to be the foremost scholar of his generation.

It is unclear whether he married Rabbi Akiva's daughter at all, or whether he married and separated from her a short while later. Due to his great passion for Torah he dedicated himself entirely to its study. It is therefore said about him that when ben Azzai died diligence in Torah study ceased (*Sota* 49a). His teachings of *halakha* and *aggada* are cited in the Mishna, in *baraitot*, and in the Talmud. It seems that he even established a body of students of his own in his hometown of Tiberias.

Ben Azzai also studied esoteric wisdom, and is listed as one of the four Sages who entered the orchard, i.e., the deepest secrets of Torah knowledge. He is said to have: Glimpsed at the Divine Presence and died (*Hagiga* 14b), and the verse "Precious in the eyes of the Lord is the death of His pious ones" (Psalms 116:15) is applied to him.

מְלַמֵּד שֶׁאֵין הַשְּׁכִינָה שׁוֹרָה עַל פָּחוֹת מִשְּׁנֵי אֲלָפִים וּשְׁנֵי רְבָבוֹת מִיִּשְׂרָאֵל. הֲרֵי שֶׁהָיוּ יִשְׂרָאֵל שְׁנֵי אֲלָפִים וּשְׁנֵי רְבָבוֹת חָסֵר אֶחָד, וְזֶה לֹא עָסַק בִּפְרִיָּה וּרְבִיָּה – לֹא נִמְצָא זֶה גּוֹרֵם לִשְׁכִינָה שֶׁתִּסְתַּלֵּק מִיִּשְׂרָאֵל?!

This teaches that the Divine Presence does not rest upon less than two thousands and two ten-thousands[N] of the Jewish people, as the terms thousands and ten-thousands are both in the plural. Consequently, if **there were two thousands and two ten-thousands of the Jewish people, less one, and this** man **did not engage in** the mitzva to be **fruitful and multiply, is he not found** to have **caused the Divine Presence to be depart from the Jewish people?**

אַבָּא חָנָן אָמַר מִשּׁוּם רַבִּי אֱלִיעֶזֶר: חַיָּיב מִיתָה, שֶׁנֶּאֱמַר ״וּבָנִים לֹא הָיוּ לָהֶם״ הָא הָיוּ לָהֶם בָּנִים – לֹא מֵתוּ. אֲחֵרִים אוֹמְרִים: גּוֹרֵם לִשְׁכִינָה שֶׁתִּסְתַּלֵּק מִיִּשְׂרָאֵל, שֶׁנֶּאֱמַר ״לִהְיוֹת לְךָ לֵאלֹהִים וּלְזַרְעֲךָ אַחֲרֶיךָ״, בִּזְמַן שֶׁזַּרְעֲךָ אַחֲרֶיךָ – שְׁכִינָה שׁוֹרָה, אֵין זַרְעֲךָ אַחֲרֶיךָ – עַל מִי שׁוֹרָה, עַל הָעֵצִים וְעַל הָאֲבָנִים?!

Abba Ḥanan said in the name of Rabbi Eliezer: A man who does not engage in procreation is **liable to death,**[N] **as it is stated** with regard to the sons of Aaron: "And Nadav and Avihu died… **and they had no children**" (Numbers 3:4). This indicates that if they would have **had children they would not have died. Others say:** He **causes the Divine Presence to depart from the Jewish people, as it is stated: "To be a God to you and to your seed after you"** (Genesis 17:7). **When your seed is after you,** i.e., when you have children, **the Divine Presence rests** upon the Jewish people, but if **your seed is not after you, upon whom** can the Divine Presence **rest? Upon wood and stones?**

מתני׳ נָשָׂא אִשָּׁה וְשָׁהָה עִמָּהּ עֶשֶׂר שָׁנִים וְלֹא יָלְדָה – אֵינוֹ רַשַּׁאי לִבְטֵל. גֵּירְשָׁהּ – מוּתֶּרֶת לִינָּשֵׂא לְאַחֵר, וְרַשַּׁאי הַשֵּׁנִי לִשְׁהוֹת עִמָּהּ עֶשֶׂר שָׁנִים. וְאִם הִפִּילָה – מוֹנֶה מִשָּׁעָה שֶׁהִפִּילָה.

MISHNA If a man **married a woman and stayed with her** for **ten years and she did not give birth,**[N] **he is no** longer **permitted to neglect** the mitzva to be fruitful and multiply. Consequently, he must either divorce her and marry someone else, or take another wife while still married to her. If **he divorced her she is permitted to marry another** man,[H] as it is not necessarily on her account that she and her first husband did not have children, **and the second** husband **is permitted to stay with her** for **ten years. And if she had a miscarriage, he counts** the ten years **from the time of the miscarriage.**

גמ׳ תָּנוּ רַבָּנַן: נָשָׂא אִשָּׁה וְשָׁהָה עִמָּהּ עֶשֶׂר שָׁנִים וְלֹא יָלְדָה – יוֹצִיא וְיִתֵּן כְּתוּבָּה, שֶׁמָּא לֹא זָכָה לְהִבָּנוֹת מִמֶּנָּה.

GEMARA **The Sages taught:** If a man **married a woman and stayed with her** for **ten years and she did not give birth,**[H] **he should divorce** her **and pay** her **marriage contract,** because **perhaps he did not merit to be built,**[N] i.e., to have children, **from her.**[B] It is not certain that their failure to have children is due to her, as it is possible that they are not a suitable match for bearing children.

HALAKHA

If he divorced her she is permitted to marry another man – גֵּירְשָׁהּ, מוּתֶּרֶת לִינָּשֵׂא לְאַחֵר: If a woman was divorced because she failed to bear a child, she is permitted to marry another man. This second husband may stay with her ten years, but if she has not had children at this point he too must divorce her or marry an additional wife (Rambam *Sefer Nashim, Hilkhot Ishut* 15:14; *Shulḥan Arukh, Even HaEzer* 154:16).

A wife who did not give birth – אִשָּׁה שֶׁלֹּא יָלְדָה: If a man remained with his wife for ten years without having children, he must divorce her and pay her marriage contract in order to marry another woman who can bear children. Even if he does not want to divorce her, he is compelled to do so. Some commentaries say that if the man has already fathered a viable child, he is not compelled to divorce his wife even if he has not fulfilled the mitzva to be fruitful and multiply (Rema, citing Rivash). The Rema adds that nowadays the custom is not to force the couple to divorce in any situation (Rambam *Sefer Nashim, Hilkhot Ishut* 15:7; *Shulḥan Arukh, Even HaEzer* 154:10 and in the comment of Rema).

BACKGROUND

He did not merit to be built from her – לֹא זָכָה לְהִבָּנוֹת מִמֶּנָּה: From a medical standpoint it is possible for both a man and a woman to be fertile and yet be unable to have children together. Certain antibodies in the woman might destroy the sperm of a particular man and prevent pregnancy, or the genetic combination of the two could create a situation in which the fetus dies before it has a chance to develop.

NOTES

Two thousands and two ten-thousands – שְׁנֵי אֲלָפִים וּשְׁנֵי רְבָבוֹת: The Maharsha notes that the verse states: "The chariots of God are ten-thousands, thousands" (Psalms 68:18), and the Jewish people are worthy of serving as a chariot for the Divine Presence by this same number. Similarly, there were twenty-two thousand Levites in the wilderness who did not participate in the sin of the Golden Calf, and in whose merit the Divine Presence rested upon the Jewish people.

Liable to death – חַיָּיב מִיתָה: This is similar to the statement cited earlier that one who is not occupied with the mitzva to be fruitful and multiply is considered a bloodshedder, and is therefore liable to death (see *Iyyun Ya'akov*).

Married a woman…and she did not give birth – נָשָׂא אִשָּׁה...וְלֹא יָלְדָה: The commentaries debate whether this means that she has not given birth to any children at all, or perhaps, as explained in the Jerusalem Talmud, it even includes a case where she had a child and the child died, and then she did not have another child for ten years. A third possibility is that this applies even to a woman who had only one child, even if that child lived, and ten years have passed since then (see Ramban and Rashba). The *Nimmukei Yosef* summarizes these opinions.

Perhaps he did not merit to be built – שֶׁמָּא לֹא זָכָה לְהִבָּנוֹת: Even if he had children from a former wife, and therefore it is clear that he is capable of having children, perhaps his present wife is also capable of having children but the two simply did not merit to have children together (Ritva). The commentaries note that this consideration is strong enough to serve as the basis for a monetary claim, and he cannot withhold the payment of her marriage contract by claiming that there is at least a doubt as to whether she is fertile (*Gilyonei HaShas*).

אַף עַל פִּי שֶׁאֵין רְאָיָה לַדָּבָר – זֵכֶר לַדָּבָר: "מִקֵּץ עֶשֶׂר שָׁנִים לְשֶׁבֶת אַבְרָם בְּאֶרֶץ כְּנָעַן" לְלַמֶּדְךָ שֶׁאֵין יְשִׁיבַת חוּץ לָאָרֶץ עוֹלָה לוֹ מִן הַמִּנְיָן. לְפִיכָךְ, חָלָה הוּא אוֹ שֶׁחָלְתָה הִיא, אוֹ שְׁנֵיהֶם חֲבוּשִׁים בְּבֵית הָאֲסוּרִים – אֵין עוֹלִין לוֹ מִן הַמִּנְיָן.

Although there is no explicit **proof**[N] **for the matter** that one must take another wife if he has not had children after ten years of marriage, there is **an allusion to the matter,** as the verse states: "And Sarai, Abram's wife, took Hagar… **after Abram had dwelled ten years in the land of Canaan,** and gave her to Abram her husband to be his wife" (Genesis 16:3). Incidentally, this verse also comes **to teach you that** the years spent **dwelling outside of Eretz Yisrael do not count** as part of **his tally.**[N] **Consequently, if he was sick**[NH] during this period **or she was sick,** or if one of **the two of them** was **imprisoned in jail,** it **does not count** as part of **his tally.**

אָמַר לֵיהּ רָבָא לְרַב נַחְמָן: וְלֵילַף מִיִּצְחָק, דִּכְתִיב "וַיְהִי יִצְחָק בֶּן אַרְבָּעִים שָׁנָה בְּקַחְתּוֹ אֶת רִבְקָה" וגו׳ וּכְתִיב "וְיִצְחָק בֶּן שִׁשִּׁים שָׁנָה בְּלֶדֶת אוֹתָם"! אָמַר לֵיהּ: יִצְחָק עָקוּר הָיָה.

Rava said to Rav Naḥman: Let us derive from Isaac that one may wait a longer period of time, **as it is written: "And Isaac was forty years old when he took Rebekah**… to be his wife" (Genesis 25:20), **and it is written** with regard to the birth of Jacob and Esau: **"And Isaac was sixty years old when she bore them"** (Genesis 25:26). This indicates that one may wait twenty years. Rav Naḥman **said to him: Isaac** knew that he **was infertile,** and therefore there was no reason for him to marry another woman, as Rebekah was not the cause of their infertility.

אִי הָכִי, אַבְרָהָם נַמִּי עָקוּר הָיָה! הַהוּא מִיבְּעֵי לֵיהּ לְכִדְרַבִּי חִיָּיא בַּר אַבָּא. דְּאָמַר רַבִּי חִיָּיא בַּר אַבָּא אָמַר רַבִּי יוֹחָנָן: לָמָּה נִמְנוּ שְׁנוֹתָיו שֶׁל יִשְׁמָעֵאל – כְּדֵי לְיַיחֵס בָּהֶן שְׁנוֹתָיו שֶׁל יַעֲקֹב.

The Gemara responds: **If so, Abraham** also should not have married another woman, as he **was also infertile.** Rather, the *tanna* **requires that** verse that states when Jacob and Esau were born **for** that which **Rabbi Ḥiyya bar Abba** taught. This is **because Rabbi Ḥiyya bar Abba said** that **Rabbi Yoḥanan said: Why were Ishmael's years counted** in the Torah, as they do not appear to be relevant to its narrative? **In order to determine through them the years of Jacob,** i.e., Jacob's age at the time that various events took place, as explained in tractate *Megilla* (17a). The verse concerning Jacob's birth was not meant to allude to a *halakha* about remaining married before having children, but to make it possible to determine Jacob's age by relating it to the age of Ishmael.

HALAKHA

If he was sick, etc. – **חָלָה הוּא וכו׳**: The ten years that one may remain married before divorcing his wife if she has not borne him children do not include periods of time when one of them was sick, even if they engaged in intercourse during this period, or time when they were imprisoned, or when one of them was out of the country, as mentioned in the Jerusalem Talmud (Rambam *Sefer Nashim, Hilkhot Ishut* 15:11; *Shulḥan Arukh, Even HaEzer* 154:11).

NOTES

Although there is no explicit proof – **אַף עַל פִּי שֶׁאֵין רְאָיָה**: See the explanations of *Tosafot* and the *Tosefot HaRosh* as to why this source is considered to merely be an allusion and not an explicit proof. Rabbi Yehuda al-Madari states that the verse does not prove he is obligated to divorce her or marry another woman, because in the case of Avraham it was Sarah who freely chose to give Hagar to her husband.

Years spent dwelling outside of Eretz Yisrael do not count as part of his tally – **אֵין יְשִׁיבַת חוּץ לָאָרֶץ עוֹלָה לוֹ מִן הַמִּנְיָן**: The commentaries discuss this issue at length. Rashi's comments that the sin of living outside Eretz Yisrael may have prevented them from having children implies that the *halakha* that one must take another wife after ten years applies only in Eretz Yisrael. Some commentaries indeed write that a husband is not compelled to divorce his barren wife outside Eretz Yisrael, due to the possibility that the reason they have no children is because they are living outside the land (*Or Zarua*). Most commentaries, however, reject this opinion, arguing that there is no reason why the mitzva to be fruitful and multiply, which is not connected to the land, cannot be fulfilled properly outside of it.

One alternative explanation is that if a man whose permanent residence is in Eretz Yisrael leaves the country, the sin of his departure might prevent him from having children (Ramban, citing Rabbi Avraham *Av Beit Din*). The majority of the commentaries explain that one who did not have children outside Eretz Yisrael and subsequently immigrated to Eretz Yisrael must wait an additional ten years, as the merit of living in Eretz Yisrael might help him bear children (see Ritva). Rabbi Avraham min HaHar states that the expression: Count as part of his tally, is referring specifically to Abraham. He lived in sorrow over the fact that he was not in Eretz Yisrael, which might have led to his failure to have children.

Consequently if he was sick – **לְפִיכָךְ חָלָה הוּא**: Rashi explains the use of the word consequently in this context: The fact that the time Abraham and Sarah spent outside of Eretz Yisrael did not count toward the ten years indicates that whenever there is an external factor that may have been responsible for the couple's childlessness, the time when that factor applied is not taken into account. Consequently, if one of them was sick or incarcerated for a period of time, that time is not included in the ten years. The Rosh explains that the Gemara's statement is not limited to situations where the couple was unable to engage in intercourse, in which case there would have been no need to state that the time does not count toward the tally. Rather, the sin for which they were punished with their illness or incarceration may also be responsible for the fact that they have not conceived, and therefore the time does not count even if they were able to engage in intercourse.

אָמַר רַבִּי יִצְחָק: יִצְחָק אָבִינוּ עָקוּר הָיָה, שֶׁנֶּאֱמַר ״וַיֶּעְתַּר יִצְחָק לַה׳ לְנֹכַח אִשְׁתּוֹ״, ״עַל אִשְׁתּוֹ״ לֹא נֶאֱמַר, אֶלָּא ״לְנוֹכַח״ מְלַמֵּד שֶׁשְּׁנֵיהֶם עֲקוּרִים הָיוּ. אִי הָכִי ״וַיֵּעָתֶר לוֹ״ ״וַיֵּעָתֶר לָהֶם״ מִיבָּעֵי לֵיהּ! לְפִי שֶׁאֵינוֹ דּוֹמֶה תְּפִלַּת צַדִּיק בֶּן צַדִּיק לִתְפִלַּת צַדִּיק בֶּן רָשָׁע.

Rabbi Yitzḥak said: Isaac our father was infertile, as it is stated: "And Isaac entreated the Lord concerning [*lenokhaḥ*] his wife[N] because she was barren" (Genesis 25:21). **It is not stated** that he entreated the Lord **for** [*al*] **his wife, but *lenokhaḥ*,** which can mean opposite, against, or corresponding to; this **teaches that they were both infertile.** The Gemara asks: **If so,** why does the verse continue: **"And the Lord let Himself be entreated of him"?** The verse **should say: And** the Lord **let Himself be entreated of them.** The Gemara answers that their prayers were answered due to Isaac, **because the prayer of a righteous individual** who is **the son of a righteous individual is not similar**[N] **to the prayer of a righteous individual** who is **the son of a wicked individual,** and Rebekah's father was the wicked Laban.

אָמַר רַבִּי יִצְחָק: מִפְּנֵי מָה הָיוּ אֲבוֹתֵינוּ עֲקוּרִים – מִפְּנֵי הַקָּדוֹשׁ בָּרוּךְ הוּא מִתְאַוֶּה לִתְפִלָּתָן שֶׁל צַדִּיקִים. אָמַר רַבִּי יִצְחָק: לָמָּה נִמְשְׁלָה תְּפִלָּתָן שֶׁל צַדִּיקִים כְּעֶתֶר – מָה עֶתֶר זֶה מְהַפֵּךְ הַתְּבוּאָה מִמָּקוֹם לְמָקוֹם, כָּךְ תְּפִלָּתָן שֶׁל צַדִּיקִים מְהַפֶּכֶת מִדּוֹתָיו שֶׁל הַקָּדוֹשׁ בָּרוּךְ הוּא מִמִּדַּת רַגְזָנוּת לְמִדַּת רַחְמָנוּת. אָמַר רַבִּי אַמִּי: אַבְרָהָם וְשָׂרָה טוּמְטְמִין הָיוּ, שֶׁנֶּאֱמַר ״הַבִּיטוּ אֶל צוּר

Rabbi Yitzḥak said: For what reason were our forefathers initially **infertile? Because the Holy One, Blessed be He, desires the prayers of the righteous,** and He therefore wanted them to pray for children. Similarly, **Rabbi Yitzḥak said: Why are the prayers of the righteous compared to a pitchfork** [*eter*],[B] as in the verse: "And He let Himself be entreated [*vaye'ater*]"? This indicates that **just as this pitchfork turns over produce from one place to another, so the prayer of the righteous turns over the attributes of the Holy One, Blessed be He,** from the **attribute of rage** to the **attribute of mercy. Rabbi Ami said: Abraham and Sarah were** originally ***tumtumin*****,**[NB] people whose sexual organs are concealed and not functional, **as it is stated: "Look to the rock**

NOTES

Concerning [*lenokhaḥ*] his wife – לְנוֹכַח אִשְׁתּוֹ: Rashi explains that the term *lenokhaḥ* indicates that Isaac and Rebekah stood opposite each other and prayed. The Maharsha states that *lenokhaḥ* can mean corresponding to. Consequently, just as Rebekah required this prayer, so did Isaac, as his status was similar to hers.

Because the prayer…is not similar, etc. – לְפִי שֶׁאֵינוֹ דּוֹמֶה תְּפִלַּת וכו׳: This means not that the prayer of a righteous individual who is the son of a righteous individual is always answered, but that it is more likely to be answered. See the *Iyyun Ya'akov*.

Abraham and Sarah were originally *tumtumin* – אַבְרָהָם וְשָׂרָה טוּמְטְמִין הָיוּ: The Meiri writes that this informs us of the power of prayer, which can change even one's physical nature.

BACKGROUND

Pitchfork [*eter*] – עֶתֶר: Rashi explains here that *eter* means a shovel, but *Tosafot* (*Sukka* 14a) prove from various sources that an *eter* is a pitchfork used to dig the earth or turn over produce in the process of winnowing, which is the way Rashi explains the word in tractate *Sukka* (14a).

Farmer winnowing with a pitchfork

Tumtum – טוּמְטוּם: A *tumtum* is one whose external sexual organs are concealed or otherwise indeterminate, and it is therefore unclear whether this person is male or female. In certain cases, the gender of the *tumtum* is later established, which is described in the language of the *halakha* as: A *tumtum* who was torn, revealing his or her gender, at which point this person is considered a full-fledged member of that gender.

חֲצַבְתֶּם וְאֶל מַקֶּבֶת בּוֹר נֻקַּרְתֶּם" וּכְתִיב "הַבִּיטוּ אֶל אַבְרָהָם אֲבִיכֶם וְאֶל שָׂרָה תְּחוֹלֶלְכֶם".

from where you were hewn, and to the hole of the pit from where you were dug" (Isaiah 51:1), **and it is written** in the next verse: **"Look to Abraham your father and to Sarah who bore you"** (Isaiah 51:2), which indicates that sexual organs were fashioned for them, signified by the words hewn and dug, over the course of time.

אָמַר רַב נַחְמָן אָמַר רַבָּה בַּר אֲבוּהּ: שָׂרָה אִמֵּנוּ אַיְלוֹנִית הָיְתָה, שֶׁנֶּאֱמַר "וַתְּהִי שָׂרַי עֲקָרָה אֵין לָהּ וָלָד" אֲפִילּוּ בֵּית וָלָד אֵין לָהּ.

Rav Naḥman said that **Rabba bar Avuh said: Our mother Sarah was** initially **a sexually underdeveloped woman [*aylonit*], as it is stated: "And Sarah was barren; she had no child"** (Genesis 11:30). The superfluous words: "She had no child," indicate that **she did not have even a place,** i.e., a womb, **for a child.**

אָמַר רַב יְהוּדָה בְּרֵיהּ דְּרַב שְׁמוּאֵל בַּר שֵׁילַת מִשְּׁמֵיהּ דְּרַב: לֹא שָׁנוּ אֶלָּא בַּדּוֹרוֹת הָרִאשׁוֹנִים, שֶׁשְּׁנוֹתֵיהֶן מְרוּבּוֹת. אֲבָל בַּדּוֹרוֹת הָאַחֲרוֹנִים שֶׁשְּׁנוֹתֵיהֶן מוּעָטוֹת – שְׁתֵּי שָׁנִים וּמֶחֱצָה, כְּנֶגֶד שְׁלֹשָׁה עִיבּוּרִים. רַבָּה אָמַר רַב נַחְמָן: שָׁלֹשׁ שָׁנִים, כְּנֶגֶד שָׁלֹשׁ פְּקִידוֹת. דַּאֲמַר מָר: בְּרֹאשׁ הַשָּׁנָה נִפְקְדוּ שָׂרָה רָחֵל וְחַנָּה.

Rav Yehuda, son of Rav Shmuel bar Sheilat, said in the name of Rav: They taught that he waits ten years **only** with regard to the people who lived **in former generations, whose years** were **numerous,** i.e., they lived longer. **However,** with regard to the people who live **in later generations, whose years are few,** he waits only **two and half years**[N] before divorcing her, **corresponding to** the time period of **three pregnancies.**[B] **Rabba said** in the name of **Rav Naḥman:** He waits **three years, corresponding to** the **three remembrances** of barren women by God, **as the Master said: On Rosh HaShana Sarah, Rachel, and Hannah were remembered,** i.e., God gave them children. Since God determines on Rosh HaShana whether barren women will conceive that year, one may remain married until three such opportunities have passed.

אֲמַר רַבָּה: לֵיתְנְהוּ לְהָנֵי כְּלָלֵי. מִכְּדִי מַתְנִיתִין מַאן תַּקֵּין – רַבִּי, וְהָא בִּימֵי דָּוִד אִימְעוּט שְׁנֵי, דִּכְתִיב "יְמֵי שְׁנוֹתֵינוּ בָהֶם שִׁבְעִים שָׁנָה".

However, **Rabba** himself **said: These principles are not** accepted as *halakha*. Why not? **Now consider, who established** the content of the **mishna? Rabbi** Yehuda HaNasi. Yet, **in the days of** King **David,** many years before the time of Rabbi Yehuda HaNasi, **the years** of an average lifespan **were** already **diminished, as it is written: "The days of our years**[N] **are seventy years,** and if with strength eighty years" (Psalms 90:10). Consequently, if Rabbi Yehuda HaNasi included in the mishna the statement that one remains married for ten years, that must apply even nowadays.

וְהַאי "שֶׁמָּא לֹא זָכָה לְהִבָּנוֹת הֵימֶנָּה" וְדִלְמָא אִיהִי דְּלָא זַכְיָא! אִיהִי, כֵּיוָן דְּלָא מִפַּקְדָא אַפְּרִיָּה וּרְבִיָּה – לָא מִיעַנְשָׁה.

The Gemara asks about the language of the *baraita*. **And** what about **this** expression: **Perhaps he did not merit to be built from her; perhaps** it was **she** who **did not merit**[N] to build a family. The Gemara answers: **She, since she is not commanded** to be **fruitful and multiply, is not punished.** Their worthiness therefore depends on him, not her.

BACKGROUND

Three pregnancies – שְׁלֹשָׁה עִיבּוּרִים: It is possible for a woman to become pregnant and give birth three times in a period of two and a half years, and this phenomenon occasionally takes place.

NOTES

Two and a half years – שְׁתֵּי שָׁנִים וּמֶחֱצָה: Since the duration of three pregnancies is twenty-seven months, why does Rav say that one remains married for two and a half years, which is thirty months? One suggestion is that the thirty months include one month for the woman to become ritually pure and permitted to her husband between each of the three time periods corresponding to a pregnancy (Rabbi Avraham min HaHar). Alternatively, Rav was not particular about the exact duration, and allowed extra time (Rabbi Yehuda al-Madari).

The days of our years – יְמֵי שְׁנוֹתֵינוּ: *Tosafot* note that even though this psalm is entitled "A prayer of Moses," it was in fact composed by David. The phrase "A prayer of Moses," means a prayer for Moses (*HaKotev* in *Ein Ya'akov*).

Perhaps it was she who did not merit, etc. – וְדִלְמָא אִיהִי דְּלָא זַכְיָא וכו׳: Rashi explains that the point of this question is that therefore she should not be entitled to the payment of her marriage contract (see Rid). Rabbi Avraham min HaHar explains similarly that since she is not obligated to have children, their inability to have children is considered a punishment for the husband, not the wife. Consequently, although it is not known whether she is fertile, she nevertheless receives payment for her marriage contract.

However, some commentaries (Ramban; Rashba; *Tosefot Ḥad MiKamma'ei*) question the connection between not being obligated to have children and receiving payment of the marriage contract. The Ramban suggests that the Gemara's initial statement that he did not merit to have children through her is meant to explain that since they are not presumed to necessarily be infertile, he must divorce her in order to marry someone else. The Gemara's question here is simply linguistic; it asks why this statement was phrased from the perspective of the husband rather than the wife (see Rashba).

איני? והא אמרו ליה רבנן לרבי אבא בר זבדא: נסיב איתתא ואוליד בני! ואמר להו: אי זכאי – הוו לי מקמייתא. התם דחוי קא מדחי להו לרבנן. דרבי אבא בר זבדא איעקר מפרקיה דרב הונא,

The Gemara challenges the mishna's statement that if one did not have children after ten years he should marry a different woman. **Is that so? Didn't the Sages say to Rabbi Abba bar Zavda: Marry a woman and have children, and he said to them: If I had merited, I would** already **have** children **from** my **first** wife? This indicates that there is no obligation to remarry if one did not have children with his first wife. The Gemara answers: **There,** Rabbi Abba bar Zavda **was** merely **putting the Rabbis off** with an excuse, **as** the real reason why he would not marry was because **Rabbi Abba bar Zavda became impotent from Rav Huna's discourse.** Rav Huna's students would hold back from relieving themselves until his lengthy sermons were finished, which caused them to become sterile.

רב גידל איעקר מפרקיה דרב הונא, רבי חלבו איעקר מפרקיה דרב הונא, רב ששת איעקר מפרקיה דרב הונא. רב אחא בר יעקב אחדתיה סוסכינתא, תליוה בארזא דבי רב ונפק מיניה כהוצא ירקא. אמר רב אחא בר יעקב: שיתין סבי הוינא, וכולהו איעקור מפרקיה דרב הונא, לבר מאנא דקיימי בנפשאי "החכמה תחיה בעליה".

The Gemara similarly relates that **Rav Giddel became impotent from Rav Huna's discourse, Rav Ḥelbo became impotent from Rav Huna's discourse,** and **Rav Sheshet became impotent from Rav Huna's discourse.** The Gemara relates: **Rav Aḥa bar Ya'akov was afflicted by** *suskhinta*, a disease caused by holding back from urinating. **They suspended him from the cedar** column that supported **the study hall, and** a substance that was as **green** as a palm **leaf emerged from him,** and he was healed. **Rav Aḥa bar Ya'akov said: We were sixty elders** present at the time, **and they all became impotent from Rav Huna's discourse, aside from me, as I fulfilled with regard to myself** the verse: **"Wisdom preserves the life of he who has it"** (Ecclesiastes 7:12). I used the above cure to avoid becoming impotent.

גירשה מותרת וכו׳. שני – אין, שלישי – לא.

§ It was taught in the mishna that if a man **divorced** his wife after ten years without children, **she is permitted** to marry a second man, who may remain married to her for ten years. The Gemara comments: **A second** husband, **yes,** but **a third** one, **no.**[H] Once she has been married to two men without children for ten years each, it is presumed that she is unable to have children.

מתניתין מני – רבי היא. דתניא: מלה הראשון ומת, שני ומת, שלישי – לא תמול, דברי רבי. רבן שמעון בן גמליאל אומר: שלישי – תמול, רביעי – לא תמול.

The Gemara comments: **Who is the** *tanna* **of the mishna? It is Rabbi** Yehuda HaNasi, who holds that a legal presumption [*ḥazaka*] is established after two occurrences. **As it is taught** in a *baraita*: If a woman **circumcised** her **first** son **and he died**[H] as a result of the circumcision, and she circumcised her **second** son **and he** also **died, she should not circumcise** her **third** son, as the deaths of the first two produce a presumption that this woman's sons die as a result of circumcision. This is **the statement of Rabbi** Yehuda HaNasi. **Rabban Shimon ben Gamliel says: She should circumcise** her **third** son, as there is not considered to be a legal presumption that her sons die from circumcision, but **she should not circumcise** her **fourth** son if her first three sons died from circumcision.

והתניא איפכא, הי מינייהו אחרינתא?

The Gemara asks: **Isn't the reverse taught** in a *baraita*, that Rabbi Yehuda HaNasi holds that the woman's third son must be circumcised and Rabban Shimon ben Gamliel holds that he is not circumcised? **Which of them** was composed **later** and is therefore presumed to be more reliable?

תא שמע, דאמר רבי חייא בר אבא אמר רבי יוחנן: מעשה בארבע אחיות בצפורי, שמלה ראשונה ומת, שניה ומת, שלישית ומת, רביעית באת לפני רבן שמעון בן גמליאל, אמר לה: אל תמולי.

The Gemara suggests: **Come** and **hear, as Rabbi Ḥiyya bar Abba said** that **Rabbi Yoḥanan said: An incident** occurred **involving four sisters in Tzippori, that** the **first** sister **circumcised** her son **and he died,**[B] and the **second** sister circumcised her son **and he died,** and the **third** one circumcised her son **and he** too **died.** The **fourth** sister **came before Rabban Shimon ben Gamliel,** who **said to her: Do not circumcise** him. This indicates that according to Rabban Shimon ben Gamliel a presumption is established only after three occurrences.

ודלמא אי אתיא שלישית – נמי הוה אמר לה? אם כן מאי אסהדותיה דרבי חייא בר אבא. ודלמא הא קא משמע לן דאחיות מחזקות!

The Gemara refutes this proof: **Perhaps if** the **third** sister had **come** before him **he would also have said to her** the same ruling. The Gemara asks: **If so, what is** the purpose **of Rabbi Ḥiyya bar Abba's testimony?** Why would he have related this incident if it does not teach us anything? The Gemara answers: **Perhaps** he comes to **teach us that sisters establish a presumption**[H] in a case like this even though the children who died were not from the same mother.

HALAKHA

A second husband yes, but a third one no – שני אין, שלישי לא: If a woman had been married twice for ten years each without bearing a child by either husband, she may not marry a third time. If she does, her husband must divorce her unless he has another wife or has already fulfilled the mitzva to be fruitful and multiply. If he divorces her, he is required to pay her marriage contract only if he was aware of her background before he married her, in which case he must pay it even if he does not have another wife and has not fulfilled the mitzva to be fruitful and multiply (Rambam *Sefer Nashim, Hilkhot Ishut* 15:14; *Shulḥan Arukh, Even HaEzer* 154:17; *Beit Shmuel*).

Circumcised her first son and he died, etc. – מלה הראשון ומת וכו׳: If a woman circumcised her first son and he died as a result of the circumcision, and she circumcised her second son and he too died, her third son is not circumcised at the usual time; rather, he is given time to grow and to become stronger. This applies regardless of whether the sons shared the same father. The same principle applies also to the sons of one father from different mothers. Some authorities disagree, but the *halakha* is in accordance with the lenient opinion in cases of potential danger (Rambam *Sefer Ahava, Hilkhot Mila* 1:18; *Shulḥan Arukh, Yoreh De'a* 263:2 and in the comment of Rema).

Sisters establish a presumption – אחיות מחזקות: If a woman circumcised her son and he died as a result, and her sister also circumcised her son and he too died, their other sisters do not circumcise their sons at the proper time (*Shulḥan Arukh, Yoreh De'a* 263:3).

BACKGROUND

The first sister circumcised her son and he died, etc. – מלה ראשונה ומת וכו׳: Apparently, this is referring to a hereditary disease that prevents the blood from clotting, e.g., hemophilia. It is transmitted through the female, who carries the offending gene, although it affects primarily males. In this case it is certain that sisters establish a presumption, as they are all likely to pass on the disease.

אֲמַר רָבָא: הַשְׁתָּא דְּאָמְרַתְּ אֲחָיוֹת מַחְזִיקוֹת – לֹא יִשָּׂא אָדָם אִשָּׁה לֹא מִמִּשְׁפַּחַת נִכְפִּין, וְלֹא מִמִּשְׁפַּחַת מְצוֹרָעִים, וְהוּא דְּאִתַּחְזַק תְּלָתָא זִימְנֵי.

Rava said: Now that you have said that **sisters establish a presumption,**[N] **a man should not marry a woman from a family of epileptics**[HB] **or from a family of lepers,** as these diseases might be hereditary. The Gemara adds: **And this** applies only if it **was established three times,** i.e., three members of the family are afflicted with the disease.

מַאי הֲוָה עֲלַהּ? כִּי אֲתָא רַב יִצְחָק בַּר יוֹסֵף אָמַר: עוּבְדָּא הֲוָה קַמֵּיהּ דְּרַבִּי יוֹחָנָן בִּכְנִישְׁתָּא דְּמָעוֹן בְּיוֹם הַכִּפּוּרִים שֶׁחָל לִהְיוֹת בְּשַׁבָּת, וּמָלָה רִאשׁוֹנָה וּמֵת, שְׁנִיָּה וּמֵת, שְׁלִישִׁית בָּאָה לְפָנָיו. אָמַר לָהּ: לְכִי וּמוּלִי.

The Gemara asks: **Which** halakhic conclusion **was about this** matter? Is a presumption established after two occurrences or only after three? **When Rav Yitzḥak bar Yosef came** from Eretz Yisrael, **he said: An incident occurred before Rabbi Yoḥanan in the synagogue of** the town of **Maon on a Yom Kippur that occurred on Shabbat.** The **first** sister had **circumcised** her son **and he died;** the **second** sister circumcised her son **and he** also **died.** The **third** sister **came before him,** and he **said to her: Go and circumcise** your son, as a presumption is not established after only two occurrences.

אֲמַר לֵיהּ אַבָּיֵי: חֲזִי דְּקָשָׁרֵית אִיסּוּרָא וְסַכַּנְתָּא!

Abaye said to Rav Yitzḥak: **See** to it that your report is accurate, **as you are permitting** an action that would otherwise constitute **a prohibition and a danger.** If the third baby should not be circumcised, doing so would be a prohibited labor and would endanger the life of the child.

סְמַךְ עֲלַהּ אַבָּיֵי, וַאֲזַל נַסְבַהּ לְחוּמָה בְּרַתָּא דְּאִיסִי בְּרֵיהּ דְּרַב יִצְחָק בְּרֵיהּ דְּרַב יְהוּדָה. דְּנַסְבַהּ רַחֲבָא דְּפוּמְבְּדִיתָא וּשְׁכִיב, רַב יִצְחָק בְּרֵיהּ דְּרַבָּה בַּר בַּר חָנָה וּשְׁכִיב, וְנַסְבַהּ הוּא וּשְׁכִיב.

The Gemara comments: **Abaye relied on this** report **and went** and **married Ḥuma, the daughter of Isi, son of Rav Yitzḥak, son of** Rav Yehuda. Ḥuma **had** previously **married Raḥava of Pumbedita, and he died,** and then she married **Rav Yitzḥak, son of Rabba bar bar Ḥana, and he died; and he,** Abaye, **married her** nevertheless, without concern that she had been established to be a woman whose husbands die; **and he died** as well while married to her.

אָמַר רָבָא: וּמִי אִיכָּא דְּעָבֵיד עוּבְדָּא בְּנַפְשֵׁיהּ כִּי הַאי, וְהָא אִיהוּ דְּאָמַר: אָבִין – דִּסְמִכָא, יִצְחָק סוּמְקָא – לָאו בַּר סָמְכָא. אָבִין – יֶשְׁנוֹ בַּחֲזָרָה, יִצְחָק סוּמְקָא – אֵינוֹ בַּחֲזָרָה. וְעוֹד: אֵימַר דִּפְלִיגִי לְעִנְיַן מִילָה, בְּנִישּׂוּאִין מִי פְּלִיגִי?

Rava said: Is there anyone **who performs an action like this** and endangers **himself** by marrying such a woman? **Wasn't it he,** Abaye, **who said** that **Avin is reliable** but **Yitzḥak the Red,** i.e., Rav Yitzḥak bar Yosef, **is not reliable?** He proceeds to explain the difference between them: **Avin returns** to Eretz Yisrael and hears whether the Sages there rescind their previous rulings, whereas **Yitzḥak the Red does not return** to Eretz Yisrael and never finds out if the Sages there rescind their rulings. **And furthermore, say that they disagree with regard to** whether a presumption is established by two or by three deaths due to **circumcision,**[N] but **do** they necessarily **argue with regard to marriage?**

אִין, וְהָתַנְיָא: נִיסֵּת לָרִאשׁוֹן וּמֵת, לַשֵּׁנִי וּמֵת, לַשְּׁלִישִׁי – לֹא תִּנָּשֵׂא, דִּבְרֵי רַבִּי. רַבָּן שִׁמְעוֹן בֶּן גַּמְלִיאֵל אוֹמֵר: לַשְּׁלִישִׁי תִּנָּשֵׂא, לָרְבִיעִי לֹא תִּנָּשֵׂא.

The Gemara responds: **Yes, and it is taught** in a *baraita*: If a woman **was married to** her **first** husband **and he died, to a second** one **and** he also **died, she may not get married to a third** husband.[N] This is **the statement of Rabbi** Yehuda HaNasi. **Rabban Shimon ben Gamliel says: She may get married to a third** husband, but if he also dies, **she may not get married to a fourth** husband.

בִּשְׁלָמָא גַּבֵּי מִילָה – אִיכָּא מִשְׁפָּחָה דְּרָפֵי דָּמָא וְאִיכָּא מִשְׁפָּחָה דְּקָמֵיט דָּמָא. אֶלָּא נִישּׂוּאִין מַאי טַעְמָא? אָמַר לֵיהּ רַב מָרְדְּכַי לְרַב אַשִׁי, הָכִי אָמַר אֲבִימִי מֵהַגְרוֹנְיָא מִשְּׁמֵיהּ דְּרַב הוּנָא: מַעְיָן גּוֹרֵם. וְרַב אַשִׁי אָמַר: מַזָּל גּוֹרֵם.

The Gemara asks: **Granted with regard to circumcision** a presumption of death due to circumcision can be established because **there are families whose blood is thin** and does not clot well, **and there are families whose blood clots. However,** in the case of **marriage, what is the reason** for concern that a subsequent husband will die? **Rav Mordekhai said to Rav Ashi: Avimi of Hagronya said in the name of Rav Huna as follows:** Her **spring** is the **cause.**[B] In other words, the woman has some sort of condition that causes those who have intercourse with her to die. **And Rav Ashi said** that her **constellation** is the **cause** of her husbands' deaths.[H]

NOTES

Sisters establish a presumption – אֲחָיוֹת מַחְזִיקוֹת: Although Rava himself maintains later in the discussion that one must be concerned that a presumption has been established after only two occurrences in the case of marriage to a woman whose previous husbands died, in this case of the sisters he admits that three occurrences are required in order to establish a presumption. The reason for the difference is that in the case of a woman whose husbands died, the presumption relates to the woman herself. Conversely, in this case the presumption is based on the experiences of other family members, and therefore more evidence is required in order to establish a legal presumption (Rashba).

Say that they disagree with regard to circumcision, etc. – אֵימַר דִּפְלִיגִי לְעִנְיַן מִילָה וכו׳: The difference between the cases is twofold. First, the presumption in the case of circumcision does not pertain to the same child, but to his brother. Secondly, the merit of the mitzva may prevent the tragedy. Therefore, even if three occurrences are required in order to establish a presumption in the case of circumcision, all should agree that if two husbands of a particular woman have died, one should not marry her (Rabbi Avraham min HaHar).

She may not get married to a third husband – לַשְּׁלִישִׁי לֹא תִּנָּשֵׂא: The Rambam rules that if she did get married, or even betrothed, her husband is not forced to divorce her. Other commentaries struggle to find a rationale for this opinion and support for it in the Gemara. The Rambam himself, in a responsum, explains that marrying a woman whose two previous husbands have died is not actually dangerous; however, if her husband thinks he is at risk, his own worry will in fact cause him to suffer a greater likelihood of harm. Therefore, if he is not concerned, he is not in danger and has committed no transgression by marrying this woman.

HALAKHA

A man should not marry a woman from a family of epileptics – לֹא יִשָּׂא אָדָם אִשָּׁה לֹא מִמִּשְׁפַּחַת נִכְפִּין: A man should not marry a woman from a family of epileptics, lepers, or the like. This applies only if three cases from the same family have been documented (Rambam *Sefer Kedusha, Hilkhot Issurei Bia* 21:30; *Shulḥan Arukh, Even HaEzer* 2:7).

Her constellation is the cause of her husbands' deaths – מַזָּל גּוֹרֵם: If a woman was married or betrothed twice and her husbands died she may not marry a third time, as there is a presumption that she was the cause of her husbands' deaths. However, if a third man married her he is not required to divorce her. Even if he has only betrothed her, he may marry her. If he was not aware of her previous history and wants to divorce her due to the fact that her previous husbands died, he is not required to pay her marriage contract.

The Rema writes that some authorities rule in accordance with the opinion that her spring is the cause, and therefore the presumption that she is the cause of her husbands' deaths is established only when they died on their own; however, if they died in accidents or due to an epidemic, no presumption is established. Therefore, many are lenient in regard to this *halakha*, and no objection to their practice is raised (Rambam *Sefer Kedusha, Hilkhot Issurei Bia* 21:31; *Shulḥan Arukh, Even HaEzer* 9:1 and in the comment of Rema).

BACKGROUND

A man should not marry a woman from a family of epileptics – לֹא יִשָּׂא אָדָם אִשָּׁה לֹא מִמִּשְׁפַּחַת נִכְפִּין: This is one of the earliest mentions in the history of medicine of the recognition that certain hereditary diseases are transmitted through a carrier. Consequently, although the woman displays no signs of the disease, the very occurrence of the hereditary disease in the family raises the possibility that she could pass it on to her children. Contemporary medicine knows of numerous such diseases, of which epilepsy is a prime example.

Her spring is the cause – מַעְיָן גּוֹרֵם: It is possible for bodily fluids to transmit infectious diseases. This applies especially to sexually transmitted illnesses, but it is true of other infectious diseases as well. It is also possible for a woman to carry a disease that does not threaten her but is deadly for a man.

מַאי בֵּינַיְיהוּ? אִיכָּא בֵּינַיְיהוּ דְּאֵירְסָהּ וּמִית, אִי נַמִּי דְּנָפַל מִדִּיקְלָא וּמִית.

The Gemara asks: **What is** the practical difference **between them?** The Gemara answers: **There is** a difference **between them** in a case **where** a man **betrothed her and died** before the wedding; **alternatively,** in a case **where he fell off a palm tree and died.** If the concern is due to intercourse, then in these cases the husband's death cannot be attributed to his wife. Conversely, if the concern is due to her bad fortune, the husband's death can be attributed to his wife even in these cases.

אָמַר לֵיהּ רַב יוֹסֵף בְּרֵיהּ דְּרָבָא לְרָבָא: בְּעִי מִינֵּיהּ מֵרַב יוֹסֵף, הֲלָכָה כְּרַבִּי? וַאֲמַר לִי: אִין. הֲלָכָה כְּרַבָּן שִׁמְעוֹן בֶּן גַּמְלִיאֵל? וַאֲמַר לִי: אִין. אַחוּכֵי אַחִיךְ בִּי?

Rav Yosef, son of Rava, said to Rava: I inquired of Rav Yosef[N] whether the ***halakha* is in accordance with** the opinion of **Rabbi** Yehuda HaNasi, **and he said to me: Yes.** I subsequently asked him if the ***halakha* is in accordance with** the opinion of **Rabban Shimon ben Gamliel, and he said to me: Yes. Was he mocking me** by issuing contradictory rulings?

אָמַר לֵיהּ: לָא, סְתָמֵי הִיא, וּפָשֵׁיט לָךְ: נִישּׂוּאִין וּמַלְקִיּוֹת – כְּרַבִּי, וְסָתוֹת וְשׁוֹר הַמּוּעָד כְּרַבָּן שִׁמְעוֹן בֶּן גַּמְלִיאֵל.

Rava **said to him: No, there are unattributed** *mishnayot* in accordance with each opinion, **and he resolved for you** that the *halakha* is in accordance with each opinion in particular cases. With regard to **marriage and lashings**[N] the *halakha* is **in accordance with** the opinion of **Rabbi** Yehuda HaNasi that two occurrences are sufficient for a presumption. Concerning **set patterns** of menstrual bleeding **and a forewarned ox,** the *halakha* is **in accordance with** the opinion of **Rabban Shimon ben Gamliel** that a presumption is established after three occurrences.

נִישּׂוּאִין – הָא דַּאֲמָרַן, מַלְקִיּוֹת – דִּתְנַן: מִי שֶׁלָּקָה וְשָׁנָה – בֵּית דִּין כּוֹנְסִין אוֹתוֹ לְכִיפָּה, וּמַאֲכִילִין אוֹתוֹ שְׂעוֹרִים עַד שֶׁתְּהֵא כְּרֵיסוֹ נִבְקַעַת. וְסָתוֹת – דִּתְנַן: אֵין הָאִשָּׁה

The Gemara identifies the aforementioned *halakhot*. **Marriage** is referring to **that which we said** with regard to a woman whose husbands have died. The case of **lashings** is **as we learned** in a mishna (*Nidda* 63b): **One who was flogged** for transgressing a Torah law, **and repeated** the same transgression[H] and was flogged again, if he then repeats the sin a third time, the **court places him in a** narrow, **vaulted chamber and they feed him barley until his stomach bursts.** Once he has sinned and been flogged twice he has established a presumption of wickedness, and when he sins again he is caused to die so that he will not continue to sin. The case of **set patterns** of menstrual bleeding is **as we learned** in a mishna (*Nidda* 63b): **A woman does not**

NOTES

Rav Yosef – רַב יוֹסֵף: When the Gemara refers to Rav Yosef without further identification, it is referring to Rav Yosef bar Ḥiyya.

Marriage and lashings, etc. – נִישּׂוּאִין וּמַלְקִיּוֹת וכו׳: The commentaries discuss why the *halakha* distinguishes between different cases. They explain that with regard to marrying a woman whose previous husbands have died, since there is a concern of danger, the *halakha* is in accordance with the more cautious opinion of Rabbi Yehuda HaNasi. Although it is not mentioned in the Gemara, the same is true in a case of circumcision; if two brothers have already died as a result of circumcision, the third is not circumcised. In the case of lashings, the *halakha* is in accordance with the opinion of Rabbi Yehuda HaNasi due to the court's responsibility to protect society from evildoers.

Conversely, the *halakhot* of set patterns of menstrual bleeding are rabbinic, and therefore the *halakha* is in accordance with the lenient opinion of Rabban Shimon ben Gamliel. In the case of a forewarned ox, which involves monetary payment, the burden of proof rests upon the claimant and therefore he is not awarded the extra payment unless he can prove that a presumption has been established. Since he cannot prove that the *halakha* is in accordance with the opinion of Rabbi Yehuda HaNasi, he is awarded the extra payment of a forewarned ox only if its owner had been warned on three separate occasions.

HALAKHA

One who was flogged and repeated the same transgression – מִי שֶׁלָּקָה וְשָׁנָה: If one was flogged for committing a transgression that carries a punishment of *karet* and repeated the sin and was flogged again, if he repeats the sin a third time he is not flogged. Rather, he is placed in a narrow, vaulted chamber until he dies (Rambam *Sefer Shofetim*, *Hilkhot Sanhedrin* 18:4).

Perek **VI**
Daf **65** Amud **a**

קוֹבַעַת לָהּ וֶסֶת עַד שֶׁתִּקְבְּעֶנָּה שָׁלֹשׁ פְּעָמִים, וְאֵין מִטַּהֶרֶת מִן הַוֶּסֶת עַד שֶׁתֵּעָקֵר מִמֶּנָּה שָׁלֹשׁ פְּעָמִים. וְשׁוֹר הַמּוּעָד – דִּתְנַן: אֵין הַשּׁוֹר נַעֲשֶׂה מוּעָד עַד שֶׁיָּעִידוּ בּוֹ שְׁלֹשָׁה פְּעָמִים.

establish a set pattern of menstrual bleeding **for herself,** so that it can be assumed that she will start bleeding at a particular time, **until she has established it three times.**[H] Similarly, **she is not purified from her set pattern until it is uprooted from her three times,** i.e., until she did not experience menstrual bleeding at the expected time according to her pattern on three occasions. **And** the case of a **forewarned ox**[HN] is **as we learned** in a mishna (*Bava Kamma* 23b): **An ox does not become forewarned until** witnesses **testify** that **it** has gored **three times.** Consequently, in the cases of set patterns and a forewarned ox, a legal presumption is created only after three occurrences, in accordance with the opinion of Rabban Shimon ben Gamliel.

HALAKHA

A set pattern of menstrual bleeding is established after three occurrences – וֶסֶת בְּשָׁלֹשׁ פְּעָמִים: A woman establishes a set pattern if she experiences menstrual bleeding at a particular interval of days, or on a particular day of the month, or after a particular physiological phenomenon, on three consecutive occasions. She must assume that she will continue to experience menstrual bleeding according to her set pattern unless it is uprooted, which occurs if she does not experience menstrual bleeding according to her pattern on three consecutive occasions (Rambam *Sefer Kedusha*, *Hilkhot Issurei Bia* 8:5; *Shulḥan Arukh*, *Yoreh De'a* 189:2).

A forewarned ox – שׁוֹר הַמּוּעָד: An ox becomes forewarned only if witnesses testify that it caused damage by goring or biting on three consecutive days. If witnesses testified about three separate incidents on the same day, it is questionable whether the ox becomes a forewarned ox. However, if fewer than three incidents occurred during a three-day period, the ox certainly maintains its status as an innocuous ox, whose owner is liable to pay only half the value of damage that it caused intentionally (Rambam *Sefer Nezikin*, *Hilkhot Nizkei Mammon* 6:1).

NOTES

A forewarned ox – שׁוֹר הַמּוּעָד: *Tosafot* contend that Rabbi Yehuda HaNasi did not disagree with regard to a forewarned ox, as this *halakha* is explicitly stated in the Torah. Rather, the Gemara is saying that in certain cases a legal presumption is established only after three occurrences, which is consistent with the general principle stated by Rabban Shimon ben Gamliel. The Ramban, however, claims that Rabbi Yehuda HaNasi disagrees in the case of a forewarned ox as well, and holds that the third time the ox gores its owner must pay for the full value of the damages caused, because after the first two occurrences it is already considered a forewarned ox.

תנו רבנן: ניסת לראשון ולא היו לה בנים, לשני ולא היו לה בנים, לשלישי – לא תנשא אלא למי שיש לו בנים. נישאת למי שאין לו בנים – תצא בלא כתובה.

The Sages taught: If a woman **was married to** her **first** husband[N] **and she did not have children,** and then she was married **to** her **second** husband **and she did not have children, she may not get married to a third** husband **unless** it is **to one who** already **has children** and has fulfilled the mitzva to be fruitful and multiply, as it is presumed that she is unable to have children. If **she got married to one who does not have children** and he had been unaware of her presumptive status, **she is divorced without** receiving payment for her **marriage contract,**[N] as he married her erroneously.

איבעיא להו: נישאת לשלישי ולא היו לה בנים, מהו דליתבעוה הנך קמאי? מי מצו אמרי לה: איגלאי מילתא דאת הוא דגרמת, או דלמא מצית אמרה להו: השתא הוא דכחשי? מסתברא מצית אמרה להו: השתא הוא דכחשי.

A dilemma was raised before the Sages: If **she was married to a third** husband **and she did not have children**[H] for ten years, **what is** the *halakha* with regard to whether **those first** husbands **can demand** the return of the money they paid for **her** marriage contracts? **Can they say to her: It has been revealed** retroactively **that it was you who caused** our inability to have children, and therefore we entered our marriages erroneously, **or perhaps** she **can say to them: It is now that** I am older that **I have become weak,** but in my youth I could have had children with a different husband. The Sages answer: It is **reasonable** that **she can say to them: It is now that I have become weak.**[BN]

איבעיא להו: נישאת לרביעי והיו לה בנים, מהו דתיתבעיה לשלישי? אמרינן לה: שתיקותיך יפה מדיבוריך, דמצי אמר לה: אנא אדעתא דהכי לא גרשתיך.

Another **dilemma was raised before** the Sages: If **she was married to a fourth** husband **and she had children**[H] with him, **what is** the *halakha* with regard to whether **she can demand** the payment of her marriage contract from her **third** husband by claiming that it is now evident that she was capable of having children? The Gemara answers: **We say to her: Your silence is preferable to your speech,** i.e., you are better off not making this claim, **as he can say to her: I did not divorce you with this understanding,** and now that I know you are capable of having children, I regret divorcing you. This would invalidate her divorce and, consequently, her marriage to her fourth husband, and would render her child a *mamzer*.

מתקיף לה רב פפא: אי איהי שתקא אנן מי שתקינן? נמצא גט בטל ובניה ממזרין! אלא אמרינן: השתא הוא דבריתא.

Rav Pappa strongly objects to this: If she was silent[N] **do we remain silent?** If there is room for concern that the divorce might be invalid, the concern exists regardless of her claim, and therefore the **bill of divorce** should be **found invalid and her children** from her fourth husband should be rendered ***mamzerin.*** **Rather, we say** that **it is now that she has become healthy.** In other words, she was previously incapable of bearing children, but she has since recovered from that disability.

HALAKHA

If she was married to a third husband and she did not have children – נישאת לשלישי ולא היו לה בנים: If a woman was married to two husbands for ten years each without children, and then marries a third husband for ten years without children, she does not have to return the money that her first two husbands paid for her marriage contract. However, if she had not yet collected the money she is no longer entitled to it. Her claim that she was fertile in her younger years is not strong enough to enable her to claim money from others (*Shulḥan Arukh, Even HaEzer* 154:18).

If she was married to a fourth husband and she had children – נישאת לרביעי והיו לה בנים: If a woman's third husband divorced her without paying her marriage contract because she did not have children after ten years of marriage, and she married a fourth husband and did bear children, she cannot claim her marriage contract from the third, as it is possible that she became fertile only after they were divorced (*Shulḥan Arukh, Even HaEzer* 154:19).

BACKGROUND

It is now that I have become weak – השתא הוא דכחשי: This statement is easily understandable, as the woman has already been married three times, for ten years each. Even if she married the first time at a very young age, she is likely to be approaching menopause. Furthermore, there is a significant drop in fertility for women in their thirties, and this weakening, as it is called here, is an expected occurrence.

NOTES

If a woman was married to her first husband, etc. – ניסת לראשון וכו׳: The commentaries point out that this *baraita* is in accordance with the opinion of Rabbi Yehuda HaNasi. A different opinion is cited in the Jerusalem Talmud which maintains that she is permitted to marry a third husband and forbidden to marry only a fourth husband.

She is divorced without receiving payment for her marriage contract – תצא בלא כתובה: The reason for this *halakha* is that the husband entered the marriage erroneously, as stated in the *Tosefta*. However, the Ramban writes that the marriage is not considered to have been entirely erroneous, because if it were, the woman would not even require a bill of divorce. He explains that with regard to this issue it is considered uncertain whether the woman is fertile, and if she is fertile, her current marriage is not erroneous, and entering a new marriage would constitute adultery. Consequently, she requires a bill of divorce before marrying someone else. However, since there is a presumption that she is infertile, he does not have to pay her marriage contract, in accordance with the general principle that in monetary law, the burden of proof is upon the claimant.

It is now that I have become weak – השתא הוא דכחשי: The commentaries ask: If this is a valid claim, why doesn't she receive payment for her marriage contract from her third husband as well, as she can claim that she was capable of having children at the time they got married? The *Tosefot HaRosh* and *Tosafot Yeshanim* explain that this claim is effective only to prevent her from having to pay back her previous husbands, but is not convincing enough to bolster claims on her part for additional money. Consequently, if for some reason her previous husbands have not yet fulfilled their obligation to pay her marriage contract, she is no longer able to force them to do so. Conversely, the Ritva explains that she cannot collect payment for her marriage contract from her third husband due to a rabbinically imposed penalty for marrying a man unsuitable for her.

If she was silent, etc. – אי איהי שתקא וכו׳: The commentaries ask why this is a reason to deprive the woman of her marriage contract; it would seem that the husband can make this claim only if he explicitly stated at the time of the divorce that he was divorcing her because she was infertile. It is explained in the *Tosefot HaRosh* that in fact the case under discussion concerns only a situation when he made such a statement at the time of the divorce. The Ramban explains that since at the time of the divorce it was not known with absolute certainty that she was infertile, as she had no external signs of infertility, he divorced her with the understanding that she might actually be fertile. Therefore, the divorce cannot be retroactively nullified.

BACKGROUND

Shoots like an arrow – יוֹרֶה כְּחֵץ: As far as fertilization is concerned, it does not matter how the sperm enters the womb. Nevertheless, if his semen does not shoot like an arrow, which is an unusual predicament, there are grounds to suspect that it is a symptom of some other problem that prevents pregnancy, even if a small chance of conception still remains.

הוּא אָמַר: מִינָּהּ, וְהִיא אָמְרָה: מִינֵּיהּ – אָמַר רַבִּי אַמִי: דְּבָרִים שֶׁבֵּינוֹ לְבֵינָהּ נֶאֱמֶנֶת. וְטַעֲמָא מַאי? הִיא – קַיְימָא לָהּ בְּיוֹרֶה כְּחֵץ, הוּא – לָא קִים לֵיהּ בְּיוֹרֶה כְּחֵץ.

§ The Gemara addresses a related case. If **he said** that the cause for their failure to have children is **from her,**[NH] i.e., it is she who is infertile, **and she said** it is **from him, Rabbi Ami said:** With regard to such **matters between him and her, she is believed.** The Gemara inquires: **What is the reason** for this ruling? **She is certain** whether his semen **shoots like an arrow,**[B] whereas **he is not certain** whether his semen **shoots like an arrow.**

אֲמַר אִיהוּ: אֵיזִיל אִינְסִיב אִיתְּתָא וְאִיבְדוֹק נַפְשַׁאי. אָמַר רַבִּי אַמִי: אַף בְּזוֹ יוֹצִיא וְיִתֵּן כְּתוּבָּה, שֶׁאֲנִי אוֹמֵר: כׇּל הַנּוֹשֵׂא אִשָּׁה עַל אִשְׁתּוֹ – יוֹצִיא וְיִתֵּן כְּתוּבָּה. רָבָא אָמַר: נוֹשֵׂא אָדָם כַּמָּה נָשִׁים עַל אִשְׁתּוֹ, וְהוּא דְּאִית לֵיהּ לְמֵיזְיינִינְהִי.

If **he says: I will go** and **marry** a different **woman and examine myself**[N] to see if I am indeed the cause, **Rabbi Ami said: Even in this** case he **must divorce** his first wife **and give** her the payment for her **marriage contract, as I say** that **whoever marries a woman in addition to his** first **wife must divorce** his first wife **and give** her the payment for her **marriage contract.** Conversely, **Rava said** that **a man may marry several women**[H] **in addition to his** first **wife, and** there is nothing wrong with this practice **as long as he has** enough **to support them** all.

NOTES

He said it is from her – הוּא אָמַר מִינָּהּ: The commentaries offer many conflicting interpretations of this passage in light of the fact that it seems to contradict the Gemara in tractate *Nedarim* (91a), in which the Sages declared that a wife who claims that her husband's semen does not shoot like an arrow is not believed, due to the possibility that she is merely trying to force him to divorce her because she has set her eyes upon another man. Some *ge'onim* claim that the Gemara here is referring to the time before the rabbinic decree mentioned in tractate *Nedarim*, and the statement of the Gemara here is not accepted as *halakha*. The Rid writes that the Gemara in tractate *Nedarim* means that the court requests of the woman to withdraw her demand for a divorce and to try again, whereas the Gemara here states that if she insists on a divorce, her claim is accepted.

The Ra'avad explains that there is no contradiction because the Gemara in tractate *Nedarim* is referring to a case where she claims that her husband is completely unable to engage in intercourse, whereas here she claims that he does not ejaculate forcefully. Others explain that she is believed in the case here because there is circumstantial support to her claim, from the fact that they have been married for ten years without children. The Rif adds that in this situation it is the court that initiates the divorce process rather than the woman, and therefore there is no concern that she has set her eyes upon another man. See the Meiri, who cites several of these explanations and explains the differences between them.

An entirely different opinion is suggested by the Razah: The wife in the Gemara here does not want to be divorced from her husband, and her claim is that since he is the cause for their failure to have children there is no point in forcing him to divorce her, as he cannot father children in any case.

I will go and marry a different woman and examine myself – אֵיזִיל אִינְסִיב אִיתְּתָא וְאִיבְדוֹק נַפְשַׁאי: According to most commentaries, this is a continuation of the previous case: Hearing his wife's claim that he is infertile, the husband suggests that he might try and have children with another woman. However, *Tosefot Ḥad MiKamma'ei* cites an alternative explanation, according to which this is a different case: The couple has not had children, and neither side is interested in a divorce. The husband claims that he wants to delay divorcing his wife until he determines that she is in fact the cause of their inability to have children. Rabbi Ami states that even in this case he must divorce her, and Rava disagrees.

HALAKHA

He said it is from her, etc. – הוּא אָמַר מִינָּהּ וכו׳: With regard to a woman who sues for divorce with the claim that she is unable to conceive because her husband does not ejaculate forcefully, if they have already been married for ten years without children and she has no other reason for demanding a divorce, then she is believed. Even if he had children from a previous marriage, it is possible that he has since become dysfunctional, and he is obligated to divorce her; however, he is required to pay only the main part of her marriage contract. This is two hundred dinars for a woman who was a virgin at the time of her marriage or one hundred dinars for a woman who was not a virgin when she married, which the Sages required a husband to include in the marriage contract. He is not required to pay any additional sum that he voluntarily included in the marriage contract. He may declare a ban on one who makes unsubstantiated claims of this kind.

If he wants to marry an additional woman in order to determine the veracity of his wife's claim before divorcing her he is permitted to do so, and if his second wife bears children he may divorce the first one without paying her marriage contract. Some commentaries state that if the second wife confirms the claim of the first wife, he must divorce them both and pay them their marriage contracts.

If the husband knows that he is infertile and his wife demands a divorce on these grounds, he must grant it at once. This is the opinion of the Rambam and the *Shulḥan Arukh*. However, the Rema rules in accordance with the opinion of the Ra'avad and the *Tur*, who contend that this *halakha* applies only to a third husband or in a case where the husband has children from a previous marriage. In other cases, the woman receives payment for her marriage contract even if she does not claim that they have been unable to have children due to her husband's dysfunction. See the *Beit Shmuel*, who cites the various opinions of the earlier halakhic commentaries on this matter (Rambam *Sefer Nashim*, *Hilkhot Ishut* 15:8–9; *Shulḥan Arukh*, *Even HaEzer* 154:6 and in the comment of Rema).

A man may marry several women – נוֹשֵׂא אָדָם כַּמָּה נָשִׁים: A man is permitted to be married to several women at once, on condition that he can provide for their sustenance, clothing, and conjugal rights. However, in a place where the custom is not to marry more than one wife he may not do so. The ban on polygamy of Rabbeinu Gershom Meor HaGola is generally accepted, and this is the binding custom of Ashkenazic Jews to this day (Rambam *Sefer Nashim*, *Hilkhot Ishut* 14:3; *Shulḥan Arukh*, *Even HaEzer* 1:9, 76:7).

הוּא אָמַר: אַפֶּלְתְּ בְּגוֹ עֶשֶׂר, וְהִיא אָמְרָה: לָא אַפְּלִית. אָמַר רַבִּי אַמִי: אַף בְּזוֹ הִיא נֶאֱמֶנֶת, דְּאִם אִיתָא דְּהִפִּילָה – נַפְשָׁהּ בְּעַקְרוּתָהּ לָא מַחְזְקָה.

The Gemara addresses another case in which the court forces a man to divorce his wife who has not had children after ten years. If **he said: You miscarried**[NH] **within** the **ten** years of our marriage, and since less than ten years have elapsed since that time he should not have to divorce her, **and she said: I did not miscarry, Rabbi Ami said: Even in this** case **she is believed, because if it is so that she miscarried she** would **not establish herself as barren** through denying his claim.

הִפִּילָה, וְחָזְרָה וְהִפִּילָה, וְחָזְרָה וְהִפִּילָה – הוּחְזְקָה לִנְפָלִים. הוּא אָמַר: אַפִּילָה תְּרֵי, וְהִיא אָמְרָה: תְּלָת. אָמַר רַבִּי יִצְחָק בֶּן אֶלְעָזָר: עוּבְדָא הֲוָה בֵּי מִדְרְשָׁא, וְאָמְרוּ: הִיא מְהֵימְנָא, דְּאִם אִיתָא דְּלָא אַפְּלָה – נַפְשָׁהּ בְּנִיפְלֵי לָא מַחְזְקָה.

If **she miscarried,** and then **miscarried again,**[N] **and miscarried again, she has been established to** be a woman who is prone to **miscarriages,**[NB] and her husband must divorce her so that he can have children with another woman. If **he said she miscarried twice,**[H] **and she said** it occurred **three** times, **Rabbi Yitzḥak ben Elazar said: There was an incident** of this kind that was adjudicated in **the study hall and they said** that **she is believed, because if it is so that** she had **not miscarried** a third time **she** would **not establish herself** as one who is prone to **miscarriages.**

מתני׳ הָאִישׁ מְצוּוֶּה עַל פְּרִיָּה וּרְבִיָּה, אֲבָל לֹא הָאִשָּׁה. רַבִּי יוֹחָנָן בֶּן בְּרוֹקָה אוֹמֵר: עַל שְׁנֵיהֶם הוּא אוֹמֵר ״וַיְבָרֶךְ אוֹתָם אֱלֹהִים וַיֹּאמֶר לָהֶם [אֱלֹהִים] פְּרוּ וּרְבוּ״.

MISHNA **A man is commanded with regard to** the mitzva to be **fruitful and multiply,**[H] **but not a woman.**[H] **Rabbi Yoḥanan ben Beroka says** that a woman is also commanded, as the verse **states with regard to both of them: "And God blessed them, and God said to them: Be fruitful and multiply"** (Genesis 1:28).

גמ׳ מְנָא הָנֵי מִילֵּי? אָמַר רַבִּי אִילְעָא מִשּׁוּם רַבִּי אֶלְעָזָר בְּרַבִּי שִׁמְעוֹן: אָמַר קְרָא ״וּמִלְאוּ אֶת הָאָרֶץ וְכִבְשׁוּהָ״ אִישׁ דַּרְכּוֹ לִכְבּשׁ, וְאֵין אִשָּׁה דַּרְכָּהּ לִכְבּשׁ.

GEMARA **From where are these matters** derived, that a woman is not obligated in the mitzva to be fruitful and multiply? **Rabbi Ile'a said in the name of Rabbi Elazar, son of Rabbi Shimon: The verse states:** "Be fruitful and multiply, **and fill the land and conquer it**" (Genesis 1:28). **It is the manner of a man to conquer and it is not the manner of a woman to conquer.** Consequently, it is evident that the entire command, including the mitzva to be fruitful and multiply, was given only to men and not to women.

אַדְּרַבָּה, ״וְכִבְשׁוּהָ״ תַּרְתֵּי מַשְׁמַע! אָמַר רַב נַחְמָן בַּר יִצְחָק: ״וְכִבְשָׁהּ״ כְּתִיב. רַב יוֹסֵף אָמַר: מֵהָכָא, ״אֲנִי אֵל שַׁדַּי פְּרֵה וּרְבֵה״ וְלֹא קָאָמַר ״פְּרוּ וּרְבוּ״.

The Gemara raises a difficulty. **On the contrary,** the plural term: **"And conquer it [*vekhivshuha*]," indicates** that the **two** of them are included. **Rav Naḥman bar Yitzḥak said: It is written** in the Torah without the letter *vav*, so that it can be read: **And conquer it [*vekhivsha*]**,[N] in the singular. **Rav Yosef said:** The proof is **from here: "**And God said to him: **I am God Almighty, be fruitful and multiply [*perei urvei*]"** (Genesis 35:11), which is in singular, **and it does not state: Be fruitful and multiply [*peru urvu*]** in the plural.

NOTES

He said, you miscarried, etc. – הוּא אָמַר אַפֶּלְתְּ וכו׳: The commentaries disagree over the context of this *halakha*. According to the *She'iltot deRav Aḥai Gaon* and other *ge'onim* it includes even a case where she is demanding a divorce. There is no concern that she is making this statement because she has set her eyes on another man, as she would presumably not publicize negative information about herself for this purpose. Others, however, claim that this *halakha* applies only if the wife did not ask for a divorce; rather, the court wanted to force the husband to divorce her and she informed them of her version of events (see Ramban; Rashba; Meiri).

If she miscarried and then miscarried again, etc. – הִפִּילָה וְחָזְרָה וְהִפִּילָה וכו׳: In this case the *halakha* is not in accordance with the opinion of Rabbi Yehuda HaNasi, and the presumption is established only after three miscarriages. Although it was stated above (64b) that the *halakha* is in accordance with the opinion of Rabbi Yehuda HaNasi with regard to marriage, since in this case it was permitted for them to marry, he is not obligated to divorce her after only two miscarriages. Furthermore, it is possible that Rabbi Yehuda HaNasi himself agrees that in this case he is obligated to divorce her only after three miscarriages (Ramban; Rashba).

She has been established to be a woman who is prone to miscarriages – הוּחְזְקָה לִנְפָלִים: In this case there is no need to wait ten years, and he must divorce her immediately (*ge'onim*; see Rid). However, just as in the case of a woman who was married for ten years without children, the woman may marry another man. This is because it has been established only that she miscarries after conceiving from her first husband; it is possible that she is capable of bearing children, but is incompatible with that man (see Meiri).

It is written, and conquer it [*vekhivshah*] – וְכִבְשָׁהּ כְּתִיב: There is a general dispute among the *tanna'im* whether the written form of the Torah's text is considered authoritative or whether it is the manner in which it is vocalized that is authoritative. Nevertheless, in this case all would agree that the written form is authoritative, because the verse implies that the purpose of procreation is for humankind to conquer the earth, and it is men who engage in conquest (Ritva).

BACKGROUND

She has been established to be a woman who is prone to miscarriages – הוּחְזְקָה לִנְפָלִים: Nowadays as well, the phenomenon of recurring miscarriages exists. While there are different reasons for this, it is clear that some women are prone to miscarry.

HALAKHA

He said, you miscarried, etc. – הוּא אָמַר אַפֶּלְתְּ וכו׳: If a husband claims that his wife had a miscarriage during their ten years of marriage without children, and she denies it, she is believed (Rambam *Sefer Nashim, Hilkhot Ishut* 15:13; *Shulḥan Arukh, Even HaEzer* 154:13).

He said she miscarried twice, etc. – הוּא אָמַר אַפִּילָה תְּרֵי וכו׳: If a husband claims that his wife miscarried only twice and she says she miscarried three times, she is believed (Rambam *Sefer Nashim, Hilkhot Ishut* 15:13; *Shulḥan Arukh, Even HaEzer* 154:14).

A man is commanded…to be fruitful and multiply – הָאִישׁ מְצוּוֶּה עַל פְּרִיָּה וּרְבִיָּה: Every man is obligated to marry in order to fulfill the mitzva to be fruitful and multiply (Rambam *Sefer Nashim, Hilkhot Ishut* 15:2; *Shulḥan Arukh, Even HaEzer* 1:1).

But not a woman – אֲבָל לֹא הָאִשָּׁה: Women are not obligated to be fruitful and multiply, and therefore they do not have to marry. Some say that a woman should not remain unmarried, in order to avoid suspicions of indecent behavior (Rambam *Sefer Nashim, Hilkhot Ishut* 15:2; *Shulḥan Arukh, Even HaEzer* 1:13 and in the comment of Rema).

וְאָמַר רַבִּי אִילְעָא מִשּׁוּם רַבִּי אֶלְעָזָר בְּרַבִּי שִׁמְעוֹן: כְּשֵׁם שֶׁמִּצְוָה עַל אָדָם לוֹמַר דָּבָר הַנִּשְׁמָע – כָּךְ מִצְוָה עַל אָדָם שֶׁלֹּא לוֹמַר דָּבָר שֶׁאֵינוֹ נִשְׁמָע. רַבִּי אַבָּא אוֹמֵר: חוֹבָה, שֶׁנֶּאֱמַר ״אַל תּוֹכַח לֵץ פֶּן יִשְׂנָאֶךָּ הוֹכַח לְחָכָם וְיֶאֱהָבֶךָּ״.

The Gemara cites other statements made by Rabbi Ile'a in the name of Rabbi Elazar, son of Rabbi Shimon. **And Rabbi Ile'a said in the name of Rabbi Elazar, son of Rabbi Shimon: Just as it is a mitzva for a person to say that which will be heeded, so is it a mitzva for a person not to say**[N] **that which will not be heeded.** One should not rebuke those who will be unreceptive to his message. **Rabbi Abba says:** It is **obligatory** for him to refrain from speaking, **as it is stated: "Do not reprove a scorner lest he hate you; reprove a wise man and he will love you"** (Proverbs 9:8).

וְאָמַר רַבִּי אִילְעָא מִשּׁוּם רַבִּי אֶלְעָזָר בְּרַבִּי שִׁמְעוֹן: מוּתָּר לוֹ לְאָדָם לְשַׁנּוֹת בִּדְבַר הַשָּׁלוֹם, שֶׁנֶּאֱמַר ״אָבִיךָ צִוָּה״ וגו׳ ״כֹּה תֹאמְרוּ לְיוֹסֵף אָנָּא שָׂא נָא״ וגו׳.

And Rabbi Ile'a further **said in the name of Rabbi Elazar, son of Rabbi Shimon: It is permitted for a person to depart** from the truth[N] **in a matter** that will bring **peace, as it is stated: "Your father commanded** before he died, saying: **So you shall say to Joseph: Please pardon** your brothers' crime, etc." (Genesis 50:16–17). Jacob never issued this command, but his sons falsely attributed this statement to him in order to preserve peace between them and Joseph.

רַבִּי נָתָן אוֹמֵר: מִצְוָה, שֶׁנֶּאֱמַר ״וַיֹּאמֶר שְׁמוּאֵל אֵיךְ אֵלֵךְ וְשָׁמַע שָׁאוּל וַהֲרָגָנִי״ וגו׳.

Rabbi Natan says: It is a **mitzva** to depart from the truth in order to preserve peace, **as it is stated: "And Samuel said: How can I go, and Saul will hear and kill me"** (1 Samuel 16:2). God responded in the next verse that Samuel should say he went to sacrifice an offering, indicating that God commands one to lie in order to preserve peace.

דְּבֵי רַבִּי יִשְׁמָעֵאל תָּנָא: גָּדוֹל הַשָּׁלוֹם שֶׁאַף הַקָּדוֹשׁ בָּרוּךְ הוּא שִׁינָּה בּוֹ. דְּמֵעִיקָּרָא כְּתִיב ״וַאדוֹנִי זָקֵן״ וּלְבַסּוֹף כְּתִיב ״וַאֲנִי זָקַנְתִּי״.

It was **taught in the school of Rabbi Yishmael: Great is peace,**[N] **as even the Holy One, Blessed be He, departed** from the truth for **it. As, initially it is written** that Sarah said of Abraham: **"And my lord is old"** (Genesis 18:12), **and in the end it is written** that God told Abraham that Sarah said: **"And I am old"** (Genesis 18:13). God adjusted Sarah's words in order to spare Abraham hurt feelings that might lead Abraham and Sarah to quarrel.

״רַבִּי יוֹחָנָן בֶּן בְּרוֹקָה אוֹמֵר״. אִתְּמַר, רַבִּי יוֹחָנָן וְרַבִּי יְהוֹשֻׁעַ בֶּן לֵוִי, חַד אָמַר: הֲלָכָה כְּרַבִּי יוֹחָנָן בֶּן בְּרוֹקָה, וְחַד אָמַר: אֵין הֲלָכָה כְּרַבִּי יוֹחָנָן בֶּן בְּרוֹקָה.

§ It is taught in the mishna that **Rabbi Yoḥanan ben Beroka says** that women are also included in the mitzva to be fruitful and multiply. **It was stated** that two *amora'im*, **Rabbi Yoḥanan and Rabbi Yehoshua ben Levi,** disagreed concerning this matter. **One said** that the ***halakha* is in accordance with** the opinion of **Rabbi Yoḥanan ben Beroka, and one said** that the ***halakha* is not in accordance with** the opinion of **Rabbi Yoḥanan ben Beroka.**

תִּסְתַּיֵּים דְּרַבִּי יוֹחָנָן הוּא דַּאֲמַר אֵין הֲלָכָה דְּיָתֵיב רַבִּי אַבָּהוּ וְקָאָמַר מִשְּׁמֵיהּ דְּרַבִּי יוֹחָנָן הֲלָכָה, וְאַהְדְּרִינְהוּ רַבִּי אַמִּי וְרַבִּי אַסִּי לְאַפַּיְיהוּ.

The Gemara comments: **Conclude that it was Rabbi Yoḥanan**[N] **who said** that the ***halakha* is not** in accordance with the opinion of Rabbi Yoḥanan ben Beroka, **as Rabbi Abbahu sat and said in the name of Rabbi Yoḥanan** that the ***halakha*** is in accordance with the opinion of Rabbi Yoḥanan ben Beroka, **and Rabbi Ami and Rabbi Asi,** who were sitting across from him, **turned their faces** as an indication that they disagreed with this report of Rabbi Yoḥanan's opinion, but did not want to explicitly contradict Rabbi Abbahu's statement out of respect for him.

NOTES

So is it a mitzva for a person not to say – כָּךְ מִצְוָה עַל אָדָם שֶׁלֹּא לוֹמַר: The commentaries question why it is permissible to remain silent when there is a mitzva to rebuke wrongdoers (see Leviticus 19:17). The Ritva answers that the Gemara is referring to addressing a group of people, whereas one is always obligated to rebuke an individual. The *Shela* explains that if the offender knows that he is acting improperly it is proper to rebuke him, but if he does not think he has transgressed the criticism is better left unsaid. Alternatively, if one rebukes another who does not accept reproof, this will only cause the latter to act willfully in the future, and it is preferable for him to remain an unwitting sinner (*Iyyun Ya'akov*).

It is permitted for a person to depart from the truth – מוּתָּר לוֹ לְאָדָם לְשַׁנּוֹת: The Gemara does not cite Sarah's reaction: "And Sarah denied, saying I did not laugh" (Genesis 18:15), as proof that one may depart from the truth, as she did so only when faced with an accusation, whereas the other verses prove that one may take the initiative in stating falsehoods for the sake of peace (*Arukh LaNer*).

It is a mitzva to depart from the truth…great is peace – מִצְוָה...גָּדוֹל הַשָּׁלוֹם: The commentaries point out that God did not command Samuel to tell an outright lie, but rather to take an animal with him and sacrifice it. In this way he would not be lying if he said that he was traveling to sacrifice an offering, even though he would be omitting the main purpose of his journey, which was to anoint David as the next king of the Jewish people. A similar claim can be made with regard to God's report to Abraham that Sarah said: And I am old; as she herself did say: "After my withering shall I have youth" (Genesis 18:12). God simply left out her additional comment: "And my lord is old" (Meiri; see *Tosafot Yeshanim*).

Conclude that it was Rabbi Yoḥanan, etc. – תִּסְתַּיֵּים דְּרַבִּי יוֹחָנָן הוּא וכו׳: It would appear that the Gemara does not prove what Rabbi Yoḥanan's opinion is, as it merely cites a dispute among his students about the matter. Perhaps that is why the Gemara continues by citing Rabbi Abbahu in the name of Rabbi Asi with regard to the incident in Caesarea; it is an attempt to prove that they actually both agree that Rabbi Yoḥanan held in accordance with the opinion of Rabbi Yoḥanan ben Beroka (*Arukh LaNer*).

וְאִיכָּא דְּאָמְרִי: רַבִּי חִיָּיא בַּר אַבָּא אֲמַר, וְאַהַדְרִינְהוּ רַבִּי אַמִי וְרַבִּי אַסִי לְאַפַּיְיהוּ. אֲמַר רַב פַּפָּא: בִּשְׁלָמָא לְמַאן דַּאֲמַר רַבִּי אַבָּהוּ אֲמָרָהּ – מִשּׁוּם כְּבוֹד בֵּי קֵיסָר לָא אָמְרוּ לֵיהּ וְלָא מִידֵי, אֶלָּא לְמַאן דְּאָמַר רַבִּי חִיָּיא בַּר אַבָּא אֲמָרָהּ – לֵימְרוּ לֵיהּ: לָא אֲמַר רַבִּי יוֹחָנָן הָכִי!

And some say a different version of the incident, that it was **Rabbi Ḥiyya bar Abba** who said this statement, **and Rabbi Ami and Rabbi Asi turned their faces. Rav Pappa said: Granted, according to the one who said** that **Rabbi Abbahu said it,** it makes sense that **due to the honor of Caesar's court,** where Rabbi Abbahu maintained close ties, Rabbi Ami and Rabbi Asi **did not say anything to him** and merely hinted at their disagreement. **However, according to the one who said** that **Rabbi Ḥiyya bar Abba said it, let them say to him explicitly: Rabbi Yoḥanan did not say this.** In any event, it is clear that according to Rabbi Ami and Rabbi Asi, Rabbi Yoḥanan disagreed with the opinion of Rabbi Yoḥanan ben Beroka.

מַאי הֲוָה עֲלָהּ? תָּא שְׁמַע, דַּאֲמַר רַבִּי אַחָא בַּר חֲנִינָא אֲמַר רַבִּי אַבָּהוּ אֲמַר רַבִּי אַסִי: עוּבְדָא הֲוָה קַמֵּיהּ דְּרַבִּי יוֹחָנָן בִּכְנִישְׁתָּא דְּקֵיסָרִי, וַאֲמַר: ״יוֹצִיא וְיִתֵּן כְּתוּבָּה״. וְאִי סָלְקָא דַּעְתָּךְ לָא מִפַּקְדָה – כְּתוּבָּה מַאי עֲבִידְתֵּיהּ?

The Gemara asks: **What** conclusion **was** reached **about** this issue? The Gemara suggests: **Come and hear, as Rabbi Aḥa bar Ḥanina said** that **Rabbi Abbahu said** that **Rabbi Asi said: There was an incident** that came **before Rabbi Yoḥanan in the synagogue of Caesarea** involving a woman who wanted a divorce from her husband after ten years of childless marriage, **and he said** that the husband **must divorce** her **and give** her the payment for her **marriage contract. If it enters your mind** to say **that she is not commanded** to be fruitful and multiply, **what is** payment for **a marriage contract doing** here? Why does she have a right to demand to be divorced and to receive the payment for her marriage contract?

דִּלְמָא בְּבָאָה מֵחֲמַת טַעֲנָה.

The Gemara responds: **Perhaps** that was **in** a case when **she came** to demand a divorce **due to** another **claim,** i.e., she wanted children for a reason other than the fulfillment of the mitzva to be fruitful and multiply. Since this claim has merit, her husband must divorce her and pay her marriage contract.

כִּי הַהִיא דַּאֲתַאי לְקַמֵּיהּ דְּרַבִּי אַמִי, אָמְרָה לֵיהּ: הַב לִי כְּתוּבָּה. אֲמַר לָהּ: זִיל, לָא מִיפַּקְדַתְּ. אָמְרָה לֵיהּ: מִסֵּיבוּ דִּילָהּ מַאי תֶּיהֱוֵי עֲלָהּ דְּהָךְ אִתְּתָא? אֲמַר: כִּי הָא – וַדַּאי כָּפֵינַן.

This is like the case of **a certain** woman **who came before Rabbi Ami** and requested a divorce due to her husband's inability to father children. **She said to** her husband: **Give me** the payment for my **marriage contract. He said to her: Go** away, as **you are not commanded** to be fruitful and multiply and have no right to demand a divorce. **She said to him: In her old age, what will be with this woman,** i.e., if I have no children, who will take care of me when I grow old? Rabbi Ami **said:** In a situation **such as this, we certainly force** the husband to divorce and her and pay her marriage contract.

הַהִיא דַּאֲתַאי לְקַמֵּיהּ דְּרַב נַחְמָן, אֲמַר לָהּ: לָא מִיפַּקְדַתְּ. אָמְרָה לֵיהּ: לָא בָּעְיָא הַךְ אִתְּתָא חוּטְרָא לִידָהּ וּמָרָה לִקְבוּרָה? אֲמַר: כִּי הָא – וַדַּאי כָּפֵינַן.

The Gemara relates a similar incident: **A certain** woman **came before Rav Naḥman** and requested a divorce due to her husband's inability to father children. **He said to her: You are not commanded** to be fruitful and multiply. **She said to him: Does this woman not require a staff for her hand and a hoe for** her **burial?** In other words, the woman said that she wanted children so that they could care for her in her old age and bury her when she would die. Rav Naḥman **said:** In a case **such as this, we certainly force** the husband to divorce her.

יְהוּדָה וְחִזְקִיָּה תְּאוֹמִים הָיוּ, אֶחָד נִגְמְרָה צוּרָתוֹ לְסוֹף תִּשְׁעָה וְאֶחָד נִגְמְרָה צוּרָתוֹ לִתְחִלַּת שִׁבְעָה. יְהוּדִית, דְּבֵיתְהוּ דְּרַבִּי חִיָּיא, הֲוָה לָהּ צַעַר לֵידָה, שְׁנַאֵי מָנָא וְאָתְיָא לְקַמֵּיהּ דְּרַבִּי חִיָּיא, אָמְרָה: אִתְּתָא מִפַּקְדָא אַפְּרִיָּה וּרְבִיָּה? אֲמַר לָהּ: לָא. אָזְלָא אִשְׁתְּיָא סַמָּא דְּעַקַּרְתָּא.

The Gemara relates that Rabbi Ḥiyya's sons, **Yehuda and Ḥizkiyya, were twins,** but **one** of them **was fully developed after nine** months of pregnancy **and one was fully developed at the beginning of the seventh** month, and they were born two months apart.[B] **Yehudit, the wife of Rabbi Ḥiyya,**[P] **had** acute **birthing pain** from these unusual deliveries. She **changed her clothes** to prevent Rabbi Ḥiyya from recognizing her **and came before Rabbi Ḥiyya** to ask him a halakhic question. **She said: Is a woman commanded** to be **fruitful and multiply? He said to her: No. She went and drank an infertility potion.**

לְסוֹף אִיגַּלַּאי מִילְּתָא. אֲמַר לָהּ: אִיכּוּ יָלַדְתְּ לִי חֲדָא כְּרֵסָא אַחֲרִיתָא! דַּאֲמַר מָר: יְהוּדָה וְחִזְקִיָּה – אַחֵי, פַּזִּי וְטַוִּי

Eventually the matter was revealed, and Rabbi Ḥiyya found out about what Yehudit had done. **He said to her: If only you had given birth to one more belly**[B] **for me,** i.e., another set of twins. **As the Master said: Yehuda and Ḥizkiyya** were twin **brothers** and became prominent Torah scholars, and **Pazi and Tavi,** Rabbi Ḥiyya's daughters,

BACKGROUND

Twins born at different times – תְּאוֹמִים שֶׁנּוֹלְדוּ בְּהֶפְרֵשׁ זְמַן: Although rare, it is possible for twins to be born at different times, occasionally with a significant interval between the births. There have been documented cases of the birth of twins separated by a gap of over fifty days, and even up to eighty-five days.

One more belly – חֲדָא כְּרֵסָא אַחֲרִיתָא: There is a hereditary tendency among certain women to give birth to twins, and therefore a woman who gave birth to two sets of twins has a considerable likelihood of having an additional set of twins. The birth of twins, and in particular the unusual occurrence of a lengthy interval between their births, explains why Rabbi Ḥiyya's wife was worried about significant labor pains.

PERSONALITIES

Rabbi Ḥiyya and his family – רַבִּי חִיָּיא וּמִשְׁפַּחְתּוֹ: Rabbi Ḥiyya ben Abba, who was from the city of Kafri, Babylonia, was among the last of the *tanna'im* and was a disciple-colleague of Rabbi Yehuda HaNasi. Rabbi Ḥiyya descended from a family of distinguished lineage that traced its ancestry back to King David and produced many Sages. While he was still in Babylonia, Rabbi Ḥiyya was considered a Torah luminary. When he ascended with his family from Babylonia to Eretz Yisrael, some, engaging in hyperbole, said that the Torah was about to be forgotten in Eretz Yisrael until he came from Babylonia and reestablished it. When he came to Eretz Yisrael, he became a disciple and a colleague of Rabbi Yehuda HaNasi, with whom he had a very close relationship. He was especially close with Rabbi Yehuda HaNasi's son Shimon, who was also his business partner.

All of the students of Rabbi Yehuda HaNasi were Rabbi Ḥiyya's colleagues, and he was close with the *tanna* Rabbi Shimon ben Ḥalafta. The younger disciples of Rabbi Yehuda HaNasi, e.g., Rabbi Ḥanina, Rabbi Oshaya, Rabbi Yannai, and others, studied Torah from Rabbi Ḥiyya and were, to a certain degree, his disciples as well. His brothers' sons, Rabba bar bar Ḥana, and above all, the great *amora*, Rav, were his primary disciples. In addition to his prominence as a Torah scholar, Rabbi Ḥiyya was outstanding in his piety, as reflected in several anecdotes throughout the Talmud. Rabbi Ḥiyya also appears as a central figure in the *Zohar*. He was buried in Tiberias and his two sons were later buried alongside him.

Rabbi Ḥiyya's sons, Yehuda, son-in-law of Rabbi Yannai, and Ḥizkiyya, were both among the leading Torah scholars in the transitional generation between the *tanna'im* and the *amora'im*. They apparently succeeded Rabbi Ḥiyya at the head of his private yeshiva in the city of his residence, Tiberias.

The *ge'onim* had a tradition, also cited in *Tosafot* (*Bava Batra* 149a), that Rabbi Ḥiyya's daughter Pazi was the mother of a large family that included several important Sages such as Rabbi Shimon ben Pazi and his son, Rabbi Yehuda. Out of respect for Rabbi Ḥiyya, they were referred to by Pazi's name rather than that of her husband. It is possible that the family of Ḥiyya's other daughter Tavi was also renowned, and for this reason the two sisters, Pazi and Tavi, are mentioned alongside their brothers, Yehuda and Ḥizkiyya, to explain why Rabbi Ḥiyya was so upset that his wife did not give birth to another set of twins.

אַחְוָותָא.

were twin **sisters,** and became the matriarchs of families of distinguished Torah scholars.

וְלָא מִיפַּקְדָי? וְהָאָמַר רַב אַחָא בַּר רַב קְטִינָא אָמַר רַבִּי יִצְחָק: מַעֲשֶׂה בְּאִשָּׁה אַחַת שֶׁחֶצְיָהּ שִׁפְחָה וְחֶצְיָהּ בַּת חוֹרִין, וְכָפוּ אֶת רַבָּהּ וַעֲשָׂאָהּ בַּת חוֹרִין! אָמַר רַב נַחְמָן בַּר יִצְחָק: מִנְהַג הֶפְקֵר נָהֲגוּ בָּהּ.

The Gemara asks: **Are** women **not commanded** to be fruitful and multiply? **Didn't Rav Aḥa bar Rav Ketina say** that **Rabbi Yitzḥak said:** There was **an incident with a certain woman who** was **half-slave**[N] **and half-free woman** and therefore could marry neither a Canaanite slave nor a Jew, **and they forced her master**[N] **and he made her a free** woman. Presumably, the reason the court forced her master to free her was so that she could fulfill the mitzva to be fruitful and multiply. **Rav Naḥman bar Yitzḥak said:** The reason they forced her master to free her was because others **treated her in a loose manner.**[H] Since she knew that she could not marry she engaged in promiscuous activity, and the court forced her master to free her in order to save her and others from sin.

הדרן עלך הבא על יבמתו

NOTES

Who was half-slave, etc. – **שֶׁחֶצְיָהּ שִׁפְחָה וכו׳**: This case can occur when a Canaanite maidservant is jointly owned by two people and one them releaser her from bondage. With regard to the case discussed here, some commentaries hold that the master is forced to free only a half-slave who acts in a promiscuous fashion, because her actions are due to the fact that she cannot marry (see *Tur*; *Shakh*). Others hold that the same would be true with regard to a full maidservant who acts promiscuously. They argue that the fact that the incident cited in the Gemara involved a half-slave does not indicate that the *halakha* is limited to this case (Rabbeinu Yeruḥam; Rambam).

A similar *halakha* applies in a case of a man who is half-Canaanite slave and half-free, and therefore cannot marry. His master is therefore forced to free him. However, in this case the reason given is so that he can fulfill the mitzva expressed in the verse: "He did not create it a waste; He formed it to be inhabited" (Isaiah 45:18).

And they forced her master – **וְכָפוּ אֶת רַבָּהּ**: The novelty here is twofold: First, the Sages required the master to forfeit his slave, who is considered his property. Additionally, it is generally prohibited to free a Canaanite slave unless one is doing so for the sake of a mitzva. Therefore, the Gemara assumed that they must have forced her master to release her so that she could fulfill a mitzva by marrying and having children. The Gemara answers that the mitzva involved was preventing people from sinning, not the mitzva to be fruitful and multiply.

HALAKHA

They treated her in a loose manner – **מִנְהַג הֶפְקֵר נָהֲגוּ בָּהּ**: If a maidservant is involved in widespread promiscuous activity, her master is forced to release her so that she can marry, thereby removing the stumbling block from the community (Rambam *Sefer Kinyan*, *Hilkhot Avadim* 9:6; *Shulḥan Arukh*, *Yoreh De'a* 267:79).

Summary of **Perek VI**

The Torah decrees that a woman is acquired by her *yavam* in levirate marriage through sexual intercourse. This chapter clarified that as long as they intended to engage in an act of intercourse it makes no difference whether they did so willingly or whether they intended only to fulfill the mitzva of levirate marriage; the very act itself serves to consummate and validate the levirate bond. With regard to the definition of the sexual act, even the first stage of sexual intercourse is considered an act of intercourse and consummates the levirate marriage.

With regard to other forbidden sexual relations, the intention of the parties involved is relevant with regard to punishment, as one is not punished unless he intentionally violates a prohibition. However, other ramifications of forbidden relations apply regardless of intent. This includes the disqualification of a *zona*, i.e., a woman who had relations with a man whom she is forbidden to marry, from marrying a priest.

With regard to women disqualified from the priesthood, the Gemara clarified that even if a woman is considered reserved for an invalid act of intercourse, she is, at least temporarily, disqualified from partaking of *teruma*. A common priest may not marry a *zona*, a divorcée, a woman who underwent *ḥalitza*, or a convert. The High Priest may marry only a minor or a maiden, i.e., a woman within the first twelve months of adulthood, who is a virgin and has never been betrothed. However, if a priest betrothed a widow and was then appointed to be High Priest, he may marry her.

All Jewish men are obligated by Torah law to marry and have children in order to fulfill the mitzva to be fruitful and multiply. One has fulfilled this mitzva if he has both a son and a daughter. If his children die after bearing children of their own, he may still be in fulfillment of the mitzva through his grandchildren. One is even required to divorce his wife in order to marry another woman and fulfill the mitzva to be fruitful and multiply, if his wife is unable to bear children. This chapter further clarified when this obligation applies, when a woman is presumed to be unable to bear children, and what the rights of a woman who cannot bear children are when she is divorced from her husband. Also included were aggadic statements pertaining to marriage in general, and the mitzva to be fruitful and multiply in particular.

Introduction to **Perek VII**

They [the priests] shall not take a woman who is a harlot, or profaned; neither shall they take a woman divorced from her husband, for he is holy to his God.

(Leviticus 21:7)

A widow, or one divorced, or a profaned woman, or a harlot, these he shall not take; but a virgin of his own people he shall take as a wife.

(Leviticus 21:14)

But if a priest buys any soul, the purchase of his money, he may eat of it; and such as are born in his house, they may eat of his bread. And if a priest's daughter be married to a common man, she shall not eat of that which is set apart from the sacred. But if a priest's daughter be a widow, or divorced, and have no child, and is returned to her father's house, as in her youth, she may eat of her father's bread; but there shall no common man eat of it.

(Leviticus 22:11–13)

One of the topics discussed in the previous chapter is the *halakha* that a woman who has intercourse with a man who is unfit for her is rendered disqualified from marrying a priest. If she is the daughter of a priest, she may no longer partake of *teruma*. This chapter discusses the matter at length, although it is connected only tangentially to the main subject of the tractate.

The Torah states that all the members of a priest's household, i.e., his wife, his sons and daughters, and their slaves, may partake of *teruma*. If the priest dies or divorces his wife, she may continue to partake of *teruma* only if she has children from him. Conversely, a priest's daughter who is married to a non-priest may not partake of *teruma*. If she is widowed or divorced from him, and has no children from him, she resumes partaking of *teruma*.

These principles raise questions with regard to different types of unions between a priest and an Israelite woman or between the daughter of a priest and an Israelite man: If a priest betroths a woman who is unfit for him but whose betrothal to him is nevertheless valid, are she and her slaves entitled to partake of *teruma*? If not, are the slaves that she brings into the marriage considered his or hers? Also, what is the ruling with regard to a levirate bond between a priest and an Israelite woman?

Precisely what constitutes the definition of a woman's having children from her husband is also discussed. Is a pregnant woman considered one who already has children from her husband, or is she still considered childless? Does the term children here refer specifically to their children, or does it apply to all of their descendants? Do children who are unfit to marry into the assembly of Israel qualify, or do only unflawed children count?

This chapter discusses these issues both in principle and in detail.

מתני׳ אַלְמָנָה לְכֹהֵן גָּדוֹל, גְּרוּשָׁה וַחֲלוּצָה לְכֹהֵן הֶדְיוֹט, הִכְנִיסָה לוֹ עַבְדֵי מְלוֹג וְעַבְדֵי צֹאן בַּרְזֶל, עַבְדֵי מְלוֹג – לֹא יֹאכְלוּ בִּתְרוּמָה, עַבְדֵי צֹאן בַּרְזֶל – יֹאכְלוּ.

MISHNA **A widow** married **to a High Priest, and a divorcée or a** *yevama* **who performed** *ḥalitza* [*ḥalutza*] married **to a common priest** are all unions prohibited by Torah law. If one of these women **brought** with her **into** the marriage **slaves of usufruct** [*melog*][L] property **or slaves of guaranteed investment,**[N] then the **slaves of usufruct** property **do not partake of** *teruma* but the **slaves of guaranteed investment do partake** of *teruma*.[H]

וְאֵלּוּ הֵן עַבְדֵי מְלוֹג: אִם מֵתוּ – מֵתוּ לָהּ, וְאִם הוֹתִירוּ – הוֹתִירוּ לָהּ, אַף עַל פִּי שֶׁהוּא חַיָּיב בִּמְזוֹנוֹתָן הֲרֵי אֵלּוּ לֹא יֹאכְלוּ בִּתְרוּמָה. וְאֵלּוּ הֵן עַבְדֵי צֹאן בַּרְזֶל: אִם מֵתוּ – מֵתוּ לוֹ, וְאִם הוֹתִירוּ – הוֹתִירוּ לוֹ, הוֹאִיל וְהוּא חַיָּיב בְּאַחֲרָיוּתָן הֲרֵי אֵלּוּ יֹאכְלוּ בִּתְרוּמָה.

And these are slaves of usufruct property: They are those with regard to whom the couple stipulated that **if** the slaves **die, their death** is **her** loss, **and if** they **increase** in value, **their increase** is **her** gain. **Although** the husband **is obligated in their sustenance,**[H] **they do not partake of** *teruma*, as they belong to her, not to him. He owns only the right of their use while he is married to her. **And these are slaves of guaranteed investment:**[H] They are those with regard to whom the couple stipulated that **if they die, their death is his** loss,[N] **and if they increase** in value, **their increase** is **his** gain. **Since he bears** financial **responsibility** for compensating her in the event of **their loss, they partake of** *teruma*, as they are considered his property.

בַּת יִשְׂרָאֵל שֶׁנִּיסֵּת לְכֹהֵן וְהִכְנִיסָה לוֹ עֲבָדִים, בֵּין עַבְדֵי מְלוֹג בֵּין עַבְדֵי צֹאן בַּרְזֶל, הֲרֵי אֵלּוּ יֹאכְלוּ בִּתְרוּמָה. וּבַת כֹּהֵן שֶׁנִּיסֵּת לְיִשְׂרָאֵל וְהִכְנִיסָה לוֹ עֲבָדִים, בֵּין עַבְדֵי מְלוֹג בֵּין עַבְדֵי צֹאן בַּרְזֶל, הֲרֵי אֵלּוּ לֹא יֹאכְלוּ בִּתְרוּמָה.

In the case of **an Israelite woman who married a priest** in a halakhic marriage **and** who **brought slaves** with her **into** the marriage, **whether** they are **slaves of usufruct** property **or slaves of guaranteed investment, they partake of** *teruma*.[H] And in the case of **the daughter of a priest who married an Israelite**[H] and who **brought slaves** with her **into** the marriage, **whether** they are **slaves of usufruct** property **or slaves of guaranteed investment, they do not partake of** *teruma*, although, as she is the daughter of a priest, it is permitted for her and her slaves to partake of *teruma* beforehand.

גמ׳ וְעַבְדֵי מְלוֹג לֹא יֹאכְלוּ בִּתְרוּמָה, אַמַּאי? לֶהֱוֵי כְּקִנְיָנוֹ שֶׁקָּנָה קִנְיָן! דְּתַנְיָא: מִנַּיִן לְכֹהֵן שֶׁנָּשָׂא אִשָּׁה וְקָנָה עֲבָדִים שֶׁיֹּאכְלוּ בִּתְרוּמָה – שֶׁנֶּאֱמַר ״וְכֹהֵן כִּי יִקְנֶה נֶפֶשׁ קִנְיַן כַּסְפּוֹ הוּא יֹאכַל בּוֹ״.

GEMARA The mishna states that if a priest married a woman forbidden to him, his wife's **slaves of usufruct** property **do not partake of** *teruma*. The Gemara asks: **Why** is this so? **Let** this case **be like** that of **his acquisition who acquired an acquisition, as it is taught** in a *baraita*: **From where** is it derived with regard **to a priest who married a woman**[H] **and acquired slaves**[H] **that they partake of** *teruma*? **As it is stated: "But if a priest buys any soul, the purchase of his money, he may eat of it"** (Leviticus 22:11).

LANGUAGE

Usufruct [*melog*] – מְלוֹג: The search after the origin of this word dates back to the early commentaries. Some claim that it stems from the root *m-l-g*, which means to scald the skin of an animal in order to remove its hair. Here too, the husband removes, so to speak, the profits from his wife's assets. Others suggest that it is derived from the Greek λόγος, *logos*, which means word or speech, indicating that the husband receives rights to these properties as the result of verbal stipulation. However, it is apparently an original Akkadian term that means assets that a woman brings with her into the marriage.

NOTES

Guaranteed investment [*tzon barzel*] – צֹאן בַּרְזֶל: This idiom existed in Roman law as well. It literally means iron sheep. The proprietorship of guaranteed property is like that of something that never dies or gets damaged, as another individual has taken upon himself responsibility for its value. This metaphor is also appropriate in the sense that these assets bring no profit to their owners; rather, they remain at a fixed value.

If they die their death is his loss – אִם מֵתוּ, מֵתוּ לוֹ: The question was raised: What is the husband's responsibility for guaranteed property in a case where a slave does not die but merely decreases in value? Most early commentaries rule that the husband does not need to reimburse his wife unless the slave dies or is incapacitated. As long as the slaves are able to work, the husband returns them to his wife without compensation for their loss in value. This *halakha* is inferred from the use of the expression: If they die, their death is his loss, i.e., he must compensate her only in cases where the guaranteed property no longer exists in its original form. This *halakha* applies not only to slaves but to any sort of guaranteed property (Rabbeinu Ḥananel; Rif).

HALAKHA

The slaves of usufruct property do not partake of ***teruma*** **but the slaves of guaranteed investment do partake of** ***teruma*** – עַבְדֵי מְלוֹג לֹא יֹאכְלוּ בִּתְרוּמָה, עַבְדֵי צֹאן בַּרְזֶל יֹאכְלוּ: If a widow married to a High Priest or a *ḥalutza* married to a common priest brought slaves with her into the marriage, her slaves of usufruct property do not partake of *teruma*. However, her slaves of guaranteed investment partake of *teruma* (Rambam *Sefer Zera'im*, *Hilkhot Terumot* 7:20).

The husband is obligated in their sustenance – חַיָּיב בִּמְזוֹנוֹתָן: The husband is obligated to sustain his slaves of usufruct property, and he must fulfill all of their needs. They must work for him, and the profits earned through their work are his (Rambam *Sefer Nashim*, *Hilkhot Ishut* 22:25; *Shulḥan Arukh*, *Even HaEzer* 85:16).

And these are slaves of usufruct property…And these are slaves of guaranteed investment – וְאֵלּוּ הֵן עַבְדֵי מְלוֹג...וְאֵלּוּ הֵן עַבְדֵי צֹאן בַּרְזֶל: If a husband does not accept financial responsibility for property a woman brings with her into a marriage, that property remains hers. As a result, if its value has increased or decreased at the conclusion of the marriage, the loss or gain is hers. On the other hand, if the husband accepts financial responsibility for this dowry, it is entirely in his possession. He must pay her the original value of the property upon the dissolution of the marriage (Rambam *Sefer Nashim*, *Hilkhot Ishut* 16:1; *Shulḥan Arukh*, *Even HaEzer* 85:2).

The slaves of a priest's wife – עַבְדֵי אֵשֶׁת כֹּהֵן: If an Israelite or Levite woman is halakhically married to a priest and brought slaves with her into the marriage, whether they are usufruct or guaranteed property they partake of *teruma* (Rambam *Sefer Zera'im*, *Hilkhot Terumot* 7:18).

The daughter of a priest who married an Israelite – בַּת כֹּהֵן שֶׁנִּיסֵּת לְיִשְׂרָאֵל: If the daughter of a priest married an Israelite and brought slaves with her into the marriage, they may no longer partake of *teruma*, whether they are slaves of usufruct property or slaves of guaranteed investment (Rambam *Sefer Zera'im*, *Hilkhot Terumot* 7:19).

The wife of a priest partakes of ***teruma*** – אֵשֶׁת כֹּהֵן אוֹכֶלֶת בִּתְרוּמָה: An Israelite woman who married a priest partakes of *teruma* as well as the breast and right hind leg of animal offerings that belong to the priests. By Torah law, she partakes of these from the time of betrothal, but the Sages decreed that she not partake of them until her marriage (Rambam *Sefer Zera'im*, *Hilkhot Terumot* 6:3).

The slaves of a priest partake of ***teruma*** – עַבְדֵי כֹּהֵן אוֹכְלִים בִּתְרוּמָה: The slaves and animals of a priest partake of *teruma* and the *teruma* of the tithe (Rambam *Sefer Zera'im*, *Hilkhot Terumot* 6:1).

וּמִנַּיִן לְאִשָּׁה שֶׁקָּנְתָה עֲבָדִים, וַעֲבָדָיו שֶׁקָּנוּ עֲבָדִים, שֶׁיֹּאכְלוּ בִּתְרוּמָה – שֶׁנֶּאֱמַר ״וְכֹהֵן כִּי יִקְנֶה נֶפֶשׁ קִנְיַן כַּסְפּוֹ הוּא יֹאכַל בּוֹ״. קִנְיָנוֹ שֶׁקָּנָה קִנְיָן – אוֹכֵל!

And from where is it derived with regard **to** both the **wife** of a priest **who acquired slaves and** a priest's **slaves who acquired slaves,**[N] **that** the acquired slaves **may** also **partake of *teruma*?**[H] **As it is stated: "But if a priest buys any soul, the purchase of his money, he may eat of it,"** which is interpreted to mean: If **his acquisition acquired an acquisition,** the latter **partakes** of *teruma*. Here too, since the **slaves of usufruct** property belong to his wife, it should be permitted for them to partake of *teruma*.

כָּל הָאוֹכֵל – מַאֲכִיל, כָּל שֶׁאֵין אוֹכֵל – אֵינוֹ מַאֲכִיל.

The Gemara answers: The principle is that **anyone who** is fit to **partake** of *teruma* can **enable** others **to partake** of *teruma*, and **anyone who does not partake** of *teruma* **cannot enable** others **to partake.** Since the priest's wife in this case does not partake of *teruma*, as her marriage is forbidden, her slaves do not partake of *teruma* either.

וְלֹא? וַהֲרֵי עָרֵל וְכָל הַטְּמֵאִים, שֶׁאֵינָן אוֹכְלִין וּמַאֲכִילִין! הָתָם פּוּמַּיְיהוּ כָּאֵיב לְהוּ.

The Gemara asks: **And** is it so that one who does not partake of *teruma* **cannot enable** others **to partake? But aren't** there the cases of a priest who is **uncircumcised** because it was considered too dangerous for him **and all impure** priests, **who do not partake** of *teruma*, **and** yet **they enable** their wives and slaves **to partake** of *teruma*? The Gemara answers: The difference is that **there,** in those cases, there is no inherent disqualification rendering them unfit to partake of *teruma*. The hindrance to their partaking of *teruma* is tantamount to a situation where **their mouths hurt,**[N] and that is why they refrain from eating *teruma*. They retain, however, the fundamental right to partake of *teruma*, and therefore they can enable others to partake as well.

וַהֲרֵי מַמְזֵר, שֶׁאֵין אוֹכֵל – וּמַאֲכִיל!

The Gemara asks: **But isn't** there the case of **a son born from an incestuous or adulterous relationship** [*mamzer*],[N] **who does not partake** of *teruma* yet **enables** others to partake? If an Israelite woman was married to a priest and was subsequently widowed or divorced, and a child from that union married a *mamzer* and then had a child, in that case, even if the woman's child is dead, she partakes of *teruma* due to her grandchild, as she has a living descendant from a priest, although that descendant is a *mamzer*. Although this child does not partake of *teruma*, he enables his grandmother to partake of it.

אֲמַר רָבִינָא: קִנְיַן אוֹכֵל קָאָמַר, קִנְיַן אוֹכֵל – מַאֲכִיל, שֶׁאֵינוֹ אוֹכֵל – אֵינוֹ מַאֲכִיל.

Ravina said that the above principle **is referring** to the case of **an acquisition who partakes** of *teruma*.[N] If the **acquisition** of a priest **partakes** of *teruma*, he **enables** others **to partake,**[H] whereas an acquisition **who does not partake,** e.g., his forbidden wife, **cannot enable** others **to partake.**

וְרָבָא אֲמַר: מִדְּאוֹרַיְיתָא מֵיכַל אָכְלֵי, וְרַבָּנַן הוּא דְּגָזְרִי בְּהוּ, כְּדֵי שֶׁתֹּאמַר: אֲנִי אֵינִי אוֹכֶלֶת, עֲבָדַי אֵינָן אוֹכְלִין, זוֹנָה הִיא אֶצְלוֹ! הִלְכָּךְ אָתֵי לְאַפּוּקָהּ.

And Rava said a different solution. **By Torah** law, the forbidden wife's slaves indeed **partake** of *teruma*, as they are included in the category of: His acquisition who acquired an acquisition. **And it was the Sages who issued a decree**[N] prohibiting **them** from partaking of *teruma*, **so that** the woman unlawfully married to a priest **would say: I do not partake** of his *teruma* and **my slaves do not partake** of it either, so that she will realize that she is not a valid wife, but rather **she is** like **a prostitute to him.** Her husband will **therefore come to divorce her,**[N] which is the desired outcome.

רַב אַשִׁי אֲמַר: גְּזֵירָה שֶׁמָּא תַּאֲכִיל לְאַחַר מִיתָה.

Rav Ashi said a different reason for the prohibition: It is a rabbinic **decree lest she have** those slaves **partake** of *teruma* even **after** the **death** of her husband the priest. As long as he is alive, they are permitted to partake of *teruma*, as she is considered his acquisition and they belong to her. Once he dies, she is no longer his acquisition.

NOTES

And a priest's slaves who acquired slaves – וַעֲבָדָיו שֶׁקָּנוּ עֲבָדִים: If whatever a slave acquires is acquired by his owner, how can a slave buy a slave for himself? This question was raised by Rashi and many other early commentaries, and it is also addressed in the Jerusalem Talmud. Rashi explains that a slave may acquire a slave when he buys him with money that was given to him under the stipulation that his master will have no access to it. *Tosefot HaRosh* adds that according to the opinion that such a stipulation is ineffective, and whatever a slave acquires always belongs to his owner, the verse from which this *halakha* is derived must be understood as referring only to wives who buy slaves. The *halakha* that whatever a wife acquires is acquired by her husband is a rabbinic ordinance, and by Torah law it is possible for a wife to acquire slaves independently. The verse teaches that such slaves would be permitted to partake of *teruma*.

Their mouths hurt – פּוּמַּיְיהוּ כָּאֵיב לְהוּ: Rashi offers an explanation different from the commentary here: Although in those cases the priests are disqualified, their disqualifications are only temporary, as they can potentially be rectified, whereas the woman is disqualified permanently.

But isn't there the case of a son born from an incestuous or adulterous relationship [*mamzer*] – וַהֲרֵי מַמְזֵר: The *halakha* is that the widow of a priest with any living descendant from the priest is permitted to partake of *teruma*. The Gemara's question is therefore not related to the fact that the descendant is specifically a *mamzer* but uses the *mamzer* as an example of a descendant who is not a priest. Rabbi Avraham min HaHar adds that the Gemara uses *mamzer* to allude to the mishna later on (69b) that elaborates on this *halakha* using the example of a *mamzer*.

Is referring to the case of an acquisition who partakes of *teruma* – קִנְיַן אוֹכֵל קָאָמַר: It appears that Ravina derived his interpretation of the principle directly from the verse that is its source: "The purchase of his money, he may eat of it." The verse is referring to an acquisition who may himself partake of *teruma*, and only if that is so does he enable his own acquisition to do so.

And it was the Sages who issued a decree – וְרַבָּנַן הוּא דְּגָזְרִי בְּהוּ: The Rambam rules in accordance with Ravina's assertion that it is Torah law that slaves of usufruct property belonging to a priest's forbidden wife do not partake of *teruma*. Other commentaries follow the other opinions in the Gemara and maintain that it is a rabbinic decree.

In the Jerusalem Talmud, both possibilities are cited, and then it is pointed out that whether or not it is a Torah law has a practical difference: If by Torah law, one who cannot partake of *teruma* cannot enable his property to do so, then slaves belonging to the uncircumcised slave of a priest will not be allowed to partake of *teruma*. If the property of property that traces back to a priest may partake of *teruma*, and the Sages restricted the slaves of an unlawful wife from doing so as a penalty, then the slaves of this slave should be allowed to partake of *teruma*. Their master did nothing wrong.

Her husband will therefore come to divorce her – הִלְכָּךְ אָתֵי לְאַפּוּקָהּ: The woman's realization will lead to a quarrel between her and her husband, which will presumably result in divorce (Meiri).

HALAKHA

The slaves of a priest's acquisition – עַבְדֵי קִנְיַן כֹּהֵן: The slaves of a priest and the slaves of the wife of a priest who themselves acquired slaves partake of *teruma* (Rambam *Sefer Zera'im*, *Hilkhot Terumot* 7:18).

Anyone who is fit to partake of *teruma* can enable others to partake of *teruma* – כָּל הָאוֹכֵל מַאֲכִיל: A priest's acquisition can enable others to partake of *teruma* only if he partakes of *teruma* himself (Rambam *Sefer Zera'im*, *Hilkhot Terumot* 7:18).

אֶלָּא מֵעַתָּה, בַּת יִשְׂרָאֵל שֶׁנִּשֵּׂאת לְכֹהֵן לֹא תַּאֲכִיל גְּזֵירָה שֶׁמָּא תַּאֲכִיל לְאַחַר מִיתָה!

The Gemara asks: **However, if** that is **so,** that the decree is lest she have those slaves partake of *teruma* after her husband's death, any **Israelite woman who marries a priest should not enable** her slaves of usufruct property **to partake**[N] of *teruma* either, due to the same rabbinic **decree, lest she have them partake** of *teruma* **after** her husband's **death.**

אֶלָּא אָמַר רַב אַשִׁי: בְּאַלְמָנָה כֹּהֶנֶת, דְּאָתְיָא לְאוֹרוּיֵי: מֵעִיקָּרָא אֲכַלֵי בִּתְרוּמָה דְּבֵי נָשָׁא, אִינְסְבִי לֵיהּ לְהַאי – אֲכַלֵי בִּתְרוּמָה דְּגַבְרַאי, וְהָשְׁתָּא הֲדַרִי לִי לְמִילְּתֵיהּ קַמַּיְיתָא, וְלָא יָדְעָה דְּמֵעִיקָּרָא לָא שַׁוְיתָהּ לְנַפְשָׁהּ חֲלָלָה, הָשְׁתָּא שַׁוְיתָהּ לְנַפְשָׁהּ חֲלָלָה.

Rather, Rav Ashi said that the decree is dealing **with a widowed priestess,** the daughter of a priest, who then married the High Priest, **as she is likely to rationalize** enabling her slaves to partake of *teruma* after the death of the High Priest as follows: **Initially,** my slaves **partook of the** *teruma* **of my father's house. I** then **married this man, and they partook of the** *teruma* **of my husband. And now** that my husband died, **I have returned to the original circumstance,** and therefore they may once again partake of my father's *teruma*. **And she does not realize that** this is not so, as **initially she did not render herself a woman disqualified from marrying a priest [*ḥalala*],** but **now,** by marrying a High Priest unlawfully, **she rendered herself a *ḥalala*,** and both she and her slaves do not partake of *teruma* even upon returning to her father's house.

תֵּינַח אַלְמָנָה כֹּהֶנֶת, אַלְמָנָה בַּת יִשְׂרָאֵל מַאי אִיכָּא לְמֵימַר – בְּאַלְמְנוּתָהּ לָא פְּלִיגִי רַבָּנַן.

The Gemara asks: This **works out well** as an explanation of the mishna, with regard to **a widowed priestess.** However, if that **widow** who married a High Priest was **an Israelite woman, what can be said?** There is no reason for the decree in that case. The Gemara answers: **With regard to widowhood, the Sages did not distinguish** between one type of widow and another. Once they issued a decree due to one widow, they applied it to all widows.

אִיתְּמַר: הַמַּכְנֶסֶת שׁוּם לְבַעְלָהּ, הִיא אוֹמֶרֶת: כֵּלַי אֲנִי נוֹטֶלֶת, וְהוּא אוֹמֵר: דָּמִים אֲנִי נוֹתֵן, הַדִּין עִם מִי? רַב יְהוּדָה אָמַר:

It was stated: With regard to a woman **who brings appraised,** guaranteed **property into her** marital contract with her **husband,** he is obligated to return it at the conclusion of the marriage. Upon collection of her marriage contract, e.g., following divorce, if **she says: I am taking my belongings,**[H] **and he says: I am willing to give you** only their **monetary** value, **the *halakha*** favors **whom?**[N] **Rav Yehuda said:**

NOTES

Any Israelite woman who marries a priest should not enable her slaves of usufruct property to partake [*ta'akhil*] – בַּת יִשְׂרָאֵל שֶׁנִּשֵּׂאת לְכֹהֵן לֹא תַּאֲכִיל: A textual variant mentioned by the early commentaries reads: Should also not partake [*tokhal*], lest she partake after her husband's death. While Rashi reads *ta'akhil*, and *Tosafot* defend Rashi's reading, the Ramban and the Rashba contend that the alternative reading is preferable, as it renders the difficulty raised by the Gemara more sensible and more pronounced.

The *halakha* favors whom – הַדִּין עִם מִי: The early commentaries addressed the opposite case: What if the husband wants to return the guaranteed assets while the wife demands their value in money? Some say that the property is in his possession and therefore she can refuse to accept it; it is her right to have the property returned to her but not her obligation (*Tosefot Ḥad MiKamma'ei*). Rivash claims that the husband may return the assets against her will, as they are not entirely in his possession, but are like a deposit. The Meiri maintains that he can compel her to accept them only if he lacks the funds to pay his debt.

HALAKHA

A wife who wants to receive her belongings – אִשָּׁה הָרוֹצָה לְקַבֵּל כֵּלֶיהָ: If a wife brought guaranteed property with her into the marriage, and upon divorce she demands to receive the actual assets she brought with her, her demand is accepted, as they are the assets of her paternal family (*Shulḥan Arukh, Even HaEzer* 88:3).

Perek **VII**
Daf **66** Amud **b**

הַדִּין עִמָּהּ, וְרַב אַמִי אָמַר: הַדִּין עִמּוֹ.

The *halakha* favors **her;** she may take the belongings. **And Rav Ami said: The *halakha*** favors **him;** he may retain the items and return their value.

רַב יְהוּדָה אָמַר: הַדִּין עִמָּהּ, מִשּׁוּם שֶׁבַח בֵּית אָבִיהָ – דִּידָהּ הָוֵי. רַבִּי אַמִי אָמַר: הַדִּין עִמּוֹ, כֵּיוָן דַּאֲמַר מָר: אִם מֵתוּ – מֵתוּ לוֹ, וְאִם הוֹתִירוּ – הוֹתִירוּ לוֹ, הוֹאִיל וְחַיָּיב בְּאַחֲרָיוּתָן – יֹאכְלוּ. אֲמַר רַב סָפְרָא: מִי קָתָנֵי "וְהֵן שֶׁלּוֹ"? "הוֹאִיל וְחַיָּיב בְּאַחֲרָיוּתָן" קָתָנֵי, וּלְעוֹלָם לָאו דִּידֵיהּ נִינְהוּ.

The Gemara explains that **Rav Yehuda said** that **the *halakha*** favors **her because** they are **the assets of her paternal family,**[N] whose prestige will suffer if they aren't returned. Therefore, **they are hers. Rabbi Ami said that the *halakha*** favors **him, since the Master said** in the mishna, with regard to guaranteed property: **If they die, their death** is **his** loss, **and if they increase** in value, **their increase** is **his** gain. **Since he bears** financial **responsibility for their** loss, **they partake** of *teruma*. Apparently, the slaves belong to the husband. Therefore, he is obligated to return only their monetary value. **Rav Safra said** in rejection of Rabbi Ami's reasoning: **Does** the mishna **teach** that **they are his?** It **teaches** only that **he bears** financial **responsibility for their** loss, **but actually they are not his.**

NOTES

The assets of her paternal family – שֶׁבַח בֵּית אָבִיהָ: The Rid explains that her family gave her these belongings for her own use, not for the use of others after her divorce.

BACKGROUND

Vetches [*karshinin*] – כַּרְשִׁינִין: The vetch, *Vicia*, is an annual of the legume family. It grows to 10–50 cm in height. Its seeds are brown, round, or oblong, and 0.25–0.5 cm in diameter. Like other legumes, vetches are high in nutritional value and are easily digested by animals.

Vetches are a winter crop in the spring fields of Mediterranean lands and are still grown nowadays in Arab villages.

The plant and its seeds are usually used as animal fodder. In order to soften the seeds, they are sometimes soaked overnight in water. Although the vetch is consumed mostly by animals, its seeds are edible for humans as well. They were eaten during years of famine and other times of need. As it is edible for humans, the vetch must be tithed, although its *teruma* was usually fed to the animals of priests.

Vetch

NOTES

Who appraised a cow upon renting it from a priest – שֶׁשָּׁם פָּרָה מִכֹּהֵן: Rashi explains that the Israelite rented a cow from the priest and appraised it due to his guarantee to return the full value of the cow. *Tosafot*, however, contend that a rental agreement of this sort is prohibited as a form of interest. Since the renter has obligated himself to give the owner its present value no matter what, his receiving the cow is viewed as a loan, and the rental fee is considered interest (see *Bava Metzia* 70a). *Tosafot* therefore contend that the case of appraisal is one where the cow is merely borrowed from the owner, and there is no rental fee.

Go free at the loss of a tooth or an eye – יוֹצְאִין בְּשֵׁן וָעַיִן: A gentile slave is set free if his owner strikes him causing his tooth to fall out; his eye to be blinded; or other extremities, e.g., his fingers and toes, to be destroyed (Exodus 21:26–27).

וְכָל הֵיכָא דְּחַיָּיב בְּאַחֲרָיוּתָן אָכְלֵי בִּתְרוּמָה? וְהָתְנַן: יִשְׂרָאֵל שֶׁשָּׂכַר פָּרָה מִכֹּהֵן – הֲרֵי זֶה יַאֲכִילֶנָּה כַּרְשִׁינֵי תְרוּמָה. כֹּהֵן שֶׁשָּׂכַר פָּרָה מִיִּשְׂרָאֵל, אַף עַל פִּי שֶׁמְּזוֹנוֹתֶיהָ עָלָיו – לֹא יַאֲכִילֶנָּה כַּרְשִׁינֵי תְרוּמָה!

The Gemara asks: **And do they partake of *teruma* wherever he bears** financial **responsibility for their loss,** even if they are not his actual possession? **But didn't we learn** in a mishna (*Terumot* 11:9): **An Israelite who rented a cow from a priest may feed it vetches** [***karshinin***][B] **of *teruma*,** since the animal belongs to a priest? With regard to **a priest who rented a cow from an Israelite, although** its feed **is** incumbent **upon him, he may not feed it vetches of *teruma*,** as it does not belong to him.[H] This indicates that the requirement for enabling an acquisition to eat *teruma* is possession, not responsibility.

וְתִסְבְּרָא? נְהִי נַמִי דְּמִחַיַּיב בִּגְנֵבָה וַאֲבֵדָה – בְּאוֹנְסֶיהָ, בְּכַחֲשָׁהּ, וּבְנִפְחַת דָּמֶיהָ מִי מִיחַיַּיב? הָא לָא דָּמְיָא אֶלָּא לְסֵיפָא: יִשְׂרָאֵל שֶׁשָּׁם פָּרָה מִכֹּהֵן – לֹא יַאֲכִילֶנָּה כַּרְשִׁינֵי תְרוּמָה, אֲבָל כֹּהֵן שֶׁשָּׁם פָּרָה מִיִּשְׂרָאֵל – יַאֲכִילֶנָּה כַּרְשִׁינֵי תְרוּמָה.

The Gemara rejects this proof: **And** how can **you understand** that the case of the rented cow is parallel to the case of guaranteed property? **Though** the renter **is indeed liable for theft and loss, is he liable for unavoidable accidents, for emaciation,** i.e., the cow became thinner or weaker for any reason, **or for** any other **decrease in its value?** Certainly he is not. In fact, the case of guaranteed property **is similar only to the latter clause** of that mishna: In the case of **an Israelite who appraised a cow** upon renting it **from a priest**[N] under an arrangement where he guaranteed its value to the owner, he **may not feed it vetches of *teruma*,** as it is considered his own. **However, a priest who appraised a cow** upon renting it **from an Israelite may feed it vetches of *teruma*.**[H] This indicates that guaranteed property is considered the acquisition of its recipient with regard to enabling it to eat *teruma*.

יָתֵיב רַבָּה וְרַב יוֹסֵף בְּשִׁילְהֵי פִּרְקֵיהּ דְּרַב נַחְמָן, וְיָתְבֵי וְקָאָמְרִי: תַּנְיָא כְּוָתֵיהּ דְּרַב יְהוּדָה, וְתַנְיָא כְּוָתֵיהּ דְּרַבִּי אַמִּי. תַּנְיָא כְּוָתֵיהּ דְּרַבִּי אַמִּי: עַבְדֵי צֹאן בַּרְזֶל יוֹצְאִין בְּשֵׁן וָעַיִן לָאִישׁ, אֲבָל לֹא לָאִשָּׁה.

Rabba and Rav Yosef sat at the conclusion of Rav Naḥman's sermon, and they sat and said: It is taught in a *baraita* **in accordance with** the opinion of **Rav Yehuda, and it is taught** in another *baraita* **in accordance with** the opinion of **Rabbi Ami. It is taught in accordance with** the opinion of **Rabbi Ami** in the following *baraita*: If a slave's owner strikes him and knocks out his tooth or blinds him in an eye, he is set free. **Slaves of guaranteed investment go free at** the loss of **a tooth or an eye**[NH] caused **by the husband, but not** at such loss caused **by the wife.** This indicates that they belong to the husband.

תַּנְיָא כְּוָתֵיהּ דְּרַב יְהוּדָה: הַמַּכְנֶסֶת שׁוּם לְבַעְלָהּ, אִם רָצָה הַבַּעַל לִמְכּוֹר – לֹא יִמְכּוֹר, וְלֹא עוֹד אֶלָּא אֲפִילּוּ הִכְנִיס לָהּ שׁוּם מִשֶּׁלּוֹ, אִם רָצָה הַבַּעַל לִמְכּוֹר – לֹא יִמְכּוֹר. מָכְרוּ שְׁנֵיהֶם לְפַרְנָסָה, זֶה הָיָה מַעֲשֶׂה לִפְנֵי רַבָּן שִׁמְעוֹן בֶּן גַּמְלִיאֵל, וְאָמַר: הַבַּעַל מוֹצִיא מִיַּד הַלָּקוֹחוֹת.

Conversely, **it is taught** in a *baraita* **in accordance with** the opinion of **Rav Yehuda:** When a woman **brings appraised,** guaranteed **property** into her marriage **to her husband, if the husband wishes to sell** it, **he may not sell** it, as it belongs to her. **And not only** that, but **even** when her husband **brought** property **into** the marriage and added it to **her** dowry as **an appraised,** guaranteed gift **of his own,**[H] even **if the husband wishes to sell** that gift **he may not sell** it. With regard to a case in which **either** the husband or wife unlawfully **sold** this property **for subsistence,** there **was an incident** like **this** that came **before Rabban Shimon ben Gamliel, and he said:** Although **the husband** executed the sale, **he may repossess** the property **from the purchasers,** as the sale is void.[H]

HALAKHA

Feeding *teruma* to a rented cow – הַאֲכָלַת תְּרוּמָה לְפָרָה שְׂכוּרָה: An Israelite who rented a cow from a priest may feed it *teruma*. On the other hand, a priest who rented a cow from an Israelite may not because it does not belong to him, even though he is responsible for its sustenance (Rambam *Sefer Zera'im*, *Hilkhot Terumot* 9:7).

Feeding *teruma* to an appraised cow – הַאֲכָלַת תְּרוּמָה לְפָרָה שֶׁנִּשּׁוֹמָה: If an Israelite received a cow from a priest and appraised it, guaranteeing its value to the original owner, in order to fatten it and share the profits, he may not feed it *teruma*, although the priest has a share in the profits. If a priest received a cow from an Israelite under the same stipulation, he may feed it *teruma* (Rambam *Sefer Zera'im*, *Hilkhot Terumot* 9:8).

Slaves of guaranteed investment go free at the loss of a tooth or an eye – עַבְדֵי צֹאן בַּרְזֶל יוֹצְאִין בְּשֵׁן וָעַיִן: Slaves of guaranteed investment brought into a marriage by the wife are set free at the loss of a tooth or an eye, if the injury was caused by the husband, not by the wife (Rambam *Sefer Kinyan*, *Hilkhot Avadim* 5:16).

Even brought property into the marriage…as an appraised, guaranteed gift of his own – אֲפִילּוּ הִכְנִיס לָהּ שׁוּם מִשֶּׁלּוֹ: In addition to her own possessions, a wife's guaranteed property includes the gifts she received from her husband (Rambam *Sefer Kinyan*, *Hilkhot Mekhira* 30:5; *Shulḥan Arukh*, *Even HaEzer* 90:15).

Selling guaranteed property – מְכִירַת נִכְסֵי צֹאן בַּרְזֶל: If a woman brought movable property into her marriage as guaranteed property, the husband does not have the right to sell it. However, if he violates this *halakha* and sells it, the sale is valid (Rav Hai Gaon). Some commentaries disagree, maintaining that the sale is void (Ramban; Rashba; Rosh; Rambam *Sefer Kinyan*, *Hilkhot Mekhira* 30:5 and *Sefer Nashim*, *Hilkhot Ishut* 22:15; *Shulḥan Arukh*, *Even HaEzer* 90:14).

אָמַר רָבָא אָמַר רַב נַחְמָן: הֲלָכָה כְּרַב יְהוּדָה. אֲמַר לֵיהּ רָבָא לְרַב נַחְמָן: וְהָתַנְיָא כְּוָתֵיהּ דְּרַבִּי אַמִי! אַף עַל גַּב דְּתַנְיָא כְּוָתֵיהּ דְּרַבִּי אַמִי, מִסְתַּבְּרָא טַעְמָא דְּרַב יְהוּדָה, מִשּׁוּם שֶׁבַח בֵּית אָבִיהָ.

Rava said that **Rav Naḥman said: The *halakha* is in accordance with** the opinion **of Rav Yehuda. Rava said to Rav Naḥman: But isn't it taught** in a *baraita* **in accordance with** the opinion **of Rabbi Ami?** He replied: **Although it is taught in accordance with** the opinion **of Rabbi Ami, Rav Yehuda's rationale,** that the wife may take the objects in question **because** they are **assets of her paternal family** and their complete removal from her domain would hurt the family's prestige, is more **reasonable.**

הַהִיא אִיתְּתָא דְּעַיְּילָה לֵיהּ לְגַבְרָא אִיצְטְלָא דְּמֵילְתָא בִּכְתוּבְּתָהּ, שְׁכֵיב, שַׁקְלוּהָ יַתְמֵי וּפַרְסוּהָ אַמִּיתְנָא.

The Gemara relates an incident: **A certain woman brought** into her marriage to her **husband a robe** [*itztela*][L] **of fine wool** [*meileta*],[L] which was deemed guaranteed property **by her marriage contract.** Her husband subsequently **died,** and **the orphans took** that robe **and spread it over the corpse** as a shroud.[N] The woman demanded that the robe be returned to her.

אָמַר רָבָא: קַנְיֵיהּ מִיתְנָא. אֲמַר לֵיהּ נָנַאי, בְּרֵיהּ דְּרַב יוֹסֵף, בְּרֵיהּ דְּרָבָא, לְרַב כָּהֲנָא: וְהָאָמַר רָבָא אָמַר רַב נַחְמָן: הֲלָכָה כְּרַב יְהוּדָה! אֲמַר לֵיהּ: מִי לָא מוֹדֶה רַב יְהוּדָה דִּמְחוּסַּר גּוּבַיְינָא? וְכֵיוָן דִּמְחוּסַּר גּוּבַיְינָא – בִּרְשׁוּתֵיהּ קָאֵי.

Rava said: The dead has acquired it,[NH] as deriving benefit from anything consecrated for the dead is prohibited. **Nanai, son of Rav Yosef, son of Rava, said to Rav Kahana: But didn't Rava say** that **Rav Naḥman said** that **the *halakha* is in accordance with** the opinion **of Rav Yehuda?** Accordingly, the woman's robe must be returned. **He said to him: Doesn't Rav Yehuda admit that** the robe **has not yet been collected? And since it has not yet been collected, it remains in his possession,** and his inheritors can render its use as a burial shroud prohibited.

רָבָא לְטַעְמֵיהּ, דְּאָמַר רָבָא: הֶקְדֵּשׁ, חָמֵץ,

The Gemara adds that in this regard **Rava** conforms **to his** standard line of **reasoning, as Rava said: Consecration** of property, the prohibition against benefiting from **leavened bread** on Passover,[N]

LANGUAGE

Robe [*itztela*] – אִיצְטְלָא: From the Greek στολή, *stolè*, meaning garment or robe.

Fine wool [*meileta*] – מֵילְתָא: Some assert that this means fine wool, named after the city Μίλητος, Milētos, where it was manufactured (Rabbi Ovadya MiBartenura). Others explain that the source of the word is the Greek μηλωτή, *mēlotē*, meaning wool.

NOTES

And spread it over the corpse as a shroud – וּפַרְסוּהָ אַמִּיתְנָא: The Gemara relates that at first taking the dead out for burial was more difficult for the relatives than the actual death, because it was customary to bury the dead in expensive shrouds, which the poor could not afford (*Moed Katan* 27b). The problem grew to the point that relatives would sometimes abandon the corpse. This lasted until Rabban Gamliel left instructions that he be taken out for burial in simple linen garments, waiving his honor. Afterward, the entire Jewish people adopted this practice and had themselves taken out for burial in linen garments.

The dead has acquired it – קַנְיֵיהּ מִיתְנָא: It is prohibited to derive benefit from a human corpse or from any object that serves its burial. Therefore, it is prohibited to use any object designated for a corpse or its burial that has been used to that end, e.g., a robe spread over the corpse as a shroud. However, one cannot render prohibited an object that belongs to someone else, even by using it for a human corpse.

Consecration of property, the prohibition against benefiting from leavened bread on Passover, etc. – הֶקְדֵּשׁ, חָמֵץ וכו׳: The Meiri explains that the *halakha* that these cannot release the property from a lien applies not only to items consecrated for the Temple, but to items consecrated for a corpse as well. The Ritva maintains that this *halakha* is a principle that applies to all items from which it is prohibited to derive benefit. In his opinion, consecrated property, leavened bread, and manumission (see 67a) are merely examples.

HALAKHA

Guaranteed property that was consecrated to the Temple or used for the dead – נִכְסֵי צֹאן בַּרְזֶל שֶׁהוּקְדְּשׁוּ אוֹ נִתְּנוּ לְמֵת: If a dead man's inheritors consecrate his widow's guaranteed property or place an object of that property on the corpse, rendering it prohibited to derive benefit from the property or item, the woman's lien is released and she receives only its value (*Shulḥan Arukh, Even HaEzer* 88:5).

Perek **VII**
Daf **67** Amud **a**

וְשִׁחְרוּר – מַפְקִיעִין מִידֵי שִׁעְבּוּד.

and the **manumission** of a slave[N] **release** the property **from a lien.** If someone placed an asset under a lien for his debt and subsequently consecrated it; or if the asset under lien is leavened bread and the festival of Passover arrived; or if the asset is a slave and he freed him, the lien is released, and the creditor must claim his debt from the debtor's other property. In the case of the robe as well, because it was placed over the corpse, it was consecrated for the dead. Consequently, it is prohibited to derive benefit from it. Therefore, it is released to the woman from under the lien.

אָמַר רַב יְהוּדָה: הִכְנִיסָה לוֹ שְׁנֵי כֵּלִים בְּאֶלֶף זוּז, וְהִשְׁבִּיחוּ וְעָמְדוּ עַל שְׁנֵי אֲלָפִים – אֶחָד נוֹטַלְתּוֹ בִּכְתוּבָּתָהּ, וְאֶחָד נוֹתֶנֶת דָּמִים וְנוֹטַלְתּוֹ, מִפְּנֵי שֶׁבַח בֵּית אָבִיהָ.

Rav Yehuda said: If the wife **brought** with her **into** the marriage **two belongings**[NH] of guaranteed investment worth **one thousand dinars, and** they **appreciated** until **they stood at two thousand, one** of them **she collects as** payment of **her marriage contract,** as it is now worth her dowry of one thousand dinars. **And** as for the other **one, she pays its monetary** value **and takes it** from her husband **because** it is **an asset of her paternal family.**

NOTES

And the manumission of a slave – וְשִׁחְרוּר: The Ramban points out that according to this ruling, the *baraita* cited by the Gemara in support of Rabbi Ami's opinion does not in fact lend his opinion any support. The *halakha* that slaves of guaranteed investment go free at the loss of a tooth or an eye by the husband can be explained by the fact that the wife's possession of them is nullified through their manumission, and therefore it cannot prove that the slaves belong to the husband.

If the wife brought with her into the marriage two belongings, etc. – הִכְנִיסָה לוֹ שְׁנֵי כֵּלִים וכו׳: A controversy between Babylonian *amora'im* is cited in the Jerusalem Talmud with regard to this issue. However, the conclusion is the same as in this Gemara.

HALAKHA

If the wife brought with her into the marriage two belongings, etc. – הִכְנִיסָה לוֹ שְׁנֵי כֵּלִים וכו׳: If the wife brought with her into her marriage two belongings or two maidservants of guaranteed investment, and they were appraised at one thousand dinars, and over the course of the marriage their value increased to two thousand dinars, upon her divorce she takes one of them for her one thousand dinars. If she wishes, she has the right to receive the other at its price at the time of her divorce, in accordance with Rav Yehuda's ruling (Rambam *Sefer Nashim, Hilkhot Ishut* 22:26; *Shulḥan Arukh, Even HaEzer* 88:3).

מַאי קָא מַשְׁמַע לָן, שֶׁבַח בֵּית אָבִיהָ דִּידָהּ הָוֵי – הָא אָמְרָהּ רַב יְהוּדָה חֲדָא זִימְנָא! מַהוּ דְּתֵימָא: הָנֵי מִילֵּי – הֵיכָא דְּמָטְיָא לְמִשְׁקַל בִּכְתוּבְּתָהּ, אֲבָל מֵיתַן דָּמֵי וּמִישְׁקַל לָא – קָא מַשְׁמַע לָן.

The Gemara asks: **What is he teaching us?** Is it that **assets of her paternal family are hers? Rav Yehuda** already **said this once,** in his previous statement. The Gemara answers: The latter statement was necessary as well, **lest you say** that **this applies** only **where she comes to collect her marriage contract,** which is rightfully hers, **but to give money and take** assets that are worth beyond what her husband owes her, you might say that she may **not** do so, although the property in question is an asset of her paternal family. Rav Yehuda therefore **teaches us** that she may take all of the assets of her paternal family and pay for what they are worth beyond her husband's debt to her.

מתני׳ בַּת יִשְׂרָאֵל שֶׁנִּיסֵּת לְכֹהֵן וָמֵת, וְהִנִּיחָהּ מְעוּבֶּרֶת, לֹא יֹאכְלוּ עֲבָדֶיהָ בִּתְרוּמָה, מִפְּנֵי חֶלְקוֹ שֶׁל עוּבָּר. שֶׁהָעוּבָּר פּוֹסֵל, וְאֵינוֹ מַאֲכִיל, דִּבְרֵי רַבִּי יוֹסֵי.

MISHNA With regard to **an Israelite woman who married a priest and he died and left her pregnant, her slaves** of guaranteed investment **may not partake of** *teruma*[N] during her pregnancy, **due to the share of the fetus,** as an inheritor of his father, in the ownership of the slaves. In the opposite case, **where** the Israelite husband of a priest's daughter died and left her pregnant, **the fetus disqualifies** her from partaking of *teruma*. However, in the current case, the fetus **does not enable** its mother or the slaves **to partake**[N] of *teruma*,[H] despite the fact that it is the child of a priest. This is **the statement of Rabbi Yosei.**

אָמְרוּ לוֹ: מֵאַחַר שֶׁהֵעַדְתָּ לָנוּ עַל בַּת יִשְׂרָאֵל לְכֹהֵן – אַף בַּת כֹּהֵן לְכֹהֵן וָמֵת, וְהִנִּיחָהּ מְעוּבֶּרֶת – לֹא יֹאכְלוּ עֲבָדֶיהָ בִּתְרוּמָה, מִפְּנֵי חֶלְקוֹ שֶׁל עוּבָּר.

The Rabbis **said to him: Since you testified before us about** the case of **an Israelite woman** who was married **to a priest,** in the case of **the daughter of a priest** who was married **to a priest and he died and left her pregnant, her slaves should not partake of** ***teruma*** **either, due to the fetus's share.** The same *halakha* should apply whether the woman is an Israelite or the daughter of a priest.

גמ׳ אִיבַּעְיָא לְהוּ: טַעְמָא דְּרַבִּי יוֹסֵי מִשּׁוּם דְּקָסָבַר עוּבָּר בִּמְעֵי זָרָה זָר הוּא, אוֹ דִּלְמָא: יָלוּד – מַאֲכִיל, שֶׁאֵינוֹ יָלוּד – אֵינוֹ מַאֲכִיל?

GEMARA **A dilemma was raised before** the scholars: Is **the reason for** the ruling of **Rabbi Yosei because he holds that a fetus in the womb of a non-priest is a non-priest,** as it is considered part of its mother's body and it becomes a priest only upon birth, and therefore the slaves in which it owns a share will be allowed to eat *teruma* only at that stage? **Or,** is Rabbi Yosei **perhaps** of the opinion that only **one who was born enables** others **to partake** of *teruma*, whereas **one who is not** yet **born does not enable** others **to partake,** although it is considered a priest?

לְמַאי נָפְקָא מִינַּהּ – לְעוּבָּר בִּמְעֵי כֹּהֶנֶת, מַאי? אָמַר רַבָּה: הַיְינוּ טַעְמָא דְּרַבִּי יוֹסֵי: דְּקָסָבַר עוּבָּר בִּמְעֵי זָרָה – זָר הוּא. רַב יוֹסֵף אָמַר: יָלוּד – מַאֲכִיל, שֶׁאֵין יָלוּד – אֵינוֹ מַאֲכִיל.

What is the **practical difference** between the two possible reasons? It is the case of **a fetus in the womb of the priestess,** the daughter of a priest. If Rabbi Yosei's rationale is that the fetus in the womb of a non-priest is a non-priest, that is not the case here, and therefore the slaves should partake of *teruma*. **What** is the *halakha* in this case? **Rabba said** that **this is Rabbi Yosei's reasoning: He holds** that **a fetus in the womb of a non-priest is a non-priest. Rav Yosef said:** His rationale is that only **one who was born enables** others **to partake** of *teruma*, whereas **one who is not** yet **born does not enable** others **to partake.**[N]

מֵיתִיבֵי, אָמְרוּ לוֹ לְרַבִּי יוֹסֵי: מֵאַחַר שֶׁהֵעַדְתָּ לָנוּ עַל בַּת יִשְׂרָאֵל לְכֹהֵן – בַּת כֹּהֵן לְכֹהֵן מַהוּ? אָמַר לָהֶם: זוֹ שָׁמַעְתִּי, וְזוֹ לֹא שָׁמַעְתִּי.

The Gemara **raises an objection** to Rav Yosef's opinion from a *baraita* that continues the last clause of the mishna: The Rabbis **said to Rabbi Yosei: Since you testified before us about** the case of **an Israelite woman** married **to a priest,** in the case of **the daughter of a priest** married **to a priest, what is** the *halakha*? **He said to them:** With regard to the former case, **I heard** from my teachers that the slaves do not partake of *teruma*, **but** with regard to **this** one, **I did not hear** such a thing.[N]

אִי אָמְרַתְּ בִּשְׁלָמָא עוּבָּר בִּמְעֵי זָרָה זָר הוּא – הַיְינוּ דְּקָאָמַר לְהוּ: ״זוֹ שָׁמַעְתִּי, וְזוֹ לֹא שָׁמַעְתִּי״. אֶלָּא, אִי אָמְרַתְּ יָלוּד – מַאֲכִיל, שֶׁאֵין יָלוּד – אֵין מַאֲכִיל, מַאי ״זוֹ שָׁמַעְתִּי וְזוֹ לֹא שָׁמַעְתִּי״ אִיהִי הִיא! קַשְׁיָא.

Granted, if you say that Rabbi Yosei's reasoning is that **a fetus in the womb of a non-priest is a non-priest, this is** the reason **that he said to them: This** case **I heard but this** case **I did not hear.** There is a logical distinction between the two cases, as in the latter case the fetus is not in the womb of a non-priest. **However, if you say** that his rationale is that only **one who was born enables** others **to partake** of *teruma*, whereas **one who is not** yet **born does not enable** others **to partake, what** does he mean by saying: **This** case **I heard but this** case **I did not hear? It is the same** case with regard to this principle. The Gemara concludes: This is **a difficult** objection.

NOTES

Her slaves may not partake of ***teruma*** **– לֹא יֹאכְלוּ עֲבָדֶיהָ בִּתְרוּמָה:** An emendation to the text is suggested in the Jerusalem Talmud, so that it reads: His slaves may not partake of *teruma*. This is because the slaves under discussion must be slaves of guaranteed investment, which belonged to the husband, and therefore belong to the fetus after his death. On the other hand, slaves of usufruct property, who belong to the woman, partake of *teruma* if she does, i.e., in a case where the woman has other children from the husband besides the fetus. A different opinion cited there suggests that according to Rabbi Yosei, the woman does not partake of *teruma* even if they had other children, due to her pregnancy, and neither do her slaves of usufruct property. Therefore, the emendation is unnecessary.

Where the Israelite husband died the fetus disqualifies her from partaking, however in the current case the fetus does not enable them to partake – שֶׁהָעוּבָּר פּוֹסֵל וְאֵינוֹ מַאֲכִיל: Rashi explains that a fetus disqualifies its mother in the opposite case, i.e., the daughter of a priest married to an Israelite man, but does not enable her to partake of *teruma* in the case of the mishna. *Tosafot*, however, explain that in the case mentioned in the mishna, the fetus disqualifies the slaves of guaranteed investment from partaking of *teruma* but does not enable its mother or her slaves of usufruct property to partake. This explanation is supported by the fact that the principle that a fetus can disqualify its mother but cannot enable her to partake is stated in the next mishna (67b), so its mention in both *mishnayot* is superfluous unless here it carries a slightly different meaning.

Only one who was born enables others to partake of ***teruma*****, whereas one who is not yet born does not enable others to partake – יָלוּד מַאֲכִיל, שֶׁאֵין יָלוּד אֵינוֹ מַאֲכִיל:** This principle is derived by the Gemara (*Nidda* 44b) from the verse "And such as are born in his house, they may eat [*yokhlu*] of his bread" (Leviticus 22:11). One who was not born may not, so to speak, feed [*ya'akhilu*] others either (Rashi).

The former case I heard, but with regard to this one I did not hear such a thing – זוֹ שָׁמַעְתִּי וְזוֹ לֹא שָׁמַעְתִּי: According to Rashi, Rabbi Yosei means that he heard from his teachers that in this case the slaves do partake of *teruma*. However, the Ritva raises several problems with this explanation and prefers a simpler understanding of Rabbi Yosei's statement: He did not hear what the *halakha* is in the latter case, and therefore he has nothing to say on the matter.

HALAKHA

A fetus does not enable others to partake of ***teruma*** **– עוּבָּר אֵינוֹ מַאֲכִיל:** If an Israelite woman married a priest, and he subsequently died and left her pregnant, her slaves may not partake of *teruma*, as only one who was born enables others to partake of *teruma*, but a fetus does not. Conversely, a fetus does not disqualify its mother from partaking of *teruma*. Therefore, if the fetus is categorized as a priest disqualified due to flawed lineage [*ḥalal*], and it has non-*ḥalal* brothers, the mother partakes of *teruma* until it is born. This ruling apparently follows the Rabbis' opinion (Rambam *Sefer Zera'im, Hilkhot Terumot* 8:4; *Tur, Yoreh De'a* 331).

אָמַר רַב יְהוּדָה אָמַר שְׁמוּאֵל: זוֹ דִּבְרֵי רַבִּי יוֹסֵי, אֲבָל חֲכָמִים אוֹמְרִים: יֵשׁ לוֹ בָּנִים – אוֹכְלִים מִשּׁוּם בָּנִים, אֵין לוֹ בָּנִים – אוֹכְלִים מִשּׁוּם אַחִים. אֵין לוֹ אַחִים – אוֹכְלִים מִשּׁוּם מִשְׁפָּחָה כּוּלָּהּ.

Rav Yehuda said that Shmuel said: **This is the statement of Rabbi Yosei. However, the Rabbis say** that if the dead husband **has children,** the slaves **partake of** *teruma* **due to** the **children,** as they inherit the slaves. If **he does not have children, they partake** of *teruma* **due to** his **brothers,** who inherit his property. If **he does not have brothers** either, **they partake due to** the **entire family,** which inherits his property. The fetus does not disqualify them, as it does not yet own its share of the inheritance.

״זוֹ״ וְלָא סְבִירָא לֵיהּ?! הָא אָמַר לֵיהּ שְׁמוּאֵל לְרַב חָנָא בַּגְדָתָאָה: פּוּק אַיְיתֵי לִי בֵּי עֲשָׂרָה, דְּאֵימָא לָךְ בְּאַנְפַּיְיהוּ: הַמְזַכֶּה לְעוּבָּר – קָנָה! אֶלָּא: ״זוֹ״ וּסְבִירָא לֵיהּ. מַאי קָא מַשְׁמַע לָן, דִּפְלִיגִי רַבָּנַן עֲלֵיהּ דְּרַבִּי יוֹסֵי.

The Gemara asks: By saying that **this** is only Rabbi Yosei's stance, Shmuel seemingly indicates that **he** himself **does not maintain** that opinion. However, **Shmuel said to Rav Ḥana of Baghdad:**[P] **Go and bring me an assembly of ten** men[N] **and I will say to you before them** a *halakha* that I seek to disseminate: **One who transfers ownership** of an object **to a fetus,** the fetus **acquires** it.[N] Consequently, according to Shmuel, a fetus can own property, which is the premise of Rabbi Yosei's stance that a fetus shares the inheritance even before he is born. The Gemara answers: **Rather,** although Shmuel said that **this** is only Rabbi Yosei's stance, **he holds** likewise. **What is** Shmuel **teaching us** by saying so? He is teaching us **that the Rabbis disagree with Rabbi Yosei.**

וּמִי פְּלִיגִי? מְתִיב רַבִּי זַכַּאי: זוֹ עֵדוּת הֵעִיד רַבִּי יוֹסֵי מִפִּי שְׁמַעְיָה וְאַבְטַלְיוֹן, וְהוֹדוּ לוֹ. אֲמַר רַב אַשִׁי: מִי קָתָנֵי ״וְקִבְּלוּ״? ״וְהוֹדוּ לוֹ״ קָתָנֵי, דְּמִסְתַּבֵּר טַעְמֵיהּ.

The Gemara asks: **But do they** really **disagree? Rabbi Zakkai raised an objection** to this statement from a *baraita*: **This** was **a testimony** that **Rabbi Yosei testified** that he heard **from the mouths of Shemaya and Avtalyon, and** the Rabbis **acknowledged** his testimony. Apparently, they accepted his opinion. **Rav Ashi said: Does** that *baraita* **state: And** the Rabbis **accepted** his testimony?[N] **It states: And they acknowledged** his testimony, which indicates **that his opinion is reasonable.** However, they did not accept his ruling.

תָּנוּ רַבָּנַן: הִנִּיחַ בָּנִים – אֵלּוּ וְאֵלּוּ אוֹכְלִים. הִנִּיחָהּ מְעוּבֶּרֶת – אֵלּוּ וְאֵלּוּ אֵין אוֹכְלִים. הִנִּיחַ בָּנִים וְהִנִּיחָהּ מְעוּבֶּרֶת, עַבְדֵי מְלוֹג אוֹכְלִים, כְּדֶרֶךְ שֶׁהִיא אוֹכֶלֶת. עַבְדֵי צֹאן בַּרְזֶל לֹא יֹאכְלוּ, מִפְּנֵי חֶלְקוֹ שֶׁל עוּבָּר, שֶׁהָעוּבָּר פּוֹסֵל וְאֵינוֹ מַאֲכִיל, דִּבְרֵי רַבִּי יוֹסֵי.

The Sages taught in a *baraita*: If the priest who was married to an Israelite woman and died **left children,**[H] both the slaves of usufruct property **and** the slaves of guaranteed investment **may partake** of *teruma*. The slaves of guaranteed investment are owned by the children, who are priests, and the slaves of usufruct property are owned by the woman, who partakes of *teruma* due to her children. If **he left** his wife **pregnant** and did not leave children, both **these** slaves **and those** slaves **may not partake** of *teruma*. If **he left children and left her pregnant,**[H] the **slaves of usufruct** property who belong to her **partake** of *teruma* **just as she partakes** due to her children. However, the **slaves of guaranteed investment,** who are inherited by the children, **may not partake, due to the fetus's share,** as it too inherits them, **as a fetus can disqualify** one from partaking of *teruma* **but it cannot not enable** one **to partake.** This is **the statement of Rabbi Yosei.**

רַבִּי יִשְׁמָעֵאל בְּרַבִּי יוֹסֵי אוֹמֵר מִשּׁוּם אָבִיו: הַבַּת – מַאֲכֶלֶת, הַבֵּן – אֵינוֹ מַאֲכִיל. רַבִּי שִׁמְעוֹן בֶּן יוֹחַי אוֹמֵר: זְכָרִים – יֹאכְלוּ, כּוּלָּן נְקֵבוֹת – לֹא יֹאכְלוּ, שֶׁמָּא יִמָּצֵא עוּבָּר זָכָר, וְאֵין לְבָנוֹת בִּמְקוֹם הַבֵּן כְּלוּם.

Rabbi Yishmael, son of Rabbi Yosei, says in the name of his father: If the priest left behind **a daughter,** she **enables** the slaves **to partake** of *teruma*; however, **a son does not enable** them **to partake. Rabbi Shimon ben Yoḥai says:** If among the priest's children there are **males,** the slaves **partake** of *teruma*. But if they are **all females, they do not partake, lest the fetus be found** to be **a male, and daughters do not** receive **any** of the inheritance **where** there is **a son.** The male fetus would be the sole inheritor, and it does not enable slaves to partake of *teruma*.

מַאי אִירְיָא שֶׁמָּא יִמָּצֵא עוּבָּר זָכָר? תֵּיפוֹק לֵיהּ דִּנְקֵבָה נַמִי פָּסְלָה! חֲדָא וְעוֹד קָאָמַר; חֲדָא – דִּנְקֵבָה נַמִי פָּסְלָה, וְעוֹד: שֶׁמָּא יִמָּצֵא עוּבָּר זָכָר, וְאֵין לְבָנוֹת בִּמְקוֹם הַבֵּן כְּלוּם.

The Gemara asks: **Why** does Rabbi Shimon ben Yoḥai **specifically** explain that if the children are females, the slaves may not partake of *teruma*, **lest the fetus be found** to be **a male? Derive** the ruling that the slaves do not partake of *teruma* from the *halakha* **that a female** fetus **also disqualifies** its slaves from partaking of *teruma*. Since the priest has only daughters, they inherit from him, and the female fetus receives a share in the inheritance too. The Gemara answers: Rabbi Shimon ben Yoḥai **stated one** reason **and another. One** reason is **that a female also disqualifies** its slaves from partaking of *teruma*, **and another** reason is **lest the fetus be found** to be **a male, and daughters have no** share in the inheritance **at all in a place** where there is **a son.**

PERSONALITIES

Rav Ḥana of Baghdad [*Bagdata'a*] – רַב חָנָא בַּגְדָתָאָה: Rav Ḥana of Baghdad was a second-generation Babylonian *amora*. He was Shmuel's preeminent disciple and transmitted several *halakhot* in his teacher's name. He was also a colleague of Rav Yehuda, another disciple of Shmuel.

Rav Ḥana was apparently from the city of Baghdad, called in those days Bagdat, which was on the border of the Jewish settlement in Babylonia, and a small city at the time.

NOTES

Bring me an assembly of ten men – אַיְיתֵי לִי בֵּי עֲשָׂרָה: Although it is a legal principle that anything said in the presence of three is considered publicized, making a statement in front of a gathering of ten constitutes a special declaration before a bona fide assembly, which serves to emphasize the importance of the announcement.

One who transfers ownership of an object to a fetus, it acquires it – הַמְזַכֶּה לְעוּבָּר קָנָה: The Gemara in several places reaches the conclusion that a fetus cannot acquire or own anything. The early commentaries discuss the apparent contradiction between that ruling and the *halakha* that one may grant property to his child while the latter is still a fetus. One opinion is that a parent's grant carries more weight than an ordinary acquisition or inheritance, due to the emotional closeness of a parent to his child. The Ramban, on the other hand, claims that the *halakha* that a parent may grant property to a fetus is not Torah law but a rabbinical ordinance that applies only to someone on his deathbed, as it is designed to calm the mind of such an individual.

Does that *baraita* state: And the Rabbis accepted his testimony, etc. – מִי קָתָנֵי, וְקִבְּלוּ וכו׳: If the Rabbis acknowledged Rabbi Yosei's testimony, why didn't they accept his ruling? The Ritva explains that while the Rabbis conceded that Rabbi Yosei's opinion is both reasonable and an accepted tradition, they had their own conflicting tradition, which they were unwilling to disregard in favor of his. Others explain that although they accepted his opinion, the wording indicates that they had initially disagreed with him (Rabbi Avraham min HaHar). Another explanation is that while they acknowledged Rabbi Yosei's tradition, they interpreted it differently than he did (*Tosafot*).

HALAKHA

If the priest who died left children – הִנִּיחַ בָּנִים: If a priest married an Israelite woman and subsequently died, and she has descendants from him and is not pregnant, she and her slaves, both slaves of usufruct property and of slaves of guaranteed investment, partake of *teruma* (*Tur, Yoreh De'a* 331).

If he left children and left her pregnant – הִנִּיחַ בָּנִים וְהִנִּיחָהּ מְעוּבֶּרֶת: The Rambam rules that if a priest married an Israelite woman and died, leaving her pregnant, if she has other children from him she and her slaves of usufruct property may partake of *teruma*. However, her slaves of guaranteed investment may not, due to the fetus's share in their ownership. Alternatively, the Rosh follows Rabbi Shimon's ruling that if they had sons, both types of slaves may partake of *teruma*. However, if they had only daughters, the slaves of guaranteed investment may not partake of *teruma* due to the fetus's share. The *Tur* concurs with this ruling (Rambam *Sefer Zera'im, Hilkhot Terumot* 8:4; *Yoreh De'a* 331).

זְכָרִים יֹאכְלוּ. וְהָאִיכָּא עוּבָּר! קָסָבַר:

The Gemara asks with regard to the first clause of Rabbi Shimon's statement, that if among the priest's children there are **males**, the slaves **may partake** of *teruma*: **But** even though sons inherit from their father, **isn't there a fetus** to be accounted for, as perhaps he too is a male, and therefore has a share in the inheritance? The Gemara answers: Rabbi Shimon **holds**

Perek **VII**
Daf **67** Amud **b**

אֵין חוֹשְׁשִׁין לְמִיעוּטָא. וְאִיבָּעֵית אֵימָא: לְעוֹלָם קָסָבַר חוֹשְׁשִׁין לְמִיעוּטָא, דְּעָבְדִינַן לֵיהּ תַּקַּנְתָּא כְּרַב נַחְמָן אָמַר שְׁמוּאֵל.

that **we are not concerned about the minority**[N] of cases. Only a minority of fetuses are male inheritors, as roughly half are female, and some are stillborn. Therefore, the majority of fetuses will not become male children. **And if you wish, say** that **actually he holds** that **we are concerned about the minority.** However, **we make an arrangement for** the slaves, **in accordance with** what **Rav Naḥman** said that **Shmuel said.**

דְּאָמַר רַב נַחְמָן אָמַר שְׁמוּאֵל: יְתוֹמִים שֶׁבָּאוּ לַחֲלוֹק בְּנִכְסֵי אֲבִיהֶם, בֵּית דִּין מַעֲמִידִין לָהֶם אַפּוֹטְרוֹפּוֹס וּבוֹרֵר לָהֶם חֵלֶק יָפֶה. הִגְדִּילוּ – יְכוֹלִין לִמְחוֹת. וְרַב נַחְמָן דִּידֵיהּ אָמַר: הִגְדִּילוּ – אֵין יְכוֹלִין לִמְחוֹת. דְּאִם כֵּן – מָה כֹּחַ בֵּית דִּין יָפֶה?

This is **as Rav Naḥman said** that **Shmuel said:** With regard to minor **orphans who came to** court to **divide up their father's property,**[H] the **court appoints for** each of **them a steward** [*apotropos*],[LN] **and he selects for them a fine share.** When the orphans **have grown up, they may object** to the manner in which the property was divided and redistribute it. **And Rav Naḥman himself said** that when **they have grown up they may not object, as, if** they may object, **what good is the power of the court?** Here too, an appointed steward selects a share of the inheritance on behalf of the fetus, and this share does not include any of the slaves. Therefore, the slaves may partake of *teruma*. However, if all of the children are females, this arrangement is impossible because if the fetus is a son all the property belongs to him.

לֵימָא, דְּרַב נַחְמָן תַּנָּאֵי הִיא! לָא, דְּכוּלֵּי עָלְמָא אִית לְהוּ דְּרַב נַחְמָן, וְהָכָא בְּחוֹשְׁשִׁין לְמִיעוּטָא קָמִיפַּלְגִי.

Based on the use of Rav Naḥman's ruling to explain Rabbi Shimon's opinion, the Gemara suggests: **Let us say** that **Rav Naḥman's** opinion **is** corresponding to one side of a dispute between ***tanna'im***, as the Rabbis disagree with Rabbi Shimon. The Gemara rejects this suggestion: **No;** it is possible **that everyone** in the dispute **accepts Rav Naḥman's** ruling, **and here they disagree** only **with regard** to whether **we are concerned about the minority,** as previously suggested, in a case where the arrangement was not made.

רַבִּי יִשְׁמָעֵאל בְּרַבִּי יוֹסֵי אוֹמֵר מִשּׁוּם אָבִיו: הַבַּת – מַאֲכִיל, הַבֵּן – אֵינוֹ מַאֲכִיל. מַאי שְׁנָא בֵּן דְּלָא מַאֲכִיל – מִשּׁוּם חֶלְקוֹ שֶׁל עוּבָּר, בַּת נַמִי לָא תַּאֲכִיל – מִפְּנֵי חֶלְקוֹ שֶׁל עוּבָּר!

It was taught in the previous clause of the *baraita* that **Rabbi Yishmael, son of Rabbi Yosei, says in the name of his father:** If the priest left behind **a daughter,** she **enables** the slaves **to partake** of *teruma*; however, **a son does not enable** them **to partake** of it. The Gemara asks: **What is different** about **a son, who does not enable** them **to partake, due to the fetus's share,** as it owns a share of the property if it is a male? **A daughter should not enable** them **to partake either, due to the fetus's share.**

HALAKHA

Minor orphans who came to court to divide up their father's property, etc. – **יְתוֹמִים שֶׁבָּאוּ לַחֲלוֹק בְּנִכְסֵי אֲבִיהֶם וכו׳**: With regard to sons, some of whom are adults and others of whom are minors, whose father dies and who want to divide up their father's property so that the adults can receive their share, the court appoints a steward for the minors, who selects for them a suitable share. The minors cannot object, even when they come of age, as the division was performed under the auspices of the court. This ruling follows Rav Naḥman's own opinion. However, the Ritva rules in accordance with Shmuel (*Shakh*; Rambam *Sefer Mishpatim*, *Hilkhot Naḥalot* 10:4; *Shulḥan Arukh*, *Ḥoshen Mishpat* 289:1).

LANGUAGE

Steward [*apotropos*] – **אַפּוֹטְרוֹפּוֹס**: From the Greek ἐπίτροπος, *epitropos*, meaning one with the power of attorney, a trustee. It generally refers to anyone who has the right to run the properties or affairs of another.

NOTES

We are not concerned about the minority – **אֵין חוֹשְׁשִׁין לְמִיעוּטָא**: With regard to Rabbi Yosei's opinion toward less probable possibilities, the early commentaries raise a contradiction between the Gemara here, which indicates that Rabbi Yosei is not concerned about the minority of cases, and other statements of his that indicate that he does take such possibilities into account.

Some commentaries claim that what is indicated here should be seen as a local ruling and not a principle (Meiri). Others differentiate between uncertainties with regard to the present reality, as is the case here, and uncertainties with regard to the future (see Ramban; *Tosefot HaRosh*). A third opinion distinguishes between ritual and monetary matters, as the former field often demands stringency, whereas with regard to monetary matters there is no such thing as stringency, since a stringent ruling for one party is a lenient one for the other.

The court appoints for them a steward – **בֵּית דִּין מַעֲמִידִין לָהֶם אַפּוֹטְרוֹפּוֹס**: According to Rashi, the court appoints a private steward for each orphan to select his share. The Ritva argues that there is no need to divide up the property between the minor orphans at this stage. Rather, a steward is appointed only if there are both minor and adult orphans, and the adults demand to receive their share. In that case, the court appoints one steward for all the minors. He selects a fine share for all of them, and when they come of age they can divide it up among themselves.

There is also a dispute as to whether a steward has the authority to select property according to its monetary value, or whether he may participate only in the distribution of identical items. The Gemara here apparently supports the opinion that lends him the authority to select property according to its monetary value, as the steward here selects land for the fetus in exchange for slaves. Those who hold otherwise explain that a steward should prefer land for the orphan that he is representing, as the value of slaves is likely to depreciate over time. Therefore, this is an exchange that he may perform (*Nimmukei Yosef*).

אֲמַר אַבַּיֵי: הָכָא בִּנְכָסִים מוּעָטִים עָסְקִינַן, וּכְגוֹן דְּאִיכָּא בֵּן בַּהֲדֵי בַּת,

Abaye said: Here we are dealing with a case of an inheritance of **insufficient property** that is enough only to sustain the daughters until they come of age. With regard to this case, the Sages instituted that the daughters receive their sustenance while the sons get nothing.[NH] This is **also** a case **where there is** a surviving **son together with** the **daughter.**

מַה נַּפְשָׁךְ: אִי הַאי דְּמִעַבְּרָא בֵּן הוּא – לָא עֲדִיף מֵהַאי דְּקָאֵי, אִי בַּת הִיא – אַמַּאי אָכְלָה, בְּתַקַּנְתָּא דְּרַבָּנַן – כַּמָּה דְּלָא נָפֵק לַאֲוִיר הָעוֹלָם לָא תַּקִּינוּ רַבָּנַן.

Therefore, **no matter what,** the slaves do not partake of *teruma*. **If this** fetus, **with which she is pregnant, is a son, it is no better than this** son who already **exists.**[N] Just as the existing son does not inherit the insufficient property, the same applies to the male fetus. **If it is a daughter,** it does not yet receive a share of the inheritance. This can be explained: **Why does** the daughter **partake** of the inheritance? It is **by** virtue of **a rabbinic ordinance.** Therefore, **as long as** the fetus **has not emerged into the atmosphere of the world, the Sages did not establish** that it should receive the inheritance. Consequently, the slaves partake of *teruma* by virtue of the existing daughter, as only she inherits them.

בְּמַאי אוֹקִימְתָּא – בִּנְכָסִים מוּעָטִים, אֵימָא סֵיפָא: שֶׁמָּא יִמָּצֵא הָעוּבָּר זָכָר, וְאֵין לְבָנוֹת בִּמְקוֹם בֵּן כְּלוּם, אַדְּרַבָּה, נְכָסִים מוּעָטִים דְּבָנוֹת נִינְהוּ! סֵיפָא אֲתַאן לִנְכָסִים מְרוּבִּין.

The Gemara asks: **In what** manner **did you establish** the *baraita*? You established it as referring **to insufficient property.** However, **say the latter clause** of the *baraita*: **Lest the fetus be found** to be a **male, and daughters do not** receive **any** of the inheritance **where** there is **a son.** Yet according to Abaye's explanation, **on the contrary,** the **insufficient property is the daughters',** whether or not there are any sons. The Gemara answers: In **the latter clause we have come to** a different case, in which there is **sufficient property.**

וּנְכָסִים מוּעָטִים דְּבָנוֹת נִינְהוּ? וְהָאָמַר רַבִּי אַסִּי אָמַר רַבִּי יוֹחָנָן: יְתוֹמִין שֶׁקָּדְמוּ וּמָכְרוּ בִּנְכָסִים מוּעָטִים, מַה שֶּׁמָּכְרוּ מָכְרוּ!

The Gemara raises another objection to Abaye's explanation: Does an inheritance of **insufficient property** belong **to the daughters? Didn't Rabbi Asi say** that **Rabbi Yoḥanan said:** If the male **orphans proceeded to sell** the **insufficient property,**[H] although by rabbinic ordinance it is designated for the daughters' sustenance, **what they sold was sold.** Apparently, the Sages did not expropriate the properties from the male inheritors, but merely designated them for the daughters' sustenance. How, then, can the sons' ownership be disregarded with regard to the slaves' partaking of *teruma*?

וְאֶלָּא מַאי בַּת דְּקָתָנֵי – אֵם – אִי הָכִי, הַיְינוּ רַבִּי יוֹסֵי! כּוּלָּהּ רַבִּי יִשְׁמָעֵאל בְּרַבִּי יוֹסֵי קָתָנֵי לַהּ.

Rather, what is the meaning of the word **daughter** in the context of the ruling **that is taught** by Rabbi Yishmael? It means female and is referring to the **mother** of the fetus. She enables her slaves of usufruct property to partake of *teruma*, as her husband's heirs have no share in them, whereas the son does not enable the slaves guaranteed investment to partake, due to the fetus's share. The Gemara asks: **If so, this is** the same as **Rabbi Yosei's** statement in the first clause. What was added by Rabbi Yishmael? The Gemara answers: Indeed, the **entire** *baraita* **is taught by Rabbi Yishmael, son of Rabbi Yosei.** There are not conflicting versions of Rabbi Yosei's opinion. Rather, Rabbi Yishmael is clarifying that he is the author of that *baraita*.

מתני׳ הָעוּבָּר, וְהַיָּבָם, וְהָאֵירוּסִין, וְהַחֵרֵשׁ, וּבֶן תֵּשַׁע שָׁנִים וְיוֹם אֶחָד – פּוֹסְלִין וְלֹא מַאֲכִילִין.

MISHNA With regard to **the fetus**[H] of a divorcée or a widow whose husband left her pregnant; **and a man whose married brother died childless** [*yavam*];[H] **and betrothal; and** a married **deaf-mute;**[N] **and a nine-year-and-one-day-old** boy[B] who engaged in intercourse with a woman; if any of these men are Israelites and the woman is the daughter of a priest, they **disqualify** her from partaking of *teruma*. **But** if she is an Israelite and they are priests, they **do not enable**[N] her **to partake** of *teruma*.

NOTES

The distribution of an inheritance – חֲלוּקַּת יְרוּשָּׁה: According to Torah law, if a man passes away, leaving sons and daughters, only the males inherit from him. Daughters inherit from him only if there are no sons. However, the Sages instituted as one of the stipulations of a marriage contract that the daughters of the married couple receive their sustenance from their father's property until they come of age or marry. As a marriage contract is essentially a promissory note, this stipulation places a lien on the inheritance. Consequently, the daughters' right to the property takes precedence over the sons', to the extent that if the property is meager and is sufficient only for the daughters' sustenance, the sons get nothing, not even their own sustenance. Nevertheless, since the sons are the inheritors, if they unlawfully sell the property, the sale is valid.

It is no better than this son who already exists – לָא עֲדִיף מֵהַאי דְּקָאֵי: The Rashba asks how it is possible that a rabbinical ordinance overrules the Torah law that the slaves do not partake of *teruma*. He leaves this difficulty unresolved. In the Jerusalem Talmud, it is answered that according to Rabbi Yosei, by Torah law there is no obligation to separate *teruma* and tithes after the destruction of the First Temple; rather, the obligation is by rabbinic law.

Deaf-mute [*ḥeresh*] – חֵרֵשׁ: When the unmodified term *ḥeresh* is employed, the reference is to one who can neither hear nor speak. In earlier times, these deaf-mutes were considered uneducable and were often placed in the same category as imbeciles and minors, who are exempt from all of the mitzvot in the Torah. In contemporary times, great strides have been made in the education of the deaf. Consequently, many rabbinic commentaries rule that those who can communicate intelligently are considered obligated in mitzvot like any Jew.

Disqualify but do not enable to partake – פּוֹסְלִין וְלֹא מַאֲכִילִין: Rabbi Shimon is cited in the Jerusalem Talmud as claiming that this principle is unjust, as any sexual relationship that disqualifies the daughter of priest from partaking of *teruma* should enable the wife of a priest to partake of *teruma*, and vice versa.

HALAKHA

An inheritance of insufficient property goes to the daughters – נְכָסִים מוּעָטִים לַבָּנוֹת: If a person died and left property, his daughters receive their sustenance from the estate until they come of age, and the rest is divided up among the sons. If the inheritance is sufficient only for the daughters' sustenance, they receive their sustenance from the property until they come of age or get betrothed, even if the sons are forced to beg for their livelihood (Rambam *Sefer Nashim*, *Hilkhot Ishut* 19:19; *Shulḥan Arukh*, *Even HaEzer* 112:14).

If the male orphans proceeded to sell the insufficient property, etc. – יְתוֹמִין שֶׁקָּדְמוּ וּמָכְרוּ בִּנְכָסִים מוּעָטִים וכו׳: If the father left only a meager inheritance and the sons proceeded to sell it, their sale is valid (Rambam *Sefer Nashim*, *Hilkhot Ishut* 19:17; *Shulḥan Arukh*, *Even HaEzer* 112:14).

A fetus disqualifies but does not enable to partake – עוּבָּר פּוֹסֵל וְאֵינוֹ מַאֲכִיל: An Israelite woman who is pregnant from a priest may not eat *teruma* due to the fetus, and the daughter of a priest who is pregnant from an Israelite does not partake of *teruma* either, even if she has no other child from him (Rambam *Sefer Zera'im*, *Hilkhot Terumot* 8:2).

The fetus and a…*yavam*, etc. – הָעוּבָּר וְהַיָּבָם וכו׳: With regard to a fetus, a *yavam*, betrothal, a married deaf-mute, and a nine-year-and-one-day-old boy who engaged in intercourse with a woman, if any of these are Israelites and the woman is the daughter of a priest, they disqualify her from partaking of *teruma*. If they are priests and she is an Israelite, they do not enable her to partake of *teruma* (Rambam *Sefer Zera'im*, *Hilkhot Terumot* 8:1).

BACKGROUND

A nine-year-and-one-day-old boy – בֶּן תֵּשַׁע שָׁנִים וְיוֹם אֶחָד: Although most boys do not experience a significant bodily change at the age of nine, the development of the testicles begins to accelerate at around this time, with the attending increase in the capacity for intercourse. Though it roughly corresponds to the average age of this development, this specification, like other specific ages the Sages established for different levels of maturity, is somewhat arbitrary.

NOTES

There is uncertainty as to whether he is nine years and one day old, etc. – סָפֵק שֶׁהוּא בֶּן תֵּשַׁע שָׁנִים וְיוֹם אֶחָד וכו׳: The commentaries point out that this cannot be referring to a case where it is currently uncertain whether or not the boy is nine years old, as in such a case the court would have had to follow his presumptive physical status, i.e., that of a minor under the age of nine. Rather, the reference is apparently to a case where he is currently at least nine years old, and the court must determine in retrospect what his age was at the time of the incident. Since he no longer has the presumptive status of a minor under the age of nine, his status at the time of the incident is deemed uncertain (see Maharshal, Rabbi Ovadya MiBartenura, and *Tosefot Yom Tov*).

If the house fell, etc. – נָפַל הַבַּיִת וכו׳: This clause appears unrelated to the rest of the mishna. One suggestion is that since the mishna includes cases of uncertainty in which the ruling is stringent, it adds this similar case as well (Rid; Rabbi Avraham min HaHar). In the Jerusalem Talmud, it is explained that the previous case of uncertainty, i.e., a boy whose adulthood is in doubt, is taught with regard to both the matter discussed in the first clause of the mishna, i.e., the partaking of *teruma*, and the rival wife's issue of her levirate bond, which is discussed in the latter clause. If there is uncertainty as to whether the first wife was betrothed before or after the husband reached adulthood, then after the husband's death the rival wife performs *ḥalitza* and does not enter into levirate marriage. Therefore, the mishna cites this clause as well.

And this woman is his brother's acquisition – וְהָא קִנְיַן דְּאָחִיו הוּא: The early commentaries disagree whether the *halakha* that the *yevama* of a priest may not partake of *teruma* is Torah law (*Tosafot Yeshanim*) or rabbinic law (*Tosafot*, citing Rabbeinu Tam). According to the latter opinion, the verse that is cited is not a proper derivation from the Torah, but rather a support of the rabbinic law.

סָפֵק שֶׁהוּא בֶּן תֵּשַׁע שָׁנִים וְיוֹם אֶחָד סָפֵק שֶׁאֵינוֹ, סָפֵק הֵבִיא שְׁתֵּי שְׂעָרוֹת וְסָפֵק שֶׁלֹּא הֵבִיא.

Likewise, in the case of a boy with regard to whom there is **uncertainty** as to **whether he is nine years and one day old**[NH] and **uncertainty** whether **he is not,** who engaged in intercourse with a woman; and in the case of a boy who betrothed a woman, with regard to whom there is **uncertainty** as to **whether he has grown two** pubic **hairs** and is considered an adult **and uncertainty whether he has not grown,** they too can disqualify the woman from partaking of *teruma* and cannot enable her to partake, as in the previous cases.

נָפַל הַבַּיִת עָלָיו וְעַל בַּת אָחִיו וְאֵין יָדוּעַ אֵי זֶה מֵת רִאשׁוֹן – צָרָתָהּ חוֹלֶצֶת וְלֹא מִתְיַבֶּמֶת.

If **the house fell**[N] **upon** a man **and upon his brother's daughter,**[H] to whom he was married, **and it is unknown which** of them **died first, her rival wife performs *ḥalitza* and does not enter into levirate marriage.** Entering into levirate marriage is not possible, as, if the wife died after her husband, the surviving wife would be rendered the rival wife of a forbidden relative, since the *yavam* is the father of the wife who died. This status prevents the creation of a levirate bond between him and the surviving wife as well. On the other hand, *ḥalitza* is necessary in case the wife died before her husband, thereby allowing the creation of a levirate bond between her rival wife and her father, the *yavam*.

גמ׳ ״הָעוּבָּר״. אִי בַּת כֹּהֵן לְיִשְׂרָאֵל הִיא פָּסֵיל לַהּ, ״כִּנְעוּרֶיהָ״ – פְּרָט לִמְעוּבֶּרֶת. אִי בַּת יִשְׂרָאֵל לְכֹהֵן הִיא לָא מַאֲכִיל לַהּ, יָלוּד מַאֲכִיל, שֶׁאֵינוֹ יָלוּד אֵינוֹ מַאֲכִיל.

GEMARA It is taught in the mishna that **the fetus** disqualifies its mother from partaking of *teruma* and does not enable her to do so. The Gemara explains: **If she is the daughter of a priest** married **to an Israelite,** and her husband died and left her pregnant, the fetus **disqualifies her** from partaking of *teruma*, as it is stated: "But if a priest's daughter be a widow, or divorced, and have no child, and is returned to her father's house, as in her youth, she may eat of her father's bread" (Leviticus 22:13). The phrase **"as in her youth" excludes a pregnant woman,** whose body has changed from her youth. **If** she **is an Israelite woman** married **to a priest,** the fetus **does not enable her to partake,** as **one who was born enables** others **to partake** of *teruma*, whereas **one who is not** yet **born does not enable** others **to partake.**

״הַיָּבָם״. אִי בַּת כֹּהֵן לְיִשְׂרָאֵל הִיא פָּסֵיל לַהּ, ״וְשָׁבָה אֶל בֵּית אָבִיהָ״ פְּרָט לְשׁוֹמֶרֶת יָבָם, אִי בַּת יִשְׂרָאֵל לְכֹהֵן הִיא לָא מַאֲכִיל לַהּ, ״קִנְיַן כַּסְפּוֹ״ אָמַר רַחֲמָנָא, וְהָא קִנְיַן דְּאָחִיו הוּא.

It is taught in the mishna that the same principle applies to a *yavam*. The Gemara explains: **If she is the daughter of a priest** who has a levirate bond **to an Israelite, he disqualifies her,** as it is stated in the verse cited above: **"And is returned to her father's house,"** which **excludes a widow waiting for her *yavam*,** who has not returned to her father's house, as a levirate bond was created with her *yavam*. **If she is an Israelite woman** with a levirate bond **to a priest, he does not enable her to partake** of *teruma*, as **the Merciful One states** in the Torah: **"The purchase of his money,** he may eat of it" (Leviticus 22:11), **and this** woman **is his brother's acquisition.**[N] The bond with her *yavam* ensued from his late brother's marriage to her, not through any action of his own.[H]

״וְהָאֵירוּסִין״. אִי בַּת כֹּהֵן לְיִשְׂרָאֵל הִיא, פָּסֵיל לַהּ,

The mishna teaches that the same principle **also** applies to **betrothal.** The Gemara explains: **If she is the daughter of a priest** betrothed **to an Israelite, he disqualifies her,**

HALAKHA

Uncertainty as to whether he is nine years and one day old, etc. – סָפֵק שֶׁהוּא בֶּן תֵּשַׁע שָׁנִים וְיוֹם אֶחָד וכו׳: In the case of a boy with regard to whom there is uncertainty as to whether or not he is nine years old who engaged in intercourse with a woman, and similarly in the case of one who married a woman and with regard to whom there is uncertainty as to whether or not he has grown two pubic hairs, they disqualify the woman from partaking of *teruma* and cannot enable her to partake of it (Rambam *Sefer Zera'im*, *Hilkhot Terumot* 8:11).

If a house fell upon a man and upon his brother's daughter – נָפַל הַבַּיִת עָלָיו וְעַל בַּת אָחִיו: If a man had two wives, one who was related to the *yavam* and the other who was not, and the man and the wife related to the *yavam* both died and it is unknown which of them died first, the rival wife performs *ḥalitza* and not levirate marriage (*Shulḥan Arukh*, *Even HaEzer* 173:8).

A *yavam* disqualifies and does not enable to partake of *teruma* – יָבָם פּוֹסֵל וְאֵינוֹ מַאֲכִיל: An Israelite widow waiting for her *yavam*, who is a priest, does not partake of *teruma*, despite their bond. The daughter of a priest waiting for an Israelite *yavam* does not partake of *teruma* either, due to their bond (Rambam *Sefer Zera'im*, *Hilkhot Terumot* 8:5).

דְּהָא קָנֵיהּ בַּהֲוָיָה, וְאִי בַּת יִשְׂרָאֵל לְכֹהֵן הִיא – לָא מַאֲכִיל לַהּ מִשּׁוּם דְּעוּלָּא.

as he acquired her by means of betrothal.[N] **And if she is an Israelite woman** betrothed **to a priest, he does not enable her to partake** of *teruma* **due to** the reason given by **Ulla:**[N] Although by Torah law a priest's betrothed partakes of *teruma*, the Sages rendered it prohibited for her to do so, lest she allow other members of her family to eat it.[H]

"וְהַחֵרֵשׁ". אִי בַּת כֹּהֵן לְיִשְׂרָאֵל הִיא – פָּסֵיל לַהּ, דְּהָא קָנֵיהּ בְּתַקַּנְתָּא דְרַבָּנַן, וְאִי בַּת יִשְׂרָאֵל לְכֹהֵן הִיא – לָא מַאֲכִיל, "קִנְיַן כַּסְפּוֹ" אָמַר רַחֲמָנָא, וְהַאי לָאו בַּר קִנְיָן הוּא.

It is **also** taught in the mishna that **a deaf-mute**[N] disqualifies a woman from partaking of *teruma* and does not enable her to do so.[H] The Gemara elaborates: **If she is the daughter of a priest** married to a deaf-mute **Israelite, he disqualifies her, as he acquired her through** marriage sanctioned by **an ordinance of the Sages.** Although the marriage of a deaf-mute is invalid by Torah law, the Sages instituted an ordinance validating this type of marriage. **And if she is an Israelite woman** married **to** a deaf-mute **priest, he does not enable** her **to partake** of *teruma*, as **the Merciful One states** in the Torah: **"The purchase of his money,** he may eat of it" (Leviticus 22:11), **and this** deaf-mute **is not capable of acquisition** by Torah law, as he is not legally competent.

"וּבֶן תֵּשַׁע שָׁנִים" וכו׳. קָא סָלְקָא דַּעְתָּן בְּשׁוֹמֶרֶת יָבָם לְבֶן תֵּשַׁע וְיוֹם אֶחָד. לְמַאי? אִי לְמִיפְסַל – קָטָן נַמִי מִיפְסַל פָּסֵיל, אִי לַאֲכוֹלֵי – גָּדוֹל נַמִי לָא מַאֲכִיל!

§ It is **also** taught in the mishna that **a nine-year-old** boy disqualifies a woman from partaking of *teruma* and does not enable her to partake. **It enters our mind** that the mishna is referring **to a widow waiting for her** ***yavam,*** who is **nine** years **and one day old.** The Gemara therefore inquires: With regard **to what** is this taught? **If** it is with regard **to disqualifying** her from partaking of *teruma*, **a younger** ***yavam*** **also disqualifies** her, as a levirate bond was created and she cannot return to her father's house. And **if** it was with regard **to enabling** her **to partake** of *teruma*, **an older** ***yavam*** **does not enable** her **to partake either,** as discussed above.

אָמַר אַבָּיֵי: הָכָא בְּיָבָם בֶּן תֵּשַׁע שָׁנִים וְיוֹם אֶחָד הַבָּא עַל יְבִמְתּוֹ עָסְקִינַן, דְּמִדְּאוֹרַיְיתָא קָנְיָא לֵיהּ. סָלְקָא דַּעְתָּךְ אָמֵינָא: הוֹאִיל וּמִדְּאוֹרַיְיתָא קָנְיָא לֵיהּ, וּבִיאָתוֹ בִּיאָה, אֵימָא לוֹכִיל – קָא מַשְׁמַע לַן: עָשׂוּ בִּיאַת בֶּן תֵּשַׁע שָׁנִים וְיוֹם אֶחָד כְּמַאֲמָר בְּגָדוֹל.

Abaye said: Here we are dealing with a nine-year-and-one-day-old ***yavam*** who already **engaged in intercourse with his** ***yevama,***[N] **as she was** thereby **acquired by him by Torah** law.[N] It might **enter your mind to say that since by Torah** law **she was acquired by him, as** the legal status of **his** act of **intercourse is** that of **intercourse,** perhaps **he enables** her **to partake** of *teruma*. The mishna therefore **teaches us** that the Sages **rendered the** legal status of the **intercourse of a nine-year-and-one-day-old** boy **like** that of **levirate betrothal** by means of money or a document performed **by an adult man,**[H] which is not sufficient for her to partake of *teruma*. Since levirate betrothal is effective only by rabbinic law, the *yevama* is not considered the acquisition of his money by Torah law and may not partake of *teruma*.

NOTES

As he acquired her by means of betrothal [*havaya*] – דְּהָא קָנֵיהּ בַּהֲוָיָה: *Tosafot* note that the use of the word *havaya* indicates that this *halakha* is derived from the verse "And if a priest's daughter be [*tihye*] married to a common man" (Leviticus 22:12). However, it appears from the Gemara later on that it is derived from a different verse. *Tosafot* conclude that the Gemara hints to this verse because it is a clearer source. The Gemara is not particular about referring to the accurate source because it is inconsequential here. The Ramban discusses the Gemara's tendency to cite inaccurate sources from the Torah for incidentally mentioned *halakhot* when the quoted source is clearer than the actual one.

Due to the reason given by Ulla – מִשּׁוּם דְּעוּלָּא: Ulla's rationale is that the woman is not yet accustomed to the priesthood, as she is still living in her father's house, and she is likely to forget that she may not allow members of her Israelite family to partake of the *teruma*. It should be noted that another *amora* suggests a different rationale for this ordinance (see *Ketubot* 57b): The priest might discover a blemish in the woman following their marriage, which would render the betrothal mistaken and annul it retroactively. However, Ulla's rationale is the one usually quoted.

And a deaf-mute – וְהַחֵרֵשׁ: The Jerusalem Talmud explains this case differently. It says that the mishna is referring to a woman who engaged in intercourse with a deaf-mute who is either her *yavam* or who is unfit to enter the assembly. Accordingly, he disqualifies her by Torah law, and not by rabbinic law as is explained by the Gemara.

The difference between the explanations in the Babylonian Talmud and the Jerusalem Talmud with regard to the case of a deaf-mute corresponds to the dispute between Abaye and Rava with regard to the case of a nine-year-old boy.

A nine-year-and-one-day-old *yavam* who engaged in intercourse with his *yevama* – יָבָם בֶּן תֵּשַׁע שָׁנִים וְיוֹם אֶחָד הַבָּא עַל יְבִמְתּוֹ: By Torah law, an act of intercourse performed by a boy is recognized from the age of nine. Any adult who engaged in forbidden intercourse with him is liable, but he is exempt from punishment, as he is a minor. He is also unable to acquire property or betroth a woman, as he is not legally competent. The complexity of a minor's levirate marriage stems from the fact that levirate marriage is an acquisition created exclusively through intercourse.

As she was thereby acquired by him by Torah law – דְּמִדְּאוֹרַיְיתָא קָנְיָא לֵיהּ: Most commentaries maintain that the levirate marriage of a minor *yavam* is invalid by Torah law and is no more effective than betrothal of a *yevama*, which is a rabbinic institution (see *Tosafot*). Therefore, they claim that this phrase is inaccurate and refers not to acquisition but to the preexisting levirate bond between them (Ritva). Accordingly, the rationale that the mishna rejects is that the combination of the levirate bond, which exists by Torah law, and the levirate betrothal might enable the woman to partake of *teruma*.

Rashi (*Kiddushin* 19a) and Rabbi Avraham min HaHar, however, hold that a *yavam* who is a minor can perform levirate marriage by Torah law, and it was the Sages who instituted that it should be equivalent only to levirate betrothal.

HALAKHA

Betrothal disqualifies and does not enable her to partake – הָאֵירוּסִין פּוֹסְלִין וְלֹא מַאֲכִילִין: The daughter of a priest who is betrothed to an Israelite is disqualified from partaking of *teruma*, as she is considered like his wife. Although an Israelite woman betrothed to a priest may partake of *teruma* by Torah law, the Sages decreed that she not do so, lest she allow other members of her family to partake of *teruma*, as stated by Ulla (Rambam *Sefer Zera'im, Hilkhot Terumot* 8:7).

A deaf-mute disqualifies and does not enable her to partake – חֵרֵשׁ פּוֹסֵל וְאֵינוֹ מַאֲכִיל: The daughter of a priest who married a deaf-mute Israelite is disqualified from partaking of *teruma* due to this marriage, as it is valid by rabbinic ordinance. An Israelite woman married to a deaf-mute priest does not partake of *teruma*, as he has not acquired her by Torah law (Rambam *Sefer Zera'im, Hilkhot Terumot* 8:9).

The intercourse of a nine-year-old *yavam* – בִּיאַת יָבָם בֶּן תֵּשַׁע: If a minor *yavam* aged nine years and one day engaged in intercourse with his *yevama*, the intercourse does not fully consummate the levirate marriage. Rather, it is equivalent to an adult's betrothal to his *yevama* (Rambam *Sefer Nashim, Hilkhot Yibbum* 5:18; *Shulḥan Arukh, Even HaEzer* 167:1).

אמר ליה רבא: אי הכי, סיפא דקתני: ספק בן תשע שנים ויום אחד ספק שאינו, השתא ודאי בן תשע לא מאכיל – ספק מיבעיא?!

Rava said to him: If so, consider **the latter clause** of the mishna, **which teaches** that a boy with regard to whom there is **uncertainty** whether **he is nine years and one day old** and **uncertainty** whether **he is not,** disqualifies a woman from partaking of *teruma,* and he does not enable her to partake. **Now** that, according to your explanation, one who is **definitely nine** years **old does not enable** her **to partake** of *teruma,* **is it necessary** to teach the same concerning a boy with regard to whom there is **uncertainty** as to whether or not he reached that age?

אלא אמר רבא: בבן תשע שנים ויום אחד דהנך פסולים קתני, דפסלי בביאתן. וכדתניא: בן תשע שנים ויום אחד גר עמוני ומואבי, מצרי ואדומי, כותי, נתין, חלל וממזר, שבאו על כהנת לויה וישראלית – פסלוה.

Rather, Rava said that the mishna **is teaching** this *halakha* **with regard to a nine-year-and-one-day-old** boy who is one **of those unfit** males listed in a *baraita,*[H] **who disqualify** a woman from marrying a priest **by their intercourse,** as they are unfit to enter the assembly of Israel through marriage, **as it is taught** in a *baraita*: **A nine-year-and-one-day-old** boy who is **an Ammonite or a Moabite convert;** or who is **an Egyptian or an Edomite** convert; or who is either **a Samaritan** [***kuti***], **a Gibeonite, a** ***ḥalal,*** **or a** ***mamzer,*** when he **engaged in intercourse with a priestess,** i.e., the daughter of a priest, **a Levite, or an Israelite,** he thereby **disqualified her** from marrying a priest,[H] and, in the case of the daughter of a priest, from partaking of *teruma.*

והא מדקתני סיפא: אם אינן ראוין לבא בישראל הרי אלו פוסלים, מכלל דרישא לאו בפסולים עסקינן! רישא פסולי קהל, סיפא פסולי כהונה.

The Gemara raises a difficulty **from** the fact **that the latter clause,** the next mishna (69a), **teaches** that **if** men who **are unfit to enter** the assembly of **Israel** by marriage engage in extramarital intercourse with women, **they disqualify** them from marrying into the priesthood: **It may be inferred that** in **the first clause,** the mishna above, **we are dealing not with unfit** individuals but with men fit to marry Jews of unflawed lineage. The Gemara answers: That inference is incorrect. **The first clause** of the mishna is dealing with those **unfit to** enter **the assembly**[N] of Israel by marriage, while **the latter clause** is dealing with those who are merely **unfit for the priesthood.** That is why the mishna is referring to them separately. Accordingly, Rava's explanation that the mishna is referring to an unfit nine-year-old boy is viable.

גופא, בן תשע שנים ויום אחד גר עמוני ומואבי מצרי ואדומי כותי נתין חלל וממזר שבאו על כהנת לויה וישראלית – פסלן.

§ The Gemara addresses the matter **itself** and cites the complete *baraita.* **A nine-year-and-one-day-old** boy who is **an Ammonite or a Moabite convert;**[N] or who is **an Egyptian or an Edomite** convert;[N] or who is either **a Samaritan,**[N] **a Gibeonite,**[N] **a** ***ḥalal,*** **or a** ***mamzer,*** when he **engaged in intercourse with a priestess, or a Levite, or an Israelite,** he thereby **disqualified her** from marrying into the priesthood.

רבי יוסי אומר: כל שזרעו פסול – פוסל, כל שאין זרעו פסול – אינו פוסל. רבן שמעון בן גמליאל אומר: כל שאתה נושא בתו – אתה נושא אלמנתו, וכל שאין אתה נושא בתו – אי אתה נושא אלמנתו.

Rabbi Yosei says: Of the individuals mentioned above, **anyone whose offspring is unfit** to enter the assembly of Israel, **disqualifies** a woman with whom he engaged in intercourse from marrying into the priesthood. However, **anyone whose offspring is not unfit does not disqualify** a woman through intercourse. **Rabban Shimon ben Gamliel says: Anyone whose daughter you may marry, you may marry his widow,** even if you are a priest. Anyone whose daughter may marry a Jew of unflawed lineage does not disqualify a woman with whom he engaged in intercourse from marrying into the priesthood. **And anyone whose daughter you may not marry, you may not marry his widow** if you are a priest.

NOTES

The first clause is dealing with those unfit to enter the assembly, etc. – **רישא פסולי קהל וכו׳**: According to Rabbeinu Ḥananel's version of the text, which is accepted by most early commentaries, the Gemara states the opposite: The first clause is dealing with those unfit for the priesthood, and the latter clause is referring to those who are unfit to enter the assembly.

Most commentaries agree with Rashi's interpretation that the expression: Those unfit for the priesthood, is referring only to a *ḥalal*, whereas the expression: Those unfit to enter the assembly, is referring to all those who are unfit.

An Ammonite or a Moabite convert – **גר עמוני ומואבי**: Torah law prohibits a male convert from these nations and his male descendants to ever marry freely among the Jewish people (see Deuteronomy 23:4).

An Egyptian or an Edomite convert – **גר מצרי ואדומי**: A convert of Egyptian or Edomite descent, whether male or female, may not marry a Jew by birth. This restriction applies for two generations (see Deuteronomy 23:8–9).

Samaritan – **כותי**: The Samaritans are the descendants of the nations displaced by Sennacherib, King of Assyria, and brought to settle in Eretz Yisrael. Eventually, they accepted upon themselves several mitzvot (II Kings, chapter 17). At the beginning of the Second Temple period, during the times of Ezra and Nehemiah, relations between the Samaritans and the Jews deteriorated. Later, the Samaritans established a center of worship on Mount Gerizim, as they claimed that the sanctity of that mountain was established by one of the Ten Commandments. Some generations of Sages recognized Samaritans as half-Jewish. They went so far as to say that the Samaritans are extremely exacting in the fulfillment of the mitzvot they adopted, even more so than Jews. Ultimately, as the Samaritans continued to distance themselves from the Jewish people in virtually every regard, they were accorded the legal status of gentiles.

Gibeonite – **נתין**: A Gibeonite is a descendant of the nation that tricked the Jewish people into making a covenant with them in the time of Joshua. According to most commentaries, by Torah law, the Gibeonites could have been treated as ordinary converts, but first Joshua and then King David decreed that they be treated as *mamzerim*, and therefore it became prohibited for Jews to marry them.

HALAKHA

The intercourse of an unfit nine-year-old boy – **ביאת פסול בן תשע**: If the intercourse of a male disqualifies a woman from marrying into the priesthood, it does so from the time the male is nine years and one day old. The woman with whom he engaged in intercourse is thereby disqualified from marrying a priest, and if she is the daughter of a priest she may no longer partake of *teruma* (Rambam *Sefer Zera'im, Hilkhot Terumot* 8:11).

Individuals who disqualify women from marrying into the priesthood – **הפוסלים לכהונה**: If a woman engaged in intercourse with a gentile; a Gibeonite, a *mamzer*, an Ammonite or a Moabite convert, an Egyptian or an Edomite convert of the first or second generation, or a *ḥalal*, she is disqualified from marrying into the priesthood, and if she is the daughter of a priest she may no longer partake of *teruma*. Some commentaries claim that she is disqualified from marrying into the priesthood only if she engaged in forbidden intercourse that renders her liable to receive *karet* (*Tosafot*; Rosh; Rambam *Sefer Kedusha, Hilkhot Issurei Bia* 18:3; *Shulḥan Arukh, Even HaEzer* 6:8).

מְנָא הָנֵי מִילֵּי? אָמַר רַב יְהוּדָה אָמַר רַב: אָמַר קְרָא "וּבַת כֹּהֵן כִּי תִהְיֶה לְאִישׁ זָר", כֵּיוָן שֶׁנִּבְעֲלָה לְפָסוּל לָהּ – פְּסָלָהּ.

The Gemara asks: **From where are these matters** derived, that intercourse with an unfit man renders a woman unfit to partake of *teruma* and marry a priest? **Rav Yehuda said** that **Rav said: The verse states: "And if a priest's daughter be married to a common man** [*ish zar*]**,** she shall not eat of that which is set apart from the sacred" (Leviticus 22:12). It may be derived that **since she engaged in intercourse with one who is unfit for her, he disqualified her**[N] from marrying into the priesthood, as the literal meaning of the expression *ish zar* is a man who is excluded.

הַאי מִיבְּעֵי לֵיהּ דְּקָאָמַר רַחֲמָנָא: בַּת כֹּהֵן דְּמִינַּסְבָא לְזָר לָא תֵּיכוּל!

The Gemara asks: **That** verse **is necessary** to teach the *halakha* **that the Merciful One says: The daughter of a priest who marries a non-priest,** even one that she is permitted to marry, **may not partake** of *teruma*. Therefore, it cannot be the source for the *halakha* that intercourse with an unfit man renders a woman unfit to partake of *teruma* and marry a priest.

הַהִיא מִ"וְּשָׁבָה אֶל בֵּית אָבִיהָ כִּנְעוּרֶיהָ מִלֶּחֶם אָבִיהָ תֹּאכֵל" נָפְקָא, מִדְּקָאָמַר רַחֲמָנָא: "וְשָׁבָה אֶל בֵּית אָבִיהָ תֹּאכֵל" מִכְּלָל דְּמֵעִיקָּרָא לָא אָכְלָה!

The Gemara answers: **That** prohibition **is derived from** the verse "But if a priest's daughter be a widow, or divorced, and have no child, **and is returned to her father's house, as in her youth, she may eat of her father's bread"** (Leviticus 22:13). **From the fact that the Merciful One says: "And is returned to her father's house… she may eat," it may be inferred that initially,** while married to a non-priest, **she** was **not** permitted to **eat.** Therefore, the prohibition against a woman who engaged in intercourse with an unfit man partaking of *teruma* may be derived from the former verse, as it is not necessary for this *halakha*.

אִי מֵהַהִיא הֲוָה אָמֵינָא לָאו הַבָּא מִכְּלַל עֲשֵׂה – עֲשֵׂה, כְּתַב רַחֲמָנָא הַאי לְלָאו. [לָאו] מִ"וְכָל זָר לֹא יֹאכַל קֹדֶשׁ" נָפְקָא.

The Gemara rejects this answer: **If** the prohibition against the daughter of a priest who married a non-priest partaking of *teruma* had been derived only **from that** latter verse, **I would have said** that it is a prohibition that stems from a positive mitzva, as it is stated in positive form, and according to the principle that **a prohibition that stems from a positive mitzva is a positive mitzva,** she would not be liable to receive a court-imposed punishment. **The Merciful One** therefore **writes that** former verse, **to** establish an explicit **prohibition.** The Gemara counters: The **prohibition** against the wife of a non-priest partaking of *teruma* **is derived from** a different verse: **"No common man may eat of the sacred"** (Leviticus 22:10).

NOTES

Since she engaged in intercourse with one who is unfit for her, he disqualified her – כֵּיוָן שֶׁנִּבְעֲלָה לְפָסוּל לָהּ, פְּסָלָהּ: Most commentaries maintain that any man unfit to enter the assembly of Israel who engaged in intercourse with a woman rendered her a *zona*, and it is prohibited for a priest to marry her, as the verse states: "They shall not take a woman who is a harlot [*zona*]" (Leviticus 21:7). The commentaries therefore ask why the Gemara derives this *halakha* from Leviticus 22:12. The Rashba answers that the *halakha* under discussion relates to a woman who was raped and therefore cannot be deemed a harlot. He adds that the derivation is clearly necessary according to an opinion mentioned previously, that only a woman who engaged in forbidden intercourse that renders her liable to receive *karet* has the status of a *zona* (61a).

Perek **VII**
Daf **68** Amud **b**

הַהוּא מִיבְּעֵי לֵיהּ לְגוּפֵיהּ! תְּרֵי "וְכָל זָר" כְּתִיבִי.

The Gemara rejects this assertion: **That** verse **is necessary to** teach **its own** basic *halakha*, that a non-priest is prohibited from partaking of *teruma*. The Gemara responds: **Two** prohibitions with regard to a **"common man" are written,** one in the verse previously cited and the other in Leviticus 22:13: "But there shall no common man eat of it." One of them prohibits a non-priest from partaking of *teruma*, while the other is referring to the daughter of a priest married to a non-priest.

וְאַכַּתִּי מִיבְּעֵי לֵיהּ לְכִדְרַבִּי יוֹסֵי בְּרַבִּי חֲנִינָא. דְּאָמַר רַבִּי יוֹסֵי בְּרַבִּי חֲנִינָא: "וְכָל זָר" – זָרוּת אָמַרְתִּי לְךָ, וְלֹא אֲנִינוּת! דְּרַבִּי יוֹסֵי בְּרַבִּי חֲנִינָא מִן "זָר" "וְכָל זָר" נָפְקָא.

The Gemara asks: One of these verses **is still necessary to** teach another *halakha* **that** is taught **by Rabbi Yosei, son of Rabbi Ḥanina, as Rabbi Yosei, son of Rabbi Ḥanina, said** that the phrase **"no common man"** indicates that **I,** God, **said to you** that **commonness,** i.e., non-priesthood, renders one unfit to partake of *teruma*, **but acute mourning,** i.e., mourning on the day when one's close relative died, does **not** render one unfit to eat *teruma*. The Gemara answers: This teaching **of Rabbi Yosei, son of Rabbi Ḥanina, is derived from** a superfluous word in the verse, as it could have stated: **A common man** may not eat of the holy thing, and it actually states: **"No common man."**

NOTES

If so, let the verse merely write, etc. – אִם כֵּן לִכְתּוֹב קְרָא וכו׳: *Tosafot* explain this statement as follows: If the verse intended to disqualify the woman only from partaking of *teruma*, it should have simply referred to the sacred, and it would have been clear that this expression is referring to *teruma*, as that is the topic under discussion. Therefore, the expression "that which is set apart from the sacred" indicates that the prohibition pertains to other consecrated foods as well.

Derivation of *halakhot* from the prefix *vav* – דְּרִישַׁת וָוִין: Apparently, all the Sages derived *halakhot* from the prefix *vav* in various contexts. The Rabbis that the Gemara is referring to must therefore be Rabbis who interpret the prefix *vav* as only connecting between a phrase and the statement previous to it, whereas Rabbi Akiva maintains that it also implies the inclusion of additional cases relevant to the subject at hand (see *Tosafot*).

וְאַכַּתִּי מִיבְּעֵי לֵיהּ לְכִדְתַנְיָא: כְּשֶׁהִיא חוֹזֶרֶת – חוֹזֶרֶת לִתְרוּמָה, וְאֵינָהּ חוֹזֶרֶת לֶחָזֶה וָשׁוֹק, וַאֲמַר רַב חִסְדָּא אֲמַר רָבִינָא בַּר רַב שֵׁילָא: מַאי קְרָא? דִּכְתִיב: "וּבַת כֹּהֵן כִּי תִהְיֶה לְאִישׁ זָר הִיא בִּתְרוּמַת הַקֳּדָשִׁים לֹא תֹאכֵל" – לֹא תֹאכַל בַּמּוּרָם מִן הַקֳּדָשִׁים.

The Gemara asks: The verse "And if a priest's daughter be married to a common man" (Leviticus 22:12), from which Rav derived the *halakha* being discussed, that intercourse with an unfit man renders a woman unfit to partake of *teruma* and marry a priest, **is still necessary for that which is taught** in a *baraita*: **When** a priest's daughter **returns** to her father's house after the death of her Israelite husband, **she resumes** partaking of ***teruma*, but she does not resume** partaking of the **breast and** the right **hind leg**[H] of sacrificial offerings. **And Rav Ḥisda said** that **Ravina, son of Rav Sheila, said: What is the verse** from which this is derived? **As it is written: "And if a priest's daughter be married to a common man, she may not eat of that which is set apart from the sacred"** (Leviticus 22:12). This implies that even after her husband's death, **she may not partake of the** portion **separated from consecrated** offerings. Therefore, the verse cannot be the source for the above *halakha*.

אִם כֵּן לִכְתּוֹב קְרָא "הִיא בַּקֳּדָשִׁים לֹא תֹאכֵל", מַאי "בִּתְרוּמַת הַקֳּדָשִׁים" – שְׁמַעַתְּ מִינָּהּ תַּרְתֵּי.

The Gemara answers: **If so,** if this is the only *halakha* derived from this verse, **let the verse** merely **write:**[N] **She may not eat of the sacred. What is** the significance of the seemingly superfluous expression **"that which is set apart from the sacred"? Conclude from this** that the prohibition is referring to **two** deeds:[H] The daughter of a priest who engaged in intercourse with an unfit man may not partake of *teruma*, and if she weds a non-priest she may not partake of the priestly portion of offerings, the breast and right hind leg.

אַשְׁכְּחַן כֹּהֶנֶת, לְוִיָּה וְיִשְׂרְאֵלִית מְנָלַן? כִּדְאָמַר רַבִּי אַבָּא אֲמַר רַב: "בַּת" "וּבַת", הָכָא נַמִי "בַּת" "וּבַת".

The Gemara asks: **We found** a source for **a priestess; from where do we** derive the same *halakha* with regard to **a Levite or an Israelite** woman[H] who engaged in intercourse with an unfit man, i.e., that they do not partake of *teruma* even if they marry a priest? The Gemara answers that it is **as Rabbi Abba** said that **Rav said:** The verse states: "**But** if a priest's **daughter** be a widow, or divorced" (Leviticus 22:13). It could have begun: If a priest's **daughter.** The word "but," the prefix *vav*, is seemingly superfluous, and therefore it may indicate the expansion of the prohibition to include additional women. **Here too,** it may be derived from the distinction between the phrase: If a priest's **daughter,** and the phrase: **"And** if a priest's **daughter,"** which utilizes the prefix *vav*, that Levite and Israelite women are subject to the prohibition as well.

כְּמַאן – כְּרַבִּי עֲקִיבָא, דְּדָרֵישׁ וָוִין! אֲפִילּוּ תֵּימָא רַבָּנַן, כּוּלֵּיהּ "וּבַת" קְרָא יְתֵירָא הוּא.

The Gemara asks: **In accordance with whose** opinion is this exposition possible? It is **in accordance** only **with** the opinion of **Rabbi Akiva, as he derives** *halakhot* from the prefix ***vav***, which means "and" or "but." The Gemara responds: **Even if you say** it is in accordance with **the Rabbis,** who do not derive *halakhot* from the prefix *vav*,[N] **the entire** phrase: **"And** if a priest's **daughter," is superfluous** in the **verse,** as the previous verse already mentioned the priest's daughter. Therefore, the inclusion of Levite and Israelite women in the prohibition may be derived from the entire expression.

HALAKHA

But she does not resume partaking of the breast and the right hind leg – וְאֵינָהּ חוֹזֶרֶת לֶחָזֶה וָשׁוֹק: If the daughter of a priest married a non-priest and was widowed or divorced without any surviving children from her husband, she may resume partaking of *teruma*. However, she may not partake of the breast and the right hind leg of offerings (Rambam *Sefer Zera'im*, *Hilkhot Terumot* 6:8–9).

Conclude from this that the prohibition is referring to two deeds – שְׁמַעַתְּ מִינָּהּ תַּרְתֵּי: Two prohibitions are derived from the verse "And if a priest's daughter be married to a common man, she may not eat of that which is set apart from the sacred" (Leviticus 22:12). The first is that a woman who engaged in sexual intercourse with a man forbidden to her is rendered a *zona* or a *ḥalala*, and she is permanently prohibited from partaking of *teruma*. The second is that the daughter of a priest who was married to a priest and subsequently widowed or divorced may resume partaking of *teruma*, but she may not eat the breast and the right hind leg of offerings (Rambam *Sefer Zera'im*, *Hilkhot Terumot* 6:7).

From where do we derive the same *halakha* with regard to a Levite or an Israelite woman – לְוִיָּה וְיִשְׂרְאֵלִית מְנָלַן: Not only is the daughter of a priest prohibited from partaking of *teruma* if she engaged in intercourse with a man unfit for her, but even a Levite or an Israelite woman who has a child from a priest is prohibited from eating *teruma* if she engaged in intercourse with a man forbidden to her (Rambam *Sefer Zera'im*, *Hilkhot Terumot* 6:10).

אַשְׁכְּחַן לִתְרוּמָה, לִכְהוּנָּה מְנָלַן? אַטּוּ לְוִיָּה וְיִשְׂרְאֵלִית לָא לִכְהוּנָּה מְרַבִּינַן לְהוּ? דְּאִי לִתְרוּמָה – בְּנוֹת מֵיכַל תְּרוּמָה נִינְהוּ?

The Gemara asks: **We found** a source for the woman's disqualification from partaking of ***teruma*; from where do we** derive that she is disqualified **from** marrying into the **priesthood?** The Gemara counters: **Is that to say that we did not include a Levite and an Israelite woman** in the verse "But if a priest's daughter be a widow, or divorced, etc." (Leviticus 22:13), with regard to their marriage **to** a member of **the priesthood?** The derivation that a Levite and an Israelite woman are included in this verse was clearly with regard to their marriage to a priest; **as if** the inclusion was with regard **to *teruma*, are** these women **fit to partake of *teruma*** at all, regardless of their having engaged in intercourse with an unfit man? Clearly, their inclusion pertains to their marriage to a priest and their partaking of *teruma* as his wife.

אַלְמָה לָא? מַשְׁכַּחַתְּ לָהּ דְּקָאָכְלָה בִּשְׁבִיל בְּנָהּ!

The Gemara rejects this assertion: **Why not?** Why can't the inclusion be referring to the partaking of *teruma* exclusively? **You find that** possibility **when she partakes** of *teruma* **due to her son.** If an Israelite woman has a son from a priest, she may partake of *teruma*. Therefore, it is necessary to include a Levite or Israelite woman in the prohibition against partaking of *teruma* if she engaged in intercourse with an unfit man.

בִּשְׁבִיל בְּנָהּ – קַל וָחוֹמֶר: וּמַה כֹּהֶנֶת, דְּבִקְדוּשָּׁה דְּנַפְשָׁהּ אָכְלָה, פָּסֵיל לָהּ, לְוִיָּה וְיִשְׂרְאֵלִית דְּלָא אָכְלָה אֶלָּא בִּשְׁבִיל בְּנָהּ – לֹא כׇּל שֶׁכֵּן?!

The Gemara responds: The *halakha* that this woman does not partake of *teruma* **due to her son is** deduced through **an *a fortiori* inference: If a priestess, who partakes** of *teruma* **by** virtue of **her own sanctity, is disqualified** from partaking of *teruma* by an unfit man who engaged in intercourse with her, then with regard to a **Levite or Israelite woman, who partakes** of *teruma* **only due to her son,** is it **not all the more so** that it should be prohibited for her to partake of *teruma* after this act?

וְהִיא הַנּוֹתֶנֶת: כֹּהֶנֶת דְּקָדֵישׁ גּוּפָהּ – פָּסֵיל לָהּ, הָא דְּלָא קָדֵישׁ גּוּפָהּ – לָא פָּסֵיל לָהּ. אֶלָּא לִכְהוּנָּה, קַל וָחוֹמֶר מִגְּרוּשָׁה! וּמַה גְּרוּשָׁה שֶׁמּוּתֶּרֶת בִּתְרוּמָה – אֲסוּרָה לִכְהוּנָּה, זוֹ שֶׁאֲסוּרָה בִּתְרוּמָה – אֵינוֹ דִּין שֶׁפְּסוּלָה לִכְהוּנָּה?

The Gemara rejects that response: **But that provides** support for the contrary reasoning. It is logical that **a priestess, who is herself sacred, is disqualified** by intercourse with an unfit man. However, with regard to **this** woman, **who is not sacred herself,** and who eats *teruma* only due to her son, intercourse with an unfit man should **not disqualify her. Rather,** the prohibition against these women marrying **into the priesthood** is derived by **an *a fortiori*** inference **from** the case of **a divorcée:**[N] **If a divorcée** who is the daughter of a priest, **who is permitted to** partake of ***teruma*,**[H] **is** nevertheless **prohibited** from marrying **into the priesthood,** as is written in the Torah (Leviticus 21:7), then with regard to **this** woman, for **whom** it **is prohibited to** partake of ***teruma*, is it not right that** she should be **disqualified** from marrying **into the priesthood?**

וְכִי מַזְהִירִין מִן הַדִּין? גִּלּוּי מִילְּתָא בְּעָלְמָא הוּא.

The Gemara raises an objection to that inference: **But do we warn,** i.e., do we deduce a prohibition through **logical derivation?** The Gemara answers: This is not a new prohibition; rather, **it is merely a revelation**[N] of the above prohibition's scope. In other words, the prohibition against marrying a priest is subsumed under the prohibition against partaking of *teruma*.

וְאֵימָא: נִבְעֲלָה לְפָסוּל לָהּ – חַיָּיבֵי כְּרֵיתוֹת! "כִּי תִהְיֶה" אֲמַר רַחֲמָנָא, הָנָךְ דְּאִית בְּהוּ הֲוָיָה, חַיָּיבֵי כְּרֵיתוֹת – לָאו בְּנֵי הֲוָיָה.

Now that the source has been established, the Gemara asks: **And** perhaps you should **say** that this *halakha* pertaining to a woman who **engaged in intercourse with** a man **unfit for her** applies only to **those liable to receive *karet***[N] for their act of intercourse, but not to intercourse with a man who is unfit to marry into the assembly of Israel. The Gemara answers that **the Merciful One states** in the Torah: **"If a priest's daughter be married"** (Leviticus 22:12), indicating that this *halakha* is referring to **those who** can **have** a valid **marriage,** while **those liable to receive *karet*** for their act of intercourse **are not fit for marriage.**[N]

NOTES

An *a fortiori* inference from a divorcée – קַל וָחוֹמֶר מִגְּרוּשָׁה: The *Tosefot HaRosh* argues that the case of an Israelite or a Levite woman should serve as a rebuttal of this inference, as she does not partake of *teruma* but she may marry a priest. He answers that the latter woman's unfitness to partake of *teruma* is inherent, and it is therefore irrelevant to the discussion. The case under discussion is a woman who was disqualified from marrying into the priesthood by an action. He continues to argue that the inference can be rebutted with the case of a daughter of a priest who was widowed by a non-priest and has children from him, as she does not partake of *teruma* but she may marry a priest. He answers that the prohibition against her partaking of *teruma* is only circumstantial; if her Israelite descendants die, she may resume partaking of *teruma*.

It is merely a revelation – גִּילּוּי מִילְּתָא בְּעָלְמָא הוּא: The commentaries offer various interpretations of this answer. The *Ḥazon Ish* explains that the prohibition against this woman partaking of *teruma* shows that she is rendered a *zona*. Once that has been established, all *halakhot* pertaining to a *zona* apply to her as well, e.g., her unfitness to marry a priest.

And perhaps you should say that it…applies only to those liable to receive *karet* – וְאֵימָא...חַיָּיבֵי כְּרֵיתוֹת: The Ritva explains that since the verse does not identify this "common man," perhaps it is referring to the type of man least suitable for her. Although those liable to receive the death penalty for their acts of intercourse are presumably less suitable than those liable to receive *karet*, they are not considered a separate legal category from those liable to receive *karet*.

Those liable to receive *karet* are not fit for marriage – חַיָּיבֵי כְּרֵיתוֹת לָאו בְּנֵי הֲוָיָה: If so, what is the source of the *halakha* that those liable to receive *karet* also disqualify the woman from marrying a priest? *Tosafot* answer that the primary meaning of the phrase *ish zar*, translated as common man, refers to a man who renders a woman liable to receive to *karet* through intercourse. The Gemara merely proves from the wording of the verse that the verse is referring to less severe acts of intercourse as well. Rashi, on the other hand, maintains that the source is Rabbi Yishmael's teaching that any man who cannot render a woman a widow or a divorcée, i.e., his marriage to her is invalid, also disqualifies her from marrying into the priesthood.

HALAKHA

A divorcée who is permitted to partake of *teruma* – גְּרוּשָׁה שֶׁמּוּתֶּרֶת בִּתְרוּמָה: The daughter of a priest who got divorced from a non-priest and does not have children with him is permitted to partake of *teruma* (Rambam *Sefer Zera'im*, *Hilkhot Terumot* 8:8).

אִי הָכִי, גּוֹי וְעֶבֶד לָא לִיפְסְלוּ! הָנָךְ פָּסְלֵי מִדְּרַבִּי יִשְׁמָעֵאל. דְּאָמַר רַבִּי יוֹחָנָן מִשּׁוּם רַבִּי יִשְׁמָעֵאל: מִנַּיִן לְגוֹי וְעֶבֶד שֶׁבָּא עַל בַּת יִשְׂרָאֵל, וְעַל כֹּהֶנֶת וּלְוִיָּה, שֶׁפְּסָלוּהָ – שֶׁנֶּאֱמַר "וּבַת כֹּהֵן כִּי תִהְיֶה אַלְמָנָה וּגְרוּשָׁה" וגו׳.

The Gemara asks: **If so, a gentile or a slave** who engaged in intercourse with a Jewish woman **should not have disqualified** her from marrying into the priesthood, as they cannot marry her. The Gemara answers: **These disqualify** her, as derived **by Rabbi Yishmael, as Rabbi Yoḥanan said in the name of Rabbi Yishmael: From where** is it derived with regard **to a gentile or a slave who engaged in intercourse with an Israelite woman, or with a priestess, or a Levite woman, that they have disqualified her? As it is stated: "But if a priest's daughter be a widow, or divorced,** and have no child, and is returned to her father's house, as in her youth, she may eat of her father's bread" (Leviticus 22:13).

Perek **VII**
Daf **69** Amud **a**

NOTES

But perhaps you should say, one who has, etc. – וְאֵימָא מִי שֶׁיֵּשׁ לוֹ וכו׳: *Tosafot* ask why the Gemara suggests a lenient interpretation, contrary to the principle that whenever a Torah juxtaposition can be interpreted in either a stringent or a lenient manner, the stringent interpretation is accepted. *Tosefot HaRosh* writes that since a Jewish woman's marriage to a gentile or a slave is invalid, and any child of theirs is considered the child of his mother only, it makes sense that the child should not cause her to be disqualified.

מִי שֶׁיֵּשׁ לוֹ אַלְמְנוּת וְגֵירוּשִׁין בָּהּ, יָצְאוּ גּוֹי וְעֶבֶד שֶׁאֵין לוֹ אַלְמְנוּת וְגֵירוּשִׁין.

This verse is referring to a man **who has** potential **widowhood and divorce with her, excluding a gentile and a slave, who do not have widowhood and divorce** with her, as they cannot marry Jews at all. Therefore, they disqualify a woman from marrying into the priesthood through sexual intercourse, even if she does not have a child with them.

אַשְׁכַּחַן כֹּהֶנֶת, לְוִיָּה וְיִשְׂרְאֵלִית מְנָא לָן? כְּדַאֲמַר רַבִּי אַבָּא אֲמַר רַב: "בַּת" "וּבַת" הָכָא נַמִי "בַּת" "וּבַת".

The Gemara asks: **We have found** a source for the *halakha* that a gentile and a slave disqualify **a priestess. From where do we** derive this with regard to **a Levite and an Israelite woman?** The Gemara answers: It is **as Rabbi Abba** said that **Rav said:** The verse **"But** if a priest's **daughter** be a widow, or divorced" (Leviticus 22:13) could have begun with the words: If a priest's **daughter.** The word "but," the prefix *vav*, expands the prohibition to include additional women. **Here too,** it may be derived from the distinction between the phrase: If a priest's **daughter,** and the phrase as it actually appears in the verse: **"But** if a priest's **daughter,"** that Levite and Israelite women are subject to the prohibition as well.

כְּמַאן, כְּרַבִּי עֲקִיבָא, דְּדָרֵישׁ וָוֵי? אֲפִילּוּ תֵּימָא רַבָּנַן, כּוּלָּהּ "וּבַת" קְרָא יְתֵירָא הוּא.

The Gemara asks: **In accordance with whose** opinion is this exposition possible? It is **in accordance** only **with** the opinion of **Rabbi Akiva, as he derives** *halakhot* from the prefix ***vav*****.** The Gemara responds: **Even if you say** it is accordance with **the Rabbis, the entire** phrase: **"But** if a priest's **daughter," is superfluous** in the **verse,** as the previous verses had already mentioned the priest's daughter. Therefore, the inclusion of Levite and Israelite women in the prohibition may be derived from the entire expression.

וְאֵימָא: מִי שֶׁיֵּשׁ לוֹ אַלְמְנוּת וְגֵירוּשִׁין בָּהּ, כִּי לֵית לֵיהּ זֶרַע – קָאָכְלָה, כִּי אִית לֵיהּ זֶרַע – לָא אָכְלָה, מִי שֶׁאֵין לוֹ אַלְמְנוּת וְגֵירוּשִׁין בָּהּ, אַף עַל גַּב דְּאִית לֵיהּ זֶרַע – נַמִי תֵּיכוּל!

The Gemara suggests: **But** perhaps you should **say** a different interpretation of the mention of widowhood and divorce in the verse: In the case of **one who has**[N] potential **widowhood and divorce with her, if he does not have offspring** from her **she may partake** of *teruma* upon her widowhood or divorce, whereas **if he does have offspring** from her **she does not partake.** However, in the case of **one who does not have widowhood and divorce with her, even if she has offspring** from him, **she should** be allowed to **partake** of *teruma*, as the offspring is not considered his.

אִם כֵּן רִבּוּיֵי לְוִיָּה וְיִשְׂרְאֵלִית לָמָּה לִי?

The Gemara answers: **If so, why do I** need to **include a Levite and an Israelite woman?** If the daughter of a priest is not disqualified from *teruma* due to intercourse with a gentile or slave, certainly a Levite or Israelite woman is not. The fact that the verse indicates inclusion of Levite and Israelite women proves that the *halakha* that is derived from it is a stringency and not a leniency.

וּלְרַבִּי עֲקִיבָא, דְּאָמַר: אֵין קִדּוּשִׁין תּוֹפְסִין בְּחַיָּיבֵי לָאוִין, וּמַאי ״כִּי תִהְיֶה לְאִישׁ זָר״ כִּי תִּיבָּעֵל, ״אַלְמָנָה וּגְרוּשָׁה״ לָמָּה לִי?

The Gemara asks: **And according to Rabbi Akiva, who said** that **betrothal of those** who may not engage in intercourse, as they are **liable for** violating **a prohibition, does not take effect, and** therefore the meaning of the phrase **"And if** a priest's daughter **be** [*tihye*] **to a common man"** (Leviticus 22:12) is not: If she marries him, but rather: **If she engages in intercourse** with him,[N] **why do I** need the Torah to mention the phrase **"a widow, or divorced"** in the verse: "But if a priest's daughter be a widow, or divorced… she may eat of her father's bread" (Leviticus 22:13)? It is not necessary for this phrase to teach that a gentile and a slave disqualify a woman from marrying into the priesthood through sexual intercourse, as suggested by Rabbi Yishmael, as they are included in the prohibition proscribing a woman who engaged in intercourse with a man who is unfit for her.

אַלְמָנָה לְהַחְמִיר עָלֶיהָ, וּגְרוּשָׁה לְהָקֵל עָלֶיהָ. וּצְרִיכָא, דְּאִי אַשְׁמְעִינַן אַלְמָנָה – אַלְמָנָה הוּא דְּכִי לֵית לָהּ זֶרַע אָכְלָה, מִשּׁוּם דַּחֲזְיָא לִכְהוּנָּה, אֲבָל גְּרוּשָׁה דְּלָא חַזְיָא לִכְהוּנָּה – אֵימָא אַף עַל גַּב דְּלֵית לָהּ זֶרַע לָא אָכְלָה. וְאִי אַשְׁמְעִינַן גְּרוּשָׁה – גְּרוּשָׁה הוּא דְּכִי אִית לָהּ זֶרַע לָא אָכְלָה, מִשּׁוּם דְּלָא חַזְיָא לִכְהוּנָּה, אֲבָל אַלְמָנָה, דַּחֲזְיָא לִכְהוּנָּה, אֵימָא: אַף עַל גַּב דְּאִית לָהּ זֶרַע נַמִי תֵּיכוּל – צְרִיכָא.

The Gemara answers: **A widow** is mentioned **to be stringent with her, and a divorcée to be lenient with her, and** both **are necessary. As,** had the Torah **taught us** only the case of **a widow,** you might have assumed that **specifically** if this daughter of a priest is **a widow** she **partakes** of *teruma* **when she does not have offspring because she is fit for the priesthood,** as she may marry a common priest, **but** with regard to **a divorcée, who is not fit for the priesthood** at all, you might **say** that **even if she does not have offspring she does not partake** of *teruma*. **And** had **it taught us** only the case of **a divorcée,** you might have assumed that only **a divorcée does not partake** of *teruma* **when she has offspring** from a non-priest **because she is not fit for the priesthood, but** with regard to **a widow, who is fit for the priesthood,** you might **say** that **even if she has offspring she should also partake** of *teruma*. It is therefore **necessary** for both cases to be stated.

וְאֵימָא: נִבְעֲלָה לְפָסוּל לָהּ – אַף מַחֲזִיר גְּרוּשָׁתוֹ! ״לְאִישׁ זָר״ אָמַר רַחֲמָנָא, מִי שֶׁזָּר אֶצְלָהּ מֵעִיקָּרָא, לְאַפּוּקֵי הַאי דְּלָא זָר אֶצְלָהּ מֵעִיקָּרָא הוּא.

The Gemara asks: **And** perhaps you should **say** that the category of a woman **who engaged in intercourse with** a man who is **unfit for her** and is therefore disqualified from the priesthood applies **even** to the case of a man **remarrying his divorcée** after she had been married to another man in the meantime, which is prohibited. The Gemara answers: **The Merciful One states** in the Torah: **"To a common man** [*ish zar*]**,"** literally, a man who is a stranger, "she shall not eat of that which is set apart from the sacred." The Gemara understands the notion of a stranger to be one whom she was forbidden to marry and interprets homiletically: Only marriage to one **who was a stranger,** i.e., forbidden, **to her from the outset** precludes her from partaking of *teruma,* **to the exclusion of one who was not a stranger to her from the outset,** such as her ex-husband.

אִי הָכִי, חָלָל דְּלָאו זָר הוּא מֵעִיקָּרָא, לָא לִפְסוֹל! אָמַר קְרָא: ״לֹא יְחַלֵּל זַרְעוֹ בְּעַמָּיו״, מַקִּישׁ זַרְעוֹ לוֹ: מַה הוּא פּוֹסֵל, אַף זַרְעוֹ נַמִי פּוֹסֵל.

The Gemara asks: **If so, a *ḥalal,* who was not excluded at the outset,** as he may marry even the daughter of a priest, **should not disqualify** a woman from marrying into the priesthood. The Gemara answers that **the verse states,** with regard to a priest who marries a woman unfit for the priesthood: **"He shall not profane his seed among his people"** (Leviticus 21:15), thereby **juxtaposing his seed to him.**[N] **Just as he,** a priest who married a woman forbidden to him, **disqualifies** her from the priesthood, **so too, his seed,** the *ḥalal,* **also disqualifies** a woman with whom he engaged in intercourse.[H]

וְאֵימָא: מִשְּׁעַת הֲוָיָה? דּוּמְיָא דְּכֹהֵן גָּדוֹל בְּאַלְמָנָה, מַה כֹּהֵן גָּדוֹל בְּאַלְמָנָה – בְּבִיאָה, אַף הַאי נַמִי – בְּבִיאָה.

The Gemara asks: **And** perhaps you should **say** that a woman who engaged in intercourse with a man unfit for her is disqualified **from the time of** their **betrothal,** even before they engaged in intercourse. The Gemara answers that this is **similar to a High Priest** who engaged in intercourse **with a widow: Just as a High Priest** who engaged in intercourse **with a widow**[H] has disqualified her **through intercourse,** not betrothal, **so too, this** unfit man has **also** disqualified her **through intercourse.**

NOTES

And the meaning of, If a priest's daughter be [*tihye*] to a common man is: If she engages in intercourse with him – וּמַאי ״כִּי תִהְיֶה לְאִישׁ זָר״, כִּי תִּיבָּעֵל: Some commentaries ask why the verse must be interpreted according to Rabbi Akiva as referring to intercourse alone, as there is an amoraic opinion that even according to Rabbi Akiva's opinion, there are several forbidden unions with regard to which betrothal does take effect, such as those that do not involve close relatives and those prohibited only due to positive mitzvot. The Rashba and the Ritva answer that the Gemara's question applies only to the amoraic opinion that, according to Rabbi Akiva, betrothal never takes effect in any forbidden union.

Juxtaposing his seed to him – מַקִּישׁ זַרְעוֹ לוֹ: The *Shela* explains that in the case discussed by the verse, the priest has not yet fathered a child. Therefore, the phrase "his seed" is superfluous.

HALAKHA

A *ḥalal* disqualifies – חָלָל פּוֹסֵל: Although it is permitted for any Jewish woman, even the daughter of a priest, to marry a *ḥalal*, their intercourse permanently disqualifies her from marrying into the priesthood and from partaking of *teruma* (Rambam *Sefer Kedusha, Hilkhot Issurei Bia* 18:1; *Shulḥan Arukh, Even HaEzer* 6:8).

A High Priest who engaged in intercourse with a widow – כֹּהֵן גָּדוֹל בְּאַלְמָנָה: A High Priest who engages in intercourse with a widow is liable to receive lashes even if he did not betroth her beforehand. As for her, she becomes a *ḥalala* and is disqualified from marrying into the priesthood (Rambam *Sefer Kedusha, Hilkhot Issurei Bia* 17:3).

HALAKHA

A second-generation Egyptian and a second-generation Edomite – מִצְרִי שֵׁנִי וַאֲדוֹמִי שֵׁנִי: It is prohibited for an Egyptian or Edomite convert and his son to enter the assembly of Israel by marriage, however, his grandson may marry an Israelite (Rambam *Sefer Kedusha*, *Hilkhot Issurei Bia* 12:19).

וְאֵימָא: עַד דְּאִיכָּא הֲוָיָה וּבִיאָה! דּוּמְיָא דְּכֹהֵן גָּדוֹל בְּאַלְמָנָה, מַה כֹּהֵן גָּדוֹל בְּאַלְמָנָה – בְּבִיאָה לְחוּדָהּ, אַף הַאי נַמִּי בְּבִיאָה לְחוּדָהּ.

The Gemara asks: **And** perhaps you should **say** that he does not disqualify her **until there is** both **betrothal and intercourse.** The Gemara again answers that this is **similar to a High Priest** who engaged in intercourse **with a widow: Just as a High Priest** who engaged in intercourse **with a widow** disqualifies her **through intercourse alone,**[N] **so too, this** man **also** disqualified her **through intercourse alone.**

״וְרַבִּי יוֹסֵי אוֹמֵר: כָּל שֶׁזַּרְעוֹ פָּסוּל – פּוֹסֵל, וְכָל שֶׁאֵין זַרְעוֹ פָּסוּל – אֵינוֹ פּוֹסֵל״. מַאי אִיכָּא בֵּין תַּנָּא קַמָּא לְרַבִּי יוֹסֵי?

§ It was taught in the *baraita* under discussion (68a) that **Rabbi Yosei says:** Of the men unfit to enter the assembly of Israel, **anyone whose offspring are** also **unfit disqualifies** a woman with whom he engaged in intercourse from the priesthood. However, **anyone whose offspring are not unfit does not disqualify** her. The Gemara asks: **What** difference **is there between the first** ***tanna*** of the *baraita* **and Rabbi Yosei?**

אֲמַר רַבִּי יוֹחָנָן: מִצְרִי שֵׁנִי וַאֲדוֹמִי שֵׁנִי אִיכָּא בֵּינַיְיהוּ.

Rabbi Yoḥanan said: The practical difference **between them** pertains to **a second**-generation **Egyptian and a second**-generation **Edomite.**[H] The children of these men, i.e., the third generation, may marry Jews of unflawed lineage. Therefore, according to Rabbi Yosei, they too do not disqualify a woman from the priesthood through intercourse with them. The first *tanna*, however, holds that they have the same status as a first-generation Egyptian or Edomite convert, in that they disqualify a woman from the priesthood through intercourse.

וּשְׁנֵיהֶם לֹא לְמָדוּהָ אֶלָּא מִכֹּהֵן גָּדוֹל בְּאַלְמָנָה. תַּנָּא קַמָּא סָבַר: מַה כֹּהֵן גָּדוֹל בְּאַלְמָנָה, שֶׁבִּיאָתוֹ בַּעֲבֵירָה – וּפוֹסֵל, אַף הַאי נַמִּי פּוֹסֵל.

And both ***tanna'im*** **derived** their respective opinions **only from** the case of **a High Priest** who engaged in intercourse **with a widow,** although they reached different conclusions. **The first** ***tanna*** **reasoned: Just as** with regard to **a High Priest** who engaged in intercourse **with a widow, his** act of **intercourse** with her **is a transgression, and** therefore **he disqualifies** her from the priesthood, **so too, this** man, a second-generation Egyptian or Edomite, **also disqualifies** her.

וְרַבִּי יוֹסֵי סָבַר: כְּכֹהֵן גָּדוֹל, מַה כֹּהֵן גָּדוֹל – שֶׁזַּרְעוֹ פָּסוּל וּפוֹסֵל, אַף כָּל שֶׁזַּרְעוֹ פָּסוּל פּוֹסֵל, לְאַפּוֹקֵי מִצְרִי שֵׁנִי דְּאֵין זַרְעוֹ פָּסוּל, דִּכְתִיב: ״בָּנִים אֲשֶׁר יִוָּלְדוּ לָהֶם דּוֹר שְׁלִישִׁי יָבֹא לָהֶם בִּקְהַל ה׳״.

And Rabbi Yosei also **reasoned:** This is **like a High Priest** who engaged in intercourse with a widow. **Just as** the **High Priest's children are unfit** for the priesthood, **and he** himself **disqualifies** the widow from marrying into the priesthood, **so too, any** man **whose children are unfit** to marry Jews of unflawed lineage **disqualifies** a woman with whom he engaged in intercourse from marrying into the priesthood. This inference comes **to exclude a second**-generation **Egyptian, whose children are not unfit, as it is written: "The children of the third generation that are born to them may enter into the assembly of the Lord"** (Deuteronomy 23:9).

״רַבָּן שִׁמְעוֹן בֶּן גַּמְלִיאֵל אוֹמֵר: כָּל שֶׁאַתָּה נוֹשֵׂא בִּתּוֹ אַתָּה נוֹשֵׂא אַלְמְנָתוֹ״ וכו׳. מַאי אִיכָּא בֵּין רַבִּי יוֹסֵי לְרַבָּן שִׁמְעוֹן בֶּן גַּמְלִיאֵל?

It is taught in the *baraita* under discussion that **Rabban Shimon ben Gamliel says: Anyone whose daughter you may marry, you may marry his widow;** anyone whose daughter you may not marry, you may not marry his widow. The Gemara asks: **What** difference **is there between Rabbi Yosei and Rabban Shimon ben Gamliel?** They appear to be stating the same principle, that a man disqualifies a woman from the priesthood only if his children are unfit to marry Jews of unflawed lineage as well.

אֲמַר עוּלָּא: גֵּר עַמּוֹנִי וּמוֹאָבִי אִיכָּא בֵּינַיְיהוּ. וּשְׁנֵיהֶם לֹא לְמָדוּהָ אֶלָּא מִכֹּהֵן גָּדוֹל בְּאַלְמָנָה. רַבִּי יוֹסֵי סָבַר: מַה כֹּהֵן גָּדוֹל בְּאַלְמָנָה – שֶׁזַּרְעוֹ פָּסוּל וּפוֹסֵל, אַף כָּל שֶׁזַּרְעוֹ פָּסוּל – פּוֹסֵל.

Ulla said: The practical difference **between them** is in the case of **an Ammonite and a Moabite convert. And both of them derived** their respective opinions **from none other than** the case of **a High Priest with a widow. Rabbi Yosei reasoned: Just as** with regard to **a High Priest** who engaged in intercourse **with a widow, his children are unfit** for the priesthood **and** he himself **disqualifies** the widow, **so too, any** man **whose children are unfit disqualifies** a woman with whom he engaged in intercourse.

NOTES

Just as a High Priest who engaged in intercourse with a widow disqualifies her through intercourse alone – מַה כֹּהֵן גָּדוֹל בְּאַלְמָנָה בְּבִיאָה לְחוּדָהּ: *Tosefot HaRosh* asks why the Gemara assumes that a High Priest disqualifies a widow through intercourse, even if he did not betroth her. It is answered that from the juxtaposition in the verse (Leviticus 21:14–15) between the prohibition against a High Priest marrying a widow and the disqualification of his child from the priesthood as a result, it is derived that just as the child is disqualified whether or not his parents were betrothed, so too, the High Priest transgresses the prohibition and disqualifies the widow through intercourse alone, even without betrothal.

רַבָּן שִׁמְעוֹן בֶּן גַּמְלִיאֵל סָבַר: מָה כֹּהֵן גָּדוֹל בְּאַלְמָנָה – שֶׁכׇּל זַרְעוֹ פָּסוּל וּפוֹסֵל, אַף שֶׁכׇּל זַרְעוֹ פָּסוּל וּפוֹסֵל, לְאַפּוּקֵי עַמּוֹנִי וּמוֹאָבִי דְּאֵין כׇּל זַרְעוֹ פָּסוּל, דְּאָמַר מָר: עַמּוֹנִי וְלֹא עַמּוֹנִית, מוֹאָבִי וְלֹא מוֹאָבִית.

Rabban Shimon ben Gamliel reasoned: Just as in the case of **a High Priest** who engaged in intercourse **with a widow, where all of his children** from her **are unfit** for the priesthood **and he disqualifies** her as well, **so too,** in the case of a man **all of whose children are unfit, he disqualifies** a woman with whom he engaged in intercourse. This is **to the exclusion of an Ammonite or a Moabite** convert, **as not all of his children are unfit** to marry Jews of unflawed lineage, **as the Master said: An Ammonite man** is unfit to enter the assembly **but not an Ammonite woman; a Moabite man** is unfit **but not a Moabite woman.**[NH] Since only the sons of an Ammonite or Moabite convert are unfit, they do not disqualify a woman with whom they engaged in intercourse from marrying into the priesthood.

מתני׳ הָאוֹנֵס וְהַמְפַתֶּה וְהַשּׁוֹטֶה – לֹא פּוֹסְלִין וְלֹא מַאֲכִילִין, וְאִם אֵינָן רְאוּיִין לָבֹא בְּיִשְׂרָאֵל – הֲרֵי אֵלּוּ פּוֹסְלִין. כֵּיצַד? (הָיָה) יִשְׂרָאֵל שֶׁבָּא עַל בַּת כֹּהֵן – תֹּאכַל בִּתְרוּמָה.

MISHNA In the case of **one who rapes** a woman without marrying her; **or one who seduces** a woman[H] without marrying her; **or an imbecile**[N] who engages in intercourse with a woman, even if he did marry her, if they are non-priests **they do not disqualify** the daughter of a priest from partaking of *teruma,* **and** if they are priests **they do not enable** an Israelite woman **to partake** of *teruma.* **And if they are not fit to enter** the assembly of **Israel** through marriage, **they disqualify** the daughter of a priest from partaking of *teruma.* **How so? If it was an Israelite who engaged in** extramarital **intercourse with the daughter of a priest, she may partake of** *teruma,* as this act of intercourse does not disqualify her.

NOTES

An Ammonite man but not an Ammonite woman, a Moabite man but not a Moabite woman – עַמּוֹנִי וְלֹא עַמּוֹנִית, מוֹאָבִי וְלֹא מוֹאָבִית: This ruling was introduced upon Ruth the Moabite's arrival in Bethlehem. It was not well known and was a cause of her rejection by her relatives before Boaz, the head of the Sanhedrin, married her (*Yalkut Shimoni*).

One who rapes, or one who seduces, or an imbecile, etc. – הָאוֹנֵס וְהַמְפַתֶּה וְהַשּׁוֹטֶה וכו׳: *Tosafot* ask why the mishna does not list a minor as well, as he too does not disqualify a woman from partaking of *teruma* through intercourse, nor can he enable her to partake of *teruma* if he is a priest. They answer that since the mishna subsequently discusses the case of a pregnant woman, it cannot list a minor, as he is incapable of impregnating a woman.

HALAKHA

An Ammonite man but not an Ammonite woman, a Moabite man but not a Moabite woman – עַמּוֹנִי וְלֹא עַמּוֹנִית, מוֹאָבִי וְלֹא מוֹאָבִית: Ammonite and Moabite men are permanently prohibited from entering the assembly of Israel by marriage. This includes their sons and their sons' sons until the end of time. However, an Ammonite or Moabite female convert is permitted to marry into the assembly immediately, just like converts from other nations (Rambam *Sefer Kedusha, Hilkhot Issurei Bia* 12:18; *Shulḥan Arukh, Even HaEzer* 4:2).

One who rapes or one who seduces a woman, etc. – הָאוֹנֵס וְהַמְפַתֶּה וכו׳: If the daughter of a priest was raped or seduced by an Israelite man, or if she engaged in intercourse with an imbecile Israelite, she is not disqualified from partaking of *teruma*, unless the intercourse was prohibited. If an Israelite woman had one of those experiences with a priest, the priest does not enable her to partake of *teruma* (Rambam *Sefer Zera'im, Hilkhot Terumot* 8:13).

Perek **VII**
Daf **69** Amud **b**

עִיבְּרָה – לֹא תֹּאכַל בִּתְרוּמָה, נֶחְתַּךְ הָעוּבָּר בְּמֵעֶיהָ – תֹּאכַל. הָיָה כֹּהֵן שֶׁבָּא עַל בַּת יִשְׂרָאֵל – לֹא תֹּאכַל בִּתְרוּמָה, עִיבְּרָה – לֹא תֹּאכַל, יָלְדָה – תֹּאכַל. נִמְצָא כֹּחוֹ שֶׁל בֵּן גָּדוֹל מִשֶּׁל אָב.

If **he impregnated her, she may not partake of** *teruma,*[N] as she is carrying an Israelite fetus. If **the fetus was cut in her womb,**[H] i.e., she miscarried, **she may partake** of *teruma.* If the man **was a priest who engaged in** intercourse **with an Israelite woman, she may not partake of** *teruma.* If **he impregnated her, she** still **may not partake** of *teruma,* as a fetus does not enable its mother to partake. If **she gave birth she may partake** due to her child, a priest.[H] It is therefore **found** in this case that **the power of the son is greater than** that **of the father,** as the father of this child does not enable the woman to partake of *teruma,* but the son does.

NOTES

If he impregnated her she may not partake of *teruma* – עִיבְּרָה לֹא תֹּאכַל בִּתְרוּמָה: This is not because the fetus is a non-priest, but because she partakes of *teruma* only as long as her body doesn't change due to pregnancy, as derived by the Gemara (67b) from the verse "As in her youth, she may eat of her father's bread" (Leviticus 22:13). Her body cannot be described as being "as in her youth" if she is pregnant (see Ritva).

HALAKHA

If the fetus was cut in her womb – נֶחְתַּךְ הָעוּבָּר בְּמֵעֶיהָ: If the daughter of a priest married an imbecile Israelite, or if she was raped or seduced by an Israelite, and she was impregnated, she may not partake of *teruma* due to the fetus. If she miscarried, she may partake of *teruma* (Rambam *Sefer Zera'im, Hilkhot Terumot* 8:14).

An Israelite woman impregnated by a priest – יִשְׂרְאֵלִית מְעוּבֶּרֶת מִכֹּהֵן: If an Israelite woman married an imbecile priest, or if she was raped or seduced by a priest, she may not partake of *teruma*, even if she is impregnated by him. However, once she has borne him a child, she may partake of *teruma* due to her child (Rambam *Sefer Zera'im, Hilkhot Terumot* 8:14).

הָעֶבֶד פּוֹסֵל מִשּׁוּם בִּיאָה, וְאֵינוֹ פּוֹסֵל מִשּׁוּם זֶרַע. כֵּיצַד? בַּת יִשְׂרָאֵל לְכֹהֵן, בַּת כֹּהֵן לְיִשְׂרָאֵל, וְיָלְדָה הֵימֶנּוּ בֵּן, וְהָלַךְ הַבֵּן וְנִכְבַּשׁ עַל הַשִּׁפְחָה, וְיָלְדָה הֵימֶנּוּ בֵּן – הֲרֵי זֶה עֶבֶד. הָיְתָה אֵם אָבִיו בַּת יִשְׂרָאֵל לְכֹהֵן – לֹא תֹּאכַל בִּתְרוּמָה, בַּת כֹּהֵן לְיִשְׂרָאֵל – תֹּאכַל בִּתְרוּמָה.

A slave disqualifies[N] a woman from partaking of *teruma* **due to** his engaging in **intercourse** with her, **and he does not disqualify** a woman **because** he is her **offspring. How so?** In what case would a slave theoretically disqualify a woman because he is her offspring? If **an Israelite woman** was married **to a priest,** or **the daughter of a priest** was married **to an Israelite; and she a bore him a son; and the son went and pressed himself onto a maidservant,** an epithet for intercourse used in this context due to the shame involved in having intercourse with a maidservant; **and she bore him a son,** then **this** son **is a slave.** If the latter's **father's mother was an Israelite** who was married **to a priest,** and her husband died, **she may not partake of *teruma*** due to her grandson, as he is not a priest but a slave. On the other hand, if **she was the daughter of a priest** married **to an Israelite,** and he died, leaving only this grandson, **she may partake of *teruma*,** as the grandson is not considered his father's offspring.[H]

מַמְזֵר פּוֹסֵל וּמַאֲכִיל. כֵּיצַד? בַּת יִשְׂרָאֵל לְכֹהֵן, וּבַת כֹּהֵן לְיִשְׂרָאֵל, וְיָלְדָה הֵימֶנּוּ בַּת, וְהָלְכָה הַבַּת וְנִישֵּׂאת לְעֶבֶד אוֹ לְגוֹי וְיָלְדָה הֵימֶנּוּ בֵּן – הֲרֵי זֶה מַמְזֵר. הָיְתָה אֵם אִמּוֹ בַּת יִשְׂרָאֵל לְכֹהֵן – תֹּאכַל בִּתְרוּמָה. בַּת כֹּהֵן לְיִשְׂרָאֵל – לֹא תֹּאכַל בִּתְרוּמָה.

A ***mamzer*** **disqualifies** a woman from partaking of *teruma*, **and** he also **enables** a woman **to partake** of *teruma*.[NH] **How so?** If **an Israelite woman** was married **to a priest, or the daughter of a priest** was married **to an Israelite, and she bore him a daughter, and the daughter went and married a slave or a gentile and bore him a son, this son is a *mamzer*.**[N] If **his mother's mother was an Israelite woman** married **to a priest,** even if her husband died, **she may partake of *teruma*,** as she has surviving offspring from a priest. Conversely, if she is **the daughter of a priest** married **to an Israelite, she may not partake of *teruma*,** even after her Israelite husband's death, as she has offspring from him.

כֹּהֵן גָּדוֹל, פְּעָמִים שֶׁהוּא פּוֹסֵל, כֵּיצַד? בַּת כֹּהֵן לְיִשְׂרָאֵל וְיָלְדָה הֵימֶנּוּ בַּת, וְהָלְכָה הַבַּת וְנִיסֵּת לְכֹהֵן וְיָלְדָה הֵימֶנּוּ בֵּן – הֲרֵי זֶה רָאוּי לִהְיוֹת כֹּהֵן גָּדוֹל עוֹמֵד וּמְשַׁמֵּשׁ עַל גַּבֵּי הַמִּזְבֵּחַ, מַאֲכִיל אֶת אִמּוֹ, וּפוֹסֵל אֵם אִמּוֹ. זֹאת אוֹמֶרֶת: לֹא כִּבְנִי כֹּהֵן גָּדוֹל שֶׁהוּא פּוֹסְלֵנִי מִן הַתְּרוּמָה.

Even with regard to **a High Priest, sometimes he disqualifies**[H] his grandmother from partaking of *teruma*. **How so?** If **the daughter of a priest** was married **to an Israelite, and she bore him a daughter, and the daughter went and married a priest and bore him a son, this son is fit to be a High Priest,** who **stands and serves on the altar.** This son **enables his mother to partake** of *teruma*, as he is a priest. **And** yet, **he disqualifies his mother's mother** from partaking of *teruma*, as he is her offspring from her Israelite husband. **This** grandmother can **say** in disapproval: Let there **not** be many **like my** daughter's **son,** the **High Priest, as he disqualifies me from** partaking of ***teruma*.**

גמ׳ תְּנֵינָא לְהָא דְּתָנוּ רַבָּנַן: שׁוֹטֶה וְקָטָן שֶׁנָּשְׂאוּ נָשִׁים וָמֵתוּ – נְשׁוֹתֵיהֶן פְּטוּרוֹת מִן הַחֲלִיצָה וּמִן הַיִּיבּוּם.

GEMARA **We** already **learned that** the marriage of an imbecile is invalid, **as the Sages taught** in a *baraita*: With regard to **an imbecile and a minor** boy **who married women and died, their wives are exempt from *ḥalitza* and from levirate marriage.**[H]

NOTES

A slave disqualifies, etc. – **הָעֶבֶד פּוֹסֵל וכו׳**: A slave disqualifies a woman with whom he engaged in intercourse from partaking of *teruma*, but he does not disqualify his Jewish mother. This principle applies to a gentile as well. In addition, both a slave and a gentile whose paternal grandparents are a priest and an Israelite woman do not enable their grandmother to partake of *teruma*. Why, then, is this principle stated specifically with regard to a slave? The novel element of this case is explained in *Arukh LaNer*: Even the slave of a priest, who partakes of *teruma* himself, does not enable his Israelite grandmother to partake of *teruma*.

A *mamzer* disqualifies and enables a woman to partake of *teruma* – **מַמְזֵר פּוֹסֵל וּמַאֲכִיל**: The commentaries disagree as to whether a *mamzer* who is the son of a priest partakes of *teruma* himself. The Rambam holds that he is a *mamzer* priest. Others maintain that his mother became a *ḥalala* due to the forbidden intercourse through which he was conceived, and he is therefore rendered a *ḥalal*, who is unfit for the priesthood (Rosh; Ritva).

This son is a *mamzer* – **הֲרֵי זֶה מַמְזֵר**: This mishna is of the opinion that the child of an Israelite woman and a slave or a gentile man is a *mamzer*. The commentaries do not follow this opinion. However, the principle that a *mamzer* whose maternal grandfather is a priest enables his maternal grandmother to partake of *teruma* is accepted unanimously (Rambam's Commentary on the Mishna).

HALAKHA

The son of a slave is not considered his offspring – **בֶּן הָעֶבֶד אֵינוֹ נֶחְשָׁב לְזֶרַע**: If an Israelite woman was married to a priest, or the daughter of a priest was married to an Israelite, and she bore a son, and that son engaged in intercourse with a maidservant and fathered a son, the son is rendered a slave. If the woman's son died and her grandson, the slave, is still alive, he is not considered his father's offspring. Therefore, if the woman is an Israelite who was married to a priest, she may not partake of *teruma* due to this grandson; if she is the daughter of a priest who was married to an Israelite, she is not disqualified from partaking of *teruma* because of him (Rambam *Sefer Zera'im*, *Hilkhot Terumot* 6:16).

A *mamzer* disqualifies and enables a woman to partake of *teruma* – **מַמְזֵר פּוֹסֵל וּמַאֲכִיל**: If the daughter of a priest was married to an Israelite, or an Israelite woman was married to a priest, and she bore him a daughter, and that daughter engaged in forbidden intercourse that renders her child a *mamzer*, the child is still considered the offspring of his grandparents. Therefore, if she is an Israelite woman married to a priest, she may partake of *teruma*; if she is the daughter of a priest married to an Israelite, she may not partake of *teruma* (Rambam *Sefer Zera'im*, *Hilkhot Terumot* 6:13–14).

A High Priest, sometimes he disqualifies – **כֹּהֵן גָּדוֹל פְּעָמִים שֶׁהוּא פּוֹסֵל**: If the daughter of a priest married an Israelite and bore him a daughter, and the daughter later married a priest and bore him a son, even if the daughter dies, her mother may not partake of *teruma* due to her grandson, who is her offspring from an Israelite. This is so even if the grandson becomes the High Priest (Rambam *Sefer Zera'im*, *Hilkhot Terumot* 6:15).

The wife of an imbecile or a minor – **אֵשֶׁת שׁוֹטֶה וְקָטָן**: The wife of an imbecile or a minor whose husband died is exempt from *ḥalitza* and levirate marriage, as their marriage was invalid (Rambam *Sefer Nashim*, *Hilkhot Yibbum* 6:8; *Shulḥan Arukh*, *Even HaEzer* 172:16).

כֵּיצַד? הָיָה יִשְׂרָאֵל שֶׁבָּא עַל בַּת כֹּהֵן – תֹּאכַל בִּתְרוּמָה. עִיבְּרָהּ – לֹא תֹּאכַל. כֵּיוָן דְּעִיבְּרָהּ לֹא תֹּאכַל – לֵיחוּשׁ שֶׁמָּא עִיבְּרָהּ! מִי לָא תְּנַן: מַפְרִישִׁין אוֹתָן שְׁלֹשָׁה חֳדָשִׁים שֶׁמָּא מְעוּבָּרוֹת הֵן!

§ It is stated in the mishna: **How so? If an Israelite engaged** in extramarital **intercourse with the daughter of a priest, she may partake of *teruma*.** If **he impregnated her, she may not partake** of *teruma*. The Gemara asks: **Since** if **he impregnated her she may not partake, let us be concerned** in any case of intercourse between an Israelite and the daughter of a priest **lest he impregnated her,**[N] thereby rendering it prohibited for her to partake of *teruma*. **Didn't we learn** in a mishna that if two men betrothed two women, and then at the time that they entered the wedding canopy, they accidently switched wives, and engaged in relations with each other's wives that night, in this case, after the accident is discovered, the court **removes** the wives from their husbands **for three months, lest they are pregnant** from the men they presumed to be their husbands and the fetus is therefore a *mamzer*, although they engaged in intercourse only once (33b)?

אָמַר רַבָּה בַּר רַב הוּנָא: לְיוּחֲסִין חָשְׁשׁוּ, לִתְרוּמָה לֹא חָשְׁשׁוּ. וְלִתְרוּמָה לֹא חָשְׁשׁוּ? וְהָתַנְיָא: "הֲרֵי זֶה גִּיטֵּיךְ שָׁעָה אַחַת קוֹדֶם לְמִיתָתִי" – אֲסוּרָה לֶאֱכוֹל בִּתְרוּמָה מִיָּד!

The Gemara answers that **Rabba, son of Rav Huna, said: About lineage** the Sages **were concerned,** and they therefore decreed a three-month separation of the husbands and wives, to prevent the possibility of a child being of uncertain lineage. However, **about** the prohibition against a non-priest eating ***teruma* they were not concerned.**[N] The Gemara asks: **And for *teruma* were they not concerned? Isn't it taught** in a *baraita* that if a husband says to his wife: **This is your bill of divorce**[H] **one hour before my death,** if she is an Israelite woman married to a priest **it is prohibited for her to partake of *teruma* immediately,** as the Sages were concerned that her husband might die within the hour?

אֶלָּא אֲמַר רַבָּה בַּר רַב הוּנָא: בְּנִישּׂוּאִין – חָשְׁשׁוּ, בִּזְנוּת – לֹא חָשְׁשׁוּ.

Rather, Rabba, son of Rav Huna, said: About impregnation through an act of **marriage they were concerned,** but **about** impregnation through **licentious intercourse they were not concerned,**[N] as the woman generally takes precautions to ensure that she will not become pregnant.

וּבְנִישּׂוּאִין מִי חָשְׁשׁוּ? וְהָתַנְיָא: בַּת כֹּהֵן שֶׁנִּישֵּׂאת לְיִשְׂרָאֵל וָמֵת – טוֹבֶלֶת וְאוֹכֶלֶת בִּתְרוּמָה לָעֶרֶב!

The Gemara asks: **And about marriage were they concerned? Isn't it taught** in a *baraita*: In the case of **the daughter of a priest who married an Israelite and** her husband **died** on that same day, **she immerses** to purify herself, as she is ritually impure due to their intercourse, **and she may partake of *teruma*** that same **evening?** Evidently, the Sages were not concerned that she became pregnant from the initial act of intercourse, even that of marriage.

אֲמַר רַב חִסְדָּא: טוֹבֶלֶת וְאוֹכֶלֶת עַד אַרְבָּעִים, דְּאִי לָא מִיעַבְּרָא – הָא לָא מִיעַבְּרָא, וְאִי מִיעַבְּרָא – עַד אַרְבָּעִים מַיָּא בְּעָלְמָא הִיא.

Rav Ḥisda said: She immerses and partakes of *teruma* only **until forty** days after her husband's death, when there is still no reason for concern, **as if she is not pregnant** then **she is not pregnant. And if she is pregnant, until forty** days[B] from conception the fetus **is merely water.** It is not yet considered a living being, and therefore it does not disqualify its mother from partaking of *teruma*.

NOTES

Let us be concerned lest he impregnated her – לֵיחוּשׁ שֶׁמָּא עִיבְּרָהּ: The Ritva asks why the Gemara raises this question with regard to this clause of the mishna and not with regard to the first clause, which states that a man who rapes or seduces a woman does not disqualify her from partaking of *teruma*. He answers that the first clause can be interpreted as referring to a virgin, as that is the case of rape and seduction that is discussed in the Torah, and the Sages did not factor into their ruling the possibility of a virgin becoming pregnant from her first experience of intercourse.

About lineage the Sages were concerned, about *teruma* they were not concerned – לְיוּחֲסִין חָשְׁשׁוּ, לִתְרוּמָה לֹא חָשְׁשׁוּ: Apparently, temporary problems relating to *teruma* were less of a concern than the lasting stain of defective lineage. A principle is indicated in the Jerusalem Talmud that the Sages were not concerned about possible occurrences that would disqualify a woman from partaking of *teruma*. For example, an Israelite woman married to a priest whose husband went overseas may continue to partake of *teruma* in his absence, without worrying that he might have passed away.

About impregnation through licentious intercourse they were not concerned – בִּזְנוּת לֹא חָשְׁשׁוּ: Why does the mishna permit the wife of an imbecile to partake of *teruma*? *Tosafot* maintain that she also takes precautions to avoid pregnancy, and therefore the Sages were not concerned that she might be pregnant. The Maharsha infers from Rashi that perhaps there is concern that she is pregnant, and therefore she should partake of *teruma* only if she knows that she is not. However, it is stated in the Jerusalem Talmud that since the marriage of an imbecile is invalid, she is considered unmarried for all intents and purposes.

HALAKHA

This is your bill of divorce, etc. – הֲרֵי זֶה גִּיטֵּיךְ וכו׳: If a priest said to his Israelite wife: This is your bill of divorce one hour before my death, it is prohibited for her to partake of *teruma* immediately, lest he die within the hour (Rambam *Sefer Zera'im, Hilkhot Terumot* 9:1).

BACKGROUND

Until forty days – עַד אַרְבָּעִים: The Sages established this date as the definitive point in time from when a fetus is considered a human being, not only a growth of tissue. From the fortieth day onward, the human fetus no longer resembles that of animals, as the tail disappears, and the head, arms, and legs have a human shape to them. Although it is still very small and undeveloped, it can be visually recognized as human, and it can therefore be considered a human being. At one month, the human embryo has no visible, distinctly human characteristics.

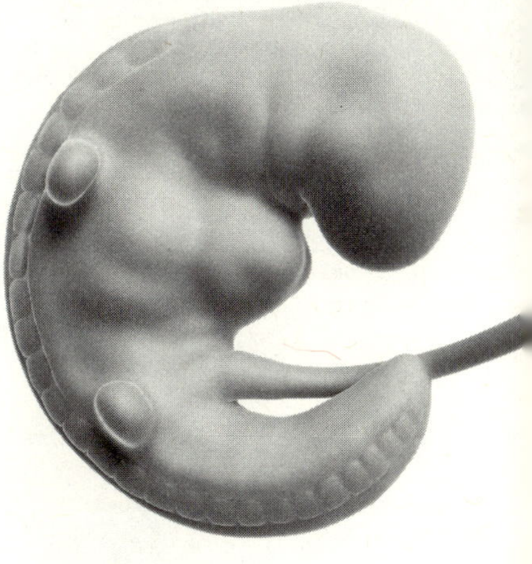

Digital rendering of a human embryo at one month

HALAKHA

The daughter of a priest who might be pregnant – בַּת כֹּהֵן סָפֵק מְעוּבֶּרֶת: If the daughter of a priest engaged in intercourse with an Israelite, there is no concern that she might have been impregnated, and she may immerse herself and eat *teruma* that evening, as stated by Rabba, son of Rav Huna. However, if she was married to an Israelite and her husband died, she may immerse and partake of *teruma* only for forty days. If she continues to partake of *teruma* after the forty days and it becomes noticeable that she is pregnant, she is retroactively considered to have sinned from after the forty days. However, during those forty days the fetus is considered merely water and does not disqualify her from partaking of *teruma* (Rambam *Sefer Zera'im, Hilkhot Terumot* 8:3).

A man who engaged in intercourse with his betrothed in his father-in-law's house – הַבָּא עַל אֲרוּסָתוֹ בְּבֵית חָמִיו: If a betrothed woman became pregnant while still living with her parents, and the couple agrees that the betrothed is the father, or if the woman claims that he is the father and he is unavailable for comment or says that he does not remember, the child is unflawed (Rema). This ruling follows the second version of the dispute between Rav and Shmuel, according to which Rav agrees with Shmuel in this case (Rambam *Sefer Kedusha, Hilkhot Issurei Bia* 15:17; *Shulḥan Arukh, Even HaEzer* 4:27).

אֲמַר לֵיהּ אַבַּיֵי: אִי הָכִי, אֵימָא סֵיפָא: הוּכַּר עוּבָּרָהּ בְּמֵעֶיהָ – תְּהֵא מְקוּלְקֶלֶת לְמַפְרֵעַ! מַאי מְקוּלְקֶלֶת: עַד אַרְבָּעִים.

Abaye said to him: If so, say the latter clause of the *baraita*: Once **her fetus in her womb is noticeable,** she **is ruined retroactively.**[N] Her prior consumption of *teruma* is retroactively prohibited. Evidently, pregnancy immediately disqualifies her from partaking of *teruma*. Therefore, the reason that she may partake of *teruma* immediately after her husband's death is that the Sages were not concerned that she became pregnant. Rav Ḥisda responded: **What is** the period in which she is retroactively **ruined?** It is from the moment the fetus is noticeable and back in time **until forty** days from the beginning of her pregnancy. During the first forty days of the pregnancy, she is not retroactively ruined, as the fetus is not yet considered a living being.[H]

אִיתְּמַר, הַבָּא עַל אֲרוּסָתוֹ בְּבֵית חָמִיו. רַב אָמַר: הַוָּלָד מַמְזֵר, וּשְׁמוּאֵל אָמַר: הַוָּלָד שְׁתוּקִי. אָמַר רָבָא: מִסְתַּבְּרָא מִילְּתֵיהּ דְּרַב – דְּדַיְימָא מֵעָלְמָא, אֲבָל לָא דַּיְימָא מֵעָלְמָא – בָּתְרָא דִּידֵיהּ שָׁדֵינַן לֵיהּ.

It was stated: With regard to a man **who engaged in intercourse with his betrothed in his father-in-law's house,**[H] i.e., before they got married, **Rav said** that **the offspring is a *mamzer*,**[N] as the future husband is not considered his father. **And Shmuel said** that **the offspring is a *shetuki*,**[N] a child of unknown paternity. **Rava said: Rav's statement stands to reason** in a case **where she is rumored** to have engaged in intercourse **with others. However,** if **she is not rumored** to have engaged in intercourse **with others, we cast** the child **after him,** i.e., we assume that the child is the betrothed's son.

אָמַר רָבָא: מְנָא אָמֵינָא לַהּ – דְּקָתָנֵי: יָלְדָה תֹּאכַל. הֵיכִי דָּמֵי? אִילֵימָא דְּדַיְימָא מֵעָלְמָא – יָלְדָה אַמַּאי תֹּאכַל? אֶלָּא לָאו – מִינֵּיהּ דַּיְימָא וְלָא דַּיְימָא מֵעָלְמָא.

Rava said: From where do I say that? What is the source for my assertion? The source is the mishna, which **teaches** that if a priest engaged in extramarital intercourse with an Israelite woman and she **gave birth, she may partake** of *teruma* due to her child, who is a priest. **What are the circumstances? If we say that she is rumored** to have engaged in intercourse **with others,** even if **she gave birth, why may she partake** of *teruma*? Shouldn't there be concern that the child's father is not the priest? **Rather, is it not** a case where **she is rumored** to have engaged in intercourse **with him and is not rumored** to have engaged in intercourse **with others?**

וּמָה הָתָם, דִּלְהַאי אִיסּוּרָא וּלְהַאי אִיסּוּרָא – בָּתְרָא דִּידֵיהּ שָׁדֵינַן לֵיהּ, הָכָא, דִּלְהַאי אִיסּוּרָא וּלְהַאי הֶיתֵּירָא – לֹא כׇּל שֶׁכֵּן?!

And if there, in the case of the mishna, **where** for her **to** engage in intercourse with **this** priest is **a prohibition, and to** engage in intercourse with **that** non-priest, with whom she is not rumored to have engaged in intercourse, is **a prohibition** of the same degree, nevertheless, **we cast** the child **after** the priest, then **here, where** for her **to** engage in intercourse with **that** man who is not her betrothed is a Torah **prohibition, and to** engage in intercourse with **this** man, her betrothed, **is permitted** by Torah law, is it **not all the more so** that her betrothed should be considered the father? Therefore, Rav's statement stands to reason only if the woman is rumored to have engaged in intercourse with others as well.

NOTES

Ruined retroactively – מְקוּלְקֶלֶת לְמַפְרֵעַ: In what way is she ruined? Rashi explains that she must pay for the *teruma* she consumed and add a fifth. Rabbi Avraham min HaHar and other commentaries argue that the daughter of a priest is never obligated to pay for consumption of *teruma*, even *teruma* that she consumed unlawfully, as stated in *Torat Kohanim*. Accordingly, her ruin must be her transgression of a Torah prohibition.

The offspring is a *mamzer* – הַוָּלָד מַמְזֵר: According to Rashi, the child is rendered a definite *mamzer*. However, the Rashba cites the Gemara in *Kiddushin* (75b), which indicates that Rav meant that the child is rendered a *mamzer* of uncertain status, who may not marry a Jew of unflawed lineage or a *mamzeret*.

A child whose father's identity is unknown [*shetuki*] – שְׁתוּקִי: A child whose father's identity is not known is referred to as a *shetuki*, from the Hebrew root *sh-t-k*, which means to silence. The Gemara explains that when a *shetuki* calls his father, his mother silences him (*Kiddushin* 70a).

אָמַר לֵיהּ אַבָּיֵי: לְעוֹלָם אֵימָא לָךְ: כׇּל הֵיכָא דְּדַיְימָא מִינֵּיהּ אַף עַל גַּב דְּלָא דַּיְימָא מֵעָלְמָא – אָמַר רַב הַוָּלָד מַמְזֵר, מַאי טַעְמָא? דְּאָמְרִינַן: מִדְּאַפְקְרָא נַפְשָׁהּ לְגַבֵּי אָרוּס – אַפְקְרָא נַפְשָׁהּ לְעָלְמָא. וּמַתְנִיתִין – שֶׁהָיוּ שְׁנֵיהֶם חֲבוּשִׁים בְּבֵית הָאֲסוּרִין.

Abaye said to him in rejection of his proof: **Actually, I could say to you** that **anywhere that she is rumored** to have engaged in intercourse **with him,** her betrothed, **even if she is not rumored** to have engaged in intercourse **with others, Rav said** that **the offspring is a *mamzer*. What is the reason?** It is **that we say** that **since she exposed herself to her betrothed,**[N] although they were not married yet, **she** apparently **exposed herself to others** as well. **And the mishna** that you cited as support for your assertion is referring to a situation **where they were both incarcerated** alone together **in prison.** Therefore, there is no concern that she engaged in intercourse with another man. This is one version of the dispute between Rav and Shmuel.

איכָּא דְּאָמְרִי: בְּבָא עָלֶיהָ – כּוּלֵּי עָלְמָא לָא פְּלִיגִי דְּבָתְרֵיהּ דִּידֵיהּ שָׁדֵינַן לֵיהּ, וְהָכִי אִיתְּמַר: אֲרוּסָה שֶׁעִיבְּרָה, רַב אָמַר: הַוָּלָד מַמְזֵר, וּשְׁמוּאֵל אָמַר: הַוָּלָד שְׁתוּקִי. אָמַר רָבָא: מִסְתַּבְּרָא מִילְּתֵיהּ דְּרַב – דְּלָא דַּיְימָא מִינֵּיהּ וְדַיְימָא מֵעָלְמָא.

Some say that **when** the betrothed admits that **he engaged in intercourse with her, everyone agrees that we cast** the child **after him.** Rather, their dispute **was stated as follows:** In the case **of a betrothed woman who became pregnant,**[H] if her betrothed denies that he engaged in intercourse with her, **Rav said** that **the offspring is a *mamzer*, and Shmuel said** that **the offspring is a child whose father's identity is not known. Rava said: Rav's statement stands to reason** in a case **where** the woman **is not rumored** to have engaged in intercourse **with him and she is rumored** to have engaged in intercourse **with others.** Therefore, it is assumed that the child is a *mamzer*.

NOTES

Since she exposed herself to her betrothed – מִדְּאַפְקְרָא נַפְשָׁהּ לְגַבֵּי אָרוּס: Sexual intercourse between a betrothed couple is prohibited only by rabbinic law. Accordingly, the blessing over betrothal: Blessed are You...Who prohibited us from incest, and forbade the betrothed to us, and permitted those married to us through a canopy and betrothal, is referring both to Torah and rabbinic prohibitions.

Early commentaries question Abaye's rationale, as intercourse between a betrothed couple is prohibited but the lineage of the child conceived through this act is completely untainted. This leads some commentaries to accept Rava's distinction and others to accept Shmuel's opinion.

HALAKHA

A betrothed woman who became pregnant – אֲרוּסָה שֶׁעִיבְּרָה: If a betrothed woman became pregnant while still living with her parents, and her betrothed denies having engaged in intercourse with her, the child is rendered a definite *mamzer*. If she is unavailable for questioning, or if she says that she does not know the father's identity, the child is rendered a *mamzer* of uncertain status.

If there are rumors that a betrothed woman engaged in licentious intercourse with her betrothed and with others, the child is rendered a *mamzer* of uncertain status, even if her betrothed admits that he engaged in intercourse with her. If she is questioned and says that she engaged in intercourse only with her betrothed, the child is rendered unflawed. It goes without saying that the child is unflawed if it is known that she engaged in intercourse with her betrothed and there are no rumors with regard to others. This ruling follows Shmuel's opinion as cited in the second version of the dispute. Some commentaries (Rosh; Rashba; *Beit Shmuel*) add that even if there were rumors that she engaged in intercourse with others, if it is known that she engaged in intercourse with her betrothed, or if he acknowledges the same, the child is unflawed, as stated by Rava (Rambam *Sefer Kedusha, Hilkhot Issurei Bia* 15:17–18; *Shulḥan Arukh, Even HaEzer* 4:27–28).

Perek **VII**
Daf **70** Amud **a**

אֲבָל דַּיְימָא מִינֵּיהּ, אַף עַל גַּב דְּדַיְימָא מֵעָלְמָא, בָּתְרֵיהּ דִּידֵיהּ שָׁדֵינַן לֵיהּ,

However, if **she is rumored** to have engaged in intercourse **with him,**[N] **even if she is** also **rumored** to have engaged in intercourse **with others, we cast** the child **after him.**

אָמַר רָבָא: מְנָא אָמֵינָא לַהּ, דְּקָתָנֵי: יָלְדָה – תֹּאכַל. הֵיכִי דָּמֵי? אִילֵימָא דְּדַיְימָא מִינֵּיהּ וְלָא דַּיְימָא מֵעָלְמָא – צְרִיכָא לְמֵימַר דְּתֵיכוֹל?! אֶלָּא לָאו – דְּדַיְימָא נָמֵי מֵעָלְמָא,

Rava said: From where do I say that? My source is the mishna that **teaches** that if a priest engaged in extramarital intercourse with an Israelite woman and she **gave birth, she may partake** of *teruma* due to her child. **What are the circumstances? If we say that she is rumored** to have engaged in intercourse **with him and she is not rumored** to have engaged in intercourse **with others, need it be said that she may partake** of *teruma*? It can easily be assumed that the priest is the father. **Rather, is it not** a case **where she is rumored** to have engaged in intercourse **with others as well?**

וּמָה הָתָם, דִּלְהַאי אִיסּוּרָא וּלְהַאי אִיסּוּרָא, בָּתְרֵיהּ דִּידֵיהּ שָׁדֵינַן לֵיהּ, הָכָא דִּלְהַאי אִיסּוּרָא וּלְהַאי הֶיתֵּירָא – לֹא כׇּל שֶׁכֵּן?!

And if there, where for her **to** engage in intercourse with **this** priest is in violation of **a prohibition and to** engage in intercourse with **that** non-priest is in violation of **a prohibition** of the same degree, and she is rumored to have engaged in intercourse with both, nevertheless, **we cast** the child **after** the priest, then **here, where** for her **to** engage in intercourse with **that** man who is not her betrothed is in violation of a Torah **prohibition and to** engage in intercourse with **this** man, her betrothed, **is permitted** by Torah law, is it **not all the more so** that he should be considered the father?

NOTES

Rumored to have engaged in intercourse with him – דַּיְימָא מִינֵּיהּ: *Tosafot* explain that she is known to have engaged in intercourse with him. Otherwise, Rava's proof from the mishna, which discusses a case of definite sexual intercourse with an Israelite, is problematic. However, the wording of Rava's statement is difficult according to this opinion. Rabbi Avraham min HaHar explains that she is rumored to have had an extensive affair with him, which raises the probability that the child is his in the mishna's case.

אָמַר לֵיהּ אַבַּיֵי: לְעוֹלָם אֵימָא לָךְ, כָּל הֵיכָא דְּדַיְימָא מֵעָלְמָא, אַף עַל גַּב דְּדַיְימָא מִנֵּיהּ אֲמַר רַב הַוָּלָד מַמְזֵר, וּמַתְנִיתִין בִּדְלָא דַּיְימָא כְּלָל.

Abaye said to him: Actually, I could **say to you** that **anywhere that she is rumored** to have engaged in intercourse **with others, even if she is** also **rumored** to have engaged in intercourse **with him, Rav said** that **the offspring is a *mamzer*. And the mishna,** which you cited as support for your claim, is referring to a situation **where she is not rumored** to have engaged in intercourse with anyone **at all.** Therefore, if they both concur that he is the father, the child is considered his.

״הָעֶבֶד פּוֹסֵל מִשּׁוּם בִּיאָה״ כו׳. מַאי טַעֲמָא? אָמַר קְרָא ״הָאִשָּׁה וִילָדֶיהָ תִּהְיֶה״ וגו׳.

§ It is stated in the mishna that **a slave disqualifies** a woman from partaking of *teruma* **due to** his engaging in **intercourse** with her, but not due to his being her offspring. The Gemara asks: **What is the reason** that he does not disqualify a woman whose offspring he is? **The verse states** with regard to a maidservant married to a Hebrew slave, that when he is released, **"the wife and her children shall be** her master's" (Exodus 21:4). This indicates that the maidservant's children are considered her own and are not considered their father's offspring at all. Therefore, a maidservant's child does not disqualify his paternal grandmother from partaking of *teruma*.

״מַמְזֵר פּוֹסֵל וּמַאֲכִיל״. תָּנוּ רַבָּנַן: ״וְזֶרַע אֵין לָהּ״, אֵין לִי אֶלָּא זַרְעָהּ, זֶרַע זַרְעָהּ מִנַּיִן? תַּלְמוּד לוֹמַר ״וְזֶרַע אֵין לָהּ״, מִכָּל מָקוֹם.

§ It is stated in the mishna that **a *mamzer* disqualifies** a woman from partaking of *teruma*, **and he** also **enables** a woman **to partake** of *teruma*. **The Sages taught:** The Torah states, "But if a priest's daughter be a widow, or divorced, **and have no child** … she may eat of her father's bread" (Leviticus 22:13). **I have** derived **only** that **her** own **child** disqualifies her from partaking of *teruma*; **from where** do I derive that **her child's child** disqualifies her as well? **The verse states: "And she has no child [*zera*]" at all,** indicating that even her grandchild disqualifies her, as *zera* means offspring.[H]

אֵין לִי אֶלָּא זֶרַע כָּשֵׁר, זֶרַע פָּסוּל מִנַּיִן? תַּלְמוּד לוֹמַר ״וְזֶרַע אֵין לָהּ״ – עַיֵּין עָלֶיהָ.

I have derived **only** that **an unflawed child** disqualifies her; **from where** do I derive that **an unfit child** disqualifies her[N] as well? **The verse states: "And she has no [*ein la*] child,"** which can be homiletically interpreted as **examine her [*ayyein ala*]** to check if she has any offspring, fit or unfit.

וְהָא אַפִּיקְתֵּיהּ לְזֶרַע זַרְעָהּ! זֶרַע זַרְעָהּ לָא אִיצְטְרִיךְ קְרָא, בְּנֵי בָנִים הֲרֵי הֵן כְּבָנִים, כִּי אִיצְטְרִיךְ קְרָא – לְזֶרַע פָּסוּל.

The Gemara asks: **But didn't you** already **derive** from that phrase **that her child's child** disqualifies her? The Gemara answers: To derive the *halakha* with regard to **her child's child, no verse was necessary,** as **the children of children** are considered **like children.** **The verse was** therefore **necessary for** deriving the *halakha* of **an unfit child.**

אָמַר לֵיהּ רֵישׁ לָקִישׁ לְרַבִּי יוֹחָנָן: כְּמַאן, כְּרַבִּי עֲקִיבָא, דְּאָמַר: יֵשׁ מַמְזֵר מֵחַיָּיבֵי לָאוִין? אֲפִילּוּ תֵּימָא רַבָּנַן, בְּעוֹבֵד כּוֹכָבִים וְעֶבֶד מוֹדוּ. דְּכִי אֲתָא רַב דִּימִי אָמַר רַבִּי יִצְחָק בַּר אַבְדִּימִי מִשּׁוּם רַבֵּינוּ: גּוֹי וְעֶבֶד הַבָּא עַל בַּת יִשְׂרָאֵל – הַוָּלָד מַמְזֵר.

Reish Lakish said to Rabbi Yoḥanan: In accordance with whose opinion is the assumption of the mishna that the child of a Jewess and a slave or a gentile is a *mamzer*? Is it **in accordance** only **with** the opinion of **Rabbi Akiva, who said** that the offspring of relations **for which** one **is liable** for violating **a prohibition is a *mamzer*?** The Gemara answers: **You** can **even say** that it is in accordance with **the Rabbis,** who hold that the offspring is a *mamzer* only if the parents are liable to receive *karet*. This is because **they concede with regard to a slave and a gentile, as when Rav Dimi came** from Eretz Yisrael to Babylonia, he said that **Rabbi Yitzḥak bar Avdimi said in the name of Rabbi** Yehuda HaNasi: With regard to **a gentile or a slave who engaged in intercourse with a Jewish woman, the offspring is a *mamzer*.**

״כֹּהֵן גָּדוֹל פְּעָמִים שֶׁפּוֹסֵל״. תָּנוּ רַבָּנַן: הֲרֵינִי כַּפָּרַת בֶּן בִּתִּי כּוּזָא – שֶׁמַּאֲכִילַנִי בִּתְרוּמָה, וְאֵינִי כַּפָּרַת בֶּן בִּתִּי כַּדָּא – שֶׁפּוֹסְלַנִי מִן הַתְּרוּמָה.

§ It was taught in the mishna that even **a High Priest sometimes disqualifies** his grandmother from partaking of *teruma*. **The Sages taught** that she can say in disapproval: **I am hereby atonement**[N] **for my daughter's son, the small jug [*kuza*],**[L] i.e., the *mamzer*. He is dear to me and I am willing to suffer to atone for him, **as he** is my offspring from a priest and therefore **enables me to partake of *teruma*. However, I am not** willing to be **atonement for my daughter's son, the large jug [*kada*],** the High Priest, **as he** is my offspring from an Israelite and therefore **disqualifies me from** partaking of ***teruma*.**

הדרן עלך אלמנה

HALAKHA

Her child and her child's child – זַרְעָהּ וְזֶרַע זַרְעָהּ: If an Israelite woman has a child from a priest she may partake of *teruma*, whether the child is male or female, or even if the child is a *tumtum*, one whose sexual organs are concealed, or a hermaphrodite. She may likewise partake of *teruma* due to her child's child, even if he is not a priest, or even if he is unfit to marry into the assembly of Israel (Rambam *Sefer Zera'im*, *Hilkhot Terumot* 6:12–13).

NOTES

From where do I derive that an unfit child disqualifies her – זֶרַע פָּסוּל מִנַּיִן: The commentaries ask how the mother of one who is unfit to marry into the assembly of Israel could possibly be allowed to partake of *teruma* as the daughter of a priest; the intercourse through which she conceived of him was prohibited, and it therefore rendered her a *zona*. In *Tosefot HaRosh*, it is answered that the *baraita* is referring to a grandchild. In *Tosafot Yeshanim*, it is suggested that the reference is to a woman who engaged in intercourse with an Egyptian or Edomite convert, which does not render her a *zona*.

I am hereby atonement, etc. – הֲרֵינִי כַּפָּרַת וכו׳: The *ge'onim* explain that this is an expression of affection. Rabbi Avraham min HaHar associates it with the expression one uses in relation to the deceased that he is mourning: I am hereby atonement for his resting-place. He therefore interprets the woman's statement to mean that she will mourn only her grandson the *mamzer* after his death and not the High Priest.

In *Arukh LaNer*, it is explained how a woman can partake of *teruma* due to one grandson and then be disqualified from partaking of *teruma* due to another grandson: She marries a priest and they have a son, and the son engages in forbidden intercourse, rendering his son a *mamzer*. After the woman is widowed, she marries an Israelite, and they have a daughter who marries a priest, and the couple's son is appointed as the High Priest. Before her daughter is born, she partakes of *teruma* due to her *mamzer* grandson. Afterward, even if her daughter dies, she does not partake of *teruma* due to her grandson the High Priest.

LANGUAGE

Small jug [*kuza*] – כּוּזָא: Apparently from the Middle Persian kūz, jug. In Hebrew and Arabic, it is called a كوز, *kūz*.

The sources that mention this term indicate that it is referring to a small jug, as opposed to a *kada*, which is a barrel, used mainly for storing drinks. A *kuza* was occasionally made out of metal but was usually ceramic, and it was used for drinking wine or water.

Summary of **Perek VII**

There is a principle, discussed in this chapter, that in a forbidden marriage between a priest and an Israelite woman, the wife may not partake of *teruma*, even if the marriage is valid. Therefore, her slaves may not partake of *teruma* either. However, her slaves of guaranteed investment may partake of *teruma*, as they are considered to be in the husband's possession.

This chapter also dealt with the principle that the daughter of a priest can be disqualified from partaking of *teruma* more easily than an Israelite woman can be entitled to partake of it. The daughter of a priest is disqualified from partaking of *teruma* by having a levirate bond with an Israelite, being impregnated by an Israelite, or engaging in intercourse with a man who is unfit for her, even if he is only nine years old. Only actual marriage to an adult priest or bearing his child entitle her to partake of *teruma*.

With regard to the definition of a woman who has children from a priest or a non-priest, any living Jewish offspring counts. This includes descendants and those who are unfit to marry into the assembly of Israel. However, descendants from gentile women or maidservants are excluded.

Index of **Background**

Index of **Background**

Index of **Language**

Index of **Personalities**

Image **Credits**

תלמוד בבלי

— מהדורת נאה —

יבמות א

Shefa

ירושלים

KOREN

תלמוד בבלי

הוצאת קורן ירושלים

— מהדורת נאה —

יבמות א

COMMENTARY BY

Rabbi Adin Even-Israel Steinsaltz

EDITOR-IN-CHIEF

Rabbi Dr Tzvi Hersh Weinreb

EXECUTIVE EDITOR

Rabbi Joshua Schreier

•

SHEFA FOUNDATION
KOREN PUBLISHERS JERUSALEM

חֲמֵשׁ*

אעֶשְׂרֵה נָשִׁים פּוֹטְרוֹת צָרוֹתֵיהֶן וְצָרוֹת צָרוֹתֵיהֶן מִן הַחֲלִיצָה וּמִן הַיִּבּוּם, עַד סוֹף הָעוֹלָם. וְאֵלּוּ הֵן: בִּתּוֹ, וּבַת בִּתּוֹ, וּבַת בְּנוֹ. בַּת אִשְׁתּוֹ, וּבַת בְּנָהּ, וּבַת בִּתָּהּ. חֲמוֹתוֹ, וְאֵם חֲמוֹתוֹ וְאֵם חָמִיו. אֲחוֹתוֹ מֵאִמּוֹ, וַאֲחוֹת אִמּוֹ, וַאֲחוֹת אִשְׁתּוֹ, וְאֵשֶׁת אָחִיו מֵאִמּוֹ, וְאֵשֶׁת

חֲמֵשׁ עֶשְׂרֵה נָשִׁים פּוֹטְרוֹת צָרוֹתֵיהֶן. כִּדְתָנֵי [סֵיפָא]: שֶׁאִם הָיְתָה אַחַת מֵהֶן נְשׂוּאָה לְאָחִיו, וְלוֹ אִשָּׁה אַחֶרֶת, וּמֵת בְּלֹא בָּנִים – שְׁתֵּיהֶן פְּטוּרוֹת. וְטַעְמָא יָלֵיף בַּגְּמָרָא. וְצָרוֹת צָרוֹתֵיהֶן עַד סוֹף הָעוֹלָם. בְּמַתְנִי' מְפָרֵשׁ. חֲמוֹתוֹ. שֶׁמֵּת בַּעְלָהּ, וּנְשָׂאָהּ אָחִיו וּמֵת בְּלֹא בָּנִים. וְאֵם חֲמוֹתוֹ וְאֵם חָמִיו. שֶׁתֵּיהֶן אֲסוּרוֹת לוֹ מִשּׁוּם עֶרְוָה, כִּדְכְתִיב (ויקרא יח) "עֶרְוַת אִשָּׁה וּבִתָּהּ לֹא תְגַלֵּה, אֶת בַּת בְּנָהּ וְאֶת בַּת בִּתָּהּ", וְיֵשׁ בִּכְלַל זֶה חֲמוֹתוֹ וְאֵם חֲמוֹתוֹ וְאֵם חָמִיו, כִּדְמְפָרֵשׁ (וְאָזִיל) בְּ"אֵלּוּ הֵן הַנִּשְׂרָפִין" (סנהדרין ד' עה.). וּבִתּוֹ (וּבַת בִּתּוֹ וּבַת בְּנוֹ) דְּהָכָא – בְּבִתּוֹ מֵאֲנוּסָתוֹ קָמַיְירֵי, וְכֵן בַּת בִּתּוֹ וּבַת בְּנוֹ. דְּאִילּוּ בִּתּוֹ מֵאִשְׁתּוֹ – הַיְינוּ בַּת אִשְׁתּוֹ, דְּכֵיוָן דִּכְתִיב (שם) "אִשָּׁה וּבִתָּהּ" – לָא שָׁנָא מִמֶּנּוּ, לָא שְׁנָא מֵאִישׁ אַחֵר. אֲבָל בִּתּוֹ מֵאֲנוּסָתוֹ לָא יָלְפָא לֵיהּ מֵהָכָא, דְּאִשָּׁה – ע"י קִדּוּשִׁין מַשְׁמַע, שֶׁהוּא אִישׁוּת, וּמִקְרָא אַחֲרִינָא נָפְקָא, כִּדְמְפָרֵשׁ בַּגְּמָרָא. אֲחוֹתוֹ מֵאִמּוֹ. שֶׁנִּשֵּׂאת לְאָחִיו מֵאָבִיו, וּמֵת. וְכֵן אֲחוֹת אִמּוֹ שֶׁנְּשָׂאָהּ אָחִיו מֵאָבִיו. שֶׁאֵין חִיּוּב יִבּוּם אֶלָּא בְּאָחִיו מִן הָאָב, דִּכְתִיב (דברים כה) "כִּי יֵשְׁבוּ אַחִים יַחְדָּו", וְיָלְפִינַן "אַחֲוָה" "אַחֲוָה" מִבְּנֵי יַעֲקֹב: מַה לְּהַלָּן מִן הָאָב אַע"פ שֶׁאֵין מִן הָאֵם – ה"נ ל"ש. וְאֵשֶׁת אָחִיו מֵאִמּוֹ. שֶׁמֵּת וּנְשָׂאָהּ אָחִיו מֵאָבִיו, שֶׁהָיְתָה נָכְרִית אֶצְלוֹ, וּמֵת בְּלֹא בָּנִים, וְנָפְלָה לִפְנֵי יָבָם זֶה לְיִיבּוּם – אֲסוּרָה לוֹ, לְפִי שֶׁהָיְתָה אֵשֶׁת אָחִיו מֵאִמּוֹ תְּחִלָּה, וַאֲסוּרָה לוֹ עוֹלָמִית, דִּכְתִיב (ויקרא יח) "עֶרְוַת אֵשֶׁת אָחִיךָ", וְדָרְשִׁינַן לָהּ בְּפ' "הַבָּא עַל יְבִמְתּוֹ" (לקמן ד' נה.): אָחִיךָ – בֵּין מִן הָאָב בֵּין מִן הָאֵם.

חמש עשרה נשים פוטרות. אר"י: דלא מלי למינקט "עריות" כדקתני בסיפא: אחת מכל העריות האלו, שש עריות חמורות מאלו (לקמן ד' יג.). משום דאמרינן בגמ' (לקמן ד' ג:): מנינא אתא למעוטי לרת סוטה, ולרת אילונית, וממאנת, ומחזיר גרושתו. ואי הוה תני "עריות" הוה משמע דלמעוטי עריות דלא קא חשיב קאתיא).

עד סוף העולם. הכא לא שייך למיפרך: כיון דתנא "עד סוף העולם", "לרות לרותיהן" ל"ל? כדפריך ב"הכותב" (כתובות ד' פג.): כיון דתנא "עד סוף העולם", "פירות פירותיהן" ל"ל? דהתם ודאי ב"הכותב" לא היה לריך לכתוב שניהם, אבל הכא – אורחיה דתנא למיתני לא זו אף זו. וא"ת: וכיון דתני "לרות לרותיהן", "עד סוף העולם" למה לי? דהכי דייק בתמורה פרק "אלו קדשים" (ד' יז:*): כיון דתנא "ולד ולדן", "עד סוף העולם" ל"ל? ואר"י: דהתם, כיון דאשמועינן דולד ולדן קרב שלמים – ממילא שמעינן דה"ה עד סוף העולם, כיון דלא חייש לשמא יגדל מהם עדרים, כדחייש התם ר"א. אבל הכא, ס"ד דלרות לרותיהן אסירי טפי, (לא) משום דמ"לצרור" דרשינן להו, ו"לצרור" משמע תרתי, שני רישי"ן. ואפי' לרב אשי, דנפקא ליה לרת לרה מסברא, לקמן בפירקין (ד' יג.) – מ"מ איצטריך לתנא לאשמועינן, דלא תיסק אדעתין למימר דמ"לצרור" נפקן. ועוד: אמרי' דלרב אשי נמי לרת לרה נפקא מ"לצרור", דהא בגמ' קתני בהדיא בשמעתין (לקמן דף ג:): לרות לרותיהן מנין – ת"ל "לצרור" ולא לצור. ולקמן (ד' יג.) דקא בעי מנה"מ – לא אלרות לרותיהן קאמר, דבהדיא דריש להו בברייתא מ"לצרור", אלא על "אפי' הן מאה" דמתניתין קאי, ואמר רב יהודה דכולהו משתמעי מ"לצרור", ורב אשי סבר דמ"לצרור" לא משמע אלא תרי, ואפילו הן מאה – מסברא נפקי. דלרתה מ"ט אסורה כל כך שאוסרת גם לרתה – דבמקום ערוה קיימא, לרת לרתה נמי תאסור לרה אחרת דבמקום ערוה קיימא. **בתו.** פי' בקונטרס: בתו מאנוסתו, דאי מנשואתו – היינו בת אשתו, דלא גרעה מפני שהיא בתו. ולפי זה, הא דקאמר בגמ' (לקמן דף ט:): רב יהודה מתרגם מחמותו ואילך. הא דתני ר' חייא בכולן אני קורא בהן: האסורה לזה מותרת לזה. אבל שיתא בבי דרישא – לא, משום דבתו כיון דבאונסין קא משכחת לה ובנשואין לא משכחת לה – בנשואין קמיירי, באונסין לא קמיירי. לא כמו שפירש בקונטרס דאמתניתין קאי הא דקאמר בנשואין קמיירי ולא באונסין – דא"כ היינו בת אשתו, וכדאמר נמי לקמן (ד' י.): מאי אמו? אילימא נשואת אביו – היינו אשת אביו. ועוד: דבהדיא אמר בגמרא בתו הואיל ואתי מדרשא חביבא ליה, והיינו בתו מאנוסתו. ועוד, לאביי דאמר דרבי חייא אכולה מתניתין קאי – ע"כ איירי באונסין. אלא יש לפרש: בנשואין קמיירי ר' חייא, דהכי משמע מילתיה דרבי חייא: בכולן אני מוצא בהם בהיתר וברגילות האסורה לזה מותרת לזה, אבל מתניתין – איירי שפיר באונסין ב). ונראה לר"י: דליכא למימר דמתניתין דקתני בתו איירי באונסין ולא בנשואין, דא"כ – מאי קאמר בגמרא כיון דבתו בנשואין לא משכחת לה, אפי' משכחת לה בנשואין – לא מצי קאי אכולהו בבי דמתני' דאיירי באונסין! אלא אר"י: דהך בתו איירי בין מאונסין בין מן הנשואין. **אשת** אחיו מאמו. משמע הכא דבאשת אחיו מאמו ✪יש בה כרת, דבחייבי לאוין סבר תנא דמתני' דחולצת, כדתנן בפ"ב (לקמן ד' כ.): איסור מצוה ואיסור קדושה חולצת ולא מתייבמת, ובהדיא תניא בגמרא: מה אחות אשתו מיוחדת – שהיא ערוה וחייבין על זדונה כרת כו'. והקשה רבינו שמואל: דבת"כ משמע שאין בה כרת, דקתני התם: "ואיש אשר יקח את אשת אחיו" – באשת אחיו מאביו הכתוב מדבר, אתה אומר באשת אחיו מאביו, או אינו אלא באשת אחיו מאמו? והדין נותן: הואיל ואסר אחות אביו ואחות אמו, ואסר אשת אחיו, מה אחות אביו ואחות אמו – בין מן האב בין מן האם וכו', ת"ל "נדה היא", מה נדה יש לה היתר ויש לה איסור – אף אשת אח יש לה היתר ויש לה איסור, וזו היא אשת אחיו מאביו שיש לה איסור ויש לה היתר. אם יש לה בנים – אסורה, אין לה בנים – מותרת. משמע דאתא למעוטי אשת אחיו מאמו דאין בה כרת! ודוחק לומר ולפרש דדרשא דת"כ לא אתא למעוטי אשת אחיו מאמו, אלא אתא למימר דאיכא כרת אף באשת אחיו מאביו באין לה בנים בחיי בעלה, אע"ג דיש לה היתר לאחר מיתה, דמה נדה אע"ג שיש לה היתר לאחר מכאן, בשעת איסורה – בכרת, אף אשת אח כן. והכי דריש בריש "הבא על יבמתו" (לקמן נד.). דאין הלשון משמע כלל כן. ועוד: דבירושלמי דפרק "כלל גדול" קאמר דאחותו יצאת לחלק, ודודתו יצאת לידון בערירי. והדר פריך מאשת אח למה יצאת? ומשני: לידון בערירי. והדר קאמר ר' יוסי: דודתו לצורך יצאתה, למעט אשת אחיו מאמו. דמה דודתו – באשת אחי אביו מאביו, כדיליף התם ערות דודו מ"דודו או בן דודו" דאיירי באחי אביו [מאביו] – אף אשת אחיו באחיו מאביו. ובתר הכי דריש לה מ"נדה היא" כמו בת"כ. משמע בהדיא דלמעט אשת אחיו מאמו אתא! ותירץ ה"ר משה: דלא אתא למעוטי אלא מערירי, דכתיב בההוא קרא. אבל כרת – יש בה. והא דבעי למילף מאחות אב ואחות אם, דבין מן האב בין מן האם, אע"ג דבאחות אב ואחות אם לא כתיב ערירי – אהקישא דר' יונה דָּרֵיש "הבא על יבמתו" (ג"ז שם:) סמיך, דמהקישא דאשת אחיו מן האב נקיש כל העריות לחומרא, ולא נקיש לאשת אחיו מאמו לקולא, דממעט מ"נדה היא". ולא יתכן פירוש זה לרש"י, שאומר* דכל כרת – הוא וזרעו נכרת, דהיינו דאיכא בין כרת למיתה בידי שמים, אלא לריב"א, שאומר דאין נכרת הוא וזרעו אלא בעריות, דכתיב בהו "עריריי". וחילוק יש בין מיתה לכרת, כדאמר בירושלמי (פ"ב דבכורים): דכרת בן נ', ומפיק ליה מדכתיב "אל תכריתו את שבט... הקהתי" (במדבר ד) ועבודתם עד נ', ומיתה היא בס' כמתי מדבר, דכתיב (שם יד) "יתמו ושם ימותו". וחולק על הש"ס שלנו, דבמ"ק (ד' כח. ושם) אמרינן: מנ' ועד ס' – זו היא מיתת כרת! ונוכל לומר לפי התלמוד שלנו דמיתה בידי שמים – אחר ס', וקודם – זמן כרת. ג) וא"ת: לפי' ריב"א דבריש "הבא על יבמתו" (לקמן נה.), מאי פריך: "עריריי" דכתיב בדודתו למה לי? כיון דמכרת לא שמעי' עריריי! ואי משום דמאשת אח שמעי' "עריריי" – בכל העריות, אם כן ה"ל לאקשויי א"עריריי" דאשת אח – למה לי? דכתיב לבסוף! ואר"י: משום דבההיא שמעתא לעיל יליף כל העריות מנדה להעראה, להכי פריך: "עריריי" דכתיב בדודתו למה לי? לילף הא נמי מנדה, דכתיב גבי אשת אחיו "נדה היא"*. **ואחות** אשתו. אין להקשות: דנדה תאסר ליבם, אע"פ שמטהרה אח"כ, כמו אחות אשתו שאין מתייבמת אפי' מתה אשתו אחרי כן! דלא דמי: דאחות אשה ושאר עריות האיסור עומד על היבם טפי משאר בני אדם. אבל נדה – לכ"ע אסירא. ואפילו בנדתה משמע בפסחים ס"פ "אלו דברים" (ד' עב:): דבת ייבום היא, דקאמר ר' יוחנן: אשתו נדה, בעל – חייב. יבמתו נדה, בָּעַל – פטור. ופריך עלה: מאי שנא יבמתו – דקעביד מצוה כו'. ד) משמע דקני לה. ועוד נראה לחלק: דאחות אשה, אע"פ שמתה אשתו אחרי כן – שוב לא תזקק לייבום. כיון שנפטרה שעה אחת, משום שנאמר "דרכיה דרכי נועם" (משלי ג) כדאמר ב"יש מותרות" (לקמן ד' פז:). ואפי' היכא דלא מידחייא מהאי ביתא לגמרי, כגון שיש אחים אחרים – אסורה לזה שמתה אשתו, כדאמר בפ' "ד' אחין" (לקמן דף כז:): כל יבמה שאין אני קורא בה בשעת נפילה "יבמה יבא עליה" – הרי היא כאשת אח שיש לה בנים, ואסורה, דאין זה דרכי נועם אם יש לה להזדקק לזה שנפטרה הימנו. אבל נדה – דרכי נועם היא, דלבעלה נמי צריכה להמתין עד שתטהר. וגבי קטן לקמן בפרק "ב"ש" (ד' קיא:) דקאמר *רבה בלאו הכי נמי לא מצית אמרת, מי איכא מידי דהשתא אסורה ליה ובתר הכי שריא ליה! והא אמר רב כו' – התם נמי אין זה דרכי נועם אם צריכה להמתין עד שיגדיל. אבל מה שממתנת מחמת שהוא קטן ואינו ראוי לביאה – הוי שפיר דרכי נועם, דאינו מחמת איסורא, והוי כאילו הלך יבם למדינת הים.

או

א א מיי' פ"ו מהל' יבום הלכה יד סמג עשין לא טוש"ע אה"ע סימן קעג סעיף א

[עי' תו' מ"ק כח: ד"ה כלעו]

ס"א אינו מהרש"ל

[וע"ש בתוס' ד"ה לא מיבעיא וכו']

[בשבת דף כה.]

[וע"ע תוס' שבת כה. ד"ה כרת]

[לפנינו הגירסא רבא]

תוספות ישנים

חמש עשרה נשים פוטרות לרותיהן. יש מקשים אמאי מתחיל סדר נשים ביבמות דהא אתחולי פורענותא לא מתחלינן ואדרבה היה לנו להתחיל קדושין וכתובות וגיטין ואח"כ יבמות. ונראה משום דכתיב והיה אמונת עתך חוסן ישועות ואמרו עתך זה סדר מועד חוסן זה סדר נשים וא"כ סדר נשים הוא בתר סדר מועד דמסיים במסכת מועד קטן א) דהוי פורענותא לכך התחיל סדר נשים במסכת יבמות ומסמיך פורענותא לפורענותא כדאמרינן פרק השותפין דמסמיך מלכים דסופיה פורענות לירמיה דכוליה פורענות. ב) אי נמי מפרש תחלה איזו אשה אסורה ואיזו אשה מותרת והדר מפרש כולהו מילי דנשים. ועוד י"ל משום דהיא מצוה ראשונה שאירעה בנשים כדכתיב בתמר בא אל אשת אחיך ויבם אותה: **א)** ועוד י"ל משום דבעי למתני לקמן שש עריות חמורות מאלו קרי להו נשים א"נ לא מצי למתני עריות משום דאי הוה תני עריות לא הוה ידעינן למעוטי דרב ורב אסי דאיכא למימר דהאי דלא תני להו משום דלאו עריות נינהו לכך תנא חמש עשרה נשים: **ב)** א"נ לקמן רוצה לומר הכי בנשואין קמיירי כלומר במקום דשייך נשואין קמיירי אבל במקום דלא שייך רק אונסין לא קמיירי ובתו שייכא בנשואין וא"כ קמיירי בה מתני' וא"ת מנא לן הא דפריש בין ממנו בין מאחר דלמא דווקא אשה ובתה אבל לא בתו ואין לומר דנפקא ליה מכל שכן דהא אמרינן בפ"ב אין עונשין מן הדין גבי אחותו דלא ילפינן בת אביו ובת אמו מכ"ש דבת אביו או בת אמו. וי"ל שאני (הכא) [התם] דכתיב מולדת בית או מולדת חוץ ומתרגמינן בת אביך דילידא מן אבוך מן אתתא אחרינא או בת אמך דאיתלידא מגבר אוחרן. משמע דקרא לא מיירי רק בבת אביו או בת אמו לחוד אבל הכא לא כתיב מעוטא וא"כ שפיר נפקא לן בתו מאשתו מכ"ש דבת אשתו שאינה בתו

גליון הש"ס

רש"י ד"ה אחותו מאמו וכו' וילפינן. לקמן ד' יז ע"ב: **תום'** ד"ה אשת אחיו מאמו וכו' יש בה כרת. עיין כריתות דף יד ע"ב תד"ה אשת אחיו:

ואין זה רק גלויי מלתא בעלמא ג) דודאי משמע בכל ענין: **ג)** ותמה בירושלמי זקן שאכל חלב מי מודיעו שחייב כרת פירוש משום שכבר עבר חמשים ומשני דמית פתאום וכו' ומאי פריך לימא שבניו יהיו נכרתים לפירוש הקונטרס דכרת הוי כמו עריריי אבל לפירוש דפריטית ניחא ויש לדחות דמיירי התם באין לו בנים או שיש לו בנים גדולים ד) שאין מתים בעון אביהם לפי שאין אוחזים מעשה אבותיהם בידיהם ותו לא חזי להוליד. ועוד יש להביא [ראיה] מדאמרינן במו"ק כי הוינא בן חמשים עבידנא יומא טבא לרבנן דאמינא נפיקנא מכרת ופריך התם נהי דנפק מכרת דשני מכרת דיומי מי נפיק. פירוש ימות פתאום. ותימה לפירוש הקונטרס אמאי לא פריך מכרת דבני מי נפק. ויש לדחות כדפרישית. דמיירי בשאין לו בנים או שיש לו בנים גדולים שאין אוחזין מעשה אבותיהם בידיהם: **ד)** א"נ כיון שיש לה היתר ע"י טבילה מקרי יבמה יבא עליה אבל הני אין להם היתר:

א) עי' בתוס' במו"ק כח: ד"ה בלע המות שכתבו כן בשם הרב ר' יעקב מאורלייאנש. ב) עי' בהקדמת התוי"ט לסדר נשים. ג) עי' סנהדרין דף ע"ו ע"א. ד) עי' בשבת דף כה בתוס' ד"ה כרת שתרצו כן.

ב א מיי' פ"ו מהל' יבום הלכה טז סמג עשין נא טוש"ע אה"ע סימן קעג סעיף יב:
ג ב מיי' שם הל' כא טוש"ע שם סעיף ז:
ד ג מיי' שם הלכה יד טוש"ע שם סעי' א:
ה ד מיי' שם הלכה כב טוש"ע שם סעי' ז:

[א]וְאֵשֶׁת אָחִיו שֶׁלֹּא הָיָה בָּעוֹלָמוֹ, וְכַלָּתוֹ. הֲרֵי אֵלּוּ פּוֹטְרוֹת צָרוֹתֵיהֶן וְצָרוֹת צָרוֹתֵיהֶן מִן הַחֲלִיצָה וּמִן הַיִּיבּוּם עַד סוֹף הָעוֹלָם. *[ב]וְכוּלָּן, אִם מֵתוּ, אוֹ מֵיאֲנוּ, אוֹ נִתְגָּרְשׁוּ, אוֹ שֶׁנִּמְצְאוּ אַיְלוֹנִית – צָרוֹתֵיהֶן מוּתָּרוֹת. וְאִי אַתָּה יָכוֹל לוֹמַר בַּחֲמוֹתוֹ וּבְאֵם חֲמוֹתוֹ וּבְאֵם חָמִיו שֶׁנִּמְצְאוּ אַיְלוֹנִית אוֹ שֶׁמֵּיאֲנוּ. [ג]כֵּיצַד פּוֹטְרוֹת צָרוֹתֵיהֶן? הָיְתָה בִּתּוֹ אוֹ אַחַת מִכׇּל הָעֲרָיוֹת הָאֵלּוּ נְשׂוּאוֹת לְאָחִיו, וְלוֹ אִשָּׁה אַחֶרֶת, וּמֵת – כְּשֵׁם שֶׁבִּתּוֹ פְּטוּרָה כָּךְ צָרָתָהּ פְּטוּרָה. הָלְכָה צָרַת בִּתּוֹ וְנִשֵּׂאת לְאָחִיו הַשֵּׁנִי וְלוֹ אִשָּׁה אַחֶרֶת, וּמֵת – כְּשֵׁם שֶׁצָּרַת בִּתּוֹ פְּטוּרָה כָּךְ צָרַת צָרָתָהּ פְּטוּרָה. אֲפִילּוּ הֵן מֵאָה. כֵּיצַד אִם מֵתוּ צָרוֹתֵיהֶן מוּתָּרוֹת? הָיְתָה בִּתּוֹ אוֹ אַחַת מִכׇּל הָעֲרָיוֹת הָאֵלּוּ נְשׂוּאוֹת לְאָחִיו, וְלוֹ אִשָּׁה אַחֶרֶת, מֵתָה בִּתּוֹ אוֹ נִתְגָּרְשָׁה, וְאַחַר כָּךְ מֵת אָחִיו – צָרָתָהּ מוּתֶּרֶת. *[ד]וְכׇל הַיְכוֹלָה לְמָאֵן וְלֹא מֵיאֲנָה – צָרָתָהּ חוֹלֶצֶת וְלֹא מִתְיַיבֶּמֶת.§

גמ' מִכְּדֵי, כּוּלְּהוּ מֵאֲחוֹת אִשָּׁה יָלְפִינַן, לִיתְנֵי אֲחוֹת אִשָּׁה בְּרֵישָׁא! וְכִי תֵּימָא תַּנָּא חוּמְרֵי חוּמְרֵי נָקַט, וְרַבִּי שִׁמְעוֹן הִיא, דְּאָמַר שְׂרֵיפָה חֲמוּרָה – אִי הָכִי, לִיתְנֵי חֲמוֹתוֹ בְּרֵישָׁא, דְּעִיקַּר שְׂרֵיפָה בַּחֲמוֹתוֹ כְּתִיבָא! וְעוֹד: בָּתַר חֲמוֹתוֹ לִיתְנֵי כַּלָּתוֹ, דְּבָתַר שְׂרֵיפָה סְקִילָה חֲמוּרָה! אֶלָּא: בִּתּוֹ, *כֵּיוָן דְּאָתְיָא מִדְּרָשָׁא – חֲבִיבָא לֵיהּ. כּוּלְּהוּ

ואשת אחיו שלא היה בעולמו. כְּגוֹן רְאוּבֵן שֶׁמֵּת בְּלֹא בָּנִים, וְנוֹלַד לוֹ אָח לְאַחַר מִיתָה וּשְׁמוֹ לֵוִי, וְעָמַד שִׁמְעוֹן וְיִיבֵּם אִשְׁתּוֹ, וְלוֹ אִשָּׁה אַחֶרֶת, וּמֵת בְּלֹא בָּנִים, וְנָפְלוּ שְׁתֵּיהֶן לִפְנֵי לֵוִי – שְׁתֵּיהֶן פְּטוּרוֹת. לְפִי שֶׁאֵשֶׁת רְאוּבֵן שֶׁנִּשֵּׂאת לְשִׁמְעוֹן אֲסוּרָה לְלֵוִי וְעָנוּשׁ כָּרֵת עָלֶיהָ, לְפִי שֶׁאֵשֶׁת אָח בְּכָרֵת, כִּשְׁאָר עֲרָיוֹת שֶׁבַּפָּרָשָׁה, דִּכְתִיב בְּכוּלְּהוּ "כִּי כׇּל אֲשֶׁר יַעֲשֶׂה מִכֹּל הַתּוֹעֵבוֹת הָאֵלֶּה וְנִכְרְתוּ", וּבִמְקוֹם מִצְוַת יִבּוּם כְּשֶׁמֵּת בְּלֹא בָּנִים – שַׁרְיָא רַחֲמָנָא. וְאֵשֶׁת אָחִיו שֶׁלֹּא הָיָה בְּעוֹלָמוֹ, שֶׁמֵּת קוֹדֶם לֵידָתוֹ – לָא שַׁרְיָא לֵיהּ, דִּכְתִיב "כִּי יֵשְׁבוּ אַחִים יַחְדָּיו" – שֶׁהָיְתָה לָהֶם יְשִׁיבָה אַחַת בָּעוֹלָם. וְהִלְכָּךְ, מִשֶּׁמֵּת רְאוּבֵן נֶאֶסְרָה עַל לֵוִי אִיסּוּר עוֹלָם כְּאֵשֶׁת אָח שֶׁיֵּשׁ לָהּ בָּנִים. וַאֲפִילּוּ עַכְשָׁיו, שֶׁנָּפְלָה לְפָנָיו מִכֹּחַ נִשּׂוּאֵי אָחִיו שִׁמְעוֹן שֶׁהָיָה בְּעוֹלָמוֹ – אֲסוּרָה לוֹ בִּשְׁבִיל רְאוּבֵן, וּכְשֵׁם שֶׁהִיא אֲסוּרָה לוֹ – כָּךְ צָרָתָהּ, אֵשֶׁת שִׁמְעוֹן הָאַחֶרֶת, אֲסוּרָה, דְּיָלְפִינַן לְקַמָּן עַל כׇּל הָעֲרָיוֹת הָעוֹמְדוֹת עָלָיו בְּכָרֵת שֶׁנָּפְלוּ לְפָנָיו לְיִיבּוּם עִם צָרוֹתֵיהֶן שֶׁשְּׁתֵּיהֶן פְּטוּרוֹת, וְאִם נְשָׂאָן עָנוּשׁ כָּרֵת, שֶׁמֵּאַחַר שֶׁפְּטָרָן הַכָּתוּב עוֹמְדוֹת עָלָיו בְּאִיסּוּר אֵשֶׁת אָח שֶׁיֵּשׁ לוֹ בָּנִים. וְכַלָּתוֹ. שֶׁמֵּת בְּנוֹ וְנָשָׂא אָחִיו כַּלָּתוֹ, אֲסוּרָה לוֹ לְעוֹלָם, וַאֲפִילּוּ לְאַחַר מִיתַת בְּנוֹ. וְכוּלָּן שֶׁמֵּתוּ. שֶׁמֵּתָה בִּתּוֹ קוֹדֶם לְאָחִיו אוֹ מֵיאֲנָה. וְהֵיכִי מַשְׁכַּחַת לָהּ מֵיאוּן בְּבִתּוֹ, וַהֲרֵי הוּא קַיָּים, וְאֵין מֵיאוּן אֶלָּא בִּיתוֹמָה? מַשְׁכַּחַת לָהּ כְּגוֹן שֶׁאָבִיהָ הִשִּׂיאָהּ לְאֶחָד, וְנִתְגָּרְשָׁה כְּשֶׁהִיא קְטַנָּה, וְשׁוּב אֵין לְאָבִיהָ רְשׁוּת בָּהּ, וְהָלְכָה וְנִשֵּׂאת לְאָחִיו בְּעוֹדָהּ קְטַנָּה, וְיָצְאָה בְּמֵיאוּן. וּבְפֶּ' ב"ש (לקמן קט.) קָרֵי לָהּ יְתוֹמָה בְּחַיֵּי הָאָב. וְאִם נִתְגָּרְשָׁה מֵאָחִיו, אוֹ מֵיאֲנָה בְּאָחִיו, אוֹ נִמְצֵאת אַיְלוֹנִית, שֶׁמִּקָּחוֹ מִקַּח טָעוּת וְלָא הָוְיָא אֵשֶׁת אָחִיו, וּכְשֶׁמֵּת אָחִיו הֲרֵי הִיא כְּמוֹ שֶׁאֵינוֹ אִשְׁתּוֹ, וּמִתְיַיבֶּמֶת צָרָתָהּ. **וְאִי אַתָּה יָכוֹל לוֹמַר כו'.** שֶׁכְּבָר יָלְדוּ מֵאַחַר קוֹדֶם שֶׁנִּישְּׂאוּ לְאָחִיו, הִלְכָּךְ לָאו אַיְלוֹנִית הִיא. וּמֵיאוּן נַמִי לֵיכָּא, שֶׁהֲרֵי גְּדוֹלוֹת הֵן, וְאֵין מְמָאֶנֶת אֶלָּא יְתוֹמָה קְטַנָּה, כִּדְמְפָרֵשׁ לְקַמָּן בְּפֶ' ב"ש. **כְּשֵׁם שֶׁבִּתּוֹ פְּטוּרָה.** שֶׁהֲרֵי אֲסוּרָה לוֹ, וְאֵין שָׁם אָח אֶלָּא הוּא – כָּךְ צָרָתָהּ פְּטוּרָה, כִּדְיָלֵיף בַּגְּמָרָא. **הָלְכָה צָרַת בִּתּוֹ וְנִשֵּׂאת לְאָחִיו הַשֵּׁנִי.** דְּהֵיכָא דְּיֵשׁ אָח אַחֵר שֶׁשְּׁתֵּיהֶן מוּתָּרוֹת לוֹ – אֵינָן פְּטוּרוֹת, שֶׁהֲרֵי יֵשׁ כָּאן מִצְוַת יִבּוּם, וּמִתְיַיבֶּמֶת הָאַחַת וְהַשְּׁנִיָּה פְּטוּרָה, דִּכְתִיב "אֶת בֵּית אָחִיו" (דברים כה) – בַּיִת אֶחָד הוּא בּוֹנֶה, וְלֹא שְׁתַּיִם. וְאִם יִיבֵּם הָאֶחָד אֶת צָרַת בִּתּוֹ, וְלוֹ אִשָּׁה אַחֶרֶת, וּמֵת בְּלֹא בָּנִים, וְחָזְרוּ וְנָפְלוּ לְפָנָיו. **כְּשֵׁם שֶׁצָּרַת בִּתּוֹ פְּטוּרָה.** שֶׁנֶּאֶסְרָה עָלָיו מִשְּׁעַת נְפִילַת אָחִיו הָרִאשׁוֹן, שֶׁנָּפְלָה עִם בִּתּוֹ לְפָנָיו, וּפְטַרְתָּהּ בִּתּוֹ הֵימֶנּוּ, וַהֲרֵי הִיא עָלָיו כְּאֵשֶׁת אָח שֶׁיֵּשׁ לוֹ בָּנִים, וַאֲסוּרָה לוֹ עוֹלָמִית. **כָּךְ צָרַת צָרָתָהּ.** אֵשֶׁת אָחִיו הַשֵּׁנִי הָאַחֶרֶת פְּטוּרָה, שֶׁזּוֹ פּוֹטַרְתָּהּ. וְטַעְמָא יָלֵיף בַּגְּמָרָא מִ"לִּצְרוֹר" (ויקרא יח), שֶׁצָּרַת עֶרְוָה פּוֹטֶרֶת צָרָתָהּ. **וַאֲפִי' הֵם ק'.** אַחִים, וְהָלְכָה צָרַת צָרָתָהּ שֶׁל בִּתּוֹ וְנִתְיַיבְּמָה לְאָחִיו הַשְּׁלִישִׁי, וְלוֹ אִשָּׁה אַחֶרֶת, וּמֵת בְּלֹא בָּנִים – שְׁתֵּיהֶן נֶאֱסָרוֹת עַל זֶה. וְכֵן לְעוֹלָם. **צָרָתָהּ מוּתֶּרֶת.** לְהִתְיַיבֵּם לוֹ, שֶׁהֲרֵי בִּשְׁעַת זִיקַת יִיבּוּם אֵינָהּ צָרָתָהּ. **וְכׇל הַיְכוֹלָה לְמָאֵן.** כְּגוֹן שֶׁהָעֶרְוָה קְטַנָּה וִיכוֹלָה לְמָאֵן וְלֹא מֵיאֲנָה, וּמֵת אָחִיו – הוֹאִיל וְקִידּוּשֶׁיהָ אֵינָהּ אֶלָּא מִדְּרַבָּנַן, וְזִיקַת נְפִילָתָהּ מִדְּרַבָּנַן, אֵינָהּ פּוֹטֶרֶת צָרָתָהּ מִן הַחֲלִיצָה. וּלְהִתְיַיבֵּם אֲסוּרָה, כִּדְמְפָרֵשׁ טַעְמָא בַּגְּמָרָא: שֶׁנִּרְאֵית צָרַת עֶרְוָה. **גמ' מִכְּדִי כּוּלְּהוּ.** עֲרָיוֹת, מַה שֶּׁפְּטוּרוֹת מִן הַיִּיבּוּם. **מֵאֲחוֹת אִשָּׁה יָלְפִינַן.** לְקַמָּן בְּשַׁמַּעְתִּין. **וְר"ש הִיא.** דְּאָמַר בְּפֶ' "ד' מִיתוֹת" (סנהדרין מט:): שְׂרֵיפָה חֲמוּרָה, וּלְהָכִי תָּנָא רֵישָׁא בִּתּוֹ וּבַת בִּתּוֹ, כּוּלְּהוּ עַד אֵם חָמִיו בִּשְׂרֵיפָה. **בַּחֲמוֹתוֹ כְּתִיב.** "וְאִישׁ אֲשֶׁר יִקַּח אֶת אִשָּׁה וְאֶת אִמָּהּ זִמָּה הִיא בָּאֵשׁ יִשְׂרְפוּ" (ויקרא כ). **כַּלָּתוֹ** בִּסְקִילָה. בְּפֶ' "ד' מִיתוֹת" (שם דף נג.). וְכׇל שְׁאָר עֲרָיוֹת דְּמַתְנִי' אֵינָן בְּמִיתַת בֵּית דִּין אֶלָּא בְּכָרֵת. **כֵּיוָן דְּאָתְיָא מִדְּרָשָׁא.** לֵיאָסֵר עָלָיו, חֲבִיבָא לֵיהּ לְתַנָּא, וְאַקְדְּמֵיהּ בְּרֵישָׁא. וּלְקַמָּן מְפָרְשִׁי לָהּ. כּוּלְּהוּ

או שנמצאו אילונית. דְּאַילוֹנִית קִדּוּשֵׁי טָעוּת הֵן, וְלֹא הָיְתָה אֵשֶׁת אָחִיו. וּתְמִיהּ: [דְּאָמְרִינַן] (לקמן ד' סא.): קָטָן וּקְטַנָּה לֹא חוֹלְצִין וְלֹא מְיַיבְּמִין כו', קְטַנָּה – שֶׁמָּא תִּמָּצֵא אַיְלוֹנִית. וְאַמַּאי? תִּתְיַיבֵּם מִמָּה נַפְשָׁךְ: דְּאִם אֵינָהּ אַיְלוֹנִית – שַׁפִּיר מְיַיבֵּם, וְאִם הִיא אַיְלוֹנִית – נַמִי שָׁרֵי, דְּלֹא הָיְתָה אֵשֶׁת אָחִיו! וְאוֹמֵר ר"ת: דְּהַהִיא בְּקַבָּלָה עִילָּוֵיהּ. וְכֵן ה"ג מְשַׁנֵּי בְּרֵישׁ "בֵּן סוֹרֵר" (סנהדרין סט:) [א]. וְה"ר אַבְרָהָם מִבּוֹרְגְוִוילָא תֵּירֵץ: בְּנִמְצֵאת אַיְלוֹנִית בְּחַיֵּי הָאָח וְהִקְפִּיד. אֲבָל לְאַחַר מִיתָה, דִּלְמָא אִם הָיָה קַיָּים – לֹא הָיָה מַקְפִּיד. וְלֹא נְהִירָא, דְּהָדְיָא קָתָנֵי בְּתוֹסֶפְתָּא (פ"א): נִמְצְאוּ אַיְלוֹנִית, בֵּין בְּחַיֵּי הַבַּעַל בֵּין לְאַחַר מִיתָה – צָרוֹתֵיהֶן מוּתָּרוֹת. וּבַגְּמ'* מְפָרֵשׁ בְּעַל כָּרְחָךְ לְמַאן דְּשָׁרֵי צָרַת בִּתּוֹ אַיְלוֹנִית אֲפִי' בְּהִכִּיר בָּהּ, מַאי חִידּוּשׁ הִשְׁמִיעָנוּ בְּתוֹסֶפְתָּא בֵּין מֵחַיִּים בֵּין אַחַר מִיתָה. וְא"ת: דְּהָכָא מַשְׁמַע דְּאַיְלוֹנִית לֹא בָּעֵי גֵּט [אֲפִי' מִדְּרַבָּנַן], דְּאִי בָּעְיָא – הָיְתָה צָרָתָהּ חוֹלֶצֶת וְלֹא מִתְיַיבֶּמֶת, כִּדְתְנַן בְּמַתְנִי': כׇּל שֶׁיְּכוֹלָה לְמָאֵן וְלֹא מֵיאֲנָה כו'. וּבִכְתוּבּוֹת בְּפֶרֶק "אַלְמָנָה" (דף ק:) תְּנַן: הַמְמָאֶנֶת וְהַשְּׁנִיָּה וְהָאַיְלוֹנִית אֵין לָהֶם כְּתוּבָּה, מַשְׁמַע: הָא גִּיטָּא – בָּעְיָא! דְּהָכִי דַּיֵּיק בְּ"הַמַּדִּיר" (כתובות דף עג. ושם). וי"ל: דְּהָתָם נָקַט הַאי לִישָּׁנָא מִשּׁוּם דְּלָא מָצֵי לְמִנְקַט אֵינָן צְרִיכִין גֵּט מִשּׁוּם שְׁנִיָּה דְּקָתָנֵי בַּהֲדַיְיהוּ. תֵּדַע, דְּע"כ מְמָאֶנֶת לֹא בָּעְיָא גִּיטָּא. א"נ בְּ"הַמַּדִּיר" לֹא דַּיֵּיק הָכִי אֶלָּא מִשּׁוּם דְּבְרֵישָׁא קָתָנֵי אֵינָהּ מְקוּדֶּשֶׁת וּבְסֵיפָא – תֵּצֵא שֶׁלֹּא בִּכְתוּבָּה, וְהָא דִּתְנַן בְּ"הַשּׁוֹלֵחַ" (גיטין דף מו: ושם): הַמּוֹצִיא אִשְׁתּוֹ מִשּׁוּם אַיְלוֹנִית לֹא יַחֲזִיר. וּמְפָרֵשׁ: מִשּׁוּם קִלְקוּלָא, דִּשְׁמָא תִּנָּשֵׂא לְאַחֵר וְיִהְיוּ לָהּ בָּנִים וְיֹאמַר כו', וְנִמְצָא גֵּט בָּטֵל וּבָנֶיהָ מַמְזֵרִים. דְּמַשְׁמַע בָּעְיָא גֵּט! אוֹמֵר ר"י: דְּהָתָם – בְּמוֹצִיאָהּ מִשּׁוּם סָפֵק אַיְלוֹנִית שֶׁאֵין הַסִּימָנִים נִיכָּרִים יָפֶה. תֵּדַע, דְּקָתָנֵי סֵיפָא: נִשֵּׂאת לְאַחֵר וְהָיוּ לָהּ בָּנִים, וְאִילּוּ וַדַּאי אַיְלוֹנִית – אֵין לָהּ רְפוּאָה, דִּבְ"הֶעָרֵל" (לקמן עט:) פְּלִיגִי ר"ע ור"א בִּסְרִיס חַמָּה, אִם חוֹלִין וְחוֹלְצִין לְאִשְׁתּוֹ, שֶׁיֵּשׁ לוֹ רְפוּאָה. וּבְאַיְלוֹנִית לֹא אַשְׁכְּחַן דִּפְלִיגִי, אַף עַל גַּב דְּקִידְּשָׁהּ עַל תְּנַאי וּכְנָסָהּ סְתָם אִיכָּא לְמ"ד בְּ"הַמַּדִּיר" (כתובות עג:) דְּבָעְיָא גֵּט – הַיְינוּ דַּוְקָא בִּשְׁאָר מוּמִין, דְּאִיכָּא דְּמָחֵיל. אֲבָל אַיְלוֹנִית – שׁוּם אָדָם אֵין מוֹחֵל. וַאֲפִי' לְאַבַּיֵי דִּמְפָרֵשׁ טַעְמָא מִשּׁוּם דְּאֵין אָדָם בּוֹעֵל בְּעִילַת זְנוּת – הַיְינוּ בִּשְׁאָר מוּמִין, דְּמַסִּיק אַדַּעְתֵּיהּ, וּבְדַעְתּוֹ אֲפִי' יִהְיוּ בָּהּ מוּמִין בּוֹעֵל לְשֵׁם קִדּוּשִׁין. אֲבָל אַיְלוֹנִית, דְּלָא שְׁכִיחַ – לָא מַסִּיק אַדַּעְתֵּיהּ, וּמִשּׁוּם חֲשַׁשׁ אַיְלוֹנִית לֹא יְהֵא בּוֹעֵל לְשֵׁם קִדּוּשִׁין.

ואי אתה יכול לומר בחמותו שמיאנה. וְא"ת: מַשְׁכַּחַת לָהּ מֵיאוּן בְּקִדּוּשֵׁי טָעוּת, דְּתָנָא דְּבֵי ר' יִשְׁמָעֵאל: אֲפִי' בְּנָהּ מוּרְכָּב עַל כְּתֵיפָהּ – מְמָאֶנֶת וְהוֹלֶכֶת לָהּ! וְתֵירֵץ רִיבָ"ן: דְּמַתְנִי' אַיְּירֵי בִּקְטַנּוּת. וְעוֹד אָמַר ר"י: דְּבְקִדּוּשֵׁי טָעוּת מָצֵי לְמֵימַר דַּאֲפִי' מֵיאוּן אֵינָהּ צְרִיכָה, וְלָא הָוֵה מָצֵי לְמִיתְנֵי בְּסֵיפָא כׇּל שֶׁיְּכוֹלָה לְמָאֵן כו'. וּמְמָאֶנֶת דְּר' יִשְׁמָעֵאל לָאו דַּוְקָא, דַּאֲפִי' לֹא מֵיאֲנָה – לָאו אִשְׁתּוֹ הִיא. וְאִם עֶרְוָה הִיא – צָרָתָהּ מוּתֶּרֶת. מִיהוּ, בְּפֶרֶק "בָּא סִימָן" (נדה נב. ושם) מַשְׁמַע דְּבְקִדּוּשֵׁי קְטַנּוּת [נַמִי] אַיְּירֵי ר' יִשְׁמָעֵאל, גַּבֵּי בִּתּוֹ שֶׁל ר' יִשְׁמָעֵאל שֶׁבָּאת לְמָאֵן בְּבֵית הַמִּדְרָשׁ וּבְנָהּ מוּרְכָּב עַל כְּתֵיפָהּ, וְרָאתָה בָּכְיָה בְּבֵית הַמִּדְרָשׁ, וְאָמְרוּ: דָּבָר שֶׁאָמַר אוֹתוֹ צַדִּיק יִכָּשֵׁל בּוֹ זַרְעוֹ! וְנִמְנוּ וְגָמְרוּ: עַד מָתַי הַבַּת מְמָאֶנֶת – עַד שֶׁתָּבִיא ב' שְׂעָרוֹת. וּמִשּׁוּם ר' יִשְׁמָעֵאל קָאָמַר דְּנִמְנוּ, דְּלֵיכָּא לְמֵימַר מִשּׁוּם דְּר' יְהוּדָה נִמְנוּ, דְּאָמַר: עַד שֶׁיִּרְבֶּה הַשָּׁחוֹר עַל הַלָּבָן – דְּהָא מוֹדֶה רַבִּי יְהוּדָה בְּנִבְעֲלָה, דְּאֵינָהּ יְכוֹלָה לְמָאֵן, וְהָא דְּפָרֵיךְ בְּפֶרֶק "נוֹשְׂאִין עַל הָאֲנוּסָה" (לקמן ק: ושם) וּמְמָאֶנֶת מִי קָא יָלְדָה? וּמְשַׁנֵּי: בְּקִדּוּשֵׁי טָעוּת כְּר' יִשְׁמָעֵאל. הָא דְּשָׁבֵיק קִידּוּשֵׁי קְטַנּוּת דְּאַיְּירֵי בְּהוּ – לָאו מִשּׁוּם דְּמוֹדֵי ר' יִשְׁמָעֵאל בְּקִידּוּשֵׁי קְטַנּוּת, אֶלָּא מִשּׁוּם דְּהַהִיא סוּגְיָא אַלִּיבָּא דִּשְׁמוּאֵל, וּשְׁמוּאֵל לָא סָבַר לָהּ כְּרַבִּי יִשְׁמָעֵאל בְּקִדּוּשֵׁי קְטַנּוּת, כִּדְמוּכָח בְּפֶרֶק "מִי שֶׁמֵּת" (ב"ב קנו: ושם) אֲבָל בְּקִדּוּשֵׁי טָעוּת – סָבַר כְּוָותֵיהּ, כִּדְאָמַר בְּ"הַמַּדִּיר" (כתובות עד. ושם): קִידֵּשׁ עַל תְּנַאי וּבְעָלָהּ – אֵינָהּ צְרִיכָה הֵימֶנּוּ גֵּט, וְהַיְינוּ כְּרַבִּי יִשְׁמָעֵאל. וְצָרִיךְ לוֹמַר מַתְנִי' לָא כְּרַבִּי יִשְׁמָעֵאל. וְהָא דְּקָאָמַר בַּגְּמָרָא (דף ט.) בִּפְלוּגְתָּא לָא קָמַיְּירֵי – הַיְינוּ דַּוְקָא אַמִּנְיָנָא דְּט"ו נָשִׁים. **דלבתר שריפה סקילה חמורה.** בְּחִנָּם נָקַט הָכִי, דַּאֲפִילּוּ הָיְתָה סְקִילָה קַלָּה בְּכׇל ד' מִיתוֹת בֵּית דִּין ה"ל לְמִיתְנֵי כַּלָּתוֹ בָּתַר חֲמוֹתוֹ, דְּבְכׇל הַנָּךְ לֵיכָּא מִיתָה אֶלָּא כָּרֵת לְחוּדֵיהּ. **בתו כיון דאתיא מדרשא חביבא ליה.** הַיְינוּ בִּתּוֹ מֵאֲנוּסָתוֹ כִּדְפֵי' בְּקוּנְטְרֵס. אֲבָל בִּתּוֹ מִנְּשׂוּאָתוֹ – מִ"עֶרְוַת אִשָּׁה וּבִתָּהּ" נָפְקָא, דְּלָא גָּרְעָא מִבַּת אִשְׁתּוֹ. וְא"ת: וְהֵיכִי נָפְקָא? וְהָא אֵין מַזְהִירִין מִן הַדִּין, כִּדְאָמַר לְקַמָּן בְּפ"ב (דף כב:) גַּבֵּי "אֲחוֹתְךָ בַּת אָבִיךָ (הִיא) אוֹ בַת אִמֶּךָ" דְּצָרִיךְ לְמִכְתַּב "אֲחוֹתְךָ הִיא" לְחַיֵּיב עַל אֲחוֹתוֹ בַּת אָבִיו וּבַת אִמּוֹ, לוֹמַר שֶׁאֵין מַזְהִירִין מִן הַדִּין! וְאר"י: דְּלָא דָּמֵי, דְּהָתָם לָא אַיְּירֵי קְרָא אֶלָּא בַּאֲחוֹתוֹ שֶׁאֵינָהּ מִן הָאָב וּמִן הָאֵם, "דְּבַת אָבִיךָ אוֹ בַת אִמֶּךָ" מַשְׁמַע מִן הָאָב שֶׁלֹּא מִן הָאֵם וּמִן הָאֵם שֶׁלֹּא מִן הָאָב, וְכִדְמְפָרֵשׁ קְרָא בְּהֶדְיָא "מוֹלֶדֶת בַּיִת אוֹ מוֹלֶדֶת חוּץ" (ויקרא יח) דְּמְתַרְגְּמִינַן דִּילִידָא

תוספות ישנים

וכולן אם מתו. הך מתני' הו"ל לא זו אף זו לא זו מתו דבדין הוא לצרותיהן מותרות דאין הערוה קיימת בשעת יבום אלא אפילו מיאנו דאיתא הערוה קמן מ"מ צרותיהן מותרות ול"מ מיאנו דכמו שלא נשאת מעולם לו דמי דהמיאון קא עקר קדושי קמאי ופשיטא דצרותיהן מותרות אלא אפילו נתגרשו דעשה מעשה קדושין גמורים אפ"ה צרותיהן מותרות ול"מ נתגרשו דבשעה שמת לא היתה ערוה עמו בתורת אישות לפי שעשה מעשה לעקור קדושי' אלא אפילו נמצאת אילונית דבשעה שמת היתה הערוה עמו בתורת אישות לפי שלא עשו מעשה לעקור הקדושין אלא הם בסוף כמו שהם בתחלה אפ"ה צרותיהן מותרות משום דהוי כמי שלא היתה אשתו: **א)** וה"ר ר' יעקב מקורביל מפרש דמאי אמרת דלמא איילונית היא וא"כ לא היתה אשת אחיו. לפי שאילו היה יודע שהיא איילונית לא קדשה. כמו כן נמי אם היה יודע בבירור שימות כשהיא קטנה לא יקפיד בזמן מועט כ"כ אם היא איילונית. ועוד י"ל דהא דאמרינן קטנה אינה מתייבמת שמא תמצא איילונית היינו לפטור צרתה להנשא לשוק דשמא תמצא איילונית ונמצא שיש לו לייבם הצרה לפי שהצרה זקוקה לו והיינו כי הכא: **ליתני** לאחות אשה ברישא. וקשה הא דאמרי' פ' ד' מיתות כל מקום ששנו חכמים דרך מנין אין מוקדם ומאוחר והלכך מאי קשיא ליה הכא ליתני אחות אשה כו'. ואית דמתרצי' דכי אמרי' אין מוקדם ומאוחר ה"מ היכא דקא חשיב המנין לגבי מעשה כגון ז' סמנים וקאמר דכל מקום לאמר דרך מנין אין מוקדם ומאוחר חוץ מז' סמנים וסדר יומא כדקאמר התם. וא"נ י"ל דנהי דאמרינן אין מוקדם ומאוחר שאם עשה מהמאוחר מוקדם לא קפדינן בה. מיהו מ"מ צריך לתת טעם בדבר למה הקדים המאוחר והכא נמי נהי דאין מוקדם מיהו מ"מ כיון דמן הדין הוה ליה למתני' לאחות אשה ברישא צריך לתת טעם למה לא הקדימה ומש"ה קא מיבעיא ליה דליתני לאחות אשה ברישא:

[לקמן יב. ד"ה תני שהיו]

קדושין מד: ולקמן יב. ל.

[לקמן קז:]

ב"ב קח: נדרים ג. נזיר ב: ב"ק יז: זבחים מח. בכורות יג. לקמן ל. לב. ר"ה יב.

ו א מיי' פ"א מהל' יבום הלכה יט:

תורה אור

כּוּלְּהוּ נַמִי מִדְּרָשָׁא אָתוּ! נְהִי דִּלְעִנְיַן יִיבּוּם אָתְיָין מִדְּרָשָׁא, עִיקַּר אִיסּוּרַיְיהוּ בְּהֶדְיָא כְּתִיב בְּהוּ, בִּתּוֹ — עִיקַּר אִיסּוּרָא מִדְּרָשָׁא. *דַּאֲמַר רָבָא: אָמַר לִי רַב יִצְחָק בַּר אַבְדִּימִי: אָתְיָא °"הֵנָּה" °"הֵנָּה", אָתְיָא °"זִמָּה" °"זִמָּה". הָשְׁתָּא דְּאָמְרַתְּ כָּל מִלְּתָא דְּאָתְיָא מִדְּרָשָׁא חֲבִיבָא לֵיהּ, לִיתְנֵי לַאֲחוֹת אִשָּׁה לְבַסּוֹף! אַיְּידֵי דְּאַיְירֵי בְּאִיסּוּר אַחְוָותָא תָּנָא אֲחוֹת אִשְׁתּוֹ. וְלִיתְנְיַיא לְהַאי בָּבָא לְבַסּוֹף! אֶלָּא: תַּנָּא קוּרְבֵי קוּרְבֵי נָקַט; תָּנָא בִּתּוֹ וּבַת בִּתּוֹ וּבַת בְּנוֹ דִּקְרוֹבֵי עַצְמוֹ, וְאַיְּידֵי דְּתָנָא שְׁלֹשָׁה דוֹרוֹת לְמַטָּה דִּידֵיהּ, תָּנָא נַמִי שְׁלֹשָׁה דוֹרוֹת לְמַטָּה דִּידָהּ. וְאַיְּידֵי דְּתָנָא *שְׁלֹשָׁה דוֹרוֹת לְמַטָּה דִּידָהּ — תָּנָא שְׁלֹשָׁה דוֹרוֹת לְמַעְלָה דִּידָהּ. וְתָנָא אֲחוֹתוֹ וַאֲחוֹת אִמּוֹ דִּקְרוֹבֵי עַצְמוֹ, וְאַיְּידֵי דְּאַיְירֵי בְּאִיסּוּר אַחֲוָה — תָּנָא אֲחוֹת אִשְׁתּוֹ. וּבְדִין הוּא דְּלִיקַדְּמָהּ לְכַלָּתוֹ מִקַּמֵּי אֵשֶׁת אָחִיו שֶׁלֹּא הָיָה בְּעוֹלָמוֹ, דְּלָא מִשּׁוּם קוּרְבָא הוּא דַּאֲסִירָא, אֶלָּא אַיְּידֵי דְּאַיְירֵי בְּאִיסּוּר אַחֲוָה — תָּנָא אֵשֶׁת אָחִיו שֶׁלֹּא הָיָה בְּעוֹלָמוֹ, וַהֲדַר תָּנָא כַּלָּתוֹ וּמַאי אִירְיָא דְּתָנָא "פּוֹטְרוֹת", לִיתְנֵי "אוֹסְרוֹת"! אִי תָּנָא אוֹסְרוֹת הֲוָה אָמִינָא: אָסוּר לְיַיבֵּם, אֲבָל מִיחְלַץ חָלְצָה, קמ"ל. וְלִיתְנֵי אֲסוּרָה לַחֲלוֹץ! מַאי קָעָבֵיד? אַלְּמָה לָא? •אִם אַתָּה אוֹמֵר חוֹלֶצֶת — מִתְיַיבֶּמֶת! כֵּיוָן דִּבְמָקוֹם מִצְוָה הוּא דַּאֲסִירָה צָרָה, וְשֶׁלֹּא בְּמָקוֹם מִצְוָה שַׁרְיָא, מִשּׁוּם הָכִי תָּנֵי "פּוֹטְרוֹת". וּמַאי אִירְיָא דְּתָנֵי "מִן הַחֲלִיצָה וּמִן הַיִּיבּוּם", לִיתְנֵי "מִן הַיִּיבּוּם" לְחוּדֵיהּ! אִי תָּנָא מִן הַיִּיבּוּם הֲוָה אָמִינָא: מִיחְלַץ חָלְצָה, יַבּוּמֵי לָא מְיַיבְּמָה, קמ"ל: *אכָּל הָעוֹלֶה לְיִיבּוּם עוֹלֶה לַחֲלִיצָה וְכָל שֶׁאֵינוֹ עוֹלֶה לְיִיבּוּם — אֵינוֹ עוֹלֶה לַחֲלִיצָה. וְלִיתְנֵי מִן הַיִּיבּוּם וּמִן הַחֲלִיצָה, א"נ מִן הַחֲלִיצָה לְחוּדָהּ! אַבָּא שָׁאוּל הִיא, דְּאָמַר: *מִצְוַת חֲלִיצָה קוֹדֶמֶת לְמִצְוַת יִיבּוּם. מִנְיָנָא דְּרֵישָׁא לְמַעוּטֵי מַאי, וּמִנְיָנָא דְּסֵיפָא לְמַעוּטֵי מַאי?

לְמַעוּטֵי

ויקרא יח | שם שם | שם כ

חגיגה יח: סנהדרין נא. עה: פו: כריתות ה.

[לקמן נג. סוטה כ. סנהדרין נג: נדה ל.]

[לקמן כ. לו. מה. מד.]

[לקמן לט: קט.]

[לקמן ד' נד.]

רש"י

כּוּלְּהוּ נַמִי. לְעִנְיַן פְּטוּר יִיבּוּם מִדְּרָשָׁא אָתְיָין, מֵאֲחוֹת אִשָּׁה. עִיקַּר אִיסּוּרַיְיהוּ. שֶׁאֲסוּרִים מִשּׁוּם עֶרְוָה בְּכָל מָקוֹם — בְּהֶדְיָא כְּתִיב בְּהוּ. אֲבָל בִּתּוֹ מֵאֲנוּסָתוֹ דְּאַיְירֵי בָּהּ בְּמַתְנִי', עִיקַּר אִיסּוּרָהּ מִדְּרָשָׁא אָתְיָא. אָתְיָא "הֵנָּה" "הֵנָּה". לְאִיסּוּרָא, אָתְיָא "זִמָּה" "זִמָּה" לִשְׂרֵיפָה. דְּבִתּוֹ מֵאִשְׁתּוֹ, וְכֵן בַּת בִּתּוֹ וּבַת בְּנוֹ, יָלְפָא מֵ"עֶרְוַת אִשָּׁה וּבִתָּהּ לֹא תְגַלֵּה", וַהֲרֵי בִּתּוֹ מֵאִשְׁתּוֹ בִּכְלַל בַּת אִשְׁתּוֹ. אֲבָל בִּתּוֹ מֵאֲנוּסָתוֹ — לָא מִשְׁתַּמְּעָא, דִּכְתִיב "עֶרְוַת אִשָּׁה" וּלְשׁוֹן אִישׁוּת — דְּעַל יְדֵי קִידּוּשִׁין מַשְׁמַע. וְגַלֵּי רַחֲמָנָא בְּבַת בִּתּוֹ וּבַת בְּנוֹ מֵאֲנוּסָתוֹ בְּהַאי קְרָא "עֶרְוַת בַּת בִּנְךָ אוֹ בַת בִּתְּךָ", וְהָכָא לְשׁוֹן אִישׁוּת לָא כְּתִיב. וְאַכַּתִּי בִּתּוֹ לָא כְּתִיב הָכָא, וְיָלְפִינַן בג"ש: כְּתִיב הָכָא בִּקְרָא דַּאֲנוּסָה "כִּי עֶרְוָתְךָ הֵנָּה", וּכְתִיב בִּקְרָא אַחֲרִינָא דְּאִישּׁוּת "שַׁאֲרָה הֵנָּה", מַה הָתָם בִּתּוֹ כְּבַת בִּתּוֹ — אַף כָּאן בִּתּוֹ כְּבַת בִּתּוֹ. אָתְיָא "זִמָּה" "זִמָּה". לִשְׂרֵיפָה, כְּתִיב הָכָא בְּבִתּוֹ מֵאִשְׁתּוֹ "זִמָּה הִיא", וּכְתִיב בִּשְׂרֵיפָה "זִמָּה הִיא בָּאֵשׁ יִשְׂרְפוּ", מַה לְהַלָּן שְׂרֵיפָה — אַף כָּאן שְׂרֵיפָה. וּבִתּוֹ מֵאֲנוּסָתוֹ הָא יָלְפִינַן מֵ"הֵנָּה" "הֵנָּה" מִבַּת אִשְׁתּוֹ. לִיתְנֵי אֲחוֹת אִשָּׁה לְבַסּוֹף. דְּכוּלְּהוּ מִינָּהּ יָלְפִי' לְעִנְיַן פְּטוּר יִיבּוּם, לְקַמָּן. לְהַאי בָּבָא. כָּל אִיסּוּר [אַחְוָותָא] לִיתְנֵי לְבַסּוֹף, וְיַקְדִּים כַּלָּתוֹ לַאֲחוֹתוֹ, כִּי הֵיכִי דְּתֶיהֱוֵי אֲחוֹת אִשָּׁה לְבַסּוֹף. קוּרְבֵי קוּרְבֵי. הָנָךְ דְּקָרֵיב לֵיהּ טְפֵי נָקַט בְּרֵישָׁא. דִּקְרוֹבֵי עַצְמוֹ. וְאֵין בְּכוּלָּן קְרוֹבוֹת כָּאֵלּוּ. לְמַטָּה דִּידָהּ. דְּאִשְׁתּוֹ. וְאע"ג דְּהָנָךְ לָאו מִשּׁוּם קוּרְבָה דִּידֵיהּ אֲסִירָן לֵיהּ. לְמַעְלָה דִּידָהּ. חֲמוֹתוֹ. וּלְמַעְלָה דִּידֵיהּ לָא מָצֵי לְמִיתְנֵי מִידֵי, דְּהָא אִמּוֹ לָא אָתְיָא לֵיהּ לְיִיבּוּם, שֶׁהֲרֵי אֲסוּרָה לְאָחִיו מֵאָבִיו מִשּׁוּם אֵשֶׁת אָבִיו: וְתָנֵי אֲחוֹתוֹ וַאֲחוֹת אִמּוֹ דִּקְרוֹבֵי עַצְמוֹ. טְפֵי מִכַּלָּתוֹ. דְּכַלָּתוֹ לָאו קוּרְבָתוֹ הִיא, אֶלָּא מִכֹּחַ קִדּוּשֵׁי בְּנוֹ נֶאֶסְרָה עָלָיו. וּבְדִין הוּא דְּלִיקַדְּמָהּ לְכַלָּתוֹ. מִקַּמֵּי אֵשֶׁת אָחִיו שֶׁלֹּא הָיָה בְּעוֹלָמוֹ. דְּלָאו מִשּׁוּם קוּרְבָא הוּא דַּאֲסוּר. כְּלוֹמַר: וְכֵיוָן דִּקְרוֹבִין נָקַט וְאָזֵיל, וְכַלָּתוֹ וְאֵשֶׁת אָחִיו שֶׁלֹּא הָיָה בְּעוֹלָמוֹ וְאֵשֶׁת אָחִיו מֵאִמּוֹ — לָאו מִשּׁוּם קוּרְבָה דִּידֵיהּ הוּא דַּאֲסִירָן לֵיהּ, בְּדִין הוּא דְּלִיתְנֵי כַּלָּתוֹ מִקַּמֵּי אֵשֶׁת אָחִיו שֶׁלֹּא הָיָה בְּעוֹלָמוֹ, וּמִקַּמֵּי אֵשֶׁת אָחִיו מֵאִמּוֹ נַמִי מִשּׁוּם דְּכַלָּתוֹ חֲמִירָא טְפֵי מִינַּיְיהוּ, וַהֲוָה לֵיהּ לְמִנְקַט חוּמְרֵי, כֵּיוָן דְּלָא מָצֵי לְמִינְקַט קוּרְבֵי. מַאי אִירְיָא דְּקָתָנֵי פּוֹטְרוֹת. דְּמַשְׁמַע פְּטוּרוֹת הֵן, וְאִי בָּעֵי — מְיַיבֵּם. לִיתְנֵי אֲסוּרוֹת. דְּהָא וַדַּאי אֲסוּרוֹת הֵן, מֵאַחַר שֶׁאֵינָן זְקוּקוֹת לְיִיבּוּם וְקָיְימִי בְּאִיסּוּר אֵשֶׁת אָח. ה"א אוֹסְרוֹת. לְיִיבּוּם. וַחֲלִיצָה לָא מִשְׁתַּמְּעָא מֵהָכָא, שֶׁאֵין אִיסּוּר בַּחֲלִיצָה. וַהֲוָה אָמִינָא: מִיחְלַץ חָלְצֵי עַל כָּרְחוֹ, שֶׁאֵין אֵשֶׁת אָח מֵת בְּלֹא בָּנִים נִפְטֶרֶת בְּלֹא חֲלִיצָה. מַאי קָעָבֵיד. וְהִלְכָּךְ לֹא שַׁיָּיךְ לְשׁוֹן אִיסּוּר בַּחֲלִיצָה, אֶלָּא לְשׁוֹן פְּטוּר. אַלְּמָה לָא. שַׁיָּיךְ [לְשׁוֹן] אִיסּוּר, הָא וַדַּאי שַׁיָּיךְ, שֶׁאִם אַתָּה אוֹמֵר חוֹלֶצֶת — אָתֵי לְמֵימַר מִתְיַיבֶּמֶת. כֵּיוָן דִּבְמָקוֹם מִצְוַת יִבּוּם הוּא דַּאֲסִירָה. צָרַת הַבַּת, וּכְדִמְפָרֵשׁ בְּמַתְנִי', דְּמִפְּטְרָהּ הַכָּתוּב מִזִּיקַת יִיבּוּם — קָיְימָא לֵיהּ בְּאֵשֶׁת אָח שֶׁיֵּשׁ לוֹ בָּנִים. שֶׁלֹּא בְּמָקוֹם מִצְוָה שַׁרְיָא. כְּגוֹן נָכְרִי שֶׁנַּעֲשָׂה חֲתָנוֹ, וְלוֹ אִשָּׁה אַחֶרֶת, וּמֵת — מוּתֶּרֶת אִשְׁתּוֹ לְחָמִיו, כִּדְתְנַן לְקַמָּן (דף יג.) גַּבֵּי שֵׁשׁ עֲרָיוֹת חֲמוּרוֹת מֵאֵלּוּ, בְּמַתְנִי'. מִשּׁוּם הָכִי תָּנָא פּוֹטְרוֹת. דְּאִי תָּנָא אוֹסְרוֹת — מַשְׁמַע שֶׁאֲסַרְתָּהּ עָלָיו לִיקַּח, [וְק"ו] שֶׁלֹּא בְּמָקוֹם מִצְוָה. אֲבָל פּוֹטְרוֹת — לָא מִשְׁתַּמַּע אִיסּוּרָא מִשּׁוּם צָרָתָהּ שֶׁל בַּת, אֶלָּא הַבַּת פּוֹטַרְתָּהּ מִיִּיבּוּם, וְאִיסּוּרָא שְׁכִיב עֲלָהּ מֵאֵילָא, דְּהָוְיָא בְּאִיסּוּר אֵשֶׁת אָח שֶׁיֵּשׁ לָהּ בָּנִים. וּמִשּׁוּם אֵשֶׁת אָח הוּא דְּמִיתְסַר — שֶׁלֹּא בְּמָקוֹם מִצְוָה, דְּלֵיכָּא אִיסּוּר אֵשֶׁת אָח עֲלָהּ, שַׁרְיָא. וְלִיתְנֵי מִן הַיִּיבּוּם לְחוּדֵיהּ. דְּהָא עִיקַּר מִצְוָה הִיא, וַחֲלִיצָה מֵאֵילָא מִשְׁתַּמַּע. ה"א מִיחְלַץ חָלְצָה. שֶׁלֹּא לְהַפְקִיעַ מִצְוַת יִיבּוּם, אֲבָל יַבּוּמֵי — לָא, מִשּׁוּם גְּזֵירַת הַכָּתוּב דִּ"לִצְרוֹר". קמ"ל מַתְנִי', הוֹאִיל וּפְטָרָהּ הַבַּת מִזִּיקַת יִבּוּם — פְּטוּרָה מִן הַחֲלִיצָה; דְּכָל הָעוֹלָה לְזִיקַת יִיבּוּם עוֹלָה לְזִיקַת חֲלִיצָה, וְכָל שֶׁאֵין עוֹלָה לְזִיקַת יִיבּוּם — פְּטוּרָה מִן הַחֲלִיצָה.• וְכָל הֵיכָא דְּאָמְרִינַן חוֹלֶצֶת וְלֹא מִתְיַיבֶּמֶת — מִשּׁוּם סְפֵקָא הוּא. וְנִיתְנֵי יִיבּוּם בְּרֵישָׁא. דְּהוּא עִיקָּר, דְּהָא כְּתִיב "אִם לֹא יַחְפּוֹץ הָאִישׁ לָקַחַת... וְחָלְצָה" (דברים כה), הָא אִם חָפֵץ לְיַיבֵּם — מְיַיבֵּם, *אַלְמָא: מִצְוַת יִיבּוּם בְּרֵישָׁא. אַבָּא שָׁאוּל הִיא. בְּפֶ' "הַחוֹלֵץ" (לקמן לט:), אַבָּא שָׁאוּל אוֹמֵר: הַכּוֹנֵס יְבִמְתּוֹ לְשׁוּם נוֹי וּלְשׁוּם אִישׁוּת — כְּאִילּוּ פּוֹגֵעַ בְּעֶרְוָה, וְקָרוֹב בְּעֵינַי לִהְיוֹת הַוָּלָד מַמְזֵר. מִנְיָנָא דְּרֵישָׁא. דְּמַשְׁמַע: ט"ו וְתוּ לָא. מִנְיָנָא דְּסֵיפָא. הֲרֵי אֵלּוּ פּוֹטְרוֹת, דְּמַשְׁמַע: אֵלּוּ וְתוּ לָא.

דְּרַב

תוספות

דילדה מן אבוך מן איתתא אוחרת או מן אמך מן גבר אוחרא. ואע"ג דדרשינן (לקמן כג.) "מולדת בית" וגו': בין שאומרים לאביך קיים, בין שאומרים לאביך הוצא — מ"מ אין מקרא יוצא מידי פשוטו. ואם היא בת שניסס — מק"ו הוא דילפת. אבל בכלל אשה ובתה הוי שפיר בת שהיא בת אשתו, כדאשכחן בפ' "ד' מיתות" (סנהדרין נג.). דאמו שהיא אשת אביו. הויא בכלל אשת אביו. ובת אשתו, היכא דנכנסה לחופה ולא נבעלה — נראה לר"י דחייב על בתה, אע"ג ד"ערות אשה ובתה לא תגלה" כתיב, דמשמע ביאה, דסברא הוא דאין תלוי בביאה, דהא לא מיחייב על בת אנוסתו, אלמא בקידושין תליא מלתא. ואין סברא לומר דבתרוייהו תליא מלתא, והא דלא מיחייב על בת אנוסתו, כמו שפי' בקונטרס — משום ד"אשה ובתה" כתיב, דמשמע לשון אישות, מדלא כתב "אם ובת". ומיהו, בהדיא בריש "נושאין על האנוסה" (לקמן ד' נז.) מפרש הש"ס טעמא אחרינא: דעריות "שאר" כתיב בהו, בנשואין איכא שאר, באונסין — ליכא שאר. **דאמר** רבא אמר לי רב יצחק בר אבדימי. יש מגיהין רב, משום דרב יצחק בר אבדימי היה רבו של רב, כדאמר בפרק "כל הבשר" (חולין דף קי. ושם): איכא תנא דאתנייה לרב כחל, אחוי ליה לרב יצחק בר אבדימי. ובפ' "כירה" (שבת מ: ושם): א"ר יצחק בר אבדימי, פעם אחת נכנסתי אחר רבי לבית המרחץ כו'. ולא היה רבא בימיו, דביום שמת רב יהודה נולד רבא, בפ' בתרא דקידושין (ד' עב:). ואר"ת: דע"כ גרסי' הכא רבא, שהיה בר פלוגתיה דאביי, ואמר בפ' "הנשרפין" (סנהדרין עו.) בתו מאנוסתו מנלן? אמר אביי: ק"ו, על בת בתו ענש — על בתו לא כ"ש? רבא אמר רב יצחק בר אבדימי כו'. וצ"ל דתרי יצחק בר אבדימי היו*). **מקמי** אשת אחיו שלא היה בעולמו. וה"ה מקמי אשת אחיו מאמו. וחדא מנייהו נקט, דתרוייהו לאו קרובי עצמו נינהו אלא ע"י קידושין. וכלתו שהיא אשת בנו קרובה מנייהו טפי. אבל אין לומר דוקא לגבי אשת אחיו שלא היה בעולמו כלתו קרובה טפי, לפי שלא היה בעולמו, אבל לגבי אשת אחיו מאמו — לא, דבאשת בנו איפלג דרא, כדאשכחן לענין עדות בב"ב (ד' קכח.), דאפי' מאן דמכשר באבא דאבא — פסיל בן אחיו. דע"כ לענין עריות אשת בנו קרובה טפי מאשת אח, שהבן כרעיה דאבוה הוא, דקחשיב בתו ובת בתו קרובי עצמו טפי מאחותו. **מאי** אירייא דתנא פוטרות. פי', דמשמע: אבל אי בעי מייבם — ליתני: אסורות לייבם. **אבל** מיחלץ חלצה קמ"ל. אע"ג דמסיפא שמעינן דרישא לא בעיא חליצה, דקתני בסיפא: כל שיכולה למאן כו' — מ"מ ניחא ליה נמי לאשמועינן ברישא גופיה**). **כיון** דבמקום מצוה הוא דאסירה צרה. ואי הוה תני אסורות הוה משמע כל שכן שלא במקום מצוה, כיון דאיסור צרה מחמת ערוה קאתי, מש"ה קתני פוטרות, דהשתא במקום מצוה הוא דאסור, משום דממילא קאי באיסור אשת אח. **דמצות** חליצה קודמת. השתא דקתני תרוייהו, ושונה חליצה ברישא, משמע דחליצה קודמת. אבל אי לא הוה תני אלא חליצה לחודה — לא הוה משמע מידי.

למעוטי

*) [וע' תוס' חגיגה יח: ד"ה לאמר וכו' ותוס' כתובות נו. ד"ה אמר ותוס' ב"ב פז. ד"ה מי כאן ותוס' מנחות נג. ד"ה רב חסדא ותוס' חולין קי. ד"ה איכא]

**) [וע"ע תוס' מנחות נג. ד"ה הכל סומכין]

גליון הש"ס

גמ' אם אתה אומר חולצת מתייבמת. לקמן דף לא ע"א קדושין דף סו ע"א: רש"י ד"ה ה"א מיחלץ חלצה וכו' וכל היכא דאמרי'. עי' לקמן ד' כא ע"א ועי"ק:

תוספות ישנים

אמר רבא אתיא הנה הנה לאיסורא. בבתו מאנוסתו מבתו מנשואתו ובקרא לערות אשה ובתה לא תגלה את בת בנה ואת בת בתה כתיב אישות ולשון אישות ע"י קדושין משמע. וא"כ (ס"ל) [היינו] נשואין. וקשה דאישות משמע שיש בה ביאה וא"כ נכנסה לחופה ולא נבעלה לא יהא בה איסור וזה לא יתכן. לכן נ"ל משום דגבי אשה כתיב שאר דכתיב א) שארה הנה ואין שאר אלא מן הנשואין אבל בלא ביאה שפיר קרויה שאר כיון שיש בה נשואין. הלכך מרבינן שפיר נכנסה לחופה ולא נבעלה כיון שיהיה יורש אותה משום קרא לשארו אע"ג דלא נבעלה דנשואין קורבה הן ומקרו שאר: **ואתיא** זמה זמה בתו מנשואתו מחמותו לשריפה ובתו מאנוסתו לשריפה מבתו מנשואתו מהנה הנה: ואין להקשות א"כ הול"ל ואתיא הנה הנה. וי"ל דיליף בתו מאנוסתו מבתו מנשואתו מה להלן הנה וזמה עמו אף כאן הנה וזמה עמו: **אי** תנא אוסרות הוה אמינא מחלץ חלצה. וא"ת היכי מצי למימר כן דלמא הוה תני אוסרות מן החליצה ומן הייבום. וי"ל דרוצה לומר ולתני אוסרות לבד והדר פריך ולתני אוסרות לחלוץ וקאמר לחלוץ מאי קעביד הלא לא שייך איסור בחליצ' [והדר] קאמר אלמה לא שייך בה שפיר איסור שאם אתה אומר חולצת מתייבמת וקאמר כיון דבמקום מצוה אסירא צרה היכא שהערוה נשאת לאחיו ושלא במקום מצוה כגון שנשאת לאדם מן השוק שאינו אחיו צרתה שריא מש"ה תני פוטרת דאי תניא אוסרות משמע שאיסור ערוה עומדת לעולם על הצרה והוה אסרינן [גם] שלא במקום מצוה דאמרינן השתא במקום מצוה אסירא שלא במקום מצוה לא כ"ש אבל השתא דתני פוטרות משמע שהערוה פוטרת הצרה ממצות יבום ועושה אותה כמאן דליכא מצוה ואסירא כאשת אחיו שלא במקום מצוה אבל היכא דליכא יבום לא עביד ערוה מידי ושריא צרה. ואם תקשי היאך נוכל לומר דאי היה תני אוסרות דאפילו שלא במקום מצוה נמי אסירי הא תני במתני' מן החליצה ומן הייבום אלמא דלא מיירי אלא במקום מצוה אלא ב) כלפי' הקונטרס דילפינן לה מכ"ש קמ"ל הא דתני פוטרות דמשמע שבשביל הערוה אין הצרה נאסרת כלל שלא במקום מצוה: וא"ת אפילו תנא מן הייבום לחודיה הוה ידענא דאינה חולצת מדתני פוטרות כדאמר לעיל וי"ל דה"פ לעיל אי תנא אוסרות הוה אמינא אוסרות לייבם. אבל מחלץ חלצה בעל כרחה קמ"ל פוטרות דאינן חולצות והכא ה"פ הוה אמינא מחלץ חלצה אם היא רוצה קמ"ל כל העולה וכו' דאינה חולצת מן התורה דהכי משמע קרא דאם לא יחפוץ וגו' ובאו הטערה אבל אם אינו יכול ליבם אין לב"ד לעסוק בזה אפי' אם היא רוצה. וכל היכא דקאמר חולצות ולא מתייבמות מיירי מדרבנן למעטם ספק אין לפוטרה בלא חליצה: **ולתני** מן הייבום ומן החליצה א"נ מן החליצה לחודה וקשה דהא אדרבה פסק ליה השתא דיבום הוי עיקר ואי גריס ליה יש ליישבו א"נ מן החליצה לחודה ומינה שמעינן דפטורה מיבום דאי לא מפטרא מחליצה לא מפטרא מיבום דכל העולה ליבום עולה לחליצה ומשני אבא שאול היא ולהכי תנא מן החליצה ומן הייבום להודיענו דמצות חליצה קודמת למצות יבום: **מניינא** דסיפא ורישא

א) נ"ע דשארה קאי על בתה ואמנם בתוס' לקמן (נ"ז) ד"ה עריות איתא כיון דכתיב שאר בקרא והיינו דכתיב בריש הפרשה אל כל שאר בשרו וגו'. ב) נראה דצ"ל הנה כבר פירש הקונטרס דהוי ילפינן לה מכ"ש וכו'.

ז א מיי' פ"י מהל' טומאת צרעת הל"ה ופ"ו מהל' יבום הלכה י:

לְמַעוּטֵי דְּרַב *וּדְרַב אַסִי. לְרַב וּלְרַב אַסִי לְמַעוּטֵי מַאי? אִי סְבִירָא לְהוּ דַּהֲדָדֵי — חֲדָא לְמַעוּטֵי צָרַת מְמָאֶנֶת, וַחֲדָא: לְמַעוּטֵי צָרַת מַחֲזִיר גְּרוּשָׁתוֹ. וְאִי לָא סְבִירָא לְהוּ דַּהֲדָדֵי — חֲדָא לְמַעוּטֵי דְּחַבְרֵיהּ, וַחֲדָא לְמַעוּטֵי אוֹ צָרַת מְמָאֶנֶת אוֹ צָרַת מַחֲזִיר גְּרוּשָׁתוֹ. לְרַב וּלְרַב אַסִי לִיתְנִינְהוּ! לְפִי שֶׁאֵינָהּ בְּצָרַת צָרָה. מנה"מ? דְּת"ר: °"אִשָּׁה אֶל אֲחוֹתָהּ לֹא תִקָּח לִצְרוֹר לְגַלּוֹת עֶרְוָתָהּ עָלֶיהָ בְּחַיֶּיהָ". "עָלֶיהָ" מַה ת"ל? לְפִי שֶׁנֶּאֱמַר °"יְבָמָהּ יָבֹא עָלֶיהָ" שׁוֹמֵעַ אֲנִי אֲפִי' בְּאַחַת מִכׇּל עֲרָיוֹת הָאֲמוּרוֹת בַּתּוֹרָה הַכָּתוּב מְדַבֵּר, נֶאֱמַר כָּאן "עָלֶיהָ" וְנֶאֱמַר לְהַלָּן "עָלֶיהָ", מַה לְּהַלָּן בִּמְקוֹם מִצְוָה — אַף כָּאן בִּמְקוֹם מִצְוָה, וְאָמַר רַחֲמָנָא "לֹא תִקָּח". וְאֵין לִי אֶלָּא הִיא, צָרָתָהּ מִנַּיִן? ת"ל "לִצְרוֹר"[א]. *וְאֵין לִי אֶלָּא צָרָתָהּ, צָרַת צָרָתָהּ מִנַּיִן? ת"ל "לִצְרוֹר" וְלֹא "לָצוּר". וְאֵין לִי אֶלָּא אֲחוֹת אִשָּׁה, שְׁאָר עֲרָיוֹת מִנַּיִן? אָמַרְתָּ: מָה אֲחוֹת אִשָּׁה מְיוּחֶדֶת — שֶׁהִיא עֶרְוָה, וְחַיָּיבִין עַל זְדוֹנָהּ כָּרֵת וְעַל שִׁגְגָתָהּ חַטָּאת, וַאֲסוּרָה לְיַבֵּם, אַף כׇּל שֶׁהִיא עֶרְוָה, וְחַיָּיבִין עַל זְדוֹנָהּ כָּרֵת וְעַל שִׁגְגָתָהּ חַטָּאת — אֲסוּרָה לְיַבֵּם. וְאֵין לִי אֶלָּא הֵן, צָרוֹתֵיהֶן מִנַּיִן? אָמַרְתָּ: מָה אֲחוֹת אִשָּׁה מְיוּחֶדֶת — שֶׁהִיא עֶרְוָה וְחַיָּיבִין עַל זְדוֹנָהּ כָּרֵת וְעַל שִׁגְגָתָהּ חַטָּאת, וַאֲסוּרָה לְיַבֵּם, וְצָרָתָהּ אֲסוּרָה — אַף כׇּל שֶׁהִיא עֶרְוָה וְחַיָּיבִין עַל זְדוֹנָהּ כָּרֵת וְעַל שִׁגְגָתָהּ חַטָּאת וַאֲסוּרָה לְיַבֵּם צָרָתָהּ אֲסוּרָה. מִכָּאן אָמְרוּ חֲכָמִים: חֲמֵשׁ עֶשְׂרֵה נָשִׁים פּוֹטְרוֹת צָרוֹתֵיהֶן וְצָרוֹת צָרוֹתֵיהֶן מִן הַחֲלִיצָה וּמִן הַיִּיבּוּם עַד סוֹף הָעוֹלָם. יָכוֹל שֶׁאֲנִי מְרַבֶּה אַף שֵׁשׁ עֲרָיוֹת *חֲמוּרוֹת מֵאֵלּוּ שֶׁיְּהוּ צָרוֹתֵיהֶם אֲסוּרוֹת! אָמַרְתָּ: מָה אֲחוֹת אִשְׁתּוֹ מְיוּחֶדֶת, שֶׁהִיא עֶרְוָה, וְחַיָּיבִין עַל זְדוֹנָהּ כָּרֵת וְעַל שִׁגְגָתָהּ חַטָּאת, וְאֶפְשָׁר לִינָּשֵׂא לָאַחִים וַאֲסוּרָה לְיַבֵּם — וְצָרָתָהּ אֲסוּרָה, אַף כׇּל שֶׁהִיא עֶרְוָה, וְחַיָּיבִין עַל זְדוֹנָהּ כָּרֵת וְעַל שִׁגְגָתָהּ חַטָּאת וְאֶפְשָׁר לִינָּשֵׂא לָאַחִים וַאֲסוּרָה לְיַבֵּם — צָרָתָהּ אֲסוּרָה. יָצְאוּ שֵׁשׁ עֲרָיוֹת חֲמוּרוֹת מֵאֵלּוּ, הוֹאִיל דְּאִי אֶפְשָׁר לִינָּשֵׂא לָאַחִים — צָרוֹתֵיהֶן מוּתָּרוֹת, שֶׁאֵין צָרָה אֶלָּא מֵאָח. אַזְהָרָה שָׁמַעְנוּ, עוֹנֶשׁ מִנַּיִן? אָמַר קְרָא °"כִּי כׇּל (אִישׁ) אֲשֶׁר יַעֲשֶׂה מִכֹּל הַתּוֹעֵבוֹת וגו'". טַעְמָא דִּכְתַב רַחֲמָנָא "עָלֶיהָ", הָא לָאו הָכִי ה"א אֲחוֹת אִשָּׁה מִיַּיבֶּמֶת, מַאי טַעְמָא? [א]דְּאָמְרִינַן: אָתֵי עֲשֵׂה וְדָחֵי לֹא תַעֲשֶׂה, אֵימַר דְּאָמְרִינַן אָתֵי עֲשֵׂה וְדָחֵי לֹא תַעֲשֶׂה — לֹא תַעֲשֶׂה גְּרֵידָא, לֹא תַעֲשֶׂה שֶׁיֵּשׁ בּוֹ כָּרֵת מִי דָּחֵי? וְתוּ: לֹא תַעֲשֶׂה גְּרֵידָא מְנָלַן דְּדָחֵי — דִּכְתִיב

(ויקרא יח; דברים כה; ויקרא יח)

רש"י

דְּרַב וּדְרַב אַסִי. דְּאָמַר רַב: צָרַת סוֹטָה אֲסוּרָה, שֶׁאִם זִינְּתָה אִשְׁתּוֹ וְלוֹ אִשָּׁה אַחֶרֶת, וּמֵת בְּלֹא בָּנִים — שְׁתֵּיהֶן פְּטוּרוֹת. וְרַב אַסִי אָמַר: צָרַת אַיְלוֹנִית אֲסוּרָה, שֶׁאִם הָיָה נָשׂוּי אַיְלוֹנִית וְאִשָּׁה אַחֶרֶת, וּמֵת בְּלֹא בָּנִים — שְׁתֵּיהֶן פְּטוּרוֹת. וְתַרְוַויְיהוּ בְּפִירְקִין (דף יא.). צָרַת מְמָאֶנֶת. הֲרֵי שֶׁהָיָה לְאָחִיו יְתוֹמָה קְטַנָּה וְאִשָּׁה אַחֶרֶת, וּמֵת, וּמֵיאֲנָה הַקְּטַנָּה בְּיָבָם זֶה — הִיא וְצָרָתָהּ אֲסוּרָה לוֹ. וּמַתְנִי' אַשְׁמְעִי' דְּאַף ע"ג דַּאֲסִירָא עֲלֵיהּ — לָא מִיפַּטְרָה מֵחֲלִיצָה. דְּהָךְ אִיסּוּרָא מִדְּרַבָּנַן הִיא, כִּדְאִיתָא בְּפִירְקִין: גְּזֵירָה מִשּׁוּם צָרַת בִּתּוֹ מְמָאֶנֶת. מַחֲזִיר גְּרוּשָׁתוֹ. אָחִיו שֶׁגֵּירֵשׁ אַחַת מִשְּׁתֵּי נָשָׁיו, וְנִשֵּׂאת לְאַחֵר, וְעָבַר וְהֶחֱזִירָהּ לְאַחַר מִיתַת בַּעֲלָהּ, וּמֵת בְּלֹא בָּנִים — שְׁתֵּיהֶן אֲסוּרוֹת א] לְהִתְיַיבֵּם. וְאַשְׁמוּעִינַן מִיעוּטָא דְּמַתְנִי' דַּחֲלִיצָה בָּעְיָא. לִיתְנִינְהוּ. לְסוֹטָה וְאַיְלוֹנִית בַּהֲדֵי הָנָךְ דְּמַתְנִי', הוֹאִיל וּפוֹטְרוֹת צָרוֹתֵיהֶן: לְפִי שֶׁאֵינָן בְּצָרַת צָרָה. דְּכׇל הָנָךְ דְּמַתְנִי' אִיכָּא לְמִיתְנֵי הִלְכָּה צָרָתָהּ וְנִשֵּׂאת לְאָחִיו הַשֵּׁנִי כו' — שֶׁהֲרֵי אֵינָהּ עֶרְוָה אֶלָּא לָזֶה, אֲבָל לְאָחִיו הַשֵּׁנִי רְאוּיוֹת הֵן. וְאִם יִיבֵּם אֲפִי' אֶת הַנׇּכְרִיָּה וְלוֹ אִשָּׁה אַחֶרֶת, וּמֵת, וְנָפְלוּ לִפְנֵי זֶה — פְּטוּרָה אַף הַנׇּכְרִית, מִפְּנֵי שֶׁהִיא צָרַת צָרָתָהּ שֶׁל בִּתּוֹ. אֲבָל בְּסוֹטָה וְאַיְלוֹנִית לֵיכָּא לְמִיתְנֵי הִלְכָה צָרָתָהּ וְנִשֵּׂאת לְאָחִיו הַשֵּׁנִי, דְּהָא עַל כׇּל הָאַחִין הִיא אֲסוּרָה, וְשֶׁהָאִיסּוּר בָּא לָהּ מִכֹּחַ קִדּוּשֵׁי בַּעְלָהּ הָרִאשׁוֹן, וְכוּלָּן שָׁוִין בָּהֶן. מנה"מ. דְּעֶרְוָה וְצָרָתָהּ וְצָרַת צָרָתָהּ לְעוֹלָם פְּטוּרוֹת. עָלֶיהָ מַה תַּלְמוּד לוֹמַר. לִכְתּוֹב "לְגַלּוֹת עֶרְוָתָהּ בְּחַיֶּיהָ", וְתִשְׁמַע נַמִי שֶׁבְּחַיֵּי אִשְׁתּוֹ נֶאֱסֶרֶת עָלָיו אֲחוֹתָהּ, וּלְאַחַר מִיתָה מוּתֶּרֶת. שׁוֹמֵעַ אֲנִי. אֲפִי' נָפְלָה לְפָנָיו לְיִיבּוּם אַחַת מִן הָעֲרָיוֹת — תִּתְיַיבֵּם: לִצְרוֹר. צָרוֹת הַרְבֵּה מַשְׁמַע, מִדְּלָא כְּתִיב "לָצוּר". זְדוֹנָהּ כָּרֵת. בְּפָרָשַׁת עֲרָיוֹת (ויקרא יח) כְּתִיב בָּתַר כּוּלְּהוּ "וְנִכְרְתוּ הַנְּפָשׁוֹת הָעוֹשׂוֹת", וְכׇל שֶׁזְּדוֹנוֹ כָּרֵת — שִׁגְגָתוֹ חַטָּאת, כִּדְיָלֵיף בְּפִירְקִין (דף ט.). ט"ו נָשִׁים. תּוּ לֵיכָּא עֲרָיוֹת בְּכָרֵת, חוּץ מִשֵּׁשׁ עֲרָיוֹת שֶׁל מִשְׁנָתֵינוּ שֶׁאֵין בָּהֶם צַד יִיבּוּם לְעוֹלָם. יָכוֹל שֶׁאֲנִי מְרַבֶּה כו'. שֶׁנְּשׂוּאוֹת לַאֲחֵרִים, שֶׁיְּהוּ צָרוֹתֵיהֶן אֲסוּרוֹת לִינָּשֵׂא לָזֶה. שֶׁאֵין צָרָה אֶלָּא מֵאָח. הוֹאִיל וּפְטָרָהּ הַכָּתוּב מִזִּיקָתוֹ — הֲרֵי הִיא עָלָיו בְּאִיסּוּר אֵשֶׁת אָח שֶׁיֵּשׁ לָהּ בָּנִים, שֶׁהִיא בְּכָרֵת, דִּכְתִיב "עֶרְוַת אֵשֶׁת אָחִיךָ", אֲבָל בְּעָלְמָא — לָא רָמְיָ' אִיסּוּר אֵשֶׁת אָח עֲלָהּ, וְשַׁרְיָא לֵיהּ. עוֹנֶשׁ מִנַּיִן. אִם יִיבֵּם עֶרְוָה אוֹ צָרָתָהּ. ה"א אֲחוֹת אִשָּׁה מִיַּיבֶּמֶת. מִיַּיבֵּם. מַאי טַעְמָא. וַהֲלֹא בְּכָרֵת קָאֵי עֲלָהּ. דְּאָתֵי עֲשֵׂה. דְּיִיבּוּם. וְדָחֵי אֶת לֹא תַעֲשֶׂה. דְּמִקְּרָא יָלְפִינַן דְּאָתֵי עֲשֵׂה וְדָחֵי ל"ת, כִּדְמְפָרֵשׁ וְאָזֵיל. לֹא

תוספות

למעוטי דרב ודרב אסי. וא"ת: לימעט תרוייהו ממניינא דרישא, דכיון דתנן ט"ו נשים ליכא למימר שייר, וממעטי כולהו מדלא קתני להו, כדאמר בפ"ק דקדושין (דף טז:) וכ"ת תנא ושייר — והא ארבעה קתני! *וי"ל: דהכא לא מצי למיתנינהו, כדמסיק, לפי שאינן בצרת צרה, וליכא למעוטי מדלא קתני להו, אלא מייתורא דמתני'. וטעמא דרב אסי ודפליג עליה אפרש לקמן (א) בע"ה.

לפי שאינן בצרת צרה. וא"ת: דמשכחת לה צרת צרה לענין בועל, שנשאת לאחיו (ב) ולו אשה אחרת ומת בלא בנים, דפוטרת צרתה מן הבועל. דלענין בועל נמי טומאה בה כמו לענין בעל, ואם הלכה הצרה ונשאת לאחיו השני, ולו אשה אחרת, ומת, כשם שהיא פטורה כך צרתה פטורה! וי"ל: דכיון דלגבי בעל לא משכחת צרת צרה אין לנו להחמיר בטומאה דגבי בועל יותר מטומאה דגבי הבעל. ועוד אר"י: דדוקא בטומאה דכתיב גבי בעל הוי כעריות, דכתיב בלשון לאו "לא יוכל בעלה וגו'" (דברים כד), אבל בבועל לא כתיב לאו, אלא "ונסתרה והיא נטמאה" (במדב' ה). והא דפריך לקמן (ד' יא:) (ג): נבעלה טומאה כתיבה בה "ונסתרה והיא נטמאה", דמשמע דמהאי לחודיה דריש "טומאה" כתיב בה כעריות — מצית למימר דלמאי דמשני למיקם עלה בלאו לא סגי בההוא ד"ונסתרה והיא נטמאה".

מה אחות אשה מיוחדת כו'. וא"ת: מה לאחות אשה — שכן בידו לרבות, כדפריך בפ' "הבא על יבמתו" (לקמן דף נד. ושם)! וי"ל: דאהיקש דר' יונה דסוף שמעתין (דף ח.) סמיך. **יכול** שאני מרבה אף שש עריות חמורות מאלו. הה"ל: יכול שאני מרבה אף שלא במקום מצוה.

טעמא דכתב רחמנא "עליה" הא לאו הכי הוה אמינא אחות אשה מייבמת. ותימה לר"י דמנא ליה הא? נימא דאי לאו "עליה" נמי אחות אשה לא מתייבמת, דאין עשה דוחה לא תעשה שיש בו כרת, ואיצטריך "עליה" למיסר לאשמעינן דבעלמא דחי! דכה"ג אמר לקמן: טעמא דכתב רחמנא "את שבתותי תשמורו" הא לאו הכי — דחי. וכ"ת דאשומע אני דברייתא קפריך, דמשמע לישנא דאי לאו עליה ה"א דדחי — א"כ מאי משני רבא בסוף מסקנא ערוה גופיה לא צריכא קרא, דאין עשה דוחה ל"ת שיש בו כרת? אלא ע"כ שומע אני לאו דוקא, והכי קאמר(ד): אם ת"ל דדחי — הא כתיב "עליה". ומיהו, עיקרא לאו להכי אתא. ואר"י: דאי בעלמא אין עשה דוחה לא תעשה שיש בו כרת — לא ה"ל לתנא למדרש "עליה" לאיסורא, ולא יצטרך לגופיה, אלא לאשמעינן דבעלמא דחי. אלא ה"ל למידרש להיתירא: נאמר כאן "עליה" ונאמר להלן "עליה" מה להלן באחות אשה אף כאן באחות אשה, ואמר רחמנא "יבמה יבא עליה". דמסתבר טפי למדרש הכי ולאוקמי קרא לגופיה. אלא ודאי סבר האי תנא עשה דוחה לא תעשה שיש בו כרת, ולא צריך קרא להיתירא. ולהכי דריש ליה לגופיה לאיסורא. ורב אשי דפריך לקמן (דף ח:): ממאי דהאי "עליה" לאיסורא, דילמא להיתירא — ארבא, דמסיק דאין עשה דוחה ל"ת שיש בו כרת פריך, כמו שפי' ר"י ברבי מאיר. אבל כל כמה דס"ד דדחי — לא מצי למיפרך הכי. ורבא לא הוה ס"ל אלא להיתירא לא מצית אמרת, דא"כ לגלות ערותה דחדא היכי משכחת לה? כדמשני לקמן אקושיא דרב אשי. דעיקר דקדוק הש"ס הוא מכח דלא דריש להיתירא, אלא לפי דעתו של מקשה היה פשוט דעשה דוחה לא תעשה שיש בו כרת, השיב לו רבא האמת, דאינו כן. **לא** תעשה שיש בו כרת מי דחי. וא"ת: ואמאי לא ילפינן דלידחי מעשה דייבום דדחי לא תעשה דכרת דאשת אח? וכ"ת דהיינו הא דקאמר לקמן (דף ז.) אלא איצטריך, סד"א תיתי אחות אשה במה מצינו מאשת אח, דא"כ היכי דחי עלה: מי דמי? התם חדא איסורא, הכא תרי איסורי. הא לא מפלגינן בשום מקום וילפינן מכלאים בציצית — אפי' תרי איסורי. היכי בעי למילף? ועוד: דלקמן, כי בעי למילף מפסח תמיד ומילה, לא פרכינן הכי. ועוד: דשביק הש"ס אשת אח דקאי בה, ולא מסיק לה אלא לבסוף. ועוד: דחדא איסורא מיהא נילף מאשת אח! אלא, על כרחך לקמן לאו בכל דוכתי בעי למילף מאשת אח קאמר, אלא דוקא אחות אשה. כדמסיק

תוספות ישנים

... שאין צרה אלא מאח. ואי ק"ל אמאי אצטריך למימר שאין צרה אלא מאח ולא סגי ליה בהואיל וא"א להנשא לאחין וכו'. דהא ודאי שמעינן מינה דאלו שש עריות חמורות הואיל ולא אפשר להנשא לאחין צרותיהן ... בק דאצטריך דאי לא הוה אמר אלא יצאו שש עריות כו' הוה אמינא הני שש עריות הוא לצרותיהן מותרות משום דלא אפשר להו למיהוי במקום מצוה כלל אבל הנך ט"ו הוה אמינא דהואיל והוו במקום ... שלא במקום מצוה צרותיהן אסורות ומעיקרא נמי כי אמר יכול שאני מרבה אף שש עריות חמורות מה טעם מפני שהוקשו כל העריות זו לזו וכיון דמקשינן הני שש לט"ו דהם כולם אסורות נקיט נמי ט"ו לשש מה ... מצוה אף הכא נמי שלא במקום מצוה ואמינא דהני ט"ו אפילו שלא במקום מצוה אסורות ולהכי אצטריך ליה למימר שאין צרה אלא מאח ב) ט"ו אינן אסורות אלא במקום מצוה אבל שלא במקום מצוה שרו:
... ס"ל לשמואל לצרת ממאנת כו'. ב) נ"ל כדי לאשמעינן דאפילו אלו הט"ו אינן אסורות כו'.

הגהות הב"ח

הגהות הגר"א

[א] גמ' ...

גליון הש"ס

גמ' לפי שאינה בצרת צרה. ...

הגהות מהר"ב רנשבורג

א] רש"י ד"ה מחזיר גרושתו וכו' שתיהן אסורות להתייבם. נ"ב עי' חדושי רמב"ן ורשב"א ולקמן דף יא ע"ב ודף יב ע"א וצ"ע ודו"ק:

(דברים כב) דכתיב °"לא תלבש שעטנז גדלים תעשה לך", ואמר רבי אלעזר: *סמוכים מן התורה (תהלים קיא) מנין — שנאמר °"סמוכים לעד לעולם עשוים באמת וישר". *ואמר רב ששת אמר ר' אלעזר משום רבי אלעזר בן עזריה: אמנין ליבמה שנפלה לפני מוכה שחין שאין חוסמין אותה (דברים כה) — שנאמר °"לא תחסום שור בדישו" וסמיך ליה "כי ישבו אחים יחדיו". *ואמר רב יוסף: אפילו למאן דלא דריש סמוכים בעלמא — במשנה תורה דריש, דהא ר' יהודה בעלמא *לא דריש, ובמשנה תורה דריש. ובעלמא מנלן דלא (שמות כב) דריש? דתניא, *בן עזאי אומר: נאמר °"מכשפה לא תחיה" ונאמר "כל שוכב עם בהמה מות יומת", סמכו ענין לו, מה שוכב עם בהמה בסקילה — באף מכשפה בסקילה. א"ל ר' יהודה: וכי מפני שסמכו ענין לו נוציא זה לסקילה? אלא אוב וידעוני בכלל מכשפים היו, ולמה יצאו — להקיש להם, ולומר לך: מה אוב וידעוני בסקילה — אף מכשפה בסקילה. ובמשנה תורה מנלן דדריש — דתנן: *גנושא אדם אנוסת אביו ומפותת אביו, אנוסת בנו ומפותת בנו. רבי יהודה אוסר באנוסת אביו ומפותת אביו ואמר רב גידל אמר רב: מ"ט דרבי יהודה (דברים כג) — דכתיב °"לא יקח איש את אשת אביו ולא יגלה כנף אביו" *כנף שראה אביו לא יגלה. וממאי דבאנוסה כתיב — מעילויה דקרא, דכתיב (שם כב) °"ונתן האיש השוכב עמה לאבי הנערה חמשים כסף" וסמיך ליה "לא יקח איש וגו'". ורבנן: אי הוה סמיך ליה — כדקאמרת, השתא דלא סמיך ליה (דכתיב "לא יקח איש את אשת אביו" בנתים) — בשומרת יבם הכתוב מדבר, *ולעבור עליו בשני לאוין. ובמשנה תורה מאי טעמא דדריש? איבעית אימא משום דמוכח, ואיבעית אימא משום דמופני. איבעית אימא משום דמוכח — דאם כן, לכתביה רחמנא גבי עריות. ואיבעית אימא משום דמופני, דאם כן, לכתוב רחמנא "לא יקח איש את אשת אביו", "לא יגלה כנף אביו" למה לי? ש"מ

רש"י

לא תלבש שעטנז. וסמיך ליה "גדילים תעשה לך", ודרשינן סמוכין, ושרינן כלאים בציצית — אלמא אתי עשה ודחי לא תעשה. שאין חוסמין. אין (א) [סותמין] טענותיה לכופה להתייבם לו, אלא כופין אותו וחולץ. חוסמין — לישנא דקרא קא נקט, דיליף לה מ"לא תחסום". וסמיך ליה כו'. אלמא: דרשינן סמוכין. וגבי כלאים בציצית נמי דרשינן. במשנה תורה דריש. והאי סמוכים דכלאים בציצית — במשנה תורה הוא, ודרשינן: סמכו ענין לו. ענין הפרשה (ב), סמוכה פרשת מכשף אצל שוכב עם בהמה, דגבי הדדי כתיבי. מכשפה לא תחיה. בספר "ואלה שמות". מה שוכב עם בהמה בסקילה. דכתיב באשה הנרבעת לבהמה "דמיהם בם", וכל "דמיהם בם" בסקילה היא, דגמרינן (סנהדרין דף נד.) מאוב וידעוני, דכתיב בהו "ירגמו אותם דמיהם בם" (ויקרא כ): נוציא זה. מכשף: לסקילה. שהיא מיתה חמורה מכולן: בכלל מכשפה היו. שנאמר "לא תחיה". להקיש אליהן. שזו מדה בתורה: כל דבר שהיה בכלל ויצא מן הכלל ללמד — לא ללמד על עצמו יצא, אלא ללמד על הכלל כולו יצא. נושא אדם אנוסת אביו. שלא נאסרה עליו עולמית אלא אשת אביו, כדכתיב (ויקרא יח) "ערות אשת אביך", ו"אשת" משמע ע"י אישות דקדושין. אנוסת בנו. לאו כלתו היא, דאין כלה אלא מקודשת וראויה לחופה (ג): ה"ג. ורבנן אי הוה סמיך ליה כדקאמרת, השתא דלא סמיך ליה בשומרת יבם כו'. לא סמיך ליה, דכתיב "לא יקח איש את אשת אביו" בנתים. דמוכח. מוכח למדרשינהו אהדדי סמכינהו. לכתביה רחמנא. להאי "לא יגלה כנף אביו" לגבי עריות — אי לאפנויי לאוי גבי אשת אב קאתי.

לאפנויי

תוספות

כדמסיק טעמא הואיל ואישתרי — אישתרי. ולהכי קאמר תיתי אחות אשה מאשת אח, ולא קאמר תיתי מאשת אח, כדאמר בכל הני דלקמן: תיתי ממילה, תיתי מכיבוד אב, ואינו מזכיר אחות אשה, משום דלמילף בכל דוכתין קאתי. ואומר ר"י: דמאשת אח לא מצי למילף בעלמא דלידחי עשה לא תעשה שיש בו כרת, דשאני אשת אח דמצותו בכך, ואי אפשר בענין אחר לקיים מצות יבום, דאל"כ — בטלה מצות יבום. אבל מכלאים בציצית ילפי' שפיר בעלמא, דאי לא מקיימת מצות תכלת בפשתי' — מקיימת בצמר, ואפ"ה דחי. וכן "וגלח את כל שערו" דמצורע מיקיים בשער דהיתר, ד"כל שערו" קרינא ביה, כמו "כל מלאכה לא תעשו" דשבת, דלא קאי אלא אמלאכות דלא דחו שבת. א"נ: "כל שערו" ממש, ובנמרטו פאת ראשו וזקנו, וכן כל הני דמייתו — מיקיימי בדוכתא אחריתי.

דכתיב לא תלבש שעטנז וסמיך ליה גדילים וכו'. ואיפכא ליכא למימר, דבמקום גדילים לא תלבש שעטנז כדאמר בסמוך במקום "כי ישבו" "לא תחסום" — דא"כ לשתוק קרא מיניה וממילא ידעינן דלא דחי עשה דציצית לאו דכלאים. וגבי יבמה נמי בסמוך ליכא למידרש כי הכא, דבלאו קרא ה"א דחוסמין אותה, ולא יחלוץ לה על כרחו. הקשה ה"ר יעקב דאורליינ"ש: דליחייבו נשים בציצית, דאית לן למימר כל שישנו ב"לא תלבש שעטנז" ישנו ב"גדילים". אף ע"ג דלאו היקש הוא אלא סמוכים דתרי קראי נינהו — מ"מ דרשינן הכי בפ"ק דערכין (דף ג:) וב"התכלת" (מנחות מג.) דקאמר: הכל חייבין בציצית כהנים לוים וישראלים, ומסיק דכהנים איצטריך ליה, סד"א: הואיל ואישתרי גבייהו כלאים — בציצית נמי לא לחייבו, קמ"ל: נהי דאישתרי בעידן עבודה, שלא בעידן עבוד' — לא אישתרי. דמשמע דאי אישתרי לגמרי — הוו מיפטרי בציצית, דהוה דרשינן: כל שאינו בלא תלבש שעטנז — אינו בגדילים, כ"ש שיש לנו לדרוש לחומרא ולחייב נשים בציצית! וי"ל: דהא דנשים פטורות בצילי' — היינו משום דיליף לה (קדושין לה.) רב אחא בר יעקב דמ"ע שהזמן גרמא נשים פטורות, דהוקשה כל התורה לתפילין, והקישא עדיף מסמוכים. ולמ"ד דתפילין לאו מ"ע שהזמן גרמא נינהו — אפשר דלדידיה נשים חייבות בציצית מסמוכין, דבלא"ה נמי לרבנן דר' *ישמעאל בפ' "התכלת" (מנחות מג. ושם) סבר נשים חייבות בציצית, דמחייבי ציצית בלילה, והוי שלא הזמן גרמא. וקשה: הא דדייק בפ' "התכלת" דרב יהודה סבר דציצית מ"ע שלא הזמן גרמא מדרמי תכלת לפורזומא דאינשי ביתיה, וממאי? דלמא אע"ג דסבר דהוי הזמן גרמא — מיחייב נשים מסמוכין! וי"ל: דעדיפא מינה משני ליה התם. ומיהו, קשה למאן דפטר נשים מציצית — ה"ל למיפטרינהו מכלאים, וע"כ נשים חייבות בכלאים, דאמר ספ"ק דבילה (דף יד:) כלאים למאי חזו? ושמא איכא שום ריבוי לענין כלאים*א). **וכי** מפני שסמכו ענין לו כו'. וא"ת: דלמא הכא הוא דלא דריש סמוכים משום ג"ש דדריש ר' יוסי הגלילי בפ' "ד' מיתות" (סנהדרין סז. ושם) דמפקא [מסמוכים] דדריש מ"לא תחיה כל נשמה" דבסייף! תדע, דאטו ר"ע דגמר התם דבסקילה מ"אם בהמה אם איש לא יחיה", מי נימא דלא סבר כרבנן דדרשי סמוכים בכל מקום? אלא איצטריך ע"כ משום ג"ש דמפקא מסמוכים! וי"ל: דהכא דייק מלישנא דר' יהודה, דקאמר "וכי מפני שסמכו", משמע דלא דריש סמוכים בעלמא. והא דדריש ר' יהודה סמוכים בפ"ב דקידושין (דף נג.) דקתני: יכול לא יחלקו בקדשי קדשים אבל יחלקו בקדשים קלים, ת"ל "איש כאחיו" וסמיך ליה "אם על תודה" וקאמר *התם: סיפרא מני — ר' יהודה! איכא למימר דהתם וי"ו מוסיף על ענין ראשון דריש, דכתיב "וזאת תורת זבח השלמים". א"נ: משום דמוכח דמדלא כתיב בפרשת ויקרא. א"נ: משום מופנה, ד"איש כאחיו" מיותר, דה"ל למיכתב "לכל בני אהרן תהיה" ותו לא. והא דקאמר במשנה תורה דריש א]ה"ה בעלמא, אלא דבמשנה תורה קים ליה דכולהו מוכח או מופנה, ולא חש להביא אלא אחד מהם. **וסמיך** ליה "לא יקח איש את אשת אביו". ורבנן לא דרשי, משום ד"לא יקח" מפסיק בין פרשת אונס ל"לא יגלה". **דא"כ** לכתביה גבי עריות. דאע"ג דאיצטריך למיכתביה הכא להיקישא ל"לא יבא ממזר", דמהכא דרשינן ממאי הוה ממזר, בין לר"ע בין לרבנן. בפרק "החולץ" (לקמן דף מט.) — התם נמי סמוכין נינהו, ודרשינן מטעם דמוכח או מופנה. וא"ת: גבי מכשפה נמי לדרוש ר' יהודה, דמוכחא מילתא מדלא כתיב "כל שוכב עם בהמה" גבי עריות! וי"ל: דלא שייך גבי עריות, דאין זנות לבהמה. א"נ: לא חשיב מוכח, כיון שהלמד נכתב במקומו. ומיהו, לענין מופנה לא איכפת לן בהי מינייהו. **אם** כן לכתוב רחמנא "לא יקח איש" וגו' "לא יגלה כנף אביו" למה לי. מדנקט לא יגלה בלא וי"ו — משמע דאכוליה קרא בעי למה לי, וקשה: דלמא מיבעי ליה לשומרת יבם, כדדרשי ליה רבנן לקמן: ואית דגרסי: "ולא יגלה כנף אביו" למה לי, ומפרש דאאביו קא בעי למה לי, דפשיטא ליה דלאביו קאי. אבל "לא יגלה" — מצי למימר דדרשי ליה לשומרת יבם כמו רבנן. וריב"ן פי': דשפיר גרס "לא יגלה" בלא וי"ו, ואכוליה קרא קבעי למה לי, דמשמע ליה להש"ס דלא מוקי ליה בשומרת יבם של אביו, כיון דבלאו הכי איכא איסור יבמה לשוק ואיסור דודתו, ולא מוקמינן ליה בלאוי יתירא היכא דאיכא למידרש. ובפ' "נושאין על האנוסה" (לקמן נז.) אמרי' נמי דלרבנן לא איצטריך לשומרת יבם אלא לעבור עליה בג' לאוין.

מכדי

עין משפט נר מצוה

ח א מיי' פ"ב מהל' יבום הלכה יד סמג עשין נא טוש"ע אה"ע סימן קסה סעיף ד [וברב אלפס פרק ז דכתובות דף קא:]:

ט ב מיי' פי"א מהל' עבודת כוכבים הל' טו סמג לאוין נה טוש"ע י"ד סימן קעט:

י ג מיי' פ"ב מהל' איסורי ביאה הל' יג:

תוספות ישנים

א) ועוד י"ל כיון דאיכא קרא דממעט להו בני ישראל ולא בנות [ישראל] וש"מ דאין להקשות [להדדי] דלימא כל שישנו בלא תלבש ישנו בגדילים וכן איפכא. משום דלאו בחד זימנא הוו תרוייהו חד הוי הזמן גרמא וחד אין הוי הזמן גרמא ואין להשוותם לא בחיובם ולא בפטורם. ולא דמי להא דאמרינן כל שישנו בבל תאכל חמץ ישנו בקום אכול מצה דבחד זימנא אתנהו ובכלהו [הוי] זמן גרמא: **אלא** אוב וידעוני בכלל מכשפים היו כו'. והקשה הר' יעקב מאורליינ"ש אמאי לא אמרינן אוב וידעוני הוה דבר שהיה בכלל ויצא מן הכלל דמכשפה לידון בדבר החדש בסקילה וא"כ אי אתה רשאי להחזירו לכללו עד שיחזירנו הכתוב לכללו בפירוש וא"כ איך קאמר שמלמד על הכלל לומר מה אוב וידעוני בסקילה אף מכשפה בסקילה [וי"ל] דלא דמי לאשם מצורע דעוקרו ממש מן כלל שאר אשמות להיות כל דמו קרב על גבי המזבח ויצא למתן בהונות שלא תמצא כלל דין זה בשאר אשמות אבל בכאן מיתה היתה לו ויצא לידון לתוספת מיתה. ועי"ל דלא הוי דבר חדש כיון דחנק אינה מפורשת אלא אתא לאשמעינן דלא תיסק אדעתין לומר דהוא בחנק כמו שאר מיתה סתם האמורה בתורה אלא אתא אוב וידעוני לגלויי דהויא בסקילה וי"ל דאין זה נקרא דבר החדש כיון שאינו סותר הכלל שאינו רק מוסיף מיתה חמורה. וכן פי' הקונטרס לקמן גבי אשם מצורע:

[ועין תוס' פסחים מג: ד"ה ס"ד אמינא ותוס' ערכין ג: ד"ה הני כהנים]

[נ"ל סתם]

הגהות מהר"ב רנשבורג

א] תוס' ד"ה וכי מפני שסמכו ענין לו וכו' ה"ה בעלמא אלא דבמשנה תורה וכו'. נ"ב אבל הרא"ש סי' לד דף יד ע"ד בסופו כתב דדוקא במשנה תורה דריש ולא בכל התורה וטעמא משום דכל התורה מפי הגבורה נאמרה ואין מוקדם ומאוחר אבל משה שסידר משנה תורה פרשה אחר פרשה לא סידר אלא להדרש עכ"ל:

מסורת הש"ס

ברכות י. [ע"ש]

[מכות כב.]

ברכות כא:

[פסחים כח:]

סנהדרין סז.

ברכות כא: לקמן נז.

לקמן מט. [נז.]

רש"ל מ"ז

עיין תוספות חגיגה י: ד"ה לעבור

[נ"ל שמעון]

הגהות הב"ח

(א) רש"י ד"ה שאין חוסמין אין כו'. נ"ב עיין במכות דף כב ע"א [illegible] (ב) ד"ה סמכו ענין לו כו' [illegible] (ג) ד"ה אנוסת בנו וכו' [illegible]

ש"מ לְאַפְנוּיֵי. וְגַבֵּי צִיצִית נַמִי, אִיבָּעֵית אֵימָא מִשּׁוּם דְּמוּכָח, וְאִיבָּעֵית אֵימָא מִשּׁוּם דְּמוּפְנֶה. אִיבָּעֵית אֵימָא מִשּׁוּם דְּמוּכָח – דְּא"כ לִכְתְּבֵיהּ רַחֲמָנָא גַּבֵּי פָּרָשַׁת צִיצִית, לְמַאי הִלְכְתָא כְּתָבֵיהּ הָכָא. וְאִיבָּעֵית אֵימָא מִשּׁוּם דְּמוּפְנֶה, מִכְּדִי כְּתַב °"וּבֶגֶד כִּלְאַיִם שַׁעַטְנֵז לֹא יַעֲלֶה עָלֶיךָ" (ויקרא יט), "לֹא תִלְבַּשׁ שַׁעַטְנֵז" ל"ל? ש"מ לְאַפְנוּיֵי. הָנֵי מִצְרַךְ צְרִיכִי; דְּאִי כְּתַב רַחֲמָנָא "לֹא יַעֲלֶה עָלֶיךָ" הֲוָה אָמִינָא: כָּל דֶּרֶךְ הַעֲלָאָה אָסַר רַחֲמָנָא, וַאֲפִילּוּ מוֹכְרֵי כְּסוּת – כְּתַב רַחֲמָנָא "לֹא תִלְבַּשׁ שַׁעַטְנֵז" [א]דּוּמְיָא דִּלְבִישָׁה דְּאִית בֵּיהּ הֲנָאָה, וְאִי כְּתַב רַחֲמָנָא "לֹא תִלְבַּשׁ" ה"א: דַּוְקָא לְבִישָׁה דְּנָפֵישׁ הֲנָיָיתָהּ, אֲבָל הַעֲלָאָה לָא – [ב]כְּתַב רַחֲמָנָא "לֹא יַעֲלֶה עָלֶיךָ" – א"כ לִכְתּוֹב רַחֲמָנָא "לֹא תִלְבַּשׁ שַׁעַטְנֵז", "צֶמֶר וּפִשְׁתִּים" לָמָּה לִי? מִכְּדִי כְּתַב "וּבֶגֶד כִּלְאַיִם שַׁעַטְנֵז לֹא יַעֲלֶה עָלֶיךָ" *וְתָנָא דְּבֵי רַבִּי יִשְׁמָעֵאל: הוֹאִיל וְנֶאֶמְרוּ בַּתּוֹרָה סְתָם "בְּגָדִים" וּפָרַט לְךָ הַכָּתוּב בְּאֶחָד מֵהֶן "צֶמֶר וּפִשְׁתִּים" [ג]אַף כָּל צֶמֶר וּפִשְׁתִּים. צֶמֶר וּפִשְׁתִּים דִּכְתַב רַחֲמָנָא ל"ל? ש"מ לְאַפְנוּיֵי. וְאַכַּתִּי אִיצְטְרִיךְ, סד"א: הַעֲלָאָה הִיא, דְּלָא נָפֵישׁ הֲנָאָתָהּ, אֲבָל לְבִישָׁה דְּנָפֵישׁ הֲנָיָיתָהּ – כָּל תְּרֵי מִינֵי אָסַר רַחֲמָנָא, [ד]כְּתַב רַחֲמָנָא "צֶמֶר וּפִשְׁתִּים". א"כ לִשְׁתּוֹק קְרָא מִינֵּיהּ, וְתֵיתֵי "שַׁעַטְנֵז" "שַׁעַטְנֵז" מֵהַעֲלָאָה. וְתַנָּא דְּבֵי ר' יִשְׁמָעֵאל, טַעְמָא דִּכְתַב רַחֲמָנָא צֶמֶר וּפִשְׁתִּים, הָא לָאו הָכִי – כִּלְאַיִם בְּצִיצִית ה"א דְּאָסַר רַחֲמָנָא? וְהָכְתִיב °"וְעָשׂוּ לָהֶם צִיצִית עַל כַּנְפֵי בִגְדֵיהֶם" (במדבר טו), וְתָנָא דְּבֵי רַבִּי יִשְׁמָעֵאל: כָּל בְּגָדִים צֶמֶר וּפִשְׁתִּים הֵם, וְאָמַר רַחֲמָנָא: עֲבֵיד לֵיהּ תְּכֵלֶת, וּתְכֵלֶת עַמְרָא הוּא. וּמִמַּאי דִּתְכֵלֶת עַמְרָא הוּא? מִדְּשֵׁשׁ כִּיתָּנָא – תְּכֵלֶת עַמְרָא הוּא. אִיצְטְרִיךְ, סד"א כְּדְרָבָא. *דְּרָבָא רָמֵי: כְּתִיב "הַכָּנָף" – מִין כָּנָף, וּכְתִיב "צֶמֶר וּפִשְׁתִּים"! הָא כֵּיצַד? [ה]צֶמֶר וּפִשְׁתִּים פּוֹטְרִין בֵּין בְּמִינָן בֵּין שֶׁלֹּא בְּמִינָן, [ו]שְׁאָר מִינִין, בְּמִינָן פּוֹטְרִין, שֶׁלֹּא בְּמִינָן – אֵין פּוֹטְרִין. וְהָא תַּנָּא דְּבֵי רַבִּי יִשְׁמָעֵאל לֵית לֵיהּ דְּרָבָא! אִיצְטְרִיךְ, סד"א כִּי דִּיּוּקָא דְּרָבָא "הַכָּנָף" – מִין כָּנָף, וְה"ק רַחֲמָנָא: עֲבֵיד לֵיהּ צֶמֶר לְצֶמֶר וּפִשְׁתִּים לְפִשְׁתִּים, וְכִי עֲבֵידַתְּ צֶמֶר לְצֶמֶר – צְבָעֵיהּ, אֲבָל צֶמֶר לְפִשְׁתִּים וּפִשְׁתִּים לְצֶמֶר – לָא, כְּתַב רַחֲמָנָא "צֶמֶר וּפִשְׁתִּים" דַּאֲפִילּוּ צֶמֶר לְפִשְׁתִּים, וּפִשְׁתִּים לְצֶמֶר.

הֲדַרַן עֲלָךְ חֲמֵשׁ עֶשְׂרֵה נָשִׁים (printed as: תִּינַח)

רש"י

לְאַפְנוּיֵי. לַאֲנוּסָתוֹ שֶׁל אָבִיו, דְּיָלֵיף מִסְּמוּכִים דִּלְעֵיל. **לֹא תִלְבַּשׁ** שַׁעַטְנֵז לָמָּה לִי. שְׁמַע מִינַּהּ לְאַפְנוּיֵי וּלְמִדְרַשׁ סְמוּכִים. **וַאֲפִי'** מוֹכְרֵי כְּסוּת. שֶׁאֵין מִתְכַּוְּונִים לַהֲנָאַת חִימּוּם. **צֶמֶר וּפִשְׁתִּים** לָמָּה לִי. אִי לְאַשְׁמוּעִינַן דְּכִלְאַיִם צֶמֶר וּפִשְׁתִּים הוּא דְּקָאָסַר – לָא צְרִיךְ, דְּמִכְּדִי בְּכִלְאַיִם כְּתִיב "בֶּגֶד", וְתַנָּא דְּבֵי ר' יִשְׁמָעֵאל כו'. **בְּאֶחָד** מֵהֶם. גַּבֵּי נְגָעִים "בְּבֶגֶד צֶמֶר אוֹ בְּבֶגֶד פִּשְׁתִּים" (ויקרא יג). **וְאַכַּתִּי אִיצְטְרִיךְ.** לְמִכְתַּב צֶמֶר וּפִשְׁתִּים הָכָא גַּבֵּי לְבִישָׁה, וְאַע"ג דִּכְתִיב בֶּגֶד בְּהַעֲלָאָה דְּמַשְׁמַע צֶמֶר וּפִשְׁתִּים, דְּס"ד כו'. **וְתַנָּא דְּבֵי רַבִּי יִשְׁמָעֵאל.** דְּיָלְפִינַן אַלִּיבֵּיהּ כִּלְאַיִם בְּצִיצִית מִדְּאִייתַּר צֶמֶר וּפִשְׁתִּים לְמִיסְמְכֵיהּ "גְּדִילִים תַּעֲשֶׂה לָּךְ". **טַעְמָא דִּכְתַב רַחֲמָנָא כו'** כָּל בְּגָדִים צֶמֶר וּפִשְׁתִּים הֵם. וְהַאי "בִּגְדֵיהֶם" דְּצִיצִית מַשְׁמַע בֵּין שֶׁל צֶמֶר בֵּין שֶׁל פִּשְׁתִּים, וְאָמַר רַחֲמָנָא עֲבֵיד וּתְכֵלֶת נַמִי לְפִשְׁתִּים. **וּתְכֵלֶת עַמְרָא.** מִדְּשֵׁשׁ כִּיתָּנָא, דִּכְתִי' (שמות לט) "מִכְנְסֵי בַּד שֵׁשׁ מָשְׁזָר", וּבַד הַיְינוּ פִּשְׁתִּים, כִּדְמְפָרֵשׁ בְּ"בָא לוֹ כ"ג" בְּמַסֶּכֶת יוֹמָא (דף עא:): "בַּד" – דָּבָר הָעוֹלֶה בַּד בְּבַד; "תְּכֵלֶת" – עַמְרָא; וְכֵן שְׁאָר צְבָעִים הָאֲמוּרִים בְּבִגְדֵי כְהוּנָּה, אַרְגָּמָן וְתוֹלַעַת שָׁנִי; שֶׁאֵין בְּבִגְדֵי כְהוּנָּה אֶלָּא מִצֶּמֶר וּפִשְׁתִּים, דִּכְתִיב בְּסֵפֶר יְחֶזְקֵאל (מד) בְּיוֹה"כ "בִּגְדֵי פִשְׁתִּים יִלְבָּשׁוּ וְלֹא יַעֲלֶה עֲלֵיהֶם צֶמֶר", ש"מ שֶׁעֲבוֹדוֹת הַחִיצוֹנוֹת יֵשׁ בָּהֶם צֶמֶר עִם פִּשְׁתָּן וְלֹא מִין אַחֵר, וּמִדְּמְפָרֵשׁ קְרָא "שֵׁשׁ" בְּאֶחָד מִן הַמִּינִין, שְׁמַע מִינַּהּ שְׁאָר הַמִּינִין צֶמֶר הָיוּ. **סד"א כִּדְרָבָא.** אִי לָא כָּתַב רַחֲמָנָא צֶמֶר וּפִשְׁתִּים הֲוָה דָּרְשִׁי' "הַכָּנָף" – מִין כָּנָף, כְּרָבָא, לְמֵימַר דִּלְבֶגֶד פִּשְׁתִּים עֲשֵׂה פִּשְׁתָּן וּלְצֶמֶר עֲשֵׂה צֶמֶר וְלִבְעֵי' תְּכֵלֶת, אֲבָל כִּלְאַיִם לֹא, קמ"ל דְּרָשָׁא דִּסְמוּכִין דַּאֲפִילּוּ כִּלְאַיִם, וְהָכִי הָוֵי מַסְקָנָא דְּמִילְּתָא, אֶלָּא דְּקָא מְפָרֵשׁ וְאָזֵיל מִילְּתֵי' דְּרָבָא. **כְּתִיב הַכָּנָף.** עֲשֵׂה צִיצִית מִמִּין הַכָּנָף, וְאִם טַלִּית שֶׁל מֶשִׁי עֲשֵׂה צִיצִית שֶׁל מֶשִׁי, וּכְתִיב צֶמֶר וּפִשְׁתִּים גְּדִילִים תַּעֲשֶׂה לָּךְ, דְּמַשְׁמַע עֲשֵׂה צִיצִית מִצֶּמֶר וּפִשְׁתִּים. **וְהָא תַּנָּא** דְּבֵי ר' יִשְׁמָעֵאל **לֵית לֵיהּ דְּרָבָא.** דְּדָרֵישׁ "הַכָּנָף" מִין כָּנָף, דְּהָא לְתַנָּא דְּבֵי רַבִּי יִשְׁמָעֵאל טַלִּית שֶׁל שְׁאָר מִינִין אֵינָהּ חַיֶּיבֶת בְּצִיצִית, דְּהָא "בֶּגֶד" כְּתִיב, וְתַנָּא דְּבֵי רַבִּי יִשְׁמָעֵאל קָאָמַר כָּל בֶּגֶד צֶמֶר וּפִשְׁתִּים. **אִיצְטְרִיךְ.** צֶמֶר וּפִשְׁתִּים אע"ג דְּלָא דָּרֵישׁ תַּנָּא דְּבֵי ר' יִשְׁמָעֵאל מִין כָּנָף לִשְׁאָר מִינִין. **סד"א.** לְגַבֵּי טַלִּית שֶׁל צֶמֶר וּפִשְׁתִּים דָּרֵישׁ כִּי דִּיּוּקָא דְּרָבָא דְּדָרֵישׁ צִיצִית מִין כָּנָף. **וְהָכִי אָמַר רַחֲמָנָא כו'.** קמ"ל דְּרָשָׁא דִּסְמוּכִין לְמִישְׁרֵי כִּלְאַיִם בְּצִיצִית.

תִּינַח

תוספות

מכדי כתיב ובגד כלאים וגו'. ההוא קרא דגדילים לא מצית לאייתורי ולמימר: מכדי כתיב פרשת ציצית – למאי הילכתא כתביה? דכולה איצטריך, כדדרשינן לקמן (דף ה:): "גדילים" – ארבעה, ודרשינן נמי על "ד' כנפות" ולא על ג' וה', "כסותך" ולא של אחרים, "אשר תכסה בה" *פרט לכסות סומא, ולמעט שאין מכסה רובו.

אבל לבישה כל תרי מיני אסר רחמנא. וא"ת: אפילו חד מינא ה"א דאסור, ובלבד שיהא שוע טווי ונוז! וי"ל: דשעטנז משמע נמי תערובות. **אם** כן לשתוק קרא מיניה ותיתי שעטנז שעטנז מהעלא'. וא"ת: בפ' "במה מדליקין" (שבת כז: ושם) קאמר רב פפא: אף כל צמר ופשתים דקאמר רבי ישמעאל – לאיתויי כלאים. וקאמר התם דהא דרב פפא בדותא היא, דכלאים צמר ופשתים בהדיא כתב בהו. ומאי קושיא? והא איצטריך אף כל לאפנויי צמר ופשתים, כדקאמר הכא! וי"ל: דבמסקנא דנפקא לן הפנאה לרבנן משעטנז, לר' ישמעאל נמי תיפוק מהתם, ותו לא איצטריך אף כל לאפנויי צמר ופשתים דכלאים.

ותנא דבי ר' ישמעאל וכו'. וא"ת: בלא תנא דבי ר' ישמעאל נמי יוכל לדקדק דבגדים משמע כל בגדים, דלכולהו אמר רחמנא עביד להו תכלת – אלמא בבגדי פשתן נמי שרי תכלת! וכ"ת: דה"א דלאו אכולהו אמר רחמנא דליעבד תכלת – השתא נמי נימא דלא אמר דוקא אמר רחמנא דליעבד תכלת, ולא אפשתים! וי"ל: דודאי אי לאו תנא דבי ר' ישמעאל ה"א (א) דשאר מיני אמר רחמנא דליעבד תכלת, ולא אפשתים, אבל לתנא דבי רבי ישמעאל דכל בגדים צמר ופשתים – משמע דאתרוייהו קאי, דאפי' נימא בעלמא דבגד הוי או צמר או פשתים – הכא "בגדיהם" כתב, דמשמע תרי. **ואמר** רחמנא עביד להו תכלת. וא"ת: והיכי משמע מהכא דשרי כלאים בציצית? נימא דעביד להו תכלת בלא שוע טווי ונוז! וי"ל: דחוטי ציצית בעינן שיהא שוע טווי ונוז, דדריש בספרי: "פתיל תכלת" – טווי ושזור, וה"ה שוע, דבעינן. ויליף התם לבן מתכלת. ושתם בגדים שלהן היו נמי שוע טווי, וגם נוזין פירוש "שזורים" כמו שפי' ר"ת לקמן (ד' ה: ד"ה עד) נוז שזורי, היינו שזורים בסוף הטלית, מקום הנחת ציצית, כדאמרינן בריש "המוצא תפילין" (עירובין צו:): ודלמא אדעתא דשיפתא דגלימא עייפינהו. אבל קשיא: דאכתי נימא דאמר רחמנא לעביד להו תכלת בלא קשירה, דלא הוי כלאים, דתוכף תכיפה אחת אין חיבור. ובמנחות (דף לט.) דקדק דקשר עליון דאורייתא מדשרי רחמנא כלאים בציצית. ושמעתי בשם ר"י קלנו': דע"כ אמר רחמנא ליעביד להו תכלת בענין דהוי כלאים, דאי דוקא בלא כלאים – א"כ לישתוק קרא מ"יחדו", ומדאמר רחמנא עביד להו תכלת – ידעי דתוכף תכיפה אחת אינו חיבור. אלא ודאי בענין דהוי כלאים אמר רחמנא ליעביד תכלת, ולא שמעינן להו מהכא מידי אי תוכף תכיפה אחת חיבור אי לא, להכי איצטריך יחדו. א).

ותכלת עמרא הוא. לא היה צריך לכך, דבין הוא כיתנא ובין הוא עמרא יכול לדקדק דכלאים בציצית שרי, דאמר רחמנא לבגדיהם דהוו צמר ופשתים – ליעביד תכלת, שהוא או כיתנא או עמרא, שאין בבגדי כהונה אלא צמר ופשתים, מדכתב בהו "בגדיהם"! אלא האמת אומר. **מדשש** כיתנא תכלת עמרא. וליכא למימר דתכלת נמי כיתנא, אלא צבוע הוא תכלת. וארגמן ותולעת שני עמרא, דסברא הוא דכל הצבועים מין אחד הוא, מדלא חילק בהן אלא בצבע. **סלקא** דעתך אמינא כדרבא. לאו דוקא, דרבא איירי בתר דכתיב צמר ופשתים, והשתא איירי אי לא כתב צמר ופשתים. אלא כלומר, כדיוקא דרבא. וה"ק קרא: ועשו להם ציצית על כנפי בגדיהם, דלבגדיהם שהם צמר ופשתים עביד ציצית. אבל תכלת דבתר הכי – לא קאי אבגדים, אלא א"הכנף" מין כנף. והמקשה דפריך והא תנא דבי ר' ישמעאל – לית ליה דרבא, וסבור דכרבא ממש קאמר – היה יכול להקשות: והא רבא לבתר דכתיב צמר ופשתים קאמר. **והא** תנא דבי ר' ישמעאל לית ליה דרבא. דליכא למימר דמ"הכנף" מרבה שאר בגדים, כדאשכחן בפ' "במה מדליקין" (שבת כז. ושם) דמרבה שאר בגדים גבי שרלים מ"או בגד", *דהכנף לאו ריבויא הוא. **ואפילו** צמר לפשתים ופשתים לצמר. משמע הכא דתנא דבי ר' ישמעאל לית ליה דרבא. וקשה, דבפ' "במה מדליקין" (ג"ז שם) קאמר התלמוד: הדר ביה רבא מההיא, וסבר דאף כל לאתויי שרלים. וסבר שפיר כתנא דבי ר' ישמעאל! וצ"ל דסוגיא דהכא כר"נ בר יצחק דהתם, דקאי אף כל לאיתויי ציצית, א"כ הוי דלא כרבא. **דאפילו** צמר לפשתן ופשתן לצמר כו'. נראה דאפילו שני חוטין לבן של צמר שרי בפשתים, כדאמר במנחות, אף על גב דאפשר במינו, כדקאמר התם: מגו דתכלת פטרה לבן נמי פוטר, ולבן של

תוספות ישנים

ואפילו מוכרי כסות כו'. פירש הקונטרס שאין מתכוונים ול"נ דלר' יהודה קיימינן ואיהו קאמר דבר שאין מתכוין אסור על כן צריך לומר ואפילו מוכרי כסות בלא שום הנאה ויש דלא גרים ליה: **ואי** כתב רחמנא לא תלבש. להך צריכותא דלא יעלה אין המקשה צריך כלל דהא להפנאה דאמרי' לעיל היינו קרא דלא תלבש דמיניה דרשי' סמוכין אבל מקרא דלא יעלה לא איירי מידי דהא לית ליה מיניה סמוכין כלל אלא משום שפי' צריכותא דלא תלבש מפרש ואזיל למאי אצטריך לא יעלה: **ומדשש** כיתנא תכלת עמרא. פי' דכתיב ומכנסי בד שש משזר איזהו דבר העולה בד בבד הוי אומר זה כיתנא: תכלת עמרא א) וי"ל שמא הוא מין אחר דכתי' לא יעלה על הכהנים צמר בבאם אל החצר הפנימית. משמע אבל בחצר החיצונה יעלה עליהם צמר ומשמע דליכא תו מינים [אחרים] רק אותם למפרש אותו הפסוק צמר ופשתים דכתיב פארי פשתים ילבשו ולא יעלה עליהם כו' ועוד י"ל דכתיב בבגדי כהונה בגדי אהרן ובגדי בניו וא"כ לא אית בהו רק צמר ופשתים דבגדים האמורי' בתורה [סתם] צמר ופשתים הם. וא"ת דלמא תכלת הוא פשתים צבוע. וי"ל דא"כ הול"ל שש לבן (וצמר) [ושש] צבוע. (והא דכתיב ארגמן ותולעת שני צ"ל ב) דצמר ופשתים ועל שם הצבעים יקראו): **א)** אבל מ"מ קשה דנוכל לומר דשמא יצטרך יחדו לשוע טווי ונוז אבל יש לומר כי המדקדק התם בפירוש רש"י ניחא הכא דה"פ התם ש"מ קשר העליון דאורייתא הלל"מ וה"פ דאי ס"ד לאו דאורייתא אמאי אצטריך כמה משניות וברייתות למשרי סדין בציצית אבל מן הסמוכין לא הוה קשה ג) ליה לאוקמא לכדרבא והשתא ניחא שפיר הא דקאמר הכא עביד להו תכלת וא"כ כלאים בציצית מותר דקשר העליון דאורייתא ואין צריך למדרש סמוכין כי הלל"מ הוא: **צמר** לפשתים ופשתים לצמר. וא"ת מנא לן הא דפשתים פוטרה לצמר התינח צמר לפשתים דכתיב ונתנו על ציצית הכנף פתיל תכלת ותכלת עמרא הוא וסברא הוא שאם יש לו בגד מפשתים שילבשנו ויניח בו תכלת כדקאמר קרא והיינו צמר לפשתים אבל פשתים לצמר מנין הלא יכול לעשות תכלת דהיינו צמר לצמר. וי"ל כדקאמרינן במנחות דלבן פטר דמגו דתכלת פטר לבן נמי פטר אע"ג דבקרא כתוב תכלת כמו כן נימא מגו דצמר פטר לפשתים ואע"ג דהוי כלאים כמו כן פטר פשתים לצמר:

א) נראה דצ"ל אין להקשות דשמא הוא מין אחר די"ל דכתיב כו'. ב) נראה דצ"ל לצמר ופשתים הם ועל שם הצבעים יקראו כך. ג) נ"ל לא הוי קשה ליה דיש לאוקמא לכדרבא.

עין משפט נר מצוה

[נ"ל לרבות וע' במנחות מג.]

יא א ב מיי' פ"י מהל' כלאים הל' יב ט"ז סמג לאוין רפג טוש"ע י"ד סי' שא סעי' א ו:

יב ג מיי' פ"ג מהל' ציצית הלכה ב:

יג ד מיי' פ"י מהל' כלאים ה"א סמג לאוין רפג טוש"ע י"ד סי' רצח סעי' א:

יד ה מיי' פ"ג מהל' ציצית הלכה ה סמג עשין כו טוש"ע א"ח סימן ט סעי' ב:

טו ו מיי' שם (ופ"י מהל' כלאים) סמג עשין כו טוש"ע שם סעיף ג:

מסורת הש"ס

שבת דף כו: מנחות ד' לט:

שבת דף כז: נזיר דף נח. מנחות ד' לט:

הגהות הב"ח

(א) תוס' ד"ה ותנא וכו' ה"א דאשאר מיני אמר רחמנא:

גליון הש"ס

תוס' ד"ה והא תנא דבי ר"י כו' דהכנף לאו ריבויא הוא. עיין יומא דף עא ע"ב תד"ה ולאותה עמרא.

תֵּינַח לְתַנָּא דְּבֵי ר' יִשְׁמָעֵאל, לְרַבָּנַן מְנָא לְהוּ? נָפְקָא לְהוּ מֵ"רֹאשׁוֹ". *דְּתַנְיָא: °"רֹאשׁוֹ" מַה תַּלְמוּד לוֹמַר? לְפִי שֶׁנֶּאֱמַר °"לֹא תַקִּיפוּ (אֶת) פְּאַת רֹאשְׁכֶם" שׁוֹמֵעַ אֲנִי אַף מְצוֹרָע כֵּן, תַּלְמוּד לוֹמַר "רֹאשׁוֹ", וְקָא סָבַר הַאי תַּנָּא: אהַקָּפַת כָּל הָרֹאשׁ שְׁמָהּ הַקָּפָה. אִיכָּא לְמִיפְרַךְ: מַה לְּלָאו דְּהַקָּפָה — שֶׁכֵּן לָאו שֶׁאֵין שָׁוֶה בַּכֹּל! אֶלָּא, אָתְיָא מִ"זְּקָנוֹ", *דְּתַנְיָא: °"זְקָנוֹ" מַה תַּלְמוּד לוֹמַר? לְפִי שֶׁנֶּאֱמַר °"וּפְאַת זְקָנָם לֹא יְגַלֵּחוּ" שׁוֹמֵעַ אֲנִי אַף כֹּהֵן מְצוֹרָע כֵּן — ת"ל "זְקָנוֹ". וְאִם אֵינוֹ עִנְיָן לְלָאו שֶׁאֵין שָׁוֶה בַּכֹּל — תְּנֵהוּ עִנְיָן לְלָאו הַשָּׁוֶה בַּכֹּל. וְאַכַּתִּי אִיצְטְרִיךְ, סד"א: שֶׁאֲנִי כֹּהֲנִים, *הוֹאִיל וְרִיבָּה בָּהֶן הַכָּתוּב מִצְוֹת יְתֵירוֹת, אֲפִילּוּ לָאו שֶׁאֵין שָׁוֶה בַּכֹּל לָא דָּחֵי — קמ"ל דְּדָחֵי? אֶלָּא: אָתְיָא מֵ"רֹאשׁוֹ" דְּהַהוּא תַּנָּא, *דְּתַנְיָא: "רֹאשׁוֹ" מַה ת"ל? לְפִי שֶׁנֶּאֱמַר °"תַּעַר לֹא יַעֲבוֹר עַל רֹאשׁוֹ" שׁוֹמֵעַ אֲנִי אַף *מְצוֹרָע וְנָזִיר כֵּן, ת"ל "רֹאשׁוֹ" — אִיכָּא לְמִיפְרַךְ: מַה לְּנָזִיר מְצוֹרָע — •שֶׁכֵּן יֶשְׁנוֹ בִּשְׁאֵלָה. דְּאִי לָא תֵּימָא הָכִי, הָא דְּקַיְימָא לָן בדְּאֵין עֲשֵׂה דּוֹחֶה לֹא תַעֲשֶׂה וַעֲשֵׂה — לִיגְמַר מִנָּזִיר! אֶלָּא, מִנָּזִיר מ"ט לָא גָּמְרִינַן, דְּאִיכָּא לְמִיפְרַךְ שֶׁכֵּן יֶשְׁנוֹ בִּשְׁאֵלָה — ה"נ אִיכָּא לְמִיפְרַךְ שֶׁכֵּן יֶשְׁנוֹ בִּשְׁאֵלָה. אֶלָּא לְעוֹלָם מִקְּרָא

תורה אור: ויקרא יד; שם יט; שם יד; שם כא; במדבר ו

רש"י

תֵּינַח לְתַנָּא דְּבֵי רַבִּי יִשְׁמָעֵאל. דְּאַיְיתוּר לֵיהּ "צֶמֶר וּפִשְׁתִּים", אֶלָּא לְרַבָּנַן, דְּלֵית לְהוּ כָּל בְּגָדִים צֶמֶר וּפִשְׁתִּים, וְהָא "צֶמֶר וּפִשְׁתִּים" לָא מְיַיתַּר, מְנָא לְהוּ דְּאָתֵי עֲשֵׂה וְדוֹחֶה לֹא תַעֲשֶׂה? רֹאשׁוֹ מַה ת"ל. בִּמְצוֹרָע כְּתִיב "יְגַלַּח אֶת כָּל שְׂעָרוֹ", הֲרֵי רֹאשׁוֹ בִּכְלָל, לָמָּה לִי דִּכְתִיב רֹאשׁוֹ? וְקָסָבַר הַאי תַּנָּא. דְּאִיצְטְרִיךְ לֵיהּ "רֹאשׁוֹ" לִדְחוֹת לָאו דְּ"לֹא תַקִּיפוּ", דְּהַקָּפַת כָּל הָרֹאשׁ שְׁמָהּ הַקָּפָה, וְלָא אָמְרִינַן "פְּאַת" כָּתַב רַחֲמָנָא. הִלְכָּךְ, אִי לָאו דְּרַבֵּי קְרָא ה"א לָא לִיקוֹף. אַלְמָא אַשְׁמְעִינַן קְרָא דְּאָתֵי עֲשֵׂה וְדָחֵי לֹא תַעֲשֶׂה, וּמֵהָכָא נָפְקָא, הִלְכָּךְ אִיצְטְרִיךְ "עָלֶיהָ" לְמֵיסַר עֶרְוָה לְיִיבּוּם, דְּלָא תֵּימָא אָתֵי עֲשֵׂה דְּיִיבּוּם וְדָחֵי לָאו דַּאֲחוֹת אִשָּׁה. שֶׁאֵין שָׁוֶה בַּכֹּל. דְּנָשִׁים אֵינָן בְּלָאו דְּהַקָּפָה, בְּפ"ק דְּקִידּוּשִׁין (דף לה:). תֹּאמַר בְּלָאו דַּאֲחוֹת אִשָּׁה, שֶׁכְּשֵׁם שֶׁהוּא מוּזְהָר עָלֶיהָ כָּךְ הִיא מוּזְהֶרֶת עָלָיו, דִּכְתִיב "הַנְּפָשׁוֹת הָעוֹשׂוֹת" (ויקרא יח) — שְׁנֵיהֶם בְּמַשְׁמַע. וּפְאַת זְקָנָם. בְּכֹהֲנִים כְּתִיב. תַּלְמוּד לוֹמַר זְקָנוֹ. לְרַבּוֹת זְקַן כֹּהֵן מְצוֹרָע, דְּאָתֵי עֲשֵׂה וְדָחֵי לֹא תַעֲשֶׂה. *(וְאַע"ג דְּהַאי נַמִי לָאו שֶׁאֵין שָׁוֶה בַּכֹּל — יָלְפִינַן מִינֵּיהּ דְּכָל לֹא תַעֲשֶׂה נַמִי דָּחֵי, דְּאִם אֵינוֹ עִנְיָן לְלָאו שֶׁאֵין שָׁוֶה בַּכֹּל דְּאָתֵי עֲשֵׂה וְדָחֵי לֵיהּ, דְּהָא נָפְקָא לָן מֵ"רֹאשׁוֹ", תְּנֵהוּ עִנְיָן כו'). וְאַכַּתִּי אִיצְטְרִיךְ. לְגוּפֵיהּ, לְאַשְׁמוֹעִינַן דְּלָאו דִּפְאַת זְקַן כֹּהֲנִים מִידְחֵי, דְּלָא נָפְקָא לָן מֵ"רֹאשׁוֹ", וְאַע"ג דְּאֵין שָׁוֶה בַּכֹּל הוּא. דְּסד"א: שָׁאנֵי לָאוֵי דְּכֹהֲנִים דַּחֲמִירֵי, שֶׁרִיבָּה בָּהֶן הַכָּתוּב מִצְוֹת רַבּוֹת, אַכַּתִּי לָאו הַשָּׁוֶה בַּכֹּל מְנָלַן דְּדָחֵי? רֹאשׁוֹ מַה ת"ל. בְּ"רֹאשׁוֹ" דִּמְצוֹרָע נַמִי קָאֵי. ת"ל רֹאשׁוֹ. אַלְמָא אָתֵי עֲשֵׂה וְדָחֵי ל"ת. וְאַע"ג דְּלָאו שֶׁאֵינוֹ שָׁוֶה בַּכֹּל הוּא, אִם אֵינוֹ עִנְיָן לְלָאו שֶׁאֵין שָׁוֶה בַּכֹּל, דְּהָא; נָפְקָא לָן מִ"זְּקָנוֹ" דְּאִידָךְ תַּנָּא — תְּנֵהוּ עִנְיָן לְלָאו הַשָּׁוֶה בַּכֹּל. מִנָּזִיר. בְּנָזִיר עֲשֵׂה וְלֹא תַעֲשֶׂה אִיכָּא: "תַּעַר לֹא יַעֲבוֹר עַל רֹאשׁוֹ", "קָדוֹשׁ יִהְיֶה גַּדֵּל פֶּרַע". שֶׁכֵּן יֶשְׁנוֹ בִּשְׁאֵלָה. לִשְׁאוֹל לְחָכָם וְיַתִּיר לוֹ, הִלְכָּךְ אָתֵי עֲשֵׂה וְדָחֵי לֵיהּ. מִקְּרָא

תוספות

של פשתים נמי פוטר הצמר על(א) מגו, דמגו דלבן של צמר פוטר בפשתים, לבן של פשתים נמי פוטר בצמר. ודוקא במקום תכלת, אבל במקום שאין תכלת – אסור, כיון *דלא כשר במינו. דהא במנחות (דף מ.) אסר סדין בציצית משום קלא אילן, ופריך: ולא יהא אלא לבן? ומשני: משום דאפשר במינן, כדר"ל.

לרבנן מנא להו. הוה מצי למימר דלא סברי כר' יהודה, ולא בעי שיהא מוכח או מופנה. אלא ניחא ליה לשנויי אפילו אי סברי כר' יהודה. וא"ת: ומאן (ב) ניהו דפליג עליה דתנא דבי רבי ישמעאל – ר' שמעון בן אלעזר, והא רשב"א ואידך תנא דבי רבי ישמעאל דפ' "במה מדליקין" (שבת כז.) מודו דבלא ריבוי הוו סתם בגדים צמר ופשתים! ואר"י: דהיינו ההיא ברייתא דפ' "התכלת" (מנחות לט:) דאמר רב נחמן התם: השיראין פטורה מן הציצית. איתיביה רבא לרב נחמן: השיראין והכלך והסריקין כולן חייבין בציצית! ומשני: מדרבנן. אבל רבא, דפריך התם לרב נחמן לטעמא דמחייב – מדאורייתא, וסבר לה כי ההיא ברייתא, ולית ליה שינוייא דרב נחמן דמשני התם מדרבנן.

מה ללאו דהקפה שכן אינו שוה בכל. בפ' "שני נזירין" (נזיר נח. וסס) מפרש דהאי תנא דמוקי "ראשו" לנזיר סבר דהקפת כל הראש לא שמה הקפה. ולהכי לא מצי לאוקמי כשאינו נזיר. והך תנא דמוקי "ראשו" ללאו גרידא סבר דשמה הקפה. ואיבעית אימא: דלכולי עלמא שמיה הקפה, ותנא מוקי לה לנזיר דהוי לא תעשה ועשה – משום דללאו גרידא לא איצטריך לאשמעינן דדחי, דמ"גדילים" נפקא. והאי תנא דמוקי לה לראשו גרידא סבר דמגדילים לא ילפינן, משום דאיצטריך לכדרבא לאשמועינן דצמר ופשתים פוטרים בשאר מינים, ולאו לדחות לאו דכלאים קאתי, ומ"ראשו" מסייע להאי תנא דעשה דחי לא תעשה בעלמא. וקשה: היכי יליף "מראשו"? דאיכא למיפרך כדפרכינן הכא: שכן לאו שאין שוה בכל. וע"כ פירכא גמורה היא, דאם לא כן – נילף מזקנו לידחי לא תעשה ועשה! וי"ל: דסוגיא דנזיר סברה דאפילו לא כתיב "ראשו" הוה מוקמינן "זקנו" בכהן, ד"זקנו" משמע בין כהן בין ישראל. אע"ג דראשו לא משמע בין נזיר ובין שאינו נזיר – משום דקרא איירי בסתם בני אדם, שאינן נזירים, ולהכי, כיון דכתיב "זקנו", דדחי לא תעשה ועשה, תו לא איצטריך "ראשו" ללאו שאין שוה בכל, ואם אינו ענין ללאו שאין שוה בכל – תנהו לענין שהוא בכל. אבל סוגיא דשמעתין סברה ד"זקנו" לא הוה מוקמינן בכהנים אי לאו דכתיב "ראשו" ואיצטריך ראשו לגלויי אזקנו דאיירי בכהנים, ודחי לא תעשה ועשה, ולא מצי למילף מ"ראשו" מידי. א"נ: סוגיא דהכא סברה דאיצטריך ראשו לאשמועינן דהקפת כל הראש שמה הקפה, אבל ההיא ד"שני נזירים" (נזיר נז:) סוברת דמסברא ידעינן דשמה הקפה: **זקנו** מה תלמוד לומר. וא"ת: והא איצטריך ראשו וזקנו לכלל ופרט וכלל, כדאמרי' בסוטה בפ' "היה מביא" (דף טז.): מה הפרט מפורש מקום כינוס שער כו'! ויש לומר: דההיא מילתא מצי למידרש מגבות עיניו.

ואכתי איצטריך סד"א שאני כהנים כו'. הוה מצי למימר דאיצטריך זקנו למידחי עשה ולא תעשה, דמראשו לא שמעינן אלא לאו גרידא, ומהכא לא מצי למילף בעלמא דליתי עשה ולידחי לא תעשה ועשה, דשאני הכא דהוי לאו ועשה שאין שוה בכל, כדאמרינן בפרק "שני נזירים" (נזיר דף נח:). וא"ת: ונלמוד מהכא לידחי לאו ועשה שאין שוה בכל, וא"כ מאי פריך בפרק "אלו מציאות" (ב"מ ל. וסס) גבי "והתעלמת" – פעמים שאתה מתעלם, כהן והיא בבית הקברות פשיטא דאין עשה דוחה לא תעשה ועשה א], והא לאו ועשה שאין שוה בכל! ואר"י: דהתם עיקר פירכא סמיך(ג) אמי דחינן איסורא מקמי ממונא. ועוד קשיא: דקאמר התם בסוף פירקין (דף לג.) יכול אמר לו אביו היטמא או אל תחזיר אבדה – יכול ישמע לו, ת"ל כו'! ופריך: תיפוק ליה דאין עשה דוחה לא תעשה ועשה! ומאי פריך? והא לאו ועשה דטומאה אינו שוה אלא בכהנים! ואר"י: דלא פריך אלא אמאי תחזיר אבדה, דלמה לי קרא להכי, דלאו ועשה שוה בכל הוא. ועוד קשה: דלקמן בפ"ב (דף כ.) גבי אלמנה לכ"ג דחולצת ולא מתייבמת, פריך: בשלמא מן הנשואין – לא אתי עשה ודחי לא תעשה ועשה, אלא מן האירוסין – ליתי עשה ולידחי ל"ת מן הנשואין – נמי, אמאי ניחא ליה? והא לאו ועשה שאין שוה בכל הוא! וכן שם גבי פלוגתא *דר' אחא ור' אלעזר (לקמן כא.) בביאת כ"ג באלמנה, קאמר: מן הנשואין – כ"ע לא פליגי דלא פטרה, דאין עשה דוחה ל"ת ועשה! •ואר"י, דלא דמי: דלאו ועשה דגילוח הוה טפי אין שוה בכל, שאין שוה בכל נשים. אבל גבי אלמנה לכ"ג – האשה עושה איסורא כמו כהן הבא עליה, דקרי ביה "לא יקחו" "לא תקח", ולא מדחי ליה עשה דיבום אע"ג דאינו שוה אלא בכהנים. וי"מ: דמ"זקנו" לא ילפינן בעלמא אפילו אין שוה בכל, משום דעשה דמצורע עדיף משאר עשה, דגדול השלום, דע"י שיטהר מותר בתשמיש, כדאמרינן ב"שילוח הקן" (חולין ד' קמא.) דאי לאו "שלח תשלח" ה"א דמצורע דחי עשה דשילוח, משום דעדיף, דגדול השלום. ובשמעתין ה"ל למימר דלא ילפינן מעשה דמצורע משום דגדול השלום, אלא דבלאו הכי דחי שפיר. ועוד: דהכא דחי דאפילו עשה כי האי לא נגמר מהכא לידחי. ומיהו, לא יתיישב טעם זה אלא למאן דאסר במ"ק (דף ז:) מצורע בימי חלוטו בתשמיש המטה, אבל למאן דשרי – לא.

ליגמר מנזיר. דדחי. וא"ת: אדרבה, נילף מכיבוד אב ואם דלא דחי לאו ועשה דהיטמא ואל תחזיר אבידה! וי"ל: דמה לכבוד אב ואם – שכן הכשר מצוה, כדלקמן. וא"ת: אכתי, אם באת ללמוד מכאן דדחי – א"כ איצטריך לן שפיר "והתעלמת" בפרק "אלו מציאות" (ב"מ ל. וסס) לכהן והיא בבית הקברות, דמתעלם, ומאחר דהתם לא דחי, אדרבה: נילף בעלמא דלא דחי! וי"ל: דהתם לא צריך קרא להכי, דפשיטא דלא דחי, כדקאמר התם: ותו מי דחינן איסורא מקמי ממונא:

שכן ישנו בשאלה. וא"ת: וניגמר במה הצד מכהן ונזיר דלידחי בעלמא עשה את לאו ועשה? ובפרק "ב' נזירים" (נזיר דף נח: וסס) בתר דקאמר וכהן ונזיר לא גמרינן מהדדי, קאמר: ובעלמא לא ילפינן מינייהו משום דאיכא למיפרך כדאמרן, פי': מה לנזיר שכן ישנו בשאלה, וכהן אינו שוה בכל. ותימה: דאמאי לא נגמר מינייהו במה הצד? וי"ל: דעל מה הצד פרכינן כל דהו, דאינו לא קולא ולא חומרא, ואיכא למיפרך: מה להצד השוה שבהן (ד) שיש בהן איסור גילוח, זה בראשו וזה בזקנו. ואית דלא גרסי כדאמרן, ומפרש דקאי איכא למפרך אהא דאמר בתר הכי אמר רב וכו', פי': (ה) ומפרש דאיכא למיפרך דאמר רב מיקל אדם כל גופו בתער, ומסיק כעין תער. וכיון דאיסור דידהו קל – אתי עשה ודחי להו. אבל קשיא: נילף מכהן ונזיר ומילה דדחיא צרעת, דהוי עשה ולא תעשה. כדאמר בפרק "ר' אליעזר אם לא הביא" (שבת קלב:)! ונראה דהוו כמו שני כתובים הבאים כאחד, דממילה וחד מהני איכא למילף נמצא חד דלא איצטריך. ועוד: אי ילפינן מינייהו למה לי קרא דכלאים בציצית ללאו גרידא? ותירוץ זה יש לדחות כמו שאפרש בסמוך. ובפרק "שני נזירים" היה יכול לומר כן כדפרישית, אלא דלא חש לדקדק ולהאריך [וע' היטיב תוס' נזיר נח: סד"ה הר"ף].

גדילים

תוספות ישנים

אלא לרבנן מנא להו. אית דגרסי אלא כי אצטריך קרא לכדרבא כלומר לעולם כדקאמרת דצמר ופשתים לא צריך א) דועשו להם ציצית חזי מיניה כלאים וכי אצטריך צמר ופשתים לכדרבא אצטריך וכו' דצמר ופשתים פוטרים וכו' וקא מקשי ליה היכי מצי למימר דסמוכין אתו לכדרבא דהא תנא דבי ר' ישמעאל לית ליה דרבא וקא משני כלוקיא דרבא והשתא קאמר כאידך גיסא דלא כדקאמרינן מעיקרא דסמוכין לכדרבא אתו דהא לא מצינן למימר אלא לעולם סמוכין ב) דלא מצי למשרי כלאים מועשו להם ציצית משום דאנא דייקנא כדרבא דדריש הכנף מין כנף וכו' אבל כלאים לא חזי מש"ה אצטריכו סמוכין לצמר ופשתים דכלאים שרי בציצית וא"ת אי לאו סמוכין הכנף למין כנף לא צריך דפשיטא דכלאים בציצית אסור דמסברא אין עשה דוחה ל"ת וכיון שכן דוקיא דרבא לא צריך קרא וי"ל דה"ק סד"א כדוקיא דרבא דבעינן מין כנף כלומר צמר לצמר הוא לגבעיה בתכלת אבל לפשתים בעינן נמי ציצית לבן של פשתים ודלא יהא לבוע למראה אחר דמין כנף לגמרי בעינן קמ"ל סמוכין ולא דרשינן הכנף דודאי אליבא דתנא דבי ר' ישמעאל כיון דלא מחייב בציצית אלא בגד של צמר ופשתים ודאי אין לן למימר דלא דריש הכנף. והראב"ד גרים כהך גי' בתרא והגיה בספרו כך וזהו לשונו פי' לתנא דבי ר' ישמעאל האי צמר ופשתים לאו למישרא כלאים בציצית אתא דלא צריך אלא לאפוקי מדרבא דמרבה שאר מינים קמ"ל צמר ופשתים אין מידי אחרינא לא. ואקשינן והא תנא דבי ר' ישמעאל לית ליה דרבא כלומר רבא גופיה דמרבה שאר מינים מהכא מייתי להו משום דכתיב הכנף ולתנא דבי ר' ישמעאל כיון דאמר כל בגדים אינן אלא צמר ופשתים הכנף גופיה אינו אלא צמר ופשתים א"כ צמר ופשתים למעוטי שאר מינין לא צריך ע"כ. ומשמע נמי לדידיה דכי קאמר אלא סד"א כלוקיא דרבא מתפרש ג) כדפרשי' ליה אנן לעיל הדר. וקי"ל כר' ישמעאל דמן התורה לא מחייב בציצית אלא של צמר ופשתים ושאר מינים אינם חייבין אלא מדרבנן ומהכא משמע ד) מ"ש הרי"ף ז"ל שיכול אדם לעשות ציצית מפשתים דקאמר הכא כתב רחמנא צמר ופשתים דאפילו צמר לפשתים ופשתים לצמר. וא"ת מה קא בעי לרבנן מנא להו לימא דשמא רבנן יסברו דדרשינן סמוכין אף היכא דלא מוכח ולא מופנה. וי"ל דקא בעי הכא לר' יהודה דלא דרש סמוכין במשנה מוכח או מופנה אי ס"ל כרבנן מנא ליה וניחא שפיר: **מה** ללאו דהקפה שאינו שוה בכל הנשים תאמר באחות אשה שהיא חייבת כמו האיש דכתיב ונכרתו הנפשות העושות תרי משמע. ותימה דמשמע הכא ראשו למצורע [וגרידא] לא יליף עשה דוחה ל"ת מהקפה משום שאינו שוה בכל ותימה דאמרינן בפ' שני נזירים לימא הקפת הראש תנאי היא דת"ר ראשו מה ת"ל כו' יכול אף מצורע כן ת"ל ראשו. ותניא אידך ראשו מה תלמוד וכו' יכול אף נזיר מצורע כן ת"ל וכו' מאי לאו תנאי היא דמר סבר הקפת כל הראש שמה הקפה כו' עד דמסיק דכ"ע הקפת כל הראש שמה הקפה ומקשה מאן דמוקים לקרא למדחי לאו תעשה ועשה לאו גרידא מנא ליה. לא"ל נימא מכ"ש דאיכא למפרך מה לנזיר שכן ישנו בשאלה ומשני יליף מגדילים ומשמע אבל למאן דמוקים לקרא למדחי לאו גרידא דהיינו הך דמוקים ראשו למצורע לחוד לא קשה לתלמודא מנא ליה דדחי לאו גרידא דיליף ליה מהכא וא"כ קשה דהכא משמע דלא ילפינן מיניה משום שאינו שוה בכל. וי"ל דודאי לעולם הך תנא דראשו למצורע נ"ל דיליף עשה דחי לאו גרידא מהכא ומגדילים דאי מגדילים לחוד ה"א כדרבא לעיל להכי אצטריך ראשו דמצורע ואי מראשו למצורע הוה פרכינן ליה מה ללאו דהקפה שאינו שוה בכל. אבל כיון דחזינן לאו שאינו שוה בכל דחי מהקפה מעתה יש לנו לומר דגם בשוה בכל דחי מגדילים ולא נדרוש גדילים לכדרבא והתם קאמר למדחי לא תעשה ועשה דהיינו אידך תנא דלקמן דמוקים ראשו לנזיר מצורע לאו גרידא מנא ליה יליף מגדילים לחוד: **לפי** שנאמר ופאת זקנם לא יגלחו. והאי דנקט האי קרא דכתיב גבי כהנים ולא נקט ולא תשחית את פאת זקנך דכתיב גבי ישראל אל משום דגבי ישראל לא כתיב גלוח אבל גבי כהנים דכתי' גלוח נקט ההוא קרא משום דקיי"ל דאינו חייב אלא בגילוח שיש בו השחתה ואע"ג דגבי ישראל נמי בעינן גילוח שיש בו השחתה דילפינן מכהנים. מיהו התנא לא צריך לכלאים דמועטו להם ציצית ילפינן מיניה דכלאים בציצית שרי וכי איצטריך וכו'. ב) נ"ל לעולם סמוכין לכלאים אתא. ג) נראה דל"ל כדפרשינן ליה אנן לעיל דהדר ביה מהא דאמר מעיקרא ד) אולי נ"ל ומהכא משמע ראיה למש"כ הרי"ף ז"ל שיכול אדם לעשות ציצית מפשתים דהא קאמר הכא כו'.

עין משפט נר מצוה

[נ"ל דאפשר במינו דהוא כו']

טז א מיי' פי"ב מהל' עבודת כוכבים הל' א סמג לאוין מה טוש"ע י"ד סי' קפא סעיף ב:

יז ב מיי' פ"ו מהל' יבום הלכה יז:

מסורת הש"ס

נזיר מא. ע"ש ודף נז

שם נח.

[לקמן קיד: קדושין כט: לה: לו. סנהדרין נח. מכות כ. תמורה ד:]

בס"א ל"ג

נזיר מא. ע"ש נח.

גירסת רש"ל נזיר מצורע

לפנינו איתא ר' יוחנן

הגהות הב"ח

(א) תוס' ד"ה לאפילו וכו' הצמר על ידי מגו: (ב) ד"ה לרבנן וכו' ומאן ניהו רבנן דפליגי עליה וכו' לרב נחמן לטעמיה דמחייב: (ג) ד"ה ואכתי וכו' עיקר פירכא סמיך על (ל"א) [ותו] מי דחינן: (ד) ד"ה שכן וכו' מה להצד השוה שבהן שכן יש בהן איסור גילוח: (ה) בא"ד בתר הכי אמר רב וכו' פי' דאיכא כצ"ל ותיבת ומפרש נמחק:

גליון הש"ס

גמ' שכן ישנו בשאלה. עי' טורי אבן ר"ה דף כח ע"ב ד"ה טובה: **תוס'** ד"ה ואכתי איצטריך וכו' ואר"י דלא דמי. ע' מכות דף טו ע"א תד"ה אם כהן:

הגהות מהר"ב רנשבורג

א] תוס' ד"ה ואכתי וכו' והא לאו ועשה שאין שוה בכל. נ"ב גם הראב"ן הקשה כך יעו"ש דף קמא ע"א שתירץ דשאני אלמנה לכה"ג דחמיר איסוריה דהיא מתחללת וזרעה מתחלל ולכן אע"ג דאינו שוה בכל כיון דחמיר איסוריה הוי כלאו השוה בכל אבל מן האירוסין דליכא אלא ל"ת דהא פסולה היא לידחי דהא עשה דוחה אפי' ל"ת השוה בכל אבל שאר לאוין שאין שוין בכל כגון דנזיר וכיוצא בו דלא חמיר איסוריה אתי עשה ודחי עשה ול"ת שאין שוה בכל עכ"ל יעו"ש היטב:

עין משפט נר מצוה

יח א מיי' פ"א מהל' ציצית הלכה י סמג עשין כו טוש"ע א"ח סימן יא סעיף יב:

יט ב מיי' פ"י מהל' כלאים הלכה ג סמג לאוין רפג טוש"ע י"ד סימן ש סעיף ב:

כ ג מיי' שם הלכה ב סמג שם טוש"ע שם סעיף א:

כא ד מיי' פ"ו מהל' ממרים הל' יב סמג עשין קיב טוש"ע יו"ד סימן רמ סעי' טו:

תורה אור

מִקְרָא קַמָּא: אִם כֵּן לֵימָא קְרָא "צִיצִית תַּעֲשֶׂה לְּךָ", "גְּדִילִים" לָמָּה לִי? ש"מ לְאַפְנוּיֵי.. הַאי לְשִׁיעוּרָא הוּא דַּאֲתָא: *[א]"גְּדִיל" — שְׁנַיִם, "גְּדִילִים" — אַרְבָּעָה, עֲשֵׂה גְּדִיל וּפוֹתְלֵהוּ מִתּוֹכוֹ! א"כ לֵימָא קְרָא "לֹא תִלְבַּשׁ שַׁעַטְנֵז", "צֶמֶר וּפִשְׁתִּים יַחְדָּו" ל"ל? ש"מ לְאַפְנוּיֵי. וְאַכַּתִּי מִיבָּעֵי לֵיהּ: [ב]לְתוֹכֵף שְׁתֵּי תְכִיפוֹת — חִיבּוּר, *וּתְכִיפָה אַחַת — אֵינוֹ חִיבּוּר! א"כ לִכְתּוֹב רַחֲמָנָא "לֹא תִלְבַּשׁ צֶמֶר וּפִשְׁתִּים יַחְדָּו", "שַׁעַטְנֵז" ל"ל? ש"מ לְאַפְנוּיֵי. וְאַכַּתִּי מִיבָּעֵי לֵיהּ: [ג]עַד שֶׁיְּהֵא שׁוּעַ טָווּי וְנוּז! אֶלָּא כּוּלָּהּ מִ"שַּׁעַטְנֵז" נָפְקָא. אַשְׁכַּחַן דְּאָתֵי עֲשֵׂה וְדָחֵי לֹא תַעֲשֶׂה גְּרֵידָא, לֹא תַעֲשֶׂה שֶׁיֵּשׁ בּוֹ כָּרֵת הֵיכָא אַשְׁכַּחַן דְּדָחֵי דְּאִיצְטְרִיךְ "עָלֶיהָ" לְמֵיסְרָה? וְכִי תֵּימָא נֵילַף מִמִּילָה — מַה לְּמִילָה שֶׁכֵּן נִכְרְתוּ עָלֶיהָ שְׁלֹשׁ עֶשְׂרֵה בְּרִיתוֹת, מִפֶּסַח — מַה לְּפֶסַח שֶׁכֵּן כָּרֵת, מִתָּמִיד — מַה לְּתָמִיד שֶׁכֵּן תָּדִיר. מֵחֲדָא לָא אָתְיָא תֵּיתֵי מִתַּרְתֵּי. מֵהֵי תֵּיתֵי? מִמִּילָה וּפֶסַח — שֶׁכֵּן כָּרֵת, מִפֶּסַח וְתָמִיד — שֶׁכֵּן צוֹרֶךְ גָּבוֹהַּ, מִמִּילָה וְתָמִיד — שֶׁכֵּן(א) יֶשְׁנוֹ לִפְנֵי הַדִּבּוּר. וְאַלִּיבָּא דְּמ"ד *[א] עוֹלָה שֶׁהִקְרִיבוּ יִשְׂרָאֵל בַּמִּדְבָּר עוֹלַת תָּמִיד הֲוָה. וּמִכּוּלְּהוּ נַמִי — שֶׁכֵּן יֶשְׁנָן לִפְנֵי הַדִּבּוּר. אֶלָּא אִיצְטְרִיךְ, סד"א תֵּיתֵי מִכִּבּוּד אָב וָאֵם, דְּתַנְיָא: [ד]יָכוֹל יְהֵא כִּבּוּד אָב וָאֵם דּוֹחֶה שַׁבָּת, ת"ל °"אִישׁ אִמּוֹ וְאָבִיו תִּירָאוּ וְאֶת שַׁבְּתוֹתַי תִּשְׁמוֹרוּ" — כּוּלְּכֶם חַיָּיבִין בִּכְבוֹדִי, מַאי לָאו דְּאָמַר לֵיהּ: "שְׁחוֹט לִי" "בַּשֵּׁל לִי", וְטַעְמָא — דִּכְתַב רַחֲמָנָא "אֶת שַׁבְּתוֹתַי תִּשְׁמוֹרוּ" הָא לָאו הָכִי — דָּחֵי! לָא לָאו

[חגיגה ו.] | ויקרא יט

רש"י

מִקְרָא קַמָּא. דְּכִלְאַיִם בְּצִיצִית. וּדְקָאָמְרַתְּ לְרַבָּנַן דְּלָא אִיַּיתַּר לְהוּ "צֶמֶר וּפִשְׁתִּים" מְנָא לְהוּ דְּכִלְאַיִם בְּצִיצִית שָׁרֵי, דְּלֵיתֵי עֲשֵׂה וְדָחֵי לֹא תַעֲשֶׂה. א"כ. דְּלָאו לְאַפְנוּיֵי, לִכְתּוֹב צִיצִית כו'. לְשִׁיעוּרָא אֲתָא. לְמִנְיַן חוּטִין. גְּדִיל שְׁנַיִם. אִי אֶפְשָׁר לַעֲשׂוֹת גְּדִיל בְּפָחוֹת מִשְּׁנֵי חוּטִין. גְּדִילִין אַרְבַּע. חוּטִין, דְּמִיעוּט גְּדִילִין שְׁנַיִם, וּכְתִיב (במדבר טו) "וְנָתְנוּ עַל צִיצִית הַכָּנָף פְּתִיל", אָמְרָה תּוֹרָה עֲשֵׂה מֵהֶנָךְ אַרְבַּע חוּטִין גְּדִיל אֶחָד, דְּהָווּ לְהוּ ח' חוּטִין כְּשֶׁתּוֹחֲבָן בִּכְנַף הַבֶּגֶד. וּפוֹתְלֵהוּ מִתּוֹכוֹ. שֶׁיִּהְיוּ תְּלוּיִין פְּתִילִין, שֶׁלֹּא יַעֲשֶׂה כּוּלּוֹ גְּדִיל, אֶלָּא קְצָת גְּדִיל וּקְצָת עָנָף. תְּכִיפָה. פוינ"ט, שֶׁתּוֹחֵב תְּחִיבָה אַחַת בְּמַחַט וְחִיבֵּר כִּלְאַיִם בֶּגֶד צֶמֶר וּבֶגֶד פִּשְׁתִּים יַחַד — אֵינוֹ חִיבּוּר בְּפָחוֹת מִשְּׁתֵּי תְּכִיפוֹת, לְהָכִי כְּתִיב "יַחְדָּיו", עַד שֶׁיִּתְחַבְּרוּ יַחַד יָפֶה. שׁוּעַ טָווּי וְנוּז. מִן הַתּוֹרָה אֵינוֹ חַיָּיב עַד שֶׁיִּהְיֶה הַצֶּמֶר וְהַפִּשְׁתָּן מְתוּקָּן יַחַד הֵיטֵב בְּמַסְרֵק: שׁוּעַ. לְשׁוֹן "חָלָק", שֶׁמְּתַרְגְּמִינַן שְׁעִיעַ (בראשית כז). נוּז. אָרוּג. כּוּלָּהּ מִשַּׁעַטְנֵז נָפְקָא. דְּאִי לְאַפְנוּיֵי לְחוּד — נִכְתּוֹב לֹא תִלְבַּשׁ כִּלְאַיִם צֶמֶר וּפִשְׁתִּים, וּמִדְּאַפֵּיק רַחֲמָנָא בִּלְשׁוֹן שַׁעַטְנֵז — דְּרוֹשׁ בֵּיהּ נַמִי הָא. מִמִּילָה. שֶׁדּוֹחֶה עֲשֵׂה שֶׁלָּהּ לֹא תַעֲשֶׂ' דְּשַׁבָּת, שֶׁיֵּשׁ בָּהּ כָּרֵת. שְׁלֹשׁ עֶשְׂרֵ' בְּרִיתוֹת. אֲמוּרִים בְּפָרָשַׁת מִילָה: מִפֶּסַח. שֶׁדּוֹחֶה שְׁחִיטָתוֹ אֶת הַשַּׁבָּת: שֶׁכֵּן צוֹרֶךְ גָּבוֹהַּ. לַמִּזְבֵּחַ, תֹּאמַר בְּעֲשֵׂ' דְּיִיבּוּם דְּלֵיכָּא כָּל הָנֵי. מִילָה וְתָמִיד שֶׁכֵּן יֶשְׁנָן לִפְנֵי הַדִּבּוּר. לִפְנֵי מַתַּן תּוֹרָה. וְאַלִּיבָּא דְּמ"ד. בְּמַסֶּ' חֲגִיגָה (ד' ו.). עוֹלָה שֶׁהִקְרִיבוּ יִשְׂרָאֵל בַּמִּדְבָּר. דִּכְתִיב (שמות כד) "וַיַּעֲלוּ עוֹלוֹת", עוֹלַת תָּמִיד הֲוָה. סד"א. אִי לָא כְּתִיב "עָלֶיהָ" לִדְרָשָׁא, תֵּיתֵי עֲשֵׂה וְדָחֵי לֹא תַעֲשֶׂ' שֶׁיֵּשׁ בּוֹ כָּרֵת מִכִּיבּוּד אָב וָאֵם. כּוּלְּכֶם. אַתָּה וְאָבִיךָ וְאִמְּךָ חַיָּיבִים בִּכְבוֹדִי. מֵ"אֲנִי ה'" דָּרֵישׁ לֵיהּ. שְׁחוֹט לִי. דְּהָוֵי אַב מְלָאכָה שֶׁחַיָּיבִין עָלֶיהָ כָּרֵת. לָאו

תוספות

גדילים ארבעה. במנחות (ד' מב.) ותימה: מנלן שכופל כל אחד ואחד לשנים? שמא יקשור כל אחד בראשו בטלית! ואי הוה מפרשינן עשה גדיל ופותלהו מתוכו, היינו: שעושה אותו כעין פתילה, וכופלין באמצע — הוה ניחא. אבל בקונט' פי': פותלהו מתוכו — היינו שני שלישי ענף, שלא יעשה הכל גדילים.

ואכתי מיבעי לי' לתוכף תכיפה אחת דאין חיבור. בלאו הכי מיבעי לי', דאי לאו "יחדו" ה"א דאסור ללבוש צמר ופשתים, אע"פ שאין מחוברים כלל זה עם זה.

עד שיהא שוע טווי ונוז. אין לפרש כמו שפי' ריב"ן: שוע וטווי יחד צמר ופשתים (ב) — א"כ כלאים בציצית היכי משכחת לה? שהרי צריך שיהיו ב' חוטין של תכלת צמר לבדו בלא פשתן! אלא שוע — כל אחד לבדו. ונוז נמי, אר"ת: דאין לפרש דהיינו אריג, כדפי' בקונט', דמאי שנא שוע וטווי דהוי כל אחד לבדו, ונוז קאי אצמר ופשתים יחד? ועוד, דבנדה פרק "האשה" (ד' סא:) גבי האי מאן דרמי חוטא דכיתנא בגלימא דעמרא כו' — ופריך: ואימא או שוע או טווי או נוז? ולפי' הקונט' — בלא נוז אי אפשר שיהא כלאים. ואין לומר דהכי פריך: ואימא או שוע ונוז או טווי ונוז או נוז לחודיה — דא"כ, דנוז לחודיה סגי, שוע וטווי דכתב רחמנא למה לי? אלא נראה לר"ת: דנוז היינו שזור, ונוז נמי כל אחד לבדו. ועל שעטנז של צמר לבד ושל פשתים לבד הזהיר הכתוב, שלא יעשה מהם בגד ביחד, ומ"יחדו" נפקא. והר' רבי יצחק הלבן הקשה לו מהא דתנן במס' כלאים (פ"ט מ"ח): אין חייבין משום כלאים אלא על טווי וארוג, שנאמר שעטנז שוע טווי ונוז. אלמא דנוז היינו ארוג! ואר"ת: דע"כ לאו למדרש כל שעטנז קאתי, מדלא קאמר אלא על שוע טווי וארוג, ולא מייתי שעטנז, אלא משום טווי (ג) ונוז לחודיה, אבל אריג — מ"יחדו" נפקא. **כולה** משעטנז נפקא. מדכתיב "שעטנז", ולא כתיב כלאים, שמעינן שוע וטווי ונוז. ומדלא כתיב שוע וטווי ונוז בהדיא שמעינן דלאפנויי קאתי, למידרש סמוכין. ואם תאמר: ודלמא לכדרבא לחוד קאתי, למדרש סמוכין דצמר ופשתים פוטרים אף שלא במינן, ומנלן דאתא למישרי כלאים? ויש לומר דהכי משמע: דלא תלבש שעטנז צמר ופשתים יחדו, גדילים תעשה לך מהם, והכי איתא בפ' "שני נזירים" (נזיר ד' נח. ושם). וא"ת: והיכי ילפינן בעלמא מהכא? שאני כלאים דהותרו מכללו אצל בגדי כהונה? ואר"י דהתם נמי משום דאתי עשה דבגדי כהונה ודחי לאו דכלאים, ואין זה הותר מכללו. ומיהו, אי לאו כלאים מבגדי כהונה לא הוה מצי למילף בעלמא, משום דמצותו בכך, ובענין אחר אי אפשר לקיים מצותו. כמו שפירשתי לעיל (ד) דלא ילפינן מאשת אח. ועוד, דצורך עבודה שאני. וא"ת: אדילפינן מכלאים בציצית דדחי, נילף משריפת קדשים דלא דחי, כדדרשינן פ' "כיצד צולין" (פסחים פג:) דאין שריפת קדשים דוחה יו"ט מ"והנותר ממנו עד בקר" (שמות יב) בא הכתוב ליתן בקר שני לשריפתו! ⊕וי"ל: דשאני התם דלא בטלה מצותו בכך, ויכול לשורפו אחר יו"ט. ומ"מ, אי לאו דבקר שני — לא הייתי מחלק, וה"א דדחי. ומיהו קשה: לקמן (דף ו:) גבי שריפת בת כהן קאמר: או אינו אלא בשבת, דהוה גמרינן מכלאים בציצית דלדחי, אי לאו "לא תבערו", אפי' לא תעשה שיש בו כרת, דמה לי חומרא רבה ומה לי חומרא זוטא, והתם, כיון דיכול להמתין עד למחר — נילף (ה) מיניה שריפת קדשים? וי"ל: דהתם נמי אי אפשר להמתין, שיש לה לידון מיד ולשרוף, שלא יְעַנּוּ הדין ושלא ישתכחו הדברים. וא"ת: ולמה לן קרא למילף מכלאים בציצית? נילף משריפת קדשים, מדאיצטריך התם לומר קרא דלא דחי, משום דיכול להמתין — מכלל דבעלמא דחי! ואר"י: דהתם איצטריך קרא, שלא תאמר דדחי משום דאפילו אוכל נפש שרי. ולמ"ד נדרים ונדבות אין קרבין בי"ט לא איצטריך הכא קרא, אלא אליבא דמ"ד קריבין. **ומכולהו** נמי שכן ישנן לפי הדיבור. וא"ת: ונילף משאר קרבנות דדחי שבת, כדדרשינן בפ' "כיצד צולין" (פסחים עז. ושם) *מ"במועדו", ואפי' עומר ושתי הלחם, כדדרשינן התם! ואר"י: דחשיבי (ו)התם כולהו תדיר, כיון דהוי בכל שנה, ואיכא למיפרך על מילה ושאר קרבנות שכן תדיר. ובש"ס לא חש לדקדק כל כך, דה"נ לא מסיק מידי למ"ד *עולה שהקריבו ישראל במדבר עולת ראייה הוה. **כולכם** חייבין בכבודי. מ"אני ה'" דסיפא דקרא קדריש. וא"ת: ומנלן דקאי טפי אשבתות מכבוד אב ואם? וכן בסמוך גבי מקדש? וי"ל: דכבוד הקב"ה הוי טפי בשמירת שבת מבשאר מצות, דמעיד על המקום שברא העולם. כדאמר בעירובין (דף סט:) ובחולין (דף ה.) דמחלל שבת ככופר במעשה בראשית. ועוד, "אני ה'" משמע דקאי א"מורא" דכתיב באב ואם ובמקדש, כלומר: מוראי למעלה ממוראכם, כדאמר במדרש: "והתקדשתם והייתם קדושים" יכול כמוני — ת"ל "כי קדוש אני" — קדושתי למעלה מקדושתכם. וא"ת: ולמה לי קרא בכבוד אב ואם דלא דחי שבת, דבלאו קרא נמי לא דחי, שהוא ואביו מוזהרין על השבת, כדאמר בפ"ק דקדושין (ד' לא.) גבי: אביו אומר השקני ואמו אומרת השקני — הנח כיבוד אמך ועשה כבוד אביך, שאתה ואמך חייבין בכבוד אביך. וכן: אביך אומר השקני ומצוה לעשות — הנח כבוד אביך ועשה מצוה, שאתה ואביך חייבין לעשות מצוה! וי"ל: דמהכא ילפינן התם.

טעמא דכתב רחמנא "את שבתותי תשמורו", הא לאו הכי דחי. פירוש: דמהכא ילפינן דבעלמא דחי. דלא איצטריך הכא למכתב דלא דחי, דמהיכא תיתי? דמפסח ומילה ותמיד לא אתי, דמה לכבוד אב ואם שכן הכשר מצוה. ועוד, דאדרבה: נילף ממקדש והבערת בת כהן דלא דחי. והא דקתני יכול יהא כיבוד אב ואם דוחה שבת, דמשמע דאי לאו קרא ה"א דדחי — לאו דוקא, אלא כלומר: אפילו את"ל דדחי, הא כתיב "אני ה'" כדפי' לעיל גבי שומע אני. ואם תאמר: היכי מוכח מהכא דבעלמא דחי, ואיצטריך "עליה" למיסר, דהשתא קרא דהכא לא איצטריך לגופיה אלא לאשמועינן דבעלמא דחי, נימא "עליה" להיתירא, והשתא איצטריך קרא דהכא לגופיה, ולא נילף מעשה דייבום! וי"ל: דאפי' נימא ד"עליה" להיתירא — לא איצטריך קרא דהכא, דלא מצינו למילף מעשה דייבום, דמה לכבוד אב ואם — שכן הכשר מצוה. ועוד(ז), אדרבה: ממקדש והבערת בת כהן הוה ילפי' דלא דחי. ועוד: מייבום ליכא למילף, דבשבת איכא סקילה. אע"ג דבעריות נמי איכא בחמותו וכלתו שריפה וסקילה, כי נימא "עליה" להיתירא לא נימא אלא באחות אשה ודכוות', דליכא סקילה ושריפה, דלא הוקשו להיתירא אלא לאיסורא. וכן סבר רבא לפר"י ⊕(לעיל ד' ג) וא"ת: אכתי, הא איצטריך לגופיה, דסד"א דהואיל והוקש כבודם לכבוד המקום לידחי

תוספות ישנים

קרא דכתיב ביה בהדיא בעי למנקט: **מה** לפסח שכן כרת שאם לא יעשה אותו בי"ד יתחייב כרת. אבל במילה לא יתחייב כרת אם לא מל בשמיני ומ"מ פריך למסקנא מה למילה ופסח שכן כרת שאם לא יעשה אותם לעולם יתחייב כרת דכתיב וערל זכר אשר לא ימול ונכרתה מעמיו: **ת"ל** את שבתותי תשמרו ומקדשי תיראו אני ה' וא"כ ר"ל דאע"ג דאיש אמו ואביו תיראו ואת שבתותי תשמורו. וא"ת ואימא איפכא דאע"ג דאת שבתותי תשמורו איש אמו ואביו תיראו ויהיה כבוד דוחה את השבת. וכ"ת דכל היכא דאיכא לאקושי לקולא ולחומרא לחומרא מקשינן הא חומרא דאתי לידי קולא היא דדרשינן מיניה הא בעלמא דחי ולחומרא דידיה לא אצטריך. וכ"ת דאית לן למדרש טפי מרישיה לסיפיה ולא מסיפיה לרישא דהא הכא בסמוך גבי מקדש דריש מסיפיה לרישיה. וי"ל דהכא דריש ליה הכי משום דכתיב אני ה' דמשמע שיהיה מוראי למעלה ממוראכם כדאמרי' במדרש והתקדשת' והייתם קדושים יכול כמוני ת"ל אני ה' קדושתי למעלה מקדושתכם. טעמא דכתב רחמנא את שבתותי תשמורו הא לאו הכי דחי אין לפרש אם לא כתב ואת שבתותי דחי דאדרבה מסברא אית לן למימר דאין עשה דוחה ל"ת שיש בו כרת אלא ה"ק ואת שבתותי תשמורו מיותר להשמיעו הא בעלמא דחי דאי אמרינן בעלמא לא דחי לשתוק קרא משבתותי תשמורו ואנא ידענא דלא דחי מסברא אלא ודאי מייתר קרא לאשמעינן דבעלמא דחי. ואין להקשו' מאי שנא לעיל דאמרינן תיתי מפסח ומילה ולא אמרינן מדאנטריך והכא אמרינן מדאנטריך. וי"ל דשאני לעיל דפסח ומילה היתירא הוא וזה לא ידעינן מסברא אבל הכא דאתא קרא לאיסורא אין לומר נילף מיניה דא"כ לשתוק קרא מיניה דלעול' נימא מסברא דאין עשה דוחה ל"ת שיש בו כרת. וא"ת א"כ מאי האי דקאמר לעיל יכול יהא כבוד אב ואם דוחה שבת מנין לומר כן כיון דלא ידעינן קרא דאת שבתותי תשמורו הא לעולם בלא פסוק יש לנו לומר דלא דחי. ופי' הר' יוסף קמנון א) דנימא הכי יכול יהא כבוד אב ואם דוחה את השבת דנימא עליה להיתירא מה להלן יבום אף כאן יבום. ונימא הכי נאמר כאן עליה ונאמר להלן עליה מה להלן ערוה אף כאן ערוה וכתב רחמנא יבמה יבא עליה ונילף מיניה בעלמא ת"ל את שבתותי תשמורו וא"כ לא מצינו למימר עליה להיתירא דא"כ לשתוק קרא מעליה ואנן הוי ידעינן מאת שבתותי תשמורו דמשמע הא בעלמא דחי ומדאצטריך עליה ודאי לאיסורא:

א) נראה דל"ל דהכי קאמר יכול יהא וכו'.

מסורת הש"ס

[מנחות לט:]

כלאים פ"ט מ"ח שבת נד. מנחות לט.

ג"ל מכמועדיכם

[חגיגה ו.]

הגהות הב"ח

(א) גמ' ותמיד שכן ישנן לפני: (ב) תום' ד"ה עד וכו' דא"כ כלאים: (ג) בא"ד אלא משום טווי לחודיה כצ"ל ותיבת ונוז נמחק: (ד) ד"ה כולה וכו' שפירשתי לעיל. נ"ב ריש דף ד': (ה) בא"ד עד למחר ניל משריפת קדשים וי"ל כצ"ל ותיבת מיניה נמחק: (ו) ד"ה ומכולהו וכו' ואר"י דחשיבי כולהו כצ"ל ותיבת התם נמחק: (ז) ד"ה טעמא וכו' ועוד לאדרבה וכו' ועוד למיכוס וכו' אע"ג דבעריות נמי בחמותו וכלתו איכא שריפה וכו':

הגהות הגר"א

[א] גמ' ואליבא דמ"ד עולה כו'. נ"ב ר"ל ב"ה דהן אוסרין הנדרות (ולכן ל"ל דהכריתא דעליה אתיא כב"ש דאמרי עולת ראייה הוה דהא ב"ש מתירין הנדרות):

גליון הש"ס

גמ' יכול יהא כבוד אב ואם. עי' כתובות ד' מ ע"א תוס' ד"ה אי אמרה: **תום'** ד"ה טולה וי"ל דש"ה דלא בטלה מצותו. עיין שבועות דף ג ע"א תד"ה ועל: **תום'** ד"ה טעמא כו'. לפר"י (לעיל דף ג. ל"ל לקמן ד' ח ע"א ד"ה רבה:

גמרא

לאו דמחמר, ואפי' הכי לא דחי. אלא דקיימא לן דאתי עשה ודחי לא תעשה, ליגמר מהכא דלא לידחי! וכ"ת: שאני לאוי דשבת דחמירי – והא תנא בעלמא קאי ולא קפריך! דתניא: *יכול אמר לו אביו: היטמא! או שאמר לו: אל תחזיר! יכול ישמע לו, ת"ל °"איש אמו ואביו תיראו ואת שבתותי תשמורו" (ויקרא יט) – *כולכם חייבין בכבודי. אלא משום דאיכא למיפרך: מה להנך – שכן הכשר מצוה, אלא סד"א: תיתי מבנין בית המקדש. דתניא *יכול יהא בנין בית המקדש דוחה שבת, ת"ל °"את שבתותי תשמורו ומקדשי תיראו" (שם) – כולכם חייבין בכבודי. מאי לאו בבונה וסותר, וטעמא דכתב רחמנא "את שבתותי תשמורו", הא לאו הכי – דחי! לא, לאו דמחמר, ואפילו הכי לא דחי. ואלא דקיימא לן דאתי עשה ודחי ל"ת, ליגמר מהכא דלא דחי! וכ"ת: שאני לאוי דשבת דחמירי – והא תנא בעלמא קאי ולא קא פריך! דתניא: יכול אמר לו אביו: היטמא! או שאמר לו: אל תחזיר! יכול ישמע לו תלמוד לומר "איש אמו ואביו תיראו וגו'" – כולכם חייבים בכבודי. אלא, משום דאיכא למיפרך: מה להנך – שכן הכשר מצוה. הכשר מצוה תיפוק לי מהתם? אין הכי נמי. "ואת שבתותי תשמורו ומקדשי תיראו" למה לי? מיבעי ליה לכדתניא: יכול יתיירא אדם ממקדש – תלמוד לומר "את שבתותי תשמורו ואת מקדשי תיראו" – נאמרה שמירה בשבת ונאמרה מורא במקדש, מה שמירה האמורה בשבת לא

רש"י

לאו דמחמר. אחר בהמה, שהוא בלאו ד"לא תעשה כל מלאכה אתה ובהמתך" (שמות כ). ובהאי לאו ליכא כרת, דלא עביד מעשה בגופיה, וכמ"ד בפ' "מי שהחשיך" (שבת דף קנד.): המחמר אחר בהמתו בשבת פטור. ואפ"ה לא דחי. בתמיה. וליגמר מהכא. דלא דחי אפילו לאו גרידא. וכי תימא שאני לאוי דשבת דחמירי. דקי"ל (עירובין דף סט:): מחלל שבת כעובד עבודה זרה, ומשום הכי אפי' לאו גרידא לא דחי, ומינייהו לא גמרינן. והא תנא בעלמא קאי ולא פריך. והא אשכחן תנא בעלמא דיליף שאר לאוי, כגון לאו ד"לא יטמא" דכהן, ולאו ד"לא תוכל להתעלם", מלאו דשבת לחומרא, ולא פרכינן שאני לאוי דשבת דחמירי. [ב"מ לב.] אמר לו אביו. לכהן. היטמא. בבית הקברות להשיב אבידה, או שהיתה עומדת בחוץ ואמר לו אל תחזיר, יכול ישמע לו – ת"ל "איש אמו ואביו". וילפינן לאו דטומאה ולאו דהשבת אבדה מלאוי דשבת. אלא. לעולם דאמר ליה שחוט לי, בשל לי, ואפ"ה לא איצטריך "עליה", דאיכא למיפרך: מה להנך שחוט לי בשל לי – שכן הכשר מצוה בחילול שבת, בעקירת לא תעשה הוא מקיים עשה דכיבוד, וזהו הכשר קיומו, ואי אפשר לקיימו בלא עקירת לאו. הלכך, אי לא כתב "את שבתותי תשמורו" – ה"א לידחי. אבל ייבום – לא זה בלבד הכשר קיום העשה, שהרי יכול לחלוץ ולא יעקור לאו של ערוה, ולא איצטריך "עליה". מאי לאו בבונה וסותר. איצטריך למיסר, אף על גב דאב מלאכה הוא ואיכא כרת, אי לאו דאשמועינן ה"א אתי עשה ד"ועשו לי מקדש" ודחי לאו דשבת. והא תנא בעלמא (א) גמר. לאוי דטומאה והעלם אבדה מלאוי דשבת, ולא פריך. תיפוק לי מהתם. מ"איש אמו ואביו תיראו" דהכשר מצוה הוא, ולא דחי. למה ליה למיהדר למכתב הכא "את שבתותי תשמורו", אלא לאו דתילף מיניה דאפילו בלא הכשר מצוה, אי לא כתיב קרא בהדיא דלא דחי – אמרינן דדחי, אם כן איצטריך "עליה". נאמר שמירה בשבת ומורא במקדש. והקישן הכתוב בפסוק אחד.

תוספות

לידחי כדאמר בסוף "אלו מציאות" (ב"מ דף לב.), דה"א אי לאו קרא – לידחי ל"ת ועשה מהאי טעמא! וי"ל: דעשה ול"ת דקיל ה"א דלידחי, אבל ל"ת שיש בו כרת – לא ה"א דדחי (ב). ולהכי ל"ת ועשה ליכא למידק: הא בעלמא דחי, כדדייק, אלא תעשה שיש בו כרת, דדוקא ל"ת שיש בו כרת, דבלאו קרא ה"א דלא דחי – איכא למידק: הא בעלמא דחי. וא"ת: וכיון דהשתא בעי למימר דבעלמא דחי ל"ת שיש בו כרת – כ"ש דלידחי בעלמא ל"ת ועשה! וא"ל דה"נ, דא"כ ה"ל למיפרך אלא הא דקי"ל דאין עשה דוחה ל"ת ועשה – נגמר מהכא דדחי, כדפרי' לעיל (דף ה.)! וי"ל: דהשתא דילפינן דבעלמא דוחה ל"ת שיש בו כרת – ע"כ גרע מל"ת ועשה, דאי אפשר שידחה עשה ל"ת ועשה, דמאי אולמיה דהאי עשה מהאי עשה. והא דהוה בעי למימר בסוף "אלו מציאות" (ב"מ דף לב.) דעשה דכיבוד לידחי ל"ת ועשה – היינו משום דעדיף, דהוקש כבודם לכבוד המקום. וא"ת: אי בעלמא דחי – א"כ קרא דכלאים בציצית למה לי? ויש לומר: דאיצטריך לכדרבא. ולתנא דבי רבי ישמעאל נמי איצטריך, דלא נדרוש הכנף מין כנף דוקא למר לצמר ופשתים לפשתים. ועוד: ס"ד דלא לידחי עשה דציצית לאו דכלאים שאין שוה בנשים, למ"ד נשים פטורות מציצית. ולעיל דהוה בעי למילף מעשה דמצורע דלידחי עשה את ל"ת (ועשה), משמע דבעי למילף מהתם אפילו כלאים בציצית – ע"כ אכתי לא אסיק אדעתיה שיש חילוק בין שוה בכל, עד דפריך ליה. ובפ' "שני נזירים" (נזיר ד' נח. ושם) דיליף לגמרי בעלמא מראשו – איכא למימר סבר דנשים חייבות בציצית. וא"ת: "ראשו" למה לי? כיון דדחי אפילו לאו שיש בו כרת! וי"ל: דאיצטריך לאשמעינן דהקפת כל הראש שמה הקפה. ומפסח ומילה ותמיד לא קשיא מידי אמאי איצטריך קרא, כיון דבעלמא דחי – דס"ד למילף לענין שבת מכיבוד אב ואם דלא דחי, וה"א דשבת לא דחי אע"ג דבעלמא דחי.

ניגמר מהכא דלא דחי. משמע דאיירי בשחיטה וביטול – ניחא. ותימה: דמנא ליה לתנא לאוקמי קרא בשחיטה וביטול לאשמועינן דבעלמא דחי? אדרבה, נוקמה בלאו דמחמר ונגמר מהכא דבעלמא לא דחי, אפילו לאו גרידא! וי"ל: דדייק תנא מדלא אשמועי' קרא בשאר דברים, דליכא אלא לאו גרידא, דלא הוה אתי למיטעי. וא"ת: והיכי נגמר מהכא דלא דחי, דלמא שאני הכא דהוי עשה ולא תעשה! דהא כתיב *("למען ינוח שורך וחמורך וביום השביעי תשבות") (שמות כג) ומש"ה הוא דלא דחי, אבל לאו גרידא – לעולם נילף מכלאים בציצית דדחי? ואר"י: דעשה דכיבוד, הואיל ועדיף כולי האי, דהוקש כבודם לכבוד המקום – חשיב עשה דשבת כמאן דליתיה לגמרי, והוי כמאן דליכא אלא לאו גרידא. וכמו כן עשה דמקדש ועשה דבת כהן עדיפי מעשה דשבת, משום מורא ומשום כפרה דבת כהן. וא"ת: מנלן דלא דחי עשה דכיבוד אפי' לאו גרידא? דהא שבת וטומאה והשבת אבדה – כולהו עשה ולא תעשה נינהו! וי"ל: כיון דגלי לן קרא דלא אלימא לן טעמא דהוקש כבודם לכבוד המקום לידחי – א"כ אפילו לאו גרידא לא דחי, דמכלאים לא מצי גמיר, משום דכיבוד הוי הכשר מצוה.

והא תנא בעלמא קאי ולא קפריך. קשה: דמשמע דאיירי בשחיטה וביטול ניחא ליה, ואדרבה: כ"ש, דקשה טפי, דהיכי יליף דהיטמא ולא תחזיר, דליכא כרת, משבת דאיכא כרת וסקילה? דנהי דהתם לא דחי – הכא דחי, אע"ג דאיכא לאו ועשה, משום דהוקש כבודם! ויש לומר: כיון דגלי קרא דגרע מעשה דעלמא, דבעלמא דחי לאו שיש בו כרת והאי לא דחי – תו לא מהני טעמא דהוקש כבודם לכבוד המקום.

שכן הכשר מצוה. פירוש בקונטרס: לעולם בשחוט לי בשל לי, והא בעלמא דחי – מ"מ לא נילף מהכא דלידחי עשה דייבום לאו דאחות אשה, משום דאיכא למיפרך: שכן הכשר מצוה – דאי אפשר לקיים הכיבוד בלא דחיית הלאו, אבל גבי ייבום – יכול לקיים המצוה בלא דחיית הלאו, דאפשר בחליצה. וקשה לר"י: דאין זה אפשר, דאי אסור לייבם משום כרת חליצה נמי לא בעי, דכל שאין עולה לייבום אין עולה לחליצה. ולקמן בפ"ב (דף כ. ושם) ילפי' מקרא. ועוד אמרי' בההיא שמעתא (דף כא.) דלא חשבינן גבי יבום אפשר לקיים שניהם ע"י חליצה, משום דחליצה במקום ייבום לאו מצוה היא. *(ועוד: דלקמן לפי האמת דאיכא קרא בכלאים – ל"ל קרא כיון דהכשר מצוה דוחה אפי' ל"ת שיש בו כרת) א). ועוד: דמסקינן דבשום מקום אין עשה דוחה ל"ת שיש בו כרת – משמע אפילו בהכשר מצוה. ולקמן דפריך הכשר מצוה תיפוק לי מהתם, דפי' הקונט': תיפוק לי מהתם – מכיבוד אב דלא דחי, אלא ודאי ההוא דמקדש אתא למימר הא בעלמא דחי – אפי' בלא הכשר מצוה. ואין זה דיוק, דדלמא לגופיה איצטריך, משום דמכיבוד ילפינן דבעלמא דחי, איצטריך למיכתב גבי מקדש דלא דחי. ומיהו, הא איכא למימר אף על גב דבעלמא דחי – גבי מקדש ה"א דלא דחי כמו בכיבוד, דבכל מילי דשבת ה"א דלא דחי, ולהכי איצטריך מילה ופסח ותמיד, וכן אומר מהרר"י. ונראה לר"י, וכן פירש רבינו חננאל: דבלאו דמחמר מוקי לה, ומהכא לא נילף בעלמא דלא לידחי לאו גרידא, דמה לכיבוד – שכן הכשר מצוה כשמחמר ומטמא ומניח מלהחזיר אבדה כדי להביא גוזלות לאביו, בשעת דחיית הלאו אין מאכילו ומלבישו. אבל בעלמא, דעביד גוף המצוה – ילפינן מכלאים בציצית דדחי. ואר"י: דכיבוד אב, אפי' עוסק בגוף מצוה לא דחי, דבכל ענין קא פסיק שלא ישמע לו. והיינו משום דברוב ענייני כיבוד רגילים להיות על ידי הכשר מצוה, קאמר רחמנא דלא דחי בכל ענין, והשתא לקמן פריך שפיר: הכשר מצוה תיפוק לי מהתם דלא דחי, ואם אינו ענין להכשר מצוה – תניהו ענין לגוף מצוה.

יכול

עין משפט נר מצוה

כב א מיי' פ"א מהל' בית הבחירה הלכה יב:

[צ"ל אני ה' כולכם כו']:

תוספות ישנים

אלא לאו דמחמר. וא"ת למאי ס"ד למימר בשחוט לי ובשל לי מעיקרא יותר מבלאו דמחמר. וי"ל משום דכתיב שבתותי תשמורו דמשמע דבעיקר שמירה איירי והיינו במלאכה שבגופו דהיינו שחוט לי בשל לי אבל לאו דמחמר אינו אלא מלאכה בנחלתו: א) חזו היכא פריך למה לי עליה הא שמא בא לומר דאף מחלילה פטורה:

הגהות הב"ח

(א) רש"י ד"ה והא תנא בעלמא קאי ולא פריך. והא תנא בעלמא גמר לאוי וכו': (ב) תום' ד"ה (בכלף הקודס) טעמא וכו' ה"א דדחי דלהכי אל"ת ועשה ליכא כו':

גליון הש"ס

גמ' יכול יהא בנין בית המקדש דוחה שבת. עיין שבועות דף טו ע"ב רש"י ד"ה אין בנין:

[צ"ל וביום השביעי תשבות למען ינוח שורך וחמורך]

רש"ל מ"ז

כג א מיי' פ"ז מהלכות בית הבחירה הל' א:
כד ב מיי' שם ה"ב:
כה ג מיי' שם הל' ז:
כו ד מיי' פי"א מהל' סנהדרין הלכה ב ופכ"ד מהל' שבת הל' ז:

תורה אור

לֹא מִשַּׁבָּת אַתָּה מִתְיָרֵא, אֶלָּא מִמִּי שֶׁהִזְהִיר עַל הַשַּׁבָּת. אַף מוֹרָא הָאֲמוּרָה בַּמִּקְדָּשׁ, [א] לֹא מִמִּקְדָּשׁ אַתָּה מִתְיָרֵא אֶלָּא מִמִּי שֶׁהִזְהִיר עַל הַמִּקְדָּשׁ. [ב] וְאֵי זוֹ הִיא מוֹרָא מִקְדָּשׁ? *לֹא יִכָּנֵס אָדָם בְּהַר הַבַּיִת בְּמַקְלוֹ, בְּמִנְעָלוֹ, בְּפוּנְדָּתוֹ, וּבְאָבָק שֶׁעַל גַּבֵּי רַגְלָיו, וְלֹא יַעֲשֶׂנּוּ קַפֶּנְדַּרְיָא, וּרְקִיקָה מק"ו. וְאֵין לִי אֶלָּא בִּזְמַן שֶׁבהמ"ק קַיָּים, [ג] בִּזְמַן שֶׁאֵין בהמ"ק קַיָּים? מִנַּיִן ת"ל °"אֶת שַׁבְּתוֹתַי תִּשְׁמוֹרוּ וּמִקְדָּשִׁי תִּירָאוּ" (ויקרא יט), מַה שְּׁמִירָה הָאֲמוּרָה בַּשַּׁבָּת — לְעוֹלָם, אַף מוֹרָא הָאֲמוּרָה בַּמִּקְדָּשׁ — לְעוֹלָם. אֶלָּא סד"א: תֵּיתֵי מֵהַבְעָרָה, *דְּתָנָא דְּבֵי רַבִּי יִשְׁמָעֵאל: °"לֹא תְבַעֲרוּ אֵשׁ בְּכֹל מוֹשְׁבֹתֵיכֶם" (שמות לה), מַה ת"ל? מַה ת"ל?! אִי לְרַבִּי יוֹסֵי — לְלָאו, אִי לְרַ' נָתָן — לְחַלֵּק! *דְּתַנְיָא: הַבְעָרָה לְלָאו יָצְתָה, דִּבְרֵי רַ' יוֹסֵי. רַבִּי נָתָן אוֹמֵר: לְחַלֵּק. וַאֲמַר רָבָא: תַּנָּא — מוֹשָׁבוֹת קָא קַשְׁיָא לֵיהּ: "מוֹשָׁבוֹת" מַה ת"ל? מִכְּדִי שַׁבָּת חוֹבַת הַגּוּף הִיא, וְחוֹבַת הַגּוּף נוֹהֶגֶת בֵּין בָּאָרֶץ בֵּין בְּח"ל, מוֹשָׁבוֹת דִּכְתַב רַחֲמָנָא בְּשַׁבָּת לָמָּה לִי? *מִשּׁוּם רַבִּי יִשְׁמָעֵאל אָמַר תַּלְמִיד אֶחָד: לְפִי שֶׁנֶּאֱמַר °"וְכִי יִהְיֶה בְאִישׁ חֵטְא מִשְׁפַּט מָוֶת וְהוּמָת" (דברים כא) •שׁוֹמֵעַ אֲנִי בֵּין בַּחוֹל בֵּין בַּשַּׁבָּת, וּמָה אֲנִי מְקַיֵּים °"מְחַלְלֶיהָ מוֹת יוּמָת" (שמות לא) — בִּשְׁאָר מְלָאכוֹת, חוּץ מִמִּיתַת ב"ד. אוֹ אֵינוֹ אֶלָּא אֲפִילּוּ מִיתַת ב"ד, וּמָה אֲנִי מְקַיֵּים "וְהוּמָת" — בַּחוֹל, וְלֹא בַּשַּׁבָּת, אוֹ אֵינוֹ אֶלָּא אֲפִילּוּ בְּשַׁבָּת? ת"ל: "לֹא תְבַעֲרוּ אֵשׁ בְּכֹל מוֹשְׁבֹתֵיכֶם" וּלְהַלָּן הוּא אוֹמֵר °"וְהָיוּ אֵלֶּה לָכֶם לְחֻקַּת מִשְׁפָּט לְדֹרֹתֵיכֶם בְּכֹל מוֹשְׁבֹתֵיכֶם" (במדבר לה) מַה מוֹשָׁבוֹת הָאֲמוּרִים לְהַלָּן בְּב"ד — אַף מוֹשָׁבוֹת הָאֲמוּרִים כָּאן בְּב"ד, [ד] וְאָמַר רַחֲמָנָא "לֹא תְבַעֲרוּ". מַאי לָאו רַבִּי נָתָן הִיא, דְּאָמַר לְחַלֵּק יָצְתָה, וְטַעְמָא דִּכְתַב רַחֲמָנָא "לֹא תְבַעֲרוּ", הָא לָאו הָכִי דָּחֵי! לָא, רַבִּי יוֹסֵי. וְתֶיהֱוֵי נַמִּי רַ' יוֹסֵי, אֵימַר דְּאָמַר רַבִּי יוֹסֵי הַבְעָרָה לְלָאו יָצְתָה — הַבְעָרָה גְּרֵידְתָּא, הַבְעָרָה דְּב"ד בִּישּׁוּל פְּתִילָה הוּא, וְא"ר שֵׁשֶׁת: *מַה לִּי בִּישּׁוּל פְּתִילָה מַה לִּי בִּישּׁוּל סַמָּנִין! אֲמַר רַב שִׁימִי בַּר אַשִׁי: הַאי תַּנָּא לָא מִשּׁוּם דְּאָתֵי עֲשֵׂה וְדָחֵי ל"ת, אֶלָּא מִשּׁוּם דְּמַיְיתֵי(א) מק"ו, וְה"ק: מָה אֲנִי מְקַיֵּים "מְחַלְלֶיהָ מוֹת יוּמָת" בִּשְׁאָר מְלָאכוֹת, חוּץ מִמִּיתַת ב"ד, אֲבָל מִיתַת ב"ד — דָּחְיָא שַׁבָּת מק"ו

וּמָה

לֹא מִשַּׁבָּת אַתָּה מִתְיָרֵא. דְּלָא כְּתִיב בֵּיהּ מוֹרָא. פּוּנְדָּתוֹ. אַרְנָקִי שֶׁאוֹזֵר בּוֹ מָתְנָיו. קַפֶּנְדַּרְיָא. לְקַצֵּר הִילּוּכוֹ, שֶׁלֹּא לְהַקִּיף, וְיִכָּנֵס בְּפֶתַח זֶה וְיֵצֵא בְּשֶׁכְּנֶגְדּוֹ, וְלֹא לְשֵׁם עֲבוֹדָה אֶלָּא לַעֲשׂוֹת צְרָכָיו. מק"ו. מְפָרֵשׁ בִּבְרָכוֹת בְּפֶ' "הָרוֹאֶה" (דף סב:) מ"כִּי אֵין לָבֹא אֶל שַׁעַר הַמֶּלֶךְ בִּלְבוּשׁ שָׂק" שֶׁאֵינוֹ מָאוּס — ק"ו לָרוֹק, שֶׁהוּא מָאוּס לִפְנֵי הקב"ה. מַה ת"ל. וַהֲלֹא כְּבָר נֶאֱמַר "לֹא תַעֲשֶׂה כָל מְלָאכָה". לְלָאו יָצְאתָה. לוֹמַר שֶׁאֵין חַיָּיבִין עָלֶיהָ כָּרֵת וּסְקִילָה, אֶלָּא לָאו בְּעָלְמָא. לְחַלֵּק. שֶׁלֹּא תֹּאמַר אֵינוֹ חַיָּיב סְקִילָה עַד שֶׁיְּחַלֵּל שַׁבָּת בְּכָל מְלָאכוֹת, לְכָךְ יָצְתָה הַבְעָרָה מִן הַכְּלָל לְחַלֵּק: מַה הַבְעָרָה מְיוּחֶדֶת שֶׁהִיא אַב מְלָאכָה וְחַיָּיב עָלֶיהָ כָּרֵת וּסְקִילָה בִּפְנֵי עַצְמָהּ — אַף כֹּל שֶׁהוּא אַב מְלָאכָה כו'. ה"ג: וַאֲמַר רָבָא כו'. מוֹשְׁבוֹתֵיכֶם. בְּכָל מָקוֹם שֶׁאַתֶּם יוֹשְׁבִים, אֲפִילּוּ בְּחוּצָה לָאָרֶץ. חוֹבַת הַגּוּף הִיא. וְאֵינָהּ תְּלוּיָה בְּקַרְקַע, כְּכִלְאַיִם וְעָרְלָה וּתְרוּמוֹת וּמַעַשְׂרוֹת. אוֹ אֵינוֹ כו'. לְקַמָּן מְפָרֵשׁ. וְהָיוּ אֵלֶּה לָכֶם. גַּבֵּי מִיתַת ב"ד כְּתִיב, בְּפָרָשַׁת רוֹצְחִים. ה"ג: מַה מּוֹשָׁבוֹת הָאֲמוּרִים לְהַלָּן בְּמִיתַת ב"ד הַכָּתוּב מְדַבֵּר אַף כָּאן כו'. מַאי לָאו ר' נָתָן הִיא. דְּאָמַר הַבְעָרָה אַב מְלָאכָה הִיא, וּבְכָרֵת. וְאַפְּ"ה, אִי לָאו דְּאַשְׁמוֹעִינַן — ה"א אָתֵי עֲשֵׂה דְּ"וְהוּמָת" וְדָחֵי לֵיהּ. פְּתִילָה. שֶׁל אֵבָר, מַתִּיךְ וְזוֹרְקָהּ לְתוֹךְ פִּיו וְיוֹרֶדֶת לְתוֹךְ מֵעָיו. וְהַאי בִּישּׁוּל גָּמוּר הוּא, וְאַב מְלָאכָה הוּא, דְּמִמִּשְׁכָּן יָלְפִינַן, וּבִישּׁוּל סַמָּנִין הָיָה בִּמְלֶאכֶת הַמִּשְׁכָּן לִצְבֹּעַ תְּכֵלֶת וְתוֹלַעַת שָׁנִי. אֲמַר רַב שִׁימִי הַאי תַּנָּא. דְּאִיצְטְרִיךְ, דִּנְסִיב לָהּ קְרָא לְמֵיסַר מִיתַת בֵּית דִּין בְּשַׁבָּת — לָאו מִשּׁוּם דְּאִי לָא דְּאַשְׁמוֹעִינַן ה"א דָּחְיָא מִשּׁוּם טַעְמָא דַּעֲשֵׂה דָּחֵי, אֶלָּא מִשּׁוּם דַּהֲוָה מַיְיתִי לֵיהּ בְּקַל וָחוֹמֶר דְּדָחֵי שַׁבָּת.

רְצִיחָה

יכול יתיירא אדם מבית המקדש. גבי אביו לא הוצרך לומר כן, דפשיטא שלא ישתחוה לו לשם אלהות. אבל גבי המקדש איצטריך, משום דהוי דבר שבקדושה. א"נ: גבי אביו שייך מורא שלא יכעיסנו, אבל במקדש — אין יכול למצוא אלא בדוחק, כמו שמפרש והולך.

מושבות דכתב רחמנא למה לי. והא דדרשינן בפ"ק דשבת (דף כ.): בכל מושבות אי אתה מבעיר, אבל אתה מבעיר במדורת בית המוקד – היינו משום דהוי ליה למכתב "מושבות" וכתיב "מושבותיכם". ומדלא כתיב "לא תבערו" (ב) לכם וכתב "מושבות" – משמע דאתא לכדהכא. ובסוף פ"ק דקידושין (דף לז: ושם) דקאמר "מושבות" דכתב רחמנא גבי שבת ל"ל, סד"א הואיל ובענין דמועדות כתיב, ליבעי בה קידוש ב"ד כמועדות – לא מ"דלא תבערו אש בכל מושבותיכם" קדריש, אלא מקרא אחרינא ד"אמור אל הכהנים" דכתיב "שבת היא לה' בכל מושבותיכם" דההוא קרא בענינא דמועד כתיב: (ג) **או אינו אלא אפילו בשבת.** משום מה לי חומרא רבה מה לי חומרא זוטא. הקשה ה"ר יהודה כהן: היכא בעי לאוקמי רבי ישמעאל כר' יוסי דאמר הבערה ללאו יצתה? והא בפ"ק דשבת (דף יב: ושם) אמר דרבי ישמעאל קרא והטה, ואמר: לכשיבנה בהמ"ק אביא חטאת שמנה, אלמא דהבערה יש כרת! ועוד קשה, דנהי נמי רבי יוסי היא – מ"מ אי לאו "לא תבערו" הוי אמינא דמיתת ב"ד נמי דחיא שבת, משום מה לי חומרא רבה כו', אע"ג דנטילת נשמה אב מלאכה הוא. וא"כ, כי כתב "לא תבערו" אצטריך נמי "עליה" באחות אשה דליכא סקילה, דלא נימא מה לי חומרא כו'! וי"ל: דבלא"ה פריך שפיר טפי. **טעמא** דכתב רחמנא לא תבערו הא לאו הכי דחי. בסמוך מוכח דלא בעי למימר השתא מדאיצטריך "לא תבערו" לאסור מכלל דבעלמא דחי. דמפרש דאי לאו "לא תבערו" ה"א דלידחי כמו בכלאים בציצית, דמה לי חומרא רבה ומה לי חומרא זוטא, ואיצטריך "לא תבערו" לגופיה. וא"ת: וכיון דלגופיה איצטריך, אדרבה: נילף מהכא דלא דחי, דלא אמרינן מה לי חומרא רבה מה לי כו'! וי"ל: דלא מצי למילף אלא לאו שיש בו מיתה כמו בשבת, דאיכא סקילה. אבל לאו שיש בו כרת גרידא – התם אמרינן מה לי חומרא רבה מה לי חומרא זוטא, וה"ה דדחי לאו דכרת כמו אחות אשה, ולא לאו דמיתה כמו כלתו וחמותו, דלהכי לא הוה מקשינן להו אהדדי. א"נ: השתא נמי. מדאצטריך כדלעיל ואין חושש על "או אינו". וכל סוגיא זו לא אתיא כר"ש, דלר"ש איצטריך "לא תבערו" לאשמועינן דמקלקל בהבערה חייב, דמדאסר רחמנא הבערת שריפת בת כהן נפקא ליה בפרק "האורג" (שבת דף קו. ושם). אלא הך סוגיא אתיא כרבי יהודה דחשיב תיקון תקוני גברא, כמו מילה וקריעה על מת. ורבי יוסי ורבי נתן נמי דלא כר"ש, דלדידיה ליכא למידרש ללאו ולחלק כיון דאצטריך למקלקל בהבערה. ור"ש נפקא ליה לחלק מהיכא דנפקא ליה לשמואל בפ' "כלל גדול" (שם דף ע.). ועוד אר"י: דאי ללמוד על מקלקל בהבערה לחוד קאתי – הוה ליה לאשמועינן במקום שאין מצוה בהבערה. וא"ת: והיכי דרשינן ללאו או לחלק, כיון דאיצטריך "לא תבערו" למיתת ב"ד דלא דחי שבת! וי"ל: דדרשינן מדכתיב "הבערה", דאי למיתת ב"ד לחוד אתא – ה"ל למכתב "לא תעשו מלאכה בכל מושבותיכם". *וא"ת: נהי דהבערה דבישול פתילה לא דחיא שבת, דהוי הכשר מצוה – רציחה עצמה, כשנתבשלה הפתילה מאתמול, או חנק וסייף, תדחה שבת מטעם מה לי חומרא רבה מה לי חומרא זוטא? ומיהו, למאי דיליף מק"ו – ע"כ לא אתי "לא תבערו" אלא לרציחה עצמה, דהק"ו עצמו הוא על הרציחה, דעל הרציחה כתיב "מעם מזבחי תקחנו" ו"לא תבערו" אתא לאפוקי הק"ו. (וי"ל: כיון דגלי לן דלא אמרינן מה לי חומרא רבה מה לי חומרא זוטא בהכשר מצוה – ה"ה במצוה עצמה לא אמרינן. א"נ: (אפילו) הכשר מצוה נפקא לן מדלעיל, ואם אינו ענין לפתילה – תנהו ענין לרציחה עצמה, ע"כ). וי"ל: דבכל דוכתין משוינן מכשירי מצוה שאי אפשר לעשותה מע"ש כמצוה עצמה, כדתנן בפרק "רבי אליעזר דמילה" (שבת דף קל. ושם) אם לא הביא, ובפסחים פ' "אלו דברים" (דף סט:) כלל אמר רבי עקיבא כו' והכא באי אפשר לעשות הפתילה מע"ש, מדאצטריך קרא למעוטי*.

לא רבי יוסי. ו"או אינו" דקאמר – משום דשבת עשה ול"ת, (וה"ק: או אינו אלא אפי' מיתת ב"ד). א"נ: משום דשאני לאוי דשבת, דחמירי (ד).

ומה

תוספות ישנים

וטעמא דכתב רחמנא לא תבערו הא לאו הכי דחי. פי' הא בעלמא דחי ואינו ר"ל דאי לא כתב לא תבערו ה"א דדחי. דזה אינו דודאי אי לא כתב שום קרא ה"א מסברא דלא דחי אלא ה"פ מדאצטריך לא תבערו מכלל דבעלמא דחי דאי בעלמא לא דחי. לשתוק מלא תבערו דלעולם ידעינן מסברא דלא דחי. אלא מדאצטריך לא תבערו מכלל דבעלמא דחי. וא"ת היכי לישתוק קרא מלא תבערו הא אצטריך לגופיה למימר דלחלק יצאת. וי"ל דממושבותיכם קא סמיך וה"ק טעמא דכתב רחמנא לא תבערו אש בכל מושבותיכם. וא"ת א"כ היכי מפיק מיניה ר' נתן לחלק הא אצטריך לומר מה להלן מיתת ב"ד אף כאן מיתת ב"ד *) וי"ל דא"כ לכתוב קרא לא תעשו אש בכל מושבותיכם ומדשני בלשון לא תבערו נפקא לן לחלק. אבל מ"מ קשה דהא אצטריך קרא דמושבותיכם למימר בכל מושבותיכם אי אתה מבעיר אבל אתה מבעיר בבית המוקד. וי"ל דאי אתא לדרשא דהתם לכתוב קרא לא תבערו אש לכם. ואי לג"ש דהכא אתא לא לכתוב אלא מושבות מאי מושבותיכם ש"מ כולהו. וקשה להר"ס אימא מושבות להיתירא נאמר כאן מושבות ונאמר להלן מושבות מה להלן שבת אף כאן שבת וקאמר רחמנא והיו אלה לכם לדליכא למימר כל היכא דאיכא לאקולי לקולא ולחומרא לחומרא מקשינן דטפי עדיף לאקולי לקולא דהוי חדוש בדידיה ואשמעינן חומרא בדוכתא אחריתי ואי מקשינן לחומרא לעולם לא הוי חדוש דלעולם מסברא יש לנו לומר לא דחי. ועוד דאי מקשינן לחומרא משמע קולא בדוכתא אחריתי דמשמע הא בעלמא דחי. וצ"ל דקים ליה דהכי נאמר הג"ש דמושבותיכם לאיסורא: **לא** ר' יוסי היא וא"כ ל"ל עליה. וא"ת וכי מוקמת לה כר' יוסי להקשות למה לי עליה. וי"ל [illegible]

*) ע' כאן בתוס' ד"ה טעמא

ברכות נד.

סנהדרין לה:

שם: סב. שבת ע. לקמן לג:

מכילתא פרשה ויקהל

הגהות הב"ח

(א) גמ' דמייתי ליה מק"ו וה"ק: (ב) תוס' ד"ה מושבות וכו' ומדלא כתיב לא תבערו בכל גבולכם וכתב מושבות וכו' כמועדות לא דמלא תבערו אש: (ג) ד"ה (או אינו אלא וכו' חומרא זוטא) תא"מ ונ"ב ס"א נמחק זה והאי הקשה כו' שייך בסוף העמוד ולי נראה דא"צ למחקו אלא כל דבור זה שייך בסוף העמוד: (ד) ד"ה לא ר' יוסי וכו' דשבת דחמירי נ"ב כאן שייך ד"ה או אינו כו' הכתוב למעלה:

[שבת קו. ע"ש]

גליון הש"ס

גמ' שומע אני בין בחול בין בשבת. ע' פסחים ד' עה ע"א תד"ה למעוטי:

[וע"ע תוס' שבת ע. ד"ה הבערה וכו' ומש"כ בגליון]

גליון

[וע' תוס' פסחים עה. ד"ה למעוטי]

רש"י

רְצִיחָה דּוֹחָה אוֹתָהּ. שֶׁאִם הָיָה רוֹצֵחַ כֹּהֵן, וְרוֹצֶה לַעֲבוֹד עֲבוֹדָה – בֵּ"ד שׁוֹלְחִים וּמְבִיאִין אוֹתוֹ לָמוּת, אֲפִלּוּ א"כ הָיָה עַל(ד) גַּגּוֹ שֶׁל מִזְבֵּחַ וַעֲבוֹדָה בְּיָדוֹ. שֶׁנֶּאֱמַר מֵעִם מִזְבְּחִי תִּקָּחֶנּוּ לָמוּת. וְלֹא מֵעַל מִזְבְּחִי. וּמַאי אוֹ אֵינוֹ דְּקָאָמַר. הוֹאִיל וּמִקַּל וָחוֹמֶר אָתְיָא דְּדָחְיָא, הֵיכִי מָצִינוּ לְמֵימַר אוֹ אֵינוֹ אֶלָּא אֲפִי' מִיתַת בֵּ"ד לָא דָּחְיָא? קְבוּרַת מֵת מִצְוָה דָּחְיָא עֲבוֹדָה. מִ"וְּלַאֲחוֹתוֹ" בְּפ"ק דִּמְגִילָּה (דף ג:), וְאֵינוֹ דּוֹחֶה אֶת הַשַּׁבָּת, אַף אֲנִי אָבִיא רְצִיחָה, דְּאַף עַל פִּי שֶׁדּוֹחָה עֲבוֹדָה – לֹא תִּדְחֶה שַׁבָּת. וְהַאי דַּהֲדַר אָמַר אוֹ אֵינוֹ אֶלָּא אֲפִילּוּ בְּשַׁבָּת – הָכִי הֲדַר וְאָמַר: קְבוּרַת מֵת מִצְוָה גּוּפָהּ תִּדְחֶה שַׁבָּת כו'. וּלְמַאי דְּסָלֵיק אַדַּעְתֵּיהּ לְמֵימַר מֵעִיקָּרָא. דְּהַאי דְּאִיצְטְרִיךְ לֵיהּ קְרָא מִשּׁוּם דְּאִי לָא כְּתָבֵיהּ – ה"א אָתֵי עֲשֵׂה וְדָחֵי לֹא תַעֲשֶׂה. מַאי אוֹ אֵינוֹ. הֵיכִי מָצֵי לְמֵימַר אוֹ אֵינוֹ, דְּלָא דָּחֵי, בְּמַאי פֵּיתֵי לָן דְּלֹא תִּדְחֶה? אֵימוּר דְּאָמְרִינַן כו'. הַיְינוּ דַּהֲדַר וְאָמַר: אוֹ אֵינוֹ אֶלָּא אֲפִי' בְּמִיתַת בֵּ"ד לָא תִּדְחֵי לָאו דְּשַׁבָּת, שֶׁהֲרֵי יֵשׁ בּוֹ כָּרֵת. הֲדַר אָמַר אַטּוּ עֲשֵׂה דָּדָחֵי וכו'. הַיְינוּ דַּהֲדַר וְאָמַר אוֹ אֵינוֹ אֶלָּא אֲפִילּוּ בְּשַׁבָּת. לָאו לֹא תַעֲשֶׂה חָמוּר מִינֵּיהּ. שֶׁהֲרֵי לוֹקִין עָלָיו. אֶלָּא סָלְקָא דַּעְתָּךְ. לְעֵיל קָאֵי, דְּאוֹקִימְנָא דְּהָא דְּאִיצְטְרִיךְ "לֹא תְבַעֲרוּ", מִשּׁוּם דְּאִי לָא כָּתַב רַחֲמָנָא – הֲוָה מַיְיתִינַן בְּק"ו, וְלָאו מִשּׁוּם דְּאָתֵי עֲשֵׂה וְדָחֵי ל"ת דְּכָרֵת, וְ"עָלֶיהָ" לָמָּה לִי? אֶלָּא סד"א כו'. שֶׁהָיָה בִּכְלָל. "כִּי כָּל אֲשֶׁר יַעֲשֶׂה מִכֹּל הַתּוֹעֵבוֹת הָאֵלֶּה וְנִכְרְתוּ" כָּלַל בְּכָל הָעֲרָיוֹת כָּרֵת. וְיָצָא מִן הַכְּלָל לְלַמֵּד. שֶׁאִם אֵין לָהּ בָּנִים – תִּתְיַיבֵּם. בִּכְלַל כָּל הַקֳּדָשִׁים הָיוּ. שֶׁכְּבָר כָּלַל כָּרֵת בְּכוּלָּן "כָּל אִישׁ אֲשֶׁר יִקְרַב מִכָּל זַרְעֲכֶם אֶל הַקֳּדָשִׁים אֲשֶׁר יַקְדִּישׁוּ" וגו'. וְלָמָּה יָצְאוּ. בְּפָסוּק זֶה שֵׁנִי. יָצְאוּ קָדְשֵׁי בֶּדֶק הַבַּיִת. שֶׁאִם אֲכָלָן בְּטוּמְאַת הַגּוּף – פָּטוּר. לָמָּה יָצְתָה. "יְבָמָהּ יָבֹא עָלֶיהָ". מִי דָּמֵי הָתָם כְּלָל בְּאִיסּוּר וכו'. אִיכָּא לְמִיתְנֵי לָמָּה יָצְתָה. הָכָא פְּרָט בְּהֶיתֵּר וּכְלָל בְּאִיסּוּר. וְלָאו לְהָךְ דְּרָשָׁא דָּמֵי, דְּהָא בְּדָבָר הֶחָדָשׁ יָצָא לִידּוֹן. אֶלָּא. לְהָךְ דְּרָשָׁא: דָּבָר שֶׁהָיָה בִּכְלָל וְיָצָא לִידּוֹן בְּדָבָר הֶחָדָשׁ. אִי אַתָּה יָכוֹל לְהַחֲזִירוֹ. וּלְהַשְׁווֹתוֹ לִכְלָלוֹ, וְלֹא לְהַשְׁווֹת כְּלָלוֹ לוֹ. עַד שֶׁיַּחֲזִירֶנּוּ לְךָ הַכָּתוּב. הִילְכָּךְ בְּלָאו "עָלֶיהָ" נַמִי לָא אָתֵי לָן שְׁאָר עֲרָיוֹת לְיִיבּוּם. וְשָׁחַט אֶת הַכֶּבֶשׂ. בְּאָשָׁם מְצוֹרָע כְּתִי'. כִּי כַּחַטָּאת הָאָשָׁם הוּא. כְּדִין הַחַטָּאת כָּךְ דִּין אָשָׁם זֶה. שֶׁאֵין ת"ל כַּחַטָּאת. דְּהָא אָשָׁם זֶה, אִם לִשְׁחִיטָה בַּצָּפוֹן – הֲלֹא כְּבָר נֶאֱמַר בּוֹ "וְשָׁחַט אֶת הַכֶּבֶשׂ בִּמְקוֹם אֲשֶׁר יִשְׁחַט אֶת הַחַטָּאת", וְאִם לְמַתַּן דָּמִים וַאֲכִילָתוֹ – הֲרֵי הוּא כְּכָל אֲשָׁמוֹת, בִּכְלַל "זֹאת תּוֹרַת הָאָשָׁם", בְּ"נֵי אֶת אַהֲרֹן". לְפִי שֶׁיָּצָא אֲשַׁם מְצוֹרָע. מִכְּלַל שְׁאָר אֲשָׁמוֹת. לִידּוֹן בְּדָבָר הֶחָדָשׁ. שֶׁאֵינוֹ בִּשְׁאָר אֲשָׁמוֹת, בְּבֹהֶן יָד וּבְבֹהֶן רֶגֶל, וְהוֹאִיל וְיָצָא מִכְּלָלוֹ – יָכוֹל לֹא יְהֵא טָעוּן מַתַּן דָּמִים וְאֵימוּרִים לְגַבֵּי מִזְבֵּחַ, ת"ל כו'.

תְּרֵי

גמרא

וּמָה עֲבוֹדָה שֶׁהִיא חֲמוּרָה וְדוֹחָה שַׁבָּת – רְצִיחָה דּוֹחָה אוֹתָהּ, שֶׁנֶּאֱמַר °"מֵעִם מִזְבְּחִי תִּקָּחֶנּוּ לָמוּת", שַׁבָּת, שֶׁנִּדְחֵית מִפְּנֵי עֲבוֹדָה, אֵינוֹ דִּין שֶׁתְּהֵא רְצִיחָה דּוֹחָה אוֹתָהּ? וּמַאי "אוֹ אֵינוֹ" דְּקָאָמַר? ה"ק: קְבוּרַת מֵת מִצְוָה תּוֹכִיחַ, שֶׁדּוֹחָה אֶת הָעֲבוֹדָה וְאֵין דּוֹחָה אֶת הַשַּׁבָּת. הֲדַר אֲמַר: קְבוּרַת מֵת מִצְוָה תִּדְחֶה שַׁבָּת מִק"ו; וּמָה עֲבוֹדָה שֶׁהִיא דּוֹחָה שַׁבָּת, קְבוּרַת מֵת מִצְוָה דּוֹחָה אוֹתָהּ, מִ"וּלְאֲחוֹתוֹ", שַׁבָּת, שֶׁנִּדְחָה מִפְּנֵי עֲבוֹדָה, אֵינוֹ דִּין שֶׁתְּהֵא קְבוּרַת מֵת מִצְוָה דּוֹחָה אוֹתָהּ? ת"ל °"לֹא תְבַעֲרוּ". וּלְמַאי דְּסָלֵיק אַדַּעְתֵּיהּ מֵעִיקָּרָא דְּאָתֵי עֲשֵׂה וְדָחֵי ל"ת – מַאי "אוֹ אֵינוֹ" דְּקָאָמַר? ה"ק: מָה אֲנִי מְקַיֵּים °"מְחַלְלֶיהָ מוֹת יוּמָת" בִּשְׁאָר מְלָאכוֹת, חוּץ מִמִּיתַת בֵּ"ד, אֲבָל מִיתַת בֵּ"ד דָּחֵי שַׁבָּת, דְּאָתֵי עֲשֵׂה וְדָחֵי ל"ת. הֲדַר אֲמַר: אֵימַר דְּאָמְרִינַן דְּאָתֵי עֲשֵׂה וְדָחֵי לֹא תַעֲשֶׂה – לֹא תַעֲשֶׂה גְּרֵידָא, ל"ת שֶׁיֵּשׁ בּוֹ כָּרֵת – מִי שָׁמְעַתְּ לֵיהּ דְּדָחֵי? הֲדַר אֲמַר: אַטּוּ עֲשֵׂה (א) דּוֹחֶה אֶת ל"ת, •לָאו לֹא תַעֲשֶׂה חָמוּר מִינֵּיהּ, וְקָאָתֵי עֲשֵׂה וְדָחֵי לֵיהּ, מַה לִּי חוּמְרָא זוּטָא, וּמַה לִּי חוּמְרָא רַבָּה? ת"ל "לֹא תְבַעֲרוּ". אֶלָּא [אִיצְטְרִיךְ]: סד"א, תֶּיהֱוֵי הַאי אֵשֶׁת אָח דָּבָר שֶׁהָיָה בִּכְלָל וְיָצָא מִן הַכְּלָל לְלַמֵּד, לֹא לְלַמֵּד עַל עַצְמוֹ יָצָא אֶלָּא לְלַמֵּד עַל הַכְּלָל כּוּלּוֹ יָצָא. דְּתַנְיָא: *דָּבָר שֶׁהָיָה בִּכְלָל וְיָצָא מִן הַכְּלָל וכו' כֵּיצַד? °"וְהַנֶּפֶשׁ אֲשֶׁר תֹּאכַל בָּשָׂר מִזֶּבַח הַשְּׁלָמִים וְטוּמְאָתוֹ עָלָיו", וַהֲלֹא שְׁלָמִים בִּכְלַל (ב) קֳדָשִׁים הָיוּ, וְלָמָּה יָצְאוּ – לְהַקִּישׁ אֲלֵיהֶן, וְלוֹמַר לְךָ: מַה שְּׁלָמִים מְיוּחָדִים קָדְשֵׁי מִזְבֵּחַ – אַף כָּל קָדְשֵׁי מִזְבֵּחַ, יָצְאוּ קָדְשֵׁי בֶּדֶק הַבַּיִת. הָכָא נַמִי(ג): הָא אֵשֶׁת אָח בִּכְלַל כָּל הָעֲרָיוֹת הָיְתָה, וְלָמָּה יָצְתָה – לְהַקִּישׁ אֵלֶיהָ וְלוֹמַר לְךָ: מָה אֵשֶׁת אָח שַׁרְיָא – אַף כָּל עֲרָיוֹת נַמִי שַׁרְיָין. מִי דָּמֵי? הָתָם כְּלָל בְּאִיסּוּר וּפְרָט בְּאִיסּוּר. הָכָא – כְּלָל בְּאִיסּוּר וּפְרָט בְּהֶיתֵּר! הָא לָא דָּמֵי אֶלָּא לְדָבָר שֶׁהָיָה בִּכְלָל וְיָצָא לִידּוֹן בְּדָבָר הֶחָדָשׁ, שֶׁאִי אַתָּה יָכוֹל לְהַחֲזִירוֹ לִכְלָלוֹ עַד שֶׁיַּחֲזִירֶנּוּ לְךָ הַכָּתוּב בְּפֵירוּשׁ. דְּתַנְיָא: *דָּבָר שֶׁהָיָה בִּכְלָל וְיָצָא לִידּוֹן בְּדָבָר הֶחָדָשׁ אִי אַתָּה רַשַּׁאי לְהַחֲזִירוֹ לִכְלָלוֹ עַד שֶׁיַּחֲזִירֶנּוּ לְךָ הַכָּתוּב בְּפֵירוּשׁ. כֵּיצַד? °"וְשָׁחַט אֶת הַכֶּבֶשׂ בִּמְקוֹם אֲשֶׁר יִשְׁחַט אֶת הַחַטָּאת וְאֶת הָעוֹלָה בִּמְקוֹם הַקֹּדֶשׁ כִּי כַּחַטָּאת הָאָשָׁם הוּא לַכֹּהֵן" שֶׁאֵין ת"ל "כַּחַטָּאת הָאָשָׁם", וּמָה ת"ל "כַּחַטָּאת הָאָשָׁם" – [א]לְפִי שֶׁיָּצָא אֲשַׁם מְצוֹרָע לִידּוֹן בְּדָבָר הֶחָדָשׁ, בְּבֹהֶן יָד וּבֹהֶן רֶגֶל הַיְמָנִית, [ב]יָכוֹל לֹא יְהֵא טָעוּן מַתַּן דָּמִים וְאֵימוּרִים לְגַבֵּי מִזְבֵּחַ

תַּלְמוּד

תוספות

ומה עבודה שהיא חמורה ודוחה שבת, רציחה דוחה אותה. הקשה הר"ר יעקב דאורלינ"ש: נימא דיו, מה רציחה אינו דוחה עבודה אלא בשב ואל תעשה – שבת נמי לא תדחה אלא בשב ואל תעשה! וי"ל: דאתיא כרבי טרפון, דאמר (ב"ק כה.): היכא דמיפרך ק"ו לא אמרינן דיו. והא דאמר ליה ריש לקיש לר' יוחנן בפ' "אחד דיני ממונות" (סנהדרין דף לה.): ותהא קבורת מת מצוה דוחה שבת מקל וחומר – לא משום דסבר כר"ט. אלא (ה) לא מסיק אדעתיה לחלק בין קום עשה לשב ואל תעשה, כי היכי דלא מסיק אדעתיה הש"ס בפ' "מי שמתו" (ברכות דף כ. ושם). ורבי יוחנן דלא מהדר ליה דיו – משום דמהדר ליה שפיר טפי: רציחה תוכיח, דאפילו לרבי טרפון ליכא ק"ו. ועוד נראה לומר, דהכא דיינין הכי: ומה עבודה דקילא – דחיא שבת, רציחה וקבורת מת מצוה דחמירא – לא כל שכן. ובמה הם חמורים – דעבודה נדחית מפניהם. ובפ' "כיצד הרגל" (ב"ק דף כה. ושם) דאמרו רבנן לר"ט דיו, ולא דיינין: ומה שן ורגל דקילי חייבים ברשות הניזק נזק שלם, קרן לא כ"ש – משום דאי נעביד קל וחומר הכי איכא למפרך טובא דאיכא בשן ורגל וליכא בקרן, כגון יש הנאה להזיקן.

שנאמר מעם מזבחי. ואפי' אם אין שם כהן אחר ראוי לעבודה, שהעבודה נדחית. וא"ת: ודלמא התם לאו משום דרציחה דחיא עבודה, אלא משום דגברא הוא דלא חזי, כדאמרי' (ברכות דף לב:): כהן שהרג נפש – לא ישא את כפיו, שנאמר "ידיכם דמים מלאו" וכ"ש עבודה! וי"ל: דע"כ חזי, דאין מחלל עבודה, ד"מעם מזבחי", ולא מעל מזבחי, ולא ישא את כפיו – חומרא בעלמא הוא. ועוד: דוקא לא ישא את כפיו, לפי *שהרגו בידו, ואין קטיגור נעשה סניגור, וכדכתיב בההוא קרא "ובפרישכם כפיכם*)".

תלמוד לומר לא תבערו. וא"ת: אמאי אילטריך בפרק "אחד דיני ממונות" (סנהדרין דף לו.) מזבחי המיוחד לי למילף דרציחה דוחה אפילו קרבן צבור, תיפוק ליה מדאילטריך "לא תבערו" לאפוקי מק"ו – ש"מ דרציחה דוחה אפי' קרבן צבור דדחי שבת. דאי קרבן יחיד – א"כ ליכא קל וחומר! וי"ל: דאי לאו דכתיב "מזבחי" לא הוה מוקמינן קרא מסברא בקרבן צבור(ו) דכדי לדרוש "לא תבערו" לאפוקי מק"ו, אלא הוה מוקמינן קרא בקרבן יחיד, ו"לא תבערו" הוה דרשינן ע"כ לשום דרשא אחריתי. *א"נ: השתא דכתב "לא תבערו" הוה מוקמינן קרא בקרבן יחיד מק"ו דאביי, דאמר בפ' "אחד דיני ממונות" (שם דף לה:): השתא דאמרת אין רציחה דוחה שבת – אין רציחה דוחה עבודה מק"ו: ומה שבת שנדחית מפני עבודה אין רציחה דוחה אותה כו'.

לפי שיצא אשם מצורע לידון בדבר החדש. מה שחטאת מצורע טעונה נסכים ושאר חטאות אין טעונות – לא חשיב דבר חדש, ואין קרוי דבר חדש אלא כשסותר כללו, כי הכא דשאר אשמות טעונות כל הדם לגבי מזבח, ואשם מצורע נותן ממנו לבהונות. וכגון אשת אח שנאסרו כל העריות וזו הותרה, שסותר כללו. אבל מה שחטאת מצורע טעונה נסכים – אין סותר את כללו. וא"ת: ולמ"ד בריש "איזהו מקומן" (זבחים דף מט:) דכללו גמר מיניה – יהיו כל אשמות טעונות מתן בהונות, ולילפו נמי כולהו עריות מאשת אח! וי"ל: דלא גמר מיניה אלא דבר דלא חדש בו, כגון שחיטת לפון לעכב. אבל לענין חידוש לא גמר מיניה, כדפרש"י התם, *דאם כן היה יוצא לידון בדבר החדש כיוצא בו ללמד על הכלל כולו – [ואין זה חידוש].

ת"ל

*) [וע"ע תוס' סנהדרין לה:]

עין משפט נר מצוה

כו א ב מיי' פ"ד מהל' מחוסרי כפרה הל' ב:

תוספות ישנים

מה לי חומרא רבה מה לי חומרא זוטא. תימה דהסברות הפוכות מלמעלה דלעיל אמרינן דאי לאו קרא אמרינן מסברא לא דחי והכא משמע איפכא. ועו"ק דא"כ מה קאמר לעיל היכא אשכחינן דדחי דאצטריך עליה למיסרה וטרי *) אלא אצטריך לימא מדאצטריך עליה דאי לאו עליה ה"א דדחי דמה לי חומרא רבה מה לי חומרא זוטא. וזה לא קשה כ"כ דהאי משא ומתן אינו כי אם למאי דסליק אדעתין מעיקרא. אכן דוחק הוא דמ"מ משמע שהסברא מועלת וא"כ הדר קושין לדוכתיה. וא"ר דה"פ ממאי דעליה לאיסורא דלמא עליה להיתירא ונילף מינה בעלמא דדחי ל"ת שיש בו כרת דהכי נימא נאמר כאן עליה ונאמר להלן עליה מה להלן ערוה אף כאן ערוה וקאמר רחמנא יבמה יבא עליה ומינה נילף בעלמא דמ"ל חומרא רבה מ"ל חומרא קולא תו אמר [ת"ל] לא תבערו וא"כ נאמר ע"כ עליה לאיסורא דאי עליה להיתירא אמאי אצטריך עליה תיפוק לי מלא תבערו דמשמע הא בעלמא דחי אלא ודאי מדאצטריך עליה ש"מ לאיסורא הוא. וא"ת ואימא איפכא דודאי עליה להיתירא ולא תבערו לא אתא למימר הא לאו הכי דחי אלא לגופיה אילטריך דסד"א ניליף מעליה דדחי כתב רחמנא לא תבערו דלא דחי. וי"ל דאפי' עליה להיתירא לא אצטריך לא תבערו דהא אין לנו ללמוד הבערה שהיא מיתת ב"ד מאחות אשה ומאשת אח שאין בה רק איסור כרת. אבל השתא כי כתב לא תבערו ודאי אמרינן עליה לאיסורא דאי עליה להיתירא לא אצטריך דהא ניליף מלא תבערו דמשמע הא בעלמא דחי דודאי כל דבר שיש בו כרת נוכל למילף מכ"ש דמיתת ב"ד.

*) נ"ל הלא אילטריך למכתב עליה דאי לאו עליה כו'.

נ"ל א"כ

הגהות הב"ח

(א) גמ' אטו עשה דדוחה את: (ב) שם בכלל כל הקדשים היו: (ג) שם הכא נמי ה"א אשת אח בכלל: (ד) רש"י ד"ה רציחה וכו' היה על גבי מזבח ועבודה בידו שנאמר כצ"ל והד"א: (ה) תוס' ד"ה ומה וכו' כר' טרפון אלא דלא מסיק: (ו) ד"ה תלמוד וכו' בקרבן צבור כדי כצ"ל ואות ו' נמחק:

גליון הש"ס

גמ' לאו ל"ת חמור מיניה. עיין רמב"ן פרשת יתרו בפסוק זכור את יום השבת: תוס' ד"ה לפי כו' דא"כ היה יוצא לידון בדבר החדש. עיין תשובת רשד"ם ח"א סימן לג:

מסורת הש"ס

שמות כא | שם לה | שם לה | ויקרא ו | שם יד | [כריתות ב:] | זבחים מט. | [ברכות לב:] | תורה אור

תַּלְמוּד לוֹמַר °"כִּי כַּחַטָּאת הָאָשָׁם הוּא", מַה חַטָּאת טְעוּנָה מַתַּן דָּמִים וְאֵימוּרִים לְגַבֵּי מִזְבֵּחַ – אַף אָשָׁם טָעוּן מַתַּן דָּמִים וְאֵימוּרִים לְגַבֵּי מִזְבֵּחַ. וְאִי לָא אַהַדְרֵיהּ קְרָא ה"א: לְמַאי דְּנָפֵק נָפַק, וּלְמַאי דְּלָא נָפֵק – לָא נָפַק. ה"נ ה"א: אֵשֶׁת אָח דְּאִישְׁתְּרָא אִישְׁתְּרַאי, שְׁאָר עֲרָיוֹת – לָא. אֶלָּא סד"א: תֵּיתֵי(א) בְּמָה מָצִינוּ מֵאֵשֶׁת אָח; מָה אֵשֶׁת אָח מִיַּיבְּמָה אַף אֲחוֹת אִשָּׁה תִּתְיַיבֵּם. מִי דָּמֵי? הָתָם חַד אִיסּוּרָא, הָכָא – תְּרֵי אִיסּוּרֵי! מַהוּ דְּתֵימָא: הוֹאִיל וְאִישְׁתְּרֵי – אִישְׁתְּרֵי. וּמְנָא תֵּימְרָא דְּאָמְרִינַן הוֹאִיל וְאִישְׁתְּרֵי אִישְׁתְּרֵי? דְּתַנְיָא: *מְצוֹרָע שֶׁחָל שְׁמִינִי שֶׁלּוֹ בְּעֶרֶב הַפֶּסַח וְרָאָה קֶרִי בּוֹ בַּיּוֹם וְטָבַל, אָמְרוּ חֲכָמִים: אע"פ שֶׁאֵין טְבוּל יוֹם אַחֵר נִכְנָס, זֶה – נִכְנָס, מוּטָב שֶׁיָּבֹא עֲשֵׂה שֶׁיֵּשׁ בּוֹ כָּרֵת וְיִדְחֶה עֲשֵׂה שֶׁאֵין בּוֹ כָּרֵת. *וְאָמַר רַ' יוֹחָנָן: דְּבַר תּוֹרָה אֲפִי' עֲשֵׂה לֵית בֵּיהּ, שֶׁנֶּאֱמַר °"וַיַּעֲמֹד יְהוֹשָׁפָט בִּקְהַל יְהוּדָה לִפְנֵי הֶחָצֵר הַחֲדָשָׁה". מַאי חָצֵר הַחֲדָשָׁה? אָמַר *(רַ' יוֹחָנָן): שֶׁחִידְּשׁוּ בָּהּ דְּבָרִים, וְאָמְרוּ: טְבוּל יוֹם לֹא יִכָּנֵס לְמַחֲנֵה לְוִיָּה. וְאָמַר עוּלָּא: מַה טַּעַם – הוֹאִיל וְהוּתַּר לְצָרַעְתּוֹ הוּתַּר לְקִרְיוֹ – מִי דָּמֵי לְדְעוּלָּא?

תֵּינַח

תורה אור: ויקרא יד | ד"ה ב כ

תְּרֵי אִיסּוּרֵי. אֵשֶׁת אָח וַאֲחוֹת אִשָּׁה. הוֹאִיל וְאִישְׁתְּרֵי. אִיסּוּר אֵשֶׁת אָח שֶׁהָיָה עָלֶיהָ כְּשֶׁמֵּת אָחִיו בְּלֹא בָנִים – אִישְׁתְּרֵי נַמִּי אִיסּוּר אֲחוֹת אִשָּׁה. שְׁמִינִי שֶׁלּוֹ. שֶׁהוּא יוֹם הֲבָאַת קָרְבְּנוֹתָיו, וְצָרִיךְ לָבֹא בְּהַר הַבַּיִת וְלַעֲמוֹד בְּשַׁעַר נִקָּנוֹר וּלְהַכְנִיס יָדָיו לָעֲזָרָה לִיתֵּן מִן הַדָּם לִבְהוֹנוֹת(ב). וְרָאָה קֶרִי. לְהָכִי נָקַט קֶרִי וְלֹא טוּמְאַת שֶׁרֶץ וּנְבֵלָה: דְּטְמֵא שֶׁרֶץ, וַאֲפִי' טְמֵא מֵת, נִכְנָסִין לְהַר הַבַּיִת, כִּדְמְפָרֵשׁ בְּ"אֵלּוּ דְּבָרִים" (פסחים דף סז.), שֶׁנֶּאֱמַר "וַיִּקַּח מֹשֶׁה אֶת עַצְמוֹת יוֹסֵף עִמּוֹ". וְשַׁעֲרֵי נִקָּנוֹר לֹא נִתְקַדְּשׁוּ בִּקְדוּשַּׁת עֲזָרָה, כִּדְאָמְרִינַן בְּ"כֵּילַד צוֹלִין" (שם דף פה:), וַהֲרֵי הֵן כְּהַר הַבַּיִת, וְיָכוֹל טְמֵא מֵת לִיכָּנֵס לְשָׁם. אֲבָל בַּעַל קֶרִי – מִשְׁתַּלֵּחַ חוּץ לִשְׁנֵי מַחֲנוֹת כְּזָב, כִּדְמְפָרֵשׁ בְּ"אֵלּוּ דְּבָרִים": זָב, וְכָל זָב – לְרַבּוֹת בַּעַל קֶרִי. וְטָבַל. לְקִרְיוֹ. אע"פ. דִּטְבוּל יוֹם אַחֵר דְּקֶרִי אֵינוֹ נִכְנָס לְהַר הַבַּיִת, דְּכָל טְבוּל יוֹם הֲרֵי הוּא בְּטוּמְאָה עֲדַיִין לִתְרוּמָה וּלְקָדָשִׁים וְלַמִּקְדָּשׁ. זֶה. יָבֹא לְהַר הַבַּיִת, וְיַכְנִיס יָדָיו לִבְהוֹנוֹת, וְיִטְהַר לֶאֱכוֹל פִּסְחוֹ לָעֶרֶב. שֶׁיָּבֹא עֲשֵׂה דְּפֶסַח שֶׁיֵּשׁ בּוֹ כָּרֵת. דְּאִם לֹא יַכְנִיס יָדָיו לִבְהוֹנוֹת לֹא יִטְהַר לֶאֱכוֹל פִּסְחוֹ לָעֶרֶב. וְיִדְחֶה עֲשֵׂה. דְ"וִישַׁלְּחוּ מִן הַמַּחֲנֶה" שֶׁאֵין בּוֹ כָּרֵת. שֶׁאֵין עָנוּשׁ כָּרֵת אֶלָּא עַל בִּיאַת עֲזָרָה, וְזֶה לֹא יִכָּנֵס לָעֲזָרָה אֶלָּא לְשַׁעֲרֵי נִיקָּנוֹר שֶׁלֹּא נִתְקַדְּשׁוּ, וְיַכְנִיס יָדָיו לִבְהוֹנוֹת וְיִטְהַר מִצָּרַעְתּוֹ. וְיִשְׁלַח פִּסְחוֹ לָעֲזָרָה לִשְׁחוֹט, וְלָעֶרֶב יַעֲרִיב שִׁמְשׁוֹ וְיִטְהַר מִקִּרְיוֹ. וַיַּעֲמֹד יְהוֹשָׁפָט. אוֹתוֹ הַיּוֹם נִטְהֲרוּ יִשְׂרָאֵל מִטּוּמְאָה שֶׁבִּידֵיהֶם, כְּדִבְרֵי הַיָּמִים. לְמַחֲנֵה לְוִיָּה. לְהַר הַבַּיִת. וְאָמַר עוּלָּא. בְּמַסֶּכֶת זְבָחִים (דף לב:), דְּאָמַר עוּלָּא: בִּיאָה בְּמִקְצָת שְׁמָהּ בִּיאָה, וְאוֹתְבִינֵיהּ מֵהָא דְּקָתָנֵי: זֶה נִכְנָס וּמַכְנִיס יָדוֹ לִבְהוֹנוֹת. וְאִי אָמְרַתְּ בִּיאָה בְּמִקְצָת שְׁמָהּ בִּיאָה, נְהִי נַמִּי דְּנִכְנָס לְהַר הַבַּיִת, מִשּׁוּם דַּעֲשֵׂה שֶׁאֵין בּוֹ כָּרֵת הוּא, לִבְהוֹנוֹת הֵיכִי מָצֵי מְעַיֵּיל יְדֵיהּ? אִידִי וְאִידִי עֲשֵׂה שֶׁיֵּשׁ בּוֹ כָּרֵת הוּא, דְּקַיְימָא לָן בִּמְנָחוֹת בְּ"הַקּוֹמֵץ" רַבָּה (דף כז:) מְחוּסַּר כִּפּוּרִים שֶׁנִּכְנָס לַמִּקְדָּשׁ עָנוּשׁ כָּרֵת, וְאֵין צָרִיךְ לוֹמַר טְבוּל יוֹם וּשְׁאָר כָּל הַטְּמֵאִים, וְשַׁנֵּי עוּלָּא: שָׁאנֵי מְצוֹרָע הוֹאִיל וְהוּתְּרָה לוֹ בִּיאָה בְּמִקְצָת לְצָרַעְתּוֹ, שֶׁהֲרֵי עֲדַיִין מְחוּסַּר כִּפּוּרִים הוּא, וּבְכָרֵת, וְהוּתְּרָה לוֹ מִן הַתּוֹרָה בִּיאָה זוֹ בְּמִקְצָת – הוּתַּר נַמִּי לְקִרְיוֹ. אַלְמָא, הוֹאִיל וְאִישְׁתְּרַאי חַד אִיסּוּרָא – אִישְׁתְּרַאי נַמִּי אִידָךְ דַּהֲוָה גַּבֵּיהּ.

תֵּינַח

ת"ל כי כחטאת האשם הוא. והשתא לא צריך קרא ד"ושחט את הכבש" דכולה מילתא מיניה גמר מהיקשא, ובריש "איזהו מקומן" (זבחים דף מט.) מוקי ליה לעכב.

למאי דנפק נפק. דהיינו מתן בהונות ושחיטת לפון שכתוב בהדיא. ולמאי דלא נפק, כגון מתן דמים ואימורים – לא נפק, ולא יהיה בו מתן דמים ואימורים עד שיכתב בהדיא.

וראה קרי בו ביום וטבל. פירש בקונטרס: להכי נקט קרי, ולא טמא שרץ ונבילה, דטמא שרץ ואפי' טמא מת נכנסים במחנה לויה, כדאמר בפר' "אלו דברים" (פסחים דף סז.) דאפי' מת עצמו נכנס, שנאמר "ויקח משה את עצמות יוסף עמו" – עמו במחיצתו. ואין נראה לר"י: דהא דאמר וידחה עשה שאין בו כרת – היינו עשה דרבנן. [כדמפרש ר' יוחנן. וטמא מת אין נכנס בחיל – נמי מדרבנן], כדתנן במסכת כלים (פ"א מ"ח): החיל מקודש הימנו, שאין גוים וטמאי מתים נכנסים לשם. עזרת נשים מקודשת הימנו – שאין טבול יום נכנס לשם. ובכל טבול יום איירי, בין דבעל קרי, בין דטמא מת, שרץ ונבילה, דקא איירי בהו התם לעיל! ואר"י: דנקט בעל קרי לרבותא, דאע"ג דאשתלח חוץ לב' מחנות – התירו לו חכמים ליכנס, דבמקום כרת לא העמידו דבריהם. וא"ת: בפ' "היה נוטל" (סוטה דף כ: ושם) דקתני גבי סוטה: והם אומרים הוליאוה הוליאוה שלא תטמא העזרה. ופריך מהא דאפילו מת עצמו שרי. ומאי קושיא? והא מדרבנן אסור! ותירץ ר"ת: שלא גזרו אלא שלא יכנס, אבל אם הוא כבר שם – לא גזרו עליו שילא, כיון דמדאורייתא שרי ליכנס שם. ודקדק מהא דאמרינן בפרק "הנשרפים" (סנהדרין דף פא:): כהן ששימש בטומאה – אחיו הכהנים מוציאין אותו חוץ לעזרה, ומפלעין מוחו בגיזרין. משמע דאין מוציאין אלא מחוץ לעזרה, שהוא מחנה שכינה, וממיתין אותו בעזרת נשים, כיון שכבר היה שם. ור"י מפרש, דבסוטה דייק מדקתני הוציאוה הוציאוה תרי זימני, דאי לאו דהוי איסור דאורייתא לא היו ממהרין כל כך. ואין להאריך כאן. זה נכנס. שהיה צריך לבא להר הבית לעמוד בשער נקנור, ולהכניס ידיו לעזרה וליתן לו מן הדם בבהונות. ושערי נקנור לא נתקדשו, כדאמרינן ב"כילד צולין" (פסחים דף פה: ושם) שכל השערים נתקדשו חוץ משערי נקנור, ששם מצורע עומד ומכניס ידיו לבהונות. וא"ת: למה נמנעו בשביל כך מלקדשם? יעמוד בעזרת נשים ויכניס ידיו לשער נקנור! ופירש ריב"ן: דאין זה "לפני ה'", דלא הוי באויר העזרה. ואין נראה: דאי הוה קדוש כקדושת העזרה – הוי שפיר "לפני ה'"! ואומר רבינו תם: דעשו בשביל תקנת מצורעים, שיעמדו שם, שיגין עליהם השער בחמה מפני החמה ובגשמים מפני הגשמים.

מוטב יבא עשה שיש בו כרת כו'. לאו מילתא דפסיקא היא, דיש מקומות שהעמידו דבריהם במקום כרת, כדאמרינן בפסחים בפרק "האשה" (דף צב.), אלא כאן לא היה נראה לחכמים להחמיר.

רבי יוחנן אמר דבר תורה אפילו עשה אין בו. רבי יוחנן לא אתא לפלוגי אברייתא, דלאו תנא הוא, כדמוכח בפרק קמא דכתובות (דף ח.), דמשני אהרב: תנא הוא ופליג, ולא בעי לשנויי הכי לר' יוחנן, אע"ג דיש לדחות דר' יוחנן (ג) כמתני' דכלים (פ"א מ"ח), דתנן: עזרת נשים מקודשת הימנו, שאין טבול יום נכנס לשם. והיינו מדרבנן, דאי מדאורייתא אסור ליכנס במחנה לויה, אם כן בהר הבית נמי ליתסר, דמפתח הר הבית עד שער נקנור מחנה לויה, כדתניא בתוספתא ובספרי. מכל מקום, אין נראה דפליגי ברייתא דהכא אמתני' דכלים. אלא רבי יוחנן לפרושי ברייתא אתא, דעשה דקתני – לאו דוקא. ולאו משום דסבר רבי יוחנן טבול יום דזב לאו כזב דמי, דהא רבא אית ליה דרבי יוחנן בסוף "האשה" (פסחים צב.), ורבא אית ליה בפ"ב דכריתות (דף י.) דמחוסר כפורים דזב כזב דמי! אלא דוקא לענין פסח הבא בטומאה דלא יאכלו ממנו זבין וזבות ונדות ויולדות קאמר, דכזב דמי – להכי מייתי לה בכריתות. אבל לענין ביאת מקדש – לאו כזב דמי. וניחא השתא בריש פ"ב דזבחים (דף יז:) מסיק לכ"ע דמחוסר כפורים דזב כזב דמי, ובפרק "ג' מינים" (נזיר דף מה.) מסיק דאפילו טבול יום דזב לאו כזב דמי! אלא ההיא דזבחים לענין פסח הבא בטומאה, וההיא דנזיר לענין ביאת מקדש. והא דמשמע בההיא סוגיא ד"ג' מינים" דאפילו נאמר טבול יום דזב לאו כזב דמי אסור ליכנס למחנה לויה, ומקרא דריש התם – אר"י: דהתם בזב בעל ג' ראיות, דאיכא תרתי" שהוא טבול יום ומחוסר כפורים. ואע"ג דבשמעתין נמי בראה קרי בו ביום, דהוי טבול יום ומחוסר כפורים, שרי מדאורייתא – היינו משום דאינו על טומאה אחת, אלא על טבול יום משום קריו ומחוסר כפורים משום לרעתו: [וע"ע תוספות זבחים לב: ד"ה ור"י].

שחדשו בה דברים ואמרו טבול יום אל יכנס למחנה לויה. וא"ת: מנא ליה שחדשו מטבול יום? דלמא חדשו מטמאת מת עצמו! ויש לומר: דמשמע ליה שלא חדשו אלא על החצר, וחצר היינו עזרת נשים כדמוכח ביחזקאל (מד), ואילו טמא מת אסור אפי' בחיל.

ואמר עולא מה טעם כו'. פירוש: כיון דביאה במקצת שמה ביאה מה טעם התירו חכמים להכניס ידיו לבהונות? ואם תאמר: וכיון דשמה ביאה, ואפילו הכי שרי מקצתו, משום דאי אפשר בענין אחר – א"כ כולו נמי לישתרי! וי"ל: דלא ניחא שידחה ביאת כולו, דכתיב בהדיא "ואל המקדש לא תבא". אבל ביאה במקצת – לא כתיב בהדיא, אלא מהיקשא גמר לה עולא התם: מה נגיעה במקצת שמה נגיעה – אף ביאה במקצת כו'. ועוד יש לומר: כיון דאפשר על ידי ביאה במקצת, אם יכנס כולו – חייב, מידי דהוה אהיה לו דרך קצרה ובא לו בארוכה.

מי

עין משפט נר מצוה

כח א מיי' פ"ו מהל' קרבן פסח הל' ה:

תוספות ישנים

הואיל והותר לצרעתו הותר לקריו. וא"ת א"כ מאי קאמר לעיל מוטב יבא עשה שיש בו כרת וידחה כו' לימא טעמא דהואיל והותר. וי"ל דלעיל לא יוכל לומר כן דמאי לימא הואיל והותר וכו'. משמע שהוא היה נאסר מקודם לכן ולעולם יכול המצורע ליכנס בשערי נקנור שהוא מחנה לויה אבל הכא [שייך] הואיל והותר דהא עד עתה נאסר להכניס ידו לבהונות:

הגהות הב"ח

(א) גמ' אלא סד"א תיתי אחות אשה במה מצינו מאשת אח: (ב) רש"י ד"ה שמיני שלו וכו' הדם לבהונות נ"ב ס"א שעומד שם המצורע ומכניס ידיו לבהונות שאעפ"י שמשתלח חוץ לג' מחנות בשמיני שלו הותר לבא בשתי מחנות אבל בעזרה אינו נכנס כדאיתא במס' מכות דף ח טמא יהיה לרבות טבול יום עוד טומאתו בו לרבות מחוסר כפורים ובטמאת מקדש כתיב בפ' פרה אדומה וחוץ לעזרה אי אפשר שלא יפסל ביוצא והכנסת ידיו ביאה מקצת היא במצורע ולא שמה ביאה הלכך מזה עליו והוא עומד בשער נקנור: (ג) תום' ד"ה ר"י דר"י סבר כמתני':

מסורת הש"ס

פסחים לב. זבחים לב:

פסחים לב: הוריות ה. זבחים לב: ע"ש

[נ"ל רבי כ"א בזבחים]

גליון הש"ס

גמ' תיתי במה מצינו. עי' יומא דף מ ע"ב תד"ה מה במקום: שם במה מצינו מאשת אח. בתוס' לעיל ג ע"ב ד"ה לא תעשה שיש בה כרת היה להם הגי' פה תיתי אחות אשה מאשת אח: תום' ד"ה רבי יוחנן אמר וכו' דרבי יוחנן כמתני' דכלים. וכן ראיה ממתני' פ"א מ"א דתמיד בא ויושב לו אצל אחיו הכהנים:

תֵּינַח הֵיכָא דְּנָשָׂא מֵת וְאַחַר כָּךְ נָשָׂא חַי, דְּמִגּוֹ דְּאִישְׁתְּרֵי אִיסּוּר אֵשֶׁת אָח – אִישְׁתְּרֵי נַמִי אִיסּוּר אֲחוֹת אִשָּׁה. אֶלָּא, נָשָׂא חַי וְאח"כ נָשָׂא מֵת, אִיסּוּר אֲחוֹת אִשָּׁה קָדֵים! וַאֲפִי' נָשָׂא מֵת נַמִי, תֵּינַח הֵיכָא דְּנָשָׂא מֵת וּמֵת, וְאח"כ נָשָׂא חַי, דְּחַזְיָא לֵיהּ דְּבֵינֵי בֵּינֵי. אֶלָּא, נָשָׂא מֵת וְלֹא מֵת, וְאַחַר כָּךְ נָשָׂא חַי – לָא אִיתַּחְזְיָא לֵיהּ כְּלָל! מִי לָא מוֹדֵי עוּלָּא שֶׁאִם רָאָה קֶרִי בְּלֵיל שְׁמִינִי – שֶׁאֵין מַכְנִיס יָדָיו לְבְהוֹנוֹת?! שֶׁלֹּא יָצָא בְּשָׁעָה שֶׁהִיא רְאוּיָה לְהָבִיא בָּהּ קָרְבָּן! אֶלָּא: כִּי אִיצְטְרִיךְ "עָלֶיהָ" הֵיכָא *דְּנָשָׂא מֵת, וּמֵת, וְאח"כ נָשָׂא חַי. וְאִי בָּעֵית אֵימָא: אָתְיָא בְּהֶיקֵּישָׁא מִדְּרַבִּי יוֹנָה. דְּאָמַר רַבִּי יוֹנָה, וְאִיתֵּימָא רַב הוּנָא בְּרֵיהּ דְּרַב יְהוֹשֻׁעַ: אָמַר קְרָא °"כִּי כָּל אֲשֶׁר יַעֲשֶׂה מִכֹּל הַתּוֹעֵבוֹת הָאֵלֶּה וְנִכְרְתוּ" *הוּקְשׁוּ כָּל הָעֲרָיוֹת כּוּלָּן לְאֵשֶׁת אָח; מָה אֵשֶׁת אָח שַׁרְיָא אַף כָּל עֲרָיוֹת נַמִי שַׁרְיָין – כָּתַב רַחֲמָנָא "עָלֶיהָ". אֲמַר לֵיהּ רַב אַחָא מִדִּפְתִּי לְרָבִינָא: מִכְּדִי, כָּל עֲרָיוֹת אִיכָּא לְאַקּוּשִׁינְהוּ לְאֵשֶׁת אָח וְאִיכָּא לְאַקּוּשִׁינְהוּ לַאֲחוֹת אִשָּׁה, מַאי חֲזֵית דְּאַקַּשְׁתְּ לַאֲחוֹת אִשָּׁה – אַקְשִׁינְהוּ לְאֵשֶׁת אָח! אִיבָּעֵית אֵימָא: *לְקוּלָּא וְחוּמְרָא – לְחוּמְרָא מַקְשִׁינַן, אִיבָּעֵית אֵימָא: הָכָא תְּרֵי אִיסּוּרֵי וְהָכָא תְּרֵי אִיסּוּרֵי, וּתְרֵי מִתְּרֵי יָלְפִינַן; אֲבָל הָכָא חֲדָא אִיסּוּרָא – וּתְרֵי מֵחֲדָא לָא יָלְפִינַן. רָבָא אֲמַר: עֶרְוָה(א) לָא צְרִיכָא קְרָא, דְּאֵין עֲשֵׂה דּוֹחֶה לֹא תַעֲשֶׂה שֶׁיֵּשׁ בּוֹ כָּרֵת. כִּי אִיצְטְרִיךְ קְרָא – לְמֵיסַר צָרָה. וְעֶרְוָה לָא צְרִיכָא קְרָא?! וְהָא(ב) תַּנְיָא: אֵין לִי אֶלָּא הִיא! מִשּׁוּם צָרָתָהּ. וְהָא קָתָנֵי: אֵין לִי אֶלָּא הֵן! מִשּׁוּם צָרוֹתֵיהֶן. ת"ש: רַבִּי אוֹמֵר, °"וְלָקַח" "וּלְקָחָהּ" °"וְיִבֵּם" "וְיִבְּמָהּ", לֶאֱסוֹר צָרוֹת וַעֲרָיוֹת! אֵימָא: לֶאֱסוֹר צָרוֹת שֶׁל עֲרָיוֹת. וְהָא תְּרֵי קְרָאֵי קָנְסֵיב לֵיהּ, מַאי לָאו: חַד לְעֶרְוָה וְחַד לְצָרָה! לָא, אִידִי וְאִידִי לְצָרָה, חַד לְמֵיסַר צָרָה בִּמְקוֹם מִצְוָה, וְחַד לְמִישְׁרֵי צָרָה שֶׁלֹּא בִּמְקוֹם מִצְוָה. מַאי טַעֲמָא – "וְיִבֵּם" "וְיִבְּמָהּ", בִּמְקוֹם יִיבּוּם הוּא דַּאֲסִירָא צָרָה, שֶׁלֹּא בִּמְקוֹם יִיבּוּם – שַׁרְיָא צָרָה. אֲמַר רַב אַשִׁי: מתני' נַמִי דַּיְקָא: דְּקָתָנֵי, חֲמֵשׁ עֶשְׂרֵה נָשִׁים פּוֹטְרוֹת צָרוֹתֵיהֶן, וְאִילּוּ "פְּטוּרוֹת וּפוֹטְרוֹת" – לָא קָתָנֵי, שְׁמַע מִינַּהּ. וּמַאי שְׁנָא עֶרְוָה דְּלָא צְרִיכָא קְרָא – דְּאֵין עֲשֵׂה דּוֹחֶה לֹא תַעֲשֶׂה שֶׁיֵּשׁ בּוֹ כָּרֵת – צָרָה נַמִי לָא תִּיבָּעֵי קְרָא מִשּׁוּם דְּאֵין עֲשֵׂה דּוֹחֶה לֹא תַעֲשֶׂה שֶׁיֵּשׁ בּוֹ כָּרֵת! א"ל רַב אַחָא בַּר בֵּיבַי מָר לְרָבִינָא: ה"ק מִשְּׁמֵיהּ דְּרָבָא, צָרָה נַמִי לָא אִיצְטְרִיךְ קְרָא, כִּי אִיצְטְרִיךְ קְרָא לְמִישְׁרֵי

רש"י

תֵּינַח הֵיכָא דְּנָשָׂא הַמֵּת. אֶת אִשָּׁה זוֹ תְּחִילָּה, וְנַעֲשֵׂית אֵשֶׁת הָאָח עַל זֶה: וְאח"כ נָשָׂא חַי. אֶת אֲחוֹתָהּ, וְנִיתּוֹסְפַת אִיסּוּר אֲחוֹת אִשָּׁה עַל יְבִמְתּוֹ. וּכְשֶׁמֵּת אָחִיו בְּלֹא בָּנִים, וְאִישְׁתְּרַאי אִיסּוּר אֵשֶׁת אָח הַמּוּקְדָּם – אִישְׁתְּרַאי נַמִי אֲחוֹת אִשָּׁה הַמְאוּחָר, כְּדְעוּלָּא, דְּאָמַר: הוֹאִיל וְהוּתַּר לְצָרַעְתּוֹ, שֶׁהִיא רִאשׁוֹנָה – הוּתַּר לְקֶרְיוֹ, שֶׁהִיא אַחֲרוֹנָה. תורה אור אֶלָּא נָשָׂא הַחַי. אִשְׁתּוֹ תְּחִילָּה, וְעָמְדָה עָלָיו בְּאִיסּוּר אֲחוֹת אִשָּׁה, וְאח"כ נְשָׂאָהּ אָחִיו הַמֵּת וְנִיתּוֹסֵף אִיסּוּר אֵשֶׁת אָח, אִיסּוּר אֲחוֹת אִשָּׁה קָדֵים. וְאַף עַל גַּב דְּהוּתַּר אִיסּוּר אַחֲרוֹן – עוֹמֵד רִאשׁוֹן בִּמְקוֹמוֹ. וַאֲפִי' נָשָׂא מֵת נַמִי. בְּרֵישָׁא, דְּקָדֵים לֵיהּ אִיסּוּר אֵשֶׁת אָח – לָא דָּמְיָא לְדְעוּלָּא, דְּהָתָם הָרוֹאֶה קֶרִי בַּשְּׁמִינִי שֶׁלּוֹ – כְּבָר הָיָה מוּתָּר מֵאִיסּוּר הָרִאשׁוֹן קוֹדֶם רְאִיַּית הַקֶּרִי, מִשֶּׁהֶאִיר הַמִּזְרָח. וְהָכָא נַמִי, תֵּינַח הֵיכָא דְּנָשָׂא מֵת וּמֵת תְּחִילָּה, וְהוּתַּר אִיסּוּר אֵשֶׁת אָח, וְאח"כ נָשָׂא חַי אֶת אֲחוֹתָהּ. אֶלָּא נָשָׂא מֵת וְלֹא מֵת. עַד שֶׁנָּשָׂא חַי אֶת אֲחוֹתָהּ, הָא לָא אִיתְחֲזַאי כְּלָל. וּמִי לָא מוֹדֶה עוּלָּא בִּכְהַאי גַּוְונָא, שֶׁאִם רָאָה קֶרִי בְּלֵיל יוֹם שְׁמִינִי – שֶׁאֵין מַכְנִיס יָדָיו מָחָר לִבְהוֹנוֹת, מִשּׁוּם קֶרִי דִּמְעַכֵּב עֲלֵיהּ, הוֹאִיל וְלֹא יָצָא מִצָּרַעְתּוֹ לְשָׁעָה הָרְאוּיָה לַהֲבָאַת קָרְבְּנוֹתָיו. דְּקוֹדֶם שֶׁהוּתַּר מִצָּרַעְתּוֹ – בָּא עָלָיו קֶרִי. הָכִי גָּרְסִינַן: כִּי אִיצְטְרִיךְ "עָלֶיהָ" לְנָשָׂא מֵת וּמֵת וְאח"כ נָשָׂא חַי: וְאִיבָּעֵית אֵימָא. אִיצְטְרִיךְ "עָלֶיהָ", דְּאִי לָא כְּתָבֵיהּ הֲוָה אָמֵינָא: תֵּיתֵי יִיבּוּם אֲחוֹת אִשָּׁה לְהַתִּיר בְּהֶיקֵּישָׁא דְּר' יוֹנָה, דְּאָמַר רַבִּי יוֹנָה: "כִּי כָּל אֲשֶׁר יַעֲשֶׂה מִכֹּל הַתּוֹעֵבוֹת הָאֵלֶּה" – הוּקְשׁוּ כָּל הָעֲרָיוֹת זוֹ לָזוֹ. וּלְעִנְיַן הָעֲרָאָה קָנָסֵיב לֵיהּ ר' יוֹנָה בְּ"הַבָּא עַל יְבִמְתּוֹ". הָכִי נַמִי ה"א: הוּקְשׁוּ כּוּלָּן לְאֵשֶׁת אָח, וְאע"ג דְּהָכָא חַד אִיסּוּרָא וְהָכָא תְּרֵי אִיסּוּרֵי – אֵין מְשִׁיבִין עַל הַהֶיקֵּשׁ, לְהָכִי אִיצְטְרִיךְ "עָלֶיהָ". מִכְּדִי כָּל הָעֲרָיוֹת. דְּמַתְנִי'. אִיכָּא לְאַקּוּשִׁינְהוּ לְאֵשֶׁת אָח. לְהַתִּיר יִיבּוּם. וְאִיכָּא לְאַקּוּשִׁינְהוּ לַאֲחוֹת אִשָּׁה. דַּאֲסִירֵי לְיִיבּוּם, דִּפְרַט בָּהּ קְרָא "עָלֶיהָ". מַאי חֲזֵית דְּאַקַּשְׁתְּ לְהוּ לַאֲחוֹת אִשָּׁה. כִּדְקָתָנֵי בְּרֵישׁ פִּרְקִין: מָה אֲחוֹת אִשָּׁה מְיוּחֶדֶת כו'. מִשּׁוּם צָרָתָהּ. מִשּׁוּם דְּבָעֵי לְמִיתְנֵי צָרָתָהּ מְנַיִן. וּלְקָחָהּ לוֹ לְאִשָּׁה וְיִבְּמָהּ. הַמ"ל וְלָקַח אִשָּׁה וְיִיבֵּם, וּכְתִיב "וּלְקָחָהּ", מַשְׁמַע מִיעוּט: זוֹ וְלֹא אַחֶרֶת. וְחַד לְמִישְׁרֵי צָרַת עֶרְוָה שֶׁלֹּא בִּמְקוֹם מִצְוָה. מֵרִבּוּיָא דִּקְרָא יְתֵירָא דְּ"וְיִבְּמָהּ" דָּרְשִׁינַן הָכִי: בִּמְקוֹם "וְיִבְּמָהּ" הוּא דְּאָמֵינָא לָךְ מִיעוּטָא "וּלְקָחָהּ" דְּמִיעֵט צָרָה; אֲבָל שֶׁלֹּא בִּמְקוֹם יִבּוּם, כְּגוֹן צָרַת בִּתּוֹ מִנָּכְרִי – שַׁרְיָא: מַתְנִי' נַמִי דַּיְקָא. כְּרָבָא, דְּעֶרְוָה פְּשִׁיטָא לָן. צָרָה נַמִי לָא תִּיבָּעֵי. "עָלֶיהָ" קְרָא לְדְרָשָׁא דְּאֵין עֲשֵׂה דּוֹחֶה לֹא תַעֲשֶׂה שֶׁיֵּשׁ בָּהּ כָּרֵת, דִּכְתִיב "לִצְרוֹר", דְּמַשְׁמַע: לֹא אֲחוֹת אִשָּׁה וְלֹא צָרָתָהּ, וּכְתִיב כָּרֵת בְּסוֹף הָעֲרָיוֹת. לְמִישְׁרֵי צָרָה שֶׁלֹּא בִּמְקוֹם מִצְוָה. דְּאִי לָא כְּתִיב "עָלֶיהָ", הֲוָה יָלְפִינַן מִ"לִּצְרוֹר" דְּצָרַת אֲחוֹת אִשָּׁה אֲסוּרָה בְּכָל מָקוֹם. מַאי

תוספות

מי לא מודה עולא בהא שאם ראה קרי בליל שמיני שאין מכנים ידיו לבהונות. ק"ק: דמנא ליה דמודה עולא בהא? וגם בפרק "כל הפסולים" (זבחים לג: ושם) דמהדר עולא למאן דפריך ליה מהך ברייתא: ומטונך, דמצורע הואיל והותר לצרעתו כו'. דמשמע: ומטונך ממשא שאתה בא להכביד עליו אביא ראייתי משם. ומה ראיה יש לו מן הברייתא? ונראה לרבינו יצחק דדייק עולא מדנקט וראה קרי בו ביום, משמע: בו ביום, אבל בלילה – לא. שמע מינה דטעמא משום דהותר לצרעתו הותר נמי לקריו. ולהכי פשיטא ליה הכא דמודי עולא בראה קרי בליל ח'.

תרי איסורי [מחד איסורא לא ילפינן]. (*אבל שלא במקום ייבום כגון צרת בתו ילפי'). וא"ת: ולרב אסי, אמאי פוטרת איילונית צרתה? והא חד איסורא הוא! וי"ל: דממה נפשך איהי אסירא, דילפי' מ"אשר תלד" – פרט לאיילונית. ולהכי צרתה נמי אסורה, וכן אשת אחיו שלא היה בעולמו. אבל קשיא: מאי טעמא דמאן דפליג אדרב אסי? וי"ל: דכיון דאיילונית לאו בת ייבום היא בשום מקום – חשיבא צרתה כצרת ערוה שלא במקום מצוה, דשריא. ולא דמיא איילונית לחייבי עשה, דילפינן בפרק שני (לקמן דף כ.)(ג) לחליצה. דאיילונית מיעטה הכתוב בהדיא, דלא הויא בכלל היתר אשת אח.

רבא אמר ערוה גופה לא צריכא קרא. וא"ת: והא לכל הפחות איצטריך(ד) לינשא מת ומת, ואח"כ נשא חי, דלא תימא הואיל ואישתרי – אשתרי! *וי"ל: דרבא לית ליה דעולא, וסבר דביאה במקצת לא שמה ביאה. ועוד אר"י דיש לחלק: דגבי בעל קרי, דשם טומאה אחת היא, אמרי': הואיל ואשתרי אישתרי, דחד לאו הוא בבעל קרי ומצורע, אבל הכא, דשני שמות הן – לא אמרינן הואיל ואישתרי אישתרי. וא"ת: מאי טעמא לא צריכא קרא? וכי לית ליה לרבא היקישא דרבי יונה?! וי"ל: דקסבר דלענין איסורא הוא דאקשינהו רחמנא, דבהכי איירי קרא, ולא לענין היתירא.

כי איצטריך קרא למיסר צרה. ותימה: דהיכי טעי(ה) למימר דאיצטריך למיסר צרה טפי מן הערוה, כיון דצרה מ"לצרור" נפקא, ויש כרת בצרה כמו בערוה! ואומר רבינו יצחק: דהשתא נמי בעי למימר לאיסור צרה, ולמידק דשלא במקום מצוה שריא, כדמסיק רב אחא לבסוף. והא דקאמר נמי אין לי אלא היא משום צרתה – לא משום דצריך קרא לאיסור, אלא למידק היתירא שלא במקום מצוה. והא דפריך: מאי שנא ערוה דלא צריכא קרא כו' – גמרא טעי במילתיה דרבא, שלא פירש בהדיא למישרי שלא במקום מצוה אתא "עליה".

ואילו פטורות ופוטרות לא קתני. אע"ג דמסקינן דלאסור צרתה נמי לא צריך קרא – מ"מ תנא פוטרות, דהוצרך להשמיענו איסור בצרה, שעדיין לא השמיענו בשום מקום. אבל איסור ערוה, דכבר נשנו כל העריות בפרק קמא דכריתות (דף ב.) (ו) – שלא איצטריך כאן להשמיענו דאסורה במקום מצוה, דפשיטא דאין עשה דוחה ל"ת שיש בו כרת. למישרי

תוספות ישנים

כי אצטריך קרא לנשא מת ומת ואח"כ נשא חי. וא"ת היכי מקרי אחות זקוקתו י"ל שאינה אלא מדרבנן אבל קשה היכא משכחת לה דפוטרת צרתה הלא כיון דלא נעשית אחות אשתו עד שמת אחיו א"כ לא היתה מעולם צרת ערוה שהרי כשנשא חי לא היתה צרת ערוה לייבם שעדיין לא נשא אחות אשתו. וי"ל דאה"נ דאערוה לבד קיימינן הכא דנפקא לן מקרא דעליה ומקרא דלצרור אם אתה רוצה למצוא צרה עמה משכחת לה בנשא חי ואח"כ מת אחיו שהיה נשוי אחות אשתו: הוקשו כל העריות לאשת אח. ומעתה אין להקשות הכא חד איסורא התם תרי איסורי דאין משיבין על ההיקש: ת"ש ר' אומר ולקח ולקחה. ונהי נמי דר' לית ליה עליה מ"מ סברא הוא דכי היכי דאצטריך קרא לדידיה כמו כן לדידן ואי לדידן לא צריכא קרא דעליה לדידיה נמי לא ליבעי קרא דולקחה: צרה נמי לא צריכא קרא. וא"ת א"כ הא ק"ל ת"ש ר' אומר ולקח ולקחה ויבם ויבמה כיון דלא אצטריך קרא לא לצרה ולא לערוה. וי"ל דנימא (לאסור) [דאתי להתיר] צרות כל עריות דוקא במקום יבום אבל שלא במקום יבום צרותיהן מותרות וכן לעיל צרותיהן מנין ר"ל צרותיהן דוקא במקום יבום אבל שלא במקום יבום צרותיהן מותרות מנין והקשה הר' יחיאל כיון דצרה לא צריכא תקשי לר' למה לי תרי קראי ולקחה ויבמה. ונראה לרשב"י דחד אתי למיסר צרה במקום מצוה וחד למשרי שלא במקום מצוה דדוקא לרבנן דמפקי מלצרור צרות וכתיב בתריה ונכרתו א"כ לא צריכא קרא לצרה אבל ר' דמפיק לצרור כר' שמעון ולא כתיב בה כרת בהדיא אצטריך שפיר קרא למיסרא במקום מצוה ואע"ג דפרשתי בסמוך דנפיק לר' עונש מלצרור היינו כאשר נכתב ולקחה דמיניה שמעינן אזהרה בצרות כדאמרינן בסמוך כל היכא דאיכא תרין לקוחין וכו' ואז מדמינן צרות להדדי צרת ערוה לצרה בזיקה אבל אי לא כתב ולקחה לא שמעינן איסור בצרת ערוה במקום מצוה. כ"נ לרשב"י:

מסורת הש"ס

[לקמן יג:]

לקמן נד: קדושין סז: כריתות ב:

[קדושין סח. ע"ז מו:]

ויקרא יח

דברים כה שם

הגהות הב"ח

(א) גמ' רבא אמר ערוה גופה לא צריכא: (ב) שם והא קתני אין לי אלא היא: (ג) תוס' ד"ה תרי וכו' בפרק שני דחולצת דאיילונית מיעטה: (ד) ד"ה רבא וכו' איצטריך לנשא מת: (ה) ד"ה כי וכו' דהיכי טעי רבא למימר: (ו) ד"ה ואילו וכו' דכריתות לא איצטריך:

גליון הש"ס

תוס' ד"ה רבא אמר וכו' וי"ל דרבא לית ליה דעולא. עיין טורי אבן מגילה ד' ג ע"ב ד"ה מולאחותו:

לְמִישְׁרֵי צָרָה שֶׁלֹּא בְּמָקוֹם. מִצְוָה מַאי טַעֲמָא? אָמַר קְרָא "עָלֶיהָ", בִּמְקוֹם "עָלֶיהָ" הוּא דַּאֲסִירָא, שֶׁלֹּא בִּמְקוֹם "עָלֶיהָ" – שַׁרְיָא. א"ל רָמִי בַּר חָמָא לְרָבָא: אֵימָא עֶרְוָה גּוּפַהּ שֶׁלֹּא בִּמְקוֹם מִצְוָה תִּישְׁתְּרֵי! וְלָאו קַל וָחוֹמֶר הוּא? בִּמְקוֹם מִצְוָה – אֲסִירָא, שֶׁלֹּא בִּמְקוֹם מִצְוָה – שַׁרְיָא?! אֲמַר לֵיהּ: צָרָה תּוֹכִיחַ, דִּבְמְקוֹם מִצְוָה – אֲסִירָא, וְשֶׁלֹּא בִּמְקוֹם מִצְוָה – שַׁרְיָא! אֲמַר לֵיהּ: עָלֶיךָ אָמַר קְרָא "בְּחַיֶּיהָ" – כָּל שֶׁבְּחַיֶּיהָ. הַאי "בְּחַיֶּיהָ" מִיבָּעֵי לֵיהּ [א]לְמַעוּטֵי לְאַחַר מִיתָה! הַהִיא °מִ"וְאִשָּׁה אֶל אֲחוֹתָהּ" נָפְקָא. אִי מִ"וְאִשָּׁה אֶל אֲחוֹתָהּ" ה"א: נִתְגָּרְשָׁה שַׁרְיָא, ת"ל "בְּחַיֶּיהָ" – [ב]כָּל שֶׁבְּחַיֶּיהָ, דְּאע"ג דְּנִתְגָּרְשָׁה – לָא. אֶלָּא אָמַר רַב הוּנָא בַּר תַּחְלִיפָא מִשְּׁמֵיהּ דְּרָבָא: תְּרֵי קְרָאֵי כְּתִיבֵי: כְּתִיב "אִשָּׁה אֶל אֲחוֹתָהּ לֹא תִקָּח לִצְרוֹר" וּכְתִי' "לְגַלּוֹת עֶרְוָתָהּ", דַּחֲדָא מַשְׁמַע, הָא כֵּיצַד? בִּמְקוֹם מִצְוָה – שְׁתֵּיהֶן אֲסוּרוֹת, שֶׁלֹּא בִּמְקוֹם מִצְוָה – הִיא אֲסוּרָה וְצָרָתָהּ מוּתֶּרֶת. אֵיפוֹךְ אֲנָא: בִּמְקוֹם מִצְוָה – הִיא אֲסוּרָה וְצָרָתָהּ מוּתֶּרֶת, וְשֶׁלֹּא בִּמְקוֹם מִצְוָה – שְׁתֵּיהֶן אֲסוּרוֹת! א"כ, לֹא יֹאמַר "עָלֶיהָ". א"ל רַב אַשִׁי לְרַב כָּהֲנָא: מִמַּאי דְּהַאי "עָלֶיהָ" לְאִיסּוּרָא? דִּלְמָא לְהֶתֵּירָא, וְה"ק רַחֲמָנָא: "אִשָּׁה אֶל אֲחוֹתָהּ לֹא תִקָּח לִצְרוֹר" – לֹא הִיא וְלֹא צָרָתָהּ, שֶׁלֹּא בִּמְקוֹם "עָלֶיהָ", אֲבָל בִּמְקוֹם "עָלֶיהָ" שְׁתֵּיהֶן מוּתָּרוֹת! א"כ "לְגַלּוֹת עֶרְוָה" דַּחֲדָא הֵיכִי מַשְׁכַּחַת לַהּ? אִי בִּמְקוֹם מִצְוָה – שְׁתֵּיהֶן מוּתָּרוֹת, אִי שֶׁלֹּא בִּמְקוֹם מִצְוָה – שְׁתֵּיהֶן אֲסוּרוֹת.§ גּוּפָא, רַבִּי אוֹמֵר: "וְלָקַח" "וּלְקָחָהּ" "וְיִבֵּם" "וְיִבְּמָהּ" – לֶאֱסוֹר צָרוֹת וַעֲרָיוֹת. מִידֵי צָרוֹת כְּתִיבָא הָכָא? וְעוֹד: צָרוֹת – מִ"לִּצְרוֹר" נָפְקָא! "לִצְרוֹר" מַפֵּיק לֵיהּ רַבִּי לִכְדְרַבִּי שִׁמְעוֹן. צָרָה *הָכָא כְּתִיב? ה"ק: א"כ לֵימָא קְרָא "וְלָקַח", מַאי "וּלְקָחָהּ" – כָּל הֵיכָא דְּאִיכָּא תְּרֵי לְקוּחִין, דְּאִי בָּעֵי נָסֵיב הַאי וְאִי בָּעֵי נָסֵיב הַאי – שַׁרְיָא, וְאִי לָא – תַּרְוַיְיהוּ אֲסִירָן. "וְיִבְּמָהּ", בִּמְקוֹם יִיבּוּם – הוּא דַּאֲסִירָא צָרָה, שֶׁלֹּא בִּמְקוֹם יִיבּוּם – שַׁרְיָא צָרָה. וְרַבָּנַן, הַאי "וּלְקָחָהּ" מַאי עָבְדֵי לֵיהּ? מִיבָּעֵי לְהוּ לִכְדְרַבִּי יוֹסֵי בַּר חֲנִינָא. *דְּאָמַר רַבִּי יוֹסֵי בַּר חֲנִינָא: "וּלְקָחָהּ", מְלַמֵּד [ג]שֶׁמְּגָרְשָׁהּ בְּגֵט וּמַחֲזִירָהּ. "וְיִבְּמָהּ" – [ד]עַל כׇּרְחָהּ. וְרַבִּי? דְּרַבִּי יוֹסֵי בַּר חֲנִינָא מִ"לְאִשָּׁה" נָפְקָא. עַל כׇּרְחָהּ מִ"יְּבָמָהּ יָבֹא עָלֶיהָ" נָפְקָא. וְרַבִּי, הַאי "עָלֶיהָ" מַאי עָבֵיד לֵיהּ? מִיבָּעֵי לֵיהּ *לִכְדְתַנְיָא: *[ה]אֵין חַיָּיבִין ב"ד אֶלָּא עַל דָּבָר שֶׁזְּדוֹנוֹ כָּרֵת וְשִׁגְגָתוֹ חַטָּאת, וְכֵן הַמָּשִׁיחַ. וְלֹא

רש"י

מאי טעמא. כלומר, היכי מידרשא היתר מהכא. במקום עליה הוא. דכתיב "לצרור" למיסר צרה, ולא במקום אחר. אימא ערוה גופה שלא במקום מצוה תשתרי. מדכתיב "עליה", דקאי נמי אאחות אשה. כל שבחייה. אשתך, לא תשא את אחותה. תרי קראי כתיבי. מעיקרא כתיב "לצרור", דמשמע לא היא ולא צרתה, והדר כתיב "לגלות ערותה", דמשמע חדא הוא דאסירא. במקום מצוה שתיהן אסורין. כדכתיב "עליה", דמשמע במקום "עליה". ואיפוך אנא במקום מצוה היא אסורה וצרתה מותרת. דהא "עליה" אַ"לגלות ערותה" סמיך, דמשמע חדא למדרש הכי: במקו' עליה הוא דלא אסיר לן אלא חדא, וקרא ד"לצרור" – אשלא במקום מצוה. א"כ לא יאמר עליה. דבלא "עליה" נמי, כי קשו לן קראי אהדדי – משנינן להו מסברא הכי: היתירא – למצוה, ואיסורא – שלא במקום מצוה, הלכך "עליה" לחדושי אתא, למדרשיה א"לצרור", ולמיסר צרה במקום מצוה כערוה. ממאי דהאי עליה לאיסורא. אצרה ולא לערוה? דלמא למישרי תרווייהו במקום מצוה אתא, והכי משמע: "ואשה אל אחותה לא תקח לצרור" – לא היא ולא צרה, ואם "עליה" דמקום מצוה היא – אפי' בחייה יתקיים (כמו) "יבמה יבא עליה" דייבום. לכדר' שמעון. בפרק "ד' אחים" (לקמן דף כח:), ג' אחין, שנים מהם נשואין שתי אחיות, או אשה ובתה, ומתו, ונפלו לפני השלישי, הרי אלו חולצות ולא מתייבמו', לפי ששתיהן זקוקות לו מקדושי שני אחיו. וזיקה הוי כקצת קדושין, ואי מייבם חדא מנייהו קנסיב אחות זקוקתו בחייה, וזקוקתו הויא כאשתו. אבל חליצה בעיא, דלא אלים למיהוי כאחות אשה ממש להפטר בלא כלום, ותניא בברייתא: רבי שמעון פוטר בשתיהן מן החליצה ומן הייבום, ויליף טעמא מ"לצרור", בשעה שנעשו צרות זו לזו, כגון הכא – דנעשו האחיות צרות זו לזו בזיקה – לא יהא לך ליקוחין אפילו באחת מהן: א"כ. דהאי "ולקחה" לגופיה הוא דאתא, נימא קרא "ולקח", מאי "ולקחה" דמשמע דשתים נפלו לו מאחיו, ואמר רחמנא "ולקחה" לאחת ולא לשתיהן, אי קרינא "ולקחה" בכל חדא מינייהו – שריין כל חדא מינייהו, ואי לא קרינן "ולקחה" בכל חדא מינייהו, כגון שהאחת ערוה – תרווייהו אסורין. וצרות צרותיהן נמי מהכא נפקא, דמשנפלה לו צרת ערוה מאחיו הראשון ונדחית הערוה ממנו – נאסרה עליו עולמית משום אשת אח, וכשנתייבמה לאחיו השני ולו אשה אחרת ומת וחזרה ונפלה לפני זה – לא קרינא בה, בזו שנאסרה עליו, "ולקחה", הלכך תרווייהו אסורים. וכן לעולם. מלמד שמגרשה בגט ומחזירה. לאחר שנשאה נעשית כאשתו, ואם רצה לגרשה – מגרשה בגט, ואינה צריכה חליצה. ומחזירה. אם רצה להחזיר, ולא אמרינן: מצוה רמא רחמנא עליה ועבדה, ומהשתא תיקום עליה באיסור אשת אח, להכי כתיב "ולקחה לו לאשה", דכיון שלקחה נעשית כאשתו לכל דבר. בעל כרחה. שאם בא עליה יבם, אפילו בעל כרחה – קנאה, ויורשה, ומטמא לה, ולכל דבר היא אשתו בכך ביאה. אין חייבין בית דין. להביא פר על העלם דבר. ולא

תוספות

למישרי צרה שלא במקום מצוה. וא"ת להנהו שינויי דלעיל דמוקמי קרא לערוה גופה, מנא להו למישרי צרה שלא במקום מצוה? וי"ל: דנפקא להו מהיכא דנפקא ליה לרבי. מאי ולקחה כו'. מצינו למימר דמייתורא דה"א דרשי' תרין ליקוחין, כדדרשינן בפ"ב דקדושין (דף מא.): "ושלח" "ושלחה" – מלמד שהשליח עושה שליח. אבל בקונט' פי' ד"ולקחה" משמע דנפלו לו שתים, ואמר רחמנא "ולקחה" – לאחת ולא לשתיהן. וליכא להקשות לפירושו: דלמא להא גופא איצטריך, לכשנפלו לו שתי יבמות מבית אחד, שלא ייבם אלא אחת, מנא ליה למידרש כל היכא דאיכא תרין לקוחין כו'? דהא דרשינן לה ב"החולץ" (לקמן דף מד.) מ"את בית אחיו" – בית אחד הוא בונה ואינו בונה שתי בתים. וא"ת: ודלמא אתא קרא למימר שֶׁיְּיַבֵּם הצרה ולא הערוה? ולמ"ד ערוה (א) לא צריכא קרא – ניחא.

כל היכא דאיכא תרין לקוחין כו'. וא"ת: חייבי עשה נמי ליתסרי צרה, דליכא למימר דאי בעי האי נסיב ואי בעי האי נסיב! ועוד תימה: דהשתא ליכא בצרת ערוה כרת, וא"כ תיבעי חליצה כמו חייבי עשה, דמרבינן להו מ"יבמתו" בפרק שני (לקמן כ.)! וי"ל דחייבי עשה דאיתרבו לחליצה, ואית בהו זיקה קצת – הוו בכלל "ולקחה". וא"כ צרת ערוה ע"כ לא בעיא חליצה, דאי בעיא הוי בכלל "ולקחה". ועוד "ולקחה" משמע לשון תפיסת קידושין, הלכך חייבי עשה דתפסי בהו קדושין הוו בכלל "ולקחה":

מלמד שמגרשה בגט ומחזירה. בפרק "החולץ" (לקמן דף לט.) אמרינן דאיצטריך, דס"ד מצוה דרמא רחמנא עליה עבדה, השתא תיקום עליה באיסור אשת אח. ותימה: דמשמע דלביאה שניה לא צריך קרא להתיר, ואמאי? והא מצוה דרמא רחמנא עליה עבדה מביאה ראשונה, דהא ביאה שניה לא דחיא חייבי לאוין כדאמר בפרק שני (לקמן כ: ושם)! וי"ל: דביאה שניה לא צריכא קרא, דסברא הוא דלא אמר רחמנא יבא עליה לגרשה אחר ביאה ראשונה, ומ"מ, ביאה שניה לא דחיא חייבי לאוין, דרשות היא וליכא עשה אלא בביאה ראשונה(א). ויבמה בעל כרחה. הכא משמע דמה"א דריש לה. ותימה: דבפ"ק דקידושין (דף יד. ושם) משמע דדריש מה"א: ביאה גומר בה ואין כו'! דפריך התם: והא מיבעי ליה ויבמה על כרחה, א"כ לימא קרא ויבם! וי"ל דהתם הכי *פריך: א"כ, דלביאה גומרת בה גרידא אתא, לימא קרא "ויבם"! *וכענין זה יש לקמן בפרק "אלמנה" (דף סח: ושם) א"כ לימא קרא "והיא בקדשים לא תאכל". *וקשה: לקמן בפ"ב (דף יט:) דרשינן מ"יבמה": עדיין יבומין הראשונים עליה! וא"ר יצחק דדרשינן הני תלתא דרשות מ"יבם" "ויבם" "ויבמה" וכענין זה בריש "האיש מקדש" (קדושין דף מא.) דריש שלשה דרשות מ"ושלחה": שלח, ושלח, ושלחה. אין חייבין אלא על דבר שזדונו כרת. למעוטי חייבי לאוין, ועל שגגתו חטאת למעוטי פסח ומילה דלית בהו חטאת, כדתנן בפ"ק דכריתות (דף ג.): ולא בעבודה זרה אלא על דבר שזדונו כרת, למעוטי מגפף ומנשק ושגגתו חטאת למעוטי דבר שאין בו מעשה. מה

עין משפט נר מצוה

כט א מיי' פ"ב מהל' איסורי ביאה ה"ט סמג לאוין קח טוש"ע אה"ע סימן טו סעי' כו:
ל ב מיי' וסמג וטוש"ע שם:
לא ג מיי' פ"א מהל' יבום הל' טו סמג עשין נא טוש"ע אה"ע סימן קסח סעיף א:
לב ד מיי' שם פ"ב הל' י סמג עשין שם טוש"ע שם סי' קסו ס"ז:
לג ה מיי' פי"ב מהלכות שגגות הלכה א:

תוספות ישנים

איפוך אנא דסברא היא להחמיר יותר שלא במקום מצוה ועוד דלגלות ערותה דמשמע דקרא סמיך אעליה דהוי לשון יבום שהוא במקום מצוה וא"כ יש לנו לומר במקום מצוה היא אסורה וצרתה מותרת. וקרא אשה אל אחותה לא תקח דמשמע שתיהם אסורות נוקים שלא במקום מצוה. א"כ לא יאמר עליה מסברא כי פרכינן מרישיה דקרא לסיפיה דכתיב ואשה אל אחותה לא תקח דמשמע שתיהן אסורות. וכתב לגלות ערותה דמשמע ערותה דוקא ודאי משנינן מסברא במקום מצוה היא אסורה וצרתה מותרת ושלא במקום מצוה שתיהן אסורות וא"כ כשנאמר עליה בא לחדש דבר שאין לנו לומר מסברא והיינו במקום מצוה שתיהן אסורות שלא במקום מצוה היא אסורה וצרתה מותרת: לצרור מפיק ליה רבי לכדר' שמעון. וא"ת כיון דר' לא מפיק צרות מלצרור ומפיק ליה לצרת ערוה בזיקה לכדר' שמעון א"כ אזהרה שמענו עונש מנין דה"נ אמרינן לעיל וקאמר ת"ל ונכרתו וא"כ השתא דלא מפקינן מלצרור צרות לא כתיב כרת גבייהו וא"כ עונש מנין וא"ל דליכא רק אזהרה דא"כ לא לפטרו מחליצה כמו דאמרינן לקמן דחייבי לאוין חולצות. וי"ל דכיון דמפיק מלצרור שום צרות כדקאמר לצרור כר' שמעון א"כ מיירי בצרת ערוה בזיקה מעתה בכל צרות נמי יש לנו להחשיבן ערוה להיות בכלל כרת דכתיב כי כל איש אשר יעשה מכל התועבות האלה ונכרתו:
א) ועוי"ל שאני התם דביאה ראשונה לא שריא רק על ידי דחיית הלאו אבל הכא דביאה ראשונה היתה בהיתר גמור א"כ לא נוה הכתוב ליקחנה ולהוציאה מיד לאחר ביאה:

[וכן פרש"י שם בקידושין להדיא והוכיח פירוש זה מברייתא דיבמות כד.]

הגהות הב"ח

(א) תוס' ד"ה מאי וכו' ולמ"ד ערוה גופה לא צריכא:

מסורת הש"ס / תורה אור

ויקרא יח

היכא כתיבא. יעב"ץ

כתובות פב: לקמן יט: לט.

נ"ל לכדתנן *הוריות ח. ע"ש

[נ"ל פירקין]

תורה אור

וְלֹא בַּעֲבוֹדָה זָרָה, אֶלָּא עַל דָּבָר שֶׁחַיָּיבִין עַל זְדוֹנוֹ כָּרֵת וְשִׁגְגָתוֹ חַטָּאת. *וּתְנַן נַמִּי: [א]כָּל מִצְוָה שֶׁבַּתּוֹרָה שֶׁחַיָּיבִין עַל זְדוֹנוֹ כָּרֵת וְעַל שִׁגְגָתוֹ חַטָּאת — יָחִיד מֵבִיא כִּשְׂבָּה אוֹ שְׂעִירָה, נָשִׂיא מֵבִיא שָׂעִיר, מָשִׁיחַ וּב"ד מְבִיאִין פַּר. וּבַעֲבוֹדָה זָרָה — יָחִיד, נָשִׂיא וּמָשִׁיחַ מְבִיאִין שְׂעִירָה. *צִבּוּר מְבִיאִים פַּר וְשָׂעִיר, פַּר לְעוֹלָה וְשָׂעִיר לְחַטָּאת. מה"מ? *דְּת"ר: °"וְנוֹדְעָה הַחַטָּאת אֲשֶׁר חָטְאוּ עָלֶיהָ", רַבִּי אוֹמֵר: נֶאֱמַר כָּאן "עָלֶיהָ" וְנֶאֱמַר לְהַלָּן "עָלֶיהָ", מַה לְּהַלָּן — דָּבָר שֶׁחַיָּיבִים עַל זְדוֹנוֹ כָּרֵת וְעַל שִׁגְגָתוֹ חַטָּאת, אַף כָּאן — דָּבָר שֶׁחַיָּיבִין עַל זְדוֹנוֹ כָּרֵת וְעַל שִׁגְגָתוֹ חַטָּאת. אַשְׁכַּחַן צִבּוּר, מָשִׁיחַ מְנָלַן? דִּכְתִיב בְּמָשִׁיחַ °"לְאַשְׁמַת הָעָם" — הֲרֵי מָשִׁיחַ כְּצִבּוּר. יָחִיד וְנָשִׂיא — אָתְיָא "מִצְוֹת" "מִצְוֹת". וְלֹא בַּעֲבוֹדָה זָרָה אֶלָּא עַל דָּבָר שֶׁחַיָּיבִין עַל זְדוֹנוֹ כָּרֵת וְעַל שִׁגְגָתוֹ חַטָּאת. צִבּוּר בַּעֲבוֹדָה זָרָה יָלֵיף "מֵעֵינֵי" "מֵעֵינֵי". יָחִיד, נָשִׂיא וּמָשִׁיחַ — °מִ"וְאִם נֶפֶשׁ אַחַת", אֶחָד יָחִיד וְאֶחָד נָשִׂיא וְאֶחָד מָשִׁיחַ בְּמַשְׁמָע, *וָי"ו מוֹסִיף עַל עִנְיָן רִאשׁוֹן, וְיִלְמַד תַּחְתּוֹן מִן הָעֶלְיוֹן. וְרַבָּנַן, הַאי סְבָרָא מְנָא לְהוּ? — נָפְקָא לְהוּ *מִדְּמַקְרֵי לֵיהּ רַ' יְהוֹשֻׁעַ לִבְרֵיהּ: °"תּוֹרָה אַחַת יִהְיֶה לָכֶם לָעוֹשֶׂה בִּשְׁגָגָה... °וְהַנֶּפֶשׁ אֲשֶׁר תַּעֲשֶׂה בְּיָד רָמָה" הוּקְשָׁה כָּל הַתּוֹרָה כּוּלָּהּ לַעֲבוֹדָה זָרָה, מָה עֲבוֹדָה זָרָה — דָּבָר שֶׁחַיָּיבִין עַל זְדוֹנוֹ כָּרֵת וְעַל שִׁגְגָתוֹ חַטָּאת, אַף כָּל דָּבָר שֶׁחַיָּיבִין עַל זְדוֹנוֹ כָּרֵת וְעַל שִׁגְגָתוֹ חַטָּאת. אַשְׁכַּחַן יָחִיד וְנָשִׂיא וּמָשִׁיחַ, בֵּין בַּעֲבוֹדָה זָרָה וּבֵין בִּשְׁאָר מִצְוֹת, צִבּוּר בַּעֲבוֹדָה זָרָה מְנַיִן? אָמַר קְרָא "וְאִם נֶפֶשׁ", וְיִלְמַד עֶלְיוֹן מִתַּחְתּוֹן. אֶלָּא צִבּוּר בִּשְׁאָר מִצְוֹת מְנָלַן? יָלֵיף "מֵעֵינֵי" "מֵעֵינֵי". וְרַבִּי, הַאי "תּוֹרָה אַחַת" מַאי עָבֵיד לֵיהּ? מִיבְּעֵי לֵיהּ לִכְדְתַנְיָא: *לְפִי שֶׁמָּצִינוּ שֶׁחִלֵּק הַכָּתוּב בֵּין יְחִידִים לִמְרוּבִּים, [ב]יְחִידִים — בִּסְקִילָה, לְפִיכָךְ מָמוֹנָן פָּלֵט, מְרוּבִּין — בְּסַיִף, לְפִיכָךְ מָמוֹנָן אָבֵד. יָכוֹל נַחֲלוֹק בְּקָרְבְּנוֹתֵיהֶן? תַּלְמוּד לוֹמַר "תּוֹרָה אַחַת יִהְיֶה לָכֶם". *מַתְקִיף לָהּ רַב חִלְקִיָּה מֵהַגְרוֹנְיָא: טַעֲמָא דִּכְתַב רַחֲמָנָא "תּוֹרָה אַחַת יִהְיֶה לָכֶם", הָא לָאו הָכִי — ה"א נַחֲלֹק, מַאי לַיְיתוּ? לַיְיתוּ פַּר — צִבּוּר בִּשְׁאָר מִצְוֹת הוּא דְּמַיְיתוּ, כִּשְׂבָּה — יָחִיד בִּשְׁאָר מִצְוֹת הוּא דְּמַיְיתִי, שָׂעִיר — נָשִׂיא בִּשְׁאָר מִצְוֹת הוּא דְּמַיְיתִי, פַּר לְעוֹלָה וְשָׂעִיר לְחַטָּאת — צִבּוּר בַּעֲבוֹדָה זָרָה הוּא דְּמַיְיתוּ. וְאֶלָּא מַאי, שְׂעִירָה — יָחִיד נַמִּי הַיְינוּ קָרְבָּנוֹ! אִיצְטְרִיךְ, ס"ד אָמִינָא: הוֹאִיל וְצִבּוּר בְּהוֹרָאָה מַיְיתוּ פַּר לְעוֹלָה וְשָׂעִיר לְחַטָּאת — אִינְהוּ נַמִּי נַיְתוּ אִיפְּכָא. א"נ: *צָרִיךְ וְאֵין לוֹ תַּקָּנָה, קמ"ל. א"ל לֵוִי לְרַבִּי: מַאי אִירְיָא דְּתָנֵי ט"ו? לִיתְנֵי ט"ז! א"ל: *כִּמְדוּמֶּה לִי שֶׁאֵין לוֹ מוֹחַ בְּקָדְקֳדוֹ. מַאי דַּעְתָּךְ — אִמּוֹ אֲנוּסַת אָבִיו? אִמּוֹ אֲנוּסַת אָבִיו פְּלוּגְתָּא דְּרַבִּי יְהוּדָה וְרַבָּנַן הִיא, וּבִפְלוּגְתָּא לָא קָא מַיְירֵי. וְלָא? וַהֲרֵי אִיסּוּר מִצְוָה וְאִיסּוּר קְדוּשָּׁה, דִּפְלִיגִי רַבִּי עֲקִיבָא וְרַבָּנַן, וְקָתָנֵי! בְּפִרְקִין קָא אָמְרִינַן, וְהָא *בֵּית שַׁמַּאי מַתִּירִין אֶת הַצָּרוֹת לָאַחִין וּבֵית הִלֵּל אוֹסְרִין! *בֵּית שַׁמַּאי בִּמְקוֹם בֵּית הִלֵּל — אֵינָהּ מִשְׁנָה. וַהֲרֵי אֵשֶׁת אָחִיו שֶׁלֹּא הָיָה בְּעוֹלָמוֹ, דִּפְלִיגִי

רש"י

וְלֹא בַּעֲבוֹדָה זָרָה. אֵין חַיָּיבִין צִבּוּר לְהָבִיא פַּר לְעוֹלָה וְשָׂעִיר לְחַטָּאת. אֶלָּא עַל דָּבָר שֶׁחַיָּיבִין עַל זְדוֹנוֹ כָּרֵת וְעַל שִׁגְגָתוֹ חַטָּאת. כְּגוֹן זִיבּוּחַ וְקִיטּוּר וְנִסּוּךְ וְהִשְׁתַּחֲוָאָה, אֲבָל מְחַבֵּק וּמְנַשֵּׁק – לָא. וְהָךְ דְּרָשָׁא מֵ"עָלֶיהָ" נָפְקָא, כִּדְמְפָרֵשׁ וְאָזֵיל. וְנֶאֱמַר לְהַלָּן "עָלֶיהָ". בְּחַיֶּיהָ, שֶׁהוּא מוּפְנֶה לִדְרָשָׁא. לְאַשְׁמַת הָעָם. כְּלוֹמַר אַשְׁמָתוֹ כְּאַשְׁמַת צִבּוּר. [וְלֹא בַּעֲבוֹדָה זָרָה]. קָרְבַּן עֲבוֹדָה זָרָה בְּפָרָשַׁת "שְׁלַח לְךָ": "וְכִי תִשְׁגּוּ". מֵעֵינֵי מֵעֵינֵי. מִסַּפֵּר הֶעְלֵם דָּבָר. וְאִם נֶפֶשׁ אַחַת. הָתָם כְּתִיב, בְּפָרָשַׁת "שְׁלַח לְךָ". מֵעֶלְיוֹן. מִצִּבּוּר, וְהָתָם יָלְפִינַן לְהוּ מִסַּפֵּר הֶעְלֵם. תּוֹרָה אַחַת. לְעִנְיַן קָרְבָּן כְּתִיב (א) בְּסֵפֶר עֲבוֹדָה זָרָה, תּוֹרָה — כָּל הַתּוֹרָה בְּמַשְׁמַע, הוּקְשָׁה כָּל הַתּוֹרָה לְעִנְיַן קָרְבָּן לַעֲבוֹדָה זָרָה. מָה עֲבוֹדָה זָרָה (ב) עַל דָּבָר שֶׁזְּדוֹנוֹ כָּרֵת וְשִׁגְגָתוֹ חַטָּאת. כִּדְכְתִיב הָתָם "וְהַנֶּפֶשׁ אֲשֶׁר תַּעֲשֶׂה בְּיָד רָמָה וְנִכְרְתָה", אַלְמָא כּוּלָּהּ פָּרָשָׁתָא בְּדָבָר שֶׁזְּדוֹנוֹ כָּרֵת וְשִׁגְגָתוֹ חַטָּאת מִישְׁתָּעֵי. אַשְׁכַּחַן יָחִיד וְנָשִׂיא וּמָשִׁיחַ. בְּהַךְ הֶיקֵּישָׁא לָא מַשְׁמַע אֶלָּא הָנֵי דִּכְתִיב "וְהַנֶּפֶשׁ", וְאֵלּוּ לְכֻלָּן בְּמַשְׁמַע, שֶׁהֵן יְחִידִין, דְּהָנֵי קְרָאֵי כְּתִיבִי בְּפָרָשַׁת "וְאִם נֶפֶשׁ אַחַת" בַּעֲבוֹדָה זָרָה. אָמַר קְרָא. גַּבֵּי יָחִיד וְנָשִׂיא וּמָשִׁיחַ. וְאִם נֶפֶשׁ. וָי"ו מוֹסִיף עַל עִנְיָן רִאשׁוֹן. וְיִלְמַד עֶלְיוֹן מִתַּחְתּוֹן. צִבּוּר מִיְּחִידִים. יָלֵיף מֵעֵינֵי מֵעֵינֵי. שְׁאָר מִצְוֹת מֵעֲבוֹדָה זָרָה. מְרוּבִּים. עִיר הַנִּדַּחַת. יָכוֹל נַחֲלֹק בְּקָרְבְּנוֹתֵיהֶם. אִם עָבְדוּ בְּנֵי עִיר אַחַת עֲבוֹדָה זָרָה בְּשׁוֹגֵג — יְהוּ חֲלוּקִים בְּקָרְבָּנָם, שֶׁלֹּא יָבִיא כָּל אֶחָד קָרְבָּנוֹ שָׂעִיר כְּיָחִיד. ת"ל כו'. אֵין חֲלוּקִים מִתּוֹרַת יָחִיד אֶלָּא רוֹב יִשְׂרָאֵל אוֹ כּוּלָּן, כִּדְכְתִיב "וְאִם מֵעֵינֵי הָעֵדָה" (במדבר טו), אֲבָל בְּנֵי עִיר אַחַת — יְחִידִים הֵם. בְּהוֹרָאָה. הַיְינוּ הֶעְלֵם דָּבָר, שֶׁהוֹרוּ ב"ד שֶׁהָעֲבוֹדָה זָרָה מוּתֶּרֶת וְעָשׂוּ צִבּוּר עַל פִּיהֶם. א"נ. אֲפִי' לָא מַשְׁכַּחַת לָהּ קָרְבָּן לְחַלֵּק, נֵימָא: צְרִיכִים הָנֵי מְרוּבִּים חִילּוּק בֵּין יָחִיד וְלֵיכָּא, הִלְכָּךְ אֵין לָהֶם כַּפָּרָה, קמ"ל. אִמּוֹ אֲנוּסַת אָבִיו. שֶׁנְּשָׂאָהּ אָחִיו מֵאָבִיו אַחֲרֵי כֵן וּמֵת בְּלֹא בָּנִים, וְנָפְלָה לִפְנֵי בְּנָהּ לְיִיבּוּם. בִּפְלוּגְתָּא דְּר' יְהוּדָה וְרַבָּנַן. כִּדְאָמְרִי' לְעֵיל (דף ד.): וְרַבִּי יְהוּדָה אוֹסֵר בַּאֲנוּסַת אָבִיו. וּלְר' יְהוּדָה לָא מַשְׁכַּחַת לָהּ אִם נוֹפֶלֶת לִפְנֵי בְּנָהּ לְיִבּוּם אֶלָּא לְרַבָּנַן, וּבַאֲנוּסָה. וּלְהָכִי לָא תָּנָא לָהּ, דִּבְפְלוּגְתָּא לָא קָא מַיְירֵי. וַהֲרֵי אִיסּוּר מִצְוָה וְאִיסּוּר קְדוּשָּׁה. לְקַמָּן בְּפֶרֶק "כֵּיצַד" כו' (דף כ.) כָּל שֶׁאִיסּוּרוֹ אִיסּוּר עֶרְוָה – לֹא חוֹלֶצֶת וְלֹא מִתְיַיבֶּמֶת. אִיסּוּר מִצְוָה – כְּגוֹן שְׁנִיּוֹת מִדְּ"ס כִּדְמְפָרֵשׁ לְקַמָּן בְּפ"ב (כא.), אוֹ אִיסּוּר קְדוּשָּׁה – כְּגוֹן שֶׁנָּפְלָה לְפָנָיו מַמְזֶרֶת אוֹ נְתִינָה, שֶׁהִיא בְּלָאו, חוֹלֶצֶת וְלֹא מִתְיַיבֶּמֶת. חוֹלֶצֶת – דְּלָא אָתֵי אִיסּוּר לָאו בְּלֹא כָּרֵת לְאַפְקוֹעֵי יִיבּוּם לְגַמְרֵי, וְלֹא מִתְיַיבֶּמֶת – דְּהָא אֲסוּרָה לֵיהּ. וּפָלֵיג ר"ע, דְּאָמַר בְּפֶ' "הַחוֹלֵץ" (לקמן דף מט.) חַיָּיבֵי לָאוִין כְּחַיָּיבֵי כְּרֵיתוֹת, דְּקָתָנֵי: אֵיזֶהוּ מַמְזֵר – כָּל שְׁאֵר בָּשָׂר שֶׁהוּא בְּ"לֹא יָבֹא", דְּיֵשׁ מַמְזֵר מֵחַיָּיבֵי לָאוִין. וּלְר"ע הָוֵי לָאו לְמִיפְטְרָהּ בְּלֹא כְּלוּם כְּעֶרְוָה גְּמוּרָה. אֶת הַצָּרוֹת. צָרַת עֶרְוָה מִתְיַיבֶּמֶת. רַבִּי

תוספות

מה להלן דבר שחייבין על זדונו כרת ושגגתו חטאת. אגב שיטפיה נקט לישנא דמתני' דהוריות (דף ח.) דאייתי לעיל, דשגגתו חטאת לא קיס ליה בשאות אשה אלא מהכא.

בעבודה זרה אתיא "מעיני" "מעיני". לא מצינו למימר אתיא "מצות", "מצות" ד"כל מצות" דכתיב בעבודה זרה איצטריך לכדדריש בספרי: "כל מצות" – זו עבודה זרה ששקולה כנגד כל המצות.

וילמד תחתון מעליון. וא"ת: תיפוק לי דכתיב התם כרת בהדיא, כדדרשי רבנן בסמוך! וי"ל: דלר' ההוא כרת במברך את השם, דהכי כתיב "את ה' הוא מגדף ונכרתה", ובפ' "מי שהיה טמא" (פסחים דף צג:) אית לי' לרבי מגדף היינו מברך את השם.

ורבנן האי סברא מנא להו. וא"ת: כולה מילתא תיפוק לי מ"עליה" דג"ש ניתנה לידרש לכל מילי! וי"ל: ד"עליה" דכתיב גבי אחות אשה וגבי חטאת לא מופנה, וההוא דיבוס מופנה. ור"ת אומר: דאפילו מופנה ההיא דאחות אשה, כיון דההוא דחטאת לאו מופנה – שבקינן ליה למופנה מצד אחד ודרשינן ממופנה משני צדדין, כדאמרינן ב"המפלת" (נדה דף כב: ושם). **מה** עבודה זרה דבר שחייבים על זדונה כרת. וא"ת, ואימא: מה עבודה זרה שחייבים על זדונה סקילה? וי"ל: דלא גמרינן אלא מה דכתיב בההוא קרא, דלא כתיב התם אלא כרת. דקסבר: מגדף היינו עובד עבודה זרה, וה"נ לרבנן דלא גמרי מה עבודה זרה שיש בה לאו וכרת, ולא בעו לאו, כיון דלא כתיב בההוא פרשה. תדע, דבפרק בתרא דמכות (ד' יג: ושם) ממעט פסח ומילה משום דבעינן דומיא דעבודה זרה, דאמר רחמנא לא תעביד – והני קום עשה נינהו ולא ממעט להו, משום דלית בהו לאו כמו בעבודה זרה. ומיהו, לרבי דנפקא ליה חטאת מ"עליה" בעי לאו וכרת כמו באחות אשה. ואתי שפיר, דבשבועות (דף יג.) דריש רבי דבפורק עול ומפר ברית ומגלה פנים אית בהו כרת, ולא חשיב להו בהדי ששה ושלשים כריתות – משום דלא אשכחן בהו לאו*.

***ורבנן** לית להו כרת בפורק עול ומפר *ברית ומגלה פנים, אלא מוקמי ג' כריתות בעבודה זרה בסוף פרק "ארבע מיתות" (סנהדרין דף סד:). ע"כ גליון. **מאי** לייתו לייתו פר כו'. קסבר דכיון שחלקם מכל חייבי מיתות ב"ד, דממונן פלט – חלקינן להו מכל מתכפרים. וקשיא: דליתו כבש או איל, ואפי' אינא שום מתכפר דמייתי – מ"מ הוה ליה לאקשויי.

והרי איסור מצוה ואיסור קדושה דפליגי ר"ע ורבנן. בכל דוכתי פשיטא ליה להתלמוד דחייבי לאוין לר"ע, דאמר אין קידושין תופסין בחייבי לאוין – לאו בני חליצה וייבום נינהו כמו חייבי כריתות, הכא וב"הערל" (לקמן דף עט:) גבי פצוע דכא וכרות שפכה, ובפרק "ד' מיתות" (סנהדרין דף נג:) ותימה לר"י: דאמאי לא אמרינן נמי לר"ע דליתי עשה ולידחי לא תעשה? בתו

עין משפט נר מצוה

לד א מיי' פ"א מהל' שגגות הל' א ב ד:

לה ב מיי' פ"ד מהלכות ע"ז הלכה ו:

תוספות ישנים

מאי נחלוק דמשמע קרבן משונה לייתי פר לצבור בשאר מצות הוא דמייתי. וא"ת ולימא לייתי כבש או איל דליתיה באיניך וי"ל דאין לנו לבדות מדעתנו קרבן חדש. וא"ת א"כ למה לו להאריך כדקאמר לייתי פר כו' הו"ל למפרך מאי נחלוק אי לייתי קרבן דאיתיה במקום אחר אין זה נחלוק ואי מייתי קרבן דליתיה בשום מקום אין לנו לבדות מדעתנו ונ"ע:

שבת סח: [הוריות ח.]

הגהות הב"ח

(א) רש"י ד"ה תורה וכו' כתיב בפרשת עבודה זרה: (ב) ד"ה מה עבודה זרה דבר כצ"ל ותיבת על נמחק:

[וע"ע תוס' יומא פו.]

גליון

עיין מהרש"א

מסורת הש"ס

הוריות ט.

[נ"ל וב"ד מביאים כו' כן איתא במשנה דהוריות ט.]

ויקרא ד

הוריות קד ח.

שם

במדבר טו

[פסחים ה. קידושין יז: ב"מ לה. שבועות י. זבחים מח. חולין עח. כריתות כב.]

שם

שם

הוריות ח.

שם

[ברכות טו: וש"נ]

[מנחות פ:]

לקמן יג. [ודף כז. עדיות פ"ד מ"ח] [ברכות לו: ביצה יח:]

דִּפְלִיגִי ר"ש וְרַבָּנַן, וְקָתָנֵי! בְּנוֹלָד וּלְבַסּוֹף יִיבֵּם לָא פָּלֵיג ר"ש. וְהָאָמַר *רַ' אוֹשַׁעְיָא: חָלוּק הָיָה ר"ש אַף בָּרִאשׁוֹנָה! הָא אִיתּוֹתַב רַ' אוֹשַׁעְיָא. *וְהָאָמַר רַב יְהוּדָה אָמַר רַב, וְכֵן תָּנֵי רַ' חִיָּיא: בְּכוּלָּן אֲנִי קוֹרֵא בָּהֶן הָאֲסוּרָה לָזֶה מוּתֶּרֶת לָזֶה, וְהָאֲסוּרָה לָזֶה מוּתֶּרֶת לָזֶה, וַאֲחוֹתָהּ שֶׁהִיא יְבִמְתָּהּ חוֹלֶצֶת אוֹ מִתְיַיבֶּמֶת. וְרַב יְהוּדָה מְתַרְגֵּם מֵחֲמוֹתוֹ וְאֵילָךְ, אֲבָל שִׁיתָּא בָּבֵי דְּרֵישָׁא — לָא, מ"ט? כֵּיוָן דְּבִתּוֹ, בְּאוֹנָסִין מַשְׁכַּחַת (א) בְּנִשּׂוּאִין לָא מַשְׁכַּחַת לָהּ, בְּנִשּׂוּאִין קָמַיְירֵי בְּאוֹנָסִין — לָא קָא מַיְירֵי. וְאַבַּיֵי מְתַרְגֵּם אַף בִּתּוֹ מֵאֲנוּסָתוֹ, כֵּיוָן דְּאַשְׁכּוּחֵי מַשְׁכַּחַת לָהּ, אִי בָּעֲיָא מִן הָאוֹנָסִין — תֶּהֱוֵי. [אִי בָּעֲיָא מִן הַנִּשּׂוּאִין — תֶּהֱוֵי], אֲבָל אֵשֶׁת אָחִיו שֶׁלֹּא הָיָה בְּעוֹלָמוֹ — לָא, מַאי טַעְמָא? כֵּיוָן דְּלר"ש הוּא דְּמַשְׁכַּחַת לָהּ לְרַבָּנַן לָא מַשְׁכַּחַת לָהּ — בִּפְלוּגְתָּא לָא קָא מַיְירֵי. וְרַב סַפְרָא מְתַרְגֵּם אַף אֵשֶׁת אָחִיו שֶׁלֹּא הָיָה בְּעוֹלָמוֹ, וּמַשְׁכַּחַת לָהּ בְּשִׁיתָּא אַחִים, וְאַלִּיבָּא דְּרַ' שִׁמְעוֹן וְסִימָנֵיךְ

רַבִּי שִׁמְעוֹן פָּלֵיג בְּאֵשֶׁת אָחִיו שֶׁלֹּא הָיָה בָּעוֹלָם בְּפֶ' שֵׁנִי (לקמן דף יח:) וּמַצְרִיךְ לֵיהּ חֲלִיצָה, וְאַפְ"ה קָתָנֵי לָהּ בְּמַתְנִי' דִּפְטוּרָה: וּמְשַׁנֵּי. **בְּנוֹלַד וּלְבַסּוֹף יִיבֵּם לָא פָּלֵיג ר"ש.** הֵיכָא דְּמֵת רְאוּבֵן בְּלֹא בָּנִים, וְעַד שֶׁלֹּא יִבְּמָהּ שִׁמְעוֹן נוֹלַד לֵוִי אֲחִיהֶם וְעוֹדָהּ זְקוּקָה לְיָבָם, וְהָיְתָה לוֹ אֲסוּרָה בִּנְפִילָה זוֹ מִשּׁוּם אֵשֶׁת אָחִיו שֶׁלֹּא הָיָה בְּעוֹלָמוֹ, וְיִבְּמָהּ שִׁמְעוֹן וּמֵת בְּלֹא בָּנִים — מוֹדֶה ר"ש שֶׁאֲסוּרָה לְלֵוִי, הוֹאִיל וְנֶאֶסְרָה עָלָיו שָׁעָה אַחַת בִּנְפִילָה רִאשׁוֹנָה. וְכִי פָּלֵיג ר"ש — כְּגוֹן שֶׁיִּבֵּם שִׁמְעוֹן אֶת אֵשֶׁת רְאוּבֵן, וְאַחַ"כ נוֹלַד לֵוִי, וּמֵת שִׁמְעוֹן — דְּהָתָם שָׁרֵי לֵיהּ ר"ש לְיַיבּוּמֵי, דְּלֹא נָפְלָה לְפָנָיו מִכֹּחַ רְאוּבֵן אָחִיו שֶׁמֵּת כְּבָר וְלֹא נֶאֶסְרָה עָלָיו כְּלוּם, שֶׁכְּשֶׁנָּפְלָה לְפָנָיו — מִכֹּחַ שִׁמְעוֹן שֶׁהָיָה בְּעוֹלָמוֹ נָפְלָה. **וְהָאָמַר ר' אוֹשַׁעְיָא.** בְּפֶ' שֵׁנִי (לקמן יח:). **חָלוּק הָיָה ר"ש אַף בָּרִאשׁוֹנָה.** בְּנוֹלַד וּלְבַסּוֹף יִיבֵּם. **וְהָאָמַר רַב יְהוּדָה אָמַר רַב.** בְּפֶרֶק "ד' אַחִין", דִּתְנַן: ד' אַחִין, שְׁנַיִם נָשְׂאוּ שְׁתֵּי אֲחָיוֹת, וּמֵתוּ הַנְּשׂוּאִין אֶת הָאֲחָיוֹת — הֲרֵי אֵלּוּ חוֹלְצוֹת וְלֹא מִתְיַיבְּמוֹת. לְפִי שֶׁשְּׁתֵּיהֶן זְקוּקוֹת לָזֶה וּשְׁתֵּיהֶן זְקוּקוֹת לָזֶה, וְאִי נָסֵיב הַאי — קָא פָּגַע בַּאֲחוֹת זְקוּקָתוֹ, וְדָמְיָא לַאֲחוֹת אִשָּׁה בְּחַיֶּיהָ. וְקָתָנֵי הָתָם: הָיְתָה אַחַת מֵהֶן אֲסוּרָה עַל הָאֶחָד אִיסּוּר עֶרְוָה, כְּגוֹן שֶׁהָיְתָה חֲמוֹתוֹ אוֹ כַּלָּתוֹ, אָסוּר בָּהּ וּמוּתָּר בַּאֲחוֹתָהּ, דְּלָאו אֲחוֹת זְקוּקָתוֹ הִיא. מִשּׁוּם דְּהָךְ עֶרְוָה הִיא וְלֹא זְקוּקָה לֵיהּ, דְּרַחֲמָנָא פַּטְרָהּ מִינֵּיהּ מִדְּרָשַׁת "עָלֶיהָ" "עָלֶיהָ", וְהַשֵּׁנִי אָסוּר בִּשְׁתֵּיהֶן. הָיְתָה הַשְּׁנִיָּה אֲסוּרָה עַל הַשֵּׁנִי אִיסּוּר עֶרְוָה, כְּגוֹן שֶׁהָיְתָה חֲמוֹתוֹ — הָאֲסוּרָה לָזֶה מוּתֶּרֶת לָזֶה. כְּגוֹן, רָחֵל וְלֵאָה שְׁתֵּי אֲחָיוֹת, וְנָפְלוּ לִפְנֵי לֵוִי וִיהוּדָה, רָחֵל חֲמוֹתוֹ שֶׁל לֵוִי וְלֵאָה חֲמוֹתוֹ שֶׁל יְהוּדָה, רָחֵל אֲסוּרָה לְלֵוִי וּמוּתֶּרֶת לִיהוּדָה, דְּלָאו אֲחוֹת זְקוּקָתוֹ הִיא, דְּלֵאָה לֹא זְקוּקָה לֵיהּ, דְּהָא חֲמוֹתוֹ הִיא, וְלֵאָה אֲסוּרָה לִיהוּדָה וּמוּתֶּרֶת לְלֵוִי (ב), וְאֵינָהּ אֲחוֹת זְקוּקָתוֹ, דְּרָחֵל לֹא זְקוּקָה לֵיהּ דְּהָא חֲמוֹתוֹ הִיא. וְקָתָנֵי הָתָם: זוֹ הִיא שֶׁאָמְרוּ אֲחוֹתָהּ כְּשֶׁהִיא יְבִמְתָּהּ אוֹ חוֹלֶצֶת אוֹ מִתְיַיבֶּמֶת. שְׁתֵּי אֲחָיוֹת שֶׁהֵן יְבָמוֹת זוֹ לָזוֹ, שֶׁנִּשְּׂאוּ לִשְׁנֵי אַחִין וְנָפְלוּ לִפְנֵי שְׁנֵי אַחִים — אוֹ חוֹלְצוֹת אוֹ מִתְיַיבְּמוֹת, רְאוּיוֹת לַחֲלִיצָה אוֹ לְיִיבּוּם, וּכְגוֹן שֶׁהָיְתָה כָּל אַחַת אֲסוּרָה עַל הָאֶחָד אִיסּוּר עֶרְוָה, כִּדְפָרֵישִׁית. וְקָאָמַר רַב יְהוּדָה: בְּכוּלָּן, ט"ו עֲרָיוֹת, אֲנִי קוֹרֵא בָּהֶם מִשְׁנָה זוֹ הָאֲסוּרָה לָזֶה מוּתֶּרֶת לָזֶה כו', כְּלוֹמַר: אֶפְשָׁר לְהִתְקַיֵּים, וּמַשְׁכַּחַת בְּכוּלָּן שֶׁיְּהוּ ב' אֲחָיוֹת נוֹפְלוֹת לִפְנֵי ב' אַחִים, וְזוֹ אֲסוּרָה לָזֶה מִשּׁוּם בִּתּוֹ וְזוֹ אֲסוּרָה לָזֶה מִשּׁוּם בִּתּוֹ, וְכֵן בַּת בִּתּוֹ וְכֵן כּוּלָּן, וּתְהֵא הָאֲסוּרָה לָזֶה מוּתֶּרֶת לָזֶה וְהָאֲסוּרָה לָזֶה מוּתֶּרֶת לָזֶה וְיִתְיַיבְּמוּ שְׁתֵּיהֶן אַעַ"פ שֶׁהֵן שְׁתֵּי אֲחָיוֹת, וְלֹא אָמְרִינַן אֲחוֹת זְקוּקָתוֹ הִיא. **בִּתּוֹ** — לֹא מַשְׁכַּחַת לָהּ אֶלָּא בִּתּוֹ מֵאֲנוּסָתוֹ, שֶׁאִי אֶפְשָׁר לְבִתּוֹ שֶׁל רְאוּבֵן וּבִתּוֹ שֶׁל שִׁמְעוֹן לִהְיוֹת אֲחָיוֹת מִן הָאֵם, שֶׁהֲרֵי אֵשֶׁת רְאוּבֵן שֶׁיָּלְדָה לוֹ בַּת וְגֵירְשָׁהּ — לֹא יִשָּׂאֶנָּה שׁוּב לְשִׁמְעוֹן, שֶׁגְּרוּשַׁת אָחִיו הִיא. אֶלָּא הָכִי מַשְׁכַּחַת לָהּ: רְאוּבֵן אָנַס אִשָּׁה וְיָלְדָה לוֹ בַּת, וְחָזַר שִׁמְעוֹן וְאָנַס אֶת אֲנוּסַת אָחִיו, שֶׁמּוּתֶּרֶת לוֹ, דְּלֹא אָסְרָה תּוֹרָה אֶלָּא אֵשֶׁת אָח עַל יְדֵי קִידּוּשִׁין, וְחָזְרָה וְיָלְדָה לוֹ בַּת לְשִׁמְעוֹן, הֲרֵי בַּת רְאוּבֵן וּבַת שִׁמְעוֹן אֲחָיוֹת מִן הָאֵם, וְנִישְּׂאוּ לְלֵוִי וִיהוּדָה אֲחֵי אֲבִיהֶן, וּמֵתוּ, וְנָפְלוּ לִפְנֵי רְאוּבֵן וְשִׁמְעוֹן — בַּת שִׁמְעוֹן מִתְיַיבֶּמֶת לִרְאוּבֵן, דְּלָאו אֲחוֹת זְקוּקָתוֹ הִיא, וּבַת רְאוּבֵן לְשִׁמְעוֹן. וְכֵן בַּת בִּתּוֹ שֶׁל רְאוּבֵן וּבַת בִּתּוֹ שֶׁל שִׁמְעוֹן שֶׁהָיוּ אֲחָיוֹת מִן הָאָב, וְנִישְּׂאוּ לְלֵוִי וִיהוּדָה. וְכֵן בַּת בְּנוֹ שֶׁל רְאוּבֵן [וְכֵן בַּת בְּנוֹ שֶׁל] שִׁמְעוֹן שֶׁהָיוּ אֲחָיוֹת מִן הָאֵם. וְכֵן בַּת אִשְׁתּוֹ שֶׁל רְאוּבֵן וּבַת אִשְׁתּוֹ שֶׁל שִׁמְעוֹן שֶׁהָיוּ אֲחָיוֹת מִן הָאָב, כְּגוֹן: נַחְשׁוֹן שֶׁנָּשָׂא ב' נָשִׁים וְיָלְדוּ לוֹ ב' בָּנוֹת, וּמֵת נַחְשׁוֹן וְנִישְּׂאוּ ב' נָשָׁיו לִרְאוּבֵן וְשִׁמְעוֹן וּב' בְּנוֹתָיו לְלֵוִי וִיהוּדָה, וּמֵתוּ לֵוִי וִיהוּדָה — בַּת אֵשֶׁת שִׁמְעוֹן תִּתְיַיבֵּם לִרְאוּבֵן, וַאֲחוֹתָהּ לְשִׁמְעוֹן. וְכֵן בַּת בִּתָּהּ שֶׁל אֵשֶׁת רְאוּבֵן וּבַת בִּתָּהּ שֶׁל אֵשֶׁת שִׁמְעוֹן שֶׁהָיוּ אֲחָיוֹת מִן הָאָב, וְכֵן בַּת בְּנָהּ שֶׁל אֵשֶׁת זֶה וְשֶׁל אֵשֶׁת זֶה שֶׁהָיוּ אֲחָיוֹת מִן הָאֵם, וְכֵן חֲמוֹתוֹ שֶׁל רְאוּבֵן וַחֲמוֹתוֹ שֶׁל שִׁמְעוֹן שֶׁהָיוּ אֲחָיוֹת, וְכֵן אֵם חֲמוֹתוֹ וְכֵן אֵם חָמִיו, וְכֵן אֲחוֹתוֹ שֶׁל רְאוּבֵן מֵאִמּוֹ וַאֲחוֹת שִׁמְעוֹן מֵאִמּוֹ הָיוּ אֲחָיוֹת מִן הָאָב, וְנָפְלוּ לִפְנֵיהֶם מִלֵּוִי וִיהוּדָה, כְּגוֹן: רְאוּבֵן וְלֵוִי בְּנֵי יַעֲקֹב מֵרָחֵל הָיוּ, וְלָהּ בַּת מִנַּחְשׁוֹן, וְכֵן שִׁמְעוֹן וִיהוּדָה בְּנֵי יַעֲקֹב מִבִּלְהָה, וְגַם לָהּ הָיָה בַּת מִנַּחְשׁוֹן. וְנָשָׂא לֵוִי בַּת בִּלְהָה מִנַּחְשׁוֹן, וִיהוּדָה נָשָׂא בַּת רָחֵל מִנַּחְשׁוֹן, וְהֵן שְׁתֵּי אֲחָיוֹת. וּמֵתוּ לֵוִי וִיהוּדָה, וְנָפְלוּ לִפְנֵי רְאוּבֵן וְשִׁמְעוֹן. בַּת בִּלְהָה אֵשֶׁת לֵוִי אֲחוֹת שִׁמְעוֹן מֵאִמּוֹ וַאֲסוּרָה לוֹ — מִתְיַיבֶּמֶת לִרְאוּבֵן, וּבַת רָחֵל אֵשֶׁת יְהוּדָה אֲחוֹת רְאוּבֵן מֵאִמּוֹ — [אֲסוּרָה לוֹ] וּמוּתֶּרֶת לְשִׁמְעוֹן. וְכֵן אֲחוֹת אִמּוֹ שֶׁל רְאוּבֵן וַאֲחוֹת אִמּוֹ שֶׁל שִׁמְעוֹן הָיוּ אֲחָיוֹת מִן הָאָב, כְּגוֹן: כָּלֵב שֶׁנָּשָׂא שְׁתֵּי נָשִׁים *חֶלְאָה וְנַעֲרָה (דה"א ד), וְיָלְדוּ לוֹ שְׁתֵּי בָּנוֹת וּמֵת. וְנָשָׂא יַחְלְאֵל לְאַחַר מִיתָתוֹ אֶת שְׁתֵּי נָשָׁיו, וְיָלְדוּ לוֹ שְׁתֵּי בָּנוֹת, וְנָשָׂא יַעֲקֹב אֶת שְׁתֵּי בְּנוֹת יַחְלְאֵל זוֹ לְאַחַר מִיתַת אֲחוֹתָהּ. וְיָלְדָה לוֹ בַּת חֶלְאָה מִיַּחְלְאֵל אֶת רְאוּבֵן, וּבַת נַעֲרָה מִיַּחְלְאֵל אֶת שִׁמְעוֹן. וְלֵוִי בֶּן יַעֲקֹב מֵאִשָּׁה אַחֶרֶת נָשָׂא אֶת בַּת כָּלֵב מֵחֶלְאָה, שֶׁהִיא אֲחוֹת אִמּוֹ שֶׁל רְאוּבֵן מִן הָאֵם, וִיהוּדָה נָשָׂא אֶת בַּת כָּלֵב מִנַּעֲרָה שֶׁהִיא אֲחוֹת אִמּוֹ שֶׁל שִׁמְעוֹן מִן הָאֵם, וּמֵתוּ לֵוִי וִיהוּדָה — אֵשֶׁת לֵוִי אֲחוֹת אֵם רְאוּבֵן מוּתֶּרֶת לְשִׁמְעוֹן, שֶׁהִיא בַּת כָּלֵב מֵחֶלְאָה, וְאֵם שִׁמְעוֹן הָיְתָה בַּת יַחְלְאֵל מִנַּעֲרָה, וְאֵשֶׁת יְהוּדָה אֲחוֹת אֵם שִׁמְעוֹן — מוּתֶּרֶת לִרְאוּבֵן. וְכֵן אֵשֶׁת אָחִיו מֵאִמּוֹ, כְּגוֹן: יַעֲקֹב שֶׁנָּשָׂא בִּלְהָה וְלָהּ נַפְתָּלִי מֵאִישׁ אַחֵר, וְהוֹלִיד מִמֶּנָּה רְאוּבֵן וְלֵוִי. וְעוֹד נָשָׂא זִלְפָּה, וְלָהּ יִשָּׂשכָר מֵאִישׁ אַחֵר, וְיָלְדָה לְיַעֲקֹב שִׁמְעוֹן וִיהוּדָה, וְנָשְׂאוּ נַפְתָּלִי וְיִשָּׂשכָר שְׁתֵּי אֲחָיוֹת, וּמֵתוּ, וְעָמַד לֵוִי וְנָשָׂא אֵשֶׁת יִשָּׂשכָר בֶּן זִלְפָּה שֶׁלֹּא הָיָה קָרוֹב לוֹ, וִיהוּדָה נָשָׂא אֵשֶׁת נַפְתָּלִי בֶּן בִּלְהָה, שֶׁהֲרֵי נָכְרִית אֶצְלוֹ, וּמֵתוּ בְּלֹא בָּנִים, וְנָפְלוּ לִפְנֵי רְאוּבֵן וְשִׁמְעוֹן. אֵשֶׁת לֵוִי אֲסוּרָה לְשִׁמְעוֹן מִפְּנֵי יִשָּׂשכָר בַּעְלָהּ שֶׁהָיָה אָחִיו מֵאִמּוֹ, וּמוּתֶּרֶת לִרְאוּבֵן, וְאֵשֶׁת יְהוּדָה אֲסוּרָה לִרְאוּבֵן מִפְּנֵי נַפְתָּלִי בַּעְלָהּ הָרִאשׁוֹן, שֶׁהָיָה אָחִיו מֵאִמּוֹ, וּמוּתֶּרֶת לְשִׁמְעוֹן. וְכֵן אֲחוֹת אִשְׁתּוֹ. [כְּגוֹן] נַפְתָּלִי שֶׁהָיוּ לוֹ שְׁתֵּי נָשִׁים עָדָה וְזִלָּה, וְיָלְדָה לוֹ עָדָה אֶת דִּינָה, וְזִלָּה יָלְדָה אֶת נַעֲמָה, וּמֵת, וְנִישְּׂאוּ נָשָׁיו לְאַחֵר, וְיָלְדוּ שְׁתֵּי בָּנוֹת, וְנָשְׂאוּ רְאוּבֵן וְשִׁמְעוֹן אֶת הַבָּנוֹת הָאַחֲרוֹנוֹת: רְאוּבֵן נָשָׂא אֶת בַּת עָדָה, וְשִׁמְעוֹן בַּת זִלָּה, וְלֵוִי וִיהוּדָה נָשְׂאוּ אֶת שְׁתֵּי בְּנוֹת נַפְתָּלִי, לֵוִי דִּינָה בַּת עָדָה וִיהוּדָה נַעֲמָה בַּת זִלָּה, וּמֵתוּ בְּלֹא בָּנִים, וְנָפְלוּ אֲחָיוֹת הַלָּלוּ לִפְנֵי רְאוּבֵן וְשִׁמְעוֹן, וְנִמְצֵאת אֵשֶׁת לֵוִי אֲחוֹת אִשְׁתּוֹ שֶׁל רְאוּבֵן מוּתֶּרֶת לְשִׁמְעוֹן, וְאֵשֶׁת יְהוּדָה אֲחוֹת אִשְׁתּוֹ שֶׁל שִׁמְעוֹן מוּתֶּרֶת לִרְאוּבֵן. **אֵשֶׁת אָחִיו שֶׁלֹּא הָיָה בָּעוֹלָם.** לֹא מַשְׁכַּחַת לָהּ אֶלָּא אַלִּיבָּא דְּר"ש דְּשָׁרֵי בְּיִיבֵּם וּלְבַסּוֹף נוֹלַד, וְסִימָנֵיךְ: מֵת נוֹלַד וְיִיבֵּם. כְּגוֹן: רְאוּבֵן וְשִׁמְעוֹן וְלֵוִי וִיהוּדָה בְּנֵי יַעֲקֹב, וְנָשְׂאוּ רְאוּבֵן וְשִׁמְעוֹן שְׁתֵּי אֲחָיוֹת, וּמֵת רְאוּבֵן בְּלֹא בָּנִים וְנוֹלַד יִשָּׂשכָר לְיַעֲקֹב, וּמְלָאָהּ לִיבִמְתּוֹ זְקוּקָה לְיִיבּוּם — אֲסוּרָה לוֹ מִשּׁוּם אֵשֶׁת אָחִיו שֶׁלֹּא הָיָה בְּעוֹלָמוֹ, וְיִבְּמָהּ לֵוִי, וּמֵת שִׁמְעוֹן אַחֲרֵי כֵן, וְנוֹלַד זְבוּלוּן, וּמְלָאָהּ עָלָיו בְּאִיסּוּר, וְיִבְּמָהּ יְהוּדָה, וּמֵתוּ לֵוִי וִיהוּדָה, וְנָפְלוּ אֲחָיוֹת הַלָּלוּ לִפְנֵי יִשָּׂשכָר וּזְבוּלוּן — אֵשֶׁת לֵוִי אֲסוּרָה לְיִשָּׂשכָר, מִפְּנֵי שֶׁבָּא וּמְלָאָהּ בְּאִיסּוּר נְפִילַת רְאוּבֵן שֶׁהָיָה אָחִיו שֶׁלֹּא הָיָה בְּעוֹלָמוֹ, וּמוּתֶּרֶת לִזְבוּלוּן שֶׁבָּא וּמְלָאָהּ בְּהֶיתֵּר, דִּכְשֶׁנּוֹלַד זְבוּלוּן כְּבָר נִתְיַיבְּמָה זוֹ לְלֵוִי. וּדְיִיבֵּם וּלְבַסּוֹף נוֹלַד שָׁרֵי רַבִּי שִׁמְעוֹן. וְאֵשֶׁת יְהוּדָה אֲסוּרָה לִזְבוּלוּן, מִפְּנֵי שֶׁבָּא וּמְלָאָהּ בְּאִיסּוּר נְפִילַת נִישּׂוּאֵי שִׁמְעוֹן אָחִיו שֶׁלֹּא הָיָה בָּעוֹלָם, וּמוּתֶּרֶת לְיִשָּׂשכָר שֶׁרָאָהּ שִׁמְעוֹן וִיהוּדָה; כַּלָּתוֹ — כְּגוֹן בֶּן רְאוּבֵן וּבֶן שִׁמְעוֹן נָשְׂאוּ שְׁתֵּי אֲחָיוֹת וּמֵתוּ, וְנָשְׂאוּ לֵוִי וִיהוּדָה אֲחֵי רְאוּבֵן וְשִׁמְעוֹן וּמֵתוּ בְּלֹא בָּנִים — כַּלָּתוֹ שֶׁל זֶה מוּתֶּרֶת לָזֶה, וְשֶׁל זֶה מוּתֶּרֶת לָזֶה, וְנִמְצְאוּ שְׁתֵּי אֲחָיוֹת מִתְיַיבְּמוֹת. **וְרַב יְהוּדָה מְתַרְגֵּם.** לְהָא דְּרַב מֵחֲמוֹתוֹ וְאֵילָךְ. אֲבָל שֵׁשׁ עֲרָיוֹת דְּבָבָא דְּרֵישָׁא — לֹא תָּנֵי בּוֹ אֲנִי קוֹרֵא בָּהֶן. וְאַף עַל גַּב דִּבְכוּלְּהוּ מַשְׁכַּחְתְּ לָהּ. **כֵּיוָן דְּבִתּוֹ.** לֹא מִיתּוֹקְמָא אֶלָּא בְּבַת אֲנוּסָה, וְכִדְפָרְשִׁינַן: בְּאוֹנָסִין — לֹא קָא מַיְירֵי מַתְנִיתִין. וְאַיְּידֵי דְּלָא תָּנֵי בִּתּוֹ, לֹא תָּנֵי לְהוּ לְכוּלְּהוּ עֲרָיוֹת מִשּׁוּם לַד בִּתּוֹ. **וְסִימָנֵיךְ**

בתו מאנוסתו. נ"ל דשניהם אנוסות, דאי אנסה ראובן, ושמעון נשאה — א"כ לשמעון אסירי תרווייהו, אחת משום בתו ואחת משום בת אשתו. **באונסין** לא קמיירי. דבכולן אני קורא בהן — משמע כרגיל להיות. **משכחת** לה בשיתא אחים. בפ' "ארבעה אחין" (לקמן ד' כח.) פריך: בחמשה נמי משכחת להו! לעולם

והאמר ר' אושעיא חלוק היה ר' שמעון אף בראשונה. וא"ת ולישני דמיירי בחד אחא ומית ולא יבם אי נמי בתרי ולא מית דבהא מודה ר' אושעיא דר' שמעון מודה בהא כדקאמר לקמן וי"ל דהא לא מצינן למימר דהא בפ"ב מפרש כילד אשת אחיו שלא היה בעולמו ולא מיירי בכי האי גוונא:

הגהות הב"ח

(א) גמ' משכחת לה בנשואין: (ב) רש"י ד"ה והאמר רב יהודה וכו' ומותרת ללוי דאינה אחות:

[לקמן יח:]

לקמן כח:

וי"ג מחלה ונועה

וסימניך: מת נולד ויבם, מת נולד ויבם. (א) אלא, לרבי – הני כללי לית ליה. רב אדא קרחינא קמיה דרב כהנא אמר משמיה דרבא: לעולם אית ליה לרבי הני כללי, והכי קא"ל: אמו אנוסת אביו – בחדא משכחת לה, בתרתי – לא קמשכחת לה. אי יעקב ב' אחיות אנס, אחותה שהיא יבמתה – משכחת לה, האסורה לזה מותרת לזה – לא משכחת (ב), ואי ב' נכריות אנס – האסורה לזה מותרת לזה משכחת לה, אחותה שהיא יבמתה – לא משכחת לה. רב אשי אמר: לעולם לית ליה לרבי הני כללי, ובפלוגתא קמיירי. ומאי "כמדומה אני שאין לו מוח בקדקדו" דקאמר ליה – ה"ק ליה: מ"ט לא דייקת מתני'? דמתני' ר' יהודה היא, [דאסר באנוסת אביו]. דקתני: *שש עריות חמורות מאלו מפני שהן נשואות לאחרים צרותיהן מותרות: אמו, ואשת אביו, ואחות אביו. מאי אמו? אילימא נשואת אביו – היינו אשת אביו! אלא לאו – אנוסת אביו, וקתני: מפני שהן נשואות לאחרים, לאחרים – אין, לאחין – לא. מאן שמעת ליה דאית ליה האי סברא – ר' יהודה, דאסר באנוסת אביו, משום הכי לא תני ליה. א"ל רבינא לרב אשי: לר' יהודה נמי משכחת לה. *דאי עבר ונסיב! *"דאי" לא קתני. א"ל רב אשי לרב כהנא: בלא "דאי" נמי משכחת לה: יעקב אנס כלתו והוליד ממנה בן, ומת [ראובן] בלא בנים, ונפלה לה קמי ברה, ומיגו דאיהי אסירה – צרתה נמי אסירה. א"ל[א]: באחותה דהתירא – קמיירי, באחותה דאיסורא – לא קמיירי. ואף על פי כן *בדקה לוי במתני', דתני לוי: אמו, פעמים פוטרת צרתה ופעמים אינה פוטרת צרתה. כיצד? היתה אמו נשואת אביו, ונשאת לאחיו מאביו ומת – זו היא אמו שאין פוטרת צרתה, היתה

וסמניך מת נולד ויבם כו'. כלפי', אלמא מדתני רבי חייא בכולן אני קורא בהן, ואפילו באשת אחיו שלא היה בעולם – אלמא תנא דמתני' תני פלוגתא, דהא רבי חייא אמתני' קאי. לרבי לית ליה הני כללי. דר' חייא, הלכך לא מוקמי מתני' בפלוגתא, אלא בנולד ולבסוף ייבם לדברי הכל. אמו אנוסת אביו בחדא משכחת לה. להכי לא נקט לה במתני', שאי אתה קורא בה האסורה לזה מותרת לזה, ואחותה כשהיא יבמתה מתייבמת, שיהו ב' אחיות נופלות להתייבם ותהא זו אסורה לזה משום אמו, וכן זו על זה, ומותרת לשני. אלא חדא משכחת לה: או האסורה לזה מותרת לזה, או אחותה כשהיא יבמתה. אי יעקב שתי אחיות אנס. וילדה לו האחת לוי והאחת יהודה, ונשא ראובן אנוסת אביו, אמו של לוי, ושמעון נשא אנוסת אביו, אמו של יהודה. אחותה כשהיא יבמתה. נופלת לייבום לפני לוי ויהודה בניה, משכחת לה. האסורה לזה מותרת לזה לא משכחת לה. לפי ששתיהן אסורות על שניהם: אמו של לוי אסורה לו משום אמו, ואחותה משום אחות האם, וכן ליהודה. ושתיהן פטורות מן החליצה ומן הייבום. ואי שתי נכריות אנס. וילדו לו ב' בנים, ונשאום ב' בנים מאשה אחרת, ונפלו לפני בניהם – האסורה לזה מותרת לזה משכחת לה, אבל לאו אחיות נינהו. ועיקר מילתיה דרבי חייא משום ייבום שתי אחיות נקט: ה"ג. רב אשי אמר לעולם לית ליה לר' הני כללי, ובפלוגתא קא מיירי. כלומר: לא תימא דהא דלא תני אמו אנוסת אביו משום דלא משכחת [בה] הני כללי, דלרבי ל"ל הני כללי. ולא תימא להכי שבקיה דלא מיירי בפלוגתא, דבפלוגתא ודאי קמיירי, ומאי אין לו מוח דקאמר ליה – ה"ק ליה כו'. דאסר באנוסת אביו. ולא משכחת לה שתפול אם לפני בנה לייבום מאחיו ומאביו. דאי עבר ונסיב. את אנוסת אביו, ונפלה לייבום לפני בנה, וליתני. בלא דאי נמי משכחת. שלא עבר זה המת בנישואיה. אנס כלתו. ועבר על דת: ואע"פ דמהדר ליה רבי ללוי: כמדומה אני שאין לו מוח בקדקדו. בדקה לוי במתני'. הגיה והוסיפה לאמו אנוסת אביו במשנתו. היתה אמו נשואת אביו ונשאת לאחיו מאביו ומת. לא תפסי קידושין בה, שהרי אשת אב בכרת, ואמרינן לקמן: אין קידושין תופסין בחייבי כריתות דברי הכל. הלכך, כשמת רשע זה לא נפלה זו לייבום לפני בנה, דלאו אשת אח הואי, ואינה פוטרת צרתה.

לעולם לית ליה לרבי הני כללי ובפלוגתא קמיירי. וא"ת: ליתני אשת איש שפוטרת צרתה, כגון דאמר לה הרי זה גיטך ע"מ שלא תנשאי לפלוני, דפליגי ב"המגרש" (גיטין דף פב.) ר"א ורבנן, דלר"א הוי גט ואסורה לפלוני, ואם נשאת לאחיו ומת פוטרת צרתה, ואע"ג דאסורה לכל אדם, אפי' לרבי אליעזר מדרבנן, עד שימות המגרש או הפלוני, דחיישינן שמא תנשא לו לאחר שתתאלמן או תתגרש מזה, ונמצאו בניה ממזרים. כדחיישינן ב"המגרש" (שם דף פד.) ע"מ שלא תבעלי לפלוני שמא תבעל לו אחר שתתאלמן או אחר שתתגרש, ובעודה תחתיו ליכא למיחש יותר מאבא ואביך – מ"מ לוי דקתני נמי "דאי", כדאמרינן לקמן – קשה, דליתני נמי להך! ולמאן דנפקא ליה מאחות אשה – ניחא, דלא דמי הך לאחות אשה. דע"מ שלא תנשאי שריא ליה בזנות, וע"מ שלא תבעלי – יכולה היא להתקדש לו, ולא דמיא לאחות אשה. ובע"מ שלא תנשאי ולא תבעלי נמי, אי חשיב שיור כמו ב"חוץ מפלוני" – א"כ שריא ליה כי נשאת לאחיו קודם. ואפי' אי לא חשיב שיור – מ"מ לא דמי לאחות אשה, דהתם בשעת נפילה הוי אחות אשתו, אבל הכא, בשעת נפילה אינה אשת איש עד שתבעל לו. ואפי' תחשבנה אשת איש כיון שמטעם אשת איש אסורה ליבעל לו – מ"מ לא דמי, כיון שאם תבעל ליבם שנאסרה עליו – הויא אשת איש, ולא היתה אשת אחיו מעולם, הלכך לא פטרה צרתה. ומיהו, למאן דנפקא ליה מ"ולקחה" כל היכא דאיכא תרי ליקוחין – קשה! וי"ל, אע"ג דלוי תני "דאי", ובפלוגתא קמיירי – לא קמיירי אלא בפלוגתא דס"ל לתנא דמתני' כוותיה. תדע, דלא תני לוי חייבי לאוין, אע"ג דלר"ע לאו בני חליצה וייבום נינהו. ומאן דמוסיף לעיל אשת אחיו שלא היה בעולמו, ומשכחת לה כר"ש, אע"ג דשמא תנא דמתני' לא סבר לה כר"ש – היינו משום דבכולן אני קורא בהן – משמע ליה דקאי אכולהו, אבל אי מודו רבנן לר"א בקידושין, דמספקא ליה לאביי מדקאמר בריש "המגרש" (שם דף פג: ושם) דאם איתא לר' אבא קשיא: ליתני אשת איש, דמשכחת לה אפילו לרבנן, כגון שבא ראובן וקדשה חוץ משמעון, ובא שמעון וקדשה סתם, ומת שמעון [ונפלה לפני לוי אחיו]. וצרת צרה נמי משכחת לה, כגון שקדשה ראובן חוץ משני אחין! וי"ל: דלא קרינא לגביה אשת המת, דכבר נאסרה [עליו לפני קדושי אחים] משום אשת [אח], ולא חשיב ערוה במקום מצוה. ומיהו, אי אשת שני מתים דאורייתא, כדמשמע ב"המגרש" (שם דף פג: ושם) ליתני הכא אשת ב' מתים, כגון שבא ראובן וקדשה חוץ משמעון ולוי אחיו, ובא שמעון וקדשה סתם ומת כו', או בענין שאמר ר' יוחנן בפ' "האומר" (קדושין דף ס.) דאפילו הן ק' – תופסין, ומשכחת בהן נמי צרת צרה! ומיהו, בפ"ג (לקמן לא: ושם ד"ה מדרבנן) ובפ"ב (לקמן יח. ושם) משמע דאשת שני מתים גזירה דרבנן, ושם אפרש. ובירושלמי בריש "המגרש" פריך לה: מתיב ר' חנינא בשם רבי פנחס: ליתני ט"ז נשים כר"א! ומשני: תמן התורה אסרה עליו (ג), הכא – הוא אסרה עליו. ופי' רבינו יצחק: תמן התורה אסרה עליו, ומשנשאה המת אין לה היתר להתייבם כשימות, מפני שאין איסור שבה תלוי בשום אדם, אלא בתורה שאסרה עליו. אבל אשת איש האיסור תלוי במגרש שאם ירצה – יתירנה ליבם קודם שימות אחיו שנשאה, ולהכי לא תני להו, דלא דמו להו, לפי שביד המגרש להתירה*. **דקתני** שש עריות חמורות מאלו כו'. ותימה: דמאי ס"ד דהנהו. דלעיל דלא דייקי מסיפא? וממ"נ, כיון דתני לה גבי שש עריות – לא אפשר למיתנייה ברישא! וי"ל: דקשיא ליה ללוי, דה"ל למיתני ברישא ט"ז ובסיפא לא הוה ליה למיתני אלא ה', ואע"ג דאתי כרבי יהודה – ה"ל למיתני ששה עשרה, דאי עבר ונסיב, ושני ליה: רבי בפלוגתא לא קא מיירי, ודאי לא קא מיירי. **לרבי** יהודה נמי משכחת לה דאי עבר ונסיב. תימה: דבלא "דאי עבר ונסיב" נמי משכחת לה (ד) שקידש ולא בעל, דאפילו אביי דאמר בפרק בתרא דקידושין (דף עח.), גבי אלמנה לכ"ג: קידש לוקה – היינו משום דכתיב "לא יקח", אבל הכא "לא יגלה" כתיב! וי"ל: דשמא אסור לקדש מדרבנן שמא יבעול, ואפילו יהא מותר לקדשה – חשיב "דאי" מטעם שאסור לבוא עליה. וא"ת: אפילו ע"י "דאי", היכי משכחת לה? הא ר' יהודה סבר כר"ע בפרק "ד' מיתות" (סנהדרין דף נג.) דאמר: אין קידושין תופסין בחייבי לאוין! וי"ל: דלא סבר לה התלמוד כברייתא דהתם, אלא כמתני' דפליג עלה. ועוד, דעל כרחך מתני' דהכא לא סברה בהא כרבי יהודה, דהא קתני בפ"ב (לקמן דף כ.): איסור מצוה ואיסור קדושה – חולצת ולא מתייבמת. ואי אין קידושין תופסין בחייבי לאוין – חליצה נמי לא תיבעי. וא"ת: בחייבי לאוין דאמר, מנלן דלא סבר מתני' כרבי יהודה? דאיסור מצוה ואיסור קדושה מפרש לקמן כגון אלמנה לכ"ג גרושה וחלוצה לכהן הדיוט ממזרת ונתינה לישראל. ופר"י: דע"כ מתני'

לקמן יג.

[לקמן עח.]

[גירסת הערוך בערך פתק פתקה]

[פסחים קה. מנחות נב.]

[וע"ע תוס' גיטין פג: ד"ה אפילו לא]

(א) גמ' מת נולד ויבם לר' כצ"ל ותיבת אלא נמחק: (ב) שם מותרת לזה לא משכחת לה ואי ב': (ג) תוס' ד"ה לעולם וכו' אסרה עליו ברם הכא הוא: (ד) ד"ה לר' יהודא וכו' משכחת לה כגון שקידש:

הגהות מהר"ב רנשבורג

א] גמ' באחותה דהיתירא קמיירי באחותה דאיסורא לא קמיירי כצ"ל:

הָיְתָה אִמּוֹ אֲנוּסַת אָבִיו, וְנִשֵּׂאת לְאָחִיו מֵאָבִיו וּמֵת – זוֹ הִיא אִמּוֹ שֶׁפּוֹטֶרֶת צָרָתָהּ. וְאע"פ שֶׁשָּׁנוּ חֲכָמִים בְּמִשְׁנָתֵנוּ "חֲמֵשׁ עֶשְׂרֵה", יֵשׁ לָנוּ לְהוֹסִיף שֵׁשׁ עֶשְׂרֵה, כְּגוֹן זוֹ. א"ל ר"ל לְרַבִּי יוֹחָנָן: לְלֵוִי דְּאָמַר "דְּאִי" נַמִי קָתָנֵי, לִתְנֵי: הַחוֹלֵץ לִיבִמְתּוֹ וְחָזַר וְקִדְּשָׁהּ וּמֵת בְּלֹא בָּנִים, דְּמִגּוֹ דְּאִיהִי אֲסוּרָה – צָרָתָהּ נַמִי אֲסִירָא! א"ל: °לְפִי שֶׁאֵינָהּ בְּצָרַת צָרָה. וְלֵימָא לֵיהּ: חַיָּיבֵי לָאוִין הִיא, וְחַיָּיבֵי לָאוִין בְּנֵי חֲלִיצָה וְיִבּוּם נִינְהוּ? לְדְבָרָיו קָאָמַר לֵיהּ: לְדִידִי חַיָּיבֵי לָאוִין הֵם, וְחַיָּיבֵי לָאוִין בְּנֵי חֲלִיצָה וְיִבּוּם נִינְהוּ, אֶלָּא לְדִידָךְ חַיָּיבֵי כְּרֵיתוֹת נִינְהוּ, לְפִי שֶׁאֵינָן בְּצָרַת צָרָה. אִיתְּמַר, הַחוֹלֵץ לִיבִמְתּוֹ וְחָזַר וְקִדְּשָׁהּ. *אָמַר ר"ל: הוּא אֵין חַיָּיב עַל הַחֲלוּצָה כָּרֵת, וְהָאַחִין חַיָּיבִין עַל הַחֲלוּצָה כָּרֵת. עַל הַצָּרָה – בֵּין הוּא וּבֵין הָאַחִים חַיָּיבִין עַל הַצָּרָה כָּרֵת. *וְרַבִּי יוֹחָנָן אָמַר: [א]בֵּין הוּא וּבֵין הָאַחִין אֵינָן חַיָּיבִין לֹא עַל הַחֲלוּצָה כָּרֵת וְלֹא עַל הַצָּרָה כָּרֵת. מ"ט דר"ל? אָמַר קְרָא °"אֲשֶׁר לֹא יִבְנֶה" (דברים כה) *כֵּיוָן שֶׁלֹּא בָּנָה – שׁוּב לֹא יִבְנֶה. אִיהוּ הוּא דְּקָאֵי בְּ"לֹא יִבְנֶה", אֲבָל אֶחָיו – כִּדְקַיְימֵי קָיְימֵי, וַעֲלָהּ דִּידָהּ הוּא דְּקָאֵי בְּ"לֹא יִבְנֶה", הָא צָרָה – כִּדְקַיְימֵי קָיְימֵי. וְרַבִּי יוֹחָנָן: מִי אִיכָּא מִידֵי דְּמֵעִיקָּרָא, אִי בָּעֵי הַאי חָלֵיץ וְאִי בָּעֵי הַאי חָלֵיץ, וְאִי בָּעֵי (א) לְהַאי חָלֵיץ וְאִי בָּעֵי לְהַאי חָלֵיץ, וְהַשְׁתָּא קָאֵי עֲלָהּ בְּכָרֵת? אֶלָּא: אִיהוּ שְׁלִיחוּתָא דְּאַחִים קָעָבֵיד, אִיהִי שְׁלִיחוּתָא דְּצָרָה קָעָבְדָה. אֵיתִיבֵיהּ רַ' יוֹחָנָן לְר"ל: הַחוֹלֵץ לִיבִמְתּוֹ וְחָזַר וְקִדְּשָׁהּ, וּמֵת – צְרִיכָה חֲלִיצָה מִן הָאַחִין. בִּשְׁלָמָא לְדִידִי דְּאָמִינָא חַיָּיבֵי לָאוִין נִינְהוּ, הַיְינוּ דִּצְרִיכָה חֲלִיצָה מִן הָאַחִין. אֶלָּא לְדִידָךְ, אַמַּאי צְרִיכָה חֲלִיצָה? וּלְטַעֲמָיךְ, אֵימָא סֵיפָא: עָמַד אֶחָד מִן הָאַחִין וְקִדְּשָׁהּ – אֵין לָהּ עָלָיו כְּלוּם. וְאִי חַיָּיבֵי לָאוִין נִינְהוּ – אַמַּאי אֵין לָהּ עָלָיו כְּלוּם? אָמַר רַב שֵׁשֶׁת: סֵיפָא אֲתָאן לְר"ע, דְּאָמַר: *אֵין קִידּוּשִׁין תּוֹפְסִין בְּחַיָּיבֵי לָאוִין. וְלִיתְנֵי: לְדִבְרֵי ר"ע אֵין (ב) לוֹ עָלָיו כְּלוּם! קַשְׁיָא

רש"י

היתה אמו אנוסת אביו ונשאת לאחיו מאביו. קידושין תופסין בה. ואפילו לר' יהודה הקידושין תופסין בחייבי לאוין, וכשמת – נמצאת צרתה צרת ערוה, ופטורה. **ללוי דאמר דאי נמי קתני.** דהא מתני' רבי יהודה (ג), ובדיק לה לוי: אמו אנוסת אביו. **וחזר וקדשה.** וקידושין תופסין לו בה, דאינה עליו אלא בלאו, דכתיב "אשר לא יבנה את בית אחיו" – כיון שלא בנה שוב לא יבנה. **ומת בלא בנים.** ולו אשה אחרת. **דמיגו דהיא אסורה לאחים.** דקיימא עלייהו בכרת לר"ל, דאמר לקמן בשמעתין: האחין של חולץ חייבין על החלוצה כרת, צרתה נמי אסורה. **לפי שאינה בצרת צרה.** דליכא למיתני בה הלכה צרתה ונשאת לאחד מן האחין – דהא לכולהו אסירא, דכל עריות דמתני' על האחד מהם ערוה ועל שאר אחין מותרות, ומצי למיתני בה "הלכה צרתה ונשאת לאחיו השני". אבל הכא כולהו אחין אסירי בתרוייהו. **ולימא ליה.** רבי יוחנן לר"ל: חייבי לאוין נינהו האחין על חלוצה זו, שחזרה ונפלה לפניהם, ולא קיימא עלייהו בכרת. דהא איהו פליג עליה דר"ש בן לקיש לקמן, ואמר: בין שאר האחים בין החולץ אין חייבין על החלוצה כרת ולא על הצרה כרת. **וחייבי לאוין בני חליצה ויבום נינהו.** כלומר, זקוקה היא להתייבם, ואין איסור לאו פוטרת מן החליצה, דהא מאחות אשה ילפינן שהיא ערוה וחייבין על זדונה כרת, והלכך לא מצי למיתנייה במתני'. **על הצרה.** אם היתה לה צרה, ונפטרה בחליצתה של זו, דכתיב "בית חלוץ הנעל" – בית אחד הוא חולץ, ואין חולץ שני בתים (ד). ואותה צרה חמורה לעמוד על כולן באיסור אשת אח בכרת שנפטרה מהן, כדמפרש טעמא. **כדקיימי קיימי.** באיסור אשת אח. **ור' יוחנן.** אמר לך: מי איכא מידי דמעיקרא אי בעי האי את חליץ ואי בעי האי את חליץ, שהרשות ביד כולן. ולענין צרתה נמי, (ה) מעיקרא – אי בעי להאי חליץ ואי בעי להאי חליץ, והשתא, משום דחליץ חד לחדא, קאי על צרה בכרת, וכן אחיו על כולהו בכרת. **האי שליחותא דידהו עבד.** דמעיקרא היה הרשות ביד כולן. וכן היא, שליחותא דצרה עבדה. וכי היכי דהוא עלה בלא יבנה, כן על צרתה בלא יבנה, וכן האחים על שתיהם. **אמאי צריכה חליצה.** נהי נמי דקידושין תפסי בה, דאיהו לא קאי עלה בכרת, מיהו כשמת – תיפטר ותצא מן האחים משום ערוה, הואיל ובכרת היא עלייהו. **עמד אחד מן האחין וקדשה.** שלא קדשה החולץ, אלא אחד מן האחין. **אין לה עליו כלום.** דאין קידושין תופסין לו בה, ואינה צריכה הימנו גט, דאין קידושין תופסין בחייבי כריתות. **סיפא אתאן לרבי עקיבא.** ורישא רבנן. ומיהו, חייבי לאוין הוא דברי הכל. קשיא

תוספות

מתני' סבר דאפי' בחייבי לאוין דשאר קידושין תופסין, מדקתני שש עריות ולא קתני ח' עריות גרושתו וחלוצתו, דאם היו יכולות לינשא לאחיו היו פוטרות צרותיהן כחייבי כריתות, כיון דאין קידושין תופסין. אלא ודאי קידושין תופסין בהו, ולהכי לא שייך למיתנינהו, דאפי' היו יכולות לינשא לאחיו – לא היו פוטרות צרותיהן. ועוד יש לדקדק: מדנקט אנוסת אביו שהיא אמו, ולא נקט אנוסת אביו סתם. וא"ת: כיון דמתני' סבר כרבי יהודה דאסר באנוסת אביו, א"כ ע"כ סבר נמי דאין קידושין תופסין בחייבי לאוין, דהא בהא תליא, כדמוכח בסוף "החולץ" (לקמן דף מט. ושם) דמפרש טעמא דר"ע דאמר: יש ממזר מחייבי לאוין, משום דסבר לה כרבי יהודה דמוקי "לא יגלה" באנוסת אביו, וסמיך ליה "לא יבא ממזר", וא"כ למתני' נמי הוי ממזר, וכל היכא דהוי ממזר – אין קידושין תופסין, כדמוכח בכמה דוכתי! וי"ל: דאע"ג דמתני' מוקמה לקרא באנוסת אביו מ"מ לא הוי ממזר, כמו לרבי יהושע דמוקי "לא יגלה" בשומרת יבם של אביו – אפ"ה סבר דלא הוי ממזר אלא מחייבי מיתות ב"ד, ודרשינן מ"לא יקח" דהוי חייבי מיתות ב"ד עד "לא יגלה" דהוי חייבי כריתות הוי ממזר, ולא חייבי כריתות. וה"נ לתנא דמתני' מ"לא יקח" עד "לא יגלה" שהוא חייבי לאוין – הוי ממזר, ולא חייבי לאוין בכלל.

לפי (ו) **שאינן בצרת צרה.** הקשה הר"ר משה כהן: לר"ש איתא בצרת צרה, כגון שנולדו אחים להן אחר שחלץ ליבמתו וקדשה, דלא קיימין עלה ב"לא יבנה" כדאמרינן לקמן בסמוך, ולוי מיירי בפלוגתא, כיון דקתני אנוסת אביו גבי שש עריות בסיפא, דהיינו כרבי יהודה! וי"ל: דבפלוגתא דלא סבר לה – לא קמיירי. כדפי' לעיל. ולוי לא סבר כר"ש באשת אחיו שלא היה בעולמו.

החולץ ליבמתו וחזר וקדשה. וליכא למימר דנקט וחזר וקדשה לאשמועינן דהוא אינו חייב על החלוצה כרת, אבל לאו איכא – לפי שקדשה, דאמרינן בקידושין (דף עח.): מודים במחזיר *גרושתו, שאם קידש ולא בעל – שאין לוקה, דרך בנין בית אסרה תורה. אלא נקט קדשה משום דאם מת פליגי רבי יוחנן ור"ל אם זקוקה ליבם לאחיו אי לאו. ולא נקט וחזר ובא עליה – דבהא לא פליגי רבי יוחנן ור"ל, דלכולי עלמא אינו חייב על החלוצה כרת. וה"ה דהוה מצי למנקט וחזר ובא עליה אחד מן האחין. **איהו הוא דקאי בלא יבנה.** אי לא הוה כתיב "לא יבנה" הוה אמינא דאפילו הוא על החלוצה בכרת, והשתא אייתר "לא יבנה" לנתקה מכרת ללאו, אבל אחין וצרה – כדקיימי קיימי, ולא קאי לא יבנה עלייהו. ותימה: דב"החולץ" (לקמן דף מד. ושם) משמע דלא אייתר קרא דלא יבנה אלא איצטריך דלא לחלוץ לחדא ולייבם לחדא. דהתם פריך אמתני' דמי שהיה נשוי ב' נשים כו' ולייבם לתרוייהו! אמר קרא "בית אחיו" – בית אחד הוא בונה, ואינו בונה שתי בתים. וליחלוץ לתרוייהו! אמר קרא "בית חלוץ" – בית אחד הוא חולץ כו'. וליחלוץ לחדא ולייבם לחדא! אמר קרא "אשר לא יבנה וכו'". ולייבם לחדא ולחלוץ לחדא! אמר קרא "אם לא יחפוץ", הא אם חפץ – מייבם, וכל שאינו עולה לייבום אינו עולה לחליצה. ומיהו, אית ספרים דלא גרסינן להו. ואף לספרים דגרסינן איכא למימר דכי משני בתר הכי הא חפץ מייבם, וכל שאין עולה לייבום כו' – תו לא איצטריך "לא יבנה" דלא ליחלוץ לחדא ולייבם לחדא, דכיון דאין עולה לחליצה, דאין חולץ שתי בתים – אינו עולה נמי לייבום. והשתא אייתר "לא יבנה" לנתק מכרת ללאו. ובפ' "ד' אחין" (לקמן דף לב.) דקאמר אי דמייבם והדר חליץ – ה"נ, אלא דלמא חליץ ברישא והדר מייבם, וקם ליה ב"לא יבנה" – התם היינו אליבא דרבי יוחנן, דמוקי לא יבנה נמי אצרה, אבל לר"ל קם ליה בכרת. **וליתני לר"ע אין לו עליו כלום.** תימה: דבפרק "המדיר" (כתובות דף עה:) איכא כי האי גוונא, דתנן: היו בה מומים ועודה בבית אביה – האב צריך להביא ראיה, נכנסה לרשות הבעל – הבעל צריך להביא ראיה, ומסיק בגמרא דרישא ר' יהושע וסיפא ר"ג, ולא פריך ולימא לדברי ר"ג נאמנת ועל הבעל להביא ראיה, ולא הוה צריך למיתני תרי בבי!

מאן

עין משפט נר מצוה

לו א מיי' פ"א מהל' יבום הלכה כב טוש"ע אה"ע סי' קסב סעיף ב:

תוספות ישנים

החולץ ליבמתו וחזר וקדשה למאי נקט וחזר וקדשה. ונראה דלרבותא נקטיה דאע"ג דקדשה והוו האחין באין מכחו ובדידיה ליכא אלא לאו בעלמא מ"מ אמר ריש לקיש דאיכא בדידהו כרת: **סיפא** אתאן לר' עקיבא דאמר אין קדושין תופסין בחייבי לאוין. ותימה דנקט א' מן האחים ה"ה דה"מ למימר הוא עצמו דהא בדידיה נמי איכא לאו ושמא דה"נ דקאמר כן דמן האחים ר"ל אחי המת:

תוספות חד מקמאי

איתמר החולץ ליבמתו וחזר וקדשה אר"ל הוא אינו חייב כרת על החלוצ' והאחין חייבין עליה כרת ובין הוא ובין אחיו חייבין על צרתה כרת ור"י אמר בין הוא ובין אחיו אין חייבין על חלוצה ולא על הצרה כרת והלכתא כר"י דאיתמר הבא על יבמתו וחזר ובא הוא או אחד מאחיו [על צרתה] רב אחא ורבינא חד אמר בעשה וחד אמר בכרת מ"ד בעשה כר"י מ"ד בכרת כר"ל וקיימא לן דכל היכא דפליגי רב אחא ורבינא רב אחא לחומרא ורבינא לקולא והלכתא כרבינא לקולא וק"ל דר"י ור"ל הלכה כר"י הלכך הלכתא כותיה דר"י ואע"ג דרב אשי סבר כר"ל וכן פסק הרב בפרק החולץ:

ס"א חלוצתו

הגהות הב"ח

(א) גמ' ואי בעי לההיא חליץ ואי בעי לההיא חליץ והשתא קאי: (ב) שם לדברי ר"ע אין לה עליו: (ג) רש"י ד"ה ללוי וכו' ר' יהודה היא ובדיק: (ד) ד"ה על הצרה וכו' אותה צרה חמורה הימנה לעמוד וכו' משנפטרה מהן: (ה) ד"ה ור' יוחנן וכו' דמעיקרא אי בעי לההיא חליץ ואי בעי לההיא חליץ: (ו) תום' ד"ה לפי שאינה בצרת וכו' כגון שנולדו לו אחין אחר:

מסורת הש"ס

(לקמן נג.)

(לקמן מ: נג.)

(לקמן לב.)

(לקמן נב: סט. לב: כתובות כט: קידושין סז. סח. סוטה יח: סנהדרין נג. תמורה כט:)

גליון הש"ס

גמ' לפי שאינה בצרת צרה. לעיל דף ג ע"ב:

תורה אור: דברים כה

קַשְׁיָא. רַב אַשִׁי סָבַר לָהּ כְּרֵישׁ לָקִישׁ, וּמְתָרֵץ לָהּ כְּרַ' שִׁמְעוֹן. רָבִינָא סָבַר לָהּ כְּרַ' יוֹחָנָן, וּמְתָרֵץ כְּרַבָּנַן. רַב אַשִׁי סָבַר לָהּ כְּרֵישׁ לָקִישׁ וּמְתָרֵץ לָהּ כְּרַ' שִׁמְעוֹן: הַחוֹלֵץ לִיבִמְתּוֹ וְחָזַר וְקִדְּשָׁהּ צְרִיכָה חֲלִיצָה מִן הָאַחִין. מַאן אַחִין – אַחִין הַיְלוּדִים, כְּמַאן – כְּר"ש. עָמַד אֶחָד מִן הַנּוֹלָדִים וְקִדְּשָׁהּ – אֵין לָהּ עָלָיו כְּלוּם, כְּמַאן – כְּר"ל. רָבִינָא סָבַר לָהּ כְּרַבִּי יוֹחָנָן וּמְתָרֵץ לָהּ אַלִּיבָּא דְּרַבָּנַן: הַחוֹלֵץ לִיבִמְתּוֹ וְחָזַר וְקִדְּשָׁהּ צְרִיכָה חֲלִיצָה מִן הָאַחִין, מַאן אַחִין – אַחִין הַנּוֹלָדִים, כְּמַאן – כְּרַ' יוֹחָנָן. עָמַד אֶחָד מִן הַיְלוּדִים וְקִדְּשָׁהּ – אֵין לָהּ עָלָיו כְּלוּם, כְּמַאן – כְּרַבָּנַן. אִיתְּמַר, הַבָּא עַל יְבָמָה, וּבָא אֶחָד מִן הָאַחִין עַל צָרָתָהּ. פְּלִיגִי בָּהּ רַב אַחָא וְרָבִינָא, חַד אָמַר: בְּכָרֵת; [א]וְחַד אָמַר: בַּעֲשֵׂה. מ"ד בְּכָרֵת – כְּרֵישׁ לָקִישׁ, וּמ"ד בַּעֲשֵׂה – כְּרַ' יוֹחָנָן. אָמַר רַב יְהוּדָה אָמַר רַב: *[ב]צָרַת סוֹטָה – אֲסוּרָה, (א)טוּמְאָה כְּתִיב בָּהּ, כַּעֲרָיוֹת. מְתִיב רַב חִסְדָּא: *רַבִּי שִׁמְעוֹן אוֹמֵר: בִּיאָתָהּ אוֹ חֲלִיצָתָהּ מֵאָחִיו שֶׁל רִאשׁוֹן פּוֹטֶרֶת צָרָתָהּ! [אָמַר לָךְ רַב]: אָמֵינָא לָךְ אֲנָא סוֹטָה דְּאוֹרַיְיתָא, וְאַתְּ אָמְרַתְּ לִי סוֹטָה דְּרַבָּנַן?! •וּדְקָאָרֵי לָהּ מַאי קָאָרֵי לָהּ! קָסָבַר: *כָּל דְּתַקּוּן רַבָּנַן – כְּעֵין דְּאוֹרַיְיתָא תַּקּוּן. מְתִיב רַב אַשִׁי: *נִכְנְסָה עִמּוֹ לְסֵתֶר וְשָׁהֲתָה עִמּוֹ כְּדֵי טוּמְאָה – [ג]אֲסוּרָה לְבֵיתָהּ, וַאֲסוּרָה לֶאֱכוֹל בִּתְרוּמָה. [ד]וְאִם מֵת – חוֹלֶצֶת

וְלֹא

רש"י

קַשְׁיָא. לְרַב שֵׁשֶׁת דְּשַׁנְיֵיהּ הָכִי. רַב אַשִׁי סָבַר לָהּ כְּרֵישׁ לָקִישׁ. דְּאָמַר בְּכָרֵת, וְסֵיפָא נִיחָא. וּמְתָרֵיץ לָהּ. לְרֵישָׁא דְּבָרַיְיתָא דְּקָתָנֵי צָרִיךְ חֲלִיצָה – בְּאַחִין שֶׁנּוֹלְדוּ לְאַחַר חֲלִיצָה וְקִדּוּשִׁין שֶׁל שֵׁנִי, וּכְר' שִׁמְעוֹן, דְּאָמַר: יִיבֵּם וּלְבַסּוֹף נוֹלַד לָא מְהַנְיָא נְפִילָתָהּ מִן הָרִאשׁוֹן לְמֶהֱוֵי עֲלָהּ אֵשֶׁת אָחִיו שֶׁלֹּא הָיָה בְּעוֹלָמוֹ, הִלְכָּךְ זִיקַּת הַהִיא נְפִילָה לָא אָסְרָה לָהּ עֲלֵיהּ דְּהַאי, הוֹאִיל וּכְשֶׁנּוֹלַד (ב) כְּבָר קִדְּשָׁהּ זֶה. רָבִינָא סָבַר לָהּ כְּרַבִּי יוֹחָנָן. דְּאָמַר: חַיָּיבֵי לָאוִין נִינְהוּ, וְרֵישָׁא נִיחָא. וּמְתָרֵץ לְסֵיפָא דְּקָתָנֵי אֵין לָהּ עָלָיו כְּלוּם – בְּאַחִין שֶׁנּוֹלְדוּ לְאַחַר מִכָּאן, וּכְרַבָּנַן דְּאָמְרֵי אֵשֶׁת אָחִיו שֶׁלֹּא הָיָה בְּעוֹלָמוֹ הִיא, וְלָא תִּקְשֵׁי רֵישָׁא לְסֵיפָא. הַיְלוּדִים. שֶׁנּוֹלְדוּ אַחַר קִדּוּשִׁין שֶׁל זֶה, וְלָא אִיתְּסַרָא עֲלַיְיהוּ בַּחֲלִיצָתוֹ, דְּהָא זִיקָה קַמַּיְיתָא לָא (ג) רָמְאִי קַמַּיְיהוּ לְיַיבּוּמֵי. וּמִשּׁוּם אֵשֶׁת אָחִיו שֶׁלֹּא הָיָה בְּעוֹלָמוֹ – לָא מִיתַּסְרָא, כְּר"ש, דְּאָמַר יִיבֵּם וּלְבַסּוֹף נוֹלַד שָׁרְיָא. עָמַד אֶחָד מִן הַנּוֹלָדִים. שֶׁהָיוּ בִּשְׁעַת חֲלִיצָה רִאשׁוֹנָה. אֵין לָהּ עָלָיו כְּלוּם. כְּר"ל, דְּאָמַר הָאַחִין חַיָּיבִין עַל הַחֲלוּצָה כָּרֵת. עָמַד אֶחָד מִן הַיְלוּדִים. אַחַר חֲלִיצָה, אוֹ אֲפִילּוּ אַחַר קִדּוּשִׁין, וּכְשֶׁמֵּת זֶה הַחוֹלֵץ קִדְּשָׁהּ אוֹתוֹ יָלוּד, אֵין לָהּ עָלָיו כְּלוּם. וְלָאו מִשּׁוּם חֲלִיצָה, אֶלָּא מִשּׁוּם דְּהָוְיָא אֵשֶׁת אָחִיו שֶׁלֹּא הָיָה בְּעוֹלָמוֹ מִנְּפִילָה רִאשׁוֹנָה. כְּמַאן כְּרַבָּנַן. דְּאָמְרֵי: אֲפִילּוּ יִיבֵּם וּלְבַסּוֹף נוֹלַד אֲסִירָא. בַּעֲשֵׂה. בַּיִת אֶחָד הוּא בּוֹנֶה, וְאֵין בּוֹנֶה ב' בָּתִּים, וְלָאו הַבָּא מִכְּלַל עֲשֵׂה – עֲשֵׂה. מ"ד בַּעֲשֵׂה כְּרַבִּי יוֹחָנָן. דְּאָמַר אִיהוּ שְׁלִיחוּתָא דְּאַחִין קָעָבֵיד, וְכִי הֵיכִי דִּלְדִידֵיהּ הָוְיָא צָרָה בַּעֲשֵׂה – לְאַחִים נַמִי הָוְיָא בַּעֲשֵׂה. וּמ"ד בְּכָרֵת כְּר"ל. דְּאָמַר לָאו שְׁלִיחוּת דְּאַחִים קָעָבֵיד. הִלְכָּךְ, הוּא נִיהוּ דְּקָאֵי עֲלָהּ בַּעֲשֵׂה, אֲבָל אַחִים כִּדְקָיְימִי קָיְימִי – בְּאִיסּוּר אֵשֶׁת אָח. צָרַת סוֹטָה אֲסוּרָה. הָיָה נָשׂוּי ב' נָשִׁים וְזִינְּתָה הָאַחַת תַּחְתָּיו, וְיֵשׁ עֵדִים, וּמֵת בְּלֹא בָּנִים – הִיא וְצָרָתָהּ פְּטוּרוֹת אַף מִן הַחֲלִיצָה. מַאי טַעְמָא – טוּמְאָה כְּתִיב בָּהּ, "וְנִסְתְּרָה וְהִיא נִטְמָאָה" (במדבר ה). כַּעֲרָיוֹת. דִּכְתִיב "אַל תִּטַּמְּאוּ בְּכָל אֵלֶּה" (ויקרא יח). בִּיאָתָהּ אוֹ חֲלִיצָתָהּ וכו'. הָאִשָּׁה שֶׁהָלַךְ בַּעְלָהּ לִמְדִינַת הַיָּם, וּבָאוּ וְאָמְרוּ לָהּ: מֵת בַּעֲלֵיךְ, וְנִשֵּׂאת, וְאח"כ בָּא בַּעְלָהּ – תֵּצֵא מִזֶּה וּמִזֶּה. מֵתוּ – אָחִיו שֶׁל זֶה וְאָחִיו שֶׁל זֶה חוֹלְצִין וְלֹא מְיַיבְּמִין. רַבִּי שִׁמְעוֹן אוֹמֵר: בִּיאָתָהּ אוֹ חֲלִיצָתָהּ מֵאָחִיו שֶׁל רִאשׁוֹן פּוֹטֶרֶת הִיא לְכַתְּחִלָּה אֶת צָרָתָהּ, שֶׁהֲרֵי הִיא כִּשְׁאָר נָשִׁים לְגַבֵּי יָבָם, דְּלָא קְנָסוּהָ רַבָּנַן מִיַּיבֵּם, דְּוַדַּאי שַׁרְיָא לֵיהּ, שֶׁאֲנוּסָה הָיְתָה, (ד) שֶׁשָּׁמְעָה שֶׁמֵּת. אַלְמָא: נִבְעֲלָה תַּחַת בַּעְלָהּ – שַׁרְיָא צָרָתָהּ לְיַיבֵּם. וַאֲפִי' רַבָּנַן לָא פְּלִיגִי אר"ש אֶלָּא בְּדִידָהּ, אֲבָל בְּצָרָתָהּ – מוֹדוּ. סוֹטָה דְּאוֹרַיְיתָא. שֶׁזִּינְּתָה, וְהַתּוֹרָה אָסְרָה בָּהּ. וְאַתְּ אָמְרַתְּ לִי סוֹטָה דְּרַבָּנַן. דְּהָא מִדְּאוֹרַיְיתָא שַׁרְיָא, שֶׁנִּישֵּׂאת ע"פ ב"ד בְּעֵד אֶחָד, וַאֲנוּסָה הִיא וְרַחֲמָנָא שַׁרְיָא, דִּכְתִיב (במדבר ה) "וְעֵד אֵין בָּהּ", תְּרֵי אֶלָּא אֶחָד, וְהִיא לֹא נִתְפָּשָׂה אֲסוּרָה, הָא נִתְפְּשָׂה מוּתֶּרֶת, וְרַבָּנַן הוּא דִּגְזָרוּ בָּהּ כִּי הֵיכִי דְּתֵידוּק שַׁפִּיר שְׁמַת בַּעְלָהּ עַד שֶׁלֹּא תִּנָּשֵׂא. וּדְקָאָרֵי לָהּ מַאי קָאָרֵי לָהּ. הָא לָא אָמַר רַב אֶלָּא בְּסוֹטָה דְּאוֹרַיְיתָא, דִּכְתִיב בָּהּ טוּמְאָה. קָסָבַר. הַאי דְּפָרֵיךְ: כָּל דְּתַקּוּן רַבָּנַן כְּעֵין דְּאוֹרַיְיתָא תַּקּוּן, וְאִי סוֹטָה דְּאוֹרַיְיתָא הִיא וְצָרָתָהּ אֲסוּרָה – הָכִי נַמִי הֲווּ אָסְרִי רַבָּנַן צָרָה מִיַּיבּוּם, וּמַצְרְכִי לָהּ חֲלִיצָה. נִכְנְסָה עִמּוֹ. הַמְקַנֵּא לְאִשְׁתּוֹ, וְאָמַר לָהּ: אַל תִּסָּתְרִי עִם אִישׁ פְּלוֹנִי. לְבֵיתָהּ. לְבַעְלָהּ, שֶׁמָּא זִינְּתָה. שֶׁרְגָלַיִם לַדָּבָר, שֶׁהֲרֵי קִינֵּא לָהּ וְנִסְתְּרָה. וְאִם כֹּהֶנֶת הִיא – אֲסוּרָה בִּתְרוּמָה, כִּדְיָלֵיף בְּמַסֶּכֶת סוֹטָה (דף כח.): "נִטְמְאָה" "נִטְמָאָה" "וְנִטְמָאָה", ג' פְּעָמִים: אֶחָד לַבַּעַל, וְאֶחָד לַבּוֹעֵל, וְאֶחָד לִתְרוּמָה.

וְלָא

[לעיל ג.] לקמן פז: [פסחים לב: וש"נ] סוטה ב.

תוספות

מאן אחין אחין הנולדים. אומר ר"י דנולדים קרי לאותן העתידין להולד. בלשון הש"ס, כדאמרינן בפרק "ד' נדרים" (נדרים ל:) למימרא דנולדים העתידים משמע? ובספ"ק דגיטין (דף יג: ושם) קאמר: אלא מעתה הקנה לנולדים דלא הוו בשעת מתן מעות, ה"נ כו'. צריכה חליצה מן האחין. (ה) מתייבמת אינה, מאחר דאסירה לבעלה, דהשתא במותר לה אסורה – באסור לה לא כ"ש. כמאן כרבנן. הוה מצי לאוקומי כר"ש. כגון שנולד קודם שקדשה. אלא ניחא ליה לאוקמי כרבנן, ונולד אפילו אחר שקדשה. חד אמר בעשה. כן גירסת הקונטרס. ופי' בקונטרס משום דדרשינן: בית אחד הוא בונה ואינו בונה שתי בתים, ולאו הבא מכלל עשה – עשה. וקשה: כיון דאיצטריך קרא לגופיה, שלא ייבם את שתיהן, מנלן דאתיא קרא א) לנתקו מכלל כרת ללאו? ואמר ר"ת, דגרסינן חד אמר בלאו. וכן פר"ת, דכשייבם אחת קאי אצרה ב"לא יבנה", דקרינא בצרה כיון שלא בנאה – שוב לא יבנה אותה. וכן האחים לא קיימא עלה אלא בלאו לרבי יוחנן. וגרסינן שפיר: וחזר ובא הוא או אחד מן האחין על צרתה. אבל לפ"ה דגרסינן בעשה ב) – לא פליגי אלא באחין, אבל איהו – לכ"ע בעשה*. צרת סוטה אסורה. לאו דוקא אסורה, דאף מחליצה פטורה, כדפירש בקונטרס. ודוקא סוטה ודאי, אבל סוטה – ספק בעי חליצה, כדמייתי בסמוך. ו"קרא דונסתרה והיא נטמאה" – בנבעלה ודאי איירי, כדמסיק לקמן. אבל סוטה ספק לא כתב בה טומאה. וא"ת: והא תנן נכנסה עמו לבית הסתר אסורה לביתה ואסורה לתרומה, ודרשינן בפרק "כשם" (סוטה דף כח. ושם): שלשה פעמים "ונטמאה" כתיב, אחד לבעל ואחד לבועל ואחד לתרומה! וי"ל: דלא אסרה הכתוב אלא משום ספק, שמא נבעלה ונטמאה, ולעולם לא כתיב טומאה אלא על הודאי נבעלה. וא"ת: כיון שלא (ו) נכתב שם טומאה אלא על הודאי – אמאי אסורה לביתה ולתרומה? וי"ל: דעשה ספק כודאי כדאמר בפרק "כשם" (ג"ז שם): אם נטמאה למה שותה, ואם לא נטמאה – למה נשקית? מגיד לך הכתוב שהספק אסורה כודאי. ולהכי ספק סוטה בעיא חליצה, דדוקא להחמיר עשה הכתוב ספק כודאי, ולא להקל לפטרה בלא חליצה. (ז) ולמאי דפרישית לעיל (דף ג: ד"ה "לפי") דלמסקנא דשמעתין טומאה כעריות כתיב בה, דאמר רב, היינו במקום לאו – ניחא, דההוא טומאה לא כתיבא אלא על ודאי נבעלה. אבל מ"מ קשה: כיון דסוטה ודאי חשיב לה רב כערוה, א"כ סוטה ספק הוה לה ליחשב כספק ערוה, וא"כ היכי פריך *ותתייבם ייבומי?. רבי שמעון אומר ביאתה או חליצתה כו'. וא"ת: ואמאי לא מקשה מת"ק, דאמר אחיו של זה ואחיו של זה חולצין, ולרב לא בעינן חליצה! וי"ל: דהא אתי ליה שפיר דחולצת, דמדאורייתא בעיא חליצה, דסוטה דרבנן היא. ולא פריך מר' שמעון אלא משום דכל דתקון רבנן כעין דאורייתא תקון, והיה לנו לאוסרה להתייבם. וא"ת: ודלמא ר' שמעון לא קאמר אלא דבדיעבד פוטרת צרתה, אבל לכתחלה לא? ואמר ר"י דבדיעבד מודה ת"ק, דלא אשכחן דפליגי. והא דלא נקט אחיו של ראשון רצה חולץ רצה מייבם, דמשמע לכתחלה – אמר ר"י: דמילתא אגב אורחיה קמ"ל, דאע"ג דאיכא צרה דשייך בה ייבום טפי – אפ"ה ביאתה או חליצה שלה פוטרת לכתחילה צרתה. דס"ד דלא פטרה, דנראה כאשתו דשני. וא"ת: לרב חסדא, שרוצה לדקדק דסוטה דאורייתא שריא, תקשי ליה מתני' דפרק קמא דסוטה (דף ב. ודף ו. ושם) דמייתי בסמוך, דספק סוטה אינה מתייבמת! וי"ל: דהוה אמינא דהא דקתני שאין מתייבמת – היינו מדרבנן. אע"ג דהתם מוכח דאסירא מדאורייתא – מכל מקום מכח משנה עצמה אין להוכיח עליו כלום. ועוד אמר רבי יצחק: דדוקא לרב פריך, דמשוי ליה כערוה לסוטה דאורייתא, ופטורה אף מן החליצה, ולכך, בסוטה דרבנן סברא היא דיש לאוסרה להתייבם. אבל בההיא דסוטה, דספק סוטה חולצת – אין תימה אם נאמר דבסוטה דרבנן אפילו מתייבמת. ועוד פירש רבינו יצחק: דלרבי שמעון אסורה להתייבם לכתחלה, מדקתני סיפא: ואין הולד ממזר. דאי שרי לייבם לכתחלה – פשיטא דאין הולד ממזר. ועוד: בירושלמי קורא לההיא דרבי שמעון חליצה פסולה, ואם היתה מותרת להתייבם – חליצה כשרה היא. ופריך מהא דקאמר ר"ש דפוטרת צרתה, דכיון דאמר בסוטה דאורייתא דלאו בת חליצה וייבום היא – בסוטה דרבנן אין לחליצה להועיל לפטור צרתה. וכ"ת: ממה נפשך תועיל, דאם חשיבא כסוטה גמורה צרתה נמי לא בעי חליצה, ואי לא חשיבא כסוטה – א"כ שפיר פטרה צרתה, דמסתבר ליה להש"ס דכיון דדמיא לסוטה דאורייתא חליצתה כמאן דליתא, ואין לה לפטור צרתה.

לרבות

[פ"ק דסוטה דף ה:]

עין משפט נר מצוה

לז א מיי' פ"א מהל' יבום הלכה יב טוש"ע אה"ע סימן קסב סעי' א:

לח ב מיי' פ"ו מהלכות יבום הלכה יט טוש"ע אה"ע סימן קעג סעיף יא:

לט ג מיי' פ"א מהל' סוטה הלכה ח ומיי' פכ"ד מהל' אישות הל' כד טוש"ע אה"ע סימן קטו סעיף ח:

מ ד מיי' פ"ו מהל' יבום הלכה יט:

תוספות ישנים

א) וע"ק מאי האי דמספקא ליה בקדושין אי ר' יעקב טעמא דנפשיה קאמר ואפילו חייבי עשה או לאפוקי מר' סימאי קאתי תפסוק דטעמא דנפשיה קאמר מדאמרינן לקמן פ' ר"ג אין לאחר ביאה כלום בשתי יבמות ומוקים לה כר' עקיבא דאמר אין קדושין תופסין וכו' ואי סבר ר' עקיבא קדושין תופסין בחייבי עשה אמאי אין לאחר ביאה כלום הלא ליכא רק עשה דבית א' הוא בונה כדפ"ה הכא: ב) וא"ת א"כ לא הוצרך קרא לר' יוחנן דבית א' בונה ואינו בונה ב' בתים דמלא יבנה נפקא דאינו בונה צרתה. וי"ל דסד"א דמייבם לא מייבמה אבל מחלץ חלצה להכי איצטריך לא יבנה א) דאפילו מחלץ נמי לא חלצה. ועי"ל דר' יוחנן סבר דאצטריך בית א' הוא בונה לייתר קרא דלא יבנה לנתוקה מכרת דאשת אח ולאוקמי אלאו. ומ"ד בכרת כריש לקיש כדפרי' דסבר דלא מיירי מן הצרה. עוד פי' ר"ס מ"ד בכרת כריש לקיש משום שיש לנו לעשות פטור לצרה בביאת חברתה כמו פטור לצרה בחליצת חברתה והיכא דמפטרה הצרה בחליצת [חבירתה] אמרינן לעיל דהוי בכרת כמו כן אמרינן הכא דמיפטרה בביאת חברתה דחליצה ויבום א' הם:

א) נ"ל להכי אצטריך בית אחד הוא בונה וכו' דאפילו מחלץ לא חלצה.

הגהות הב"ח

(א) גמ' צרת סוטה אסורה מ"ט טומאה: (ב) רש"י ד"ה ומתרץ וכו' וכשנולד זה כבר: (ג) ד"ה הילודים וכו' לא רמאי קמייהו: (ד) ד"ה ביאתה וכו' שאנוסה היתה שסבורה ששמעה שמת: (ה) תוס' ד"ה צריכה וכו' ומתייבמת: (ו) ד"ה כרת וכו' וא"ת כיון שלא נקרא שם טומאה: (ז) בא"ד ולא להקל לפטרה בלא חליצה ומיהו קשה היכי פריך בפ"ק דסוטה תתייבם ספק סוטה ולמאי דפרישית לעיל דלמסקנא דשמעתין טומאה:

גליון הש"ס

גמ' ודקארי לה מאי קארי לה. כתובות עז ע"א וש"נ:

תוספות חד מקמאי

תניא החולץ ליבמתו וחזר וקדשה ומת צריכה חליצה מן האחים הנולדים א) אבל לא מן הילודים כרבנן דאמרי אפלו כנס ולבסוף נולד אסורה משום אשת אחיו שלא היה בעולמו עמד אחד מן האחים וקדשה צריכה חליצה מן האחים עמד אחד מן הילודים וקדשה אין לו עליו כלום ואפי' ילוד לאחר שקדשה החולץ כרבנן דאסרי אפי' כנס ולבסוף נולד: אמר רב יהודה אמר רב צרת סוטה אסורה טומאה כתיב בה כעריות פירוש דאפי' חליצה לא בעיא ממאי מדפרכינן בריש מכלתין ולרב אסי ליתנהו ואם היתה צריכה [חליצה] אליבא דרב מאי קושיא והא קתני במתניתין פטורות מן החליצה ועוד דהא אותביה רב יוסף מהא דתנן נכנסה עמו לחורבה ושהתה כדי טומאה אסורה לביתה ובתרומה ואם מת חולצת ולא מתייבמת ש"מ דאליבא דרב אינה חולצת מיהו רב יוסף ס"ל דצריכה חליצה אפי' סוטה ודאית כיון דאילו איתיה לבעל בעיא גט השתא נמי תבעי חליצה והכי שמעינן ליה לרב יוסף בפ"ק דסוטה ורב יוסף לא שני ליה בין סוטה ודאית לספק סוטה דתרוייהו טומאה כתיב בהו וכיון דסוטה מספקא בעיא חליצה משום דאיתיה לבעל בעיא גיטא הכי נמי בסוטה ודאית לא בעיא חליצה וקי"ל דסוטה טומאה כתיב בה כעריות אבל גבי ספק סוטה לא כתיב בה טומאה ובעיא חליצה והא

א) גירסת רבינו הוא כגירסת תוס' דגרסינן מאן אחין הנולדים.

עין משפט נר מצוה

מא א מיי' פי"א מהל' גירושין הלכ' יב סמג לאוין פב טוש"ע אה"ע סי' י סעיף א:
מב ב ג מיי' שם הלכ' יד סמג עשין מח:
מג ד מיי' פט"ו מהל' אסורי ביאה הלכה ב סמג לאוין קיז:
[ועי' תוס' סוטה כח. ד"ה מה ת"ל]
מד ה מיי' פ"א מהלכו' יבום הלכה י סמג עשין נא טוש"ע אה"ע סימן קסא סעיף ב:
מה ו מיי' שם פ"ו הלכה יג סמג שם טוש"ע אה"ע סימן קעד סעיף ב:

מסורת הש"ס

ולא מתייבמת! [אמר לך רב]: אמינא לך אנא סוטה ודאי. ואמרת לי את סוטה ספק! ומ"ש סוטה ודאי (מ"ט), משום דכתיב בה טומאה — סוטה ספק נמי טומאה כתיבא בה! דתניא: *ר' יוסי בן כיפר אומר משום רבי אלעזר: המחזיר גרושתו מן הנישואין — אסורה, מן האירוסין — מותרת, משום שנאמר °"אחרי אשר הוטמאה", [א]וחכ"א: אחת זו ואחת זו — אסורה. אלא מה אני מקיים "אחרי הוטמאה" — לרבות סוטה שנסתרה. [ב]ומאי נסתרה — נבעלה, ואמאי קרי ליה נסתרה — *לישנא מעליא נקט. נבעלה, טומאה בהדיא כתיב בה °"ונסתרה והיא נטמאה"! — [ג]למיקם עלה בלאו. ור' יוסי בן כיפר לאו בסוטה לית ליה[א], ואפי' זנאי נמי מאי. טעמא — הויה ואישות כתיב בה. בעא מיניה רב יהודה מרב ששת: המחזיר גרושתו משניסת, ומת, צרתה מהו? אליבא דרבי יוסי בן כיפר לא תיבעי לך, כיון דאמר ר' יוסי בן כיפר טומאה במחזיר גרושתו הוא דכתיבא — צרתה כמותה. ואי משום דכתיב בה °"תועבה היא", *[ד]"היא תועבה ואין בניה תועבין — הא צרתה תועבה. כי תיבעי לך — אליבא דרבנן, אע"ג דאמור רבנן טומאה בסוטה הוא דכתיב — *אין מקרא יוצא מידי פשוטו, או: דלמא, כיון דאיעקר — איעקר? איכא דאמרי: אליבא דרבנן לא תיבעי לך, כיון דאיתעקר — איעקר. כי תיבעי לך — אליבא דרבי יוסי בן כיפר, מאי? אע"ג דאמר ר' יוסי בן כיפר טומאה במחזיר גרושתו הוא דכתיבא — מיעט רחמנא(א) "היא תועבה" ואין צרתה תועבה, או: דלמא, היא תועבה ואין בניה תועבין, הא צרתה — תועבה! א"ל, תניתוה: *[ה]היתה אחת כשרה ואחת פסולה, אם היה חולץ — חולץ לפסולה, ואם היה מייבם — מייבם לכשרה. מאי כשרה ומאי פסולה? אילימא כשרה — כשרה לעלמא, פסולה — פסולה לעלמא, כיון דלדידיה חזיא מאי נפקא ליה מינה? אלא לאו: כשרה — כשרה ליה, פסולה — פסולה ליה. ומאי ניהו — מחזיר גרושתו. וקתני: ואם היה מייבם — מייבם לכשרה! לא, לעולם כשרה — כשרה לעלמא, פסולה — פסולה לעלמא. ודקאמרת כיון דלדידיה חזיא מאי נפקא ליה מינה — משום דרב יוסף. *דאמר רב יוסף, כאן שנה רבי: לא ישפוך אדם מי בורו ואחרים צריכים להם. ת"ש: המחזיר גרושתו משנשאת — היא וצרתה חולצת היא. *וצרתה ס"ד?! [אלא] אימא: או היא או צרתה. ולאו תרוצי קמתרצת לה? תריץ הכי: [ו]היא חולצת, צרתה — או חולצת או מתייבמת. אמר רבי חייא בר אבא, רבי יוחנן בעי: המחזיר גרושתו משניסת, צרתה מהו? אמר ליה רבי אמי: ותיבעי לך היא גופה! היא גופה לא קמיבעיא לי, •דאמרינן: *קל וחומר: במותר לה (ב) אסורה, באסור לה — לא כל שכן?! כי קא מיבעיא לי — צרתה מאי? מי אלים ק"ו למידחי צרה, או לא? רב נחמן בר יצחק מתני הכי: אמר ר' חייא בר אבא, בעי ר' יוחנן: המחזיר גרושתו משניסת מהו? א"ל ר' אמי: ותיבעי לך צרתה? צרתה לא קמיבעיא לי, דלא אלים קל וחומר למידחי צרה. אלא, כי קמיבעיא לי — היא גופה מאי, מי אלים קל וחומר במקום מצוה, או לא?

אמר

ולא מתייבמת. טעמא מפרש בפ"ק דסוטה. [קתני מיהא] חולצת, קשיא לרב. מן הנשואין. משניסת לאחר, ומת או גירשה. אסורה לחזור. לראשון. מן האירוסין. שנתארסה לאחר ומת, מותרת לחזור לראשון. הוטמאה. ונבעלה. אחת זו ואחת זו אסורה. תורה אור דכתיב "והיתה לאיש אחר", והויה היינו קידושין, וכתיב "לא יוכל בעלה הראשון אשר שלחה" וגו'. ורבי יוסי. דמוקי כולה קרא במחזיר גרושתו. לאו בסוטה. המזנה תחת בעלה לית ליה, ואפילו פשיטא לן דזנאי. מ"ט הויה ואישות כתיב בה. באותה (ג) הנאסרה לבעלה יש בה הויה, דכתיב "והיתה לאיש אחר", אישות דכתיב "או כי ימות האיש האחרון, לא יוכל בעלה הראשון", משניסת לאחר על ידי קידושין ואישות, וכגון דגירשה הראשון, הוא דקאי קמא ב"לא יוכל", אבל מזנה תחתיו — לא. צרתה מהו. להתייבם צרתה כמותה, וגמיר טומאה מעריות. ואי משום דכתיב בה "תועבה היא". דמשמע מיעוטא: "היא" ולא צרתה, איכא למידרש מיעוטא אבניה, דאין בתה הימנו פסולה לכהונה (ד). היתה אחת כשרה. מי שנפלו לפניו שתי יבמות מאח אחד, ביאתה או חליצתה של אחת מהן פוטרת צרתה. היתה אחת כשרה ואחת פסולה וכו'. כשרה לעלמא. מיוחסת וכשרה לכהונה. פסולה לעלמא. כגון שהיתה גרושה או חלוצה מבעל אחר, ופסולה לכהונה. כיון דלדידיה חזיא. דהוא ישראל. מאי נפקא ליה מינה. הי דליבעי לחלוץ, ואי בעי לייבם — הי דליבעי לייבם. פסולה פסולה ליה. וכשרה (ה) לעלמא לכל העולם. ומאי ניהו — כגון שהחזיר אחיו גרושתו ולו אשה אחרת ומת, דהוי הגרושה פסולה לזה שאינה ראויה לאחיו. ואשמועינן דאע"ג דכתיב בה טומאה — צרתה כשרה, דכתיב "היא תועבה". דאי שאר חייבי לאוין, כגון אלמנה לכ"ג וגרושה לכהן הדיוט — מאי אתא לאשמועינן? פסולה לעלמא. לכהונה. כאן שנה רבי. במשנה זו, דקתני חולץ לפסולה, למדנו רבי: לא ישפוך אדם מי בורו אע"פ שאין צריך להם, ואחרים צריכים להם, כגון הכא, מכיון דיכול לחלוץ לפסולה ותפטר הכשרה — לא יחלוץ לכשרה ויפסלנה לכהונה. והא דרב יוסף בפ' "החולץ" (לקמן מד.) עלה דהא משנה. היא וצרתה ס"ד. חליצה לתרוייהו למה לי? צרתה מהו. לייבום. במותר לה. (ו) בעלה, זה שמת נאסרה תחלה כשנשאת לשני, וחזר הראשון והחזירה באיסור, ולמחר מת. באסור לה. כגון יבמה, לא כ"ש. מי אלים ק"ו. האי ק"ו דאמרן: במותר לה נאסרה.

א"ל

לרבות סוטה שנסתרה. וא"ת: והיכי מפקי רבנן קרא מפשטיה? דפשטיה דקרא במחזיר גרושתו כתיב! וי"ל: דלא מסתבר להו למיקרי טומאה לנישואי גרושה, כיון דבעילתה היתר היא. **מאי** נסתרה נבעלה. וא"ת וכיון דלא כתיב לאו בסוטה ספק, אמאי אמר בסוטה (דף ז.) •דאם בא עליה בעלה בדרך לוקה? *וי"ל: דלחומרא עשה הכתוב ספק כודאי, כדפרישית לעיל. **הויה** ואישו' כתיב בה. פי' בקונטרס: דההוא ענינא במחזיר גרושתו כתיב. ותימה: דפשיטא דבמחזיר גרושתו איירי קרא, ואפילו רבנן לא פליגי! ונראה לרשב"א לפרש: דהויה ואישות כתיב בה, פירוש: או"הוטמאה" דכתיב "לא יוכל בעלה הראשון אשר שלחה לשוב לקחתה להיות לו לאשה אחרי אשר הוטמאה" — אלמא במחזיר גרושתו איירי, ד"אחרי אשר הוטמאה" — א"להיות לו לאשה" קאי, דבסוטה לא שייך הויה ואישות, שהרי לא גירשה מעולם. **צרתה** מהו. היא גופה לא מיבעי ליה, דלר' יוסי בן כיפר — ודאי פטורה מן החליצה ומן הייבום, דטומאה כתיב בה כעריות. ולרבנן נמי, היא גופה פשיטא דחולצת ולא מתייבמת. דאפי' אם תמצא לומר כיון דאיתעקר איתעקר — אינה מתייבמת מק"ו: דהשתא במותר לה נאסרה, באסור לה לא כ"ש?! ואת"ל נמי דאין מקרא יוצא מידי פשוטו — אין לפוטרה מן החליצה, כיון דעיקר קרא דטומאה בסוטה כתיב ולא במחזיר גרושתו, משום דלא מסתברא למיקרי טומאה נישואי גרושה, כדפרישית לעיל. וכן משמע לקמן דקאמר: אלא או היא או צרתה חולצת, ובעי למיפשט דלרבנן אין מקרא יוצא מידי פשוטו, ואפילו הכי אין פוטרתה מחליצה, כדפרישית. אבל צרתה בעי לר' יוסי בן כיפר אם פטורה מן החליצה, או אפילו מתייבמת. ולרבנן בעי אי מתייבמת, דפשיטא(ז) ליה דלא אלים קל וחומר למידחי צרה. או חולצת ולא מתייבמת משום דאין מקרא יוצא מידי פשוטו. **אמר** ליה תניתוה. למיפשט בעיא קמייתא הוא דאתא. דלאיכא דאמרי דפשיטא ליה לרבנן כיון דאיתעקר איתעקר — איכא למימר דאתיא •כרבנן. **אן** היא או צרתה. אע"ג דחליצה פסולה צריך לחזור [על כל האחין]* — היינו דוקא כגון חלץ לאחיות, דלא נפטרו צרות. וכן חלץ לבעלת הגט לא נפטרה צרה, דהורע הזיקה וקלשה לה. אבל בשאר דוכתי, דאע"ג דאסורה להתייבם, כיון שהזיקה •שלימה — פוטרת. **לאו** תרוצי קא מתרצת לה תריץ הכי. תימה: במאי מתרץ להו? דאע"ג דבעי למימר או היא או צרתה — שייך למיתני שפיר היא וצרתה, כמו *אלך ועשה בה מאמר. ובפ' "נערה" בנדרים (דף סו:) דקתני: אביה ובעלה מפירין נדריה, איצטריך למתני סיפא: הפר האב ולא הפר הבעל הפר הבעל, ולא הפר האב, אין מופר, דלא תימא אביה ובעלה — אביה או בעלה קאמר. **מי** אלים ק"ו למידחי לצרה. לאוסרה לייבום קא מיבעיא ליה. דלפוטרה מן החליצה לא מהני קל וחומר אפילו להיא

תוספות חד מקמאי

והא דתנינן מה אני מקיים אשר הוטמאה לרבות סוטה שנסתרה מאי נסתרה נבעלה ולישנא מעליא נקט: **תנן** שתי יבמות הבאות מבית אחד היתה אחת כשרה וא' פסולה אם היה חולץ חולץ לפסולה ואם היה מיבם מיבם לכשרה לא מבעיא אם פסולה לו וכשרה לעלמא כגון מחזיר גרושתו משנשא' שמיבם לכשירה שהיא כשרה לו וחולץ לפסולה שהיא הגרושה שאסורה לו מק"ו אם נאסרה במותר לה באסור לה מבעיא אלא אפילו שתיהן כשירות לו כגון שהוא ישראל והאחת גרושה שהיא פסולה לכהן חולץ לפסולה ולא לכשרה משום דרב יוסף דאמר כאן שנה ר' לא ישפוך אדם מי בורו ואחרים צריכים לו:

הגהות הב"ח

(א) גמ' מיעט רחמנא היא היא תועבה: (ב) שם במותר לה נאסרה באסור לה: (ג) רש"י ד"ה מ"ט הויה וכו' באותה אשה הנאסרה: (ד) ד"ה ואי משום וכו' לכהונה הס"ד ואח"כ נ"ל ד"ה אין מקרא יוצא מידי פשוטו. דהא כתיב גבי מחזיר גרושתו וכיון דכתיב בה טומאה צרתה כמותה או דלמא כיון דאיעקר איעקר דכיון דדרשינן להאי אחרי אשר הוטמאה לסוטה איעקר ליה ממחזיר גרושתו ולא כתיב בה טומאה ולא הוי צרתה אסורה לייבם הס"ד: (ה) ד"ה פסולה וכו' וכשרה לכל העולם כצ"ל ותיבת לעלמא נמחק: (ו) ד"ה במותר לה כגון בעלה: (ז) תוס' ד"ה צרתה וכו' דפשיטא להו דלא אלים

[לקמן נ: ועי' היטב שם ומצוה להסביר]

לקמן פח:

כתובות יג. [ודף סה: ברכות יא: פסחים ג. יומא עה. לקמן קג. גיטין עו: פ: ב"מ לא: סנהדרין נד. תמורה ל.]

קידושין עז. [לקמן מד: נדה ע.]

[שבת סג. לקמן כד.]

לקמן מד.

לקמן כו: מא.

לקמן יב. מד. נג

[לקמן קטו.]

[סוטה ו.]

הגהות הגר"א

[א] גמ' ואפילו זנאי נמי. נ"ב גרסת הגאון אבל הכא על הגרושה ואפילו זנאי מותרת לבעלה מ"ט הויה כו'. הגהות מרדכי ועי' רי"ף (ועמ"ש רבינו בא"ע ר"ס יו"ד)

גליון הש"ס

גמ' דאמרי' ק"ו כו'. עיין לקמן פד ע"ב תד"ה שייר פלוע דכה: תוס' ד"ה מאי וכו' דאם בא עליה וכו' לוקה. עיין לקמן סט ע"א תד"ה כי תהיה: ד"ה א"נ וכו' כרבנן. עי' לקמן ע"ב תד"ה כ"ע לא פליגי: ד"ה אן היא וכו' שלימה פוטרת. עי' לקמן כו ע"ב תד"ה וחליצה פסולה

אָמַר לֵיהּ: תְּנֵיתוּהָ, הָיְתָה אַחַת כְּשֵׁרָה וְאַחַת פְּסוּלָה, אִם הָיָה חוֹלֵץ — חוֹלֵץ לַפְּסוּלָה, וְאִם הָיָה מְיַיבֵּם — מְיַיבֵּם לַכְּשֵׁרָה. מַאי כְּשֵׁרָה וּמַאי פְּסוּלָה? אִילֵימָא כְּשֵׁרָה — כְּשֵׁרָה לְעָלְמָא, פְּסוּלָה — פְּסוּלָה לְעָלְמָא, כֵּיוָן דִּלְדִידֵיהּ חַזְיָא מַאי נָפְקָא לֵיהּ מִינַּהּ? אֶלָּא לָאו: כְּשֵׁרָה — כְּשֵׁרָה לֵיהּ, פְּסוּלָה — פְּסוּלָה לֵיהּ, וּמַאי נִיהוּ — מַחֲזִיר גְּרוּשָׁתוֹ, וְקָתָנֵי: אִם הָיָה מְיַיבֵּם — מְיַיבֵּם לַכְּשֵׁרָה! לָא, כְּשֵׁרָה לְעָלְמָא, פְּסוּלָה לְעָלְמָא. וּדְקָאָמְרַתְּ: כֵּיוָן דִּלְדִידֵיהּ חַזְיָא מַאי נָפְקָא לֵיהּ מִינַּהּ — מִשּׁוּם דְּרַב יוֹסֵף. דְּאָמַר רַב יוֹסֵף: *כָּאן שָׁנָה רַבִּי לֹא יִשְׁפּוֹךְ אָדָם מֵי בּוֹרוֹ וַאֲחֵרִים צְרִיכִים לָהֶם. ת"ש: הַמַּחֲזִיר גְּרוּשָׁתוֹ מִשֶּׁנִּיסֵּת — הִיא וְצָרָתָהּ חוֹלֶצֶת. הִיא וְצָרָתָהּ ס"ד? אֶלָּא אֵימָא: אוֹ הִיא אוֹ צָרָתָהּ. וְלָאו תֵּרוּצֵי קָא מְתָרְצַתְּ לָהּ? תָּרֵיץ הָכִי: הִיא חוֹלֶצֶת, צָרָתָהּ — אוֹ חוֹלֶצֶת אוֹ מִתְיַיבֶּמֶת. אָמַר רַב לִילִי בַּר מָמָל אָמַר מַר עוּקְבָא אָמַר שְׁמוּאֵל: [א]צָרַת מְמָאֶנֶת אֲסוּרָה. לְמַאן? אִילֵימָא לְאַחִים — הָשְׁתָּא הִיא גּוּפַהּ שַׁרְיָא, דְּאָמַר שְׁמוּאֵל: *[ב]מֵיאֲנָה בְּזֶה מוּתֶּרֶת בְּזֶה, צָרָתָהּ מִיבָּעֲיָא? אֶלָּא לְדִידֵיהּ, וּמַאי שְׁנָא מְמָאֶנֶת דְּשַׁרְיָא לְאַחִין — דְּלָא עָבְדָא בְּהוּ מַעֲשֶׂה, צָרָה נַמִי לָא עָבְדָא בְּהוּ מַעֲשֶׂה! גְּזֵירָה מִשּׁוּם צָרַת בִּתּוֹ מְמָאֶנֶת. וְצָרַת בִּתּוֹ מְמָאֶנֶת מִי אֲסִירָא? וְהָתְנַן: וְכוּלָּן, אִם מֵתוּ אוֹ מֵיאֲנוּ (א) צָרוֹתֵיהֶן מוּתָּרוֹת! דְּמֵיאֲנָה בְּמַאן? אִילֵימָא דְּמֵיאֲנָה בְּבַעַל — הַיְינוּ גְּרוּשָׁה, אֶלָּא לָאו בְּיָבָם! לָא, לְעוֹלָם בְּבַעַל, וּתְרֵי גַּוְונֵי גֵּירוּשִׁין, וּמ"ש כִּי מֵיאֲנָה בְּבַעַל, דְּעָקְרִינְהוּ לְנִשּׂוּאִין, כִּי מֵיאֲנָה בְּיָבָם נַמִי נִשּׂוּאִין קַמָּאֵי קָא עָקְרָא! מִשּׁוּם *דְּתָנֵי רָמִי בַּר יְחֶזְקֵאל. דְּתָנֵי רָמִי בַּר יְחֶזְקֵאל: [ג]מֵיאֲנָה בְּבַעַל — מוּתֶּרֶת לְאָבִיו, בְּיָבָם — אֲסוּרָה לְאָבִיו. אַלְמָא: מִשְּׁעַת נְפִילָה נִרְאֵית כְּכַלָּתוֹ, ה"נ — מִשְּׁעַת נְפִילָה נִרְאֵית כְּצָרַת בִּתּוֹ. *אָמַר רַב אַסִי: צָרַת אַיְלוֹנִית אֲסוּרָה, שֶׁנֶּאֱמַר °"וְהָיָה הַבְּכוֹר *אֲשֶׁר תֵּלֵד" — [ד]פְּרָט לְאַיְלוֹנִית שֶׁאֵינָהּ יוֹלֶדֶת. מְתִיב רַב שֵׁשֶׁת: *שְׁלֹשָׁה אַחִין נְשׂוּאִין שָׁלֹשׁ נָשִׁים נָכְרִיּוֹת, וּמֵת אֶחָד מֵהֶם, וְעָשָׂה בָּהּ שֵׁנִי מַאֲמָר וּמֵת — הֲרֵי אֵלּוּ חוֹלְצוֹת וְלֹא מִתְיַיבְּמוֹת, שֶׁנֶּאֱמַר °"וּמֵת אֶחָד מֵהֶם יְבָמָהּ יָבֹא עָלֶיהָ" — מִי שֶׁעָלֶיהָ זִיקַת יָבָם אֶחָד, וְלֹא זִיקַת שְׁנֵי יְבָמִין. וְקָתָנֵי עֲלָהּ, *אָמַר רַב יוֹסֵף: זוֹ הִיא צָרַת אֵשֶׁת אָח מֵאָב, שֶׁאִיסּוּר נְפִילָה גָּרַם לָהּ, שֶׁלֹּא מָצִינוּ בְּכָל הַתּוֹרָה כּוּלָּהּ כְּגוֹן זֹאת. "זוֹ הִיא" לְמַעוּטֵי מַאי? לָאו לְמַעוּטֵי צָרַת אַיְלוֹנִית דְּשַׁרְיָא? לָא, לְמַעוּטֵי צָרַת אַיְלוֹנִית דַּאֲסִירָא, וּמַאי "זוֹ הִיא" — זוֹ הִיא דְּאִיסּוּר נְפִילָה גָּרַם לָהּ — צָרָתָהּ בָּעֲיָא חֲלִיצָה, אַיְלוֹנִית — אֲפִילּוּ חֲלִיצָה לָא בָּעֲיָא. מ"ט? הָא — דְּאוֹרָיְיתָא, הָא — דְּרַבָּנַן. תְּנַן: וְכוּלָּן, אִם מֵתוּ אוֹ מֵיאֲנוּ אוֹ נִתְגָּרְשׁוּ אוֹ שֶׁנִּמְצְאוּ אַיְלוֹנִית — צָרוֹתֵיהֶן מוּתָּרוֹת! לָא קַשְׁיָא: כָּאן שֶׁהִכִּיר בָּהּ, כָּאן — שֶׁלֹּא הִכִּיר בָּהּ. דַּיְקָא נַמִי, דְּקָתָנֵי: שֶׁנִּמְצְאוּ, וְלֹא קָתָנֵי שֶׁהָיוּ. שְׁמַע מִינַּהּ. אָמַר רָבָא:

הִלְכְתָא

רש"י

א"ל תניתוה. אתרוייהו ליתני מהדר, דקתני: אחת כשרה ואחת פסולה, אלמא היא אסורה וצרתה מותרת. צרת ממאנת. נפלו לפניו ב' יבמות מאח אחד, גדולה וקטנה, ומיאנה בו הקטנה – צרתה אסורה. למאן אסורה. אילימא אף לשאר אחין, השתא היא גופה מותרת לזה. אלא לדידיה. ליבם שמיאנה בו אסורה, דמיאון עקר ליה לזיקה, וקאי עליה באשת אח. וא"ת: מיאון נישואין קמאי עקר, והרי היא נכרית אצלו ומותרת לו! גזירה דרבנן היא, הואיל ולא מיאנה בראשון, ומכח נישואין (ב) נפלה להתייבם – נראית כאשת אחיו. והכי אמרי' לקמן: משעת נפילה נראית ככלתו כו'. והא דשמואל – בפ' ב"ש (לקמן דף קז:). משום צרת בתו ממאנת. דאתי למישרי צרת בתו קטנה שנפלה לו לייבום ומיאנה בו, דאמרינן: נישואין קמאי קא עקרא, ואין זו צרת ערוה. וה"ד מיאון בבתו, הואיל והוא קיים, דאין מיאון אלא ביתומה שלא קיבל אביה קידושיה? משכחת לה ביתומה בחיי האב, כדתנן בפרק ב"ש: קטנה שהשיאה אביה ונתגרשה – הרי היא יתומה בחיי האב, דפקע (ג) לה זכותיה מינה משיצאתה מרשותו. ואם הלכה ונשאת לאחי אביה – יכולה למאן ביבם בחיי אביה. מיאנה בבעל. קטנה יתומה נכרית שמיאנה בבעל – מותרת לחמיה, לפי שעקרתה לקדושין, והרי היא כמפותה, ולא כלתו היא. ביבם אסורה לאביו. דכיון דאהנו נישואין קמאי לזקקה ליבם – נראית כאשתו גמורה, ונראית ככלתו של זה. ה"נ. בבתו ממאנת. משעת נפילה. שנפלה בתו לפניו לייבום, והוצרכה למאן בו – נראית כאשת אחיו, ונראית צרתה צרת הבת. צרת אילונית. הרי שהיה נשוי ב' נשים, והא' אילונית. אילונית = דוכרניתא דלא ילדה, לשון איל זכר מן הצאן (ד). ומת בלא בנים. שתיהן אסורות להתייבם, ופטורות מן החליצה. שנאמר והיה הבכור אשר תלד בראויה לילד פרט לאילונית. וכיון דפטורה קיימא עליה באשת אח, וצרתה צרת ערוה. ואע"ג דהאי "והיה הבכור אשר תלד" מיתוקם במכילתין לקמן (דף כד.) בגדול האחים, ומהכא נפקא לן מצוה בגדול לייבם – מ"מ דרשינן נמי פרט לאילונית מ"אשר תלד", דקרא יתירא הוא, כיון דהבכור ביבם גופיה משתעי. מאמר. קדושי יבמה. הרי אלו. שתי נשים. חולצות. דאילו כנסה הוה פקעה זיקה קמייתא, ולא הוה עלה אלא זיקת נשואי האחרון, אבל מאמר – לא מפקע זיקה, והויא עלה קצת זיקת ראשון וקצת זיקת האחרון. דכתיב ומת אחד מהם. ולא זו שמתו ב' בעליה וזיקת שניהם עליה, ושתיהן אסורות מדרבנן. וקרא אסמכתא בעלמא. כדמפרש בפ' "ד' אחין". ובחליצה נמי חדא לא מיפטרא אידך, דלאו מבית אחד קאתו, הואיל ולא כנסה. ואי לא עבד בה מאמר – לא הואי עלה אלא זיקת ראשון. והוו להו שתי יבמות הבאות מב' בתים, ושתיהן מתייבמות. שאיסור נפילה גרם לה. שנפלה ב' פעמים מזיקה אחת. שלא מצינו בכל התורה. שתיאסר, אלא מדרבנן הוא דמיתסרא. שאין כאן איסור ערוה, ואסורה צרתה (ה). הא דאורייתא. "תלד" – למעוטי צרת אילונית דאסירא, ואפילו חליצה לא בעיא. והא דרבנן. כדמפרש טעמא בפ' "ד' אחין", וקאסרי לה על השלישי. כאן שהכיר בה. דרב אסי בשהכיר בה כשנשאה שהיא אילונית, ואין כאן מקח טעות, והרי היא אשתו. וצרתה הויא צרת אילונית, ורחמנא פטרה מ"אשר תלד". ומתני' בשלא הכיר בה כשנשאה שתהא אילונית, ומקחו מקח טעות, ולאו אשתו היא. לפיכך צרתה מותרת, דלאו צרת אילונית היא. שנמצאו. לאחר נישואין.

הלכתא

תוספות

להיא גופא, כדאמרינן פ"ק דסוטה (דף ו. וסס) דספק סוטה חולצת ולא מתייבמת משום ק"ו. מי אמרינן ק"ו במקום מצוה כו'. וא"ת: תפשוט מפ"ק דסוטה (דף ג.) דקתני: חולצת ולא מתייבמת, ומפרש בגמ' *משום ק"ו! וי"ל: דאיכא התם טעמא אחרינא, כדמפרש התם. צרתה נמי לא עבדה ביה מעשה. תימה: נהי דלא עבדה ביה מעשה, מ"מ כיון דהממאנת אסורה ליה – הוי צרתה כצרת ערוה, והיכי מדמה לה לממאנת דשריא לאחין. אלא לאו ביבם וקתני צרותיהן מותרות. שהמיאון עוקר לנישואין קמאי. תימה: למאי דס"ד השתא תקשה ליה סיפא, דקתני: כל שיכולה למאן ולא מיאנה – צרתה חולצת ולא מתייבמת, ואם איתא דעקרה נישואין קמאי – תמאן השתא ותתייבם צרתה, דהכי פריך עלה לקמן! וי"ל: דלמאי דסלקא דעתך השתא מצי למימר דמתני' בדליתא קמן שתמאן, או בגדולה. ולקמן דפריך עלה, משום דבעי לאוקמי מתני' אפילו היא קטנה ואיתה קמן. מאי לאו למעוטי צרת אילונית דשריא. וא"ת: אמאי לא פריך מינה לעיל, למאן דאסר צרת מחזיר גרושתו, ולימא ליה: מאי לאו למעוטי צרת מחזיר גרושתו דשרי? וי"ל: דלא משמע ליה למעוטי מזו היא אלא כיוצא בה, דאילונית דמיא לאשת שני מתים, דזו וזו מותרות לבעליהן. אבל מחזיר גרושתו – נאסרה לבעלה. תני שהיו. וא"ת: לרבא, דשרי צרת בתו אילונית אפי' הכיר בה – מה חידוש הוא לשנות בתוספתא: וכולן שנמצאו אילונית, בין בחיי הבעל בין לאחר מיתה? בשלמא לרב אסי – אילטריך לאשמועינן בחיי בעל, דסד"א הואיל ובחייו נמצאת אילונית – דלמא קיבלה. וי"ל: דס"ד למיסרה כשנמצאת אחר מיתה משום דבשעת נפילה נראית כצרת בתו, כדאסר לעיל צרת בתו ממאנת. וא"ת: מ"ש אילונית ממאנת! ויש לומר: דהתם מיתסרא מיאון, הכא לא מיתסרא מידי. א"נ: ממאנת אין לה קול, ובשעת מיאון נראית כצרת בתו, אבל אילונית – יש לה קול, וידוע שלא היתה צרת בתו. וא"ת: מאי פריך הכא לרבא מדקתני שנמצאו? נימא דנקט נמצאו לרבותא! וי"ל: דבהכיר בה איכא רבותא טפי, להכי משני: תני שהיו.

שלם

לעיל יח: וש"נ | לקמן קח: | לקמן יג. קז: | [לעיל ג: לקמן כ.] | [לקמן כד. ע"ש] | דברים כה | לקמן יח: לח: | שם

הגהות הב"ח

(א) גמ' מתו או מיאנו או נתגרשו צרותיהן מותרות: (ב) רש"י ד"ה אלא לדידיה וכו' ומכח נישואין שלו נפלה לפניו להתייבם: (ג) ד"ה משום וכו' דפקע ליה זכותיה מינה: (ד) ד"ה צרת איילונית הכ"ל עם ד"ה ומת בלא: (ה) ד"ה שלא מצינו וכו' צרתה הס"ד ואח"כ מ"ה לא למעוטי צרת וכו' לא בעיא הס"ד ואח"כ מ"ה לאיילונית תלד:

[תוספתא לפנינו לא מצאתי רק בפרק ה דמכילתין תניא בזה"ל ג' אחין נשואין ג' נשים נכריות ומת אחד מהן ועשה בה שני מאמר ומת הרי אלו חולצות ולא מתייבמות היא צרת אשת אחיו שחולצת ולא מתייבמת דברי ר' יוסי]

עין משפט נר מצוה

מו א מיי' פ"ו מהל' יבום הלכה כב טוש"ע אה"ע סימן קעג סעי' ז:

מז ב ג מיי' פי"א מהל' גירושין הלכה עז יז סמג עשין נ טוש"ע אה"ע סימן קנה סעיף יא וסימן קעג סעיף יד:

מח ד מיי' פ"ז מהלכות יבום הלכה ח סמג עשין נא טוש"ע אה"ע סימן קעב סעיף א.

תוספות ישנים

מיאנה בזה מותרת בזה. כלומר באחיו לפי שהמיאון עוקר הזיקה. וא"ת אף לאותן שמיאנה נמי תשתרי שהמיאון יעקור הקדושין מאחיו ראשון ותהיה כמו נכרית בעלמא. וי"ל דטעמא משום דמשעת נפילה נראית כאשת אח דמכיון שנצטרך לה ליצא ממנו ע"י מיאון נראית כאשת אחיו כדאמרינן לקמן מיאנה ביבם אסורה לאביו משום דמשעת נפילה נראית ככלתו. בבעל מותרת לאביו שהמיאון עוקר הקדושין ונמצא שלא היתה מעולם כלתו ולא נחשבת כ"א כמפותת בנו: מאי לאו למעוטי צרת אילונית דשריא. אבל א"ל צרת סוטה וצרת מחזיר גרושתו דאין לנו למעט אלא דכוותה כגון שאסורה משום אשת אח מאב ולא משום ערוה אחרת. וא"ת דלמא אתא למעוטי צרת ממאנת א) שלא היתה מעולם אשת אחיו ואינה אסורה רק משום גזרה משום צרת בתו ממאנת:

א) חסר כאן ונראה דל"ל צרת ממאנת וי"ל דממאנת נמי לא הוה ערוה דכוותה דכיון דמיאנה נמצא שלא היתה כו'.

תוספות חד מקמאי

והלכתא צרת ממאנת [מותרת אפילו לזה] שמיאנה בו ולא גזרינן משום בתו ממאנת שאסורה משום דבשעת נפילה נראית כצרת בתו והממאנת עצמה אסורה לזה שמיאנה בו ומותרת לאחיו כשמואל דאמר מיאנה לזה מותרת לזה: גרסינן בנדה פרק בנות כותים קטן וקטנה לא חולצין ולא מייבמין קטן שמא [ימצא] סרים קטנה שמא תמצא אילונית ואקשינן כי תמצא אילונית מאי הוי והא מקח טעות הוא ואין כאן אסור אשת אח ואפי' גט לא בעיא דהא תנן וכולן אם נמצאו אילונית צרותיהן מותרות להתייבם ואם אילונית היתה צריכה גט מספק אמאי מותרת להתייבם ודלמא צרת ערוה היא אלא לאו ש"מ דאילונית לא בעיא גט ועוד תניא בפ' הזורק כל עריות שאמרו צרותיהן מותרות הלכו הצרות האלו ונישאו ונמצאו אילונית תצא מזה ומזה שמא כיון דנמצאו העריות אילונית לאו צרת ערוה היא כלל ומותרת להתייבם ותנן נמי התם הכונס יבמתו והלכה צרתה ונשאת לאחר ונמצאת אילונית תצא מזה ומזה וכל הדרכים האלו בה. אמר רבא צרת בתו אילונית אפי' הכיר בה מותרת כל אילונית שלא הכיר בה בעלה בשעת קידושין צריכה גט מספק שמא לא יקפיד בה הבעל ואין לה כתובה דאוקי' ממונא בחזקת מריה וזו היא ששנינו הממאנת והשניה והאילונית אין להן כתובה משמע הא גט בעיא כדדייקינן בפ' המדיר כנסה סתם אין לה כתובה כתובה הוא דלא בעיא הא גט בעיא. והכי נמי איכא למימר גבי אילונית כתובה הוא דלית לה הא גט בעיא ועוד דקתני אילונית דומיא דשניה מה שניה צריכה גט אף אילונית שלא הכיר בה צריכה גט או מדרבנן או משום ספק שמא לא יקפיד הבעל בשעת קדושין ואע"פ שמקפיד עתה שנודע לו שהיא אילונית וכיון דצריכה גט אמרינן התם שמא תמצא אילונית והיא אשת אחיו שלא במקום מצוה. ומתני' דהכא ודפרק הזורק לא קשה לרבא כלל דהא ס"ל לרבא דאפילו צרת בתו אילונית דהכיר בה בשעת קדושין ונשואין צרתה מותרת להתייבם אבל לרב אשי צרת אילונית שהכיר בה אפי' אשה בעלמא שאינה ערוה אסורה להתייבם ואזלא לעלמא בלא חליצה ומתני' דהכא ודפרק הזורק דאמר צרותיהן מותרת להתייבם דוקא נמצאו לאחר קדושין מפני שהוא מקח טעות א) ולרבה ודאי כיון שמותרת להתייבם כשנמצאו אילונית אין כאן קדושין כלל וא"כ קשיא ההיא דפ' בנות כותיים דאמר קטנה שמא תמצא איילונית והא אמרת דאין כאן קדושין כלל ואם נמצאת איילונית אין כאן איסור אשת אח ואי לאו מתני' דהכא ההיא דפ' הזורק ל"ק מידי דאיכא למימר (דלרבה) [דלרב אשי] נמי ספק מקח טעות הוא שמא לא יקפיד וחולצת ולא מתייבמת ומפני שהלכו צרותיהן ונשאו בלא חליצה תצא מזה ומזה וכל הדרכים האלו בה אבל מתני' הכא קתני נמצאו איילונית צרותיהן מותרות להתייבם ש"מ דודאי מותרות וי"ל (כרבה) [דרב אשי] מוקים לה למתני' דהכא כגון שאמר הבעל בפירוש שיקפיד אם תמצא אילונית ותוספתא שכתב הרב אלפסי וכולן שנמצאו איילונית או שהיו נשואות לאחרים בין בחיי הבעל בין לאחר מיתה כגון שגילה הבעל בחייו שיקפיד אם תמצא איילונית ורבינו יעקב תריץ אליבא דרב אשי כל זמן שלא הכיר בה הראשון הרי היא כאשתו ואע"פ שאם היה מכיר בה והיה מקפיד יוצאה בלא גט ואעפ"כ כל זמן שלא הקפיד לא מחזקינן לה בהכי וההיא דתנן בפ' הזורק מיירי שהכיר בהן הבעל שאינן איילונית והקפיד והצרות לא ידעו בקפידת הבעל ונשאו ולפיכך תצא מזה ומזה וכל הדרכים האלו ומתני' דהכא נמי דקתני נמצאו אילונית מותרות כגון שהקפיד הבעל בחייו שאמר אם תמצא איילונית אגרשנה והתוספתא שכתב הרב אלפסי בין בחיי הבעל בין לאחר מיתת הבעל כגון שאמר הבעל בחייו שיקפיד אם תמצא אילונית אבל כל זמן שלא יקפיד וכן אם מת ולא הכיר בה לא מחזיקים ליה שיקפיד והרי היא כאשתו ולפיכך אמרו קטנה שמא תמצא אילונית ועוד יש לפרש אליבא

דרבא

א) נ"ל ולדידיה ולאי וכו' ור"ל לרב אשי.

תורה אור

[א] הִלְכְתָא, צָרַת אַיְלוֹנִית מוּתֶּרֶת, וַאֲפִי' הִכִּיר בָּהּ, וַאֲפִילּוּ צָרַת בִּתּוֹ אַיְלוֹנִית. וְאֶלָּא הָא דְּקָתָנֵי שֶׁנִּמְצְאוּ? תְּנֵי שֶׁהָיוּ. כִּי אֲתָא רָבִין אֲמַר רַ' יוֹחָנָן: אַחַת צָרַת מְמָאֶנֶת וְאַחַת צָרַת אַיְלוֹנִית, וְאַחַת צָרַת מַחֲזִיר גְּרוּשָׁתוֹ — כּוּלָּן מוּתָּרוֹת. *תָּנֵי רַב בֵּיבָי קַמֵּיהּ דְּרַב נַחְמָן: שָׁלֹשׁ נָשִׁים מְשַׁמְּשׁוֹת בְּמוֹךְ: קְטַנָּה, מְעוּבֶּרֶת, וּמֵנִיקָה. קְטַנָּה — שֶׁמָּא תִתְעַבֵּר וְשֶׁמָּא תָמוּת, מְעוּבֶּרֶת — שֶׁמָּא תַּעֲשֶׂה עוּבָּרָהּ סַנְדָּל, מֵנִיקָה — שֶׁמָּא תִּגְמוֹל בְּנָהּ וְיָמוּת. וְאֵיזוֹ הִיא קְטַנָּה — מִבַּת י"א שָׁנָה וְיוֹם אֶחָד עַד י"ב שָׁנָה וְיוֹם אֶחָד, פָּחוֹת מִכָּאן וְיָתֵר עַל כֵּן מְשַׁמֶּשֶׁת כְּדַרְכָּהּ וְהוֹלֶכֶת, דִּבְרֵי ר"מ, וְחכ"א: אַחַת זוֹ וְאַחַת זוֹ מְשַׁמֶּשֶׁת כְּדַרְכָּהּ וְהוֹלֶכֶת, וּמִן הַשָּׁמַיִם יְרַחֲמוּ. מִשּׁוּם שֶׁנֶּאֱמַר °"שׁוֹמֵר פְּתָאִים ה'" (תהלים קטז). מִדְּקָאָמַר שֶׁמָּא תִתְעַבֵּר וְשֶׁמָּא תָמוּת, מִכְּלָל דְּאִיכָּא קְטַנָּה דְּמִיעַבְּרָא וְלָא מֵתָה, א"כ מָצִינוּ חֲמוֹתוֹ מְמָאֶנֶת, וּתְנַן: אִי אַתָּה יָכוֹל לוֹמַר בַּחֲמוֹתוֹ וְאֵם חֲמוֹתוֹ וְאֵם חָמִיו שֶׁנִּמְצְאוּ אַיְלוֹנִית אוֹ שֶׁמֵּיאֲנוּ! אֵימָא: שֶׁמָּא תִתְעַבֵּר וְתָמוּת. דְּאָמַר רַבָּה בַּר לִיוַאי: גְּבוּל יֵשׁ לָהּ: קוֹדֶם הַזְּמַן הַזֶּה אֵינָהּ מִתְעַבֶּרֶת כָּל עִיקָּר, תּוֹךְ הַזְּמַן הַזֶּה הִיא מֵתָה וְעוּבָּרָהּ מֵת, לְאַחַר זְמַן הַזֶּה — הִיא חַיָּה וְעוּבָּרָהּ חַי. אִינִי? וְהָא תָּנֵי רַבָּה בַּר שְׁמוּאֵל: אִי אַתָּה יָכוֹל לוֹמַר בַּחֲמוֹתוֹ וְאֵם חֲמוֹתוֹ וְאֵם חָמִיו שֶׁנִּמְצְאוּ אַיְלוֹנִית אוֹ שֶׁמֵּיאֲנוּ, שֶׁכְּבָר יָלְדוּ! אֶלָּא, לְעוֹלָם — שֶׁמָּא תִתְעַבֵּר וְשֶׁמָּא תָמוּת. וְאֶלָּא קַשְׁיָא הָךְ! אָמַר רַב סַפְרָא: [ב] בָּנִים הֲרֵי הֵם כְּסִימָנִים. וְאִית דְּאָמְרִי: בָּנִים עֲדִיפֵי מִסִּימָנִים. לְמַאי נָפְקָא מִינָּהּ? דַּאֲפִילּוּ לְרַבִּי יְהוּדָה, דְּאָמַר: *עַד שֶׁיִּרְבֶּה הַשָּׁחוֹר, בְּבָנִים מוֹדֶה. וְרַב

רש"י

הִלְכְתָא צָרַת אַיְלוֹנִית מוּתֶּרֶת. וְאע"ג דְּהִכִּיר בָּהּ אָחִיו וְקַיְּימָהּ וְהָוְיָא אִשְׁתּוֹ — לָא מִיתַּסְרָא צָרָתָהּ מִשּׁוּם צָרַת הַבַּת, דְּכִי אָסַר רַחֲמָנָא צָרַת עֶרְוָה — בִּמְקוֹם מִצְוָה הוּא דַּאֲסָרָהּ. וְהָא, כֵּיוָן דְּאַיְלוֹנִית הִיא — דִּבְלָאו עֶרְוָה נַמִי לָא חַזְיָא לְיִיבּוּם — הָוֵי צָרָתָהּ צָרַת עֶרְוָה שֶׁלֹּא בִּמְקוֹם מִצְוָה. וְכָךְ מְפוֹרָשׁ בַּהֲלָכוֹת גְּדוֹלוֹת. צָרַת מְמָאֶנֶת. בַּיְּבָם. מַחֲזִיר גְּרוּשָׁתוֹ. מִשֶּׁנִּיסֵּאת. מְשַׁמְּשׁוֹת בְּמוֹךְ. מוּתָּרוֹת לָתֵת מוֹךְ בִּמְקוֹם תַּשְׁמִישׁ כְּשֶׁהֵן מְשַׁמְּשׁוֹת, כְּדֵי שֶׁלֹּא יִתְעַבְּרוּ. סַנְדָּל. וָלָד שֶׁאֵין לוֹ צוּרַת פָּנִים. וְקַיְימָא לָן בְּמַסֶּכֶת נִדָּה (דף כה:): אֵין סַנְדָּל שֶׁאֵין עִמּוֹ וָלָד, מָשָׁל לְאָדָם שֶׁסָּטַר אֶת חֲבֵירוֹ וְהֶחֱזִיר צוּרָתוֹ לַאֲחוֹרָיו. דִּכְשֶׁהִיא מְעוּבֶּרֶת וְחוֹזֶרֶת וּמִתְעַבֶּרֶת דּוֹחֵק הָאֶחָד אֶת חֲבֵירוֹ וּפוֹחֵת צוּרָתוֹ. שֶׁמָּא תִּגְמוֹל אֶת בְּנָהּ. אִם תִּתְעַבֵּר תְּהֵא צְרִיכָה לִגְמוֹל אֶת בְּנָהּ מִלְּהָנִיק כְּמוֹ "וַיִּגָּמַל" (בראשית כא) — לְשׁוֹן הַבְדָּלָה. וְאֵיזוֹ הִיא. (א) הָרְאוּיָה לְהִתְעַבֵּר וְלָמוּת. מִבַּת י"א שָׁנָה כו'. פָּחוֹת מִי"א וַדַּאי לֹא תִּתְעַבֵּר, וְיוֹתֵר מִי"ב — אִם תִּתְעַבֵּר לֹא תָמוּת. מְשַׁמְּשׁוֹת. בְּלֹא מוֹךְ, כְּדַרְכָּן, וְהוֹלְכוֹת. וּמִדְּקָאָמַר שֶׁמָּא תָמוּת. וְלָא קָאָמַר וְתָמוּת, דְּהָא הֲוֵי מַשְׁמַע שֶׁאִם תִּתְעַבֵּר תָּמוּת וַדַּאי: מָצִינוּ חֲמוֹתוֹ מְמָאֶנֶת. כְּגוֹן שֶׁיָּלְדָה בְּקַטְנוּ', בְּתוֹךְ זְמַן הָאָמוּר לְמַעְלָה בִּשְׁנַת י"ב, שֶׁנִּתְעַבְּרָה וְלֹא מֵתָה, וְקִידֵּשׁ *אָדָם אֶת בִּתָּהּ, וְנִמְלֵאת זֹאת חֲמוֹתוֹ קְטַנָּה, וּרְאוּיָה לְמָאֵן עַד י"ב שָׁנָה. קוֹדֶם הַזְּמַן הַזֶּה. הָאָמוּר לְמַעְלָה, קוֹדֶם י"א. אַחַר הַזְּמַן הַזֶּה. אַחַר י"ב. שֶׁכְּבָר יָלְדוּ. וּמִדְּתָלֵי טַעְמָא בְּוָלָד, מִכְּלָל דִּקְטַנָּה הִיא. דְּאִי לָאו קְטַנָּה הִיא, לִיתְנֵי שֶׁכְּבָר גָּדְלוּ. הֲרֵי הֵן כְּסִימָנִים. הִלְכָּךְ אֵין לְךָ יוֹלֶדֶת מְמָאֶנֶת, אֲפִי' הִיא קְטַנָּה. וַאֲפִי' לְר"י דְּאָמַר. בְּמַסֶּכֶת נִדָּה, אַף מִשֶּׁהֵבִיאָה שְׁתֵּי שְׂעָרוֹת מְמָאֶנֶת עַד שֶׁיִּרְבֶּה הַשָּׁחוֹר, שֶׁיִּהְיוּ שָׁם שְׂעָרוֹת הַרְבֵּה. אֵין

תוספות

שלש נשים משמשות במוך. פי' הקונטרס: מותר לשמש במוך, אבל שלא נשים — אסור, משום השחתת זרע, אע"ג דלא מיפקדה אפריה ורביה. וכן משמע בנדה (דף יג. ושם) דתנן בפ' "כל היד": המרבה לבדוק בנשים — משובחת, באנשים — תקצץ. ומפרש בגמרא משום דנשים לאו בנות הרגשה נינהו. משמע דאי הוו בנות הרגשה — הוי אסור. ומיהו, מצינו לפרש דלאו בנות איסור הרגשה נינהו. ור"ת אומר: דלפני תשמיש ודאי אסור ליתן שם מוך, דאין דרך תשמיש בכך, והרי הוא כמטיל זרע על העצים ועל האבנים כשמטיל על המוך. אבל אם נותנת מוך אחר תשמיש — אין נראה לאסור, דהאי גברא כי אורחיה משמש, מידי דהוה אקטנה ואילונית דלא איתסרו בתשמיש משום דלאו בנות בנים נינהו. והאשה שנותנת אח"כ מוך — לא הוזהרה אהשחתת זרע, כיון דלא מיפקדה אפריה ורביה. ומשמשות במוך דקתני הכא, היינו — צריכות לשמש במוך. **שמא** תעשה עוברה סנדל. פירש בקונטרס: דכשהיא מתעברת וחוזרת ומתעברת דוחק האחד את חבירו, ופוחת צורתו. והא דאמר ב"המפלת" (נדה דף כז.) דאין אשה מתעברת וחוזרת ומתעברת — צ"ל דהיינו דוקא בן קיימא. ור"ת מפרש: דסנדל הוא כשהאשה מתעברת תאומים. אם משמשת בלא מוך — נכנס השכבת זרע בין שני הולדות ודוחק אותם ועושה את האחד סנדל. וכן משמע ב"המפלת" (שם דף כה:) דבעיבור אחד הוי, דקאמרינן: ולמה הוזכר סנדל, והלא אין סנדל שאין עמו ולד? ומשני: אי דאתיליד נקבה בהדיה — ה"נ, הב"ע דאתיליד זכר בהדיה, מהו דתימא: הואיל ואמר רבי יצחק אשה מזרעת תחלה יולדת זכר, ומדהאי זכר — האי נמי זכר הוא, קמ"ל, אימור: שניהם הזריעו בבת אחת. ואם סנדל בשני עיבורים — למה ה"ל למימר מדהאי זכר האי נמי זכר? ולמה לי נמי למימר שניהם הזריעו בבת אחת*? **שמא** תתעבר ותמות. ולא בעי לשנויי דנקט שמא תמות משום דאינה ודאי מתה אלא כשילדה בְּקַטְנוּת, אבל ילדה בְּגַדְלוּת, אע"פ שנתעברה בקטנות, פעמים חיה, ולא משכחת חמותו ממאנת, דאי ילדה בקטנות ודאי מתה, ואי ילדה בגדלות שוב אינה יכולה למאן — משום דברייתא דרב ביבי לא מיפלגא מידי בעיבור שנת י"ב בין ילדה בגדלות בין ילדה בקטנות. ועוד: לא מסתברא ליה שתגרום הלידה בקטנות מיתה אלא העיבור. ועוד: דמתרץ האמת כרבה בר ליואי, דכל תוך הזמן היא מתה ועוברה מת. **אחר** הזמן הזה היא חיה ועוברה חי. ואומר ר"י: דאין לפרש: אחר הזמן — אחר שנת י"ב ויום א', אפילו בלא הבאת ב' שערות, דא"כ מצינו חמותו ממאנת, דעד רוב שנותיה יכולה למאן אם לא הביאה ב' שערות — למ"ד אין חוששין שמא נשרו. ואפילו למאי דפסקי' התם בפ' "יוצא דופן" (נדה דף מו.) דחוששין היכא דבעל אחר זמן, דהויא ליה ספיקא דאורייתא — משכחת חמותו ממאנת כגון שפירש כשבעל אחר זמן, שאין בועל לשם קידושין, דהשתא לא הויא ספיקא דאורייתא. אלא כשהביאה ב' שערות איירי, ולא חש לפרש, משום דאורחא הוא דאיכא שערות אחר זמן. וכן נמצא בירושלמי דתלי טעמא דרבה בר ליואי בשערות, ולא בשנים. **שכבר** ילדו. ומדקאמר שכבר ילדו — משמע דבלא הביאה ב' שערות. דאי איכא שערות — כי לא ילדה נמי נפקא מתורת קטנות ואילונית ע"י שערות, וא"כ איכא קטנה דמיעברא ולא מתה. וא"ת: מאי ס"ד דמקשה? תקשה ברייתא דרבה בר שמואל גופיה, דכיון דבלא הביאה ב' שערות איירי — כי ילדה מאי הוי? מ"מ תמאן! ואר"י: דסבר המקשה דאע"ג דבקטנה איירי — לית בה מיאון מדרבנן, לפי שנראית גדולה, וסבורים העולם שהביאה ב' שערות. ולא פריך אלא לרבה בר ליואי דוקא, דאמר דליכא קטנה דמיעברא ולא מתה. אבל לברייתא דרב ביבי — לא קשיא מידי, דאע"ג דקתני שמא תמות, דמשמע דאיכא קטנה דמיעברא ולא מתה — מ"מ לא מצינו חמותו ממאנת, שהלידה מונעתה מלמאן אע"פ שהיא קטנה, כדפרישית. אבל אין לפרש דלמקשה ניחא ליה ברייתא גופא דמסיק אדעתיה שפיר דלידה הרי הוא כסימנים, ולכך אינה יכולה למאן, ולא פריך אלא לרבה בר ליואי, ומשני: דבנים הרי הן כסימנים משעת העיבור, כמו שאפרש, דא"כ הל"ל בהדיא: עיבור בנים הרי הם כסימנים, כיון דמעיקרא נמי אסיק אדעתיה דלידה הרי היא כסימנים. **הרי** הם כסימנים. פי': משעת העיבור. ושפיר תני רב ביבי שמא תמות, דבשנת י"ב פעמים חיה אפי' לרבה בר ליואי, ואז היתה גדולה משעת ההריון. ואע"פ דקי"ל בנדה דתוך הזמן כלפני הזמן, ולא הויא גדולה בהביאה שערות בשנת י"ב — מ"מ עיבור בנים, בני קיימא, תוך הזמן — כסימנים אחר הזמן. והא דקאמר רבה בר ליואי תוך הזמן היא מתה ועוברה מת — לא קאי אשנת י"ב, דאז פעמים חיה כשהיא גדולה בשעת ההריון, כדפרישית. אלא ה"פ דמלתא: קודם הזמן, פי', קודם — שנה שלפני גדלות, תוך הזמן — היינו תוך שנה שלפני גדלות, אחר זמן — היינו אחר שגדלה, כדפי' ר"י בתחלת הסוגיא. **דאפי'** לר' יהודה דאמר כו'. משום דבעי לאוקמי מתני' כר"י דלא מצינו חמותו ממאנת קאמר הכי. וא"ת: אמאי קאמר דעדיפי מסימנים? אפי' לא הוו משעת עיבור אלא כסימנים — לא מצינו חמותו ממאנת לר' יהודה, דמשעת עיבור עד הלידה יש זמן מרובה יותר ממה שיש מהבאת שערות עד שירבה השחור. ומיהו, למ"ד התם דרבוי שחור היינו עד שיקיפו השערות משפה אל שפה — אפשר שריבוי השחור מאחר יותר מזמן עיבור עד שעת לידה. אבל למ"ד שערות שוכבות, ונראה כמו שריבה השחור — קשיא! ונראה דאם הביאה שערות ונשרו יכולה לְמָאֵן אפילו שהה כדי ריבוי שחור, דאין הזמן גורם אלא ריבוי שחור ממש בעינן, שתהא נראית גדולה לַכֹּל ע"י כך. וא"ת: אכתי בלא "בנים עדיפי מסימנים" מיתוקמא מתני' שפיר כר"י, דהא מודה רבי יהודה כשבָּעַל אחר גדלות דאינה יכולה למאן, כדאמר בפ' "בא סימן" (נדה דף נב.), וזאת החמותו שנבעלה בגדלות כשנתעברה, דבנים הרי הם כסימנים משעת ההריון — תריץ דאי לאו דבנים עדיפי מסימנים משכחת חמותו ממאנת כגון שעיברה באמבטי, או שבעל בפירוש שלא לשם קידושין.

רב

עין משפט נר מצוה

מט א מיי' פ"ו מהל' יבום הלכה כ כא טוש"ע אה"ע סימן קעב ס"א וסי' קעג סעיף ט:

נ ב מיי' פ"כ מהל' איסורי ביאה הלכה ט סמג עשין כ טוש"ע אה"ע סימן קנה סעיף יב:

תוספות ישנים

צרת אילונית מותרת ואפילו הכיר בה ואפילו צרת בתו דכיון דלאו בת ייבום היא הויא צרתה צרת ערוה שלא במקום מצוה ושריא:

תוספות חד מקמאי

דרבא ההיא שמא תמצא איילונית דלמפטר צרתה קאמר כלומר שמא תמצא אילונית ותלך צרתה לעלמא ביבום זה ושמא תמצא אילונית ואינה פוטרת צרתה (אמר רבא הלכתא צרת אילונית מותרת) וכיוצא בזה אמר רבה בפ' האשה הא דאמרו רבנן זיקת שני יבמין מחלין [חלצה] יבומי לא מייבמי גזרה משום שתי יבמות הבאות מבית אחד. לא תימא ה"מ היכא דאיכא צרה דאיכא למיגזר משום צרה [דהא] הכא ליכא צרה מחלץ חלצה יבומי לא מייבמה: אמר רבא הלכתא צרת אילונית מותרת ואפי' הכיר בה ואפי' צרת בתו אילונית טעמא דמילתא דכיון דלא רמייה כלל ליבום אחד מן האחים הו"ל כצרת ערוה שלא במקום מצוה משא"כ בצרת עריות דמתני' וצרת אשת אחיו שלא היה בעולמו שאם לזה שאינה ערוה אינה ראויה ראויה היא לאחים אבל אילונית אינה ראויה לא' מן האחים וקי"ל כרבא כל אילונית שלא הכיר בה בעלה בשעת קידושין ונמצאת איילונית לאחר קדושין ומקפיד בה בעלה צריכה גט מספק או מדרבנן ויוצאים שלא בכתובה דאוקי ממונא בחזקת מאריה הרב אלפס כתב מילתא דרב זביד דאמר אין בנים בלא סימנים ולכאורה נראה דרב זביד ס"ל (אין בתוך) [דתוך] זמן כלאחר זמן וכן פרש"י ז"ל ואנן קי"ל תוך זמן כלפני זמן משום הכי אית לן לפרש דרב זביד לעולם ס"ל תוך זמן כלפני זמן משום הכי אית לן לפרש דאמאי דתני רבה בר שמואל קאי ובלאחר זמן וה"ק לעולם שמא תתעבר ותמות שאין קטנה יולדת והא דתני רבה בר שמואל שכבר ילדו ולא קתני שכבר הגדילו דאתא לאשמועינן אפי' למ"ד אין חוששין שמא נשרו משום צער לידה חיישינן ולפיכך תלה הטעם בלידה ולא תלה הטעם בגדלות דמשום לידה הוא דחיישינן שמא נשרו ואי לאו לידה אע"פ שהגיעה לכלל שנותיה איכא מ"ד אין חוששין שמא נשרו אבל בלידה לכ"ע חיישינן משום צער לידה וההיא דפרק אלו נערות דפריך התם ומי מעברא והא תני רב ביבי וכו' משמע התם דלא מעברא והכא אסיק' שמא תתעבר ושמא תמות וקשיין אהדדי ולמאי דפריש' איכא למימר (דהתם איכא למימר) דהתם אליבא דרב זביד קא פריך דס"ל שמא תתעבר ותמות דקטנה לא מעברא ואיכא לפרושי נמי ההיא דפ' [אלו] נערות דאליבא דרבנן קא פריך דאמר אחת זו ואחת זו משמשת כדרכה והולכת וס"ל לרבנן דקטנה לא מעברא. א"נ אליבא דרב ספרא והכי קאמר בנים הרי הן כסימנים בשעת עבורה קאמר להכי פריך ליה התם כיון דבשעת עבורה ה"ל כסימנים אישתכח דבשעת לידה הרי היא בוגרת שהרי אין בין נערות לבגרות אלא ששה חדשים וא"כ מאי קא מבעיא ליה יש בוגרת בקבר והרי קודם שמתה היתה בוגרת. מ"מ לא מפרשה מילתא דרב זביד לדעת הרב אלפסי אלא כדפריש' וכן נראה שפירש הראב"ד ז"ל ואיכא לעיוני דרב זביד גופיה אם בדקוה קודם לידה ולא הביאה ולאחר לידה ולא הביאה אי אמרינן דבההיא פורתא דבשעת לידה הביאה סימנין ונשרו ומיהו אליבא דהללו דחוששין שמא נשרו אפי' בלא בנים כ"ש בבנים. א) ולמ"ד אין חוששין בעלמא הכא משום צער לידה חוששין שמא בההיא פורתא הביאה סימנים ונשרו דאלת"ה למ"ד אין חוששין שמא נשרו מצינו. ושמא אם בדיקנא קודם לידה ולאחר לידה ולא הביאה. ואי אמרינן אין בנים בלא סימן לגבי מיאון אמרינן לחומרא שאינה ממאנת אבל לקולא שלא תחלוץ לא. ומסתברא מדקאמר חיישינן אלמא לחומרא קאמר שלא תמאן ולא לקולא שתחלוץ כדאמרינן בפ' יוצא דופן מכלל דלמ"ד חיישינן חלצ' והא חיישינן בעלמא קא': כי אתא רבין אר"י א' צרת ממאנת וא' צרת אילונית וא' צרת מחזיר

א) נראה דל"ל אבל למ"ד וכו' ונשרו לאלתר מצינו לומר אם בדיקנא וכו' ולא הביאה אין חוששין שמא נשרו ועוד איכא לעיוני אי אמרינן אין בנים בלא סימן לגבי חליצה וכו'.

מסורת הש"ס

כתובות לט. לקמן יב: נדה מה. נדרים לה: [תוס' נדה פ"ב]

נ"ל אחיו

כתובות לו. ב"ב קנו. נדה נב. חולין כו:

[ועי' תוס' נדה כה: ד"ה קמ"ל]

הגהות הב"ח

(א) רש"י ד"ה ואיזו היא קטנה הראויה:

וְרַב זְבִיד אָמַר: אֵין בָּנִים בְּלֹא סִימָנִים. וְנִבְדּוֹק! חָיְישִׁינַן שֶׁמָּא נָשְׁרוּ. הָנִיחָא לְמ"ד חוֹשְׁשִׁין, אֶלָּא לְמ"ד אֵין חוֹשְׁשִׁין מַאי אִיכָּא לְמֵימַר? אֲפִי' לְמ"ד אֵין חוֹשְׁשִׁין, מִשּׁוּם צַעַר לֵידָה – חָיְישִׁינַן.§ "כֵּיצַד פּוֹטְרוֹת צָרוֹתֵיהֶן וכו'".§ מְנָהָנֵי מִילֵּי? אֲמַר רַב יְהוּדָה: דְּאָמַר קְרָא ויקרא יח "לִצְרוֹר", *הַתּוֹרָה רִיבְּתָה צָרוֹת הַרְבֵּה. רַב אַשִׁי אֲמַר: סְבָרָא הִיא, צָרָה מ"ט אֲסִירָא – דְּבִמְקוֹם עֶרְוָה קַיְימָא, צָרַת צָרָה נַמִי – בִּמְקוֹם עֶרְוָה קַיְימָא.§ "כֵּיצַד אִם מֵתוּ הֵן כו'".§ [א]וַאֲפִילּוּ כָּנַס וּלְבַסּוֹף גֵּירֵשׁ? וּרְמִינְהוּ: *ג' אַחִים, שְׁנַיִם מֵהֶן נְשׂוּאִים ב' אֲחָיוֹת וְאֶחָד נָשׂוּי נָכְרִית, גֵּירֵשׁ אֶחָד מִבַּעֲלֵי אֲחָיוֹת *אִשְׁתּוֹ וּמֵת הַנָּשׂוּי נָכְרִית, וּכְנָסָהּ הַמְגָרֵשׁ וּמֵת – זוֹ הִיא שֶׁאָמְרוּ: שֶׁאִם מֵתוּ אוֹ נִתְגָּרְשׁוּ – צָרוֹתֵיהֶן מוּתָּרוֹת. טַעְמָא דְּגֵירֵשׁ וְאח"כ כָּנַס, אֲבָל כָּנַס וְאח"כ גֵּירֵשׁ – לָא! *א"ר יִרְמְיָה: *תַּבְרָא, מִי שֶׁשָּׁנָה זוֹ לֹא שָׁנָה זוֹ. הַאי תַּנָּא סָבַר: מִיתָה מַפֶּלֶת, וְהַאי תַּנָּא סָבַר: נִשּׂוּאִין הָרִאשׁוֹנִים מַפִּילִים. רָבָא אֲמַר: לְעוֹלָם חַד תַּנָּא הוּא, *"וְזוֹ וְאֵין צָרִיךְ לוֹמַר זוֹ" קָתָנֵי.§ "וְכָל שֶׁיְּכוֹלָה לְמָאֵן".§ *וּתְמָאֵן הַשְׁתָּא וְתִתְיַבֵּם! [לקמן קז:] לֵימָא מְסַיְּיעָא לֵיהּ לְרַבִּי אוֹשַׁעְיָא, *דא"ר אוֹשַׁעְיָא: מְמָאֶנֶת לְמַאֲמָרוֹ וְאֵינָהּ מְמָאֶנֶת לְזִיקָתוֹ! לָא, צָרַת עֶרְוָה שָׁאנֵי. *דְּתָנֵי רָמִי בַּר יְחֶזְקֵאל: מֵיאֲנָה בְּבַעַל – מוּתֶּרֶת לְאָבִיו, מֵיאֲנָה בְּיָבָם – אֲסוּרָה לְאָבִיו, אַלְמָא: מִשְּׁעַת נְפִילָה נִרְאֵית כְּכַלָּתוֹ, הָכָא נַמִי מִשְּׁעַת נְפִילָה נִרְאֵית כְּצָרַת בִּתּוֹ.§

מתני' *שֵׁשׁ עֲרָיוֹת חֲמוּרוֹת מֵאֵלּוּ, מִפְּנֵי שֶׁנְּשׂוּאוֹת לַאֲחֵרִים, [ב]צָרוֹתֵיהֶן מוּתָּרוֹת: אִמּוֹ, וְאֵשֶׁת אָבִיו, וַאֲחוֹת אָבִיו, אֲחוֹתוֹ מֵאָבִיו, וְאֵשֶׁת אֲחִי אָבִיו, וְאֵשֶׁת אָחִיו מֵאָבִיו. *בֵּית שַׁמַּאי מַתִּירִין הַצָּרוֹת לָאַחִים, וּבֵית הִלֵּל אוֹסְרִים.

חלצו

רש"י

אין בנים בלא סימנים. והיולדת בקטנות חזקה הביאה סימנים. ומשהביאה סימנים בתוך י"ב – לא תמאן, דהני סימנים גמורים נינהו. דס"ל לרב זביד: תוך זמן כלאחר זמן לענין סימן, ולא אמרינן שומא נינהו: **הניחא** למ"ד כו'. פלוגתא בפ' "יוצא דופן" (נדה דף מו.). **מנא הני מילי.** דצרת צרתה פטורה. **נתגרשו** צרותיהן מותרות. **ואפי'** כנס אחיו את הנכרית, ולבסוף גירש את בת אחיו, דהוו להו צרות זו לזו קודם גירושין – אפ"ה קשרינן ליה ליבומי, כדקתני: ומתה בתו או נתגרשה, הואיל ובשעת נפילה לא הוו צרות זו לזו. **וכנסה המגרש ומת.** ונפלה נכרית לפני שלישי שנשוי אחות אשתו של (א) זו הראשונה, דהויא להו צרת אחות אשה, משנתגרשה. **צרותיהן מותרות.** הואיל ולא היתה אחות אשתו של זה צרה לנכרית זו שקודם נשואים של זו נתגרשה. **תברא.** קשיין אהדדי. **האי תנא.** דמתני' סבר מיתת הבעל מפלת נשיו לייבום, הלכך אפי' כנס ולבסוף גירש, כיון דבשעת מיתה לאו צרת הבת היא – שריא. **ותנא.** *דברייתא סבר: נישואין הראשונים שהאשה נשאת לבעלה מפילים אותה לייבום. הלכך, משנעשית צרת ערוה שעה אחת – אסורה עולמית. **זו.** דמתני' דהכא דכנס ולבסוף גירש מותרת, כדקתני: ומתה בתו או נתגרשה, ואין צ"ל זו דג' אחים דגירש ולבסוף כנס. **ותמאן.** הערוה השתא, ותאמר: אי איפשי בקדושין שקדשוני אמי ואחי לבעלי המת, ותעקור קידושין הראשונים, ותתייבם צרתה. **ממאנת למאמרו.** הא דתנא לקמן בפ' ב"ש: וב"ה אומרים בבעל וביבם. **למאמרו.** הוא דממאנת, שאם עשה היבם מאמר ביבמה קטנה ומיאנה בו – מפקיע מיאון את המאמר, וחוזרה לזיקה לבדה, וחולצת. ואע"ג דגדולה שעשה בה מאמר ולא רצה לכנוס, קי"ל בפ' ר"ג (לקמן דף נ:) (ב) צריכה גט למאמרו וחליצה לזיקתו – הכא מיאון עקר למאמרו, ולא בעיא גיטא. **ואין ממאנת לזיקתו.** לעקור נשואים ראשונים, ולהפקיע זיקת ייבום, ולצאת בלא חליצה. ה"נ גבי ערוה – לא עקר ליה מיאון דהשתא לנשואין קמאי למישרי צרתה. **צרת ערוה שאני.** רבנן גזרו שלא תמאן ליבומי צרתה, דלא לזלזולי בצרת ערוה, דלמא אתי למישרי. **מיאנה.** כלתו בבעלה מותרת לחמיה. דעקרתה לנישואיה, והויא כמפותת בנו, ומותרת לו. אבל מת בנו, בעלה הראשון, ומיאנה בזיקת יבם, אע"ג דנשואין קמאי עקרה – אסורה לאביו. אלמא: משעת נפילה כלתו היא, משעה שנפלה להתייבם ונזקקה ליבם מחמת נישואין הראשונים – נראים אותם נישואין גמורים למיהוי אשת המת וכלתו של זה. **ה"נ.** בצרת ערוה, משעת נפילה שנזקקה הבת ליבם (ג) למאן בו מחמת קידושי ראשון – נראים נישואים גמורים, למיהוי אשת המת וצרתה צרת הבת, ואי שרית ליה – אתי למישרי צרת הבת בעלמא. **מתני' שש עריות.** יש שחמורות מאלו, ומהו חומר שלהן – שנשואות לאחרים, ואינן יכולין להנשא לאחיו מאביו. ואם מתו בעליהן, שהן (ד) נכריות אצל זה – צרותיהן מותרות להנשא לזה. **אמו.** אינה יכולה להנשא לאחיו של זה מאביו, שהרי היא לו אשת האב. וכן אשת האב ואחות אביו (ה) ואשת אחיו מאביו שהיו לו בנים ואשת אחי אביו – כולן אסורות לאחיו מאביו כשם שאסורות עליו, ואין בהן צד ייבום על זה לעולם. ואם נישאו לאחרים, ולהם נשים אחרות, ומתו – מותרות ליגשא לזה, שאין צרת ערוה אסורה אלא כשנפלה לייבום *עם הערוה פעם אחת. שכיון שפטרה לצרת ערוה – עמדה עולמית באיסור אשת אח שיש לה בנים. **ב"ש מתירים.** צרת ערוה להתייבם לאחיו, דלית להו הך דרשה ד"לצרור".

חללו

תוספות

(ו) **רב** זביד אמר אין בנים בלא סימנים. אומר ר"י דצריך לפרש דאין עיבור בנים של קיימא מצוי להיות בלא סימנים. ומיהו, זמנין אתו. מדפריך: וניבדוק. וכן אלא למ"ד אין חוששין מאי איכא למימר. ואם אין בנים כלל בלא סימנים – ודאי נשרו. וגם לשון חוששין נמי משמע דליכא אלא חששא בעלמא, ולא שודאי נשרו, ומשום דלא שכיח עיבור בלא סימנים לא מצינו חמותו ממאנת, דחוששים לסימנים, כדמסיק ואזיל ולהכי קאמר נמי רבה בר ליואי: תוך הזמן הזה היא מתה ועוברה מת, אע"פ דפעמים חיה, כיון דלא שכיח. ובברייתא דרב ביבי דנקט שמא תמות – בשביל המיעוט, ואע"ג דרבה בר ליואי לא חש למינקט שמא בשביל מיעוטא. וא"ת: ומנין לו לגמרא דרב זביד לא בעי למימר דאין בנים כלל בלא סימנים כדמשמע במילתיה? וי"ל: דאם אין בנים כלל בלא סימנים בא למימר, א"כ במאי אתא לפלוגי אדרב ספרא? כיון דלדידיה נמי אין בנים כלל בלא סימנים כמו לרב ספרא! אלא ודאי אתא למימר דאין הבנים סימן גדלות אלא השערות, וכי ליכא שערות – לא מחזקינן לה ודאי גדולה. ולהכי פריך: ולבדוק? ומשני: חוששין שמא נשרו ותוששין לה בספק גדולה לענין חליצה וקדושין דאורייתא, ולענין עונשין ומילי טובא. ובקונטרס פי': דסבר רב זביד דתוך הזמן כלאחר הזמן, דלא כהלכתא. נראה לר"י דבעלמא מודה רב זביד דתוך הזמן כלפני הזמן, ושאני הכא דע"י בנים חשבינן לסימנים כאילו הם לאחר זמן, כדפרישית נמי לרב ספרא. **משום** צער לידה חיישינן. וא"ת: כיון דאין בנים בלא סימנים – משעת העיבור נבדוק קמי לידה, ואי ליכא סימנין – ליכא למיחש שמא נשרו, דאכתי לא בא צער לידה! וי"ל: דלאו דוקא נקט צער לידה, דה"ה נמי דמשום צער עיבור חיישינן שמא נשרו. ולא נקט צער לידה אלא משום דאקשי ליה ונבדוק את החמות כדי למאן, דהיינו אחר לידה – להכי נקט צער לידה. וה"ה דאי בדקינן קמי לידה ולא אשכחן, דאיכא למיחש דנשרו משום צער עיבור. ואי היה מפרש מילתיה דרב זביד דאין לידת בנים בלא סימנים קאמר – הוי אתי שפיר הא דנקט צער לידה, ולא היינו צריכים לומר משום צער עיבור חיישינן. אבל אי אפשר לומר כן, דא"כ לא הוי משני מידי לרבה בר ליואי. **מתה** בתו או נתגרשה. הא דלא נקט מיאנה או שנמצאת אילונית, משום דמתני' אתא לאשמועינן אפילו כנס ולבסוף גירש, ומיאנה או שנמצאת אילונית אין שום חדוש, דבטלו להו קידושי קמאי. וכך לי כנס ולבסוף מיאנה כמו מיאנה ולבסוף כנס. א"נ: משום דקאי אאחת מכל העריות האלו ומיאנה או שנמצאת אילונית לא שייך בכל העריות. **שלשה** אחים שנים וכו'. לקמן בפרק "ד' אחים" (דף ל. ד"ה גירש) אפרש לה אמאי נקט שלשה אחים. **נשואין** הראשונים מפילים. הכא לא הוה שייך למינקט הראשונים, דליכא הכא תרי נישואין, ומשום ההיא דבפרק "ב"ש" (לקמן קח:) נקט הכי, דתנן: המגרש האשה והחזירה מותרת ליבם ור"א אוסר ומפרש התם טעמא דר"א משום דמספקא ליה אי מיתה מפלת אי נישואים הראשונים מפילים. **תמאן** השתא ותתייבם כו'. ואפי' לר"ג דלית ליה מלמדין את הקטנה שתמאן, לקמן בפ' "ב"ש" (דף קט.) היינו להוציאה מבעלה. א"נ: פריך דהיכא דמיאנה – תתייבם צרתה, ומתני' משמע דאין לה תקנה אלא בחליצה. **לא** צרת ערוה שאני כו'. ה"נ בשעת נפילה נראית כצרת בתו. וא"ת: ומנא ליה דטעמא דרמי בר יחזקאל משום דבשעת נפילה נראית ככלתו? דלמא טעמא דרמי בר יחזקאל גופיה משום דרבי אושעיא, דאינה ממאנת לזיקתו! וי"ל דע"כ טעמא דרמי בר יחזקאל משום דבשעת נפילה נראית ככלתו, מדנקט אסורה לאביו – מכלל דלעלמא שריא, ואי טעמא משום דאינה ממאנת לזיקתו – אסורה נמי לעלמא. וא"ת: א"כ תקשה ברייתא דרמי בר יחזקאל לר' אושעיא! ותירץ הר"ר משה כהן: דאיכא למימר דמיירי כשחלצה, ולהכי שריא לעלמא, ולא משום דממאנת לזיקתו. א"נ: כשמיאנה ביבם אחר שנתייבמה, דליכא זיקה. ומ"מ אסורה לאביו – משום דבשעת נפילה נראית ככלתו.

מאי

מסורת הש"ס

לעיל ג. | לקמן ל. | [נ"ל את אשתו] | נ"א בתרא | [לקמן ל:] | [שם עירובין עו. ר"ה לב: לג. כתובות נח. הוריות ב:] | לקמן קז. קידושין מה. ע"ש | לעיל יב. לקמן קז: | [לעיל ג:.] | [לעיל ט.] לקמן כז. עדיות פ"ד מ"ח | לעיל ח.

עין משפט נר מצוה

נא א מיי' פ"ו מהלכות יבום הלכה כא טוש"ע אה"ע סימן קעג סעי' ז:

נב ב מיי' שם הלכה יב טוש"ע אה"ע שם סעיף ב:

[שבת לב: וש"נ ועי' תוס' כתובות עה: ד"ה תברא]

תוספות חד מקמאי

מחזיר גרושתו כולן מותרות: **מתני'** ב"ש מכשירין וב"ה פוסלין לכהונה דנבעלה לפסול לה דכתיב ובת כהן כי תהיה לאיש זר [היא] בתרומת הקדשים לא תאכל כגון שנבעלה לזר אצלה פסלה לתרומה ולכהונה מק"ו הגרושה דמותרת בתרומה אסורה לכהונה זו שאסורה [בתרומה] אינו דין שאסורה בכהונה והכי אי' בפ' אלמנה לכהן גדול והתם אסיק' דזר אצלו מעיקרא בעי' לאפוקי מחזיר גרושתו דלאו זר מעיקרא הוא ולא פסלה לא לתרומה ולא לכהונה דהא פסול כהונה מתרומה קאתי אבל בחייבי כריתות אע"ג דלאו זר מעיקרא הוה פסלה לתרומה ולכהונה מק"ו וה"נ אמרינן בשלהי פרקין נהי נמי דעשו והא"ר יהושע אין ממזר מחייבי כריתות ומאי מפסלא. א) והלכה כב"ה נהי דממזר לא הוי פגום מיהא הוי דאתי בק"ו מאלמנה ולא פריך מה לאלמנה שכן היא עצמה מתחללת כדפריך בהא שמעתתא גבי מחזיר גרושתו וש"מ דבחייבי כריתות היא עצמה מתחללת ואע"ג דלאו זר מעיקרא הוא:

א) נראה דצ"ל ומאי מפסלא אפי' אם הלכה כב"ה:

הגהות הב"ח

(א) רש"י ד"ה וכנסה וכו' של זה הראשונה דהויא לה צרת: (ב) ד"ה למאמרו וכו' בפ' ר"ג דצריכה: (ג) ד"ה הכא נמי וכו' ליבם והוצרכה למאן בו: (ד) ד"ה שם וכו' שהן נכרים אצל זה: (ה) ד"ה אמו וכו' ואחות אביו ואחותו מאביו ואשת אחיו: (ו) תוס' ד"ה ורב זביד וכו' ומיהו זימנין איתא מדפריך.

גליון הש"ס

גמ' רב אשי אמר סברא היא. ע' לעיל דף ג ע"א תד"ה על סוף: **שם** נשואין הראשונים מפילים. לקמן דף פד ע"ב: **שם** ה"נ משעת נפילה. עיין לקמן דף כט ע"א תד"ה אי כרבי אלעזר.

חלצו, ב"ש פוסלין מן הכהונה, ובית הלל מכשירין. נתייבמו, בית שמאי מכשירין ובית הלל פוסלין. אע"פ שאלו *אוסרים ואלו מתירין, אלו פוסלין ואלו מכשירין — לא נמנעו בית שמאי מלישא נשים מבית הלל, ולא בית הלל מבית שמאי. כל הטהרות והטמאות שהיו אלו מטהרים ואלו מטמאין — לא נמנעו עושין טהרות אלו על גבי אלו.§ **גמ'** אמר רבי שמעון בן פזי: מאי טעמא דבית שמאי — דכתיב °"לא תהיה אשת המת החוצה לאיש זר", — "חוצה" מכלל דאיכא פנימית. ואמר רחמנא: "לא תהיה". ובית הלל: מיבעי להו לכדרב יהודה אמר רב. *דאמר רב יהודה אמר רב מנין שאין קידושין תופסין ביבמה, שנאמר "לא תהיה אשת המת החוצה לאיש זר" — לא תהיה בה הויה(א) לזר. ובית שמאי: מי כתיב "לחוץ"? "חוצה" כתיב. ובית הלל: כיון דכתיב "חוצה" כמאן דכתיב "לחוץ" דמי. דתניא, ר' נחמיה אומר: כל תיבה שצריכה למ"ד בתחלתה — הטיל לה הכתוב ה"א בסופה. ותנא דבי ר' ישמעאל: כגון "אלים" °"אלימה" "מחנים" °"מחנימה", "מצרים" °"מצרימה", °"דבלתימה", °"ירושלימה(ב)" °"מדברה". ובית שמאי, דרב יהודה אמר רב מנא להו? מ"לאיש זר" נפקא. ובית הלל נמי, תיפוק להו מ"לאיש זר"! אין הכי נמי "חוצה" למה לי — לרבות הארוסה. ואידך: מ"חוצה" "החוצה" — ואידך: "חוצה" "החוצה" לא משמע להו. רבא אמר: טעמייהו דבית שמאי, *אדאין איסור חל על איסור. תינח היכא *דנשא מת ואחר כך נשא חי — לא אתי איסור אחות אשה וחייל אאיסור אשת אח, אלא נשא חי ואחר כך נשא מת, אחות אשה קדים! כיון דלא אתי איסור אשת אח וחייל אאיסור אחות אשה — הויא לה צרת ערוה שלא במקום מצוה, ושריא.§ "חלצו, בית שמאי פוסלים וכו'".§ פשיטא! לאפוקי מדרבי יוחנן בן נורי, דאמר: *בואו ונתקן להם לצרות שיהו חולצות ולא מתייבמות — קמ"ל דבית הלל מכשירים.§ "נתייבמו בית הלל פוסלין כו'".§ הא תו למה לי? איידי דתנא חלצו, תנא נמי נתייבמו. תנן התם: *במגילה נקראת באחד עשר ובשנים עשר ובשלשה עשר ובארבעה עשר ובחמשה עשר, לא פחות ולא יותר. אמר ליה ר"ל לר' יוחנן: איקרי כאן °"לא תתגודדו" — לא תעשו אגודות אגודות! האי "לא תתגודדו" מיבעי ליה לגופיה, דאמר רחמנא: גלא תעשו חבורה על מת! א"כ לימא קרא "לא תגודדו", מאי(ג) "תתגודדו" — שמע מינה להכי הוא דאתא. ואימא כוליה להכי הוא דאתא? אם כן לימא קרא "לא תגודו" מאי "לא תתגודדו" — שמע מינה תרתי. א"ל: עד כאן לא שנית *דמקום שנהגו לעשות מלאכה בערבי פסחים עד חצות — עושין, מקום שנהגו שלא לעשות — אין עושין? א"ל: *אמינא לך אנא איסורא, *דאמר רב שמן בר אבא אמר ר' יוחנן: °"לקיים את ימי הפורים בזמניהם", זמנים הרבה תיקנו להם חכמים, ואת אמרת לי מנהגא! והתם לאו איסורא הויא? *והתנן: (*בלילה) בית שמאי אוסרין ובית הלל מתירין! אמר ליה: *התם הרואה אומר מלאכה הוא דלית ליה. והא בית שמאי מתירין הצרות לאחים, ובית הלל אוסרים!

מי

תורה אור

דברים כה | שמות טו | ש"ב יז | בראשית יג | במדבר לג | יחזקאל ח | דה"א ה | דברים יד | אסתר ט

חלצו. הצרות מן האחין. ב"ש פוסלין מן הכהונה. שחליצתה חליצה. וב"ה מכשירין. לפי שחליצתן שלא לצורך, והרי כחולצת מן הנכרי. נתייבמו. לאחים. בית שמאי מכשירין. אותן לכהנים, אם נתאלמנו מיבמיהן. ובית הלל פוסלין. שנבעלו לאסור להן, והנבעלה לפסול לה עשאה זונה, והזונה אסורה לכהונה. לא נמנעו כו'. אע"פ שבני הצרה שנתייבמו כב"ש ממזרים [הם לב"ה], שהרי באיסור אשת אח היא עליהם, ואשת אח בכרת, ובני עריות שהן חייבי כריתות ממזרים הם, כדאמרינן בפירקין — אפ"ה לא נמנעו ב"ה מלישא נשים מב"ש, לפי שהיו מודיעים להם אותן הבאות מן הצרות, ופורשים. אלו על גבי אלו. אלו משאילים כליהם לאלו. גמ' לא תהיה אשת המת החוצה. החיצונה, שהיא נכרית ליבם, לא תהיה לזר. מכלל דאיכא פנימית. בהדה, קרובה ליבם. שאין קידושין תופסין ביבמה. יבמה שלא חלצה, מנין אם נתקדשה לשוק שאין קידושין תופסין (ד) — אע"ג דחייבי לאוין בעלמא תפסי בהו קידושין. ת"ל כו' לא תהא בה הויה. אינן תופסין. חוצה כתיב. דמשמע חיצונה. לרבות ארוסה. שאם נתארמלה מן האירוסין צריכה ליבם כנשואה. וחוצה משמע חיצונה, שלא נתקרבה עדיין לביאה. אין איסור. אשת אח חל על בתו של זה אצל אביה, הלכך לא רמיא קמיה לייבומי, והויא כמאן דליתא. וכן באחות אשה, וכולן. והכי מפרשא מילתיה דרבא במסקנא דמילתא. ומיהו, הא דפריך: תינח היכא דנשא כו' — לא ידע מילתיה דרבא, וסבר דרבא באחות אשה וכיוצא בה לחודייהו קאי, שקורבתו ע"י קדושין. דלא אתי איסור אחות אשה וחייל אאיסור אשת אח. והויא כנכרית. פשיטא. כיון דלב"ש זקוקות ליבם, פשיטא אם חלצו פסולות. ולב"ה, כיון דפטרי להו מזיקת יבום — אם חלצו כשרות לכהונה, דלאו חליצה היא. דר' יוחנן. לקמן (דף יד:) בברייתא. בואו ונתקן לצרות. העריות שיהו חולצות. וכיון דבעו חליצה — חליצתה פוסלת אפי' לב"ה. קמ"ל דב"ה אפי' תקנתא דרבנן לית להו בצרות דליחלצו. וב"ה פוסלין. דזונה היא, ופסולה לכהונה. אבל מתרומה דבי נשא לא מיפסלא בבעילת כרת, אלא בבעילת חלל ונתין וממזר וגוי ועבד, בפרק "אלמנה לכ"ג" (לקמן סח:). לא תעשו אגודות. דנראה כנוהגין ב' תורות, כשקורין כפרים את המגילה ביום כניסה, ועיירות גדולות בי"ד, ומוקפין חומה בט"ו. א"כ לכתוב קרא לא תגודדו. דמשמע לשון גדידה וחבורה. ואימא כוליה להכי הוא דאתא. שלא תעשו אגודות. א"כ לכתוב לא תגודו. מדלא כתיב תגודו, לשון אגודה. לא שנית ע"כ מקום שנהגו כו'. היה לך להשיב תשובה זו. אמינא לך אנא איסורא. דאסרי להו רבנן לבני הכרכים, דאי בעו למיקרא בחמיסר — לא מצו, וכן בני ט"ו בי"ד, ודמיא לשתי תורות. ואת אמרת לי מנהגא. דהתם לכ"ע שרי, ומיהו באתרא דאתמור — לא ישנה את דרכו, מפני המחלוקת. ופרכינן והתם איסורא ליכא. בתמיה. והא קתני התם בלילה. בליל בדיקת חמץ, ב"ש אוסרים וב"ה מתירים לעשות מלאכה, ואיכא דעבדי כב"ה ואיכא דעבדי כבית שמאי, והרי כאן אגודות! א"ל התם. לא דמי לשתי תורות, דהרואה את זה שאין עושה מלאכה אומר דאין לו מה לעשות.

בת

מאי טעמא דב"ש. וא"ת: ומאי קנעי ליה? דלמא מוקמי "לצרור" לכדר"ש (לעיל דף ח:). "ועליה" לכדרבי! ואומר רבינו יצחק: משום דמסתברא ליה לדרוש ל"צרור" לענין צרות — אי לאו דשמעיה בשום דוכתא דשריא. וא"ת: אכתי, כי דרשי נמי חוצה מכלל דאיכא פנימית — נדרוש מ"לצרור" למיסר צרה שלא במקום מצוה! וי"ל: דליכא למדרש הכי. דהא כתיב "לגלות ערותה" — דחדא. ולמקום מצוה לא איצטריך דמ"חוצה" נפקא, אלא לשלא במקום מצוה. **לכדרב** יהודה אמר רב כו'. ה"נ המ"ל לכדשמואל, דפליג עליה דרב, ב"האשה רבה" (לקמן דף צב: ושם) ומוקי קרא דלצאו הוא דאתא. **כיון** דכתיב חוצה כמאן דכתיב לחוץ דמי. ואע"ג דכתיב נמי" ה"א בתחלה, דכתיב "החוצה" — היינו נמי אל החוץ, כמו "המדברה" (שמות ד) דהוי אל המדבר: **לרבות** את הארוסה. אר"י, דאיצטריך *לרבויי ארוסה משום דכתיב "בית אחיו", ובפ"ק דיומא (דף יג.) משמע ד"בית" נשואה משמע. **דלא** אתי איסור אחות אשה וחייל אאיסור אשת אח. וא"ת: כיון דאיסור אחות אשה לא חייל — תתייבם ערוה גופה! וי"ל: דאיסור אחות אשה מיתלא תלי וקאי, אי פקע איסור אשת אח — אתי וחייל, הלכך לא פקע*: א) **בית** הלל פוסלים. פי' בקונטרס: מכהונה, ולא מתרומה. וא"א לומר כן, (ה) דמחייבי כריתות זונה היא, כדאמרינן ב"החולץ" (לקמן מד:) גבי הנושא את חלוצתו, וזונה אסורה בתרומה, כמו שנפרש שם בע"ה (ד"ה "הכא"). ורש"י עצמו חזר בסוף פירקא (דף טו: ד"ה "היא עצמה") גבי מה לאלמנה שכן היא עצמה מתחללת: **דאמר** רחמנא לא תעשו חבורה על מת. והא דאמרינן בסוף פרק "ד' מיתות" (סנהדרין דף סח. ושם) גבי ר"ע שהיה מכה עצמו על ר"א שנפטר עד שהיה דמו שותת לארץ! ואומר רבינו יצחק: דאיכא למימר דדרך שריטה אסר רחמנא דוקא. א"נ: אתורה היה מצטער, כדאמרינן התם: הרבה מעות יש לי ואין שולחני כו'.

תוספות ישנים

א) וא"ת מ"ט דב"ה. וא"ל דסברי איסור חל על איסור משום דגלי קרא ללצרור דמשמע שהצרה אסורה דא"כ אמאי אמרינן בכולא תלמודא דאין איסור חל על איסור נילף מהכא שיחול. ואין סברא לומר דנפלוג כלהו אמוראי דאמרינן אין איסור חל על איסור אבית הלל דסבירא לן הלכתא כוותייהו. וי"ל דודאי סברי ב"ה דאין איסור חל על איסור אכן ידחו ויאמרו דכיון דהך טעמא לא מהניא מידי גבי ערוה כדפרי' איסור אחות אשה מתלא תלי וקאי וכו' מעתה יש לנו לומר צרתה כמו כן דהיא חשובה צרת ערוה מקרא דלצרור. וא"כ היא תיתסר מהאי טעמא דפרישית באחות אשה. ותימה לפי פירושא דפרישית לעיל דכל זמן דאיכא לאוקמי לצרור בצרות מוקמינן כיון דליכא קרא לאפוקי וא"כ קשה מאי טעמא דב"ש הלא אין זו רק סברא דאין איסור חל על איסור ומצינו למימר דחייל מקרא דלצרור דמשמע צרות דליכא לאוקמי במלתא אחריתי וליכא שום קרא למעט צרות ולהתירן כ"א אותה סברא דאין איסור חל על איסור. ואין סברא לומ' שאותה הסברא תדחה הפסוק כיון דליכא לאוקמי במלתא אחריתי ותירץ הקדוש מרא"ש דאיכא לאוקמי קרא דלצרור כשבאו בבת אחת אשת אח ואחות אשה וכלהו עריות דמתני' נמי משכחת לה כבת אחת כגון בתו שקדש בתו לאחיו פחותה מבת ג' שנים וחלו אשת אח ובתו יחד שאינה חשובה ערוה עד שתהא בת ג"ש וכלהו בכה"ג. ותימה דנשא מת ומת ואח"כ נשא חי ומ"ט דב"ש דהא ליכא למימר דאין איסור חל על איסור שהרי בשעה היתה אשת אח במקום מצוה וא"כ אתי איסור אחות אשה חייל. וי"ל בכי האי גוונא ב"ה נמי שרי דלא היו צרות ערוה מעולם: תינח היכא דנשא מת וכו' המקשה היה סבור דרבא אמר למלתיה גבי אחות אשה ולהכי פריך ליה כלפריך ולפום מסקנא לגבי כלהו עריות מצי למימר טעמא שפיר

נג א מיי' פי"ז מהל' איסורי ביאה הל' ח:
נד ב מיי' פ"א מהל' מגילה הלכה ד ו ז סמג עשין ד טוש"ע א"ח סי' תרפח:
נה ג מיי' פי"ב מהל' עבודת כוכבים הל' יא סמג לאוין סב טוש"ע י"ד סימן קפ סעיף ו:
נו ד מיימן פ"ח מהל' י"ט הל' יח סמג לאוין עה טוש"ע א"ח סי' תסח סעיף ג ד:

[וכך מבואר להדיא בגמ' יומא יג: אלא מעתה ארוסה לא תתייבם [וע"ש ברש"י] ומשני הס"ם החוצה לרבות הארוסה וכבר מלוה לייבם על סוס וכו' דלא קאמרי הכי משמיה דגמרא]

[וכ"ה בסוגיא דלקמן לב. להדיא ככל מ"ש תוס' הכא ומלוה לייבם]

כרי"ף ורא"ש לא גרס' אוסרים ומתירים וכן בעדיות פ"ד מ"ח ליתא

לקמן לב: [ונזכר ג"כ לקמן מט: נז.]

[חולין קיג.]

לעיל ח.

[לקמן יד: כז.]

מגילה ב.

פסחים נ.

[נדה סו.]

מגילה ב.

פסחים נה. [נ"ל הלילה] שם נה:

הגהות הב"ח

(א) גמ' לא תהיה בה הויה וב"ש כנ"ל ותיבת לזר נמחק: (ב) שם המדברה: (ג) שם מאי לא תתגודדו ש"מ להכי: (ד) רש"י ד"ה שאין וכו' תופסין בה אע"ג לחייבי לאוין בעלמא דליכא כרת תפסי בהו קידושין ת"ל כו' הס"ד ואח"כ מ"ה לא תהא וכו' תופסין בה הס"ד: (ה) תוס' ד"ה בית הלל וכו' דמחייבי כריתות. נ"ב עיין פ' אלמנה דף ס"ח:

גליון הש"ס

תום' ד"ה מאי טעמא וכו' דלמא מוקמי לצרור וכו'. ק"ל על לשונם הזהב דלמא ולא הקשו ביותר דהא גם לפי האמת דיליף ב"ש מן החוצה ע"כ דרשי' לצרור לכדר"ש ועליה לכדר' וצ"ע:

מִי סָבְרַתְּ עָשׂוּ ב"ש כְּדִבְרֵיהֶם? לֹא עָשׂוּ ב"ש כְּדִבְרֵיהֶם. וְר' יוֹחָנָן אָמַר: עָשׂוּ וְעָשׂוּ, וּבִפְלוּגְתָּא [דְּרַב וּשְׁמוּאֵל], דְּרַב אוֹמֵר: לֹא עָשׂוּ ב"ש כְּדִבְרֵיהֶם, וּשְׁמוּאֵל אָמַר: עָשׂוּ וְעָשׂוּ. אֵימַת? אִילֵימָא קוֹדֶם בַּת קוֹל – מ"ט דְּמ"ד לֹא עָשׂוּ? וְאֶלָּא לְאַחַר בַּת קוֹל – מ"ט דְּמ"ד עָשׂוּ? אִי בָּעֵית אֵימָא קוֹדֶם בַּת קוֹל, וְאִי בָּעֵית אֵימָא לְאַחַר בַּת קוֹל. אִי בָּעֵית אֵימָא קוֹדֶם בַּת קוֹל: וּכְגוֹן דְּב"ה רוּבָּא, לְמ"ד לֹא עָשׂוּ דְּהָא ב"ה רוּבָּא, וּמ"ד עָשׂוּ – כִּי אָזְלִינַן בָּתַר רוּבָּא הֵיכָא דְּכִי הֲדָדֵי נִינְהוּ, הָכָא – בֵּית שַׁמַּאי מְחַדְּדֵי טְפֵי. וְאִי בָּעֵית אֵימָא לְאַחַר בַּת קוֹל: מ"ד לֹא עָשׂוּ – דְּהָא נָפְקָא בַּת קוֹל, וּמ"ד עָשׂוּ – רַבִּי יְהוֹשֻׁעַ הִיא, *דַּאֲמַר: אֵין מַשְׁגִּיחִין בְּבַת קוֹל. וּמ"ד עָשׂוּ, קָרֵינַן כָּאן °"לֹא תִתְגּוֹדְדוּ" – לֹא תַּעֲשׂוּ אֲגוּדּוֹת אֲגוּדּוֹת! אָמַר אַבָּיֵי: [א]כִּי אָמְרִינַן "לֹא תִתְגּוֹדְדוּ" – כְּגוֹן שְׁתֵּי בָּתֵּי דִינִים בְּעִיר אַחַת, הַלָּלוּ מוֹרִים כְּדִבְרֵי ב"ש וְהַלָּלוּ מוֹרִים כְּדִבְרֵי ב"ה. אֲבָל שְׁתֵּי בָּתֵּי דִינִים בִּשְׁתֵּי עֲיָירוֹת – לֵית לָן בָּהּ. אֲמַר לֵיהּ רָבָא: וְהָא ב"ש וּב"ה כִּשְׁתֵּי בָּתֵּי דִינִים בְּעִיר אַחַת דָּמֵי! אֶלָּא אֲמַר רָבָא: כִּי אָמְרִינַן "לֹא תִתְגּוֹדְדוּ" – כְּגוֹן ב"ד בְּעִיר אַחַת, פֶּלֶג מוֹרִין כְּדִבְרֵי ב"ש וּפֶלֶג מוֹרִין כְּדִבְרֵי ב"ה. אֲבָל שְׁתֵּי בָּתֵּי דִינִין בְּעִיר אַחַת – לֵית לָן בָּהּ. תָּא שְׁמַע: *בִּמְקוֹמוֹ שֶׁל רַבִּי אֱלִיעֶזֶר הָיוּ כּוֹרְתִים עֵצִים לַעֲשׂוֹת פֶּחָמִים בְּשַׁבָּת, לַעֲשׂוֹת בַּרְזֶל. בִּמְקוֹמוֹ שֶׁל ר' יוֹסֵי הַגְּלִילִי הָיוּ אוֹכְלִים בְּשַׂר עוֹף בְּחָלָב. בִּמְקוֹמוֹ שֶׁל רַבִּי אֱלִיעֶזֶר אִין, בִּמְקוֹמוֹ שֶׁל רַבִּי עֲקִיבָא – לָא. *דְּתַנְיָא, *[ב]כְּלָל אָמַר רַבִּי עֲקִיבָא: כָּל מְלָאכָה שֶׁאֶפְשָׁר לַעֲשׂוֹתָהּ מֵעֶ"ש – אֵין דּוֹחָה אֶת הַשַּׁבָּת. וְהַאי מַאי תְּיוּבְתָּא? מְקוֹמוֹת מְקוֹמוֹת שָׁאנֵי! °וּדְקָאָרֵי לָהּ מַאי קָאָרֵי לָהּ? ס"ד אָמִינָא: מִשּׁוּם חוּמְרָא דְּשַׁבָּת כְּמָקוֹם אֶחָד דָּמֵי – קמ"ל. ת"ש, דְּרַבִּי אַבָּהוּ, כִּי אִיקְלַע *לְאַתְרֵיהּ דְּרַבִּי יְהוֹשֻׁעַ בֶּן לֵוִי הֲוָה מְטַלְטֵל שְׁרָגָא, וְכִי אִיקְלַע לְאַתְרֵיהּ דְּר' יוֹחָנָן – לָא הֲוָה מְטַלְטֵל שְׁרָגָא. וְהַאי, מַאי קוּשְׁיָא? וְלָא אָמְרִינַן (א)מְקוֹמוֹת שָׁאנֵי? אֲנַן הָכִי קָאָמְרִינַן: ר' אַבָּהוּ, הֵיכִי עָבֵיד הָכָא הָכִי וְהֵיכִי עָבֵיד הָכָא הָכִי? רַבִּי אַבָּהוּ כְּר' יְהוֹשֻׁעַ בֶּן לֵוִי סְבִירָא לֵיהּ, וְכִי מִקְּלַע לְאַתְרֵיהּ דְּרַבִּי יוֹחָנָן – לָא הֲוָה מְטַלְטֵל, מִשּׁוּם כְּבוֹדוֹ דְּרַבִּי יוֹחָנָן. וְהָאִיכָּא שַׁמָּעָא! דְּמוֹדַע לֵיהּ לְשַׁמָּעָא. ת"ש: אע"פ שֶׁאֵלּוּ אוֹסְרִים וְאֵלּוּ מַתִּירִים, לֹא נִמְנְעוּ ב"ש מִלִּישָּׂא נָשִׁים מִבּ"ה, וְלֹא ב"ה מִבּ"ש. אִי אָמְרַתְּ בִּשְׁלָמָא לֹא עָשׂוּ, מִשּׁוּם הָכִי לֹא נִמְנְעוּ. אֶלָּא אִי אָמְרַתְּ עָשׂוּ – אַמַּאי לֹא נִמְנְעוּ? בִּשְׁלָמָא ב"ש מִבּ"ה לֹא נִמְנְעוּ – דִּבְנֵי חַיָּיבֵי לָאוִין נִינְהוּ. אֶלָּא ב"ה מִבֵּית שַׁמַּאי – אַמַּאי לֹא נִמְנְעוּ? בְּנֵי חַיָּיבֵי כָּרֵיתוֹת מַמְזֵרִים נִינְהוּ! וְכִי תֵּימָא קָסָבְרִי ב"ה דְּאֵין מַמְזֵר מֵחַיָּיבֵי כָּרֵיתוֹת – *וְהָאֲמַר רַבִּי אֶלְעָזָר: אַף עַל פִּי שֶׁנֶּחְלְקוּ ב"ש וּב"ה בְּצָרוֹת – מוֹדִים שֶׁאֵין מַמְזֵר אֶלָּא מִמִּי שֶׁאִיסּוּרוֹ אִיסּוּר עֶרְוָה, וְעָנוּשׁ כָּרֵת! אֶלָּא לָאו שְׁמַע מִינָּהּ – לֹא עָשׂוּ! לָא, לְעוֹלָם עָשׂוּ, דְּמוֹדְעֵי לְהוּ וּפָרְשִׁי. וְהָכִי נַמִּי מִסְתַּבְּרָא, דְּקָתָנֵי סֵיפָא: כָּל הַטְּהָרוֹת וְכָל הַטֻּמְאוֹת שֶׁהָיוּ אֵלּוּ מְטַהֲרִין וְאֵלּוּ מְטַמְּאִין – לֹא נִמְנְעוּ עוֹשִׂים טְהָרוֹת אֵלּוּ עַל גַּבֵּי אֵלּוּ.

אי

רש"י

בת קול. בְּעֵירוּבִין בְּפ"ק (דף יג.): יָצְאתָה בַּת קוֹל וְאָמְרָה הֲלָכָה כְּב"ה. דְּכִי הֲדָדֵי נִינְהוּ. בְּחָכְמָה. ר' יְהוֹשֻׁעַ הִיא. בְּפֶ' "הַזָּהָב". הָיוּ כּוֹרְתִים עֵצִים בְּשַׁבָּת לַעֲשׂוֹת פֶּחָמִים. לְבוֹ בַּיּוֹם, כְּדֵי לַעֲשׂוֹת בַּרְזֶל, אִיזְמֵל שֶׁל מִילָה. דְּקָסָבַר ר"א: מַכְשִׁירֵי מִצְוָה דּוֹחִין שַׁבָּת כְּמִצְוָה עַצְמָהּ. בְּשַׂר עוֹף בְּחָלָב. שֶׁהָיָה דּוֹרֵשׁ: "בַּחֲלֵב אִמּוֹ" – מִי שֶׁיֵּשׁ לוֹ חֲלֵב אֵם, יָצָא בְּשַׂר עוֹף שֶׁאֵין לוֹ חֲלֵב אֵם. וְהָכִי אָמְרִי' בְּפֶ' "כָּל הַבָּשָׂר". כְּלָל אָמַר ר"ע. לְגַבֵּי מִילָה בְּאִיסּוּר שַׁבָּת. מַאי קָאָרֵי לָהּ. הָא כְּבָר שָׁנוּ לְעֵיל: כִּי אָמְרִינַן לֹא תִתְגּוֹדְדוּ כו'. מְטַלְטֵל שְׁרָגָא. נֵר שֶׁהִדְלִיקוּ בּוֹ בַּשַּׁבָּת וְכָבָה. דְּסָבַר לָהּ רַבִּי יְהוֹשֻׁעַ כְּר"ש דְּלֵית לֵיהּ מוּקְצֶה. וְר' יוֹחָנָן סָבַר לָהּ כְּר' יְהוּדָה דְּאִית לֵיהּ מוּקְצֶה, אֲפִי' שֶׁלֹּא מֵחֲמַת אִיסּוּר. וְהָא אִיכָּא שַׁמָּעָא. דְּרַבִּי אַבָּהוּ דְּלָא מַסֵּיק אַדַּעְתֵּיהּ וּמְטַלְטֵל בְּאַתְרֵיהּ דְּר' יוֹחָנָן, הוֹאִיל וַחֲזִי לְר' אַבָּהוּ בְּעָלְמָא דִּמְטַלְטֵל. בְּנֵי חַיָּיבֵי לָאוִין נִינְהוּ. הָנָךְ דְּב"ה, שֶׁהַצָּרוֹת נִישָּׂאוֹת לַשּׁוּק בְּלֹא חֲלִיצָה, אֲפִי' לְב"ש דְּאָמְרִי חֲלִיצָה בָּעֵי – בְּלָאו בְּעָלְמָא נִינְהוּ "לֹא תִהְיֶה אֵשֶׁת הַמֵּת", וְאֵין מַמְזֵר אֶלָּא מֵחַיָּיבֵי כְּרֵיתוֹת, כִּדְאָמְרִי' לְקַמָּן בְּ"הַחוֹלֵץ" (דף מט.). חַיָּיבֵי כְּרֵיתוֹת נִינְהוּ. כֵּיוָן דְּצָרַת הַבַּת פְּטוּרָה, הַמְיַיבְּמָהּ עוֹמֵד בְּאִיסּוּר אֵשֶׁת אָח בְּכָרֵת. אֵין מַמְזֵר מֵחַיָּיבֵי כְּרֵיתוֹת. אֶלָּא מֵחַיָּיבֵי מִיתוֹת ב"ד, כְּגוֹן אִמּוֹ וַחֲמוֹתוֹ וְכַלָּתוֹ וְכַיּוֹצֵא בָּהֶן. וְכָל הָנָךְ דְּאִיסּוּר אַחֲוָה – לֵית בְּהוּ מִיתָה. דְּמוֹדְעֵי לְהוּ. ב"ש לְב"ה: דְּעוּ שֶׁהַמִּשְׁפָּחָה זוֹ מִצָּרַת עֶרְוָה שֶׁנִּתְיַיבְּמָה בָּאָה, וּפִרְשׁוּ. ע"ג אֵלּוּ. מַשְׁאִילִין כֵּלִים אֵלּוּ לָאֵלּוּ, וּב"ה מַחְמִירִין בְּטָהֳרוֹת טְפֵי.

ומאי

תוספות

מי סברא עשו וכו'. תימה: שלא הקשה רבי יוחנן לר"ל מההיא דמייתי בסמוך: במקומו של ר' אליעזר היו כורתין כו'! וי"ל: דאין חוששין לדקדק כל כך על דבריו, דממילא הוה מוקשה ממגילה, כמו שהקשה בעצמו. לא עשו ב"ש כדבריהם. תימה: הא אשכחן דעשו, דהטה ר' טרפון כדברי ב"ש (ברכות דף י:). והלל שהביא עולתו לעזרה, וחברו עליו תלמידי שמאי (ביצה דף כ.). ותניא בפרק "אלו טרפות" (חולין דף מד.): הרוצה לעשות כדברי ב"ש – עושה, ומוקי לה קודם בת קול. ומיהו, בלאו הכי מוכח בשמעתין דעשו. רבי יהושע היא דאמר אין משגיחין בבת קול. וא"ת: ומ"ש דלא קי"ל כבת קול דר"א*, אלא אמרינן בכל דוכתי דשמותי הוא ואין הלכה כמותו. וכבת קול דב"ה קי"ל, דהלכה כב"ה! וי"ל: משום דבת קול דר"א לא יצאה אלא לכבודו, שאמר מן השמים יוכיחו, כדאמר התם. א"נ: בההיא בת קול שהיתה כנגד רבים, דרבנן הוו רובא(ב) – דודאי אין הלכה. אבל כבת קול דב"ה קי"ל, משום דהוו ב"ה רובא, אלא דב"ש מחדדי טפי. וא"ת: ודלמא רבי יהושע נמי, דוקא התם קאמר דאין משגיחין, כדפירשנו, אבל בעלמא לא? וי"ל: מדנקט ר' יהושע האי לישנא, ואמר לא בשמים היא – ש"מ דבכל דוכתא אית ליה דאין משגיחין. כי אמרי' לא תתגודדו כגון שתי בתי דינין בעיר אחת כו'. וא"ת: מה תירץ ממגילה דבעיר אחת היו קורין לבני העיר בי"ד ולבני כפרים היו מקדימים ליום הכניסה! ואומר הרב רבי חיים(ג): דבני כפרים היו קורין *בעירם. כדמוכח בירושלמי. והשתא הוו שתי בתי דינים בב' עיירות, דבכי האי גוונא לא שייך "לא תתגודדו" אפילו לאביי. והא דקרי ליה יום הכניסה – לפי שבעירם היו מתאספים לבא לבית הכנסת בשני ובחמישי לקרות התורה. וכן נראה, דאמר בירושלמי דבן עיר אין מוציא בן (ד)כרך, דכל שאין מחויב בדבר אין מוציא אחרים ידי חובתם. וכיון שבני הכפרים היו בקיאים לקרות – ודאי היו קורין בעירם. במקומו של רבי אליעזר כו'. במתכוין היו מביאים עצמם שיהיו צריכים לכך, משום חיבוב מצוה. לא הוה מטלטל שרגא. וא"ת: התם משום דהרואה אומר אין צריך לטלטל! וי"ל: דאפילו היה נופל על טליתו לא היה מטלטל. לא הוה מטלטל משום כבודו של רבי יוחנן. ואע"ג דבסוף שבת (דף קנו: ושם) פסיק רבי יוחנן כר"ש במוקצה מחמת איסור, הכא בהדליקו בו אותה שבת איירי, כדפיר' בקונטרס, דחמיר טפי משום דדחייה בידים. אבל אין לפרש דהכא איירי במוקצה מחמת מיאוס, דהא מוקצה מחמת איסור חמיר טפי, לפירוש ר"ת שפירש בספ"ק דשבת (דף יט: ושם) גבי כרכי דזוזי. ועוד: דעל מוקצה מחמת מיאוס א"ר יוחנן בפ' "כירה" (ד' מה:*) אנו אין לנו בנר אלא כר"ש. בשלמא ב"ש לא נמנעו כו'. וא"ת: ואמאי לא נמנעו משום צרה עצמה, כדאמרי' לקמן בשמעתין? וי"ל: דצרה עצמה לא שכיחא כולי האי כמו בני הצרות, שהאחת יולדת כמה בנים.

בשלמא

תוספות ישנים

אין משגיחין בבת קול. פי' בעירובין: והא איכא שמעא. פ"ה דמטלטל ליה באתרי' דר' יוחנן ומשני דמודע ליה הזהר בכבוד ר' יוחנן ואל תהי מטלטל הנר במקומו ותימה מה ענין זאת הקושיא בכאן גבי אגודות אגודות בשבת הו"ל למפרך ועוד פשיטא דמודע לשמעא שיעשה כמוהו. ונראה לפרש והא איכא שמעא שיסבור דשרי לעשות אגודות אגודות לפי שראה רבו מטלטל במקום אחד ובמקום אחר לא היה מטלטל. ומשני דמודע ליה לשמעא ואומר אל תעשה אגודות. דהא שראית שאין אני מטלטלה במקומו של ר' יוחנן אין זה משום איסור טלטול אלא משום כבודו של ר' יוחנן: בני חייבי לאוין כשרים נינהו. וא"ת משכחת לה דב"ה לב"ש חייבי כריתות לר' שמעון דפטר אחיות בזיקה מחלוצה ומיבום כגון צרת בתו ויבמה אחרת דנפול קמי שמעון והם אחיות שנפלו משני אחין ור' שמעון אמר א) לקמן כיון שהם אחיות בזיקה לא יהא לו לקוחין אפילו באחת מהן דלב"ה מייבם שמעון יבמתו הראשונה אחות זקוקתו לצרת ערוה אינה זקוקה לו דהיא אסורה לו ולב"ש לא יוכל לייבמה שהיא אשת אח שלא במקום מצוה שהרי אחות זקוקתו היא דלצרת ערוה שרי' לה אליבא דב"ש וי"ל דפריך הכי אפילו לרבנן תקשי לן אמאי לא נמנעו (ב"ש מב"ה) [ב"ה מב"ש] והה"נ דלר' שמעון תקשי לן אף מב"ה לב"ש אמאי לא נמנעו הא בני חייבי כריתות נינהו כדפרי':

א) נ"ל ור"ש אמר לקמן דף כח ע"ב שכל שתי אחיות שנפלו לצרות זו לזו בזיקה כו'.

תוספות חד מקמאי

ובפלוגתא רב אמר לא עשו ב"ש כדבריהם ושמואל אמר עשו מ"ד לא עשו דב"ה רובא מ"ד עשו כי אזלינן בתר רובא היכא דכי הדדי נינהו הכא ב"ש מחדדי טפי ואב"א לאחר כך ואמר עשו ר' יהושע היא דאמר אין משגיחין בב"ק ומסיק עשו ב"ש כדבריהם ולא הוו מצות אגודות אגודות אלא ב"ד אחד בעיר אחת פלגו מורו כב"ש ופלגו מורו כב"ה אבל שתי ב"ד בעיר אחת לית לן בה:

עין משפט נר מצוה

נז א מיי' פי"ב מהל' עבודת כוכבים הל' יד:

נח ב מיי' פ"ב מהל' מילה הלכה ו סמג עשין נח טוש"ע א"ח סימן שלא סעיף ו טוש"ע י"ד סימן רסו סעיף ב:

הגהות הב"ח

(א) גמ' ולא אמרינן מקומות מקומות שאני: (ב) תוס' ד"ה ר' יהושע וכו' הוו רובא בודאי אין הלכה כבת קול אבל: (ג) ד"ה כי אמרינן וכו' הרב רבי חיים הכהן דבני: (ד) בא"ד דבן עיר אין מוציא בן כפר דכל:

גליון הש"ס

גמ' ודקארי לה מאי קארי לה. כעין זה כתובות עז ע"א ועו ע"ב:

מסורת הש"ס

ברכות נב. ערובין ז. פסחים קיד. [ב"מ נט:] חולין מד.

[ב"מ נט: ושם]

דברים יד

שבת קל. חולין קטז.

עיין בהרא"ש דכתב דהוו כשני ב"ד בעיר אחת

שבת קל. פסחים סו. סנ: מנחות עב. ע.

נ"ל דתנן

שבת מו ע"ש

קידושין עה: [תוספ' פ"א]

[וע"ש היטב תוספות סד"ה אין לנו]

אי אמרת בשלמא דמודעי להו — משום הכי לא נמנעו. אלא אי אמרת דלא מודעי להו, בשלמא ב"ש מב"ה לא נמנעו. דטמאות דב"ה — לב"ש טהרות נינהו, אלא, ב"ה מב"ש למה לא נמנעו? טהרות דב"ש לב"ה טמאות נינהו! אלא לאו דמודעי להו — שמע מינה. ומאי אולמיה דהך מהך? מהו דתימא: צרה — קלא אית לה, קמ"ל. גופא, אמר רבי אלעזר: אע"פ שנחלקו ב"ש וב"ה בצרות — מודים שאין ממזר אלא ממי שאיסורו איסור ערוה וענוש כרת. מאן מודים? אילימא ב"ש לב"ה — פשיטא, בני חייבי לאוין כשרים נינהו! אלא ב"ה לב"ש — היא גופא חייבי כריתות היא! לעולם ב"ש לב"ה, ולאפוקי מדר' עקיבא, דאמר: יש ממזר מחייבי לאוין, קמ"ל דאין ממזר מחייבי לאוין. ת"ש: *אע"פ שנחלקו ב"ש וב"ה בצרות, ובאחיות, בגט ישן, ובספק אשת איש, ובמגרש את אשתו ולנה עמו בפונדק, בכסף ובשוה כסף, בפרוטה ובשוה פרוטה — לא נמנעו ב"ש מלישא נשים מבית הלל, ולא ב"ה מבית שמאי, ללמדך שחיבה וריעות נוהגים זה בזה, לקיים מה שנאמר °"האמת והשלום אהבו" (זכריה ח). ר"ש אומר: נמנעו הן מן הודאי, ולא נמנעו מן הספק. אי אמרת בשלמא עשו — משום הכי נמנעו, אלא אי אמרת לא עשו — אמאי נמנעו? ותסברא, נהי נמי דעשו, בשלמא בית הלל נמנעו מבית שמאי, דחייבי כריתות נינהו, וממזרים הם לב"ה. אלא ב"ש אמאי נמנעו מב"ה? בני חייבי לאוין נינהו, וכשרים נינהו! כדאמר רב נחמן בר יצחק: לא נצרכה אלא לצרה עצמה — ה"נ לא נצרכה אלא לצרה עצמה. ומ"ש מן הודאי — דאיסורא הוא, ספק נמי איסורא הוא! לא תימא מן הספק, אלא אימא: מן הסתם, דמודעי להו ופרשי, ומאי קמ"ל — דאהבה וריעות נוהגים זה בזה — היינו רישא! הא קמ"ל דכולה ר"ש היא. תא שמע, *דאמר רבי יוחנן בן נורי: היאך הלכה זו רווחת בישראל? נעשה כדברי ב"ש — הולד ממזר לדברי ב"ה, נעשה כדברי ב"ה — הולד פגום לדברי ב"ש, *בואו ונתקן להן לצרות שיהו

ומאי אולמיה דהאי מהאי. דקאמר: ה"נ מסתברא דמודעי להו, מהאי, היכי מסתברא טפי? קלא אית לה. ולא צריך לאודועי, ומהתם לא תילף דמודעי: ה"ג: פשיטא בני חייבי לאוין כשרים נינהו. מדר"ע. לקמן בפרק "החולץ" (דף מט.). בצרות. במתני'. ובאחיות. בפרק "ד' אחין" (לקמן כו.). ובספק אשת איש. בפרק ב"ש (לקמן קז.), דתנן: ב"ש אין ממאנים אלא ארוסות וכו', והקטנה בת מיאון קרי ספק אשת איש, דלמא ממאנת ונפקא. לישנא אחרינא נראה: שכיב מרע שכתב לאשה "זה גיטיך מהיום אם מתי מחולי זה", כל אותם הימים נקראת ספק אשת איש, (א) כדתנן (גיטין דף עד.): מה היא כל אותן הימים? ר' יוסי אומר: בעילתו ספק, ר"מ אומר: בעילתו תלויה. ותנן: לא תתייחד עמו אלא ע"פ עדים, אע"פ שלא שנינו בה מחלוקת ב"ש וב"ה — על כרחך נחלקו בה אותו מחלוקת שנחלקו במגרש את אשתו ולנה עמו בפונדק (שם דף פא.). לב"ש דאמרי לא אמרי' הן הן עדי ייחוד הן הן עדי ביאה — אינה צריכה הימנו גט שני, ולב"ה דאמרי הן הן עידי ייחוד הן הן עדי ביאה — צריכה הימנו גט שני (ב). ובפ' "מי שאחזו קורדייקוס" (שם עג:) איפליגו בה ר' יוסי בר' יהודה ורבנן, דקתני: ראוה שנתייחדה עמו באפילה כו'. ומוקמינן התם דאליבא דב"ה, דמגרש אשתו ולנה עמו בפונדקי הוא דאיפליגו בה, דאמר: כמאן אזלא הא דא"ר יוחנן מחלוקת כשראוה כשנבעלה כו'. והיא דר' יוחנן — גבי פלוגתא דב"ש וב"ה איתמר. גט ישן. (ג) המגרש את אשתו ולנה עמו בפונדקי במס' גיטין ב"הזורק" (ד' פא.). בכסף ושוה כסף בפרוטה ושוה פרוטה. לענין קידושי אשה, ב"ש אומרים: בדינר ושוה דינר, וב"ה: בפרוטה ושוה פרוטה. ודינר הוא כסף צורי, ופרוטה היא של נחושת. וה"ק הכא: בכסף ובשוה כסף לב"ש, בפרוטה ובשוה פרוטה לב"ה. ובפ"ק דקדושין (דף יא.) קרי לדינר דב"ש כסף, דאמר רב אסי: כל כסף האמור בתורה סתם — כסף צורי, ואותבינן: והרי קידושי אשה כו', לימא רב אסי דאמר כב"ש. מן הספק. קא ס"ד השתא באיסור ספק, כגון מגרש ולנה עמו בפונדקי, דליכא אלא ספק דשמא בא עליה לשם קידושין. לצרה עצמה. הא דקתני נמנעים — מצרה עצמה, ולעולם ב"ש נמי נמנעים מב"ה מלישא צרת הבת בלא חליצה. מן הסתם. כל כמה דלאו מודעי להו — לא היו פרשי מספיקא, דודאי אי הוי מההך דלא סבירא להו — הוו מודעי להו. הולד פגום לדברי ב"ש. דאם היה כהן — פסול לכהונה. ואע"ג דבני חייבי לאוין כשרים לקהל — חללים הם לענין כהונה, דאתיא בק"ו מאלמנה לכ"ג, לקמן בשמעתין.
שיהו

תורה אור

[תוספתא פ"א]

[תוספתא פ"א]

[לעיל יג: לקמן כז.]

בשלמא ב"ש לא נמנעו מב"ה כו'. להאי גירסא לא מוכח מהכא אלא דלמ"ד עשו – אודועי מודעי להו. אבל ר"ח גרים איפכא: בשלמא ב"ה לא נמנעו מב"ש – דטומאות דב"ש לב"ה טהורות נינהו. וזאת הגירסא נראית, דבכל מקום ב"ש מחמיר לענין טומאה. דכי חשיב בעדיות (פ"ה) קולי דב"ש וחומרי דב"ה – לא חשיב אלא תרי מילי דטומאה וטהרה, אבל כל שאר מילי דטומאה וטהרה, כגון שדרה וגולגולת ושוקת יהוא – הוו ב"ש לחומרא. והשתא, לפי האי גירסא מוכח שפיר דאודועי מודעי להו [אפי' לא עשו], דליכא למימר דלא נמנעו ב"ש מב"ה משום דלא עשו ב"ש כדבריהם, והיו עושין בכל דבר כב"ה ואפי' לקולא, כדמוכח לקמן. דהא טעמא דלא עשו משום אגודות ובטומאה ובטהרה דב"ש לחומר' – היה להם לב"ש למנוע מלעשו' טהרות אגב כלים דב"ה, דליכא אגודות, דהרואה אומר לא צריכי לכלים דידהו, כדאמר גבי שוקת בית יהוא: הרואה אומר לאפושי מיא הוא דעבדי. אלא ודאי, ע"כ אודועי הוו מודעי להו אפילו למ"ד לא עשו. והא דקאמר בשלמא בית הלל לא נמנעו מב"ש, דטומאות דב"ש – לב"ה טהורות נינהו, ואע"ג דבתרי מילי ב"ש לקולא – הני תרי מילי לא שכיחי. א"נ: נקט בשלמא משום איכא דמ"ד לא עשו א).

פשיטא בני חייבי לאוין כשרים נינהו. תימה: דלא מסיק אדעתי' דאתא לאפוקי מדר"ע, ואי הוה האי ר' אלעזר אמורא – הוה א"ש, דפשיטא ליה דאין הלכה כר"ע. אבל הוא רבי אלעזר בן שמוע שהוא תנא, כדמוכח ב"עשרה יוחסין" (קדושין עה:)! ונראה דס"ד דלשום תנא לא הוי ממזר מיבמה לשוק אלא דוקא מחייבי לאוין דשאר, כדתנן ב"החולץ" (לקמן מט. ושם): איזהו ממזר – כל שאר בשר שהוא ב"לא יבא". והא דתנן ב"האשה רבה" (לקמן ד' צב. ושם): האשה שהלך בעלה ובנה למד"ה ואמרו מת בעלה, ואח"כ מת בנה ונשאת, ואח"כ אמרו לה: חילוף היו הדברים – תצא (מזה ומזה) והולד ממזר (מזה ומזה). משמע דהוי ממזר מיבמה לשוק! קס"ד דקנסא בעלמא הוא. אע"ג דתניא בגמ' זו דברי ר"ע, דאמר אין קידושין תופסין בחייבי לאוין – ההיא ברייתא לא שמיע ליה.

ובספק אשת איש. לשון אחר שפי' בקונט', דהיינו: שכיב מרע שכתב גט לאשתו, ואע"ג דאין שם מחלוקת ב"ש וב"ה – הא נחלקו במגרש אשתו ולנה עמו בפונדקי – לא נהירא, דבהדיא חשיב הכא ההיא פלוגתא דהמגרש אשתו ולנה עמו בפונדקי. **בגט** ישן. תימה למ"ד בפ' ["הזורק"] בגיטין (ד' עט: ושם) דאם פטרה בגט ישן – תנשא לכתחלה, למה היה להם למנוע? דמשמע דלא נמנעו משום דלא עשו כדבריהם, או משום דהוו מודעי להו ופרשי. **אלא** ב"ש אמאי נמנעים מב"ה. וא"ת: ודלמא משום ממאנת, ומשום ההיא דשוה כסף ככסף היו נמנעים? דאם נתקדשה לראשון בפרוטה ולשני בדינר, לב"ש – מקודשת לשני, ובניה מן הראשון ממזרים! ואומר ר"י: דעיקר הך ברייתא משום צרות קתני לה, [ולכך קתני לה גבי מתני' דהכא], דלגבי הכי קתני לה מתני'. ומשמע משום צרות גרידא היו נמנעים. **ומאי** שנא ודאי כו'. לא אשנוייה קאי, אלא בתר דאסיק קושייתו בא לפרש הברייתא. **נעשה** כדברי ב"ה הולד פגום לדברי ב"ש. פי' בקונט': דאע"ג דבני חייבי לאוין כשרים לקהל – חללים הם לענין כהונה, דאתי בק"ו מאלמנה כדלקמן. ופליג אדר' יהושע, ולית ליה פירכא דמה לאלמנה שכן היא עצמה מתחללת. ועוד י"ל: דשפיר אית ליה הך פירכא, ומ"מ הולד פגום, מדאיצטריך במחזיר גרושתו "היא תועבה ואין בניה תועבין" (קידושין דף עו.) ול"ל קרא? דהא לא אתי מק"ו דאלמנה, דאיכא למיפרך: שכן היא עצמה מתחללת, אלא דאתי למידק הא כיוצא בזאת, דהיינו יבמה לשוק – בניה תועבין. אבל קשה: דבסוף נדה (ע. ושם) מסיק ר' יהושע דולד מחזיר גרושתו כשר, משום היא תועבה ואין בניה תועבין, ול"ל קרא? דליכא למימר דאתי למידק אבני יבמה לשוק – דהא לקמן קאמר רבי יהושע בני צרות מעיד אני לכם דכשרים לכהונה לב"ש, משום פירכא
דשכן

א) ומאי דפריך [מאי אולמיה דהך מהך א) דהא מההיא דלעיל נמי דייקי' שפיר (ע"פ) דמודעי להו אפי' אי אמרינן דלא עשו דאלו"ה קשיא לן ב"ש מב"ה אמאי לא נמנעו דאין לנו לומר (דלמא) דהאי דלא נמנעו ב"ש משום דלא עשו כדבריהם דהיכא אמרינן דלא עשו היכא דשייך אגודות אגודות אבל הכא לא שייך דהרואה יאמר לאתתא לא צריכי שהרי הרבה נשים אחרות ימצאו וא"כ אפי' לא עשו ב"ש כדבריהם צ"ל דמודעי להו וא"כ פריך שפיר מאי אולמיה דהך מהך ומשני מהו דתימא צרה קלא אית לה ולא צריכי למימר לעיל [גבי] צרה דמודעי (נהי) דליכא למפרך אמאי לא נמנעו היה להם להמנע משום הצרות דהתם ודאי עשו ב"ש כדבריהם דלא שייך אגודות אגודות דהרואה יאמר לאתתא לא צריכי דזה לא קשה מידי דהיינו משום דצרה קלא אית לה ולהכי לא נמנעו קמ"ל מההיא דטהרות דצ"ל ע"כ דמודעי להו אפי' אי אמרי' לא עשו: **בספק** אשת איש. י"מ ספק אשת איש היינו מגרש אשתו ולנה עמו בפונדקי וחדא מלתא היא דמגרש אשתו וכו' ספק אשת איש היא ופליגי ב"ש וב"ה אי צריכא גט שני:

א) נ"ל ומאי דפריך מאי אולמיה דהך מהך היינו משום דגם בההיא דלעיל נמי דייקינן שפיר דע"כ דמודעי להו כו'.

הגהות הב"ח

(א) רש"י ד"ה ובספק וכו' אשת איש כדתניא בפ' מי שאחזו מה היא כל וכו' (ב) שם בא"ד גט שני דהתם איפלגו בה ר' יוסי כצ"ל ותיבות ובפ' מי שאחזו קורדייקוס נמחק (ג) ד"ה גט ישן והמגרש

שֶׁיְּהוּ חוֹלְצוֹת וְלֹא מִתְיַיבְּמוֹת, לֹא הִסְפִּיקוּ לִגְמוֹר אֶת הַדָּבָר עַד שֶׁנִּטְרְפָה הַשָּׁעָה. א"ל רַשְׁבַּ"ג: מַה נַּעֲשֶׂה לָהֶם לַצָּרוֹת הָרִאשׁוֹנוֹת מֵעַתָּה? אִי אָמְרַתְּ בִּשְׁלָמָא עָשׂוּ — הַיְינוּ דְּקָאָמַר "מַה נַּעֲשֶׂה", אֶלָּא אִי אָמְרַתְּ לֹא עָשׂוּ — מַאי "מַה נַּעֲשֶׂה"? אָמַר רַב נַחְמָן בַּר יִצְחָק: לָא נִצְרְכָה אֶלָּא לַצָּרָה עַצְמָהּ, וּמַה נַּעֲשֶׂה — הָכִי קָאָמַר: הָנָךְ צָרוֹת דְּב"ה לְב"ש הֵיכִי נַעֲבֵיד לְהוּ? לִיחָלְצוּ — מִימָּאֲסֵי אַגַּבְרַיְיהוּ, וְכִי תֵּימָא לִימָּאֲסָן — °"דְּרָכֶיהָ דַרְכֵי נוֹעַם וְכָל נְתִיבוֹתֶיהָ שָׁלוֹם"! ת"ש, *דא"ר טַרְפוֹן: *תְּאֵבְנִי, מָתַי תָּבֹא צָרַת הַבַּת לְיָדִי וְאֶשָּׂאֶנָּה! אֵימָא: וְאַשִּׂיאֶנָּה. וְהָא "תְּאֵבְנִי" קָאָמַר! לְאַפּוּקֵי מִדְּרַבִּי יוֹחָנָן בֶּן נוּרִי. ת"ש: מַעֲשֶׂה בְּבִתּוֹ שֶׁל רַבָּן גַּמְלִיאֵל שֶׁהָיְתָה נְשׂוּאָה לְאַבָּא אָחִיו, וּמֵת בְּלֹא בָנִים, וְיִיבֵּם רַבָּן גַּמְלִיאֵל אֶת צָרָתָהּ. וְתִסְבְּרָא, רַבָּן גַּמְלִיאֵל מִתַּלְמִידֵי ב"ש הוּא?! אֶלָּא: שָׁאנֵי בִּתּוֹ שֶׁל רַבָּן גַּמְלִיאֵל דְּאַיְילוֹנִית הֲוַאי. הָא מִדְּקָתָנֵי סֵיפָא: אֲחֵרִים אוֹמְרִים בִּתּוֹ שֶׁל רַבָּן גַּמְלִיאֵל אַיְילוֹנִית הָיְתָה, מִכְּלָל דְּתַנָּא קַמָּא סָבַר לָאו אַיְילוֹנִית הָיְתָה! הִכִּיר בָּהּ וְלֹא הִכִּיר בָּהּ אִיכָּא בֵּינַיְיהוּ. וְאִיבָּעֵית אֵימָא: כָּנַס וּלְבַסּוֹף גֵּירֵשׁ אִיכָּא בֵּינַיְיהוּ. אִיבָּעֵית אֵימָא: יֵשׁ תְּנַאי בְּבִיאָה אִיכָּא בֵּינַיְיהוּ. מְתִיב רַב מְשַׁרְשְׁיָא: *מַעֲשֶׂה בְּרַ' עֲקִיבָא שֶׁלִּיקֵּט אֶתְרוֹג בְּאֶחָד בִּשְׁבָט, וְנָהַג בּוֹ ב' עִשּׂוּרִין; אֶחָד כְּדִבְרֵי ב"ש וְאֶחָד כְּדִבְרֵי ב"ה, ש"מ: עָשׂוּ! רַ' עֲקִיבָא גְּמָרֵיהּ אִסְתַּפֵּק לֵיהּ, וְלָא יָדַע אִי ב"ה בְּאֶחָד בִּשְׁבָט אָמוּר אוֹ בְּט"ו בִּשְׁבָט אָמוּר. מְתִיב מָר זוּטְרָא: *מַעֲשֶׂה וְיָלְדָה כַּלָּתוֹ שֶׁל שַׁמַּאי הַזָּקֵן וּפִיחֵת אֶת הַמַּעֲזִיבָה, וְסִיכֵּךְ עַל גַּבֵּי מִטָּה בִּשְׁבִיל קָטָן. ש"מ: עָשׂוּ! הָתָם הָרוֹאֶה אוֹמֵר לְאַפּוּשֵׁי אֲוִיר קָעָבֵיד. מְתִיב מָר זוּטְרָא: *מַעֲשֶׂה בְּשׁוֹקֶת יְהוּא שֶׁהָיְתָה בִּירוּשָׁלַיִם וְהָיְתָה נְקוּבָה לַמִּקְוֶה, וְכָל טְהָרוֹת שֶׁהָיוּ בִּירוּשָׁלַיִם נַעֲשִׂים עַל גַּבָּהּ. וְשָׁלְחוּ בֵּית שַׁמַּאי וְהִרְחִיבוּהָ, שֶׁבֵּית שַׁמַּאי אוֹמְרִים: עַד שֶׁתִּיפָּחֵת בְּרוּבָּהּ. וּתְנַן: *א עֵירוּב מִקְוָאוֹת בִּשְׁפוֹפֶרֶת הַנּוֹד, בְּעוֹבְיָיהּ, וּבַחֲלָלָהּ כִּשְׁתֵּי אֶצְבָּעוֹת חוֹזְרוֹת לִמְקוֹמָן. שְׁמַע מִינָּהּ: עָשׂוּ! הָתָם הָרוֹאֶה

°משלי ג

רש"י

שֶׁיְּהוּ חוֹלְצוֹת. וְיִנָּשְׂאוּ לַשּׁוּק בְּהֶכְשֵׁר לְדִבְרֵי הַכֹּל. מַה נַּעֲשֶׂה לַצָּרוֹת הָרִאשׁוֹנוֹת. שֶׁנִּתְיַיבְּמוּ, וּבְנֵיהֶם מַמְזֵרִים אִם נִגְמוֹר הֲלָכָה שֶׁלֹּא יִתְיַיבְּמוּ. לַצָּרָה עַצְמָהּ. וְהַצָּרוֹת דְּב"ה שֶׁנִּישְּׂאוּ לַשּׁוּק קָאֵי. וְהַאי "וּמַאי נַעֲשֶׂה" לָאו אַבָּנִים קָאֵי, דְּהָא אֲפִי' לְב"ש כְּשֵׁרִים לַקָּהָל, אֶלָּא אַצָּרָה עַצְמָהּ. רַבִּי טַרְפוֹן. מִתַּלְמִידֵי ב"ש הָיָה. מָתַי תָּבֹא צָרַת הַבַּת. מֵאָחִי לְיָדִי. וְאֶשָּׂאֶנָּה. אֲיַיבֵּם אוֹתָהּ, כְּדִבְרֵי ב"ש. וְאַשִּׂיאֶנָּה. לַשּׁוּק כְּדִבְרֵי ב"ה. וְהָא תְּאֵבְנִי קָאָמַר. וְאִם כְּב"ה, מַה חִידּוּשׁ? כ"ע הָכִי נָהֲגוּ. לְאַפּוּקֵי מִדְּר' יוֹחָנָן בֶּן נוּרִי. דְּאָמַר תַּקַּנְתָּא דְּחוֹלְצוֹת. מִתַּלְמִידֵי ב"ש הוּא. בִּתְמִיָּה: וַהֲלֹא מִבְּנֵי בָנָיו שֶׁל הִלֵּל הוּא! אַיְילוֹנִית הָיְתָה. וּתְנַן: אוֹ שֶׁנִּמְצְאוּ אַיְילוֹנִית — צָרוֹתֵיהֶן מוּתָּרוֹת: ה"ג. הִכִּיר בָּהּ וְלֹא הִכִּיר בָּהּ אִיכָּא בֵּינַיְיהוּ. וְל"ג אֶלָּא לְת"ק דַּוְקָא דְּלֹא הִכִּיר בָּהּ הוּא דַּהֲוֵי מִקַּח טָעוּת, אֲבָל הִכִּיר בָּהּ צָרָתָהּ אֲסוּרָה. וְלַאֲחֵרִים אֲפִי' הִכִּיר בָּהּ מוּתֶּרֶת, דְּקָתָנֵי הָיְתָה וְלֹא קָתָנֵי נִמְצֵאת. כָּנַס וּלְבַסּוֹף גֵּירֵשׁ אִיכָּא בֵּינַיְיהוּ. לְת"ק עַל יְדֵי שֶׁגֵּירֵשׁ אָחִיו אֶת בִּתּוֹ קוֹדֶם מִיתָה, אע"פ שֶׁכְּבָר כָּנַס הַנָּכְרִית וְהָיוּ צָרוֹת זוֹ עַל זוֹ — מוּתֶּרֶת, הוֹאִיל וְגֵירֵשׁ אֶת הָעֶרְוָה לְבַסּוֹף. וְלַאֲחֵרִים, הוֹאִיל וְכָנַס אֶת הַנָּכְרִית קוֹדֶם גֵּירוּשִׁין דְּעֶרְוָה — אֲסוּרָה. אֶלָּא בִּתּוֹ שֶׁל ר"ג אַיְילוֹנִית הָיְתָה. יֵשׁ תְּנַאי בְּבִיאָה. הַכּוֹנֵס אִשָּׁה עַל תְּנַאי שֶׁאֵין עָלֶיהָ מוּמִין אוֹ נְדָרִים, וְנִמְצָא שֶׁיֵּשׁ עָלֶיהָ, לְת"ק מְהַנֵּי תְּנַאי, וַהֲוֵי מִקַּח טָעוּת. וּתְנַאי הָיָה לוֹ לְאָחִיו שֶׁל ר"ג בְּבִתּוֹ, וְלֹא נִתְקַיֵּים. הִילְכָּךְ — לָאו אִשְׁתּוֹ הִיא, וְצָרָתָהּ מוּתֶּרֶת. וַאֲחֵרִים סָבְרֵי דְּאֵין תְּנַאי מוֹעִיל בְּבִיאָה, דְּכֵיוָן דְּבָעֵיל אַחוּלֵי אַחֵיל, כִּדְאָמְרִינַן בִּכְתוּבּוֹת בְּ"הַמַּדִּיר" (ד' עג.): אֵין אָדָם עוֹשֶׂה בְּעִילָתוֹ בְּעִילַת זְנוּת, אֶלָּא מִשּׁוּם דְּאַיְילוֹנִית הָיְתָה. בְּאֶחָד בִּשְׁבָט. וְשָׁנָה שְׁנִיָּה הַנִּכְנֶסֶת לִשְׁלִישִׁית הָיְתָה, וְנָהַג בָּהּ שְׁנֵי עִישּׂוּרִין: מַעֲשֵׂר שֵׁנִי, כְּב"ה דְּאָמְרִי ט"ו בִּשְׁבָט ר"ה לָאִילָנוֹת, וַאֲכַתִּי שְׁנִיָּה הִיא; וּמַעֲשַׂר עָנִי, כְּב"ש דְּאָמְרִי בְּא' בִּשְׁבָט ר"ה לָאִילָנוֹת, וּשְׁלִישִׁית הִיא. מַעֲזִיבָה. טִיחַ טִיט שֶׁעַל הַתִּקְרָה. בִּשְׁבִיל קָטָן. דִּסְבִירָא לֵיהּ לְשַׁמַּאי: קָטָן הַצָּרִיךְ לְאִמּוֹ — חַיָּיב בְּסוּכָּה. שׁוֹקֶת. אֶבֶן חֲלוּלָה שֶׁתַּחַת לִנּוֹר הַמְקַלֵּחַ מַיִם מִן הָהָר, וְהָיְתָה נִקְרֵאת שׁוֹקֶת יֵהוּא. נַעֲשִׂים עַל גַּבָּהּ. מַטְבִּילִים בְּתוֹכָהּ, וְאֵין בָּהּ מ' סְאָה. אֲבָל מִקְוֶה שָׁלֵם הֲוָה בַּמַּיִם שֶׁבְּגַלְדָּהּ, וּמִתְעָרְבִין מַעְיַין הַשּׁוֹקֶת דֶּרֶךְ נֶקֶב כִּשְׁפוֹפֶרֶת הַנּוֹד. הִרְחִיב לוֹ אֶת הַנֶּקֶב. הִרְחִיבוּ וּפִיחֲתוּ רוּבָּהּ לְעָרֵב הַמִּקְוֶה יָפֶה. עֵירוּב מִקְוָאוֹת. מִקְוֶה חָסֵר שֶׁבְּצַד מִקְוֶה שָׁלֵם, וּמִתְעָרְבִים הַמַּיִם דֶּרֶךְ חָרִיץ וָנֶקֶב. וְשִׁיעוּר הַנֶּקֶב לְצָרֵף הַמִּקְוָאוֹת וּלְהַכְשִׁיר הֶחָסֵר. כִּשְׁפוֹפֶרֶת הַנּוֹד. קָנֶה שֶׁנּוֹתְנִים בְּפִי הַנּוֹד, שֶׁיְּהֵא שִׁיעוּר חֲלַל הֶחָרִיץ כְּעוֹבְיָהּ וַחֲלָלָהּ שֶׁל שְׁפוֹפֶרֶת, דְּהַיְינוּ כִּשְׁתֵּי אֶצְבָּעוֹת. הַחוֹזְרוֹת לִמְקוֹמָן. מִתְהַפְּכוֹת בַּחֲלַל הַנֶּקֶב בְּרֶיוַח, וְהַיְינוּ כְּבֵית הִלֵּל, אֲבָל לְבֵית שַׁמַּאי — עַד שֶׁתִּפָּחֵת רוּבָּהּ. הָרוֹאֶה

תוספות

דשכן היא עצמה מתחללת! וי"ל: דלר' יהושע איצטריך היא תועבה ואין בניה תועבין דלא תימא בניה תועבין משום דכתיב בה טומאה כעריות. ואפי' לרבנן דרבי יוסי בן כיפר דמוקמי לה (לעיל ד' יא:) אסוטה — הא אמרן דאין מקרא יוצא מידי פשוטו. ואפילו למ"ד כיון דאיתעקר איתעקר — מ"מ איצטריך היא תועבה דלא תימא אמחזיר גרושתו נמי קאי. ועוד: דאיצטריך ליה "היא" למעוטי, דלא תדרוש מלשון תועבה שבניה תועבין. וקצת קשה: דקאמרי' לקמן דבעו מר' יהושע: בני צרות דב"ה, לב"ש מהו? למאי נפקא מינה למיפסל ולד מחזיר גרושתו, והיכי איכא למיפסל מינה? דלמא ולד מחזיר גרושתו יש לפסול מטעם טומאה דכתיב בה, או משום תועבה. ואי נמי בני יבמה לשוק פסולים — יש להכשיר בני מחזיר גרושתו, דהיא תועבה ואין בניה תועבין, איכא למימר דאתא למידק דיבמה לשוק בניה תועבין! וי"ל: דאינהו לא מסקי אדעתייהו הנך דרשות, ולא בעו אלא אי אמרינן ק"ו גבי יבמה לשוק או לא. **ונהג** בו שני עשורין. בירושלמי מפרש דהפריש מעשר שני ופדאו, וחלק המעשר לעניים, והמעות אכל בירושלים.

גמריה איסתפק ליה. הוה מצי למימר: וליטעמיך, היכי עביד כחומרי דמר וכחומרי דמר? והכתיב (קהלת ב) "הכסיל בחשך הולך", דהכי פריך עלה בפ"ק דעירובין (דף ז.) ובפ"ק דר"ה (דף יד:).

וסיכך על גבי מטה ש"מ עשו. מכאן משמע דמ"ד לא עשו, אפי' היכא דב"ש לחומרא — היו עושים כב"ה לקולא.

עירוב מקואות כשפופרת הנוד כו'. וא"ת: והא תנן במס' טהרות (פ"ח מ"ט), ומייתי לה בריש פ"ב דגיטין (דף טז. ושם): הנצוק והקטפרס ומשקה טופח אינן חיבור לא לטומאה ולא לטהרה, אבל טופח להטפיח — חיבור! ואמר ר"ת: דנקב בעינן כשפופרת הנוד, אבל במים הבאים תוך הנקב סגי בטופח להטפיח. ואין נראה לר"י, דתנן במס' מקואות בפ' ששי (מ"ט): כותל שבין ב' מקואות שנסדק, לשתי — מצטרף, לערב — אין מצטרף, עד שיהא במקום אחד כשפופרת הנוד. רבי יהודה אומר: חילוף הדברים, נפרצו זה לתוך זה על רוס כקליפת השום, על רוחבו — כשפופרת הנוד. משמע דלמעלה, כשאין דבר מפסיק, צריך שיהא צף על רומו כקליפת השום וברוחב שפופרת, ולא סגי בטופח להטפיח, ובנקובה זו לזו ומפסיק הכותל משמע דצריך מים כשפופרת! ועוד: דאם אין במים הבאים דרך הנקב אלא טופח להטפיח — אין כאן נקב רוחב מים כשפופרת, שאין הנקב מרובע אלא עגול, כדקאמרינן כשתי אצבעות חוזרות למקומן. אלא ודאי נקב מלא בעינן, וכשצפין למעלה סגי בקליפת השום כרוחב שפופרת! ונראה לר"י דההיא דנצוק וקטפרס — לא לענין חיבור מקואות איירי, אלא לענין הַשָּׁקָה. דאם יש כאן מים טמאים ומשיקן בנהר, ומחברן ע"י נצוק וקטפרס ומשקה טופח — אין חיבור, אבל בטופח להטפיח — הוי חיבור, והשתא הוי לטהרה דומיא דלטומאה. ובהדיא מיתנייא לענין השקה במס' טהרות בסוף פרק שמיני, ובריש פרק שני דגיטין (דף טז. ושם) מסיק עלה: דלמא לענין מקואות ורבי יהודה היא, מכלל דעד השתא לא הוי מוקי לה לענין מקואות. והשתא נמי, דמוקי לה לענין מקואות — מוקי לה דוקא כר' יהודה, אבל לרבנן — לא הוי חיבור בטופח להטפיח. ולר' יהודה נמי, טופח להטפיח לא הוי חיבור אלא משום גוד אחית, כההיא ד"אם היו רגליו נוגעות במים" דאיירי בה רבי יהודה. אבל היכא דלא שייך גוד אחית, כמו בקרקע שוה — לא הוי טופח להטפיח חיבור, אלא בעי מים צפים כקליפת השום. וכן משמע דנפרצו זה לתוך זה על רוס כקליפת השום אתי כרבי יהודה דהוזכר שם ברישא. ומה שקשה על זה בכל שאר הדבור פרשנו פרק שני דגיטין, ואין להאריך כאן.

אמר

מסורת הש"ס: [תוספתא פ"א] | [גי' רש"ל תאב אני (וכ"ה בתוספתא)] | עירובין ז. ר"ה יד. | סוכה כח. | מקואות פ"ד מ"ה ע"ש | חגיגה כב: מקואות פ"ו מ"ז

עין משפט נר מצוה: **נט א** מיי' פ"ח מהל' מקואות הלכה א סמג עשין רמח טוש"ע י"ד סי' רא סעיף מ וסעיף נב:

תוספות ישנים

ת"ש ר' טרפון אומר תאבני מתי תבא צרת הבת לידי ואשאנה אלמא עשו ב"ש כדבריהם. ומשני ואשיאנה לאחרים כב"ה. והא תאבני קאמר [ופ"ה] ואין זה חדוש לעשות כב"ה דפשיטא דהלכה כב"ה בכל מקום. ולא נהירא דמאי פריך הלא אשמעינן חדוש להורות דלא כב"ש שהרי ר' טרפון מתלמידי ב"ש הוא. לכך נראה דגרסינן אפכא ת"ש תאבני מתי תבא צרת הבת לידי ואשיאנה אלמא לא עשו וכו' ומשני אימא ואשאנה כב"ש. והא תאבני קאמר ואין זה חדוש לעשות כמו רבו ומשני לאפוקי מדר' יוחנן וכו': **ונהג** בו שני עשורין וא"ת והא אמרינן המרבה במעשרות מעשרותיו מקולקלים מפו' שהמעשר הוא טבל והכא נמי איכא טבל בגווייהו. וי"ל דמפריש על תנאי ואומר אם זה מעשר עני הרי הוא לעניים ואם זה מעשר שני הרי הן מחוללין על מעות הללו והמעות יביאם לירושלים ויקנה מהן צרכי סעודה וכן יעשה משני העשורין א):

א) אינו מובן דבעושה כסדר הזה בחד מעשר סגי וכ"מ בתוס' כאן בשם הירושל' ואולי דט"ס נפל בכאן וצ"ל וכן יעשה בכל שני עשורין ועדיין צ"ע.

תוספות חד מקמאי

תנן התם במסכת מקואות פ"ד שוקת שבסלע אין מלאין בה ואין קדשים בה ואין מזין ממנה ואינה צריכה צמיד פתיל ואינה פוסלת את המקוה היתה כלי וחברתה בסיד ממלאין בה ומקדשין בה ומזין ממנה וצריכה צמיד פתיל ופוסלת את המקו' ניקבה מלמטה או מן הצד אם אינה יכולה לקבל המים כל שהוא כשרה כמה יהא בנקב כשפופרת [הנוד]. תני ר"י בן בתירא מעשה בשוקת יהוא שהיתה בירושלי' כתבתי משנה זו מפני שהיא בקצת פירושי ר"ש ז"ל על לא נכון:

הָרוֹאֶה אוֹמֵר: לְאַפּוּשֵׁי מַיָּא הוּא דְּקָא עָבֵיד. ת"ש, דְּא"ר אֶלְעָזָר בַּר צָדוֹק: כְּשֶׁהָיִיתִי לוֹמֵד תּוֹרָה אֵצֶל רַ' יוֹחָנָן הַחוֹרָנִי רָאִיתִי שֶׁהָיָה אוֹכֵל פַּת חֲרֵיבָה בְּמֶלַח בִּשְׁנֵי בַּצּוֹרֶת. בָּאתִי וְהוֹדַעְתִּי אֶת אַבָּא. אָמַר לִי: הוֹלֵךְ לוֹ זֵיתִים, וְהוֹלַכְתִּי לוֹ. רָאָה אוֹתָן שֶׁהֵן לַחִין, אָמַר לִי: אֵין אֲנִי אוֹכֵל זֵיתִים. בָּאתִי וְהוֹדַעְתִּי אֶת אַבָּא. אָמַר לִי: לֵךְ וֶאֱמוֹר לוֹ: חָבִית נְקוּבָה הָיְתָה, אֶלָּא שֶׁסְּתָמוּהָ שְׁמָרִים. וּתְנַן: *חָבִית שֶׁל זֵיתִים מְגוּלְגָּלִים, בֵּית שַׁמַּאי אוֹמְרִים אֵין צְרִיכָה לִנָּקֵב, וּבֵית הִלֵּל אוֹמְרִים: [א]צְרִיכָה לִנָּקֵב וּמוֹדִים, שֶׁאִם נִיקְּבָהּ וּסְתָמוּהָ שְׁמָרִים — שֶׁהִיא טְהוֹרָה. וְאע"פ שֶׁתַּלְמִיד שַׁמַּאי הָיָה — כָּל מַעֲשָׂיו לֹא עָשָׂה אֶלָּא כְּדִבְרֵי ב"ה. אִי אָמְרַתְּ בִּשְׁלָמָא עָשׂוּ — הַיְינוּ רְבוּתֵיהּ, אֶלָּא אִי אָמְרַתְּ לֹא עָשׂוּ — מַאי רְבוּתֵיהּ? ת"ש: שָׁאֲלוּ אֶת רַ' יְהוֹשֻׁעַ: צָרַת הַבַּת מַהוּ? אָמַר לָהֶם: מַחֲלוֹקֶת ב"ש וּב"ה. וַהֲלָכָה כְּדִבְרֵי מִי? אָמַר לָהֶם: מִפְּנֵי מָה אַתֶּם מַכְנִיסִין רֹאשִׁי בֵּין שְׁנֵי הָרִים גְּדוֹלִים, בֵּין שְׁתֵּי מַחֲלוֹקוֹת גְּדוֹלוֹת, בֵּין ב"ש וּבֵין ב"ה, מִתְיָירֵא אֲנִי שֶׁמָּא יָרוֹצּוּ גֻּלְגָּלְתִּי. אֲבָל אֲנִי מֵעִיד לָכֶם עַל שְׁתֵּי מִשְׁפָּחוֹת גְּדוֹלוֹת שֶׁהָיוּ בִּירוּשָׁלַיִם: מִשְׁפַּחַת בֵּית צְבוֹעִים מִבֶּן עַכְמַאי, וּמִשְׁפַּחַת בֵּית קוּפַאי מִבֶּן מְקוֹשֵׁשׁ, שֶׁהֵם בְּנֵי צָרוֹת וּמֵהֶם כֹּהֲנִים גְּדוֹלִים, וְשִׁמְּשׁוּ עַל גַּבֵּי הַמִּזְבֵּחַ. אִי אָמְרַתְּ בִּשְׁלָמָא עָשׂוּ — הַיְינוּ דְּקָאָמַר מִתְיָירֵא אֲנִי, אֶלָּא אִי אָמְרַתְּ לֹא עָשׂוּ — אַמַּאי קָאָמַר מִתְיָירֵא אֲנִי? וּנְהִי נַמִי דְּעָשׂוּ, מַאי מִתְיָירֵא אֲנִי? הָא *אָמַר רַ' יְהוֹשֻׁעַ: אֵין מַמְזֵר אֶלָּא מֵחַיָּיבֵי מִיתוֹת בֵּית דִּין! *נְהִי נַמִי דְּמַמְזֵר לָא הָוֵי, פָּגוּם מִיהוּ הָוֵי, מִק"ו מֵאַלְמָנָה: *מָה אַלְמָנָה, שֶׁאֵין אִיסּוּרָהּ נוֹהֵג בַּכֹּל — בְּנָהּ פָּגוּם, זוֹ שֶׁאִיסּוּרָהּ שָׁוֶה בַּכֹּל — כו'. קָבְעוּ מִינֵּיהּ צָרוֹת וְקָפָשֵׁיט *לֵיהּ בְּנֵי צָרוֹת! תַּרְתֵּי קָא בָּעֵי מִינֵּיהּ: צָרוֹת מַאי, וְאִם תִּמְצֵי לוֹמַר צָרוֹת כְּבֵית הִלֵּל — בְּנֵי צָרוֹת (א) דְּבֵית הִלֵּל לְב"ש מַהוּ? לְמַאי נָפְקָא מִינַּהּ? לְמִיפְשַׁט וְלַד מַחֲזִיר גְּרוּשָׁתוֹ לְבֵית הִלֵּל. מִי קָאָמְרִינַן קַל וָחוֹמֶר: וּמָה אַלְמָנָה לְכֹהֵן גָּדוֹל שֶׁאֵין אִיסּוּרָהּ שָׁוֶה בַּכֹּל — בְּנָהּ פָּגוּם, זוֹ שֶׁאִיסּוּרָהּ שָׁוֶה בַּכֹּל — אֵינוֹ דִּין שֶׁבְּנָהּ פָּגוּם? אוֹ דִּלְמָא אִיכָּא לְמִיפְרַךְ: מָה לְאַלְמָנָה — שֶׁהִיא עַצְמָהּ מִתְחַלֶּלֶת! וְאָמַר לְהוּ: צָרוֹת — מִתְיָירֵא אֲנִי, בְּנֵי

רש"י

הָרוֹאֶה אוֹמֵר כו'. וְלָא דָּמֵי לִשְׁתֵּי תוֹרוֹת. אֲבָל הֵיכָא דְּדָמֵי לַאֲגוּדּוֹת אֲגוּדּוֹת — לֹא עָשׂוּ בֵּית שַׁמַּאי כְּדִבְרֵיהֶם. שֶׁהֵן לַחִין. וְהוּכְשְׁרוּ לְקַבֵּל טוּמְאָה. וּכְלִי חֶרֶס טָמֵא עַל גַּבֵּי עַם הָאָרֶץ, וְשֶׁמָּא נָגַע בְּגַב הֶחָבִית, וּטְמֵאָה מִדְּרַבָּנַן, וְטִימְּאָתָם. חָבִית הָיְתָה נְקוּבָה. מִשּׁוּלֶיהָ הָיְתָה נְקוּבָה, כְּדֵי שֶׁיֵּצֵא מַשְׁקֶה הַזָּב מִן הַזֵּיתִים לַחוּץ. וְכֵיוָן דְּגַלֵּי דַּעְתֵּיהּ דְּלָא נִיחָא לֵיהּ בֵּיהּ — לָא מַכְשַׁר. אֶלָּא שֶׁסְּתָמוּהָ שְׁמָרִים. וְלֹא יָצְאוּ מִן הַמַּשְׁקִין, לְפִיכָךְ הֵן לַחִים. מְגוּלְגָּלִים. כְּמוֹ בֵּיצָה מְגוּלְגֶּלֶת (עוקצין פ"ב מ"ו): דְּחוּקִין וְעוֹמְדִים בֶּחָבִית. אֵין צְרִיכָה לִנָּקֵב. דְּמוֹהַל הַיּוֹצֵא מִן הַזֵּיתִים מֵי פֵּירוֹת הֵן, וְאֵין מַכְשִׁירִין. צְרִיכָה לִנָּקֵב. שֶׁמּוֹהַל מַכְשִׁיר כְּשֶׁמֶן, (ב) *[וּצְרִיכָה לִנְקוֹב] שֶׁיֵּצֵא הַמַּשְׁקֶה לַחוּץ לְגַלּוּיֵי דַּעְתֵּיהּ דְּלָא נִיחָא לֵיהּ בֵּיהּ. יָרוֹצּוּ. כְּמוֹ "וַתָּרִץ גֻּלְגָּלְתּוֹ" דַּאֲבִימֶלֶךְ (שופטים ט), לְ' רִיצּוּץ. שֶׁהֵן בְּנֵי צָרוֹת. שֶׁנִּשְּׂאוּ לַשּׁוּק כְּב"ה. וּמֵהֶן כֹּהֲנִים גְּדוֹלִים וכו'. לְקַמָּן פָּרֵיךְ: קָא בָּעוּ מִינֵּיהּ צָרוֹת, וְקָפָשֵׁיט לְהוּ בְּנֵי צָרוֹת? דַּאֲפִילּוּ לְב"ש פְּשִׁיטָא דִּכְשֵׁרִים, דִּבְנֵי חַיָּיבֵי לָאוִין בְּעָלְמָא נִינְהוּ. הַיְינוּ דְּקָאָמַר מִתְיָירֵא אֲנִי. דְּמַשְׁוֵי לְהוּ מַמְזֵרִים (ג) וְלִקְטְלֵיהּ לֵיהּ. הָא א"ר יְהוֹשֻׁעַ. לְקַמָּן בְּפֶ' "הַחוֹלֵץ" (דף מט.): אֵין מַמְזֵר אֶלָּא מֵחַיָּיבֵי מִיתוֹת ב"ד, וַאֲפִי' פְּשִׁיטָא לֵיהּ דַּהֲלָכָה כְּב"ש לָא מַשְׁוֵי לְהוּ מַמְזֵרִים. מֵאַלְמָנָה מָה אַלְמָנָה לְכה"ג שֶׁאֵין אִיסּוּרָהּ שָׁוֶה בַּכֹּל בְּנָהּ פָּגוּם. לִכְהוּנָּה, דִּכְתִיב "לֹא יְחַלֵּל זַרְעוֹ" (ויקרא כא). זוֹ שֶׁאִיסּוּרָהּ שָׁוֶה. בְּיִשְׂרְאֵלִים כִּבְכֹהֲנִים אֵינוֹ דִּין שֶׁבְּנָהּ פָּגוּם? בְּנֵי צָרוֹת דְּב"ה. דְּחַיָּיבֵי לָאוִין נִינְהוּ, מִי הָווּ פְּגוּמִין אַלִּיבָּא דְּב"ש? לְמַאי נָפְקָא מִינַּהּ. מֵאַחַר שֶׁהֲלָכָה כְּב"ה. לְמִיפְשַׁט וְלַד מַחֲזִיר גְּרוּשָׁתוֹ. מִשֶּׁנִּשֵּׂאת לְאַחֵר וְהֶחֱזִירָהּ, וְיָלְדָה לוֹ בַּת, אוֹתָהּ הַבַּת מַה הִיא לִכְהוּנָּה לְב"ה? וּמִבֵּית שַׁמַּאי בִּבְנֵי צָרוֹת נִשְׁמַע לְב"ה בְּבַת מַחֲזִיר גְּרוּשָׁתוֹ, דַּהֲוֵי נַמִי חַיָּיבֵי לָאוִין. הִיא עַצְמָהּ מִתְחַלֶּלֶת. שֶׁאִם מֵת כֹּהֵן גָּדוֹל פְּסוּלָה זוֹ לְהֶדְיוֹט, אוֹ אִם הָיְתָה בַּת כֹּהֵן נִפְסֶלֶת מִן הַתְּרוּמָה, דְּשַׁוְיֵיהּ חֲלָלָה בְּבִיאָתוֹ, דִּכְתִי' (שם) "לֹא יְחַלֵּל זַרְעוֹ בְּעַמָּיו", ●וְעַמָּיו הַיְינוּ אִשְׁתּוֹ, וּמַשְׁמַע דִּשְׁנֵיהֶם מִתְחַלְּלִים — הָאִשָּׁה וְהַזֶּרַע. תֹּאמַר בְּמַחֲזִיר גְּרוּשָׁתוֹ שֶׁאֵין מִתְחַלֶּלֶת בְּבִיאָה זוֹ, דְּאִי לִינָּשֵׂא לְכֹהֵן — כְּבָר מִיפַּסְלָא מִשְּׁעַת גֵּירוּשִׁין, וְאִי בִּתְרוּמָה דְּבֵי נָשָׂא — לָא מִיפַּסְלָה, כִּדְאָמְרִי' בְּפֶ' "אַלְמָנָה לְכה"ג" (לקמן סט.) דְּאֵין נִפְסֶלֶת בְּבִיאַת חַיָּיבֵי לָאוִין אֶלָּא בְּזָר אֶלָּא מֵעִיקָּרָא, לְאַפּוּקֵי מַחֲזִיר גְּרוּשָׁתוֹ וִיבָמָה לַשּׁוּק, דְּלָאו זָר מֵעִיקָּרָא הוּא. וּלְעֵיל גַּבֵּי חַיָּיבֵי כְרֵיתוֹת בְּנֵי צָרוֹת דְּבֵית שַׁמַּאי דְּלָא פָּרְכִינַן מַה לְאַלְמָנָה לְכֹהֵן גָּדוֹל שֶׁכֵּן הִיא עַצְמָהּ מִתְחַלֶּלֶת — הָתָם נַמִי, כֵּיוָן דְּנִבְעֲלָה לְחַיָּיבֵי כְרֵיתוֹת עֲשָׂאָהּ זוֹנָה, וּמִתְּרוּמָה דְּבֵי נָשָׂא מִיפַּסְלָא, כִּדְאָמְרִינַן בְּפֶ' "אַלְמָנָה לְכה"ג", וּלְהִנָּשֵׂא לְכֹהֵן נַמִי מִיפַּסְלָא, כִּדְתְנַן בְּמַתְנִיתִין (דף יג:): נִתְיַיבְּמוּ — ב"ה פּוֹסְלִים. צָרוֹת מִתְיָירֵא אֲנִי. לוֹמַר הֲלָכָה כְּדִבְרֵי מִי, דִּמְשַׁוֵּי לְהוּ לְצָרוֹת דְּבֵית שַׁמַּאי בְּנֵי חַיָּיבֵי כְרֵיתוֹת.

תוספות

אמר לי איני אוכל זיתים. מתוך פירוש הקונטרס משמע שהיה רבי יוחנן חושש שלא היה מקפיד ר' לדוק על מגע עם הארץ. ואף על גב דרבי לדוק כהן הוה, ובגדי פרושים מדרס לאוכלי תרומה — מ"מ היה חושש, לפי שר' לדוק מתלמידי ב"ש הוה ולכך היה חושש ר' יוחנן שמא לא הקפיד ר' לדוק לשומרה בטהרה, משום דבית שמאי אומרים אין לריך לנקוב. ולר"י נראה דודאי ידע בי' ר' יוחנן שר' לדוק קנה חבית מעם הארץ.

צריכה לנקוב. פירש בקונטרס: דמוהל של זיתים מכשיר. והכי נמי תנן בהדיא במס' מכשירין (פ"ו מ"ה): מי חלב כחלב, מוהל של זתים כשמן. וקשה: דבסוף פרק קמא דשבת (ד' יז. ד"ה "גוזרני") פירש הרב ר' יוסף: דלכך לא גזרו על המסיקה משום דלא שייכא טעמא דבצירה גבי מסיקה, דטעמא שמא יבצרו בקופות מזופפות לא שייך במסיקה, דמוהל אין מכשיר! וי"ל: דיש ג' עניני מוהל; דמוהל היוצא על ידי המסיקה — לכ"ע אינו מכשיר, והיוצא על ידי אכילה, פירוש ע"י שמתחממים בכומר ויוצא מהם מוהל, פליגי בה (שבת דף קמד:) ר' יעקב ור"ש, דר"ש מטהר ור' יעקב מטמא. והאי דהכא, שהחבית צריכה לינקב — צ"ל דחשיב כההיא דנפיק ע"י עיקול בית הבד, דמודה בה ר"ש, כי היכי דלא תיקשי מב"ה לר"ש.

למאי נפקא מינ' למיפשט מחזיר גרושתו. קלת קשה: דאמאי נקט ולד מחזיר גרושתו? דהוה ליה למיפשט ולד יבמה גמורה לשוק לב"ה, דקאי בה! וי"ל: לפי שפעם אחרת שאלו עליה לר' יהושע בסוף נדה (דף סט:) אנשי אלכסנדריא: בת משולחת מהו לכהונה, מי אמרינן ק"ו כו'. **מה** לאלמנה שכן היא עצמה מתחללת. וא"ת: היא גופה נילף דתתחלל גרושה מק"ו דאלמנה! ובקונטרס פי': דלתרומה דבי נשא לא מיפסלה, כדאמרי' לקמן בפ' "אלמנה" (דף סט.) דאינה נפסלת בביאת חייבי לאוין אלא בזר אללה מעיקרא הוא, ולאפוקי מחזיר גרושתו ויבמה לשוק דלאו זר אללה מעיקרא הוא. וקשיא: דנהי דמ"כי תהיה לאיש זר" (ויקרא כב) לא מלינו למילף אלא ההוא דזר אללה מעיקרא, מ"מ נילף בק"ו שתתחלל! וב"החולץ" (לקמן מד: מה.) נמי יליף חייבי כריתות מאלמנה, וקאמרי': וכי תימא מה לאלמנה וכו' ה"נ כיון דבא עליה עשאה זונה, ולמה לי טעם דעשאה זונה? היא גופה נילף בק"ו שתתחלל! ועוד: דלתקינן לקמן בפרק "אלמנה" (דף סח. ושם) למדרש מקרא דעמוני ומואבי ומלרי ואדומי כולן פוסלין בביאתן — תיפוק ליה מהאי ק"ו! ונראה לפרש דמהאי ק"ו לא מלינן למילף שתתחלל, דאין חילול אלא מאיסורי כהונה, כדאמרי' בפ' "עשרה יוחסין" (קדושין דף עז: ושם) א)מהאי טעמא דישראל הבא על אחותו — זונה משוי לה, חללה — לא משוי לה. ואע"ג דלקמן יליף דמתחללת בביאת גר עמוני ומואבי ומלרי ואדומי כותי חלל נתין ממזר, אף על גב דלא הויא איסור כהונה — התם מקרא דריש לה, אבל מק"ו ליכא למילף, דלהכי אייתר ליה חללה, לומר דלא ילפינן בק"ו. ולענין בנה — ודאי הוה בעי למילף מק"ו, אבל פסול האשה, דהיינו פסול חללות, שהיתה כשרה ונתחללה — לא ילפינן. וא"ת: נילף במה הלד מאלמנה וכותי ועבד, או מאלמנה ומלרי ואדומי, דבפ' "עשרה יוחסין" (שם עח. ושם) מוכח דילפינן במה הלד מאיסור כהונה, דרבי יהודה יליף התם דגר פוסל בביאתו מחלל ומלרי כו'! ומיהו, יש לומר: דדוקא ר"י אית ליה להאי סברא דילפינן במה הלד מאיסור כהונה, אבל רבנן — פליגי עליה, דלית להו בת גר זכר כבת חלל זכר. אבל קשיא: לרבי יהודה למה לן קרא דגר עמוני ומואבי כו' דפוסלים בביאתם? נילף במה הלד, או מאלמנה או מחלל כותי ועבד. דכי פרכת מה לחלל שכן איסור כהונה — כותי ועבד יוכיחו, מה לכותי ועבד דלא תפסי בה קידושין — חלל יוכיח! ●וי"ל: דר"י סבר לה כר"ע, וסבר נמי דיש ממזר מכותי ועבד. והשתא לא שייך למילף מכותי ועבד, כיון דהתם נמי הוי ממזר.

עין משפט נר מצוה

ס א מיי' פי"א מהל' טומאת אוכלין הל' ז:

תוספות ישנים

א) וא"ת כי קאמר לקמן גבי גוי ועבד ומה אלמנה וכו'. לימא גר עמוני שבא על בת ישראל יוכיח. שאיסורן שוה בכל ואין בתו פגומה לר' יוחנן דאמר התם בתו כשרה לכהונה. וי"ל לרשב"ג דאמר התם [דגר עמוני אין] פוסל אשה בביאתו משום דכל שאתה נושא בתו אתה נושא אלמנתו ניחא דליכא למימר הכא גר עמוני יוכיח דאיכא למימר מה לגר עמוני שאין פוסל אשה בביאתו וגם ליכא למימר מלרי ראשון יוכיח דשאני מלרי ראשון דליכא רק עשה. וא"ת מאי האי דקאמר הכא למפשט ולד מחזיר גרושתו הלא אין לדמות ולד יבמה לולד מחזיר גרושתו דבולד מחזיר גרושתו גלי קרא היא תועבה ואין בניה תועבין אבל ולד יבמה דלא כתיב בה מיעוטא אימא מק"ו דהוי פגום. וי"ל דאם איתא דולד מחזיר גרושתו כשר משום דגלי קרא מעתה גם גבי ולד יבמה לשוק יש לנו לומר דכשר דלא מלינו למימר דפגום הוי מק"ו דאלמנה דאיכא למימר מחזיר גרושתו יוכיח דאיסור שוה בכל הוא ואין בנה פגום:

הגהות הב"ח

(א) גמ' דב"ה לב"ש מהו נ"ב ע"ל פ' האשה רבה דף צ"ב בתוס' ד"ה אבל חכמים: (ב) רש"י ד"ה צריכה וכו' כשמן ומשום הכי נקבו שיצא המשקה: (ג) ד"ה היינו וכו' ממזרים וקטלי ליה:

גליון הש"ס

רש"י ד"ה היא עצמה מתחללת. ועמיו היינו אשתו. עי' לקמן דף סט ע"א ברש"י ד"ה מקיש זרעו: תוס' ד"ה מה לאלמנה וכו' וי"ל דר"י ס"ל כר"ע. עי' לקמן ד' מז ע"א תד"ה נאמן:

מסורת הש"ס

ומ"ה נקבו כדי שיצא רש"ל

עדיות פ"ד מ"ו

לקמן מט.

[לקמן מד:]

[לקמן מד: מה. נדה סט.]

[להו]

בני

תורה אור

בני צרות אני מעיד לכם. ת"ש: בימי רבי דוסא בן הרכינס הותרה צרת הבת לאחין. שמע מינה: עשו, שמע מינה. גופא, בימי רבי דוסא בן הרכינס התירו צרת הבת לאחין והיה הדבר קשה לחכמים, מפני שחכם גדול היה ועיניו קמו מלבא לבית המדרש. (*אמר: ומי ילך) ויודיעו? אמר להן רבי יהושע: אני אלך. ואחריו מי? רבי אלעזר בן עזריה, ואחריו מי? ר"ע. הלכו ועמדו על פתח ביתו, נכנסה שפחתו, אמרה לו: רבי, חכמי ישראל באין אצלך. אמר לה: יכנסו, ונכנסו. תפסו לרבי יהושע והושיבוהו על מטה של זהב, א"ל: רבי, אמור לתלמידך אחר וישב. אמר לו: מי הוא? רבי אלעזר בן עזריה. אמר: ויש לו בן לעזריה חבירנו? קרא עליו המקרא הזה: (תהלים לז) "נער הייתי גם זקנתי ולא ראיתי צדיק נעזב וזרעו מבקש לחם". תפסו והושיבו על מטה של זהב. א"ל: רבי, אמור לתלמידך אחר וישב. א"ל: ומי הוא? עקיבא בן יוסף. א"ל: אתה הוא עקיבא בן יוסף, ששמך הולך מסוף העולם ועד סופו? שב בני, שב, כמותך ירבו בישראל! התחילו מסבבים אותו בהלכות, עד שהגיעו לצרת הבת. אמרו ליה: צרת הבת מהו? אמר להן: מחלוקת בית שמאי ובית הלל. הלכה כדברי מי? אמר להן: הלכה כבית הלל. אמרו ליה: והלא משמך אמרו הלכה כבית שמאי! אמר להם: דוסא שמעתם, או בן הרכינס שמעתם? אמרו ליה: חיי רבי, סתם שמענו. אמר להם: אח קטן יש לי, בכור שטן הוא, ויונתן שמו, והוא מתלמידי שמאי. והזהרו שלא יקפח אתכם בהלכות. לפי שיש עמו שלש מאות תשובות בצרת הבת שהיא מותרת. אבל מעיד אני עלי שמים וארץ שעל מדוכה זו ישב חגי הנביא ואמר שלשה דברים: צרת הבת אסורה, *עמון ומואב מעשרין מעשר עני בשביעית, ומקבלים גרים מן הקרדויין ומן התרמודים. (חגיגה ג: ידים פ"ד מ"ג) תנא: כשנכנסו נכנסו בפתח אחד, כשיצאו — יצאו בשלשה פתחים. פגע בו בר"ע, אקשי ליה ואוקמיה. אמר לו: אתה הוא עקיבא ששמך הולך מסוף העולם ועד סופו? אשריך שזכית לשם, ועדיין לא הגעת לרועי בקר. אמר לו רבי עקיבא: ואפילו לרועי צאן. "עמון ומואב מעשרין מעשר עני בשביעית" *דאמר מר: (חגיגה ג:) [א]הרבה כרכים כבשו עולי מצרים ולא כבשו עולי בבל, [ב]וקדושה ראשונה קדשה לשעתה ולא קדשה לעתיד לבא, [ג]והניחום כדי שיסמכו עליהן עניים בשביעית. ומקבלים גרים מן הקרדויים והתרמודים. איני? והא תני רמי בר יחזקאל: אין מקבלים גרים מן הקרדויים! אמר רב אשי: קרתויים אתמר. כדאמרי אינשי: קרתויים פסולים. ואיכא דאמרי, תני רמי בר יחזקאל: אין מקבלים גרים מן הקרתויים. מאי לאו — היינו קרתויים היינו קרדויים? אמר רב אשי: לא, קרתויי לחוד וקרדויי לחוד. כדאמרי אינשי: קרתויי פסילי. רבי יוחנן וסביא דאמרי תרווייהו: אין מקבלים גרים מן התרמודים. ומי אמר ר' יוחנן הכי? והתנן: (ב"ק לח: נדה נו:) *[ד]כל הכתמים הבאים מן הרקם טהורים, ורבי יהודה מטמא, מפני שהם גרים וטועים, מבין הגוים טהורים. והוינן בה:

קפסיק

רש"י

בני צרות. דב"ה דקא בעיתו אי הם פגומים. מעיד אני לכם. שהם כהנים גדולים. בימי ר' דוסא הותרה. אחיו של ר' דוסא, שהיה מתלמידי ב"ש התירה, כדתני לקמן, ועשו על פיו ונהגו כן. שחכם גדול היה. וסבורים חכמים שהוא התירה. קמו. עמדו מלראות. אמר לו. רבי יהושע לר' דוסא: אמור לתלמידך אחר וישב. דוסא. התירו, שמעתם (א) אומרים? או בן הרכינס. בלא דוסא. סתם שמענו. בן הרכינס סתם, ושמו לא הוזכר. בכור שטן הוא. חריף ועומד על (ב) שמועה ועושה מעשה, ואינו שב משמועתו לעשות כרבים. עמון ומואב. ישראלים הדרים בארץ עמון ומואב, שכיבש משה מסיחון, ונתקדשו בקדושת א"י, ועכשיו בבית שני בטלה קדושתה, וזורעין בשביעית. ותקנו להן מעשר ראשון ומעשר עני בשביעית, כדמפרש לקמן, מפני פרנסת עניים שבא"י שאין להם מה לאכול בשביעית, לפי שבטל לקט שכחה ופיאה, והולכים שם ונוטלים לקט שכחה ופיאה ומעשר עני. ומקבלים גרים מן הקרדויין כו'. ולא אמרינן ממזרים הן, מבנות ישראל שבאו עליהן גוים, דאיכא רבנן דפסלי. פגע בו. יונתן בר"ע. וקדושה ראשונה. דבימי יהושע קדשה לשעתה ולא לעתיד. הלכך זורעים בהן בשביעית, שיסמכו עליהן עניים לשכור עצמן לחרוש ולקצור. ועוד: ליטול לקט שכחה ופיאה ומעשר עני. אין מקבלין גרים. מפרש לקמן שממזרים הן מישראל שנטמעו שם. הכתמים. שנמצאו בבגדים הבאים מרקם. טהורים. לפי שלא גזרו על כתמי גוים. שהם גרים. ודמם מטמא. וטועים. שהמירו דמם, וגזרו על כתמיהם, שאף על פי שחטאו, שהמירו – ישראלים הם. מבין הגוים. שאין ישראל דרים שם:

ואפי'

תוספות

בני צרות אני מעיד לכם. דכשרים אף לב"ש. וא"ת: לשמואל, דמספקא ליה ב"האשה רבה" (לקמן צב: ושם) אי קידושין תופסין ביבמ' לשוק, א"כ פשיטא דכשירה, דמיד שקדשה פקעה לה זיקה, כדאמרי' בשומרת יבם שקידש אחותה שקידושיה מפקיעין הייבום! וי"ל, דלא דמי: דהתם אין שום תקנה לעשות שתתייבם, שאין להמית אחותה. אבל היבמה שנתקדשה לשוק – אפשר לתקן ע"י גירושין שתתייבם. הלכך לא פקע זיקה. ועוד אמר רבי יצחק: ד"לא תהיה אשת המת לאיש זר" – משמע דאפילו ע"י הויה, דהיינו קידושין, לא תהיה לאיש זר, דלהכי אפקיה בלשון הויה. יצאו בג' פתחים. שלא ימצאם כולם יחד ויקפחם בהלכות, ויצטרכו לקבוע הלכה כמותו. א"נ: יצאו בג' פתחים כדי *שימצאו וישמעו תשובתו. עמון ומואב מעשרין מעשר עני בשביעית. פי' בקונטרס: ישראלים הדרים בארץ עמון ומואב שכיבש משה מסיחון, ונתקדשו בקדושת הארץ, ועכשיו בבית שני בטלה קדושתה. וקשה לר"ת: דאמר בפ' "מקום שנהגו" (פסחים נב: ושם) ג' ארצות לביעור: יהודה ועבר הירדן וגליל. ועבר הירדן היא ארץ סיחון ועוג, אלמא שקדשוה עולי בבל! ואומר ר"ת: דהתם בארץ סיחון ועוג שלא היתה של עמון ומואב, אבל ארץ סיחון שכיבש מעמון ומואב – לא קדשו עולי בבל, כדמשמע הכא. ועוד אמר ר"ת: דמצינו למימר דהכא בארץ עמון ומואב שלא כיבש סיחון מעולם, שלא קדשוהו אפילו עולי מצרים. וכן משמע במס' ידים (פ"ד משנה ג) דמדמה לה מצרים ובבל (ג). וה"פ הכא, דאמר מר: הרבה כרכים קדשו עולי מצרים ועולי בבל לא קדשום, והניחום כדי שיסמכו עליהם עניים. אלמא חששו לתקנת עניים, אע"ג דמא"י היו – נמנעו מלקדש. כל שכן בעמון ומואב, שלא נתקדש מעולם, שראוי לתקן מעשר עני בשביעית ולא מעשר שני. דבמס' ידים איכא מ"ד מעשר שני בשביעית. וכן יש לפרש במס' חגיגה (ד' ג. ושם) דקאמר נמי ר"א התם עמון ומואב מעשרין מעשר עני בשביעית. ומפרש: מה טעם – הרבה כרכים כו'. ולא בעי למימר דעמון ומואב הוא מכרכים שכבשו עולי מצרים. ותדע, דהא לר"א מספקא ליה בפ"ק דמגילה (דף י.) ובפ"ב דשבועות (טז. ושם) אי סבר קדושה ראשונה קדשה לעתיד לבא או לא, ור' יהושע ס"ל דקדשה לעתיד לבא במגילה ובשבועות, ואפ"ה אית ליה במס' ידים בעמון ומואב כר"א. אלא על כרחך, הא דקאמר התם מה טעם – לא מדברי ר"א הוא, ודברי ר"א הם במס' ידים ולא קתני לה התם, אלא הש"ס הוא שמפר' כן דלמ"ד לא קדשה – הניחו (ד) לקדש אף מא"י בשביל עניים, ולכך אין תימה אם גזרו על עמון ומואב מעשר עני ולא מעשר שני. והא דשבק הכא ובחגיגה טעמא דקאמר ר"ט בהדיא במסכת ידים מצרים – ח"ל, עמון ומואב – ח"ל, מה מצרים שהיא קרובה – עשאוה מעשר עני כדי שיסמכו עליה עניים, אף עמון ומואב כו'. משום דניחא ליה להש"ס למשכחת טעמא דאף בא"י הניחו מלקדש בשביל עניים, וכ"ש עמון ומואב שהן ח"ל. כל הכתמים הבאים מרקם טהורים. אע"ג דברקם נמי הוו ישראל, כדתנן בריש גיטין (דף ב. ושם) "אף המביא מן הרקם ומן החגר" – מ"מ, כתמים הבאים מרקם – טהורים, דלאו דישראלים נינהו. דישראל מצניעים כתמיהם, וגוים הדרים שם גוים גמורים, ולא ישראל מומרים.

רבי

עין משפט נר מצוה

סא א מיי' פ"א מהל' תרומות הל' ה ופ"ד מהל' שמיטה ויובל הלכ' כז:

סב ב מיי' פ"א מהל' תרומות הלכה ה ופ"ו מהלכות בית הבחירה הלכה טז:

סג ג מיי' פ"א מהל' תרומות הלכה ה:

סד ד מיי' פ"ד מהל' מטמא משכב ומושב הלכה י:

נ"ל שימצאוהו. יעב"ץ

תוספות ישנים

בני צרות מעידני לכם לפי שהם אף לב"ש בני יבמה לשוק וכשרים הם. ותימה עדיין הוא מכניס ראשו בין הרים גדולים לרב המנונא שאמר שומרת יבם שזינתה אסורה ליבמה וגם לכהונה נפסלה כדמשמע לקמן פרק הערל וא"כ צרה נמי הוי הולד פגום מק"ו דאלמנה וליכא למפרך מה לאלמנה שכן היא עצמה מתחללת דהא היא מתחללת נמי לרב המנונא וי"ל דסוגיא דהכא לא אתיא כרב המנונא דלרב המנונא לא אמרי' תרתי בעי מיניה דלא תקשי לן קא בעי מיניה צרות וקא פשיט ליה בני צרות דודאי מתירולא דבני צרות טובל לפשוט דין לצרות דכיון שהוא אומר שהבנים שמשו ע"ג המזבח א"כ (אמאי) [ממילא] מביא ראיה שאין הלכה ככל כב"ש דלב"ש הולדות פגומים ולא יוכלו לשמש אליבא דרב המנונא דאמר שומרת יבם שזינתה אסורה ליבמה וזאת השיאה עצמה לשוק א"כ לדברי רב המנונא בני זונה הם. וא"כ מדפשט מבני צרות דכשרים הם ושמשו ע"ג המזבח הצרות עצמן יהיו מותרות להנשא [לשוק] ודלא כב"ש דלב"ש הולד פגום: בכור שטן פ"ה כך שמו. י"מ שזה שם עירו ור"ל יש לי אח בכור שטן כדאמר התם רב אקלע לבור שטן:

מסורת הש"ס

[נ"ל אמרו מי ילדך]

הגהות הב"ח

(א) רש"י ד"ה דוסא התירו שמעתם הס"ד ותיבת אומרים נמחק: (ב) ד"ה בכור וכו' ועומד על שמועתו ועושה: (ג) תוס' ד"ה עמון וכו' דמדמה לה מצרים ובבל. נ"ב פי' עמון ומואב מדמה למצרים לר' טרפון שאמר מעשר עני [ור"א בן עזריה] פליג ומדמה עמון ומואב לבבל ומשמע דכי היכי דמצרים ובבל לא קידשום מעולם אף עמון ומואב דמדמה להו לא קידשום מעולם: (ד) בא"ד הניחו מלקדש אף מא"י בשביל:

גליון הש"ס

גמ' בני צרות אני מעיד לכם. עיין לקמן דף פא ע"א תד"ה לימא ודף לב ע"א תד"ה אבל חכמים: שם ואחריו מי ר"ע. עיין כתובות דף קה ע"א תד"ה דחשיב ליה:

מסורת הש"ס

קפסיק ותני: מבין הגוים — ואפי' מן תרמוד. ואמר רבי יוחנן: זאת אומרת: מקבלין גרים מתרמוד. וכי תימא: זאת, ולא ס"ל — *והא אמר רבי יוחנן: הלכה כסתם משנה! *אמוראי נינהו, ואליבא דר' יוחנן. מתרמוד מאי טעמא לא? פליגי בה רבי יוחנן וסבייא: חד אמר: משום עבדי שלמה, וחד אמר: משום בנות ירושלים. בשלמא למ"ד משום עבדי שלמה — קסבר: *גוי ועבד הבא על בת ישראל הולד ממזר. אלא למ"ד משום בנות ירושלים — מאי היא? פליגי בה רב יוסף ורבנן, ותרוייהו משמיה דרבה בר בר חנה. חד אמר: תריסר אלפי גברי ושיתא אלפי קשתויי, וחד אמר תריסר אלפי גברי ומנייהו שיתא אלפי קשתויי. בשעה שנכנסו גוים להיכל, הכל נפנו על כסף וזהב, והם נפנו על בנות ירושלים, שנאמר °"נשים בציון ענו בתולות בערי יהודה". אמר רבי שמואל בר נחמני (איכה ה)
אמר רבי יונתן, פסוק זה שר העולם אמרו: °"נער הייתי גם זקנתי", מאן אמריה? (תהלים לז)
אילימא קודשא בריך הוא — מי איכא זקנה קמיה? ואלא דוד אמריה — מי קשיש כולי האי? אלא ש"מ — שר העולם אמרו. ואמר רבי שמואל בר נחמני אמר רבי יונתן: מאי דכתיב: °"ידו פרש צר על כל מחמדיה" — זה עמון ומואב. בשעה (איכה א)
שנכנסו גוים להיכל הכל נפנו על כסף וזהב, והם נפנו על ס"ת. אמרו: זה שכתוב בו (דברים כג) °"לא יבא עמוני ומואבי בקהל ה'" — ישרף באש! °"צוה ה' ליעקב (איכה א)
סביביו צריו", *אמר רב: כגון הומניא לפום נהרא. אמר רב יהודה א"ר אסי: [קדושין עב: וע"ש שהוא רב יהודה]
גוי שקידש בזמן הזה — חוששין לקידושין, שמא מעשרת השבטים הוא. והא כל דפריש *מרובא פריש! בדוכתא דקביעי, דאמר רבי אבא בר [יומא פד: וש"נ]
כהנא: *°"וינחם בחלח ובחבור נהר גוזן וערי מדי". חלח — זה חלזון, וחבור — (מלכים ב יח)
זו

תורה אור

רש"י

ואפי' מתרמוד. אלמא לאו בספק ישראל קיימי. מקבלים גרים. ולא אמרי' ישראלים ממזרים הם. מתרמוד מ"ט לא. מקבלים. עבדי שלמה. שנשאו בנות ישראל (א) מחמת עושרן, ודרין שם בחזקת גוים, וקסבר: גוי ועבד הבא על בת ישראל הולד ממזר. משום בנות ירושלים. לקמיה מפרש לה בנות ירושלים בחורבנה, כשבאו גוים ונשאום. ה"ג. אלא למ"ד משום בנות ירושלים מאי היא. קשתויי. מושכי קשת. נער הייתי. איידי דאזכריה (ב) הא דלעיל נקט ליה הכא. שר העולם. מלאך. הומניא לפום נהרא. בהומניא יונים הם, ומצירין לבני פום נהרא שהם ישראל עניים. מעשרת שבטים הוא. שנשאו גויות, וקסבר דגויה שילדה מישראל הולד ממזר, וחוששין לקידושי ממזר. בדוכתא דקביעי. בני עשרת השבטים וכל קבוע כמחצה על מחצה דמי, והיכא קביעי — כדכתיב "וינחם בחלח ובחבור".
זו

נדה נו: | שבת מו. וש"נ | [גיטין פח: חולין מג. מנחות נב: נדה נו:] | [לקמן מה. לט. קידושין ע.]

תוספות

*רבי יוחנן וסביא אמרי אין מקבלין גרים מן התרמודיים. תימה: היכי פליג ר' יוחנן אחגי הנביא? ושמא סבר ר' יוחנן שלא אמרה חגי מעולם. קא פסיק ותני אפי' מתרמוד. תימה: דלמא לבד מתרמוד, כדאמרי' בפ"ק דגיטין (דף ו.): לא, לבר מבבל. אמוראי נינהו ואליבא דרבי יוחנן. דההוא דסבר אין מקבלים גרים מן התרמוד לית ליה אליבא דרבי יוחנן שתהא הלכה כסתם משנה. א"נ: סבר מן הגוים טהורים, לבד מתרמוד. ומיהו, ע"כ צ"ל דל"ל הלכה כסתם משנה, דהא קסבר גוי ועבד הבא על ישראלית הולד ממזר, וסתם מתני' ד"האומר" (קדושין דף סו:) סברה •דהולד כשר. דלר"ע דוקא, דאמר אין קידושין תופסין בחייבי לאוין, הו דהוי ממזר מגוי ועבד, כדמוכח בפרק "עשרה יוחסין" (שם עה: ושם), ומתני' ד"האומר" סוברת דקידושין תופסין בחייבי לאוין, דקתני: כל מקום שיש קידושין ויש שם עבירה, כגון ממזרת ונתינה לישראל. וא"כ אין ממזר מגוי ועבד. והא דקתני התם כל מי שאין לה עליו קידושין אבל יש עליה קידושין מעל אחרים הולד ממזר — היינו כמו שמפרש התם: ואיזו היא — כגון הבא על אחת מכל עריות שבתורה, ולא מגוי ועבד, אע"ג דגוי ועבד נמי אין לה עליו קידושין, ויש עליה קידושין מעל אחרים. וכה"ג איכא בגמרא. ואע"ג דאיכא סתמא אחרינא לקמן בפרק "אלמנה" (דף סט:) דסברה דיש ממזר מגוי ועבד — מ"מ מאי אולמיה דהך סתמא מהך סתמא? דכה"ג פריך בריש שבועות (דף ד.) וב"מרובה" (ב"ק סט:) ובכמה דוכתי. והכא דפריך: ומי א"ר יוחנן הכי? הוה מצי למיפרך מסתם דמתני' דפרק "האומר", אלא דניחא ליה למיפרך ממתני' דנדה, דאמר רבי יוחנן בהדיא דמקבלים גרים מן התרמוד, ולעיל אמר דאין מקבלים. ועוד: דמתני' דנדה אלימא טפי לאקשויי מינה, משום דהתם מוכח דלא באו עליהן גוי ועבד. דאי באו עליהם — אמאי כתמיהן טהורים? וליכא למימר משום דסברה דהולד כשר דבתר גוי ועבד שדינן ליה — דהא משמע דאתיא נמי כרבי יהודה דאיירי ברישא, ורבי יהודה על כרחך סבר דגוי ועבד הבא על בת ישראל הולד ממזר, כדפי' לעיל, גבי מה לאלמנה שכן היא עצמה מתחללת. **בשלמא** למ"ד משום עבדי שלמה קסבר כו'. וא"ת: ל"ל למיתלי טעמא משום עבדי שלמה, דעבדים אסורין בישראלית! וי"ל: דמסתמא נתייאשו הבעלים מהם, ואיכא למ"ד בפ' "השולח" (גיטין לט:) נתיאשתי מפלוני עבדי — אינו צריך גט שחרור. **קסבר** גוי ועבד הבא על בת ישראל הולד ממזר. וכן בפ' "החולץ" (לקמן מה. ושם) סוגיא דהש"ס אזלא דר' יוחנן אית ליה גוי ועבד הבא על בת ישראל הולד ממזר. מ"מ, נראה אמת דלרבי יוחנן הולד כשר. דבכל דוכתי קי"ל דרבי יוחנן אית ליה כסתם משנה, וסתם משנה ד"האומר" (קדושין סו:) סברה דהולד כשר. אע"ג דמתני' דפרק "אלמנה" (לקמן סט:) סברה דהולד ממזר מגוי ועבד — מ"מ נראה לסמוך טפי אסתמא דמתני' ד"האומר" [משום דמיתניא גבי הילכתא פסיקתא דקדושין](ג). וכיוצא בה קרי הלכתא פסיקתא ב"הגוזל קמא" (ב"ק קב.). וכל הנהו דסברי הולד ממזר אתו כר"ע, כדאמרינן ב"עשרה יוחסין" (קדושין עה:). וסברי לה כר"ע, דאמר: גוי ועבד הבא על בת ישראל — הולד ממזר. והתם נמי משמע דרבי יוחנן משום ר' ישמעאל סבר הולד כשר. וא"ת: והיכי פשיטא ליה התם דלר"ע הוי ממזר מגוי ועבד? דלמא גמר מאשת אב או מאנוסת אביו דלא תפסי בה לדידיה, [אבל לאחריני תפסי], לאפוקי הני דלא תפסי לא לדידיה ולא לאחריני, דהכי איכא מ"ד בפ' "החולץ" (לקמן מה:)! וי"ל: דתנן בהדיא בפ' "אלמנה" (לקמן סט:) דגוי ועבד הבא על בת ישראל — הולד ממזר, וע"כ ר"ע היא. וא"ת: בשלמא מעבד הוי ממזר — דבעבד איכא לאו, אלא מגוי אמאי הוי ממזר? ב"ד של שם גזרו ומדאורייתא ביאת היתר היא! וי"ל: אע"ג דביאת היתר היא מדאורייתא בלנעא, מ"מ כיון דלא תפסי בה קידושין — הוי ממזר, כמו בעבד. דאפילו ר"ש התימני היה מודה, אי לאו משום דלא תפסי בה קידושין לא לדידיה ולא לאחריני. והואיל דמעבד הוי ממזר לר"ע(ד), דאע"ג דלא תפסי בה קדושין לא לדידיה ולא לאחריני — ה"ה מגוי. א"נ מגוי לא הוי ממזר אלא מדרבנן, ובכל מקום מזכיר גוי אגב עבד, כמו שמזכיר חלוצה אגב גרושה בכל דוכתי וב"אלו הן הלוקין" (מכות יג.). והראשון עיקר. **פסוק** זה שר העולם אמרו. קשיא לר"ת: דעשה הפייט: *"השר המשרת נער נקרא הוא מטטרון הנכבד והנורא". אלמא, מטטרון הוא שר העולם שנקרא נער. ובפיוט אחר יסד: "תוקף מטטרון שר הנהפך לאש מבשר". משמע דחנוך הוא מטטרון. ואי אפשר שיהיה חנוך שר העולם, דבפרק "אלו טרפות" (חולין ס. ושם) אמר דבששת ימי בראשית פתח שר העולם ואמר "יהי כבוד ה' לעולם ישמח ה' במעשיו" וחנוך לא היה במעשה בראשית! וי"ל: דמטטרון אין זה שר העולם, והא דנקרא נער — לא משום דכתיב "נער הייתי וגם זקנתי" אלא(ה) נער, שכן היה שמו. ובפסיקתא, *בח' שמות של מטטרון מונה נמי נער. •ועוד, דאגדות חולקות זו על זו: דבבראשית רבה י"א דחנוך מת, *כדמתרגמי' "כי לקח אותו" (בראשית ה) — "אמית יתיה", ובריש מסכת דרך ארץ *משמע דנכנס לג"ע בחייו. **גוי** שקדש בזמן הזה חוששין לקידושין חיישינן כו'. פי' בקונטרס, דקסבר: גויה שילדה מישראל — הולד ממזר, וחוששין לקידושי ממזר. ותימה: דבכמה משניות מוכח דאין מתייחס אלא אחריה, דתנן לקמן בפ"ב (ד' כב.): מי שיש לו בן מכל מקום [פוטר אשת אביו מן הייבום], חוץ ממי שיש לו מן השפחה ומן הגויה! ותנן נמי בפרק "האומר" (קידושין סו: ושם) דולד שפחה וגויה כמותה, ולא הוי ממזר! ונראה דלא קשיא כל כך, דהנהו משניות סברי דגוי ועבד הבא על בת ישראל — הולד כשר, וה"ה איפכא. ורב אסי סבר כר"ע, דאמר: אין קידושין תופסין בחייבי לאוין, והולד ממזר מגוי ועבד, •והוא הדין הבא על שפחה וגויה. ונראה דטעמא דרב יהודה אמר רב אסי משום בנות, ולית ליה בנתיה דההוא דרא איגיור איגיורו. ועל כרחך רבי יוחנן דאמר וכולן לפסול — לא משום שבאו על הגויות, דהא בפ' שני (לקמן כג. ושם) בהדיא סבר כשמואל דאין בנך הבא מן הגויה קרוי בנך אלא בנה, אלא משום בנות הוא דקאמר לפסול, ולית ליה דאיגיורי איגיורו. ואע"ג דרב יהודה אית ליה ב"החולץ" (לקמן מה.) דגוי ועבד הבא על בת ישראל הולד כשר — הכא משמיה דרב אסי קאמר. **בדוכתא** דקביעי. דבדוכתייהו הוו רובא רובא מעשרת שבטים, ולא כמו שפירש בקונטרס משום דכל קבוע כמחצה על מחצה דמי. דאי אזיל איהו לגבה — כל דפריש מרובא פריש, כדאמרינן בסוף פרק קמא דכתובות (דף טו.).
ואין

[שייך לעמוד א' קודם ד"ה כל הכתמים]

תוספות ישנים

והאמר ר' יוחנן הלכה כסתם משנה. וא"ת ולימא דקאמר כאידך סתמא דאמרינן לקמן (ד' סט) גוי ועבד הבא על בת ישראל הולד ממזר ולדידיה אין מקבלין גרים מן התרמוד משום עבדי שלמה שבאו על בת ישראל. וי"ל מ"מ פריך שפיר דמאי אולמיה דהך סתמא מהך סתמא:

הגהות הב"ח

(א) רש"י ד"ה עבדי שלמה שנשאו בנות ישראל בחזקת עושרן: (ב) ד"ה נער וכו' דאזכריה להאי קרא לעיל נקט ליה הכא: (ג) תוספות ד"ה קסבר וכו' דכיוצא בה: (ד) בא"ד לר"ע אע"ג דלא כצ"ל ואות ד' נמחק: (ה) ד"ה פסוק וכו' גם זקנתי אלא שכן היה שמו נער ובפסיקתא:

[קדושין עב.]

גליון הש"ס

תום' ד"ה אמוראי וכו' דהולד כשר דלר"ע וכו'. ע' לקמן מד ע"א ודף ע ע"א ולע"ג: **ד"ה** פסוק זה וכו' ועוד דאגדות חולקות. כפי' רשב"ם ב"ב ד' קכא ע"ב ד"ה קפלו: **ד"ה** עובד כוכבים שקידש וכו' וה"ה הבא על שפחה. עיין לקמן סט ע"ב במתני' ולע"ג:

[וביוצר לשמחת תורה]

[ועי' היטב תוס' חולין ס. ד"ה פסוק וכו' מ"ש בשם יוסיפון]

באונקלוס ובירושל' ליתא

[זוטא ספ"א]

זו חדייב, נהר גוזן — זו גינזק, ועַרי מדי — זו חמדן וחברותיה, ואמרי לה: זו *ניהר וחברותיה. חברותיה מאן? אמר שמואל: כרך, מושכי, *חידקי ודומקיא. א"ר יוחנן: וכולן לפסול, כי אמריתה קמיה דשמואל: א"ל*: בנך (א) הבא מן ישראלית קרוי בנך, [א]ואין בנך הבא מן הגויה קרוי בנך — אלא בנה. והאיכא בנות, ואמר רבינא: ש"מ בן בתך הבא מן הגוי קרוי בנך! גמירי דבנתא דההוא דרא איצטרויי אצטרו. איכא דאמרי: כי אמריתה קמיה דשמואל א"ל: לא זזו משם עד שעשאום גוים גמורים, שנאמר הושע ה °"בה' בגדו כי בנים זרים ילדו". יתיב רב יוסף אחוריה דרב כהנא, ויתיב רב כהנא קמיה דרב יהודה, ויתיב וקאמר: עתידין ישראל דעבדי יומא טבא כי חרבי תרמוד. והא חריב! ההיא תמוד הואי. רב אשי אמר: היינו תרמוד היינו תמוד, אכפולי הוא דמכפל. חריב מהאי גיסא — אותיב מהאי גיסא, ואי חריב מהאי גיסא — אותיב מהאי גיסא. יתיב רב המנונא קמיה דעולא וקא הוי בשמעתא. אמר: מה גברא ומה (ב) גברא, אי לאו דהרפניא מאתיה! אכסיף. א"ל: כסף גלגלתא להיכא יהבת? א"ל: לפום נהרא. א"ל: א"כ — מפום נהרא את. מאי הרפניא? אמר ר' זירא: הר שהכל פונין בו. במתניתא תנא: כל שאין מכיר משפחתו ושבטו נפנה לשם, אמר רבא: והיא עמוקה משאול, שנאמר תהלים מט °"מיד שאול אפדם ממות אגאלם", ואילו פסול דידהו — לית להו תקנתא. פסולי דהרפניא משום פסולי דמישון ופסולי דמישון משום פסולי דתרמוד. פסולי דתרמוד משום עבדי שלמה, והיינו דאמרי אינשי: קבא רבא וקבא זוטא, מיגנדר ואזיל לשאול, ומשאול לתרמוד, ומתרמוד למישן, וממישן להרפניא.§

הדרן עלך חמש עשרה נשים

כיצד [ב]אשת אחיו שלא היה בעולמו? שני אחים, ומת אחד מהן; ונולד להן אח, ואח"כ ייבם השני את אשת אחיו ומת. הראשונה יוצאה משום אשת אחיו שלא היה בעולמו, והשניה משום צרתה. עשה בה מאמר ומת — שניה חולצת ולא מתייבמת.§ **גמ'** אמר רב נחמן: מאן דתני ראשונה לא משתבש, מאן דתני שניה לא משתבש. מאן דתני ראשונה

זו חדייב נהר גוזן וכו' מושכי חידקי ודומקיא. לפסול. רובן ממזרים, שנטמעו *עשרת השבטים בגויות, ובניהן הרי הן כישראלים, ונוהג בהן איסור ממזרות. והן לא נזהרו ונשאו זה אחותו או בתו, והרי הן ממזרים. כי אמריתה קמיה דשמואל. עד השתא מילתיה דרב יהודה *(משמיה דרב אסי (ג) קאמר, *ואחר פטירתו של רב אסי בא לפני שמואל) וקאמר: כי הדר אמריתה להא דרב אסי קמיה דשמואל, דחוששין לקידושין. אמר בנך הבא מישראלית קרוי בנך ואין בנך הבא מן הגויה קרוי בנך אלא בנה. דנפקא לן מ"כי יסיר את בנך מאחרי" (דברים ז) ולא כתיב כי תסיר את בנך — אלמא: לאו אבתו לא תקח לבנך מהדר, דא"כ היה לו לומר כי הגויה תסיר, ש"מ דאי נמי יולדת בן לעבודה זרה — לא בנך מיקרי, ולא קרינן ביה "כי תסיר את בנך". הילכך, גוים גמורים הם. והאיכא בנות. שנשבו, ונשאום גוים והולידו מהם. ואמר רבינא. לקמן בפ"ב (דף כג.) בן בתך הבא מן הגוי קרוי בנך, דכתיב "בתך לא תתן לבנו כי יסיר את בנך מאחרי". מדלא כתב כי תסיר, ש"מ דאבתך לא תתן לבנו קאי, וה"ק: שמא תלד לו בן ויסירנו האב מאחרי, וקא קרי ליה בנך, וליחוש לקידושין. דההוא דרא. דעשרת השבטים. איצטרויי איצטרו. (ד) נבקע רחמן מלקלוט זרע, ונעשו עקרות. איצטרו. לשון בקוע, כמו *טילָא חריפי דמלרי זיקי (ע"ז ד' ל.), וכמו לירא דחיטי (פסחים דף מ:). יומא טבא. משום דממזרים הם, ומטמעים בישראל ופוסלים אותן. היינו תרמוד היינו תמוד. ודקאמר הא חרוב — לא חריב כולה. דאיכפולי איכפול. כשחרבה מכאן נכפלה ונבנית מכאן. וקא הוי. מקשה. אמר. עולא עליה דרב המנונא: מה גברא ומה גברא! כמה הוא גדול. אי לאו דהרפניא מאתיה. שאינם מיוחסים. שהכל פונים שם. כל פסולין שאין מולאין אשה פונין והולכין שם. והיא עמוקה. ורעה לדבר זה יותר מגיהנם. דאילו ליורדי גיהנם איכא תקנתא, דכתיב "מיד שאול אפדם ממות אגאלם", ואילו פסולי דידהו לית להו תקנתא. משום פסולי דמישון. שקרובה לה, ומתערבין בהן. ואמר בפרק "עשרה יוחסין" (קידושין עא:) מישון מתה. והתם מפרש פסולייהו. קבא רבא וקבא זוטא. איפה גדולה ואיפה קטנה, שניהם מעוותים. כלומר: כל הפסולין מתגלגלים ויורדים לשאול, ומשאול לתרמוד. כלומר: שאול גבוה מתרמוד, ומתגלגל משאול לתרמוד. וטעמא כדלעיל: דאילו ליורדי גיהנם איכא תקנתא, ולפסול דידהו אין טהרה. מגנדר. מתגלגל.

הדרן עלך חמש עשרה נשים

כיצד אשת אחיו שלא היה בעולמו. פוטרת צרתה. ונולד להם אח. ומלאה זקוקה ליבם, ועליו אסורה משום אשת אחיו שלא היה בעולמו. ואח"כ ייבם השני את אשת אחיו. ולו אשה אחרת, ומת. הראשונה. זו היא אשת (ה) ראובן שנפלה לפניו כבר פעם אחת. יוצאה. ונפטרת מזה משום אשת אחיו שלא היה בעולמו כו'. עשה בה. זה שמת מאמר, ולא הספיק לכונסה עד שמת. שניה חולצת. ולא מיפטרא משום צרת ערוה, דלאו צרתה ממש היא. ולא מתייבמת. דמאמר קונה מקצת, והויא צרת ערוה במקצת מדרבנן. **גמ'** מאן דתני ראשונה. מאן דקרי לה ראשונה להך שנפלה לפני לוי שני פעמים — לא משתבש, ומאן דקרי לה שניה — לא משתבש. ראשונה

ואין בנך הבא מן הגויה קרוי בנך אלא בנה. פירש בקונטרס: דמדכתב "כי יסיר" ולא כתב "כי תסיר" משמע דלא קאי א"בתו לא תקח לבנך", דאי (ו) יולדת בן לעבודה זרה — לאו בנך מיקרי ולא קרינן ביה "כי תסיר את בנך". אלא אבתך לא תתן לבנו קאי, וה"ק: שמא תלד בן, ויסירנו האב מאחרי, שאותו קרוי בנך. וקשה לר"ת: לפירושו דפי' בנך* קרוי בנך — היינו בנך הבא מן הישראלית, שאביו גוי, דעליה קאי "כי יסיר", וא"כ אמאי מייתי ואמר רבינא בן בתך כו'? הרי הן ממש דברי שמואל! ורבינא נמי, מאי קאמר (ז) ש"מ מדר' יוחנן? מה שייך לומר ש"מ — דהן ממש דברי רבי יוחנן! ואומר ר"ת: ד"כי יסיר" אבתו לא תקח לבנך קאי, והכי קאמר: כי יסיר החותן את בנך מאחרי, והיינו הסרה — שאין הזרע מתייחס אחר בנך אלא אחר הגויה, דאין קרוי בנך אלא בנה. ושמואל ורבי יוחנן לא פירשו כלום בגוי הבא על בת ישראל, אלא רבינא מדקדק דבן בתך הבא מן הגוי קרוי בנך, מדלא כתב "כי יסיר את בתך" — ש"מ דלית בה הסרה, משום דמתייחס אחריה. ואין נראה לר"י, ד"כי יסיר" משמע כמו הסרה מאת הקב"ה, כדמתרגמי' "ארי יטעי יתה" ודרשי' נמי מכי יסיר לרבות כל המסירים. ועוד פירש ר"ת בע"א: דשמואל ורבי יוחנן דייקי מ"כי יסיר את בנך" — דמשמע דוקא על הסרתו הקפיד הכתוב, שלא יטעהו. ולא על הסרת בן בנו, דכיון דבא מן הגויה אין קרוי בנך אלא בנה מדלא כתיב כי יסירם, או כי יסיר בנך וזרעו מאחרי. ורבינא דייק: ש"מ בן בתך הבא מן הגוי קרוי בנך, דדוקא בבנך (ח) "כי יסיר את בנך" למעוטי זרעו, אבל בבתך — אפי' בזרעו יש לחוש להסרה.

פסולי דמישן משום פסולי דתרמוד. והא דאמר בפרק שני דקדושין (דף מט:): עשרה קבין עזות ירדו לעולם, תשעה נטלה מישן ואחת כל העולם. פי': לפי שהן ממזרים. הא דלא נקט תרמוד שפסולין יותר — שמא אשתרבוב למישן עד שגדלו יותר מתרמוד, ושמא בתרמוד היו רוב גוים, ובמישן רוב ישראל.

משאול לתרמוד. שאול קורא *בבל, לפי שתחילה גלו כולם לבבל כשרים ופסולים, ומבבל הלכו כל הפסולים לתרמוד. כדאמר ב"עשרה יוחסין" (קדושין סט:) דלא עלה עזרא מבבל עד שעשאה כסולת נקיה. ומונה כסדר שהלכו הפסולים מזו לזו, כמו שהקב הולך ומתגלגל מכאן לכאן.

הדרן עלך חמש עשרה נשים

כיצד. עשה בה מאמר. דסיפא (דף יח:) לא אצטריך, דמרישא שמעי' לה, אלא איידי דמתני ליה ברישא תנא להו נמי בסיפא.

מאן דתני ראשונה לא משתבש. הכא לא בעי: מאן דתני ראשונה אמאי לא תני שניה, כדדייק בריש מס' ע"ז (דף ב. ושם): מאן דתני אידיהן מ"ט לא תני עידיהן. דהתם בעי משום דה"ל למיתני לשון עדות, כדכתיב "יתנו עדיהן ויצדקו", ובתר דמשני דתברא עדיף — הדר פריך: מאן דתני עידיהן — מאי טעמא לא תני אידיהן? אשת

נ"ל בנות עשרת השבטים כעובדי עבודה זרה כו'

והרש"ל מקיים גירסא זו נ"ל לאחר

[ע' קידושין עב:]

[ע"ש]

לקמן כג. קידושין סח:

הושע ה

תהלים מט

פי' עמוקה כשאול

הוא יון לבן

עין משפט נר מצוה

סה א מיי' פי"ב מהל' איסורי ביאה הלכה ז:

א ב מיי' פ"ו מהל' יבום הלכה יז סמג עשין נא נב טוש"ע אה"ע סימן קעג סעיף יב:

בנך כו' קרוי. יעב"ץ

תוספות ישנים

ואמר רבינא ש"מ בן בתך הבא מן הגוי קרוי בנך וכו' פירוש מדלא קאמר כי יסירם מכלל דבן בתך הבא מן הגוי קרוי בנך ומ"ה לא רצה לכללם יחד כי הדבר אינו שוה בשניהם כלומר בנך ובתך משום דבבנך ליכא חששא כ"א ממנו אבל מבנו ליכא חששא שהוא בן הגויה ואינו קרוי בנך אבל בתך יש שם חששא ממנה ומבנה. כי בנה דין הוא שילך אחר מעשיך וא"כ בבתך יש שני הסרות אחד ממנה שמסירה לעבודה זרה וגם בנה הוא מסיר לעבודה זרה והוא קרוי בנך כי הולך אחר האם:

ביצד. ר' שמעון אומר מייבם לאחיו שירלה וחולץ לשניה. נראה דמייבם לאחיו שירלה לא קאי אעשה בה מאמר דהא ר' שמעון סבר לקמן חלץ לבעלת מאמר לא נפטרה לרתה:

הגהות הב"ח

(א) גמ' א"ל בנך (הבא מן ישראלית) תא"מ ונ"ב בתוספות מבואר דלא גרס ליה אבל בסוף פ' האומר מפורש דגרסי ליה התוס' ע"ש דף ס"ח ע"ב: (ב) שם מה גברא ומה גוברייה אי לאו: (ג) רש"י ד"ה כי אמריתה וכו' יהודה משמיה דרב אסי משמיה לאחר פטירתו של רב אסי בא לפני שמואל וקאמר כי הדר: (ד) ד"ה אלטרויי אלטרו נבקע נ"ב כמו בע"ז דף למ"ד: (ה) ד"ה הראשונה זו היא אשת ראובן הראשון שנפלה לפניו: (ו) תוס' ד"ה ואין בנך וכו' דאי נמי יולדת בן: (ז) בא"ד מאי קאמר ש"מ נ"ב לקמן דף כ"ג: (ח) בא"ד דדוקא בבנך כתיב כי יסיר את בנך למעוטי זרעו:

תוספות חד מקמאי

פרק כיצד. הא דתנן עשה בה מאמר ומת מתיבמת ה"ה אע"ג דלא עבד בה מאמר שניה מחלץ חלצה ולא מיבמה דקי"ל כשמואל דאמר יש זיקה אפי' בתרי אחי וה"ל צרת (א)אחות אשה בזיקה. והא דקתני עשה בה מאמר לאפוקי מב"ש דאמרי מאמר קונה קנין גמור קמ"ל: (א) נ"ל אשת אחיו שלא היה בעולמו בזיקה

עין משפט
נר מצוה

לקמן כד.

ב א מיי' פ"א מהל' יבום הלכה א סמג עשין נה טוש"ע אה"ע סימן קנז סעיף א:
ג ב מיי' שם הלכה יג סמג שם טוש"ע שם סימן קנט סעיף ה.

[ע' תוס' יומא ב: ד"ה הנ"מ ותו' מנחות ז. ד"ה מאי נ"מ מה שהגיהו בקושיא]

תוספות ישנים

ואי כתב רחמנא יחדו. נ"ע אמאי אצטריך למכתב אחים דלוט ויחדו לפתוק מתרוייהו דמשום דכתוב חד אצטריך אידך. וי"ל דמסברא ידעי' דמייחד באבא ואמא משום חומר דאשת אח דמישתריא גביה. וא"כ אצטריך אחים לומר דלא בעי' אחוה מיוחדת גמורה דהא אף מאחין דלוט אית לן למילף וכיון דאצטריך אחים בלוט אצטריך נמי יחדו כדמפרש תלמודא: **באחותה** אין באמה לא. וא"ת מאי קא פריך דלמא ההיא כמאן דאמר יש זיקה דהא איכא כמה תנאי דקא סברי יש זיקה וי"ל דפריך שפיר דמסתבר דהלכתא כוותה מתניתא דמייתי דהויא מחלוקת ואח"כ סתם. שהמחלוקת הוא בהחולץ גבי שומרת יבם שקדש אחיו אחותה דהיינו ר"י בן בתירה ורבנן דפליגי עליה כדקאמר שמואל הלכה מכלל דפליגי רבנן עליה וסתם ישנו בהחולץ בסוף המשנה והלכה כסתם כ"כ להר"ס: **ולימא** הלכה כדברי האומר יש זיקה. מצינן לפרש דהיינו ר"י בן בתירא דאפי' בקידש סבר יש זיקה: **והא** כי פליגי בתרי פליגי. אף בתרי פליגי וא"כ היה לו לאמורא לפרש דבריו כדי שלא יבא לטעות בהם:

תוספות חד מקמאי

אסיקנא דאחין מן האב מייבמין אע"פ שאין אחים מן האם. מן האם ולא מן האב אין מייבמין.

ראשונה לא משתבש. מאי ראשונה – ראשונה לנפילה, ומאן דתני שניה לא משתבש: מאי שניה – שניה לנשואין. מי לא עסקינן דייבם ואח"כ כנס? אלא: מאי שניה – שניה בנשואין.

אשת אחיו שלא היה בעולמו היכא כתיבא? אמר רב יהודה אמר רב: אמר קרא °"כי ישבו אחים יחדו" – שהיתה להם ישיבה אחת בעולם, פרט לאשת אחיו שלא היה בעולמו. "יחדו" – מיוחדים בנחלה, *פרט לאחיו מן האם. רבה אמר: אחין מן האב – יליף *"אחוה" "אחוה" מבני יעקב, מה להלן מן האב ולא מן האם, אף כאן מן האב ולא מן האם. ולילף "אחוה" "אחוה" מעריות! דנין "אחים" מ"אחים", ואין דנין "אחים" מ"אחיך". מאי נפקא מינה? הא *תנא דבי רבי ישמעאל: °"ושב הכהן" °"ובא הכהן" זו היא שיבה זו היא ביאה! *ה"מ היכא דליכא מידי דדמי ליה, אבל היכא דאיכא מידי דדמי ליה – מדדמי ליה ילפינן. ולילף "אחוה" "אחוה" מלוט, דכתיב °"כי אנשים אחים אנחנו"! מסתברא, מבני יעקב הוה ליה למילף, משום דמפני. מדהוה ליה למכתב "שנים עשר עבדיך בני אבינו" וכתיב "אחים" – ש"מ לאפנויי. ואיצטריך למכתב "אחים", ואיצטריך למכתב "יחדו". דאי כתב רחמנא "אחים" ה"א: לילף "אחוה" "אחוה" מלוט. וכי תימא לא מפני – לאיי, אפנויי מפני, מדהוה ליה למכתב "רעים" וכתיב "אחים", שמע מינה לאפנויי – כתב רחמנא "יחדו", המיוחדים בנחלה. ואי כתב רחמנא "יחדו", הוה אמינא: דמייחדי באבא ובאמא, צריכא. והא מהיכא תיתי? *יבום בנחלה תלא רחמנא, ונחלה מן האב ולא מן האם היא! איצטריך, סד"א: הואיל וחידוש הוא, דקמשתרי ערוה גביה – אימא עד דמייחדי באבא ובאמא, צריכא. אמר רב הונא אמר רב: שומרת יבם שמתה – מותר באמה. אלמא קסבר: *אין זיקה. ולימא: הלכה כדברי האומר אין זיקה! אי הוה אמר הכי ה"א: הנ"מ בתרי, אבל בחד יש זיקה. ולימא: הלכה כדברי האומר אין זיקה אפי' בחד?! אי אמר הכי הוה אמינא אפילו מחיים, קמשמע לן: לאחר מיתה – אין, מחיים – לא, משום *דאסור לבטל מצות יבמין. תנן: *יבמתו שמתה – מותר באחותה. באחותה אין, באמה לא! הוא הדין דאפילו באמה, ואיידי דתנא רישא אשתו שמתה מותר באחותה, באחותה – אין, אבל באמה – לא, דהויא לה איסורא דאורייתא, תנא נמי סיפא מותר באחותה. ורב יהודה אמר: [ג]שומרת יבם שמתה – אסור באמה. אלמא קסבר: *יש זיקה. ולימא: הלכה כדברי האומר יש זיקה! אי הוה אמר הכי הוה אמינא: הנ"מ בחד, אבל בתרי אין זיקה. והא כי פליגי – בתרי פליגי! אלא, אי אמר הכי הוה

אשת אחיו שלא היה בעולמו היכא כתיבא. וא"ת: תיפוק ליה מדכתיב (משלי ג) "דרכיה דרכי נועם" ומהאי טעמא עבדינן מתים כחיים לענין יבום, בפ' "יש מותרות" (לקמן פז:), אע"ג דאיצטריך למילי אחריני, כדאמר בפרקין* גבי מצוה בגדול לייבם, א"כ, אשת אחיו שלא היה בעולם דכתב רחמנא – ל"ל? ובפרק "ב"ש" (לקמן קיא:) נמי דייקינן מיני' דקטן זוקק ליבום. מ"מ, משמע דעיקריה לגופיה איצטריך. ואר"י: דאיצטריך להיכא דממותם של יבמה מעוברת, דהוי שפיר "דרכי נועם" ותמתין, שמא תלד זכר ותהא זקוקה לו: **אחוה** אחוה מבני יעקב. לענין אשת אחיו שלא היה בעולמו אין סברא למילף מבני יעקב, דלא מיקרי אחים אא"כ הם בעולם אחד כבני יעקב, דפשיטא דמיקרי אחין, ואי לאו דמיעט קרא בהדיא – לא הוה שייך למילף מבני יעקב לענין הך מילתא.

ולימא הלכה כדברי האומר אין זיקה. פי' בקונט': דרבנן דרבי יהודה בן בתירא דמייתי לקמן, דמדפסיק שמואל כר' יהוד' בן בתירא דאמר יש זיקה – מכלל דפליגי רבנן. וקש': דלמא בעלמא סברי רבנן דיש זיקה, והתם שרו ולא מצרכי להמתין שיעשה אחיו מעשה – משום דקידושין מפקעי זיקה, דהא חשיב בסוף "הערל" (לקמן דף פג.) וב"פ דמגילה (דף יח:) הסיא לדרבי יהודה בן בתירא יחידאה, דדייקינן דשמואל חייש ליחידאה מדפסיק כר' יהודה. ולמאי חשיב ליה יחידאה? והא כמה תנאים סברי דיש זיקה. ורב אשי דייק מסתם מתניתין דפ' "ד' אחין" (לקמן ל. ושם): זאת אומרת יש זיקה, ואפי' בתרי אחין! אלא ודאי בההיא דר"י מודו כולהו דע"י קדושין פקעה זיקה. ובסוף שמעתין (דף יח:) דמצריך תרי מילי דשמואל היה יכול לומר אי אשמועינן יש זיקה ה"א בההיא דר"י דקידושין מפקעי זיקה, אלא טעמא אחרינא אשכח. ואין לפרש לכדברי האומר אין זיקה היינו ר"מ, דא"כ מאי קאמר ה"א ה"מ בתרי, הא ר"מ בחד נמי קאמר דאין זיקה! וליכא למימר נמי דהיינו ר' יהושע דאמר יפר לאחד ולא לשנים – דהא בפ' "ד' אחין" מוקי פלוגתייהו בעבד בה מאמר, ופליגי אי מאמר קונה אי לאו! וי"ל: דאין נ"ל לחלק משום קידושין. ורב יוסף דקרי ליה יחידאה קסבר דכולהו תנאי סברי אין זיקה, ולית ליה דרב אשי דדייק ממתני' דפ' "ד' אחין" דיש זיקה. דה"נ פליגי עליה סתם. וכן משמע ב"החולץ" (לקמן מ.) דקרי רב יוסף משנה שאינה צריכה להא דתנן: יבמתו שמתה מותר באחותה, ואע"ג דבעי למידק מינה בשמעתין דיש זיקה. אלא דרב יוסף לא בעי למימר דלהאי לאשמועינן דיש זיקה, משום דסבר דאין זיקה לכולי עלמא.

אבל מחיים לא דאסור לבטל מצות יבמין. ואפילו ר"ג דאמר: אם מיאנה – מיאנה, מודה הכא. דהתם שסבר נשואה לו. וא"ת: ומנלן דסבר אין זיקה? דלמא לעולם יש זיקה, ולאחר מיתה שרי משום דפקעה זיקה, כדאמר בסמוך! וי"ל: דאע"פ שהעשה עומד בסמוך לריכות, האמת הוא דאי יש זיקה – אחר מיתה נמי אסור, דזיקה כבדי לא פקעה. והאי

ראשונה לנפילה. שנפלה ראשונה לייבום, קודמת לזו בפעם ראשונה. **שניה** לנישואין. לנישואין של שני, שהוא היה נשוי כבר כשנפלה זאת לפניו: ופרכינן. **מי** לא עסקינן. כלומר, מי לא מיתוקמא נמי מתני' דייבם אשת אחיו תחילה, ואח"כ כנס את האחרת, דלא הויא הך בנישואין. **אלא** שניה. יבמה שניה לנישואין. שנישאת שני פעמים, אחת לבעל ואחת ליבם. **היכא** כתיבא. לאיסורא. **המיוחדים** בנחלה. הראויין לירש זה את זה. **אחוה** אחוה. "כי ישבו אחים", "שנים עשר אחים עבדיך בני אבינו" (בראשית מב). **מעריות**. "ערות אשת אחיך", וקי"ל לקמן בפרק "הבא על יבמתו" (דף נה.), דאפילו אחיך מן האם ולא מן האב. **זו** היא שיבה כו'. דאע"ג דלא דמו קראי להדדי, כיון דתרווייהו בבית כהן משתעי – דיינינן בהו ג"ש: מה להלן חולץ וקוצה וטח כו'. **מלוט** כי אנשים אחים אנחנו. ותתייבם אשת אחי אביו, שהרי בן אחיו היה (א). **המיוחדים** בנחלה. שחולקין נחלה אחת, לאפוקי לוט שאין חולקין נחלה אחת. **והא** מהיכא תיתי. דליבעי עד דמייחדי באבא ובאמא? והא ייבום בנחלה תליא, דכתיב (דברים כה) "יקום על שם אחיו המת", ואוקמינן לקמן (דף כד.) "על שם אחיו" – לנחלה, שיירש המייבם כל נכסי המת, ואין אחין חולקין עמו. **אין** זיקה. זיקת יבמתו שמתה לא חשיבא למיהוי כארוסה, להאסר (ב) אמו עליו משום חמותו. **ולימא** הלכה כדברי האומר אין זיקה. דתנן בפ' "החולץ" (לקמן מא.): שומרת יבם שקדש אחיו את אחותה של יבמה, והלכה הייבום באחיו – משום רבי יהודה בן בתירא אמרו, אומרים לזה שקדש אחות יבמתו: המתן מלכנוס, לפי שאחות זקוקתו היא, הואיל ולאחר שנזקקה אחותה לו קדש את זו – צריך להמתין עד שתתייבם היבמה לאחיו, דפקעה זיקה. ואמר שמואל: הלכה כרבי יהודה. ומדקאמר הלכה – מכלל דפליגי עליה ואמרי: אין זיקה לאחין חשיבא לאסור עליהן קרובותיה. **ה"מ**. דלא חשיבא זיקה להיות אסורות קרובות בתרי אחין – כשנפלה לפני שני יבמין, כגון ההיא פלוגתא דר"י ורבנן, דכיון דלא ידיע קמי מאן מינייהו רמיא, לא חשיבא למיסר קרובות. **אבל** בחד. שאין שם אלא יבם אחד, דודאי עליה רמיא, אימא דמיא לכנוסה, ואיסר באמה. **ולימא** הלכה כדברי האומר אין זיקה אפילו בחד. ר"ע קא"ל בפ' "ד' אחין" (לקמן כט:): שומרת יבם שמתה אין יבמה מיפר נדריה לא לאחד ולא לשנים. כלומר: בין שנפלה לפני יבם אחד, בין שנפלה לפני שנים, דלא קרינן ביה "אישה"*. **ה"א** אפי' מחיים. (ג) יבמה מותר באמה קודם חליצה, וחלה היבמה לשוק משום בת אשתו. **דאסור** לבטל כו'. ואי נסיב אמה מחיים – מבטל למצוה לגמרי מייבום וחליצה. **יבמתו** שמתה מותר באחותה. דקתני: אשתו מתה מותר באחותה. אבל אמו, דלגבי אשתו אסורה אף לאחר מיתתה – ביבמתו נמי אסורה. **איסורא** דאורייתא. חמותו', אסר רחמנא, ולא פליג בין מחיים בין לאחר מיתה, דכתיב גבי אחות אשה, "עליה בחייה". **יש** זיקה. זיקת ייבום הויא כארוסה, ואסורה אמה על הכנס משום חמותו. **והא** כי פליגי. ר"י ורבנן בתרי [הוא] דפליגי, דקתני (לקמן דף מא.): המתן עד שיעשה אחיך מעשה.

באחותה

מסורת הש"ס

ב"ב קיז: [לקמן כב.]

עירובין נא. יומא ב: נזיר ה. מכות יג: הוריות ח: חולין פה. מנחות ז. מה: בכורות לב. נדה כב:

[לקמן כ: כד. ועי' לקמן מ.]

[לקמן כו: ל. נא. נג.]

[לקמן ושם יט:]

*לקמן מט

[עמ"ש תוס' לקמן כט: סד"ה כגון]

[לקמן ל. נא. נג.]

הגהות הב"ח

(א) רש"י ד"ה מלוט וכו' היה הס"ד ואח"כ מ"ה כתב רחמנא יחדו המיוחדין בנחלה וכו' לאפוקי אחיו דלוט שאין: (ב) ד"ה אין זיקה וכו' להאסר אמה עליו: (ג) ד"ה ה"א אפילו מחיים מחיי היבמה מותר באמה:

גליון הש"ס

תוס' ד"ה אבל מחיים וכו'. שסבר נשואה לו. עיין לקמן דף קט ע"א תד"ה אי כר"ג:

הוה אמינא: מחיים, אבל לאחר מיתה פקעה לה זיקה, קמ"ל דזיקה בכדי לא פקעה. לימא מסייע ליה: יבמתו שמתה מותר באחותה, באחותה – אין, באמה – לא. ה"ה דאפי' באמה, ואיידי דתנא רישא אשתו שמתה מותר באחותה, דוקא באחותה אבל באמה לא, דהויא לה איסורא דאורייתא – תנא נמי סיפא מותר באחותה. מתיב רב הונא בר חייא: עשה בה מאמר ומת – שניה חולצת ולא מתייבמת. טעמא – דעבד בה מאמר, הא לא עבד בה מאמר – שניה נמי יבומי מייבמה. ואי אמרת יש זיקה, הויא לה [א]צרת אשת אחיו שלא היה בעולמו בזיקה! אמר רבה: הוא הדין דאע"ג דלא עבד בה מאמר – שניה מחלץ חלצה, יבומי לא מייבמה, והא דקתני מאמר – *לאפוקי מב"ש, דאמרי: מאמר קונה קנין גמור, קמ"ל. איתיביה אביי: *שני אחין בעולם אחד, ומת אחד מהן בלא ולד, ועמד השני הזה לעשות מאמר ביבמתו, ולא הספיק לעשות בה מאמר עד שנולד לו אח, ומת, הראשונה יוצאה משום אשת אחיו שלא היה בעולמו, ושניה – או חולצת או מתייבמת. ואי אמרת יש זיקה – הויא לה צרת אשת אחיו שלא היה בעולמו בזיקה! הא מני – ר"מ היא, דאמר: אין זיקה. ומי סבירא ליה לרבי מאיר אין זיקה? והתנן: *ארבעה אחים, שנים מהן נשואים שתי אחיות, ומתו הנשואין האחיות – הרי אלו חולצות ולא מתייבמות. ואי ס"ד סבר ר"מ אין זיקה – *הני מתרי בתי קאתיין, האי לייבם חדא והאי לייבם חדא! לעולם אין זיקה, משום דקסבר: *אסור לבטל מצות יבמין, דדלמא אדמייבם חד מיית אידך, וקא בטלת מצות יבמין. ואי אין זיקה – תיבטל, דהא ר"ג אמר אין זיקה, ומותר לבטל מצות יבמין. דתנן: *ר"ג אומר: אם מאנה – מאנה, ואם לא מאנה – תמתין עד שתגדיל ותצא הלזו משום אחות אשה! אמר ליה: דרבן גמליאל אדרבי מאיר קרמית? לא, הכי(א) קאמרינן: ר"מ חייש אפי' לספיקא, ר"ג – אפילו לודאי לא חייש?! דלמא, מאן דלא חייש אפי' לודאי לא חייש, ומאן דחייש – אפי' לספיקא חייש. א"ל אביי לרב יוסף: הא דרב יהודה – דשמואל היא, דתנן:

שומרת

באחותה אין. דאפי' כנוסה שמתה מותר באחותה. **עשה בה מאמר.** מתני' היא (ב). **מחליץ חליצה.** **יבומי לא מייבמה.** דהויא צרת ערוה בזיקה. שכשנפלה לפני אחיו קודם מותו ונזקקה לו, נעשית צרה לאשתו בזיקה, והויא השתא הך נכרית לגביה צרת ערוה בשביל זיקה שהיתה לאחין בה. **מדב"ש.** בפ' "ד' אחין" (לקמן ד' כט.), ב"ש אומרים אשתו עמו והלזו תצא משום אחות אשה כו'. **קנין גמור.** ותיהוי צרת ערוה, ותיפטר אף מן החליצה, קמ"ל. **עד שנולד לו אח ומת אותו שני.** ולו אשה אחרת, ונפלו שתיהן לפני הנולד. **בזיקה.** שנזקקה לשני לפני מותו, ונעשית צרה לאשתו. **ר"מ היא.** ר"מ קאמר לה להך ברייתא בפירקין, (ג) דאמר תניא כוותיה דרב אדא, ומייתי לה להך מתניתא, וקתני סיפא דברי ר"מ. **ומתו הנשואין שתי האחיות.** ונפלו שתיהן יחד לפני האחין. **ולא מתייבמות.** משום דתרווייהו זקיקי ליה להאי, ותרווייהו זקיקי ליה להאי, ואי נסיב חד חדא – [קא] פגע באחות זקוקתו. **מתרי בתי.** משני אחין נפלו. **לעולם אין זיקה.** והא דקאמר לא מתייבמות – משום דאסור לבטל מצות יבמין, ואי אמרת לייבם האי חדא – דלמא מיית אידך אח, ולא מייבם לאידך, ונפקא מהאי משום אחות אשה מחליצה ומייבום, הלכך אמרינן ליה לקמא חלוץ, דאי נמי מיית אידך – הדר האי חולץ וחליץ לה. ומדינא לבתר חליצה דקמא מצי אידך לייבומי, דהשתא מיקיימא מצות יבמין בתרווייהו, אלא גזירה דלמא אתי לייבומי ברישא. **ואי אין זיקה.** דלית ליה איסור זיקה – תיבטל מצות יבמין ולא איכפת לן. דמאן דלית ליה איסור זיקה, לא חייש נמי לבטול מצות יבמין. **דהא** לר"ג דשמעינן ליה אין זיקה. בפ' ר"ג (לקמן דף נא.) שמעינן ליה נמי דאמר מותר לבטל מצות יבמין בפרק ב"ש (לקמן קט.). **דתנן ר"ג אומר כו'.** שני אחין נשואין שתי אחיות, אחת גדולה ואחת קטנה, ומת בעלה של גדולה ונפלה לפני בעל הקטנה, מלמדים את הקטנה למאן בבעלה ולעקור נשואיה כדי לייבם את זו, שזיקתה של זו חמורה לאסור הקטנה עליו, שלא היו נישואיה גמורים, שמא תמאן – ולכך לא תוציא את זו משום אחות אשה. **ר"ג אומר אם מיאנה מיאנה.** ותתייבם הגדולה. ואם לאו – תמתין גדולה עד שתגדיל קטנה, ויבעול, ויהיו קידושין גמורין, ותצא גדולה משום אחות אשה. אלמא: אין זיקה, מדשרי קטנה עליה, ומותר לבטל מצות יבמין. ולר"מ נמי, אי סבר אין זיקה – לימא נמי מותר לבטל מצות יבמין. **רבן גמליאל אדר"מ קרמית.** נהי נמי דבזיקה סבירא להו כי הדדי, בביטול יבמין פליגי. **אפילו לספיקא.** כי ההיא דלעיל, אדמייבם חד – מיית אידך. ורבן גמליאל, אפי' היכא דודאי בטלה, כגון הכא דתמתין עד שתגדיל – לא חייש. **הא דרב יהודה.** דאמר לעיל אסור באמה, דיש זיקה. **דשמואל היא.** משמיה דשמואל רביה שמיע ליה, ולא מרב, דהוה נמי רביה.

שומרת

והאי דקתני מאמר לאפוקי מב"ש. תימה: דמה צריך למיתני בשני מקומות לאפוקי מב"ש? דלקמן בפ' "ד' אחין" (דף ל.) גבי ג' אחים, שנים מהם נשואים שתי אחיות כו', קתני נמי: עשה בה מאמר ומת (ד) חולצת ולא מתייבמת, וקאמר רב אשי בגמ': דה"ה אע"ג דלא עשה בה מאמר, דיש זיקה. והא דקתני מאמר – לאפוקי מב"ש! וי"ל: דאי לאו משנה יתירה הוה דייקינן מתני' כפשטה, דמשמע דוקא עשה בה מאמר. ורב דאמר אין זיקה – סבר דמסברא ה"א דיש זיקה, ואי לאו משנה יתירה הוה אמרי' דנקט עשה בה מאמר לאפוקי מב"ש.

הא מני ר"מ. דקתני בסיפא דברי ר"מ. לעיל דפריך ממתני' ה"מ לשנויי נמי הא מני רבי מאיר, אלא דניחא ליה לתרולי סתמא דמתני' כוותיה.

הני מתרי בתי קאתיין. הלשון מגומגם, דמשמע דאפשר להם להיות מבית אחד, ולא ה"ל למימר טפי אלא: ואי אין זיקה האי לייבם חדא כו'.

משום דקסבר אסור לבטל מצות יבמין. הא דלא כר"ע, דלרבי עקיבא כי חליץ נמי בטיל מצות יבמין, (ה) (*מדאידך דדריש בפרק "החולץ" (לקמן מד. ושם) "בית חלוץ" – הכתוב קראו ביתו, ומדאורייתא אחות חלוצה הויא כאחות אשה.

דלמא אדמייבם חד מיית אידך כו'. וא"ת: הא רבנן למיתה לא חשו, דלית להו שמתקנין לו אשה אחרת שמא תמות אשתו (יומא ב.). ור"מ גופיה לא חייש לשמא יבקע הנוד, ולא לשמא ימות, בפרק "כל הגט" (גיטין דף כח. ושם)! וי"ל: דלאלתר דוקא לא חייש, אבל הכא – פעמים שמאחר זמן גדול מלחלוץ ומלייבם אחר חברו, ובזמן מרובה חיישינן שמא ימות לכ"ע. ואע"ג דאביי מדמה שמא מת לשמא ימות, ולשמא מת לא חייש ר"מ אפי' לזמן מרובה, דתנן (שם): בת ישראל הנשואה לכהן, והלך בעלה למדינת הים – אוכלת בתרומה בחזקת שהוא קיים. ושמעתין אתיא כאביי, דמשמע דקבלה מיניה אביי – לא מדמי להו לגמרי, אלא שמא ימות לאלתר לשמא מת לזמן מרובה. תדע דלא לגמרי מדמי, דהא לר' יהודה דחייש לשמא ימות לאלתר, אי הוה חייש נמי לשמא מת לאלתר – א"כ אשת כהן שיצא בעלה מפתח ביתו לא תאכל בתרומה אלא כשרואה בעלה בפניה חי! וא"ת: וליחלוץ חד והדר לייבם אידך, דתו ליכא למיחש לביטול יבמין! וי"ל: דגזרינן דלמא אתי לייבם ברישא. וריב"ן פי': משום דבשעת נפילה לא חזו תרווייהו, כל זמן שלא חלץ לאחת. וקשיא לפירושו: דאותה שנפלה תחילה תשתרי כי חלץ לשניה, דהוה לה יבמה שהותרה ונאסרה – דתחזור להתירה הראשון!

מיאנה מיאנה ואם לאו תמתין עד שתגדיל. ופי' בקונטרס: תמתין גדולה עד שתגדיל הקטנה. ואין הלשון משמע כן, דלא הוה ליה למימר "הלזו" אלא: ותצא משום אחות אשה, הואיל דתמתין נמי אגדולה קאי! אלא נראה דתמתין הקטנה מלבעול עד שתגדיל. אבל בקטנות אסור לבעול, אע"ג דסבר אין זיקה, דמכוער הדבר, כיון דבהאי ביאה לא מיפטרה גדולה.

שומרת

[לקמן כט: נח:] [לקמן יט.] [לקמן כו.] [לקמן קט.]

ד א טוש"ע אה"ע סימן קעג סעיף יב:

תוספות ישנים

לימא מסייע ליה יבמתו שמתה כו' אע"ג דפליגי תנאי בה מ"מ מייתי שפיר דהלכה כן משום דהוי מחלוקת ואח"כ סתם א"נ מייתי מהכא דאפילו לאחר מיתה לא פקעה ליה זיקה והכא לא איירו תנאי כלל: **ואי** אמרת יש זיקה הוה צרת אשת אחיו שלא היה בעולמו בזיקה. וא"ת ומאי קא מייתי הלא ידעי' דאיכא תנאי דסברי אין זיקה. וי"ל דהכי פריך אא"כ דאפי' למ"ד יש זיקה לאחר מיתה פקעה לה זיקה שפיר דאתיא הך אפי' למ"ד יש זיקה. אלא כיון דאמרת דמיתה לא פקעה לה זיקה תקשי מהך אי סברת יש זיקה דא"כ זיקה חזקה היא כיון דמיתה לא פקעה לה ואין לנו לחלק בין מתה היא למת הוא כיון שהזיקה חזקה כ"כ דמיתה לא פקעה לה: **לאפוקי** מב"ש. וא"ת למה לי הא ידעינן דב"ש במקום ב"ה אינה משנה וי"ל דאצטריך לאפוקי משום דאיכא דסבר כאותה ברייתא וא"ת לקמן נמי אמרינן לאפוקי מב"ש וי"ל דאי לאו יתירא דב' משניות ה"א הכא מסברא טעמא דעבד בה מאמר ולא הוה אמינא ה"ה דאע"ג דלא עבד בה מאמר: **אדמייבם** חד מיית אידך וקא מבטלא מצות יבמין. וא"ת ולחלוץ ברישא והדר לייבם דאי לא מיית אידך לייבם ואי מיית לחלוץ האי וי"ל דגזרינן דלמא מייבם ברישא:

הגהות הב"ח

(א) גמ' אדר' מאיר קרמית לא הכי קאמינא ר' מאיר וכו' ורבן גמליאל: (ב) רש"י ד"ה עשה וכו' מתני' היא נ"ב בדף יז ע"א: (ג) ד"ה ר' מאיר וכו' בפירקין דף י"ט ע"א דאמר תניא כוותיה דרב פפא ומייתי: (ד) תום' ד"ה והאי וכו' ומת נכרית חולצת: (ה) ד"ה משום וכו' בטיל מצות יבמין אי מת אידך דדריש כצ"ל להגיה:

גליון הש"ס

גמ' א"ל אביי לרב יוסף הא דר"י דשמואל היא. עירובין דף ז ע"א ד' פה ע"א כתובות ד' יב ע"ב:

עין משפט נר מצוה

ה א טוש"ע אה"ע סימן קנט סעיף ה:
ו ב מיי' פ"ו מהלכות יבום הלכה יז סמג עשין נח טוש"ע אה"ע סימן קעג סעיף יב:

גמרא

*שומרת יבם שקידש אחיו את אחותה, משום ר' יהודה בן בתירה אמרו: אומרים לו, המתן עד שיעשה אחיך מעשה. *ואמר שמואל: הלכה כר' יהודה בן בתירה. א"ל: דאי דרב מאי? (*א"ל): קשיא דרב אדרב! דלמא אמוראי נינהו, ואליבא דרב? כיון דאיתמר משמיה דשמואל בהדיא, ומשמיה דרב כאמוראי – לא שבקינן משמיה דשמואל בהדיא ומוקמינן כאמוראי ואליבא דרב. אמר רב כהנא, אמריתה לשמעתא קמיה דרב זביד מנהרדעא, אמר: אתון הכי מתניתו לה, אנן בהדיא מתנינן: (א) אמר רב יהודה אמר שמואל: שומרת יבם שמתה – אסור באמה. אלמא *קסבר: יש זיקה. ואזדא שמואל לטעמיה, דאמר שמואל: הלכה כרבי יהודה בן בתירה. וצריכי, דאי אשמעינן יש זיקה – ה"א: ה"מ – בחד, אבל בתרי – לא, אקמ"ל. ואי אשמעינן הלכה כר' יהודה בן בתירה – ה"א ה"מ מחיים, אבל לאחר מיתה – פקעה לה זיקה, קמ"ל: דזיקה בכדי לא פקעה.§

מתני' בשני אחים ומת אחד מהן, ויבם השני את אשת אחיו, ואח"כ נולד להן אח ומת – הראשונה יוצאה משום אשת אחיו שלא היה בעולמו, והשניה משום צרתה, *עשה בה מאמר, ומת – השניה חולצת ולא מתייבמת. *ר"ש אומר: מייבם לאיזו מהן שירצה, או חולץ לאיזו מהן שירצה.§

גמ' *אמר רב אושעיא: חלוק היה ר"ש אף בראשונה. ממאי – מדקתני משנה יתירה – בבא דרישא למאן קתני לה? אילימא לרבנן – השתא יבם ולבסוף נולד, דכי אשכחה בהתירא אשכחה, אסרי רבנן – נולד ואח"כ יבם מיבעיא? אלא לאו – לר"ש איצטריך, ותנא רישא להודיעך כחו דר"ש, ותנא סיפא להודיעך כחן דרבנן. ובדין הוא דנפלוג ר"ש ברישא, אלא נטר להו לרבנן עד דמסיימי למילתייהו, והדר פליג עלייהו. אלא, אשת אחיו שלא היה בעולמו, לר"ש היכי משכחת לה? בחד אחא, ומית, ונולד לו אח. אי נמי: בתרי, ולא יבם ולא מית. בשלמא יבם ואח"כ נולד – כי אשכחה בהתירא אשכחה, אלא נולד ואח"כ יבם – מאי טעמא? קסבר: יש זיקה, וזיקה כבנוסה דמיא. מתקיף לה רב יוסף: השתא זיקה ומאמר מספקא ליה לר"ש אי כבנוסה דמיא אי לאו כבנוסה דמיא, זיקה לחודה מיבעיא? מאי היא? דתנן: *שלשה אחין נשואין שלש נשים נכריות, ומת אחד מהם ועשה בה שני מאמר, ומת – הרי אלו חולצות ולא מתייבמות, שנאמר °"ומת אחד מהם יבמה יבא עליה" – מי שעליה זיקת יבם אחד, ולא שעליה זיקת שני יבמין. רבי שמעון אומר: מייבם לאיזהו מהן שירצה, וחולץ לשניה. יבומי תרווייהו לא – דדלמא יש זיקה, והוו שני יבמות הבאות

מבית

תורה אור: דברים כה

רש"י

שומרת יבם. ממתנת לייבום יבמה. שקידש אחיו. של יבם את אחותה אחר שנפלה זו לפניו. אומרים לו. למארס: המתן מלכנוס, לפי שאחות זקוקתך היא. עד שיעשה אחיך מעשה. עד שייבם אחיך את היבמה, ותפקע זיקתה ממך. אלמא: זיקה אסרה לאחותה. א"ל. רב יוסף לאביי: ואי משמיה דרב אמרה מאי קשיא לך? דרב אדרב. דא"ר הונא אמר רב לעיל מותר באמה. אמוראי נינהו. רב הונא ורב יהודה תלמידי דרב הוו, ופליגי אליביה. כיון דאיתמר משמיה דשמואל בהדיא. דיש זיקה, דשמואל עצמו אמרה ולא תלמידו משמו, ומצינו למימר דרב יהודה תלמידו מכלל אותה שמועה אמר להאי דידיה. ומשמיה דרב איתמר באמוראי. בפלוגתא, דהא פליג רב הונא – לא שבקינן כו'. הכי קמתניתו לה. לרב יהודה דלעיל, בסתמא, שלא הזכיר שם רבו. וצריכיתו למידק, הא דרב יהודה – דשמואל היא: ה"ג: אנן בהדיא מתנינן לה. ואזדא שמואל לטעמיה. כולה רב כהנא אמרה. ה"מ מחיים. כל זמן שיבמתו קיימת. **מתני'** ומת. המייבם. מייבם לאיזו שירצה. ופטורה חברתה. ולאו אעשה בה מאמר קאי, אלא ארישא, דקתני: הראשונה יוצאה כו'. דקאמר ר"ש, דכיון דכשנולד כבר נתייבמה, ולא היתה על זה בזיקת נישואי אחיו הראשון מעולם – מותרת לו. **גמ'** אף בראשונה. וקא שרי נולד ואח"כ ייבם. מדקתני משנה יתירה. לכולה ההיא בבא דרישא. דלמאן קתני לה, אי לאו דפלוגתא דר"ש עלה קיימא, ולהכי תנייה, לאשמועינן דאפי' בההיא שרי. למאן קתני לה. לאשמועינן מילתיה דמאן איצטריכא? אילימא לרבנן. לאשמועינן איסורא לרבנן, דהא לא איסור ולא היתר לר"ש שמעת מינה ברישא, דהא לא איירי בה. ונטר להו. המתין להם. והדר פליג עלייהו. בכולה מילתא. בחד אחא. דודאי מכח זיקת זה שלא היה בעולמו אסורה לזה להתייבם. אי נמי בתרי. אחים, ומת האחד, ונולד להם את השלישי. ולא ייבם. זה השני את יבמתו. ולא מת. אסורה לזה שנולד לאחר מיתה ליבמה מזיקת אח שלא היה בעולמו. אבל היכא דייבמה השני – פקעה זיקת אח הראשון, ונעשית אשתו של זה השני. אי נמי: לא יבמה האי שני, הואיל והוזקקה לו – הרי היא כנוסה כדלקמן, וכשמת – מותרת לשלישי. בהתירא אשכחה. שלא נאסרה עליו שעה אחת, שלא נזקקה לו מכח הראשון כלום. יש זיקה. כשנפלה לפני השני קודם לידתו של זה, ונזקקה לו לשני – אלימא ההיא זיקה לשוויא כנוסה, והוי ליה כייבם ולבסוף נולד. זיקת יבם אחד. כגון שלא נפלה אלא פעם אחת, או שכנסה שני ופקעה זיקה ראשונה. וכשמת אין כאן אלא זיקת ייבום של שני, או לא עשה בה מאמר ומת – אין כאן אלא זיקת ייבום ראשון, ועכשיו יש כאן זיקת ייבום של שני יבמין, שיש עליה קצת זיקה מן הראשון, דכל זמן שלא נתייבמה – לא פקע זיקתה מן השני, וצרתה, אשת השני, אסורה משום דידה. מייבם לאיזו שירצה. דלית ליה הך דרשה דזיקת שני יבמים, דאי מאמר קונה – הרי היא אשת שני, ואין כאן אלא זיקתו. ואם אין קונה – הרי הוא כמו שאינו, ואין כאן אלא זיקת ראשון. וחולץ לשניה. משום ספיקא, כדמפרש ואזיל:

מבית

תוספות

שומרת יבם שקידש אחיו את אחותה כו'. אר"י: דדוקא קידש אומרים לו המתן מלישא, משום דבשעת נישואין נראה כנושא אחות זקוקתו. אבל אם נשא כבר, שהיא אשתו גמורה – פקע לה זיקה לגמרי ואין צריך להמתין מלבעול. ודוקא קידש אחר נפילה, כדמוכח ב"החולץ" (לקמן מא. ושם) דבקידש באיסור איירי, דמסיק עלה: מתה אשתו מותר ביבמתו, משום דהואי יבמה שהותרה ונאסרה וחזרה והותרה. אבל אם קידש בהיתר קודם נפילה, שלא היתה אחות זקוקתו בשעת קידושין – א"צ להמתין כלל. **אומרים** לו המתן. וא"ת: למה צריך להמתין? דכיון דקדשה פקעה לה זיקה לגמרי, כדמוכח בפ' "ד' אחים" (לקמן כט. ושם) גבי הא דא"ר אלעזר: מאמר לב"ש אינו קונה קנין גמור אלא לדחות צרה בלבד, א"ר אבין אף אנן נמי תנינא: ב"ש אומר יקיימו, דיעבד אין, לכתחלה – לא. ואי ס"ד דמאמר קונה קנין גמור – זה יעשה מאמר ויקנה, וזה יעשה מאמר ויקנה! ומאי קושיא? אפי' קני קנין גמור, הא אמרי' הכא דצריך להמתין בקידושין דאורייתא! ולפי מאי דפרישית לעיל(ב), דמש"ה חשיב לר"י בן בתירה יחידאה – א"ש. וי"ל: דלר"י בן בתירה, דסבר יש זיקה, אין הקידושין מפקיעים הזיקה. אבל ר' אבין סבר אין זיקה, ולא אסור לייבם אלא משום ביטול מצות יבמין. ולהכי פריך אי מאמר קונה לב"ש קנין גמור זה יעשה קנין גמור – ויקנה וזה יעשה מאמר ויקנה, ויכולים לעשות ע"י שליח בבת אחת, דליכא ביטול מצות יבמין. והא דשרי הכא לקיימה, אפי' לרבי יהודה בן בתירה, ובפ' "ד' אחין(ג)" שניהם נשואים ב' אחיות דאייתי לעיל, קתני סיפא קדמו וכנסו יוציאו! אר"י: דשאני גבי ד' אחים, שהאחיות לא היו באות לעולם לכלל היתר, שכל אחת אחות זקוקתו. אבל היכא דאחות יבמה אתיא לכלל היתר, לאחר שיעשה אחיו מעשה – לא החמירו להוציא. **דאי** דרב מאי. וא"ת: דבסוף פ"ק דכתובות (דף יב:) נמי אמרינן הא דרב יהודה – דשמואל היא, ולא פריך דאי דרב מאי! וי"ל: דהכא משמע דרב יהודה משמיה דרב קאמר לה, דקאי ארב הונא דקאמר משמיה דרב שומרת יבם שמתה מותר באמה.

משכחת לה בחד אחא. וא"ת: לעיל בפ"ק (דף ט: ושם) בשמעתיה דלוי קאמר: בפלוגתא לא קמיירי, ופריך: והא א"ר אושעיא חלוק היה ר"ש אף בראשונה, הא לרבי אושעיא נמי משכחת לה בחד אחא, ולפטור צרתה וצרת צרתה נמי משכחת לה למאי דאמר לקמן דמודי ר"ש בזיקת שני יבמין דלאו ככנוסה דמיא! וי"ל: דמתני' דפרקין אתא לפרושי פרקין קמא, דקתני: כיצד אשת אחיו שלא הי' בעולמו. ולר' אושעיא דחלוק ר"ש אף בראשונה – ע"כ מתני' דפרק קמא איירי בפלוגתא.

שמא

הגהות הב"ח

(א) גמ' בהדיא מתנינן לה אמר: (ב) תוס' ד"ה אומרים וכו' דפרישית לעיל כ"ב דף יז בד"ה ולימא: (ג) בא"ד ובפ' ד' אחין שנים מהן נישואין ב':

תוספות ישנים

מאי טעמא דקסבר יש זיקה וזיקה ככנוסה. והאי דקאמר בתרי ולא ייבם ולא מית משמע דאין זיקה דאי זיקה ככנוסה אפי' לא יבם הוי כמו יבם. היינו משום דלא מית אבל במית זיקה הוי ככנוסה. וא"ת כיון דזיקה הוי ככנוסה אמאי נקט במתני' יבם בלא יבם נמי שריא ליה לר' שמעון דהוי כמו יבם ואח"כ נולד וי"ל דנקט יבם משום דמפרש הכא אשת אחיו שלא היה בעולמו דפרקין קמא וקאמר דכלהו פוטרות צרותיהן וצרות צרותיהן ואי לא ייבם לא משכחת בגוה צרה:

מסורת הש"ס

מגילה יח: לקמן מח.
שם
רש"ל מ"ז
[לקמן כז.]
עי' תוס' ריש פרקין
[לעיל ט:]
[לעיל ט: וצ"ל אמר רבי אושעיא וע' תוס' עירובין סח. ד"ה אמר ותוס' לקמן יט. ד"ה ועוד וכן איתא לעיל ט: רבי אושעיא]
לעיל יב. לקמן לח:

מבית אחד, יבומי חדא ואיפטור אידך – לא, דדלמא אין זיקה ככנוסה והוו להו שתי יבמות הבאות משני בתים. אלמא: מספקא ליה. וכי תימא: מדאורייתא ה"נ דמייבמא חדא, ומפטרא חדא, ומדרבנן הוא דאסור, גזירה משום שמא יאמרו: ב' יבמות הבאות משני בתים, חדא מייבמא ואידך מיפטרא בולא כלום, והא טעמא דר"ש משום מאמר ולאו מאמר הוא! דתניא, אמר להם רבי שמעון לחכמים: אם מאמרו של שני מאמר – אשת שני הוא בועל, ואם מאמרו של שני אינו מאמר – אשת ראשון הוא בועל. אמר ליה אביי: ולא שני לך בין זיקת יבם אחד לזיקת שני יבמים? דלמא, כי אר"ש זיקה ככנוסה דמיא – ביבם אחד, אבל בשני יבמין – לא. ומי שני ליה לר"ש? והתניא, כלל אר"ש: כל שהלידה קודמת לנשואין – לא חולצת ולא מתייבמת, נשואין קודם ללידה – או חולצת או מתייבמת. מאי לאו ביבם אחד, וקתני: לא חולצת ולא מתייבמת! לא, בשני יבמים. אבל ביבם אחד מאי, הכי נמי או חולצת או מתייבמת? אי הכי, אדתני נשואין קודמין ללידה חולצת או מתייבמת – ליפלוג וליתני בדידה: בד"א – בשני יבמים, אבל ביבם אחד – או חולצת או מתייבמת! כולה בשני יבמין קמיירי. ואלא מאי כללא? ועוד, מתיב רב אושעיא: *ג' אחין, שנים מהן נשואין שתי אחיות, או אשה ובתה, או אשה ובת בתה, או אשה ובת בנה – הרי אלו חולצות ולא מתייבמות, ור"ש פוטר. ואי ס"ד קסבר ר"ש זיקה ככנוסה דמיא – לייבם לקמייתא ותיפטר אידך! אמר רב עמרם: מאי פוטר נמי – פוטר בשניה. והתניא: *ר"ש פוטר בשתיהן! אמר רבא: שניה שבזוג זה והשניה שבזוג זה. קא טעי רבא בארבעה זוגי, חדא: ד"או" "או" קתני. ועוד: "ר' שמעון פוטר בארבעתן" מיבעי ליה. ועוד: תניא, ר"ש פוטר בשתיהן מן החליצה ומן הייבום, שנא' (ויקרא יח) "ואשה אל אחותה לא תקח לצרור" •בשעה שנעשו צרות זו לזו לא יהא לך ליקוחין אפי' באחת מהן. אלא אמר רב אשי: אי דנפול בזה אחר זה – הכי נמי. הכא במאי עסקינן – דנפול בבת אחת, ורבי שמעון סבר לה *כרבי יוסי הגלילי, דאמר: אפשר לצמצם. רב פפא אמר: בייבם ואח"כ נולד – פליג ר"ש, בנולד ואח"כ ייבם – לא פליג, ותרווייהו לרבנן איצטריך, *ו"לא זו אף זו" קתני. תניא כוותיה דרב פפא, ותיובתא דר' אושעיא: שני אחים בעולם אחד, ומת אחד מהם בלא ולד, ועמד השני הזה לעשות מאמר ביבמתו, ולא הספיק לעשות בה מאמר עד שנולד לו אח, ומת. הראשונה יוצאה משום אשת אחיו שלא היה בעולמו, ושניה או חולצת או מתייבמת. עשה בה מאמר, ואח"כ נולד אח, או שנולד לו אח ואח"כ עשה בה מאמר, ומת – הראשונה יוצאה משום אשת אחיו שלא היה בעולמו, ושניה חולצת ולא מתייבמת. ר'

מבית אחד. ורחמנא אמר "את בית אחיו" (דברים כה) – בית אחד הוא בונה, ואינו בונה שני בתים. ולמיפטרה אידך. דזיקה ככנוסה דמיא, וכ"ש זיקה ומאמר. גזירה שמא יאמרו שתי יבמות הבאות משני בתים. ונפלו בבת אחת בעולם, דליכא למימר שהראשונה הוזקקה לבעל השניה, ואתי למימר נמי תתייבם חדא ותיפטר אידך. משום מאמר ולא מאמר. ספק מאמר קונה ספק אינו קונה. ביבם אחד. כגון מתני' דהוו שני אחין, וכי מיית חד – זקוקה להאי לחודיה, ורמיא עליה. הלכך, אע"פ שלא כנסה עד שנולד השלישי – הוה ליה כייבם ולבסוף נולד. אבל בשני יבמים. כגון הך דשלשה אחין, דפשו להו תרי – לא. ומי שני ליה. ושרי ליה בנולד ולבסוף ייבם? והתניא. כל שהלידה של שלישי קודמת לנישואין של שני – לא חולצת, אלמא מודה ר"ש בהא! מאי לאו ביבם אחד. שכשמת ראשון לא נשאר אלא אח אחד, ואח"כ נולד זה. לא בשני יבמין. שהיו שלשה אחים, ומת אחד מהן, ונפלה לפני השנים, ונולד להם אח – ההיא ודאי אסירא עליו דהאי בתרא, אפילו לאחר שייבמוה שנים הראשונים ומתו. דהא ודאי נולד ולבסוף ייבם הוא, דההיא זיקה דהויא לה גבי הני קודם לידתו של זה לא אלימא לשוויה ככנוסה למהוי כייבם ולבסוף נולד. כולה בשני יבמין קמיירי. בשני יבמין בעי לאשמועינן איסורא והיתרא. אלא מאי כללא. הואיל וביבם אחד אפילו לידה קודמת לנישואין שרי, היכי מצי למיתני כל שהלידה קודמת לנישואין לא חולצת ולא מתייבמת, וקתני: כלל א"ר שמעון, הא זמנין דלא הוי הכי! חולצות. אם מתו הנשואין את הקרובות, ונפלו לפני השלישי – הרי אלו חולצות. ולא מתייבמות. הואיל ותרווייהו זקיקן ליה – קא פגע בקרובת זקוקתו. רבי שמעון פוטר. אף מן החליצה, כדקתני לקמן בשמעתין, מ"לצרור". לייבמה לקמייתא. ההיא דנפלה בריש', ואפי' לא הספיק לכונסה עד שנפלה אחותה – מאי איכפת לן דהוי זיקה קמייתא ככנוסה, ותיפטר בתרייתא משום אחות אשה, וקמייתא תתייבם, דכיבם אחד דומה! *(דהא כי נפלה מעיקרא לא נפלה אלא קמי חד, דלגבי אידך – ערוה היא משום אחות אשה, ולא רמיא קמיה כלל). בשניה. שנפלה אחרונה. שניה שבזוג זה. אם היו שלשה אחין, שנים מהן נשואין שתי אחיות ואשה ובתה, ומתו שניהם ונפלו לפני השלישי, אחת מן הראשונות מתייבמת, ושתים האחרונות פטורות. דחדא מן הראשונות חשובה ככנוסה ומתייבמת, והשניות פטורות, אחת – משום ערוה, דהי מינייהו מן הראשונות דחשבת ככנוסה אית לה חדא קרובה בשתים השניות. נמצאת האחת יוצאת משום ערוה, ושניה משום צרתה. וקטעי רבא בהנך ארבעה זוגי. דמתני', דס"ד דרבא דמיירי כשנפלו כולן לפני יבם אחד, מדמתרץ שניה שבזוג זה ושניה שבזוג זה. וטעות הוא בידיה, חדא: ד"או" "או" קתני, או אשה ובתה כו', אלמא: לאו כולהו בחד ביתא עסקינן. ועוד. א"כ, דכולהו בחד ביתא עסקינן, שהיו ג' אחים, שנים מהם נשואין שתי אחיות, ואשה ובתה ואשה ובת בתה ואשה ובת בנה – כל אחד נשוי ארבע נשים, ומתו ונפלו לפני השלישי, וקא"ר שמעון דאחת מן הראשונות מתייבמת והשניות פטורות – ארבעתן מיבעי ליה, דהא ד' שניות איכא! בשעה שנעשו אחיות צרות זו לזו. כגון הכא, שנפלו לפני יבם אחד. אלמא: תרווייהו פטורי. אפי' באחת מהן. אי דנפול בזו אחר זו ה"נ. דזיקה ככנוסה דמיא, וקמייתא מתייבמת דנפלה אפילו לאחר נפילת שניה. כרבי יוסי הגלילי. בבכורות (יז.): רחל שלא בכרה וילדה שני זכרים, ויצאו שני ראשים כאחד, ר' יוסי אומר: שניהן לכהן, וחכ"א: אחד לו ואחד לכהן, דאי אפשר לצמצם ולצאת שניהם כאחד, אלא אחד יוצא ראשון ופוטר את הרחם, והשני חולין. ומשום דלא ידיע הי מינייהו – הוו תרווייהו ספק בכורות, ונותן אחד לכהן והשני ירעה עד שיסתאב, ויאכל במומו לבעל הבית. והכא נמי סבר ר"ש אפשר לצמצם מיתת שני אחים כאחד, וליכא חדא דתיהוי ראשונה, ושתיהן פטורות, כדיליף טעם מ"לצרור". דאי לאו כר' יוסי הגלילי – הויא לה חדא ראשונה, ולא ידיע הי מינייהו, ותרווייהו ליבעו חליצה. רב פפא. לעיל מהדר, ופליג אדרבי אושעיא. ותרווייהו בבי דמתני', לאשמועי' דרבנן בתרווייהו פטרי. ודקא קשיא לך, בבא דרישא למה לי? פשיטא דבנולד ולבסוף ייבם פטרי! לא זו אף זו קתני. כלומר, אשמועינן ברישא נולד ולבסוף ייבם, והדר תנא ייבם ולבסוף נולד. לומר לך: דלא זו בלבד דנולד ולבסוף ייבם פטורה – אלא אף דייבם ולבסוף נולד נמי פטורה. כוותיה דרב פפא. דמודי ר"ש בנולד ולבסוף ייבם. ועמד השני כו'. לקמן פריך: למה לי למיתני עמד ולא הספיק? ושניה. אשתו של שני. עשה בה מאמר כו'. חולצת, דלא אלים מאמר לשוויה צרת ערוה למיפטר בולא כלום. ר"ש

שמא יאמרו שתי יבמות כו'. פירש בקונט' שנפלו בבת אחת, כר' יוסי הגלילי, דאמר אפשר לצמצם. ועי"ל: כגון שהראשונה היא ערוה לאחיו השני שמת, שלא היתה זקוקה לו כלל.

והא טעמא דר"ש משום מאמר ולאו מאמר הוא דתניא וכו'. הו"מ לשנויי דלדבריהם דרבנן קא"ל.

דתניא אמר להם ר"ש כו'. והא דאמר בפ' "ר"ג" (לקמן נא:) דר"ש סבר דמאמר קונה קנין גמור – היינו לענין שאין ביאה ומאמר אחריו, אבל לא עביד לה ככנוסה.

ועוד מתיב רב אושעיא. כאן מוכיח כפר"ת דרבי אושעיא לאו היינו רב אושעיא *דההיא דפ' "הדר" בעירובין (ד' סח. ושם) דקסבר התם ר' אושעיא דאין ברירה, ובפרק בתרא דבילה (ד' לז: ושם) אית ליה לר' אושעיא ברירה.

רבי

פוטר בארבעתן. תימה אמאי לא קאמר בשבעתן דהא כי לקח אחת מן נשי ראובן לא יקח מנשי שמעון כלום ולא מנשי ראובן. מנשי ראובן לא יקח לפי שמבית אחד אין לו לייבם אלא אחת והאחרות פטורות. וגם מנשי שמעון לא יקח כי האחת הערוה לאותה שלקח א"כ כל נשי שמעון הם צרת ערוה. ומזה נוכל לתרץ דלא חשש למתני פטור בשלש הצרות שנפלו עם אותה שמייבם דפשיטא הוא שאין לו לייבם מארבעתן אלא אחת ואותה שירצה יקח לו דכלהו חזיא ליה. אבל הד' האחרונות כלהו אסורות לו ובהני הו"ל למכתב פוטר בארבעתן כ"נ לראב"י אבל מ"מ קשה דהיכי קאמר אי דנפול בזה אחר זה הכי נמי דר' שמעון סבר הכא יש זיקה וזיקה ככנוסה דמיא הא אמרינן דבשני יבמין לא אמרינן זיקה ככנוסה וה"נ כיון דאיכא הרבה יבמות אין לנו לומר לר' שמעון דזיקה ככנוסה דמיא משום דלא ידעינן איזה מהם יקח ואין הזיקה מיוחדת וע"ק אמאי נקט דנשואין ד' זוגי (איסור) כי נמי אינם נשואין רק ב' אחיות ושאר נשותיהן נכריות אמת הדבר דכשייבם א' מהן כולן פטורות. ונראה אל הקדוש דכי קאמר שניה שבזוג זו ושניה שבזוג זו מיירי שיש שמונה אחין נשואים אותם שמנה נשים שתי אחיות ואשה ובתה ואשה ובת בתה ואשה ובת בנה כל א' וא' אחת מהן. והשתא הראשון שמת אשתו מתייבמת והשניה יוצאה משום אחות ערוה אשת מי שמת שני ערוה לאשת הראשון וכן כולן אשת מי שמת ראשון מתייבמת ואשת מי שמת אחריו ערוה. והשתא איכא ד' מהם ראויות לייבם לזה האח שנפלו כלם לפניו וד' מהן יש שאינן ראויות להתייבם וניחא דקאמר פוטר בארבעתן וכן כלהו קושיות מתורץ (ממני) [בזה]:

[לקמן כח:]

[לקמן כח: קדושין נ:]

*כל זה בס"א איתו

[לקמן כח. שבועות לב. בכורות ע. יז. יח.]

[גיטין טו: ב"מ לח. הוריות ב.]

תורה אור

ויקרא יח

גליון הש"ס

גמ' בשעה שנעשו צרות. ע' קידושין דף נ ע"ב תד"ה אי הכי:

ז א מיי' פ"ב מהלכות יבום הלכה א סמג עשין נא טוש"ע אה"ע סימן קסו סעיף ג:

ר' שִׁמְעוֹן אוֹמֵר: בִּיאָתָהּ אוֹ חֲלִיצָתָהּ שֶׁל אַחַת מֵהֶם פּוֹטֶרֶת צָרָתָהּ, חָלַץ לְבַעֲלַת מַאֲמָר לֹא נִפְטְרָה צָרָה. כְּנָסָהּ וָמֵת, וְאח"כ נוֹלַד לוֹ אָח, אוֹ שֶׁנּוֹלַד לוֹ אָח וְאח"כ כְּנָסָהּ וָמֵת — שְׁתֵּיהֶן פְּטוּרוֹת מִן הַחֲלִיצָה וּמִן הַיִּיבּוּם. כְּנָסָהּ וְנוֹלַד לוֹ אָח, וְאח"כ מֵת — שְׁתֵּיהֶן פְּטוּרוֹת מִן הַחֲלִיצָה וּמִן הַיִּיבּוּם, דִּבְרֵי ר"מ. וְר' שִׁמְעוֹן אוֹמֵר: הוֹאִיל וּבָא וּמְצָאָהּ בְּהֶיתֵּר, וְלֹא עָמְדָה עָלָיו שָׁעָה אַחַת בְּאִיסּוּר — מְיַיבֵּם לְאֵיזוֹ מֵהֶן שֶׁיִּרְצֶה, אוֹ חוֹלֵץ לְאֵיזוֹ מֵהֶן שֶׁיִּרְצֶה. הָא בָּבָא דְּסֵיפָא לְמַאן קָתָנֵי לָהּ? אִילֵימָא לְרַ' מֵאִיר קָתָנֵי לָהּ — מִכְּדִי, לָא שָׁנֵי לֵיהּ לְרַבִּי מֵאִיר בֵּין יִיבֵּם וְאח"כ נוֹלַד, בֵּין נוֹלַד וְאח"כ יִיבֵּם — לְעַרְבִינְהוּ וְלִתְנִינְהוּ! אֶלָּא, לָאו רַבִּי שִׁמְעוֹן, וּבְיִיבֵּם וְאח"כ נוֹלַד — פָּלֵיג, בְּנוֹלַד וְאַחַר כָּךְ יִיבֵּם — לָא פָּלֵיג, ש"מ. אֲמַר מָר: עָמַד הַשֵּׁנִי לַעֲשׂוֹת מַאֲמָר בִּיבִמְתּוֹ, וְלֹא הִסְפִּיק לַעֲשׂוֹת מַאֲמָר בִּיבִמְתּוֹ עַד שֶׁנּוֹלַד לוֹ אָח, וָמֵת — רִאשׁוֹנָה יוֹצְאָה מִשּׁוּם אֵשֶׁת אָחִיו שֶׁלֹּא הָיָה בְּעוֹלָמוֹ, וּשְׁנִיָּה — אוֹ חוֹלֶצֶת אוֹ מִתְיַיבֶּמֶת. מַאי עָמַד וּמַאי לֹא הִסְפִּיק? אִי עֲבַד — עֲבַד, וְאִי לֹא עֲבַד — לָא עֲבַד! אֶלָּא: עָמַד — מִדַּעְתָּהּ, וְלֹא הִסְפִּיק מִדַּעְתָּהּ, אֶלָּא בְּעַל כָּרְחָהּ. וּדְלֹא כְּרַבִּי דְּתַנְיָא: *הָעוֹשֶׂה מַאֲמָר בִּיבִמְתּוֹ שֶׁלֹּא מִדַּעְתָּהּ, רַ' אוֹמֵר: קָנָה, [א]וְחכ"א: לֹא קָנָה. מ"ט דְּרַ'? גָּמַר מִבִּיאָה דִּיבָמָה, מַה בִּיאָה דִּיבָמָה בְּעַל כָּרְחָהּ, אַף קִדּוּשִׁין דִּיבָמָה בְּעַל כָּרְחָהּ. וְרַבָּנַן גָּמְרֵי מִקִּדּוּשִׁין דְּעָלְמָא, מַה קִּדּוּשִׁין דְּעָלְמָא — מִדַּעְתָּהּ, אַף קִדּוּשִׁין דִּיבָמָה — מִדַּעְתָּהּ. בְּמַאי קָמִיפַּלְגִי? מָר סָבַר: מִילֵּי דִּיבָמָה מִמִּילֵּי דִּיבָמָה הֲוָה לֵיהּ לְמֵילַף, וּמָר סָבַר: מִילֵּי דְּקִדּוּשִׁין מִמִּילֵּי דְּקִדּוּשִׁין הֲוָה לֵיהּ לְמֵילַף. עָשָׂה בָּהּ מַאֲמָר וְאח"כ נוֹלַד לוֹ אָח, אוֹ שֶׁנּוֹלַד לוֹ אָח וְאח"כ עָשָׂה בָּהּ מַאֲמָר, וּמֵת, רִאשׁוֹנָה יוֹצְאָה מִשּׁוּם אֵשֶׁת אָחִיו שֶׁלֹּא הָיָה בְּעוֹלָמוֹ, וּשְׁנִיָּה חוֹלֶצֶת וְלֹא מִתְיַיבֶּמֶת. ר"ש אוֹמֵר: בִּיאָתָהּ אוֹ חֲלִיצָתָהּ שֶׁל אַחַת מֵהֶן פּוֹטֶרֶת צָרָתָהּ. ר"ש אַהַיְּיא קָאֵי? אִילֵימָא אַנּוֹלַד לוֹ אָח וְאח"כ עָשָׂה בָּהּ מַאֲמָר — הָא אָמַרְתְּ בְּנוֹלַד וּלְבַסּוֹף יִיבֵּם לָא פָּלֵיג ר"ש! אֶלָּא — אַעָשָׂה בָּהּ מַאֲמָר וְאח"כ נוֹלַד לוֹ אָח. חָלַץ לְבַעֲלַת מַאֲמָר לֹא נִפְטְרָה צָרָה, מ"ט? מִשּׁוּם דְּהַוְאִי צָרָה וַדַּאי וּבַעֲלַת מַאֲמָר סָפֵק, *וְאֵין סָפֵק מוֹצִיא מִידֵי וַדַּאי. יְתֵיב רַב מְנַשֶּׁה בַּר זְבִיד קַמֵּיהּ דְּרַב הוּנָא, וִיתֵיב וְקָאָמַר: מַאי טַעְמָא דְּר"ש? מ"ט דְּר"ש?! כְּדַאֲמַר טַעְמָא: הוֹאִיל וּבָא וּמְצָאָהּ בְּהֶיתֵּר, וְלֹא עָמְדָה עָלָיו שָׁעָה אַחַת בְּאִיסּוּר! אֶלָּא: מַאי טַעְמָא דְּרַבָּנַן? אֲמַר קְרָא "וּלְקָחָהּ לוֹ לְאִשָּׁה *וְיִבְּמָהּ" — עֲדַיִין יִבּוּמִים הָרִאשׁוֹנִים עָלֶיהָ. אֶלָּא, הָא דִּתְנַן: *כְּנָסָהּ — הֲרֵי הִיא כְּאִשְׁתּוֹ לְכָל דָּבָר, *וְאָמַר רַבִּי יוֹסֵי בַּר חֲנִינָא: מְלַמֵּד שֶׁמְּגָרְשָׁהּ

תורה אור

ר"ש אוֹמֵר בִּיאָתָהּ כו'. מְפָרֵשׁ לְקַמֵּיהּ דְּאַעָשָׂה בָּהּ מַאֲמָר וְאח"כ נוֹלַד לוֹ אָח קָאֵי, וּמִשּׁוּם דְּקָסָבַר מַאֲמָר סָפֵק קוֹנֶה סָפֵק אֵינוֹ קוֹנֶה כִּדְאָמַר לְעֵיל, וּמְפָרֵשׁ ר"ש וְאָזֵיל. חָלַץ לְבַעֲלַת מַאֲמָר לֹא נִפְטְרָה צָרָה. כְּלוֹמַר, הָא דְּקָאָמֵינָא בִּיאָתָהּ אוֹ חֲלִיצָתָהּ שֶׁל אַחַת מֵהֶן פּוֹטֶרֶת צָרָתָהּ — כְּגוֹן שֶׁיְּהֵא חוֹלֵץ אוֹ מְיַיבֵּם לַשְּׁנִיָּה, וְהָרִאשׁוֹנָה פְּטוּרָה ממ"נ: אִי מַאֲמָר קָנֵי — הָוֵי לֵיהּ יִיבֵּם וּלְבַסּוֹף נוֹלַד, וַאֲפִי' רִאשׁוֹנָה מוּתֶּרֶת לְר' שִׁמְעוֹן, וּבַחֲלִיצָה דְּאִידָךְ מִיפַּטְרָה, דְּהָא מַאֲמָר כִּכְנוּסָה, וְהָווּ לְהוּ מִבַּיִת אֶחָד. וְאִי מַאֲמָר לָא קָנֵי — הֲרֵי שַׁפִּיר יִיבֵּם לַשְּׁנִיָּה, דְּאֵשֶׁת אָחִיו שֶׁהָיָה בְּעוֹלָמוֹ הִיא, וְאֵינָ' צָרַת עֶרְוָה. וְרִאשׁוֹנָה תֵּצֵא מִשּׁוּם אֵשֶׁת אָחִיו שֶׁלֹּא הָיָ' בְּעוֹלָמוֹ. אֲבָל חָלַץ לְבַעֲלַת מַאֲמָר, שֶׁהִיא רִאשׁוֹנָה — לֹא נִפְטְרָה צָרָה, דְּדִלְמָא מַאֲמָר לָא קָנֵי, וּמִמֵּילָא פְּטוּרָה מִשּׁוּם אֵשֶׁת אָחִיו שֶׁלֹּא הָיָה בָּעוֹלָם, וַחֲלִיצָתָהּ אֵינָהּ חֲלִיצָה. וְהָכִי מְפָרֵשׁ לְקַמָּן. אוֹ שֶׁנּוֹלַד לוֹ אָח. דְּה"ל נוֹלַד וּלְבַסּוֹף יִיבֵּם. שְׁתֵּיהֶן פְּטוּרוֹת. בְּהָא לָא פָּלֵיג ר"ש, וּכְרַב פַּפָּא. הָךְ בָּבָא דְּסֵיפָא. יִיבֵּם וּלְבַסּוֹף נוֹלַד. לְמַאן קָתָנֵי לָהּ. כְּלוֹמַר, לְהוֹדִיעַ כֹּחוֹ שֶׁל מִי קָתָנֵי לָהּ בִּפְנֵי עַצְמָהּ, וְלֹא עֵירְבָהּ עִם נוֹלַד וּלְבַסּוֹף יִיבֵּם? אִילֵימָא לְר"מ. לְאַשְׁמוּעִינַן דִּבְהָא נַמִי אָסַר, וְלָאו לְמֵימַר דְּר"ש אַהַךְ לְחוּדָהּ הוּא דְּפָלֵיג. לְעַרְבִינְהוּ. לְבָבֵי, וְלִיתְנֵי בְּרֵישָׁא הָכִי: כְּנָסָהּ וּמֵת וְאח"כ נוֹלַד לוֹ אָח, אוֹ שֶׁנּוֹלַד לוֹ אָח וְאח"כ כְּנָסָהּ וּמֵת, אוֹ שֶׁכְּנָסָהּ וְנוֹלַד לוֹ אָח וְאח"כ מֵת — שְׁתֵּיהֶן פְּטוּרוֹת. אֶלָּא מִדְּפַלְגִינְהוּ — ש"מ מִשּׁוּם דְּאַיְירֵי בָּהּ ר"ש הִיא דְּאַשְׁמוּעִינַן דִּבְהָא לְחוּדָהּ פָּלֵיג, מִשּׁוּם דְּבָא וּמְצָאָהּ בְּהֶיתֵּר, אֲבָל בְּרֵישָׁא — מוֹדֶה. אֶלָּא בְּעַל כָּרְחָהּ. וְקמ"ל דְּמַאֲמָר בְּע"כ וַאֲפִילּוּ לְמִקְצָת לָא קָנֵי, וּשְׁנִיָּה יַבּוּמֵי נַמִי מְיַיבְּמָה. בִּיאָה דִּיבָמָה. אָמְרִי' בְּפ"ק (דף ח:): "וְיִבְּמָהּ" — בְּעַל כָּרְחָהּ; דְּאִם בָּא עָלֶיהָ, אֲפִי' בְּאוֹנֶס — קְנָאָהּ. קִדּוּשִׁין דְּעָלְמָא. "וְהָלְכָה וְהָיְתָה לְאִישׁ אַחֵר" (דברים כד) — מִדַּעְתָּהּ מַשְׁמַע. אִי נֵימָא אַנּוֹלַד לוֹ אָח. קוֹדֶם מַאֲמָר, בְּהָא לֵימָא ר"ש בִּיאַת הַשְּׁנִיָּה כְּשֵׁרָה? וְהָא דָּיְיקַתְּ מִסֵּיפָא דְּבְנוֹלַד וּלְבַסּוֹף יִיבֵּם לָא פָּלֵיג, וְהָוֵה לֵיהּ אֵשֶׁת אָחִיו שֶׁלֹּא הָיָה בְּעוֹלָמוֹ, וְדִלְמָא מַאֲמָר קָנֵי וְה"ל שְׁנִיָּה צָרַת עֶרְוָה! וְעוֹד: מַאי פּוֹטֶרֶת צָרָתָהּ אִיכָּא? הָא מִיפַּטְרָה וְקָיְימָא, דְּאֵשֶׁת אָחִיו שֶׁלֹּא הָיָה בְּעוֹלָמוֹ הִיא. אֶלָּא אַעָשָׂה בָּהּ מַאֲמָר וְאח"כ נוֹלַד אָח. וְאַשְׁמוּעִינַן בְּרֵישָׁא דְּמַאֲמָר סָפֵק קוֹנֶה לְגַמְרֵי סָפֵק לֹא קוֹנֶה, *אֲפִי' מִקְצָת לָא מְהַנֵּי, הִלְכָּךְ מְיַיבֵּם אוֹ חוֹלֵץ לַשְּׁנִיָּה ממ"נ: אִי מַאֲמָר הַמֵּת קִנְיָן גָּמוּר הוּא — הָוֵה לֵיהּ יִיבֵּם וּלְבַסּוֹף נוֹלַד, וַאֲפִילּוּ קַמַּיְיתָא חַזְיָא לְיִיבּוּמֵי, וְאִי לָאו קִנְיָן גָּמוּר הוּא — בַּתְרַיְיתָא שַׁרְיָא, דְּלָאו צָרַת עֶרְוָה הִיא, דְּקִנְיָן מִקְצָת בְּמַאֲמָר לֵית לֵיהּ לְר"ש. וּבְסֵיפָא אַשְׁמוּעִינַן דְּיִיבֵּם וּלְבַסּוֹף נוֹלַד הוּא דְּשַׁרְיָא, אֲבָל נוֹלַד וּלְבַסּוֹף יִיבֵּם — אֲסוּרָה. דְּלָא תֵּימָא בִּיאָתָהּ אוֹ חֲלִיצָתָהּ דְּקָאָמַר ר"ש בְּרֵישָׁא אַנּוֹלַד וְאח"כ עָשָׂה בָּהּ מַאֲמָר נַמִי קָאֵי. הָוְיָא צָרָה וַדַּאי. זְקוּקָה לְיַיבֵּם, דְּאִי מַאֲמָר קָנֵי — תַּרְוַיְיהוּ חֲזוּ, דְּהָוֵי לֵיהּ יִיבֵּם וּלְבַסּוֹף נוֹלַד. וְאִי מַאֲמָר לָא קָנֵי — שְׁנִיָּה חַזְיָא, דְּלָאו צָרַת עֶרְוָה הִיא, וּבַעֲלַת מַאֲמָר סָפֵק זְקוּקָה סָפֵק אֵין זְקוּקָה, דְּדִלְמָא לָא קָנֵי וְהָוֵי אֵשֶׁת אָחִיו שֶׁלֹּא הָיָה בְּעוֹלָמוֹ, וַחֲלִיצָתָהּ לָאו חֲלִיצָה לִפְטוֹר אֶת הַוַּדָּאִית. מ"ט דְּרַבָּנַן. דְּאָסְרִי בְּיִיבֵּם וּלְבַסּוֹף נוֹלַד? הֲרֵי לֹא עָמְדָה עַל זֶה בִּזִיקַּת אָחִיו שֶׁלֹּא הָיָה בְּעוֹלָמוֹ מִיָּמָיו. וּלְקָחָהּ לוֹ לְאִשָּׁה וְיִבְּמָהּ. אע"ג שֶׁכְּנָסָהּ — עֲדַיִין קְרוּיָה יְבָמָה. אִית דְּגָרַס: אִי הָכִי תִּיבָּעֵי חֲלִיצָה, אַלְּמָה תְּנַן כְּנָסָהּ הֲרֵי הִיא כְּאִשְׁתּוֹ כו' — כְּלוֹמַר, אִי הָכִי דְּאִשָּׁה שֶׁנִּתְיַיבְּמָה עֲדַיִין זִיקַּת רִאשׁוֹנָה עָלֶיהָ — תִּיבָּעֵי חֲלִיצָה, כָּל אִשָּׁה שֶׁנִּתְיַיבְּמָה וּבָא שֵׁנִי זֶה לְגָרְשָׁהּ — לָא תִּסְגֵּי לָהּ בְּגֵט.

שֶׁמְּגָרְשָׁהּ

רבי שמעון אומר ביאתה או חליצתה כו'. פי' בקונטרס: דקסבר ר' שמעון מאמר ספק קונה ספק אינו קונה, וכשייבם או חלץ לשניה – נפטרת בעלת מאמר ממ"נ. ונראה שפי' כן, דאין ר"ל שיקנה לר"ש מדרבנן – דא"כ לא היה יכול לייבם השניה, דהויא לה צרת אשת אחיו שלא היה בעולמו במאמר. אלא ודאי קסבר דקני לגמרי, או לא קני כלל. וא"ת: אכתי צרתה היא בזיקה! וי"ל: דר"ש סבר אין זיקה. ולר"י נראה: דאפילו ס"ל דיש זיקה, ומאמר קונה קצת מדרבנן – ניחא, *דאין זיקה אוסרת, ולא המאמר, אלא היכא דאם היתה נשואה היתה אוסרת. וכאן, אם היתה נשואה היא עצמה – היתה מותרת לר"ש, דשרי ייבם ואח"כ נולד. ומ"מ אמת הוא דלר"ש אי לא קני מאמר – לא קני אפילו מדרבנן, מדקאמר לעיל: אם מאמרו של שני אינו מאמר – אשת ראשון בועל. משמע דלא קני כלל.

חליץ לבעלת מאמר לא נפטרה צרתה. וא"ת: ואמאי לא דייק מהכא תיובתא לר' אושעיא, דלדידיה כיון דהוי זיקה ככנוסה, אמאי לא נפטרה הצרה? וי"ל: מדרבנן, כדאמר לעיל: גזירה משום שתי יבמות הבאות משני בתים, חדא מיחלצה וחדא מיפטרה (א) בלא כלום.

כנסה ומת ואח"כ נולד לו אח וכו'. הא מילתא דפשיטא היא, ולא הוה צריך כלל למתנייה! ואר"י: דלא שנאה אלא לאשמועי' דהאי תנא עירובי מערב ותני מילי בהדי הדדי, ולהכי דייק מינה דבנולד ולבסוף ייבם לא פליג ר"ש, מדעריב ותני להו בהדי כנסה ומת ואח"כ נולד לו אח, דמודה בה ר"ש דאי בנולד ולבסוף ייבם פליג נמי ר"ש – א"כ בהדי סיפא הוה ליה למיערבה, ולא בהדי רישא. והשתא א"ש דלא מותיב לר' אושעיא ממתני' דלא עריב ותני להו, דאברייתא שייך למידק, כדפרישית.

לערבינהו ולתנינהו. לא כמו שפירש בקונטרס דאכולהו קאי – דאכנסה ומת ואח"כ נולד ודאי ל"פ ר"ש. אלא אתרי בתראי קאי (ב).

גמרינן מביאה דיבמה. דאע"ג דמאמר אינו אלא מדרבנן, מ"מ, מר מסתבר ליה דעשאוהו חכמים כביאה ולמר מסתבר דעשאוהו כקדושין. וכה"ג איכא בפ"ק דב"מ (ד' יא. ושם) דקאמר מר יליף מציאה מגט אע"ג דלקטן לית ליה זכיה אלא מדרבנן, כדאמרי' בסוף "הניזקין" (גיטין סה. ושם).

הא

(נ"ל דאי זיקה רש"ל)

תוספות ישנים

ביאתה או חליצתה של אחת מהן פוטרת צרתה. ומפרש לה ואזיל חלץ לבעלת מאמר לא נפטרה צרתה וא"כ הא דקאמר ביאתה או חליצתה של אחת מהן פוטרת צרתה ר"ל מאותה שאינה בעלת מאמר דהויא אשת השני וטעמא דביאתה או חליצתה פוטרת צרתה היינו מ"נ דאי מאמר קונה תרווייהו חזיין דהוי יבם ואח"כ נולד וא"כ כי מייבם לחדא מפטרה צרתה. ואי מאמר אינו קונה מצי לייבומי אשת השני דהא לא הוי צרת אשת אחיו בעולמו [כלל] (אבל) דר' שמעון לא סבר מאמר קונה קצת ואינו קונה מכל וכל אלא אומר [או] קונה מכל וכל או אינו קונה כלל. אבל חלץ לבעלת מאמר לא נפטרה צרתה דשמא מאמר אינו קונה כלל ונמצא שהחליצה בחנם היתה ואינה כלום שהיא אשת אחיו שלא היה בעולמו וא"כ לא נפטרה צרתה וצריכה לייבם לזה. וא"ת היכי קאמר דמצי לייבם אותה שאינה בעלת מאמר הא מ"מ היתה זקוקה לאחיו השני והויא ליה אשת אח השני צרת אשת אחיו שלא היה בעולמו בזיקה וא"כ היכי מצי לייבמה. וי"ל דלרב פפא איירינן דסבר ר' שמעון אין זיקה וא"כ לא הוי צרת אשת אחיו שלא היה בעולמו. ואף לר' הושעיא דאמר לר' שמעון יש זיקה וזיקה ככנוסה לא קשה מידי דא"כ היא עצמה יכולה לייבם כיון דזיקה ככנוסה דהוי כמו יבם ואח"כ נולד:

הגהות הב"ח

(א) תום' ד"ה חלץ וכו' בלא כלום. נ"ב ס"א שלא יבא להתיר אשת אחיו שלא היה בעולמו: (ב) ד"ה לערבינהו וכו' בתראי קאי כפי' הס"ד:

קדושין מד.

[לקמן לח. פסחים ע. ע"ש מה: חולין י.]

לעיל ח: לקמן לט. כתובות פב:

[עיין תוספות לעיל ח: סד"ה ויבמה]

[לקמן לח. כתובות פ:]

שֶׁמְּגָרְשָׁהּ בְּגֵט וּמַחֲזִירָהּ, הָתָם נַמִי לֵימָא: "וְיִבְּמָהּ" עֲדַיִין יְבוּמִין הָרִאשׁוֹנִים עָלֶיהָ, וְתִיבָּעֵי חֲלִיצָה! שָׁאנֵי הָתָם, דְּאָמַר קְרָא °"וּלְקָחָהּ לוֹ לְאִשָּׁה", כֵּיוָן שֶׁלְּקָחָהּ נַעֲשֵׂית כְּאִשְׁתּוֹ לְכָל דָּבָר. אִי הָכִי, הָכָא נַמִי! הָא כְּתַב רַחֲמָנָא °"וְיִבְּמָהּ". וּמָה רָאִיתָ? מִסְתַּבְּרָא: שְׁדִי הֶיתֵּירָא אַהֶיתֵּירָא וּשְׁדִי אִיסּוּרָא אַאִיסּוּרָא. וּלְרַ' שִׁמְעוֹן, דְּאָמַר: הוֹאִיל וּבָא וּמְצָאָהּ בְּהֶיתֵּר וְלֹא עָמְדָה עָלָיו שָׁעָה אַחַת בְּאִיסּוּר, אֶלָּא מֵעַתָּה, אֲחוֹתוֹ מֵאִמּוֹ שֶׁנְּשָׂאָהּ אָחִיו מֵאָבִיו, וְאַחַר כָּךְ נוֹלַד אָח, וּמֵת — תִּתְיַיבֵּם, הוֹאִיל וּבָא וּמְצָאָהּ בְּהֶיתֵּר! אִיסּוּר אֲחוֹתוֹ לְהֵיכָן אָזַל?! הָכָא נַמִי, אִיסּוּר אָחִיו שֶׁלֹּא הָיָה בָּעוֹלָם לְהֵיכָן אָזַל! הַאי, אִיסּוּרָא דְּלֵית לֵיהּ הֶיתֵּירָא, הַאי — אִיסּוּרָא דְּאִית לֵיהּ הֶיתֵּירָא.§

מתני' כְּלָל אָמְרוּ בִּיבָמָה: כָּל (א) שֶׁהִיא אִיסּוּר עֶרְוָה, לֹא חוֹלֶצֶת וְלֹא מִתְיַיבֶּמֶת. *[א]אִיסּוּר מִצְוָה וְאִיסּוּר קְדוּשָּׁה — חוֹלֶצֶת וְלֹא מִתְיַיבֶּמֶת. *[ב]אֲחוֹתָהּ שֶׁהִיא יְבִמְתָּהּ — חוֹלֶצֶת אוֹ מִתְיַיבֶּמֶת. [ג]אִיסּוּר מִצְוָה: שְׁנִיּוֹת מִדִּבְרֵי סוֹפְרִים. אִיסּוּר קְדוּשָּׁה: אַלְמָנָה לְכ"ג, גְּרוּשָׁה וַחֲלוּצָה לְכֹהֵן הֶדְיוֹט, מַמְזֶרֶת וּנְתִינָה לְיִשְׂרָאֵל, וּבַת יִשְׂרָאֵל לְנָתִין וּלְמַמְזֵר.§

גמ' כְּלָל לְאַתּוֹיֵי מַאי? אָמַר רַפְרָם בַּר פַּפָּא: לְאַתּוֹיֵי צָרַת אַיְלוֹנִית, *וּכְדְרַב אַסִּי. וְאִיכָּא דְּאָמְרִי: "כָּל שֶׁאִיסּוּרָהּ אִיסּוּר עֶרְוָה" הוּא דַּאֲסִירָא צָרָתָהּ, הָא לֹא אִיסּוּרָהּ אִיסּוּר עֶרְוָה — צָרָתָהּ לֹא אֲסִירָא. לְמַעוּטֵי מַאי? אָמַר רַפְרָם: לְמַעוּטֵי צָרַת אַיְלוֹנִית, וּדְלָא כְּרַב אַסִּי.§ "אֲחוֹתָהּ שֶׁהִיא יְבִמְתָּהּ". אֲחוֹתָהּ דְּמַאן? אִילֵימָא דְּאִיסּוּר מִצְוָה, כֵּיוָן דְּמִדְּאוֹרָיְיתָא רָמְיָא קַמֵּיהּ פָּגַע בַּאֲחוֹת זְקוּקָתוֹ! אֶלָּא: אֲחוֹתָהּ דְּאִיסּוּר עֶרְוָה.§ "אִיסּוּר מִצְוָה שְׁנִיּוֹת". *אַמַּאי קָרֵי לֵיהּ אִיסּוּר מִצְוָה? אָמַר אַבַּיֵי: *מִצְוָה לִשְׁמוֹעַ דִּבְרֵי חֲכָמִים.§ "אִיסּוּר קְדוּשָּׁה אַלְמָנָה לְכֹהֵן גָּדוֹל גְּרוּשָׁה וַחֲלוּצָה לְכֹהֵן הֶדְיוֹט".§ וְאַמַּאי קָרֵי לְהוּ אִיסּוּר קְדוּשָּׁה? דִּכְתִיב °"קְדוֹשִׁים יִהְיוּ לֵאלֹהֵיהֶם". תַּנְיָא, רַבִּי יְהוּדָה מַחֲלִיף: *אִיסּוּר מִצְוָה — אַלְמָנָה לְכֹהֵן גָּדוֹל, גְּרוּשָׁה וַחֲלוּצָה לְכֹהֵן הֶדְיוֹט. וְאַמַּאי קָרֵי לֵיהּ אִיסּוּר מִצְוָה? דִּכְתִי' °"אֵלֶּה הַמִּצְוֹת" אִיסּוּר קְדוּשָּׁה — "שְׁנִיּוֹת מִדִּבְרֵי סוֹפְרִים", וְאַמַּאי קָרֵי לֵיהּ אִיסּוּר קְדוּשָׁ'? אָמַר אַבַּיֵי: כָּל הַמְקַיֵּים דִּבְרֵי חֲכָמִים נִקְרָא קָדוֹשׁ. א"ל רָבָא: וְכָל שֶׁאֵינוֹ מְקַיֵּים דִּבְרֵי חֲכָמִים, קָדוֹשׁ הוּא דְּלָא מִיקְּרֵי, רָשָׁע נַמִי לָא מִיקְּרֵי?! אֶלָּא אָמַר רָבָא: קַדֵּשׁ עַצְמְךָ בְּמוּתָּר לָךְ.§ "אַלְמָנָה לְכֹהֵן גָּדוֹל".§ *קָפְסֵיק וְתָנֵי, לֹא שְׁנָא מִן הַנִּשּׂוּאִין וְלֹא שְׁנָא מִן הָאֵירוּסִין. *) בִּשְׁלָמָא מִן הַנִּשּׂוּאִין — עֲשֵׂה וְלֹא תַעֲשֶׂה, [ד]וְאֵין עֲשֵׂה דּוֹחֶה לֹא תַעֲשֶׂה וַעֲשֵׂה. אֶלָּא מִן הָאֵירוּסִין, לֹא תַעֲשֶׂה גְּרֵידָא הוּא, יָבֹא עֲשֵׂה וְיִדְחֶה לֹא תַעֲשֶׂה! אָמַר רַב גִּידֵּל אָמַר רַב: אָמַר קְרָא °"וְעָלְתָה יְבִמְתּוֹ הַשַּׁעְרָה" שֶׁאֵין ת"ל "יְבִמְתּוֹ", מַה תַּלְמוּד לוֹמַר יְבִמְתּוֹ — יֵשׁ לְךָ יְבָמָה (ג) אַחַת שֶׁעוֹלָה לַחֲלִיצָה וְאֵינָהּ עוֹלָה לְיִיבּוּם. וְאֵיזוֹ — זוֹ חַיָּיבֵי לָאוִין. וְאֵימָא חַיָּיבֵי כָרֵיתוֹת! אָמַר קְרָא °"וְאִם לֹא יַחְפֹּץ הָאִישׁ לָקַחַת" הָא חָפֵץ — מְיַיבֵּם, *[ה]"כָּל הָעוֹלָה לְיִיבּוּם עוֹלָה לַחֲלִיצָה וְכָל שֶׁאֵין עוֹלָה לְיִיבּוּם — אֵינוֹ עוֹלָה לַחֲלִיצָה. א"ה, חַיָּיבֵי לָאוִין נַמִי! הָא רַבֵּי רַחֲמָנָא "יְבִמְתּוֹ". וּמָה רָאִיתָ? מִסְתַּבְּרָא

*) [ע' תוספות לעיל ה. ד"ה ואכתי]

רש"י

שֶׁמְּגָרְשָׁהּ בְּגֵט. וְאֵינָהּ צְרִיכָה חֲלִיצָה, וְאִם רָצָה לְהַחֲזִיר — מַחֲזִירָהּ, וְלָא אָמְרִינַן: מִצְוָה רָמְיָא רַחֲמָנָא עֲלֵיהּ וַעֲבַדָהּ, וּמֵהָשְׁתָּא תֵּיקוּ עֲלֵיהּ בְּאִיסּוּר אֵשֶׁת אָח. לֵימָא. עֲדַיִין יְבוּמִין הָרִאשׁוֹנִים עָלֶיהָ, וְתִיבָּעֵי חֲלִיצָה. שְׁדִי הֶיתֵּרָא. לְמִדְרַשׁ "וּלְקָחָהּ" דְּלָא תִּיבָּעֵי חֲלִיצָה. אַהֶיתֵּרָא. הֵיכָא דְּכוּלָּהּ מִילְּתָא הֶיתֵּר, כְּגוֹן בִּמְיַיבֵּם אֵשֶׁת אָח. וּשְׁדִי אִיסּוּרָא. לְמִדְרַשׁ "וְיִבְּמָהּ" — עֲדַיִין יְבוּמִין עָלֶיהָ. אַאִיסּוּרָא. הֵיכָא דְּאִיכָּא צַד אִיסּוּר, כְּמוֹ בְּאֵשֶׁת אָחִיו שֶׁלֹּא הָיָה בְּעוֹלָמוֹ. אֲחוֹתוֹ מֵאִמּוֹ שֶׁנְּשָׂאָהּ אָחִיו מֵאָבִיו. קוֹדֶם לֵידָתוֹ שֶׁל זֶה, וּכְשֶׁנּוֹלַד זֶה מְצָאָהּ נְשׂוּאָה לְאָחִיו — תִּתְיַיבֵּם לוֹ כְּשֶׁיָּמוּת זֶה, דְּהָא מְצָאָהּ בְּהֶיתֵּר יִיבּוּם. אִיסּוּר אֲחוֹתוֹ לֵית לֵיהּ הֶיתֵּר. אֲבָל אִיסּוּר אֵשֶׁת אָח אִית לֵיהּ הֶיתֵּר כְּשֶׁאֵין לוֹ בָּנִים, הִילְכָּךְ, כְּשֶׁמֵּת רִאשׁוֹן בְּלֹא בָּנִים — פָּקַע אִיסּוּרוֹ לְגַבֵּי שֵׁנִי וּנְשָׂאָהּ, וְהַשְּׁלִישִׁי מִכֹּחַ שֵׁנִי בָּא. **מתני'** לֹא חוֹלֶצֶת וְלֹא מִתְיַיבֶּמֶת. צָרָתָהּ וְכ"ש הִיא. אִיסּוּר מִצְוָה. מְפָרֵשׁ לְהוּ וְאָזֵיל. אֲחוֹתָהּ. שֶׁל עֶרְוָה כְּשֶׁהִיא יְבִמְתָּהּ. כְּגוֹן שֶׁנָּפְלוּ שְׁתֵּי אֲחָיוֹת מִשְּׁנֵי אַחִין, הָאַחַת אֲסוּרָה מִשּׁוּם עֶרְוָה, כְּגוֹן שֶׁהִיא כַּלָּתוֹ אוֹ חֲמוֹתוֹ. אוֹ חוֹלֶצֶת אוֹ מִתְיַיבֶּמֶת. אֲחוֹת הָעֶרְוָה. דְּלֹא פָּגַע בַּאֲחוֹת זְקוּקָתוֹ, מִשּׁוּם דְּעֶרְוָה לָאו זְקוּקָתוֹ הִיא. שְׁנִיּוֹת. שְׁנִיּוֹת לָעֲרָיוֹת שֶׁגָּזְרוּ סוֹפְרִים עֲלֵיהֶם, וּבַגְּמָ' מְפָרֵשׁ לָהּ: לְשׁוֹן מִצְוָה וּקְדוּשָּׁה מְפָרֵשׁ בַּגְּמָרָא. אַלְמָנָה לְכ"ג. שֶׁמֵּת אָחִיו הֶדְיוֹט, וְנָפְלָה אַלְמָנָתוֹ לְפָנָיו. גְּרוּשָׁה וַחֲלוּצָה לְכֹהֵן הֶדְיוֹט. שֶׁעָבַר אָחִיו הַמֵּת וְנָשָׂא חֲלוּצָה וּגְרוּשָׁה, וּכְשֶׁמֵּת צְרִיכָה חֲלִיצָה, שֶׁהֲרֵי תּוֹפְסִים לוֹ בָּהּ קִידּוּשִׁין. דְּקִידּוּשִׁין תּוֹפְסִים בְּחַיָּיבֵי לָאוִין. אֲבָל יַבּוּמֵי לָא, שֶׁהֲרֵי אֲסוּרָה לוֹ לָזֶה שֶׁהוּא כֹּהֵן. וְאַפְּטוּרֵי בְּלֹא כְלוּם — לָא, דְּלָא אֲלִים לָאו לְמִיפְטְרָהּ, דְּיָלְפִי' מֵאֲחוֹת אִשָּׁה בְּפ"ק (דף ג:). **גמ'** לְאִיתּוּיֵי צָרַת אַיְלוֹנִית כְּרַב אַסִּי. בְּפ"ק (דף יב.), דְּלָא חוֹלֶצֶת וְלָא מִתְיַיבֶּמֶת, דְּעֶרְוָה קָרֵינַן בָּהּ בְּאַיְלוֹנִית, דְּמִיעֲטָהּ קְרָא מֵ"אֲשֶׁר תֵּלֵד", וְקָיְימָא עֲלֵיהּ בְּאִיסּוּר אֵשֶׁת אָח, הִילְכָּךְ צָרָתָהּ צָרַת עֶרְוָה. אֵלֶּה הַמִּצְוֹת. בְּסוֹף סֵפֶר תּוֹרַת כֹּהֲנִים, וּמַשְׁמַע דְּאַכּוּלָּ' סִפְרָא קָאֵי, וְכָל אַזְהָרַת כֹּהֲנִים הָתָם כְּתִיבָא. קַדֵּשׁ עַצְמְךָ. לַעֲמוֹד וּלְהִזָּהֵר. אַף בַּמּוּתָּר לָךְ. לְהוֹסִיף עֲלֵיהֶם שְׁנִיּוֹת הַמּוּתָּר לְךָ עַל הָעֲרָיוֹת, כְּדֵי שֶׁלֹּא תָּבֹא לִידֵי עֲרָיוֹת הָאֲסוּרוֹת מִן הַתּוֹרָה. קָפְסֵיק וְתָנֵי. אַלְמָנָה לְכ"ג, לָא שְׁנָא נָפְלָה לְפָנָיו מִן הַנִּשּׂוּאִין — דְּהַיְינוּ תַּרְתֵּי לְגְרִיעוּתָא, חֲדָא — דְּאַלְמָנָה הִיא, וְאִיכָּא לָאו דְּ"אַלְמָנָה לֹא יִקָּח". וְעוֹד, דִּבְעוּלָה הִיא, וְאִיכָּא אִיסּוּר עֲשֵׂה לְגַבֵּיהּ, דִּכְתִיב "אִשָּׁה בִבְתוּלֶיהָ יִקָּח" וְלֹא בְּעוּלָה, וְלָאו הַבָּא מִכְּלַל עֲשֵׂה — עֲשֵׂה. וְלָא שְׁנָא. נָפְלָה לְפָנָיו מִן הָאֵירוּסִין וְעוֹדָהּ בְּתוּלָה, דְּלֵיכָּא אֶלָּא לָאו דְּאַלְמָנָה. יָבֹא עֲשֵׂה. דְּ"יְבָמָהּ יָבֹא עָלֶיהָ". וְעָלְתָה הַשַּׁעְרָה מָצֵי לְמִכְתַּב. דְּהָא כְּתִיב בְּרֵישָׁא דִּקְרָא "לָקַחַת אֶת יְבִמְתּוֹ", מַה ת"ל יְבִמְתּוֹ? יֵשׁ לְךָ יְבָמָה כו'. דְּאִם כָּתַב "וְלֹא יַחְפּוֹץ הָאִישׁ לָקַחַת אֶת יְבִמְתּוֹ וְעָלְתָה הַשַּׁעְרָה" — הֲוָה מַשְׁמַע דְּהַהִיא דְּקָרֵינָא בֵּיהּ לָקַחַת — הוּא דְּקָא מַצְרְכָהּ רַחֲמָנָא וְעָלְתָה הַשַּׁעְרָה לַחֲלוֹץ. אֲבָל חַיָּיבֵי לָאוִין, דְּלָא קָרֵינַן בְּהוּ "לָקַחַת" — לָא קָרֵינַן בָּהּ "וְעָלְתָה". לְהָכִי הֲדַר כְּתַב "יְבִמְתּוֹ", לְמֵימַר דְּיֵשׁ לְךָ יְבָמָה אַחֶרֶת שֶׁעוֹלָה הַשַּׁעְרָה לַחֲלוֹץ, וְאַע"ג דְּלָא כְּתִיב בָּהּ לָקַחַת, שֶׁאֵין עוֹלָה לְיִיבּוּם. נַמִי לֵילַף מֵהָכָא דְּלִיבָּעֵי חֲלִיצָה, וְאַמַּאי פָּטְרִינַן לְגַמְרֵי? אֵימָא חַיָּיבֵי כָרֵיתוֹת. *תָּפְסִי בָּהּ קִידּוּשִׁין. הִילְכָּךְ קָרֵינַן בֵּיהּ "לָקַחַת", בְּדִיעֲבַד, אֲבָל חַיָּיבֵי כָרֵיתוֹת לָא תָּפְסִי בְּהוּ קִידּוּשִׁין, וְאַפִּי' עָבַר הַאי יָבָם וּנְסָבָהּ — לָאו קִיחָה הִיא.

[שייך לע"ב]

לְדִדִין

תוספות

האי איסורא דאית ליה התירא. דפקע איסור אשת אח, דיכול להחזירה לאחר שגרשה. וכי היכי דפקע ליה לגבי דידיה איסור אשת אח — פקע נמי לגבי אחיו הנולד, וה"ל אשת אחיו שהיה בעולמו. **לאתויי** צרת אילונית. אע"ג דמתני' לא קתני צרה, מ"מ הוי בכלל דכל שאיסורה איסור ערוה דמשמע שאיסורה בא מחמת ערוה, דהיינו הצרה. ולא הוצרך להזכיר הצרה בהדיא, משום דאפירקין דלעיל קאי. והא דלא קאמר לאיתויי צרת סוטה וצרת מחזיר גרושה, משום דאילונית דמיא טפי לעריות, שמותרות למת ואסורות לייבם.

בשלמא מן הנשואין כו'. תימה: דמן הנשואין נמי תיקשי ליה, דאמאי חולצת? כיון דאין עולה לייבום, דלא אתי עשה ודחי לא תעשה ועשה, ותיהוי כי חייבי כריתות! וי"ל דלא קאמר בשלמא אלא ממאי דאין מתייבמת.

יבא עשה וידחה לא תעשה. הקשה ריב"א: בפ"ב דסנהדרין (דף יט. ושם): דכיון דאין אשה מתעברת מביאה ראשונה, כדאמר בסוף פ' "ד' אחין" (לקמן ד' לד. ושם), היאך תתייבם? דבביא' ראשונה ליכא הקמת שם, וביאה שניה אסירא ליה, כדאמר לקמן: גזירה ביאה ראשונה אטו ביאה שניה! ואר"י: דלא קשה מידי: דלא בעינן (ג) שתהא ראויה להקמת שם אלא שהיבמה והיבם יהו ראוין להקמת שם, ולא ממעטינן אלא אילונית וסריס שאינן ראוין לילד לעולם. אבל ביאה שאין יכולה להתעבר בה — לא ממעטי, כיון שהאשה או היבם ראוין לבסוף להוליד. דאל"כ תיקשה: היאך קטנה מתייבמת לרבנן? וגם לרבי מאיר היתה מתייבמת, אי לאו חששא דשמא תמצא אילונית. ובפרק "ב"ש" (לקמן דף קיא:) תנן: קטן הבא על הגדולה תגדלנו. ובפ' "הבא על יבמתו" (לקמן נה:) נמי מרבינן דנקנית בביאה שלא כדרכה והערא', אע"פ שאין מתעברת בה א).

אי הכי חייבי לאוין נמי. פי': כיון דאין עולים לייבום — לא יעלו לחליצה! ותימה לר"י: היכי מצי למימר דלא יעלו לחליצה? הא מ"יבמתו" דשמעינן דאין

עין משפט נר מצוה

ח א מיי' פ"ו מהלכות יבום הלכה ז טוש"ע אה"ע סימן קעד סעיף א:

ט ב מיי' שם פ"ז הלכה א טוש"ע שם סימן קעה סעיף ב וסעיף ד:

י ג מיי' פ"א מהלכות אישות הלכה ו סמג לאוין קי טוש"ע שם סימן טו:

יא ד מיי' פ"ו מהלכות יבום הלכה יא:

יב ה מיי' שם פ"א הלכה יט:

תוספות ישנים

א) ואע"ג דלקמן אצטריך קרא לקטן למימר שתגדלנו שמא מיניה ילפינן בעלמא א"נ שאני קטן דאינו בר הקמת שם כלל בעודנו קטן אבל אותה הבתולה לאחר ביאה ראשונה איכא בה הקמת שם. וא"ת היכי קאמר בשלמא מן הנשואין לא אתי עשה ודחי ל"ת ועשה. הא ודאי יש לנו לומר דהכא דחי ל"ת ועשה אע"ג דבעלמא לא דחי משום דהוי לאו שאינו שוה בכל. וי"ל דפריך הכי אפי' אי אמרינן דאין חלוק בין לאו השוה בכל ללאו שאינו שוה בכל (מ"מ) ולא תקשי לך מידי מן הנשואין מ"מ תקשי לך מן האירוסין דיכא עשה וידחה ל"ת: **ומשני** רבי רחמנא יבמתו. וא"ת א"כ מנלן דחייבי לאוין גרידי דלא מייבמה נוקי יבמתו בלאו ועשה וחייבי לאוין גרידי עדיין לא שמעינן וי"ל דמסתבר לאתא יבמתו לחלק ולאסור ליבם ואי לחייבי לאוין ועשה לא אצטריך לאין עשה דוחה ל"ת ועשה א) וא"כ אתא לאסור חייבי לאוין גרידי מיבום. וא"ת ונימא לחייבי לאוין ועשה אפי' חליצה לא צריכי ותפטר ונוקי יבמתו דמשמע לחליצה [מיהו צריך] בחייבי לאוין גרידי די"ל דסברא הוא לאוקמי יבמתו בכל הנך דתפסי בהו קדושי:

א) קצ"ע דלפי מש"כ בתחלה שפיר אילטריך לאף דהוי לאו ועשה שאינו שוה בכל ואפ"ה לא דחי.

הגהות הב"ח

(א) במשנה כל שאיסורה איסור ערוה לא: (ב) גמ' יש לך יבמה אחרת שעולה לחליצה: (ג) תוס' ד"ה יבא וכו' דלא קשה מידי דלא בעינן ביאה שתהא:

גליון הש"ס

מתני' חולצת ולא מתייבמת. עיין בר"ש פ"ב דחלה:

מסורת הש"ס

תורה אור

דברים כה

שם

סנהדרין נג. לקמן כו. וכף כח: [לקמן כח.]

[לעיל יג.]

סנהדרין נג:

סנהדרין שם קידושין נ. [ב"מ מח. הוריות ב: חולין קו.]

ויקרא כא

סנהדרין שם

שם כז

לקמן פה. סנהדרין יח:

דברים כה

שם

[לעיל ג.] לקמן מד. [ול. מח:]

יג א מיי' פ"ו מהל' יבום הלכה י סמג עשין נג טוש"ע אה"ע סימן קעד סעי' א:
יד ב מיי' שם:
טו ג מיי' שם טוש"ע שם:
טז ד מיי' פ"ג מהל' נזירות הלכה ו:
יז ה מיי' שם ופ"י מהלכות טומאת צרעת הלכה ה ופ"ו מהלכות יבום הלכה י:

[ע' תוספות סוטה כו. ד"ה אשת]

מסתברא, חייבי לאוין תפסי בהו קדושין, חייבי כריתות לא תפסי בהו קדושין. מתיב רבא: [א]איסור מצוה ואיסור קדושה, בא עליה או חלץ לה – נפטרה צרתה. ואי ס"ד חייבי לאוין מדאורייתא לחליצה רמיא, לייבום לא רמיא – כי בא עליה אמאי נפטרה צרתה? הוא מותיב לה והוא מפרק לה: לצדדין קתני, בא עליה – אאיסור מצוה, חלץ לה – אאיסור קדושה. מתיב רבא: *פצוע דכא וכרות שפכה, *סריס אדם והזקן [א] – או חולצין או מייבמין. כיצד? מתו, ולהם (א) אחים ולהם נשים, ועמדו אחין ועשו מאמר בנשותיהן, ונתנו גט, וחלצו, מה שעשו עשו, ואם בעלו קנו. מתו אחים, ועמדו הם ועשו מאמר בנשותיהן, ונתנו גט, או שחלצו – מה שעשו עשו. ואם בעלו – קנו ואסור לקיימן, משום שנאמר "לא יבא פצוע דכא". (דברים כג) ואי סלקא דעתך חייבי לאוין מדאורייתא לחליצה רמיא, לייבום לא רמיא, אם בעלו – אמאי קנו? אלא אמר רבא: אלמנה (ג) מן האירוסין נמי עשה ולא תעשה הוא, דכתיב "קדושים יהיו לאלהיהם". (ויקרא כא) ממזרת ונתינה מאי איכא למימר? כתיב "והתקדשתם" (שם יא) אי הכי, כל התורה כולה נמי עשה ולא תעשה הוא, דכתיב "והתקדשתם"! אלא אמר רבא: גזירה אלמנה מן האירוסין אטו אלמנה מן הנשואין. ממזרת ונתינה מאי איכא למימר? גזירה במקום מצוה אטו שלא במקום מצוה. אלא מעתה, אשת אחיו מאביו לא תתייבם, גזירה משום אשת אחיו מאמו! *ייבום בנחלה תלא רחמנא, מידע ידיע. אשה שאין לה בנים לא תתייבם, גזירה משום אשה שיש לה בנים! בבנים תלא רחמנא, מידע ידיע. אשת אחיו שהיה בעולמו לא תתייבם, גזרה משום אשת אחיו שלא היה בעולמו! [לעיל יז: לקמן כד.] בישיבה תלא רחמנא, מידע ידיע. כל הנשים לא תתייבמנה, גזרה משום אילונית! לא שכיחא. ממזרת ונתינה נמי לא שכיחא! אלא אמר רבא: *[ב]גזרה ביאה ראשונה אטו ביאה שניה. תניא נמי הכי: *[ג]אם בעלו – קנו בביאה ראשונה, ואסור לקיימן בביאה שניה. הדר אמר רבא, ואיתימא רב אשי: לאו מילתא היא דאמרי, דאמר *ריש לקיש: [ד]כל מקום שאתה מוצא עשה ולא תעשה, אם אתה יכול לקיים שניהם מוטב, ואם לאו [ה]יבא עשה וידחה את לא תעשה, הכא נמי אפשר בחליצה דמקיים עשה ולא תעשה. מיתיבי: ואם בעלו קנו! תיובתא. § איתמר: ביאת כהן גדול באלמנה, רבי *יוחנן ור' אלעזר: חד אמר: אינה פוטרת צרתה, וחד אמר[א] פוטרת צרתה.

באלמנה

לצדדין קתני. בא עליה קאי אאיסור מצוה, דהיינו שניות מדברי סופרים. דמדאורייתא חזיא ליה וקמיה רמיא, לפיכך נפטרה צרתה בביאתה. חלץ קאי אאיסור קדושה דרמיא לחליצה, הילכך חליצתה פוטרת צרתה. פצוע דכא וכרות שפכה. לקמן מפרש להו בפרק "הערל"*. [דף ע. עה.] סריס אדם. שסירסו אדם, ולא מחמת חולי נסתרס מאליו, והוי כלאו, דבכלל פצוע דכא וכרות שפכה הוא, ואסור לישא ישראלית, דכתיב "לא יבא פצוע דכא". או מייבמין. לאו לכתחלה קאמר, אלא ייבומן יבום, שאם בעלו קנו, כדקתני ואזיל. והזקן. שפסק מלידה. והאי לאו מחייבי לאוין הוא, אלא קמ"ל, דאע"ג דלאו בר אולודי הוא – ביאתו ביאה לקנות יבמתו, ויוצאה ממנו בגט. ונתנו גט. כלומר, או נתנו גט או חלצו. וגט ביבמה מהני למיפסל עליו ועל כל האחין, דאי בעי לייבומי – תו לא מצי, דקם ליה בשוב לא יבנה. ואם בעלו קנו. ויוצאות בגט בלא חליצה. ואסור לקיימן. אסיפא קאי, מתו אחין ובעלו הן את יבמתן, ואפצוע דכא וכיוצא בו, ולאו אזקן. אלא אמר רבא. חייבי לאוין נמי לייבום רמיא. הלכך, אם בעלו – קנו. ודקשיא לך באלמנה ארוסה שנפלה לכהן גדול תתייבם, ויבא עשה וידחה את ל"ת – אלמנה (ג) מן האירוסין נמי כו'. גזירה ביאה ראשונה. דמקיים בה עשה, ומצי למידחי. אטו ביאה שניה. דלא מצי למידחי, דהא איקיים בה עשה. לאו מילתא היא דאמרי. דבביאה ראשונה הויא שרי לכתחילה, אי לאו משום גזירת ביאה שניה, דודאי אפילו ביאה ראשונה אסורה ולא אמרי' תדחה עשה את לא תעשה, דהא אפשר להתקיים בחליצה בלא עשה ולא תעשה. אם בעלו קנו. אלמא מדאורייתא רמיא קמיה למידחי לא תעשה. תיובתא. דרבא ותיובתא *דריש לקיש ב] דאמרי לעיל אם אתה יכול לקיים את שניהם לא עקרת ליה ללאו. באלמנה. יבמתו. פוטרת. אותה ואת צרתה מן החליצה וסגי לה בגט.

דאין עולין לייבום – מהתם שמעינן דעולין לחליצה, כדדרשינן: יש לך יבמה אחרת שעולה לחליצה. ועוד: דפריך, מה ראית? פי': דאימא איפכא, ונוקי "יבמתו" לחייבי כרת, "ואם לא יחפוץ" לחייבי לאוין – היכי מצי למעוטי מאם לא יחפוץ חייבי לאוין מחליצה? הא קרינן בהו אם חפץ – יבם, דאתי עשה ודחי ל"ת, כיון דמוקמינן "יבמתו" לחייבי כריתות! וקצת היה נראה לפרש, דה"פ: א"ה, חייבי לאוין נמי נשוה חליצה וייבום מהאי קרא. ותו פריך: מה ראית, פירוש: דמהאי קרא "ולא יחפוץ" נשוה חייבי לאוין לחליצה וייבום, וליהוו בני חליצה וייבום! ואין להקשות דלמה לן קרא להכי? דליסתוק קרא מיני'. דטובא איצטריך, (ד) כדפרישית לקמן בפ' "החולץ" (דף מד.): וניייבם לחדא ונחלוץ לחדא. אבל קשה: דאם כן מאי קא משני: מיסתברא חייבי לאוין תפסי בהו קדושין, דמשמע מתוך התירוץ דהוא פריך שלא יעלו חייבי לאוין לחליצה? וי"ל בדוחק דמחייבי לאוין וחייבי עשה פריך, והכי פריך: א"ה, חייבי לאוין וחייבי עשה נשוה לחליצה וייבום מהאי קרא, וחייבי לאוין יעלו גם לייבום, וחייבי עשה לא יעלו גם לחליצה. ועיקר פירכא מחייבי עשה. **מסתברא** חייבי לאוין תפסי בהו קדושין. ותימה: מנלן לאוקמי קרא בחייבי לאוין? נוקי קרא בחייבי עשה גרידא, דאע"ג דאין מייבמין – מ"מ עולים לחליצה, כיון דתפסי בהו קידושין. אבל חייבי לאוין נימא דאתי עשה ודחי לא תעשה, ויעלו גם לייבום! וי"ל: דמשמע ליה השתא לדרוש מקרא ד"יבמתו" לאסור יבום ולהצריך חליצה. אבל קשה: א"כ, היכי הוה בעי לאוקמי קרא בחייבי כריתות? והא ל"ל דהכי פריך: ואימא חייבי כריתות נמי ליבעי חליצה מהאי קרא – דהא קאמר בתר הכי ומה ראית, דמשמע: ואימא איפכא. **פצוע** דכא וכרות שפכה וסריס אדם. פירוש: סריס אדם – לאפוקי בידי שמים, שלא היה להם שעת הכושר. **אם** בעלו קנו. ה"ה דלכתחילה נמי שרי, כדמוכח לקמן. אלא, איידי דנקט בסיפא לשון דיעבד נקט נמי ברישא לשון דיעבד. **אמר** קרא והתקדשתם. אע"ג דהאי עשה נמי הוה במצות יבום, ואיכא תרי עשה – מ"מ אין תרי עשה דוחה ל"ת ועשה. **אי** הכי, כל הנשים לא יתייבמו. כל הני פירכי לא פריך שיעקרו חכמים לגמרי מצות ייבום, והכי פי': אשת אחיו מאביו לא תתייבם, כשאינו אחיו אלא מאביו – לא תתייבם עד דמיחדי באבא ובאמא, גזיר' משום אשת אחיו מאמו. א) אשה שאין לה בנים לא תתייבם, פירוש: שאין לה עכשיו, אבל היו לה בחיי הבעל ומתו – גזירה משום אשה שיש לה בנים. אשת אחיו שהיה בעולמו כגון שבא ממדינת הים והיה מוחזק לן דלית ליה אחים, דדמי כמי שלא היה בעולמו ב), כל הנשים לא יתייבמו, פירוש: אשה שלא היה לה בנים מעולם לא מזה ולא מאחר, דדמיא לאילונית. **גזירה** ביאה ראשונה אטו כו'. אלמנה מן הנשואין וחייבי עשה נפקא לן מיבמתו, דאע"ג דאין עולין ליבום – עולין לחליצה. **אטו** ביאה שניה. לאו דוקא נקט ביאה שניה, דהא אפילו גמר ביאה ראשונה אסור, דיבמה נקנית בהערא'. והו"מ למימר גזירה אטו גמר ביאה. ואין להתיר ביאה שניה מטעם דנעשית אשתו לכל דבר – דאינה נעשית כאשתו אלא היכא דשרי ליה בלא דחייה, אבל חייבי לאוין, אפילו ביאה ראשונה לא שריא אלא משום דאתי עשה ודחי לא תעשה, וביאה שניה דלית בה עשה – לא דחיא, אע"ג דבפרק "הבא על יבמתו" (לקמן סא.) לא מצריך קרא אלא לאירס ואח"כ נתמנה להיות כהן גדול, אבל נשאה קודם שנתמנה משמע דלא צריך קרא שיכול לקיימה, משום דנשאה בהיתר – התם נמי, משום דבהיתר בלא שום דחיית איסור נשאה, אבל הכא – ביאה ראשונה לא שריא אלא משום דאתי עשה ודחי לא תעשה, ביאה דמצוה – דחיא, דלאו מצוה – לא דחיא. **מיתיבי** ואם בעלו קנו. תימה: דרבא גופי' מותיב מהך ברייתא, והשתא איתותב מינה!

תוספות ישנים

ואסור לקיימן לא קאי אזקן: אי הכי כל התורה נמי כתיב והתקדשתם. אע"ג דבפ' אלו מגלחות משמע דחשבינן ליה עשה גבי טומאה, י"ל דהיינו דווקא לגבי מלאכת דכתיבה בהאי פרשתא [illegible] אבל לגבי כל התורה לא חשבינן ליה לעשה: א) א"נ פריך הכא אפכא דקא פריך [illegible] אחיו מאביו וגם מאמו לא תתייבם גזירה משום אשת אחיו מאמו ומצות יבום תתקיים באשת אחיו מאביו בלבד דליכא [illegible] ולא שייך למגזר משום אשת אחיו מאמו: ב) א"נ יש פרק דקא בעי [illegible] היכא שיש את אחד שהיה בעולמו ואת אחר שלא היה בעולמו [illegible] לא תתייבם אשת אחר שלא היה בעולמו משום גזרה (לא"ה) [לאחר] שלא היה בעולמו ומצות יבום תתקיים היכא שאין כאן את שלא היה בעולמו:

הגהות הב"ח

(א) גמרא כיצד מתו ולהן אחין ועמדו אחין: (ב) שם אלמנה מן האירוסין נמי: (ג) רש"י ד"ה אלא [illegible] אלמנה מן האירוסין נמי: (ד) תום' ד"ה [illegible] כדפריך לקמן בפ' החולץ:

[תוס' פי"א] לקמן [illegible] ע"ש

גליון הש"ס

גמ' סריס אדם. ע' סוטה דף כו ע"ב תד"ה אשת סריס: שם גזירה ביאה ראשונה. ע' לקמן דף [illegible] תד"ה [illegible]: תום' ד"ה אם בעלו וכו' כדמוכח לקמן. ע' לקמן [illegible] ד"ה [illegible]

הגהות מהר"ב רנשבורג

א] גמ' איתמר וכו' וחד אמר פוטרת צרתה. נ"ב [illegible] פ"ו מהל' יבום הלכה [illegible] ב] רש"י ד"ה תיובתא דרבא ותיובתא דר"ל [illegible]

נ"א דרבא אתי

סנהדרין יט:

שבת קלג. נזיר מא. מנחות מ.

[לקמן סח.]

[וע' תוס' לעיל ה. ד"ה ולאכתי שנרגם ר' אחא]

הגהות הגר"א

[א] גמ' והזקן או חולצין או מייבמין. נ"ב בתוספתא (ספ"ב) גרים חולצין או מייבמין [illegible]

תוספות חד מקמאי

תניא אסור מצוה או אסור קדושה בא עליה או חלץ לה נפטרה צרתה. פצוע דכא וכרות שפכה סרים אדם והזקן או חולצין או מייבמין כיצד מתו ולהן אחים ועמדו אחים ועשו מאמר בנשותיהם נתנו גט או שחלצו מה שעשו עשו אם בעלו קנו ואסור לקיימן משום שנאמר לא יבוא פצוע דכא אלמא מדאורייתא חייבי לאוין רמיין לייבום דאתי עשה ודחי לא תעשה. והא דקתני במתני' אלמנה לכהן גדול גרושה וחלוצה לכהן הדיוט ממזרת ונתינה לישראל חולצת ולא מתייבמת מדרבנן גזרינן ביאה ראשונה אטו ביאה שניה ותניא נמי [הכי] אם בעלו קנו בביאה ראשונה ואסור לקיימן בביאה שניה וביאת כ"ג באלמנה מן הנשואין אינה פוטרת צרתה דאין עשה דוחה לא תעשה ועשה אבל ביאה באלמנה מן האירוסין ובכל חייבי לאוין פוטרת צרתה כדתנינן אם בעלו ק

באלמנה מן הנשואין כולי עלמא לא פליגי דלא פטרה, דאין עשה דוחה לא תעשה ועשה. כי פליגי – באלמנה מן הארוסין. מ"ד פוטרת, אתי עשה ודחי את לא תעשה, ומאן דאמר אינה פוטרת – לא אתי עשה ודחי את לא תעשה, כיון דאפשר בחליצה. מיתיבי: ואם בעלו – קנו! תיובתא. לימא תיהוי נמי תיובתא דר"ל! אמר לך ר"ל: כי אמינא אנא – היכא דמקיימי מצוה, אבל הכא, חליצה במקום ייבום לאו מצוה היא. [א]אמר *רבא: רמז לשניות מן התורה מנין? שנאמר °"כי את כל התועבות האל עשו אנשי הארץ". "האל" קשות, מכלל דאיכא רכות, ומאי נינהו – שניות. ומאי משמע ד"האל" לישנא דקשה הוא? דכתיב °"ואת אילי הארץ לקח". לימא פליגא דר' לוי, *דא"ר לוי: [ב]קשה עונשין של מדות יותר מעונשין של עריות, שזה נאמר בהן "אל" וזה נאמר בהן "אלה". "אל" – קשה, "ואלה" – קשה מ"אל". גבי עריות נמי, הא כתיב "אלה". ההוא למעוטי מדות מכרת. אלא, מאי חומרייהו? הני אפשר בתשובה, הני – לא אפשר בתשובה. רב יהודה אמר מהכא: °"ואזן וחקר תקן משלים הרבה" ואמר עולא *א"ר אלעזר: קודם שבא שלמה היתה תורה דומה לכפיפה שאין לה אזנים, עד שבא שלמה ועשה לה אזנים. ר' אושעיא אמר מהכא: °"פרעהו אל תעבר בו שטה מעליו ועבור". אמר רב אשי: משל דר' אושעיא למה הדבר דומה – לאדם משמר פרדס, משמרו מבחוץ – כולו משתמר, משמרו מבפנים – שלפניו משתמר, שלאחריו – אינו משתמר. והא דרב אשי *בדותא היא: התם, שלפניו מיהא משתמר, הכא, אי לאו שניות – פגע בערוה גופה. רב כהנא אמר מהכא: °"ושמרתם את משמרתי" – *עשו משמרת למשמרתי. א"ל אביי לרב יוסף: הא – דאורייתא, היא דאורייתא ופירשו רבנן. כל התורה נמי פירשו רבנן! אלא: מדרבנן, וקרא – אסמכתא בעלמא. § ת"ר: *מה הם שניות? [ג]אם אמו, [ד]ואם אביו, [ה]ואשת אבי אביו, [ו]ואשת אבי אמו, [ז]ואשת אחי האב מן האם, [ח]ואשת אחי האם מן האב, [ט]וכלת בנו, [י]וכלת בתו. [כ]ומותר אדם באשת חמיו ובאשת חורגו, ואסור בבת חורגו. [ל]וחורגו מותר באשתו ובתו. ואשת חורגו אומרת לו: אני מותרת לך, ובתי אסורה לך. בת חורגו – דאורייתא היא, דכתיב °"את בת בנה ואת בת בתה"! משום דקבעי למיתני סיפא: אשת חורגו אומרת לו: אני מותרת לך ובתי אסורה לך, ואע"ג דבתי אסורה לך מדאורייתא – בדידי לא גזור ביה רבנן, תנא רישא נמי בת חורגו. אי הכי, אשת חמיו נמי תימא: אני מותרת לך ובתי אסורה לך, דהויא אחות אשתו! הא – פסיקא ליה, הא – לא פסיקא ליה. § אמר רב: [מ]ארבע נשים יש להן הפסק. נקיט רב בידיה תלת: אשת אחי האם מן האב, ואשת אחי האב מן האם, וכלתו. וזעירי מוסיף אף אשת אבי אמו. אמר רב נחמן בר יצחק, וסימניך: דעילאי דרב. ורב, מאי טעמא לא חשיב ליה? מיחלפא ליה באשת אבי אביו. וזעירי: להתם שכיח ואזיל, להכא – לא שכיח ואזיל. כלתו –
דאורייתא

תורה אור: ויקרא יח; יחזקאל יז; קהלת יב; משלי ד; ויקרא יח; שם

רש"י

כי את כל התועבות האל. גבי עריות כתיב, ומשמע התועבות הקשות. מכלל דיש רכות. וקלות מהן, ואסורות. אלה. במדות כתיב "כי תועבת ה' כל עושה אלה כל עושה עול", ומדקאמר יותר משל עריות – מכלל דהא לאו קשה הוא. הכתיב אלה. "מכל התועבות האלה ונכרתו". עריות אפשר בתקנה. כל זמן שלא הוליד ממזר – יפרוש הימנה ויתחרט. אבל מדות – גזל את הרבים הוא, ואינו יודע למי יחזיר. ואע"ג דקיימא לן* יתקן בהם צרכי רבים – לאו תשובה מעלייתא הוא. ואזן. לשון אזנים, בית אחיזה, כדאמר בעירובין*: לימד דעת את העם – דאגמריה בסימני טעמא ואסברה בדדמי, גמר מילתא ממילתא, והזהיר על דברי סופרים, כדכתיב "ויותר מהמה בני הזהר" – הזהר בדברי סופרים יותר מדברי תורה, וגזר על השניות. אזנים. של קופה לאחוז בהן הקופה, ומשתמרת שלא תפול. ה"נ, ע"י שניות מתרחקין מן העריות. פרעהו. *הגילהו לאיסור, והוסיף עליו, כדי שלא תעבור בו, כמו "גדל פרע". ושמרתם את משמרתי. גבי עריות כתיב. אם אמו. אמו כתיבה, וגזרו רבנן על אם אמו כדי שלא יפגע באמו. וגזרו נמי באם אביו משום אם אמו. ואע"ג דגזירה לגזירה הוא, כדאמר לקמן: משום דתרווייהו אימא רבתא קרו להו. ואשת אבי אביו. משום אשת אביו הכתובה. ואשת אבי אמו. ואע"ג דאשת אבי (אם) אמו גזירה משום אשת אבי אביו – דתרווייהו אבא רבא קרו להו, והילכך חדא הוא. ואשת אחי האב מן האם. דמן התורה ערות אחי אביך כתיב, ואמרינן לקמן ב"הבא על יבמתו" דבאחי אביו מן האב קמשתעי. אבל אם היה אחיו של אביו מן האם שריא, וגזרו רבנן עלה משום אשת אחי אביו מן האב. ואשת אחי האם מן האב. כגון נפתלי אחי יוכבד מאביה, ונשא אשה – אסורה לאהרן משום שניה. דאע"ג דאשת אחי אמו לא כתיבא – גזרו בה רבנן היכא דהוא אחי אמו מן האב, גזירה משום אחי אביו מן האם דהויא נמי שנייה (א) ואיכא גד אב. אבל אם היה נפתלי אחי יוכבד מן האם ולא מן האב – מיבעי לקמן בגמרא אי גזור רבנן עלה אי לאו. וכלת בנו. גזור משום כלתו. וכלת בתו. מפרש טעמא לקמן: גזירה משום כלת בנו. חורגו. בן אשתו. ואסור בבת חורגו. לקמן פריך: הא דאורייתא היא "את בת בנה", ואמאי תני לה בהדי שניות? הא פסיקא ליה. בת חורגו לעולם אסורה לו. הא לא פסיקא ליה. בת אשת חמיו האסורה לו משום אחות אשה. הואיל ולאחר מיתת אשתו מותרת לו – לא פסיקא ליה. ד' נשים שניות יש להן הפסק. שלמעלה מהן ולמטה מהן מותר. אבל האחרות, כגון אם אמו – אין (ב) להם הפסק, שלמעלה הימנה עד סוף כל הדורות הויא נמי שנייה. וכן אשת אבי אביו ואם אבי אביו למעלה מהן עד לעולם אסור. כגון אשת אבי אבי אביו ואם אבי אבי אביו. ונקיט רב בידיה תלת. לפרושי תלת מהנך ארבעה, אבל רביעית לא הוה ידע מה היא, אבל גמרא הוה גמיר דארבע נינהו. אשת אחי האם מן האב. היא לבדה שנייה, אבל אשת אחי אם אמו – מותרת. ואשת אחי האב מן האם. לבדה שנייה. אבל אשת אחי אבי אביו מן האם – מותרת וטעמא, משום דלא שייכא בהו ערוה דאורייתא. אבל אם אמו, דשייכא בדורותיה ערוה דאורייתא, כגון אמו ואשת אבי אביו, יש בדורותיה אשת אב דאורייתא. ואם אביו נמי, אע"ג דלא שייכא בדורה ערוה דאורייתא – אין לה הפסק, ואסורה אף אם אבי אביו, דמיחלפא באם אם אמו. וכלתו. יש לה הפסק. ולקמן פריך: היכי חשיב כלתו בהדי שניות? הא דאורייתא היא! ומתרץ: אימא כלת בתו, דחשבינן לה לעיל בשניות. וקאמר רב דיש לה הפסק, הואיל ולא שייכא בה איסור כלה דאורייתא. הילכך, כלת בת בתו – שריא. אבל כלת בנו – אין לה הפסק, וכלת בן בנו נמי אסירא, הואיל ושייכא בדורות הללו איסור כלה דאורייתא. אשת אבי אמו. יש לה הפסק, ושרינן אשת אבי אבי אמו, הואיל ולא שייכא בדורות הללו אישות אב דאורייתא. וסימן. הא דאוסיף זעירי דעילאי דרב, הוא דור אחד למעלה משניות דרב דחשיב אשת אחי האם, וזו של זעירי דור אחד למעלה (ג). אשת אבי אמו מחלפא באשת אבי אביו. דאי אמרת יש לה הפסק – אתי למימר באשת אבי אביו יש לה הפסק. והתם איכא באותם דורות אישות דאורייתא. למשפחת אביו אדם רגיל לילך, ויודע שיש שם קורבה יותר מאמו, הילכך לא מיחלפי.
דאורייתא

תוספות

רב יהודה אמר (ד) ואזן וחקר. והא דאמר פרק שני דעירובין (דף כא:): בשעה שתיקן שלמה נטילת ידים ועירובין יצאת בת קול ואמרה כו' ולא חשיב שניות – שמא אחר בת קול תקנה.

ומותר באשת חמיו. ירושלמי: אשת חמיו אסורה משום* מראית העין. וא"ת: תורה היא לאסור' – הא דוד נשא רצפה בת איה! וקאמר נמי: שני חורגין שגדלו בבית – אסורה מפני מראית העין. רבי חנינא אומר: יסבון באתרא דלא חכימי להו. ומעשה בפרובינציא באחד שהיה טבחו טבות ויינו מזוג לישא אשת חמיו, ואפסדיה ר"ת לסעודתיה! ואע"ג דשמעתין שרי להו אשת חמיו וחורגו – שמא *אחר כך אסרום. ומיהו בסוף "משוח מלחמה" *מוכיח סוגיא דלא חיישינן למראית העין גבי חורגה הגדילה בין האחין.

אי הכי אשת חמיו נמי. מאם (ה) אם חמיו לא מצי למיפרך דתימא ליה אני מותרת לך כו' – דבעיא היא לקמן אם שניות דרבי חייא יש להן הפסק או לא.
לא

עין משפט נר מצוה

יח א (מיי' פ"א מהל' אישות הלכה ו סמג לאוין קי קלג טור אה"ע סימן טו):

וכ"ה בדרך ארץ רבה פ"א ומסיים ובתה מותרת לו

יט ב מיי' פ"ז מהל' גנבה הלכה יב סמג לאוין קנג טוש"ע ח"מ סימן רלא סעיף יט:

כ ג מיי' פ"א מהל' אישות הלכה ו סמג לאוין קי טוש"ע אה"ע סימן טו סעי' ב:

כא ד מיי' שם טוש"ע שם סעי' ד:

[במסכת דרך ארץ איתא בזה"ל אבל אמרו חכמים אשת חמיו אסורה מפני מראית העין ובתה מותרת לו]

כב ה מיי' שם טוש"ע שם סעיף ו:

כג ו מיי' שם טוש"ע שם סעיף ז:

כד ז מיי' שם טוש"ע שם סעיף ח:

כה ח מיי' שם טוש"ע שם סעיף ט:

כו ט מיי' שם טוש"ע שם סעיף יט:

כז י מיי' שם טוש"ע שם סעיף כ:

כח כ מיי' שם טוש"ע שם סעיף כז:

כט ל מיי' שם טוש"ע שם סעיף יח:

ל מ מיי' שם טוש"ע שם סעיף יח:

תוספות ישנים

דלא אפשר בתשובה. לאין יודע למי משלם ואין להקשות יעשה מהן צרכי רבים דמ"מ אין זו תשובה כתיקונה כיון דאינו משלם לאותו שגזל: הני אפשר בתשובה ובלבד שלא הוליד בן דאם הוליד בן הוי מעוות לא יוכל לתקון: עד שבא שלמה ועשה לה אזנים. וא"ת התם פרק עושין פסין חשיב ערובין ונט"י דקאמר בשעה שתקן שלמה ערובין וידים ואמאי לא חשיב שניות דהכא וי"ל דלא חשיב אלא דבר התלוי בחכמה ובסברת הלב. אבל הכא אין הדבר תלוי בחכמה אלא להחמיר ולעשות סייג לתורה:

תוספות חד מקמאי

תנו רבנן מה הן שניות אם אמו ואם אביו ואשת אבי אביו ואשת אבי אמו פי' כל הני אין להן הפסק דאם אמו ואם אבי אביו ואשת אבי אביו ואשת אבי (אבי) אמו [אסור] עד סוף כל הדורות. אמר רב [ארבע נשים] יש להן הפסק. ונקט רב בידיה תלת אשת אחי האם מן האב ואשת אחי האב מן (האב) [האם] וכלת בתו אבל כלת בנו וכלת בן בנו עד סוף כל הדורות אין להן הפסק. וזעירי מוסיף אף אשת אבי אמו.

מסורת הש"ס

[ביצה כט.]
דף כח:
[בשאלתות פ' אחרי סי' נז איתא רב הונא]
[ס"א הגדילהו]
ב"ב דף פח:
עירובין כא:
[עי' פסחים יא. ומ"ש שם על הגליון]
[מ"ק ה.]
[מס' ד"א פ"א ע"ש]

הגהות הב"ח

(א) רש"י ד"ה ואשת אחי האם מן האב וכו' דהויא נמי שנייה משום דבתרוייהו איכא גד אב: (ב) ד"ה ד' נשים וכו' אין להם הפסק שלמעלה וכו' הויא נמי שנייה הואיל ואמו מן התורה וכן אשת אבי אביו הואיל ואשת אב הויא לדאורייתא וכן אם אביו למעלה מהן וכו' ואם אבי אביו כנ"ל ותיבת אבי נמחק פעמים: (ג) ד"ה וסימן וכו' למעלה מאשת אחי אמו הס"ד: (ד) תום' ד"ה רב יהודה אמר מהכא ואוזן: (ה) ד"ה אי הכי וכו' מאם אם חמיו לא. נ"ב כן הגיה מהרש"ל ועיין בש"ת הב"ח סי' ז:

גליון הש"ס

גמ' ומאי משמע דהאל לישנא דקשה הוא. עי' מדרש רבה פרשה תולדות פ' סד בפסוק את כל הארצות האל:

דְּאוֹרַיְיתָא הִיא, דִּכְתִיב "עֶרְוַת כַּלָּתְךָ לֹא תְגַלֵּה"! אֵימָא: כַּלַּת בְּנוֹ. וְכַלַּת בְּנוֹ יֵשׁ לָהּ הֶפְסֵק? *וְהָא תַּנְיָא: כַּלָּתוֹ — עֶרְוָה, כַּלַּת בְּנוֹ — שְׁנִיָּה, וְכֵן אַתָּה אוֹמֵר [א]בִּבְנוֹ, וּבֶן בְּנוֹ, עַד סוֹף כָּל הַדּוֹרוֹת! אֶלָּא אֵימָא: כַּלַּת בִּתּוֹ. דְּאָמַר רַב חִסְדָּא: הָא מִילְּתָא מִגַּבְרָא רַבָּה שְׁמִיעַ לִי, וּמַנּוּ — רַבִּי אַמִי: לֹא אָסְרוּ כַּלָּה אֶלָּא מִפְּנֵי כַּלָּה. וְאָמְרוּ לִי כַּלְדָּאֵי: מַלְפָנָא הָוֵית. אָמֵינָא: אִי גַּבְרָא רַבָּה הָוֵינָא — אַסְבְּרָא מִדַּעְתִּי, אִי מַקְרֵי דַרְדְּקֵי הָוֵינָא — אַשְׁיילָה מֵרַבָּנַן דְּאָתוּ לְבֵי כְּנִישְׁתָּא. הַשְׁתָּא סְבַרְתָּהּ מִדַּעְתִּי: לֹא אָסְרוּ כַּלַּת בִּתּוֹ אֶלָּא מִשּׁוּם כַּלַּת בְּנוֹ. אֲמַר לֵיהּ אַבַּיֵי לְרָבָא: אַסְבְּרָהּ לָךְ, כְּגוֹן כַּלָּתָה דְּבֵי בַּר צִיתַאי. רַב פַּפָּא אָמַר: כְּגוֹן כַּלָּתָה דְּבֵי רַב פַּפָּא בַּר אַבָּא. רַב אַשִׁי אָמַר: כְּגוֹן כַּלָּתָה דְּבֵי מָרִי בַּר אִיסַק.§ אִיבַּעְיָא לְהוּ: [ב]אֵשֶׁת אֲחִי הָאֵם מִן הָאֵם, מַהוּ? אֵשֶׁת אֲחִי הָאָב מִן הָאֵם, וְאֵשֶׁת אֲחִי הָאֵם מִן הָאָב, דְּאִיכָּא צַד אָב — הוּא דְּגָזְרוּ רַבָּנַן, אֲבָל הֵיכָא דְּלֵיכָּא צַד אָב לָא גָּזְרוּ בְּהוּ רַבָּנַן, אוֹ דִּלְמָא לָא שְׁנָא? אֲמַר רַב סַפְרָא: הִיא *גּוּפָהּ גְּזֵירָה, וַאֲנַן נֵיקוּם וְנִגְזוֹר גְּזֵירָה לִגְזֵירָה?! אֲמַר רָבָא: אַטּוּ כּוּלְּהוּ לָאו גְּזֵירָה לִגְזֵירָה נִינְהוּ? אִמּוֹ — עֶרְוָה, [ג]אֵם אִמּוֹ — שְׁנִיָּה, וְגָזְרוּ עַל אֵם אָבִיו מִשּׁוּם אֵם אִמּוֹ. וְטַעֲמָא מַאי? כּוּלְּהוּ "דְּבֵי אִימָּא רַבָּתִי" קָרוּ לֵיהּ. אֵשֶׁת אָבִיו — עֶרְוָה, אֵשֶׁת אֲבִי אָבִיו — שְׁנִיָּה, וְגָזְרוּ עַל אֵשֶׁת אֲבִי אִמּוֹ מִשּׁוּם אֵשֶׁת אֲבִי אָבִיו, וְטַעֲמָא מַאי? כּוּלְּהוּ "דְּבֵי אַבָּא רַבָּה" קָרוּ לֵיהּ. [ד]אֵשֶׁת אֲחִי הָאָב מִן הָאָב — עֶרְוָה, אֵשֶׁת אֲחִי הָאָב מִן הָאֵם — שְׁנִיָּה, וְגָזְרוּ עַל אֵשֶׁת אֲחִי הָאֵם מִן הָאָב מִשּׁוּם אֵשֶׁת אֲחִי הָאָב מִן הָאֵם, וְטַעֲמָא מַאי — מִשּׁוּם דְּכוּלְּהוּ "דְּבֵי דוֹדֵי" קָרֵי לְהוּ. מַאי? תָּא שְׁמַע: דְּכִי אֲתָא רַב יְהוּדָה בַּר שֵׁילָא אֲמַר: אָמְרִי בְּמַעַרְבָא: כָּל שֶׁבִּנְקֵבָה עֶרְוָה — בְּזָכָר גָּזְרוּ עַל אִשְׁתּוֹ מִשּׁוּם שְׁנִיָּה. וְאָמַר רָבָא: וּכְלָלָא הוּא? [ה]חֲמוֹתוֹ — עֶרְוָה, אֵשֶׁת חָמִיו מוּתֶּרֶת. בַּת חֲמוֹתוֹ — עֶרְוָה, אֵשֶׁת בֶּן חֲמוֹתוֹ מוּתֶּרֶת. בַּת חָמִיו — עֶרְוָה, אֵשֶׁת בֶּן חָמִיו — מוּתֶּרֶת. חוֹרַגְתּוֹ — עֶרְוָה, אֵשֶׁת חוֹרְגוֹ — מוּתֶּרֶת! בַּת חוֹרַגְתּוֹ עֶרְוָה אֵשֶׁת בֶּן חוֹרְגוֹ מוּתֶּרֶת וְהָא דְּרַב יְהוּדָה בַּר שֵׁילָא לְאִיתּוּיֵי מַאי? לָאו לְאִיתּוּיֵי אֵשֶׁת אֲחִי הָאֵם מִן הָאֵם, דְּכָל שֶׁבִּנְקֵבָה עֶרְוָה — בְּזָכָר גָּזְרוּ *אִשְׁתּוֹ מִשּׁוּם שְׁנִיָּה! מַאי שְׁנָא הָנֵי וּמַאי שְׁנָא הָא? הָא — בְּחַד קִידּוּשִׁין מִקָּרַב לָהּ, הָנֵי — עַד דְּאִיכָּא תְּרֵי קִידּוּשִׁין לָא מִקָּרַב לְהוּ. שְׁלַח לֵיהּ רַב מְשַׁרְשְׁיָא מִתּוֹסְנְיָא לְרַב פַּפִּי: יְלַמְּדֵנוּ רַבֵּינוּ, אֵשֶׁת אֲחִי אֲבִי הָאָב, וַאֲחוֹת אֲבִי הָאָב, מַהוּ? מִדִּלְמַטָּה עֶרְוָה — לְמַעְלָה נַמִי גָּזְרוּ בֵּיהּ, אוֹ דִּלְמָא, הָא אִיתְפְּלִיג דַּרְגָּא? ת"ש: "מַה הֵן שְׁנִיּוֹת", וְלָא קָחָשֵׁיב לְהוּ בַּהֲדַיְיהוּ. *תָּנָא וְשַׁיֵּיר. מַאי שַׁיֵּיר דְּהַאי שַׁיֵּיר? שַׁיֵּיר שְׁנִיּוֹת דְּבֵי רַבִּי חִיָּיא*. אֲמֵימַר [ו]אַכְשַׁר בְּאֵשֶׁת אֲחִי אֲבִי אָבִיו, וּבַאֲחוֹת אֲבִי אָבִיו. א"ל רַב הִלֵּל לְרַב אַשִׁי: לְדִידִי חֲזֵיא לִי שְׁנִיּוֹת מָר בְּרֵיהּ דְּרַבָּנָא, וּכְתִיבָן שֶׁיִּתְסָרֵי לְאִיסּוּרָא. מַאי לָאו תְּמָנֵי דְּמַתְנִיתָא וְשִׁית דְּבֵי רַבִּי חִיָּיא, וְהָנָךְ תַּרְתֵּי — הָא שִׁיתְסָרֵי! וּלְטַעְמִיךְ שִׁיבְסָרֵי הָוְיָין, דְּהָא אִיכָּא אֵשֶׁת אֲחִי הָאֵם מִן הָאֵם, דְּפָשְׁטִינַן לְאִיסּוּרָא! הָא לָא קַשְׁיָא, הָנָךְ

תורה אור: ויקרא יח (עֶרְוַת כַּלָּתְךָ לֹא תְגַלֵּה)

רש"י

דאורייתא היא. והיכי חשיב לה רב בהדי שניות. **אלא אימא כלת** בתו. וטעמא פרישנא לעיל, לפי שאין בגדה לד כלות דאורייתא. **לא אסרו כלה.** סתם משמע. **אמרו לי כלדאי.** החוזים בכוכבים. **מלפנא הוית.** חכם תהיה. **ואמינא.** אי האי מלפנא דאמרו לי גברא רבא בתלמוד משמע — אסברא להא דר' אמי דלא אסרו כלה מדעתי, ולא אשאלנה בבית המדרש: ואי האי מלפנא מקרי דרדקי הוא — ולאו תלמיד, אשיילה מרבנן — כלומר, אהיה צריך לשאול, דלא אבינה מדעתי. **לא אסרו** כלת בתו. דהא ליתא בבת לד כלה דאורייתא, אלא משום כלת בנו, דיש בבן לד כלה דאורייתא, כגון אשת בנו. **כגון כלתה דבר ציתאי.** שהיתה לו כלת הבן וכלת הבת, ואתו לאיחלופי, וכן כולהו. **דאיכא צד אב.** ואיכא למיגזר משום אשת אחי האב מן האב דאורייתא. **או דלמא לא שנא.** אשת אחי האם מן האם מאשת אחי האם מן האב. **היא גופה.** אשת אחי האם מן האב. **אטו כולהו כו'.** הא כולהו לאו דוקא. **אם אמו שניה.** שסמוכה לערוה. **וגזרו רבנן על אם אביו.** שאין בה לד ערוה, משום אם אמו. **וטעמא מאי וכו'.** אשת אבי אביו שניה, שסמוכה לאשת אב. **וגזרו רבנן על אשת אבי אמו.** אע"ג דלא שייך לד אישות אב דאורייתא לא למעלה ולא למטה משום אשת אבי אביו: ה"ג. **כולהו דבי דודי קרו** ליה ול"ג רבתי. **כל שבנקבה** ערוה. שאם היתה נקבה היתה ערוה לזה, גזרו בזכר על אשתו. וכולהו מפרש ואזיל להו: ה"ג. **ואמר רבא וכללא הוא.** בתמיה. **בת חמותו** ערוה. שהיא אחות אשתו. **לאו לאיתויי אשת אחי האם מן האם.** דבנקבה ערוה, דאחות האם מן האם ערוה, דכתיב "ערות אחות אמך", ודרשינן ב"הבא על יבמתו": בין מן האב בין מן האם, הילכך בזכר גזרו על אשתו. **מאי שנא האי ומאי שנא** הנך. דלעיל אשת חמיו ואשת בן חמיו ובן חמותו ואשת חורגו ובן חורגו. ואע"ג דנקבה ערוה — בזכר מותר באשתו. **הא אשת אחי האם** בחד קידושין מיקרבא. לגבי דהאי, בקידושין שקדשה אחי אמו. אבל כל הנך דלעיל — לא איקרבו לגביה עד דאיכא תרתי קידושין. כגון אשת חמיו — בקידושין שקדש (א) את אשתו נתקרב חמיו אצלו, ועדיין אשת חמיו רחוקה לזה כל זמן שלא קדשה חמיו. וכן אשת בן חמיו, בקדושין שלו באשתו נתקרב בן חמיו, וקידושין בן חמיו באשתו, וכן כולם. **אשת אחי אבי האב מן האב.** דאמרן לעיל: אשת אחי האב מן האם יש לה הפסק, דהיינו היתירא לאשת אחי אבי האב מן האם, דלמטה דידה לאו ערוה היא אלא שנייה. וכי קמיבעיא ליה — באשת אחי אבי האב מן *האב, דלמטה דידה ערוה. אשת אחי האב מן האב, וכן אחות אבי האב בין מן האב בין מן האם, דלמטה דידה ערוה, כגון אחות האב. **איתפליג.** נתרחקה קורבה. **מה הן שניות.** ברייתא דלעיל. **שניות דרבי חייא.** לקמן במתניתין. הנך

תוספות

לא אסרו כלת בתו אלא משום כלת בנו. ותימה: דאמאי לא אסרינן לה משום כל שבנקבה ערוה — בזכר גזרו על אשתו משום שנייה, כדלקמן? דטעם גמור הוא, ולא סימנא בעלמא, מדפריך עלה: מ"ש הני ומ"ש (ב) הני *), הא בחד קדושי מקרב לה כו'! ועוד: מדפשיט מינה אשת אחי האם מן האם, ולא מוקי לה בכלת בתו! ואור"י: דתנא דברייתא לית ליה ההוא טעמא, אבל בדורות האחרונים גזרו, ולהכי, כי פריך מאי שייר דהאי שייר. לא בעי למימר דשייר אשת אחי האם מן האם דפשטנא לאיסור. ואם תאמר: מאי פריך וכללא הוא חמותו ערוה כו'? דלמא בהני נמי גזרו בתר הכי מהאי טעמא? וי"ל: דקים ליה בהנהו — דשרו. והא דפריך לקמן ולטעמיך שבסרי הויין, אע"ג דבתר הכי גזרו, כדפי' — יודע הוא דשניות דמר בריה דרבנא בדורות אחרונים הוה.

רב אשי אמר כגון כלה דבי רב מרי בר איסק. כל חד נקיט אותו שהיה בימיו. וצ"ל דתרי מרי בר איסק הוו: אחד בימי רב אשי, כדמשמע הכא ובפרק "אלו מציאות" (ב"מ דף כב.): אמימר ורב אשי ומר זוטרא איקלעו לבוסתני' דבי מרי בר איסק, ואחד היה בימי רב חסדא, דאמר ב"המפקיד" (שם דף לט: ושם) מרי בר איסק *ואיכא דאמרי חנה בר איסק, אתא ליה אחוה מבי חוזאי, אתא לקמיה דרב חסדא. ורב חסדא נפטר בימי רבא, כדאמר בפ' בתרא דיומא (ד' עה: ושם). וביום שמת רבא נולד רב אשי, כדאיתא בפרק "עשרה יוחסין" (קידושין דף עב:).

אשת אחי אבי האב ואחות אבי האב מהו. הוה מצי למיבעי אחות אם האם, והיא בכלל אחות אבי האב דלמטה דידה ערוה. ואית ספרים דגרסינן לה בהדיא.

מאי שייר דהאי שייר. אף על גב דתרתי נינהו — חדא חשיב להו, כדקאמר בסמוך: הנהו תרתי דדמיין להדדי (ג) חדא חשיב להו. ופירש בקונטרס דהנך תרתי היינו: אשת אחי אבי האב ואחות אבי האב, ולא כמו שפירש רבינו יצחק בן רבינו מאיר דקאי אאשת אחי האם מן האם ואשת אחי האם מן האב — דכולהו אחי אמו קרו להו.

אמימר אכשר כו'. פסק רבינו חננאל דהלכה כאמימר, וכן בשאלתות דרב אחאי*. וכן משמע דסבר רב אשי, דקאמר: השתא נמי דכתיבי לאיסורא — לאו מר בריה דרבנא חתים עלייהו. ולר"י נראה דאין הלכה כאמימר, דסוגיא דגמרא ב"החולץ" (לקמן דף מ: ושם) *דלא כוותיה. (ד) וקאמר נמי: אמימר מוקי לה משום חולץ, וקסבר: גזרו שניות בחלוצה. ואין התלמוד רוצה לפשוט בעיא שלו מדברי אמימר (ה).

*) נ"ל ומשני הא בחד כו'

[פי' אחרי סי' נז]

שניות

עין משפט נר מצוה

לא א מיי' פ"א מהל' אישות הלכה ו טוש"ע אה"ע סימן טו סעיף יט:
לב ב מיי' שם טוש"ע שם:
לג ג מיי' שם טוש"ע שם סעיף ב:
לד ד מיי' שם טוש"ע שם סעיף יח:
לה ה מיי' שם טוש"ע שם סעיף טו:
לו ו מיי' שם טוש"ע שם סעיף יח:

תוספות ישנים

אשת אחי האם מן האם מהו. וא"ת אמאי לא קא פשיט ליה דשרי מדלא חשבה בהדי שניות וי"ל דלא חשש לשנותה משום דתנא כבר אשת אחי האם מן האב: **לאתויי** מאי לאתויי אשת אחי האם מן האם. וא"ת אמאי לא קאמר דאתא לאתויי כלת בתו אך לא אשת אחי האם מן האם. וי"ל דפסיקא ליה שנאמר זה הכלל לאחר שנשנית הברייתא דשניות וא"כ לא אתא לרבויי כלת בתו שהרי כבר תנינן לה עם השניות אלא ודאי בא לחדש דבר שלא פירש כגון אשת אחי האם מן האם:

[שם ליתא לפנינו א"ך אבל בכתובות כז: איתא]

תוספות חד מקמאי

אבעיא להו אשת אחי האם מן האם מהו אשת אחי האב מן האם ואשת אחי האם מן האב דאיכא צד אב הוא דגזור רבנן אבל היכא דליכא צד אב לא או דלמא לא שנא ופשיט לאסור דכי אתא רב שילא אמר אמרי במערבא כל שבנקבה ערוה בזכר גזרו על אשתו משום שניה והא ודאי לאו כללא הוא דאילו חמותו ערוה אשת חמיו מותרת. בת חמותו ערוה אשת בן חמיו מותרת חורגתו ערוה אשת חורגו מותר' בת חורגו ערוה אשת בן חורגו מותרת. על כרחין דרב שילא לאתויי אשת אחי האם מן האם. אמימר אכשר באשת אחי [אבי] אביו ובאחות אבי אביו. הר' אלפס לא פסק בשניות כר' חייא. יש להן הפסק או אין להן הפסק ומסתברא לקולא דבשל סופרים הלך אחר המקל

דלא כוותיה דקאמר מאי לאו משום חולץ דהויא לי' אשת אבי אביו לא משום מיתנא דהויא לי' אשת אחי אבי אביו וקאמר נמי והא אמימר מכשיר כו' אמימר מוקי להו כו' בעיא שלו מתוך דברי אמימר משום דלא סבירא ליה כוותיה כו' מהרש"ל

מסורת הש"ס

כריתות יד:

ביצה ג. [שבת יא: קא. עירובין ד: נט. יומא יא. מד: סוכה ו: ע"ז כח. חולין פה: וקד. נדה סז. לקמן קט.]

[נ"ל על אשתו]

[סוכה נב. וש"נ]

[נ"ל האם) לקמן מ:

הגהות הב"ח

(א) רש"י ד"ה הא אשת וכו' שקדש זה את אשתו נתקרב חמיו וכו' בקדושין שלו נתקרב בן חמיו אלא וקידושין: (ב) תוס' ד"ה לא אסרו וכו' מ"ש הני ומאי שנא הא הא בחד: (ג) ד"ה מאי וכו' להדדי כחדא חשיב: (ד) ד"ה אמימר וכו' דקאמר אמימר מוקי כנ"ל ותיבת נמי נמחק: (ה) בא"ד שלו מדברי אמימר משום דלא סבירא ליה כוותיה הס"ד

הָנָךְ תַּרְתֵּי דְּדָמְיָין לַהֲדָדֵי — כַּחֲדָא חָשֵׁיב לְהוּ, וְהָא שִׁיתְסְרֵי. וְהָא מִכָּל מָקוֹם לְדִידִי חַזְיָין לָן דִּכְתִיבָן לְאִיסּוּרָא! אֲמַר לֵיהּ: וְלִיטַעֲמִיךְ, אִי הֲוָה כְּתִיב לְהֶיתֵּירָא — מִי הֲוָות סָמְכַת עֲלַיְיהוּ? דְּמָר בְּרֵיהּ דְּרַבָּנָא — מִי חָתִים עֲלַיְיהוּ? הָשְׁתָּא נַמִי דִּכְתִיב לְאִיסּוּרָא — לָאו מָר בְּרֵיהּ דְּרַבָּנָא חָתִים עֲלַיְיהוּ. תָּנֵי דְּבֵי רַבִּי חִיָּיא: [א]שְׁלִישִׁי שֶׁבִּבְנוֹ וְשֶׁבְּבִתּוֹ, [ב]וְשֶׁבְּבֶן אִשְׁתּוֹ וְשֶׁבְּבַת אִשְׁתּוֹ — שְׁנִיָּה, [ג]רְבִיעִי שֶׁבַּחֲמִיו וְשֶׁבַּחֲמוֹתוֹ — שְׁנִיָּה. א"ל רָבִינָא לְרַב אַשִׁי: מַאי שְׁנָא לְמַעְלָה, דְּקָחָשֵׁיב לָהּ לְאִשְׁתּוֹ, וּמַאי שְׁנָא לְמַטָּה, דְּלָא קָחָשֵׁיב לָהּ לְאִשְׁתּוֹ? לְמַעְלָה, דְּאִיסּוּרָא מִכֹּחַ אִשְׁתּוֹ קָא אָתֵי, חָשֵׁיב לָהּ. לְמַטָּה, דְּאִיסּוּרָא לָאו מִכֹּחַ אִשְׁתּוֹ קָאָתֵי — לָא קָחָשֵׁיב לָהּ. וְהָא [א]בֶּן אִשְׁתּוֹ וּבַת אִשְׁתּוֹ, דְּאִיסּוּרָא מִכֹּחַ אִשְׁתּוֹ קָאָתֵי וְלָא חָשֵׁיב לָהּ! אַיְּידֵי דְּתָנָא שְׁלֹשָׁה דּוֹרוֹת לְמַטָּה[ב] דִּידֵיהּ, וְלָא חָשְׁבָהּ, תָּנָא נַמִי ג' דּוֹרוֹת לְמַטָּה דִּידָהּ וְלָא חָשְׁבָהּ. א"ל רַב אַשִׁי לְרַב כָּהֲנָא: [ד]שְׁנִיּוֹת דְּבֵי רַבִּי חִיָּיא יֵשׁ לָהֶן הֶפְסֵק אוֹ אֵין לָהֶם הֶפְסֵק? ת"ש, דְּאָמַר רַב: ד' נָשִׁים יֵשׁ לָהֶם הֶפְסֵק. וְתוּ לָא. דִּלְמָא, כִּי קָאָמַר רַב — לְהַהִיא מַתְנִיתָא: ת"ש, "שְׁלִישִׁי" "וּרְבִיעִי". שְׁלִישִׁי וּרְבִיעִי — אִין, טְפֵי — לָא! דִּלְמָא מִשְּׁלִישִׁי וְאֵילָךְ, מֵרְבִיעִי וְאֵילָךְ. אֲמַר לֵיהּ רָבָא לְרַב נַחְמָן: חֲזִי מָר הַאי מֵרַבָּנַן דַּאֲתָא מִמַּעַרְבָא וְאָמַר: בָּעוּ בְּמַעַרְבָא, גָּזְרוּ שְׁנִיּוֹת בְּגֵרִים אוֹ לֹא גָּזְרוּ שְׁנִיּוֹת בְּגֵרִים? אֲמַר לֵיהּ: הָשְׁתָּא, וּמָה עֶרְוָה גּוּפָהּ, [ה]אִי לָאו שֶׁלֹּא יֹאמְרוּ בָּאִין מִקְּדוּשָּׁה חֲמוּרָה לִקְדוּשָּׁה קַלָּה לֹא גָּזְרוּ בְּהוּ רַבָּנַן — [ו]שְׁנִיּוֹת מִיבַּעְיָא?! אֲמַר רַב נַחְמָן: גֵּרִים, °הוֹאִיל וְאָתוּ לִידַן נֵימָא בְּהוּ מִלְּתָא: אַחִין מִן הָאֵם לֹא יָעִידוּ, וְאִם הֵעִידוּ — עֵדוּתָן עֵדוּת. אַחִין מִן הָאָב מְעִידִין לְכַתְּחִלָּה. [ז]אַמֵימָר אָמַר: אֲפִילּוּ אַחִין מִן הָאֵם נַמִי מְעִידִין לְכַתְּחִלָּה. וּמ"ש מֵעֲרָיוֹת? עֶרְוָה לַכֹּל מְסוּרָה, *עֵדוּת — לְבֵית דִּין מְסוּרָה, *[ח]וְגֵר שֶׁנִּתְגַּיֵּיר כְּקָטָן שֶׁנּוֹלַד דָּמֵי. §

מתני' [ט]מִי שֶׁיֵּשׁ לוֹ אָח מִכָּל מָקוֹם — זוֹקֵק אֶת אֵשֶׁת אָחִיו לְיִבּוּם, וְאָחִיו הוּא לְכָל דָּבָר, חוּץ מִמִּי שֶׁיֵּשׁ לוֹ אָח מִן הַשִּׁפְחָה וּמִן הַנׇּכְרִיָּה. [י]מִי שֶׁיֵּשׁ לוֹ בֵּן מִכָּל מָקוֹם — פּוֹטֵר אֵשֶׁת אָבִיו מִן הַיִּבּוּם, [כ]וְחַיָּיב עַל מַכָּתוֹ וְעַל קִלְלָתוֹ, וּבְנוֹ לְכָל דָּבָר — [ל]חוּץ מִמִּי שֶׁיֵּשׁ לוֹ בֵּן מִן הַשִּׁפְחָה וּמִן הַנׇּכְרִיָּה. §

גמ' מִכָּל מָקוֹם לְאַתּוֹיֵי מַאי? אֲמַר רַב יְהוּדָה [מ]לְאַתּוֹיֵי מַמְזֵר. פְּשִׁיטָא, אָחִיו הוּא! מַהוּ דְּתֵימָא: לֵילַף *אַחֲוָה אַחֲוָה מִבְּנֵי יַעֲקֹב, מָה לְהַלָּן כְּשֵׁרִין וְלֹא פְּסוּלִין, אַף כָּאן כְּשֵׁרִין וְלֹא פְּסוּלִין — קמ"ל. *וְאֵימָא הָכִי נַמִי! כֵּיוָן דִּלְעִנְיַן יִבּוּם מִיפְּטַר נִפְטַר מִיזְקַק

רש"י

הָנָךְ תַּרְתֵּי דְּדָמְיָין לַהֲדָדֵי. אֵשֶׁת אֲחִי אֲבִי הָאָב וַאֲחוֹת אֲבִי הָאָב שֶׁהֵן לְגַבֵּי אַחֲוָה דְּאָב, וּלְמַטָּה דִּידְהוּ עֶרְוָה. שְׁלִישִׁי שֶׁבִּבְנוֹ. בַּת בֶּן בְּנוֹ, דְּהָא בַּת בְּנוֹ עֶרְוָה. וְשֶׁבְּבִתּוֹ. בַּת בֶּן בִּתּוֹ, שֶׁהֲרֵי בַּת בִּתּוֹ עֶרְוָה. הִלְכָּךְ בַּת בֶּן בִּתּוֹ שְׁנִיָּה, וְכֵן בַּת בֶּן בְּנָהּ שֶׁל אִשְׁתּוֹ אוֹ בַּת בֶּן בִּתָּהּ. רְבִיעִי שֶׁבַּחֲמִיו. דּוֹר רְבִיעִי שֶׁבַּחֲמִיו, הַיְינוּ אֵם אֵם חָמִיו, וְהוּא דּוֹר רְבִיעִי לְאִשְׁתּוֹ, וְאִשְׁתּוֹ בַּכְּלָל. וְשֶׁבַּחֲמוֹתוֹ. אֵם אֵם חֲמוֹתוֹ. שְׁנִיָּה. דְּאֵם חָמִיו וְאֵם חֲמוֹתוֹ עֶרְוָה, שֶׁהֵן בִּכְלַל אִשָּׁה וּבַת בְּנָהּ אִשָּׁה וּבַת בִּתָּהּ, הִלְכָּךְ אִמּוֹ שְׁנִיָּה. מַאי שְׁנָא לְמַעְלָה. דְּקָרֵי לְאֵם אֵם חָמִיו וְאֵם אֵם חֲמוֹתוֹ רְבִיעִי, וְקָא חָשֵׁיב לְאִשְׁתּוֹ בְּחוּשְׁבְּנָא דְּדָרֵי. וּמַאי שְׁנָא לְמַטָּה. דְּקָרֵי לְבַת בֶּן בְּנוֹ דּוֹר שְׁלִישִׁי, וְלָא חָשֵׁיב אִשְׁתּוֹ, דְּתֶהֱוֵי רְבִיעִי. לָאו מִכֹּחַ אִשְׁתּוֹ קָאָתֵי. אֶלָּא מִכֹּחַ דִּידֵיהּ, דְּבִבְנוֹ מֵאֲנוּסָה עָסְקִינַן. לְהַהִיא מַתְנִיתָא. הָא דְּקָתָנֵי לְעֵיל מַה הֵן שְׁנִיּוֹת, בְּהַהִיא אַיְירֵי רַב וְאָמַר: אַרְבַּע יֵשׁ לָהֶן הֶפְסֵק וְתוּ לָא, אֲבָל בְּהָנָךְ דְּר' חִיָּיא — אִיכָּא. ת"ש. דְּתָנֵי בִּשְׁנִיּוֹת דְּר' חִיָּיא שְׁלִישִׁי שֶׁבִּבְנוֹ וּרְבִיעִי שֶׁבַּחֲמִיו וְתוּ לָא, אַלְמָא יֵשׁ לָהֶם הֶפְסֵק. בְּגֵרִים. גָּזְרוּ שְׁנִיּוֹת, שֶׁאִם הָיָה גֵּר נָשׂוּי אֵם אִמּוֹ — יוֹצִיא. מִקְּדוּשָּׁה חֲמוּרָה. שֶׁהַגּוֹיִם מוּזְהָרִין עַל הָעֲרָיוֹת. לֹא גָּזְרוּ בְּהוּ רַבָּנַן. דִּכְקָטָן שֶׁנּוֹלַד דָּמֵי, וְאֵין לוֹ קוּרְבָה. לֹא יָעִידוּ. לְכַתְּחִלָּה, דְּקוּרְבַת אֵם בְּגֵרִים קוּרְבָה הִיא, דְּהָא וַדַּאי אִמּוֹ הִיא. וְאִם הֵעִידוּ עֵדוּתָן עֵדוּת. דִּכְקָטָן שֶׁנּוֹלַד דָּמֵי. מְעִידִין לְכַתְּחִלָּה. דְּרַחֲמָנָא אַפְקְרֵיהּ לְזַרְעָא מִצְרִי, דִּכְתִיב "וְזִרְמַת סוּסִים זִרְמָתָם" (יחזקאל כג), הִלְכָּךְ קוּרְבַת אָב אֵינָהּ קוּרְבָה. מַאי שְׁנָא. עֵדוּת מֵעֲרָיוֹת, דְּאָמַר לְקַמָּן בְּפֶרֶק "נוֹשְׂאִין" (דף מח.): גֵּר שֶׁהָיָה נָשׂוּי אֲחוֹתוֹ מִן הָאֵם — יוֹצִיא. לַכֹּל מְסוּרָה. הַכֹּל נוֹשְׂאִין נָשִׁים, הִלְכָּךְ אִי שָׁרֵית לְקִיּוּמָהּ — אָתֵי נַמִי לְמִישְׁרֵי עֶרְוָה בְּיִשְׂרָאֵל, דְּכוּלֵּי עָלְמָא לָא יָדְעִי דְּטַעְמָא דְּגֵר מִשּׁוּם דִּכְקָטָן שֶׁנּוֹלַד דָּמֵי. לְבֵית דִּין מְסוּרָה. וְאִי נַמִי מַכְשַׁרְתְּ עֵדוּת אַחִים גֵּרִים, לָא אָתְיָא לְאַכְשׁוּרֵי אַחִין יִשְׂרָאֵל, דְּבֵית דִּין יָדְעִי דְּגֵר שֶׁנִּתְגַּיֵּיר כְּקָטָן שֶׁנּוֹלַד דָּמֵי.

מתני' אָח מִכָּל מָקוֹם. בַּגְּמָרָא מְפָרֵשׁ. וְאָחִיו לְכָל דָּבָר. מְפָרֵשׁ בַּגְּמָ'. שִׁפְחָה וְנׇכְרִיָּה וְלָדָהּ כָּמוֹהָ. וּבְתָרָהּ אָזֵיל, כְּדְיָלֵיף בַּגְּמָ'. עַל מַכָּתוֹ וְעַל קִלְלָתוֹ. אִם הִכָּה אוֹ קִלֵּל אֶת אָבִיו חַיָּיב מִיתָה. **גמ'** מִדִּלְעִנְיַן יִבּוּם מִיפְּטַר. אֶת אֵשֶׁת אָבִיו מִיִּבּוּם פּוֹטֵר, כְּגוֹן אִם הָיָה לוֹ בֵּן מַמְזֵר, וְנָשָׂא אִשָּׁה וּמֵת, וְלֹא יָלְדָה לוֹ — פְּטוּרָה מִן הַיִּבּוּם בִּשְׁבִיל הַמַּמְזֵר בֶּן בַּעְלָהּ, כְּדְיָלֵיף לְקַמָּן: "בֵּן אֵין לוֹ" — עַיֵּין עָלָיו. מִיזְקַק

תוספות

שניות דרבי חייא יש להן הפסק או לא. תימה: דלעיל תנא דכלת בן בנו אסורה עד סוף כל הדורות, ודומה דכ"ש בת בן בנו עד סוף כל הדורות שהן קורבי עצמו ולא מחמת קדושין! וי"ל: דכלת בן בנו יש (א) לאוסרו, שהן בני ירושה ושכיחא גביה. אבל בת בני בניס — לאו בת ירושה היא ולא שכיחא גביה.

ערוה לכל מסורה. תימה: דלעיל קאמר דטעמא דגרים — שלא יאמרו באנו מקדושה כו', והכא משמע טעמא משום דאתיא לאיחלופי בישראל, כדפי' בקונטרס? וכן בפ' "נושאין" (לקמן דף לז: ושם) משמע דטעמא משום איחלופי, גבי בני יודן אמתא איסתחרור, שרא להו רב אחא בר יעקב למינסב נשי דהדדי, וקאמר: מן האם ולא מן האב כולי עלמא לא פליגי דאסור, [מן האב ולא מן האם — כולי עלמא לא פליגי דמותר. כי פליגי — מן האב ומן האם]. ואי משום "שמא יאמרו" — אמאי שרי התם מן האב ומן האם? אבל אי משום איחלופי — ניחא, דכיון דאיכא נמי לד אב — לא אתי לאיחלופי, דבתר אב שדי להו ומצרים אין להם קורבת אב, דכתיב "וזרמת סוסים זרמתם", ולא שייך למיגזר אטו ישראל! ויש לומר: דהני תרי טעמי צריכין, דבקורבת אב שהיו אסורין קודם לא שייך טעמא לאיחלופי, שהכל יודעים דרחמנא אפקריה לזרעיה, כגון אשת אביו לרבי עקיבא ואחות אביו לרבי אליעזר, דאמר בפ' "ד' מיתות" (סנהדרין דף נח.): "על כן יעזב איש את אביו ואת אמו" ר' אליעזר אומר: אחות אביו, ור"ע אומר: אשת אביו. הוי טעמא שלא יאמרו כו'. אבל אשת אביו לרבי אליעזר, ואחות אביו לרבי עקיבא — שרי, דלא משום שמא יאמרו איכא ולא משום איחלופי איכא. אבל עריות שמלד אם, שלא היו אסורות קודם, יש לאסור משום איחלופי. דמשום "שמא יאמרו" — ליכא. והא דאמר בפרק "ד' מיתות" (ג"ז שם) נשא אחותו מן האם — יוציא, היינו משום איחלופי, ד"שמא יאמרו" ליכא, שלא היו נאסרות בגיותם. ומן האב יקיים — דמשום איחלופי ליכא בלד אב, כדפרישית. והיינו טעמא נמי דאמר אחין מן האם לא יעידו לכתחלה, דלמא אתי לאיחלופי. אבל מן האב — יעידו לכתחלה.

מי שיש לו אח מ"מ זוקק אשת אחיו. בגמרא מפרש לאתויי ממזר. וא"ת: מרישא שמעינן לה בת ישראל לנתין וממזר דחולצת ולא מתייבמת! ויש לומר: דאי מהתם — הוי אמינא כששניהם ממזרים, אבל כשאחיו המת כשר — אין אחיו ממזר זוקק אשתו.

פשיטא אחיו הוא. תימה: אמאי פשיטא ליה? הא אילטריך שפיר לאשמועינן דמחייבי כריתות הוי אחיו, ולא ממעטינן ליה למי שיש אישות לאביך בה, כדפריך לקמן (דף כג.) לרבי יוסי בר יהודה, ואימא למי שיש אישות לאביך בה, למעוטי חייבי כריתות! וי"ל: דה"מ לשנויי הכי, אלא דניחא ליה לשנויי דאיצטריך משום דהוה ילפינן אחוה אחוה מבני יעקב, דמשום האי טעמא איצטריך "'בן אין לו' — עיין עליו", דממזר פוטר מן היבום, דלא נימא דנילף אחוה אחוה מבני יעקב דלא זקיק, ומדלא זקיק — מיפטר נמי לא פטר. ועוד אור"י, דהכי פריך: פשיטא, כיון דתני אחיו הוא לכל דבר — פשיטא דזוקק נמי ליבום, ומשני: דס"ד אע"ג דאחיו הוא לכל דבר — ה"א [ליבום] לא זוקק, משום דילפינן אחוה אחוה מבני יעקב. ובתר הכי פריך: ואחיו הוא לכל דבר? דהיינו: ליורשו וליטמא לו — פשיטא, כיון דזוקק ליבום אף על גב דהוה ס"ד למילף מבני יעקב — כ"ש לשאר דברים. מאי

עין משפט נר מצוה

לז א מיי' פ"א מהל' אישות הלכה ו סמג לאוין קי טוש"ע אה"ע סימן טו סעיף יב:
לח ב מיי' שם וטוש"ע שם סעיף יד:
לט ג מיי' שם וטור ש"ע שם סעיף טו:
מ ד מיי' שם טוש"ע שם:
מא ה מיי' פי"ד מהל' איסורי ביאה הלכה יב טוש"ע י"ד סימן רסט סעיף א:
מב ו טוש"ע שם סעיף ח:
מג ז מיי' פי"ג מהלכות עדות הלכה ב טוש"ע ח"מ סימן לג סעיף יא וטוש"ע י"ד סימן רסט סעיף י:
מד ח מיי' שם ופי"ד מהל' איסורי ביאה הלכה יא טוש"ע שם:
מה ט מיי' פ"א מהל' יבום הלכה ו סמג עשין נא ולאוין קא טור ש"ע אה"ע סימן קנז סעיף א:
מו י מיי' שם הל' ג טוש"ע שם סי' קנו סעי' ב:
מז כ מיי' פ"ה מהלכות ממרים הל' ט טור ש"ע י"ד סימן רמא סעיף ח:
מח ל מיי' שם ופ"א מהל' יבום הלכה ד טוש"ע אה"ע סימן קנו סעיף ב:
מט מ מיי' פ"א מהלכות יבום הלכה ו טור ש"ע אה"ע סימן קנז סעיף א:

תוספות ישנים

מעידין לכתחלה. ומ"ש מעריות ופי' הקונט' דלקמן אמרי' נשא אחותו מן האם יוציא והכא אמרי' מעידין לכתחלה. ותימה לשני שנא ושנא דגבי עדות לא שייך האי טעמא דשמא יאמרו באנו מקדושה חמורה לקדושה קלה ולהכי מעידין אבל גבי ערוה יוציא שלא יאמרו באנו מקדושה חמורה לקדושה קלה. וי"ל דקא בעי משום דאמרינן לקמן טעמא משום דאתי לאחלופי ואם כן היה לנו לגזור בעדות כמו ערוה: **יבום** מפטר פטר. מדאמרינן לקמן ובן אין לו עיין עליו ואיירי הכא תלמודא כאילו ידע הדרשא דלקמן אע"ג דלקמן קאמר מכל מקום לאתויי מאי כן דרך התלמוד בכמה מקומות:

הגהות הב"ח

(א) תום' ד"ה שניות וכו' לאוסרה יותר שהן בני ירושה:

הגהות הגר"א

[א] גמ' בן אשתו ובת אשתו. נ"ב גי' הרמב"ם בנו ובתו לאיסורא כו' ופי' מכח כו' שכל לד מינה אסור (ועמ"ש רבינו באה"ע סימן טו ס"ק כג): [ב] שם למטה דידיה. נ"ב גירסת הרמב"ם להיפך איידי דתני כו' למטה דידה כו' למטה דידיה:

גליון הש"ס

גמ' הואיל ואתו לידן. שבת פא ע"ב וש"נ:

[ביצה ה:]

לקמן מח: סנ. לז: בכורות מז.]

[לעיל יז: ב"ב קי:]

[עי' תוספות סוטה כו. ד"ה וחז]

מִיזַקֵּק נַמִּי זָקִיק.§ "וְאָחִיו הוּא לְכָל דָּבָר".§ לְמַאי הִלְכְתָא? אלְיוֹרְשׁוֹ וְלִיטַּמֵּא לוֹ. פְּשִׁיטָא, אָחִיו הוּא! סד"א: הוֹאִיל וּכְתִיב °"כִּי אִם לִשְׁאֵרוֹ הַקָּרוֹב אֵלָיו" *וַאֲמַר מָר: בשְׁאֵרוֹ – *זוֹ אִשְׁתּוֹ, וּכְתִיב °"לֹא יִטַּמָּא בַּעַל בְּעַמָּיו לְהֵחַלּוֹ", יֵשׁ בַּעַל שֶׁמִּטַּמֵּא וְיֵשׁ בַּעַל שֶׁאֵין מִטַּמֵּא, הָא כֵּיצַד? גמִטַּמֵּא הוּא לְאִשְׁתּוֹ כְּשֵׁרָה, וְאֵין מִטַּמֵּא לְאִשְׁתּוֹ פְּסוּלָה, ה"נ מִטַּמֵּא הוּא לְאָח כָּשֵׁר וְאֵין מִטַּמֵּא לְאָח פָּסוּל, קמ"ל. *וְאֵימָא ה"נ! הָתָם לְאַפּוּקֵי קַיְימָא, הָכָא – אָחִיו הוּא.§ ד"חוּץ מִמִּי שֶׁיֵּשׁ לוֹ אָח מִן הַשִּׁפְחָה וּמִן הַגּוֹיָה".§ מ"ט? אָמַר קְרָא °"הָאִשָּׁה וִילָדֶיהָ תִּהְיֶה לַאֲדוֹנֶיהָ".§ "מִי שֶׁיֵּשׁ לוֹ בֵּן מ"מ פּוֹטֵר" וכו'.§ מִכָּל מָקוֹם לְאֵתוּיֵי מַאי? אָמַר רַב יְהוּדָה: הלְאֵיתוּיֵי מַמְזֵר. מַאי טַעְמָא? דְּאָמַר קְרָא °"וּבֵן *אֵין לוֹ" – *עַיֵּין עָלָיו.§ "וְחַיָּיב עַל מַכָּתוֹ",§ אַמַּאי? קְרִי כָּאן °"וְנָשִׂיא בְעַמְּךָ לֹא תָאֹר" – *ובְּעוֹשֶׂה מַעֲשֵׂה עַמְּךָ! *) כְּדַאֲמַר רַב פִּנְחָס מִשְּׁמֵיהּ דְּרַב פָּפָּא: בְּעוֹשֶׂה תְּשׁוּבָה – זהָכָא נַמִּי כְּשֶׁעָשָׂה תְּשׁוּבָה. וְהַאי בַּר תְּשׁוּבָה הוּא? וְהָתְנַן: *שִׁמְעוֹן בֶּן מְנַסְיָא אוֹמֵר: אֵיזֶהוּ °"מְעֻוָּת לֹא יוּכַל לִתְקֹן", זֶה הַבָּא עַל הָעֶרְוָה וְהוֹלִיד מִמֶּנָּה מַמְזֵר! הָשְׁתָּא מִיהָא עוֹשֶׂה מַעֲשֵׂה עַמְּךָ הוּא.§ תָּנוּ רַבָּנַן: חהַבָּא עַל אֲחוֹתוֹ וְהִיא בַּת אֵשֶׁת אָבִיו – חַיָּיב מִשּׁוּם אֲחוֹתוֹ, וּמִשּׁוּם בַּת אֵשֶׁת אָבִיו. רַבִּי יוֹסֵי *בֶּן יְהוּדָה אוֹמֵר: אֵינוֹ חַיָּיב אֶלָּא מִשּׁוּם אֲחוֹתוֹ בִּלְבַד, וְלֹא מִפְּנֵי בַּת אֵשֶׁת אָבִיו. מַאי טַעֲמַיְיהוּ דְּרַבָּנַן? אָמְרִי: מִכְּדֵי כְּתִיב °"עֶרְוַת אֲחוֹתְךָ בַת אָבִיךָ אוֹ בַת אִמֶּךָ" "עֶרְוַת בַּת אֵשֶׁת אָבִיךָ מוֹלֶדֶת אָבִיךָ אֲחוֹתְךָ הִיא" לָמָּה לִי? ש"מ: לְחַיְּיבוֹ מִשּׁוּם אֲחוֹתוֹ וּמִשּׁוּם בַּת אֵשֶׁת אָבִיו. וְרַבִּי יוֹסֵי בְּרַ' יְהוּדָה: אָמַר קְרָא "אֲחוֹתְךָ הִיא", מִשּׁוּם אֲחוֹתוֹ אַתָּה מְחַיְּיבוֹ וְאִי אַתָּה מְחַיְּיבוֹ מִשּׁוּם בַּת אֵשֶׁת אָבִיו – וְרַבָּנַן, הַאי "אֲחוֹתְךָ הִיא" מַאי עָבְדִי לֵיהּ? מִיבָּעֵי לְהוּ לְחַיְּיבוֹ עַל אֲחוֹתוֹ בַּת אָבִיו וּבַת אִמּוֹ, לוֹמַר *שֶׁאֵין מַזְהִירִין מִן הַדִּין. וְרַבִּי יוֹסֵי בְּרַ' יְהוּדָה? אִם כֵּן לִכְתּוֹב רַחֲמָנָא "אֲחוֹתְךָ", "הִיא" לָמָּה לִי – מִשּׁוּם אֲחוֹתְךָ אַתָּה מְחַיְּיבוֹ וְאִי אַתָּה מְחַיְּיבוֹ מִשּׁוּם בַּת אֵשֶׁת אָבִיו. וְרַבָּנַן? אַף עַל גַּב דִּכְתִיב "אֲחוֹתְךָ" אִיצְטְרִיךְ לְמִכְתַּב "הִיא", שֶׁלֹּא תֹּאמַר: בְּעָלְמָא מַזְהִירִין מִן הַדִּין, וְכ"ת: "אֲחוֹתְךָ" דִּכְתַב רַחֲמָנָא לָמָּה לִי – *מִילְּתָא דְּאָתְיָא בְּק"ו טָרַח וְכָתַב לָהּ קְרָא – כָּתַב רַחֲמָנָא "הִיא". וְרַבִּי יוֹסֵי בְּרַ' יְהוּדָה: אִם כֵּן לִיכְתְּבֵיהּ רַחֲמָנָא לַ"אֲחוֹתְךָ הִיא" בְּאִידָּךְ קְרָא. וְרַ' יוֹסֵי בְּרַ' יְהוּדָה, הַאי "בַּת אֵשֶׁת אָבִיךָ" מַאי עָבֵיד לֵיהּ? מִיבָּעֵי לֵיהּ: מִי שֶׁיֵּשׁ לוֹ אִישׁוּת לְאָבִיךָ בָּהּ, טפְּרָט לַאֲחוֹתוֹ מִשִּׁפְחָה וְגוֹיָה, שֶׁאֵין אִישׁוּת לְאָבִיךָ בָּהּ. וְאֵימָא: יפְּרָט לַאֲחוֹתוֹ מֵאֲנוּסָה? הַהִיא לָא מָצֵית אָמְרַתְּ, מִדְּרָבָא, *דְּרָבָא רָמֵי: כְּתִיב °"עֶרְוַת בַּת בִּנְךָ אוֹ בַת בִּתְּךָ לֹא תְגַלֶּה", הָא בַּת בְּנָהּ דִּידָהּ וּבַת בִּתָּהּ דִּידָהּ – שָׁרֵי, וּכְתִיב °"עֶרְוַת אִשָּׁה וּבִתָּהּ לֹא תְגַלֵּה אֶת בַּת בְּנָהּ וְאֶת בַּת בִּתָּהּ". הָא כֵּיצַד? כָּאן בְּאוֹנָסִין כָּאן בְּנִשּׂוּאִין. וְאֵימָא

*) חגיגה כו. ע"ש ב"מ סב. ע"ש ב"ק לז: ע"ש סנהדרין פה. ע"ש

רש"י

מִיזַקֵּק נַמִּי זָקִיק. לְאֵשֶׁת אָחִיו לְיִבּוּם, שֶׁאֲפִילּוּ אֵין כָּאן אָח אֶלָּא מַמְזֵר זֶה – זְקוּקָה לַחֲלִיצָה. וְלִיטַּמֵּא לוֹ. אִם כֹּהֵן הוּא, וְלוֹ אָח מַמְזֵר – מִיטַּמֵּא לוֹ. כִּי אִם לִשְׁאֵרוֹ. זוֹ אִשְׁתּוֹ: לְאַפּוּקֵי קַיְימָא הִלְכָּךְ לָאו אִשְׁתּוֹ הִיא. הָאִשָּׁה וִילָדֶיהָ. בְּשִׁפְחָה כְּתִיב. גּוֹיָה. לְקַמָּן מְפָרֵשׁ בִּשְׁמַעְתִּין מִ"כִּי יָסִיר אֶת בִּנְךָ מֵאַחֲרַי". וּבֵן אֵין לוֹ. מָצֵי לְמִכְתַּב וּבֵן אַיִן לוֹ, כִּדְאָמְרִינַן בְּקִדּוּשִׁין (דף ד.) "אֵין כֶּסֶף", וּכְמוֹ "מֵאֵן יְבָמִי" (דברים כה) "מֵאֵן בִּלְעָם" (במדבר כב). וּלְהָכִי כָּתַב "אֵין", לְמִידְרַשׁ: עַיֵּין עָלָיו! דְּאִם יֵשׁ לוֹ בֵּן בָּעוֹלָם – פּוֹטֵר. בְּעוֹשֶׂה מַעֲשֵׂה עַמְּךָ. וְהַאי אָבִיו לָאו עוֹשֶׂה מַעֲשֵׂה עַמְּךָ הוּא, שֶׁהֲרֵי בָּא עַל הָעֶרְוָה וְהוֹלִיד מִמֶּנָּה מַמְזֵר. כְּדַאֲמַר רַב פִּנְחָס. בְּפֶ' "חוֹמֶר בַּקֹּדֶשׁ". הָשְׁתָּא מִיהַת. הוֹאִיל וְשָׁב – עוֹשֶׂה מַעֲשֵׂה עַמְּךָ הוּא. וְנְהִי נַמִּי דַּעֲוֹנוֹ גָּלוּי וְנִזְכָּר כָּל זְמַן שֶׁמַּמְזֵר קַיָּים – מִיהוּ מִתְּשׁוּבָה וְאֵילָךְ בִּכְלַל "עוֹשֶׂה מַעֲשֵׂה עַמְּךָ" הוּא. וְהִיא בַּת אֵשֶׁת אָבִיו. דְּעַל יְדֵי נִשּׂוּאִין נוֹלְדָה לְאָבִיו, וְלֹא בְּאוֹנְסִין. מִכְּדֵי כְּתִיב עֶרְוַת אֲחוֹתְךָ בַּת אָבִיךָ. וּבֵין מִן הָאוֹנָסִין וּבֵין מִן הַנִּשּׂוּאִין מַשְׁמַע, "עֶרְוַת בַּת אֵשֶׁת אָבִיךָ מוֹלֶדֶת אָבִיךָ" לָמָּה לִי? הָא נַמִּי אֲחוֹתוֹ בַּת אָבִיו הִיא! שָׁמְעַתְּ מִינָּהּ לְחַיְּיבוֹ מִשּׁוּם שְׁנֵי לָאוִין הַלָּלוּ, וְאִם שׁוֹגֵג – חַיָּיב שְׁתֵּי חַטָּאוֹת. אֲחוֹתְךָ הִיא. בְּהַאי קְרָא דְּבַת אֵשֶׁת אָבִיךָ כְּתִיב. לְחַיְּיבוֹ עַל אֲחוֹתוֹ. מִן הָאוֹנָסִין בַּת אָבִיו וּבַת אִמּוֹ, כְּגוֹן נוֹלְדוּ הוּא וְהִיא מִן אֲנוּסָה. דְּמֵהַהוּא קְרָא דְּאוֹנָסִין לָא שָׁמְעִי' אֶלָּא בַּת אָבִיו שֶׁלֹּא בַּת אִמּוֹ, דִּכְתִי' "בַּת אָבִיךָ אוֹ בַת אִמֶּךָ". וְהָא דִּכְתִיב נַמִּי "בַּת אֵשֶׁת אָבִיךָ", דְּמַשְׁמַע בֵּין אִמּוֹ בֵּין שֶׁאֵין אִמּוֹ – בְּאִישׁוּת הוּא דִּכְתִיב, אֲבָל בְּאוֹנְסִין לָא שָׁמְעִינַן. לְהָכִי כְּתִיב "אֲחוֹתוֹ" – לְרַבּוֹת בַּת אָבִיו וּבַת אִמּוֹ. מִן הַדִּין. מִק"ו: אִם עַל בַּת אָבִיו שֶׁלֹּא בַּת אִמּוֹ הִזְהִיר – עַל בַּת אָבִיו וְאִמּוֹ לכ"ש. שֶׁלֹּא תֹּאמַר בְּעָלְמָא מַזְהִירִין מִן הַדִּין. וַהֲוֵי לָאו גָּמוּר. וּמֵהָכָא לָא יָלְפִינַן לְמֵימַר, מִדְּאִיצְטְרִיךְ "אֲחוֹתְךָ" – אַלְמָא אֵין מַזְהִירִין מִן הַדִּין. דְּאִיכָּא לְשַׁנּוּיֵי: מִילְּתָא דְּאָתְיָא בְּק"ו טָרַח וְכָתַב לָהּ קְרָא. לְהָכִי כָּתַב "הִיא", כְּלוֹמַר: הָכָא הוּא דְּאִיַּיתַּר קְרָא, אֲבָל אַזְהָרַת דִּין ק"ו לָאו אַזְהָרָה הִיא. בְּאִידָּךְ קְרָא. גַּבֵּי אֲחוֹתְךָ בַּת אָבִיךָ, דְּלָא הוּזְכַּר שָׁם אִישׁוּת, דְּנָפְקִי אוֹנָסִין מִינֵּיהּ. (א) דְּבְנִשּׂוּאִין אַשְׁמְעִינַן אַף בְּבַת אָבִיו וּבְבַת אִמּוֹ, מִדִּכְתִיבָא הָכָא – ש"מ לְמֵימְרָא דְּאַע"ג דְּהִיא בַּת אֵשֶׁת אָבִיו לָא מִחַיַּיב אֶלָּא מִשּׁוּם אֲחוֹתוֹ. שֶׁאֵין אִישׁוּת לְאָבִיךָ בָּהּ. בְּשִׁפְחָה וְגוֹיָה לָא תָּפְסֵי בָּהּ קִדּוּשִׁין. בְּמַסֶּכֶת קִדּוּשִׁין נָפְקָא לָן מִקְּרָאֵי בְּפֶ' "הָאוֹמֵר לַחֲבֵרוֹ" בְּסוֹפוֹ (דף סח.): שִׁפְחָה – עַם הַדּוֹמֶה לַחֲמוֹר, וְגוֹיָה, כִּדְכְתִיב "וְאַחַר כֵּן תָּבֹא עָלֶיהָ וּבְעַלְתָּהּ" (דברים כא), וּמֵעִיקָּרָא לָא. וְאֵימָא פְּרָט לַאֲחוֹתוֹ מֵאֲנוּסָתוֹ. שֶׁלֹּא הָיָה אִישׁוּת לְאָבִיךָ בָּהּ. כָּאן בְּאוֹנָסִין. עֶרְוַת בַּת בִּנְךָ מֵאֲנוּסָתוֹ לֹא תְגַלֶּה, הָא בַּת בְּנָהּ מֵאִישׁ אַחֵר – גַּלֵּה, דְּלָאו אִשְׁתְּךָ הִיא. וּמִיהוּ, בְּנוֹ מִן הָאוֹנָסִין בְּנוֹ הוּא, וְכֵן בִּתּוֹ. הִלְכָּךְ, גַּבֵּי אַחֲוָה נַמִּי אַחֲוָה הוּא.

תוספות

מאי טעמא. הכא לא פריך פשיטא דבנו הוא, כדפריך לעיל "פשיטא אחיו הוא", אלא אדרבה, בעי מאי טעמא. והיינו משום דשני לעיל נילף אחוה אחוה מבני יעקב כו', ולהכי בעי מאי טעמא לא ילפינן מבני יעקב דלא זקוקה, ואם כן – מיפטר נמי לא מיפטר.

בן אין לו עיין עליו. אע"ג דסתם אח ובן הוי אפילו ממזר, כדפריך לעיל פשיטא, אחיו הוא. והכא נמי לא איצטריך "ובן אין לו" – עיין עליו, אלא משום דלא נילף מבני יעקב. [והא דאיצטריך "וזרע אין לה", עיין עלה – היינו משום] דסתם זרע לא הוי אלא זרע כשר, כדאמר בריש קדושין (דף ד.): אין לי אלא זרע כשר, זרע פסול מנין? ולענין בני בנים הוי איפכא, דזרע משמע אפי' בני בנים, כדמשמע נמי התם, דקאמר: זרע זרעה לא צריך קרא, דבני בנים הרי הן כבנים. ובן לא משמע אלא בן לבדו, כדאמר ב"יש נוחלין" (ב"ב דף קטו. ושם): אין לי אלא בן(ב), ובן הבן ובת הבן בן בת הבן מנין? ונראה לר"י דמ"עיין עליו" דהכא גבי יבום אין לדרוש בן הבת ובת הבן שיפטור מן היבום, כיון דאפקינן לאתויי ממזר. ולהכי איצטריך לאתויי בן הבן ובת הבן לענין נחלה, ולא בעי למילף מדלענין יבום בן ובן הבן כי הדדי נינהו – לענין נחלה נמי כי הדדי נינהו, כדאמר התם (שם דף קט. ושם) גבי בת. וא"ת: ונדרוש איפכא גבי נחלה לאתויי ממזר, ומ"אין לו" דגבי יבום נדרוש בן הבן? וי"ל: דגבי נחלה א"צ לאתויי ממזר, דלכל מילי בנו הוא. אלא דלענין יבום הוה ס"ד למילף מבני יעקב, ולהכי ע"כ ההוא דנחלה אתא לרבות בן הבן. והא דפשיט ליה ב"יש נוחלין" דלענין יבום בן ובת כי הדדי נינהו – נראה לר"י דנפקא לן מ"לא ימחה" פרט לזה שאין שמו מחוי. א"נ דבת וממזר שקולים, ובת נמי נפקא מ"עיין עליו" דהכא. ומיהו, קשה לר"י: דהיכי נוכל לומר דשקולים הם בת וממזר? הא כיון דמלינו לאוקומי עיין עליו בבת – מהיכי תיתי לאוקומי אף בממזר, כיון דמאחוה אחוה משמע למעוטי ממזר! וי"ל: כיון דאחוה אחוה איצטריך לדרשא אחריתי, לית לן למעוטי מיניה ממזר לענין יבום, כיון דלכל מילי חשיב בן ואח. ולגבי יבום נמי מלי לרבויי (ג) בהדיא בת מעיין עליו, הלכך אע"ג דאיצטריך לרבויי בת – לא נניח בשביל כך מלרבויי ממזר. תדע, דהא ריש לקיש דריש לה בריש "החולץ" (לקמן לה: ושם) למילתא אחריתי, ואפ"ה מרבינן מיניה ממזר.

כשעשה תשובה. והא דאמר בפ' "הנחנקין" (סנהדרין דף פה: ושם) לַכֹּל אין הבן נעשה שליח לאביו להכותו ולקללו חוץ ממסית כו'! התם כשעשה תשובה. וא"ת: בשלמא מלקות מכשחת דמחייב אע"פ שעשה תשובה, אלא לקללו – מי שעשה תשובה אין רשאי לקללו אפילו אחר! ויש לומר: דאם הזכיר שם שמים לבטלה, או עשה דבר שנתחייב בו נדוי, אף על פי שעשה תשובה – חייב, ולא מיפטר. וכי

עין משפט נר מצוה

נ א מיי' פ"א מהלכות נחלות הלכה ז סמג עשין נו טוש"ע ח"מ סי' רעו סעיף ו:

נא ב ג מיי' פ"ב מהל' אבל הלכה ע סמג עשין כח ולאוין רלה טוש"ע י"ד סימן שעג סעיף ד:

נב ד מיי' שם הל"ג ופ"א מהלכות נחלות הל' ז טוש"ע שם וטוש"ע ח"מ סימן רעו סעיף ו:

נג ה מיי' פ"א מהלכות יבום הלכה ג טוש"ע אה"ע סימן קנו סעיף ב:

נד ו ז מיי' פ"ה מהלכות ממרים הלכה יב טור ש"ע י"ד סימן רמא סעיף ד:

נה ח מיי' פ"ב מהלכות איסורי ביאה הלכה ג ד סמג לאוין קה:

נו ט מיי' פ"א מהלכות יבום הלכה ד טוש"ע אה"ע סימן טו סעיף י:

נז י מיי' פ"ב מהלכות איסורי ביאה הלכה ד:

תוספות ישנים

ואימא פרט לאחותו מאנוסה. פי' וגם פרט לאחותו משפחה וגויה דבכולהו אין אישות: **פרט** לאחותו מאנוסה. קשה להר"ם הלא כתיב אחותך בת אביך דמיירי על כרחך באונסים דאי בנשואין תיפוק לי מאשת אביך וי"ל דה"ק ואימא דקרא דאשת אביך ימעט אנוסתו דאינה תחתיו כסדר אישות וקרא דבת אביך מוקים לה בבת שיש לו מן השפחה וגויה שיושבת תחתיו ואע"ג דאף לשפחה וגויה אין לאביו אישות בה מ"מ דרשא דאין לאביך אישות בה אין למעוטי כל אותם שאין בהם אישות אלא אחת לבד וכן משמע בסמוך דבעי קראי אחריני לשפחה ולגויה. וה"נ טוב לנו למעט אנוסתו שאינה כלל תחתיו משפחה ומגויה העומדות תחתיו:

מסורת הש"ס

[לקמן ל:] [לקמן לה: ע. קדושין ד. ב"ב קטו.] [ב"ב ד. ב"מ מח:] [חגיגה ט.]

[פירוש נכון על זה תמצא ברשב"ם ב"ב קטו: קיא וכ"א בשאלתות ריש פ... אמור שארו זו אשת כדכתיב שארה כסותה ועונתה]

[עיין תוספות סוטה כ... ד"ה וזו הואיל]

[גרסת הערוך בערך אי... אין עליו וע"ע שם בער... אן א' קלת באריכות וכ... עוד שם בערך עין וע... מ"ש הסמ"ע ריש סי... רעו לפרש בלשון אין ואפ... ע"ש קלת באריכות והתוי"... מ"ה פ"ב דמכילתין משי... עליו ע"ש]

[פסחים כב. מכות ה:] [פסחים יח: וש"נ] [לקמן נז.]

תוספות חד מקמאי

מסקנא דשמעתתא דל"ש אחותו מחייב כריתות וכ"ש מחייב לאוין וכ"ש אחות מאנוסתו אסור אחור...

הגהות הב"ח

(א) רש"י ד"ה באידך וכו' מיניה דהא בנשואין וכו' מדכתביה הכא ש"מ... (ב) תום' ד"ה בן וכו'. אי... לי אלא בן בן הבן ובת הבן ובן בת הבן מנין כל"ל (ג) בא"ד לרבויי בהד... בת:

גליון הש"ס

גמ' מ"ט אמר קר... האשה וילדיה לקמן ע... ע"א: **תום'** ד"ה בן א... לו וכו' אפילו בני בני... כדמשמע נמי התם. עי... סנהדרין פד ע"ב:

וְאֵימָא פְּרָט לְחַיָּיבֵי לָאוִין? *אֲמַר *רַב פַּפָּא: [א]חַיָּיבֵי לָאוִין תָּפְשִׂי בְּהוּ קִדּוּשִׁין, דִּכְתִיב °"כִּי תִהְיֶיןָ לְאִישׁ שְׁתֵּי נָשִׁים הָאַחַת אֲהוּבָה וְהָאַחַת שְׂנוּאָה", וְכִי יֵשׁ אֲהוּבָה לִפְנֵי הַמָּקוֹם וְיֵשׁ שְׂנוּאָה לִפְנֵי הַמָּקוֹם? אֶלָּא: אֲהוּבָה – אֲהוּבָה בְּנִישּׂוּאֶיהָ, שְׂנוּאָה – שְׂנוּאָה בְּנִישּׂוּאֶיהָ, וְאָמַר רַחֲמָנָא: "כִּי תִהְיֶיןָ". וְאֵימָא פְּרָט לְחַיָּיבֵי כְּרֵיתוֹת – אֲמַר רָבָא: אָמַר קְרָא °"עֶרְוַת אֲחוֹתְךָ בַת אָבִיךָ אוֹ בַת אִמֶּךָ מוֹלֶדֶת בַּיִת אוֹ מוֹלֶדֶת חוּץ", [ב]בֵּין שֶׁאוֹמְרִים לוֹ לְאָבִיךָ: "קַיֵּים", בֵּין שֶׁאוֹמְרִים לוֹ לְאָבִיךָ "הוֹצֵא", וְאָמַר רַחֲמָנָא: "אֲחוֹתְךָ הִיא" – אֵימָא: בֵּין שֶׁאוֹמֵר לוֹ אָבִיךָ "קַיֵּים" בֵּין שֶׁאוֹמֵר לוֹ אָבִיךָ "הוֹצֵא", וְאָמַר רַחֲמָנָא "אֲחוֹתְךָ הִיא" – לְרַבּוֹת אֲחוֹתוֹ מִשִּׁפְחָה וְגוֹיָה – אָמַר קְרָא "בַּת אֵשֶׁת אָבִיךָ", מִי שֶׁיֵּשׁ לוֹ אִישׁוּת לְאָבִיךָ בָּהּ, פְּרָט לַאֲחוֹתוֹ מִשִּׁפְחָה וְגוֹיָה. וּמָה רָאִיתָ? מִסְתַּבְּרָא, חַיָּיבֵי כְּרֵיתוֹת הֲוָה לֵיהּ לְרַבּוֹת, שֶׁכֵּן תָּפְסִי בָּהֶן קִדּוּשִׁין לְעָלְמָא. אַדְּרַבָּה, שִׁפְחָה וְגוֹיָה הֲוָה לֵיהּ לְרַבּוֹת, דְּאִי מְגַיְּירָה – לְדִידֵיהּ נַמִי תָּפְסִי בָּהּ קִדּוּשִׁין! לְכִי מְגַיְּירָה גּוּפָא אַחֲרִינָא הִיא. וְרַבָּנַן, לְמַעוּטֵי שִׁפְחָה וְגוֹיָה מְנָא לְהוּ? [ג]נָפְקָא לְהוּ °מֵ"הָאִשָּׁה וִילָדֶיהָ תִּהְיֶה לַאדֹנֶיהָ". וְרַבִּי יוֹסֵי בְּרַ' יְהוּדָה: חַד – בְּשִׁפְחָה, וְחַד – בְּגוֹיָה. וּצְרִיכִי, דְּאִי אַשְׁמְעִינַן שִׁפְחָה – מִשּׁוּם דְּאֵין לָהּ חַיִּים, אֲבָל גּוֹיָה דְּאִית לָהּ חַיִּים – אֵימָא לָא. וְאִי אַשְׁמְעִינַן גּוֹיָה – מִשּׁוּם דְּלָא שַׁיְיכָא בְּמִצְוֹת, אֲבָל שִׁפְחָה, דְּשַׁיְיכָא בְּמִצְוֹת, אֵימָא לָא – צְרִיכָא. וְרַבָּנַן, אַשְׁכַּחַן שִׁפְחָה, גּוֹיָה מְנָא לְהוּ? וְכ"ת: נֵילַף מִשִּׁפְחָה – הָנְהוּ מִצְרָךְ צְרִיכִי! *א"ר יוֹחָנָן מִשּׁוּם רַ' שִׁמְעוֹן בֶּן יוֹחַי: [ד]אָמַר קְרָא °"כִּי יָסִיר אֶת בִּנְךָ מֵאַחֲרַי", בִּנְךָ מִיִּשְׂרְאֵלִית קָרוּי בִּנְךָ, וְאֵין בִּנְךָ הַבָּא מִן הַגּוֹיָה קָרוּי בִּנְךָ, אֶלָּא בְּנָהּ. אָמַר רָבִינָא, ש"מ: בֶּן בִּתְּךָ הַבָּא מִן הַגּוֹי – קָרוּי בִּנְךָ. *לֵימָא קָסָבַר רָבִינָא *[ה]גּוֹי וְעֶבֶד הַבָּא עַל בַּת יִשְׂרָאֵל הַוָּלָד כָּשֵׁר? נְהִי דְּמַמְזֵר לָא הָוֵי – כָּשֵׁר נַמִי לָא הָוֵי, יִשְׂרָאֵל פָּסוּל מִיקְרֵי. הַאי בְּשִׁבְעָה אוּמּוֹת כְּתִיב! "כִּי יָסִיר" לְרַבּוֹת כָּל הַמְּסִירִים. הָנִיחָא לְרַבִּי שִׁמְעוֹן, דְּדָרֵישׁ טַעֲמָא דִּקְרָא, אֶלָּא לְרַבָּנַן מְנָא לְהוּ? מַאן תַּנָּא דִּפְלִיג עֲלֵיהּ דְּרַבִּי יוֹסֵי בְּרַבִּי יְהוּדָה – רַבִּי שִׁמְעוֹן הִיא.§

מַתְנִי'

(דברים כא; ויקרא יח; שמות כא; דברים ז) [לקמן מה. קדושין סח:]

רש"י

פְּרָט לְחַיָּיבֵי לָאוִין. אִם נָשָׂא אָבִיו מַמְזֶרֶת וְהוֹלִיד בַּת – לָאו אֲחוֹתוֹ הִיא, וְאֵימָא דְּלָא תָּפְסִי בְּהוּ קִדּוּשֵׁי. יֵשׁ אֲהוּבָה לִפְנֵי הַמָּקוֹם. לוֹרֶךְ הָיָה לוֹ לְהַזְכִּיר שֶׁאִם זֶה הָיָה אוֹהֵב אֶת זוֹ וְשׂוֹנֵא אֶת זוֹ אֵין הַבְּכוֹרָה מִשְׁתַּנָּה בְּכָךְ? פְּשִׁיטָא, שֶׁאִם זֶה שׂוֹנְאָהּ – אֵין הַמָּקוֹם שׂוֹנְאָהּ. שְׂנוּאָה בְּנִישּׂוּאֶיהָ. בַּעֲבֵירָה. כִּי תִהְיֶינָה. דְּאִית בְּהוּ תּוֹרַת הֲוָיָה. וְאֵימָא. דְּהַאי בַּת אֵשֶׁת אָבִיו פְּרָט לַאֲחוֹתוֹ מֵחַיָּיבֵי כְּרֵיתוֹת, דְּאֵין אִישׁוּת בָּהּ לְאָבִיךָ, דְּהָא לָא תָּפְסִי בְּהוּ קִדּוּשִׁין, דְּיָלְפִינַן מֵאֲחוֹת אִשָּׁה שֶׁהִיא בְּכָרֵת, וּכְתִיב בָּהּ "לֹא תִקָּח" – אֵין לְךָ בָּהּ לִקּוּחִין, בְּפֶ' "הָאוֹמֵר לַחֲבֵרוֹ" בְּקִדּוּשִׁין (דף סז:). שִׁפְחָה אֵין לָהּ חַיִּים. אֵין לָהּ יַחַס, דִּכְתִיב "עִם הַחֲמוֹר" (בראשית כב). וְגוֹיָה מִתְיַיחֶסֶת עַל שֵׁם אָבִיהָ, דִּכְתִיב "בַּלְאֲדָן בֶּן בַּלְאֲדָן" (מ"ב כ) *"הֲדַרִימָן בֶּן טַבְרִימּוֹן" (מ"א טו). שִׁפְחָה שַׁיְיכָא בְּמִצְוֹת. כָּל מִצְוָה שֶׁהָאִשָּׁה חַיֶּיבֶת בָּהּ – עֶבֶד חַיָּיב בָּהּ, דְּגָמַר "לָהּ" "לָהּ" מֵאִשָּׁה (חגיגה דף ד.). כִּי יָסִיר אֶת בִּנְךָ. מִדְּלָא כְּתִיב "כִּי תָסִיר" ש"מ הָכִי קָאָמַר: בִּתְּךָ לֹא תִתֵּן לִבְנוֹ כִּי יָסִיר בַּעַל בִּתְּךָ אֶת בִּנְךָ שֶׁתֵּלֵד לוֹ בִּתְּךָ מֵאַחֲרַי, אֲבָל אַ"בִּתּוֹ לֹא תִקַּח לִבְנֶךָ" לָא קָמַהְדַּר, וְלָא קָרֵינַן בֵּיהּ כִּי תָסִיר בַּת הַגּוֹי אֶת בִּנְךָ שֶׁתֵּלֵד מֵאַחֲרַי. אַלְמָא: בִּנְךָ מִן הַגּוֹי שֶׁיָּלְדָה לוֹ בִּתְּךָ – קָרוּי בִּנְךָ, וְאֵין בִּנְךָ הַבָּא מִן הַגּוֹיָה קָרוּי בִּנְךָ. ש"מ. מִדִּכְתִיב "כִּי יָסִיר אֶת בִּנְךָ", וּמוֹקְמִינַן לֵיהּ בְּבֵן שֶׁתֵּלֵד בִּתְּךָ לְגוֹי, אַלְמָא: בֵּן בִּתְּךָ הַבָּא מִן הַגּוֹי קָרוּי נַמִי בִּנְךָ. לֵימָא קָסָבַר רָבִינָא וכו' הַוָּלָד כָּשֵׁר. וּלְקַמָּן פְּלִיגֵי בָּהּ בְּ"הַחוֹלֵץ" (דף מה.) (א) (וְל"ג דְּהַוָּלָד מַמְזֵר גָּרְסִי', דְּלָא הָוֵי כְּגֵר שֶׁנִּתְגַּיֵּיר, אֶלָּא צַד יִשְׂרְאֵלִית יֵשׁ בּוֹ, וְשַׁיָּיךְ בֵּיהּ מַמְזֵרוּת). בְּשִׁבְעָה אוּמּוֹת כְּתִיב. וּשְׁאָר גּוֹיוֹת מְנָלָן דִּוְלָדָהּ כָּמוֹהָ. לְרַבִּי שִׁמְעוֹן דְּדָרֵישׁ טַעֲמָא דִּקְרָא. בְּפֶרֶק "הַמְקַבֵּל" בְּבָבָא מְצִיעָא (דף קטו.): אַלְמָנָה עֲנִיָּה אֵין מְמַשְׁכְּנִין אוֹתָהּ, אֲבָל עֲשִׁירָה מְמַשְׁכְּנִין (ב), שֶׁאֵין אַתָּה חַיָּיב לְהַחֲזִיר לָהּ, וְאֵין אַתָּה מַשִּׂיאָהּ שֵׁם רַע בִּשְׁכֵנוֹתֶיהָ. אַלְמָא דָּרֵישׁ טַעְמָא דְּ"לֹא תַחֲבוֹל בֶּגֶד אַלְמָנָה" מִשּׁוּם שֵׁם רָע, וּמוֹצִיא עֲשִׁירָה מִן הַכְּלָל. וְהָכָא נַמִי לְדִידֵיהּ נִיחָא, דְּאִי נַמִי לָא מְפָרֵשׁ קְרָא טַעְמָא – הֲוָה דָּרֵישׁ טַעְמָא דְּחִיתּוּן מִשּׁוּם "כִּי יָסִיר אֶת בִּנְךָ", וְלָא אִיצְטְרִיךְ קְרָא לְפָרוּשֵׁי טַעְמָא, וְאִייַּתַּר קְרָא "כִּי יָסִיר" לְרַבּוֹת שְׁאָר מְסִירִין. אֶלָּא לְרַבָּנַן. אִיצְטְרִיךְ קְרָא לְפָרוּשֵׁי טַעְמָא בְּז' אוּמּוֹת גּוּפַיְיהוּ, וּלְמַעוּטֵי שְׁאָר אוּמּוֹת, דְּאֵינָן אֲדוּקִין בַּעֲבוֹדָה זָרָה כְּמוֹתָן, כִּדְקַיְימָא לָן (חולין דף יג:): גּוֹיִם שֶׁבְּחוּ"ל לָאו עוֹבְדֵי עֲבוֹדָה זָרָה הֵן, אֶלָּא מִנְהַג אֲבוֹתֵיהֶן בִּידֵיהֶן, וְלָא אִייַּתַּר לֵיהּ רִבּוּיָא. וּשְׁאָר אוּמּוֹת מְנָלָן? וְדִכְוָותֵיהּ אָמְרִינַן בְּסַנְהֶדְרִין (דף כא.) גַּבֵּי "לֹא יַרְבֶּה לוֹ נָשִׁים וְלֹא יָסוּר לְבָבוֹ", דְּלְר"ש הָוֵי לֹא יָסוּר לְרִבּוּיָא, דִּבְלָאו פֵּירוּשָׁא דִּקְרָא הֲוָה דָּרְשִׁינַן בֵּיהּ טַעְמָא. וּלְרַבָּנַן דְּלָא דָּרְשֵׁי טַעְמָא דִּקְרָא בְּעָלְמָא, הָכָא קְרָא פֵּירֵשׁ טַעְמָא.

תוספות

וכי יש אהובה לפני המקום. דפשיטא דבשביל אהבת ושנאת הבעל לא יפקיע המקום זכות בנה. ואם תאמר: ונימא שנואה – היינו רשעה, דהיא שנואה לפני המקום! וי"ל: דמשמע ליה אהובה ושנואה בנישואיה, ואם ברשעה מדבר – בלא נישואיה נמי יש לשנאותה א).

ורבי יוסי ברבי יהודה חד בשפחה וחד בגויה. וא"ת: ולמה לי קרא ד"האשה וילדיה", דמ"בת אשת אביך" נפקי תרוייהו דאין אישות לאביך בהו! וי"ל: דהוה מוקמינן קרא בדמסתברא טפי, ואידך הוה מרבינן מ"מולדת חוץ" בין שאומרים לאביך הוצא, כי היכי דמרבינן מיניה חייבי כריתות. ואי אשמועינן גויה משום דלא שייכא במצות. לא הוה צריך להך צריכותא, דגויה לא מפרש בהדיא בקרא ובטעמא קמא סגי. דאי לאו אלא חד קרא – הוה מוקמינן בשפחה, משום דאין לה *חיים. וא"ת: השתא, דאיכא טעמא בגויה ואיכא טעמא בשפחה – למה לי קרא ד"האשה וילדיה" דמ"בת אשת אביך" ממעטי תרוייהו, דהי מינייהו מפקת? וי"ל: דה"א טעמא דלא שייך במצות עדיף, והוה מוקמינן לה בגויה א] ואע"ג דטעמא דגויה לא הוה אתא משפחה, כיון דאיכא בשפחה טעם כל דהו דלא הוי בגויה.

(ג) קסבר רבינא גוי ועבד הבא על בת ישראל הולד כשר. כן גיר' הקונטרס. וכן כתוב ברוב ספרים כאן. אבל בקדושין בסוף פרק "האומר" (דף סח: ושם) ברוב ספרים כתוב: הולד ממזר. וכן גורס התם. וכן נראה עיקר לר"י, דכיון דבתר ישראלית שדינן ליה – הוה טפי ממזר ממאי דהוה שדינן בתר גוי, דאין ממזרות לגוי. וכן משמע לעיל, דקא"ר יוחנן בספ"ק (דף יז. ושם): וכולן לפסול. והדר קאמר: כי אמריתה קמיה דשמואל אמר: אין בנך הבא מן הגויה קרוי בנך אלא בנה, ואין חוששין לקידושיו, דגוי הוא ולא ממזר. והא דאמרינן בפרק "יש בכור" (בכורות דף מז. ושם) גבי לויה שנתעברה מן הגוי בנה פטור מה' סלעים – לא תימא למ"ד אין מזהמין את הולד, אלא אפילו למ"ד מזהמין – לוי פסול איקרי! אומר ר"י דמ"ד אין מזהמין – היינו מ"ד הולד ממזר, דלאו בתר גוי שדינן ליה. ולשון מזהמין על שם גוים שהן מזוהמין, ובקונטרס לא פירש שם כן. ההוא בשבעה אומות כתיב. ואע"ג ד"לא תחנס" דכתיב נמי התם מוקמינן בפרק קמא דמסכת ע"ז (דף כ.) בכל אומות, עובדי עבודה זרה הכא לא מוקמינן ליה בז' אומות אלא משום ד"כי יסיר" משמע שבעה אומות, דמסירין טפי. ואי לאו "כי יסיר" – הוה מוקמינן ליה נמי בכל אומות עובדי עבודה זרה לרבנן. ולר"ש דדריש טעמא דקרא, אי לאו "כי יסיר" הוה דרשי' דטעמא דקרא משום הסרה, והוה (ד) מוקי ליה דוקא בז' אומות דמסירין טפי. וא"ת: ד"לא תתחתן בם" דכתיב נמי התם מוקמינן דוקא בז' אומות, אע"ג דאין שייך שם הסרה, דבגירותן איירי, כדאמר ב"הערל" (לקמן דף עו. ושם)! וי"ל: דעל כרחך אי אפשר לאוקומי בכל אומות, דמדאסר גר עמוני ומואבי מצרי ואדומי – מכלל דשאר גרים שרי בישראל. ואם תאמר: והיכי כרת ברית שלמה עם חירם מלך צור, דכתיב "ויכרתו ברית שניהם" (מ"א ה), והכתיב "לא תכרות להם ברית ולא תחנם" (דברים ז) ובכל האומות עובדי עבודה זרה איירי, כמו "ולא תחנם"! וי"ל: דשמא לא אסר אלא כריתת ברית לשם עבודה זרה, כדכתיב באידך קרא "לא תכרות להם ולאלהיהם ברית" (שמות כג) או שמא חירם מלך צור גר תושב היה. ועוד נ"ל: דלא מיתסר כריתת ברית אלא דוקא בשבעה אומות, מדכתיב גבי גבעונים (יהושע ט) "אולי בקרבי אתה יושב ואיך אכרות לך ברית", משמע דבשאר אומות – שרי. ואע"ג ד"לא תחנם" איירי בכל אומות – עובדי עבודה זרה כריתת ברית שאני, דמוכח עניינא דאיירי דוקא בשבעה אומות, כמו "לא תחיה כל נשמה", דדוקא ז' האומות היו מצווים להחרים, דכתיב "שבעה גוים רבים ועצומים וכו' החרם תחרים" (דברים ז) ולוה הכתוב שלא לכרות להם ברית שלום שלא להכותם כדי לכבוש ארץ ישראל.

מאן תנא דפליג עליה דרבי יוסי בר' יהודה ר"ש היא. בסוף פ' "האומר" (קדושין סח: ושם) איתא הך סוגיא, ומשני בענין אחר: דאמר קרא "כי תהיינה וילדו לו" כל היכא דקרינן ביה "כי תהיינה" קרינן ביה "וילדו לו", וכל היכא דלא קרינן ביה "כי תהיינה" – לא קרינן ביה "וילדו לו". וקאמר נמי בתר הכי: אם כן "האשה וילדיה" למה לי? ומוקי לה לדרשא אחריתי, ולא קאמר חד בשפחה וחד בגויה וצריכי.

קדמו

עין משפט נר מצוה

נח א מיי' פ"ד מהל' אישות הל' יד סמג עשין מח טוש"ע אה"ע סימן מד סעיף ז:

[בערוך גרס רבא]

נט ב מיי' פ"ב מהלכות איסורי ביאה הלכה א טוש"ע אה"ע סימן טו סעיף י:

ס ג ד מיי' פ"א מהל' יבום הלכה ז:

סא ה מיי' פט"ו מהל' איסורי ביאה הלכה ג סמג לאוין קה טוש"ע אה"ע סימן ד סעיף יט:

[ועיין היטב תוספות סנהדרין פג: סוף ד"ה וטבול יום ותוס' זבחים יז. ד"ה הג"ה וכו' ישוב על זה]

מסורת הש"ס

קדושין סח.

נ"ל הדד

רש"ל מ"ז

קדושין סח: לעיל יז.

[קדושין שם ע"ש היטב]

הגהות הב"ח

(א) רש"י ד"ה לימא וכו' ולי נראה נ"ב זה אינו מדברי רש"י: (ב) ד"ה לר' שמעון וכו' עשירה ממשכנין אותה שאין: (ג) תוספות ד"ה לימא קסבר רבינא: (ד) ד"ה ההוא וכו' משום הסרה והוה מוקמי' ליה:

הגהות מהר"ב רנשבורג

א] תוספות ד"ה ואי אשמעינן כו' ואף על גב דטעמא דעובדת כוכבים עדיף לא הוה כו' כצ"ל:

תוספות ישנים

א) ועוד דפשיטא דאין לבני' להפסיד לכך נחלתם: בין שאומרים לאביך הוצא והיינו חייבי כריתות דליכא לאוקומי בחייבי לאוין דהא ככר שמעינן להו מכי תהיינה שהרי קדושין תופסין בהם ועוד ניחא לאוקמי בחייבי כריתות דמשמע הוצא משום דהוי אשה דלא תפסי בה קדושין והיינו חייבי כריתות דאילו חייבי לאוין קדושין תופסין: חד בשפחה וחד בגויה וצריכי. ותימה דבפרק האומר משמע דלא צריך רק חד קרא לשפחה וגויה דפריך אלא האשה וילדיה למה לי ולא קאמר חד לשפחה וחד לגויה וי"ל דהכא היינו טעמא דאצטריך תרי קראי משום דחזינן הכא דאף חייבי כריתות דלית בהו קדושין מרבינן מדכתיב מולדת חוץ בין שאומרים לאביו הוצא. א"כ אי ליכא תרי קראי לשפחה ולגויה לא הוה ממעטינן רק חד מינייהו שהרי יש לנו לרבות כל מה שנוכל דהא אף חייבי כריתות מרדינן אבל התם אין לחלק ביניהם ותימה כי קאמר הכא אשכחן שפחה גויה מנלן אמאי לא משמע דנפקא מדכתיב כי תהיינה וילדו כל היכא דקרינא ביה כי תהיינה קרינא ביה וילדו לו ושפחה וגויה לא בני הויה נינהו דהכי קאמר תלמודא בפרק האומר וי"ל להא דפרישית ניחא דהכא לא מצי למימר כן משום דאף חייבי כריתות דלא קרינן בהו נמי כי תהיינה מרבינן הכא ממולדת חוץ:

תוספות חד מקמאי

היא. דולדה כמוה ולא תפסי בה קדושין ואפי' בשפחה שטבלה לשם עבדות דשייכא במצות דהא אמר בהא שמעתתא וצריכה דאי אשמעינן בגויה משום דלא שייכא במצות. ואם אנס ופתה אשה מותר לישא בתה ודוקא לאחר מיתת האשה אבל בחיי האשה אסור לישא בתה דתנן הנטען מן האשה אסור באמה ובבתה ובאחותה דנשי לגבי נשי שכיחן דאולן:

סב [א] מיי' פ"ט מהל' אישות הל"ג סמג עשין מח טוש"ע אה"ע סימן מא סעיף ב:
סג [ב] מיי' פ"ח מהלכות יבום הלכה א סמג עשין נב טוש"ע אה"ע סימן קטו סעיף א:
סד [ג] מיי' שם הלכה ב טוש"ע אה"ע שם סעיף ג:
סה [ד] מיי' פ"ט מהל' אישות הלכה ב סמג עשין מח טוש"ע אה"ע סימן מא סעיף ב וסימן קטו סעיף א:
סו [ה] מיי' פ"ח מהל' יבום הלכה א.

מתני' *[א]מִי שֶׁקִּידֵּשׁ אַחַת מִשְּׁתֵּי אֲחָיוֹת וְאֵין יוֹדֵעַ אֵי זֶה מֵהֶן קִידֵּשׁ — נוֹתֵן גֵּט לָזוֹ וְגֵט לָזוֹ. [ב]מֵת, וְלוֹ אָח אֶחָד — חוֹלֵץ לִשְׁתֵּיהֶן. הָיוּ לוֹ שְׁנַיִם — אֶחָד חוֹלֵץ וְאֶחָד מְיַיבֵּם. קָדְמוּ וְכָנְסוּ — אֵין מוֹצִיאִין מִיָּדָם. *[ג]שְׁנַיִם שֶׁקִּדְּשׁוּ שְׁתֵּי אֲחָיוֹת, זֶה אֵינוֹ יוֹדֵעַ אֵי זוֹ קִידֵּשׁ, וְזֶה אֵינוֹ יוֹדֵעַ אֵיזוֹ קִידֵּשׁ — זֶה נוֹתֵן שְׁנֵי גִיטִּין, וְזֶה נוֹתֵן שְׁנֵי גִיטִּין. מֵתוּ, לָזֶה אָח וְלָזֶה אָח — זֶה חוֹלֵץ לִשְׁתֵּיהֶן, וְזֶה חוֹלֵץ לִשְׁתֵּיהֶן. לָזֶה אֶחָד וְלָזֶה שְׁנַיִם — הַיָּחִיד חוֹלֵץ לִשְׁתֵּיהֶן. וְהַשְּׁנַיִם — אֶחָד חוֹלֵץ וְאֶחָד מְיַיבֵּם. קָדְמוּ וְכָנְסוּ — אֵין מוֹצִיאִין מִיָּדָם. לָזֶה שְׁנַיִם וְלָזֶה שְׁנַיִם — אָחִיו שֶׁל זֶה חוֹלֵץ לְאַחַת וְאָחִיו שֶׁל זֶה חוֹלֵץ לְאַחַת, אָחִיו שֶׁל זֶה מְיַיבֵּם חֲלוּצָתוֹ שֶׁל זֶה וְאָחִיו שֶׁל זֶה מְיַיבֵּם חֲלוּצָתוֹ שֶׁל זֶה. קָדְמוּ שְׁנַיִם וְחָלְצוּ — לֹא יְיַבְּמוּ הַשְּׁנַיִם, אֶלָּא אֶחָד חוֹלֵץ וְאֶחָד מְיַיבֵּם. קָדְמוּ וְכָנְסוּ — אֵין מוֹצִיאִין מִיָּדָם.§ **גמ'** שְׁמַע מִינַּהּ: *[ד]קִדּוּשִׁין שֶׁאֵין מְסוּרִין לְבִיאָה — הָווּ קִדּוּשִׁין! הָכָא בְּמַאי עָסְקִינַן — כְּשֶׁהוּכְּרוּ וּלְבַסּוֹף נִתְעָרְבוּ. דַּיְקָא נַמִי, דְּקָתָנֵי "וְאֵינוֹ יוֹדֵעַ", וְלֹא קָתָנֵי "וְאֵינוֹ יָדוּעַ", ש"מ (א). מַאי קמ"ל? סֵיפָא אִיצְטְרִיכָא לֵיהּ: מֵת וְלוֹ אָח אֶחָד — חוֹלֵץ לִשְׁתֵּיהֶן, הָיוּ לוֹ שְׁנַיִם — אֶחָד חוֹלֵץ וְאֶחָד מְיַיבֵּם. [ה]דַּוְקָא מִיחְלַץ וַהֲדַר יַבּוּמֵי, אֲבָל יַבּוּמֵי בְּרֵישָׁא — לָא, דְּקָא פָּגַע בַּאֲחוֹת זְקוּקָתוֹ.§ "שְׁנַיִם שֶׁקִּדְּשׁוּ שְׁתֵּי אֲחָיוֹת וכו'".§ שְׁמַע מִינַּהּ: קִדּוּשִׁין שֶׁאֵין מְסוּרִין לְבִיאָה הָווּ קִדּוּשִׁין! הָכָא נַמִי: כְּשֶׁהוּכְּרוּ וּלְבַסּוֹף נִתְעָרְבוּ. דַּיְקָא נַמִי, דְּקָתָנֵי "וְאֵין יוֹדֵעַ" וְלֹא קָתָנֵי "וְאֵין יָדוּעַ", ש"מ. וּמַאי קמ"ל? סֵיפָא אִיצְטְרִיכָא לֵיהּ: מֵתוּ, לָזֶה אֶחָד וְלָזֶה שְׁנַיִם — הַיָּחִיד, חוֹלֵץ לִשְׁתֵּיהֶן. וְהַשְּׁנַיִם, אֶחָד חוֹלֵץ וְאֶחָד מְיַיבֵּם". פְּשִׁיטָא, הַיְינוּ רֵישָׁא! מַהוּ דְּתֵימָא: לִיגְזוֹר תְּרֵי אַטּוּ חַד, קמ"ל. וְדַוְקָא מִיחְלַץ וַהֲדַר יַבּוּמֵי, אֲבָל יַבּוּמֵי בְּרֵישָׁא — לָא, דְּקָא פָּגַע בִּיבָמָה לַשּׁוּק.§ "לָזֶה שְׁנַיִם וְלָזֶה שְׁנַיִם וכו'".§ הָא תּוּ לָמָּה לִי, הַיְינוּ הַךְ! מַהוּ דְּתֵימָא: לִיגְזוֹר דִּלְמָא מְיַיבֵּם בְּלֹא חֲלִיצָה, קמ"ל. מ"ש מֵהָא דִּתְנַן: *אַרְבָּעָה אַחִין, שְׁנַיִם מֵהֶן נְשׂוּאִין שְׁתֵּי אֲחָיוֹת, וּמֵתוּ הַנְּשׂוּאִין אֶת הָאֲחָיוֹת — הֲרֵי אֵלּוּ חוֹלְצוֹת וְלֹא מִתְיַיבְּמוֹת? הָכִי הָשְׁתָּא?!
הָתָם

מתני' וְאֵין יוֹדֵעַ אֵי זֶה מֵהֶן קִידֵּשׁ. אָסוּר בִּשְׁתֵּיהֶן, דְּכָל חֲדָא וַחֲדָא אִיכָּא לְמֵימַר: זוֹ אֲחוֹת אִשָּׁה. חוֹלֵץ לִשְׁתֵּיהֶן. דְּלָא יָדַע אֵיזוֹ הִיא יְבִמְתּוֹ. וּמִיחֲלַץ חֲדָא וְיַיבּוּמֵי חֲדָא, לָא — דַּאֲחוֹת חֲלוּצָתוֹ אֲסוּרָה לוֹ מִדְּרַבָּנַן בְּחַיֶּיהָ. וְיַבּוּמֵי בְּרֵישָׁא, נַמִי לָא — דְּדִלְמָא לָאו זוֹ הִיא יְבִמְתּוֹ, וְקָפָגַע בַּאֲחוֹת זְקוּקָתוֹ דַּהֲוְיָא כְּאִשְׁתּוֹ. הָיוּ לוֹ שְׁנַיִם **אֶחָד חוֹלֵץ**. תְּחִלָּה לְאַחַת. וְהַשֵּׁנִי, אִם רָצָה לְיַיבֵּם לַשְּׁנִיָּה — מְיַיבֵּם, דְּאִם זוֹ יְבִמְתּוֹ — שַׁפִּיר, וְאִם אֲחוֹתָהּ הִיא — לָא קָפָגַע בַּאֲחוֹת זְקוּקָתוֹ, דַּחֲלִיצָה אַפְקְעָהּ לְזִיקָה. קָדְמוּ וְכָנְסוּ. קוֹדֶם שֶׁנִּמְלְכוּ בְּבֵית דִּין. **אֵין מוֹצִיאִין מִיָּדָם**. דְּכָל חַד וְחַד אָמַר: אֲנָא שַׁפִּיר נְסִיבִי. וְאִי נַמִי הֲוָה אִיפְּכָא, שֶׁהָרִאשׁוֹן לְיִבּוּם כָּנַס אֲחוֹת זְקוּקָתוֹ — הַהִיא שַׁעְתָּא וַדַּאי הֲוְיָא אֲסִירָא, וּמִשֶּׁבָּא אָחִיו וְיִיבֵּם הַשְּׁנִיָּה שֶׁהִיא יְבִמְתּוֹ — פָּקַע זִיקָה מֵאִידָךְ לְמַפְרֵעַ. שְׁנַיִם שֶׁקִּדְּשׁוּ ב' **אֲחָיוֹת**. וְהֵם נָכְרִים. זֶה חוֹלֵץ לִשְׁתֵּיהֶן וכו'. דְּכָל חַד וְחַד מִינַּיְיהוּ אָסוּר לְיַבּוּמֵי, דְּדִלְמָא בַּאֲחוֹת זְקוּקָתוֹ פָּגַע. הַיָּחִיד חוֹלֵץ לִשְׁתֵּיהֶן. כִּדְפָרֵישִׁית לְעֵיל, שֶׁאִי אֶפְשָׁר לוֹ לְיַיבֵּם לֹא קוֹדֶם חֲלִיצָה מִשּׁוּם אֲחוֹת זְקוּקָתוֹ, וְלֹא לְאַחַר חֲלִיצָה מִשּׁוּם אֲחוֹת חֲלוּצָה. לְפִיכָךְ, הוֹאִיל וְאָסוּר לְיַיבֵּם — יַחֲלוֹץ תְּחִלָּה לִשְׁנֵיהֶם, כְּדֵי לְהוֹצִיא אוֹתָהּ שֶׁהִיא יְבִמְתּוֹ מֵאִיסּוּר יְבָמָה לַשּׁוּק. וְהַשְּׁנַיִם **אֶחָד חוֹלֵץ**. לְאַפְקוּעֵי זִיקָה מֵאָחִיו אִם זוֹ הִיא יְבִמְתּוֹ, וְתִשְׁתְּרֵי אֲחוֹתָהּ לַשֵּׁנִי מִמַּה נַּפְשָׁךְ: אִם יְבִמְתּוֹ הִיא — שַׁפִּיר, וְאִם אֲחוֹתָהּ הִיא — הָא קָפָקְעָה זִיקַת הַיְבָמָה מִינֵּיהּ בַּחֲלִיצַת אָחִיו. **אָחִיו** שֶׁל זֶה מְיַיבֵּם חֲלוּצָתוֹ שֶׁל זֶה. מִמַּה נַּפְשָׁךְ: אִם זוֹ יְבִמְתּוֹ — שַׁפִּיר נָסֵיב, שֶׁהֲרֵי אָחִיו לֹא חָלַץ לָזוֹ אֶלָּא לַאֲחוֹתָהּ שֶׁלֹּא הָיְתָה יְבִמְתּוֹ, וְאֵינָהּ כְּלוּם. וְאִי לָאו יְבִמְתּוֹ — שַׁפִּיר נָסֵיב נָכְרִית. דְּאִי מִשּׁוּם אֲחוֹת זְקוּקָתוֹ — לֵיכָּא, שֶׁהֲרֵי חָלַץ אָחִיו לַאֲחוֹתָהּ שֶׁהִיא יְבִמְתּוֹ, וּפָקַע זִיקָה. וְאִי מִשּׁוּם יְבָמָה לַשּׁוּק — הֲרֵי חֲלָצָהּ זוֹ מִן הַיָּחִיד, שֶׁהוּא אָח בַּעְלָהּ. קָדְמוּ שְׁנַיִם. אַחִין שֶׁל אֶחָד וְחָלְצוּ לִשְׁתֵּיהֶן, מִשּׁוּם דְּלָא יָדְעִי אֵי זוֹ הִיא יְבִמְתּוֹ. **לֹא** יְיַבְּמוּ הַשְּׁנַיִם. אַחִים הָאֲחֵרִים זֶה אֶת זוֹ וְזֶה אֶת זוֹ, דְּקַמָּא דְּנָסֵיב אִיכָּא לְמֵימַר זוֹ הִיא אֲחוֹת זְקוּקָתוֹ. אֶלָּא, אֶחָד חוֹלֵץ תְּחִלָּה לְאַחַת, וְאֶחָד מְיַיבֵּם לַשְּׁנִיָּה, ממ"נ: אִם יְבִמְתּוֹ הִיא — שַׁפִּיר, וְאִי לָאו יְבִמְתּוֹ הִיא — בַּאֲחוֹת זְקוּקָתוֹ לֹא פָּגַע, שֶׁהֲרֵי חָלַץ אָחִיו לִיבִמְתּוֹ. וִיבָמָה לַשּׁוּק נַמִי לֵיכָּא, שֶׁהֲרֵי הִיא חֲלוּצָה מֵאֲחֵי בַּעְלָהּ. **וְאִם** קָדְמוּ. אֵלּוּ שְׁנַיִם הָאַחֲרוֹנִים וְכָנְסוּ אַחַר חֲלִיצַת הַשְּׁנַיִם הָרִאשׁוֹנִים, וְלֹא בָּאוּ לִימָּלֵךְ לְבֵ"ד — אֵין מוֹצִיאִין מִיָּדָם, כִּדְפָרֵישִׁית, שֶׁאֵין כָּאן אֶלָּא סְפֵק אִיסּוּר אֲחוֹת זְקוּקָה בַּנְּשׂוּאִין הָרִאשׁוֹנִים. דְּאִיכָּא לְמֵימַר קַמָּא דְּנָסֵיב — יְבִמְתּוֹ הִיא, וְשַׁפִּיר נָסֵיב. וּבַתְרָא נַמִי שַׁפִּיר נָסֵיב נָכְרִית. וְאִי נַמִי הֲוָה אִיפְּכָא, דְּקַמָּא פָּגַע בַּאֲחוֹת זְקוּקָתוֹ, כֵּיוָן שֶׁבָּא שֵׁנִי וְיִבְּמָהּ — פָּקַע זִיקָתָהּ מֵאָחִיו, וְהוּתְּרָה לוֹ אִשְׁתּוֹ, וְאִיסּוּרָא דַּעֲבַד — עֲבַד. **גמ'** שְׁמַעַתְּ מִינַּהּ קִדּוּשִׁין שֶׁאֵין מְסוּרִים לְבִיאָה. שֶׁאֵין סוֹפָן לָבֹא לִידֵי בִּיאָה. דְּקס"ד דְּמַתְנִיתִין בְּשֶׁלֹּא הוּכְּרוּ, בִּשְׁעַת קִדּוּשִׁין לָא הֲוָה יָדַע הֵי מִינַּיְיהוּ, כְּגוֹן דְּאָמַר: הֲרֵי אַחַת מִכֶּם מְקוּדֶּשֶׁת לִי, וְעָשׂוּ שְׁתֵּיהֶן שָׁלִיחַ לְקַבֵּל קִדּוּשִׁין. וְקִדּוּשִׁין אֵלּוּ אֵין סוֹפָן לְבִיאָה, דְּכָל חֲדָא קַיְימָא עֲלֵיהּ בִּסְפֵק אֲחוֹת אִשָּׁה. וּמִדְּקָתָנֵי נוֹתֵן גֵּט לָזוֹ וְגֵט לָזוֹ — מִכְּלָל דַּחֲדָא מִיהָא מְקוּדֶּשֶׁת, וּמִשּׁוּם סְפֵיקָא דְּלָא יָדַע הֵי מִינַּיְיהוּ בָּעֵי לְמֵיתַב גֵּט לְתַרְוַויְיהוּ. אַלְמָא: קִדּוּשִׁין הֵן. וּפְלוּגְתָּא דְּאַבַּיֵי וְרָבָא הִיא, בְּקִדּוּשִׁין. שֶׁהוּכְּרוּ. בִּשְׁעַת קִדּוּשִׁין, וְיוֹדֵעַ הָיָה אֶת מִי מְקַדֵּשׁ. הִלְכָּךְ מְסוּרִים לְבִיאָה נִינְהוּ, וְהָלוּ קִדּוּשִׁין. **וְאֵינוֹ** יוֹדֵעַ. מַשְׁמַע: הַשְׁתָּא אֵין יוֹדֵעַ. "אֵין יָדוּעַ" מַשְׁמַע לֹא נוֹדַע הַדָּבָר מֵעוֹלָם. **וּמַאי** קמ"ל. מַתְנִיתִין, פְּשִׁיטָא דְּתַרְוַויְיהוּ בָּעֵי גִּיטָּא, דְּלָא יָדַע הֵי מִינַּיְיהוּ. **סֵיפָא** אִיצְטְרִיכָא לֵיהּ. דְּקָתָנֵי: אֶחָד חוֹלֵץ וְאֶחָד מְיַיבֵּם. וְקָא שְׁמָעִינַן דַּוְקָא מִיחֲלַץ חַד וַהֲדַר יַבּוּמֵי אִידָךְ, מִמַּה נַּפְשָׁךְ, כִּדְפָרֵישִׁית לְעֵיל. **אֲבָל** יַבּוּמֵי. חַד בְּרֵישָׁא, וַהֲדַר מִיחֲלַץ שֵׁנִי לְאִידָךְ — לָא. דְּקַמָּא דְּיִיבֵּם דִּלְמָא פָּגַע בַּאֲחוֹת זְקוּקָתוֹ. הַיְינוּ **רֵישָׁא**. דְּהָא אַשְׁמְעִינַן בְּרֵישָׁא: הָיוּ לוֹ שְׁנַיִם — אֶחָד חוֹלֵץ וְאֶחָד מְיַיבֵּם. מַהוּ **דְּתֵימָא**. הָכָא לֹא לְיַיבֵּם, כֵּיוָן דְּחַד מִינַּיְיהוּ יֵשׁ לוֹ אָח יְחִידִי — לִגְזוֹר תְּרֵי אַחֵי דְּלָא לְיַיבֵּם חַד מִינַּיְיהוּ אַטּוּ הַהוּא אָח שֶׁאֵין לוֹ אָח שֵׁנִי, וְאָתֵי לְמִפְגַּע בַּאֲחוֹת זְקוּקָה, קמ"ל. וְדַוְקָא **מִיחֲלַץ**. הָאָח הַיְּחִידִי לִשְׁתֵּיהֶן, וַהֲדַר יַבּוּמֵי חַד מֵהַשְּׁנַיִם אַחַר חֲלִיצַת אָחִיו לַשְּׁנִיָּה. **אֲבָל** יַבּוּמֵי **בְּרֵישָׁא**. קוֹדֶם חֲלִיצַת הַיָּחִיד לִשְׁתֵּיהֶן. וַאֲפִילּוּ חָלַץ אָחִיו שֶׁל מְיַיבֵּם לַאֲחוֹתָהּ, דְּלֵיכָּא הַשְׁתָּא אִיסּוּר אֲחוֹת זְקוּקָה — לָא [מְיַיבֵּם], מִשּׁוּם שֶׁמָּא זוֹ הִיא אֲרוּסַת הַנָּכְרִי וְקָא פָּגַע בִּיבָמָה לַשּׁוּק בְּלֹא חֲלִיצָה. דְּהַיְּחִידִי הוּא הַנָּכְרִי, וְלוֹ הַיְבָמָה זְקוּקָה, וְהָא מִילְּתָא לָא אַשְׁמְעִינַן בְּרֵישָׁא. **אָחִיו** שֶׁל זֶה מְיַיבֵּם חֲלוּצָתוֹ שֶׁל זֶה **הָא** תּוּ לָמָּה לִי. הַיְינוּ הַךְ, דְּהָא אַשְׁמְעִינַן בְּרֵישָׁא: הַשְּׁנַיִם, אֶחָד חוֹלֵץ וְאֶחָד מְיַיבֵּם. וה"נ הָכִי הוּא, דְּהָנֵי תְּרֵי — חַד חָלֵיץ וְחַד מְיַיבֵּם, וְהָנֵי תְּרֵי — חַד חָלֵיץ וְחַד מְיַיבֵּם. מַהוּ **דְּתֵימָא**. נִיגְזוֹר דִּלְמָא אָתֵי לְיַבּוּמֵי אֶחָד מִשְּׁנַיִם אֵלּוּ וְאֶחָד מִשְּׁנַיִם אֵלּוּ בְּלֹא חֲלִיצָה, וְקָפָגַע כָּל חַד בִּסְפֵק יְבָמָה לַשּׁוּק וּבַאֲחוֹת זְקוּקָה. קמ"ל. דְּלָא גָּזְרִינַן. וְהָא מֵרֵישָׁא לָא שָׁמְעִינַן, דְּהָתָם לָזֶה אֶחָד וְלָזֶה שְׁנַיִם, דְּסוֹף סוֹף לֹא מְיַיבֵּם אֶלָּא חֲדָא. וְכֵיוָן דְּעוֹסְקִין בַּחֲלִיצָה דַּחֲדָא — מַדְכְּרֵי נַמִי וְלָא מְיַיבְּמֵי עַד שֶׁיַּחֲלוֹץ הַיָּחִיד לִשְׁתֵּיהֶן. אֲבָל הָכָא, כֵּיוָן דִּלְבַסּוֹף תַּרְוַויְיהוּ מְיַיבְּמִין, הָךְ לְהַאי בֵּיתָא וְהָךְ לְהַאי בֵּיתָא — אָתֵי לְמֵימַר מַה לָּנוּ וְלַחֲלִיצָה. **מַאי** **שְׁנָא** **מֵהָא** וכו' **וְלֹא** מִתְיַיבְּמוֹת. וְקָתָנֵי סֵיפָא "אִם קָדְמוּ וְכָנְסוּ יוֹצִיאוּ", וְהָכָא קָתָנֵי "אֵין מוֹצִיאִין מִיָּדָן". חוֹלְצוֹת וְלֹא מִתְיַיבְּמוֹת. וְלָא אָמְרִינַן לִיחְלוֹץ חַד מִנַּיְיהוּ וְדָחֵי לְזִיקָה דִּידָהּ מֵאָחִיו. וְהַאי מְיַיבֵּם חֲדָא, כִּי מַתְנִי' דְּקָתָנֵי מִתְיַיבְּמוֹת שְׁתֵּיהֶן — כָּל אַחַת לְאַחַר חֲלִיצַת אֲחוֹתָהּ, כִּדְקָאָמַר: אָחִיו שֶׁל זֶה מְיַיבֵּם חֲלוּצָתוֹ שֶׁל זֶה, לֵימָא כּוּלָּן חוֹלְצוֹת כִּי הָתָם, אַמַּאי מְהַדְּרִינַן לְיַיבֵּם? הָכִי הָשְׁתָּא. הָתָם זְקוּקוֹת שְׁתֵּיהֶן לָהֶן, אִי לְמ"ד בְּפֶרֶק "ד' אַחִין" טַעְמָא דְּאֵין מִתְיַיבֶּמֶת אֲפִילּוּ אַחַת מֵהֶן מִשּׁוּם דְּיֵשׁ זִיקָה, דְּמֵרֵישָׁא מִיתַּסְרָא מִשּׁוּם דְּקָפָגַע בַּאֲחוֹת זְקוּקָה, וְכִי חָלֵיץ (מְיַיבֵּם) חַד לַחֲדָא וּפָקַע זִיקָה — לָא מִשְׁתַּרְיָא אֲחוֹתָהּ לְאִידָךְ, דְּכָל יְבָמָה שֶׁנֶּאֶסְרָה שָׁעָה אַחַת עַל יְבָמָהּ, אֲפִילּוּ לְאַחַר נְפִילָה — הֲרֵי הִיא כְּאֵשֶׁת אָח שֶׁיֵּשׁ לָהּ בָּנִים, וַאֲסוּרָה לְעוֹלָם.
וְאִי

קדמו וכנסו אין מוציאין מידם. אר"י: דווקא משום דשמא לא פגע באחות זקוקתו, אבל אי ודאי הוה (ב) — זקוק להוציא, אף על גב דגבי שומרת יבם שקידש אחיו את אחותה (לקמן דף מא.) אין צריך לרבנן אפילו להמתין — היינו משום שקדש תחלה, ולא בא עליה באיסור, דכבר נפטרה היבמה [זיקתה ממנו] בקדושי אחותה, אבל הכא, דקני לה בביאה — דוקא במקום ספק הוא דאמרינן קדמו וכנסו אין מוציאין מידם, אבל בודאי — לא.

קדושין שאין מסורים לביאה. פירוש: דע"י קדושין קא מפסדה בביאה. אבל חייבי לאוין ועשה — חשיבי קדושין המסורים לביאה.

דיקא נמי דקתני אינו יודע. וא"ת: א"כ תקשה לאביי, דאמר בפ' "האיש מקדש" (קדושין דף נא. ושם) דהוי קדושין! וי"ל: דאין יודע משמע הכי ומשמע הכי.

ומאי שנא מהא דתנן. פי' בקונט': דפריך אהא דקתני במתני' קדמו וכנסו אין מוציאין מידם. וקשה: דלפי זה ה"ל לאתויי סיפא דמתניתין דד' אחין! ועוד: דבסמוך מייתי סיפא דמתני' אברייתא דשילא! ואר"י: דפריך אהא דקתני במתניתין אחד חולץ וא' מייבם, וגבי ד' אחין שתיהן (ג) חולצות.

תוספות ישנים

מהו דתימא דלמא ייבם בלא חליצה. וא"ת והא ידעינן מדלעיל דלא גזרינן דלמא ייבם קודם חליצה וי"ל דשאני הכא דכל השתים מתייבמות שהרי זה מייבם חלוצתו של זה וזה מייבם חלוצתו של זה וא"כ יטעו העולם ויאמרו אחר שזה מייבם וזה מייבם ושתיהם מתייבמות מה לנו ולחליצתם אבל לעיל אנן חזינן דאיכא אחת דמתייבמת ואחת שאינה מתייבמת יבינו העולם וישימו ללב שלא תתיבם זאת עד שיהא חולץ לאחותה וכן יהי' פוגע באחות זקוקתו:

תוספות חד מקמאי

הא דתנן שנים שקדשו שתי אחיות לזה אחד ולזה שנים היחיד חולץ לשתים והשנים א' חולץ וא' מייבם דוקא מיחלץ היחיד והדר יבומי אחד מן השנים*) והדר מיחלץ היחידי דקא פגע ביבמה

*) אולי צ"ל אבל יבומי אחד מהשנים והדר מיחלץ היחידי לא דקא כו'.

(קדושין נג:)
שם
שם
לעיל יח. לקמן כו. עדיות פ"ה מ"ה

הגהות הב"ח

(א) גמ' ש"מ ומאי קמ'
(ב) תוס' ד"ה קדמו ו... אי ודאי הוה היה זק...
(ג) ד"ה ומאי שנא ו... שתיהן חולצות. נ"ב ס... ומיהו הך פירכא ליתא ... יוחנן דאמר אחיות א... יודע מי שנאן:

התם אי למ"ד יש זיקה – יש זיקה. ואי למ"ד *אסור לבטל מצות יבמין – אסור לבטל מצות יבמין. הכא – כל חד וחד, אימור דידיה קא מתרמיא ליה. § "קדמו וכנסו אין מוציאין כו'". § תני שילא: אואפי' שניהם כהנים. מ"ט? בחלוצה דרבנן היא, וספק חלוצה – לא גזרו בהו רבנן. וחלוצה דרבנן היא? והתניא: *°"גרושה" (ויקרא כא), אין לי אלא גרושה, חלוצה מנין? ת"ל "ואשה"! מדרבנן הוא, וקרא אסמכתא בעלמא הוא. §

מתני' גמצוה בגדול לייבם דואם קדם הקטן – זכה. §

גמ' ת"ר: °"והיה הבכור" (דברים כה) – מיכן שמצוה בגדול לייבם, °"אשר תלד" (שם) – *פרט לאילונית שאין יולדת, "יקום על שם אחיו" – לנחלה. אתה אומר הלנחלה, או אינו אלא לשם, יוסף – קורין אותו יוסף, יוחנן – קורין אותו יוחנן? נאמר כאן "יקום על שם אחיו" ונאמר להלן °"על שם אחיהם יקראו בנחלתם" (בראשית מח), מה "שם" האמור להלן – נחלה, אף "שם" האמור כאן – לנחלה. "ולא ימחה שמו" – ופרט לסריס, ששמו מחוי. אמר רבא: אע"ג דבכל התורה כולה *אין מקרא יוצא מידי פשוטו, הכא אתאי גזרה שוה אפיקתיה מפשטיה לגמרי. ואי לאו גזרה שוה הוה אמינא "שם" שם ממש? למאן קמזהר רחמנא, ליבם – "יקום על שם אחיך" מיבעי ליה! אי לבי דינא – "יקום על שם אחי אביו" מיבעי ליה! ודלמא הכי קאמר להו רחמנא לבית דין: אמרו ליה ליבם "יקום על שם אחיו!". אלא, אתאי גזרה שוה אפיקתיה לגמרי. השתא דאמרת קרא בגדול כתיב, אימא: בכור – לייבם, פשוט – לא לייבם. א"כ, אשת אחיו שלא היה בעולמו דמיעט רחמנא – למה לי? *פריך רב אחא: ואימא למעוטי בוכרא דאמא! ההוא לא מצית אמרת, *דיבום בנחלה תלה רחמנא, זונחלה מן האב ולא מן האם. ואימא: כי איכא בכור תתקיים מצות יבום, כי ליכא בכור לא תתקיים מצות יבום! אמר קרא: "ומת אחד מהם", מי לא עסקינן דמית בכור, ואמר רחמנא לייבם קטן. ואימא דמית קטן, ואמר רחמנא לייבם בכור! הא מיעט רחמנא אשת אחיו שלא היה בעולמו. ואימא: כי ליכא בכור – קדם קטן זכה, ואי איכא בכור – קדם קטן לא זכה! אמר קרא: °"כי ישבו אחים יחדו" (דברים כה) – הוקשה ישיבת אחים זה לזה. ואימא: כי איכא בכור – ליהדר אגדול, כי ליכא בכור – אין חוזרין אצל גדול! אלמה תני אביי קשישא: *חמצוה בגדול לייבם. לא רצה – הולכים אצל אחיו הקטן, לא רצה – חוזרין אצל גדול! כבכור, מה בכור – בכורתו גרמה לו, אף גדול – גדולתו גרמה לו. ואימא: כי מייבם בכור – לישקול נחלה, כי מייבם פשוט לא לישקול נחלה! אמר קרא: "יקום על שם אחיו" – והרי קם. ואלא בכור דקרייה רחמנא – למאי

רש"י

ואי למ"ד. טעמא משום דאסור לבטל מצות יבמין, ואי מייבם האי חדא – דלמא מיית אידך קודם שייבם, ותיאסר אחותה משום אחות אשה, ונמצא מצות יבמין בטלה על ידינו מיבום ומחליצה הרי נאסרה *משום כך, וכיון שנאסרה שעה אחת א"נ חלץ חד לחדא ואזלא האי השניה – עומדת היא באיסור אשת אח שלא נראית ליבום מתחלה. (א) אבל הכא, זו שנאסרה משום אחות זקוקה – לאו יבמה היתה, וכי פקע איסור אחות זקוקה בחליצת אחותה הרי זו מותרת ועומדת, דלאו אשת אח הואי, הלכך, מספיקא לא מפקינן לה, דאימר כל חד וחד דידיה איתרמיא ליה. ואפילו שניהם כהנים. וחד מנייהו ודאי חלוצה נסיב, דהא ארוסת הנכרי חלוצה היא מאחד משני אחיו, כדקתני: קדמו שנים וחלצו. חלוצה. דאסורה לכהן. מדרבנן הוא. והכא, דלכל חד אינה אלא ספק, דשמא זה ייבם את יבמתו גמורה – לא גזור רבנן לאפוקה מספק. גרושה. "מאישה לא יקחו". מכאן שמצוה בגדול. הכי דריש: "ולקחה לו לאשה ויבמה, והיה הבכור" – המייבם יהיה הבכור. אשר תלד. ואותה יבמה תהא ראויה לילד, פרט לאילונית. יקום. היבם על שם אחיו לנחול נחלתו, ולא יחלקו אחיו עמו. אתה אומר לנחלה. והאי "יקום" ביבם משתעי. או אינו. אלא בבן שיולד לו משתעי, שאם היה שם המת יוסי – קורין לזה יוסי. אין מקרא יוצא מידי פשוטו. ואע"ג דדרשינן ליה לדרשא – מידי פשוטו מיהו לא נפיק לגמרי. ואפיקתיה לגמרי. שאין צריך לקרות לבנו בשם אחיו המת, והכי גמר לה מרביה: ופרכינן ואי לאו גזרה שוה הוה אמינא שם ממש בתמיה. ליבם. קאמר רחמנא: בן הנולד לך יקום על שם אחיך, מיבעי ליה. ואי לבית דין. מודע רחמנא מצות קריית שם הבן. יקום על שם אחי אביו מיבעי ליה. אלא ודאי ביבם גופיה משתעי קרא, ולבית דין קאמר רחמנא, שיקום היבם על שם אחיו המת לנחלה. אמרו לו ליבם. שיקום בנו על שם אחיו. דכל מצות יבום קא מודע קרא לב"ד, וקאמר להו להזהיר יבמה לבא עליה, והבן אשר תלד לו יקימנו ע"ש אחיו. אימא בכור. דווקא קאמר קרא, אבל פשוט – לא לייבם לגמרי, בין איכא בכור בין ליכא בכור. אם כן. דפשוט לאו בר יבום הוא, למה לי דמיעט רחמנא אשת אחיו שלא היה בעולמו? תיפוק לי משום דלאו בכור הוא זה שנולד לאחר מיתת אחיו. ואימא. האי דמיעט אשת אחיו שלא היה בעולמו – כגון שהיה זה שנולד בכור לאמו ואחיו מאביו, ולהכי אצטריך למעוטי. בנחלה תלה רחמנא. וממילא בכור הנוטל פי שנים הוא דמייבם, אבל בכור לאם – לא. ומדמעטיה – שמע מיניה בכור דקרא לאו דווקא, אלא גדול האחים. ואימא כי איכא בכור כו'. כלומר, דלמא לעולם בכור דווקא, והכי קאמר רחמנא: אי איכא בכור קמך – תתקיים מצות יבום או בבכור או בפשוט, דנפקא לן מדאימעיט אשת אחיו שלא היה בעולמו, וכי ליכא בכור – לא תתקיים, ופטורה לגמרי מן הפשוט. ומת אחד מהם. משמע שלא היו שם אלא שנים ומת אחד מהן. מי לא עסקינן. כלומר, מי לא משתמע נמי מקרא דמת בכור, וקאמר רחמנא לייבם פשוט. ואימא. על כרחך קרא דחיק ומתוקם כגון דמית פשוט, וקאמר רחמנא לייבם בכור. דהא כתיב "והיה הבכור". הא מיעט רחמנא וכו'. דהכא גבי תרי אחים כתיב מיעוט אשת אחיו שלא היה בעולמו, אלמא דמית גדול משמע, ותו ליכא בכור *קטן. אימא כי ליכא בכור קדם הקטן זכה. דהא לא רבי דלייבם פשוט אלא מ"ומת אחד מהם", ומיעוט דאשת אחיו שלא היה בעולמו, דמשמע דמית בכור ואמר רחמנא לייבם פשוט, אבל איכא בכור – לא לייבם פשוט. הוקשה כו'. שוין לייבם. ליהדר אגדול. אי לא בעו שאר אחיו – נחזור עליו לכופו, דמצוה עליה רמיא ולא על האחרים. אבל כי ליכא בכור – לא רמיא מצוה אגדול טפי משאר אחיו. הולכין אצל אחיו הקטן. משמע קטן הימנו, וגדול משאר אחיו, אלמא מהדרינן אגדול, דגדול קודם. ומדקתני חוזרין אצל גדול ליכא לאוקמי, דאיכא למימר: מאי גדול – בכור. דאי לא מצי לשנויי הכי, אדמותיב מדתני אביי – לותיב ממתניתין דקתני בפרק "החולץ" נמי: לא רצה חוזרין אצל גדול. לא לישקול נחלה. דהא "בכור" כתיב. אלא

תוספות

אי למ"ד יש זיקה. אר"י: אע"ג דלמ"ד יש זיקה ליכא למיגזר לייבם אחר חליצה משום דלמא אתי לייבם ברישא, כדמשמע בפרק "ד' אחין" (לקמן דף כז: ושם). גבי רבי יוחנן, דאמר: אחיות איני יודע מי שנאן. מ"מ ליכא למימר דליחלץ חד ולייבם חד, כיון דכל אחת נאסרה שעה אחת – אסורה עולמית, אפילו ראשונה, דלית ליה יבמה שהותרה ונאסרה וחזרה והותרה תחזור להתירה, אלא לר' יוחנן, לכך הוצרך לומר אחיות איני יודע מי שנאן. ולמ"ד אין זיקה, אף על גב דלרב דאמר אין זיקה לית ליה לקמן כיון שנאסרה שעה וכו' – מ"מ גזרינן דלא ליחלץ חד ולייבם חד אטו דלמא מייבם ברישא, דכיון דאין זיקה – אתי למטעי ולייבם ברישא, דהא לא מסקי אינשי אדעתייהו דלמא מית אידך. אבל הכא – כל חד וחד אמרינן אימא דידיה מתרמיא ליה, [וליכא למגזר דלמא מייבם ברישא, דאפילו מייבם ברישא אימא דידיה אתרמי ליה, וכי מייבם] שפיר עבד. ומשום מ"ד אין זיקה צריך לומר כל כך.

וספק חלוצה לא גזרו בהו רבנן. הקשה הר"ר משה ברבי יעקב מפיה"ס: דאמר ב"החולץ" (לקמן דף לו:), מת בתוך ל' יום, אם אשת ישראל היא חולצת, ואם אשת כהן היא אינה חולצת. ולמה לא תחלוץ, כיון דספק חלוצה מותרת לכהן? וי"ל דהתם שחולצת לאחר נשואין יאמרו קמו רבנן במילתא דנפל הוה, ולכך הוצרכו חליצה, ואתי למישרי חלוצה לכהן. אבל הכא, כל אחד כשכונס אמרי' קים ליה להאי דלאו חלוצה היא, ולכך כנסה*.

או אינו אלא לשם. ויהא כוליה קרא כפשטיה, ולא נדרוש מבכור דמצוה בגדול לייבם, אלא ה"ק: והיה הבכור. פי': הראשון שתלד היבמה יקרא שמו בשם המת. ויליף בג"ש דלאו שם ממש קאמר אלא לנחלה, וכיון דלנחלה קאמר – ליכא לאוקומי קרא אלא ביבם. דאי על הבכור שתלד היבמה קאמר קרא שיקום על שם המת לנחלה, שאותו בכור יירש את המת – דאם כן יקום על שם אחי אביו מיבעי ליה, דהשתא לא שייך למימר דה"ק: "אמרו ליה ליבם". כדקאמ' בסמוך.

ה"ג ואם לא רצה הולכין אצל אחיו הקטן. פי': אצל קטן ממנו. לא רצה הולכים אצל אחיו – פירוש: שאר פשוטין קטנים ממנו. לא רצו – חוזרין אצל גדול. ויש ספרים דלא גרסי אלא הולכין אצל קטן, ותו לא. וצריך לומר דמשמע דקטן ממנו קאמר, מדלא נקט לישנא דמתני' ד"החולץ" (לקמן דף לט.): מהלכין על כל האחין.

עין משפט נר מצוה

סז א מיי' פ"ח מהלכות יבום הלכה ב סמג עשין כב טוש"ע אה"ע סימן קעו סעיף ג:
סח ב מיי' פ"א מהלכות אישות הל' ז ופי"ז מהל' איסורי ביאה הל"ז טוש"ע אה"ע סימן ו סעיף א:
סט ג מיי' פ"ב מהלכות יבום הלכה ו סמג עשין נא טור ש"ע אה"ע סימן קסא סע"ד:
ע ד מיי' שם טוש"ע שם סעיף ז:
עא ה מיי' פ"ג מהלכות נחלות הלכה ז סמג עשין נו טוש"ע אה"ע סימן קסג סעיף א:
עב ו מיי' פ"ו מהלכות יבום הלכה ב סמג עשין נא טוש"ע אה"ע סימן קעב סעיף א:
עג ז מיי' פ"א מהלכות נחלות הלכה ו סמג עשין נ טוש"ע ח"מ סי' רעו סעיף ד:
עד ח מיי' פ"ב מהלכות יבום הלכה ד סמג עשין נא טוש"ע אה"ע סימן קסא סעיף ד:

תוספות חד מקמאי

לשוק: **הא** דתני שילא אפי' שניהם כהנים דוקא כשקדמו וכנסו שאין מוציאין אותן מידן אפילו שניהם כהנים אבל לכתחלה לא שרינן אע"ג דחלוצה דרבנן שלא שרינן לכתחלה ואי קשיא הא דגרסינן בפ' החולץ מת בתוך ל' יום ועמדה ונתקדשה אם אשת כהן אינה חולצת ומסקנא משום דאיכא רבנן דפליגי עליה דרשב"ג דאמר אע"ג דלא שהה ולד מעליא הוא אשת כהן דלא אפשר עבדינן כרבנן משמע דלרשב"ג אם אשת כהן היא שמפקינן לה מיניה והא ספק חולצת [היא] איכא למימר שאני הכא שכבר חלצה וכבר כנסה כהן ומשום הכי לא מפקינן מיניה אע"פ שהוא כהן אבל התם לכתחלה הוא דאמר לא תחלוץ ותהוי לכהן והא א) בשלא אקדמו וכנסו קאי אבל לכתחלה לא ב) והתם אי שריא לה השתא לכתחלה למיחלץ אף על פי שהוא כנסה בלכתחלה ואיכא מ"ד שאני הכא שאחת מהן בודאי אינה חלוצה אף על פי שאחת מהן בודאי חלוצה ולאו מילתא היא דהא תינח כהן שני שנשא השניה אבל הראשון ספק חלוצה נשא אמאי לא מפקינן מיניה וכי משום דנסב שני שרי לראשון דאי לא נסב שני הראשון ודאי ספק חלוצה נשא אלא ודאי כדפרישית: **תני** אביי קשישא מצוה בגדול לייבם לא רצה לייבם הולכין אצל קטן אלא בכור דקרייה רחמנא למאי הלכתא מה בכור אינו נוטל בראוי כבמוחזק אף יבם אינו נוטל בראוי

א) נ"ל והא דהכא בשאקדמו וכנסו קאי כו'. ב) אין הלשון מדוקדק ואולי צ"ל והתם אי שרינן לה השתא למחלץ אע"פ שהוא כנסה אתי נ"כ למחלץ ולכנוס אותה לכתחלה ואיכא מ"ד כו'.

מסורת הש"ס

משום כך וכו' ואין לה היתר אפילו בדיעבד כצ"ל רש"ל
[לעיל יח. וש"נ]
קדושין עח.
לעיל יב.
[לעיל יח: שבת סג.]
[קדושין יג. וש"נ]
[לעיל יז: כ.]
ביצה לז. לקמן לט.
אולי צ"ל קמן

הגהות הב"ח

(א) רש"י ד"ה ואי למ"ד וכו' מתחלה מדרבנן אבל הכא זו וכו' וכי פקע איסור אחות זקוקה ביבום אחותה:

לְמַאי הִלְכְתָא? לִגְרִיעוּתָא, [א]מַה בְּכוֹר אֵינוֹ נוֹטֵל בָּרָאוּי כִּבְמוּחְזָק – אַף הַאי אֵינוֹ נוֹטֵל בָּרָאוּי כִּבְמוּחְזָק.§ **מתני'** *[ב]הַנִּטְעָן עַל הַשִּׁפְחָה וְנִשְׁתַּחְרְרָה, אוֹ עַל הַגּוֹיָה וְנִתְגַּיְּירָה, הֲרֵי זֶה לֹא יִכְנוֹס. וְאִם כָּנַס – אֵין מוֹצִיאִין מִיָּדוֹ. הַנִּטְעָן עַל אֵשֶׁת אִישׁ וְהוֹצִיאוּהָ מִתַּחַת יָדוֹ, אע"פ שֶׁכְּנָסָהּ – יוֹצִיא.§ **גמ'** הָא גִּיּוֹרֶת מִיהָא הָוְיָא, וּרְמִינְהִי: אֶחָד אִישׁ שֶׁנִּתְגַּיֵּיר לְשׁוּם אִשָּׁה, וְאֶחָד אִשָּׁה שֶׁנִּתְגַּיְּירָה לְשׁוּם אִישׁ, וְכֵן מִי שֶׁנִּתְגַּיֵּיר לְשׁוּם שׁוּלְחַן מְלָכִים, לְשׁוּם עַבְדֵי שְׁלֹמֹה – אֵינָן גֵּרִים, דִּבְרֵי רַ' נְחֶמְיָה. שֶׁהָיָה רַבִּי נְחֶמְיָה אוֹמֵר: אֶחָד *גֵּירֵי אֲרָיוֹת וְאֶחָד גֵּירֵי חֲלוֹמוֹת, וְאֶחָד גֵּירֵי מָרְדְּכַי וְאֶסְתֵּר – אֵינָן גֵּרִים עַד שֶׁיִּתְגַּיְּירוּ בַּזְּמַן הַזֶּה. בַּזְּמַן הַזֶּה ס"ד?! אֶלָּא, אֵימָא: כְּבַזְּמַן הַזֶּה. הָא אִיתְּמַר עֲלָהּ, א"ר יִצְחָק בַּר שְׁמוּאֵל בַּר מָרְתָא מִשְּׁמֵיהּ דְּרַב: [ג]הֲלָכָה כְּדִבְרֵי הָאוֹמֵר כּוּלָּם גֵּרִים הֵם. אִי הָכִי לְכַתְּחִלָּה נַמִי! מִשּׁוּם דְּרַב אַסִּי, *דַּאֲמַר רַב אַסִּי: °"הָסֵר מִמְּךָ עִקְּשׁוּת פֶּה וּלְזוּת שְׂפָתַיִם וגו'". מִשְׁלֵי ד ת"ר: *אֵין מְקַבְּלִין גֵּרִים לִימוֹת הַמָּשִׁיחַ. כַּיּוֹצֵא בּוֹ *[ד]לֹא קִבְּלוּ גֵּרִים לֹא בִּימֵי דָּוִד וְלֹא בִּימֵי שְׁלֹמֹה. א"ר *אֱלִיעֶזֶר: מַאי קְרָא – °"הֵן גּוֹר יָגוּר אֶפֶס מֵאוֹתִי מִי גָּר אִתָּךְ עָלַיִךְ יִפּוֹל" (א) ישעיה נד אֲבָל אִידָּךְ – לָא.§ "הַנִּטְעָן עַל אֵשֶׁת אִישׁ וכו'".§ אֲמַר רַב: וּבְעֵדִים. אֲמַר רַב שֵׁשֶׁת: *אָמֵינָא כִּי נָיֵים וְשָׁכֵיב רַב אֲמַר לְהַאי שְׁמַעְתָּא. דְּתַנְיָא: *[ה]הַנִּטְעָן עַל אֵשֶׁת אִישׁ *וְהוֹצִיאוּהָ עַל יָדוֹ, וְנִתְגָּרְשָׁה מִתַּחַת יְדֵי אַחֵר, אִם כָּנַס – לֹא יוֹצִיא. ה"ד, אִי דְּאִיכָּא עֵדִים – כִּי אֲתָא אַחֵר וְאַפְסְקֵיהּ לְקָלָא מַאי הָוֵי? אֶלָּא לָאו דְּלֵיכָּא עֵדִים, וְטַעֲמָא, דַּאֲתָא אַחֵר וְאַפְסְקֵיהּ לְקָלָא, הָא לָאו הָכִי – מַפְּקִינַן! אָמַר לָךְ רַב: הוּא הַדִּין דְּאע"ג דְּלָא אֲתָא אַחֵר וְאַפְסְקֵיהּ לְקָלָא. אִי אִיכָּא עֵדִים – מַפְּקִינַן, אִי לֵיכָּא עֵדִים – לָא מַפְּקִינַן, וְהָכִי קָאָמַר: דְּאע"ג דַּאֲתָא אַחֵר וְאַפְסְקֵיהּ לְקָלָא – לְכַתְּחִלָּה לֹא יִכְנוֹס. מֵיתִיבֵי: [ו]בד"א – כְּשֶׁאֵין לָהּ בָּנִים, אֲבָל יֵשׁ לָהּ בָּנִים – לֹא תֵּצֵא. [ז]וְאִם בָּאוּ עֵדֵי טוּמְאָה – אֲפִילּוּ יֵשׁ לָהּ כַּמָּה בָּנִים תֵּצֵא. רַב מוֹקֵי לָהּ לְמַתְנִיתִין בְּיֵשׁ לָהּ בָּנִים וְיֵשׁ לָהּ עֵדִים. וּמַאי דּוּחְקֵיהּ דְּרַב לְאוֹקְמֵי לְמַתְנִיתִין בְּיֵשׁ לָהּ בָּנִים וְיֵשׁ לָהּ עֵדִים, וְטַעֲמָא דְּאִיכָּא עֵדִים – מַפְּקִינַן, וְאִי לֵיכָּא עֵדִים – לָא מַפְּקִינַן, לוֹקְמָהּ בְּשֶׁאֵין לָהּ בָּנִים, אע"ג דְּלֵיכָּא עֵדִים? אֲמַר רָבָא: מַתְנִיתִין קְשִׁיתֵיהּ: מַאי אִירְיָא דְּתָנֵי "הוֹצִיאוּהָ", לִיתְנֵי הוֹצִיאָהּ, אֶלָּא, כָּל "הוֹצִיאוּהָ" בְּבֵית דִּין, וּבֵית דִּין – בְּעֵדִים הוּא דְּמַפְּקֵי. וְאִי בָּעֵית אֵימָא: הָנֵי מַתְנְיָיתָא – רַבִּי הִיא, דְּתַנְיָא: [ח]רוֹכֵל יוֹצֵא וְאִשָּׁה חוֹגֶרֶת בְּסִינָר, אֲמַר רַבִּי: הוֹאִיל וּמְכוֹעָר הַדָּבָר – תֵּצֵא. רוֹק לְמַעְלָה מִן הַכִּילָּה, אֲמַר רַבִּי: הוֹאִיל וּמְכוֹעָר הַדָּבָר – תֵּצֵא.

מִנְעָלִים

אֶלָּא לְמַאי הִלְכְתָא קָרֵייהּ בְּכוֹר. לִיכְתּוֹב גָּדוֹל. **בְּכוֹר אֵינוֹ נוֹטֵל.** חֵלֶק בְּכוֹרָה בַּנַּחֲלָה הָרְאוּיָה לָבֹא לָהֶם אַחַר מִיתַת אֲבִיהֶן, אֶלָּא בְּמַה שֶּׁמּוּחְזָק בְּיַד אֲבִיהֶן בְּיוֹם מוֹתוֹ, דִּכְתִיב "בְּכֹל אֲשֶׁר יִמָּצֵא לוֹ" (דברים כא), אַף יָבָם הַנּוֹטֵל פִּי שְׁנַיִם [א] בְּנִכְסֵי אָבִיו – חֶלְקוֹ וְחֵלֶק אָחִיו שֶׁמֵּת [ב] – אֵינוֹ נוֹטֵל בָּרָאוּי כִּבְמוּחְזָק. **מתני'** הַנִּטְעָן. חָשׁוּד, כְּלוֹמַר: שֶׁטּוֹעֲנִים עָלָיו דִּבְרֵי לַעַז. **לֹא יִשָּׂאֶנָּה.** מִשּׁוּם לַעַז, שֶׁלֹּא יֹאמְרוּ: אֱמֶת הָיָה הַקּוֹל הָרִאשׁוֹן. **הַנִּטְעָן עַל אֵשֶׁת אִישׁ וְהוֹצִיאוּהָ.** בֵּית דִּין מִתַּחַת בַּעְלָהּ בִּשְׁבִיל זֶה שֶׁאֲסָרָהּ עָלָיו, וְהָלַךְ זֶה וּנְשָׂאָהּ. **יוֹצִיא.** דְּמִדְּאוֹרַיְיתָא אֲסוּרָה נַמִי לַבּוֹעֵל, דְּדָרְשִׁינַן "וְנִטְמְאָה" "וְנִטְמָאָה" (במדבר ה) שְׁנֵי פְעָמִים, אֶחָד לַבַּעַל וְאֶחָד לַבּוֹעֵל, בְּמַסֶּכֶת סוֹטָה (דף כז:). **גמ'** הָא גִּיּוֹרֶת מִיהָא הָוְיָא. וְאַע"ג דְּלֹא נִתְגַּיְּירָה לְשֵׁם יַהֲדוּת, אֶלָּא בִּשְׁבִיל שֶׁיִּשָּׂאֶנָּה זֶה. **עַבְדֵי שְׁלֹמֹה.** בַּעֲלֵי שְׂרָרָה הָיוּ. **גֵּירֵי אֲרָיוֹת.** ◐כְּגוֹן כּוּתִים, דִּכְתִיב בְּסֵפֶר מְלָכִים (ב' יז) "וַיְשַׁלַּח ה' בָּהֶם אֶת הָאֲרָיוֹת" וְנִתְגַּיְּירוּ, כִּדְכְתִיב הָתָם בְּגָלוּת שׁוֹמְרוֹן. **גֵּירֵי חֲלוֹמוֹת.** בַּעַל חֲלוֹמוֹת אָמַר לָהֶם לְהִתְגַּיֵּיר. **מָרְדְּכַי וְאֶסְתֵּר.** "וְרַבִּים מֵעַמֵּי הָאָרֶץ מִתְיַהֲדִים" (אסתר ח). **בַּזְּמַן הַזֶּה ס"ד.** כָּל הָנֵי מִקַּמֵּי הָכִי לָאו גֵּרִים נִינְהוּ? כְּגוֹן נְבוּזַרְאֲדָן וְכַיּוֹצֵא בּוֹ. **כְּבַזְּמַן הַזֶּה.** שֶׁלֹּא יַעֲשֶׂה מֵחֲמַת שְׂרָרָה. **אִי הָכִי.** דְּגִיּוֹרֶת מַעַלְיָיתָא הִיא. **לְכַתְּחִלָּה נַמִי.** יִכְנוֹס, וְאַמַּאי תָּנֵי לֹא יִכְנוֹס? **דַּאֲמַר רַב אַסִּי.** טַעְמָא דְּמַתְנִיתִין מִשּׁוּם דִּכְתִיב "הָסֵר מִמְּךָ עִקְּשׁוּת פֶּה וּלְזוּת שְׂפָתַיִם הַרְחֵק מִמֶּךָּ", דְּאָתוּ לְאַחֲזוּקֵי לְקָלָא קַמָּא. **הֵן גּוֹר.** הַבָּא לְהִתְגַּיֵּיר, "יָגוּר אֶפֶס מֵאוֹתִי" – בְּעוֹד שֶׁאֵין אֲנִי עִמָּכֶם יִתְגַּיֵּיר, דְּהַיְינוּ בַּזְּמַן הַזֶּה. **מִי גָּר אִתָּךְ** עָלַיִךְ יִפּוֹל. מִי גָּר אִתָּךְ בַּעֲנִיּוּתֵךְ כַּאֲשֶׁר אָמַרְתְּ. **עָלַיִךְ יִפּוֹל.** לָעוה"ב. יִפּוֹל = יָנוּחַ, כְּמוֹ "עַל פְּנֵי כָל אֶחָיו נָפָל" (בראשית כה) "יִפֹּל מִצִּדְּךָ אֶלֶף" (תהלים צא). **וּבְעֵדִים.** הָא דִּתְנַן יוֹצִיא זֶה הֶחָשׁוּד שֶׁכְּנָסָהּ – כְּגוֹן שֶׁבָּאוּ עֵדִים עַל קוֹל הָרִאשׁוֹן, שֶׁרָאוּהָ שֶׁזִּינְּתָה עִמּוֹ. **לְהָא שְׁמַעְתָּא.** בְּעֵדִים. **כִּי נָיֵים וְשָׁכֵיב רַב אֲמָרָהּ דְּתַנְיָא.** תְּיוּבְתָּא. **וְנִתְגָּרְשָׁה מִתַּחַת יְדֵי אַחֵר.** רְאוּבֵן נִטְעַן עַל דִּינָה אֵשֶׁת שִׁמְעוֹן, וְגֵירְשָׁהּ שִׁמְעוֹן וּנְשָׂאָהּ נַחְשׁוֹן, וְגֵירְשָׁהּ. אִם כְּנָסָהּ רְאוּבֵן מֵעַתָּה – לֹא יוֹצִיא. **אִי דְּאִיכָּא עֵדִים.** בִּזְנוּת קַמָּא – הֲרֵי נֶאֶסְרָה עוֹלָמִית עָלָיו. **ה"ה דַּאֲפִילּוּ דְּלָא אַפְסֵיק אַחֵר לְקָלָא.** וּכְנָסָהּ רְאוּבֵן מִגֵּירוּשֵׁי שִׁמְעוֹן לֹא תֵּצֵא, הוֹאִיל וְלֵיכָּא עֵדִים. וְהָא דְּנָקַט מִתַּחַת יְדֵי אַחֵר – הִיא גּוּפָהּ אִיצְטְרִיךְ לְאַשְׁמוּעִינַן רְבוּתָא, דִּלְכַתְּחִלָּה לֹא יִכְנוֹס, כִּדְקָתָנֵי: אִם כָּנַס – אִין, לְכַתְּחִלָּה – לָא. **בַּמֶּה דְּבָרִים אֲמוּרִים.** דְּאִם כָּנַס הַנִּטְעָן יוֹצִיא – כְּשֶׁאֵין לָהּ בָּנִים מִן הָרִאשׁוֹן. **אֲבָל יֵשׁ לָהּ בָּנִים.** מִן הָרִאשׁוֹן – לֹא תֵּצֵא. דְּכִי מַפְּקֵי לָהּ – קָא מַחְזְקִינַן לְקָלָא קַמָּא, וְעָבְדִינַן לְהוּ מַמְזֵרִים. **וְאִם בָּאוּ כו'.** אַלְמָא אֵין לָהּ בָּנִים – בְּלֹא עֵדִים נַמִי מַפְּקִינַן. רַב מוֹקֵי לְמַתְנִיתִין בְּיֵשׁ לָהּ בָּנִים. וּמִשּׁ"ה אָמַר רַב: וּבְעֵדִים. וּב"ד **בְּעֵדִים הוּא דְּמַפְּקֵי.** מִבַּעַל רִאשׁוֹן, דְּאֵין אִשָּׁה נֶאֱסֶרֶת לְבַעְלָהּ מִשּׁוּם קוֹל. וְאָתָא רַב לְמֵימַר: דַּוְקָא מַתְנִי' מִשּׁוּם כָּךְ יוֹצִיא הַנִּטְעָן, הוֹאִיל וְאִיכָּא עֵדִים. אֲבָל בְּלֹא עֵדִים, הוֹאִיל וְיֵשׁ לָהּ בָּנִים – לֹא. **וְאבע"א.** בְּלֹא בָּנִים לֹא נָפְקָא בְּלֹא עֵדִים, וְהָנֵי מַתְנִיתָא דְּאָמְרִי נָפְקָא – ר' אָמְרִינְהוּ, דְּמַפִּיק אִשָּׁה מִבַּעְלָהּ בְּקוֹל כָּל דְּהוּ. **רוֹכֵל.** מוֹכֵר בְּשָׂמִים לְנָשִׁים לְהִתְקַשֵּׁט בָּהֶן. **רוֹכֵל יוֹצֵא.** מִן הַבַּיִת, וּמָצָא זֶה אֶת אִשְׁתּוֹ שֶׁהָיְתָה חוֹגֶרֶת בְּסִינָר – מְכוֹעָר הַדָּבָר, שֶׁלֹּא הִתִּירַתּוּ מֵעָלֶיהָ אֶלָּא לִזְנוּת. **סִינָר.** הוּא כְּעֵין מִכְנָסַיִם, שֶׁהָיוּ הַנָּשִׁים חוֹגְרוֹת לִצְנִיעוּת. **רוֹק לְמַעְלָה מִן הַכִּילָּה.** אָרוֹכֵל יוֹצֵא קָאֵי, וּמָצָא בַּעַל רוֹק לְמַעְלָה בְּגַג הַכִּילָּה שֶׁעַל מִטָּתוֹ, מִי זָרַק הָרוֹק לְמַעְלָה – כ"א הַשּׁוֹכֵב וּפָנָיו לְמַעְלָה, הִלְכָּךְ זִינְּתָה זוֹ, וְרָקְקָה בִּשְׁעַת תַּשְׁמִישׁ.

מִנְעָלִים

למאי הלכתא לגריעותא. פר"י: דהוי מצי למימר לחשיבותא, שאין ירושתו חוזרת ביובל*. **גיורת** מיהא הויא. דמשמע לא יכנוס הוא, אבל אחר – שרי לכנוס לכתחלה. **הלכה** כדברי האומר כולם גרים הם. (ב) הך גירי אריות לא דמי להא דאיכא מ"ד כותים גירי אריות הן, דהתם היו עובדים אלהיהם, כדכתיב בספר מלכים. ולמ"ד גירי אמת הן – קסבר דשוב נתגיירו לגמרי*. **אי** הכי לכתחלה נמי. אי אמרת בשלמא דאינה גיורת גמורה – ניחא דלכתחלה לא יכנוס, משום דספק גיורת היא, דשמא נתגיירה לשם איש. ודיעבד אין להוציא, דאין להחמיר משום חששא זו. **משום** דרב אסי הסר ממך עקשות פה כו'. פר"י: דבנטען על הפנויה אין להחמיר מלכנוס משום לזות שפתים, דאדרבה: מלוה לכונסה, דבאנוסה כתיב "ולו תהיה לאשה" (דברים כב). **לא** בימי דוד ולא בימי שלמה. (ג) מאיתי הגיתי *ובת פרעה דבימי שלמה לא קשה, דמידי הוא טעמא – אלא משום שולחן מלכים, והני לא צריכי. אבל קשה, דאמרינן ב"הערל" (לקמן דף עט. ושם) גבי מעשה דגבעונים דבימי דוד נתוספו גרים על ישראל ק"ן אלף! וי"ל: דמעצמן נתגיירו, כדאשכחן גבי מרדכי ואסתר "ורבים מעמי הארץ מתיהדים". ויש ספרים שכתוב בהן: לא קבלו גרים לא בימי דוד ולא בימי שלמה, אלא שנעשו גרים גרורים. והיא דפ"ב דשבת (דף לא.) ההוא דאתא לקמיה דהלל ואמר: גיירני ע"מ לעשות כ"ג – בטוח היה הלל ◐דסופו לעשות לשם שמים. וכן ההיא ד"התכלת" (מנחות מד.) דאתיא לקמיה *דרבי: גיירני ע"מ שאנשא לאותו תלמיד. **אמר** רבי הואיל ומכוער הדבר תצא. אר"ת: דתלא מן הרוכל אם נשאת לו, דכל הסוגיא איירי בנטען. דאין לומר תלא מן הבעל – דאין האשה נאסרת על בעלה אלא על ידי קנוי וסתירה, *או שיראו(ד) דרך מנאפין. ועוד: דלגבי בעל הוי קלא דבתר נשואין, דאמר(ה) ב"האשה רבה" (לקמן דף לב. ושם) דלקלא דלבתר נשואין לא חיישינן. ◐ורוק למעלה בגג הכילה לא עדיף מקלא דלא פסיק, דהא בסמוך אמר דלרבי מפקינן אפי' בקלא דפסיק מכח הך ברייתא. אלא ודאי תלא מן הרוכל אם נשאה. דרוק למעלה בגג הכילה הוי קלא דקמי נישואי רוכל. וכן פר"ת. וכן נראה לר"י, דמתוך ההלכה משמע דאין מוציאין ע"י קול מבעלה, דקאמר: ובית דין בעדים הוא דמפקי. משמע לדבר פשוט הוא דמבעל לא מפקי' אלא בעדים, אע"ג דמנטען קתני בברייתא דמפקי בקול. [אף דקתני הוציאוה הדר רב נחמן דבסמוך הוציאה תנן. דמשמע על ידי בעלה – אפ"ה מבעלה לא מפקינן על ידי קול] באין בנים מן הראשון. והא דאיצטרי' בהנהו עובדי דסוף נדרים (דף צא:) להנהו

טעמי

תורה אור

מִשְׁלֵי ד

ישעיה נד

כתובות עג.

[ישוב לזה כתבו תוס' בבכורות נב: ד"ה בכור]

עה א מיי' פ"ג מהל' נחלות הלכה א סמג עשין נו טוש"ע אה"ע סימן קסג סעיף א:

[עי' תוספות חולין ג: ד"ה קסבר]

עו ב מיי' פ"י מהלכות גירושין הלכה יד סמג עשין נ טור ש"ע אה"ע סימן יא סעיף ה:

עז ג מיי' פי"ג מהל' איסורי ביאה הלכה יד סמג לאוין קיז טוש"ע י"ד סימן רסח סעיף יב:

עח ד מיי' שם הל' טו:

עט ה מיי' פ"ב מהל' סוטה הל' טו טור ש"ע אה"ע סי' יא סע"ב:

[זה שהתעוררו התוספות מבת פרעה שקיבלה שלמה דמידי הוא טעמא אלא משום שולחן מלכים חידוש קצת שהרי כל זה מבואר להדיא בש"ס לקמן עו ע"א מתיב רב יוסף וכו' והא לא קבלו וכו' מידי הוא טעמא וכו']

פ ו שם סעיף א:

פא ז מיי' שם הלכה טז וטוש"ע שם סעיף ב:

פב ח מיי' פכ"ד מהל' אישות הלכה טו ופ"ב מהל' סוטה הלכה יג טוש"ע שם סעיף א:

[תוספתא פ"ד]

[נ"ל דרבי חייא]

תוספות חד מקמאי

בבמוחזק: **תניא** אחד איש שנתגייר לשום אשה ואחד אשה שנתגיירה לשום איש וכן מי שנתגייר לשום שולחן מלכים לשם עבדי שלמה אינם גרים דברי רבי נחמיה שהיה ר"נ אומר אחד גרי אריות ואחד גרי חלומות ואחד גרי מרדכי ואסתר אינם גרים עד שיתגיירו שנית ואע"ג דכותיים אליבא דמ"ד גרי אריות הן גוים גמורים הן התם לא נתגיירו לגמרי כדכתיב את ה' היו יראים ואת אלהיהם היו עובדים אבל (התם) [הכא] שנתגיירו לגמרי הלכה כולן גרים הן רבינו יעקב ז"ל: **תניא** בד"א שתצא כשאין לה בנים אבל כשיש לה בנים לא תצא. הרב אלפס פירש כשיש לה בנים מן הנטען ור"ש פי' כשיש לה בנים מן הבעל והרב"י כתב כשיש לה בנים מן הנטען או מן הבעל לא תצא והא דתניא רוכל יוצא ואשה חוגרת בסינר ואמר רבי הואיל ומכוער הדבר תצא וקיי"ל כותיה בקלא דלא פסיק לכאורה נראה דאבעל קאי וכן נראה מפי' רש"י ז"ל דבדבר מכוער מפקינן לה מבעלה והר' אלפס כתב כל דהוא נטען מפקינן מיניה בדבר מכוער אבל מבעל לא מפקינן אלא בעדים ומסתברא כותיה דהא גמרי' דבר דבר מממון מה להלן דבר ברור ולא באמתלא אף כאן דבר ברור ולא באמתלא ולא בדבר מכוער. ובמס' סוטה איבעיא לן עוברת על דת משה ויהודית אם רשאי הבעל לקיימה או לא ולא איפשיטא ומיהו מעוברת על דת ליכא ראיה דהתם [אין] עדים בדבר מכוער של זנות אלא לדבר מכוער של חוצפא ומש"ה איבעי לן אם רשאי הבעל לקיימה ואפילו תימא דבדבר

[לקמן כה: ע"ש]

[קדושין עה: ב"ק לח: סנהדרין פה: חולין ג: נדה נו:]

כתובות כב: [עי' תוס' שם]

[ע"ז ג:]

[לקמן עו.]

[נ"ל אלעזר]

[לקמן נא. קט: ב"ק מז: סה. בכורות כג: נדה ס.]

[נ"ל והוציאה וכ"ה רש"א]

הגהות הב"ח

(א) גמ' מי גר אתך עליך יפול מי גר אתך בעניותך הוא דמליך יפול אבל אידך לא: (ב) תום' ד"ה הלכה כדברי האומר כולם גרים הם ואפי' גירי אריות הך גירי אריות: (ג) ד"ה לא וכו' מאיתי הגיתי. נ"ב עיין בפרק בתרא דקדושין דף עה: (ד) ד"ה אמר וכו' או שיראו אותם כדרך המנאפין: (ה) באד"ה בהאשה רבה. נ"ב דף לב. ועי"ש בתוס' ד"ה כל קלא:

הגהות הגר"א

[א] רש"י ד"ה בכור כו' אף יבם הנוטל פי שנים כו'. נ"ב אבל ר"ת פי' שאין נוטל חלק אחיו אלא אם מת אביו קודם לאחיו (ועמ"ש רבינו באה"ע סימן קסג ס"ק ד'): [ב] שם וחלק אחיו שמת. נ"ב תלקו שמת.

גליון הש"ס

רש"י ד"ה גירי אריות כגון כותים. עי' סנהדרין פה ע"ב ברש"י ד"ה גירי אריות: **תום'** ד"ה לא בימי דוד וכו' דסופו לעשות לש"ש. עי' לקמן דף קט ע"ב תוס' ד"ה אמר רבי וכו' ורוק למעלה בגג כו'. עיין לקמן דף לב ע"א תד"ה כל קלא:

מְנְעָלִים הֲפוּכִים תַּחַת הַמִּטָּה, אָמַר רַבִּי: הוֹאִיל וּמְכוֹעָר הַדָּבָר — תֵּצֵא. מִנְעָלִים הֲפוּכִים? לֵיחֲזֵי דְּמַאן נִינְהוּ! אֶלָּא: מְקוֹם מִנְעָלִים הֲפוּכִים (תַּחַת הַמִּטָּה א"ר: הוֹאִיל וּמְכוֹעָר הַדָּבָר — תֵּצֵא). [א]וְהִלְכְתָא כְּוָותֵיהּ דְּרַב, [ב]וְהִלְכְתָא כְּוָותֵיהּ דְּרַבִּי. קַשְׁיָא הִלְכְתָא אַהִלְכְתָא! לָא קַשְׁיָא: [ג]הָא — בְּקָלָא דְּפָסֵיק, הָא — בְּקָלָא דְּלָא פָּסֵיק. קָלָא דְּלָא פָּסֵיק וְלֵיכָּא עֵדִים — כְּרַבִּי, קָלָא דְּפָסֵיק וְאִיכָּא עֵדִים — כְּרַב. וְקָלָא דְּלָא פָּסֵיק עַד כַּמָּה? *אֲמַר אַבַּיֵי, [ד]אָמְרָה לִי אֵם: דּוּמֵי דְּמָתָא יוֹמָא וּפַלְגָא. וְלָא אֲמָרַן אֶלָּא דְּלָא פָּסַק בֵּינֵי וּבֵינֵי, אֲבָל פָּסַק בֵּינֵי וּבֵינֵי — הָא פָּסַק. וְלָא אֲמָרַן אֶלָּא דְּלָא פָּסַק מֵחֲמַת יִרְאָה, אֲבָל פָּסַק מֵחֲמַת יִרְאָה — מֵחֲמַת יִרְאָה הוּא. *וְלָא אֲמָרַן אֶלָּא דְּלֵיכָּא אוֹיְבִים, אֲבָל אִיכָּא אוֹיְבִים — אוֹיְבִים הוּא דְּאַפְּקוּ לֵיהּ לְקָלָא. *תְּנַן הָתָם: [ה]הַמּוֹצִיא אֶת אִשְׁתּוֹ מִשּׁוּם שֵׁם רַע — לֹא יַחֲזִיר. מִשּׁוּם נֶדֶר — לֹא יַחֲזִיר. שְׁלַח לֵיהּ רַבָּה בַּר *הוּנָא לְרַבָּה בַּר ר"נ: יְלַמְּדֵנוּ רַבֵּינוּ, כָּנַס מַהוּ שֶׁיּוֹצִיא? א"ל, תָּנֵינָא: הַנִּטְעָן עַל אֵשֶׁת אִישׁ וְהוֹצִיאָהּ מִתַּחַת יָדוֹ, אע"פ שֶׁכָּנַס יוֹצִיא. א"ל: מִי דָּמֵי? הָתָם "הוֹצִיאוּהָ" וְהָכָא "הוֹצִיאָהּ"! וְרַבָּה בַּר ר"נ — מַתְנִיתִין נַמִי "הוֹצִיאָהּ" תְּנַן. וְאַכַּתִּי מִי דָּמֵי? הָכָא — בַּעַל, וְהָתָם — בּוֹעֵל! א"ל: שַׁפִּיר דָּמֵי אַהֲדָדֵי: הָכָא אֲמוּר רַבָּנַן [ו]לֹא יִכְנוֹס, וְאִם כָּנַס יוֹצִיא — ה"נ אָמְרִי רַבָּנַן לֹא יַחֲזִיר, וְאִם כָּנַס — יוֹצִיא. וְלֹא הִיא, הָתָם — אַלּוּמֵי אַלְּמֵיהּ לְקָלָא, הָכָא אָמְרִינַן קָם בֵּיהּ בְּקָלָא וְלֵיתֵיהּ.§ **מתני'** [ז]הַמֵּבִיא גֵּט מִמְּדִינַת הַיָּם וְאָמַר "בְּפָנַי נִכְתַּב וּבְפָנַי נֶחְתַּם" לֹא יִשָּׂא אֶת אִשְׁתּוֹ. "מֵת", "הֲרַגְתִּיו", "הֲרַגְנוּהוּ" — לֹא יִשָּׂא אֶת אִשְׁתּוֹ. רַבִּי יְהוּדָה אוֹמֵר "הֲרַגְתִּיו" — לֹא תִּנָּשֵׂא אִשְׁתּוֹ, "הֲרַגְנוּהוּ" — תִּנָּשֵׂא אִשְׁתּוֹ.§ **גמ'** טַעֲמָא דְּמִמְּדִינַת הַיָּם — דַּעֲלֵיהּ קָסָמְכִינַן, אֲבָל מֵא"י, דְּלָאו עֲלֵיהּ קָסָמְכִינַן, יִשָּׂא אֶת אִשְׁתּוֹ, וְהָא מֵת, דְּלָאו עֲלֵיהּ קָסָמְכִינַן, דַּאֲמַר מָר: *אִשָּׁה דַּיְיקָא וּמִינַּסְבָא, וְקָתָנֵי: לֹא יִשָּׂא אֶת אִשְׁתּוֹ! הָתָם לֵיכָּא כְּתָבָא, הָכָא — אִיכָּא כְּתָבָא. דִּתְנַן: *מַה בֵּין גֵּט לְמִיתָה — שֶׁהַכְּתָב מוֹכִיחַ.§ "מֵת", "הֲרַגְתִּיו", "הֲרַגְנוּהוּ" — לֹא יִשָּׂא אֶת אִשְׁתּוֹ.§ הוּא נִיהוּ דְּלֹא יִשָּׂא אֶת אִשְׁתּוֹ, [ח]הָא לְאַחֵר — תִּנָּשֵׂא. *וְהָאֲמַר רַב יוֹסֵף: [ט]"פְּלוֹנִי רְבָעַנִי לְאוֹנְסִי" — הוּא וְאַחֵר מִצְטָרְפִין לְהָרְגוֹ. "לִרְצוֹנִי" — רָשָׁע הוּא, וְהַתּוֹרָה אָמְרָה: °"אַל תָּשֶׁת יָדְךָ עִם רָשָׁע לִהְיוֹת עֵד חָמָס". וְכ"ת שָׁאנֵי עֵדוּת אִשָּׁה דְּאַקִּילוּ בָּהּ רַבָּנַן — וְהָא"ר מְנַשֶּׁה: גַּזְלָן

רש"י

מנעלים הפוכים. פיהן למטה, ודאי של נכרי הם, והפכו כדי שלא יכיר הרואה. מקום מנעלים הפוכים. ניכר מקום הפיכתן בעפר שתחת המטה, לשון מורי. לשון אחר: מקום מנעלים מלא הפוך, שבא ומלא את מנעליה במקום שהוא רגיל לתת שלו – ודאי נכרי בא לכאן, ושם מנעליו במקום שלה ושלה במקום בעל. ולשון ראשון עיקר, דא"כ הפוך מיבעי ליה. והלכתא כוותיה דרב. דאמר: אין מחזיקין קלא אלא בעדים. דפסיק. שיצא קול אחר, לומר: שקר הוא הלעז. דומי מתא. חשודי העיר. ל"א: דומי – דלא ידעי ודאי, אלא אמרי בדדמי, לשון מורי. משום נדר לא יחזיר. וטעמא מפרש התם ב"השולח גט": שאם אתה אומר יחזיר, שמא תלך זו אצל חכם לאחר שניסת, ויתיר לה נדרה, ויאמר המגרש: אילו הייתי יודע שיש היתר לנדר שנדרה, אם היו נותנים לי מאה מנה לא הייתי מגרשה, שהיתה חביבה עלי ביותר, ונמצא זה מבטל גיטו למפרע ועוקרו, ובניה מן השני ממזרים. לפיכך אומרים לו מתחלה: הוי יודע שהמוציא את אשתו משום נדר שנדרה – לא יחזיר עולמית, ואם היא חביבה עליך – לא ובקש היתר לנדרה. ואי מגרש לה מהשתא – ודאי שנואה היא עליו, ותו לא מצי עקר (לה) גיטה בדברי שקר. ומשום שם רע. שיצא עליה לא יחזיר, כדפרישית טעמא: שמא תנשא לאחר, ויצא קול על הלעז הראשון ששקר היה, ויתחרט המגרש, ויאמר: אילו הייתי יודע שכן הוא כו'. כנס מהו שיוציא. אם החזירה, מהו שנכופנו להוציא? תנינא הנטען כו'. והתם נמי מפקיעה מבעלה, דכיון דהוציאה משום שם רע – גילה דעתו שהקול אמת ונאסרה לו, כי היכי דאסרינן לה הכא משום שהחזיק זה הקול כשכנסה. התם הוציאוה. ב"ד, שבאו עדי טומאה ואסורה לבועל מה"ת. הכא הוציאה. והאי דלא יחזיר – דרבנן הוא. ורבה בר נחמן מתני' נמי הוציאה תנן. בלא עדים, הלכך לא אסורה לבועל אלא משום לזות שפתים מדרבנן, ואפ"ה קתני: יוציא. ואכתי מי דמי הכא בעל. החזירה, ואין דבר זה מגונה הוא. התם בועל. כונס, ודבר מגונה הוא. א"ל שפיר דמי להדדי. דהכא והכא מדרבנן הוא. ולא היא התם. הוא כשכנס בועל – אלומי אלמיה לקול הראשון, שאמת היה הלעז. אבל הכא, כשהחזירה בעל – בטולי בטליה לקלא, דאמרינן: מדהחזירה – קים ליה בקלא, חזר ובדק בקול ראשון של שם רע, ומצא שאינו. **מתני'** המביא גט ממדינת הים. צריך שיאמר "בפני נכתב ובפני נחתם". וטעמא מפרש בגיטין (דף ב.): לפי שאין בקיאים לשמה. לא ישא את אשתו. הואיל ואדיבוריה סמכינן. מת הרגתיו הרגנוהו לא ישא אשתו. הואיל ועל עדותו היא נשאת – איכא לזות שפתים, שמא עיניו נתן בה והעיד שקר. אבל לאחר – תנשא, דאשה נשאת בעד אחד. ר' יהודה אומר הרגתיו לא תנשא אשתו. אפי' לאחר על פיו, לפי שהוא משים עצמו רשע, והתורה אמרה "אל תשת רשע עד". הרגנוהו תנשא אשתו. לאחר, ובגמרא בעי טעמא.

גמ' אבל מארץ ישראל. המביא גט מארץ ישראל אין צריך לומר "בפני נכתב ובפני נחתם". והא מת דלא עילויה סמכינן. דכי אמר מת בעל, הא דשרו רבנן לאינסובי לאחר – לא עליה סמכינן. דאמר מר. בפרק "האשה" רבה (לקמן דף נג:) היינו טעמא דעד אחד נאמן באשה, משום דהיא גופה דייקא, עד שיודעת שמת ודאי, ואחר כך נשאת. מה בין גט למיתה. ב"המביא" (וכן לקמן דף קיז.) תנן: אף הנשים שאין נאמנות לומר מת בעלה, כגון חמותה ויבמתה וצרתה ובת בעלה, נאמנות להביא גיטה, ואף על פי שצריכות לומר "בפני נכתב ובפני נחתם". ומה בין גט למיתה – אלא שהכתב מוכיח, ולאו עלה סמכינן כל כך. פלוני רבעני לאונסי כו' להורגו. את הרובע. גזלן

תוספות

טעמי דאיתתא שריא, דאם איתא דעבד איסורא – אירכוסי הוי מירכס, ואם איתא דעבד איסורא – ניחא ליה דליכול. נראה לר"י דהתם באומרת טמאה אני, כי מתני' דהתם דעלה קאי, ואפ"ה שריא מהנהו טעמי. אבל באומרת טהורה אני – שריא בלאו הנהו טעמי דהתם. ואין לתמוה: אמאי שריא כיון שאומרת טמאה, הא שויתה לנפשה חתיכה דאיסורא! דלפי שראו חכמים שנתקלקלו הנשים ליתן עיניהם באחר, ורוב האומרות כן משקרות, לכך נראה להם להתירן*. **הא** בקלא דפסיק. ומיהו, רב גופיה אית ליה ל"ש קלא דפסיק ול"ש קלא דלא פסיק. **ואכתי** מי דמי. בספרים ישנים לא גרסי ליה, אלא גרסי: ורבה בר (א) נחמן הוציאה תני. הכא בעל והכא *בועל, הכא אמור רבנן וכו' ועד ולא היא חד שינויא הוא. והכי פירושו: ורבה ב"ר נחמן הוציאה תני, וכיון דתני הוציאה, והכא בעל והכא בועל הוציאה ולא בית דין. ואפ"ה קתני במתני' "ואם כנס – יוציא", ה"ה דהתם בגיטין (דף מה:) נמי אם כנס מוציא. ויפה פשיט רבה ב"ר נחמן, ומסיק "ולא היא כו' קם ביה בקלא דליתיה". ומה שאסור להחזיר אינו משום שסבורים העולם שאסורה לו משום שם רע, דהא סברי דקם ביה בקלא דליתיה, אלא משום קלקול או משום פריצות, כדאמרינן בגיטין. וקשיא לר"י: דהיאך היה מדמה אותה רבה ב"ר נחמן? וכי לא היה יודע טעם זה, דבהדיא מפרש להנהו טעמי ב"השולח" (גיטין דף מו.) בברייתא! וי"ל: דלא שמיע ליה. א"נ, אומר ר"י, דרבה ב"ר נחמן יודע טעמי דקלקול ופריצות, אבל סובר דכנס יוציא מפני שהעולם אין יודעים הטעם דקלקולא ופריצות, אלא סוברים שמחמת שם רע אסורה לו כיון שגירשה ע"י כן. ולכך, אם כנס – יוציא משום רננה, כמתניתין דהכא. ומסיק: ולא היא, שיטעו העולם בזה, כי יש חילוק גדול בין מתני' דהכא למתני' דהתם – דהכא אלמיה לקלא כו'. **הכא** איכא כתבא דתנן מה בין גט כו'. ואע"ג דלאביי בסוף פ"ב דגיטין (דף כג:) איירי הך משנה בח"ל – מ"מ דייק שפיר מינה דיש לסמוך על הכתב. **מת** הרגתיו הרגנוהו. כיון דאפילו במת לא ישא את אשתו לא הוה צריך למיתני "הרגנוהו", ואפילו בהרגתיו לאחר תנשא, ולא תני ליה אלא משום דר' יהודה מפליג בין הרגתיו להרגנוהו: **הוא** ואחר מצטרפים להורגו. הקשה הר"ר חיים: דבסוף פ"ק דמכות (דף ו. ושם) פריך: הרוג ונרבע יליף! משמע דהרוג ונרבע פסולים להעיד משום שוגג, והכא משמע דכשר! וי"ל: דלא משום שוגג פסול נרבע התם, אלא בנרבע לרצונו איירי, ומשום רשע פסול. אפילו לרבא דבסמוך, דסובר דלרצונו נמי כשר – מכל מקום, כשיש עדים שנרבע לרצונו – הוי כנמצא אחד מהן קרוב או פסול. וכי פריך בתר הכי הורג ורובע יליל – פי': יעילו על עצמם, הוה מצי למינקט נרבע דקאי ביה, כיון דאיירי בנרבע לרצונו, אלא משום

עין משפט נר מצוה

פג א ב ג ד מיי' פ"ב מהלכות סוטה הלכה יג יד טוש"ע אה"ע סי' יא סעיף א:
פד ה מיי' פ"י מהל' גירושין הלכה יב סמג עשין נא טוש"ע אה"ע סימן י סעיף ג:
פה ו מיי' שם טוש"ע שם סעיף ו:
[וע' היטב תוס' כתובות סג: ד"ה אבל]
פו ז מיי' פ"י מהלכות גירושין הלכה יד טוש"ע אה"ע סימן יב סעיף א:
ס"א בעל
פז ח מיי' פי"ג מהל' גירושין הלכה י טוש"ע אה"ע סימן יז סעיף ז:
פח ט מיי' פי"ב מהל' עדות הלכה ב סמג לאוין ריד טוש"ע ח"מ סימן לד סעיף כו:
פט י מיי' שם פ"י הל' א סמג לאוין ריד טוש"ע ח"מ סימן לד סעיף א:

תוספות חד מקמאי

דבדבר מכוער של זנות מפקינן מבעל בדבר מכוער דחוצפא לא מפקינן והתם אסיקנא דלהפסידה כתובתה צריכה התראה אבל אי הדרא בה תהדר: **תנן** התם המוציא [את] אשתו משום שם רע משום נדר לא יחזיר ואיבעי לן כנס מהו שיוציא ואסיק' אינו מוציא ולא דמי למתני' דנטען דהתם כיון דנסבה נטען אלומי אלמה לקליה הכא אמר קם ביה בקלא וליתא איכא מ"ד (מיהא) דהא מילתא אליבא דלישנא בתרא הוא דקסבר טעמא מאי שלא יהיו בנות ישראל פרוצין בעריות ובנדרים אבל ללישנא קמא דסבר טעמא דמילתא משום קלקולא אם אינו מוציא כ"ש דאיכא קלקולא וכיון דקי"ל כלישנא קמא אם כנס מוציא וכ"כ הראב"ד ז"ל ואני אומר כיון א) דאמרו לה בשעת קדושין המוציא אשתו משום ש"ר לא יחזיר (עלמא) [לעולם] לא אפשר למיהוי בה קלקולא והלכך אם כנס אינו מוציא. וכן נראה מדברי הג' אלפס שפסק כלישנא קמא דאמר דמשום קלקולא הוא ופסק דכנס אינו

א) נראה דל"ל כיון דאמרי' ליה בשעת גירושין דהמוציא אשתו וכו'.

מסורת הש"ס

רס"ל מ"ז
מ"ק יח:
[עי' היטב במ"ק יח:]
גיטין מה: כתובות עב:
רב הונא כל"ל. יעב"ץ.
[לקמן נג: קטו. קטז:]
לקמן קיז. גיטין כג:
סנהדרין ט:
שמות כג

הגהות הב"ח

(א) תוס' ד"ה ואכתי וכו' לא גרסי' ורבה בר רב נחמן הוציאה:

[א]גַּזְלָן דִּדְבָרֵיהֶם — כָּשֵׁר לְעֵדוּת אִשָּׁה, גַּזְלָן דְּדִבְרֵי תוֹרָה — פָּסוּל לְעֵדוּת אִשָּׁה. נֵימָא רַב מְנַשֶּׁה דְּאָמַר כְּרַ' יְהוּדָה? אָמַר לָךְ רַב מְנַשֶּׁה: אֲנָא דַּאֲמַרִי אֲפִילּוּ לְרַבָּנַן, וְטַעֲמָא דְּרַבָּנַן הָכָא — כִּדְרָבָא, דְּאָמַר רָבָא: *[ב]אָדָם קָרוֹב אֵצֶל עַצְמוֹ, וְאֵין אָדָם מֵשִׂים עַצְמוֹ רָשָׁע. לֵימָא רַב יוֹסֵף דְּאָמַר כְּרַבִּי יְהוּדָה?! אָמַר לָךְ רַב יוֹסֵף: אֲנָא דַּאֲמַרִי אֲפִי' לְרַבָּנַן, וְשָׁאנֵי עֵדוּת אִשָּׁה דְּאַקִילוּ בָּהּ רַבָּנַן, וְרַב מְנַשֶּׁה דְּאָמַר כְּרַבִּי יְהוּדָה.§ "הֲרַגְתִּיו" כו' "הֲרַגְנוּהוּ" תִּנָּשֵׂא כו'.§ מַאי שְׁנָא הֲרַגְתִּיו וּמַאי שְׁנָא הֲרַגְנוּהוּ? אָמַר רַב יְהוּדָה: בְּאוֹמֵר "אֲנִי הָיִיתִי עִם הוֹרְגָיו". *וְהָתַנְיָא: *אָמְרוּ לוֹ לְרַבִּי יְהוּדָה, מַעֲשֶׂה בְּלִסְטִים אֶחָד שֶׁיָּצָא לֵיהָרֵג בְּמְגִיזַת קַפּוֹטְקְיָא, וְאָמַר לָהֶם "לְכוּ אִמְרוּ לָהּ לְאֵשֶׁת שִׁמְעוֹן בֶּן כֹּהֵן: אֲנִי הֲרַגְתִּי אֶת בַּעְלָהּ בִּכְנִיסָתִי לְלוֹד" וְאָמְרִי לָהּ "בִּכְנִיסָתוֹ לְלוֹד" — וְהִשִּׂיאוּ אֶת אִשְׁתּוֹ. אָמַר לָהֶם: *מִשָּׁם רְאָיָה?! *בְּאוֹמֵר: אֲנִי הָיִיתִי עִם הוֹרְגָיו — וְהָא לִסְטִים קָתָנֵי! שֶׁנִּתְפַּס ע"י לִסְטִיּוּת. וְהָא יָצָא לֵיהָרֵג קָתָנֵי! בֵּי דִּינָא דְּגוֹיִם דְּלָא דָּיְיקֵי וְקָטְלֵי.§ **מתני'** [ג]הֶחָכָם שֶׁאָסַר אֶת הָאִשָּׁה בְּנֶדֶר עַל בַּעְלָהּ — הֲרֵי זֶה לֹא יִשָּׂאֶנָּה, *מֵיאֲנָה אוֹ שֶׁחָלְצָה בְּפָנָיו — יִשָּׂאֶנָּה, מִפְּנֵי שֶׁהוּא ב"ד.§ **גמ'** הָא הִתִּירָהּ יִשָּׂאֶנָּה, בְּמַאי עָסְקִינַן? אִילֵימָא בְּחַד — חַד מִי מָצֵי מַתִּיר? וְהָאָמַר *(רַב אָמַר) רַ' חִיָּיא בַּר אָבִין אָמַר רַב עַמְרָם: [ד]תָּנָא, הַתָּרַת נְדָרִים בִּשְׁלֹשָׁה! וְאֶלָּא בִּתְלָתָא — מִי חֲשִׁידִי? וְהָתְנַן: מֵיאֲנָה אוֹ שֶׁחָלְצָה בְּפָנָיו יִשָּׂאֶנָּה, מִפְּנֵי שֶׁהוּא בֵּית דִּין! לְעוֹלָם בְּחַד, *וְכִדְאָמַר רַב חִסְדָּא אָמַר רַ' יוֹחָנָן: [ה]בְּיָחִיד מוּמְחֶה, [ו]הָכָא נַמִי — בְּיָחִיד מוּמְחֶה.§ "מֵיאֲנָה אוֹ שֶׁחָלְצָה וכו'".§ טַעְמָא דְּב"ד, הָא בִּתְרֵי — לָא. מ"ש מֵהָא *דִּתְנַן: *עֵדִים הַחֲתוּמִים עַל שְׂדֵה מִקָּח [ז]וְעַל גֵּט אִשָּׁה — לֹא חָשׁוּ חֲכָמִים לְדָבָר זֶה! הִיא גּוּפָהּ קָמַשְׁמַע לָן, לְאַפּוֹקֵי מִמ"ד מֵיאוּן *בִּפְנֵי שְׁנַיִם, קָמַשְׁמַע לָן: מֵיאוּן בְּג'. אִיבַּעְיָא לְהוּ: כָּנַס, מַהוּ שֶׁיּוֹצִיא? רַב כָּהֲנָא אָמַר: כָּנַס — מוֹצִיא, רַב אַשִׁי אָמַר: כָּנַס — אֵינוֹ מוֹצִיא. תָּנֵי לְהוּ רַב זוּטִי דְּבֵי רַב פַּפִּי כְּדִבְרֵי הָאוֹמֵר כָּנַס אֵינוֹ מוֹצִיא. אָמְרוּ לֵיהּ רַבָּנַן לְרַב אַשִׁי: *גְּמָרָא אוֹ סְבָרָא? אָמַר לְהוּ: מַתְנִי' הִיא: *הַנִּטְעָן מִשִּׁפְחָה וְנִשְׁתַּחְרְרָה, מִגּוֹיָה וְנִתְגַּיְּירָה, הֲרֵי זֶה לֹא יִכְנוֹס, וְאִם כָּנַס — אֵין מוֹצִיא. אַלְמָא בְּרְנָנָה

[גליון: [א"ז דב"ב ל.] [נדרים לה: ע"ש]]

רש"י

גַּזְלָן דְּדִבְרֵיהֶם. כְּמוֹ מַפְרִיחֵי יוֹנִים וּמְשַׂחֵק בְּקוּבְיָא. דִּתְנַן (ר"ה דף כב.): כָּל הָעֵדוּת שֶׁאֵין הָאִשָּׁה כְּשֵׁרָה לָהּ, אַף הֵן אֵינָם כְּשֵׁרִים. וַעֲלָהּ אָמַר רַב מְנַשֶּׁה: זֹאת אוֹמֶרֶת גַּזְלָן דִּדְבָרֵיהֶם כו': רָבָא פָּלֵיג עֲלֵיהּ דְּרַב יוֹסֵף וְאָמַר: אֲפִי' אָמַר "פְּלוֹנִי רְבָעַנִי לִרְצוֹנִי" — הוּא וְאַחֵר מִצְטָרֵף לְהוֹרְגוֹ לָרוֹבֵעַ. דְּכֵיוָן שֶׁזֶּה מִתְכַּוֵּין לְעֵדוּת — נֶאֱמָן הוּא אֵצֶל חֲבֵרוֹ, וְאֵין נֶאֱמָן עַל עַצְמוֹ מִמַּה שֶּׁאָמַר "לִרְצוֹנִי", דְּאָדָם קָרוֹב אֵצֶל עַצְמוֹ, וְקָרוֹב פָּסוּל לְעֵדוּת בֵּין לְטוֹבָה בֵּין לְרָעָה. הִלְכָּךְ אֵינוֹ נַעֲשֶׂה רָשָׁע בְּעֵדוּת עַצְמוֹ. וְאֵין אָדָם מֵשִׂים. אֶת (א) עֵדוּתוֹ עֵדוּת אֵצֶל עַצְמוֹ לֵיעָשׂוֹת רָשָׁע. וְהָא דְּקַיְ"ל (ב"מ דף ג:) הוֹדָאַת פִּיו כְּמֵאָה עֵדִים דָּמֵי — הנ"מ לְמָמוֹנָא, אֲבָל לִקְנָסָא וּלְעוֹנֶשׁ מַלְקוֹת וְלִיפָּסֵל — לָא. וְשָׁאנֵי עֵדוּת אִשָּׁה דְּאַקִילוּ בָּהּ רַבָּנַן. הִלְכָּךְ אֲפִילּוּ רָשָׁע נֶאֱמָן. וַאֲנָא לֵית לִי דְּרַב מְנַשְּׁיָא דְּאָמַר הָא דְּדִבְרֵי תוֹרָה פָּסוּל. אֶלָּא רַב מְנַשְּׁיָא דְּאָמַר כְּרַבִּי יְהוּדָה. וְהָכִי מִיתּוֹקַם סוּגְיָא: רַב יוֹסֵף מוֹקִים לְרַב מְנַשְּׁיָא כְּרַבִּי יְהוּדָה, וְרַב מְנַשְּׁיָא מוֹקֵי לְרַב יוֹסֵף כְּרַבִּי יְהוּדָה. אֲנִי הָיִיתִי עִם הוֹרְגָיו. אֲבָל לֹא נָגַעְתִּי בּוֹ. ע"י לִסְטִיּוּת. לְפִי שֶׁהָיָה עִמָּהֶן. **מתני'** בְּנֶדֶר. שֶׁנָּדְרָה הֲנָאָה מִבַּעְלָהּ וְלֹא הֵפֵר לָהּ, וּבָאתָה לְחָכָם לְהַתִּיר לָהּ, וְלֹא מָצָא פֶּתַח לַחֲרָטָה. לֹא יִשָּׂאֶנָּה. מִשּׁוּם חֲשָׁד. שֶׁהוּא ב"ד. כְּלוֹמַר, מֵיאוּן אוֹ חֲלִיצָה לֹא עָשָׂה חָכָם זֶה בְּיָחִידִי, דְּקַיְ"ל: חֲלִיצָה וּמֵיאוּן בְּג', וּתְלָתָא לָא חֲשִׁידִי. **גמ'** הָא הִתִּירָהּ. וְאַחַ"כ מֵת בַּעְלָהּ אוֹ גֵּירְשָׁהּ — יִשָּׂאֶנָּה, שֶׁאֵין כָּאן חֲשָׁדָא. לְעוֹלָם בְּחַד. וּדְקַשְׁיָא לָךְ: מִדְּקָתָנֵי שֶׁאָסַר, מִכְּלָל דְּבַר מִישְׁרֵי הוּא — אִין, בְּיָחִיד מוּמְחֶה, וְכִדְרַב חִסְדָּא בִּנְדָרִי' בְּפֶרֶק "נַעֲרָה הַמְאוֹרָסָה". ב"ד. ג'. לֹא חָשׁוּ חֲכָמִים לְדָבָר זֶה. לוֹמַר: לֹא יִקְחוּ שׁוּב שָׂדֶה זוֹ מִן הַלּוֹקֵחַ, וְכֵן הָעֵד שֶׁל גֵּט לֹא יִשָּׂא אֶת הָאִשָּׁה. הִיא גּוּפָהּ. כְּלוֹמַר, ה"ה דִּתְרֵי נַמִי לָא חֲשִׁידִי. וְהָא דְּקָתָנֵי שֶׁהוּא ב"ד — לָאו מִשּׁוּם לְאַפּוֹקֵי מֵחֲשָׁדָא, אֶלָּא לְאַשְׁמוּעִי' דְּאֵין מֵיאוּן בְּפָחוֹת מִג', וּלְאַפּוֹקֵי מִמַּאן דְּאָמַר בְּפֶ' [ב"ש] (לְקַמָּן קז:) מֵיאוּן בִּשְׁנַיִם. כָּנַס מַהוּ שֶׁיּוֹצִיא. אֶחָכָם וְאַמְּבִיאָה גֵּט [א] קָאֵי. גְּמָרָא אוֹ סְבָרָא. הַאי דְּאָמְרַתְּ כָּנַס אֵין מוֹצִיא. בְּרְנָנָה

תוספות

משום דעד השתא איירי בהכלת הורג ורובע, מסיק לה. והרוג נמי לא משום שנאה פסיל ליה התם, אלא אמר רבינו יצחק: דמיפסל משעה שנעשה טרפה, דטרפה פסול להעיד, כדאמרי' בסנהדרין (דף עח. ושם). וה"ר יוסף מאורלינ"ש מפרש דפריך מהרוג ונרבע שיהיו כשהם קרובים להורג ורובע. וקשה לר"י: דאין ה"נ, דנהי דבהרוג ליכא למימר דאין ה"נ שיליל, דהרי חייב הכתוב מכה אביו — מ"מ מנרבע מאי פריך? וכ"ת: בנרבע נמי, דהא דרשינן בסנהדרין (דף נד.) "ערות אביך" ממש, שרבעו, ה"מ לענין כרת, אבל מיתה — לא אשכחן. **רבא** אמר אדם קרוב אצל עצמו. הקשה ר' יצחק בן אברהם: דבפרק שני דכתובות (דף יח: ושם) מסיק *רבא גופיה, גבי הא דתנן התם: אם אין כתב ידן יוצא ממקום אחר הרי אלו נאמנים לומר אנוסים היינו, לא שנו אלא שאמרו אנוסים היינו מחמת נפשות, אבל אמרו מחמת ממון — אין נאמנים. ואמאי אין נאמנים? דהוה לן לפלוגי דיבורא ולומר דאנוסים היו ולא מחמת ממון אלא מחמת נפשות! ואומר ר"י: דלא פלגינן דיבורא כדי לפסול השטר, דמדאורייתא עדים החתומים על השטר נעשה כמי שנחקרה עדותן בב"ד. א"נ, התם בכל ענין שהם אנוסים, אם לא מחמת נפשות — הוו רשעים, הלכך לית לן למיתלי באונס מחמת נפשות, דהוי מיעוטא(א). **ואין** אדם משים עצמו רשע. היינו לפסול את עצמו, אבל נאמן הוא לומר גבי אכילת חלב: מזיד הייתי, כדאמר בכריתות (דף יב. ושם) דאין לנו לכופו להביא חולין לעזרה לפי דבריו. והא דקאמרינן ב"האיש מקדש" (קדושין דף נ. ושם), גבי הבא לי מן החלון או מן הדלוסקמא, דלא עביד איניש דמשוי נפשיה רשיעא לומר מזיד הייתי — לאו משום שלא יהא נאמן לומר מזיד הייתי, דפשיטא דנאמן, אלא כלומר: שאין ברצון אומר בענין דמשוי נפשיה רשיעא. וא"ת: דהשתא משמע דנרבע לרצונו פסול לעדות, ובפרק "זה בורר" (סנהדרין דף כו:) איכא למ"ד דחשוד על העריות כשר לעדות! וי"ל: דהתם בחשוד שהוא פרוץ, ומתייחד עם העריות, ולא ודאי בא על הערוה, כדפי' התם בקונטרס. ומאן דפריך התם עני מרי ארבעים בכתפיה וכשר? היינו משום דמלקין על "לא טובה השמועה". וא"ת: וכי ודאי בא על הערוה אמאי פסול? הא רשע דחמס בעינן, שיהא רע לשמים ולבריות, וזה אין רע לבריות, כגון אוכל נבלות להכעיס, דכשר לרבא בפרק "זה בורר" (שם כ"ז.)! וי"ל: דהוי כמו אוכל נבלות לתאבון, דפסול לכולי עלמא, אע"פ שאין רע לבריות, דכיון דחשוד לעבור בשביל הנאת עצמו — חשוד נמי להעיד שקר בשביל ממון, והכי נמי בא על הערוה. **לימא** רב יוסף דאמר כרבי יהודה. ◦תימה: דהכא לרבי יהודה לית ליה פלגינן דיבורא, ובפרק "החולץ" (לקמן דף מז. ושם) אמרינן: ההוא דאתא לקמיה דרבי יהודה ואמר נתגיירתי ביני לבין עצמי, א"ל: נאמן אתה לפסול את עצמך, ואי אתה יכול לפסול את בניך. אלמא: פלגינן דיבורא! ומיהו, י"ל: דהתם לא מטעם עדות נאמן, (דהא אדם קרוב אצל עצמו, ועוד: דאם נאמן לפסול עצמו — איך יתכן שיהו בניו כשרים?) אלא הא דפסלינן — היינו לאוסרו בבת ישראל, דשויה אנפשיה חתיכה דאיסורא. או אם נגח שור של ישראל את שורו — פטור מטעם הודאת בעל דין. והשיא דר' יהודה גופא קשיא, ושם נפרש בעזרת השם. **באומר** אני הייתי עם הורגיו. אור"י: דאע"ג דאמר הרגנוהו — נעשה כאומר אני הייתי עם הורגיו. וכענין זה מפרש ר"ת ורבינו חננאל בפ' "מי שאחזו" (גיטין עג: ד"ה "אמר") באומר מעת שאני בעולם — נעשה כאומר. **במגיזת** קפוטקיא. יש ספרים דגרסי במזיגת, והוי כמו במגיזת עבראי*, כמו שמלה שלמה. ר"י. **טעמא** דב"ד הא בי תרי לא. ואע"ג דאמרינן בריש "השולח" (גיטין דף לג: ושם) דלתרי נמי בי דינא קרו להו, מ"מ אור"י דדייק שפיר, דמדתלי טעמא בבית דין, ולא קאמר מפני שהיו ב', ש"מ דלא סגי הכא בתרי. ועוד: דומיא דחליצה, דבג', אע"ג דאיכא מאן דמכשר בפרק "מצות חליצה" (לקמן דף קד.) ביחידי — הך תנא לא סבר לה כוותיה, דחד ודאי לא מיקרי ב"ד, ואיכא נמי רננה בחד. **לא** חשו חכמים לדבר זה. ואע"ג דשרי[ב], מ"מ בעל נפש יתרחק, כדתני' עלה ב"אלו טרפות" (חולין דף מד: ושם): דן את הדין, זיכה וחייב, טימא וטיהר, וכן העדים שהעידו — כולם רשאים ליקח, אבל חכמים אמרו: התרחק מן הכיעור ומן הדומה לו. וא"ת: הא אמרינן בסוף "התקבל" (גיטין דף סז. ושם) גבי חיישינן שמא תשכור עדים: דיבורא — אמרי, מעשה — לא עבדי! וי"ל: דכשמעידים שקר חשיב נמי מעשה, כדפי' בקונטרס, כיון דעל פיהם נגמר, ולא קרי דיבורא התם אלא באומר: אמרו, שאומר מן הבעל לסופר ולעדים לכתוב ולחתום, דלא נגמר הדבר על ידיהם. **אמר** להו מתני' היא הנטען כו'. ולנטען על אשת איש לא דמי, דהתם בדין שיוציא, אם הוא אמת אסירא ליה! אבל הכא, שאסר את האשה בנדר אפילו אסרה שלא כדין, כיון שגירשה בעלה — שריא לחכם מדאורייתא ג). אגירושין

עין משפט נר מצוה

צ א מיי' פי"ב מהלכות גירושין הלכה יז סמג עשין ג טוש"ע אה"ע סימן יז סעיף ג:

צא ב מיי' פי"ב מהל' עדות הל' ב ופי"ג מהל' גירושין הלכה י סמג לאוין ריד טוש"ע ח"מ סימן לד סעיף כו:

צב ג מיי' פ"י מהלכות גירושין הלכה יד טוש"ע אה"ע סימן יב סעיף ב:

צג ד ה מיי' פ"ו מהל' שבועות הלכה א ה טוש"ע י"ד סימן רכח סעיף א:

ע"ש שהוא רמי בר חמא

צד ו מיי' שם טוש"ע אה"ע סי' יב סע"ב:

צה ז שם סעיף א:

[עי' רש"א]

תוספות ישנים

א) ועוי"ל דשאני הכא שיש לנו לומר פלגינן דבורא דכשאמר פלוני רבעני מעתה נהרג הרובע בין לאונסו בין לרצונו ולא צריך תו לומר לאונסו או לרצונו וא"כ כי אמר אחרי כן לרצונו פלגינן דבורא דמלתא דרבעו חשיבא בפני עצמה היא והוו כתרי דבורי אבל התם כי אמרו אנוסים היינו אין הדבר כלום עד שיפרשו אם מחמת ממון אם מחמת נפשות לכן לא שייך לחלק הדבור שאין זה בלא זה כלום: **באומר** אני הייתי אם הורגיו. יש גורסים בכ"ף פי' כ"ש דמהני כשאומר הרגנוהו כמו אם היה אומר אני הייתי אם הורגיו והוי כדאמרי' בגיטין כאומר מעת שאני בעולם וניחא שאינו מגיה המשנה: **ב)** ולהך פי' נ"ל דכי בעי לעיל כנס מהו שיוציא לא קאי אלא אחכם שאסר וכו' דאי קאי אכולהו כדפ"ה לעיל מאי שנא דלא מפקינן הכא ברננה ובנטען מפקינן אף ברננה. דגם הכא אם הרננה אמת שמשקר מהאי דאמר מת הרגתיו אסורה לו מן התורה שעדיין אשת איש היא אלא ודאי לא קא בעי אלא אחכם שאסר האשה בנדר על בעלה:

תוספות חד מקמאי

מוציא: **אמר** רב מנשה גזלן דדבריהם כשר לעדות הא דדברי תורה פסול לעדות אשה: **הא** דתנן החכם שאסר את האשה בנדר לא ישאנה וקי"ל ביחיד מומחה ולפום הכי אם התירה ישאנה אבל בתלתא אפילו אסרו ישאנה משום שהם ב"ד ובבכורות פרק כל פסולי המוקדשים דכי אמרי' הפרת נדרים בשלשה הדיוטות במקום שאין שם מומחה ורבי יהודה ס"ל התם ואחד מהם חכם ולית הלכתא כוותיה ומקשינן התם מכלל דהנך כל דהו ומשנינן דמסברי להו וסברי: גרסינן בשלהי נדרים ההיא איתתא דכל יומא דמשמש מקדמא ומשיא לגברא יומא חד אייתא ליה מיא לממשא א"ל הא מילתא לא הות האידנא א"ל א"כ חד מהני נכרים דהוו הכא אמר ר"נ עיניה נתנה באחר וכו':

מסורת הש"ס

כתובות יח: סנהדרין ט: כה.

[תוספתא פ"ד]

[שבת כט: וש"נ]

[תוספתא פ"ד ע"ש]

לקמן קח: בכורות לו.

[בכורות לו: ליתא וע"ש היטב]

נדרים עח: ע"ש ב"ב קכ: קכא. בכורות לו.

גיטין סז.

[לקמן קח: קז:]

[לעיל כד: ע"ש]

רש"ל מ"ז

תרגום על בעיי העבריים במדבר לג פ' מ"ד

הגהות הב"ח

(א) רש"י ד"ה ואין אדם משים את עצמו רשע אין עדותו:

הגהות הגר"א [א] רש"י ד"ה כנס מהו שיוציא אחכם ואמביא גט קאי. נ"ב וכ"כ הרמב"ם וש"ע. אבל רשב"א כתב דלא קאי רק על מתני' זו על החכם וכ"ה ברא"ש להדיא וכ"מ בתוספתא ועט"ז (ועמ"ש רבינו באה"ע סימן יב ס"ק ב'): [ב] תוס' ד"ה לא כו' מ"מ ב"נ יתרחק. נ"ב אבל לטעם הירושלמי ר"ל דאף לכתחלה מותר ואין כאן הרחק דהל"כ ל"ל שאין שנים כו' אפילו בשביל שניהם כמו במקח ועמש"ש (ע"ש בס"ק ה'):

גליון הש"ס **גמ'** והאמר (רב) אר"ח בר אבין. נ"ל [רבא] סדר הדורות בהקדמה אות ר: **תוס'** ד"ה לימא רב יוסף דאמר כר"י תימה דהכא וכו'. עיין תשובת רשד"ם חלק י"ד סימן רנד:

ברננה לא מפקינן, ה"נ ברננה לא מפקינן.§ **מתני'** [א]וכולם שהיו להם נשים ומתו – מותרות לינשא להם. [ב]וכולן שנישאו לאחרים, ונתגרשו או שנתאלמנו – מותרות לינשא להם. [ג]וכולן מותרות לבניהם או לאחיהם.§ **גמ'** מתו – אין, נתגרשו – לא. אמר ליה רב הלל לרב אשי: והתניא אפי' נתגרשו! לא קשיא; הא – דהואי קטטה, הא – דלא הואי קטטה. ואיבעית אימא: הא והא דלא הואי קטטה, ולא קשיא; [ד]הא – דארגיל הוא, הא – דארגילה היא.§ "וכולן שנישאו" וכו'.§ קס"ד מיתה אמיתה, וגירושין אגירושין, נימא מתניתין דלא כרבי, דאי כרבי – *האמר: בתרי זימני הויא חזקה! לא, מיתה אגירושין וגירושין אמיתה.§ "וכולן מותרות לבניהם או לאחיהם".§ מאי שנא מהא *דתנן: *הנטען מן האשה – אסור באמה ובבתה ובאחותה! נשי לגבי נשי – שכיחן דאזלן, גברי לגבי – גברי לא שכיחן. אי נמי: נשי דלא אסרן שכיבתן אהדדי – לא קפדי אהדדי, גברי דאסרן שכיבתן אהדדי – קפדי אהדדי. אי הכי אביו נמי! לא מיבעיא קאמר, לא מיבעי' אביו – *דבזיז בניה מיניה, אבל בנו דלא בזיז אביו מיניה – אימא לא, קמ"ל.§

הדרן עלך כיצד אשת אחיו

ארבעה *[ה]אחין, שנים מהם נשואים שתי אחיות, ומתו הנשואים את האחיות – הרי אלו חולצות ולא מתייבמות. ואם קדמו וכנסו – יוציאו. *רבי אליעזר אומר, ב"ש אומרים: *יקיימו, וב"ה אומרי': [ו]יוציאו. *[ז]היתה אחת מהן אסור' על האחד איסור ערוה – אסור בה ומותר באחות', והשני אסור בשתיהן. *[ח]איסור מצוה ואיסור קדושה – חולצת ולא מתייבמת. [ט]היתה אחת מהן אסורה על זה איסור ערוה, והשניה אסורה על זה איסור ערוה – האסורה לזה מותרת לזה, והאסורה לזה מותרת לזה. וזו היא שאמרו: *אחותה כשהיא יבמתה – או חולצת או מתייבמת.§ **גמ'** ש"מ: [י]יש זיקה. דאי *אין זיקה, מכדי הני מתרי בתי קאתיין, האי לייבם חדא והאי לייבם חדא! לעולם אימא לך: אין זיקה, ומשום דקסבר *אסור לבטל מצות יבמין; דלמא אדמייבם חד – מיית אידך, וקמבטל מצות יבמין. אי הכי, תלתא נמי! – לא מיבעיא קאמרינן; לא מיבעיא תלתא, דודאי בטלה מצות יבמין, אבל ד', למיתה לא חיישינן – קמ"ל. אי הכי, חמשה

רש"י

ברננה. מפני רינון ולעז בני אדם לא אמרינן ליה "הוצא". ולא דמי לנטען על אשת איש, דהתם הואיל והוציאה בעלה מפני זה, והלך זה ונשאה – מכוער הדבר. **מתני' וכולם.** החכם, והמביא גט, והמעיד באשה להשיאה, דתנן בהן לא יכנוס. שהיו להם נשים. בשעת מעשה, ומתו לאחר זמן – מותרות אלו לינשא להם. דהשתא ליכא חשד, שהרי בשעה שהעיד בה העד או שאסרה חכם היתה אשתו קיימת, ולא לישא את זו נתכוין. **וכולן.** הנשים הללו. **שנישאו.** לאחרים, כשאסרה חכם או כשהעיד עד במיתת בעלה, ומתו הבעלים השניים. **מותרות לינשא.** לחכם, ולעד, ולמביא גט. **וכולן.** הנשים האלו, מותרות לבניהם או לאחיהם של אלו המתירים אותן, ואין אסורות אלא להן לבדן. **גמ' נתגרשו לא.** דע"י שנתן את עיניו בזו שהתיר – גירש את אשתו. **הא.** דקתני אפי' נתגרשו – כגון דהוי להו קטטה מקמי הכי, דעדיין לא נתן דעתו על זאת: ה"ג: ואיבעית אימא אידי ואידי דלא הוו להו קטטה. **הא.** דקתני נתגרשו לא – בדארגיל הוא קטטה, שהוא התחיל להקניט את אשתו. **והא.** דקתני אפי' נתגרשו – בדארגילה היא קטטה, שהיא הקניטתו תחלה. **קס"ד מיתה אמיתה.** הא דקתני וכולן שנישאו לאחרים ומתו – קאי נמי ארישא, דקתני: מת, הרגתיו, הרגנוהו – לא ישא את אשתו. וקתני דאם נישאת לאחר על פיו, ומת השני הזה – מותרת לינשא לעד זה. ואע"פ שמתו ב' בעליה – תנשא לשלישי, ולא אמרינן הוחזקה זו קטלנית, שהנושאה מת. וגירושין דקתני נתגרשה – קאי אגירושין דלעיל, המביא גט כו'. ואשמעינן דאם נשאת לאחר באותו הגט וגירשה השני הזה – מותרת לינשא למביא גיטה הראשון. **בתרי זימני הויא חזקה.** לקמן בפ' "הבא על יבמתו" (דף סד:): נישאת לראשון ומת, לשני ומת, לשלישי לא תינשא – דברי רבי. ומתני' דלא כרבי. דאי רבי, נהי דחשד ליכא – מיהו לכל העולם אסורה, שהוחזקה להתאלמן או להתגרש. **מיתה.** דקתני הכא שנישאו לאחרים ומתו מותרות – לאו אכולהו דלעיל קאי, אלא אגירושין ואמביא גט, או חכם שאסר את האשה. **וגירושין.** דקתני – אמ"מת" "הרגתיו" "הרגנוהו". ומש"ה כשנתגרשה משני זה – מותרת לשלישי, שעדיין לא הוחזקה בחדא ריעותא תרי זימני. **אסור באמה ובתה ואחותה.** כדמפרש טעמא לקמן: שמא לאחר שישא את אמה או את בתה תזנה זו עמו. ובזנות קמא לא הוה מיתסר באמה ובקרובותיה, דקי"ל (לקמן דף צז.): נושאין על האנוסה ועל המפותה, דלא נאסרו קרובות אשה על האיש אא"כ קדשה לראשונה, דאישות כתיב בה, וקיחה – *"כי יקח איש את אשה ואת אמה" (ויקרא כ). אבל משנשא את אמה ואת בתה עומדת – הנטענת הראשונה עליו בכרת, דתנן (שם): האונס והמפתה על הנשואה – חייב. וה"נ אמאי מותרת לבניהם? ליחוש שמא עגת וזמה היה ביניהם, לישא את בנו של זה, ויהא זה רגיל אצלה. **נשי לא אסרו.** (א) שכיבת זנות הקרובה את אשתו גמורה עליו, הילכך לא קפדא אשתו ושתקה, וחיישינן. אבל גברי דאסרי שכיבתן אהדדי, דאשה המזנה אסורה לבעלה – קפיד בעל, ורחיק האי מיניה. א"ה. דבגברי לא חיישינן לזנות שיזנה קרובו עם אשתו, לאביו של מתיר, שאמאי נמי תשתרי? ואמאי תני לבניהן ולאחיהן, ולא תני נמי לאביהן? **לא מיבעיא לאביו.** של מתיר, דמותרת, ולא חיישינן שמא יזנה מתיר זה עמה. **דבזיז מיניה.** *בוש הוא מאביו, ואימתו עליו.

ארבעה אחין. **ולא מתייבמות.** מפרש טעמא בגמ' משום זיקה. דכיון דתרווייהו זקוקן להאי ולהאי, קמא דמייבם פגע באחות זקוקתו, דהויא כאשתו. **איסור ערוה.** כגון חמותו ואם חמותו. **ומותר באחותה.** דלאו אחות זקוקה היא, דערוה לאו קמיה רמיא לייבומי. **איסור מצוה.** רמיא קמיה מדאורייתא, הלכך אסור באחותה, דאחות זקוקה היא. **אחותה** (ב) **כשהיא יבמתה.** אחותה של ערוה כשהיא יבמתה, אשת אחי בעלה, כשנופלת עמה לייבום. **או חולצת או מתייבמת.** דלאו אחות זקוקתו היא, דערוה לא רמיא קמיה. **גמ' יש זיקה.** כלומר: חומרת זיקה לשוויי אחות זקוקתו כאחות אשתו. ובמס' נדרים (דף עד.) פליגי בה, איכא למ"ד: זקוקתו כאשתו להפרת נדריה ולאסור קרובות, ואיכא למ"ד: אין זיקה. ובפרקין דלעיל (דף יז:) איפליגו בה רב הונא ורב יהודה. **מתרי בתי.** משני אחין נפלו. **מיית אידך.** ונפלה קמיה דהאי, ונפקא משום אחות אשתו בלא חליצה וייבום. הלכך אמרי' להו חלוצו, דאי נמי מיית אידך את לבתר חליצה דחד – הדר האי חולץ וחלץ לה. **תלתא נמי.** מאי שנא דנקט ד' אחין? אי אמרת בשלמא יש זיקה – אשמעי' רבותא, דאע"ג דתרי אחי נינהו, ולא אלימא זיקתו דקמא דמייבם, דמצינו למימר ההיא רמיא קמיה ואחותה קמי' אחיו – ואפ"ה אסור, וכ"ש שלשה אחין, ב' מהם נשואים שתי אחיות, ומתו, ונפלו שתיהן לפני זה – שתיהן אסורות, דתרווייהו עליה רמיא, וזיקתו חמורה. וכי נסיב – הוי פגע באחות זקוקתו. אלא אי משום ביטול מצות יבמין – אפי' תלתא נמי, ומתו השנים הנשואים שתי אחיות – שתיהן חולצות, דאי מייבם חדא – נפקא אידך בולא כלום.

תוספות

אגירושין. אגב מיתה נקט גירושין – דאפי' נתגרשה כמה פעמים שריא לינשא. **אי הכי אביו נמי.** לא מצי לשנויי דנקט בנו לרבותא, אע"ג דאסור באנוסת אביו לר' יהודה* – דהתינח בניהן, אבל אחיהן אמאי נקט אי לאו לדקדק אבל לאביו – לא!

הדרן עלך כיצד אשת אחיו

חולצות ולא מתייבמות. פירשתי לעיל (דף יח. ד"ה "דלמא" וכו') ועוד נפרש בגמ' גבי פלוגתא דרב ור' יוחנן. **אי הכי תלתא נמי.** אי אמרת בשלמא יש זיקה ניחא דנקט ארבעה לאשמועינן דאפי' בתרי יש זיקה – אלא אי אין זיקה, וטעמא משום ביטול מצות יבמין – לישמעינן תלתא, דהוי רבותא טפי דאסור לבטל, אע"ג דחדא מינייהו לא חזיא לייבומי. וכל שכן בד', דשתיהן ראויות להתייבם זה אחת וזה אחת, דאסור. ועוד אר"י: דמצי לפרש, דס"ד השתא דחיישינן למיתה דתרי כמו למיתה דחד, ולהכי פריך: א"ה תלתא נמי, כיון דלא אתא לאשמועינן חידוש של חשש מיתה, מדלא נקט חמשה, דהוי רבותא טפי, אלא לאשמעינן דאסור לבטל – זה יכול להשמיענו אפילו בתלתא.

למיתה

[…]

באסורא וראיה לדבר פסק זה ממה שפירש הרב אלפס [בס"פ ר"ג] גבי פלוגתא דרבי ורבנן כשקדשה לשם יבמות דרבנן כרב ור' כשמואל וקי"ל כרבנן ורב אשי נמי אמר התם דכו"ע חליצה פסולה אינה פוטרת היינו כרב אלמא הלכתא כרב אע"ג דכתב הרב אלפס דכל הני שינויי לא סמכינן עלייהו והרב אלפס כתב דברי רב ודברי שמואל ולא פסק הלכתא כחד מנייהו ואולי סמך על הכלל שבידינו דהלכתא כרב באיסורא: ובמאי

תוספות ישנים

ש"מ יש זיקה. וא"ת א"כ לחלוץ לחדא ולייבם לחדא וי"ל גזרה דלמא מייבם והדר חליץ וכי מייבם פגע באחות זקוקתו. ולא נהירא דכיון דקאמר ש"מ יש זיקה א"כ אין לגזור דלמא מייבם ברישא דטעם של זיקה פשוט הוא ולא יטעו כמו שאפרש לקמן בע"ה. וי"ל דטעמא דכיון שנאסרה עליו שעה אחת שוב לא יבא לה היתר עולמית וא"ת לרב דלא סבר כן לקמן מאי איכא למימר. וי"ל דמ"מ מוקים לה להך משנה כר' אליעזר דאמר כיון שנאסרה פעם אחת שוב אין לה היתר אף באיסורא דרבנן כי הכא דאין האיסור רק משום אחות זקוקתו. והא דדייקינן לקמן מדסיפא ר' אליעזר רישא לאו ר' אליעזר ולרבי יוחנן אבל רב לא סבר כן א"כ לא יסבור האי דיוקא.

תוספות חד מקמאי

ארבעה אחין שנים מהם נשואים ב' אחיות ומתו הנשואין לאחיות הרי אלו חולצות ולא מתייבמות דוקא בדליכא צרות אבל בדאיכא צרות כיון דחליצת צרות מעולה מאחרות חליץ לצרות ולא לאחיות דקי"ל כשמואל דאמר ב' יבמות הבאות מב' בתים חליץ (ליבמות) [לאחיות] לא נפטרו הצרות לצרות נפטרו אחיו' דלא אלימא זיקה לשוויה צרה כערוה ומי' אי חליץ לאחיות אהני למפטר נפשה. אבל לכתחלה אמרינן ליה דיחלוץ לצרות שהיא חליצה מעולה מן האחיות. אבל היכא דליכא צרות לא אפשר דלא למחלץ לאחיות. והוי יודע דאליבא דרב דאמר חליצה פסולה צריכה לחזור על האחין שתי האחיות כל אחת מהן צריכה חליצה משני האחין. ולפי דעתי הלכתא כרב בהא אע"ג דפליג עליה שמואל דקי"ל הלכתא כרב

עין משפט נר מצוה

[לעיל ד. לקמן נג.]

צו א מיי' פ"י מהל' גירושין הלכה כח סמג עשין נ טוש"ע אה"ע סימן יב סעיף ז:

צז ב מיי' שם טוש"ע שם סעיף ג:

צח ג ד מיי' שם והל' עז טוש"ע שם סעיף ז:

א ה ו מיי' פ"ו מהלכו' יבום הלכה א טוש"ע אה"ע סי' קעה סעי' ג:

ב ז מיי' שם טוש"ע אה"ע שם סעיף ז:

ג ח ט מיימן שם הל' ב טוש"ע אה"ע שם סעיף ה:

ד י מיי' שם הלכה א טוש"ע אה"ע שם סעיף ג:

מסורת הש"ס

לקמן סד: ב"מ קו: [ערכין כז. כתובות מג:]

[נ"ל דתניא]

לקמן כו. [תוספתא פ"ד]

[גי' הערוך בזיז]

לעיל יח. כג: כז: עדיות פ"ה מ"ה

[ע' תוס' לקמן כח. ד"ה רבי אליעזר]

[לקמן כח.]

[לעיל כ. לקמן כח: סנהדרין נג.]

לעיל כ.

[לעיל יח.]

[שם]

נ"ל ואיש אשר יקח

נ"ל יקיימו

הגהות הב"ח

(א) רש"י ד"ה נשי לא אסרו שכיבת זנות הקרובה לא אסרו אשתו עליו גמורה: (ב) רש"י ד"ה אחותה של ערוה כשהיא וכו' ותיבות אחותה נמחק:

גליון הש"ס

רש"י ד"ה דבזיז מיניה בוש הוא כו'. עי' נדה טו ע"ב תוד"ה אפילו ילדה:

חֲמִשָּׁה — נַמִי לְמִיתָה דִּתְרֵי לָא חָיְישִׁינַן. אֲמַר *רָבָא בַּר רַב הוּנָא אֲמַר רַב: שָׁלֹשׁ אֲחָיוֹת יְבָמוֹת שֶׁנָּפְלוּ לִפְנֵי שְׁנֵי אַחִין יְבָמִין, זֶה חוֹלֵץ לְאַחַת, וְזֶה חוֹלֵץ לְאַחַת, וְאֶמְצָעִית צְרִיכָה חֲלִיצָה מִשְּׁנֵיהֶם. אֲמַר לֵיהּ רַבָּה: מִדְּקָאָמְרַתְּ אֶמְצָעִית צְרִיכָה חֲלִיצָה מִשְּׁנֵיהֶם — קָסָבְרַתְּ יֵשׁ זִיקָה, וְהָוְיָא לָהּ חֲלִיצָה פְּסוּלָה, *וַחֲלִיצָה פְּסוּלָה צָרִיךְ לַחֲזוֹר עַל כָּל הָאַחִין. אִי הָכִי, קַמַּיְיתָא נַמִי! — אִי דִּנְפוּל בְּבַת אַחַת — הָכִי נַמִי, לָא צְרִיכָא דִּנְפוּל בְּזוֹ אַחַר זוֹ נָפְלָה חֲדָא — חָלַץ לָהּ רְאוּבֵן, נָפְלָה אִידָךְ חָלַץ לָהּ שִׁמְעוֹן נָפְלָה אִידָךְ חָלַץ לָהּ הַאי מַפְקַע זִיקָתוֹ, חָלַץ לָהּ הַאי מַפְקַע זִיקָתוֹ. *וְהָאֲמַר רַב: אֵין זִיקָה! לְדִבְרֵי הָאוֹמֵר יֵשׁ זִיקָה קָאֲמַר. וּשְׁמוּאֵל אָמַר: אֶחָד חוֹלֵץ לְכוּלָּן. — מִכְּדִי שָׁמְעִינַן לֵיהּ לִשְׁמוּאֵל דְּאָמַר: חֲלִיצָה מְעַלְיָא בָּעֵינַן, דְּאָמַר שְׁמוּאֵל: חָלַץ

רש"י

חֲמִשָּׁה נַמִי. שְׁנַיִם נְשׂוּאִים שְׁתֵּי אֲחָיוֹת, וּמֵתוּ הַשְּׁנַיִם וְנִשְׁאֲרוּ הַשְּׁלֹשָׁה, דִּלְמָא אַדְּמְיַיבֵּם חַד מַיְיתוּ לְהוּ תְּרֵי, וּבָטְלָה מִצְוַת יְבָמִין. לִפְנֵי שְׁנֵי אַחִין יְבָמִין. כְּלוֹמַר, לִפְנֵי שְׁנֵי אֲחֵי בַּעֲלֵיהֶן שֶׁהֵן יְבָמֵיהֶן. אֶמְצָעִית. כְּלוֹמַר, שְׁלִישִׁית, וְלָאו דַּוְקָא נָקַט. צְרִיכָה חֲלִיצָה מִשְּׁנֵיהֶן. כִּדְמְפָרֵשׁ וְאָזֵיל: לָא גָּרְסִינַן מִדְּקָאָמְרַתְּ זֶה חוֹלֵץ כו', אֶלָּא ה"ג. מִדְּקָאָמְרַתְּ צְרִיכָה חֲלִיצָה מִשְּׁנֵיהֶם קָסָבְרַתְּ יֵשׁ זִיקָה וְהָוְיָא לָהּ חֲלִיצָה פְּסוּלָה וַחֲלִיצָה פְּסוּלָה צְרִיכָה לַחֲזוֹר כו'. כְּלוֹמַר, מִדְּקָאָמְרַתְּ צְרִיכָה חֲלִיצָה מִשְּׁנֵיהֶם, קָסָבְרַתְּ: אַלִּימָא מִצְוַת זִיקַת יְבָמִין לְמִירְמֵי אַתַּרְוַויְיהוּ. וְהָךְ חֲלִיצָה עַל כָּרְחָךְ חֲלִיצָה פְּסוּלָה הִיא, כְּלוֹמַר גְּרוּעָה, שֶׁאִם רָצָה לְיַיבֵּם — אֵינוֹ יָכוֹל, דַּאֲחוֹת חֲלוּצָתוֹ הִיא, הִילְכָּךְ לָאו מְעַלְיְיתָא הִיא וּצְרִיכָה לַחֲזוֹר עַל כּוּלָּן, דְּלָא מִיפַּקְעָא זִיקָה דְּתַרְוַויְיהוּ בַּחֲלִיצָה דַּחֲדָא, מִשּׁוּם דַּאֲלִימָא זִיקָה וְרַמְיָא אַתַּרְוַויְיהוּ. קַמַּיְיתָא. שְׁתַּיִם רִאשׁוֹנוֹת נַמִי לִיבָּעוּ חֲלִיצָה מִשְּׁנֵיהֶם, דַּחֲלִיצָתָן נַמִי לָאו מְעַלְיְיתָא הִיא, דְּאִי בָּעֵי לְיַיבּוּמֵי — לָא מָצֵי, הוֹאִיל וְיֵשׁ זִיקָה. בְּבַת אַחַת. כְּלוֹמַר, אִם בָּאוּ לַחֲלוֹץ כְּאַחַת, שֶׁלֹּא הִסְפִּיקָה הָרִאשׁוֹנָה לַחֲלוֹץ עַד שֶׁנָּפְלָה גַּם הַשְּׁנִיָּה וְהַשְּׁלִישִׁית — הָכִי נַמִי דְּכוּלָּן צְרִיכוֹת לַחֲזוֹר אַחַר כָּל הָאַחִין. הָכָא דִּנְפְלוּ זוֹ אַחַר זוֹ. נְפִילָתָהּ שֶׁל זוֹ אַחַר חֲלִיצָתָהּ שֶׁל זוֹ. נָפְלָה לָהּ חֲדָא חָלַץ לָהּ רְאוּבֵן. וַחֲלִיצָה כְּשֵׁרָה הָיְתָה, שֶׁאִם רָצָה — יָכוֹל לְיַיבֵּם. נָפְלָה אִידָךְ חָלַץ לָהּ שִׁמְעוֹן. וְגַם זוֹ כְּשֵׁרָה, שֶׁאִם רָצָה — מְיַיבֵּם. וְאֵין כָּאן אֲחוֹת זְקוּקָה, שֶׁכְּבָר חָלְצָה אֲחוֹתָהּ קוֹדֶם נְפִילַת זוֹ. נָפְלָה שְׁלִישִׁית, אִי בָּעֵי לְיַיבּוּמֵי — לָא מָצֵי, דַּאֲחוֹת חֲלוּצַת שְׁנֵיהֶם הִיא. וּבְלֹא כְּלוּם נַמִי לָא נָפְקָא, דַּאֲחוֹת חֲלוּצָה אֵינָהּ אֶלָּא מִדִּבְרֵי סוֹפְרִים, לְקַמָּן בְּ"הַחוֹלֵץ" (דף מ:). הִלְכָּךְ, חָלַץ הַאי חֲלִיצָה כָּל דְּהוּ, וְלָאו מְעַלְיְיתָא הִיא, שֶׁאִם חָפֵץ — לֹא יְיַבֵּם. וּמִיהוּ, חֲלִיצָתוֹ וְזִיקָתוֹ שָׁווֹת שְׁתֵּיהֶן לִגְרוֹעַ, וּפָקְעָה זִיקָתוֹ בַּחֲלִיצָתוֹ. חָלַץ הַאי מַפְקַע זִיקָה. וְהָא אָמַר רַב אֵין זִיקָה. בְּפֶרֶק "כֵּיצַד" (לעיל דף יז:): א"ר הוּנָא אָמַר רַב: שׁוֹמֶרֶת יָבָם שֶׁמֵּתָה — מוּתָּר בְּאִמָּהּ.

תוספות

למיתה דתרי לא חיישינן. תימה: דבפ"ק דיומא (דף ב.), גבי הא דאמר ר' יהודה אף אשה אחרת מתקינין לו שמא תמות אשתו, ופרכי לה רבנן: א"כ אין לדבר סוף, ומאי קושיא? הוא רבנן חיישי הכא למיתה דחד ולא דתרי! ואר"י, דהכי פרכי ליה: כיון דחיישת למיתה דזמן מועט, אע"ג דלא שכיחא – תחוש נמי למיתה דתרי אע"ג דלא שכיח, וא"כ אין לדבר סוף?! ומשני התם (דף יג.) דלר' יהודה מיתה דחדא שכיחא, פירוש אפי' לזמן מועט, דתרי – לא שכיחא. והא דקאמרי התם רבנן מיתה לא שכיחא – לאו משום שאין לדבר סוף. דהא דקאמר אין לדבר סוף – היינו משום דלא שכיח, כדפריש', כי מיתה דחד [דשכיח] יש לדבר סוף, דתרי ודאי לא שכיחי.

מדקאמרת אמצעית צריכה חליצה משניהם קא סברת יש זיקה וחליצה פסולה וכו'. ואית ספרים דגרסי: מדקאמר זה חולץ לאחת וזה חולץ לאחת קא סברת יש זיקה. ופי' בקונטרס דלא גרסי' ליה. ונראה דלא גרים ליה בקונטרס משום דלמ"ד אין זיקה – נמי, זה חולץ לאחת וזה חולץ לאחת, דאי אפשר לייבם אחת משום ביטול מצות יבמין. וליכא למימר נמי דאחד יחלוץ לשתיהן, דלמ"ד אין זיקה – נמי, אין חליצה פסולה של ראובן, שכבר חלץ לאחת, מפקעת זיקת שמעון החשובה. דהא לקמן קאמר: בשלמא צרה דרחל לא תפטר – משום דחליצת רחל חליצה פסולה היא. אלמא, אפי' למ"ד אין זיקה – אין חליצת רחל פוטרת זיקת צרתה החשובה. דהא אוקי דשמואל אליבא דמ"ד אין זיקה קאמר, וה"ה דה"נ לא תפטר חליצת ראובן השניה מאח השני, דהא אכתי לא מסיק אדעתיה לחלק בין מיפטר נפשה בין מיפטר צרה. ולר"י נראה דשפיר גרסי' ליה, דלפי האמת, למ"ד אין זיקה – חליצה גרועה פוטרת החשובה הימנה, דאמרי' בהדיא בפרק "ר"ג" (לקמן דף נא. ושם) דלמ"ד אין זיקה, חלץ לבעלת הגט – נפטרה צרתה, אע"ג דבעלת הגט חליצתה פסולה טפי משל צרה, שהרי חשובה כחלוצה אצלו למיסר בקרובותיה. וע"כ, שמואל דאמר חלץ לאחיות – לא נפטרו צרות, לבעלת הגט לא נפטרה צרה, סבר דיש זיקה. וסוגיא דבסמוך אינה לפי האמת, אלא ה"פ: בשלמא צרה דרחל לא תפטר, כלומר: אפי' אם תאמר דלמ"ד אין זיקה נמי חליצה פסולה צריכה לחזור, והשתא ניחא דצרת רחל לא תפטר, מ"מ צרה דלאה תפטר, דחליצה כשרה היא. תדע דאותה סוגיא אינה לפי האמת, דהא פריך בתר הכי: ולצרה דרחל מי מיפטרא והתנן כו', אלמא בעי למימר דלמ"ד אין זיקה לא מיפטרא רחל בחליצת צרה, אע"ג דלא אסירא צרה אלא מכחה, וכ"ש אם היו שוות. וא"כ איך מדקדק, אפילו לפי גירסת הקונט', דיש זיקה, מדקאמר אמצעית צריכה חליצה משניהם? אלא, על אותה סוגיא אין לסמוך, כדפרישי', דלא קאי הכי. וכי מפרש דשמואל אליבא דמ"ד אין זיקה קאמר, כמו שאפרש, דלדידיה חלץ לאחיות ולבעלת הגט נפטרו צרות, וגרסינן שפיר מדקאמר זה חולץ לאחת כו' קסבר יש זיקה. ומדקאמר אמצעית צריכה חליצה משניהם – קא סבר דחליצה פסולה צריכה לחזור, ואע"ג דתרוייהו יכול לדקדק מסיפא, מ"מ מה שיכול לדקדק מרישא – מדקדק. **וחליצה** פסולה צריך לחזור וכו'. לא [א] כמו שפירש בקונטרס דכל היכא שאינו יכול לייבם חשיבה חליצה פסולה, דהא אמר בפ"ק (לעיל דף יא:) גבי מחזיר גרושתו: או היא או צרתה חולצת, ולא חשיבה חליצת גרושה חליצה פסולה, אע"ג דאין יכול לייבמה. ולקמן נמי קאמר אלא צרה דלאה תפטר, דחליצתה כשרה. אלמא, חשיבא לה חליצה כשרה אע"ג דאסירא ליבמה משום ביטול מצות יבמין. דנהי דלא מבטל מצות יבמין מצרת רחל, דאע"ג דכשייבם לאה יהיה אסור בצרת רחל, כמו שאסור בצרת קרובת חלוצתו – מ"מ, חליצה מיהא בעיא דאורייתא, דאינה צרת אחות אשה לאחר שיבם לאה, [כיון שכבר] לא היתה צרת [אחות אשה] משמת בעלה. וכשיחלוץ לצרת רחל – לא מיתסרא לאה, דמותר אדם בקרובת צרת חלוצתו, מ"מ איכא ביטול מצות יבמין, אם יבא לייבם לאה – דחיישינן שמא תמות צרת רחל, וקא מבטל מרחל מצות יבמין, וליכא למימר דיש לצרת רחל צרות הרבה דליכא למיחש למיתה דכולהו, אי נמי כשחלץ ללאה קודם נפילת רחל – א"כ בחנם דחק לתרץ מאי לא נפטרו צרות אצרות רחל, ומאי צרות – צרות דעלמא דה"ל לאוקומי טפי בנפול בבת אחת, ואין כי אם צרה אחת ללאה וצרה אחת לרחל, דאז אסורה לייבם לאה משום ביטול מצות יבמין[ב]. אלא נראה לר"י דלא חשיבא חליצה פסולה אלא אחות זקוקתו למ"ד יש זיקה, או אחות חלוצתו לכ"ע, ובעלת הגט ובעלת מאמר, דבכולהו קלשא זיקה. דאחות זקוקתו דמיא לאחות אשתו דאין בה זיקה, ואחות חלוצתו כאחות גרושתו, ובעלת הגט דמיא לחלוצה, ובעלת מאמר לכנוסה דאין בה זיקה. *וכן סוטה, דרבנן דקרי ליה בירושלמי חליצה פסולה, גבי הא דא"ר שמעון ביאתה כו' דדמיא נמי לסוטה דאורייתא, דאין בה זיקה, דטומאה כתיב בה כעריות. אבל מחזיר גרושתו, ואסור לבטל מצות יבמין – לא נגרעה בהם הזיקה, ולהכי חשיבי חליצה כשרה. **דנפול** בזה אחר זה נפלה חדא חליץ לה ראובן כו'. הקשה ה"ר אברהם מבורגויי"ל: אמאי נקט שלש אחיות? דמידוש זה יכול להשמיענו אפי' בב' אחיות היכא דנפול בבת אחת, דכל אחד ואחד חולץ לשתיהן משום דיש זיקה, וחליצה פסולה צריכה לחזור על כל האחין! ותי': דהתם משכחת לה שמתייבמת אחת, דכשחלץ לשניה הויא ראשונה יבמה שהותרה ונאסרה וחזרה והותרה, דתחזור להיתירה הראשון ומתייבמת לאח השני. אע"ג דגם השני צריך לחלוץ לשניה משום דחליצה פסולה היא – מ"מ אינה אסורה לו הראשונה משום אחות חלוצתו, דכיון דחליצה זו לא עשה אלא משום היזור, כדמוכח לקמן (דף כז:) דפריך רבי יוסי בר' חנינא לר' יוחנן דאמר: מתה השניה מותר בראשונה, ממתני' דקתני חולצות שתיהן ולא מתייבמות. ואמאי? ליקו חד מינייהו ולחלוץ לשניה כו'. והשיב לו ר' יוחנן: אחיות איני יודע מי שנאן. ואמאי לא שני ליה דחולצות ולא מתייבמות משום דשניה צריכה חליצה משניהם, ולכך אסורה לשניהם הראשונה? אלא ודאי לשני שריא, כיון דלא חלץ לה אלא משום היזור. ואין ראיה, דאיכא למימר דר' יוחנן לא בעי לשנויי הכי משום דסבר כשמואל דחליצה פסולה אין צריך לחזור, ולפי סברתו היה יכול לומר דבשתי אחיות שריא אפי' שניה לשני, *אם שחלצו לראשונה. דרב לא מפליג לקמן בין ראשונה לשניה, דאמר לקמן: אפי' מתה ראשונה מותר בשניה. ואין נראה לר"י, דלעיל פ"ב (ד' יח.) משמע דלכ"ע, בין למ"ד יש זיקה בין למ"ד אין זיקה – שתיהן חולצות, אי משום ביטול מצות יבמין או משום שנאסרה עליו שעה אחת, כדפי' לעיל. ודוקא ר' יוחנן הוא דאמר אחיות איני יודע מי שנאן, ומתייבמת הראשונה: **נפלה** אידך חליץ לה כו'. והא דקרי לה אמצעית אע"פ שהיא אחרונה – משום דהאחרות כל אחת לא חלצה אלא מן האחד, וזו חולצת משניהם. **לדברי** האומר יש זיקה קאמר. ולא מסתברא ליה למימר דרב סבר יש זיקה, וההיא דשומרת יבם – לדברי האומרים אין זיקה קאמר. משום דהתם קמ"ל תרתי: דאין זיקה, ומחיים אסור משום ביטול מצות יבמין, משום הכי סבירא ליה דההיא אליבא דנפשיה:

מאי

תוספות חד מקמאי

ובמאי דאמר שמואל חלץ לאחיות לא נפטרו צרות לצרות נפטרו אחיות פסק הרב כשמואל ואליבא דרב אשי דאע"ג דלא אלימא זיקה לשווי צרה כערוה והוצרך הרב ז"ל למפסק הלכתא כשמואל ואליבא דרב אשי משום דסוגייא קמא בשמעתתא משוי לחליצה צרות כאחיות ופליגא אדרב אשי לפיכך הוצרך ליה למיפסק כשמואל ולעולם בחליצה פסולה דפליגי רב ושמואל הלכה כרב דחליצה פסולה צריכה לחזור על כל האחין. הלכך הא דתנן הכא חולצות האחיות ולא מתייבמות כל אחת ואחת צריכה חליצה משניהם והרב ז"ל ודאי הו"ל (להצריך) [לפרש] כדברי רב שאמר ג' אחיות יבמות וכו' כדאוקימנא בגמ' דנפול בזה אחר זה אבל בבת א' כל אחת צריכה חליצה משניהם אלא שקצר הרב ז"ל דבריו כמנהגו ואי איכא א) מאן דס"ל דמשום דס"ל לרב אלפס הלכתא כשמואל לכך קצר בדברי הרב. ומנ"ל לרב ז"ל דהלכתא כשמואל והא קי"ל כרב באיסורי. ואי משום דתניא כוותיה דרב אשי חלץ לאחיות לא נפטרו צרות לצרות (לא) נפטרו אחיות לא פליג רב אדשמואל בהא מלתא וכל המיקל בו צריך להביא ראיה לדבריו ואין רוח חכמים נוחה הימנו. והוי יודע דמאי דאמרי' בגמ' גבי האי מתני' דילמא אדמייבם חד מיית אידך וקא בטלה מצות יבמין כלומר דאזלא אחותה בלא חליצה דוקא אליבא דמ"ד אין זיקה אבל למ"ד יש זיקה וקי"ל כותיה ב) דלמא אדמייבם חד מיית אידך לא מפטרא אחותה בלא חליצה דתנן בפ' החולץ שומרת יבם שקדש אחיו את אחותה משום ר' יהודה בן בתירה אמרו אומרים לו המתן עד שיעשה אחיך הגדול מעשה מתה היבמה יכנוס את אשתו מת היבם צריכה חליצה ואמר נמי בר"פ כיצד אמר רב הונא אמר רב שומרת יבם שמתה מותר באמה אלמא קסבר אין זיקה ואסיקנא לאחר מיתה אין מחיים לא דאסור לבטל מצות יבמין ופרש"י ז"ל דאזלא יבמה בלא חליצה ג) כדתנן מת יבם מוציא את אשתו בגט ואת אשת אחיו בחליצה וכיון דקי"ל יש זיקה אפי' בתרי אדמייבם חד מיית אידך לא מפטרה אחותה בלא חליצה אמר רבא בר רב הונא אמר רב שלשה אחיות יבמות שנפלו לשני אחים יבמין זה חולץ לאחת וזה חולץ לאחת והאמצעית צריכה חליצה משניהם פירוש אמצעית שלישי' א"ל רבא מדקאמרת אמצעית צריכה חליצה משניהם קסבר יש זיקה ולפיכך חליצה פסולה צריכה לחזור על כל האחין אי הכי קמייתא נמי (לא) צריך אי נפיל בב"א הכי [נמי לא צריכא] דנפיל בזה אח"ז נפל חדא [חליץ] ראובן נפל אידך חליץ שמעון נפל אידך חליץ האי מיפקע זיקתו פירוש נפיל בבת א' שבאו לפני ב"ד לאחר שמתו ג' בעליהן ששלשתן צריכות חליצה אעפ"י שמתו בעליהן בזה אחר זה השתא מיהת כשבאו לפני ב"ד חליצה פסולה היא שכל אחד אחות וכל א' וא' צריכה חליצה מן האחין אבל בנפול בזה אח"ז שכל א' שמת בעלה באה לב"ד לחלוץ ועדיין לא מתו האחין האחרים וחלץ לה ראובן חליצה כשירה הוא ד) כיון שמת האחד קודם שמת השלישי וחליצה כשרה היא כשמת השלישי חליצה פסולה היא בין למ"ד יש זיקה בין למ"ד אין זיקה דאחות חלוצתו ומיהו למ"ד אין זיקה אין צריכה לחזור על כל האחין. למ"ד יש זיקה לא אלימא חליצה פסולה למפקע זיקה וכ"ת מכדי רב אתא לאשמועינן חליצה פסולה צריכה לחזור על כל האחין למה לי לאשמועינן בנפול בזה אחר זה ובאמצעית (אתא) לאשמועינן בנפול בבת אחת וכל אחת צריכה חליצה משניהם. אין הכי נמי אלא רבותא אשמועינן לא מיבעיא א דנפיל בבת אחת דזיקה אלימא היא וצריכה לחזור על האחין אלא אפילו חלץ זה לאחת וזה חלץ לאחת דקלשא ליה זיקה משום איסור [אחות] חלוצתו אפ"ה צריכה לחזור על האחין (ליבומי) [אי נמי] לא מיבעיא דנפול בבת א' דכיון דיש זיקה הו"ל חליצה פסולה דאורייתא דהיא זקוקתו ואלא אפי' בזה אח"ז שאין החליצה פסולה משום זיקה אלא משום [אחות] חלוצתו שאינה פסולה אלא מדרבנן [מ"מ] צריכה לחזור על האחין. וחליצה פסולה דאשמועי' משום דאינה ראויה להתייבם. ושמואל אמר א' חולץ לכולן. מכדי שמעינן ליה לשמואל דאמר חליצה מעולה בעיא דאמר (ש"מ) חלץ לאחיות לא נפטרו צרות היכי דקיימא חליצה דשמעון חליצה כשרה חליץ לה ראובן חליצה פסולה ומשני מאי אחד חולץ לכולן אאמצעית דהא לא מיפטר לה. והא כולן קאמר כיון דרובא גביה קרי להו כולן ואב"א כי קאמר שמואל חליצה מעולה בעיא למפטר צרה אבל אנפשה פטרה. כתבתי דברי שמואל אע"פ דהלכה כרב לאשמועינן דבמלתא דחלץ לאחיות לא פליג עליה דרב ואיכא למ"ד אליבא דרב כיון דחליצה פסולה צריכה לחזור על כל האחין הכי נמי צריכה לחזור על כל הצרות וכי דהלכה כשמואל דאמר [חלץ] לצרות נפטרו אחיות שמעינן דלית הלכתא כרב דהא בהא תליא. ולאו מילתא היא דגרסינן בפרק רבן גמליאל נתן לה גט לזו וגט לזו חולץ לראשונה וכו' לימא תהוי תיובתא לשמואל דאמר חלץ לבעלת הגט לא נפטרה צרה והדר פריך לרב דאמר חליצה פסולה צריך לחזור על כל האחין מסיפא דקתני וכן אתה אומר בשני יבמין ויבמה אחת ואילו מרישא לא פריך ליה אלמא לאו מילתא מיתליין אהדדי נינהו וללישנא קמא חלץ לאחיות אף האחיות לא נפטרו וללישנא בתרא חלץ לאחיות נפטרו אחיות ופסק הרב כלישנא בתרא: איבעיא להו בעלת הגט ובעלת מאמר איזה מהן קודמת לחליצה ואסיקנא דכי הדדי

ניתנו

א) עי' בר"א כאן. ב) נראה דל"ל אפילו אדמייבם חד מיית אידך וקא בטלה וכו'. ג) נראה דחסר כאן וצ"ל והא דתנן לאם מת יבם מוציא את אשתו בגט ואת אשת אחיו בחליצה וכו'. ד) נ"ל וכן בשמת השני.

נ"ל רבה. יעב"ץ

לקמן נח: נג.

לעיל יז: ע"ש

הגהות הגר"א

[א] תוס' ד"ה וחליצה. כמו שפירש בקונטרס. נ"ב וכ"ד הרמב"ם: [ב] שם אלא נראה לר"י דלא כו'. נ"ב וכן עיקר ועי' כ ע"ב וכ"ה בתוספתא פ"ו (ועמ"ש רבינו בא"ה סי' ק"ע ס"ק ט"ו וס"ק מ"ה):

גליון הש"ס

תוס' ד"ה וחליצה פסולה וכו' וכן סוטה דרבנן דקרי ליה בירושלמי וכו'. ע' לעיל דף יא ע"א תד"ה רש"א:

ס"א אחר

אחָלַץ לָאֲחָיוֹת לֹא נִפְטְרוּ צָרוֹת. הֵיכָא דְּקַיְימָא חֲלִיצָה דְּשִׁמְעוֹן חֲלִיצָה כְּשֵׁרָה, חָלֵיץ לָהּ רְאוּבֵן חֲלִיצָה פְּסוּלָה. מַאי "אֶחָד חוֹלֵץ לְכוּלָּן" נַמִּי דְּקָאָמַר – אַאֶמְצָעִית. וְהָא כּוּלָּן קָאָמַר! – כֵּיוָן דְּרוּבָּה גַּבֵּיהּ קָרֵי לֵיהּ "כּוּלָּן". וְאִיבָּעֵית אֵימָא: כִּי קָאָמַר שְׁמוּאֵל חֲלִיצָה מַעַלְיָא בָּעֵינַן – בה"מ לְמִיפְטַר צָרָתָהּ, אֲבָל מִפְטְרָא נַפְשָׁהּ – פָּטְרָה. גּוּפָא, אָמַר שְׁמוּאֵל: חָלַץ לָאֲחָיוֹת – לֹא נִפְטְרוּ צָרוֹת, לַצָּרוֹת – נִפְטְרוּ אֲחָיוֹת. *חָלַץ לְבַעֲלַת הַגֵּט – לֹא נִפְטְרָה צָרָה, לַצָּרָה – נִפְטְרָה בַּעֲלַת הַגֵּט. *חָלַץ לְבַעֲלַת הַמַּאֲמָר – לֹא נִפְטְרָה צָרָה, לַצָּרָה – נִפְטְרָה בַּעֲלַת מַאֲמָר. מַאי שְׁנָא לָאֲחָיוֹת דְּלָא נִפְטְרוּ צָרוֹת – דְּהָוְיָא (א) לוֹ אֲחוֹת אִשָּׁה בְּזִיקָה, – חָלַץ לַצָּרוֹת נַמִּי לָא לִיפַּטְרוּ אֲחָיוֹת, דְּהָוְיָא לְהוּ צָרוֹת אֲחוֹת אִשָּׁה בְּזִיקָה! – קָסָבַר שְׁמוּאֵל: אֵין זִיקָה. *וְהָא אָמַר שְׁמוּאֵל: יֵשׁ זִיקָה! – לְדִבְרֵי הָאוֹמֵר אֵין זִיקָה קָאָמַר. אִי הָכִי, חָלַץ לָאֲחָיוֹת אַמַּאי לֹא נִפְטְרוּ צָרוֹת? בִּשְׁלָמָא צָרָה דְּרָחֵל לָא תִּיפָּטֵר – דְּכֵיוָן דְּחָלַץ לָהּ לְלֵאָה וַהֲדַר חָלַץ לְרָחֵל – הָוְיָא לָהּ חֲלִיצָה דְּרָחֵל חֲלִיצָה פְּסוּלָה. אֶלָּא צָרָה דְּלֵאָה תִּיפָּטֵר! – מַאי "לֹא נִפְטְרוּ צָרוֹת" נַמִּי דְּקָאָמַר – אַצָּרָה דְּרָחֵל, – וְהָא "צָרוֹת" קָאָמַר! – צָרוֹת דְּעָלְמָא. – אִי הָכִי, חָלַץ "לַצָּרוֹת נִפְטְרוּ אֲחָיוֹת", – וְאַצָּרַת רָחֵל מִי מִיפַּטְרָא? וְהָא תְּנַן: *גאָסוּר אָדָם בְּצָרַת קְרוֹבַת חֲלוּצָתוֹ! – שְׁמוּאֵל נַמִּי, הִתְחִיל וְלֹא הִתְחִיל קָאָמַר: הִתְחִיל בָּאֲחָיוֹת – לֹא יִגְמוֹר בַּצָּרוֹת, דִּתְנַן: אָסוּר אָדָם בְּצָרַת קְרוֹבַת חֲלוּצָתוֹ, הִתְחִיל בַּצָּרוֹת – יִגְמוֹר אַף בָּאֲחָיוֹת, דִּתְנַן: *מוּתָּר אָדָם בִּקְרוֹבַת צָרַת חֲלוּצָתוֹ. רַב אַשִׁי אָמַר: לְעוֹלָם כִּדְקָאָמְרַתְּ, דוּמִשּׁוּם דְּלָא אַלִּימָא זִיקָה לְשַׁוּוֹיֵי לַצָּרָה כְּעֶרְוָה. תַּנְיָא כְּוָותֵיהּ דְּרַב אַשִׁי: חָלַץ לָאֲחָיוֹת – לֹא נִפְטְרוּ צָרוֹת, הָא לַצָּרוֹת נִפְטְרוּ אֲחָיוֹת – מַאי טַעְמָא, לָאו מִשּׁוּם דְּקָסָבַר יֵשׁ זִיקָה, וְלָא אַלִּימָא זִיקָה לְשַׁוּוֹיֵיהּ לַצָּרָה כְּעֶרְוָה?! א"ר אַבָּא בַּר מֶמֶל: הָא מַנִּי – ב"ש הִיא, דִּתְנַן: *בֵּית שַׁמַּאי מַתִּירִין הַצָּרוֹת לָאַחִין. – אִי הָכִי, יַבּוּמֵי נַמִּי תִּתְיַיבֵּם! – כְּרַבִּי יוֹחָנָן בֶּן נוּרִי, דְּאָמַר: *בּוֹאוּ וְנַתְקִין לָהֶם לַצָּרוֹת שֶׁיְּהוּ חוֹלְצוֹת וְלֹא מִתְיַיבְּמוֹת. – וְהָאָמַר מָר *לֹא הִסְפִּיקוּ לִגְמוֹר אֶת הַדָּבָר עַד שֶׁנִּטְרְפָה הַשָּׁעָה! אָמַר רַב נַחְמָן בַּר יִצְחָק: אַחֲרָיו חָזְרוּ וְתִקְּנוּ.§ אִיבַּעְיָא לְהוּ:

בַּעֲלַת

רש"י

חָלַץ לָאֲחָיוֹת. שְׁתֵּי אֲחָיוֹת שֶׁנָּפְלוּ לְפָנָיו מִשְּׁנֵי אַחִים, וְכָל אַחַת צָרָתָהּ עִמָּהּ, וְחָלַץ לָאֲחָיוֹת – לֹא נִפְטְרוּ צָרוֹתֵיהֶן, הוֹאִיל וְאִי בָּעֵי לְיַיבּוּמֵי – לָא מָצֵי. אֶלָּא יַחֲלוֹץ לַצָּרוֹת וְיִפָּטְרוּ אֲחָיוֹת. וְאַע"ג דְּצָרוֹת נַמִי, אִי הֲוָה בָּעֵי לָא הֲוָה מְיַיבֵּם – מִיהוּ, קַל אִיסּוּרָם מִשֶּׁל אֲחָיוֹת. הִלְכָּךְ, אַף חֲלִיצָתָם מְשׁוּבַּחוֹת מִשֶּׁל אֲחָיוֹת, וְהָכִי מְפָרֵשׁ לְקַמָּן. **הֵיכָא דְּקַיְימָא** חֲלִיצָה דְּשִׁמְעוֹן חֲלִיצָה כְּשֵׁרָה. לַחֲלוֹץ לַשְּׁנִיָּה, שֶׁהוּא לֹא חָלַץ לָרִאשׁוֹנָה. חָלֵיץ לָהּ רְאוּבֵן חֲלִיצָה **פְּסוּלָה**. בִּתְמִיָּה, רְאוּבֵן שֶׁחָלַץ לָרִאשׁוֹנָה וְהָוְיָא זוֹ אֲחוֹת חֲלוּצָתוֹ, וְלָא חֲלִיצָה מְעַלְּיָא הִיא כְּדְשִׁמְעוֹן, דִּזִיקָה גְּרִידָתָא הִיא. **אַאֶמְצָעִית**. כְּלוֹמַר, הַשְּׁלִישִׁית, לְאַחַר שֶׁחָלַץ שִׁמְעוֹן לַשְּׁנִיָּה שֶׁהִיא עַל שְׁנֵיהֶן אֲחוֹת חֲלוּצָה, וּשְׁנֵיהֶן שָׁוִין בָּהּ. (לקמן נג.) **וְקָסָבַר**: חֲלִיצָה פְּסוּלָה אֵין צְרִיכָה לַחֲזוֹר עַל כָּל הָאַחִין. **כֵּיוָן דְּרוּבָּה גַּבֵּיהּ**. שֶׁהַחוֹלֵץ לַשְּׁלִישִׁית חָלַץ לַב'. (לקמן נג.) **לְמִיפְטַר צָרָה**. כִּדְקָאָמְרִי': לֹא נִפְטְרוּ צָרוֹת. **אֲבָל מִיפַּטְרָא נַפְשָׁהּ פָּטְרָה**. בַּחֲלִיצָה דְּכָל דְּהוּ. הִלְכָּךְ אֶחָד חוֹלֵץ לַג', הֵיכָא דְּלֵיכָּא צָרוֹת בַּהֲדַיְיהוּ. **לְבַעֲלַת הַגֵּט**. ב' יְבָמוֹת מֵאָח אֶחָד, וְנָתַן יָבָם גֵּט לְאַחַת מֵהֶן – שׁוּב אֵין חֲלִיצָתָהּ הוֹגֶנֶת כָּל כָּךְ, דִּקְלִישָׁא זִיקָתָהּ, וְאִם חָלַץ לָהּ – לֹא נִפְטְרָה צָרָהּ. (לעיל יח:) **חָלֵיץ לְבַעֲלַת מַאֲמָר**. עָשָׂה מַאֲמָר בְּאַחַת מִנְּשֵׁי אָחִיו הַמֵּת, וְאַחַ"כ חָלַץ לָהּ – לֹא נִפְטְרָה צָרָהּ. שֶׁחֲלִיצָה זוֹ אֵינָהּ פּוֹטֶרֶת לְגַמְרֵי, שֶׁעֲדַיִין צְרִיכָה גֵּט לְמַאֲמָרוֹ, כִּדְתְנַן בְּפֶרֶק ר"ג (לקמן דף נ.): עָשָׂה מַאֲמָר וְחָלַץ – צְרִיכָה הֵימֶנּוּ גֵּט. וְאַע"ג דְּיָהֵיב לָהּ גֵּט אַחַר דְּחָלַץ לָהּ הוּא דְּמַהַנְיָא, אֲבָל צָרָתָהּ צְרִיכָה חֲלִיצָה, אֲבָל חָלַץ לַצָּרָה נִפְטְרָה בַּעֲלַת מַאֲמָר מֵחֲלִיצָה וְאֵינָהּ צְרִיכָה אֶלָּא גֵּט לְמַאֲמָרוֹ. (לקמן מ:) **דְּהָוְיָא אֲחוֹת אִשָּׁה בְּזִיקָה**. וְאִי הֲוָה בָּעֵי לְיַיבּוּמֵי לָא מָצֵי, וּלְהָכִי גְּרִיעָה חֲלִיצָתָהּ. **לַצָּרוֹת נַמִּי**. הָא צָרַת אֲחוֹת זְקוּקָה הִיא, וַאֲסִירָא לְיַיבּוּמֵי, דְּצָרָה בִּמְקוֹם עֶרְוָה קָיְימָא. (שם) **וְהָאָמַר שְׁמוּאֵל כו'**. בְּפ"ב. **אִי הָכִי**. דְּאֵין זִיקָה, חָלַץ לָאֲחָיוֹת שֶׁחֲלִיצָה הוֹגֶנֶת הִיא. **בִּשְׁלָמָא צָרָה דְּרָחֵל**. דְּחָלְצָה בָּאַחֲרוֹנָה – לֹא תִּפָּטֵר, דַּחֲלִיצָה דְּרָחֵל גְּרוּעָה הֲוַאי, דְּאִי בָּעֵי לְיַיבּוּמֵי – לָא מָצֵי, דַּאֲחוֹת חֲלוּצָתוֹ הִיא. (לעיל יג. עדיות פ"ד מ"ח) **אֶלָּא צָרָה דְּלֵאָה תִּיפָּטֵר**. [לעיל ט.] דַּחֲלִיצַת לֵאָה כְּשֵׁרָה הִיא, דְּאִי הֲוָה בָּעֵי מָצֵי לְיַיבּוּמֵי. [לעיל יג: יד:] **צָרוֹת דְּעָלְמָא**. כְּלוֹמַר, כָּל הֵיכָא דְּמִיתְרְמֵי כה"ג – לֹא נִפְטְרוּ צָרוֹת שֶׁל אַחֲרוֹנָה. [לעיל טו.] **אִי הָכִי**. דְּצָרוֹת דְּקָאָמַר שְׁמוּאֵל – בְּצָרָה דְּרָחֵל שֶׁחָלְצָה בָּאַחֲרוֹנָה קָאָמַר. **חָלַץ לַצָּרוֹת נִפְטְרוּ אֲחָיוֹת**. בִּתְמִיָּה, דְּכִי חָלַץ לְצָרַת אֲחוֹת הַחֲלוּצָה נִפְטְרָה אֲחוֹת הַחֲלוּצָה. **אַצָּרָה דְּרָחֵל מִי מִיפַּטְרָא**. אַחֲלִיצָה דְּצָרָה מִי מִיפַּטְרָה רָחֵל? **וְהָא תְּנַן**. בְּ"הַחוֹלֵץ". **אָסוּר אָדָם בְּצָרַת קְרוֹבַת חֲלוּצָתוֹ**. וַאֲפִילּוּ לֹא הָיְתָה צָרָתָהּ מֵאָחִיו אֶלָּא מִנָּכְרִי. וְטַעְמָא הָתָם מְפָרֵשׁ. וְהָכָא נַמִּי, אִי הֲוָה בָּעֵי לְיַיבּוּמֵי – לָא מָצֵי. **הִתְחִיל בָּאֲחָיוֹת**. שֶׁחָלַץ לְלֵאָה, לֹא יִגְמוֹר בַּצָּרוֹת, לֹא פָּטְרָה חֲלִיצַת צָרָה דְּרָחֵל אֶת רָחֵל. דִּתְנַן **אָסוּר אָדָם כו'**. וְכ"ש דְּלֹא יִגְמוֹר בָּאֲחָיוֹת, דַּחֲלִיצַת רָחֵל לֹא מִיפַּטְרָה צָרָהּ, דְּלָאו חֲלִיצָה מַעַלְיְיתָא הִיא, דַּאֲחוֹת חֲלוּצָתוֹ הִיא, אֶלָּא שְׁתֵּיהֶן צְרִיכוֹת חֲלִיצָה. **הִתְחִיל בַּצָּרוֹת**. שֶׁחָלַץ לְצָרַת לֵאָה. **יִגְמוֹר אַף בָּאֲחָיוֹת**. אִם רָצָה לַחֲלוֹץ לְרָחֵל – נִפְטְרָה צָרָתָהּ. וְאַע"ג דְּרָחֵל קְרוֹבַת לֵאָה שֶׁהִיא צָרַת חֲלוּצָתוֹ – לָא גְּרִיעַ בְּהָכִי, דִּתְנַן: מוּתָּר אָדָם בִּקְרוֹבַת צָרַת חֲלוּצָתוֹ. וְה"נ, כֵּיוָן דְּאֵין זִיקָה, אִי הֲוָה בָּעֵי לְיַיבּוּמֵי לְרָחֵל מְיַיבֵּם, וְכָל שֶׁכֵּן גָּמַר בְּצָרַת רָחֵל וְלֹא בְּרָחֵל, *דִּשְׁכִיחָא מִילְּתָא טְפֵי. **לְעוֹלָם**. כִּדְקָאָמַר שְׁמוּאֵל בְּרֵישָׁא, חָלַץ לָאֲחָיוֹת לֹא נִפְטְרוּ צָרוֹת, מִשּׁוּם דְּיֵשׁ זִיקָה, וַחֲלִיצַת הָאֲחָיוֹת גְּרוּעָה, וַאֲפִילּוּ צָרַת לֵאָה לֹא מִיפַּטְרָה – חָלַץ לַצָּרוֹת נִפְטְרוּ אֲחָיוֹת, דַּחֲלִיצָתָן מְשׁוּבַּחוֹת מִשֶּׁל אֲחָיוֹת. וּדְקַשְׁיָא לָךְ: הָוְיָא צָרַת אֲחוֹת אִשָּׁה בְּזִיקָה, וְהָוְיָא כִּי אֲחוֹת זְקוּקָה גּוּפָהּ – לָא הִיא, מִשּׁוּם דְּלָא אַלִּימָא זִיקָה לְשַׁוּוּיֵי לַצָּרָה כִּי עֶרְוָה, וְלֹא גָּזְרוּ חֲכָמִים אֶלָּא בַּאֲחוֹת זְקוּקָה. **הַצָּרוֹת לָאַחִין**. וַאֲפִילּוּ צָרַת אֲחוֹת אִשָּׁה שָׁרֵי לְיַיבּוּמֵי, וְכ"ש צָרַת אֲחוֹת זְקוּקָה. **אִי הָכִי**. אַמַּאי תָּנֵי חָלַץ? יַבּוּמֵי נַמִּי תִּתְיַיבֵּם הַצָּרָה!

בַּעֲלַת

תוספות

מאי אחד חולץ לכולן דקאמר **אאמצעית**. תימה: דלקמן מסקינן דשמואל התחיל ולא התחיל קאמר. והתחיל באחיות לא יגמור בצרות, ולא מיפטרא רחל בחליצת צרתה, וכ"ש היכא דשניהן שוין. דבעינן חליצה מתרוייהו. דלהאי שינויא לא מפלגינן בין מיפטר נפשה למיפטר צרה! ואר"י: דההוא דמפרש לקמן דשמואל התחיל ולא התחיל קאמר – סבר כשינויא דבסמוך, דמפלגינן בין מיפטר נפשה למיפטר צרה. ושינויא דהכא דאחד חולץ לכולן אאמצעית – סבר כרב אשי, דאמר לקמן: לא אלימא זיקה לשווי צרה כערוה, וחליצת צרות הויא חליצה כשרה. ולהכי חלץ לאחיות – לא נפטרו צרות. אבל הכא, דשתיהן שוין – אחד חולץ לכולן. **אלא** צרה דלאה תיפטר. דהא חליצה כשרה היא. פי' בקונט': דאי בעי מייבם לה. וא"א לומר כן, דאסירא ליה משום ביטול מצות יבמין. ומ"מ לא חשיב בהכי חליצה פסולה, כדפרישית לעיל.

א"ה חלץ לצרות נפטרו אחיות **ואצרת רחל מי מיפטרא**. פירוש: כיון דאוקמה חלץ לאחיות לא נפטרו צרות דוקא מרחל, ומשום שחלץ ללאה, בענין זה נמי שחלץ ללאה חלץ לצרות נמי לא נפטרו אחיות.

שמואל התחיל ולא התחיל קאמר. השתא לפי המסקנא לית ליה להא דשמואל לדברי האומר אין זיקה [קאמר], דלפי האמת למ"ד אין זיקה חלץ לאחיות ולבעלת גט – נפטרו צרות(ב) אחיות. אלא שמואל אליבא דנפשיה, דאית ליה זיקה, קאמר. והא דלא קאמר "אלא" – לפי שלא הוזכר שם אמורא תחלה. ומיירי כשחלץ ללאה קודם נפילת רחל וצרתה, ולהכי התחיל בצרת לאה – יגמור אף ברחל, דכשנפלה רחל כבר נפטרה לאה בחליצת צרתה, וחליצת רחל חליצה כשרה היא, דלא הויא אלא קרובת צרת חלוצתו. וקצת דוחק הוא, דה"ל לפרש בהדיא דאיירי בנפול זה אחר זה, כיון דעד השתא הוה איירי בנפול בבת אחת. ועוד אמר ר"י: דמצינו לפרש דאיירי אפי' נפול בבת אחת, כדס"ד עד השתא, ואפ"ה – התחיל בצרת לאה יגמור ברחל. ואע"ג דחליצת הצרה הויא חליצה פסולה דהויא לה צרת אחות אשה בזיקה ולא מיפטרה לאה בחליצתה מ"מ חשיב חליצת רחל חליצה כשרה ואפי' אי חלץ ללאה ברישא קודם רחל כיון דלא נשתייר בלאה אלא זיקה מועטת שכבר חלץ לצרתה – חליצה חשובה טפי. ולהכי לא חשיב רחל אחות חלוצתו, כענין שפירש ה"ר אברהם לעיל. ואע"ג דקודם שחלץ לצרת לאה כבר נאסרה רחל, ושמואל סבר ב"החולץ" (לקמן ד' מ:): כיון שנאסרה עליו שעה אחת נאסרה עולמית, מכל מקום הוי חליצת רחל חליצה כשרה, כיון דעכשיו אינה אחות זקוקתו, ואינה אסורה אלא משום שנאסרה עליו כבר.

תניא כוותיה דרב אשי. אברייתא לא שייך למימר דהתחיל ולא התחיל קאמר – דא"כ הוה ליה לפרושי הכי בהדיא. אבל שמואל, דאיירי נמי בבעלת הגט ובעלת מאמר – נקט לשון השוה בכולן. **א"ה** יבומי נמי תתייבם. וא"ת: אין ה"נ, ומ"מ נקט חליצה לאשמועינן דחליצה פסולה אינה פוטרת, כמו שמואל ללישנא דהתחיל ולא התחיל ה"מ למינקט יבום! וי"ל: דשמואל לא נקט יבום משום דמתני' היא: מותר אדם בקרובת כו', אבל ברייתא ה"ל למנקט יבום, דעדיפא טפי. אי נמי לשמעינן תרוייהו.

אחריו חזרו ותקנו. דחוק לומר כן, משום דלא מסתבר ליה למימר דלא אלימא זיקה לשווי צרה כערוה.

בעלת

עין משפט נר מצוה

ה א מיי' פ"ז מהלכות יבום הל' ט סמג עשין נא טוש"ע אה"ע סימן קע סעיף יז יח וסימן קעד סעיף א:

ו ב מיי' שם פ"ה הל' יב סמג שם טוש"ע שם סעיף יט ועי' בטור ובב"י:

ז ג מיי' שם פ"ה הל' טו ופ"ו הלכה כ טוש"ע שם סי' קסב סעיף ה:

ח ד מיי' שם פ"ה הל' יב טוש"ע שם סי' קע סעיף יח:

תוספות ישנים

לדברי האומר אין זיקה וא"ת אמאי חלץ לבעלת הגט לא נפטרה צרה הא אמרינן לקמן פרק ר"ג דלמ"ד אין זיקה חלץ לבעלת הגט נפטרה צרה. וי"ל דהך דלקמן מיירי לפי מסקנא דהכא דסבר שמואל יש זיקה ולכך לא נפטרה צרה. עוד פי' הר"מ דאף כי נמי אמרינן הכא דשמואל איירי אף לדברי האומר אין זיקה היינו דווקא רישא דמלתא דחלץ לאחיות אבל האי דקאמר חלץ לבעלת הגט לא נפטרה צרה מיירי [דוקא] למ"ד יש זיקה. והאי דנקט מלתא כתנאי. י"ל דרישא אשמעינן חדושא דאע"ג דאין זיקה מ"מ חלץ לאחיות לא נפטרו צרות אע"ג דשאר חליצה פסולה פטרה למ"ד אין זיקה פסול דאחיות חמיר טפי וסיפא אשמעינן דלמ"ד יש זיקה חלץ לבעלת הגט לא נפטרה צרה אע"ג דשאר חליצה פסולה פטרה היינו דווקא למ"ד אין זיקה אבל למ"ד יש זיקה לא פטרה:

הגהות הב"ח

(א) גמ' דהויא לה אחות אשה: (ב) תוס' ד"ה שמואל וכו' נפטרו צרות אלא שמואל כצ"ל ותיבת אחיות נמחק:

דשכיחא

ט א מיי' פ"ה מהל' יבום הל' ז טוש"ע אה"ע סימן קע סעיף יז:
י ב ג מיי' פ"ז מהלכות יבום הל' ד סמג עשין נא נב טוש"ע שם סימן קעה סעיף א:

בַּעֲלַת הַגֵּט וּבַעֲלַת מַאֲמָר — אֵיזוֹ מֵהֶן קוֹדֶמֶת? בַּעֲלַת הַגֵּט עֲדִיפָא — (א) מִשּׁוּם דְּאַתְחֵיל בָּהּ *בַּחֲלִיצָה, אוֹ דִּלְמָא בַּעֲלַת מַאֲמָר עֲדִיפָא מִשּׁוּם דִּקְרוֹבָה לְבִיאָה? אֲמַר רַב אַשִׁי, ת"ש: *וּמוֹדֶה ר"ג שֶׁיֵּשׁ גֵּט אַחַר מַאֲמָר, וּמַאֲמָר אַחַר גֵּט. אִי גֵּט עָדִיף — לָא לִיהֲנֵי מַאֲמָר אַבַּתְרֵיהּ, וְאִי מַאֲמָר עָדִיף — לָא לִיהֲנֵי גֵּט אַבַּתְרֵיהּ! אֶלָּא לָאו ש"מ כִּי [א]הֲדָדֵי נִינְהוּ, ש"מ. אָמַר רַב *הוּנָא אָמַר רַב: ב' אֲחָיוֹת יְבָמוֹת שֶׁנָּפְלוּ לִפְנֵי יָבָם אֶחָד, חָלַץ לָרִאשׁוֹנָה — הוּתְּרָה, חָלַץ לַשְּׁנִיָּה — הוּתְּרָה. מֵתָה רִאשׁוֹנָה מוּתָּר בַּשְּׁנִיָּה, וְאֵין צָרִיךְ לוֹמַר מֵתָה שְׁנִיָּה שֶׁמּוּתָּר בָּרִאשׁוֹנָה, מִשּׁוּם דַּהֲוָיָא יְבָמָה שֶׁהוּתְּרָה וְנֶאֶסְרָה וְחָזְרָה וְהוּתְּרָה — תַּחֲזוֹר לְהֶיתֵּירָהּ הָרִאשׁוֹן. וְרַבִּי יוֹחָנָן אָמַר: [ב]מֵתָה שְׁנִיָּה — מוּתָּר בָּרִאשׁוֹנָה. אֲבָל מֵתָה רִאשׁוֹנָה — אָסוּר בַּשְּׁנִיָּה. מ"ט — שֶׁכָּל יְבָמָה שֶׁאֵין אֲנִי קוֹרֵא בָּהּ בִּשְׁעַת נְפִילָה "יְבָמָהּ יָבֹא עָלֶיהָ" הֲרֵי זוֹ כְּאֵשֶׁת אָח שֶׁיֵּשׁ לָהּ בָּנִים, וַאֲסוּרָה — וְרַב לֵית לֵיהּ הַאי סְבָרָא? •וְהָאָמַר רַב: *כָּל אִשָּׁה שֶׁאֵין אֲנִי קוֹרֵא בָּהּ בִּשְׁעַת נְפִילָה "יְבָמָהּ יָבֹא עָלֶיהָ" הֲרֵי הִיא כְּאֵשֶׁת אָח שֶׁיֵּשׁ לוֹ בָּנִים וַאֲסוּרָה! — ה"מ הֵיכָא דְּקָאֵי בְּאַפַּהּ אִיסּוּר אֲחוֹת אִשָּׁה דְּאוֹרַיְיתָא, אֲבָל הָכָא — זִיקָה דְּרַבָּנַן הִיא. אֵיתִיבֵיהּ ר' יוֹסֵי בַּר חֲנִינָא לְרַבִּי יוֹחָנָן: *אַרְבָּעָה אַחִין, ב' מֵהֶם נְשׂוּאִים ב' אֲחָיוֹת, וּמֵתוּ הַנְּשׂוּאִין אֶת הָאֲחָיוֹת — הֲרֵי אֵלּוּ חוֹלְצוֹת וְלֹא מִתְיַבְּמוֹת. וְאַמַּאי? לֵיקוּ חַד מִינַּיְיהוּ לַחֲלוֹץ לָהּ לַשְּׁנִיָּה, וְתֶיהֱוֵי רִאשׁוֹנָה לְגַבֵּי אִידָךְ כִּיבָמָה שֶׁהוּתְּרָה וְנֶאֶסְרָה וְחָזְרָה וְהוּתְּרָה — תַּחֲזוֹר לְהֶיתֵּירָהּ הָרִאשׁוֹן! א"ל: [ג]אֲחָיוֹת •אֵינִי יוֹדֵעַ מִי שְׁנָאָן. — וְלֵימָא לֵיהּ: מַאי "חוֹלְצוֹת" נַמִּי דְּקָתָנֵי — חוֹלֶצֶת חֲדָא! — "חוֹלְצוֹת" קָתָנֵי. — וְלֵימָא לֵיהּ: מַאי "חוֹלְצוֹת" (ב) חוֹלְצוֹת דְּעָלְמָא! — "הֲרֵי אֵלּוּ" קָתָנֵי. — וְלֵימָא: דְּחָלֵיץ לֵיהּ לָרִאשׁוֹנָה בְּרֵישָׁא! — "חוֹלְצוֹת" לְכַתְּחִלָּה

רש"י

בַּעֲלַת הַגֵּט וּבַעֲלַת מַאֲמָר. אָחִיו שֶׁמֵּת וְלוֹ ב' נָשִׁים, וְעָשָׂה זֶה מַאֲמָר לָזוֹ וְגֵט לָזוֹ, וְשׁוּב אָסוּר לְיַיבֵּם, דְּקָם לֵיהּ בְּ"לֹא יִבְנֶה", כֵּיוָן שֶׁהִתְחִיל לְגָרֵשׁ, אֵי זוֹ מֵהֶן הֲגוּנָה לַחֲלוֹץ וְלִפְטוֹר צָרָתָהּ? וּמוֹדֶה ר"ג. דְּאָמַר לְקַמָּן בְּפ"ה אֵין גֵּט אַחַר גֵּט – מוֹדֶה הוּא שֶׁיֵּשׁ גֵּט אַחַר מַאֲמָר. כְּגוֹן ב' יְבָמוֹת מֵאָח א', וְעָשָׂה מַאֲמָר בָּזוֹ וְאַח"כ נָתַן גֵּט לָזוֹ – מְהַנֵּי גֵּט לִפְסוֹל הָרִאשׁוֹנָה עָלָיו מִשּׁוּם "לֹא יִבְנֶה" וּלְהֵאָסֵר בִּקְרוֹבוֹת שְׁנִיָּה כְּבָרִאשׁוֹנָה, וְלָא אָמְרִי' מַאֲמָר כִּכְנוּסָה, וְאִדַּחַאי שְׁנִיָּה מִינֵּיהּ וְלָא מְהַנֵּי בָּהּ גֵּט: וּמַאֲמָר אַחַר גֵּט. אִם נָתַן גֵּט לָרִאשׁוֹנָה וְאַח"כ עָשָׂה מַאֲמָר בְּצָרָתָהּ, לָא אָמְרִי': גֵּט קַמָּא בִּמְקוֹם חֲלִיצָה קָאֵי, וְתוּ לָא קָנֵי מַאֲמָר יְבָמִין בַּצָּרָה; אֶלָּא וַדַּאי מְהַנֵּי, וּצְרִיכָה גֵּט לְמַאֲמָרוֹ, וְאָסוּר גַּם בִּקְרוֹבוֹתֶיהָ: כִּי הֲדָדֵי נִינְהוּ. וְתִפְשׁוֹט בְּעַיִין שֶׁהָאַחַת פּוֹטֶרֶת חֲבֶרְתָּהּ, וְיַחֲלוֹץ לְאֵיזוֹ שֶׁיִּרְצֶה, שֶׁחֲלִיצַת שְׁתֵּיהֶן גְּרוּעָה: לָרִאשׁוֹנָה. שֶׁנָּפְלָה רִאשׁוֹן: הוּתְּרָה. לַשּׁוּק: חָלַץ לַשְּׁנִיָּה הוּתְּרָה. לַשּׁוּק, וְה"ה אִם חָלַץ לַשְּׁנִיָּה וְאַח"כ לָרִאשׁוֹנָה: מֵתָה רִאשׁוֹנָה. בְּלֹא חֲלִיצָה, מוּתָּר לְיַיבֵּם אֶת הַשְּׁנִיָּה. וְאַע"פ שֶׁבִּשְׁעַת(ג) נְפִילָתָן אֲחוֹת זְקוּקַת רִאשׁוֹנָה הָיְתָה, וְאֵין אֲנִי קוֹרֵא בָּהּ "יְבָמָהּ יָבֹא עָלֶיהָ", כִּי מֵתָה קַמַּיְיתָא – פָּקְעָה זִיקָה וְשָׁרְיָא הָךְ. וְלֵית לֵיהּ הָא דְּשַׁנֵּינַן בְּפֶ' "כֵּיצַד" (לעיל דף כג:) הָךְ מַתְנִי' דְּהָכָא אִי לְמ"ד יֵשׁ זִיקָה יֵשׁ זִיקָה כו', דְּאוֹקִימְנָא לְעֵיל דְּהוֹאִיל וְנֶאֶסְרָה עָלָיו בִּשְׁעַת נְפִילָה – תּוּ לָא מִשְׁתַּרְיָא. וְאִיכָּא לְאוֹתוּבֵי מִמַּתְנִי' דְּקָתָנֵי חוֹלְצוֹת וְלֹא מִתְיַבְּמוֹת, אַמַּאי? לִיחֲלוֹץ חֲדָא וְלִישְׁתְּרֵי אִידָךְ! וּלְקַמָּן מוֹתְבִינַן לֵיהּ מִינָּהּ אַסֵּיפָא דְּמִילְּתֵיהּ, וְלָא מְתָרֵץ: וְאֵין צ"ל מֵתָה שְׁנִיָּה. וְלֹא חֲלָצָהּ, שֶׁמּוּתָּר בָּרִאשׁוֹנָה. שֶׁהָיְתָה רְאוּיָה לְיַיבֵּם בִּשְׁעַת נְפִילָתָהּ, אֶלָּא שֶׁנָּפְלָה זוֹ אַחֲרֵי כֵן וַאֲסָרַתָּהּ, וְכֵיוָן שֶׁמֵּתָה זוֹ – חָזְרָה לְהֶיתֵּירָהּ הָרִאשׁוֹן: וְרַבִּי יוֹחָנָן אָמַר מֵתָה שְׁנִיָּה מוּתָּר בָּרִאשׁוֹנָה. הוֹאִיל וּבִשְׁעַת נְפִילָתָהּ הָיְתָה רְאוּיָה לוֹ: אֲחוֹת אִשָּׁה דְּאוֹרַיְיתָא. כְּגוֹן ג' אַחִים, ב' מֵהֶם נְשׂוּאִין ב' אֲחָיוֹת, וּמֵת אֶחָד מֵהֶם, וְאַח"כ מֵתָה אִשְׁתּוֹ שֶׁל ב', דַּעֲלָהּ אִיתְּמַר הָךְ דְּרַב בְּפִרְקִין (לקמן דף ל.): אֲסוּרָה יְבִמְתּוֹ עָלָיו, הוֹאִיל וּבִשְׁעַת נְפִילָה אֲחוֹת אִשְׁתּוֹ הֲוַאי: דְּרַבָּנַן הִיא. וְכֵיוָן דְּמֵתָה שָׁרְיָא: אֵינִי יוֹדֵעַ מִי שְׁנָאָן. כְּלוֹמַר, זוֹ אֵינָהּ מִשְׁנָה: וְלֵימָא לֵיהּ מַאי חוֹלְצוֹת חֲדָא. שְׁנִיָּה: חוֹלְצוֹת דְּעָלְמָא. כָּל הֵיכָא דְּמִיתְרְמֵי כה"ג – חוֹלְצוֹת הַשְּׁנִיּוֹת: הֲרֵי אֵלּוּ. מַשְׁמַע: הָנָךְ תַּרְתֵּי דְּאַיְירֵי בְּהוּ: לָרִאשׁוֹנָה בְּרֵישָׁא. דְּתוּ לָא מִשְׁתַּרְיָא שְׁנִיָּה, שֶׁלֹּא נִרְאֵית בִּשְׁעַת נְפִילָה: חוֹלְצוֹת

תוספות

בעלת הגט עדיפא. פי': שנעשה בה מעשה עדיף טפי מחברתה. אבל ריב"ן פי': בעלת הגט עדיפא דאתחיל (ד) בחליצה, ולכך יגמור בה חליצתו. ולפירושו לא יהא עדיפא דהכא פירושו כההוא דאי מאמר עדיף או גט עדיף דבסמוך. ומיהו, עדיפא משמע קצת דהיינו קודמת, דקאי אאיזו מהן קודמת דקאמר מעיקרא. **תא שמע** ומודה ר"ג כו'. מדרבנן דשמעינן להו פרק "ר"ג" (לקמן דף נ. ושם) דיש גט אחר גט ומאמר אחר הגט – אין יכול להביא ראיה, דלדידהו דיש גט אחר גט – אפי' עדיף קמא מהני גרוע בתריה לתפוס במה ששייר הראשון. אבל ר"ג, דאית ליה דאין גט אחר גט, סברא הוא דאי עדיף גט ממאמר או מאמר מגט לא מהני הגרוע לתפוס אחר קמא דעדיף, כמו שאין מועיל גט אחר גט ומאמר אחר מאמר. **אי** גט עדיף **לא** תיהני **מאמר** בתריה. אע"ג דאפילו אחר חליצה קידושין תופסין – היינו משום דהוי קידושין דאורייתא. אבל ביבמה, דלא הוי מאמר אלא מדרבנן – אין לו להועיל אחר הגט אי גט עדיף. א"כ אומר ר"י: דבריית' דמודה ר"ג קיימא אמתני' דפ' "ר"ג" (לקמן ד' נ.) דמוקמינן לה כר"ע התם בגמ' (דף נג:), ולא מהני קידושין אחר חליצה, וה"ה דאין להם להועיל אחר הגט אי גט עדיף, דגט במקום חליצה קאי.

אלא כי הדדי נינהו. ותפשוט דאחת פוטרת חברתה, והיינו כשמואל, וכלישנא דקאמר דאחד חולץ לכולן אאמצעי', וכרב אשי. אבל ללישנא דהתחיל ולא התחיל קאמר, היכי דכי הדדי נינהו צריכות שתיהן חליצה, דהא התחיל באחיות לא יגמור אפי' בצרות, ולא מיפטרה רחל בחליצת צרתה דעדיפא. והכא הך בעיא על כרחין אליבא דמ"ד יש זיקה איירי דלמ"ד אין זיקה – אפילו חלץ לבעלת הגט נפטרה צרה.

חליץ לראשונה הותרה. וא"ת: מאי קמ"ל? פשיטא דהותרה! וא"ר"י: דקמ"ל דהותרה אפי' צרתה, דרב אית ליה אין זיקה, וחלץ לאחיות נפטרו צרות כדפרישית לעיל. **ורב** לית ליה האי **סברא והאמר** רב כל יבמה כו'. •ממתני' הוה מלי למיפרך, דבהדיא תנן בפירקין (לקמן דף לג.): ב' אחין נשואין ב' אחיות ומת אחד מהן, ואח"כ מתה אשתו של שני – הרי זו אסורה עליו עולמית, הואיל ונאסרה עליו! אלא ניחא להקשות דבהדיא אמר רב אותו לשון עצמו שאמר ר' יוחנן. שכל יבמה שאין אני קורא כו'. ועוד נראה: דממתני' לא הוה מלי לאקשויי, דהתם הוא משום דכבר נפטרה לשוק, ומשום דמתה אשתו אח"כ לא תחשב עוד זקוקה(ה) עדיין לחליצה. אבל היכא דעדיין זקוקה לחליצה – לא. אבל מדרב פריך שפיר, דרב איירי אפילו היכא דאיכא אחין, דלא מידחיא מהאי ביתא *) (לגמרי) כדאמר לקמן (ג"ז שם). **אבל** הכא זיקה דרבנן היא. פר"ח דרב: לטעמיה, דאמר אין זיקה, דאע"ג דאסיר משום ביטול מצות יבמין – לא חשיב הך איסור לאוסרה עולמית אף כשתבא לכלל היתר. אבל למ"ד יש זיקה – ראוי לאסור משום שנאסרה עליו שעה אחת. **איתיביה** רבי יוסי בר חנינא לרבי יוחנן. לעיל פי' בקונטרס דלרב נמי פריך. אבל ריב"ן פירש דלא פריך לרב משום דרב ס"ל חליצה פסולה צריכה לחזור על כל האחים, דהאחת צריכה חליצה משניהן, ושוב השנית א"א לייבס משום דלכל אחד הויא אחות חלוצתו. אבל רבי יוחנן סבר כשמואל, דאינה צריכה לחזור, ולהכי פריך ליה. ואע"ג דרב דאמר צריכה לחזור – היינו אליבא דמ"ד יש זיקה, וליה לא ס"ל – מ"מ מלינו למימר דרב מוקי לה כמ"ד יש זיקה, דפלוגתא דתנאי היא. ואע"ג דלעיל בריש פ' "כילד" (דף יח.) מוקי לה סתמא דהש"ס כר"מ, דאמר אין זיקה – רב לא מוקי לה כוותיה. ולר"ח נמי, דפי' לעיל דרב דלית ליה הואיל ונאסרה עליו שעה אחת, לטעמיה דאמר אין זיקה אתי שפיר נמי דלא פריך לרב, דמוקי למתני' כמ"ד יש זיקה. אבל ר' יוחנן סבר דעל כרחך יש זיקה, דאי אין זיקה, א"כ ב' אחיות שנפלו לפני שני אחין – יתייבמו שתיהן, דהא ר' יוחנן לא חייש למיתה. ומפירכא דפריך רבי יוסי בר חנינא: ואמאי וליקו חד מנייהו כו' – משמע דלא שרי רבי יוחנן לייבס אלא חדא – על כרחך סבר יש זיקה, ואפ"ה שרי לראשונה, ולית ליה הואיל ונאסרה שעה א' שתאסר עולמית, מש"ה פריך לה. ומיהו, נראה לר"י כדפרישית לעיל (דף כד. ד"ה א) דלרב *דחייש למיתה(ו) – לא מלי פריך, דגזרי' דלמא אתי לייבס ברישא, אבל לעיל במתה אחת מהן ליכא למיגזר דלמא אתי לייבס בלא מתה אחת מהן, כיון דליכא אלא אח אחד ולא אתי לבטל מצות יבמין להדיא. אבל רבי יוחנן היה יודע רבי יוסי בר חנינא דלא הוי חייש למיתה, להכי *(לא) פריך ליה. *(א"נ, לפי שהיה אצל ר' יוחנן הקשה לו**). **ולימא** ליה דלמא קדים וחליץ לראשונה. פי' ר"י לפי שיטת הקונטר': שכשבאין לפנינו לימלך לא אמרינן להו לחלוץ שניה ולייבס את הראשונה, דגזרינן דלמא אתי למיעבד איפכא באלו [היבמות] עצמן. אבל אם כבר חלץ האחד לשנייה – שרי אידך לייבס הראשונה, כמו במתה שנייה, כיון דבאלו

*) ס"א אינו

**) שייך לקמן כח ע"א

תוספות ישנים

בעלת הגט עדיפא. פ"ה עדיפא שחליצה תפטור צרתה. ולא נהירא דא"כ מאי קאמר בעלת מאמר עדיפא משום דקרובה לביאה. אדרבה משו"ה הוי חליצה פסולה דאיקלישא לה הזיקה. אלא נראה לפרש איפכא בעלת הגט עדיפא להפטר בחליצת חברתה וניחא הכל: **זיקה** דרבנן היא. פר"ח דרב לטעמיה דסבר אין זיקה אבל אין לפרש דיש זיקה מ"מ לא החמירו כבאחות (זקוקתו) [אשתו] דלקמן בהחולץ משמע דלמ"ד יש זיקה הוי כמו אחות אשתו גמורה. ואין להקשות נהי נמי דאין זיקה מ"מ נאסרה שעה אחת משום ביטול מצות יבמין דלא קרינן אסרה שעה אחת כיון שאין האיסור משום ערוה רק משום גזרה:

תוספות חד מקמאי

נינהו: ופסק הרב אלפס כר' יוחנן בשתי אחיות יבמות שנפלו לפני יבם א' מתה השניה מותר בראשונה אבל מתה ראשונה אסור בשניה ואקשינן לר"י דאמר מותר בראשונה מהא דתנן ארבעה אחין שנים מהן נשואין ב' אחיות ומתו הנשואין את האחיות הרי אלו חולצות ולא מתייבמות ואמאי ליקום חד מינייהו ולחלוץ לשניה ותהוי ראשונה לגבי אידך כיבמה שהותרה ונאסרה ותחזור להיתרה הראשון א"ל ר"י אחיות איני יודע מי שנאן כלומר זו אינה משנה ולימא ליה מאי חולצת חדא חולצות קתני. [ולימא] חולצות דעלמא הרי אלו קתני ולימא ליה דחליץ לראשונה ברישא חולצות לכתחלה קתני. ולימא גזרו דלמא קדם וחלץ לראשונה ברישא ולא מתייבמת קתני דליכא הכא דין יבום כלל ולימא ליה שמא ימות ואסור לבטל מצות יבמין. פירוש וקעבדא חליצה פסולה. ר"י למיתה לא חייש ולימא ליה דלא ידעינן הי נפיל ברישא אי הכי היינו דקתני אם קדמו וכנסו יוציאו. בשלמא ראשון אמרי' [ליה] מאן שרא ליה אלא שני א) אמרי' חבראי שני יבום האיכא ראשון ראשון ש"מ יבמי היינו דקתני אחיות איני יודע מי שנאן:

א) נ"ל אלא שני אמר חבראי שנייה ייבם אנא ראשונה מייבם והיינו דקאמר אחיות וכו'.

(טעות הדפוס) ס"א ל"ג

מסורת הש"ס

גירסת רש"ל בגירושין

לקמן נח.

גירסת הרא"ש יהודה

[לקמן ל. ע"ש קיא: ע"ש]

[לעיל כו. וש"נ]

הגהות הב"ח

(א) גמ' בעלת הגט עדיפא (משום דאתחיל בה בגירושין) תא"מ ונ"ב בתוספות משמע דלא גרסינן ליה: (ב) שם [illegible] חולצות דעלמא נ"ב [illegible]: (ג) רש"י ד"ה מתה וכו' שבשעת נפילתה [illegible]: (ד) תוס' ד"ה בעלת וכו' עדיפא דאתחיל בה בגירושין ולכך יגמור בה חליצתו: (ה) ד"ה ורב וכו' לא תחשוב [illegible]: (ו) [illegible] דחייש למיתה לא מלי פריך דגזרי' דלמא אתי לייבס בריש[illegible] אדעתייהו [illegible] כצ"ל

גליון הש"ס

גמ' והאמר רב כל אשה. עי' לעיל [illegible] ואחות אשתו [illegible] תוד"ה [illegible] איני יודע מי שנאן. [illegible] קמא ע"ב: תד"ה וכו' ממתני' הוה מלי למפרך וכו'. [illegible] נה ע"ב [illegible] מרע [illegible] תוד"ה [illegible] תד"ה [illegible]

לְכַתְּחִלָּה קָתָנֵי. [א]וְלֵימָא לֵיהּ גְּזֵירָה דִּלְמָא קָדֵים וְחָלֵיץ לָרִאשׁוֹנָה בְּרֵישָׁא! — "וְלֹא מִתְיַיבְּמוֹת" קָתָנֵי, דְּלֵיכָּא דִּין יִבּוּם הָכָא כְּלָל. — וְלֵימָא לֵיהּ גְּזֵירָה שֶׁמָּא יָמוּת, *וְאָסוּר לְבַטֵּל מִצְוַת יְבָמִין! — רַ' יוֹחָנָן לְמִיתָה לָא חָיֵישׁ. — וְלֵימָא לֵיהּ רַבִּי (א) אֶלְעָזָר הִיא, *דְּאָמַר: כֵּיוָן שֶׁעָמְדָה עָלָיו שָׁעָה אַחַת בְּאִיסּוּר נֶאֶסְרָה עָלָיו עוֹלָמִית! — מִדְּסֵיפָא רַ' אֶלְעָזָר רֵישָׁא לָאו רַבִּי אֶלְעָזָר. וְנֵימָא *לְהוּ דִּנְפוּל בְּבַת אַחַת וְרַבִּי יוֹסֵי הַגְּלִילִי הִיא, *דְּאָמַר: אֶפְשָׁר לְצַמְצֵם! — לָא סָתַם לָן תַּנָּא כְּרַ' יוֹסֵי הַגְּלִילִי. — וְלֵימָא לֵיהּ [ב]דְּלָא יָדְעִינַן הֵי נְפוּל בְּרֵישָׁא! — אִי הָכִי, הַיְינוּ דְּקָתָנֵי "קָדְמוּ וְכָנְסוּ יוֹצִיאוּ"? בִּשְׁלָמָא (ב) רִאשׁוֹנָה אָמְרִינַן לֵיהּ: מַאן שַׁרְיָא לָךְ? אֶלָּא שְׁנִיָּה, אָמַר: חַבְרָאי שְׁנִיָּה יִיבֵּם, אֲנָא רִאשׁוֹנָה מְיַיבֵּם! — הַיְינוּ דְּקָאָמַר לֵיהּ: אֲחָיוֹת אֵינִי יוֹדֵעַ מִי שְׁנָאָן. § תְּנַן: *הָיְתָה אַחַת מֵהֶן אֲסוּרָה עַל הָאֶחָד אִיסּוּר עֶרְוָה — אָסוּר בָּהּ וּמוּתָּר בַּאֲחוֹתָהּ, וְהַשֵּׁנִי אָסוּר בִּשְׁתֵּיהֶן. ס"ד דְּנָפְלָה חֲמוֹתוֹ תְּחִלָּה, וְאַמַּאי? לֵיקוּ חָתָן לְיַיבֵּם הַךְ דְּאֵינָהּ חֲמוֹתוֹ בְּרֵישָׁא, וְתֶהֱוֵי חֲמוֹתוֹ לְגַבֵּי אִידָךְ כִּיבָמָה שֶׁהוּתְּרָה וְנֶאֶסְרָה וְחָזְרָה וְהוּתְּרָה — תַּחֲזוֹר לְהֶיתֵּרָהּ הָרִאשׁוֹן. [ג]א"ר פַּפָּא: כְּגוֹן דְּנָפְלָה הַךְ דְּאֵינָהּ חֲמוֹתוֹ בְּרֵישָׁא. § "ר"א אוֹמֵר: בש"א וכו'". § תַּנְיָא: *ר"א אוֹמֵר ב"ש אוֹמְרִים: יְקַיְּימוּ, וּבה"א: יוֹצִיאוּ. רש"א: יְקַיְּימוּ. אַבָּא שָׁאוּל אוֹמֵר: קַל הָיָה לָהֶם לְב"ה בְּדָבָר זֶה, שֶׁבֵּית שַׁמַּאי אוֹמְרִים יוֹצִיאוּ וּבה"א יְקַיְּימוּ. ר"ש כְּמַאן? אִי כְּב"ש — הַיְינוּ ר"א, אִי כְּב"ה — הַיְינוּ אַבָּא שָׁאוּל! — *ה"ק לֹא נֶחְלְקוּ ב"ש וּב"ה בְּדָבָר זֶה. § "הָיְתָה אַחַת מֵהֶם כו'". § הָא תָּנֵינָא חֲדָא זִימְנָא: *אֲחוֹתָהּ כְּשֶׁהִיא יְבִמְתָּהּ אוֹ חוֹלֶצֶת אוֹ מִתְיַיבֶּמֶת! — צְרִיכָא, דְּאִי אַשְׁמוּעִינַן הָתָם מִשּׁוּם דְּלֵיכָּא לְמִיגְזַר מִשּׁוּם שֵׁנִי, אֲבָל הָכָא דְּאִיכָּא לְמִיגְזַר מִשּׁוּם שֵׁנִי — אֵימָא לָא. וְאִי אַשְׁמוּעִינַן הָכָא — מִשּׁוּם דְּאִיכָּא שֵׁנִי דְּקָא מוֹכַח, אֲבָל הָתָם דְּלֵיכָּא שֵׁנִי — אֵימָא לָא, צְרִיכָא. § "אִיסּוּר מִצְוָה כו'". § הָא נַמִּי תָּנֵינָא: אִיסּוּר

רש"י

חולצות לכתחלה. משמע, כלומר: אין כאן תקנה אחרת: ה"ג. ולימא ליה גזירה דלמא קדים וחליץ לראשונה ברישא. אי אמרת להו חלוצו לשנייה ויבמו ראשונה – גזירה דלמא קדים חד וחליץ לראשונה, ואתי ליבומי אידך שנייה, דסברי: מה איכפת בין זו לזו. אבל בדיעבד, שחלץ לשנייה תחלה, שריא ליה לאידך ליבומי קמייתא. דמאן דחזי דחלץ לשנייה ברישא וחזר וייבם קמייתא – אסיק אדעתיה, ולא אתי למחלץ לקמייתא וליבומי שנייה: ומשני. ולא מתייבמות קתני. דאי נמי חלץ לשנייה אין כאן יבום. ולימא ליה גזירה שמא ימות ואסור לבטל מצות יבמין. וה"פ: לימא ליה רבי יוחנן, תנא דמתני' טעמיה לאו משום זיקה קא אסר לייבם ב' אחיות, דס"ל אין זיקה. דאי טעמא משום זיקה – מכי חליץ לשנייה ופקע זיקתה שרי ליבומי ראשונה, כדאמרי אנא. אלא טעמא משום שמא ימות, כדאמר בריש פירקין: דלמא אדמייבם חד מיית אידך כו', ומשו"ה שקול רבנן דין יבום מאחיות לגמרי. ואפילו חלץ לחדא מינייהו, דלא בטלי תו מצות יבמין – כי היכי דלא ירגילו יבום באחיות, ואתי ליבומי לכתחלה קמי חליצה, ואדמייבם חד מיית אידך. אבל לגבי מיתה דלעיל, דאיירי בה ר' יוחנן – ליכא למיגזר הכי. ר' אלעזר היא. בפ' ב"ש (לקמן קט.), ואנא דאמרי כרבנן. מדסיפא. דמתני' ר"א, דקתני: ר"א אומר, ב"ש אומרים יקיימו (כו'), ב"ה אומרים יוציאו. ולימא ליה. דלא ידעינן הי נפול ברישא דלימא ליה חלוץ לשנייה. א"ה. דמשום דלא ידעינן הוא, הא אי הוה ידעינן – מתייבמת ראשונה. היינו דקתני. כלומר, הא דקתני יוציאו אמאי? בשלמא לראשון אמרי' ליה. אפיק, דודאי באיסורא אתא לידך. דא"כ ראשונה היא, מאן שריא ניהלך? הלא אחות זקוקה היא, ומי מאחיך חלץ לאחותה לאפקועי זיקה מינה? אלא שני – לימא: *אחר שייבם ראשון, שנייה אירע לחלקו, והויא זו ראשונה יבמה שהותרה ונאסרה וחזרה והותרה. דהכי אמר בפ' "כילד" (לעיל כד.): קדמו וכנסו – אין מוציאין מידם, משום דליכא אלא ספק פגע באחות זקוקה, והא נמי לשני ספק הוא. היינו דקאמר ליה אחיות איני יודע מי שנאן. דלא מצי לתרוצי כשמעתיה כלל. איסור ערוה. כגון חמותו או ערוה אחרת. דנפלה חמותו ברישא. *זו שאסרה את האחרת נפלה תחלה. והאי דנקט חמותו – חדא מעריות נקט, וניחא למינקטיה מילתא דשכיחא, ושאר עריות טריחא מילתא לאשכוחי. אמאי. שני אסור בשתיהן? ליקו חתן של ראשונה, ולייבם לשנייה דאינה חמותו ואינה אחות זקוקה, ותיהוי חמותו לגבי אידך את – יבמה שהותרה בשעת נפילה כו'. כגון דנפלה הך דאינה חמותו ברישא. ואי במייבם לה האיך ברישא – פקיעא שנייה, שנאסרה משעת נפילתה (הוי), הלכך תו לא מהני לה היתר. קל היה להן לב"ה. כלומר: ב"ה לקולא אמרי. ר"ש כמאן. אליבא דמאן. אי. אתא למימר בית שמאי אומרים יקיימו – היינו ר"א. ואי אב"ה. קא מסהיד – היינו אבא שאול. והא ליכא למימר דטעמא דנפשיה קאמר, דלאו בר פלוגתייהו דבית שמאי ובית הלל הוא. תנינא חדא זימנא. בפרק "כילד": אחותה של ערוה כשהיא יבמתה, או חולצת כו'. והיינו נמי אסור בה ומותר באחותה. התם. הוא דליכא אלא חד אחא לקמן, וליכא למיגזר מידי. אבל הכא דאיכא למיגזר דלמא אתא שני ליבומי *כאחיו, וקא פגע באחות זקוקתו, דקמי דידיה הוו רמיין תרווייהו – אימא אפילו האי דלא רמיא ערוה קמיה לא לייבם, קא משמע לן. דקא מוכח. דמדלא מייבם האי *כאחיו – איכא היכרא דאחות זקוקתו אסורה, והאי דייבם האי – משום טעמא דערוה לא רמיא קמיה, ולא אתי למישרי אחות זקוקתו בעלמא. אבל התם. דליכא אלא חד את – אימא לא לייבם, דלמא אתי למישרי אחות זקוקתו בעלמא. איסור

תוספות

דבאלו יבמות ליכא שום חששא. והא לא חיישינן שאם נתיר כאן לייבם הראשונה כשכבר חלץ לשניה אתי בעלמא למיעבד איפכא – שאינה חששא גדולה כ"כ, שלא יטעו להתיר השניה שלא הותרה מתחלה בשביל שנתיר הראשונה שהותרה, אבל באו לימלך בפנינו מתחלה – יש לגזור, כיון שהיו *הצרות עצמן יכול לבא לידי קלקול. ומשני: ולא מתייבמות קתני, דליכא דין ייבום כלל, אפי' קדם וחלץ כבר לשניה. ופריך: ולימא ליה שמא ימות וכו', ויעמיד המשנה כמ"ד אין זיקה, דלדידיה ודאי אפילו קדם וחלץ לשניה דליכא למיחש טפי באלו יבמות – מ"מ אסור לייבם ראשונה, שאם נתיר כאן לייבם אחר חליצה – יבוא בעלמא לייבם ברישא, דלא מסקי אדעתייהו טעמא דלמא אדמייבם חד מיית אידך, שאין זה טעם ידוע. ועוד אר"י דיש לפרש בענין אחר: ולימא ליה דלמא קדים וחליץ לראשונה ברישא, ואפי' חלץ כבר מעצמו לשניה – אסרינן ראשונה ליבם, דלמא אתי למישרי בעלמא שניה נמי כשקדם וחלץ לראשונה, אבל במיתת שניה – לא שייך למיגזר כי האי גוונא! ומשני: ולא מתייבמות קתני, דליכא דין ייבום כלל אפילו מתה שניה. ופריך: ולימא ליה גזירה שמא ימות, ולהכי אסרה מתני' אפילו מתה שניה, דאי שריא לייבם בשני יבמים – אחר מיתת שניה יבא להתיר בלא מיתה! אבל ר' יוחנן לא איירי אלא ביבם אחד, דביבם אחד לא אתי להתיר בלא מיתה, דאם כן היה מבטל מיד מצות יבמין, אבל בשני יבמין, דאין מבטל מיד, אלא דגזירה שמא ימות אידך ויבוא לטעות ולייבם. וחזר בו ר"י מפירוש זה, דביבם א' נמי קתני במתני' ולא מתייבמות, דמשמע דליכא דין ייבום כלל, ואפי' מתה שניה. דקתני לקמן: ג' אחין, ב' מהן נשואין ב' אחיות, ומתו הנשואין את האחיות – הרי אלו חולצות ולא מתייבמות. **ולימא** ליה ר"א היא. היינו ר' אלעזר ד"החולץ" (לקמן דף מא. ושם) דתני גבי שומרת יבם שקידש אחיו את אחותה: מתה יבמתו – מותר באשתו, מתה אשתו – אותה יבמה חולצת ולא מתייבמת, ובקונטרס פי': דהיינו ר"א בפרק "ב"ש" (לקמן דף קט. ושם) דתנן: המגרש את אשתו והחזירה – מותרת לייבם, ור' אלעזר אוסר. **לא** סתם לן כר' יוסי הגלילי. לר' יוחנן הוא דמסקינן הכי, אבל רב חסדא מוקי מתניתין ד"שבועת העדות" (שבועות לב. ושם) דכפרו שניהם בבת אחת כר' יוסי הגלילי. ור' יוחנן מסיק התם: אפי' תימא רבנן, והיינו לטעמיה דהכא. ובפ"ק דעירובין (דף ה: ד"ה "וספק") פירשתי דקיימא לן דבידי אדם אפשר לצמצם, ובידי שמים נמי משמע לרבא דאית ליה פרק בתרא דבכורות[א] (דף ס: ושם) דאפשר לצמצם, גבי יצאו שנים בעשירי. ובפרק "בהמה המקשה" (חולין ע. ושם) גבי בעיא אם הלכו באברים אחר הרוב, דמוקי לה שילא חליו ברוב אבר, ואי אמרת דא"א לצמצם – מאי קמיבעיא ליה? דממה נפשך טעון קבורה דשמא יצא רובו. ואין להאריך, כי שם הארכתי. **הך** דאין חמותו ברישא. וא"ת: מ"מ תקשה לרב דשרי אפילו שניה! וי"ל: דרב אית ליה אין זיקה, ולא מיתסר אלא משום ביטול מצות יבמין, וגזרינן דלמא מייבם אידך ברישא:[ב] **רבי אליעזר** אומר ב"ש אומרים יקיימו. וא"ת: וכי טעמא דב"ש אתא לאשמועינן?! דהכי פריך בפרק "רבי אליעזר דמילה" (שבת דף קלה.) וי"ל: דאיצטריך הכא לאפוקי מברייתא דאבא שאול, דאמר: קל היה להם לב"ה בדבר זה. אבל

א) [ע"ש היטב וע"ע תוס' שם יז: סוף ד"ה אפשר]. ב) [שייך לעיל במשנה כו.]

עין משפט נר מצוה

יא א מיי' פ"ז מהל' יבום הלכה א סמג עשין נא נב טוש"ע אה"ע סימן קעה סעי' א:

כ"א היבמות

יב ב מיי' שם טוש"ע שם סעיף ב:

יג ג מיי' שם הל' ה טוש"ע שם סעיף א:

מסורת הש"ס

[לעיל יח. וש"נ]

לקמן מא. קט.

ליה יעב"ץ

לעיל יט. בכורות ע. יז. יח. [שבועות לב.]

לעיל כו.

[תוספתא פ"ה]

[שבת מב. קלה. סוכה טו. ב"ק לד.]

לעיל כ.

[בכת"י אחיו]

[זו שאסורה על האחד נפלה כצ"ל רש"ל]

ס"א באחת

ס"א באחת

הגהות הב"ח

(א) גמ' ר' אליעזר היא כצ"ל וכן בכל העמוד: (ב) שם בשלמא ראשון אמרינן ליה מאן שרא לך אלא שני אמר:

תוספות ישנים

דנפלה הך דאינה חמותו ברישא. פ"ה דלאו דווקא נקט חמותו ה"ה ערוה אחרת. א"נ פי' ה"ר ריב"ן דנקט חמותו משום דחמותו הויא ערוה ראשונה לגבי כללא דרבי חייא דהאסורה לזה מותרת לזה כדקאמר (לקמן) [לעיל דף ט] רב [יהודה] מתרגם מחמותו ואילך.

תוספות חד מקמאי

הדר אקשינן לר"י מהא דתנן היתה אחת מהן אסורה עליו אסור ערוה אסור בה ומותר באחותה והשני [אסור] בשתיהן קס"ד דנפול חמות ברישא ואמאי ליקום חתן ולייבם הך דאינה חמות ותהוי חמות ליבם אידך כיבמה שהותרה ונאסרה וחזרה והותרה תחזור להיתירא הראשון אמר רב פפא כגון שנפל הך דאינה חמות תחילה כך היא הצעת הגמרא. וה"ר אלפס כתב משנתנו כפשוטה. ור"י דקי"ל כוותיה אמר זו אינה משנה וסיפא נמי דקא' השני אסור בשתיהן אוקמה רב פפא אליבא דר"י כגון דנפל הך דאינה חמות תחילה והוא ז"ל לא כתב דברי רב פפא והוא דבר תימה נשוב ונאמר כי דברי הרב ברורים ונכונים וכולה מתני' הלכה היא והא דתנינן ולא מתייבמת משום גזרה דלמא קדים וחליץ ברישא הראשונה כדאמרן בהאי פירקא גבי (חזקת) א) יבמין דגזרינן מיבם והדר חליץ דלמא חליץ והדר מייבם הכא נמי לא שנא. ואע"ג דבפרק כיצד אמר קדש א' משתי אחיות ואינו יודע איזה מהן קדש דוקא מחלץ והדר יבומי אבל יבומי והדר מחלץ לא ולא גזרינן דלמא עביד הא אטו הא. שאני התם דספק הוא דהא אם קדמו וכנסו אין מוציאין אותה מידו אבל הכא דודאי אחות זקוקתו הוא גזרינן הא אטו הא ואע"ג דלר"י שנינן ולא מתייבמות קתני למימר דליכא דין יבום כלל. מיהו ר"י מודה דגזרינן דלמא קדים וחליץ לראשונה ברישא והא דקתני בסיפ' אסור בשתיהן אפילו נפלה חמות ברישא ובדין הוא דליקום חתן ולייבם הא דאינה חמות

אלא גזרינן דלמא מייבם הך דאינו חתן ברישא. ורב פפא לא שני ליה הכי דמשמע ליה מדקתני אסור בשתיהן ב) אסור שנה ומשום הכי אוקמה כגון שנפל הך דאינה חמות ברישא. מיהו מ"מ אפלו נפל חמות ברישא אסור בשתיהן או משום גזרה דלמא נפל הך דאינה חמות ברישא או משום דגזרינן דלמא קדים ומייבם הך חתן ברישא. וזו אותה סברת הרב שכתב משנתנו כפשטה ודאתו ג) עלה לרב פפא דאמר ג' כגון דנפל דאינה חמות ברישא. דתינח לר"י אלא לרב מתני' היכי מתרצא. איכא מ"ד דלא קשיא מתני' לרב אלא רישא דקתני ולא מתייבמת ולא סיפא דקתני השני אסור בשתיהן דרב לא קאמר אלא במתה. אבל לר"י דאמר אסור בשניה לא שני ליה בין מתה ללא מתה. ואפ"ה מותר בראשונה מפני שהותרה בשעת נפילה ומשום הכי אקשינן ליה ממתני'. ולדידי מסתברא דלא קשיא ממתני' דרב לטעמיה דאמר אין זיקה כדקאמרן לעיל ורב לית ליה האי סברא וכו' ומשני ה"מ היכא דקאי באפה אסור אחות אשה אבל הכא זיקה דרבנן הוא וס"ל לרב דמתניתין ס"ל יש זיקה וה"ל כמ"ד דקאי באפה אסור אחות אשה דאורייתא מדקאמרן כל יבמה

א) נ"ל כדאמרינן בהך פירקא (דף לא ע"ב) גבי זיקת ב' יבמין. ב) נ"ל מדקתני אסור בשתיהן משמע דהוא איסור שוה ומשו"ה וכו'. ג) אולי צ"ל ומה דקשה עליה דרב פפא דאמר כגון דנפלה וכו'.

*איסור מצוה ואיסור קדושה חולצת ולא מתייבמת! — התם איסור מצוה לחודה. הכא איסור מצוה ואחותה, ס"ד אמינא: ליקום איסור מצוה במקום איסור ערוה, ותתייבם, קמ"ל. ותתייבם! — כיון דמדאורייתא רמיא קמיה קא פגע באחות זקוקתו, סד"א: משום מצוה עבוד רבנן — קמ"ל. § "היתה אחת מהן כו'". § הא תו ל"ל? היינו הך, מה לי לחד מה לי לתרי! — צריכא, דאי אשמועינן התם — משום דאיכא שני דמוכח, אבל הכא דליכא שני דקא מוכח — אימא לא. ואי אשמועינן הכא — אדרבה, תרווייהו מוכחי אהדדי. אבל אידך לא — צריכא. § "זו היא שאמרו וכו'". § זו היא למעוטי מאי? — למעוטי איסור מצוה לזה ואיסור מצוה לזה. — הא תו ל"ל? היינו הך, מה לי לחד מה לי לתרי! — מהו דתימא: כי לא אמרינן אוקי איסור מצוה במקום איסור ערוה — היכא דאיכא למיגזר משום שני, אבל היכא דליכא למיגזר משום שני — אימא: להאי אוקימנא איסור מצוה במקום איסור ערוה ולהאי [אוקימנא] איסור מצוה במקום איסור ערוה, וליבמו. קמ"ל אמר רב יהודה אמר רב. וכן תני ר' חייא: *בכולן אני קורא בהן האסורה לזה מותרת לזה, ואחותה כשהיא יבמתה — או חולצת או מתייבמת. ורב יהודה מתרגם מחמותו ואילך, אבל שיתא בבי דרישא — לא. מ"ט? כיון דבתו באונסין הוא דמשכחת לה, בנשואין לא משכחת לה, בנשואין — קמיירי, באונסין — לא קא מיירי. ואביי מתרגם אף בתו (באה) מאנוסתו, כיון דאשכוחי משכחת לה, אי בעיא באונסין — תיהוי, אי בעיא בנשואין — תהוי. אבל אשת אחיו שלא היה בעולמו — לא, כיון דאליבא דר"ש הוא דמשכחת לה — אליבא דרבנן לא משכחת לה בפלוגתא לא קמיירי. ורב ספרא מתרגם אף אשת אחיו שלא היה בעולמו, ומשכחת לה בשיתא אחי, ואליבא דר"ש. וסימניך: מת נולד וייבם, מת נולד וייבם; ראובן ושמעון נשואין שתי אחיות, לוי ויהודה נשואין שתי נכריות. מת ראובן נולד יששכר וייבם לוי, מת שמעון נולד זבולן וייבם יהודה. מתו לוי ויהודה בלא בנים, ונפלו להו קמי יששכר וזבולן — האסורה לזה מותרת לזה, והאסורה לזה מותרת לזה, — ואחותה שהיא יבמתה. — ל"ל ייבם יהודה? בלא ייבם יהודה נמי משכחת לה! — משום צרה. — הא תינח צרה, צרה דצרה מאי איכא למימר? — כגון דהדר ויבמינהו נמי גד ואשר. § **מתני'** *א שלשה אחין, שנים מהן נשואין שתי אחיות, או אשה ובתה, או אשה ובת בתה, או אשה ובת בנה — הרי אלו חולצות ולא מתייבמות, ור"ש פוטר. היתה אחת מהן אסורה עליו איסור ערוה — אסור בה, ומותר באחותה. *איסור מצוה או איסור קדושה — חולצות ולא מתייבמות. § **גמ'** *תניא: ר"ש פוטר בשתיהן מן החליצה ומן הייבום, שנאמר °"ואשה אל אחותה לא תקח לצרור" (ויקרא יח) — *"בשעה שנעשו צרות זו לזו לא יהא לך ליקוחין אפי' באחת מהן. § "היתה אחת מהן כו'". § הא תו למה לי? היינו הך! — לר"ש איצטריך: סד"א: הואיל ואמר ר"ש שתי אחיות לא חולצות ולא מתייבמות — לגזור משום ב' אחיות דעלמא, קמשמע לן. § "איסור מצוה כו'". § והא

רש"י

איסור מצוה. אם היתה האחת אסורה על האחד איסור מצוה — אינו מותר באחותה, הואיל והיא מדאורייתא רמיא קמיה הואי אידך אחות זקוקתו, הלכך בעו חליצה. **התם.** בפרק "כילד". **איסור מצוה לחודה.** לא אשמעינן אלא יבמה שנפלה לפניו, שהיא אסורה עליו איסור מצוה — חולצת. **והכא אשמועינן איסור מצוה ואחותה.** שנפלו לו משני אחין, דאחותה לא מתייבמת. דלא תימא אוקי איסור מצוה במקום ערוה, ותתייבם אחותה, ולא תיהוי כאחות זקוקתו. **משום מצוה עבוד רבנן.** שתתקיים מצות יבום, ולא העמידו איסור זיקה, שהוא מדבריהם, לאסור את אחותה היכא דהיא עליו איסור מצוה, קמ"ל. **הכא ליכא שני דמוכח.** שהרי שתיהן מתייבמות, ואתי למישרי אחות זקוקה בעלמא, ואימא לא ליבמן, קמ"ל. **תרווייהו מוכחי אהדדי.** שזה לא יכול לישא את האחרת אלא זו, וכן זו — מוכחא מילתא שזו אסורה על זה, וזו על זה. לפיכך ליכא אחות זקוקתו. **היינו הך.** דהא בהדיא קתני לה לעיל: איסור מצוה ואיסור קדושה חולצת. **כי לא אמרינן אוקי איסור מצוה במקום ערוה.** להתייבם אחותה — היכא דאין איסור מצוה אלא באחת על האחד, ולשני שתיהן זקוקות. דאי שרית לייבומי להאי שהאחת אסורה עליו — אתי שני נמי לייבומי, וקא פגע באחות זקוקתו. **בכולן אני קורא בהן.** בכל חמש עשרה עריות דבפ"ק, אפשר להן להיות שתי אחיות נופלות לשני אחין, והאחת אסורה על זה משום אחת מכל העריות הללו, ומותרת לזה, והשניה אסורה על זה משום אותו שם ערוה עצמו, ומותרת לזה. ומתוך כך נמצאו שתי אחיות מתייבמות, ולא פגעו באחות זקוקה. וכולן פירשתי בפ"א (דף ט:). **באונסין.** בבתו מאנוסתו, כגון: ראובן אנס אשה והוליד בת, ובא שמעון ואנס אנוסת אחיו והוליד בת, וניסאו בת ראובן ובת שמעון ללוי ויהודה אחיהן, והרי הן אחיות מן האם — בת שמעון מותרת לראובן, ובת ראובן מותרת לשמעון, ונמצאו שתי אחיות מתייבמות. וכן בת בתו, וכן כולן, אע"ג דכל חמשה בבי דרישא משתכחי בנשואין, הואיל ובתו לא משתכחא שיהו שתי בנות של שני אחין אחיות מן האם, שאי אפשר שנשא יבמתו שיש לה בת — לא תני בהו האסורה לזה כו', הואיל וכולן איסור שם בת הן. **דאליבא** דרבי שמעון היא דמשכחת בה. האסורה לזה, כדמפרש רב ספרא לקמיה. **בפלוגתא לא איירי.** רבי חייא. **האסורה לזה.** אשת לוי האסורה ליששכר שבאה ומצאה אסורה עליו מזיקת ראובן שלא היה בעולמו, ומותרת לזבולן. שכשנולד כבר נתייבמה ללוי, וכייבם ולבסוף נולד שרי ר"ש. ואשת יהודה אסורה לזבולון משום שמעון שלא היה בעולמו, וכשנולד מצאה באיסור, ומותרת ליששכר. **בלא ייבם יהודה נמי.** שרי ליששכר. ובחמשה אחי משכחת לה: מת ראובן נולד יששכר ייבם לוי, מת שמעון נולד זבולון ומת לוי בלא בנים, ונפלו אשת לוי ואשת שמעון לפני יששכר וזבולון. אשת לוי אסורה ליששכר מפני ראובן בעלה הראשון, ומותרת לזבולון, ואשת שמעון מותרת ליששכר, שהרי בעולמו היה, ואסורה לזבולון. **ומשום צרה.** האי דנקט ייבם יהודה — משום צרה, דבעי אשכוחי נמי בצרה האסורה לזה מותרת לזה, אם באו יששכר וזבולון לייבם לנשי לוי ויהודה הראשונה — אשת לוי אסורה ליששכר משום צרת אשת אחיו שלא היה בעולמו, וכן אשת יהודה על זבולון. וכגון שהיו הצרות אחיות זו לזו. ונכריות קרי להו אצל נשי ראובן ושמעון, דאיכא נמי השתא בצרות האסורה לזה מותרת לזה ואחותה כשהיא יבמתה כו'. ואי לא ייבם יהודה לא מיתוקם מילתא דרבי חייא באיסור צרתה, דאם נפלו שתי נשים משמעון — שתיהן אשת אח שלא היה בעולמו הן. **צרה דצרה מאי איכא למימר.** היכי קרית האסורה לזה מותרת לזה באיסור וצרות צרה? דהא צרות צרותיהן נמי תנן בפ"ק. **כגון דהדר יבמינהו גד ואשר.** לנשי לוי ויהודה הראשונות, ולהם נשים, וייבם גד את אשת יהודה, ואשר ייבם אשת לוי, ומתו גד ואשר ונפלו לפני יששכר וזבולון. ואם באים לייבם נשי גד ואשר הראשונות — אשת גד צרת אשת יהודה שהיתה צרת אשת שמעון שלא היה בעולמו אסורה לזבולון ומותרת ליששכר. וכן אשת אשר על יששכר, ומותרת לזבולון. **בשעה שנעשו צרות זו לזו.** כגון (א) השתא, שנפלו לפניו ונעשו שתי אחיות צרות זו לזו בזיקה. **ליגזור משום שתי אחיות דעלמא.** אע"ג דהא נמי מרישא שמעינן התם הוא לרבנן לא גזרינן. דאי נמי אתי למישרי אחיות דעלמא — ליכא אלא איסור אחות זקוקה דרבנן. אבל לר"ש דאמר איסור אחות זקוקה ערוה גמורה היא, דרחמנא פטרה, וקיימא עליה באיסור אשת אח — ליגזור היכא דאחותה אסורה משום ערוה ולא זקוקה ליה, ונימא לא לייבם לאחותה, דלא ליתי לייבומי אחות זקוקה דעלמא, קמ"ל. והאמר

תוספות

אבל הכא דליכא שני דמוכח. ואם תאמר: הא נמי ידעינן מההיא דפ"ב כדאמרינן לעיל (דף כ.)! ויש לומר: דהתם איכא ערוה דקמוכח שאינה לא חולצת ולא מתייבמת, אבל הכא — שתיהן מתייבמות, וליכא הוכחה. **שנעשו** צרות זו לזו כו'. היינו דוקא כשנפלו לפני יבם אחד, אבל כשנפלו לפני שני יבמין — מודה רבי שמעון, כדתניא לעיל: רבי שמעון אומר יקיימו. אחותה

עין משפט נר מצוה

יד א מיי' פ"ו מהלכות יבום הלכה כה סמג עשין נא טוש"ע אה"ע סימן קעה סעיף ו:

תוספות ישנים

לגזור משום שתי אחיות דעלמא ונהי דלעיל חזינן דלא גזרינן היינו דווקא לרבנן אבל לר"ש דסבר דאלימא כל כך זיקה דאמר דשתי אחיות לא חולצות ולא מתייבמות סד"א ליגזור משום שתי אחיות דעלמא:

תוספות חד מקמאי

יבמה שאין אני קורא לה בשעת נפילה יבמה יבוא עליה הרי היא כאשת אח שיש לה בנים אלמא ס"ל יש זיקה: הא דקתני במתני' איסור מצוה או איסור קדושה חולצת ולא מתייבמת פרכינן עלה בגמ' הא נמי תנינן אסור מצוה או איסור קדושה חולצת ולא מתייבמת. התם איסור מצוה לחודיה. והכא איסור מצוה ואחותה. ומאי דקתני זו היא שאמרו אחותה שהיא יבמתה חולצת או מתייבמת פרשינן בגמ' למעוטי איסו' מצוה לזה ואיסור מצוה לזה:

מסורת הש"ס

לעיל כ. [כו.] סנהדרין נג.

לעיל ט.

לעיל יט.

[לעיל כ. וש"נ]

לעיל יט. קידושין נ:

[לעיל יט. ונזכר ר"ש ז' עוד לעיל יח:]

תורה אור — ויקרא יח

הגהות הב"ח

(א) רש"י ד"ה בשעה וכו' כגון הכא שנפלו:

טו א מיי' פ"ז מהלכות יבום הלכה ו סמג עשין נא טוש"ע אה"ע סימן קעה סעיף ו:

וְהָא א"ר שִׁמְעוֹן: שְׁתֵּי אֲחָיוֹת לֹא חוֹלְצוֹת וְלֹא מִתְיַבְּמוֹת! — גְּזֵירָה מִשּׁוּם אִיסּוּר מִצְוָה דְּעָלְמָא. הָא תֵּינַח אִיהִי, אֲחוֹתָהּ מַאי אִיכָּא לְמֵימַר? — גְּזֵירָה אֲחוֹתָהּ מִשּׁוּם לָתָא דִּידָהּ. — וְהָא גַּבֵּי עֶרְוָה לָא גָּזְרִינַן! — שָׁאנֵי עֶרְוָה דְּמִגְמַר גְּמִירִי לָהּ אֱינָשֵׁי, וְקָלָא אִית לָהּ.§ **מתני'** *שְׁלֹשָׁה אַחִין, שְׁנַיִם נְשׂוּאִים שְׁתֵּי אֲחָיוֹת, וְאֶחָד מוּפְנֶה; מֵת אֶחָד מִבַּעֲלֵי אֲחָיוֹת וְעָשָׂה בָּהּ מוּפְנֶה מַאֲמָר, וְאַחַ"כ מֵת אָחִיו הַשֵּׁנִי — בש"א: אִשְׁתּוֹ עִמּוֹ, וְהַלָּזוּ תֵּצֵא מִשּׁוּם אֲחוֹת אִשָּׁה. וב"ה אוֹמְרִים: [א]מוֹצִיא אֶת אִשְׁתּוֹ בְּגֵט וּבַחֲלִיצָה, וְאֵשֶׁת אָחִיו בַּחֲלִיצָה. זוֹ הִיא שֶׁאָמְרוּ: *אוֹי לוֹ עַל אִשְׁתּוֹ, וְאוֹי לוֹ עַל אֵשֶׁת אָחִיו.§ **גמ'** "זוֹ הִיא" לְמַעוּטֵי מַאי? — לְמַעוּטֵי הָךְ דְּרַ' יְהוֹשֻׁעַ, דְּלָא עָבְדִינַן כְּוָותֵיהּ, אֶלָּא אִי כְּרַ"ג אִי כְּרַ"א. *א"ר אֶלְעָזָר: לָא תֵּימָא מַאֲמָר לְב"ש קוֹנֶה קִנְיָן גָּמוּר, דְּאִי בָּעֵי לְאַפּוּקֵי סַגִּי לָהּ בְּגִיטָּא, אֶלָּא: מַאֲמָר לְב"ש אֵינוֹ קוֹנֶה אֶלָּא לִדְחוֹת בְּצָרָה בִּלְבַד. אֲמַר רַבִּי אָבִין, אַף אֲנַן נַמִּי תָּנֵינָא: בש"א: יְקַיְּימוּ, יְקַיְּימוּ — אִין, לְכַתְּחִלָּה — לָא, וְאִי

רש"י

וְהָאָמַר ר' שִׁמְעוֹן שְׁתֵּי אֲחָיוֹת לֹא חוֹלְצוֹת וְלֹא מִתְיַבְּמוֹת. וְהָכָא אַמַּאי בָּעֵי חֲלִיצָה? הָא כֵּיוָן דְּמִדְּאוֹרַיְיתָא חַזְיָא לְיַבּוּמֵי – זְקוּקָה הִיא, וְהָווּ לְהוּ כִּשְׁאָר ב' אֲחָיוֹת שֶׁנַּעֲשׂוּ צָרוֹת זוֹ לָזוֹ, וְר"ש פּוֹטֵר אֲחוֹת זְקוּקָה מֵחֲלִיצָה. גְּזֵירָה מִשּׁוּם אִיסּוּר מִצְוָה דְּעָלְמָא. אִי פָּטְרַתְּ לְהוּ לְגַמְרֵי, מַאן דַּחֲזֵי סָבַר: טַעְמָא לָאו מִשּׁוּם אֲחוֹת זְקוּקָה, אֶלָּא מִשּׁוּם דְּאִיסּוּר מִצְוָה הָוְיָא כְּעֶרְוָה וּפְטוּרָה מֵחֲלִיצָה, וְאָתֵי לְמִיפְטַר אִיסּוּר מִצְוָה דְּעָלְמָא, דְּלָאו אֲחָיוֹת, מֵחֲלִיצָה. תֵּינַח אִיהִי. אִיסּוּר מִצְוָה. אֲחוֹתָהּ. אַמַּאי חָלְצָה? תִּיפָּטֵר מִשּׁוּם אֲחוֹת זְקוּקָה, דְּהָכָא מַאי אָמְרַתְּ. מִשּׁוּם לָתָא דִּידָהּ. מִשּׁוּם מַזָּל דִּידָהּ, דְּאִיסּוּר מִצְוָה. הַאי "לָתָא" – יִתּוּר לָשׁוֹן הוּא. וְהָא גַּבֵּי עֶרְוָה לָא גָּזְרִינַן. דְּאִם הָיְתָה אַחַת מֵהֶן אֲסוּרָה עָלָיו אִיסּוּר עֶרְוָה – אָסוּר בָּהּ וּמוּתָּר בַּאֲחוֹתָהּ, הָעֶרְוָה יוֹצְאָה בְּלֹא חֲלִיצָה, וְלָא אָמְרִינַן תַּחֲלוֹץ עֶרְוָה גְּזֵירָה מִשּׁוּם אֲחוֹתָהּ שֶׁאֵין עֶרְוָה וּרְאוּיָה לְיִיבּוּם. וְהָא נַמִּי לְרַבִּי שִׁמְעוֹן עֶרְוָה הִיא מִשֶּׁנַּעֲשׂוּ צָרוֹת, וְאַמַּאי מַצְרְכַתְּ לָהּ חֲלִיצָה מִשּׁוּם גְּזֵרַת אֲחוֹתָהּ? דְּמִגְמַר גְּמִירֵי לָהּ אֱינָשֵׁי. וְהַכֹּל יוֹדְעִין שֶׁאֵין צְרִיכָה חֲלִיצָה, וַאֲחוֹתָהּ לָאו אֲחוֹת זְקוּקָה הִיא, וְלָא אָתֵי לְמִשְׁרֵי אֲחוֹתָהּ בְּלֹא חֲלִיצָה. אֲבָל עֶרְוָה דְּנַעֲשׂוּ צָרוֹת דְּר"ש – לָא כ"ע גְּמִירֵי הִלְכְתָא דְּאִיסּוּר שְׁתֵּיהֶן שָׁווֹת. וְאִי מַפְקַתְּ לָהּ בְּלֹא חֲלִיצָה – אָתֵי נַמִּי לְמֵיפַּק אֲחוֹתָהּ שֶׁהִיא אִיסּוּר מִצְוָה בְּלֹא חֲלִיצָה, וְנָפְקָא מִינָּהּ חוּרְבָּה לְאִיסּוּר מִצְוָה בְּעָלְמָא: *מִגְמַר גְּמִירֵי אֱינָשֵׁי. וְיָדְעֵי דְּלָא רַמְיָא קַמֵּיהּ, וַאֲחוֹתָהּ לָאו אֲחוֹת זְקוּקָה הִיא, וְלָא אָתֵי לְמִישְׁרֵי אֲחוֹת זְקוּקָה דְּעָלְמָא. **מתני'** אִשְׁתּוֹ עִמּוֹ. דְּמַאֲמָר כִּכְנוּסָה דָּמְיָא, וְכִי נָפְלָה אֲחוֹתָהּ לָא מִיתַּסְרָא הָךְ עֲלֵיהּ מִשּׁוּם אֲחוֹת זְקוּקָה. וְהַלָּזוּ תֵּצֵא. אַף מִן הַחֲלִיצָה מִשּׁוּם אֲחוֹת אִשָּׁה. **גמ'** הָךְ דְּרַבִּי יְהוֹשֻׁעַ. בְּפֶרֶק ב"ש, דְּקָאָמַר נַמִּי: אִי לוֹ עַל אִשְׁתּוֹ אִי לוֹ עַל אֵשֶׁת אָחִיו, וּפְלִיגִי עֲלָהּ רַבָּן גַּמְלִיאֵל וְרַבִּי אֱלִיעֶזֶר. לָא תֵּימָא מַאֲמָר לְב"ש קוֹנֶה קִנְיָן גָּמוּר. וְתֶהֱוֵי כְּאִשְׁתּוֹ, וְאִי בָּעֵי לְאַפּוֹקֵי – תִּיסְגֵּי לָהּ בְּגִיטָּא. אֶלָּא מַאֲמָר לְב"ש אֵין קוֹנֶה אֶלָּא לִדְחוֹת בְּצָרָה. כְּלוֹמַר: לִדְחוֹת אֲחוֹתָהּ שֶׁלֹּא תֵּאָסְרֶנָּה לָזוֹ מִשּׁוּם אֲחוֹת זְקוּקָה. יְקַיְּימוּ. אִם קָדְמוּ וְכָנְסוּ, בְּרֵישׁ פִּירְקִין. לְכַתְּחִילָּה לָא. מְיַיבְּמוּ, מִשּׁוּם אֲחוֹת זְקוּקָתוֹ. וְאִי

תוספות

אחותה משום לתא דידה. דאי נפקא בלא חליצה, משום דנעשו צרות זו לזו – אתי לאפוקי מהאי טעמא נמי ההיא דאיסור מצוה, ואתי למישרי נמי איסור מצוה דעלמא, ופרכינן: והא גבי ערוה לא גזרו שתהלך אלא יוצאה בלא חליצה, ולא חיישינן שמא יסברו דמטעם (א) אחותה יוצאה, ואתי לאפוקי אידך בלא חליצה. **ב"ש** אומרים אשתו עמו כו'. בגמ' גבי השתא ארוסה דעלמא כו' עשה בה מאמר מיבעיא פירש בקונטרס דמאמר יבמין מדרבנן, אפילו לבית שמאי, דמדאורייתא "יבמה יבא עליה" כתיב. ואין נראה לריב"ס, דא"כ אמאי תצא הלזו משום אחות אשה במאמר זה? ומיהו, י"ל: דתצא משום אחות אשה – היינו אחר שיבעול [בעלת המאמר]. אבל קשה, דלעיל פ"ב (דף יח. ושם) דקאמר: הא דקתני מאמר – לאפוקי מב"ש, משמע דלב"ש (ב) יוצאה שניה משום צרת אשת אחיו שלא היה בעולמו. וכן נמי קאמרינן לקמן בפירקין (דף ל.) גבי אחות אשה אלמא מאמר קני דאורייתא לב"ש, וכולה סוגיא דגמרא מוכח הכי. והא דקאמר השתא ארוסה דעלמא כו' עבד בה מאמר מיבעיא – אע"ג דמאמר נמי מדאורייתא, מ"מ קאמר מאמר מיבעיא, משום דהא דמאמר קני – מדאורייתא היינו משום דגמרינן מקידושין דעלמא, הלכך לא עדיף מקידושין. ודיו לבא מן הדין להיות כנדון. **אוי** לו על אשתו כו'. אר"י: דבכל הני דפ' "חרש" (לקמן קיג: קיד:) דתנן מוציא את אשתו בגט ואת אשת אחיו בחליצה לא קתני "אוי לו" כי הכא, משום ד"אוי לו" משמע לשון צער, כלומר: ראוי לו להצטער שהפסיד אשתו בלא פשיעתו. והכא והא דאייתי בגמ' פלוגתא דר"א ור' יהושע דקטנה וגדולה – לא פשע, להכי קתני "אוי לו". אבל התם פשע, שהכניס עצמו בספק חרשות, שלא היה לו לישא חרשת. וכן ההיא ד"ההולך" (לקמן דף מא. ושם) דשומרת יבם שקידש אחיו את אחותה כו' להכי נמי קאמר בגמרא למעוטי דר' יהושע, דשייך התם לשון "אוי לו" כי הכא, ולא קאמר למעוטי כל הני. **אי** כר"ג. דאמר תמתין עד שתגדיל ויבעול ותצא הלזו משום אחות אשה, אע"ג דקדושי קטנה דרבנן – מ"מ הקילו בה מבבעלת מאמר, משום דכנוסה היא אצלו קודם זמן גדולה. והא דפריך מינה לעיל בריש פ"ב (דף יח.) אהא דר"מ אוסר לבטל מצות יבמין, ור"ג שרי לבטל מצות יבמין, אע"ג דהכא כנוסה אצלו מעיקרא – מ"מ פריך אהא דר"מ חייש לספיקא, ור"ג אפילו לודאי לא חייש. **אי** כרבי אלעזר. דאמר: מלמדין הקטנה שתמאן, ומותר בגדולה לייבם. וא"ת: ואמאי שרי? והא בשעת נפילה נראית כאחות אשה, כדאמרינן לעיל בפ"ק (דף יב.) גבי צרת בתו הממאנת, דבשעת נפילה נראית כצרת בתו, ובשעת נפילה נראית ככלתו! וי"ל: דלא דמי, דהתם, כשהבעל מת, אין דומה כ"כ עוקרת נישואין קמאי כי הכא, שהבעל קיים(א). **לא** תימא מאמר לב"ש קונה קנין גמור כו'. אע"ג דאין קונה קנין גמור, מ"מ אמרי' לעיל (ג) ולקמן (דף ל.) גבי אחות אשה דפוטרת [צרתה] לב"ש ע"י מאמר. תימה: מאי קאמר ר"ש לעיל בפ"ב (דף יט.): אם מאמרו של שני מאמר – אשת שני הוא בועל, כי הוי נמי מאמר – אשת שניהם בועל, דהא אפילו לב"ש דמאמר קונה אינו קונה לגמרי, אלא קונה ומשייר! וכ"ת דלר"ש אי קני – קני לגמרי, טפי מלב"ש – א"כ מנא ליה לר' אלעזר דלא קני לגמרי לב"ש כמו לר"ש? **אלא** לדחות בצרה בלבד. פי' בקונטרס: צרה דכולהו שמעתין – אחותה שנופלת עמה. וקשה: לרב אשי דאמר דוחה ומשייר היא וצרתה בעיא חליצה, הא קתני במתני' תצא משום אחות אשה, משמע דיוצאה בלא חליצה! ועוד: אי בעיא חליצה – היאך מקיים את זו? וי"ל: דסבר רב אשי דמהני מאמר להסיר הזיקה, ודחי לצרה לענין שלא תאסור את זו משום אחות זקוקתו, ואחר שיבעול בעלת המאמר – קאמר דתצא אחותה משום אחות אשה. וא"ת: והיכי מייתי לה סייעתא ממתניתין יקיימו – אין, לכתחלה – לא, הא מהני מאמר לרב אשי לכל הפחות דדחי לצרה ושריא בעלת מאמר לכתחלה? וי"ל: דהכי מייתי, דאי ס"ד דבמאמר דהיתירא (ד) דוחה דחייה גמורה לפטור צרתה בלא חליצה – א"כ מאמר דאיסור דחי נמי לצרה לענין שלא תאסור את זו משום אחות זקוקה וזה יעשה מאמר וידחה כו'. ופריך: ואלא הא קתני בש"א אשתו עמו כו' – משמע דדוחה דחייה גמורה, אלא יבמה דחזיא לכולהו כו'. פי': דמאמר דהיתירא – דחי דחייה גמורה. יבמה דלא חזיא לכולהו, דהיינו מאמר דאיסור – לא דחי למקצתה, ולא דחי ההוא מאמר כלל. כן צריך לפרש לפי' הקונטרס. אבל קשה: דצרה דבכל דוכתי היינו – שנופלת עמה מבית אחד. ועוד: שמגיה הספרים אלא יבמה דחזיא לכולהו כו', שלא היה כתוב בספרים "אלא". ועוד: דלמה שינה הלשון יבמה דחזיא כו', ולא נקט לישנא דנקט מעיקרא מאמר דהיתירא קני דאיסורא לא קני! ונראה לר"י: דצרה – היינו שעמה בבית אחד. וה"פ: לא תימא מאמר לב"ש כו' אלא לדחות צרה בלבד, שאם נתן מאמר לא' מב' יבמות שנפלו מבית אחד, אע"ג דבעלת מאמר לא סגי לה בגט – צרתה מיהו פטורה לגמרי בלא חליצה, דכיון שהתחיל הקנין לעשות בזו, אע"פ שלא נגמר – קרינן ביה בית אחד הוא בונה ואינו בונה ב' בתים. וטעמא דב"ש דסברי דאהני קרא דדרשינן *ביאה גומרת בה ואין כסף ושטר גומרין בה, לענין דאי בעי לאפוקי, דלא סגי לה בגט. ורב אשי סבר דלא מהני מאמר לפטור צרתה בלא חליצה, אלא דוחה הצרה ממנו, שאסור לייבמה, ומשייר קצת זיקה לאוסרה לשוק עד שתחלוץ. ואע"ג דלענין אחותה *דחי מאמר לגמרי לפוטרה לשוק, כדקתני מתני': והלזו תצא משום אחות אשה – התם אחותה נפלה אחר המאמר, כמו שפירשתי בסמוך. וקאמר: אף אנן נמי תנינא, שכשקדמה זיקה למאמר שאין המאמר מפקיע לגמרי – זה יעשה מאמר וידחה כו'. ופריך: אלא הך דקתני בש"א אשתו עמו כו', אלמא ע"י המאמר מידחי אחותה לגמרי, ה"נ תדחה צרתה לגמרי! ומשני: יבמה דחזיא לכולהו, ול"ג "אלא", וה"פ: יבמה דחזיא לכולהו מילי דיבום, כגון ב' יבמות שנפלו מבית אחד, שכל אחת ראויה לחלוץ ולייבם בשעת נפילה, וכן הא דבש"א יקיימו, דבשעת נפילה חזיא כל אחת לכל מילי דיבום מן התורה, דהא חזיא [אף] ליבום מן התורה – חזיא נמי למקצתו, פי': למקצת מילי דיבמה, דהיינו חליצה. דכיון דבהך זיקה איחזיא ליבום – לא מפיק מאמר להאי זיקה לגמרי, ובעי חליצה. אבל יבמה דלא איחזיא לכולהו מילי דיבום, כגון ההיא דבש"א אשתו עמו, שלא נראית ליבום בשעת נפילה שכבר עשה המאמר באחותה – לא חזיא למקצתו. פי': חליצה, ואידחיא ע"י מאמר חברתה לגמרי. והשתא לא מצי לשנויי כדשני לעיל מאמר דהיתירא דחי כו' – שאפי' במאמר דהיתירא קאמר דלא מפקע הזיקה לגמרי להתיר צרה לשוק(ב). הקשה ה"ר יעקב דאורלינ"ש: מנא לן דטעמא דב"ש משום דמאמר קונה? דלמא קסברי אין זיקה, ומותר לבטל מצות יבמין, ונקט מאמר משום ב"ה? וי"ל: דלא מסתבר שיהא שום תנא מיקל לבטל בהדיא מצות יבמין. ועוד: דהא אמר לעיל בש"א יקיימו לכתחלה לא. ועוד הקשה: דלמא טעמא דב"ש משום דזיקה ככנוסה? וי"ל: דלא מסתבר ליה למימר דלא נקט מאמר אלא משום ב"ה, כיון שיכול לומר דלב"ש נמי איצטריך.

יעשה

תוספות ישנים

והאמר ר"ש וכו' וא"כ אמאי אמרינן במתני' חולצות. וא"ת ודלמא משום דאיסור מצוה פקעה קצת זיקה. ונראה לר"ס דפריך מאיסור מצוה גופה אמאי חולצת דממה נפשך היה לנו לומר דלא תחלוץ דאי איסור מצוה משוי לה ערוה א"כ פטורה היא גם מחליצה ואי לא משוי לה כערוה א"כ יש בהן זיקה כמו שתי אחיות דעלמא דאינן חולצות. והא דקא פריך אחותה מאי איכא למימר אין זה ממה נפשך דהא אי איסור מצוה ערוה היא א"כ מותר באחותה דאינה אחות זקוקתו. אבל מ"מ פריך שפיר דכיון דלא מחזקינן איסור מצוה לערוה ולא אמרי' אלא משום גזרה משום איסור מצוה בעלמא. א"כ אחותה הוי אחות זקוקה: **והא** גבי ערוה לא גזרינן. פי' דאמרינן אסור בה ומותר באחותה ואמאי לא אמרינן דתחלוץ גזרה משום אחותה דשמא יאמרו העולם דכי היכי דפטורה איהי תפטר אחותה וזה אינו דהא מותר בה. א"כ לא היה לנו להתיר אחותה היכא דאיכא נמי איסור ערוה גזרה משום שתי אחיות שאין בהם ערוה ומשני ערוה מגמר גמרי אינשי: **שנים** מהם נשואים שתי אחיות וא' מופנה האי דלא נקט הכא וא' נשוי נכרית כמו במשנה דבסמוך. נראה משום דבעי למימר זו היא שאמרו אוי לו על אשתו ועל אשת אחיו לכך מוקים לה דהוי מופנה דהשתא הוי בלא אשה כלל: **אשתו** עמו משום דקסבר ב"ש מאמר קונה ומשמע מדאורייתא הוא מדקאמר והלזו תצא משום אחות אשה ונפקא לן מדכתיב ולקחה לו לאשה כאשה מה אשה בשטר אף יבמה בשטר ולא כפ"ה דפי' בגמרא עביד בה מאמר מיבעיא. ופ"ה דמאמר אינו אלא מדרבנן ולפי' שפיר י"ל דהוי מדאורייתא וכדפרשתי לקמן דהכי קאמר השתא ארוסה בעלמא דהוו קדושין מפורשים בהדיא בקרא וכו' עביד בה מאמר דלא ידעינן אלא מקדושין מיבעיא: **א)** ועוי"ל דלא דמי ללעיל איירי שמיאנה ביבם לבד ולא בבעל ואינו נראה כעוקרת נשואי המת אבל הכא שממאנת הקטנה בבעלה ורואין העולם שיוצאה מבעלה במיאון יודעין העולם שלא היו נשואיה נשואין ולא היתה אחות אשה: **ב)** והקשה הרב רבינו נתנאל חדא דלפי הך פירושא הך צרה ר"ל באשה אחרת ובהא לא איירי במתני' כי אם באחותה שנפלה מאח אחר. ועוד דפי' דדוחה צרתה משום בית א' הוא בונה קשה אטו מאמר בנין מקרי הא אמרינן בעשרה יוחסין הכל מודים במחזיר גרושתו בקידש ולא בעל דאינו לוקה מאי טעמא דרך ליקוחין אסרה תורה אלמא לא מקרי בנין אלא ביאה. לכן נראה לרבינו נתנאל לפרש שיטה אחרת מראש ועד סוף מאמר אינו קונה אלא לדחות צרה בלבד כלומר לצרתה מאחיו שהיא אחותה של בעלת מאמר לא בעיא חליצה אבל איהי לא סגיא בגט וב"ש לטעמייהו דהכי מפרש בירושלמי אמר ר' אליעזר בן ערך גירש לבעלת מאמר לא תהא צריכה חליצה א"ר הילא בשם ר' אליעזר מודה ב"ש שאם גירש לבעלת מאמר צריכה הימנו חליצה אלמא לב"ש לא סגי לה בגט. וא"ת כיון דלא אלים כח בעלת מאמר לפטור בגט היכי אלימא לפטור צרתה מחליצה י"ל דלא גרע מקדושין דעלמא דהכא נמי כתיב ולקחה זו מאמר ואם קדש אשה ואח"כ מת אחיו נשוי אחותה פשיטא דלא תצא המאורסת הכא נמי הא בעלת מאמר ומ"מ ההיא גופה לא סגי לה בגט אע"ג דאלים בעלת מאמר כקדושין דעלמא לענין שלא תהא צרה צריכה חליצה מ"מ הכא לא סגי לה בגט דביאה גומרת בה דכתיב יבמה יבא עליה וזיקה דבהדי מאמר לא פקעה בגט לבד אי ליכא חליצה בהדיה.

הגהות הב"ח

(א) תוס' ד"ה אחותה וכו' דמטעם אחות אשה יוצאה ואתי: (ב) ד"ה ב"ש וכו' משמע דלב"ש במאמר לחוד יוצאת שניה: (ג) ד"ה לא תימא וכו' מ"מ אמרינן לעיל דפוטר גבי אשת אחיו שלא היה בעולמו ולקמן גבי אחות אשה: (ד) ד"ה אלא וכו' דהיתירא דחיא לחייא גמורה:

מסורת הש"ס: לקמן נה: עדיות פ"ד מ"ט | לקמן קט. | לקמן לט. [נדרים עז.] | נ"א לישנא אחרינא | [לקמן נב. קדושין יג.] | מאמר חברתה דחי לגמרי כצ"ל

טז א מיי' פ"ב מהל' אבל הלכה ג סמג לאוין רלה טוש"ע י"ד סימן שעג סעיף ד וטוש"ע אה"ע סימן נד סעיף ה:
יז ב מיי' פכ"ב מהל' איסורי ביאה הלכה כג סמג עשין מח טוש"ע אה"ע שם (וסימן נז):
יח ג מיי' שם הלכה יא סמג שם טוש"ע אה"ע סימן נד סעיף ו:
יט ד מיי' פ"א מהל' נדרים הלכה כב סמג לאוין רמב טוש"ע י"ד סימן רלד סעיף ז:
כ ה מיי' שם הלכה ט טוש"ע י"ד שם סעי' ה:

וְאִי ס"ד מַאֲמָר לְב"ש קוֹנֶה קִנְיָן גָּמוּר — זֶה יַעֲשֶׂה מַאֲמָר וְיִקְנֶה, וְזֶה יַעֲשֶׂה מַאֲמָר וְיִקְנֶה! אֶלָּא מַאי — דּוֹחֶה דְּחִיָּיה גְּמוּרָה? זֶה יַעֲשֶׂה מַאֲמָר וְיִדְחֶה, וְזֶה יַעֲשֶׂה מַאֲמָר וְיִדְחֶה. אֶלָּא מַאי אִית לָךְ לְמֵימַר: מַאֲמָר דְּהֶתֵּירָא — דָּחֵי, דְּאִיסּוּרָא — לָא דָּחֵי — ה"נ: מַאֲמָר, אֲפִילּוּ לְמ"ד מַאֲמָר קוֹנֶה קִנְיָן גָּמוּר, מַאֲמָר דְּהֶתֵּירָא — קָנֵי דְּאִיסּוּרָא — לָא קָנֵי. רַב אַשִׁי מַתְנֵי הָכִי, אֲמַר ר"א: לָא תֵּימָא מַאֲמָר לְב"ש דָּחֵי דְּחִיָּיה גְּמוּרָה, וְצָרָתָהּ חֲלִיצָה נַמִּי לָא בָּעֲיָא, אֶלָּא דּוֹחֶה וּמְשַׁיֵּיר הוּא. א"ר אָבִין: אַף אֲנַן נַמִּי תָּנֵינָא: ב"ש אוֹמְרִים: יְקַיְּימוּ. יְקַיְּימוּ — אִין, לְכַתְּחִלָּה — לָא. וְאִי ס"ד מַאֲמָר לְב"ש דּוֹחֶה דְּחִיָּיה גְּמוּרָה — זֶה יַעֲשֶׂה מַאֲמָר וְיִדְחֶה, וְזֶה יַעֲשֶׂה מַאֲמָר וְיִדְחֶה! — וְאֶלָּא הָא קָתָנֵי, בש"א: אִשְׁתּוֹ עִמּוֹ, וְהַלָּזוּ תֵּצֵא מִשּׁוּם אֲחוֹת אִשָּׁה! — אֶלָּא: יְבָמָה דְּחַזְיָא לְכוּלְּהוּ — חַזְיָא לְמִקְצָתָהּ. יְבָמָה דְּלָא חַזְיָא לְכוּלְּהוּ — לָא חַזְיָא לְמִקְצָתָהּ. *בָּעֵי רַבָּה: מַאֲמָר, לְב"ש, נִישּׂוּאִין עוֹשֶׂה אוֹ אֵירוּסִין עוֹשֶׂה? אֲמַר לֵיהּ אַבָּיֵי: לְמַאי הִלְכְתָא? אִילֵימָא לְיוֹרְשָׁהּ וְלִיטַּמֵּא לָהּ וּלְהָפֵר נְדָרֶיהָ — הַשְׁתָּא אֲרוּסָה בְּעָלְמָא תָּנֵי רַ' חִיָּיא: *אִשְׁתּוֹ [א]אֲרוּסָה לֹא אוֹנֵן וְלֹא מִטַּמֵּא לָהּ, וְכֵן הִיא לֹא אוֹנֶנֶת וְלֹא מִטַּמֵּאת לוֹ, [ב]מֵתָה — אֵינוֹ יוֹרְשָׁהּ, מֵת [ג]הוּא — גּוֹבָה כְּתוּבָּתָהּ, — עָבַד בָּהּ מַאֲמָר מִיבָּעֲיָא? וְאֶלָּא לְעִנְיַן מְסִירָה לְחוּפָּה, מַאי? נִישּׂוּאִין עוֹשֶׂה — וְלֹא בָּעֲיָא מְסִירָה לְחוּפָּה, אוֹ דִּלְמָא אֵירוּסִין עוֹשֶׂה — וּבָעֲיָא מְסִירָה לְחוּפָּה! א"ל: הַשְׁתָּא, לָא עֲבַד בָּהּ מַאֲמָר כְּתִיב °"יְבָמָהּ יָבֹא עָלֶיהָ", בְּעַל כָּרְחָהּ, עֲבַד בָּהּ מַאֲמָר מִיבָּעֲיָא? א"ל: (א) שֶׁאֲנִי אוֹמֵר *כָּל הָעוֹשֶׂה מַאֲמָר בִּיבִמְתּוֹ — פָּרְחָה מִמֶּנּוּ זִיקַת יְבָמִין, וְחָלָה עָלֶיהָ זִיקַת אֵירוּסִין. מַאי? ת"ש: *שׁוֹמֶרֶת יָבָם, בֵּין יָבָם אֶחָד בֵּין שְׁנֵי יְבָמִין, ר"א אוֹמֵר: יָפֵר, רַ' יְהוֹשֻׁעַ אוֹמֵר: לְאֶחָד וְלֹא לִשְׁנַיִם, [ד]רַ' עֲקִיבָא אוֹמֵר: לֹא לְאֶחָד וְלֹא לִשְׁנַיִם. וְהָוֵינַן בָּהּ: *בִּשְׁלָמָא ר"ע סָבַר: אֵין זִיקָה אֲפִי' לְחַד, לְרַ' יְהוֹשֻׁעַ: לְחַד — יֵשׁ זִיקָה, לִתְרֵי — אֵין זִיקָה. אֶלָּא לְר"א, נְהִי נַמִּי דְּקָסָבַר יֵשׁ זִיקָה. בִּשְׁלָמָא לְחַד — מֵיפֵר, אֶלָּא לִתְרֵי — אַמַּאי? וְא"ר אַמִּי (*בַּר אַהֲבָה): הָכָא בְּמַאי עָסְקִינַן — כְּגוֹן דַּעֲבַד בָּהּ מַאֲמָר, *וּב"ש הִיא, דְּאָמַר: מַאֲמָר קוֹנֶה קִנְיָן גָּמוּר. אִי אָמְרַתְּ בִּשְׁלָמָא נִישּׂוּאִין עוֹשֶׂה — מִשּׁוּם הָכִי מֵיפֵר, אֶלָּא אִי אָמְרַתְּ אֵירוּסִין עוֹשֶׂה — הֵיכִי מָצֵי מֵיפֵר? וְהָתְנַן: *[ה]נַעֲרָה הַמְאוֹרָסָה אָבִיהָ וּבַעְלָהּ מְפִירִים נְדָרֶיהָ! אֲמַר רַב נַחְמָן בַּר יִצְחָק: מַאי מֵיפֵר — מֵיפֵר בְּשׁוּתָּפוּת. וְלר"א, דְּאָמַר: מַאֲמָר לְב"ש אֵינוֹ קוֹנֶה אֶלָּא לִדְחוֹת לַצָּרָה בִּלְבַד, אַמַּאי מֵיפֵר בְּשׁוּתָּפוּת? אָמַר לָךְ רַ' אֶלְעָזָר: אֵימַר דַּאֲמָרִי אֲנָא אֵינוֹ קוֹנֶה אֶלָּא לִדְחוֹת לַצָּרָה בִּלְבַד — דְּלָא סַגִּי לָהּ בְּגִיטָּא אֶלָּא בָּעֵי נַמִּי חֲלִיצָה, לְהָפֵר נְדָרֶיהָ — מִי אָמְרִינַן? וְאִיבָּעֵית אֵימָא, אָמַר לָךְ רַבִּי אֶלְעָזָר: וּלְרַב נַחְמָן בַּר יִצְחָק מִי נִיחָא? מִי קָתָנֵי "יָפֵרוּ"? "יָפֵר" קָתָנֵי. אֶלָּא הָכָא בְּמַאי עָסְקִינַן — (ב) שֶׁעָמְדָה בְּדִין וּפָסְקוּ לָהּ מְזוֹנוֹת מִשֶּׁלּוֹ, וְכִדְרַב פִּנְחָס מִשְּׁמֵיהּ דְּרָבָא, דְּאָמַר רַב פִּנְחָס מִשְּׁמֵיהּ דְּרָבָא: *כָּל הַנּוֹדֶרֶת — עַל דַּעַת בַּעְלָהּ הִיא נוֹדֶרֶת.§
מתני'

דברים כה

רש"י

וְאִי מַאֲמָר לְב"ש קוֹנֶה קִנְיָן גָּמוּר. זֶה יַעֲשֶׂה מַאֲמָר בְּזוֹ וְיִקְנֶה אוֹתָהּ קִנְיָן גָּמוּר לִהְיוֹת אִשְׁתּוֹ, דְּהָא אֵין אִיסּוּר בְּמַאֲמָר, (ג) וְתָלֵא אֲחוֹתָהּ מֵעָלָיו, וְלָא הָוְיָא הָךְ אֲחוֹת זְקוּקָתוֹ — וְיִכְנוֹס אֶת אִשְׁתּוֹ. אֶלָּא מַאי כו'. נְהִי נַמִּי דְּלָא קָנֵי קִנְיָן גָּמוּר — הָא אָמְרַתְּ דּוֹחֶה בְּצָרָה. וְתִקְשֶׁה לָךְ נַמִּי: יַעֲשֶׂה מַאֲמָר בְּזוֹ, וְתִדָּחֶה אֲחוֹתָהּ, וְיִכְנוֹס אֶת אִשְׁתּוֹ. דְּהֶיתֵּירָא דָּחֵי. מַאֲמָר שֶׁנַּעֲשָׂה בְּהֶיתֵּר, דְּאִי הֲוָה בָּעֵי לְיַיבּוּמֵי בִּשְׁעַת מַאֲמָר הֲוָה מָצֵי לְיַיבּוּמֵי, כְּגוֹן בְּמַתְנִי', דַּעֲדַיִין לֹא נָפְלָה אֲחוֹתָהּ. דְּאִיסּוּרָא. כְּגוֹן דְּנָפְלוּ שְׁתֵּי הָאֲחָיוֹת קוֹדֶם מַאֲמָר. הָכִי נַמִּי. לְעִנְיַן קְנִיָּה. וְצָרָתָהּ. אֲחוֹתָהּ שֶׁנַּעֲשֵׂית לָהּ צָרָה בְּזִיקָה חֲלִיצָה נַמִּי לָא תִּיבָּעֵי (ד) דְּתָלֵא מִשּׁוּם אֲחוֹת אִשָּׁה. אֶלָּא דּוֹחֶה. אוֹתָהּ מִלֶּאֱסוֹר (ה) אֵשֶׁת בַּעַל הַמַּאֲמָר עָלָיו. וּמְשַׁיֵּיר. דְּבָעְיָא חֲלִיצָה אִם בָּאת לִינָּשֵׂא עַד שֶׁלֹּא כָּנַס הַיָּבָם אֶת בַּעֲלַת הַמַּאֲמָר. וּלְקַמֵּיהּ פָּרֵיךְ לֵיהּ: הָא קָתָנֵי הַלָּזוּ תֵּלֵא מִשּׁוּם אֲחוֹת אִשָּׁה, דְּמַשְׁמַע אַף מֵחֲלִיצָה. זֶה יַעֲשֶׂה מַאֲמָר וְיִדְחֶה. אֶת אֲחוֹתָהּ מֵעָלָיו, וְאַחַ"כ יִשָּׂא אֶת זוֹ. אֶלָּא לָאו מִשּׁוּם דְּלָא דָּחֵי דְּחִיָּיה גְּמוּרָה, וְכָל כַּמָּה דְּרַמְיָא עֲלֵיהּ לַחֲלִיצָה — זְקוּקָתוֹ הִיא, וְאוֹסֶרֶת אֶת זוֹ עָלָיו: ה"ג. אֶלָּא יְבָמָה דְּחַזְיָא כו'. כְּלוֹמַר, אֶלָּא לְעוֹלָם דּוֹחֶה דְּחִיָּיה גְּמוּרָה, וּדְקַשְׁיָא לָךְ: הָתָם נַמִּי לִידְחֵי — לָא דָּמְיָא לְמַתְנִיתִין דְּהָכָא, דְּכִי נָפְלָה וַעֲבַד מַאֲמָר — הֲוָה חַזְיָא לְכוּלְּהוּ מִילֵּי דִּיבָמָה, לְהִתְיַיבֵּם וְלַחֲלוֹץ, הִלְכָּךְ חַזְיָא לְמִקְלְטֵיהּ לְמַאֲמָר, דְּמַאֲמָר דְּחַיָּא אֲחוֹתָהּ לִכְשֶׁתִּפּוֹל. אֲבָל הָתָם, דִּתְרַוַיְיהוּ נָפְלוּ קוֹדֶם מַאֲמָר, וְלָא חַזְיָא לְכוּלְּהוּ מִילֵּי דִּיבָמָה — לָא חַזְיָא לְמִקְלְטֵיהּ, לְפִיכָךְ אֵין מַאֲמָר דּוֹחֶה אֲחוֹתָהּ. הַשְׁתָּא אֲרוּסָה. דְּקִידּוּשִׁין דִּידָהּ דְּאוֹרַיְיתָא, תָּנֵי רַבִּי חִיָּיא: אֵינוֹ יוֹרְשָׁהּ וְאֵינוֹ מִטַּמֵּא לָהּ, מַאֲמָר יְבָמִין מִדְּרַבָּנַן הוּא, דְּהָא מִדְּאוֹרַיְיתָא "יְבָמָהּ יָבֹא עָלֶיהָ" כָּתַב רַחֲמָנָא — מִיבַּעְיָא?! לֹא אוֹנֵן. לֵיאָסֵר בְּקָדָשִׁים (ו). וְלֹא מִיטַּמֵּא. אִם כֹּהֵן הוּא, דְּהָא לָאו שְׁאֵרוֹ הַקָּרוֹב אֵלָיו הִיא. וְכֵן הִיא לֹא אוֹנֶנֶת. לִהְיוֹת אֲסוּרָה בְּקָדָשִׁים. וְלֹא מִיטַּמְּאַת. אֵינָהּ צְרִיכָה לְהִתְעַסֵּק בּוֹ (ז). וְלָאו דַּוְקָא נָקַט וְלֹא מִיטַּמְּאַת, דְּהָא בְּנוֹת אַהֲרֹן לֹא הוּזְהֲרוּ עַל הַטּוּמְאָה. אֶלָּא אַיְּידֵי דְּנָקַט לֹא אוֹנֶנֶת, דְּאִיצְטְרִיךְ לֵיהּ, נָקַט וְלֹא מִיטַּמְּאַת דְּבָעֵי לְמִתְנֵי תַּרְתֵּי, בְּדִידֵיהּ וּבְדִידָהּ. כָּךְ שָׁמַעְתִּי. וְלִי נִרְאֶה: וְלֹא מִיטַּמְּאָה — כְּגוֹן בָּרֶגֶל, שֶׁיִּשְׂרְאֵלִים מוּזְהָרִים עַל הַטּוּמְאָה (ח) מִ"וּבְנִבְלָתָם לֹא תִגָּעוּ", בְּמַסֶּ' ר"ה (דף טז:). גּוֹבָה כְּתוּבָּתָהּ. וּדְכָתַב לָהּ מִן הָאֵירוּסִין מִיתוֹקְמָא בִּכְתוּבּוֹת בְּפֶרֶק "הַכּוֹתֵב" (דף פט:). וְלָא בָּעֲיָא מְסִירָה לְחוּפָּה. דְּאִם בָּא עָלֶיהָ בְּעַל כָּרְחָהּ בְּלֹא חוּפָּה — קָנֵי. וְאִי בָּעֵי תּוּ לְאַפּוֹקֵי בְּגִיטָּא — סַגְיָא לָהּ. בְּעַל כָּרְחָהּ. דְּקָנֵי לָהּ וְנַעֲשֵׂית כְּאִשְׁתּוֹ לְכָל דָּבָר בְּבִיאָה בע"כ שֶׁאֵין בָּהּ חוּפָּה. וְחָלָה עָלָיו זִיקַת אֵירוּסִין. וְנִשּׂוּאִין שֶׁל שְׁאָר נָשִׁים. וְאִם בָּא עָלֶיהָ לְאַחַר מַאֲמָר בְּלֹא חוּפָּה — לֹא קָנָה. יָפֵר. אֶחָד מֵהֶן אֶת נִדְרָהּ. לְאֶחָד וְלֹא לִשְׁנַיִם. שׁוֹמֶרֶת יָבָם א' — יָפֵר, אֲבָל שׁוֹמֶרֶת לִשְׁנֵי יְבָמִין — לֹא יָפֵר לֹא זֶה וְלֹא זֶה. אֵין זִיקָה. דְּתֶיהֱוֵי כִּכְנוּסָה. וַאֲפִילּוּ בְּחַד. הֵיכָא דְּלֵיכָּא אֶלָּא חַד, דְּוַדַּאי עֲלֵיהּ רַמְיָא — אפ"ה אֵין זִיקָה. לִתְרֵי אֵין זִיקָה. דְּלָא יָדְעִינַן לְהֵי מִינַּיְיהוּ רַמְיָא, וַאֲפִילּוּ שְׁנֵיהֶם כְּאֶחָד — אֵין הֲפָרָתָן הֲפָרָה, דִּקְלִישָׁא זִיקָתָן. אֶלָּא לִתְרֵי אַמַּאי. נְהִי נַמִּי דְּיֵשׁ זִיקָה אֲפִי' לִתְרֵי, מִיהוּ יָפֵרוּ שְׁנֵיהֶם מִיבָּעֵי לֵיהּ: וַאֲמַר רָמִי בַּר (ט) אַבָּא גָּרְסִינַן. בְּשׁוּתָּפוּת. הוּא וְאָבִיהָ כַּאֲרוּסָה. לִדְחוֹת בַּצָּרָה. בַּאֲחוֹתָהּ שֶׁנָּפְלָה לְפָנָיו אַחַר מַאֲמָר זוֹ. דְּלָא סַגִּי לָהּ בְּגֵט. הָעוֹשֶׂה מַאֲמָר בִּיבָמָה, וּבָא לְהוֹצִיאָהּ — בָּעֲיָא חֲלִיצָה וְגֵט, וְלָא אָמְרִינַן כִּכְנוּסָה הִיא, וְסַגִּי לָהּ בְּגֵט. אָמַר לָךְ רַבִּי אֶלְעָזָר וּלְרַב נַחְמָן מִי נִיחָא. כְּלוֹמַר, נְהִי נַמִּי דְּקוֹנֶה, בִּשְׁלָמָא אִי נִישּׂוּאִין עוֹשֶׂה — שַׁפִּיר. אֶלָּא לְרַב נַחְמָן דְּאָמַר לָא עָבֵיד אֶלָּא אֵירוּסִין — מִי נִיחָא? הָא בְּשׁוּתָּפוּת לֵיכָּא לְמֵימַר דְּיָפֵר קָתָנֵי, יָפֵרוּ מִיבָּעֵי לֵיהּ. אֶלָּא הָכָא בְּמַאי עָסְקִינַן שֶׁעָמְדָה בְּדִין. לְדִידִי [אֲפִילּוּ] בְּלֹא מַאֲמָר. וּלְרַב [אַמִּי] אַחַר מַאֲמָר וְלֹא רָצָה לִכְנוֹס וְלֹא לִפְטוֹר. וּפָסְקוּ לָהּ מְזוֹנוֹת מִשֶּׁלּוֹ. כְּדִתְנַיָא לְקַמָּן בְּ"הַחוֹלֵץ" (דף מא:): עָמַד בַּדִּין וּבָרַח — נִזּוֹנֵית מִשֶּׁל יָבָם, דְּמֵהַשְׁתָּא בַּעְלָהּ הוּא, וְעַל דַּעְתּוֹ נוֹדֶרֶת עַל מְנַת שֶׁיִּרְצֶה.
מתני'

תוספות

יעשה מאמר ויקנה כו'. ומשום ביטול מלות יבמין ליכא למיחש כדפרישית בפ' שני (לעיל דף יח:)(י).
לא מיטמאה לו. פירוש ברגל שהוזהרו על הטומאה כדאמרינן בר"ה (דף טז:)(כ) ועוד י"ל דאין מטמאה לו היינו דאינה חייבת ליטמא לו למאן דאמר בסוטה (דף ג.) לה יטמא חובה.
עבד בה מאמר מיבעיא. וא"ת דמשמע דלא עדיפא בעלת מאמר מארוסה ובהחולץ (לקמן דף לט. ושם) קאמר רבא גופיה מאמר לב"ש עושה ודאי ארוסה לדחות בצרה וספק נשואה לחלוק בנכסים אלמא מהני ליורשה וי"ל דהכא גרס רבה רבו של אביי דמסיק עלה אמר ליה אביי ולקמן גרס רבא שהוא אחר אביי.
אלא לענין מסירה לחופה. וא"ת: מאי משני? דהשתא נמי תקשי: השתא ארוסה בעלמא בעיא מסירה לחופה, עבד בה מאמר — מיבעיא? וי"ל: דעבד בה מאמר ובא עליה, והביאה עושה אותה ככנוסה.
אביה ובעלה מפירים נדריה. ואם אין לה אב או שאינה ברשות אב — לא מצי מיפר, כדאמרינן בנדרים (דף עא.).
כגון (ל) שעמדה בדין כו'. לפי מסקנא שאיירי דעבד בה מאמר, כדמוכח בנדרים בפ' "נערה המאורסה" (שם עד.) דלר' אליעזר כיון דעביד בה מאמר ופסקו לה מזונות משלו — נודרת על דעתו. ולר' יהושע דוקא בחד יבם, אבל בתרי, כיון דאי בעי אחוה פסיל לה עליה בביאה או בגיטא — אינה נודרת על דעתו. ולר"ע, אפילו ביבם אחד קאמר דלא יפר, אפילו עבד בה מאמר, משום דאין חייבים עליה סקילה כנערה המאורסה. ולא יתכן לפי זה מה שפי' בקונטרס בריש פ"ב (לעיל יז: ד"ה ולימא) דמאן דאמר אין זיקה אפי' בחד — היינו ר"ע. דמלי סבר דיש זיקה, ואפי' הכי לא יפר — משום דאין חייבין עליה סקילה.

תוספות ישנים

ואי אמרת מאמר לב"ש קונה קנין גמור זה יעשה מאמר ויקנה אלא מאי דוחה דחייה גמורה זה יעשה מאמר וידחה. [illegible]

הגהות הב"ח

(א) גמ' א"ל אין שאני אומר: (ב) שם שעמדה בדין ופסקו: (ג) רש"י ד"ה ואי מאמר וכו' אין איסור במאמר והואיל ותלא אחותה: (ד) ד"ה דלא וכו' ותלא אחותה: (ה) ד"ה אלא וכו' מלאסור את בעלת המאמר: (ו) ד"ה לא אונן לאסור בקדשים דכתיב לא אכלתי באוני ממנו מכאן ס"ד: (ז) ד"ה ולא מיטמאת וכו' ולאו דוקא: [illegible]

[נדרים עד:]
לקמן מג: כתובות נג. פטו: ע"ש בבא מציעא יח. ע"ש סנהדרין כח. [ע"ש היטב]
[לקמן נב.]
נדרים עד
[שם ע"ש]
[בנדרים ליתא]
[לעיל יח. לקמן ל. נח.]
כתובות לט. מו: קדושין ד. נדרים סו.
שבת מו: גיטין פג. נדרים עג: עד נדה מו:

תוספות חד מקמאי

ת"ר שומרת יבם בין ליבם א' בין לשנים ר"א [אומר] יפר ר"י אומר לא' ולא לשנים ר"ע אומר לא לאחד ולא לשנים [illegible] בתרי והוינן בה לר"א נהי נמי דיש זיקה אפילו בתרי בשלמא לא' מיפר אלא לתרי אמאי מפיר כ"א לבדו ואוקימנא כגון שעמדה בדין עם א' מהן ופסקו לה מזונותיה משלו וכדרבי פנחס משמיה דרבא דאמר כל הנודרת ע"ד בעלה היא נודרת ואיכא דמפרש אע"ג דעמדה בדין

מתני' שְׁלֹשָׁה אַחִין, שְׁנַיִם מֵהֶם נְשׂוּאִים שְׁתֵּי אֲחָיוֹת וְאֶחָד נָשׂוּי נָכְרִית. מֵת אֶחָד מִבַּעֲלֵי אֲחָיוֹת, וְכָנַס נְשׂוּי נָכְרִית אֶת אִשְׁתּוֹ, וָמֵת – הָרִאשׁוֹנָה יוֹצְאָה מִשּׁוּם אֲחוֹת אִשָּׁה, וּשְׁנִיָּה מִשּׁוּם צָרָתָהּ. עָשָׂה בָּהּ מַאֲמָר וָמֵת – נָכְרִית חוֹלֶצֶת וְלֹא מִתְיַיבֶּמֶת.§ **גמ'** טַעְמָא דַּעֲבַד בָּהּ מַאֲמָר, הָא לָא עֲבַד בָּהּ מַאֲמָר – נָכְרִית יַבּוּמֵי נַמִי מְיַיבְּמָה. אָמַר רַב נַחְמָן: זֹאת אוֹמֶרֶת *אֵין זִיקָה, וַאֲפִילּוּ בְּחַד אַחָא.§

מתני' [א]שְׁלֹשָׁה אַחִים, שְׁנַיִם מֵהֶם נְשׂוּאִים שְׁתֵּי אֲחָיוֹת וְאֶחָד נָשׂוּי נָכְרִית. מֵת הַנָּשׂוּי נָכְרִית, וְכָנַס אֶחָד מִבַּעֲלֵי אֲחָיוֹת אֶת אִשְׁתּוֹ וָמֵת – הָרִאשׁוֹנָה יוֹצֵאת מִשּׁוּם אֲחוֹת אִשָּׁה, וּשְׁנִיָּה מִשּׁוּם צָרָתָהּ. עָשָׂה בָּהּ מַאֲמָר וָמֵת – נָכְרִית חוֹלֶצֶת וְלֹא מִתְיַיבֶּמֶת.§ **גמ'** הָא תּוּ לָמָּה לִי? הַיְינוּ הַךְ! הַשְׁתָּא, וּמַה הָתָם דַּאֲחוֹת אִשָּׁה הָוְיָא צָרָה לְנָכְרִית אָמַרְתְּ: נָכְרִית אֲסוּרָה, הָכָא, דְּנָכְרִית הָוְיָא צָרָה לַאֲחוֹת אִשָּׁה – לֹא כָּל שֶׁכֵּן? – תַּנָּא הַךְ תָּנָא בְּרֵישָׁא, וְהַךְ (א) חַזְיָא לְהֶיתֵּירָא, וְשַׁרְיָא. וַהֲדַר חַזְיָא לְאִיסּוּרָא. וְאַיְּידֵי *דַּחֲבִיבָה לֵיהּ – אַקְדְּמַהּ, *וּמִשְׁנָה לֹא זָזָה מִמְּקוֹמָהּ.§

מתני' [ב]שְׁלֹשָׁה אַחִין, שְׁנַיִם מֵהֶם נְשׂוּאִים שְׁתֵּי אֲחָיוֹת וְאֶחָד נָשׂוּי נָכְרִית. מֵת אֶחָד מִבַּעֲלֵי אֲחָיוֹת, וְכָנַס נָשׂוּי נָכְרִית אֶת אִשְׁתּוֹ, וּמֵתָה אִשְׁתּוֹ שֶׁל שֵׁנִי, וְאַחַר כָּךְ מֵת נָשׂוּי נָכְרִית – [ה]הֲרֵי זוֹ אֲסוּרָה עָלָיו עוֹלָמִית, הוֹאִיל וְנֶאֶסְרָה עָלָיו שָׁעָה אַחַת.§ **גמ'** *אָמַר רַב יְהוּדָה אָמַר רַב: [ג]כָּל יְבָמָה שֶׁאֵין אֲנִי קוֹרֵא בָּהּ בִּשְׁעַת נְפִילָה °"יְבָמָהּ יָבֹא עָלֶיהָ" – הֲרֵי הִיא כְּאֵשֶׁת אָח שֶׁיֵּשׁ לָהּ בָּנִים, וַאֲסוּרָה. מַאי קָמַשְׁמַע לַן? תְּנֵינָא: הֲרֵי זוֹ אֲסוּרָה עָלָיו עוֹלָמִית, הוֹאִיל וְנֶאֶסְרָה עָלָיו שָׁעָה אַחַת! – מַהוּ דְּתֵימָא: הָנֵי מִילֵּי – הֵיכָא דְּלָא אִיחַזְיָא לָהּ בִּנְפִילָה רִאשׁוֹנָה, אֲבָל הֵיכָא דְּאִיחַזְיָא לָהּ בִּנְפִילָה רִאשׁוֹנָה – אֵימָא תִּישְׁתְּרֵי, קָמַשְׁמַע לַן. הָא נַמִי תְּנֵינָא: *שְׁנֵי אַחִין נְשׂוּאִין שְׁתֵּי אֲחָיוֹת, מֵת אֶחָד מֵהֶם וְאַחַר כָּךְ מֵתָה אִשְׁתּוֹ שֶׁל שֵׁנִי – הֲרֵי זוֹ אֲסוּרָה עָלָיו עוֹלָמִית, הוֹאִיל וְנֶאֶסְרָה עָלָיו שָׁעָה אַחַת! – מַהוּ דְּתֵימָא: הָתָם הוּא דְּאִידְּחִי לָהּ מֵהַאי בֵּיתָא לְגַמְרֵי. אֲבָל הָכָא, דְּלָא אִידְּחִי לָהּ מֵהַאי בֵּיתָא לְגַמְרֵי, אֵימָא: מִיגּוֹ דְּחַזְיָא לְהַאי נָשׂוּי נָכְרִית חַזְיָא נַמִי לְהַאי, קָמַשְׁמַע לַן.§

מתני' *[ד]שְׁלֹשָׁה אַחִים, שְׁנַיִם מֵהֶם נְשׂוּאִין שְׁתֵּי אֲחָיוֹת, וְאֶחָד נָשׂוּי נָכְרִית. גֵּירֵשׁ אֶחָד מִבַּעֲלֵי אֲחָיוֹת אֶת אִשְׁתּוֹ, וּמֵת נָשׂוּי נָכְרִית, וּכְנָסָהּ הַמְגָרֵשׁ וָמֵת – זוֹ הִיא שֶׁאָמְרוּ: וְכוּלָּן שֶׁמֵּתוּ אוֹ נִתְגָּרְשׁוּ – צָרוֹתֵיהֶן מוּתָּרוֹת.§ **גמ'** [ה]טַעְמָא דְּגֵירֵשׁ וְאַחַר כָּךְ מֵת, אֲבָל מֵת וְאַחַר כָּךְ גֵּירֵשׁ – אֲסוּרָה. אָמַר רַב אַשִׁי; זֹאת אוֹמֶרֶת *יֵשׁ זִיקָה, אֲפִילּוּ בִּתְרֵי אַחֵי. – וּלְרַב אַשִׁי קַשְׁיָא דְּרַב נַחְמָן! – אָמַר לָךְ רַב אַשִׁי: [ו]ה"ה דְּאַף עַל גַּב דְּלָא עֲבַד בָּהּ מַאֲמָר נָכְרִית – מִיחֲלַץ חָלְצָה, יַבּוּמֵי לָא מְיַיבְּמָה. וְהָא דְּקָתָנֵי מַאֲמָר – *לְאַפּוּקֵי (ג) ב"ש, דְּאָמְרִי: מַאֲמָר קוֹנֶה

קִנְיָן

רש"י

מתני' הָרִאשׁוֹנָה. לִנְפִילָה. **גמ'** נָכְרִית יַבּוּמֵי נַמִי מְיַיבְּמָה. וְלָא אָמְרִינַן מִשֶּׁמֵּת בַּעַל הָאֲחָיוֹת וְנָפְלָה לְיַיבֵּם הוּזְקְקָה לְנָשׂוּי נָכְרִית לְבַדּוֹ, דְּהָא עַל בַּעַל אֲחָיוֹת לָא רַמְיָא וְנַעֲשֵׂית (ג) זוֹ צָרָתָהּ בְּזִיקָה, וּכְשֶׁמֵּת תֵּאָסֵר הַנָּכְרִית עַל הַנִּשְׁאָר מִשּׁוּם צָרַת אֲחוֹת אִשָּׁה. וַאֲפִילּוּ בְּחַד אַחָא. כִּדְפָרֵישִׁית. דְּאַף עַל גַּב דִּתְרֵי אַחִין נִינְהוּ – אֵין זוֹ זְקוּקָה אֶלָּא לְנָשׂוּי נָכְרִית לְבַדּוֹ. **מתני'** הָרִאשׁוֹנָה. לְנִישּׂוּאִין. **גמ'** הַיְינוּ הַךְ. וְכָל שֶׁכֵּן הוּא; דְּהַשְׁתָּא, וּמַה הָתָם דְּנָכְרִית עִיקַּר נְשׂוּאָה הִיא, דַּאֲחוֹת אִשָּׁה נָפְלָה עָלֶיהָ וְנַעֲשֵׂית צָרָתָהּ בְּמַאֲמָר אֲסַרְתָּהּ. הָכָא. דַּאֲחוֹת אִשָּׁה עִיקַּר נְשׂוּאָה הִיא – לֹא כָּל שֶׁכֵּן דְּאוֹסֶרֶת נָכְרִית שֶׁהִיא טְפֵלָה. הָא תָּנָא בְּרֵישָׁא. מִשְׁנָה אַחֲרוֹנָה זוֹ שָׁנָה תְּחִלָּה, וְהַהִיא דִּלְעֵיל לָא הֲוֵי בְּדַעְתֵּיהּ לְמִיתְנֵי מִשּׁוּם דְּחַזְיָא (ד) לְהֶיתֵּירָא, הוֹאִיל וְנָכְרִית עִיקָּר. וַהֲדַר חַזְיָא לְאִיסּוּרָא, מִשּׁוּם דְּמִכָּל מָקוֹם צָרָתָהּ הִיא, וּתְנָיֵיהּ. וְאַיְּידֵי דְּקָא חֲבִיבָה לֵיהּ. דְּחִידּוּשׁ הוּא. אַקְדְּמַהּ. וְתוּ לָא הֲוָה צָרִיךְ לְמִיתְנֵי סֵיפָא, אֶלָּא הוֹאִיל וְנִשְׁנֵית לֹא זָזָה מִמְּקוֹמָהּ. [**מתני'**] שָׁעָה אַחַת. בִּנְפִילָה רִאשׁוֹנָה, כְּשֶׁנָּפְלָה מֵאָחִיו הָרִאשׁוֹן. **גמ'** הֲרֵי הִיא כְּאֵשֶׁת אָח כו'. וְאַף עַל גַּב דַּהֲדַר אִיחַזְיָא. בִּנְפִילָה רִאשׁוֹנָה. כָּל זְמַן נְפִילָה רִאשׁוֹנָה הָיְתָה אִשְׁתּוֹ קַיֶּימֶת, שֶׁהִיא אֲחוֹתָהּ. אֲבָל הֵיכָא דְּאִיתַּחְזְיָא בִּנְפִילָה רִאשׁוֹנָה. כְּגוֹן שֶׁמֵּתָה אִשְׁתּוֹ אַחַר מִיתַת אָחִיו וְלֹא כְּנָסָהּ נָשׂוּי נָכְרִית. דְּאִידַּחְיָא לָהּ מֵהַאי בֵּיתָא לְגַמְרֵי. (ה) שֶׁנָּפְלָה, וְאֵין כָּאן אַחֵר אֶלָּא זֶה בַּעַל אֲחוֹתָהּ – נִדְחֵית וְנִפְטֶרֶת לַשּׁוּק, וְאֵין עָלֶיהָ צַד זִיקָה עוֹד. אֲבָל הֵיכָא דְּלָא אִידַּחְיָא מֵהַאי בֵּיתָא לְגַמְרֵי. בִּשְׁעַת נְפִילָה, שֶׁהָיָה שָׁם נָשׂוּי נָכְרִית וּזְקוּקָה לְיַיבֵּם. אֵימָא מִיגּוֹ דַּחֲזָיָא לְנָשׂוּי נָכְרִית עֲדַיִין זִיקָתָהּ עָלֶיהָ, וְכִי מֵתָה אֲחוֹתָהּ וְעוֹדָהּ בִּנְפִילָה – תִּתְיַיבֵּם לָזֶה בִּנְפִילָה. קָמַשְׁמַע לַן. רַב יְהוּדָה דְּלָא. **מתני'** וּכְנָסָהּ הַמְגָרֵשׁ וָמֵת. מוּתֶּרֶת זוֹ לְהִתְיַיבֵּם, שֶׁהֲרֵי עַד שֶׁלֹּא כְּנָסָהּ גֵּירֵשׁ אֶת הָרִאשׁוֹנָה שֶׁהִיא עֶרְוָה, וְלֹא הָיְתָה צָרָתָהּ מֵעוֹלָם. וְזֶהוּ שֶׁאָמְרוּ. בְּפֶרֶק רִאשׁוֹן: נִתְגָּרְשׁוּ הָעֲרָיוֹת צָרוֹתֵיהֶן מוּתָּרוֹת. **גמ'** טַעְמָא דְּגֵירֵשׁ. בַּעַל הָאֲחָיוֹת תְּחִלָּה, וְאַחַר כָּךְ מֵת נָשׂוּי נָכְרִית, דַּאֲפִילּוּ בְּזִיקָה לֹא נַעֲשֵׂית צָרָתָהּ מֵעוֹלָם. הָא מֵת נָשׂוּי נָכְרִית, וְהוּזְקְקָה נָכְרִית לְבַעֲלֵי אֲחָיוֹת, וְאַחַר כָּךְ גֵּירֵשׁ וּנְשָׂאָהּ לָזוֹ, הוֹאִיל וְקוֹדֶם שֶׁגֵּירֵשׁ נַעֲשֵׂית צָרָתָהּ בְּזִיקָה – אֲסוּרָה עַל אָחִיו, כְּשֶׁיָּמוּת הַמְגָרֵשׁ, מִשּׁוּם צָרַת אָחוֹת. אִשָּׁה בִּשְׁלָמָא אִי לָא כְּנָסָהּ – הָוְיָא מוּתֶּרֶת לָזֶה מֵחֲמַת זִיקַּת אָחִיו הָרִאשׁוֹן, אֲבָל מִשֶּׁכְּנָסָהּ וְעַכְשָׁיו זְקוּקָה לָזֶה מֵאֵת בַּעַל הָעֶרְוָה אֲסוּרָה, וְאַף עַל גַּב דְּלֹא הָיְתָה צָרָתָהּ אֶלָּא בְּזִיקָה. בִּתְרֵי אַחֵי. כְּגוֹן הָכָא, דְּכִי מֵת נָשׂוּי נָכְרִית קוֹדֶם גֵּירוּשִׁין שֶׁל זֶה – הָיְתָה זוֹ זְקוּקָה לִשְׁנֵי בַּעֲלֵי הָאֲחָיוֹת, וּמְהַנְּיָא בָּהּ זִיקָה זוֹ לְאוֹסְרָהּ עַל הַשֵּׁנִי. קַשְׁיָא דְּרַב נַחְמָן. דְּדָיֵיק לְעֵיל מִסֵּיפָא מַתְנִי': "זֹאת אוֹמֶרֶת: אֵין זִיקָה אֲפִי' בְּחַד אַחָא". אָמַר לָךְ רַב אַשִׁי. הַהִיא דִּיּוּקָא דִּלְעֵיל לָאו דַּוְקָא, דְּה"ה אַף עַל גַּב דְּלָא עֲבַד מַאֲמָר בַּעַל הַנָּכְרִית בַּאֲחוֹת (אִשָּׁה) אֵשֶׁת אָחִיו כְּשֶׁיָּמוּת – נָכְרִית אִשְׁתּוֹ מִיחֲלַץ חָלְצָה, וְלֹא מִתְיַיבֶּמֶת, הוֹאִיל וְעֶרְוָה עַל בַּעְלָהּ לְבַדּוֹ הָוְיָת רַמְיָא, (ו) נַעֲשָׂה צָרָתָהּ בְּזִיקָה.

קִנְיָן

תוספות

שלשה אחין. בהך רישא גרסינן "הראשונה יוצאה משום אחות אשה" וראשונה לנפילה קאמר דומיא דההיא דפרק ב' (לעיל יז.) ובבבא *בתרא ה"ג השניה יוצאה כו'. **אמר** רב נחמן זאת אומרת אין זיקה. תימה שלא דקדק רב נחמן על מתני' דריש "כילד" (לעיל יז.)? **דחביבה** ליה אקדמה. בשאר מקומות אין דוחק לומר כן, אלא אמר: זו ואין צריך לומר זו קתני. וכאן (ז) דחק לומר כן, לפי שבבא שלימה דלא צריכה היא. (ח) **ונאסרה** עליו שעה אחת. בהך בבא הו"מ למינקט ואחד מופנה. אלא נקט הכי, משום דנכרית נמי מתסרא, לפי שהיתה צרת אחות אשה שעה אחת. וקצת קשה: שאינו מזכיר הצרה כלל! וא"ת: לרבי ירמיה דאמר (לעיל דף יג.) דהאי תנא דפירקין סבר נישואין מפילין, אמאי לא נקט דמתה אחת מן האחיות תחלה ואח"כ מת בעלה של שניה, וכנס נשוי נכרית את אשתו ומת – אסורה, שנאסרה עליו שעה אחת, כיון דנישואין מפילין! וכן בבבא דלקמן ב' אחין – ה"ל למתני שמתה אחת מהן תחלה, ואח"כ מת בעלה של שניה! וי"ל: דלא מהני למימר נישואין מפילין אלא לענין שאם היתה צרת ערוה שעה אחת – שוב אין לה היתר, אע"פ שבשעת נפילה כבר אינה צרת ערוה. אבל כאן, משום נישואין מפילין – לא נחשבנה כאילו נפלה בחיי אשתו ויצאה ממנו באותה שעה משום אחות אשה. **גירש** אחד מבעלי אחיות את אשתו. תימה: אמאי נקט ג' אחין? ה"ל למימר ב' אחין נשואין ב' אחיות וגירש האחד את אשתו ונשא אשה אחרת (ט) ומת! ולרבי ירמיה ניחא, כיון דאיצטריך לאשמועינן דיש זיקה, כדדייק רב אשי בגמרא. ולרבא נמי נקט הכי למעוטי מת ולא גירש, אבל לרב נחמן דקסבר אין זיקה – קשיא: אמאי נקט ג' אחין? וי"ל: דלרב נחמן נקט הכי אגב אורחיה לאשמועינן דאין זיקה, דכר' ירמיה ס"ל דנישואין מפילין ואם יש זיקה – תיתסר, אע"ג דגירש ואח"כ מת. דמקודם שגירשה חשובה נכרית כזקוקה לו משעה שנשאת לאחיו, דנישואין הראשונים מפילין. ורב אשי דדייק מינה דיש זיקה, סבר דלא אסרינן לה, משום דא"א לה ליאסר אא"כ תרי נישואין מפילין. **זאת** אומרת יש זיקה. וא"ת: והיאך נסבה המגרש? והא הויא לה צרת אחות אשתו בזיקה! וי"ל: דלא חשיב צרת אחות אשתו בזיקה אלא כשמת אחיו ונפלו שתיהן לפניו. אבל כשהוא חי – לא. ומה שכתב בעל ה"ג דאם מת ולא גירש אסירא לתרווייהו – לא בעוד ששניהם חיים, אלא לכל אחד כשימות אחיו – תהיה אסורה.

כתב

קנין

עין משפט נר מצוה

כא א מיי' פ"ז מהלכות יבום הלכה ז סמג עשין נא נב טוש"ע אה"ע סימן קעה סעיף ז:

כב ב ג מיי' שם הלכה יא טוש"ע שם סעיף א:

כג ד ה מיי' שם הלכה יב טוש"ע שם סעי' ח:

כד ו מיי' שם טוש"ע שם סעיף ז:

תוספות ישנים

זאת אומרת אין זיקה ואפילו בחד. וא"ת הא מפרק כילד לעיל דייקינן הכי וי"ל דאיצטריך לאפוקי מב"ש דלעיל. וא"ת הא נמי ידעינן בבבא בתרייתא בסמוך. י"ל דתרתי אצטריך למתני כדפרישי' לעיל א) דמסברא אמינא יש זיקה: **אבל** הכא דלא אדחי לה מהאי ביתא לגמרי אימא לא. וא"ת הא ממתני' דלעיל דארבעה אחין שמעינן לה. וי"ל דשאני התם דנהי דלא אדחי מהאי ביתא לגמרי מ"מ לא איחזיא בנפילה ראשונה אבל היכא דלא אדחי לה מהך ביתא לגמרי ואיחזיא בנפילה ראשונה אימא לא:

א) עי' לעיל י"ח בתוס' ד"ה והאי.

תוספות חד מקמאי

בדין ופסקו לה מזונותיה אינו מפיר אלא א"כ עשה בה מאמר ומ"מ שניהם מפירין ולא הועמדה בדין: הרב אלפס פסק צרת ערוה דכנס ואח"כ גירש מותרת הצרה להתייבם דמיתה מפילה וכיון דבשעת ערוה לא הוי צרת ערוה מותרת וג"כ מתני' דג' אחין שניהן מהם נשואין ב' אחיות וא' נשוי נכרית וגרש א' מבעלי אחיות את אשתו ומת נשוי נכרית וכנסה המגרש פסק דבמת ואח"כ גירש אסור' ויהיב טעמא למילתיה דגזרי' הכא משום זיקה דעלמא. א"נ הכי גבי נכרית כיון דבשעת נפילה באיסור זיקה נפלה קמיה לא מהני לה גרושין אלו דברי הרב ז"ל ויש בהן כמה תמיהות חדא דאם אתמר להני טעמי למה ליה לר' ירמיה לשנויי תברא מי ששנה זו לא שנה זו. ולרבא למה ליה למימר זו ואצ"ל זו קתני לישני ליה דשאני הכא דגזרינן משום זיקה דעלמא. א"נ בשעת נפילה אתסרא ליה למה ליה למימר הכא אליבא דרבא זו היא למעוטי מת ולא גירש ולא כנס לוקמה אפי' דכנס וגירש. ומאי דכתב נמי הכא גבי נכרית כיון דבשעת נפילה באיסור זיקה נפלה קמיה לא מהנו לה גירושין לא ירדנו לסוף דעתו דמאי איסור זיקה איכא בנכרית והרי ב' אחין הנשואין ב' אחיות הוו קיימין בשעת נפילת נכרית ואין כאן איסור [אחות] זקוקתו שהרי שניהם קיימין והרי משנה שלימה שנינו ג' אחין שנים מהן נשואין ב' אחיות וא' נשוי (א') נכרית ומת נשוי נכרית וכנס א' מבעלי אחיות את אשתו וכו' ולא קתני עבר וכנס ועוד אם עבר וכנס מוציא כדקתני רישא בה"א יוציאו אלא ודאי ליתנהו להני טעמי דכתב הרז"ל ומיהו אפשר דרב אשי לית ליה דרבא דאליבא דהאי [תנא] נישואין הראשונים מפילין מת א) ואחד כנס גירש אסורה ואפ"ה הלכתא כת"ק דמתני' דפ"ק דכנס ואח"כ [גירש] מותרת דמיתה מפלת חדא דהא רבא ס"ל דלא פליגי אהדדי. ועוד דתנן נפל הבית עליו ועל אשתו שהיא בת אחיו ואין ידוע איזה מהן [מת] ראשון צרתה חולצת ולא מתייבמת אלמא האי תנא ס"ל מיתה מפלת ועוי"ל דרב אשי לא שמעינן ליה בהדיא דלימא מת ואח"כ גירש אסורה אלא ש"מ זאת אומרת יש זיקה ואפי' בתרי אחי וא"נ ס"ל כרבא דאמר זו היא למעוטי מת דלא גירש ולא כנס ש"מ דיש זיקה אפלו בתרי אחי:

א) נראה דצ"ל ואח"כ גירש או דצ"ל מת וכנס ואח"כ גירש.

מתניתין

מסורת הש"ס

[לעיל יז: כו: לקמן נא. נג.]

[לעיל ב: וש"נ] [לקמן לב. קדושין כה. ע"ז לה: שבועות ד. חולין לב: קטז:]

לעיל כז: ע"ש לקמן קיא:

דברים כה

[לקמן לב:]

[לעיל יז: וש"נ]

[לעיל יח. כט: נח:]

הגהות הב"ח

(א) גמ' חזיא להתירא ושריא. נ"ב ע"ל בדף לב ע"א בכהאי סוגיא: (ב) שם לאפוקי מב"ש: (ג) רש"י ד"ה נכרית וכו' ונעשית נכרית זו לרתה וכו' אחות אשה בזיקה הס"ד: (ד) ד"ה הא תנא וכו' משום דחזיה בדעתיה להתירה: (ה) ד"ה דאידחיא וכו' משנפלה ואין: (ו) ד"ה אמר לך וכו' הוית רמיא ונעשית צרתה: (ז) תוס' ד"ה דחביבה וכו' וכאן דוחקא דוחק לומר כן: (ח) ד"ה הואיל ונאסרה וכו' ומת אסורה הואיל שנאסרה עליו: (ט) ד"ה גירש וכו' אשה אחרת נכרית ומת:

גליון הש"ס

מתני' הרי זו אסורה עליו עולמית. עי' לקמן דף לב ע"א תד"ה לא פקע:

כה א מיי' פ"ו מהלכות יבום הלכה כב סמג עשין יא טוש"ע אה"ע סימן קעג סעיף ג:
כו ב מיי' פ"ד מהל' אישות הלכה כב טוש"ע אה"ע סי' ל סעיף ה.

קִנְיָן גָּמוּר, קמ"ל דְּלָא כְּבַ"שׁ. וּלְרַב נַחְמָן קַשְׁיָא דְּרַב אַשִׁי! וְכ"ת: הוּא הַדִּין דַּאֲפִי' מֵת וְאַחַר כָּךְ גֵּירֵשׁ צָרָתָהּ מוּתֶּרֶת, אֶלָּא "זוֹ הִיא" לְמַעוּטֵי מַאי — לְמַעוּטֵי כָּנַס וְאח"כ גֵּירֵשׁ, — הָנִיחָא אִי סָבַר לָהּ כְּרַבִּי יִרְמְיָה, דְּאָמַר: *תַּבְרָא, מִי שֶׁשָּׁנָה זוֹ לֹא שָׁנָה זוֹ, וְהַאי תַּנָּא סָבַר מִיתָה מַפֶּלֶת, וְהַאי תַּנָּא סָבַר נִישּׂוּאִין הָרִאשׁוֹנִים מַפִּילִים — "זוֹ הִיא" לְמַעוּטֵי כָּנַס וּלְבַסּוֹף גֵּירֵשׁ. אֶלָּא אִי סָבַר לָהּ כְּרָבָא, דְּאָמַר לְעוֹלָם חַד תַּנָּא הוּא, *וְ"זוֹ וְאֵין צ"ל זוֹ" קָתָנֵי — "זוֹ הִיא" לְמַעוּטֵי מַאי? — עַל כָּרְחָךְ כְּרַבִּי יִרְמְיָה סְבִירָא לֵיהּ. וּלְרָבָא, הָנִיחָא אִי סָבַר לָהּ כְּרַב אַשִׁי — "זוֹ הִיא" לְמַעוּטֵי[א] מֵת בְּלֹא גֵּירֵשׁ, אֶלָּא אִי סָבַר לָהּ כְּרַב נַחְמָן, "זוֹ הִיא" לְמַעוּטֵי מַאי? — ע"כ כְּרַב אַשִׁי סְבִירָא לֵיהּ.§

מתני' **אוְכוּלָּן שֶׁהָיוּ בָּהֶן קִדּוּשִׁין אוֹ גֵּרוּשִׁין בְּסָפֵק — הֲרֵי אֵלּוּ הַצָּרוֹת חוֹלְצוֹת וְלֹא מִתְיַיבְּמוֹת. כֵּיצַד סְפֵק קִדּוּשִׁין? בזָרַק לָהּ קִדּוּשִׁין, סָפֵק קָרוֹב לוֹ סָפֵק קָרוֹב לָהּ — זֶהוּ סְפֵק קִדּוּשִׁין. סְפֵק גֵּרוּשִׁין — כָּתַב בִּכְתַב יָדוֹ וְאֵין עָלָיו עֵדִים, יֵשׁ עָלָיו עֵדִים וְאֵין בּוֹ זְמַן, יֵשׁ בּוֹ זְמַן וְאֵין בּוֹ אֶלָּא עֵד אֶחָד — זֶהוּ סְפֵק גֵּרוּשִׁין.§ **גמ'** וְאִילּוּ בְּגֵרוּשִׁין סָפֵק קָרוֹב לוֹ סָפֵק קָרוֹב לָהּ — לָא קָתָנֵי, מַאי טַעְמָא? אֲמַר רַבָּה: אִשָּׁה זוֹ בְּחֶזְקַת הֶיתֵּר לַשּׁוּק עוֹמֶדֶת, וּמִסָּפֵק אַתָּה בָּא לְאוֹסְרָהּ — אַל תַּאַסְרֶנָּה מִסָּפֵק. אֲמַר לֵיהּ אַבַּיֵי: אִי הָכִי בְּקִדּוּשִׁין נָמֵי, נֵימָא: אִשָּׁה זוֹ בְּחֶזְקַת הֶיתֵּר לַיָּבָם עוֹמֶדֶת, וּמִסָּפֵק אַתָּה בָּא לְאוֹסְרָהּ — אַל תַּאַסְרֶנָּה מִסָּפֵק! — הָתָם לְחוּמְרָא. הַאי — חוּמְרָא דְּאָתֵי לִידֵי קוּלָּא הוּא; זִימְנִין דְּאָזֵיל הוּא וּמְקַדֵּשׁ לָהּ לַאֲחוֹתָהּ קִדּוּשֵׁי וַדַּאי, וְאִי נָמֵי זִימְנִין דְּאָתָא אַחֵר וּמְקַדֵּשׁ לָהּ לְדִידָהּ קִדּוּשֵׁי וַדַּאי, וְכֵיוָן דְּאָסַר לָהּ מָר לַצָּרָה לְיַיבּוּמֵי, אָמְרִי: דְּקַמָּא — קִדּוּשִׁין וּדְבַתְרָא — לָאו קִדּוּשִׁין

כֵּיוָן

קִנְיָן גָּמוּר. וַאֲפִי' חֲלִיצָה לָא תִּיבְּעֵי נָכְרִית, אֶלָּא תֵּיזֵל מִשּׁוּם צָרַת אֲחוֹת אִשָּׁה — קמ"ל חוֹלֶצֶת. ה"ה דַּאֲפִי' מֵת. נָשׂוּי נָכְרִית וְאח"כ גֵּירֵשׁ אֶחָד מִבַּעֲלֵי אֲחָיוֹת אֶת אִשְׁתּוֹ וּכְנָסָהּ, מוּתֶּרֶת לַשְּׁלִישִׁי כְּשֶׁיָּמוּת זֶה, וְלָא אָמְרִי' צָרַת אֲחוֹת אִשְׁתּוֹ שֶׁל זֶה בְּזִיקָה הֲוַאי מֵעִיקָּרָא, קוֹדֶם גֵּירוּשִׁין. כָּנַס. הַנָּכְרִית וְאח"כ גֵּירֵשׁ אֶת אִשְׁתּוֹ וּמֵת, דַּאֲסוּרָה נָכְרִית מִשּׁוּם צָרַת אֲחוֹת אִשָּׁה, וְאע"ג דְּהַשְׁתָּא בִּשְׁעַת נְפִילָה לָאו צָרוֹת נִינְהוּ. הָנִיחָא אִי סָבַר לָהּ. רַב נַחְמָן כְּר' יִרְמְיָה, דַּאֲמַר בְּפ"ק: כִּי רָמֵינַן הָא מַתְנִי' דְּ"זוֹ הִיא" דִּמְמַעֵט כָּנַס וּלְבַסּוֹף גֵּירֵשׁ אַהַהִיא דְּקָתָנֵי "וְכוּלָּן אִם נִתְגָּרְשׁוּ צָרוֹתֵיהֶן מוּתָּרוֹת", וְאע"ג דְּכָנַס וּלְבַסּוֹף גֵּירֵשׁ, וְאָמַר רַבִּי יִרְמְיָה: תַּבְרָא כו'. אֶלָּא אִי סָבַר לָהּ כְּרָבָא. דְּזוֹ וְאֵין צָרִיךְ לוֹמַר זוֹ קָתָנֵי, אַלְמָא כָּנַס וּלְבַסּוֹף גֵּירֵשׁ שַׁרְיָא אֲפִי' לְתַנָּא דְּהָכָא, וְ"זוֹ הִיא" לָאו לְמַעוּטֵי אָתָא. זוֹ הִיא לְמַעוּטֵי מַאי. אִי לְמַעוּטֵי מֵת אָחִיו וְאח"כ גֵּירֵשׁ אִשְׁתּוֹ וְכָנַס יְבִמְתּוֹ, הַשְׁתָּא כָּנַס וְאח"כ גֵּירֵשׁ — שַׁרְיָא, גֵּירֵשׁ וְאח"כ כָּנַס מִיבַּעְיָא? וְאִי לְמַעוּטֵי מֵת נָשׂוּי נָכְרִית וְלֹא גֵּירֵשׁ בַּעַל אֲחוֹת אִשָּׁה אִשְׁתּוֹ וּמֵת, דַּאֲסוּרָה נָכְרִית לְיַיבּוּמֵי, מִשּׁוּם דַּהֲוַאי צָרָה בְּזִיקָה לָזוֹ שֶׁנָּפְלָה עַכְשָׁיו בְּעוֹד בַּעְלָהּ חַי, וַהֲרֵי לֹא נִתְגָּרְשָׁה, וּבִשְׁעַת מִיתָה צָרוֹת הֵן, וּבְהָא מוֹדֵי רָבָא — הָא לְר"נ לֵיכָּא לְמֵימַר הָכִי, דְּהָא אֵין זִיקָה סְבִירָא לֵיהּ. וְהִלְכָּךְ, עַל כָּרְחָךְ כְּרַבִּי יִרְמְיָה סְבִירָא לֵיהּ, וּלְמַעוּטֵי כָּנַס וְאח"כ גֵּירֵשׁ, דְּאָמַר נִישּׂוּאִין מַפִּילִין, וְהַאי שַׁעְתָּא צָרַת עֶרְוָה הָוְיָא. וּלְרָבָא. דְּאָמַר מִיתָה מַפֶּלֶת, וְכָנַס וְאח"כ גֵּירֵשׁ — שַׁרְיָא. הָנִיחָא אִי סָבַר [לָהּ] כְּרַב אַשִׁי. דְּיֵשׁ זִיקָה. זוֹ הִיא לְמַעוּטֵי מֵת בְּלֹא גֵּירֵשׁ. וְלָא דָּיֵיק לְמַתְנִיתִין כְּרַב אַשִׁי דְּאָמַר הָא מֵת וְאח"כ גֵּירֵשׁ אֲסוּרָה, דְּהָא רָבָא מִיתָה מַפֶּלֶת סְבִירָא לֵיהּ, וְכֵיוָן דְּגֵירֵשׁ — שַׁרְיָא. אֶלָּא הָכִי דָּיֵיק: טַעְמָא דְּגֵירֵשׁ, דְּבִשְׁעַת מִיתָה לָאו צָרוֹת הֲווּ — זוֹ הִיא דְּנָכְרִית מוּתֶּרֶת. אֲבָל מֵת שֵׁנִי זֶה אַחַר רִאשׁוֹן, וְלֹא גֵּירֵשׁ אֶת אִשְׁתּוֹ, וַאֲפִי' לֹא כָּנַס אֶת הַנָּכְרִית — אֲסוּרָה, דַּהֲוַאי צָרַת אֲחוֹת אִשָּׁה בְּזִיקָה, וַאֲפִילּוּ בִּשְׁעַת מִיתָה. דְּכֵיוָן דְּיֵשׁ זִיקָה הָוֵי כְּאִילּוּ בָּאָה אַף מִכֹּחַ הַשֵּׁנִי. וְא"ת: הוֹאִיל וְזִיקָה חֲשִׁיבָא לִהְיוֹת עָלֶיהָ כֹּחַ הַשֵּׁנִי — הָוְיָא אֵשֶׁת ב' מֵתִים, דִּבְלָאו אִיסּוּר דַּאֲחָיוֹת נָמֵי אֲסִירָא! לָא הִיא, דְּזִיקַת שְׁנֵי יְבָמִין דַּאֲסִירָא לֵיתָא מִדְּאוֹרַיְיתָא, וְלָא גְּזוּר רַבָּנַן אֶלָּא הֵיכָא דַּעֲבַד בָּהּ מַאֲמָר, גְּזֵירָה שֶׁמָּא יֹאמְרוּ שְׁתֵּי יְבָמוֹת הַבָּאוֹת מִבַּיִת אֶחָד מִתְיַיבְּמוֹת. אֶלָּא אִי סָבַר לָהּ כְּרַב נַחְמָן. דְּאֵין זִיקָה, וְהָא שַׁרְיָא — זוֹ הִיא לְמַעוּטֵי מַאי? הָא כּוּלְּהוּ שַׁרְיָין בַּר מְכָנֵס וְלֹא גֵּירֵשׁ, וְהַהִיא פְּשִׁיטָא, דְּהָא בְּהֶדְיָא תָּנֵינָא לָהּ, וְלָא אֲתָא "זוֹ הִיא" לְמַעוּטָהּ.

מתני' וְכוּלָּן. ט"ו עֲרָיוֹת. שֶׁהָיוּ בָּהֶן. לְאָחִיו הַמֵּת. קִידּוּשֵׁי סָפֵק אוֹ גֵּירוּשֵׁי סָפֵק. הָוְיָא צָרָתָהּ סְפֵק צָרַת עֶרְוָה, דִּלְמָא אִיגָּרְשָׁה עֶרְוָה, וּלְגַבֵּי קִידּוּשִׁין דִּלְמָא לָא מִיקַּדְּשָׁה. הֲרֵי אֵלּוּ הַצָּרוֹת חוֹלְצוֹת. וְלָא מִפַּטְרָן בְּלָא כְּלוּם, דִּלְמָא לָאו צָרַת עֶרְוָה הִיא. וְלֹא מִתְיַיבְּמוֹת. דִּלְמָא צָרַת עֶרְוָה הִיא. סָפֵק קָרוֹב לוֹ. שֶׁהָיוּ ח' אַמּוֹת מְלוּמְלָמוֹת בֵּינֵיהֶן בִּר"ה, וְד' אַמּוֹת קוֹנוֹת שָׁם, וּזְרָקוֹ, סָפֵק בְּד' אַמּוֹת הַקָּרוֹב לָהּ, סָפֵק בְּד' אַמּוֹת הַקָּרוֹב לוֹ. כָּתַב בִּכְתַב יָדוֹ. דְּקַיְ"ל (ב"ב דף קעה:): הוֹצִיא עָלָיו כְּתַב יָדוֹ שֶׁהוּא חַיָּיב לוֹ — גּוֹבֶה מִנְּכָסִים בְּנֵי חוֹרִין. אַלְמָא: כְּתַב יָדוֹ בְּלֹא עֵדִים מִילְּתָא הִיא. יֵשׁ עָלָיו עֵדִים וְאֵין בּוֹ זְמַן. כָּתוּב, אוֹ יֵשׁ בּוֹ זְמַן וְאֵין בּוֹ אֶלָּא עֵד א' וְאֵינוֹ כְּתַב יָדוֹ שֶׁל בַּעַל — זֶהוּ סְפֵק גֵּירוּשִׁין. דְּאָמְרִינַן בְּמַסֶּ' גִּיטִּין (דף פו.): ג' גִּיטִּין פְּסוּלִין וְאִם נִשֵּׂאת הַוָּלָד כָּשֵׁר, וְאֵלּוּ הֵן: כָּתַב בִּכְתַב יָדוֹ כו'. וְה"נ חוֹלֶצֶת צָרָתָהּ כֵּיוָן דְּגִיטָּא הוּא. דְּאִם נִיסֵּת — הַוָּלָד כָּשֵׁר וְלֹא מִתְיַיבֶּמֶת, כֵּיוָן דְּלָאו גִּיטָּא מַעַלְיָא הוּא, דְּקָרֵי לְהוּ פְּסוּל לְכַתְּחִלָּה. הִלְכָּךְ, אִי שָׁרֵית לֵיהּ, אָמְרֵי אֱינָשֵׁי: צָרַת עֶרְוָה מִתְיַיבֶּמֶת. וּבִגְמָרָא בָּעֵי, אַמַּאי לָא נָקַט נָמֵי בְּגֵירוּשִׁין סָפֵק קָרוֹב לוֹ כו'. **גמ'** וְאִילּוּ בְּגֵירוּשִׁין סָפֵק קָרוֹב לָהּ סָפֵק קָרוֹב לוֹ לָא קָתָנֵי. דְּהָתָם אֲפִי' חֲלִיצָה נָמֵי לָא בָּעְיָא צָרָתָהּ, מ"ט? אֲמַר רַבָּה אִשָּׁה זוֹ בְּחֶזְקַת הֶיתֵּר לַשּׁוּק עוֹמֶדֶת. קוֹדֶם לָכֵן, אִם יָמוּת בַּעְלָהּ, שֶׁהֲרֵי צָרַת עֶרְוָה הִיא. וּמִסָּפֵק אַתָּה בָּא לְאוֹסְרָהּ. שֶׁמָּא נִתְגָּרְשָׁה הָעֶרְוָה. אַל תַּאַסְרֶנָּה מִסָּפֵק. אֲבָל בְּהָנָךְ ג' גִּיטִּין לָאו מִסָּפֵק אָסְרִינַן לָהּ, דְּהָא גִּיטָּא הוּא, אֶלָּא שֶׁאֵין מִן הַמּוּבְחָר. בְּקִידּוּשִׁין נָמֵי. אַמַּאי אָסְרִינַן לָהּ לְיַיבּוּמֵי? לֵימָא: אִשָּׁה זוֹ קוֹדֶם שֶׁקִּידֵּשׁ בַּעְלָהּ אֶת בַּת אָחִיו בְּחֶזְקַת הֶיתֵּר לְיִבּוּם עוֹמֶדֶת כְּשֶׁיָּמוּת, וּמִסָּפֵק אַתָּה בָּא כו'. לְחוּמְרָא. שְׁנוּיָא הוּא: וּפָרְכִינַן. הָא חוּמְרָא דְּאָתֵי לִידֵי קוּלָּא הוּא. דְּאָזֵיל הַאי מְקַדֵּשׁ בְּסָפֵק וְקָמְקַדֵּשׁ לַאֲחוֹתָהּ שֶׁל זוֹ שֶׁקִּידֵּשׁ בִּסְפֵק קִידּוּשִׁין וַדַּאי. אִי נָמֵי אָתֵי אִינִישׁ אַחֲרִינָא וּמְקַדֵּשׁ לָהּ. לְהָךְ מְקוּדֶּשֶׁת בְּקִידּוּשֵׁי סָפֵק. קִידּוּשֵׁי וַדַּאי. בְּחַיֵּי בַּעְלָהּ. וְכֵיוָן דְּקָאָסַר מָר לְצָרָתָהּ לְיַיבּוּמֵי. לַאֲבִיהָ שֶׁל זוֹ, מִשּׁוּם צָרַת הַבַּת. אָמְרֵי. אֱינָשֵׁי: קִידּוּשֵׁי קַמָּא וַדַּאי הָווּ קִידּוּשִׁין גְּמוּרִין. וּדְבַתְרָא לָאו קִידּוּשִׁין. שֶׁאֵשֶׁת אִישׁ קִידֵּשׁ, וְאֵינָהּ צְרִיכָה הֵימֶנּוּ גֵּט. וּלְגַבֵּי קִידּוּשֵׁי אֲחוֹתָהּ נָמֵי, דַּאֲמַרַן דְּאָזֵיל הוּא וּמְקַדֵּשׁ לַאֲחוֹתָהּ, אָתוּ לְמֵימַר לְאַחַר מִיתָתוֹ כִּי אָסְרִינַן לַצָּרָה לְיַיבּוּמֵי, אָמְרֵי דְּקַמַּיְיתָא קִידּוּשִׁין [דְּבַתְרַיְיתָא] לָאו קִידּוּשִׁין, שֶׁאֵין קִידּוּשִׁין תּוֹפְסִין בַּאֲחוֹת אִשָּׁה, וְיִשָּׂאֶנָּה אָחִיו מֵאַחַר כְּנָכְרִית בְּעָלְמָא, וּפָגַע בְּעֶרְוָה.

כֵּיוָן

כתב בכתב ידו. מפרש ר"י בר' מאיר: אפי' אין כאן אלא חתימת ידו. (א) והא דתנן (ב"ב דף קעה:) הוציא עליו כתב ידו כו' — היינו חתימת ידו, וכן מוכח בפרק שני דכתובות (דף כא. ושם), דאמר אביי: לא ליחוי איניש חתימת ידיה אלא אחספא או אריסא דמגילתא, דלמא משכח איניש דלא מעלי, ותנן הוציא כתב ידו כו'(ב). אר"י: דכתב בכתב ידו ואין עליו עדים — פסול משום זמן, דיכול להקדים זמן כמו שירצה. וא"ת: [מאחר שדעתו לגרשה למה חיישינן לקנוניא ועוד]: אם הוא חשוד להקדים זמן ולעשות עם האשה קנוניא על הלקוחות בפירות שמכר מזמן הכתוב עד עכשיו, א"כ אנן לא נסמוך על הזמן הכתוב, ואמאי פסול? וי"ל: דאע"פ שבא לגרשה חיישינן לקנוניא, כדחיישינן בסוף פרק "שנים אוחזין" (ב"מ דף יט: ושם) גבי שובר, ולא סמכינן אזמן הכתוב בו. ופעמים תפסיד האשה שלא כדין בשלא הקדים הזמן, ואנו חושדין אותו שביוש הנתינה כתב והקדים הזמן, ומפסדת האשה שלא כדין פירות שמשעת הזמן עד הנתינה. אבל כשנפסלנו — לא תפסיד שלא כדין, דבדין הוא שלא תטרוף, דהא דאין לבעל פירות משעת כתיבה ותתימה — היינו דווקא בגט כשר. **יש** בו זמן ואין בו אלא עד אחד וכו'. הנך ג' גיטין פסולין ואם נשאת הולד כשר, כדתנן בפ' בתרא דגיטין (דף פו. ושם). ולמאן דמפרש התם דכתב ידו ועד אחד שנינו — איצטריך רישא כתב ידו ואין עליו עדים *לאשמועינן דאפילו הכי הולד כשר, וסיפא דאין בו אלא עד אחד איצטריך לאשמועינן דאפ"ה לא תנשא לכתחלה. וא"ת: ולמ"ד דכתב סופר ועד שנינו, ניחוש שמא הסופר כתבו להתלמד וזרקו לאשפה והחתימה עליו האשה עד אחד? וי"ל: שהסופרים חוששים שיבא לידי מכשול ונזהרים בכך. ומ"מ לא חשיב סופר ועד כשני עדים לגרש בו לכתחלה. **אשה** זו בחזקת היתר לשוק עומדת. וא"ת: תינח כנס ואח"כ גירש, שכבר הויא צרת ערוה. אבל גירש ואח"כ כנס — הא לא הויא בחזקת היתר לשוק! ועוד: (ג) לר"י דוקא בגירש ולבסוף כנס איירי! וי"ל: דמ"מ היא בחזקת היתר לשוק, דמוקמינן הערוה בחזקה שלא נתגרשה. וא"ת: דהכא מוקמינן אשה בחזקת היתר לשוק, אע"פ שבשעה שנולד הספק היתה עומדת בחזקת איסור שבעלה עדיין חי, ובפ"ק דחולין (דף ט. ושם) אמרינן: בהמה בחייה בחזקת איסור עומדת, עד שיודע לך במה נשחטה. נשחטה — בחזקת היתר עומדת, עד שיודע לך במה נטרפה. ומשמע: דוקא לענין ריעותא דאתיליד אחר שחיטה הויא בחזקת היתר, כגון בא זאב ונטל בני מעים והחזירם כשהם נקובים, דלא חיישינן שמא במקום נקב נקבו. אבל אם נולד הספק מחיים, כגון ספק דרוסה — לא, משום דבשעה שנולד הספק היתה עדיין בחזקת איסור! ואר"י: דהתם חיישי' לספק דרוסה משום דשכיחא, ומוכחא מילתא לאיסורא טפי מדלהיתרא. וכן ההיא דישב לה קוץ בושט דחיישינן שמא הבריא,

למאן

רש"ל

[לאשמועינן דהולד כשר וסיפא אתא לאשמועינן כצ"ל רש"ל]

לעיל יג.

[לעיל יג. וש"נ]

גיטין פו:

תוספות ישנים

בחזקת היתר לשוק עומדת ואע"ג דבחזקת אשת איש היתה מ"מ כיון דסופו למות ולבסוף נמי מת קרינן לה שפיר בחזקת היתר לשוק. וא"ת ומאי שנא מספק דרוסה דאסרינן והלא אית לה חזקת היתר דסופה להשחט ואולי דהתם חיישינן דשמא תמות הבהמה: **בחזקת** היתר ליבם. וא"ת התינח היכא שכנס זו קודם הקדושין של ספק אבל היכא שהקדושין של ספק קדמו מאי קאמר בחזקת היתר ליבם הלא לא היתה מעולם בחזקת היתר ליבם דשמא הקדושין גמורים היו וא"כ היתה זו צרת ערוה ואסורה ליבם. וי"ל דמ"מ בחזקת היתר ליבם היא דאוקמה לערוה בחזקת פנויה והויא זו מותרת ליבם:

הגהות הב"ח

(א) תוס' ד"ה כתב וכו' חתימת ידו וכן הא דתנן: (ב) בא"ד ואר"י דכתב וכו' וא"ת אם הוא חשוד להקדים זמן ולעשות עם האשה קנוניא על הלקוחות בפירות שמכר מזמן הכתוב עד עכשיו דאע"פ שבא לגרשה חיישינן לקנוניא כדחיישי' בסוף שנים אוחזין גבי שובר א"כ אנן לא נסמוך על הזמן הכתוב ואמאי פסול וי"ל דודאי איטו נאמן ולא סמכינן אזמן הכתוב בו ולכך פסלוהו דלפעמים תפסיד האשה וכו' שמשעת כתיבת הזמן עד כו' כצ"ל. ונ"ב עיין בתוס' פ"ק דגיטין דף ג: (ג) ד"ה אשה וכו' ועוד לר' ירמיה דוקא:

הגהות הגר"א

[א] גמ' מת בלא גירש. נ"ב גירסת הגאונים והרי"ף מת ואח"כ גירש וכ"ש במת ולא גירש וכתב הטור דווקא בלא כנס והרשב"א כתב להיפך דווקא בכנס והרמב"ן אמר (אליבא דהרי"ף) בין בזה ובין בזה (ועמ"ש רבינו באה"ע סי' קעה ס"ק יח):

תוספות חד מקמאי

מתניתין כיצד ספק קדושין זרק לה קדושין ספק קרוב לו ספק קרוב לה כיצד ספק גירושין כתב בכתב ידו ואין עליו עדים וכו' מסקנא דשמעתא דבגירושין נמי זרק לה גטה ספק קרוב לו ספק קרוב לה ל"ש כת אחת ול"ש ב' כתי עדים א' אומר קרוב לו וא' אומר קרוב לה חולצת ולא מתייבמת וקדושין נמי בכתב ידו ואין עליו עדים או אין עליו אלא עד א' לרב כדאית ליה כתב ידו ועד אבל כתב סופר שאינו מובהק ועד הולד פסול ולשמואל אפי' בסופר שאינו מובהק הולד כשר כדאיתא בפ' המגרש וגבי קידושין נמי חולצת ולא מתייבמת כללא

כֵּיוָן דְּקָא מַצְרְכַתְּ חֲלִיצָה — מֵידַע יָדְעִי דְּחוּמְרָא בְּעָלְמָא הוּא. — א"ה גֵּירוּשִׁין נַמִי לִיתְנֵי, ו וְלִיצְרְכָהּ חֲלִיצָה, וּמֵידַע יָדְעִי דְּחוּמְרָא בְּעָלְמָא הוּא! — אִם אַתָּה אוֹמֵר חוֹלֶצֶת — מִתְיַיבֶּמֶת. — הָכָא נַמִי: אִם אַתָּה אוֹמֵר חוֹלֶצֶת — מִתְיַיבֶּמֶת! — וְתִתְיַיבֵּם, וְאֵין בְּכָךְ כְּלוּם — אַחֲזָקָה קָא קַיְימָא. אֵיתִיבֵיהּ אַבַּיֵי: *נָפַל הַבַּיִת עָלָיו וְעַל בַּת אָחִיו, וְאֵין יָדוּעַ אֵיזֶה מֵהֶם מֵת רִאשׁוֹן — צָרָתָהּ חוֹלֶצֶת וְלֹא מִתְיַיבֶּמֶת. אַמַּאי? הָכָא נַמִי נֵימָא: אִשָּׁה זוֹ בְּחֶזְקַת הֶיתֵּר לַשּׁוּק עוֹמֶדֶת, וּמִסָּפֵק אַתָּה בָּא לְאוֹסְרָהּ — אַל תַּאַסְרֶנָּה מִסָּפֵק! וְכִי תֵּימָא: ה"נ לְחוּמְרָא — חוּמְרָא דְּאָתֵי לִידֵי קוּלָּא הוּא, שֶׁאִם אַתָּה אוֹמֵר חוֹלֶצֶת — מִתְיַיבֶּמֶת! — גֵּירוּשִׁין דִּשְׁכִיחִי גָּזְרוּ בְּהוּ רַבָּנַן, *מַפּוֹלֶת דְּלָא שְׁכִיחִי — לָא גָּזְרוּ בְּהוּ רַבָּנַן. אִי נַמִי: גֵּירוּשִׁין דְּקַיְימָא עֶרְוָה דְּקָא מוּכָח, וְצָרָתָהּ קָמַצְרְכַתְּ לָהּ חֲלִיצָה — אָמְרִי: קָמוּ בֵּיהּ רַבָּנַן בְּגִיטָּא דְּגִיטָּא מַעַלְיָא הוּא, וְאָתוּ לְיַיבּוּמֵי לַצָּרָה. מַפּוֹלֶת — מִי קָמוּ בְּהוּ רַבָּנַן בְּמַפּוֹלֶת? — וְגַבֵּי גֵּירוּשִׁין מִי לָא תְּנַן? וְהָתְנַן: *[א] הָיְתָה עוֹמֶדֶת בּרה"ר וְזָרְקוֹ לָהּ, קָרוֹב לָהּ — מְגוֹרֶשֶׁת, קָרוֹב לוֹ — אֵינָהּ מְגוֹרֶשֶׁת. מֶחֱצָה עַל מֶחֱצָה — מְגוֹרֶשֶׁת וְאֵינָהּ מְגוֹרֶשֶׁת. וְאָמְרִינַן: לְמַאי הִלְכְתָא — דְּאִי כֹּהֵן הוּא אֲסוּרָה לֵיהּ, וְאִי עֶרְוָה הִיא — צָרָתָהּ בָּעֲיָא חֲלִיצָה. וְלָא אָמְרִינַן שֶׁאִם אַתָּה אוֹמֵר חוֹלֶצֶת מִתְיַיבֶּמֶת! — הָא אִיתְּמַר עֲלָהּ, *רַבָּה וְרַב יוֹסֵף דְּאָמְרִי תַּרְוַויְיהוּ: הָכָא בִּשְׁתֵּי כִּיתֵּי עֵדִים עָסְקִינַן, אַחַת אוֹמֶרֶת: קָרוֹב לָהּ, וְאַחַת אוֹמֶרֶת: קָרוֹב לוֹ, דַּהֲוָה לֵיהּ סְפֵיקָא דְּאוֹרַיְיתָא. וּמַתְנִיתִין דְּהָכָא בְּכַת אַחַת, דְּהָוֵי סְפֵיקָא דְּרַבָּנַן. — וּמִמַּאי דְּמַתְנִיתִין דְּהָכָא בְּכַת אַחַת? — דּוּמְיָא דְּקִדּוּשִׁין, מַה קִּדּוּשִׁין בְּכַת אַחַת — אַף גֵּרוּשִׁין בְּכַת אַחַת. וְקִדּוּשִׁין גּוּפַיְיהוּ מִמַּאי דִּבְכַת אַחַת, דִּלְמָא בְּב' כִּיתֵּי עֵדִים? — אִי בְּב' כִּיתֵּי עֵדִים — תִּתְיַיבֵּם, וְאֵין בְּכָךְ כְּלוּם. — קַיְימֵי עֵדִים וְקָאָמְרִי "קָרוֹב לָהּ" וְאַתְּ אָמְרַתְּ תִּתְיַיבֵּם וְאֵין בְּכָךְ כְּלוּם?! וְתוּ: בִּשְׁתֵּי כִּיתֵּי עֵדִים נַמִי סְפֵיקָא דְּרַבָּנַן הִיא, דְּאָמְרִי': אוֹקֵי תְּרֵי לְבַהֲדֵי תְּרֵי, וְאִשָּׁה אוֹקְמָהּ אַחֲזָקָה. מִידֵי דַּהֲוָה אַנִּכְסֵי דְּבַר שְׁטְיָא. *דְּבַר שְׁטְיָא זַבֵּין נִכְסֵי, אָתוּ בֵּי תְּרֵי וְאָמְרִי: כְּשֶׁהוּא חָלִים זַבֵּין, וַאֲתוּ בֵּי תְּרֵי וְאָמְרוּ כְּשֶׁהוּא שׁוֹטֶה זַבֵּין. וַאֲמַר רַב אַשִׁי: [ב]אוֹקֵי תְּרֵי לַהֲדֵי תְּרֵי וְאַרְעָא

רש"י

כֵּיוָן דְּקָמַצְרְכַתְּ חֲלִיצָה לַצָּרָה מֵידַע יָדְעִי. דְּקִידּוּשֵׁי דְּבַת אָחִיו לָאו קִידּוּשִׁין, וְהַאי דְּלָא מִתְיַיבֶּמֶת צָרָתָהּ — חוּמְרָא בְּעָלְמָא הוּא. לִיתְנֵי. סָפֵק קָרוֹב לוֹ. מֵידַע יָדְעִי דְּחוּמְרָא בְּעָלְמָא הוּא. כְּלוֹמַר, אִי חָיְישַׁתְּ דְּלָא לֵימְרוּ אִינָשֵׁי מִדְּחָלְצָה וַדַּאי גֵּירוּשִׁין גְּמוּרִין נִינְהוּ, דְּאִי קָדֵישׁ לָהּ לִמְגוֹרֶשֶׁת אִינִישׁ דְּעָלְמָא וַהֲדַר קָדֵישׁ לַאֲחוֹתָהּ, דְּקַמַּיְיתָא (א) קָדֵישׁ, דְּבַתְרַיְיתָא לָאו קִידּוּשִׁין — לָא חֵיישׁ לְהָכִי. דְּמִדְּלָא מִתְיַיבֶּמֶת צָרָתָהּ, מֵידַע יָדְעִי דַּחֲלִיצָה חוּמְרָא בְּעָלְמָא הוּא. מִתְיַיבֶּמֶת. וְקָמְיַיבֵּם צָרַת עֶרְוָה, דְּאוֹקְמָהּ אַחֲזָקָה, וּפָגַע בְּכָרֵת. הָכָא נַמִי. גַּבֵּי קִידּוּשִׁין, אַמַּאי חוֹלֶצֶת? הָא אָתֵי לְיַיבּוּמֵי, וְדִלְמָא קִידּוּשֵׁי עֶרְוָה קִידּוּשֵׁי הֲווּ, וְקָמְיַיבֵּם לְצָרַת עֶרְוָה. אַחֲזָקָה קַיְימָא. בְּחֶזְקַת הֶיתֵּר לְיַיבֵּם. וְעַל בַּת אָחִיו. וְהִיא אִשְׁתּוֹ, צָרָתָהּ חוֹלֶצֶת — לָא מִיפַּטְרָא בְּלָא כְּלוּם מִשּׁוּם צָרַת עֶרְוָה, שֶׁמָּא הִיא מֵתָה רִאשׁוֹנָה וְאַחַ"כ מֵת הוּא. וּתְנַן: וְכוּלָּן, אִם מֵתוּ הָעֲרָיוֹת קוֹדֶם לְבַעֲלֵיהֶן — צָרוֹתֵיהֶן מוּתָּרוֹת, בְּפ"ק. וְלֹא מִתְיַיבֶּמֶת. שֶׁמָּא הוּא מֵת רִאשׁוֹן, וְהָוְיָא לָהּ הָךְ צָרַת בִּתּוֹ: ה"ג: חוּמְרָא דְּאָתֵי לִידֵי קוּלָּא הוּא, שֶׁאִם אַתָּה אוֹמֵר חוֹלֶצֶת מִתְיַיבֶּמֶת. גָּזְרוּ בְּהוּ רַבָּנַן. דְּסָפֵק גֵּירוּשִׁין בְּעֶרְוָה לֹא תַּחֲלוֹץ הַצָּרָה, שֶׁאִם אַתָּה אוֹמֵר חוֹלֶצֶת — מִתְיַיבֶּמֶת: דְּקַיְימָא עֶרְוָה. קַמָּן, וְקָמוֹכַחַת, דְּהַכֹּל רוֹאִין שֶׁזּוֹ צָרַת עֶרְוָה הָיְתָה, וְאַתָּה מַצְרְכַתְּ חֲלִיצָה — אָתוּ לְמֵימַר קָמוּ בֵּיהּ רַבָּנַן בְּגִיטָּא, וְגִיטָּא מְעַלְיָא הוּא, וְאֵין זוֹ צָרַת עֶרְוָה — וְאָתָא לְיַיבּוּמֵי. אֲבָל מַפּוֹלֶת. אע"ג מַצְרְכַתְּ לָהּ חֲלִיצָה, מִי אָתֵי לְמֵימַר קָמוּ בְּהוּ רַבָּנַן בְּמַפּוֹלֶת? אֵלּוּ הַדַּיָּינִים הַמַּצְרִיכִים אוֹתָהּ חֲלִיצָה, נְבִיאִים הֵם וְיָדְעוּ שֶׁהִיא מֵתָה רִאשׁוֹנָה, דְּלֵיתֵי לְיַיבֵּם לַצָּרָה? וּמֵידַע יָדְעִי דְּהַאי דַּחֲלָצָה — מִשּׁוּם סְפֵיקָא הָיָה. קָרוֹב לוֹ כו'. מְפָרֵשׁ בְּמַסֶּכֶת גִּיטִּין. לְמַאי הִלְכְתָא. קָתָנֵי מְגוֹרֶשֶׁת. דְּהָוֵי לָהּ סְפֵקָא דְּאוֹרַיְיתָא. כֵּיוָן דִּתְרֵי אָמְרֵי קָרוֹב לָהּ — לָא מָצֵי לְאוֹקְמִי נָרָה אַחֲזָקָה וּלְמִיפְטְרָא לְעָלְמָא בְּלָא חֲלִיצָה. וּמַתְנִי' דְּהָכָא בְּכַת אַחַת. עֵד אוֹמֵר קָרוֹב לוֹ וְעֵד אוֹמֵר קָרוֹב לָהּ. הִלְכָּךְ, בְּקִידּוּשִׁין הוּא דְּאִיכָּא לְמִיתְנְיֵיהּ — מִשּׁוּם דְּבְחֶזְקַת הֶיתֵּר לְיַיבֵּם קַיְימָא, וּמִשּׁוּם עֵד אֶחָד דְּאָמַר קָרוֹב לָהּ לָא מַפְּקִינַן לָהּ מֵחֲזָקָה, וְחָלְצָה. אֲבָל בְּגֵירוּשִׁין לֵיכָּא לְמִתְנְיֵיהּ דִּבְחֶזְקַת הֶיתֵּר לַשּׁוּק קַיְימָא, וְעֵד א' דְּאָמַר קָרוֹב לָהּ — בָּעֵי לְאַפּוֹקֵי מֵחֲזָקָה, וְכֵיוָן דְּלֵיכָּא עֵדוּת שָׁלֵם — אָזְלִינַן לְקוּלָּא וְקָא מוֹקְמִינַן אַחֲזָקָה, וְלָא בָּעֲיָא חֲלִיצָה, שֶׁאִם אַתָּה אוֹמֵר חוֹלֶצֶת — מִתְיַיבֶּמֶת. אַף גֵּירוּשִׁין בְּכַת אַחַת. כְּלוֹמַר, אִי הֲוָה תָּנֵי לְהוּ, דְּע"כ הֲוָה מִיתוֹקְמָא דּוּמְיָא דְּקִידּוּשִׁין, מִשּׁוּם הָכִי לָא תָּנֵי לָהּ: הָכִי גָּרְסִינַן. וְקִידּוּשִׁין גּוּפַיְיהוּ מִמַּאי דִּבְכַת אַחַת דִּלְמָא בִּשְׁתֵּי כִּיתֵּי עֵדִים אִי בִּשְׁתֵּי כִּיתֵּי עֵדִים תִּתְיַיבֵּם צָרָתָהּ וְאֵין בְּכָךְ כְּלוּם קַיְימֵי עֵדִים וְאָמְרֵי קָרוֹב לָהּ וְאַתְּ אָמְרַתְּ תִּתְיַיבֵּם וְאֵין בְּכָךְ כְּלוּם. וְתוּ, בִּשְׁתֵּי כִּיתֵּי עֵדִים נַמִי סְפֵיקָא דְּרַבָּנַן הוּא דְּאָמְרִינַן אוֹקֵי תְּרֵי כו'. וְהָכִי פֵּירוּשׁוֹ: אִי בִּשְׁתֵּי כִּיתֵּי עֵדִים לָא הֲוָה תָּנֵי "וְלֹא מִתְיַיבֶּמֶת", אֶלָּא תִּתְיַיבֵּם וְאֵין בְּכָךְ כְּלוּם, דְּהָא אוֹקְמַתְּ אַחֲזָקָה דְּמוּתֶּרֶת לְיַיבֵּם הֲוַאי. וּפָרְכִינַן: קַיְימֵי עֵדִים כו' וְהָאָמְרַתְּ שְׁתֵּי כִּיתֵּי עֵדִים סְפֵיקָא דְּאוֹרַיְיתָא הִיא! וְתוּ: בִּשְׁתֵּי כִּיתֵּי עֵדִים נַמִי סְפֵיקָא דְּרַבָּנַן הוּא. וּבְגֵירוּשִׁין גּוּפַיְיהוּ, אע"ג דְּכַת אַחַת אוֹמֶרֶת קָרוֹב לָהּ — לָא הֲוָה לָן לְאַפּוֹקֵי מֵחֶזְקַת הֶיתֵּר לַשּׁוּק, כֵּיוָן דְּאִיכָּא כַּת אַחֲרִיתִי דְּאָמְרָה קָרוֹב לוֹ, וְאַמַּאי קָתָנֵי חוֹלֶצֶת? וְאִית דִּמְפָרְשֵׁי הָכִי: אִי בִּשְׁתֵּי כִּיתֵּי עֵדִים — מִי הֲוָה אָמְרִינַן לְעֵיל בְּסָפֵק קִידּוּשִׁין תִּתְיַיבֵּם וְאֵין בְּכָךְ כְּלוּם? קַיְימֵי עֵדִים וְאָמְרֵי קָרוֹב לָהּ וּמְקוּדֶּשֶׁת, וְנַעֲשֵׂית הָרִאשׁוֹנָה צָרַת עֶרְוָה, וְאַתְּ אָמְרַתְּ תִּתְיַיבֵּם? אֶלָּא וַדַּאי בְּכַת א', וּמִשּׁוּם דְּלֵיכָּא אֶלָּא חַד דְּאָמַר קָרוֹב לָהּ — אָמְרִינַן אוֹקֵי נָרָה אַחֶזְקָתָהּ דִּשְׁרְיָא לְיַבֵּם. וְכָךְ שָׁמַעְתִּי. וְקָשֶׁה בְּעֵינַי: מִשּׁוּם דְּמַיְיתֵי סַיְיעְתָּא לְמִילְּתֵיהּ מִדְּנַפְשֵׁיהּ, דְּהַהוּא "תִּתְיַיבֵּם וְאֵין בְּכָךְ כְּלוּם" דִּלְעֵיל — הוּא גּוּפֵיהּ פֵּירֵשׁ הָכִי. תָּנָא

תוספות

למאן דחייש לספק דרוסה. כדאמר בריש "אלו טרפות" (חולין דף מג: ושם), ואחרי שנכנס לבין השוורים, ופסק התם אמימר* הלכתא דחוששין לספק דרוסה, אע"ג דאמרינן התם איכא למימר הכי ואיכא למימר הכי, מ"מ מסתברא טעמא לאיסורא טפי מלהתירא. תדע, דהא בספק כלבא ספק שונרא אמרינן התם (דף נג:) אימור כלבא, אפי' לשמואל דחייש לספק דרוסה. **הכא** נמי אם אתה אומר חולצת מתייבמת. תימה: דמעיקרא פריך ואל תאסרנה מספק, ורוצה להתירה ליבם לכתחילה, והשתא פריך דאפילו חליצה לא תיבעי, גזרה שמא תתייבם! ויש לומר: דהכא הכי קאמר: מה מועיל שאתה אוסרה לייבם? וכיון דחולצת יבוא מתוך כך לייבם! ומשני דחולצת ממה נפשך, ואם יבא בא(ק)ראי בעלמא לייבם — אין בכך כלום. **נפל** הבית וכו'. כאן יש תימה: אמאי חשיב לה טפי בחזקת היתר לשוק מלייבם? דהא קמן שניהם מתו, וכן יכול להיות שהיא מתה תחלה כמו הבעל! וי"ל: דמשום הכי חשיב לה טפי בחזקת היתר לשוק מלייבם, משום דבמיתת הבעל משתריא לשוק, אבל במיתת הערוה אינה ניתרת לייבם עד שימות הבעל עמה. **ואין** ידוע איזה מהם מת ראשונה. קסבר האי תנא דמיתה מפלת.

(ב) **למאי** הלכתא. תימה: דמשנה זו בגיטין ב"הזורק" (דף עח.*) ולא מסיק התם בגמרא למאי הלכתא. **אי** בשתי כיתי עדים תתייבם ואין בכך כלום. פ"ה דחוק הוא: דאיך עלה על דעת המתרץ לומר כן? ועוד, דבספרים ישנים גרס "ודלמא", והוא מוחק וגרס "ותו"! ונראה לר"י דה"פ: דומיא דקידושין, וקידושין משמע ליה דמיירי אף בכת אחת, ואע"ג דבכת אחת דאורייתא מתייבמת, כיון דבב' כיתי עדים הויא ספיקא דאורייתא — גזרו רבנן שלא תתייבם בכת אחת אטו ב' כיתי עדים. ופריך: וקידושין גופייהו, ממאי דמיירי בכת אחת? דלמא דוקא בב' כיתי עדים, אבל בכת אחת — מותרת להתייבם, ולא גזרינן אטו ב' כיתי עדים משום דב' כיתי עדים גופייהו הויא ספיקא דרבנן, ומדאורייתא' מתייבמת, דמוקים לה אחזקה. אלא מדרבנן חולצת ולא מתייבמת לחומרא — דווקא בשתי כיתי עדים, אבל בכת אחת — לא החמירו. ומוכיח דשתי כיתי עדים ספיקא דרבנן, כמו שמפורש לבסוף. והשתא קאמר: אי בב' כיתי עדים דוקא אתה רוצה להעמידו, אבל בכת אחת מתייבמת, ולא גזרינן אטו שתי כיתי עדים, דשתי כיתי עדים גופייהו אינה חולצת אלא לחומרא, ואם תתייבם אין בכך כלום, והיכי מצינן למימר דתתייבם ואין בכך כלום(ג)? קיימי עדים ואמרי כו'! ומסיק: ודלמא בשתי כיתי עדים גופייהו הויא ספיקא דרבנן, כמו שהקשה בתחלה. והשתא, לפי מסקנא זו בקידושין בכת אחת — שריא להתייבם. ומיהו ודלמא בעלמא קאמר. ועוד אר"י, דמצינן לפרש: דמשמע ליה דבקידושין איירי בכת אחת, משום דבשתי כיתי עדים לא איצטריך, דפשיטא, שהוא ספיקא דאורייתא, ותנן לה בגיטין (ג"ז שם) גבי ספק גירושין דחולצת. אבל(ד) אי הוה בקידושין מיירי בשתי כיתי עדים — הוה מיירי נמי בגירושין בשתי כיתי עדים, אע"ג דלא איצטריך וכבר תנן לה בגיטין. ולהכי קאמר דומיא דקידושין, דקידושין נמי בכת אחת. ופריך: וקידושין גופייהו דלמא בשתי כיתי עדים, דשתי כיתי עדים נמי ספיקא דרבנן, וכת א' ושתי כיתי עדים הכל הוה שוה, שהכל ספיקא דרבנן, כדמפרש ואזיל. **שתי** כיתי עדים נמי ספיקא דרבנן. וא"ת: וכיון דמסקינן דבשתי כיתי עדים הוי ספיקא דרבנן — למה דחקו רבה ורב יוסף לאוקמי ההיא

תוספות ישנים

שאם אתה אומר חולצת מתייבמת. וא"ת לעיל שאמרנו בפ' כילד חולצת ולא מתייבמת אמאי לא אמרינן שאם אתה אומר חולצת מתייבמת. וי"ל דהתם נמי אינה אסורה לייבם אלא מדרבנן וא"כ תתייבם ואין בכך כלום כדאמר הכא. וא"ת ולר' שמעון דאסר שתי אחיות בזיקה מדאורייתא וכשהאחת איסור מצוה אמרינן לעיל חולצת ולא מתייבמת ואמאי לא גזרינן שאם אתה אומר חולצת מתייבמת דהא מדאורייתא היא וא"א לומר תתייבם ואין בכך כלום. וי"ל דאחיות בזיקה והאחת איסור מצוה מלתא דלא שכיחא היא ולא גזור בה רבנן: **נפל** הבית עליו ועל בת אחיו וכו' ואמאי נימא אשה זו בחזקת היתר לשוק עומדת. וא"ת אדרבה נימא בחזקת היתר לייבם שמתה הערוה מתחלה מספק אתה בא לאוסרה לומר שמת האיש קודם ואל תאסרנה מספק וי"ל דסברא הוא להחזיקה בחזקת היתר לשוק יותר מלייבם משום דלשוק משתרייא במיתת הבעל לבד אבל להתירה לייבם צריך מיתת הבעל והערוה: **ומתניתין** דהכא ממאי דבכת אחת. נראה דאמתני' קפריך אמאי נקט מלתיה בכת אחת ומ"ה גזרינן חליצה אטו יבום והחליצה הוא חומרא בעלמא ליתני בשתי כתי עדים והוי התחלה כדין ולא נגזור אטו יבום ומשני משום דבעי למתני קדושין דמשום גירושין לא תנייה דהא כבר תנינן לה בגיטין אלא משום קדושין תנינן לה וא"כ צריך למתני דומיא דקדושין דמיירי בכת אחת:

עין משפט נר מצוה

כז א מיי' פ"ה מהל' גירושין הלכה יג סמג עשין כ טוש"ע אה"ע סימן קלט סעיף יג:

כח ב מיי' פכ"ט מהל' מכירה הלכה ה סמג עשין פב טוש"ע ח"מ סימן רלה סעיף כא בהג"ה:

[חולין נג:]

[עי' תוס' ב"ב קסט: ד"ה בחזקה]

מסורת הש"ס

לקמן מז:

[עירובין סג: וש"נ]

גיטין עח.

[שם:]

כתובות כ.

הגהות הב"ח

(א) רש"י ד"ה מידע וכו' דקמייתא קידושין דבתרייתא: (ב) תוס' ד"ה ולמאי למאי הלכתא: (ג) ד"ה אי בשתי וכו' ואין בכך כלום והא קיימי עדים: (ד) בא"ד אבל אי בקידושין הוה מיירי וכו' דכבר תנן לה וכו' קידושין מיירי נמי בכת אחת:

עין משפט נר מצוה

כט א מיי' פי"ב מהל' אישות הלכ' א ג סמג עשין מח טוש"ע אה"ע סימן סט סעי' א ג:
ל ב מיי' פ"א מהל' גירושין הלכה כד סמג עשין כ טוש"ע אה"ע סימן קכז סעיף א:
לא ג מיי' פ"ג מהלכות עדות הל' ד ופ"ח הלכה ה סמג עשין קט טוש"ע ח"מ סימן כח סעיף יג וסימן מו סעיף י:
לב ד מיי' פ"ז מהלכות יבום הלכה כז סמג עשין נ טוש"ע אה"ע סימן קעד סעיף ד:
לג ה מיי' שם הלכ' כז:

וְאַרְעָא אוּקְמָא בְּחֶזְקַת בַּר שַׁטְיָא. אֶלָּא אֲמַר *אַבַּיֵי: °"יַגִּיד עָלָיו רֵיעוֹ"; תָּנָא בְּקִידּוּשִׁין – וְה"ה לְגֵירוּשִׁין, תָּנָא בְּגֵירוּשִׁין – וה"ה לְקִידּוּשִׁין. א"ל רָבָא: אִי יַגִּיד עָלָיו רֵיעוֹ – מַאי "זֶהוּ" דְּקָתָנֵי? אֶלָּא אָמַר רָבָא: כָּל שֶׁיֵּשׁ בְּקִידּוּשִׁין – יֵשׁ בְּגֵירוּשִׁין, וְיֵשׁ בְּגֵירוּשִׁין מַה שֶּׁאֵין בְּקִידּוּשִׁין. וְ"זֶהוּ" דְּגֵירוּשִׁין לָאו דַּוְקָא, אֶלָּא מִשּׁוּם דְּתָנָא "זֶהוּ" בְּקִידּוּשִׁין – תָּנָא נַמִי "זֶהוּ" בְּגֵירוּשִׁין. וְ"זֶהוּ" דְּקִידּוּשִׁין לְמַעוּטֵי מַאי? – לְמַעוּטֵי זְמַן, דְּלֵיכָּא בְּקִידּוּשִׁין. – וּמִפְּנֵי מָה לֹא תִּקְּנוּ זְמַן בְּקִידּוּשִׁין? – הָנִיחָא לְמ"ד מִשּׁוּם פֵּירֵי – אֲרוּסָה לֵית לָהּ פֵּירֵי. אֶלָּא לְמ"ד מִשּׁוּם בַּת אֲחוֹתוֹ – לִיתְקִין זְמַן! – מִשּׁוּם דְּאִיכָּא דִּמְקַדֵּשׁ בְּכַסְפָּא וְאִיכָּא דִּמְקַדֵּשׁ בִּשְׁטָרָא – לָא תְּקוּן רַבָּנַן זְמַן. א"ל רַב אַחָא בְּרֵיהּ דְּרַב יוֹסֵף לְרַב אַשִׁי: וְהָא עַבְדָּא, דְּאִיכָּא דְּקָנֵי בְּכַסְפָּא וְאִיכָּא בִּשְׁטָרָא, וּתְקוּן רַבָּנַן זְמַן! – הָתָם רוּבָּא בִּשְׁטָרָא, הָכָא – רוּבָּא בְּכַסְפָּא. אב"א: מִשּׁוּם דְּלָא אֶפְשָׁר. הֵיכִי לִיעֲבִיד? לִינְחָהּ גַּבֵּי דִּידָהּ – מָחֲקָה לֵיהּ. לִינְחָהּ גַּבֵּי דִּידֵיהּ – זִמְנִין דְּבַת אֲחוֹתוֹ הִיא, וּמְחַפֶּה עֲלָהּ. לִינְחָהּ גַּבֵּי עֵדִים, (א) אִי דְּזָכְרִי – לֵיתוּ לִיסְהוּד, וְאִי לָא – זִמְנִין דְּחָזוּ מִכְּתָבָא, וַאֲתוּ מְסַהֲדִי. וְרַחֲמָנָא אָמַר: *"מִפִּיהֶם", וְלֹא מִפִּי כְּתָבָם. – אִי הָכִי בְּגֵירוּשִׁין נַמִי נֵימָא הָכִי! – הָתָם לְהַצָּלָה דִּידָהּ קָאָתֵי, הָכָא – לְחוֹבָה דִּידָהּ קָאָתֵי.§ **מתני'** *ג' אַחִין נְשׂוּאִין ג' נָכְרִיּוֹת, וּמֵת אֶחָד מֵהֶן, וְעָשָׂה בָּהּ הַשֵּׁנִי מַאֲמָר וָמֵת – הֲרֵי אֵלּוּ חוֹלְצוֹת וְלֹא מִתְיַבְּמוֹת. שֶׁנֶּאֱמַר °"וּמֵת אַחַד מֵהֶן יְבָמָהּ יָבֹא עָלֶיהָ" (ב) שֶׁעָלֶיהָ זִיקַת יָבָם אֶחָד וְלֹא שֶׁעָלֶיהָ זִיקַת ב' יְבָמִין. רַבִּי שִׁמְעוֹן אוֹמֵר: מְיַיבֵּם לְאֵיזוֹ שֶׁיִּרְצֶה, וְחוֹלֵץ לַשְּׁנִיָּה.§ **גמ'** וְאִי זִיקַת ב' יְבָמִין דְּאוֹרַיְיתָא, חֲלִיצָה נַמִי לָא תִּיבָּעֵי! אֶלָּא מִדְּרַבָּנַן, וּגְזֵירָה שֶׁמָּא יֹאמְרוּ ב' יְבָמוֹת הַבָּאוֹת מִבַּיִת אֶחָד מִתְיַבְּמוֹת. – וְנִיַיבֵּם לַחֲדָא וְנִיחֲלוֹץ לַחֲדָא! – גְּזֵירָה *) שֶׁמָּא יֹאמְרוּ: בַּיִת אֶחָד, מִקְצָתוֹ בָּנוּי וּמִקְצָתוֹ

תורה אור: איוב לו; דברים כה

רש"י

תָּנָא בְּקִידּוּשִׁין. סָפֵק קָרוֹב לוֹ כו', וְה"ה בְּגֵירוּשִׁין. וְתָנָא בְּגֵירוּשִׁין. כָּתַב בִּכְתַב יָדוֹ וכו', וְה"ה לְקִידּוּשִׁין: ה"ג. כָּל שֶׁיֵּשׁ בְּקִידּוּשִׁין יֵשׁ בְּגֵירוּשִׁין וְיֵשׁ בְּגֵירוּשִׁין מַה שֶּׁאֵין בְּקִידּוּשִׁין. וְ"זֶהוּ" דְּגֵירוּשִׁין לָאו דַּוְקָא, וּמִשּׁוּם דְּתָנָא "זֶהוּ" בְּקִידּוּשִׁין – תָּנָא נַמִי "זֶהוּ" בְּגֵירוּשִׁין. כָּל שֶׁיֵּשׁ בְּקִידּוּשִׁין. כְּגוֹן סָפֵק קָרוֹב לוֹ וכו' הָוֵי נַמִי סָפֵק בְּגֵירוּשִׁין. וְיֵשׁ בְּגֵירוּשִׁין. שֶׁאֵין סָפֵק לְעִנְיַן קִידּוּשִׁין, כְּגוֹן זְמַן. כִּדְמְפָרֵשׁ לְקַמָּן, דְּבִשְׁטַר קִידּוּשִׁין כְּגוֹן הַמְקַדֵּשׁ בִּשְׁטָר – לֹא תִּקְּנוּ זְמַן. וְ"זֶהוּ" דְּגֵירוּשִׁין לָאו דַּוְקָא. דְּמַשְׁמָעוֹ: זֶהוּ דְּהָוֵי סָפֵק בְּגֵירוּשִׁין, אֲבָל סָפֵק קָרוֹב – לֹא הָוֵי סָפֵק לְגֵירוּשִׁין. וְאַיְּידֵי דְּתָנָא "זֶהוּ" בְּקִידּוּשִׁין, דְּדַוְקָא זֶהוּ, דְּקמ"ל זֶהוּ סָפֵק קָרוֹב, הוּא דְּשַׁיָּיךְ בְּקִידּוּשִׁין, אֲבָל סָפֵק זְמַן – לֹא שַׁיָּיךְ בְּהוּ. הָנִיחָא לְמ"ד. בְּגִיטִּין בְּפֶ' *"כָּל הַגֵּט" (דף כו:): מִפְּנֵי מָה תִּקְּנוּ חֲכָמִים זְמַן בְּגִיטִּין – מִשּׁוּם פֵּירֵי, לֵידַע מֵאֵימָתַי תִּגְבֶּה מִבַּעְלָהּ פֵּירוֹת שֶׁאָכַל מִנִּכְסֵי מְלוֹג שֶׁלָּהּ, דְּקָסָבַר: מִשָּׁעָה שֶׁנָּתַן עֵינָיו בָּהּ לְגָרְשָׁהּ שׁוּב אֵין לוֹ לַבַּעַל פֵּירוֹת. אֲרוּסָה לֵית לָהּ פֵּירֵי. לְפִיכָךְ לֹא תִּקְּנוּהוּ בִּשְׁטַר קִידּוּשִׁין, שֶׁאֵין הַבַּעַל אוֹכֵל פֵּירוֹת עַד שֶׁתִּכָּנֵס לַחוּפָּה. דְּכִי תַּקּוּן רַבָּנַן פֵּירֵי לַבַּעַל מִשּׁוּם פִּרְקוֹנָהּ, וּפִרְקוֹנָהּ לָא קָא מְחַיֵּיב בָּהּ אֶלָּא מִכְּתוּבָּה וְאֵילָךְ, דִּתְנַאי כְּתוּבָּה הוּא: דְּאִם תִּשְׁתַּבַּאי אֶפְרְקִינָךְ, בִּכְתוּבּוֹת פֶּ' "נַעֲרָה" (דף נא.). מִשּׁוּם בַּת אֲחוֹתוֹ. שֶׁמָּא יְהֵא נָשׂוּי בַּת אֲחוֹתוֹ וְתִזְנֶה תַּחְתָּיו, וְיִרְאֶה עֵדִים מְמַשְׁמְשִׁין וּבָאִין, וְיָחוּס עָלֶיהָ וִיגָרְשֶׁנָּה, וְיֹאמַר: קוֹדֶם זְנוּת שֶׁאַתֶּם מְעִידִים – כְּבָר נִתְגָּרְשָׁה. לִיתְקִין זְמַן. נַמִי בִּשְׁטַר קִידּוּשִׁין, שֶׁמָּא תִּזְנֶה, וְיֹאמַר: קוֹדֶם קִידּוּשִׁין הֲוָה. וְהָא עַבְדָּא. מְכִירַת עֶבֶד. וּתְקוּן רַבָּנַן זְמַן. בְּכָל שְׁטָרֵי מְכִירָה [שֶׁל עֶבֶד, כְּדֵי] לֵידַע מֵאֵיזֶה זְמַן יֹאכַל פֵּירוֹת, (ג) שֶׁזֶּה קָנָה נִכְסֵי עַבְדּוֹ: מָחֲקָה לֵיהּ. (ד) לִזְמַן, וְתֹאמַר: קוֹדֶם קִידּוּשִׁין הָיָה זְנוּת זֶה. לִינְחֵיהּ גַּבֵּי עֵדִים. מַאי מְהַנֵּי? אִי דְּכִירֵי אֵימַת הֲוָה קִידּוּשִׁין – אֲפִי' אֵינוֹ כָּתוּב בִּשְׁטָר מָצוּ לְאַסְהוּדֵי! אֶלָּא לְהָכִי אָמְרַתְּ דִּמְהַנֵּי, דְּזִימְנִין דְּלָא דְּכִירֵי וְחָזוּ מִכְּתָבָא וְאָתוּ וּמְסַהֲדֵי – וְהַאי לָאו עֵדוּת הוּא, דְּרַחֲמָנָא אָמַר "עַל פִּי שְׁנַיִם עֵדִים" (דברים יט), וְלֹא שֶׁיָּעִידוּ עַל פִּי כְּתָבָם. גַּבֵּי גֵּירוּשִׁין נַמִי. אַמַּאי תִּקְּנוּ זְמַן מִשּׁוּם בַּת אֲחוֹתוֹ. גַּבֵּי מַאן נִינְחֵיהּ? לְהַצָּלָה דִּידָהּ קָאָתֵי. וְלֵיכָּא לְמֵיחַשׁ דִּלְמָא מָחֲקָה לֵיהּ. דְּכִי אָתוּ סָהֲדֵי דְּזִינְּתָה, אִי לָא מַיְיתָא שְׁטָרָא דְּאִיגָּרְשָׁה מִקַּמֵּי הָכִי – מוֹקְמִינַן לָהּ בְּחֶזְקַת אֵשֶׁת אִישׁ. וּמִיהוּ, אִי לָא תְּקוּן רַבָּנַן זְמַן – הֲוָה מָצֵי לְאַחְפּוּיֵי עֲלָהּ, וּמִסְּפֵיקָא לָא קָטְלִינַן לָהּ. אֲבָל הַשְׁתָּא דִּתְקוּן רַבָּנַן, (ה) אִי לָא מַיְיתָא לֵיהּ מוֹקְמִינַן לָהּ אַחֲזָקָה וְקָטְלִינַן לָהּ. הָכָא לְחוֹבָה דִּידָהּ קָאָתֵי. זְמַן דְּקִידּוּשִׁין, וְאִי תְּקוּן לָהּ רַבָּנַן זְמַן וְזִינְּתָה – כָּבְשָׁה לֵיהּ לִשְׁטָרָא, אוֹ מָחֲקָה לֵיהּ, וְקַיְימָא אַחֶזְקַת פְּנוּיָה כִּדְמֵעִיקָּרָא. **מתני'** זִיקַת שְׁנֵי יְבָמִין. דְּכָל זְמַן שֶׁלֹּא כְּנָסָהּ זֶה – עֲדַיִין זִיקַת רִאשׁוֹן עָלֶיהָ, וְנִתּוֹסֶפֶת עָלֶיהָ זִיקַת מַאֲמָרוֹ, הֲרֵי כְּשֶׁמֵּת זֶה – נוֹתְרוּ עֲלָהּ זִיקַת שְׁנֵיהֶם, וְאִילּוּ כְּנָסָהּ – הֲוָה פָּקְעָה זִיקָה דְּקַמָּא, וְכִי מָיֵית – לָא הֲוָה עֲלָהּ אֶלָּא זִיקַת שֵׁנִי. א"נ לָא עָבַד בָּהּ מַאֲמָר לָא הֲוָה עֲלָהּ אֶלָּא זִיקַת רִאשׁוֹן. מְיַיבֵּם לְאֵיזוֹ שֶׁיִּרְצֶה. כִּדְקָתָנֵי טַעְמָא בְּפֶרֶק שֵׁנִי בְּבָרַיְיתָא: אִם מַאֲמָרוֹ שֶׁל שֵׁנִי מַאֲמָר – אֵשֶׁת שֵׁנִי הוּא בּוֹעֵל, וְאִם אֵינוֹ מַאֲמָר – אֵשֶׁת רִאשׁוֹן הוּא בּוֹעֵל. וְחוֹלֵץ לַשְּׁנִיָּה. דַּחֲדָא לָא מִיפַּטְרָא בְּבִיאָה דְּאִידָךְ, דִּלְמָא מַאֲמָר לָא קָנֵי, וְהָווּ לְהוּ ב' יְבָמוֹת הַבָּאוֹת מִב' בָּתִּים. וְיַיבּוּמֵי תַּרְוַויְיהוּ נַמִי לָא – דִּלְמָא מַאֲמָר קָנֵי, וְהָווּ לְהוּ ב' יְבָמוֹת הַבָּאוֹת מִבַּיִת אֶחָד. **גמ'** אִי זִיקַת שְׁנֵי יְבָמִין דְּאוֹרַיְיתָא כו'. לְרַבָּנַן פָּרֵיךְ. אֶלָּא מִדְּרַבָּנַן. דְּמִדְּאוֹרַיְיתָא מַאֲמָר לָא קָנֵי, וְהָווּ לְהוּ שְׁתֵּי יְבָמוֹת מִב' בָּתִּים, וְתַרְוַויְיהוּ מָצֵי לְיַיבּוּמֵי. וְרַבָּנַן הוּא דְּגָזְרוּ, שֶׁמָּא יֹאמְרוּ: ב' יְבָמוֹת הַבָּאוֹת מִבַּיִת א' – מִתְיַיבְּמוֹת. וּמִקְצָתוֹ

תוספות

ההיא דגיטין בשתי כיתי עדים! י"ל: דלשון מחלה על מחלה דקתני התם במתני' שייך טפי בשתי כיתי עדים. ובפ"ב דכתובות (דף כו: ד"ה "אנן") ובפ' "חזקת הבתים" (ב"ב לג. ד"ה "אנן") הארכתי. **וארעא** אוקמא בחזקת בר שטיא. לא דמי להא דאמר בקידושין (דף עט:) ובבבא בתרא (דף קנג: ושם): אם בריא הוא – עליו להביא ראיה שכיב מרע היה, ואם שכיב מרע הוא כו'. דהכא, כיון שדרכו להיות עתים חלים ועתים שוטה – לא שייך להעמידו אחזקה כמו שהוא עתה. **אי** יגיד עליו ריעו מאי זו היא דקתני. הוה מצי למיפרך אי יגיד עליו ריעו (ו) ליתני כולהו בחד וליתני חד מינייהו באידך כדפריך בפרק לא יחפור (ב"ב דף יט.). **למעוטי** זמן דליתיה בקידושין. מספקא לר"י: כתב בכתב ידו ואין עליו עדים, אי מהני בקידושין אי לא? דכיון שאין צריך זמן – מה לנו אם אין עליו עדים? **והא** עבדא דאיכא דקני בכספא כו'. פירש בקונטרס: שטר קניית עבד. וקשה לר"י: דא"כ מ"ש דנקט עבד? דהו"מ למינקט שטר מכירת קרקע, וכל שטרי מקח וממכר! ועוד: דהתם לא תיקון רבנן זמן! ונראה דאשטר שיחרור קאי, דתיקון (ז) זמן לידע מתי נאסר בשפחה והותר בבת ישראל. וה"ק: והא עבדא – איכא דקני נפשיה בכספא ואיכא דקני בשטרא. והשתא ניחא הא דמשני התם רובא וכו'. וא"ת: בפ"ק דגיטין (דף ט.) דתנן: בג' דרכים שוו גיטי נשים לשחרורי עבדים, ליתני נמי זמן, ששוו גיטי נשים לשחרורי עבדים וליתיה בקידושין! וי"ל: דכל מילי דחשיב התם ודפריך התם – הוי חד טעמא בגיטי נשים ושחרורי עבדים, אבל [זמן (ח) דשחרורי עבדים – בא] להתירו בבת ישראל, וגיטי נשים – משום פירי*: **דחזו** בכתבא ואתו ומסהדי כו'. קשה לר"י: דב"הגוזל קמא" (ב"ק דף לח. ושם:), גבי השורף שטרותיו של חבירו, פריך: ואי דאיכא סהדי דידעי – ליכתבו ליה שטרא אחרינא, ואמאי? הא אמר הכא דמפיהם ולא מפי כתבם! ואר"י: דה"נ, אם היו מעידים שכך ראו בשטר – שפיר הוו עדי, דהרי הם כאילו מעידים: ראינו עדות שנתקבל בב"ד, דעדים החתומים על השטר נעשה כמי שנחקרה עדותן בב"ד. אבל חיישינן שמא לא יעידו שכך ראו בשטר, אלא שמא יעידו על המעשה עצמו כאילו הם זוכרים, והם אינן זוכרין אלא על פי הכתב. וכן הא דאמרינן בפ"ב דכתובות (דף כ.): כותב אדם עדותו על השטר ומעיד עליה אפילו אחר כמה שנים, והוא – שזוכרה מעצמו, אבל אין זוכרה מעצמו – לא. התם נמי לא איירי במעיד שכך ראה כתוב, אלא במעיד על מעשה עצמו. ועוד: דהתם לא הוה שטר, אלא שכותב לזכרון דברים בעלמא, ולא שייך למימר נעשה כמי שנחקרה עדותו בב"ד. ואר"י דשמע מר"ת: שנוהגין עכשיו ששולחין העדים עדותן בכתב ידם לב"ד, ולא קרינן ביה "מפיהם ולא מפי כתבם" כיון שהם זוכרין עדותן. והא דתניא ב"מי שאחזו" (גיטין דף עא.) "ואם לא יגיד" – פרט לאלם, שאין יכול לדבר. ופריך: ואמאי? והרי יכול לדבר מתוך הכתב! שאני עדות, דרחמנא אמר "מפיהם ולא מפי כתבם" – שאני אלם שאין ראוי להגיד, כדאמרינן (מנחות דף קו:): כל שאין ראוי לבילה כו'. אבל אחר – מועיל כתב ידו כשזוכר העדות. ומיהו, בפירוש חומש (דברים יט) פרש"י "ע"פ שנים עדים" – פרט שלא ישלחו כתבם לב"ד. **להצלה** דידה קאתי. פי' בקונט': דהשתא דתיקון זמן, אי לא מייתא שטרא דאיגרשה מקמי הכי – מוקמינן לה אחזקת אשת איש, וקטלינן לה. ואין נראה, דההיא אמר בפ' שני דגיטין (דף יז:): גזייה לזמן ויהביה ניהלה – מה הועילו חכמים בתקנתן? ומשני: לרמאי לא חיישינן. אלמא, כי ליכא זמן – לא קטלינן לה! ואר"י: דה"פ: להצלה דידה קאתי, שהגט בא להצילה ולהגיד שהיא מגורשת, ולכך יראה למחוק הזמן כי סבורה שיפסול בכך וגרע כחו טפי. אבל ודאי, אי הוה מחקת ליה – לא הוה קטלינן לה. הכא לחובה דידה קאתי דהקידושין באין להעיד שהיא מקודשת, ומחקה ליה לעולם לזמן. **שלשה** אחין נשואין ג' נשים נכריות. הו"מ למנקט ואחד מופנה. (ט) **מדרבנן** וגזירה כו'. משמע דאשת ב' מתים בשום מקום לא הויא אלא מדרבנן, דאי לאו גזירה דהכא – היתה מתייבמת אפי' בעלת מאמר

א) [וע"ע תוס' ב"ב לט: ד"ה מחאה וכו']

תוספות ישנים

ואי זיקת ב' יבמין לאוריי' חליצה נמי לא תבעי. וקשה דהא אין מאמר אלא מדרבנן והזיקה אינה אלא מחמת המאמר. וי"ל דבעי הכי אי סבירא לן כב"ש דאמר מאמר קונה קנין גמור וזיקת שני יבמין חליצה נמי לא תיבעי. וא"ת הא לעיל מייתי קרא ויבמה מי שעליה זיקת יבם אחד ולא שעליה זיקת שני יבמין. וי"ל דלא הוי אלא אסמכתא בעלמא: **ונגזור** דלמא חליץ והדר מייבם. משמע הא אי לאו הך גזרה שריין תרוייהו לייבם ותימה דאמרינן לקמן פרק האשה גבי יבם קטן שבא על יבמתו ומשהגדיל נשא אחרת ומת אם לא ידע הראשונה משהגדיל יבמתו חולצת ולא מתייבמת ואשתו או חולצת או מתייבמת וכו' ופליגי אי גזרינן משום צרה כי הכא או לא ותנא דהתם לא גזר משום צרה וא"כ קשה לתנא דהתם דלא גזר גזרה דהכא אמאי אין אשת שני מתים גופה מתייבמת וי"ל נהי דלא גזר גזרה דהכא מ"מ לא מייבמה לאשת שני מתים גזרה אטו אשת שני מתים דבפרק המגרש שבא ראובן וגרשה חוץ משמעון ובא שמעון וקדשה סתם וסבירא לתנא דלקמן דההיא אשת שני מתים דפרק המגרש הויא לאורייתא והכא דלא גזרינן משום אשת שני מתים דהתם לא סבירא להך דהכא אשת שני מתים דהתם ליסווי [לאורייתא]. ואין להקשות כיון דהך לא סבירא אשת שני מתים מאי האי דאמרינן יבמה יבא עליה שיש עליה זיקת יבם אחד ולא שיש עליה זיקת שני יבמין. וי"ל דטעמא כדקאמר הכא וקרא אסמכתא בעלמא הוא וכן פי' לעיל. ותימה דאמרינן לעיל א"ר שמעון אם מאמרו של ראשון מאמר אשת ראשון בועל וכו' משמע דאית ליה גופיה אשת שני מתים. לכן נראה לפרש הכא דולאי ס"ל הכא אשת שני מתים דפרק המגרש וגזרה דהכא לא אצטריכא משום בעלת מאמר גופה אלא משום צרתה דאי לאו גזרה לא חמירא כל כך לאסור גם את הצרה. והשתא נמי האי דקאמר ר' שמעון אם מאמרו של ראשון מאמר ניחא לטעמייהו משום אשת שני מתים:

תוספות חד מקמאי

כללא דמילתא כל דאיתיה בקדושין איתיה בגירושין וכל דאיתיה נמי בגרושין איתיה בקדושין לבר מזמן דלא תקנו בקדושין. מאי דכתב הרב אלפס גבי מפיהם ולא מפי כתבם דכל שטר היוצא מתחת ידי מלוה או מלוקה לאו מפי כתבם הוא דמעידנא דמסהדי סהדי נעשה כמי שנחקרה עדותן בב"ד איכא דקשי ליה הא דגרסינן בגיטין פ' מי שאחזו אם לא יגיד פרט לאלם דאינו יכול להגיד ואמאי הא יכול להגיד מתוך הכתב למסרו למלוה (אם הלוה) אם לא [היה] כתובה בשעת הלואה. ולא היא דשבועת העדות אינו חייב אלא בכפירה בב"ד וכיון דהשתא דבשעת כפירה היא לפני ב"ד אם מסרו לה מפי כתב' הוא ומצאתיו כתוב בכתב ידי הראב"ד ז"ל שכתב בזה הלשון אמר אברהם מדברי הרב ז"ל עדים שחתמו על השטר ונשתהא השטר בידם זמן ארוך עד ששכחו את העדות אותו השטר בטל אע"פ שמסרו אח"כ ליד בעליו דהשתא הוא דקאמרי בהדי סהדי בשעת מסירת השטר וההיא שעתא מפי כתבם הוא וזו תימה גדולה וכמה שטרות יהיו נפסלין בכך אלא כל שטר דאי בעי לממסריה ביד בעליו מצו מסרי לה אף על גב דאישתהי גבייהו זמן גדול ושכחו העדות כיון שמסרוהו ליד בעליו שטרא מעליא הוא ואפי' לא מסרוהו עד שעת העמדה בדין ולא עוד אלא שאומרין לו תנו לו שטרו ויתקיים בב"ד ושני הכא שאין שטר הזה ראוי למוסרו לידו דלמא מחקא ליה לזמן הלכך ה"ל ההיא שעתא כעדות על פה ומשום הכי בעיא מפיהם ולא מפי כתבם וההיא שמעתתא דכתובות לא מיפרשא כהאי ענינא אלא במוכרת

בדפרי' התם וכן עקר בפ' שנים אוחזין כתבתי דעת ר' יעקב ז"ל בענין מפיהם. הא דאמר רבא נתן גט למאמרו הותרה צרתה ואיכא דאמר הותרה אפילו היא א) דוקא ליה ולא לזיקתו והכי איתא בפ' רבן גמליאל:

א) נ"ל דוקא דנתן גט למאמרו ולא לזיקתו.

מסורת הש"ס

[ב"מ לא. ב"ב יט. ע"ז ע. וע' תוס' שם נד. ד"ה אמר חזקיה]

[ובפרק המביא גט יח.]

גיטין עא.

לעיל יב. יח:

הגהות הב"ח

(א) גמ' גבי עדים אי דכירי ליתו: (ב) שם במשנה אחד מהם יבמה יבא עליה מי שעליה: (ג) רש"י ד"ה ותקון רבנן וכו' מכירה של עבד כדי לידע מאיזה זמן יאכל פירות שדה ויקנה נכסי עבדו: (ד) ד"ה מחקה ליה אם תזנה מחקה ליה לזמן והאמר: (ה) ד"ה להצלה וכו' דתקון רבנן זמן אי לא: (ו) תוס' ד"ה אי יגיד וכו' ליתנינהו לכולהו בחדא וליתני חדא מינייהו באידך והוא הדין לאידך כדפריך בפ' לא יחפור: (ז) ד"ה והא וכו' דתקון רבנן זמן לידע וכו' עבדא דאיכא דקני וכו' דקני נפשא בשטרא וכו' התם רובא בשטרא וא"ת: (ח) בא"ד אבל זמן לאו חד טעמא לשיחרורי עבדים להתירו בבת ישראל. נ"ב ועיין בתוס' לגיטין דף י"ז ע"א בד"ה מפני מה תקנו זמן בגיטין כתבו לתקון זמן בגט שיחרור דחיישינן שמא ימכור אותו ואח"כ יתן לו גט שיחרור בלא זמן והיינו טעמא דמשום פירי ועיין בפ"ק דגיטין דף י' בתוס' ד"ה כי שקלינן קושיא זו דליתני נמי זמן ותירלי ע"ש: (ט) ד"ה אלא מדרבנן כו' לא הויא. נ"ב עיין לעיל בדף יו"ד בד"ה לעולה.

ומקצתו חלוץ. ואתי למימר בב' יבמות הבאות מבית אחד: חדא מתייבמת ואחרת חלוצה. נתן גט למאמרו. אמתניתין קאי, שאם נתן זה שעשה מאמר גט למאמרו, ולא לזיקתו, ואח"כ מת – הותרה אשתו הראשונה, שהיא צרתה, להתייבם לשלישי, דמאמר דעבד – שקליה, ולאו צרות נינהו. והשתא לא אתי למימר

מאמר ולא גזרינן לה אטו אשת שני מתים, וא"כ מי שעליה זיקת יבם אחד כו' לא הויא דרשא גמורה אלא אסמכתא בעלמא. וקשה: דבפרק בתרא דגיטין (דף פב: ושם) אמרי': אלא אשת ב' מתים היכי משכחת לה? משמע דהוי דאורייתא, ואפי' בחד דוכתא! וי"ל: דפלוגתא דתנאי היא,

גמרא

ומקצתו חלוץ. – ויאמרו! – אי דמייבם והדר – חליץ הכי נמי, אלא גזירה *דילמא חליץ ברישא והדר מייבם, וקם ליה ב"אשר לא יבנה", ורחמנא אמר: *כיון שלא בנה – שוב לא יבנה. *אמר רבא: נתן גט למאמרו – הותרה צרתה, אבל היא אסורה, דמחלפה בבעלת גט. *אאיכא דאמרי, אמר רבא: נתן גט למאמרו – הותרה אפי' היא, מאי טעמא? מאי דעבד בה – שקליה.§ מתני' *בשני אחין נשואין שתי אחיות, ומת אחד מהן, ואחר כך מתה אשתו של שני – הרי זו אסורה עליו עולמית, הואיל ונאסרה עליו שעה אחת.§ גמ' פשיטא! השתא, ומה התם דלא מידחיא מהאי ביתא לגמרי – אמרת לא, הכא דקא מידחיא מהאי ביתא לגמרי – לא כ"ש?! – תנא הא תנא ברישא, והך חזיא להיתירא (א) ושריא, והדר חזיא לאיסורא. ואיידי *דחביבה ליה – אקדמה, *ומשנה לא זזה ממקומה. ת"ר: בא עליה – חייב עליה משום אשת אח, ומשום אחות אשה, דברי רבי יוסי. רבי שמעון אומר: אינו חייב אלא משום אשת אח בלבד. והא תניא, ר"ש אומר: אינו חייב אלא משום אחות אשה בלבד! – לא קשיא: כאן – שנשא חי ואח"כ נשא מת, כאן – שנשא מת ואח"כ נשא חי. °ור' שמעון, היכא דנשא מת ואח"כ נשא חי, כיון דאיסור אחות אשה לא חייל – תתייבם יבומי! אמר רב אשי: איסור אחות אשה מיתלא תלי וקאי, אי פקע איסור אשת אח – אתי איסור אחות אשה וחייל, והילכך לא פקע. – וסבר רבי יוסי איסור חל על איסור? והא תניא: *געבר עבירה שיש בה שתי מיתות – נידון בחמורה, רבי יוסי אומר: נידון בזיקה הראשונה הבאה עליו. ותניא: *כיצד אמר רבי יוסי נידון בזיקה הראשונה הבאה עלי? חמותו ונעשית אשת איש – נידון בחמותו, אשת איש ונעשית חמותו – נידון באשת איש.
אמר

רש"י

בשתי יבמות מבית אחד חדא חלוצה וחדא מייבמא, דהכא לאו מבית אחד מיהו. אבל היא אסורה. ולא משום דקם ליה ב"לא יבנה" דפוסלה על אחיו הנשאר, שהרי לא נתן גט לזיקה, אלא משום דאתי לאיחלופי בבעלת הגט, היכא דעבד גט למאמרו ולזיקתו, דהיא ודאי מידחיא, אבל גט למאמרו – לא דחי אלא מאמר, ונשארה זיקה ראשונה במקומה. הותרה אפילו היא. לשלישי, כשיימות שני. מאי דעבד שקליה. והויא כמו שלא עשה בה מאמר, ואתיא ומתייבמת לשלישי מחמת זיקת אחיו הראשון. ודוקא שפירש למאמרו ולא לזיקתו קאמר, אבל סתמא – קיימא ב"לא יבנה" אכולהו אחין. והכי מוכחא מילתא דרבא בפרק "רבן גמליאל" (לקמן ד' נג:) דלמאמרו ולא לזיקתו קאמר. פשיטא השתא ומה התם דלא אידחיא מהאי ביתא. לעיל (דף ל.), גבי שלשה אחים, שנים מהם נשואים שתי אחיות ואחד נשא נכרית, ומת אחד מבעלי אחיות, וכנס נשוי נכרית את אשתו, ומתה אשתו של שני, ואח"כ מת נשוי נכרית – הרי זו אסורה עליו עולמית משום אשת אח, הואיל ונאסרה עליו שעה אחת בנפילה ראשונה משום אחות אשה. ואע"ג דבההיא נפילה קמייתא לא אידחיא לה לגמרי, דהא קאי נשוי נכרית שזוקקה לייבום, וקורא אני בה בשעת נפילה "יבמה יבא עליה" – אפי' הכי חשבינן לה לגבי בעל אחותה כאשת אח שיש לה בנים לאיתסורי עליה אפילו לאחר מיתת אחותה. הכא. דבשעת נפילה אידחיא מהאי ביתא לגמרי, דאין כאן אלא בעל אחותה, ומשעה שנפלה לפניו אין זיקת יבום עליה – מיבעיא?! תנא הא. מתני' דהכא תנא ברישא. והך. דשלשה אחים, דלא אידחיא מהאי ביתא לגמרי, חזיא מעיקרא להיתרא, ושריא, [משום הכי לא תנייא]. הדר חזיא לאיסורא. דמ"מ לדידה לא קרינא ביה משעת נפילה "יבמה יבא עליה". דחביבה ליה. משום דחידוש הוא. ומשנה הראשונה. שמשנית זו, הואיל והיתה שנויה מתחלה. לא זזה ממקומה. לעוקרה לגמרי. בא עליה. בחיי אשתו. משום אשת אח. דהא רחמנא פטרה מייבום, וקמה עליה כמי שיש לו בנים. אלא משום אשת אח. כדמוקי טעמא לקמן. בנשא מת ואח"כ נשא חי. דאיסור אשת אח קדים, ותו לא אתי איסור אחות אשה וחייל עלה, דקסבר: אין איסור חל על איסור. נשא חי ואח"כ נשא מת. איסור אחות אשה קדים, דקודם שנשאה אחיו המת היתה עומדת עליו באיסור אחות אשה. מיתלא תלי. דאי הוה פקע איסור אשת אח – הוה חייל איסור אחות אשה. דהאי דלא חייל מעיקרא – משום טעמא דאיסור אשת אח דהוה קאי קמיה. הלכך, הואיל ואיסור אחות אשה מוכן ועומד לחול עליה פטורה מן (ב) היבם – לא פקע איסור אשת אח, וחייב משום אשת אח. שתי מיתות. כגון חמותו והיא אשת איש, דחמותו שריפה ואשת איש חנק. נידון בחמורה. בשריפה. חמותו ונעשית אשת איש. שהיתה אלמנה כשנשא בתה. נידון באשת איש. ואע"ג דקיל הוא. אלמא: לא אתי איסור חמותו וחייל אאשת איש, דאי חיילי תרווייהו עליה – הוה לן למדייניה בחמורה.
אמר

תוספות

כדמוכח לקמן בסוף "האשה רבה" (דף צו:) גבי בן תשע שבא על יבמתו, ומשהגדיל נשא אשה אחרת, ומת, השניה חולצת או מתייבמת, הראשונה שהיא בעלת זיקת שני יבמין – חולצת ולא מתייבמת. ופריך בגמרא: ויעשו ביאת בן תשע כמאמר בגדול ותדחה צרה מיבום. פירוש: כי הכא! ומסיק לרבי יוחנן דעשו ועשו, ופליג תנא דשמעתין אההוא תנא, דהאי תנא דשמעתין גזר משום צרה. פירוש: הא דקא אסר בעלת מאמר משום דאיכא צרה בהדה, כדגזר בשמעתין דלמא חליץ והדר מייבם, כדפירש בקונטרס. אבל משום זיקת שני יבמין – לא מיתסרא, דלאו דאורייתא. ומיהו, כי ליכא צרה בהדה – נמי אסורה אטו היכא דאיכא צרה, כדקאמר התם רבא לעיל, דאפי' היכא דליכא צרה בהדה – מיחלץ חלצה, יבומי לא מייבמא. ותנא דהתם לא גזר משום צרה, פי': הא דקא אסר לבעלת ביאת בן תשע לייבומי – לאו משום צרה, אלא אטו אשת שני מתים, דהוי בעלמא דאורייתא. ודוקא בדידה גזרו, אבל בצרתה לא, דלא רצו להחמיר גם בצרתה אטו אשת שני מתים. וההיא דריש "המגרש" (גיטין פב:) כההוא תנא. וריב"ן פירש שם: דלכולי עלמא אשת שני מתים דאורייתא, ותנא דהכא גזר אף באשת השני משום צרה – דהיינו בעלת מאמר, דקא סבר כיון דבעלמא אשת שני מתים דאורייתא – מחמירי אפי' באידך. ותנא דהתם לא מחמיר כולי האי, ולא גזר באשתו של בן תשע אטו בעלת זיקת שני יבמים. וקשה: דהכא מסיק דטעמא דהך תנא משום הנך גזירות דמפרש הכא! ועוד: דהתם(ג) קרי רבא לאשתו צרה, וקאמר נמי ויעשו ביאת בן תשע כמאמר בגדול ותדחה צרה כו', והכא קרי לבעלת מאמר צרה! וריב"ן הקשה לעצמו שתי קושיות הללו. ופר"י עיקר.

גט למאמרו כו'. הקשה ריב"ן: דתנן בפר"ג (לקמן דף נ.) דיש מאמר אחר מאמר, ואם עשה מאמר בזו ובזו – צריכה ב' גיטין וחליצה, בין יבם אחד לב' יבמות בין ב' יבמין ליבמה אחת, אבל יבומי חד מינייהו – לא, ולרבא, יתן גט למאמרו ולא לזיקתו, וליבומי אידך! ותירץ: דלכתחלה אין לעשות כן, דגזרינן גט למאמרו אטו גט לזיקתו, ודוקא בדיעבד קאמר הכא רבא דהותרה אפי' היא, דכיון דתו ליכא למיגזר בהאי מאמר אטו שאר מאמרות דעלמא – לא גזרינן, דלא שכיחי כולי האי. אבל לכתחלה – גזרינן משום האי מאמר גופיה.

דאידחיא מהאי ביתא לגמרי לא כ"ש. אע"ג דמהאי בבא שמעינן דאסירא, אע"ג דאיחזיא בהך נפילה, דלא שמעינן מבבא דלעיל, כדאמר לעיל (דף ל.) – מ"מ, כיון דאידחיא מהאי ביתא לגמרי פשיטא דאסירא, אע"ג דחזיא בהא נפילה. ולעיל דקאמר טעמא דאיחזיא בהך נפילה (אהאי מתניתין) – משום דאכתי לא אסיק אדעתיה טעמא דאידחיא מהאי ביתא.

שנשא חי ואח"כ נשא מת.(ד) אע"ג דבכי האי גוונא שרו ב"ש צרה לייבומי, לעיל בפ"ק (דף ח.) דכיון דלא חייל איסור אשת אח – חשבי שלא במקום מצוה, ר"ש לית ליה האי סברא, דמכל מקום הרי היא אשת אחיו. **לא** פקע. ואע"ג דלא חייל איסור אחות אשה – אסורה נמי הצרה לייבומי, כיון דלא פקע איסור אשת אח, כמו אילונית דאוסרת צרתה אע"ג דאין בה אלא איסור אשת אח לחודה. וא"ת: לר"ש משכחת לה אשת אח מן האב דפוטרת צרתה, וליתשבה בהדי ט"ו נשים בפ"ק (דף ב. ודף י.) למ"ד בפלוגתא קא מיירי! וכן האי דלעיל דקתני נאסרה עליו עולמית גם היא פוטרת צרתה – וליתשבה! וי"ל: דהני, כיון דמכח אחות אשה אסירא – בכלל אחות אשה נינהו. **ונעשית** אשת איש נידון בחמותו. ואין זה מכח זיקה ראשונה, דבלאו הכי מי שנתחייב ב' מיתות נידון בחמורה.
איסור

עין משפט נר מצוה

לד א מיי' פ"ו מהלכות יבום הלכה כט טוש"ע אה"ע סימן קעד סעיף ה:

לה ב מיי' שם הל' יב טוש"ע אה"ע סימן קעה סעיף ח:

לו ג מיי' פי"ד מהל' סנהדרין הלכה ז:

תוספות ישנים

נתן גט למאמרו הותרה אפילו היא ולא הוי גרושת אחיו כיון שלא נתן גט אלא להפקיע המאמר ומאמר דעבד שקליה ונמצא כאילו לא היתה אשתו מעולם. ודוקא שפירש שנתן גט למאמרו אבל נתן גט סתם אסור ליבמה דכיון שלא בנה שוב לא יבנה. תימה דאמרינן לקמן ובשתי יבמות שנפלו לפני יבם אחד ועשה מאמר בזו ומאמר בזו נותן גט לזו וגט לזו וחליצה אחת לכולן א"כ משמע דלא מצי לייבמה אחר הגט ואמאי לא אמרינן מה דעבד שקליה. וי"ל דלקמן מיירי שנתן הגט סתם ולא פירש למאמרו דלכתחלה לא אמרינן ליה לתת גט להפקיע המאמר. ותימה אמאי לא גזרינן שמא לא יפרש להפקיע המאמר כדאמרינן דמחלפא בבעלת הגט. ונראה להריב"ן דדוקא שנפלו שתי יבמות גזרינן אפילו פירש שהגט להפקיע בעלת המאמר אטו האחרת שיתן לה סתם. אבל הכא דליכא אלא יבמה אחת היכא שפירש בדיעבד שהגט להפקיע המאמר הותרה לייבם. ולא גזרינן מידי כיון דליכא אחרת בהדה: **ביצד** א"ר יוסי נדון בזיקה (שניה) [הראשונה] הבאה עליו חמותו וכו' ומייתי מהא דקאמר אשת איש ונעשית חמותו נדון באשת איש דאי איסור חל על איסור היה נידון בחמותו בחמורה אבל לא מייתי מחמותו ונעשית אשת איש דנדון בחמותו דאפי' איסור חל על איסור מ"מ נדון בחמותו דהא בתרי קטלי לא קטלן ליה וא"כ נידון בחמותו.

הגהות הב"ח

(א) גמ' חזיא להתירא ושריא כ"ב ס"א ושיירא: (ב) רש"י ד"ה מיתלא וכו' מן היבום ולא פקע: (ג) תד"ה (בעמוד הקודם) מדרבנן וגזרה כו' ועוד דהתם לעיל מינה קרי רבא: (ד) ד"ה שנשא וכו' ואע"ג דבכי וכו' לעיל בפ"ק משום דכיון וכו' חשבי לה שלא במקום:

גליון הש"ס

גמ' ור"ש היכא דנשא מת. עיין בספר המקנה לקידושין דף עז ע"ב בתוס' ד"ה פרט לכ"ג:

[לקמן מד.]
[לעיל יז:]
[לעיל ל.]
[לעיל ב: וש"נ]
[לעיל ל. וש"נ]
לקמן נב:
סנהדרין פא. כריתות יד: [תוספתא סנהדרין פי"ב]
כריתות יד:

אָמַר רַ׳ אַבָּהוּ: מוֹדֶה רַ׳ יוֹסֵי [א]בְּאִיסּוּר מוֹסִיף. תֵּינַח — הֵיכָא דְּנָשָׂא חַי וְאח״כ נָשָׂא מֵת, מִגּוֹ דְּאִתּוֹסַף אִיסּוּר לְגַבֵּי אַחִים — אִתּוֹסַף אִיסּוּר לְגַבֵּי דִּידֵיהּ. אֶלָּא, הֵיכָא דְּנָשָׂא מֵת וְאח״כ נָשָׂא חַי, מַאי אִיסּוּר מוֹסִיף אִיכָּא? וְכ״ת: מִגּוֹ דְּאִיתְּסַר בְּכוּלְּהוּ אַחְוָותָא — הַאי אִיסּוּר כּוֹלֵל הוּא! אֶלָּא אָמַר רָבָא: מַעֲלֶה אֲנִי עָלָיו כְּאִילּוּ עָשָׂה שְׁתַּיִם, וְאֵינוֹ חַיָּיב אֶלָּא אַחַת. וְכֵן כִּי אֲתָא רָבִין א״ר יוֹחָנָן: מַעֲלֶה אֲנִי עָלָיו כְּאִילּוּ עָשָׂה ב׳, וְאֵינוֹ חַיָּיב אֶלָּא אַחַת. מַאי נָפְקָא מִינָּהּ? — *לְקָבְרוֹ בֵּין רְשָׁעִים גְּמוּרִים. וּבִפְלוּגְתָּא, דְּאִיתְּמַר: זָר שֶׁשִּׁימֵּשׁ בְּשַׁבָּת, רַבִּי חִיָּיא אוֹמֵר: [ב]חַיָּיב שְׁתַּיִם, בַּר קַפָּרָא אוֹמֵר: אֵין חַיָּיב אֶלָּא אַחַת. *קָפַץ רַבִּי חִיָּיא וְנִשְׁבַּע: הָעֲבוֹדָה! כָּךְ שָׁמַעְתִּי מֵרַבִּי: שְׁתַּיִם. קָפַץ בַּר קַפָּרָא וְנִשְׁבַּע: הָעֲבוֹדָה! כָּךְ שָׁמַעְתִּי מֵרַבִּי: אַחַת. הִתְחִיל רַבִּי חִיָּיא לָדוּן: שַׁבָּת לַכֹּל נֶאֶסְרָה, כְּשֶׁהוּתְּרָה בַּמִּקְדָּשׁ — אֵצֶל כֹּהֲנִים הוּתְּרָה, לְכֹהֲנִים הוּתְּרָה וְלֹא לְזָרִים, יֵשׁ כָּאן מִשּׁוּם זָרוּת, וְיֵשׁ כָּאן מִשּׁוּם שַׁבָּת. הִתְחִיל בַּר קַפָּרָא לָדוּן: שַׁבָּת לַכֹּל נֶאֶסְרָה, כְּשֶׁהוּתְּרָה — בַּמִּקְדָּשׁ הוּתְּרָה, אֵין כָּאן אֶלָּא זָרוּת. בַּעַל מוּם שֶׁשִּׁימֵּשׁ בְּטוּמְאָה, רַבִּי חִיָּיא אוֹמֵר: [ג]חַיָּיב שְׁתַּיִם, בַּר קַפָּרָא אוֹמֵר: אֵין חַיָּיב אֶלָּא אַחַת. קָפַץ רַ׳ חִיָּיא וְנִשְׁבַּע: הָעֲבוֹדָה! כָּךְ שָׁמַעְתִּי מֵרַבִּי: שְׁתַּיִם, קָפַץ בַּר קַפָּרָא וְנִשְׁבַּע: הָעֲבוֹדָה! כָּךְ שָׁמַעְתִּי מֵרַבִּי: אַחַת. הִתְחִיל ר״ח לָדוּן: טוּמְאָה לַכֹּל נֶאֶסְרָה, כְּשֶׁהוּתְּרָה בַּמִּקְדָּשׁ — אֵצֶל כֹּהֲנִים תְּמִימִים הוּתְּרָה, לְכֹהֲנִים תְּמִימִים הוּתְּרָה וְלֹא לְבַעֲלֵי מוּמִין, יֵשׁ כָּאן מִשּׁוּם בַּעֲלֵי מוּמִין, וְיֵשׁ כָּאן מִשּׁוּם טוּמְאָה. הִתְחִיל בַּר קַפָּרָא לָדוּן: טוּמְאָה לַכֹּל נֶאֶסְרָה, כְּשֶׁהוּתְּרָה בַּמִּקְדָּשׁ — הוּתְּרָה, אֵין כָּאן אֶלָּא מִשּׁוּם בַּעַל מוּם, זָר שֶׁאָכַל מְלִיקָה, רַ׳ חִיָּיא אוֹמֵר: [ד]חַיָּיב שְׁתַּיִם, בַּר קַפָּרָא אוֹמֵר: אֵין חַיָּיב אֶלָּא אַחַת. קָפַץ רַבִּי חִיָּיא וְנִשְׁבַּע: הָעֲבוֹדָה! כָּךְ שָׁמַעְתִּי מֵרַבִּי: שְׁתַּיִם. קָפַץ בַּר קַפָּרָא וְנִשְׁבַּע: הָעֲבוֹדָה! כָּךְ שָׁמַעְתִּי מֵרַבִּי: אַחַת. הִתְחִיל רַבִּי חִיָּיא לָדוּן: נְבֵלָה לַכֹּל נֶאֶסְרָה, כְּשֶׁהוּתְּרָה בַּמִּקְדָּשׁ — אֵצֶל כֹּהֲנִים הוּתְּרָה, לְכֹהֲנִים הוּתְּרָה וְלֹא לְזָרִים. יֵשׁ כָּאן מִשּׁוּם זָרוּת, וְיֵשׁ כָּאן מִשּׁוּם מְלִיקָה. הִתְחִיל בַּר קַפָּרָא לָדוּן: נְבֵלָה לַכֹּל נֶאֶסְרָה, כְּשֶׁהוּתְּרָה בַּמִּקְדָּשׁ — הוּתְּרָה, אֵין כָּאן אֶלָּא מִשּׁוּם זָרוּת בְּמַאי

רש״י

אָמַר רַבִּי אַבָּהוּ מוֹדֶה ר׳ יוֹסֵי בְּאִיסּוּר מוֹסִיף. שֶׁהוּא חָל עַל אִיסּוּר, כְּגוֹן אִיסּוּר אֵשֶׁת אָח, דְּמוֹסִיף הוּא; שֶׁבַּתְּחִלָּה כְּשֶׁנָּשָׂא זֶה אֶת אֲחוֹתָהּ, וְזוֹ פְּנוּיָה, נֶאֶסְרָה עָלָיו מִשּׁוּם אֲחוֹת אִשָּׁה, וּמוּתֶּרֶת לְכָל אֶחָיו. נִשֵּׂאת לְאֶחָד מֵהֶן — נֶאֶסְרָה עַל כּוּלָּן מִשּׁוּם אֵשֶׁת אָח, וְעַכְשָׁיו נִיתּוֹסֵף אִיסּוּר עָלֶיהָ לְגַבֵּי שְׁאָר אֶחָיו, וּמִגּוֹ דְּחָיֵיל שֵׁם אֵשֶׁת אָח עֲלָהּ לְגַבֵּי שְׁאָר אֶחָיו שֶׁהָיְתָה מוּתֶּרֶת לָהֶם — חָל נַמִּי הַשֵּׁם הַזֶּה לְגַבֵּי דִּידֵיהּ, וְאע״ג דַּאֲסִירָא עֲלֵיהּ וְקַיְימָא. אֲבָל אֵשֶׁת אִישׁ וְנַעֲשֵׂית חֲמוֹתוֹ, מִתְּחִלָּה הָיְתָה אֲסוּרָה לְכָל הָעוֹלָם מִשּׁוּם אֵשֶׁת אִישׁ, נָשָׂא זֶה אֶת בִּתָּהּ — אֵין אִיסּוּר זֶה רָאוּי לְהוֹסִיף עָלֶיהָ עִם אֲחֵרִים, דְּנֵימָא מִגּוֹ דְּחָיֵיל עֲלַיְיהוּ לֵיחוּל נַמִּי עֲלֵיהּ דְּהַאי. דַּחֲמוֹתוֹ וְנַעֲשֵׂית אֵשֶׁת אִישׁ (א) וַדַּאי אִיסּוּר מוֹסִיף הוּא, שֶׁמִּתְּחִלָּה אֲסוּרָה לָזֶה וּמוּתֶּרֶת לְכָל הָעוֹלָם; נַעֲשֵׂית אֵשֶׁת אִישׁ — אִיתּוֹסַף הַאי שֵׁם עֲלָהּ לְגַבֵּי כ״ע, וּמִגּוֹ דְּחָיֵיל עֲלַיְיהוּ חָיֵיל נַמִּי לְגַבֵּי דְּהַאי. וְהַאי דְּקָאָמַר רַבִּי יוֹסֵי נִידּוֹן בַּחֲמוֹתוֹ — מִשּׁוּם דְּבְמִיתוֹת עָסְקִינַן, וְאִי חַטָּה יָכוֹל לַהֲמִיתוֹ בְּב׳ מִיתוֹת, הוֹאִיל וּשְׁתֵּיהֶן עָלָיו — יִדּוֹן בַּחֲמוּרָה. אֲבָל אִם הָיָה שׁוֹגֵג — הָיָה חַיָּיב ב׳ חַטָּאוֹת. **תֵּינַח נָשָׂא חַי.** דַּאֲחוֹת אִשָּׁה קָדֵים, וְאח״כ נָשָׂא מֵת, אָתֵי אִיסּוּר אֵשֶׁת אָח חָיֵיל, כִּדְפָרִישִׁית: מִגּוֹ דְּאִיתּוֹסַף אִיסּוּרָא דְּהַאי שֵׁם לְגַבֵּי אֶחָיו כו׳. **אֶלָּא הֵיכָא דְּנָשָׂא מֵת.** דְּאִיסּוּר אֵשֶׁת אָח קָדֵים עֲלֵיהּ דְּהַאי, וְאח״כ נָשָׂא אֲחוֹתָהּ, מַאי תּוֹסֶפֶת אִיכָּא עֲלָהּ דְּקַמַּיְיתָא לְגַבֵּי אַחֲרִינֵי דְּנֵימָא מִגּוֹ? וְכִי תֵּימָא מִגּוֹ. דִּבְהָנָךְ נִישּׂוּאִין דְּבַתְרַיְיתָא מִתְּסַר הַאי גַּבְרָא בְּכוּלְּהוּ אַחְוָותָא מִשּׁוּם אֲחוֹת אִשָּׁה דְּעַד הָשְׁתָּא הֲווּ שְׁרְיָין לֵיהּ, אִיתְּסַר נַמִּי מִשּׁוּם הַאי שְׁמָא גּוּפֵיהּ עֲלָהּ דְּקַמַּיְיתָא, שֶׁהִיא אֵשֶׁת אָחִיו. הַאי לָאו אִיסּוּר מוֹסִיף הוּא, דְּהָא עֲלָהּ דְּקַמַּיְיתָא לָא אִיתּוֹסַף אִיסּוּר לְגַבֵּי אַחֲרִינָא, אֶלָּא אִיסּוּר כּוֹלֵל הוּא, דְּכָיֵיל לָהּ לְקַמַּיְיתָא בְּשֵׁם אֲחוֹת אִשָּׁה, מִגּוֹ דְּחָיֵיל עַל אֲחוֹתָהּ. **אִיסּוּר מוֹסִיף.** כְּשֶׁהָאִיסּוּר מוֹסִיף עַל הַחֲתִיכָה לְאוֹסְרָהּ עַל מִי (ב) שֶׁמּוּתֶּרֶת עָלָיו. אִיסּוּר כּוֹלֵל — שֶׁהָאִיסּוּר חָל עַל חֲתִיכוֹת אֲחֵרוֹת, וְאוֹתָהּ גּוֹרֶרֶת לָזוֹ עִמָּהֶם עַל יְדֵי מִגּוֹ: וְאִית דְּגָרְסִי הָכָא. וְתוּ חֲמוֹתוֹ וְנַעֲשֵׂית אֵשֶׁת אִישׁ אִיסּוּר מוֹסִיף הוּא. וְשִׁיבּוּשׁ הוּא בְּיָדָם. וְאע״ג דְּוַדַּאי אִיסּוּר מוֹסִיף הוּא — לָאו פִּירְכָא הִיא, דְּוַדַּאי אִית לֵיהּ לְר׳ יוֹסֵי אִיסּוּר מוֹסִיף, כְּגוֹן אֵשֶׁת אִישׁ חָל עַל אִיסּוּר חֲמוֹתוֹ, וְתַרְוַיְיהוּ אִיסּוּרֵי עֲלֵיהּ. וְהָא דְּקָאָמַר וְנִידּוֹן בַּחֲמוֹתוֹ — מִשּׁוּם דְּזוֹ הִיא הַחֲמוּרָה, דְּאִי אָמְרַתְּ נִידּוֹן בְּאֵשֶׁת אִישׁ — אִם כֵּן אֵין זֶה אִיסּוּר חָל עַל אִיסּוּר אֶלָּא אִיסּוּר מְבַטֵּל אִיסּוּר. **אֶלָּא אָמַר רָבָא.** לְעוֹלָם לֵית לֵיהּ לְר׳ יוֹסֵי אִיסּוּר חָל עַל אִיסּוּר. וְהָא דְּקָאָמַר לְעֵיל חַיָּיב עֲלָהּ מִשּׁוּם אֵשֶׁת אָח וּמִשּׁוּם אֲחוֹת אִשָּׁה — לָאו בְּשׁוֹגֵג, לְחַיְּיבוֹ שְׁתֵּי חַטָּאוֹת, אֶלָּא בְּמֵזִיד וְלֵיעָשׂוֹת רָשָׁע גָּמוּר וּלְקָבְרוֹ בֵּין רְשָׁעִים (ג) גְּמוּרִים. שֶׁהָרָשָׁע נִקְבָּר אֵצֶל רְשָׁעִים, דִּתְנַן בְּסַנְהֶדְרִין (דף מו.): שְׁתֵּי קְבָרוֹת הָיוּ מְתוּקָּנִין לְב״ד, א׳ לַנֶּהֱרָגִין וְלַנֶּחֱנָקִין וְא׳ לַנִּסְקָלִין וְלַנִּשְׂרָפִין. וְהָכָא נַמִּי, אע״ג דְּהַאי לָאו מְחַיְּיבֵי ב״ד הוּא, הוֹאִיל וַעֲבַד תַּרְתֵּי — קָבְרִינַן לֵיהּ גַּבֵּי נִסְקָלִין וְנִשְׂרָפִין. **חַיָּיב ב׳.** ב׳ אִיסּוּרֵי קָחָשֵׁיב. דְּהָא מִשּׁוּם זָרוּת אֵין כָּאן חַטָּאת, דְּהָא עַל זְדוֹנוֹ מִיתָה בִּידֵי שָׁמַיִם הוּא, וְאֵין חַיָּיב חַטָּאת אֶלָּא עַל שִׁגְגַת כָּרֵת. **מֵרַבִּי.** רַבֵּינוּ הַקָּדוֹשׁ. **כְּשֶׁהוּתְּרָה בַּמִּקְדָּשׁ הוּתְּרָה.** סְתָם, הִלְכָּךְ אֵין כָּאן אֶלָּא מִשּׁוּם זָרוּת. **שֶׁשִּׁימֵּשׁ בְּטוּמְאָה.** בְּקָרְבַּן צִבּוּר קָאָמַר, שֶׁדּוֹחֶה הַטּוּמְאָה. וְכֵן זָר שֶׁשִּׁימֵּשׁ בְּשַׁבָּת וְיֵשׁ כָּאן מִשּׁוּם טוּמְאָה, וְאַזְהַרְתֵּיהּ מִ״וְיִנָּזְרוּ מִקָּדְשֵׁי בְנֵי יִשְׂרָאֵל וְלֹא יְחַלְּלוּ״ (ויקרא כב). **אֵצֶל תְּמִימִים הוּתְּרָה.** דִּרְאוּיִם לַעֲבוֹד, דִּיְלָפִינַן מִ״בְּמוֹעֲדוֹ״ — אֲפִי׳ בְּטוּמְאָה (פסחים דף עז.). **זָר שֶׁאָכַל מְלִיקַת.** הַכֹּהֲנִים. **חַיָּיב שְׁתַּיִם.** מִשּׁוּם זָרוּת וּמִשּׁוּם נְבֵלָה, דְּקָרְבָּן הַנֶּאֱכָל לְכֹהֲנִים זָר הָאוֹכְלוֹ עוֹבֵר מִשּׁוּם ״וְזָר לֹא יֹאכַל כִּי קֹדֶשׁ הֵם״ (שמות כט), וְלָאו הַיְינוּ אַזְהָרָה דִּמְעִילָה, דְּכָל שֶׁיֵּשׁ בּוֹ שְׁעַת הֶיתֵּר לְכֹהֲנִים — אֵין בּוֹ מְעִילָה. **לְכֹהֲנִים הוּתְּרָה.** בְּחַטַּאת הָעוֹף. בְּאִיסּוּר

תוספות

איסור כולל הוא. וא״ת: ולדמא ר׳ יוסי אית ליה נמי איסור כולל? ואומר ר״י, דקסבר דאשת איש ונעשית חמותו נמי איסור כולל הוא, דמגו דאיתסר בשאר קרובות, וקתני דנידון באשת איש. ומיהו, אר״י, דלההוא לישנא דלקמן דסבר רבי חייא דרבי יוסי מחייב תרתי באיסור כולל — צ״ל דאשת איש ונעשית חמותו לא חשיב איסור כולל, אע״ג דאיתסר בשאר קרובות, כיון שאין (ד) שם אחד — כי היכי דלא תקשה דרבי יוסי אדר׳ יוסי. והא דחשיב איסור כולל בעל מום שימש בטומאה, דמעיקרא שרי באכילה ואסור בעבודה, איטמי ליה — מגו דאיתסר באכילה איתסר נמי בעבודה — אכילה ועבודה חשיב נמי שם אחד, דשניהם נאסרו בלשון קריבה. דבעבודה כתיב ״כל איש אשר בו מום לא יגש להקריב לחם״ וגו׳ (ויקרא כא) ובאכילה בטומאה כתיב ״איש (איש) אשר יקרב מכל זרעכם״ וגו׳ (שם כב) דמיירי באכילה, כדאמרינן בפ״ב דמעילה (דף י:) ובזבחים (דף מה:) ומיהו, איסור מוסיף, אומר ר״י דחשיב אפילו כשאין השמות שוין, כדמוכח בפ׳ ״אמרו לו״ (כריתות יד:) גבי הבא על בת בתו חייב משום כלתו כו׳. ואין להאריך כאן.

ותו חמותו ונעשית אשת איש איסור מוסיף הוא. בקונטרס לא גרס ליה, דאפילו חייל עליה איסור אשת איש — נידון (ה) בחמורה. וליכא למימר דמשמע ליה נידון בחמותו ולא חל כלל איסור אשת איש, ואם לא התרו בו משום חמותו אלא משום אשת איש פטור — דהא בפרק ״הנשרפים״ (סנהדרין דף פא. ושם) פריך רב אדא בר אהבה: וליתרו נמי משום איסור אשת איש, דהא א״ר אבהו: מודה רבי יוסי באיסור מוסיף! ומשני ליה התם: אדא ברי, אטו בתרי קטלי קטלת ליה? משמע בהדיא דחל איסור אשת איש, אלא משום דנידון בחמורה. ור״ת אומר: דשפיר גרס ליה, וטעי הכא כדהוה טעי התם רב אדא בר אהבה, והוה סבור דנידון בחמותו משום דלא חייל עליה איסור אשת איש. ולא חש לתרץ, כיון דע״כ צריך לשינויא אחרינא משום קושיא קמייתא.

אלא אמר רבא מעלה כו׳. לפי המסקנא דהכא לא איצטריך לר׳ אבהו למימר דמודה ר׳ יוסי באיסור מוסיף. מ״מ בהנשרפים (ג״ז שם) מייתי מדרבי אבהו משום דהאמת הוא דמודה ר׳ יוסי באיסור מוסיף, כדמשמע בפ׳ ״אמרו לו״ (כריתות דף יד: ושם) גבי א״ר יוסי: אם עבר זקן ונשאה — חייב עליה משום אשת אב, משום הכי איצטריך ליה לרבי אבהו לאסוקי הכי. **בין** רשעים גמורים. פירוש: אצל רשעים כמותו, לפי שאין קוברין רשע אצל צדיק. ולא כמו שפירש בקונטרס לקוברו אצל נסקלים ונשרפין. ור״ש סבר: דאע״פ שיש בעבירה זו שני איסורין, כיון דלא מיחייב אלא חדא — אין קוברין אותו אצל רשעים גמורים. **בעל** מום ששימש בטומאה. הא דלא נקט זר כדנקט לעיל — היינו משום דאטומאה לא הוזהרו זרים אלא כהנים, דכתיב ״דבר אל אהרן ואל בניו וינזרו״ וגו׳ (ויקרא כב). והא דקאמר טומאה לכל נאסרה — היינו אפי׳ בעלי מומין. במאי

[לקמן לג:]

שבועות כו.

לז א מיי׳ פי״ז מהל׳ איסורי ביאה הלכה ח ופ״ד מהלכות שגגות הלכה א:

לח ב ג מיי׳ פ״ט מהלכות ביאת מקדש הל׳ יב:

לט ד מיי׳ פי״א מהלכו׳ מעשה קרבנות הל׳ ט סמג לאוין שכו:

הגהות הב״ח

(א) רש״י ד״ה אמר ר׳ אבהו וכו׳ אשת איש הא ודאי איסור: (ב) ד״ה איסור מוסיף וכו׳ על מי שהיתה מותרת עליו: (ג) ד״ה אלא וכו׳ רשעים גמורים: (ד) תוס׳ ד״ה איסור וכו׳ שאין זה שם אחד: (ה) ד״ה ותו וכו׳ אשת איש נידון בחמותו התמורה וליכא:

בְּמַאי קָמִיפַּלְגִי? בְּאִיסּוּר כּוֹלֵל, וְאַלִּיבָּא דְּרַ' יוֹסֵי: רַבִּי חִיָּיא סָבַר, רַבִּי יוֹסֵי [א]בְּאִיסּוּר כּוֹלֵל מִיחַיֵּיב תַּרְתֵּי; בַּר קַפָּרָא סָבַר, לָא מִיחַיֵּיב אֶלָּא חֲדָא. וּמַאי אִיסּוּר כּוֹלֵל אִיכָּא הָכָא? בִּשְׁלָמָא זָר, מֵעִיקָּרָא שָׁרֵי בִּמְלָאכָה וְאָסוּר בַּעֲבוֹדָה, אָתְיָא לָהּ שַׁבָּת — מִגּוֹ דְּקָא מִיתְּסַר בִּמְלָאכָה מִיתְּסַר נַמִי בַּעֲבוֹדָה. בַּעַל מוּם, מֵעִיקָּרָא שָׁרֵי בַּאֲכִילָה וְאָסוּר בַּעֲבוֹדָה, אִיטַּמֵּי לֵיהּ, מִגּוֹ דְּקָא מִיתְּסַר בַּאֲכִילָה מִיתְּסַר נַמִי בַּעֲבוֹדָה, אֶלָּא מְלִיקָה — בְּבַת אַחַת הִיא דְּמַשְׁכַּחַת לָהּ, בְּאִיסּוּר כּוֹלֵל לָא מַשְׁכַּחַת לָהּ! אֶלָּא קָמִיפַּלְגִי בְּאִיסּוּר בְּבַת אַחַת וְאַלִּיבָּא דְּרַ' יוֹסֵי: רַבִּי חִיָּיא סָבַר, רַבִּי יוֹסֵי [ב]בְּאִיסּוּר בַּת אַחַת מִיחַיֵּיב תַּרְתֵּי, וּבַר קַפָּרָא סָבַר, לָא מִיחַיֵּיב אֶלָּא חֲדָא. וְהָכָא — מַאי אִיסּוּר בַּת אַחַת אִיכָּא הָכָא? זָר שֶׁשִּׁימֵּשׁ בְּשַׁבָּת, כְּגוֹן דְּאַיְיתֵי שְׁתֵּי שְׂעָרוֹת בְּשַׁבָּת, דְּהָוְיָא לְהוּ זָרוּת וְשַׁבָּת בַּהֲדֵי הֲדָדֵי. בַּעַל מוּם נַמִי — כְּגוֹן דְּאַיְיתֵי שְׁתֵּי שְׂעָרוֹת וְאִיטַּמֵּי לֵיהּ, דְּהָוְיָא לֵיהּ בַּעַל מוּם וְטוּמְאָה בַּהֲדֵי הֲדָדֵי. א"נ: שֶׁחָתַךְ אֶצְבָּעוֹ בְּסַכִּין טְמֵאָה. בִּשְׁלָמָא לְרַבִּי חִיָּיא, כִּי אַתְנְיֵיהּ לְדִידֵיהּ — אַלִּיבָּא דְּרַ' יוֹסֵי, כִּי אַתְנְיֵיהּ לְבַר קַפָּרָא — אַלִּיבָּא דְּר"ש, אֶלָּא לְבַר קַפָּרָא — °רַ' חִיָּיא שַׁקּוּרֵי קָא מְשַׁקֵּר?! אֶלָּא: קָמִיפַּלְגִי בְּאִיסּוּר בַּת אַחַת, וְאַלִּיבָּא דְּר"ש. בִּשְׁלָמָא לְרַ' חִיָּיא, קָא מִישְׁתַּבַּע לְאַפּוּקֵי לְרַ' שִׁמְעוֹן מֵחֶזְקֵיהּ, אֶלָּא לְבַר קַפָּרָא — לָמָּה לֵיהּ לְאִשְׁתַּבּוּעֵי? — קַשְׁיָא. בִּשְׁלָמָא לְבַר קַפָּרָא, כִּי אַתְנְיֵיהּ רַבִּי לְדִידֵיהּ — אַלִּיבָּא דְּרַ' שִׁמְעוֹן, כִּי אַתְנְיֵיהּ לְרַבִּי חִיָּיא — אַלִּיבָּא דְּרַבִּי יוֹסֵי. אֶלָּא לְרַבִּי חִיָּיא, בַּר קַפָּרָא שַׁקּוּרֵי קָא מְשַׁקֵּר? אָמַר לָךְ רַ' חִיָּיא: כִּי אַתְנְיֵיהּ רַבִּי לְדִידֵיהּ — תַּרְתֵּי לִפְטוּר אַתְנְיֵיהּ

וְאִיסּוּר

רש"י

בְּאִיסּוּר כּוֹלֵל. לְקַמֵּיהּ מְפָרֵשׁ מַאי אִיסּוּר כּוֹלֵל אִיכָּא. **וְאַלִּיבָּא** דְּרַ' יוֹסֵי. דְּאָמַר: בִּשְׁאָר אִיסּוּרֵי אִיסּוּר חָל עַל אִיסּוּר, ע"י מִגּוֹ. **בְּאִיסּוּר כּוֹלֵל** מִיחַיֵּיב תַּרְתֵּי. דְּקָתָנֵי: חַיָּיב מִשּׁוּם אֵשֶׁת אָח וּמִשּׁוּם אֲחוֹת אִשָּׁה, אֲפִילּוּ נָשָׂא מֵת וְאח"כ נָשָׂא חַי, דְּלֵיכָּא אִיסּוּר מוֹסִיף בְּהַאי בַּתְרָא אֶלָּא אִיסּוּר כּוֹלֵל, מִגּוֹ דְּמִיתְּסַר בְּכוּלְּהוּ אַחֲוָותָא כּוֹלֵל גַּם אֶת זוֹ עִמָּהֶן. **לָא** מִיחַיֵּיב אֶלָּא חֲדָא. וְכִי חַיְּיבֵיהּ רַבִּי יוֹסֵי תַּרְתֵּי — בְּנָשָׂא חַי וְאח"כ נָשָׂא מֵת, דְּאִיסּוּר מוֹסִיף הוּא. וְהָא דְּקָתָנֵי ר"ש אוֹמֵר אֵינוֹ חַיָּיב אֶלָּא מִשּׁוּם אֵשֶׁת אָח, דְּאוֹקִימְנָא בְּנָשָׂא מֵת וְאח"כ נָשָׂא חַי — רַבִּי חִיָּיא תָּנֵי לָהּ, בַּר קַפָּרָא לָא תָּנֵי לָהּ. **מֵעִיקָּרָא.** קוֹדֶם שַׁבָּת זוֹ. **מִגּוֹ** דְּמִתַּסְרָא בִּמְלָאכָה. מִשּׁוּם שַׁבָּת, כּוֹלֵל אֶת הָעֲבוֹדָה בִּכְלַל הָאִיסּוּר מִשּׁוּם שַׁבָּת. וְהָכָא לָא שַׁיָּיךְ מוֹסִיף, שֶׁלֹּא נִיתּוֹסֵף אִיסּוּר עַל הַחֲתִיכָה דְּהַיְינוּ עֲבוֹדָה. וְהֵיכִי דָּמֵי מוֹסִיף — כְּגוֹן אִי הֲוָה מָצֵינוּ לְמֵימַר הָכִי: עֲבוֹדָה מֵעִיקָּרָא אֲסוּרָה לְזָרִים וּמוּתֶּרֶת לְכֹהֲנִים, הֲוֵה לֵיהּ שַׁבָּת, מִגּוֹ דְּאִיתּוֹסַף עֲלָהּ אִיסּוּר לְגַבֵּי כֹּהֲנִים מִשּׁוּם שַׁבָּת — אִיתּוֹסַף נַמִי לְגַבֵּי דִּידֵיהּ מִשּׁוּם שַׁבָּת. וְהָכִי לֵיכָּא לְמֵימַר, דְּהָא מִשּׁוּם שַׁבָּת לָא מִיתַּסְרֵי כֹּהֲנִים. **שָׁרֵי בַּאֲכִילָה.** בְּקָדָשִׁים, דִּכְתִיב "וּמִן הַקֳּדָשִׁים יֹאכֵל" (ויקרא כא). **מִגּוֹ** דְּמִיתְּסַר בַּאֲכִילָה. מִשּׁוּם טוּמְאָה, חָיֵיל נַמִי שֵׁם טוּמְאָה עַל הָעֲבוֹדָה. **אֶלָּא** מְלִיקָה. כּוֹלֵל לָא מַשְׁכַּחַתְּ לָהּ, דְּהָא בִּשְׁעַת מְלִיקָה חָיְילֵי תַּרְוַויְיהוּ. דְּכָל זְמַן שֶׁלֹּא נִמְלְקָה הָיָה עָלֶיהָ אִיסּוּר (א) מְעִילָה, וְלֹא זֶהוּ אִיסּוּר זָרוּת הָאָמוּר בַּקָּרְבָּן שֶׁנִּיתַּר לַאֲכִילַת כֹּהֲנִים. וּכְשֶׁנִּמְלְקָה וְנִרְאֵית לַכֹּהֲנִים פָּקַע מִינָּהּ אִיסּוּר אַזְהָרַת מְעִילָה, וְחָיֵיל עָלֶיהָ אִיסּוּר זָרוּת דְּ"זָר לֹא יֹאכַל" וְאִיסּוּר מְלִיקָה בְּאִיסּוּר בַּת אַחַת. **מִיחַיֵּיב** תַּרְתֵּי. דְּהָא דְּקָאָמַר לְעֵיל חַיָּיב שְׁתַּיִם — כְּגוֹן שֶׁבָּא עָלָיו אִיסּוּר דְּאֵשֶׁת אָח וַאֲחוֹת אִשָּׁה כְּאֶחָד, וּמַשְׁכַּחַתְּ לָהּ כְּגוֹן (ב) דְּשַׁוְּויִנְהוּ שָׁלִיחַ שְׁנֵי אַחִין לְקַדֵּשׁ שְׁתֵּי אֲחָיוֹת, וְהֵן עָשׂוּ שָׁלִיחַ לְקַבֵּל קִידּוּשֵׁיהֶן, וּפָגַע שָׁלִיחַ בְּשָׁלִיחַ. **לָא** מִיחַיֵּיב אֶלָּא חֲדָא. וְכִי חַיָּיב (ג) בְּאִיסּוּר מוֹסִיף — בְּנָשָׂא חַי וְאח"כ נָשָׂא מֵת, כִּדְמְפָרֵשׁ לְעֵיל. **כְּגוֹן** דְּאַיְיתֵי שְׁתֵּי שְׂעָרוֹת. הַיּוֹם בְּשַׁבָּת זוֹ, דְּהַשְׁתָּא לֵיכָּא לְמֵימַר כִּדְלְעֵיל מֵעִיקָּרָא שָׁרֵי בִּמְלָאכָה וְאָסוּר בַּעֲבוֹדָה, דְּהָא לֹא חָל שׁוּם אִיסּוּר עָלָיו עַד הַיּוֹם, דְּאִיסּוּר זָרוּת וְאִיסּוּר שַׁבָּת יַחַד בָּאוּ, אֲבָל הֵבִיא שְׁתֵּי שְׂעָרוֹת בְּחוֹל קָדֵים זָרוּת עָלֵיהּ. **בַּעַל מוּם** נַמִי כְּגוֹן דְּאַיְיתֵי שְׁתֵּי שְׂעָרוֹת **וְאִיטַּמֵּי** לֵיהּ. כְּלוֹמַר, דְּאִיטַּמֵּי קוֹדֶם (ד) ב' שְׂעָרוֹת, וּבְתוֹךְ טוּמְאָתוֹ וּמוּמוֹ הֵבִיא שְׁתֵּי שְׂעָרוֹת, וּבִשְׁעַת הֲבָאָה חָלוּ שְׁנֵיהֶן, שֶׁהֲרֵי שְׁנֵיהֶן הָיוּ תְּלוּיִין עָלָיו. **שֶׁחָתַךְ אֶצְבָּעוֹ.** וְהוּא הַמּוּם, וְנִטְמְאָה בַּחֲתִיכָתוֹ בַּסַּכִּין. **בִּשְׁלָמָא** לְרַ' חִיָּיא. מָצֵי לְאוֹקְמֵי גְּמָרֵיהּ וּדְבַר קַפָּרָא הָכִי. **כִּי אַתְנְיֵיהּ.** [רַבִּי] לְדִידֵיהּ כְּרַבִּי יוֹסֵי, וּלְבַר קַפָּרָא כְּר"ש. וּבַר קַפָּרָא הוּא דְּטָעָה, וְסָבַר דְּרַ' אַלִּיבָּא דְּרַ' יוֹסֵי אַתְנְיֵיהּ. **אֶלָּא לְבַר** קַפָּרָא. דְּאָמַר רַבִּי אַלִּיבָּא דְּרַ' יוֹסֵי אַתְנְיֵיהּ קוּלָּא, א"כ, אַלִּיבָּא דְּמַאן אַתְנְיֵיהּ לְרַ' חִיָּיא חוּמְרָא? וְכִי לְבַר קַפָּרָא שַׁקּוּרֵי מְשַׁקֵּר רַבִּי חִיָּיא, דְּלָא אַתְנְיֵיהּ רַבִּי [*לר"י] מְחַיֵּיב שְׁתַּיִם? **וְאַלִּיבָּא** דְּר"ש. וְה"ק רַבִּי חִיָּיא: אע"ג דְּפָלֵיג ר' שִׁמְעוֹן וּפָטַר, הנ"מ בְּכוֹלֵל, אֲבָל בְּבַת אַחַת — מוֹדֶה, הוֹאִיל וְלָא קָדֵים חַד לַחֲבְרֵיהּ. וּבַר קַפָּרָא אָמַר: בְּבַת אַחַת נַמִי פָּלֵיג ר"ש. **לְאַפּוּקֵי** לְר"ש מֵחֶזְקֵיהּ. דַּהֲוָה מַחְזְקִינַן לֵיהּ לְרַבִּי שִׁמְעוֹן לְקוּלָּא, וְאִישְׁתַּבַּע לָן ר' חִיָּיא דִּבְבַת אַחַת מוֹדֵי. **בִּשְׁלָמָא** לְבַר קַפָּרָא. מָצֵי לְתָרוּצֵי לִגְמָרֵיהּ וּגְמָרֵיהּ דְּרַבִּי חִיָּיא וּלְמֵימַר: כִּי אַתְנְיַין רַבִּי פְּטוּר — אַלִּיבָּא דְּר"ש, וְכִי אַתְנְיֵיהּ לְרַ' חִיָּיא חִיּוּבָא — אַלִּיבָּא דְּרַ' יוֹסֵי. וְרַבִּי חִיָּיא הוּא דְּטָעָה וְסָבַר דְּרַבִּי אַלִּיבָּא דְּר"ש אַתְנְיֵיהּ. **אֶלָּא** לְרַ' חִיָּיא. דְּאָמַר אַלִּיבָּא דְּר"ש אַתְנְיֵיהּ רַבִּי חִיּוּבָא, הָלָא פְּטוּרָא דְּאַתְנְיֵיהּ לְבַר קַפָּרָא — אַלִּיבָּא דְּמַאן? וְכִי שַׁקּוּרֵי מְשַׁקֵּר בַּר קַפָּרָא דְּלָא אַתְנְיֵיהּ ר' פְּטוּרָא כְּלָל?! **אָמַר לָךְ רַבִּי** חִיָּיא. וַדַּאי בַּר קַפָּרָא לָא מְשַׁקֵּר אֶלָּא טָעֵי. דְּרַבִּי וַדַּאי פְּטוּרָא אַתְנְיֵיהּ, וְלָא בְּכוּלְּהוּ אֶלָּא בְּתַרְתֵּי: בְּזָר שֶׁשִּׁימֵּשׁ בְּשַׁבָּת וּבַעַל מוּם שֶׁשִּׁימֵּשׁ בְּטוּמְאָה, דְּמִשְׁתַּכַּח בֵּין ע"י כּוֹלֵל בֵּין ע"י בַּת אַחַת, כִּדְאָמַר לְעֵיל.

וְאִיסּוּר

[*] נ"ל דר"י. יעב"ץ.

תוספות

במאי קמיפלגי באיסור כולל. הו"מ לאקשויי: בשלמא לבר קפרא משתבע לאפוקי ר' יוסי מחזקיה, אלא לר' חייא – למה ליה אשתבועי? דכה"ג דייק בסמוך. אלא כאן לא חש לדקדק, משום דלא קאי הכי(ה). **לא** מיחייב אלא חדא. פי' בקונטרס: והא דקתני ר"ש אומר אינו חייב אלא משום אשת אח בלבד, דאוקימנא בנשא מת ואח"כ נשא חי, דהוי איסור כולל – רבי חייא תני לה ולא בר קפרא. ונראה דבר קפרא נמי תני לה, ולקברו בין רשעים גמורים.

אלא מליקה בבת אחת הוא דמשכחת לה. וא"ת: היכי הויא בבת אחת? והא מיד כי נמלקה הויא לה נבילה, ואיסור זרות לא חייל עד אחר זריקה, שיש היתר לכהנים, כדאמר בפרק בתרא דמכות (דף יח: ושם) דכל היכא דקרינן "ואכלו אותם אשר כופר בהם" קרינן ביה "וכל זר לא יאכל (ו) קודש"! וי"ל: דאיסור נבילה נמי לא חייל עד אחר הזריקה, דנפקא איסור מעילה, דלא חייל איסור נבילה על איסור מעילה דחמיר מיניה, כי היכי דחמיר איסור מעילה מאיסור גיד, כדאמר בפרק "גיד הנשה" (חולין דף קא. ושם). ואע"ג דבר קפרא דשמעתין אית ליה בריש מעילה (ד' ה.) דהיתר זריקה שנינו. ומשנראה לזריקה נפיק מידי מעילה – מ"מ איסור(ז) איכא עד שיזרוק, הלכך לא חייל איסור נבלה עד אחר זריקה. א) ועוי"ל: [דבר קפרא סבר] דר"ש דשמעתין לטעמיה דאית ליה איסור זרות לפני זריקה דאמר התם במכות (דף יז:) דזר שאכל עולה לפני זריקת דמים לוקה חמש, ולא משום זרות דכתיב גבי "ואכלו אותם אשר כופר בהם" – דמשום ההוא לא לקי אפי' לר"ש, כדאיתא בהדיא התם, אלא מההוא קרא ד"לא תוכל לאכול בשעריך" (דברים יב).

באיסור בת אחת מיחייב תרתי. פי' בקונטרס: דהא דקאמר לעיל חייב שתים – כגון שבא עליו איסור אשת אח ואחות אשה כאחד, ומשכחת לה ע"י שליח, כדלקמן (דף לד.). והשתא הא דפליג עליה ר"ש דאמר אין חייב אלא משום אשת אח בלבד אע"ג דבבת אחת (ח) אשת אח דחמור חייל, דאין לה היתר אחר מיתה אלא במקום יבום, אבל אחות אשה שרי לאחר מיתת אשתו. וברייתא דקתני אינו חייב אלא משום אחות אשה – לא איירי בבת אחת, דא"כ היה חייב משום אשת אח. אלא בנשא חי ואח"כ נשא מת איירי. והא דקאמר ר' חייא דר' יוסי בבת אחת מחייב תרתי – לאו דוקא באיסור בת אחת, אלא אפילו באיסור מוסיף, כדמוכח בפ' "אמרו לו" (כריתות דף יד:).

(ט) **בר** קפרא סבר לא מיחייב אלא חדא. והיא דקתני ר"ש אומר אינו חייב אלא משום אשת אחיו [בלבד, דמשמע דמחייב ר' יוסי תרתי – היינו לקוברו בין רשעים גמורים ובאידך ברייתא דמיירי בנשא חי ואח"כ נשא מת מודה בה בר קפרא דלר' יוסי חייב שתים דמודה ר' יוסי באיסור מוסיף כמו שפירש בקונטרס כדמוכח ממתני' דפ' אמרו לו וקשה לר"י דמשמע דבאיסור מוסיף חל טפי איסור על איסור מבאיסור בת אחת וכי מסקינן דמיפלגו באיסור בת אחת ואליבא דר"ש, וחייב לר' חייא שתים – באיסור בת אחת לר"ש, ואפ"ה לית ליה איסור מוסיף, דקתני לעיל אין חייב אלא משום אחות אשה! ואר"י: דבודאי איסור בת אחת עדיף, אלא דסבר בר קפרא דדוקא באיסור בת אחת דהכא, כגון אחות אשה, וטומאה, ושבת, ונבילה, (י) דלא חיילא – היינו משום דהותרה בהדי ההיא דלא הותרה, שכן משמע לישנא דקאמר בר קפרא: שבת לכל הותרה, טומאה לכל הותרה – משמע משום דהותרו לא חיילי. ורבי חייא לית ליה האי סברא, כדקאמר: לכהנים הותרה ולא לזרים. הלכך קאמר בסמוך דבבת אחת מחייב ר"ש שתים, אע"ג דבאיסור מוסיף לא מחייב אלא אחת. וכן משמע קצת לקמן דאיסור בת אחת עדיף טפי, דקאמר: השתא משום כולל מיחייב – משום בת אחת מיבעיא! ומאן דמחייב באיסור כולל, היינו משום דמידי דהוה אאיסור מוסיף, כדאמר בפ"ג דשבועות (דף כד: ושם), וא"כ עדיף נמי מאיסור מוסיף. **אצבעו** בסכין טמאה. שהיתה אצבעו חתוכה עד משהו אחרון דכשנגע בו הסכין נטמא ונעשה בעל מום.

ואיסור

עין משפט נר מצוה

מ א ב מיי' פי"ז מהל' איסורי ביאה הל' ח ופ"ד מהלכות שגגות הל' א ופ"ח מהלכות מאכלות אסורות הלכה ו:

תוספות ישנים

במאי קמיפלגי. דמאי דקאמר כשהותרה וכו' אין זה עיקר טעם דהא אפשר לומר בשני לדדין: **באיסור** כולל מחייב תרתי. וא"כ הא דר' יוסי דלעיל דמחייב באשת אח ובאחות אשה מיירי בין נשא חי ואח"כ נשא מת בין נשא מת ואח"כ נשא חי. וא"ת והא קאמר אשת איש ונעשית חמותו נדון באשת איש ואמאי איסור כולל הוא וא"כ לחייב בחמותו החמורה. וי"ל דלאו כר' חייא אתיא כי אם לבר קפרא. א"נ י"ל דהא דמחייב ר' יוסי באיסור כולל תרתי היינו (כשהיו) [כשהם] משם אחד כמו אשת אח ואחות אשה שהכל משום אחוה הוא. אבל בשני שמות כמו חמותו ואשת איש לא מחייב ר' יוסי. וא"ת והלא קאמר ר' יוסי גבי עבר זקן ונשאה חייב שתים אע"ג דשתי שמות הן וי"ל דהיינו דווקא גבי איסור מוסיף דאין חילוק באיסור מוסיף בין שם אחד לשתי שמות אבל באיסור כולל דגרע מיניה אין חייב שתים רק כשהם משם אחד: **מגו** דמתסר באכילה אתסר נמי בעבודה. ולפי' שפי' נ"ל דשם אחד הוא דעבודה אקרי קריבה דכתיב המקריב ואכילה אקרי קריבה דכתיב איש [איש] אשר יקרב אל הקדשים והיינו אכילה ואי נמי כיון דאיסורא דאית בהו משום טומאה שם אחד הוא [ועי' בתוס' לעיל עמוד ב' ד"ה איסור] ומיירי הכי בקרבן צבור דהותרה בו טומאה ושבת ולהכי הוי איסור כולל ולא איסור מוסיף דלא נוסף בו איסור בגבר שהי' בו היתר אבל בקרבן יחיד היה איסור מוסיף דקודם שבת הותרו כהנים להקריב [illegible] נאסרו מגו דלא נתוסף [illegible] לגבי כהנים [illegible] קודם [illegible] איסורא לגבי [illegible] בעל מום [illegible] אי בקרבן [illegible] איסור [illegible] תמימים [illegible] אטמי נאסרו בו [illegible] תמימים [illegible] מגו דאתוסף [illegible] התמימים איתוסף [illegible] לגבי בעל מום [illegible] ודאי בקרבן [illegible]: **א)** [illegible] נתנאל [illegible] היתר זריקה [illegible] מידי מעילה [illegible] בבהמה [illegible] שריא משום [illegible] מליקה [illegible] אסירה [illegible] הכא לא [illegible] עד לאחר [illegible] אמרינן [illegible] עליה [illegible] וטמא [illegible] מעילה הזאה [illegible]: **רבי** חייא סבר רבי יוסי באיסור בת אחת מחייב תרתי [פי' בקונטרס] והא דאמרינן לעיל דמחייב ר' יוסי תרתי באשת אח ואחות אשה מיירי בבת אחת דשוו אינהו ואינהי שליח ופגשו שליח בשליח ואין צריך לומר כן. ונראה דהא דאמרי' לעיל דר' יוסי מחייב שתים היינו לקברו בין רשעים חמורים. וא"ת הלא גבי עבר זקן ונשאה משמע דר' יוסי מחייב שתים באיסור מוסיף וא"כ כ"ש באיסור בת אחת והכא קאמר בר קפרא דלא מחייב ר' יוסי אלא חדא. וי"ל דשאני התם דאיסור חמור הוא דאיכא סקילה. והכא בזר ששימש בשבת לא מחייב רק משום זרות ולא משום שבת אע"ג דאיכא סקילה משום דהותרה מכללה בקרבן צבור. וכן בעל מום ששימש בטומאה מחייב משום בעל מום ולא משום טומאה דהותרה מכללה בצבור. וכן מליקה מחייב משום זרות אבל לא משום נבלה שהותרה מכללה: **שחתך** אצבעו בסכין טמאה. וא"ת מ"מ לא הוי בת אחת דמיד שנגע לסכין אטמי. ובעל מום לא הוי עד שחתך. וי"ל כיון דליכא רק זמן מועט בינתים חשבינן ליה בבת אחת. וכן מפורש גבי דמצי לאהדורי ע"י הדחק א) עוד י"מ דמיירי שחתך אצבעו סמוך לעצם הרבה ועתה שחתך העצם בסכין טמאה מיד אטמי ונעשה בעל מום: **באיסור** בת אחת ואליבא דר' שמעון דר' חייא סבר דר' שמעון מחייב תרתי בבת אחת והא דאמר ר' שמעון לעיל אינו חייב אלא אחת ב) אף באיסור בת אחת ולעולם סבר דמחייב על

החמור

א) בכתובות דף ל' ע"ב וע"ש בתוס' ד"ה לא נריכא בשם הריצב"א. ב) נראה דחסר כאן וצ"ל אינו חייב אלא אחת מיירי בזה אחר זה ובר קפרא סובר דאף באיסור בת אחת לעולם סבר וכו'.

הגהות הב"ח

(א) רש"י ד"ה אלא וכו' איסור לאזהרת וכו' איסור לאזהרת מעילה: (ב) ד"ה מיחייב וכו' כגון דשוו שני אחין שליח לקדש וכו' שליח בשליח כדלקמן הס"ד: (ג) ד"ה לא מיחייב אלא חדא וכי חייב תרתי באיסור: (ד) ד"ה בעל מום וכו' קודם שהביא ב' שערות: (ה) תוס' ד"ה במאי וכו' דלא קאי הכי. נ"ב ומהר"ר משה תירץ להכי הוצרך ר' חייא לאשתבועי דלא נימא אשת איש ונעשה חמותו איסור כולל הוא ודוחק ע"ל דף לב ע"ב בתוס' ד"ה איסור: (ו) ד"ה אלא וכו' קרינן ביה וכל זר לא יאכל כי קדש הם וי"ל: (ז) בא"ד מ"מ איסור מעילה איכא עד שיזרוק: (ח) ד"ה באיסור וכו' דבבת אחת כן אשת: (ט) ד"ה ובר קפרא וכו' אשת אח דעלמא דמחייב ר' יוסי: (י) בא"ד ושבת ונבילה הוא דלא חיילא ההיא דהותרה בהדי:

גליון הש"ס

גמ' אי נמי שחתך אצבעו. עיין כתובות דף ל ע"ב תד"ה לא נריכא: **שם** ר' חייא שקורי קא משקר. עיין שבועות דף כו ע"א תד"ה את לבך:

וְאִיסּוּר כּוֹלֵל אַתְנְיָיהּ, וְאַלִּיבָּא דְּרַ׳ שִׁמְעוֹן, וְחַזְיָא לְבַר קַפָּרָא לְזָר שֶׁאָכַל מְלִיקָה, וְאַיְּידֵי דְּדָמְיָא לָהּ — עֲרָבָהּ בַּהֲדַיְיהוּ, וְעַיֵּין בָּהּ, וְלֹא אַשְׁכַּח אֶלָּא בְּבַת אַחַת. וְסָבַר: מִדְּהָא בְּבַת אַחַת — הָא נַמִי בְּבַת אַחַת, וּמִדְּהָנָךְ לִפְטוֹר — הָנָךְ נַמִי לִפְטוֹר. מֵיתִיבֵי: *זָר שֶׁשִּׁימֵּשׁ בְּשַׁבָּת, וּבַעַל מוּם שֶׁשִּׁימֵּשׁ בְּטוּמְאָה — יֵשׁ כָּאן מִשּׁוּם זָרוּת, וּמִשּׁוּם שַׁבָּת, וּמִשּׁוּם בַּעַל מוּם, וּמִשּׁוּם טוּמְאָה, דִּבְרֵי רַבִּי יוֹסֵי. ר״ש אוֹמֵר: אֵין כָּאן אֶלָּא מִשּׁוּם זָרוּת וּבַעַל מוּם בִּלְבַד. וְאִילּוּ מְלִיקָה שַׁיְּירָהּ. לְמַאן שַׁיְּירָהּ? אִילֵימָא לְרַבִּי יוֹסֵי — הַשְׁתָּא רַ׳ יוֹסֵי בְּאִיסּוּר כּוֹלֵל מִיחַיֵּיב שְׁתַּיִם, בְּאִיסּוּר בַּת אַחַת מִיבַּעְיָא? אֶלָּא לָאו — לְרַ׳ שִׁמְעוֹן וּבְאִיסּוּר כּוֹלֵל הוּא דְּפָטַר — אֲבָל בְּאִיסּוּר בְּבַת אַחַת מִיחַיֵּיב, תְּיוּבְתָּא דְּבַר קַפָּרָא! תְּיוּבְתָּא. ״זָר שֶׁשִּׁימֵּשׁ בְּשַׁבָּת״, בְּמַאי? אִי בִּשְׁחִיטָה — שְׁחִיטָה בְּזָר כְּשֵׁרָה, א] וְאִי בְּקַבָּלָה וְהוֹלָכָה — •טִלְטוּל בְּעָלְמָא הוּא. אִי בְּהַקְטָרָה — •*וְהָא״ר יוֹסֵי: הַבְעָרָה לְלָאו יָצָאתָה! אָמַר רַב אַחָא בַּר יַעֲקֹב: בִּשְׁחִיטַת פָּרוֹ שֶׁל כֹּהֵן גָּדוֹל, וּכְדִבְרֵי הָאוֹמֵר: שְׁחִיטַת פָּרוֹ שֶׁל כֹּהֵן גָּדוֹל בְּזָר — פְּסוּלָה. — אִי הָכִי מַאי אִירְיָא זָר, אֲפִילּוּ כֹּהֵן הֶדְיוֹט נַמִי! — שֶׁזָּר אֶצְלוֹ קָאָמַר. מַתְקִיף לָהּ רַב אַשִׁי: מִידֵי חַטָּאוֹת קָתָנֵי, אוֹ לָאוֵי קָתָנֵי? אֶלָּא: אִיסּוּרֵי בְּעָלְמָא קָא חָשֵׁיב. לְמַאי נָפְקָא מִינָּהּ — *לְקוֹבְרוֹ בֵּין רְשָׁעִים (א) גְּמוּרִים.§

מתני׳ אשְׁנַיִם שֶׁקִּידְּשׁוּ שְׁתֵּי נָשִׁים, וּבִשְׁעַת כְּנִיסָתָן לְחוּפָּה הֶחֱלִיפוּ אֶת שֶׁל זֶה לָזֶה וְאֶת שֶׁל זֶה לָזֶה — הֲרֵי אֵלּוּ חַיָּיבִין מִשּׁוּם אֵשֶׁת אִישׁ. וְאִם הָיוּ אַחִין — מִשּׁוּם אֵשֶׁת אָח, וְאִם הָיוּ אֲחָיוֹת — מִשּׁוּם אִשָּׁה אֶל אֲחוֹתָהּ, וְאִם הָיוּ נִדּוֹת — מִשּׁוּם נִדָּה. *ב וּמַפְרִישִׁין אוֹתָן שְׁלֹשָׁה חֳדָשִׁים, שֶׁמָּא מְעוּבָּרוֹת הֵן, *וְאִם הָיוּ קְטַנּוֹת שֶׁאֵינָן רְאוּיוֹת לֵילֵד — מַחֲזִירִים אוֹתָן מִיָּד, וְאִם הָיוּ כֹּהֲנוֹת — נִפְסְלוּ *מִן הַתְּרוּמָה.§ **גמ׳** ״הֶחֱלִיפוּ״, מִידֵי *בִּרְשִׁיעֵי עָסְקִינַן?! וְתוּ: הָא דְּתָנֵי רַבִּי חִיָּיא: הֲרֵי כָּאן שֵׁשׁ עֶשְׂרֵה חַטָּאוֹת. אִי בְּמֵזִיד — מִי אִיכָּא קָרְבָּן? אָמַר רַב יְהוּדָה, תְּנֵי: הוּחְלְפוּ. הָכִי נַמִי מִסְתַּבְּרָא, דְּקָתָנֵי סֵיפָא: אִם הָיוּ קְטַנּוֹת שֶׁאֵינָן רְאוּיוֹת לֵילֵד — מַחֲזִירִין אוֹתָן מִיָּד. וְאִי בְּמֵזִיד — מִי שַׁרְיָא? — הָא לָא קַשְׁיָא: •*פִּיתּוּי קְטַנָּה — אוֹנֶס נִינְהוּ, גוְאוֹנֶס בְּיִשְׂרָאֵל מִישְׁרָא שָׁרֵי. אֶלָּא דְּקָתָנֵי: מַפְרִישִׁין אוֹתָן שְׁלֹשָׁה חֳדָשִׁים שֶׁמָּא מְעוּבָּרוֹת הֵן, הָא לָאו מְעוּבָּרוֹת — שָׁרְיָין, וְאִי בְּמֵזִיד — מִי שָׁרֵי? אֶלָּא לָאו שְׁמַע מִינָּהּ: הוּחְלְפוּ, שְׁמַע מִינָּהּ.

וּמַאן

[לקמן סא:]

רש״י

וְאִיסּוּר כּוֹלֵל אַתְנְיָיהּ. כְּלוֹמַר, הֵיכִי דְּאִיתְרַמֵּי עַל יְדֵי כּוֹלֵל אַתְנְיֵין רַבִּי פְּטוּרָה, וְאַלִּיבָּא דר״ש, וְהֵיכָא דְּאִיתְרַמּוּ בְּבַת אַחַת — אַתְנְיֵין חִיּוּבָא. אֲבָל מְלִיקָה לָא אַתְנְיֵי׳ לִפְטוּר כְּלָל, דְּלָא מַשְׁכַּחַתְּ לָהּ בְּכוֹלֵל אֶלָּא בְּבַת אַחַת, וְהָתָם ר׳ שִׁמְעוֹן מוֹדֵי. **וְחַזְיָא בַּר קַפָּרָא לְזָר שֶׁאָכַל מְלִיקָה.** דְּדָמְיָא לְהוּ, דְּהָווּ נַמִי כְּקָדָשִׁים: אֲדָא דְּמִיחַיֵּיב עֲלֵיהּ תַּרְתֵּי, וַעֲרָבָהּ בַּהֲדַיְיהוּ לִפְטוּרָא. וְכִי עֲרָבָהּ — לָא אַסֵּיק אַדַּעְתֵּיהּ דְּהָא לָא מִשְׁתַּכְּחַת בְּכוֹלֵל. **וְעַיֵּין בָּהּ.** לְאַחַר זְמַן, כְּשֶׁנִּתְקַיְּימָה בְּיָדוֹ, וְהָיָה שׁוֹנֶה שְׁלָשְׁתָּן כְּיַחַד, וְאַשְׁכַּח דְּלָא מִיתּוֹקְמָא אֶלָּא בְּבַת אַחַת, וְשָׁכַח דְּהוּא עֲרָבָהּ. וְסָבַר דְּר׳ אַתְנְיֵיהּ, וְאָמַר: מִדְּהָא בְּבַת אַחַת וּפְטוּרָה — הָנָךְ נַמִי דְּאַתְנְיֵיהּ רַבִּי לִפְטוּרָא — אֲפִי׳ הֵיכָא דְּמִיתְרַמּוּ בְּבַת אַחַת אַתְנְיֵין. **לְמַאן שַׁיְּירָא.** כְּלוֹמַר, (ב) לְמַאן מִינַּיְיהוּ מוֹדֶה בָּהּ דְּלָא בָּעֵי לְאִיפְּלוּגֵי. **אִילֵימָא ר׳ יוֹסֵי.** מוֹדֶה בָּהּ, הַשְׁתָּא בְּאִיסּוּר כּוֹלֵל, דְּחַד מִינַּיְיהוּ קָדֵים, א״ר יוֹסֵי אַחֲרוֹן חָל — בְּבַת אַחַת מִיבַּעְיָא? **אֶלָּא לָאו לר״ש.** וּמִדְּמוֹדֶה בִּמְלִיקָה — ש״מ דְּהָא דְּפָלֵיג בְּהָנָךְ הֵיכָא דְּאִיתְרַמּוּ בְּכוֹלֵל הוּא דְּפָלֵיג, אֲבָל בְּאִיסּוּר בַּת אַחַת — מִיחַיֵּיב תַּרְתֵּי, וּתְיוּבְתָּא דְּבַר קַפָּרָא תְּיוּבְתָּא. **שְׁחִיטָה בְּזָר כְּשֵׁרָה.** וְאֵין כָּאן זָרוּת. **טִלְטוּל בְּעָלְמָא הוּא.** וְאֵין כָּאן א] שְׁבוּת. **אִי בְּהַקְטָרָה.** רַבִּי יוֹסֵי הֵיכִי מִיחַיֵּיב חַטָּאת מִשּׁוּם שַׁבָּת, דְּקס״ד חַטָּאת מִיחַיֵּיב לֵיהּ: **הָאָמַר ר׳ יוֹסֵי.** בְּפ״ק: הַבְעָרָה לְלָאו יָצָאת. **בִּשְׁחִיטַת פָּרוֹ שֶׁל כ״ג.** בְּיוֹם הַכִּפּוּרִים. דִּשְׁחִיטָה אַב מְלָאכָה הִיא, וּמִשּׁוּם זָרוּת נַמִי אִיכָּא, כְּדִבְרֵי הָאוֹמֵר בְּיוֹמָא בְּפֶרֶק ״טָרַף בַּקַּלְפִּי״ (דף מב.): שְׁחִיטַת פָּרוֹ בְּזָר פְּסוּלָה. **אֲפִי׳ כֹּהֵן הֶדְיוֹט נַמִי.** דְּהָא מַאן דְּפָסֵיל יָלֵיף טַעְמָא מֵאַהֲרֹן, וְחוּקָּה, דִּכְתִיב ״וְהִקְרִיב אַהֲרֹן״ (ויקרא טז), וּכְתִיב בְּסוֹף הַפָּרָשָׁה ״לְחֻקַּת עוֹלָם״, וְכָל הֵיכָא דִּכְתִיב חוּקָּה — עִיכּוּבָא הוּא, אַלְמָא: אַהֲרֹן דַּוְקָא: הָכִי גָּרְסִי׳. **מִידֵי חַטָּאוֹת קָתָנֵי אוֹ לָאוֵי קָתָנֵי.** אִיסּוּרֵי הוּא דְּקָחָשֵׁיב: **מתני׳ וּמַפְרִישִׁין אוֹתָן ג׳ חֳדָשִׁים.** שֶׁלֹּא לַחֲזוֹר לְבַעֲלֵיהֶן, שֶׁמָּא מְעוּבָּרוֹת הֵן וּבְנֵיהֶם מַמְזֵרִים, וּבָעֵינַן הַבְחָנָה בֵּין זֶרַע כָּשֵׁר לְזֶרַע פָּסוּל, שֶׁלֹּא יִתְלוּ הָעוּבָּרִים בְּבַעֲלֵיהֶן. **אִם הָיוּ כֹּהֲנוֹת.** בַּגְּמָ׳ מְפָרֵשׁ. **גמ׳ שֵׁשׁ עֶשְׂרֵה חַטָּאוֹת.** לְכָל אֶחָד אַרְבַּע, וְכֵן לַנָּשִׁים. דְּעַל שְׁנֵיהֶם הוּא אוֹמֵר ״וְנִכְרְתוּ הַנְּפָשׁוֹת הָעוֹשׂוֹת״ (ויקרא יח). **וְאוֹנֶס בְּיִשְׂרָאֵל מִישְׁרָא שָׁרֵי.** לְבַעְלָהּ, דְּיָלְפִינַן (כתובות דף נא:) מִ״וְהִיא לֹא נִתְפָּשָׂה״, הָא נִתְפְּשָׂה — מוּתֶּרֶת. **מַפְרִישִׁין אוֹתָן שֶׁמָּא מְעוּבָּרוֹת הֵן.** וּלְאַחַר שְׁלֹשָׁה חֳדָשִׁים מוּתָּרוֹת, אע״ג שֶׁגְּדוֹלוֹת הֵן.

תוספות

ואיסור כולל אתניין ואליבא דר״ש. אבל לר׳ יוסי מחייב תרתי באיסור כולל, דלא מצי למימר דאליבא דרבי יוסי נמי אתנייה לפטורא — דא״כ לא הוה טעי בר קפרא לערב מליקה בהדייהו. דבבת אחת פשיטא ליה לבר קפרא דלר׳ יוסי מיחייב תרתי, ולהכי פשיטא ליה בסמוך דלר׳ יוסי מיחייב תרתי באיסור כולל, שעל כרחו צ״ל דאליבא דר״ש אתנייה, ולא אליבא דר׳ יוסי. ופליג רבי יוחנן ארבי חייא ובר קפרא. (ג) **אמר** ר׳ יוסי הבערה ללאו יצאה. תימה: דאטו מי לא מני לאוי גרידי? והרי זר שאכל מליקה, דליכא אלא לאו דנבלה! וי״ל: דאע״ג דבאיסור מוסיף לר׳ יוסי חייל איסור קל על איסור חמור, כדפריך רב אדא בפרק ״הנשרפין״ (סנהדרין דף פא. ושם): ולידון נמי באיסור אשת איש, דהא מודה רבי יוסי כו׳, אע״ג דאיסור אשת איש קל מאיסור חמותו, ובפרק ״אמרו לו״ (כריתות יד: ושם) גבי הא דאמר ר׳ יוסי אם (ד) זקן נשאה כו׳, משמע דמודה ר׳ יוסי דאיסור כרת חייל על חייבי מיתות ב״ד משום איסור מוסיף — מ״מ, באיסור כולל סבירא ליה לגמרא דלא חייל קל על חמור, כדאמר בסוף ״גיד הנשה״ (חולין קא. ושם): מאן האי תנא דאיסור כולל באיסור חמור אית ליה כו׳. ולהכי פריך: והאמר רבי יוסי הבערה ללאו יצאה, ואם כן היכי חיילא אאיסור זרות? הקשה ה״ר יעקב דאורליינ״ש: דאמאי לא מוקי לה בהכנסת האליתא, דעבודה היא, ובעיא כהונה, ואין בה מיתה אלא לאו גרידא לפי שאין עבודה תמה, כדאמר בפ״ב דיומא (דף כד:)? דהשתא לא הוי קל על חמור, דתרוייהו לאוי נינהו! ואר״י: דמ״מ איסור שבת קיל, לפי שהותרה במקדש. אבל אי הוה מיתה בהבערה — הוה חשיב איסור חמור, אע״ג דהותר במקדש. ואיסור טומאה נמי, אע״ג דהותר — חל על איסור בעל מום משום (ה) טמא ששימש במיתה, ובעל מום ששימש באזהרה לרבנן דרבי בסוף ״אלו הן הנשרפין״ (סנהדרין פג.), אע״ג דכולה שמעתין בר קפרא ורבי חייא אליבא דרבי פליגי — מודה רבי דלר׳ יוסי בעל מום ששימש באזהרה, כרבנן דידיה. ואם תאמר, דאמר בחולין (דף קג.): התורה אמרה יבא איסור נבלה ויחול על איסור חֵלֶב, והיינו קל על חמור באיסור כולל! ואר״י: דחלב קל, דהותר מכללו אצל חיה, כדאמר בס״פ ״גיד הנשה״ (שם). ואע״ג דנבלה נמי הותר במליקה — שאני קדשים, דכהנים משולחן גבוה קזכו, כדאמר ב״העור והרוטב״ (שם דף קכ.). ועוד: דיש חומרא בנבלה, שכן מטמאה. ואע״ג דיש חומרא בחֵלֶב דליכא בנבלה — אין לחוש בכך, כדאמרינן בפרק ״גיד הנשה״ (שם דף קא.) מאי חזית דטומאת הגוף חמירא — שכן כרת, דלמא טומאת בשר חמירא דלית לה טהרה במקוה. וא״ת: דאמר לקמן, מאן האי תנא דאית ליה איסור כולל ואיסור מוסיף ואיסור בת אחת, ומשמע דאיסור אחות אשה חייל באיסור כולל אאיסור אשת איש דחמיר מיניה! וי״ל: דאיסור אשת איש קיל, דיש לה היתר בחיי אוסרה, דחשבינן ליה קולא ב״הבא על יבמתו״ (לקמן דף נד.). ואע״ג דבפ׳ ״גיד הנשה״ (חולין דף קג. ושם) איכא מאן דאמר דאיסור טריפה חל על איסור אבר מן החי, אע״ג דחמיר מיניה, דחשיב משהו בשר גידים ועצמות אע״ג דלית ביה כזית, ונוהג בבני נח, וחייל עלייהו איסור טריפה דקיל אפי׳ בלא כוללו! ואור״י: דיש חומרא בטריפה, דכשנטרפה — שוב אין לה היתר אפי׳ נשחטה. אבל איסור אבר מן החי — אתיא שחיטה ומפקע ליה. **מידי** חטאות קתני או לאוי קתני איסורי בעלמא קחשיב. וכן גרס ר״ח, דאין כאן לא חטאת ולא לאו, כיון דלא חייל איסור קל על חמור. ומ״מ פריך שפיר לעיל לבר קפרא, דמשייר מליקה — מכלל דמודה בה ר״ש. דאין לומר דשיירא לרבי יוסי משום דבהסיא חייב תרתי, ולא חשיב אלא הנהו דמעלה עליו כאילו עשה שתים, **לקוברו** בין רשעים כו׳ — דהא חשיב בעל מום ששימש, אע״ג דחייב לגמרי שתים, כיון דקסבר *)רבי חייא דרבי יוסי אית ליה איסור כולל.

אם

*) גי׳ רש״ל בר קפרא

עין משפט נר מצוה

מא מיי׳ פ״ד מהל׳ שגגות הלכה א:

מב ב מיי׳ פי״א מהל׳ גירושין הלכה יח סמג עשין נ טוש״ע אה״ע סימן יג סעיף א:

מג ג מיי׳ פי״א מהל׳ איסורי ביאה הל׳ ז סמג לאוין קכא ועשין מח טוש״ע שם סימן ו סעיף יא:

תוספות ישנים

החמור. וא״ת מאי טעמא דאית תנא דתני דקאמר ר׳ שמעון אינו חייב אלא משום אשת אח ואית תנא דתני דר׳ שמעון אמר אינו חייב אלא משום אחות אשה. דליכא לתרץ כדמתרץ לעיל כאן שנשא מת וכו׳ דהא לא איירי כלל באיסור מוסיף ובאיסור כולל אלא באיסור בת אחת. וא״כ בבת אחת היכי נתרץ הקושיא. וי״ל לעולם סבר דמחייב על החמורה. ובהא פליגי דחד אמר דאשת אח חמירא משום דאסירא אף לאחר מיתה משא״כ באחות אשה דהא שריא לאחר מיתה וחד סבר דאחות אשה חמירא משום דאחות אשה לא הותרה אף בשאין לה בנים ואשת אח הותרה באין לה בנים: **באיסור** בת אחת מיבעיא. וא״ל דלמא באיסור כולל דאיכא תרתי היינו לקברו בין רשעים חמורים אבל באיסור בת אחת ר״ל חיוב גמור דלא מסתבר ליה לחלק. וכן לקמן דקאמר אלמא ר׳ שמעון באיסור בת אחת מחייב תרתי לא משני לקוברן בין רשעים חמורים. דלא מיסתבר לר׳ שמעון הך מילתא דלאי לקברו בין רשעים חמורים אפי׳ באיסור כולל יהיה כן: **מידי** חטאות קתני או לאוי קתני איסורי קתני פ״ה לעולם בקבלה והולכה. ואי פרכת טלטול בעלמא הוא. הא לא קשה מידי דהא לא קתני אלא חייב שתים ואיכא למימר איסורי קתני. ולא נהירא דהא אין זה איסורא כיון דאינו אלא טלטול דאסור מדרבנן. לכן נראה דקאי אהא דאמרי לעיל אי בהבערה הא אמר ר׳ יוסי ללאו יצאת. ועל זה מקשה מידי חטאות קתני או לאוי קתני איסורי קא חשיב. וא״כ נהי נמי דללאו יצאת נימא דאיסורא למלאוריית׳ הוא:

תוספות חד מקמאי

מתניתין שנים שקדשו שתי נשים ובשעת כניסתן לחופה החליפו את של זה בזה ואת של זה בזה חייבין משום א״א ואם היו אחים חייבים אף משום אשת אח ואם היו אחיות חייבים אף משום אשה אל אחותה. ואם היו נדות חייבין משום נדה וכולן מפרישין אותן ג׳ חדשים שמא מעוברות הן אוקימ׳ הוחלפו אבל בהחליפו אפילו אינן מעוברות אסורות שהרי זינתה ברצון ואם היו קטנות אפי׳ ברצון שרו לגברייהו דקטנה היא ואוקימנא שמתני׳ כר״מ דאית ליה איסור כולל ואיסור מוסיף ואיסור בת אחת א״נ כר״ש ובאיסור בת אחת ואקשי׳ בשלמא כולהו משכחת ליה דשוו אינהו שליח ושוו (עלייהו) [אינהי] שליח ופגעו שליח בשליח אלא נדות היכי משכחת לה אמר רב עמרם אמרי בי רב בשופעות מתוך י״ב לאחר י״ב לחיובי אינהי ומתוך י״ג לאחר י״ג לחיובי אינהו וכ״ת אם קדשו בתוך י״ג או ביום סוף י״ג קדושי קטן הוא ואין קדושיו קדושין אפי׳ גט לא צריכה איכא למימר משכחת לה כגון שקדש לסוף י״ג שהיא מקודשת לאחר י״ג ואליבא דר״מ היא דאמר אדם מקנה דבר שלא בא לעולם ואית דגרס בשופעת מתוך שלשה לאחר שלשה לחיובי אינהי פירוש כגון שהיו גדולים וקדשו בנות קטנות פחותות מבת שלשה ונתנו קדושין לאביהן שהן קדושי תורה ושפעו הבנות מתוך שלש [לאחר שלש] דפחותות מבנות שלש אין חייבין עליהן לא משום אשת אח ולא משום חיוב א) וכשהיו אחר ג׳ הן עליהן חיובן בבת א׳ וכשהיו הן לאחר י״ג חייבין ז׳ חטאות הן:

אמר

א) נראה דצ״ל ולא משום אחות אשה וא״א ונדה וכשהיו אחר שלש חלו עליהן כולן בבת אחת וכשהיו הן לאחר י״ג חייבין הן ט״ז חטאות.

מסורת הש״ס

[תוספתא פ״ה]

שבת ע. סנהדרין לה: סב. לעיל ו:

[לעיל לב:]

לקמן סט.

[לקמן לה.]

מן הכהונה רש״ל

[יומא ו. כתובות קה. קדושין לג. גיטין ל:]

הגהות הב״ח

(א) גמ׳ בין רשעים גמורים. נ״ב ס״א חמורים: (ב) רש״י ד״ה למאן שיירא כלומר מאן מינייהו: (ג) תוס׳ ד״ה האמר ר׳ יוסי וכו׳ בפ׳ הנשרפין וליתרו נמי משום איסור אשת איש: (ד) בא״ד ר׳ יוסי אם עבר זקן ונשאה: (ה) בא״ד משום דטמא ששימש במיתה:

הגהות מהר״י לנדא

א] רש״י ד״ה טלטול בעלמא הוא ואין כאן שבת כצ״ל:

גליון הש״ס

גמ׳ טלטול בעלמא הוא. עיין סוכה דף מב ע״ב תד״ה טלטול: **שם** והאמר ר״י הבערה ללאו יצאתה. עיין ירושל׳ פ״ב דשבת סוף הל׳ ה דמשני כיון דהוא רוצה בעיכולם כמבשל הוא: **שם** פיתוי קטנה אונס. עי׳ כתובות ט ע״א תד״ה ואב״א:

הגהות מהר״ב רנשבורג

א] גמ׳ ואי בקבלה והולכה טלטול בעלמא הוא. נ״ב עי׳ שער המלך פ״ז מהלכות לולב סוף הלכה כ״ה ד״ה ומצאתי וכו׳ יעוש״ה דף נא ע״ד:

וּמַאן הַאי תַּנָּא דְּאִית לֵיהּ [א]אִיסּוּר כּוֹלֵל וְאִיסּוּר מוֹסִיף וְאִיסּוּר בַּת אַחַת? אֲמַר רַב יְהוּדָה אֲמַר רַב: ר"מ הִיא. *דְּתַנְיָא: *[ב]יֵשׁ אוֹכֵל אֲכִילָה אַחַת וְחַיָּיב עָלֶיהָ אַרְבַּע חַטָּאוֹת וְאָשָׁם אֶחָד: טָמֵא שֶׁאָכַל חֵלֶב וְהוּא נוֹתָר מִן מוּקְדָּשִׁין בְּיוה"כ. ר' מֵאִיר אוֹמֵר: אִם הָיְתָה שַׁבָּת וְהוֹצִיאוֹ בְּפִיו — חַיָּיב. אָמְרוּ לוֹ: אֵינוֹ מִן הַשֵּׁם. וְר"מ אַלִּיבָּא דְּמַאן? אִי אַלִּיבָּא דְּרַבִּי יְהוֹשֻׁעַ — הָאָמַר: [ג]טָעָה בִּדְבַר מִצְוָה פָּטוּר. אֶלָּא אַלִּיבָּא דְּרַבִּי אֱלִיעֶזֶר. אִיבָּעֵית אֵימָא: לְעוֹלָם אַלִּיבָּא דְּרַבִּי יְהוֹשֻׁעַ, כִּי קָאָמַר רַבִּי יְהוֹשֻׁעַ טָעָה בִּדְבַר מִצְוָה פָּטוּר — הנ"מ גַּבֵּי תִּינוֹקוֹת, [ד]דִּזְמַנּוֹ בָּהוּל. אֲבָל הַאי, כֵּיוָן דְּאֵין זְמַנּוֹ בָּהוּל — לָא. — וַהֲרֵי תְּרוּמָה דְּאֵין זְמַנּוֹ בָּהוּל, וְקָפָטַר! דִּתְנַן: *[ה]הָיָה אוֹכֵל בִּתְרוּמָה, וְנוֹדַע שֶׁהוּא בֶּן גְּרוּשָׁה אוֹ בֶּן חֲלוּצָה — רַבִּי אֱלִיעֶזֶר מְחַיֵּיב קֶרֶן וָחוֹמֶשׁ, וְרַבִּי יְהוֹשֻׁעַ פּוֹטֵר. *הָא אִיתְּמַר עֲלָהּ, אֲמַר רַב בֵּיבָי בַּר אַבָּיֵי: הָכָא בִּתְרוּמָה בְּעֶרֶב הַפֶּסַח עָסְקִינַן, דִּזְמַנָּהּ בָּהוּל. וְאִי בָּעֵית אֵימָא: בְּאִיסּוּר בַּת אַחַת, וְאַלִּיבָּא דְּרַ' שִׁמְעוֹן. בִּשְׁלָמָא *כּוּלְּהוּ — מַשְׁכַּחַת לְהוּ, דְּשָׁוִינְהוּ שָׁלִיחַ, וְשָׁווּ אִינְהוּ שָׁלִיחַ, וּפָגַע שָׁלִיחַ בְּשָׁלִיחַ. אֶלָּא נִדּוֹת — הֵיכִי מַשְׁכַּחַת לַהּ? אָמַר רַב עַמְרָם אָמַר רַב: בְּשׁוֹפְעוֹת מִתּוֹךְ י"ג לְאַחַר שְׁלֹשָׁה עָשָׂר לְאִחַיּוּבֵי אִינְהוּ, מִתּוֹךְ שְׁנֵים עָשָׂר לְאַחַר שְׁנֵים עָשָׂר — לְחַיּוּבֵי אִינְהִי.§ "מַפְרִישִׁים אוֹתָן".§ וְהָא אֵין אִשָּׁה מִתְעַבֶּרֶת בְּבִיאָה רִאשׁוֹנָה! אָמַר ר"נ אָמַר רַבָּה בַּר אֲבוּהּ: שֶׁבָּעֲלוּ וְשָׁנוּ. — [א] וְאֶלָּא הָא דְּתָנָא רַ' חִיָּיא: הֲרֵי כָּאן ט"ז חַטָּאוֹת, תְּלָתִין וְתַרְתֵּין הָוְיָין! — וְלִיטַעְמִיךְ, לְרַ' אֱלִיעֶזֶר, דִּמְחַיֵּיב עַל כָּל כֹּחַ וְכֹחַ, טוּבָא הָוְיָין! אֶלָּא, דְּבְכֹחַ רִאשׁוֹן קָחָשֵׁיב — ה"נ דְּבִיאָה רִאשׁוֹנָה קָחָשֵׁיב. א"ל רָבָא לְרַב נַחְמָן: וְהָא

רש"י

וּמַאן הַאי תַּנָּא. דְּמַתְנִי', דְּאִית לֵיהּ אִיסּוּר חָל עַל אִיסּוּר, בֵּין עַל יְדֵי כּוֹלֵל, בֵּין בְּאִיסּוּר מוֹסִיף, בֵּין עַל יְדֵי בַּת אַחַת, כְּגוֹן אֵלּוּ שֶׁחַיָּיבִין אַרְבַּע חַטָּאוֹת. (א) וּכְשֶׁקִּידֵּשׁ רְאוּבֵן אֶת רָחֵל תְּחִלָּה נֶאֶסְרָה עַל שִׁמְעוֹן מִשּׁוּם אֵשֶׁת אָח וְאֵשֶׁת אִישׁ — וְהַיְינוּ בַּת אַחַת, וְקָמְחַיֵּיב לֵיהּ תַּנָּא דִּידַן אַתַּרְוַויְיהוּ. חָזַר שִׁמְעוֹן וְקִידֵּשׁ לֵאָה, מִיגּוֹ דְּאָסְרֵי לֵיהּ הָנָךְ קִדּוּשִׁין בְּכוּלְּהוּ שְׁאָר אַחְוָותָא מִשּׁוּם אֲחוֹת אִשָּׁה, אָסְרֵי לֵיהּ נַמִי בְּאֵשֶׁת אָחִיו מִשּׁוּם אֲחוֹת אִשָּׁה, וְאע"ג דַּאֲסוּרָה עֲלֵיהּ וְקַיְימָא, וְהַיְינוּ אִיסּוּר כּוֹלֵל. וַעֲדַיִין רָחֵל זוֹ מוּתֶּרֶת לִרְאוּבֵן בַּעְלָהּ. פֵּירְסָה נִדָּה, מִיגּוֹ דְּאִיתּוֹסַף אִיסּוּר עֲלָהּ לְגַבֵּי בַּעְלָהּ מִשּׁוּם נִדָּה — אִיתּוֹסַף בָּהּ נַמִי אִיסּוּר לְגַבֵּי שִׁמְעוֹן, הֲרֵי אִיסּוּר מוֹסִיף. **אַרְבַּע חַטָּאוֹת.** מִשּׁוּם טוּמְאָה דְּאוֹכֵל קָדָשִׁים בְּטוּמְאַת הַגּוּף כְּכָרֵת, וּמִשּׁוּם חֵלֶב, וּמִשּׁוּם נוֹתָר, וּמִשּׁוּם יוה"כ. וַאֲשַׁם מְעִילוֹת, דַּאֲפִילּוּ כֹּהֵן לְגַבֵּי אֵימוּרִים זָר הוּא. **אִם הָיְתָה שַׁבָּת כו'.** אֲבָל מִשּׁוּם יוה"כ לָא הָוֵי מְחַיֵּיב אַהוֹצָאָה, דְּקָסָבַר: אֵין עֵירוּב וְהוֹצָאָה לְיוה"כ. וְהָכִי מְפָרֵשׁ בִּכְרֵיתוֹת. אַלְמָא אִית לֵיהּ לְרַבִּי מֵאִיר כּוּלְּהוּ, דְּהָא הָכָא, מִשֶּׁנּוֹלְדָה בְּהֵמָה זוֹ וְהִיא חוּלִּין — נֶאֶסְרָה חֶלְבָּהּ בַּאֲכִילָה וּמוּתָּר בַּהֲנָאָה. הוּקְדְּשָׁה, מִיגּוֹ דְּאִתּוֹסַף אִיסּוּר הֲנָאָה עַל הַחֵלֶב מִשּׁוּם [קָדָשִׁים] — אִיתּוֹסַף בֵּיהּ נַמִי אִיסּוּר אֲכִילָה מִשּׁוּם זָרוּת, וְאע"ג דְּאָסוּר וְקָאֵי בַּאֲכִילָה. הָוֵה לֵיהּ נוֹתָר, מִיגּוֹ דְּאִיתּוֹסַף אִיסּוּר לַמִּזְבֵּחַ מִשּׁוּם נוֹתָר — אִיתּוֹסַף נַמִי לַכֹּהֵן מִשּׁוּם נוֹתָר, הֲרֵי הָנָךְ תְּרֵי מִשּׁוּם אִיסּוּר מוֹסִיף. נִטְמָא, זֶה שֶׁעַד עַכְשָׁיו הָיָה מוּתָּר בַּחֲתִיכוֹת בְּשַׂר קֹדֶשׁ וְעַכְשָׁיו נֶאֱסַר בָּהֶן, מִיגּוֹ דְּמִיתְּסַר בִּשְׁאָר חֲתִיכוֹת מִשּׁוּם טוּמְאָה — נֶאֱסָר נַמִי בָּזוֹ מִשּׁוּם טוּמְאָה, וְהַיְינוּ אִיסּוּר כּוֹלֵל. ה"ל יוה"כ, מִיגּוֹ דְּמִיתְּסַר בְּחוּלִּין מִשּׁוּם יוה"כ — אָסוּר נַמִי בְּקָדָשִׁים מִשּׁוּם יוה"כ, וְהַיְינוּ נַמִי אִיסּוּר כּוֹלֵל. וּמִדִּמְחַיֵּיב לֵיהּ רַבִּי מֵאִיר מִשּׁוּם הוֹצָאַת שַׁבָּת — אַלְמָא אִית לֵיהּ אִיסּוּר בַּת אַחַת חָיֵיל, דִּכְשֶׁקִּידֵּשׁ הַיּוֹם חָלוּ עָלָיו אִיסּוּר אֲכִילַת יוה"כ וְאִיסּוּר שַׁבָּת. **וְר"מ אַלִּיבָּא דְּמַאן.** כְּלוֹמַר, נְהִי דְּסָבַר רַבִּי מֵאִיר אִיהוּ כה"ג אִיסּוּר חָל עַל אִיסּוּר, מִיהוּ הֵיכָא דְּקָא מִתְכַּוֵּין לִדְבַר מִצְוָה לִישָּׂא אִשָּׁה, כְּמַאן מֵרַבּוֹתָיו סְבִירָא לֵיהּ לְרַבִּי מֵאִיר בְּטָעָה בִּדְבַר מִצְוָה וְלֹא עָשָׂה מִצְוָה? אִי אַלִּיבָּא דְּר' יְהוֹשֻׁעַ — הָאָמַר פָּטוּר בְּמַסֶּ' שַׁבָּת, בְּפֶרֶק "ר' אֱלִיעֶזֶר דְּמִילָה" (דף קלז.), דְּתַנְיָא הָתָם בְּגְמָ': מִי שֶׁהָיוּ לוֹ שְׁנֵי תִינוֹקוֹת, אֶחָד לָמוּל בַּשַּׁבָּת וְאֶחָד לָמוּל בְּא' בַּשַּׁבָּת, וְשָׁכַח וּמָל אֶת שֶׁל אֶחָד בְּשַׁבָּת בַּשַּׁבָּת, דְּהַיְינוּ נַמִי טָעָה בִּדְבַר מִצְוָה וְלֹא עָשָׂה מִצְוָה, שֶׁעֲדַיִין לֹא הִגִּיעַ זְמַנּוֹ — פּוֹטֵר ר' יְהוֹשֻׁעַ. **דִּזְמַנּוֹ בָּהוּל.** שֶׁהָיָה טָרוּד לָמוּל אֶת שֶׁל שַׁבָּת, כְּדֵי שֶׁלֹּא יַעֲבוֹר זְמַנּוֹ. **אֲבָל הָכָא.** גַּבֵּי נִשּׂוּאִין, אֵין זְמַנּוֹ בָּהוּל, דְּאֵין זְמַן קָבוּעַ לַמִּצְוָה, וְה"ל לְמֵידַק. **תְּרוּמָה בְּעֶרֶב הַפֶּסַח** זְמַנּוֹ בָּהוּל. שֶׁלֹּא תִּשָּׂרֵף. **וְאִיבָּעֵית אֵימָא.** כּוּלָּהּ מַתְנִי' לָאו ר' מֵאִיר הִיא, אֶלָּא אֲפִילּוּ לְר"ש דְּמֵיקֵל הָכָא מוֹדֵי, וּכְגוֹן דְּחָלוּ כּוּלְּהוּ בְּבַת אַחַת. **דְּשָׁווּ אִינְהוּ.** שְׁנֵי הָאַחִין שָׁלִיחַ אֶחָד לְהוֹלִיךְ אֶת הַקִּדּוּשִׁין לִשְׁתֵּי אֲחָיוֹת, וְהֵן עָשׂוּ שָׁלִיחַ אֶחָד לְקַבֵּל קִדּוּשִׁין. **וּפָגַע שָׁלִיחַ בְּשָׁלִיחַ.** וְחָלוּ יַחַד זֶה עַל זֶה וְזֶה עַל זֶה, אִיסּוּר אֵשֶׁת אִישׁ, וְאִיסּוּר אֵשֶׁת אָח, וַאֲחוֹת אִשָּׁה. **אֶלָּא נִדּוֹת הֵיכִי מַצֵי מַשְׁכַּחַת לַהּ.** בְּבַ"א עִם קִדּוּשִׁין? אִי קִדּוּשִׁין קָדְמוּ לְנִדּוּת זֶה — הֲרֵי אֵשֶׁת אִישׁ וַאֲחוֹת אִשָּׁה וְאֵשֶׁת אָח קָדְמוּ, וְתוּ לָא אָתֵי נִדּוּת וְחָיֵיל. וְאִי נִדּוּת קָדֵים תּוּ לָא אָתֵי אִיסּוּר אַחֲרִינָא וְחָיֵיל. **אָמַר רַב עַמְרָם אָמְרֵי בֵּי רַב.** מַשְׁכַּחַת לָהּ ט"ז חַטָּאוֹת בְּאִיסּוּר בַּת אַחַת, בְּשׁוֹפְעוֹת מִתּוֹךְ י"ג שָׁנָה לְאַחַר י"ג. **לְאִחַיּוּבֵי אִינְהוּ.** כְּלוֹמַר: טַעַם זֶה כְּדֵי לְחַיֵּיב הַזְּכָרִים, שֶׁחָלוּ כּוּלָּן עֲלֵיהֶן בבת אחת, דִּבְהָהוּא יוֹמָא אָתוּ לִכְלַל עוֹנָשִׁין. **וּמִתּוֹךְ י"ב לְאַחַר י"ב לְאִיחַיּוּבֵי אִינְהִי.** שֶׁהָאִשָּׁה בָּאָה לִכְלַל עוֹנָשִׁין בַּת י"ב שָׁנָה וְיוֹם אֶחָד, וְהַזָּכָר לְי"ג וְיוֹם אֶחָד. וּמַשְׁכַּחַת לָהּ שֶׁנּוֹלְדוּ הַזְּכָרִים בְּאֶחָד בְּתִשְׁרֵי וְהַנְּקֵבוֹת בְּאֶחָד בְּתִשְׁרֵי לְשָׁנָה הַבָּאָה, וּבְיוֹם אֶחָד מַשְׁלִים י"ב לַנְּקֵבוֹת שֶׁהֵן י"ג לַזְּכָרִים. וּמָסְרוּ קִדּוּשִׁין שֶׁיָּחוּלוּ לְיוֹם הַמָּחֳרָת כְּשֶׁהֵן נַעֲשִׂין גְּדוֹלִים, דְּיוֹם אֶחָד בִּשְׁנַת י"ג בָּעֵינַן לַנְּקֵבוֹת, וְיוֹם אֶחָד בִּשְׁנַת י"ד לַזְּכָרִים. וְהִתְחִילוּ שׁוֹפְעוֹת בְּסוֹף י"ב לַלֵּידָה עַד לְמָחָר. וְאע"ג שֶׁהַנִּדּוּת קָדַם — לֹא הָיוּ הֵן אֲסוּרוֹת לְאֵלּוּ, לְפִי שֶׁאֵינָן בִּכְלַל מִצְוֹת, וְלֹא אֵלּוּ אֲסוּרִים בָּהֶן, לְפִי שֶׁאֵינָן בְּנֵי מִצְוֹת, נִמְלְאוּ הַקִּדּוּשִׁין וְאִיסּוּר עוֹנֶשׁ נִדּוּת חָל עֲלֵיהֶם כְּשֶׁחֲשֵׁכָה ר"ה שֶׁל י"ג לַנְּקֵבוֹת, שֶׁהִיא שְׁנַת י"ד לַזְּכָרִים. שֶׁהַקִּדּוּשִׁין וְהַנִּדּוּת קָדְמוּ לְגַדְלוּתָן, וּתְלוּיִן וְעוֹמְדִין לָחוּל כְּשֶׁיִּגְדְּלוּ, וּבְשָׁעָה אַחַת חָלוּ כּוּלָּן. וּלְהָכִי נָקַט שׁוֹפְעוֹת, דְּאִי אֶפְשָׁר לְנַמְלֵס פְּרִישַׁת נִדָּה וּתְפִיסַת קִדּוּשִׁין בְּשָׁעָה אַחַת, אא"כ קָדְמוּ שָׁעָה אַחַת בְּקַטְנוּתָן. תְּלָתִין וְתַרְתֵּין הָוְיָין. דְּהָא מַתְנִיתִין כְּר' אֱלִיעֶזֶר אוֹקְמִינַן לְעֵיל, וְשָׁמְעִינַן לֵיהּ דְּאָמַר: חַיָּיב עַל כָּל בִּיאָה וּבִיאָה, לְקַמָּן (דף נג.) וּבְמַסֶּכֶת כְּרֵיתוֹת (דף טו.). **עַל כָּל כֹּחַ וְכֹחַ.** שֶׁל בִּיאָה, לְקַמָּן בְּפֶרֶק "הָאִשָּׁה" (דף נג.), וְהָתָם הָכִי תַּנְיָא: בָּא עָלֶיהָ, חָזַר וּבָא עָלֶיהָ — חַיָּיב עַל כָּל אַחַת, דִּבְרֵי רַבִּי אֱלִיעֶזֶר. וְכֵיוָן דְּשָׁמְעִינַן לֵיהּ לְרַבִּי אֱלִיעֶזֶר דִּמְחַיֵּיב אַשְּׁתֵּי בִּיאוֹת בְּהֶעְלֵם אַחַת — עַל כָּרְחָךְ שָׁמְעַתְּ לֵיהּ נַמִי בְּבִיאָה אַחַת כַּמָּה חִיּוּבִין, דְּכָל כֹּחַ וָכֹחַ — הֲנָאָה שֶׁל בִּיאָה בִּפְנֵי עַצְמָהּ הִיא. וּלְרַבָּנַן הוּא דְּלָא מְחַיֵּיב אֶלָּא אַחַת מִשּׁוּם דְּכוּלָּן בְּהֶעְלֵם אַחַת הֵן. וּבִשְׁתֵּי בִיאוֹת נַמִי לָא הָווּ מִיחַיְּיבֵי אֶלָּא חֲדָא. אֲבָל אִי הֲוָה יְדִיעָה בֵּין כֹּחַ לְכֹחַ — הֲוָה מְחַיֵּיב אַכָּל חַד וְחַד, כִּדְתְנַן בִּשְׁבוּעוֹת (דף יד:) וּבְמַסֶּכֶת (ב) הוֹרָיוֹת *(דף ו): הָיָה מְשַׁמֵּשׁ עִם הַטְּהוֹרָה וְאָמְרָה לוֹ נִטְמֵאתִי, וּפֵירַשׁ מִיָּד — חַיָּיב, שֶׁיְּצִיאָתוֹ הֲנָאָה לוֹ כְּבִיאָתוֹ, וּלְרַ' אֱלִיעֶזֶר דְּאָמַר בִּיאוֹת מְחַלְּקוֹת — אִית לֵיהּ נַמִי כּוֹחוֹת מְחַלְּקִין. וּמַתְנִי' כְּרַבִּי אֱלִיעֶזֶר אוֹקִימְנָא לְעֵיל, וְהֵיכִי תָּנֵי רַבִּי חִיָּיא שֵׁשׁ עֶשְׂרֵה וְתוּ לָא. וְהָא

תוספות

אם היתה שבת והוציאו כו'. בפרק "אמרו לו" (כריתות דף יד.) רצה לדקדק מכאן דאין עירוב והוצאה ליום הכפורים, מדאיצטריך למנקט אם היתה שבת כו', דהוה ליה למיתני: ואם הוציאו — חייב. ומסיק — דיש עירוב והוצאה ליוה"כ, ולאפוקי חיובי נקט שבת, וחייב משום שבת ויוה"כ. וא"ת: והיכי חשיב רבי מאיר חיובי הוצאה בהדי חיובי דאכילה? מה ענין זה אצל זה! דכמו כן היה יכול לומר אם עשה מלאכה בשבת חייב! ואר"י: משום דבשעת בליעה אתי נמי חיוב הוצאה, אע"ג דאכתי לא נח, משום דבליעתן זו היא הנחתן. כדאמר רבא בפרק "המוציא יין" (שבת דף פ.): הוציא ב' אותיות וכתבן כשהוא מהלך — חייב, דכתיבתן זו היא הנחתן*.

והוציאו בפיו חייב. והא דאמר ב"המצניע" (שם דף צב.) המוציא בפיו ובמרפקו פטור, שלא הוציא כדרך המוציאים — במידי דבר אכילה הוי שפיר דרך הוצאה בכך. פי' הקונטרס דאיכא הכא איסור בת אחת, דכשקידש היום חל עליו איסור אכילת יוה"כ ואיסור הוצאת שבת. וקשיא לרבינו יצחק: דמה ענין זה לאיסור חל על איסור? דאפילו למ"ד אין איסור חל על איסור אפילו בבת אחת — הכא חל לכולי עלמא אפילו בזה אחר זה, ואפי' יעשה אכילה והוצאה בזה אחר זה, ואפילו חלו שבת ויום הכפורים בזה אחר זה, שבשביל איסור מלאכת שבת אם הוא תחלה — לא ימנע איסור אכילת יום הכפורים לחול אחריו, שעדיין לא נאסר זה מחמת השבת, וכן איפכא! ואמר רבי יצחק: דאיסור בבת אחת היינו איסור הוצאה דשבת ואיסור הוצאה דיוה"כ, כדפרישית, דנקט שבת לאפוקי חיובי.

טעה בדבר מצוה פטור. וא"ת: והא בפסחים בפרק "אלו דברים" (דף עב. ושם) מוקי רבי מאיר פלוגתייהו בשתי תינוקות, אחד למול בשבת ואחד למול באחד בשבת, דפטר ר' יהושע כשקדם ומל של אחד בשבת בשבת אע"ג דלא עשה מצוה, משום דנתנה שבת לדחות אצל תינוק אחד. אבל בשתי תינוקות, אחד למול בשבת ואחד למול בע"ש, וקדם ומל של שבת בע"ש ושל ע"ש מל בשבת — חייב, אע"ג דעשה מצוה, משום דלא נתנה לדחות. וה"נ גבי שתי נשים — לחייב, דלא ניתנה ערוה לדחות! וי"ל: דהתם לא בדחיה תליא מילתא, אלא משום דטריד בתינוק שיש לו למול בשבת, וטועה בו. וה"נ — הרי טועה באשתו.

בערב הפסח כו'. המ"ל משום דאכילת תרומה איקרי עבודה וטעמא דרבי יהושע משום דכתיב(ג) "ופועל ידיו תרצה" — אפילו חללים, כדאמר פרק "אלו דברים" (פסחים דף עב: ושם).

באיסור בת אחת ואליבא דרבי שמעון. ואתי שפיר אפילו כרבי יהושע. דרבי שמעון אית ליה בפרק "אלו דברים" (שם) דלרבי יהושע טעה בדבר מצוה ולא עשה מצוה — חייב.

מתוך שלשה עשר לאחר שלשה עשר לאיחיובי אינהו. כן גירסת הקונטרס. וקשה: דלא הוי בבת אחת, דנדות חל

מסורת הש"ס

[נ"ל דרתנן]

תרומות פ"ח מ"א פסחים עב: מכות יח:

[פסחים עב:]

[עי' תוספות ב"מ עח: ד"ה כגון]

[ליתא [שם] ועי' ש"פ ב"ה מ"ה בפי' המשניות להרמב"ם

שבת קב. שבועות כד: כריתות יג:

[ועי' תוספות כריתות יד. ד"ה אם ותוספות שבת יא. ד"ה לא יעמוד ותוס' ערובין כ. ד"ה לא]

עין משפט נר מצוה

מד א מיי' פ"ד מהל' שגגות הלכה א:

מה ב מיי' פ"ו שם הלכה ד:

מו ג ד מיי' שם פ"ב הלכה ח:

מז ה מיי' פ"י מהל' תרומות הלכה יב:

תוספות ישנים

ומאן האי תנא דאית ליה איסור כולל ואיסור מוסיף ואיסור בת אחת א"ר יהודה אמר רב ר"מ היא. ה"נ הוי מצי למימר רבי יוסי היא דאית ליה איסור כולל וכ"ש דאית ליה איסור מוסיף ואיסור בת אחת אלא נקט רבי מאיר משום דאית ליה בהדיא כל הני יחד כולל ומוסיף ובת אחת:

הגהות הב"ח

(א) רש"י ד"ה ומאן וכו' דכשקידש ראובן: (ב) ד"ה על כל כח וכו' ובמסכת כריתות היה משמש: (ג) תוספות ד"ה בערב וכו' משום דכתיב ברך ה' חילו ופועל ידיו:

הגהות הגר"א

[א] גמ' (ואלא הא כו' עד דביאה ראשונה קחשיב) תא"מ:

מח א מיי' פכ"א מהל' איסורי ביאה הלכה יח סמג לאוין קכו טור ש"ע אה"ע סימן כג סעיף א:
מט ב מיי' פ"ה מהל' אבות הטומאה הלכה ט:
נ ג מיי' שם הלכה י:
נא ד מיי' פי"א מהל' גירושין הלכה כב סמג עשין נ טור ש"ע אה"ע סימן יג סעיף ו:
נב ה מיי' שם והלכה כ טוש"ע אה"ע שם סעיף א:

תורה אור

•וְהָא תָּמָר בְּבִיאָה רִאשׁוֹנָה אִיעַבְּרָא! א"ל: תָּמָר •בְּאֶצְבַּע מָעֲכָה. דְּאָמַר רַבִּי יִצְחָק: כָּל מוֹעֲכוֹת שֶׁל בֵּית רַבִּי תָּמָר שְׁמָן, וְלָמָּה נִקְרָא שְׁמָן תָּמָר? ע"ש תָּמָר שֶׁמָּעֲכָה בְּאֶצְבָּעָהּ. — וְהָא הָווּ עֵר וְאוֹנָן! — עֵר וְאוֹנָן שִׁמְּשׁוּ שֶׁלֹּא כְּדַרְכָּן. מֵיתִיבֵי: כָּל עֶשְׂרִים וְאַרְבָּעָה חֹדֶשׁ דָּשׁ מִבִּפְנִים וְזוֹרֶה מִבַּחוּץ, דִּבְרֵי רַ' אֱלִיעֶזֶר. א"ל: אהַלָּלוּ אֵינוֹ אֶלָּא כְּמַעֲשֵׂה עֵר וְאוֹנָן! — כְּמַעֲשֵׂה עֵר וְאוֹנָן, וְלֹא כְּמַעֲשֵׂה עֵר וְאוֹנָן. כְּמַעֲשֵׂה עֵר וְאוֹנָן — דִּכְתִיב °"וְהָיָה אִם בָּא אֶל אֵשֶׁת אָחִיו וְשִׁחֵת אַרְצָה", וְלֹא כְּמַעֲשֵׂה עֵר וְאוֹנָן, דְּאִילּוּ הָתָם — שֶׁלֹּא כְּדַרְכָּהּ, וְהָכָא — כְּדַרְכָּהּ. (בראשית לח) בִּשְׁלָמָא אוֹנָן — דִּכְתִיב בֵּיהּ "וְשִׁחֵת אַרְצָה", אֶלָּא עֵר מְנָלַן? — אָמַר רַב נַחְמָן בַּר יִצְחָק: דִּכְתִיב °"וַיָּמֶת גַּם אוֹתוֹ", אַף הוּא בְּאוֹתוֹ מִיתָה מֵת. (שם) בִּשְׁלָמָא אוֹנָן — מִשּׁוּם "לֹא לוֹ יִהְיֶה הַזָּרַע", אֶלָּא עֵר מ"ט עֲבַד הָכִי? — כְּדֵי שֶׁלֹּא תִּתְעַבֵּר וְיַכְחִישׁ יָפְיָהּ. ת"ר: °"אוֹתָהּ" פְּרָט לְכַלָּה, דִּבְרֵי רַבִּי יְהוּדָה. (ויקרא טו) וְחכ"א: בפְּרָט לְשֶׁלֹּא כְּדַרְכָּהּ. אֲמַר לֵיהּ הוֹן בְּרֵיהּ דְּרַב נַחְמָן לְרַב נַחְמָן: לֵימָא קָא סָבַר רַבִּי יְהוּדָה הַתּוֹרָה חָסָה עַל תַּכְשִׁיטֵי כַלָּה? — אֲמַר לֵיהּ: לְפִי שֶׁאֵין אִשָּׁה מִתְעַבֶּרֶת מִבִּיאָה רִאשׁוֹנָה. בְּמַאי קָמִיפַּלְגִי? רַבָּנַן סָבְרִי "שִׁכְבַת זֶרַע" פְּרָט גלְהַעֲרָאָה, "אוֹתָהּ" פְּרָט לְשֶׁלֹּא כְּדַרְכָּהּ. וְרַבִּי יְהוּדָה סָבַר: שֶׁלֹּא כְּדַרְכָּהּ וְהַעֲרָאָה — מִ"שִּׁכְבַת זֶרַע" נָפְקָא, "אוֹתָהּ" פְּרָט לְכַלָּה. כִּי אֲתָא *רָבִין א"ר יוֹחָנָן: כָּל שֶׁשָּׁהֲתָה אַחַר בַּעֲלָהּ עֶשֶׂר שָׁנִים וְנִשֵּׂאת — שׁוּב אֵינָהּ יוֹלֶדֶת. אָמַר רַב נַחְמָן: לֹא שָׁנוּ אֶלָּא שֶׁאֵין דַּעְתָּהּ לְהִנָּשֵׂא, •אֲבָל דַּעְתָּהּ לְהִנָּשֵׂא — מִתְעַבֶּרֶת. אֲמַר לֵיהּ רָבָא לְבַת רַב חִסְדָּא: קָא מְרַנְּנֵי רַבָּנַן אֲבַתְרִיךְ. — אֲמָרָה לֵיהּ: אֲנָא דַּעְתַּאי עִלָּוָךְ הֲוַאי. הַהִיא דַּאֲתְיָא לְקַמֵּיהּ דְּרַב יוֹסֵף, אָמְרָה לוֹ: רַ', אֲנָא שֶׁהָיִיתִי אַחַר בַּעֲלִי עֶשֶׂר שָׁנִים וְיָלַדְתִּי. — א"ל: בִּתִּי, אַל תּוֹצִיאִי לַעַז עַל דִּבְרֵי חֲכָמִים. — אָמְרָה לֵיהּ: לְגוֹי נִבְעַלְתִּי. אָמַר שְׁמוּאֵל: וְכוּלָּן צְרִיכוֹת לְהַמְתִּין שְׁלֹשָׁה חֳדָשִׁים, חוּץ מִגִּיּוֹרֶת וּמְשׁוּחְרֶרֶת קְטַנָּה. אֲבָל קְטַנָּה בַּת יִשְׂרָאֵל — צְרִיכָה לְהַמְתִּין ג' חֳדָשִׁים. וּבְמַאי? אִי בְּמֵיאוּן — וְהָאָמַר שְׁמוּאֵל דְּלָא בָּעְיָא. וְאִי בְּגֵט — הָאָמְרָהּ שְׁמוּאֵל חֲדָא זִימְנָא. דְּאָמַר שְׁמוּאֵל: *ד מֵיאֲנָה בּוֹ — אֵינָהּ צְרִיכָה לְהַמְתִּין שְׁלֹשָׁה חֳדָשִׁים, הנָתַן לָהּ גֵּט — צְרִיכָה לְהַמְתִּין שְׁלֹשָׁה חֳדָשִׁים! — אֶלָּא בִּזְנוּת. וְגָזְרוּ

רש"י

וְהָא תָּמָר אִיעַבְּרָא בְּבִיאָה רִאשׁוֹנָה. מִיהוּדָה, כִּדְאָמַר לְקַמָּן דְּעֵר וְאוֹנָן שֶׁלֹּא כְּדַרְכָּן שִׁמְּשׁוּ. בְּאֶצְבַּע מִיעֲכָה. קוֹדֶם בִּיאָה, וּפִתְחָהּ פָּתוּחַ, וְהָווּ לֵיהּ כְּבִ' בִּיאוֹת. כָּל מוֹעֲכוֹת שֶׁל בֵּית רַבִּי. הַמְשִׁירוֹת בְּתוּלֵיהֶן בְּאֶצְבְּעוֹתֵיהֶן תָּמָר שְׁמָן. כָּל כ"ד חֹדֶשׁ. שֶׁתִּינוֹק יוֹנֵק. דָּשׁ מִבִּפְנִים וְזוֹרֶה מִבַּחוּץ. כְּדֵי שֶׁלֹּא תִּתְעַבֵּר, וְתִגְמוֹל אֶת בְּנָהּ, וְיָמוּת. אֶלָּא כְּמַעֲשֵׂה עֵר וְאוֹנָן. אַלְמָא, תָּמָר פֶּתַח פָּתוּחַ הָיָה לָהּ. אוֹתָהּ. "וְאִשָּׁה (כִּי) [אֲשֶׁר] יִשְׁכַּב אִישׁ אוֹתָהּ שִׁכְבַת זֶרַע וְרָחֲצוּ בַמַּיִם", "אוֹתָהּ" מִיעוּטָא הוּא. פְּרָט לְכַלָּה. דְּלָא בָּעְיָא טְבִילָה מִשּׁוּם טוּמְאַת בִּיאָה רִאשׁוֹנָה, כִּדְמְפָרֵשׁ טַעְמָא לְקַמָּן. הוֹן. שֵׁם חָכָם. עַל תַּכְשִׁיטֵי כַלָּה. כְּחָל וּשְׂרָק שֶׁנּוֹתֶנֶת עַל פָּנֶיהָ, וְאִם תִּטְבּוֹל יַעֲבִירוּם הַמַּיִם. לְפִי שֶׁאֵין אִשָּׁה מִתְעַבֶּרֶת מִבִּיאָה רִאשׁוֹנָה. וְלָא "שִׁכְבַת זֶרַע" קָרֵינַן בֵּיהּ, דְּאֵין רָאוּי לְהַזְרִיעַ. וּמִיהוּ, מִיעוּטָא מִ"שִּׁכְבַת זֶרַע" לָא נָפְקָא, הוֹאִיל וְהַאי מָקוֹם רָאוּי לְהַזְרִיעַ הוּא בְּבִיאָה שְׁנִיָּה. וּמִשּׁוּם נוֹגֵעַ בְּשִׁכְבַת זֶרַע נַמִי לָא מִיטַּמְּיָא, דְּטוּמְאַת בֵּית הַסְּתָרִים לָא מְטַמְּאָה, אֶלָּא שֶׁגְּזֵרַת הַכָּתוּב הִיא בְּבִיאָה, וְכֵן הוּא בְּמַסֶּכֶת נִדָּה (דף מא:). לְהַעֲרָאָה. שֶׁלֹּא הִזְרִיעַ, אִי לְמ"ד נְשִׁיקָה, אִי לְמ"ד הַכְנָסַת עֲטָרָה. שֶׁלֹּא כְּדַרְכָּהּ וְהַעֲרָאָה מִשִּׁ"ז נָפְקָא. שֶׁלֹּא כְּדַרְכָּהּ אֵינוֹ מְקוֹם זֶרַע, הַעֲרָאָה — לָאו שִׁכְבַת זֶרַע הוּא, דְּאֵין כָּאן זֶרַע. הִלְכָּךְ תַּרְוַיְיהוּ מִ"שִּׁכְבַת זֶרַע" מִימְעֲטִי. לְבַת רַב חִסְדָּא. אִשְׁתּוֹ דְּרָבָא. אַבַּתְרִיךְ. שֶׁשָּׁהִית עֶשֶׂר שָׁנִים אַחַר בַּעֲלֵיךְ הָרִאשׁוֹן, וְרָמֵי בַּר חָמָא הֲוָה. אָמַר שְׁמוּאֵל וְכוּלָּן. הַנָּשִׁים שֶׁנִּבְעֲלוּ. צְרִיכוֹת לְהַמְתִּין. מִלְּהִנָּשֵׂא שְׁלֹשָׁה חֳדָשִׁים אַחַר בִּיאָתָן, חוּץ מִגִּיּוֹרֶת וּמְשׁוּחְרֶרֶת קְטַנָּה, וְאַע"ג דִּסְתָם גּוֹיוֹת וְשִׁפְחָה זוֹנוֹת הֵן — לֹא גָּזְרוּ רַבָּנַן בִּקְטַנָּה לְהַמְתִּין אַחַר טְבִילַת גִּיּוֹרֶת וּמְשׁוּחְרֶרֶת כְּלוּם. וּמִדְּקָאָמַר שְׁמוּאֵל חוּץ מִגִּיּוֹרֶת קְטַנָּה — מִכְּלָל דְּכוּלָּן דְּקָאָמַר אַקְּטַנּוֹת נַמִי קָאֵי, דִּקְטַנָּה בַּת יִשְׂרָאֵל צְרִיכָה לְהַמְתִּין. וְאַע"ג דְּלָאו בַּת בָּנִים הִיא, וְאֵין כָּאן הַבְחָנָה בֵּין זַרְעוֹ שֶׁל רִאשׁוֹן לְזַרְעוֹ שֶׁל שֵׁנִי — גְּזוּר בָּהּ רַבָּנַן מִשּׁוּם גְּדוֹלָה. וּבְמַאי. נָפְקָא מִבַּעְלָהּ קַמָּא. אִי בְּמֵיאוּן הָאָמַר שְׁמוּאֵל דְּלָא בָּעְיָא. אַמְּתוּנֵי, דְּלֵיכָּא לְמִיגְזַר מִשּׁוּם גְּדוֹלָה דְּאֵין גְּדוֹלָה יוֹצֵאת בְּמֵיאוּן. וְגָזְרוּ

תוספות

חל עליו תחלה שאין יכול לקדש ולא לעשות שליח עד שיגדיל, דאין מעשה קטן כלום. ואר"ת: דבכל ספרים קדמונים כן, (א) אבל בספר "בשר על גבי גחלים" גרס בשופעות מתוך ג' לאחר ג' לאיתויי אינהו, דלאחר ג' שנים ויום אחד חזיא לביאה, ואתו כולהו איסורי וחיילי. ומתוך י"ב לאחר י"ב לאיתויי אינהו. ואם בעלו כשכולן בגדלות איכא ט"ז חטאות, ודין לגירסת הקונטרס ודין לגירסא זו שופעות לאו דוקא, אלא שראתה ולא טבלה בינתים. ולגירסת ר"ת שראתה בתוך ג' ולא טבלה עד לאחר י"ב. **ולא** כמעשה ער ואונן דאילו התם שלא כדרכה. משמע דאסור לשמש שלא כדרכה. ותימה: דבפ"ב דנדרים (דף כ:) אמר: ההיא דאתיא לקמיה דרבי ואמרה ליה שולחן ערכתי לו והפכו, אמר לה: בתי, התורה התירתך לו. ומסיק דהלכתא הכי. והפכו – היינו שלא כדרכה, לפי שמצטערת בכך, שנא' (בראשית לד) "וישכב אותה ויענה" שעינה אותה שלא כדרכה. וכן "אם תענה את בנותי" (שם לא) שלא כדרכן. דאי הפכו היא למעלה והוא למטה – לא היתה קובלת על כך. וכן בפ' "ארבע מיתות" (סנהדרין דף נח:) אמר: גוי הבא על אשתו שלא כדרכה – חייב מיתה. ופריך: מי איכא מידי דישראל לא מיחייב וגוי מיחייב? (ב) והיינו האי לא מחייב היינו דבישראל שרי. דאי איכא איסור בישראל – ניחא דמחייב בגוי מיתה, דאזהרתן זו היא מיתתן כמו בגזל ושאר דברים! ואר"י: דהתם מיירי בלא הוצאת זרע, דשרי, דכיון דליכא השחתת זרע לא הוי כמעשה ער ואונן. עוד אמר ר"י: דלא חשוב כמעשה ער ואונן אלא כשמתכוין להשחית זרע, ורגיל לעשות כן תמיד. אבל באקראי בעלמא, ומתאוה לבא על אשתו שלא כדרכה – שרי, כדאמרי' בנדרים (דף כ:): כל מה שאדם רוצה לעשות באשתו יעשה, משל לבשר הבא מן הטבח, ודג מן הציד, רצה – אוכלו צלי, רצה – אוכלו מבושל, רצה – שלוק. **התורה** חסה על תכשיטי כלה. שלא יפול שרק מעל פניה אע"ג דמיד שתעמוד תפלוט ותצטרך לטבול – מ"מ נימא שהתורה חסה כל זמן שלא תעמוד, או שתתן מוך קודם שתעמוד, כדי שלא תפלוט. **דעתאי** עלך הואי. אמר רבינו תם: משום ההיא עובדא דפ"ק דב"ב (דף יב:), דאמרה בת רב חסדא: תרווייהו קבעינא, והיתה מצפה שתתקיים נבואתה. לפי שהיה לרבא אשה אחרת איחרה לינשא לו, ואפ"ה היתה מצפה לו. **אמר** שמואל וכולן צריכות כו'. אכל נשים דתנן ב"החולץ" (לקמן דף מא.) ובברייתא התם בגמר' (דף מג:) קאי. **אבל** קטנה בת ישראל צריכה להמתין. דגזרינן זנות דקטנה בת ישראל אטו גדולה. אבל בגיורת קטנה לא שייך למגזר אטו גיורת גדולה, דגדולה גופה כיון דדעתה לאיגיורי מינטרא נפשה, כדאמר לקמן, ולא אסירא אלא אטו בת ישראל. וא"ת: ושמואל דאמר כמאן? בשלמא בקטנה בת ישראל – סבר לה כר"מ, דגזר ב"החולץ" (שם דף מג:) בברייתא דרדופה קטנה בנישואין אטו גדולה, וקסבר שמואל דה"ה בזנות. אלא בגיורת, כמאן סבר לה? אי כר' יהודה – אפילו גיורת קטנה לגזור, כדתניא בסמוך: הגיורת והשפחה כו', יתירות על בנות שלש שנים, צריכות להמתין שלשה חדשים, דברי ר"י. ואע"פ דהכא ברוב ספרים לא גרסי' יתירות על בנות שלש שנים, בפרק "אלו נערות" (כתובות דף לז.) גרסינן לה בכל הספרים. ואי כרבי יוסי – אפילו גדולה נמי תשתרי, דר' יוסי שרי אפילו בגיורת גדולה לינשא מיד. דהא באידך לישנא דשמואל דשרי גדולה אמרי' הוא דאמר כרבי יוסי. ועוד: דסברת שמואל הפוכה מדר' יהודה, דהא בברייתא דרדופה לא גזר ר"י בקטנה בת ישראל אפילו בנישואין, ובגיורת גזר אפילו בקטנה, כדקתני: יתירות על בנות ג', ושמואל איפכא: דבקטנה בת ישראל גזר ובגיורת לא גזר. ומיהו, לספרים דגרסי בברייתא דרדופה רבי יוסי ולא רבי יהודה אתי שפיר. ולקמן *נמי נפרש בע"ה. ואר"י: דל"ג בשמעתין יתירות, ובתוספתא ליתיה. ובגדולה דוקא אסר ר"י, אבל בקטנה שרי ושמואל כרבי יהודה סבירא ליה בגיורת.

נתן לה גט צריכה להמתין. הקשה ה"ר משה כהן: הא אמרה שמואל חדא זימנא בפרק "אע"פ" (כתובות דף ס: ושם), דפסיק שמואל הלכה כרבי מאיר בגזירותיו אברייתא דרדופה! ואר"י: דעיקר מילתיה דשמואל לא איצטריך הכא אלא משום ממאנת, ועיקר מילתיה דשמואל דהכא בסוף "אלמנה" בכתובות (דף ק: ושם). והא דפריך עלה התם: כולהו תנינא, ומשני: צריכה להמתין שלשה חדשים איצטריך ליה, דלא תנן – הכי פירושו: דין דשלשה חדשים איצטריך ליה. אבל היא גופה לא איצטריך אלא משום ממאנת, דאין צריכה להמתין, כדפרישית.

חוץ

תוספות חד מקמאי

אמר רב נחמן אמר שמואל כל שנשתהה עשר שנים אחר בעלה ונשאת שוב אין נתעברת. ולא אמרן אלא שאין דעתה להנשא אבל דעתה להנשא מתעברת:

[עי' תוס' סוטה כז. ד"ה שאינה]

גליון הש"ס

גמ' והא תמר. עיין פי' רש"י בחומש בראשית יט לו ובר"ח שם בשם מדרש רבה: **שם** באצבע מיעכה. עיין לקמן עו ע"א תד"ה שלא ראה: **שם** אבל דעתה להנשא. עיין כתובות דף סב ע"ב ברש"י ד"ה איעקרה.

הגהות הב"ח

(א) תוס' ד"ה בעל מתוך וכו' דבכל ספרי קדמונים כן אבל בספר נ"ב מ"א וכן בספר כו (ב) ד"ה ולא וכו' ועוד כוכבים מיחייב ועל כרך האי לא מיחייב:

[כתובות ק:]

[דף מב. ד"ה רבי יוסי]

וְגָזְרוּ רַבָּנַן קְטַנָּה מִשּׁוּם גְּדוֹלָה. — וּמִי גָּזְרִינַן קְטַנָּה מִשּׁוּם גְּדוֹלָה? וְהָתְנַן: *[א]אִם הָיוּ קְטַנּוֹת שֶׁאֵינָן רְאוּיוֹת לֵילֵד — מַחֲזִירִין אוֹתָן מִיָּד! אָמַר רַב גִּידֵּל אָמַר רַב: הוֹרָאַת שָׁעָה הָיְתָה. — מִכְּלָל דַּהֲוַאי?! אֶלָּא כְּהוֹרָאַת שָׁעָה הָיְתָה, וְחִילּוּף לָא שְׁכִיחַ. לִישָּׁנָא אַחֲרִינָא אָמְרִי לָהּ, אָמַר שְׁמוּאֵל: כּוּלָּן צְרִיכוֹת לְהַמְתִּין שְׁלֹשָׁה חֳדָשִׁים, חוּץ מִגִּיּוֹרֶת וּמְשׁוּחְרֶרֶת גְּדוֹלָה. [אֲבָל] קְטַנָּה בַּת יִשְׂרָאֵל — אֵינָהּ צְרִיכָה לְהַמְתִּין ג' חֳדָשִׁים. בְּמַאי? אִי בְּמֵיאוּן — הָאֲמָרָהּ שְׁמוּאֵל חֲדָא זִימְנָא, אִי בְּגֵט — הָא קָאָמַר שְׁמוּאֵל דְּבָעְיָא, דְּאָמַר שְׁמוּאֵל: מֵיאֲנָה בּוֹ — אֵינָהּ צְרִיכָה לְהַמְתִּין שְׁלֹשָׁה חֳדָשִׁים, נָתַן לָהּ גֵּט — צְרִיכָה לְהַמְתִּין שְׁלֹשָׁה חֳדָשִׁים! — אֶלָּא בִּזְנוּת, וּזְנוּת בִּקְטַנָּה לָא שְׁכִיחַ. — גִּיּוֹרֶת וּמְשׁוּחְרֶרֶת, דִּשְׁכִיחַ בְּהוּ זְנוּת, לִיגְזוֹר! — הוּא דְּאָמַר כְּרַבִּי יוֹסֵי. דְּתַנְיָא: *[ב]הַגִּיּוֹרֶת וְהַשְּׁבוּיָה וְהַשִּׁפְחָה שֶׁנִּפְדּוּ וְשֶׁנִּתְגַּיְּירוּ וְשֶׁנִּשְׁתַּחְרְרוּ — צְרִיכוֹת לְהַמְתִּין ג' חֳדָשִׁים, דִּבְרֵי רַבִּי יְהוּדָה. רַבִּי יוֹסֵי מַתִּיר לֵיאָרֵס וְלִינָּשֵׂא מִיָּד. אָמַר רַבָּה: מ"ט דְּרַבִּי יוֹסֵי — קָסָבַר: אִשָּׁה מְזַנָּה מְשַׁמֶּשֶׁת בְּמוֹךְ כְּדֵי שֶׁלֹּא תִּתְעַבֵּר. א"ל אַבַּיֵי: בִּשְׁלָמָא גִּיּוֹרֶת, כֵּיוָן דְּדַעְתָּהּ לְאִיגַּיּוּרֵי — מְנַטְּרָה נַפְשָׁהּ. כְּדֵי לְהַבְחִין בֵּין זֶרַע שֶׁנִּזְרַע בִּקְדוּשָּׁה וּבֵין זֶרַע שֶׁנִּזְרַע שֶׁלֹּא בִּקְדוּשָּׁה. שְׁבוּיָה וְשִׁפְחָה נַמִי, דְּשָׁמְעֵי מִמָּרַיְיהוּ וּמְנַטְּרֵי נַפְשַׁיְיהוּ. אֶלָּא יוֹצֵאת בְּשֵׁן וָעַיִן — הֵיכִי מַשְׁכַּחַתְּ לָהּ? וְכִי תֵּימָא: כָּל דְּמִמֵּילָא מוֹדֶה רַ' יוֹסֵי — *וְהָתְנַן: אֲנוּסָה וּמְפוּתָּה צְרִיכָה לְהַמְתִּין ג' חֳדָשִׁים, דִּבְרֵי רַ' יְהוּדָה. רַבִּי יוֹסֵי [ג]מַתִּיר לֵיאָרֵס וְלִינָּשֵׂא מִיָּד! — אֶלָּא אָמַר *אַבַּיֵי: אִשָּׁה מְזַנָּה מִתְהַפֶּכֶת, שֶׁלֹּא תִּתְעַבֵּר. — וְאִידָךְ: חָיְישִׁינַן שֶׁמָּא לֹא נִתְהַפְּכָה יָפֶה יָפֶה.§

"וְאִם הָיוּ כֹּהֲנוֹת כו'".§ כֹּהֲנוֹת — אִין, יִשְׂרְאֵלִית — לָא?! אֵימָא: אִם הָיוּ נְשֵׁי כֹּהֲנִים. — נְשֵׁי כֹּהֲנִים — אִין, נְשֵׁי יִשְׂרְאֵלִים — לָא? *וְהָאָמַר *רַב עַמְרָם: הָא מִילְּתָא אֲמַר לָן רַב שֵׁשֶׁת, וְאַנְהֲרִינְהוּ לְעַיְינִין מִמַּתְנִיתִין: [ד]אֵשֶׁת יִשְׂרָאֵל שֶׁנֶּאֶנְסָה, אַף עַל פִּי שֶׁמּוּתֶּרֶת לְבַעְלָהּ — פְּסוּלָה לִכְהוּנָּה! — אָמַר רָבָא, הָכִי קָאָמַר: [ה]אִם הָיוּ כֹּהֲנוֹת נְשׂוּאוֹת לְיִשְׂרָאֵל — נִפְסְלוּ מִן הַתְּרוּמָה דְּבֵי נְשַׁיְיהוּ.§

הדרן עלך ארבעה אחין

רש"י

וְגָזְרוּ רַבָּנַן קְטַנָּה וכו'. וְגַבֵּי גִּיּוֹרֶת קְטַנָּה לֹא גְּזוּר, מִשּׁוּם דְּלָא שְׁכִיחָא. **מִכְּלָל דַּהֲוַאי.** בִּתְמִיָּה: וְכִי מַעֲשֶׂה כָּזֶה אֵירַע בִּימֵי חֲכָמִים? וְהָא שְׁנַיִם שֶׁקִּידְּשׁוּ קָתָנֵי, וְלָא תָּנֵי מַעֲשֶׂה. **אֶלָּא כְּהוֹרָאַת שָׁעָה הָיְתָה.** (א) וְלֹא הָיְתָה, דְּלָא גָּזְרִינַן בָּהּ, מ"ט — חִילּוּף לָא שְׁכִיחַ. **חוּץ מִגִּיּוֹרֶת וּמְשׁוּחְרֶרֶת גְּדוֹלָה.** מִדְּקָתָנֵי בְּהַאי חוּץ גְּדוֹלָה, מִכְּלָל דִּצְרִיכוֹת לְהַמְתִּין דְּקָאָמַר — בִּגְדוֹלוֹת קָמַיְירֵי. **גִּיּוֹרֶת וּמְשׁוּחְרֶרֶת גְּדוֹלָה דִּשְׁכִיחָא** בְּהוּ זְנוּת לִגְזוֹר. **שֶׁיַּמְתִּינוּ,** כְּדֵי לְהַבְחִין בֵּין זֶרַע שֶׁנִּזְרַע שֶׁלֹּא בִּקְדוּשָּׁה לְזֶרַע שֶׁנִּזְרַע בִּקְדוּשָּׁה. **הוּא דְּאָמַר כְּרַבִּי יוֹסֵי.** דְּלָא גָּזַר. דִּמְפָרֵשׁ טַעְמָא, דְּאִשָּׁה מְזַנָּה מִתְהַפֶּכֶת כְּדֵי שֶׁלֹּא תִּתְעַבֵּר. וּמִיהוּ, בְּיִשְׂרְאֵלִית גָּזַר שְׁמוּאֵל זְנוּת אַטּוּ נְשׂוּאִין שֶׁמִּתְעַבֶּרֶת, וְלֹא סָבַר כְּר' יוֹסֵי דְּלָא גָּזַר בְּהוּ, כִּדְאָמַר לְקַמָּן בַּאֲנוּסָה וּמְפוּתָּה, אֲבָל בְּגִיּוֹרֶת לֹא גְּזוּר זְנוּת שֶׁבְּנָכְרִית מִשּׁוּם נְשׂוּאִין דְּנָכְרִית. דַּאֲפִילּוּ גִּיּוֹרֶת נְשׂוּאָה, כֵּיוָן דְּדַעְתָּהּ לְאִיגַּיּוּרֵי — מִתְהַפֶּכֶת נַמִי, כְּדֵי לְהַבְחִין בֵּין זֶרַע קְדוּשָּׁה לְזֶרַע שֶׁלֹּא בִּקְדוּשָּׁה כִּדְלְקַמָּן. **מְנַטְּרָא נַפְשָׁהּ.** וּמַמְטְיָא מוֹךְ בַּהֲדָהּ, וּמְזוּמָּן לָהּ. **אֶלָּא יוֹצְאָה בְּשֵׁן וָעַיִן.** דְּלָא הֲוַת יָדְעָה מֵעִיקָּרָא דַּעֲתִידָה לְהִשְׁתַּחְרֵר, לָא מִיטַּרְחָא וּמִזְדַּהֲרָא לְאַתּוּיֵי מוֹךְ בַּהֲדָהּ. **אֲנוּסָה וּמְפוּתָּה.** יִשְׂרְאֵלִית. וַהֲרֵי אוֹנֶס מִמֵּילָא הוּא, וְאֵין לָהּ מוֹךְ. **מִתְהַפֶּכֶת.** וְאַף יוֹצְאָה בְּשֵׁן וָעַיִן נַמִי לֵיכָּא הַשְׁתָּא לְמִפְרַךְ, דְּכֵיוָן דְּהִיפּוּךְ קַל הוּא לָהּ וְאֵין בּוֹ טוֹרַח — מִתְהַפֶּכֶת הִיא, דְּכָל אִשָּׁה מְזַנָּה אֵינָהּ רוֹצָה לְהִתְעַבֵּר. **כֹּהֲנוֹת.** בְּנוֹת כֹּהֲנִים. **יִשְׂרְאֵלִית לָא.** בִּתְמִיָּה: הוֹאִיל וְאֵשֶׁת כֹּהֵן הִיא, אֲפִילּוּ בַּת יִשְׂרָאֵל נַמִי אֲסוּרָה לְבַעְלָהּ כֹּהֵן! **נְשֵׁי כֹּהֲנִים.** אִם בַּעֲלֵיהֶן כֹּהֲנִים נִפְסְלוּ לָהֶן, דְּאֵשֶׁת כֹּהֵן שֶׁנֶּאֶנְסָה אֲסוּרָה לְבַעְלָהּ. **נְשֵׁי יִשְׂרְאֵלִים לָא.** בִּתְמִיָּה: וְכִי אִם בַּעֲלֵיהֶם שֶׁל אֵלּוּ יִשְׂרְאֵלִים — מִי לָא מִיפַּסְלוּ נַמִי לִכְהוּנָּה? שֶׁאִם יָמוּתוּ אֵלּוּ — לֹא יִנָּשְׂאוּ לְכֹהֲנִים. **וְהָאָמַר רַב עַמְרָם כו' וְאַנְהֲרִינְהוּ** לְעַיְינִין מִמַּתְנִיתִין. כְּלוֹמַר: הֵבִיא לָנוּ רְאָיָה מִמִּשְׁנָתֵנוּ. וְאוֹתָהּ מִשְׁנָה לְקַמָּן בְּ"הַבָּא עַל יְבִמְתּוֹ" (דף נו.). **אֵשֶׁת יִשְׂרָאֵל שֶׁנֶּאֶנְסָה אַף עַל פִּי שֶׁמּוּתֶּרֶת** לְבַעְלָהּ. מִ"וְהִיא לֹא נִתְפָּשָׂה" (במדבר ה), הָא נִתְפְּשָׂה מוּתֶּרֶת, אַפ"ה — פְּסוּלָה לִכְהוּנָּה אִם יָמוּת בַּעְלָהּ. **אִם הָיוּ כֹּהֲנוֹת.** בְּנוֹת כֹּהֲנִים, וַאֲפִילּוּ נְשׂוּאוֹת לְיִשְׂרָאֵל. דְּלָא מְהַנֵּי הַאי זְנוּת לְאָסְרָן לְבַעֲלֵיהֶן. **נִפְסְלוּ מִתְּרוּמָה דְּבֵי נְשַׁיְיהוּ.** שֶׁאִם יָמוּת בַּעְלָהּ וְזֶרַע אֵין לָהּ — אֵינָהּ שָׁבָה אֶל בֵּית אָבִיהָ כִּנְעוּרֶיהָ, דְּפָסֵיל לָהּ הַאי זְנוּת, כִּדְתַנְיָא לְקַמָּן בְּ"אַלְמָנָה לְכֹהֵן גָּדוֹל" (דף סח.): כֹּהֶנֶת לְוִיָּה וְיִשְׂרְאֵלִית שֶׁבָּא עָלֶיהָ גֵּר עַמּוֹנִי כו', וְיָלֵיף טַעְמָא מִ"וּבַת כֹּהֵן כִּי תִהְיֶה לְאִישׁ זָר", כֵּיוָן שֶׁנִּבְעֲלָה לְפָסוּל לָהּ — פְּסָלָהּ. וְאַע"ג דְּמוֹתְבִינַן: וְאֵימָא נִבְעֲלָה לְפָסוּל חַיָּיבֵי כְּרֵיתוֹת? וּמְשַׁנֵּינַן: "כִּי תִהְיֶה" כְּתִיב, הָנָךְ דְּאִית בְּהוּ הֲוָיָיה, אַלְמָא זְנוּת דְּחַיָּיבֵי כְּרֵיתוֹת לָא פָּסֵיל מֵאֲכִילַת תְּרוּמָה — הָא הֲדַר מַיְיתִינָא הָתָם קְרָא אַחֲרִינָא "כִּי תִהְיֶה אַלְמָנָה וּגְרוּשָׁה" — לְמַעוּטֵי כּוּתִי וְעֶבֶד שֶׁאֵין לוֹ אַלְמָנוּת וְגֵירוּשִׁין בָּהּ, וּמֵהַהוּא קְרָא נַמִי נָפְקָא לָן חַיָּיבֵי כְּרֵיתוֹת, דְּהָא אֵין לוֹ אַלְמָנוּת וְגֵירוּשִׁין בָּהּ. וּמֵעִיקָּרָא פָּרְכִינַן הָכִי. וְאֵימָא חַיָּיבֵי כְּרֵיתוֹת וְלֹא חַיָּיבֵי לָאוִין.

הדרן עלך ארבעה אחין

תוספות

חוץ מגיורת ושפחה משוחררת גדולה. והא דתניא ב"החולץ" (לקמן דף מב.) לפיכך גר וגיורת צריכין להמתין שלשה חדשים – כר' יהודה אתיא, דחייש שמא לא נתהפכה יפה יפה. א"נ, אפילו כרבי יוסי, וה"ק: לפיכך גר וגיורת צריכין להמתין, אם ידוע שנבעלה ולא נתהפכה. ועוד אר"י, דיש לחלק: דלא מינטרא נפשה כלל – כשמתגיירת עם בעלה, כיון שכל הזרע מאותו איש ואין חוששת להבחין בין זרע שנזרע מבעלה זה בקדושה לשלא נזרע בקדושה.

גיורת ומשוחררת דשכיחא (ב) לגזור. פירוש: לגזור שיהיו צריכות להמתין. ולא לגזור אטו בת ישראל קאמר, דמהא לא הוה משני מידי.

אשה מזנה מתהפכת. וכן גיורת ומשוחררת, כיון דדעתה לאיגיורי. אבל יוצאה בשן ועין – מודה בה רבי יוסי.

כהנות אין ישראלית לא. ובכתובות (דף נא.), גבי הא דתנן: ובכהנת אהדרינתיך למדינתיך, לא דייק הכי. אלא דוקא הכא, משום דכי משני אימא נשי כהנים – אכתי אית ליה פירכא אחריתי: נשי כהנים – אין, נשי ישראלים – לא.

אע"פ שמותרת לבעלה פסולה לכהונה. פי' בקונט': טעמא דשמעתין משום "ובת כהן כי תהיה לאיש זר". ולר"י נראה דמ"בת איש כהן" לא שמעינן אשת איש וכל חייבי כריתות הנאסרות ע"י קדושין, משום דלא הוי זר אלא מעיקרא. והכי משמע ב"הבא על יבמתו" (לקמן דף נו:) דקאמר רבא: אשת כהן שנאנסה ובא עליה – לוקה משום זונה ומשום טומאה. ואי מ"בת כהן כי תהיה לאיש זר" שמעינן נמי אשת איש, א"כ יהא לוקה נמי מהאי קרא, דלכהונה נמי אסורות מק"ו דלקמן בפרק "אלמנה" (דף סח: ושם) דלא חשיב לה התם אזהרה מן הדין, אלא גילוי מלתא בעלמא הוא. וה"נ משמע כן קצת מדקאמר: אף על פי שמותרת לבעלה – פסולה לכהונה. ואי פסולה מקרא דבת כהן – פשיטא, דאין לחלק בין אונס לרצון. ואי היא גופה אתא לאשמועינן דשייך קרא דבת כהן בחייבי כריתות דע"י קדושין, כיון דשייך בהו ממזרות, אע"ג דלא הוי זר אלא מעיקרא – אם כן לישמעינן הכי בהדיא וממילא ידענו דלא שייך בהאי קרא לפלוגי בין אונס לרצון באשת איש טפי מבשאר [פסולי כהונה]. אלא (ג) לר"י נראה דפסולה מן הכהונה מטעם טומאה וזונה, כדאמר ב"הבא על יבמתו" (לקמן דף נו: ושם). וללישנא דאמר התם דכל באונס לא מיקריא זונה – פסולה לכהונה משום טומאה גרידא. ומיהו, קשה לר"י: (ד) כיון דלא חשיב טומאה אאשת ישראל שנבעלה באונס, דכתיב "והיא לא נתפשה", הא נתפשה מותרת, אם כן, אמאי פסולה לכהונה? דבכלל איסור טומאה הוי בעל ובועל ותרומה וגם כהונה, וכי שרי לבעלה – תשתרי נמי לכהונה! ואמר ר"י: דההוא קרא ד"לא נתפשה" לא מיירי אלא בטומאה דבעל גרידא, דנטמאה קמא אית לן לאוקמי לבעל, ולענין בעל שרי אונס בישראל. אבל ונטמאה בתרא, דנפקא לן מינה איסור תרומה וכהונה – לא מפליג בה בין אונס לרצון. בין אשת כהן לאשת ישראל, ויש לאסור בכל ענין. דכיון דאשכחן באשת כהן דאפילו באונס – אסורה – אין לנו לחלק בין אונס לרצון לענין תרומה וכהונה אפילו באשת ישראל. ומיהו, גבי בועל אע"ג דלא כתיב ביה "לא נתפשה" יש לחלק בין אונס לרצון באשת ישראל, דסברא הוא דלא נאסרה על הבועל. אלא כשנאסרה על הבעל. ולפי פר"י אין פסולה זונה לתרומה מקרא ד"בת כהן", אלא שמא מטעם דכלליה קרא בהדי חללה – פסולה לתרומה כמו חללה, ובפרק "החולץ" (לקמן דף מד: ד"ה הכא) כתב ר"י מזה:

הדרן עלך ארבעה אחין

עין משפט נר מצוה

נג א מיי' פי"א מהל' גירושין הלכ"ג סמג עשין נ טוש"ע אה"ע סימן יג סעיף ח:

נד ב מיי' שם הלכה כה טוש"ע אה"ע שם סעיף ה:

נה ג מיי' שם הלכה כב טוש"ע שם סעיף ו:

נו ד מיי' פי"ח מהלכות איסורי ביאה הלכה ז סמג לאוין קכח טוש"ע אה"ע סימן ו סעיף יא:

נז ה מיי' פ"ו מהלכות תרומות הל' ג והל' ו:

מסורת הש"ס

[לעיל לג:]

כתובות לו. כל הסוגיא ע"ש

[נ"ל והתניא]

[שם איתא רבה וכרב אלפס דהכא איתא רבא]

[לקמן נו.]

הגהות הב"ח

(א) רש"י ד"ה אלא היתה (ולא היתה) וכו' היתה (ולא היתה) תא"מ ונ"ב ס"א אין זה: (ב) תוס' ד"ה גיורת ומשוחררת דשכיחא בהו זנות לגזור: (ג) ד"ה אע"פ וכו' אלא נראה לר"י: (ד) באד"ה ומיהו קשה לר"י בר אברהם כיון דלא כתיב:

גליון הש"ס

גמ' והאמר רב עמרם. הא מילתא כעין זה לקמן דף נח ע"א ועי' ב"ב דף יג ע"ב: שם ואנהרינהו לעיינין. עיין לקמן דף ל ע"ב תד"ה היתה בת ישראל:

תוספות ישנים

אבל קטנה בת ישראל אינה צריכה להמתין. פי' מדקאמר חוץ מגיורת ומשוחררת גדולה משמע דהאי דקאמר דבת ישראל צריכה להמתין מיירי בגדולה מכלל אבל קטנה אינה צריכה להמתין [illegible] וכולן צריכות להמתין אפילו קטנות חוץ מגיורת ומשוחררת ואף גדולה אינה צריכה להמתין וי"ל דאי הכי [illegible] מיירי קודם לכן בקטנה [illegible]

מאנוסה ומפותה נימא כלמתרץ תלמודא דודאי מתהפכת היא שלא תתעבר ואין טורח גדול בדבר: **אע"פ** שמותרת לבעלה פסולה לכהונה דכתיב ובת איש כהן כי תהיה לאיש זר כיון שנבעלה לפסול לה פסלה. ואע"ג דאמרינן לקמן ואימא בחייבי כריתות אמר קרא כי תהיה בהנך דאית הויה ולא למעט חייבי כריתות אתא דגלי קרא (בזר) [דכי תהיה לאיש זר] הכא ובת כהן כי תהיה אלמנה וגרושה מי שיש לו אלמנות וגירושין בה ומחייבי כריתות לית בהו אלמנות וגירושין אלא ה"ק ואימא חייבי כריתות ולא חייבי לאוין אמר קרא כי תהיה וגו' לרבות חייבי לאוין:

תוספות חד מקמאי

אמר שמואל כולן צריכות להמתין שלשה חדשים חוץ מגיורת ומשוחררת גדולה וקטנה בת ישראל בזנות דזנות בקטנה [לא שכיח] אבל קטנה יוצאה בגט או במיאון צריכה להמתין שלשה חדשים [illegible] אין צריכה להמתין ג' חדשים ואף על גב דר"ס אנוסה ומפותה אינה צריכה להמתין ג' חדשים דאשה מזנה מתהפכת כדי שלא תתעבר וקי"ל דר' יהודה ור"י הלכה כר"י הכא כיון דקאי שמואל באנוסה ומפותה כוותיה דר' יהודה מסתברא דהלכה כותיה בהא ואע"ג דאמרינן בשלהי פרק אלמנה לכהן גדול בנשואין חששו לזנות לא חששו דמשמע [דהלכה] כר' יוסי לתרומה קא' אבל לא ליוחסין אבל הגיורת ומשוחררת גדולה ס"ל לשמואל דכיון דדעתה לאגיורי מנטרא נפשה בין זרע כשר לזרע פסול כך פרש"י ז"ל והראב"ד פי' דבגיורת ומשוחררת איכא תרי ספיקא ספק זינתה ספק לא זינתה ואת"ל זינתה שמא נתהפכה יפה יפה אבל באנוסה ומפותה ליכא למימר אלא חד ספק ולפום האי טעמא יוצאה במיאון צריכה להמתין ג' חדשים ומאי דאמר שמואל דאמר כר' יוסי סבר לה ס"ל כוותיה בחדא ופליג עליה בחדא ס"ל כוותיה בגיורת ומשוחררת גדולה ופליג עליה בחדא בבת ישראל ומסתברא דלית הלכתא לא כר' יהודה ולא כר"י אלא כשמואל וזה שלא כדברי הרב ז"ל ואף לדברי הרב אלפס בזנות הוא הלכה כר"א כל מן הנשואין כל הנשים אפי' קטנות ואפילו עקרות ואפילו איילונית לא ינשאו ולא יתארסו הגזרינן הא אטו הא. הא דתנן כהנות פסולות מן התרומה ה"ה לישראלית וה"ה לנשי ישראל דאשת ישראל שנאנסה אע"פ שמותרת לבעלה פסולה לכהונה אלא ה"ק אם היו

הַחוֹלֵץ [א]לִיבִמְתּוֹ וְנִמְצֵאת מְעוּבֶּרֶת. וְיָלְדָה. בִּזְמַן שֶׁהַוָּלָד שֶׁל קַיָּימָא – הוּא מוּתָּר בִּקְרוֹבוֹתֶיהָ וְהִיא מוּתֶּרֶת בִּקְרוֹבָיו, וְלֹא פְּסָלָהּ מִן הַכְּהוּנָּה. אֵין הַוָּלָד שֶׁל קַיָּימָא – הוּא אָסוּר בִּקְרוֹבוֹתֶיהָ וְהִיא אֲסוּרָה בִּקְרוֹבָיו, וּפְסָלָהּ מִן הַכְּהוּנָּה. [ב]הַכּוֹנֵס אֶת יְבִמְתּוֹ וְנִמְצֵאת מְעוּבֶּרֶת וְיָלְדָה, בִּזְמַן שֶׁהַוָּלָד שֶׁל קַיָּימָא – יוֹצִיא, [ג]וְחַיָּיבִין בְּקָרְבָּן. וְאִם אֵין וָלָד שֶׁל קַיָּימָא – יְקַיֵּים. *[ד]סָפֵק בֶּן תִּשְׁעָה לָרִאשׁוֹן, סָפֵק בֶּן שִׁבְעָה לָאַחֲרוֹן – יוֹצִיא, וְהַוָּלָד כָּשֵׁר, [ה]וְחַיָּיבִין בְּאָשָׁם תָּלוּי.§ **גמ'** אִיתְּמַר, הַחוֹלֵץ לִמְעוּבֶּרֶת וְהִפִּילָה. רַבִּי יוֹחָנָן אָמַר: אֵינָהּ צְרִיכָה חֲלִיצָה מִן הָאַחִין, ר"ל אָמַר: [ו]צְרִיכָה חֲלִיצָה מִן הָאַחִין. *ר' יוֹחָנָן אָמַר: א"צ חֲלִיצָה מִן הָאַחִין – חֲלִיצַת מְעוּבֶּרֶת שְׁמָהּ חֲלִיצָה, וּבִיאַת מְעוּבֶּרֶת שְׁמָהּ בִּיאָה. ור"ל אָמַר: צְרִיכָה חֲלִיצָה מִן הָאַחִין – חֲלִיצַת מְעוּבֶּרֶת לָא שְׁמָהּ חֲלִיצָה, [ז]וּבִיאַת מְעוּבֶּרֶת לָא שְׁמָהּ בִּיאָה. בְּמַאי קָמִפַּלְגִי? *אִיבָּעֵית אֵימָא קְרָא, וְאִיבָּעֵית אֵימָא סְבָרָא. (א) אִיבָּעֵית אֵימָא סְבָרָא, רַבִּי יוֹחָנָן סָבַר: אִם יָבֹא אֵלִיָּהוּ וְיֹאמַר דְּהָא דְּאִיעַבְּרָא מַפּוּלֵי מַפְּלָה – מִי לָאו בַּת חֲלִיצָה וְיִבּוּם הִיא? הַשְׁתָּא נַמִי, תִּגְלֵי מִילְּתָא לְמַפְרֵעַ. ור"ל אָמַר: תִּגְלֵי מִילְּתָא לְמַפְרֵעַ לָא אָמְרִינַן. וְאִיבָּעֵית אֵימָא קְרָא; רַבִּי יוֹחָנָן סָבַר °"וּבֵן אֵין לוֹ" אָמַר רַחֲמָנָא, (דברים כה) וְהָא לֵית לֵיהּ. ור"ל סָבַר: "וּבֵן אֵין לוֹ" *עַיֵּין עָלָיו. אֵיתִיבֵיהּ ר' יוֹחָנָן לר"ל: אֵין הַוָּלָד שֶׁל קַיָּימָא – הוּא אָסוּר בִּקְרוֹבוֹתֶיהָ, וְהִיא אֲסוּרָה בִּקְרוֹבָיו. וּפְסָלָהּ מִן הַכְּהוּנָּה. בִּשְׁלָמָא לְדִידִי, דְּאָמֵינָא חֲלִיצַת מְעוּבֶּרֶת שְׁמָהּ חֲלִיצָה – מִשּׁוּם הָכִי פְּסָלָהּ. אֶלָּא לְדִידָךְ, דְּאָמְרַתְּ חֲלִיצַת מְעוּבֶּרֶת לָא שְׁמָהּ חֲלִיצָה – אַמַּאי פְּסָלָהּ מִן הַכְּהוּנָּה? א"ל: מִדְּרַבָּנַן, וּלְחוּמְרָא בְּעָלְמָא. א"ד, אֵיתִיבֵיהּ רֵישׁ לָקִישׁ לְרַ' יוֹחָנָן: אֵין הַוָּלָד שֶׁל קַיָּימָא – הוּא אָסוּר בִּקְרוֹבוֹתֶיהָ, וְהִיא אֲסוּרָה בִּקְרוֹבָיו, וּפְסָלָהּ מִן הַכְּהוּנָּה. בִּשְׁלָמָא לְדִידִי, דְּאָמֵינָא חֲלִיצַת מְעוּבֶּרֶת לָא שְׁמָהּ חֲלִיצָה – הַיְינוּ דְּקָתָנֵי פְּסָלָהּ מִן הַכְּהוּנָּה לְחוּמְרָא, וְלָא קָתָנֵי: אֵינָהּ צְרִיכָה חֲלִיצָה מִן הָאַחִין. אֶלָּא לְדִידָךְ, אֵינָהּ צְרִיכָה חֲלִיצָה מִן הָאַחִין מִיבְּעֵי לֵיהּ! – א"ל: אִין הָכִי נַמִי, וְאַיְּידֵי דִּתְנָא רֵישָׁא לֹא פְּסָלָהּ – תְּנָא *סֵיפָא פְּסָלָהּ. אֵיתִיבֵיהּ רַבִּי יוֹחָנָן לר"ל: אֵין הַוָּלָד שֶׁל קַיָּימָא – יְקַיֵּים. בִּשְׁלָמָא לְדִידִי דְּאָמֵינָא חֲלִיצַת מְעוּבֶּרֶת שְׁמָהּ חֲלִיצָה וּבִיאַת מְעוּבֶּרֶת שְׁמָהּ בִּיאָה – מִשּׁוּם הָכִי קָתָנֵי יְקַיֵּים. אֶלָּא לְדִידָךְ, דְּאָמְרַתְּ חֲלִיצַת מְעוּבֶּרֶת לָא שְׁמָהּ חֲלִיצָה, וּבִיאַת מְעוּבֶּרֶת לָא שְׁמָהּ בִּיאָה – יַחֲזוֹר וְיִבְעוֹל וִיקַיֵּים מִיבְּעֵי לֵיהּ! – מַאי יְקַיֵּים – יַחֲזוֹר וְיִבְעוֹל וִיקַיֵּים, דְּלָא *סַגִּי. אִיכָּא דְּאָמְרִי, אֵיתִיבֵיהּ ר"ל לְרַבִּי יוֹחָנָן: אֵין הַוָּלָד שֶׁל קַיָּימָא – יְקַיֵּים. בִּשְׁלָמָא לְדִידִי, דְּאָמֵינָא חֲלִיצַת מְעוּבֶּרֶת לָא שְׁמָהּ חֲלִיצָה וּבִיאַת מְעוּבֶּרֶת לָא שְׁמָהּ בִּיאָה, הַיְינוּ דְּקָתָנֵי יְקַיֵּים – יַחֲזוֹר וְיִבְעוֹל וִיקַיֵּים, דְּלָא סַגִּי בְּלָאו הָכִי. אֶלָּא לְדִידָךְ, רָצָה – יוֹצִיא, רָצָה – יְקַיֵּים, מִיבְּעֵי לֵיהּ! – אה"נ, אַיְּידֵי דִּתְנָא רֵישָׁא יוֹצִיא – תְּנָא נַמִי סֵיפָא יְקַיֵּים. מֵיתִיבִי: הַכּוֹנֵס אֶת יְבִמְתּוֹ וְנִמְצֵאת מְעוּבֶּרֶת – הֲרֵי זוֹ לֹא תִּנָּשֵׂא צָרָתָהּ, שֶׁמָּא יְהֵא וָלָד בֶּן קַיָּימָא. אַדְּרַבָּה, כִּי הָוֵי הַוָּלָד בֶּן קַיָּימָא מִיפַּטְרָה צָרָתָהּ! אֶלָּא אֵימָא: שֶׁמָּא לֹא יְהֵא הַוָּלָד בֶּן קַיָּימָא. וְאִי ס"ד בִּיאַת מְעוּבֶּרֶת שְׁמָהּ בִּיאָה – אַמַּאי לֹא תִּנָּשֵׂא צָרָתָהּ? תִּיפָּטֵר בְּבִיאָה שֶׁל חֲבֵירְתָּהּ! אָמַר אַבַּיֵי: בְּבִיאָה – כּוּלֵּי עָלְמָא לָא פְּלִיגִי דְּלָא פָּטְרָה, כִּי פְּלִיגִי – בַּחֲלִיצָה. רַבִּי יוֹחָנָן סָבַר: חֲלִיצַת מְעוּבֶּרֶת שְׁמָהּ חֲלִיצָה, בִּיאַת מְעוּבֶּרֶת לָא שְׁמָהּ בִּיאָה. ר"ל סָבַר: בִּיאַת מְעוּבֶּרֶת – לָא שְׁמָהּ בִּיאָה, וַחֲלִיצַת מְעוּבֶּרֶת – לָא שְׁמָהּ חֲלִיצָה. אֲמַר לֵיהּ רָבָא: מַה נַּפְשָׁךְ: אִי בִּיאַת מְעוּבֶּרֶת שְׁמָהּ בִּיאָה – חֲלִיצַת מְעוּבֶּרֶת שְׁמָהּ חֲלִיצָה, וְאִי בִּיאַת מְעוּבֶּרֶת לָא שְׁמָהּ בִּיאָה – חֲלִיצַת מְעוּבֶּרֶת נַמִי לָא שְׁמָהּ חֲלִיצָה. דְּהָא קי"ל

דְּכָל

הַחוֹלֵץ הוּא מוּתָּר בִּקְרוֹבוֹתֶיהָ. דְּלָאו חֲלִיצָה הִיא, דְּהָא לָא בָּעְיָא. קְרוֹבוֹתֶיהָ וּקְרוֹבָיו. מְפָרֵשׁ לְקַמָּן בְּמַתְנִי' הָנָךְ דְּנֶאֱסָרוֹת עַל הָאִישׁ מֵחֲמַת אִשְׁתּוֹ, וּקְרוֹבָיו שֶׁנֶּאֱסָרִים עַל הָאִשָּׁה מֵחֲמַת בַּעְלָהּ. **אִם אֵין** הַוָּלָד שֶׁל קַיָּימָא. שֶׁהָיָה נֵפֶל. וְחַיָּיבִין בְּקָרְבָּן. שֶׁבָּעַל אֵשֶׁת אָח שֶׁלֹּא בִּמְקוֹם מִצְוָה. (תורה אור) הַוָּלָד כָּשֵׁר. מִמָּה נַפְשָׁךְ. **גמ'** אֵינָהּ צְרִיכָה חֲלִיצָה מִן הָאַחִין. דְּהָךְ חֲלִיצָה מַעַלְיָיתָא הִיא. שְׁמָהּ חֲלִיצָה. הֵיכָא דְּהִפִּילָה, דְּאִיגַּלַּאי מִילְּתָא דְּבַת חֲלִיצָה הֲוַאי. מִדְּרַבָּנַן **וּלְחוּמְרָא**. דִּלְמָא אָתֵי לְמִישְׁרֵי חֲלוּצָה לִכְהוּנָּה, דְּלָא יָדְעֵי דַּהֲוַאי מְעוּבֶּרֶת. הַיְינוּ דְּקָתָנֵי פְּסוּלָה **וּלְחוּמְרָא**. וְלָא קָתָנֵי בְּהֶדְיָא אֵין צְרִיכָה חֲלִיצָה מִן הָאַחִין. **אֶלָּא** לְדִידָךְ. דְּאָמְרַתְּ חֲלִיצָה מַעַלְיָיתָא הִיא, לִישְׁמְעִינַן הָא דְּאֵינָהּ צְרִיכָה חֲלִיצָה, וַאֲנָא יָדַעְנָא דַּאֲסוּרָה בִּקְרוֹבָיו וּפְסָלָהּ מִן הַכְּהוּנָּה. **וְאַיְּידֵי דִּתְנָא רֵישָׁא לֹא** פְּסָלָהּ. וְלָא תָּנָא חֲלִיצָה, דְּהָתָם לָא מָצֵי לְמֵימַר: וּצְרִיכָה חֲלִיצָה, תָּנָא נַמִי סֵיפָא פְּסָלָהּ, וְלָא אַיְירֵי בַּחֲלִיצָה. **אֵין** הַוָּלָד שֶׁל **קַיָּימָא** יְקַיֵּים. הַכּוֹנֵס יְבִמְתּוֹ וְנִמְצֵאת מְעוּבֶּרֶת. הַיְינוּ דְּקָתָנֵי יְקַיֵּים. דְּלָא מַצְרִיךְ בִּיאָה לְאַחַר שֶׁהִפִּילָה. וְאִם בָּא לְגָרְשָׁהּ בְּגֵט – מְגָרְשָׁהּ, דְּאִיפַּטְרָה לָהּ בְּבִיאָה קַמַּיְיתָא. וּבִיאַת מְעוּבֶּרֶת שְׁמָהּ בִּיאָה, דְּקס"ד יְקַיֵּים דְּקָתָנֵי מַתְנִי' לָאו חוֹבָה הִיא, אֶלָּא הֶתֵּירָא, מִשּׁוּם דִּתְנָא רֵישָׁא: אִם הַוָּלָד שֶׁל קַיָּימָא יוֹצִיא. דְּלָא סַגִּי בְּלא"ה. דְּלָא מִיפַּטְרָה בְּלֹא בִּיאָה לְאַחַר שֶׁהִפִּילָה. דְּאִם לֹא יַחֲזוֹר וְיִבְעוֹל לָא מָצֵי לְמִפְטְרָהּ בְּגֵט, דְּאֵין אָדָם יָכוֹל לְהוֹצִיא אֶת יְבִמְתּוֹ בְּגֵט אא"כ כְּנָסָהּ תְּחִלָּה, וּבִיאַת מְעוּבֶּרֶת לָאו שְׁמָהּ בִּיאָה. וּבַחֲלִיצָה נַמִי לָא אֶפְשָׁר לְמִפְטְרָהּ, הוֹאִיל וּמ"מ בָּא עָלֶיהָ. רָצָה **יוֹצִיא**. בְּגֵט, רָצָה יְקַיֵּים מִיבָּעֵי לֵיהּ. **אֶלָּא שֶׁמָּא לֹא יְהֵא** וָלָד שֶׁל **קַיָּימָא**. וְנִמְצֵאת זְקוּקָה לַיָּבָם, וּבִיאַת מְעוּבֶּרֶת לָא שְׁמָהּ בִּיאָה.

החולץ ליבמתו ונמצאת מעוברת. הא דלא נקט החולץ למעוברת כדנקט בגמ' – משום דרבותא היא, דאע"ג דלא היה עוברה ניכר בשעת חליצה, ונראית חליצה מעולה – אפילו הכי לא פסלה בזמן שהולד של קיימא. ובגמ' נקט נמי למעוברת לרבותא, דאע"פ שהוכר עוברה, כיון שהפילה – חליצה מעלייתא הויא. א"נ, נקט ונמצאת משום סיפא, דהתם לא מצי למיתני הכונס ליבמתו מעוברת – דא"כ מזיד הוא, ולא מיחייב קרבן, דלא שב מידיעתו הוא.

ונמצאת מעוברת. בחולץ תוך ג' חדשים איירי, דומיא דסיפא דהכונס יבמתו דאיירי תוך ג', דאי לאחר ג' – אמאי חייב קרבן? כיון דרוב נשים עוברן ניכר לשליש, וזו, הואיל ולא הוכר עוברה – מאי הוה ליה למיעבד? וכה"ג אמרינן בשבועות (דף יח. ושם): פרט לאנוס, גבי שלא בשעת וסתה. וא"ת: אם כן, אם אין הולד של קיימא, אמאי אסור בקרובותיה? דתוך שלשה חדשים לאו חליצה היא, דהא תנן לקמן: היבמה לא תחלוץ ולא תתייבם עד שיהיו לה ג' חדשים. ומפרש בגמ' טעמא, דכיון דאינה עולה ליבום – אינה עולה לחליצה! ואר"י: דנהי דלאו חליצה היא מ"מ אסור בקרובותיה, כיון דמדאורייתא הויא חליצה. [א] ועוד: דדיעבד, אם חלצה – אפילו מדרבנן אינה צריכה חליצה אחרת. דאמר לקמן: יבמה שחלצו לה אחין בתוך ג' – צריכה להמתין ג' חדשים, משמע דלא בעיא חליצה.

צריכה חליצה מן האחין. לאו דוקא מן האחין, דה"ה דלא פקעה זיקת החולץ[ב]. אי נמי: מן האחין של מת קאמר. **והא** לית ליה. כיון דהפילה לבסוף. אבל בר קיימא לא. א"נ, כשהוא בר קיימא נפקא לן מ"להקים שם" ומ"לא ימחה" – פרט לזה שאין שמו מחוי. **וריש** לקיש סבר בין אין לו עיין עליו. הואיל ובאותה שעה היה ראוי להתקיים. וא"ת: א"כ, תפטר לשוק בלא חליצה כמו בזרע פסול, דנפקא לן (לעיל דף כב:) נמי מ"אין לו", ואמאי נמי אמרינן לקמן דולד אינו פוטר עד שיצא לאויר העולם! ויש לומר, דאמרינן נמי: עיין עליו שלא תחלוץ ולא תנשא כל זמן שעומדת בספק. **תגלי** מילתא למפרע לא אמרינן. אע"ג דלקמן (דף מא:), גבי ספקות שקידש אחת משתי אחיות חשבינן לה בת חליצה ויבום, כיון דאם יבוא אליהו ויאמר דהא קדיש – לא דמי, דהכא אין זה ספק ראוי להתברר עכשיו, שא"א לידע העתידות. אבל התם א"ל לידע אלא מה שבאותה שעה. וא"ת: לריש לקיש הכונס יבמתו מעוברת והפילה, אמאי פטור מן הקרבן? כיון דביאת מעוברת לא שמה ביאה, א"כ אשת אח שלא במקום מצוה היא! ואר"י: דאפ"ה לא מחייב, מידי דהוה אקטן שבא על יבמתו גדולה, דאמר לקמן (דף לט) דתגדלנו.

רצה יוציא רצה יקיים מיבעיא ליה. והא דקתני לעיל גבי ד' אחין: ב"ש אומרים יקיימו, ולא קתני רצו – משום דהתם ליכא למיטעי. **הרי** זו לא תנשא צרתה. כ"ש היא שלא תנשא ושלא תבעל, אלא צרתה איצטריך, שלא תאמר תנשא ממה נפשך. **כולי** עלמא לא פליגי. הא דקאמר לעיל איתיביה הכונס יבמתו – להד"מ, וכה"ג איכא בפרק "המפלת" (נדה דף כד.) גבי פניו ממוסמסין, וכמה דוכתין*. **כי** פליגי בחליצה. ובביאה מודה, שלא יבא לידי איסור.

בשלמא

עין משפט נר מצוה

א א מיי' פ"א מהלכות יבום הלכה כ סמג עשין נא טוש"ע אה"ע סימן קסד סעיף ב:
ב ב מיי' שם הלכה כא טור ש"ע שם סעי' ה:
ג ג מיי' פ"א מהלכות שגגות הלכה א:
ד ד מיי' פ"א מהלכות יבום הלכה כג סמג עשין נא טוש"ע אה"ע סימן קסד סעיף ו:
ה ה מיי' פ"ח מהלכות שגגות הלכה א:
ו ו מיי' פ"א מהלכות יבום הלכה כ סמג שם טוש"ע אה"ע סימן קסד סעיף ב:
ז ז מיי' שם טור ש"ע שם סעיף ג:

תוספות ישנים

החולץ ליבמתו ונמצאת מעוברת. ומיירי שחלץ לה תוך שלשה חדשים דאי לאחר ג' חדשים לא מצי למימר לקמן בזמן שהולד של קיימא חייבין בקרבן שהרי אנוס הוא אחרי שעשה כתקנת חכמים אלא מיירי תוך שלשה חדשים ומזיד לא הוי דסבור הוא שאינה מעוברת ואע"ג דאמרינן היבמה לא תחלוץ ולא תתייבם עד שיעברו ג' חדשים מ"מ דיעבד שפיר דמי והכי נקט [בגמ'] החולץ למעוברת משום דאשמעינן רבותא דאע"ג דידע שפיר שהיא מעוברת קאמר ר' יוחנן דאינה צריכה חליצה מעולה.

תוספות חד מקמאי

היו כהניות נשואות לישראל פסולין לתרומה דבי נשייהו:
פ"ד איתמר החולץ למעוברת והפילה ר"י אומר אינה צריכה חליצה מן האחין ר"ל אמר צריכה חליצה מן האחים חליצת מעוברת לאו שמה חליצת והלכתא כר"ל ומודה ר"ל דפסולה לכהונה לחומרא ופסלה מן האחים וצרתה פסולה לו ולאחין ולחומרא כללא דמילתא חליצת מעוברת שהפילה לאו שמה חליצה לחומרא אבל החולץ למעוברת והולד בן קיימא תרוייהו מודו דלאו שמה חליצה כלל ולא פסלה מן הכהונה תניא הכונס את יבמתו ונמצאת מעוברת הרי זו לא תנשא צרתה [שמא] לא יהיה הולד בן קיימא וביאת מעוברת לאו שמה ביאה וא"ת הלך אחר רוב נשים ורוב נשים וולד של קיימא ילדן ולד אינו פוטר עד שיצא לאויר העולם והא דקתני רישא שמא לא יהא ולד של קיימא לאו דוקא שמא דבין יהא ולד של קיימא ובין לא יהא ולד של קיימא לא תנשא צרתה:

מסורת הש"ם

[כריתות יז:]
[לקמן מח:]
[ברכות ז: קדושין לה: ב"ב ח: ט. ע"ז לז: סנהדרין ל. שבועות כב: וע"ש בתוס' ד"ה אב"א זבחים ב. ז: מנחות ב. יג: עג: חולין קיח: תמורה ל:]
[לעיל כב: וש"נ ועי' מ"ש שם בשם הערוך והסמ"ע והתי"ט]
בדפו"י תנא נמי
[ועי' תוס' ב"ב קנד: ד"ה ברם ותוס' בכורות ז: ד"ה אלא]

הגהות הב"ח

(א) גמרא איבעית אימא קרא ואיבעית אימא סברא איבעית אימא קרא ר' יוחנן סבר ובן אין וכו' עיין עליו ואיבעית אימא סברא ר' יוחנן סבר אם יבא וכו' לא אמרי' איתיביה רבי יוחנן כל"ל:

הגהות הגר"א

[א] תום' ד"ה ונמצאת. ועוד דדיעבד כו'. נ"ב וג"ח הכל לכתחלה דדיעבד אף יבום מהני (עמ"ש רבינו באה"ע סי' קסד ס"ק ב') אלא דבירושלמי אמר בהדיא דצריך חליצה אחרת אבל גמרא דידן פליגא כמ"ש תוס' ועמש"ש בדברי הירושלמי (ע"ש בס"ק ה): [ב] שם ד"ה צריכה. א"נ מן האחין כו'. נ"ב וע"ל עט ב' במתני' (איילונית שחלצו לה אחין כ"כ רבינו להדיא באה"ע שם ס"ק ת' בכי"ק ונשמט בדפוס):

גליון הש"ס

תום' ד"ה תגלי מילתא וכו' דאמר לקמן דף לט וכו'. נ"ל דף קיא ע"ב:

*[א] דכל העולה ליבום עולה לחליצה, וכל שאין עולה ליבום – אינו עולה לחליצה! אלא אמר רבא, הכי קאמר: [ב] הכונס יבמתו ונמצאת מעוברת – הרי זו לא תנשא צרתה, שמא יהא ולד בן קיימא, וביאת מעוברת לא שמה ביאה, וחליצת מעוברת לא שמה חליצה, והולד אינו פוטר עד שיצא לאויר העולם. תניא כוותיה דרבא: הכונס יבמתו ונמצאת מעוברת – הרי זו לא תנשא צרתה, שמא יהא ולד בן קיימא, ואין ביאה וחליצה פוטרת, אלא ולד פוטר, והולד אין פוטרה עד שיצא לאויר העולם. טעמא – דשמא יהא ולד בן קיימא הוא, הא לא הוי ולד בן קיימא – מיפטר צרתה. לימא תיהוי תיובתא דר"ל! – אמר לך ר"ל, הכי קתני: הכונס יבמתו ונמצאת מעוברת – הרי זו לא תנשא צרתה, שמא לא יהא הולד בן קיימא, וחליצת מעוברת לא שמה חליצה, וביאת מעוברת לא שמה ביאה. וא"ת: הלך אחר רוב נשים, ורוב נשים ולד מעליא ילדן? – ולד אין פוטר עד שיצא לאויר העולם. א"ר אלעזר: אפשר, איתא להא דריש לקיש ולא תנן לה במתניתין?! – נפק, דק ואשכח, דתנן: *האשה שהלך בעלה וצרתה למדינת הים, ובאו ואמרו לה: "מת בעלך" – הרי זו לא תנשא ולא תתייבם, עד שתדע שמא מעוברת היא צרתה. בשלמא יבומי לא – שמא יהא ולד בן קיימא, ויפגע באיסור אשת אח דאורייתא. אלא לא תחלוץ, אמאי? בשלמא תחלוץ בתוך ט' ותנשא בתוך ט' – לא, היינו ספק. אלא תחלוץ בתוך תשעה, ותנשא לאחר תשעה! – ולטעמיך: תחלוץ ותנשא לאחר ט'! אלא: בר מינה דההיא, *דאביי בר *אבא ורב חיננא בר *אביי דאמרי תרוייהו: *שמא יהא ולד בן קיימא, ונמצא אתה מצריכה כרוז לכהונה. – ולצרכה! – דלמא איכא איניש דהוי בחליצה ולא הוי בהכרזה, ואתי למימר: קשרי חלוצה לכהן. א"ל אביי: מידי לא תחלוץ ולא תתייבם קתני? לא תנשא ולא תתייבם קתני, בלא חליצה, אבל אי חליץ לה – הכי נמי דשריא. תניא כוותיה דריש לקיש: [ג] החולץ למעוברת והפילה – צריכה חליצה מן האחין. *אמר רבא: *הלכתא כוותיה דר"ל בהני תלת: חדא – הא דאמרן. אידך – דתנן: *[ד] המחלק נכסיו על פיו, ריבה לאחד ומיעט לאחד, והשוה להם את הבכור – דבריו קיימין. ואם אמר משום ירושה – לא אמר כלום. כתב, בין בתחלה בין בסוף בין באמצע, משום מתנה – דבריו קיימין. ואמר

רש"י

דכל העולה לייבום כו'. דביאתה פוטרתה. **עולה לחליצה.** דכתיב (דברים כה) "אם לא יחפוץ האיש לקחת יבמתו (א) וחלצה" וכו'. **שמא יהא הולד של קיימא וביאת מעוברת.** בולד של קיימא לדברי הכל לא שמה ביאה, דטעמא דרבי יוחנן משום שמא יבא אליהו ויאמר נפל הואי, והכא ליכא למימר הכי. **והולד אין פוטר עד שיצא לאויר העולם. הא לא יהא ולד של קיימא.** דלמפרע בת יבום היא, הוה מיפטרא צרתה, ואין צריך לחזור ולבעול לאחר שהפילה. **אמר לך ר"ל הכי קתני.** כלומר, לא קתני שמא יהא, אלא שמא לא יהא. והאי דקתני סיפא ולד אינו פוטר כו', דמשמע דבשל קיימא מיירי – הכי קאמר: וא"ת, הלך אחר רוב נשים, ורוב נשים ולד מעליא ילדן, ונהי דביאתה לא פטרה, מיהו פטורה משום הולד – הולד אין פוטר עד שיצא לאויר העולם. **שהלך בעלה.** ואין לו בנים. **לא תנשא.** קס"ד אפילו ע"י חליצה קאמר, דלא תנשא לשוק לעולם. **היא צרתה.** אותה צרתה שהלכה עמו. אבל אי שמעה עליה שאינה מעוברת – תתייבם, ולא חיישינן שמא נשא בעלה אחרת במדינת הים. ולהכי תנן היא צרתה, והכי מפרש בפ' "האשה". **אלא לא תחלוץ.** ותנשא לשוק. **אמאי.** אי חליצת מעוברת שמה חליצה תחלוץ ממה נפשך, דבין צרתה מעוברת ובין אינה מעוברת – הרי חליצה פוטרתה. **בשלמא תחלוץ בתוך ג' ותנשא בתוך ג'.** שמת לא אפשר דהיינו ספק – דבן ט' לראשון או בן ז' לאחרון, דאפילו נשאת ב' ימים (ב) בתוך ג' חדשים וילדה בסוף ט' לבעל הראשון – אכתי איכא למימר שמא בן ז' לאחרון הוא. ואע"פ שאין אלא ו' חדשים וב' ימים, דקי"ל (ר"ה דף יא.): יולדת לז' יולדת למקוטעין. ואע"ג דהיא לאו ודאי מעוברת, דהא מדקתני שמא מעוברת צרתה, מכלל דאחר זמן מרובה שהלך בעלה למדינת הים קמיירי – לא פלוג רבנן בנשים, אלא כולן צריכות להמתין: א) **אלא תחלוץ בתוך ג' ותנשא לאחר** כו'. וקשה לי: היכי מצי לאותובי הכי? נהי נמי דחליצת מעוברת שמה חליצה, הני מילי – בנפל, אבל הכא – הא איכא למיחש שמא צרתה מעוברת בולד בן קיימא, ואין ביאה וחליצה פוטרת בה לדברי הכל, אלא ולד. והולד אין פוטר עד שיצא לאויר העולם! ונראה בעיני דה"ג: בשלמא תחלוץ בתוך ט' ותנשא בתוך ט' לא דהיינו ספק שמא יהא ולד צרתה בן קיימא, ואין ביאה וחליצה פוטרת אלא ולד, והולד אין פוטר עד שיצא לאויר העולם. ול"ג "אי בן ט' לראשון", ופירושו היה בספרים משובשים. אלא תחלוץ בתוך ט' ותנשא לאחר ט' ממה נפשך: אי מיעברא צרתה והפילה, או לא מעוברת הואי – הרי חלצה זו. ואי ולד של קיימא הוה – הרי יצא לאויר העולם. אלא לאו, משום שמא מעוברת צרתה היתה בשעת חליצה, ואין הולד של קיימא, והיא חליצה לא פטרה כר"ל, הואיל ואחת מהן מעוברת לא שייכא חליצה היא שעתא, דאמרינן עיין עליו. **ולטעמיך.** אי טעמא דלא תחלוץ משום ספק מעוברת צרתה בשעת חליצה היא – תחלוץ לאחר ט', דהשתא ודאי לאו מעוברת היא, ותנשא. ומ"ט קתני עד שתדע, ואפי' לסוף כמה שנים? **אלא בר מינה דההיא.** כלומר, מההיא לא תידוק סייעתא לר"ל. דהא דקתני לא תחלוץ בתוך ט' ותנשא לאחר ט', התם טעמא לאו משום ספק יבמה לשוק הוא, אלא כדאביי בר אבין כו'. **שמא יהא ולד.** צרתה. **בן קיימא.** ונמצא חליצתה שלא לצורך, וכשרה לכהונה. ומי שראה בחליצה מחזיקה כפסולה לכהונה, ואתה צריך להכריז: דעו שזו לא פסלתה חליצתה. **[א"ל] אביי מידי לא תחלוץ ולא תתייבם קתני.** דתידוק מינה סייעתא לר"ל? **לא תנשא** קתני. דלא תנשא לשוק בלא חליצה לסמוך ולומר צרתי ילדה לבעלי, אע"פ שרוב נשים יולדות. אבל אי חלצה, אפי' בתוך ט' – ה"נ דמשתריא לאחר ט'. דביאת מעוברת וחליצתה – שמה ביאה וחליצה. **על פיו.** אחרי דברי פיו, ולא בסתם ירושה בשתיקה. **ריבה לאחד ומיעט לאחד או שהשוה לו את הבכור דבריו קיימים.** דלכולן נתן בחייו, ואין כאן ירושה ליטול בכורה, ולא הפשוטים ליטול בשוה, אלא מה שריבה – ריבה, ומה שמיעט – מיעט. **ואם אמר משום ירושה.** פלוני יירש שדה פלונית, ופלוני שדה פלונית. **לא אמר כלום.** שהתנה על מה שכתוב בתורה, ותנאו בטל, הואיל ולא חילק לפשוטים בשוה, ולבכור פי שנים. **בתחלה.** תנתן שדה פלונית לפלוני ויירשנה. **באמצע.** יירשה ותנתן לו ויירשה. **בסוף.** יירשה ותנתן לו.

לעולם

תוספות

בשלמא בתוך ג' חדשים כו'. אין גירסא זו נכונה, כדפירש בקונטרס. ועוד: דאי אפשר כלל לדקדק מדאינה חולצת תוך ג' לינשא אחר ג', דחליצת מעוברת לא שמה חליצה. דהא ודאי תוך ג' מודה ר' יוחנן דאין חולצת, כדתנן: היבמה לא תחלוץ עד שיהיו לה ג' חדשים. וטעמא, משום דאינה עולה לייבום, דאפי' יבא אליהו ויאמר דלא מיעברא – לאו בת ייבום היא, ולכך אינה עולה לחליצה. אבל בתוך ט' – בת ייבום היא אם יבא אליהו ויאמר דלא מיעברא, או אפילו הפילה. לכך דייק שפיר, אלא ה"ג: תחלוץ בתוך ט' ותנשא לאחר ט'. **ותנשא** לאחר ט'. תימה: דלא מסיק אדעתיה האי ולטעמיך דפריך! **ונמצא** אתה מצריכה כרוז לכהונה. ודוקא בשאר נשים דלאו גרושות איירי. וכן מוקי לה בהדיא בפרק בתרא (לקמן קיט: וש"נ). והא דפריך לקמן (דף מא:) גבי והיבמה לא תחלוץ עד שיהא לה ג' חדשים, ומפרש בגמרא מעיקרא טעמא שמא יהא ולד של קיימא ונמצא מצריכה כרוז לכהונה, תינח אלמנה, גרושה מאי איכא למימר? אר"י: משום דהתם בא להשמיענו דין כל הנשים שנופלות לייבום, ואם היה דין אחר לגרושה – ה"ל לפרושי. אבל הכא, דאיירי אם אירע בו מעשה באשה שהלך בעלה וצרתה למדינת הים, איירי שפיר דוקא בשאר נשים דלאו גרושות. ועדיפא מינה בפרק בתרא, דמוקי ההיא ד"האשה שלום" דוקא בגרושה, דפריך מינה אההיא דמייתי הכא. **הלכתא** כר"ל בהני תלת. הא דפליגי בפרק ב' דחולין (דף כט: וש"נ) גבי ישנה שחיטה מתחלה ועד סוף – לא חשיב הכא, אע"ג דסבירא ליה כוותיה בפ' ב' דזבחים (דף ל. וש"נ) – היינו משום דר"ל משמיה דלוי סבא אמרה. ותימה, דלא חשיב הא דפ"ק דמסכת ע"ז (דף ו: וש"נ). דתניא כותיה דר"ל דנשא ונתן מותר, כיון דחשיב הכא מידי דתניא כוותיה! ואור"י: דמ"מ, התם הלכתא כר' יוחנן, דהתם, גבי הא דתנן וחכ"א לפניהם אסור לאחריהם מותר, פריך: חכמים היינו ת"ק! ומשני: נשא ונתן איכא בינייהו. ובפרק קמא דסנהדרין (דף טו: וש"נ) גבי זאב וארי, דתניא כוותיה דר"ל – התם פליגי אליבא דר"א ולא סבירא להו כוותיה*. **משום** ירושה לא אמר כלום. טעמא (ג) מפרש התם במתניתין: לפי שהתנה על מה שכתוב בתורה. ורבי יוחנן בן ברוקא פליג בפרק "יש נוחלין" (ב"ב קל.) ואמר: דאם אמר על מי שראוי ליורשו – דבריו קיימים. וטעמא מפרש התם, משום דכתיב "והיה ביום הנחילו את בניו" – התורה נתנה רשות לאב להנחיל לכל מי שירצה. והא דכתיב "לא יוכל לבכר" – היינו דוקא חלק בכורה, אבל חלק פשיטות – יכול. ורבנן – "ביום הנחילו את בניו" מוקמי לדרשא אחריתי, "ולא יוכל לבכר" איצטריך, משום דהורע כחו, שאין נוטל בראוי כבמוחזק, וס"ד דהורע כחו נמי בהא. א"נ איצטריך, דס"ד כיון דשנואה בנישואיה – דיכול לבכר.

ואמר

עין משפט נר מצוה

ח א מיי' פ"א מהלכות יבום הלכה יט:

ט ב מיי' פ"א שם הלכה כב סמג עשין נ טוש"ע אה"ע סימן קסד סעיף ג:

י ג מיי' שם הלכה כ טוש"ע שם סעיף ב:

יא ד מיי' פ"ו מהלכות נחלות הלכה ה סמג עשין נו טוש"ע ח"מ סימן רפא סעיף ז:

מסורת הש"ס

[לעיל ג. וש"נ]

לקמן קיט.

[לקמן קיט:]

נ"ל אבין

ב"ב קכט: חולין עז.

ב"ב קכו:

נ"ל אבין

[לקמן מח.]

[וע"ע תוס' ב"מ מח. ד"ה נתנה וכו' ותוס' ע"ז עא. ובכורות יג: ד"ה רב אשי]

[עי' תוס' שבת ע: סוף ד"ה נודע לו]

הגהות הב"ח

(א) רש"י ד"ה עולה לחליצה וכו' לקחת יבמתו ועלתה וגו' הא חפץ מייבם הס"ד: (ב) ד"ה לא אפשר וכו' ב' ימים בסוף ג' חדשים: (ג) תוס' ד"ה משום וכו' טעמא דמתני' מפרש התם לפי:

תוספות ישנים

א) **ועוד** דהו"ל לאתויי בהדיא הא דתנן לקמן לא תחלוץ עד שיעברו עליה ג' חדשים ולפרוך לר' יוחנן תחלוץ בתוך שלשה ותנשא לאחר שלשה. ונהי נמי דלקמן פריך לה הכי הכא הו"ל לאתויי ועוד מאי קאמר ולטעמיך תחלוץ לאחר ג' ותנשא וכו' היכי מצי להנשא לאחר ג' הא שמא צרתה מעוברת מולד בן קיימא ואין החליצה כלום ומשום ולד לא מפטר דולד אינו פוטר עד שיצא לאויר העולם:

תוספות חד מקמאי

תנן האשה שהלך בעלה למ"ה ובאו ואמרו לה מת בעלך ה"ז לא תנשא ולא תתיבם עד שתדע שמא מעוברת היא צרתה. בשלמא מייבם לא דלמא מעברא וקא פגע באיסור אשת אח דאורייתא אלא לא תנשא אמאי בשלמא חליצה בתוך ט' חדשים ונשואין בתוך ט' חדשים לא דהיינו ספיקא שמא יהיה הולד של קיימא ולד אינו פוטר עד שיצא לאויר העולם ותחלוץ בתוך ט' ותנשא לאחר ט' ואסיקנן שמא יהיה ולד של קיימא ונמצאת מצריכה כרוז לכהונה. ולפום האי טעמא אם היתה גרושה שפסולה לכהונה תחלוץ ותנשא לאחר ט' חדשים ודוקא לכתחלה הוא דחיישינן לכרוז אבל דיעבד לא דהא תנן החולץ ליבמתו ונמצאת מעוברת וילדה בזמן שהולד של קיימא הוא מותר בקרובותיה והיא מותרת בקרוביו ולא פסלה מן הכהונה אמר רבא הלכתא כותיה דר"ל בהני תלת ואיכא נמי אחריני בפ"ק דע"ז בנשא ונתן לפני אידיהם ר"י אמר אסור ר"ל אמר מותר ותניא כותיה דר"ל אלא באסור [לא] קמיירי אבל החולץ למעוברת מאי איסורא איכא בחליצה.

איתמר

יב א מיי' פ"ו מהלכות נחלות הלכה ו סמג עשין נו טוש"ע ח"מ סי' רפא סעיף ז:
יג ב מיי' פי"ב מהל' זכיה הלכה יג סמג עשין פב טוש"ע שם סי' רנז סעיף ה:
יד ג מיי' שם טוש"ע שם סעיף ג:
טו ד ה מיי' שם טוש"ע שם סעיף ה:
טז ו מיי' פי"א מהל' גירושין הלכה כה סמג עשין נ טוש"ע אה"ע סי' יג סעיף יא:
יז ז ח מיי' שם הלכה כח טוש"ע שם סעי' יב:
יח ט מיי' פ"א מהלכות מילה הל' יג (ופכ"ה מהל' שבת) ופ"א מהל' יבום הלכה ה ופי"ב מהל' רוצח הלכה ה ופ"א מהל' אבל הל' ו סמג עשין נא ועשין מד"ס ב טוש"ע יו"ד סי' שמ סעי' ל וסי' שעד סעיף ח וטוש"ע אה"ע סימן קנו סעיף ז:
[ועי' היטב תוס' ב"ק פח: ד"ה באושא ותוס' כתובות נ. ד"ה הכותב ותוס' ב"ב קנו: ד"ה ר"ין]
יט י מיי' פ"ב מהלכות יבום וחליצה הלכה כא סמג עשין נו טוש"ע אה"ע סי' קסד סעי' ז:
[נ"ל תניא ועי' תוספות חולין פז: ד"ה תנן וכן בעתיקי תוס' בכורות מט. ד"ה מת וכו' את הסוגיא דהכא ובזה"ל התם תניא רשב"ג אומר וכו']
[בשבת איתא שרביא]
עי' בהרא"ש

*אואמר ר"ל: לְעוֹלָם לֹא קָנָה עַד שֶׁיֹּאמַר "פְּלוֹנִי וּפְלוֹנִי יִרְשׁוּ שָׂדֶה פְּלוֹנִית וּפְלוֹנִית שֶׁנְּתַתִּים לָהֶם בְּמַתָּנָה וְיִרָשׁוּם". וְאִידָךְ — דִּתְנַן: *בהַכּוֹתֵב כָּל נְכָסָיו לִבְנוֹ לְאַחַר מוֹתוֹ, הָאָב אֵינוֹ יָכוֹל לִמְכּוֹר — מִפְּנֵי שֶׁנְּתָנָן לַבֵּן, וְהַבֵּן אֵינוֹ יָכוֹל לִמְכּוֹר — מִפְּנֵי שֶׁהֵן בִּרְשׁוּת הָאָב — גמָכַר הָאָב מְכוּרִין עַד שֶׁיָּמוּת הוּא. מָכַר הַבֵּן — אֵין לַלּוֹקֵחַ כְּלוּם עַד שֶׁיָּמוּת הָאָב. *וְאִיתְּמַר, מָכַר הַבֵּן בְּחַיֵּי הָאָב, וּמֵת הַבֵּן בְּחַיֵּי הָאָב, רַ' יוֹחָנָן אָמַר: לֹא קָנָה לוֹקֵחַ, וְרֵישׁ לָקִישׁ אָמַר: דקָנָה לוֹקֵחַ. רַ' יוֹחָנָן אָמַר: לֹא קָנָה לוֹקֵחַ, *קִנְיַן פֵּירוֹת כְּקִנְיַן הַגּוּף דָּמֵי. וְר"ל אָמַר: קָנָה לוֹקֵחַ, הקִנְיַן פֵּירוֹת לָאו כְּקִנְיַן הַגּוּף דָּמֵי.§ "אֵין הַוָּלָד שֶׁל קַיָּימָא כו'".§ תָּנָא: מִשּׁוּם רַבִּי אֱלִיעֶזֶר אָמְרוּ: יוֹצִיא בְּגֵט. אָמַר רָבָא: רַ' מֵאִיר וְרַ' אֱלִיעֶזֶר אָמְרוּ דָּבָר אֶחָד. רַבִּי אֱלִיעֶזֶר — הָא דַּאֲמָרַן, ר"מ — דְּתַנְיָא: *ולֹא יִשָּׂא אָדָם מְעוּבֶּרֶת חֲבֵירוֹ וּמֵינֶקֶת חֲבֵירוֹ, וְאִם נָשָׂא — יוֹצִיא, וְלֹא יַחֲזִיר עוֹלָמִית, דִּבְרֵי רַ' מֵאִיר. וַחֲכָמִים אוֹמְרִים: זיוֹצִיא, וְלִכְשֶׁיַּגִּיעַ זְמַנּוֹ לִכְנוֹס — יִכְנוֹס. א"ל אַבַּיֵי: מִמַּאי? דִּלְמָא לָא הִיא, עַד כָּאן לָא קָאָמַר רַ' אֱלִיעֶזֶר הָכָא — אֶלָּא מִשּׁוּם דְּקָפָגַע בְּאִיסּוּר אֵשֶׁת אָח דְּאוֹרַיְיתָא, אֲבָל הָתָם דְּרַבָּנַן — כְּרַבָּנַן סְבִירָא לֵיהּ. אִי נַמִי: עַד כָּאן לָא קָאָמַר רַבִּי מֵאִיר הָתָם — אֶלָּא מִשּׁוּם דְּרַבָּנַן, *וַחֲכָמִים עָשׂוּ חִיזּוּק לְדִבְרֵיהֶם יוֹתֵר מִשֶּׁל תּוֹרָה. אֲבָל הָכָא — מִדְּאוֹרַיְיתָא, מִפְרָשׁ פָּרְשִׁי מִינָּהּ. אָמַר רָבָא: וּלְדִבְרֵי חֲכָמִים חיוֹצִיאָהּ בְּגֵט. אָמַר מָר זוּטְרָא: דַּיְקָא נַמִי, דְּקָתָנֵי יוֹצִיא, וְלֹא קָתָנֵי יַפְרִישׁ, ש"מ. א"ל רַב אַשִׁי לְרַב הוֹשַׁעְיָא בְּרֵיהּ דְּרַב אִידִי: הָתָם *תְּנַן, *) רשב"ג אוֹמֵר: טכָּל שֶׁשָּׁהָא בְּאָדָם ל' יוֹם — אֵינוֹ נֵפֶל. הָא לֹא שָׁהָא — סְפֵיקָא הָוֵי. וְאִיתְּמַר, *מֵת בְּתוֹךְ ל' יוֹם, וְעָמְדָה וְנִתְקַדְּשָׁה. רָבִינָא מִשְּׁמֵיהּ דְּרָבָא אָמַר: יאִם אֵשֶׁת יִשְׂרָאֵל הִיא — חוֹלֶצֶת, וְאִם אֵשֶׁת כֹּהֵן הִיא — אֵינָהּ חוֹלֶצֶת. רַב *מְשַׁרְשְׁיָא מִשְּׁמֵיהּ דְּרָבָא אָמַר: אַחַת זוֹ וְאַחַת זוֹ חוֹלֶצֶת. אֲמַר לֵיהּ רָבִינָא לְרַב מְשַׁרְשְׁיָא: בְּאוֹרְתָא

*) שבת קלה: לקמן פ: נדה מד: [תוספתא דשבת פט"ז]

רש"י

לְעוֹלָם לֹא קָנָה כו'. לָאו אַמַּתְנִיתִין פָּלֵיג, אֶלָּא הָתָם בְּ"יֵשׁ נוֹחֲלִין" פְּלִיגִי אַמּוֹרָאֵי בְּדִיּוּקָא דְּמַתְנִי'. דְּכִי אֲתָא רָבִין אֲמַר: יָרַשׁ פְּלוֹנִי שָׂדֶה פְּלוֹנִי, וְתִנָּתֵן שָׂדֶה פְּלוֹנִי לִפְלוֹנִי, רַבִּי יוֹחָנָן אָמַר: קָנָה אֲפִילּוּ הַאי דִּירוּשָּׁה, דְּמִדְּאַדְכַּר לְשׁוֹן מַתָּנָה בְּהַאי שְׁטַר נְוָוֹה לְחַד מִינַּיְיהוּ — כּוּלְּהוּ נַמִי מַתָּנָה נִינְהוּ. וְר"ל אָמַר: לְעוֹלָם לֹא קָנָה הַהוּא דִּירוּשָּׁה, דְּאָמְרִינַן: לְהַאי הָוֵה מַתָּנָה וּלְהַאי יְרוּשָּׁה, עַד שֶׁיֹּאמַר כו', דְּתֵיקוּ לְשׁוֹן מַתָּנָה אַתַּרְוַיְיהוּ. לְאַחַר מוֹתוֹ. שֶׁכָּתַב: מֵהַיּוֹם וּלְאַחַר מִיתָה, וְאֵין לָאָב בָּהֶן אֶלָּא אֲכִילַת פֵּירוֹת בְּחַיָּיו. מָכַר הָאָב מְכוּרִין. לֶאֱכוֹל הַלּוֹקֵחַ פֵּירוֹת כָּל יְמֵי חַיֵּי הָאָב, שֶׁזָּכָה בִּזְכוּת שֶׁהָיָה לוֹ לָזֶה בָּהֶן. וּמֵת הַבֵּן בְּחַיֵּי הָאָב רַבִּי יוֹחָנָן אָמַר לֹא קָנָה לוֹקֵחַ. אֲפִילּוּ לִכְשֶׁיָּמוּת הָאָב. דְּקִנְיַן פֵּירוֹת שֶׁהָיָה לוֹ לָאָב בַּנְּכָסִים הַלָּלוּ כְּקִנְיַן הַגּוּף דָּמֵי, וְאֵין מְכִירַת הַבֵּן מְכִירָה. וּמַתְנִיתִין דְּקָתָנֵי אֵין לַלּוֹקֵחַ בָּהֶן כְּלוּם עַד שֶׁיָּמוּת הָאָב, הָא כְּשֶׁיָּמוּת הָאָב יֵשׁ לוֹ — הָתָם דְּמִית הָאָב בְּחַיֵּי הַבֵּן, וְנִתְקַיְּימָה הַמַּתָּנָה. וּמַה מָּכַר רִאשׁוֹן לַשֵּׁנִי — כָּל זְכוּת שֶׁתָּבֹא לְיָדוֹ. אֲבָל מֵת הַבֵּן — לֹא בָּא זְכוּת לְיָדוֹ. תָּנָא מִשּׁוּם ר"א כו'. ר' אֱלִיעֶזֶר פָּלֵיג אַסֵּיפָא דְּמַתְנִי', וְקָאֵי אַאֵין הַוָּלָד שֶׁל קַיָּימָא יְקַיֵּים, וְקָאָמַר אִיהוּ: אע"פ שֶׁאֵין הַוָּלָד שֶׁל קַיָּימָא קָנְסִינַן לֵיהּ דְּיוֹצִיא (א) בְּגֵט, מִשּׁוּם דְּנִכְנַס לִסְפֵק אִיסּוּר אֵשֶׁת אָח. וְאע"ג דְּהַשְׁתָּא אִיגַּלַּאי מִילְּתָא דְּיִיבּוּם מְעַלְיָא הֲוַאי. וּמִיהוּ, בְּגֵט בְּלֹא חֲלִיצָה סַגִּי. דָּבָר אֶחָד. דְּר"מ נַמִי קָנֵיס אֶת הַנּוֹשֵׂא מְעוּבֶּרֶת חֲבֵרוֹ וּמֵינֶקֶת חֲבֵרוֹ (ב) — לְגָרְשָׁהּ. אִשָּׁה שֶׁמֵּת בַּעְלָהּ, וְהִיא מְעוּבֶּרֶת אוֹ מֵינִיקָה, אֲסוּרָה לְהִנָּשֵׂא עַד עֶשְׂרִים וְאַרְבָּעָה חֹדֶשׁ, שֶׁכֵּן תִּינוֹק יוֹנֵק. וְלִכְשֶׁיַּגִּיעַ זְמַנּוֹ לִכְנוֹס. לְסוֹף כ"ד חֹדֶשׁ, יִכְנוֹס. בְּאִיסּוּר אֵשֶׁת אָח. כְּלוֹמַר, שֶׁהֵיקֵל לְהִכָּנֵס לִסְפֵק אֵשֶׁת אָח שֶׁיֵּשׁ לוֹ בָּנִים, דְּדִלְמָא הָוֵי וָלָד שֶׁל קַיָּימָא, הִלְכָּךְ קָנְסִינַן לֵיהּ. אֶלָּא [מִשּׁוּם] דְּרַבָּנַן. דִּמְעוּבֶּרֶת חֲבֵרוֹ מִדְּרַבָּנַן הִיא, וְקָא מְזַלְזְלֵי בָּהּ. וּמִשּׁוּם הָכִי קָנְסוּהוּ דְּלָא לֵיתֵי אַחֲרִינָא לְמֶיעֱבַד הָכִי. אֲבָל הָכָא. יְבָמָה מְעוּבֶּרֶת דְּאוֹרַיְיתָא הִיא, וּבְדִילֵי מִינָּהּ, וְלָא בָּעֵי לְמִיקְנְסֵיהּ לְהַאי אַטּוּ אַחֲרִינֵי. וּלְדִבְרֵי חֲכָמִים. דְּאָמְרֵי לִכְשֶׁיַּגִּיעַ זְמַנּוֹ לִכְנוֹס יִכְנוֹס. מִיהוּ, עַד שֶׁיַּגִּיעַ הַזְּמַן יוֹצִיא בְּגֵט, וְלָא סַגִּי לֵיהּ בְּהַפְרָשָׁה בְּעָלְמָא. דְּקָתָנֵי יוֹצִיא. וַחֲכָמִים אוֹמְרִים יוֹצִיא. הָתָם תְּנַן וכו'. מִשּׁוּם דְּקָבָעֵי לְמִבְּעֵי הָכָא מַאי. כָּל שֶׁשָּׁהָה שְׁלֹשִׁים יוֹם. מִשֶּׁנּוֹלַד חַי שְׁלֹשִׁים יוֹם. בְּאָדָם אֵין נֵפֶל. לְהָכִי נָקַט בְּאָדָם, דְּתָנֵי סֵיפָא: וּבִבְהֵמָה ח' יָמִים. אֵינוֹ נֵפֶל. וּפוֹטֵר אֶת אִמּוֹ מִן הַחֲלִיצָה. סְפֵיקָא הוּא. וְחוֹלֶצֶת וְלֹא מִתְיַיבֶּמֶת. וְדַוְקָא אִי מְסַפְּקָא לָן אִי כָּלוּ לוֹ חֳדָשָׁיו אִי לָא, אֲבָל אִי קִים לָן דְּכָלוּ לוֹ חֳדָשָׁיו — תְּנַן בְּמַסֶּכֶת נִדָּה (דף מג:): תִּינוֹק בֶּן יוֹמוֹ פּוֹטֵר מִן הַיִּיבּוּם. מֵת בְּתוֹךְ שְׁלֹשִׁים. בֶּן הַיְּבָמָה, וְנִתְקַדְּשָׁה לַשּׁוּק בְּחֶזְקַת שֶׁפְּטוּרָה מִשּׁוּם בְּנָהּ. אִם אֵשֶׁת יִשְׂרָאֵל הִיא. אִם זֶה שֶׁקִּדְּשָׁהּ יִשְׂרָאֵל הוּא, שֶׁאִם תַּחֲלוֹץ מִן הַיָּבָם לְאַחַר קִדּוּשִׁין לֹא תֵּיאָסֵר עַל בַּעְלָהּ — חוֹלֶצֶת. וְאִם זֶה שֶׁקִּדְּשָׁהּ כֹּהֵן הוּא. שֶׁאִם תַּחֲלוֹץ תֵּיאָסֵר עָלָיו — אֵינָהּ חוֹלֶצֶת, וְסָמְכִינַן אַוָּלָד. בְּאוֹרְתָא

תוספות

ואמר ריש לקיש לעולם לא קנה כו'. אע"ג דרבא גופיה קאמר ב"יש נוחלין" (ב"ב דף קל.) דהלכה כרבי יוחנן בן ברוקה — מ"מ נפקא מינה דהלכה כר"ל לענין (ג) [אחר] שאין ראוי ליורשו. ורבי יוחנן אמר לא קנה לוקח. וא"ת: לרבי יוחנן, אפי' לא מת הבן בחיי האב נמי לא ליקני, דהוי כמו (ב"מ טז.): מה שאירש מאבא מכור לך, כיון דאלים קנין פירות כקנין הגוף! וי"ל: דלגבי הכי לא אלים קנין פירות לבטל לגמרי קנין הגוף דבן, וכיון דלבסוף אתיא שדה לידי דבן — חשיב מכר. קנין פירות כקנין הגוף דמי. מה שהתקינו באושא דאשה שמכרה בנכסי מלוג בחיי בעלה, ומתה, דהבעל מוציא מיד הלקוחות — לרבי יוחנן לא איצטריך (א). וכן משמע ב"החובל" (ב"ק דף פח: ושם) דמסיק: תקנת אושא לר"ל. א"נ, קנין הגוף דאשה עדיף, שאין לבעל פירות אלא מכחה. ועוד: דאין לבעל פירות אלא בתקנתא דרבנן. וה"ר יעקב דאורליינ"ש תירץ: דאיצטריך תקנתא דאושא להיכא דכתב לה "דין ודברים אין לי בפירות נכסייך"*. חיזוק לדבריהם יותר משל תורה. והיא ד"הזהב" (ב"מ נה:) גבי חמשה חומשין דלא עשו אלא כשל תורה — משום דלא איצטריך [לחיזוק]. והכא גבי איסורא הוא דקניס ר"מ, אבל גבי ממונא כגון כתובה — לא עשו חיזוק אפי' כשל תורה, דקאמר ר"מ בפ' "אע"פ" (כתובות נו: ושם): כל המַתְנֶה על מה שכתוב בתורה — תנאו בטל, הא בדרבנן — תנאו קיים. וקשה תימה: אי רבנן דהכא היינו ר' יהודה — הא סבירא ליה גבי כתובה דעשו חיזוק לדבריהם יותר משל תורה! וי"ל: דבמילתא דשכיחא עבדו חיזוק, אבל הכא — מילתא דלא שכיחא היא שישא אדם מעוברת חברו ומינקת חברו. ולא קתני יפריש. והא דתני בסוטה בפ' "ארוסה" (דף כד. ושם) גבי מעוברת חברו ומינקת חברו יכול הוא להפרישה ולהחזירה לאחר זמן — לשון הפרשה משמע הכי ומשמע הכי, אבל יוציא לא משמע אלא בגט. א"נ: התם, שקינא לה ונסתרה — לא חיישינן שיבא עליה, כיון דאסירא ליה מדאורייתא ולא בעיא גט. והר"ר יוסף מאורליינ"ש הורה מטעם זה באחד שקידש מינקת חברו שלא להצריך גט אלא הפרשה בעלמא (אפילו לרבי מאיר), כיון דבלאו הכי אסורה ליה, דכלה בלא ברכה אסורה לבעלה כנדה. ודוקא בנשא הוא דאמר הכא דבעיא גיטא. אע"ג דקדש תוך ג' וברח, אי לאו דערוקיה מסתייה היה צריך ליתן גט — במעוברת ומינקת חבירו לא החמירו. ואין נראה: דמאי חומרא דכלה בלא ברכה ממינקת חבירו, דתרווייהו מדרבנן. (ד) וקשה היה מדקדק ר"י מהא דתניא התם (כתובות דף ס.): מינקת שמת בעלה — הרי זו לא תארס ולא תנשא, ואם כשאירס צריך ליתן גט — לא איצטריך תו למימר לא תנשא! ומיהו, י"ס דגרסי לא תנשא ולא תארס, ואיכא למימר דזו אף זו קתני. ואפילו גרסינן לא תארס ולא תנשא — מצי למימר דנקט ולא תנשא משום רבי יהודה, דאפילו לינשא שרי בתר י"ח חדש. ובשאלתות דרבי אחאי בפרשה וירא (סימן יג) כתוב גבי מעוברת ומינקת חברו, דהיכא דעבר וקדיש — מפקיע לה בגט מיניה, ואפילו אי הוה כהן — מפסדינן לה מיניה. הא לא שהא ספיקא הויא. ב) לא כמו שפי' הקונטרס דפיהק ומת וולד איירי, [דבהא] אפילו רבנן מודו בפיהק ומת דנפל הוא. אלא כשנפל מן הגג או אכלו ארי איירי, כדאמר בס"פ "ר' אליעזר דמילה" (שבת דף קלו. ושם), והתם פסקינן כרשב"ג. וא"ת: ואמאי לא אזלינן בתר רוב נשים דולד מעליא ילדן? ואר"י: דחיישינן למיעוט מצוי כזה, כמו במים שאין להם סוף (לקמן קכא.) דאשתו אסורה, וגוסס *שאין מעידים עליו להשיא אשתו, אע"ג דשמא התם משום ערוה החמירו, מ"מ כיון דמיעוט של נפלים מצוי — מחמירים ביה. ומחמירים נמי שלא לאכול בהמה תוך ח' ימים, כדאמרינן בס"פ "ר' אליעזר דמילה" (ג"ז שם). ומיהו, לענין אבילות לא החמירו, שיש להקל באבלות כדאמר בפ' "יש בכור" (בכורות מט.): הכל מודים לענין אבלות שאין מתאבלים, דאמר שמואל: הלכה כדברי המיקל באבל. והא דתנן במסכת שמחות: *הספקות אוננים ומתאבלים עליהם — נראה דבספק בן ט' לראשון או ז' לאחרון איירי, דגבאי הדבר שלא יתאבלו לא זה ולא זה, מאחר שודאי קרוב לאחד. מת בתוך שלשים יום כו'. נראה דהכי גרסי'. ולא כרש"י *דגרים בפ' "ר"א דמילה" (שבת קלו. ושם): "מת בסוף שלשים יום", כיון דבפרק "יש בכור" (בכורות מט. ושם) אמרינן דיום ל' כשלפניו — מה לי ביום שלשים מה לי תוך שלשים, ולמה ליה למינקט ביום שלשים טפי? ומיהו בה"ג כתב דביום שלשים אפי' פיהק ומת לרבנן לא הוי נפל, דדוקא תוך שלשים הוא דאמר בשבת (ג"ז שם): פיהק ומת לד"ה מת הוא. משמע דגרסינן הכא "מת ביום שלשים", דאי לאו הכי — מנין היה להם חילוק זה? ועוד יש מקיים גירסא זאת אפילו בנפל מן הגג או אכלו ארי, וביום שלשים דוקא סמכי ארבנן. ושמא לענין אבילות נמי חשיב בר קיימא. מי

תוספות ישנים

א) וי"מ דרבי יוחנן יליף מהתם דבקנין הגוף דמי. ואינו נראה דא"כ היכא פליג ריש לקיש עליה הא הוא ודאי לא פליג אתקנת אושא לכן נראה כדפרישית: יוציא בגט. פ"ה דקנסינן ליה אבל חליצה לא צריך ותימה דהא פסקינן הלכה כריש לקיש דאמר ביאת מעוברת לא שמה ביאה וא"כ גם חליצה (לא) צריך שהביאה לא פטרה דלא הועילה שום דבר. לכן נ"ל יוציא בגט וחליצה עמו. ועי"ל יוציא בגט אחר ביאה ראשונה ואע"ג דאשתו גמורה היא קנסינן לה כדפ"ה: הא לא שהה ספיקא הוא. ומיירי דלא קים לן שלא כלו לו חדשיו. דאי קים לן אפי' בן יום א' פוטר מיבום אלא פליגי בסתם [וולדות] דלרבנן הלך אחר רוב נשים דולד מעליא ילדן: ב) והא דפליגי הכא ר"ג ורבנן בתרתי פליגי. פליגי בספק אם כלו לו חדשיו אם לא. דר"ג סבר דספק הוא כי לא שהה ורבנן סברי דולד מעליא הוא. גם פליגי בשידעתו בבירור שלא כלו לו חדשיו דר"ג סבר איתו נפל כיון ששהה שלשים יום באדם ורבנן סברי דנפל הוי כיון שלא שהה והכי משמע דפליגי בתרתי מדקאמר כל ששהה וכו' משמע דפליגי א) כל ששהה רבנן דקאמר ר"ג איתו נפל ואינהו קאמרי (איתו) [דהוי] נפל בשידעתו בודאי דלא כלו לו חדשיו דאי לא פליגי כי אם ב... לומר אם שהה וכו' אבל מדתנא כל ששהה ודאי בתרווייהו פליגי:

א) נ"ל משמע דפליגי רבנן גם בשהה דקאמר ר"ג איתו נפל כו'.

תוספות חד מקמאי

איתמר מת בתוך שלשים יום או ביום ל' ועמדה ונתקדשה אמר רבינא משמיה דרבא אם אשת ישראל חולצת אם אשת כהן אינה חולצת ושריא לבעלה דכיון דאיכא רבנן דפליגי עליה דרשב"ג (קאי) [דאמרי דהוי] ולד מעלי' אע"ג דלא שהא גבי אשת כהן עבדינן (לחומרא) [לקולא] כרבנן. ודוקא בנפל מן הגג או אכלו ארי אבל פיהק ומת אף אשת כהן חולצת ואסרינן לה אגברא דקי"ל בפר"א דמילה דפיהק

מסורת הש"ס

ב"ב קכט.
ב"ק פח: ב"ב קנו.
[ב"ק שם ב"ב שם]
[שם: שבת קלה: גיטין מז:]
לקמן מב. סוטה כו.
[עירובין עז. פה. כתובות נו. פג: פד. ב"מ נה: זבחים קא.]
[ועי' תוס' לקמן קכא. ד"ה ולא היא]
[פ"ד ה"ז]
[ברש"י שלפנינו שם איתא בתוך ועי' היטב תוס' בכורות מט. ד"ה לאחר]

הגהות הב"ח

(א) רש"י ד"ה תנא וכו' דיוציא בגט. נ"ב ס"א כדי שלא יחזירנה עולמית: (ב) ד"ה דבר אחד וכו' חבירו לגרשה. נ"ב ס"א ולא יחזירנה עולמית: (ג) תוס' ד"ה ואמר וכו' לענין אחר שאין ראוי ליורשו: (ד) ד"ה ולא קתני וכו' מדרבנן. ועוד הביא ר' יוסף ראיה מההיא דפ' אע"פ דף ס ע"ב מאריסה לאביי שהתיר לו לאחר כ"ד חודש וכו' ומגנו שהגריס לתינוק ... שאותה שמועה ... בגט לא הזכירו ... מדקדק ר"י:

גליון הש"ס

גמ' התם תנן. עיין בכלבו שבע פ"א דהוריות סימן לז: שם ואם אשת כהן היא אינה חולצת. עיין לעיל כד ע"א תוס' ד"ה וספק חלוצה:

*באורתא אמר רבא הכי, ובצפרא הדר ביה. א"ל: *שריתו? יהא רעוא דתשתרו אף תרבא. הכא גבי מעוברת חבירו ומינקת חבירו הנשואה לכהן, מאי? מי עבוד רבנן תקנתא לכהן, או לא? אמר ליה: [א]הכי השתא! בשלמא התם, כיון דאיכא רבנן דפליגי עליה דרשב"ג, דאמרי: אע"ג דלא שהא ולד מעליא הוי, – גבי אשת כהן, כיון דלא אפשר, עבדינן כרבנן. אבל הכא, כמאן נעביד? אי כר' מאיר – הא אמר יוציא ולא יחזיר עולמית, ואי כרבנן – האמרי בגט. איתמר, קדשה בתוך שלשה וברח פליגי בה רב אחא ורפרם, חד אמר: משמתינן ליה, וחד אמר: עירוקיה מסתייה. הוה עובדא, ואמר להו רפרם: [ב]עירוקיה מסתייה.§ "ספק בן תשע וכו'".§ אמר ליה רבא לרב נחמן: לימא הלך אחר רוב נשים, ורוב נשים לתשעה ילדן! אמר ליה: נשי דידן – לשבעה ילדן. א"ל: נשי דידכו הוו רובא דעלמא? א"ל: הכי קאמינא, רוב נשים ילדן לתשעה ומיעוט לשבעה, וכל היולדת לתשעה – *עוברה ניכר לשליש ימיה. וזו, הואיל ולא הוכר עוברה לשליש ימיה – איתרע ליה רובא. אי כל היולדת לתשעה עוברה ניכר לשליש ימיה, הא' מדלא הוכר לשליש ימיה – עוברה ודאי בר שבעה לבתראה הוא! – אלא אימא: רוב היולדת לתשעה עוברה ניכר לשליש ימיה, והאי מדלא הוכר לשליש ימיה – איתרע ליה רובא. ת"ר: *ראשון ראוי להיות כהן גדול, ושני ממזר מספק. רבי אליעזר בן יעקב אומר: *אין ממזר מספק. מאי קאמר? אמר אביי: הכי קאמר, ראשון ראוי להיות כהן גדול, ושני – ספק ממזר, ואסור בממזרת. ר' אליעזר (א) אומר: אינו ספק ממזר אלא ודאי ממזר, ומותר בממזרת. רבא אמר, [ג]הכי קאמר: ראשון – ראוי להיות כהן גדול, ושני – ממזר ודאי מספק, ומותר בממזרת. ורבי אליעזר בן יעקב אומר: אין ודאי ממזר מספק, אלא ספק ממזר, ואסור בממזרת. וקמיפלגי בדרבי אלעזר. דתנן, *רבי אלעזר אומר: [ד]ודאן בודאן – מותר. ודאן בספקן, וספקן בודאן, וספקן בספקן – אסור. [ה]ואלו הן ספקן: שתוקי ואסופי וכותי, *ואמר רב יהודה אמר רב: הלכה כר' אלעזר. כי אמריתה קמיה דשמואל אמר לי: הלל שנה עשרה יוחסין עלו מבבל: כהני, לויי, וישראלי, חללי, גירי, חרורי, ממזרי, נתיני, שתוקי, ואסופי. וכולן מותרין לבא זה בזה – ואת אמרת הלכה כרבי אלעזר?! אביי סבר לה כשמואל דאמר הלכה כהלל, ומוקי לה רבי אליעזר בן יעקב אליבא דהלכתא כי היכי דלא תקשי הלכתא אהלכתא. רבא סבר לה כרב, דאמר הלכה כר' אלעזר, ומוקי לה לדרבי אליעזר בן יעקב אליבא דהלכתא, כי היכי דלא תקשי הלכתא

רש"י

באורתא אמר רבא הכי. כדקאמרת. לצפרא הדר ביה. ושמעתי מפיו שאינה חולצת. הכא מאי. לר' יהושע בריה דרב אידי קבעי לה. מי עביד רבנן תקנתא לכהן. דאע"ג דלישראל בעינן יוציא בגט עד שיגיע זמנו, התם הוא דלכשיגיע זמנו מצי להדורה, אבל הכא, דאי מגרש לה לא מצי מהדר לה – תסגי בהפרשה בעלמא. עבדינן כרבנן. וסמכינן אולד. קידשה בתוך שלשה. שום אלמנה או גרושה. עירוקיה מסתייה. לא בעי למיכפייה דלכתוב גט, דגלי דעתיה דלא בעי לכנוס עד זמנו. ורוב נשים לט' ילדן. ולייתי חטאת, דודאי בר קמא הוא, ואשת אח בת בנים בעל. וזו הואיל ולא הוכר עוברה לשליש ימיה. דאי הוכר לא הוה מספקא לן. לשליש ימיה. דכתיב "ויהי כמשלש חדשים" (בראשית לח). איתרע לה רובא. דלא תשדייה בתר רוב נשים, אלא ספק בתר מיעוט, ספק בתר רוב. ראשון. דספק הוה ראוי להיות כהן גדול ממה נפשך. והשני. אם קיימה עד שילדה לו בן ודאי ממזר מספק שמא ראשון בן המת הוה, וקאי עליה בכרת, ואישתכח האי שני ולד חייבי כריתות, וממזר. מאי קאמר. ר"א בן יעקב, היכי מצי לאפוקי מספק ממזר? אמר אביי כו' ספק ממזר הוי. ואסור בממזרת ובכשרה. ר"א (ב) אומר אין ממזר מספק. אלא כודאי ממזר הוי, ומותר בממזרת. דקסבר: ספיקן בודאן מותר. ושני ממזר ודאי הוי מספק. כלומר, מתוך ספק זה נעשה כודאי ממזר, ומותר בממזרת. וקמיפלגי. אביי ורבא, דמר מוקי רבי אליעזר בן יעקב להיתרא, ומר מוקי ליה לאיסורא, פליגי בדרבי *אליעזר. ודאן בספיקן אסור. שמא הספק כשר הוא, ונמצא בא ממזר בקהל. וכן ספק ממזר בספק ממזרת, דשמא זה פסול וזה כשר. שתוקי. שקורא אביו, ואמו משתקתו. אסופי. שנאסף מן השוק. ובכולהו איכא למיחש שמא מפסול נתעברה. כותי. אין מקפיד על קידושי כסף ושטר, דלית ליה גזירה שוה דקיחה קיחה, וכי מקדש חד – מנסבא לאידך. לפיכך כולן ספק ממזרים הם, שמא נתקדשה אמו לאחר. כי אמריתה. רב יהודה מסיים למילתיה ואזיל: כי אמריתה להא שמעתא דרב אמר הלכה כר"א, קמיה דשמואל, אמר לי כו'. וכולן מותרין לבא זה בזה. אי אמרת (ג) ספיקן בודאן מותר, וכ"ש ספיקן בספיקן – היינו דמשכחת ליה כולן מותרין זה בזה. כהנים לוים וישראלים – מותרין זה בזה, לויי, וישראלי, חללי, גירי, וחרורי, עבדים משוחררים – מותרים זה בזה, גירי, חרורי, ממזרי, ונתיני, שתוקי, ואסופי – מותרים זה בזה, דקהל גרים לא איקרי קהל, לפיכך ממזרים מותרים בהן, וכסדר הזה שנויים בקידושין (דף סט.). ואת אמרת הלכה כר"א. שאין ממזר מותר בשתוקי, ולא שתוקי בשתוקי, ולא שתוקי באסופי (א"כ לא משכחת לה כולהו מעורבים). נתיני. גבעונים שנתגיירו בימי יהושע בערמה, ויש כהן לך עבדות, דכתיב (יהושע ט) "ויתנם יהושע חוטבי עצים ושואבי מים לעדה". הלכתא

תוספות

מי עביד רבנן תקנתא או לא. בעיא זו אליבא דרבנן ולא אליבא דר' מאיר. ומכאן מדקדק בה"ג ובשאלתות דהא דאמר בפ' "אע"פ" (כתובות דף ס: ושם) דהלכה כר"מ בגזרותיו – היינו דוקא בגזרותיו ולא בקנסותיו*. אי כל היולדת כו'. כה"ג דייק ברפ"ב דכתובות (דף טז:) גבי כל הנישאת בתולה יש לה קול כו', ובפ' "המפלת" (נדה דף כט.) גבי כל היולדות מטנפות. אבל בפרק "ואלו טריפות" (חולין דף נג.), גבי כל הדורס אין לפרנו נשמטת, לא דייק (אע"ג) ד"כל" לאו דוקא. רוב היולדת לט' כו'. וא"ת: מה מועיל המתנת ג' חדשים משום הבחנה? אכתי יכול לבא לידי ספק אם תנשא מיד ותלד לו' חדשים ויום אחד, או אפילו ג' ימים, דיש להסתפק אם הוא בנו של ראשון ולא נקלט הזרע עד יום ג', או הוא בנו של שני, דיולדת לשבעה יולדת למקוטעים! וזהו תימה לומר שתהא האשה צריכה להמתין ג' חדשים וג' ימים, דלקמן משמע דג' חדשים דוקא, דאמר: חוץ מיום שמת בו ויום שנתארסה בו! ואין לומר כיון דהמתינה ג' חדשים שריא לינשא, ולא חיישינן שמא תלד מעֵי לסוף ששה חדשים וג' ימים או ג', דסמכינן ארובא דלט' ילדן, וא"כ דסמכינן ארובא דלט' ילדן – א"כ אפילו תוך ג' חדשים תנשא, דסמכינן ארובא, ואין צריך להמתין אלא חדש אחד, ושוב אין ספק, דאם תלד לסוף ט' ממיתת ראשון – אין להסתפק שמא הוא מז' לאחרון, דאזלינן בתר רוב נשים דלט' ילדן, אלא ע"כ, כל מקום שיכול לבא לידי ספק – החמירו חכמים! וי"ל: דכ"כ לא היה משתהא הכרת העובר של ראשון עד שליש ימיה מן השני. וזו הואיל ולא הוכר. תימה: דאמאי לא מוקמינן לה בחזקת היתר ליבם, ולא יתחייב באשם תלוי, ויהא נמי ולד שני כשר, דסמוך מיעוט יולדת לשבעה אחזקה, ואיתרע ליה רובא, ונסמוך ארובא דעוברה ניכר לשליש ימיה, דלעיל בפ' "ד' אחין" (דף ל:) חשבינן לה חזקה גבי ספק קידושין, ולקמן בפ' בתרא (דף קיט. ושם) אפילו היתה צרתה מעוברת חשבינן לה בחזקת זקוקה? וכ"ת דאיכא רובא אחרינא, דרוב נשים מתעברות ויולדות, לפיכך יש להחזיקה כמעוברת מן הראשון – דאין סברא כלל לומר בנשים ששהו עם בעליהן כמה שנים ולא עיברו ומתו בעליהם דרוב מעוברות, ולקמן (דף קיט.) הוא דאמר לה גבי האשה שהלך בעלה וצרתה למדינת הים! ראשון ראוי להיות כה"ג. והא דאמר בפ"ק דכתובות (דף יג: ושם) גבי עשר כהנים שפירש אחד מהן ובעל הולד שתוקי, שמשתקין אותו מדין כהונה, דבעינן זרעו מיוחס אחריו – לקמן בפ' "נושאין" (דף ק:) פריך לה, ומשני: זרעו מיוחס אחריו דרבנן, וכי גזור רבנן – בזנות, בנישואין – לא גזור. סבר לה כרב דאמר הלכה כר' אלעזר. והא דפריך ב"עשרה יוחסין" (קידושין דף עג. ושם) גבי הא דאמר רבא דבר תורה כו' שתוקי כשר: אלא מעתה שתוקי – שתוקית לא ישא! לאו משום דלרבא שרי שתוקי בשתוקית, אלא משום דגם אליבא דרבנן אמר רבא מילתיה דהתם, להכי פריך דלרבנן נמי שתוקי שתוקית לא ישא.

יהודי

עין משפט נר מצוה

כ א ב מיי' פי"ד מהל' גירושין הלכה כח סמג עשין נ טוש"ע אה"ע סימן יג סעיף יב:

[וע"ע תוס' ב"ק ל: סד"ה וחכמים ותוס' ב"מ עב. ד"ה קונסין ותוס' ב"ב לד: ד"ה וחכ"א ותוס' בכורות כח. ד"ה ר"מ ותוס' זבחים קד. ד"ה אמר ר"ע]

כא ג מיי' פ"א מהלכות יבום הלכה כג סמג לאוין קיז טוש"ע שם סימן ד סעיף כה וסימן קסד סעיף ו:

כב ד מיי' פט"ו מהל' איסורי ביאה הלכה כא סמג שם טוש"ע שם סימן ד סעיף כד:

כג ה מיי' שם וטוש"ע שם סעיף לו וסעיף לא:

תוספות חד מקמאי

דפיהק ומת ד"ה (מותר) [נפל] הוא. עמד וקדשה בתוך ג' חדשים וברח פליגי רב אחא ורפרם חד אמר משמתין ליה עד שיוציאה בגט (ושמואל) [וחד אמר] ערקויי מסתייה דגלי דעתיה שאין דעתו לכנסה עד אחר שלשה חדשים והלכתא ערקויי מסתייה אבל לא ברח יוציא בגט אפי' קדשה ביום השלמת שלשה חדשים דקי"ל צריכה להמתין ג' חדשים חוץ מיום שמת בו וחוץ מיום שנתארסה בו. הרב אלפס כתב לאלמנת חבירו ולגרושת חבירו בתוך ג' חדשים משמע דהא אם קדש אלמנת אחיו א) לא איבעיא ג' חדשים אלא אמר ערקויי מסתייה והראב"ד כתב דה"ה אם קדש אשת אחיו דהא לא פסקא דמתני' אתמהא הא שמעתא:

א) נראה דצ"ל בתוך ג' חדשים לא אמרינן דערוקיה מסתייה דהא אפסקא דמתניתין אתמר הא שמעתא.

הגהות הב"ח

(א) גמ' ר' אליעזר בן יעקב אומר אינו ספק ממזר אלא ודאי: (ב) רש"י ד"ה ר' אליעזר בן יעקב אומר אין ממזר: (ג) ד"ה וכולן וכו' אי אמרת בשלמא ספקן:

מסורת הש"ס

שבת קלו:
[ס"א שריתוה]
[סנהדרין סט.]
ל"ל אלעזר
קדושין עד.
[שם עה.]
ס"א אינו ספק

הלכתא אהלכתא. אמר אביי: מנא אמינא לה דכל ספיקא לר' אליעזר בן יעקב כודאי משוי ליה – דתניא, *ר' אליעזר בן יעקב אומר: אהרי שבא על נשים הרבה ואין יודע על איזו מהן בא. וכן היא, שבאו עליה אנשים הרבה ואינה יודעת מאיזה מהן קבלה, נמצא אב נושא את בתו ואח נושא את אחותו, ונתמלא כל העולם כולו ממזרין, ועל זה נאמר °"ומלאה הארץ זמה". ורבא אמר לך: הכי קאמר: *"זו מה היא". יתר על כן אמר ר' אליעזר בן יעקב: *בלא ישא אדם אשה במדינה זו, וילך וישא אשה במדינה אחרת, שמא יזדווגו זה לזה ונמצא אח נושא את אחותו. איני? והא *רב, כי איקלע לדרדשיר [מכריז] ואמר: מאן הויא ליומא. ורב נחמן, כי איקלע לשכנציב [מכריז] ואמר: מאן הויא ליומא! – גשאני רבנן דפקיע שמייהו. והאמר רבא: *דתבעוה לינשא ונתפייסה – צריכה לישב שבעה נקיים! רבנן שלוחייהו הוו משדרי, ומודעי להו, ואיבעית אימא: לרבנן יחודי בעלמא הוא דמייחדי להו, דאמר מר: *אינו דומה מי שיש לו פת בסלו למי שאין לו פת בסלו. תנא, רבי אליעזר בן יעקב אומר: הלא ישא אדם אשה *אשתו *ודעתו לגרשה, משום שנאמר °"אל תחרש על רעך רעה והוא יושב לבטח אתך". § ספק ויבם שבאו לחלוק בנכסי מיתנא. ספק אמר: אנא בר מיתנא הוא, ונכסי דידי הוא. ויבם אמר: את בראי דידי את, ולית לך ולא מידי בנכסי. והוי ממון המוטל בספק, וממון המוטל בספק – חולקין. וספק ובני יבם שבאו לחלוק בנכסי מיתנא, ספק אמר: ההוא גברא בר מיתנא הוא, ונכסי דידי הוא. בני יבם אמרי: את אחינו את, ומנתא הוא דאית לך בהדן. סבור רבנן קמיה דרב משרשיא למימר: מתניתין היא, דתנן: *הוא אינו יורש אותם, והם יורשין אותו. והכא איפכא, התם אמרי ליה: אייתי ראיה ושקול. הכא אמר להו: אייתו ראיה ושקולו. אמר להו רב משרשיא: מי דמי? התם – אינהו ודאי, ואיהו ספק. הכא – אידי ואידי ספק. אלא, אי דמיא למתני' – [להא] דמיא: לספק ובני יבם שבאו לחלוק בנכסי יבם גופיה, דהתם אמרי ליה: אייתי ראיה דאחונא את ושקול. ספק ובני יבם שבאו לחלוק בנכסי יבם, לבתר דפלג יבם בנכסי מיתנא. בני יבם אמרי: אייתי ראיה דאחונא את ושקול. אמר להו ספק: מה נפשייכו, אי אחוכון אנא – הבו לי מנתא בהדייכו, ואי בר מיתנא אנא – הבו לי פלגא דפלג אבוכון בהדאי. ר' אבא אמר רב: חקם דינא. ר' ירמיה אמר: הדר דינא. לימא בפלוגתא דאדמון ורבנן קמיפלגי, דתנן: *מי שהלך למדינת הים ואבדה לו דרך שדהו, אדמון אומר: ילך בקצרה. וחכ"א: יקח לו דרך במאה מנה, או יפרח באויר. והוינן בה לרבנן; טשפיר קאמר אדמון! ואמר רב יהודה אמר רב: הכא במאי עסקינן – יכגון שהקיפוה ארבעה בני אדם מארבע רוחות. א"ה, מ"ט דאדמון? ואמר רבא: כבארבעה דאתו מכח ארבעה, וארבעה דאתו מכח חד – כולי עלמא לא פליגי, דמצו מדחי ליה. כי פליגי – בחד דאתי מכח ארבעה. אדמון סבר: מצי א"ל: מכל מקום דרכי גבך הוא. ורבנן סברי, דא"ל: לאי שתקת – שתקת, ואי לא – מהדרנא שטרא למרייהו, ולא מצית לאשתעויי דינא בהדייהו. לימא ר' אבא דאמר כרבנן, ור' ירמיה דאמר כאדמון! אמר לך ר' אבא: אנא דאמרי אפילו כאדמון. עד כאן לא קאמר אדמון התם – אלא משום דא"ל: ממה נפשך דרכי

רש"י

הלכתא אהלכתא. דקיימא לן: משנת ר"א ב"י קב ונקי, במסכת גיטין (דף סז.). קבלה. נתעברה. ונתמלא כל העולם כולו ממזרים. מספק קרו להו ממזרים. זו מה היא. לשון ספק. יתר על כן. דלפי שהכל, דע"י נישואין הוה והדבר מפורסם, גזר ר"א בן יעקב. מאן הויא ליומי. מי חפצה לינשא לימים שאתעכב כאן. דפקיע. כ"ע בשמייהו, וקולין לבתו על שמו. ואם ילד בנו ממקום אחר – ישמע שהיא בת אביו, ויפרוש. שבעה נקיים. שמא מחמת חימוד פירסה נדה, בשעה שנתפייסה. שלוחייהו הוו משדרי. שבעה יומי קודם דיתהן. ממון המוטל בספק. שאין זה מוחזק (א) בזה יותר מזה. דאם זה בן המת – אין ליבם בהן כלום, ואם בן היבם הוא – אין לו בהן כלום. הלכך אין כאן מוציא מחבירו להטיל עליו הראיה. ספק ובני יבם. הספק מוחזק בהן ביותר, דממה נפשך אית ליה זכיה בנכסייהו. אבל בני יבם – שמא אין להם חלק בהם, שזה בן ראשון הוא וכולה שלו. ומשום הכי סבור רבנן למימר היינו מתניתין בפ' "נושאין על האנוסה", דקתני ספק בן תשעה לראשון ספק בן שבעה לאחרון, הוא לא יורש אותן לא זה ולא זה, דבני ראשון מדחו ליה אצל בני אחרון, ובני אחרון – אצל בני ראשון, והם יורשין אותו בין כך ובין כך. והכא אמרינן איפכא. דהוא מוחזק יותר. דהתם לבני מדחו ליה, דאמרי ליה: אייתי ראיה דאחונא את ושקול. והכא נמי אמר להו הכי: אייתו ראיה דאחוכון אנא ושקולו. מי דמי התם אינהו ודאי. שהן יודעין מאת מי הן באין לירש. אידי ואידי ספיקא נינהו. שאפילו הספק אין טוענת ודאי, ואינו יודע מאת מי הוא בא לירש. בנכסי יבם גופיה. התם מיתוקמא מתניתין, דהוא לא יורש אותן, דאמרי ליה: אייתי ראיה ושקול. אבל בההיא דלעיל – שניהם ספק. ונראה בעיני דההיא מנתא דקמודו ליה – שקיל, ואידך הוי ממון המוטל בספק וחולקין, הוא נוטל חציו ובני יבם כולם חציו. לבתר דפלג יבם. עם ספק בנכסי מיתנא, כדאמרינן לעיל חולקין. אי אחוכון אנא הבו לי מנתא בהדייכו. ואי משום דשקלי הנה פלגא בנכסי מיתנא – מהדרנא לכו ההוא פלגא, ונחלוק הכל בשוה, בין נכסי הראשון בין נכסי האחרון. וכגון שהיו נכסי היבם מרובין, והניו מועטין. קם דינא. אחר שנעשה דין בנכסי המת אין זה יכול לחזור ולערער עליהם, ומה שהוא שואל בנכסי היבם – אמרי ליה: אייתי ראיה. הדר דינא. ומהדרי ליה פלגא דנכסי מיתנא, או פלג כולהו נכסי בשוה. ואבדה דרך שדהו. שהיתה שדהו מוקפת משדות אחרים, והיה לו דרך על אחת מן השדות ואבדה, שנשכחו על איזה מן השדות היתה. ילך בקצרה. יתנו ביניהם דרך קצרה, ולקמן מפרש לה.

שפיר קאמר אדמון. קסלקא דעתא שהקיפוה אדם אחד מכל רוחותיו, דקאמר: אורחיה גביה הוא. ארבעה בני אדם. דכל חד וחד מדחי ליה. דאתו מכח ארבעה. שארבעה אנשים מכרום לאלו. אי שתקת שתקת. ולא אעלה עליך בדמים יקרים. דרכי

תוספות

יחודי בעלמא הוו מיחדי. ויש כאן פת בסלו, כיון שאם היה רוצה (ב) היה בא עליה. וכיון שפעמים לא היה בא עליה – לא מיתחלא ולא חזיא. דאי לא תימא הכי – גם להתיחד הוה אסור, כדאמר בפ"ק דכתובות (דף ד. ושם) גבי חתן, אם פרסה אשתו נדה – הוא ישן בין האנשים ואשתו ישנה בין הנשים. ומשום נושא אשה במדינה אחרת נמי ליכא למיחש, שאם היה אירע שבא עליה ונתעברה ממנו היה מוליכה עמו לעירו*.

וממון המוטל בספק חולקים. אפילו רבנן דסומכוס (ב"ק לה:) מודו הכא, דלא שייך כאן המוציא מחבירו עליו הראיה, שאין זה מוחזק יותר מזה, והוי כמו הללו באין לירש והללו באין לירש, דאמר ב"מי שמת" (ב"ב דף קנז:) דיחלוקו. אמר רבי אבא קם דינא. דוקא בתר דפלג, אבל מקמי דפלג – לא. דאמר ליה אי שתקת שתקת. פי': ולא תטול כלום. ולא כמו שפירש בקונט' אי שתקת ומוזילנא לך, דהא קתני יקח לו דרך במאה מנה. ובפ"ק דב"ק (דף ח.) גבי מכרן לאחד כולן נכנסו תחת הבעלים, והויא אשה בזיבורית אע"פ שלקח עידית באחרונה, משום אי שתקת כו' ולא מצי אמרה ליה: לכי תהדר. כיון שאין בא להפקיע מדינא. ובחד דאתי מכח חד לא מצי למימר ואי לא מזבינא לארבעה – דהא פשיטא, כיון דלא אתי מכח ארבעה – לא שבקינן ליה. ואם תאמר: וארבעה דאתו מכח חד, ליהדר ההוא חד דמי קרקע! וי"ל: דמצי אמר ליה: לא מכרתי אלא מה שיש לי בה.

הוי

עין משפט נר מצוה

כד א מיי' פט"ו מהל' איסורי ביאה הלכה כט:

כה ב מיי' פ"א שם הלכה כט סמג לאוין קכו טוש"ע אה"ע סימן ב סעיף יח:

[ועי' תוס' יומא יח: ד"ה יחודי]

כו ד מיי' פ"א שם הלכה ט סמג לאוין קיח ועשין רמג טוש"ע יד סימן קלב סעיף ח:

כז ה מיי' פ"ו מהל' גרושין הלכה כב סמג עשין נ טוש"ע אה"ע סימן ב סעיף ו וסימן קיט סעיף ה:

כח ו מיי' פ"ה מהל' נחלות הלכה ד סמג עשין צ טוש"ע שם סימן קמב סעיף ג:

כט ז מיי' שם טוש"ע שם סעיף ד:

ל ח מיי' שם הלכה ה טוש"ע שם סעי' ה:

לא ט מיי' פכ"ו מהל' טוען ונטען הלכה יא טוש"ע ח"מ סימן קמח סעיף ב:

לב י כ ל מיי' שם טוש"ע שם וסעיף ה:

נ"ל אשה

מסורת הש"ס

[תוספתא דקידושין פ"א] | ויקרא יט | [נדרים נא.] | [יומא יח: ע"ש] | שם | ג"ז שם נדה סו. | יומא יח: סז. עג: כתובות סב: סג. | [גיטין ל. ע"ש הוטיב] | משלי ג | לקמן ק: | כתובות קט: כה"ע

תוספות ישנים

כי פליגי בחד דאתי מכח ארבעה ולא קאמר א) משום דמצי למוכרים לארבעה דאין לנו להעמיד הדבר אלא במה שהוא או כמו שהיה: אי שתקת פ"ה ותקח לך דרך במאה מנה. ותימה דה"ל לכשתהדר שהרי מה יכול להפסידו יותר וה"ל מוזיל גביה דהא קאמר לעיל יקח לו דרך במאה מנה ואין זה זול. וה"ל דכיון שלקחת מהארבעה תתבעוני כלום מוחזק הספק כבר ולא שייך לכשתהדר וה"ל קאמר ליה אי שתקת שתקת ותקנה ממני בזוקף:

א) חסר כאן וצ"ל ולא קאמר בחד דאתי מכח חד משום דמצי למוכרים וכו' וכ"ה בחד דאתי מכח חד לא מצי למימר וכו'.

תוספות חד מקמאי

ספק ובני יבם שבאו לחלוק בנכסי מיתנא ספק אמר בר מיתנא אנא ונכסי דידי הוו. ובני יבם אמרי ליה את אחינו את ומנתא הוא דאית לך. כתב ר"ש ז"ל דמאי דמודו ליה שקיל והשאר הוי ממון המוטל בספק וחולקין והכי משמע במסקנא דשמעתתא. ספק ובני יבם שבאו לחלוק בנכסי יבם בתר דפלג יבם בנכסי (אלמנה) מיתנא. אמר להו ספק אי אחוכון אנא הבו לי

הגהות הב"ח

(א) רש"י ד"ה ממון וכו' מוחזק בנכסי יותר מזה: (ב) תוס' ד"ה יחודי וכו' היה בא עליה נ"ב ועיין ביאור דיבור זה בתשובות ב"ח סימן פ':

לי א) נכסי דפליג אבוכון בנכסי. ר' אבא אמר קם דינא. ר' ירמיה אמר הדר דינא. משמע לכאורה מדקאמר לבתר דפלג יבם בנכסי מיתנא הא מקמי דפליג בנכסי מיתנא דכ"ע אמר להו מ"ג דלא שייך למימר קם דינא כיון דלא פלג בנכסי ומיהו בפלוגתא דאדמון ורבנן איכא לעיוני בהא מילתא דהא לא קם דינא בהדיה ואפ"ה אמרו רבנן קם דינא. ופסק הרב אלפס כר' אבא דאמר קם דינא כיון דקאי כרבנן. ואע"ג דאמרי' אמר לך ר' ירמיה אנא דאמרי אפילו לרבנן שנויא דחיקא היא. ואע"ג דאיתא בפ' בית כור שני אחים שחלקו ובא להן אח ממדינת הים רב אמר בטלה מחלוקת וקי"ל כוותיה אלמא הדר דינא שאני התם דהחלוקה בטעות הוא והרב ר' אפרים (מה') פסק כר' ירמיה: ספק ויבם שבאו לחלוק בנכסי סבא בספק א' אנא בר מיתנא ופלגא דידי ויבם אמר את ברי ולית ליך ולא מידי הוה יבם ודאי וספק ספק ואין ספק מוציא מידי ודאי. סבא ויבם שבאו לחלוק בנכסם ספק

דְּרַבִּי חַד גַּבְרָא הוּא, אֲבָל הָכָא — מִי אִיכָּא לְמֵימַר? הָכִי וְרַבִּי יִרְמְיָה אָמַר לָךְ: אֲנָא דְּאָמְרִי אֲפִי' לְרַבָּנַן, עַד כָּאן לָא קָאָמְרִי רַבָּנַן הָתָם אֶלָּא מִשּׁוּם דְּא"ל: אִי שָׁתְקַתְּ — שָׁתְקַתְּ, וְאִי לָא — מַהַדְרְנָא שְׁטָרָא לְמָרֵייהוּ, וְלָא מָצֵית לְאִשְׁתַּעוּיֵי דִּינָא בַּהֲדַיְיהוּ. אֲבָל הָכָא — מִי אִיכָּא לְמֵימַר הָכִי? ספק וְיָבָם שֶׁבָּאוּ לַחֲלוֹק בְּנִכְסֵי סָבָא, סָפֵק אָמַר: הַאי גַּבְרָא בַּר מִיתְנָא הוּא, וּפַלְגָא דִּידִי הוּא. יָבָם אָמַר: אַתְּ בְּרַאי דִּידִי אַתְּ, וְלֵית לָךְ וְלָא מִידֵי, הָוֵי יָבָם וַדַּאי, וְסָפֵק סָפֵק — וְאֵין סָפֵק מוֹצִיא מִידֵי וַדַּאי. ספק וּבְנֵי יָבָם שֶׁבָּאוּ לַחֲלוֹק בְּנִכְסֵי סָבָא, סָפֵק אָמַר: הַהוּא גַּבְרָא בַּר מִיתְנָא הוּא, וּפַלְגָא דִּידִי הוּא. וּבְנֵי יָבָם אָמְרִי: אֲחוּנָא אַתְּ, וּמַנְתָּא אִית לָךְ בַּהֲדַן. פַּלְגָא דְּקָמוֹדֵי לְהוּ — שָׁקְלִי, תִּילְתָּא דְּקָא מוֹדוּ לֵיהּ — שָׁקֵל, פָּשׁ לְהוּ דַּנְקָא, הָוֵי מָמוֹן הַמּוּטָּל בְּסָפֵק — וְחוֹלְקִין. סָבָא וְיָבָם בְּנִכְסֵי סָפֵק, אוֹ סָבָא וְסָפֵק בְּנִכְסֵי יָבָם — הָוֵי מָמוֹן הַמּוּטָּל בְּסָפֵק, וְחוֹלְקִין.

מתני' שׁוֹמֶרֶת יָבָם שֶׁנָּפְלוּ לָהּ נְכָסִים, מוֹדִים ב"ש וּב"ה שֶׁמּוֹכֶרֶת וְנוֹתֶנֶת וְקַיָּים. מֵתָה — מָה יַעֲשֶׂה בִּכְתוּבָּתָהּ וּבִנְכָסִים הַנִּכְנָסִים וְיוֹצְאִין עִמָּהּ? ב"ש אוֹמְרִים: יַחֲלוֹקוּ יוֹרְשֵׁי הַבַּעַל עִם יוֹרְשֵׁי הָאָב, וּב"ה אוֹמְרִים: נְכָסִים בְּחֶזְקָתָן: כְּתוּבָּה בְּחֶזְקַת יוֹרְשֵׁי הַבַּעַל, נְכָסִים הַנִּכְנָסִים וְיוֹצְאִין עִמָּהּ בְּחֶזְקַת יוֹרְשֵׁי הָאָב. כְּנָסָהּ — הֲרֵי הִיא כְּאִשְׁתּוֹ לְכָל דָּבָר, וּבִלְבַד שֶׁתְּהֵא כְּתוּבָּה עַל נִכְסֵי בַעְלָהּ הָרִאשׁוֹן.

גמ' מ"ש רֵישָׁא דְּלָא פְּלִיגִי, ומ"ש סֵיפָא דִּפְלִיגִי? אָמַר עוּלָּא: רֵישָׁא — דְּנָפְלָה כְּשֶׁהִיא אֲרוּסָה, וְסֵיפָא — דְּנָפְלָה כְּשֶׁהִיא נְשׂוּאָה. וְקָסָבַר עוּלָּא: זִיקַת אֲרוּסָה — עוֹשָׂה סָפֵק אֲרוּסָה, זִיקַת

דְּרַבִּי חַד אִית לִי גַּבָּךְ. וְטַעֲנַת בָּרִי הוּא, דְּיָדַע מַאי קָתָבַע מִינֵּיהּ. **מִי אִיכָּא לְמֵימַר הָכִי.** הָא לָא יָדַע מַאי קָא תָּבַע מִינֵּיהּ, אִי פַּלְגָּא בְּנִכְסֵי מִיתְנָא (א) אִי פַּלְגָּא מִנָּתָא בְּנִכְסֵי יָבָם. וּמִכָּאן שְׁתֵּי טְעָנוֹת הֵן בָּא עֲלֵיהֶם, בְּכָל אַחַת וְאַחַת אוֹמְרִים לוֹ: הָבֵא רְאָיָה. **סָבָא.** אֲבִי הַמֵּת וְהַיָּבָם. **הָוֵי יָבָם וַדַּאי.** יוֹרֵשׁ, וְיוֹדֵעַ מִכֹּחַ מִי הוּא בָּא וּמוּחְזָק בַּנְּכָסִים, וְלָא דָּמֵי לְהָהִיא דְּרַב מְשַׁרְשְׁיָא דִּלְעֵיל, דְּהָתָם, אע"ג דְּסָפֵק אִית לֵיהּ זְכִיָּה בַּנְּכָסִים מִמָּה נַפְשָׁךְ, אֲפִילּוּ הָכִי לָא חָשִׁיב וַדַּאי, דְּלָא יָדַע מִכֹּחַ מִי הוּא בָּא לִירַשׁ, מִכֹּחַ מַה הוּא בָּא עֲלֵיהֶן. **פַּלְגָא דְּקָא מוֹדֶה לְהוּ שָׁקְלִי.** מִשִּׁשָּׁה זְהוּבִים נוֹטְלִין שְׁלֹשָׁה. **תִּילְתָּא דְּקָא מוֹדוּ לֵיהּ.** שְׁנֵי זְהוּבִים תִּילְתָּא דְּכוּלְּהוּ נִכְסֵי. **שָׁקֵיל.** דְּהָא אָמְרוּ לֵיהּ אָחוּנָא אַתְּ, וְאִינְהוּ הָווּ תְּרֵי וְאִיהוּ שְׁלִישִׁי. **פָּשׁ דַּנְקָא.** דִּקְמַיְּיתָא עֲלֵיהּ. הַאי אָמַר: כּוּלֵּיהּ דִּידִי, וְהָנֵי אָמְרִי: כּוּלֵּיהּ דִּידָן. הוּא נוֹטֵל חֶצְיוֹ, וְהֵן שְׁנֵיהֶם חֶצְיוֹ. **סָבָא וְיָבָם בְּנִכְסֵי סָפֵק.** סָבָא אָמַר: הָאִי בַּר מִיתְנָא הוּא, וְכֵיוָן דְּאֵין לוֹ יוֹרֵשׁ אֲנִי קוֹדֵם, דִּתְנַן (ב"ב דף קטו.): הָאָב קוֹדֵם לְכָל יוֹצְאֵי יְרֵכוֹ, וְיָבָם אָמַר בְּנִי הוּא וַאֲנִי יוֹרְשׁוֹ דְּהָאָב קוֹדֵם. **אוֹ סָבָא וְסָפֵק בְּנִכְסֵי יָבָם.** שֶׁאֵין לַיָּבָם בֵּן אַחֵר. סָבָא אָמַר: אַתְּ בַּר מִיתְנָא, וַאֲנִי יוֹרֵשׁ אֶת בְּנִי מָקוֹם שֶׁאֵין לוֹ בֵּן, וְסָפֵק אָמַר: בְּנוֹ אֲנִי, וַאֲנִי יוֹרְשׁוֹ. **חוֹלְקִין.** דִּלְמָא כּוּלְּהוּ דְּהַאי וּדְלְמָא כּוּלְּהוּ דְּהַאי. וְאֵין לוֹמַר הָאָב וַדַּאי מוּחְזָק, דְּאִם זֶה בְּנוֹ — אֵין כָּאן לָאָב כְּלוּם.

מתני' שׁוֹמֶרֶת יָבָם. הַמַּמְתֶּנֶת וּמְצַפָּה לַיָּבָם, כְּמוֹ: עֵינֶיהָ זוֹ לַשָּׁוְא שָׁמָרָה, בְּ'אַף עַל פִּי' בִּכְתוּבּוֹת (דף סג:). **שֶׁנָּפְלוּ לָהּ נְכָסִים.** מֵאָבִיהָ. וְסָלְקָא דַּעְתָּךְ שֶׁנָּפְלוּ לָהּ כְּשֶׁהִיא שׁוֹמֶרֶת יָבָם. **וּבִנְכָסִים הַנִּכְנָסִים וְיוֹצְאִים עִמָּהּ.** הַיְינוּ נִכְסֵי מְלוֹג, שֶׁהַקֶּרֶן שֶׁלָּהּ קַיָּים, וּכְשֶׁהִיא נִכְנֶסֶת נִכְנָסִין עִמָּהּ, וּכְשֶׁהִיא יוֹצְאָה יוֹצְאִין עִמָּהּ: ה"ג. **ב"ש אוֹמְרִים יַחֲלוֹקוּ יוֹרְשֵׁי הַבַּעַל עִם יוֹרְשֵׁי הָאָב.** דִּסְפֵק נְשׂוּאָה הִיא, וְזָכָה הַיָּבָם בְּחַיֵּי יְרֻשָּׁתוֹ מִסָּפֵק. שֶׁהַבַּעַל יוֹרֵשׁ אֶת אִשְׁתּוֹ, וְזוֹ שֶׁמִּסָּפֵק נְשׂוּאָה הִיא אֵינוֹ זוֹכֶה אֶלָּא בְּפַלְגָּא. אֲבָל בִּכְתוּבָּתָהּ מוֹדִים ב"ש דִּבְחֶזְקַת הַבַּעַל הִיא, וְלָא פָּלְגֵי בָּהּ יוֹרְשֵׁי הָאָב, וְטַעְמָא דְּכוּלָּהּ מַתְנִיתִין מְפָרֵשׁ בַּגְּמָ'. **גמ' מַאי שְׁנָא רֵישָׁא דל"פ ומ"ש סֵיפָא דִּפְלִיגִי ב"ש.** מַאי שְׁנָא רֵישָׁא כְּשֶׁהִיא קַיֶּימֶת דְּלָא פְּלִיגִי ב"ש, אֶלָּא בְּכוּלָּהּ דִּילָהּ מַחֲזִיקִינַן לְנִכְסֵי, דְּקָאָמְרִי: מוֹכֶרֶת וְנוֹתֶנֶת לְכַתְּחִלָּה, וּמַאי שְׁנָא סֵיפָא, דִּפְלִיגִי כְּשֶׁמֵּתָה לָא מוֹקְמֵי נִכְסֵי מְלוֹג בְּחֶזְקַת יוֹרְשֶׁיהָ? ה"ג. **אָמַר עוּלָּא רֵישָׁא דְּנָפְלָה כְּשֶׁהִיא אֲרוּסָה.** שֶׁנָּפְלָה לְיִיבּוּם מֵאֵירוּסִין, וְנָפְלוּ הַנְּכָסִים לָהּ כְּשֶׁהִיא שׁוֹמֶרֶת יָבָם. **סֵיפָא דְּנָפְלָה.** לְפָנָיו לְיִיבּוּם. **כְּשֶׁהִיא נְשׂוּאָה.** הִלְכָּךְ רֵישָׁא דִּלְגַבֵּי אֲרוּסָה מַמָּשׁ קי"ל לב"ש תִּמְכּוֹר, כִּדְתְנַן לְקַמָּן, כ"ש זוֹ שֶׁאֵינָהּ אֶלָּא זְקוּקָה לְבַעְלָהּ. וּב"ה דְּאָמְרִי בַּאֲרוּסָה וַדַּאי לֹא תִּמְכּוֹר לְכַתְּחִלָּה, אֲבָל אִם מָכְרָה וְנָתְנָה קַיָּים, הָכָא מִשּׁוּם דִּסְפֵק אֲרוּסָה הִיא דַּאֲגִידָא בֵּיהּ, וְלָאו אִשְׁתּוֹ מַמָּשׁ הִיא — מוֹדוּ ב"ה דְּמוֹכֶרֶת וְנוֹתֶנֶת לְכַתְּחִלָּה. סֵיפָא

הוי יבם ודאי וספק ספק. פי' בקונטרס: ודאי – שיודע מאיזה כח הוא בא, ומוחזק בנכסים, ולא דמי להההוא דרב משרשיא לעיל, דהתם אע"ג דספק אית ליה בנכסים זכיה ממה נפשך – אפ"ה לא חשיב ודאי, דלא ידע מכח מי הוא בא עליהם. משמע מתוך פירושו דקרי ודאי מה שודאי נוטל חלק בנכסים, ובפרק "מי שמת" (ב"ב דף קנח: ושם), גבי הא דתנן נפל הבית עליו ועל אמו (ב) אלו ואלו מודים שיחלוקו, פירש רבינו שמואל שיחלוקו יורשי האם, דהיינו: אחי האם מאביה, עם יורשי הבן, היינו: אחי הבן מן האב ראובן. ולא רצה לפרש יורשי האם – בני האם דהיינו אחי הבן מן האם דהיינו בנימין – דא"כ ה"ל בנימין ודאי וראובן ספק ואין ספק מוציא מידי ודאי. ואין נראה כלל, דאטו מפני שהוא ודאי במקצת הנכסים יהא ודאי בכולן? ועוד: דאמר התם, ומייתי ליה לקמן גבי נפל הבית עליו ועל אביו [עליו] ועל מורישיו, והיתה עליו כתובת אשה וב"ח כו', ומסיק דיורשי האב – אחי הבן. אלמא, אע"ג דיש לאב בנים אחרים לא חשבינן להו ודאי. וכן בפ"ק דב"ק (דף ט. ושם) גבי אחים שחלקו ובא ב"ח ונטל חלקו של אחד מהן, דאמר רב אסי: נוטל רביע בקרקע או רביע במעות, משום דמספקא ליה אי כיורשים דמו אי כלקוחות, ולא אמרי' שלא יטול כלום – שהרי זה המוחזק הוא ודאי במקצת נכסים. וכן זה אומר כולה שלי וזה אומר חציה שלי גבי "שנים אוחזים בטלית" (ב"מ דף ב.). אלא הא דקרי הכא יבם ודאי, היינו: משום שהיבם הוא ודאי יורשו של סבא, אבל ספק – הוא ספק אם הוא יורשו כלל. אבל התם, בנפל עליו ועל אמו – לא הוי בנימין ודאי יורש בכל חלקי האחר. דאם מתה רחל קודם יוסף – הוי ראובן נמי יורשו. וכן בנפל הבית עליו ועל אביו, אם מת האב קודם – הוי בעל חוב יורש, ולא בן האחר. **ובית הלל אומרים הנכנסים בחזקתן.** בפרק "מי שמת" (ב"ב קנח. ושם) פליגי בכהאי גוונא ב"ש וב"ה, גבי נפל הבית עליו ועל אשתו, וקאמר בגמ' בחזקת מי? פירוש: בית הלל דקאמרי נכסים בחזקתן, דהיינו נכסי צאן ברזל – בחזקת מי? ר' אלעזר אומר: בחזקת יורשי האשה, רבי יוחנן אמר: בחזקת יורשי הבעל. וריש לקיש אמר: יחלוקו. ופי' בקונטרס בפרק "האשה שנפלו" (כתובות דף פ: ושם): דכי היכי דפליגי התם – הכי נמי פליגי אמתניתין דהכא. ורבינו תם אומר דלא דמיא הך להתם. דהכא לא פליגי ב"ש בכתובה אלא בנכסי מלוג, כדאמר בגמ' דכתובה שיירה, מדקתני יחלוקו יורשי הבעל עם יורשי האב כו', אבל התם קתני סתמא יחלוקו, משמע דבכתובה נמי פליגי. והיינו טעמא: דהתם, אם הבעל מת תחלה – הויא האשה כמו שגבתה כתובתה, אבל הכא כשהיא זקוקה ליבם – אין לאשה כלום בנכסי הבעל עד אחר החליצה, דלא ניתנה כתובה לגבות מחיים, ומפשר דכולהו אמוראי מודו הכא דנכסי צאן ברזל הוי בחזקת יורשי הבעל. והא דלא ערבינהו עם כתובה – כדי ליתן טעם לדבר. כלומר: בחזקת מי שהיו עד עתה, דהיינו בחזקת הבעל. אבל בכתובה – דבר פשוט הוא יותר שהיא בחזקת הבעל מנכסי צאן ברזל שהיא הביאה מבית אביה ושמה אותם לבעל. וכן נ"ל למאן דאמר התם בחזקת יורשי הבעל. ואם תאמר: ולמאן דאמר בחזקת יורשי האשה – מ"ש מנפל הבית עליו ועל אמו, דמודים בית הלל שיחלוקו ולא מוקמינן להו בחזקת יורשי האם? ויש לומר: דשמא קסבר הואיל תנא דירושת יורשי הבעל לרבנן. א"נ: אפילו קסבר דהוי דאורייתא, כיון דלאו מכח קורבה קאתין – מוקמינן להו בחזקת האשה טפי. א"נ: משום הכי לא מוקמינן להו התם בחזקת יורשי האם, משום דרגילות הוא שהאם היא מתה קודם, דקא חשיב בריש "יש נוחלין" (ב"ב דף קח.) פורענות כשהבן מת תחלה, לפיכך לא החזיקום בחזקת האם. ואם תאמר: ויורשי האשה היכי גבו כתובה? (ג) הא קי"ל כרב ושמואל דאמרי בפרק "כל הנשבעין" (שבועות דף מז.) דאין אדם מוריש שבועה לבניו! ומיהו, לב"ש ניחא, דאית להו: שטר העומד לגבות כגבוי דמי, והוו כמוחזקין בממון. דכמה ברייתות דפריך מינייהו לרב ושמואל בשבועות (ד) משני התם דאתאי כב"ש. ולר"א דאמר בחזקת יורשי האשה – ניחא, דאיהו פליג דהיא בשבועות (דף מח.), דלרב ושמואל, אבל לר' יוחנן, דאמר בחזקת יורשי הבעל, ופי' דנכסים שהכניסה בחזקת הבעל הוא טעם לדבר – למה לי' תיפוק ליה דאין אדם מוריש שבועה לבניו! ויש לומר, דהיא הנותנת: לפי שהנכסים בחזקת הבעל (ה) אינה מורשת. שאם היו בחזקת האשה היתה מורשת, כמו לבית שמאי דאמרי כגבוי דמי. אי נמי, אר"י: דאיכא לאוקמי במטלטלי, ואיתנהו בעינייהו, שנוטל בלא שבועה. והא דלא משני הכי בשבועות, אלא דוחק להעמידה כב"ש, משום דהתם בכתובה איירי, אבל הכא הוא דאיירי בנכסי צאן ברזל שהביאה מבית אביה, דרגילין להיות בעיינייהו, דאין דרך לבעלה למכרן. ואיכא למ"ד לקמן (דף סו:) המכנסת שום לבעלה, אם רצה הבעל למכור – לא ימכור. זיקת

לג א מיי' פ"ה מהלכות נחלות הלכה ד ה סמג עשין צו טוש"ע אה"ע סימן קסג סעיף ו:
לד ב מיי' שם טוש"ע שם סעיף ז:
לה ג מיי' שם טוש"ע שם סעיף ח:
לו ד מיי' פכ"ב מהל' אישות הלכה י ופ"ג מהלכות נחלות הלכה י סמג עשין נו טוש"ע אה"ע סימן קס סעיף ה:
לז ה טוש"ע שם ס"ע:
לח ו מיי' שם טוש"ע אה"ע סי' קסח ס"ח:
לט ז מיי' פ"ו מהלכות יבום הל' ה טוש"ע אה"ע שם סעיף ג וסימן קסו סעיף ד:

תוספות חד מקמאי

ספק או סבא וספק בנכסי יבם חולקין: **מתניתין** שומרת יבם שנפלו לה נכסים מודים ב"ש וב"ה שמוכרת ונותנת וקיים מתה מה יעשו בכתובתה ובנכסים הנכנסים והיוצאין עמה ב"ש אומרים יחלוקו וב"ה אומרים נכסים בחזקתן וכתובה בחזקת יורשי הבעל נכסים הנכנסים והיוצאים עמהן בחזקת יורשי האב וה"ה לנצ"ב שהן בחזקת יורשי הבעל כדין כתובתה ואע"ג דגבי נפל הבית עליו ועל אשתו נצ"ב יחלוקו יורשי הבעל עם יורשי האב שאני הכא כיון דשומרת יבם היא יבם במקום בעל קאי וכשם שהוא מוחזק בכתובה כך הוא מוחזק בנצ"ב והרמב"ם כתב גבי שומרת יבם נמי יחלוקו מספקא דשמעתתא אליבא דהלכתא שומרת יבם מן הארוסין כל הנכנסים בחזקתן ל"ש נפלו לה בחיי ארוס ל"ש נפלו לה כשהיא שומרת יבם ל"ש עבד בה מאמר ול"ש לא עבד בה מאמר ל"ש בחייה ולפירות ול"ש מתה ולגוף הנכסים ואם היתה שומרת יבם מן הנשואין ונפלו לה נכסים כשהיא שומרת יבם מוכרת ונותנת וקיים ואפלו עשה בה מאמר ואם מתה נכסים בחזקתן כתובה ונצ"ב בחזקת יורשי הבעל. נ"מ בחזקת יורשי האב ואפי' עשה בה מאמר ואם היתה שומרת יבם מן הנשואין ונפלו לה נכסים כשהיא תחת בעלה קי"ל כרבא דאמר ידו עדיפא מידה ל"ש עבד בה מאמר ול"ש לא עביד בה מאמר והשתא כשמת הבעל קלישא ליה ידו כידה ויחלוקו הנכנסים והיוצאין עמה. אבל לאביי ורבא אליבא דב"ה דידו כידה השתא כשמת הבעל קלישא ליה ידו ונכסים בחזקת יורשי האב. מיהו קי"ל כרבא ויחלוקו ואע"ג דאמר רב פפא דייקא מתני' כותיה דאביי הלכתא כותיה דרבא דקי"ל כל היכא דפליגי אביי ורבא הלכה כרבא בר מיע"ל קג"ם הלכך הלכתא כרבא ויחלוקו. וי"מ אליבא דרבא דאמר ידו עדיפא מידה דנכסים

לעיל יט: פסחים ע. וש"נ

כתובות פ:

[לעיל יט: כתובות פ:]

לקמן נב. ופס. כתובות נג: פ:

הגהות הב"ח

(א) רש"י ד"ה מי איכא וכו' פלגא בנכסי מיתנא אי מנתא כל"ל ותיבת פלגא נמחק: (ב) תום' ד"ה הוי יבם וכו' עליו ועל אמו כגון יוסף ורחל אלו ואלו מודים שיחלוקו פי' רבינו שמואל שיחלוקו יורשי האם והיינו אחי האם מן האב לבן עם יורשי הבן: (ג) ד"ה ובית הלל וכו' והיכי גבו כתובה. נ"ב כלומר דהא מחויבת שבועה היא וכיון שמתה ולא נשבעה הוי מוריש שבועה לבניו: (ד) בא"ד לרב ושמואל בשבועות וקא משני התם. נ"ב כלומר על הדא ברייתא דקא מקשה מבריתא קא משני הא מני ב"ש היא דאמר שטר העומד לגבות כגבוי דמי אלמא לב"ש ניחא דיכולה להוריש שבועה כיון דהוי כמו שמוחזקין בממון: (ה) בא"ד בחזקת הבעל לכך אינה מורשת שאם היו בחזקת וכו' ואין דרך בעלה למכרן:

בחזקת יבם. ורש"י כתב ויחלוקו והא דאמר ואע"ג דקשיא מתה לאביי ה"ה לרבא נמי קשיא אדמפלגי לאחר מיתה לפלגו בחייה ולפירות דאליבא דב"ש יחלוקו. וי"מ דלרבא לא קשיא מתה א) דבמתה ה"ה יחלוקו לב"ש הואיל והללו באים לירש אבל בחייה נכסים בחזקתן אפי' לב"ש אפי' עבד לה מאמר ב) ולפי הפירוש הזה לא הוה צריך לאוקמי רישא בדלא עבד לה מאמר. וה"ל לאוקמי רישא וסיפא בחד טעמא בדעבד לה מאמר: כתב

א) נ"ל דנפלו לה נכסים תחתיו דבעל ול"ש נפלו לה כשהיא שומרת יבם לב"ש יחלוקו. ב) עי' תוס' לקמן לט ד"ה אע"ג.

מ א ב מיי' פכ"ב מהל' אישות הל' ז סמג לאוין פא טוש"ע אה"ע סי' צ סעיף יא וסימן קס סעיף ה:

[ניחא ליה]

מא ג מיי' שם טוש"ע שם סימן ל סעיף ט:

מב ד מיי' פי"ח מהל' נחלות הלכה ח סמג עשין צו טוש"ע ח"מ סי' רפ סעיף יב:

מג ה מיי' פ"ב מהל' סוטה הל' ז סמג עשין מח טוש"ע אה"ע סימן קטו וסימן קעח:

דבארוסה ושומרת יבם יש לתוספה כצ"ל מהר"ם

תורה אור

זִיקַּת נְשׂוּאָה עוֹשָׂה סָפֵק נְשׂוּאָה. זִיקַּת אֲרוּסָה עוֹשָׂה סָפֵק אֲרוּסָה, דְּאִי ס"ד וַדַּאי אֲרוּסָה — מוֹדִים ב"ה שֶׁמּוֹכֶרֶת וְנוֹתֶנֶת וְקַיָּים?! וְהָתְנַן: *נָפְלוּ לָהּ נְכָסִים מִשֶּׁנִּתְאָרְסָה, ב"ש אוֹמְרִים: תִּמְכּוֹר, וב"ה אוֹמְרִים: [א]לֹא תִּמְכּוֹר. אֵלּוּ וְאֵלּוּ מוֹדִים [ב]שֶׁאִם מָכְרָה וְנָתְנָה — קַיָּים. אֶלָּא ש"מ: זִיקַּת אֲרוּסָה — עוֹשָׂה סָפֵק אֲרוּסָה. זִיקַּת נְשׂוּאָה עוֹשָׂה סָפֵק נְשׂוּאָה, דְּאִי ס"ד וַדַּאי נְשׂוּאָה ב"ש אוֹמְרִים יַחֲלוֹקוּ יוֹרְשֵׁי הַבַּעַל עִם יוֹרְשֵׁי הָאָב?! וְהָתְנַן: *נָפְלוּ לָהּ נְכָסִים מִשֶּׁנִּישֵּׂאת — אֵלּוּ וְאֵלּוּ מוֹדִים [ג]שֶׁאִם מָכְרָה וְנָתְנָה שֶׁהַבַּעַל מוֹצִיא מִיַּד הַלָּקוֹחוֹת. אֶלָּא שְׁמַע מִינָּהּ: זִיקַּת נְשׂוּאָה עוֹשָׂה סָפֵק נְשׂוּאָה. אֲמַר לֵיהּ רַבָּה: אַדְּמִפַּלְגִי בְּגוּפָהּ וּלְאַחַר מִיתָה, לִפְלְגוּ בְּחַיֶּיהָ וְלַפֵּירוֹת! אֶלָּא אֲמַר רַבָּה: אִידִי וְאִידִי דְּנָפְלָה כְּשֶׁהִיא נְשׂוּאָה, וְזִיקַּת נְשׂוּאָה — עוֹשָׂה סָפֵק נְשׂוּאָה. רֵישָׁא דְּאִיהִי קַיְּימָא — הָוֵה לָהּ אִיהִי וַדַּאי וְאִינְהוּ סָפֵק *וְאֵין סָפֵק מוֹצִיא מִידֵי וַדַּאי. סֵיפָא דְּמֵתָה — הַלָּלוּ בָּאִין לִירַשׁ וְהַלָּלוּ בָּאִין לִירַשׁ, וְיַחֲלוֹקוּ. אֵיתִיבֵיהּ אַבַּיֵּי: וּלְב"ש אֵין סָפֵק מוֹצִיא מִידֵי וַדַּאי?! וְהָתְנַן: *נָפַל הַבַּיִת עָלָיו וְעַל אָבִיו, עָלָיו וְעַל מוֹרִישָׁיו, וְהָיוּ עָלָיו כְּתוּבַּת אִשָּׁה וּב"ח, יוֹרְשֵׁי הָאָב אוֹמְרִים: הַבֵּן מֵת רִאשׁוֹן וְאַחַר כָּךְ מֵת הָאָב. וּב"ח אוֹמֵר: הָאָב מֵת רִאשׁוֹן וְאח"כ מֵת הַבֵּן, ב"ש אוֹמְרִים: יַחֲלוֹקוּ, וּב"ה אוֹמְרִים: [ד]נְכָסִים בְּחֶזְקָתָן. וְהָא הָכָא, יוֹרְשֵׁי הָאָב — וַדַּאי, וּב"ח — סָפֵק, וְקָאָתֵי סָפֵק וּמוֹצִיא מִידֵי וַדַּאי! קָסָבְרִי ב"ש: *שְׁטָר הָעוֹמֵד לִגְבּוֹת כְּגָבוּי דָּמֵי. וּמְנָא תֵּימְרָא — דִּתְנַן: *מֵתוּ בַּעֲלֵיהֶן עַד שֶׁלֹּא שָׁתוּ, ב"ש אוֹמְרִים: נוֹטְלוֹת כְּתוּבָּתָן וְאֵינָן שׁוֹתוֹת, וּב"ה אוֹמְרִים: אוֹ שׁוֹתוֹת אוֹ לֹא נוֹטְלוֹת כְּתוּבָּתָן. אוֹ שׁוֹתוֹת?! °"וְהֵבִיא הָאִישׁ אֶת אִשְׁתּוֹ" אָמַר רַחֲמָנָא, וְלֵיכָּא! אֶלָּא: [ה]מִתּוֹךְ שֶׁלֹּא שׁוֹתוֹת לֹא נוֹטְלוֹת כְּתוּבָּתָן. וְהָא הָכָא, דְּסָפֵק הוּא, סָפֵק זַנַּאי סָפֵק לֹא זַנַּאי, וְקָאָתֵי סָפֵק וּמוֹצִיא מִידֵי וַדַּאי! אֶלָּא ש"מ: *שְׁטָר הָעוֹמֵד לִגְבּוֹת כְּגָבוּי דָּמֵי. וְאַבַּיֵּי, לוֹתְבֵיהּ מֵהָא! דִּלְמָא כְּתוּבַּת אִשָּׁה שָׁאנֵי, מִשּׁוּם *חִינָּא. וְלוֹתְבֵיהּ כְּתוּבָּה דְּמַתְנִיתִין! לָא פְּלִיגִי. וְלָא? וְהָא *)קָתָנֵי: מֵתָה, מַה יַּעֲשֶׂה בִּכְתוּבָּתָהּ וּבַנְּכָסִים הַנִּכְנָסִים וְיוֹצְאִין עִמָּהּ? ב"ש אוֹמְרִים: יַחֲלוֹקוּ יוֹרְשֵׁי הַבַּעַל עִם יוֹרְשֵׁי הָאָב, וּב"ה אוֹמְרִים: נְכָסִים בְּחֶזְקָתָן! הָכִי קָאָמַר: מֵתָה, מַה יַּעֲשֶׂה בִּכְתוּבָּתָהּ, וּשְׁבָקָהּ. נְכָסִים הַנִּכְנָסִים וְהַיּוֹצְאִים עִמָּהּ, ב"ש אוֹמְרִים: יַחֲלוֹקוּ יוֹרְשֵׁי הַבַּעַל עִם יוֹרְשֵׁי הָאָב וּב"ה אוֹמְרִים נְכָסִים בְּחֶזְקָתָן. [א] אֲמַר רַב אַשִׁי: מַתְנִי' נַמִי דַּיְקָא, דְּקָתָנֵי: יַחֲלוֹקוּ יוֹרְשֵׁי הַבַּעַל עִם יוֹרְשֵׁי הָאָב, *וְלָא קָתָנֵי יוֹרְשֵׁי הָאָב עִם יוֹרְשֵׁי הַבַּעַל — ש"מ. אַבַּיֵּי אֲמַר: רֵישָׁא דְּנָפְלוּ לָהּ כְּשֶׁהִיא שׁוֹמֶרֶת יָבָם, סֵיפָא דְּנָפְלוּ לָהּ כְּשֶׁהִיא תַּחְתָּיו דְּבַעַל. וְקָסָבַר

*) כתובות פ:

במדבר ה

סיפא. דגבי נשואה בעלמא אמרי' לקמן דברי הכל מכרה ונתנה, אפי' בדיעבד — הבעל מוציא מיד הלקוחות, הכא, לגבי זיקת נשואה, דספק היא ולא כנשואה ממש — קיימי נכסי בספק. הלכך, לב"ש חלוקה עדיפא, [ולב"ה חזקה עדיפא]. זיקת ארוסה. זיקת יבמה שנפלה מן האירוסין. ספק ארוסה ולא ודאי ארוסה. ואע"ג דלגבי נכסים אין לו שום כח בהן, ונמלא שזיקת ארוסה אינה כלום — קרי לה ספק ארוסה, דלא מצי למימר קסבר עולא זיקת ארוסה אינה כלום, דהא בעיא חליצה. מודים ב"ה כו'. בתמיה. אלא ש"מ: כספק ארוסה היא, הלכך תמכור לכתחלה. עושה ספק נשואה. כדפרישית לעיל, דכיון דודאי נשואה — הבעל מוציא מיד הלקוחות, הכא דספק נשואה היא — הוו נכסים בספק, ולב"ש חלוקה עדיפא, דאין לה בהם חזקה יותר ממנו, דידו כידה. ולב"ה חזקה עדיפא, דאין ידו כידה, הואיל ולא נפלו לה כשהיא תחת הבעל. אמר ליה רבה. לעולא: אי טעמא משום חלוקה עדיפא הוא, אדמיפלגי בגופה של קרקע ולאחר מיתה — ליפלגו בחייה ולפירות, דלב"ש פליג יבם פירי בהדה, דספק נשואה היא. דאילו ודאי נשואה הואי — הוה שקיל להו בעל כרחה (א), ולב"ה נכסים בחזקתה, ולא שקיל מידי! ומדנקט מתני' מיתה בסיפא — ש"מ טעמייהו דב"ש ברישא דאלמוה לחזקה דילה, משום דהיא קיימא. אלא אמר רבה אידי ואידי דנפלה. ליבום כשהיא נשואה כו'. איהי ודאי. שהקרן שלה מתה נפשך, הלכך אלימא חזקה דילה. סיפא. הואיל ומתה, הללו באים וטוענים מכח ירושה, והיבם טוען מכח ירושה. הלכך שניהם ספק לב"ש, דאי זיקה ככנוסה — אין כאן ליורשי האב כלום, שהבעל יורש שלה. ואי לאו ככנוסה — אין כאן ליבם כלום, לפיכך ספק וספק הוא ויחלוקו. ולב"ה, הואיל ואלו קרובין ודאין הם, והוחזקה נחלה זו כבר בחזקת משפחתן, אמרינן: אוקי אחזקתה. אבל בחייה ולפירות — אפי' ב"ש מודו דנכסים בחזקתייהו, ולא שקיל בעל מידי: עליו ועל יורשיו ל"ג. נפל הבית כו'. לו אין נכסים, ולמורישים יש נכסים. הבן מת ראשון. ולא זכה בנכסי האב, ואין לב"ח מה לגבות. יורשי האב ודאי. מוחזקים, שבאין מכח ירושה ודאית, שאפי' (ב) האב מת ראשון — נכסי הבן מסתמא נופלים לפני יורשין. דאילו ב"ח מיחסר גוביינא, עד שיחזיקוהו ב"ד בהם. ובעל חוב ספק. דלא הוחזק שטרו עליהן, וקאתי ספק ומוציא את החלי מידי ודאי. כגבוי דמי. כלומר, גדול כח השטר, וכמו שמוחזק בנכסים (ג), והרי הן קמו במקום הבן ומוחזקים בנכסים דמי. הלכך, ספק וספק הוא, ואין כאן חזקה לזה יותר מזה. אם האב מת ראשון — הוחזק ב"ח מיד, ולא אמרינן הא מחוסר גוביינא. ואם בן מת ראשון — הוחזקו יורשים. מתו בעליהן. כל אשה שקינא לה בעלה ונסתרה, ומת עד שלא שתתה — נוטלת כתובתה. ואע"פ שספק זינתה ואין לה כתובה — לא שותות, דבעינן והביא האיש את אשתו, וליכא. מידי ודאי. מידי יורשי הבעל, שהן מוחזקין ודאי, מוליאה זו כתובה מספק. אלא. לאו ש"מ קסברי ב"ש: שטר העומד לגבות — כגבוי דמי, וכיון שמת — עמדו הנכסים מיד בחזקת האשה, ויורשים קאתו לאפוקי מינה משום ספק זנאי, ולא אתי ספק ומוליא מידי ודאי. דאי לא כגבוי דמי, וטעמא משום דאתי ספק ומוליא מידי ודאי הוא — הוה להו למימר יחלוקו, ונשווי ספק כודאי. אבל לעלויי מינה — ליכא למ"ד. וגבי נפל הבית קאמר יחלוקו, דכי נמי אמרי' כגבוי דמי — לא מלינו לב"ח לשווי ודאי טפי מיורשין, שהרי לא הוחזק בו זה בנכסים, והשטר זה יולא עליו ולא על האב, הלכך ספק וספק הוא: אם האב מת ראשון — נמלא ב"ח ודאי, דהאי שטר כגבוי דמי, ויורשים אינם כלום, ואם הבן מת ראשון — נמלאו יורשין ודאין, וב"ח אין כלום. ואביי. דלא אסיק אדעתיה מעיקרא משום טעמא דשטר העומד לגבות, כי אותביה לרבה מנפל הבית, דתנן ב"מי שמת" בבבא בתרא בסדר ישועות. לותביה מהא. דמתני' היא בסדר נשים, דהכא נמי ספק מוליא מידי ודאי. ואביי. להכי לא אותביה מכתובה, דקסבר: שאני כתובה משום חינא, שיהיו נושאין חן בעיני האנשים ויתרצו להנשא, לפיכך החזיקוה מספק. ולותביה מכתובה דמתני'. דאמרי ב"ש יחלוקו. דקס"ד השתא דב"ש נמי אכתובה אמרי יחלוקו, וקאתו יורשין דידה (ד) מספק וגבו פלגא דכתובה מיבם דהוי ודאי. והתם ליכא למימר משום חינא, דהתם מתה, וגבי יורשין לא חיישינן לחינא, כדאמר ב"אלמנה ניזונת" (כתובות נז:), אא"כ היו יורשיה נקבות. לא פליגי. דמודו ב"ש שהיא בחזקת יורשי הבעל, דלא ניתנה כתובה לגבות מחיים. וכל שהיא מתה בחייו של יבם — לא גבו יורשים דילה כתובה, דיבם במקום בעל קאי. ואע"ג דשמעינן ליה לאביי בכתובות פרק "האשה" (דף פא.) ניתנה כתובה לגבות מחיים לב"ש — הני מילי להתחייב יבם בקבורתה, דאמר: מינה קא ירית כתובה ולא מאחיו. אבל דליםקלו יורשין דילה כתובתה — לא שמעינן ליה. דיקא נמי כו'. וטעמא לאו משום דשטר העומד לגבות הוא, דלא ניתנה כתובה לגבות מחיים. יורשי הבעל עם יורשי האב. נכסי מלוג. אביי. מהדר אחרישא דשמעתין לתרולי, מאי שנא רישא דלא פליגי ומאי שנא סיפא דפליגי. ותרליה: לאו משום דברישא היא קיימת וסיפא משום דליתא, דודאי סיפא נמי אי כשהיא שומרת יבם נפלו לה מודו ב"ש דיורשי האב ודאין ונכסים בחזקתן. אלא: רישא דנפלו לה כשהיא שומרת יבם לפיכך מוכרת לכתחלה. וה"ה אם מתה — יורשיה יורשין אותה, דלא מהניא זיקה למיקני נכסי דהשתא. סיפא. דנפלו לה כשהיא תחת בעלה הראשון. וקסבר

זיקת נשואה עושה ספק נשואה. ואפ"ה, לב"ה הוו בחזקת יורשי האב. דחזקה עדיפא, שיש לנו להחזיק נחלה בחזקת אותו השבט. דאי ס"ד ודאי נשואה והתנן נפלו לה כו'. מכמה משניות דתנן פרק "יש נוחלין" (ב"ב דף קח.) שהבעל יורש את אשתו הוה מצי למיפרך! אלא מסיפא דההוא דאייתי לעיל *כ"ל לאיתויי. הויא לה איהי ודאי. שהגוף (ה) שלה. קסברי ב"ש שטר העומד לגבות כגבוי דמי. אביי גופיה אית ליה הכי בפרק "האשה שנפלו" (כתובות דף פא. ושם), דלבתר דשמע מרבה סברה. בש"א נוטלות כתובה ולא שותות. והא דתנן בריש פ' "ארוסה" (סוטה דף כג:): ארוסה ושומרת יבם לא שותות ולא נוטלות כתובתן, ולא פליגי ב"ש! אור"י: דהתם היא נתנה אצבע בין שיניה, שנסתרה ואסרה עצמה על בעלה. אבל הכא, בשעה שנסתרה היתה יכולה ליבדק בשתיה. ועוד: *דבארוסה ושומרת יבם אין לתוספה כעוברת על דת, כיון שאינה יכולה ליבדק, כדקאמר התם בגמ'. בה"א או שותות או לא נוטלות כו'. הא דגרס במסכת סוטה (דף כד.) לא שותות ולא נוטלות כתובה*) — כתבו שם כמו שמגיה הש"ס כאן. ואביי לותביה מהא. וא"ת: אדרבה, תקשי ליה למה נוטלת כל הכתובה מספק?! וי"ל: לפי שהיא באה בטענת ברי, והיורשין בטענת ספק. וספק

*) לפנינו ליתא הכי גירסא

לותביה מהא מאי טעמא נוטלת כתובה כיון דלא ידע דשטר העומד לגבות כגבוי דמי: ואביי לותביה מכתובה דמתני' דהא ליכא למימר משעבד משום חינא אי לאו אם היו היורשים נקבות: בכתובה דמתני' לא פליגי. דלא נתנה [...] מחיי הבעל וה"ה מחיי היבם דיבם במקום בעל קאי ואף למ"ד נתנה כתובה לגבות מחיים ה"מ להתחייב בקבורה דחשבינן ליה כאילו ירית כתובה מינה וצריך לקוברה אבל במידי אחרינא אמרי' לא נתנה

תוספות ישנים

ליפלגו בחייה ולפירות. [...]

הגהות הב"ח

(א) רש"י ד"ה אמר לי' וכו' בעל כרחה כולהו ולב"ה וכו': (ב) ד"ה יורשי האב וכו' שאפי' אם האב: (ג) ד"ה כגבוי וכו' בנכסים דמי והכי הוו: (ד) ד"ה ולותביה מכתובה וכו' יורשין דידיה דספק הן וגבו: (ה) תום' ד"ה הויא לה איהו ודאי וכו' שהגוף שלה. [...]

גליון הש"ס

גמ' ולא קתני יורשי האב עם יורשי הבעל. ע' יומא דף פה ע"ב בתוס' ישנים ד"ה תשובה וכר"ש פ"ז מ"ב דטהרות:

כתובות עח.

ג"ז שם

[לעיל יט: פסחים ע. וש"נ]

ב"ב קנז.

[סוטה כה. וש"נ]

סוטה כד. כתובות פא.

גיטין לו. כתובות פא. שבועות מח: סוטה כה. [ב"מ סב.]

[פירוש דכיון שיודעת שאפי' מספק נוטלת כתובתה משמשת לבעלה ויעלת חן בעיני בעלה ערוך ערך חן ב ועי' תוס' כתובות פד. ד"ה לכתובה וכו']

[בתו' ישנים יומא פה: ד"ה תשובה בעיא יוה"כ וכו' האריכו קצת בפירושו של סוגיא דהכא]

הגהות מהר"ב רנשבורג א] אמר רב אשי מתני' נמי דיקא דקתני יחלוקו יורשי הבעל עם יורשי האב. נ"ב עי' יומא פה ע"ב בתוס' ישנים ד"ה תשובה בעיא יוה"כ וכו' ובתוי"ט פ"ב דאבות מ"ב בד"ה יפה ת"ת עם ד"א וכו':

וְקָסָבַר אַבַּיֵי יָדוֹ כְּיָדָהּ. מִדְּאוֹקִי פְּלוּגְתַּיְיהוּ כְּנָפְלוּ לָהּ (ב) תַּחְתָּיו, וַאֲפִי׳ הָכִי לְבֵית הִלֵּל נְכָסִים בְּחֶזְקָתָן – קָסָבַר אַבַּיֵי: נְשׂוּאָה יָדוֹ כְּיָדָהּ, וְלֹא יוֹתֵר. הִלְכָּךְ, כְּשֶׁמֵּת וְאֵין לַיָּבָם בָּהּ אֶלָּא זִיקָה – יָדוֹ גְּרִיעָא מִיָּדָהּ, וּנְכָסִים בְּחֶזְקָתָהּ. וּבֵית שַׁמַּאי פָּלְגִי וְאָמְרִי: נְשׂוּאָה, יָדוֹ עֲדִיפָא מִיָּדָהּ, וּכְשֶׁמֵּת – יַד הַיָּבָם כְּיָדָהּ, וְיַחֲלוֹקוּ. וּבִכְתוּבּוֹת בְּ״הַכּוֹתֵב״ (דף פג.) נַמִּי פְּלִיגִי אַבַּיֵי וְרָבָא, דְּקָאָמַר אַבַּיֵי: יָדוֹ כְּיָדָהּ, וְרָבָא אָמַר: יָדוֹ עֲדִיפָא מִיָּדָהּ. וְאָמְרִינַן הָתָם: נָפְקָא מִינָּהּ לְשׁוֹמֶרֶת יָבָם. **דְּיָדוֹ עֲדִיפָא מִיָּדָהּ.** וַאֲפִילוּ בֵּית הִלֵּל מוֹדוּ דְּשָׁקְלֵי יוֹרְשֵׁי הַבַּעַל בִּנְכָסִים: הָכִי גָּרְסִינַן. **אֶלָּא אִידִי וְאִידִי דְּנָפְלוּ לָהּ כְּשֶׁהִיא שׁוֹמֶרֶת יָבָם רֵישָׁא דְּלָא עֲבַד בָּהּ מַאֲמָר.** קוֹדֶם שֶׁנָּפְלוּ לָהּ הַנְּכָסִים, הִלְכָּךְ זִיקָה לָא מְהַנְּיָא וְלָא מִידֵי בִּנְכָסִים. **וְסֵיפָא דַּעֲבַד בָּהּ מַאֲמָר.** וּבֵית שַׁמַּאי לְטַעְמַיְיהוּ, דְּאָמְרִי: מַאֲמָר קָנֵי, בְּפֶרֶק ״אַרְבָּעָה אַחִין״ (לעיל כט.) בֵּית שַׁמַּאי אוֹמְרִים: אִשְׁתּוֹ עִמּוֹ כו׳, וּב״ה לְטַעְמַיְיהוּ, דְּאָמְרִי: לָא קָנֵי. **וְקָסָבַר רָבָא.** קִנְיַן מַאֲמָר לְבֵ״שׁ קָנֵי כְּוַדַּאי אֲרוּסָה וּכְסָפֵק נְשׂוּאָה. כְּלוֹמַר, אַע״ג דְּבֵ״שׁ (ג) וַדַּאי אֲרוּסָה מְשַׁוֵּי לָהּ לִדְחוֹת בְּצָרָה אֲחוֹתָהּ מִשּׁוּם אֲחוֹת אִשָּׁה, כִּדְקָתָנֵי: אִשְׁתּוֹ עִמּוֹ, מִיהוּ לָא כְּוַדַּאי נְשׂוּאָה מְשַׁוֵּי לָהּ, לְמִיקְנֵי יָבָם כּוּלָּהּ יְרוּשָּׁה דִּילָהּ, אֶלָּא כִּסְפֵק נְשׂוּאָה, וְיַחֲלוֹקוּ. **כְּוָותֵיהּ דְּאַבַּיֵי.** דְּסֵיפָא בִּדְנָפְלוּ לָהּ כְּשֶׁהִיא תַּחַת הַבַּעַל. **דְּקַשְׁיָא מֵתָה.** לְקַמָּן מְפָרֵשׁ. **וְיוֹצְאִין מֵרְשׁוּת הַבַּעַל** כְּשֶׁמֵּתָה. אַלְמָא דְּנָפְלוּ לָהּ תַּחַת בַּעְלָהּ. **אַדְּמִפַּלְגִי בְּגוּפָהּ.** שֶׁל קַרְקַע, וּלְאַחַר מִיתָהּ. לִיפַלְגוּ בְּחַיֶּיהָ וּלְפֵירוֹת. הוֹאִיל וְטַעְמָא מִשּׁוּם דְּיָדוֹ כְּיָדָהּ. **וְתוּ לָא מִידֵי.** אֵין לְהָשִׁיב עַל כָּךְ, דְּוַדַּאי דַּיְקָא כְּוָותֵיהּ, וְקַשְׁיָא לֵיהּ מֵתָה. **שֶׁמְּגָרְשָׁהּ** בְּגֵט. וְלָא בָּעֵי חֲלִיצָה. **וּמַחֲזִירָהּ.** אִם רָצָה, וְלָא מִיתַּסְרָא עֲלֵיהּ. **וִיבָּמָהּ.** אַע״פ שֶׁלְּקָחָהּ קָרֵי לֵיהּ ״וִיבְּמָהּ״. **וְאֵימָא הָכִי נַמִּי.** אֲכוּלָּהּ מִילְּתָא קָאֵי. **וּלְקָחָהּ לוֹ.** וִיבְּמָהּ מָצֵי לְמִכְתַּב, לָמָּה לִי דִּכְתִיב ״לְאִשָּׁה״? ש״מ: הֲרֵי הִיא כְּאִשְׁתּוֹ. ״וִיבְּמָהּ״, אִי לְכִדְרַבִּי בְּפ״ק (לעיל דף ח.) לֶאֱסוֹר צָרוֹת וַעֲרָיוֹת, אִי לְכִדְרַבָּנַן – וִיבָמָהּ בְּעַל כָּרְחָהּ. **אִשָּׁה הִקְנוּ לוֹ.** לַיָּבָם. מִן הַשָּׁמַיִם. וְלֹא שֶׁיִּשְׁתַּעְבְּדוּ נְכָסָיו לִכְתוּבָּתָהּ, וְיָכוֹל לְמוֹכְרָן בְּכָל עֵת שֶׁיִּרְצֶה. **וְאִי לֵית לָהּ מֵרִאשׁוֹן.** דְּלֵית לֵיהּ נְכָסִים. **מתני׳ מִצְוָה בְּגָדוֹל.** מִ״וְהָיָה הַבְּכוֹר״ (דברים כה). **לֹא רָצָה כו׳.** מְפָרֵשׁ בַּגְּמָ׳. **תָּלָה בְּקָטָן.** קָטָן מַמָּשׁ. **וּבְגָדוֹל.** (ד) שֶׁהָיָה גָּדוֹל הָאַחִים בִּמְדִינַת הַיָּם, וְיֵשׁ לוֹ אָח כָּאן הַגָּדוֹל מִן הָאַחִין שֶׁלְּפָנֵינוּ. וְתָלָה גָּדוֹל הָאַחִין שֶׁלְּפָנֵינוּ בּוֹ, לוֹמַר: הַמְתִּינוּ לוֹ, שֶׁהוּא גָּדוֹל מִמֶּנִּי, שֶׁמָּא יְיַבֵּם אוֹתָךְ. וְהָכִי מוּכַח בַּגְּמָ׳, דְּאָמְרִי, ת״ש: וּבְגָדוֹל עַד שֶׁיָּבֹא מִמְּדִינַת הַיָּם – אֵין שׁוֹמְעִין לוֹ. וְאִי ס״ד חֲלִיצַת גָּדוֹל עֲדִיפָא – אַמַּאי אֵין שׁוֹמְעִין לוֹ? נִיגְטַר דִּלְמָא אָתֵי וְחָלֵיץ. אַלְמָא אוֹתוֹ שֶׁבִּמְדִינַת הַיָּם גָּדוֹל שֶׁבְּכָל הָאַחִין הוּא. **עָלֶיךָ מִצְוָה.** שֶׁאַע״פ שֶׁאָחִיךָ שֶׁבִּמְדִינַת הַיָּם גָּדוֹל מִמְּךָ, כֵּיוָן דְּאַתָּה גָּדוֹל הָאַחִין שֶׁלְּפָנֵינוּ – עָלֶיךָ מִצְוָה, דְּשִׁהוּיֵי מִצְוָה לָא מַשְׁהִינַן, וְהָכִי מְפָרֵשׁ בַּגְּמָרָא. **גמ׳ בִּיאַת קָטָן וַחֲלִיצַת גָּדוֹל.** גָּדוֹל רוֹצֶה לַחֲלוֹץ וְקָטָן [מִמֶּנּוּ] רוֹצֶה לְיַיבֵּם. וְהַאי קָטָן – לָאו קָטָן מַמָּשׁ הוּא, דְּקָטָן לָאו בַּר חֲלִיצָה וְיִיבּוּם הוּא, שֶׁמָּא יִמָּצֵא סָרִיס. וַאֲפִי׳ מַאן דְּלָא חָיֵישׁ לְמִיעוּט, וְקָטָן מוּתָּר לְיַיבֵּם – הָכָא וַדַּאי סוּגְיָא דִּשְׁמַעְתִּין מוֹכְחָא דְּלָאו קָטָן מַמָּשׁ הוּא, מִדְּקָפָרֵיךְ לְקַמָּן: תָּלָה בְּקָטָן עַד שֶׁיַּגְדִּיל, וְשַׁנֵּי לֵיהּ: שִׁהוּיֵי מִצְוָה לָא מַשְׁהִינַן. אַלְמָא: בְּקָטָן מַמָּשׁ כּוּלְּהוּ מוֹדוּ. **בִּמְקוֹם גָּדוֹל בִּיאַת קָטָן לָאו כְּלוּם הוּא.** דְּהָא מִצְוָה בַּגָּדוֹל רָמְיָא. **אֶלָּא** לַחֲלוֹץ וְקָתָנֵי מְהַלְּכִין עַל כָּל הָאַחִין. אוּלַי יְיַבְּמָהּ. **וְאַמַּאי חוֹזְרִין אֵצֶל גָּדוֹל.** אִי אָמְרַתְּ בִּשְׁלָמָא דְּכָל לֹא רָצָה וְרָצוּ דְּמַתְנִיתִין אַיִּיבּוּם קָאֵי – לְהָכִי חוֹזְרִין אֵצֶל גָּדוֹל; דְּכֵיוָן דְּכוּלְּהוּ בָּעוּ לְמִיחֲלַץ, וְאִיהוּ נַמִּי בָּעֵי לְמִיחֲלַץ – אִיהוּ קָדֵים. אֶלָּא אִי אָמְרַתְּ אֲפִילּוּ מִיחֲלַץ לָא בָּעֵי, אַמַּאי חוֹזְרִין אֵצֶל גָּדוֹל? פְּשִׁיטָא דִּלְמִכְפְּיֵיהּ לְמִיחֲלַץ, וְנִכְפִּינַן לְדִידְהוּ, וְלָא נִטְרַח ב״ד כּוּלֵּי הַאי. הָתָם

תורה אור

וְקָסָבַר *אַבַּיֵי יָדוֹ כְּיָדָהּ. [א] א״ל רָבָא. אִי דְּנָפְלִי לָהּ כְּשֶׁהִיא תַּחְתָּיו דְּבַעַל – דְּכ״ע לָא פְּלִיגִי דְּיָדוֹ עֲדִיפָא מִיָּדָהּ. אֶלָּא: אִידִי וְאִידִי דְּנָפְלוּ לָהּ כְּשֶׁהִיא שׁוֹמֶרֶת יָבָם, רֵישָׁא – דְּלָא עֲבַד בָּהּ מַאֲמָר, אסֵיפָא – דַּעֲבַד בָּהּ מַאֲמָר. וְקָסָבַר רָבָא: מַאֲמָר לְב״ש עוֹשֶׂה וַדַּאי אֲרוּסָה וּסְפֵק נְשׂוּאָה, וַדַּאי אֲרוּסָה – לִדְחוֹת בְּצָרָה, וּסְפֵק נְשׂוּאָה – לַחֲלוֹק בִּנְכָסִים. אִיתְּמַר מִשְּׁמֵיהּ דְּרַ׳ אֶלְעָזָר כְּוָותֵיהּ דְּרָבָא וְאִיתְּמַר מִשְּׁמֵיהּ דְּרַבִּי יוֹסֵי בְּרַבִּי חֲנִינָא כְּוָותֵיהּ דְּאַבַּיֵי. וּמִי אָמַר רַבִּי אֶלְעָזָר הָכִי? וְהָא אָמַר רַבִּי אֶלְעָזָר: *מַאֲמָר לְב״ש אֵינָהּ קוֹנָה אֶלָּא לִדְחוֹת בְּצָרָה בִּלְבָד! אֵיפוּךְ. וְאִי בָּעֵית אֵימָא: לְעוֹלָם לֹא תֵּיפוּךְ, אָמַר לָךְ רַבִּי אֶלְעָזָר: כִּי אֲמַרִי אֲנָא – דְּלָא סַגִּי לָהּ בְּגֵט, אֶלָּא דְּבָעֵי נַמִּי חֲלִיצָה, לַחֲלוֹק בִּנְכָסִים דְּלָא קָנֵי – מִי אֲמַרִי? אָמַר רַב פַּפָּא: דִּיוּקָא דְּמַתְנִיתִין כְּוָותֵיהּ דְּאַבַּיֵי. וְאע״ג דְּקַשְׁיָא ״מֵתָה״, דְּקָתָנֵי: ״נְכָסִים הַנִּכְנָסִים וְיוֹצְאִים עִמָּהּ״, מַאי נִכְנָסִין וּמַאי יוֹצְאִין? לָאו נִכְנָסִין: לִרְשׁוּת הַבַּעַל, וְיוֹצְאִים: מֵרְשׁוּת הַבַּעַל לִרְשׁוּת הָאָב, וְאע״ג דְּקַשְׁיָא מֵתָה, אַדְּמִפַּלְגִי בְּגוּפָהּ וּלְאַחַר מִיתָה לִפְלְגוּ בְּחַיֶּיהָ וְלַפֵּירוֹת. *וְתוּ לָא מִידֵי.§ ״כְּנָסָהּ הֲרֵי הִיא כו׳״.§ לְמַאי הִלְכְתָא? א״ר יוֹסֵי בַּר חֲנִינָא: *בלוֹמַר שֶׁמְּגָרְשָׁהּ בְּגֵט וּמַחֲזִירָהּ. מְגָרְשָׁהּ בְּגֵט פְּשִׁיטָא! סד״א: הוֹאִיל וּכְתִיב °״וּלְקָחָהּ לוֹ לְאִשָּׁה וְיִבְּמָהּ״ (דברים כה) אָמַר רַחֲמָנָא, וַעֲדַיִין יִבּוּמֵי הָרִאשׁוֹן עָלֶיהָ. בַּחֲלִיצָה – אִין, בְּגֵט – לָא, קמ״ל. ״מַחֲזִירָהּ״. פְּשִׁיטָא! סד״א: מִצְוָה דְּרָמְיָא רַחֲמָנָא עֲלֵיהּ *עֲבַדָהּ. הָשְׁתָּא תֵּיקוּם עֲלֵיהּ בְּאִיסּוּר אֵשֶׁת אָח – קמ״ל. וְאֵימָא הָכִי נַמִּי! אָמַר קְרָא: ״וּלְקָחָהּ לוֹ לְאִשָּׁה״, כֵּיוָן שֶׁלְּקָחָהּ – הֲרֵי הִיא כְּאִשְׁתּוֹ לְכָל דָּבָר.§ ״וּבִלְבַד שֶׁתְּהֵא כְּתוּבָּתָהּ כו׳״.§ מ״ט? *אִשָּׁה הִקְנוּ לוֹ מִן הַשָּׁמַיִם, גוְאִי לֵית לָהּ מִן הָרִאשׁוֹן – תַּקִּינוּ לָהּ מִשֵּׁנִי, כְּדֵי שֶׁלֹּא תְּהֵא קַלָּה בְּעֵינָיו לְהוֹצִיאָהּ.§

מתני׳ *דמִצְוָה בְּגָדוֹל לְיַיבֵּם, לֹא רָצָה – מְהַלְּכִין עַל כָּל הָאַחִין, לֹא רָצוּ – חוֹזְרִין אֵצֶל גָּדוֹל, וְאוֹמְרִים לוֹ: עָלֶיךָ מִצְוָה, אוֹ חֲלוֹץ אוֹ יַבֵּם. התָּלָה בְּקָטָן עַד שֶׁיַּגְדִּיל. (א) אוֹ בְּגָדוֹל עַד שֶׁיָּבֹא מִמְּדִינַת הַיָּם, אוֹ חֵרֵשׁ אוֹ שׁוֹטֶה – אֵין שׁוֹמְעִין לוֹ, אֶלָּא אוֹמְרִים לוֹ: עָלֶיךָ מִצְוָה, אוֹ חֲלוֹץ אוֹ יַבֵּם.§ **גמ׳** אִיתְּמַר, בִּיאַת קָטָן וַחֲלִיצַת גָּדוֹל, פְּלִיגִי בָּהּ רַ׳ יוֹחָנָן וְרַ׳ יְהוֹשֻׁעַ בֶּן לֵוִי, חַד אָמַר: ובִּיאַת קָטָן עֲדִיפָא, וְחַד אָמַר: חֲלִיצַת גָּדוֹל עֲדִיפָא. מַאן דְּאָמַר בִּיאַת קָטָן עֲדִיפָא – דְּהָא מִצְוָה בְּיִיבּוּם, וּמַאן דְּאָמַר חֲלִיצַת גָּדוֹל עֲדִיפָא – בִּמְקוֹם גָּדוֹל – בִּיאַת קָטָן לָאו כְּלוּם הִיא. תְּנַן: לֹא רָצָה – מַחֲזִירִין עַל כָּל הָאַחִין. מַאי לָאו: לֹא רָצָה לְיַיבֵּם אֶלָּא לַחֲלוֹץ, וְקָתָנֵי: מְהַלְּכִין אֵצֶל הָאַחִין, שְׁמַע מִינָּהּ בִּיאַת קָטָן עֲדִיפָא – לָא, לֹא רָצָה לַחֲלוֹץ וְלֹא לְיַיבֵּם, דִּכְוָותָהּ גַּבֵּי הָאַחִין לֹא רָצוּ – לֹא לַחֲלוֹץ וְלֹא לְיַיבֵּם, אַמַּאי חוֹזְרִים אֵצֶל הַגָּדוֹל, זלְמִיכְפְּיֵיהּ – לִכְפְּיֵיהּ לְדִידְהוּ! כֵּיוָן דְּמִצְוָה עֲלֵיהּ דִּידֵיהּ רַמְיָא – לְדִידֵיהּ כָּיְיפִינַן. תְּנַן: תָּלָה בְּקָטָן עַד שֶׁיַּגְדִּיל – אֵין שׁוֹמְעִין לוֹ. וְאִי בִּיאַת קָטָן עֲדִיפָא, אַמַּאי אֵין שׁוֹמְעִין לוֹ? נִינְטַר דִּלְמָא גָּדֵיל וּמְיַיבֵּם! וְלִיטַעְמִיךְ, וּבְגָדוֹל עַד שֶׁיָּבֹא מִמְּדִינַת הַיָּם אֵין שׁוֹמְעִין לוֹ, אַמַּאי? נִינְטַר, דִּלְמָא אָתֵי *וְחָלֵיץ! אֶלָּא: כָּל *) שִׁהוּיֵי מִצְוָה לָא מַשְׁהִינַן. אית

*) [לקמן מז:]

וספק נשואה לחלוק בנכסים. לעיל פ׳ ״ד׳ אחין״ (דף כט: ושם) גרס רבה, גבי מאמר לב״ש נישואין עושה או אירוסין עושה, דמתוך תשובתו משמע דמודה דאין יורשה. **אע״ג** דקשיא מתה. לרבא ניחא, דדוקא לאחר מיתה מהני מאמר לחלוק בנכסים, אבל מחיים – לא, דהויא לה איהי ודאי ואינהו ספק. ומ״מ לא בעי רישא לאוקמי בעבד בה מאמר, דמשום דהויא איהי ודאי אין נראה לרבא דתמכור לכתחלה, להכי מוקי לה בלא עבד בה מאמר. אע״ג דלרבה דלעיל מוכרת לכתחלה משום האי טעמא, משום דהויא איהי ודאי – רבא לית ליה האי סברא, בהלכות פסוקות דרב יודאי גאון פסיק כאביי, ⊕דרב פפא בתראה קאי כוותיה. והא דלא חשיב ביע״ל קג״ם – משום דאיירי בה אמוראי*. **אשה** הקנו לו מן השמים. וא״ת: ומה מרויח בכך היבם? כיון דאי לית לה מראשון תקינו לה רבנן משני! וכ״ת: שאם מכר הראשון נכסיו טורפא מלקוחות, אע״פ שיש בני חורין לשני – א״כ תהא קלה בעיניו להוציאה! א) ואר״י: דנפקא מינה שיכול היבם למכור שדותיו, ואפילו אשתדוף אחר כך שדות של מת – לא טורפא ממשעבדי. ואם היתה אשתו – טורפת מהן. ומיהו, למאי דבעי למימר בס״פ ״מי שהיה נשוי״ (כתובות צה. ושם) דאי אשתדוף בני חרי לא טרפא ממשעבדי – קשה! וי״ל: דנפקא מינה אם גירשה ואח״כ אשתדוף שדותיו של מת, דלא גביא מבני חרי דשני. **ובחרש** ושוטה. מדלא קאמר עד שיתרפא, משמע דאפי׳ תלה לייבם לאלתר – אין שומעין, לפי שאין סומכין אותה. וה״ה דה״מ למינקט מוכה שחין. **גבי** אחין **לא** רצו **לא** לייבם ולא לחלוץ **אמאי** חוזרין כו׳. אפילו לא רצו לייבם אלא לחלוץ ה״מ למיפרך. אמר

עין משפט נר מצוה

מד א מיי׳ פ״ג מהלכות נחלות הלכה ז טוש״ע אה״ע סימן קם סעיף ה:
מה ב מיי׳ פ״א מהל׳ יבום הלכה טו סמג עשין נא טוש״ע שם סימן קסח סעי׳ א:
מו ג מיי׳ פכ״ב מהל׳ אישות הלכה יא סמג שם טוש״ע שם סעיף ח וסעיף ט בהגה״ה:
מז ד מיי׳ פ״ב מהלכו׳ יבום הלכה ו סמג עשין נא טוש״ע שם סימן קסח סעיף ז:
מח ה מיי׳ שם הל׳ ח טוש״ע שם סעיף ח:
מט ו מיי׳ שם הל׳ יג טוש״ע שם סעיף ו:
נ ז מיי׳ שם הלכה ז טוש״ע שם סעיף ז:

[ודומה לזה כתבו תוס׳ מגילה כב: ד״ה והלכתא]
[סוכה לו. וש״נ]

תוספות ישנים

כתובה לגבות מחיים: **וקסבר** אביי ידו כידה. ובהלכות פסוקות דרב יהודאי פסק כאביי ולא נמנו ביע״ל קג״ם משום דאמוראי בתראי סבר כוותיה וא״ל לפסוק כוותיה: **א)** אומר הש״ר דהא דקאמר אשה הקנו לו מן השמים זהו ליתן טעם למה אין לה שתי כתובות אחת מהיבם שהיא אשתו ואין אשה בלא כתובה ואחת מבעלה הראשון שנשתעבדו לה נכסיו. ומשני [אשה] הקנו לו מן השמים בלא כתובה ואין לה כי אם כתובה ראשונה ואי לית לה מראשון אף הכתובה ראשונה תקנו לה וכו׳ שלא תהא קלה וכו׳ והרבה יש פירושים ודחוקים: **ובגדול** עד שיבא ממדינת הים. פי׳ שיש גדול ממנו במדה״י ואומר לנו להמתין ואין שומעין לו משום דאח שהוא עומד לפנינו מוטלת עליו המצוה וכן משמע בגמ׳:

מסורת הש״ס

[כתובות פג.]
לעיל כט. [נדרים עד.]
לעיל ח: יט: כתובות פב:
נ״א עברה
לקמן פה. כתובות פב:
ביצה לו. לעיל כד.
[נ״ל ומייבם]

הגהות הב״ח

(א) במשנה עד שיגדיל כצ״ל ותיבת או נמחק: (ב) רש״י ד״ה וקסבר וכו׳ כנפלו לה כשהיא תחתיו: (ג) ד״ה וקסבר רבא וכו׳ כודאי ארוסה משוי לה לענין לדחות: (ד) ד״ה ובגדול או שהיה וכו׳ שמא ייבם אותה והכי מוכח:

הגהות הגר״א

[א] גמ׳ א״ל רבא אי כו׳. ב לדברי רש״י לרבא אף ב״ה מודו דיחלוקו. וכו׳ פרש״י דהכל לבעל. רמב״ם מפרש כל אוקימתות הכל לב״ש אבל ב״ה לעולם לאשה עמש״ו ועי׳ רמב״ם וכתב ד״ה למכירה ולפירי אבל רמב״ם פסק דל״ל לייבם ירות ועי׳ רמב״ם פ״ד כתובות סי׳ כב וכו׳ רבא״א ועמש״ס רבינו באה״ע סי׳ ק״ס:

גליון הש״ס

גמ׳ ד״ה אע״ג. דרב פפא בתראה. ע׳ מס׳ כ״ב ע״ב תד״ה אר״פ ובהרא״ש שם:

נא א טוש"ע אה"ע סי' קסא סעיף ו:
נב ב מיי' פ"א מהלכות יבום הל' ב ופ"ב הלכה ז סמג עשין נב טוש"ע שם סימן קסה סעיף א:
נג ג שם סעיף א בהג"ה וסימן קסא סעיף ו בהג"ה:
נד ד טוש"ע שם סימן קסה סעיף א בהג"ה:
נה ה ו מיי' פ"ד מהלכו' יבום הלכה ל סמג עשין נב טור אה"ע סימן קסט:
נו ז מיי' שם הל' לא טוש"ע אה"ע סי' קסט ס"א וקנז ס"ב ובפירוש סדר חליצה סעיף לא:
נז ח מיי' פ"א מהלכות יבום הלכה ב סמג עשין נא טוש"ע שם סימן קנו סעיף א:

אמר רב אין כופין. פירש בקונטרס: כי ניחא לתרוייהו לייבם – אין כופין (ב) לחלוץ משום מצוה, דנימא דלאו למצוה מכווני. אבל אם לא תרצה לייבם מחמת שתתן אמתלא לדבריה, אם אין יכולין להטעותו – כפינן ליה, וחליץ. וממוכה שחין ובורסי שהביא בקונט' נראה דאין ראיה, שהן מאותם שכופין להוציא מן הבעל. אבל בשאר אמתלא – אין נראה לומר דכופין. דא"כ – למה היו טורחין לקמן בפרק "מצות חליצה" (דף קו.) להטעותו? יכפוהו לחלוץ! ומאגרת מרד אין ראיה, דא"כ – בלא אמתלא נמי, והתם הוי טעמא משום דמצות חליצה קודמת, כדמסיק. (ג) ועוד: דקאמר התם רבי יוחנן תבע לייבם – אין נזקקין לו. השתא לחלוץ כופין – ואין נזקקין לייבם מבעיא? ועוד: מדקאמר בדידך תלה רחמנא – משמע אפי' בזמן הזה, דמצות חליצה קודמת, ור"ת גריס: מצות יבום קודמת למצות חליצה, אמר רב: אין כופין. וקאי אבראשונה שהיו מתכוונין לשם מצוה, וקאמר דאין כופין לייבם. וכי הוו אתו לקמיה דרב, אותן שהיו מתכוונים לשם מצוה. ורב יהודה נמי דאתקין אי צבית לייבומי – באותן שבאין לפנינו לחלוץ איירי, שאותן אם היו מייבמין היו מכוונים לשם מצוה, שהרי לא היו מתכוונים לשם נוי ולשם אישות, שלא היו חוששים לייבם אלא לחלוץ. אבל אחריני – אין מניחין לייבם, אלא אדרבה כופין[א] לחלוץ. ואר"ת: דהלכה כאבא שאול, כסתם מתני' דבכורות (דף יג.), ולא כרמי בר חמא דאמר חזרו לומר דמצות ייבום קודמת כרבנן. ועוד: *דבריש מכילתין אוקי מתניתין דפ"ק (דף ג. ושם) כאבא שאול, ובפרק "בית שמאי" (לקמן דף קט. ושם) תני בר קפרא: לעולם ידבק אדם בחליצה, כאבא שאול. וסתמא דגמרא בפרק "אע"פ" (כתובות דף סד. ושם) כאבא שאול. ולעיל בשמעתין דמשמע דביאה עדיפא – במתכוין לשם מצוה איירי. ור"ח פסק כאן דמצות יבום קודמת, וחזר בו בפ' "מצות חליצה", ופסק דמצות חליצה קודמת. **דמתחזיא** לן בבי דינא **על ארעא**. נראה דל"ג על ארעא, דלא צריך. כדאמר בפרק "מצות חליצה" (לקמן דף קו: ושם) גבי הוא ארוך והיא גוצא וקלטתו הרוח*).

ולשום אישות. דתיפוק ליה עליה שם אישות. אר"י: כי אין פירושו כההיא דבסמוך רצה לשם נוי – כונסה, רצה לשם אישות – כונסה, דההוא לשם אישות – היינו לשם מצות יבום. וכה"ג איכא בפרק "הבא על יבמתו" (לקמן דף נג: ושם) אפילו שניהם שוגגין או מזידים, דההוא מזיד – *לשם זנות, ולא הוי כההוא דקאמר התם *דרבי רחמנא ביאת שוגג כמזיד, דההוא מזיד במתכוין לשם מצוה, וכן אפילו הוא שוגג והיא מזידה. רצה

*) [ועי' תוס' לקמן קו: ד"ה עד דמטי]

נ"ל דבריש מכילתין דף ג. אוקי מתניתין דפ"ק כאבא שאול וכו'.

תוספות ישנים

נינטר דלמא אתי וחליץ. וא"ל אפי' לדידיה תקשי דלמא אתי ומייבם דהא כ"ע מודים דביאת גדול עדיפא דאיכא למימר שמעתו ממנו שלא היה רוצה לייבם: **למה** חוזרין אצל גדול למכפייה וכו'. פי' אא"ב דר"ל לא רצה לייבם אלא לחלוץ וכן האחים לא רצו לייבם אלא לחלוץ ניחא שחוזרין אצל גדול לחלוץ כי חליצתו טובה מהם. אא"א שלא רצה לייבם ולא לחלוץ ודכוותה גבי אחין. א"כ אמאי חוזרין אצל גדול היינו ודאי למכפייה וכן נמי נכפייה לדידהו:

התם תנן. במסכת בכורות. אמר רב אין כופין. ואי ניחא לתרוייהו לייבומי, אין כופין אותו לחלוץ, דנימא לאו למצוה מכווני ופגע באיסור אשת אח. אלא, אי בעי – מייבם. ומיהו, היכא דהוא בעי לייבומי ואיהי אמרה לא בעינא ליה, ואמרה דברים ניכרים, אי מצינו לאטעוייה ולומר לו: חלוץ לה ע"מ שתתן לך מאתים זוז – מטעינן ליה, ואי לא – כפינן ליה וחליץ. דאמר רב ששת (לעיל ד.): מנין ליבמה שנפלה לפני מוכה שחין שאין חוסמין אותה, ולא תימא מוכה שחין דוקא, אלא כל אמתלא שתתן לדבריה, דאמר ב"המדיר" (כתובות עז.) מעשה בצידן בבורסי שמת ולו אח בורסי, ואמרו חכמים: יכולה שתאמר: לאחיך הייתי יכולה לקבל, ולך איני יכולה לקבל. ועוד: פסקינן הלכתא בא"ע"פ (שם סד.): כותבין אגרת מרד על ארוסה, ואין כותבין אגרת מרד על שומרת יבם. ומכל הלין טעמי כפינן ליה דחליץ, ושקלה כתובה. וכל הני אין כופין דהכא, היכא דתרווייהו ניחא להו: **איקרבת**. הקריבה. **אטלע**. נדד לה רגל ימין. **דאיתחזי לנא**. דבעינן רוק הנראה לעיני דיינין, בפרק "מצות חליצה" (לקמן דף קו:). **ואקרינהו**. "לא חפצתי לקחתה". **בעדים**. שצריך להביא שני עדים שהוא אחי המת מאביו: **אכשור דרי**. בתמיה: וכי נתכשרו הדורות?! **יבמה יבא עליה מצוה**. גרסינן: ולא גרס הכא למצוה, אלא לקמן בתירוצא דרב יצחק בר אבדימי: **שבתחלה**. עד שלא קדשה אחיו: **נאסרה**. כשקדשה אחיו. **וחזרה והותרה**. כשמת בלא בנים. **יכול תחזור להיתירה הראשון**. מפרש לקמן: **מאן תנא**. ומאי קאמר. **אבא שאול היא**. וה"ק: יבמה יבא עליה למצוה, משמע: לשם מצות יבום, דכתב "ויבמה". **רבא אמר אפי' תימא רבנן**. ולא תיתני למצוה, אלא מצוה: **יבמה יבא עליה מצוה**. מצוה עליו ליבמה, יותר מן החליצה. **יכול תחזור להיתירה הראשון**. ותו לא. דאי בעי – לא כניס לה, ת"ל: יבמה יבא עליה – מצוה. **בכדי תיפוק**. בתמיה. **מצות תאכל**. קרא יתירא הוא, דכתיב ברישא דקרא "והנותרת מן המנחה יאכלו". שבתחלה

איכא דאמרי: בביאה – כולי עלמא לא פליגי דביאת קטן עדיפא. כי פליגי – בחליצת קטן, והכי איתמר: חליצת קטן וחליצת גדול – פליגי בה ר' יוחנן ור' יהושע בן לוי. חד אמר: [א]חליצת גדול עדיפא, וחד אמר: כי הדדי נינהו. מאן דאמר חליצת גדול עדיפא – דהא מצוה בגדול. ואידך: כי אמרינן מצוה בגדול – לענין יבום, אבל לענין חליצה – כהדדי נינהו. תנן: לא רצו – חוזרין אצל גדול, מאי לאו: לא רצו לייבם אלא לחלוץ, וקתני חוזרין אצל גדול, וש"מ: חליצת גדול עדיפא! לא, לא רצו – לא לחלוץ ולא לייבם. דכוותיה גבי גדול – לא רצה לא לחלוץ ולא לייבם, אלא אמאי חוזרין אצל גדול, למכפייה? לכפייהו לדידהו! כיון דמצוה עליה דידיה רמיא – לדידיה כייפינן. ת"ש: תלה בגדול עד שיבא ממדינת הים – אין שומעין לו. ואי ס"ד חליצת גדול עדיפא, אמאי אין שומעין לו? נינטר דלמא אתי וחליץ! ולטעמיך, בקטן עד שיגדיל אין שומעין לו, אמאי? נינטר דלמא גדיל ומייבם, (אי נמי (א) אתי איהו ומייבמה). [ס"א ל"ג] אלא כל *שהויי מצוה לא שהינן. תנן התם: *[ב] מצות יבום קודמת למצות חליצה – בראשונה שהיו מתכוונין לשם מצוה, [ג]עכשיו שאין מתכוונין לשם מצוה – אמרו: מצות חליצה קודמת למצות יבום. אמר רב: [ד]אין כופין: כי אתו לקמיה דרב אמר להו: אי בעית – חלוץ, אי בעית – ייבם, בדידך תלא רחמנא, °"ואם לא יחפוץ האיש", הא אם חפץ – אי בעי חליץ, אי בעי ייבם. [דברים כה] ואף רב יהודה סבר אין כופין. [ה]מדאתקין רב יהודה בגיטא דחליצה: איך פלונית בת פלוני אקרבת ית פלוני יבמה קדמנא לבי דינא, ואשתמודעינהו *דאחוה דמיתנא מאבא ניהו, ואמרי ליה: אי צבית ליבם – יבם, *ואי לא – איטלע לה רגליך דימינא. ואיטלע לה רגלא דימינא, ושרת סיניה מעל רגלוהי, וירקת באנפוהי רוקא דמתחזיא לבי דינא על ארעא.

[ו]ורבי חייא בר אויא מסיים בה משמיה דרב יהודה: ואקרינהו מה דכתיב בספר אורייתא דמשה. אשתמודעינהו, פליגי בה רב אחא ורבינא. חד אמר: בעדים, וחד אמר: אפילו קרוב, אפילו אשה. [ז]והלכתא: גלויי מילתא בעלמא הוא, ואפילו קרוב ואפילו אשה.§ בראשונה שהיו מתכוונין לשם מצוה – מצות יבום קודמת למצות חליצה, ועכשיו שאין מתכוונין לשם מצוה – אמרו: מצות חליצה קודמת למצות יבום. אמר רמי בר חמא א"ר יצחק: חזרו לומר מצות יבום קודמת למצות חליצה. א"ל רב נחמן בר יצחק: *אכשור דרי?! מעיקרא סברי לה כאבא שאול, ולבסוף סברי לה כרבנן. דתניא, *אבא שאול אומר: *הכונס את יבמתו לשם נוי, ולשום אישות, ולשום דבר אחר – כאילו פוגע בערוה, וקרוב אני בעיני להיות הולד ממזר. וחכמים אומרים: °"יבמה יבא עליה" – מכל מקום. [דברים כה] מאן תנא להא דתנו רבנן: *"יבמה יבא עליה" מצוה. שבתחלה היתה עליו בכלל היתר, נאסרה, וחזרה והותרה, יכול תחזור להתירה הראשון – ת"ל "יבמה יבא עליה" מצוה. מאן תנא? אמר רבי יצחק בר אבדימי: אבא שאול היא, וה"ק: "יבמה יבא עליה" מצוה, שבתחלה היתה עליו בכלל היתר, רצה לשם נוי – כונסה, רצה לשום אישות – כונסה. נאסרה, חזרה והותרה, יכול תחזור להתירה הראשון – ת"ל "יבמה יבא עליה", למצוה. רבא אמר: אפי' תימא רבנן, והכי קאמר: "יבמה יבא עליה" – מצוה. שבתחלה היתה בכלל היתר. רצה – כונסה, רצה – אינו כונסה. נאסרה, חזרה והותרה, יכול תחזור להתירה הראשון; רצה – כונסה, רצה – אינו כונסה. רצה אינו כונסה? הא אגידה ביה, בכדי תיפוק?! אלא אימא: רצה – כונסה, רצה – חולץ לה. ת"ל: "יבמה יבא עליה" – [ח]מצוה. אימא *) רישא: °"מצות תאכל במקום קדוש" – מצוה, [ויקרא ו] שבתחלה

*) ס"א סיפא [אבל לע שבת"כ היא רישא ע"ש וכן בילקוט איתא אימא רישא]

[לקמן מז:]
כתובות סד. בכורות יג.

הגהות הב"ח

(א) גמ' אי נמי דלמא אתי איהו ומייבם: (ב) תוס' ד"ה אמר וכו' אין כופין אותו לחלוץ: (ג) בא"ד כדמסיק התם ועוד:

[לקמן קו.]
[גירסת הערוך ערך טלע ואם לאו איטלע לך ריגלא דימינא ואטלע ליה ריגלא דימינא פי' איש טלע נעלו תרגום טלע גבר ית נרתיק ימיניה וכו']
[חולין נג:]
[לקמן קט. לעיל ג.]
[תוספתא פ"ו ע"ש]
[לקמן קט:]
[תורת כהנים סוף פ"ב]
[דף נד.]

הגהות הגר"א

[א] תוס' ד"ה אמר כו' אלא אדרבה כופין. נ"ב ר"ל במילי. תוס' בכתובות (ס"ד א' סד"ה ודיני) ועמ"ש רבינו בא"ה ע סי' קס"ה ס"ק ט'):

תוספות חד מקמאי

כתב הרב אלפס ואשתמודעינן דאחוה [דמיתנא] מאבא הוא אפי' מפי אשה ואפי' מפי קרוב וכיון דמודעי ליה הכי איתחזק גבי [ההוא] סהדא מפומא דהאי קרוב או מפומא דהאי איתתא דהאי ניהו פלניא והא ניהי פלניתא הלכך שרי ליה לסהדא למסמך אפומיה ולמסהד עלוי דההוא [גברא]. או עלוי הך אתתא בין לענין ממונא בין לענין איסורא והוא א) כמ"ש הה"ל ברבי מדבריו שאם היו קרוב או אשה מעידין עכשיו בשעת חליצה דאחוה דמיתנא הוא לא סמכינן עלייהו. וכי סמיכנא עלייהו כגון שכבר קודם מעשה אמרו קמיה דהך סהדי שלא ע"י מעשה דאחוה דהאי הוא ולפיכך כתב הרב שאותו העד יש לסמוך ולהעיד בב"ד על אותו קרוב או אותה אשה שאמרו לו שלא ע"י מעשה דהוא אחוה דהאי גברא ב). ומיהו עיקר הדבר ג) שע"י מעשה קרוב או אשה נאמן דגלויי מלתא בעלמא הוא. והלשון שכתב הרב ז"ל [דלא] שרי לסהדא למסמך אפומייהו ד) משום עובדא דרבה בר חנן דאייתיה מיניה ראיה הוא דכתב עד לפי דברי הרב שכך פירש אמר לה אף אנא. ומיהו אמרי להו דלאו איהי היא ואמרו לי קרובים מקשא הוא דאקשו לה קלא ועתה אני מכיר כי האמת אתך והמניה אביי (לרבא) [לרבה] בר חנן ואילו היו שם עדים כשרים בודאי לא היה נאמן רבה בר חנן. אלמא במקום חשדא אין קרוב [נאמן] אבל לעולם בודאי קרוב או אשה בשעת מעשה נאמן אפי' לדעת הרב אלפס ז"ל: מתניתין

א) נראה דל"ל כמש"כ הרב ז"ל למדבריו נראה שאם כו'. ב) וכ"כ בריב"ש סימן קפ"ב שדעת הרי"ף דבעת מעשה אין נאמן אשה או קרוב ע"ש. ג) נ"ל נראה שגם בעת מעשה כו'. ד) נ"ל במקום לאוכח חששא לחששא משום כו' דמייתי מיניה ראיה לפי דברי הרב כך פירושו שאמר לה

שֶׁבַּתְּחִלָּה. קוֹדֶם שֶׁהוּקְדְּשָׁה מִנְחָה זוֹ, הָיְתָה עָלָיו בִּכְלַל הֶיתֵּר. וְנֶאֶסְרָה. כְּשֶׁהוּקְדְּשָׁה, וְחָזְרָה וְהוּתְּרָה בְּהַקְטָרַת הַקּוֹמֶץ. יָכוֹל תַּחֲזוֹר וכו'. כִּדְמְפָרֵשׁ. בִּשְׁלָמָא לְרָבָא דְּאָמַר רַבָּנַן הִיא. וּמִצְוָה קָתָנֵי, וְלָא קָתָנֵי לְמִצְוָה. ה"ק כו' וְאָכְלוּ אוֹתָם. אֶת הַקֳּדָשִׁים אֲשֶׁר כּוּפַּר בָּהֶם, כִּי הֵיכִי דְּתֶהֱוֵי כַּפָּרָה שְׁלֵימָה. רָצָה הוּא. כֹּהֵן שֶׁעָבַד עֲבוֹדָתָהּ. אֶלָּא לְרַב יִצְחָק. דְּתָנֵי לְמִצְוָה, וְאַבָּא שָׁאוּל הִיא. הָכָא מַאי תְּרֵי גַּוְונֵי אִיכָּא. דְּקָא מְמַעֵט תַּנָּא יָכוֹל תַּחֲזוֹר לְהֶיתֵּירָהּ הָרִאשׁוֹן – ת"ל דְּלָא. וְהָא לֵיכָּא לְמֵימַר תַּחֲזוֹר לְהֶיתֵּירָהּ הָרִאשׁוֹן, רָצָה לְשֵׁם מִצְוָה אוֹכְלָהּ, רָצָה שֶׁלֹּא לְשֵׁם מִצְוָה אוֹכְלָהּ, ת"ל דְּלָא – דְּהָא כָּל כַּמָּה דְּבָעֵי לֵיכְלָהּ, דְּהָתָם הוּא כִּי בָּעֵיל שֶׁלֹּא לְשֵׁם מִצְוָה פָּגַע בְּעֶרְוָה, אֲבָל הָכָא – מַאי קָעָבֵיד? וע"כ בִּתְרֵי גַּוְונֵי בָּעֲיָא לְאוֹקְמֵי, דּוּמְיָא דְּרֵישָׁא. אֲכִילָה גַּסָּה מִי מִקַּרְיָא אֲכִילָה וְהָאָמַר ר"ל כו'. וְכֵיוָן דְּלָאו אֲכִילָה הִיא, מִ"וְאָכְלוּ אַהֲרֹן וּבָנָיו" דְּרֵישָׁא נָפְקָא. פָּטוּר. דְּלָא עָבַר עַל "אֲשֶׁר לֹא תְעוּנֶּה", שֶׁאַף זֶה עִינּוּי הוּא, שֶׁמַּזִּיק אֶת עַצְמוֹ. אֶלָּא. תְּרֵי גַּוְונֵי הָכִי תִּיבָּעֵי לְמֵימַר: רָצָה מַצָּה אוֹכְלָהּ רָצָה חָמֵץ אוֹכְלָהּ, ת"ל "מַצּוֹת תֵּאָכֵל" – וְלֹא חָמֵץ. לֹא תֵאָפֶה חָמֵץ חֶלְקָם נָתַתִּי אוֹתָהּ. לְהָכִי סָמֵיךְ "חֶלְקָם" לְ"לֹא תֵאָפֶה חָמֵץ", לוֹמַר: אֲפִי' שְׁיָרֵי מִנְחָה, שֶׁהֵם חֶלְקָם שֶׁל כֹּהֲנִים – לֹא תֵאָפֶה חָמֵץ, וּמֵהָתָם נָפְקָא. חָלוּט. בְּרוֹתְחִים. רָצָה חָלוּט אוֹכְלָהּ. ת"ל: מַצּוֹת, וְלֹא חָלוּט. אִי מַצָּה הִיא* מַצָּה הִיא. וְהֵיכִי מִימְעִיט מִמַּשְׁמָעוּת דְּ"מַצּוֹת תֵּאָכֵל". וְאִי לָאו מַצָּה הִיא מַצּוֹת אָמַר רַחֲמָנָא. בִּשְׁיָרֵי מִנְחַת חוֹבָה, דִּכְתִיב (א) בְּ"צַו אֶת אַהֲרֹן" "וַאֲכָלוּהָ מַצּוֹת", וְה"ה לִשְׁאָר מְנָחוֹת, וְלָמָּה לִי "מַצּוֹת תֵּאָכֵל". מתני' הֲרֵי הוּא כְּאֶחָד כו'. וְלֹא הִפְסִיד חֶלְקוֹ בְּנִכְסֵי אָחִיו. זָכָה בְּנִכְסֵי הָאָח. וַאֲפִילּוּ גֵּירְשָׁהּ לְמָחָר. גמ' פְּשִׁיטָא. דְּלֹא אִיבֵּד זְכוּתוֹ. מַהוּ דְּתֵימָא. כְּלוֹמַר, לָאו לְאַשְׁמוֹעִינַן דְּלֹא אִיבֵּד זְכוּתוֹ תַּנְיָא לֵיהּ, אֶלָּא לְאַשְׁמוֹעִינַן דְּלֹא שָׁקֵיל כּוּלְּהוּ נִכְסֵי. אִי הָכִי. דְּלְגָרוּעֵי אָתָא, הֲוָה לֵיהּ לְמִיתְנֵי: אֵינוֹ אֶלָּא כְּאֶחָד כו': ה"ג. אֶלָּא סָלְקָא דַּעְתָּךְ אָמִינָא לִיקְנְסֵיהּ הוֹאִיל וְאַפְסְדָהּ מִיִּבּוּם. שֶׁפְּסָלָהּ עַל הָאַחִין. אַף הַאי נַמִי. לְאַחַר מִיתַת הָאָב, אִם מֵת הָאָב לְאַחַר יִבּוּמוֹ שֶׁל זֶה – מוֹדֶה ר"י דְּנוֹטֵל זֶה חֶלְקוֹ וְחֵלֶק אָחִיו. עַל שֵׁם אָחִיו כְּתִיב. וְלֹא עַל שֵׁם אָבִיו כְּתִיב, וְכֵיוָן דִּבְשָׁעָה שֶׁקָּם עַל שֵׁם אָחִיו לֹא שָׁקַל – תּוּ לֹא שָׁקֵיל. [דְּאִי שָׁקֵיל הַשְׁתָּא – לֹא מִנִּכְסֵי אָחִיו שָׁקֵיל, אֶלָּא מִנִּכְסֵי אָבִיו, דְּהָא יָרְתִינְהוּ]. הֵיכָא דְּאִיכָּא אָב דְּלָא שָׁקֵיל. יָבָם נַחֲלָה – לֹא תִּתְקַיֵּים מִצְוַת יִבּוּם. אִיסְמְיֵיהּ. לְכוּלָּהּ מַתְנִי', דְּמִשְׁנָה שֶׁאֵינָהּ צְרִיכָה הִיא. אֲמַר לֵיהּ לָא. תִּסְמְיֵיהּ, דְּאַתְּ הֲלָכָה כְּרַבִּי יְהוּדָה אַתְנְיָיךְ, וּמִשְׁנָה צְרִיכָה הֲוַאי. וּמִיקְשָׁה הוּא דְּקַשְׁיָא לָךְ. הֵיכִי שָׁבֵיק רַבָּנַן וְעָבֵיד כְּרַבִּי יְהוּדָה, וְאַפַּכְתְּ לָהּ, וְשַׁפִּיר עֲבַדְתְּ דְּאַפַּכְתְּ לָהּ. מתני' אָסוּר בִּקְרוֹבוֹתֶיהָ. כְּאִילּוּ הִיא אִשְׁתּוֹ, וְכָל קְרוֹבוֹת הַנֶּאֱסָרוֹת מֵחֲמַת אִשָּׁה גְּמוּרָה – אֲסוּרוֹת מִדְּרַבָּנַן בַּחֲלוּצָה.
הוא

תורה אור

שֶׁבַּתְּחִלָּה הָיְתָה עָלָיו בִּכְלַל הֶיתֵּר, נֶאֶסְרָה, וְחָזְרָה וְהוּתְּרָה, יָכוֹל תַּחֲזוֹר לְהֶיתֵּירָהּ הָרִאשׁוֹן – ת"ל "מַצּוֹת תֵּאָכֵל בְּמָקוֹם קָדוֹשׁ" [א]מִצְוָה. בִּשְׁלָמָא לְרָבָא, דְּאָמַר הָא מַנִּי רַבָּנַן הִיא – הָכָא הָכִי קָאָמַר: "מַצּוֹת תֵּאָכֵל בְּמָקוֹם קָדוֹשׁ" מִצְוָה. שֶׁבַּתְּחִלָּה הָיְתָה עָלָיו בִּכְלַל הֶיתֵּר, רָצָה – אוֹכְלָהּ, רָצָה – אֵינוֹ אוֹכְלָהּ. (נֶאֶסְרָה, חָזְרָה וְהוּתְּרָה, יָכוֹל תַּחֲזוֹר לְהֶיתֵּירָהּ הָרִאשׁוֹן) – רָצָה אוֹכְלָהּ, רָצָה אֵינוֹ אוֹכְלָהּ. רָצָה אֵינוֹ אוֹכְלָהּ?! וְהָכְתִיב °"וְאָכְלוּ אֹתָם אֲשֶׁר כֻּפַּר בָּהֶם" *[ב]מְלַמֵּד שֶׁהַכֹּהֲנִים אוֹכְלִים וּבְעָלִים מִתְכַּפְּרִין! אֶלָּא: רָצָה – הוּא אוֹכְלָהּ, רָצָה – כֹּהֵן אַחֵר אוֹכְלָהּ, ת"ל "מַצּוֹת תֵּאָכֵל בְּמָקוֹם קָדוֹשׁ" – מִצְוָה. אֶלָּא לְרַב יִצְחָק בַּר אַבְדִּימִי, דְּאָמַר אַבָּא שָׁאוּל הִיא – הָכָא מַאי תְּרֵי גַּוְונֵי אִיכָּא? וְכִי תֵּימָא: רָצָה – לְתֵאָבוֹן אוֹכְלָהּ, רָצָה – אֲכִילָה גַּסָּה אוֹכְלָהּ, אֲכִילָה גַּסָּה מִי שְׁמָהּ אֲכִילָה? וְהָאָמַר ר"ל: *[ג]הָאוֹכֵל אֲכִילָה גַּסָּה בְּיוה"כ – פָּטוּר מִ"לֹּא תְעֻנֶּה"! אֶלָּא: רָצָה – מַצָּה אוֹכְלָהּ, רָצָה – חָמֵץ אוֹכְלָהּ, וְהָכְתִיב °"לֹא תֵאָפֶה חָמֵץ חֶלְקָם", *וְאָמַר רֵישׁ לָקִישׁ: [ד]וַאֲפִילּוּ חֶלְקָם לֹא תֵאָפֶה חָמֵץ! אֶלָּא: רָצָה – מַצָּה אוֹכְלָהּ, רָצָה – חָלוּט אוֹכְלָהּ. הַאי חָלוּט הֵיכִי דָּמֵי? אִי מַצָּה הִיא – הָא מַצָּה הִיא, וְאִי לָא מַצָּה הִיא – "מַצּוֹת" אָמַר רַחֲמָנָא! לָא, לְעוֹלָם אֵימָא לָךְ מַצָּה הִיא, וּלְהָכִי *תְּנָא בֵּיהּ קְרָא – לְעַכֵּב. אֶלָּא חָלוּט מַצָּה הִיא דְּקָאָמְרִינַן, לְמַאי הִלְכְתָא? לוֹמַר [ה]שֶׁאָדָם יוֹצֵא בָּהּ יְדֵי חוֹבָתוֹ בְּפֶסַח, אע"פ דְּחָלְטֵיהּ מֵעִיקָּרָא, כֵּיוָן דַּהֲדַר אֲפָייֵהּ בְּתַנּוּר – "לֶחֶם עוֹנִי" קָרֵינָא בֵּיהּ, וְאָדָם יוֹצֵא בָּהּ יְדֵי חוֹבָתוֹ בְּפֶסַח.§ מתני' [ו]הַחוֹלֵץ לִיבִמְתּוֹ – הֲרֵי הוּא כְּאֶחָד מִן הָאַחִין לְנַחֲלָה, וְאִם יֵשׁ שָׁם אָב – נְכָסִים שֶׁל אָב. [ז]הַכּוֹנֵס אֶת יְבִמְתּוֹ זָכָה בַּנְּכָסִים שֶׁל אָחִיו. רַ' יְהוּדָה אוֹמֵר: בֵּין כָּךְ וּבֵין כָּךְ, אִם יֵשׁ שָׁם אָב – נְכָסִים שֶׁל אָב.§ גמ' פְּשִׁיטָא! סד"א: חֲלִיצָה בִּמְקוֹם יִבּוּם קַיְימָא, וְנִשְׁקוֹל כּוּלְּהוּ נִכְסֵי, קמ"ל. אִי הָכִי "הֲרֵי הוּא כְּאֶחָד מִן הָאַחִים"? אֵינוֹ אֶלָּא כְּאֶחָד מִן הָאַחִים מִיבְּעֵי לֵיהּ! אֶלָּא, סד"א: הוֹאִיל וְאַפְסְדָהּ מִיִּבּוּם לִקְנְסֵיהּ, קמ"ל.§ "אִם יֵשׁ שָׁם אָב".§ *דַּאֲמַר מָר: [ח]אָב קוֹדֵם לְכָל יוֹצְאֵי יְרֵכוֹ.§ "הַכּוֹנֵס אֶת יְבִמְתּוֹ וכו'".§ מ"ט? °"יָקוּם עַל שֵׁם אָחִיו" אָמַר רַחֲמָנָא, וַהֲרֵי קָם.§ "רַ' יְהוּדָה אוֹמֵר וכו'".§ אָמַר עוּלָּא: הֲלָכָה כְּרַ' יְהוּדָה. וְכֵן א"ר יִצְחָק נַפָּחָא: הֲלָכָה כְּרַ' יְהוּדָה. וַאֲמַר עוּלָּא וְאִיתֵימָא רַ' יִצְחָק נַפָּחָא: מ"ט דְּרַ' יְהוּדָה – דִּכְתִיב °"וְהָיָה הַבְּכוֹר אֲשֶׁר תֵּלֵד", כִּבְכוֹר: מָה בְּכוֹר אֵין לוֹ בְּחַיֵּי הָאָב – אַף הַאי נַמִי אֵין לוֹ בְּחַיֵּי הָאָב. אִי מָה בְּכוֹר נוֹטֵל פִּי שְׁנַיִם לְאַחַר מִיתַת הָאָב – אַף הַאי נוֹטֵל פִּי שְׁנַיִם לְאַחַר מִיתַת הָאָב! מִידֵי "יָקוּם עַל שֵׁם אָבִיו" כְּתִיב? "יָקוּם עַל שֵׁם אָחִיו" כְּתִיב, וְלֹא "עַל שֵׁם אָבִיו"! אֵימָא: הֵיכָא דְּלֵיכָּא אָב דְּלִשְׁקוֹל נַחֲלָה – תִּתְקַיֵּים מִצְוַת יִבּוּם, הֵיכָא דְּאִיכָּא אָב, [דְּלָא] שָׁקֵיל נַחֲלָה – לֹא תִּתְקַיֵּים מִצְוַת יִבּוּם! מִידֵי *יִבּוּם בְּנַחֲלָה תָּלָה רַחֲמָנָא? יַבּוּמֵי מְיַבְּמֵי, וְאִי אִיכָּא נַחֲלָה – שָׁקְלֵי, וְאִי לָא – לָא שָׁקֵיל. יָתֵיב רַ' חֲנִינָא קָרָא קַמֵּיהּ דְּרַ' יַנַּאי, וְיָתֵיב וְקָאָמַר: הֲלָכָה כְּרַ' יְהוּדָה. א"ל: *פּוּק קְרִי קְרָיָיךְ לְבָרָא, אֵין הֲלָכָה כְּרַ' יְהוּדָה. תָּנֵי תַּנָּא קַמֵּיהּ דְּרַב נַחְמָן: אֵין הֲלָכָה כְּרַ' יְהוּדָה. א"ל: אֶלָּא כְּמַאן, כְּרַבָּנַן? פְּשִׁיטָא, *יָחִיד וְרַבִּים הֲלָכָה כְּרַבִּים! א"ל: אִסְמְיֵיהּ?! א"ל: לָא, אַתְּ "הֲלָכָה" אַתְנְיָיךְ, וּמוּקְשֶׁה הוּא דְּאַקְשֵׁי לָךְ, וְאַפְּכַתְּ, וּלְמַאי דְּאַפְּכַתְּ – שַׁפִּיר אַפְּכַתְּ.§ מתני' [ט]הַחוֹלֵץ לִיבִמְתּוֹ – הוּא אָסוּר בִּקְרוֹבוֹתֶיהָ, וְהִיא אֲסוּרָה בִּקְרוֹבָיו.
הוא

רצה כהן אחר אוכלה. והא דדרשינן בפ"ב דקדושין (דף נג.) "לכל בני אהרן תהיה איש כאחיו" – היינו של אותו משמר, או של אותו בית אב. א"נ: הכא מרבוי [ילפינן], דכהן המקריב צריך שיאכל ממנה ולא כולה. מאי תרי גווני איכא. דליכא למימר רצה לשם סעודה אוכלה רצה לשם מצוה, דאין צריך שיתכוין לשם מצוה, אלא שלא יהא אוכלה אכילה גסה.

אכילה גסה ביוה"כ פטור. וא"ת: דאמר בפרק "מי שאמר הריני נזיר" (נזיר דף כג. ושם): "כי ישרים דרכי ה' צדיקים ילכו בם ופושעים יכשלו בם" (הושע יד) משל לב' בני אדם שצלו פסחיהן, אחד אכלו לשם פסחו ואחד אכלו אכילה גסה, ומשמע התם דתרוייהו נפקי, אלמא הויא אכילה! וי"ל: דתרי ענייני אכילה גסה הם א)*.

מצות אמר רחמנא. פי' בקונט': "ואכלוה מצות אצל המזבח" וגו', ובשמיני של מלואים כתיב. ואפילו לשמואל דאמר בריש "הקומץ רבה" (מנחות דף יט:) דלא ילפינן דורות משעה – שמא הכא איכא שום יתור.

שנה בה קרא לעכב. הך דהכא לא הוי כמו "שנה עליו הכתוב לעכב" דעלמא, דמהיכא תיתי לעכב? דדלמא למצוה הוא, דאמר רחמנא דלא ליעבד חלוט. אלא לעכב. כלומר: דבעינן מצה מעלייתא, ולא חלוט*.

כיון דהדר אפייה בתנור. או באילפס, לחם איקרי, ואדם יוצא בה ידי חובתו בפסח. והא דאמר בפ' "כל שעה" (פסחים דף לו:): "לחם עוני" – פרט לחלוט ואשישה – אר"ת: דהתם בלא הדר אפייה בתנור. ועוד אר"ת: דהתם בחלוט גדול, דומיא דאשישה, ולא חשיב לחם עוני לפי שהוא גדול, ולא משום דחלוט. א"נ: התם בבלילתו קשה, והכא בבלילתו רכה, כגון סופגנין או חלת המַשְׂרֵת, דמפרש התם דהיינו חלוט של בעלי בתים, דלא מחייב בחלה, ולא חשיב לחם אלא על ידי אפיה. ולהכי חשיב שפיר לחם עוני, אע"ג דחלטיה. אבל בלילתו עבה – מיפסל לעשות, דחשיב לחם עשירות אפי' לא הדר אפייה. ובפ' "כל שעה" (שם ד"ה פרט) הארכתי.
אבל

תוספות ישנים

א) וי"ל א) דתרי ענייני הוו מאכילה גסה היכא שאכל כל צרכו והסיח דעתו מלאכול עוד כשאכל יותר לא מקרייא אותה אכילה אכילה גסה אבל היכא דלא הסיח דעתו אכן אוכל הוא יותר מדאי שהיה שבע בפחות מקרי אותה אכילה אכילה גסה עוד י"ל דשאני אכילת פסחים דלא מיעכבא דהא לא ממעטינן מקרא דלפי אוכלו כי אם חולה וזקן שאינו ראוי כלל לאכילה אבל אפילו אכילה גסה גמורה מותרת דפסח מיהא קעביד אבל בכל מקום אכילה גסה לא שמה אכילה ואין חילוק באכילה גסה: מצות אמרה רחמנא פ"ה דכתיב ואכלוה מצות. ולא נהירא דהא בשמיני של מילואים כתיב ודורות משעה לא ילפינן אלא נראה מצות אמר רחמנא דכתיב לא תאפה חמץ חלקם א"נ משום דכתיב מצה תהיה ובזה ניחא דקאמר להכי תנא ביה קרא לעכב וקשה לאין זה לעכב ממש שהרי קרא אחרינא לא כתיב למעוטי חלוט דהא אמרי' לעולם מצה היא ולא חזינן בשום מקום לעכב אם לא כתיבי תרי קראי דמשמע שִׁנָּה הכתוב לעכב ונ"ל לעכב לאו דוקא אלא ר"ל לעכב שלא יביא חלוט אבל זה אינו לעכב ממש כי אם למצוה ולמאי דפרישית ניחא דודאי לעכב הוי מקרא דמצות תאכל דכבר כתיב קרא אחרינא למעוטי חלוט דכתיב מצה תהא

נח א מיי' פ"י מהלכות מעשה קרבנות הל' ב סמג עשין קפד קפה:
נט ב מיי' שם הלכה א:
ס ג מיי' פ"ב מהלכות שביתת עשור הלכה ז סמג לאוין סט טוש"ע א"ח סימן תריב סעיף ו:
סא ד מיי' פי"ב מהל' מעשה קרבנות הל' יד סמג לאוין של:
סב ה מיי' פ"ו מהל' חמץ ומצה הלכה ו סמג עשין מ טוש"ע א"ח סימן תנד סעיף ג:
סג ו טוש"ע אה"ע סימן קסג סעיף ב:
סד ז מיי' פ"ג מהלכות נחלות הלכה ז סמג עשין צו טוש"ע ח"מ סי' רעז סעי' א:
סה ח מיי' שם הל' ב סמג עשין צו טור ש"ע ח"מ סי' רעו סעי' ה:
סו ט מיי' פ"ב מהלכות יבום הלכה יג סמג עשין נב ולאוין קי טור ש"ע אה"ע סמן קסב סעיף ג:

[וע"ע תוס' פסחים קז: ד"ה דלמא ותוספות נזיר כג. ד"ה פסח ותוספות ב"ק קי. ד"ה אכילה]

[ועי' היטב תוס' מנחות נג. ד"ה ת"ל תהיה]

שמות כט | ויקרא ו | [נ"ל הא] | דברים כה | שם

[לעיל ל. פסחים נט: יומא סח:] | יומא פ: | [שבועות טו: סוטה טו. מנחות נה.] | [מנחות יט: וש"נ] | ב"ב קטו. | [עי' לעיל יז: כ: כד.] | [ברכות ל: כתובות נו.] | [שבת ס: וש"נ]

הגהות הב"ח

(א) רש"י ד"ה ואי לאו וכו' דכתיב בסדר שמיני ואכלוה מצות:

והכי איתא במנחות בריש פ' כל המנחות דף נג ע"א: מידי יבום בנחלה תלה רחמנא והא דאמרינן [דף יז] יבום בנחלה תלה רחמנא ר"ל ב) היכי דמי שראוי לנחלה מייבם איידך לא אבל אם אין נחלה משום הכי לא פקע מצות יבום: תנא
א) נ"ל וי"ל לתרי ענייני אכילה גסה הוו היכא וכו'. ב) נ"ל ר"ל דהיכי שראוי לנחל [כגון אח מן האב] מייבם איידך לא.

הוא אָסוּר בְּאִמָּהּ, וּבְאֵם אִמָּהּ, וּבְאֵם אָבִיהָ, וּבְבִתָּהּ, וּבְבַת בִּתָּהּ, וּבְבַת בְּנָהּ, וּבַאֲחוֹתָהּ בִּזְמַן שֶׁהִיא קַיֶּימֶת, וְהָאַחִין מוּתָּרִין. וְהִיא אֲסוּרָה בְּאָבִיו, וּבַאֲבִי אָבִיו, וּבִבְנוֹ, וּבְבֶן בְּנוֹ, בְּאָחִיו, וּבְבֶן אָחִיו. *[א]מוּתָּר אָדָם בִּקְרוֹבַת צָרַת חֲלוּצָתוֹ, *[ב]וְאָסוּר בְּצָרַת קְרוֹבַת חֲלוּצָתוֹ.§

גמ' אִיבַּעְיָא לְהוּ: גָּזְרוּ שְׁנִיּוֹת בַּחֲלוּצָה אוֹ לָא? בְּעֶרְוָה דְּאוֹרַיְיתָא גָּזְרוּ בְּהוּ רַבָּנַן שְׁנִיּוֹת, בַּחֲלוּצָה לָא גָּזְרוּ רַבָּנַן שְׁנִיּוֹת, אוֹ דִּלְמָא לָא שְׁנָא? ת"ש: "הוּא אָסוּר בְּאִמָּהּ וּבְאֵם אִמָּהּ", וְאִילּוּ "אֵם אֵם אִמָּהּ" — לָא קָתָנֵי. דִּלְמָא הַיְינוּ טַעֲמָא דְּלָא תָּנֵי — מִשּׁוּם דְּקָבָעֵי לְמִיתְנֵי סֵיפָא "וְהָאַחִין מוּתָּרִין", וְאִי תָּנָא "אֵם אֵם אִמָּהּ" ה"א: הָאַחִין מוּתָּרִין דַּוְקָא בְּאֵם אֵם אִמָּהּ, אֲבָל בְּאֵם אִמָּהּ וּבְאִמָּהּ לָא. וְלִיתְנֵי "אֵם אֵם אִמָּהּ" וְלִיתְנֵי "הָאַחִין מוּתָּרִין בְּכוּלָּן"! קַשְׁיָא. ת"ש: הִיא אֲסוּרָה בְּאָבִיו וּבַאֲבִי אָבִיו. קָתָנֵי מִיהָא אֲבִי אָבִיו, מַאי לָאו — מִשּׁוּם חוֹלֵץ, דְּהָוְיָא לָהּ כַּלַּת בְּנוֹ! לָא, מִשּׁוּם מִיתְנָא, דְּהָוְיָא לָהּ כַּלַּת בְּנוֹ. ת"ש: וּבְבֶן בְּנוֹ. מַאי לָאו — מִשּׁוּם חוֹלֵץ, דְּהָוְיָא לָהּ (מִשּׁוּם) אֵשֶׁת אֲבִי אָבִיו! לָא, מִשּׁוּם מִיתְנָא, וְהָוְיָא לָהּ אֵשֶׁת אֲחִי אֲבִי אָבִיו. הָא *אֲמֵימַר מַכְשַׁר בְּאֵשֶׁת אֲחִי אֲבִי אָבִיו! אֲמֵימַר מוֹקֵי לָהּ בְּבַר בְּרָא דְּסָבָא. אִי הָכִי, הַיְינוּ אָחִיו וּבֶן אָחִיו! תָּנָא אָחִיו מִן הָאָב, וְקָתָנֵי אָחִיו מִן הָאֵם ת"ש, דְּתָנֵי רַ' חִיָּיא: אַרְבַּע מִדִּבְרֵי תוֹרָה, וְאַרְבַּע מִדִּבְרֵי סוֹפְרִים. אָב וּבְנוֹ, אָחִיו וּבֶן אָחִיו — מִדִּבְרֵי תוֹרָה, אֲבִי אָבִיו וַאֲבִי אִמּוֹ, בֶּן בְּנוֹ, וּבֶן בִּתּוֹ — מד"ס. קָתָנֵי מִיהָא אֲבִי אָבִיו, מַאי לָאו מִשּׁוּם חוֹלֵץ, וְהָוְיָא לָהּ כַּלַּת בְּנוֹ! לָא, מִשּׁוּם מִיתְנָא, דְּהָוְיָא לָהּ כַּלַּת בְּנוֹ. ת"ש: אֲבִי אִמּוֹ — מַאי לָאו מִשּׁוּם חוֹלֵץ, דְּהָוְיָא לָהּ כַּלַּת בִּתּוֹ! לָא, מִשּׁוּם מִיתְנָא, דְּהָוְיָא לָהּ כַּלַּת בִּתּוֹ. ת"ש: וּבֶן בְּנוֹ, מַאי לָאו מִשּׁוּם חוֹלֵץ, דְּהָוְיָא לָהּ אֵשֶׁת אֲבִי אָבִיו! לָא, מִשּׁוּם מִיתְנָא דְּהָוְיָא לָהּ אֵשֶׁת אֲחִי אֲבִי אָבִיו. וְהָא אֲמֵימַר מַכְשִׁיר בְּאֵשֶׁת אֲחִי אֲבִי אָבִיו! אֲמֵימַר מוֹקִים לָהּ מִשּׁוּם חוֹלֵץ, וְקָסָבַר גָּזְרוּ שְׁנִיּוֹת בַּחֲלוּצָה. ת"ש: וּבְבֶן בִּתּוֹ, מַאי לָאו מִשּׁוּם חוֹלֵץ, דְּהָוְיָא לָהּ אֵשֶׁת אֲבִי אִמּוֹ! לָא, מִשּׁוּם מִיתְנָא דְּהָוְיָא לָהּ אֵשֶׁת אֲחִי אֲבִי אִמּוֹ. וְהָא גַּבֵּי שְׁנִיּוֹת דְּעֶרְוָה לָא גָּזְרוּ! אֶלָּא לָאו מִשּׁוּם חוֹלֵץ, [ג]וּשְׁמַע מִינַּהּ: גָּזְרוּ שְׁנִיּוֹת בַּחֲלוּצָה, שְׁמַע מִינַּהּ.§ "מוּתָּר אָדָם וכו'".§ אָמַר רַב טוֹבִי בַּר קִיסְנָא אָמַר שְׁמוּאֵל: הַבָּא עַל צָרַת חֲלוּצָה — הַוָּלָד מַמְזֵר. מַאי טַעֲמָא — בְּאִיסּוּרָהּ קַיְימָא. אָמַר רַב יוֹסֵף: אַף אֲנַן נַמִי תְּנֵינָא: מוּתָּר אָדָם בִּקְרוֹבַת צָרַת חֲלוּצָתוֹ. אִי אָמְרַתְּ בִּשְׁלָמָא צָרָה אַבָּרַאי — מִשּׁוּם הָכִי מוּתָּר בַּאֲחוֹתָהּ. אֶלָּא אִי אָמְרַתְּ צָרָה כַּחֲלוּצָה דָּמְיָא — אַמַּאי מוּתָּר? לֵימָא תֶּיהֱוֵי תְּיוּבְתָּא דְּרַבִּי יוֹחָנָן, דְּאָמַר: *בֵּין הוּא בֵּין אַחִין אֵין חַיָּיבִין לֹא עַל הַחֲלוּצָה כָּרֵת, וְלֹא עַל צָרָתָהּ כָּרֵת! אָמַר לָךְ רַבִּי יוֹחָנָן: וְתִסְבְּרָא אֲחוֹת חֲלוּצָה דְּאוֹרַיְיתָא? וְהָאָמַר ר"ל: *כָּאן שָׁנָה רַבִּי: אֲחוֹת גְּרוּשָׁה — מִדִּבְרֵי תוֹרָה, אֲחוֹת חֲלוּצָה — מִדִּבְרֵי סוֹפְרִים. מַאי שְׁנָא הַאי, וּמַאי שְׁנָא הַאי?

הך

רש"י

הוא אָסוּר כו'. כָּל הָנָךְ עֲרָיוֹת דְּאוֹרַיְיתָא נִינְהוּ בְּאִשְׁתּוֹ, וְגָזְרִינְהוּ רַבָּנַן בַּחֲלוּצָתוֹ. **בִּזְמַן שֶׁהִיא קַיֶּימֶת.** אַאֲחוֹתָהּ קָאֵי, וְלָא אַשְּׁאָר עֲרָיוֹת. **בְּאָבִיו.** מִשּׁוּם כַּלָּתוֹ. **וּבַאֲבִי אָבִיו.** מִשּׁוּם כַּלַּת בְּנוֹ, אע"ג דְּבְאִשְׁתּוֹ גְּמוּרָה אֵין אֲסוּרָה לַאֲבִי אָבִיו אֶלָּא מִדִּבְרֵי סוֹפְרִים, דְּהָא כַּלַּת בְּנוֹ מִשְּׁנִיּוֹת דְּרַבָּנַן הִיא — וַאֲפִילּוּ הָכִי גְּזָרוּהָ רַבָּנַן נַמִי בַּחֲלוּצָה. **בִּבְנוֹ.** מִשּׁוּם אֵשֶׁת אָב. **בְּבֶן בְּנוֹ.** מִשּׁוּם אֵשֶׁת אֲבִי אָבִיו, שֶׁהִיא מִן הַשְּׁנִיּוֹת. **בְּאָחִיו.** מִשּׁוּם אֵשֶׁת אָח. **בְּבֶן אָחִיו.** מִשּׁוּם אֵשֶׁת אֲחִי אָבִיו. **מוּתָּר אָדָם בִּקְרוֹבַת צָרַת חֲלוּצָתוֹ.** וְלָא אָמְרִינַן צָרָה כַּחֲלוּצָה, וְאָסוּר בִּקְרוֹבוֹתֶיהָ. **וְאָסוּר בְּצָרַת קְרוֹבַת חֲלוּצָתוֹ.** רְאוּבֵן חָלַץ לְלֵאָה, וְרָחֵל נְשׂוּאָה לְנָכְרִי וְלָהּ צָרָה, וּמֵת הַנָּכְרִי — אֲסוּרָה הַצָּרָה לִרְאוּבֵן. וְטַעְמָא מְפָרֵשׁ בַּגְּמָרָא.

גמ' גָּזְרוּ שְׁנִיּוֹת בַּחֲלוּצָה אוֹ לָא. כְּגוֹן אֵם אֵם אִמָּהּ וְאֵם אֵם אָבִיהָ, דְּגַבֵּי אִשְׁתּוֹ מִיתַּסְרוּ עֲלֵיהּ מִשּׁוּם שְׁנִיּוֹת, כִּדְתָנֵי רַבִּי חִיָּיא בְּפֶרֶק "כֵּיצַד" (לעיל דף כא.): רְבִיעִי שֶׁבַּחֲמָיו וְשֶׁבַּחֲמוֹתוֹ. שְׁנִיָּה הָכָא מַאי? בְּעֶרְוָה דְּאוֹרַיְיתָא. כְּלוֹמַר, בְּאִשְׁתּוֹ, דְּאִמָּהּ וְאֵם אִמָּהּ הָוֵה עֶרְוָה דְּאוֹרַיְיתָא — גָּזְרוּ רַבָּנַן שְׁנִיּוֹת, אֲבָל בַּחֲלוּצָה, דַּאֲפִילּוּ עֲרָיוֹת דִּידַהּ דְּרַבָּנַן — לֹא גָּזְרוּ שְׁנִיּוֹת בָּהֶן. **אוֹ דִּלְמָא לָא שְׁנָא.** וּמִמַּתְנִי' לָא דָּיֵיק. דְּקָתָנֵי הִיא אֲסוּרָה בַּאֲבִי אָבִיו מִשּׁוּם כַּלַּת בְּנוֹ דְּהָוֵי שְׁנִיָּה — הָא קַמַּיְיתִינַן לַהּ לְקַמָּן עֲלַהּ דְּהָא מִילְּתָא, וּמַדְחֵי לֵיהּ, לְמֵימַר: לָאו מִשּׁוּם חוֹלֵץ, אֶלָּא בִּשְׁבִיל הַמֵּת שֶׁהָיְתָה זוֹ אִשְׁתּוֹ גְּמוּרָה, לְפִיכָךְ אֲבִי אָבִיו אָסוּר בָּהּ מִשּׁוּם כַּלַּת בְּנוֹ. **ה"א הָאַחִין מוּתָּרִין.** לָא קָאֵי אֶלָּא אַאֵם אֵם אִמָּהּ, דְּלָא גָּזְרוּ שְׁנִיּוֹת בִּזִיקָה. אֲבָל אִמָּהּ וְאֵם אִמָּהּ, דְּהָווּ לְהוּ עֲרָיוֹת דְּאוֹרַיְיתָא לְגַבֵּי אִשָּׁה גְּמוּרָה — לָא מִשְׁתַּרוּ אַחִין, דְּגָזְרוּ עֲרָיוֹת בִּזִיקָה וַאֲפִי' לְאַחַר חֲלִיצָה. נֵימָא דְּאִיהוּ שְׁלִיחוּתַיְיהוּ עֲבַד, מִשּׁוּם הָכִי לָא תַּנְיֵיהּ. ת"ש מִבֶּן בְּנוֹ מַאי לָאו מִשּׁוּם חוֹלֵץ דְּהָוֵי לֵיהּ אֵשֶׁת אֲבִי אָבִיו. וְהִיא מִן הַשְּׁנִיּוֹת. **לָא מִשּׁוּם מִיתְנָא.** שֶׁהָיְתָה זוֹ אִשְׁתּוֹ גְּמוּרָה, וַאֲסוּרָה עַל בֶּן בְּנוֹ שֶׁל חוֹלֵץ, דְּהָוְיָא לַהּ אֵשֶׁת אֲחִי אֲבִי אָבִיו. וְקס"ד דְּהָא נַמִי מִשְּׁנִיּוֹת הִיא. **וְהָא אֲמֵימַר מַכְשַׁר כו'.** בְּפֶרֶק "כֵּיצַד" (לעיל דף כא:). **אֲמֵימַר מוֹקֵי לָהּ.** לְהַאי בֶּן בְּנוֹ דְּמַתְנִי' אַסָּבָא, אֲבִיהֶן שֶׁל מֵת; וְחוֹלֵץ דְּתָנָא בְּרֵישָׁא, דְּקָתָנֵי: הִיא אֲסוּרָה בְּאָבִיו, וַהֲדַר תָּנֵי וּבִבְנוֹ שֶׁל אָבִיו — שֶׁהוּא אֲחִי הַמֵּת וְהַחוֹלֵץ, וְקָמָה עֲלֵיהּ בְּלָא יִבְנֶה מִשֶּׁחָלַץ לָהּ הָאֶחָד, וּלְבֶן בְּנוֹ שֶׁל אֲבִיהֶם, דְּהָוְיָא לֵיהּ אֵשֶׁת אֲחִי אָבִיו. **וְקָתָנֵי אָחִיו מִן הָאֵם.** שֶׁהָיָה זֶה אָחִיו מִן הָאֵם, אוֹ בֶּן אָחִיו מִן הָאֵם, וְלָאו מִשּׁוּם חוֹלֵץ — דְּא"כ הָוְיָא לָהּ שְׁנִיּוֹת בַּחֲלוּצָה, דְּהָא לֵיתָא. אֶלָּא אֵשֶׁת אֲחִי הָאָב מִן הָאֵם, וְהָא בִּשְׁנִיּוֹת תָּנֵינַן לָהּ. אֶלָּא מִשּׁוּם מִיתְנָא, דְּהָוֵי שְׁנִיָּה מִשּׁוּם עֶרְוָה דְּאוֹרַיְיתָא, דְּאִשְׁתּוֹ מַעַלְיְיתָא הֲוָה. וּכְגוֹן שֶׁהָיוּ (א) הַיָּבָם וְהַחוֹלֵץ אַחִין מִן הָאָב וּמִן הָאֵם, וְלִשְׁנֵיהֶם אָח מִן הָאֵם שֶׁלֹּא מִן הָאָב. **דְּתָנֵי רַבִּי חִיָּיא.** בַּחֲלוּצָה. **אַרְבַּע מִדִּבְרֵי תוֹרָה.** כְּלוֹמַר, דִּלְגַבֵּי אִשְׁתּוֹ הָוְיָין דְּאוֹרַיְיתָא. **אָב.** שֶׁל חוֹלֵץ, אָסוּר בָּהּ מִן הַתּוֹרָה מִפְּנֵי הַמֵּת, דְּהָוְיָא לֵיהּ כַּלָּתוֹ שֶׁל אָב. **וּבְנוֹ.** שֶׁל חוֹלֵץ, שֶׁהָיָה הַמֵּת אֲחִי אָבִיו, וְעֶרְוָה הִיא לְגַבֵּיהּ. **וְאָחִיו.** שֶׁל חוֹלֵץ, דְּהָוֵה נַמִי אֲחִי הַמֵּת, וְקָם לֵיהּ בְּ"לֹא יִבְנֶה". **וּבֶן אָחִיו.** שֶׁל חוֹלֵץ, שֶׁהָיָה הַמֵּת אֲחִי אָבִיו. **אֲבִי אָבִיו.** מִשּׁוּם כַּלַּת בְּנוֹ. **וַאֲבִי אִמּוֹ.** מִשּׁוּם כַּלַּת בִּתּוֹ. **וּבֶן בְּנוֹ.** קס"ד מִשּׁוּם חוֹלֵץ, דְּהָוְיָא לֵיהּ אֵשֶׁת אֲבִי אָבִיו. **וּבֶן בִּתּוֹ.** דְּהָוְיָא לֵיהּ אֵשֶׁת אֲבִי אִמּוֹ, וְכָל הָנָךְ שְׁנִיּוֹת נִינְהוּ: הָכִי גָּרְסִינַן: ת"ש וּבַאֲבִי אִמּוֹ מַאי לָאו מִשּׁוּם חוֹלֵץ דְּהָוְיָא לֵיהּ כַּלַּת בִּתּוֹ לָא מִשּׁוּם מִיתְנָא דְּהָוְיָא לֵיהּ כַּלַּת בִּתּוֹ וּכְגוֹן שֶׁהָיוּ אַחִין אַף מִן הָאֵם. **אֲמֵימַר מוֹקֵי לָהּ.** וְאִי כְּדְקָאָמְרַתְּ מִשּׁוּם חוֹלֵץ, וְקָסָבַר גָּזְרוּ שְׁנִיּוֹת בַּחֲלוּצָה אֲבָל מַאן דְּאָסַר בְּאֵשֶׁת אֲחִי אֲבִי הָאָב — מָצֵי לְאוֹקְמֵי מִשּׁוּם מִיתְנָא, וְתִיבָּעֵי לָךְ אִי גָּזְרוּ שְׁנִיּוֹת בַּחֲלוּצָה אוֹ לָא. **בְּאִיסּוּרָהּ קַיְימָא.** חֲלוּצָה הִיא דְּקַיְימָא בְּ"לֹא יִבְנֶה" וְתוּ לָא, אֲבָל צָרָתָהּ קַיְימָא עֲלֵיהּ בְּאִיסּוּר אֵשֶׁת אָח בְּכָרֵת, וְהַוָּלָד מַמְזֵר. **אִי אָמְרַתְּ בִּשְׁלָמָא צָרָה אַבָּרַאי קַיְימָא.** בְּאִיסּוּרָא קַמָּא, וְלָא אָמְרִינַן חֲלוּצָה שְׁלִיחוּתָא דִּידַהּ עָבְדָא. **מִשּׁוּם הָכִי שָׁרֵי בַּאֲחוֹתָהּ.** דְּלָאו אֲחוֹת חֲלוּצָה הִיא. וּלְגַבֵּי דִּידַהּ נַמִי, כֵּיוָן דַּחֲלוּצָה לָאו שְׁלִיחוּת דִּידַהּ עָבְדָא — לָא מְשַׁוְּיָא לֵיהּ בְּ"לֹא יִבְנֶה", אֶלָּא בְּאִיסּוּרָא קַמָּא קַיְימָא. **אֶלָּא אִי אָמְרַתְּ צָרָה כַּחֲלוּצָה דָּמְיָא.** דַּחֲלוּצָה שְׁלִיחוּתָא דִּידַהּ עָבְדָא, וּמְשַׁוֵּי לָהּ בְּ"לֹא יִבְנֶה" — א"כ הָוְיָא לָהּ צָרָה כַּחֲלוּצָה, וְאַמַּאי שָׁרֵי בַּאֲחוֹתָהּ? **דר' יוֹחָנָן.** בְּפֶרֶק קַמָּא (לעיל י:). **וְלֹא עַל צָרָתָהּ כָּרֵת.** הַחוֹלֵץ לִיבִמְתּוֹ, וְחָזַר וּבָא הוּא אוֹ אֶחָד מִן הָאַחִין עַל צָרָתָהּ. **וְתִסְבְּרָא.** דְּהָא רְאָיָה דְּרַב יוֹסֵף דְּאַיְיתִי מִמַּתְנִיתִין — רְאָיָה הִיא? וְכִי *חֲלוּצָה גּוּפָהּ דְּאוֹרַיְיתָא (דְּרַבָּנַן הִיא), דְּכִי אָמְרִינַן צָרָה כַּחֲלוּצָה יֵאָסֵר בַּאֲחוֹת הַצָּרָה. **וְהָאָמַר ר"ל.** לְקַמָּן אַמַּתְנִיתִין דִּלְקַמָּן. **כָּאן שָׁנָה רַבִּי.** בְּמִשְׁנָה זוֹ לִמְּדָנוּ רַבִּי: אֲחוֹת גְּרוּשָׁה מִדִּבְרֵי תוֹרָה וכו'. וּלְקַמָּן מְפָרֵשׁ לָהּ. וְכֵיוָן דַּאֲחוֹת חֲלוּצָה גּוּפָהּ דְּרַבָּנַן, בַּחֲלוּצָה — גְּזוֹר בַּאֲחוֹתָהּ, בַּצָּרָה — לָא גְּזוֹר. **מַאי שְׁנָא.** רֵישָׁא קְרוֹבַת צָרַת חֲלוּצָה דִּשְׁרֵיָא, וּמַאי שְׁנָא סֵיפָא צָרַת קְרוֹבַת חֲלוּצָתוֹ שֶׁנְּשׁוֹתֵיהֶן נָכְרִיּוֹת, הִיא וְצָרָתָהּ נְשׂוּאוֹת לְנָכְרִי, וְקָתָנֵי אָסוּר?

הך

תוספות

אבל אמה ואם אמה לא. והא דתנן בפרק ב' (לעיל כג:) אחד חולץ ואחד מייבם, אלמא שרי באחותה! שאני התם משום דאימור דידיה איתרמי ליה. והא נמי דתנן לקמן בפרקין (דף מא.): החולץ ליבמתו ונשא אחיו את אחותה — היינו דיעבד. **וליתני אחין מותרין בכולן קשיא.** הא דלא קאמר אלא שמע מינה דלא גזרו שניות בחלוצה, היינו משום דלקמן מסיק דגזרו. ולא שייך לשנויי תנא ושייר, כיון דלא תנא שום שניה אלא הני דאורייתא לחוד. **אמימר** מוקי לה כו'. כל סוגיא דשמעתין דלא כאמימר, כדפרשתי לעיל (דף כא: ד"ה "אמימר"). **בבן** בתו לאו משום חולץ. לא בעי לאוקמי בבן בתו דסבא דומיא דבן בנו — דלא מיירי בבן בנו דסבא, דא"כ הויא ליה אשת אחי אביו דאורייתא. **שמע** מינה גזרו שניות בחלוצה. והא דלא תני במתניתין אבי אמו ובן בתו — משום דתנא ושייר. ומיהו רבי חייא, דקתני מנינא, קשה דלא תנא בן אחותו ובן אחיו מן האם! ויש לומר: דלא תנא אלא ארבע, כנגד ארבע של דברי תורה.

הך

עין משפט נר מצוה

סז א מיי' פ"א מהל' יבום הלכה יג וסמג עשין נ"ב וטוש"ע אה"ע סי' קסב סעיף ז:

סח ב מיי' שם פ"ו הל' כ סמג שם טוש"ע שם סעיף ה:

סט ג מיי' שם פ"א הל' יב סמג שם טוש"ע שם סעיף ג:

תוספות ישנים

תנא אחיו מן האב ותנא אחיו מן האם פי' הא דקאמר ובן אחיו ר"ל אחיו מן האם וא"ת א"כ לפשוט דגזרו שניות בחלוצה דהא אשת אחי האב מן האם היינו שניה וי"ל דזהו משום מיתנא דמיירי שאותו בן אחיו דמיירי בה מתני' שהוא אח מן האם למיתנא ולחולץ אבל החולץ והמיתנא אחין מן האב ומן האם וזה בן אחיו ר"ל שהוא בן אחי האב מן האם לשניהם וא"כ לא תפשוט שניות בחלוצה דהיינו משום מיתנא: **אמימר** מוקים לה בבר ברא לחולץ וקסבר כו' אבל לא קאמר בבר ברא דסבא כלעיל וא"כ לא תפשוט דגזרו שניה בחלוצה דדוקא לעיל מצינן למימר הכי דהא קאי אהיא אסורה באביו ור"ל בן בנו של אותו אב אבל ר' חייא דהכא לא קתני אביו ועוד נלע"ד דלא מצי מוקי לה בבר ברא דסבא כלעיל דא"כ בן בנו הוי מן התורה דהיינו לכל הפחות אשת אחי אביו ור' חייא תני ליה בן בנו עם הארבעה שמדברי סופרים: **ותסברא** אחות חלוצה לאורייתא היא. פי' אלא ודאי לאו סיועא היא דלעולם מצינן למימר דצרה כחלוצה וליכא להקשות אמאי מותר כי יש טעם גדול בדבר דהא אפי' אי הוי הצרה עצמה חלוצה אחותה אינה אסורה אלא מדרבנן וא"כ לא גזור רבנן באחות הצרה דכי גזור רבנן באחות חלוצה עצמה אבל באחות צרת חלוצה לא גזור:

מסורת הש"ס

[לעיל כז.] | שם | לעיל כח: | [לעיל י:] | לקמן מח. מד. קדושין סה. | ס"א אחות חלוצה

הגהות הב"ח

(א) רש"י ד"ה וקתני אחיו וכו' וכגון שהיו המת והחולץ אחים מן האב:

תוספות חד מקמאי

מתני' (א) אסור בקרובת חלוצתו ומותר בקרובת חלוצתו פירוש אי חליץ לצרת לאה מותר אף ברחל אי חליץ ללאה אסור בצרת רחל ופי' רש"י ז"ל אע"פ שרחל נשואה לנכרי ולה צרה ומת הנכרי אסורה הצרה לראובן החולץ ומפורש טעמא בגמ' הך דאזלא לב"ד גזרו בהו רבנן כלומר כשלאה חולצת מוליכה רחל אחותה עמה לב"ד וכ"ע לא ידעי הי מינייהו יבמתו ואיכא דסברי ב) דרחל חליץ ואנסיב צרת רחל דהיינו צרת אחות חלוצתו אמרי צרת אחות חלוצתו נסיב ואינהו סברי דרחל וצרת האחין הוו. הך דלא אזלא לב"ד לא גזרו בהו רבנן כשהיבמה חולצת אין צרתה הולכת עמה דמסתפק דלמא חליץ לה הלכך כי נסיב אחות הצרה לא אמרי אחות חלוצתו נסיב כך פירש"י ז"ל ולפי דבריו מצינו חלוצה שהיא מדברי סופרים חמורה מערוה שהיא מד"ת דאילו צרת ערוה שלא במקום מצוה היא שריה וצרת אחות חלוצה שלא במקום מצוה אסורה וי"מ שלא אסרו צרת קרובת חלוצתו אלא במקום יבום כגון שלאה ורחל נשואים לראובן ושמעון ומתו שניהם וכההיא דאמר בפרק ד' אחין התחיל באחיות לא יגמור אפילו בצרות דתנן אסור אדם בצרת קרובת חלוצתו התחיל בצרות יגמור אף באחיות דתנן מותר אדם בקרובת צרת חלוצתו ועל הפירוש הזה איכא לעיוני כיון דרחל אזלא בתרה (דינא) לב"ד וכי חליץ לאה סברי חליץ רחל אלא מעתה תפסול רחל לכהונה ותפסלה רחל לאחי החולץ אלמא תנן החולץ ליבמתו אסור הוא בקרובותיה והאחין מותרים ונפסלת רחל לאחר מיתת לאה אלמה תנן מתה מותר באחותה אלא כיון דאחות חלוצה אינה אסורה אלא מדברי סופרים לא גזרו בה רבנן כולי האי אע"פ שגזרו בצרתה: הא דאמר נפלה לפני יבם קטן לית לה מזוני מבעל מסתברא הני מילי לאחר שלשה חדשים אבל תוך שלשה חדשים אית לה מזוני מבעל:

גרים

א) נ"ל אסור אדם בצרת קרובת חלוצתו ומותר בקרובת צרת חלוצתו. ב) נ"ל ואיכא דסברי דלרחל חלץ ואי נסיב צרת רחל דהיינו צרת אחות חלוצתו אמרי צרת חלוצתו נסיב דאינהו סברי דרחל חלוצת האחין הוואי.

הַךְ דְּאָזְלָא בַּהֲדָהּ לְבֵי דִינָא — גָּזְרוּ בְּהוּ רַבָּנַן, הַאי דְּלָא אָזְלָא בַּהֲדָהּ לְבֵי דִינָא — לָא גָּזְרוּ בְּהוּ רַבָּנַן.§ **מתני'** [א]הַחוֹלֵץ לִיבִמְתּוֹ, וְנָשָׂא אָחִיו אֶת אֲחוֹתָהּ, וָמֵת — חוֹלֶצֶת וְלֹא מִתְיַבֶּמֶת. [ב]וְכֵן הַמְגָרֵשׁ אֶת אִשְׁתּוֹ, וְנָשָׂא אָחִיו אֶת אֲחוֹתָהּ וָמֵת — הֲרֵי זוֹ פְּטוּרָה. *[ג]שׁוֹמֶרֶת יָבָם שֶׁקִּידֵּשׁ אָחִיו אֶת אֲחוֹתָהּ, מִשּׁוּם רַבִּי יְהוּדָה בֶּן בְּתֵירָא אָמְרוּ: אוֹמְרִים לוֹ: הַמְתֵּן עַד שֶׁיַּעֲשֶׂה אָחִיךָ מַעֲשֶׂה. חָלַץ לָהּ אָחִיו אוֹ כְּנָסָהּ — יִכְנוֹס אֶת אִשְׁתּוֹ. מֵתָה הַיְבָמָה — יִכְנוֹס אֶת אִשְׁתּוֹ. [ד]מֵת יָבָם — יוֹצִיא אֶת אִשְׁתּוֹ בְּגֵט, וְאֵשֶׁת אָחִיו בַּחֲלִיצָה.§ **גמ'** מַאי "וְכֵן"? אֵימָא: אֲבָל הַמְגָרֵשׁ. אָמַר רֵישׁ לָקִישׁ: *כָּאן שָׁנָה רַבִּי: [ה]אֲחוֹת גְּרוּשָׁה — מִדִּבְרֵי תוֹרָה, [ו]אֲחוֹת חֲלוּצָה — מִדִּבְרֵי סוֹפְרִים.§ "שׁוֹמֶרֶת יָבָם שֶׁקִּידֵּשׁ וכו'".§ *אָמַר שְׁמוּאֵל: הֲלָכָה כְּדִבְרֵי רַבִּי יְהוּדָה בֶּן בְּתֵירָא. אִיבַּעְיָא לְהוּ: מֵתָה אִשְׁתּוֹ, מַהוּ בִּיבִמְתּוֹ? רַב וְרַבִּי חֲנִינָא דְּאָמְרִי תַּרְוַיְיהוּ: [ז]מֵתָה אִשְׁתּוֹ מוּתָּר בִּיבִמְתּוֹ, שְׁמוּאֵל וְרַב אַסִּי דְּאָמְרִי תַּרְוַיְיהוּ: מֵתָה אִשְׁתּוֹ אָסוּר בִּיבִמְתּוֹ. אָמַר רָבָא: מַאי טַעְמָא דְּרַב — מִשּׁוּם דְּהָוֵאי יְבָמָה שֶׁהוּתְּרָה, וְנֶאֶסְרָה, וְחָזְרָה וְהוּתְּרָה — תַּחֲזוֹר לְהֶיתֵּירָהּ הָרִאשׁוֹן. מְתִיב רַב הַמְנוּנָא: *ג' אַחִין, ב' נְשׂוּאִין ב' אֲחָיוֹת וְאֶחָד מוּפְנֶה, מֵת אֶחָד מִבַּעֲלֵי אֲחָיוֹת וְעָשָׂה בָּהּ מוּפְנֶה מַאֲמָר, וְאַחַר כָּךְ מֵת אָחִיו הַשֵּׁנִי, וְאַחַר כָּךְ מֵתָה אִשְׁתּוֹ אַחֲרָיו — אוֹתָהּ יְבָמָה חוֹלֶצֶת וְלֹא מִתְיַבֶּמֶת. וְאַמַּאי? תֶּיהֱוֵי כִּיבָמָה שֶׁהוּתְּרָה, וְנֶאֶסְרָה, וְחָזְרָה וְהוּתְּרָה — תַּחֲזוֹר לְהֶיתֵּירָהּ הָרִאשׁוֹן! אִישְׁתִּיק. לְבָתַר דְּנָפַק אֲמַר: אַמַּאי לָא אֲמַרְתְּ לֵיהּ רַבִּי אֱלִיעֶזֶר הִיא, דַּאֲמַר: *כֵּיוָן שֶׁעָמְדָה עָלָיו שָׁעָה אַחַת בְּאִסּוּר נֶאֶסְרָה עָלָיו עוֹלָמִית? הֲדַר אֲמַר: אֵימוּר דְּא"ר אֱלִיעֶזֶר — הֵיכָא דְּלָא חֲזָיָא בִּשְׁעַת נְפִילָה, אֲבָל הֵיכָא דַּחֲזָיָא בִּשְׁעַת נְפִילָה — מִי אֲמַר? הֲדַר אֲמַר: אִין, וְהָתַנְיָא: רַבִּי אֱלִיעֶזֶר אוֹמֵר: מֵתָה יְבִמְתּוֹ — מוּתָּר בְּאִשְׁתּוֹ, מֵתָה אִשְׁתּוֹ אוֹתָהּ יְבָמָה חוֹלֶצֶת וְלֹא מִתְיַבֶּמֶת. לֵימָא שְׁמוּאֵל וְרַב אַסִּי דְּאָמְרִי כְּר' אֱלִיעֶזֶר! אֲפִי' תֵּימָא כְּרַבָּנַן, עַד כָּאן לָא קָמִיפַּלְגִי רַבָּנַן עֲלֵיהּ דְּרַבִּי אֱלִיעֶזֶר — אֶלָּא מִשּׁוּם דְּמִנְּפִילָה וְאֵילָךְ לָא מִיתְּסַר עֲלַיְיהוּ, אֲבָל הָכָא דְּאִיתְּסַר — אֲפִילוּ רַבָּנַן מוֹדוּ.§ **מתני'** *[ח]הַיְבָמָה לֹא תַּחֲלוֹץ וְלֹא תִּתְיַבֵּם עַד שֶׁיֵּשׁ לָהּ שְׁלֹשָׁה חֳדָשִׁים. [ט]וְכֵן כָּל שְׁאָר הַנָּשִׁים לֹא יִתְאָרְסוּ וְלֹא יִנָּשְׂאוּ עַד שֶׁיְּהוּ לָהֶן שְׁלֹשָׁה חֳדָשִׁים אֶחָד בְּתוּלוֹת וְאֶחָד בְּעוּלוֹת, אֶחָד גְּרוּשׁוֹת וְאֶחָד אַלְמָנוֹת, אֶחָד נְשׂוּאוֹת וְאֶחָד אֲרוּסוֹת. רַבִּי יְהוּדָה אוֹמֵר: הַנְּשׂוּאוֹת יִתְאָרְסוּ, וְהָאֲרוּסוֹת יִנָּשְׂאוּ, חוּץ מִן הָאֲרוּסוֹת שֶׁבִּיהוּדָה, מִפְּנֵי שֶׁלִּבּוֹ גַּס בָּהּ. *ר' יוֹסֵי אוֹמֵר: כָּל הַנָּשִׁים יִתְאָרְסוּ, חוּץ מִן הָאַלְמָנָה, מִפְּנֵי

רש"י

הַךְ דְּאָזְלָא בַּהֲדָהּ לְבֵי דִינָא. כְּשֶׁלָּאָה חוֹלֶצֶת מוֹלִיכָה אֲחוֹתָהּ עִמָּהּ לְבֵ"ד, וְכ"ע לָא יָדְעֵי הֵי מִנַּיְיהוּ יְבִמְתּוֹ, וְאִיכָּא דְּסָבַר דִּלְרָחֵל חָלַץ. וְכִי נָסֵיב צָרַת רָחֵל, דְּהַיְינוּ צָרַת קְרוֹבַת חֲלוּצָתוֹ, אָמְרִי: צָרַת חֲלוּצָתוֹ נָסֵיב. דְּאִינְהוּ סָבְרִי שֶׁרָחֵל וְצָרָתָהּ נְשֵׁי אָחִיו הֲווּ, שֶׁהֲרֵי חָלַץ לְרָחֵל. הַאי דְּלָא אָזְלָא בַּהֲדָהּ לְבֵי דִינָא. כְּשֶׁהַיְבָמָה חוֹלֶצֶת אֵין צָרָתָהּ הוֹלֶכֶת עִמָּהּ. הִלְכָּךְ, כִּי נָסֵיב אֲחוֹת צָרָה — לָא אָמְרִינַן אֲחוֹת חֲלוּצָתוֹ נָסֵיב. **מתני'** וְלֹא מִתְיַיבֶּמֶת. דְּהָוְיָא לָהּ אֲחוֹת חֲלוּצָתוֹ. וּמִיהוּ, מֵחֲלִיצָה לָא מִפַּטְרָא, דְּמִדְּאוֹרַיְיתָא רַמְיָא קַמֵּיהּ, וְאַע"ג דַּאֲחוֹתָהּ קַיֶּימֶת. דַּאֲחוֹת חֲלוּצָה אֵינָהּ אֶלָּא מִדִּבְרֵי סוֹפְרִים. וְכֵן הַמְגָרֵשׁ. בַּגְּמָרָא בָּעֵי: מַאי "וְכֵן"? פְּטוּרָה. אַף מִן הַחֲלִיצָה, דְּיוֹצְאָה מִשּׁוּם אֲחוֹת אִשָּׁה, הוֹאִיל וְאִשְׁתּוֹ קַיֶּימֶת. וַאֲחוֹת גְּרוּשָׁה מִדִּבְרֵי תוֹרָה, דִּכְתִיב (ויקרא יח) "עָלֶיהָ בְּחַיֶּיהָ" — כָּל שֶׁבְּחַיֶּיהָ. שׁוֹמֶרֶת יָבָם שֶׁקִּידֵּשׁ. אֶחָד מִן הָאַחִין אֶת אֲחוֹתָהּ לְאַחַר שֶׁנָּפְלָה זוֹ לִפְנֵיהֶם, וְהוּזְקְקָה לְכוּלָּן. הַמְתֵּן. מִלִּכְנוֹס, דְּקָא פָּגַעְתְּ בַּאֲחוֹת זְקוּקָה. עַד שֶׁיַּעֲשֶׂה מַעֲשֶׂה. שֶׁיִּכְנְסוּ הָאַחִין אֶת הַיְבָמָה אוֹ יַחְלְצוּ, וְתֵעָקֵר זִיקָּתָהּ מִמְּךָ. מֵתָה הַיְבָמָה יִכְנוֹס אֶת אִשְׁתּוֹ. דַּאֲפִילּוּ כְּנָסָהּ וּמֵתָה — מוּתָּר בַּאֲחוֹתָהּ. מֵת הַיָּבָם. וְלֹא נוֹתַר לוֹ אָח אֶלָּא זֶה. וְאֶת אֵשֶׁת אָחִיו בַּחֲלִיצָה. אֲבָל יִבּוּמֵי לָא, דַּאֲחוֹת גְּרוּשָׁתוֹ הִיא. **גמ'** הֲלָכָה כְּרַבִּי יְהוּדָה. דְּיֵשׁ זִיקָה, וְאַלִּימָא לְמֵיסְרָא עָלָיו. מַהוּ בִּיבִמְתּוֹ. מִי אָמְרִינַן: כֵּיוָן דְּמֵתָה — פָּקַע אִיסּוּר אֲחוֹת אִשָּׁה, וְשַׁרְיָא, אוֹ דִּלְמָא, אע"ג דְּפָקַע אִיסּוּר אֲחוֹת אִשָּׁה, קָם עָלֶיהָ בְּאִיסּוּר אֵשֶׁת אָח, הוֹאִיל וְנֶאֶסְרָה עָלָיו שָׁעָה אַחַת בְּשָׁעָה שֶׁהָיְתָה זְקוּקָה לְיַבֵּם, וְאֵין אֲנִי קוֹרֵא בָּהּ "יְבָמָהּ יָבֹא עָלֶיהָ" — הֲרֵי הִיא כְּאֵשֶׁת אָח שֶׁיֵּשׁ לָהּ בָּנִים, וַאֲסוּרָה עוֹלָמִית עָלָיו. מ"ט דְּרַב. דְּשָׁרֵי, הֲרֵי נֶאֶסְרָה עָלָיו שָׁעָה אַחַת! שֶׁהוּתְּרָה. בִּשְׁעַת נְפִילָתָהּ. נֶאֶסְרָה. כְּשֶׁקִּידֵּשׁ זֶה אֲחוֹתָהּ. וְאח"כ מֵת אָחִיו. הַב', וְנָפְלָה אֲחוֹתָהּ, וַאֲסָרַתָּהּ לָרִאשׁוֹנָה עָלָיו מִשּׁוּם אֲחוֹת זְקוּקָה. וְאַע"ג דַּעֲבַד בָּהּ מַאֲמָר, כְּדִתְנַן בְּפֶ' "אַרְבָּעָה אַחִין", ב"ה אוֹמְרִים: אוֹי לוֹ עַל אִשְׁתּוֹ, וְאוֹי לוֹ עַל אֵשֶׁת אָחִיו. וְאח"כ מֵתָה אִשְׁתּוֹ שֶׁל שֵׁנִי אַחֲרָיו. וְנִשְׁאֲרָה בַּעֲלַת מַאֲמָר זוֹ. ר' אֱלִיעֶזֶר הִיא. בְּפֶרֶק ב"ש: הַמְגָרֵשׁ אֶת הָאִשָּׁה וְהֶחֱזִירָהּ — מוּתֶּרֶת לְיַבֵּם, רַבִּי אֱלִיעֶזֶר אוֹסֵר, הוֹאִיל וְעָמְדָה עָלָיו שָׁעָה אַחַת בְּאִיסּוּר גְּרוּשַׁת אָח. דִּבְשְׁעַת נְפִילָה לָא אִיתְחֲזַאי. דְּמִקַּמֵּי נְפִילָה אִיתַּסְרָא עֲלֵיהּ. מֵתָה יְבִמְתּוֹ. אַמְקַדֵּשׁ אֲחוֹת יְבִמְתּוֹ קָאֵי. חוֹלֶצֶת. כִּשְׁמוּאֵל וְרַב אַסִּי. עַד כָּאן לָא פְּלִיגִי רַבָּנַן עֲלֵיהּ דְּרַבִּי אֱלִיעֶזֶר. בְּפֶרֶק "בֵּית שַׁמַּאי" אֶלָּא גַּבֵּי מְגָרֵשׁ אִשָּׁה וְהֶחֱזִירָהּ, מִשּׁוּם דְּמִנְּפִילָה וְאֵילָךְ לָא אִיתַּסְרָא עֲלֵיהּ, וְאִיסּוּר שֶׁבְּחַיֵּי אָחִיו לָא מְהַנֵּי. הַשְׁתָּא, לֵיכָּא לְמֵימַר אֵין אֲנִי קוֹרֵא בָּהּ בִּשְׁעַת נְפִילָה — דְּלָאו בִּשְׁעַת נְפִילָה הֲוַאי. אֲבָל בְּבָרַיְיתָא דִּמְקַדֵּשׁ אֲחוֹת יְבִמְתּוֹ, דְּמִנְּפִילָה וְאֵילָךְ אִיתַּסְרָא עֲלֵיהּ, וַהֲרֵי אֵין אֲנִי קוֹרֵא בָּהּ בִּשְׁעַת זִיקַּת יִבּוּם "יְבָמָהּ יָבֹא עָלֶיהָ", לָא פְּלִיגֵי. **מתני'** לֹא תַחֲלוֹץ. מְפָרֵשׁ טַעְמָא בַּגְּמָרָא. בְּתוּלוֹת וּבְעוּלוֹת אֲרוּסוֹת וּנְשׂוּאוֹת. בַּגְּמָרָא בָּעֵי: מַאי הֶפְרֵשׁ אִיכָּא בֵּין בְּתוּלוֹת לַאֲרוּסוֹת, בֵּין נְשׂוּאוֹת לִבְעוּלוֹת? הַנְּשׂוּאוֹת יִתְאָרְסוּ. דְּטַעְמָא מִשּׁוּם לְהַבְחִין בֵּין זֶרַע רִאשׁוֹן לְזֶרַע שֵׁנִי הוּא. שֶׁלֹּא תֵּלֵד סָפֵק בֶּן ט' לָרִאשׁוֹן סָפֵק בֶּן ז' לָאַחֲרוֹן, וּבְאֵירוּסִין לֵיכָּא לְמֵימַר הָכִי. וְהָאֲרוּסוֹת יִנָּשְׂאוּ. מִיָּד, דְּהָא לָא אִיעַבְּרָא מִן הָרִאשׁוֹן. חוּץ מֵאֲרוּסָה שֶׁבִּיהוּדָה. דִּתְנַן פֶּרֶק קַמָּא דִּכְתוּבּוֹת (דף יב.): בִּיהוּדָה הָיוּ מְיַיחֲדִים הֶחָתָן וְהַכַּלָּה קוֹדֶם כְּנִיסָתָן לַחוּפָּה כְּדֵי שֶׁיְּהֵא לִבּוֹ גַּס בָּהּ — כְּלוֹמַר: רָגִיל וּמְלַחֵק עִמָּהּ — שֶׁלֹּא יְהוּ בּוֹשִׁין זֶה מִזֶּה בִּבְעִילַת מִצְוָה. הִלְכָּךְ, חָיְישִׁינַן דִּלְמָא בָּעֵיל. כָּל הַנָּשִׁים יִתְאָרְסוּ. רַבִּי יוֹסֵי אַנְּשׂוּאוֹת קָאֵי, וְהָכִי *(קא"ל ר' יְהוּדָה): כָּל הַנָּשִׁים נְשׂוּאוֹת יִתְאָרְסוּ, כִּדְקָאָמְרַתְּ, וְלָא גָּזְרִינַן אֵירוּסִין אַטּוּ נִשּׂוּאִין. וּמִיהוּ, בְּהָא פְּלִיגְנָא עֲלָךְ, שֶׁלֹּא חִלַּקְתָּ בֵּין אַלְמָנָה לִגְרוּשָׁה, וְהִתַּרְתָּ אַלְמָנָה לֵיאָרֵס בְּתוֹךְ יְמֵי אֶבְלָהּ — וַאֲנָא סְבִירָא לִי: אַלְמָנָה מִן הַנִּשּׂוּאִין לֹא תִּתְאָרֵס כָּל שְׁלֹשִׁים יְמֵי אֶבְלָהּ. מִפְּנֵי

תוספות

הך דאזלא בהדה לבי דינא. פי' בקונטרס: כשלאה חולצת מוליכה רחל אחותה עמה לב"ד, ואיכא דסברי שרחל חלצה ולהכי אסורה גם צרתה, אפילו שתיהן נשואות לנכרי, דאינהו סברי שרחל וצרתה נשי אחיו היו, שהרי חלץ לרחל. ותימה גדולה פירש: דהא תנן במתניתין: ובאחותה בזמן שהיא קיימת, הא מתה — שריא! ותנן נמי לקמן (דף מט.): חלץ לה ומתה מותר באחותה. ואמאי? והא סברי שלאחותה חלץ! ועוד, דתנן: האחין מותרין, אע"ג דאזלי בהדיה לבי דינא! ועוד: דלא מיתסר צרה אלא דוקא במצוה, כדאמרינן בפ' קמא (לעיל ח.), ולעיל בריש "ארבעה אחין" (דף כו. ושם) גבי התחיל באחיות מייתי לה למתני' דהכא, דהיינו ששניהן נשואות לאחיו. ופ"ה יש ליישב קצת בנשואה לאחיו ולא לנכרי. א) ונראה לר"י דגרסי': הא דאזלא בהדיה לבי דינא, פי': שהולכת לחלוץ, וכיון דחלצה — דמיא לגרושה טפי, ואסרו גם צרת קרובתה כנשואה לאחין, דדמיא לצרת ערוה. אבל כשחולצת צרת לאה ולא לאה — לא דמיא לאה לגרושה, ואפילו רחל שהיא קרובת צרת חלוצה שריא. ויש ספרים דלא גרסי לא בהדיה ולא בהדה, אלא: הא דאזלא לבי דינא והא דלא אזלא. **יוציא** את אשתו בגט. בפ' "ארבעה אחין" (לעיל כט.) לא בעי למימר ד"זו היא" למעוטי הך דהכא דפשע, כדפרישית לעיל(א). **מתה** אשתו מותר ביבמתו. ומתני' דקתני מתה יבמתו, ולא נקט מתה אשתו, דהוי רבותא טפי — איידי דבעי למיתני מת היבם תנא נמי מתה היבמה. **מאי** טעמא דרב משום דהוי יבמה שהותרה. ואע"פ דבפ' "ארבעה אחין" (שם דף כז:) שרי רב אפילו לא הותרה לכתחלה, דקאמר: מתה הראשונה מותר בשניה — היינו דוקא בזיקה דרבנן, אבל הכא — אחות אשה דאורייתא, דוקא משום דהותרה. **עשה** בה מופנה מאמר. לא אצטריך אלא לאפוקי מב"ש, דאמר (לעיל דף כט.): מאמר קונה קנין גמור. אי נמי: נקט עשה בה מאמר לאשמועינן דאע"ג דאין זיקת השניה גמורה — אפילו הכי אוסרת את זו. **ואמאי** תיהוי יבמה שהותרה כו'. תימה: דלא פריך מהך ברייתא לרב בריש פרק "ארבעה אחין" (לעיל דף כח.), ולישני דרבי אלעזר היא, כדמשני הכא. **הדר** אמר אימור דאמר רבי אלעזר כו'. אכתי הוה מצי למימר דטעמא דר' אלעזר כדמפרש לקמן בפרק "ב"ש" (דף קט. ושם), אבל בהך ברייתא דלמא לא פליגי. אמאי

ע א מיי' פ"ו מהלכות יבום הלכה כ טוש"ע אה"ע סימן קעד סע"ג:

עא ב מיי' שם הלכה ט סמג עשין נא נב טוש"ע אה"ע סימן קעג סעיף א:

עב ג מיי' פ"א מהלכות יבום הלכה יד ופ"ג הלכה ח סמג עשין נא טוש"ע אה"ע סימן קנט סעיף ה:

עג ד מיי' שם טוש"ע אה"ע שם סעיף ז:

עד ה מיי' פ"ב מהלכות איסורי ביאה הלכה ז סמג לאוין קח טוש"ע אה"ע סימן טו סעיף כו:

עה ו מיי' פ"א מהלכות יבום הלכה יג סמג עשין נב ולאוין קי טוש"ע אה"ע סימן קעד סע"ג:

עו ז מיי' פ"ז שם הלכה ח סמג עשין נא טוש"ע אה"ע סימן קנט סעיף ז:

עז ח מיי' פ"א מהלכות יבום הלכה יט סמג עשין נג טוש"ע אה"ע סימן קסד סעיף א:

עח ט מיי' פי"א מהל' גירושין הלכה יח סמג עשין כ טור ש"ע אה"ע סי' יג סעיף א:

תוספות ישנים

א) ועוד קשה דלפ"ה היכא דנולדה לאחר חליצת אחותה תשתרי צרתה דהא לא אתיא בהדה לב"ד וא"כ מתני' לא מיירי בכל ענין ועוד קשה דפ"ה דאף בנשואות לנכרי אסירן ליה ואמאי הלא אף אם היתה צרה עמה ממש שריא ליה כיון דאינה מאחין דאין צרה אלא מאח וגם לפ"ה קשה הלשון דנקט במתני' לצרת קרובת חלוצה דהא לא מקרייא צרה אלא מאח ונראה לפרש דה"ק הך דאזלא בהדיה לבי דינא כלומר שהולכת עם האיש לב"ד לחלוץ ולייבם גזרו בה רבנן לאסור קרובותיה כמו קרובי גרושתו ואם כן אסור בצרתה כמו בצרת גרושתו ובנשואות [לנכרי] לא מיירי אבל הך דלא אזלא לב"ד בהדיה דהיינו הצרה שאינה הולכת עמו לב"ד שהרי לא עשה בה מעשה לא גזור רבנן לאסור קרובותיה ולכך מותר בקרובת צרת חלוצתו: **היכא** דחזיא בשעת נפילה מי אמר. תימה א"כ לא מצי אתיא אפילו כרבנן ודלא כרבי אליעזר כדמפרש ואם כן מאי קאמר הדר אמר דמשמע דעדיין קשה ליה הך דמייתי רב המנונא ומשום הכי אשתיק הא ודאי לא קשיא ליה דהא משבשתא היא שהיה רוצה לומר דלא אתיא כרבי אליעזר וא"כ הך ברייתא ליתא כמאן דכיון דלא אתיא אפי' לר' אליעזר וכ"ש אליבא דרבנן לא מצי אתיא דהא רבנן שרו לה לגמרי וי"ל דידע שפיר שטויא לקמן דעד כאן לא שרו רבנן אלא משום דנפילה ואילך לא מתסר עלויה אבל היכא דמנפילה ואילך אתסר אפילו רבנן מודו דאסירא ומש"ה ניחא הא דקאמר ולא מתייבמת וא"כ שפיר קאמר הדר אמר דודאי היה מתחרט ממה שאמר דלא אתיא אליבא דרבי אליעזר דודאי אתיא כרבנן כדפי' וא"כ אשתיק בדין שהרי לא ידע מה (היה) לתרץ ממה שאמר תחזור להתירה הראשון הכא חזינן דהכא מתייבמת ולא אמרינן תחזור להתירה הראשון: כל

מסורת הש"ס: לעיל יח: מגילה יח: | לעיל מ: לקמן מד.] קדושין מה. | [לעיל יח: מגילה יח:] | לעיל כט. | [לעיל כח.] לקמן קט. | עירובין מז. | תוספות לקמן מב: ד"ה ר' יוסי] | [צ"ל קאמר לר' יהודה]

הגהות הב"ח: (א) תוס' ד"ה יוצא וכו' פרישית לעיל. דף כ"ט. [illegible]

מִפְּנֵי הָאִיבּוּל.§ **גמ'** בִּשְׁלָמָא לֹא תִתְיַיבֵּם — שֶׁמָּא יִהְיֶה הַוָּלָד בֶּן קַיָּימָא, וְקָא פָּגַע בְּאִיסּוּר אֵשֶׁת אָח דְּאוֹרָיְיתָא. אֶלָּא לֹא תַחֲלוֹץ — אַמַּאי? לֵימָא תֶּיהְוֵי תְּיוּבְתָּא דר"י דְּאָמַר: *חֲלִיצַת מְעוּבֶּרֶת שְׁמָהּ חֲלִיצָה! וְלָאו מִי אוֹתְבִינֵיהּ לְרַ' יוֹחָנָן חֲדָא זִימְנָא? לֵימָא מֵהָא נַמִּי תֶּיהְוֵי תְּיוּבְתָּא! לָא, הָכָא הַיְינוּ טַעֲמָא *שֶׁמָּא יְהֵא וָלָד בֶּן קַיָּימָא, וְנִמְצֵאת אַתָּה מַצְרִיכָהּ כָּרוֹז לִכְהוּנָּה. וְנִצְרְכָהּ! דִּלְמָא אִיכָּא דַּהֲוָאי בַּחֲלִיצָה וְלָא הֲוֵי בַּהַכְרָזָה, וּמִפְסְלוּהָ מִן הַכְּהוּנָּה. תֵּינַח אַלְמָנָה, גְּרוּשָׁה מַאי אִיכָּא לְמֵימַר? מִשּׁוּם דְּמַפְסִיד לָהּ מְזוֹנוֹת. תֵּינַח נְשׂוּאָה, אֲרוּסָה גְּרוּשָׁה מַאי אִיכָּא לְמֵימַר? אֶלָּא מִשּׁוּם דְּרַבִּי יוֹסֵי. דְּתַנְיָא: *מַעֲשֶׂה בְּאָדָם אֶחָד שֶׁבָּא לִפְנֵי רַבִּי יוֹסֵי, א"ל: מַהוּ לַחֲלוֹץ בְּתוֹךְ ג'? א"ל: לֹא תַחֲלוֹץ. וְתַחֲלוֹץ וּמָה בְּכָךְ? קָרָא עָלָיו מִקְרָא זֶה: °"וְאִם לֹא יַחְפֹּץ" הָא אִם חָפֵץ — יַבֵּם, *[א]כָּל הָעוֹלֶה לְיִיבּוּם — עוֹלֶה לַחֲלִיצָה כו'. מְתִיב רַב חִינְּנָא: הַסְּפֵיקוֹת חוֹלְצוֹת וְלֹא מִתְיַבְּמוֹת. מַאי סְפֵיקוֹת? אִילֵּימָא סְפֵק קִדּוּשִׁין אַמַּאי לֹא מִתְיַבְּמוֹת? [ב]תִּתְיַיבֵּם וְאֵין בְּכָךְ כְּלוּם! אֶלָּא לָאו — סָפֵק שֶׁקִּידֵּשׁ אַחַת מִשְּׁתֵּי אֲחָיוֹת וְאֵינוֹ יוֹדֵעַ אֵיזוֹ מֵהֶן קִידֵּשׁ, וְקָתָנֵי: חוֹלֶצֶת! •הָכִי הַשְׁתָּא?! הָתָם, אִם יָבֹא אֵלִיָּהוּ וְיֹאמַר דְּהָא קִידֵּשׁ — בַּת חֲלִיצָה וְיִיבּוּם הִיא, הָכָא אִם יָבֹא אֵלִיָּהוּ וְיֹאמַר דְּהָא לָא אִיעַבְּרָה — מִי מַשְׁגַּח בֵּיהּ וְיַבְּמִינַן לַהּ? [ג]הָא קְטַנָּה דְּלָאו בַּת אִיעַבּוּרֵי הִיא, וְאפ"ה צְרִיכָה לְהַמְתִּין ג' חֳדָשִׁים *ת"ר: [ד]יְבָמָה, שְׁלֹשָׁה חֳדָשִׁים הָרִאשׁוֹנִים — נִזּוֹנֶת מִשֶּׁל בַּעַל, מִכָּאן וְאֵילָךְ — אֵינָהּ נִזּוֹנֶת לֹא מִשֶּׁל בַּעַל וְלֹא מִשֶּׁל יָבָם. עָמַד בַּדִּין וּבָרַח — נִזּוֹנֶת מִשֶּׁל יָבָם, נָפְלָה לִפְנֵי יָבָם קָטָן (מַאי)? מִיָּבָם — לֵית לָהּ, מִבַּעַל — מַאי? פְּלִיגִי בָּהּ רַב אַחָא וְרָבִינָא; חַד אָמַר: אִית לָהּ, וְחַד אָמַר: לֵית לָהּ, [ה]וְהִלְכְתָא: לֵית לָהּ, מִשְּׁמַיָּא קְנָסוּהָ. ת"ר: [ו]יְבָמָה שֶׁחָלְצוּ לָהּ אַחִים בְּתוֹךְ שְׁלֹשָׁה — צְרִיכָה לְהַמְתִּין שְׁלֹשָׁה חֳדָשִׁים לְאַחַר

תורה אור: דברים כה

מפני האיבול. אבילות. והאי כל הנשים יתארסו – לאו למעוטי ארוסה לינשא, דהתם כר' יהודה סבירא ליה. דגבי הבחנה רבי יוסי מקיל טפי מרבי יהודה, כדאמר בשלהי גמ' ד"ארבעה אחים" (לעיל דף לה.), אלא באבילות אתי לפלוגי עליה. **גמ'** אלא לא תחלוץ אמאי. ולאחר ג', אם אינה מעוברת – תנשא, או אם הפילה – תנשא, דהא חלצה. לימא תיהוי תיובתיה דר' יוחנן. ומשום הכי לא תחלוץ שמא תפיל ותנשא בחליצה זו, וחליצת מעוברת לא שמה חליצה. ולאו מי אותביניה. בריש פירקין (דף לה:). לימא מהא נמי תיהוי תיובתא. ונפקא מינה דאי מיתרצא קמייתא – תיקום הך. גרושה מאי איכא למימר. אמאי לא תחלוץ, אם היתה גרושה מאחר קודם שנשאה אחיו של זה, דהא פסולה היא לכהונה וקיימא, מאי איכא למימר? אמאי לא תחלוץ? משום מזוני. דאית לה כל שלשה מנכסי בעלה, כדתניא בברייתא בשמעתין. ואי חלצה – לית לה מזוני. ואיהי לא מצי מינסבא עד לאחר שלשה, ומפסיד לה. ארוסה וגרושה. גרושה שנתארסה ומת בעלה, ונפלה ליבום מן האירוסין – תחלוץ בתוך שלשה. דהכא לאו משום מזוני איכא – דארוסה לית לה מזוני מבעל, ולא משום כרוז לכהונה – דהא פסולה היא משום גרושין קמאי. אלא משום דרבי יוסי. כל העולה ליבום כו', וזו הואיל ואינה עולה ליבום בתוך ג', כדאמרן לעיל שמא יפגע באשת אח – אינה עולה השערה לפני הזקנים לחליצה. ולרבי יוחנן לא תיקשי, דאי חלצה – ודאי חליצה, (א) דהאי אינה עולה לחליצה – לאו חליצה פסולה משמע, שהרי כמה נשים שנינו חולצות ולא מתייבמות היכא דלא אפשר, אלמא חליצה היא. ומיהו, היכא דאפשר לאמתוני עד שתראה ליבום מחינן. אילימא ספק קידושין. כגון זרק לה אחיו קידושין, ספק קרוב לו ספק קרוב לה. אמאי לא מתייבמת. תתייבם ממ"נ: אי היא יבמתו – שפיר מייבם, ואי לאו קידושין הוו – נכרית בעלמא נסיב. שקידש אחת משתי אחיות ואין יודע איזה מהן קידש. ומת, שתיהן חולצות ולא מתייבמות, דלא מצי לייבומי, דלמא פגע באחות זקוקה. והא הכא דאינה עולה לייבום ועולה לחליצה, ולא אמרי' ממתין עד שיבואו עדים ויבררו את יבמתו. הכי השתא. התם עולה לייבום היא, אי הוה ידעינן לה. אבל הכא, אם יבא אליהו ויאמר לא מיעברא – מי משגחינן ביה ותתיבם. הרי קטנה דלאו בת איעבורי היא כו'. הלכך לא חלצה. וכל הנך דאמרו רבנן חולצות ולא מתייבמות, כגון אחות חלוצתו ואחות זקוקתו וספק צרת ערוה – התם (ב) משום דלא אפשר הוא, דאם כן לעולם תתעגן. הלכך, כיון דמדאורייתא בת ייבום היא – חלצה. אבל הכא, דאפשר לשהויי – משהינן, ויגלה הדבר בהיתר. שלשה חדשים הראשונים. שאינה יכולה להנשא מחמת בעלה. נזונת משל בעלה. שכן כתב לה "את תהא יתבא בביתי ומתזנא מנכסי כל יומי מיגר ארמלותיך". מכאן ואילך אינה נזונת לא משל בעל ולא משל יבם. ואינה דומה לשאר אלמנה. דהתם, כל זמן שלא נשאת לאחר ואומרת מחמת פלוני בעלי שכבודו גדול עלי – יש לה מזונות. אבל הך – אגידא ביבם, לפיכך אין לה על נכסי בעל מזונות. ולא משל יבם – עד שיכנסנה לחופה. עמד בדין. שתבעתו בדין: או כונס או פוטר, וברח. נזונת משל יבם. דקנסינן ליה. צריכה להמתין. עד שיהיו לה ג' חדשים מיום מיתה. הוי

אמאי לימא תיהוי תיובתא דרבי יוחנן. וא"ת: דלמא לא תחלוץ משום שמא תסמוך על אותה חליצה לינשא לשוק, וחיישינן שמא תמלא מעוברת וולד של קיימא, וולד אינו פוטר עוד שילא לאויר העולם! וי"ל: דלהא ליכא למיחש, דתוך שלשה ודאי לא תנשא, ולאחר ג' נמי, אם תמלא מעוברת לא יבא לטעות. ועוד: שלא ישא אדם מעוברת חברו: משום דמפסיד לה מזוני. לפי טעם זה לא תחלוץ דמתני' – עלה טובה קמ"ל. אלא ארוסה גרושה מאי איכא למימר. וא"ת: לר"ש לקיש ארוסה, כיון דלא מיעברא, אמאי לא תחלוץ? וי"ל: דלר"ל גזרו ארוסה אטו נשואה. אבל לר' יוחנן, דנשואה גופה משום כרוז בעלמא, ליכא למגזר. ותימה: דאמאי נקט גרושה? דמארוסה גרידא הוה מצי למיפרך. קרא עליו המקרא הזה. וא"ת: לר"ל תקשי ליה מרבי יוסי! וי"ל: דלר"ל נמי אינה עולה תוך ג', משום דאינה עולה ליבום. הספקות חולצות ולא מתיבמות. מהסיא דבפ' שני (לעיל כו:), [מי] שקידש אחת מב' אחיות ואינו יודע איזו קידש, ה"מ למיפרך, אלא שהיה צריך להאריך. אבל מהסיא דריש "ארבעה אחין" (לעיל דף כו.) דחולצות ולא מתיבמות – לא ה"מ למיפרך, דלעולם אין לה ליבם ולהתעגן, אבל הכא – יכולה להמתין עד שיתברר הספק, כהסיא דלעיל שיכולה להמתין עד אחר הג'. ומיהו, מהסיא דספק קידושין דבפ' "ד' אחין" (לעיל דף ל:) הוה מצי למיפרך. אילימא ספק קדושין תתייבם ואין בכך כלום. ולא בעי למימר שנולד ספק קידושין בערוה, דהוי ספק אם היא צרת ערוה או לא – דא"כ הוה ליה למימר הספיקות צרותיהן חולצות ולא מתיבמות. ובספק גירושין ה"מ לאוקמי דלא מתיבמות, שמא היא גרושת אחיו. הא קטנה דלאו בת איעבורי. ואפילו למאן דלא גזר לקמן (דף מב:) קטנה אטו גדולה – ה"מ לענין הבחנה בשאר נשים, אבל לענין יבמה – מודה. עמד בדין וברח. לאו בברח בשבילה איירי, שרוצה לעגנה ואין רוצה לא לייבם ולא לחלוץ. דהא בפרק בתרא דכתובות (דף קז:) פריך מינה לשמואל דמחייב לגררי, ואם בשבילה ברח – אמאי אית לן למיחש לגררי? אלא בברח מחמת מרדין או מחמת ממון איירי. ולאו דוקא ברח, דהוא הדין חלה. דכיון דלא בשבילה ברח, אלא מחמת אונס שאירע לו – מה לי ברח מה לי חלה. ובהדיא אמר בירושלמי בפרק "אע"פ" דה"ה חלה. ולא כמו שפירש בקונטרס התם דוקא ברח, אבל חלה לא. והא דבעיא בריש כתובות (דף ב.) חלה מאי – היינו שחלה מיד בהגעת זמן, אבל הכא – שחלה אחר שעמד בדין, דהוה לו לכונסה לאחר קודם שאירע לו אונס. ונראה לר"י: דוקא בנתרצה ליבום וברח, אבל אם לא נתרצה אלא לחלוץ – אין נראה שיתקנו לה חכמים מזונות מיבם, כיון דאין סופו לייבם אלא לחלוץ. ודוקא ברח תקנו לה מזונות משלו, אבל לא ברח – לא, משום דלא שכיח שיאמר מליבם, כיון דלאימיה קמן ונתרצה, דמשום זמן מועט שרגיל לאחר לא תקנו לה מזונות. ומיהו בפרק "ד' אחין" (לעיל דף כט: ושם) משמע קצת דכי לא ברח נמי חייב במזונות. דקאמר: כשעמד בדין ופסקו לה מזונות משלו, ואינו מזכיר כלל ברח. אף על גב דהתם איירי בעבד בה מאמר, כדפרישית לעיל – לענין זה אין שום סברא לחלק בין עשה בה מאמר ללא עשה אלא כשיש שני יבמין, דאי לא עשה מאמר לא זה ולא זה לא – מחייב במזונות, לא זה ולא זה, אפילו נתרצה אחד מהם ליבם וברח. ואצטריך התם לאוקמי בעבד בה מאמר, משום דבעניין אחר לא הוה מצי מיפרך. וקצת נראה דמחמת קנס שקנסוהו חכמים שלא כנסה – תקנו לה מזונות. דהא אין מעשה ידיה שלו. כדאמר בפרק בתרא דכתובות (דף קז: ושם) "אי משום מעשה ידיה לא משעבדא ליה". ולמאי דפרישית דבשלא ברח אין לה מזונות – איכא ראיה דמעשה ידיה אינו שלו, דאין לחוש שמא תאמר לה לאי עשה מעשה ידיך למזונותיך – דלאכתי לא משעבדא ליה עד שיברח ויפסקו לה מזונות. ומיהו, אר"י: דלפירוש זה טפי הוי ליה למימר דלא מיחייב במזונותיה. לאחר

עין משפט נר מצוה

עט א מיי' פ"א מהל' יבום הלכה יט:

פ ב מיי' פ"ו מהלכות יבום הלכה ז סמג עשין נא טוש"ע אה"ע סימן קנו סעיף טו:

פא ג מיי' פ"א מהל' גרושין הלכה כ סמג עשין נ טוש"ע אה"ע סימן יג סעיף א:

פב ד מיי' פי"א מהל' אישות הלכה טו סמג עשין מח טוש"ע אה"ע סימן קס סעיף א:

פג ה מיי' שם הלכה יז וטוש"ע שם סע"ג:

פד ו מיי' פ"א מהלכות יבום הלכה יט סמג עשין נב טור ש"ע אה"ע סימן קסח סעיף א:

תוספות ישנים

כל שאינה עולה לייבום [אינה] עולה לחליצה. ואין להקשות א"כ איך קאמר ר' יוחנן חליצת מעוברת שמה חליצה הא אינה עולה לייבום משום שמא יהא הולד בן קיימא וא"כ הא תהא עולה לחליצה. וי"ל דדוקא לכתחלה אין לחלוץ מעוברת משום דלא מצי לייבמה אבל דיעבד מהניא החליצה כי חזינן דהשתא לאו חזיא לייבום.

מסורת הש"ס

[לעיל לה:]

לקמן קיט: [לעיל לו.]

[תוספתא פ"ו]

[לעיל ג. כ. לו. לקמן ...]

כתובות קז:

הגהות הב"ח

(א) רש"י ד"ה אלא כו' וכו' חליצה היא אינה: (ב) ד"ה הרי וכו' משום דלא אפשר ע"ל דף ג ע"ב

גליון הש"ס

גמ' הכי השתא התם יבא אליהו. עיין לקמן ס"ז ע"ב תוס' ד"ה דאפשר תושבין

לְאַחַר ג' — אֵין צְרִיכָה לְהַמְתִּין ג' חֳדָשִׁים. הֱוֵי הַג' חֳדָשִׁים שֶׁאָמְרוּ — מִשְּׁעַת מִיתַת הַבַּעַל, וְלֹא מִשְּׁעַת חֲלִיצַת הַיָּבָם. מ"ש מִגֵּט, *דְּרַב אֲמַר מִשְּׁעַת נְתִינָה וּשְׁמוּאֵל אֲמַר משְּׁעַת כְּתִיבָה? אֲמַר רָבָא: ק"ו: *אִיסּוּר כָּרֵת הִתַּרְתָּ, אִיסּוּר לָאו לֹא כ"ש? § "וְכֵן שְׁאָר כָּל הַנָּשִׁים". בִּשְׁלָמָא יְבָמָה — כְּדַאֲמָרַן. אֶלָּא שְׁאָר כָּל הַנָּשִׁים אַמַּאי? אָמַר *רַב נַחְמָן אֲמַר שְׁמוּאֵל: מִשּׁוּם דְּאָמַר קְרָא "לִהְיוֹת לְךָ לֵאלֹהִים וּלְזַרְעֲךָ אַחֲרֶיךָ" לְהַבְחִין בֵּין זַרְעוֹ שֶׁל רִאשׁוֹן לְזַרְעוֹ שֶׁל שֵׁנִי. מְתִיב רָבָא: לְפִיכָךְ *גֵּר וְגִיּוֹרֶת צְרִיכִין לְהַמְתִּין ג' חֳדָשִׁים, הָכָא מַאי לְהַבְחִין אִיכָּא? ה"נ: אִיכָּא לְהַבְחִין בֵּין זֶרַע שֶׁנִּזְרַע בִּקְדוּשָּׁה לְזֶרַע שֶׁלֹּא נִזְרַע בִּקְדוּשָּׁה. רָבָא אָמַר: גְּזֵירָה שֶׁמָּא יִשָּׂא אֶת אֲחוֹתוֹ מֵאָבִיו, וְיִיַבֵּם אֵשֶׁת אָחִיו מֵאִמּוֹ, וְיוֹצִיא אֶת אִמּוֹ לַשּׁוּק, וְיִפְטוֹר אֶת יְבִמְתּוֹ לַשּׁוּק. מְתִיב רַב חֲנַנְיָה: בְּכוּלָּן אֲנִי קוֹרֵא בָּהֶן מִשּׁוּם תַּקָּנַת עֶרְוָה, וְכָאן מִשּׁוּם תַּקָּנַת וָלָד. וְאִם אִיתָא — כּוּלְּהוּ מִשּׁוּם תַּקָּנַת עֶרְוָה! הַאי מִשּׁוּם תַּקָּנַת וָלָד דְּלָא לִפְגַּע בְּהוּ עֶרְוָה. בִּשְׁלָמָא תַּמְתִּין ב' חֳדָשִׁים וְתִנָּשֵׂא, לָא — דְּהַיְינוּ סְפֵיקָא, אִי בַּר תִּשְׁעָה לְקַמָּא אִי בַּר שִׁבְעָה לְבַתְרָא. אֶלָּא, תַּמְתִּין חֹדֶשׁ אֶחָד וְתִנָּשֵׂא: וְאִי לְשִׁבְעָה יָלְדָה — הַאי בַּר שִׁבְעָה לְבַתְרָא הוּא, וְאִי לִתְמַנְיָא יָלְדָה — הַאי בַּר תִּשְׁעָה לְקַמָּא הוּא. אִי נַמִי לִתְמַנְיָא יָלְדָה — אִיכָּא לְמֵימַר דְּבַתְרָא הוּא, דִּלְמָא אִישְׁתַּהוּיֵי אִישְׁתָּהָא חֹדֶשׁ אֶחָד וְאִיעַבַּר. וְתַמְתִּין שְׁנֵי חֳדָשִׁים וּמֶחֱצָה וְתִנָּשֵׂא, דְּאִי לְשִׁבְעָה יָלְדָה — הַאי בַּר שִׁבְעָה לְבַתְרָא הוּא. וְאִי לְשִׁיתָּא וּפַלְגָּא יָלְדָה — הַאי בַּר תִּשְׁעָה לְקַמָּא הוּא, דְּאִי בַּר בַּתְרָא הוּא — בַּר שִׁיתָּא וּפַלְגָּא לָא חַיֵּי! א"נ לְשִׁיתָּא וּפַלְגָּא יָלְדָה — אִיכָּא לְמֵימַר דְּבַתְרָא הוּא, *דְּאָמַר מָר זוּטְרָא: אֲפִילּוּ לְמַאן דְּאָמַר *יוֹלֶדֶת לְט' אֵינָהּ יוֹלֶדֶת לְמְקוּטָּעִין — יוֹלֶדֶת לְז' יוֹלֶדֶת לִמְקוּטָּעִין, שֶׁנֶּאֱמַר "וַיְהִי לִתְקֻפוֹת הַיָּמִים", *מִעוּט "תְּקוּפוֹת" — ב', מִעוּט "יָמִים" — ב'. וְתַמְתִּין מַשֶּׁהוּ וְתִנָּשֵׂא, וְכִי מָלוּ שְׁלֹשָׁה חֳדָשִׁים לִבְדְּקָהּ! אָמַר רַב סָפְרָא: אֵין בּוֹדְקִין אֶת הַנְּשׂוּאוֹת, שֶׁלֹּא יִתְגַּנּוּ עַל בַּעֲלֵיהֶן. וְנִבְדְּקָהּ בְּהִלּוּכָהּ? אָמַר רָמִי בַּר חָמָא: אִשָּׁה מְחַפָּה עַצְמָהּ, כְּדֵי שֶׁיִּירַשׁ בְּנָהּ בְּנִכְסֵי בַעְלָהּ. הֵיכָא דְּקִים לָן דִּמְעוּבֶּרֶת הִיא תִּנָּשֵׂא, אַלְמָה תַּנְיָא: *לֹא יִשָּׂא אָדָם מְעוּבֶּרֶת חֲבֵרוֹ וּמֵינֶקֶת חֲבֵרוֹ, וְאִם נָשָׂא יוֹצִיא וְלֹא יַחֲזִיר עוֹלָמִית. גְּזֵירָה שֶׁמָּא תֵּעָשֶׂה עוּבָּרָהּ סַנְדָּל, אִי הָכִי — דִּידֵיהּ נַמִי, אִי לְמ"ד בְּמוֹךְ בְּמוֹךְ — וְאִי לְמ"ד מִן הַשָּׁמַיִם יְרַחֲמוּ — מִן הַשָּׁמַיִם יְרַחֲמוּ, הָכָא נַמִי: אִי לְמַאן דְּאָמַר בְּמוֹךְ — בְּמוֹךְ, אִי לְמַאן דְּאָמַר מִן הַשָּׁמַיִם יְרַחֲמוּ — מִן הַשָּׁמַיִם יְרַחֲמוּ! אֶלָּא מִשּׁוּם דְּחָסָה. אִי הָכִי דִּידֵיהּ נַמִי! דִּידֵיהּ חָיֵיס עִילָּוֵיהּ. הָכָא נַמִי חָיֵיס עִילָּוֵיהּ! *אֶלָּא: סְתָם מְעוּבֶּרֶת לִמְנִיקָה קַיְימָא, דִּלְמָא

רש"י

הֱוֵי. כְּלוֹמַר, הֱוֵי לוֹמֵד מִכָּאן שְׁלֹשָׁה חֳדָשִׁים שֶׁאָמְרוּ כו'. וּמ"ש מִגֵּט דְּרַב אֲמַר מִשְּׁעַת נְתִינָה. וְאַף עַל גַּב דְּמִשְּׁעַת כְּתִיבָה לֹא נִתְיַיחֵד עִמָּהּ, דְּאִם כֵּן הָוֵה לֵיהּ גֵּט יָשָׁן, וַאֲפִילּוּ הָכִי מִשְּׁעַת נְתִינָה מָנֵינַן, ה"נ נִמְנֵי מִשְּׁעַת חֲלִיצָה. לְאִיסּוּר כָּרֵת. לְיַבֵּם, הִתַּרְתָּ לְאַחַר ג' חֳדָשִׁים מִיָּד. לְאִיסּוּר לָאו. לַשּׁוּק לֹא כ"ש דְּמוּתֶּרֶת לְאַחַר חֲלִיצָה מִיָּד, הוֹאִיל וְעָבְרוּ שְׁלֹשָׁה חֳדָשִׁים מִיּוֹם מִיתָה. וּלְזַרְעֲךָ אַחֲרֶיךָ. שֶׁאֵין הַשְּׁכִינָה שׁוֹרָה אֶלָּא עַל הַוַּודָּאִים, שֶׁזַּרְעוֹ מְיוּחָס אַחֲרָיו. וְהָכִי נַמִי קָיְימָא לָן בִּנְדָרִים (דף כ:) "וּבָרוֹתִי מִכֶּם הַמּוֹרְדִים וְהַפּוֹשְׁעִים בִּי" — אֵלּוּ בְּנֵי עִרְבּוּבְיָא. גֵּר וְגִיּוֹרֶת. גֵּר שֶׁנִּתְגַּיֵּיר וְאִשְׁתּוֹ עִמּוֹ — צְרִיכִים לְהַמְתִּין ג' חֳדָשִׁים, לִפְרוֹשׁ זֶה מִזֶּה. וְהָכָא מַאי לְהַבְחִין אִיכָּא? הֲרֵי אֵין כָּאן רִאשׁוֹן וְשֵׁנִי. רָבָא אָמַר שֶׁמָּא יִשָּׂא אֲחוֹתוֹ מֵאָבִיו. אִם נִשֵּׂאת תּוֹךְ שְׁלֹשָׁה וְיָלְדָה, וְהוּא בֶּן ט' לָרִאשׁוֹן וְנוֹלַד בְּבֵיתוֹ שֶׁל שֵׁנִי, וְסָבוּר שֶׁהוּא בְּנוֹ וְיִשָּׂא אֶת בַּת בַּעְלָהּ הָרִאשׁוֹן שֶׁיֵּשׁ לוֹ מֵאִשָּׁה אַחֶרֶת, וְהִיא אֲחוֹתוֹ מִן הָאָב. וּמְיַיבֵּם אֵשֶׁת אָחִיו מֵאִמּוֹ. שֶׁאִם תֵּלֵד לָאַחֲרוֹן בֵּן אַחֵר, וְיִשָּׂא אִשָּׁה וְיָמוּת בְּלֹא בָּנִים, וִייַבְּמֶנָּה זֶה, כְּסָבוּר שֶׁהוּא אָחִיו מֵאָבִיו, וְנִמְצָא מְיַיבֵּם אֵשֶׁת אָחִיו מֵאִמּוֹ שֶׁלֹּא מֵאָבִיו, וְחַיָּיב כָּרֵת. וְיוֹצִיא אֶת אִמּוֹ לַשּׁוּק. אִם לֹא תֵּלֵד אִמּוֹ לַשֵּׁנִי וְיָמוּת, וּכְסְבוּרִים שֶׁזֶּה בְּנוֹ, וְתִנָּשֵׂא אִמּוֹ לַשּׁוּק בְּלֹא חֲלִיצָה. וְיִפְטוֹר אֶת יְבִמְתּוֹ לַשּׁוּק. אִם יֵשׁ לוֹ אָח מֵאָבִיו הָרִאשׁוֹן, וְלֹא הָיוּ לוֹ בָּנִים וּמֵת, וְאֵין שָׁם אָח אֶלָּא הוּא, וְהוּא סָבוּר שֶׁהוּא בֶּן הָאַחֲרוֹן, וְנִמְצֵאת אֵשֶׁת בְּנוֹ שֶׁל רִאשׁוֹן הַזְּקוּקָה לוֹ נִשֵּׂאת לַשּׁוּק בְּלֹא חֲלִיצָה. וְגַבֵּי גֵּר וְגִיּוֹרֶת לַחֲדָא מֵהָנֵי הוּא דְּאִיכָּא לְמֵיחַשׁ, כְּגוֹן לְשֶׁמָּא יְיַבֵּם אֵשֶׁת אָחִיו מֵאִמּוֹ, שֶׁמָּא מְעוּבֶּרֶת הָיְתָה, וּכְשֶׁתֵּלֵד סְבוּרָה הִיא שֶׁבֶּן ז' הוּא, וּבִקְדוּשָּׁה נִזְרַע, וְתַחֲזוֹר וְתֵלֵד בֵּן אַחֲרָיו וְיִשָּׂא אִשָּׁה וְיָמוּת בְּלֹא בָּנִים, וִייַבֵּם זֶה אֶת אִשְׁתּוֹ, דְּסָבוּר שֶׁגַּם הוּא נִזְרַע בִּקְדוּשָּׁה. וְכֵיוָן שֶׁזֶּה נִזְרַע שֶׁלֹּא בִּקְדוּשָּׁה, וּסְתָם גּוֹיָה זוֹנָה הִיא — אִיכָּא לְמֵימַר שֶׁמָּא אֵינוֹ בְּנוֹ שֶׁל זֶה, וְנִמְצָא נוֹשֵׂא אֵשֶׁת אָחִיו מֵאִמּוֹ. בְּכוּלָּן אֲנִי קוֹרֵא בָּהֶן. כָּל נָשִׁים שֶׁאָסְרוּ חֲכָמִים לְהִנָּשֵׂא אוֹ לְהִתְיַיבֵּם, קוֹרֵא אֲנִי בָּהֶן תַּקָּנַת עֶרְוָה, כְּדֵי שֶׁלֹּא יָבֹאוּ לִידֵי עֶרְוָה. וְכָאן. בְּהַמְתָּנָה שֶׁל ג' חֳדָשִׁים שֶׁאָסְרוּ חֲכָמִים לִשְׁאָר נָשִׁים אֵין כָּאן תַּקָּנַת עֶרְוָה, אֶלָּא תַּקָּנַת הַוָּלָד, לְהַבְחִין בֶּן מִי הוּא. וְאִם אִיתָא. דְּחָשׁוּ חֲכָמִים לְשֶׁמָּא יִשָּׂא אֲחוֹתוֹ מִן אָבִיו — הָא נַמִי תַּקָּנַת עֶרְוָה הִיא. דְּלָא לִפְגַּע וָלָד. בְּעֶרְוָה. אֲבָל כָּל שְׁאָר הַנֶּאֱסָרוֹת — אִיכָּא (א) תַּקָּנְתָּא הִיא וּבַעַל עַצְמוֹ דְּלָא לִפְגְּעוּ בְּעֶרְוָה. הָא בַּר ז' לְבַתְרָא הוּא. דְּאִי מִקַּמָּא אִיעַבְּרָא כְּשֶׁמֵּת — אִישְׁתַּכַּח דְּבַר תְּמַנְיָא הוּא, וּבַר תְּמַנְיָא לָא חַיֵּי. א"נ לִתְמַנְיָא יָלְדָה כו'. תֵּירוּצָא הוּא. אִישְׁתַּהֵי. לְאַחַר שֶׁנִּשֵּׂאת. וְה"ה נַמִי דְּמָצֵי לְתָרוּצֵי אִי נַמִי לְשִׁבְעָה יָלְדָה — אִיכָּא לְמֵימַר בַּר תִּשְׁעָה לְקַמָּא הוּא, מֵעִיקָּרָא חֹדֶשׁ אֶחָד אִיעַבְּרָא קוֹדֶם מִיתָתוֹ. אֶלָּא הוֹאִיל וְתֵירֵץ לְמִילְּתֵיהּ בַּחֲדָא, וְאוֹקֵי דְּאַכַּתִּי אִיכָּא סָפֵק — סַגִּי לֵיהּ בְּהָכִי. אֲפִילּוּ לְמ"ד. בְּמַסֶּכֶת נִדָּה, בְּפֶרֶק "בְּנוֹת כּוּתִים". וַיְהִי לִתְקֻפוֹת הַיָּמִים. הֲרֵי שִׁשָּׁה חֳדָשִׁים וּב' יָמִים. וְתַמְתִּין מַשֶּׁהוּ. שָׁבוּעַ אוֹ שְׁבוּעַיִם. וְכִי מָלוּ ג' חֳדָשִׁים. לְיוֹם מִיתַת בַּעְלָהּ, שֶׁדֶּרֶךְ עוּבָּר לִהְיוֹת נִיכָּר — לִיבְדְּקָהּ בְּדַדֵּיהּ, כְּדֶרֶךְ נָשִׁים. וְאִי מִיעַבְּרָא — וַדַּאי בַּר קַמָּא הוּא, דְּאִי בַּר בַּתְרָא הוּא אַכַּתִּי לֹא הֲוָה מִינְכַּר, דְּלֹא מָלוּ שְׁלֹשָׁה חֳדָשִׁים לְנִישּׂוּאֶיהָ, דְּחָסֵר לֵיהּ הַהוּא מַשֶּׁהוּ שֶׁהִמְתִּינָה. וְאִי לָא מִינְכַּר וּלְבָתַר הָכִי מִינְכַּר (ב) — וַדַּאי בַּר בַּתְרָא הוּא. בְּהִילּוּכָהּ. מוֹלִיכִין אוֹתָהּ בֶּעָפָר תִּיחוּחַ, אִי מְעוּבֶּרֶת הִיא — פְּסִיעוֹתֶיהָ נִיכָּרוֹת וּמַעֲמִיקוֹת יוֹתֵר מִשְּׁאָר נָשִׁים, שֶׁהַוָּלָד מַכְבִּידָהּ. כָּךְ מָצָאתִי בִּתְשׁוּבַת הַגְּאוֹנִים. מְחַפָּה עַצְמָהּ. שֶׁלֹּא תֵּרָאֶה מְעוּבֶּרֶת, כְּדֵי שֶׁלֹּא יָבִינוּ שֶׁבֶּן הָרִאשׁוֹן הוּא, וְיִירַשׁ בְּנִכְסֵי בַּעְלָהּ שֵׁנִי. הֵיכָא דְּקִים לָן כו'. הוֹאִיל וְטַעַם הַמְתָּנָה מִשּׁוּם וָלָד הוּא, שֶׁלֹּא יְהֵא סָפֵק, כְּשֶׁאָנוּ יוֹדְעִים וַדַּאי שֶׁהִיא מְעוּבֶּרֶת מֵרִאשׁוֹן — תִּנָּשֵׂא! וּמְשַׁנֵּי: גְּזֵרָה שֶׁמָּא תֵּעָשֶׂה כו'. דִּידֵיהּ נַמִי. לֹא יְשַׁמֵּשׁ עִם אִשְׁתּוֹ מְעוּבֶּרֶת, שֶׁמָּא תַּחֲזוֹר וְתִתְעַבֵּר, וְיִדְחוֹק אָחִיו וְיִמָּעֵךְ צוּרַת פָּנָיו, כְּסַנְדָּל הַזֶּה שֶׁאֵין לוֹ צוּרָה. אִי לְמ"ד בְּמוֹךְ. פְּלוּגְתָּא הִיא בְּפ"ק (לעיל דף יב:). דְּחָסָה. שֶׁמְּמָעֲכוֹ בִּשְׁעַת תַּשְׁמִישׁ. דְּחָסָה — לְשׁוֹן לַחַץ, שֶׁלּוֹחֲצוֹ, כִּדְאָמַר לְקַמָּן (דף קג.) גַּבֵּי חֲלִיצָה: צָרִיךְ לְמִידְחַסֵּיהּ לְכַרְעֵיהּ. ה"נ חָיֵיס עִילָּוֵיהּ. שֶׁאֵין אָדָם מִתְכַּוֵּין לַהֲרוֹג הַנֶּפֶשׁ. לִמְנִיקָה קַיְימָא. כְּשֶׁתֵּלֵד מְנִיקַתּוֹ. וְאִי

תוספות

לאחר שלשה חדשים אין צריכה להמתין. אמר ר"ת: דוקא חלץ. שהחליצה מוכחת שלא בא עליה, כדאמר בממאנת דמיאונה מוכיח עליה שהיא קטנה. אבל אם מת היבם לאחר ג' — צריכה להמתין שלשה חדשים, דיותר יבמה קרובה לביאה מארוסה, דגזרינן אטו נשואה. אע"ג דאמר לקמן בפ' "ב"ש" (דף קיב.) ובפסחים פרק "אלו דברים" (דף עג:) יבמתו — בזיז מינה, אשתו — לא בזיז מינה, היינו לענין לאוקמי אנפשיה עד שלשים, אבל לענין גזרה שמא ישא אחותו כו' — איכא למימר יבמתו קרובה לביאה טפי. **מאי** שנא מגט דרב אמר משעת נתינה. אע"ג דודאי לא בא עליה מקמי כתיבה — דאם כן לא היה פוטרה בגט זה, דהוה ליה גט ישן. וטעמא מפרש בפרק שני דגיטין (דף יח. ושם) שלא יאמרו: ב' נשים בחצר אחת זו אסורה וזו מותרת, שהעולם סוברים שכתיבת שניהם היתה סמוך לנתינה, ויבא להתיר תוך שלשה. והכא גבי חליצה נמי יסברו ששתיהן סמוך למיתה חלצו, ויבא להתיר תוך שלשה. ומשני: לאיסור כרת התרת, דאם היה רוצה לייבם אחר שלשה — היה מייבם, לאיסור לאו לא כ"ש? דהיאך אפשר לאסרה להנשא לשוק אחר חליצה, שזה דומה לחוכא ואיטלולא, ולא ישמעו לנו העולם על כך. **לזרעך** אחריך. לקמן בפ' "נושאין" (דף ק:) דריש מהאי קרא דאזהר ליה רחמנא לאברהם: לא תינסיב גויה ושפחה, דלא יתייחס זרעך בתרה. **גר** וגיורת. מכאן משמע דגר מותר בגיורת, ודלא כאוסרים כשנשאה מקודם דלא יחזרו לסורם. **בכולן** אני קורא כו'. איבמה לחוד קאי, ונקט לשון כולן — משום דאיירי בכל יבמות, בין ארוסות בין נשואות, בין להתייבם או להנשא לשוק. אם חלצה תוך ג' — כולן צריכות להמתין שלשה חדשים. **ותמתין** משהו ותנשא. לאו דוקא משהו, שצריכה להמתין שלשה ימים של קליטת הזרע. **סתם** מעוברת למניקה קיימא. רבינו שמשון זקנו של רשב"א היה אומר דגרושה מינקת מותרת לינשא. משום דלא משעבדא להניק, כדאמרי' בפ' "אע"פ" (כתובות נט: ושם) נתגרשה — אינו כופה. ואין נראה לר"ת, דהא למאי דהוה בעי למימר דטעמא משום סנדל, או משום דיחסא — לא היה חילוק בין אלמנה לגרושה. וה"ה להאי טעמא, דאינו חוזר בו אלא מהטעם בלבד. ועוד: אלמנה גופה, אי אמרה איני ניזונית ואיני עושה, או תבעה כתובתה — לא משעבדא, וכן פוסק בשאלתות דרב אחאי* דלא שנא גרושה ולא שנא אלמנה.

עין משפט נר מצוה

פה א מיי' פי"א מהל' גירושין הל' יט סמג עשין נב טוש"ע אה"ע סי' יג סעיף א:
פו ב ג ד מיי' שם וטור ש"ע שם סעיף ה:
פז ה מיי' שם הל' כה טוש"ע שם סעיף יא:
פח ו מיי' שם הל' כה:

תוספות ישנים

אלא שאר כל הנשים מאי טעמא. תימה אמאי [לא] קאמר משום דלמא היא מעוברת ואמרי' לא ישא אדם מעוברת. וי"ל דהיינו דווקא כשהיא ודאי מעוברת אבל כשאינה אלא ספק אם היא מעוברת אם לאו [לא אסרינן לה] משום לא ישא אדם מעוברת חבירו אם לא מקרא כדמייתי: **ויפטור** את יבמתו לשוק. אבל בגר וגיורת לתנהו לכלהו טעמי דהכא אלא משום דשמא ייבם אשת אחיו מאמו לפי שזה יחשוב כי הוא נזרע בקדושה וא"כ ייבם אשת אחיו הנזרע בודאי בקדושה כי הוא יחשוב כי הוא אחיו מן האב ביהדות והוא נזרע בקדושה ושמא הוא אינו אלא אחיו מאמו כי שמא נזרע שלא בקדושה וסתם גויה זונה היא ואין לו קורבה לאבות אף אם הגר נתגייר עם אשתו: **לפיכך** גר וגיורת צריכות להמתין וכו' מכאן קשה למאי דאיתא בהגדה גר לא ישא גיורת שמא יחזרו לסורן דהכא משמע דשרי: **א"נ** לתמניא ילדה איכא למימר דבתרא הוא. ה"נ ה"מ למימר א"נ לשבעה ילדה איכא למימר אימור בר תשעה לקמא הוא דשמא נתעברה חדש אחד לפני מותו:

הגהות הב"ח

(א) רש"י ד"ה דלא ליפגע וכו' איכא תקנת היא: (ב) ד"ה וכי מלו ג' וכו' ולבתר הכי מינכר כ"ב ואין להקשות דלמא לא יהא ניכר עובר כלל לשליש כדאיתא לעיל דף ל"ז דאין כולם ניכר רק רובן ובכיל זה נקרא האי דאין ניכר ספק דיש ספק אם הולכין אחר רוב היולדות לט' והוה מן הראשון או אזלינן בתר רוב להכיר לשליש וזו הואיל ולא ניכר הוא מן שני א"כ ע"כ לא תנשא עכשיו [והשאר חסר]:

[שייך לעיל במשנה מח.]

פט א מיי' פי"א מהל' גירושין הלכה כה:
צ ב ג מיי' שם הל' כ סמג עשין נ טוש"ע אה"ע סימן יג סעיף א:

אדלמא איעברה, ומעבר חלבה, וקטלה ליה. אי הכי דידיה נמי! דידיה ממסמסא ליה בביצים וחלב. דידה נמי ממסמסא ליה בבצים וחלב! לא יהב לה בעל. וליתבעיניה ליורשים! אמר אביי: אשה בושה לבא לבית דין, והורגת את בנה. § "אחת בתולות ואחת בעולות". הי ניהו בתולות והי ניהו ארוסות, הי ניהו בעולות והי ניהו נשואות? א"ר יהודה הכי קאמר: אחת בתולות ואחת בעולות שנתארמלו או שנתגרשו, בין מן הארוסין בין מן הנשואין. *ר' אלעזר לא על לבי מדרשא, אשכחיה לרב אסי, אמר ליה: מאי אמור רבנן בבי מדרשא? אמר ליה, הכי א"ר יוחנן: הלכה כר' יוסי. מכלל דיחידאה פליג עליה? אין, והתניא: *בהרי שהיתה רדופה לילך לבית אביה, או שהיה לה כעס בבית בעלה, או שהיה בעלה חבוש בבית האסורין[א], או שהיה בעלה זקן או חולה, או שהיתה היא חולה, או שהפילה אחר מיתת בעלה, או שהיתה עקרה, או זקנה, או קטנה, או אילונית, או שאינה ראויה לילד (א) – צריכה להמתין ג' חדשים, דברי ר' מאיר. *ר' [ב] יהודה מתיר ליארס ולינשא מיד. אמר רבי חייא בר אבא: חזר בו רבי יוחנן. אמר רב יוסף: אי הדר ביה – ממתני' דכרמא הדר ביה. דתניא, *אמר ר' ישמעאל בנו של ר' יוחנן בן ברוקה: שמעתי מפי חכמים בכרם ביבנה: גכולן צריכות להמתין שלשה חדשים. אמר ליה ר' ירמיה לר' זריקא: כי עיילת לקמיה דר' אבהו רמי ליה: מי אמר רבי יוחנן הלכה כרבי יוסי? והאמר ר' יוחנן: *הלכה כסתם משנה, ותנן: כל הנשים לא ינשאו ולא יתארסו עד שיהו להם שלשה חדשים, אחת בתולות ואחת בעולות! אמר ליה: *דרמא לך הא – לא חש לקמחיה; סתם ואח"כ מחלוקת היא, ואין הלכה כסתם. דאמר רב פפא ואיתימא ר' יוחנן: *מחלוקת ואחר כך סתם – הלכה כסתם, סתם ואחר כך מחלוקת – אין הלכה כסתם מסתמיך ואזיל ר' אבהו אכתפיה דרבי נחום שמעיה, מנקיט ואזיל הלכתא מיניה. בעא מיניה: מחלוקת ואחר כך סתם מאי? א"ל: הלכה כסתם. סתם ואחר כך מחלוקת מאי? אמר ליה: אין הלכה כסתם. סתמא דמתני' ומחלוקת בברייתא מאי? א"ל: הלכה כסתם. מחלוקת במתני' וסתמא בברייתא מאי? א"ל:

וכי

רש"י

ואי מינסבא דלמא מיעברא. לאחר לידתה, ומיעכר עליה חלבה, וקטלה לברה ברעב. ממסמסא ליה. מאכילתו. לא יהב לה בעל. משום דלאו בריה הוא. וליתבעיניה ליורשים. של בעל ראשון. אשה בושה לבא לב"ד. ולתבוע יורשים בשביל בנה. והורגת את בנה. על כרחה מת בנה ברעב. הי ניהו בתולות הי ניהו ארוסות. הא חדא היא, דהיכי משכחת לה בתולה יבמה אם לא ארוסה? הכי קאמר. כלומר, לא תתני אחת ואחת, דמשמע תרי מילי, אלא כולה חדא קתני. ופרושי קמפרש: אחת בתולות ואחת בעולות, וכגון שנתארמלו או נתגרשו בין מן האירוסין, דהיינו בתולות, בין מן הנשואין, דהיינו בעולות. הלכה כר' יוסי. דשרי ארוסות לינשא, הואיל וליכא למיחש לזרע ראשון, ונשואה ליארס. והאי דנקט ר' יוסי ולא רבי יהודה, דהא רבי יהודה נמי שרי ארוסה לינשא בהדיא, אלא משום דר' יוסי נימוקו עמו. מכלל דיחידאה פליג עליה. תנא קמא דאמר לא ינשאו ולא יתארסו אחת ארוסות ואחת בתולות, דאסר אפי' ארוסות ליארס כ"ש לינשא – יחידאה היא, ולאו סתמא דרבים היא. ה"ג אין והתניא. בניחותא. רדופה. רגילה. וגם סמוך למיתתו עמדה בבית אביה זמן מרובה, דליכא למימר מעוברת היא. או שהיה לה כעס. ולא שימשה: עקרה. שנעקר רחמה, וניטלה האם שלה. אילונית. מתמעי אמה לקויה היא, ואין לה סימני שער ודדים. או שאינה ראויה לילד. לאיתויי [מחמת] סמא או חולי. כולן צריכות להמתין. דגזרו שאינה ראויה אטו ראויה. ממתני' דכרמא. שנשנית בכרם ביבנה, מחמת אותה משנה חזר בו. בכרם ביבנה. שהיו יושבים שורות שורות כעין (ב) הכרם. לא חש לקימחיה. למה שהוא טוחן ומוציא מפיו, כלומר לדיבורו: סתם ואח"כ מחלוקת היא. דהא איפלגו עלה ר' יוסי ור' יהודה: מחלוקת ואחר כך סתם. בין שסתם אחריה מיד (ג) באחד מהם, בין שסתם אחריה במסכת אחרת באותו הסדר. כגון: נתן למר לצבע, דמחלוקת בב"ק ב"הגוזל" (דף ק:), וסתם בב"מ (ד עו.): כל המשנה ידו על התחתונה, וסתם לן כר"י, דאמר: אם השבח יתר על היציאה כו' – הלכה כסתם. סתם ואחר כך מחלוקת. כי מתני'. מנקיט. מלקט ממנו הלכות פסוקות, הלכה כפלוני ופלוני.

תוספות

*רבי יוסי אומר כל הנשים יתארסו. בעירובין (דף מז.) פי' בקונט' דאפילו ארוסות דוקא יתארסו. אבל ינשאו – לא, דגזר רבי יוסי ארוסה אטו נשואה. ואין נראה. דאי גרס בברייתא דרדופה רבי יוסי מתיר ליארס ולינשא מיד – א"כ קשיא דרבי יוסי אדרבי יוסי, דהכא גזר אפילו ארוסה אטו נשואה, כ"ש דהוה ליה למיגזר נשואה רדופה אטו שאינה רדופה! ואפילו גרס בברייתא דרדופה רבי יהודה – מ"מ קשיא, דהיכי מוכח בפרק "מי שהוליאוהו" (ג"ז שם) ובגמ' דיחידאה פליג עליה מברייתא דרדופה, ותנא קמא דמתניתין הוא ר"מ? דלמא ר"מ דרדופה הוא כר' יוסי דמתניתין, דלא שרי אלא ליארס, אבל לינשא – לא, וצריכות להמתין שלשה חדשים דקאמר ר"מ, היינו: מלינשא, אבל ליארס – מיד שרי, ואף על גב דקתני סתמא צריכות להמתין, הכי נמי קתני בפרק "ד' אחין" (לעיל דף לה. ושם) גבי גיורת ושבויה ואנוסה ומפותה צריכות להמתין סתמא, דברי רבי יהודה. וע"כ היינו דוקא לינשא, דליארס אפי' נשואה שרי הכא ר"י. ועוד: היכי מוכח בגמ' דהדר ביה ר' יוחנן ממתני' דכרמא, דקתני כולן צריכות להמתין. דלמא לינשא קאמר, אבל ליארס שרי? ונראה כמו [שפי' רש"י] כאן, דרבי יוסי שרי נמי ארוסה לינשא, ולא פליג ארבי יהודה אלא באיבול לחודיה ומיהו, מה שהביא ראיה דשמעינן לרבי יוסי דמיקל בהבחנה טפי מרבי יהודה בסוף פרק "ד' אחין" (ג"ז שם) – אינה ראיה, דדלמא בגיורת ואנוסה מיקל, משום דמתהפכת שלא תתעבר, כדאמרינן לעיל (דף לה.). אבל לעולם גזר ארוסה אטו נשואה. ומברייתא דרדופה היה יכול לדקדק אי גרס בה ר' יוסי, דלא גזר אפי' נשואה רדופה – אטו שאין רדופה כ"ש דלא גזר ארוסה אטו נשואה. והא דפסיק רבי יוחנן כר' יוסי, ולא נקט ר' יהודה, כיון דשניהם שוין – משום שבא לפסוק כרבי יוסי גם באיבול. או נקט ר' יוסי כדפי' בקונטרס משום דנימוקו עמו. וא"ת: כשמגיה בגמרא (לקמן מג.) אימא רבי יוסי אומר כל הנשים ינשאו, ופריך: ולית ליה לרבי יוסי להבחין? ומאי קשיא ליה! נימא דכל הנשים לאו דוקא, ואארוסות דוקא קאי, ולא אנשואות, דמעיקרא נמי לא הוי כל דוקא, דלא הוי קאי אלא אנשואות, דארוסות שרי אפילו לינשא! וי"ל: דלא דמי, דהשתא הוי כל דוקא, וקאי שפיר בין אארוסות בין אנשואות, אלא שהדיוק דמשמע יתארסו – אין, ינשאו – לא, לא קאי אכל נשים אלא אנשואות לחוד. אבל פשטא דמתניתין אכל נשים. קאי אבל קשה לר"ת: דקתני לקמן בברייתא: וכולן לא ינשאו עד שיהו להם שלשה חדשים. משמע אפילו ארוסות כמו כל הנשים. ודוחק לחלק בין וכולן לכל הנשים. ואר"ת: דגרס בברייתא דרדופה רבי יוסי מתיר ליארס, ול"ג לינשא. וגזר ר' יוסי ארוסה אטו נשואה. ודוחק הוא למחוק הספרים, דבכולהו גרס לינשא. ועוד, דליארס אפילו נשואה שרי. הלכה כרבי יוסי. ול"ג כרבי יהודה, דהא בפ' "מי שהוליאוהו" (עירובין דף מו:) קאמר רבי יעקב בר אידי אמר רבי יוחנן: רבי מאיר ורבי יהודה – הלכה כר"י, ר"י ורבי יוסי – הלכה כרבי יוסי, ואין צ"ל רבי מאיר ורבי יוסי – הלכה כרבי יוסי. ודייק דליתנהו להני כללי מדאיצטריך רבי יוחנן לפסוק כרבי יוסי, אף על גב דיחידאה פליג עליה. ואי גרס הלכה כרבי יהודה – שפיר איצטריך לפסוק הלכה כר' יהודה, לאפוקי מר' יוסי דפליג עליה. סתם ואח"כ מחלוקת היא. וא"ת: והא אמרינן בריש מסכת ביצה (דף ב.) גבי שבת סתם לן תנא כר"ש. דתנן: מחתכין הדלועין כו', אע"ג דפליג ר' יהודה בסיפא, וקאמר אם לא היתה נצילה מערב שבת כו'! ויש לומר: דנהי דלא חשיב סתם גמור – מ"מ חשיב כרבים לגבי יחיד. וא"ת: בפ' "המוציא יין" (שבת פה: ושם) דפריך: ומי סבר רבי יוחנן דבר שאין מתכוין אסור? והאמר ר' יוחנן הלכה כסתם משנה, ותנן: נזיר חופף ומפספס אבל לא סורק! ומאי קושיא? דסתמא בנזיר (דף מב.) ופלוגתא בפ"ב דביצה (דף כג.) גבי קירוד וקרצוף, ובתרי מסכתי אמר בפ"ק דמס' ע"ז (דף ז. ושם) אין סדר למשנה! וליכא למימר דר' יוחנן אית ליה הלכה כסתם, אפי' בסתם ואח"כ מחלוקת – דהא קאמר הכא בהדיא אליבא דר' יוחנן סתם ואח"כ מחלוקת היא! וי"ל: דודאי בסתם ואח"כ מחלוקת מודה ר' יוחנן דאין הלכה כסתם, אבל בתרי מסכתי – אית ליה לר' יוחנן דהלכתא כסתם. וטעמא דר' יוחנן משום דמסתמא אית לן למימר דמחלוקת ואח"כ סתם הוא, ולא סתם ואח"כ מחלוקת, דאין לנו לומר שחזר בו רבי מפסקו עד שנראה בפירוש. ומיהו, שאר אמוראי אית להו דבתרי מסכתי אין סדר למשנה ואין הלכתא כסתם. וא"ת: דבפ' "כל גגות" (עירובין דף צב. ושם) פסק ר' יוחנן כר"ש, בין עירבו בין לא עירבו. ופריך: והא אמר ר' יוחנן הלכה כסתם משנה ומייתי מסתם משנה! דבפרק "חלון" (שם דף עו:) והיינו סתם ואח"כ מחלוקת! ותירץ ה"ר אהרן כהן: דעיקר קושיא לרבי יוחנן אינה אלא דלא גזר בעירבו, ובזה הדבר הוי מחלוקת ואח"כ סתם, מחלוקת בשלש חצירות ב"מי שהוציאוהו" (שם דף מה:) וסתם בפרק "חלון". אבל בפרק "כל גגות" לא פליגי בגזירה. ומיהו קשה, דבסוף פרק קמא דמסכת ע"ז (דף כא.), גבי שכירות בתים, פסק שמואל כרבי יוסי, אע"ג דסתם לן תנא בתר הכי כרבי מאיר!

במקום

מסורת הש"ס

[עירובין מז.]
שם ע"ש כתובות ס: ע"ש [תוספתא פ"ו]
[בעירובין ובכתובות א"ר יוסי וכ"א בשאלתות פ' וירא ס"ס יג אכן רבי יהודה איתא וכן בתוספתא ועיין תוספות לעיל לו: סד"ה אבל]
[תוספתא שם]
[שבת מו. וש"נ]
[פסחים פד. יומא מו. סוכה נז.]
[ב"ק קב. ע"ז ז. נדה יח:]

תוספות ישנים

הלכה כרבי יוסי וה"ה דה"מ למימר כר' יהודה אלא נקט כר' יוסי משום דנימוקו עמו: ורבי יוסי מתיר ליארס ולינשא מיד ל"ג ר' יוסי דהא משמע לקמן דמיקל בהבחנה אף בנשואה אלמנה כדמשמע דקאמר (לקמן מג ע"א) אלא אימא כל הנשים ינשאו פי' אף נשואות והכא משמע דלא מתיר לינשא אלא זקנה ואילונית אבל אשה דעלמא לא. א"כ שפיר גרסינן ליה א) דהכי משמע בעירובין (דף מו) דמייתי מהכא ב) דר' יוסי ליתיה להני כללי אלא ודאי גרסי' ליה והאי דנקט מתיר ליארס ולינשא על זקנה ואיילונית וכו' לאו למעוטי שאר נשים אלא משום דלא מיירי ת"ק אלא בהכי לא קאמר מתיר ר' יוסי בכל הנשים משום דת"ק לא איירי בהו אכן ה"נ בשאר נשים ופירש רבינו נתנאל לעיל גרסי' הלכה כר' יהודה דאי גרסי' ר' יוסי לא הוה ליה למפסק הלכתא כוותיה אלא לקמן על משנת ר' יוסי שרמז הספר לקמן ר' יוסי אומר כל הנשים וכו' א"כ לעיל מיניה הוי ר' יהודה וא"ת אמאי לא בעינן שלשה חדשים וג' ימים להמתין כי שמא לא נקלט הזרע עד לאחר ג' ימים וא"כ אם תנשא מיד לאחר ג' חדשים ותלד לשלשה חדשים ויום אחד לא נדע אם מן הראשון או מן האחרון דהא יכול להיות דף מן הראשון והוא נקלט עד יום א' לאחר מיתת הבעל וי"ל דהא לאו אנו מלגלגין כולי האי בבדיקות אם בדיקנן אותה אחרת ג' חדשים כי בדקינן אותה לחלבה כדמשמע לקמן פי' מה שהיא מכבדת על עפר מיתות ופסיעותיה כבדין יותר מאשה אחרת:

א) וכ"כ התוספות עירובין שם. ב) אולי צ"ל דמייתי מהכא דלר"י יוחנן הלכה כרבי יוסי דלהנייהו להני כללי.

הגהות הב"ח

(א) גמ' שאינה ראויה לילד כולן צריכות להמתין ג' (ב) רש"י ד"ה בכרם וכו' כעין נטיעות הכרם (ג) ד"ה מחלוקת וכו' אחריה מיד באותה מסכת בין שסתם אחריה במסכת אחרת:

הגהות הגר"א

[א] גמ' בבית האסורין נ"ב בתוספתא וירושלמי איתא או שהלך בעלה למדינת הים וכו' בכתובות ס ע"ב: [ב] שם ר' יהודה. נ"ב בכתובות שם הגירסא רבי יוסי ובזה מתורץ קושית רש"י ד"ה הלכה דנקיט רבי יוסי משום הברייתא:

גליון הש"ס

גמ' א"ל הל' כסתם. עיין חידושי הרשב"א ב"ק קב ע"א ד"ה אלא הלכה: תוס' ד"ה סתם ואח"כ מחלוקת וכו' וא"ת והא אמרי' וכו'. עיין תשובת הרשב"א סי' קיד:

וְכִי *רַבִּי לֹא שְׁנָאָהּ *רַ' חִיָּיא מִנַּיִן לוֹ? אֲמַר לֵיהּ: וְהָא תְּנַן: *[א]מַסְרֵק שֶׁל פִּשְׁתָּן שֶׁנִּיטְּלוּ שִׁינָּיו, וְנִשְׁתַּיְּירוּ בּוֹ שְׁתַּיִם — טְמֵאוֹת, וְאַחַת — טְהוֹרָה. וְכוּלָּן שֶׁנִּיטְּלוּ אַחַת אַחַת בִּפְנֵי עַצְמָן — טְמֵאוֹת. [ב]שֶׁל צֶמֶר שֶׁנִּיטְּלוּ שִׁינָּיו אַחַת מִבֵּינְתַיִם — טָהוֹר, נִשְׁתַּיְּירוּ בּוֹ ג' בְּמָקוֹם אֶחָד — טָמֵא, הָיְתָה הַחִיצוֹנָה אַחַת מֵהֶן — טָהוֹר. נִיטְּלוּ ב' וַעֲשָׂאָן לְמַלְקֵט — טְמֵאוֹת, אַחַת וְהִתְקִינָהּ לְנֵר אוֹ לְמִיתּוּחַ — טְמֵאָה. וְקי"ל דְּאֵין הֲלָכָה כְּאוֹתָהּ מִשְׁנָה! אֲמַר לֵיהּ: בַּר מִינַּהּ דְּהַהִיא, דְּרַ' יוֹחָנָן וְר"ל דְּאָמְרִי תַּרְוַיְיהוּ: זוֹ אֵינָהּ מִשְׁנָה. מ"ט? אֲמַר רַב הוּנָא בַּר מָנוֹחַ מִשְּׁמֵיהּ דְּרַב אִידִי בְּרֵיהּ דְּרַב אִיקָא: מִשּׁוּם דְּקַשְׁיָא רֵישָׁא לְסֵיפָא. דְּקָתָנֵי: שֶׁל צֶמֶר שֶׁנִּיטְּלוּ שִׁינָּיו אַחַת מִבֵּינְתַיִם — טָהוֹר, הָא נִשְׁתַּיְּירוּ בּוֹ שְׁתַּיִם בְּמָקוֹם אֶחָד — טָמֵא, וַהֲדַר תָּנֵי: נִשְׁתַּיְּירוּ בּוֹ ג' — טָמֵא, ג' — אִין, שְׁתַּיִם — לָא! וּמַאי קוּשְׁיָא? דִּלְמָא הָא בְּגַוָּויָתָא הָא בְּבָרָיָיתָא! אֶלָּא מֵהָכָא, דְּקָתָנֵי: וְכוּלָּן שֶׁנִּיטְּלוּ אַחַת אַחַת בִּפְנֵי עַצְמָן טְמֵאוֹת, וְאע"ג דְּלָא הִתְקִינָהּ. אֵימָא סֵיפָא: אַחַת וְהִתְקִינָהּ לְנֵר אוֹ לְמִיתּוּחַ — טְמֵאָה. הִתְקִינָהּ — אִין, לֹא הִתְקִינָהּ — לָא! אֲמַר אַבַּיֵּי: וּמַאי קוּשְׁיָא? דִּלְמָא הָא בְּקַתַּיְיהוּ, הָא בְּלָא קַתַּיְיהוּ. א"ר פַּפָּא: [ג]וּמַאי קוּשְׁיָא? וְדִלְמָא הָא — בְּקַטִּינָתָא, הָא — בְּאַלִּימְתָּא. אֶלָּא: מִשּׁוּם דִּמְסַיְּימִי בָּהּ דַּוְוקָנֵי: זוֹ דִּבְרֵי ר"ש. שָׁלַח רַ' חִיָּיא בַּר אָבִין: מְאָרְסִין תּוֹךְ ג', וְכֵן עוֹשִׂים מַעֲשֶׂה. וְכֵן הָיָה רַ' אֶלְעָזָר מְלַמְּדֵנוּ מִשּׁוּם רַבִּי חֲנִינָא הַגָּדוֹל: רוּבּוֹ שֶׁל רִאשׁוֹן, וְרוּבּוֹ שֶׁל שְׁלִישִׁי, וְאֶמְצָעִי שָׁלֵם. אֲמֵימַר שְׁרָא לְיָאֳרֵס בְּיוֹם תִּשְׁעִים. אֲמַר לֵיהּ רַב אַשִׁי לַאֲמֵימַר: וְהָא רַב וּשְׁמוּאֵל דְּאָמְרִי תַּרְוַיְיהוּ: צְרִיכָה לְהַמְתִּין ג' חֳדָשִׁים, חוּץ מִיּוֹם שֶׁמֵּת בּוֹ וְחוּץ מִיּוֹם שֶׁנִּתְאָרְסָה בּוֹ! הַהוּא לְעִנְיַן מֵינֶקֶת אִיתְּמַר. דְּרַב וּשְׁמוּאֵל דְּאָמְרִי תַּרְוַיְיהוּ: *צְרִיכָה לְהַמְתִּין כ"ד חֹדֶשׁ, חוּץ מִיּוֹם שֶׁנּוֹלַד בּוֹ וְחוּץ מִיּוֹם שֶׁנִּתְאָרְסָה בּוֹ. וְהָא הַהוּא דַּעֲבַד סְעוּדַת אֵירוּסִין בְּיוֹם תִּשְׁעִים, וְאַפְסְדֵיהּ רָבָא לִסְעוּדָתֵיהּ! הַהִיא סְעוּדַת נִשּׂוּאִין הֲוַאי. [ד]וְהִלְכְתָא: צְרִיכָה לְהַמְתִּין כ"ד חוֹדֶשׁ, חוּץ מִיּוֹם שֶׁנּוֹלַד בּוֹ וְחוּץ מִיּוֹם שֶׁנִּתְאָרְסָה בּוֹ. וּצְרִיכָה לְהַמְתִּין ג' חֳדָשִׁים, חוּץ מִיּוֹם שֶׁמֵּת בּוֹ וְחוּץ מִיּוֹם שֶׁנִּתְאָרְסָה בּוֹ.§ "חוּץ מִן הָאַלְמָנָה וכו'".§ אָמַר רַב חִסְדָּא: ק"ו, וּמַה בְּמָקוֹם שֶׁאָסוּר לְכַבֵּס — מוּתָּר לְיָאֳרֵס, מָקוֹם שֶׁמּוּתָּר לְכַבֵּס — אֵינוֹ דִּין שֶׁמּוּתָּר לְיָאֳרֵס! מַאי הִיא? דִּתְנַן: *[ה]שַׁבָּת שֶׁחָל תִּשְׁעָה בְּאָב בְּתוֹכָהּ — אָסוּר לְסַפֵּר וּלְכַבֵּס, וּבַחֲמִישִׁי מוּתָּר מִפְּנֵי כְּבוֹד הַשַּׁבָּת. וְתַנְיָא: [ו]קוֹדֶם הַזְּמַן הַזֶּה הָעָם מְמַעֲטִין בְּעִסְקֵיהֶם מִלִּישָּׂא וּמִלִּיתֵּן, מִלִּבְנוֹת וְלִנְטוֹעַ, [ז]וּמְאָרְסִין אֲבָל לֹא כּוֹנְסִין, וְאֵין עוֹשִׂין סְעוּדַת אֵירוּסִין. כִּי תַּנְיָא הַהִיא — קוֹדֶם דְּקוֹדֶם (תַּנְיָא). אֲמַר רָבָא: וְקוֹדֶם דְּקוֹדֶם נַמִי, ק"ו: וּמַה בְּמָקוֹם שֶׁאָסוּר לִישָּׂא וְלִיתֵּן — מוּתָּר לְיָאֳרֵס, מָקוֹם שֶׁמּוּתָּר לִישָּׂא וְלִיתֵּן — אֵינוֹ דִּין שֶׁמּוּתָּר לְיָאֳרֵס?! לָא תֵּימָא דְּרַבִּי יוֹסֵי אוֹמֵר כָּל הַנָּשִׁים יִתְאָרְסוּ, אֶלָּא אֵימָא: כָּל הַנָּשִׁים יִנָּשְׂאוּ.

וְלִית

רש"י

רַבִּי לֹא שְׁנָאָהּ. רַבִּי שֶׁסִּידֵּר אֶת הַמִּשְׁנָה לֹא שְׁנָאָהּ שֶׁתְּהֵא מִשְׁנָה, שֶׁלֹּא רָצָה לְסוֹתְמָהּ. **רַבִּי חִיָּיא.** תַּלְמִידוֹ מִנַּיִן לוֹ שֶׁהֲלָכָה כְּמוֹתָהּ, שֶׁסְּתָמָהּ בְּבָרַיְיתָא? **שְׁתַּיִם טְמֵאוֹת.** דַּחֲזוּ לְמִילְּתַיְהּ. **אַחַת טְהוֹרָה.** דְּלָא חֲזֵי לְמִידֵּי. **אַחַת בִּפְנֵי עַצְמָהּ.** שֶׁאֵינָהּ תְּחוּבָה בְּמַסְרֵק. **טְמֵאָה.** שֶׁרְאוּיָה לְנֵר, אוֹ לְמִיתּוּחַ, לִפְרוֹשׂ בְּגָדִים אוֹ חוּט זוֹ מִזּוֹ. **אַחַת מִבֵּינְתַיִם.** שֶׁמִּכָּל ג' הַסְּמוּכוֹת נִיטְּלָה הָאֶמְצָעִית — תּוּ לָא חֲזֵי. **הָיְתָה הַחִיצוֹנָה.** אַחַת מֵהַשְּׁלֵימוֹת הַלָּלוּ, שֶׁנִּשְׁתַּיְּירוּ ג' עִם הַחִיצוֹנוֹת. וְאֵין חִיצוֹנָה רְחָבָה הִיא, כְּעֵין חִיצוֹנוֹת שֶׁבְּמַסְרֵק שֶׁל עֵץ שֶׁלָּנוּ — הִלְכָּךְ לָא מְהַנְּיָא בַּהֲדַיְיהוּ, וְטָהוֹר. **לְמַלְקֵט.** מֶלְקָחַיִם, שֶׁקּוֹרִין טנל"ש. **לְנֵר.** לְנַקֵּר אֶת הַנֵּר. **וּלְמִיתּוּחַ.** לִפְרוֹשׂ בֶּגֶד, כְּעֵין הַחַיָּיטִים שֶׁמּוֹתְחִין עוֹרוֹת בְּמַסְמְרִים: **טְמֵאָה.** לְקַמָּן פָּרֵיךְ: דְּהָא תָּנָא רֵישָׁא כּוּלָּן (א) אַחַת אַחַת בִּפְנֵי עַצְמָן טְמֵאוֹת, וְאע"ג דְּלֹא הִתְקִינָהּ. **הָא.** דְּקָתָנֵי שְׁתַּיִם טָמֵא בְּגַוָּויָתָא אֶמְצָעִיּוֹת, דַּחֲזֵין טְפֵי, שֶׁהֵן כְּנֶגֶד בֵּית יַד הַמַּסְרֵק, וּכְשֶׁהוּא אוֹחֵז בּוֹ מְכוּוָּנוֹת הֵן לִסְרוֹק. **וְהָא.** דְּקָתָנֵי שָׁלֹשׁ אִין שְׁתַּיִם לָא — בְּבָרַיְיתָא. וְלָא בַּחִיצוֹנוֹת [מַמָּשׁ], דְּהָא אָמְרִינַן הָיְתָה חִיצוֹנָה אַחַת מֵהֶן טָהוֹר, אֶלָּא אוֹתָן הַמְּשׁוּכוֹת כְּלַפֵּי הָרֹאשׁ, דְּאֵינָן מְכוּוָּנוֹת כְּנֶגֶד בֵּית יַד הַמַּסְרֵק, וְלָא חֲזוּ כּוּלֵּי הַאי — הִלְכָּךְ ג' הוּא דַּחֲזוּ בְּמִקְצָת, אֲבָל שְׁתַּיִם — לָא חֲזוּ וְלָא מִידֵּי. ל"א, וְהוּא עִיקָּר: בְּגַוָּויָתָא וּבָרַיְיתָא — שְׁתֵּי שׁוּרוֹת שִׁינַּיִם יֵשׁ לְמַסְרֵק שֶׁל צֶמֶר, חִיצוֹנוֹת וּפְנִימִיּוֹת. הַחִיצוֹנִיּוֹת — עִיקַּר הַמְּלָאכָה תְּלוּיָה בָּהֶן, וּפְנִימִיּוֹת — לִקְלוֹט הַצֶּמֶר שֶׁלֹּא יִפּוֹל. וְהִלְכָּךְ, בַּחִיצוֹנוֹת צָרִיךְ ג' בְּמָקוֹם אֶחָד, וְהַפְּנִימִיּוֹת — דַּיָּין בְּב': **בְּקַתַּיְיהוּ.** שֶׁנָּטַל עִמָּהּ חֲתִיכַת עֵץ, וְהִיא נַעֲשֵׂית לָהּ בֵּית יָד, וְאֵינָהּ צְרִיכָה תִּיקּוּן אַחֵר. **אַלִּימְתָּא.** עָבוֹת, וְאֵינָם צְרִיכוֹת בֵּית יָד. **זוֹ דִּבְרֵי ר"ש.** וְלָאו סְתָמָא הוּא. **וְכֵן עוֹשִׂין מַעֲשֶׂה.** כְּלוֹמַר: כָּךְ רָאִיתִי מִנְהַג חֲכָמִים עוֹשִׂים. **רוּבּוֹ.** שֶׁל חֹדֶשׁ רִאשׁוֹן, וְרוּבּוֹ שֶׁל אַחֲרוֹן, וְאֶמְצָעִי (ב) שָׁלֵם. **וְהִלְכְתָא.** מֵינִיקָה צְרִיכָה לְהַמְתִּין כ"ד חֹדֶשׁ חוּץ מִיּוֹם שֶׁנּוֹלַד בּוֹ, וְאִשָּׁה שֶׁאֵינָהּ מֵינִיקָה צְרִיכָה לְהַמְתִּין ג' חֳדָשִׁים, חוּץ מִיּוֹם שֶׁמֵּת בַּעְלָהּ וְחוּץ מִיּוֹם שֶׁנִּתְאָרְסָה בּוֹ (כָּל הַנָּשִׁים יִתְאָרְסוּ — אַנְּשׂוּאוֹת קָאֵי, חוּץ מִן הָאַלְמָנָה — אָתָא לְאַשְׁמוּעִינַן וְלָא אַאֲרוּסוֹת וּלְמַעוּטִינְהוּ מִלִּינָּשֵׂא. דְּגַבֵּי הַבְחָנָה רַבִּי יוֹסֵי מֵיקֵל טְפֵי מִכּוּלְּהוּ, כִּדְאָמַר בְּ"אַרְבָּעָה אַחִין"). **ק"ו.** רַב חִסְדָּא מַתְמִיהַּ עַל דִּבְרֵי רַבִּי יוֹסֵי שֶׁאוֹסֵר לְיָאֳרֵס מֵחֲמַת אֲבֵילוּת כָּל ל', כִּדְקָתָנֵי לְקַמָּן: כַּמָּה אִיבּוּל שֶׁלָּהּ — שְׁלֹשִׁים יוֹם. **בְּמָקוֹם שֶׁאָסוּר לְכַבֵּס.** שַׁבָּת שֶׁחָל ט' בְּאָב לִהְיוֹת בְּתוֹכָהּ. **מוּתָּר לְיָאֳרֵס.** דְּאֵירוּסִין לָאו שִׂמְחָה נִינְהוּ. **מָקוֹם שֶׁמּוּתָּר לְכַבֵּס.** תּוֹךְ ל' יוֹם שֶׁל אֵבֶל, דְּאָבֵל אֵין אָסוּר בְּתִכְבּוֹסֶת אֶלָּא שִׁבְעָה יָמִים, דְּכָל שְׁלֹשִׁים יוֹם לְגִיהוּץ תְּנַן בְּפֶ' "וְאֵלּוּ מְגַלְּחִין" (מו"ק דף כג.) אֲבָל כִּיבּוּס — לָא, דְּהָא תִּסְפּוֹרֶת גּוּפָהּ, אִי לָאו דְּאָתְיָא "פֶּרַע" "פֶּרַע" מִנָּזִיר — לָא מִיתַּסְרָא. **קוֹדֶם הַזְּמַן הַזֶּה.** קָא ס"ד: קוֹדֶם ט' בְּאָב, דְּהַיְינוּ כָּל הַשַּׁבָּת שֶׁחָל לִהְיוֹת בְּתוֹכָהּ מְמַעֲטִין כו'. **וּמְאָרְסִין.** דְּלָאו שִׂמְחָה הִיא, וּמִצְוָה קָעָבֵיד. **כִּי תַּנְיָא הַהִיא.** דִּמְאָרְסִין. **קוֹדֶם דְּקוֹדֶם.** קוֹדֶם שַׁבָּת שֶׁחָל ט"ב בְּתוֹכָהּ, דְּהָתָם מוּתָּר לְכַבֵּס. אֲבָל תּוֹךְ הַשַּׁבָּת, כְּשֵׁם שֶׁאָסוּר לְכַבֵּס — אָסוּר נַמִי לְיָאֳרֵס, וְלֵיכָּא ק"ו.

אֶלָּא

תוספות

במקום שמותר לכבס. גרסי', ול"ג לספר. דהא אמרינן [בירושלמי] במועד קטן: לגיהוץ ולתספורת שלשים יום. והר"ר יעקב מאורליינ"ש הביא מהך גרסא דאשה מותרת בנטילת שער, [וכן איתא בה"ג]. ועוד מלינו למימר: דהתם אליבא דר' יוסי קיימי, דשרי תספורת באבל. דהכי כתב בעל ה"ג: כשם שאסור לגלח במועד כך אסור *לגלח בימי אבלו, דברי רבי יהודה. רבי יוסי מתיר, כל ל' יום אסור לתספורת, אחד זקנו, אחד שער ראשו, ואחד כל שער שבו. וכשם שאסור *ליטול לפרנים במועד — כך אסור בימי אבלו, דברי רבי יהודה, ר' יוסי מתיר. והאשה מותרת בנטילת שער לאחר ז'. ומיהו, אין נראה: דשמא אשה, דשריא באבלה — שריא נמי בתשעה באב. וכן ר' יוסי, דשרי לספר באבילות — שרי נמי בתשעה באב. ועוד נראה: דלרבי יוסי נמי אסור לספר, דמסתמא יליף "פרע" "פרע": מנזיר, וכל ראשו הוא דשריא לגלח — דניוול הוא, אבל לספר — אסור. וכן משמע מתוך הלכות גדולות שהבאתי, וא"כ לא גרסינן הכא לספר, דגילוח כל הראש לא מיקרי סיפור*. **שמותר** לכבס. אחר שבעה ותוך ל'. והא דמשמע בפ' "ואלו מגלחין" (מו"ק דף כג.) דאבל אסור לכבס כסותו במים — היינו תוך ז', דדוקא גיהוץ אסור תוך שלשים יום. ומיהו, גיהוץ דידן שרי, כדאמרינן בפ"ק דכתובות (דף י:) דגיהוץ שלנו ככיבוס שלהם. ואין להאריך*. **מאי** היא דתנן. למאי דפרישית דבאיבול פליגי רבי יהודה ורבי יוסי קשה, דנוקי הא דשרי לארס בתשעה באב כרבי יהודה, דשרי נמי באבל! וכי תימא: מ"מ תקשה ליה, שסברת רבי יוסי הפוכה מדרבי יהודה, דר' יהודה מחמיר טפי בכיבוס מבאירוסין, ולרבי יוסי איפכא — ע"כ אין הש"ס חושש בכך, דהא לקמן בעי למימר דתנאי היא! וי"ל: דאין נראה להש"ס שום תנא יחלוק אמתני' דשרי לארס בט' באב אם לא ימצא ברייתא בפירוש, דהא לקמן כשמצא ברייתא נמי בהדיא דקתני ממעטין מליארס — דוחק ומוקי לה בסעודת אירוסין כי היכי דלא תפלוג אמתני' [דהתם]. **מלישא** וליתן מלבנות ולנטוע. בפרק בתרא דתענית [בירושלמי] מוקי בבנין ונטיעה של שמחה, כגון אבורנקי של מלכים. וי"מ דמשא ומתן נמי איירי בשל שמחה, כגון צרכי חופה. ואין נראה: דלא אסר אלא סעודה עצמה. ונראה דריבוי משא ומתן קא אסר, שימעטו יותר מבשאר ימים*). **ומה** במקום שאסור לישא וליתן. וא"ת: מה לקודם דקודם — שמותר לספר! ועוד תימה: דתספורת יהא אסור בקודם דקודם מק"ו דשלשים יום דאבילות, שמותר לישא וליתן! או משא ומתן ליתסר בשלשים יום דאבילות מק"ו דתספורת בקודם דקודם! או תספורת לישרי בשלשים יום של אבילות! ולפי המסקנא ניחא.

*) [ועיין תוספות מגילה ה: ד"ה ממעטין]

תוספות ישנים

והא בברייתא. פי' הא דאמרי' שלש א) (או שתים) מיירי בברייתא פי' ולא בחיצונות ממש דהא אמרי' (קמייתא) [דהיתה] החיצונה אחת מהן טהורה אלא באותן המשוכות כלפי הראש (כזה). י"מ בברייתא בשורה החיצונה ובגוייתא מיירי בשורה הפנימית דאינם משוכות כלפי בית יד המסרק ולא חזו כולי האי הלכך שלשה ב) (לא) דחזו במקצת אבל שתים לא חזו מידי כי שתי שורות יש למסרק של צמר חיצונה ופנימית והחיצונה עיקר המלאכה תלויה בהם והפנימית לקלוט את הצמר שלא יפול הלכך בחיצונות צריך שלש במקום אחד והפנימית דיין בשתים: **מתני'** כל הנשים יתארסו אנשואות קאי וחוץ מן האלמנה אתא לאשמעינן ולאו אארוסות ולמעוטינהו מלינשא דגבי הבחנה ר' יוסי מיקל טפי מכלהו כדאמרינן בד' אחין: **מה** במקום שאסור לכבס ולספר כגון בשבת שחל ט' באב להיות בתוכה מותר לארס נראה דל"ג לספר שהרי איך אמרי' מקום שמותר לספר כגון ג) כל ימי אבלות א"א לומר כן שהרי אסור לספר כל שלשים יום כדילפינן פרע פרע מנזיר ולפי הספרים שגורסים לספר י"ל דמיירי באשה דשריא בנטילת שער כל ל' יום ודוחק הא דמנא לן דאסירא נטילת שער באשה בשבת שחל ט' באב להיות בתוכה הלא אין זה לה אלא ניוול לגלח שערה וי"מ דמוכחינן [מהא] דמותר לספר תוך ל' יום בתכפוהו אבליו אבל בשבת שחל ט' באב להיות בתוכו סברא הוא לאסור משום דלא צריך רק להמתין מעט שיעבור ט' באב אבל באבלות שרי להקל שערו בתכפוהו אבליו. משמע הכא בתוך ל' יום מותר לכבס וא"ת הא אמרינן אבל אסור לכבס כסותו במים וי"ל התם איירי תוך שבעה אבל לאחר שבעה שרי ועתה אף גיהוץ שלנו שרי דגיהוץ שלנו ככיבוס שלהם דהכי אמרינן התם וא"ת הא אמרינן דא"ר שמעון בן אלעזר לא אסרו אלא לכלים חדשים וגם קאמר התם אביי נפק בחומרתא סומקתי ורבא נפק בגילא דסרבלא משמע דגיהוץ בבבל לא שרי וי"ל דהתם מיירי שהיו שם הכלים מגוהצים מארץ ישראל א"נ יכול להיות שיש מקומות בבבל שיש בהם אומנים כמו בארץ ישראל ועתה יש לנו לאסור כל שלשים יום דאמרינן בתוספתא כל שלשים לתכבוסת וא"כ נהי נמי דגיהוץ שלנו ככיבוס שלהם מ"מ אסור דהא אף כיבוס שלהם אסור ועתה יש להזהר בכיבוס שלנו דהוי לבן ביותר והוי כגיהוץ ואסור ככיבוס שלהם ולכן יש להחמיר ולאת חלוק לבן שלו לחברו ללבשו טרם ילבשנו וכן נהגו העולם: **לישא** וליתן ר"ל משא ומתן של שמחה דומיא דלבנות ולנטוע דמפרש התם כגון אבורנקי של מלכים: וקודם דקודם נמי ק"ו ומה במקום שאסור לישא וליתן דהיינו קודם דקודם מותר ליארס וא"ת וליפרך מה לקודם דקודם שמותר לספר תאמר באבלות שאסור לספר וי"ל דלמסקנא ניחא ד) דאבלות ישנה מתחלה ועד סוף אבל אין להקשות דלשתרי תספורת כל ל' יום מק"ו דקודם דקודם שאסור לישא וליתן ומותר לספר ל' יום של אבלות כו' איטו דין שמותר לספר דזה איטו יכול להיות דהא ילפינן פרע פרע מנזיר לאסור כל ל' יום ואם תאמר ותספורת תיאסר בקודם דקודם בק"ו דאבלות שמותר לישא וליתן ואסור לספר וכן נמי משא ומתן לתסר כל שלשים יום של אבלות מק"ו מקודם דקודם דמותר בתספורת ואסור לישא וליתן וגם בזה יש לומר דלמסקנא ניחא הכל:

א) נ"ל הא דאמרינן שלש אבל לא שתים מיירי בחיצונות. ב) נראה דל"ל הלכך אם נשתיירו שלש במקום אחד טמא דחזו במקצת וכו'. ג) אולי דל"ל כגון בל' יום של אבילות א"א לומר כן שהרי אסור לספר כל ל' יום. ד) נ"ל דשאני אבילות חדשה מאבילות ישנה.

עין משפט נר מצוה

צא א מיי' פי"א מהל' כלים הלכה ז:

צב ב ג מיי' שם הלכה ג ועיין שם בכ"מ:

[ליטול לפרנים במועד רש"ל]

[ולגלח בימי אבלו כך אסור ליטול לפרנים בימי אבלו. רש"ל]

צג ד מיי' פי"א מהלכות גירושין הל' כו סמג עשין נ טוש"ע אה"ע סי' יג סעיף א וסעיף יא:

צד ה מיי' פ"ה מהל' תעניות הלכה ו סמג עשין מד"ס ג טוש"ע א"ח סימן תקנא סעיף ג:

[והאריכות בזה מבואר בתוס' מ"ק כג. ד"ה כל]

צה ו מיי' וסמג שם טוש"ע א"ח סימן תקנא סעיף ב [בהמג"א ליתא גם ברי"ף והרא"ש השמיטוהו ועי' ב"י סימן תקנ"א טעם להשמטה זו]

צו ז מיי' פ"י מהלכות אישות הלכה יד טור ש"ע שם:

[ועי' ארוכות בתוספות מו"ק כג. ד"ה כל שלשים וכו']

מסורת הש"ס

[עירובין לב. נדה סב:] [עי' תוס' נדה סב: ד"ה ר"ח] כלים פי"ג מ"ח

כתובות ס:

תענית כו:

תוספות חד מקמאי

גרים הרב אלפס אמר רב נחמן ק"ו ומה במקום שאסור לספר ולכבס מותר לארם מקום שמותר לספר ולכבס אינו דין שמותר לארם ומוכח מהכא שהאשה מותרת לספר בשבעת האיבול והכי איתא באבל רבתי ורש"י ז"ל גרים ומה במקום שאסור לכבס מותר לארם במקום שמותר לכבס אינו דין שמותר לארם ול"ג לספר: ומאי דאיסתפקא לרב אלפס בעובד כוכבים ועבד הבא על בת ישראל אם הולד פגום לכהונה או לא תימה הוא מאי ספיקא איכא דמילתא פסיקא הוא ק"ו מאלמנה ועוד הגרים בפ' כיצד לימא קסבר רבינא גוי ועבד הבא על בת ישראל הולד כשר נהי דממזר מיהא לא הוי. ישראל פסול מיהא ליקרי הלכך מילתא פשוטה היא שהולד פגום לכהונה:

הגהות הב"ח

(א) רש"י ד"ה טמאה וכו' ריישא כולן שניטלו אחת אחת: (ב) ד"ה רובו וכו' של שלם הס"ד ואח"כ נ"ל ד"ה ביום תשעים. יום השלמת ג' חדשים הס"ד:

גליון הש"ס

רש"י ד"ה מקום שמותר וכו' אבל כבוס לא. עי' מו"ק דף יט ע"א ברש"י ד"ה שמנה ימים ול"ע:

וְלֵית לֵיהּ לְרַבִּי יוֹסֵי לְהַבְחִין? (א) לֵית לֵיהּ. וְאִיבָּעֵית אֵימָא: לְעוֹלָם אִית לֵיהּ, וְאֵימָא, רַבִּי יוֹסֵי אוֹמֵר: כָּל אֲרוּסוֹת גְּרוּשׁוֹת יִנָּשְׂאוּ. אִי הָכִי הַיְינוּ רַ' יְהוּדָה! אִיכָּא בֵּינַיְיהוּ נְשׂוּאָה לֵיאָרֵס; רַבִּי יְהוּדָה סָבַר: נְשׂוּאָה מוּתֶּרֶת לֵיאָרֵס, וְרַבִּי יוֹסֵי סָבַר: נְשׂוּאָה אֲסוּרָה לֵיאָרֵס. וְסָבַר רַ' יוֹסֵי נְשׂוּאָה אֲסוּרָה לֵיאָרֵס? וְהָתַנְיָא, רַבִּי יוֹסֵי אוֹמֵר: כָּל הַנָּשִׁים יִתְאָרְסוּ, חוּץ מִן הָאַלְמָנָה מִפְּנֵי הָאִיבּוּל, וְכַמָּה אִיבּוּל שֶׁלָּהּ — שְׁלֹשִׁים יוֹם. וְכוּלָּן לֹא יִנָּשְׂאוּ עַד שֶׁיְּהוּ לָהֶן ג' חֳדָשִׁים! הַאי מַאי קוּשְׁיָא? אִילֵימָא דְּקָתָנֵי, רַבִּי יוֹסֵי אוֹמֵר: כָּל הַנָּשִׁים יִתְאָרְסוּ — מִי אַלִּימָא מִמַּתְנִי' דְּאוֹקִימְנָא בַּאֲרוּסוֹת גְּרוּשׁוֹת יִנָּשְׂאוּ — ה"נ כָּל אֲרוּסוֹת גְּרוּשׁוֹת יִנָּשְׂאוּ. אֶלָּא מִסֵּיפָא, דְּקָתָנֵי: וְכוּלָּן לֹא יִנָּשְׂאוּ עַד שֶׁיְּהוּ לָהֶן ג' חֳדָשִׁים. אִינְּסוּבֵי הוּא — דְּלָא, הָא אִיתְרוּסֵי — שַׁפִּיר דָּמֵי. אֲמַר רָבָא, תְּרֵיץ וְאֵימָא הָכִי: רַ' יוֹסֵי אוֹמֵר כָּל אֲרוּסוֹת גְּרוּשׁוֹת יִנָּשְׂאוּ, חוּץ מִן הָאַלְמָנָה מִפְּנֵי הָאִיבּוּל, וְכַמָּה אִיבּוּל שֶׁלָּהּ — שְׁלֹשִׁים יוֹם. וּנְשׂוּאוֹת לֹא יִתְאָרְסוּ עַד שֶׁיְּהֵא לָהֶן שְׁלֹשָׁה חֳדָשִׁים. וְאַלְמָנָה מִן הָאֵירוּסִין מִי אִית לָהּ אִיבּוּל? וְהָתָנֵי רַבִּי חִיָּיא בַּר אַמִּי: *אִשְׁתּוֹ אֲרוּסָה — לֹא אוֹנֵן וְלֹא מִיטַּמֵּא לָהּ, וְכֵן הִיא לֹא אוֹנֶנֶת וְלֹא מִיטַּמְּאָה לוֹ. מֵתָה — אֵינוֹ יוֹרְשָׁהּ, מֵת הוּא — גּוֹבָה כְּתוּבָּתָהּ. אֶלָּא תַּנָּאֵי הִיא. דְּתַנְיָא: מֵרֹאשׁ חֹדֶשׁ וְעַד הַתַּעֲנִית הָעָם מְמַעֲטִין מֵעִסְקֵיהֶן, מִלִּישָּׂא וּמִלִּיתֵּן, מִלִּבְנוֹת וְלִנְטוֹעַ, וּמִלֵּיאָרֵס וּמִלִּישָּׂא. *שַׁבָּת שֶׁחָל תִּשְׁעָה בְּאָב בְּתוֹכָהּ — אָסוּר לְסַפֵּר וּלְכַבֵּס (וְאָסוּר לֵיאָרֵס). וי"א: *כָּל הַחֹדֶשׁ אָסוּר. מַתְקִיף לָהּ רַב אַשִׁי: מִמַּאי דְּלֵיאָרֵס — לֵיאָרֵס מַמָּשׁ? [א]דִּלְמָא לְמֶיעֱבַד סְעוּדַת אֵירוּסִין הוּא דְּאָסוּר, הָא לֵיאָרֵס — שַׁפִּיר דָּמֵי. אִי הָכִי, מִלִּישָּׂא? לִינָּשֵׂא נָמֵי לְמֶיעֱבַד סְעוּדַת נִשּׂוּאִין הוּא דְּאָסוּר, הָא לִישָּׂא — שַׁפִּיר דָּמֵי! הָכִי הַשְׁתָּא! בִּשְׁלָמָא נִשּׂוּאִין בְּלֹא סְעוּדָה — אִיכָּא שִׂמְחָה, אֶלָּא אֵירוּסִין בְּלֹא סְעוּדָה — מִי אִיכָּא שִׂמְחָה? אֶלָּא אֲמַר רַב אַשִׁי: שָׁאנֵי אֲבֵילוּת חֲדָשָׁה מֵאֲבֵילוּת יְשָׁנָה, וְשָׁאנֵי אֲבֵילוּת דְּרַבִּים מֵאֲבֵילוּת דְּיָחִיד.§

מתני' [ב]אַרְבָּעָה אַחִין נְשׂוּאִין אַרְבַּע נָשִׁים, וָמֵתוּ. אִם רָצָה הַגָּדוֹל שֶׁבָּהֶם לְיַיבֵּם אֶת כּוּלָּן — הָרְשׁוּת בְּיָדוֹ. [ג]מִי שֶׁהָיָה נָשׂוּי לִשְׁתֵּי נָשִׁים וָמֵת — בִּיאָתָהּ אוֹ חֲלִיצָתָהּ שֶׁל אַחַת מֵהֶן פּוֹטֶרֶת צָרָתָהּ.

הָיְתָה

אֶלָּא אֵימָא רַבִּי יוֹסֵי אוֹמֵר כָּל הַנָּשִׁים יִנָּשְׂאוּ. חוּץ מֵאַלְמָנָה. וְרַבִּי יוֹסֵי לָאו אִיבּוּל אָתָא לְאַשְׁמוּעִינַן. דִּבְנִישּׂוּאִין אֲפִילּוּ רַבִּי יְהוּדָה מוֹדֶה דְּאָסוּר בִּימֵי אִיבּוּל, דְּהָא שִׂמְחָה הִיא. אֶלָּא יִנָּשְׂאוּ אָתָא לְאַשְׁמוּעִינַן, וּפָלֵיג אַדְּרַבִּי יְהוּדָה, דְּאָמַר כָּל הַנְּשׂוּאוֹת יִתְאָרְסוּ. וְאָתָא ר' יוֹסֵי לְמֵימַר: אֲפִילּוּ נְשׂוּאוֹת יִנָּשְׂאוּ. וג' מַחֲלוֹקוֹת בַּדָּבָר: דְּת"ק אָסַר אֲפִילּוּ אֲרוּסוֹת לֵיאָרֵס, דְּגָזְרוּ אֲרוּסַת רִאשׁוֹן אַטּוּ נְשׂוּאָה, וְגָזְרִינַן אֵרוּסִין דְּאַחֲרוֹן אַטּוּ נִשּׂוּאִין דְּאַחֲרוֹן. וְר' יְהוּדָה סָבַר: הַנְּשׂוּאוֹת יִתְאָרְסוּ, וְלָא גָּזַר אֵירוּסִין אַטּוּ נִשּׂוּאִין, וְהָאֲרוּסוֹת יִנָּשְׂאוּ, וְלָא גָּזַר אֲרוּסָה אַטּוּ נְשׂוּאָה. אֲבָל הַבְחָנָה מִיהָא אִית לֵיהּ, וּנְשׂוּאָה לֹא תִּנָּשֵׂא. וְרַבִּי יוֹסֵי — אֲפִילּוּ הַבְחָנָה לֵית לֵיהּ. **וְאִי בָּעֵית אֵימָא אִית לֵיהּ.** וְאַפְּ"ה יִנָּשְׂאוּ קָתָנֵי. [וְלָא אַנְּשׂוּאוֹת קָאֵי] אֶלָּא אַאֲרוּסוֹת קָאֵי, וְה"ק: כָּל הָאֲרוּסוֹת שֶׁנִּתְגָּרְשׁוּ — יִנָּשְׂאוּ חוּץ מִן הָאֲרוּסוֹת אַלְמָנוֹת מֵחֲמַת הָאִיבּוּל. וּלְקַמָּן פָּרֵיךְ: מִי חָיֵיל אִיבּוּל אַאֲרוּסָה? **אִי הָכִי הַיְינוּ ר' יְהוּדָה.** דְּרַבִּי יְהוּדָה נָמֵי שָׁרֵי אֲרוּסָה לִינָּשֵׂא. וְלֵיכָּא לְמֵימַר הָכָא כִּדְלְעֵיל, דְּרַבִּי יוֹסֵי אִיבּוּל אָתָא לְאַשְׁמוּעִינַן, דְּנִשּׂוּאִין אָסוּר כָּל ל' יוֹם — דְּהָא בְּנִשּׂוּאִין כ"ע מוֹדוּ דְּשִׂמְחָה הִיא. וְיִנָּשְׂאוּ דְּקָאָמַר רַבִּי יְהוּדָה — אַגְּרוּשָׁה, דְּלֵיכָּא אִיבּוּל, קָאָמַר. **אִיכָּא בֵּינַיְיהוּ נְשׂוּאָה לֵיאָרֵס.** דְּקָאָמַר רַבִּי יְהוּדָה הַנְּשׂוּאוֹת יִתְאָרְסוּ, דְּלָא גָּזַר אֵירוּסִין אַטּוּ נִשּׂוּאִין. וְאָתָא רַבִּי יוֹסֵי לְמֵימַר: כָּל אֲרוּסוֹת [גְּרוּשׁוֹת] יִנָּשְׂאוּ, הוֹאִיל וְלֵיכָּא אִיבּוּל — שָׁרֵי. וּמִשּׁוּם הַבְחָנָה — לָא מִיתַּסְרָא, דְּהָא לָאו מְעוּבֶּרֶת הִיא. וַאֲרוּסָה אַטּוּ נְשׂוּאָה לָא גָּזְרִינַן. אֲבָל נְשׂוּאוֹת לֹא יִתְאָרְסוּ, דְּאִיכָּא לְמֵיחַשׁ שֶׁמָּא מְעוּבֶּרֶת הִיא, וְאִי שָׁרֵית לָהּ לְהִתְאָרֵס — אָתֵי לְאִינְּסוּבֵי. **כָּל הַנָּשִׁים יִתְאָרְסוּ.** וַאֲפִילּוּ נְשׂוּאוֹת. **וְכוּלָּן.** הַנְּשׂוּאוֹת, בֵּין גְּרוּשָׁה בֵּין אַלְמָנָה — לֹא יִנָּשְׂאוּ, מִשּׁוּם הַבְחָנָה עַד שְׁלֹשָׁה חֳדָשִׁים. **הָכָא נָמֵי.** תְּנִי הָכִי: כָּל אֲרוּסוֹת גְּרוּשׁוֹת יִנָּשְׂאוּ, חוּץ מִן הָאַלְמָנָה אֲפִי' אֲרוּסָה, מִפְּנֵי הָאִיבּוּל. וְכוּלָּן. הַנְּשׂוּאוֹת לֹא יִנָּשְׂאוּ, אֲפִי' גְּרוּשָׁה דְּלֵיכָּא אִיבּוּל, דְּחָיְישִׁינַן לְהַבְחָנָה. **אֶלָּא מִסֵּיפָא** דְּקָתָנֵי וְכוּלָּן לֹא יִנָּשְׂאוּ. דְּעַל כָּרְחָךְ אַנְּשׂוּאוֹת לֹא יִנָּשְׂאוּ קָאֵי, דְּהָא אוֹקְמָא רֵישָׁא אַאֲרוּסוֹת יִנָּשְׂאוּ, וְלָא גָּזְרִינַן מִשּׁוּם הַבְחָנָה דִּנְשׂוּאוֹת. הִלְכָּךְ, סֵיפָא אַנְּשׂוּאוֹת קָאֵי, דְּקָתָנֵי לֹא יִנָּשְׂאוּ, דְּבָעֵינַן הַבְחָנָה. אֲבָל אִיתְרוּסֵי — שַׁפִּיר דָּמֵי, וְלָא גָּזְרִינַן אֵירוּסִין אַטּוּ נִשּׂוּאִין. **תְּרֵיץ וְאֵימָא הָכִי כו'.** דְּוַדַּאי סֵיפָא אַנִּשּׂוּאִין קָאֵי כִּדְקָאָמְרַתְּ, וּמִיהוּ לָא תִּיתְנֵי לֹא יִנָּשְׂאוּ, אֶלָּא לֹא יִתְאָרְסוּ. **וְלֹא מִיטַּמְּאָה.** (ב) כְּלוֹמַר, אֵינָהּ מְלוּוָּה לְהִתְעַסֵּק בּוֹ. **גּוֹבָה כְּתוּבָּתָהּ.** וּכְגוֹן דְּכָתַב לָהּ מִן הָאֵירוּסִין: ה"ג. **אֶלָּא תַּנָּאֵי הִיא.** אֶלָּא לְעוֹלָם כִּדְקָתָנֵי מַתְנִי' כָּל הַנָּשִׁים יִתְאָרְסוּ, וְכִדְפָרְשִׁינַן בְּרֵישׁ שְׁמַעְתִּין דְּאַנְּשׂוּאוֹת קָאֵי. וְאִיבּוּל אִיכָּא בֵּינַיְיהוּ, וְאַשְׁמְעִינַן דְּאֵירוּסִין בִּימֵי אֵבֶל אָסוּר. וּדְקַשְׁיָא לָךְ: קוֹדֶם הַזְּמַן דְּקָתָנֵי וּמְאָרְסִין — תַּנָּאֵי הִיא, דְּאִיכָּא לְמַאן דְּאָסַר. וְהַהִיא דְּקָתָנֵי מְאָרְסִין — לָאו דִּבְרֵי הַכֹּל הִיא, וְלָא סְבִירָא לֵיהּ לְרַבִּי יוֹסֵי. **אֶלָּא אָמַר רַב אַשִׁי.** לָא תּוֹקְמָא כְּתַנָּאֵי, וְרַבִּי יוֹסֵי מוֹדֶה בְּהַהִיא דִּמְאָרְסִין. וּדְקַשְׁיָא לָךְ: ק"ו הוּא — שָׁאנֵי בֵּין אֲבֵילוּת חֲדָשָׁה, *דְּתִשְׁעָה בְּאָב דַּהֲוֵי אֲבֵילוּת יְשָׁנָה וַאֲבֵלוּת דְּרַבִּים, הִלְכָּךְ קִילָּא. **מתני'**

הָיְתָה

ולית ליה לרבי יוסי להבחין לית ליה. ודלופה וחברותיה דנקט לעיל – משום ר"מ. **אי** הכי היינו רבי יהודה. השתא לא בעי למימר דאיכא בינייהו איבול – דלא מסתברא ליה למימר שלא יחוש רבי יהודה באיבול לענין נישואין, כדפי' בקונטר'. אע"ג דלפי המסקנא ליכא איבול בארוסה, מ"מ, למאי דס"ד השתא דאיכא איבול בארוסה – אין סברא לומר שלא יחוש ר' יהודה לענין נישואין. **שאני** בין אבילות חדשה. פי' בקונט': דאבילות דתשעה באב דהוי ישנה, ודרבים – קילא. וקשיא: דאכתי תקשי ק"ו, כדמעיקרא! ומפרש ר"ת: שאני בין אבילות חדשה שאסרו ליארס, לפי שבחדשה יש להחמיר מבישנה, משא"כ באבילות ישנה ובאבילות דרבים יש להחמיר טפי לענין משא ומתן מאבילות דיחיד. דמשא ומתן שהוא דבר של פרהסיא, אם יעסקו בפרקמטיא כל היום – יבאו ויאמרו שאין חוששין להתאבל על ירושלים. ולא דמי לאירוסין שאין אלא שעה אחת, וכדאוקמי' בקודם דקודם. אבל בשבת שחל תשעה באב להיות בתוכה – אסור ליארס, דאי שרי – אכתי איכא ק"ו דכיבוס. ומיהו, במגילת סתרים מתיר ליארס אפילו בט' באב, שלא יקדמנו אחר ברחמים. והביא ראיה מירושלמי. וצ"ל: דבאבילות דרבים יש להחמיר נמי בכיבוס, דכיבוס נמי דבר של פרהסיא, שלא יהו כולם עוסקים לכבס ולספר וליפות עצמם, ונראים שאין חוששין להתאבל כלל. וא"ת: דהכא אסרי' ליארס תוך שלשים. ובפרק בתרא דמו"ק (דף כג. ושם) תני: כל שלשים יום לנישואין, משמע ליארס שרי! וי"ל: דההיא כרבי יהודה דשרי. אי נמי, נשואין נקט, לאשמועינן דאפילו נשואין שרי מיד לאחר שלשים יום. אע"פ שבאשתו קתני דצריך להמתין ג' רגלים. ונראה לר"ת: דאע"ג דאסרינן באביו ובאמו בית השמחה עד י"ב חדש – מ"מ מותר לישא אחר שלשים, משום מצות פריה ורביה. דכל ל' יום לנשואין סתמא קתני, אפילו באביו ובאמו, דלא מפליג אלא באשתו. ואע"ג דקיים פריה ורביה – שרי, דהלכה כר' יהושע דאמר ב"הבא על יבמתו": *ישא אשה בזקנותו, שנאמר "בבקר זרע את זרעך" (קהלת יא). ואם יש לו בנים קטנים – מותר לכנוס אפילו תוך ז'. או שאין לו בנים כלל, או לכל הפחות אחר שבעה כדמשמע בעובדא *דר' יוסף הכהן (מו"ק דף כג.), דבעוד שהיה בבית הקברות אמר לאחותה לכי וגדלי בני אחותך – ומשמע דכנסה לאלתר, מדקתני: אעפ"כ לא בא עליה אלא לזמן מרובה. ומפרש התם דהיינו ל'. ומשמע דלא בא עליה, אבל נשואין – הוו. ור"ח הביא הירושלמי, דקתני: אע"פ שכנסה – לא הכיר בה עד לאחר שלשים. ומעשה באחת משודכת שמת אחיה לאחר הזמנת קרואים סמוך לחופה, והתיר לכונסה תוך שלשים משום פריה ורביה דבעל, מאחר שאם לא ישא את זו – לא ישא אחרת. ושמא אפי' אם לא היתה משודכת היה מתיר, מאחר שחפץ בה יותר מאחרת, כדאשכחן *ברבי יוסף הכהן דמשום פרנסת בניו אשתראי, אע"פ שהיתה אבילה מאחותה. ומיהו, התם לא אפשר באחרת לפי שמרחמת על בני אחותה יותר משאר נשים. והא דאסר במתני' ליארס תוך שלשים, ולא מפליג אפילו רוצה לינשא למי שיש לו בנים קטנים, או למי שאין לו בנים כלל – לפי שצריכה להמתין עדיין לינשא עד שלשה חדשים משום הבחנה. ועוד אומר ר"ת: דמי שאין לו בנים מותר לישא ולבעול תוך ל', דלא מקיימא מצות פריה ורביה אלא בבעילה. אבל תוך ז' ימי אבילות – אסור לכנוס, כדמוכח בריש כתובות (דף ד. ושם) דלא שרי אלא בטבחו טבוח ויינו מזוג, ובמת אביו של חתן או אמה של כלה דוקא. ובשאין לו בנים מיירי התם, מדקאמרינן התם דאביו של חתן קטרח. *ורבי יוסף הכהן אף על פי שדבר עמה בבית הקברות – לא כנס עד אחר שבעה. או שמא משום פרנסת בנים שרי לכנוס אפילו תוך שבעה. וק"ק לפירוש רבינו תם מדתני במסכת שמחות פרק ז' גבי אשתו דצריך להמתין שלש רגלים כשיש לו בנים, אבל אין לו בנים או שיש לו בנים קטנים – מותר לישא אחרת לאחר שלשים יום, ומותר לישא – צריך לומר דלישא ולבעול קאמר, דלכנוס גרידא

אפילו

עין משפט נר מצוה

צז א מיי' פ"י מהלכות אישות הלכה י"ד טור שו"ע א"ח סימן תקנ"א סעיף א:

צח ב מיי' פ"א מהלכות יבום הלכה יא סמג עשין נ טוש"ע אה"ע סימן קסא סעיף א:

צט ג מיי' שם הלכה ט טור ש"ע שם סעיף א:

הגהות הב"ח

(א) גמ' להבחין איבעית אימא לית ליה ואיבעית אימא: (ב) רש"י ד"ה ולא מיטמאה כלומר אינה מלווה. נ"ב עיין לעיל דף כט ע"ב:

מסורת הש"ס

לעיל כט: ב"מ יח. כתו' נג. ע"ש פט: ע"ש סנה' כח: [וע"ש וצ"ע]

תענית כו:

[שם כט:]

[לקמן סב:]

[צ"ל ליוסף הכהן]

[צ"ל כיוסף הכהן]

[צ"ל ויוסף הכהן]

צ"ל לתשעה באב. יעב"

[גמרא]

תורה אור

*[א]הָיְתָה אַחַת כְּשֵׁרָה וְאַחַת פְּסוּלָה, אִם הָיָה חוֹלֵץ — חוֹלֵץ לַפְּסוּלָה, וְאִם הָיָה מְיַיבֵּם — מְיַיבֵּם לַכְּשֵׁרָה.§ **גמ'** אַרְבָּעָה אַחִין ס"ד? אֶלָּא אֵימָא: אַרְבָּעָה מֵאַחִין.§ "הָרְשׁוּת בְּיָדוֹ".§ וְשָׁבְקִי לֵיהּ? וְהַתַנְיָא: *°"וְקָרְאוּ לוֹ זִקְנֵי עִירוֹ" — [ב]הֵן וְלֹא שְׁלוּחָן, "וְדִבְּרוּ אֵלָיו" — מְלַמֵּד שֶׁמַּשִּׂיאִין לוֹ עֵצָה הַהוֹגֶנֶת לוֹ, שֶׁאִם הָיָה הוּא יֶלֶד וְהִיא זְקֵנָה, הוּא זָקֵן וְהִיא יַלְדָּה — אוֹמְרִין לוֹ: מַה לְּךָ אֵצֶל יַלְדָּה, מַה לְּךָ אֵצֶל זְקֵנָה? כְּלַךְ אֵצֶל שֶׁכְּמוֹתְךָ, וְאַל (א) תָּשִׂים קְטָטָה בְּבֵיתְךָ. לָא צְרִיכָא, דְּאֶפְשָׁר לֵיהּ. א"ה, אֲפִילּוּ טוּבָא נַמִי! [ג]עֵצָה טוֹבָה קמ"ל: ד' — אִין, טְפֵי — לָא, כִּי הֵיכִי דְּנִמְטְיֵיהּ עוֹנָה בְּחֹדֶשׁ.§ "מִי שֶׁהָיָה נָשׂוּי וכו'".§ וְנִיַיבֵּם לְתַרְוַיְיהוּ! א"ר חִיָּיא בַּר אַבָּא א"ר יוֹחָנָן: אָמַר קְרָא °"אֲשֶׁר לֹא יִבְנֶה אֶת בֵּית אָחִיו" — [ד]בַּיִת אֶחָד הוּא בּוֹנֶה, וְאֵין בּוֹנֶה שְׁנֵי בָתִּים. וְנַחֲלוֹץ לְתַרְוַיְיהוּ! אָמַר מָר זוּטְרָא בַּר טוֹבִיָּה: אָמַר קְרָא °"בֵּית חֲלוּץ הַנָּעַל" — בַּיִת אֶחָד הוּא חוֹלֵץ, וְאֵין חוֹלֵץ שְׁנֵי בָתִּים. (ב) וְנִיַיבֵּם לַחֲדָא וְנַחֲלוֹץ לַחֲדָא! — אָמַר קְרָא °"אִם לֹא יַחְפּוֹץ" הָא חָפֵץ — יַיבֵּם, *כָּל הָעוֹלָה לְיִבּוּם — עוֹלָה לַחֲלִיצָה, כָּל שֶׁאֵין עוֹלָה לְיִבּוּם — אֵין עוֹלָה לַחֲלִיצָה. וְעוֹד: *שֶׁלֹּא יֹאמְרוּ בַּיִת מִקְצָתוֹ בָּנוּי וּמִקְצָתוֹ חָלוּץ. וְיֹאמְרוּ! אִי דִּמְיַיבֵּם וַהֲדַר חָלֵיץ — הָכִי נַמִי, אֶלָּא [דִּלְמָא] חָלֵיץ וַהֲדַר מְיַיבֵּם, וְקָם לֵיהּ בְּ"לֹא יִבְנֶה". וְאֵימָא: כִּי אִיכָּא חֲדָא — תִּתְקַיֵּים מִצְוַת יִבּוּם, כִּי אִיכָּא תַּרְתֵּי — לֹא תִּתְקַיֵּים מִצְוַת יִבּוּם! א"כ, צָרַת עֶרְוָה דְּאָסַר רַחֲמָנָא לָמָּה לִי? הַשְׁתָּא, ב' בְּעָלְמָא אָמְרַתְּ לָאו בְּנֵי חֲלִיצָה וְיִבּוּם נִינְהוּ, צָרַת עֶרְוָה מִיבַּעְיָא? אַלְמָה לָא? אִצְטְרִיךְ, סד"א עֶרְוָה אַבָּרָאֵי קַיְימָא, וְתִתְיַיבֵּם צָרָתָהּ — קמ"ל דַּאֲסִירָא, אֶלָּא: "יְבִמְתּוֹ... יְבַמְּתוֹ" — רִיבָּה.§ "הָיְתָה אַחַת כְּשֵׁרָה".§ אָמַר רַב יוֹסֵף: *כָּאן שָׁנָה רַבִּי: לֹא יִשְׁפּוֹךְ אָדָם מֵי בוֹרוֹ וַאֲחֵרִים צְרִיכִים לָהֶם.§ **מתני'** הַמַּחֲזִיר גְּרוּשָׁתוֹ, וְהַנּוֹשֵׂא חֲלוּצָתוֹ, וְהַנּוֹשֵׂא קְרוֹבַת חֲלוּצָתוֹ — יוֹצִיא, וְהַוָּלָד מַמְזֵר, דִּבְרֵי ר"ע. וְחכ"א: אֵין הַוָּלָד מַמְזֵר. וּמוֹדִים בְּנוֹשֵׂא קְרוֹבַת גְּרוּשָׁתוֹ, שֶׁהַוָּלָד מַמְזֵר.§ **גמ'** וְסָבַר רַ' עֲקִיבָא הַנּוֹשֵׂא קְרוֹבַת חֲלוּצָתוֹ הַוָּלָד מַמְזֵר? וְהָאָמַר רֵישׁ לָקִישׁ, *כָּאן שָׁנָה רַבִּי: אֲחוֹת גְּרוּשָׁה — מִדִּבְרֵי תוֹרָה, אֲחוֹת חֲלוּצָה — מִדִּבְרֵי סוֹפְרִים! תְּנִי: קְרוֹבַת גְּרוּשָׁתוֹ. הָכִי נַמִי מִסְתַּבְּרָא, דְּקָתָנֵי סֵיפָא: וּמוֹדִים בְּנוֹשֵׂא קְרוֹבַת גְּרוּשָׁתוֹ שֶׁהַוָּלָד מַמְזֵר. אִי אָמְרַתְּ בִּשְׁלָמָא אַיְירֵי בָּהּ — הַיְינוּ דְּקָתָנֵי "וּמוֹדִים", אֶלָּא אִי אָמְרַתְּ לָא אַיְירֵי בָּהּ — מַאי "וּמוֹדִים"? וְדִלְמָא הָא קָא מַשְׁמַע לָן: דְּיֵשׁ מַמְזֵר מֵחַיָּיבֵי כְּרֵיתוֹת. הָא קָתָנֵי לָהּ לְקַמָּן: *אֵיזֶהוּ מַמְזֵר — כָּל שְׁאֵר בָּשָׂר שֶׁהוּא בְּ"לֹא יָבֹא" דִּבְרֵי ר"ע, *ר"ש הַתִּימְנִי אוֹמֵר: כָּל שֶׁחַיָּיבִין עָלָיו כָּרֵת בִּידֵי שָׁמַיִם, וַהֲלָכָה כִּדְבָרָיו. וְדִלְמָא קְסָתֵים לָן תַּנָּא *כְּר"ש הַתִּימְנִי. א"כ לִיתְנֵי שְׁאָר חַיָּיבֵי כְּרֵיתוֹת, קְרוֹבַת גְּרוּשָׁתוֹ לָמָּה לִי? אֶלָּא ש"מ אַיְירֵי בָּהּ. [וְדִלְמָא] לְעוֹלָם לָא אַיְירֵי בָּהּ, וְאַיְּידֵי דְּתָנָא מַחֲזִיר גְּרוּשָׁתוֹ וְנוֹשֵׂא חֲלוּצָתוֹ וּקְרוֹבַת חֲלוּצָתוֹ — תָּנֵי נַמִי קְרוֹבַת גְּרוּשָׁתוֹ. אֶלָּא קְרוֹבַת חֲלוּצָתוֹ לְרַבִּי עֲקִיבָא הָוֵי מַמְזֵר. אָמַר רַ' חִיָּיא בַּר אַבָּא א"ר יוֹחָנָן: הַיְינוּ טַעְמָא דְּר"ע, דְּאָמַר קְרָא "בֵּית חֲלוּץ הַנָּעַל" — הַכָּתוּב קְרָאוֹ בֵּיתוֹ. אָמַר רַב יוֹסֵף אָמַר ר"ש ב"ר: הַכֹּל מוֹדִים בְּמַחֲזִיר גְּרוּשָׁתוֹ שֶׁהַוָּלָד

שכן

[רש"י]

הָיְתָה אַחַת כְּשֵׁרָה. לִכְהוּנָּה, וְאַחַת פְּסוּלָה, כְּגוֹן שֶׁנִּתְגָּרְשָׁה מֵאִישׁ אַחֵר. אִם בָּא יָבָם לַחֲלוֹץ חוֹלֵץ לַפְּסוּלָה. וְלֹא יִפְסוֹל אֶת הַכְּשֵׁרָה לִכְהוּנָּה. דְּלֹא יִשְׁפּוֹךְ אָדָם מֵי בוֹרוֹ וַאֲחֵרִים צְרִיכִים לָהֶם, אע"ג דְּהוּא אֵין צָרִיךְ לָהֶם. **גמ'** אַרְבָּעָה אַחִין ס"ד. כֵּיוָן דְּלָא הֲווּ אֶלָּא ד' וְכוּלָּן מֵתוּ, כִּדְקָתָנֵי מֵתוּ, מַאן מְיַיבֵּם? וְשָׁבְקִינַן לֵיהּ. בִּתְמִיָּה: וּבַמֶּה יְפַרְנֵס כּוּלָּן? דְּאֶפְשָׁר לֵיהּ. שֶׁעָשִׁיר הוּא, וְיָכוֹל לְזוּנָן. עוֹנָה בְּחֹדֶשׁ. עוֹנָה שֶׁל ת"ח מֵעֶרֶב שַׁבָּת לְעֶרֶב שַׁבָּת, וְזֶהוּ "אֲשֶׁר פִּרְיוֹ יִתֵּן בְּעִתּוֹ" בִּכְתוּבּוֹת (דף סב:), דְּמָטֵי לְכָל חֲדָא עוֹנָה בְּחֹדֶשׁ. וְנִיַיבֵּם לַחֲדָא. בְּרֵישָׁא, וַהֲדַר נַחֲלוֹץ לַחֲדָא. כָּל שֶׁאֵינוֹ עוֹלֶה. לְבֵית דִּין לְיִיבּוּם, שֶׁאֵינָהּ זְקוּקָה לְהִתְיַיבֵּם, דְּרַחֲמָנָא פַּטְרַהּ, דִּכְתִיב "אֶת בֵּית אָחִיו" — בַּיִת אֶחָד הוּא בּוֹנֶה, וְלֹא שְׁנֵי בָתִּים — אֵינוֹ עוֹלֶה לַחֲלִיצָה. אַלְמָה לָא. בִּתְמִיָּה, כְּלוֹמַר: וְאִי שְׁתֵּי בָתִּים בְּעָלְמָא פְּטוּרָה — מִי לָא אִיצְטְרִיךְ לְמֵיסַר צָרַת עֶרְוָה? וְהָא אִיצְטְרִיךְ, סד"א עֶרְוָה אַבָּרָאֵי קַיְימָא וְלָא רָמְיָא קַמֵּיהּ, וְהָוְיָא לָהּ צָרַת בַּיִת אֶחָד וְתִתְיַיבֵּם, קמ"ל. כָּאן שָׁנָה רַבִּי. בְּמִשְׁנָה זוֹ לִמְּדָנוּ רַבִּי לֹא יִשְׁפּוֹךְ כו'. **מתני'** הַמַּחֲזִיר גְּרוּשָׁתוֹ. מִשֶּׁנִּישֵּׂאת. וְהַנּוֹשֵׂא אֶת חֲלוּצָתוֹ. דְּקַיְימָא עָלָיו בְּלָאו, דְּשׁוּב לֹא יִבְנֶה. וְהַנּוֹשֵׂא אֶת קְרוֹבַת חֲלוּצָתוֹ. לְקַמָּן בָּעֵי לָן בַּגְּמָרָא: הָא קְרוֹבַת חֲלוּצָתוֹ לָאו דְּאוֹרַיְיתָא הִיא! יוֹצִיא וְהַוָּלָד מַמְזֵר. דְּסָבַר ר"ע: יֵשׁ מַמְזֵר מֵחַיָּיבֵי לָאוִין. קְרוֹבַת גְּרוּשָׁתוֹ. דִּגְרוּשָׁתוֹ כְּאִשְׁתּוֹ, וַאֲחוֹתָהּ אוֹ אִמָּהּ חַיָּיבֵי כְּרֵיתוֹת נִינְהוּ לְגַבֵּיהּ. **גמ'** אֵימָא קְרוֹבַת גְּרוּשָׁתוֹ. וְרַבָּנַן אַמַּחֲזִיר גְּרוּשָׁתוֹ וְנוֹשֵׂא חֲלוּצָתוֹ פְּלִיגֵי. וְדִלְמָא הָא קמ"ל דְּיֵשׁ מַמְזֵר מֵחַיָּיבֵי כְּרֵיתוֹת. וְה"ק: אע"ג דִּפְלִיגֵי רַבָּנַן בְּחַיָּיבֵי לָאוִין, מוֹדִים הֵם בְּחַיָּיבֵי כְּרֵיתוֹת שֶׁהַוָּלָד מַמְזֵר. וְדִלְמָא לְעוֹלָם לָא אַיְירֵי בָּהּ. וּדְקָאָמְרַתְּ לְאַשְׁמוּעִינַן שְׁאָר חַיָּיבֵי כְּרֵיתוֹת. אַיְּידֵי דְּתָנָא רֵישָׁא מַחֲזִיר גְּרוּשָׁתוֹ וְנוֹשֵׂא חֲלוּצָתוֹ וּקְרוֹבַת חֲלוּצָתוֹ. וּפְלִיגֵי רַבָּנַן עֲלֵיהּ, תָּנָא נַמִי וּמוֹדִים בִּקְרוֹבַת גְּרוּשָׁתוֹ. (ג) אֲבָל קְרוֹבַת חֲלוּצָתוֹ — ה"נ דְּלר"ע הָוֵי מַמְזֵר. הַכָּתוּב קְרָאוֹ בֵּיתוֹ. וְלֵית לֵיהּ סְתָמָא דְּמַתְנִי' בְּרֵישׁ פִּרְקִין (מא.) דְּקָתָנֵי: הַחוֹלֵץ לִיבִמְתּוֹ וְנָשָׂא אָחִיו אֶת אֲחוֹתָהּ וּמֵת — חוֹלֶצֶת. דְּלר"ע פְּטוּרָה לְגַמְרֵי.

[תוספות]

אפילו תוך שלשים שרי, כדמוכח בעובדא *דר' יוסף, דמשמע אע"פ שאין לו בנים כלל – אין מותר לבעול עד לאחר שלשים. ושמא מילתא דפסיקא לתרווייהו נקט, ולעולם באין לו בנים שרי אפילו תוך שלשים. ולר"י נראה: באין לו בנים כלל – אסור אפילו לכנוס תוך שלשים, כיון דאינו יכול לבעול עד לאחר שלשים. ואתי שפיר דנקט במס' שמחות לישא, משום דאין לו בנים נקטיה, דאפילו לישא אסור, והר"ר יוסף אומר, דהא דאסרינן בית השמחה – היינו דוקא שמחה של רשות, דאמרינן במסכת שמחות (פ"ט): על כל המתים אסור לילך לבית השמחה עד שלשים יום, ועל אביו ועל אמו שנים עשר חדש, אא"כ היתה סעודה של מצוה. דאפשר דלא שרי בסעודה של מצוה אלא אחר שלשים, וקאי אאביו ואמו. אך קצת משמע דשרי אפילו תוך שלשים.

ונייבם לחדא ונחלוץ לחדא אמר קרא "אם לא יחפוץ כו'". אית ספרים (ד) דגרסי מקמי הכי: ונחלוץ לחדא ונייבם לחדא, אמר קרא "אשר לא יבנה" – כיון שלא בנה שוב לא יבנה. ונראה דל"ג. (ה) דלא צריך קרא להכי, דכיון דחליץ לחדא – א"א לייבם שניה, כיון דאין עולה לחליצה, כדאמר לעיל דאינו חולץ שני בתים. [ועוד, דאינו חולץ שני בתים] משמע דהשניה מותרת לשוק בולא כלום. וקרא ד"לא יבנה" אייתר לכדדרשינן פ"ק (לעיל דף י. ושם) לנתק החלוצה מכרת ללאו. **כל** שאינו עולה כו'. וא"ת: והרי חרש וחרשת, דאינן עולים לחליצה ועולים לייבום כדאמר בפרק "חרש" (לקמן דף קיב:)! ויש לומר: דהתם בני חליצה נינהו, אלא דפומייהו הוא דכאיב להו. **ועוד.** לא גרסינן: ועוד גזרה שמא יאמרו בית מקצתו כו', דאי מדאורייתא מייבם לחדא וחליץ לחדא – משום גזרה לא ינית. **כי** איכא תרתי לא תתקיים מצות ייבום. תימה: דא"כ למה לי קרא דאין חולץ לשני בתים? **אלמה** לא איצטריך סד"א ערוה אבראי קיימא. הקשה הר"ר יו"ט בר' יצחק: אכתי צרת צרה היכי משכחת לה? שהרי צרת ערוה אינה יכולה לינשא לאחיו השני, דאסורה לו מדאורייתא, דגבי דידיה ערוה לאו אבראי קיימא! וי"ל: דמשכחת לה כגון שהערוה היא מחייבי עשה או ל"ת ועשה לכל האחין, דלאו בת יבום היא, וצרתה שריא(א). **ודלמא** קסתים לן תנא כשמעון התימני. תימה: דסתם ואח"כ מחלוקת היא. דכהאי גוונא פריך בפרק "יש נוחלין" (ב"ב דף קכב:): וכי תאמר סתם לן תנא כרבי יוחנן בן ברוקא – סתם ואח"כ מחלוקת היא! וי"ל: דנהי דאין חשיב סתם, מ"מ חשיב כרבים לגבי יחיד, כדפרישית לעיל*. ובפ' "יש נוחלין" סמיך אקושיא אחריתי, דקאמר: ועוד מאי אלא. **אם** כן לשמעינן שאר חייבי כריתות. אכתי ה"מ למיפרך תנינא, דסתם לן תנא כוותיה בקדושין בפרק "האומר" (דף סו:): כל מקום שאין קדושין כו' ואיזה זה – הבא על אחת מכל העריות. **הכל** מודים במחזיר גרושתו. לרבותא נקט מחזיר גרושתו טפי משאר חייבי לאוין, דאף על גב דכתיב "היא" "תועבה" ואין בניה תועבין – פגום מיהא הוי.

[עין משפט נר מצוה]

נ"ל דיוסף

ק א מיי' פ"א מהלכות יבום הלכה י סמג עשין נ טור ש"ע אה"ע סי' קסא סעיף ב:

קא ב מיי' פ"ד שם הלכה א סמג עשין נב טוש"ע שם סימן קסו סעיף א:

קב ג מיי' פי"ד מהלכות איסורי ביאה הלכה א סמג עשין מה ולאוין פא טור ש"ע שם סימן טו סעיף ז:

קג ד מיי' פ"א מהלכות יבום הלכה ט:

תוספות ישנים

כי איכא תרתי לא תתקיים מצות יבום. וא"ת איך אפשר לומר כן הלא אמרינן בית אחד הוא בונה ואינו בונה שני בתים אם כן הרי מצינו יבום אף בשני בתים שמייבם האחת וי"ל דנימא הכא בית אחד הוא בונה פירוש כי ליכא אלא בית א' אז הוא בונה אבל אינו בונה כלל בשיש שני בתים: א) [ועוד י"ל] כגון שגירש הערוה ולמ"ד נשואין הראשונים מפילין דאסורה לשמעון ומותרת ללוי: **אלא** אי אמרת לא איירי בה מאי ומודים. ואע"ג דבפרק האשה שנפלו (דף ע"ח) קאמר ומודים אף על גב דלא איירי בה שאני הכא כיון דלא אשמעינן שום חדוש לא הו"ל למתני ומודים הואיל ולא איירי בה אבל התם אשמעינן חדוש: **בית** חלוץ הנעל הכתוב קראו ביתו. וא"כ לא סבר כמו ההיא דלעיל (דף מ"א) דמגיה המשנה דאימא אבל המגרש ושפיר גרסינן במתני' וכן וניתני בכלהו באחות חלוצה ובאחות גרושתו (פסולה) דהרי זו פטורה: **הכתוב** קראו ביתו. וא"כ לרבי עקיבא אם בא עליה כהן חייב מן התורה וגם נפקא לן מואשה לרבות חלוצה והא א) דקאמרינן באלו הן הלוקין וקחשיב גרושה וחלוצה לכהן הדיוט היינו כר"ע דלרבנן לא לקי אחלוצה דקרא ב) דהא דכתיב ואשה לא הוי אלא אסמכתא בעלמא אי נמי שפיר אתיא אליבא דרבנן ואגב גרושה נקט חלוצה א"נ בחלוצה נפרש דלוקין ר"ל מדרבנן מכת מרדות: **הכל** מודים במחזיר גרושתו. ל"ע אמאי נקט מחזיר גרושתו טפי מאינך חייבי לאוין נראה משום דס"ד דאין הולד פגום משום דכתיב היא תועבה דמשמע ואין בניה תועבין קמ"ל דהולד פגום ונימא דהיא תועבה אבל אין צרתה

א) והא דקחשיב בר"פ אלו הן הלוקין גרושה וחלוצה כו'. כצ"ל:

ב) נראה דצ"ל והא דילפינן מואשה לרבות חלוצה לא הוי אלא כו':

[מסורת הש"ס]

לעיל יח.

לקמן קח:

דברים כה

שם

שם

שם

[לעיל כ. וש"נ]

[לעיל לח:]

לעיל יח: [יב. לקמן נג.]

לעיל מ: וש"נ

לקמן מט. וש"נ

נ"ל שמעון התימני]

נ"ל כשמעון התימני]

[קדושין סז. ב"ב קכג:]

הגהות הב"ח

(א) גמ' ואל תכניס קטטה בביתך: (ב) שם ואין חולץ שני בתים ונחלוץ לחדא ונייבם לחדא אמר קרא אשר לא יבנה כיון שלא בנה שוב לא יבנה ונייבם לחדא ונחלוץ לחדא: (ג) רש"י ד"ה איידי דתנא וכו' בקרובת גרושתו הס"ד ואח"כ מ"ה אלא קרובת חלוצתו: (ד) תוס' ד"ה ונייבם וכו' אית ספרים. נ"ב ע"ל דף י ע"ב בתוס' ... איתו: (ה) בא"ד דל"ג ... ליה דלא צריך:

שֶׁהַוָּלָד פָּגוּם לִכְהוּנָּה. מַאן "הַכֹּל מוֹדִים" — שִׁמְעוֹן הַתִּימְנִי. דְּאע"ג דְּאָמַר שִׁמְעוֹן הַתִּימְנִי: אֵין מַמְזֵר מֵחַיָּיבֵי לָאוִין — נְהִי דְּמַמְזֵר לָא הָוֵי, פָּגוּם — מִיהָא הָוֵי, מִק"ו מֵאַלְמָנָה. *וּמָה אַלְמָנָה לְכ"ג, שֶׁאֵין אִיסּוּרָהּ שָׁוֶה בַּכֹּל — בְּנָהּ פָּגוּם, זוֹ שֶׁאִיסּוּרָהּ שָׁוֶה בַּכֹּל — אֵינוֹ דִּין שֶׁבְּנָהּ פָּגוּם? אִיכָּא לְמִיפְרַךְ: מַה לְאַלְמָנָה — שֶׁכֵּן הִיא עַצְמָהּ מִתְחַלֶּלֶת, וְעוֹד: *"הִיא תוֹעֵבָה" כְּתִיב, וְאֵין בָּנֶיהָ תּוֹעֲבִין. וְעוֹד, תַּנְיָא: הַמַּחֲזִיר גְּרוּשָׁתוֹ, וְהַנּוֹשֵׂא חֲלוּצָתוֹ, וְהַנּוֹשֵׂא קְרוֹבַת חֲלוּצָתוֹ. ר"ע אוֹמֵר: אֵין לוֹ בָּהּ קִדּוּשִׁין, וְאֵינָהּ צְרִיכָה הֵימֶנּוּ גֵּט, וְהִיא פְּסוּלָה וּוְלָדָהּ פָּסוּל, [א]וְכוֹפִין אוֹתוֹ לְהוֹצִיא. וְחכ"א: יֵשׁ לוֹ בָּהּ קִדּוּשִׁין, וּצְרִיכָה הֵימֶנּוּ גֵּט, וְהִיא כְּשֵׁרָה וּוְלָדָהּ כָּשֵׁר. לְמַאן — לָאו לִכְהוּנָּה? לָא, לַקָּהָל. אִי הָכִי, הִיא כְּשֵׁרָה — לְמַאן? אִילֵימָא לַקָּהָל — פְּשִׁיטָא, מִשּׁוּם דִּזְנַיָא אִפַּסְלָה לַקָּהָל? אֶלָּא לָאו — לִכְהוּנָּה, וּמִדְּהִיא לִכְהוּנָּה — וְלָדָהּ נַמִי לִכְהוּנָּה. מִידֵּי אִירְיָא? הָא כִּדְאִיתָא וְהָא כִּדְאִיתָא. הָכִי נַמִי מִסְתַּבְּרָא, דְּקָתָנֵי רֵישָׁא: הִיא פְּסוּלָה וּוְלָדָהּ פָּסוּל. הִיא פְּסוּלָה לְמַאן? אִילֵימָא לַקָּהָל — מִשּׁוּם דִּזְנַיָא אִפַּסְלָה *לֵיהּ לַקָּהָל? אֶלָּא לָאו — לִכְהוּנָּה, וּוְלָדָהּ פָּסוּל, לְמַאן? אִילֵימָא לִכְהוּנָּה — הָא לַקָּהָל כָּשֵׁר? הָאָמַר רַבִּי עֲקִיבָא הַוָּלָד מַמְזֵר! אֶלָּא פְּשִׁיטָא — לַקָּהָל, וּמִדְּרֵישָׁא הָא כִּדְאִיתָא וְהָא כִּדְאִיתָא — סֵיפָא נַמִי הָא כִּדְאִיתָא וְהָא כִּדְאִיתָא. וְ"הִיא תוֹעֵבָה" נַמִי, הִיא תוֹעֵבָה — וְאֵין צָרָתָהּ תּוֹעֵבָה, אֲבָל בָּנֶיהָ — תּוֹעֲבִין. אֶלָּא אַלְמָנָה קַשְׁיָא: מַה לְאַלְמָנָה שֶׁכֵּן הִיא עַצְמָהּ מִתְחַלֶּלֶת! אֶלָּא אִי אִתְּמַר הָכִי אִתְּמַר: אָמַר רַב יוֹסֵף אָמַר רַ' שִׁמְעוֹן בְּרַבִּי: הַכֹּל מוֹדִים בְּבָא עַל חַיָּיבֵי כְּרֵיתוֹת שֶׁהַוָּלָד פָּגוּם. מַאן "הַכֹּל מוֹדִים" — רַבִּי יְהוֹשֻׁעַ, דְּאע"ג דְּאָמַר רַ' יְהוֹשֻׁעַ אֵין מַמְזֵר מֵחַיָּיבֵי כְּרֵיתוֹת, *נְהִי דְּמַמְזֵר לָא הָוֵי — פָּגוּם מִיהָא הָוֵי, מִק"ו מֵאַלְמָנָה. וּמָה אַלְמָנָה לְכ"ג, שֶׁאֵין אִיסּוּרָהּ שָׁוֶה בַּכֹּל — בְּנָהּ פָּגוּם, זוֹ שֶׁאִיסּוּרָהּ שָׁוֶה בַּכֹּל — אֵינוֹ דִּין שֶׁבְּנָהּ פָּגוּם. וְכ"ת: מַה לְאַלְמָנָה שֶׁכֵּן הִיא עַצְמָהּ מִתְחַלֶּלֶת — הָכָא נַמִי, כֵּיוָן שֶׁבְּעָלָהּ — עֲשָׂאָהּ זוֹנָה. אָמַר רַבָּה בַּר בַּר חָנָה א"ר יוֹחָנָן: הַכֹּל מוֹדִים בְּעֶבֶד וְגוֹי הַבָּא עַל בַּת יִשְׂרָאֵל שֶׁהַוָּלָד מַמְזֵר. מַאן "הַכֹּל מוֹדִים" שִׁמְעוֹן הַתִּימְנִי. דְּאע"ג דְּאָמַר *שִׁמְעוֹן הַתִּימְנִי אֵין מַמְזֵר מֵחַיָּיבֵי לָאוִין — ה"מ מֵחַיָּיבֵי

שֶׁהַוָּלָד פָּגוּם. וְאִם יָלְדָה בַּת – פְּסוּלָה לִכְהוּנָּה כַּחֲלָלָה. שֶׁכֵּן הִיא עַצְמָהּ מִתְחַלֶּלֶת. שֶׁאִם מֵת כֹּהֵן גָּדוֹל – אֲסוּרָה אֲפִילּוּ לְכֹהֵן הֶדְיוֹט, שֶׁפְּסָלָהּ זֶה בְּבִיאָתוֹ וַעֲשָׂאָהּ חֲלָלָה, דִּכְתִיב "לֹא יְחַלֵּל זַרְעוֹ" (ויקרא כא) וְלָא כְּתִיב "וְלֹא יָחֵל". וּמַשְׁמַע: ב' חִילּוּלִים, אֶחָד לָהּ וְאֶחָד לְזַרְעוֹ, וְהָכִי מְפָרֵשׁ בְּקִדּוּשִׁין (דף עז.). אוֹ אִם בַּת כֹּהֵן הִיא פְּסָלָהּ מִן הַתְּרוּמָה, כִּדְאָמַר בִּמְכִילְתִּין לְקַמָּן (דף סח.): תֹּאמַר בְּמַחֲזִיר גְּרוּשָׁתוֹ שֶׁאֵין הִיא עַצְמָהּ מִתְחַלֶּלֶת. דְּאִי לְמִפְסְלָהּ לְכֹהֵן לָא מִפַּסְלָה בְּהַאי חֲזָרָה, דְּהָא פְּסוּלָה וְקָיְימָא מִשְּׁעַת גֵּירוּשִׁין, וְאִי לִתְרוּמָה – לָא מִתַּסְרָא בְּהָכִי, כִּדְאָמַר בְּפֶרֶק "אַלְמָנָה לְכֹהֵן גָּדוֹל" (לקמן דף סט.): הַמַּחֲזִיר גְּרוּשָׁתוֹ. מִשֶּׁנִּשֵּׂאת. אֵין לוֹ בָּהּ קִדּוּשִׁין. דְּקָסָבַר ר"ע אֵין קִדּוּשִׁין תּוֹפְסִין בְּחַיָּיבֵי לָאוִין. וְהִיא פְּסוּלָה. לְכֹהֵן, דְּזוֹנָה הִיא. וּוְלָדָהּ פָּסוּל. מַמְזֵר הוּא. לְמַאן. קָתָנֵי וְלָדָהּ כָּשֵׁר, לָאו לִכְהוּנָּה? הָא כִּדְאִיתָא וְהָא כִּדְאִיתָא. הִיא כְּשֵׁרָה לִכְהוּנָּה, וְלָדָהּ כָּשֵׁר לָבֹא בַּקָּהָל, אֲבָל לִכְהוּנָּה פָּגוּם. ה"נ מִסְתַּבְּרָא. דְּהָא כִּדְאִיתָא וְהָא כִּדְאִיתָא: וְהִיא תוֹעֵבָה. דְּקָא פָּרְכַתְּ הִיא תּוֹעֵבָה וְאֵין בָּנֶיהָ תּוֹעֲבִין — לָא תֵּידוֹק הָכִי, אֶלָּא: הִיא תּוֹעֵבָה וְאֵין צָרָתָהּ תּוֹעֵבָה, לֵיאָסֵר לְיִיבּוּם, אֶלָּא מִתְיַיבֶּמֶת. ר' יְהוֹשֻׁעַ. דְּאָמַר בְּמַתְנִיתִין (לקמן דף מט.): אֵין מַמְזֵר אֶלָּא מֵחַיָּיבֵי מִיתוֹת. עֲשָׂאָהּ זוֹנָה. וּפְסָלָהּ לִכְהוּנָּה. אֲבָל לְעֵיל, גַּבֵּי מַחֲזִיר גְּרוּשָׁתוֹ, לֵיכָּא לְשַׁנּוּיֵי הָכִי, דְּאָמַר בְּפֶרֶק אַלְמָנָה לְכ"ג לְקַמָּן (דף סט.): וְאֵימָא נִבְעֲלָה לְפָסוּל לָהּ מַחֲזִיר גְּרוּשָׁתוֹ? וּמְשַׁנֵּי: זָר אֶלָּלָה מֵעִיקָּרָא בָּעֵינַן.

חַיָּיבֵי

שכן היא עצמה מתחללת. ליכא למימר דהיא נמי מתחלל מק"ו, דהא אמר בקדושין (דף עז:) דאין חללה אלא מאיסורי כהונה. ולעיל בפ"ק (דף טו: ד"ה "מה") פירשתי. **היא** כשרה. לכהונה איירי, כדמסיק היינו לתרומה, דלכהן אסירא דגרושה היא. וא"ת: לרבי עקיבא, אמאי מיפסלה לתרומה? הא לאו זר אללה מעיקרא הוא! דלקמן בפרק "אלמנה" (דף סט. ושם) פריך: ואימא נבעלה לפסול לה מחזיר גרושתו, ומשני: זר אללה מעיקרא בעינן! וי"ל: דסוגיא דהתם אליבא דרבנן, אבל ר"ע לא בעי זר אללה מעיקרא, כדאמר בפ' "עשרה יוחסין" (קדושין עה:): השתא ממזר הוי, מיפסיל בביאתו מיבעיא? וקצת תימה לר"י: דמאי דריש ר"ע מ"היא תועבה"? דלא דריש ואין בניה תועבין — דהא ממזר הוי, ולא מצי למדרש נמי ואין צרתה תועבה — דלא שייך בה צרתה, דאין קדושין תופסין בחייבי לאוין אליבא דר"ע). **הכא** נמי כיון דבא עליה עשאה זונה. משמע הכא דזונה פסולה לתרומה, דמתחללת כמו אלמנה. וכן בפ"ק דסוטה (א) (דף ו.) אמתני' דואלו אסורות לאכול בתרומה דקאמר: אילימא מקמי דתשתי — זונה היא, ופשיטא דאסורה בתרומה ב). ותימה לר"י: מנא לן דאסורה בתרומה? ד"אשה זונה לא יקחו" כתיב, אבל לתרומה לא אשכחן! ועוד: לקמן בפ' "אלמנה" (דף סח:) דפריך: ואימא נבעלה לפסול לה — חייבי כריתות, ולמה לי קרא ד"כי תהיה לאיש זר" לחייבי כריתות? כיון דבחייבי כריתות הויא זונה, וזונה אסורה בתרומה! והיה נראה לר"י ד"מכי תהיה לאיש זר" הוא דנפקא לן דזונה אסורה בתרומה. וכל חייבי כריתות, אפילו אותה דע"י קדושין דלא הוי זר אללה מעיקרא, וכן חייבי לאוין לר"ע, ואפי' מחזיר גרושתו, דלא הוי זר אללה מעיקרא, כדמשמע לעיל דמיפסלה לר"ע מתרומה — הוי בכלל "לאיש זר", כדאמרינן ב"עשרה יוחסין" (קדושין עה. ושם): השתא ממזר הוי, מפסיל בביאתו מיבעיא? ואפילו לרבי יהושע דלא הוי ממזר, כיון דחמירי (ג) דזרים אללה חשיבי. והא דבעינן בפרק "אלמנה" (לקמן דף סט. ושם) זר אללה מעיקרא — היינו דוקא בחייבי לאוין, ולרבנן, ולא ממעטו מ"כי תהיה" דמשמע הנך דאית בהו הויה חייבי כריתות דחמירי, אלא דוקא (ג) גוי ועבד. ולהכי איצטריך קרא ד"אלמנה וגרושה" — מי שיש לו אלמנות וגרושין, לאתויי גוי ועבד. ולרבי עקיבא דמגוי ועבד הוי ממזר, ונפיק מ"לאיש זר" — דריש "אלמנה וגרושה" לקמן (דף סט.) לדרשה אחריתי. ומכל הנהו דלא תפסו בהו קדושין הויא זונה, כדאמר בפרק "כל האסורין" (תמורה דף כט: ושם): מה עריות דלא תפסי בהו קדושין והויא זונה כו', דלשון זונה משמע שא"א להיות בה אלא ביאת זנות — לא לאו דמלקות. ואין להקשות: למה לי דכתב רחמנא "זונה לא יקחו" כיון דזונה אסורה בתרומה — ק"ו דאסורה לכהונה, מגרושה דשריא בתרומה ואסורה לכהן? דמהאי ק"ו נפקא לן (לקמן דף סח:) דגר עמוני ומואבי פסלי לכהונה, אע"ג דאין מזהירין מן הדין — קאמר התם דגילוי מילתא בעלמא הוא! דאיצטריך לאו דזונה דלקי תרתי. ועוד איצטריך לזונה מגוי ועבד לרבנן דר"ע, דליכא בה *לאו בתרומה מ"לאיש זר" אלא מ"אלמנה וגרושה", דמאלמנה וגרושה נפקא. אי נמי: משום גיורת ומשוחררת איצטריך לאו דזונה. ואפילו לאביי דאמר בפ' "כל האסורין" (תמורה כט:) דכהן הבא על הזונה גויה אינו לוקה משום זונה, אם נתגיירה — מודה דלקי, דהוי זרעו מיוחס אחריו. ועוד: דמטעם שנעשה זונה ואסרה רחמנא משום זונה — הוא דהוי חייבי כריתות בכלל "לאיש זר", כדמשמע הכא ובכל דוכתי, דשם זונה גורם לה ליפסל. ומיהו מגוי ועבד, אע"ג דהויא זונה, דהא לא תפסי בה קדושין מינייהו — לא הוי בכלל "לאיש זר", אלא דוקא חייבי כריתות דחמירי. וקצת קשה: דבפרק "עשרה יוחסין" (קדושין דף עה: ושם) דפריך: השתא ממזר הוי, מפסיל בביאתו מיבעיא? משמע, היכא דהוי ממזר פשיטא דהוי בכלל "לאיש זר" אפילו לא הויא זונה. ומיהו, לרבי יהושע דלא הוי ממזר מחייבי כריתות, ושם זונה גרם לה דהויא בכלל "לאיש זר". וזהו דוחק, דבכל דוכתין משמע דשם זונה גורם לה ליפסל מתרומה אתי כר' יהושע. ולעיל בסוף פ' "ד' אחין" (דף לה. ד"ה "אע"פ") הביא ר"י דכל הנך דע"י קדושין, כיון דלא הוי זר אללה מעיקרא — לא הוי בכלל "לאיש זר", וזונה דפסולה לתרומה — משום דכללה קרא בהדי חללה, להכי פסולה כחללה. ולפי זה צריך ליישב הא דפריך בפ' "אלמנה" (לקמן דף סח:) ואימא נבעלה לפסול לה — חייבי כריתות. **עשאה** זונה. משמע דלר' יהושע אין קדושין תופסין בחייבי כריתות, דבתפיסת קדושין תלוי שם זנות, כדמשמע בפרק "כל האסורין" (שם), וכן בס"פ "ר"ג" (לקמן נג. ושם) איצטריך לאשמועינן דאין קדושין תופסין בחייבי כריתות, משמע דליכא מאן דפליג. והא דמשמע בסמוך דממזרות תלוי בתפיסות קדושין, וכן לקמן (דף מה:) דקאמר: מה אשת [אב] דלא תפסי קדושין והולד ממזר, משמע דכל היכא דלא תפסי קדושין — הוי ולד ממזר. היינו לשמעון התימני ולר"ע, משום דגלי לן קרא שיש ממזר מחייבי כריתות, כדילפינן בסוף פירקין (דף מט.). וגלי לן נמי דלא תפסי בהו קדושין, כדאמרינן בס"פ "האומר" (קדושין סח. ושם), משום הכי אית לן למימר דהא בהא תליא. אבל לר' יהושע, אע"ג דאין קדושין תופסין בחייבי כריתות — לא הוי ממזר, כדיליף ר' יהושע בסוף פירקין דאין ממזר אלא מחייבי מיתות ב"ד. ולהכי בסמוך, דקאמר: הכל מודים שמעון התימני, לא קאמר: הכל מודים ר' יהושע — אע"ג דאמר ר' יהושע אין ממזר מחייבי כריתות ה"מ כו', דלרבי יהושע אין קדושין תופסין בחייבי כריתות אף על גב דאין הולד ממזר. אבל קצת קשה, דבפ"ק דתמורה (דף ה: ושם) פריך: לרבא דאמר כל היכא דאמר רחמנא לא תעביד אי עביד לא מהני — והרי אלמנה לכהן גדול, דרחמנא אמר "לא יקח" ותנן: כל מקום שיש קדושין ויש עבירה, כגון אלמנה לכהן גדול כו'!

ומשני

קד א מיי' פי"א מהל' גירושין הלכה יב סמג לאוין פב:

תוספות ישנים

תועבה: **היא** פסולה וולדה פסול נראה היא פסולה לתרומה אע"ג דבעינן זר אללה מעיקרא כיון דר' עקיבא אומר אין קדושין תופסין בחייבי לאוין אמרינן כיון שבעלה עשאה זונה אע"ג דבעינן זר אללה מעיקרא כיון שאין קדושין תופסין א"כ הוי כמו חייבי כריתות וחייבי כריתות הוי כמו זר אללה מעיקרא אבל י"מ היא פסולה לכהן ולא נהירא דהא מקודם לכן איפסילא ליה משום גרושה וי"ל דר"ל לכהונה וקאי אקרובי חלוצתו וכן פר"ח: **היא** כשרה. פר"ח ז"ל דלא קאי אמחזיר גרושתו דנהי נמי דולדה כשר משום דכתיב היא תועבה ואין בניה תועבין מ"מ איהי אפסלה מתרומה דבי נשא וכירושלמי מפרש כן ולא עת עתה להאריך: **א)** ושמעתי מתרלים כי רבי עקיבא מפיק מקרא דהיא תועבה למימר ואין צרת סוטה תועבה ובהא שפיר איצטריך דליכא למימר דלא שייך בה צרה דהא מקודם שסטתה היתה זאת צרתה כי קדושי הסוטה היו טובים בתחלה וא"ת ולמה לי קרא דכי תהיה אלמנה וגרושה דגוי ועבד פסלי אשה בביאתן הא ידעת ליה שפיר מלאיש זר אליבא דר"ע דס"ל דאין קדושין תופסין וכיון דאין קדושין תופסין הולד ממזר והשתא ממזר הוי מפסיל בביאתו מבעיא דהא גוי ועבד חייבי לאוין נינהו וזר מעיקרא נינהו וי"ל דס"ד דהואיל ולא תפסי בה קדושי כלל דלא הוי בכלל אשה בביאתן ולהכי איצטריך קרא דוקא כהן כי תהיה אלמנה וגרושה: **ב)** גם בפרק כשם משמע כן דקאמר תרומה נמי עשה בה ספק זונה כשרה לכהונה וקשה ומנלן דזונה פסולה לתרומה [illegible]

כריתות דיש מביאתו ממזר וגם לר' יהושע דאמר אין ממזר מחייבי כריתות מ"מ שמעינן דפסלה לתרומה מכ"ש דחייבי לאוין דפסלי לה לקמן: **מאן** הכל מודים שמעון התימני. וא"ת אמאי לא קאמר מאן הכל מודים דר' יהושע דאמר ר' יהושע אין ממזר מחייבי כריתות ה"מ חייבי כריתות דתפסי בהו קדושי אבל גוי ועבד לא וי"ל דפשיטא דר' יהושע סבר דאין קדושין תופסין בחייבי כריתות ואע"ג דסבר דאין ממזר מהם מ"מ לא תפסי בהו קדושי ס"ל הא תליא בהא וכן משמע בריש מכילתין ט"ו נשים פוטרות צרותיהן מחליצה ומיבום וקחשיב חייבי כריתות ואי קדושין תופסין בהן לר' יהושע א"כ בני חלילה נינהו כמו חייבי לאוין לרבנן דאמרי חולצות ולא מתייבמות קדושה וכאיך חייבי לאוין ואין סברא לומר דפליג רבי יהושע על מתני' דלעיל דהא אמרינן לעיל דבפלוגתא לא קא מיירי ועוד דאמרינן בפרק ארבע מיתות חייבי כריתות מי איכא למ"ד דתפסי בהו קדושי משמע דליכא מאן דפליג וגם משמע כן מהא דאמרינן בכל דוכתא אין קדושין תופסין באחותו והיא חייבי כריתות וליכא מאן דפליג וא"כ משמע דר' יהושע לא סבר הא תליא בהא וקשה דאמרינן פ"ק דתמורה גבי כל מלתא דאמר רחמנא לא תעביד אי עביד לא מהני ופריך מאלמנה לכה"ג ומשני שאני התם דאמר קרא לא יקח [ולא יחלל] חללין הוא עושה ממזרים אינו עושה ולהכי תפסי בהו קדושין משמע דהא תליא בהא וגם הכא קאמר תלמודא לר"ש התימני הא תליא בהא

א) לאו משום הכי לא שמעינן.

דקאמר

לעיל טו: לקמן סה. נדה סט:

לעיל יא: וש"נ

הגהות הב"ח

(א) תוס' ד"ה הכא וכו' בפ"ק דסוטה. נ"ב דף ו ועי"ש בפרש"י דכתוב זונה היא ופשיטא דאסור בתרומה דהא תנן ליה האומרת טמאה אני: (ב) בא"ד כיון דחמירי כזרים אללה מעיקרא חשיבי וכו' ולא ממעטי מכי תהיה לאיש זר בתרומת הקדשים להם לכך למשמע הנך דאית להו הויה כמו: (ג) בא"ד אלא דוקא וגוי ועבד) תא"מ וג"כ ס"ה חייבי לאוין:

נ"ל לה. יעב"ץ

[לעיל טו:]

[הכונה לקמן מט.]

דלא ילפינן מלאיש זר אלא מאלמנה וגרושה א"נ וכו' כל"ל רש"ל

מחייבי לאוין דתפסי בהו קידושין, אבל הכא — גוי ועבד, כיון דלא תפסי בהו קידושין — כחייבי כריתות דמי. מיתיבי: *גוי ועבד הבא על בת ישראל — הולד ממזר, רבי שמעון בן יהודה אומר: אין ממזר אלא ממי שאיסורו איסור ערוה, וענוש כרת. אלא אמר רב יוסף: מאן "הכל מודים" — רבי. אף על גב דרבי אומר: *אין הדברים הללו אמורים אלא לדברי ר"ע, שהיה עושה חלוצה כערוה, וליה לא סבירא ליה — בגוי ועבד מודה. *דכי אתא רב דימי אמר רב יצחק בר אבודימי משום רבינו: גוי ועבד הבא על בת ישראל — הולד ממזר. רבי אחא שר הבירה ור' תנחום בריה דרבי חייא איש כפר עכו פרוק הנהו שבויתא דאתו מארמון לטבריא. הוה חדא דאעברא מגוי, ואתו לקמיה דר' אמי. אמר להו: ר' יוחנן ור' אלעזר ור' חנינא דאמרי, גוי ועבד הבא על בת ישראל הולד ממזר. אמר רב יוסף: *רבותא למחשב גברי?! הא רב ושמואל בבבל, ורבי יהושע בן לוי ובר קפרא בארץ ישראל, ואמרי לה: חלופי בר קפרא ועיילי זקני דרום, דאמרי: *גוי ועבד הבא על בת ישראל — הולד כשר. אלא אמר רב יוסף: רבי היא. *דכי אתא רב דימי אמר רבי יצחק בר אבודימי משום רבינו אמרו: גוי ועבד הבא על בת ישראל — הולד ממזר. רבי יהושע בן לוי אומר: הולד מקולקל. למאן? אילימא לקהל — הא אמר רבי יהושע הולד כשר, אלא לכהונה — דכולהו אמוראי דמכשרי מודו שהולד פגום לכהונה *מק"ו מאלמנה: מה אלמנה לכהן גדול, שאין איסורה שוה בכל — בנה פגום, זו שאיסורה שוה בכל — אינו דין שבנה פגום. מה לאלמנה לכהן גדול שכן היא עצמה מתחללת! הכא נמי, כיון שנבעלה פסלה. *דאמר רבי יוחנן משום רבי (א) שמעון: מנין לגוי ועבד הבא על הכהנת ועל הלויה ועל הישראלית שפסלוה — שנאמר "ובת כהן כי תהיה אלמנה וגרושה" (ויקרא כב), מי שיש לו אלמנות וגירושין בה, יצאו גוי ועבד שאין להם אלמנות וגירושין בה. אמר ליה אביי: מאי חזית דסמכת אדרב דימי? סמוך אדרבין! דכי אתא רבין אמר: רבי נתן ורבי יהודה הנשיא מורים בה להיתירא, ומאן *רבי יהודה הנשיא — רבי ואף רב מורה בה היתירא, דההוא דאתא לקמיה דרב, אמר ליה: גוי ועבד הבא על בת ישראל מהו? אמר לו: הולד כשר. אמר ליה: הב לי ברתך! לא יהיבנא לך. אמר שימי בר חייא לרב: אמרי אינשי: גמלא במדי אקבא רקדא, הא קבא והא גמלא והא מדי — ולא רקדא! א"ל: אי (ג) נ(י)הוי כיהושע בן נון לא יהיבנא ליה ברתי. א"ל: אי הוה כיהושע בן נון, אי מר לא יהיב ליה — אחריני יהבי ליה. האי, אי מר לא יהיב ליה — אחריני לא יהבי ליה. לא הוה קאזיל מקמיה, יהיב ביה עיניה ושכיב. ואף רב מתנה מורה בה להיתירא, ואף רב יהודה מורה בה להיתירא. דכי אתא לקמיה דרב יהודה א"ל: זיל איטמר, או נסיב בת מינך. וכי אתא לקמיה דרבא א"ל: *או גלי, או נסיב בת מינך. שלחו ליה בני בי מיכסי לרבה: מי שחציו עבד וחציו בן חורין הבא על בת ישראל מהו? א"ל: השתא עבד כולו אמרי' כשר — חציו מיבעיא? אמר רב יוסף: מרא דשמעתא מנו

רש"י

חייבי לאוין דתפסי בהו קידושין. דנפקא לן בפרק "כילד" (לעיל דף כג.) מ"כי תהיין לאיש שתי נשים" וגו', ועבד וגוי לאו בני קידושין נינהו, דכתיב (בראשית כב) "שבו לכם פה עם החמור" — עם הדומה לחמור. וגוי נמי ליתיה בכלל קידושין, דכתיב (דברים ז) בז' אומות "לא תתחתן בם" — לא יהא לך בהן חיתון. ובשאר אומות כתיב (שם כא) "ואחר כן תבא" — מכלל דמעיקרא לית בה הויה. ומהני קראי נפקא לן בקדושין (דף סח:) דלא תפסי קידושין בגויה, וגוי נמי מהי למילף מינייהו. הלכך, אין ביאתו ביאה לשם קידושין, ודמיא לחייבי כריתות. ובשאלתות דרב אחאי* מפיק מהא "והיא בעולת בעל" (בראשית כ) ודרשינן בסנהדרין (דף מז:): בעולת בעל יש להם, נכנסה לחופה ולא נבעלה — אין להם, וכל שכן דארוסה לית להו. וביאה לשם קידושין נמי לית להו, דאיתקוש הויות להדדי*. אין ממזר וכו'. והא האי תנא כשמעון התימני סבירא ליה, וקתני בגוי ועבד דאין ממזר. אף על גב דקאמר רבי. בפרק ר"ג אין ביאה אחר חליצה, דאם חלץ לזו ובעל את זו — אינה צריכה הימנו גט. וקאמר: אין הדברים הללו אמורים, דביאה אחר חליצה לא תפסה, אלא לדברי ר"ע כו', אבל לדידיה לא סבירא ליה, אפילו הכי, בגוי ועבד — מודים. דכי אתא רב דימי כו' משום רבינו. רבי. שבוייתא מן ארמון. לאנטוכי. אלא אמר רב יוסף רבי היא. לא תחשוב גברי. דהאי משום רבותא דרבים לא תפסיל ליה, דהא נמי רבים אכשרי, אלא משום ההיא דר' איכא למיפסליה, דהלכה כמותו. והאמר רבי יהושע בן לוי. לעיל, הולד כשר. זו שאיסורה שוה בכל. גוי אסור בין בכהנת בין בלויה בין בישראלית. שבנה פגום. בנה פגום לאו דוקא, דהא פשיטא בן הגויה לאו כהן הוא. ואי משום דלא ישא כהנת, כיון דמותר בישראלית — מותר נמי בכהנת, שאין קדושה בנשים, דאפילו כשרות מותרות לפסולים, דקיימא לן (קדושין דף עג.): לא הוזהרו כשרות מלינשא לפסולים. אלא משום בתה נקט, דאם תלד בת — פסולה לכהונה. פסלה. אפי' מתרומה דבי נשא, וכ"ש מלהנשא לכהן. שפסלוה. כהנת מתרומת אביה, ולויה וישראלית כגון שנישאו לכהן וילדו לו בנים, וכשמתו בעליהן היו אוכלות בתרומה בשביל בניהם. ואם בא עליה גוי ועבד — פסלה מתרומה, וכ"ש מכהונה. מי שיש לו אלמנות וגירושין בה. כגונא] ישראלית, הוא דכי מת וזרע אין לה — "ושבה אל בית אביה" וגו' (ויקרא כב). יצאו גוי ועבד שאין לו אלמנות וגירושין בה. שאין קידושין תופסין. א"ל אביי. לרב יוסף. מאי חזית דסמכת אדרב דימי. דאמר משמיה דרבי הולד ממזר, סמוך אדרבין דמכשרי ליה משמיה דרבי. דההוא דאתא. בן גוי מישראלית. אמרי אינשי גמלא במדי אקבא רקדא. גמל גדול מרקד בתוך קב קטן בד' רגליו במלכות מדי, וגוזמא. הא קבא והא גמלא והא מדי. יבא וירקד לפנינו. כלומר: אתה שהתרת דבר חידוש — האמת דבריך ותן לו בתך. לא הוה אזיל מקמיה. אותו בן הגוי דקא א"ל הב לי ברתך. זיל איטמר. לך במקום שלא יכירוך, ושא בת ישראל. שאילו יכירוך — לא יתנוה לך. אלמא לא ממזר הוא, מדאכשר ליה בת ישראל, שהרי ממזר מוזהר על הכשרה. בת מינך. בת ישראל מן הגוי, הכשרה כמותך. אבל ממזרת ושפחה — לא תשא, אלמא כשר הוא. גלי. לך לגלות במקום שלא יכירוך, ויתנו לך בת ישראל כשרה. בני בי מיכסי. מקום. מרא דשמעתא. דאמר: גוי ועבד הבא על בת ישראל — בנו כשר. מנו

תוספות

ומשני: שאני התם דאמר רחמנא: "לא יחלל" — חילולים הוא עושה, ואין עושה ממזרים. פי': וכיון דלא הוי ממזר — תפסו בה קידושין. א"כ לרבי יהושע לא תפסי קידושין באלמנה אליבא דרבא, דלרבי יהושע ליכא לאוקומי מידי דתפסי בה קידושין מדלא הוי ממזרת! ואם תאמר: בקדושין ב"האומר" (דף סח: ושם) אמאי דוחק למצוא שאר עריות דלא תפסי בהו קדושין מנלן, כיון דכבר אשכחן דלא תפסי באשת אב קדושין? דמהשתא תיפוק לן כל עריות דהוי מינייהו ממזר(ג)! וי"ל: דממזרים גופייהו לא שמעינן בכל חייבי כריתות כל כמה דלא מייתי היקישא דרבי יונה. דמ"לא יקח" "ולא יגלה" דמייתי בסוף פירקין (לקמן דף מט.) דכתיבי באשת אב ובשומרת יבם של אביו — לא שמעינן ממזרות בשאר עריות, כגון אשת איש שיש לה היתר בחיי אוסרה, ואחות אשה וכל דכוותייהו. אבל בסוף, דמייתי היקישא — איכא למילף בעלמא, כדפרשי'.

יצאו גוי ועבד שאין לו אלמנות וגירושין בה. וא"ת: והא רבי יוחנן אית ליה לעיל דגוי ועבד הבא על בת ישראל הולד ממזר, אם כן למה לי קרא? דהשתא ממזר הוי, מפסיל בביאתו מיבעיא? וי"ל: הא דידיה והא דרביה. ועוד: דאמוראי נינהו, ואליבא דרבי יוחנן, כדאמרינן ספ"ק (לעיל טז:). ושם פירשתי אמאי הוי ממזר מגוי, כיון דביאת היתר היא מדאורייתא*. **זיל** איטמר. וישאוך מיוחסת. וא"ת: והא בעי ראיה, כדאמר בפ"ב בכתובות (דף כד: ושם) דמעלין מתרומה ליוחסין! ויש לומר: דהתם להשיא בתו לכהן העובד על גבי המזבח, כמו שמוכיח שם רבינו תם. א"נ: התם כר"מ, אבל חכמים אומרי' כל משפחות בחזקת כשרות הם עומדות, בפרק "עשרה יוחסין" (קדושין דף עז:). משום

עין משפט נר מצוה

קה א מיי' פ"ד מהלכות אישות הל' טו סמג עשין מח טוש"ע אה"ע סימן מד סעיף ח:

קו ב טוש"ע אה"ע סי' ד סעי' ה וסעיף יט:

קז ג מיי' פי"ח מהלכות איסורי ביאה הלכה ג טוש"ע אה"ע סימן ו סעיף ח:

תוספות ישנים

דקאמר אבל גוי ועבד דלא תפסי בהו קדושי הולד ממזר וצ"ל דלר"ש התימני וגם לר' עקיבא הא תליא בהא אבל לרבי יהושע לא אמרינן הא תליא בהא וכן מפורש בקדושין: **מיתיבי** גוי ועבד וכו' ר' [שמעון בן] יהודה אמר אין ממזר אלא ממי שאיסורו איסור ערוה וענוש (מיתה) [כרת] א) וכמו האי קאמר ר' שמעון התימני דאין ממזר אלא מחייבי מיתות וכו' וכמו דהך דר"ל דאין ממזר אלא מחייבי כריתות סבר דגוי ועבד הבא וכו' הולד כשר דהכי משמע דפליג את"ק דלעיל מיניה כמו כן יש לנו לומר לרבי שמעון התימני: **זיל** גלי או נסיב בת מינך. וא"ת ומה מועיל לו זה הא אמרינן כשאומר אני כהן אינו נאמן להשיאו אשה וע"ק התם אמאי אינו נאמן להשיאו אשה הא אמרינן כל המשפחות בחזקת כשרות הן עומדות וי"ל דהתם מיירי להשיאו אשה מיוחסת מד' אמהות וזה אינו כן דזה לא מצי להיות בנו כהן דחיישינן ליה משום חללות ובתו פסולה מספק היא דשמא חלל הוא ובת חלל פסולה לכהונה. עי"מ דהתם מיירי בדנפק עליה קלא דבן גרושה ולהכי אמרי' דאינו נאמן להשיאו אשה ולהכי קאמר זיל איטמר דלא ליפוק עליה קלא ודוחק וז"ל מורי לעולם נימא דהא דקאמר אינו נאמן להשיאו אשה ר"ל אף ישראלית אף להנשא בתו לישראל ומיירי בדנפק עליה קלא דממזרות וא"כ נוכל לומר

א) נראה דל"ל וכמו האי דקאמר שמעון התימני דאין ממזר אלא במי שחייבין עליו כרת בידי שמים וכו'

תוספות חד מקמאי

ואם נשא כהן בת עבד ועובד כוכבים הבא על בת ישראל מוציאין אותה מידו אבל בנו ינשא לכהונה לכתחלה שלא החזרו כשרות לינשא לפסולין לכהונה וחציו עבד וחציו בן חורין שבא על בת ישראל הולד פגום לכהונה שהיא עצמה מתחללת ואע"פ שיש אלמנות וגירושין בה מצד החירות אין לה אלמנות וגירושין מצד

גליון הש"ס

גמ' ה"נ כיון שנבעלה פסלה. עיין לקמן עז ע"א תד"ה רבי יוחנן אמר כשרה: **שם** דאמר רבי יוחנן משום ר"ש מנין לגוי וכו'. לקמן סח ע"ב ובסוטה דף כו ע"ב ובקדושין דף עה ע"ב איתא משום רבי ישמעאל:

מסורת הש"ס

[לעיל עז: לקמן נט. קדושין ע.] — [פ' וישלח סימן כה] — לקמן נב: — [לקמן ע.] — [עי' היטב לקמן סח: ברש"י ד"ה עבד] — [כ"ב לו:] — [לעיל כג. קדושין עח:] — [לקמן ע. ע"ש] — [לעיל טו: מד: נדה סט:] — [לקמן סח: סוטה כו: קדושין עה:] — [שבת לב: קדושין סג.]

הגהות מהר"ב רנשבורג

רש"י ד"ה מי שיש לו כגון ישראלית הוא כו' ישראלית נמחק וצ"ב ישראל:

תוס' לקמן מז. ד"ה ... ותוס' פסחים ג: ד"ה ואנא]

הגהות הב"ח

(א) גמ' דאמר ר' יוחנן משום ר' שמעון. נ"ב עיין לקמן סח ע"ב דמשמע דהתוספות דגרסי' ר' ישמעאל ע"ש ד"ה ... (ב) שם ולא ... א"ל אי הוי כיהושע: (ג) תוס' ד"ה עשאה וכו' דהוי מינייהו ממזר לא ... בהו קדושין וי"ל דממזרים:

תורה אור

מַנּוּ — רַב יְהוּדָה וְהָא אָמַר רַב יְהוּדָה: [א]מִי שֶׁחֶצְיוֹ עֶבֶד וְחֶצְיוֹ בֶּן חוֹרִין הַבָּא עַל בַּת יִשְׂרָאֵל — אוֹתוֹ וָלָד אֵין לוֹ תַּקָּנָה. כִּי אִיתְּמַר דְּרַב יְהוּדָה כְּגוֹן דְּקַדֵּישׁ בַּת יִשְׂרָאֵל, דְּנִמְצָא צַד עַבְדוּת שֶׁבּוֹ מִשְׁתַּמֵּשׁ בְּאֵשֶׁת אִישׁ. וְהָאָמְרִי נְהַרְדְּעֵי מִשְּׁמֵיהּ דְּרַבִּי יַעֲקֹב: לְדִבְרֵי הַפּוֹסֵל — פּוֹסֵל אֲפִילּוּ בִּפְנוּיָה, לְדִבְרֵי הַמַּכְשִׁיר — מַכְשִׁיר אֲפִי' בְּאֵשֶׁת אִישׁ. וּשְׁנֵיהֶם לֹא לָמְדוּהָ אֶלָּא מֵאֵשֶׁת אָב — מַאן דְּפָסֵיל סָבַר: מָה אֵשֶׁת אָב דְּלָא תָּפְסֵי בָּהּ קִדּוּשִׁין [הַוָּלָד מַמְזֵר] — אַף כָּל דְּלָא תָּפְסֵי בָּהּ קִדּוּשִׁין הַוָּלָד מַמְזֵר. וּמַאן דְּמַכְשַׁר סָבַר: מָה אֵשֶׁת אָב, דִּלְדִידֵיהּ לָא תָּפְסֵי בָּהּ קִדּוּשִׁין לַאֲחֵרִינֵי תָּפְסֵי בָּהּ קִדּוּשִׁין — לְאַפּוֹקֵי גּוֹי וְעֶבֶד דְּלָא תָּפְסֵי בְּהוּ קִדּוּשִׁין כְּלָל. אֶלָּא, כִּי אִיתְּמַר דְּרַב יְהוּדָה — [ב]כְּגוֹן שֶׁבָּא עַל אֵשֶׁת אִישׁ וְנִמְצָא צַד חֵירוּת שֶׁבּוֹ מִשְׁתַּמֵּשׁ בְּאֵשֶׁת אִישׁ. אֲמַר רָבִינָא אֲמַר לִי רַב גְּזָא: אִיקְלַע רַ' יוֹסֵי בַּר אָבִין לְאַתְרִין, וַהֲוָה עוּבְדָא בִּפְנוּיָה — וְאַכְשַׁר, בְּאֵשֶׁת אִישׁ — וּפְסִיל. א"ר שֵׁשֶׁת: לְדִידִי אֲמַר לִי רַב גְּזָא: לָא רַ' יוֹסֵי בַּר אָבִין הֲוָה, אֶלָּא רַבִּי יוֹסֵי בְּרַבִּי זְבִידָא הֲוָה, וְאַכְשַׁר בֵּין בִּפְנוּיָה בֵּין בְּאֵשֶׁת אִישׁ. א"ל רַב אַחָא בְּרֵיהּ *דְּרַבָּה לְרָבִינָא: אִיקְלַע אֲמֵימַר לְאַתְרִין. וְאַכְשַׁר בֵּין בִּפְנוּיָה בֵּין בְּאֵשֶׁת אִישׁ. [ג]וְהִלְכְתָא: גּוֹי וְעֶבֶד הַבָּא עַל בַּת יִשְׂרָאֵל — הַוָּלָד כָּשֵׁר, בֵּין בִּפְנוּיָה בֵּין בְּאֵשֶׁת אִישׁ. *רָבָא אַכְשְׁרֵיהּ לְרַב מָרִי בַּר רָחֵל וּמַנְיֵיהּ בְּפוּרְסֵי דְּבָבֶל. וְאע"ג *דְּאָמַר מָר °"שׂוֹם תָּשִׂים עָלֶיךָ מֶלֶךְ", (א) [ד]כָּל מְשִׂימוֹת שֶׁאַתָּה מֵשִׂים אַל יְהוּ אֶלָּא מִקֶּרֶב אַחֶיךָ, הַאי כֵּיוָן דְּאִמּוֹ מִיִּשְׂרָאֵל — "מִקֶּרֶב אַחֶיךָ" קָרֵינַן בֵּיהּ. עַבְדֵּיהּ דְּרַבִּי חִיָּיא בַּר אַמִּי אַטְבְּלָהּ לְהַהִיא גּוֹיָה לְשֵׁם אִנְתְּתָא. אֲמַר רַב יוֹסֵף: יָכֵילְנָא לְאַכְשׁוּרֵי בָּהּ וּבִבְרַתָּהּ. בָּהּ — כִּדְרַב אַסִּי, דַּאֲמַר רַב אַסִּי: מִי לֹא טָבְלָה לְנִדּוּתָהּ? בִּבְרַתָּהּ — גּוֹי וְעֶבֶד הַבָּא עַל בַּת יִשְׂרָאֵל הַוָּלָד כָּשֵׁר. הַהוּא דְּהָווּ קָרוּ לֵיהּ בַּר אֲרַמַיְיתָא. אֲמַר רַב אַסִּי: [ה]מִי לֹא טָבְלָה לְנִדּוּתָהּ? הַהוּא דְּהָווּ קָרוּ לֵיהּ בַּר אַרְמָאָה, אֲמַר ריב"ל: [ו]מִי לָא טָבַל לְקִרְיוֹ? אֲמַר רַב חָמָא בַּר גּוּרְיָא אָמַר רַב: [ז]הַלּוֹקֵחַ עֶבֶד מִן הַגּוֹי, וְקָדַם וְטָבַל לְשֵׁם בֶּן חוֹרִין — קָנָה עַצְמוֹ בֶּן חוֹרִין. מַאי טַעְמָא?

גּוֹי

דברים יז

רש"י

מַנּוּ רַב יְהוּדָה. כִּדְאָמַר, וְאַף רַב יְהוּדָה מוֹרֶה בָּהּ לְהֶיתֵּירָא. וְהָאָמַר רַב יְהוּדָה. גַּבֵּי חֶצְיוֹ עֶבֶד הַבָּא עַל בַּת יִשְׂרָאֵל. הַוָּלָד אֵין לוֹ תַּקָּנָה. בְּבַת יִשְׂרָאֵל, כְּלוֹמַר: מַמְזֵר הוּא. כִּי אִיתְּמַר. הַהִיא דְּאֵין לוֹ תַּקָּנָה. כְּגוֹן דְּקַדֵּישׁ. מִי שֶׁחֶצְיוֹ עֶבֶד וְחֶצְיוֹ בֶּן חוֹרִין אֶת בַּת יִשְׂרָאֵל, וְאַחַר כָּךְ בָּא עָלֶיהָ. דְּכֵיוָן דְּקִדְּשָׁהּ הָוְיָא מְקוּדֶּשֶׁת לְצַד חֵירוּת, אֲבָל לֹא לְצַד עַבְדוּת, וְנִמְצָא צַד עֶבֶד שֶׁבּוֹ מִשְׁתַּמֵּשׁ בְּא"א, וּלְפִיכָךְ הַוָּלָד מַמְזֵר. דְּכָל הָנֵי דְּמַכְשְׁרִי — בִּפְנוּיָה מַכְשְׁרִי, אֲבָל בְּאֵשֶׁת אִישׁ — אֲפִילּוּ בְּיִשְׂרָאֵל הַוָּלָד מַמְזֵר, וְכ"ש גּוֹי וְעֶבֶד. אֲבָל הֵיכָא דְּבָא עָלֶיהָ בְּלֹא קִדּוּשִׁין — כָּשֵׁר: ה"ג: דְּנִמְצָא צַד עַבְדוּת שֶׁבּוֹ מִשְׁתַּמֵּשׁ בְּאֵשֶׁת אִישׁ. לְדִבְרֵי הַמַּכְשִׁיר. בְּעֶבֶד הַבָּא עַל בַּת יִשְׂרָאֵל, מַכְשִׁיר אֲפִי' בְּא"א. וְטַעְמָא מְפָרֵשׁ וְאָזֵיל. אֶלָּא מֵאֵשֶׁת אָב. דְּמַמְזֵרוּת לְגַבָּהּ כְּתִיב, דִּכְתִיב "לֹא יִקַּח אִישׁ אֶת אֵשֶׁת אָבִיו" וּסְמִיךְ לֵיהּ "לֹא יָבֹא מַמְזֵר" (דברים כג). כְּגוֹן שֶׁבָּא עַל אֵשֶׁת אִישׁ. וּמִשּׁוּם הָכִי הַוָּלָד אֵין לוֹ תַּקָּנָה בְּבַת יִשְׂרָאֵל, דְּנִמְצָא צַד חֵירוּת שֶׁל עֶבֶד, כְּשֶׁבָּא עָלֶיהָ, מִשְׁתַּמֵּשׁ בְּאֵשֶׁת אִישׁ. וְאע"ג דְּאִי כּוּלּוֹ עֶבֶד הַוָּלָד כָּשֵׁר, כִּדְאָמַרַן לְדִבְרֵי הַמַּכְשִׁיר מַכְשִׁיר אֲפִי' בְּא"א — הָכָא מַמְזֵר מִשּׁוּם צַד חֵירוּת דְּהָוֵי כִּשְׁאָר יִשְׂרָאֵל הַבָּא עַל אֵשֶׁת אִישׁ, דְּהַוָּלָד מַמְזֵר: רַב גְּזָא גָּרְסִי'. הֲוָה עוּבְדָא. בְּעֶבֶד גָּמוּר. בֵּין בְּאֵשֶׁת אִישׁ. כִּדְאָמַרַן, שֶׁאֵין עוֹשֶׂה מַמְזֵר אֶלָּא מִי שֶׁיֵּשׁ לוֹ קִדּוּשִׁין עַל אֲחֵרִים. רַב מָרִי בַּר רָחֵל. מִגּוֹי הַבָּא עַל יִשְׂרְאֵלִית הֲוָה. בְּפוּרְסֵי דְּבָבֶל. גַּבָּאִים מְמוּנִּים עַל יִשְׂרָאֵל. וְאע"ג דְּגֵר בְּעָלְמָא אָסוּר לְמַנּוֹתוֹ פַּרְנָס עַל יִשְׂרָאֵל, דְּאָמַר מָר כו', הַאי, כֵּיוָן דְּאִמּוֹ מִיִּשְׂרָאֵל — "מִקֶּרֶב אַחֶיךָ" קָרֵינַן בֵּיהּ. אַטְבְּלָהּ לְשֵׁם אִנְתְּתָא. לְשֵׁם טְבִילַת נִדָּה, וְלֹא לְשֵׁם טְבִילַת גֵּירוּת. יָכֵילְנָא לְאַכְשׁוּרֵי בָּהּ. לִהְיוֹת גִּיוֹרֶת גְּמוּרָה, וְאע"פ שֶׁלֹּא טָבְלָה לְשֵׁם גֵּירוּת. וְאָמַר לְקַמָּן (דף מו:): לְעוֹלָם אֵינוֹ גֵּר עַד שֶׁיָּמוֹל וְיִטְבּוֹל. דִּטְבִילַת נִדָּה סָלְקָא לָהּ לְשֵׁם גֵּירוּת, דְּגוֹיָה לֹא טָבְלָה לְנִדּוּתָהּ. וּבִבְרַתָּהּ. וְאע"ג דְּבַת עֶבֶד הַבָּא עַל בַּת יִשְׂרָאֵל הִיא, דְּהָא נִתְגַּיְּירָה זוֹ, וּכְבַת יִשְׂרָאֵל הִיא — אפ"ה כְּשֵׁרָה בִּתָּהּ. בָּהּ כִּדְרַב אַסִּי. דְּאָמַר בִּשְׁמַעְתִּין: הַהוּא דַּהֲווּ קָרוּ לֵיהּ בַּר אֲרַמַּיְיתָא, שֶׁלֹּא טָבְלָה אִמּוֹ לְשֵׁם גֵּירוּת, וַאֲמַר רַב אַסִּי: מִי לָא טָבְלָה לְנִדּוּתָהּ? אַלְמָא: טְבִילַת נִדָּה סָלְקָא לָהּ לְשֵׁם גֵּירוּת. ל"א: לְשֵׁם אִנְתְּתָא — לְשֵׁם אִישּׁוּת. וּטְבִילַת גֵּירוּת הֲוָה, אֶלָּא שֶׁאֵינָהּ טְבִילָה, דְּאָמַר בְּ"הַבָּא" (לעיל דף כד:) אֶחָד אִישׁ שֶׁנִּתְגַּיֵּיר לְשׁוּם אִשָּׁה וְאֶחָד אִשָּׁה שֶׁנִּתְגַּיְּירָה לְשׁוּם אִישׁ — אֵינָן גֵּרִים. יָכֵילְנָא לְאַכְשׁוּרֵי בָּהּ ע"י טְבִילוֹת אֲחֵרוֹת שֶׁטָּבְלָה אח"כ לְנִדּוּתָהּ. כָּךְ שָׁמַעְתִּי, וְקַשְׁיָא לִי: חֲדָא, דְּקָבָעֵינַן הִלְכְתָא הָתָם הֲלָכָה כּוּלָּן גֵּרִים. וַאֲפִי' לְמִשְׁנָה רִאשׁוֹנָה נַמִי, אִי קַמַּיְיתָא לָא סָלְקָא לָהּ — בַּתְרָא נַמִי לָא סָלְקָא לָהּ, דְּלָאו לְשֵׁם שָׁמַיִם נִתְגַּיְּירָה. וְלָשׁוֹן רִאשׁוֹן עִיקָּר, וְנִרְאֶה בְּעֵינַי. בַּר אֲרַמַּיְיתָא. שֶׁלֹּא טָבְלָה אִמּוֹ כְּשֶׁנִּתְגַּיְּירָה. מִי לֹא טָבְלָה לְנִדּוּתָהּ. וְאוֹתָהּ טְבִילָה עוֹלָה לָהּ לִטְבִילַת גֵּירוּת, דְּדַת יְהוּדִית הִיא. וְכֵן מִי לָא טָבַל לְקִרְיוֹ.

גּוֹי

תוספות

משום דאתי צד עבדות ומשתמש באשת איש. והא דמשמע בפ"ק דקדושין (דף ז. ושם) דהתקדשי לחציי לא אמר כלום, אי לאו משום דלאי(ב) בעינן למינסב אחריתי נסיבנא קאמר – היינו משום דשייר בקניינו, כדאמר ב"השולח" (גיטין דף מג. ושם) והכא לא שייר. **מה** אשת אב כו'. וא"ת: מה לאשת אב שכן כרת ומיתה! ויש לומר! דממזרות תלוי בתפיסת קדושין, כדפרישית לעיל. **רבא** אכשריה לרב מרי בר רחל. רבא גרסי' ולא רב, דרב מרי בריה דאיסור גיורא הוה, שהיה בימי רבא, כדמוכח בפ' "מי שמת" (ג) (ב"ב קמט. ושם*). **פורסי** דבבל. ממונה, כדאמר בפ"ק דיומא (דף ט.): מאי פרהדרין – פורסי. **כיון** דאמו מישראל מקרב אחיך קרינן ביה. מכאן קשה לפי' הקונטרס: דפירש "באלו נאמרין" (סוטה דף מא. ושם) גבי אגריפס המלך, שאמרו לו אחינו אתה, וקאמר בגמרא דבאותה שעה נתחייבו שונאיהם של ישראל כלייה, שהחניפו לאגריפס, ופי' בקונטרס: שקראוהו אחינו לפי שהיתה אמו מישראל, ולפירושו אמאי נענשו? הא אמרינן הכא כיון דאמו מישראל "מקרב אחיך" קרינן ביה! ואע"ג דתניא בתוספתא (דסנהדרין פ"ד) דאין מעמידין מלך אלא מן המשיאים לכהונה – מ"מ תימה הוא לומר דמשום איסורא דרבנן נתחייבו כלייה! ואומר רבינו שמואל: דהורדוס לא נשא בת ישראל, שעשה תשובה, כדאמרינן בפ"ק דב"ב (דף ד.), ולכך נענשו. ואע"פ שהיה עבד קראוהו אחינו, לפי שהיה אחיהם במצות. ואתי שפיר הא דאמר שמואל בפ' "עשרה יוחסין" (קדושין ע:): כל דאמר מבית חשמונאי קאתינא – עבדא הוא, ושמואל גופיה אית ליה (לעיל עמוד א) דגוי ועבד הבא על בת ישראל הולד כשר. אלא ודאי לא נשא ישראלית. וא"ת: מ"מ אמאי עבדא הוא? והלא מסתמא כשמלך הורדוס נתייאשו בעליו, ושמואל אית ליה (לקמן דף מח.): המפקיר עבדו יצא לחירות, ואין צריך גט שחרור! וי"ל: דשמא היו מלפים שתהא גאותו מושפלת. וא"ת: דהכא משמע דגר שאין אמו מישראל אין כשר לדון, ובפ' "אחד דיני ממונות" (סנהדרין דף לו: ושם) תנן: הכל כשרים לדון, ופריך: תנינא! [ומשני]: חדא לאתויי גר, וחדא לאתויי ממזר. משמע דגר, אע"פ שאין אמו מישראל, אלא שנתגייר בעצמו – דכשר לדון, דקרינן ליה בא מטיפה פסולה דקאמר התם, אבל גר מטיפה פסולה לא! וי"ל: דהתם מיירי לדון גר חברו, כדאמר בפ' "מצות חליצה" (לקמן דף קב. ושם): גר דן את חברו דבר תורה, ואם היתה אמו מישראל – דן אפילו ישראל. וא"ת בפ' "עשרה יוחסין" (קדושין עו:) אמרינן: מי שהוחזקו אבותיו משוטרי הרבים, למימרא דלא מוקמינן פסולים, ורמינהו: הכל כשרים לדון כו', ואמר רב יהודה: לאתויי ממזר. ומאי קושיא? דהתם היינו לדון את חברו! וי"ל: דממזר, כיון דאביו ואמו מישראל – "מקרב אחיך" קרינן ביה. תדע, דהא דרשינן "עליך" הוא דבעינן מקרב אחיך, וחברו ממזר מיקרי שפיר עליך, שבא מזרע ישראל, ואי מיפסל ממזר לדון את ישראל – מיפסל נמי לחברו, ובפרק "אחד דיני ממונות" (סנהדרין דף לו:) דקעביד צריכותא בין גר לממזר, אע"פ שגר וממזר חלוקין, דגר אינו דן אלא חברו – מ"מ נקט צריכותא, לפי שהמשנה שנויה סתם, ואין חילוק זה מפורש בהא. **אטבלה** להההיא גויה לשום אנתתא. שהיה רוצה לייחדה לו, והיה מטבילה כדרך כל בנות ישראל שטובלות משנתבעות לינשא. וטועה היה, דבעבד לא גזרו נשג"ז, כדאמרינן בנדה] (דף כ). **מי** לא טבלה לנדותה. תימה: דאמר לקמן (דף מו:) דגר צריך שלשה, דמשפט כתיב ביה. ואפילו למאן דאמר בריש סנהדרין (דף ג.) דבר תורה חד נמי כשר – מכל מקום אין דרך נשים להביא איש עמהן בשעת טבילה, ואשה אינה ראויה לדון, כדתנן (נדה דף מט:): כל הכשר לדון כשר להעיד. וההיא איתא בירושלמי דיומא: מעתה שאין אשה מעידה אינה דנה. ודבורה לא היתה דנה, אלא מלמדת להן שידונו. אי נמי על פי הדיבור שאני! וי"ל: האי דבעינן שלשה – היינו לקבלת המצות, אבל לא לטבילה. ג) אף על גב דאמרינן לקמן (דף מז:) דשני ת"ח עומדים מבחוץ – היינו לכתחלה, דעדיף טפי. *ויש מפרשים: דכיון דידוע לַכֹּל שטבלה – כאילו עומדים שם דמי. ומיהו קשיא: דטבילת נדה בלילה, ולקמן (דף מו:) אמר: אין מטבילין גר בלילה! אבל אי לאו כתיב משפט אלא אקבלת מצוה – אתי שפיר והא דאין מטבילין – היינו לכתחלה, מדרבנן.

הקדש

לעיל ולא נוכרית דהא מסקינן הלכה כולם גרים וא"כ הטבילה לשם אישות מהניא ואם לא מהניא משום דלא נתכוונה לשם יהודות כלל א"כ מה אהנו הטבילות של נדות שטבלה אחרי כן אחרי שלא נתכוונה לשם יהודות [ולכן נראה עיקר] כפי' קמא: ב) ונ"ל דהכי מיירי כשקבלה כבר המצות והודיעוה מצות קלות וחמורות דאל"ה לא סגי בטבילת נדותן:

עין משפט נר מצוה

קח א ב מיי' פט"ו מהל' איסורי ביאה הלכה ה סמג לאוין קיז טוש"ע אה"ע סי' ד סעי' יז:

קט ג מיי' שם ה"ג טוש"ע שם סעיף ה וסעיף יט:

קי ד מיי' פ"א מהלכות מלכים הלכה ד:

קיא ה ו מיי' פי"ג מהל' איסורי ביאה הלכה ט סמג לאוין קטז קיז טוש"ע יו"ד סימן רסח סעיף ג:

[וע"ע שבת קנד. ובתוס' שם ובתוס' ב"מ עג: ד"ה רב מרין]

קיב ז מיי' שם ה"א ופ"ח מהל' עבדים הי"ט סמג שם טוש"ע שם סי' רכז סעיף ע:

תוספות ישנים

[illegible]

מסורת הש"ס

דרבא. יעב"ץ

[שבת קנד. ע"ש]

קדושין עו:

[וע"ע תוס' קדושין סב: ד"ה גר]

הגהות הב"ח

(א) גמ' תשים עליך מלך מקרב אחיך כל משימות: (ב) תוס' ד"ה משום וכו' לאי בעינא: (ג) ד"ה רבא וכו' בפרק מי שמת כ"ב ע"ש בתוספו' קמט ע"א ובפ' א"נ עג רע"ב במה שפי' רש"י ועיין עוד בתוס' פרק מי שהחשיך קנד ע"א:

הגהות מהר"ב רנשבורג

[illegible]

תוספות חד מקמאי

עבודות: עבדיה דר' חייא בר אמי אטבלה להההיא גויה לשום אנתתא אמר רב יוסף יכילנא לאכשורי בה ובברתה בה כדרב אסי דאמר רב [אסי] מי לא טבלה לנדותה פירוש עבדיה דר' חייא גיירה לההיא גויה וקבלה עליה מקצת מצות קלות ומקצת מצות חמורות ובשעת גירותה לא טבלה לשם גירות אלא שטבלה לאחר ימי נדותה לטהרה לבעלה משום הכי אמר רב אסי מי לא טבלה לנדותה דכיון שטבלה לנדותה או האיש שטבל לקריו ש"מ בקבלת המצות שקבלו עליהם הם עומדים. וכן ההוא דהוו קרו ליה בר ארמאה ואריב"ל מי לא טבל לקריו הכי הוא מעשה שנתגייר ומל וקבל מקצת מצות קלות ומקצת מצות חמורות ולא טבל בשעת גירותו עד לאחר מכאן שטבל לקריו ולפיכך אמרינן כיון דנתגייר וקבל עליו מקצת מצות קלות ומקצת מצות חמורות אף על פי שבשעת הקבלה לא נזדמן להיות שם שלשה ואחר כך טבל לקריו עלתה לו טבילה והא דאמרינן גר צריך שלשה הני מילי לכתחלה כל שיודיעוהו מקצת מצות קלות ומקצת מהחמורות בשעת מילה ובשעת טבילה והכי תניא (לקמן מז:) נתרפא מטבילין אותו מיד ושני תלמידי חכמים עומדים על גביו ומודיעין וכו' ופרכינן עלה והא אנן תנן שלשה הא אמר ליה ר"י לתנא תני ג' אבל דיעבד כגון שהודיעוהו מקצת מצות קלות ומקצת מצות חמורות אע"פ שלא נזדמן לו לטבול בשעה שהודיעוהו ואח"כ טבל לקריו או אשה לנדותה גרים גמורים הם ומותרים לבוא בקהל ישראל לכתחלה אבל כשנתגייר בינו לבין עצמו שלא הודיעוהו מקצת מצות קלות וחמורות גוי גמור הוא ואפילו נמול ולפיכך אמר גר שנתגייר בינו לבין עצמו אינו גר ומעשה באחד שבא לפני רבי יהודה וכו' ומסקנא לדבריך גוי אתה והרב אלפס כתב דהא דרבי אסי ודריב"ל בדיעבד דלא פסלין ליה לבריה הואיל ונמול והא דר' יוחנן לכתחלה דלא נהיגנא ביה מנהג גר ולא מנסבין ליה בת ישראל עד דטבל בפני ג' ת"ח והראב"ד כתב והוא דחזו ליה בי תרי דטבל לקריו אבל לא חזו ליה בי תרי לאו כלום הוא ע"כ ואני אומר דוקא בדאיתחזק בגוי אבל לא איתחזק בגוי אם אמר טבל לקריו נאמן במגו:

תניא

גוי גופא לא קני ליה, מאי דקני ליה — הוא דמקני ליה לישראל, וכיון דקדם וטבל לשם בן חורין — אפקעיה לשעבודיה, כדרבא. *דאמר רבא: אהקדש, חמץ, בושחרור — מפקיעין מידי שעבוד. מתיב רב חסדא: *גמעשה בבלוריא הגיורת שקדמו עבדיה וטבלו לפניה. ובא מעשה לפני חכמים ואמרו: קנו עצמן בני חורין. לפניה — אין, לאחריה — לא! אמר רבא: דלפניה — בין בסתם בין במפורש. לאחריה, במפורש — אין, בסתם — לא. אמר רב אויא: לא שנו אלא בלוקח מן הגוי, אבל הגוי גופיה — קני, דכתיב °"וגם מבני התושבים הגרים עמכם מהם תקנו" — *אתם קונים מהם, ולא הם קונים מכם, ולא הם קונים זה מזה. ולא הם קונים מכם, למאי? אילימא למעשה ידיו — אטו גוי לא קני ליה לישראל למעשה ידיו? והכתיב °"או לעקר משפחת גר" ואמר מר: *"משפחת גר" — זה הגוי! אלא לאו — לגופיה, וקאמר רחמנא "אתם קונין מהם" — אפילו גופיה. *פריך רב אחא: אימא בכספא ובטבילה! קשיא. אמר שמואל: זוצריך לתקפו במים. חכי האי דמנימין, עבדיה דרב אשי, בעא לאטבולי, מסריה ניהליהו לרבינא ולרב אחא בריה דרבא, אמר להו: חזו דמינייכו *קבעית ליה. רמו ליה *ארויסא בצואריה, ארפו ליה. וצמצמו ליה. ארפו ליה — כי היכי דלא להוי חציצה, צמצמו ליה — כי היכי דלא לקדים ולימא (א) להו: לשם בן חורין אני טובל. בהדי דדלי רישיה ממיא, אנחו ליה זולטא דטינא ארישיה. ואמרו ליה: זיל אמטי לבי מרך. א"ל רב פפא לרבא: חזי מר הני דבי פפא בר אבא דיהבי זוזי לאינשי לכרגייהו, ומשעבדי בהו. *כי נפקי, צריכי גיטא דחירותא או לא? *א"ל: איכו שכיבי לא אמרי לכו הא מילתא, טהכי א"ר ששת: מוהרקייהו דהני בטפסא דמלכא מנח, ומלכא אמר: מאן דלא יהיב כרגא — משתעבד למאן דיהיב כרגא. *ר' חייא בר אבא איקלע לגבלא. חזא בנות ישראל דמעברן מגרים שמלו ולא טבלו, וחזא חמרא דישראל דמזגי גוים ושתו ישראל, וחזא תורמוסין דשלקי גוים ואכלי ישראל, ולא אמר להו ולא מידי. אתא לקמיה דר' יוחנן. א"ל: צא והכרז על בניהם שהם ממזרים, ועל יינם משום יין נסך, ועל תורמוסן משום בישולי גוים, לפי שאינן בני תורה. על בניהן שהם ממזרים — ר' יוחנן לטעמיה, דאמר ר' חייא בר אבא אמר ר' יוחנן: ילעולם אין גר עד שימול ויטבול, וכיון דלא טביל — גוי הוא. ואמר רבה בר בר חנה א"ר יוחנן: גוי ועבד הבא על בת ישראל — הולד ממזר. כועל יינם משום יין נסך — משום *"לך לך", אמרין נזירא, סחור סחור, לכרמא לא תקרב". ועל תורמוסן משום בשולי גוים — לפי שאינן בני תורה, הא בני תורה שרי? *והאמר רב שמואל בר רב יצחק משמי' דרב: לכל הנאכל כמות שהוא חי — אין בו משום בשולי גוים, והא תורמוס אינו נאכל כמות שהוא חי, ויש בו משום בשולי גוים! ר' יוחנן כאידך לישנא סבירא ליה דאמר רב שמואל בר רב יצחק משמי' דרב: מכל שאין עולה על שולחן מלכים לאכול בו את הפת — אין בו משום בשולי גוים. וטעמא דאינן בני תורה, הא בני תורה — שרי. ת"ר: גר שמל ולא טבל, ר"א אומר הרי זה גר, שכן מצינו באבותינו שמלו ולא טבלו. טבל ולא מל, ר' יהושע אומר: הרי זה גר, שכן מצינו באמהות שטבלו ולא מלו. וחכמים אומרים: טבל ולא מל, מל ולא טבל — [מ] אין גר עד שימול ויטבול. ורבי יהושע נמי — נילף מאבות, ור"א נמי — נילף מאמהות! וכי תימא: אין דנין אפשר משאי אפשר — והתניא, *ר"א אומר: גמנין לפסח דורות שאין בא אלא מן החולין — נאמר פסח במצרים ונאמר פסח בדורות, מה פסח האמור במצרים — אין בא אלא מן החולין, אף פסח האמור לדורות — אין בא אלא מן החולין. א"ל ר' עקיבא: *וכי דנין אפשר משאי אפשר? א"ל: אע"פ שאי אפשר — ראיה גדולה היא, ונלמד הימנה. אלא
בטבל

תורה אור: ויקרא כה · שם

גוי גופא לא קני. גוי לא קנאו לגופו של זה מתחלה, כדאמר לקמן: ולא הם קונים זה את זה. **הקדש חמץ ושחרור.** עשה שורו אפותיקי והקדישו למזבח, דהויא קדושת הגוף — פקע שיעבודא דקמא. אבל קדושת בדק הבית לא מפקעא, כדתנן בערכין (דף כג:): מוסיף עוד דינר ופודה הנכסים כולן. או אם עשה חמצו אפותיקי לגוי, והרי הוא מופקד בידו של ישראל, ובאו שש שעות של ערב הפסח — פקע שיעבוד הגוי, הואיל ולא הוי ממש דידיה, וחייב זה לבערו. **ושחרור.** עשה עבדו אפותיקי לחבירו ושחררו — משוחרר, ופקע ממונו של מלוה. **בבלוריא כו' לפניה אין.** לפי שהן גרים, והיא גויה, והגוי — ישראל לא קני לגופיה. **לאחריה לא.** אלמא גבי ישראל לא אמרינן קנה עבד עצמו בן חורין. **בין בסתם.** שלא פירש, הרי אנו תולין לשם בני חורין. **במפורש.** כדרב חמא בר גוריא, דקתני: וקדם וטבל לשם בן חורין. **אבל גוי גופיה.** גוי שמכר עצמו לישראל — קנהו ישראל לגופיה, ואם קדם וטבל לשם בן חורין — לא קנה עצמו בן חורין. **אלא גוי מי לא קני ליה לישראל.** למעשה ידיו, והכתיב "או לעקר משפחת גר", ואמר מר: משפחת גר — זה הגוי. **אימא בכספא ובטבילה.** לשום עבדות הוא דקאמר רחמנא ליקני, אבל אם קדם וטבל לשם בן חורין — ה"נ דבן חורין הוא. **לתקפו במים.** כשמטבילו לשם יהדות לעבדות, צריך שיתקפנו, לתת עליו עול מלאכה במים, כדי שתהא נראית כטבילת עבדות. שאפילו יאמר הוא לשם בן חורין — לא קנה עצמו בן חורין, ולא יהא ממשות בדבריו. **בעי לאטבולי.** לשם יהדות לעבד. **מינייכו קא בעינא ליה.** אם יקדים ויאמר לשם בן חורין. **ארויסא.** קיסטרי. **וצמצמו.** דחקוהו לקשור בצוארו, משום לתוקפו במים. **ארפו ליה וצמצמו ליה.** שהיה לו ענידה, וכשרוצים מושכין ראש החבל והוא דוחק מאליו, וכשאין מושכין — רפוי, והמים נכנסים על בשרו. **זולטא דטינא.** כלי מלא טיט. **דיהבי זוזי לאינשי לכרגייהו.** כשאין נותנין כסף גולגולת למלך תופסים אותם גבאי המלך. והני דבי פפא עשירים היו, ופורעים המס לגבאי המלך, וקונין אותם לעבדים מהם. וגוים היו אותן הנקנין, וקא מיבעיא ליה אי הוי קנין, דלכי נפקי מיניה ליבעי גיטא דחירותא, או לא. **מוהרקייהו דהני.** חותמן של אלו. **בטפסא דמלכא.** (ב) שהן לו לעבדים. **טפסא.** ארגז, אשקרי"ן בלע"ז. **ומלכא אמר כו'.** הילכך מכר הוא, ובעו גיטא דחירותא אי בעו לאיגיורי ולאשתרויי בבת ישראל. **לפי שאינם בני תורה.** אתורמוסין קאי, דאין בו משום בישולי גוים כדמפרש לקמן, אלא לפי שאינן בני תורה לא ואסור עליהן, שלא יזלזלו בבשולי גוים. **ועל יינם משום יין נסך.** דאע"ג דלא נגעי, אלא כמו בעלמא הוא — אסור משום לך לך אמרין לנזירא כו': **תורמוס אינו עולה על שלחן מלכים. באבותינו שמלו.** בימי משה, כשיצאו ממצרים, ויצאו מכלל בני נח לקבל התורה ולקבל פני השכינה. **באמהות.** נשותיהם שטבלו כדמפרש לקמן, דאם לא טבלו — במה נכנסו תחת כנפי שכינה? **משאי אפשר.** אמהות אי אפשר למול. **אלא מן החולין.** ולא מדמי מעשר שני, דהכתי מעשר שני לא הוה. **אין בא אלא מן החולין.** למעוטי מדמי מעשר שני: ה"ג במנחות בהתודה (דף פג.). **א"ל רבי עקיבא וכי דנין אפשר כו'.** ומאן דגריס רבי יהושע קשיא, דהאמר רבי יהושע דנין מאמהות. **משאי אפשר.** מפסח מצרים, דהאי דלא בא מן המעשר — דאי אפשר הוא, דהכתי מעשר לא הוה.
במקום

הקדש חמץ ושחרור. מפורש ב"השולח" (גיטין דף מ:). **כי נפקי** צריכי גיטא דחירותא או לאו. מספקא ליה אי דינא דמלכותא דינא (ג) או לא. ואע"ג דלא קני גופיה — הכא קני. או דלמא, הכא נמי לא קני אלא למעשה ידיו. ובגויותן איירי, אם היו באין להתגייר.

רבי יוחנן כאידך לישנא ס"ל. אומר ר"ת: דכולהו מודו דכשנאכל כמות שהוא חי — דאין בו משום בישולי גוים, דאמר ב"אין מעמידין" (ע"ז דף לח.) דאיכא בינייהו דגים קטנים ארזי ודייסא, היינו: דברים שאין עולים על שלחן מלכים ואין נאכלים כמות שהן חיין. ולא נקט כמה דברים הנאכלים כשהן חיין ועולים על שלחן מלכים, כמו פירות וגבינה וכיוצא בהן. והא דאסר רבי יוחנן התם בילה, אע"ג דראוי לגומעה חיה — אין זו אכילה חשובה, דהכי נמי בשר מליח מותר לטלטלו בשבת (שבת קכח.), דחזי לאכילה. ואפ"ה יש בו משום בישולי גוים.

אמר ליה ר' עקיבא וכי דנין אפשר משאי

לקמן סו: כתובות נט: גיטין מ: נדרים פו: ב"ק פט:
[גיטין לז:]
[קדושין כ. ב"ק קיג: ב"מ עא. ערכין ל:] [קדושין יג. וש"נ]
נ"ל קבעינא
ברא"ש ובכ"י גרסי עבידתא יתירתא וע"ש בכ"י
[ב"מ עג.]
ע"ז נט.
[שבת יג. וש"נ]
ע"ז לז. נט. שבת קלט. מ"ק יב:
מנחות פב.
[מנחות סה. יט. לקמן סח. סוכה נ: הוריות ו: זבחים לא. תמורה טז: יח: נדה לז:]

קיג א מיי' פ"ז מהל' ערכין הל' יד ופי"ח מהלכות מלוה ולוה הל' ו ז וסמג עשין לד טוש"ע ח"מ סימן קיז סעיף ז:
קיד ב מיי' פ"ח מהל' עבדים הלכה טז סמג עשין פז טוש"ע שם סעיף ו טוש"ע י"ד סימן רסז סעיף סח:
קטו ג מיי' פ"ח מהל' עבדים הל' כא:
מכילת' פרשת בא פ' טו
קטז ד מיי' שם הל' יט ומיי' פי"ג מהל' איסורי ביאה הלכה יא:
קיז ה טוש"ע י"ד סימן רסו סעיף ט:
קיח ו מיי' פ"א מהל' עבדים הלכה ג סמג עשין פג:
קיט ז ח מיי' פי"ג מהל' איסורי ביאה הל' יא טוש"ע י"ד סימן רסז סעיף ט:
קכ ט מיי' פ"ה מהל' גזילה הל' טז ופ"א מהל' עבדים הל' ח סמג עשין עג טוש"ע ח"מ סי' שסט סעי' יא:
קכא י מיי' פי"ג מהל' איסורי ביאה הל' ו סמג לאוין קטז:
קכב כ מיי' פי"א מהל' מאכלות אסורות הל' ג סמג לאוין קמח טוש"ע י"ד סי' קכג סעיף א:
[נ"ל ארוסיה פירוש שלשלת ערוך ערך ארסה]
קכג ל מ מיי' פי"ז מהל' מאכלות אסורות הלכה יד סמג לאוין קמב טוש"ע י"ד סימן קיג ס"א: [מ] [מיי' פי"ג מהל' איסורי ביאה סמג ל"ת קטז טוש"ע י"ד סימן רסח]:
קכד נ מיי' פט"ז מהל' מעשה הקרבנות הלכה טו:

הגהות הב"ח

(א) גמ' ולימא לשם בן חורין כצ"ל ותיבת להו נמחק: (ב) רש"י ד"ה בטפסא דמלכא (שהן) תז"מ ונ"ב ס"א שהיו: (ג) תוס' ד"ה כי וכו' דינא ואע"ג כצ"ל ותיבות או לא נמחק:

תוספות ישנים

הקדש חמץ ושחרור מפקיעים וכו'. פירשתי פרק כל שעה בפסחים. וא"ת מאי קא מדמה האי דהכא להאי דשחרור מפקיע מידי שעבוד הא לא דמי דהתם איירי כשהרב עצמו משחרר עבדו. אבל הכא איירי שהוא משחרר עצמו כשטובל לשם בן חורין. וי"ל דמ"מ מדמי שפיר דהכא נמי כיון שטבל אפקע ליה שם עבדות ולא איתא לרב אלא מעשה ידיו דהא גוי גופיה לא קני והעבד יכתוב לו שטר על חצי דמיו ולא יהיה לרב כלום לד עבדות עליו: (לעיל) **מי** לא לא טבלה לנדותה. וא"ת הלא טבילתה בלילה וגר צריך לטבול ביום דמשפט כתיב ביה. וי"ל דאיכא טבילת נדות דהוי שפיר ביום כגון טבילה שלא בזמנה: **ומשתעבד** בהו עבידתא ל"ג יתירתא רק בבבא מציעא גבי רבית ואי גרסינן ליה הכא יש לייתבו משום דאז מוכחא מלת' שגופם קנוי לעבדים:

תוספות חד מקמאי

תניא מעשה בבלוריא הגיורת שקדמו עבדיה וטבלו לפניה ובא מעשה לפני חכמים ואמרו קנו עצמן בן חורין ואסיק רבא בפניה בין בסתם בין במפורש לאחריה במפורש אין בסתם לא ופירוש לפניה הוא קודם שנתגיירה לאחריה לאחר שנתגיירה והרב אלפס לא גרים לאחריה אלא שלא בפניה במפרש אין בסתם לא פירוש בפניה כיון שראתה ושתקה בין בסתם בין במפורש. שלא בפניה שלא ראתה כדטבלה במפרש אין בסתם לא וגירסת מכילתא מסייע א) לרב ז"ל דגרס' התם בפ' בא אל פרעה ר' נתן אמר מה ת"ל המול לו כל זכר ואז יקרב לעשותו להביא את העבד שטבל בפני רבו שיצא בן חורין ומעשה בבלוריא הגיורת שטבלו שפחותיה בפני' ומקצתן לאחריה ובא מעשה לפני חכמים ואמרו את שטבלו בפני' בנות חורין ואת [שטבלו] לאחריה משועבדים ואעפ"כ משמשות אותה עד יום מיתה: **אמר** שמואל וצריך לתקפו במים פירוש שיראה שלשום עבדות טובלין ולא לשום בן חורין והרב ז"ל פירש כדי שתעלה לו טבילה ומסתברא (בפ"ק) כפר"ש ז"ל א"ר יוחנן לעולם אינו גר עד שימול ויטבול דוקא מילה והדר טבילה אבל איפכא לא. וצריך לטבול (עד) אחר המילה וכן נעשה מעשה בלוניל מפי אבא מארי וחבריו ז"ל שהצריכוהו טבילה לאחר המילה. תניא הרי שבא ואמר מלתי ולא טבלתי מטבילין אותו ומה בכך דברי ר"י ור' יוסי אמר אין מטבילין. ומסקנא בהא פליגי דר"י סבר בחד מינייהו סגי או מילה או טבילה ור' יוסי תרתי בעי. והלכתא כר' יוסי דתרתי בעי. ושמעי' מהא דגר שנתגייר כשהוא מהול צריך להטיף ממנו דם ברית
וכבר

א) נראה דצ"ל וגירסת מכילתא מסייע לפי' רש"י ז"ל.

קכה א מיי' פי"ג מהל' איסורי ביאה הל' ו סמג לאוין קטז טוש"ע י"ד סי' רסח סעיף ד:
קכו ב ג מיי' שם וטוש"ע שם וסעיף ג:

בטבל ולא מל — כולי עלמא לא פליגי דמהני. כי פליגי — במל ולא טבל. רבי אליעזר יליף מאבות, ורבי יהושע: באבות נמי טבילה הוה. מנא ליה? אילימא מדכתיב °"לך אל העם וקדשתם היום ומחר וכבסו שמלתם", ומה במקום שאין טעון כבוס — טעון טבילה, מקום שטעון כבוס — אינו דין שטעון טבילה? ודלמא נקיות בעלמא? אלא מהכא: °"ויקח משה את הדם ויזרק על העם" וגמירי *דאין הזאה בלא טבילה. ורבי יהושע, טבילה באמהות מנלן? סברא הוא, דאם כן — במה נכנסו תחת כנפי השכינה? *א"ר חייא בר אבא א"ר יוחנן: לעולם אינו גר עד שימול ויטבול. פשיטא, *יחיד ורבים הלכה כרבים! מאן חכמים — *רבי יוסי. דתניא: הרי שבא ואמר מלתי ולא טבלתי — מטבילין אותו, ומה בכך, דברי ר' יהודה. רבי יוסי אומר: אין מטבילין. לפיכך מטבילין גר בשבת, דברי ר' יהודה. ור' יוסי אומר: [א]אין מטבילין. אמר מר: לפיכך מטבילין גר בשבת, (א) פשיטא, כיון דא"ר יהודה בחדא סגיא, היכא דמל לפנינו — מטבילין, מאי לפיכך? מהו דתימא: לרבי יהודה טבילה עיקר, וטבילה בשבת — לא, דקא מתקן גברא, קמ"ל דר' יהודה או הא או הא בעי. ר' יוסי אומר אין מטבילין. פשיטא, דכיון דאמר רבי יוסי תרתי בעינן — תקוני גברא בשבת לא מתקנינן! מהו דתימא: לר' יוסי מילה עיקר, והתם הוא דלא הואי מילה בפנינו, אבל היכא דהויא מילה בפנינו — אימא ליטבל זה בשבתא, קמ"ל דרבי יוסי תרתי בעי. אמר רבה: עובדא הוה בי רבי חייא בר רבי, ורב יוסף מתני רבי אושעיא *בר רבי, ורב ספרא מתני ר' אושעיא בר' חייא, דאתא לקמיה גר שמל ולא טבל. א"ל שהי כאן עד למחר ונטבלינך. ש"מ תלת: [ב]ש"מ גר צריך שלשה וש"מ: אינו גר עד שימול ויטבול, וש"מ: [ג]אין מטבילין גר בלילה. וניזמא: ש"מ נמי בעינן מומחין! דלמא דאיקלעו. אמר רבי חייא בר אבא אמר רבי יוחנן: *גר צריך ג' "משפט" כתיב ביה. ת"ר: מי שבא ואמר: "גר אני", יכול נקבלנו — ת"ל "אתך" — במוחזק לך. בא ועדיו עמו מנין — ת"ל °"וכי יגור (ב) אתך גר בארצכם".

אין

רש"י

במקום שאין טעון כיבוס. כגון בעל קרי בעלמא, דכתיב "ורחץ במים וטמא עד הערב" (ויקרא טו) ולא כתיב יכבס בגדיו. מקום שטעון כיבוס. כגון בקבול תורה, דכתיב "וכבסו שמלותם". דלמא נקיות בעלמא. ההוא כיבוס לאו משום טומאה הוה דלטעון טבילה מק"ו, אלא שיהיו בגדיהם לבנים והגונים לקבל פני שכינה. ויזרוק על העם. הזאה הוא. מטבילים אותו. והוי כישראל מעליא, ואין צריך לבדוק בעדים אם מילתו לשם מצות מילה. ומה בכך. אם אין מילתו לשם מילה, הואיל וטבל — בטבילה סגי. אין מטבילים. שמא ערבי מהול* וגבעוני מהול הוא, וצריך להטיף ממנו דם ברית. דר' יוסי תרתי בעי. לפיכך. הואיל ולר' יהודה בחדא סגיא — מטבילין בשבת גר שמל אתמול לפנינו, דבמילה סגי ליה, וכי מטבלי ליה בשבתא — לא מתקני גברא. הכי גרסינן: אמר מר לפיכך מטבילין גר בשבת דברי רבי יהודה פשיטא כיון דלרבי יהודה בחדא סגי היכא דמל לפנינו מטבילים. טבילה עיקר. דהא אמילה שמעינן ליה דקאמר ומה בכך. ר' יוסי אומר אין מטבילין. תרתי בעי, ואע"ג דמל בפנינו — טבילתו תקנתו. עובדא הוה בי ר' חייא בר רבי ורב יוסף מתני בר' אושעיא ב"ר. כלומר, ר' אושעיא נמי הוה בהדי ר' חייא. ורב ספרא מתני. דאף רבי אושעיא בר' חייא הוה בהדייהו. שהי האידנא. ליליה היה. ש"מ. מדרב ספרא, דאמר תלתא הוו — גר צריך שלשה. דבעינן מומחין. כי הנך תלתא גברי רבנן רברבי. דלמא דאיקלעו. הכי הוה מעשה דאיתרמו רבנן כי הני. אבל ג' ודאי שמעינן, מדקפליג רב ספרא ומוסיף עד דהוו תלתא. משפט כתיב ביה. "משפט אחד יהיה לכם ולגר" (במדבר טו) ואין משפט פחות מג'. יכול מקבלין אותו. לא נצריכנו הטפת דם ברית וטבילה. בא ועדיו עמו. שנאמן. תלמוד לומר וכי יגור. מכל מקום. ולקמן פריך: כיון דעדיו עמו — פשיטא, ומי בעי קרא?

בכל

תוספות

משאי אפשר. תימה: לר' עקיבא, מנלן דאין משלשין במכות? דבפרק קמא דמכות (דף ה.) ילפינן לה ממיתה, והיינו אי אפשר! ואין לומר דהתם דגזירה שוה היא מודה ר"ע דדנין משאי אפשר, משום דאין ג"ש למחצה. אבל הכא, בנין אב הוא. דהא הכא נמי היקישא הוא, כדמסיק בסוף "התודה" (מנחות דף פג: ושם) דדריש רבי אליעזר מ"ועבדת" (שמות יג) — שיהו כל העבודות שוות זה כזה, ולא קיבל ר"ע, אף על גב דאין היקש נמי למחצה*א).

בשטבל ולא מל כולי עלמא לא פליגי. ואם תאמר: ור' יהושע, אדמודי ליה אודויי — לפלוג עליה לפלוגי, דנקט טבל דמודי ר' אליעזר, ולא נקט מילתא דפליג בה! וכי האי גוונא פריך בסוף "שבועת הפקדון" (שבועות דף לח.). וי"ל: דהתם לא דייק אלא משום דהתנא הראשון הזכיר הכל. אבל הכא נקט שפיר ר' יהושע טבל ולא מל, כיון דלא דבר בו ר' אליעזר. כי פליגי במל ולא טבל. תימה: דלקמן בריש "הערל" (דף עא.) ממעט ר"ע גר שמל ולא טבל מפסח, מדכתיב "תושב ושכיר", והשתא כמאן סבר ר"ע? אי כר' יהושע — למה לי קרא? פשיטא דלא אכיל בפסח, דגוי גמור הוא! ואי כר' אליעזר, כיון דגר מעליא הוא — אין סברא למעטו מפסח, כדמשמע התם! וי"ל: דלעולם כרבי יהושע סבירא לי', ולאו מטעמיה. דאיהו סבר דבאבות נמי טבילה הוה, ורבי עקיבא סבר מדמעטיה קרא מפסח — שמע מינה דאין גר עד שימול ויטבולב).

דאין הזאה בלא טבילה. מפרש ר"ת: בלא טבילה לפני הזאה, כדי לקבל הזאה. כדאמר בפרק "ארבעה מחוסרי כפרה" (כריתות דף ט.): מה אבותינו לא נכנסו לברית אלא במילה וטבילה והזאת דמים. ואותה טבילה כשרה אף בלילה, כדתנן במסכת פרה (פי"ב מי"א): אבל הוא עצמו טובל בלילה ומזה ביום. ולענין טומאה יש עוד טבילה אחרת אחר הזאה, שהיא כדי לטהר מטומאה, כדכתיב בקרא "והזה" ברישא והדר "ורחץ במים", ואותה טבילה אינה כשרה אלא ביום, כדתנן בפרק ב' דמגילה (דף כ. ושם): אין טובלין ואין מזין אלא ביום. ויש מפרשים דהתם בטבילת אזוב איירי — אין טובלים אזוב אלא ביום, כדאמרינן בסוף מסכת פרה שאם טבל את האזוב בלילה אפי' הזה ביום הזאתו פסולה. והשתא אתי שפיר הא דתנן טבילה קודם להזאה. והא דקאמר התם בגמ' לא מזין אלא ביום, דכתיב (במדבר יט) "והזה הטהור על הטמא ביום השלישי וגו'" ואיתקש טבילה להזאה — היינו בקרא דלקמיה, דכתיב "ולקח אזוב וטבל במים איש טהור והזה על האהל וגו'". וכן משמע בירושלמי דמגילה דאמר: וטבל והזה, מה הזאה ביום אף טבילה ביום. ואין לתמוה כיון דבעי הזאה היאך מקבלים גרים בזמן הזה? דבפ' ["ארבעה] מחוסרי כפרה" נפקא לן מקרא דלא בעינן*. ורבי יהושע טבילה באמהות מנא ליה. אע"ג דאית ליה דאין הזאה בלא טבילה — שמא הנשים לא היו בכלל אותה הזאה. אי נמי, משום רבי אליעזר איצטריך האי טעמא, דמסיק משום דאיהו נמי מודה דבטבילה לחוד סגי, כדאמר לעיל בטבל ולא מל — כולי עלמא לא פליגי דלית ליה, דאין הזאה בלא טבילהג).

כיון דאמר רבי יהודה דבחדא סגי כו'. תימה: דפריך פשיטא, דמנא ליה דסגי במילה לחודה? דלמא כר' יהושע סבר ליה דטבילה בלא מילה — מהניא, אבל מילה בלא טבילה — לא מהני. תקוני גברא בשבתא לא מתקנינן. ואע"ג דלענין טומאה שרי לטבול בשבת משום דנראה כמיקר — שאני הכא, דבעי שני ת"ח לעמוד שם בשעת טבילה להודיעו המצות, כדאמרינן לקמן (דף מז:). דרבי יוסי תרתי בעי. כתב בה"ג דגר שנתגייר כשהוא מהול צריך להטיף ממנו דם ברית, וקטן שנולד כשהוא מהול אין צריך להטיף. וטעמא: דקטן, שלא היתה לו ערלה מעולם, אין צריך, אבל גר שהיתה לו ערלה ומילתו אינה מילה — צריך להטיף דם ברית. ד) ומיהו, אם נכרת לו כל הגיד ובא להתגייר — אין דומה שמילתו מעכבתו מלהתגייר. ומודי רבי יוסי בההיא דסגי בטבילה לחודה. ור"ח פסק במסכת שבת איפכא מה"ג, וכן משמע בפרק "ר"א דמילה" (שבת דף קלה. ושם) דקאמר: לא נחלקו בית שמאי ובית הלל על נולד כשהוא מהול שצריך להטיף ממנו דם ברית, על מה נחלקו — על גר שנתגייר כשהוא מהול. ונראה שעל זה סמכו ה"ג, דסברי להו כאמוראי דהתם, דאית להו דקטן אין צריך, ובגר סברי כר' יוסי דשמעתין, דמשמע דהלכתא כוותיה. ובפרק "הערל" (לקמן דף עב.) פליגי רבי אלעזר בר"ש ורבנן בגר שנתגייר כשהוא מהול אם נמול ביום או אפי' בלילה, אבל כולהו מודו דצריך הטפת דם ברית. שמע מינה דגר צריך שלשה. וא"ת: ודלמא דאיקלעו? וי"ל: דמרב ספרא דייק, שהרי ר' חייא הזכירו לפי שהיה בעל מעשה וראש, ורב יוסף הזכיר רבי אושעיא חברו, אבל רב ספרא — למה הזכיר ר' אושעיא בר' חייא. אינו גר עד שימול ויטבול. מהכא לא מצי לדקדק דלא תיסגי בטבילה לחודה, ולא בא לדקדק אלא דמילה בלא טבילה לא מהניא. אין מטבילין גר בלילה. דמשפט כתיב ביה, ואע"פ שכבר מל — חשיב ליה כתחילת דין. משפט כתיב ביה. "ושפטתם צדק בין איש ובין אחיו ובין גרו" (דברים א). אי נמי — "משפט אחד יהיה לכם ולגר" (במדבר טו). ואפי' למ"ד בסנהדרין (דף ג. ושם)

דבר

[וע"ע תוס' מנחות פב: ד"ה והשתא ותוס' בכורות ט. ד"ה ומה בכך]

מסורת הש"ס

ס"א גבנוני

[כריתות ט. ע"ש]

ברכות מז: ע"ש

[שם ט. וש"נ]

[לקמן קה: עירובין פג. וש"נ]

[נ"ל בריבי וכ"א ברב אלפס]

קידושין סב: [לקמן מז.]

ויקרא יט

[וע"ע תוס' מגילה כ.]

הגהות הב"ח

(א) גמ' מטבילין גר בשבת דברי רבי יהודה פשיטא כיון: (ב) שם ת"ל וכי יגור באזרחכם כצ"ל ותיבות אתך גר נמחק:

גליון הש"ס

תוס' ד"ה תקוני גברא כו' משום דנראה כמיקר. כלאי' בכלים דף יח ע"א:

תוספות ישנים

א) וי"ל דהתם היינו טעמא משום דמלקות תחת מיתה עומדת ולכך אין משלשין בו כמו במיתה וילפינן מינה אע"ג דלא אפשר: ב) עוד פירש רבינו נתנאל דודאי ר' עקיבא פליג עלייהו וקמפלגי בגר שבא להתגייר בזמן הזה דר' אליעזר סבר דהוי גר שהרי כשאכלו בפסח אבותינו עדיין לא טבלו ומ"מ נפקו מתורת ערל מדאכלו בפסח א"כ מל ולא טבל הוי גר ור' יהושע סבר דלא הוי גר שהרי טבלו במתן תורה וכיון שנצטוו לטבול לא הוי גר אם לא טבל. ור' עקיבא סבר דמדאכלו בפסח טבלו דאל"ה הוו אסורים בו כדמרבינן מקרא מל ולא טבל שאינו אוכל וכו'. ובזה ניחא מ"ש לקמן בסמוך: טבל ולא מל כ"ע לא פליגי. ותימה אמאי קאמר לעיל טבל ולא מל ר' יהושע אומר וכו' דמשמע מהאי לישנא דפליגי בטבל ולא מל הול"ל על מלתיה דת"ק ר' יהושע אומר אינו גר ואין עוד וי"ל דניחא לי' להזכיר מילה בלא טבילה וטבילה בלא מילה משום דרבנן פליגי על הכל ואמרי דמצריכין מילה וטבילה: ויקח משה את הדם ויזרוק על העם וגמירי דאין הזאה בלא טבילה. פי' דהיינו הזאה דקודם מתן תורה שעדיין לא הוו יודעין שמזין ממי חטאת והזו מן הדם על העם. ואליבא דר' אליעזר נימא דהאי קרא אינו ר"ל הזאה. ופי' הפסוק כמו דמתרגמי' וזרק על מדבחא לכפרא על עמא וא"כ אינו ר"ל שהזה על העם כי אם על המזבח לכפר על העם וזה הדוחק אין נ"ל לפי' רבינו נתנאל: ורבי יהושע טבילה באמהות מנא ליה. תימה לימא מויזרוק משה את הדם על העם וגמירי דאין הזאה בלא טבילה ונשים בכלל. וי"ל דפסיקא ליה דעם לא אקרו נשים. עוי"ל לשיטת רבינו נתנאל ניחא דהכי פריך טבילה באמהות מנא ליה כלומר בשעה שאכלו הפסח מנא ליה שהאמהות עשו טבילה דמסברא כל העם אכלו פסח בין אנשים בין נשים דא"ל דטבלו מדכתיב ויזרוק שהרי אותו הפסוק במתן תורה כתיב אבל בפסח היכי אכלו עדיין כיון שלא טבלו הא אינו גר עד שיטבול. וכיון דבאמהות לא שייכא בהו מילה מהיכא נפקו מתורת ערל דבשלמא באבות אע"ג דלא טבלו עד מתן תורה מ"מ כיון שמלו נפקו מתורת ערל כדי לאכול פסח אע"ג שלא היו יהודים גמורים עד שטבלו כדמשמע ליה לר' יהושע: ג) וה"ה דהוה מצי למפרך לר' אליעזר גופיה מיהו פריך לר' יהושע מפני שהזכיר בהדיא שכן מצינו באמהות שטבלו ולא מלו: רבי יוסי אומר אין מטבילין. פירוש דשמא ערבי מהול הוא ולא היתה מילה לשמה וצריך להטיף ממנו דם ברית. ותימה דמשמע דהלכה כן דהכי איתא במסקנא דהלכה כר' יוסי ובשבת משמע דגר שנתגייר כשהוא מהול ב"ה אומרים א"צ להטיף ממנו דם ברית גבי לא נחלקו על קטן כשהוא מהול וכו' וקיי"ל דהלכה כב"ה לכן נראה דודאי אין צריך. וטעמא דר' יוסי משום דבעי טבילה עם מילה וזה שמא לא מל לשמה אבל נתגייר כשהוא מהול מודה דא"צ להטיף ממנו דם ברית דהכא גרע משום דמל שלא לשמה מנולד מהול דהוי סתמא דלא עבד ולא מידי לכן נראה דגר [שנתגייר כשהוא מהול] אין צריך להטיף כדאמרי ב"ה בשבת וקטן שנולד מהול צריך להטיף כדקאמר התם לא נחלקו שצריך להטיף בנולד מהול: ד) וצריך ליתן טעם לפ' ההלכות גדולות דדוקא גר כשבא לתורת יהודות אין לו ליכנס תחת כנפי השכינה כשנתגייר מהול אם לא בהטפת דם ברית אבל קטן שלא הוחזק בערלות לא צריך ודוחק הוא. אכן יש טעם ברור דמן הדין היו שניהם גר וקטן צריכין הטפת דם ברית אלא בקטן א"צ להטיף דדרשינן מדכתיב ערלתו וכיון שנולד מהול לא הוי ערלה וא"צ להטיף ודוקא בקטן אבל בגר דלא גלי לא גלי: לפיכך מטבילין גר בשבת. פי' היכא שמל בפנינו מטבילין לפי שהטבילה אינה עיקר תיקון: לפיכך אין מטבילין. תימה דאמרינן כל חייבי טבילות טובלין כדרכן בין בשבת בין ביוה"כ. י"ל דלא דמי דהתם לאו תיקון גדול כמו הכא שבא על ידי כן לתורת יהודות: קמ"ל דר' יוסי תרתי בעי. משמע הכא דר' יוסי בעי מילה לשמה ותימה דבפרק אין מעמידין משמע דקאמר ר' יוסי והיכן מצינו מילה לשמה אלא מל והולך עד

שתלא

אין לי אלא בארץ, בח"ל מנין? תלמוד לומר "אתך" — בכל מקום שאתך. אם כן מה ת"ל "בארץ" — בארץ צריך להביא ראיה, בח"ל — אין צריך להביא ראיה. דברי ר' יהודה. וחכמים אומרים: בין בארץ בין בחוצה לארץ — צריך להביא ראיה. בא הוא ועדיו עמו — קרא למה לי? אמר רב ששת, דאמרי: שמענו שנתגייר בב"ד של פלוני. סד"א: לא ליהמנייהו, קמ"ל. (א) "בארץ", אין לי אלא בארץ, בח"ל מנין? ת"ל "אתך" — בכל מקום שאתך. והא אפיקתיה! חדא מ"אתך" וחדא[א] מ"עמך". וחכ"א: בין בארץ בין בח"ל צריך להביא ראיה. ואלא, הא כתיב (ב) "בארץ"! ההוא מיבעי ליה דאפילו בארץ מקבלים גרים. דסד"א: משום טיבותא דארץ ישראל קמגיירי, והשתא נמי דליכא טיבותא — איכא לקט שכחה ופאה ומעשר עני, קמ"ל. א"ר חייא בר אבא אמר ר' יוחנן: [א]הלכה, בין בארץ בין בח"ל — צריך להביא ראיה. פשיטא, *יחיד ורבים הלכה כרבים! מהו דתימא: מסתבר טעמא דרבי יהודה, דקמסייעי ליה קראי, קמ"ל. ת"ר: °"ושפטתם צדק בין איש ובין אחיו ובין גרו" מכאן א"ר יהודה: גר שנתגייר בב"ד — הרי זה גר, בינו לבין עצמו — אינו גר. מעשה באחד שבא לפני רבי יהודה, ואמר לו: נתגיירתי ביני לבין עצמי. א"ל רבי יהודה: יש לך עדים? אמר ליה: לאו. יש לך בנים? א"ל: הן. א"ל: [ב]נאמן אתה לפסול את עצמך, ואי אתה נאמן לפסול את בניך. — [ומי] א"ר יהודה אבנים לא מהימן? *והתניא: °"יכיר" — יכירנו לאחרים. מכאן א"ר יהודה: [ג]נאמן אדם לומר: זה בני בכור. [ד]וכשם שנאמן לומר זה בני בכור כך נאמן לומר: בני זה בן גרושה הוא, או בן חלוצה הוא. וחכ"א: אינו נאמן. א"ר נחמן בר יצחק, ה"ק ליה: לדבריך גוי אתה, ואין עדות לגוי. רבינא אמר: הכי קאמר ליה: יש לך בנים? הן, יש לך בני בנים? הן. א"ל: נאמן אתה לפסול בניך, ואי אתה נאמן לפסול בני בניך. תניא נמי הכי, ר' יהודה אומר: [ה]נאמן אדם לומר על בנו קטן, ואין נאמן על בנו גדול. ואמר ר' חייא בר אבא א"ר יוחנן: לא קטן קטן ממש, ולא גדול גדול ממש, אלא, קטן ויש לו בנים — זהו גדול, גדול ואין לו בנים — זהו קטן. והלכתא כוותיה דרב נחמן בר יצחק. והתניא כוותיה דרבינא! [ו]ההוא לענין "יכיר" איתמר. תנו רבנן: [ז]גר שבא להתגייר בזמן הזה אומרים לו: מה ראית שבאת להתגייר? אי אתה יודע שישראל בזמן הזה דוויים, דחופים, סחופים ומטורפין, ויסורין באין עליהם? אם אומר: יודע אני ואיני כדאי — מקבלין אותו מיד. ומודיעין אותו מקצת מצות קלות, ומקצת מצות חמורות, ומודיעין אותו עון לקט שכחה ופאה ומעשר עני, ומודיעין אותו ענשן של מצות, אומרים לו: הוי יודע שעד שלא באת למדה זו, אכלת חלב — אי אתה ענוש כרת, חללת שבת — אי אתה ענוש סקילה. ועכשיו, אכלת חלב — ענוש כרת, חללת שבת — ענוש סקילה. וכשם שמודיעין אותו ענשן של מצות, כך מודיעין אותו מתן שכרן. אומרים לו: הוי יודע שהעולם הבא אינו עשוי אלא לצדיקים, וישראל בזמן הזה אינם יכולים לקבל

לא

רש"י

בכל מקום שאתך. ולקמן פריך הא אפיקתיה. צריך להביא ראיה. שבב"ד נתגייר, שמא גבעוני מהול הוא, ומשום שבחא דא"י הוא דקאמר הכי, ומשקר: ה"ג: מהו דתימא לא ניהמניהו: [ב] מעמך. "גר ותושב וחי עמך" (ויקרא כה). דליכא טובה. דפסק חלב ודבש. דקמסייעי קראי. דהא עמך — כל מקום שאתך משמע, ואפילו בארץ. "ובארצכם" למה לי? אלא לאו אראיה קאי. דבארץ צריך להביא ראיה, ולא בחוצה לארץ: מדכתיב (ג) גר אצל "ושפטתם", מכאן אמר ר' יהודה: גר בעי בית דין. יכיר. "את הבכור בן השנואה יכיר". יכירנו לאחרים. שאם אין ב"ד מכירים אותו — נאמן עליו אביו לומר: זה בני בכור ליטול פי שנים. בן גרושה הוא. וכהן חלל הוא. ואין עדות לגוי. הואיל ובניך מוחזקין בכשרות — אין אתה נאמן להעיד עליהן ולפוסלן. לפסול את בניך. דנפקא לן מ"יכיר", ואי אתה נאמן לפסול את בני בניך. והלכתא כרב נחמן. דאמר לדבריו גוי הוא, ואין עדות לגוי, ואפילו אבנים לא מהימן. והתניא כרבינא. דנאמן הוא על בנו קטן שאין לו בנים. וקס"ד דהא מתני' בגר שבא ואמר גר אני קמיירי. ההיא. דקתני נאמן הוא על בנו קטן. לענין יכיר. תניא, אההיא מתני' דיכיר קאי, דקתני וכשם שנאמן אדם לומר זה בני בכור כך נאמן לומר זה בני בן גרושה. ועלה קתני דנאמן הוא על הקטן, דהא ישראל הוא ויש לו עדות, והתורה האמינתו על בנו, ולא על בן בנו. אבל גבי גר — אפילו אבנו לא מהימן, דאין עדות לגוי. וסחופין. שפלים וכפויין. כמו סחופי כסא (שבת דף סו:) — כפיית הכלי. ואיני כדאי. ואיני ראוי להשתתף בצרתן, ומי יתן ואזכה לכך. ומודיעים אותו. לקמן מפרש טעמא דכולה מתני'.

תוספות

דבר תורה חד נמי כשר — הכא מדמין לגזילות וחבלות, דבעינן שלשה לכ"ע. ור' יוחנן דהכא אית ליה בהדיא (ד) בירושלמי דשנים שדנו אין דיניהם דין. וא"ת: ואנן היכי מקבלין גריס? הא בעינן מומחין! וי"ל: דשליחותייהו עבדינן, כדמשמע נמי בשילהי "המגרש" (גיטין דף פח: ושם). וכמו שחשו לנעילת דלת בפני לווין חשו נמי לנעילת דלת בפני גרים*.

*במוחזק לך. אומר רבינו תם דדוקא בדידעינן דהוה גוי מעיקרא, דאי לא הוה ידעינן — מהימן, מגו דאי בעי אמר, ישראל אני, דמהימן, כדמשמע בריש מסכת פסחים (דף ג: ושם) גבי ההוא גוי דהוה סליק ואכיל פסחים בירושלים. ואין לומר שאני התם דהוו סמכי ארובא דהוו ישראל — דהא בכל מקום נמי איכא רובא, [ו]דרוב הבאין לפנינו בתורת יהדות ישראל הם. ועוד ראיה משמעתין, דאמר ליה ר"י: אי אתה נאמן לפסול את בניך. ואיהו גופיה כשר, אלא דשוי נפשיה חתיכה דאיסורא. אבל אם בא על בת כהן לא פסלה, כדפי' לעיל. (ה) ומההיא דלעיל (דף מה.) דא"ל: זיל גלי — אין ראיה, דשמא לא היו בודקים אלא אם הוא ישראל אם לאו, אבל במשפחתו לא היו בודקין.

אין לי אלא בארץ. פי': דמקבלין גרים. ולא"ג דחובת הגוף היא — בעיא ריבויא, כיון דכתיב "בארץ". כדאשכחן בסוף פ"ק דקידושין (דף לח:) גבי שילוח עבדים והשמטת כספים. אי נמי: בארץ לא חיישינן דלמא הדרי בהו, משום דאיכא שבחא דארץ ישראל.

מהו דתימא לא להימניהו. ויש ספרים דגרסי: מהו דתימא ליהמניהו, וה"פ: ליהמניהו כעד מפי עד. יש לך עדים. פירוש: שנתגיירת בינך לבין עצמך. ותימה: מיהא, אי הא דבעינן ג' היינו דוקא לכתחלה, אבל דיעבד חד נמי כשר — א"כ אם יש לו עדים לאו בינו לבין עצמו הוא.

נאמן אתה לפסול עצמך כו'. היינו דוקא במילי [ו]דמשוי נפשיה חתיכה דאיסורא, אבל אם בא על בת כהן — לא פסלה, כדפרישית לעיל בסוף פ' שני (דף כה: ושם). וא"ת: היכי דמי? אם אשתו גויה — ממה נפשך בניו פסולים, דאין קרוי בנך אלא בנה. ואם היתה אשתו ישראלית — ממה נפשך בניו כשרים, דקי"ל (לעיל דף מה.): גוי ועבד הבא על בת ישראל — הולד כשר. וכי תימא נהי דממזר לא הוי — פגום מיהא הוי, הא השתא נמי דאין נאמן פגומין הם, דר"י אית ליה בפרק "עשרה יוחסין" (קדושין עז.) דבת גר זכר כבת חלל זכר! וי"ל: דקסבר ר"י גוי ועבד הבא על בת ישראל הולד ממזר, דבפרק "ד' מיתות" (סנהדרין דף נג. ושם) אמר דר' יהודה סבר לה כרבי עקיבא דאמר אין קידושין תופסין בחייבי לאוין.

כך נאמן אדם לומר זה בן גרושה. ר' אליהו מפרי"ש מפרש דנפקא לן מדכתיב "בן השנואה יכיר" (דברים כא). וכן משמע בירושלמי בפרק בתרא דקידושין. ולשון הש"ס לא משמע הכי, דקתני: כשם שנאמן אדם לומר זה בני בכור — משמע דמינה גמר. וי"מ דטעמא דר' יהודה, דמשמע ליה קרא דנאמן אדם לומר זה בני בכור אפי' על תינוק בין הבנים. וכשאומר על הקטן שהוא בכור — א"כ הראשון ממזר, אלמא דנאמן לפוסלו. וה"נ דנאמן לומר שהוא בן גרושה.

ואין עדות לגוי. ועל עצמו נאמן, משום דשוי נפשיה חתיכה דאיסורא. ואין אתה נאמן לפסול בני בניך. אומר ר"י דה"פ: נאמן אתה לפסול בניך, פי': כשאין לו אלא בנים ואין לו בני בנים, ואי אתה נאמן לפסול בני בניך — כשיש לו בני בנים אין נאמן לפסול אפי' בניו, דאין סברא לומר שיהיו בניו פסולים ובני בניו כשרים. וכן משמע בסמוך, דקאמר: ואין אדם נאמן על בנו גדול, ומפרש כשיש לו בנים, משמע דאבנו נמי לא מהימן. והלכתא כוותיה דרב נחמן בר יצחק. משמע דהלכה כר"י, דנאמן אף לפסול בניו, דדוקא משום דאין עדות לגוי דאין יכול לפוסלן. ולא כמו שמפרש רבינו תם דאין הלכה כרבי יהודה אלא כשפוסל אחרים על ידי הכרת בכור, אבל בלא הכרת בכור לא. ובשאלתות בפרשת *"וירא" נמי דקדק מהך דשמעתין דבכל ענין הלכה כרבי יהודה.

מטבילין

עין משפט נר מצוה

קכז א מיי' פי"ג מהל' איסורי ביאה הל' ז סמג לאוין קטז טוש"ע י"ד סי' רסח סעיף י:

[ועי' תוס' קידושין סב: ד"ה גר] *שייך לעמוד הקודם

קכח ב מיי' שם הלכה ח טוש"ע שם סי"א:

קכט ג מיי' פ"ב מהל' נחלות הלכה יד סמג עשין נו טוש"ע ח"מ סימן רעז סעי' יב:

קל ד מיי' פט"ו מהל' איסורי ביאה הל' טז סמג לאוין קטז:

קלא ה ו מיי' שם הל' טז וסמג שם טוש"ע אה"ע סימן ד סעיף כט:

קלב ז מיי' פי"ג שם הל' יד ופי"ד הל' א סמג לאוין קטז טוש"ע י"ד סימן רסח סעיף ב:

תוספות חד מקמאי

וכבר כתבתי מזה כל הצורך בפר"א דמילה: א"ר יוחנן בין בארץ בין בחוצה לארץ צריך להביא ראיה כשהוא מוחזק בעובד כוכבים אבל אם אינו מוחזק א"צ להביא ראיה. הפה שאסר הוא הפה שהתיר דאי בעי אמר ישראל אני מאבותי. וראיה לדבר ההוא גוי דהוה אכיל פסחים בירושלים בפרק קמא דפסחים: מעשה באחד שבא לפני ר' יהודה וא"ל נתגיירתי ביני לבין עצמי וכו' פי' לא היו מוחזקים בו שהוא גוי דא"כ היה צריך להביא ראיה עליו ועל בניו אלא היו מוחזקים בו שהיה גר. ושאל לו ר' יהודה יש לך עדים כלו' יש לך עדים שנתגיירת בינך לבין עצמך אפילו בניו פסולים ואם יש עדים שנתגיירת בפני ב"ד או א) בפניהם קבל עליו עול מצות שהודיעוהו [הרי] הוא גר גמור והוא עצמו כשר ומיירי שנתגייר הוא ובניו דאם נתגייר הוא לבדו ובא אח"כ על גיורת או על בת ישראל הרי בניו כשרים. דקי"ל גוי ועבד הבא על בת ישראל הולד כשר ואם לבתה האמר ר' יהודה בת גר זכר כבת חלל זכר. והיכא דאמרי סהדי שמענו שנתגייר בב"ד פלוני מהימנין ליה. תניא א"ר יהודה נאמן הוא על בנו קטן לאמר שהוא בן גרושה או בן חלוצה ואינו נאמן על בנו גדול. א"ר חייא בר אבא א"ר (שמעון) [יוחנן] לא קטן קטן ממש ולא גדול גדול ממש אלא קטן ויש לו בנים זהו גדול גדול ואין לו בנים זהו קטן כלומר נאמן הוא על בנו כשאין לו בנים אבל אם יש לו בנים אינו נאמן אפלו אבנו דאבריה המניה רחמנא ולא אבר בריה:

א) דעתו דבדיעבד אפי' דקבלת עול מצות בלבד הי' בפני ב"ד נמי סגי ועי' בטוש"ע יו"ד סימן רס"ח סעיף ג'.

מסורת הש"ס

[ברכות ע. וש"נ]

קידושין עד עח: ב"ב קכז:

[נ"ל וארא מ"ם מ"א]

הגהות הב"ח

(א) גמ' קמ"ל בארצכם אין לי: (ב) שם הא כתיב בארצכם ההוא: (ג) רש"י ד"ה מדכתיב גרו אצל: (ד) תוס' ד"ה משפט (בעמוד הקודם) אית ליה בהדיא. נ"ב עי' סנהדרין ב' ע"ב תוד"ה דברי הכל: (ה) ד"ה במוחזק וכו' כדפי' לעיל. נ"ב בפ' שני דף כה ע"ב בד"ה לימא:

הגהות הגר"א

[א] גמ' מעמך. נ"ל מאתכם (דכתיב בתר וכי יגור כו' הגר אתכם וכ"ה בתורת כהנים ומ"ש רש"י הוא תמוה): [ב] רש"י ד"ה מעמך כו' עד סה"ד. נמחק:

גליון הש"ס

גמ' א"ל נאמן אתה לפסול את עצמך. ע' כתובות כה ע"ב תד"ה הרי שאמר: שם ואי אתה נאמן לפסול את בניך. ע' לעיל כה ע"ב תד"ה לימא רב יוסף: תום' ד"ה במוחזק לך וכו' דרוב הבאין וכו' עיין ירושלמי רפ"ב דר"ה ובקרבן עדה שם: ד"ה נאמן אתה לפסול וכו' דמשוי נפשיה חתיכה לאיסורא. ע' במרדכי סוף פירקין:

לא רוב טובה ולא רוב פורענות. ואין מרבין עליו, ואין מדקדקין עליו. קיבל — מלין אותו מיד. נשתיירו בו ציצין המעכבין את המילה — חוזרים ומלין אותו שניה. נתרפא — מטבילין אותו מיד. ושני ת"ח עומדים על גביו, ומודיעין אותו מקצת מצות קלות ומקצת מצות חמורות. טבל ועלה — הרי הוא כישראל לכל דבריו. אשה — נשים מושיבות אותה במים עד צוארה, ושני ת"ח עומדים לה מבחוץ, ומודיעין אותה מקצת מצות קלות ומקצת מצות חמורות. אחד גר ואחד עבד משוחרר. ובמקום שנדה טובלת — שם גר ועבד משוחרר טובלין. וכל דבר שחוצץ בטבילה — חוצץ בגר ובעבד משוחרר ובנדה. אמר מר: גר שבא להתגייר אומרים לו: מה ראית שבאת להתגייר? ומודיעים אותו מקצת מצות קלות ומקצת מצות חמורות. מ"ט? דאי פריש — נפרוש. *דא"ר חלבו: קשים גרים לישראל כספחת, דכתיב "ונלוה הגר עליהם ונספחו על בית יעקב". § "ומודיעים אותו עון לקט שכחה ופאה ומעשר עני". § מ"ט? א"ר חייא בר אבא א"ר יוחנן: *בן נח נהרג על פחות משוה פרוטה, ולא ניתן להשבון. (*ומודיעים אותו עון שכחה ופאה). § "ואין מרבים עליו ואין מדקדקים עליו". § אמר רבי אלעזר: מאי קראה — דכתיב "ותרא כי מתאמצת היא ללכת אתה ותחדל לדבר אליה", אמרה לה: אסיר לן תחום שבת — "באשר תלכי אלך", אסיר לן יחוד — "באשר תליני אלין", מפקדינן שש מאות וי"ג מצות — "עמך עמי", אסיר לן עבודה זרה — "ואלהיך אלהי", *ארבע מיתות נמסרו לב"ד — "באשר תמותי אמות", *ב' קברים נמסרו לב"ד — "ושם אקבר". מיד — "ותרא כי מתאמצת היא וגו'". § "קיבל — מלין אותו מיד". § מ"ט? *שהויי מצוה לא משהינן. § "נשתיירו בו ציצין המעכבין המילה וכו'". § כדתנן: *אלו הן ציצין המעכבין המילה: בשר החופה את רוב העטרה, ואינו אוכל בתרומה. וא"ר ירמיה בר אבא אמר רב: בשר החופה רוב גובהה של עטרה. § "נתרפא מטבילין אותו מיד", § נתרפא — אין, לא נתרפא — לא. מאי טעמא? משום *דמיא מרזו מכה. § "ושני ת"ח עומדים על גביו". § והא *א"ר חייא א"ר יוחנן: גר צריך שלשה! הא א"ר יוחנן לתנא: תני שלשה. § "טבל ועלה הרי הוא כישראל לכל דבריו". § למאי הלכתא? דאי הדר ביה, ומקדש בת ישראל — ישראל מומר קרינא ביה, וקידושיו קידושין. § "אחד גר ואחד עבד משוחרר". § קסלקא דעתך לקבל עליו עול מצות, ורמינהו: במה דברים אמורים — בגר, אבל בעבד משוחרר — אין צריך לקבל! אמר רב ששת: לא קשיא, הא — ר"ש בן אלעזר, הא — רבנן. דתניא, "ובכתה את אביה ואת אמה וגו'" בד"א — שלא קבלה עליה, אבל קבלה עליה — מטבילה, *ומותר בה מיד. ר"ש בן אלעזר אומר: אע"פ שלא קבלה עליה — כופה, ומטבילה לשם שפחות, וחוזר ומטבילה לשם שחרור, ומשחררה, ומותר

רש"י

לא רוב הטובה. לפי שיצר הרע מחזר אחריהן, כדאמרי' במס' סוכה (דף נב:), ושמא תזוח דעתן עלייהו, ויחטאו. ואין מרבין עליו. דברים, לחייס עליו שיפרוש. ציצין. חתיכות בשר, שלא נפרעת המילה כהלכתה. ומודיעין אותו מקצת מצות. דהשתא, ע"י טבילה, הוא נכנס לכלל גירות, הלכך בשעת טבילת מצוה צריך לקבל עליו עול מצות. אחד גר ואחד עבד משוחרר. לקמן מפרש למאי הלכתא אקשינהו. ובמקום שנדה טובלת. בארבעים סאה. שם גר ועבד משוחרר טובלין. ואע"פ שאין טבילתו משום טומאה וטהרה כשאר טבילות. חוצץ בגר ועבד משוחרר ובנדה. לבעלה, ואע"פ שאין טבילתן לענין מגע טהרות כשאר טבילות. דאי פריש. שלא יתגייר. נפרוש. ולא איכפת לן. דאמר מר קשים גרים לישראל כספחת דכתיב ונלוה הגר עליהם ונספחו על בית יעקב. לשון ספחת, שאוחזין מעשיהם הראשונים, ולומדים ישראל מהם, או סומכין עליהם באיסור והיתר. ומודיעין אותו עון לקט שכחה ופאה. שלא יאמרו: עניים הללו הלוקטין פאת שדה — גזלנים הם, ועומד עליהם והורגם בדיניהם, שבני נח הוזהרו על הגזל, בסנהדרין (דף נו.), ואזהרתן זו היא מיתתן, דלא בעו התראה. לפיכך בן נח נהרג על פחות משוה פרוטה, דגוי קפיד על דבר מועט, ולגבי ישראל הויא מחילה. ולא ניתן להשבון. אינו בחזרה, אלא נהרג. דגבי ישראל כתיב "והשיב את הגזלה אשר גזל" (ויקרא ה), אבל בני נח אמרינן בסנהדרין (דף נח:): אזהרתן זו היא מיתתן. וכיון שעבר על אחת מז' מצות — נהרג. לישנא אחרינא: מודיעים אותו עון לקט שכחה ופאה. הואיל והן מקפידים על הממון כ"כ, כדאמר דנהרג על פחות משוה פרוטה — מודיעין אותו עון לקט כו' שמא יחזור בו מלהתגייר. ולשון זה עיקר, דאי משום טעמא קמא — מאי לשון עון לקט שכחה ופאה? יודיעוהו (א) שילקטו עניים בשדהו. אסיר לן יחוד. להתייחד עם אשת איש. ב' קברים. אחד לנסקלים ולנשרפים שהרשיעו בעבירות חמורות, ואחד לנהרגים ולנחנקים שאין מיתתן חמורה, ואינם רשעים כל כך. עטרה. שורה גבוהה שסביב הגיד, וממנה הולך ומשפע למעלה ולמטה. רוב גובהה. של אותה שורה, ולא תימא רוב היקיפה. ואין אוכל בתרומה. אם כהן הוא. דכהן ערל אסור בתרומה, כדאמר לקמן בפרק "הערל". מרזו מכה. מכבידין את חולי המכה, כמו מטרא רזיא לאילני במסכת תענית (דף ג:). דאי הדר ביה. לקדמותו, ואח"כ קידש בת ישראל — מקודשת, וצריכה גט. דישראל מומר קידושיו קידושין, דישראל הוא. קס"ד. דהאי דאקיש שיחרור של עבד לגירות הגוי לקבל קאמר, שבשעת טבילת שחרור העבד צריך להודיעו מקצת מצות. אבל עבד אין צריך לקבל. בשעת שחרור, דמשעה שטובל לשם עבדות שייך במצות, דכתיב (דברים ה) "למען ינוח עבדך ואמתך". ועוד: דגמרי' (חגיגה דף ד.) "לה" "לה" מאשה. שלא קבלה עליה. להתגייר. כופה ומטבילה לשם שפחות. דכל טבילות עבדים על כרחן היא. ומשחררה. ומטבילה לשם שחרור בע"כ. ומותר

תוספות

מטבילין אותו מיד. משמע שהמילה קודם טבילה, וכדאמר: אין גר עד שימול ויטבול. ותימה: דאמר ב"הערל" (לקמן דף עח.) מעוברת שנתגיירה בנה אין צריך טבילה! ואר"י: דשאני התם, דאכתי לא חזי למילה. במקום שהנדה טובלת. טבילת נדה לא כתב קרא בהדיא, ופי' רב יהודה גאון דנפקא לן בק"ו ממגעה דטעון טבילה — וכ"ש היא עצמה. ור"ת מפרש דנפקא לן מהא דדרשינן בע"ז (דף עה:): "אך במי נדה יתחטא" — מים שהנדה טובלת בהם, וכמה הם — מ' סאה. ורבינו יצחק פירש: דנפקא מהא דדרשינן בפ' "במה אשה" (שבת דף סד:) תהיה בנדתה — תהא בנדתה עד שתבא במים*א). שם גר ועבד טובלים. בכולי שמעתין משמע דעבד בעי טבילה כשמשתחרר, ולא סגי ליה בטבילה קמייתא. וקשה: דב"השולח" (גיטין דף מ.) אמרינן: הכותב שטר אירוסין לשפחתו, ואמר לה נאי בו והתקדשי בו — משמע דמקודשת, אע"ג דלא טבלה! וי"ל: דאיירי כגון שטבלה מקודם לשם שחרור, שהטבילה של שחרור קודמת לגט, כדמשמע לקמן, דקתני: ומטבילה לשם שחרור ומשחררה, ומותר בה מיד. וכל דבר שחוצץ בטבילה כו' ובנדה. תימה: דלענין הכשר מקוה פשיטא ליה שאין לחלק בין נדה לבעלה, ובין טהרות, דקאמר: במקום שהנדה טובלת. ולענין חציצה תלי נדה בטבילת טומאה וטהרה! וי"ל: דבחציצה דאיכא מילי טובא דלא הוי אלא מדרבנן, כגון רובו ואינו מקפיד, או מיעוטו ומקפיד, איצטריך לאשמועינן דבחציצה דרבנן נמי אין לחלק בין לבעלה לטהרות, ואיכא מילי דחציצה דאמר בפ' בתרא דנדה (דף סז. ושם): ה"מ — לטהרות, אבל לבעלה — לא, והיינו ספק חציצה, אבל ודאי חציצה, אפילו דרבנן — לא הקילו לבעלה יותר מלטהרות. ובקונטרס לא גרס ליה במסכת נדה משום הא דהכא. קשים גרים לישראל (ג) כספחת. לפי שאין בקיאין בדקדוקי מצות, וישראל למדין ממעשיהם. ובמס' נדה (דף יג: ושם) פירש בקונטרס עוד לשון אחר: משום דכל ישראל ערבים זה בזה. *וקשה: דבפרק "אלו נאמרים" (סוטה דף לז:) משמע שלא היו ערבין על הגרים, דלא חשיב התם ערבות של ערב רב! ועוד י"ל: דקשים גרים לישראל — לפי שמתערבין בהם, ואין שכינה שורה אלא על משפחות המיוחסות שבישראל. וי"מ: לפי שביותר הוזהרו ישראל על הגרים, ואין יכולין להזהר מאונאתן*ב). אלא

תוספות ישנים

שתלא נפשו גבי ימול גוי ואל ימול כותי לפי שהוא מל לשם הר גריזים וי"ל דהתם עדיף טפי לפי שהישראל עומד ע"ג של כותי: **א)** עי"מ מק"ו דכתיב יכבס בגדיו כ"ש היא עצמה שצריכה טבילה וי"מ דכתיב ומזה מי הנדה מכאן לנדה שצריכה מים: **ב)** עי"מ לפי שהקב"ה מעניש אותנו על ידם כשמטיבים מעשיהם ואומר כי הוא רואה שאין אנו נזהרים במצות כמותם אע"פ שאינם מזרע כשר כמונו: **ומודיעין** אותן עון לקט שכחה חוששין פן יראו העניים באים בשדותיהם ללקוט לקט שכחה ופאה ויהרגו אותם כמו שהם עושים בדיניהם מפני שבן נח נהרג על פחות משוה פרוטה ולא ניתן להשבון שאזהרה שלהם זו היא מיתתן ולא קרינן בהו ונהרגין בלא התראה דבן נח א"ל התראה. י"מ מודיעין אותן עון לקט מפני שמקפידים על ממון מועט וחיישינן שמא יחזרו לסורן ומהשתא מודיעין אותו לו שינית ואל יקפיד ואי פריש מהשתא נפרוש לפי שיהיה עינו צרה אבל פירוש קמא לא נהירא דא"כ דלא חיישינן אלא שמא יהרגו בדיניהם העניים. מה לנו להודיעם עון לקט שכחה ופאה נאמר להם הזהרו שלא תהרגו עניים כשיבואו ללקוט בשדותיכם כי דינים בזה אבל השתא ניחא

עין משפט נר מצוה

קלג א מיי' פי"ד מהל' איסורי ביאה הל' ב סמג לאוין קטז טוש"ע י"ד סימן רסח סעיף ב:
קלד ב מיי' שם הל' ט סמג שם טוש"ע שם סימן רסח סעיף ג:
קלה ג מיי' שם פי"ג הל' יג ופ"ב מהל' מקוואות הל' כב סמג שם טוש"ע שם סימן רסח סעיף ב:
קלו ד מיי' פי"ג מהל' איסורי ביאה הל' יח:
קלז ה מיי' פ"ט מהל' מלכים הלכה ט:
[ע' תוספות חגיגה יח. ד"ה לא נצרכה ותו' יומא עח. ד"ה מכאן]
קלח ו ז מיי' פ"ב מהל' מילה הל' ג סמג עשין כח טוש"ע י"ד סי' רסד סעיף ה:
קלט ח מיי' פי"ג מהל' איסורי ביאה הל' יז סמג לאוין קטז טוש"ע שם סימן רסח סעיף ב:
קמ ט מיי' שם הל' יב סמג שם טוש"ע שם סעיף ז:
קמא י מיי' פ"ח מהל' מלכים הלכה ה:

[וע"ע תוס' קידושין ע: ובנדה יג: ד"ה קשים]

גליון הש"ס

גמ' קשים גרים לישראל כספחת. וברמב"ם פי"ג הל' י"ח מהל' א"ב איתא כנגע צרעת:

מסורת הש"ס

קידושין ע: ע"ש נדה יג: לקמן קט:
ע"ז עא: ערכין כב.
רש"ל מ"ז
[סנהדרין מט:]
[שם מו.]
[לעיל לט.]
לקמן עח: שבת קלז.
[לקמן קב: קכח.]
[לעיל מו:]
[ואין הפירוש שמותר לבא עליה מיד דהא בעינן להמתין ג' חדשים ע' ב"מ פ"ח מהל' מלכים דין ה]

הגהות הב"ח

(א) רש"י ד"ה לישנא אחרינא וכו' יודיעוהו שסופו שילקטו: (ב) תוס' ד"ה קשים גרים לישראל כספחת. נ"ב עיין בתוס' פ' י' יוחסין דף עב:

ומותר בה מיד. אמר רבא: מאי טעמא דרבי שמעון בן אלעזר — דכתיב °"כל עבד איש מקנת כסף", עבד איש ולא עבד אשה?! אלא: עבד איש אתה מל בעל כרחו, ואי אתה מל בן איש בעל כרחו. ורבנן? אמר עולא: כשם שאי אתה מל בן איש בעל כרחו כך אי אתה מל עבד איש בעל כרחו. ואלא, הכתיב "כל עבד איש"! ההוא מיבעי ליה לכדשמואל. *דאמר שמואל: [א]המפקיר עבדו יצא לחירות, ואין צריך גט שחרור, שנאמר "כל עבד איש מקנת כסף", עבד איש ולא עבד אשה? אלא: עבד שיש לו רשות לרבו עליו — קרוי עבד, ושאין רשות לרבו עליו — אין קרוי עבד. מתקיף לה רב פפא: אימור דשמעת להו לרבנן ביפת תואר, דלא שייכא במצות. אבל עבד דשייך במצות — הכי נמי דאפי' רבנן מודו. דתניא: אחד גר ואחד לוקח עבד מן הגוי צריך לקבל. הא לוקח מישראל — אין צריך לקבל, מני? אי רבי שמעון בן אלעזר — האמר לוקח מן הגוי נמי אין צריך לקבל. אלא לאו — רבנן, וש"מ: [ב]דלוקח מן הגוי צריך לקבל, אבל לוקח מישראל — אין צריך לקבל. ואלא קשיא אחד גר ואחד עבד משוחרר! [ג]כי תניא ההיא — לענין טבילה תניא. תנו רבנן: °"וגלחה את ראשה ועשתה את צפרניה" רבי אליעזר אומר: תקוץ, רבי עקיבא אומר: [ד]תגדיל. אמר רבי אליעזר: נאמרה עשיה בראש ונאמרה עשיה בצפרנים, מה להלן העברה — אף כאן העברה. רבי עקיבא אומר: נאמר עשיה בראש, ונאמר עשיה בצפרנים. מה להלן ניוול — אף כאן ניוול. וראיה לדברי רבי אליעזר °"ומפבשת בן שאול ירד לקראת המלך לא עשה רגליו ולא עשה שפמו". מאי עשיה — העברה. ת"ר: °"ובכתה את אביה ואת אמה", ר'

שמות יב | דברים כא | שמואל ב יט | דברים כא

רש"י

ומותר בה מיד. אלמא: לר' שמעון עבד אין צריך לקבל בשעת טבילת שחרור. ולרבנן, דלא הוי תקנתא בהכי — סברי צריך לקבל. עבד איש ולא עבד אשה. בתמיה. ואשה שקנתה עבדים ולא מלו, מי לא הוו כשאר עבדים? אלא ע"כ, האי איש — אגוי שמכרו קאי, ולמעוטי בן איש. וה"ק: עבד שלקחת מן הגוי אתה מל בעל כרחו של עבד, ואי אתה מל בן גוי בעלמא, דלאו עבד, בעל כרחו. ומדכתב רחמנא "איש", קרא יתירא, למעוטי בן איש, ש"מ "ומלתה אותו" בעל כרחו משמע, דאי מדעתו — היכי ממעט לבן איש? ואי לא כתיב איש ה"א האי עבד לאו למעוטי בן אמה, אלא היא גופא איצטריך לאשמועינן — דמילת עבדים מעכבא בפסח. לשון אחר, ועיקר: "עבד איש" ה"ק: עבד שהוא איש, אע"פ שהוא גדול ובן דעת — "ומלתה אותו" בעל כרחו. ואי אתה מל בן [שהוא] איש, גר הבא להתגייר אין לו כח למול בנו גדול בעל כרחו, דגבי בנים כתיב "המול לו כל זכר", ולא כתיב בהו "איש", וגבי עבד כתיב "איש" למעוטי בן. ורבנן. כשם שאין אתה מל בן איש [בע"כ], דהא לא כתיב בהו איש. כך אי אתה מל כו'. ומילתא בעלמא היא, ולא הקישא, אלא ה"ק ליה: כי היכי דמודית לן בבן — ה"ה לעבד נמי, דאין מגיירין בן דעת אלא מרצונו. אימור דקא שמעת לרבנן. דפליגי אדרבי שמעון, דלא הויא תקנתא. ביפת תואר. דלא שייכא במצות. אבל עבד. שאשה אצלו כמה ימים, ויהג עליו מצות הנוהגות בעבד — מי שמעת להו דצריך לקבל? לענין טבילה תניא. שניהם שוים בטבילה, שצריכים לטבול כשבאין לכלל ישראל גמור. אבל לענין קבלה לא הושוו, דעבד אין צריך לקבל בשעת טבילת שחרור. תקוץ. הצפרנים קאי, ואע"ג דלאו ניוול גזירת הכתוב היא. עשיה בראש. כלומר, נאמר שם תיקון מצוה בראש, דכתיב "וגלחה". לא עשה רגליו. לא קצץ צפרני רגליו. ולא עשה שפמו. לא גלח שער שפמו. אלמא: עשיה קרי להעברה. כי

תוספות

אלא עבד איש אתה מל בעל כרחו. פי' בקונט' בלשון שני: דעבד איש, אע"ג שהוא גדול ובן דעת – "ומלתה אותו וגו'" בעל כרחו, ואי אתה מל בן איש, גר הבא להתגייר אין לו כח למול בנו גדול בעל כרחו. דגבי בנים כתיב "המול לו כל זכר" ולא כתיב בהו "כל איש" כמו גבי עבד. ודבר תימה פירש; דקרא ד"המול לו כל זכר" מוקמינן למילת זכריו, שמעכבתו מלאכול בפסח, וזה לא שייך אלא בבנים שנולדו בקדושה. אבל מילת בניו שלא נולדו בקדושה – אינה מעכבתו מלאכול בפסח! ונראה דלא צריך קרא למידרש מיניה "ואי אתה מל בן איש בעל כרחו", דממילא ידעינן שלא יגיירוהו בעל כרחו. ועוד: דמיפת תואר שמעינן דאין מלין גר בעל כרחו, דהא יפת תואר אין מטבילין אותה בעל כרחה, מדאיצטריך רחמנא להמתין לה שלשים יום. ובקבלה עליה – אין צריך להמתין. ולא נקטיה אלא לפרושי מילתיה דרשב"א, דקאמר דמתחלה כופין לשם שפחות ולא לשם גירות. אי נמי, משום דנקט לה במילתיה דרבנן "כשם שאי אתה מל בן איש" נקט נמי בדרבי שמעון בן אלעזר, לאשמועינן דאע"פ שאי אתה מל בן איש בעל כרחו – עבד אתה מל בעל כרחו. תימה: דרשב"א קאמר לקמן דאין משהין אותו בא"י מפני הפסד טהרות – עבד שאינו רוצה למול, ומשמע דזקוק למוכרו, ולמאי? ימהלנו בעל כרחו! וכן קשה, דרבי יהושע בן לוי אית ליה ב"השולח" (גיטין דף לט: ושם): נתיאשתי מפלוני עבדי, אותו העבד אין לו תקנה אלא בשטר. אלמא, לית לי' ההיא דשמואל דבסמוך, וא"כ דריש: עבד איש אתה מל בעל כרחו, ולקמן קאמר: הלוקח עבד מן הגוי ולא רצה למול – מגלגל עמו עד י"ב חודש וימול אותו בעל כרחו! ואומר ר"י: דתקנת חכמים היא שלא יכשיל את רבו באיסור והיתר, כיון דאין מקבל עליו עול מצות. ועוד: דאין טוב לחייבו במצות, מאחר דאין חפץ לקיימם. **המפקיר** עבדו יצא לחירות ואין צריך גט שחרור. תימה: לשמואל תקשי ליה: למה ליה שטרא בעבד כנעני? יפקירנו ולימא ליה באפי בי תרי "זיל", דהכי דייק בפ"ק דקידושין (דף טז. ושם) גבי עבד עברי למה לי שטרא, לימא ליה באפי בי תרי זיל. ומשני: עבד עברי גופו קנוי! ואר"י: דהכי פריך(א): למה לי שטרא, דאותו לשון עצמו הכתוב בשטר "הרי את בן חורין" "הרי את לעצמך" – יאמר לו בעל פה! דס"ד דאין צריך אלא מחילה מחוב שעליו, ומסיק דגופו קנוי ואין הלשון הכתוב בשטר מועיל בעל פה, אבל הפקר, שמסלק רשותו, מועיל אפי' בעל פה לשמואל. וא"ת: אמאי לא חשיב הפקר גבי קניים של עבד בפ"ק דקידושין? (*גז"ש). וי"ל: דלא חשיב אלא קניים שמקנה הרב לעבד עצמו, והפקר אינו אלא סילוק בעלמא, שהרב מסלק עצמו מן העבד. ועוד יש לומר: דמילתא דאיתא בכל מילי לא קתני, כדקאמר התם לענין חליפין, ותנא דידן – מילתא דאיתא במטלטלין לא קתני. **לא** עשה רגליו. פי' בקונטרס: צפרני רגליו. ולר"י נראה דהיינו שער בית הערוה, דהכי משמע פרק "מצות חליצה" (לקמן קג.) גבי "מן הארכובה ולמעלה חליצתה פסולה", למימרא דלא מיקרי רגל מן הארכובה ולמעלה? תא שמע: ולא עשה את רגליו, ומשני: לישנא מעליא. מכאן אין ראיה דשרי לגלח שער של בית הערוה, דשמא מדרבנן אסור. אבל בריש פרק "ב' נזירים" (נזיר נח:) קאמר רב בהדיא: מיקל אדם כל גופו בתער, אפילו שער בית השחי ובית הערוה, כדמשמע התם דפריך עלה: והתניא המעביר שער בית השחי ובית הערוה הרי זה לוקה! ומשני: כי קאמר רב – במספרים. והא בתער קאמר! כעין תער. וא"ת דבתר הכי קאמר בעי מיניה רב מרבי חייא: מהו לגלח? א"ל: אסור. והא קא גדיל? א"ל: גדול יש לו. משמע דבמספרים בעא מיניה אי שרי, דאי בתער – מאי פריך והא קא גדיל? והלא יכול לגלח במספרים! ושמא רב לא קבלה מרבי חייא. ור"ת מפרש: דבתער בעא מיניה, והא דפריך: והא קא גדיל – ה"פ: והלא אין זה תיקון, ואין דומה כלל לתיקוני אשה, שאין זה משום ייפוי אלא משום צער, שגדל יותר מדאי. ואפילו בתער אית לן למישרי! ולפי זה צריך לומר שלא היה יודע ברייתא דלעיל שאוסרת. ובה"ג גרים הכי, אמר רב: מיקל אדם כל גופו בתער, והתניא המעביר כו' – כי קאמר רב בשאר אברים. ובשאר אברים מי שרי? והתניא העברת שער אינו מדברי תורה אלא מדברי סופרים, ומשמע ליה דאיירי ההיא ברייתא אף *(בשאר אברים, אע"ג דבבית השחי ובבית הערוה נמי איירי, כדמוכח בתר הכי דכי קאמר רב במספרים כי תניא ההיא בתער, ולפי זה בשאר אברים לא שרי אלא במספרים. ובית השחי ובית הערוה – אפי' במספרים אסור, ומדרבנן, דלא תקשי הך דהכא. מיהו, בה"ג של אספמיא כתוב: אלא, הא בתער והא במספרים, והדר ביה משינויא קמא דשני כי קאמר רב בשאר אברים). ולגירסא זו שאר אברים ודאי אסור לגלח בתער, אבל במספרים שרי אף בית השחי ובית הערוה. ובערוך בערך גינוסטרא גורס כגירסת ספרים שלנו. ובתשובת הגאונים שרי לגלח בית השחי ובית הערוה כי מגלח כל גופו מראשו ועד רגליו. ולא משמע דאיירי במצורע, דפשיטא הוא \ אלא במגלח לרפואה, כיון דמגלח כל גופו – אין זה ייפוי אלא ניוול. ותדע, דלא משתמיט בשום דוכתא גבי מצורע שיהא עשה דמצורע דוחה לאו דלא ילבש גבר, אלא לאו דהקפת הראש וזקן גרידא.

רבי

עין משפט נר מצוה

קמב א מיי' פ"ח מהל' עבדים הלכה יג טוש"ע י"ד סימן רסז סעיף סד:

קמג ב מיי' פי"ד מהל' איסורי ביאה הל' ט סמג לאוין קיז טוש"ע שם סימן רסח סעיף ג:

קמד ג מיי' שם פי"ג הל' יג סמג שם טוש"ע שם:

קמה ד מיי' פ"ח מהל' מלכים הלכה ה סמג עשין קנב:

תוספות ישנים

א) והא דלא משני תלמודא התם דבשאר אברים שרי לגמרי בתער והא דקאמר העברת שער אינה אלא מד"ס דמשמע דהא מדברי סופרים מיהא איתא מיירי בבית השחי ובבית הערוה. והא דקאמר המעביר בית השחי ובית הערוה ה"ז לוקה ר"ל מכת מרדות מדרבנן. כדמשני תלמודא התם גבי ר' יוחנן דאמר המעביר בית השחי ובית הערוה ה"ז לוקה. ופריך מהא דהעברת שער אינה אלא מד"ס. ומשני מאי לוקה מכת מרדות מדרבנן. וי"ל משום דס"ל דהעברת שער מיירי בכל אברים מדלא מפרש בית השחי ובית הערוה כמו דמפרש גבי המעביר בית השחי ובית הערוה לוקה:

[גיטין לח. נזיר סב: קידושין עב:]

הגהות הב"ח

(א) תוס' ד"ה המפקיר [...]' ואר"י דהכי פריך. נ"ב [...]נתו בתירוץ זה למה [...]ירצו התוס' בקידושין [...] טז בד"ה לימא ליה [...]ם ועיין עוד בפרק [...]ולח דף לח בתוס' ד"ה המפקיר:

גליון הש"ס

[...]' ולא עבד אשה. עיין [...]רש"א לקמן עא ע"ב [...]ה כגון שהיה אביו: שם [...] דאפילו רבנן מודו. [...] קידושין דף סב ע"ב [...]"ה אלא מעתה: תוס' [...] אלא עבד כו'. ולמאי [...]לנו בעל כרחו. עיין [...] נז ע"ב תד"ה נוד:

[אולי צ"ל דף כב:]

[בשאר אברים ומשני ...ואמר רב כו' מהרש"ל]

קמו א ב מיי׳ פ״ח מהל׳ מלכים הלכה ה סמג עשין קנב:
קמז ג מיי׳ פ״א מהלכות מילה הל׳ ו ופי״ד מהל׳ איסורי ביאה הל׳ ט סמג עשין סז טוש״ע י״ד סימן רסז סעיף ד:
קמח ד מיי׳ וסמג שם טוש״ע שם בהג״ה:

ר׳ אליעזר*אומר: ״אביה״ – אביה ממש, ״אמה״ – אמה ממש. ר״ע אומר: א״אביה ואמה״ – זו עבודה זרה, וכן הוא אומר °״אומרים לעץ אבי אתה וגו׳״. ״ירח ימים״ – ב״ירח שלשים יום. ר״ש בן אלעזר אומר: תשעים יום, ״ירח״ – שלשים, ״ימים״ – שלשים, ״ואחר כן״ – שלשים. מתקיף לה רבינא: אימא ״ירח״ - שלשים, ״ימים״ - שלשים, ״ואחר כן״ - כי הני! – קשיא. ת״ר: מקיימין עבדים שאינם מלין, דברי רבי ישמעאל. רבי עקיבא אומר: אין מקיימין. אמר ליה ר׳ ישמעאל: הרי הוא אומר °״וינפש בן אמתך״! א״ל: בלוקח עבד בין השמשות ולא הספיק למולו הכתוב מדבר. דכ״ע מיהת ״וינפש בן אמתך״ בעבד ערל כתיב, מאי משמע? דתניא: *״וינפש בן אמתך״ – בעבד ערל הכתוב מדבר. אתה אומר בעבד ערל, או אינו אלא בעבד מהול? כשהוא אומר: °״למען ינוח עבדך ואמתך כמוך״ – הרי עבד מהול אמור, הא מה אני מקיים ״וינפש בן אמתך״! – בעבד ערל. ״והגר״ – זה גר תושב, אתה אומר זה גר תושב. או אינו אלא גר צדק? כשהוא אומר ״וגרך אשר בשעריך״ – הרי גר צדק אמור, הא מה אני מקיים ״והגר״ – זה גר תושב. אמר רבי יהושע בן לוי: גהלוקח עבד מן הגוי ולא רצה למול, מגלגל עמו עד י״ב חדש. לא מל – חוזר ומוכרו לגוים. אמרוה רבנן קמיה דרב פפא: כמאן – דלא כר׳ עקיבא, דאי ר״ע – האמר אין מקיימין! אמר להו רב פפא: אפילו תימא ר׳ עקיבא, הני מילי – היכא דלא פסקא למילתיה, אבל היכא דפסקא למילתיה – פסקא. אמר רב כהנא: אמריתא לשמעתא קמיה דרב זביד מנהרדעא, אמר לי: אי הכי, כי אמר ליה ר״ע בלוקח עבד בין השמשות – לישני ליה הא! חדא מתרי טעמי קאמר. שלח רבין משמיה דרבי אילעאי, וכל רבותי אמרו לי משמו: דאיזהו עבד ערל שמותר לקיימו – זה שלקחו רבו על מנת שלא למולו. אמרוה רבנן קמיה דרב פפא: כמאן – דלא כרבי עקיבא, דאי ר״ע – האמר: אין מקיימין! אמר להו רב פפא: אפילו תימא רבי עקיבא, ה״מ – היכא דלא אתני בהדיה, אבל היכא דאתני – אתני. אמר רב כהנא: אמריתא לשמעתא קמיה דרב זביד מנהרדעא, וא״ל: אי הכי, כי קאמר ליה רבי עקיבא בלוקח עבד בין השמשות ולא הספיק למולו – לישני ליה הא! ולטעמיך – לישני ליה הך! אלא: *חד מתרי ותלת טעמי קאמר. יתיב רבי חנינא בר פפי ורבי אמי ור׳ יצחק נפחא אקילעא דרבי יצחק נפחא, ויתבי וקאמרי: עיר אחת היתה בארץ ישראל ולא רצו עבדיה למול, וגלגלו עמהם עד שנים עשר חדש, וחזרו ומכרום לגוים. כמאן – כי האי תנא. דתניא: הלוקח עבד מן הגוי ולא רצה למול – מגלגל עמו עד שנים עשר חדש, לא מל – חוזר ומוכרו לגוים. ר׳ שמעון בן אלעזר אומר: אין משהין אותו בארץ ישראל, מפני הפסד טהרות. ובעיר הסמוכה לספר – אין משהין אותו כל עיקר, שמא ישמע דבר, וילך ויאמר לחברו גוי. תניא, רבי חנניא בנו של רבן גמליאל אומר: מפני מה גרים בזמן הזה מעונין, ויסורין באין עליהן – מפני שלא קיימו שבע מצות בני נח. רבי יוסי אומר: *גר שנתגייר כקטן שנולד דמי. אלא מפני מה מעונין – לפי שאין בקיאין בדקדוקי מצות כישראל, אבא חנן אומר משום ר׳ אלעזר: לפי שאין עושין מאהבה אלא מיראה. אחרים אומרים: מפני ששהו עצמם להכנס תחת כנפי השכינה. אמר ר׳ אבהו ואיתימא ר׳ חנינא: מאי קראה – °״ישלם ה׳ פעלך ותהי משכרתך שלמה מעם ה׳ אלהי ישראל אשר באת לחסות״ וגומר.§

מתני׳

ירמיה ב | שמות כג | דברים ה | רות ב

רש״י

כי הני. שבים. (א) ״ואחר כן תבא אליה״ – אחר שיעור אחר כזה תבא אליה. הרי הוא אומר וינפש בן אמתך. והאי בעבד ערל כתיב, כדמפרש לקמן. בין השמשות של ע״ש ולא הספיק למולו. ומזהירו הכתוב לרבו על עבדו לנוח ביום השבת. ולא על שבת הבאה, שהרי צריך למולו בשבת זו. וכיון דמל – מקרא אחר נפקא מ״למען ינוח עבדך״, דלקמן מוקי לה בעבד שמל. גר תושב. שקבל עליו שלא לעבוד עבודה זרה, ואוכל נבלות. והזהירו הכתוב על השבת, דמחלל את השבת כעובד עבודה זרה. האמר אין מקיימין. אפילו יום אחד. ה״מ. דאין מקיים. היכא דלא פסקא למילתיה. דלא קיבל מעולם להתגייר, ולא פסק מגיותו. אבל היכא דפסקא למילתיה. בשעת לקיחתו, ונתפייס להתגייר, ואחר כך חזר בו – מגלגלין, שמא יחזור ויתרצה, לשון מורי. לישנא אחרינא: ה״מ – דאין מקיימין, היכא דלא פסק למילתיה, שמקיימין סתם, אבל היכא דפסק דאמר לו הריני מגלגל עמך י״ב חדש, ואם לא תמול אמכור אותך – מותר, דהוי גביה כשכיר בעלמא. לשמעתא. האי תרוצא דרב פפא דהיכא דפסק למילתיה – משהינן. לישני ליה הא. כגון דפסק למילתיה, דיכול לקיימו כל י״ב חדש. חד מתרי טעמי. שני ליה. וכל רבותי אמרו לי משמיה. דרבי אלעאי. הפסד טהרות. שמטמא את התרומות. דגוי גזרו עליו שיהא טמא כזב לכל דבריו. לספר. מרק״א בלע״ז, כרך המבדיל בין ארץ ישראל לארץ העמים. שלא קיימו ז׳ מצות. בעודן גוים. ועד השתא לא איפרעו מינייהו, דפורענות גנוזה להם לעתיד לבא. אבל כשמתגיירין – נפרעין מהם כדי למרק חובתן. כקטן שנולד. ואינו נענש על שעבר. מיראה. מיראת גיהנם והפורענות האמורה עליהם. אשר באת. שמיהרת ולא איחרת.

מתני׳

תוספות

רבי אליעזר אומר אביה כו׳. למיסבר קראי פליגי. אי נמי נפקא מינה אם מתו אביה ואמה או נתגיירו. וריב״ן פירש דלר״ע צריכה שתכפור בעבודה זרה קודם שתבעל לו. ולפירושו לא אתי כר״ע הא דקתני לעיל בד״א שלא קיבלה עליה.

ירח שלשים יום. וכן בפ״ק דנזיר (דף ה. ושם): ואימא שלשים יום כדכתיב ״עד חדש ימים״. משמע דסתם חדש שלשים. והא דאמרי׳ בר״ה (דף יט:) ובסנהדרין (דף יא. ושם) כמה עיבור שנה – שלשים יום, רשב״ג אומר – חודש! היכא דמוכח – שאני* א).

אין מקיימין. פירש ריב״ן: שלא ינסך יינו. וקשיא לר״י: דא״כ, כי אתני בהדיה נמי! ועוד: דמתשובתו של ר׳ ישמעאל משמע דמדאורייתא פליגי! ונראה לר״י דטעמא דר׳ עקיבא לפי שצוה הקב״ה לאברהם למול עבדיו, לכך אסור לקיים שאינם מולין.

זה גר תושב. פירש בקונטרס: שקבל עליו שלא לעבוד עבודה זרה, ומחלל שבת כעובד עבודה זרה. וקשה: דאם כן נפישי להו משבע מצות! ובמסכת ע״ז (דף סד:) משמע דבשבע מצות שקבלו בני נח איקרי גר תושב! ועוד, דבפרק ״ארבע מיתות״ (סנהדרין דף נח:) אמרי׳ דגוי ששבת חייב מיתה אפילו בחול, כל שכן בשבת. ובפרק ״ד׳ מחוסרי כפרה״ (כריתות דף ט. ושם) קאמר ר״ע דגר תושב אין מוזהר על השבת! ונראה דהכא בעושה מלאכה לצורך ישראל, דומיא ד״וינפש בן אמתך״.

היכא דלא פסקא וכו׳. פר״ת: דהני מילי אדר׳ יהושע קאי. ולא פסקא למילתיה – היינו שכל שעה דוחה אותו מיום ליום שימול. אבל היכא דפסקא למילתיה שלא ימול כלל – התם אין מקיימין. ולא משמע כן, דה״מ אדר״ע קאי! ונראה לר״י כפירושו, אבל אדר״ע קאי, דהיכא דנתרצה למול ודוחהו – התם אין מקיימין, הואיל ומצוה למול, דשהויי מצוה לא משהינן. אבל היכא דפסק שלא ימול – אינו מחויב למולו בעל כרחו, ומגלגל י״ב חדש עמו, אולי יתרצה. וכן פי׳ בשערי דרב האי בשער *רביעי. [נ״ל שבועי]

שאין עושין מאהבה אלא מיראה. בפרק *״נוטל״ [נ״ל היה נוטל] (בסוטה דף כב: ושם) משמע שניהם רעים, ובפרק ״כשם״ (שם דף לא. ושם) משמע דשניהם לשבח! ואומר ר״י דמאהבת המקום ומיראת המקום – הוו תרווייהו לשבח, מאהבת אדם ומיראת אדם – תרווייהו לגריעותא. או כמו שפירש שם בקונט׳: מאהבת שכר, וכגון שאם לא יהיה לו שכר – תוהא על הראשונות ואין עושה אלא על מנת לקבל פרס. ומיראה – היינו מיראת עונש. אבל הכא קשה, דנקט מאהבה לשבח ומיראה לגריעותא, והוי מצי למימר איפכא: או תרווייהו לגריעותא, או תרווייהו לשבח! אשר באת לחסות. פירוש: שמיהרת. ותימה: דבפ׳ ״מי שאמר הריני נזיר ושמע חבירו ואמר ואני״ (נזיר דף כג: ושם) אומר: רות בת בנו של עגלון בנו של בלק מלך מואב היתה, וכשתחשוב שנותיו של אהוד שהרג עגלון עד סוף ימים של אבצן, דהיינו: בועז, תמצא יותר ממאתים שנה, ולעת זקנתו נשאה, דכתיב ״לבלתי לכת אחרי הבחורים״! וי״ל: דבת בנו של עגלון לאו דוקא, אלא כלומר דמזרעו היתה, כמו בן בנו של נמרוד הרשע (חגיגה דף יג.), ובקרא קרי לה נערה.

שמעון

תוספות ישנים

א) נראה לומר דירח דקרא ר״ל מלא משום שאין חדשה של לבנה פחותה מכ״ט י״ב תשל״ג וכיון שנכנס ביום שלשים מקצת היום ככולו והוי משלשים. אבל חדש דלשון חכמים הוי שפיר מכ״ט יום: זה גר תושב ולא הספיק למולו בין השמשות. פי׳ ומן שבת ראשון קאמר דאילו מן שבת שני פשיטא דכיון שהיה לו שהות למולו ולא מל לא ישבות. אכן משמע דהשתא ישבות ואם ירצה לחייב עצמו משביתת שבת הרשות בידו. ותימה דאמרינן גוי ששבת חייב וי״ל דזה כיון דדעתו להתגייר מצי לשבות. וא״כ דאף כי אינו מצווה על שבת מ״מ אנחנו מצווים שלא לחלל שבת על ידינו לצוות לו ישראל לעשות מלאכתו: ה״מ היכא דלא פסקא למלתיה. פ״ה דוקא כי לא אמר מתחלה שימול עצמו אין מקיימין אבל היכא דפסקא למלתיה שאמר מתחלה שהוא רוצה למול ואח״כ חזר בו מגלגלין עמו אולי יתרצה למול כמקודם. י״מ היכא דלא פסקא למלתיה שלא פי׳ שום דבר אז מקיימים אבל פסקא פירוש פסק הקונה עמו שאם רוצה למול יגלגל עמו ואם לא ימול ימכרנו לגוי פסקא ומגלגל עמו דהוי גביה כשכיר בעלמא. וקשה דלקמן משמע דהיכא דאמר שאינו רוצה למול מקיימין א) הכא נמי היינו רב פפא אבל היכא דאתני אתני וכ״מ ה״מ היכא דלא פסקא שלא אמר איני רוצה למול אז אין מקיימין ומלין אותו מיד דשהויי מצוה לא משהינן אבל היכא דפסקא שאינו רוצה למול ב) א״כ אינו עם הישראל רק כשכיר יום מקיימין ומגלגלין עמו אולי יתרצה למול וקשה לי דלמה שינה לשונו. ונראה כפ״ה אך לא אסיק אדעתיה דהיכא דאתני אתני עד דשמעיה להא דשלח רבין: גר שנתגייר כקטן שנולד דמי. ואינו נענש על אשר עשה בגיותו ובדיני שמים איירי נמי הכא. אבל בדיני אדם אמרינן בן נח שברך את השם בגיותו ונתגייר היה נהרג. וכמו כן אינו אסור בקרובות מטעם הזה דכקטן שנולד דמי רק היכא דשייך שמא יאמרו באנו מקדושה חמורה לקדושה קלה: שאין עושין מאהבה אלא מיראה. משמע היכא דמיראה אינו טוב ובמגילה (כ״ה) משמע דאף מאהבה אינו טוב דקאמר דלמא אתי למעבד מאהבה ומיראה. וגם (בסמוך) [בסוטה (כ״ב)] נמי משמע דמאהבה נמי אינו טוב (דקאמר חשיב) [דקחשיב ליה] גבי ז׳ פרושין הם וכולן כגנת. ובסוף כשם משמע דאף מיראה קא חשיב דקאמר תרווייהו צדיקי גמורי נינהו מר מאהבה ומר מיראה משמע מהתם דאף מיראה צדיק הוא. ונראה לפרש דדוקא מאהבת המקום ומיראת המקום הוו צדיקי אבל מיראת העונש ומאהבת השכר לאו צדיקי נינהו והכא ר״ל שאין עושין מאהבת המקום אלא מיראת העונש והמבין יבין:

א) נראה דל״ל והתם נמי רב פפא הוא דאמר כן דהיכא דאתני אתני ולכן נראה דה״ק היכא דלא פסיקא וכו׳.
ב) אולי צ״ל א״נ דאמר דאינו רוצה להיות אלא כישראל רק כשכיר יום.

מסורת הש״ס

(סנהדרין יא) ספרי פרשה כי תצא

מכילתא פרשת משפטים פ״כ

(יומא עה: סוטה ח. ב״ק קו: זבחים יג: לג: מנחות פט: כריתות ג:)

[לעיל כב. וש״נ]

(ועי׳ תוס׳ כתובות מז: ד״ה ואין. ועוד שם תוס׳ ד״ה ר׳ יהודה)

הגהות הב״ח

(א) רש״י ד״ה כי הני שבים וכו׳ק ואחר כן:

גליון הש״ס

גמ׳ גר שנתגייר כקטן. עיין סנהדרין דף עא ע״ב תד״ה כי תנא:

תוספות חד מקמאי

תניא וינפש בן אמתך בעבד ערל הכתוב מדבר למען ינוח עבדך ואמתך כמוך בעבד המל. והגר זה גר תושב. וגרך אשר בשעריך זה גר צדק. ודוקא במלאכת ישראל הוא דאסור עבד ערל אבל לעצמו מותר. והכי איתא בכריתות פרק מחוסרי כפרה. דגרים התם גר תושב עושה מלאכה לעצמו כישראל בחולו של מועד ר״ע אומר כישראל בי״ט ר״י אומר גר תושב עושה מלאכה לעצמו כישראל בחולו של מועד. עבד ואמה התושבים עושין מלאכה לעצמן בשבת כישראל בחול ר״ש אומר א׳ גר תושב וא׳ עבד ואמה התושבים עושין מלאכה לעצמן בשבת כישראל בחש״מ. אמר רב אידי בר גרשום אמר רב אדא בר אהבה הלכה כר״ש: הא ה) דאר״ש הא גופה ומטבילה לשם עבדות כתב הראב״ד דרבנן פליגי עליה ואמרי אף לשום עבדות צריך לקבל ואינו כופהו והלכתא כרבנן דר״ש ור״ע קיימי כותיה לקמן גבי מקיימין עבדים שאינן מהולים ויש אומרים דלא פליגי רבנן עליה דר״ש אלא בשחרור אבל לשום עבדות כופהו כדי שלא יטבול לשום בן חורין. ור״ש ור״ע פליגי אם אינו רוצה לכופן אם רשאי לקיימן או לא: הכל

ה) נ״ל להראב״ד כופה.

מתני' איזהו *ממזר? כל שאר בשר שהוא ב"לא יבא", דברי ר"ע. *שמעון התימני אומר: א*כל שחייבים עליו כרת בידי שמים. והלכה כדבריו. ורבי יהושע אומר: כל שחייבין עליו מיתת בית דין. אמר *רבי שמעון בן עזאי: מצאתי מגלת יוחסין בירושלים וכתוב בה: איש פלוני ממזר מאשת איש, לקיים דברי רבי יהושע. *באשתו שמתה — מותר באחותה, גרשה ומתה — מותר באחותה. נשאת לאחר ומתה — מותר באחותה. *יבמתו שמתה — מותר באחותה, חלץ לה ומתה — מותר באחותה, נשאת לאחר ומתה — מותר באחותה.§ **גמ'** מ"ט דרבי עקיבא? דכתיב °"לא יקח איש את אשת אביו ולא יגלה כנף אביו" — *כנף שראה אביו לא יגלה, וסבר לה כר' יהודה, דאמר: באנוסת אביו הכתוב מדבר, דהויא לה חייבי לאוין. וסמיך ליה °"לא יבא ממזר בקהל ה'". אלמא: מהני הוי ממזר. *ולרבי סימאי דמרבה שאר חייבי לאוין דלאו ד"שאר", ולרבי ישבב דמרבה אפילו חייבי עשה — נפקא להו מ"ולא". ושמעון התימני סבר לה כרבנן, דאמרי: בשומרת יבם של אביו הכתוב מדבר, דהויא לה חייבי כריתות, וסמיך ליה "לא יבא ממזר", אלמא: מחייבי כריתות הוי ממזר. ורבי יהושע: לכתוב רחמנא "לא יגלה", "לא יקח" ("ולא יגלה") למה לי? אלא לאו הכי קאמר: מ"לא יקח" עד "לא יגלה" — הוי ממזר, טפי — לא הוי ממזר. *)אמר אביי: הכל מודים בבא על הנדה ועל

*) [קדושין סח. ע"ש]

דברים כג | שם | רש"ל מ"ז

רש"י

מתני' כל שאר בשר שהוא בלא יבא. כל קורבה שהיא בלאו, ואפי' אין בה כרת, כגון אנוסת אביו, וכרבי יהודה דהויא בלאו ד"לא יגלה כנף אביו". ומחמת קורבה,(א) כגון נושא חלוצתו, דהוי ב"לא יבנה" והוי לאו דקורבה בלא כרת. כל שחייבין עליו כרת. אבל נושא חלוצתו לא הוי ממזר. לקיים דברי רבי יהושע. לא היה כתוב במגלה, אלא אריישא קאי: אמר ר"ש בן עזאי לקיים דברי ר' יהושע כו'. מאשת איש. חייבי מיתות כו'. **גמ'** וכתיב לא יבא ממזר. וסמיך ליה "לא יגלה". דר' יהודה ורבנן. בפרק "נושאין על האנוסה" (לקמן דף נז.). ולרבי סימאי. בכתובות (דף כט:) וקידושין (דף סח.) מן הכל היה עושה ר"ע ממזרים, חוץ מאלמנה לכ"ג שעושה חללין ולא ממזרי". מדקאמר חוץ מאלמנה — אלמא אפי' חייבי לאוין שלא מחמת קורבה מרבה, כגון מחזיר גרושתו משנישאת, וכגון נתינה לישראל, דקיימא ב"לא תתחתן בם" (דברים ז), ומשבעה אומות הוא, וכגון עמוני שנשא בת ישראל בניו ממזרים. חייבי עשה. מצרי או אדומי קודם ג' דורות, דכתיב (דברים כג) "דור שלישי יבא להם" — ולא שני, ולאו הבא מכלל עשה — עשה. והא דר' ישבב נמי בכתובות (שם): בואו ונקרא על עקיבא בן יוסף, שהיה אומר: כל שאין לו ביאה בישראל הולד ממזר. סבר לה כרבנן. דפליגי אדרבי יהודה ב"נושאין על האנוסה" (לקמן דף נז.) ואמרי: האי "לא יגלה כנף אביו" — בשומרת יבם של אביו הכתוב מדבר, דהויא ליה אשת אחי אביו, ובכרת. והאי דהדר כתבה במשנה תורה — משום למסמך ליה "לא יבא ממזר", ולאשמועינן דיש ממזר מחייבי כריתות: ה"ג. ורבי יהושע לכתוב רחמנא לא יגלה. כלומר, אי בשומרת יבם של אביו משתעי, או באנוסת אביו משתעי — לכתוב "לא יגלה כנף אביו" לחודיה, ולאשמועינן דיש ממזר מחייבי כריתות לרבנן, או מחייבי לאוין לרבי יהודה, וכל שכן מאשת אב דהויא בכרת ומיתה. "לא יקח. איש את אשת אביו" למה לי למכתב? אלא ש"מ מדכתביה, הא קמ"ל: ד"לא יבא ממזר" עלה קאי, דמינה הוא דהוי ממזר, משום דחייבי מיתות הוא.(ב) ואי "לא יגלה כנף אביו" לא קאי. ואי קשיא: כנף אביו למאי כתביה? אי בשומרת יבם, לעבור עליו בשני לאוין — "ערות אחי אביך לא תגלה", ולאו ד"לא יגלה כנף אביו", ואי באנוסת אביו — אשמעינן דאסורה. מ"לא יקח עד לא יגלה". דהיינו אשת אב הכתובה בין "לא יקח" ל"לא יגלה". הכל מודים. ואפילו שמעון התימני. בבא על הנדה. אע"ג דקאי בכרת — אין הולד ממזר. והבא

תוספות

שמעון התימני אומר כו' והלכה כדבריו. אע"ג דאין למדין הלכה מפי גמרא(ג) — *הכא הלכתא כוותיה, דסתמא דפרק "האומר" (קדושין דף סו: ושם) נראה עיקר, דבהאי גוונא קרי הלכתא פסיקתא בבבא קמא (ד' קב.) ובמסכת ע"ז (דף ז: ושם) בההיא דכל המשנה ידו על התחתונה, ולעיל בפ' קמא (דף יד. ושם) אמר: פשיטא, בני חייבי לאוין כשרים נינהו. ובפרק שני (לעיל כג.) קאמר רב פפא: מסתברא, חייבי לאוין תפסי בהו קידושין. ולעיל (דף מה.) פסקינן דגוי ועבד הבא על בת ישראל הולד כשר. וכמה אמוראי דאיירי בגרת מחזיר גרושתו. ולר"ע לא משכחת לה גרה דאין קידושין תופסין בחייבי לאוין. וכרבי יהושע נמי יש להוכיח דלא קי"ל כוותיה, דאמר לעיל (שם:): ושניהם לא למדוה אלא מאשת אב, וחייבי כריתות דמו לאשת אב לכולי עלמא. ולעיל בריש פירקין (דף לז.) קאמר ראב"י דהלכתא כוותיה דאין ממזר מספק, משמע דהויא ממזר מאשת אח. ולעיל (ד' מ:) אמר רב טובי בר קיסנא: הבא על גרת חלוצתו הולד ממזר. ואפילו רבי יוחנן לא פליג אלא משום דגרה כחלוצה בלאו). **רבי** יהושע אומר כל שחייבין עליו כו'. יש מגיהים ר' יהודה במקום רבי יהושע, דבפרק "עשרה יוחסין" (קדושין דף עד:) גבי כל האסורין לבא בקהל מותרים לבא זה בזה. ור' יהודה אוסר. ומפרש עלה דר' יהודה סבר דממזר מאחותו לא הוי ממזר, אלא מאשת איש. ופריך עלה: תנינא, מהך דהכא. ואין נראה, דהיאך היה בן עזאי אומר לקיים מילתיה דר' יהודה? והא קשיא מיניה טובא, דהא בן עזאי תלמיד חבר הוה לרבי עקיבא, כדאמר ב"מי שמת" (ב"ב ד' קנח:), ור' יהודה מתלמידי בתראי דר' עקיבא הוה! ועוד: דר' יהודה סבר כרבי עקיבא דיש ממזר מחייבי לאוין, כדפרישית לעיל (ד' מז.) גבי ההוא דאתא לקמיה דרבי יהודה, וכדאמר בפ' "ארבע מיתות" (סנהדרין ד' נג: ושם). אלא ודאי ר' יהושע גרסינן. והתם פריך תנינא — משום דהוה ליה למיתני: וכן היה רבי יהודה אומר כדבריו, אי הוה סבר כר' יהושע. ומיהו, התם דפריך תנינא הוה מצי למיפרך טפי שפיר דלא אפשר לומר דלר' יהודה ממזר מאחותו לא הוי ממזר, כיון דמוקי קרא באנוסת אביו, וסבר כר"ע דיש ממזר מחייבי לאוין. **איש** פלוני ממזר מאשת איש כו'. תימה: דלא נקט חייבי מיתות ב"ד סתם. ואי משום דמעשה שהיה כך היה — א"כ מנ"ל דהוי כר' יהושע? וי"ל: דנקט אשת איש לרבותא, דאע"פ שהוא קל משאר חייבי מיתות, דהוי בחנק ויש לה היתר בחיי אוסרה.

וכתיב לא יבא ממזר. וא"ת: והא מפסיק קרא ד"לא יבא פלוע דכא" בינתים! וי"ל: דכיון דלאו בני בנים נינהו, ולא שייך מינייהו ממזר — לא חשיב הפסק. **לכתוב** רחמנא או לא יקח או לא יגלה. בקונטרס גרס: לכתוב רחמנא "לא יגלה", ופי': דמלא יגלה לחודיה שמעינן דיש ממזר מחייבי כריתות לרבנן, או מחייבי לאוין לר' יהודה לא יקח איש את אשת אביו למה לי למכתב? אלא, ש"מ מדכתביה — דלא יבא ממזר עליה קאי, דמיניה הוא דהוי ממזר, משום דחייבי מיתות ב"ד הוא. אבל א"לא יגלה" לא קאי, ובין לא יקח עד לא יגלה היינו אשת אב הכתובה בין לא יקח ללא יגלה. וקשה: חדא, שמוחק הספרים. ועוד: דבין לא יקח עד לא יגלה לא משמע כפירושו דקאי על אשת אב הכתובה בינתים, ועוד: אמאי כתב לא יגלה גבי ממזרות? ועוד: בחייבי מיתות דקילי, כמו אשת איש, מנ"ל דהוי ממזר? ועוד: דליליף ר' יהושע שאר חייבי כריתות מהיקישא דר' יונה! ונראה לר"י כגירסת הספרים, דגרסי: לכתוב רחמנא או לא יקח או לא יגלה, דמ"לא יקח" נמי שמעינן כריתות, דהא דומיא דאשת אב דלא תפסי בה קידושין, דהא בהא תליא, כדפיר' לעיל (ד' מד: ד"ה "עשאה"), או מהיקישא דרבי יונה אתו דאיתקיש כל העריות, כדאמרי' בריש "הבא על יבמתו" (לקמן ד' נד:). ומדכתב תרוייהו — ש"מ דמ"לא יקח" היינו חייבי סקילה, עד "לא יגלה" דהיינו חייבי כריתות — הוי ממזר. ואתא לרבויי כל חייבי [כריתות] ומיתות קלות. וסבר כרבנן דבשומרת יבם הכתוב מדבר, ולא הוי לא יגלה בכלל, דאי הוי בכלל — לא לכתוב אלא לא יגלה, ושמעון התימני נמי ה"מ למימר דסבר כר' יהודה, דאמר באנוסת אביו הכתוב מדבר, ומלא יקח עד לא יגלה הוי הולד ממזר, ואין לא יגלה בכלל. אלא דניחא ליה למימר דסבר כרבנן. ❂ולפירוש ר"י נ"ל לתנא דפירקין קמא דסבר כרבי יהודה(ד) דאמר באנוסת אביו הכתוב מדבר, וסבר נמי דאין ממזר מחייבי לאוין, דמלא יקח עד לא יגלה הוי ממזר, ואין לא יגלה בכלל. **הכל** מודים בבא על הנדה ועל הסוטה. פירש בקונטרס: אפי' לר' עקיבא דפליג ארבנן דמתניתין במחזיר גרושתו, וקאמר דהולד ממזר, אע"ג דלאו חייבי לאוין ד"שאר" — הוא הכא בסוטה מודה. וקשה לר"ת: דא"כ ה"ל לאתויי לעיל (ד' מד.) גבי משנה דמחזיר גרושתו! ועוד: אי קאי הכל מודים למ"ד אליבא דר' עקיבא דהוי ממזר אפילו מחייבי לאוין שאין דשאר, הא ע"כ הוי ממזר לרבי עקיבא מיבמה לשוק לשום תנא, כדאמר בפ"ק (לעיל ד' יד.) דאמר ר' אלעזר: אע"פ שנחלקו ב"ש וב"ה בצרות — מודים שאין ממזר כו', וקאמר: לאפוקי מדרבי עקיבא, דאמר אין קידושין תופסין בחייבי לאוין. משמע בהדיא דלר' עקיבא הוי ממזר משומרת יבם! ועוד אמר בפרק "עשרה יוחסין" (קדושין דף עה:), גבי כותים שהיו מייבמים את הארוסות ופוטרים הנשואות, ורבי עקיבא לטעמיה דאמר אין קידושין תופסין בחייבי לאוין. ובפרק "האשה רבה" (לקמן ד' צב. ושם), גבי אשה שהלך בעלה ובנה למדינת הים קאמר: זו דברי רבי עקיבא, דאמר אין קידושין תופסין בחייבי לאוין. אבל חכמים אומרים דאין ממזר מיבמה. ולימא אין ממזר מחייבי לאוין! האי תנא הך תנא דר"ע הוא, דמחייבי לאוין דשאר הוא דהוי ממזר, מחייבי לאוין גרידא — לא הוי ממזר. משמע בהדיא דלמאן דלא בעי אליבא דרבי עקיבא שיהא לאו דשאר הוי ממזר מיבמה לשוק. ושם נפרש בעזרת השם מנא ליה דאתיא כרבי עקיבא, דלמא אתיא אפילו כרבנן והוי ממזר מדרבנן? ונראה לר"ת דמחזיר גרושתו וסוטה הוו חייבי לאוין דשאר, שאינם אסורים אלא משום אישות, ואליבא דתנא דמתני'

קדושין עד: לעיל מד. [לקמן פה:]
[ע' בפי' הרב מברטנורה ריש פ"ד לאבות]
[לעיל יז: יח.]
לעיל יז:
לעיל ז. [לקמן נז.]
[כתובות כט: קידושין סד. סח.]
[כלאיתא ב"ב קל: נדה ז:]
[לעיל מד.]

עין משפט נר מצוה

קמט א מיי' פט"ו מהל' איסורי ביאה הל' א סמג לאוין קיז טוש"ע אה"ע סימן ד סעיף יג:

קנ ב מיי' שם פ"ב הל' ט סמג לאוין שם טוש"ע שם סי' טו סעיף כז:

תוספות ישנים

א) ועוד ראיה דאמר רב נחמן (בקדושין ע"ו) גבי כותי ממזר מאחותו וממזר מאשת איש נתערבו בהם משמע שיש ממזר מאחותו דהוי חייבי כריתות ויש לדחות דהתם קאי אליבא דר' אלעזר ולר' אלעזר אין ראיה דהא ודאי איהו סבר דיש ממזר מחייבי כריתות כדאמרי' לעיל א"ר אלעזר אע"פ שנחלקו ב"ש וב"ה בצרות מודים שאין ממזר אלא ממי שאיסורו איסור ערוה וענוש כרת:

הגהות הב"ח

(א) רש"י ד"ה כל שאר וכו' ומחמת קורבה לאביו וכגון נושא: (ב) ד"ה לא יקח וכו' דמחייבי מיתות הוא אבל אלא יגלה: (ג) תום' ד"ה שמעון וכו' מפי גמרא. נ"ב בפרק יש נוחלין דף קל ע"ב: (ד) ד"ה לכתוב וכו' דפרקין קמא דסבר כרבי יהודה. נ"ב ע"ל דף י' בתוספות ד"ה לרבי יהודה:

גליון הש"ס

תום' ד"ה לכתוב רחמנא וכו' ולפיר"י נ"ל וכו'. וכפיר"י נ"ל כנ"ל:

תוספות חד מקמאי

הכל מודים בבא על הנדה ועל הסוטה ועל שומרת יבם שאין הולד ממזר הא דאמר הבא על הסוטה דאין הולד ממזר ה"מ דרך זנות א"נ מדאורייתא אבל דרך נישואין הולד ממזר מדרבנן. וזו היא ששנינו האשה שהלך בעלה למד"ה וא"ל מת בעלך ואח"כ בא בעלה תצא מזה ומזה והולד ממזר מזה [ומזה]. פירוש משני דאוריית' ומראשון דרבנן משום קנסא שמא יאמרו גרש זה ונשא זה ומ"מ אסור בממזרת שאין ב"ד מתנין לעקור דבר מן התורה. ומאי ממזר דקאמר שאחור בבת ישראל והכי איתא בפרק האשה רבה שאסור בממזרת. אלמא אינו ממזר אלא מדרבנן אלא לאו א) ש"מ דברי הכל הוי ממזר ואפי' לר"ש התימני ב) הא דאתמר לעיל לענין טבילה איתמר כתב הראב"ד פי' לענין טבילה שהוא צריך טבילה אעפ"י שטבל כבר לשם עבדות אבל לקבל עליו עול מצות א"צ שכבר קבל עליו מתחלה מדעתו הלכך משחררין אותו בע"כ אבל מתחלה אין מטבילין אותו לשם עבדות אא"כ קבל מדעתו לשום עבדות חוזר ומשחררו אח"כ בע"כ ומ"מ אין צריך ג' לטבילת שחרור מדאמרי' בקדושין פ' האומר כל שבידו לאו כמחוסר מעשה דמי ואמר' התם גר נמי לאו בינו [לבינו] הוא דאמרי' א"ר יוחנן גר צריך ג' ואקשי' אלא מעתה הנותן פרוטה לשפחתו וא"ל הרי את מקודשת לאחר שאשחרריך שבידו הוא ה"נ דהוו קדושין ש"מ דגבי משוחררת לא בעינא ג' ע"ג ג) וי"ל דהיינו טעמא (דאין) [דהוי] ממזר מראשון (אלא) מדרבנן שנשאה ע"פ ב"ד וכיון דאם זינתה ברצון הוי ממזר מדאורייתא לכ"ע אם בא עליה בעל השתא שנשאת ע"פ ב"ד בעד א' הוי ממזר מדרבנן אבל לרבנן אפילו זינתה ברצון אינו ממזר דחייבי לאוין הן עכשיו שנשאה ע"פ ב"ד אינו ממזר אפילו מדרבנן שאין בו איסור כלל. אלא משמע דבין לרבנן בין לר"ע

תוספות חד מקמאי

לר"ע הוי ממזר מדרבנן ע"י נשואין שמא יאמרו גרש זה ונשא זה אבל ע"י זנות אינו ממזר אפי' מדרבנן והא דאמרי' בשומרת יבם שאין הולד ממזר פרש"י משום דכתיב לא תהיה אלמא יש בה הויה ואע"ג דכתיב נמי ואשה אל אחותה לא תקח ולא יקח איש את אשת אביו דמשמע דאית ביה קיחה ובמסכת קדושין פ' האומר ילפינן מהני תרי קראי דלא תפסי בה קדושין לא דמי לא יקח ללא תהיה. ומיהו קשיא לי להאי פירוש דהא בפרק הזורק תנן בתרתי בבי דיש ממזר מיבמה דתנן התם כל ערוה שאמרו צרותיהן מותרות וכו' הכונס ליבמתו והלכה צרתה ונשאת וכו' תצא מזה ומזה וכל הדרכים האלו בה וכו' ובפרק האשה רבה נמי תנן בהדיא דיש ממזר מיבמה אלא ודאי אליבא דר"ע דבריית' דלא בעי שאר יש ממזר מיבמה ומתני' בפרק הזורק ובפ' האשה רבה אליבא דר' עקיבא (דמתני' דבעי) [דברייתא דלא בעי] שאר והכל מודים דקא' הכא אליבא דר' עקיבא דמתני' דבעי שאר קאמר ולדידיה אין הולד ממזר ואע"ג דכתיב לא תהיה לא מפרשינן מניה דלא תפסי בה קדושי' וללאו הוא דאתא. והכי איתא בפ' האשה [רבה] דתניא התם זו דר"ע דאמר אין קידושי' תופסי' בחייבי לאוין אבל חכ"א אין ממזר מיבמה. ולימא אין ממזר מחייבי לאוין האי תנא דר"מ הוא דאמר מחייבי לאוין דשאר הוי ממזר מחייבי לאוין גרידי לא הוי ממזר ד) ורבנן דאמרין אין קדושין תופסי' איכא למימר דרב תנא הוא ופליג א"נ אמר ה) לך רב הונא אנא דאמר ביבמה כה"ג דתנינן הרי את מקודשת לי ע"מ שיחלוץ לך יבמך וכו' אינה מקודשת אלמא אין קדושין תופסין ביבמה שאילו היו קדושין תופסין ביבמה לא הוי דבר שלא

א) נראה דצ"ל ומשמע דמן הנשואין הוי ממזר מדרבנן לר"ה ואפי' לשמעון התימני. ב) מתיבת הא דאתמר עד בעינא ג' שייך לעיל מ"ז ע"ב. ג) אולי צ"ל ויש מפרשים דהיינו טעמא וכו' שאין בו איסור כלל ולא נהירא אלא משמע דבין לרבנן וכו'. ד) צ"ל ורב דאמר לקמן (צ"ב) אין קדושין תופסין בימה. ה) נ"ל אמר לך רב הונא דאמרי כתנא דליבמה כהלה דתנינן בקדושין (ס"ב).

קנא א מיי' פ"ד מהל' איסורי ביאה הל' יב סמג עשין מח טוש"ע אה"ע סימן קנט סעיף ו:
קנב ב מיי' פט"ו מהל' איסורי ביאה הלכה א סמג לאוין קיז טוש"ע שם סימן ד סעיף יג:
קנג ג מיי' פ"ז מהלכו' יסודי התורה הל' ו:
קנד ד ה מיי' פ"ב מהל' תשובה הל' ו:

וְעַל הַסּוֹטָה שֶׁאֵין הַוָּלָד מַמְזֵר. [א]נִדָּה — דְּהָא תָּפְסִי בָּהּ קִידּוּשִׁין, שֶׁנֶּאֱמַר "וּתְהִי נִדָּתָהּ עָלָיו" (ויקרא טו) — אֲפִי' בִּשְׁעַת נִדָּתָהּ — תָּפְסֵי בָּהּ קִידּוּשִׁין. סוֹטָה נַמִי — דְּהָא תָּפְסֵי בָּהּ קִידּוּשִׁין. תַּנְיָא נַמִי הָכִי: *[ב]הַכֹּל מוֹדִים בְּבָא עַל הַנִּדָּה, וְעַל הַסּוֹטָה, וְעַל שׁוֹמֶרֶת יָבָם — שֶׁאֵין הַוָּלָד מַמְזֵר. וְאַבַּיֵי: שׁוֹמֶרֶת יָבָם מְסַפְּקָא לֵיהּ, אִי *כְּרַב אִי כִּשְׁמוּאֵל.§ "א"ר שִׁמְעוֹן בֶּן עַזַּאי כו'".§ תָּנֵי, שִׁמְעוֹן בֶּן עַזַּאי אוֹמֵר: מָצָאתִי מְגִלַּת יוֹחֲסִין בִּירוּשָׁלַיִם, וְכָתוּב בָּהּ: אִישׁ פְּלוֹנִי מַמְזֵר מֵאֵשֶׁת אִישׁ. וְכָתוּב בָּהּ: *מִשְׁנַת ר' אֱלִיעֶזֶר בֶּן יַעֲקֹב קַב וְנָקִי. וְכָתוּב בָּהּ: מְנַשֶּׁה הָרַג אֶת יְשַׁעְיָה. אֲמַר רָבָא: מֵידָן דַּיְינֵיהּ וְקַטְלֵיהּ. אֲמַר לֵיהּ: מֹשֶׁה רַבָּךְ אָמַר "כִּי לֹא יִרְאַנִי הָאָדָם וָחָי" (שמות לג) וְאַתְּ אָמְרַתְּ "וָאֶרְאֶה אֶת ה' יוֹשֵׁב עַל כִּסֵּא רָם וְנִשָּׂא" (ישעיה ו), מֹשֶׁה רַבָּךְ אָמַר "מִי כַּה' אֱלֹהֵינוּ בְּכָל קָרְאֵנוּ אֵלָיו" (דברים ד) וְאַתְּ אָמְרַתְּ "דִּרְשׁוּ ה' בְּהִמָּצְאוֹ" (ישעיה נה). מֹשֶׁה רַבָּךְ אָמַר "אֶת מִסְפַּר יָמֶיךָ אֲמַלֵּא" (שמות כג) וְאַתְּ אָמְרַתְּ "וְהוֹסַפְתִּי עַל יָמֶיךָ חֲמֵשׁ עֶשְׂרֵה שָׁנָה" (מ"ב כ)! אָמַר יְשַׁעְיָה: יָדַעְנָא בֵּיהּ דְּלָא מְקַבֵּל מַה דְּאֵימָא לֵיהּ, וְאִי אֵימָא לֵיהּ — אִישַׁוְיֵיהּ מֵזִיד. אָמַר שֵׁם, אִיבְלַע בְּאַרְזָא. אַתְיוּהָ לְאַרְזָא וְנַסְרוּהָ. כִּי מְטָא לַהֲדֵי פּוּמָא — נָח נַפְשֵׁיהּ, מִשּׁוּם דְּאָמַר "וּבְתוֹךְ עַם טְמֵא שְׂפָתַיִם אָנֹכִי יוֹשֵׁב" (ישעיה ו). מִכָּל מָקוֹם קָשׁוּ קְרָאֵי אַהֲדָדֵי! "וָאֶרְאֶה אֶת ה'" — כִּדְתַנְיָא: [ג]כָּל הַנְּבִיאִים נִסְתַּכְּלוּ *בְּאַסְפַּקְלַרְיָא שֶׁאֵינָהּ מְאִירָה, מֹשֶׁה רַבֵּינוּ נִסְתַּכֵּל בְּאַסְפַּקְלַרְיָא הַמְּאִירָה. "דִּרְשׁוּ ה' בְּהִמָּצְאוֹ" — *[ד]הָא בְּיָחִיד הָא בְּצִבּוּר. וְיָחִיד אֵימַת? אָמַר רַב נַחְמָן אָמַר רַבָּה בַּר אֲבוּהּ: [ה]אֵלּוּ עֲשָׂרָה יָמִים שֶׁבֵּין רֹאשׁ הַשָּׁנָה לְיוֹם הַכִּפּוּרִים. "אֶת מִסְפַּר יָמֶיךָ אֲמַלֵּא" — תַּנָּאֵי הִיא. דְּתַנְיָא: "אֶת מִסְפַּר יָמֶיךָ אֲמַלֵּא" אֵלּוּ

רש"י

וְהַבָּא עַל הַסּוֹטָה. אֵשֶׁת אִישׁ שֶׁזִּינְּתָה, וְקַיְימָא לָן דַּאֲסוּרָה לְבַעְלָהּ, בְּפ"ק (לעיל דף יא:) מָה אֲנִי מְקַיֵּים "אֲשֶׁר הוּטַּמָּאָה" (דברים כד) — לְרַבּוֹת סוֹטָה שֶׁנִּסְתְּרָה. וְאַע"ג דְּחַיָּיבֵי לָאוִין הִיא — מוֹדֶה בָּהּ רַבִּי עֲקִיבָא, דְּפָלֵיג אַדְּרַבָּנַן בְּמַתְנִי' (לעיל מד.) בְּמַחֲזִיר גְּרוּשָׁתוֹ, וְקָאָמַר דְּהַוָּלָד מַמְזֵר אַע"ג דְּלָאו חַיָּיבֵי לָאוִין דִּ"שְׁאֵר" הוּא — הָכָא מוֹדֵי דְּאֵין וָלָד מַמְזֵר. וְכָל שֶׁכֵּן לְאִידָךְ רַבִּי עֲקִיבָא בַּר פְּלוּגְתָּא דְּשִׁמְעוֹן הַתֵּימְנִי לָא הָוֵי מַמְזֵר, מִשּׁוּם דְּסוֹטָ' לָאו מְחַיְּיבֵי לָאוִין דִּשְׁאֵר הִיא. דְּהָא תָּפְסִי בָּהּ קִידּוּשִׁין. לְאִשָּׁה, דְּאַף לְאַחַר שֶׁזִּינְּתָה לָא פָּקְעוּ מִינָּהּ קִידּוּשֶׁיהָ הָרִאשׁוֹנִים. נִדָּה דִּכְתִיב וּתְהִי נִדָּתָהּ עָלָיו. "תְּהִי" — לְשׁוֹן הֲוָיָה דְּקִידּוּשִׁין עָלָיו. שׁוֹמֶרֶת יָבָם.(א) לְאֶחָד מִן הַשּׁוּק בְּלֹא חֲלִיצָה, שֶׁאֵין הַוָּלָד מַמְזֵר. וַאֲפִילּוּ לְרַבִּי עֲקִיבָא דְּפָלֵיג אַדְּרַבָּנַן בְּמַתְנִי'. וְטַעְמָא — מִשּׁוּם דְּקִידּוּשִׁין תּוֹפְסִין בָּהּ, מִדְּאַפְקֵיהּ רַחֲמָנָא לְלָאו דִּידָהּ בִּלְשׁוֹן הֲוָיָה, דִּכְתִיב (דברים כה) "לֹא תִהְיֶה" — בַּת הֲוָיָה הִיא. וְהָכִי קָאָמַר: לֹא תִהְיֶה אֵשֶׁת הַמֵּת — לֹא תִּתְקַדֵּשׁ אֵשֶׁת הַמֵּת בְּקִידּוּשִׁין לְאִישׁ זָר, אַלְמָא: קִידּוּשִׁין תָּפְסִי בָּהּ. וְאַבַּיֵי מְסַפְּקָא לֵיהּ. הַאי לֹא תִהְיֶה לְאִישׁ זָר. אִי כְּרַב. דְּאָמַר בְּפֶרֶק "הָאִשָּׁה רַבָּה" (לקמן דף צב:) מִנַּיִן שֶׁאֵין קִידּוּשִׁין תּוֹפְסִין בִּיבָמָה — דִּכְתִיב "לֹא תִהְיֶה אֵשֶׁת הַמֵּת לְאִישׁ זָר" — לֹא תְּהֵא בָּהּ הֲוָיָה לְזָר, וְהַוָּלָד מַמְזֵר. אִי כִּשְׁמוּאֵל. דְּאָמַר (שם): בַּעֲנִיּוּתֵינוּ, בַּעֲנִיּוּת דַּעְתֵּינוּ, צְרִיכָה גֵּט. דִּמְסַפְּקָא לָן אִי לְהָכִי הוּא דְּאָתָא כִּדְקָאָמַר רַב, אוֹ דִּלְמָא לְאוֹקְמָהּ בְּלָאו אָתָא, וְקִידּוּשִׁין תָּפְסִי בָּהּ, מִדְּאַפֵּיק לָאו דִּידֵיהּ בִּלְשׁוֹן הֲוָיָה. מִשְׁנַת רַבִּי אֱלִיעֶזֶר ב"י קַב וְנָקִי. קַב מִדָּה קְטַנָּה, כְּלוֹמַר: בִּמְקוֹמוֹת מוּעָטִים הוּא נִזְכָּרָא] בַּמִּשְׁנָה [אוֹ בַּבָּרַיְיתָא]. וְנָקִי. בְּכָל מָקוֹם שֶׁנִּזְכָּר — הֲלָכָה כְּמוֹתוֹ. בְּהִמָּצְאוֹ. מַשְׁמַע: פְּעָמִים שֶׁאֵינוֹ מָצוּי. אֲמַלֵּא. לָאו לְשׁוֹן תּוֹסֶפֶת, אֶלָּא מַשְׁלִים וְלֹא יוֹתֵר. יָדַעְנָא בֵּיהּ. בִּמְנַשֶּׁה דְּלָא מְקַבֵּל תֵּירוּצָא דְּטַעְמָא דִּקְרָאֵי, אֶלָּא קָטֵיל לִי. וְאִי אֵימָא לֵיהּ וְלָא מְקַבֵּל — אִישַׁוְיֵי' לֵיהּ מֵזִיד בַּהֲרִיגָתִי, דְּעַכְשָׁיו הוּא סָבוּר לְהוֹרְגֵנִי בְּדִין — מוּטָב שֶׁאֶעֱבַרְתּ מִפָּנָיו. כִּי מְטָא. נִרְגָּא. לַהֲדֵי פּוּמָא. דִּישַׁעְיָה. נְסָרוּהָ לְפוּמֵיהּ וְנָח נַפְשֵׁיהּ. וּמִשּׁוּם הָכִי אִיעֲנַשׁ לְנָסוֹרֵי פּוּמֵיהּ, מִשּׁוּם דְּקָרְיֵנְהוּ לְיִשְׂרָאֵל "עַם טְמֵא שְׂפָתַיִם" מִדַּעְתּוֹ, שֶׁלֹּא נִוָּה לוֹ הקב"ה, וְלֹא מֵחֲמַת תּוֹכֵחָה, דִּכְתִיב "וָאוֹמַר אוֹי לִי כִּי נִדְמֵיתִי". נִסְתַּכְּלוּ בְּאַסְפַּקְלַרְיָא שֶׁאֵין מְאִירָה. וּכְסְבוּרִים לִרְאוֹת וְלֹא רָאוּ. וּמֹשֶׁה נִסְתַּכֵּל בְּאַסְפַּקְלַרְיָא הַמְּאִירָה, וְיָדַע שֶׁלֹּא רָאָהוּ בְּפָנָיו.

שְׁנֵי

תוספות

דמתני' קאי, דלא אסר אלא חייבי לאוין ד"שאר". וא"ת: א"כ, אמאי איצטריך למנקט הכל מודים בשומרת יבם? אמאי תיסק אדעתא למימר דהוי ממזר טפי מבשאר חייבי לאוין דלאו דשאר? וי"ל: דאליבא דרב, דאמר אין קידושין תופסין ביבמה, איצטריך לאשמועינן שפיר דלא הוי ממזר. וטעמא, אר"ת: דהוי כגוי ועבד, שאין בה קידושין לשום אדם. וליבם נמי לאו בת קידושין היא, אלא ביאה הוא דאית בה. ואפי' למ"ד דהוי ממזר מגוי ועבד — מ"מ אין ממזר מיבמה, דכיון דיבמה עומדת לחלוץ כמו ליבם — חשיבא בת תפיסת קידושין. וא"ת: לשמואל תפשוט מהך ברייתא דאין קידושין תופסין ביבמה, דאי תופסין — לא הוה צריך לאשמועינן דאין הולד ממזר! וי"ל: דשמואל מספקא ליה, דלמא ברייתא היא גופה אתא לאשמועינן דקידושין תופסין ביבמה. וא"ת: היכי קמ"ל דתפסי, הא אפי' לא תפסי לא הוי ממזר, דשמואל אית ליה לעיל (דף מה.) דגוי ועבד הבא על בת ישראל הולד כשר! וי"ל: דשפיר משמע דתפסי בה קידושין, מדכייל לה בהדי סוטה ונדה — משמע דכולהו לא הוי הולד ממזר, משום דתפסי בהו קידושין. והא דקאמר ואביי מספקא ליה אי כרב אי כשמואל — לא כפירוש הקונטרס דאפי' לרב אין הולד ממזר, כדפי', אלא להכי לא נקט שומרת יבם — משום דשמא תפסי בה קידושין כדשמואל, ופשיטא דלא הוי ממזר, ואין שום חידוש להשמיענו. וא"ת: ואמאי הוי ממזר משומרת יבם לשום תנא (ג)כיון דהוי כגוי ועבד דלא תפסי קדושין לא לדידיה ולא לאחריני? וברייתא ד"האשה רבה" (לקמן דף צב. ושם) נמי, דקתני זו דברי ר' עקיבא דאמר אין קידושין תופסין בחייבי לאוין אבל חכמים אומרים כו' — משמע דלרבנן לא הוי ממזר משום דקידושין תופסין, ולפי' ר"ת אפי' אין קידושין תופסין לא הוי ממזר? ואר"י: דלמ"ד דהוי ממזר לר' עקיבא מחייבי לאוין דלאו דשאר — נמי הוי ממזר מיבמה לשוק ומגוי ועבד, אע"ג דלא דמו לאשת אב, דהא מוי"ו ד"ולא יגלה" נפקי כולהו, וסמיך ליה לא יבא ממזר. ולא ילפינן מידי מאשת אב, אלא בהדיא כתיב בכולהו ממזרות. אבל לתנא דמתניתין, דאין ממזר לר' עקיבא אלא מחייבי לאוין דשאר, ולא דריש וי"ו ד"ולא יגלה" — לא נפקי שום חייבי לאוין אלא מאשת אב, בעינן דליהוי דומיא דאשת אב דלא תפסי בה קידושין לדידיה ותפסי בה לאחריני. וה"פ דברייתא ד"האשה רבה" (ג"ז שם): זו דברי ר' עקיבא דאמר אין קדושין נמי תפסי בכל חייבי לאוין דלאו דשאר. פי': מוי"ו ד"ולא יגלה" שמעינן בכולהו דהוה ממזר, ולהכי אין קידושין תופסין נמי בכולן, ולהכי אין לחלק בין לאו יבמה לשוק לשאר לאוין, כדפירשתי. אבל חכמים אומרים אין ממזר מיבמה, דכיון דקידושין תופסין בחייבי לאוין דלאו דשאר, ולא הוי ממזר מינייהו — לא הוי ממזר נמי מיבמה לשוק, אע"ג דאין קידושין תופסין בה, כיון דלא דמיא לאשת אב. **סוטה** נמי דהא תפסי בה קדושין. פי' בקונט': דאף לאחר שזינתה לא פקעי מינה קידושיה הראשונים. וק' לר"י: דנדה נמי לא פקעי קידושיה ואפילו הכי איצטריך קרא לאתויי דתפסי בה קידושין! ואר"י: דגרס, וכן ברוב ספרים, סוטה נמי הא כתיב בה הויה ותפסי בה קידושין. פי': שגרשה ומחזירה, והויה דכתיב בה היינו קרא "להיות לו לאשה" דמוקמינן בפ"ק (לעיל יא: ושם) לרבות סוטה. וכן משמע בפרק "יש מותרות" (לקמן ד' פה:) דבסוטה ודאי תפסי קידושין. ולא פליגי אלא אי אית לה כתובה אי לאו, דקאמר: סוטה ודאי איכא בינייהו, דמ"ד דאורייתא — הא נמי דאורייתא, ואית לה כתובה כו'. והיינו על כרחך במחזיר סוטה אחר שגירשה, דאי לא גירשה, כיון דזנתה — הפסידה כתובתה. ובפרק "עשרה יוחסין" (קדושין ד' עח.) נמי משמע ד"להיות לו" משמע לשון הויה, דקאמר: ושניהם מודים במחזיר גרושתו, שאם בעל ולא קידש — שאין לוקה, דרך הויה אסרה תורה. וא"ת: בסוף "האומר" בקידושין (ד' סח. ושם) ור' עקיבא "כי תהיין" במאי מוקי להו? לוקמה במחזיר סוטה! וכ"ת דכי תהיין מיותר, וסוטה נפקא לן מקרא ד"להיות לו לאשה" — א"כ היכי מוקי לה באלמנה לכ"ג וכדר' סימאי, הא כתיב "לא יחלל" — חילולין הוא עושה, ואין עושה ממזרים! וי"ל: דלא בעי לאוקמא בסוטה, משום דשנואה משמע שהיא שנואה בתחלת נישואין. וא"ת: ולוקמה בסוטה ולבועל! וי"ל: דמי כתיב כי תהיין לבועל, כדקאמר התם מי כתיב כי תהיין לכהן? א"נ: בבועל לא כתיב הויה, ולא תפסי בה קידושין. פר"ת: דמסוטה, נהי דלא הוי ממזר מדאורייתא — מדרבנן מיהא הוי ממזר, מידי דהוי (לקמן פז:) אאשה שהלך בעלה למדינת הים, ואמרו לה מת בעליך ונישאת, ואח"כ בא בעלה, דהולד ממזר ותלא מזה ומזה. ואין ראיה, דהתם קנסוה כי היכי דתידוק, אבל הכא — אין צריך לקונסה כדי שלא תזנה תחת בעלה. ועוד דבריש "יש מותרות" (לקמן ד' פה: ושם) קאמר גבי סוטה למ"ד דמרגלא ליה — הא איהי מרגליתו, ואי הוי ממזר — אפילו מדרבנן לא מרגלא ליה, כדאמר התם גבי חלוצה(א). **אי** כרב אי כשמואל. מתוך פי' הקונט' משמע דלרב ליכא לאו ביבמה. דפי': אי כרב, דאמר ב"האשה רבה" (לקמן ד' צב:) מנין שאין קידושין תופסין ביבמה, שנאמר "לא תהיה וגו'" — לא תהא בה הויה לזר, והולד ממזר, ואי כשמואל דמספקא ליה אי להכי הוא דאתא כדקאמר רב, או לאוקומי ללאו הוא דאתא, וקידושין תפסי בה, מדאפיק לאו דידה בלשון הויה. ואין נראה, דאמרינן ב"האומר" בקידושין (ד' סח. ושם) מאי יבמה שהיא בלאו *לא תפסי בה קידושין. אלמא איכא לאו אפילו למ"ד דלא תפסי בה קידושין — ובכל מקום חשיב יבמה לשוק חייבי לאוין! ואותם ששאלו לר' יהושע בני צרות דבית הלל לב"ש (לעיל ד' טו:) דקבעי למילף יבמה לשוק בקל וחומר מאלמנה, משמע דאיכא לאו! ואומר רבינו תם: דלכולי עלמא אית בה לאו, וה"ק לקמן: ושמואל מספקא ליה אי ללאו הוא דאתא, ותהיה אורחיה *דקרא(ג), או לאשמועינן דלקי אקידושין, או לקידושין דלא תפסי נמי הוא דאתא. **אשוייה** מזיד. פר"ת: שרצה להשיבו דבמשה *)כתיב "ויראו את אלהי ישראל" (שמות כד).

*) נ"ל דבמשה נמי כתיב. יעב"ץ

מוסיפין

קדושין סח.
[לעיל יג. לקמן נב: נו.]
[[לעיל לז.] לקמן ס. עירובין סב: גיטין פז. בכורות כג.]
[שני פרוקים אמלא זו תמלא כתי"ע פ' ר' דכלים מ"כ]
לקמן קה. ר"ה יח.

הגהות הב"ח

(א) רש"י ד"ה שומרת יבם שנשאה אחד מן וכו' במתניתין במחזיר גרושתו וטעמא: (ב) תוס' ד"ה (בעמוד הקודם) הכל מודים וכו' מידי דהוי אגוי ועבד כו': (ג) ד"ה אי כרב וכו' אורחיה דקרא ולאשמועינן דלקי אקידושין או אתי נמי לאשמועינן דלא תפסי קידושין הס"ד:

תוספות חד מקמאי

שלא ב"ל. וס"ל לרב דלא מתוקמא התם מתניתא כר"מ דהא לר"מ אדם מקנה דשלב"ל כדתניא קונם שאיני עושה לפיך א"ע להפר ר"מ אומר יפר שמא תעדיף עליו יותר מן הראוי לו ולא ס"ל לרב התם אוקימתא דאוקמה רבה בר רב הונא בריה דר"ה באומר יקדשו ידים לעושיהם. ושמואל מספקא ליה וס"ל אין ממזר מיבמה ממזר ודאי אבל ספק ממזר הוי וכיון דקי"ל כשמואל יש ממזר ספק מיבמה והא דתניא הכל מודים בבא על הנדה ועל הסוטה ועל שומרת יבם שאין הולד ממזר. (בנדרים) [לצדדין] קתני בנדה אינו ממזר כלל אפי' בספק בשומרת יבם אינו ממזר ודאי אבל ממזר ספק הוי. ואסור בממזרת ואסור בישראלית. ואית דבעי מימר דאע"ג דס"ל לרב דאין קדושין תופסין מודה הוא דאין הולד ממזר ולא פליג אמתניתא. ושמואל נמי אע"ג דמספקא ליה אם קדושין תופסין בה אי לא מודה הוא דאין הולד ממזר [ואמנם] מאי דאמר הכא דלאביי מספקא בשומרת יבם או כרב או כשמואל לא משמע הכי אלא משמע דהא בהא תליא אם אין קדושין תופסין בה הולד ממזר ואם קדושין תופסין בה הולד כשר:

(נ"ל ולא תפסי כו')

גירסת רש"ל ולאשמועינן דלקי לקידושין או לאתויי למה לא תפסי קידושין הס"ד:

תוספות ישנים

א) והקשה הר' נתנאל כיון דנפקא לן מחזיר סוטתו מלא יוכל בעלה הראשון וכו' ואמרינן הכא דהולד כשר א"כ מאי טעמא דרבי עקיבא דאמר במחזיר גרושתו הולד ממזר. בשלמא לפ"ה ניחא דנימא דקרא דלא יוכל לא איירי כלל במחזיר סוטתו [אלא] במקיים סוטתו איירינן הכא דאית בה ראיה דאין הולד ממזר מטעם דלא פקעי קדושי ואפי' החזירה אין הולד ממזר לר"ע נמי כיון דאנתק לאו דלא יוכל לגבי מקיים סוטתו דהא אית בה הויה משום דלא פקעי קדושי מעתה נאמר הואיל ואשתראי הלאו אישתרי ואפילו החזירה לא יהיה הולד ממזר אבל במחזיר גרושתו יהא הולד ממזר אבל לפי הר"י דמקרא דלא יוכל שמעי' דאית הויה במחזיר סוטתו ואין הולד ממזר מאי שנא מחזיר גרושתו ממחזיר סוטתו. הא כולהו נפקי מחד קרא מלא יוכל וכו' וכתיב בתר כן הויה להיות לו לאשה. וי"ל דר"ע יתרץ שאני מחזיר גרושתו דכתיב בגופה תועבה אבל בסוטה לא. ואומר ראב"י כי מזה נוכל לתרץ קושיא דלעיל דפריך לעיל לר' עקיבא למאי איצטריך היא תועבה וכו' וצ"ע לעיל. והשתא נוכל לומר דשפיר איצטריך היא תועבה להיא גופה למימר דלא תפסי בה קדושי. דאי לא כתיב בגופה תועבה ה"א דתפסי בה [illegible]

הגהות מהר"ב רנשבורג

א] רש"י ד"ה משנת ראב"י קב ונקי וכו'. במשנה או בברייתא עכ"ל. [illegible]

אֵלּוּ שְׁנֵי דּוֹרוֹת, זָכָה — מַשְׁלִימִין לוֹ, לֹא זָכָה — פּוֹחֲתִין לוֹ. דִּבְרֵי רַ' עֲקִיבָא. וַחֲכָמִים אוֹמְרִים: זָכָה — מוֹסִיפִים לוֹ, לֹא זָכָה — פּוֹחֲתִין לוֹ. אָמְרוּ לוֹ לְרַבִּי עֲקִיבָא: הֲרֵי הוּא אוֹמֵר "וְהוֹסַפְתִּי עַל יָמֶיךָ חֲמֵשׁ עֶשְׂרֵה שָׁנָה"! אָמַר לָהֶם: מִשֶּׁלּוֹ הוֹסִיפוּ לוֹ. תֵּדַע, שֶׁהֲרֵי נָבִיא עוֹמֵד וּמִתְנַבֵּא (מ"א יג) "הִנֵּה בֵן נוֹלָד לְבֵית דָּוִד יֹאשִׁיָּהוּ שְׁמוֹ" וַעֲדַיִין לֹא נוֹלַד מְנַשֶּׁה. וְרַבָּנַן: מִי כְּתִיב מֵחִזְקִיָּה? "לְבֵית דָּוִד" כְּתִיב, אִי מֵחִזְקִיָּה נוֹלַד, אִי מֵאֱינָשׁ אַחֲרִינָא. § "אִשְׁתּוֹ שֶׁמֵּתָה וכו' יְבִמְתּוֹ שֶׁמֵּתָה וכו'". § אָמַר רַב יוֹסֵף: כָּאן שָׁנָה רַבִּי מִשְׁנָה שֶׁאֵינָהּ צְרִיכָה. §

הדרן עלך החולץ

רַבָּן גַּמְלִיאֵל אוֹמֵר: אֵין גֵּט אַחַר גֵּט, וְלֹא מַאֲמָר אַחַר מַאֲמָר, וְלֹא בְּעִילָה אַחַר בְּעִילָה, וְלֹא חֲלִיצָה אַחַר חֲלִיצָה. וַחֲכָמִים אוֹמְרִים: [א]יֵשׁ גֵּט אַחַר גֵּט, [ב]וְיֵשׁ מַאֲמָר אַחַר מַאֲמָר, [ג]אֲבָל לֹא אַחַר בְּעִילָה וְלֹא אַחַר חֲלִיצָה כְּלוּם. [ד]כֵּיצַד? עָשָׂה מַאֲמָר בִּיבִמְתּוֹ, וְנָתַן לָהּ גֵּט — צְרִיכָה הֵימֶנּוּ חֲלִיצָה. עָשָׂה מַאֲמָר וַחֲלִיצָה — צְרִיכָה הֵימֶנּוּ גֵּט. עָשָׂה מַאֲמָר וּבָעַל — הֲרֵי זוֹ כְּמִצְוָתָהּ. [ה]נָתַן גֵּט וְעָשָׂה מַאֲמָר — צְרִיכָה גֵּט וַחֲלִיצָה. נָתַן גֵּט וּבָעַל — צְרִיכָה גֵּט וַחֲלִיצָה. נָתַן גֵּט וְחָלַץ — [ו]אֵין אַחַר חֲלִיצָה כְּלוּם. חָלַץ וְעָשָׂה מַאֲמָר, נָתַן גֵּט וּבָעַל, אוֹ בָּעַל וְעָשָׂה מַאֲמָר, נָתַן גֵּט וְחָלַץ — אֵין אַחַר חֲלִיצָה כְּלוּם.

אַחַת

רש"י

שְׁנֵי דּוֹרוֹת. שָׁנִים שֶׁפּוֹסְקִין לְאָדָם בִּשְׁעַת לֵידָתוֹ. זָכָה מוֹסִיפִין לוֹ. וְהַאי "אַמַלֵּא" — לְשׁוֹן תּוֹסֶפֶת הוּא. מִשֶּׁלּוֹ הוֹסִיפוּ לוֹ. אֶלָּא שֶׁמִּתְּחִלָּה הָיוּ רוֹצִים לִפְחוֹת מִשָּׁנָיו. תֵּדַע. שֶׁמִּתְּחִלָּה כְּשֶׁנּוֹלַד נִפְסְקוּ לוֹ כָּל אוֹתוֹ תּוֹסֶפֶת. שֶׁהֲרֵי נָבִיא נִתְנַבֵּא. בִּימֵי יָרָבְעָם שָׁנִים הַרְבֵּה קוֹדֶם "הִנֵּה בֵן נוֹלָד לְבֵית דָּוִד יֹאשִׁיָּהוּ שְׁמוֹ", וּבִשְׁעַת תורה אור חָלְיוֹ שֶׁל חִזְקִיָּה עֲדַיִין לֹא נוֹלַד מְנַשֶּׁה שֶׁמִּמֶּנּוּ יָצָא יֹאשִׁיָּהוּ, הֱוֵי אוֹמֵר: בִּשְׁעַת חָלְיוֹ גָּזְרוּ לִפְחוֹת מִשָּׁנָיו, וּכְשֶׁזָּכָה — הִשְׁלִימוּ לוֹ. מִשְׁנָה שֶׁאֵינָהּ צְרִיכָה. דְּזִיל קְרֵי בֵּי רַב הוּא "עָלֶיהָ בְּחַיֶּיהָ", שֶׁלֹּא נֶאֶסְרָה אֲחוֹתָהּ אֶלָּא בְּחַיֶּיהָ.

הדרן עלך החולץ

רַבָּן גַּמְלִיאֵל אוֹמֵר. סֵדֶר מִשְׁנָה זוֹ — שֶׁלֹּא תִּטְעֶה לְשַׁבֵּשׁ הַגִּירְסָא שֶׁבַּסְּפָרִים — סֵדֶר יָבָם אֶחָד וִיבָמָה אַחַת: תְּחִלָּה מְפָרֵשׁ דִּין גֵּט וַחֲלִיצָה וּבִיאָה שֶׁאַחַר מַאֲמָר, וְאַחַר כָּךְ מְפָרֵשׁ דִּין מַאֲמָר וּבִיאָה וַחֲלִיצָה שֶׁאַחַר הַגֵּט, וְאַחַר כָּךְ דִּין מַאֲמָר וְגֵט וּבִיאָה שֶׁאַחַר הַחֲלִיצָה, וְאַחַר כָּךְ דִּין מַאֲמָר וְגֵט וַחֲלִיצָה שֶׁאַחַר הַבִּיאָה. וְכֵן סֵדֶר יָבָם א' וּשְׁתֵּי יְבָמוֹת. **אֵין גֵּט אַחַר גֵּט.** שְׁתֵּי יְבָמוֹת לְאָדָם אֶחָד מֵאָח אֶחָד, וְנָתַן גֵּט לָזוֹ וְגֵט לָזוֹ — אֵינוֹ אָסוּר בִּקְרוֹבוֹת שְׁנִיָּה, דְּאִי קַמָּא אַהֲנֵי — הָא פָּקְעָה זִיקָה דְּתַרְוַיְיהוּ, וְהָוֵי כִּמְגָרֵשׁ נָכְרִית. וְאִי קַמָּא לָא אַהֲנֵי לְמִידְחֵי — בַּתְרָא נַמִי לָא אַהֲנֵי, וְהִלְכָּךְ לָאו גְּרוּשָׁתוֹ הִיא. וְכֵן שְׁנֵי יְבָמִין לִיבָמָה אַחַת, וְנָתַן זֶה גֵּט וְזֶה גֵּט — הָאַחֲרוֹן אֵינוֹ כְּלוּם, וּמוּתָּר בִּקְרוֹבוֹתֶיהָ. וְטַעְמָא כְּדְפָרִישִׁית. **וְלֹא מַאֲמָר אַחַר מַאֲמָר.** בֵּין בְּיָבָם אֶחָד לִשְׁתֵּי יְבָמוֹת, בֵּין שְׁנֵי יְבָמִים לִיבָמָה אַחַת — הָאַחֲרוֹן אֵין כְּלוּם לִפְסוֹל אֶת הָרִאשׁוֹנָה עָלָיו, וְאֵינָהּ צְרִיכָה הֵימֶנּוּ גֵּט, וְלֹא לֵיאָסֵר בִּקְרוֹבוֹת הַשְּׁנִיָּה. **וְלֹא בְּעִילָה אַחַר בְּעִילָה.** בָּא עַל זוֹ וְחָזַר וּבָא הוּא אוֹ אָחִיו עַל צָרָתָהּ — בִּיאַת זְנוּת בְּעָלְמָא הוּא, וְאֵין אָסוּר בִּקְרוֹבוֹתֶיהָ. **יֵשׁ גֵּט אַחַר גֵּט.** דְּקַמָּא לָא דָּחֵה לְגַמְרֵי, הִלְכָּךְ הַכָּא אִיכָּא פַּלְגָּא זִיקָה, דְּהָא בָּעְיָא חֲלִיצָה. הִלְכָּךְ, אַהֲנֵי בַּתְרָא וְהָוְיָא גְּרוּשָׁתוֹ, וְאָסוּר בִּקְרוֹבוֹתֶיהָ. **כֵּיצַד.** לָאו אַפְּלוּגְתָּא קָאֵי, אֶלָּא מִלְּתָא בְּאַנְפֵּי נַפְשָׁהּ הִיא, וְאַיָּבָם אֶחָד וְאַיְּבָמָה אַחַת קָאֵי. וְהָכִי קָאָמַר: כֵּיצַד דִּין יָבָם וִיבָמָה, וְהָכִי מְפָרֵשׁ בַּגְּמָ'. **צְרִיכָה הֵימֶנּוּ חֲלִיצָה.** וְאִם רָצָה לִכְנוֹס — לֹא יִכְנוֹס, דְּכֵיוָן דְּהִתְחִיל בְּגֵירוּשִׁין — קַיְימָא עֲלֵיהּ בְּ"לֹא יִבְנֶה". **צְרִיכָה הֵימֶנּוּ גֵּט.** דַּחֲלִיצָה אַפְקַעְתַּהּ לְזִיקָתָהּ, וּבָעֵי גֵּט לְאַפְקוּעֵי קִדּוּשִׁין דִּילֵיהּ, דַּחֲלִיצָה לָא מַפְקַעַת קִידּוּשִׁין. **הֲרֵי זוֹ כְּמִצְוָתָהּ.** מְפָרֵשׁ בַּגְּמָרָא: אַף זוֹ כְּמִצְוָתָהּ. **נָתַן גֵּט וְעָשָׂה מַאֲמָר.** בַּאֲחוֹתָהּ יְבָמָה עַצְמָהּ, אֲפִי' ר"ג מוֹדֶה דְּיֵשׁ מַאֲמָר אַחַר הַגֵּט. דְּמִסְפְּקָא לֵיהּ אִי גֵּט דָּחֵי אִי לָא, וְדִלְמָא גֵּט לָא דָּחֵי, וְאַהֲנֵי מַאֲמָר יְבָמִין בָּהּ. וְכ"ש לְרַבָּנַן דְּאָמְרִי גֵּט דּוֹחֶה קְצָת וּמְשַׁיֵּיר קְצָת — אַהֲנֵי מַאֲמָר לְמִיקְנֵי שִׁיּוּרָא דְּגֵט, וְצָרִיךְ גֵּט לְמַאֲמָרוֹ וַחֲלִיצָה לְזִיקָתוֹ. וְיִבּוּמֵי — לָא, דְּמִגֵּט קַמָּא קַיְימָא עֲלֵיהּ בְּ"לֹא יִבְנֶה". **נָתַן גֵּט וּבָעַל.** אָסוּר לְקַיְּימָהּ, דְּקָמָה עֲלֵיהּ בְּ"לֹא יִבְנֶה", וּצְרִיכָה גֵּט לְבִיאָתוֹ וַחֲלִיצָה לְזִיקָתוֹ. גֵּט לְבִיאָתוֹ, וַאֲפִילּוּ לְר' עֲקִיבָא דְּאָמַר אֵין קִידּוּשִׁין תּוֹפְסִין בְּחַיָּיבֵי לָאוִין, דְּהָא הָךְ מַתְנִי' כּוּלָּהּ ר' עֲקִיבָא הִיא, כִּדְמְפָרֵשׁ בַּגְּמָ', הָכָא מוֹדֵי דְּתָפְסִי קִידּוּשֵׁי בִּיאָה. דְּגֵט לָאו כַּחֲלִיצָה דָּמֵי (א) לְאַפְקוּעֵי כּוּלָּהּ זִיקָה, הִלְכָּךְ לָא עָמְדָה עָלָיו בְּלָאו גָּמוּר. **וַחֲלִיצָה.** לְזִיקָתוֹ. וּבְגֵט לְחוּדֵיהּ לָא מִפַּטְרָא (ב), [כְּמוֹ] שֶׁאַחֵר כּוֹנֵס אֶת יְבִמְתּוֹ שֶׁיָּכוֹל לְפוֹטְרָהּ בְּגֵט. מִשּׁוּם דְּהָוֵי בִּיאָה פְּסוּלָה מִשּׁוּם גֵּט קַמָּא, וְלָא קַנְיָא לְגַמְרֵי. **אֵין לְאַחַר חֲלִיצָה כְּלוּם.** וְאַע"ג דַּחֲלִיצָה פְּסוּלָה הִיא. דְּאִי הֲוָה בָּעֵי לְיַיבּוּמֵי — לָא מָצֵי, וְאַפ"ה דָּחְיָא לְגַמְרֵי, וְאֵין אַחֲרֶיהָ כְּלוּם. דְּאִי הָדַר וּמְקַדֵּשׁ לָהּ בְּמַאֲמָר אוֹ בְּבִיאָה — לָא בָּעֵינַן גֵּט, וּכְדְרַבִּי עֲקִיבָא דְּאָמַר אֵין קִידּוּשִׁין תּוֹפְסִין בְּחַיָּיבֵי לָאוִין. וְהָכִי מְפָרֵשׁ בַּגְּמָ', דְּמַתְנִי' ר"ע הִיא. **חָלַץ וְעָשָׂה בָּהּ מַאֲמָר.** אוֹ נָתַן גֵּט אַחַר חֲלִיצָה, אוֹ בָּעַל אַחַר חֲלִיצָה — אֵינוֹ כְּלוּם, כִּדְתָנֵי בְּסֵיפָא: אֵין אַחַר חֲלִיצָה כְּלוּם. שֶׁאֵין מַאֲמָר וּבִיאָה תּוֹפְסִין בָּהּ אַחַר חֲלִיצָה כְּר' עֲקִיבָא, וְגֵט דְּאַחַר חֲלִיצָה לָא הֲוָה צָרִיךְ לְמִיתְנֵי לְאַשְׁמוּעִינַן דְּאֵין כְּלוּם, דִּלְמַאי לִיהֲנֵי? לְיִתְסוּרֵי בִּקְרוֹבוֹתֶיהָ — הָא מִיתְּסַר וְקָאֵי מֵחֲמַת חֲלִיצָה. אֶלָּא אַיְּדֵי דְּבָעֵי לְמִיתְנֵי גֵּט דְּאַחַר בְּעִילָה, כְּדְקָתָנֵי אוֹ בָּעַל וְעָשָׂה מַאֲמָר וְנָתַן גֵּט, לְאַשְׁמוּעִינַן דְּאֵין לְאַחַר בִּיאָה כְּלוּם זִיקַת יִבּוּמִים, וּבְהַאי גֵּט סַגֵּי לֵיהּ בְּלֹא חֲלִיצָה — תָּנָא נַמִי גֵּט דְּאַחַר חֲלִיצָה, וְהָכִי מְפָרֵשׁ בַּגְּמָ'. **אוֹ בָּעַל וְעָשָׂה מַאֲמָר.** אוֹ נָתַן גֵּט אַחַר בִּיאָה, אוֹ חָלַץ אַחַר בִּיאָה — אֵין לְאַחַר בִּיאָה כְּלוּם. זִיקַת יְבָמִים דְּגֵט שֶׁנָּתַן אַחַר בִּיאָה מְגָרֵשׁ לָהּ כְּאִשְׁתּוֹ גְּמוּרָה, וְלָא בָּעְיָא חֲלִיצָה. וְאִם רָצָה לְהַחֲזִיר — מַחֲזִירָהּ. וַחֲלִיצָה שֶׁעָשָׂה אַחַר בִּיאָה — אֵינָהּ מוֹעֶלֶת כְּלוּם, דְּאֵין עָלֶיהָ זִיקַת יְבָמִין. וּמַאֲמָר דְּאַחַר בִּיאָה לָא הֲוָה צָרִיךְ לְמִיתְנֵי, דִּפְשִׁיטָא לַן דְּלָא מְהַנֵּי. דִּלְמַאי לִיהֲנֵי? הָא אֲפִילּוּ מַאֲמָר אַחַר מַאֲמָר בְּיָבָם אֶחָד וִיבָמָה אַחַת — בַּתְרָא כְּמַאן דְּלֵיתֵיהּ דָּמֵי, דְּמַאי קָעָבֵיד? הָא מִיתְּסַר וְקָאֵי בִּקְרוֹבוֹתֶיהָ. אֶלָּא אַיְּדֵי דְּתָנָא רֵישָׁא חָלַץ וְעָשָׂה מַאֲמָר, דְּאִיצְטְרִיךְ לְאַשְׁמוּעִינַן כְּר' עֲקִיבָא דְּאֵין קִידּוּשִׁין תּוֹפְסִין בַּחֲלוּצָתוֹ — תָּנָא נַמִי בָּעַל וְעָשָׂה מַאֲמָר, וְהָכִי מְפָרֵשׁ בַּגְּמָ'. **אֵין אַחַר חֲלִיצָה כְּלוּם.** אַרֵישָׁא קָאֵי, וּכְדְפָרִישִׁית לְעֵיל. וְאַלִּישָּׁנָא דְּסֵיפָא, דְּקָתָנֵי אוֹ בָּעַל וְעָשָׂה מַאֲמָר אוֹ נָתַן גֵּט וְחָלַץ, הֲוָה שַׁיָּיךְ לְמִיתְנֵי אֵין אַחַר בִּיאָה כְּלוּם, וּבַגְּמָרָא קָא בָּעֵי לֵיהּ.

אַחַת

תוספות

מוסיפין לו. והא דאמר במועד קטן (דף כח. ושם): בני חיי ומזוני לאו בזכותא תליא מילתא אלא במזלא תליא מילתא – פשיטא דזכות גדול מועיל, כדאמר בשבת (דף קנו: ושם): אין מזל לישראל. ומיהו, לא שכיח שישתנה המזל, כדמוכח בתענית (דף כה.) גבי עובדא דר"א בן פדת.

משלו הוסיפו לו. וקרי ליה תוספת – לפי מה שנגזר לפחות ע"י עון. והא דאמר בפ"ק דחגיגה (דף ד: ושם) גבי איתתא מגדלא נשיא כי חזינן צורבא מרבנן דמעבר אמיליה מוסיפין ליה – אר"י ניחא אפילו לר"ע, דאין זה תוספת, כיון שנגזרו לשום אדם.

תדע שהרי נביא עומד. וא"ת: והלא אם לא התפלל חזקיהו על עצמו היה מת, והיתה נבואה בטלה! אלא ע"כ אין הנביא מתנבא אלא מה שראוי להיות אם לא היה חוטא. א"כ, היכי מוכח מכאן דמשלו הוסיפו לו? אפי' לא הוסיפו לו משלו, והיה כבר כל שנותיו שנגזרו לו – מה שלא נתקיימה הנבואה לפי שחטא, ואילו לא חטא ונשא אשה בשנים הראשונים – היה מוליד! ואר"י: דשמא הדורות נגזרו להוולד באותו הזמן ובאותו הפרק שהם נולדים. ובשני התוספת נגזר לו להוליד מנשה.

שנה רבי משנה שאינה צריכה. פ"ה: דזיל קרי בי רב הוא. וקשה: דבכמה מקומות שונה התנא מה שבפסוק בפירוש! ועוד: דגרשה ומתה מותר באחותה איצטריך למידק, הא לא מתה – אסירא, דלא כתיב בהדיא, ודרשינן לה בפ"ק (דף ח:) מ"עליה בחייה" – כל שבחייה, אפילו נתגרשה! אלא נראה לר"י דיבמתו היא משנה שאין צריכה, דכיון דתנא אשתו – כ"ש יבמתו[א].

הדרן עלך החולץ

רבן גמליאל. אין מאמר אחר מאמר. אתי אפי' כרבנן דרבי עקיבא, אע"ג דקידושין לדידהו תופסין בחייבי לאוין. ותפסי קידושין אחר ביאה – התם הוא משום דהוו קדושין דאורייתא, דע"י ביאה פקעה זיקה. אבל הכא, שהיא זקוקה לו – אין לו לתפוס אלא מדרבנן, ולא תקון רבנן שיהא מאמר אחר מאמר. ולהכי לא קאמר בגמרא עלה זו דברי ר' עקיבא. ולא כמו שפי' ריב"ן דר"ג כר"ע.

ולא בעילה אחר בעילה. היינו אחר בעילה כשרה, אבל אחר בעילה פסולה, כגון ביאה שאחר הגט – יש אחריה ביאה, כי היכי דיש אחריה מאמר, כמו שמפרש בגמ'.

ולא חליצה אחר חליצה. היינו אפילו אחר חליצה פסולה.

עשה מאמר ביבמתו ונתן לה גט צריכה חליצה. היינו בנתן גט סתם, אף לזיקתו. אבל אם נתן גט למאמרו – שריא אף ליבם, דאמר בפ' "ד' אחין" (לעיל דף לב.) דהותרה אפי' היא, דמאי דעבד – שקליה.

עשה מאמר וחליץ צריכה הימנו גט. הכא לא תני אין אחר חליצה כלום – משום דאכתי צריכה גט למאמר שכבר ולא תני ליה אלא היכא דאחר חליצה אין צריך לעשות כלום.

חליץ ועשה מאמר כו'. אומר ריב"ן: לא הוה צריך למיתני כלל, דכיון דתנא נתן גט וחלץ אין אחר חליצה כלום, אע"פ שהיא חליצה פסולה – כ"ש דאחר חליצה כשירה אין אחריה כלום, אלא כל העניינים שונה.

עשה

עין משפט נר מצוה

א א מיי' פ"ה מהלכות יבום הלכה יד טוש"ע אה"ע סימן קע סעיף ג:

ב ב מיי' שם טוש"ע שם סעיף ו:

ג ג מיי' שם טוש"ע שם סעיף יב:

ד ד מיי' שם הלכה ד טוש"ע שם סעי' ב:

ה ה מיי' שם הלכה ז טוש"ע שם סעיף ט וסעיף י:

ו ו מיי' שם טוש"ע שם סעיף יד:

הגהות הב"ח

(א) רש"י ד"ה נתן גט וכו' לאפקועי. נ"ב ע"ל דף נב ע"ב דיש לאו בגט ג"כ רק דהוא אסמכתא: (ב) ד"ה וחליצה וכו' לא מפטרא כשאר יבם שכונס את יבמתו:

תוספות ישנים

א) ואע"ג דגבי יבמה איכא למידק באחותה אין באמה לא כדדייקי' בפ"ב. ר' יוסף לית ליה ההוא דיוקא דקסבר אין זיקה אבל בבא דאשתו צריכה שלא תדרוש כל שבחייה לדרשא אחריתא כדבעיא למדרשיה בפ"ק [דף ח ע"ב] ונשאת לאחר נמי אצטריך דלא תימא כי לא מתה נמי כיון שנשאת לאחר כמתה דמיא. מאחר דאסור להחזיר גרושתו משנשאת והוה אמינא דשרי באחותה:

אַחַת יְבָמָה אַחַת לְיָבָם אֶחָד, וְאַחַת שְׁתֵּי יְבָמוֹת לְיָבָם אֶחָד. [א]כֵּיצַד? עָשָׂה מַאֲמָר בָּזוֹ וּמַאֲמָר בָּזוֹ — צְרִיכוֹת שְׁנֵי גִיטִּין וַחֲלִיצָה. [ב]מַאֲמָר בָּזוֹ וְגֵט לָזוֹ — צְרִיכָה גֵּט וַחֲלִיצָה. [ג]מַאֲמָר בָּזוֹ וּבָעַל אֶת זוֹ — צְרִיכוֹת ב' גִּיטִּין וַחֲלִיצָה. [ד]מַאֲמָר בָּזוֹ וְחָלַץ לָזוֹ — הָרִאשׁוֹנָה צְרִיכָה גֵּט. [ה]גֵּט לָזוֹ וְגֵט לָזוֹ — צְרִיכוֹת הֵימֶנּוּ חֲלִיצָה. [ו]גֵּט לָזוֹ וּבָעַל אֶת זוֹ — צְרִיכָה גֵּט וַחֲלִיצָה. [ז]גֵּט לָזוֹ וּמַאֲמָר בָּזוֹ — צְרִיכָה גֵּט וַחֲלִיצָה. [ח]גֵּט לָזוֹ וְחָלַץ לָזוֹ — אֵין אַחַר חֲלִיצָה כְּלוּם. [ט]חָלַץ וְחָלַץ, אוֹ חָלַץ וְעָשָׂה מַאֲמָר, נָתַן גֵּט וּבָעַל, אוֹ בָּעַל וּבָעַל, אוֹ בָּעַל וְעָשָׂה מַאֲמָר, נָתַן גֵּט וְחָלַץ — אֵין אַחַר חֲלִיצָה כְּלוּם, בֵּין יָבָם אֶחָד לִשְׁתֵּי יְבָמוֹת. בֵּין שְׁנֵי יְבָמִין לִיבָמָה אַחַת. חָלַץ וְעָשָׂה מַאֲמָר, נָתַן גֵּט וּבָעַל, אוֹ בָּעַל וְעָשָׂה מַאֲמָר, וְנָתַן גֵּט וְחָלַץ — אֵין אַחַר חֲלִיצָה כְּלוּם, בֵּין בַּתְּחִלָּה בֵּין בָּאֶמְצַע בֵּין בַּסּוֹף. [י]וְהַבְּעִילָה, בִּזְמַן שֶׁהִיא בַּתְּחִלָּה — אֵין אַחֲרֶיהָ כְּלוּם. בָּאֶמְצַע וּבַסּוֹף — יֵשׁ אַחֲרֶיהָ כְּלוּם. *רַבִּי נְחֶמְיָה אוֹמֵר: אַחַת בְּעִילָה וְאַחַת חֲלִיצָה, בֵּין בַּתְּחִלָּה בֵּין בָּאֶמְצַע בֵּין בַּסּוֹף — אֵין אַחֲרֶיהָ כְּלוּם.§ **גמ'** עַד כָּאן לָא פְּלִיגִי אֶלָּא בְּגֵט אַחַר גֵּט וּמַאֲמָר אַחַר מַאֲמָר, [כ]אֲבָל גֵּט אֶחָד בִּיבָמָה [וּמַאֲמָר אֶחָד בִּיבָמָה] — מְהַנֵּי, מ"ט אֲמוּר רַבָּנַן גֵּט בִּיבָמָה מְהַנֵּי — מִשּׁוּם דִּמְהַנֵּי בְּעָלְמָא. דְּאִי אָמְרַתְּ לָא מְהַנֵּי, אָמְרִי: גֵּט לְהוֹצִיאָהּ וַחֲלִיצָה לְהוֹצִיאָהּ וּמִדְּגֵט לָא מְהַנֵּי — חֲלִיצָה נַמִּי לָא מְהַנֵּי, וְאָתֵי לְמִיבְעַל אַחַר חֲלִיצָה. וּמַאי טַעְמָא [ל]אֲמוּר רַבָּנַן מַאֲמָר בִּיבָמָה מְהַנֵּי — מִשּׁוּם דִּמְהַנֵּי בְּעָלְמָא. דְּאִי אָמְרַתְּ לָא מְהַנֵּי, אָמְרִי: מַאֲמָר לִקְנוֹת וּבִיאָה לִקְנוֹת, וּמִדְּמַאֲמָר לָא מְהַנֵּי — בִּיאָה נַמִּי לָא מְהַנְיָא וְאָתֵי לְמִבְעַל אַחַר בִּיאָה. וּמ"ט אֲמוּר רַבָּנַן [מ]בִּיאָה פְּסוּלָה יֵשׁ אַחֲרֶיהָ כְּלוּם — אָמְרִי: אִי בִּיאָה אַחַר הַגֵּט הִיא — גְּזֵירָה בִּיאָה אַחַר הַגֵּט מִשּׁוּם בִּיאָה אַחַר חֲלִיצָה, וְאִי בִּיאָה אַחַר מַאֲמָר הִיא — גְּזֵירָה בִּיאָה אַחַר מַאֲמָר מִשּׁוּם בִּיאָה אַחַר בִּיאָה. וּמ"ט אֲמוּר רַבָּנַן [נ]הַאי חֲלִיצָה פְּסוּלָה אֵין אַחֲרֶיהָ כְּלוּם — אָמְרִי: מַאי לִגְזוֹר? נִגְזוֹר חֲלִיצָה אַחַר הַגֵּט מִשּׁוּם חֲלִיצָה אַחַר חֲלִיצָה — כָּל כִּי הָנֵי תַּחֲלוֹץ וְתֵיזִיל?! לִיגְזוֹר חֲלִיצָה אַחַר מַאֲמָר מִשּׁוּם חֲלִיצָה אַחַר בִּיאָה — אַטּוּ חֲלִיצָה אַחַר מַאֲמָר מִי לָא בָּעֲיָא גֵּט לְמַאֲמָרוֹ? חֲלִיצָה אַחַר בִּיאָה נַמִּי — בָּעֲיָא גֵּט לְבִיאָתוֹ. אֲמַר רָבָא: מ"ט

רש"י

אחת יבמה אחת ליבם אחד ואחת שתי יבמות ליבם אחד. שוין, כמו שאמרנו, שיש אחר גט ראשון או אחר מאמר ראשון כלום, ואין אחר ביאה שבתחלה, או אחר חליצה, כלום. כיצד. בשתי יבמות ליבם אחד. צריכות שני גיטין. כרבנן, דיש מאמר אחר מאמר. ויבומי לא, דהיכי ליעביד? אי לייבומי לתרוייהו – הוו להו שני בתים. ואי לחדא, הואיל וחברתה ביה אגידא – הוה ליה בונה שני בתים. וחליצה. לאחת מהן, ופוטרת צרתה. מאמר לזו וגט לזו. פסל גט של אחרונה את הראשונה, דקם ליה ב"לא יבנה", וצריכה גט למאמרו וחליצה לזיקתו. דחליצה לא מפקעא קידושין, וגט לא מפקע זיקה. מאמר לזו ובעל את זו. אסור לקיימה, דהואיל וקמייתא אגידא ביה – הוו להו שני בתים. וצריכות שני גיטין: זו גט למאמרו, וזו גט לביאתו, וחליצה לאחת מהן, ופוטרת צרתה. אבל בגט לחודיה לא נפקא בעלת ביאה, הואיל דביאה פסולה היא. מאמר בזו וחלץ לזו. בעלת מאמר הראשונה צריכה גט למאמר, דחליצה דאידך לא מפקעה למאמרו. צריכות הימנו חליצה. אחת, ואסור בקרובות שניה. דרבנן הוא דאמרי: יש גט אחר גט. גט לזו ובעל את זו צריכה גט וחליצה. ואסור לקיימה, דקמה עליה ב"לא יבנה", משום גט דראשונה. ובגט לחודיה לא נפקא, משום דביאה פסולה היא. אין לאחר חליצה כלום. דאי הדר מקדש לה לצרתה לא תפסי בה קידושין, כרבי עקיבא. חלץ וחלץ או חלץ ועשה מאמר ונתן גט ובעל וקתני סיפא אין לאחר חליצה כלום. והכי פירושו: חלץ לזו וחלץ לזו – מותר בקרובות שניה, שאין אחר חליצה ראשונה שום זיקת יבמין, וחליצה בתרייתא לאו כלום היא. וכן חלץ לזו ומאמר לזו, וכן נתן גט לזו אחר חליצת זו, וכן בעל לזו אחר חליצה של זו – אין מעשה האחרון כלום. או בעל. תחלה, וחזר ובעל לשניה. או בעל ועשה מאמר. בשניה, או נתן גט לשניה, או חלץ לשניה – אין אחר ביאה ראשונה כלום, ומעשה אחרון לא חשיב, ומותר בקרובות שניה.

אין אחר חליצה כלום. ארישא קאי. ואסיפא שייך למימר אין אחר ביאה כלום, ובגמרא קמיבעיא לה. בין שני יבמין ליבמה אחת. בכל הדין האמור למעלה, ביבם א' וב' יבמות. איבם א' ואיבמה אחת קמהדר. חלץ ועשה מאמר ונתן גט ובעל כו'. ואע"ג דתניא לעיל – הדר תניא הכא משום סיפא, דבעי לפלוגי בין ביאה לחליצה, כדקתני: חליצה, בין בתחלה בין באמצע בין בסוף אין אחריה כלום, והבעילה בזמן שהיא בתחלה כו'. ולאשמועינן פלוגתא דרבי נחמיה ורבנן. בין בתחלה בין באמצע. בין מאמר לגט, כגון גט לזו וחלץ לזו, וחזר ועשה בה מאמר, או בבעלת הגט – לא מהני מאמר, ולא בעיא גט למאמרו. בסוף. אחר מאמר וגט חלץ – אין אחריה כלום, וחליצה גמורה היא. ואי הדר עביד מאמר – לא בעיא גט, דחליצה גירושין גמורים היא, וקמה בלאו גמור עליה, ואע"ג דחליצה פסולה הואי. הביאה באמצע. כגון גט לזו ובעל לזו, וחזר ועשה מאמר בשלישית – אסור בקרובותיה. ובסוף. גט לזו ומאמר לזו, וחזר ובא על האחת – יש אחר ביאה זו זיקת יבמין, וכי מפיק לה – בעיא חליצה, ולא סגי לה בגט. אין אחריה כלום. ונפקא בגט ובלא חליצה. ואי הדר קדיש לאידך אחר ביאה – לא מהני. גמ' אבל גט אחד ביבמה. או מאמר אחד ביבמה – מהני גט ביבמה למיקם עליה ב"לא יבנה", ושוב לא ייבם. ומאמר ביבמה מהני לה להצריכה גט למאמרו, אי בעי לאפוקה. מ"ט אמור רבנן גט ביבמה מהני. הא מדאורייתא חליצה הוא דמהני בה, ומשום גט לא קרינא בה שלא בנה. משום דבעלמא מהני. בכל הנשים להתגרש, ואי אמרת הכא לא מהני, ואם רצה לכונסה אחר הגט יכנוס. אמרי אינשי: גט להוציא, וחליצה נמי להוציא, מדגט לא מהני ליה כו'. ומ"ט אמור רבנן מאמר ביבמה מהני. לאסור חברתה עליו? הא מן התורה קנין לא הוי ביבמה אלא בביאה. משום דמהני בעלמא. קידושי אשה קונים אותה, ואתי למבעל אחר ביאה, והוה ליה בונה שתי בתים, דאיסורא דאורייתא. ומ"ט אמור רבנן ביאה פסולה יש אחריה. זיקת יבמין, כדתנן לעיל: מאמר בזו ובעל לזו צריכות שני גיטין וחליצה, ולא אמרינן תיסגי לבעלת ביאה בגט בלא חליצה, ותיפטר אף חברתה בביאתה מן החליצה. אי ביאה אחר הגט היא. כגון גט לזו ובעל לזו, דאמרינן צריכה גט וחליצה, ולא סגי בגט לחודיה כשאר יבמה שכונסה. גזירה ביאה אחר הגט משום ביאה אחר חליצה. דאי אמרת תיסגי לה בגט – אתי למימר: מדקניא ביאה אחר הגט בביאה גרידתא, אלמא מעליותא היא, ואתי למיבעל לכתחלה אחר חליצה. ואי ביאה אחר מאמר היא. כגון מאמר לזו ובעל לזו, להכי תנן צריכות(א) שנים גט וחליצה. דאי אמרת בגט סגי לה – אמרי: ביאה של זו אחר קנין של זו מעליותא היא, ואתי למעבד ביאה אחר ביאה, וקא פגע באיסור אשת אח. שאחר גט או אחר מאמר. חליצה פסולה. אין אחריה כלום. דאי הדר עבד מאמר או גט לשלישית – לא מהני. משום חליצה אחר חליצה. דלא ליתי למיחלץ לשתי יבמות זו אחר זו, או שני יבמין ליבמה אחת זה אחר זה. כל כי הני תחלוץ ותיזיל. כלומר, מאי איכפת לן? כל ימיה תחלוץ. משום חליצה אחר ביאה. דלא ליתי למימר: יבמה כנוסה יוצאת בחליצה בלא גט – לא אתו למימר הכי, דהא חליצה אחר מאמר מי לא בעיא גט למאמרו? והא דאמרינן אין אחריה כלום – בדבר העשוי אחריה קאמר, דאי הדר עביד גט או מאמר או חליצה בחברתה, לא מיתסר בקרובותיה.

מאי

תוספות

עשה מאמר בזו ומאמר בזו צריכות ב' גיטין וחליצה. הכא שייך להקשות: דיתן גט לאחת מהן למאמרו ותשתרי אידך. ולעיל פי' (דף לב. ד"ה "גט"). **צריכות** ב' גיטין וחליצה. למ"ד חליצה פסולה צריכה לחזור – הכא בעו ב' חליצות, וקאי נמי צריכות אחליצה. ובסמוך דקתני עשה מאמר ונתן גט צריכה גט וחליצה, הא דלא קתני וצריכות חליצה לשון רבים – איידי דקתני צריכה גט, לשון יחיד, נקט נמי גבי חליצה לשון יחיד. **מדגט** לא מהני חליצה נמי לא מהניא. באשה דעלמא ליכא למיחש שמא יאמרו: מדחליצה לא מהני – גט נמי לא מהני, דבאשה לא שייך חליצה וקריאה. ואין לומר דתיבעי יבמה גט וחליצה משום דלא יאמרו מדחליצה לחודה מהניא גט נמי מהני – דהא לא יטעו שיפטרוה בלא חליצה, דבהדיא הצריך הכתוב חליצה. אבל הכא, חיישינן שיאמרו מה שהצריך הכתוב חליצה, היינו מלבד הגט שהוא בכל הנשים, ויאמרו: מדגט לחודיה לא מהני – חליצה נמי לא מהניא, ואתי למיבעל אחר חליצה. **ואתי** למיבעל אחר ביאה. אבל השתא דמהני לא חיישינן שמא יאמרו: כי היכי דמהני ביאה אחר גט ומאמר – מהני נמי אחר ביאה וחליצה, ואתי למיבעל אחר ביאה כמו אחר מאמר. דאחר מאמר נמי אסור למיבעל.

דמספקא

עין משפט נר מצוה

ז א מיי' פ"ה מהלכות יבום הלכה יד טוש"ע אה"ע סימן קע סעיף ו:
ח ב מיי' שם הלכה ו טוש"ע שם סעיף ז:
ט ג מיי' שם טוש"ע שם סעיף ח:
י ד מיי' שם טוש"ע שם סעיף ז:
יא ה מיי' שם הלכה טו טוש"ע שם סעיף א וסעיף ה:
יב ו טוש"ע שם סעיף יד:
יג ז שם סעיף יא:
יד ח שם סעיף יד:
טו ט שם סעיף יג:
טז י מיי' שם הלכה ט טוש"ע שם סעיף יד:
יז כ מיי' שם הלכה ז טוש"ע שם סעי' א:
יח ל מיי' שם הלכה ב טוש"ע שם סעי' ב:
יט נ מיי' שם הלכה ט טוש"ע שם סעיף יד:

תוספות ישנים

ומדגט לא מהני חליצה נמי לא מהניא. ואם תאמר והלא כתיבא בקרא בהדיא חליצה וי"ל שיאמרו דצריך חליצה עם גט דשאר נשים ויצטרך ביבמה גט וחליצה אבל אין לומר דבאשה בעלמא נמי תועיל חליצה דאי חליצה לא מהניא יאמרו דגט נמי לא מהניא והא דכתב בהדיא גט נאמר דהיינו עם חליצה כמו דאמרינן בחליצה שביבמה. וי"ל דדוקא ביבמה שייך שפיר גט וחליצה אבל בשאר נשים לא שייך קריאה כמו ביבמה ולא שייך בהו חליצה כלל ולא אתי למטעי שלא יועיל גט בשאר נשים:

[לקמן נא: קיא.]

הגהות הב"ח

(א) רש"י ד"ה ואי ביאה וכו' להכי תנן צריכות גיטין וחליצה:

מ"ט דר"ג – דמספקא ליה: גט, אי דחי אי לא דחי, מאמר, אי קני אי לא קני. גט אי דחי אי לא דחי, אי קמא דחי – בתרא מאי קעביד? אי קמא לא דחי – בתרא נמי לא דחי. מאמר אי קני אי לא קני, אי קמא קני – בתרא מאי קעביד? ואי קמא לא קני – בתרא נמי לא קני. איתיביה אביי: *ומודה ר"ג שיש גט אחר מאמר, ומאמר אחר הגט, וגט אחר ביאה ומאמר, ומאמר אחר ביאה וגט. ואי מספקא ליה לר"ג – תהוי כביאה דלכתחלה, ותקני! דהא תנן: הבעילה, בזמן שהיא בתחלה – אין אחריה כלום. אלא אמר אביי: לעולם פשיטא ליה לר"ג בגט דדחי, ומאמר דקני. מיהו, אמור רבנן: הא יבמה, בחד צד מהני בה גט, ובחד צד מהני בה מאמר. גט אחר גט – לא דחי, דהא דחה ליה קמא, ומאמר אחר מאמר – לא קני, דהא קני ליה קמא. גט אחר מאמר, ומאמר אחר הגט – האי מילתא קא דחי, והאי מילתא קא קני. ורבנן: כל חד וחד תקינו ליה רבנן גט ומאמר ביבמה. והאי ביאה פסולה עדיפא ממאמר, וגריעא ממאמר. עדיפא ממאמר, דאילו מאמר אחר מאמר לא מהני, ואילו ביאה אחר מאמר – מהני. וגריעא ממאמר, דאילו מאמר אחר הגט קני לכוליה שיורא דגט, ואילו ביאה אחר הגט – לא קניא ליה לכוליה שיורא דגט. ת"ר: כיצד אר"ג אין גט אחר גט? שתי יבמות שנפלו לפני יבם אחד, ונתן גט לזו וגט לזו – ר"ג אומר: חולץ לראשונה ואסור בקרובותיה, ומותר בקרובות שניה. וחכמים אומרים: [א]נתן גט לזו וגט לזו – אסור בקרובות שתיהן, וחליצה לאחת מהן. וכן אתה אומר בשני יבמים ויבמה אחת, כיצד אמר ר"ג אין מאמר אחר מאמר? שתי יבמות שנפלו לפני יבם אחד ועשה מאמר בזו ומאמר בזו, רבן גמליאל אומר: נותן גט לראשונה, וחולץ לה, ואסור בקרובותיה, ומותר בקרובות שניה. וחכמים אומרים: [ב]נותן גט לשתיהן, ואסור בקרובות שתיהן, וחליצה לאחת מהן. וכן אתה אומר בשני יבמים ויבמה אחת. אמר מר: נותן גט לזו וגט לזו, ר"ג אומר: חולץ לראשונה ואסור בקרובותיה, ומותר בקרובות שניה. לימא תיהוי תיובתא דשמואל, דאמר שמואל: *חלץ לבעלת הגט – לא נפטרה צרה! אמר לך שמואל: כי אמרי אנא – אליבא דמאן דאמר יש זיקה, ור"ג סבר *אין זיקה. ומדר"ג סבר אין זיקה – רבנן

מאי טעמא דר"ג. דאמר אין גט אחר גט בשתי יבמות או בשני יבמין, דלא מיתסר בתרא בקרובותיה. **שיש גט אחר מאמר.** מאמר לזו וגט לזו, פסל את הראשונה ואסור בקרובות שתיהן. **ומאמר אחר גט.** גט לזו ומאמר לזו, בעלת מאמר צריכה גט.(א) **וגט אחר ביאה ומאמר.** אחר ביאה שאחר מאמר, כגון מאמר לזו ובעל לזו וגט לשלישית – מהני גט ואסור בקרובותיה: (דביאה פסולה היא בשניה, דמאחר שעשה מאמר בראשונה – פסולות בשניה). **ומאמר אחר ביאה וגט.** גט לזו ובעל לזו ומאמר לשלישית – קונה מאמר, וצריכה גט ואסור בקרובותיה. **ואי אמרת מספקא ליה.** בדחיית הגט וקניית מאמר. **תיהוי.** הך ביאה אמצעית כביאה בתחלה, ותיקני, ולא תיהני מעשה שלישית, בין בגט אחר ביאה ומאמר, בין במאמר אחר ביאה וגט – ממה נפשך: גט אחר ביאה ומאמר לא ליהני, דאי מאמר קמא קני לגמרי – תו לא מהני ביאה וגט אבתריה, ואי מאמר לא קני מידי – נמצאת ביאה של אחריו ביאה בתחלה וכשרה, ותו לא מהני גט בשלישית. דהא תנן: הבעילה בזמן שהיא בתחלה – אין אחריה כלום. וכן במאמר אחר ביאה וגט, דאי גט קמא דחי – תו לא מהני ביאה ומאמר אבתריה, ואי גט לא דחי מידי – נמצא ביאה שלאחריהן בתחלה, וכשרה היא, וקונה, ומאמר דבתריה לאו כלום היא. **אלא.** פשיטא ליה דגט דחי קצת ומאמר קני קצת. הלכך, ביאה של אחריהן אינה תחלה. ומיהו, מ"ט יש מאמר אחר גט וגט אחר מאמר, ואין מאמר אחר מאמר ולא גט אחר גט – דאמור רבנן: בחד צד מהני בה גט לדחות אגידה, וחד צד מהני בה מאמר לקנות אגידה. **גט אחר גט לא דחי דהא דחה ליה קמא.** כל את גט. הלכך לאו כלום הוא, ומותר בקרובותיה. וכן מאמר אחר מאמר, דהא קנה קמא כל את מאמר. **האי מילתא כו'.** גט אחר מאמר, מאי דשייר מאמר מן קמייתא – דחי גט בבתרייתא. וכן בשני יבמין, מאי דשייר מאמר דקמא – דחי גט דבתרא. **מאמר אחר הגט.** מאי דשייר גט דקמא מן הזיקה, דלא דחייה – קני מאמר דבתרא. **ורבנן.** דפליגי עליה דר"ג, דאמרי: יש גט אחר גט, אמרי לך. **כל חד וחד.** מן היבמין תיקנו ליה רבנן גט ומאמר בכל היבמות. הלכך, ליכא למימר קמא דחה כל את הגט, דקמא, כל את הגט דידיה דאית ליה בהך יבמה הוא דדחה, אבל את גט דאחוה בהך יבמה, וכן גיטא דידיה בצרתה – לא דחה, וכן לענין מאמר. **והאי ביאה פסולה כו'.** כלומר, להכי אמר ר"ג יש גט אחר ביאה שאחר מאמר ויש מאמר אחר ביאה וגט, דהא ביאה אמצעית, שהיא פסולה, עדיפא ממאמר וגריעא ממאמר. **עדיפא ממאמר כו'.** דאילו ביאה אחר מאמר מהניא, כדקתני: גט אחר ביאה ומאמר, אלמא יש ביאה אחר מאמר. **וגריעא ממאמר דאילו מאמר אחר הגט** קני ליה לכוליה **שיורא** דגט. כל מה ששייר גט למאמר, ואין מאמר אחר מועיל כלום אחריו, אם חזר ועשה מאמר בשלישית, כדקאמר רבן גמליאל: אין מאמר אחר מאמר, ולא שנא אי הוה מאמר ראשון אחר גט אי לא – אין מאמר אחריו, ולא פלוג בין שהיה מאמר ראשון בתחלה, בין שהיה אחר הגט, מדלא קתני: מודה רבן גמליאל שיש מאמר אחר מאמר וגט. **ואילו ביאה אחר הגט לא קניא** ליה לכוליה **שיורא** דגט. כל מה ששייר גט לביאה, דיש מאמר אחר ביאה וגט, כדתנן: הבעילה בזמן שהיא בתחלה אין אחריה כלום, אבל באמצע יש אחריה כלום, וכדאמר טעמא לעיל: מ"ט אמור רבנן ביאה פסולה יש אחריה כלום כו': ה"ג: ונתן גט לזו וגט לזו ר"ג כו'. **חולץ לראשונה.** וכ"ש דאי חלץ לשניה הוי חליצה מעלייתא לאיפטורי קמייתא, דכיון דגט דשניה(ב) אין גט – חליצה דידה מעלייתא היא. אלא עצה טובה אשמועינן, שלא יאסור עצמו בקרובות שניה, שאם יחלוץ לה – נמצא זו גרושתו וזו חלוצתו, ואסור בקרובות שתיהן. **וכן אתה אומר בשני יבמין ויבמה אחת.** נתן זה גט וזה גט, ר"ג אומר חולץ לה הראשון והשני מותר בקרובותיה, ולדברי חכמים שניהם אסורין בקרובות. **מאמר בזו ומאמר בזו ר"ג אומר נותן גט לראשונה כו'.** לקמן פריך: כיון דאין מאמר אחר מאמר, ייבומי נמי תתייבם קמייתא, דהא לא איפסלה עליה! **לימא תיהוי תיובתא דשמואל דאמר שמואל** חלץ לבעלת הגט. נפלו לפניו שתי יבמות, ונתן גט לאחת מהן, ואח"כ חלץ לה – לא נפטרה צרתה, משום דקלישא זיקתה, ולא חלימא חליצה לאפקועי זיקה חלימתא דצרתה. והא הכא, כיון דאמר ר"ג אין גט אחר גט – נמצאת זיקה שניה שלימה, וקתני: חולץ לראשונה, וקשה לשמואל. ומדרבנן ליכא לאותובי לשמואל, אע"ג דאמרי רבנן וחליצה לאחת מהן, אלמא חליצת בעלת גט פוטרת צרתה – לא קשה לשמואל, דהכא היינו טעמא דתרוייהו זיקתא קלישא, דהא אמרי רבנן: יש גט אחר גט. **יש זיקה.** אלימא זיקתה, ולא פקעה זיקה שלימה אלא בחליצה מעלייתא. **ר"ג סבר אין זיקה.** כדאמר בפרק ב"ש (לקמן דף קט.): אם מיאנה – מיאנה כו'. הלכך, כיון דלאו אלימא זיקה – פקעה בחליצה כל דהו.

רבנן

דמספקא ליה גט אי דחי אי **לא** דחי. לא מצי למימר דפשיטא ליה דגט ודאי דחי ומאמר ודאי קונה – דא"כ אמאי מהני מאמר אחר הגט וגט אחר מאמר? ואע"ג דאכתי לא ידע ברייתא דבסמוך דמודה ר"ג דיש גט אחר מאמר כו' – מתניתין משתמע ליה דיש גט אחר מאמר לר"ג, דדוקא נקט גט אחר גט ומאמר אחר מאמר דלא מהני, אבל מאמר אחר הגט או איפכא – מהני.

עדיפא ממאמר דאילו מאמר כו'. דמאמר האחרון אין יכול לתפוש במקום שתפס הראשון, וביאה פסולה תופסת אחר מאמר אותו צד עצמו שתפס המאמר, דסברא הוא שאין תופס אלא אותו צד שתופס המאמר, דתרוייהו לקנות. והיינו משום דעדיף ממאמר, לפי שהיא דאורייתא וגריעא ממאמר – דאילו מאמר אחר הגט קני לכוליה שיורא דגט. שהרי אין מאמר מועיל אחריו, אבל ביאה לא קני לכוליה שיורא דגט, שהרי מאמר מועיל אחריה, ואם היתה קונה כל השיור – לא היה מאמר מועיל אחריה לתפוש מה שתפשה הביאה. דביאה עדיפא ואלימא לפי שהיא דאורייתא, כדפרישית. ואתי לפרושי טעמא דלא תקשה הא דביאה עדיפא ממאמר, אע"ג דגריעא נמי ממאמר. ובקונטרס פירש: דאילו ביאה אחר גט לא קניא לכוליה שיורא דגט, דיש ביאה אחר ביאה פסולה. ותימה: דלא אשכחן בהדיא להאי מילתא שתהא לר"ג ביאה אחר ביאה פסולה! מיהו, יש לדקדק דיש ביאה אחר ביאה פסולה לר"ג. דאי אין ביאה אחרי ביאה פסולה, משום שכל קנין הראוי לביאה עשתה ביאה הראשונה ואין האחרונה יכולה לתפוש אחריה אע"ג דראשונה לא קניא כוליה שיורא דגט, א"כ – מנא ליה שמאמר קונה כוליה שיורא דגט? שמא גט ומאמר משייר אלא שאין במאמר אחר כח לחול אחריו במה ששייר, כמו שאין ביאה אחר ביאה פסולה אף על פי ששייר לקונה מאמר אחריה.

כולהו

ס"א כל זה איתו
לעיל כז:
לעיל כז.
[לעיל יז: וש"נ]

כ א מיי' פ"ה מהלכות יבוס הלכה טו טוש"ע אה"ע סימן קע סעי' ג ד:
כא ב מיי' שם וטוש"ע שם סעיף ו:

הגהות הב"ח
(א) רש"י ד"ה וגט אחר וכו' הכ"א עם ד"ה לביאה וכו' פסול בשניה הס"ד: (ב) ד"ה חולץ וכו' לשניה איתו גט:

תוספות ישנים

עדיפא ממאמר. אין להקשות ומאי עדיפותא הוא הלא כמו כן יש גט אחר מאמר אע"ג דלא עדיף ממאמר אלא דכותיה די"ל שאני גט ומאמר דזה דוחה וזה קונה אבל הכא הכי פירושא עדיפא ממאמר דמאמר אחר מאמר לא מהני דלא עדיף מאמר בתרא ממאמר קמא ואינו יכול לתפוס במה שתפס מאמר ראשון. וביאה פסולה אע"פ שאינה יכולה לתפוס מסברא רק בצד שתפס המאמר שלפניה שהרי כיון דתרווייהו לקנות סברא הוא דההוא צד דחזי למאמר חזי לביאה ואפ"ה מהניא אחר מאמר ותופסת באותו צד עצמו א"כ אלימא היא ממאמר וגריעא ממאמר דאילו מאמר אחר הגט קני לכולא שיורא דגט שאין מאמר מועיל אחריו דכי אמרי' במתני' אין מאמר אחר מאמר ר"ל בין לאחר מאמר כשר בין לאחר מאמר פסול מדלא מפליג בין כשר לפסול כמו גבי ביאה וחליצה. ואילו ביאה לא קניא ליה לכולא שיורא דגט שהרי מאמר מועיל אחריה ואם הוה קני לכולא שיורא דגט כמו מאמר לא היה מועיל מאמר אחריה שאין מאמר יכול לתפוס הצד שהביאה תפסה: **הא** אמר שמואל חלץ לבעלת הגט לא נפטרה צרה. פ"ה דדוקא לר"ג קא פריך דאמר חולץ לראשונה ומפטרא אידך אבל לרבנן לא פריך אע"ג וכו' ותימה דלעיל משמע דאף בפסולות קאמר שמואל דבחדא לא מפטרא אידך גבי התחיל באחיות לא יגמרו בצרות וצ"ל דה"ה דהוי מצי למפרך לרבנן אכן פריך בהדיא לר"ג דפטר שניה דמצית לחלוץ חליצה כשרה בחליצה ראשונה שהיא פסולה:

תוספות חד מקמאי

פרק ר"ג ת"ר (כיוצא בו) [כיצד] אמר ר"ג אין גט אחר גט ב' יבמות שנפלו לפני יבם א' ונתן גט לזו וגט לזו ר"ג אומר חולץ ראשונה ואסור בקרובותיה ומותר בקרובות שניה. וחכ"א אסור בקרובות שתיהן וחולץ לאחת וכן אתה מוצא בב' יבמין ויבמה אחת פי' כשתחלוץ לאחת מהן ופרכינן מיניה לרב דאמר חליצה פסולה צריכה לחזור על כל האחין. ופריק דבין לר"ג בין לרבנן אין זיקה ס"ל ובגט אחר גט ובמאמר אחר מאמר נמי פליגי וכיון דקי"ל יש זיקה לפום מאי דפסיקנא בפ' ד' אחין כרב דאמר חליצה פסולה צריכה לחזור על כל האחין לית הלכתא כי הא מתני' דקתני וכן אתה מוצא בב' יבמין ויבמה אחת ומדאקשינן לרב מסיפא דשני יבמין ולא מקשינן מרישא דשתי יבמות דקתני חליצה לא' מהן אלמא לרב לא פליג בהדי שמואל דאמר חלץ לבעלת הגט לא נפטרת צרה. לצרה נפטרת בעלת הגט ולא מילתא דתליין אהדדי נינהו והא דאמר נמי חולץ לראשונה לית הלכתא כותיה דאיהו ס"ל אין זיקה. וקי"ל דיש זיקה וקי"ל כשמואל חלץ לבעלת הגט לא נפטרת צרה:

בעא

רבנן סברי יש זיקה. וקתני סיפא: וכן אתה אומר בשני יבמין ויבמה אחת. לימא תיהוי תיובתא דרבה בר רב הונא אמר רב. דאמר רבה בר רב הונא אמר רב: *חליצה פסולה – צריכה לחזור על כל האחין! אמר לך רבה בר רב הונא: בין לר"ג בין לרבנן סברי אין זיקה, והכא בגט אחר גט ומאמר אחר מאמר קמיפלגי. אמר מר: עשה מאמר בזו ומאמר בזו, רבן גמליאל אומר: נותן גט לראשונה וחולץ לה, ואסור בקרובותיה, ומותר בקרובות שניה. מכדי קסבר רבן גמליאל אין מאמר אחר מאמר – ראשונה נמי תתייבם! גזירה דלמא אתי לייבומי לשניה. אמר רבי יוחנן: רבן גמליאל, וב"ש, *ור"ש, ובן עזאי ורבי נחמיה – כולהו סבירא להו: מאמר קונה קנין גמור. רבן גמליאל – הא דאמרן. ב"ש – דתנן(א): *שלשה אחין, שנים מהם נשואין לשתי אחיות ואחד מופנה, מת אחד מבעלי אחיות ועשה בה מופנה מאמר, ואח"כ מת אחיו השני, ב"ש אומרים: אשתו עמו, והלזו תצא משום אחות אשה. ר"ש – דתניא, *אמר(ב) להו ר"ש לחכמים: אם ביאת ראשון ביאה – ביאת שני אינה ביאה, אם ביאת ראשון אינה ביאה – ביאת שני נמי אינה ביאה. והא ביאת בן תשע, דכמאמר שויוה רבנן, וקאמר ר' שמעון אינה ביאה. בן עזאי – דתניא, *בן עזאי אומר: יש מאמר אחר מאמר בשני יבמין ויבמה אחת, ואין מאמר אחר מאמר בשתי יבמות ויבם אחד. ר' נחמיה – דתנן, *ר' נחמיה אומר: אחת בעילה ואחת חליצה, בין בתחלה בין באמצע בין בסוף – אין אחריה כלום. והא ביאה פסולה, דכמאמר שויוה רבנן וקתני: אין אחריה כלום.§ "כיצד עשה מאמר כו'".§ האי

[ועי' תוס' ר"ה מה:] [לקמן נג:]

רבנן סברי יש זיקה. לאקשויי אתי, כלומר: קס"ד דכי היכי דפליגי רבנן אדרבן גמליאל בגט אחר גט, הכי פליגי בזיקה. ואע"ג דממילתייהו לא שמעינן ליה. וקתני סיפא וכן אתה אומר בשני יבמין. דאם נתנו שניהם גט – חולץ לה אחד מהם. ואפילו לרבנן דאמרי יש זיקה – סגי לה בהך חליצה רעועה דחד מינייהו. לימא תיהוי תיובתא כו'. דהא נמי חליצה פסולה היא, שאחר הגט באה: הכי גרסינן. בין לרבן גמליאל בין לרבנן אין זיקה והכא כו'. והנא דאמרי – אליבא דמאן דאמר יש זיקה. קנין גמור. לא גמור ממש, אלא קנין חשוב. הא דאמרן. אין מאמר אחר מאמר – אלמא חשיב קמא למיקני כל כח מאמר. אשתו עמו. דקנייה במאמר, וכי נפלה אחותה – לא רמיא קמיה, דאחות אשה היא, ולא מיתסרא קמייתא עליה משום אחות זקוקה. והלזו תצא. אף מן החליצה. הלזו. כמו "הארץ הלזו הנשמה" (יחזקאל לו). אמר להם ר"ש כו'. לקמן בפרק "האשה רבה": בן תשע שנים ויום אחד הבא על יבמתו, וחזר ובא אחיו בן תשע שנים ויום אחד עליה – פסולה על ידו, דביאת בן תשע שנים כמאמר שויוה רבנן, והוה ליה מאמר אחר מאמר, ומקודשת אף לשני, ופסלה אף על ראשון, כרבנן דאמרי יש מאמר אחר מאמר. ר"ש אומר: לא פסלה. אמר להם ר' שמעון אם ביאת ראשון ביאה. קנייה לגמרי. ביאת שני אינה ביאה. דהביאה בזמן שהיא בתחלה – אין אחריה כלום, ואינה מקודשת לשני, ולא פסלה על הראשון. ואי משום דזינתה, דקי"ל ביאתו ביאה, דתנן (נדה דף מה.): בא על אחת מכל העריות שבתורה – מומתים על ידו, אפילו הכי לא מיתסרא על בעלה, דקיימא לן (כתובות דף ט.) אין האשה נאסרת על בעלה אלא על עיסקי קינוי וסתירה. כמאמר שויוה רבנן. דהכי תניא בפרק "האשה": עשו ביאת בן תשע כמאמר בגדול. וקאמר רבי שמעון: ביאת שני אינה ביאה, אלמא: מאמר ראשון חשוב לקנות כל כח מאמר: ה"ג. יש מאמר אחר מאמר בשני יבמין ויבמה אחת. דכל חד וחד תקינו ליה רבנן מאמר בה. ואין מאמר אחר מאמר בשתי יבמות ויבם אחד. דכל כח שתקנו חכמים במאמר – קנה במאמר ראשון, לשון מורי. ל"א ה"ג: אין מאמר אחר מאמר בשני יבמין ויבמה אחת דדומיא דקידושין בעלמא תקינו רבנן למאמר, ואין קידושין אחר קידושין באשה אחת. ויש מאמר אחר מאמר בשתי יבמות ויבם אחד – דהא תרווייהו קמיה רמיין, וכל חדא אית לה כח יבמין, דלא כח ביאה יהבי רבנן למאמר למיקני לגמרי. *ולא פקע זיקה דחברתה, דביאה הוא דפטרה. ולשון ראשון עיקר, דלקמן מוכחא מילתא בפירקין. והא ביאה פסולה במאמר שויוה רבנן. דלא נפקא מיניה בגט, דקא בעיא נמי חליצה לזיקתו. האי

כולהו סבירא להו. אין התנאים כולן שוין, דלבית שמאי קונה מדאורייתא, כדמשמע בפ' "ד' אחין" (לעיל דף כט. ושם) ולכולהו תנאי לא קני אלא מדרבנן, ולר"ג לא קני אלא בהא דלא מהני מאמר בתריה, ובן עזאי מפליג בין שני יבמין ויבמה אחת ובין יבם אחד ושתי יבמות, ולר"ש מספקא ליה אי קני אי לא קני. וכה"ג איכא בפ"ק(ג) דסוטה (דף ז: ושם)*. אי ביאת ראשון ביאה כו'. משנה היא לקמן ב"האשה רבה" (דף נו:) וקאמר תנא קמא דשני פוסל על ידו לראשון. ואם תאמר: לרבי שמעון נמי תיאסר לראשון, משום דזינתה תחתיו, ובקונטרס פירש דאין נאסרת על בעלה אלא על ידי קינוי וסתירה! ואר"י: שהוא טעות סופר, ולא פירשו רש"י מעולם. דבעד אחד ודאי אינה נאסרת אלא בקינוי וסתירה, אבל בעדי טומאה – נאסרת בלא קינוי. ואין לומר משום דהני נשואין דרבנן נינהו לא חשו לאוסרה – דכל דתיקון רבנן כעין דאורייתא תיקון. ועוד, דתיתסר משום דרב המנונא, דאמר: *שומרת יבם שזינתה אסורה ליבמה! ואר"י: דמיירי בבא עליה בשוגג, שאינה נאסרת. אי נמי בקטנה, דפיתוי קטנה אונס הוא. אי נמי בבא עליה בעל כרחה. ונאמר אע"ג דביאת בן תשע כמאמר, ומאמר בעל כרחה לא מהני. כדאמר בפ"ב (לעיל יט:) – עשו חכמים ביאת בן תשע בעל כרחה כמאמר מדעת, דלא שני לן בביאה דיבמה בין מדעת לבע"כ. בן עזאי אומר כו'. בקונט' נראה לו עיקר דגרסינן אין מאמר אחר מאמר בשתי יבמות ויבם אחד, משום דלקמן (דף נג.) אמתני' בעשה מאמר בזו ומאמר בזו כו' קאמר: מתני' דלא כבן עזאי. ור"י אומר דשפיר גרים איפכא, ולקמן סמיך אסיפא, דקתני בין שני יבמין ויבמה אחת, ולהכי נקטיה אמתניתין דעשה מאמר בזו ומאמר בזו, לפרושי דעלה קאי מתניתין, דלא כבן עזאי, וכה"ג איכא לקמן, דקתני גט לזו וגט לזו צריכות הימנו חליצה, ומסיק: לימא מסייע ליה לרבה בר רב הונא דאמר חליצה פסולה צריכה לחזור על כל האחין. ומהיא ליכא סייעתא, שיש לחלק בין מיפטר נפשה למיפטר צרה, כדאמר בריש פ' "ד' אחין" (לעיל דף כז.) אלא אסיפא סמיך, דקתני בין שני יבמין ויבמה אחת. ויש ספרים שכתוב בהם: כילד עשה מאמר ביבמתו כו' עד בין שני יבמין ליבמה אחת, ועלה מסיק מתניתין דלא כבן עזאי. ביאה פסולה כמאמר שויוה רבנן וקתני דאין אחריה כלום. פי': וה"ה אחר מאמר. תימה: דבסוף פירקין מפרש טעמא דרבי נחמיה דליכא למיגזר ביאה שאחר הגט ומאמר אטו ביאה שאחר חליצה וביאה, כיון דחליצה וביאה מדאורייתא – מידע ידיע. ואם כן, מנלן דלא יהא כלום אחר מאמר? ואומר ה"ר יצחק ב"ר ברוך דע"כ לרבי נחמיה גט ומאמר דאורייתא, דילפינן מק"ו משאר נשים. ולית ליה הני מיעוטי דבפ"ק דקידושין (דף יד.). דאי אפשר לומר שיהא מדרבנן לרבי נחמיה, דכיון דאית ליה דביאה וחליצה דאורייתא מידע ידיע, דאם כן לא שייך למיגזר הני גזירות דאמר לעיל: גט להוציא וחליצה להוציא, וביאה לקנות ומאמר לקנות. ותימה גדולה הוא לומר כן(ד), ולא מישתמיט שום תנא ולימא דגט פוטר ביבמה. ועוד: דא"כ הוה ליה למימר נמי דאין אחר הגט כלום! ועוד: דלישנא דהש"ס לא משמע שבא לדקדק מכח זה. א)ונראה לר"י, דה"פ: והא ביאה(ה) כמאמר שויוה רבנן, שיהא אחריה כלום משום גזירות דלעיל, ואל אחריה מאמר. [ומשום הכי תקינו נמי] רבנן שיהא מאמר אחר מאמר, אע"ג דמסברא הוה לן למימר כר"ג דאין מאמר אחר מאמר, לפי שקנה המאמר הראשון כל מה שיש למאמר לקנות. אלא טעמא דרבנן, דאי אמרינן דאין מאמר אחר מאמר – אתי למימר נמי דאין מאמר אחר ביאה פסולה, דלא גרעא ביאה ממאמר, לכך תיקנו שיהא מאמר אחר מאמר וגט אחר גט. דגט ומאמר ענין אחד, דשניהן דרבנן. ואי אמרת דאין גט אחר גט – אתי למימר נמי דאין מאמר אחר מאמר, ולא מאמר אחר ביאה פסולה. אם כן לרבי נחמיה אין מאמר אחר מאמר, דלדידיה ליכא למגזר מידי, דהא לית ליה נמי מאמר אחר ביאה פסולה, דקתני: (ביאה פסולה) אין אחריה כלום. ואם תאמר: אמאי תקינו רבנן לר' נחמיה גט ומאמר כלל ביבמה? כיון דביאה וחליצה מידע ידיע – ליכא למיגזר דגט להוציא וחליצה להוציא כו'! ויש לומר: דהעולם סוברים דגט ומאמר מהני מן התורה מקל וחומר דבפרק קמא דקידושין (ג"ז שם). ואע"ג דאימעוט – מכל מקום אהני קצת, כמו מאמר לבית שמאי. ולהכי, אי שרית למיבעל אחר גט ומאמר – אתי למיבעל אחר חליצה וביאה. אבל בהא לא טעו שיאמרו אחר הגט ומאמר בשביל שתקנה ביאה קנין גמור תקנה כמו כן קנין גמור אחר ביאה וחליצה, ויבא לבעול אחריה, דהא ודאי ידעי דחליצה וביאה עדיפא מגט ומאמר, שכתובין בהדיא, וגט ומאמר נתמעטו.ב) ר"י. אם

לימא תהוי תיובתא דרבה בר רב הונא דאמר חליצה פסולה צריכה לחזור על כל האחין. וא"ת ואמאי לא פריך מיבם א' ושתי יבמות דאמרו חכמים (חלצה) [דחולץ] לאחת מהם ואמאי הלא יש לנו לומר צריכה לחזור על כל הבית כמו על כל האחין. וי"ל דניחא ליה לאתוביה שפיר בהדיא מחיזור דאחין לחיזור דאחין: א) ונראה א) דקאמר והא ביאה פסולה וכו' דפריך מכח שאין לנו לומר שמועיל ביאה יותר ממאמר לשום תנא שהרי ר"ג סבר אין מאמר אחר מאמר ואפ"ה מהני מאמר וביאה אחר ביאה פסולה כדפרישית בריש פרקין וכן לרבנן לא גרע מאמר מביאה פסולה ושוין הם דיש מאמר אחר מאמר וכן יש ביאה אחר ביאה פסולה וא"כ אין לנו לומר לר' נחמיה שתועיל ביאה פסולה יותר ממאמר וקאמר דאין מאמר אחר ביאה פסולה וא"כ כמו כן אין מאמר אחר מאמר. ולא נהירא שהרי סברא גדולה יש לחלק דהא ביאה פסולה דיש ב) אומרים לר"ג ולרבנן היינו משום דאיכא למגזר כדמפרש תלמודא בריש פרקין ור' נחמיה לא ס"ל משום דביאה וחליצה הוו מדאורייתא ומידע ידע: ב) גם נ"ל דטעמא רבא איכא דאין לטעות למבעל אחר ביאה דאדרבה סברי כ"ע דחשיבות דביאה היא ואפילו פסולה אין אחריה כלום וכ"ש דביאה כשרה ואין לה שיור דאין אחריה כלום ולא אתי למבעל אחר ביאה. ורבנן לית להו האי טעמא דקסברי דכיון שתקנו חכמים גט ומאמר לתודייהו ביבמה דלא ליתי למיבעל אחר ביאה. כמו כן תקנו דביאה פסולה יש אחריה דלא ליתו למטעי בביאה אחר ביאה והמוסיף יוסיף:

לעיל כו: לקמן נג.

[עי' תוספות לעיל יט. ד"ה דתניא]

עדיות פ"ד מ"ט

לקמן נו:

[לקמן נג. נו:]

(נדה דף מה.)

[לעיל נ: לקמן קיא.]

ס"א ולמפקע

רש"ל מ"ז

הגהות הב"ח

(א) גמ' ב"ש דתנן. נ"ב ... כט ע"א: (ב) שם ... להם ר' שמעון: (ג) ר... ד"ה כולהו וכו' ב... דסוכה דף ז הס... (ד) ד"ה ביאה וכו' ... מישתמיט וכו': (ה) ב... והא ביאה פסולה כמא...

האי גט אחר גט הוא! אמר רב יהודה, הכי קאמר: גט אחר הגט ומאמר אחר מאמר כדאמרן, יבם אחד ויבמה אחת כיצד(א) התרתן? עשה מאמר ביבמתו ונתן לה גט — צריכה הימנו חליצה. § "עשה מאמר ובעל הרי זו כמצותה". § לימא מסייע ליה לרב הונא, דאמר רב הונא: [א]מצות יבמה — מקדש ואח"כ בועל. אימא: אף זה כמצותה. פשיטא! סד"א: (ב)כיון דאמר מר: *העושה מאמר ביבמתו — פרחה הימנו זיקת יבמין, וחלה עליו זיקת ארוסין ונשואין, אימא לאו מצוה קעביד — קמ"ל. גופא, אמר רב הונא: מצות יבמין מקדש ואחר כך בועל, ואם בעל ועשה מאמר — קנה. אם בעל ועשה מאמר — פשיטא, דהא קניה בביאה! אלא אימא: [ב]אם בעל בלא מאמר — קנה. והתניא: לוקה! *מכת מרדות [ג]מדרבנן. *דרב מנגיד [ד]מאן דמקדש בביאה, [ה]ומאן דמקדש בשוקא, [ו]ומאן דמקדש בלא שדוכי, [ז]ומאן דמבטל גיטא, [ח]ומאן דמסר מודעא אגיטא, [ט]ומאן דפקיר שליחא דרבנן, [י]ומאן דשהי שמתא דרבנן עליה תלתין יומין ולא אתי לבי דינא ותבע לשמתיה, [כ]ועל חתנא דדאיר בבי חמוהי. דדאיר — אין, דחליף — לא. והא ההוא דחליף אבבא דבי חמוהי, ונגדיה רב ששת! [ל]ההוא — מידם הוה דיים מחמתיה. נהרדעי אמרי: בכולהו לא מנגיד רב אלא למקדש בביאה ובלא שדוכי. ואיכא דאמרי: אפילו בשדוכי נמי, משום פריצותא. ת"ר: [מ]כיצד מאמר — נתן לה כסף או שוה כסף, ובשטר כיצד? בשטר כיצד?! כדאמרן: *[נ]כתב לה על הנייר או על החרס, אע"פ שאין בו שוה פרוטה, "הרי את מקודשת לי"! אמר אביי, ה"ק: [ס]שטר כתובת יבמין כיצד — כתב לה: אנא פלוני בר פלוני קבילית ית פלונית יבמתי עלי לזון ולפרנסה כראוי, *ובלבד שתהא כתובתה על נכסי בעלה הראשון. *ואי לית לה מראשון — תקינו לה רבנן משני, כדי שלא תהא קלה בעיניו להוציאה. בעא מיניה אביי מרבה: נתן לה גט, ואמר: הרי את מגורשת הימני, ואי את מותרת לכל אדם, מהו? גט יבמה דרבנן הוא, גט דמהני באשת איש מהני ביבמה. גט דלא מהני באשת איש — לא מהני ביבמה. או דלמא אתי לאחלופי בגיטא? [א"ל: חיישינן דלמא אתי לאחלופי בגיטא]. מתקיף לה רבה בר חנן: אלא מעתה, יהיב לה ניירא בעלמא ה"נ דפסלה? א"ל: התם לא פסיל בכהונה, [ע]הכא — קפסיל בכהונה. דתניא: "°ואשה גרושה *מאישה לא יקחו" [פ]אפילו לא נתגרשה אלא מאישה — לא יקחו, והיינו ריח הגט שפוסל בכהונה. אמר רמי בר חמא: *הרי אמרו, [צ]אמר אחד ללבלר "כתוב גט לארוסתי, לכשאכנסנה אגרשנה" הרי זה גט, מפני שבידו לגרשה. ולאשה

רש"י

האי גט אחר גט הוא. בתמיה: וכי זהו גט אחר גט? דקתני רישא וחכמים אומרים יש גט אחר כו'? ומפרש כיצד עשה מאמר כו' — דהיינו גט אחר מאמר. כדאמרן. בברייתא דלעיל, כיצד אר"ג כו' ובמתני' לא פירש. הואיל דאמר מר. בפרק "ד' אחין" (לעיל דף כט:). והתניא לוקה. ואין מלקות ארבעים אלא על דברי תורה. אלמא דאורייתא היא, והיכי אמרת קנה? וקמשני: האי לוקה לאו מלקות ארבעים הוא, אלא מכת מרדות, מכת רידוי מדרבנן, שנהג קלות ראש בעצמו, ולעולם קנה. דרב מנגיד. מכת מרדות. אמאן דמקדש בביאה. משום פריצותא. ואמאן דמקדש בשוקא. אפילו בכספא, דמנהג זילות ופריצות היא. דמתפקר. לשון חוצפא, שמעיז פניו להתרים עם שליח ב"ד. מידם הוה דיימא חמתיה מיניה. חשודה היתה חמותו ממנו. נתן לה כסף או שוה כסף. ואמר לה: התקדשי לי במאמר יבמין. ואע"ג דיהב לה מידי — לאו קידושין גמורים הן כקידושי תורה, שהרי אין קידושין תופסין באשת אח, והתורה לא התירתה לו ליעשות כאשה נכרית אלא כסדר המצוה, וביאה הוא דכתבה בה רחמנא. ובשטר כיצד. ואם קידש בשטר כיצד כתב בו? והוינן: כיצד?! בתמיה. והא כיון דקידושי כסף אמרת נתן לה כסף כשאר נשים, ממילא שמעינן שטר נמי כשאר כל שטר אירוסין בעלמא, כדאמר בקידושין: כתב על הנייר או על החרס, אע"פ שאין בו שוה פרוטה, הרי את מקודשת כו'. אמר אביי. האי תנא לאו אשטר מאמר קאי, אלא אשטר כתובה קאי. על נכסי בעלה הראשון. ולא על של יבם. מאי טעמא — כדאמר ב"החולץ" (לעיל דף לט.) אשה הקנו לו מן השמים. נתן לה גט. יבם ליבמתו. מהו. לפוסלה על אחיו ועליו בהאי גיטא, דתיקום עליה ב"לא יבנה". האי גט לא מהני באשת איש להתירה ליגשא, והכא נמי — לאו גירושין למיקם בלא יבנה. לאיחלופי בגיטא. ולכנוס יבמה אחר הגט. הכא פסיל בכהונה. כהן שנתן גט כזה לאשתו אסורה עליו, והלכך תיבעי לן (ג) אי מהני מדרבנן. אלא מאישה. ולא התירה לכל אדם. הרי זה גט. ואם נתנו (ד) משכנסה — הרי זו מגורשת, הואיל ובידו לגרשה משנכתב. ואי משום גט ישן, דקי"ל (גיטין דף עט:) בית הלל פוסלין, ותנן: איזהו גט ישן — כל שנתייחד עמה אחר כתיבה, הא איתמר בפרק "הזורק" (שם): אם נתגרשה — תנשא לכתחלה. ולאשה

תוספות

אם בעל ועשה מאמר פשיטא דהא קניה בביאה. הא לא פריך פשיטא דקניה בביאה לחודה — דמהא לא הוה משני מידי. אלא הכי פריך: פשיטא שמאמר אחר ביאה אינו מגרע, ואם בביאה לחוד קנה — בשביל מאמר שאחריו לא גרע! ומשני: אימא אם בעל בלא מאמר קנה, דס"ד לא קני אלא אם כן עושה כמצותה: מקדש ואחר כך בועלה. וממתניתין דתנן בריש קידושין (דף ב.): היבמה נקנית בביאה — לא שמעינן ליה, דדלמא היינו מדאורייתא, וכן הא דתנן הכא במתני' (לעיל נ:) הבעילה, בזמן שהיא בתחילה אין אחריה כלום — דלמא נמי היינו משום דמדאורייתא קני ופריך: והתניא לוקה! וידע שפיר דמדרבנן לוקה, אלא דס"ד דלוקה מדרבנן משום דעשאוהו חכמים כפוגע באשת אח שלא במקום מצוה, וא"כ מדרבנן לא קני לה בלא מאמר. ומשני: מכת מרדות מדרבנן, ומשום פריצותא בעלמא, כדרב.

דמבטל גיטא. אע"ג דרב משמע דסבירא ליה בריש "השולח" (גיטין דף לג.) דביטלו אינו מבוטל *כר"ג, גבי הא דאמר רב יוסף ניחזי אנן, מ"מ קאמר הכא דלקי — משום דמוציא לעז על הגט.

דמסר מודעא אגיטא. אפילו היה מבטל כל מודעי, מ"מ היה מלקה אותו, משום דמוציא לעז על הגט, דאיכא דשמע במודעא ולא שמע בביטול.

דמתפקר בשליח דבי דינא. כך גירס' הקונטרס. ויש ספרים שכתוב בהן: מאן דמצער שליחא דרבנן. וכן כתוב בכל הספרים בפ"ק דקידושין (דף יב:). ומיהו, גם שם פי' בקונטרס: שליחא דרבנן — שליח ב"ד. ונראה דבכל שליחא דרבנן יש ללקות, אע"ג דלא הוי שליח ב"ד. כדאשכחן בפ' "עשרה יוחסין" (קדושין ע.) דשמתיה רב יהודה לההוא *טבחא דליצר שלוחו. ואע"ג דשמתא חמור מנגדא, כדמוכח ב"מקום שנהגו" (פסחים דף נב.) — שמא החמיר עליו משום שביזה את רב יהודה עצמו.

דמקדש בביאה. אר"ת דאפי' ביבמה דצריך ביאה — דפרילותא הוא שעושה תחלת קנינו בביאה.

הדר בבית חמיו. אנן סמכינן אנהרדעי, דאמרי: בכולהו לא מנגיד רב אלא אמאן דמקדש בביאה, דבשל סופרים הלך אחר המיקל.

על הנייר או על החרס. אר"ת: כר' אליעזר אתיא, דלרבי מאיר, דאמר עדי חתימה כרתי — לא מהני, דדבר שיכול להזדייף הוא, דבשטר קידושין נמי בעי ר' מאיר עדי חתימה, כדמוכח בפ"ב דקידושין (דף מח.). ובפ"ק דקידושין (דף ט. ד"ה "כתב") פירשתי.

שאין בו שוה פרוטה. פירוש: ואינה מתקדשת משום כסף — מקודשת מטעם שטר, גבי שדי מכורה לך בפרק קמא דקידושין (דף כו. ושם) שהמוכר נותן שטר. תימה: אמאי נקט אע"פ שאין בו שוה פרוטה דאין בו שוה פרוטה כמו אין שוה פרוטה! ויש לומר: דמשום דכתב ביה נתינה אחרי תיבת את ספר המקנה, ס"ד דליבעי שוה פרוטה*.

לכשאכנסנה אגרשנה הרי זה גט. תימה דבפרק "כל הגט" (גיטין דף כו:) אמרינן דאינו גט, שלא יאמרו גטה קודם לבנה ובקונטרס פי': דהכא נמי לא קאמר דהוי גט אלא בדיעבד, שכבר נתגרשה בו. ואין נראה: דהתם דקאמר אין גט משמע דלא הוי גט כלל! ואר"ת דהכא כשכתב בו זמן שאחר נשואין, שהוא זמן נתינה — דאפילו גט ישן לא הוי, שלא נתייחד עמה אחר זמן הכתוב בגטה. והרי

עין משפט נר מצוה

כב א ב ג מיי' פ"א מהל' יבום ה"א ופ"ב הלכה א ב סמג עשין נא טוש"ע אה"ע סימן קסו סעיף ב:

כג ד ה ו מיי' פ"ג מהל' אישות הלכה כא כב ופכ"א מהלכו' איסורי ביאה הלכה יד סמג עשין מח טוש"ע שם סימן כו סעיף ד:

כד ז ח מיי' פ"ו מהל' גירושין הלכה כו סמג שם טוש"ע שם סי' קמא סעיף סז:

כה ט מיי' פכ"ה מהל' סנהדרין הלכה ה סמג לאוין רח טוש"ע ח"מ סי' ח סעיף ה:

כו י מיי' פ"א מהלכו' טוען ונטען הלכה ה טוש"ע שם סי' פז ס"ט:

כז כ מיי' פכ"א מהל' איסורי ביאה הלכה טו סמג לאוין קפו:

כח ל מיי' פ"ב מהל' איסורי ביאה הל' יב:

כט מ מיי' פ"ב מהלכות יבום הלכה א סמג עשין נא טוש"ע אה"ע סי' קסו סעי' ב:

[נ"ל כרשב"ג]

ל נ מיי' פ"ג מהלכות אישות הלכה ג סמג עשין מח טוש"ע שם סימן לב סעיף א ב:

לא ס מיי' פ"ד מהלכות יבום הלכה לב:

לב ע מיי' פ"ה שם הלכה א סמג עשין נא נב טוש"ע שם סי' קע סעיף א:

לג פ מיי' פ"י מהל' גרושין הלכה א סמג לאוין קכג טוש"ע שם סימן ו סעיף א:

לד צ מיי' פ"ג שם הל' ו סמג עשין נ טוש"ע שם סי' קלב סעיף א:

נ"ל גברא

תוספות ישנים

ועל דמצער שליחא דרבנן. לאו שליחא ממש אלא צורבא מרבנן ולאו מצער דוקא אלא מחרף כדאמרי' בעשרה יוחסין גבי רבי יהודה דקריא ליה ההוא גברא [יהודה בר] שויסקאל:

תוספות חד מקמאי

בעא מניה אביי מרב' נתן לה גט ואמר לה הרי את מגורשת ממני ואי את מותרת לכל אדם מהו גט יבמ' מדרבנן הוא [גט] דמהני בא"א מהני ביבמה גט דלא מהני בא"א לא מהני ביבמה או דלמא אתי לאחלופי בגיטא מעליא ולא איפשיטא: תניא ואשה גרושה מאישה אפילו לא נתגרשה אלא מאישה פסולה לכהונה וזהו ריח הגט שפוסל בכהונה אמר רמי בר חמא הרי אמר ללבלר כתוב גט לארוסתי לכשאכנסנה אגרשנה ה"ז גט מפני שבידו לגרשה. לאשה דעלמא אינו גט. ובפ' כל הגט אמרינן אמר ללבלר כתוב גט לארוסתי לכשאכנסנה אגרשנה אינו גט מפני תקנת ולד שמא יאמרו גטה קודם לבנה התם כגון דכתב בו זמן מהשתא דאיכא משום תקנת ולד הכא דכתיב זמן דשעת גירושין דליכא תקנת ולד. א"נ הכא מדאורייתא קא' ה"ז גט א"נ כגון שנתגרשה דקי"ל אין מגרשין בגט ישן גזרה שמא

מסורת הש"ס (שוליים)

[לעיל כט:] | [שבת מ: וש"נ] | קידושין יב: | לעיל לח. [וש"נ] | שם לט. | קידושין ע. ע"ש ב"ב נח. | ויקרא כא | [גיטין פב: לקמן צ"ב] | גיטין כו: | ע"ע תוס' קידושין ט. ד"ה אע"פ

הגהות הב"ח

(א) גמ' כיצד מצות התרתן: (ב) שם פשיטא סד"א הואיל דאמר מר: (ג) רש"י ד"ה הכא וכו' תיבעי לן אי מהני: (ד) ד"ה הרי וכו' נתנו לה משכנסה:

לה א ב מיי' פ"ג מהל' גירושין הלכ' ו סמג עשין נ טוש"ע אה"ע סי' קלב סעיף ב:
[וע"ע תוס' ב"ב קלה: ד"ה כל]
לו ג מיי' פ"ה מהלכות יבום הלכה ד סמג עשין נא נב טוש"ע שם סי' קע סעיף טו:
לז ד ה מיי' שם הלכה א טוש"ע שם ס"א:
לח ו ז מיי' שם הלכה טו טוש"ע שם סעיף יג:
לט ח מיי' פ"ב מהלכו' זכייה ומתנה הלכה יג סמג עשין פב טוש"ע ח"מ סי' רעה סעי' כה:
מ ט מיי' שם טוש"ע שם סעיף כו:
מא י טוש"ע אה"ע סימן קע סעי' יד:

ולאשה בעלמא — אין גט, מפני שאין בידו לגרשה. בעי רמי בר חמא: ליבמתו מהו? כיון דאגידא ביה — כארוסתו דמיא, או דלמא: כיון דלא עבד בה מאמר — לא? תיקו. בעי רב חנניה: כתב גט לזיקתו ולא למאמרו, למאמרו ולא לזיקתו, מהו? מאמר עילוי זיקה קא רמי, והוה ליה כמגרש חצי אשה, והמגרש חצי אשה לא עשה ולא כלום, או דלמא: האי לחודיה קאי והאי לחודיה קאי? ותפשוט ליה מדרבא, דאמר רבא: *נתן גט למאמרו — הותרה צרתה! לרבא — פשיטא ליה, לרב חנניה — מיבעיא ליה, מאי? תיקו. § "חלץ ועשה מאמר". § אמר רב יהודה אמר רב: זו דברי *ר' עקיבא, דאמר: אין קדושין תופסין בחייבי לאוין. אבל חכ"א: יש אחר חליצה כלום. ומי מצית מוקמת לה כרבי עקיבא? והא קתני רישא: נתן גט ועשה מאמר — צריכה גט וחליצה, ואי רבי עקיבא — כיון דיהב לה גט מי מהני בה מאמר? והתניא, רבי עקיבא אומר: מנין לנותן גט ליבמתו שנאסרה עליו עולמית — שנאמר "לא יוכל בעלה הראשון אשר שלחה" אחר שילוח. (דברים כד) אמר רב אשי: גט יבמין מדרבנן. וקרא — אסמכתא בעלמא. תניא נמי הכי, אמר רבי: *אין הדברים הללו אמורים אלא לדברי ר' עקיבא, שהיה עושה חלוצה כערוה. אבל חכמים אומרים: יש אחר חליצה כלום. ואני אומר: אימתי — בזמן שקידשה לשום אישות, אבל קידשה לשום יבמות — אין אחר חליצה כלום. תניא אידך: החולץ ליבמתו, וחזר וקידשה. רבי אומר: אם קידשה לשום אישות — צריכה הימנו גט, לשום יבמות — אין צריכה הימנו גט. וחכמים אומרים: בין שקידשה לשום אישות, בין שקידשה לשום יבמות — צריכה הימנו גט. אמר רב יוסף: מ"ט דרבי — עשאוה כעודר בנכסי הגר וכסבור שלו הן דלא קני. א"ל אביי: מי דמי? התם — לא קא מכוין למיקני, הכא — קא מכוין למיקני. הא לא דמיא אלא לעודר בנכסי גר זה, וכסבור של גר אחר הוא, דקני. אלא אמר אביי: הכא במאי עסקינן — כגון דאמר לה "התקדשי לי במאמר יבמין". רבי סבר: מאמר עילוי זיקה קא רמי, ואתאי חליצה אפקעתה לזיקה. ורבנן סברי: האי לחודיה קאי והאי לחודיה קאי. מעיקרא, אילו אמר לה "התקדשי לי במאמר יבמין" מי לא מהני? השתא נמי מהני. רבא אמר: אי דאמר לה "במאמר יבמין" כולי עלמא לא פליגי דמהניא, והכא במאי עסקינן — כגון דאמר לה "התקדשי לי בזיקת יבמין". רבי סבר:

יש

רש"י

ולאשה בעלמא. וכנסה וגירשה בו — אינו גט, הואיל כשנכתב לא היה ראוי לגירושין. ליבמתו מהו. כתבו קודם שכנסה, וכשכנסה נתנו לה, מהו שתתגרש בו? כתב גט לזיקתו ולא למאמרו או למאמרו ולא לזיקתו. והוא עשה בה מאמר תחלה, מהו שתיפסל עליו בכך? מאמר (תורה אור) עילוי זיקה רמי. כשעשה מאמר נדבק עם הזיקה, וניתוסף עליה — ואין גט מועיל לזה בלא זה. וכיון שנכתב בתוך הגט שלא עשאו אלא לאחד מהן — הוה ליה מגרש חצי אשה, ולא כלום היא, ומותרת לו. או דלמא האי לחודיה קאי והאי לחודיה קאי. ומהני. והיכא דכתב לזיקתו ולא למאמרו — אסורה עליו ועל אחיו, דפקע זיקה, וקמה ב"לא יבנה", ואי כתב למאמרו ולא לזיקתו — אסורה לו ומותרת לאחיו, דמאמר דעבד שקליה, ופשה ליה זיקה כמעיקרא. נתן גט למאמרו. ולא לזיקתו, ב"ארבעה אחין" (לעיל לג.) גבי זיקת [ב'] יבמין — ג' אחין נשואין ג' נכריות, ומת אחד מהן, ועשה בה השני מאמר ומת — הרי אלו חולצות כו', וקאמר(א) רבא עלה: נתן גט למאמרו ואח"כ מת — הותרה אשתו הראשונה שהיא צרתה לאחיו השני, דאי לאו גט הוה אסורה עליו משום זיקת שני יבמין. אלמא, האי לחודיה קאי, מדמהני גט לאישתרויי צרתה לאחיו השני. והוא הדין דהיא גופה נמי שריא לאחיו, אלא דמחלפא בבעלת גט גמור לזיקה דמקמי מאמר, או לזיקה ומאמר. והכי אמרינן ב"ארבעה אחין". זו דברי רבי עקיבא. אחלץ ועשה בה מאמר קאי, דקתני: לא תפיס מאמר. אחר שילוח. כלומר, מדכתיב "אשר שלחה" קרא יתירא דלא צריך, הכי קאמר: יש לך משלח שאסור להחזיר אחר שילוח אפילו לא נישאת, ואיזו — זו יבמה. וכיון דבלאו קאי — היכי מהני בה תו מאמר? אימתי. יש אחר חליצה תפיסת קידושין. בזמן שקידשה לשום אישות. בקידושין גמורים, ולא במאמר יבמין. דודאי קידושין תופסין בחייבי לאוין. אבל קידשה לשום יבמות. אינן קידושין, שהרי אין כאן לד ייבום, והוו להו קידושי טעות. כעודר. חופר וכסבור שלו הן. שהיה קרקע הגר סמוך לקרקעו, ומת הגר ואין לו יורשין, והמחזיק בנכסיו קנה. וזה חופר בקרקע הגר, וכסבור שזה קרקע שלו, ולא נתכוון להחזיק — דלא קני. והאי נמי סבור שקידושי יבמה תופסין בה, ולא נתכוון לקנות אלא מכח ייבומי אחיו — והא פקעו להו. התם לא קמיכוין למיקני. דהא סבור שלו הן. הכא מכוין למיקני. מ"מ. הא לא דמיא כו'. אביי הוא דאקשי ואזיל. וכסבור של גר אחר הוא. ומתכוין לקנות מכל מקום. והאי נמי קסבר לקנות מכח אחיו, ואינו קונה אלא מכחו — ומ"מ קנין הוא. מאמר עילוי זיקה רמי. מאמר דתקינו רבנן לכל היבמין, לא תקון אלא היכא דקיימא זיקה, ואתא מאמר ואיתוסף עלה. והכא ליכא למימר הכי, דאתיא חליצה מפקעה לזיקה. האי לחודיה קאי כו'. ולא מהני זיקה למאמר. הילכך, השתא כמעיקרא: מעיקרא, אילו אמר לה התקדשי לי במאמר יבמין, מי לא קני? ואף על גב דלא מהניא ליה זיקה, דהאי לחודה קיימא — השתא נמי מהני.

יש

תוספות

והרי זה גט* [דקאמר, היינו:] לגרש בו לכתחלה. והיא ד"כל הגט" — שכתב זמן דקודם נישואין, וגרע טפי מגט ישן. דבגט ישן ליכא אלא ייחוד בעלמא, לכך אם נתגרשה בו תנשא לכתחלה. אבל התם דכנסה, ואיכא ודאי ביאה — אינו גט כלל* א). ולאשה בעלמא אין גט. ואפילו כתוב בו זמן דאחר נשואים. כיון דאין בידו לגרשה בשעה שעשאו שלית. ונראה לר"י דהיינו דוקא למ"ד אין אדם מקנה דבר שלא בא לעולם, אבל למאן דאמר אדם מקנה — הוי גט, דבידו לגרשה, כמו בשחרור דמהני לוקח עבד על מנת לשחררו וכתב לו לכשאקחך הרי עצמך קנוי לך מעכשיו, כדאמר ב"האשה רבה" (לקמן דף צג:) ובקידושין בפרק "האומר" (דף סג.). וגט שחרור וגט אשה שוים לכל דבר, דהא ילפינן "לה" "לה" מאשה. ליבמתו מהו. אין לפרש דמיבעיא ליה אם גירשה בגט זה לאחר שיבמה יבומין גמורין אי הוי גט אי לא — דפשיטא דאין ניתרת בגט זה לשוק. דהא בההיא שעתא לא היה בידו לגרשה ולהתירה לשוק על ידי גט זה. ומאי קאמר נמי או דלמא כיון דלא עבד בה מאמר לא, אי בלא מאמר לא מהני — עבד בה מאמר נמי לא מהני להתגרש אחר שתתייבם, דמאמר לא הוי אלא מדרבנן. ואמר ר"י: דלפוסלה מכהונה מיבעיא ליה, אי חשיב ריח הגט דפסיל לכהונה אי לא. ב)וריב"ם הגיה בפירושיו דמיבעיא ליה אי כְּתָבוֹ קודם מאמר, ועשה מאמר וגירש בו, מהו שיפקיע את מאמר. או דלמא האי לחודיה קאי כו'. פירש בקונטרס: ואי כתב גט למאמרו ולא לזיקתו — אסורה לו ומותרת לאחיו, דמאמר דעבד ליה שקליה, ופשה ליה זיקה כמעיקרא. ולר"י נראה דללישנא דאמר רבא — הותרה אפילו היא. ואם כן, הכא נמי שריא לדידיה. וללישנא דהיא אסורה, דמיחלפא בבעלת הגט, הכא נמי אסורה אפי' לאחיו, דהא בעלת הגט אסורה על כל האחין. והא דשרי רבא צרתה בנתן גט למאמרו — משום דבאות משני בתים הן, ואפילו היה נותן גט גם לזיקתו היתה צרתה מותרת. כעודר בנכסי הגר. אר"י: דמיירי לרב יוסף כגון דאמר לה התקדשי לי סתם, ולשם יבמות היינו — דגלי אדעתיה שבתורת יבמין מקדשה. דאי באמר לה בהדיא במאמר יבמין — לא הוי פריך ליה אביי מי דמי, דהא אביי קאמר בסמוך דהיכא דאמר לה במאמר יבמין — דלא קני לרבי, אלא בסתם איירי. א"נ: באמר לה התקדשי לי לשם יבמות, ולא משמע בתורת מאמר יבמין. דבמאמר יבמין משמע — בתורת מאמר ולא בתורת קידושין. אבל לשם יבמות — לא משמע בתורת יבמות, אלא שסבור שעדיין היא זקוקתו. אי אמר לה התקדשי לי בזיקת (ג) מאמר יבמין מי לא מהני. דאפילו למ"ד אין זיקה — היינו לענין אחות זקוקתו וכיוצא בה, אבל פשיטא דמהני לשון זיקה, שהרי היא זקוקתו ועומדת בפניו.

רבינא

תוספות ישנים

א) א"נ שאני הכא שלא רצה שיחול הגט עד לאחר שכנסה [illegible] ב) וא"ת [illegible]

נאסרה אלא מטעם האחרת שעשה בה בעלה מאמר וכשנתן גט פקע ליה למאמרו וזו שלא עשה בה מידי מותרת לאחין אבל היא אסורה על כולן דמחלפא בבעלת הגט. אבל הכא דליכא אלא חדא שקידש תחלה במאמרו ואח"כ נתן גט אי שריא לה באחיו משום דמאי דעבד שקליה כ"ש לדידיה ואי אסרי' לה עליה משום דמחלפא כ"ש על האחין. וא"כ נ"ל דהכי אמרינן האי לחודיה קאי והאי לחודיה קאי כשכתב גט למאמרו ולא לזיקתו אסורה בין לו בין לאחיו ומייתי ראיה מסוף דברי [רבא] דאמר נתן גט למאמרו הותרה צרתה אבל היא אסורה משום דמחלפא בבעלת הגט ור"ל לאסרה על האחין: מנין לנותן גט ליבמתו שנאסרה עליו עולמית שנאמר לא יוכל בעלה הראשון לשוב לקחתה לו לאשה. ומוכח מדקאמר לא יוכל בעלה לשוב לקחתה אחרי אשר הוטמאה ויש לך אחרת אע"ג דלא הוטמאה אסורה ואיזו זו מגרש יבמתו דכיון ששלחה שוב אינה חוזרת: וכסבור שלו הן דלא קני. וקשה דמשמע הכא דלקניה בעינן כוונה ובב"ק [כ"ע ע"ב] אמרינן לוקמה בלמעלה משלשה ובשלא מתכוין וי"ל דהתם בקנין מטלטלין א"נ כוונה דלא אליס חזקת הבעלים עליהם דהם נכסים שאין להם אחריות ונקנים בקל. אבל בקרקע [אליס] חזקת הבעלים וצריך כוונה לקנותה קודם שתצא מרשות הבעלים: אלא אמר אביי הב"ע כגון דאמר לה התקדשי במאמר יבמין. והא דאביי קא מתמה לעיל שמן הדין היתה קנויה לו והשתא פשיטא ליה דאינה נקנית היינו טעמא משום דלא אמר לה לשום מאמר יבמין בהדיא ודין הוא שיקנה להיות אשתו:

א) נ"ל והאי לחודיה קאי ומהני. ופי' הקונטרס דהיכא דכתב גט לזיקתו ולא למאמרו אסורה עליו ועל אחיו דפקעה זיקה וכו'.

הגהות הב"ח

(א) רש"י ד"ה נתן גט וכו' וקאמר רבא. נ"ב דף לב ע"א: (ב) תוס' ד"ה מאי אמר וכו' דזיקת יבמין כצ"ל ותיבת מאמר נמחק:

גליון הש"ס

גמ' ליבמתו מהו. עיין נזיר דף יב ע"א תד"ה מאי טעמא:

לעיל לב. [לעיל י: וש"נ] לעיל מה.

תוספות חד מקמאי

שמא יאמר גיטה קודם לבנה. ומודים שאם נתגרשה תנשא לכתחלה: בעי רמי בר חמא ליבמתו מהו כיון דאגידה גביה כארוסתו דמיא או דלמא כיון דלא עבד בה מאמר לא תיקו: ואי כתב גט לזיקתו ולא למאמרו למאמרו ולא לזיקתו מהני דקי"ל כרבא דאמר נתן גט למאמרו הותרה צרתה. תניא אידך החולץ ליבמתו וחזר וקדשה רבי אומר אם קדשה לשום אישות צריכה הימנו גט לשום יבמות אינה צריכה הימנו גט מ"ט דרבי אמר רב יוסף עשאוה כעודר בנכסי הגר וסבור שלו הן דלא קני א"ל אביי מי דמי התם לא מכוין למקני הכא מכוין למקני הא לא דמי אלא לעודר בנכסי הגר [זה] וכסבור של גר [אחר] הן דקני. אלא אמר אביי הב"ע כגון דא"ל התקדשי לי במאמר יבמין פירוש מעיקרא הוה קס"ד כגון שא"ל בשעת קדושין לשום יבמות והשתא שני אביי כגון שאמר במאמר יבמין א"נ מעיקרא קס"ד שקדשה סתם ומסתמה לשום יבמות קדשה. והראב"ד פירש דמעיקר' דהוה מדמי לה לעודר בנכסי הגר הוא קס"ד כגון דאמר פלונית יבמתי התקדשי לי ולא תלי הקידושין במאמר יבמין וזיקת יבמין ודלמא הכי קאמר פלונית שהיתה יבמתי תתקדשי לי והשתא שני אביי כגון דא"ל התקדשי במאמר יבמין וס"ל לרבנן האי לחודיה קאי והאי לחודיה קאי מעיקרא אי א"ל התקדשי לי במאמר מי לא מהני השתא נמי מהני וכיון דקי"ל כרבא דאמר נתן לה גט למאמרו הותרה צרתה אלמא הלכתא כרבנן והיינו דאמר רבא אי דא"ל במאמר יבמין דכ"ע לא פליגי דרבא לטעמיה דאמר הותרה צרתה אלא הכא במ"ע כגון דא"ל התקדשי לי בזיקת יבמין. ר' סבר יש זיקה אתאי חליצה ואפקעיה לזיקה

*יש זיקה, ואתאי חליצה אפקעתיה לזיקה. ורבנן סברי, *אין זיקה. מעיקרא אילו אמר לה "התקדשי לי בזיקת יבמין" מי לא מהני? השתא נמי מהני. רב שרביא אמר: בחליצה כשירה, אי דאמר לה "התקדשי לי בזיקת יבמין" כ"ע לא פליגי דלא מהני. והכא בחליצה פסולה קמיפלגי. מר סבר: חליצה פסולה פוטרת, ומר סבר: חליצה פסולה אינה פוטרת. רב אשי אמר: דכ"ע חליצה פסולה אינה פוטרת. והכא ביש תנאי בחליצה קמיפלגי. מר סבר: יש תנאי בחליצה, ומר סבר: [א]אין תנאי בחליצה. רבינא אמר: דכ"ע יש תנאי בחליצה. והכא *בתנאי כפול קמיפלגי; מר סבר: [ב]בעינן תנאי כפול, ומר סבר: לא בעינן תנאי כפול.§ "חלץ ועשה מאמר ונתן גט ובעל וכו'".§ וניתני נמי אין אחר ביאה כלום (א) אביי ורבא דאמרי תרוייהו, תני: [ג]אין אחר ביאה כלום. ותנא דידן — התרת יבמה לשוק עדיפא ליה.§ "אחד יבמה אחת אחד שתי יבמות".§ מתני' דלא כבן עזאי. דתניא, *בן עזאי אומר: יש מאמר אחר מאמר בשני יבמין ויבמה אחת, ואין מאמר אחר מאמר בשתי יבמות ויבם אחד.§ "כיצד מאמר לזו וכו'".§ לימא מסייע ליה לשמואל, דאמר שמואל: *חלץ לבעלת מאמר לא נפטרה צרתה, ותיובתא *דרב יוסף! מי קתני "חולץ"? "חלץ" קתני, דיעבד.§ "גט לזו וגט לזו כו'".§ לימא מסייע ליה לרבה בר רב הונא, דאמר *רבה בר רב הונא: [ד]חליצה פסולה — צריכה לחזור על כל האחין. מאי "צריכות" צריכות דעלמא.§ "גט לזו וחלץ לזו".§ לימא מסייע ליה לשמואל ותהוי תיובתא דרב יוסף! מי קתני "חולץ"? "חלץ" קתני, דיעבד.§ "חלץ וחלץ או חלץ וכו'".§ וליתני נמי אין אחר ביאה כלום (א)! אביי ורבא דאמרי תרוייהו, תני: אין אחר ביאה כלום. ותנא דידן — התרת יבמה לשוק עדיפא ליה.§ "בין יבם אחד לשתי יבמות כו'".§ בשלמא *לרבי יוחנן, דאמר: כולה ביתא בלאו קאי, איצטריך לאשמועינן דאין קדושין תופסין בחייבי לאוין. אלא לר"ל, דאמר: כולה ביתא בכרת קאי — איצטריך לאשמועינן [ה]דאין קדושין תופסין בחייבי כריתות?! אמר לך ר"ל: ולטעמיך, סיפא דקתני: בעל ועשה מאמר, איצטריך לאשמועינן דאין קדושין תופסין באשת איש? אלא: איידי דתנא התרת יבם אחד ויבמה אחת — תנא נמי שתי יבמות ויבם אחד, *ואיידי דתנא שתי יבמות ויבם אחד — תנא נמי שתי יבמין ויבמה אחת.§

הדרן עלך רבן גמליאל

רש"י

יש זיקה. האי דתפיס מאמר בעלמא בכי האי לישנא — משום דיש זיקה, והשתא אתאי חליצתה פקעתה, וליכא למימר הכי. אין זיקה. אין כאן לזיקה. ואפי' הכי מעיקרא הוי מאמר. רב שרביא אמר. אי דאמר לה בזיקת יבמין — כ"ע לא פליגי דלא מהני, דיש זיקה, ואתיא חליצה ואפקעתה. והכא בחליצה פסולה. כגון שחלץ אחר הגט קמיפלגי, רבנן סברי: לא אפקעתה שפיר, ויש אחריה כלום, הלכך קני מאמר. יש תנאי בחליצה. שחלץ לה על מנת שתתן לו מאתים זוז. רבי סבר: אין תנאי מועיל בחליצה, ואפילו לא נתנה לו אין תנאי מועיל, והוי חליצה. הלכך לא תפיס מאמר שעשה בלשון זיקת יבמין אבתרה, דהא אפקעתה לזיקתו. ולרבנן יש תנאי, וכל כמה דלא קיימא לא פקע זיקה. וכי אמר לה התקדשי לי ע"י כסף זה בזיקת יבמין — קני: ה"ג. רבינא אמר דכ"ע יש תנאי בחליצה. אע"ג דקי"ל (לקמן דף קו.) חליצה מוטעת כשירה — הני תנאי לא סבירא להו. והכא בתנאי כפול קמיפלגי. וכגון דלא כפליה לתנאי. לרבי בעינן תנאי כפול כתנאי בני גד ובני ראובן, והאי דלא כפליה: אם תתני תהא חליצה, ואם לא תתני לא תהא חליצה — לא הוי תנאי לבטולי לחליצה. וניתני נמי אין לאחר ביאה כלום. דהא ביאה שייכא למימר בסיפא, דקתני: או בעל ועשה מאמר ונתן גט וחלץ, דהא או או קתני. ובבעל ועשה מאמר, או בבעל ונתן גט, מאי חליצה איכא? תני אין לאחר ביאה כלום. ולא צריך למיתני נמי אין לאחר חליצה כלום, דכיון דתנא אין אחר ביאה כלום — ה"ה נמי דאין אחר חליצה כלום. ולישנא קלילא הוא למיתני חדא, או ביאה או חליצה. ותנא דידן. דלא נקט ביאה, ואע"ג דאיירי בה בסיפא — משום דהיתר יבמה לשוק חביבא ליה לאורויי, ומינה שמעינן דאין אחר ביאה כלום. וטריחא לתנא למיתני תרתי: אין אחר ביאה, ואין אחר חליצה כלום. מתניתין. דקתני אחת שתי יבמות עשה מאמר בזו ומאמר בזו צריכות שני גיטין. דלא כבן עזאי. דאמר: אין מאמר אחר מאמר בשתי יבמות ויבם אחד. ומתני' בשתי יבמות ויבם אחד קא מיירי. וללישנא בתרא דגרסינן למילתיה דבן עזאי איפכא, קיימא הך אתקפתא אסיפא דמתני', דקתני: בין יבם אחד לשתי יבמות בין שני יבמין ויבמה אחת. ומיסתברא כלישנא קמא, דא"כ לא הוה לן לאיתויי הך אתקפתא הכא, אלא בגמרא דסיפא דלקמן. לימא מסייע ליה לשמואל. אמאמר לזו וחלץ לזו קאי, מדלא נקט חליצה אבעלת מאמר — מסייע לשמואל, דאמר: חלץ לבעלת מאמר לא נפטרה צרתה, דכיון דבעי גט למאמרו — לא הויא חליצה מעלייתא לאפוקי זיקה דחברתה. ותיובתא דרב יוסף. דאמר ב"החולץ" (לעיל דף מד.) לא ישפוך אדם מי בורו ואחרים צריכים להם. דהא הכא דחלץ לחברתה, וקמייתא בעיא גט, ונמצא פוסל את שתיהן מן הכהונה, ולא אמרינן ליחלוץ לקמייתא ותהא חברתה כשירה. צריכות. משמע חליצה לכל אחת, דכיון דחליצת שתיהן רעועה — אין אחת מהן פוטרת חברתה, וקתני סיפא: וכן שני יבמין ליבמה אחת. דאם נתן זה גט וזה גט צריכה חליצה משניהן: לימא מסייע ליה לרבה כו': ה"ג. גט לזו וחלץ לזו לימא מסייע ליה לשמואל. מדלא נקט חליצה לבעלת הגט אלא לחברתה — מסייע ליה לשמואל דאמר בפ' "ד' אחין": חלץ לבעלת הגט — לא נפטרה צרה. וליתני נמי אין אחר ביאה כלום. בסיפא, דקתני או בעל ובעל או בעל ועשה מאמר כו', דהא משום הכי נקט לה, דהתם לא שייך למיתני אין אחר חליצה כלום — דהא ליכא חליצה. כולה ביתא. כל האמור על החלוצה ועל צרתה בלאו בעלמא, כחולץ עצמו, דשליחות דידהו עבד. איצטריך לאשמועינן. מתני' חלץ לזו ועשה מאמר בזו אינו כלום, דאע"ג דלאו בעלמא היא גביה לא תפסי קידושין. וסתים לן כהולכן כר' עקיבא, וכן בשני יבמין ויבמה אחת. אלא לר"ש בן לקיש דאמר. בפ"ק (דף י:): כוליה ביתא בכרת קאי, לבד מחולץ בחלוצה. אבל חולץ לגבי צרה, וכל האחין, בין בחלוצה בין בצרה, בכרת, מאי איצטריך למיתני גבי ב' יבמות ויבם אחד, וב' יבמין ויבמה אחת דאין מאמר השני תופס אחר חליצה? ולטעמיך סיפא. בב' יבמין ויבמה אחת, דקתני: בעל הראשון ועשה השני מאמר — אין אחר ביאה כלום, מי איצטריך לאשמועינן דאין קידושין תופסין בא"א? הרי כנסה, וכאשתו היא לכל דבר. אלא איידי דתני התרת יבם ויבמה אחת. דאיצטריך לאשמועינן אפילו לר"ל דאין מאמר אחר חליצה, דהא ליתא גביה אלא בלאו ד"לא יבנה", ואיצטריך לאשמועינן כרבי עקיבא, תנא נמי כו'.

מראי מקומות בשולי רש"י: [לעיל יז: וש"נ] [שם] [קידושין סא.] [לעיל נא: לקמן נו:] [לעיל כז.] [לעיל יח: יב. מד.] [לעיל כו: נא.] [לעיל י:] [לעיל ג. וש"נ]

תוספות

רבינא אמר דכ"ע יש תנאי בחליצה. תימא לר"י: דהני אמוראי אתו דלא כהלכתא, דקי"ל בפרק "מצות חליצה" (לקמן דף קו.) וב"המדיר" (כתובות דף עד. וסס) דחליצה מוטעת כשירה, דאין תנאי בחליצה, משום דגמרינן מתנאי בני גד ובני ראובן, דבעינן דאיפשר לקיימו ע"י שליח. דאי סבירא להו דאין תנאי — לא הוה להו לאוקמי פלוגתא דרבי ורבנן בהכי! ועוד: אדמיפלגי ביש תנאי בחליצה לענין מאמר שאחריה — ליפלגו לענין התרה לשוק! ואר"י דלענין התרה לשוק לכ"ע הויא חליצה, כדקי"ל דאין תנאי בחליצה. אלא לענין דהויא חליצה פסולה דלא מפקע לה זיקה לגמרי, שלא יועיל אחריה מאמר בלשון זיקת יבמין קאמר דיש תנאי. ושוב מצא ר"י בשם ר"ת א).

לימא מסייע ליה לשמואל ותיובתא לרב יוסף. אמאמר לזו וחלץ לזו קאי. ואם תאמר: אמאי הוי תיובתא לרב יוסף? דהא דאין חולץ לבעלת מאמר — משום דשמואל, דחלץ לבעלת מאמר לא נפטרה צרה! וי"ל דה"ק: לימא מסייע ליה לשמואל, או תיהוי תיובתא דרב יוסף. דאי לא תסייע לשמואל ומיפטרה צרה בחליצת בעלת מאמר — א"כ, האי דנקט מאמר לזו וחלץ לזו לאשמועינן דחולץ לאיזו שירצה, לאפוקי מדרב יוסף, דקאמר לא ישפוך מי בורו ואחרים צריכים לו.

איצטריך לאשמועינן דאין קידושין תופסין בחייבי לאוין. אע"ג דככר אשמועינן לעיל — קתני לה נמי הכא אגב שאר גווני. כיון דלאו מילתא דפשיטא היא.

איצטריך לאשמועינן דאין קידושין תופסין באשת איש. פירוש: דקתני סיפא: וכן בשני יבמין ויבמה אחת. ותימא: דלמא הא דנקט בעל ועשה מאמר — משום שתי יבמות ויבם אחד נקטיה.

*סלקא דעתך אמינא ליגזור מאמר דבתר חליצה כו'. תימה: מה צריך לטעם זה? דלעיל הוה ניחא לר' יוחנן דאיצטריך לאשמועי' דאין קידושין תופסין בחייבי לאוין, אע"ג דככר אשמועינן ליה מרישא. והכי נמי תינח ליה הכא, מהאי טעמא גופיה.

עין משפט נר מצוה

מב א מיי' פ"ד מהלכות יבום הלכה כד סמג עשין נב טוש"ע אה"ע סימן קסט סעיף נ:

מג ב מיי' פ"ו מהל' אישות הלכה ב סמג עשין מח טוש"ע שם סימן לח סעי' ב:

מד ג מיי' פ"ה מהלכות יבום הלכה יד טוש"ע שם סימן קע סעיף יב:

מה ד מיי' שם הלכה יא טוש"ע שם סעיף ה:

מו ה מיי' פ"ד מהל' אישות הלכה יב סמג עשין מח טוש"ע שם סימן מד סעי' ו:

תוספות ישנים

א) ועוד דקאמר לעיל דכ"ע חליצה פסולה אינה פוטרת ובשלהי מתני' אמרינן אין אחר חליצה כלום וכן הא דקאמר רב אשי דכו"ע חליצה פסולה אינה פוטרת היינו לענין דחייל מאמר אבתרה: לימא מסייעא ליה לרבה בר רב הונא פי' לעיל בהאי פרקא: אביי ורבא דאמרי תרווייהו תני אין אחר ביאה כלום ותנא דידן התרת יבמה לשוק עדיפא ליה והקשה הר' נתנאל למאי קאמר ותנא דידן הא אמר תני במתני' וא"כ אינו כ"א מגיה המשנה ואין זה תנא אחר ותירץ דה"ג תנא אין אחר ביאה כלום דברייתא היא בתוספתא א) והשתא ניחא דקאמר ותנא דידן דלא תני במתני' הכי ומשני התרת יבמה לשוק עדיפא ליה וכו':

א) כ"ה באמת בתוספתא פ"ז חלץ את זו וכו' אין אחר בעילה כלום אך דיש שם ט"ס דבבבא קמייתא גבי בעל את זו צריך לסיים אין אחר בעילה כלום ע"ש.

תוספות חד מקמאי

לזיקה ורבנן סברי אין זיקה מעיקרא כו' (וקי"ל יש זיקה): רב שרביא אמר בחליצה פסולה קא מיפלגי רבי סבר חליצה פסולה פוטרת ורבנן סברי חליצה פסולה אינה פוטרת [פי' רבי סבר דפוטרת] ושריא לעלמא ודחי' לה מהאי ביתה ואין (כלל) [כאן] יבמות כלל. ולפיכך אינה צריכה הימנו גט ורבנן סברי אינה פוטרת ולא אידחיא מהאי ביתא ויש כאן יבמות. והרב אלפס פי' דבחליצה פסולה צריכה לחזור על כל האחין קמיפלגי וס"ל לרבנן צריכה לחזור על כל האחין וכל זה סיוע למפסק הלכתא כרב דאמר חליצה פסולה צריכה לחזור אחר כל האחין דהא רבנן קיימי כותיה אעפ"י שפסק הרב אלפס דכל הני טעמי דאתמר (בהו) [גבי] פלוגתא דרבי ורבנן לא סמכינן עלייהו איכא מינייהו דסמכינן כגון האי טעמי דאיתמר לעיל מתוקמ' כרבי דלא סמכינן אדרבנן דקי"ל דיש זיקה כדפרישנא. רב [אשי] אמר ביש תנאי בחליצה קא מיפלגי רבי סבר אין תנאי בחליצה ורבנן סברי יש תנאי בחליצה וכיון דלא נתקיים התנאי אין כאן חליצה ויש כאן יבמות רבינא אמר דכ"ע דיש תנאי בחליצה והכא בתנאי כפול קמיפלגי דרבנן סברי דלא בעי תנאי כפול ואע"ג דלא כפילנא לתנאיה התנאי תנאי וצריך לקיימו וכיון שלא קיימו אין כאן חליצה ויש כאן יבמות. א) הכי אוקימנא דרב אסי ורבינא הוו להו לרבנן דלא כהלכתא דקי"ל אין תנאי בחליצה דתניא חליצה מוטעת כשרה ואוקימנא בפרק המדיר דאין תנאי בחליצה. דמכדי כל תנאי מהיכא גמרינן ליה מתנאי בני גד ובני ראובן תנאה דאפשר לקיומי ע"י שליח כי התם הוי תנאיה תנאה דלא אפשר לקיומי ע"י שליח לא הוי תנאיה תנאה. ומיהו מעיקרא קס"ד בפ' המדיר דהיינו טעמא דחליצה מוטעת כשירה דכיון דעבד מעשה אחולי אחליה לתנאיה ולהאי טעמא אי אדכר תנאיה בשעת חליצה הוי תנאיה תנאה ואפ"ה הלכתא כטעמא בתראה כהאי מסקנא ואפי' אידכר התנאי בשעת חליצה לא הוי תנאיה תנאה דלא אפשר לקיומי ע"י שליח: הא דתנן מאמר לזו וחלץ לזו צריכה גט ואמר עלה בגמ' לימא (תהוי תיובתא) [מסייע ליה] לשמואל דאמר חלץ לבעלת מאמר לא נפטרת צרתה ותיובתא דרב יוסף דאמר לא ישפוך אדם מי בורו ואחרים צריכים לו מי קתני חולץ חלץ קאמר דיעבד וכיון דקי"ל כשמואל לכתחלה נמי אית ליה למעבד אם עשה מעשה לזו חולץ לאחרת ונפטרת בעלת מאמר לא נפטרת צרה ב) וכי חליץ לאחרת לא הוי תיובתא דרב יוסף כלומר לית ליה לשמואל דאם חלץ לבעלת מאמר נפטרת צרתה וה"ל למחלץ לבעלת מאמר שאחרים פסולין לה בלא חליצה ולא לצרתה שאחרים כשירים לה בלא חליצה והשתא נפסלה לאחרים בחליצה זו ג):

הגהות הב"ח

(א) גמ' (אביי ורבא דאמרי תרוייהו תני) תא"מ ונ"ב ס"א אביי ורבא תנו:

א) נראה דצ"ל ולכך אוקימתא דרב אשי ורבינא. ב) אינו מובן ונראה דצ"ל לאחרת וכו' חולץ לאחרת [illegible] ג) הדבר צ"ע [illegible]

"חָלַץ וְעָשָׂה מַאֲמָר וְנָתַן וכו'". § בִּשְׁלָמָא חָלַץ וְעָשָׂה מַאֲמָר אִיצְטְרִיךְ, סד"א: נִגְזוֹר מַאֲמָר דְּבָתַר חֲלִיצָה אַטּוּ מַאֲמָר דְּקַמֵּי חֲלִיצָה – קמ"ל דְּלָא גָּזְרִינַן. אֶלָּא חָלַץ וְנָתַן גֵּט לָמָּה לִי? וּלְטַעְמִיךְ אֵימָא סֵיפָא: בָּעַל וְעָשָׂה מַאֲמָר, בָּעַל וְנָתַן גֵּט – בִּשְׁלָמָא בָּעַל וְנָתַן גֵּט אִיצְטְרִיךְ, סד"א: נִגְזוֹר גֵּט דְּבָתַר בְּעִילָה אַטּוּ גֵּט דְּקַמֵּי בְּעִילָה, קמ"ל דְּלָא גָּזְרִינַן. אֲבָל בָּעַל וְעָשָׂה מַאֲמָר לָמָּה לִי? אֶלָּא: אַיְּידֵי דְּתָנָא חָלַץ וְעָשָׂה מַאֲמָר – תָּנָא נַמִי בָּעַל וְעָשָׂה מַאֲמָר, וְאַיְּידֵי דְּבָעֵי לְמִיתְנֵי בָּעַל וְנָתַן גֵּט – תָּנָא נַמִי חָלַץ וְנָתַן גֵּט. § "בִּזְמַן שֶׁהִיא וכו'". מַתְנִיתִין דְּלָא כִּי הַאי תַּנָּא. דְּתַנְיָא, אַבָּא יוֹסֵי בֶּן יוֹחָנָן אִישׁ יְרוּשָׁלַיִם אוֹמֵר מִשּׁוּם רַבִּי מֵאִיר: אַחַת בְּעִילָה וְאַחַת חֲלִיצָה, בַּתְּחִלָּה – אֵין אַחֲרֶיהָ כְּלוּם, בָּאֶמְצַע וּבַסּוֹף – יֵשׁ אַחֲרֶיהָ כְּלוּם. *וְשָׁלֹשׁ מַחֲלוֹקוֹת בַּדָּבָר, תַּנָּא קַמָּא סָבַר: בִּיאָה דְּאִיכָּא לְמִיגְזַר – גָּזְרִינַן, חֲלִיצָה דְּלֵיכָּא לְמִיגְזַר – לָא גָּזְרִינַן. וְר' נְחֶמְיָה סָבַר: בִּיאָה נַמִי לֵיכָּא לְמִיגְזַר. וּדְקָאָמְרַתְּ: לִיגְזוֹר בִּיאָה אַחַר הַגֵּט מִשּׁוּם בִּיאָה אַחַר חֲלִיצָה – כֵּיוָן דַּחֲלִיצָה דְּאוֹרַיְיתָא, מֵידַע יָדְעִי. וּדְקָאָמְרַתְּ לִיגְזוֹר בִּיאָה אַחַר מַאֲמָר מִשּׁוּם בִּיאָה אַחַר בִּיאָה – כֵּיוָן דְּבִיאָה דְּאוֹרַיְיתָא, הָא מֵידַע יָדִיעִי. וְאַבָּא יוֹסֵי בֶּן חָנָן סָבַר לָהּ כְּרַבָּנַן דְּגָזְרִי בְּבִיאָה, וְגָזַר חֲלִיצָה מִשּׁוּם בִּיאָה.§

הדרן עלך רבן גמליאל

הַבָּא [א]עַל יְבִמְתּוֹ, בֵּין בְּשׁוֹגֵג בֵּין בְּמֵזִיד בֵּין בְּאוֹנֶס בֵּין בְּרָצוֹן, אֲפִי' הוּא שׁוֹגֵג וְהִיא מְזִידָה, הוּא מֵזִיד וְהִיא שׁוֹגֶגֶת, הוּא אָנוּס וְהִיא לֹא אֲנוּסָה, הִיא אֲנוּסָה וְהוּא לֹא אָנוּס. אֶחָד הַמְעָרֶה וְאֶחָד הַגּוֹמֵר – קָנָה, וְלֹא חִילֵּק בֵּין בִּיאָה לְבִיאָה. [ב]וְכֵן הַבָּא עַל אַחַת מִכָּל הָעֲרָיוֹת שֶׁבַּתּוֹרָה, אוֹ פְּסוּלוֹת, כְּגוֹן: אַלְמָנָה לְכ"ג, גְּרוּשָׁה וַחֲלוּצָה לְכֹהֵן הֶדְיוֹט, מַמְזֶרֶת וּנְתִינָה לְיִשְׂרָאֵל, בַּת יִשְׂרָאֵל לְמַמְזֵר וּלְנָתִין – פְּסָלָהּ, וְלֹא חִילֵּק בֵּין בִּיאָה לְבִיאָה.§

גמ' מַאי אֲפִי'? לָא מִיבַּעְיָא קָאָמַר: לָא מִיבַּעְיָא הוּא שׁוֹגֵג וְהִיא קָמְכַוְּונָה לְמִצְוָה, אִי נַמִי הוּא מֵזִיד וְהִיא קָמְכַוְּונָה לְמִצְוָה, אֶלָּא אֲפִי' הוּא שׁוֹגֵג וְהִיא מְזִידָה(א), דְּתַרְוַיְיהוּ לָא קָמְכַוְּונֵי לְשֵׁם מִצְוָה – אֲפִילּוּ הָכִי קָנָה. תָּנֵי רַ' חִיָּיא: אֲפִי' *שְׁנֵיהֶם שׁוֹגְגִים, שְׁנֵיהֶם מְזִידִים, שְׁנֵיהֶם אֲנוּסִים. אָנוּס דְּמַתְנִיתִין הֵיכִי דָּמֵי? אִילֵימָא כְּשֶׁאֲנָסוּהוּ גּוֹיִם וּבָא עָלֶיהָ – וְהָאָמַר רָבָא: [ג]אֵין אוֹנֶס לְעֶרְוָה, לְפִי שֶׁאֵין קִישּׁוּי אֶלָּא לְדַעַת. אֶלָּא בְּיָשֵׁן – וְהָאָמַר רַב יְהוּדָה: יָשֵׁן

הבא על יבמתו בין בשוגג בין במזיד. איכא למימר דמזיד ורצון תרי גווני נינהו. דרצון היינו דמכוין למצוה, אע"ג דפשיטא הוא – קתני ליה, דהכי אורחיה בכל דוכתא. אבל בפ"ב דב"ק (דף כו: *ושם) גבי אדם מועד לעולם קשה: מה בין מזיד לרצון? וי"מ דה"ק: בין שיהא אותו שוגג ומזיד באונס, שאנסו לעשות כן, בין שיהא ברצון*.

הוא אנוס והיא לא אנוסה. תימה: דהוה ליה למינקט שניהם אנוסים, דהוי רבותא טפי! וי"ל: דאגב דנקט ברישא הוא שוגג והיא מזידה – נקט נמי הכא הוא אנוס והיא לא אנוסה. א"נ: לא קאמר והיא לא אנוסה אלא ברצון, אלא היא לא אנוסה אבל מזידה או שוגגת, דהשתא תרוייהו לא מיכווני לשם מצוה. **ולא** חילק בין ביאה לביאה. פי' בקונטרס: בין העראה לגמר ביאה. ובבבא שניה פירש: ולא חילק בין ביאה לביאה – בין כדרכה לשלא כדרכה. ואין נראה לר"י: דכיון דתנא סבר אחד המערה ואחד הגומר – למה ליה תו למיתני ולא חילק בין העראה לגמר ביאה? ועוד: דבגמ' (לקמן דף נו:) מפרש "מאי וכן" אשלא כדרכה בחייבי לאוין, מכלל דלא חילק דרישא איירי בשלא כדרכה! ונראה לר"י שהסופרים טעו וכתבו איפכא. ומיהו, ההיא דבבא שניה אפשר לפרשו כמו הראשון בין כדרכה לשלא כדרכה, ולפרושי "וכן" קאתי.

שאנסוהו גוים ובא עליה. אין לפרש שאנסוהו – היינו שאיימו עליו להרגו אם לא יבא עליה – דא"כ מאי פריך מרבא דאמר: אין קישוי אלא לדעת? פירוש: דאין זה אונס, שקישוי עושה מדעת, ואין דוחקין אותו לבעול בקישוי, ולוקמא כגון שמאיימין עליו לבעול בקישוי! ועוד: דמילתא דרבא אי אפשר לפרש במאיימין עליו להורגו אם לא שיבעול הערוה מעצמו, כמו שאפרש. אלא כל דבר שעושה מעצמו, אפילו ע"י אונס פחד מיתה לדעת חשיב. והאי שאנסוהו גוים ובא עליה דקאמר – היינו שהביאוהו עליה והדביקוהו ביבמתו, ולא שבא עליה מעצמו, כמו תקפתו יבמתו ובא עליה דבסמוך. והשתא פריך שפיר דאין אונס, דקישוי לא הוי אלא לדעת. ואר"י: דיש לדקדק מכאן דאין יבמה נקנית אלא בבא עליה בקישוי, מדלא מוקמי שהדביקוהו בלא קישוי. ואיכא למימר דאתי הך סוגיא כמ"ד: *משמש מת בעריות פטור, וילפינן קיחה מעריות דאינה נקנית אלא בקישוי. ועוד אר"י: דאתיא שפיר אפילו למאן דאמר משמש מת בעריות חייב, ולענין יבום – בעינן ביאה דרך הקמת שם.

אין אונס לערוה שאין קישוי אלא לדעת. אין לפרש במאיימין עליו להורגו אם לא יבא בעצמו על הערוה – דאם כן אפילו יש קישוי שלא לדעת תיפוק ליה דאגילוי עריות יהרג ואל יעבור, כדאמר בפרק "בן סורר" (סנהדרין דף עד. ושם), אלא איירי כשגוים מדביקים אותו על הערוה, וא"א לו להשמט אם לא ע"י שיהרג. וקאמר רבא דיש לו למסור עצמו ליהרג אם יודע שאי אפשר לו אם לא יתקשה, דאין קישוי אלא לדעת(א), וחשיב כעושה מעשה. אבל אם יש קישוי שלא לדעת, או שהיה כבר מקושה, או שיודע שלא יתקשה – אין חייב למסור עצמו, כיון שהוא אינו עושה שום מעשה, והוי כקרקע עולם, כדאמר ב"בן סורר" (ג"ז שם) גבי אסתר, דקרקע עולם היתה. וטעמא, משום דנערה המאורסה ילפינן התם מרוצח

חָלַץ וְעָשָׂה מַאֲמָר. אִיבָּם אֶחָד וִיבָמָה אַחַת קָאֵי. דְּאוֹקְמֵיהּ דְּצָרִיךְ לְמִתְנְיֵיהּ. בִּשְׁלָמָא חָלַץ וְעָשָׂה מַאֲמָר אִיצְטְרִיךְ. לְמִיתְנֵי דְּאֵינוֹ כְּלוּם. סד"א. אֲפִי' לְר' עֲקִיבָא. לִיגְזוֹר מַאֲמָר דְּבָתַר חֲלִיצָה. דְּלִיבָּעֵי גֵּט אַטּוּ מַאֲמָר דְּמִקַּמֵּי חֲלִיצָה, קמ"ל דְּלָא גָּזְרִינַן. אֶלָּא חָלַץ וְנָתַן גֵּט. בְּיָבָם אֶחָד וִיבָמָה אַחַת, לָמָּה לִי כו'? לְמַאי לִיהֲנֵי הַאי גֵּט? אִי לְמֵיסְרָהּ – הָא אִיתַּסְרָא הִיא וּקְרוֹבוֹתֶיהָ עָלָיו. וּלְטַעְמִיךְ בָּעַל וְעָשָׂה מַאֲמָר. בְּיָבָם וִיבָמָה אַחַת לָמָּה לִי? בִּשְׁלָמָא בָּעַל וְנָתַן גֵּט – אִילְטְרִיךְ לְמִתְנֵי אֵין אַחַר בִּיאָה כְּלוּם, דְּנָפְקָא בְּהַאי גִּיטָּא וְלָא בָּעְיָא חֲלִיצָה, דְּבִיאָה קַמַּיְיתָא אַפְקַעְתָּהּ לְזִיקָה. סד"א לִגְזוֹר גֵּט דְּבָתַר בִּיאָה. דְּלָא תִּיסְגֵּי לֵיהּ בְּגֵט בְּלָא חֲלִיצָה – אַטּוּ גֵּט דְּמִקַּמֵּי בִּיאָה, דְּלָא לֵימְרוּ גֵּט סַגִּי בִּיבָמָה בִּמְקוֹם חֲלִיצָה. אֶלָּא בָּעַל וְעָשָׂה מַאֲמָר. לְמַאי קָבָעֵי אִיתְנוּיֵי? הֲלָא אִשְׁתּוֹ הִיא. אֶלָּא. אַיְּידֵי דְּתָנָא חָלַץ וְעָשָׂה מַאֲמָר דְּאִילְטְרִיךְ לֵיהּ, כְּדַאֲמַרַן, תָּנָא נַמִי כו'. וְשָׁלֹשׁ מַחֲלוֹקוֹת בַּדָּבָר תַּנָּא קַמָּא. דְּמַתְנִיתִין, דְּאָמַר חֲלִיצָה פְּסוּלָה אֵין אַחֲרֶיהָ כְּלוּם, אֲבָל בִּיאָה פְּסוּלָה יֵשׁ אַחֲרֶיהָ כְּלוּם. וְרַבִּי נְחֶמְיָה. דְּאָמַר: אַחַת זוֹ וְאַחַת זוֹ אֵין אַחֲרֶיהָ כְּלוּם. וְאַבָּא יוֹסֵי בַּר חָנָן. דְּאָמַר: אַחַת זוֹ וְאַחַת זוֹ יֵשׁ אַחֲרֶיהָ כְּלוּם בָּאֶמְצַע וּבַסּוֹף. כִּדְפָרִישְׁנָא לֵיהּ בְּמַתְנִיתִין. בִּיאָה – דְּאִיכָּא לְמִיגְזַר כְּדַאֲמַרַן בְּרֵישׁ פִּירְקִין (לעיל נ:), אִי בִּיאָה אַחַר הַגֵּט הִיא – גְּזֵירָה בִּיאָה אַחַר הַגֵּט מִשּׁוּם בִּיאָה אַחַר חֲלִיצָה, דְּלָא לֵיתֵי לְמִיבְעַל אַחַר חֲלִיצָה. וְאִי בִּיאָה אַחַר מַאֲמָר כו' חֲלִיצָה לֵיכָּא לְמִיגְזַר, כִּדְאָמַר בְּרֵישׁ פִּירְקִין (שם).

הדרן עלך רבן גמליאל

הַבָּא עַל יְבִמְתּוֹ שׁוֹגֵג. כְּסָבוּר שֶׁהִיא אִשְׁתּוֹ, אוֹ אִשָּׁה אַחֶרֶת. מֵזִיד. לְשֵׁם זְנוּת, וְלֹא לְשׁוּם מִצְוָה. אֲפִי'. מְפָרֵשׁ בַּגְּמָרָא. הַמְעָרֶה. שֶׁלֹּא גָּמַר בִּיאָתוֹ. קָנָה. וְזָכָה בַּנַּחֲלָה, וְיוֹצִיאָהּ בְּגֵט אִם בָּא לְהוֹצִיאָהּ. בֵּין בִּיאָה לְבִיאָה. [בֵּין בִּיאָה כְּדַרְכָּהּ לְשֶׁלֹּא כְּדַרְכָּהּ, וּבֵין הַעֲרָאָה לִגְמַר בִּיאָה]. וְכֵן הַבָּא עַל אַחַת מִכָּל הָעֲרָיוֹת. בְּאַחַת מִכָּל הַבִּיאוֹת הַלָּלוּ. אוֹ פְּסוּלוֹת. לִכְהוּנָּה, כְּגוֹן אַלְמָנָה כו'. פְּסָלָהּ לִכְהוּנָּה. מִשּׁוּם זוֹנָה. [וּגְרוּשָׁה מִיפַּסְלָא (ג) מִתְּרוּמָה דְּבֵי נָשָׁא אִם הִיא בַּת כֹּהֵן, דְּשַׁוְיָהּ חֲלָלָה]. וְדַוְקָא עֲרָיוֹת אוֹ פְּסוּלוֹת, אֲבָל בִּיאַת זְנוּת דִּפְנוּיָה – לָא מְשַׁוְּיָה לָהּ זוֹנָה, וְלֹא פְּסָלָהּ מִן הַכְּהוּנָּה. דְּלָא אַשְׁכַּחְנָא תַּנָּא דְּפָסַל אֶלָּא רַבִּי אֶלְעָזָר, דְּאָמַר: פָּנוּי הַבָּא עַל הַפְּנוּיָה שֶׁלֹּא לְשֵׁם אִישׁוּת עֲשָׂאָהּ זוֹנָה, לְקַמָּן בְּפִירְקִין*. מַמְזֶרֶת וּנְתִינָה. לָאו אַפְּסוּלָה לִכְהוּנָּה קָאֵי – דְּהָא פְּסוּלָה וְקַיְימָא. וּלְעִנְיַן תְּרוּמָה דְּבֵי נָשָׁא נַמִי לֵיכָּא לְמֵימַר. וְעוֹד, בִּיאַת כָּשֵׁר מַאי מְגַרְעָא לָהּ? אֶלָּא לְעִנְיַן הַעֲרָאָה נְקָטָהּ, וּלְמִילְקֵי עָלֶיהָ הַאי יִשְׂרָאֵל בְּהַעֲרָאָה כִּגְמַר בִּיאָה.

גמ' אֶלָּא אֲפִילּוּ הוּא שׁוֹגֵג. כְּסָבוּר אִשָּׁה אַחֶרֶת הִיא. וְהִיא מְזִידָה. לְבִיאַת זְנוּת מְכַוֶּונֶת. דְּתַרְוַיְיהוּ לָא מִיכַּוְּונֵי לְמִצְוָה. אֲפִילּוּ הָכִי קָנֵי. אֶלָּא בְּיָשֵׁן. שֶׁנִּתְקַשָּׁה כְּשֶׁהוּא יָשֵׁן. יָשֵׁן

א א מיי' פ"ב מהלכות יבום הלכה ג סמג עשין כא טוש"ע אה"ע סי' קסו סעי' ז:

[עמ"ש שם על הגליון]

[ועי' פרש"י במס' ע"ז נג. ד"ה מזיד כו' ובפרש"י פסחים עז: ד"ה בין ביחיד וברש"י מנחות כה: ד"ה שוגג]

ב ב מיי' פ"א מהלכות איסורי ביאה הלכה יז ופי"ח הלכה ו סמג לאוין קטו טוש"ע שם סימן ו סעי' ט וסימן כ סעיף א:

ג ג מיי' פ"א מהלכות איסורי ביאה הל' ט:

תוספות ישנים

א) וא"ת ולמה ליה קישוי הלא אמרי' משמש מת בעריות חייב וי"ל דס"ל פטור. א"נ א) אפי' למ"ד חייב היינו משום שהיה לו לפרוש בהנאה מועטת ופירש בהנאה מרובה אבל הכא שהדביקו גוים כבר לא מתחייב עד שיקשה שהרי נאנס הוא ולא יכול לפרוש.

א) לכאורה אינו מובן דמה ענין בכאן שהיה לו לפרוש בהנאה מועטת ולא שייך זה רק גבי משמש עם הטהורה ואמרה לו נטמאתי ופירש מיד ועי' בשבועות י"ח.

תוספות חד מקמאי

פרק הבא על יבמתו. הא דתנן הבא על יבמתו פרישנא בגמ' ה"ק ל"מ הוא שוגג והיא מכוונה למצוה. א"נ הוא מזיד והיא מכוונה למצוה. [אלא] אפילו הוא שוגג והיא מזידה פירוש לזנות דתרווייהו לא מכווני למצוה קנה. תני רבי חייא אפילו שניהם מזידין שניהם אנוסים. אנוס דמתני' ה"ד אילימא שאנסוהו גוים ובא עליה. והא אמר [רבא] אין אונס בערוה שאין קישוי אלא לדעת אלא בישן והאמר רב יהודה ישן לא קנה ביבמתו

שבועות יח. לקמן נה:

[עירובין עה. וש"נ]

הגהות הב"ח

(א) גמ' אפילו הוא ש... והיא מזידה הוא מ... והיא שוגגת דתרווייהו ... (ב) רש"י ד"ה פס... מיפסלא בהך בי... מתרומה:

רש"ל

רש"ל

[עי' תוס' מעילה ב. ד"ה ... שמחון]

[דף נט:]

יָשֵׁן לֹא קָנָה. דְּיָשֵׁן לָאו בַּר דַּעַת, וְלָא הָוֵה קִנְיָנוֹ קִנְיָן. בְּנִתְקַע. שֶׁנִּתְקַשָּׁה לְאִשְׁתּוֹ, וְנָפַל מִן הַגַּג וְנִתְקַע בִּיבִמְתּוֹ. חַיָּיב בְּד' דְּבָרִים. בְּנֶזֶק וְצַעַר וְרִפּוּי וָשֶׁבֶת, כִּדְאָמַר בְּ"הַחוֹבֵל" (ב"ק דף פה:) "פֶּצַע תַּחַת פָּצַע" – לְרַבּוֹת הַשּׁוֹגֵג כְּמֵזִיד, וְאוֹנֶס כְּרָצוֹן. אֲבָל בְּבוֹשֶׁת – לָא, כִּדְמְפָרֵשׁ לְקַמָּן. וּבִיבִמְתּוֹ לֹא קָנָה. דְּלָא אִכַּוֵּין לְבִיאָה. שֶׁנִּתְכַּוֵּין לְאִשְׁתּוֹ. וְנִתְקַשָּׁה לָהּ. מִצְוָה. כְּלוֹמַר, בְּבִיאָה יוֹתֵר מִבַּחֲלִיצָה. הָא חָפֵץ. מִצְוָה לְיַבּוּמֵי. וּלְקָחָהּ שֶׁלֹּא כְּדַרְכָּהּ. לְרַבּוֹת שֶׁאִם בָּא עָלֶיהָ שֶׁלֹּא כְּדַרְכָּהּ – קָנָה: בְּמָקוֹם שֶׁמֵּקִים שֵׁם גָּרְסִינַן. עַד דִּמְכַוֵּין לָהּ. לְשֵׁם בִּיאָה בְּעוֹלָם. נֵזֶק. שָׁמִין אוֹתָהּ כְּאִילּוּ הִיא שִׁפְחָה נִמְכֶּרֶת:(ב) כַּמָּה הָיְתָה יָפָה וְכַמָּה הִיא יָפָה. לְהַטִּיחַ בְּכוֹתֶל. לָאו לְשׁוּם בִּיאָה מִיכַּוֵּין. שֶׁכֵּן מְטַמְּאָה אֶת בּוֹעֲלָהּ. לִהְיוֹת כְּמוֹתָהּ טָמֵא ז', דִּכְתִיב "וּתְהִי נִדָּתָהּ עָלָיו וְטָמֵא שִׁבְעַת יָמִים" (ויקרא טו). וְכִי אֵשֶׁת אָחִיו לְעוֹלָם נִדָּה הִיא. וְאֵינָהּ פּוֹסֶקֶת. שֶׁכֵּן בְּיָדוֹ. שֶׁל אָדָם לְרַבּוֹת נָשִׁים הַרְבֵּה עַל אָחִיו בְּאִיסּוּר אֵשֶׁת אָח. דְּאִי בָּעֵי מְקַדֵּשׁ וְאָזֵיל כִּי אַלְפָּא. וְתִפְשׁוֹט מִינָּהּ כָּל עֲרָיוֹת הַנֶּאֱסָרוֹת עָלָיו מֵחֲמַת אִישׁוּת, כְּגוֹן אֵשֶׁת אָב וְכַלָּתוֹ וַחֲמוֹתוֹ וַאֲחוֹת אִשְׁתּוֹ. אֲבָל אִמּוֹ וַאֲחוֹתוֹ וּבִתּוֹ וְכַיּוֹצֵא בָּהֶן, דְּאֵין בְּיָדוֹ לְרַבּוֹת – מְנָלַן? שֶׁכֵּן אִיסּוּר הַבָּא מֵאֵלָיו. וּפְשׁוֹט מִינָּהּ אִמּוֹ וַאֲחוֹתוֹ וּבִתּוֹ וְכַיּוֹצֵא בָּהֶן, וְלָא תִּפְשׁוֹט מִינָּהּ עֲרָיוֹת הַנֶּאֱסָרוֹת לוֹ מֵחֲמַת קִידּוּשִׁין. מֵאֵשֶׁת אָח וַאֲחוֹת אָב וָאֵם. דְּכִי פָּרְכַתְּ: מַה לַּאֲחוֹת אָב וָאֵם שֶׁכֵּן אִיסּוּר הַבָּא מֵאֵלָיו – אֵשֶׁת אָח תּוֹכִיחַ. מַה לְּאֵשֶׁת אָח שֶׁכֵּן בְּיָדוֹ לְרַבּוֹת – אֲחוֹת אָב וָאֵם תּוֹכִיחַ. וְחָזַר הַדִּין. הַצַּד הַשָּׁוֶה שֶׁבָּהֶן, שֶׁהֵן אֲסוּרוֹת עָלָיו מִשּׁוּם עֶרְוָה, וְעָשָׂה בָּהֶן הַעֲרָאָה כִּגְמַר בִּיאָה – אַף אֲנִי אָבִיא כָּל הָעֲרָיוֹת בַּדִּין הַזֶּה. שֶׁכֵּן אִיסּוּרָן מִשּׁוּם שְׁאֵר. וְתִפְשׁוֹט כָּל הָאֲסוּרוֹת מִשּׁוּם שְׁאֵר. אֲבָל אֵשֶׁת אִישׁ דְּלָאו מִשּׁוּם שְׁאֵר – מְנָא תֵּיתֵי? בְּחַיֵּי אוֹסְרָן. כָּל זְמַן* שֶׁאָדָם חַי וְהִיא שׁוֹפַעַת. וְכֵן אֵשֶׁת אָח אֵין הֶיתֵּר בְּחַיֵּי אָחִיו, שֶׁאֲפִילּוּ הוּא מְגָרְשָׁהּ אֲסוּרָה לָזֶה. אֵשֶׁת אִישׁ יֵשׁ לָהּ הֶיתֵּר בְּחַיָּיו עַל יְדֵי גֵט.

תורה אור

א יָשֵׁן לֹא קָנָה בִּיבִמְתּוֹ! אֶלָּא — בְּנִתְקַע? וְהָא אָמַר *רַבָּה: ב נָפַל מִן הַגַּג וְנִתְקַע — חַיָּיב בְּאַרְבָּעָה דְּבָרִים, ג וּבִיבִמְתּוֹ לֹא קָנָה! אֶלָּא: כְּגוֹן שֶׁנִּתְכַּוֵּין לְאִשְׁתּוֹ, וּתְקָפָתוֹ יְבִמְתּוֹ, וּבָא עָלֶיהָ, שְׁנֵיהֶם אֲנוּסִים דְּבֵי רַבִּי חִיָּיא הֵיכִי דָּמֵי? כְּגוֹן שֶׁנִּתְכַּוֵּין לְאִשְׁתּוֹ, וּתְקָפוּהוּ גּוֹיִם וְדִבְּקוּם זֶה בָּזֶה, וּבָא עָלֶיהָ. מְנָא הָנֵי מִילֵּי? (דברים כה) דְּתָנוּ רַבָּנַן: "°יְבָמָהּ יָבֹא עָלֶיהָ" מִצְוָה. דָּבָר אַחֵר: "יְבָמָהּ יָבֹא עָלֶיהָ" בֵּין בְּשׁוֹגֵג בֵּין *בְּמֵזִיד, בֵּין בְּאוֹנֶס בֵּין בְּרָצוֹן. וְהָא אַפִּיקְתֵּיהּ לְמִצְוָה! (שם) לְמִצְוָה °מִ"וְּאִם לֹא יַחְפֹּץ הָאִישׁ" נָפְקָא, הָא חָפֵץ — יַבֵּם, וְכִי אֲתָא קְרָא — בֵּין בְּשׁוֹגֵג בֵּין בְּמֵזִיד בֵּין בְּאוֹנֶס בֵּין בְּרָצוֹן. תַּנְיָא אִידָךְ: *"יְבָמָהּ יָבֹא עָלֶיהָ" כְּדַרְכָּהּ, "וּלְקָחָהּ" שֶׁלֹּא כְּדַרְכָּהּ. *"וְיִבְּמָהּ" ד בִּיאָה גּוֹמֶרֶת בָּהּ ה וְאֵין כֶּסֶף וּשְׁטָר גּוֹמְרִין בָּהּ. "וְיִבְּמָהּ" בְּעַל כָּרְחָהּ.(א) ד"א: "יְבָמָהּ יָבֹא עָלֶיהָ" בֵּין בְּשׁוֹגֵג כו'. וְהָא אַפִּיקְתֵּי' לְכַדַּרְכָּהּ! (שם) הַהוּא °מִ"לְּהָקִים לְאָחִיו שֵׁם" נָפְקָא, בְּמָקוֹם שֶׁמֵּקִים שֵׁם. וְכִי אֲתָא קְרָא — בֵּין בְּשׁוֹגֵג בֵּין בְּמֵזִיד בֵּין בְּאוֹנֶס בֵּין בְּרָצוֹן. גּוּפָא, אָמַר רַב יְהוּדָה: יָשֵׁן לֹא קָנָה בִּיבִמְתּוֹ, דְּאָמַר קְרָא "יְבָמָהּ יָבֹא עָלֶיהָ" עַד דִּמְכַוֵּין לָהּ לְשֵׁם בִּיאָה. וְהָתַנְיָא: בֵּין עֵר [בֵּין יָשֵׁן! אֵימָא: בֵּין עֵרָה בֵּין יְשֵׁנָה. וְהָתַנְיָא: בֵּין עֵר] הוּא בֵּין יָשֵׁן הוּא. ו בֵּין עֵרָה הִיא בֵּין יְשֵׁנָה הִיא! הָכָא בְּמַאי עָסְקִינַן — בְּמִתְנַמְנֵם. *ה"ד מִתְנַמְנֵם? אָמַר רַב אַשִׁי: נִים וְלָא נִים, תִּיר וְלָא תִּיר, כְּגוֹן דְּקָרוּ לֵיהּ וְעָנֵי, וְלָא יָדַע לְאַהֲדוּרֵי סְבָרָא, וְכִי מַדְכְּרוּ לֵיהּ מִדְּכַר. גּוּפָא, אָמַר רַבָּה: נָפַל מִן הַגַּג וְנִתְקַע חַיָּיב בְּאַרְבָּעָה דְּבָרִים, וּבִיבִמְתּוֹ לֹא קָנָה: בְּנֶזֶק, בְּצַעַר, בְּשֶׁבֶת, בְּרִפּוּי, אֲבָל בּוֹשֶׁת לָא מִיחַיַּיב, *דְּאָמַר מָר: ז אֵין חַיָּיב עַל הַבּוֹשֶׁת עַד שֶׁיִּתְכַּוֵּין. אָמַר רָבָא: ח נִתְכַּוֵּין לְהַטִּיחַ בְּכוֹתֶל וְהִטִּיחַ בִּיבִמְתּוֹ — לֹא קָנָה. לְהַטִּיחַ בִּבְהֵמָה וְהִטִּיחַ בִּיבָמָה — קָנָה, דְּהָא קָמְכַוֵּין לְשֵׁם בִּיאָה בְּעוֹלָם.§ "אֶחָד הַמְעָרֶה".§

(ויקרא כ) אָמַר עוּלָּא: מִנַּיִן לְהַעֲרָאָה מִן הַתּוֹרָה? שֶׁנֶּאֱמַר °"וְאִישׁ אֲשֶׁר יִשְׁכַּב אֶת אִשָּׁה דָּוָה וְגִלָּה אֶת עֶרְוָתָהּ אֶת מְקֹרָהּ הֶעֱרָה" מִכָּאן לְהַעֲרָאָה מִן הַתּוֹרָה. אַשְׁכַּחַן נִדָּה, שְׁאָר עֲרָיוֹת מִנַּיִן? וְכ"ת: נֵילַף מִנִּדָּה — ט מַה לְנִדָּה שֶׁכֵּן מְטַמְּאָה אֶת בּוֹעֲלָהּ! (שם) אֶלָּא: אָתְיָא מֵאֵשֶׁת אָח, דִּכְתִיב °"וְאִישׁ אֲשֶׁר יִקַּח אֶת אֵשֶׁת אָחִיו נִדָּה הִיא", וְכִי אֵשֶׁת אָחִיו [לְעוֹלָם] נִדָּה הִיא? אֶלָּא: כְּנִדָּה, מַה נִּדָּה בְּהַעֲרָאָה — אַף אֵשֶׁת אָח בְּהַעֲרָאָה. מַה לְּאֵשֶׁת אָח שֶׁכֵּן בְּיָדוֹ לְרַבּוֹת, דְּאִי בָּעֵי מְקַדֵּשׁ וְאָזֵיל כִּי אַלְפָּא! (שם) אֶלָּא אָתְיָא מֵאֲחוֹת אָב וַאֲחוֹת אֵם, דִּכְתִיב °"וְעֶרְוַת אֲחוֹת אִמְּךָ וַאֲחוֹת אָבִיךָ לֹא תְגַלֵּה כִּי אֶת שְׁאֵרוֹ הֶעֱרָה" אִיכָּא לְמִיפְרַךְ: מַה לַּאֲחוֹת אָב וַאֲחוֹת אֵם — שֶׁכֵּן אִיסּוּר הַבָּא מֵאֵלָיו! מֵחֲדָא לָא אָתְיָא, תֵּיתֵי [חֲדָא] מִתַּרְתֵּי. מְהֵי תֵּיתֵי? תֵּיתֵי מֵאֵשֶׁת אָח וַאֲחוֹת אָב וַאֲחוֹת אֵם — מַה לְהָנָךְ, שֶׁכֵּן אֲסוּרִין מִשּׁוּם שְׁאֵר! אֶלָּא תֵּיתֵי מִנִּדָּה וַאֲחוֹת אָב וַאֲחוֹת אֵם — מַה לְּהָנָךְ, שֶׁכֵּן אִיסּוּר הַבָּא מֵאֵלָיו! אֶלָּא תֵּיתֵי מִנִּדָּה וְאֵשֶׁת אָח, דְּמַאי פָּרְכַתְּ? מַתְקִיף לָהּ רַב אַחָא בְּרֵיהּ דְּרַב אִיקָא: מַה לְּנִדָּה וְאֵשֶׁת אָח — שֶׁכֵּן אֵין לָהֶם הֶיתֵּר בְּחַיֵּי אוֹסְרָן, תֹּאמַר בְּאֵשֶׁת אִישׁ שֶׁכֵּן יֵשׁ לָהּ הֶיתֵּר בְּחַיֵּי אוֹסְרָהּ! אֲמַר לֵיהּ רַב אַחָא מִדִּפְתִּי לְרָבִינָא: אַטּוּ נִדָּה וְאֵשֶׁת אָח בְּחַיֵּי אוֹסְרָן הוּא דְּאֵין לָהֶם הֶיתֵּר, אֲבָל לְאַחַר מִכָּאן יֵשׁ לָהֶם הֶיתֵּר? נִדָּה בְּיוֹמֵי

מרוצה ורוצה גופיה קאמר התם דסברא הוא, דמאי חזית דדמא דידך סומקא טפי כו'. וזה לא שייך אלא במאנסין אותו להרוג בידים, אבל אם רוצים לזורקו על התינוק ויתמעך – בזה אדרבה, איכא למימר איפכא: מאי חזית דדמא דחבריה סומקא טפי כו', כיון שאין הורג בידים, ולא הוי אלא קרקע עולם בעלמא, ואין מצווה להציל חברו בגופו, דאדרבה: חייו קודמין, וההיקש דקרא – בהורג בידים כתיב "כי כאשר יקום איש על רעהו וגו'". והשתא גרסינן בכל דוכתא: מה רוצח יהרג ואל יעבור. אף נערה המאורסה יהרג ואל יעבור. פירוש: יהרג הבועל, ולא גרסינן תיהרג, דקרקע עולם היא. אי נמי אר"י, דאפי' גרסינן תיהרג יש לפרש דהכי קאמר: תיהרג קודם שתעשה מעשה ותביא עליה את הערוה. וא"ת: במסכת ע"ז בפרק "רבי ישמעאל" (דף נד. ושם) דנעבד באונס אסור, ומפרש: כגון דאנסוהו גוים והשתחוה לבהמה דידיה. ופריך עלה רבי זירא: אונס רחמנא פטריה, דכתיב "ולנערה לא תעשה דבר" (דברים כב), ומאי קושיא? הא האי קרא דוקא בקרקע עולם איירי, אבל עשה מעשה חייב למסור עצמו, כדפרישי', ומשתחוה לעבודה זרה עושה מעשה הוא, דליכא לאוקמה כשכפוהו גוים לעבודה זרה, דאין זה משתחוה! ואר"י: דהכי פריך: אונס רחמנא פטריה ממיתה – אפי' בעושה מעשה, דנהי דחייב למסור עצמו, מ"מ אם לא מסר עצמו לא מיחייב מיתה. ד"ולנערה לא תעשה דבר" – אפילו בעשתה מעשה קאמר קרא דפטורה ממיתה, דבעשיית מעשה איירי היקישא דקרא. ועוד: דכיון דאפילו ברצון מיחייב מיתה, אע"ג דלא עביד מעשה, דהא אשה חייבת ברצון אע"ג דהויא קרקע עולם – ה"נ כשפטר הכתוב אונס במיתת בית דין. כדכתיב "ולנערה לא תעשה דבר" – פטר בכל ענין, לא שנא עביד לא שנא לא עביד. ולהכי פריך: כיון דפטור ממיתה לא חשיב נעבד ליאסר בהן עבודה. ומהדר ליה התם דחשיב שפיר נעבד באונס, אע"ג דפטו' ממית' בדיעבד, כיון דחייב למסור עצמו [וע"ע תוס' יומא פב. האריכו טובא].

ישן לא קנה. פי' בקונטרס: משום דלא הוי בר דעת. וקשיא: דהא קטן, אע"ג דלא הוי בר דעת הוה קונה אי לאו דמיעטיה קרא! אלא טעמא משום דלא איכוין לביאה כלל, והוי כ"מתכוין להטיח בכותל" דבסמוך.

וכי איצטריך קרא בין בשוגג כו'. וא"ת: והא איצטריך לאשמועינן ביאה ביבמה, דלא כתיב אלא הכא! וי"ל: דמ"להקים לאחיו שם" נפקא. וא"ת: והא אכתי איצטריך לג"ש דלקמן: יבמה מנין – אתיא ביאה ביאה! וי"ל: דביאה דחייבי לאוין מופנה, וה"ל מופנה מצד אחד.

דמכוין לה. לאו דוקא נקט דמכוין לה, דהא בסמוך אמר דנתכוון להטיח בבהמה והטיח ביבמתו – קנה.

שכן בידו לרבות. וא"ת: דבקדושין פרק "האומר" (דף סז:) בעי למילף כל העריות דלא תפסי בהו קידושין מאחות אשתו, וקאמר התם: בשלמא כולהו אתיין. והיכי אתיין? הא איכא למיפרך: מה לאחות אשה – שכן בידו לרבות! וי"ל: דבלאו הכי פריך שפיר. א"נ: דדוקא באשת אח חשיב יש בידו לרבות לאומרה, שכן יש בידו לרבות איסור על אחרים. אבל מה שבידו לרבות על עצמו – לא חשיב פירכא. **מה** לאחות אב ואחות אם שכן איסור הבא מאליו. הקשה ריב"ן: דמאחות אב ואם נילף איסור הבא מאליו, ומאשת אח נילף היכא דעל ידי קידושין! וי"ל: דאשת איש לא אתי, כדפריך בסמוך: מה להנך שכן שאר.

אלא

עין משפט נר מצוה

ד א מיי' פ"ב מהל' יבום הלכה ג ד סמג עשין נא טוש"ע אה"ע סימן קסו סעיף ח:

ה ב מיי' פ"א מהל' חובל ומזיק הלכה יב סמג עשין ע טוש"ע ח"מ סימן תכא סעיף יא:

ו ג מיי' פ"ב מהל' יבום הלכה ג סמג עשין נא טוש"ע אה"ע סימן קסו סעי' ח:

ז ד מיי' פ"ב שם ה"א ופ"ה שם הלכה ט טוש"ע שם סימן קע סעיף יב:

ח ה מיי' שם וטוש"ע שם סעיף ב וסימן קסו סעיף ב:

ט ו מיי' שם פ"ב הל' ג טוש"ע שם סימן קסו סעיף ז:

י ז מיי' פ"א מהל' חובל ומזיק הלכה י סמג עשין ע טוש"ע ח"מ סימן תכא סעיף א:

יא ח מיי' פ"ב מהלכות יבום הלכה ד סמג עשין נא טוש"ע אה"ע סימן קסו סעיף ח:

יב ט מיי' פ"ג מהל' מטמא משכב ומושב הל' א סמג עשין רמג:

תוספות ישנים

ישן לא קנה ביבמתו פ"ה משום דלא הוי בן דעת. ולא נהירא דאפילו חרש דלא הוי בר דעת אמרי' לקמן קנה. ונראה טעמא משום דבעינן כוונה וניחא דחרש יש לו כל הכוונה שיכול. אבל בישן אין לו כוונה שיש לו כמו שהוא ער. וכן נמי משמע לקמיה דמפיק ליה מיבא עליה עד דמכוין לה: **מה** לאשת אח שכן יש בידו לרבות. ותימה בקדושין (ס"ז) דיליף כל העריות [דאין קדושין תופסין] מאחות אשה נפרוך מה לאחות אשה שכן יש בידו לרבות שיקדש הרבה נשים וירבה עליו איסור אחות אשה וי"ל דהא לא קרי בידו לרבות אלא כשהוא מרבה איסור על אחרים כמו באשת אח דאי מקדש אלף כולן אסורות על אחיו משום אשת אח אבל אין זה חשיבות אם יכול להרבות איסור על עצמו: **מה** לאחות אב שכן איסור הבא מאליו והקשה ה"ר יהודה בר נתן אמאי לא שמעינן כל שאיסורו בא מאליו ולא ע"י קדושין מאחות אב והני דעל ידי קדושין שבידו לרבות ניליף מאשת אח. וי"ל כיון דמ"מ אצטריכו תרווייהו למילף עדיפא לן לאתויי מבינייא ועוי"ל דהא אי קאמר הכי הוה פרכינן אשת איש מנ"ל דמאשת אח לא מצינן למילף אשת איש שיש לה היתר בחיי בעלה משא"כ באשת אח אבל לקמן בסמוך בעי למילף מבינייא דנדה ואשת אח דנדה יש לה היתר בחיי בעלה ומ"מ פריך שפיר תלמודא מה לנדה ואשת

תוספות חד מקמאי

אלא בנתקע והאמר רבה נפל מן הגג פירוש ברוח מצויה ונתקע חייב בד' דברים [וביבמתו] לא קנה. אלא כגון שנתכוון לאשתו ותקפתו יבמתו ובא עליה שניהם אנוסים ה"ד כגון שנתכוון לאשתו ותקפוהו גוים ודבקום זו לזו. והא דאמר ישן לא קנה דוקא ישן אבל מתנמנם קנה בין היא ערה בין היא ישנה קנה: אמר רבה נתכוון להטיח (באשתו) [בכותל] והטיח ביבמתו לא קנה להטיח בבהמה והטיח ביבמתו קנה דהא קא מכוון לשום ביאה בעלמא

מסורת הש"ס

ב"ק כז.

[עי' תוספות לעיל לט: ד"ה ולשום]

קדושין יז.

נ"ל ויבמה. יעב"ץ

הגהות הב"ח

(א) גמ' בעל כרחה אמר מר ד"א יבמה יבא עליה: (ב) רש"י ד"ה נזק וכו' נמכרת בשוק כמה:

פסחים קכ: תענית יב. מגילה יח: חגיגה יח: נדה סג.

[נ"ל שהוא] ב"ק פו.

גליון הש"ס

גמ' ויבם ביאה גומרת. עיין לעיל דף ח ע"ב תד"ה ויבמה ובקדושין יד ע"א רש"י ד"ה א"כ:

עין משפט
נר מצוה

יג א מיי' פ"ד מהל' איסורי ביאה הלכה א סמג לאוין קיד ועשין רמג:
יד ב מיי' פ"א שם הל' א ופ"ב הל' א:
טו ג מיי' פ"א שם הל' יד:
טז ד מיי' שם הל' טז:
יז ה מיי' פ"ב שם הל' ה סמג לאוין קד טוש"ע אה"ע סימן טו סעי' טז:
יח ו מיי' שם הל' ב טוש"ע שם סעי' י:
יט ז מיי' שם טוש"ע שם סעיף ח:
כ ח מיי' פ"א מהלכות נחלות הלכה ו סמג עשין לו טוש"ע ח"מ סימן רעו סעיף ד:

אלא רמז ליבמה שאסורה בחיי בעלה מנין. דכיון דשריא רחמנא אחר מיתה – אין סברא לומר דאסירא בחיי בעלה, דלא מיסתבר שהיה בא הכתוב לומר דאתי עשה ודחי לא תעשה שיש בו כרת, אי לאו דמוכח קרא בהדיא.

בזכור מהו. הא דלא יליף זכור ובהמה מהקישא דרבי יונה משום ד"את מקורה הערה" כתיב, והנהו לא שייך בהו מקור. ועוד, דאפסקינהו בקרא דמולך. אי נמי משום דזכור ובהמה לא חשיב ביאה, דאין דרך ביאה בכך. ולהכי בפרק "ארבע מיתות" (סנהדרין נד:) לריך אזהרה ועונש לשוכב ונשכב בזכור, אע"ג דבעלמא לא בעי קרא לחייב האשה הנשכבת. **אמרו** לו מתה אשתך כו'. בתלתא הוה סגי, אלא קמ"ל דאף על פי שיש ערבוב, שכל חמשתן שלשלת אחוה, וצריך להוציא האסורות – לא גזרינן הנך דשרינן אטו הנך דאסירן.

צרותיהן איצטריך, אע"ג דס"ד דמוטב שיחלוץ הצרות – גזירה שלא יחלוץ לשניה או רביעית.

תורה אור

ביומי תליא מילתא. אשת אח – בבנים תליא רחמנא. אלא פריך הכי: מה לנדה ואשת אח – שכן אין אוסרן מתירן, תאמר באשת איש – שאוסרה! מתירה! אלא *אמר ר' יונה ואיתימא רב הונא בריה דרב יהושע: אמר קרא °"כי כל אשר יעשה מכל התועבת האלה ונכרתו הנפשות העשת" הוקשו כל העריות כולן לנדה, מה נדה בהעראה – אף כל בהעראה. ואלא נדה דכתיבא גבי אשת אח למה לי? לכדרב הונא. דאמר רב הונא: רמז ליבמה מן התורה מנין? מנין?! הא כתיב "יבמה יבא עליה"! אלא: רמז ליבמה שאסורה בחיי בעלה מנין? האי – סברא היא, מדאמר רחמנא: לאחר מיתת בעלה שריא – מכלל דבחיי בעלה אסורה! ודלמא: לאחר מיתת בעלה – מצוה, בחיי בעלה – רשות? אי נמי: לאחר מיתת בעלה – אין, בחיי בעלה – לא, *ולאו הבא מכלל עשה – עשה! אמר קרא: °"ואיש אשר יקח את אשת אחיו נדה היא", וכי אשת אחיו נדה היא? אלא כנדה, מה נדה, אף על פי שיש לה היתר לאחר מכאן – [א]בשעת איסורא בכרת, אף אשת אח [נמי], אף על פי שיש לה היתר לאחר מכאן – [ב]בחיי בעלה בכרת. אלא העראה דכתיבא גבי אחות אב ואחות אם למה לי? לכדבעא מיניה רבינא מרבא: [ג]המערה *בזכור, מהו? בזכור – "משכבי אשה" כתיבא! אלא: המערה בבהמה מהו? אמר ליה: אם אינו ענין להעראה, דכתיבא גבי אחות אב ואחות אם, דאתיא בהקישא מדרבי יונה – [ד]תנהו ענין להעראה דבהמה. מכדי בהמה חייבי מיתות בית דין היא, מאי טעמא כתיב להעראה דידה גבי חייבי כריתות? לכתוב גבי מיתת בית דין, ונילף מיתת ב"ד ממיתת ב"ד! *איידי דכוליה קרא לדרשא אתי – כתיב ביה נמי הא מילתא לדרשא. מאי דרשא – דתניא: °"ערות אחות אביך לא תגלה" [ה]בין מן האב בין מן האם. אתה אומר בין מן האב בין מן האם, או אינו אלא מן האב ולא מן האם? ודין הוא: חייב כאן – וחייב באחותו. מה אחותו – [ו]בין מן האב בין מן האם, אף כאן – בין מן האב בין מן האם. או כלך לדרך זו: חייב כאן וחייב בדודתו, מה דודתו – [ז]מן האב ולא מן האם, אף כאן – מן האב ולא מן האם. נראה למי דומה: דנין איסור הבא מאליו מאיסור הבא מאליו, ואל תוכיח דודתו – שאין איסור הבא מאליו. או כלך לדרך זה: דנין קרובי האב מקרובי האב, ואל תוכיח אחותו שקרובי עצמו? תלמוד לומר "ערות אחות אביך לא תגלה" בין מן האב בין מן האם. "ערות אחות אמך לא תגלה" בין מן האב בין מן האם. למה לי למכתבא באחות אב, למה לי למכתבא באחות אם? אמר רבי אבהו: צריכי, דאי כתב רחמנא באחות אב – שכן יש לה חיים, אבל אחות אם – אימא לא. ואי כתב רחמנא באחות אם – שכן ודאית, אבל אחות אב – אימא לא, צריכא. ודודתו, דפשיטא ליה לתנא דמן האב ולא מן האם, מנא ליה? אמר רבא: אתיא "דודו" "דודו", כתיב הכא °"ערות דדו גלה" וכתיב התם °"או דדו או בן דדו יגאלנו" מה להלן מן האב ולא מן האם – אף כאן מן האב ולא מן האם. והתם מנלן? אמר קרא "ממשפחתו יגאלנו", *משפחת אב – קרויה משפחה, [ח]משפחת אם – אינה קרויה משפחה. והדתנן: *אמרו לו: מתה אשתך, ונשא אחותה מאביה. מתה, ונשא אחותה מאמה. מתה, ונשא אחותה מאביה. מתה, ונשא אחותה מאמה – מותר בראשונה ובשלישית ובחמישית, ופוטרות צרותיהן. ואסור בשניה וברביעית, ואין ביאת אחת מהן פוטרת צרתה. ואם בא על השניה לאחר מיתת הראשונה – מותר בשניה וברביעית, ופוטרות צרותיהן, ואסור בשלישית ובחמישית.
אלמא

ביומי תליא מילתא. אפי' אם מת האוסרה, שפסקה דם בראייה ראשונה – אסורה כל שבעה. בבנים תליא. אם יש לה בנים אפילו מת אחיו. אין אוסרן מתירן. אין כח באוסר להתיר, אלא דבר אחר מתירה: ימים מתירין את הנדה, ואשת אח – כשהוא ערירי. הוקשו כל העריות לנדה. שהרי כאן הוקשו כולן זו לזו, ונדה כתובה בפרשת עריות, הלכך בהעראה ילפינן כולהו מנדה. נדה דכתיב גבי אשת אח. דילפינן מיניה לעיל העראה לאשת אח מנדה. בחיי בעלה. אם גירשה אחיו. ולאו הבא מכלל עשה עשה. אבל כרת ליכא. משכבי אשה. וכיון דבאשה הוי העראה משכב, ממילא איתפרשא בזכור, דהא בזכור כתיב "משכבי אשה". המערה בבהמה. שלא גמר ביאתו. ואחות אב ואחות אם. לאו מחייבי מיתות הן, דלא כתיבא בהו מיתה. ליכתבה במיתת בית דין. כגון באמו וחמותו, וליימא נמי: אם אינו ענין להו, דאתיא בהיקישא דר' יונה, תנהו ענין לבהמה. איידי דכוליה קרא. דכתיב באחות אב ואחות אם בפרשת "קדושים תהיו" לדרשא אתא, כדתניא לקמן כתיב ביה נמי העראה, בלא צורך, לדרשא דבהמה. ערות אחות אביך. קרא ד"אחרי מות" קמא נקט. בין שהיא אחות אביך. מן האב בין מן האם. מה אחותו בין מן האב בין מן האם. דכתיב "בת אביך או בת אמך". מה דודתו מן האב ולא מן האם. שאם היה דודו אחי אביו מן האם ולא מן האב – אין אשתו עליו ערוה, ולקמן בעי מנלן. דודתו אין איסורה בא עליו מאליו. אלא על ידי קדושי דודו, ולא תוכיח אחותו. וכיון דלא נפקא לן מדינא, תלמוד לומר מקרא שני בפרשת "קדושים תהיו": "ערות אחות אביך ואחות אמך לא תגלה". ואין צריך להזהיר – שכבר הזהיר, ולא הוה ליה לאשמועינן אלא עונש, כדעבד באשת אח ובאחותו: "איש כי יקח אחות אביו ואחות אמו עונם ישאו", וקרא יתירא הוא, לרבות אחות אביו מן האם ואחות אמו מן האם. למה לי למכתב. האי קרא יתירא בתרוייהו? לכתוב בחדא, ותיתי אידך מינה. יש לה חיים. דמשפחת אב קרויה משפחה, דכתיב "ויתילדו על משפחתם לבית אבתם" (במדבר א). אחות אם ודאי. קרובתו. אבל אחות אב, שמא ח"ו אין זה אביו? מה להלן מן האב. אם אחי אביו מן האב הוא – הוי קרוב לענין גאולה יותר, ומצות גאולה מוטל עליו יותר מקרובי האם, אף כאן – מן האב ולא מן האם: ה"ג. ממשפחתו יגאלנו משפחת אב קרויה משפחה כו'. והא דתנן אמרו לו מתה אשתך כו'. כגון דינה בת לאה מיעקב, ויוכבד בת לאה מחצרון, ושרה בת חצרון מקטורה, ורבקה בת קטורה מבתואל, ומלכה בת בתואל מחנה. וראובן נשא את מלכה, והלך למדינת הים. אמרו לו מתה אשתך, ונשא את רבקה, שהיא אחותה מאביה. חזרו ואמרו לו מתה רבקה, ונשא את שרה אחותה מאמה. אמרו לו מתה שרה, ונשא את יוכבד אחותה מאביה. אמרו לו מתה יוכבד, ונשא את דינה אחותה מאמה. חזרו ואמרו לו: כולן קיימות. מותר בראשונה. במלכה אשתו. ובשלישית. שרה, לפי שרבקה לא היו קדושיה קידושין, וביאתה באונס הוא. ומותר בשרה אחותה, דתנן (לקמן דף נז.): נושאין על האנוסה. ובחמישית. דינה, ואע"פ שהיא אחות יוכבד הרביעית. לפי שביאת יוכבד פיתוי היא, ואינה קידושין, מפני שהשלישית היו קידושיה קידושין. ופוטרות צרותיהן. אם מת והללו האחין לאחת מהן – פוטרות צרותיהן. ואסור בשניה. מפני הראשונה, וברביעית מפני השלישית.
אלמא

תוספות ישנים

את שאין להם היתר בחיי אוסרן. נדה בשעת הדם ואשת אח בחיי בעלה: **מותר** בראשונה ובשלישית ואינו אסור בה מטעם דנשואין [דשניה] לא הוו כלום מטעם הראשונה וביאתה הוי כמו אנוסה ואמרי' נושאין על האנוסה דאם אנס אשה אינו אסור בקרובותיה והשתא מייתי מהכא דאף מן האם אסורה מדקאמר אסור בשניה דוקא ובשלישית שרי משום דאין קדושי שניה כלום. הא אי הוה שרי בשניה הוי אסור בשלישית מפני שהיא אחותה אע"ג דשלישית הוי אחות שניה מן האם לבד. וה"ה דה"מ לאתויי ולאוכוחי בהדיא בלא דוחק מסיפא דמשמע דאף מן האם אסורה. דקאמר מתה הראשונה מותר בשניה וברביעית ואסור בשלישית

תוספות חד מקמאי

בעלמא: **תניא** ערות אחות אמך לא תגלה בין מן האב בין מן האם. (ומן האם). אשה אל אחותה לא תקח בין מן האב בין מן האם ערות אחי אביך לא תגלה אל אשתו לא תקרב דודתך היא מן האב ולא מן האם דאתייא דודו [דודו] כתיב הכא דודתך היא וכתיב התם או דודו או בן דודו יגאלנו מה להלן מן האב ולא מן האם דכתיב ממשפחתו יגאלנו ומשפחת אב קרויה משפחה ומשפחת אם אינה קרויה משפחה ומה שכתב הרב אלפס בענין העראת אשה לבעלה כבר כתבתי בקדושין סברת האחרים תוספת על סברת הרב ז"ל ולפי סברת הרב ז"ל משמע דביאה בלא חופה קונה ליורשה וליטמא לה ובפ' נערה שנתפתתה (מ"ח:) תניא נמי או שהיתה לה חצר בדרך ונכנסה עמו לשם נשואין אע"פ שכתובתה בבית אביה ומתה בעלה יורשה. בר"א לירושתה אבל

מסורת הש"ס

לעיל ח. קידושין כריתות ב:
[לקמן נו: סח. ענ: פס מח: זבחים לד. חולין
סנהדרין נה
[פסחים סז: לקמן סוטה ג. ב"ק נא. פח. וע"ע שבועות ז. סנהדרין ענ:]
[ב"ב קטו: קיז:]
לקמן נו.

ויקרא יח
שם כ
שם יח
שם כ
שם כה

גמרא

תורה אור

אַלְמָא [א]אֲחוֹת אִשְׁתּוֹ. בֵּין מִן הָאָב בֵּין מִן הָאֵם אֲסוּרוֹת. מְנָלַן? יָלֵיף מֵאֲחוֹתוֹ, מָה אֲחוֹתוֹ — בֵּין מִן הָאָב בֵּין מִן הָאֵם, אַף כָּאן בֵּין מִן הָאָב בֵּין מִן הָאֵם. וְלֵילַף מִדּוֹדָתוֹ, מַה דּוֹדָתוֹ — מִן הָאָב וְלֹא מִן הָאֵם, אַף כָּאן — מִן הָאָב וְלֹא מִן הָאֵם! מִסְתַּבְּרָא, מֵאֲחוֹתוֹ הֲוָה לֵיהּ לְמֵילַף, שֶׁכֵּן קְרוֹבֵי עַצְמוֹ מִקְּרוֹבֵי עַצְמוֹ. אַדְּרַבָּה, מִדּוֹדָתוֹ הֲוָה לֵיהּ לְמֵילַף שֶׁכֵּן דָּבָר עַל יְדֵי קִדּוּשִׁין מִדָּבָר שֶׁעַל יְדֵי קִדּוּשִׁין! אֶלָּא: מֵאֵשֶׁת אָח יָלְפִינַן, דְּשֶׁכֵּן דָּבָר עַל יְדֵי קִדּוּשִׁין, וּקְרוֹבֵי עַצְמוֹ. וְאֵשֶׁת אָח גּוּפָהּ מנ"ל? דְּתַנְיָא: °"עֶרְוַת אֵשֶׁת אָחִיךָ לֹא תְגַלֵּה" [ב]בֵּין מִן הָאָב בֵּין מִן הָאֵם. אַתָּה אוֹמֵר בֵּין מִן הָאָב בֵּין מִן הָאֵם, אוֹ אֵינוֹ אֶלָּא מִן הָאָב וְלֹא מִן הָאֵם? וְדִין הוּא: חַיָּיב כָּאן, וְחַיָּיב בַּאֲחוֹתוֹ. מָה אֲחוֹתוֹ — בֵּין מִן הָאָב בֵּין מִן הָאֵם, אַף כָּאן — בֵּין מִן הָאָב בֵּין מִן הָאֵם. אוֹ כְּלָךְ לְדֶרֶךְ זוֹ: חַיָּיב כָּאן וְחַיָּיב בְּדוֹדָתוֹ. מַה דּוֹדָתוֹ — מִן הָאָב וְלֹא מִן הָאֵם, אַף כָּאן — מִן הָאָב וְלֹא מִן הָאֵם? נִרְאֶה לְמִי דּוֹמֶה; דָּנִין קְרוֹבֵי עַצְמוֹ מִקְּרוֹבֵי עַצְמוֹ, וְאַל תּוֹכִיחַ דּוֹדָתוֹ שֶׁקְּרוֹבֵי הָאָב. אוֹ כְּלָךְ לְדֶרֶךְ זוֹ: דָּנִין דָּבָר שֶׁעַל יְדֵי קִדּוּשִׁין מִדָּבָר שֶׁעַל יְדֵי קִדּוּשִׁין, וְאַל תּוֹכִיחַ אֲחוֹתוֹ שֶׁאִיסּוּר הַבָּא מֵאֵלָיו? ת"ל "עֶרְוַת אָחִיךָ הִיא" בֵּין מִן הָאָב בֵּין מִן הָאֵם. וְאֵימָא: אִידִי וְאִידִי בְּאֵשֶׁת אָח מִן הָאָב, חֲדָא — דְּיֵשׁ לָהּ בָּנִים בְּחַיֵּי בַּעְלָהּ, וַחֲדָא — דְּאֵין לָהּ בָּנִים בְּחַיֵּי בַּעְלָהּ. אֵין לָהּ בָּנִים בְּחַיֵּי בַּעְלָהּ — מִדְּרַב הוּנָא נָפְקָא! וְאֵימָא: אִידִי וְאִידִי בְּאֵשֶׁת אָח מִן הָאָב, חֲדָא — דְּיֵשׁ לָהּ בָּנִים בְּחַיֵּי בַּעְלָהּ, וַחֲדָא — דְּיֵשׁ לָהּ בָּנִים לְאַחַר מִיתַת בַּעְלָהּ! יֵשׁ לָהּ בָּנִים לְאַחַר מִיתַת בַּעְלָהּ לָא צְרִיכָא קְרָא, מִדְּאָמַר רַחֲמָנָא שֶׁאֵין לָהּ בָּנִים מוּתֶּרֶת — הָא יֵשׁ לָהּ בָּנִים אֲסוּרָה. וְדִלְמָא: אֵין לָהּ בָּנִים — אֲסוּרָה לְעָלְמָא וְשַׁרְיָא לְיָבָם. יֵשׁ לָהּ בָּנִים — שַׁרְיָא לְעָלְמָא וְשַׁרְיָא לְיָבָם! אִי נַמִי: אֵין לָהּ בָּנִים — מִצְוָה, יֵשׁ לָהּ בָּנִים — רְשׁוּת, אִי נַמִי: אֵין לָהּ בָּנִים — אִין, יֵשׁ לָהּ בָּנִים — לָא, *וְלָאו הַבָּא מִכְּלַל עֲשֵׂה — עֲשֵׂה! כְּתַב קְרָא אַחֲרִינָא: °"עֶרְוַת אָחִיו גִּלָּה". וְאֵימָא אֵשֶׁת אָח מִן הָאֵם כְּאֵשֶׁת אָח מִן הָאָב: מָה אֵשֶׁת אָח מִן הָאָב — לְאַחַר מִיתַת בַּעְלָהּ שַׁרְיָא, אַף אֵשֶׁת אָח מִן הָאֵם — לְאַחַר מִיתַת בַּעְלָהּ שַׁרְיָא! אָמַר קְרָא "הִיא" [ג]בַּהֲוָיָיתָהּ תְּהֵא. אֲחוֹתוֹ דִּכְתַב בָּהּ כָּרֵת לָמָּה לִי? לִכְדְרַבִּי יוֹחָנָן. דְּאָמַר ר' יוֹחָנָן: שֶׁאִם *עֲשָׂאָן כּוּלָּם בְּהֶעְלֵם אֶחָת — חַיָּיב עַל כָּל אַחַת וְאַחַת. וּלְרַבִּי יִצְחָק, דְּאָמַר: כָּל חַיָּיבֵי כָּרֵיתוֹת בִּכְלָל הָיוּ, וְלָמָּה יָצְתָה כָּרֵת בַּאֲחוֹתוֹ — לְדוּנוֹ בְּכָרֵת וְלֹא בְּמַלְקוֹת, לְחַלֵּק מְנָלַן? נָפְקָא לֵיהּ: °מ"וְאֶל אִשָּׁה בְּנִדַּת טוּמְאָתָהּ" לְחַיֵּיב עַל כָּל אִשָּׁה וְאִשָּׁה. דּוֹדָתוֹ דִּכְתַב בָּהּ רַחֲמָנָא "עֲרִירִים יִהְיוּ" ל"ל? לִכְדְרַבָּה. דְּרַבָּה רָמֵי: כְּתִיב °"עֲרִירִים יִהְיוּ" וּכְתִיב °"עֲרִירִים יָמֻתוּ"! הָא כֵּיצַד? יֵשׁ לוֹ בָּנִים — קוֹבְרָן, אֵין לוֹ בָּנִים — הוֹלֵךְ עֲרִירִי. וְאִיצְטְרִיךְ לְמִכְתַּב "עֲרִירִים יִהְיוּ" וְאִיצְטְרִיךְ לְמִכְתַּב "עֲרִירִים יָמֻתוּ". דְּאִי כָּתַב רַחֲמָנָא "עֲרִירִים יִהְיוּ" ה"א: עַד חֶטְאֵיהּ, אֲבָל מֵחֶטְאֵיהּ וְאֵילָךְ — לָא כָּתַב רַחֲמָנָא "עֲרִירִים יָמֻתוּ". וְאִי כָּתַב רַחֲמָנָא "עֲרִירִים יָמֻתוּ" ה"א: מֵחֶטְאֵיהּ וְאֵילָךְ, אֲבָל מֵעִיקָּרָא — לָא, צְרִיכָא. § [ד]הַעֲרָאָה דְּחַיָּיבֵי לָאוִין מְנָלַן? מִדְּגַלֵּי רַחֲמָנָא °"שִׁכְבַת זֶרַע" גַּבֵּי שִׁפְחָה חֲרוּפָה — מִכְּלָל דְּחַיָּיבֵי לָאוִין בְּהַעֲרָאָה. אַדְּרַבָּה, מִדְּגַלֵּי רַחֲמָנָא הַעֲרָאָה בְּחַיָּיבֵי כָּרֵיתוֹת — מִכְּלָל דְּחַיָּיבֵי לָאוִין בִּגְמַר בִּיאָה! אָמַר רַב אַשִׁי: אִם כֵּן לִשְׁתּוֹק קְרָא מִשִּׁפְחָה חֲרוּפָה, הַעֲרָאָה [ה]דְּחַיָּיבֵי לָאוִין דִּכְהוּנָּה מְנָלַן? אָתְיָא °"קִיחָה" °"קִיחָה". [ו]דְּחַיָּיבֵי עֲשֵׂה מְנָלַן? אָתְיָא

רש"י

אַלְמָא אֲחוֹת אִשָּׁה בֵּין מִן הָאָב בֵּין מִן הָאֵם. דְּהָא שְׁלִישִׁית אֲחוֹתָהּ שֶׁל שְׁנִיָּה מֵאִמָּהּ הִיא. וְטַעְמָא – דִּשְׁנִיָּה לָאו אִשְׁתּוֹ הִיא, מִשּׁוּם הָכִי מוּתָּר בַּשְּׁלִישִׁית. הָא אִם הֲווּ קִידּוּשֵׁי שְׁנִיָּה קִידּוּשִׁין – הֲוָה אָסוּר בַּשְּׁלִישִׁית: אֲחוֹת אִשָּׁה קְרוֹבֵי עַצְמוֹ חָשֵׁיב לָהּ, שֶׁמֵּחֲמַת עַצְמוֹ נֶאֶסְרָה עָלָיו וְלֹא מֵחֲמַת אָבִיו. וּלְאַפּוֹקֵי דּוֹדָתוֹ, דִּקְרוֹבַת אָבִיו הִיא: ה"ג הָכָא: ת"ל עֶרְוַת אָחִיךָ הִיא. בְּחַיֵּי בַעְלָהּ. אִם גֵּירְשָׁהּ. מִדְּרַב הוּנָא. דִּכְתִיב "אֵשֶׁת אָחִיו נִדָּה הִיא" כִּדְלְעֵיל (דף נד:). וְלָאו הַבָּא מִכְּלַל עֲשֵׂה. "יְבָמָהּ יָבֹא עָלֶיהָ", אֲבָל כָּרֵת לֵיכָּא. הָכִי גָּרְסִינַן: כְּתִיב קְרָא אַחֲרִינָא עֶרְוַת אָחִיו גִּלָּה. אַף אֵשֶׁת אָח מִן הָאֵם לְאַחַר מִיתַת בַּעְלָהּ. בְּלֹא בָּנִים שַׁרְיָא. וְא"ת: הָא יָלְפִינַן (לעיל דף יז:) "אַחֲוָה" "אַחֲוָה" מִבְּנֵי יַעֲקֹב! אִיכָּא לְמֵימַר: אַחִים מִן הָאָב – מִצְוָה, מִן הָאֵם – רְשׁוּת. עֶרְוַת אָחִיךָ הִיא. וּמֵהַאי קְרָא מְרַבִּינַן אֵשֶׁת אָח מִן הָאֵם. אֲחוֹתוֹ דִּכְתַב בָּהּ כָּרֵת לָמָּה לִי. כֵּיוָן דְּדָרְשַׁתְּ הַעֲרָאָה, וּקְרָאֵי יְתֵירֵי, דְּכוּלְּהוּ כָּרֵת דַּאֲחוֹתוֹ מַאי תִּדְרוֹשׁ בֵּיהּ? הָא כְּבָר נִכְתַּב בְּכָל הָעֲרָיוֹת "וְנִכְרְתוּ הַנְּפָשׁוֹת הָעוֹשׂוֹת". חַיָּיב עַל כָּל אַחַת וְאַחַת. וְאִי לָא כָּתַב אֶלָּא חַד כָּרֵת אַכּוּלְּהוּ, הֲוֵי אָמֵינָא: הֵיכָא דַּעֲבָדִינְהוּ לְכוּלְּהוּ בְּהֶעְלֵם אֶחָד – לָא מִחַיֵּיב אֶלָּא חֲדָא, הַשְׁתָּא הָוֵי דָּבָר שֶׁהָיָה בִּכְלָל וְיָצָא מִן הַכְּלָל לְלַמֵּד עַל הַכְּלָל כּוּלּוֹ; דְּמָה אֲחוֹתוֹ מְיוּחֶדֶת שֶׁהִיא עֶרְוָה וְחַיָּיבִין עָלֶיהָ בִּפְנֵי עַצְמָהּ, אַף כָּל שֶׁהִיא עֶרְוָה – חַיָּיבִין עָלֶיהָ בִּפְנֵי עַצְמָהּ. לְכָרֵת נִתְּנָה וְלֹא לְמַלְקוֹת. דְּאִי הִתְרוּ בּוֹ לְמַלְקוֹת אֵינוֹ לוֹקֶה, דְּלָאו שֶׁנִּיתַּן לְאַזְהָרַת כָּרֵת הוּא, לְפִיכָךְ אֵין לוֹקִין עָלָיו. •דְּלָא הֲוָה לֵיהּ לְעוֹנְשׁוֹ כָּרֵת אא"כ הִזְהִיר עָלֶיהָ, הִלְכָּךְ אַזְהָרָה לָאו לְמַלְקוֹת נִתְּנָה. מוֹאֶל אִשָּׁה. לְחַלֵּק עַל כָּל אִשָּׁה וְאִשָּׁה שֶׁבְּפָרָשָׁה זוֹ, דַּהֲוָה לֵיהּ לְמִכְתַּב: וְנִדָּה לֹא תִקְרַב. עֲרִירִים. הַיְינוּ נַמִי כָּרֵת, שֶׁזַּרְעוֹ נִכְרָת. עֲרִירִים יִהְיוּ. לִשְׁעַת מִיתָתָן. מַשְׁמַע, סוֹפָן לָבֹא לִידֵי עֲרִירִי, דְּאִם יֵשׁ לוֹ בָּנִים – קוֹבְרָן. עֲרִירִים יָמוּתוּ. מַשְׁמַע דְּאִם הֵן עַכְשָׁיו עֲרִירִים – כֵּן יָמוּת, וַאֲפִי' יִוָּלְדוּ לָהֶם לְאַחַר מַעֲשֶׂה. דְּאִי כָּתַב רַחֲמָנָא עֲרִירִים יִהְיוּ הֲוֵי אָמֵינָא דַּהֲווּ לֵיהּ עַד חֶטְאֵיהּ. וְהָכִי מַשְׁמַע: סוֹפָם לִהְיוֹת עֲרִירִים, שֶׁיָּמוּתוּ בְּנֵיהֶם שֶׁיֵּשׁ לָהֶם עַתָּה, וְיִהְיוּ עֲרִירִים. אֲבָל בִּשְׁעַת מִיתָתָם לֹא יָמוּתוּ עֲרִירִים, דְּבָנִים דַּהֲווּ לֵיהּ מֵחֶטְאֵיהּ וְאֵילָךְ – לָא מָיְיתִי. וְאִי כָּתַב רַחֲמָנָא עֲרִירִים יָמוּתוּ הֲוֵי אָמֵינָא מֵחֶטְאֵיהּ וְאֵילָךְ. דְּהָכִי מַשְׁמַע: מֵ"חֶטְאָם יִשָּׂאוּ" וְאֵילָךְ – עֲרִירִים יָמוּתוּ; אֲבָל בָּנִים דִּמְעִיקָּרָא – לָא מָיְיתִי. כָּתַב רַחֲמָנָא "עֲרִירִים יִהְיוּ" – סוֹפָן לָבֹא לִידֵי עֲרִירִים, דְּמִדִּכְתִיב "עֲרִירִים יִהְיוּ" – מִכְּלָל דְּהַשְׁתָּא לָאו עֲרִירִים נִינְהוּ. שִׁפְחָה חַיָּיבֵי לָאוִין הִיא. דִּכְתִיב בָּהּ "לֹא יִהְיֶה קָדֵשׁ" (דברים כג). וְגַלֵּי בָּהּ רַחֲמָנָא דְּלָא מַיְיתִי אָשָׁם עַד שֶׁיִּגְמוֹר בָּהּ בִּיאָתוֹ, דִּכְתִיב "שִׁכְבַת זֶרַע". מִכְּלָל דְּחַיָּיבֵי מַלְקוֹת דְּלָאו דְּאָשָׁם, כְּגוֹן מַמְזֵר וּשְׁפָחָה שֶׁאֵין חֲרוּפָה – בְּהַעֲרָאָה מִיחַיֵּיב. שִׁפְחָה חֲרוּפָה. שִׁפְחָה כְּנַעֲנִית הַמְאוֹרֶסֶת לְעֶבֶד עִבְרִי, שֶׁמּוּתָּר בָּהּ, כִּדְכְתִיב (שמות כא) "אִם אֲדוֹנָיו יִתֶּן לוֹ אִשָּׁה". לִשְׁתּוֹק קְרָא. דְּלָא לִגְלֵי שִׁכְבַת זֶרַע בְּשִׁפְחָה חֲרוּפָה, וַאֲנָא אָמֵינָא (א) כִּשְׁאָר חַיָּיבֵי לָאוִין – בִּגְמַר בִּיאָה. דִּכְהוּנָּה מְנָלַן. דְּמִשִּׁפְחָה לָא גָּמְרִינַן אֶלָּא לָאו הַשָּׁוֶה בַּכֹּל, דּוּמְיָא דְּשִׁפְחָה חֲרוּפָה. קִיחָה קִיחָה. כְּתִיב גַּבֵּי חַיָּיבֵי כָּרֵיתוֹת (ויקרא כ) "אִישׁ אֲשֶׁר יִקַּח אֶת אֲחוֹתוֹ", וּכְתִיב בְּחַיָּיבֵי לָאוִין דִּכְהוּנָּה "לֹא יִקָּחוּ" (שם כא). דְּחַיָּיבֵי עֲשֵׂה. כְּגוֹן מִצְרִי וַאֲדוֹמִי עַד דּוֹר שְׁלִישִׁי, מְנָלַן דַּאֲסִירָא הַעֲרָאָה דִּידְהוּ בְּיִשְׂרְאֵלִית? וְקָאֵי בַּעֲשֵׂה, כִּדְכְתִיב "דּוֹר שְׁלִישִׁי יָבֹא" (דברים כג) וְלֹא שֵׁנִי. וְלָאו הַבָּא מִכְּלַל עֲשֵׂה עֲשֵׂה. בִּיאָה

תוספות

מאשת אח ילפינן. ואפילו למאי דפרישית לעיל דאחות אשה לא חשיב חומרא מה שבידו לרבות, מ"מ ליכא למיפרך: מה לאשת אח שכן בידו לרבות – דהכא לא יליף, אלא דשייך אחוה מן האם באחות אשה כמו באשת אח.

דיש לה בנים לאחר מיתת בעלה. תימה: הכא מצרכינן קרא לאסור לאחר מיתה, וכן בפ' "ד' מיתות" (סנהדרין נג. נד.) גבי אשת אב וכלתו, ופ"ק דקדושין (דף יג: ושם) קבעי: אשת איש מנלן דשריא אחר מיתת בעלה? וי"ל: דבכל הני צריך קרא לאסור, דלא נילף מאשת איש דשריא לאחר מיתה, כדיליף התם. וקשה: דב"האשה רבה" (לקמן דף צד: ושם) קאמר גבי חמותו לאחר(ב) מיתה דממעט לה רבי עקיבא מדכתיב "ישרפו אותו ואתהן" – ואת שתיהן, כלומר ששתיהן קיימות. נהי דמעטיה קרא משרפה, מאיסורא מי מיעטיה? משמע דאי לאו קרא – היתה בשרפה! וי"ל: דבכולהו צריך קרא לאסור ולהתיר, דלא נילפו מהדדי.

בהוייתה תהא. ומכל מקום איצטריך לעיל (דף יז:) למילף אחוה(ג) מבני יעקב, דלא נימא דבעינן דמיחדי באבא ובאימא משום דכתיב "יחדו". (ד)

דכתב רחמנא גבי דודתו למה לי. אפילו למאי דמפרש (בה) דאין ערירי בכל חייבי כריתות אלא היכא דמפרש קרא בהדיא – אתי שפיר, כדפרישית בריש מכילתין (דף ב. ד"ה "אשת").

לישתוק קרא משפחה חרופה. וא"ת: השתא דחייבי לאוין בהעראה, אם כן לישתוק קרא בחייבי כריתות! ותירץ ה"ר משה כהן: דאי לאו קרא בחייבי כריתות הוה אמינא: מדגלי רחמנא בשפחה – מכלל דחייבי כריתות בהעראה, אבל חייבי לאוין – בגמר ביאה. דילפינן משפחה חרופה. אבל השתא דכתיב העראה בחייבי כריתות, אי כל חייבי לאוין בגמר ביאה, א"כ לישתוק קרא משפחה חרופה(א).

אתיא

תוספות ישנים

ובחמישית: **מדגלי** רחמנא שכבת זרע בשפחה חרופה מכלל דחייבי לאוין בהעראה. וא"ת אדרבה נימא דנילף מינה דמה שפחה חרופה בגמר ביאה אף חייבי לאוין וכו' וא"ל א"כ לשתוק קרא משפחה חרופה דהא עדיין לא מסקינן אדעתין הך קושיא עד לקמן. וי"ל דהא מסיק אדעתיה שפיר דאם איתא דחייבי לאוין בגמר ביאה לשתוק משפחה חרופה דשפחה חרופה נמי חייבי לאוין היא דכתיב לא יהיה קדש אבל לקמן גבי חייבי כריתות לא הוה מסקינן אדעתין לומר ישתוק קרא משפחה חרופה כיון דלא ידעינן ליה רק מדיוקא מדגלי רחמנא בחייבי כריתות מכלל דחייבי לאוין בגמר ביאה. עוי"ל דאין להקשות הכא נילף מיניה דהא ודאי מיניה בעי' למילף דהכי פירושא מדגלי רחמנא בשפחה חרופה ש"ז גבי חיוב האשם מכלל לחיוב הלאו הוי קודם גמר ביאה וא"כ חייבי לאוין הוו בהעראה: **א)** ולפי' זה קשה את שפרשתי דשמעינן מש"ז דכתיב גבי אשם לחיוב הלאו הוי משעת העראה וא"כ אפילו אי לא כתיב העראה בחייבי כריתות ידעינן דחייבי לאוין בהעראה ומגינן לתרץ כתירוץ שתלתי בתי'

עין משפט נר מצוה

כא א מיי' פ"ב מהל' איסורי ביאה הל' ט סמג לאוין קח טוש"ע אה"ע סימן טו סעי' כו:

כב ב שם סעיף כב:

כג ג מיי' פ"א מהלכות יבום ה"א טוש"ע שם סי' קנז סעי' א:

כד ד ה ו מיי' פ"א מהלכות איסורי ביאה הלכה ז:

ס"א איתו

מסורת הש"ס

ויקרא יח | שם כ | שם יח | שם כ | שם | שם יט | שם כ

[לעיל נד: וש"נ]

מכות יד. כריתות ב:

הגהות הב"ח

(א) רש"י ד"ה לשתוק וכו' כשאר חייבי לאוין נמי לא מיחייב בהעראה אלא בגמר ביאה: (ב) תוס' ד"ה ויש וכו' לאחר מיתת אשתו דממעט לה ר"ע: (ג) ד"ה בהווייתה וכו' למילף אחוה אחוה מבני: (ד) ד"ה דכתב כך צריך להתחיל ודלתו דכתב רחמנא גבי ערירים למה לי אפי' למאן דמפרש כצ"ל:

גליון הש"ס

רש"י ד"ה לכרת ניתנה כו' דלא הוי"ל לעונשו כרת א"כ הזהיר עליה. עיין מכות דף יג ע"ב:

כה א מיי' פ"ג מהל' איסורי ביאה הל' טו סמג לאוין קפה טור אה"ע סי' כ:

כו ב ג מיי' שם פ"א הל' יא יב סמג שם טור אה"ע שם:

כז ד מיי' שם הלכה י וסמג שם טוש"ע אה"ע סימן כ סעיף א בהג"ה:

אָתְיָא "בִּיאָה" "בִּיאָה". יְבָמָה לַשּׁוּק מְנָלַן? אִי לְמַאן דַּאֲמַר לָאו – לָאו, אִי לְמַאן דַּאֲמַר עֲשֵׂה – עֲשֵׂה. אֶלָּא יְבָמָה לַיָּבָם מְנָלַן? אָתְיָא "בִּיאָה" "בִּיאָה". אִשָּׁה לְבַעְלָהּ מְנָלַן? אָתְיָא "קִיחָה" "קִיחָה". אָמַר רָבָא: לָמָּה לִי דִּכְתַב רַחֲמָנָא "שִׁכְבַת זֶרַע" בְּשִׁפְחָה חֲרוּפָה, "שִׁכְבַת זֶרַע" בְּאֵשֶׁת אִישׁ, "שִׁכְבַת זֶרַע" בְּסוֹטָה, דְּשִׁפְחָה חֲרוּפָה – [א]כְּדַאֲמָרַן. דְּאֵשֶׁת אִישׁ – פְּרָט לִמְשַׁמֵּשׁ מֵת. הָנִיחָא לְמַאן דַּאֲמַר *מְשַׁמֵּשׁ מֵת בָּעֲרָיוֹת [ב]פָּטוּר, אֶלָּא לְמ"ד חַיָּיב – מַאי אִיכָּא לְמֵימַר? אֶלָּא [ג]פְּרָט לִמְשַׁמֵּשׁ מֵתָה. דְּסד"א: [הוֹאִיל] לְאַחַר מִיתָה נַמִּי אִיקְרֵי שְׁאֵרוֹ, אֵימָא לִיחַיֵּיב עָלֶיהָ בְּאֵשֶׁת אִישׁ – קמ"ל. דְּסוֹטָה לָמָּה לִי? לְכִדְתַנְיָא: *"שִׁכְבַת זֶרַע" פְּרָט לְדָבָר אַחֵר. מַאי דָּבָר אַחֵר? אֲמַר רַב שֵׁשֶׁת: פְּרָט לְשֶׁקִּינֵּא לָהּ שֶׁלֹּא כְּדַרְכָּהּ. א"ל רָבָא: "מִשְׁכְּבֵי אִשָּׁה" כְּתִיב! אֶלָּא אֲמַר רָבָא: פְּרָט לְשֶׁקִּינֵּא לָהּ דֶּרֶךְ אֵבָרִים. א"ל אַבַּיֵי: פְּרִיצוּתָא אֲסַר רַחֲמָנָא? אֶלָּא אֲמַר אַבַּיֵי: פְּרָט לְשֶׁקִּינֵּא לָהּ בִּנְשִׁיקָה. הָנִיחָא לְמ"ד *הַעֲרָאָה זוֹ הַכְנָסַת עֲטָרָה, אֶלָּא לְמ"ד זוֹ נְשִׁיקָה – מַאי אִיכָּא לְמֵימַר? אֶלָּא, לְעוֹלָם לְשֶׁקִּינֵּא לָהּ דֶּרֶךְ אֵבָרִים, וְאִיצְטְרִיךְ: סד"א: בְּקְפֵידָא דְּבַעַל תָּלָה רַחֲמָנָא, וְהָא קָא קָפֵיד, קמ"ל. אָמַר שְׁמוּאֵל: *הַעֲרָאָה זוֹ נְשִׁיקָה, מָשָׁל לְאָדָם שֶׁמַּנִּיחַ אֶצְבָּעוֹ עַל פִּיו – אִי אֶפְשָׁר שֶׁלֹּא יִדְחוֹק הַבָּשָׂר. כִּי אֲתָא רַבָּה בַּר בַּר חָנָה אָמַר רַבִּי יוֹחָנָן: גְּמַר בִּיאָה בְּשִׁפְחָה חֲרוּפָה – זוֹ הַכְנָסַת עֲטָרָה. מְתִיב רַב שֵׁשֶׁת: "שִׁכְבַת זֶרַע" אֵינוֹ חַיָּיב אֶלָּא עַל בִּיאַת הַמֵּירוּק. מַאי לָאו – מֵירוּק גִּיד? לָא, מֵירוּק עֲטָרָה. כִּי אֲתָא רַב דִּימִי א"ר יוֹחָנָן: [ד]הַעֲרָאָה – זוֹ הַכְנָסַת עֲטָרָה. אָמְרוּ לֵיהּ: וְהָא רַבָּה בַּר בַּר חָנָה לָא אָמַר הָכִי? אֲמַר לְהוּ: אוֹ אִיהוּ שַׁקְרַאי אוֹ אֲנָא שַׁקְרִי. כִּי אֲתָא רָבִין א"ר יוֹחָנָן: הַעֲרָאָה זוֹ הַכְנָסַת עֲטָרָה. אַדְּרַבָּה בַּר בַּר חָנָה – וַדַּאי פְּלִיג, אַדִּשְׁמוּאֵל מִי לֵימָא פְּלִיג?! לָא, מִנְּשִׁיקָה וְעַד הַכְנָסַת עֲטָרָה – הַעֲרָאָה קָרֵי לָהּ. כִּי אֲתָא רַב שְׁמוּאֵל בַּר יְהוּדָה א"ר יוֹחָנָן הַעֲרָאָה – זוֹ הַכְנָסַת עֲטָרָה, גְּמַר בִּיאָה – גְּמַר בִּיאָה מַמָּשׁ.

מִכָּאן

בִּיאָה בִּיאָה. מֵחַיָּיבֵי לָאוִין, דִּכְתִיב בְּהוּ "לֹא יָבֹא מַמְזֵר". **יְבָמָה לַשּׁוּק.** בְּלֹא חֲלִיצָה, מִנַּיִן דְּהַעֲרָאָה דִּידָהּ כִּגְמַר בִּיאָה? **אִי לְמַאן דַּאֲמַר לָאו.** דִּכְתִיב "לֹא תִהְיֶה אֵשֶׁת הַמֵּת" (דברים כה) יָלְפִינַן הַעֲרָאָה לְחַיָּיבֵי לָאוִין. **אִי לְמַאן דַּאֲמַר עֲשֵׂה.** דִּכְתִיב (שם) "יְבָמָהּ יָבֹא עָלֶיהָ" וְלֹא אַחֵר, וְלָאו הַבָּא מִכְּלַל עֲשֵׂה – עֲשֵׂה. וְהַאי "לֹא תִהְיֶה" מַפֵּיק לָהּ לְאֵין קִידּוּשִׁין תּוֹפְסִין בָּהּ. וְה"ק: לֹא יְהֵא בָּהּ הֲוָיָה לְזָר. וּפְלוּגְתָּא דְּרַב וּשְׁמוּאֵל הִיא בְּ"הָאִשָּׁה קַמָּא" (לקמן צב:). **אֶלָּא יְבָמָה לַיָּבָם מְנָלַן.** דְּקָנֵי לָהּ בְּהַעֲרָאָה. **אִשָּׁה לְבַעְלָהּ.** לְעִנְיַן מְקַדֵּשׁ בְּבִיאָה, מְנָלַן דִּבְהַעֲרָאָה מְקַדְּשָׁהּ? **קִיחָה קִיחָה.** "כִּי יִקַּח אִישׁ אִשָּׁה וּבְעָלָהּ" (דברים כד) וּמֵהָכָא יָלְפִינַן קִידּוּשֵׁי בִּיאָה: כְּתִיב הָכָא קִיחָה וּכְתִיב הָתָם בְּחַיָּיבֵי כְרֵיתוֹת קִיחָה (ויקרא כ). **לָמָּה לִי לְמִיכְתַּב שִׁכְבַת זֶרַע בְּאֵשֶׁת אִישׁ.** "וְאֶל אֵשֶׁת עֲמִיתְךָ לֹא תִתֵּן שְׁכָבְתְּךָ לְזָרַע" (ויקרא יח) וְהָא אִיתְרַבֵּי בָּהּ הַעֲרָאָה מֵהֶקֵּישָׁא דְּר' יוֹנָה? **שִׁכְבַת זֶרַע בְּסוֹטָה.** הַנִּסְתָּרָה, דְּנֶאֱסֶרֶת מִסָּפֵק, כְּתִיב "וְשָׁכַב אִישׁ אוֹתָהּ שִׁכְבַת זֶרַע" (במדבר ה). **כִּדַאֲמָרַן.** דְּבָעֵינַן גְּמַר בִּיאָה. דְּלָא תֵּימָא כִּי הֵיכִי דְּמִחַיֵּיב מַלְקוּת בְּהַעֲרָאָה לִיחַיֵּיב נַמִּי אָשָׁם בְּהַעֲרָאָה. **לִמְשַׁמֵּשׁ מֵת.** בְּאֵבֶר מֵת בְּלֹא קִישּׁוּי, דְּאֵין רָאוּי לְהַזְרִיעַ. **הָנִיחָא לְמ"ד.** בִּשְׁבוּעוֹת בְּפֶרֶק "יְדִיעוֹת הַטּוּמְאָה". **לִמְשַׁמֵּשׁ מֵתָה.** אֵשֶׁת אִישׁ לְאַחַר מִיתָתָהּ. **סד"א הוֹאִיל וּלְאַחַר מִיתָתָהּ שְׁאֵרוֹ.** דְּבַעְלָהּ מִיקְרֵי, דִּכְתִיב גַּבֵּי טוּמְאָה "כִּי אִם לִשְׁאֵרוֹ" (ויקרא כא) וְאָמְרִי': *שְׁאֵרוֹ זוֹ אִשְׁתּוֹ, לִיחַיֵּיב עָלֶיהָ. **לְשֶׁקִּינֵּא לָהּ שֶׁלֹּא כְּדַרְכָּהּ.** שֶׁהָיָה חוֹשְׁדָהּ עִמּוֹ בְּכָךְ, וּכְשֶׁאָמַר אַל תִּסָּתְרִי עִמּוֹ – יָדוּעַ לַכֹּל דִּלְדַעַת כֵּן הִזְהִירָהּ, דְּלֹא הָיָה חוֹשְׁדָהּ עִמּוֹ בְּבִיאָה אַחֶרֶת. לִישָּׁנָא אַחֲרִינָא: לְשֶׁקִּינֵּא לָהּ שֶׁלֹּא כְּדַרְכָּהּ – אַל תִּסָּתְרִי עִמּוֹ לִיבָּעֵל לוֹ שֶׁלֹּא כְּדַרְכָּהּ. **מִשְׁכְּבֵי אִשָּׁה כְּתִיב.** הוּקְשׁוּ שְׁנֵיהֶן. **דֶּרֶךְ אֵבָרִים.** מִיעוּךְ דַּדִּים, וְדָשׁ מִבַּחוּץ בִּשְׁאָר אֵבָרִים. **פְּרִיצוּתָא קָאָסַר רַחֲמָנָא.** בִּתְמִיָּה. כְּלוֹמַר, פְּשִׁיטָא דְּלָאו קִינּוּי הוּא, דְּמִשּׁוּם פְּרִיצוּתָא לָא מִיתַּסְרָא עֲלֵיהּ. **בִּנְשִׁיקָה.** אֵבֶר נוֹשֵׁק בִּמְקוֹם תַּשְׁמִישׁ. **הָנִיחָא לְמ"ד.** לְקַמָּן בִּשְׁמַעְתִּין: הַעֲרָאָה זוֹ הַכְנָסַת עֲטָרָה, אֲבָל נְשִׁיקָה לָאו הַעֲרָאָה הִיא, וְלָא מִיתַּסְרָא לְבַעְלָהּ בְּהָכִי – שַׁפִּיר קָאָמְרַתְּ (דְּלָא מִיתַּסְרָא לְבַעְלָהּ), דְּלָאו קִינּוּי הוּא. **אֶלָּא לְמ"ד נְשִׁיקָה הַעֲרָאָה הִיא.** הֵיכִי מְמַעֵט לָהּ. **גְּמַר בִּיאָה זוֹ הַכְנָסַת עֲטָרָה.** מִכְּלָל דִּנְשִׁיקָה הַעֲרָאָה הִיא, כִּשְׁמוּאֵל. **שִׁכְבַת זֶרַע.** בְּשִׁפְחָה חֲרוּפָה קָאֵי. **עֲטָרָה.** רֹאשׁ הַגִּיד הִיא, וְאֵינָהּ מִן הַגִּיד אֶלָּא בָּשָׂר. **מֵירוּק.** שֶׁמַּזְרִיעַ. **וַדַּאי פְּלִיגָא.** דְּהָא אָמַר: הַכְנָסַת עֲטָרָה זוֹ הִיא גְּמַר בִּיאָה, וְהָכָא קָרֵי לָהּ הַעֲרָאָה. **אַדִּשְׁמוּאֵל.** דְּאָמַר: נְשִׁיקָה הָוֵי הַעֲרָאָה. **מִי לֵימָא פְּלִיג.** דְּלִשְׁמוּאֵל הָוֵי הַכְנָסַת עֲטָרָה גְּמַר בִּיאָה, וּלְרָבִין נְשִׁיקָה לָאו כְּלוּם הִיא. אוֹ דִּלְמָא תַּרְוַיְיהוּ, בֵּין לְרָבִין בֵּין לִשְׁמוּאֵל הַעֲרָאָה נִינְהוּ, וּמַר אָמַר חֲדָא וּמַר אָמַר חֲדָא וְלָא פְּלִיגֵי.

מִכָּאן

אתיא ביאה ביאה. והוי כאילו כתיב דור שלישי יבא, משמע הא דור שני – לא יבא, ולא שייך לאקשויי מהא דאמר בסוף "הנשרפין" (סנהדרין פד.) דבר הבא מן הכלל אין דנין אותו בגזירה שוה, דהכא ביאה דאתיא לגזירה שוה כתיבא בהדיא, ולא מן הכלל אתי, כי ההיא דהתם דלא ילפינן חילול חילול מתרומה כהן העובד באנינות, דלא כתיב חילול אלא דנפיק מכלל דכתב בכהן גדול "ומן המקדש לא יצא ולא יחלל" (ויקרא כא) הא אחר שעבד – חלל. **אי** למאן דאמר עשה. ל"ג לי', וברוב ספרים ליתא, דבין לרב ובין לשמואל איכא לאו, כדפרישי' בסוף "החולץ" (לעיל מט: ד"ה "אי כרב"). **אשה** לבעלה מנין **אתיא** קיחה קיחה. פירוש: דנקנית בהעראה. הקשה ה"ר נסים: דבפ"ק דקדושין (דף י. ושם) בעי: תחלת ביאה קונה או סוף ביאה קונה? למאי נפקא מינה – שהערה בה וקבלה קידושין מאחר כו'. ומסיק רבא דכל הבועל דעתו על גמר ביאה, ולא קני בהעראה! ותירץ הר' שמעון הזקן: דהא דאמר הכא דקני בהעראה – היינו בשלא עשה כי אם העראה ופירש מיד, ולא גמר ביאתו. אבל התם איירי כשעושה כל הביאה, דלא קני בהעראה, כיון שדעתו על גמר ביאה. וכן מוכח הלשון, דקאמר התם: כל הבועל – דעתו על גמר ביאה, ולא קאמר כל המערה. וה"ר יצחק בן ה"ר מאיר פירש: דכשמפרש שרוצה לקנות בהעראה – קני בהעראה אפי' אם גומר ביאתו, אבל בסתם – דעתו על גמר ביאה. ור"ת פירש שם בע"א, ושם פירשתיא). **קיחה** קיחה. תימה: דנפקא לן בפרק קמא דקדושין (דף ט:) דאשה נקנית בביאה מדכתיב "ובעלה", ותיפוק ליה מקיחה קיחה! וי"ל: אי לאו דכתיב ובעלה – מקיחה דעריות לא הוה גמרינן עיקר ביאה, כיון דקיחה דעריות לא משתעי בקנין כלל, אבל לענין שתיחשב העראה כגמר ביאה – ילפינן שפיר מהתם. ואם תאמר: ונילף מקיחה דיבמה דאיירי בקנין, דכתיב "ולקחה לו לאשה"! וי"ל: דאינו מופנה לג"ש. וא"ת: ונילף מקיחה דחייבי לאוין דכהונה, דקיחה דידהו איירי בקנין, כדאמר בפרק בתרא דקידושין (דף עח.): קדש לוקה משום "לא יקח", ודרשינן ליה נמי לג"ש! וי"ל: דלא איירי בקיחה דביאה, אלא בסתם קידושין, כדאמר התם: בעל – לוקה משום "לא יחלל", ועוד י"ל: דאי לאו "ובעלה" לא הוה גמרינן קידושי כסף מקיחה קיחה דשדה עפרון. אלא הוה מוקמינן קיחה דקרא בקידושי ביאה, משום דמסתבר למגמר טפי קיחה דאשה מקיחה דאשה. אבל השתא דכתיב "ובעלה" – ע"כ גמרינן קיחה משדה עפרון קידושי כסף, דליכא למימר דאיצטריך קיחה להעראה – דא"כ לשתוק מ"ובעלה", ונילף כולה מילתא מעריות. **לאחר** מיתה נמי שארו **איקרי** כו'. והא דפשיטא לן בפרק "יש נוחלין" (ב"ב דף קיד:) *דאין הבעל יורש את אשתו כשהוא בקבר, וקאמר נמי התם: כשם שאין האיש יורש את אשתו בקבר להנחיל לקרוביו, כך הבן לא יירש את אמו בקבר להנחיל לאחיו מן האב. הא דפשיטא ליה בבעל טפי מבבן – היינו מהך דרשא דהכא דאשמועינן דלאחר מיתה לא מיקרי שארו. וא"ת: דבפרק "ד' מיתות" (סנהדרין סו:) ממעט משמש מתה מקרא אחרינא. דדריש התם "ומתו גם שניהם" – פרט למעשה הורדוס. והיינו משמש מתה, כדאמר בבבא בתרא (דף ג:): דהטמין בדובשא ינוקתא דבי חשמונאי, והיה בא עליה לייתובי יצריה! ואר"י: דאיצטריך דרשא דשמעתין למאן דדריש התם "ומתו גם שניהם" – עד שיהו שניהם שוים. והא דקאמר התם ואידך מעשה הורדוס לאו כלום הוא – המ"ל דנפקא ליה מקרא דהכא, אלא דניחא ליה לאוקמי ההוא תנא דדריש עד שיהו שניהם שוים אפילו כמ"ד משמש מת בעריות פטור. ויש ספרים דגרסי התם: פרט למעשה אידודין. וכן גורס בערוך*: ופי' רש"י שם דמעשה אידודין היינו דרך אברים, וקשה: דהכא פשיטא ליה לאביי דדרך אברים לאו כלום הוא? וי"ל: דהיינו כמ"ד התם דמעשה אידודין לאו כלום הוא, ואפילו למאן דממעט התם מקרא – איכא למימר דמקרא התם פשיטא ליה לאביי הכא. **לשקינא** לה דרך **אברים**. ואם תאמר: הא אפילו אמר לה אל תסתרי סתם הוי קינוי, ואם כן מה בכך אם הזכיר נמי דרך אברים? כיון דאמר לה נמי אל תסתרי! ויש לומר דהכי פירושו: שקינא לה דרך אברים, שאמר לה: איני חושדך אלא דרך אברים, וכן שלא כדרכה. **אינו** חייב **אלא על ביאת** מירוק. נראה דמחייב בשפחה חרופה אפילו בלא הוצאת זרע. [אלא שתהא] ביאה הראויה להזריע. כמו באשת איש, דלא בעינן הוצאת זרע, אף על גב דכתיב בה ש"ז. ולא אתא למעוטי בשפחה חרופה אלא העראה ושלא כדרכה בספ"ב דכריתות (דף יא:). ונראה דלמ"ד העראה זו הכנסת עטרה אין ראויה להתעבר בהעראה אלא במירוק גיד, שאם היתה ראויה להתעבר – לא הוה מוקמי קרא למעוטי העראה שלא כדרכה.

לדברים

[סנהדרין נה.] שבועות יח. | סוטה כו: | גז"ש [סנהדרין עג:] | סוטה כו: | [לעיל כב:] | ס"א איזו | [וע"ש היטב בתוס' ד"ה מה אשה] | [ערך הרדום]

תוספות ישנים

הראשון: א) עוד פר"ת לאחרי שרבינו העראה כגמר ביאה מעתה ביאה נקראת אע"ג דליכא אלא העראה ור"ל התם תחלת העראה קונה או סוף העראה קונה ומסיק כל הבועל דעתו על גמר העראה וכמ"ד העראה זו הכנסת העטרה דלמ"ד זו נשיקה לא שייך בה תחלה וסוף ומקשינן מהא דאמרינן לעיל אלא מן האירוסין יבא עשה וידחה ל"ת ומאי קאמר הלא [ביבמה] דעתו על גמר ביאה ממש דאי לאו הכי לא קני ליה ליבמתו דבעינן שיהא ראוי להקמת שם ומקודם שגמר ביאתו עשה בה העראה ונקראת בעולה בהכי וא"כ איכא עשה ול"ת אף [באלמנה] מן האירוסין עשה דבתולה ולא בעולה דלאו הבא מכלל עשה עשה ולאו דאלמנה. וי"ל דלעיל ס"ל כתלמודא כמ"ד העראה זו נשיקה ולא שייך בה תחלה סוף וא"כ לא הוי א) בעולה בסוף העראה. עוי"ל דכיון דלא הוי בעולה רק מעצמו ליכא עשה דבעולת עצמו אינה רק מדרבנן וא"ת הא אמרינן לקמן ולו תהיה לאשה פרט לאלמנה לכ"ג דכיון דלא חזיא למיקס קמיה וכו' וקאמר היכי דמי אילימא כדרכה תיפוק ליה דהויא לה בעולה. ומאי קאמר הלא אמרינן דבעולת עצמו לא הוי אלא מדרבנן וי"ל דה"ק תיפוק ליה דהויא בעולה וכחלוצה שוה רבנן וא"כ אין לה קנס דלא חזיא למיקס קמיה. עוד יש מתרצים דהא דאמרינן הכא דהעראה קונה מקיחה קיחה היינו לאחר קדושי כסף לחשוב העראה כחופה והא דאמרינן דעתו על גמר ביאה היינו בלא קדושי כסף. וא"ת למה לי קרא בקדושין ובעלה מלמד שנקנית בביאה תיפוק ליה מקיחה קיחה וי"ל אי לאו ובעלה דמשמע דביאה גמורה קונה באשה לא הוה ידעינן מקיחה קיחה. ורבינו נתנאל תירץ דלפי' לעיל מכוון הדבר הזה דובעלה משמע דביאה גמורה מיירי בלא קדושין כסף ותחלת קנינו בביאה בעי' ביאה גמורה ומעתה ידעינן מקיחה קיחה דהעראה לאחר קדושי כסף קונה כמו חופה: **פרט** לשקינא א) נראה לר"י דכ"ע לא מקרי בעולה על ידי העראה.

תוספות חד מקמאי

לתרומה אין האשה אוכלת בתרומה עד שתכנס לחופה: אמר רבה שכבת זרע דכתב גבי שפחה חרופה למעט מינה דכל חייבי לאוין בהעראה דא"כ לישתוק קרא מיניה דשפחה חרופה. שכבת זרע דאשת איש למ"ד משמש מת בעריות חייב פרט למשמש מתה. שכבת זרע דסוטה לאו למעקרה קינא לה שלא כדרכה דהא משכבי אשה [כתיב]. אלא פרט שקנא לה דרך אבריה ואע"ג דפריצות בעלמא איצטריך ס"ד בקפידא דבעל תלה רחמנא והא קפיד קמ"ל. ולמ"ד העראה זו הכנסת עטרה פרט לשקנא לה בנשיקה מהו: רב

מִכָּאן וְאֵילָךְ אֵינוֹ אֶלָּא נְשִׁיקָה, וּפָטוּר עָלֶיהָ. וּפָלֵיג אַדִּשְׁמוּאֵל.§ "אֶחָד הַמְעָרֶה וְאֶחָד הַגּוֹמֵר קָנָה".§ מַאי קָנָה? *רַב אָמַר: קָנָה לַכֹּל. וּשְׁמוּאֵל אָמַר: לֹא קָנָה אֶלָּא לַדְּבָרִים הָאֲמוּרִים בַּפָּרָשָׁה: לִירַשׁ בְּנִכְסֵי אָחִיו, וּלְפוֹטְרָהּ מִן הַיִּבּוּם. [א]מִן הַנִּשּׂוּאִין לְד"ה אָכְלָה, דְּהָא הֲוַת קָאָכְלָה מֵעִיקָּרָא. כִּי פְּלִיגִי — מִן הָאֵירוּסִין. רַב אָמַר: אוֹכֶלֶת, דְּהָא רַבֵּי רַחֲמָנָא בִּיאַת שׁוֹגֵג כְּמֵזִיד. וּשְׁמוּאֵל אָמַר: כִּי רַבֵּי רַחֲמָנָא — לְאוֹקְמֵיהּ בִּמְקוֹם בַּעַל, לְאַלּוּמֵי מִבַּעַל — לָא. וְאַזְדָּא שְׁמוּאֵל לְטַעְמֵיהּ, דְּאָמַר רַב נַחְמָן אָמַר שְׁמוּאֵל: כָּל שֶׁהַבַּעַל מַאֲכִיל — יָבָם מַאֲכִיל, וְכָל שֶׁאֵין הַבַּעַל מַאֲכִיל — יָבָם אֵינוֹ מַאֲכִיל. מֵיתִיבֵי: בַּת יִשְׂרָאֵל פִּקַּחַת שֶׁנִּתְאָרְסָה לְכֹהֵן פִּקֵּחַ, וְלֹא הִסְפִּיק לְכוֹנְסָהּ עַד שֶׁנִּתְחָרֵשׁ — אֵינָהּ אוֹכֶלֶת. מֵת, וְנָפְלָה לִפְנֵי יָבָם חֵרֵשׁ — אוֹכֶלֶת. וּבְזוֹ יָפֶה כֹּחַ הַיָּבָם מִכֹּחַ הַבַּעַל. בִּשְׁלָמָא לְרַב — נִיחָא, אֶלָּא לִשְׁמוּאֵל — קַשְׁיָא! אָמַר לָךְ שְׁמוּאֵל: אֵימָא הָכִי: וְלֹא הִסְפִּיק לְכוֹנְסָהּ עַד שֶׁנִּתְחָרֵשׁ — אֵינָהּ אוֹכֶלֶת בִּתְרוּמָה. כְּנָסָהּ וְאח"כ נִתְחָרֵשׁ — אוֹכֶלֶת, מֵת וְנָפְלָה לִפְנֵי יָבָם חֵרֵשׁ — אוֹכֶלֶת. וּמַאי "בְּזוֹ" דְּאִילּוּ בַּעַל חֵרֵשׁ מֵעִיקָּרָא — לֹא אוֹכֶלֶת, וְאִילּוּ יָבָם חֵרֵשׁ מֵעִיקָּרָא — אָכְלָה. וְאִיכָּא דְּאָמְרִי: מִן הָאֵירוּסִין — ד"ה לָא אָכְלָה, דְּהָא לָא אָכְלָה בְּחַיֵּי בַּעַל. כִּי פְּלִיגִי — מִן הַנִּשּׂוּאִין. רַב אָמַר: [ב]אוֹכֶלֶת, דְּהָא הֲוַת אָכְלָה מֵעִיקָּרָא. וּשְׁמוּאֵל אָמַר: אֵינָהּ אוֹכֶלֶת, כִּי רַבֵּי רַחֲמָנָא בִּיאַת שׁוֹגֵג כְּמֵזִיד — לַדְּבָרִים הָאֲמוּרִים בַּפָּרָשָׁה, אֲבָל לְכָל מִילֵּי — לָא. וְהָאָמַר רַב נַחְמָן אָמַר שְׁמוּאֵל: כָּל שֶׁהַבַּעַל מַאֲכִיל — יָבָם מַאֲכִיל! אֵימָא: כָּל בִּיאָה שֶׁהַבַּעַל מַאֲכִיל בָּהּ — יָבָם מַאֲכִיל בָּהּ — וְכָל בִּיאָה שֶׁאֵין הַבַּעַל מַאֲכִיל בָּהּ — אֵין הַיָּבָם מַאֲכִיל בָּהּ. מֵיתִיבֵי [ג]בַּת יִשְׂרָאֵל פִּקַּחַת שֶׁנִּתְאָרְסָה לְכֹהֵן פִּקֵּחַ, וְלֹא הִסְפִּיק לְכוֹנְסָהּ עַד שֶׁנִּתְחָרֵשׁ — אֵינָהּ אוֹכֶלֶת. מֵת וְנָפְלָה לִפְנֵי יָבָם חֵרֵשׁ — אוֹכֶלֶת, וּבְזוֹ יָפֶה כֹּחַ יָבָם מִכֹּחַ בַּעַל. בִּשְׁלָמָא לְרַב — מְתָרֵץ [ד]כִּדְתָרֵיץ מֵעִיקָּרָא. אֶלָּא לִשְׁמוּאֵל קַשְׁיָא! קַשְׁיָא.§ ת"ר: בַּת יִשְׂרָאֵל פִּקַּחַת שֶׁנִּתְאָרְסָה לְכֹהֵן פִּקֵּחַ, וְלֹא הִסְפִּיק לְכוֹנְסָהּ עַד שֶׁנִּתְחָרֵשׁ — אֵינָהּ אוֹכֶלֶת, [ה]נוֹלַד לָהּ בֵּן — אוֹכֶלֶת. מֵת הַבֵּן, רַבִּי נָתָן אוֹמֵר: אוֹכֶלֶת, וַחֲכָמִים אוֹמְרִים: אֵינָהּ אוֹכֶלֶת. מַאי טַעְמָא דְּרַבִּי נָתָן? אָמַר רַבָּה: הוֹאִיל שֶׁכְּבָר אָכְלָה. א"ל אַבַּיֵי: אֶלָּא מֵעַתָּה בַּת יִשְׂרָאֵל שֶׁנִּיסֵּת לְכֹהֵן וּמִית לֵיהּ — תֵּיכוּל, שֶׁכְּבָר אָכְלָה! אֶלָּא, כֵּיוָן דְּמִית לֵיהּ פָּקַע לֵיהּ קְדוּשָּׁתֵיהּ מִינַּהּ — הָכָא נַמִי, כֵּיוָן דְּמִית לֵיהּ פָּקַע קְדוּשָּׁתֵיהּ מִינַּהּ! אֶלָּא אֲמַר רַב יוֹסֵף: קָסָבַר ר' נָתָן נִשּׂוּאֵי חֵרֵשׁ מַאֲכִילִין בִּתְרוּמָה, וְלָא גָּזְרִינַן נִשּׂוּאֵי חֵרֵשׁ אַטּוּ קִדּוּשֵׁי חֵרֵשׁ. א"ל אַבַּיֵי: אִי הָכִי, נוֹלַד לָהּ בֵּן לָמָּה לִי! מִשּׁוּם רַבָּנַן. וְלִיפְלוֹג רַבִּי נָתָן עֲלַיְיהוּ בְּרֵישָׁא — שָׁבֵיק לְהוּ לְרַבָּנַן עַד דִּמְסַיְּימִי מִילְּתַיְיהוּ, וַהֲדַר פָּלֵיג עֲלַיְיהוּ. אִי הָכִי לִיתְנֵי: מֵת הַבֵּן אֵינָהּ אוֹכֶלֶת, רַבִּי נָתָן אוֹמֵר: אוֹכֶלֶת! קַשְׁיָא.§ "וְכֵן הַבָּא עַל אַחַת מִכָּל הָעֲרָיוֹת".§ *אֲמַר רַב עַמְרָם: הָא מִלְּתָא אֲמַר לָן רַב שֵׁשֶׁת, וְאַנְהָרִינְהוּ

רש"י

מִכָּאן וְאֵילָךְ. מֵהַכְנָסַת עֲטָרָה וּלְמַטָּה אֵינוֹ אֶלָּא נְשִׁיקָה, וּפָטוּר, וּמִדְּפָטַר בִּנְשִׁיקָה — וַדַּאי פָּלֵיג אַדִּשְׁמוּאֵל, דִּנְשִׁיקָה קָרֵי לָהּ הַעֲרָאָה, וְהַעֲרָאָה רַבִּינַן לָהּ לְחִיּוּבֵי. קָנָה לַכֹּל. בְּאֶחָד מִן הַבִּיאוֹת גְּרוּעוֹת הַלָּלוּ קָנָה לָהּ לְכָל דָּבָר, וְאוֹכֶלֶת בִּתְרוּמָה מִיַּד אִם כֹּהֵן הוּא, אֲפִי' הָלַךְ לִמְדִינַת הַיָּם וְלֹא בָּא עָלֶיהָ בִּיאָה גְּמוּרָה. הָאֲמוּרִים בַּפָּרָשָׁה. בְּפָרָשַׁת יְבָמִים, שֶׁכָּתַב בָּהּ מִקְרָא זֶה "יְבָמָהּ יָבֹא עָלֶיהָ", דְּדָרְשִׁינַן לֵיהּ: בֵּין בְּשׁוֹגֵג בֵּין בְּמֵזִיד בֵּין בְּאוֹנֶס בֵּין בְּרָצוֹן. לִירַשׁ. דִּכְתִיב "יָקוּם עַל שֵׁם אָחִיו" (דברים כה). וּלְפוֹטְרָהּ מִיִּבּוּם. דְּאִם מֵת וְלוֹ בָּנִים מֵאִשָּׁה אַחֶרֶת מוּתֶּרֶת לַשּׁוּק, אוֹ אִם הוֹצִיאָהּ בְּגֵט לֹא בָּעְיָא חֲלִיצָה, אוֹ אִם הָיְתָה לָהּ צָרָה נִפְטְרָה בְּבִיאָתוֹ שֶׁל זוֹ. מִן הַנִּשּׂוּאִין. הֵיכָא דְּנָפְלָה לְפָנָיו מִן הַנִּשּׂוּאִין שֶׁכְּבָר הָיְתָה אוֹכֶלֶת בִּימֵי אָחִיו, וּכְשֶׁמֵּת וּבָטַל קִנְיָנוֹ פָּסְקָה מִלֶּאֱכוֹל. דְּכ"ע לָא פְּלִיגֵי דְּקַנְיָא לָהּ הָךְ בִּיאָה גְּרוּעָה לְהַאֲכִילָהּ. לְאוֹקְמֵיהּ בִּמְקוֹם בַּעַל. שֶׁאִם הָיְתָה אוֹכֶלֶת בְּחַיָּיו תֹּאכַל בִּשְׁבִיל זֶה. אֲבָל לְאַלּוּמֵי מִבַּעַל, דִּבְחַיֵּי הַבַּעַל לֹא הָיְתָה אוֹכֶלֶת, דְּאֵין הָאִשָּׁה אוֹכֶלֶת בִּתְרוּמָה עַד שֶׁתִּכָּנֵס לַחוּפָּה, הַאי נַמִי לָא אַלִּים מִינֵּיהּ. וְדַוְקָא בְּבִיאָה בְּלֹא דַּעַת קִנְיָן, אֲבָל בְּבִיאָה גְּמוּרָה — אִשְׁתּוֹ גְּמוּרָה הִיא, וְאוֹכֶלֶת אֲפִי' לִשְׁמוּאֵל. אֵין הַיָּבָם מַאֲכִיל. בְּבִיאָה גְּרוּעָה. אֵינָהּ אוֹכֶלֶת. (דְּהָךְ חוּפָּה לָאו חוּפָּה הִיא), דְּגָזְרִינַן נִשּׂוּאֵי חֵרֵשׁ אַטּוּ קִידּוּשֵׁי חֵרֵשׁ, כִּדְאָמְרִינַן לְקַמָּן. מֵת. חֵרֵשׁ זֶה לְאַחַר שֶׁכְּנָסָהּ, וְנָפְלָה לִפְנֵי יָבָם חֵרֵשׁ. אוֹכֶלֶת. דְּלָא גָּרְעָה בִּיאַת חֵרֵשׁ מִבִּיאַת שׁוֹגֵג וּזְנוּת וְאוֹנֶס שֶׁאֵין מִתְכַּוֵּין לִקְנוֹת, וְרַבְּיָהּ רַחֲמָנָא לְגַבֵּי יָבָם. לִשְׁמוּאֵל קַשְׁיָא. דְּהָא לָא הֲוָה אָכְלָה מֵעִיקָּרָא, וְקָאָכְלָה הַשְׁתָּא. אֵימָא כְּנָסָהּ וְאח"כ נִתְחָרֵשׁ אוֹכֶלֶת. מֵת אַחַר שֶׁכְּנָסָהּ וְנִתְחָרֵשׁ וְנָפְלָה כו' — אוֹכֶלֶת, דְּהָא אָכְלָה מֵעִיקָּרָא. וּמַאי בְּזוֹ. יָפֶה כֹּחוֹ, וּמַאי יִיפּוּי כֹּחַ אִיכָּא? הָא בַּעַל נַמִי חֵרֵשׁ הוּא, וּמַאֲכִילָהּ. חֵרֵשׁ מֵעִיקָּרָא. קוֹדֶם שֶׁכְּנָסָהּ. דְּהָא אָכְלָה מֵעִיקָּרָא. וְהַשְׁתָּא הָדְרָא בְּהַךְ בִּיאָה, דְּהָא רַחֲמָנָא רַבְּיָהּ. כָּל בִּיאָה שֶׁהַבַּעַל מַאֲכִיל. כְּגוֹן בִּיאַת חוּפָּה. בִּשְׁלָמָא לְרַב. אע"ג דְּהָא מַתְנִי' פְּרִיכָא לֵיהּ, דְּקָתָנֵי אָכְלָה וְאע"ג דְּלָא אָכְלָה מֵעִיקָּרָא, וְהָוְיָא כְּנוֹפֶלֶת מִן הָאֵירוּסִין, דַּאֲמַרַן לָא אָכְלָה אֲפִי' לְרַב. מְתָרֵץ לָהּ כִּדְמְתָרְצִינַן מֵעִיקָּרָא. אַלִּיבָּא דִּשְׁמוּאֵל, חַסּוּרֵי מִחַסְּרָא וְהָכִי קָתָנֵי: כְּנָסָהּ וְאח"כ נִתְחָרֵשׁ — אוֹכֶלֶת, מֵת וְנָפְלָה לִפְנֵי יָבָם חֵרֵשׁ — אוֹכֶלֶת, דְּהָא אָכְלָה מֵעִיקָּרָא. אֶלָּא לִשְׁמוּאֵל. דַּאֲפִי' הָאוֹכֶלֶת בְּחַיֵּי בַּעְלָהּ אֵינָהּ אוֹכֶלֶת בִּשְׁבִיל הַיָּבָם, בְּבִיאָה גְּרוּעָה. קַשְׁיָא. דְּהָא בִּיאַת חֵרֵשׁ כְּבִיאַת שׁוֹגֵג וְאוֹנֶס הִיא, בְּלֹא כַּוָּונַת קִנְיָן, וְאָכְלָה. נוֹלַד לָהּ בֵּן אוֹכֶלֶת. בִּשְׁבִיל בְּנָהּ, כִּדְכְתִיב "וִילִיד בֵּיתוֹ הֵם יֹאכְלוּ בְלַחְמוֹ" (ויקרא כב) קְרֵי בֵּיהּ: "יַאֲכִילוּ". מֵת הַבֵּן. וְהָאָב קַיָּים. ר' נָתָן אוֹמֵר אוֹכֶלֶת. בִּשְׁבִיל בַּעְלָהּ. וּמִית לֵיהּ. בְּלֹא בֵּן. קָסָבַר ר' נָתָן נִשּׂוּאֵי חֵרֵשׁ. דְּקִדְּשָׁהּ כְּשֶׁהוּא פִּקֵּחַ מַאֲכִילִין בִּתְרוּמָה, דְּמִדְּאוֹרַיְיתָא מִשְּׁעַת אֵירוּסִין אוֹכֶלֶת, דִּכְתִיב (שם) "וְכֹהֵן כִּי יִקְנֶה נֶפֶשׁ קִנְיַן כַּסְפּוֹ הוּא יֹאכַל בּוֹ" מִיָּד, וְרַבָּנַן הוּא דִּגְזָרֵי עַד שֶׁתִּכָּנֵס לַחוּפָּה, מִשּׁוּם גְּזֵירָה, שֶׁמָּא יִמְזְגוּ לָהּ כּוֹס בְּבֵית אָבִיהָ וְתַשְׁקֶה לְאָחִיהָ וְלַאֲחוֹתָהּ, כִּדְאָמְרִינַן בִּכְתוּבּוֹת בְּאע"פ (דף נז:). הִלְכָּךְ, כֵּיוָן דְּהַאי בִּשְׁעַת קִנְיָן הֲוֵי בֶּן דַּעַת, וְהַשְׁתָּא הִכְנִיסָהּ לַחוּפָּה, וְלֵיכָּא לְמִיגְזַר *שֶׁמָּא תַּשְׁקֶה — אָכְלָה. אֲבָל לָא גָּזְרִינַן נִשּׂוּאֵי חֵרֵשׁ אַטּוּ קִידּוּשֵׁי חֵרֵשׁ, דְּלָאו בַּר קִנְיָן הוּא. וְרַבָּנַן דְּאָסְרֵי גָּזְרֵי נִשּׂוּאֵי חֵרֵשׁ דַּהֲוֵי בֶּן דַּעַת בִּשְׁעַת קִידּוּשִׁין אַטּוּ הֵיכָא דְּקִדְּשָׁהּ כְּשֶׁהוּא חֵרֵשׁ, דְּקִנְיָנוֹ לָאו קִנְיָן. נוֹלַד לָהּ בֵּן לָמָּה לִי. בְּלֹא בֵּן נַמִי אָכְלָה לְרַבִּי נָתָן. מִשּׁוּם רַבָּנַן. לְאַשְׁמוּעִינַן הֵיכָא דְּנוֹלַד לָהּ בֵּן מוֹדוּ. וַהֲדַר פָּלֵיג עֲלַיְיהוּ. וְאוֹכֶלֶת דְּקָאָמַר רַבִּי נָתָן — אַכּוּלָּהּ מִילְּתָא קָאֵי, בֵּין אַרֵישָׁא קוֹדֶם שֶׁנּוֹלַד לָהּ בֵּן, דְּקָאָמְרֵי רַבָּנַן אֵינָהּ אוֹכֶלֶת, בֵּין אַסֵּיפָא דְּמֵת הַבֵּן. אִי הָכִי. דְּרַבִּי נָתָן אַרֵישָׁא נַמִי פָּלֵיג, וּמְנַטַּר הוּא דְּנָטַר לְרַבָּנַן עַד סִיּוּמָא. לִיתְנֵי מֵת הַבֵּן אֵינָהּ אוֹכֶלֶת רַבִּי נָתָן אוֹמֵר אוֹכֶלֶת. דְּתֶיהֱוֵי כּוּלָּהּ מִילְּתָא דְּרַבָּנַן בַּחֲדָא, וַהֲדַר לִיפְלוֹג רַבִּי נָתָן אַכּוּלָּהּ. אֲבָל הַשְׁתָּא — לֵיכָּא לְמֵימַר דְּנָטַר לְהוּ אַסִּיּוּמָא, וּבְמֵת הַבֵּן לְחוּדָא פָּלֵיג. וְאַנְהָרִינְהוּ

תוספות

לדברים האמורים. אע"ג דכל שאר דברים כתובים נמי בפרשה, כדדרשינן: כיון שלקחה – נעשית כאשתו לכל דבר – כיון דביאת שוגג לא קני בעלמא סברא הוא דלא רבייה אלא לדברים המפורשים בפרשה בהדיא, כגון לירש בנכסי אחיו, דכתיב "יקום על שם אחיו" לנחלה, ולפטור אשת אחיו מן היבום, דכתיב "לו לאשה" ולא לאחיו לאשה, דפקע מינה זיקת אחיו, ולפטור צרתה, דכתיב "בית אחיו" – בית אחד הוא בונה ואינו בונה שני בתים, דהנהו דברים הוו לאוקמיה במקום בעל. אבל בתרומה לא אכלה ע"י ביאה גרועה, ולא יורשה, ולא מיטמא לה, ולא מיפר נדריה, דהיינו לאלומי מבעל. אבל מן הנשואין – זכאי בכולהו, דלא הוי אלא לאוקמיה במקום בעל, דילפינן מהני דכתיבי, ולא פליגי אלא בביאת שוגג וכיוצא בה. אבל בהעראה דקניא נמי בעלמא, וביאה היא לכל דבר – לא פליגי בה. א)ומה שקבע מחלוקתן כאן אמתני' דאחד הגומר ואחד המערה – לאו משום דעלה פליגי, אלא משום דמסיים בה "קנה", דקאי נמי אביאת שוגג. כן נראה לר"י. ובירושלמי איכא פלוגתייהו. ואיכא דמוקי פלוגתייהו בהעראה.

מן הנשואין כ"ע לא פליגי דאכלה. ע"י ביאה. וה"ה דהוה מצי למינקט לענין ליורשה, ולהטמא לה, ולהפר נדריה. אלא נקט אכילת תרומה לרבותא, וכ"ש לשאר דברים. דזימנין שהיא כאשתו לכל דבר ולא אכלה בתרומה, כדאמר בכתובות בפ' "נערה" (דף מח: ושם): מסורה לכל חוץ לתרומה, גבי מסר האב לשלוחי הבעל. [וע' היטב תוס' סוטה כד: ד"ה דהאמר רב].

מת ונפלה לפני יבם חרש אוכלת. וא"ת: ואמאי אוכלת? וניחוש לסימפון, שהרי לא בדקה, שלא הספיק לכונסה עד שנתחרש, וא"כ אינה זקוקה לו! ולקמן נמי דקאמר דגזרינן נישואין דחרש אטו קידושין – תיפוק ליה משום סימפון, ולר' נתן נמי אמאי אוכלת! ואור"י דלא חיישינן לסימפון אלא כשיכול הדבר להתגלות שיש סימפון ויהיו קידושי טעות. אבל הכא, דנתחרש, לא חיישינן שמא יתפקח וימצא סימפון.

כל ביאה שהבעל מאכיל בה. אי (א) ביאה אירוסין עושה – אר"י דכל ביאה שהבעל מאכיל בה, ע"י חופה שאחריה קאמר.

*)**ממזרת** ונתינה לישראל פסלה. לשון פסלה נקט משום אחריני, דממזרת ונתינה הם פסולות ועומדות.

מאי

*) שייך למתני' לעיל נג:

עין משפט נר מצוה

כח א ב מיי' פ"ח מהל' תרומות הל' ו:
כט ג מיי' שם הל' ט:
ל ד ה מיי' שם הל' י:

מסורת הש"ס

[לקמן נח:] סוטה כד:

כמ"ס אין

[לעיל לה.]

ס"א שמא תשקה ותאכל ולא גזרינן

הגהות הב"ח

(א) תוס' ד"ה כל וכו' אי ביאה. נ"ב בפ"ק דקדושין דף י ע"א קא מיבעיא ליה ביאה אי נישואין עושה אי אירוסין עושה וע"ש:

תוספות ישנים

לה שלא כדרכה. ואין להקשות ומי גרע מקינא לה סתם דודאי גרע דגלי בדעתיה שאינו חושדה אלא בשלא כדרכה ומ"מ פריך משכבי אשה כתיב וא"כ קנוי גמור הוא: **לדברים** האמורים בפרשה. ואע"ג דבפרשה משמע דהויא כאשתו לכל דבר דאמרינן כיון שלקחה נעשית כאשתו לכל דבר מ"מ לא שמעינן מהתם ביאת שוגג ואונס (הא) [רק מיירי] בביאה גמורה אבל ביאת שוגג ואונס לא הוי כאשתו לכל דבר אלא לדברים האמורים בהדיא בפרשה: **מן** הנשואין דברי הכל אכלה ע"י ביאת שוגג דבלא ביאה לא דאמרינן ולא היבמה עד שתבעל: **לאלומי** מבעל לא. וה"ה דהוה מצי למימר דאיכא בינייהו ליורשה וליטמא לה דלשמואל כיון דלא אלימא מבעל לא ירית לה ולא מיטמא כמו בעל גופיה באשתו ארוסה: **א)** ובירושלמי לא משמע כן וז"ל הירושלמי קנה ולא חילק בין ביאה לביאה מאי קנה שמואל אמר לא קנה לכל אלא לדברים האמורים בפרשה לירש בנכסי המת ולהתיר צרתה לשוק ור' יוחנן אומר קנה לכל. א"ר יצחק ב"ר אליעזר פליגין בשמערה בה אבל אם גמר הביאה כ"ע מודו וא"כ משמע דרב ושמואל דהכא קיימי אהעראה וניחא שסתם התלמוד פלוגתייהו דרב ושמואל אחר מתני' אחד המערה ואחד הגומר קנה דעלה קיימי כן פירש רבינו נתנאל אך התוספות לא פירשו כן. ופירשו דקיימי אביאת שוגג וראיה לדבריהם דקאמר בסמוך כי רבי רחמנא ביאת שוגג כמזיד וכו' משמע דבביאת שוגג איירי אבל בהעראה לא פליגי דביאה היא לכל דבר וקניא נמי בעלמא ואע"פ שקבע כאן מחלוקתן על משנה אחד המערה ואחד הגומר לאו משום דקאי עלה אלא משום דמסיים קנה דקאי נמי אשוגג כ"כ לר' שנ"ז: **ולא** הספיק לכונסה עד שנתחרש. לקמן מפרש טעמא דגזרינן נשואי חרש אטו קדושי חרש וא"ת בלא האי טעמא לא תאכל משום סמפון דשמא יש בה מום וקדושי טעות הוו דלא ידע לבודקה הבעל לפי שלא הספיק לכונסה עד שנתחרש וי"ל טעמא מאי קדושי טעות הוו כשנמצא בה מום משום דאימר אם היה יודע שכן הוא לא היה מקדשה וזה החרש לא היה לו דעת להקפיד בדבר ולא חיישינן שמא יתפקח וימצא סמפון: **נשואי** חרש מאכילין בתרומה. דלא איכא משום סמפון כיון דהוה בר דעת כשקדשה ולשמא ימזגו ליכא דאינה בבית אביה ואטו קדושי חרש לא גזר רבי נתן: **הבא** על אחת מכל העריות האמורות בתורה או פסולות ודוקא הני אבל ביאת זנות דפנויה לא פסיל לה לכהן ולא משויא לה זונה דלית דסבר פנוי הבא על הפנויה שלא לשם אישות עשאה זונה אלא לר' אלעזר ולא קי"ל כוותיה: **ממזרת** ונתינה לישראל פסל לאו לפוסלה לכהונה מיירי דבלא"ה אפסלא וקיימא ולתרומה דבי נשא ליכא למימר דאינה בת כהן אלא ר"ל לענין מלקות למלקי הבא עליה אם בעל בהעראה

תוספות חד מקמאי

רב אמר קנה לכל ושמואל אמר לא קנה אלא לדברים האמורים בפרשה אבל להאכילה בתרומה לא קנה באונס ובשוגג. והלכתא כרב ודוקא באונס ובשוגג דה"ל כביאה אבל בלא ביאה לא אכלה מן הנשואין אע"פ שכבר אכלה בחיי בעלה. ושמעינן מהא דהא דתנן בפ' אע"פ ובפ' אלמנה לכ"ג היבם אינו מאכיל בתרומה אע"פ שכבר אכלה בחיי בעלה ולאפוקי (מהמ"פ תוין) [מהמפרשים] שפרשוה כשלא אכלה בחיי הבעל אבל אם אכלה בחיי הבעל אוכלת שומרת יבם בתרומה. ת"ר בת ישראל פקחת שנתארסה לכהן פקח ולא הספיק לכונסה עד שנתחרש אינה אוכלת מת ונפלה לפני יבם חרש אינה אוכלת כנסה הבעל ואח"כ נתחרש אוכלת מת ונפלה לפני

וַאֲנְהֲרִינְהוּ לְעַיְינִין מִמַּתְנִיתִין: [א]אֵשֶׁת יִשְׂרָאֵל שֶׁנֶּאֶנְסָה, אע"פ שֶׁמּוּתֶּרֶת לְבַעֲלָהּ – פְּסוּלָה לִכְהוּנָּה. וְתַנָּא תּוּנָא: וְכֵן הַבָּא עַל אַחַת מִכָּל הָעֲרָיוֹת הָאֲמוּרוֹת בַּתּוֹרָה, אוֹ פְּסוּלוֹת. מַאי "וְכֵן"? מַאי לָאו: לָא שְׁנָא בְּשׁוֹגֵג וְלָא שְׁנָא בְּמֵזִיד וְלָא שְׁנָא בְּאוֹנֶס וְלָא שְׁנָא בְּרָצוֹן. וְקָתָנֵי "פְּסָלָהּ". לָא, מַאי "וְכֵן" – אַהַעֲרָאָה. הַעֲרָאָה דְּמַאן? אִילֵימָא דַּעֲרָיוֹת – לְמֵימְרָא דַּעֲרָיוֹת יָלְפִי' מִיבָמָה? אַדְּרַבָּה, יְבָמָה יָלְפִינַן מֵעֲרָיוֹת, דְּעִיקַּר הָעֲרָאָה בַּעֲרָיוֹת כְּתִיב! אֶלָּא מַאי "וְכֵן" – אַשֶּׁלֹּא כְּדַרְכָּהּ דַּעֲרָיוֹת – אַדְּרַבָּה, עִיקַּר "מִשְׁכְּבֵי אִשָּׁה" בַּעֲרָיוֹת כְּתִיב? אֶלָּא מַאי "וְכֵן" אַשֶּׁלֹּא כְּדַרְכָּהּ דְּחַיָּיבֵי לָאוִין. אָמַר *רָבָא: אֵשֶׁת כֹּהֵן שֶׁנֶּאֶנְסָה – בַּעֲלָהּ לוֹקֶה עָלֶיהָ מִשּׁוּם זוֹנָה. מִשּׁוּם זוֹנָה – אִין, מִשּׁוּם טוּמְאָה – לָא? אֵימָא: אַף מִשּׁוּם זוֹנָה. מְתִיב רַבִּי זֵירָא: °"וְהִיא לֹא נִתְפָּשָׂה" – אֲסוּרָה, *הָא נִתְפְּשָׂה – מוּתֶּרֶת. וְיֵשׁ לְךָ אַחֶרֶת שֶׁאע"פ שֶׁנִּתְפְּשָׂה אֲסוּרָה, וְאֵי זוֹ – זוֹ אֵשֶׁת כֹּהֵן, וְלָאו *הַבָּא מִכְּלַל עֲשֵׂה – עֲשֵׂה! אָמַר רַבָּה: הַכֹּל הָיוּ בִּכְלַל זוֹנָה, כְּשֶׁפָּרַט לְךָ הַכָּתוּב גַּבֵּי אֵשֶׁת יִשְׂרָאֵל "וְהִיא לֹא נִתְפָּשָׂה" אֲסוּרָה, הָא נִתְפְּשָׂה – מוּתֶּרֶת, מִכְּלָל דְּאֵשֶׁת כֹּהֵן – כִּדְקַיְימָא קַיְימָא. וְאִיכָּא דְּאָמְרִי, אָמַר רַבָּה: [ב]אֵשֶׁת כֹּהֵן שֶׁנֶּאֶנְסָה – בַּעֲלָהּ לוֹקֶה עָלֶיהָ מִשּׁוּם טוּמְאָה. מִשּׁוּם טוּמְאָה – אִין, מִשּׁוּם זוֹנָה – לָא, אַלְמָא: בְּאוֹנֶס לָא קָרֵינָא בֵּיהּ זוֹנָה, מְתִיב רַבִּי זֵירָא: "וְהִיא לֹא נִתְפָּשָׂה" – אֲסוּרָה, [ג]הָא נִתְפְּשָׂה – מוּתֶּרֶת, [ד]וְיֵשׁ לְךָ אַחֶרֶת שֶׁאַף עַל פִּי שֶׁנִּתְפְּשָׂה אֲסוּרָה, וְאֵיזוֹ זוֹ – אֵשֶׁת כֹּהֵן, וְלָאו הַבָּא מִכְּלַל עֲשֵׂה – עֲשֵׂה! אָמַר(א) רָבָא: [ה]הַכֹּל הָיוּ בִּכְלַל °"אַחֲרֵי אֲשֶׁר הֻטַּמָּאָה", כְּשֶׁפָּרַט לְךָ הַכָּתוּב גַּבֵּי אֵשֶׁת יִשְׂרָאֵל "וְהִיא לֹא נִתְפָּשָׂה" אֲסוּרָה" הָא נִתְפְּשָׂה – מוּתֶּרֶת, מִכְּלָל דְּאֵשֶׁת כֹּהֵן כִּדְקַיְימָא קַיְימָא.§ **מתני'** [ו]אַלְמָנָה לְכֹהֵן גָּדוֹל, גְּרוּשָׁה וַחֲלוּצָה לְכֹהֵן הֶדְיוֹט מִן הָאֵירוּסִין – לֹא יֹאכְלוּ בִּתְרוּמָה, *רַבִּי אֶלְעָזָר וְרַבִּי שִׁמְעוֹן מַכְשִׁירִין. *נִתְאַרְמְלוּ אוֹ נִתְגָּרְשׁוּ, מִן הַנִּשּׂוּאִין – פְּסוּלוֹת, מִן הָאֵירוּסִין – כְּשֵׁרוֹת.§ **גמ'** תַּנְיָא, אָמַר ר"מ: ק"ו, וּמַה קִּדּוּשֵׁי רְשׁוּת – אֵין מַאֲכִילִין, קִדּוּשֵׁי עֲבֵירָה – לֹא כ"ש?! אָמְרוּ לוֹ: לֹא, אִם אָמַרְתָּ בְּקִידּוּשֵׁי רְשׁוּת – שֶׁכֵּן אֵין לוֹ לְהַאֲכִיל בְּמָקוֹם אַחֵר, תֹּאמַר בְּקִדּוּשֵׁי עֲבֵירָה – שֶׁכֵּן יֵשׁ לוֹ לְהַאֲכִיל בְּמָקוֹם אַחֵר. א"ר אֶלְעָזָר א"ר אוֹשַׁעְיָא: פְּצוּעַ דַּכָּא כֹּהֵן שֶׁקִּדֵּשׁ בַּת יִשְׂרָאֵל – בָּאנוּ לְמַחֲלוֹקֶת ר"מ וְרַבִּי אֶלְעָזָר וְר"ש. לְר"מ דְּאָמַר מִשְׁתַּמֶּרֶת לְבִיאָה פְּסוּלָה דְּאוֹרַיְיתָא לָא אָכְלָה – [ז]הָא נַמִּי לָא אָכְלָה, לְרַ' אֶלְעָזָר וְרַ' שִׁמְעוֹן דְּאָמְרִי מִשְׁתַּמֶּרֶת לְבִיאָה פְּסוּלָה דְּאוֹרַיְיתָא אָכְלָה

הָא

רש"י

וַאֲנְהֲרִינְהוּ לְעַיְינִין מִמַּתְנִיתִין. מִמִּשְׁנָתֵנוּ הֵבִיא רְאָיָה לִדְבָרָיו, וְהֵאִיר עֵינָיו בָּהּ. **אע"פ** שֶׁמּוּתֶּרֶת לְבַעְלָהּ. דִּכְתִיב (במדבר ה) "וְהִיא לֹא נִתְפָּשָׂה" – אֲסוּרָה, הָא נִתְפְּשָׂה – מוּתֶּרֶת. פְּסוּלָה לִכְהוּנָּה. אִם מֵת בַּעְלָהּ, לֹא תִּנָּשֵׂא לְכֹהֵן. **וְתַנָּא תּוּנָא.** תַּנָּא דִּידַן, כְּמוֹ: אֲבוּנָא, אֲחוּנָא. **מַאי וְכֵן.** לָאו אַאוֹנֶס וְאַשּׁוֹגֵג דִּלְעֵיל קָאֵי, וְקָתָנֵי: הַבָּא עַל אַחַת מִכָּל הָעֲרָיוֹת פְּסָלָהּ לִכְהוּנָּה, וְאֵשֶׁת אִישׁ בִּכְלַל עֲרָיוֹת הִיא. **לָא אַהַעֲרָאָה.** וּבְרָצוֹן, דְּהָוְיָא זוֹנָה: וּפָרְכִינַן עִיקַּר הָעֲרָאָה בַּעֲרָיוֹת **כְּתִיבָא.** וְהֵיכִי מְדַמֶּה לָהּ מַתְנִי' לִיבָמָה, כְּאִילּוּ מִיבָמָה גָּמַר לָהּ? **אַשֶּׁלֹּא כְּדַרְכָּהּ.** דְּקָתָנֵי גַּבֵּי יְבָמָה: וְלֹא חִילֵּק בֵּין בִּיאָה לְבִיאָה – דְּהַיְינוּ בֵּין כְּדַרְכָּהּ לְשֶׁלֹּא כְּדַרְכָּהּ, וַעֲלָהּ תָּנֵי: וְכֵן הַבָּא עַל אַחַת מִכָּל הָעֲרָיוֹת פְּסָלָהּ לִכְהוּנָּה מִשּׁוּם זוֹנָה. וּלְעוֹלָם בְּרָצוֹן, וְגָמַר "בִּיאָה" "בִּיאָה" מִיבָמָה, דְּרַבִּינַן בָּהּ "וּלְקָחָהּ" – שֶׁלֹּא כְּדַרְכָּהּ: ה"ג. **אֶלָּא מַאי וְכֵן אַשֶּׁלֹּא כְּדַרְכָּהּ דְּחַיָּיבֵי לָאוִין.** אַלְמָנָה לְכ"ג, גְּרוּשָׁה וַחֲלוּצָה לְכֹהֵן הֶדְיוֹט, דְּלָא כְּתִיב בְּהוּ "מִשְׁכְּבֵי אִשָּׁה". אֲבָל מִשּׁוּם הַעֲרָאָה לָא אִיצְטְרִיךְ לְמִיתְנְיֵיהּ, דְּהָא רַבִּינַן לְעֵיל הַעֲרָאָה דְּחַיָּיבֵי לָאוִין מִ"קִּיחָה" "קִיחָה" דַּעֲרָיוֹת. **בַּעְלָהּ לוֹקֶה עָלֶיהָ מִשּׁוּם זוֹנָה.** דִּכְתִיב "זוֹנָה לֹא יִקָּחוּ" (ויקרא כא), וּסְתָם זוֹנָה הַיְינוּ מְנָאֶפֶת תַּחַת בַּעְלָהּ, שֶׁטָּעֲתָה מֵאַחַר בַּעְלָהּ לְזָרִים. וְזוֹ, אע"ג דְּנֶאֶנְסָה, גַּבֵּי כֹּהֵן לָא פָּלֵיג רַחֲמָנָא בֵּין אוֹנֶס בֵּין רָצוֹן, כִּדְגָמְרִי' מִ"וְהִיא לֹא נִתְפָּשָׂה", דְּ"הִיא" מִיעוּטָא מַשְׁמַע: "הִיא" אֵשֶׁת יִשְׂרָאֵל – הוּא דְּיֵשׁ חִילּוּק בֵּין נִתְפְּשָׂה לְלֹא נִתְפְּשָׂה, אֲבָל אֵשֶׁת כֹּהֵן אֵין חִילּוּק. **מִשּׁוּם טוּמְאָה לָא.** בִּתְמִיָּה. הָא אָמְרִי' בְּפ"ק (דף יא:), הָא מָה אֲנִי מְקַיֵּים "אַחֲרֵי אֲשֶׁר הוּטַּמָּאָה" – לְרַבּוֹת סוֹטָה שֶׁנִּבְעֲלָה, דִּכְתִיב "לֹא יוּכַל בַּעְלָהּ" (דברים כד). **הַכֹּל הָיוּ בִּכְלַל זוֹנָה.** כָּל הַנִּבְעָלוֹת תַּחַת בַּעֲלֵיהֶן, בֵּין בְּאוֹנֶס בֵּין בְּרָצוֹן, בִּכְלַל "זוֹנָה לֹא יִקָּחוּ" הֵן, שֶׁהֲרֵי כּוּלָּן נִבְעֲלוּ בְּעִילַת זְנוּת, וְהוֹצִיא לְךָ הַכָּתוּב אֵשֶׁת יִשְׂרָאֵל אֲנוּסָה מִן הַכְּלָל, אֲבָל אֵשֶׁת כֹּהֵן – כִּדְקַיְימָא קַיְימָא. **מִשּׁוּם טוּמְאָה.** "אַחֲרֵי אֲשֶׁר הוּטַּמָּאָה" – לְרַבּוֹת סוֹטָה שֶׁנִּבְעֲלָה. **מתני' מִן הָאֵירוּסִין לֹא יֹאכְלוּ בִּתְרוּמָה.** מִשָּׁעָה שֶׁנִּתְקַדְּשׁוּ לְאֵלּוּ קִדּוּשֵׁי עֲבֵירָה – נִפְסְלָה מִלֶּאֱכוֹל בִּתְרוּמָה דְּבֵי נָשָׁא, אִם בַּת כֹּהֵן הִיא. **ר' אֶלְעָזָר וְר"ש מַכְשִׁירִין.** עַד שֶׁתִּבָּעֵל לוֹ וְתֵעָשֶׂה חֲלָלָה, כִּדְכְתִיב "לֹא יְחַלֵּל" – שְׁנֵי חִלּוּלִין, אֶחָד לָהּ וְאֶחָד לְזַרְעָהּ. **נִתְאַרְמְלוּ אוֹ נִתְגָּרְשׁוּ.** מִן הַכֹּהֲנִים הַלָּלוּ. **מִן הַנִּשּׂוּאִין פְּסוּלוֹת.** דְּשַׁוְּיֵיהּ חֲלָלָה בְּבִיאָתוֹ. **מִן הָאֵירוּסִין כְּשֵׁרוֹת.** דַּאֲפִילּוּ ר"מ לָא פָּסֵיל מִן הָאֵירוּסִין אֶלָּא בְּחַיֵּיהֶן, דְּמִשְׁתַּמֶּרֶת לְבִיאָה פְּסוּלָה, אֲבָל מֵתוּ – לֹא. **גמ' מַה קִּידּוּשֵׁי רְשׁוּת.** כְּגוֹן יִשְׂרָאֵל שֶׁקִּידֵּשׁ בַּת כֹּהֵן, שֶׁאֵין קִידּוּשֶׁיהָ עֲבֵירָה. **אֵין מַאֲכִילִין.** כְּלוֹמַר אֵין מַנִּיחִין אוֹתָן לֶאֱכוֹל, דִּתְנַן לְקַמָּן: הָאֵירוּסִין פּוֹסְלִין, בְּפ' אַלְמָנָה לְכה"ג (דף סז:). **תֹּאמַר בְּקִידּוּשֵׁי עֲבֵירָה שֶׁיֵּשׁ לוֹ.** לְכֹהֵן זֶה לְהַאֲכִיל בְּמָקוֹם אַחֵר בִּרְאוּיָה לוֹ. כָּךְ שָׁמַעְתִּי, וְלִבִּי מְגַמְגֵּם. חֲדָא, דְּאֵין זֶה לְשׁוֹן הַשַּׁ"ס, וְהָכִי אִיבַּעְיָא לֵיהּ לְמֵימַר: וּמַה קִּידּוּשֵׁי רְשׁוּת פּוֹסְלִין כו'. וְעוֹד, מִדְּקָאָמַר ר' אוֹשַׁעְיָא פְּצוּעַ דַּכָּא כֹּהֵן שֶׁקִּדֵּשׁ בַּת יִשְׂרָאֵל בָּאנוּ לְמַחֲלוֹקֶת ר"מ ור"א, וְלָא קָתָנֵי פְּצוּעַ דַּכָּא כֹּהֵן שֶׁקִּידֵּשׁ בַּת כֹּהֵן – ש"מ דִּפְלוּגְתָּא דְּמַתְנִי' לָאו בְּבַת כֹּהֵן לְחוֹדָהּ הִיא, דְּא"כ הֵיכִי מָצֵי רַבִּי אוֹשַׁעְיָא לְמֵימַר לְרַבִּי *אֱלִיעֶזֶר וְר' שִׁמְעוֹן אָכְלָה? אֵימַר דְּאָמְרִי ר' אֶלְעָזָר ור"ש בְּבַת כֹּהֵן, בְּבַת יִשְׂרָאֵל מִי אָמְרִי? לָשׁוֹן אַחֵר, וְהוּא עִיקָּר: אַלְמָנָה לְכ"ג גְּרוּשָׁה וַחֲלוּצָה לְכֹהֵן הֶדְיוֹט מִן הָאֵירוּסִין לֹא יֹאכְלוּ בִּתְרוּמָה – בֵּין בְּבַת כֹּהֵן בֵּין בְּבַת יִשְׂרָאֵל קָמַיְירֵי. בְּבַת כֹּהֵן – כְּדְפָרֵישִׁית, בְּבַת יִשְׂרָאֵל וְאַלִּיבָּא דְּמִשְׁנָה רִאשׁוֹנָה, דְּקָאָמַר בִּכְתוּבּוֹת (דף נז.): הִגִּיעַ זְמַן וְלֹא נִישְּׂאוּ – אוֹכְלוֹת מִשֶּׁלּוֹ וְאוֹכְלוֹת בִּתְרוּמָה. וְקָאָמַר ר' מֵאִיר: אַלְמָנָה לְכ"ג, אע"פ דְּקִידּוּשָׁיו קִידּוּשִׁין וְקִנְיַן כַּסְפּוֹ הִיא – לֹא תֹּאכַל בִּתְרוּמָה כִּשְׁאָר הָאֲרוּסוֹת לְכֹהֵן שֶׁאוֹכְלוֹת מִן הַתּוֹרָה. מ"ט – דְּמִשְׁתַּמֶּרֶת לְבִיאַת עֲבֵירָה. וְר' אֶלְעָזָר ור"ש מַכְשִׁירִין, דְּהָא קִנְיַן כַּסְפּוֹ הִיא. וְאִי מִשּׁוּם חֲלָלָה – הֲרֵי כָּל זְמַן שֶׁלֹּא בָּא עָלֶיהָ לֹא נִתְחַלְּלָה. **נִתְאַרְמְלוּ אוֹ נִתְגָּרְשׁוּ.** מִן הַכֹּהֲנִים הַלָּלוּ, מִן הָאֵרוּסִין – כְּשֵׁרוֹת לִינָּשֵׂא לְכֹהֲנִים אִם נִתְאַלְמְנוּ. וְגַבֵּי גְּרוּשָׁה, אִם בַּת כֹּהֵן הִיא – כְּשֵׁרָה לִתְרוּמָה. **מִן הַנִּשּׂוּאִין פְּסוּלָה.** דְּשַׁוְיוּהָ חֲלָלָה. **וּמַה קִּידּוּשֵׁי רְשׁוּת.** יִשְׂרָאֵל שֶׁקִּדֵּשׁ בַּת יִשְׂרָאֵל, אֵין מַאֲכִילָהּ בִּתְרוּמָה. **קִידּוּשֵׁי עֲבֵירָה.** כְּגוֹן אֵלּוּ לְכ"ש. **בְּמָקוֹם אַחֵר.** אֲפִילּוּ נִשֵּׂאת, תֹּאמַר בְּקִדּוּשֵׁי עֲבֵירָה שֶׁיֵּשׁ לוֹ לְהַאֲכִיל בִּרְאוּיָה לוֹ. **פְּצוּעַ דַּכָּא.** מִשְׁתַּמֶּרֶת לְבִיאָה פְּסוּלָה דְּאוֹרַיְיתָא הִיא.

הָא

תוספות

מאי וכן מאי לאו לא שנא בשוגג כו' וקתני פסלה. וליכא למימר משום אחרים נקט פסלה ולא משום אשת איש – דעיקר חידוש דאונס ורצון לא הוי אלא באשת איש. אבל בשאר עריות – אין חידוש טפי באונס מברצון לענין פסולי כהונה(ב). **עיקר** הערוה בעריות כתיב. ואית ספרים דגרסי: אדרבה, יבמה הוא דילפינן מעריות, ויש לפרש בדוחק: דאע"ג דיבמה מחייבי לאוין הוא דילפינן, ולא מעריות – חשיב ליה כאילו ילפינן מעריות, דע"י עריות ושפחה חרופה שמעינן לה בחייבי לאוין. **וכן** אשלא כדרכה דחייבי לאוין. פי' בקונטרס: אלמנה לכ"ג, גרושה וחלוצה לכהן הדיוט. אבל משום העראה – לא איצטריך למיתנייה, דהא מרבינן ליה לעיל מקיחה קיחה דעריות. וקשה לר"י: דאי משום חייבי לאוין דכהונה נקט לה – לשלא כדרכה נמי לא איצטריך, דאיכא למילף נמי קיחה קיחה מעריות, דכתיב בהו "משכבי אשה"! אלא נראה לר"י: דקאי אשאר חייבי לאוין דלאו דכהונה, דלא כתיב בהו קיחה, דלא שמעינן בהו שלא כדרכה אלא מג"ש ד"ביאה" "ביאה" מיבמה, כי היכי דילפינן לעיל מינייהו יבמה לענין העראה. **ואי** זו זו אשת כהן. מ"והיא" קדריש. וא"ת: והא קדרשינן לה בכתובות בפרק "נערה" (דף נא: ושם) לדרשא אחריתי, לתחלתה באונס וסופה ברצון, דשריא! וא"ר"י: דהתם אסמכתא היא, דמסברא היא דשריא, דחשיב אונס, אע"ג דסופה ברצון – דיצרה אלבשה, כי היכי דהוי אסמכתא הא דקאמר (לקמן דף ק:) ואי זו זו שקדושיה טעות.

מן האירוסין לא יאכלו. פי' בקונט' בלשון שני, ונראה לו עיקר, דאיירי בין בבת כהן בין בבת ישראל. דר"מ פסיל אפי' בבת כהן, ור"א ור' שמעון מכשירין אפי' בבת ישראל. ונתארמלו או שנתגרשו מן האירוסין כשרות – ולא שייך כשרות בבת ישראל אלא לינשא לכהונה, דבתרומה לא אכלה. ובנתגרשה לא שייך אפי' לינשא, ויש לפרש בנתגרשה, אם בת כהן היא – כשרה לתרומה. ובגמ' דקאמר מה קדושי רשות אין מאכילים – בישראל שקדש בת ישראל קאמר. וקשה לר"י: דמה ק"ו הוא זה? דכיון דליכא לד כהונה כלל – מאין להם להאכיל לאותם הקידושין? ועוד הקשה ה"ר משה כהן: דהיאך יאכיל בת ישראל בהגעת זמן? דבפסולות לא שייך אוכלות משלו ואוכלות בתרומה, כדאמרי' ב"יש מותרות" (לקמן פה.): "בעמוד והוצא קאי – מזוני אית לה"! א)ונראה דבבת כהן איירי, כדפי' בקונטרס בלשון ראשון. ובגמ' גרים: מה קדושי רשות פוסלין. וכן גירסת ר"ח. וגבי פצוע דכא גרסי' שקדש בת כהן, וכן ר"ח, ולא כמו שכתוב בספרים "שקידש בת ישראל". ולפי שהגירסא היתה כתובה בספר רש"י פי' כן, אבל הגירסא כתובה בספר ר"ח כמו שפירשתי.

והא

עין משפט נר מצוה

לא א מיי' פי"ח מהלכו' איסורי ביאה הל' ח סמג לאוין קכא ועשין מח טוש"ע אה"ע סימן ו סעיף יא:

לב ב מיי' שם הלכה א ז סמג לאוין שם:

לג ג מיי' פכ"ד מהל' אישות הלכה יט:

לד ד מיי' שם הל' כא וסמג שם וטוש"ע שם סעיף י:

לה ה מיי' פי"ח מהל' איסורי ביאה הל' ז סמג שם:

לו ו מיי' פ"ז מהלכות תרומות הלכה כא:

לז ז מיי' שם הלכה יד:

תוספות ישנים

בהעראה לבד: **ומאי** וכן לא שנא בשוגג לא שנא במזיד ובאונס וברצון וקתני פסולות. וא"ת היכי מוכח מהכא דאשת ישראל שנאנסה אסורה לכהן דלמא הא דתני פסל באונס קאי אפסולות לכהונה ולומר שנעשות חללות באונס דע"כ פסול לא קאי אכולה מלתא דמתני' דהא ממזרת ונתינה מפסלי וקיימי וי"ל דהא לאו חדוש הוא לומר דפסולות לכהונה שמתחללות באונס דמה לנו לחלק אכן תימה אמאי לא משני דפסל לא קאי אאשת איש אלא (באשתו נאמן) [נקטיה] לענין התראה (לקנוס) [ללקות וכמו] כדפ"ה גבי ממזרת ונתינה וי"ל דפסיקא ליה דקאי אאשת איש דומיא דשאר עריות דר"ל פסל לכהונה: **אדרבה** יבמה ילפינן מעריות דעיקר העראה (ביבמה) [בעריות] כתיבא. ואע"ג דיבמה ילפינן לעיל מביאה ביאה מחייבי לאוין קאמר הכא הכי כלומר לא שייך למימר וכן מן העיקר לטפל דהא בעריות כתיבא בהדיא העראה: **וכן** אשלא כדרכה דחייבי לאוין אבל לא קאמר אהעראה דחייבי לאוין דאדרבה ילפינן לעיל יבמה משאר חייבי לאוין וא"כ חייבי לאוין עיקר ויבמה טפל: **א)** ולא נהירא הך פירושא דא"כ הול"ל ומה קדושי רשות פוסלין ועוד כיון דפרשינן דמתני' לא איירי בבת ישראל אלא בבת כהן היכי קא מייתי לקמן בסמוך מפצוע דכא כהן שנשא בת ישראל באנו למחלוקת דמתני' הלא במתני' לא איירי אלא בבת ישראל. אלא ודאי נראה כפירוש אחר במתני' ונימא דמתני' איירי בבת ישראל והכי פירושא אלמנה לכ"ג מן האירוסין לא יאכלו בתרומת הכהן הגדול ואף כי הגיע זמנו לינשא. דבת ישראל שנתארסה לכהן אמרי' כי הגיע זמנו לינשא אוכלת בתרומה והכא כיון שהיא משמרת לביאה פסולה לא אכלה ור' אליעזר ור' שמעון מכשירים דאמרי משמרת לביאה פסולה אכלה וכיון דהגיע זמנו יאכלו דקנין כספו הוא:

תוספות חד מקמאי

לפני יבם חרש אוכלת נולד לה בן אוכלת מת הבן אינה אוכלת. אמר רבה אשת כהן שנאנסה בעלה לוקה עליה משום טומאה אבל משום (אונס) [זונה] לא כל באונס לא קרינן לה זונה מסתברא דלא פליג רב' אדרב עמרם דאמר אשת ישראל שנאנסה פסולה לכהונה ע"כ לא פליגי בה אלא לענין מלקות

מסורת הש"ס

[נ"ל רבה]

לקמן קי: כתובות נא: עד. נדה נב.

[לעיל נד: וש"נ]

[לקמן עה.]

[לקמן נט.]

[נ"ל אלעזר]

הגהות הב"ח

(א) גמ' אמר רבה הכל היו: (ב) תוס' ד"ה מאי וכן וכו' כהונה ס"ד ואח"כ מ"ה ה"ג אדרבה עיקר הערוה.

גליון הש"ס

גמ' אמר רבה אשת כהן שנאנסה. עיין לעיל דף נו ע"א תד"ה אע"פ.

מיהו אם [נאנסה מודה] שפסלוה לכהונה שהרי נבעלה לפסול לה דכתיב ובת איש כהן כי תהיה לאיש זר היא בתרומת הקדשים לא תאכל. ומינה ילפינן בפרק אלמנה לכ"ג כיון שנבעלה לפסול פסלה מהתרומה ומהכהונה ק"ו מגרושה שמותרת בתרומה פסלה לכהונה זו שאסורה בתרומה אינו דין שפסולה לכהונה והכי איתא בפ' אלמנה לכ"ג והיינו דתנן בפ"ק דכתובות מעשה בתינוקת שירדה למלאות מים מן המעיין ונאנסה אר"י בן נורי אם רוב העיר משיאין לכהונה תנשא זו לכהונה ואם אין רוב העיר משיאין לכהונה פסולה שהרי נבעלה לפסול לה דלא חיישי באונס ולא בזנות לכהונה כדפרישנא אבל לעולם זונה לא הויא אליבא דלישנא בתרא. ולא פליג רב' אדרב עמרם ואפי' לישנא בתרא. והאי דלא אגהר רב ששת עיינין מתניתן דכתובות דתינוקת. דדלמא שאני התם דזר דמעיקרא הוא אבל באשת איש לאו זר דמעיקרא הוא. ולא כדכתב הרב בעל התוספות: הא דתנן אלמנה לכ"ג גרושה וחלוצה לכהן הדיוט מן האירוסין לא יאכלו בתרומה אפי' באלמנה כהנת שכבר אכלה כיון שמשמרת לביאה פסולה משוו לה רבנן כאילו נבעלה ונפסלה מלאכול בתרומה אבל כשנתארמלה ונתגרשה מן הנשואין כשרה שהרי לא נבעלה לפסול לה. מן האירוסין כשרה שהרי לא נבעלה לפסול לה ואינה משמרת לביאה פסולה. וא"ר א"ר אושעיא פצוע דכא כהן שקדש בת ישראל באנו

הא נמי אכלה. ממאי? דלמא עד כאן לא קאמרי רבי אלעזר ורבי שמעון התם אלא דיש לו להאכיל במקום אחר, אבל הכא, דאין לו להאכיל במקום אחר – לא. וכי תימא: הכא נמי יש לו להאכיל בבת גרים – והא מיבעיא בעי לה רבי יוחנן מרבי אושעיא, ולא פשיט ליה. איתמר, אביי אמר: הואיל ומאכילה בלא *ידעה, רבא אמר: הואיל ומאכילה בעבדיו ושפחותיו הכנענים. אביי לא אמר כרבא, קנין דאישות מקנין דאישות – ילפינן, ולא ילפינן קנין דאישות מקנין דעבדים. ורבא לא אמר כאביי – שאני התם שכבר אכלה. ואביי: *שכבר אכלה לא אמרינן, דאי לא תימא הכי – בת ישראל שניסת לכהן ומית – תיכול, שכבר אכלה. ורבא: *התם – פקע קנייניה, הכא – לא פקע קנייניה. גופא, בעא מיניה רבי יוחנן מרבי אושעיא: פצוע דכא כהן שנשא בת גרים, מהו שיאכילנה בתרומה? אישתיק ולא אמר ליה ולא מידי. לסוף אתא גברא רבה אחרינא, ובעא מיניה מילתא [אחריתא], ופשט ליה. ומנו – ריש לקיש. א"ל רבי יהודה נשיאה לר' אושעיא: אטו ר' יוחנן לאו גברא רבה הוא? אמר ליה: דקבעי מינאי מילתא דלית לה פתרי. למאן? אי לרבי יהודה – בין בקדושתיה קאי בין לאו בקדושתיה קאי – לא אכלה. אי בקדושתיה קאי לא אכלה, דהא *אמר מר: בת גר זכר כבת חלל זכר. אי לאו בקדושתיה קאי – לא אכלה, דהא אמרינן: קהל גרים איקרי קהל, ואי לר' יוסי, בין בקדושתיה קאי בין לאו בקדושתיה קאי – אכלה. בקדושתיה קאי אכלה – דהא אמר: *אף גר שנשא גיורת בתו כשרה לכהונה. אי לאו בקדושתיה קאי אכלה – דהא אמר: קהל גרים לא איקרי קהל. אלא אליבא דהאי תנא. דתנן, רבי אליעזר בן יעקב אומר: *אשה בת גרים לא תנשא לכהונה עד שתהא אמה מישראל. והכי קמיבעיא ליה: כשרות מיתוספא בה ואכלה, או דלמא קדושה מיתוספא בה ולא אכלה? תא שמע: כי אתא רבי אחא בר חיננא מדרומא, אתא ואייתי מתניתא בידיה: מנין לפצוע דכא כהן שנשא בת גרים שמאכילה בתרומה – שנאמר °"וכהן כי יקנה נפש קנין כספו וגו' יאכל בו", למאן? אילימא לרבי יהודה – האמר: בין בקדושתיה קאי בין לאו בקדושתיה קאי – לא אכלה. ואי לרבי יוסי – ל"ל קרא? האמר: בין בקדושתיה קאי, בין לאו בקדושתיה קאי – אכלה. אלא לאו – לרבי אליעזר בן יעקב, וש"מ: כשרות איתוספא בה, ואכלה. ש"מ. איתמר, רב אמר:
יש

תורה אור

רש"י

הא נמי אכלה. דקנין כספו היא, ואוכלת דבר תורה. ועד דבעיל לה דשוייה חללה – אכלה. הכא אין לו להאכיל במקום אחר. שאין לך אשה שמותרת לו. בבת גרים. דקסבר: קהל גרים לא אקרי קהל, ואינן בכלל "לא יבא פצוע דכא", ונושאה בהיתר, ומאכילה תרומה. והא בעי מיניה ר' יוחנן מרבי אושעיא. לקמן בשמעתין, ולא פשיט ליה אי מאכילה בתרומה או לא. איתמר. לשנויי קושיין אתא. הואיל ומאכילה (א) בלא ידעה. היה נשוי כהן אשה ואוכלת בתרומה, ונעשה פצוע דכא ובא עליה – לא תאכל בתרומה, דשוייה חללה, דנבעלה לפסול לה. ואם לא ידעה משנעשה פצוע דכא – הרי זו אוכלת, משנה היא בפ' "הערל" (לקמן ע.). אלמא מצינו פצוע דכא כהן מאכיל במקום אחר, הלכך, בקידושי עבירה נמי מאכיל כל זמן שלא עשאה חללה. שכבר אכלה. כשהוא בריא. דלית ליה פתרי. שאין (ב) יודע לפרשה. למאן אי לר' יהודה כו'. הש"ס הוא דקא בעי לה, ומפרש ואזיל עד סיפא, ופשטה. אבל ר' אושעיא לא פשט בה מידי, כדאמרן לעיל: הא בעא מיניה כו'. ואית דמפרשי דלית ליה פתרי – אינה צריכה לפרש. דלמאן קבעי לה, אי לר' יהודה כו' – ושבוש הוא, מפני שני דברים: חדא – דאמרן לעיל ולא פשט ליה, ואם כן, דרבי אושעיא קאמר לה לכולה מילתא – הא פשטה במסקנא. ועוד: דקנסיב ואזיל לפרושי דלא צריכה ליה למיבעיא לן, וקא נסיב בסיפא תא שמע, אלמא צריכה רבה. בין בקדושתיה קאי כו'. לקמן בפרק "הערל" (דף עו.) מיבעיא לן: כהן פצוע דכא מהו בגיורת? בקדושתיה קאי ואסור כו'. והכא, בין בקדושתיה קאי – כהן הנעשה פצוע דכא, בין בקדושת כהן קאי – ואסור בכל האסורות לכהונה, בין לאו בקדושתיה קאי, ואינו מוזהר מלישא אשה פגומה – לא אכלה. אי בקדושתיה קאי לא אכלה דהא אמר מר בת גר זכר כבת חלל זכר. ובת חלל פסולה לכהונה, בפרק "עשרה יוחסין". וכיון דבקדושתיה קאי – לא אכלה, דאמרינן: הרי זו פסולה לו, ועשאה חללה בביאתו. ואי לאו בקדושתיה קאי. ואינה אסורה לו משום קדושת כהן – אפי' הכי לא אכלה, שאסורה לו משום פצוע דכא, דהאמרת קהל גרים איקרי קהל. פלוגתא דר' יהודה ור' יוסי בפרק "עשרה יוחסין". אליבא דהאי תנא קמיבעיא ליה. לר' יוחנן, וכגון דאמה מישראל. כשרות איתוספא בה. וראויה לכהונה, ולאו קדושה לאקרויי קהל. ומותרת לפצוע דכא, ואוכלת ממה נפשך, דאי נמי בקדושתיה קאי – הרי זו מותרת לו, ומשום פצוע דכא לא מיתסר בה, דהא לא איקרי קהל. או דלמא קדושה נמי איתוספא בה. וקהל איקרי, ואסורה לפצוע דכא ולא אכלה.א) לישנא אחרינא מפי המורה: בת גר וגיורת קמיבעיא ליה, אליבא דראב"י מאי? כשרות איתוספא בהך דאמה מישראל לאקרויי קהל, אבל בת גר וגיורת לאו קהל היא, ואכלה, שמותרת לפצוע דכא, והאי לאו בקדושה קאי דתיתסר עליה משום כהונה. או דלמא קדושה איתוספא בה. ליגשא לכהונה. והך דאין אמה מישראל, נהי דקדושה לית בה – כשרות מיהא אית בה, ובכלל קהל היא, ואסורה לפצוע דכא, ולא אכלה. ולשון ראשון נראה עיקר. לרבי יוסי. לא איצטריך נפש יתירה, כדאמר לעיל דממה נפשך אכלה.
יש

תוספות

והא בעא רבי יוחנן מר' אושעיא ולא פשיט ליה. מדרבי אושעיא אדרבי אושעיא פריך. ותימה: דלקמן מסקינן דרבי יוחנן בעי אליבא דר' אליעזר בן יעקב, אבל אליבא דר' אלעזר ור' שמעון אפשר דמאכיל בבת גרים, דר"ש מכשיר גיורת פחותה מבת ג' לכהן, ודלמא סבר נמי דקהל גרים לא מיקרי קהל. ומיהו, בקונטרס פי' דכולה סוגיא דהש"ס מסיק לה, אבל ר' אושעיא לא פשט מידי. אביי אמר הואיל ומאכילה בלא ידעה. תימה: דבלא ידעה גופה אמאי מאכיל לאביי? דמשתמרת לביאה פסולה! היא וטעמא שכבר אכלה לית ליה לאביי, כדקאמר בסמוך. ורבא נמי, היכי קאמר שאני התם שכבר אכלה, הא אליבא דרבי *אליעזר קיימא הכא, ורבי *אליעזר אית ליה ב"הערל" (לקמן עה.) שכבר אכלה לא אמרינן, אההיא מתנית' גופה דלא ידעה, דקאמר: מאן תנא משתמרת לביאה פסולה דאורייתא אכלה – אמר ר' אלעזר: במחלוקת שנויה, ור' אלעזר ור' שמעון היא. ורבי יוחנן אמר: אפילו תימא רבי מאיר, שאני התם שכבר אכלה! ויש לומר: דטעמא שכבר אכלה מהני לכ"ע לענין זה שאוכלת לרבי אלעזר ור' שמעון, אע"פ שאין מאכיל במקום אחר. ולא פליג ר"א *ורבי יוחנן אלא במאי דקאמר ר' יוחנן דאוכלת אפי' לרבי מאיר מטעם שכבר אכלה, דלא חשיבא משתמרת לביאה פסולה, כיון דתחילת אכילתה הוו נישואי כשרות והוי כאילו הן קיימין ועומדין עדיין שתאכל מכאן. ומייתי אביי אפצוע דכא שקידש, דחשיב יש לו להאכיל במקום אחר, כיון שמאכיל בלא ידעה. ורבא סבר דלא חשיב יש לו להאכיל במקום אחר, כיון דאין מאכיל התם על ידי מעשה של עכשיו אלא ע"י שכבר אכלה. אתא גברא רבה אחרינא ובעא מיניה מילתא אחריתי. כאן משמע שהיה ר"ל גדול כשבא לפני רבי יוחנן, כמו שפירש ר"ת בב"מ (דף פד. ד"ה אי), שהיה לומד תורה לפני ר' אושעיא רבו של רבי יוחנן. [וע"ע תוס' עירובין סה: ד"ה ר"ל]. ואי לאו בקדושתיה קאי לא אכלה דהא אמר קהל גרים איקרי קהל. תימה: דהוה ליה למימר בין בקדושתיה קאי בין לא קאי – לא אכלה מהני תרי טעמי, דבת גר זכר כבת חלל זכר, ועוד דקהל גרים איקרי קהל. דהא אפילו לא בקדושתיה קאי – לא אכלה נמי, מטעם דבת גר זכר כבת חלל זכר, דהרי היא כחללה, וחללה אינה אוכלת בתרומה. כדמוכח בפרק בתרא דקדושין (דף עז.) ואי הוה טעמא דר' יהודה בבת גר זכר משום דכתיב "מזרע ישראל" כדמוכח התם – הוה מצי למימר דלא הויא ממש כחללה אלא דוקא לינשא לכהונה. אבל התם משמע דעיקר טעמא דרבי יהודה מק"ו: ומה חלל שבא מטיפה כשרה כו', ולפי זה – אית לן לשוייה כחללה לגמרי. דהא אמר אף גר שנשא גיורת בתו כשרה לכהונה. אכתי צריך לטעמא, דאית ליה קהל גרים לא אקרי קהל, ולא חש להזכיר, אלא נטר עד דקאמר אי לאו בקדושתיה קאי אכלה כו'. דאי לא קאי – סגי לה בטעם דקהל גרים לא איקרי קהל לחודיה. הכי גרסינן דתנן רבי אליעזר בן יעקב אומר אשה בת גרים כו'. דמשנה היא במסכת ביכורים (פ"א משנה ה). ולא קשיא דלא מייתי מתניתין דפרק בתרא דקדושין – (דף עז.) דהך נמי משנה היא.
רב

עין משפט נר מצוה

לח א מיי' פט"ו מהל' איסורי ביאה הל' ז סמג לאוין קיז טוש"ע אה"ע סימן ה סעיף כב:
לט ב מיי' שם פי"ט הל' ו סמג לאוין קנב טוש"ע שם סימן ז סעיף כא:
מ ג מיי' פ"ז מהל' תרומות הלכה יג:

[אלעזר] [אלעזר]

מסורת הש"ס

[מלשון והאדם ידע וגו' בראשית ד עוד שם יש אשר לא ידעו איש עוד שם כל ולא ידעה]
[לקמן עה.]
[גז"ש]
קדושין עז.
שם
בכורים פ"א מ"ה
רש"ל
ויקרא כב

הגהות הב"ח

(א) רש"י ד"ה הואיל ומאכילה בלא כו' פי' כשלא בא עליה לאחר שנעשה פצוע דכא ע"ל ר"פ הערל: (ב) ד"ה דלית וכו' שאין אני יודע:

תוספות ישנים

א) ודוחק הוא דקרי לקדושה קריאת קהל ולכשרות היתר כהונה. הלא לישנא דקדושה משמע כהונה כדאמרינן לעיל איסור קדושה אלמנה לכה"ג ופ"ה לשון אחר דבת גר וגיורת קא מיבעיא ליה ואליבא דר' אליעזר בן יעקב ובעי מאי כשרות איתוספא ביה פירוש בההיא שאמה מישראל ליקרא קהל פירוש אף כשרות דקהל עם היתר כהונה אבל בת גר וגיורת דלית בה כל כך אלא כשרות דקהל ולא קדושה לכהונה א"כ לא נקראת קהל ומותרת לפצוע דכא אם אמת הדבר דלאו בקדושתיה קאי ולא תיאסר עליו משום כהונה דאי בקדושתיה קאי אסורה ליה כדאמרינן דבת גר כבת חלל אליבא דר' אליעזר נמי כדקאמר דבת גר וגיורת לא תנשא לכהונה או דלמא קדושה אתוספא בה בההיא דאמה מישראל יותר מבת גר וגיורת דמותרת לכהונה והך דאין אמה מישראל נהי דקדושה לית בה להנשא לכהן מ"מ כשרות אית בה להיות בכלל קהל ואסירא בפצוע דכא ולא אכלה בין בקדושתי' קאי בין לאו בקדושתיה קאי ורש"י פי' דראשון עיקר:

תוספות חד מקמאי

באנו למחלוקת ר"מ ור"ש ור"א לר"מ דאמר משמרת לביאה פסולה לא אכלה הא נמי לא אכלה לר"א ור"ש אכלה. ממאי דלמא ע"כ לא אמר ר"א ורבי שמעון אלא היכא דיש לו להאכיל במקום אחר אבל פצוע דכא דאין לו להאכיל במקום אחר לא. אביי אמר הואיל ומאכיל בלא ידיעה. פירוש אליבא דר"א ור"ש אבל אליבא דר"מ אינו מאכיל בלא ידיעה שהרי משתמרת לביאה פסולה. רבא אמר הואיל ומאכיל בשפחותיו ועבדיו. רבא לא אמר כאביי שאני התם שכבר אכלה פירוש אפילו לר"מ אכלה משום טעמא שכבר אכלה והכי איתא בפ' הערל: בעא מניה רבי יוחנן מר' אושעיא פצוע דכא כהן שנשא בת גרים מהו שתאכל בתרומה ואסיקנא אליבא דרבי יוסי דקי"ל כותיה בין בקדושתיה קאי בין לאו בקדושתיה קאי אכלה. דהא אמר גר שנשא גיורת בתו כשרה לכהונה ואי לאו בקדושתיה קאי [אכלה] דהא אמר קהל גרים לא אקרי קהל ור' יוחנן דקא מיבעיא ליה אליבא דראב"י קמיבעיא ליה דאמר אשה בת גרים לא תנשא לכהונה עד שתהא אמה מישראל וקמיבעיא ליה כשרות אתוספא בה ואכלה או דלמא קדושה איתוספא בה ולא אכלה ראב"י נמי ס"ל כר' יוסי בהא דקהל גרים לא איקרי קהל וקמיבעיא ליה כשאמו מישראל כשרות לחודה איתוספא בה שכשרה לכהונה ולא קדושה וכשם שאם אין אמה מישראל לא איקרי קהל כך כשאמה מישראל לא איקרי קהל ואכלה או דלמא כשאמה מישראל קדושה נמי אתוספא דאקרי קהל ולא אכלה. ואית דמפרשי לה כשאין אמה מישראל והכי קמיבעיא ליה כשאמו מישראל כשרות אתוספא בה לאקרויי קהל אבל כשאין אמו מישראל לא אקרי קהל ואכלה או דלמא קדושה אתוספא בה למשרייא לכהונה אבל לאקרויי קהל אע"פ שאין אמו מישראל איקרי קהל ואסורה לפצוע דכא:
גרסי'

מא א מיי' פ"ז מהל' תרומות הלכה כא:
מב ב מיי' פ"ג מהל' אישות הלכה יא טוש"ע אה"ע סימן לז סעיף א:
מג ג טוש"ע שם סימן קסז סעיף ד:
מד ד מיי' פ"ג מהל' איסורי ביאה ה"ב:
מה ה מיי' פ"ג מהל' מטמא משכב ומושב הלכה ג:
מו ו מיי' פ"ו מהל' תרומות הל' ג:
מז ז מיי' פי"ח מהל' איסורי ביאה הלכה יז ופי"ט ה"ב טוש"ע אה"ע סי' ו סעיף ט וסי' ז סעיף יב:

^א^יֵשׁ חוּפָּה לִפְסוּלוֹת, וּשְׁמוּאֵל אָמַר: אֵין חוּפָּה לִפְסוּלוֹת. אָמַר שְׁמוּאֵל: וּמוֹדֶה לִי אַבָּא בְּתִינוֹקֶת פְּחוּתָה מִבַּת שָׁלֹשׁ שָׁנִים וְיוֹם אֶחָד, הוֹאִיל וְאֵין לָהּ בִּיאָה — אֵין לָהּ חוּפָּה. אָמַר רָבָא: אַף אֲנַן נַמִי תָּנֵינָא, *^ב^בַּת שָׁלֹשׁ שָׁנִים וְיוֹם אֶחָד מִתְקַדֶּשֶׁת בְּבִיאָה ^ג^וְאִם בָּא עָלֶיהָ יָבָם קְנָאָהּ, ^ד^וְחַיָּיבִין עָלֶיהָ מִשּׁוּם אֵשֶׁת אִישׁ, ^ה^וּמְטַמְּאָה אֶת בּוֹעֲלָהּ לְטַמֵּא מִשְׁכָּב תַּחְתּוֹן כְּעֶלְיוֹן. ^ו^נִשֵּׂאת לְכֹהֵן — אוֹכֶלֶת בִּתְרוּמָה, ^ז^בָּא עָלֶיהָ אֶחָד מִכׇּל הַפְּסוּלִין — פְּסָלָהּ. בַּת שָׁלֹשׁ שָׁנִים וְיוֹם אֶחָד הוּא דְּמִפַּסְלָה בְּבִיאָה — מִפַּסְלָה בְּחוּפָּה, הָא פְּחוּתָה מִבַּת שָׁלֹשׁ שָׁנִים וְיוֹם אֶחָד, דְּלָא מִפַּסְלָה בְּבִיאָה — לָא מִפַּסְלָה נַמִי בְּחוּפָּה, שְׁמַע מִינַּהּ. אָמַר רָמִי בַּר חָמָא: יֵשׁ חוּפָּה לִפְסוּלוֹת — בָּאנוּ לְמַחֲלוֹקֶת רַבִּי מֵאִיר וְרַבִּי אֶלְעָזָר וְרַבִּי שִׁמְעוֹן, לְרַבִּי

רש"י

יֵשׁ חוּפָּה לִפְסוּלוֹת. כה"ג שֶׁהִכְנִיס אַלְמָנָה בַּת כֹּהֵן לַחוּפָּה וְלֹא בָּא עָלֶיהָ, וּמֵעִיקָּרָא נַמִי לֹא קִידְּשָׁהּ — אֲפִילּוּ הָכִי פְּסָלָהּ מִתְּרוּמָה דְּבֵי נָשָׁא, דְּחוּפָּה כִּכְנִיסַת בְּעִילָה דָּמְיָא. וּמוֹדֶה לִי אַבָּא. מִשּׁוּם דְּקָשִׁישׁ מִינֵּיהּ קָרֵי לֵיהּ אַבָּא, כְּמוֹ לְשׁוֹן נְשִׂיאֵי וְרַבֵּי. הוֹאִיל וְאֵין לָהּ בִּיאָה. אֵין בִּיאָתָהּ פּוֹסַלְתָּהּ מִתְּרוּמַת אָבִיהָ — אֵין חוּפָּתָהּ פּוֹסַלְתָּהּ. אַף אֲנַן נַמִי תָּנֵינָא. דְּאֵין בִּיאָתָהּ פּוֹסַלְתָּהּ, וְכֵיוָן דְּאֵין בִּיאָתָהּ פּוֹסַלְתָּהּ — כ"שׁ דְּאֵין חוּפָּתָהּ פּוֹסַלְתָּהּ. דְּהָא חֲשִׁיבוּת חוּפָּה אֵינָהּ אֶלָּא מִשּׁוּם שֶׁהִיא קְרוֹבָה לְבִיאָה, וְהֵיכָא דְּבִיאָה לָא חֲשִׁיבָא — כׇּל שֶׁכֵּן חוּפָּה. וּמְטַמְּאָה אֶת בּוֹעֲלָהּ. אִם נִדָּה הִיא, לְטַמֵּא בּוֹעֲלָהּ מִשְׁכָּב תַּחְתּוֹן כְּעֶלְיוֹן. בְּמַסֶּכֶת נִדָּה מְפָרֵשׁ לָהּ: שֶׁיְּהֵא תַּחְתּוֹן שֶׁל בּוֹעֵל נִדָּה כְּעֶלְיוֹנוֹ שֶׁל זָב, שֶׁמְּטַמֵּא אוֹכָלִין וּמַשְׁקִין. וְאֵין מְטַמֵּא אָדָם וְכֵלִים, כְּתַחְתּוֹן שֶׁל נִדָּה עַצְמָהּ שֶׁהוּא קָרוּי מִדְרָס וְאַב הַטּוּמְאָה. מִן הַפְּסוּלִין. כְּגוֹן חָלָל נָתִין וּמַמְזֵר, אוֹ אַלְמָנָה לְכֹהֵן גָּדוֹל. פְּסָלָהּ. מִתְּרוּמַת בֵּית אָבִיהָ.

תוספות

רב אמר יש חופה לפסולות. נראה לר"י לפרש לפי שיטת הקונטרס, דפליגי בחופה בלא כסף. דרב ושמואל סברי כרב הונא, דאית ליה בריש קידושין (דף ה.) דחופה קונה, וקאמר רב דכי היכי דקנו קידושי חופה בכשרות — הכא נמי קני בפסולות. ועדיפא מקידושי כסף, דאפי' ר"א ור"ש דאמרי דקידושי כסף לא פסלי — בחופה דקרובה לביאה מודו, כדקאמרינן בדיחויא דמילתא דרמי בר חמא. ולא שייך כאן דיו, דהא דמשתמרת לביאה פסולה דאורייתא — לא אכלה מדרבנן, והחמירו חכמים בחופה יותר, לפי שקרובה לביאה. וטעמא דרב, משום דסבר דבפסולות נמי שייך שארו, וכי היכי דקרינן בה "שארו" על ידי חופה שאחר קידושין, לשויה נשואה לענין השקאת סוטה, דבעינן "תחת אישך" דהיינו נשואה. ולענין נערה המאורסה לאפוקי מסקילה לחנק — קניה נמי בלא כסף לשויה ארוסה. ושמואל אמר: אין חופה לפסולות, דחופה לא מהני אלא בכשרות, דחופה קירוב ביאה הוא ולא מהניא אלא בראויות לביאה, אבל בפסולות שאין ראויות לביאה — לא. וחופה דלאחר קידושין נמי לא מהניא בפסולות לשמואל, א) דלא שייך בהו שארות וקירוב ביאה מדמייתי מההוא שלא שטיתי ארוסה כו' סייעתא לרב דמיירי בחופה שאחר הקידושין. ורמי בר חמא דקאמר דיש חופה לפסולות באנו למחלוקת כו' — פליג אדרב ושמואל, ואתא למימר דליתיה לדרב דפסל לכולי עלמא, וליתא דשמואל דאמר דלכולי עלמא לא פסלה, אלא כי היכי דפליגי בקידושין — ה"נ פליגי בחופה. כן צריך לפרש לפי שיטת הקונטרס. ב) ולא רצה לפרש דאיירי בחופה שאחר הקידושין — דא"כ לא מצי שמואל למימר דלכולי עלמא לא פסלה, דהא פסולה וקיימא משעת קידושין לר' מאיר. ואין לפרש בחופה שאחר קידושין, וכגון שלא היה הפסול בשעת קידושין, כגון שנעשה פצוע דכא אחר הקידושין, או כהן גדול שקידש קטנה ובגרה תחתיו — דבכהאי גוונא נמי מיפסלא, כדמוכח בבעיא דלקמן (דף נט.) בכהן שקידש קטנה ובגרה תחתיו לפירוש ר"י (שם ד"ה "מהו"). ומתאי דאמר ב"הערל" (לקמן עה.) דאפי' לרבי יוחנן, דמוקי מתניתין דאם לא ידעה אפילו כר"מ משמע דוקא בנשואה שכבר אכלה, אבל ארוסה לא — אין ראיה, דהתם בבת ישראל מיירי שאינה אוכלת אלא מכחו, ולכך לא תתחיל לאכול על ידי נישואין פסולין. אבל בת כהן לכהן, איכא למימר: כיון דאכלה מקודם — אוכלת נמי לאחר שנפצע. ולא מסתבר נמי לאוקמי בארוסה שכבר אכלה בהגעת זמן, כמשנה ראשונה, וכר' יוחנן דאמר היכא דכבר אכלה דלא מפסלא משום שימור ביאה פסולה לר"מ — דדוחק להעמיד פלוגתא כמשנה ראשונה. ועוד: דמשמע דאיירי רב ושמואל בפסולות דמתני': אלמנה לכהן גדול, גרושה וחלוצה לכהן הדיוט. וקשיא לר"י על פירוש הקונטרס: דלישנא דקאמר רמי בר חמא לר"מ דאמר קידושין פסלי חופה נמי פסלה — משמע דאיירי בחופה שאחר קידושין, דאי בחופה בלא כסף — הא חופה נמי קידושין היא, ולא הוה ליה למימר סתם קידושין אלא כסף ושטר. ועוד הקשה ר"ת: דלפירוש הקונטרס אתו רב ושמואל דלא כהלכה, דלא קיימא לן כרב הונא, מדאמר בריש קידושין (דף ג. ושם): מניינא דרישא למעוטי חופה, ולרב הונא דאמר חופה קונה למעוטי מאי? וקאמר נמי בגמרא התם (דף ה:): ורב הונא — כסף באישות לא אשכחן כו'. משמע דאין הלכה כמותו. ועוד הקשה ה"ר י"ט מיוני: דלשמואל דאמר אין חופה לפסולות, אבל לכשרות יש חופה — ואמאי? הא רב הונא יליף דחופה קונה מהצד השוה דכסף ושטר וביאה, והשתא איכא למפרך: מה להצד השוה — שכן קונין בפסולות, תאמר בחופה שאף אחר שתלמוד שקונה — אין קונה בפסולות! ◐דבכי האי גוונא שייכא פירכא כדאשכחן בפרק קמא דמנחות (דף ו.) גבי טריפה לגבוה ובבבא קמא (דף מ:) גבי שור האיצטדין ואין לומר דלא חשיבא פירכא משום דחופה דפסולות אינה קרויה חופה — דמכל מקום פירכא היא, כדפריך התם — מה לכסף שכן פודין בו הקדשות ומעשר שני, תאמר בביאה כו'. ונראה לר"י כפירוש ר"ת: דבחופה שאחר קידושין איירי רב ושמואל, ובנתאלמנה או נתגרשה דמתניתין קיימי. רב אמר: יש חופה לפסולות, ואם נתאלמנו או נתגרשו אחר חופה — פסולות לכולי עלמא, כיון דיש חופה, וחופה חשיבא כביאה לפסול לעולם. ושמואל אמר: אין חופה לפסולות, והוי נתאלמנו או נתגרשו מן האירוסין, דכשרות אפילו לר"מ. והא דלא קבעי ליה אמתניתין דנתאלמנו או נתגרשו — משום דאפלוגתא דר"מ ור"א ור"ש קיימי. והא דאמר רמי בר חמא לרבי מאיר דאמר קידושין פסלי — ה"פ: כיון שמחמיר כל כך, דאפי' בקידושין לא אכלה — כמו כן יחמיר בחופה בנתאלמנה או נתגרשה שלא תאכל לעולם וכו'. ולפירושו נמי רמי בר חמא פליג אדרב ושמואל. **אמר** שמואל ומודה לי **אבא.** לא כמו שפירש בקונטרס לשון חשיבות, אלא כך היה שמו של רב, כדפירש בערוך בערך 'אבא'. כדאמרינן בברכות (דף מז.): אילו מייתו אהדליא וגוזליא לאבא. ורב כהנא דאמר (שם דף סב.): דמי פומיה דאבא כדלא טעים תבשילא, וב"ראשית הגז" (חולין קלז:) נמי אמר: מאן ריש סידרא בבבל, אמר ליה: אבא אריכא. וקצת קשיא על רב כהנא שהיה תלמידו של רב היאך היה קורא לרב בשמו? וב"חלק" (סנהדרין ק.) אמר: מפני מה נענש גחזי — מפני שקרא רבו בשמו. ושמא משום דרב כהנא תלמיד חבר דרב הוה, כדאמרינן בפרק "אחד דיני ממונות" (שם לו:): כגון רב כהנא ורב אסי, דלגמריה דרב הוו צריכי. ולסבריה דרב לא הוו צריכי. ובסוף בבא קמא (דף קיז:) נמי אמר דשייליה רבי יוחנן כל ספיקי דהוו ליה*. **וחייבין** עליה משום אשת איש. פירוש: אם קבל בה אביה קידושין. ותימה: דלמאי איצטריך למתני? דמסיפא שמעינן לה, דקתני: ואם בא עליה אחד מכל העריות — מומתין על ידה, ואשת איש בכלל, כדמוכח בפרק "בן סורר ומורה" (סנהדרין דף סט. ושם). ואפילו בהמה בכלל, כדמוכח בפרק "ארבע מיתות" (שם נה: ושם) בשמעתא דתקלה וקלון! ונראה לר"י: דקאי אאם בא עליה יבם קנאה, וקמ"ל דקנאה קנין גמור מדאורייתא, ולא הוי כביאת בן תשע, דקתני בההיא משנה (נדה מה.), דהתם לא קנה אלא מדרבנן כדאמרינן (שם): עשו ביאת בן תשע כמאמר בגדול, דממעטינן לה מדאורייתא בפרק "ארבע מיתות" (סנהדרין דף נב:) ובפרק קמא דקידושין (דף יט.) מ"אשר ינאף את אשת איש" — פרט לאשת קטן. וקשה, דבפ' "בן סורר" (סנהדרין סט.) דייק מינה שהולכין בדיני נפשות אחר הרוב, דאי לא אזלינן — ניחוש דלמא אילונית היא, ואדעתא דהכי לא קדיש. ולהאי פירושא דקאי אאם בא עליה יבם — אמאי פריך ניחוש דלמא אדעתא דהכי לא קדיש — היינו אחיו הראשון. ויצטרך לומר והאי נמי אדעתא דהכי לא יבם, ה"ל למיפרך טפי: ניחוש דלמא אדעתא דהכי קדיש אחיו הראשון, דשוב אינה אשת יבם. או ה"ל להקשות בסתם: ניחוש דלמא אילונית היא, ובכל ענין בין אדעתא דהכי קדיש אחיו הראשון או לא קדיש — אינה אשת יבם! וי"ל: דנקט אדעתא דהכי לא קדיש — משום דמסיפא נמי בעי למיפרך, ואם בא עליה אחד מכל העריות כו'. דמרישא היה יודע דמצי לשנויי: מאי חייבין דקתני — קרבן, כדמשני ליה. ופריך: הא מומתין קתני. ומכח זה הקשה בתחלה, ומשני: בדקבלה עילויה. פירוש: בסיפא, אבל ברישא לעולם נ"ל מאי חייבין דקתני — קרבן. דהתם לא מהני מידי מה שקבלה עילויה, כדפירשנו. וריב"א פירש: דאצטריך וחייב עליה משום אשת איש, דאי לאו דקתני לה — הוה מוקמינן ואם בא עליה אחד מכל העריות דוקא בעריות, ולא בבהמה. אבל השתא, דקתני וחייב עליה משום אשת איש והוא הדין כל העריות — תו לא איצטריך סיפא, אלא משום בהמה. ומכח זה דייק בפרק "ד' מיתות" (שם דף נה:) דכל העריות אפילו בהמה. תדע, דבסיפא גבי בן תשע קתני כל העריות שבתורה מומתין על ידו, ואפילו הכי קתני: ונסקלת בהמה על ידו, אלמא: לא הוי בהמה בכלל כל העריות. **נשאת** לכהן אוכלת בתרומה. אבל פחותה מבת ג', כיון דלאו בת ביאה היא — לא בדיק לה, ◐ואיכא למיחש לסמפון, *וגם חוזר ומשלחה לבית אביה, ולהכי לא אכלה. דהני

קדושין י. סנהדרין נה: סט. נדה מד:

גליון הש"ס

תוס' ד"ה רב אמר דבכה"ג שייכא פירכא כדאשכחן בפ' קמא דמנחות. עיין בב"מ דף מב ע"א תד"ה אמר: **ד"ה** נשאת לכהן וכו' ואיכא למיחש לסמפון וכו' עיין לקמן דף סב ע"א תד"ה מכתון:

[וע"ע היטב תוס' חולין לח. ד"ה איצטריך]

נ"א אם

תוספות ישנים

א) ותימה מאי קאמר אבל חופה דלא קני לה ...

... שבבעל ירית לה שלא כדין כגון לקמן גבי קטנה שאין לבעל בה קדושין רק מדרבנן א"כ כיון שהוא יורשה ואין קרוביה יורשין אותה קריא ולא עגו לה והויא מת מצוה אבל היכא דבדין ... מקפידים וקרייא שפיר ועגו לה כיון שאין מפסידים שום דבר מדינם. וא"ת הכא נמי שלא כדין ירית לה דהא ירושת הבעל דרבנן וי"ל דכיון שאין זאת האשה חלוקה מאחרות שהרי כל העולם הורו ... מדרבנן נראה לקרובים שיורשה בדין ושפיר עגו לה קרוביה ולא הויא מת מצוה אבל בקטנה הכל יודעים כי קדושיה אינם כלום רק מפני שמא נהגו בה מנהג הפקר וא"כ לא עגו לה כיון ...

תוספות חד מקמאי

גרס' בפ' עשרה יוחסין בא לימלך מורין לו כרבא' אבל אין מוציאין מידו כר' יוסי: אתמר רב אמר יש חופה לפסולות ושמואל אמר אין חופה לפסולות. פירוש חופה בלא קידושין והכי משמע לקמן דאמר רמי בר חמא יש חופה לפסולות באנו למחלוקת ר"מ ור"ש ור"א עד ודלמא לא היא ע"כ לא קאמר ר"מ אלא בקדושין דקני לה אבל חופה דלא קנה לה. אלמא בחופה בלא קידושין עסקינן והפירוש הנכון בחופה דאחר קדושי' איירי וכהן שנפצע אחר קדושין ונכנסת לחופה לאחר שנפצע. ומסתברא כיון דקי"ל הלכתא כרב באיסור ... בן ברוקה ... לחופה עם פסול לה אע"פ שלא נבעלה כמי שנבעלה דמי ונפסלה מלאכול בתרומה ובחלה:

לְרַבִּי מֵאִיר דְּאָמַר קִדּוּשִׁין פָּסְלִי — חוּפָּה נַמִי פָּסְלָה, לְרַ' אֶלְעָזָר וְרַ' שִׁמְעוֹן דְּאָמְרִי קִדּוּשִׁין לָא פָּסְלִי — חוּפָּה נַמִי לָא פָּסְלָה. וּמִמַּאי? דִּלְמָא עַד כָּאן לָא קָאָמַר ר"מ הָתָם אֶלָּא בְּקִדּוּשִׁין דְּקָנֵי לָהּ. אֲבָל חוּפָּה דְּלָא קָנָה לָהּ — לָא. א"נ, עַד כָּאן לָא קָאָמְרִי רַבִּי אֶלְעָזָר וְרַבִּי שִׁמְעוֹן הָתָם — אֶלָּא בְּקִדּוּשִׁין, דְּלָא קְרִיבִי לְבִיאָה, אֲבָל חוּפָּה דִּקְרִיבָא לְבִיאָה — הָכִי נַמִי דְּפָסְלָה. אֶלָּא אִי אִיכָּא לְמֵימַר — בִּפְלוּגְתָּא דְּהָנֵי תַּנָּאֵי, דְּתַנְיָא: נִישְּׂאוּ זוֹ וָזוֹ, כְּשֵׁרוֹת וּפְסוּלוֹת, אוֹ שֶׁנִּכְנְסוּ לְחוּפָּה וְלֹא נִבְעֲלוּ — אוֹכְלוֹת מִשֶּׁלּוֹ וְאוֹכְלוֹת בִּתְרוּמָה. נִכְנְסוּ, מִכְּלָל דְּנִישְּׂאוּ — נִישְּׂאוּ מַמָּשׁ? אֶלָּא לָאו — כְּגוֹן שֶׁנִּכְנְסוּ לְחוּפָּה וְלֹא נִבְעֲלוּ. וְקָתָנֵי: אוֹכְלוֹת מִשֶּׁלּוֹ וְאוֹכְלוֹת בִּתְרוּמָה. רַבִּי יִשְׁמָעֵאל בְּנוֹ שֶׁל רַ' יוֹחָנָן בֶּן בְּרוֹקָה אוֹמֵר: כָּל שֶׁבִּיאָתָהּ מַאֲכִילָתָהּ — חוּפָּתָהּ מַאֲכִילָתָהּ, וְכָל שֶׁאֵין בִּיאָתָהּ מַאֲכִילָתָהּ — אֵין חוּפָּתָהּ מַאֲכִילָתָהּ. מִמַּאי? דִּלְמָא רַבִּי יִשְׁמָעֵאל בְּנוֹ שֶׁל רַבִּי יוֹחָנָן בֶּן בְּרוֹקָה כְּרַ' מֵאִיר סְבִירָא לֵיהּ, דְּאָמַר: קִדּוּשִׁין לָא אָכְלָה. הַאי "כָּל שֶׁאֵין בִּיאָתָהּ מַאֲכִילָתָהּ אֵין חוּפָּתָהּ מַאֲכִילָתָהּ"? "כָּל שֶׁאֵין בִּיאָתָהּ מַאֲכִילָתָהּ אֵין כַּסְפָּהּ מַאֲכִילָתָהּ" מִיבָּעֵי לֵיהּ! דִּלְמָא, אַיְּידֵי דַּאֲמַר ת"ק חוּפָּה — אֲמַר אִיהוּ נַמִי חוּפָּה. אֲמַר רַב עַמְרָם: הָא מִילְּתָא אֲמַר לָן רַב שֵׁשֶׁת, וְאַנְהְרִינְהוּ לְעַיְינִין מִמַּתְנִיתִין: יֵשׁ חוּפָּה לִפְסוּלוֹת, וְתַנָּא תּוּנָא: *"אָמֵן [א]שֶׁלֹּא שָׂטִיתִי אֲרוּסָה, וּנְשׂוּאָה, שׁוֹמֶרֶת יָבָם, וּכְנוּסָה". הַאי אֲרוּסָה הֵיכִי דָּמֵי? אִילֵימָא דְּקָנֵי לָהּ כְּשֶׁהִיא אֲרוּסָה, (א) וְקָא מַשְׁקֶה לָהּ כְּשֶׁהִיא אֲרוּסָה — אֲרוּסָה בַּת מִשְׁתְּיָא הִיא? וְהָא תְּנַן: *[ב]אֲרוּסָה וְשׁוֹמֶרֶת יָבָם לֹא שׁוֹתוֹת וְלֹא נוֹטְלוֹת כְּתוּבָּה! אֶלָּא דְּקָנֵי לָהּ כְּשֶׁהִיא אֲרוּסָה, וְאִיסְתַּתְּרָה, וְקָמַשְׁקֶה לָהּ כְּשֶׁהִיא נְשׂוּאָה — מִי בָּדְקִי לָהּ מַיָּא? וְהָתַנְיָא: *°"וְנִקָּה הָאִישׁ מֵעָוֹן" [ג]בִּזְמַן שֶׁהָאִישׁ מְנוּקֶּה מֵעָוֹן הַמַּיִם בּוֹדְקִין אֶת אִשְׁתּוֹ, אֵין הָאִישׁ מְנוּקֶּה מֵעָוֹן — אֵין הַמַּיִם בּוֹדְקִין אֶת אִשְׁתּוֹ! אֶלָּא דְּקָנֵי לָהּ כְּשֶׁהִיא אֲרוּסָה, וְאִיסְתַּתְּרָה וְנִכְנְסָה לְחוּפָּה וְלֹא נִבְעֲלָה, וּשְׁמַע מִינָּהּ: יֵשׁ חוּפָּה לִפְסוּלוֹת. אֲמַר רָבָא: וְתִסְבְּרָא דְּהָא מִתָּרְצְתָּא הִיא? וְהָא כִּי אֲתָא רַבִּי אַחָא בַּר חֲנִינָא מִדָּרוֹמָא, אֲתָא וְאַיְיתֵי מַתְנִיתָא בִּידֵיהּ: °"מִבַּלְעֲדֵי אִישֵׁךְ" [ד]מִי *שֶׁקָּדְמָה שְׁכִיבַת בַּעַל לְבוֹעֵל, וְלֹא שֶׁקָּדְמָה שְׁכִיבַת בּוֹעֵל לְבַעַל. אֲמַר רָמִי בַּר חָמָא: מַשְׁכַּחַת לָהּ כְּגוֹן שֶׁבָּא עָלֶיהָ אֲרוּסָהּ בְּבֵית אָבִיהָ. דִּכְוָותָהּ גַּבֵּי שׁוֹמֶרֶת יָבָם — שֶׁבָּא עָלֶיהָ יָבָם בְּבֵית חָמִיהָ?

שׁוֹמֶרֶת

רש"י

לְרַבִּי מֵאִיר דְּאָמַר קִידּוּשִׁין פָּסְלִי. חוּפָּה בְּלֹא קִידּוּשִׁין נַמִי פָּסְלָה. חוּפָּה. אֵינָהּ קוֹנָה בְּלֹא כֶּסֶף אוֹ שְׁטָר אוֹ קִידּוּשֵׁי בִיאָה, כִּדְאִיתָא בְּפ"ק דְּקִדּוּשִׁין (דף ה:). נִישְּׂאוּ. לְכֹהֵן זוֹ וָזוֹ, וּמַאי זוֹ וָזוֹ כְּשֵׁרוֹת וּפְסוּלוֹת. מִכְּלָל דְּנִישְּׂאוּ מַמָּשׁ. בִּבְעִילָה?! בִּתְמִיָּה: וְכִי בִּיאָה בִּפְסוּלָה מִי אִיכָּא לְמ"ד דְּלָא פָּסְלָה מִתְּרוּמָה דְּבֵי נָשָׂא? אֶלָּא פֵּירוּשֵׁי קָא מְפָרֵשׁ: נִישְּׂאוּ כֵּיצַד — כְּגוֹן שֶׁנִּכְנְסוּ לְחוּפָּה וְלֹא נִבְעֲלוּ. אוֹכְלוֹת מִשֶּׁלּוֹ כו'. דְּחוּפָּה לָא פָּסְלָה. אֵין חוּפָּתָהּ מַאֲכִילָתָהּ. אִם בַּת יִשְׂרָאֵל הִיא. וְאַלִּיבָּא דְּמִשְׁנָה אַחֲרוֹנָה, דִּתְנַן (כתובות דף נז.): ב"ד שֶׁל אַחֲרֵיהֶם אָמְרוּ: אֵין הָאִשָּׁה אוֹכֶלֶת בִּתְרוּמָה עַד שֶׁתִּכָּנֵס לַחוּפָּה. וְאָמַר ר' יִשְׁמָעֵאל: חוּפָּה פְּסוּלָה אֵינָהּ מַאֲכֶלֶת, וְה"ה בִּיאָה, מִדְּמַקִּישׁ חוּפָּה לְבִיאָה מַשְׁמַע דְּאִם בַּת כֹּהֵן הִיא חוּפָּה פּוֹסַלְתָּהּ כְּבִיאָתָהּ. מִמַּתְנִי'. דְּמַסֶּכֶת סוֹטָה. אָמֵן. אָמֵן, תְּרֵי זִימְנֵי, לְרַבּוֹת כָּל הָנֵי. שׁוֹמֶרֶת יָבָם וּכְנוּסָה. כְּלוֹמַר — וְאִם הָיְתָה יְבִמְתּוֹ וּכְנָסָהּ — הַיָּבָם מַשְׁקֶה אוֹתָהּ, וּמַשְׁבִּיעָהּ אַף עַל סְתִירָה שֶׁנִּסְתְּרָה בְּעוֹדָהּ שׁוֹמֶרֶת יָבָם, וּמַיִם בּוֹדְקִין אוֹתָהּ עַל שְׁתֵּיהֶן, דְּהָא אִי זַנַּאי בְּעוֹדָהּ שׁוֹמֶרֶת יָבָם — אֲסוּרָה עָלָיו, וּכְר' עֲקִיבָא מוֹקְמִינַן לָהּ בְּמַסֶּכֶת סוֹטָה (דף יח:), דְּאָמַר: אֵין קִידּוּשִׁין תּוֹפְסִין בְּחַיָּיבֵי לָאוִין, דְּמַשְׁוֵי לָהּ יְבָמָה לַשּׁוּק כְּאֵשֶׁת אִישׁ. וְכִי הֵיכִי דְּאֵשֶׁת אִישׁ מִיתַּסְרָא אַגַּבְרָא בִּזְנוּת — שׁוֹמֶרֶת יָבָם נַמִי מִיתַּסְרָא אַיְּבָמָהּ. וְכֵיוָן דְּמִיתַּסְרָא עֲלֵיהּ — בַּת קִינּוּי הִיא. דְּקַנֵּי לָהּ. קִינֵּא לָהּ וְהִתְרָה בָּהּ: אַל תִּסָּתְרִי עִם אִישׁ פְּלוֹנִי. לֹא שׁוֹתוֹת. דְּבָעֵינַן "תַּחַת אִישֵׁךְ". וְלֹא נוֹטְלוֹת כְּתוּבָּה. אִם קִינֵּא לָהּ וְנִסְתְּרָה שֶׁהִיא גָּרְמָה לֶאֱסוֹר אֶת עַצְמָהּ עָלָיו. אֶלָּא דְּקַנֵּי לָהּ כְּשֶׁהִיא אֲרוּסָה וְקָא אִיסְתַּתְּרָה. בְּאֵירוּסֶיהָ, וּנְשָׂאָהּ, וּמַשְׁקֶה לָהּ. וּמִי בָּדְקִי לָהּ. וְהָתַנְיָא כו'. מְנוּקֶּה מֵעָוֹן. שֶׁלֹּא בָּא עָלֶיהָ לְאַחַר שֶׁנִּסְתְּרָה, שֶׁהַתּוֹרָה אֲסָרָהּ עָלָיו, דִּכְתִיב (במדבר ה) "וְהִיא נִטְמָאָה". וש"מ. מִדְּמַשְׁקֶה לָהּ — יֵשׁ חוּפָּה לִפְסוּלוֹת, וְקָרֵינַן בֵּיהּ "תַּחַת אִישֵׁךְ", דְּקָנֵי לָהּ חוּפָּה. וְאַף עַל גַּב דְּלָא חַזְיָא לְבִיאָה, דְּהָא אֲסוּרָה לוֹ מִשֶּׁנִּסְתְּרָה: אֲמַר רָבָא וְתִסְבְּרָא דְּהָא מַתְנִי' מִתָּרַצְתָּא הִיא וְהָא כִּי אֲתָא כו'. שֶׁבָּא עָלֶיהָ אֲרוּסָהּ בְּבֵית אָבִיהָ. קוֹדֶם סְתִירָה, וּלְעוֹלָם מִתָּרַצְתָּא הִיא: וּפָרְכִינַן. דִּכְוָותָהּ גַּבֵּי שׁוֹמֶרֶת יָבָם שֶׁבָּא עָלֶיהָ. לְשֵׁם זְנוּת בְּבֵית חָמִיהָ בְּלֹא מְנוּתָהּ, וַהֲדַר קִינֵּא לָהּ וְאִיסְתַּתְּרָה, וְהִכְנִיסָהּ לְחוּפָּה וְלֹא נִבְעֲלָה, וּמַשְׁקֶה לָהּ, וּמַשְׁבִּיעָהּ שֶׁלֹּא שָׂטִית בַּסְּתִירָה הָרִאשׁוֹנָה.

שׁוֹמֶרֶת

תוספות

דהני תנאי. דתנא קמא סבר: אוכלות משלו ואוכלות בתרומה, דאין חופה פוסלתה מלאכול בתרומה, דאין חופה לפסולות. ורבי ישמעאל סבר: דיש חופה, דקאמר: כל שאין ביאתה מאכילתה – חופה נמי פוסלתה מן התרומה, אפילו היא בת כהן. דאי בבת ישראל קאמר *דאין חופה מאכילתה – בהא לא הוה פליג תנא קמא, לפי מה שפירשתי דמתני' איירי בבת כהן. ולפי מה שפי' בקונטרס דבבת ישראל נמי פליגי דאלכה לרבי אלעזר ורבי שמעון בהגעת הזמן אפילו היא פסולה – יש לפרש כאן שמדקדק מדמקשינן חופה לביאה, כדפי' בקונטרס, דמשמע *שאותה חופה כביאה. וא"ת: לת"ק, כיון דאין חופה לפסולות – אמאי אוכלות משלו? וי"ל: דלא גרע מהגעת זמן. ואוכלות בתרומה – כיון דנכנסה לחופה, דליכא למיחש למזיגת כוס ולסימפון. ואם תאמר: דאכתי פסולות אמאי אוכלות משלו? בעמוד והוצא קאי, מזוני אית להו?! כדאמרינן בריש "יש מותרות" (לקמן פה.)! וי"ל: דללדדין קתני, אוכלות משלו – לאחר מיתה, ואוכלות בתרומה – מחיים.

שומרת יבם וכנוסה. וא"ת: היאך מתנה על זנות דיבמה? הא תנן (סוטה דף יח:): כל שאילו תיבעל ולא תהא אסורה לו – לא היה מתנה עמה! וי"ל דהכא נמי נאסרה כדרב המנונא, דאמר: שומרת יבם שזינתה אסורה ליבמה. ובפ' שני דסוטה (דף יח: ושם) מייתי מינה סייעתא לרב המנונא, ודחי: הא מני ר' עקיבא היא, דאמר: אין קידושין תופסין בחייבי לאוין. וא"ת: והיכי מפיק כולהו מחד "אמן" יתירא: אמן על האלה, אמן על השבועה, אמן אם מאיש זה, אמן אם מאיש אחר, וארוסה ונשואה, ושומרת יבם, וכנוסה? וי"ל: דחד "אמן" קאי אכל מה דכתיב בפרשה, ואָלָה ושבועה כתיב בהדיא, וכן מאיש אחר – דכתיב "מבלעדי אישך", ואמן יתירא – לשומרת יבם וארוסה קאתי*.

אלא דקני לה כשהיא ארוסה(ב) ומשקה לה כשהיא נשואה. דהשתא לא ממעטינן מ"תחת אישך", כיון דהשתא בשעת השקאה היא תחת בעלה. וא"ת: ומנלן דקרא משמע שהסתירה היא כשהיא נשואה? דטומאה "תחת אישך" כתיב! וי"ל: דכי היכי דמרבה מאיש איש קינוי דאירוסין, בריש "ארוסה" (סוטה כד. ושם) ה"נ נרבה סתירה.

ונקה האיש מעון. וא"ת: ונוקמה כגון שבא עליה בשוגג, וכשבא עליה – לא ידע עדיין שנסתרה? דכי האי גוונא חשיב מנוקה מעון, דהא כי מוקי לה ע"י גלגול לא חשיב אין מנוקה מעון אם זינתה באירוסין! וי"ל: דהכא, כיון דבשעת השקאה יודע שבא עליה באיסור, אפילו בא עליה שוגג – לא חשיב מנוקה מעון. אבל על ידי גלגול, שאינו יודע בשעת השקאה – מנוקה מעון קרינן ביה.

דכוותה גבי שומרת יבם כו'. פי' בקונטרס בלישנא אחרינא: דמוקי לה הכי כי היכי דלא תיקשי: שומרת יבם בת משתיא היא? אבל משום קדמה שכיבת בעל לבועל לא פריך, דמה שקדמה שכיבת המת – כשכיבת בעל היא. ולשון דכוותה לא משמע הכי, דמשמע דמאותו הטעם שאנו מעמידים דארוסה – בבא עליה ארוסה בבית אביה, דהיינו: מטעם דבעינן שתקדים שכיבת בעל, יש לנו להעמיד בשומרת יבם בבית חמיה. ועוד, דבריש פרק "ארוסה" (סוטה כד: ושם) קאמר בהדיא דכוותה שומרת יבם כו' אקושיא דקדמה שכיבת בעל לבועל, דקאמר: טעמא דכתיבי הני קראי, הא לאו הכי – הוה אמינא: ארוסה שותה, והא כי אתא כו' ולא שקדמה שכיבת בועל לבעל, אמר רמי בר חמא: משכחת לה כגון שבא עליה ארוס בבית אביה, ודכוותה גבי שומרת יבם כו'. ונראה לר"י כפירוש ראשון שבקונטרס: דמטעם שתקדום שכיבת בעל קאמר דכוותה בשומרת יבם – שבא עליה יבם בבית חמיה, דכרבי יאשיה אתיא מתניתא: דשלא סטיתי שומרת יבם וכנוסה, דלדידיה שומרת יבם בת משתיא היא, כדיליף התם. ולא צריך לאוקמא כשבא עליה יבם בבית חמיה אלא משום דליקדום שכיבת בעל. דלרבי יונתן דפליג עליה התם אפילו בא עליה יבם בבית חמיה לא שתיא, כדאמרינן התם. ומוקי כוותיה ההיא דארוסה ושומרת יבם לא שותות כו'. וא"ת: וכיון דהני מתני' פליגי אהדדי, א"כ, מאי פריך לעיל אלא דקינא לה ומשקה לה כשהיא ארוסה, והתנן ארוסה ושומרת יבם כו'! ויש לומר: דלא פליגי רבי יאשיה ורבי יונתן אלא בשומרת יבם, אבל בארוסה – ליכא מאן דפליג.

שומרת

עין משפט נר מצוה

מח א מיי' פ"ד מהלכ' סוטה הלכה טז:
מט ב מיי' פ"ב שם הלכה ג:
נ ג מיי' שם הל' ח ופ"ג הלכ' יז:
ס"א משום דלא קניא האי חופה כלל
נא ד מיי' שם פ"ב הלכה ה:
ס"א שעושה

מסורת הש"ס

קדושין כז: סוטה יח.
סוטה כג: קדושין כז: ספרי פ' נשא
סוטה כח. מז: שבועות ה. קדושין כז: ספרי פ' נשא
סוטה כד:

תורה אור: במדבר ה

תוספות ישנים

אמן שלא שטיתי ארוסה ונשואה וכו' האי ארוסה היכי דמי אלימא שקינא לה כשהיא ארוסה ואסתתרה וקא משקה לה כשהיא ארוסה והשתא ארוסה ונשואה בחד שבועה מפיק א) דאיירי דנקט איידי הקנוי בארוסים וההשקאה בנשואים והשתא לא הוי דומיא דסיפא אמן מאיש זה אמן מאיש אחר דמיירי בתרתי ולמסקנא ניחא שפיר דמוקמי' לה ע"י גלגול והוי ארוסה ונשואה בתרתי:

א) אולי צ"ל דאיידי דנקט דהיה הקינוי וההשקאה באירוסין נקט נמי הקינוי באירוסין וההשקאה בנשואים.

הגהות הב"ח

(א) גמ' כשהיא ארוסה ואיסתתרה וקא משקה לה כשהיא ארוסה: (ב) תוס' ד"ה אלא וכו' ארוסה ואיסתתרה ומשקה:

[וע"ע תוס' קדושין כז: ד"ה אמן]

נב א מיי' פ"ד מהל' סוטה הל' יז:
נג ב מיי' פ"ז מהל' תרומות הל' כב:
נד ג ד מיי' שם הל' כג:

*שומרת יבם קרית לה?! אשתו מעליא היא! דהא *אמר רב: קנה לכל. כשמואל דאמר: לא קנה אלא לדברים האמורים בפרשה. מידי הוא טעמא – אלא לרב, הא אמר רב קנה לכל! הכא במאי עסקינן, כגון דעבד בה מאמר, וב"ש היא, דאמרי: *מאמר קונה קנין גמור. אי הכי, היינו ארוסה! ולטעמיך, נשואה וכנוסה לאו חדא מילתא היא? אלא: נשואה – דידיה, וכנוסה – דחבריה. הכא נמי: ארוסה – דידיה, ושומרת יבם – דחבריה. רב פפא אמר: האי תנא הוא, דתניא: *אין מקנין לה לארוסה להשקותה כשהיא ארוסה, אבל מקנין אותה להשקותה כשהיא נשואה. רב נחמן בר יצחק אמר: *[א]על ידי גלגול. שלח רב חנינא משמיה דרבי יוחנן: העושה מאמר ביבמתו, [ויש לו אח], אפילו הוא כהן והיא כהנת – פסלה מן התרומה. למאן? אילימא לרבי מאיר, אימר דאמר רבי מאיר משתמרת לביאה פסולה לא אכלה – מדאורייתא, דרבנן מי אמר? ואלא לרבי אלעזר ורבי שמעון, השתא משתמרת לביאה פסולה דאורייתא אכלה, דרבנן מיבעיא? אלא כי אתא רבין אמר: עשה בה מאמר ביבמתו – דברי הכל אכלה, [ב]יש לו אח חלל – דברי הכל אינה אוכלת. לא נחלקו אלא שנתן לה גט, רבי יוחנן אמר: אוכלת, ריש לקיש אמר: אינה אוכלת. רבי יוחנן אמר: [ג]אוכלת, אפילו לרבי מאיר דאמר אינה אוכלת – הני מילי משתמרת לביאה פסולה דאורייתא, [ד]אבל דרבנן – אכלה. וריש לקיש אמר: אינה אוכלת, אפילו לר"א ורבי שמעון דאמרי אוכלת – הני מילי דיש לו להאכיל במקום אחר, אבל הכא, כיון דאין לו להאכיל במקום אחר – לא. וכי תימא: הכא נמי יש לו להאכילה בחוזרת – חוזרת פסקה מיניה, וקרובה לבי נשא, אבל הא אגידא ביה. § "נתארמלו או נתגרשו וכו'". § בעא מיניה רבי חייא בר יוסף משמואל: כהן גדול שקידש את הקטנה ובגרה תחתיו, מהו

רש"י

שומרת יבם קרית לה. קנה לכל. בביאת שוגג ומזיד. מידי הוא טעמא אלא לרב. הא דמייתינן יש חופה לפסולות – לסיועה לרב מייתינן לה, דאמר לעיל: יש חופה לפסולות, ורב – קאמר לעיל קנה לכל, ולדידיה לא מיתרצתא היא. כגון דעבד מאמר. ואח"כ בא עליה בזנות בבית חמיה. וב"ש היא דאמרי. בפרק "ד' אחין" (לעיל דף כט:) מאמר קונה קנין גמור – ליעשות ארוסה גמורה, והפריש את זיקת היבום, ותו לא מקנייא ליה בביאת מזיד אלא במסירת חופה כאשה בעלמא. כדאמרינן בד' אחין" (שם). ומשום הכי קרי לה שומרת יבם אפילו לאחר ביאה, דאי לב"ה – לא אלים מאמר להפריש זיקת יבמין וליחול זיקת אירוסין ונישואין, והוי קני לה בביאת זנות לגמרי. אי הכי היינו ארוסה. גמורה, וארוסה – הא תנא לה. נשואה דידיה. אשתו, שלא היתה יבמתו. דחבריה. אחיו. דיבמתו שייך לשון כניסה. לישנא אחרינא, ועיקר: דכוותה גבי שומרת יבם דקשיא לך נמי בה: הא לאו בת אשקויי היא – מוקמת לה נמי כגון שבא עליה, דהא כשנכנסה לחופה ליכא לאוקומה, דהא חופה ביבמה לא שייכא. שומרת יבם קרית כו'. אלא לא תוקמה לשומרת יבם כשבא עליה, אלא כגון דעבד בה מאמר. ולשקדמה שכיבת בעל לא קפדינן, דהא קדמה שכיבת בעל הראשון שהיא באה מכחו, ומאמר קונה קנין גמור וקרינן בה "תחת אישך". רב פפא אמר. לעולם לא תדוק מינה דיש חופה, והכא כגון דקינא לה כשהיא ארוסה ונשאה ובא עליה והדר איסתתרה, ומשקה לה על ידי אותו קינוי, והאי תנא הוא כו': לישנא אחרינא: אמר רב פפא – לעולם דקינא לה כשהיא ארוסה, ואיסתתרה, ומשקה לה כשהיא נשואה. [הג"ה עד שלא נבעלה, ודקשיא לך משקדמה שכיבת בעל לבועל, האי תנא וכו'. עכ"ה]. ודקשיא לך אין מנוקה מעון – האי תנא הוא, דלית ליה הך דרשא. וזה הוא לשון מורי, והוא נראה עיקר. דללישנא קמא איכא למיפרך: אם כן מאי לא שטיתי ארוסה? ואדרבה, הא לא כשהיא ארוסה איסתתרה. רב נחמן אמר. מתניתין בדלא קינא ולא איסתתרה כשהיא ארוסה, אלא קינא לה משנשאה ואיסתתרה, ומשקה לה ע"י קינוי של עכשיו, ומגלגל עליה שבועה כל ימים שהיתה תחתיו משנתארסה ונבדקה, ומכאן לגלגול שבועה מן התורה. פסלה מן התרומה. עד שיכנוס. משתמרת לביאה פסולה. שיש ביד אחיו לבא עליה, וביאתו ביאה. וכי היכי דהיא משתמרת לביאתו, כך היא משתמרת לביאת אחיו, שהיא פסולה מדרבנן, דיש ביאה אחר מאמר, כדתנן (לעיל דף נ:): מאמר לזו ובעל לזו כו', וכן בב' יבמין ויבמה אחת. דאורייתא. ביאה שהיא פסולה דאורייתא, כגון אלמנה לכהן גדול. דברי הכל. בין לרבי יוחנן בין לריש לקיש אכלה בתרומה דבי נשא, דהא אפילו לרבי מאיר לא פסיל אלא במשתמרת לביאה פסולה דאורייתא. יש. לזה היבם אח חלל. לדברי הכל לא אכלה. אפי' היא בת כהן. ואע"ג דעבד בה מאמר כהן כשר – אכתי משתמרת לביאה פסולה היא, לביאת החלל, דהויא פסולה דאורייתא ולא אכלה. ואפי' לרבי אלעזר ורבי שמעון, כי מכשרי – באלמנה לכ"ג קמכשרי, שיש לו להאכיל במקום אחר. אבל משתמרת ליבם חלל, דאין לו להאכיל, דהא כהן חלל זר הוא – פסל לה, ולא אכלה. אלא שנתן לה גט. כהן ליבמתו כהנת. ואכתי, לביאתו היא משתמרת, וביאתה פסולה מדרבנן היא, דגט מהני בה מדרבנן. אפילו לרבי אלעזר דאמר אוכלת. הני מילי על ידי קידושין, דיש לו להאכיל כי האי גוונא במקום אחר. אבל על ידי גירושין. דאין לו להאכיל על ידי גירושין במקום אחר – לא. ואם תאמר. הכא נמי יש לו להאכיל על ידי גירושין גמורים בחוזרת, דאם היה מגרשה לגמרי – היתה חוזרת לבית אביה, ואוכלת בתרומה. כדאמרינן במתניתין. ובגרה תחתיו. בימי אירוסין. וכ"ג אסור בבוגרת, כדאמרינן במתניתין, ומצותו בקטנה או בנערה. מהו

תוספות

שומרת יבם קרית לה אשתו מעלייתא היא דהא אמר רב קנה לכל. ואע"ג דקרי לה שומרת יבם במילתיה דרבי יאשיה ורבי יונתן, דאיירו בבא עליה יבם בבית חמיו, ובלא עבד בה מאמר – התם משום דלאו אשתו מעליא היא לענין השקאה קרי לה שפיר שומרת יבם, אפילו לרב דאמר קנה לכל, דהא ממעט לה רבי יונתן בברייתא מ"תחת אישך". ורבי יאשיה קרי לה נמי שומרת יבם, דקתני: יכול שאני מוציא שומרת יבם כו' – משום דאי לאו רבויא ד"איש איש" הוה ממעט לה. וכן מסיק התם. אבל הכא לא הזכיר שום טעם שהיה ראוי לקרותה על ידו שומרת יבם. ועוד: כיון דקונה לכל – לא הוה ליה למימר שומרת יבם וכנוסה, דהך נמי כנוסה היא.

דהא אמר רב קנה לכל. ונפל מן הגג ונתקע, או בנתכוון להטיח בכותל, ליכא לאוקמה – ד"ויתן איש בך את שכבתו מבלעדי אישך" דמשמע מבלעדי אישך שנתן בך את שכבתו, משמע דבעינן בבעל כוונת שכיבה. רב פפא אמר האי תנא. פי' בקונטרס בלשון שני: לעולם דקינא לה ואיסתתרה כשהיא ארוסה, והאי תנא הוא דלית ליה הך דרשא ד"ונקה האיש מעון" ולית ליה הך דרשא שקדמה שכיבת בעל. וקשה לר"י: דבריש שבועות (דף ה. ושם) ובסוטה (דף כח.) ובכמה דוכתי פריך: ומי בדקי לה מיא, והתניא: ונקה האיש וכו'. ולא משני: האי תנא הוא. משמע דליכא מאן דפליג. ועוד: מנא ליה דהאי תנא לא בעי שתקדום שכיבת בעל? דלמא כשבא עליה ארוסה בבית אביה איירי! ונראה כלשון ראשון שבקונטרס, ושלא שטית ארוסה דקאמר – לא שנסתרה באירוסין קאמר, אלא ה"ק: שלא שטית להיות נבדקת עליה בקינוי דאירוסין. מיהו, גם ללשון זה קצת קשה: כיון שצריך להביא ראיה על זה שמועיל קינוי דאירוסין להשקותה בסתירה דנישואין – מנא ליה דהאי תנא אית ליה האי סברא? הא איכא לפרושי מקנין לארוסה להשקותה כשהיא נשואה – היינו דקינא לה כשהיא ארוסה ואיסתתרה ונכנסה לחופה ולא נבעלה, כדפי' מתניתין דלעיל.

על ידי גלגול. לא בעי*) לאפוקי גלגול מגלגול דאיש אחר, דלא דמי, דגלגול דאיש אחר ראוי להשקות על ידו אם היה מקנא על ידו, אבל קרקעות – לאו בנות שבועה נינהו כלל. אבל מגלגול דארוסה יליף שפיר, דלאו בת השקאה היא כלל – ואפי' הכי מגלגל זנות דאירוסין. וא"ת: ולמאי דדייקינן מיניה לעיל דיש חופה לפסולות, ולא מוקמינן על ידי גלגול – מנלן גלגול שבועה? וי"ל: דנפקא ליה מ"איש אחר" ולא הוה מפליג בין קרקעות לאיש אחר. אי נמי דמשמע ליה מ"איש אחר" – אפילו קטן, דדמי לקרקעות, שאין מקנין על ידו, כדתנן בסוף פרק "ארוסה" (סוטה דף כו: וכן בריש פ' שם כד.).

אימור דאמר רבי מאיר כו'. גם מכאן ראיה דחשיב משתמרת לביאה פסולה, אף על פי שלא היו הקידושין בעבירה.

*) ס"א לאתויי

סוטה כד:
[לעיל נו.]
[לעיל כט: וש"נ]
סוטה כה.
קדושין כז:

תוספות ישנים

שומרת יבם קרית לה אשתו מעלייתא היא. הכא פריך משום דקאמר בתר הכי וכנוסה [אבל] בסוטה לא נוכל לפרש כן וא"ת ולוקמה שנתכוין להטיח בכותל והטיח ביבמתו דאמרינן לעיל לא קנה וי"ל דא"כ הדרא קושיא לדוכתין דלא קדמה שכיבת בעל לבועל דלאו שכיבה מקרייא: דעבד בה מאמר והשתא פרחה מינה זיקת יבמין וחלה עליו זיקת ארוסין ונשואין דמאמר קונה קנין גמור לב"ש והשתא לא קנאה בביאה דמחסרא מסירה לחופה ולעולם מיירי שבא עליה יבם בבית חמיה: ע"י גלגול פי' ומיירי דקינא לה בנשואין ומשקה לה בנשואין אבן על ידי גלגול נשבעת שלא זנתה בארוסין והשתא נימא לארוסה ונשואה תרתי מילי נינהו והוי כמו אמן מאיש זה אמן מאיש אחר וא"ת מ"מ תקשי לאם אמת הדבר שזנתה כשהיא ארוסה היכי בדקי לה מיא בנשואין הלא אינו מנוקה מעון וי"ל דמ"מ כיון שאינו מזיד בדבר בדקי ליה שפיר מיא. וא"ת א"כ לעיל כי פריך ומי בדקי לה מיא והלא אין האיש מנוקה מעון ליתני דמיירי כשבא עליה בשוגג וי"ל דלעיל לא מצי לשנויי הכי דכיון דמיירי דקני לה בארוסין יש לו להשמר שלא יבא עליה וכאשר בא עלי' קרוב למזיד ואינו מנוקה מעון שקרי תשלם מזונות מדקני לה אבל הכא לא קני לה בארוסין כלל ואינו מנוקה מעון ואפילו אם זנתה כי לא [עלה] על דעתו לא תהא אסורה עליו האיש מנוקה מעון: כ"ג שקדש את הקטנה ובגרה תחתיו מהו בתר אירוסין אזלינן ושריא ליה או בתר נשואין אזלינן ואסורה. ופשיט מן האירוסין כשרות אלמנה מאירוסין דבתר נשואין אזלינן ולקמן פשיטא ליה דבתר אירוסין אזלינן מההוא דנתמנה להיות כ"ג יכנוס. וע"ק לשנויי חללה לא קא מבעיא ליה משמע דר' יוחנן היה סובר דרבי חייא הלכה לא מיירי לשנויי כלל לאיסור קיחה והו"ל שאני איסור חללה מאיסור קיחה ונראה דודאי ס"ד לר' יוחנן דר' חייא קא בעי לענין חללות ופשיטא ליה לאסור לכונסה. אכן דכאן קבעי לר' מאיר לאמר משמרת לביאה פסולה לא אכלה ולכך קבעי היכא דקדשה קטנה ובגרה אי בתר נשואין אזלי' והויא ביאה פסולה ותשבינן לה משעת אירוסין משמרת לביאה פסולה ולא אכלה או דלמא לא. ופשיט לה מגופה דמתני' דאזלינן בתר נשואין וקא"ל לשנויי חללה לא קא מיבעיא ליה א) כיון דס"ד דפשיטא ליה שאסור לכונסה דודאי בזה אנכי מסופק אי שרי לכונסה אי לא אי קיחה דאירוסין או קיחה דנשואין ופשיט ליה מההוא דיכנוס דקיחת אירוסין קאמר קרא וא"כ מ"מ הדרן קושיין לדוכתא דמעיקרא פשיט לה ר' יוחנן מההיא דמתני' דבתר נשואין אזלינן ולכן פשיט ליה לאסור לכונסה והשתא קא פשיט מההיא דיכנוס דשרי לכונסה וי"ל דלעיל לא קא פשיט אלא לדבריו לאסר עלה בדעתו דרבי חייא היה שואלו ממנו לשוויה חללה ועל כן היה ר' יוחנן סבור שהיה פשוט לר' חייא שאסור לכונסה ומיבעיא לך אי תשבינן לה לפסול מתרומה כיון דהאירוסין הוו

א) נראה דצ"ל ולא כס"ד דפשיטא ליה שאסור לכונסה אלא דבזה אנכי מסופק.

תוספות חד מקמאי

כי אתא רבין אמר כהן שעשה מאמר ביבמתו לר"ג אכלה ואפי' לר"מ דאמר משמרת לביאה פסולה לא אכלה ה"מ ביאה פסולה מדאורי' אבל ביאה פסולה מדרבנן כגון זה שאם בא עליה אחר אין בה פסולות אלא מדרבנן אכלה. יש לו אח חלל ד"ה אינה אוכלת לא נחלקו אלא בנתן לה גיטו דר"י אומר אוכלת אע"פ שאינו מאכיל במקום אחר אפילו לר"מ דאמר אינה אוכלת ה"מ דיש לו להאכיל במקום אחר אבל הכא כיון דאינו מאכיל במקום אחר לא. וכ"ת להאכיל בחוזרת חוזרת פסקה מניה וחזרה לבי נשא הוא ואינה גביה והלכתא כר' יוחנן:

מַהוּ? בָּתַר נִישּׂוּאִין אָזְלִינַן, אוֹ בָּתַר אֵירוּסִין אָזְלִינַן? א"ל: תְּנֵיתוּהָ, *נִתְאַרְמְלוּ אוֹ נִתְגָּרְשׁוּ, מִן הַנִּשּׂוּאִין — פְּסוּלוֹת, מִן הָאֵירוּסִין — כְּשֵׁרוֹת. אֲמַר לֵיהּ: לְשַׁוּוֹיָהּ חֲלָלָה — לָא קָמִיבַּעְיָא לִי דְּבִיאָה הִיא דִּמְשַׁוְּיָא חֲלָלָה. כִּי קָמִיבַּעְיָא לִי °"וְהוּא אִשָּׁה בִבְתוּלֶיהָ יִקָּח" מַאי? קִיחָה דְּקִדּוּשִׁין בָּעֵינַן, אוֹ קִיחָה דְּנִישּׂוּאִין בָּעֵינַן? אֲמַר לֵיהּ, הָא נַמִי תְּנֵיתוּהָ: *[א]אֵירֵס אֶת הָאַלְמָנָה וְנִתְמַנָּה לִהְיוֹת כֹּהֵן גָּדוֹל — יִכְנוֹס. שָׁאנֵי הָתָם, דִּכְתִיב °"יִקַּח אִשָּׁה". הָכָא נַמִי כְּתִיב "אִשָּׁה". אַחַת וְלֹא שְׁתַּיִם. וּמָה רָאִיתָ? [ב]הָא אִישְׁתַּנֵּי גּוּפָהּ, וְהָא לָא אִישְׁתַּנֵּי גּוּפָהּ.§ **מתני'** [ג]כֹּהֵן גָּדוֹל לֹא יִשָּׂא אַלְמָנָה, [ד]בֵּין אַלְמָנָה מִן הָאֵירוּסִין בֵּין אַלְמָנָה מִן הַנִּשּׂוּאִין. [ה]וְלֹא יִשָּׂא אֶת הַבּוֹגֶרֶת, רַ' אֶלְעָזָר וְרַ' שִׁמְעוֹן מַכְשִׁירִין בְּבוֹגֶרֶת. [וְלֹא יִשָּׂא אֶת מוּכַּת עֵץ].§ **גמ'** תָּנוּ רַבָּנַן: °"אַלְמָנָה לֹא יִקָּח", בֵּין אַלְמָנָה מִן הָאֵירוּסִין, בֵּין אַלְמָנָה מִן הַנִּשּׂוּאִין. פְּשִׁיטָא! מַהוּ דְּתֵימָא: לֵילַף אַלְמָנָה אַלְמָנָה מִתָּמָר, מָה לְהַלָּן — מִן הַנִּשּׂוּאִין, אַף כָּאן — מִן הַנִּשּׂוּאִין, קמ"ל. וְאֵימָא הָכִי נַמִי! דּוּמְיָא דִּגְרוּשָׁה, מָה גְּרוּשָׁה [ו]בֵּין *מִן הַנִּשּׂוּאִין בֵּין מִן הָאֵירוּסִין, אַף אַלְמָנָה בֵּין מִן הָאֵירוּסִין בֵּין מִן הַנִּשּׂוּאִין.§ "וְלֹא יִשָּׂא אֶת הַבּוֹגֶרֶת".§ *תָּנוּ רַבָּנַן: "וְהוּא אִשָּׁה בִבְתוּלֶיהָ יִקָּח", פְּרָט לְבוֹגֶרֶת שֶׁכָּלוּ לָהּ בְּתוּלֶיהָ, דִּבְרֵי רַ' מֵאִיר. רַ' אֶלְעָזָר וְרַ' שִׁמְעוֹן מַכְשִׁירִין בְּבוֹגֶרֶת. בְּמַאי קָא מִיפַּלְגִי? *רַבִּי מֵאִיר סָבַר: "בְּתוּלָה" אֲפִילּוּ מִקְצָת בְּתוּלִים מַשְׁמַע, "בְּתוּלֶיהָ" עַד דְּאִיכָּא כָּל הַבְּתוּלִים, "בִּבְתוּלֶיהָ" בִּכְדַרְכָּהּ אִין, שֶׁלֹּא כְּדַרְכָּהּ לָא. וְרַבִּי אֶלְעָזָר וְרַבִּי שִׁמְעוֹן סָבְרִי: "בְּתוּלָה" בְּתוּלָה שְׁלֵימָה מַשְׁמַע, "בְּתוּלֶיהָ" וַאֲפִי' מִקְצָת בְּתוּלִים, "בִּבְתוּלֶיהָ" עַד שֶׁיִּהְיוּ כָּל בְּתוּלֶיהָ קַיָּימִין, בֵּין בִּכְדַרְכָּהּ בֵּין שֶׁלֹּא כְּדַרְכָּהּ. אָמַר רַב יְהוּדָה אָמַר רַב: [ז]נִבְעֲלָה שֶׁלֹּא כְּדַרְכָּהּ — פְּסוּלָה לִכְהוּנָּה. מְתִיב רָבָא: °"וְלוֹ תִהְיֶה לְאִשָּׁה" [ח]בְּאִשָּׁה הָרְאוּיָה לוֹ, פְּרָט לְאַלְמָנָה לְכֹהֵן גָּדוֹל, גְּרוּשָׁה וַחֲלוּצָה לְכֹהֵן הֶדְיוֹט. הֵיכִי דָּמֵי? אִילֵימָא בִּכְדַרְכָּהּ — מַאי אִירְיָא מִשּׁוּם אַלְמָנָה? תֵּיפוֹק לֵיהּ מִשּׁוּם דַּהֲוְיָא לָהּ בְּעוּלָה. אֶלָּא לָאו שֶׁלֹּא כְּדַרְכָּהּ. וּמִשּׁוּם אַלְמָנָה — אִין, מִשּׁוּם בְּעוּלָה — לָא. הָא

רש"י

מַהוּ. לְכוֹנְסָהּ מִשֶּׁבָּגְרָה, אוֹ לָא. בָּתַר קִיחָה דְּאֵירוּסִין אָזְלִינַן וְשַׁרְיָא לֵיהּ, אוֹ בָּתַר נִישּׂוּאִין אָזְלִינַן, וְכֵיוָן דְּבָגְרָה — אֲסִירָא לֵיהּ. מִן הָאֵירוּסִין כְּשֵׁרוֹת. אַלְמָא בִּפְסוּל כְּהוּנָּה בָּתַר נִישּׂוּאִין אָזְלִינַן מִדְּלָא פָּסֵיל אַלְמָנָה שֶׁנִּתְאָרְסָה לְכ"ג וּמֵת. יִכְנוֹס. אַלְמָא בָּתַר אֵירוּסִין אָזְלִינַן. שָׁאנֵי הָתָם דִּכְתִיב אִשָּׁה. "כִּי אִם בְּתוּלָה מֵעַמָּיו יִקַּח אִשָּׁה", וְהַאי אִשָּׁה קְרָא יְתֵירָא הוּא, וּמִינֵּיהּ מְרַבִּינַן לְקַמָּן בְּפִירְקִין (דף סא.) דְּאִם אֵירֵס אַלְמָנָה וְנִתְמַנָּה לִהְיוֹת כֹּהֵן גָּדוֹל יִכְנוֹס. אַחַת וְלֹא שְׁתַּיִם. אֵירוּצָא הוּא: אַחַת יֵשׁ לְךָ לְרַבּוֹת, וְלֹא שְׁתַּיִם. הָא אִישְׁתַּנֵּי גּוּפָהּ. בּוֹגֶרֶת נִשְׁתַּנָּה גּוּפָהּ מִן אֵירוּסִין לְנִישּׂוּאִין, אַלְמָנָה לֹא נִשְׁתַּנֵּית. **מתני'** וְלֹא יִשָּׂא אֶת הַבּוֹגֶרֶת. פְּלוּגְתַּיְיהוּ מְפָרֵשׁ בַּגְּמָ'. **גמ'** פְּשִׁיטָא. אַלְמָנָה סְתָמָא מַשְׁמַע. מִתָּמָר. "שְׁבִי אַלְמָנָה" (בראשית לח). דּוּמְיָא דִּגְרוּשָׁה. וּבִגְרוּשָׁה פְּשִׁיטָא לֵיהּ; דִּסְתָמָא הִיא, דְּלֵית לָךְ לְמֵילַף כִּדְיָלְפִינַן ג"ש בְּאַלְמָנָה. בְּתוּלָה. אִי הֲוָה כְּתִיב "בְּתוּלָה יִקַּח" — מִקְצָת בְּתוּלִים מַשְׁמַע, וַהֲוַאי מִיכַּשְׁרֵי בּוֹגֶרֶת. הַשְׁתָּא דִּכְתִיב "בְּתוּלֶיהָ" — מִיפַּסְלָא בּוֹגֶרֶת, דְּמַשְׁמַע דְּבָעֵינַן כָּל בְּתוּלֶיהָ. בִּבְתוּלֶיהָ. בֵּי"ת יְתֵירָא, דְּמַשְׁמַע הָכִי: לְמִדְרַשׁ בִּמְקוֹם בְּתוּלֶיהָ, דְּהַיְינוּ כְּדַרְכָּהּ, אִם נִבְעֲלָה — נִפְסְלָה לְכ"ג, אֲבָל בִּבְעִילָה שֶׁלֹּא כְּדַרְכָּהּ — לָא. דִּלְמֵיסַר בְּעוּלָה שֶׁלֹּא כְּדַרְכָּהּ לֵיכָּא לְמֵימַר מֵהַאי קְרָא, וּלְמִידְרַשׁ עַד שֶׁיִּהְיוּ כָּל בְּתוּלֶיהָ קַיָּימִין, וַאֲפִילּוּ שֶׁלֹּא כְּדַרְכָּהּ, כִּדְדָרְשִׁינַן לֵיהּ אַלִּיבָּא דְּרַבִּי אֶלְעָזָר — כֵּיוָן דִּ"בְתוּלָה" מְמַעֵט בּוֹגֶרֶת, כ"ש בְּעוּלָה שֶׁלֹּא כְּדַרְכָּהּ. הִלְכָּךְ, כִּי אָתָא קְרָא — לְמִישְׁרֵי אָתָא, וְכִדְדָרְשִׁינַן. וְרַבִּי אֶלְעָזָר וְרַבִּי שִׁמְעוֹן סָבְרִי. אִי הֲוָה כְּתִיב בְּתוּלָה — שְׁלֵימָה מַשְׁמַע, וּמִיפַּסְלָא בּוֹגֶרֶת. הַשְׁתָּא דִּכְתִיב "בְּתוּלֶיהָ" — אֲפִילּוּ מִקְצָת בְּתוּלִים מַשְׁמַע, לְרַבּוֹת בּוֹגֶרֶת. בִּבְתוּלֶיהָ. ב' יְתֵירָה מַשְׁמַע שֶׁתְּהֵא בִּבְתוּלֶיהָ, שֶׁלֹּא אִבְּדָה מֵהֶם כְּלוּם עַל יְדֵי בְעִילָה, בֵּין כְּדַרְכָּהּ בֵּין שֶׁלֹּא כְּדַרְכָּהּ. וְכֵיוָן דְּאִיתְרַבַּאי בּוֹגֶרֶת לְהֶיתֵּירָא, אִיצְטְרִיךְ לְמֵיסַר בְּעוּלָה שֶׁלֹּא כְּדַרְכָּהּ. פְּסוּלָה לִכְהוּנָּה. לְכ"ג שֶׁמְּצוּוֶּה עַל הַבְּתוּלָה. אֲבָל לְהֶדְיוֹט אֲפִילּוּ כְּדַרְכָּהּ כְּשֵׁרָה. וְאֵין זוֹנָה אֶלָּא הַנִּבְעֶלֶת לְאָסוּר לָהּ. וְלוֹ תִהְיֶה לְאִשָּׁה. בִּמְאַנֵּס נַעֲרָה בְּתוּלָה כְּתִיב. פְּרָט לְאַלְמָנָה. מִן הָאֵירוּסִין, וְזֶה הַמְאַנֵּס כ"ג הוּא. אוֹ גְּרוּשָׁה אוֹ חֲלוּצָה מִן הָאֵירוּסִין הִיא, אִם כֹּהֵן הֶדְיוֹט הוּא. הֵיכִי דָּמֵי. הָךְ בִּיאַת אוֹנֵס, שֶׁבָּא עָלֶיהָ כֹּהֵן גָּדוֹל זֶה. תֵּיפוֹק לֵיהּ דַּהֲוְיָא לָהּ בְּעוּלָה. וְתַנְיָא לְקַמָּן: אֲנוּסַת עַצְמוֹ וּמְפוּתַּת עַצְמוֹ — לֹא יִשָּׂא.

תוספות

מהו בתר נישואין אזלינן. מתוך פירוש הקונטרס משמע דשמואל ידע דמיבעיא ליה אם מותר לכונסה משבגרה או לא, אע"ג דמתניתין לא איירי באיסור קיחה — מ"מ שמואל הוה מדמי איסור קיחה לאיסור חללה. וקשה לר"י: דמעיקרא פשט ליה שמואל דבתר נישואין אזלינן, ובתר הכי פשט ליה דבתר אירוסין אזלינן? ועוד: דלא הוה ליה למימר לשוויה חללה לא קמיבעיא לי, כיון דאיהו נמי ידע דלא קמיבעיא ליה אלא לענין קיחה, אלא שהיה מדמה זה לזה. והכי הוה ליה למימר: שאני איסור קיחה מאיסור חללה! ונראה לר"י: דשמואל היה סבר דמיבעיא ליה אי חשיב ליה לר"מ משתמרת לביאה פסולה, כיון שהקידושין היו בהיתר, או לא. והיה יכול להשיבו דזו ביאה כשרה היא, דמותר לכנוס, כדקאמר בסמוך. אלא לפי דבריו, שסבור דאסור לכנוס, משיב לו: תנינא דמן הנישואין פסולות. וכיון דעיקר חללות מן הנשואין — סברא הוא דבתר נישואין אזלינן. אפי' הוי הקידושין בהיתר. **הא** לא אישתני גופה. קודם נישואין, אחר שנתמנה להיות כ"ג. וה"ה אם אירס בוגרת, או קטנה ובגרה, ואח"כ נתמנה להיות כ"ג. דדוקא נתמנה ואח"כ בגרה הוא דלא יכנוס, דנשתנה הגוף אחר שנתמנה. וצ"ע אם אחר שנתמנה נעשית מוכת עץ או בעולה, אי הוי נשתנה הגוף ולא יכנוס, או לא? וקצת משמע בפ"ק דקדושין (דף י.) דלא חשיבא בעולה אישתני גופה, דקאמר: אי תחלת ביאה קונה יכול כ"ג לקדש בביאה, ואי חשוב כאישתני גופה — היאך יכנוס? והלא בעולה היא בשעת נישואין, אם תאמר דביאה אירוסין (א) עושה! ומיהו, בפ' "אלו נערות" (כתובות לח: ושם) חשיב בעולה שינוי הגוף, גבי הא דפריך: אדרבה "בתולה" "בתולה" לגזירה שוה, שהרי אני קורא בה "נערה אשר לא אורסה", ומשני: הא — אישתני גופה, הא — לא אישתני גופה. והא דאמרי' בפ' "נערה" בכתובות (דף מה. ושם) ודלמא כי חדית רחמנא — היכא דלא אישתני גופה, שלא בגרה — התם שהיתה כבר בעולה מן הבועל, לא חשיב שינוי הגוף בבעילת בעל. ובעילת בועל, אע"ג דהוי שינוי הגוף — התם לא איירי אלא בנשתנה הגוף אחר העבירה. [וע"ע תוס' כתובות מה. ד"ה דלמא]. **דומיא** דגרושה. וא"ת: אדרבה, גרושה דומיא דאלמנה, דדוקא מן הנשואין! וי"ל: דלחומרא מקשינן. ועוד אר"י: דגרושה הויא אף מן האירוסין, כמו גרושה דכהן הדיוט, ואע"ג דב"השולח" (גיטין מח. ושם) אמרי': לא, דכולי עלמא ג"ש עדיפא מהקישא — שאני התם, דעיקר שטר נפקא לן מגזרה שוה. [וע"ע תוס' זבחים מח. ד"ה דכ"ע]. **פרט** לבוגרת שכלו בתוליה. לאו דוקא כלו, אלא כלומר: נתמעטו קצת. **אפי'** מקצת בתולים. לא מצי למימר: לרבי מאיר בתולה שלימה משמע, בין כדרכה בין שלא כדרכה "בתוליה" — להכשיר שלא כדרכה, "בבתוליה" — למעוטי בוגרת — דלא משמע ליה למדרש מבי"ת אלא לענין שלא כדרכה, "בבתוליה" — במקום בתוליה. ועוד: דע"כ לר"מ "בתולה" — מקצת בתולה, דשמעינן ליה לר"מ בפרק "אלמנה ניזונת" (כתובות נז: ושם) דאמר: מקצת כסף ככל כסף. ועוד: דאי אפשר דבתולה — שלימה משמע, למעוטי שלא כדרכה, דמ"בתולה" ליכא למעוטי שלא כדרכה, דהא בקנס של נערה כתיב בתולה, ואפילו הכי יש לה קנס, כדאמר בפרק קמא דקידושין (דף י.): מודה רבי לענין קנס דכולהו משלמי. וכן לענין סקילה בנערה המאורסה — לא פליג רבי אלא משום דכתיב "לבדו". ומיהו קשה לר"י: למאן דאמר "בתולה" שלימה משמע, אמאי איצטריך גבי קנס למעוטי בוגרת? תיפוק ליה מדכתיב "בתולה" דמשמע שלימה. וכן גבי נערה המאורסה. ומיהו, בתולה דגבי קנס איכא למימר דאיצטריך לכדדרשינן בפרק "אלו נערות" (כתובות לח: ושם). **אילימא** בכדרכה תיפוק ליה דהויא בעולה. משמע דאסירא ליה, אע"פ שהיא בעולת עצמו. והא דקאמר בריש "אלו נערות" (שם ל. ושם): איכא בינייהו בעולה לכהן גדול — היינו בעולה מאותה בעילה עצמה שנאנסה בה. וכן פירש ר"ת. ולא כמו שדוחק שם בקונטרס לפרש שנבעלה לאחר שלא כדרכה. ועוד: דא"כ הוה ליה למיפרך: הניחא לר"א דאמר נבעלה שלא כדרכה פסולה, אלא לר"מ — מאי איכא למימר. **אלא** לאו שלא בדרכה. משמע דמשלם קנס אביאה שלא כדרכה. וכן בפ"ק דקידושין (דף י. ושם) דקאמר: מודה רבי לענין קנס, דכולהו משלמין. הקשה ריב"א מכאן על פירוש רש"י בפ' "בן סורר ומורה" (סנהדרין עג. ושם), גבי רדף אחר חייבי לאוין ואחר חייבי כריתות, דניתן להציל בנפשו, ופריך: ואלו נערות שיש להם קנס הבא

תוספות חד מקמאי

אמר רב יהודה אמר רב נבעלה שלא כדרכה פסולה לכהונה פי' לכ"ג מתיב רבה ולו תהיה לאשה באשה הראויה לו פרט לאלמנה לכ"ג גרושה וחלוצה לכהן הדיוט ה"ד אלימא כדרכה מאי איריא משום אלמנה תיפוק ליה דה"ל בעולה. פירוש הא תניא לקמן אנוסת עצמו ומפותת עצמו לא (תצא) [ישא אלא] לאו בשלא כדרכה ומשום אלמנה אין משום בעולה לא. הא מני ר"מ היא ורב דאמר כר"א ושמעינן מהא מתניתא שלא כדרכה יש לה קנס. ואקשינן אי כר"א מאי איריא משום בעולה. וקשה לן ומאי קושיא דלמא רב ס"ל כר"א בשלא כדרכה ופליג עליה בפנוי הבא על הפנויה. ועוד לישני ליה רב דאמר כר"ש. ועוד לישני ליה דבאנס מיירי דבכה"ג לא עשה זונה בפנוי הבא על הפנויה (ועוד לישני ליה) דאלת"ה קשיא דרב אדרב דהא אמר רב בפ"ק דכתובות הלכה כר' יוסי דאמר אם רוב העיר משיאין לכהונה ה"ז תנשא לכהונה א) דראב"י גבי אנוסת עצמו ומפותת עצמו הולד חלל. ג)ואוקימנא דראב"י במפותה אבל באנוסה ליכא משום זונה בפנוי הבא על הפנויה (ואנוסת חברו דקתני משום לה דאמר לא ישא) לכך נראה מה שפירש הראב"ד דהכי פריך אי רב כיחידאה ס"ל ה"ל לאשמועינן הא דר"א אלא לאו ש"מ דאליבא דר"ה אמר למילתיה ושני ליה בממאנת ודכ"ע בעל א' עושה אותה בעולה שלא כדרכה כדאית' בפ"ק דקידושין: אמר רב שימי בר חייא נבעלה לבהמה כשרה לכהונה ואפי' לכ"ג דאין זנות לבהמה. וקטנה שנתפתתה תחת בעלה אסורה לבעלה כהן ומותרת לבעלה ישראל דפיתוי קטנה אונס הוא ואונס בישראל משרא שרי. הא דתניא אי אתה עושה חלל מנדה ה"ק אפילו בא עליה ב' פעמים דאילו ראשונה לא צריך דהא [אין חלל אלא] מאסור כהונה אלא כגון שחזר עליה ביאה שניה כיון דנדה שביח לבעלה בתר יומי נדותה אינה מתחללת. ג) נראה בפרק עשרה יוחסין אמר רב אסי הלכך כהן שבא על אחותו זונה עשה לה חללה לא עשה לה חזר ובא עליה עשאה חללה: והא

נראה דצ"ל ועוד דלקמן פסק רב הלכה כראב"י גבי אנוסת חבירו ומפותת חבירו הולד חלל כו'. ב) לפנינו בגמ' לא אמרינן שום חילוק בין מפותה לאנוסה אליבא דר"א וצ"ע. ג) נראה דצ"ל גרסינן בפ' עשרה יוחסין דף עז ע"ב.

עין משפט נר מצוה

נה א מיי' פי"ז מהל' איסורי ביאה הל' יב סמג לאוין קכה ועשין כו:
נו ב מיי' שם הל' יז:
נז ג מיי' שם הלכה א:
נח ד מיי' שם הל' יא:
נט ה מיי' שם הל' יג:
ס ו מיי' שם הל' יח טוש"ע אה"ע סימן ו סעיף א:
סא ז מיי' שם הלכה יד:
סב ח מיי' פ"א מהל' נערה בתולה הל' ה סמג לאוין פד טוש"ע אה"ע סי' קעז סעיף ד:

מסורת הש"ס

[לעיל נו:]
[לקמן סא.]
רש"ל וס"א
נ"ל מן האירוסין בין מן הנישואין אף וכו' וכ"א בילקוט
כתובות לז:
[לקמן ס.]

הגהות הב"ח

(א) תוס' ד"ה אלא לאו וכו' דשתני וכו' דביאה ירוסין. נ"ב בפ"ק קידושין קא מיבעיא ליה ועי' לקמן דף י ע"א:

עין משפט נר מצוה

סג א מיי' פי"ז מהל' איסורי ביאה הל' יד:
סד ב מיי' שם הל' יח:
סה ג ד מיי' פי"ח שם הל' א סמג לאוין קפא טוש"ע אה"ע סימן ו סעיף ח:
סו ה מיי' פ"ד מהל' איסורי מזבח הל' יח:
סז ו מיי' פ"א מהל' נערה בתולה הל' ו ופי"ז מהלכות איסורי ביאה הל' טו טז:
סח ז מיי' פי"ט מהל' איסורי ביאה הל' ז טוש"ע אה"ע סימן סעיף יב:
סט ח מיי' שם פי"ז הל' טו טז ופ"א מהלכות נערה בתולה הלכה ו:

הָא מַנִּי – רַ' מֵאִיר הִיא, וְרַב דְּאָמַר כְּרַ' אֶלְעָזָר. אִי כְּרַבִּי אֶלְעָזָר, מַאי אִירְיָא מִשּׁוּם בְּעוּלָה? תֵּיפּוֹק לֵיהּ דְּהָוְיָא לָהּ זוֹנָה, דְּהָא א"ר אֶלְעָזָר: *פָּנוּי הַבָּא עַל הַפְּנוּיָה שֶׁלֹּא לְשֵׁם אִישׁוּת עֲשָׂאָהּ זוֹנָה! אֲמַר רַב יוֹסֵף: כְּגוֹן שֶׁנִּבְעֲלָה לִבְהֵמָה, דְּהָתָם, מִשּׁוּם בְּעוּלָה – אִיכָּא, מִשּׁוּם זוֹנָה – לֵיכָּא. אֲמַר לֵיהּ אַבַּיֵי: מִמָּה נַפְשָׁךְ, אִי בְּעוּלָה הָוְיָא – זוֹנָה נַמִי הָוְיָא, וְאִי זוֹנָה לָא הָוְיָא – [א]בְּעוּלָה נַמִי לָא הָוְיָא. וְכִי תֵּימָא: מִידֵּי דְּהָוְיָא אַמּוּכַּת עֵץ שֶׁלֹּא כְּדַרְכָּהּ – אִם כֵּן אֵין לְךָ אִשָּׁה שֶׁכְּשֵׁרָה לִכְהוּנָּה שֶׁלֹּא נַעֲשֵׂית מוּכַּת עֵץ עַל יְדֵי צְרוֹר. אֶלָּא אֲמַר רַבִּי זֵירָא: [ב]בִּמְמָאֶנֶת. אָמַר רַב שִׁימִי בַּר חִיָּיא: [ג]נִבְעֲלָה לִבְהֵמָה – כְּשֵׁרָה לִכְהוּנָּה. תַּנְיָא נַמִי הָכִי: [ד]נִבְעֲלָה לְמִי שֶׁאֵינוֹ אִישׁ, אע"פ שֶׁבִּסְקִילָה – כְּשֵׁרָה לִכְהוּנָּה. כִּי אֲתָא רַב דִּימִי אֲמַר: מַעֲשֶׂה בְּרִיבָה אַחַת בְּהִיתְלוּ שֶׁהָיְתָה מְכַבֶּדֶת אֶת הַבַּיִת, וּרְבָעָהּ כֶּלֶב כּוּפְרִי מֵאַחֲרֶיהָ, וְהִכְשִׁירָהּ רַבִּי לִכְהוּנָּה. אֲמַר שְׁמוּאֵל: וּלְכֹהֵן גָּדוֹל. בִּימֵי רַבִּי כֹּהֵן גָּדוֹל מִי הֲוָה? אֶלָּא: רְאוּיָה לְכֹהֵן גָּדוֹל. א"ל רָבָא *מְפַּרְקִין לְרַב אַשִׁי: מְנָא הָא מִילְּתָא דַּאֲמוּר רַבָּנַן *אֵין זְנוּת לִבְהֵמָה – דִּכְתִיב °"לֹא תָבִיא אֶתְנַן זוֹנָה וּמְחִיר כֶּלֶב", דברים כג וּתְנַן: *[ה]אֶתְנַן כֶּלֶב וּמְחִיר זוֹנָה מוּתָּרִין, (מִשּׁוּם) שֶׁנֶּאֱמַר °"גַּם שְׁנֵיהֶם" שְׁנַיִם וְלֹא אַרְבָּעָה. שם ת"ר: [ו]אֲנוּסַת עַצְמוֹ וּמְפוּתַּת עַצְמוֹ – לֹא יִשָּׂא, וְאִם נָשָׂא – נָשׂוּי. אֲנוּסַת חֲבֵירוֹ וּמְפוּתַּת חֲבֵירוֹ – לֹא יִשָּׂא, וְאִם נָשָׂא, רַ' אֱלִיעֶזֶר בֶּן יַעֲקֹב אוֹמֵר: [ז]הַוָּלָד חָלָל, וַחֲכָמִים אוֹמְרִים: הַוָּלָד כָּשֵׁר. § "אִם נָשָׂא – נָשׂוּי". § אָמַר רַב הוּנָא אָמַר רַב: [ח]וּמוֹצִיא בְּגֵט. וְאֶלָּא הָא דְּקָתָנֵי: "אִם נָשָׂא – נָשׂוּי"! אָמַר רַב אַחָא בַּר יַעֲקֹב: לוֹמַר שֶׁאֵין

רש"י

הָא מַנִּי ר"מ. דְּקָאָמַר: "בְּתוּלֶיהָ" – עַד שֶׁיְּהוּ כָּל בְּתוּלֶיהָ קַיָּימִין, פְּרָט לְבוֹגֶרֶת. וְאִיַּיתַּר לֵיהּ "בִּבְתוּלֶיהָ" לְמַעוּטֵי בְּעוּלָה שֶׁלֹּא כְּדַרְכָּהּ, דְּשַׁרְיָא. וְרַב. דְּאָמַר פְּסוּלָה – כְּרַבִּי אֶלְעָזָר, דַּאֲמַר לְעֵיל: "בְּתוּלֶיהָ" – מִקְצָת בְּתוּלִים, לְרַבּוּיֵי בּוֹגֶרֶת. וְאָתָא "בִּבְתוּלֶיהָ" לְמַעוּטֵי בְּעוּלָה שֶׁלֹּא כְּדַרְכָּהּ, כִּדְלְעֵיל. דְּהָוְיָא לָהּ זוֹנָה. וַאֲפִי' לְכֹהֵן הֶדְיוֹט אֲסוּרָה. דְּהָא אָמַר רַבִּי אֶלְעָזָר כו'. לְקַמָּן בְּפִירְקִין (דף סא:). אִיסּוּר זוֹנָה לֵיכָּא. דְּיָלְפִינַן לְקַמָּן בִּשְׁמַעְתִּין: אֵין זְנוּת לִבְהֵמָה. אִי זוֹנָה לָא הָוְיָא. א"כ לָאו בִּיאָה הִיא, וַאֲפִי' לְכֹהֵן גָּדוֹל תִּשְׁתְּרֵי. וְכ"ת מִידֵּי דְּהָוְיָא אַמּוּכַּת עֵץ. דְּהָא רַבִּי אֶלְעָזָר קָאָמַר בְּמַתְנִי', לֹא יִשָּׂא אֶת מוּכַּת עֵץ, וְתִיבָּעֵי לְמֵימַר דַּאֲפִי' בְּמוּכַּת עֵץ שֶׁלֹּא כְּדַרְכָּהּ פְּסוּלָה. א"כ אֵין לְךָ אִשָּׁה שֶׁכְּשֵׁרָה לִכְהוּנָּה גְּדוֹלָה שֶׁלֹּא נַעֲשֵׂית מוּכַּת עֵץ עַל יְדֵי צְרוֹר. שֶׁל קִינּוּחַ בֵּית הַכִּסֵּא. אֶלָּא א"ר זֵירָא. מַשְׁכַּחַתְּ לָהּ לְהָא דְּרַב אַלִּיבָּא דְּרַבִּי אֶלְעָזָר דְּהָוְיָא בְּעוּלָה, וְלֹא זוֹנָה וְלֹא אַלְמָנָה וְלֹא גְּרוּשָׁה – בִּקְטַנָּה יְתוֹמָה הַמְּאֻשֶּׂאֶת לְבַעַל, וּבְעָלָהּ שֶׁלֹּא כְּדַרְכָּהּ וּמֵיאֲנָה בּוֹ. דְּאֵין כָּאן פְּסוּל זְנוּת וְאַלְמְנוּת וְגֵירוּשִׁין, וְאַשְׁמְעִינַן רַב דְּיֵשׁ כָּאן פְּסוּל בְּעוּלָה לְכֹהֵן גָּדוֹל. כְּשֵׁרָה לִכְהוּנָּה. אֲפִי' לְכֹהֵן גָּדוֹל, דְּמוּכַּת עֵץ בְּעָלְמָא הִיא. וּמַאן דְּשָׁרֵי בְּמוּכַּת עֵץ – שָׁרֵי בָּהּ. לְמִי שֶׁאֵינוֹ אִישׁ. בְּהֵמָה. שֶׁבִּסְקִילָה. אִם יֵשׁ עֵדִים וְהַתְרָאָה – הֵיכָא דְּלֵיכָּא עֵדִים וְהַתְרָאָה – כְּשֵׁרָה לִכְהוּנָּה. בְּהִיתְלוֹ. שֵׁם מָקוֹם. כּוּפְרִי. כְּלָבִים גְּדוֹלִים שֶׁצָּדִין בָּהֶן חַיּוֹת*. מֵאַחֲרֶיהָ. שֶׁלֹּא כְּדַרְכָּהּ. דְּאִי כְּדַרְכָּהּ – לֹא גָּרְעָה מִמּוּכַּת עֵץ: רַבִּי לְאַחַר חוּרְבַּן הַבַּיִת הָיָה כַּמָּה דּוֹרוֹת, שֶׁהוּא סוֹף הַתַּנָּאִים, וּבִימֵי רַבָּן יוֹחָנָן בֶּן זַכַּאי חָרַב הַבַּיִת, דִּתְנַן (ר"ה דף כט:): מִשֶּׁחָרַב בֵּית הַמִּקְדָּשׁ הִתְקִין רַבָּן יוֹחָנָן בֶּן זַכַּאי וכו'. אֶתְנַן כֶּלֶב. (א) שֶׁאִם אָמַר אָדָם לְזוֹנָה הֵילָךְ טָלֶה זֶה וְהִבָּעֲלִי לְכַלְבִּי, וּמְחִיר זוֹנָה שֶׁהֶחֱלִיף זוֹנָה בְּטָלֶה – מוּתָּרִים לַמִּזְבֵּחַ. וּמִדְּשָׁרֵי אֶתְנַן כֶּלֶב – אַלְמָא לָאו זְנוּת הוּא. לֹא יִשָּׂא. כֹּהֵן גָּדוֹל, דִּכְתִיב "בְּתוּלָה יִקָּח" (ויקרא כא) – בִּשְׁעַת לִיקּוּחִין תְּהֵא בְּתוּלָה.

שֶׁאֵין

תוספות

הבא על אחותו – ומשני: משעת הערלה הוא דפגמה, איפטר ליה מקטלא, ממונא לא משלם עד גמר ביאה. ופירש בקונטרס: דאין משלם קנס עד גמר ביאה, שיש שם הסרת בתולים. ומפרש ר"ת וריב"א: דודאי משלם קנס אהערלה ואשלא כדרכה, אע"ג דאין מסיר בתולים. והתם דוקא קאמר דלא משלם עד גמר ביאה – משום דמעיקרא קם לי' בדרבה מיניה, דניתן להצילה בנפשו. והא דנקט התם כגון שבא עליה שלא כדרכה וחזר ובא עליה בכדרכה – הוה מצי למינקט וחזר ובא עליה שלא כדרכה, כיון דחייב קנס אשלא כדרכה. ועוד מצינו למימר: דאע"ג דיש קנס בשלא כדרכה – בהערלה אין קנס, לפי שלא נתרבתה הערלה להיות כגמר ביאה לענין קנס. דהא לעריות וחייבי לאוין וחייבי עשה ואשה לבעלה ויבמה מצרכינן קראי לעיל (דף נה.) לרבות הערלה וכן משמע מתוך הך דשמעתין, דאי יש קנס בהערלה – הוה ליה לשנויי כגון שלא עשה אלא נשיקה ובנשיקה אינו מסיר בתולים כדמשמע בפרק בן סורר (סנהדרין דף עג: ושם) וא"ת ואי אין קנס בהערלה היאך איש מתחייב קנס למאן דאמר הערלה זו הכנסת עטרה? דבהכנסת עטרה הוא מסיר בתוליה, כדמוכח ב"בן סורר" (ג"ז שם), ואז היא כבר בעולה, ורחמנא אמר "בתולה" ולא בעולה! וי"ל: דבהכי חייב רחמנא, הואיל ובבעילה זו נעשית בעולה, אע"ג דלא מתחיל חיוב קנס עד אח"כ. דאי לא תימא הכי – למה ליה למכתב הערלה כלל? לילף הערלה מנערה המאורסה בכל העריות, דאיתקוש כולם להדדי, כדאמרי' בריש פירקין (דף נה.)! ובנערה המאורסה ע"כ מיחייב בהערלה, דאי בגמר ביאה – כבר הסיר בתוליה בהכנסת עטרה, ורחמנא אמר "בתולה" ולא בעולה, כדדרשינן בפ' "ד' מיתות" (סנהדרין סו:) אלא ע"כ, אפי' לא מחייב אלא עד גמר ביאה, כיון דבביאה זו נעשית בעולה – חייב רחמנא. אבל קשה: אי לא מחייב קנס בהערלה, א"כ מאי פריך ב"בן סורר": הניחא למ"ד הערלה זו נשיקה, אלא למאן דאמר הערלה זו הכנסת עטרה – מאי איכא למימר? הא לדידיה נמי אתי שפיר, דהא לא מיחייב קנס בהכנסת עטרה אלא בגמר ביאה ממש!.

הא מני ר' מאיר. – אע"ג דלר' מאיר חייבי לאוין וכריתות בני קנס, דרב גופיה מוקי מתניתין דריש "אלו נערות" (כתובות דף כט.) כרבי מאיר – הכא לאו מקנס ממעט להו, אלא לענין שאין ראויה לקיימה. כדקתני נמי סיפא ב"אלו נערות" (שם לט.): אם לא היתה ראויה לבא בישראל אינו רשאי לקיימה, שנאמר "ולו תהיה לאשה" – באשה הראויה לו. תימה: דהתם (דף מ.) פריך עלה וליתי עשה ולידחי לא תעשה, ומאי פריך? שאני הכא דגלי קרא! וי"ל, דפריך הכי: וניתי עשה, וכי תימא שאני הכא דגלי קרא – אם כן נגמר מהכא בכל מקום דלא דחי! א"נ, פריך: דלא הוה ליה לאוקמי קרא בחייבי לאוין אלא בחייבי כריתות דוקא, דהוה אמינא שמותר לקיימה הואיל ואיתרבו לקנס מהבתולות ומנערות, בריש "אלו נערות" (שם דף כט:) דקראי משתמעי דהיכא דאיכא קנס איכא נישואין. אבל בחייבי לאוין – נימא דאתי עשה ודחי לא תעשה. אבל קשה: דמשני, היכא אמרינן דדחי – כגון מילה בצרעת, אבל הכא אי אמרה לא בעינא ליה – מי איתיה לעשה כלל. א"כ למה לי קרא למעוטי שלא ישאנה? ונראה לר"י: דהכא לאו מיתורא קדריש, אלא הכי פירושו: "ולו תהיה לאשה" – באשה הראויה לו, פרט לאלמנה. משום דדרשינן ב"אלו נערות" (שם דף לח.) "תהיה" – מדעתה, וכיון דבעינן אשה הראויה לו, דלא חשיב עשה, דהא אי אמרה לא בעינא ליה – מי איתיה לעשה כללו! ומעיקרא דפריך וניתי עשה ונדחי לא תעשה – סלקא דעתך דכי אמרה: מיהא בעינא ליה – ידחה עשה את לא תעשה, דלא מסיק אדעתיה דלא אתי עשה ודחי לא תעשה אלא כגון מילה בצרעת כו'. א"נ: מעיקרא ס"ד כדפי', דמייתורא קא דריש. **ורבי** דאמר כרבי אלעזר. לא שסבר רב כרבי אלעזר, דהא רב ושמואל דאמרי תרוייהו: בוגרת ומוכת עץ לא ישא, ורבי אלעזר מכשיר בוגרת. אלא הכי קאמר: דרב דאמר לרבי אלעזר נבעלה שלא כדרכה פסולה לכהונה, כיון דמכשיר בוגרת, וליה לא סבירא ליה. והשתא ניחא דפריך: אי כר' אלעזר – מאי איריא משום בעולה, תיפוק ליה דהויא זונה, דהא אמר רבי אלעזר פנוי כו'. ואי אליבא דנפשיה קאמר – מאי פריך? דאטו משום דסבר לה כר' אלעזר בחדא סבר לה כותיה בכל מילי?! דאין שני הדברים הללו תלויין זה בזה, דמה ענין זה אצל זה? ועוד: דעל כרחך לא סבר כוותיה בהא, דאמר: "פנוי הבא על הפנויה עשאה זונה" מדפריך ארב בסמוך, ובהא אמר רב עמרם, דאין הלכה כר' אלעזר; ובסוף פ"ק דכתובות (דף טו. ושם) גבי תינוקת שנאנסה – פסיק לשם כר' יוסי, דמכשיר. והיכי הוה מכשיר, אפילו בתרי רובי, אי סבר "פנוי הבא על הפנויה עשאה זונה"! ודוחק לומר, דלא אצטריך לפסוק אלא לבא עליה לשום אישות, אלא אליבא דר' אלעזר קאמר, וליה לא סבירא ליה. **שנים** ולא ארבעה. וא"ת: ומהיכא תיסק אדעתיה למיסר דאיצטריך קרא למעוטי. וי"ל, דסלקא דעתך לאסור משום דאיתקוש, וכי תימא: אם איתא דהני נמי אסור, לכתוב רחמנא: "אתנן ומחיר כלב וזונה"! – א"כ הוה אמינא דכל חד לחוד שרי. ומיהו,(ב) למאן דאמר (ב"מ לד: ובשאר דוכתי) "משמע שניהם כאחד ומשמע אחד בפני עצמו, עד שיפרוט לך הכתוב: 'יחדו'" – ה"ל למכתב הכי. ובפ' "כל האסורין" (תמורה דף ל: ושם) מהאי דרשא דשנים ולא ד', נפקא לן דאין זונות לבהמה.

שאינו

תוספות ישנים

הוו בכשרות הא ודאי בתר נשואין אזלינן והוו נשואי פסולות אבל ר' יוחנן אליבא דנפשיה סבר דשרי לכונסה כמו שהטיב לו לבסוף דקיחה דאירוסין קאמר קרא: **אי** כר"א מאי איריא. ותימה דאטו משום דס"ל כרבי אלעזר במלתי' דשלא כדרכה יסבור כמותו מכל וכל. וא"כ מאי פריך מאי אריא משום בעולה תיפוק לי' דהוה לה זונה דאמר ר"א פנוי הבא על הפנויה עשאה זונה דלמא לא סבר לה כותיה במילתא דפנוי הבא על הפנויה עשאה זונה וע"ק דהלכה כרב באיסורי וא"כ הלכה כר' אלעזר דבתולה שלימה משמע וא"כ היכי הוי מנהג שאנו כותבין בכתובות בוגרת כסף זוזי מאתן דחזו ליכי מדאורייתא הלא כתיב כי יפתה איש נערה בתולה דבתולה שלימה משמע ומינה שמעינן מוהר הבתולות שהוא מאתים וא"כ אין בוגרת כבתולה. וע"ק דודאי רב לא מצי סבר כרבי אלעזר דבפ"ק דכתובות פסק רב כר' יוסי דאמר אם רוב העיר משיאין לכהונה תנשא לכהונה ולא אמרינן עשאה זונה משום פנוי הבא על הפנויה שלא לשם אישות ועוד דלקמן קאמר רב בוגרת לא ישא אלמא לאו כר' אלעזר ס"ל דמכשר בבוגרת וע"ק דהלכה כרב ולקמן פסקינן הלכה כראב"י דלא ס"ל כר"א בההיא דפנוי הבא על הפנויה וא"כ קשה הלכתא אהלכתא לכנ"ל דרב כר"א ר"ל דאליבא דר"א קאמר אבל לא סבר כן ולהכי פריך לר' אלעזר מאי אריא משום בעולה תיפוק ליה דהויא לה זונה: **גם** שניהם שנים ולא ארבעה. מפורש במהר"

מסורת הש"ס

לקמן סא: עו. סנהדרין [...] תמורה ל.

[מפרזקיא]

[ובערוך פי' כלב [...] שצווח בלילה במלברות כפרים]

[תמורה ל. ע"ש ל: [...] בסוטה כו:]

הגהות הב"ח

(א) רש"י ד"ה אתנן [...] כ"ב ובמסכת תמורה דף [...] פרש"י הילך טלה זה [...] כלבתך אלי אלא דסוג [...] דהכא ורבעה כלב כוף [...] כו' משמע דמיירי בנבע[...] לכלב וכן בסוטה דף [...] ע"ב: (ב) תוס' ד"ה שנ[...] וכו' ומיהו ודאי למ[...] לאמר משמע וכו' ובפ' האיסורין בלאו האי דרש[...]

גליון הש"ס

גמ' ורב דאמר כ[...] אלעזר. עיין תמ[...] הרשב"א סי' אלף רל"[...]

שֶׁאֵין מְשַׁלֵּם קְנָס בִּמְפוּתָּה. אֱזַל רַב גְּבִיהָה מִבֵּי כְּתִיל, אֲמָרָהּ לִשְׁמַעְתָּא קַמֵּיהּ דְּרַב אַשִׁי. אֲמַר לֵיהּ: וְהָא רַב וְרַ' יוֹחָנָן דְּאָמְרִי תַּרְוַיְיהוּ: [א]בּוֹגֶרֶת [ב]וּמוּכַּת עֵץ — לֹא יִשָּׂא, [ג]וְאִם נָשָׂא — נָשׂוּי. אַלְמָא: סוֹפָהּ לִהְיוֹת בּוֹגֶרֶת תַּחְתָּיו, סוֹפָהּ לִהְיוֹת מוּכַּת עֵץ תַּחְתָּיו, הָכָא נַמִי — סוֹפָהּ לִהְיוֹת בְּעוּלָה תַּחְתָּיו! קַשְׁיָא. § "אֲנוּסַת חֲבֵירוֹ וּמְפוּתַּת חֲבֵירוֹ — לֹא יִשָּׂא, וְאִם נָשָׂא, רַ' אֶלְעָזָר בֶּן יַעֲקֹב אוֹמֵר: הַוָּלָד חָלָל, וַחֲכָמִים אוֹמְרִים: הַוָּלָד כָּשֵׁר". § אָמַר רַב הוּנָא אָמַר רַב: *הֲלָכָה כְּרַ' אֱלִיעֶזֶר בֶּן יַעֲקֹב. וְכֵן אָמַר רַב גִּידֵּל אָמַר רַב: הֲלָכָה כְּרַבִּי אֱלִיעֶזֶר בֶּן יַעֲקֹב. אִיכָּא דְּאָמְרִי, אָמַר רַב הוּנָא אָמַר רַב: מַאי טַעֲמָא דְּרַבִּי אֱלִיעֶזֶר בֶּן יַעֲקֹב — סָבַר לָהּ כְּרַבִּי אֶלְעָזָר. וּמִי סָבַר לָהּ כְּוָתֵיהּ? וְהָא קַיְימָא לָן: *מִשְׁנַת רַ' אֱלִיעֶזֶר בֶּן יַעֲקֹב קַב וְנָקִי, וְאִילּוּ בְּהָא *אָמַר רַב עַמְרָם (א) אָמַר רַב: אֵין הֲלָכָה כְּרַבִּי אֶלְעָזָר! קַשְׁיָא. רַב אַשִׁי אָמַר: בְּיֵשׁ חָלָל מֵחַיָּיבֵי עֲשֵׂה קָמִיפַּלְגֵי. רַבִּי אֱלִיעֶזֶר בֶּן יַעֲקֹב סָבַר: *יֵשׁ חָלָל מֵחַיָּיבֵי עֲשֵׂה, וְרַבָּנַן סָבְרִי: אֵין חָלָל מֵחַיָּיבֵי עֲשֵׂה. מ"ט דְּרַאבַ"י — דִּכְתִיב (ויקרא כא) "אַלְמָנָה וּגְרוּשָׁה וַחֲלָלָה זוֹנָה אֶת אֵלֶּה לֹא יִקָּח כִּי אִם בְּתוּלָה וגו'", וּכְתִיב "וְלֹא יְחַלֵּל זַרְעוֹ בְּעַמָּיו" אַכּוּלְּהוּ. וְרַבָּנַן "אֵלֶּה" הִפְסִיק הָעִנְיָן. וְרַבִּי אֱלִיעֶזֶר בֶּן יַעֲקֹב — אָמַר "אֵלֶּה" [ד]לְמַעוּטֵי נִדָּה. כְּמַאן אָזְלָא הָא דְּתַנְיָא: מֵ"אֵלֶּה" אַתָּה עוֹשֶׂה חָלָל, וְאִי אַתָּה עוֹשֶׂה חָלָל מִנִּדָּה, כְּמַאן — כְּרַבִּי אֱלִיעֶזֶר בֶּן יַעֲקֹב. וְרַבִּי אֱלִיעֶזֶר בֶּן יַעֲקֹב, נִכְתְּבֵיהּ לְ"אֵלֶּה" לְבַסּוֹף! קַשְׁיָא. תָּנוּ רַבָּנַן: אֲחוֹתוֹ אֲרוּסָה, רַבִּי מֵאִיר וְרַ' יְהוּדָה אוֹמְרִים: מִטַּמֵּא לָהּ, רַבִּי יוֹסֵי וְרַבִּי שִׁמְעוֹן אוֹמְרִים: [ה]אֵין מִטַּמֵּא לָהּ. אֲנוּסָה וּמְפוּתָּה — ד"ה אֵין מִטַּמֵּא לָהּ, וּמוּכַּת עֵץ — אֵין מִטַּמֵּא לָהּ, דִּבְרֵי רַ' שִׁמְעוֹן. שֶׁהָיָה רַ' שִׁמְעוֹן אוֹמֵר: רְאוּיָה לְכ"ג מִטַּמֵּא לָהּ, שֶׁאֵין רְאוּיָה לְכ"ג — אֵין מִטַּמֵּא לָהּ. וּבוֹגֶרֶת מִטַּמֵּא לָהּ — דִּבְרֵי כָּל אָדָם. מַאי טַעֲמָא דְּר"מ וְרַ' יְהוּדָה? דְּדָרְשִׁי הָכִי: (שם) "וְלַאֲחוֹתוֹ הַבְּתוּלָה" [ה]פְּרָט לַאֲנוּסָה וּמְפוּתָּה. יָכוֹל שֶׁאֲנִי מוֹצִיא אַף מוּכַּת עֵץ — ת"ל (שם) "אֲשֶׁר לֹא הָיְתָה לְאִישׁ", מִי שֶׁהֲוָיָיתָהּ עַל יְדֵי אִישׁ, [ו]יָצְאָה זוֹ שֶׁאֵין הֲוָיָיתָהּ עַל יְדֵי אִישׁ. "הַקְּרוֹבָה" לְרַבּוֹת הָאֲרוּסָה. [ז]"אֵלָיו" לְרַבּוֹת הַבּוֹגֶרֶת. הָא לָמָּה לִי קְרָא? וְהָאָמַר *רַבִּי מֵאִיר: "בְּתוּלָה" אֲפִילּוּ מִקְצָת בְּתוּלָה מַשְׁמַע! אִיצְטְרִיךְ, סָלְקָא דַּעְתָּךְ אָמִינָא: נֵילַף "בְּתוּלָה" "בְּתוּלָה" מֵהָתָם, מַה לְּהַלָּן נַעֲרָה — אַף כָּאן נַמִי נַעֲרָה, קָא מַשְׁמַע לָן. וְרַבִּי יוֹסֵי וְרַבִּי שִׁמְעוֹן, מַאי טַעֲמַיְיהוּ? דָּרְשִׁי הָכִי: "וְלַאֲחוֹתוֹ הַבְּתוּלָה" פְּרָט לַאֲנוּסָה וּמְפוּתָּה וּמוּכַּת עֵץ, "אֲשֶׁר לֹא הָיְתָה" פְּרָט לַאֲרוּסָה, "הַקְּרוֹבָה" [ח]לְרַבּוֹת אֲרוּסָה שֶׁנִּתְגָּרְשָׁה, "אֵלָיו" לְרַבּוֹת אֶת הַבּוֹגֶרֶת. "הַקְּרוֹבָה" לְרַבּוֹת אֲרוּסָה שֶׁנִּתְגָּרְשָׁה? וְהָא

רש"י

שֶׁאֵין מְשַׁלֵּם קְנָס בִּמְפוּתָּה. שֶׁאִם מְפוּתָּה הִיא, אֲהֲנוּ לֵיהּ נִשּׂוּאִין לְמִפְטְרֵיהּ מִקְּנָסָא. שֶׁהַמְפַתֶּה אֵין מְשַׁלֵּם קְנָס אֶלָּא כְּשֶׁאֵין כּוֹנְסָהּ, דִּכְתִיב "אִם מָאֵן יְמָאֵן" (שמות כב). אֲבָל אִם מָהוֹר יִמְהָרֶנָּה לּוֹ לְאִשָּׁה — לֹא יִתֵּן כְּלוּם. אֲבָל אוֹנֵס נוֹתֵן מִיָּד, אֲפִילּוּ הוּא כּוֹנְסָהּ, דִּכְתִיב (דברים כב) "וְנָתַן הָאִישׁ הַשּׁוֹכֵב עִמָּהּ... וְלוֹ תִהְיֶה לְאִשָּׁה". אֲמָרָהּ לִשְׁמַעְתָּא. לְהָא דְּרַב הוּנָא דְּאָמַר וּמוֹלִיאָהּ בְּגֵט. סוֹפָהּ לִהְיוֹת מוּכַּת עֵץ תַּחְתָּיו. כְּלוֹמַר: סוֹפָהּ לִיבָּעֵל לוֹ, וּלְאַבֵּד בְּתוּלֶיהָ. סוֹפָהּ לִהְיוֹת בְּעוּלָה תַּחְתָּיו. וְאִם נָשָׂא נָשׂוּי דְּקָתָנֵי — לְגַמְרֵי קָאָמַר, דְּמוּתָּר לְקַיְּימָהּ, הוֹאִיל וּלְעַצְמוֹ נִבְעֲלָה, וְסוֹפָהּ לִהְיוֹת בְּעוּלָה לוֹ. סָבַר לָהּ כְּר' אֶלְעָזָר. דְּאָמַר (לקמן דף סא:): פְּנוּי הַבָּא עַל הַפְּנוּיָה שֶׁלֹּא לְשֵׁם אִישׁוּת — עֲשָׂאָהּ זוֹנָה, וְקָיְימָה עֲלֵיהּ בְּלָאו. וּמְחַיְּיבֵי לָאוִין דִּכְהוּנָּה הָוֵי הַוָּלָד חָלָל. דְּרַב עַמְרָם. לְקַמָּן בְּפִירְקִין (שם). בְּיֵשׁ חָלָל מֵחַיָּיבֵי עֲשֵׂה. *ר' אֱלִיעֶזֶר ב"י לָאו כְּר' אֶלְעָזָר סְבִירָא לֵיהּ, וְלָאו זוֹנָה הִיא, וְלָא קָיְימָא עֲלֵיהּ בְּלָאו אֶלָּא בַּעֲשֵׂה, דִּכְתִיב "בְּתוּלָה יִקַּח" וְלֹא בְּעוּלָה, וְלָאו הַבָּא מִכְּלַל עֲשֵׂה — עֲשֵׂה. וּכְתִיב לֹא יְחַלֵּל אַכּוּלְּהוּ. וַאֲפִי' אַ"בְּתוּלָה יִקַּח וְלֹא בְּעוּלָה", דַּעֲשֵׂה הוּא. אֵלֶּה הִפְסִיק הָעִנְיָן. דִּכְתִיב "אֵלֶּה" בָּתַר חַיָּיבֵי לָאוִין, לְאַשְׁמוּעִינַן: אֵלֶּה שֶׁהֵן חַיָּיבֵי לָאוִין חֲלוּקִין מִדִּין חַיָּיבֵי עֲשֵׂה. לְמַעוּטֵי נִדָּה. שֶׁאִם בָּא כֹּהֵן עַל אִשְׁתּוֹ נִדָּה — אֵין הַוָּלָד חָלָל. וְלִכְתְּבֵיהּ לְבַסּוֹף. הוֹאִיל וְלָאו לְפַלּוּגִינְהוּ אָתֵי. קַשְׁיָא. לְרַב אַשִׁי דְּמוֹקֵי פְּלוּגְתַּיְיהוּ בְּטַעְמָא דְּהָנֵי קְרָאֵי. אֲחוֹתוֹ אֲרוּסָה. שֶׁל כֹּהֵן הֶדְיוֹט. אֲבָל נְשׂוּאָה — פְּשִׁיטָא לָן דְּאֵין מִטַּמֵּא, דִּכְתִיב "וְלַאֲחוֹתוֹ הַבְּתוּלָה". אֲנוּסָה וּמְפוּתָּה. אֲחוֹתוֹ שֶׁנֶּאֶנְסָה אוֹ שֶׁנִּתְפַּתְּתָה. דִּבְרֵי הַכֹּל אֵין מִטַּמֵּא לָהּ. וְטַעְמָא דְּכוּלְּהוּ מְפָרֵשׁ לְקַמָּן. וּמוּכַּת עֵץ אֵין מִטַּמֵּא לָהּ דִּבְרֵי ר"ש. ר"ש לְטַעְמֵיהּ, דְּאָמַר בְּמַתְנִיתִין: מוּכַּת עֵץ אֲסוּרָה לְכ"ג, אַלְמָא: לָאו בִּכְלַל בְּתוּלָה הִיא. שֶׁאֵינָהּ רְאוּיָה לְכ"ג אֵין מִטַּמֵּא לָהּ. דְּהָכָא וְהָכָא "בְּתוּלָה" כְּתִיב. דִּבְרֵי כָּל אָדָם. וַאֲפִי' לְרַבִּי מֵאִיר, דְּפָסֵיל בּוֹגֶרֶת לְכֹהֵן גָּדוֹל — הָכָא לְעִנְיַן טוּמְאָה אִיתְרַבַּי, כִּדְלְקַמָּן. פְּרָט לַאֲנוּסָה וּמְפוּתָּה. שֶׁאֵינָהּ בְּתוּלָה. יָכוֹל שֶׁאֲנִי מוֹצִיא אַף מוּכַּת עֵץ. שֶׁאֵינָהּ בְּתוּלָה. לְרַבּוֹת אֶת הָאֲרוּסָה. וְאִיצְטְרִיךְ לְרַבּוּיָא, דְּלָא תֵּימָא "אֲשֶׁר לֹא הָיְתָה" — פְּרָט לַאֲרוּסָה שֶׁהָיְתָה לְאִישׁ, דַּהֲוָיָה לְשׁוֹן קִידּוּשִׁין הִיא: ה"ג. לָמָּה לִי קְרָא וְהָא אֲמַר ר"מ בְּתוּלָה מִקְצָת בְּתוּלִים מַשְׁמַע. לְעֵיל אֲמַר הָכִי: מִדְּאִיצְטְרִיךְ לְמִכְתַּב "בִּבְתוּלֶיהָ" לְגַבֵּי כ"ג לְהוֹצִיא אֶת הַבּוֹגֶרֶת לר"מ — מִכְּלַל דִּבְתוּלָה — בּוֹגֶרֶת נַמִי מַשְׁמַע. מֵהָתָם. "כִּי יִמְצָא אִישׁ נַעֲרָה בְתוּלָה" (דברים כב). מִדְּשָׁבְקֵיהּ

תוספות

שאינו משלם קנס במפותה. ואם תאמר: וכיון דבעיא גט, ואית לה כתובה, כמו אלמנה לכ"ג דיש לה כתובה, כדאמרינן ב"יש מותרות" (לקמן דף פה. ושם) אע"ג דאסורה מן התורה, וא"כ — מאי נפקא מינה דאין משלם קנס? הרי יש לה כתובה, ומה לי קנס ומה לי כתובה! ואמר ר"י: דנפקא מינה אם מחלה לכתובה. ועוד נפקא מינה: דלא משלם מן העידית כדין קנס, אלא מן הזיבורית כדין כתובת אשה. ועוד: דכתובת בעולה דרבנן. ועוד נראה: דהא דאמר רב מוליא בגט — היינו מדרבנן. ולהכי נקט פלוגתא *דרבי באנוסת חבירו, דבאנוסת עצמו — מודה דלא הוי חלל. ומיהו, מלינן למימר דנקט אנוסת חבירו להודיעך כוחן דרבנן דמכשרי. **סופה** להיות בעולה תחתיו. ואין לומר דמוליאה בגט דקאמר רב — היינו לרבי אלעזר, דאמר: פנוי הבא על הפנויה עשאה זונה. דהא רב אברייתא קאי, ובריייתא דלא כרבי אלעזר, דהא אמרי רבנן הולד כשר. **חלל** מחייבי עשה. תימה: כיון ד"לא יחלל" קאי נמי אבעולה לרבי אליעזר בן יעקב, אם כן אין זה חייבי עשה גרידא, ד"לא יחלל" לאו הוא, כדקאמר בפרק [בתרא] דקידושין (דף עח.): בעל — לוקה משום "לא יחלל"!. **אלה** הפסיק הענין. ולא מוקמינן "לא יחלל" אבעולה, אע"ג דמינה סליק — משום דמיסתבר טפי לאוקמי אחייבי לאוין. **ואי** אתה עושה חלל מנדה. בתורת כהנים מפרש, דאיצטריך דלא נילף דליהוי חלל מקל וחומר מהני שהם חייבי לאוין. תימה: דמה לאלמנה וכיולא בה — שכן הן עצמן מתחללות? וכי תימא ה"נ, כיון דבא עליה עשאה זונה — הא לא הוי זונה, כיון דתפסי בה קידושין!. **אליו** לרבות הבוגרת. וא"ת: למה לי "אליו"? נרבי בוגרת מ"ולא היתה לאיש" כדמרבינן מיניה מוכת עץ! וי"ל: דאי לאו "אליו" הוה מוקמינן "לא היתה" לבוגרת גרידא, דבוגרת מסתבר לרבות טפי ממוכת עץ. משום דמוכת עץ איתעביד בה מעשה, ולהכי מוקי "אליו" דכתיב ברישא לרבות בוגרת, ו"לא היתה לאיש" דכתיב בסוף מוקי למוכת עץ. וכן משמע דבוגרת עדיפא ממוכת עץ, דהא בבוגרת לא פליגי, כדקתני: ובוגרת מטמא לה דברי כל אדם. ועוד נראה: דממשמעות "בתולה" מימעטא מוכת עץ אפילו לרבי מאיר, מדפריך גבי בוגרת: והא למה לי קרא. וגבי מוכת עץ לא פריך הכי, ולהכי מוקי קרא קמא בבוגרת. וניחא נמי השתא הא דדרשינן דרשא ד"אשר לא היתה לאיש" ברישא, אע"ג דכתיב בסוף — משום דממשמעות "בתולה" הוה לן למעוטי מוכת עץ, הולרך לפרש דמתרבי מ"אשר לא היתה לאיש". **נילף** "בתולה" "בתולה" מהתם. אומר ר"ת: מהתם — היינו מכ"ג, ולא כמו שפירש בקונטרס דמ"בתולה" דאונס ומפתה קאמר. וכן נראה לר"י, דהא בכולה שמעתא לא איירי באונס ומפתה, ולא ה"ל למימר מהתם, אלא ה"ל למימר בהדיא: מאונס ומפתה, אלא מהתם — היינו כ"ג, כדפירש ר"ת, דאיירי ביה, ומשום דרבי שמעון גמרה מהתם, קא סלקא דעתך נילף מהתם, כדקאמר: ראויה לכהן גדול מטמא לה כו', ועל כרחך לא לסימנא בעלמא נקטיה, מדפריך בסמוך: והא אמר רבי שמעון ראויה לכ"ג כו'. ואי פריך משום דאין הכלל אמת — מהא לא הוה מסני מידי, אלא ודי פריך דמכ"ג ה"ל למילף. ומוכת עץ מהתם גמר לה רבי שמעון, כדקתני בהדיא בברייתא: הראויה לכ"ג כו', דאי לאו דמיעטיה רחמנא מוכת עץ מ"בבתוליה" עד שיהו כל בתוליה קיימין, וגמר מהתם — ה"ל למידרש הכא: מי שהווייתה על ידי איש, יצתה מוכת עץ, והוה ילפינן התם מהכא. והא

תוספות ישנים

אלה למעוטי נדה. כמאן אזלא כר' אליעזר בן יעקב. משמע אבל לרבנן לא אתי וסברי דיש חלל מנדה וא"ת ומהיכא נילף לומר דעושה חלל מנדה אי מק"ו דגרושה שאין בה לאו שאינו גרושה שהיא עצמה מתחללת ופסלה בביאתו מתרומה דבי נשא אחר בנדה דלא פסלה דהא איש בה הויא וא"ל כיון דבעלה עשאה זונה דהא כיון דתפסי בה קדושי לא הויא כשאר חייבי כריתות ואי מאלמנה לכהן גדול מה לאלמנה שכן היא עצמה מתחללת כדלעיל דא"ל הויא עצמה מתחללת מק"ו דלימא איסור כהונה שאינו כדפריכינן לעיל וי"ל יליף מאלמנה ומגרשה שני ספוסלים וכנו פגום קף אני אביא נדה. וקשה תאי תנא דעבדינן ספיר לך השוה הוכל לחדא הוי איסור לכהונה ולידך אינו איסור כהונה כדפריכית לעיל. ולר"א בן יעקב ניחא דאצטריך קרא למימר דאתי אתה עושה חלל מנדה דס"ד דנילף מחייבי עשה דיש חלל מהם אליבא דידיה: **אליו** לרבות הבוגרת. תימה לי למה לי קרא כיון דרבנן מוכת עץ משום שאין הווייתה ע"י איש הה"ה בוגרת נמי אין הווייתה ע"י איש. וגם כי עיישא יותר בוגרת ממוכת עץ משום דלא אתעביד בה מעשה וא"כ כיון דחזינן מוכת עץ כ"ש בוגרת וי"ל דס"ד דבוגרת גריעא ממוכת עץ משום דאשתני גופה ומלא היתה לאיש לא נפקא דשמא קרא לא איירי אלא בדבר שבא ע"י מעשה:

עין משפט נר מצוה

ע א מיי' פי"ז מהל' איסורי ביאה הלכ' יג:
עא ב מיי' שם הלכ' יד:
עב ג מיי' שם הלכה טו:
עג ד מיי' שם פי"ט הל' ו סמג לאוין קנב טוש"ע אה"ע סימן ו סעיף ח:
עד ה ו ז ח מיי' פ"ב מהל' אבל הלכה י יא סמג עשין נח ולאוין רלה טוש"ע יו"ד סימן שעג סעיף ד:
עד [ה] מיי' שם הלכה י טוש"ע שם:
[נ"ל דר"א בן יעקב]

מסורת הש"ס

[עי' תוספות בכורות כג: ד"ה משנת]
[נ"ל ורבי אליעזר כו' מהרש"ל]
[לעיל מט. וש"נ]
[לקמן סא: וע"ש]
[לקמן עז: פה:]
[לעיל נט.]

הגהות הב"ח

(א) גמ' בהא אמר רב עמרם אין הלכה כו' כצ"ל ותיבות אמר רב נמחק:

גליון הש"ס

גמ' אמר רב הלכה כראב"י. עיין תוס' בכורות דף כג ע"ב ד"ה משנת: שם ואילו בהא אמר רב עמרם אמר רב. דברי תוס' לעיל דף נט ע"ב ד"ה ורב מבואר דל"ג אין אמר רב וכן הוא לקמן דף עז ע"ב: שם ראב"י יש חלל מחייבי עשה. עיין לקמן דף עז ע"ב תד"ה מחלל.

עה א מיי' פי"ח מהל' איסורי ביאה הלכה ג סמג לאוין קלא טוש"ע אה"ע סימן ו סעיף ח:

וְהָא אָמַר רַבִּי שִׁמְעוֹן: רְאוּיָה לְכֹהֵן גָּדוֹל – מְטַמֵּא לָהּ, שֶׁאֵין רְאוּיָה לְכֹהֵן גָּדוֹל – אֵין מְטַמֵּא לָהּ! שָׁאנֵי הָתָם דְּרַבֵּי רַחֲמָנָא "קְרוֹבָה". א"ה מוּכַּת עֵץ נַמִי [רַבֵּי]! "קְרוֹבָה" אַחַת וְלֹא שְׁתַּיִם. וּמָה רָאִיתָ? הָא אִתְעֲבִיד בָּהּ מַעֲשֶׂה, הָא לָא אִתְעֲבִיד בָּהּ מַעֲשֶׂה. וְרַבִּי יוֹסֵי, *מִדְּשָׁבְקֵיהּ (א) לְבַר זוּגֵיהּ – מִכְּלָל דִּבְמוּכַּת עֵץ כְּרַבִּי מֵאִיר סְבִירָא לֵיהּ, מְנָא לֵיהּ? מִ"לֹּא הָיְתָה לְאִישׁ". וְהָא אַפִּיקְתֵּיהּ! חַד מִ"לֹּא הָיְתָה" וְחַד מִ"לְּאִישׁ". "אֵלָיו" לְרַבּוֹת הַבּוֹגֶרֶת. וְהָא אָמַר ר' שִׁמְעוֹן: "בְּתוּלָה" בְּתוּלָה שְׁלֵימָה מַשְׁמַע! טַעֲמָא דִּידֵיהּ נַמִי הָתָם מֵהָכָא, דְּדָרֵישׁ הָכִי: מִדְּ"אֵלָיו" לְרַבּוֹת הַבּוֹגֶרֶת, מִכְּלָל דִּ"בְתוּלָה" בְּתוּלָה שְׁלֵימָה מַשְׁמַע. *תַּנְיָא, ר' שִׁמְעוֹן בֶּן יוֹחַי אוֹמֵר: גִּיּוֹרֶת פְּחוּתָה מִבַּת שָׁלֹשׁ שָׁנִים וְיוֹם אֶחָד כְּשֵׁירָה לִכְהוּנָּה, שֶׁנֶּאֱמַר במדבר לא °"וְכֹל הַטַּף בַּנָּשִׁים אֲשֶׁר לֹא יָדְעוּ מִשְׁכַּב זָכָר הַחֲיוּ לָכֶם" וַהֲרֵי פִּנְחָס עִמָּהֶם. וְרַבָּנַן: לַעֲבָדִים וְלִשְׁפָחוֹת. – אִי הָכִי – בַּת שָׁלֹשׁ שָׁנִים וְיוֹם אֶחָד נַמִי! כִּדְרַב הוּנָא. דְּרַב הוּנָא רָמֵי: כְּתִיב שם °"כָּל אִשָּׁה יֹדַעַת אִישׁ לְמִשְׁכַּב זָכָר הֲרֹגוּ". הָא אֵינָהּ יוֹדַעַת – קַיְּימוּ, מִכְּלָל דְּהַטַּף בֵּין יָדְעוּ בֵּין לֹא יָדְעוּ – קַיְּימוּ, וּכְתִיב שם °"וְכֹל הַטַּף בַּנָּשִׁים אֲשֶׁר לֹא יָדְעוּ מִשְׁכַּב זָכָר הַחֲיוּ לָכֶם", הָא יָדְעִי – הֲרוֹגוּ. הֱוֵי אוֹמֵר: בִּרְאוּיָה לִיבָּעֵל הַכָּתוּב מְדַבֵּר. תַּנְיָא נַמִי הָכִי: "וְכָל אִשָּׁה יוֹדַעַת אִישׁ" בִּרְאוּיָה לִיבָּעֵל הַכָּתוּב מְדַבֵּר. אַתָּה אוֹמֵר בִּרְאוּיָה לִיבָּעֵל, אוֹ אֵינוֹ אֶלָּא נִבְעֲלָה מַמָּשׁ? כְּשֶׁהוּא אוֹמֵר "וְכֹל הַטַּף בַּנָּשִׁים אֲשֶׁר לֹא יָדְעוּ מִשְׁכַּב זָכָר" הֱוֵי אוֹמֵר בִּרְאוּיָה לִיבָּעֵל הַכָּתוּב מְדַבֵּר. מְנָא יָדְעִי? אָמַר רַב *הוּנָא בַּר בִּיזְנָא אָמַר ר' שִׁמְעוֹן חֲסִידָא: הֶעֱבִירוּם לִפְנֵי הַצִּיץ, כָּל שֶׁפָּנֶיהָ מוֹרִיקוֹת – בְּיָדוּעַ שֶׁהִיא רְאוּיָה לִיבָּעֵל, כָּל שֶׁאֵין פָּנֶיהָ מוֹרִיקוֹת – בְּיָדוּעַ שֶׁאֵינָהּ רְאוּיָה לִיבָּעֵל. אָמַר רַב נַחְמָן: *סִימָן לְעֲבֵירָה הַדְּרוֹקָן. כַּיּוֹצֵא בַּדָּבָר אַתָּה אוֹמֵר: שופטים כא °"וַיִּמְצְאוּ מִיּוֹשְׁבֵי יָבֵישׁ גִּלְעָד אַרְבַּע מֵאוֹת נַעֲרָה בְתוּלָה אֲשֶׁר לֹא יָדְעוּ אִישׁ לְמִשְׁכַּב זָכָר". מְנָא יָדְעִי? אָמַר רַב כָּהֲנָא: הוֹשִׁיבוּם עַל פִּי חָבִית שֶׁל יַיִן, *בְּעוּלָה – רֵיחָהּ נוֹדֵף, בְּתוּלָה – אֵין רֵיחָהּ נוֹדֵף. וְנַעַבְרִינְהוּ לִפְנֵי צִיץ! אָמַר רַב כָּהֲנָא בְּרֵיהּ דְּרַב נָתָן: שמות כח °"לְרָצוֹן לָהֶם" כְּתִיב, לְרָצוֹן וְלֹא לְפוּרְעָנוּת. אִי הָכִי בְּמִדְיָן נַמִי! אָמַר רַב אָשֵׁי: "לָהֶם" כְּתִיב, לָהֶם לְרָצוֹן וְלֹא לְפוּרְעָנוּת, וּלְגוֹיִם – אֲפִילּוּ לְפוּרְעָנוּת. אָמַר רַבִּי יַעֲקֹב בַּר אִידִי אָמַר רַבִּי יְהוֹשֻׁעַ בֶּן לֵוִי: הֲלָכָה כְּרַבִּי שִׁמְעוֹן בֶּן יוֹחַאי. אֲמַר לֵיהּ רַבִּי זֵירָא לְרַבִּי יַעֲקֹב בַּר אִידִי: *בְּפֵירוּשׁ שְׁמִיעַ לָךְ, אוֹ מִכְּלָלָא שְׁמִיעַ לָךְ? מַאי כְּלָלָא? דַּאֲמַר ר' יְהוֹשֻׁעַ בֶּן לֵוִי: עִיר אַחַת הָיְתָה בְּאֶרֶץ יִשְׂרָאֵל שֶׁקָּרָא עָלֶיהָ עַרְעָר, וְשִׁגֵּר רַבִּי אֶת רַבִּי רוֹמָנוּס וּבְדָקָהּ, וּמָצָא בָּהּ בַּת גִּיּוֹרֶת פְּחוּתָה מִבַּת שָׁלֹשׁ שָׁנִים וְיוֹם אֶחָד – וְהִכְשִׁירָהּ רַבִּי לִכְהוּנָּה. אֲמַר לֵיהּ: בְּפֵירוּשׁ שְׁמִיעַ לִי. *וְאִי מִכְּלָלָא מַאי? דִּלְמָא שָׁאנֵי הָתָם, הוֹאִיל וְאִנְסִיב – אִנְסִיב. דְּהָא רַב וְרַבִּי יוֹחָנָן דְּאָמְרִי תַּרְוַיְיהוּ: בּוֹגֶרֶת וּמוּכַּת עֵץ – לֹא יִשָּׂא, וְאִם נָשָׂא – נָשׂוּי. הָכִי הַשְׁתָּא?! בִּשְׁלָמָא הָתָם – סוֹפָהּ לִהְיוֹת בּוֹגֶרֶת תַּחְתָּיו, סוֹפָהּ לִהְיוֹת בְּעוּלָה תַּחְתָּיו. הָכָא – סוֹפָהּ לִהְיוֹת זוֹנָה תַּחְתָּיו?! רַב סַפְרָא מַתְנֵי לָהּ מִכְּלָלָא, וְקַשְׁיָא לֵיהּ, וּמְשַׁנֵּי לֵיהּ הָכִי. הַהוּא כָּהֲנָא דְּאִנְסִיב גִּיּוֹרֶת פְּחוּתָה מִבַּת שָׁלֹשׁ שָׁנִים וְיוֹם אֶחָד. אֲמַר לֵיהּ ר"נ בַּר יִצְחָק: מַאי הַאי? אֲמַר לֵיהּ: דַּאֲמַר רַבִּי יַעֲקֹב בַּר אִידִי אָמַר ר' יְהוֹשֻׁעַ בֶּן לֵוִי: הֲלָכָה כְּר"ש בֶּן יוֹחַאי. אֲמַר לֵיהּ: אזִיל אַפֵּיק, וְאִי לָא – מַפֵּיקְנָא לָךְ רַ' יַעֲקֹב בַּר אִידִי מֵאוּנָךְ. תַּנְיָא וְכֵן הָיָה ר"ש בֶּן יוֹחַאי אוֹמֵר

קִבְרֵי

רש"י

מִדְּשָׁבְקֵיהּ (ב) לְבַר זוּגֵיהּ. דְּגַבֵּי מוּכַּת עֵץ לָא פָּלֵיג אֶלָּא ר' שִׁמְעוֹן לְחוּדֵיהּ, וְשָׁבְקֵיהּ ר' יוֹסֵי דַּהֲוָה בַּר זוּגֵיהּ בַּאֲרוּסָה. מִכְּלָל דִּבְמוּכַּת עֵץ כְּר' מֵאִיר סְבִירָא לֵיהּ לְר' יוֹסֵי, דִּמְטַמֵּא לָהּ. מִ"לֹּא הָיְתָה". דְּדָרֵישׁ לֵיהּ לְר' מֵאִיר: מִי שֶׁהֲוָיָיתָהּ עַל יְדֵי אִישׁ. וְהָא אַפְּקֵיהּ. ר' יוֹסֵי לְהוֹצִיא אֶת הָאֲרוּסָה. חַד מִ"לֹּא הָיְתָה". לְהוֹצִיא אֶת הָאֲרוּסָה. מִ"לְּאִישׁ". לְמִישְׁרֵי מוּכַּת עֵץ, שֶׁאֵין מְקוּלְקֶלֶת עַל יְדֵי אִישׁ. וְהָא אָמַר ר' שִׁמְעוֹן. לְעֵיל: "בְּתוּלָה" – שְׁלֵימָה מַשְׁמַע, מִדְּאִיצְטְרִיךְ "בְּתוּלֶיהָ" לְמִישְׁרֵי בּוֹגֶרֶת לְכ"ג. כְּשֵׁרָה לִכְהוּנָּה. לָא מַחֲזְקִינַן לָהּ כְּזוֹנָה. אִי הָכִי אֲפִילּוּ בַּת ג' שָׁנִים. נַמִי לִיתַּכְשַׁר לְרַבִּי שִׁמְעוֹן, וּבִלְבַד שֶׁלֹּא תְּהֵא נִבְעֶלֶת. דְּהָא קְרָא אַנִּבְעֲלָה הוּא דְּקָא קָפֵיד לֵיהּ, וְקָאָמַר: כָּל שֶׁאֵין נִבְעֶלֶת – הַחֲיוּ לָכֶם. כִּדְרַב הוּנָא. לָא מָצֵית אָמְרַתְּ דְּבַת ג' שָׁנִים לֵימָא קְרָא "הַחֲיוּ". דְּרַב הוּנָא רָמֵי. "אִשָּׁה" מַשְׁמַע גְּדוֹלָה, וְקָאָמַר קְרָא: יוֹדַעַת – הֲרוֹגוּ, וְשֶׁאֵינָהּ יוֹדַעַת – הַחֲיוּ, מִכְּלָל דְּטַף, לָא שְׁנָא הָכִי וְלָא שְׁנָא הָכִי – הַחֲיוּ, וּכְתִיב וְכָל הַטַּף וגו'. הֱוֵי אוֹמֵר. מִדְּקָשׁוּ קְרָאֵי אַהֲדָדֵי עַל כָּרְחָךְ "יוֹדַעַת" דִּקְרָא וַ"אֲשֶׁר לֹא יָדְעוּ" – לָאו יְדִיעָה מַמָּשׁ קָאָמַר, דְּאִם כֵּן – לָא מִיתָּרְצָא דּוּקְיָא דִּקְרָא. אֶלָּא בִּרְאוּיָה לִיבָּעֵל הַכָּתוּב מְדַבֵּר – דְּכָל אִשָּׁה הָרְאוּיָה לֵידַע – הֲרוֹגוּ, וְהַשְׁתָּא מַשְׁמַע: אִשָּׁה – אֲפִילּוּ טַף בַּת ג' דִּרְאוּיָה לֵידַע. וְלָא תֵּידוֹק: הָא טַף בֵּין יָדְעִי בֵּין לָא יָדְעִי – הַחֲיוּ, דְּהָא בִּרְאוּיָה קָא מִישְׁתַּעֵי קְרָא. אֶלָּא "הַחֲיוּ לָכֶם" דְּקָאָמַר רַחֲמָנָא – בִּפְחוּתָה מִבַּת שָׁלֹשׁ קָאָמַר. בִּרְאוּיָה לִיבָּעֵל. אַע"פ שֶׁלֹּא נִבְעֲלָה. כְּשֶׁהוּא אוֹמֵר וְכָל הַטַּף אֲשֶׁר לֹא יָדְעוּ הַחֲיוּ. הָא אִשָּׁה, אַע"פ שֶׁלֹּא יָדְעָה – הֲרוֹגוּ הֲוֵי בִּרְאוּיָה לִיבָּעֵל קָמִשְׁתַּעֵי קְרָא. פָּנֶיהָ מוֹרִיקוֹת. נֵס הָיָה. הַדְּרוֹקָן. פְּנֵיהֶן שֶׁל עוֹבְרֵי עֲבֵירָה מוֹרִיקִין. מֵאַנְשֵׁי יָבֵשׁ גִּלְעָד. בִּימֵי פִּלֶגֶשׁ בַּגִּבְעָה, שֶׁנֶּהֶרְגוּ כָּל אַנְשֵׁי יָבֵשׁ גִּלְעָד לְפִי שֶׁלֹּא בָּאוּ לְהִלָּחֵם בְּשֵׁבֶט בִּנְיָמִין כִּשְׁאָר אַחִים. וְהֶחֱיוּ כָּל שֶׁלֹּא נִבְעֲלָה, וּנְתָנוּם לַנּוֹתָרִים מִשֵּׁבֶט בִּנְיָמִין לְנָשִׁים. בְּפֵירוּשׁ שְׁמִיעַ לָךְ. מִינֵּיהּ דְּרַבִּי יְהוֹשֻׁעַ בֶּן לֵוִי. אוֹ מִכְּלָלָא. דְּשָׁמַעְתְּ מִינֵּיהּ מִילְּתָא דְּדָיְיקַתְּ מִינֵּיהּ דִּסְבִירָא לֵיהּ כְּר' שִׁמְעוֹן. מַאי כְּלָלָא. מֵאֵיזֶה כְּלָל הָיָה לוֹ לוֹמַר. עַרְעָר. לִפְסוֹל מִשְׁפַּחַת הָעִיר. רוֹמָנוּס גָּרְסִינַן. וְהִכְשִׁירָהּ. הַנִּיסָה תַּחַת בַּעְלָהּ כֹּהֵן. וְאִי מִכְּלָלָא מַאי. וְאִי מֵהַאי כְּלָלָא שְׁמִיעַ לֵיהּ לְר' יַעֲקֹב, מַאי אִית לֵיהּ לְרַבִּי זֵירָא לְאוֹתְבֵיהּ, דְּקָא בָּעֵי מִינֵּיהּ: בְּפֵירוּשׁ שְׁמִיעַ לָךְ אוֹ מִכְּלָלָא? הָכָא סוֹפָהּ לִהְיוֹת זוֹנָה תַּחְתָּיו? בִּתְמִיָּה. אִי סְבִירָא לֵיהּ דִּפְסוּל – מִשּׁוּם זְנוּת סְבִירָא לֵיהּ, וְאִם כֵּן – לָא שְׁנָא לְכַתְּחִלָּה וְלָא שְׁנָא דִּיעֲבַד – אֲסִירָא. וְקַשְׁיָא לֵיהּ. כִּדְמַקְשֵׁי: דִּלְמָא הָתָם הוֹאִיל וְאִינְסִיב אִינְסִיב. וּמְשַׁנֵּי הָכִי. כִּדְשַׁנֵּינַן: בִּשְׁלָמָא הָתָם סוֹפָהּ לִהְיוֹת בְּעוּלָה תַּחְתָּיו כו'. מַפֵּיקְנָא לָךְ ר' יַעֲקֹב מֵאוּנָךְ. כְּלוֹמַר: מְשַׁמְּתִינַן לָךְ, וְתַפֵּיק עַל כָּרְחָךְ. אֵין

תוספות

והא אמר רבי שמעון בתולה שלימה משמע. תימה: דלעיל פריך: למה לי לרבות הבוגרת – והא אמר רבי מאיר "בתולה" – אפילו מקצת בתולים [משמע]. משמע דאי הוה סבר בתולה שלימה – לא הוה קשה לן מידי. והשתא פריך איפכא! ואומר ר"י: דהכא פריך הכי: והאמר רבי שמעון בתולה שלימה משמע, ולהכי מכשיר התם בכהן גדול בוגרת – ואם כן למה לי הכא "אליו" לרבות בוגרת? נילף "בתולה" "בתולה" מהתם! ומשני: טעמא דידיה נמי מהכא. ואם תאמר: מאחר דמרבינן הכא בוגרת, למה לי יו"ד ד"בתוליה" לעיל להכשיר בוגרת? נילף מהכא! ואומר ר"י: דצריך למכתב התם בתוליה ביו"ד, משום דבענין אחר לא אפשר למכתב יתור של בי"ת, דבבתוליה, למדרש מיניה עד שיהו כל בתוליה קיימין, למעוטי שלא כדרכה ומוכת עץ, כדפרישית לעיל. **הא** אינה יודעת יקיימוה. לא היה צריך למידק הכי, אלא: הא טף, אפי' יודעת – יקיימו כו'. אלא שרוצה להקשות משניהם ד"כל אשה יודעת" משמע: דאינה יודעת – קיימו, וטף נמי, אפילו יודעת – קיימו. ובאידך קרא ד"טף אשר לא ידעו" משמע הא ידעו, או גדולה ואפי' לא ידעה – הרוגו. **בראויה** ליבעל הכתוב מדבר. ו"יודעת איש" היינו ראויה לדעת איש. והא דכתיב "אשה" דמשמע דוקא גדולה – היינו משום דליקשו קראי, ומתוך כך מוקמינן דבראויה ליבעל הכתוב מדבר. דאי לא כתיב אשה אלא סתם וכל "יודעת איש" הוה אמינא דהאי קרא נמי בטף איירי. ובטף, יודעת – הרוגו, ושאינה יודעת – יקיימו. אבל גדולה – אפילו אין יודעת הרוגו. **סימן** לעבירה הדרוקן. ע"י העבירה בא הדרוקן, כדאמרינן ב"במה מדליקין" (שבת דף לג.) והדרוקן לאו היינו ירקון, כדאמר ב"הרואה" (ברכות דף סב:) אבל קצת יש להדרוקן ירוקת פנים, כדאמר. דכל שפניה מוריקות*.

[וע' בתוספות בכורות מד: ד"ה לידי כו']

תוספות ישנים

והאמר ר' שמעון בתולה שלמה משמע. וא"ת ומאי פריך אדרבה היא הנותנת דסד"א בתולה שלמה משמע אילטריך אליו לרבות בוגרת. דהכי משמע לעיל הך סברא דפריך לר"מ האמר [בתולה] מקצת בתולה משמע הא אי אמרינן בתולה שלמה משמע ניחא דאלטריך אליו לרבות בוגרת ונראה לפרש דה"ק והאמר ר"ש בתולה שלמה משמע ואינו מייתי [רק] תחלת דבר ור"ל בתולה שלמה משמע ובבתולה מקצת בתולים דהיינו מלתיה דלעיל וא"כ למה לי אליו לרבות בוגרת תיפוק ליה דניליף מהתם ודוחק הוא דהא לא מייתי קרא דבבתוליה. ונ"ל דה"ק והאמר רבי שמעון בתולה שלמה משמע ואמאי קאמר ר' שמעון כן הו"ל למגמר מהכא דלאו שלמה משמע דהא אמרינן אליו לרבות את הבוגרת: **טעמא** דידי נמי מהכא מדאלטריך אליו לרבות את הבוגרת א"כ בתולה משמע בתולה שלמה והקשה הר' ידידיה היכי קאמר ר"ש מדאלטריך לרבות הבוגרת א"כ בתולה משמע בתולה שלמה דלמא לעולם אימא לך מקצת בתולים משמע ומ"מ אילטריך אליו לרבות בוגרת דלא ניליף בתולה בתולה מהתם דלדריש בתולה מקצת בתולים משמע בבתוליה עד שיהיו כל בתוליה קיימין כמו דאמר ר"מ לעיל ונראה לרשב"י דהא לא קשה מידי דהכי נמי מצי להקשות אמאי לא קאמר ר"ש כר"מ בהדיא ובהא ודאי מצינו שפיר למימר טעם דדלמא ר' שמעון ניחא ליה א) שפיר לומר בתולה שלמה ואצטריך אליו למעט ממשמעותיה דקרא משנאמר כר' מאיר דבתולה משמע ואצטריך אליו דלא ניליף בתולה מהתם דהתם נמי משמע בתולה מקצת בתולים רק דמפקינן מבתוליה עד דאיכא כל בתולים. ועוד ב) מדקא"ל לר' שמעון למצוא טעם להעמיד דבתולה שלמה משמע מלומר מקצת בתולים ועוד אינו ר"ל בתולה מקצת בתולים משמע בבתוליה עד שיהיו כל בתוליה קיימין דא"כ לא מצינו לאסור שלא כדרכה דלא מצינו למדרש בבתוליה בין בכדרכה בין שלא כדרכה דא"כ לשתוק קרא מיניה ומבתוליה שמעינן לה דבעינן לעולם כל בתולים כדפרישית לעיל לר' מאיר וא"כ היינו נריכים לדרוש בבתוליה כדרכה אין שלא כדרכה לא בעינן כל בתולים ור' שמעון לא ניחא לדורשה שלא כדרכה כיון דמצינו לומר איפכא ולפסול שלא כדרכה:

א) אולי צ"ל ניחא ליה טפי לומר בתולה שלמה משמע מדאצטריך אליו למעט ממשמעותיה דקרא משנאמר כר"מ דבתולה מקצת בתולה משמע כו'. ב) אולי צ"ל ועוד דניחא ליה טפי למצוא טעם לר"ש להעמיד דבתולה וכו'.

הגהות הב"ח

(א) גמ' ורבי יוסי מדשבקיה בר זוגיה כצ"ל ואות ג' נמחק: (ב) רש"י ד"ה מדשבקיה בר זוגיה וכו' ושבקיה לרב יוסי דהוה:

מסורת הש"ס

[לקמן סג.] קידושין (עח:) עח. שבת לג. [כתובות י:] [שבת לג: עירובין מו. ועי' ברכות ט.] [ברכות יב. וש"נ]

קברי *[א]גוים אינן מטמאין באהל, שנא' °"ואתן צאני צאן מרעיתי אדם אתם" ⊕אתם קרויין "אדם", ואין הגוים קרויין "אדם", מיתיבי: °"ונפש אדם ששה עשר אלף"! משום בהמה. °"אשר יש בה הרבה משתים עשרה רבוא אדם אשר לא ידע בין ימינו לשמאלו (ובהמה רבה)". משום בהמה. °"כל הורג נפש וכל נוגע בחלל תתחטאו"! דלמא איקטיל חד מישראל. ורבנן: "לא נפקד ממנו איש". ור' שמעון בן יוחי: "לא נפקד ממנו איש" לעבירה. רבינא אמר: [ב]נהי דמעטינהו קרא מאטמויי באהל, דכתיב °"אדם כי ימות באהל", ממגע ומשא מי מעטינהו קרא?. §**מתני'** *⊕[ג]אירס את האלמנה ונתמנה להיות כהן גדול — יכנוס. ומעשה ביהושע בן גמלא שקידש את מרתא בת ביתוס, ומנהו המלך להיות כה"ג, וכנסה. שומרת יבם שנפלה לפני כהן הדיוט, ונתמנה להיות כה"ג, אע"פ שעשה בה מאמר — הרי זה לא יכנוס. §**גמ'** ת"ר: מנין שאם אירס את האלמנה ונתמנה להיות כהן גדול שיכנוס — ת"ל °"יקח אשה". א"ה שומרת יבם נמי! "אשה ולא יבמה". §"מעשה ביהושע וכו'". § מנהו — אין, נתמנה — לא. אמר רב יוסף: ⊕קטיר קחזינא הכא. *דאמר רב אסי: תרקבא דדינרי עיילה ליה מרתא בת ביתוס לינאי מלכא, עד דמוקי ליה ליהושע בן גמלא בכהני רברבי. §**מתני'** [ד]כהן גדול שמת אחיו — חולץ ולא מייבם. §**גמ'** *קא פסיק ותני, [ה]לא שנא מן האירוסין ולא שנא מן הנשואין. בשלמא מן הנשואין — עשה ולא תעשה הוא, [ו]ואין עשה דוחה לא תעשה ועשה. אלא מן האירוסין, [ז]יבא עשה וידחה את לא תעשה! [ח]גזירה ביאה ראשונה אטו ביאה שניה. §**מתני'** [ט]כהן הדיוט לא ישא אילונית, אלא א"כ יש לו *אשה ובנים. רבי יהודה אומר: אע"פ שיש לו אשה ובנים — *לא ישא אילונית, שהיא זונה האמורה בתורה. וחכמים אומרים: [י]אין זונה אלא גיורת, ומשוחררת, ושנבעלה בעילת זנות. §**גמ'** א"ל ריש גלותא לרב הונא: מ"ט — משום פריה ורביה, אפריה ורביה כהנים הוא דמפקדי, וישראל לא מפקדי?! אמר ליה: משום דקא בעי למיתני סיפא, רבי יהודה אומר: אע"פ שיש לו אשה וי֯ש

(מקראות בגליון: יחזקאל לד; במדבר לא; יונה ד; במדבר לא; שם יט; ויקרא כא; לקמן סא.)

רש"י

אין מטמאין. את המאהיל עליהם. אתם קרוים אדם. וגבי טומאת אהל כתיב "אדם כי ימות באהל" (במדבר יט). נפש אדם. במדין כתיב. ומשני: הא דקרי להו אדם – משום דבעי למכתב בהמה גבייהו, כדכתיב "וחמורים ובקר", וגבי בהמה מיקרו אדם. אבל אדם סתמא – לא מיקרו: אנשי נינוה גוים היו. כל הורג נפש. במדין כתיב, ומדבעו טומאת שבעה – אלמא מיטמו. ממגע ומשא מי מעטינהו. וגבי מגע אשכחן נוגע בעצם או בחלל דלא כתיב אדם. הלכך, אע"ג דלא מיקרו אדם מטמו במגע ובמשא. ת"ל בתולה מעמיו יקח אשה. האי "אשה" לא איצטריך אלא לדרשא. מינהו אין. כלומר: המלך מינהו, אבל אחיו הכהנים וסנהדרין לא מנוהו. נתמנה לא. נתמנה לא קתני, דהוי משמע דראוי היה לכך. קטיר קחזינא הכא. קשר של רשעים אני רואה כאן, שלא היה ראוי לכך, אלא שנתן ממון ומינוהו. **מתני'** חולץ. כהן גדול. ולא מייבם. דאלמנה היא ואסורה לו. **גמ'** לא תעשה ועשה. "אלמנה לא יקח", "בתולה יקח" (ויקרא כא) ולא בעולה. **מתני'** אלא אם כן יש לו בנים. משום דמצווה על פריה ורביה, וה"ה לישראל. ובגמרא מפרש אמאי נקט כהן. שהיא זונה האמורה בתורה. ובגמרא מפרש לה. אלא הגיורת והמשוחררת. דביאת עכו"ם ועבד פסלה. ושנבעלה בעילת זנות. כגון ישראלית הנבעלת לפסול לה.

תוספות

קברי גוים אינן מטמאין באהל. תימה: למה ליה לרבי בנאה לציוני מערתא דאברהם אבינו ואדם הראשון (ב"ב נח.)? אף דאיקרו "אדם" אדם ואברהם, או אפי' לרבנן דאמרי קברי גוים מטמאין באהל – הא לא מטמא באהל אפילו קברי ישראל אלא אותם שמתו משעה שנאמרה אותה פרשה ד"אדם כי ימות באוהל", דכי ימות משמע באותם העתידים למות עדיין, ומדאיצטריך נמי בנזיר (דף נד. ושם) קרא לרבות קבר שלפני הדבור למגע – מכלל דבאהל לא מטמא*.

ואין הגוים קרוים אדם. תימה: דבריש מס' ע"ז (ג. ושם) ופ' "ד' מיתות" (סנהדרין דף נט. ושם) דרשינן: דגוי העוסק בתורה הרי הוא ככהן גדול, שנאמר "אשר יעשה אותם האדם" וגו', כהנים לוים וישראלים – לא נאמר, אלא: "האדם", ופי' בקונטרס בסנהדרין (ג"ז שם ד"ה "האדם") דההוא לית ליה הך דר"ש דהכא? ויתכן לפי ספרים דגרסי התם רבי ירמיה, אבל לספרים דגרסי התם ר' מאיר – קשיא, דשמעינן ליה לר"מ בפ' קמא דכריתות (דף ו:) דסך שמן המשחה לגוי – פטור, ומשמע דטעמא משום דכתיב "על בשר אדם" ואין גוי קרוי אדם! ומיהו, מצי למימר דטעמא דרבי מאיר דפטור הוי מטעם דכל שהוא בסך – הרי הוא בלא ייסך, וכל שאין בסך – אין בלא ייסך. ור"ת מפרש: ⊕דיש חילוק בין "אדם" ל"האדם", דגוים בכלל "האדם" נינהו, והא דקאמר כהנים לוים וישראלים לא נאמר – ה"ק: אדם לא נאמר, דהוי משמע כהנים לוים וישראלים, אלא "האדם". וכל הני קראי דמייתי כתיב "אדם". דלא פריך מקראי דכתיב "האדם". וה"ר משולם היה אומר: דגבי פורענות דוקא קאמר "אתם קרוין אדם" דלא רצה לכתוב ישראל בהדיא גבי פורענות, אבל גבי "האדם וחי" – הוה ליה למכתב בהדיא כהנים לוים וישראלים, כמו שרגיל בכל מקום. והא דפריך מהני קראי, אע"ג דגוים נמי קרוין אדם – מ"מ פריך, כיון דגבי פורענות ישראל קרוין אדם, היכא דלא איירי אלא בגוים דוקא – לא הוה ליה למיקרינהו אדם. והא דכתיב (תהלים קכד) "בקום עלינו אדם" – היינו לפי שהזכיר השם, וכן "ואתה אדם ולא אל" גבי חירם (יחזקאל כח). והא דכתיב "ואתן אדם תחתיך" (ישעיה מג) – הא דרשינן בברכות (דף סב:) אל תקרי אדם וכו'. והא דכתיב "והארץ נתן לבני אדם" (תהלים קטו) ודרשינן מיניה (גיטין מז.) דיש קנין לגוים – ⊕היינו בני אדם הראשון*.

ממגע ומשא מי מעטינהו. ואע"ג דכתיב "וכל אשר יגע על פני השדה וגו' או בעצם אדם" (במדבר יט) – הא דרשינן בנזיר פרק "כ"ג" (דף נג. ושם) לענין אהל. ואר"י: דאין הלכה כר"ש, דרשב"ג פליג עליה. כדתנן במס' אהלות (פרק יח מ"ט, כתובות עז.), והלכה כמותו במשנתנו. ואריכים כהנים ליזהר מקברי גוים. ובפרק "המקבל" (ב"מ קיד:) בעובדא דאליהו דהשיב לרבה בר אבוה כר' שמעון בן יוחי דהכא – לדחויי קא מדחי לה. ועיקר טעמא שהיה סומך על רוב ארונות שיש בהן פותח טפח. וכן היה רגיל בכל מקום לדחות, כמו שמצינו כשהיה קובר רבי עקיבא ואמר ליה: לאו כהן ניהו מר? אמר ליה: צדיקים אינם מטמאים. ועיקר טעמא לפי שהיה מת מצוה, שהיה מהרוגי מלכות והיו יראים לקברו. ומיהו, בבתי גוים מותרים ליכנס, כדתניא בתוספתא דאהלות: מדורות הגוים – טמאים, בחוצה לארץ – טהורים:

עיילה ליה מרתא בת ביתוס לינאי מלכא. לאו היינו ינאי כ"ג דבפרק "האומר" בקידושין (דף סו.), דאם כן – לא היה מושיב אחר במקומו(א).

כהן גדול שמת אחיו חולץ ולא מייבם. ג) וא"ת: מרישא שמעי' לה, דקתני שומרת יבם(א) לכהן הדיוט ונתמנה להיות כ"ג לא יכנוס? ואר"י: דהכא – חולץ אתא לאשמועינן, דס"ד משום בזיון דכ"ג שרוקקת לפניו לא תחלוץ. אע"ג דכבר תנן לה לעיל(ב) ובפרק "כ"ג" בסנהדרין (דף יח.).

אין זונה אלא גיורת ומשוחררת. אפי' נתגיירה פחותה מבת ג' שנים אסורה מטעם זונה, כדאמר לעיל (דף ס:) גבי עיר אחת שהיתה בא"י כו'. וטעמא – לפי שבאה מן הגוים השטופים בזימה. אע"ג דבפרק בתרא דקידושין (דף עח.) דריש לה מקרא דיחזקאל, למר כדאית ליה ולמר כדאית ליה, מ"מ, בין למר ובין למר אסירא מטעם זונה, ואתא יחזקאל ואסמכה אקראי. והקשה ה"ר משה מפונטייש"א: דהכא משמע דגיורת אסורה לכהן מדאורייתא מטעם זונה, ובפרק "אין מעמידין" (ע"ז דף לו:) אמר: דב"ד של חשמונאי גזרו דהבא על הגויה חייב משום "נשג"ז". פי': אם הוא כהן חייב משום זונה. ואיכא למ"ד משום "נש"ג", אבל משום זונה – לא, דנשייהו לא מפקרי? ולאביי (בתמורה כט:) ניחא, דלגויה לא מחייב משום דכתיב "לא יקח ולא יחלל", ובגויה לא קרינן בה "לא יקח" דלא תפסי בה קידושין, ולא שייך נמי בה חלול זרע, שאין הזרע מתייחס אחריו, אבל לרבא דפליג עליה וקאמר: אחד זה ואחד זה, פירוש בין זונה גויה בין זונה ישראלית אתננה אסור, וכהן הבא עליה לוקה משום זונה – קשה! ויש לומר: דרבא לא פליג אלא היכא דזינתה, דיליף לה מזונה ישראלית, כדקאמר רבא. אבל לא זינתה – מודה דלא מיתסרא משום זונה. כדקאמר אביי, משום דכתיב "לא יחלל". והיכא דלא זינתה הוצרכו לגזור. אבל גיורת דשייך בה קיחה וחילול – אסורה משום זונה, אע"ג דלא זינתה.

שנבעלה בעילת זנות. פירוש בקונטרס: ישראלית שנבעלה לפסול לה. וא"א לומר כן, דמחייבי לאוין דתפסי בה קידושין לא הוי זונה, ⊕אלא מחייבי כריתות, כדפי' ב"החולץ" (לעיל דף מט.).

כל

עין משפט נר מצוה

עו א ב מיי' פ"ג מהל' אבל הלכה ג ופ"א מהל' טומאת מת הלכה יג סמג לאוין רלא טוש"ע י"ד סימן שעב סעי' ב:
עז ג מיי' פי"ז מהל' איסורי ביאה הל' יב:
עח ד מיי' שם ופ"ה מהלכות כלי המקדש הלכה י:
עט ה מיי' פי"ז מהל' איסורי ביאה הלכה יג:
פ ו מיי' פ"ו מהלכות יבום הלכה יח:
פא ז ח מיי' שם הלכ' ו:
פב ט מיי' פט"ו מהלכות אישות הלכה ז סמג עשין מט טוש"ע אה"ע סי' א סעי' ח:
פג י מיי' פי"ח מהל' איסורי ביאה הלכה ב סמג לאוין קכא טוש"ע שם סי' ו סעי' ח:

(ועי' תוס' ב"ב נח. כתבו ישוב לזה ותוס' נדה ע: ד"ה ולאו נגיעה)

תוספות ישנים

ואין הגוים כו'. פרשתי בב"ק בפרק שור שנגח: **דלמא** אקטיל חד מישראל. י"מ דר"ש מוכיח מכאן דכל קבוע כמחצה על מחצה מדקאמר תתחטאו דלמא אקטיל חד מישראל אע"ג דגוים רובא אכן לא נהירא דלמסקנא אין הדבר מיושב דקאמר ממגע ומשא מי מעטינהו קרא וש"מ הוצרכו חטוי משום טומאת מגע ומשא עוי"ל דאין ראיה מכאן דדלמא הכי פירושא דלמא אקטיל חד מישראל והם היו פושטים ידיהם על החללים ונמצא שנגעו בכולם א) האהלות ואפי' אי ליכא אלא חד מישראל אטמו מחמתיה. ובכתובות פי' דנפקא ליה מוחרב לו וקם עליו והקשינו מנא ליה לר' שמעון דמפיק לדרשא אחרינא בפרק ואלו הן הנשרפים (דף ע"ט) מגליה ופי' שם ור"ת פסק דלא כר"ש דאמר קברי ישמעאלים אין מטמאים באהל דכל מקום ששנה רשב"ג הלכה כמותו ורשב"ג פליג עליה דר"ש דאמר ב) מדורות גוים מטמאין באהל מפני שקוברין שם נפליהם. ובמסכת אהלות (פי"ח מ"ט) נמי רשב"ג פליג עליה דקאמר עיר גוים שחרבה אין בה משום מדורות הגוים משמע אבל ישובה אית בה ומטמאה באהל: **ממגע** ומשא מי אמעיט. וא"ת הא כתיב נמי או בעצם אדם דמשמע ישראל ולא גוים וי"ל דבנזיר מוקמינן לכולי קרא בטומאת אהל אבל ממגע ומשא לא אמעוט גוים: **א)** וגם אין זה יהושע בן

מסורת הש"ס

ב"מ קיד: [כריתות ו:]
רש"ל מ"ז
יומא יח.
סנהדרין יח: לעיל כ.
[לעיל נט.]

הגהות הב"ח

(א) תוס' ד"ה כהן וכו' שומרת יבם שנפלה לפני כהן הדיוט: (ב) בא"ד תנן לה לעיל. נ"ב בפרק כ' דף כ:

פי' או אשה לפרות ולרבות שמא או בנים קו"ע בשם הרמב"ם ומתוך פרש"י משמע דגרס אשה יש לו בנים ולא הוא ברכתו אשה כלל

[ע' תוספות נזיר נג. ב"ק לח. ב"ב נח. מס' ע"ז ג. סנהדרין נט: ובנדה ע:]

גליון הש"ס

גמ' אתם קרוין אדם. עי' תוי"ט רפ"ג דנגעי' ובתוי"ט שם רפי"ב: **מתני'** אירס את האלמנה. עי' לעיל דף כ ע"ב תד"ה אטו ביאה: **גמ'** קטיר קחזינא הכא. עיין ב"ב דף כ"א ע"א ד"ה זכור: **תוס'** ד"ה אין וכו' דיש חילוק בין אדם להאדם. עי' ירמיה ל"ב: כ' ובישראל ובאדם: **בא"ד** בסוף הדבור היינו בני אדם הראשון. עיין ברמב"ן סימן שי"ז: **ד"ה** שנבעלה וכו' אלא מחייבי כריתות וכו'. עיין עין ד' פט ע"א תד"ה בעולה ובמהרש"א שם:

אלא ג) שהיה בב"ב שתקן כמה תקנות שאלותו לדיק היה אלא אחר הוא זה ד): ב) וא"ת והא כבר תנינא לעיל אלמנה לכה"ג חולצת ולא מתייבמת גבי איסור מצוה ואיסור קדושה וי"ל דהכא עיקר ולעיל תנייא שם כללא דכייל ותני: נראה דצ"ל או שאלתיה בכולם. ב) לפנינו במשנה דאהלות פי"ח משנה ז' תנן סתמא ולא הוזכר בה רשב"ג. ג) נ"ל שהוזכר בב"ב שם לשון. ד) ועי' תוס' ב"ב שם ד"ה זכור.

וְיֵשׁ לוֹ בָּנִים לֹא יִשָּׂא אַיְלוֹנִית, שֶׁהִיא זוֹנָה הָאֲמוּרָה בַּתּוֹרָה. דְּאַזּוֹנָה כֹּהֲנִים הוּא דְּמִפַּקְּדִי, וְיִשְׂרָאֵל לָא מִפַּקְּדִי, מִשּׁוּם הָכִי קָתָנֵי כֹּהֵן. אָמַר רַב הוּנָא: מַאי טַעֲמָא דְּרַ' יְהוּדָה — דִּכְתִיב "אָכְלוּ וְלֹא יִשְׂבָּעוּ הִזְנוּ וְלֹא יִפְרֹצוּ", כָּל בִּיאָה שֶׁאֵין בָּהּ[א] (א) פִּירְצָה — אֵינָהּ אֶלָּא בְּעִילַת זְנוּת. תַּנְיָא, רַבִּי אֱלִיעֶזֶר אוֹמֵר: כֹּהֵן לֹא יִשָּׂא אֶת הַקְּטַנָּה. אָמַר לֵיהּ רַב חִסְדָּא לְרַבָּה: פּוּק עַיֵּין בָּהּ, דִּלְאוֹרְתָא בָּעֵי לָהּ רַב הוּנָא מִינָּךְ. נָפַק עַיֵּין בָּהּ: רַבִּי אֱלִיעֶזֶר סָבַר לָהּ כְּרַבִּי מֵאִיר, וְסָבַר לָהּ כְּרַבִּי יְהוּדָה. סָבַר לָהּ כְּרַבִּי מֵאִיר — דְּחָיֵישׁ לְמִיעוּטָא, וְסָבַר לָהּ כְּרַבִּי יְהוּדָה — דְּאָמַר: אַיְלוֹנִית זוֹנָה הָוְיָא. וּכְרַבִּי מֵאִיר מִי סָבַר לָהּ? וְהָתַנְיָא: קָטָן וּקְטַנָּה — לֹא חוֹלְצִין וְלֹא מְיַבְּמִין, דִּבְרֵי רַבִּי מֵאִיר. אָמְרוּ לוֹ לְרַבִּי מֵאִיר: יָפֶה אָמַרְתָּ שֶׁאֵין חוֹלְצִין "אִישׁ" כְּתִיב בַּפָּרָשָׁה, וּמַקְשִׁינַן אִשָּׁה לְאִישׁ. אֶלָּא מַאי טַעְמָא אֵין מְיַבְּמִין? [א"ל]: קָטָן — שֶׁמָּא יִמָּצֵא סָרִיס, קְטַנָּה — שֶׁמָּא תִּמָּצֵא אַיְלוֹנִית, וְנִמְצְאוּ פּוֹגְעִין בָּעֶרְוָה, וְתַנְיָא: קְטַנָּה — מִתְיַיבֶּמֶת וְאֵינָהּ חוֹלֶצֶת, דִּבְרֵי רַבִּי אֱלִיעֶזֶר. וּכְרַבִּי יְהוּדָה מִי סָבַר לָהּ? וְהָתַנְיָא: "זוֹנָה" זוֹנָה כִּשְׁמָהּ, דִּבְרֵי רַבִּי אֱלִיעֶזֶר. רַבִּי עֲקִיבָא אוֹמֵר: "זוֹנָה" זוֹ מוּפְקֶרֶת. רַבִּי מַתְיָא בֶּן חָרָשׁ אוֹמֵר: אֲפִי' הָלַךְ בַּעְלָהּ לְהַשְׁקוֹתָהּ, וּבָא עָלֶיהָ בַּדֶּרֶךְ — עֲשָׂאָהּ זוֹנָה. רַבִּי יְהוּדָה אוֹמֵר: "זוֹנָה" זוֹ אַיְלוֹנִית. וַחֲכָמִים אוֹמְרִים: אֵין זוֹנָה אֶלָּא גִּיּוֹרֶת וּמְשׁוּחְרֶרֶת וְשֶׁנִּבְעֲלָה בְּעִילַת זְנוּת. ר' אֱלִיעֶזֶר אוֹמֵר: פָּנוּי הַבָּא עַל הַפְּנוּיָה שֶׁלֹּא לְשֵׁם אִישׁוּת — עֲשָׂאָהּ זוֹנָה. אֶלָּא אָמַר רַב אַדָּא בַּר אַהֲבָה: הָכָא בְּכֹ"ג עָסְקִינַן, לְאֵימַת קָנֵי לָהּ — לְכִי גָּדְלָה, בְּעוּלָה הִיא. אֲמַר רָבָא: מִכְּדֵי לֵב! אִי דְּקִדְּשָׁהּ אֲבוּהָ — מֵהַהִיא שַׁעְתָּא הוּא דְּקָנֵי לָהּ, וְאִי דְּקִדְּשָׁה נַפְשָׁהּ — הָא רַבִּי אֱלִיעֶזֶר הִיא וְלָא רַבָּנַן! אֶלָּא אָמַר רָבָא: לְעוֹלָם בְּכֹהֵן הֶדְיוֹט, וְחָיְישִׁינַן שֶׁמָּא תִּתְפַּתֶּה עָלָיו. א"ה יִשְׂרָאֵל נַמִי! פִּתּוּיֵי קְטַנָּה אוֹנֶס הוּא, וְאוֹנֶס בְּיִשְׂרָאֵל מִישְׁרָא שָׁרֵי. רַב פַּפָּא אֲמַר: בְּכֹ"ג, וְהַאי תַּנָּא הוּא, דְּתַנְיָא: "בְּתוּלָה" יָכוֹל קְטַנָּה — ת"ל "אִשָּׁה". אִי "אִשָּׁה" יָכוֹל בּוֹגֶרֶת — ת"ל "בְּתוּלָה". הָא כֵּיצַד? יָצְתָה מִכְּלַל קְטַנּוּת, וְלִכְלַל בַּגְרוּת לֹא בָּאתָה. רַב נַחְמָן בַּר יִצְחָק אָמַר: הַאי תַּנָּא הוּא, דְּתַנְיָא "בְּתוּלָה" אֵין בְּתוּלָה אֶלָּא נַעֲרָה, וְכֵן הוּא אוֹמֵר "וְהַנַּעֲרָה טֹבַת מַרְאֶה מְאֹד בְּתוּלָה". ר' אֶלְעָזָר אוֹמֵר: פָּנוּי הַבָּא עַל הַפְּנוּיָה שֶׁלֹּא לְשֵׁם אִישׁוּת — עֲשָׂאָהּ זוֹנָה. אָמַר רַב עַמְרָם: אֵין הֲלָכָה כְּרַבִּי אֶלְעָזָר.§

מתני' לֹא יִבָּטֵל אָדָם מִפְּרִיָּה וּרְבִיָּה אֶלָּא אִ"כ יֵשׁ לוֹ בָּנִים. ב"ש אוֹמְרִים: שְׁנֵי זְכָרִים, וּב"ה אוֹמְרִים: זָכָר וּנְקֵבָה, שֶׁנֶּאֱמַר "זָכָר וּנְקֵבָה בְּרָאָם".§

גמ' הָא יֵשׁ לוֹ בָּנִים, מִפְּרִיָּה וּרְבִיָּה — בָּטֵיל, מֵאִשָּׁה — לָא בָּטֵיל. מְסַיְּיעָא לֵיהּ לְרַב נַחְמָן אָמַר שְׁמוּאֵל, דְּאָמַר: אע"פ שֶׁיֵּשׁ לוֹ לְאָדָם כַּמָּה בָּנִים — אָסוּר לַעֲמוֹד בְּלֹא אִשָּׁה, שֶׁנֶּאֱמַר "לֹא טוֹב הֱיוֹת הָאָדָם לְבַדּוֹ". וְאִיכָּא דְּאָמְרִי: הָא יֵשׁ לוֹ בָּנִים — בָּטֵיל מִפְּרִיָּה וּרְבִיָּה, וּבָטֵיל נַמִי מֵאִשָּׁה. נֵימָא תֶּיהֱוֵי תְּיוּבְתָּא דְּרַב נַחְמָן אָמַר שְׁמוּאֵל! לָא, אֵין לוֹ בָּנִים — נוֹשֵׂא אִשָּׁה בַּת בָּנִים, יֵשׁ לוֹ בָּנִים — נוֹשֵׂא אִשָּׁה דְּלָאו בַּת בָּנִים. נָפְקָא מִינָּהּ — לִמְכּוֹר סֵפֶר תּוֹרָה בִּשְׁבִיל בָּנִים.§ "בֵּית שַׁמַּאי אוֹמְרִים שְׁנֵי זְכָרִים".§ מַאי טַעֲמַיְיהוּ דְּבֵית שַׁמַּאי — יָלְפִינַן מִמֹּשֶׁה, דִּכְתִיב "בְּנֵי מֹשֶׁה גֵּרְשׁוֹם וֶאֱלִיעֶזֶר", וּבֵית הִלֵּל — יָלְפִינַן מִבְּרִיָּיתוֹ שֶׁל עוֹלָם. וּבֵית שַׁמַּאי, לִילְפֵי מִבְּרִיָּיתוֹ שֶׁל עוֹלָם! אֵין דָּנִין אֶפְשָׁר מִשֶּׁאִי

גמ' פּוּק עַיֵּין בָּהּ. אַמַּאי לֹא יִשָּׂא אֶת הַקְּטַנָּה. רַבִּי מֵאִיר חָיֵישׁ לְמִיעוּטָא. כִּדְתַנְיָא לְקַמָּן: קָטָן שֶׁמָּא יִמָּצֵא כו' — ה"נ חָיֵישׁ רַבִּי אֱלִיעֶזֶר דְּשֶׁמָּא תִּמָּצֵא קְטַנָּה זוֹ אַיְלוֹנִית. קָטָן וּקְטַנָּה. אוֹ קָטָן אוֹ קְטַנָּה. אִישׁ כְּתִיב. בְּפָרָשַׁת חֲלִיצָה "וְאִם לֹא יַחְפֹּץ הָאִישׁ לָקַחַת אֶת יְבִמְתּוֹ". פּוֹגְעִים בָּעֶרְוָה. כֵּיוָן דְּלָאו בְּנֵי הֲקָמַת שֵׁם נִינְהוּ — פָּגַע בְּאֵשֶׁת אָח שֶׁלֹּא בִּמְקוֹם מִצְוָה, דְּרַחֲמָנָא פַּטְרֵיהּ, דִּכְתִיב "אֲשֶׁר תֵּלֵד" (דברים כה) — פְּרָט לְאַיְלוֹנִית. וְאֵינָהּ חוֹלֶצֶת. דְּאֵינָהּ נִפְטֶרֶת לַשּׁוּק בַּחֲלִיצָתָהּ, דְּאֵין מַעֲשֵׂה קְטַנָּה כְּלוּם. אֲבָל מִתְיַיבֶּמֶת, וְתִגְדַּל אֶצְלוֹ, וְתִתְקַיֵּים מִצְוַת יִבּוּם. כִּשְׁמָהּ. לְשׁוֹן טוֹעָה, שֶׁטּוֹעָה מִתַּחַת בַּעְלָהּ לַאֲחֵרִים. דִּלְרַבִּי אֱלִיעֶזֶר אֵין זוֹנָה אֶלָּא אֵשֶׁת אִישׁ. מוּפְקֶרֶת. וַאֲפִי' פְּנוּיָה, מֵאַחַר שֶׁהִפְקִירָה עַצְמָהּ לַכֹּל — קְרוּיָה זוֹנָה. אֲבָל מִשּׁוּם בְּעִילָה אַחַת — לָא הָוְיָא זוֹנָה הַפְּנוּיָה. הָלַךְ בַּעְלָהּ. לְבֵ"ד הַגָּדוֹל, וְהוֹלִיכָהּ לְהַשְׁקוֹתָהּ מֵי הַמָּרִים, שֶׁקִּינֵּא לָהּ וְנִסְתְּרָה, וַאֲסוּרָה לוֹ עַד שֶׁתִּשְׁתֶּה — עֲשָׂאָהּ זוֹנָה, הוֹאִיל וְנִבְעֲלָה לְפָסוּל לָהּ. וְאִם מֵת — אֲסוּרָה לְכֹהֵן. אֶלָּא גִּיּוֹרֶת. דְּנִבְעֲלָה בְּגֵיוּתָהּ לְגוֹיִם, וְכֵן מְשׁוּחְרֶרֶת. דְּגוֹי וְעֶבֶד, הוֹאִיל וְלָאו בְּנֵי קִדּוּשִׁין נִינְהוּ — פָּסְלֵי. וְשֶׁנִּבְעֲלָה. לְפָסוּל לָהּ, כְּגוֹן אֶ' מִכָּל הָעֲרָיוֹת, וּכְגוֹן בַּת יִשְׂרָאֵל לְנָתִין וּמַמְזֵר. לְכִי גָּדְלָה. דְּקִידּוּשֵׁי קְטַנָּה לָאו כְּלוּם הֵן, וְהָוְיָא לֵיהּ כַּאֲנוּסַת עַצְמוֹ וּמְפוּתַּת עַצְמוֹ. מִכְּדֵי לֵב. כְּמוֹ מִכְּלֵי לֵב. [אִי דְּקִדְּשָׁהּ אֲבוּהָ כו']. הָאָב זַכַּאי לְקַדֵּשׁ בִּתּוֹ קְטַנָּה, בְּפ"ק דְּקִידּוּשִׁין (דף ג:): "אֶת בִּתִּי נָתַתִּי לָאִישׁ הַזֶּה". הָא רַבִּי אֱלִיעֶזֶר הִיא וְלָא רַבָּנַן. בִּתְמִיָּה, דְּקָתָנֵי לְעֵיל: רַבִּי אֱלִיעֶזֶר אוֹמֵר כֹּהֵן לֹא יִשָּׂא אֶת הַקְּטַנָּה, וּמַשְׁמַע דִּפְלִיגֵי רַבָּנַן עֲלֵיהּ, וכה"ג מִי פְּלִיגֵי רַבָּנַן(ג)? תִּתְפַּתֶּה. וְתִזְנֶה עָלָיו, לְפִי שֶׁאֵין בָּהּ דַּעַת(ג) כְּלוּם. רַב פַּפָּא אֲמַר בְּכֹהֵן גָּדוֹל וְהַאי תַּנָּא הוּא. דְּאָסַר קְטַנָּה מִגְּזֵירַת הַכָּתוּב. בְּתוּלָה. "מֵעַמָּיו יִקַּח אִשָּׁה". [מֵאִשָּׁה לָא בָּטֵיל]. מִדְּקָתָנֵי לֹא יִבָּטֵל אָדָם מִפְּרִיָּה וּרְבִיָּה אֶלָּא א"כ יֵשׁ לוֹ בָּנִים, וְלָא קָתָנֵי לֹא יִבָּטֵל אָדָם מֵאִשָּׁה אֶלָּא אִם כֵּן יֵשׁ לוֹ בָּנִים — שְׁמַע מִינָּהּ: הָא יֵשׁ לוֹ בָּנִים, מֵאִשָּׁה לָא בָּטֵיל, דְּצָרִיךְ לִישָּׂא אִשָּׁה, אֲבָל אֵין צָרִיךְ לַחֲזוֹר אַחַר רְאוּיָה לְבָנִים. לִמְכּוֹר ס"ת. כְּדֵי לִישָּׂא בַּת בָּנִים, וְאִם יֵשׁ לוֹ בָּנִים — לֹא יִמְכּוֹר, אֶלָּא יִשָּׂא עֲקָרָה אוֹ זְקֵנָה. ב"ש אוֹמְרִים שְׁנֵי זְכָרִים. אֲבָל לֹא זָכָר וּנְקֵבָה. יָלְפִינַן מִמֹּשֶׁה. שֶׁכֵּיוָן שֶׁהָיוּ לוֹ שְׁנֵי בָּנִים — פֵּירֵשׁ מִן הָאִשָּׁה. מִבְּרִיָּיתוֹ שֶׁל עוֹלָם. אָדָם וְחַוָּה. מִשֶּׁאִי

כל בִּיאָה שֶׁאֵין בָּהּ פִּירְצָה. קטנה אתיא לכלל פירצה לכשתתגדל, ולא ממעט אלא היכא דלא אתיא לעולם לכלל פירצה. **אין** בתולה אלא נערה. קשה: דלהאי תנא אמאי איצטריך בשום מקום לכתוב נערה בתולה?. **וכן** הוא אומר והנערה טובת מראה מאד. תימה: דהכא משמע דרבקה נערה היתה, ובסדר עולם (פ"א) תניא בהדיא: שהיתה בת שלש כשנשאה יצחק. ואי אפשר להגיה, דהא תניא התם יצחק אבינו כשנעקד על גבי המזבח היה בן שבעה ושלשים שנה, ובו בפרק נולדה רבקה, וכתיב "ויהי יצחק בן ארבעים שנה וגו'" — נמצאת שהיתה בת ג'. וה"ר שמואל חסיד מספיר"א הוכיח שהיתה בת י"ד. מדתניא בספרי: ו' זוגות שנותיהן שוות: וקחשיב קהת ורבקה. וקהת היה קל"ג, כדכתיב בקרא. ואם היתה בת י"ד כשנשאה — אז החשבון מכוון, דכשנולד יעקב היתה בת ל"ד,(א) ויעקב היה בן צ"ט כשמתה רבקה — הרי קל"ג. שהרי כשנתברך היה בן ס"ג, שאז מת ישמעאל, וכל שנותיו של ישמעאל קל"ז, כדכתיב וישמעאל (גדול מיצחק י"ד שנה, ויצחק בן ס' שנה בלדת אותם, א"כ ישמעאל) בן ע"ד. ונשאר מלידת יעקב עד סוף שני ישמעאל ס"ג, וי"ד נטמן בבית עבר, כדאמרינן במגילה (דף יז.). ועשרים שנה בבית לבן, ושתי שנים בדרך, ואז מתה רבקה כדדרשינן (מדרש רבה קהלת פ"ג): אלון בכות — שתי בכיות, של רבקה ומניקתה — הרי צ"ט! וצריך לומר דמדרשות חלוקים זה על זה. **פנוי** הבא על הפנויה כו'. לאו דוקא נקט פנוי, דכ"ש נשוי שמזנה על אשתו דחשובה זונה. **לא** יבטל אדם מפריה ורביה. אע"ג דמרישא שמעינן לה, דקתני: כהן הדיוט לא ישא אילונית, ולאו דוקא כהן, כדאמרינן לעיל — מ"מ איצטריך הכא להנך דיוקי דגמרא. או משום פלוגתא דבית שמאי ובית הלל הדר תני לה. **מאשה** לא בטיל. פירש בקונטרס: מדלא קתני לא יבטל מאשה. **א"ד** מאשה בטיל. להאי לישנא דייק מדלא קתני "לא ישא אדם אשה שאינה בת בנים" אלא אם כן יש לו בנים. **נפקא** מינה למכור ספר תורה בשביל בנים. כלומר, להאי מילתא נמי נפקא מינה. ול"ג למאי נפקא מינה — דהא טובא נפקא מינה, כדקאמר בהדיא: אין לו בנים — נושא אשה בת בנים, יש לו בנים — נושא אשה דלאו בת בנים. ועוד אר"י: דמצי למימר דאפילו יש לו בנים לעולם מצוה לישא בת בנים, אלא מודו היכא דצריך למכור ספר תורה בשביל בת בנים, כיון דיש לו בנים — לא ימכור, מאחר שמוצא שאינה בת בנים, ולא יצטרך למכור.

מדעתיה

עין משפט נר מצוה

פד א מיי' פ"א מהלכות יבום הלכה טז יח סמג עשין נא טוש"ע אה"ע סי' קסז סעי' ג ד:
פה ב ג מיי' פי"ז מהל' איסורי ביאה הלכ' יג:
פו ד מיי' פט"ו מהל' אישות הלכה א סמג עשין מט טוש"ע אה"ע סימן א סעיף א:
פז ה מיי' שם הלכה ד טוש"ע שם סעיף ה:
פח ו ז ח מיי' שם הלכ' טז ופכ"א מהל' איסורי ביאה הלכה כו טוש"ע שם סעי' ח:

תוספות ישנים

פנוי הבא על הפנויה שלא לשם אישות עשאה זונה. ואיכא בינו לרבי עקיבא דר' עקיבא אומר זונה זו מופקרת רגילה בזנות כמה פעמים אבל בביאה ראשונה לא עשאה זונה ולר' אליעזר עשאה זונה בפעם אחת: **א)** ובזה ניחא דפריך לקמן ולילף מיצחק פי' שנשתהה כ' שנה ואי כפ"ה שבת ג' שנים היתה א"כ משעה שהיתה ראויה להריון דהיינו מי"ג (בסמוך) [שנה] לא שהתה רק עשר שנים אלא ודאי בת י"ד שנה כדפרישית ומ"מ קשה להכא דמשמע שלא היתה בוגרת ופרשנו שהיתה בת י"ד שנה ושמא יש הרבה מדרשים חלוקים זה מזה: **הא** יש לו בנים בטיל מפריה ורביה בטיל נמי מאשה מדקאמר הכי ולא קאמר לא יבטל אדם מאשה בת בנים אבל אשה בעלמא נסיב מדלא קאמר הכי משמע דאף מאשה נמי בטיל כי יש לו בנים:

תוספות חד מקמאי

והא דתנן וב"ה אומרים זכר ונקבה. וב"ש בשני זכרים מקיים מצות פריה ורביה דזכרים עדיפי מנקבות מדאמר לקמן בני בנים הרי הם כבנים סבר אביי למימר ברא לברא וברתא לברתא אבל ברתא לברא לא וכו' אלמא זכרים עדיפי מנקבות.

גליון הש"ס

גמ' א"ל רב חסדא לרבה פוק. עיין גיטין דף כז ע"א: **שם** ר"ע אומר זונה זו מופקרת. עי' סנהדרין דף נ ע"ב תד"ה ת"ל ובת כהן: **שם** פתויי קטנה אונס הוא. וכן הוא בירושלמי פ"א דסוטה הובא בתוס' בסוטה דף כ"ח ע"ב ד"ה מכאן עיין כתובות דף ט ע"א תד"ה ואב"א ושם דף מ ע"ב תד"ה הא לאו:

הגהות מהר"ב רנשבורג

א] גמ' ככל ביאה שאין בה פירצה. נ"ב מלשון ופרצת ימה וקדמה:

מסורת הש"ס

[לקמן קיט. וש"נ]
לקמן קיא: קיט. בכו' יט: נדה לב.
[לקמן קה: קיט.]
[עי' תוס' נדה לב. ... שמא ותוס' לעיל ב: ... או ותוס' גיטין מו: ... המוליא]
לקמן פה:
[לעיל נט: וש"נ]
[לעיל לג:]
[לעיל ס: ע"ש]
בראשית ה
שם ב

הגהות הב"ח

(א) גמ' כל ביאה שאין ... פרילה אינה: (ב) ... ד"ה הא רבי אליעזר ... רבנן עליה הס"ד: (ג) ... תתפתה וכו' לפי שאין ... דעת ...

משאי אפשר. ובית הלל נמי, לילפו ממשה! אמרי לך: משה מדעתיה הוא דעבד. דתניא: *שלשה דברים עשה משה מדעתו, והסכימה דעתו לדעת המקום: פירש מן האשה, ושיבר הלוחות, והוסיף יום אחד. פירש מן האשה, מאי דרש? אמר: ומה ישראל שלא דברה עמהם שכינה אלא לפי שעה, וקבע להם זמן — אמרה תורה °"אל תגשו אל אשה", אני שמיוחד לדבור בכל שעה ושעה, ולא קבע לי זמן — על אחת כמה וכמה. והסכימה דעתו לדעת המקום, שנאמר °"לך אמור להם שובו לכם לאהליכם ואתה פה עמוד עמדי". שיבר את הלוחות, מאי דרש? אמר: ומה פסח, שהוא אחד משש מאות ושלש עשרה מצות, אמרה תורה °"כל בן נכר לא יאכל בו", התורה כולה וישראל משומדים — על אחת כמה וכמה. והסכימה דעתו לדעת המקום, דכתיב °"אשר שברת", ואמר ריש לקיש: אמר ליה הקב"ה למשה: *יישר כחך ששברת. הוסיף יום אחד מדעתו, מאי דרש? דכתיב °"וקדשתם היום ומחר" היום כמחר, מה מחר לילו עמו — אף היום לילו עמו. ולילה דהאידנא נפק ליה. ש"מ: תרי יומי, לבר מהאידנא. והסכימה דעתו לדעת המקום — דלא שריא שכינה עד שבתא. תניא, *רבי נתן אומר, ב"ש אומרים: שני זכרים ושתי נקבות, ובה"א: זכר ונקבה. א"ר הונא: מ"ט דרבי נתן אליבא דב"ש — דכתיב °"ותוסף ללדת את אחיו את הבל" הבל ואחותו, קין ואחותו. וכתיב °"כי שת לי אלהים זרע אחר תחת הבל כי הרגו קין". ורבנן אודויי הוא דקא מודית. תניא אידך, *ר' נתן אומר: ב"ש אומרים: זכר ונקבה, ובה"א: או זכר או נקבה. אמר רבא מ"ט דר' נתן אליבא דב"ה — *שנא' °"לא תהו בראה לשבת יצרה" והא עבד לה שבת. איתמר, *היו לו בנים בגיותו ונתגייר, ר' יוחנן אמר: קיים פריה ורביה, וריש לקיש אמר: לא קיים פריה ורביה. רבי יוחנן אמר: קיים פריה ורביה, דהא הוו ליה. וריש לקיש אמר: לא קיים פריה ורביה — *גר שנתגייר כקטן שנולד דמי. ואזדו לטעמייהו, דאיתמר, *היו לו בנים בגיותו ונתגייר, רבי יוחנן אמר: אין לו בכור לנחלה, דהא הוה ליה "ראשית אונו". וריש לקיש אמר: יש לו בכור לנחלה, גר שנתגייר כקטן שנולד דמי. וצריכא, דאי אשמעינן בההיא קמייתא — בההיא קאמר רבי יוחנן, משום דמעיקרא נמי בני פריה ורביה נינהו, אבל לענין נחלה, דלאו בני נחלה נינהו, אימא מודי ליה לריש לקיש. ואי איתמר בהא — בהא קאמר ריש לקיש, אבל בההיא — אימא מודה ליה לר' יוחנן, צריכא. איתיביה ר' יוחנן לר"ל: °"בעת ההיא שלח בראדך בלאדן בן בלאדן מלך בבל וגו'"! א"ל: בגויותן — אית להו חיים, נתגיירו — לית להו חיים. אמר *רב: הכל מודין בעבד שאין לו חיים, דכתיב °"שבו לכם פה עם החמור", עם *הדומה לחמור. מיתיבי: °"ולציבא חמשה עשר בנים ועשרים עבדים"! אמר רב אחא בר יעקב: כ"פר בן בקר". א"ה, ה"נ! שאני התם דיחסינהו בשמייהו ובשמא דאבוהון, והכא לא מפרש. ואיבעית אימא: יחסינהו בדוכתא אחריתי באבוהון ובאבא דאבוהון, דכתיב °"וישלח המלך אסא אל בן הדד בן טברימון בן חזיון מלך ארם היושב בדמשק לאמר". איתמר, היו לו בנים ומתו, רב הונא אמר: קיים פריה ורביה, רבי יוחנן אמר: לא קיים. רב הונא אמר: קיים — משום דרב אסי, דאמר *רב אסי: *) אין בן דוד בא עד שיכלו כל נשמות שבגוף, שנאמר °"כי רוח מלפני יעטוף וגו'". ורבי יוחנן אמר: לא קיים פריה ורביה, "לשבת יצרה" בעינן — והא ליכא. מיתיבי

בני

*) ע"ז ה. נדה יג: לקמן סג:

רש"י

משאי אפשר. דאי לא איברא חוה — לא הוה נקבה אחריתי. אבל הכא, מי שיש לו שני זכרים — נקבות הרבה בעולם. מדעתיה. משום שכינה, ואסור לשאר כל אדם לעשות כן. הוסיף יום אחד. הקב"ה אמר לו "וקדשתם היום ומחר", והוא אמר "היו נכונים לשלשת ימים". ולא קבע לי זמן. אימתי ידבר עמי, שאפרוש יום אחד קודם. לאהליכם. לנשיכם. אשר. לשון יישר. עד שבתא. במס' שבת, בפרק ר"ע (דף פו.) גמרינן לה, דעבוד פרישה בארבע בשבתא, ופירשו חמישי וששי שלימים, ובשבתא שריא שכינה והוא שלישי לימים השלמים, ויום ראשון לא חשיב, שלא היה לילו עמו. את קין את הבל. אתין רבויין *[הן], לומר: נקבות היו עמהן. כי שת לי זרע אחר תחת הבל. אלמא תשלומין בעי, ולא סגיא בלא שני זכרים ושתי נקבות. תרי תנאי. אליבא דר' נתן. מ"ט דר' נתן אליבא דב"ה. או זכר או נקבה, ולא מברייתו עולם יליף, ולא ממשה. לא תהו בראה. לא ברא עולמו לתוהו, אלא לשבת — להיות עסוקים ביישובו של עולם. אין לו בכור לנחלה. בן בכור שיולד לו משיתגייר — אינו נוטל פי שנים. בני נח. בני פריה ורביה נינהו — דכתיב "ויאמר להם פרו ורבו" (בראשית ט). בגויותן. לאו בני דין נחלה נינהו, דבת כהן, ובכור כפשוט. אבל ירושה — נהגא בהו, כדאמרינן בקדושין (דף יז:): גוי יורש אביו דבר תורה. בלאדן בן בלאדן. אלמא: בנים מיקרו. חיים. מתייחסין אחרי אביהם. נתגיירו אין להם חיים. מראשונים, דכקטן שנולד דמי. שבו לכם פה. אליעזר עבד אברהם הוה. ציבא. עבד כנעני של מפיבושת הוה. שאני הכא דיחסינהו בשמייהו. שהזכיר שמו [ושמו] של אביו "בלאדן בן בלאדן", אלמא בנים איקרו, אבל הכא לא הוזכרו בשמותן. משום דרב אסי. כלומר, טעמא דפריה ורביה משום דרב אסי. והאי, כיון דנטלו על ידו מנשמות שבאוצר ששמו גוף — הרי קיים מצות פריה ורביה.

בני

תוספות

מדעתיה הוא דעבד. אע"ג דק"ו קאמר — אין זה ק"ו גמור. דאטו מפני שלוה פעם אחד לבטל לבטל יבטל לעולם פרו ורבו? אי נמי דוקא אז אמר לבטל, משום עשרת הדברות.

וקבע להם זמן. וא"ת: אדרבה, משום דקבע להם זמן(א) וידבר עמהם — בודאי יש לפרוש יותר מעל הספק? ויש לומר: *דהכא פי' וקבע להם זמן (*משה) שלשה ימים ולא היו צריכים לפרוש אלא יום אחד משום קרי, אלא משום ספק פליטה הוזקקו לפרוש שלשה ימים. ק"ו אני, שלא קבע לי זמן, ויש ספק שיתיחד הדבור בשעת תשמיש או ביום תשמיש.

דכתיב אמור להם. וא"ת: ומנלן שפירש מדעתו? והלא משעה שנאסר במתן תורה עם ישראל — שוב לא הותר לו, כדכתיב "ואתה פה עמוד עמדי"! ויש לומר: דאי לאו דפירש מדעתו — למה כעסו עליו אהרן ומרים? אלא ודאי כששמע מפי הגבורה "אל תגשו אל אשה" נשא ק"ו בעצמו. וגלה לה דעתו, ועשה לה אהל בפני עצמו או נתן לה גט — ולפיכך כעסו עליו. וא"ת: ולמה המתינו כל כך, שלא כעסו עליו אלא בחצרות שהוא זמן גדול אחר מתן תורה? וי"ל: שלא נתגלה להם אלא באותה שעה. כדתניא בסיפרי: שבשעה שאמר הקב"ה למשה ליקח ע' זקנים מישראל, אמרה מרים: אשרי נשותיהן של אלו שנתבקשו לגדולה. אמרה צפורה: אוי להן לנשותיהן של אלו, שמיום שדברה השכינה עם אחיך פירש ממני. וא"ת: ולמה כעסו עליו, מאחר שהסכים לו המקום? וי"ל: משום דאמרינן (במכות דף י:) בדרך שאדם רוצה לילך מוליכין אותו, וסייעוהו בבא לטהר.

התורה כולה וישראל משומדים כו'. אין זה ק"ו *גמור, דשאני פסח משום דקדשים. אבל כל התורה כולה — אדרבה, יש לו ללמדם ולהחזירם בתשובה.

אף היום לילו עמו. אין זו דרשה גמורה, ד"היום" משמע: היום ממש.

רבי יוחנן אמר קיים פריה ורביה. אע"ג דלענין כמה דברים אמרינן (לעיל כב.) גר שנתגייר כקטן שנולד דמי, מכל מקום מסתברא ליה לר' יוחנן הכא, כיון דבגיותו קיים דזרעו מיוחס אחריו באותה שעה — מפטר נמי כשנתגייר.

בני פריה ורביה נינהו. וא"ת: דבפ' "ד' מיתות" (סנהד' נט: ושם) משמע דבני נח לא מיפקדו אפריה ורביה! וי"ל: דהכא לאו בני חיוב אפריה ורביה קאמר, אלא כלומר שבניהם נקראים על שמם, כדאמרינן בסמוך.

דלאו בני נחלה נינהו. כלומר: נחלת בכורה. אבל גוי יורש את אביו דבר תורה, כדאמרינן בפ"ק דקדושין (דף יז:).

הכל מודים בעבד שאין לו חיים כו'. ואם נשתחרר לא קיים פריה ורביה. וא"ת: הא דאמרינן גבי חציו עבד וחציו בן חורין לישא שפחה אינו יכול, משמע דאם היה יכול לישא שפחה — הוה סגי ליה בהכי, ואמאי? והא לא *מיפקד אפריה ורביה, ולא מיפטר בהכי? ויש לומר: דאם היה יכול לישא שפחה — לא הוה כפינן לרבו לשחררו, כיון דשבת מיהא היה יכול לקיים, אף על גב דפריה ורביה לא מקיים בהכי. ואף על גב דלעיל משמע דפריה ורביה תלי בשבת, דקאמר רבא מאי טעמא דרבי נתן אליבא דבית הלל — "לא תהו בראה לשבת יצרה" והא עבד ליה שבת — מכל מקום לא הוה כפינן לרבו, כיון דיכול לקיים כל דהו.

וכל

עין משפט נר מצוה

פט א מיי' פט"ו מהל' איסורי ביאה הלכה ו סמג עשין מט טוש"ע אה"ע סימן א סעיף ז:

צ ב מיי' פ"ב מהלכות נחלות הלכה יב סמג עשין צו טוש"ע ח"מ סי' רעז סעיף ט:

צא ג מיי' שם ופט"ו מהל' אישות הל' ו סמג שם (וסימן ע') טור ש"ע שם וטוש"ע אה"ע סימן א סעיף ז:

צב ד מיי' פט"ו מהל' אישות הלכה ה סמג עשין מח טוש"ע אה"ע סימן א סעיף ו:

נ"ל דהכי

רש"ל מ"ז

תוספות ישנים

אין בן דוד בא עד שיכלו נשמות שבגוף. תימה דאמרי' (שבת קי"ח) אלמלא ישראל משמרים שתי שבתות מיד נגאלין והלא צריך שיכלו כל הנשמות שבגוף וי"ל שהיו יולדות ששה בכרס אחד ויכלו הנשמות שבגוף מיד:

עיין אדר"נ פ"ב איתא ק"ו אחר

תוספות חד מקמאי

והא דמקשינן בגמרא וב"ה לילפו ממשה. ומאי קושיא דהא ב"ה ילפי מברייתו של עולם זכר ונקבה בראם ובזכר ונקבה נמי קיים מצות פריה ורביה. ה"ק כיון דמשה אשכחן שהיו לו שני זכרים לילפי ממשה ולא מברייתו של עולם דהא אי אפשר: הא דאמר אין ישיבה בחו"ל עולה לו ה"מ למי שדר בארץ אבל למי שלא דר בא"י כגון בשאר ארצות ודאי ישיבת ח"ל עולה לו וכ"כ הראב"ד ז"ל:

[כתובות קיא. קדושין סח. ב"ק מט. נדה יז.]

נ"ל לא מיפטר מפ"ו מהרש"ל

גליון הש"ס

גמ' קין ואחותו. עיין סנהדרין דף נח ע"ב תד"ה ויכלו ובסוטה דף ט ע"ב רש"י ד"ה קין ובב"ב דף קכג ע"א ובמהרש"א חדושי אגדות שם: שם ר' יוחנן אמר קיים כו'. עיין טורי אבן ר"ה דף כח ע"א תד"ה אילימא: שם מיתיבי ולציבא. עיין טורי אבן חגיגה דף ב ע"א ד"ה כאן כמשנה ראשונה.

מסורת הש"ס

שבת פז.

כ"ה בדפו"י

הגהות הב"ח

(א) תוס' ד"ה וקבע וכו' זמן לדבר עמהם:

שבת פז. ב"ב יז: מנחות לט.

[תוס' פ"ח ע"ש נ"ע]

[תוספתא שם]

עדיות פ"א מי"ג

[בכורות מז.]

לעיל כב. וש"נ

[בכורות מז.]

מ"ב כ

[נ"ל רבי אבא כך איתא בהלפס ובהרא"ש] ברכות כב

מ"א טו

[בע"ז ה. ובנדה יג: איתא ר' יוסי]

עין משפט נר מצוה

צג א מיי' פט"ו מהל' אישות הלכה ה וסמג עשין מח טוש"ע אה"ע סימן א סעיף ו:
צד ב מיי' שם הלכה ד טוש"ע שם ס"ה:
צה ג ד מיי' שם הלכה ה טור שו"ע שם סעיף ו:
צו ה טוש"ע שם סי' א סעיף א בהג"ה:
צז ו ז טוש"ע א"ח סי' ר מ סעי' א וטוש"ע י"ד סימן קפד סעיף י:
צח ח מיי' פ"ד מהל' איסורי ביאה הלכה יב ופ"ח הלכה ג טוש"ע י"ד שם סעיף ב:
צט ט (טור) שו"ע שם סעיף י [בהג"ה] וטוש"ע א"ח סימן רמ סעיף א:
ק י מיי' פט"ו מהלכות אישות הלכה יט:
קא כ מיי' פכ"א מהל' איסורי ביאה הלכה כה סמג לאוין קכו טור אה"ע סימן א:
קב ל מיי' פ"ב מהלכות איסורי ביאה הי"ד:

גמרא

תורה אור

*בני בנים הרי הן כבנים! כי תניא ההיא – להשלים. מיתיבי: *[א]בני בנים הרי הם כבנים, מת אחד מהם, או שנמצא סריס, לא קיים פריה ורביה. תיובתא דרב הונא! תיובתא.§ "בני בנים הרי הם כבנים".§ סבר אביי למימר: ברא לברא [א] וברתא לברתא, וכ"ש ברא לברתא, אבל ברתא לברא – לא. א"ל רבא: "לשבת יצרה" בעיא, והא איכא. דכולי עלמא מיהת תרי מחד לא. ולא?! והא אמרי ליה רבנן *לרב ששת: נסיב איתתא ואוליד בני! ואמר להו: בני ברתי בני נינהו. התם דחויי קמדחי להו, *דרב ששת איעקר מפירקיה דרב הונא. [לקמן סד:] אמר ליה רבה לרבא בר מארי: מנא הא מילתא דאמור רבנן בני בנים הרי הן כבנים? אילימא מדכתיב "הבנות בנותי והבנים בני" (בראשית לא) אלא מעתה, "והצאן צאני" הכי נמי? אלא – דקנית מינאי, הכא נמי – דקנית מינאי! אלא מהכא: "ואחר בא חצרון אל בת מכיר אבי גלעד (דה"א ב) ותלד לו את שגוב", וכתיב: "מני מכיר ירדו (שופטים ה) מחוקקים" וכתיב "יהודה מחוקקי" (תהלים ס וקח). מתניתין דלאו כרבי יהושע. דתניא, רבי יהושע אומר: נשא אדם אשה בילדותו – ישא אשה בזקנותו, היו לו בנים בילדותו – יהיו לו בנים בזקנותו, שנא' "בבקר זרע את זרעך ולערב אל תנח (קהלת יא) ידך כי אינך יודע אי זה יכשר הזה או זה ואם שניהם כאחד טובים". ר"ע אומר: למד תורה בילדותו – ילמוד תורה בזקנותו, היו לו תלמידים בילדותו – יהיו לו תלמידים בזקנותו, שנא' "בבקר זרע את זרעך וגו'". אמרו: שנים עשר אלף זוגים תלמידים היו לו לרבי עקיבא מגבת עד אנטיפרס, וכולן מתו בפרק אחד, מפני שלא נהגו כבוד זה לזה. והיה העולם שמם, עד שבא ר"ע אצל רבותינו שבדרום ושנאה להם: ר"מ, ור' יהודה, ור' יוסי, ורבי שמעון, ורבי אלעזר בן שמוע. והם הם העמידו תורה אותה שעה. תנא: כולם מתו מפסח ועד עצרת. אמר רב חמא בר אבא ואיתימא ר' חייא בר אבין: כולם מתו מיתה רעה. מאי היא? א"ר נחמן: אסכרה. א"ר מתנא: הלכה כרבי יהושע. אמר רבי תנחום א"ר חנילאי: כל אדם שאין לו אשה שרוי בלא שמחה, בלא ברכה, בלא טובה. בלא שמחה – דכתיב "ושמחת אתה וביתך", בלא ברכה – דכתיב "להניח ברכה אל ביתך" (דברים יד), בלא טובה – דכתיב "לא טוב היות האדם לבדו" (בראשית ב). במערבא אמרי: בלא תורה, בלא חומה. בלא תורה – דכתיב "האם אין עזרתי בי ותושיה נדחה ממני" (איוב ו), בלא חומה – דכתיב "נקבה תסובב גבר" (ירמיה לא). רבא בר עולא אמר: בלא שלום, דכתיב "וידעת כי שלום אהלך ופקדת נוך ולא תחטא" (איוב ה). אמר ריב"ל: כל היודע באשתו שהיא יראת שמים, ואינו פוקדה – נקרא חוטא, שנאמר "וידעת כי שלום אהלך וגו'". ואמר ריב"ל: חייב אדם לפקוד את אשתו בשעה שהוא יוצא לדרך שנא' "וידעת כי שלום אהלך וגו'". הא מהכא נפקא? מהתם נפקא: "ואל *אישך תשוקתך" מלמד שהאשה משתוקקת על בעלה בשעה שהוא יוצא לדרך! א"ר יוסף: לא נצרכה אלא *) סמוך לווסתה. (עירובין ק:) וכמה? אמר **) רבא: עונה. והני מילי – לדבר הרשות, אבל לדבר מצוה – מיטרידי. *ת"ר: (סנהדרין עו:) האוהב את אשתו כגופו, והמכבדה יותר מגופו, והמדריך בניו ובנותיו בדרך ישרה, והמשיאן סמוך לפירקן – עליו הכתוב אומר "וידעת כי שלום אהלך". *האוהב את שכניו, והמקרב את קרוביו, והנושא את בת אחותו, (ג"ז שם) והמלוה

*) שבועות יח: נדה סג: **) [נ"ל רבה]

רש"י

בני בנים הרי הן כבנים. קס"ד שמת הזכר או הנקבה, והיה לו בן, שילטרף עם אחות אביו או עם אחי אמו – אין אבי האב חייב עוד בפריה ורביה. וטעמא, שהיה לו למת בן, הא לאו הכי לא קיים, דשבת בעינן, וקשיא לרב הונא. כי תניא ההיא להשלים. כגון שלא היה לו לזקן אלא בן אחד, ונשא הבן אשה והוליד בת – פטור הזקן, שהרי השלים זה את חובתו. [לקמן ע. קדושין ז.] אבל אי הוה ליה מעיקרא זכר ונקבה, ואפילו מתו בלא בנים – קיים פריה ורביה. [תוספתא פ"ח] דכולי עלמא. בין לאביי בין לרבא. תרי מחד. והשני מת בלא בנים – לא קיים הזקן פריה ורביה. איעקר מפרקיה דרב הונא. שהיה מאריך בדרשיו, ולריכים למי רגלים, ומעמידים עצמן ונעקרים, (א) כדתניא בבכורות (דף מד:). מנא הא מילתא כו'. אבני בתו קאי, דבן בנו פשיטא לן. [ובשאלתות פרשת הבו איתא לר' אבא בר זב] מני מכיר ירדו מחוקקים. ולא מצינו למימר מבני בניו אלא מבני בתו, דהא כתיב קרא אחרינא "יהודה מחוקקי", ולא משכחת לה דליתו מתרוייהו אלא הכי, דנפקו מחוקקים מחצרון מבתו של מכיר, אלמא: בני בתו כבניו. מתניתין. דקתני אא"כ כו', הא אם יש לו – יבטל, דלא כר' יהושע. לערב. לעת זקנתו. אי זה יכשר. איזה זרע יהא הגון וירא שמים, ומתקיים. מגבת עד אנטיפרס. [בין העיירות הללו היו כולם]. שמם. שנשתכחה תורה. ביתך. אשה. האם אין עזרתי בי. אשתי, דכתיב (בראשית ב) "עזר כנגדו", מיד "תושיה נדחה ממני", שצריך לעסוק בצרכי ביתו, ותלמודו משתכח. וידעת כי שלום אהלך. בזמן שיש לך אהל, ואין אהלו אלא אשתו,* שנאמר "שובו לכם לאהליכם". [מ"ק ז:] ואין פוקדה. בתשמיש, בעת עונתה. כי שלום אהלך. שלימה ביראת שמים. בשעה שיוצא לדרך. משום שמתאוה לו באותה שעה יותר. תשוקתך. תאותך. ה"ג. לא נצרכה אלא סמוך לווסתה. [אע"ג] דאמור רבנן (שבועות דף יח:) חייב אדם לפרוש מאשתו וכו', ואפ"ה כשיוצא לדרך – יפקדנה. עונה. אם רגילה לראות ביום – אסורה כל היום, ואם רגילה לראות בלילה – אסורה כל הלילה. וה"מ. דחייב לפוקדה, כי אזיל לדבר הרשות. אבל לדבר מצוה – לא, משום דטריד במצוה, אי נמי: מיטריד בתשמיש, ויבטל ממצוה. יותר מגופו. דזילותא דאיתתא קשה מדגברא. והנושא בת אחותו. געגועי (יחזקאל מד) אדם רבין על אחותו יותר מן אחיו, ומתוך כך נמלא מחבב את אשתו.

תוספות

וכל שכן ברא לברתא. אע"ג דאמרינן לעיל אין שני זכרים חשובים כבן ובת! הכא שבא מכח מי שפטרתו מפריה ורביה – פשיטא דקאי שפיר הבן במקום הבת. **חייב** אדם לפקוד את אשתו. אומר ר"ת: דפקידה זו אינו תשמיש, אלא כשהוא רוצה לצאת בדרך, אם הוא רחוק ממנה – לא יצא לדרך אא"כ ישוב אליה ויפקדנה, (ב) או בתשמיש או בשאר דברים, וידבר על לבה. ופריך: מהתם נפקא ליה, מלמד שהאשה משתוקקת על בעלה כשיוצא לדרך, ומסתמא כיון שמתאוה לו – יש לו לפוקדה, דהמכבד אשתו עליו הכתוב אומר "אז תקרא וגו'"! ומשני, אמר רב יוסף: לא נצרכה אלא לאשתו נדה. ה"ג בכל הספרים ישנים. והכי פי': דהד קרא אתא דאפילו באשתו נדה יש לו לפוקדה, וכמה – עונה. אע"פ שאסור לשמש, מ"מ שמחה ותענוג הוא לה, הואיל ורוצה לצאת בדרך. והכי אמרי' בריש "הדר" (עירובין סג: ושם): הישן בקילעא שאיש ואשתו ישנים – שם עליו הכתוב אומר "נשי עמי תגרשון מבית תענוגיה". ואמר רב יוסף התם: ואפילו אשתו נדה. ומה שהגיהו בספרים "לא נצרכה אלא סמוך לוסתה" – אין נראה כלל. דהגיהו כן לפי שרוצין לפרש דפקידה היינו תשמיש, ובשבועות (דף יח: ושם) מוכיח דסמוך לוסתה מדאורייתא, מ"והזרתם את בני ישראל וגו'" ועוד: דמוקי לה ביוצא לדבר הרשות, וא"כ, אפילו למאן דאמר (נדה דף טו.) ווסתות דרבנן – אם כן סמוך לווסתה נמי דרבנן – מכל מקום למה יהא מותר ביוצא לדבר הרשות?. **סמוך** לפירקן. אבניו נמי קאי, כדאמרי' ב"הנשרפין" (סנהד' דף עו: ושם) ואע"ג דקטן לא תקינו ליה רבנן נשואין, כדאמרינן לקמן (ג) בפרק "אלמנה" (דף סח.) מ"מ להכי תקינו ליה נשואין, דלא הויא בעילתו בעילת זנות*. [ועי' היטב תוס' לקמן נו: ד"ה נשא ותוספות סנהדרין עו: ד"ה סמוך] **והנושא** את בת אחותו. פירש רשב"ם: דה"ה בת אחיו. אבל אחותו נקט לפי שמשדלתו בדברים, ושכיח שנושא בתה. ור"ת אומר: דדוקא נקט בת אחותו, לפי שהיא בת מזלו כדאמרי': *רוב בנים דומין לאחי האם*): [ב"ב קי. מס' סופרים ספט"ו]

*) [עיין תוס' לקמן נט. ד"ה ספק]

תוספות ישנים

חייב אדם לפקוד אשתו בשעה שיוצא לדרך. פ"ה שהפקידה היא בתשמיש ולא נהירא דהא מוקי לה תלמודא בסמוך לוסתה וכיון דמדאוריית' אסור דכתיב והזרתם את בני ישראל אזהרה לבני ישראל שיפרשו מנשותיהן סמוך לווסתן ואיך שרו רבנן משום שהוא רוצה לילך בדרך וע"ק דקאמר לקמן אבל לדבר מצוה טריד ומאי קאמר השתא איסורא דאוריית' דוהזרתם שרינן כל שכן שלא יניח משום טרדתו דמצוה לפוקדה וע"ק דיש ספרים שכתוב בהם לא נצרכה אלא אפילו לאשתו נדה ואח"כ אין יכול להיות תשמיש לכן נ"ל לפוקדה בדברי ריצוי והכי ר"ל וכמה יש לפוקדה עונה וכ"מ (בנדרים) [בעירובין ס"ג] דשייך פקידה בדברים אפילו באשתו נדה דקאמר כל הישן בקילעא ואשתו ישנים עליו הכתוב אומר ואת נשי עמי תגרשון מבית תענוגיה ומוקים לה תלמודא אפילו באשתו נדה דסד"א דחיישינן שמא ירגילנו בדבר עבירה קמ"ל דלא חיישינן וגם ר"ל [כאן] הכי אע"ג דאמור רבנן חייב אדם לפרוש מ... סמוך לווסתה וסד"א שמא יבעל מתוך רבוי דברים ויעבור על דת מלות חכמים [קמ"ל]: **והמלוה** סלע לעני בשעת דחקו פירשתי בסנהדרין פרק אלו הנשרפין: **והנושא** בת אחותו לפי שהיא בת גילו כדאמרינן רוב בנים לא...

הגהות הב"ח

(א) רש"י ד"ה איעקר ונעקרים כדאיתא לקמן סד ע"ב הס"ד: (ב) ר... ד"ה חייב וכו' ויפקדנה בתשמיש או) תא"מ. ... ס"א אינו ואפשר לו... דה"פ זה אינו תש... עכ"פ ואפילו ס... לווסתה אלא או בתש... כשהווסת רחוק או ב... דברים [סמוך לווס... (ג) ד"ה סמוך כדאמרינן לקמן נ"ב סט ע"ב והעיקר... חרש דף קיג בד"ה ש...

הגהות הגר"א

[א] גמ' וברתא לבר... נ"ב גי' הרמב"ם אבל לברתא וברתא לברא... א"ל כו' וכזה מ... קושיות תוס' ד"ה ו...

גליון הש"ס

גמ' מנא הא מי' לאמור רבנן דבני הרי הן כבנים. עיין דף סו ע"ב ולעיל ד... ע"א ובפי' רש"י בו... בראשית כ י"ב וכמ... כו ובכד"ק שם וכמ"ש... י וג"ע ובראשית כ"... ש"ב יט כה ובמהר... ח"א סוף סוטה ד"ה אשקיין:

עין משפט נר מצוה

קג א טוש"ע אה"ע סי' א סעיף א בהג"ה:
קד ב מיי' פ"ה מהלכות דעות הלכה י:

גמרא

וְהַמַּלְוֶה סֶלַע לְעָנִי בִּשְׁעַת דָּחְקוֹ – עָלָיו הַכָּתוּב אוֹמֵר (ישעיה נח) °"אָז תִּקְרָא וַה' יַעֲנֶה תְּשַׁוַּע וְיֹאמַר הִנֵּנִי".§ סי' אִשָּׁ"ה וְקַרְקַ"ע עֵזֶ"ר זֹא"ת שְׁתֵּ"י הַבְּרָכוֹ"ת תַּגָּרֵ"י פָּחֵתֵ"י.§ א"ר אֶלְעָזָר: אכָּל אָדָם שֶׁאֵין לוֹ אִשָּׁה – אֵינוֹ אָדָם, שֶׁנֶּאֱמַר (בראשית ה) °"זָכָר וּנְקֵבָה בְּרָאָם וַיִּקְרָא אֶת שְׁמָם אָדָם". וְאָמַר רַבִּי אֶלְעָזָר: כָּל אָדָם שֶׁאֵין לוֹ קַרְקַע – אֵינוֹ אָדָם, שֶׁנֶּאֱ' (תהלים קטו) °"הַשָּׁמַיִם שָׁמַיִם לַה' וְהָאָרֶץ נָתַן לִבְנֵי אָדָם". וְאָמַר רַבִּי אֶלְעָזָר: מַאי דִּכְתִיב (בראשית ב) °"אֶעֱשֶׂה לּוֹ עֵזֶר כְּנֶגְדּוֹ", *זָכָה – עוֹזַרְתּוֹ, לֹא זָכָה – כְּנֶגְדּוֹ. וְאִיכָּא דְּאָמְרִי: רַ' אֶלְעָזָר רָמֵי, כְּתִיב "כְּנַגְדּוֹ" וְקָרֵינַן "כְּנֶגְדּוֹ", זָכָה – כְּנֶגְדּוֹ, לֹא זָכָה – מְנַגַּדְתּוֹ. אַשְׁכְּחֵיהּ רַבִּי יוֹסֵי לְאֵלִיָּהוּ, א"ל: כְּתִיב "אֶעֱשֶׂה לּוֹ עֵזֶר", בַּמָּה אִשָּׁה עוֹזַרְתּוֹ לְאָדָם? א"ל: אָדָם מֵבִיא חִטִּין – חִטִּין כּוֹסֵס? פִּשְׁתָּן – פִּשְׁתָּן לוֹבֵשׁ? לֹא נִמְצֵאת מְאִירָה עֵינָיו וּמַעֲמִידָתוֹ עַל רַגְלָיו?! וְא"ר אֶלְעָזָר: מַאי דִּכְתִיב (שם ב) °"זֹאת הַפַּעַם עֶצֶם מֵעֲצָמַי וּבָשָׂר מִבְּשָׂרִי" מְלַמֵּד שֶׁבָּא אָדָם עַל כָּל בְּהֵמָה וְחַיָּה וְלֹא נִתְקָרְרָה דַּעְתּוֹ עַד שֶׁבָּא עַל חַוָּה. וְאָמַר רַ' אֶלְעָזָר: מַאי דִּכְתִיב (שם יב) °"וְנִבְרְכוּ בְךָ כֹּל מִשְׁפְּחֹת הָאֲדָמָה" אֲמַר לֵיהּ הקב"ה לְאַבְרָהָם: שְׁתֵּי בְּרָכוֹת טוֹבוֹת יֵשׁ לִי לְהַבְרִיךְ בְּךָ: רוּת הַמּוֹאֲבִיָּה וְנַעֲמָה הָעַמּוֹנִית. "כֹּל מִשְׁפְּחֹת הָאֲדָמָה" אֲפִילּוּ מִשְׁפָּחוֹת הַדָּרוֹת בַּאֲדָמָה אֵין מִתְבָּרְכוֹת אֶלָּא בִּשְׁבִיל יִשְׂרָאֵל. (שם יח) °"כֹּל גּוֹיֵי הָאָרֶץ" – אֲפִילּוּ סְפִינוֹת הַבָּאוֹת מִגַּלְיָא לְאַסְפַּמְיָא אֵינָן מִתְבָּרְכוֹת אֶלָּא בִּשְׁבִיל יִשְׂרָאֵל. וְאָמַר רַבִּי אֶלְעָזָר: עֲתִידִים כָּל בַּעֲלֵי אוּמָנִיּוֹת שֶׁיַּעַמְדוּ עַל הַקַּרְקַע, שֶׁנֶּאֱמַר (יחזקאל כז) °"וְיָרְדוּ מֵאֳנִיּוֹתֵיהֶם כֹּל תֹּפְשֵׂי מָשׁוֹט מַלָּחִים כֹּל חֹבְלֵי הַיָּם *עַל הָאָרֶץ יַעֲמֹדוּ". וְאָמַר רַ' אֶלְעָזָר: אֵין לְךָ אוּמָנוּת פְּחוּתָה מִן הַקַּרְקַע, שֶׁנֶּאֱמַר "וְיָרְדוּ" רַבִּי אֶלְעָזָר חֲזָיָא לְהַהִיא אַרְעָא דִּשְׁדִי בֵּיהּ כְּרָבָא לְפוּתְיָא, א"ל: אִי תִּשְׁדְּיֵיהּ לְאוֹרְכֵּיךְ – הַפּוּכֵי בְּעִיסְקָא טַב מִינָּךְ, רַב עָל לְבֵינֵי שִׁיבְלֵי, חָזַנְהוּ דְּקָא נָיְיפָן. אֲמַר לְהוּ: אִי נָיְיפַתְּ אִיתְנוּפֵי, הַפּוּכֵי בְּעִיסְקָא טַב מִינָּךְ. אֲמַר רָבָא: במֵאָה זוּזֵי בְּעִיסְקָא – כָּל יוֹמָא בִּשְׂרָא וְחַמְרָא, מֵאָה זוּזֵי בְּאַרְעָא – מִילְחָא וַחֲפוּרָה. וְלֹא עוֹד אֶלָּא מְגַנְּיָא לֵיהּ אַאַרְעָא וּמְרַמְיָא לֵיהּ תִּיגְרֵי. אֲמַר רַב פַּפָּא: זְרַע וְלָא תִּזְבֵּין. אע"ג דְּכִי הֲדָדֵי נִינְהוּ – הָנֵי מְבָרְכָן. זַבֵּין וְלָא *תֵּיזוּל, הָנֵי מִילֵּי – בִּיסְתַּרְקֵי. אֲבָל גְּלִימָא – לָא מִיתַּרְמְיָא לֵיהּ. (א) טוּם וְלָא תְּשַׁפֵּיץ, שַׁפּוּץ וְלָא תִּיבְנֵי, *שֶׁכָּל הָעוֹסֵק בְּבִנְיָן מִתְמַסְכֵּן. קְפוֹץ זַבֵּין אַרְעָא, מְתוּן נְסֵיב אִיתְּתָא, נְחֵית דַּרְגָּא נְסֵיב אִיתְּתָא, סַק דַּרְגָּא בְּחַר שׁוּשְׁבִינָא. א"ר אֶלְעָזָר *בַּר אֲבִינָא: (צפניה ג) *אֵין פּוּרְעָנוּת בָּאָה לָעוֹלָם אֶלָּא בִּשְׁבִיל יִשְׂרָאֵל, שֶׁנֶּאֱמַר °"הִכְרַתִּי גוֹיִם נָשַׁמּוּ פִּנּוֹתָם הֶחֱרַבְתִּי חוּצוֹתָם" וּכְתִיב (שם) °"אָמַרְתִּי אַךְ תִּירְאִי אוֹתִי תִּקְחִי מוּסָר". רַב הֲוָה מִיפַּטַר מֵרַבִּי חִיָּיא, אֲמַר לֵיהּ: רַחֲמָנָא לִיצְּלָךְ מִמִּידֵי דְּקָשֶׁה מִמּוֹתָא. וּמִי אִיכָּא מִידֵי דְּקָשֶׁה מִמּוֹתָא? נְפַק, דַּק וְאַשְׁכַּח (קהלת ז) °"וּמוֹצֶא אֲנִי מַר מִמָּוֶת אֶת הָאִשָּׁה וגו'". רַב הֲוָה קָא מְצַעֲרָא לֵיהּ דְּבֵיתְהוּ, כִּי אֲמַר לָהּ "עֲבִידִי לִי *טְלוֹפְחֵי" עָבְדָא לֵיהּ "חִימְצֵי", "חִימְצֵי" – עָבְדָא לֵיהּ טְלוֹפְחֵי. כִּי גָּדַל חִיָּיא בְּרֵיהּ, אַפֵּיךְ לָהּ. אֲמַר לֵיהּ: אִיעַלְיָא לָךְ אִמָּךְ! אֲמַר לֵיהּ: אֲנָא הוּא דְּקָא אַפֵּיכְנָא לָהּ. אֲמַר לֵיהּ: הַיְינוּ דְּקָא אָמְרִי אֱינָשֵׁי: דְּנָפֵיק מִינָּךְ – טַעֲמָא מַלְפָךְ. אַתְּ לָא תַּעֲבֵיד הָכִי, (ירמיה ט) *שֶׁנֶּאֱמַר °"לִמְּדוּ לְשׁוֹנָם דַּבֶּר שֶׁקֶר הַעֲוֵה וגו'". רַבִּי חִיָּיא הֲוָה קָא מְצַעֲרָא לֵיהּ דְּבֵיתְהוּ. כִּי הֲוָה מַשְׁכַּח מִידֵי – צָיֵיר לֵיהּ בְּסוּדָרֵיהּ, וּמַיְיתֵי נִיהֲלָהּ. אֲמַר לֵיהּ רַב: וְהָא קָא מְצַעֲרָא לֵיהּ לְמָר! א"ל: דַּיֵּינוּ שֶׁמְּגַדְּלוֹת בָּנֵינוּ, וּמַצִּילוֹת אוֹתָנוּ

מִן

רש"י

אז תקרא. לעיל מיניה כתיב "כי תראה ערום וכסיתו" – היינו דוחק עני. "ומבשרך לא תתעלם" – היינו אוהב את שכניו שהן כקרוביו, ומקרב את קרוביו, ונושא בת אחותו. כנגדו. חלוקה עליו וסותרת דבריו. מנגדתו. מדלא כתיב יו"ד, לשון נגדא דמלקות(ב). חטים כוסס. בתמיה(ג). זאת הפעם. מכלל דפעמים אחרים שמש, ולא עלו בדעתו. שתי ברכות. כמו: מבריך את הגפן (כלאים פ"ז מ"א). רות המואביה ונעמה העמונית. יצאו מהם מלכים ונביאים. נעמה – אמו של רחבעם, ויצא ממנה חזקיה ואסא ויהושפט דהוו צדיקים גמורים, וישעיהו הנביא. דאמר מר: אמוץ ואמציה אחים הוו (מגילה דף י:). שיעמדו על הקרקע. יניחו אומנותם לעסוק בחריש ובקציר: וירדו מאניותיהם כל תופשי משוט אל הארץ יעמדו. וירדו. לשון ירידת עניות. דשדי בה כרבא. זרע כרוב. לישנא אחרינא: כרבא – חרישה, כמו: כרוב ותני (ב"ב דף יב.), כמה דמסיק תעלא מבי כרבא (נדה דף סה:). לפותיא. לרוחב הערוגה. אי תשדייה לאורכיך. כלומר: אפילו תחזור ותחרשנה – לא יועיל כלום לפי עסקא. דהפוכי בעסקא טוב. להרויח יותר. דקא נייפן. הרוח מנשבת זו בזו. אי תניפנו. כמה שתרצו תנופפו, אין תועלת בהן לפי פרקמטיא. תניפנו – לשון הניפי לי במניפה (ב"מ דף פו.). חפורה. שמת ששכרה מועט ואוכל עבדים וחזיז במלח. חפורה. ירק מן התבואה עד שלא הביאה שליש. מגניא ליה אארעא. [משכבת אותו על הארץ], לשמור כל הלילה: [ומרמיא ליה תיגרי. בשבילה מתקוטט עם בני אדם]. זרע. תבואה לאכילת ביתך. ולא תזבון. לא תקנה תבואה מן השוק. ואע"ג דכי הדדי נינהו. אפילו חיטין בזול וקרקעך אינו חשוב, ואין לך שכר(ד) לפי השעה – אפ"ה הני מתברכין, ברכה מלויה בדבר שאין לוקח בדמים ואין כלה מהר. ברכה. פליסו"ן בלע"ז. זבן ולא תיזול. מכור כלי תשמישך והשתמש בדמים בפרקמטיא, קודם שתבא לידי עניות. ביסתרקי. כלי הבית, טאפי"ט בלע"ז. אבל גלימא. שהיא להתכבד בלבישתה – לא ימכור, דלמא כי הדר בעי לה לא מתרמיא ליה הגונה כמותה. טום. תרגום של סתום, כמו "סתמום פלשתים" (בראשית כו) – טומינון פלשתאי טום ולא תשפוץ אם יש לך חור קטן בכותל רעוע – סתום אותו מיד, ולא תרחיב בנקב לשפץ בו טיט ולבנים הרבה ליפותו. שפוץ. פלסטי"ר בלע"ז. ואם בעל נפש אתה להנאות בנייניך – הרחב הנקב ושפליהו להיות יפה. ולא תיבני. לא תפיל את כל הכותל ותבנהו. מתון נסיב איתתא. המתן עד שתבדוק מעשיה, שלא תהא רעה וקנטרנית. נחית דרגא ונסיב איתתא. לא תקח אשה חשובה ממך, שמא לא תתקבל עליה. שושבינא. אוהב טוב, בחר לך אדם חשוב להדבק אחריו. בשביל ישראל. ליראם, כדי שיחזרו בתשובה. חימצי. מין קטנית. אפיך לה. היה אומר האב לבנו: אמור לאמך לעשות עדשים, והוא אומר לה: עשי חימצי, והיא עושה עדשים. טעמא מלפך. פעמים שהבן מחכים את אביו, אני היה לי לעשות כן(ה). אבל אתה. דבר שקר הוא, וכתיב "למדו לשונם דבר שקר". כי הוה משכח מידי. דבר הראוי לה.

תוספות

המלוה סלע לעני בשעת דחקו. מקשה ר"ת: דבפ"ק דחגיגה (דף ה. ושם) אמר "ומלאוהו (ו) צרות רבות ורעות" – זה הממציא מעות לעני בשעת דחקו? ואומר ר"ת: דהתם מיירי שעושה ממנו המושל מס, וזקוק למכור ביתו או שדהו על כך, וזה ממציא לו מעות. ואם לא היה מוצא למכור היו מקילין מעליו. והיינו צרות רבות, שצריך למכור בזול ומפסיד הכל. ומסיק עלה: דהיינו דאמרי אינשי: זוזא לעללא לא שכיח, כלו': לקנות תבואה אין ממציאין לו מעות, לתליתא שכיח – כשדוחקין אותו למכור, כמו תליוהו וזבין (ב"ב דף מז:). ורש"י פירש שם בענין אחר.

אפילו ספינות הבאות מגליא לאספמיא. מ"כל" דריש, שבא לרבות אפילו הנך שאין עומדים אלא מעט בארץ. שאין לך אומנות פחותה כו. אף על גב דרבי אלעזר גופיה קאמר לעיל כל אדם שאין לו קרקע אינו אדם – צריך לומר קרקע לבנות עליו, שידור בו, וגם לצורך מזונותיו, כדאמר רב פפא בסמוך: זרע ולא תזבון והכא מיירי באדם שעיקר אומנותו בקרקע. זבין ולא תיזול. פי' בקונטרס לשון דלות, כלומר: מכור כלי תשמישך קודם שתעני. וקשה: דמאי שנא דנקט ביסתרקי טפי משאר מילי? ונראה לר"ת כפירוש ר"ח: דתיזול ענין אריגה, כמו סתר זוללי בשוקא (חולין ס.) כלומר: קנה בגדים ולא תארוג, כי יותר תרויח בקנין מבאריגה. אבל גלימא – טוב לארוג, דאימור לא מיתרמי ליה כרצונו.

לרתה

תוספות ישנים

לאחי האם י"מ [דנקט אחותו] דאחותו לא מצויא למטרח להשיאה אבל לא נקט בת אחיו דאחיו טרח ומשיאה וי"מ דווקא בת אחותו אבל לא בת אחיו דאתי להפקיע מצות יבום: אין לך [אומנות] פחותה מקרקע וא"ת והא איהו קאמר לעיל כל אדם שאין לו קרקע אינו אדם י"ל לדירתו יש לו לקנות או גם להשתכר למזונות (בנין) [ביתו] אבל להיות בה כל אומנתו אינו עושה כהוגן שאין לך אומנות פחותה מקרקע להיות בה כל עיקר מלאכתו: זבין ולא תידול. פי' מכור כלי תשמישך קודם שתהיה עני ולא נהירא דמאי קאמר ה"מ ביסתרקי אבל גלימא לא הרי יש לו למכור כל אשר לו קודם שיהיה עני ונראה לפרש כדאמרינן באלו טרפות סתר דולי בשוקא ור"ל זבין ולא תידול כלומר קנה בגדים ארוגים ולא תארוג שרגילות יותר למצוא בזול לקנות מלארוג וה"מ ביסתרקי אבל גלימא לא דודאי גלימא יש לו לארוג בביתו דלמא לא מתרמיא לה עשויה כתיקנה היטב כפי מדתו:

מסורת הש"ס ומראי מקומות

[נ"ל אל]

[גירסת הערוך תיזיל ע"ש דמביא ראיה כמו זוללא בשוקא חולין ס.]

[בילקוט ליתא ואם כן שפיר טולל הך מימרא דרבי אלעזר בהדי הנך מימרות דר"א לעיל וצ"ל ואמר ר"א אין וכו']

[ונזיר עדשים תרגום ובבבל דטלופחין]

...רובין נג. פרש"י ד"ה ...ה אם יש לו מזל טוב]

[סוטה יא.]

...קלט. ע"ש ב"ב ח. ע"ש]

סוכה מו:

הגהות הב"ח

(א) גמ' לא מתרמיא ליה ...עי טום ולא: (ב) רש"י ... מנגדתו וכו' דמלקות הס"ד: (ג) ד"ה חיטין ... בתמיה וכו' אדם ... חיטין כמות שהן ... פשתן כמות שהוא ... (ד) ד"ה ולאע"ג ... שכר ... (ה) ד"ה טעמא וכו' אבל ... שקר הוא לך וכתיב ... (ו) תוס' ד"ה ומלאוהו רעות ... רבות ולרות זה:

עין משפט נר מצוה

קה א טוש"ע אה"ע סי' א סעיף א בהג"ה:
קו ב ג שם סעיף א:
קז ד מיי' פט"ו מהלכות אישות הלכה ג טור ש"ע שם סעיף ז:

רש"י

מן החטא. הרהור עבירה. עבורי מיעברא במלה. נוחה לרצות, ומעברת על מדותיה. פומא. לקלל ולגדף עד זמן סעודה, כדי לצערו. ומהדרא ליה גבא. שלא לאכול עמו, ולצערתו. מתפקקין. נסתמין. לשון "ויפק", כמו "פוקקין הנקבים" (שבת דף קכה:). צרתה בצדה. ישא אחרת אללה. בחברתה. מקבלת תוכחה יותר. בסילתא. קוץ. סגריר. יום גשם ורוח. דלף טורד וגו' ואשת מדינים נשתוה. שוין הן. תלוין בכספו. שאין לו זריעה בקרקע, דכל שעה מיצר ודואג שמא תייקר התבואה או ינעלו שערי שבר. אין אלהים. מי שאמר "אין אלהים" קרי תורה אור נבל. חברי. פרסיים רשעים ומבזין, ואינם מכירים כבודם של ישראל. שגא. כסף נפל, מרוב צער שהיו בני הישיבה מסורים בידם. אמרו ליה מקבלי שוחדא. לבטל גזירתא. תריץ. יתיב, *ושמח. אמרו ליה על שלשה גזרו. אמר להם: מפני שלשה עבירות שהיו ביד בני בבל. גזרו על הבשר. שלא יאכלו בשר שחוטה: אמר להם – מפני עבירה שבידם, שהיו גוזלים מתנות כהונה, זרוע ולחיים וקיבה. [ועל המרחצאות מפני הטבילה. שלא היו זהירין בה. מחטטי שכבי. מוציאים הנקברים מקבריהם]. ששמחים ביום אידם. באה עליהם זו הגזרה להתאבל בה. בכם ובאבותיכם. ואבותם כבר מתו, ומה מכה יש בהן? [אלא] חטוטי שכבי. וכתיב ונבחר מות מחיים. בתריה דההוא קרא, דהואיל ואין ניתנים לקבורה – היאך יבחרו החיים למות? א"ל. האי נבחר לא קאמר שיהו הן בוחרין מות מחיים, אלא נביא הוא דקאמר להו: מוטב להן לרשעים שימותו ממה שיחטאו ויחיו. מספר ימיו כפלים. כלומר: שמח בחלקו, ודומה לו כאילו ימיו כפלים. מאשת חן. של אחרים. רוכל. המוכר בשמים לנשים להתקשט בהן, ומלוי בו ניאוף, ובא בעלה ופלעו. כניצוץ אש המבעיר גחלת. כן יגרו מבעירו. ככלוב. קן עופות. מחר מת. ואיננו בעולם, ולא יראה אותה דאגה שהוא מיצר וירא ודואג עליה, ונמצא שנצטער אתמול על עולם שאין שלו. גוף. פרגוד שחוצץ בין שכינה למלאכים, ושם רוחות ונשמות נתונות, שנבראו מששת ימי בראשית העתידות להנתן בגופים העתידים להבראות. שנאמר כי רוח מלפני יעטוף. הגאולה, ונשמות שאני עשיתי (ג). יעטוף. לשון עכבה, כדכתיב (בראשית ל) "והיה העטופים ללבן". ורישיה משתעי בגאולה – "כי לא לעולם אריב" וגו'. ואתם פרו ורבו. בתריה דתרוייהו כתיב, הלכך – כמו שעשה שתיהן הוא.

תוספות

צרתה בצדה. רצה לטעמיה דאמר בסוף פירקין (לקמן סה.): נושא אדם כמה נשים על אשתו.

שיתקיים ע"י אחרים. אע"ג דמשמע בפרק "אע"פ" (כתובות דף סג. ושם) שנשא בתו של ר"ע. דקאמר התם ברתיה של ר"ע עבדא ליה לבן עזאי הכי – הא אמר בפ"ק דסוטה (דף ד:) דנשא וגירש. יולא

גמרא

מן החטא. *מקרי ליה רב יהודה לרב יצחק בריה: °"ומוצא אני מר ממות את האשה". א"ל: כגון מאן? כגון אמך. (א) והא *מתני ליה רב יהודה לרב יצחק בריה: אין אדם מוצא קורת רוח אלא מאשתו ראשונה, שנאמר °"יהי מקורך ברוך ושמח מאשת נעוריך". וא"ל: כגון מאן? כגון אמך. מתקיף תקיפא, ועבורי מיעברא במלה. היכי דמי אשה רעה? אמר אביי: מקשטא ליה תכא, ומקשטא ליה פומא. רבא אמר: מקשטא ליה תכא, ומהדרא ליה גבא. אמר רבי חמא בר חנינא: [א]כיון שנשא אדם אשה – עונותיו מתפקקין, שנאמר °"מצא אשה מצא טוב ויפק רצון מה'". *במערבא, כי נסיב אינש איתתא אמרי ליה הכי: מצא או מוצא? מצא – דכתיב "מצא אשה מצא טוב", "מוצא" – דכתיב "ומוצא אני מר ממות את האשה". אמר רבא: אשה רעה מצוה לגרשה, דכתיב °"גרש לץ ויצא מדון וישבות דין וקלון". ואמר רבא: אשה רעה וכתובתה מרובה – צרתה בצדה, דאמרי אינשי: בחברתה ולא בסילתא. ואמר רבא: קשה אשה רעה כיום סגריר, שנאמר °"דלף טורד ביום סגריר ואשת מדינים נשתוה". ואמר רבא: בא וראה כמה טובה אשה טובה – וכמה רעה אשה רעה. כמה טובה אשה טובה – דכתיב "מצא אשה מצא טוב". אי בגוה משתעי קרא – כמה טובה אשה טובה שהכתוב משבחה, אי בתורה משתעי קרא – כמה טובה אשה טובה שהתורה נמשלה בה. כמה רעה אשה רעה – דכתיב "ומוצא אני מר ממות את האשה". אי בגוה משתעי קרא – כמה רעה אשה רעה שהכתוב מגנה, אי בגיהנם משתעי קרא – כמה רעה אשה רעה, שגיהנם נמשלה בה. °"הנני מביא רעה אשר לא יוכלו לצאת ממנה". אמר רב נחמן אמר רבה בר אבוה: זו אשה רעה וכתובתה מרובה. °"נתנני ה' בידי לא אוכל קום" אמר רב חסדא אמר מר עוקבא בר חייא: זו אשה רעה וכתובתה מרובה. במערבא אמרו: זה שמזונותיו תלוין בכספו. °"בניך ובנותיך נתונים לעם אחר" *אמר רב חנן בר רבא אמר רב: זו אשת האב. °"בגוי נבל אכעיסם" אמר רב חנן בר רבא אמר רב: זו אשה רעה וכתובתה מרובה. רבי אליעזר אומר: אלו המינים. וכן הוא אומר °"אמר נבל בלבו אין אלהים וגו'". במתניתא תנא: אלו אנשי ברברי‌א ואנשי מרטנאי, שמהלכין ערומים בשוק. שאין לך משוקץ ומתועב לפני המקום יותר ממי שמהלך בשוק ערום. רבי יוחנן אמר: אלו חברים. אמרו ליה לר' יוחנן: אתו חברי לבבל, שגא נפל. אמרו ליה: מקבלי שוחדא. תריץ יתיב. גזרו על ג' מפני ג'; גזרו על הבשר – מפני המתנות, גזרו על המרחצאות – מפני הטבילה, קא מחטטי שכבי – מפני ששמחים ביום אידם, שנאמר °"והיתה יד ה' בכם ובאבותיכם", אמר רבה בר שמואל: זו חטוטי שכבי, דאמר מר: בעון חיים – מתים מתחטטין. א"ל רבא לרבה בר מארי: כתיב °"לא יאספו ולא יקברו לדומן על פני האדמה יהיו" וכתיב °"ונבחר מות מחיים". אמר ליה: נבחר מות לרשעים, שלא יחיו בעולם הזה ויחטאו ויפלו בגיהנם. *כתוב בספר בן סירא: "אשה טובה – מתנה טובה(ב) לבעלה". וכתיב "טובה בחיק ירא אלהים תנתן. אשה רעה – צרעת לבעלה". מאי תקנתיה – יגרשנה ויתרפא מצרעתו. "אשה יפה אשרי בעלה, מספר ימיו כפלים". "העלם עיניך מאשת חן פן תלכד במצודתה. אל תט אצל בעלה למסוך עמו יין ושכר, כי בתואר אשה יפה רבים הושחתו, ועצומים כל הרוגיה". "רבים היו פצעי רוכל המרגילים לדבר ערוה, כניצוץ מבעיר גחלת, ככלוב מלא עוף כן בתיהם מלאים מרמה", "אל תצר צרת מחר כי לא תדע מה ילד יום, שמא מחר בא ואיננו, נמצא מצטער על העולם שאין שלו". "מנע רבים מתוך ביתך, ולא הכל תביא ביתך. רבים יהיו דורשי שלומך, גלה סוד לאחד מאלף". *אמר רבי אסי: אין בן דוד בא עד שיכלו כל הנשמות שבגוף שנאמר °"כי רוח מלפני יעטוף ונשמות אני עשיתי". תניא, רבי אליעזר אומר: [ב]כל מי שאין עוסק בפריה ורביה – כאילו שופך דמים שנאמר °"שופך דם האדם באדם דמו ישפך" וכתיב בתריה "ואתם פרו ורבו". רבי *יעקב אומר: [ג]כאילו ממעט הדמות, שנאמר °"כי בצלם אלהים עשה את האדם" וכתיב בתריה "ואתם פרו וגו'". בן עזאי אומר: כאילו שופך דמים, וממעט הדמות, שנאמר "ואתם פרו ורבו". אמרו לו לבן עזאי: יש נאה דורש ונאה מקיים, נאה מקיים ואין נאה דורש. ואתה – נאה דורש ואין נאה מקיים! אמר להן בן עזאי: ומה אעשה [ד]שנפשי חשקה בתורה, אפשר לעולם שיתקיים על ידי אחרים. תניא אידך, רבי אליעזר אומר: כל מי שאין עוסק בפריה ורביה – כאילו שופך דמים, שנאמר "שופך דם האדם" וסמיך ליה "ואתם פרו וגו'". רבי אלעזר בן עזריה אומר: כאילו ממעט הדמות, בן עזאי אומר: וכו'. אמרו לו לבן עזאי יש נאה דורש וכו'. *ת"ר: °"ובנחה יאמר שובה ה' רבבות אלפי ישראל" מלמד

תורה אור

קהלת ז; משלי ה; שם יח; שם כב; שם כז; ירמיה יא; איכה א; דברים כח; שם לב; תהלים יד; ש"א יב; ירמיה ח; שם; ישעיה נז; בראשית ט; שם; במדבר י

מסורת הש"ס

[סנהדרין כב:]; שם; ס"א וסמך; ברכות ח.; שם נו. ע"ש; [סנהדרין ק: ע"ש]; לעיל סב. ע"ז ה. נדה יג:; [בילקוט ובע"י איתא רבי עקיבא וכן איתא בשאלתות פ' נח סימן ה וע"ע תוספתא פ"ח]; [ב"ק פג. ע"ש]

תוספות ישנים

אתו חברי לבבל שגא פל מפורש בשבת (פ"ק) [דף מה:]

הגהות הב"ח

(א) כגון אמך איני והא מתני: (ב) שם מתנה טובה בחיק ירא כצ"ל ותיבות לבעלה וכתיב טובה נמחק: (ג) רש"י ד"ה שנאמר כי רוח וכו' שאני עשיתי יעטוף ומסיפא לרישיה מידרש:

מתני' אֵינוֹ רַשַּׁאי לְבַטֵּל. אֶלָּא: אוֹ יְגָרְשֶׁנָּה, אוֹ יִשָּׂא אַחֶרֶת עִמָּהּ. מוּתֶּרֶת לִינָּשֵׂא לְאַחֵר. וְלָא אָמְרִינַן עֲקָרָה הִיא, דְּשֶׁמָּא הָרִאשׁוֹן לֹא זָכָה לִיבָּנוֹת מִמֶּנָּה. **גמ'** מִקֵּץ עֶשֶׂר שָׁנִים. בָּא עַל הָגָר. וְהַאי דְּלָא נְסֵיב לָהּ בְּהָנָךְ שְׁנֵי קַמָּאֵי, עַד שֶׁלֹּא בָּא לְאֶרֶץ כְּנַעַן שֶׁהָיוּ שָׁנִים מְרוּבּוֹת כְּשֶׁהָיָה בְּחָרָן — לְלַמֶּדְךָ שֶׁאֵין יְשִׁיבַת חוּצָה לָאָרֶץ עוֹלָה לוֹ, דִּלְמָא מִשּׁוּם עֲוֹן חוּצָה לָאָרֶץ הֵם עֲקוּרִים. לְפִיכָךְ. הוֹאִיל וְקָא חָזֵינַן שֶׁאֵין יְשִׁיבַת חוּצָה לָאָרֶץ מִן הַמִּנְיָן, דְּתָלֵינַן בְּכָל דָּבָר הַמּוֹנְעָן מִן הַהֵרָיוֹן חָלָה הוּא אוֹ חָלְתָה הִיא כו'. וְלֵילַף מִיִּצְחָק. שֶׁשָּׁהָה עֶשְׂרִים שָׁנָה וְלֹא נָשָׂא אַחֶרֶת. עָקוּר הָיָה. וְיוֹדֵעַ שֶׁמֵּחֲמַת עַצְמוֹ הוּא, וּלְקַמָּן נָפְקָא לָן דְּעָקוּר הָיָה. אַבְרָהָם נַמִי עָקוּר הָיָה. כִּדְאָמְרִינַן לְקַמָּן, וְהֵיכִי יָלְפַתְּ מִינֵּיהּ? הַהוּא מִיבָּעֵי לֵיהּ כו'. כְּלוֹמַר: יִצְחָק עָקוּר הָיָה, מִשּׁוּם הָכִי לָא נְסֵיב אַחֲרִיתִי. וּקְרָא דְּיִצְחָק בֶּן שִׁשִּׁים שָׁנָה לָא יְתֵירָא הוּא, דְּתֵימָא לְהָכִי כְּתָבֵיהּ רַחֲמָנָא לְמִיגְמַר מִינֵּיהּ שְׁהִיַּית עֶשְׂרִים שָׁנָה, דְּהַהוּא מִיבָּעֵי לֵיהּ כו'. אֲבָל מִקֵּץ עֶשֶׂר שָׁנִים דְּאַבְרָהָם, אע"ג דְּעָקוּר הֲוָה — יָלְפִינַן מִינֵּיהּ. דְּאִי לָאו לִדְרָשָׁא, לְמַאי הִלְכְתָא קַמַּשְׁמְעִינַן קְרָא "מִקֵּץ עֶשֶׂר שָׁנִים"? לְיַיחֵס בָּהֶן. לֵידַע שְׁנוֹתָיו שֶׁל יַעֲקֹב, בֶּן כַּמָּה שָׁנִים הָיָה כְּשֶׁהָלַךְ לְבֵית עֵבֶר, וּכְשֶׁעָמַד עַל הַבְּאֵר. וּבִשְׁלְהֵי *גְּמָרָא דִּמְגִילָּה (דף יז.) מְפָרֵשׁ לָהּ. וְהַאי קְרָא דְּ"יִצְחָק בֶּן שִׁשִּׁים שָׁנָה" מַיְיתֵי לֵיהּ הָתָם, דְּיָלְפִינַן מִינֵּיהּ דְּגָדוֹל תַּלְמוּד תּוֹרָה מִכִּיבּוּד אָב וָאֵם, שֶׁכָּל אוֹתָן שָׁנִים שֶׁהָיָה יַעֲקֹב בְּבֵית עֵבֶר לֹא נֶעֱנַשׁ עֲלֵיהֶם. וַיֶּעְתַּר לָהֶם מִיבָּעֵי לֵיהּ. בִּשְׁלָמָא אִי אָמְרַתְּ תְּפִלַּת יִצְחָק עַל אִשְׁתּוֹ הָיְתָה — הַיְינוּ דִּכְתִיב "וַיֵּעָתֶר לוֹ" כְּמוֹ שֶׁהָיָה מִתְפַּלֵּל עָלֶיהָ, "וַתַּהַר רִבְקָה אִשְׁתּוֹ". אֶלָּא אִי אָמְרַתְּ עַל עַצְמוֹ הָיָה מִתְפַּלֵּל, וּ"לְנוֹכַח אִשְׁתּוֹ" מַשְׁמַע שֶׁשְּׁנֵיהֶם הָיוּ צוֹעֲקִים זֶה מוּל זֶה, וַיֶּעְתַּר לָהֶם מִיבָּעֵי לֵיהּ. לְפִי שֶׁאֵינוֹ דּוֹמֶה. תְּפִלָּתוֹ, שֶׁהָיָה צַדִּיק בֶּן צַדִּיק, לִתְפִלָּתָהּ, שֶׁהָיְתָה צַדֶּקֶת בַּת רָשָׁע. לְפִיכָךְ תָּלָה בּוֹ הַכָּתוּב. עָתָר. פל"א (א) בְּלַעַ"ז. חולבתס

[תוספתא פ"ח] [נ"ל פ"א] מגילה יז. ישעיה נא [חולין ס: ע"ש] [נ"ל ואמר רבי]

תורה אור

מְלַמֵּד שֶׁאֵין הַשְּׁכִינָה שׁוֹרָה עַל פָּחוֹת מִשְּׁנֵי אֲלָפִים וּשְׁנֵי רְבָבוֹת מִיִּשְׂרָאֵל. הֲרֵי שֶׁהָיוּ יִשְׂרָאֵל שְׁנֵי אֲלָפִים וּשְׁנֵי רְבָבוֹת חָסֵר אֶחָד, וְזֶה לֹא עָסַק בִּפְרִיָּה וּרְבִיָּה — לֹא נִמְצָא זֶה גּוֹרֵם לַשְּׁכִינָה שֶׁתִּסְתַּלֵּק מִיִּשְׂרָאֵל?! אַבָּא חָנָן אָמַר מִשּׁוּם רַבִּי אֱלִיעֶזֶר: חַיָּיב מִיתָה, שֶׁנֶּאֱמַר °"וּבָנִים לֹא הָיוּ לָהֶם" הָא הָיוּ לָהֶם בָּנִים — לֹא מֵתוּ. אֲחֵרִים אוֹמְרִים: גּוֹרֵם לַשְּׁכִינָה שֶׁתִּסְתַּלֵּק מִיִּשְׂרָאֵל, שֶׁנֶּאֱמַר °"לִהְיוֹת לְךָ לֵאלֹהִים וּלְזַרְעֲךָ אַחֲרֶיךָ", בִּזְמַן שֶׁזַּרְעֲךָ אַחֲרֶיךָ — שְׁכִינָה שׁוֹרָה, אֵין זַרְעֲךָ אַחֲרֶיךָ — עַל מִי שׁוֹרָה, עַל הָעֵצִים וְעַל הָאֲבָנִים?!. § **מתני'** [א]נָשָׂא אִשָּׁה וְשָׁהָה עִמָּהּ עֶשֶׂר שָׁנִים וְלֹא יָלְדָה — אֵינוֹ רַשַּׁאי לְבַטֵּל. [ב]גֵּירְשָׁהּ — מוּתֶּרֶת לִינָּשֵׂא לְאַחֵר, וְרַשַּׁאי הַשֵּׁנִי לִשְׁהוֹת עִמָּהּ י' שָׁנִים. וְאִם הִפִּילָה — מוֹנֶה מִשָּׁעָה שֶׁהִפִּילָה. § **גמ'** ת"ר: *נָשָׂא אִשָּׁה וְשָׁהָה עִמָּהּ עֶשֶׂר שָׁנִים וְלֹא יָלְדָה — יוֹצִיא וְיִתֵּן כְּתוּבָּה, שֶׁמָּא לֹא זָכָה לְהִבָּנוֹת מִמֶּנָּה אע"פ שֶׁאֵין רְאָיָה לַדָּבָר — זֵכֶר לַדָּבָר: °"מִקֵּץ עֶשֶׂר שָׁנִים לְשֶׁבֶת אַבְרָם בְּאֶרֶץ כְּנָעַן" לְלַמֶּדְךָ שֶׁאֵין יְשִׁיבַת חו"ל עוֹלָה לוֹ מִן הַמִּנְיָן. [ג]לְפִיכָךְ, חָלָה הוּא אוֹ שֶׁחָלְתָה הִיא, אוֹ שְׁנֵיהֶם חֲבוּשִׁים בְּבֵית הָאֲסוּרִים — אֵין עוֹלִין לוֹ מִן הַמִּנְיָן. א"ל רָבָא לְרַב נַחְמָן: וְלֵילַף מִיִּצְחָק, דִּכְתִיב °"וַיְהִי יִצְחָק בֶּן אַרְבָּעִים שָׁנָה בְּקַחְתּוֹ אֶת רִבְקָה וגו'" וּכְתִיב °"וְיִצְחָק בֶּן שִׁשִּׁים שָׁנָה בְּלֶדֶת אוֹתָם"! א"ל: יִצְחָק עָקוּר הָיָה. — א"ה, אַבְרָהָם נַמִי עָקוּר הָיָה! הַהוּא מִיבָּעֵי לֵיהּ לִכְדְרַ' חִיָּיא בַּר אַבָּא. *דְּא"ר חִיָּיא בַּר אַבָּא א"ר יוֹחָנָן: לָמָּה נִמְנוּ שְׁנוֹתָיו שֶׁל יִשְׁמָעֵאל — כְּדֵי לְיַיחֵס בָּהֶן שְׁנוֹתָיו שֶׁל יַעֲקֹב. אָמַר רַבִּי יִצְחָק: יִצְחָק אָבִינוּ עָקוּר הָיָה, שֶׁנֶּאֱמַר °"וַיֶּעְתַּר יִצְחָק לַה' לְנֹכַח אִשְׁתּוֹ", "עַל אִשְׁתּוֹ" לֹא נֶאֱמַר, אֶלָּא "לְנוֹכַח" מְלַמֵּד שֶׁשְּׁנֵיהֶם עֲקוּרִים הָיוּ. א"ה "וַיֵּעָתֶר לוֹ" "וַיֵּעָתֵר לָהֶם" מִיבָּעֵי לֵיהּ! לְפִי שֶׁאֵינוֹ דּוֹמֶה תְּפִלַּת צַדִּיק בֶּן צַדִּיק לִתְפִלַּת צַדִּיק בֶּן רָשָׁע. א"ר יִצְחָק: מִפְּנֵי מָה הָיוּ אֲבוֹתֵינוּ עֲקוּרִים — *מִפְּנֵי שֶׁהקב"ה מִתְאַוֶּה לִתְפִלָּתָן שֶׁל צַדִּיקִים. *א"ר יִצְחָק: לָמָּה *) נִמְשְׁלָה תְּפִלָּתָן שֶׁל צַדִּיקִים כְּעֶתֶר — מָה עֶתֶר זֶה מְהַפֵּךְ הַתְּבוּאָה מִמָּקוֹם לְמָקוֹם, כָּךְ תְּפִלָּתָן שֶׁל צַדִּיקִים מְהַפֶּכֶת מִדּוֹתָיו שֶׁל הקב"ה מִמִּדַּת רַגְזָנוּת לְמִדַּת רַחְמָנוּת. אָמַר רַבִּי אַמִּי: אַבְרָהָם וְשָׂרָה טוּמְטְמִין הָיוּ, שֶׁנֶּאֱמַר °"הַבִּיטוּ אֶל צוּר חֻצַּבְתֶּם

במדבר ג | בראשית יז | שם טז | שם כה | שם

*) סוכה יד. ע"ש

יוציא ויתן כתובה. בסוף "המדיר" (כתובות עז. ושם) איכא פלוגתא דאמוראי כשנשא אשה ושהה עמה עשר שנים, אם כופין אותו להוציא אם לאו. וקשה: דלמ"ד אין כופין — תקשי ליה מהכא דקתני "יוציא", ולשון יוציא — משמע בכפיה, כדמשמע התם, דאמר רב: האומר איני זן ואיני מפרנס — יוציא ויתן כתובה. ופריך עליה שמואל: עד שכופין אותו להוציא יכפוהו לזון.(א) ונראה דלא משמע יוציא *לכפיה — אלא היכא שעושה לאשה שלא כדין, אבל הכא שאינו אלא משום דאינו רשאי לבטל מפריה ורביה — לא משמע לשון כפיה. וכל הנהו ד"המדיר" (גז"ש) דתנן בהו: יוציא ויתן כתובה — בכפיה קאמר, כיון שמתנהג עמה שלא כדין. ולעיל ב"החולץ" (דף לט.) נמי אמרי' כשאין רוצה לא לייבם ולא לחלוץ דחוזרין אצל גדול למיכפייה, לפי שמתנהג עמה שלא כדין, שאינו רוצה לא לכנוס ולא לפטור. ונראה דכופין אותו בשוטים. דאי במילי — הא אמר בסוף "המדיר" (כתובות עז. ושם) ד"בדברים לא יוסר עבד". ותימה: דכי פריך ב"המדיר" למאן דאמר כופין בנשא אשה ושהה עמה עשר שנים, דלתניי' בהדי אלו שכופין אותו להוציא — תקשי ליה נמי מכל הנהו דתנן ב"המדיר" (ג"ז שם), והיא ד"נערה שנתפתתה" (שם מח.) דהאומר אי אפשי אלא אני בבגדי והיא בבגדה — יוציא ויתן כתובה, וההוא דסוף פירקין (לקמן דף סה.) דאמר ר' אמי: הנושא אשה על אשתו — יוציא ויתן כתובה? וי"ל: דלא קתני הנך דאתייה כפייה דידהו על ידי פשיעת בעל, אלא הנהו דאתיין ממילא, כגון מוכה שחין ובעל פוליפוס. והא דקתני מצרף ומקמץ ובורסי, אע"פ שנעשו אחר שנשאו — הנהו אינן מתכוונים להקניט ולצער את האשה. ומיהו, קשיא: דליתני בהא מחמת טענה, דאמר בסוף פרקין (שם:) דכופין אותו להוציא, אע"פ שאין פושע — דמה יכול לעשות שהוא עקור? ונראה לפרש: דקתני סיפא בין שהיו עד שלא נישאו בין משנישאו, בכולן אמר ר' מאיר יכולה היא שתאמר: סבורה הייתי לקבל כו'. והכא לא שייך למיתני בה סבורה הייתי שאני יכולה לקבל. ורובן מיתרצי בההיא שנויא. ובירושלמי משמע דאין כופין *בהנהו דתנן ב"המדיר" (כתובות עז.) ור"ת הביאו בשילהי "אע"פ" (שם סג:) *וזה לשונו: בירושלמי דסוף "אלמנה ניזונית" תנינן: גט המעושה, בישראל כשר, בגוים פסול. אמר שמואל: פסול ופוסל לכהונה. ואמר שמואל: אין מעשים אלא לפסולות. *(אמר שמואל) והתנינן המדיר אשתו מלהנות כו', ומשני: שמענו שמוציא, שמענו שכופין? בתמיה. ש"מ דאין כופין אלא היכא דקתני כופין, אבל היכא דאמור רבנן יוציא, ולא פירשו כופין — אומרים לו: חייבוך רבנן להוציא, ואם לא הוציא — מותר לקרותו עבריינא, אבל לכפותו בשוטים — לא. וגר"ח כדברי האומר איני זן ואיני מפרנס — כופין אותו להוציא, ויתן כתובה. והיא ד"החולץ" (לעיל לט.) דחוזרים אצל גדול למכפייה — היינו טעמא דכופין לפי שמונעה מכל ענייני אישות, בין תשמיש בין מזונות. אבל משום תשמיש המטה לחודיה, או משום מזונות לחודייהו — אין כופין. ומההוא עובדא דבי נשיאה בקיסרי דסוף פירקין (לקמן סה:), דקאמר רבי יוחנן: יוציא ויתן כתובה, דמשמע התם דכופין ליה — אין ראיה דכופין כל היכא דקאמר יוציא, דהתם לאו מימרא היא, אלא כשבא מעשה לפניו נוה להם שיוציא. משמע שאמר להם לכפותו, וכל היכא דלא קאמר בהדיא כופין — אין כופין, שלא יהא גט מעושה בישראל שלא כדין, ופסול. **יוציא** ויתן כתובה. נראה דבכל הנהו דתנן (כתובות עז.) שכופין אותו להוציא — שנותן כתובה אע"פ שמגרש בעל כרחו. מדפריך התם דליתני בהדייהו הך דשהה י' שנים, וקאמר הכא דאית לה כתובה. ומשמע נמי התם (שם) דהוה תני בהדייהו אלמנה לכ"ג גרושה וחלוצה לכהן הדיוט אי לאו משום דאורייתא לא קתני. והנהו אית להו כתובה, כדאמר ב"יש מותרות" (לקמן פה.) ובאה מחמת טענה אמרינן לקמן (שם) דיש לה כתובה, אע"פ שכופין אותו לגרש. ורבינו גרשום כתב בתשובה דמוכת שחין אין לה כתובה. ודקדק מדקתני גבי בורסי שנשא אשה, יכולה שתאמר כסבורה הייתי לקבל ועכשיו איני יכולה לקבל. ואם היו כופין ליתן כתובה — אם כן כל שעה תערים ותנשא ותאמר כן כדי לגבות כתובה לאלתר? וי"ל: דשמא אותה אין לה כתובה. כיון שיכולה להערים. אבל אחריני — יש להם כתובה. ובהדיא תני בתוספתא יוציא ויתן כתובה. **אע"פ** שאין ראיה לדבר. ראיה גמורה אינה, דמשם אין ללמוד שיהא זקוק לגרש אשתו אפילו אם אי אפשר בלא גירושין. ואדרבה, ראוי ללמוד מכאן דאפי' את"ל בעלמא הנושא אשה על אשתו יוציא ויתן כתובה — היכא דשהה עמה י' שנים שרי להכניס צרתה, כמו שמצינו באברהם, אולי ירחמו מן השמים ויזכה עדיין ליבנות ממנה, כמו שלבסוף זכה אברהם משרה. **ולילף** מיצחק. ואם תאמר: יצחק נמי לא שהה יותר מי', לפי מה שפי' שלא היתה רבקה אלא בת ג' כשנשאה, ועד שהיתה בת י"ב לא היתה ראויה להוליד? ויש לומר: דמדרשים חלוקין, כדפרישי' לעיל.* ועוד: דמוכח בפרק "בן סורר ומורה" (סנהדרין סט:) שדורות הראשונים היו ראויין להוליד הרבה קודם הזמן הזה. **אי** הכי אברהם נמי עקור היה. כדאמר לקמן אברהם ושרה טומטמים היו. ואע"פ שמסתמא כבר נקרע כשנשא שרה הכא אליבא דרבי יהודה פריך, דאמרינן ב"הערל" (לקמן פא.) טומטום שנקרע — אין מוליד. ועוד: דאפי' לרבנן נמי דפליגי עליה — לא שכיח שיוליד.

ימי

[רש"ל מ"ז] [דף סה: ד"ה וכן] [ליתא שם] [גליון]

קח א מיי' פט"ו מהל' אישות הלכה ז סמג עשין מט טוש"ע אה"ע סימן קנד סעיף י:

קט ב ג מיי' שם הלכה יא יב יד טוש"ע שם סעיף יא יב יז:

בכפיה כצ"ל. יעב"ץ

תוספות ישנים

א) וא"ת ומאי א) מקשה התם לרב תחליפא ליתיב מהך ברייתא דתני נשא אשה ושהה עמה וכו' יוציא ויתן כתובה וכל יוציא ר"ל כופין. לכ"נ דודאי יוציא לא משמע כופין אם לא שהתלמוד מפרש בהדיא [ונראה דאין כופין] אלא בדבר שמתנהג עם האשה שלא כדין. אבל הכא אינו מתנהג שלא כדין לטעמא דאמרינן יוציא היינו משום דנכריה אותו משום שאינו רשאי ליבטל מפריה ורביה וגם ניחא דהתם פליגי אי ר"ל כופין אי לאו. ב) דודאי הכא לא ידעינן דיוציא ר"ל כופין כדפרישית ובהכי פליגי דחד אמר אין כופין ורב תחליפא אמר כופין א"נ י"ל דלכ"ע לא אמרינן יוציא כופין בשום מקום אם אינו מפרש בהדיא וגרסי' באיני זן ואיני מפרנס כופין וניחא הכל וכן משמע בירושלמי גבי גט המעושה תמן תנינן כו' עי' בתוס' מטו"ד: **מה** עתר זה מהפך את התבואה. פ"ה עתר פילא. ולא נהירא ג) דאמרי' שהמהפכת הקש מעל התבואה וא"כ הוי פורקא ורחת היינו פיל"א:

א) נראה דצ"ל ועוד קשה דמאי מקשה התם לרב תחליפא ממתני' ליתיב מהך ברייתא אמתני' דתני הכא דיוציא ויתן כתובה וכו'. ב) אולי צ"ל הרי הכא לא ידעינן אי ר"ל כופין ובהכי פליגי וכו'. ג) אולי צ"ל ולא נהירא דאמרינן בסוכה (י"ד) דעתר מהפך את התבואה בגורן וכו' וא"כ היינו פורק"א

תוספות חד מקמאי

והא דתניא שמא [לא] זכה להבנות ממנה. מקשי' עלה בגמ' ודילמא איהי היא דלא זכיא כלומר לא יתן לה כתובה ומשני איהי כיון דלא מפקדה אפריה ורביה לא מיענשא. משמע דלר' יוחנן בן ברוקא דאמר מפקדה לית לה כתובה ובשלהי פירקין גרסינן עובדא הוה קמיה ר"י בבנישתא דקסרין ואמר יוציא ויתן כתובה ואי ס"ד דלא מפקדה כתובה מאי עבידתה אלמא אי מפקדה יש לה כתובה קשיא הך. י"ל ולפרש דההיא דהבעל היה עקור תליה בדידיה ולא בדידה ואי מפקדה יש לה כתובה אבל היכא דאין הבעל עקור דאיכא למיתלא בדידה ובדידיה אמרי' אוקי

הגהות הב"ח

(א) רש"י ד"ה עתר פל"א בלע"ז. נ"ב רחת והתוספות פ"ק דסוכה השיגו על פירושו וכתבו דהעיקר כמו שפי' רש"י לשם עתר פורק"א בלע"ז דהיינו שופי"ל בלשון אשכנז שיש לו שוקלים וע"ש בדף יד ע"א:

ממונא בחזקת מריה ואיהי היא דלא זכאי ואין לה כתובה אי הוה מפקדה ואי לא מפקדה לא מענשא ואית לה כתובה והראב"ד פירש בהגהת ספריו דהא דמקשינן הכא ודלמא איהי היא דלא זכאי לישנא בעלמא הוא דקשיא ליה דקתני שמא לא זכה ליבנות הימנה ולא משום כתובה אקשי ליה: הוא אמר מינה והיא אמרה מיניה א"ר אמי דברים שבינו לבינה היא נאמנת מ"ט איהו קים לה בגווה כחץ איהו לא קים ליה. ה"ר אלפס פרשה בבאין לדון על עסקי כתובה וכן פרש"י ז"ל. הוא אמר מינה ולית לה כתובה והיא אמרה מיניה ואית לי כתובה (והא) וא"ר אמי היא נאמנת ויש לה כתובה. והקשה עליו הרב ר' אברהם אב"ד ואבא מרי וב"ה למה ליה למימר לאנתתיה מיניה דאינו יורה כחץ אפי' יורה כחץ יש לה כתובה שמא לא זכה ליבנות הימנה ואיהו דמפקיד מענש איהי דלא מפקדה לא מענשא וכתב הראב"ד ז"ל איכא דמתריץ דהאי גברא הוה ליה בני וכיון דאית ליה ליכא למימר לא זכה ליבנות הימנה ואיהי כיון דלא מפקדה לא איכפת ליה ולא ענשינן ליה במידי דלא איכפת ליה. לכך פי' אבא מארי ז"ל דבבאה מחמת טענה מיירי כגון ששהתה עמו עשר שנים ולא ילדה לו והבעל יש לו בנים ולא מפקינן מניה מידי. אלא היא בעיא למיפק מיניה דבעינא חוטרא לידה ומרה לקבורה ובעיא למיפק בלא כתובה דליכא למימר שמא עיניה נתנה באחר ולפיכך אמר ר' אמי איהי מהימנא ומפקינן לה מיניה בלא כתובה. אבל כתובה לא יהבין לה שמא עיניה נתנה באחר ובלא כתובה נמי לא מפקינן מיניה אלא לאחר ששהתה עשר שנים אבל בתוך עשר שנים אע"פ שבאה מחמת טענה לא מפקינן מיניה אפי' בלא כתובה שמא עיניה נתנה באחר. ורב אחא משבחה פירש אפילו בתוך עשר שנים כיון שבאת מחמת טענה מפקינן לה מיניה בכתובה ולא מסתברא כותיה

עין משפט נר מצוה

קי א מיי' פט"ו מהל' אישות הלכה יד טוש"ע אה"ע סימן קכד סעיף יז:

קיא ב מיי' פ"א מהלכות מילה הלכה יח סמג עשין כח טוש"ע י"ד סימן רסג סעיף ב:

קיב ג טוש"ע שם סעיף ג:

קיג ד מיי' פכ"א מהל' איסורי ביאה הלכה ל טוש"ע אה"ע סי' ב סעי' ז:

קיד ה ו מיי' שם הל' לא סמג לאוין קכו טוש"ע שם סימן יט סעיף א:

קטו ז מיי' פי"ח מהל' סנהדרין הלכה ד:

קטז ח מיי' פ"ח מהל' איסורי ביאה הלכה ה סמג לאוין קיא טוש"ע י"ד סימן קפט סעיף ב:

ימי שנותינו בהם שבעים שנה. אע"ג דהאי קרא בתפלת משה כתיב – מסתמא דוד אמרו, שמצינו שחי כך, אבל משה מצינו שחי יותר:

בעי מיניה מרב יוסף. פר"י: דנראה ששאלו: הלכה כרבי או כרשב"ג, והשיבו דהלכה כשניהם.

דתנן מי שלקה ושנה כו'. הקשה ה"ר משה: דב"הנשרפים" (סנהדרין פא: ושם) מוקי לה אפילו כרשב"ג, ועבירות מחזקות! ואמר ר"י: דאע"ג דאיכא תנא התם דאמר עבירות מחזקות, מתוך לשון המשנה משמע ליה לרב יוסף דקסבר מלקיות מחזקות. דנראה לו דוחק דלא נקט מי שלקה ושנה אלא לאשמועינן דאיירי בעבירה שיש בה מלקות. ואפי' את"ל דקסבר עבירות מחזקות – שמא סבר רב יוסף דכיפה צריכה התראה.

ושור

חצבתם ואל מקבת בור נקרתם" וכתיב "הביטו אל אברהם אביכם ואל שרה תחוללכם" (ישעיה נא). אמר רב נחמן אמר רבה בר אבוה: שרה אמנו *אילונית היתה, שנאמר "ותהי שרי עקרה אין לה ולד" (בראשית יא) אפי' בית ולד אין לה. אמר רב יהודה בריה דרב שמואל בר שילת משמיה דרב: לא שנו אלא בדורות הראשונים, ששנותיהן מרובות. אבל בדורות האחרונים ששנותיהן מועטות – שתי שנים ומחצה, כנגד שלשה עיבורים. רבה אמר רב נחמן: שלש שנים, כנגד שלש פקידות. *דאמר מר: בר"ה נפקדו שרה רחל וחנה. אמר רבה: ליתנהו להני כללי. מכדי מתני' מאן תקין – רבי, והא בימי דוד אימעוט שני, דכתיב "ימי שנותינו בהם שבעים שנה" (תהלים צ). והאי "שמא לא זכה להבנות הימנה" ודלמא איהי דלא זכיא! איהי, כיון דלא מפקדא אפריה ורביה – לא מיענשה. איני? והא אמרו ליה רבנן לר' אבא בר זבדא: נסיב איתתא ואוליד בני! ואמר להו: אי זכאי – הוו לי מקמייתא. התם דחוי קא מדחי להו לרבנן. דר' אבא בר זבדא איעקר מפרקיה דרב הונא, רב גידל איעקר מפרקיה דרב הונא, רבי חלבו איעקר מפרקיה דרב הונא, *רב ששת איעקר מפרקיה דרב הונא. רב אחא בר יעקב אחדתיה *סוסכינתא, תליוה בארזא דבי רב ונפק מיניה כהוצא ירקא. אמר רב אחא בר יעקב: שיתין סבי הוינא, וכולהו איעקור מפרקיה דרב הונא, לבר מאנא דקיימי בנפשאי "החכמה תחיה בעליה" (קהלת ז). § גירשה מותרת וכו'. § [א]שני – אין, שלישי – לא. מתניתין מני – *רבי היא. דתניא: [ב]מלה הראשון ומת, שני ומת, שלישי – לא תמול, דברי רבי. רבן שמעון בן גמליאל אומר: *שלישי – תמול, רביעי – לא תמול. והתניא איפכא, *הי מינייהו אחרינתא? ת"ש, דאמר ר' חייא בר אבא א"ר יוחנן: [ג]מעשה בארבע אחיות בצפורי, שמלה ראשונה ומת, שניה ומת, שלישית ומת, רביעית באת לפני רבן שמעון בן גמליאל, אמר לה: אל תמולי. ודלמא אי אתיא שלישית – נמי הוה אמר לה? א"כ מאי אסהדותיה דר' חייא בר אבא. ודלמא הא קמ"ל דאחיות מחזקות! אמר רבא: השתא דאמרת אחיות מחזקות – [ד]לא ישא אדם אשה לא ממשפחת נכפין, ולא ממשפחת מצורעים, והוא דאתחזק תלתא זימני. מאי הוה עלה? כי אתא רב יצחק בר יוסף אמר: עובדא הוה קמיה דר' יוחנן בכנישתא דמעון ביוה"כ שחל להיות בשבת, ומלה ראשונה ומת, שניה ומת, שלישית באה לפניו. – אמר לה: לכי ומולי. א"ל אביי: חזי דקשרית איסורא וסכנתא! סמך עלה אביי, ואזל נסבה לחומה ברתא דאיסי בריה דרב יצחק בריה דרב יהודה. דנסבה רחבא דפומבדיתא ושכיב, רב יצחק בריה דרבה בר בר חנה ושכיב, ונסבה הוא ושכיב. אמר רבא: ומי איכא דעביד עובדא בנפשיה כי האי, והא איהו דאמר: אבין – דסמכא, יצחק סומקא – לאו בר סמכא. אבין – ישנו בחזרה, יצחק סומקא – אינו בחזרה. ועוד: אימר דפליגי לענין מילה, בנישואין מי פליגי? אין, והתניא: *[ה]ניסת לראשון ומת, לשני ומת, לשלישי – לא תנשא, דברי רבי. רבן שמעון בן גמליאל אומר: לשלישי תנשא, לרביעי לא תנשא. בשלמא גבי מילה – איכא משפחה דרפי דמא ואיכא משפחה דקמיט דמא. אלא נישואין מ"ט? א"ל רב מרדכי לרב אשי, הכי אמר אבימי מהגרוניא משמיה דרב הונא: מעין גורם. ורב אשי אמר: [ו]מזל גורם. מאי בינייהו? °איכא בינייהו דאירסה ומית, אי נמי דנפל מדיקלא ומית. א"ל רב יוסף בריה דרבא לרבא: בעי מיניה מרב יוסף, הלכה כרבי? ואמר לי: אין. הלכה כרבן שמעון בן גמליאל? ואמר לי: אין. אחוכי אחיך בי? א"ל: לא, סתמי *היא, ופשיט לך: נישואין ומלקיות – כרבי, וסתות ושור המועד כרבן שמעון בן גמליאל. נישואין – הא דאמרן, מלקיות – דתנן: *[ז]מי שלקה ושנה – ב"ד כונסין אותו לכיפה, ומאכילין אותו שעורים עד שתהא כריסו נבקעת. וסתות – דתנן: *[ח]אין האשה

קובעת

רש"י

חוצבתם. נעשה לו זכרות. **נוקרתם.** נעשה לה נקבות, כמו "אני קרתי ושתיתי מים" (ישעיהו לז). **אין לה ולד.** קרא יתירא הוא, דהא כתיב עקרה. **לא שנו.** דשוהה עשר שנים. **שלשה עיבורים.** כ"ז חדשים לימי הולד, וחדש לכל עיבור ועיבור לימי טומאה וטהרה, דאשה מתעברת סמוך לוסתה. **שלש פקידות.** שהקב"ה פוקד העקרות לשמוע תפלתן בר"ה, וגוזר עליהן הריון. **להני כללי.** דקאמר כל דורות של עכשיו שתי שנים ומחצה שהייתן. **ודלמא איהי דלא זכיא.** ולא תטול כתובה. **כיון דלא מיפקדא אפריה ורביה.** לא איכפת לה, ולא ענש לה קודשא בריך הוא על עונותיה. **איני והא אמרו ליה כו'.** אמתני' פריך, דקתני: ישא אחרת שמא לא זכה להבנות ממנה, ויזכה להבנות מן השניה. **סוסכינתא.** חולי מעוצר השתן, ואדם נעקר הימנו. **כהוצא ירקא.** ירוק ככף תמר. **שלישי לא.** דהוחזקה עקרה. **הי מינייהו אחרינתא.** איזו מהמשניות נשנית אחרונה, דנסמוך עלה אמלתא דמר ודמר? דכל חד וחד הדר משיטתיה קמייתא ונקט שיטתיה דחבריה, ובתרייתא עיקר, דהדור בהו מקמייתא. **אמר לה אל תמולי.** אלמא: מתניתא קמייתא אחרינתא, דהאי מעשה בסוף ימיו של רשב"ג הוה, מדקא מסהיד עליה ר' יוחנן שהיה אמורא, וסוף התנאים, והוא ראה את המעשה. **דאחיות מחזקות.** דכי היכי דאשה מוחזקת בג' פעמים – כך היא מוחזקת בשלש אחיותיה. **נכפין.** חולין. **איסורא וסכנתא.** שאם חזקה בשני פעמים והשלישי ניתן לדחות ממנה – הויא מילה שלא בזמנה, ואינה דוחה את השבת. **וסכנתא.** סכנת נפשות. **סמך עלה אביי.** על הא דרב יצחק, דאמר משמיה דרבי יוחנן: בתלת זימני הוא דהויא חזקה. **בנפשיה.** בסכנת נפשו. **אבין דסמכא.** מה שאמר אבין משום רבי יוחנן – יש לסמוך עליו. **ישנו בחזרה.** חוזר על תלמודו. לשון אחר: מצוי כל שעה לפני רבי יוחנן, ואם חזר בו רבי יוחנן משום דבר שאמר תחלה – שומע אבין וחוזר גם הוא בו. אבל רב יצחק אינו מצוי לפניו, ופעמים ששמע דבר מרבי יוחנן ולמחר חזר בו רבי יוחנן, והוא אינו יודע. **דאירסה.** השלישי ומת. **אי נמי.** דנסבה וסליק לדיקלא ונפל ומת. למ"ד מעין גורם – לא הוחזקה זו, שהרי מעיינה לא גרם לו שימות, שהרי לא מת מחולי: ה"ג. **בעי מיניה מרב יוסף הלכה כרבי ואמר לי אין הלכה כרשב"ג ואמר לי אין אחוכי אחיך בי.** שאלתי מרב יוסף אם הלכה כרבי, ואמר לי: הלכה, ופעם אחרת שאלתיו אם הלכה כרשב"ג, ואמר לי: הלכה. וכמדומה אני שמשחק בי: ה"ג. **אמר ליה סתמי הוא ופשיט לך.** לא שיחק בך, סתומות של משנה הן: יש שסתמה כרבן שמעון בן גמליאל, ויש שסתמה כרבי. דאיכא מילתא דמחזקינן לה בתרי זימני, ואיכא מילתא דבעינן תלתא זימני. ומשום הכי פשט לך כמר וכמר, *כסתומים. **נישואין הא דאמרן.** דסתם לן תנא דידן כרבי, דקתני: רשאי השני, שני – אין, שלישי – לא. **כונסין אותו לכיפה.** אם חזר וחטא בשלישית, דמחזקינן ליה ברשיעא מתרי זימני שלקה.

קובעת

מסורת הש"ס

[עי' תוס' גיטין מו: ד"ה המוציא וכו']

ר"ה יא: [ברכות כט.]

[לעיל סב:]

[גירס' הערוך ססגוניתא פי' שנלטייר בשרו גוונים מן החולי]

[עירובין לז. לעיל כו. כתובות מג:]

ב"מ קו: סנהדרין פא:

[מנחות נב. חולין פו:]

נדה סד.

נ"ל נינהו. יעב"ץ

סנהדרין פא:

נדה סג:

נ"ל כסתמי. יעב"ץ

גליון הש"ס

שם א"ב לאירסה ומית עיין לקמן דף קח ע"א וכתו' שם ד"ה קטנה:

תוספות ישנים

אבין ישנו בחזרה. פי' שהיה תדיר חוזר תלמודו ומתקיים בידו אבל יצחק סומקא לא היה בקי כל כך א"נ י"מ אבין ישנו בחזרה פי' שהיה תמיד אצל ר' יוחנן ויודע כשהיה ר' יוחנן חוזר מדבריו אבל יצחק לא היה תמיד אצל רבו ולא ידע כשר' יוחנן מתחרט מדבורו: **מלקיות** דתנן מי שלקה ושנה ב"ד מכניסין אותו לכיפה. וא"ת למ"ד עבירות מחזיקות היכי מייתי דסתם לן תנא כר' דלמא היינו משום שעבר ג' פעמים והוחזק בעבירות וי"ל דדייק מדנקט מי שלקה ושנה משמע דבתרי הויא חזקה שנראה לו דוחק לפרש דלא נקט לקה אלא לאשמעינן דאיירי בעבירה שיש בה מלקות. ואפי' את"ל דקסבר עבירות מחזיקות שמא ס"ל כמ"ד כיפה צריכה התראה ומייתי שפיר דהא התרינו לו משום כיפה אחרי ב' מלקיות א"כ משמע דבתרי זמני הויא חזקה:

תוספות חד מקמאי

וב"ה פירש דלאחר עשר שנים דמפקינן לה מיניה היינו בכתובה ולאבא מרי ז"ל מסתברא דלא מפקינן בכתובה לעולם ואפי' לאחר כמה שנים ואפי' באה מחמת טענה. ואע"ג דאמרי' לקמן בשמעתי' אתא עובדא קמיה דר' יוחנן בבי כנשתא דקסרי ואמר יוציא ויתן כתובה ומסקנא מוקמי' לה בבא מחמת טענה [א] ההיא לאו טענה כגון דידעינן בבעל שהוא עקור ולא שייך למימר בה שמא עיניה נתנה באחר אבל הכא דבעינא למיפק מתותיה בטענה דאינו יורה כחץ לא מהמנינן לה למיפק מיניה בכתובה דאמרי' שמא עיניה נתנה באחר ומשקרה במאי דטענה. הרי כאן ג' סברות בבאה מחמת טענה דלדעת ר' אחא מפקינן מיניה אפי' בתוך עשר ובכתובה ולדעת הרב בעל (התוספות) [הלכות] [ב] לאחר עשר שנים מפקינן לה מיניה ובכתובה ולדעת אבא מרי ז"ל לא מפקינן לה מיניה לעולם בכתובה אפילו לאחר עשר אבל בלא כתובה מפקינן לה מיניה בעל כרחו בבא מחמת טענה ולאחר עשר שנים ויש לדחוק ולפ' בפי' הרב אלפס [ג] ובודאי אי לא הוא הוא דמר איהו מינה לא הוה איהי צריכה למימר מיניה. אלא כגון דאמר איהו בודאי מינה שהיא עקרה וסתותיה ומעיינה שאינה כשאר נשים ומשום הכי איצטריכה איהי למי' שאינו יורה כחץ אבל בודאי אם היתה אילונית ידועה ואמרה איהי שאינו יורה כחץ לא מהמנינן לה. ויש דמפרשי' דאשלישית וארביעית לרשב"ג קאי דאמר תצא בלא כתובה ואמרה איהי מיניה אית לה כתובה וא"ר אמי היא נאמנת ולא נהירא דא"כ לא משכחת לה שתצא בלא כתובה אם תרצה לטעון מיניה. אלא ודאי במקרה אי אמרה מיניה לא מהימנא ואין לה כתובה. והא דא' אם נשאת לג' [אנשים] לרשב"ג תצא בלא כתובה. איכא מאן דאמר בתוך עשר אם שהתה עמו כדי שלש עיבורין. ומסתברא בלאחר עשר אבל בתוך עשר יש לה כתובה שמא עדיין יזכה ליבנות הימנה. והראב"ד פירש אפי' בתוך עשר אם שהה כדי עבור תצא משלישי בלא כתובה. ודאתן עלה מיהת דאשה לא מפקדה אפריה ורבי'. איכא לעיוני מה ששנינו בנדרים [השמים] ביני לבינך למשנה ראשונה יוצאה בכתובה למשנה אחרונה יעשו דרך בקשה שמא עיניה נתנה באחר והא לא מפקדה וי"ל משנה ראשונה ודאי ס"ל דמפקדה ומשנה אחרונה דקא' שמא עיניה נתנה באחר לדברי המשנה ראשונה קאמ' שמא עיניה נתנה באחר ולמשנה אחרונה אטמאה אני לך ואנוטלה אני לך מן היהודים קאי אבל השמים ביני ובינך לא היה צריך לטעם שמא עיניה נתנה באחר דבלאו הכי נמי אינה יוצאה אליבא דהלכתא דלא מפקדה. ועוד יש להעמיד משנת נדרים כבאת מחמת טענה ולפיכך היה צריך לטעם שמא עיניה נתנה באחר וזה שלא כדברי רב אחא משבחה. ויש לפרש שיש מי שאומר שכיון שאינו יורה כחץ כמי שאינו יכול להזקק עמה דמי ולפיכך אי לאו משום טעמא דשמא עיניה נתנה באחר כופין אותו להוציא ולאו מילתא היא והראב"ד פי' השמים ביני ובינך שאינו נזקק עמה ומאמינין לה מגו דאי בעיא אמרה אינו יורה כחץ. ומאי דאתמר עלה בגמ' בנדרים צריך הביאור למדחק להאי פירושה ודוק ותשכח:

א) אולי צ"ל ההיא לאו בטענה דבעינא הוטרא לידה אלא כגון וכו'. ב) הוא בבה"ג בהלכות כתובות סי' ל"ז. ג) נראה דצ"ל דוודאי אי לאו דאמר איהו דמינה לא הוה איהי וכו'.

קוֹבַעַת לָהּ וֶסֶת עַד שֶׁתִּקְבְּעֶנָּה שָׁלֹשׁ פְּעָמִים, וְאֵין מְטַהֶרֶת מִן הַוֶּסֶת עַד שֶׁתֵּעָקֵר מִמֶּנָּה שָׁלֹשׁ פְּעָמִים. וְשׁוֹר הַמּוּעָד — דִּתְנַן: *א אֵין הַשּׁוֹר נַעֲשֶׂה מוּעָד עַד שֶׁיָּעִידוּ בּוֹ שְׁלֹשָׁה פְּעָמִים.§ ת"ר: ב נִיסֵּת לָרִאשׁוֹן וְלֹא הָיוּ לָהּ בָּנִים, לַשֵּׁנִי וְלֹא הָיוּ לָהּ בָּנִים, לַשְּׁלִישִׁי — לֹא תִּנָּשֵׂא אֶלָּא לְמִי שֶׁיֵּשׁ לוֹ בָּנִים. נִישֵּׂאת לְמִי שֶׁאֵין לוֹ בָּנִים — תֵּצֵא בְּלֹא כְּתוּבָּה. אִיבַּעְיָא לְהוּ: נִישֵּׂאת לַשְּׁלִישִׁי וְלֹא הָיוּ לָהּ בָּנִים, מַהוּ דְּלִיתְבְּעוּהָ הָנָךְ קַמָּאֵי? מִי מָצוּ אָמְרִי לָהּ: אִיגַּלַּאי מִילְּתָא דְּאַתְּ הוּא דְּגָרְמַתְּ, אוֹ דִּלְמָא מָצֵית אָמְרָה לְהוּ: הַשְׁתָּא הוּא דְּכָחֲשִׁי? ג מִסְתַּבְּרָא מָצֵית אָמְרָה לְהוּ: הַשְׁתָּא הוּא דְּכָחֲשִׁי. אִיבַּעְיָא לְהוּ: נִישֵּׂאת לָרְבִיעִי וְהָיוּ לָהּ בָּנִים, מַהוּ דְּתִיתְבְּעֵיהּ לַשְּׁלִישִׁי? אָמְרִינַן לָהּ: שְׁתִיקוּתִיךְ יָפָה מִדִּיבּוּרִיךְ, דְּמָצֵי אָמַר לָהּ: אֲנָא אַדַּעְתָּא דְּהָכִי לָא גַּרַשְׁתִּיךְ. מַתְקִיף לָהּ רַב פָּפָּא: אִי אִיהִי שָׁתְקָא אֲנַן מִי שָׁתְקִינַן? נִמְצָא גֵּט בָּטֵל וּבָנֶיהָ מַמְזֵרִין! ד אֶלָּא אָמְרִינַן: הַשְׁתָּא הוּא דִּבְרִיתָא.§ ה הוּא אָמַר: מִינָּהּ, וְהִיא אָמְרָה: מִינֵּיהּ — אָמַר רַבִּי אַמִי: דְּבָרִים שֶׁבֵּינוֹ לְבֵינָהּ נֶאֱמֶנֶת. וְטַעְמָא מַאי? ° הִיא — קַיְימָא לָהּ בְּיוֹרֶה כְּחֵץ, הוּא — לָא קִים לֵיהּ בְּיוֹרֶה כְּחֵץ. ו אֲמַר אִיהוּ: אֵיזִיל אִינְסִיב אִיתְּתָא וְאִיבְדּוֹק נַפְשַׁאי. אָמַר רַבִּי אַמִי: אַף בְּזוֹ יוֹצִיא וְיִתֵּן כְּתוּבָּה, שֶׁאֲנִי אוֹמֵר: כָּל הַנּוֹשֵׂא אִשָּׁה עַל אִשְׁתּוֹ — יוֹצִיא וְיִתֵּן כְּתוּבָּה. רָבָא אָמַר: ז נוֹשֵׂא אָדָם כַּמָּה נָשִׁים עַל אִשְׁתּוֹ, וְהוּא דְּאִית לֵיהּ לְמִיזַיְינִינְהִי.
הוא

רש"י

קוֹבַעַת לָהּ וֶסֶת. לִסְמוֹךְ עָלֶיהָ לִהְיוֹת דַּיָּהּ שְׁעָתָהּ, דִּתְנַן (נדה דף ב.): כָּל אִשָּׁה שֶׁיֵּשׁ לָהּ וֶסֶת – דַּיָּהּ שְׁעָתָהּ, וְלָא מְטַמְּאִינַן לָהּ לְמַפְרֵעַ מֵעֵת לְעֵת. וְעוֹד: דְּאִם קוֹבַעַת לָהּ וֶסֶת וְהִגִּיעַ זְמַן וְסְתָּהּ וְלֹא בָּדְקָה – טְמֵאָה, דְּאוֹרַח בִּזְמַנּוֹ בָּא. וְאֵינָהּ מְטַהֶרֶת מִן הַוֶּסֶת. אֲפִילּוּ נֶעֶקְרָה פַּעֲמַיִם, שֶׁבָּדְקָה בב' וְסָתוֹת וְלֹא רָאֲתָה, וְשִׁינְּתָה רְאִיָּיתָהּ לְיוֹם אַחֵר ב' פְּעָמִים – אֲפִילּוּ הָכִי מַחְזְקִינַן וְסְתָּהּ לִכְשֶׁיַּגִּיעַ, וְאִם לֹא בָּדְקָה – טְמֵאָה, דְּאוֹרַח בִּזְמַנּוֹ בָּא. אַדַּעְתָּא דְּהָכִי לָא גַּרַשְׁתִּיךְ. אִילּוּ הָיִיתִי יוֹדֵעַ שֶׁאַתְּ בַּת בָּנִים – לֹא גֵּרַשְׁתִּיךְ, וְנִמְצָא גֵּט בָּטֵל לְמַפְרֵעַ. מַתְקִיף לָהּ רַב פָּפָּא. וְאִי מָצֵי בַּעְלָהּ לְבַטּוּלֵי גֵּט בְּהָכִי, כִּי שָׁתַק מַאי הָוֵי? אֲנַן מִי שָׁתְקִינַן? הָא וַדַּאי אַדַּעְתָּא דְּהָכִי לֹא גֵּירְשָׁהּ. אֶלָּא מִדְּשָׁתְקִינַן – וַדַּאי לָא מָצֵי לְבַטּוּלֵי, דְּאָמְרִינַן לֵיהּ: מִסְּפֵיקָא קָא מְגָרַשְׁתְּ לָהּ, וְלָא אִיכְפַּת לָךְ בָּהּ, וְגָמַרְתְּ בְּדַעְתָּךְ לְגֵרוּשִׁין. אֶלָּא. אִי אִיכָּא לְמִפְטְרֵיהּ, הָכִי פָּטְרִינַן לֵיהּ; דְּאָמְרִינַן לֵיהּ: הַשְׁתָּא הִיא דְּאִיבְּרִית, שֶׁחָזְרָה לִהְיוֹת בְּרִיאָה מֵחוּלְיָיהּ. מִינָּהּ. יוֹדֵעַ אֲנִי שֶׁמֵּחֲמָתָהּ הוּא שֶׁאֵין לִי בָּנִים, וְלֹא אֶתֵּן כְּתוּבָּה: כָּל שִׁכְבַת זֶרַע שֶׁאֵינוֹ יוֹרֶה כְּחֵץ אֵינָהּ מַזְרַעַת*.
הוא

תוספות

ושור המועד. רבי לא פליג אקרא, אלא כלומר: התם מתקיימין דברי רשב"ג דלא מיתחזיק אלא בתלת זימני*:

נישאת למי שאין לו בנים תצא בלא כתובה. משמע דמן השני יש לה כתובה. וכן משמע בסמוך. דקאמר: נישאת לשלישי ולא היו לה בנים מהו דליתבעוה הנך קמאי? משמע שהשני נתן לה כתובה. ותימה לר"י: דאמאי יש לה כתובה מן השני? הא כיון דאסר לה לשלישי – א"כ סבר דבתרי זימני הויא חזקה? וכ"ת משום דאמרה ליה השתא הוא דכחשי ונסתחפה שדהו – אם כן מאי קבעי נישאת לשלישי כו', מי מצי אמרי לה דאיגלאי מילתא דאת גרמת, או דלמא מציא אמרה השתא הוא דכחשי, הלא אע"ג דלא נישאת לשלישי – אין לה כתובה מן השני אלא מטעם דמצי אמרה השתא הוא דכחשי! ואר"י: דלענין ממון מודה רבי דלא הוי חזקה עד דאיתחזיק בג' זימני, כדאשכחן בשור המועד. דבשור המועד לא פליג, כדפירשתי לעיל. ומיהו, תימה: דהשתא לענין איסורא לא סמכינן ארוב נשים דחזיין לבנים – משום דאיתרע רובא ע"י דאיתחזק בתרי זימני, ולענין ממון סמכינן אהאי רובא אע"ג דאיתרע בתרי זימני? ובעלמא* אמרי' איפכא: דאזלינן בתר רובא לענין איסורא, ולענין ממונא לא אזלינן(א).

תצא בלא כתובה. לכאורה נראה דוקא כששהתה עם השלישי, דומיא דנשאת לשלישי ולא היו לה בנים דבסמוך. וטעמא, דלענין ממון לא מחזקינן לה בעקרה עד דאיתחזק בתלת זימני. וא"ת: מן השלישי נמי לא תפסיד כתובה, דתימא ליה: השתא הוא דכחשי, כמו שאומרת לראשון ולשני! י"ל: דטענה דהשתא הוא דכחשי לא מהני להוציא, אלא לענין שלא תחזיר מה שגבתה מראשון ומשני. אבל קשה: דאי בשהה עמה י' שנים – היכי קאמר בסמוך גבי נישאת לרביעי והיו לה בנים, או דלמא מצי אמר לה אדעתא דהכי לא גרשתיך, והא אע"ג שהיא בת בנים – על כרחו הוא צריך לגרשה, כיון דלא זכה ליבנות ממנה! לכך נראה לר"י דלאלתר תצא שלא בכתובה, ולא משום קנס, דקנסוה כמו בשניות לפי שנישאת באיסור, מדקבעי בסמוך נישאת לרביעי והיו לה בנים מהו דתיתבעיה לשלישי. ואי קנס הוא – היכי תיתבע לשלישי? אלא נראה לר"י דבשלא הכיר בה איירי, ותצא שלא בכתובה – משום דהוי מקח טעות. ומ"מ, כשיש לה בנים מן הרביעי – חוזרת ותובעת לשלישי, דאיגלאי מילתא דלאו מקח טעות הוא. וכן מצא ר"י בהלכות דרב יהודאי גאון דבלא הכיר בה איירי. אבל הכיר בה – יש לה כתובה. והא דקתני בתוספתא נישאת למי שאין לו בנים תצא שלא בכתובה, מפני שנישואיה נישואי מינות – נראה שהסופרים טעו וכתבו מינות במקום טעות, דלא שייך כאן לשון מינות כלל.

אי איהי שתקא אנן מי שתקינן. וא"ת: דתנן ב"השולח" (גיטין מו: ושם): המוציא אשתו משום אילונית, רבי יהודה אומר לא יחזיר כו'. נשאת לאחר והיו לה בנים, והיא תובעת כתובתה, א"ר יהודה, אומר לה: שתיקותיך יפה מדבוריך. והשתא תקשה התם: אי היא שתקה – אנן מי שתקינן? וי"ל: דהתם, כיון דתקינן לרבי יהודה דלא יחזיר – ליכא למיחש לקלקולא. ורבנן, אע"ג דיחזיר – לא חיישינן התם לקלקולא, כיון דלא(א) חשיב לבדוק יפה בסימני אילונית – גמר בדעתו לגרש בכל ענין, ולהכי שתקינן. וכי תובעת כתובתה – מצי אמר לה: אדעתא למיתב כתובה לא גירשתיך. אבל הכא, דליכא תקנה דלא יחזיר – פריך שפיר: היכי שתקינן. ואפי' רבנן דלא חיישי התם לקלקולא – היינו דוקא בספק אילונית, דכיון דלא חשש לבדוק יפה – גמר לגרש בכל ענין. אבל הכא – אין בידו לבדוק ומוכיח הדבר שמשום בנים מוציאה, שכבר נישאת לשנים ולא היו לה בנים – איכא קילקולא, ולהכי פריך לכ"ע: אנן מי שתקינן. ואתי נמי שפיר הא דמשמע ב"השולח" דלא מצי מקלקל לה אלא כשאמר לה משום שם רע ונדר ואילונית אני מוציאך. והכא אע"ג דלא אמר לה משום עקרות אני מוציאך – מצי מקלקל לה, כדפי'. ומשני: דהכא לא שייך קילקולא, דאמרינן: השתא הוא דבריית, ובשעה שגירשה לא היתה ראויה. אבל בשם רע ונדר ואילונית – איכא קלקולא כשנתגלה לבסוף שהשם רע היה שקר, ולא היתה אילונית גם מתחלה. דאם – היתה לא הוה בריאה לעולם. ונדר נמי, כיון שיכול להפר – כאילו לא היה נדר. ואם תאמר: דבפ"ק דנדה (דף יב: ושם) אמר גבי אשה שאין לה וסת לא יחזיר אפי' הדר ואיתקן – משום קלקולא, והשתא והא אין יכול לקלקלה, דלאמר השתא הוא דבריאת, כדאמרי' הכא? ואר"י: דלא דמי, דקלקול בנים – אין רפואה מועלת כ"כ, ולכך בשעה שגירשה לא היתה בת בנים, דלא שכיח(ב) שתרפא – לגמרי מגרש לה. אבל קלקול דוסת – שכיח להתרפאות ולא גמר ומגרש, דיאמר אילו הייתי יודע שסם מועיל לה – לא הייתי מגרשה. וה"ר שלמה מדריו"ש תירץ: דהתם יש לחוש שתקבע וסת, כמו שהתחילה לקבוע סמוך לגירושין. דליכא למימר השתא הוא דבריאת – דהא איגלאי מילתא למפרע דבעוד שהיתה תחתיו איבריאת.

שבינו לבינה היא נאמנת. תימה: דבמאי איירי? דאי בשהתה עשר שנים עמו – למה לי טעמא דאין יורה כחץ? אפילו יורה כחץ נמי יוציא ויתן כתובה, לפי שלא זכה ליבנות ממנה. ואי לא שהה – ניחוש שמא עיניה נתנה באחר, כמשנה אחרונה דסוף נדרים (דף צ:) דתנן: בראשונה היו אומרים ג' נשים יוצאות ונוטלות כתובה: השמים ביני לבינך, פי': גלוי לשמים שאין יורה כחץ. דהכי משמע התם בגמרא כו', חזרו לומר: שלא תהא אשה נותנת עיניה באחר ומקלקלת על בעלה, אלא השמים ביני לבינך – יעשו דרך בקשה: יבקשו שניהם רחמים. או כמו שפר"ת: שיעשו סעודה ויתפייסו. וכ"ת: דהתם באינה באה מחמת טענה, והכא בבאה מחמת טענה – מ"מ ניחוש שמא נתנה עיניה באחר! ועוד: דהתם אם אין באה מחמת טענה – מאי נפקא לה מיניה. ובמשנה ראשונה למה אמרו יוציא ויתן כתובה? והיא דסוף שמעתין דכופין בבאה מחמת טענה, ולא חיישי' שמא עיניה נתנה באחר – איכא לאוקמא בידוע שהוא עקור, או בשהתה עמו י' שנים ויש לו בנים מאשה אחרת. דאי לאו דבאה מחמת טענה – לא היו כופין משום ביטול פריה ורביה, כיון דיש לו בנים. והך דהכא – ליכא לאוקמה בשהה י' שנים ויש לו בנים ובאה מחמת טענה – דא"כ אפי' יורה כחץ נמי כופין, כיון דלא זכה ליבנות ממנה. ומיהו, י"ל קצת: דכיון דיש לו בנים – אין לתלות *)באונס שלו, אלא אית לן למימר דאדרבה: איהי היא דלא זכתה, כדאמר לעיל. ולכך צריכה טעם דיורה כחץ. ואע"פ שיש לו בנים מאשה אחרת – שמא אח"כ נתקלקל. ויש להאמינה, דמוכח מילתא דשהה י' שנים ולא ילדה. ומה שלא אמרה מיד – משום דעד י' שנים לא הייתו חוששין לדבריה, דהוה תלינן בעיניה נתנה באחר. א"נ: איכא לאוקמא בדלא שהה עמה י' שנים ובאה מחמת טענה, דכיון שיש לה טענה מעליא – לא רצו להפסידה, ואוקמוה אדין משנה ראשונה, דלא חשו לעיניה נתנה באחר. והיא דנדרים – באינה באה מחמת טענה, ומ"מ, למשנה ראשונה – יוציא ויתן כתובה משום דשמא אין לה הנאת תשמיש כ"כ כשאין יורה כחץ. שטוענת שרוצה שיהא לה זכר, דמי שאין לו בנים חשוב כמת. והר"ר יצחק בן רבינו מאיר פירש: דהכא אניסת לשלישי קאי, דאמרו תצא בלא כתובה, וקמ"ל דאי אמרה דאין יורה כחץ דנאמנת ולא תפסיד כתובתה ממנו, דחזא ליה כיון דאין ראוי לבנים. וקשה לר"י: דמתוך הלשון משמע דהוא אמר מינה והיא אמרה מיניה, דמחמת שהיו יחד הרבה ולא הולידו מחמת כן באים לב"ד. ועוד ק"ק: דלמה אין לחוש שטוענת כן ומשקרת בשביל כתובה? וה"ר שמואל ב"ר חיים פירש: דהכא איירי כששהתה עם השלישי י' שנים, וכרשב"ג דאמר בתלת זימני הויא חזקה, דמסקנא דשמעתין כוותיה אתיא, כדקאמר: הוא אומר אפילה

*) אולי צ"ל בעונש.

תוספות חד מקמאי

אמר אזול ואנסיב אתתא ואבדוק נפשאי אמר רב [אמי] אף בזו יוציא ויתן כתובה לפי' רב אחא משבחא ולפי' המאור איכא לפרושי דאמילתא דלעיל קאי דאמרה איהי מיניה ואמר איהו אזול ואבדוק נפשאי דאנסיב אתתא ואם יהיה לו בנים ממנה נמצאו דבריה בדאים. אבל לפי אבא מרי ז"ל לאו אמילתא דלעיל קאי דא"כ היכי קאמר ר' אמי אף בזו יוציא ויתן כתובה דהא במילתי' דלעיל לית לה כתובה אלא אמתני' קאי דקתני שהה עמה עשר שנים אינו רשאי ליבטל ויוציא ויתן כתובה. אמר הבעל לא אגרשנה אלא אזול ואבדוק נפשאי ואם יהיו לו בנים ממנה א"ר [אמי] יוציא ויתן כתובה. הוא אומ' הפילה בתוך עשר ולא אוציא והיא אומרת לא הפלתי ויש לב"ד לכופו ולהוציא מידו א"ר אמי אף בזו היא נאמנת דאם איתה דאפלה נפשה בעקרתא לא מחזקא ואם נשאת לשלישי ואמרה איהי אפילו' ויש לי כתובה והוא אומר לא הפילה ולית לה כתובה בכה"ג מאי בעל מהימן. א)ואי אמרת נמי הפלית כלומר ויש לה כתובה והוא אומר לא הפילה כלל מסת' דאיהו נאמן ולא אמרי' בהא נפשה בנפלנית לא מחזקה להוציא כתובה מידו. ומאי דפי' הרב אלפס בהיא אמרה מיניה לענין כתובה קא' כדין מנה לי בידך והלה אומר איני יודע. לא נהיר דהיכא דאמר הוא מינה דבעי לאפוקי בלא כתובה ודאי כגון דאומר מינה קודם נישואין דאי בשעת נישואין היתה ראויה לבנים ולבתר הכי אינה ראויה לא מפסדה כתובה בהם דנסתחפה שדהו [וא"כ] איכא לעיוני דהא קי"ל כרב נחמן ור' יוחנן דאמרי מנה לי בידך והלה אמר איני יודע פטור אע"ג דקי"ל כר"ג גבי מוכת עץ אני והוא אומר לא כי אלא דרוסת איש את דאיהי מהימנא דברי ושמא ברי עדיף. הא אסיקנא בפ"ק דכתובות שאני התם דאיכא חזקה מגופיה אי נמי משום דאיכא למימר מיגו אבל הכא כי היכי דאיכא חזקה לדידה דבת בנים איכא חזקה לדידיה דיורה כחץ הוא ואמאי מפקי' מיניה כתובה. וגבי מתני' דנדרים נמי ששנינו דשלש נשים יוצאות ונוטלות כתובה איכא לעיוני הכי דאפי' משנה אחרונה לא פליג למשנה ראשונה אלא משום עיניה נתנה באחר הא לאו הכי כייפי' לאפוקי ויהיב לה כתובה ומ"ש מנה לי בידך והלה או' איני יודע פטור. וי"ל כיון דנתחייב לו בשעת נשואין בכתובה

(א) נראה דצ"ל ככה"ג מאי אי בעל מהימן או דהוה מהימנא ומשכבר לאו מהימן וכו'.

תוספות ישנים

שור מועד דתנן. וא"ת היאך יחלוק רבי על זה הלא מקראי שמעינן לה בפרק כילד הרגל וליכא מאן דפליג גבי תמול חד שלשום תרי וכו' דמשמעות דורשים איכא בינייהו וי"ל אה"נ ומ"מ מייתי ראיה ומוכח מקרא כרשב"ג דבתלתא זמני הויא חזקה. וא"כ יש לנו לומר דהדין עמו בכל מקום דבג' זמני הויא חזקה: **א**) ומסופק הר"י אם הא דקאמר תצא ר"ל לאלתר או לאחר עשר שנים. ונראה דר"ל לאלתר מדאמרינן לקמן דאמר לה אדעתא דהכי לא גרשתיך. ואי מיירי לאחר עשר שנים מאי קאמר אדעתא דהכי לא גרשתיך הלא בעל כרחו מגרש לה כדאמרינן במתני' אלא ודאי לאלתר תצא וטעמא משום דכיון שעברה על דברי חכמים שאסרוה לינשא לו קנסינן לה. א"נ מ"ה אמרינן תצא משלישי בלא כתובה דמקח טעות דמצי למימר אני לא ידעתי שהיתה עם שני אנשים עשר שנים ולא ילדה ואילו הייתי יודע כן לא נשאתיה. וקשה דאמר לקמן את הוא דגרמת ואי לאלתר מאי קאמר דלמא אם תשהה עמו עשר שנים תלד. לכ"נ דלאחר עשר שנים קאמר תצא. והא דקאמר לקמן דאמר לה אדעתא דהכי לא גרשתיך. ה"ק אם יבא אליהו ויאמר דבת בנים היא לא הייתי מגרשה וכל אשר כפוהו ב"ד להוציא כפיית טעות היתה. ור"ל תצא בלא כתובה ובלא תוספת דנשים שאמרו חכמים דיוצאות ואין להם כתובה אין להם תוספת: **השתא** הוא דכחשי. ואין להקשות א"כ משלישי נמי אמאי אין לה כתובה תאמר השתא הוא דכחשי וי"ל דטענת השתא הוא דכחשי מועלת לענין שלא יוציאו שני בעליה את הכתובה שנתנו בידה אבל אינה מועלת להוציא הכתובה מיד השלישי: **שתיקותיך** יפה ליך מדבוריך. משום דאמר לה אלו הייתי יודע שכן הוא אפי' אם נותנים לי מאה מנה לא הייתי מגרשך ונמצא גט בטל ובניה ממזרים ותימה דבגיטין משמע דלא מצי אמר לה הכי אלא כשאומר לה משום שם רע אני מוציאך. אבל הכא לא פירש לה דמשום עקרות הוא מוציאה וא"כ מציא אמרה ליה לא גרשתני משום עקרות כי לא פירשת כשנתת לי גט דמשום עקרות אתה נותן גט דודאי משום שנאה גרשתני. וי"ל דה"נ מיירי שפי' דמשום עקרות הוא מוציאה ועוי"ל דמיירי שפיר שלא פירש ואעפ"כ יש הוכחה בדבר דמשום עקרות הוציאה שהרי יצתה בלא כתובה ויכול לומר אילו הייתי יודע שלא היתה עקרה לא הייתי מוציאה אכן לא הייתי יכול לבודקה. אבל המוציא אשתו משום שם רע צריך לפרש לאם
לא

עין משפט נר מצוה

[עי' בתוספות בדיבור שלאחר זה ד"ה נשאת כו' דבשור המועד לא פליג כדפירשתי לעיל כו']

קיז א מיי' פ"ו מהלכות נזקי ממון הלכה ה:
קיח ב מיי' פט"ו מהלכות אישות הלכה יד סמג עשין מח טוש"ע אה"ע סימן קנד סעיף יז [וברב אלפס עוד סוף פ"ח דכתובות דף קכ.]:
קיט ג טוש"ע שם סעיף יח:
קכ ד שם סעיף יט:
קכא ה ו מיי' שם טוש"ע שם סעיף ו:
קכב ז מיי' פי"ד שם סמג שם טוש"ע אה"ע סימן א סעיף ט וסימן עו סעיף ז:

מסורת הש"ס

ב"ק כג: ע"ש
[חגיגה טו.]
[ב"ק מו: ב"ב כב:]

הגהות הב"ח

(א) תוס' ד"ה אי איהי וכו' כיון דלא חשש לבדוק יפה: (ב) בא"ד דלא שכיח שתתרפא וגמר ומגרש לה:

גליון הש"ס

גמ' הוא קיימא לה ביורה כחץ. עיין נדה דף מג ע"א תד"ה כיורה:

אהוא אָמַר: אַפֶּלַת בְּגוֹ עֶשֶׂר, וְהִיא אָמְרָה: לָא אַפֵּלִית. א"ר אַמִי: אַף בְּזוֹ הִיא נֶאֱמֶנֶת, דְּאִם אִיתָא דְּהִפִּילָה – נַפְשָׁהּ בְּעַקְרוּתָהּ לָא מַחְזְקָה. הִפִּילָה, וְחָזְרָה וְהִפִּילָה, וְחָזְרָה וְהִפִּילָה – הוּחְזְקָה לִנְפָלִים. בהוּא אָמַר: אַפִּילָה תְּרֵי, וְהִיא אָמְרָה: תְּלָת. אָמַר רַבִּי יִצְחָק בֶּן אֶלְעָזָר: עוּבְדָּא הֲוָה בֵּי מִדְרְשָׁא, וְאָמְרוּ: הִיא מְהֵימְנָא, דְּאִם אִיתָא דְּלָא אַפְּלָה – נַפְשָׁהּ בְּנִיפְלֵי לָא מַחְזְקָה.§ מתני' גהָאִישׁ מְצוּוֶּה עַל פְּרִיָּה וּרְבִיָּה, דאֲבָל לֹא הָאִשָּׁה. רַבִּי יוֹחָנָן בֶּן בְּרוֹקָה אוֹמֵר: עַל *שְׁנֵיהֶם הוּא אוֹמֵר °"וַיְבָרֶךְ אוֹתָם אֱלֹהִים וַיֹּאמֶר לָהֶם [אֱלֹהִים] פְּרוּ וּרְבוּ".§ גמ' מְנָא הָנֵי מִילֵּי? אָמַר ר' אִילְעָא מִשּׁוּם ר' אֶלְעָזָר בְּר' שִׁמְעוֹן: אָמַר קְרָא °"וּמִלְאוּ אֶת הָאָרֶץ וְכִבְשׁוּהָ" אִישׁ דַּרְכּוֹ לִכְבֹּשׁ, וְאֵין אִשָּׁה דַּרְכָּהּ לִכְבֹּשׁ. אַדְּרַבָּה, "וְכִבְשׁוּהָ" תַּרְתֵּי מַשְׁמַע! אָמַר רַב נַחְמָן בַּר יִצְחָק: "וְכִבְשָׁהּ" כְּתִיב. רַב יוֹסֵף אָמַר: מֵהָכָא, °"אֲנִי אֵל שַׁדַּי פְּרֵה וּרְבֵה" וְלָא קָאָמַר "פְּרוּ וּרְבוּ". וְאָמַר רַבִּי אִילְעָא מִשּׁוּם רַ' אֶלְעָזָר בְּרַ' שִׁמְעוֹן: כְּשֵׁם שֶׁמִּצְוָה עַל אָדָם לוֹמַר דָּבָר הַנִּשְׁמָע – כָּךְ מִצְוָה עַל אָדָם שֶׁלֹּא לוֹמַר דָּבָר שֶׁאֵינוֹ נִשְׁמָע. רַבִּי אַבָּא אוֹמֵר: חוֹבָה, שֶׁנֶּאֱמַר °"אַל תּוֹכַח לֵץ פֶּן יִשְׂנָאֶךָּ הוֹכַח לְחָכָם וְיֶאֱהָבֶךָּ". וְא"ר אִילְעָא מִשּׁוּם רַבִּי אֶלְעָזָר בְּרַ' שִׁמְעוֹן: מוּתָּר לוֹ לְאָדָם לְשַׁנּוֹת בְּדָבָר הַשָּׁלוֹם, שֶׁנֶּאֱמַר °"אָבִיךָ צִוָּה וגו' כֹּה תֹאמְרוּ לְיוֹסֵף אָנָּא שָׂא נָא וגו'. רַ' נָתָן אוֹמֵר: מִצְוָה, שֶׁנֶּאֱמַר °"וַיֹּאמֶר שְׁמוּאֵל אֵיךְ אֵלֵךְ וְשָׁמַע שָׁאוּל וַהֲרָגָנִי וגו'". *דְּבֵי רַבִּי יִשְׁמָעֵאל תָּנָא: גָּדוֹל הַשָּׁלוֹם שֶׁאַף הַקָּדוֹשׁ בָּרוּךְ הוּא שִׁינָּה בּוֹ. דְּמֵעִיקָּרָא כְּתִיב °"וַאדֹנִי זָקֵן" וּלְבַסּוֹף כְּתִיב "וַאֲנִי זָקַנְתִּי".§ "רַבִּי יוֹחָנָן בֶּן בְּרוֹקָה אוֹמֵר".§ אִתְּמַר, רַבִּי יוֹחָנָן וְרַ' יְהוֹשֻׁעַ בֶּן לֵוִי, חַד אָמַר: הֲלָכָה כְּרַבִּי יוֹחָנָן בֶּן בְּרוֹקָה, וְחַד אָמַר: אֵין הֲלָכָה כְּרַבִּי יוֹחָנָן בֶּן בְּרוֹקָה. תִּסְתַּיֵּים דְּרַבִּי יוֹחָנָן הוּא דְּאָמַר אֵין הֲלָכָה" דְּיָתֵיב רַ' אַבָּהוּ וְקָאָמַר מִשְּׁמֵיהּ דְּרַבִּי יוֹחָנָן הֲלָכָה, וְאַהַדְרִינְהוּ רַבִּי אַמִי וְרַבִּי אַסִי לְאַפַּיְיהוּ. וְאִיכָּא דְּאָמְרִי: רַבִּי חִיָּיא בַּר אַבָּא אֲמַר, וְאַהַדְרִינְהוּ רַבִּי אַמִי וְרַבִּי אַסִי לְאַפַּיְיהוּ. אָמַר רַב פַּפָּא: בִּשְׁלָמָא לְמַאן דְּאָמַר רַבִּי אַבָּהוּ אֲמָרָהּ – מִשּׁוּם כְּבוֹד בֵּי קֵיסָר לָא אָמְרוּ לֵיהּ וְלָא מִידֵי, אֶלָּא לְמַאן דְּאָמַר רַבִּי חִיָּיא בַּר אַבָּא אֲמָרָהּ – לֵימְרוּ לֵיהּ: לָא אָמַר רַבִּי יוֹחָנָן הָכִי! מַאי הֲוָה עֲלַהּ? ת"ש, דְּאָמַר רַ' אַחָא בַּר חֲנִינָא אָמַר רַ' אַבָּהוּ אָמַר רַ' אַסִי: עוּבְדָּא הֲוָה קַמֵּיהּ דְּרַבִּי יוֹחָנָן בִּכְנִישְׁתָּא דְּקֵיסָרִי, וַאֲמַר: "יוֹצִיא וְיִתֵּן כְּתוּבָּה". וְאִי ס"ד לָא מִפַּקְדָה – כְּתוּבָּה מַאי עֲבִידְתֵּהּ? דִּלְמָא בְּבָאָה מֵחֲמַת טַעֲנָה. כִּי הַהִיא דַּאֲתַאי לְקַמֵּיהּ דְּרַ' אַמִי, אָמְרָה לֵיהּ: ההַב לִי כְּתוּבָּה. אֲמַר לָהּ: זִיל, לָא מִיפַּקְדַתְּ. אָמְרָה לֵיהּ: מְסִיבוּ דִּילַהּ מַאי תֶּיהֱוֵי עֲלַהּ דְּהָךְ אִתְּתָא? אֲמַר: כִּי הָא – וַדַּאי כָּפֵינַן. והַהִיא דַּאֲתַאי לְקַמֵּיהּ דְּרַב נַחְמָן, אֲמַר לַהּ: לָא מִיפַּקְדַתְּ. אָמְרָה לֵיהּ: לָא בָּעֲיָא הַךְ אִתְּתָא *חוּטְרָא לִידָהּ וּמָרָה לִקְבוּרָה? אֲמַר: כִּי הָא – וַדַּאי כָּפֵינַן. *יְהוּדָה וְחִזְקִיָּה תְּאוֹמִים הָיוּ, אֶחָד נִגְמְרָה צוּרָתוֹ לְסוֹף תִּשְׁעָה וְאֶחָד נִגְמְרָה צוּרָתוֹ לִתְחִלַּת שִׁבְעָה. יְהוּדִית, דְּבֵיתְהוּ דְּרַ' חִיָּיא, הֲוָה לַהּ צַעַר לֵידָה, שַׁנַּאי מָנָא וַאֲתַיָא לְקַמֵּיהּ דְּרַ' חִיָּיא, אָמְרָה: אִתְּתָא מִפַּקְדָא אַפְּרִיָּה וּרְבִיָּה? אֲמַר לַהּ: לָא. אֲזַלָא אִשְׁתְּיָא סַמָּא דְּעַקַרְתָּא. לְסוֹף *אִיגַּלַּאי מִילְּתָא. אֲמַר לַהּ: אִיכּוּ יָלַדְתְּ לִי חֲדָא כְּרֵסָא אַחֲרִיתָא! דַּאֲמַר מָר: יְהוּדָה וְחִזְקִיָּה – אַחֵי, פַּזִּי וְטַוִי. אַחְוָותָא

תורה אור

הוּא אָמַר אַפֶּלַת בְּגוֹ עֶשֶׂר. כְּשֶׁבָּאוּ בָּאִין לְכוֹפוֹ לְהוֹצִיא, הוּא אוֹמֵר: "הִפִּילָה בְּתוֹךְ עֶשֶׂר", וַעֲדַיִין אֵין זְמַן לְהוֹצִיא, דִּתְנַן: מוֹנֶה מִשָּׁעָה שֶׁהִפִּילָה. וְהִיא אָמְרָה לָא אַפֵּלִית. אֶלָּא עֲקָרָה אֲנִי. הוּחְזְקָה לִנְפָלִים. וְיוֹצִיא וְיִתֵּן כְּתוּבָּה, שֶׁמָּא לֹא זָכָה לִיבָּנוֹת מִמֶּנָּה. אַפִּילָה תְּרֵי. וְלֹא הוֹצִיא. הִיא מְהֵימְנָא. וְכוֹפִין אוֹתוֹ. וְלֹא שֶׁהִיא תּוֹבַעַת גֵּירוּשִׁין, אֶלָּא שֶׁעָלֵינוּ לְכוֹפוֹ לְקַיֵּים פְּרִיָּה וּרְבִיָּה. מתני' אֲבָל לֹא הָאִשָּׁה. וְטַעְמָא מְפָרֵשׁ בַּגְּמָרָא. גמ' לוֹמַר דָּבָר הַנִּשְׁמָע. דִּכְתִיב (ויקרא יט) "הוֹכֵחַ תּוֹכִיחַ" – לְהוֹכִיחַ מִי שֶׁמְּקַבֵּל הֵימֶנּוּ. אָבִיךָ צִוָּה. יַעֲקֹב לֹא צִוָּה, אֶלָּא הֵם שִׁינּוּ מִפְּנֵי דַּרְכֵי שָׁלוֹם. אֵיךְ אֵלֵךְ. וּכְתִיב "וַיֹּאמֶר ה' עֶגְלַת בָּקָר תִּקַּח בְּיָדֶךָ וְאָמַרְתָּ לִזְבּוֹחַ" וגו' – הקב"ה צִוָּה לְשַׁנּוֹת. וַאדֹנִי זָקֵן. שָׂרָה אָמְרָה לְשׁוֹן בִּזּוּי, וּכְשֶׁגִּלָּה הקב"ה הַדָּבָר לְאַבְרָהָם, כְּתִיב: "לָמָּה זֶה צָחֲקָה שָׂרָה וגו' וַאֲנִי זָקַנְתִּי", וְשִׁינָּה הַדָּבָר מִפְּנֵי הַשָּׁלוֹם. מִשְּׁמֵיהּ דְּרַבִּי יוֹחָנָן. הֲלָכָה כְּר' יוֹחָנָן בֶּן בְּרוֹקָה. וְאַהַדְרִינְהוּ לְאַפַּיְיהוּ. דְּלֹא אֲמָרָהּ רַבִּי יוֹחָנָן מֵעוֹלָם. וְחָלְקוּ לוֹ כָּבוֹד, וְלֹא רָצוּ לְהַכְחִישׁוֹ: רַבִּי אַבָּהוּ קָרוֹב לַמַּלְכוּת הֲוָה, כִּדְאָמַר בְּסַנְהֶדְרִין (דף יד.) וּבִכְתוּבּוֹת (דף יז.): דִּמְשָׁרַן אַמְהָתָא דְּבֵי קֵיסָר: רַבָּא דְּעַמֵּיהּ, מְדַבְּרָנָא דְּאוּמָּתֵיהּ. עוּבְדָּא הֲוָה. וְהִיא תּוֹבַעְתּוֹ לְגָרְשָׁהּ, לְפִי שֶׁלֹּא הָיוּ לָהּ בָּנִים. דַּאֲתַאי לְקַמֵּיהּ דְּרַבִּי אַמִי. וְתוֹבַעְתּוֹ לְגָרְשָׁהּ. לָא מִפַּקְדַתְּ. וְאִם רוֹצָה אַתְּ לָצֵאת – אֵין לָךְ כְּתוּבָּה. מְסִיבוּ דִּילַהּ. בְּזִקְנָתָהּ מַה תְּהֵא עָלֶיהָ? חוּטְרָא לִידָהּ. עַד שֶׁתִּשָּׁעֵן עָלָיו לְעֵת זִקְנָתָהּ, וְאִם תָּמוּת יִקְבְּרֶנָּה. אִיכּוּ יָלַדְתְּ לִי חֲדָא כְּרֵסָא. וּמִי יִתֵּן שֶׁלֹּא שָׁתִית, וְתֵלְדִי לִי עוֹד כֶּרֶס אֶחָד, שְׁנֵי בָנִים. אַחֵי. תְּאוֹמִים. אַחְוָותָא

אפילה תרי, והיא אמרה תלתא. והשתא ניחא הא דקאמר הוא אומר מינה, שהרי עכשיו הוחזקה בתלת זימני, ויש לה להפסיד כתובתה. והיא אמרה מיניה. ומסיק דנאמנת. ואם טוענת דאין יכול להזקק – פסקו רבותינו דנאמנת אפילו למשנה אחרונה. דדוקא כשטוענת שאין יורה כחץ חיישינן שמא משקרת, לפי שבעלה לא ידע בה דמשקרת, כדאמרי' בסוף נדרים (דף צא.). אבל במילתא דידע בה דמשקרא – נאמנת מדרב המנונא, *לפי שאין האשה מעיזה פניה בפני בעלה א).

ולא קאמר פרו ורבו. אע"ג דלאדם הראשון קאמר "פרו ורבו" – ההוא ברכה בעלמא, ולא למצוה*.

ואי סלקא דעתך דלא מיפקדא כתובה מאי עבידתה. משמע דאי מיפקדא – ניחא דיש לה כתובה. ותימה: דאי מפקדא, א"כ מיענשא אפריה ורביה, ואית לן למימר לאדרבה: איהי היא דלא זכתה, כדמוכח לעיל! ותירץ ר"י בן ר' מאיר: דהכא בידוע שהוא עקור. אבל ק"ק: אמאי פריך כתובה מאי עבידתה, ולא פריך נמי: אמאי יוציא.

כי הא ודאי כפינן. פר"ח: דכל הנך דכופין מחמתה – דוקא מנה ומאתים אית לה, אבל תוספת – לית לה, דאדעתא למיפק לא אוסיף לה. ודייק מהא דאמר בריש "אע"פ" (כתובות דף נד:) תנאי כתובה ככתובה, נפקא מינה למורדת כו', ולא קאמר נפקא מינה לבאה מחמת טענה, וכיוצא בה. והא דלא קאמר נ"מ לשהה עמה עשר שנים, שיש לה נמי תוספת, דלא גרעה מאילונית, דאמר בסוף "אלמנה ניזונת" (שם ד' קא.) דיש לה תוספת – מילתא דפשיטא היא, כיון דלא מחמתה כופין, דמה היא יכולה אם ב"ד כופין אותו משום פריה ורביה. ור"ת מפרש: דלכל מילי הוי תנאי כתובה [ככתובה]. וממאנת וחברותיה דאין להם כתובה אע"פ שיש להם תוספת – התם משום דאיגלאי מילתא דלא נתקדשה מעולם. ולא יתכן דלענין "פרעתי" לא הוי תנאי כתובה ככתובה, דאכתובה – לא אמר כלום, ובתוספת – נאמן לומר "פרעתי", כדמוכח בעובדא דשבתאי בריה דרבי מריניס (ב"מ יז.) ויש לדחות: דהתם לא הוסיף חתן עצמו, כ"א שבתאי אביו, ולא חשיב כשאר תוספת. ואין להאריך כאן. כן מצאתי בתשובה אחת שפסק ריצב"א על אשה שהיתה טוענת על בעלה כי אין לאיש גבורתו. והאיש היה טוען כי היה לו גבורת אנשים, אך היא בועטת וגורמת שאין יכול לבעול, דלא מהימנא מדרב המנונא*, כיון שהיתה תובעת כתובה. והיכא שהודה הבעל שאין יכול לבעול – פסק דצריך ליתן גט וכתובה אפילו אינה באה מחמת טענה, כיון דאין יכול כלל לקיים לה עונה. ודוקא מנה ומאתים, אבל תוספת – לא יתן. דהא בנכנסה לחופה ולא נבעלה עמד בתיקו בריש ""אע"פ" (כתובות דף נו. ושם) דשמא לא כתב אלא ע"מ תיבת. ביאה ולרב האי גאון, דכל תיקו חולקין – שייך כאן דין חולקין. אבל נדוניתה שהכניסה לו – יחזיר הכל מה שידעו שהכניסה לו אבל מה שכותבין נדוניא גדולה לכבוד הכלה – נראה לו דהוי כעין תוספת. ומיהו, אם יכול להתקשות, ויש(א) כאן לכל הפחות הכנסת עטרה. אבל אין לו כח למרק – על זה נראה לו דיש תוספת, דיש כאן חיבת ביאה בהכנסת עטרה. ואם אין יכול לבעול מחמת שרחמה צר – כתב דאם המתין ג' שנים – דימתין עוד שנה. ואף על הקשוי כתב שאין לה למהר לסתור בניינה, כי רחמי שדי מרובים. ומטעם דפסק ר"ת דאין תוספת בבאה מחמת טענה משום דאדעתא למיפק לא כתב לה – זה הטעם אין שייך באין יכול ליבעול, דמידע ידיע דנישאת לו מתחילה לכך:

הדרן עלך הבא על יבמתו

קכג א מיי' פט"ו מהל' אישות הלכה יג טוש"ע אה"ע סימן קנד סעיף יג:

קכד ב מיי' שם טוש"ע שם סעיף יד:

קכה ג מיי' שם הלכה ב טוש"ע שם סימן א סעיף א:

קכו ד מיי' שם טוש"ע שם סעיף יג:

[לקמן קטז.]

קכז ה ו מיי' שם הלכה י טוש"ע שם סימן קנד סעיף ז:

[ועיין רש"א סנהדרין נט: סד"ה גמרא והרי פריה ורביה]

[בנדרים לא. וע' בהר"ן שם ובתוספות שם]

בראשית א · שם · שם לה · משלי ט · בראשית נ · שמואל א טז · בראשית יח

שבת קיא. גיטין מג: קדושין לה.

סוף מס' ר"ה [ב"מ פז.]

[כתובות סד.]

[נדה כז.]

תוספות חד מקמאי

בכתובה ה"ל כהלויתני ואיני יודע אם פרעתיך שחייב לדברי הכל כדתנן ההוא בהגוזל זוטא אבל במלתא דר"ג גבי מוכת עץ טוען הבעל שמעולם לא נתחייב לה בכתובה ולפום הכי אי לאו משום מגו א"נ משום חזקת דגופה הוה איהו מהימן:

תוספות ישנים

לא אמר משום שם רע אני מוציאה לא מצי אמר לה אילו הייתי יודע וכו' שהרי היה יכול לבודקה. ומדלא בדקה כאשר אנחנו רואים לבסוף כי שקר היה ודאי אמרינן שמחמת שנאה נתן לה גט ואפילו היה יודע בודאי שהשם רע שקר היה מגרשה. וגם כי לשם גרשה מדעתו. אבל הכא ב"ד נוו אותו לגרשה: **אי** איהי שתקה אנן מי שתקינן. וא"ת התם גבי המוציא את אשתו משום שם רע ואיילונית דאמרינן ר"י אומר אומרין לה שתיקותיך יפה ליך מדבוריך כי נשאת לאחר והיו לה בנים והיא תובעת כתובתה. אמאי לא פריך תלמודא אי איהו שתיק אנן מי שתקינן וי"ל דודאי הא דקאמר גט בטל ובניה ממזרים לא הוי אלא לעז בעלמא. וגם קשה אמאי לא קאמרי רבנן התם השתא הוא דבריאת כדאמרינן הכא וגם ר' יהודה למה לי טעמא דאמרינן שתיקותיך יפה ליך מדבוריך תיפוק לי דשמא השתא הוא דבריאת ומעיקרא הוות איילונית כשיגרשה ואין לה כתובה וצ"ל דבאיילונית לא מצי למימר השתא הוא דבריאת דלא שכיח דאיילונית תתרפא: **א)** אכן הכא קשה דלא איירי בעקר מדקאמר איהי קים לה ביורה כחץ א"כ אין אנו יודעין כלל שהוא עקר וי"ל דהכא קאי אהא דאמרינן לעיל נשאת לשלישי ולא היו לה בנים ושהתה עם שני אנשים עשר שנים עם כל אחד והיא אומרת מיניה ואין לו להוציאני בלא כתובה אע"פ שיש לו לגרשני בדין מ"מ לא הוחזקתי לעקרה כי לא שהיתי כי אם שתי פעמים עשר שנים וזאת הפעם איננה מן המספר כי בשבילך הוא וכתובה אין לי להפסיד בשתי פעמים כדפרישנא דדוקא להנשא אסירה והוא אומר מינה והויא הוחזקה לעקרה ואין לה כתובה. אכן בהלכות גדולות איתא דהכא מיירי בתוך עשר שנים ובבאה מחמת טענה והיא דנדרים מיירי באינה באה מחמת טענה ואי תקשי א"כ היכי הוה אמרינן מתחלה יוצאת ונוטלת כתובה לימא לה זיל לא מפקדת ומה לנו לדבריה. וי"ל דהתם מיירי דקאמרה שאין זרעו יורה כחץ ולא נהגיתי מביאתו: **לשנות** בדבר השלום. **א)** י"מ דאין זה שנוי גמור שהרי אמרה אחרי בלותי היתה לי עדנה בניחותא כלומר איני נבהלת אם אלד כי פרסתי נדה וחזרתי לנעורי אכן ואדוני זקן יוליד בנים. והמפרשים שאין זה שנוי גמור לפי שנוח לומר כן מפני כבוד שכינה. וגם גבי שמואל י"ל דאין זה שנוי גמור שהרי היה הולך למשוח לדוד ולזבוח זבח זבחים כאשר קרא לדוד. והשם אמר לו שלא יגלה לשאול שהולך למשוח ולזבוח רק לזבוח לבד: **ואי** ס"ד לא מפקדא כתובה מאי עבידתה. פי' הרי אמר לה אם תרצי להיות עמי הרי זה טוב ואם אין את רוצה להיות אנלי ה"ז גיטיך בלא כתובה ומשמע אבל אי מיפקדא ניחא [ותימה] לאדרבה אז תיקשי אמאי יתן לה כתובה דלמא איהי לא [זכתה] דלעיל פרכינן הכי ומשני כיון דלא מפקדא **ב)** מיענשא ולא יתן כתובה וי"ל להא דפרישית לעיל ניחא דמיירי הכא דידעינן ביה שהוא עקור וא"כ אי מיפקדא יתן לה כתובה דמיניה הוא מסתמא כיון שידוע הוא לעקור אבל פריך שפיר דאי לא מיפקדא כתובה מאי עבידתה הרי לא יבנה לעולם מאחרת ומשום האשה אין קפידא דהא לא מיפקדא:

א) נראה דצ"ל י"מ דהיה שינוי גמור שהרי אמרה וכו' ויש מפרשים שאין זה שינוי גמור לפי שנוח וכו' ועי' היטב בתוס' על התורה ובדברי הריב"א שם מה שהביא בשם תוס'. ב) נ"ל כיון דלא מפקדא לא יענשא אבל אי מפקדא א"ל ליתן כתובה וי"ל לפי מאי דפרישית וכו'.

הגהות הב"ח

(א) תוס' סד"ה כי הא וכו' אם יכול להתקשות ויש לו כח לכל הפחות וכו' דיש לה תוספת:

אַחְוָותָא. וְלָא מִיפַּקְדֵי? וְהָאָמַר רַב אַחָא בַּר רַב קְטִינָא א"ר יִצְחָק: *מַעֲשֶׂה בְּאִשָּׁה אַחַת שֶׁחֶצְיָהּ שִׁפְחָה וְחֶצְיָהּ בַּת חוֹרִין, וְכָפוּ אֶת רַבָּהּ וַעֲשָׂאָהּ בַּת חוֹרִין! אָמַר רַב נַחְמָן בַּר יִצְחָק: [א]מִנְהַג הֶפְקֵר נָהֲגוּ בָּהּ.§

הדרן עלך הבא על יבמתו

אַלְמָנָה [ב]לְכֹהֵן גָּדוֹל, גְּרוּשָׁה וַחֲלוּצָה לְכֹהֵן הֶדְיוֹט, הִכְנִיסָה לוֹ עַבְדֵי מְלוֹג וְעַבְדֵי *צֹאן בַּרְזֶל, עַבְדֵי מְלוֹג — לֹא יֹאכְלוּ בִּתְרוּמָה, עַבְדֵי צֹאן בַּרְזֶל — יֹאכְלוּ. [ג]וְאֵלּוּ הֵן עַבְדֵי מְלוֹג: אִם מֵתוּ — מֵתוּ לָהּ, וְאִם הוֹתִירוּ — הוֹתִירוּ לָהּ, אע"פ [ד]שֶׁהוּא חַיָּיב בִּמְזוֹנוֹתָן הֲרֵי אֵלּוּ לֹא יֹאכְלוּ בִּתְרוּמָה. [ה]וְאֵלּוּ הֵן עַבְדֵי צֹאן בַּרְזֶל: אִם מֵתוּ — מֵתוּ לוֹ, וְאִם הוֹתִירוּ — הוֹתִירוּ לוֹ, הוֹאִיל וְהוּא חַיָּיב בְּאַחֲרָיוּתָן הֲרֵי אֵלּוּ יֹאכְלוּ בִּתְרוּמָה. [ו]בַּת יִשְׂרָאֵל שֶׁנִּיסֵּת לְכֹהֵן וְהִכְנִיסָה לוֹ עֲבָדִים, בֵּין עַבְדֵי מְלוֹג בֵּין עַבְדֵי צֹאן בַּרְזֶל, הֲרֵי אֵלּוּ יֹאכְלוּ בִּתְרוּמָה. [ז]וּבַת כֹּהֵן שֶׁנִּיסֵּת לְיִשְׂרָאֵל וְהִכְנִיסָה לוֹ עֲבָדִים, בֵּין עַבְדֵי מְלוֹג בֵּין עַבְדֵי צֹאן בַּרְזֶל, הֲרֵי אֵלּוּ לֹא יֹאכְלוּ בִּתְרוּמָה.§ **גמ'** וְעַבְדֵי מְלוֹג לֹא יֹאכְלוּ בִּתְרוּמָה, אַמַּאי? לֶהֱוֵי כְּקִנְיָנוֹ שֶׁקָּנָה קִנְיָן! דְּתַנְיָא: מִנַּיִן לְכֹהֵן [ח]שֶׁנָּשָׂא אִשָּׁה [ט]וְקָנָה עֲבָדִים שֶׁיֹּאכְלוּ בִּתְרוּמָה — שֶׁנֶּאֱמַר °"וְכֹהֵן כִּי יִקְנֶה נֶפֶשׁ קִנְיַן כַּסְפּוֹ הוּא יֹאכַל בּוֹ". [י]וּמִנַּיִן לְאִשָּׁה שֶׁקָּנְתָה עֲבָדִים, [כ]וַעֲבָדָיו שֶׁקָּנוּ עֲבָדִים, שֶׁיֹּאכְלוּ בִּתְרוּמָה — שֶׁנֶּאֱמַר "וְכֹהֵן כִּי יִקְנֶה נֶפֶשׁ קִנְיַן כַּסְפּוֹ הוּא יֹאכַל בּוֹ". קִנְיָנוֹ שֶׁקָּנָה קִנְיָן — אוֹכֵל! כָּל הָאוֹכֵל — מַאֲכִיל, כָּל שֶׁאֵין אוֹכֵל — אֵינוֹ מַאֲכִיל. וְלָא? וַהֲרֵי עָרֵל וְכָל הַטְּמֵאִים, שֶׁאֵינָן אוֹכְלִין וּמַאֲכִילִין! הָתָם פּוּמַיְיהוּ כָּאֵיב לְהוּ. וַהֲרֵי מַמְזֵר, שֶׁאֵין אוֹכֵל — וּמַאֲכִיל! אָמַר רָבִינָא: [כ]קִנְיַן אוֹכֵל קָאָמַר, קִנְיַן אוֹכֵל — מַאֲכִיל, שֶׁאֵינוֹ אוֹכֵל — אֵינוֹ מַאֲכִיל. וְרָבָא אָמַר: מִדְּאוֹרַיְיתָא מֵיכַל אָכְלֵי, וְרַבָּנַן הוּא דִּגְזַרִי בְּהוּ, כְּדֵי שֶׁתֹּאמַר: אֲנִי אֵינִי אוֹכֶלֶת, עֲבָדַי אֵינָן אוֹכְלִין, זוֹנָה הִיא אֶצְלוֹ! הִלְכָּךְ אָתֵי לְאַפּוּקַהּ. רַב אַשִׁי אָמַר: גְּזֵירָה שֶׁמָּא תַּאֲכִיל לְאַחַר מִיתָה. אֶלָּא מֵעַתָּה, בַּת יִשְׂרָאֵל שֶׁנִּשֵּׂאת לְכֹהֵן לֹא תַּאֲכִיל גְּזֵירָה שֶׁמָּא תַּאֲכִיל לְאַחַר מִיתָה! אֶלָּא אָמַר רַב אַשִׁי: בְּאַלְמָנָה כֹּהֶנֶת דְּאָתְיָא לְאוֹרוּיֵי: מֵעִיקָּרָא אָכְלֵי בִּתְרוּמָה דְּבֵי נָשָׁא, אִינְסְבִי לֵיהּ לְהַאי — אָכְלֵי בִּתְרוּמָה דְּגַבְרַאי, וְהַשְׁתָּא הָדְרֵי לִי לְמִילְּתֵיהּ קַמַּיְיתָא, וְלָא יָדְעָה דְּמֵעִיקָּרָא לָא שָׁוְיתָהּ לְנַפְשָׁהּ חֲלָלָה, הַשְׁתָּא שָׁוְיתָהּ לְנַפְשָׁהּ חֲלָלָה. תֵּינַח אַלְמָנָה כֹּהֶנֶת, אַלְמָנָה בַּת יִשְׂרָאֵל מַאי אִיכָּא לְמֵימַר — בְּאַלְמְנוּתָהּ *לָא פְּלִיגִי רַבָּנַן. אִיתְּמַר: הַמַּכְנֶסֶת שׁוּם לְבַעְלָהּ, הִיא אוֹמֶרֶת: כֵּלַי אֲנִי נוֹטֶלֶת, וְהוּא אוֹמֵר: דָּמִים אֲנִי נוֹתֵן, הַדִּין עִם מִי? רַב יְהוּדָה אָמַר: הַדִּין

תורה אור: ויקרא כב

רש"י

אַחְוָותָא. תְּאוֹמוֹת וּבְנוֹתָיו הָיוּ. וַעֲשָׂאָהּ בַּת חוֹרִין. כְּדֵי שֶׁתְּהֵא מוּתֶּרֶת לִינָּשֵׂא וּמִדְּכָפֵינַן לְרַבָּהּ אַלְמָא מִפַּקְדָא. מִנְהַג הֶפְקֵר נָהֲגוּ בָּהּ. לְפִי שֶׁלֹּא הָיְתָה יְכוֹלָה לִינָּשֵׂא הָיְתָה מַפְקֶרֶת עַצְמָהּ וְחוֹטְאִים בָּהּ לְפִיכָךְ כָּפוּ אֶת רַבָּהּ לְשַׁחְרְרָהּ.

הדרן עלך הבא על יבמתו

אַלְמָנָה לְכֹהֵן גָּדוֹל: הִכְנִיסָה לוֹ עַבְדֵי מְלוֹג. מַה שֶּׁהָאִשָּׁה מַכְנֶסֶת לְבַעְלָהּ, וְשָׂמָה לוֹ לְקַבְּלָם עָלָיו בְּאַחֲרָיוּת כְּתוּבָּתָהּ, כְּמוֹ שֶׁכּוֹתְבִין: וְדָא נְדוּנְיָא דְּהַנְעָלַת לֵיהּ. וְהוּא מוֹסִיף כְּנֶגְדָּן וְכוֹתֵב: סַךְ הַכֹּל קִבֵּל עָלָיו פְּלוֹנִי כָּךְ וְכָךְ בִּכְתוּבָּתָהּ – קוֹרִין צֹאן בַּרְזֶל. וְיֵשׁ שֶׁמַּכְנֶסֶת מָמוֹן הַרְבֵּה וְאֵינָהּ כּוֹתֶבֶת כּוּלּוֹ בִּכְתוּבָּתָהּ, וּמְשַׁיֶּירֶת לְעַצְמָהּ – הֵן נִכְסֵי מְלוֹג. וְהַבַּעַל אוֹכֵל פֵּירוֹת, וְהַקֶּרֶן שֶׁלָּהּ קַיָּים. וְאִם מֵתוּ – מֵתוּ לָהּ, *אוֹ פָּחֲתוּ – פָּחֲתוּ לָהּ. לְשׁוֹן צֹאן בַּרְזֶל – קֶרֶן קַיָּים שֶׁאֵין פּוֹחֵת וְנִפְסָד, שֶׁאֲפִילּוּ מֵתוּ כּוּלָּן – אַחֲרָיוּתָן עָלָיו לְשַׁלֵּם לָהּ כְּשֶׁיָּמוּת אוֹ יְגָרְשֶׁנָּה. עַבְדֵי מְלוֹג לֹא יֹאכְלוּ. לְפִי שֶׁהֵן שֶׁלָּהּ, וְהִיא חֲלָלָה. וּלְקַמָּן בַּגְּמָרָא מְפָרֵשׁ טַעְמָא. בַּת יִשְׂרָאֵל שֶׁנִּיסֵּת לְכֹהֵן. אֲפִילּוּ עַבְדֵי מְלוֹג שֶׁאֵינָן שֶׁלּוֹ – יֹאכְלוּ, דְּהַיְינוּ קִנְיָנוֹ שֶׁקָּנָה קִנְיָן. וְיָלְפִינַן בַּגְּמָרָא דְּקִנְיָנוֹ שֶׁקָּנָה קִנְיָן אוֹכֵל. **גמ'** שֶׁנָּשָׂא אִשָּׁה וְקָנָה עֲבָדִים. אוֹ קָנָה עֲבָדִים. וּמִנַּיִן לְאִשָּׁה. בַּת יִשְׂרָאֵל לְכֹהֵן, שֶׁקָּנְתָה עֲבָדִים מִנִּכְסֵי מְלוֹג שֶׁלָּהּ, אוֹ עֲבָדָיו שֶׁל כֹּהֵן שֶׁקָּנוּ עֲבָדִים. וַעֲבָדָיו שֶׁקָּנוּ עֲבָדִים. וְאִ"ת: מַה שֶּׁקָּנָה עֶבֶד קָנָה רַבּוֹ, וּלְמַאי אִיצְטְרִיךְ קְרָא לְרַבּוּיֵינְהוּ? מַשְׁכַּחַתְּ לָהּ כְּגוֹן שֶׁנָּתְנוּ לוֹ לָעֶבֶד מָנֶה עַל מְנָת שֶׁאֵין לְרַבּוֹ רְשׁוּת בּוֹ. וְכֹהֵן כִּי יִקְנֶה נֶפֶשׁ קִנְיַן כַּסְפּוֹ. "קִנְיַן כַּסְפּוֹ" קְרָא יְתֵירָא, וְדָרְשִׁינַן דִּלְהָכִי אָתָא. וְהָכִי מַשְׁמַע: כֹּהֵן כִּי יִקְנֶה קִנְיַן כַּסְפּוֹ נֶפֶשׁ, שֶׁעַבְדּוֹ יִקְנֶה עֶבֶד – הוּא יֹאכַל בּוֹ. הֶעָרֵל. כֹּהֵן עָרֵל אֵינוֹ אוֹכֵל, וַעֲבָדָיו אוֹכְלִין, כְּדִתְנַן לְקַמָּן (דף ע.). פּוּמַיְיהוּ כָּאֵיב לְהוּ. כְּלוֹמַר, מְחוּסְּרֵי תַּקַּנְתָּא הֵם, אֲבָל עוֹמְדִים לִיתָּקֵן וְלֶאֱכוֹל. אֲבָל זוֹ שֶׁהִיא נַעֲשֵׂית חֲלָלָה – אֵין לָהּ תִּיקּוּן עוֹלָמִית. וַהֲרֵי מַמְזֵר. בַּת יִשְׂרָאֵל שֶׁנִּיסֵּת לְכֹהֵן וְיָלְדָה בַּת, וְהַבַּת נִיסֵּת לְמַמְזֵר וְיָלְדָה בֵּן וּמֵתָה, וְהַבֵּן קַיָּים, וַהֲרֵי אֵם אִמּוֹ אֵשֶׁת כֹּהֵן אוֹכֶלֶת בִּשְׁבִילוֹ תְּרוּמָה לְאַחַר מִיתַת בַּעְלָהּ – לְפִי שֶׁיֵּשׁ לָהּ זֶרַע מִן הַכֹּהֵן, כְּדִתְנַן בְּסֵיפָא דְּפִרְקִין (דף סט:), וְהוּא אֵינוֹ אוֹכֵל – דְּזָר הוּא. וְהוּא הַדִּין נַמִּי אִי כָּשֵׁר הֲוָה, שֶׁנּוֹלַד מִיִּשְׂרָאֵל כָּשֵׁר, נַמִּי אֵין אוֹכֵל, וּמַאֲכִיל אֶת אִמּוֹ. וְהָא דְּנָקַט לְאוֹתוּבֵי מַמְזֵר – מִשּׁוּם דְּמַתְנִיתִין הִיא. שֶׁמָּא תַּאֲכִיל. עַבְדֵי מְלוֹג שֶׁלָּהּ לְאַחַר מִיתַת הַכֹּהֵן בַּעְלָהּ. אֲבָל בְּעַבְדֵי צֹאן בַּרְזֶל לֵיכָּא לְמִגְזַר, דְּהַשְׁתָּא לָאו מִשּׁוּם דִּידָהּ אָכְלֵי אֶלָּא מִשּׁוּם כֹּהֵן שֶׁהוּא רַבָּן. אֶלָּא מֵעַתָּה בַּת יִשְׂרָאֵל שֶׁנִּישֵּׂאת לְכֹהֵן לֹא תַּאֲכִיל. עַבְדֵי מְלוֹג בִּתְרוּמָה. גְּזֵירָה שֶׁמָּא תַּאֲכִיל לְאַחַר מִיתָה. אַלְמָה תְּנַן בְּמַתְנִיתִין: בֵּין עַבְדֵי מְלוֹג בֵּין עַבְדֵי צֹאן בַּרְזֶל יֹאכְלוּ. בְּאַלְמָנָה כֹּהֶנֶת. בַּת כֹּהֵן שֶׁשָּׁבָה לִתְרוּמַת אָבִיהָ מִמִּיתַת בַּעְלָהּ. וְאִי אָמְרִינַן יֹאכְלוּ עַבְדֵי מְלוֹג בִּתְרוּמָה בְּחַיֵּי בַּעְלָהּ כֹּהֵן גָּדוֹל זֶה, מִשּׁוּם קִנְיָנוֹ שֶׁקָּנָה קִנְיָן, דְּלָא גָּרְעָה הַךְ חֲלָלָה מֵעֶבֶד שֶׁקָּנָה עֲבָדִים – אָתְיָא לְאוֹרוּיֵי הֶיתֵּירָא אַחַר מִיתָתוֹ, לְהַאֲכִילָם בִּתְרוּמָה מֵחֲמַת אָבִיהָ, דְּאָמְרָה: מֵעִיקָּרָא בְּאַלְמְנוּתִי הָרִאשׁוֹן הָיוּ עֲבָדַי אוֹכְלִין בִּתְרוּמָה דְּבֵי נָשָׁא. אִינְסְבִי לֵיהּ. לְכ"ג, אָכְלֵי עֲבָדַי בִּתְרוּמָה דְּגַבְרַאי. הַשְׁתָּא, כְּשֶׁמֵּת, הָדְרֵי לְמִילְּתָא קַמַּיְיתָא, וְיֹאכְלוּ עֲבָדַי בִּתְרוּמָה דְּבֵי נָשָׁא כִּמְעִיקָּרָא, בְּאַלְמְנוּתִי הָרִאשׁוֹן. אַלְמָנָה בַּת יִשְׂרָאֵל. דְּלָא אָתְיָא לְאוֹרוּיֵי, מַאי אִיכָּא לְמֵימַר? מַאי טַעְמָא לָא אָכְלֵי בְּחַיָּיו, הָא לָא גָּרְעָה מֵעֶבֶד שֶׁקָּנָה עֲבָדִים! לָא פְּלִיגֵי. לֹא חִילְּקוּ בֵּין אַלְמָנָה לְאַלְמָנָה. הַמַּכְנֶסֶת שׁוּם לְבַעְלָהּ. נִכְסֵי צֹאן בַּרְזֶל שֶׁשָּׂמָה לוֹ בִּכְתוּבָּתָהּ, וְהָיוּ בָּהֶן כֵּלִים וְדָבָר הַמְסוּיָּים, וּכְשֶׁגֵּירְשָׁהּ וּבָאתָה לִיטּוֹל כְּתוּבָּתָהּ. הִיא אוֹמֶרֶת כֵּלַי אֲנִי נוֹטֶלֶת וְהוּא אוֹמֵר דָּמִים אֲנִי נוֹתֵן. כְּמוֹ שֶׁקִּבַּלְתִּי עָלַי בְּשׁוּמָא, וּמֵאָז הֵן בְּאַחֲרָיוּתִי, וְשֶׁלִּי הֵן. הַדִּין

תוספות

אלמנה לכהן גדול: עבדי מלוג **לא יאכלו**. אפילו למ"ד(א) (גיטין דף מז:) קנין פירות כקנין הגוף דמי – לא חשיב בהכי קנין כספו, כיון שאין הגוף שלו, כמו שאין יוצאין בשן ועין לאיש, אפילו למ"ד קנין פירות כקנין הגוף דמי, כדאמר ב"החובל" (ב"ק דף פט: ושם). וקצת יש להביא ראיה דבתרומה אזלינן בתר קנין הגוף, דבריש פרק בתרא דכריתות (דף כד:) אמר, גבי המפקיר עבדו יצא לחירות, דמעוכב גט שחרור אוכל בתרומה, אע"פ שאין לרב פירות, אלא הגוף. ואפילו למ"ד קנין פירות כקנין הגוף דמי אתיא. **מנין** לכהן כו'. ממתניתין דקתני בסיפא "בת ישראל שניסת לכהן דעבדי מלוג שלה אוכלין" לא בעי למפרך – דה"א דאכלי מכח האשה עצמה שאוכלת, ולא מכח הבעל, משום קניינו שקנה קנין, להכי פריך מברייתא דקתני: קניינו שקנה קנין אוכל. וא"כ, אפילו אינה אוכלת – יש להם לאכול: **לכהן** שנשא **אשה** כו'. ה"ה שאירס, אלא נקט נשא משום דארוסה מדרבנן לא אכלה משום דעולא (כתובות דף נז:) או משום סמפון. **שנאמר** וכהן כי יקנה נפש. והא דדרשינן לעיל בפ' "הבא על יבמתו" (דף נז.) פלוע דכא כהן שנשא בת גרים – היינו מ"נפש" יתירא. **ועבדיו** שקנו עבדים. אפילו לרבי מאיר, דאמר (בקדושין דף כג:) אין קנין לעבד בלא רבו אפילו ע"מ שיצא בו לחירות, משכחת לה עבדים שקנו עבדים – במפקיר עבדו, דאוכל בתרומה, כדאמרינן בפרק בתרא דכריתות (ד' כד:). **גזירה** שמא תאכיל לאחר מיתה. ובעבדי צאן ברזל לא שייך למגזר, אפי' למ"ד (בסמוך) הדין עמה – דכל זמן שלא גבתה אותם בב"ד אוכלין מכחו, ואחר שגבתה ושמו לה ב"ד – הרי כאילו קנתה עבדים לאחר מיתת בעלה. **אלא** מעתה בת ישראל שניסת לכהן לא תאכיל שמא כו'. תימה: דלא דמי, דהתם ליכא למיטעי, דהא בחיי הבעל היתה אוכלת בעצמה ועכשיו אינה אוכלת. אבל כאן, אם יאכלו עבדים בחיי הבעל, אע"פ שבעצמה אינה אוכלת – איכא למגזר שמא תאכיל גם לאחר מיתה! ואית ספרים דגרסי: בת ישראל שניסת לכהן לא תאכל. ופריך: דהיא עצמה לא תאכל, שמא תאכל אחר מיתה. ולספרים דגרסי "נמי לא תאכיל" – איכא למימר דאכולי מילתא פריך: שלא תאכל ולא תאכיל, אלא דנקט לא תאכיל משום דניחא ליה לאקשויי מעבדים אעבדים.

כרשיי

עין משפט נר מצוה

קכח א מיי' פ"ט מהל' עבדים ה"ו סמג עשין פב טוש"ע יו"ד סי' רסז סעיף עט:
א ב מיי' פ"ז מהל' תרומות הל' כ טוי"ד סי' שלב:
ב ג מיי' פט"ז מהל' אישות הל' א סמג עשין מח טוש"ע אה"ע סי' פה סעי' ב:
ג ד מיי' שם פכ"ב הל' כה סמג שם טוש"ע שם סעי' טז:
ד ה מיי' שם פט"ז הל' א טוש"ע שם סעי' ב:
ה ו מיי' פ"ז מהל' תרומות הל' יח טוי"ד סי' שלב:
ו ז מיי' שם הלכה יט:
ז ח מיי' שם פ"ו הל' ג טור שם:
ח ט מיי' שם הל' א:

[וז"ל רש"י ב"מ סט: ד"ה אין מקבלין צאן ברזל וכו' ונראה לי שרוב המקבלים כך היו נוהגים לקבל בהמה דקה להכי קרי להו צאן]

ט י כ מיי' פ"ז שם הל' יח טור שם:

תוספות ישנים

עבדי מלוג לא יאכלו בתרומה. וא"ת למ"ד קנין פירות כקנין הגוף דמי אמאי לא יאכלו הא אית ליה בגווייהו פירות וי"ל דגבי תרומה כיון דהויא מן התורה בעינן קנין הגוף דכתיב כי יקנה נפש. וה"נ אמרינן מחוסר גט שחרור אוכל בתרומה אע"ג דאין (לבעל) [להאדון] בו שום פירות שהחררו מ"מ כיון דגופו קנוי לצריך גט אוכל בתרומה: **ועבדים** שקנו עבדים. פ"ה וא"ת הא למה לי קרא מה שקנה עבד קנה רבו וי"ל דאצטריך היכא שנתנו לו ע"מ שאין לרבו רשות בו וא"ת לר"מ דאמר (איהו) בקדושין (כ"ד) דאפ"ה לא קני ליה עבד דקני ליה רבו משום דאין קנין לעבד בלא רבו מאי איכא למימ' וי"ל דלר"מ נימא דעיקר קרא לאשה שקנתה עבדים ואגב אשה נקט עבדים שקנו עבדים וא"ת והא אשה נמי אמרינן מה שקנתה אשה קנה בעלה וי"ל דהכא מיירי שנתנו לה במתנה ע"מ שאין לבעלה רשות בהן ובמתנה זכתה ואין הבעל אוכל פירות. וא"ת ואמאי לא פריך מגופה דמתני' בת ישראל שנשאת לכהן והכניסה לו בין עבדי מלוג בין עבדי צאן ברזל אלמא קניינו שקנה קנין אוכל וי"ל דאי מהתם הוה ידע תלמודא שפיר דמשנינן דשאני התם שהיא אוכלת ולכך עבדיה אוכלין מכחה. אבל הכא שאינה אוכלת לא אכלי עבדיהם דהיינו כדמשני כל האוכל מאכיל וכו' אבל פריך מהא דקאמר מכח הפסוק דקנין כהן שקנה קנין אוכל וכיון דמקרא נפיק ס"ד דאין חילוק בין אוכלת לאינה אוכלת דמכח הכהן יש להם לאכול ומ"מ משני דווקא האוכל קאמר קרא דמאכיל אבל קנין שאינו אוכל אינו מאכיל: ת"ל וכהן כי יקנה נפש קנין כספו דדרשינן וכהן כי יקנה כספו נפש יאכל וכו'. וא"ת והא אצטריך לקמן לפצוע דכא כהן שנשא בת גרים. וי"ל דמיתורא דנפש קא דריש:

מסורת הש"ס

גיטין לח. [סג: ע"ש]

ס"א ואם הותירו הותירו

[לקמן קז. כתובות נב: כ"מ נג.]

תוספות חד מקמאי

אלמנה. הא דתנן אלמנה לכ"ג גרושה וחלוצה לכהן הדיוט והכניסה לו (נכסי) [עבדי] מלוג לא יאכלו אסקוה רבא ורב אשי בתראי דמדרבנן היא אבל מדאורייתא אכלי דלא גרע מקניינו שקנה קנין דתניא מנין לכהן שנשא אשה וקנה עבדים שיאכלו בתרומה שנאמר וכהן כי יקנה נפש קנין כו' אפילו קניינו שקנה קנין אוכל ומיהו רבינא ס"ל דמדאורייתא נמי לא אכלה דכל קנין שאוכל מאכיל קנין שאינו אוכל אינו מאכיל אבל מידי דלא קנין הוא אע"פ שאינו אוכל מאכיל שהרי ישראל אע"פ שאין אוכלים ומאכילין אם אמו שהיתה בת ישראל לכהן כדאיתא במתני'.

הגהות הב"ח

(א) תוס' ד"ה עבדי וכו' למ"ד קנין נ"ב פרק התולך דף לו:

גליון הש"ס

גמ' ועבדיו שקנו עבדים. עי' מז"ר דף סא ע"ב תד"ה אי הכי בעבדים נמי:

הַדִּין *עִמָּהּ, וְרַ' אַמִי אָמַר: הַדִּין עִמּוֹ. רַב יְהוּדָה אָמַר: הַדִּין עִמָּהּ, מִשּׁוּם *שֶׁבַח בֵּית אָבִיהָ — דִּידָהּ הָוֵי. רַ' אַמִי אָמַר: הַדִּין עִמּוֹ, כֵּיוָן דַּאֲמַר מָר: אִם מֵתוּ — מֵתוּ לוֹ, וְאִם הוֹתִירוּ — הוֹתִירוּ לוֹ, הוֹאִיל וְחַיָּיב בְּאַחֲרָיוּתָן — יֹאכְלוּ. אֲמַר רַב סָפְרָא: מִי קָתָנֵי "וְהֵן שֶׁלּוֹ"? "הוֹאִיל וְחַיָּיב בְּאַחֲרָיוּתָן" קָתָנֵי, וּלְעוֹלָם לָאו דִּידֵיהּ נִינְהוּ. וְכָל הֵיכָא דְּחַיָּיב בְּאַחֲרָיוּתָן אָכְלֵי בִּתְרוּמָה? וְהָתְנַן: ב יִשְׂרָאֵל *שֶׁשָּׂכַר פָּרָה מִכֹּהֵן — הֲרֵי זֶה יַאֲכִילֶנָּה כַּרְשִׁינֵי תְּרוּמָה. כֹּהֵן שֶׁשָּׂכַר פָּרָה מִיִּשְׂרָאֵל, אע"פ שֶׁמְּזוֹנוֹתֶיהָ עָלָיו — לֹא יַאֲכִילֶנָּה כַּרְשִׁינֵי תְּרוּמָה! וְתִסְבְּרָא? נְהִי נַמִי דְּמִחַיַּיב בִּגְנֵבָה וַאֲבֵדָה — בְּאוֹנָסֶיהָ, בְּכַחֲשָׁהּ, וּבְנִפְחַת דָּמֶיהָ מִי מִיחַיַּיב? הָא לָא דָּמְיָא אֶלָּא לְסֵיפָא: ג יִשְׂרָאֵל שֶׁשָּׁם פָּרָה מִכֹּהֵן — לֹא יַאֲכִילֶנָּה כַּרְשִׁינֵי תְּרוּמָה, אֲבָל כֹּהֵן שֶׁשָּׁם פָּרָה מִיִּשְׂרָאֵל — יַאֲכִילֶנָּה כַּרְשִׁינֵי תְּרוּמָה. יָתֵיב רַבָּה וְרַב יוֹסֵף בְּשִׁילְהֵי פִּרְקֵיהּ דְּרַב נַחְמָן, וְיָתְבֵי וְקָאָמְרֵי: תַּנְיָא כְּוָתֵיהּ דְּרַב יְהוּדָה, וְתַנְיָא כְּוָתֵיהּ דְּרַבִּי אַמִי. תַּנְיָא כְּוָתֵיהּ דְּרַ' אַמִי: ד עַבְדֵי צֹאן בַּרְזֶל יוֹצְאִין בְּשֵׁן וָעַיִן לְאִישׁ, אֲבָל לֹא לְאִשָּׁה. תַּנְיָא כְּוָתֵיהּ דְּרַב יְהוּדָה: ה הַמַּכְנֶסֶת שׁוּם לְבַעְלָהּ, אִם רָצָה הַבַּעַל לִמְכּוֹר — לֹא יִמְכּוֹר, וְלֹא עוֹד אֶלָּא אֲפִילּוּ הִכְנִים לָהּ שׁוּם מִשֶּׁלּוֹ, אִם רָצָה הַבַּעַל לִמְכּוֹר — לֹא יִמְכּוֹר. מָכְרוּ שְׁנֵיהֶם לְפַרְנָסָה, זֶה הָיָה מַעֲשֶׂה לִפְנֵי רשב"ג, וְאָמַר: הַבַּעַל מוֹצִיא מִיַּד הַלָּקוֹחוֹת. אָמַר רָבָא אָמַר רַב נַחְמָן: הֲלָכָה כְּרַב יְהוּדָה. א"ל רָבָא לְרַב נַחְמָן: וְהָתַנְיָא כְּוָתֵיהּ דְּרַ' אַמִי! אע"ג דְּתַנְיָא כְּוָתֵיהּ דְּרַ' אַמִי, מִסְתַּבְּרָא טַעֲמָא דְּרַב יְהוּדָה, מִשּׁוּם שֶׁבַח בֵּית אָבִיהָ. הַהִיא אִיתְּתָא דְּעַיְּילָה לֵיהּ לְגַבְרָא אִיצְטְלָא דְּמֵילְתָא בִּכְתוּבָּתָהּ, שְׁכֵיב, שְׁקַלוּהָ יַתְמֵי וּפָרְסוּהָ אַמִּיתְנָא. אָמַר רָבָא: ו קַנְיָיהּ מִיתְנָא. אֲמַר לֵיהּ נַאנַאי, בְּרֵיהּ דְּרַב יוֹסֵף, בְּרֵיהּ דְּרָבָא, לְרַב כָּהֲנָא: וְהָאֲמַר רָבָא אֲמַר רַב נַחְמָן: הֲלָכָה כְּרַב יְהוּדָה! אֲמַר לֵיהּ: מִי לָא מוֹדֶה רַב יְהוּדָה דִּמְחוּסַּר גּוּבַיְינָא? וְכֵיוָן דִּמְחוּסַּר גּוּבַיְינָא — בִּרְשׁוּתֵיהּ קָאֵי. רָבָא לְטַעֲמֵיהּ, דְּאָמַר רָבָא: *הֶקְדֵּשׁ, חָמֵץ, וְשִׁחְרוּר

רש"י

הַדִּין עִמָּהּ. וְתִטּוֹל כֵּלֶיהָ. יֹאכְלוּ. וּמִדְּאָכְלֵי בִּתְרוּמָה — ש"מ דִּידֵיהּ נִינְהוּ. שֶׁשָּׂכַר פָּרָה מִיִּשְׂרָאֵל. וְהָא שׂוֹכֵר חַיָּיב בְּאַחֲרָיוּתָהּ אִם נִגְנְבָה אוֹ נֶאֶבְדָה, וְקָתָנֵי לֹא יַאֲכִילֶנָּה כַּרְשִׁינֵי תְּרוּמָה: ה"ג. וְתִסְבְּרָא נְהִי נַמִי דְּחַיָּיב בִּגְנֵבָה וַאֲבֵדָה בְּאוֹנָסֶיהָ וּבְכַחֲשָׁה וּבְנִפְחֶתֶת דָּמֶיהָ מִי מִיחַיַּיב. שׂוֹכֵר פָּטוּר מִן הָאוֹנָסִין, וְכֵן אִם כָּחֲשָׁה וְאִם הוּזַל דָּמֶיהָ. הָא. מַתְנִיתִין לָא דָּמְיָא אֶלָּא לְסֵיפָא. אֲבָל כֹּהֵן שֶׁשָּׁם פָּרָה מִיִּשְׂרָאֵל. בְּדָמִים, כְּשֶׁשְּׂכָרָהּ הֵימֶנּוּ שָׁמָאָהּ לוֹ, *וְהִתְנָה עִמּוֹ לְהַחֲזִירָהּ לוֹ בְּדָמִים הַלָּלוּ, שֶׁאִם תִּכְחַשׁ אוֹ תָּמוּת אוֹ יוּזְלוּ פָּרוֹת בָּעוֹלָם יִתֵּן הַדָּמִים. יַאֲכִילֶנָּה כַּרְשִׁינֵי תְּרוּמָה. הוֹאִיל וְקִבְּלָהּ בְּאַחֲרָיוּתוֹ, וְאַף עַל פִּי שֶׁחוֹזֶרֶת בְּעֵינֶיהָ אִם לֹא יִפְחֲתוּ דָּמֶיהָ — כָּל כַּמָּה דְּלָא הָדְרָה דִּידֵיהּ הוּא. וְגַבֵּי עֲבָדִים נַמִי, אע"ג דְּהָדְרִי בְּעֵינַיְיהוּ, כֵּיוָן דִּלְעִנְיַן יוּקְרָא וְזוֹלָא קָיְימִי בִּרְשׁוּתֵיהּ — אָכְלֵי. בְּשִׁילְהֵי פִּירְקֵיהּ. כְּשֶׁסִּיֵּים הַדְּרָשָׁה. בְּשֵׁן וָעַיִן לְאִישׁ. אִם סִימֵּא הַבַּעַל אֶת עֵינוֹ. אֲבָל לֹא לְאִשָּׁה. אִם סִימְּתָה עֵינוֹ, דְּלָאו דִּידָהּ הוּא. לֹא יִמְכּוֹר. שֶׁאִם יְגָרְשֶׁנָּה תִּטּוֹל כֵּלֶיהָ. מָכְרוּ שְׁנֵיהֶם. אוֹ זֶה אוֹ זֶה. לְפַרְנָסָה. אוֹרְחָא דְּמִילְּתָא נָקַט, שֶׁאֵין אָדָם מוֹכֵר כְּלֵי תַּשְׁמִישָׁיו אֶלָּא לִמְזוֹנוֹת. הַבַּעַל מוֹצִיא. לָא מִיבַּעְיָא דְּאִם מָכַר הוּא בְּלֹא דַּעְתָּהּ, וּמֵת אוֹ גֵּרְשָׁהּ — דְּהִיא מוֹצִיאָה מִיַּד הַלָּקוֹחוֹת, אֶלָּא אֲפִילּוּ מֵתָה הִיא הוּא מוֹצִיא מִיַּד הַלָּקוֹחוֹת, דִּמְכִירָה לָאו מְכִירָה הֲוַאי (א), *(שֶׁמָּא יָמוּת הוּא בְּחַיֶּיהָ וְנִמְצֵאת מְכִירָה שֶׁלֹּא כַּדִּין) כָּל זְמַן שֶׁהִיא קַיֶּימֶת. קַנְיֵיהּ מִיתְנָא. תַּכְרִיכֵי הַמֵּת אִיסּוּרֵי הֲנָאָה הֵן כְּהֶקְדֵּשׁ, דְּגָמַר "שָׁם" "שָׁם" מֵעֶגְלָה עֲרוּפָה, בְּפֶ' "נִגְמַר הַדִּין" (סנהדרין דף מז:). מִי לָא מוֹדֶה רַב יְהוּדָה דִּמְחוּסַּר גּוּבַיְינָא. אע"ג דְּהַדִּין עִמָּהּ, מוֹדֶה הוּא דְּכָל כַּמָּה דְּלָא גְּבָתִינְהוּ מִינֵּיהּ — לָאו בִּרְשׁוּתָהּ קָיְימִי, אֶלָּא שִׁיעְבּוּדָא בְּעָלְמָא אִית לָהּ עֲלַיְיהוּ. דְּהָא אִם נֶאֶנְסוּ אוֹ נֶאֶבְדוּ — חַיָּיב בְּאַחֲרָיוּתָן. וְכֵיוָן דִּבְרְשׁוּת יַתְמֵי נִינְהוּ — אָתֵי הֶקְדֵּשׁ דְּאַקְדְּשׁוּהּ יַתְמֵי וּמַפְקַע לָהּ לְשִׁיעְבּוּדַיְיהוּ, וְיָהֲבִי דְּמֵי. רָבָא לְטַעֲמֵיהּ כו'. הֶקְדֵּשׁ — דַּוְקָא קְדוּשַּׁת הַגּוּף, כִּי הַאי גַּוְונָא. אֲבָל קְדוּשַּׁת דָּמִים — לָא, כִּדְתְנַן (ערכין דף כג:): מוֹסִיף עוֹד דִּינָר וּפוֹדֶה הַנְּכָסִים הַלָּלוּ כו'. חָמֵץ. גּוֹי שֶׁהִלְוָה אֶת יִשְׂרָאֵל עַל חֲמֵצוֹ אַחַר הַפֶּסַח — אָסוּר בַּהֲנָאָה, דְּאָתֵי אִיסּוּר חָמֵץ וּמַפְקַע לֵיהּ לְשִׁיעְבּוּדָא דְּגוֹי. וְהָא דִּתְנַן בְּפֶרֶק "כָּל שָׁעָה" (פסחים דף ל.): מוּתָּר בַּהֲנָאָה — רַבָּה מוֹקֵי לָהּ הָתָם כְּשֶׁהִרְהִינוֹ אֶצְלוֹ, שֶׁנְּתָנוֹ יִשְׂרָאֵל בְּבֵיתוֹ שֶׁל גּוֹי, דְּהַהוּא לָא מִיחַסַּר גּוּבַיְינָא. וְשִׁחְרוּר

תוספות

כרשיני תרומה. אר"י: דעיקרם קיימי למאכל בהמה. דאם היו עיקרם לאדם — היה אסור ליתנם לבהמה, משום הפסד תרומה. ומ"מ חזו לאדם, דאי לא חזו כלל לאדם — פטורין מתרומה ומעשר, כדאמר בריש "כלל גדול" (שבת דף סח. ושם).

לא יאכילנה כרשיני תרומה. והא דתנן (עירובין דף כו:) מערבין לישראל בתרומה, דשרי בהנאה! אר"ת דהיינו דוקא הנאה שאין של כילוי, אבל הנאה של כילוי כגון להאכיל לבהמתו — אסור. וכן להדליקה ולהסיקה תחת תבשילו, כדתנן במסכת תרומות (פי"א מ"י) מדליקין בשמן של תרומה(ב) במבואות האפילות ע"ג כהן, ברשות כהן. פי': כשיש שם כהן שצריך לאותה אורה, דנר לאחד נר למאה, אבל לא ברשות ישראל. והא דאמר ב"כל שעה" (פסחים דף לד.) אבא שאול גבל של בית רבי הוה והיה מחמם חמין *בשמן של תרומה שנטמאה — אמר ר"ת: דהיינו לכהנים שבבית רבי. וטעמא דלא אסור אלא הנאה של כילוי מפרש ר"י: משום דדרשינן בפ' "במה מדליקין" (שבת דף כו. ושם) גבי אין מדליקין בטבל טמא "את משמרת תרומותי" — בשתי תרומות הכתוב מדבר, אחת תרומה טמאה ואחת תרומה טהורה. מה תרומה טהורה — אין לך בה אלא משעת הרמה ואילך, פירוש: עיקר הנאתה, דהיינו אכילה — אף תרומה טמאה אין לך בה עיקר הנאה, דהיינו הדלקה, אלא משעת הרמה ואילך. ומהכא יליף דאין מדליקין בטבל טמא. ובטבל טהור נמי(ג) משמע גבי עובדא דרבי פנחס בן יאיר (חולין דף ז.) דאסור הנאה של כלוי, היינו משום דהדר ילפינן תרומה טהורה מטמאה. ולא כמו שפירש שם בקונטרס *דכ"ש בטבל טהור. דכל שכן לא הוי, דטהור מטמא הוא דילפינן, וכי היכי דילפינן לאסור טבל בהנאה של כילוי — הכי נמי ילפינן לאסור זו בתרומה, דמשעת הרמה לא הותרה אלא לכהנים ולא לישראל* א).

***ישראל** ששכר פרה מכהן שמאכילה כרשיני תרומה אע"פ שמזונותיה עליו. אר"י: היינו משום דבהמה האוכלת היא קנין כספו של כהן, וישראל אין נהנה אלא הדמים, והרי הוא כמוכר תרומה לכהן והדמים שלו. אבל כהן ששכר פרה מישראל — לא יאכילנה, דלאו קנין כספו דכהן הוא, דשכירות לא קניא.

דמחייב בגניבה ואבדה כו'. כאן משמע דהלכתא כמ"ד דשוכר כנושא שכר דמי ב"האומנים" (ב"ב דף פ:) וכן הלכה, כדמשמע בריש "המפקיד" (שם דף לו.) גבי שוכר ושואל פעמים שניהם באשם כו', ובפרק "השואל" (שם דף נז.) גבי ההוא דאגר כודני לבי חוזאי*. **אבל** כהן ששם פרה מישראל. פירש בקונטרס: כששכרה הימנו התנה להחזיר לו דמים אלו אם תכחש או תמות או יוזלו הפרות. ואר"י, דאסור לעשות כן משום רבית, כדמוכח בפרק "איזהו נשך" (שם דף סד.*) אלא איירי בשואל. **עבדי** צאן ברזל יוצאין בשן ועין. תימה לר"י: מה ראיה מייתי מהכא לרבי אמי? דהא רב יהודה נמי מודה דיוצאין בשן ועין לאיש, דחשיב כעבדו, כי היכי דחשיב כספו לענין תרומה, דתנן: עבדי צאן ברזל יאכלו בתרומה, דתרומה ושן ועין ענין אחד הוא, כדפי' במתני'. ועוד הקשה הר' משה כהן: דמי לא מודה רב יהודה דמיחסרי גוביינא, וא"כ ברשותיה קיימי, ושחרור מפקיע מידי שעבוד, כדאמר לקמן גבי איצטלא דמילתא דפרסוה אמיתנא, דאפי' לרב יהודה מפקיעין מידי שיעבוד. דאפי' שחרור דשן ועין, דממילא, אמרינן ב"החובל" (ב"ק דף פט: ושם) דמפקיע מידי שיעבוד? ואין לומר דרבה ורב יוסף דדייקי מהכא תניא כוותיה דרבי אמי לית להו דרבא, דאמר שיחרור מפקיע מידי שיעבוד — דהא ממתני' ד"השולח" (גיטין דף מ: ושם) דייק לה. ואין לומר לית להו ההוא טעמא דלקמן כיון דמיחסרי גוביינא ברשותיה קיימי, דהא רבא אית ליה ההוא טעמא בסמוך ואפ"ה קאמר רבא לרב נחמן: והא תניא כוותיה דרבי אמי! ותירץ ה"ר שמואל בר' חיים מוורדי"ש: דדייק מאבל לא לאשה. ומחיים לא איצטריך, דפשיטא, אלא לאחר מיתה קאמר דאין יוצאין לאשה — משום דהדין עמו. **הבעל** מוציא מיד הלקוחות. פי' בקונטרס: דאפילו מתה היא, מוציא הוא מיד הלקוחות. משמע מתוך פירושו דכל זמן שהאשה חיה — אין הבעל יכול להוציאם כשמכר הוא עצמו, אלא כשמתה האשה, דאז יורש כחה, והיא היתה יכולה למחות בחיים. ותימה הוא: דכיון שהמכירה קיימת כל זמן שהאשה שותקת — למה תוכל לבטל מכירתו במחאתה על חנם? דמחיים אין לה בהם כלום. ועוד: דאפילו אם האשה תוכל להוציא מחיים — נראה דאין הבעל יכול להוציא אחר מיתה, ולא אמרינן דבמקום אשתו קאי — כיון שמכר בעצמו, כדמשמע בפרק "מי שהיה נשוי" (כתובות דף נא:) גבי ההוא גברא דזבין כתובתה דאימיה בטובת הנאה, אמר: אי אתיא אם ומערערה — לא מפלינא לך. שכיבא אימיה, אתא איהו וקא מערער. סבר רמי בר חמא: איהו במקום אימיה קאי, א"ל רבא: נהי דלאחריות דאימיה לא קביל עילויה — אחריות דידיה קביל עילויה, ונראה כפר"ח: דאין המקח קיים כלל אפי' שעה אחת, דתקון רבנן שלא תהא אשה צריכה לטרוח ולחזור להוציא מיד הלקוחות אחר מיתת הבעל. דלא דמי לאשה הטורפת מנכסים משועבדים לכתובה — דהתם הויא מכירה, דשמא לא תהא אשה צריכה לטרוח שיפרעו לה כתובתה, או תטרוף מבני חרי. אבל היכא שאין יכולים לסלקה בשאר נכסים — תקנו שהמקח בטל לאלתר. פוסל

תוספות ישנים

הואיל וחייב באחריותן יאכלו והיינו דלא כרב יהודה. ותימה דהא כרב יהודה מצי שפיר אתיא דרב יהודה נמי מודה שהם ברשותו של בעל קודם שיגרשנה ומ"ה אכלי בתרומה וי"ל דלרב יהודה כיון דלאחר מיתה וגירושין יהיו שלה דקאמר הדין עמה וגם מחיים קאמר רב יהודה לקמן אם רצה הבעל למכור לאו כדידיה דמו ולא היה להם לאכול בתרומה דאין גופן קנוי לו: **א)** וה"ר משה תירץ דכל הנאות של תרומה מותרו' לישראל רק להאכיל לבהמתו משום דהויא בכלל נפש כדדרשינן על כל נפשות מת לא יבא שומע אני אפילו נפש בהמה כשהוא אומר לאביו ולאמו וכו' משמע דבהמה הויא בכלל נפש ולהכי אמרי' הכא דהיכא שהפרה של ישראל אין להאכילה תרומה כדכתיב וכהן כי יקנה נפש קנין כספו דבעינן שהנפש יהיה קנין כספו כשאוכל בתרומה: **יוצאין** בשן ועין לאיש. וא"כ הדין עמו דאי הדין עמה לא היה יכול להוציאם לחרות דאע"ג דרב יהודה מודה לאוכלין בתרומה

תוספות חד מקמאי

איתמר המכנסת שום לבעלה הוא אומר (כלי) [דמים] אני נותן והיא אומרת כלי אני נוטלת רב יהודה אומר הדין עמה משום שבח בית אביה והלכתא כותיה וכ"ש אם אמרה דמים אני נוטלת שהדין עמה משום דינא ולא משום שבח בית אביה תניא כותיה דרב יהודה המכנסת שום לבעלה אם רצה הבעל למכור לא ימכור מכרו שניהם לפרנסה היה מעשה לפני ר"ג ואמר הבעל מוציא מיד הלקוחות. כתב הרב אלפס הא מילתא דר"ג בעיא ולא אפשיטא שפיר ולא עבדי' בה עובדא ואבא מרי ז"ל כתב מכרו שניהם לפרנסה כיון שלקח מן האיש וחזר ולקח האשה. וכ' רש"י לא מבעיא אשה עצמה שמוציאה מן הלקוחות אפי' בחיי בעלה כיון שיכולה לומר בשעת גביית כתובה כלי אני

מסורת הש"ס: גיטין מד: | [כתובות עט:] | נ"ל התנה להחזיר לו דמים אלו אם תכחש או הוזלו דמיה שיהיו דמיה ברשותיה | ע"ז טו. [תרומות פי"א מ"ט] | כמ"ס אין זה | לעיל מו. כתובות נט: גיטין מ: נדרים פו: ב"ק פט: | [וע"ש בתוס' ד"ה אי תקפה]

עין משפט נר מצוה / הגהות הב"ח: [נ"ל בחיטין] | [שבת כו.] | [וע"ע תוספות פסחים לג: ד"ה כדי] | [וע"ע תוספות ב"ק נז: ד"ה סברוה]

ושחרור — מפקיעין מידי שעבוד. א"ר יהודה: [א]הכניסה לו שני כלים באלף זוז, ושבחו ועמדו על שני אלפים — אחד נוטלתו בכתובתה, ואחד נותנת דמים ונוטלתו, מפני שבח בית אביה. מאי קא משמע לן, שבח בית אביה דידה הוי — הא אמרה רב יהודה חדא זימנא! מהו דתימא: ה"מ — היכא דמטיא למשקל בכתובתה, אבל מיתן דמי ומישקל לא — קמ"ל.§

מתני' [ב]בת ישראל שניסת לכהן ומת, והניחה מעוברת, לא יאכלו עבדיה בתרומה, מפני חלקו של עובר. *שהעובר פוסל, ואינו מאכיל, דברי ר' יוסי. אמרו לו: מאחר שהעדת לנו על בת ישראל לכהן — אף בת כהן לכהן ומת, והניחה מעוברת — לא יאכלו עבדיה בתרומה, מפני חלקו של עובר.§

גמ' איבעיא להו: טעמא דרבי יוסי משום דקסבר עובר במעי זרה זר הוא, או דלמא: ילוד — מאכיל, שאינו ילוד — אינו מאכיל? למאי נפקא מינה — לעובר במעי כהנת, מאי? אמר רבה: היינו טעמא דרבי יוסי: דקסבר עובר במעי זרה — זר הוא. רב יוסף אמר: [ג]ילוד — מאכיל, שאין ילוד — אינו מאכיל. מיתיבי, אמרו לו לר' יוסי: מאחר שהעדת לנו על בת ישראל לכהן — בת כהן לכהן מהו? אמר להם: זו שמעתי, וזו לא שמעתי. אי אמרת בשלמא עובר במעי זרה זר הוא — היינו דקא"ל: "זו שמעתי, וזו לא שמעתי". אלא, אי אמרת ילוד — מאכיל, שאין ילוד — אין מאכיל, מאי "זו שמעתי וזו לא שמעתי" איהי היא! קשיא. אמר רב יהודה אמר שמואל: זו דברי ר' יוסי, אבל חכמים אומרים: יש לו בנים — אוכלים משום בנים, אין לו בנים — אוכלים משום אחים. אין לו אחים — אוכלים משום משפחה כולה. "זו" ולא ס"ל?! הא א"ל שמואל לרב חנא בגדתאה: *פוק איתי לי בי עשרה, דאימא לך באנפייהו: המזכה לעובר — קנה! אלא: *"זו" וס"ל. מאי קמ"ל, דפליגי רבנן עליה דרבי יוסי — ומי פליגי? (א) מתיב רבי זכאי: זו עדות העיד ר' יוסי מפי שמעיה ואבטליון, והודו לו. [עדיות פ"ה] אמר רב אשי: מי קתני "וקבלו"? "והודו לו" קתני, דמסתבר טעמיה. ת"ר:* [ד]הניח בנים — אלו ואלו אוכלים. הניחה מעוברת — אלו ואלו אין אוכלים. הניח בנים והניחה מעוברת, עבדי מלוג אוכלים, כדרך שהיא אוכלת. עבדי צאן ברזל לא יאכלו, מפני חלקו של עובר, שהעובר פוסל ואינו מאכיל, דברי ר' יוסי. רבי ישמעאל ברבי יוסי אומר משום אביו: הבת — מאכלת, הבן — אינו מאכיל. [ה]ר"ש בן יוחי אומר: זכרים — יאכלו כולן, נקבות — לא יאכלו, שמא ימצא עובר זכר, ואין לבנות במקום הבן כלום. מאי איריא שמא ימצא עובר זכר? תיפוק ליה דנקבה נמי פסלה! חדא ועוד קאמר; חדא — דנקבה נמי פסלה, ועוד: שמא ימצא עובר זכר, ואין לבנות במקום הבן כלום. זכרים יאכלו? והאיכא עובר! קסבר: אין

רש"י

ושחרור. ישראל שעיבד עבדו לב"ח, ושחררו הלוה — יצא לחירות, והמלוה גובה מלוה* ממקום אחר. בכתובתה. שהיא אלף זוז, דהא מאי דאשבחו — ברשותי' אשבחו. אבל למיתן דמי ומישקל לא. אלא שלו הן עולמי', קמ"ל.

מתני' והניחה מעוברת. אע"פ שיש לה בנים הימנו והיא אוכלת בתרומה – לא יאכלו עבדי צאן ברזל בתרומה, לפי שהן של יורשים, ויש לעובר בהן חלק, ואין לעובר כח להאכילן בתרומה. אי משום דקסבר: עובר במעי זרה זר הוא, אי משום דקסבר: ילוד – מאכיל, שאין ילוד – אין מאכיל, שנאמר (ויקרא כב) "ויליד ביתו הם יאכלו בלחמו", קרי ביה: יאכילו. שהעובר פוסל. אם בת כהן נישאת לישראל, והניחה מעוברת, ואין לה בן אחר – פוסלה מלשוב לבית אביה כנעוריה. ואינו מאכיל. אם בת ישראל לכהן היא, ומת והניחה מעוברת – אין בעובר כח להאכילה, וה"ה לעבדים. אף בת כהן לכהן. כיון דאמרת שאין ילוד אינו מאכיל, היאך העבדים אוכלין בתרומה מפני חלקו של עובר? שהרי עבדיו הן, ואין אוכלים אלא בשבילו, והוא אין בו כח להאכיל.

גמ' במעי כהנת. בת כהן מעוברת מכהן. אי אמרת משום זרות – ליכא, ואי משום שאין ילוד – איכא. וזו לא שמעתי. לאיסור, אלא להיתירא. יש לו בנים אחרים. לבד מעובר זה. אוכלים. העבדים בשביל בנים, דעובר לית ליה זכיה. בשביל משפחה. שאין אחד מישראל שאין לו יורשין, וכל זמן שלא נולד העובר זוכה הקרוב לירושת כהן, ואוכלים בגינו. זו דברי רבי יוסי. ולא סבירא ליה לשמואל דעובר אית ליה זכיה. בגדתאה. בעל אגדה. ל"א: שם מקום שהוא בבבל ששמו בגדד*. בי עשרה. לפרסם את הדבר. הניח בנים. הכהן, ולא הניחה מעוברת. אלו ואלו. עבדי מלוג ועבדי צאן ברזל אוכלין. דעבדי מלוג אוכלין בשבילה, שהיא אוכלת בשביל בניה, ועבדי צאן ברזל אוכלין בשביל בנים. הניחה מעוברת. ולא הניח לה בנים. אלו ואלו אין אוכלין. שהעובר אינו מאכיל לא את אמו ולא את העבדים. הניח בנים והניחה מעוברת עבדי מלוג אוכלים. שהם שלה ואין לעובר חלק בהן, והיא אוכלת בשביל בניה. עבדי צאן ברזל לא יאכלו מפני חלקו של עובר. שיש לו חלק בהן, דאית ליה זכייה, ולא ידעינן הי מתרמי לחלקו. לפיכך עבדים אסורים לאכול. שהעובר פוסל. בת כהן המעוברת מישראל. ואינו מאכיל. בת ישראל המעוברת מכהן, ולא את עבדיו. הבת מאכלת. לקמן מפרש לה. כולן זכרים. ל"ג "כולן", אלא ה"ג: זכרים יאכלו כולן נקבות לא יאכלו. אם יש זכר בבנים – אוכלים העבדים בשבילו, ולא חיישינן לחלקו של עובר, דשמא נקבה היא ואין לה חלק במקום בן, ואת"ל זכר הוא – שמא תפיל, שכל היולדות – מחצה זכרים ומחצה נקבות, ויש שמפילות – סמוך מיעוטא דמפילות למחצה דנקיבות, הוו להו זכרים הראוים לירש מיעוטא, ולמיעוטא לא חיישינן. כולן נקבות – לא יאכלו, שמא יהא עובר זכר כו'. תיפוק ליה. דא"נ הויא נקבה פסלה, דכיון שכל אותן שלפניו נקבות – יש לעובר חלק בהן, אפילו היא נקבה.

תוספות

פוסל ואין מאכיל. נראה לפרש שהעובר פוסל בעבדי אביו, ואין מאכיל את אמו. דתרווייהו אעבדים ליכא למימר: פוסל בעבדי אביו ואין מאכיל בעבדי אביו, דכיון דאשמועינן דפוסל – היכי משכחת שיאכיל. ובקונטרס פירש כולה מילתא אאמו, ואע"ג דאעבדים קאי – ה"ק: שהעובר פוסל ואין מאכיל את אמו וה"ה לעבדיו דפוסל.

למאי נפקא מינה לעובר במעי כהנת. אע"ג דע"כ דרשינן ההיא דרשא דילוד מאכיל, דמהאי טעמא אמרינן לקמן דבת ישראל לכהן והניחה מעוברת דלא מאכיל, דהתם לא שייך טעמא דעובר במעי זרה זר הוא, דאפילו זר מאכיל את אמו, ואפילו ממזר, כדאמרינן לקמן (ד' סט:), – מ"מ מיבעיא ליה לענין עבדים, דאיכא למימר דוקא לענין אמו דכתב בה קרא "ויליד ביתו הם יאכלו", דמינה דרשינן שמאכיל את אמו, דרשינן ילוד מאכיל. אבל עבדים שאוכלים מטעם קנין כספו – לא קאמר קרא ילוד מאכיל, שאינו ילוד לא.

היינו דקאמר זו שמעתי כו'. ורבנן שהיו אומרים לו כן הוו סברי דטעמא משום דילוד מאכיל.

אוכלין בשביל כל המשפחה כולה. ה"מ למימר דטעמא דרבנן משום דלא סבירא להו דרשא דשאין ילוד אין מאכיל לגבי עבדים, ולית להו נמי דעובר במעי זרה זר הוא. אלא קבלה היתה בידו דטעמא משום דלא זכי בהו עובר. וקשה תימה: דהא מסתמא מעשה ידיהם עד שיולד הוא לעובר ולא לבני משפחה, קשה לר"י: דתנן בפרק "יוצא דופן" (נדה ד' מד.) דבן יום אחד פוסל מן התרומה, ופריך בגמרא: מאי איריא בן יום אחד? אפי' עובר נמי! ומשני רב ששת: מתניתין בכהן שיש לו ב' נשים, אחת גרושה ואחת שאינה גרושה, ויש לו בנים משאינה גרושה ובן יום אחד מן הגרושה פוסל בעבדי אביו. ולאפוקי מדרבי יוסי, דאמר: עובר נמי פוסל, קמ"ל: בן יום אחד – אין, עובר – לא. והשתא, למה ליה לאוקמי כשיש לו שתי נשים? אפי' אין לו אלא אחת גרושה, ודוקא בן יום אחד אבל עובר – לא, דאוכלין בשביל כל המשפחה כולה לרבנן! [ב"ב קמב.] ואר"י: דרב ששת לטעמיה, דאית ליה ב"מי שמת"* המזכה לעובר קנה, ולא אכלי בשביל המשפחה. ולהכי מוקי בשיש לו בנים משאינה גרושה, ואין העובר שבמעי גרושה פוסל, משום דלא חיישינן למיעוטא, דסמוך מיעוטא דמפילות למחצה דנקבות והוו להו זכרים מיעוטא, כדלקמן, ולאפוקי מדר' יוסי, דרבי יוסי חייש למיעוטא. ואתי שפיר דבפרק "מי שמת" (ב"ב קמב. ושם) פריך למ"ד המזכה לעובר קנה מדתנן "יוצא דופן" (נדה דף מד. ושם) בן יום אחד נוחל ומנחיל, אבל עובר לא – ולא פריך מרישא דבן יום אחד פוסל, דאיכא לאוקמא בשתי נשים כו'.

זו וסבירא ליה. אע"ג דשמואל פסיק ב"אע"פ" (כתובות דף נט.) כרבי יוחנן הסנדלר, דאין אדם מקנה דשלב"ל – שמואל חשיב עובר כבא לעולם.

תוספות ישנים

רב יוסף אמר ילוד מאכיל שאינו ילוד אינו מאכיל אבל לא ס"ל שיהא הטעם משום דעובר במעי זרה זר הוא דא"כ מאי קא מיבעיא להו לרבנן מאחר שהעדת מה ענין זה לזה בת ישראל שנשאת לכהן עובר במעי זרה [הוא] ולא אכלי אבל במעי כהנת לא פסיל. [ורבה אמר לך אי] טעמא דר' יוסי משום דילוד מאכיל שאינו ילוד אינו מאכיל א"כ מה בעו מיניה רבנן בכהן במעי כהנת הלא ההיא היא כדקאמר תלמודא אלא טעמא משום דעובר במעי זרה הוא: ואימא קמייהו המזכה לעובר קנה. וא"ת והא אמר שמואל הלכה כר' יוחנן הסנדלר דאמר אין אדם מקנה דבר שלא בא לעולם וי"ל שאני הכא שהמתנה הויא בעולם ולא נהירא דהא אמרינן בגיטין דלדבר שלא בא לעולם לא קנה אף דבר שישנו בעולם. וי"ל דעובר חשוב כדבר שהוא בעולם ומיירי הכא בהוכר עוברה. וא"ת ומאי קאי דקאמר זו ולא ס"ל וכו' והאמר ליה שמואל וכו' המזכה לעובר קנה ואת אמרת דהלכה כחכמים דאין לעובר זכיה דלמא דגם רבנן [ס"ל] דמזכה לעובר קנה דאית ליה לעובר [זכיה] ובחוששין למיעוט קמיפלגי דהרבה תנאי פליגי בהא ונפרש דר' יוסי סבר חוששין למיעוט שמא יהיה (לה) זכר קיים ורבנן לא חיישי דסמוך מיעוטא דמפילות למחצה זכרים ומחצה נקבות והו"ל זכרים מיעוטא וי"ל דא"א לומר כן מדקאמר שמואל לעיל אליבא דרבנן אין לו אחין אוכלין בשביל כל המשפחה א"כ טעמייהו משום דאין מזכה לעובר קונה דא"ל משום דאין חוששין למיעוט דהא לאו מיעוט איכא דבין יהיה הולד זכר או נקבה יהיה לולד חלק בעבדים שאף נקבה תירש קודם לאחיו ולמשפחה:

כולם זכרים יאכלו. הקונטרס לא גריס כולם זכרים דאפי' אי ליכא אלא חד זכר יאכלו בגללו ולא חיישינן למיעוט שמא

תוספות חד מקמאי

אני נוטלת אשתכח דדילה נינהו ומצי למימר נחת רוח עשיתי לבעלי אלא אפילו הבעל עצמו במקום אשה קאי ומוציא מיד הלקוחות מכח האשה. ומכרו שניהם לפרנסה רבותא נקט אפילו לפרנסה ששניהם צריכין לו אפ"ה הבעל מוציא מיד הלקוחות ולא מבעי' מה שהכניסה לו מטלטלין שהאשה מוציאה מיד הלקוחות אפי' בחיי בעלה וכן הבעל מכוחה אלא אפי' הכניסה לו קרקעות וקבלם עליו הבעל נמי שיכולה לומר בשעת גביית כתובה קרקעותי אני נוטלת אשתכח דדילה נינהו ואם מכרם הבעל האשה מוציאה מיד הלקוחות אפי' בחיי בעלה וכן אם לקח מן האיש וחזר ולקח מן האשה מה שלקח מן האשה הוא בטל מיד שיכולה לומר נחת רוח עשיתי לבעלי כיון שנטל הבעל עליו. (אבל נכסי מלוג שהגוף שלה אמרי'

בפ' ח"ה שאינה יכולה לומר נחת רוח עשיתי לבעלי). ואפי' בחיי הבעל מוציאה מיד הלקוחות ולכך נהגו בנרבונה לכתוב בכתובה הוא נתן לה קרקע פלוני והיא הביאה לו בנדונייתה כדי שתוכל לטרוף מן הלקוחות בחיי הבעל אם מכרן. וכן אם לקח מן האיש וחזר ולקח מן האשה כיון שיכולה לומר נחת רוח עשיתי לבעלי נמי (א)שלקח מן האשה היא ותוציא מהלקוחות אפלו בחיי בעלה ולפיכך אמר רשב"ג שהבעל מוציא מיד הלקוחות מכח האשה. ופ' השולח פי' בדין נכסי האיש והאשה ודין אפותיקי סתם ודין אפותיקי מפורש. ומיהו מילתא פשיטא היא דנכסי הבעל אינה מוציאה מיד הלקוחות אם מכרם הבעל עד שעת גביית כתובה והיינו דאמר פ' האשה שנפלו לה. אבעי לזבוני מי לא מזבין. ורש"י פי' ל"מ אם מת הוא או גרשה שהאשה מוציאה מיד הלקוחות אם מכר הוא בלא דעתה אלא אפי' מתה היא הוא מוציא מיד הלקוחות דשעת מכירה לאו מכירה ודאית היא שמא ימות הוא ונמצאת מכירה שלא כדין והראב"ד פי' מכרו שניהם לפרנסה כגון שמכר האחד בפני חברו וקא' רשב"ג שאם מכרה האשה בפני בעלה הבעל מוציא מיד הלקוחות. וזהו לשונו מה שפסק הרב אלפס דרבנן דאמרי עובר לית ליה זכיה מסתברא כוותייהו דרבא קאי כרבנן בפ' מי שמת ואביי פליג עליה וכו' וקי"ל אביי ורבא הלכה כרבא וכבר כתבתי דבר זה בפרק מי שמת. מצאתי כתוב בחדושי שחדשתי לפני אבא מארי ז"ל שמעשה היה בלוניל לפני הראב"ד ז"ל ולפני זקני הרב ר' משולם ולפני הרב ר' שמואל ב"ר משה ע"ה באחד שנתן מתנה לבנו קודם ארבעים יום ליצירתו והיה מחלוקת ביניהם יש מהם שאמרו שהמתנה מתנה הואיל ודעתו של אדם קרובה אצל העובר ויש מהם שאמרו שאין המתנה מתנה דכיון דארבעים יום קודם ליצירתו מיא בעלמא הוא וכמו דלא עיברה כלל דמיא ונגמר הדין ע"פ רובם שהמתנה מתנה ולאבא מארי ז"ל היה מסתברא כדברי היחיד שאין המתנה מתנה:

(א) נראה דצ"ל נמי שלא שלקח מן האשה בטל הוא ותוציא מן הלקוחות.

עין משפט נר מצוה

טז א מיי' פכ"ב מהל' אישות הלכה כו טוש"ע אה"ע סי' פח סעיף ג:

יז ב ג מיי' פ"ח מהל' תרומות הל' ד טור יו"ד סי' שלא:

יח ד ה מיי' שם טור שם:

מסורת הש"ס

נ"ל מלוה שלו. יעב"ץ

ב"כ קמח: נדה מד.

[אלמנה בסוכה כג: משמע כפי' הרא"ש עי' מערכי לשון ערך דיגלת סוף הערה לא]

ב"כ קמב: כתובות ז: [זבחים לב.] [ב"ב קה.]

הגהות הב"ח

(א) גמ' ומי פליגי והאמר ר' זכאי זו עדות:

תורה אור

אֵין חוֹשְׁשִׁין לְמִיעוּטָא. וְאִיבָּעֵית אֵימָא: לְעוֹלָם קָסָבַר חוֹשְׁשִׁין לְמִיעוּטָא, דְּעָבְדִינַן לֵיהּ תַּקַּנְתָּא כְּרַב נַחְמָן אָמַר שְׁמוּאֵל. דְּאָמַר *רַב נַחְמָן אָמַר שְׁמוּאֵל: אי יְתוֹמִים שֶׁבָּאוּ לַחֲלוֹק בְּנִכְסֵי אֲבִיהֶם, ב"ד מַעֲמִידִין לָהֶם אַפּוֹטְרוֹפּוֹס וּבוֹרֵר לָהֶם חֵלֶק יָפֶה. הִגְדִּילוּ — יְכוֹלִין לִמְחוֹת. וְרַב נַחְמָן דִּידֵיהּ אוֹמֵר: בהִגְדִּילוּ — אֵין יְכוֹלִין לִמְחוֹת. דא"כ — מַה כֹּחַ ב"ד יָפֶה? לֵימָא, דְּרַב נַחְמָן תַּנָּאֵי הִיא! לָא, דְּכ"ע אִית לְהוּ דְּרַב נַחְמָן, וְהָכָא *בְּחוֹשְׁשִׁין לְמִיעוּטָא קָמִיפַּלְגִי. רַ' יִשְׁמָעֵאל בְּרַ' יוֹסֵי אוֹמֵר מִשּׁוּם אָבִיו: הַבַּת — *מַאֲכִיל, הַבֵּן — אֵינוֹ מַאֲכִיל. מ"ש בֵּן דְּלָא מַאֲכִיל — מִשּׁוּם חֶלְקוֹ שֶׁל עוּבָּר, בַּת נַמִי לֹא תַּאֲכִיל — מִפְּנֵי חֶלְקוֹ שֶׁל עוּבָּר! אֲמַר אַבַּיֵי: הָכָא בִּנְכָסִים מוּעָטִים עָסְקִינַן, וּכְגוֹן דְּאִיכָּא בֵּן בַּהֲדֵי בַּת, מַה נַּפְשָׁךְ: אִי הַאי דִּמְעַבְּרָא בֵּן הוּא — לָא עָדִיף מֵהַאי דְּקָאֵי, אִי בַּת הִיא — אַמַּאי אָכְלָה, בְּתַקַּנְתָּא דְּרַבָּנַן — כַּמָּה דְּלָא נָפַק לַאֲוִיר הָעוֹלָם לָא תַּקִּינוּ רַבָּנַן. בְּמַאי אוֹקִימְתָּא — בִּנְכָסִים מוּעָטִים, אֵימָא סֵיפָא: שֶׁמָּא יִמָּצֵא הָעוּבָּר זָכָר, וְאֵין לְבָנוֹת בִּמְקוֹם בֵּן כְּלוּם, אַדְּרַבָּה, גנְכָסִים מוּעָטִים דְּבָנוֹת נִינְהוּ! סֵיפָא אֲתַאן לִנְכָסִים מְרוּבִּין. וּנְכָסִים מוּעָטִים דְּבָנוֹת נִינְהוּ? *וְהָאָמַר רַבִּי אַסִי א"ר יוֹחָנָן: דיְתוֹמִין שֶׁקָּדְמוּ וּמָכְרוּ בִּנְכָסִים מוּעָטִים, מַה שֶּׁמָּכְרוּ מָכְרוּ! וְאֶלָּא מַאי בַּת דְּקָתָנֵי — אֵם — א"ה, הַיְינוּ רַ' יוֹסֵי! כּוּלַּהּ רַ' יִשְׁמָעֵאל בְּרַ' יוֹסֵי קָתָנֵי לַהּ.§ **מתני'** ההָעוּבָּר, וְהַיָּבָם, וְהָאֵירוּסִין, וְהַחֵרֵשׁ, וּבֶן תֵּשַׁע שָׁנִים וְיוֹם אֶחָד — פּוֹסְלִין וְלֹא מַאֲכִילִין. וסָפֵק שֶׁהוּא בֶּן ט' שָׁנִים וְיוֹם אֶחָד סָפֵק שֶׁאֵינוֹ, סָפֵק הֵבִיא ב' שְׂעָרוֹת וְסָפֵק שֶׁלֹּא הֵבִיא, *נָפַל הַבַּיִת עָלָיו וְעַל בַּת אָחִיו וְאֵין יָדוּעַ אֵי זֶה מֵת רִאשׁוֹן — זצָרָתָהּ חוֹלֶצֶת וְלֹא מִתְיַיבֶּמֶת.§ **גמ'** "הָעוּבָּר".§ חאִי בַּת כֹּהֵן לְיִשְׂרָאֵל הִיא פָּסֵיל לָהּ, °"כִּנְעוּרֶיהָ" — פְּרָט לִמְעוּבֶּרֶת. אִי בַּת יִשְׂרָאֵל לְכֹהֵן הִיא לֹא מַאֲכִיל לָהּ, יָלוּד מַאֲכִיל, שֶׁאֵינוֹ יָלוּד אֵינוֹ מַאֲכִיל.§ "הַיָּבָם".§ טאִי בַּת כֹּהֵן לְיִשְׂרָאֵל הִיא פָּסֵיל לָהּ, °"וְשָׁבָה אֶל בֵּית אָבִיהָ" פְּרָט לְשׁוֹמֶרֶת יָבָם, אִי בַּת יִשְׂרָאֵל לְכֹהֵן הִיא לֹא מַאֲכִיל לָהּ, *°"קִנְיַן כַּסְפּוֹ" אָמַר רַחֲמָנָא, וְהָא קִנְיָן דְּאָחִיו הוּא.§ "וְהָאֵירוּסִין".§ יאִי בַּת כֹּהֵן לְיִשְׂרָאֵל הִיא פָּסֵיל לָהּ, דְּהָא

ויקרא כב | שם | שם

רש"י

אֵין חוֹשְׁשִׁין לְמִיעוּטָא. לְשֶׁמָּא יְהֵא זָכָר, וְיֵשׁ לוֹ חֵלֶק בָּהֶן. דְּבָתַר רוּבָּא אָזְלִינַן, וְרוּבָּא יוֹלְדוֹת אוֹ נְקֵבוֹת אוֹ מַפִּילוֹת, כְּדְפָרֵישִׁית לְעֵיל. דְּעָבְדִינַן לֵיהּ תַּקַּנְתָּא. בּוֹרְרִין לָעוּבָּר שְׁאָר נְכָסִים לְחֶלְקוֹ, וְנִמְלְאוּ הָעֲבָדִים כּוּלָּן לְחֵלֶק הַנּוֹלָדִים. אֲבָל הֵיכָא דְּכוּלָּן נְקֵבוֹת — לָא מָצִינוּ לְמֶיעֱבַד תַּקַּנְתָּא, שֶׁמָּא יְהֵא הָעוּבָּר זָכָר וִיהֵא הַכֹּל שֶׁלּוֹ. יְתוֹמִים. קְטַנִּים שֶׁבָּאוּ לַחֲלוֹק, מַעֲמִידִין אַפּוֹטְרוֹפּוֹס לְכָל אֶחָד וְאֶחָד, וּבוֹרֵר כָּל אַפּוֹטְרוֹפּוֹס חֵלֶק אֶחָד יָפֶה לְחֶלְקוֹ. הִגְדִּילוּ. הַיְּתוֹמִים יְכוֹלִים לִמְחוֹת, וּמְהַנְיָא חֲלוּקָה לְפֵירוֹת דְּעַד מְחָאָה. לֵימָא דְּרַב נַחְמָן תַּנָּאֵי הִיא. מִדְּקָאָמַר ר' שִׁמְעוֹן זְכָרִים יֹאכְלוּ מִשּׁוּם תַּקַּנְתָּא דְּרַב נַחְמָן — מִכְּלָל דְּת"ק דְּקָאָמַר עַבְדֵי צֹאן בַּרְזֶל לֹא יֹאכְלוּ, אַפִּי' בְּתַקַּנְתָּא קָאָמַר. וְלֵית לֵיהּ דְּרַב נַחְמָן, וְאֵינָן רַשָּׁאִין לַחֲלוֹק עַד שֶׁיַּגְדִּילוּ. לָא דְּכוּלֵּי עָלְמָא אִית לְהוּ דְּרַב נַחְמָן. וְאִי דַּעֲבַד לְהוּ תַּקַּנְתָּא, הָכִי נַמִי דְּאָכְלֵי אֲפִילּוּ לְתַנָּא קַמָּא. וְהָכָא בִּדְלָא עֲבוּד תַּקַּנְתָּא פְּלִיגֵי, וְקָאָמַר רַבִּי שִׁמְעוֹן — יֹאכְלוּ, וְלָא חָיֵישׁ לְמִיעוּטָא. וְתַנָּא קַמָּא חָיֵישׁ לְמִיעוּטָא. הַבַּת מַאֲכִיל. קס"ד ה"ק: אִם יֵשׁ כָּאן בַּת וְלֹא בֵּן — מַאֲכִיל עֲבָדִים, אֲבָל אִם זְכָרִים הֵם — לֹא יֹאכְלוּ הָעֲבָדִים. בִּנְכָסִים מוּעָטִים. דְּתִיקּוּן רַבָּנַן הַבָּנוֹת יִזּוֹנוּ וְהַבָּנִים יִשְׁאֲלוּ עַל הַפְּתָחִים. וּכְגוֹן דְּאִיכָּא בֵּן בַּהֲדָהּ. דְּהָךְ בַּת, דְּהָווּ כּוּלְּהוּ בְּחֶזְקַת הַבֵּן מִדְּאוֹרַיְיתָא. דְּהַשְׁתָּא מִמָּה נַפְשָׁךְ: אִי עוּבָּר זָכָר הוּא — לָא עָדִיף מֵהַאי דְּשָׁקְלִינְהוּ רַבָּנַן מִינֵּיהּ, וְאוֹקְמִינְהוּ בִּרְשׁוּת בַּת. וְאִי עוּבָּר בַּת הִיא — כֵּיוָן דְּיֵשׁ בֵּן זָכָר לְפָנֵינוּ, אֵין לְעוּבָּר נְקֵבָה חֵלֶק בָּהֶן אֶלָּא בְּתַקַּנְתָּא דְּרַבָּנַן, וְכַמָּה דְּלָא נָפַק כו'. וּלְהָכִי נָקַט בֵּן בַּהֲדָהּ, דְּאִי לָא הֲוֵה בֵּן — אִית לֵיהּ זְכִיָּיה לְעוּבָּר נְקֵבָה מִדְּאוֹרַיְיתָא בַּנְּכָסִים בְּתוֹרַת יְרוּשָּׁה בַּהֲדֵי הָךְ בַּת. וְהָכִי מְפָרֵשׁ מִילְּתָא דְּר' יִשְׁמָעֵאל: הַבַּת עִם הַבֵּן מַאֲכֶלֶת, אֲבָל אִם יֵשׁ בֵּן בְּלֹא בַּת — אֵינוֹ מַאֲכִיל. מַה שֶּׁמָּכְרוּ מָכְרוּ. וְכֵיוָן דִּלְעִנְיַן מְכִירָה בִּרְשׁוּתַיְיהוּ קָיְימִי, הֵיכִי אָכְלֵי? אֶלָּא מַאי הַבַּת דְּקָתָנֵי אֵם. וְהָכִי קָאָמַר: הָאֵם מַאֲכֶלֶת עַבְדֵי מְלוֹג שֶׁלָּהּ כְּדֶרֶךְ שֶׁהָיְתָה אוֹכֶלֶת, וְהַבֵּן אֵינוֹ מַאֲכִיל אֶת עַבְדֵי צֹאן בַּרְזֶל מִפְּנֵי חֶלְקוֹ שֶׁל עוּבָּר. **מתני'** הָעוּבָּר פּוֹסֵל. בַּת כֹּהֵן שֶׁנִּיסֵּאת לְיִשְׂרָאֵל וּמֵת, וְהִנִּיחָהּ מְעוּבֶּרֶת. וְאֵינוֹ מַאֲכִיל. בַּת יִשְׂרָאֵל שֶׁנִּיסֵּאת לְכֹהֵן וּמֵת וְהִנִּיחָהּ מְעוּבֶּרֶת. וְהַיָּבָם. בַּת כֹּהֵן שׁוֹמֶרֶת לְיָבָם יִשְׂרָאֵל — פְּסָלָהּ מִתְּרוּמַת אָבִיהָ, וּבַת יִשְׂרָאֵל שׁוֹמֶרֶת לְיָבָם כֹּהֵן — אֵינוֹ מַאֲכִילָהּ. וְהָאֵירוּסִין. בַּת כֹּהֵן מְאוֹרֶסֶת לְיִשְׂרָאֵל — פְּסָלָהּ, וּבַת יִשְׂרָאֵל מְאוֹרֶסֶת לְכֹהֵן — אֵינוֹ מַאֲכִילָהּ. וּבֶן ט' שָׁנִים. בַּגְּמָרָא מְפָרֵשׁ לָהּ. סָפֵק שֶׁהוּא בֶּן ט' סָפֵק שֶׁאֵינוֹ. הָוֵי נַמִי כְּבֶן ט', וּפוֹסֵל. וְאַמִּילְּתָא דִּלְעֵיל קָאֵי. סָפֵק שֶׁהֵבִיא שְׁתֵּי שְׂעָרוֹת כו'. לְעֵיל קָאֵי, לְעִנְיַן הָאֵירוּסִין, דְּקָתָנֵי פּוֹסְלִין. וְהָכִי קָאָמַר: קָטָן שֶׁקִּידֵּשׁ הָאִשָּׁה, סָפֵק הֵבִיא שְׁתֵּי שְׂעָרוֹת וְקִדּוּשָׁיו קִדּוּשִׁין, סָפֵק שֶׁלֹּא הֵבִיא — פּוֹסֵל בַּת כֹּהֵן הַמְאוֹרֶסֶת לוֹ מִן הַתְּרוּמָה. נָפַל הַבַּיִת עָלָיו וְעַל בַּת אָחִיו. שֶׁהִיא אִשְׁתּוֹ, סָפֵק הוּא מֵת תְּחִלָּה וְנָפְלוּ שְׁתֵּיהֶן לִפְנֵי אָחִיו, וּפוֹטֶרֶת צָרָתָהּ מִשּׁוּם צָרַת הַבַּת, סָפֵק בַּת אָחִיו מֵתָה רִאשׁוֹנָה, וּבִשְׁעַת נְפִילָה לַיִּבּוּם לָא הֲוַאי צָרָתָהּ צָרַת עֶרְוָה, דִּתְנַן (לעיל דף ג:): וְכוּלָּן אִם מֵתוּ אוֹ מֵיאֲנוּ — צָרוֹתֵיהֶן מוּתָּרוֹת. צָרָתָהּ חוֹלֶצֶת וְלֹא מִתְיַיבֶּמֶת. אַיְּידֵי דְּאַיְירֵי בִּסְפֵק לְחוּמְרָא תָּנֵי לָהּ בַּהֲדַיְיהוּ. **גמ'** וְשָׁבָה אֶל בֵּית אָבִיהָ כִּנְעוּרֶיהָ. מַשְׁמַע בִּזְמַן שֶׁהִיא דּוֹמָה לִנְעוּרֶיהָ. יָלוּד מַאֲכִיל. יִשְׂרְאֵלִית הָאוֹכֶלֶת בִּשְׁבִיל בְּנָהּ — אֵינָהּ אוֹכֶלֶת אֶלָּא אִם בֵּן יָלוּד. בֵּן מַאֲכִיל אֶת אִמּוֹ נָפְקָא לָן בְּתוֹרַת כֹּהֲנִים (ויקרא כב) מִ"וִילִיד בֵּיתוֹ הֵם יֹאכְלוּ בְּלַחְמוֹ" — קְרֵי בֵּיהּ יַאֲכִילוּ. וּמֵהָכָא יָלוּד הוּא דְּמַשְׁמַע. וְשָׁבָה פְּרָט לְשׁוֹמֶרֶת יָבָם. שֶׁאֵינָהּ בִּרְשׁוּתָהּ לָשׁוּב, דְּהָא אֲגִידָא בֵּיהּ. דְּקַנְיֵיהּ

תוספות

אין חוששין למיעוטא כו'. הקשה הר"ר שמואל בר' חיים: הא כי הוי נמי נפל פסיל, כדמוכח בפ' "מי שמת" (ב"ב דף קמב. ושם) דלמאן דאמר המזכה לעובר קנה — זוכה העובר בנכסי אביו עד שתפיל האשה, דתניא (שם), גבי גר שמת ובזבזו ישראל נכסיו ושמעו שאשתו מעוברת, והחזירו, ואחר כך שמעו שהפילה והחזיקו, המחזיק בשניה זכה, בראשונה — לא זכה! ואר"י: דהכא יש להסתפק שמא כבר הוא נפל. וא"ת: דהכא חייש רבי יוסי למיעוטא, ובפ' "מצות חליצה" (לקמן דף קה:) קאמר דקטנה חולצת, ואמאי? הא אין עולה לייבום, כיון דחייש למיעוטא, דחיישינן שמא תמצא אילונית, וכיון דאין עולה לייבום אין עולה לחליצה! °וי"ל: דחשיב עולה לייבום, כיון דאם יבא אליהו ויאמר דאינה אילונית היתה יכולה להתייבם. ולא דמיא לחולצת תוך ג' חדשים, *(א) דאפי' יבא אליהו ויאמר דלא מיעברא לא משגחינן ביה. וא"ת: דבפ"ק דכתובות (דף יד:) לא חייש ר' יוסי למיעוטא בתינוקת שנאנסה! ואר"י: דברובא דאיתיה קמן כ"ע מודו דלא חיישינן למיעוטא. ומיהו, ל"ע בריש "המוכר פירות" (ב"ב דף צג:) דאזיל רבי יוסי בתר רובא דזריעה להוציא ממון, ואייתי מינה ראיה לרב דאמר הולכין בממון אחר הרוב, אלמא לא חייש רבי יוסי למיעוט לענין ממונא, וכל שכן לענין איסורא! °ויש לחלק. **יתומים** שבאו לחלוק כו'. מפורש "בהשולח" (גיטין דף לד.). **מועטים** עסקינן. אע"ג דפסקינן בפ' "נערה" בכתובות (דף נג.) דמזון האשה והבנות ממקרקעי ולא ממטלטלי — סוגיא דהכא סברא דעבדא כמקרקעי דמי, כרבי אלעזר דאמר בפ"ק דב"ק (דף יא: ושם) הלכה, גובין מן העבדים. ומיהו, אין הלכה כן, אלא כרב נחמן דפליג עלי', דקי"ל ככל הני שמעתתא דשלח ליה ר' אבא לרב יוסף בר חמא פרק "יש נוחלין" (ב"ב דף קכח.), דמסיק התם דשלח ליה: אין גובין, אבל אין לומר דחשיב עבדא כמטלטלי, וסבר כרבי דאמר בפרק "נערה" (כתובות דף נג.) מזון האשה והבנות בין ממקרקעי בין ממטלטלי — דא"כ, בסמוך דפריך במאי אוקימתא בנכסים מועטים, ודוחק לומר דסיפא אתא לנכסים מרובין, ה"ל למימר: דסבר לה ר"ש בן יוחאי כר"ש בן אלעזר, דקי"ל (שם) כוותיה, דמזוני מקרקעי ולא ממטלטלי. **שקדמו** ומכרו כו'. מלשון קדמו משמע דאיירי שקדמו למכור קודם שהחזיקו בהן בית דין לצורך בנות. אבל אין נראה לר"י, דא"כ, הוה ליה לאוקמי כגון שכבר החזיקו בהן בנות ע"פ ב"ד, אלא אין שום חזקה מועלת, אלא קדמו קודם שיאכלו הבנות קאמר. ומיהו אר"י דיש לדחות: דמשמע ליה דבת אוכלת מיד אחר מיתת הבעל, בלא החזקה על פי ב"ד.

מה שמכרו מכרו. והדמים שלהם, דאם לא כן — בחזקת הבנות הן. וכן משמע בסוטה (דף כא:) דחשיב ליה רשע ערום — זה המשיא עצה למכור בנכסים מועטים. **קנין** כספו אמר רחמנא והאי קנין דאחיו הוא. אמר ר"ת: דאסמכתא בעלמא הוא דמדאורייתא מיכל אכלה.א) דהא למשנה ראשונה דפרק "אף על פי" (כתובות דף נז. ושם) היכא דאכלה בחיי הבעל אכלה נמי בחזקת היבם. ודייק ר"ת מדקתני התם ואפילו כולם בפני הבעל חסר יום אחד, משמע הא כולן בפני הבעל — אוכלת. ועוד: דתניא בתוספתא (דכתובות פ"ה) זו משנה ראשונה, אבל רבותינו אמרו: אין האשה אוכלת בתרומה עד שתיכנס לחופה, ולא היבמה עד שתיבעל, משמע דלמשנה ראשונה — אוכלת. ובירושלמי דפרק "אע"פ" הגיע זמן ולא נישאו, או שמתו בעליהן — אוכלות משלו ואוכלות בתרומה. והיינו בלא ביאה, דאי אחר ביאה — פשיטא דאשתו גמורה היא, והיינו טעמא דמשנה ראשונה

עין משפט נר מצוה

יט א ב מיי' פ"י מהל' נחלות הלכה ד סמג עשין צו טוש"ע חו"מ סימן רפט סעי' א:

כ ג מיי' פי"ט מהל' אישות הלכה יז סמג עשין כו טוש"ע אה"ע סימן קיב סעי' יא:

כא ד מיי' שם הל' יט סמג עשין פא טוש"ע שם סעיף יד:

כב ה מיי' פ"ח מהל' תרומות הל' א טוי"ד סי' שלא:

כג ו מיי' שם הל' יא:

כד ז מיי' פ"ו מהלכות יבום סמג עשין נא טוש"ע אה"ע סי' קעג סעי' ח:

כה ח מיי' פ"ח מהל' תרומות הל' ב טוי"ד סי' שלא:

כו ט מיי' שם הלכה ה:

כז י מיי' שם הלכה ז:

[לעיל לה:]

מסורת הש"ס

כתובות ק: קידושין מב. גיטין לד.

לקמן קיט. וש"נ

[נ"ל מאכלת]

כתובות קג. סוטה כא: ב"ב קמ.

לעיל לה.

[כתובות נח.]

תוספות ישנים

יתומים שקדמו ומכרו בנכסים מועטים מה שמכרו מכרו. פ"ה קדמו קודם שהגבו ב"ד לבנות ולא נהירא דא"כ מה פריך הכא לוקמה כשכבר הגבו ב"ד הנכסים לבנות ולכן נ"ל קדמו ומכרו קודם שאכלו הבנות הנכסים: **א)** ור' יצחק בר' אברהם פי' דודאי דרשה גמורה היא והאי דמשמע התם דלמשנה ראשונה אוכלת כי הגיע זמנה בפני הבעל היינו דווקא בתרומ' דרבנן אבל בתרומה דאורייתא לא אכלה אפי' למשנה ראשונה דקנין כספו אמרה רחמנא והאי קנין דאחיו הוא. וכן משמע פרק נערה המאורסה (דף עג) גבי בוגרת ששהתה י"ב חדש וכו' וקאמר ר' אליעזר ומשנה ראשונה אמרו דבר אחד דתנן היבם אינו מאכיל וכו' וקאמר אביי ולמא לא היא עד כאן לא אשמעי' משנה ראשונה אלא להאכילה בתרומה דרבנן משמע דבכתובות בתרומה דרבנן מיירי: **אי** בת כהן לישראל פסל לה דהא קניה בהאי הויה ולא נהירא לגרוס כן שהרי אצטריך כי תהיה לומר בת כהן שנבעלה לפסול לה פסלה וצ"ל דטעמא משום דכתיב ושבה אל בית אביה וזו עומדת בבית בעלה ואיגררא ביה:

הגהות הב"ח

(א) תום' ד"ה אין וכו'. דאפילו יבא אליהו. נ"ב ע"ל בפרק החולץ דף מא ע"ב:

גליון הש"ס

תום' ד"ה אין חוששין וכו'. וי"ל דחשיב עולה ליבום. עיין לעיל דף מא ע"ב: **בא"ד** בסופו ויש לחלק. עי' בר"ן שבת פ' יט דף נט ע"ב ובב"י יו"ד סי' קלא בשם תשובת הר"ש ול"ע:

ראשונה

דְּהָא קָנְיָהּ בַּהֲוָיָה, וְאִי בַּת יִשְׂרָאֵל לְכֹהֵן הִיא — לָא מַאֲכִיל לָהּ מִשּׁוּם דְּעוּלָּא.§ "וְהַחֵרֵשׁ".§ [א]אִי בַּת כֹּהֵן לְיִשְׂרָאֵל הִיא — פָּסֵיל לָהּ, דְּהָא קָנְיָהּ בְּתַקַּנְתָּא דְּרַבָּנַן, וְאִי בַּת יִשְׂרָאֵל לְכֹהֵן הִיא — לָא מַאֲכִיל, "קִנְיַן כַּסְפּוֹ" אָמַר רַחֲמָנָא, וְהַאי לָאו בַּר קִנְיָן הוּא.§ "וּבֶן תֵּשַׁע שָׁנִים וכו'".§ קס"ד בְּשׁוֹמֶרֶת יָבָם לְבֶן תֵּשַׁע וְיוֹם אֶחָד. לְמַאי? אִי לְמִיפְסָל — קָטָן נַמִי מִיפְסָל פָּסֵיל, אִי לַאֲכוּלֵי — גָּדוֹל נַמִי לָא מַאֲכִיל! אֲמַר אַבַּיֵי: הָכָא בְּיָבָם בֶּן תֵּשַׁע שָׁנִים וְיוֹם אֶחָד הַבָּא עַל יְבִמְתּוֹ עָסְקִינַן, דְּמִדְּאוֹרַיְיתָא קָנְיָא לֵיהּ. סד"א: הוֹאִיל וּמִדְּאוֹרַיְיתָא קָנְיָא לֵיהּ, וּבִיאָתוֹ בִּיאָה, אֵימָא לוֹכִיל — קמ"ל: *עָשׂוּ [ב]בִּיאַת בֶּן ט' שָׁנִים וְיוֹם אֶחָד כְּמַאֲמָר בְּגָדוֹל. א"ל רָבָא: אִי הָכִי, סֵיפָא דְּקָתָנֵי: סָפֵק בֶּן ט' שָׁנִים וְיוֹם אֶחָד סָפֵק שֶׁאֵינוֹ, הַשְׁתָּא וַדַּאי בֶּן ט' לָא מַאֲכִיל — סָפֵק מִיבַּעְיָא?! אֶלָּא אֲמַר רָבָא: [ג]בְּבֶן תֵּשַׁע שָׁנִים וְיוֹם אֶחָד דְּהָנָךְ פְּסוּלִים קָתָנֵי, דְּפָסְלֵי בְּבִיאָתָן. וְכִדְתַנְיָא: *[ד]בֶּן תֵּשַׁע שָׁנִים וְיוֹם אֶחָד גֵּר עַמּוֹנִי וּמוֹאָבִי, מִצְרִי וַאֲדוֹמִי, כּוּתִי, נָתִין, חָלָל וּמַמְזֵר, שֶׁבָּאוּ עַל כֹּהֶנֶת לְוִיָּה וְיִשְׂרְאֵלִית — פְּסָלוּהָ. וְהָא מִדְּקָתָנֵי סֵיפָא: אִם אֵינָן רְאוּיִן לָבֹא בְּיִשְׂרָאֵל הֲרֵי אֵלּוּ פּוֹסְלִים, מִכְּלָל דְּרֵישָׁא לָאו בִּפְסוּלִים עָסְקִינַן! רֵישָׁא פְּסוּלֵי קָהָל, סֵיפָא פְּסוּלֵי כְהוּנָּה.§ גּוּפָא, *בֶּן ט' שָׁנִים וְיוֹם א' גֵּר עַמּוֹנִי וּמוֹאָבִי מִצְרִי וַאֲדוֹמִי כּוּתִי נָתִין חָלָל וּמַמְזֵר שֶׁבָּאוּ עַל כֹּהֶנֶת לְוִיָּה וְיִשְׂרְאֵלִית(א) — פְּסָלָן. רַבִּי יוֹסֵי אוֹמֵר: כָּל שֶׁזַּרְעוֹ פָּסוּל — פּוֹסֵל, כָּל שֶׁאֵין זַרְעוֹ פָּסוּל — אֵינוֹ פּוֹסֵל. רשב"ג אוֹמֵר: כָּל שֶׁאַתָּה נוֹשֵׂא בִּתּוֹ — אַתָּה נוֹשֵׂא אַלְמָנָתוֹ, וְכָל שֶׁאֵין אַתָּה נוֹשֵׂא בִּתּוֹ — אִי אַתָּה נוֹשֵׂא אַלְמָנָתוֹ.§ מְנָא הָנֵי מִילֵּי? אֲמַר רַב יְהוּדָה אֲמַר רַב: אָמַר קְרָא °"וּבַת כֹּהֵן כִּי תִהְיֶה לְאִישׁ זָר", [ה]כֵּיוָן שֶׁנִּבְעֲלָה לְפָסוּל לָהּ — פְּסָלָהּ. הַאי מִיבְּעֵי לֵיהּ דְּקָאָמַר רַחֲמָנָא: בַּת כֹּהֵן דְּמִינַּסְבָא לְזָר [ו]לָא תֵּיכוֹל! הַהִיא °מִ"וְשָׁבָה אֶל בֵּית אָבִיהָ כִּנְעוּרֶיהָ מִלֶּחֶם אָבִיהָ תֹּאכֵל" נָפְקָא, מִדְּקָאָמַר רַחֲמָנָא: "וְשָׁבָה אֶל בֵּית אָבִיהָ תֹּאכֵל" מִכְּלָל דְּמֵעִיקָּרָא לָא אָכְלָה! אִי מֵהַהִיא הֲוָה אָמֵינָא *לָאו הַבָּא מִכְּלַל עֲשֵׂה — עֲשֵׂה, כָּתַב רַחֲמָנָא הַאי לְלָאו. [לָאו] °מִ"וְכָל זָר לֹא יֹאכַל קֹדֶשׁ" נָפְקָא. הַהוּא

ויקרא כב | שם | שם

דְּקָנְיָה בַּהֲוָיָה. וּמִשַּׁעַת הֲוָיָה אִיפְסִילָה, כִּדְכְתִיב "וּבַת כֹּהֵן כִּי תִהְיֶה לְאִישׁ זָר". מִשּׁוּם דְּעוּלָּא. בְּמַסֶּ' כְּתוּבּוֹת, בְּפֶרֶק אע"פ (דף נז:): דְּבַר תּוֹרָה אֲרוּסָה בַּת יִשְׂרָאֵל אוֹכֶלֶת בִּתְרוּמָה, דִּכְתִיב "קִנְיַן כַּסְפּוֹ" הוּא יֹאכַל בּוֹ", וּמַה טַּעַם אָמְרוּ אֵינָהּ אוֹכֶלֶת, גְּזֵירָה שֶׁמָּא יִמְזְגוּ לָהּ כּוֹס בְּבֵית אָבִיהָ וְתֵלֵךְ וְתַשְׁקֶה לְאָחִיהָ וְלַאֲחוֹתָהּ. בְּתַקַּנְתָּא דְּרַבָּנַן. דְּחֵרֵשׁ, אע"ג דְּלָאו בַּר דַּעַת הוּא — תַּקִּינוּ בֵּיהּ רַבָּנַן נִשּׂוּאִין, לְקַמָּן בְּפֶ' "חֵרֵשׁ שֶׁנָּשָׂא" (דף קיב:). קס"ד בְּשׁוֹמֶרֶת יָבָם לְבֶן ט'. וְלֹא בָּא עָלֶיהָ, וּלְמַאי הִלְכְתָא נָקַט בֶּן ט', אִי לְמִיפְסַל, לְאַשְׁמוּעִינַן דְּכֵיוָן דַּחֲזֵי לְבִיאָה פָּסֵיל לָהּ בְּזִיקַּת יְבָמִין — מַאי אִירְיָא בֶּן ט', אֲפִילּוּ קָטָן נַמִי, דְּלָא קָרֵינַן בָּהּ "וְשָׁבָה אֶל בֵּית אָבִיהָ", וְלַשְׁמָעִינַן בָּצִיר מִבֶּן ט'. וְאִי לַאֲכוּלֵי כו'. וְאִי לְהָכִי נָקַט בֶּן ט' לְאַשְׁמוּעִינַן רְבוּתָא, דְּאע"ג דַּחֲזֵי לְבִיאָה לֹא מַאֲכִיל יְבִמְתּוֹ בְּזִיקָּתוֹ — אֲפִילּוּ גָּדוֹל מַמָּשׁ לֹא מַאֲכִיל, דְּלָאו קִנְיָנוֹ הוּא, דְּהָא אַשְׁמְעִי' בְּגָדוֹל בְּרֵישָׁא דְּמַתְנִי'. הַבָּא עַל יְבִמְתּוֹ. דְּאִילּוּ גָּדוֹל הֲוָה אָכְלִי, וְאַשְׁמוּעִינַן רְבוּתָא דְּאע"ג דְּבִיאָתוֹ בִּיאָה — לֹא מַאֲכִיל, וּפוֹסְלִין דְּקָתָנֵי בְּמַתְנִיתִין — אַשְּׁאָרָא קָאֵי, אָעוּבָּר וְיָבָם בְּלֹא בִּיאָה וְאֵירוּסִין וְחֵרֵשׁ, אֲבָל בֶּן ט' — לָא נָקַט לֵיהּ אֶלָּא מִשּׁוּם וְאֵין מַאֲכִילִין. אִי הָכִי. דְּמִשּׁוּם אֵינוֹ מַאֲכִיל נָקַט לֵיהּ, לָמָּה לִי לְמִיתְנֵי סֵיפָא, דְּקָתָנֵי סָפֵק שֶׁהוּא בֶּן תִּשְׁעָה סָפֵק שֶׁאֵינוֹ — הָוֵי נַמִי כְּבֶן ט', הַשְׁתָּא וַדַּאי בֶּן ט' כו'. פְּסוּלִין. כְּגוֹן מַמְזֵר וְנָתִין. וּמִשּׁוּם פּוֹסְלִין נָקַט לֵיהּ. וְלֹא מַאֲכִילִין — לָא אַבֶּן ט' קָאֵי, אֶלָּא אַשְּׁאָרָא: עוּבָּר וְיָבָם אֵירוּסִין וְחֵרֵשׁ. בֶּן תִּשְׁעָה. שֶׁהוּא גֵּר עַמּוֹנִי וּמוֹאָבִי וכו' — דַּאֲסוּרִין לָבֹא בַּקָּהָל. מִצְרִי וַאֲדוֹמִי. עַד דּוֹר שְׁלִישִׁי בַּעֲשֵׂה. כּוּתִי וְנָתִין. בְּ"לֹא תִתְחַתֵּן בָּם", דְּקָסָבַר:(ב) גֵּירֵי אֲרָיוֹת הֵן. חָלָל. פָּסוּל לִכְהוּנָּה. פְּסָלוּהָ. אִם בַּת כֹּהֵן — מִן הַתְּרוּמָה, וּלְוִיָּה וְיִשְׂרְאֵלִית — לִינָּשֵׂא לִכְהוּנָּה עוֹלָמִית. מִדְּקָתָנֵי סֵיפָא. דְּמַתְנִיתִין. סֵיפָא פְּסוּלֵי כְהוּנָּה. חָלָל. וְאע"ג דְּקָתָנֵי שֶׁאֵינָן רְאוּיִן לָבֹא בְּיִשְׂרָאֵל — לָא מַיְירֵי אֶלָּא בִּכְהוּנָּה. דְּמֵרֵישָׁא הֲוָה אָמֵינָא פְּסוּלֵי קָהָל הוּא דְּפָסְלִי, אֲבָל בִּיאַת חָלָל — לָא. לְהָכִי תָּנֵי סֵיפָא מִשְׁנָה יְתֵירָה, לְאַשְׁמוּעִינַן חָלָל. פְּסָלוּהָ. כֹּהֶנֶת מִתְּרוּמָה דְּבֵי נָשָׁא וּמִן הַכְּהוּנָּה, לְוִיָּה וְיִשְׂרְאֵלִית מִן הַכְּהוּנָּה. רַבִּי יוֹסֵי אוֹמֵר כו'. טַעְמָא דְּרַבִּי יוֹסֵי וְרַבָּן שִׁמְעוֹן מְפָרֵשׁ לְקַמָּן בִּשְׁמַעְתִּין, מַאי קָאָמְרִי וּמַאי פְּלוּגְתַּיְיהוּ. לָאו מִ"וְכָל זָר" נָפְקָא. "וְכָל זָר לֹא יֹאכַל קֹדֶשׁ". וְהַשְׁתָּא סָלְקָא דַּעְתָּךְ דְּקָסָבַר דְּהָךְ בַּת כֹּהֵן נַמִי מַשְׁמַע מִינֵּיהּ, הוֹאִיל וְנִישֵּׂאת לְיִשְׂרָאֵל. הַאי

לקמן ע. [נדה מה.] | קדושין עד: | [תוספתא נדה פ"ו] | [לעיל נז: וש"נ]

ראשונה דאינה אוכלת היכא דלא אכלה, משום דאין חייב במזונותיה אלא היכא דעמד בדין וברח, כדאמרינן ב"הכותב" (לעיל דף מא: ושם) ולא מייחד לה דוכתא. ומשום סימפון נמי איכא למיחש, דשמא יש סימפון ולא היתה אשתו מעולם, כיון שלא הגיע זמן בחיי הבעל ולא ברח. ואין להקשות: לעולא דאמר (כתובות דף נז:) טעמא משום שמא תשקה — כי אכלה בחיי הבעל נמי לא תיכול, כיון דאין יבם חייב במזונותיה לא מייחד לה דוכתא! — דאיכא למימר: כיון דזכתה — זכתה. אבל קשה: דא"כ מאי פריך בפרק "אע"פ" (שם דף נז: ושם) אלא מעתה לקיט כהן בבית ישראל לא יאכל בתרומה — שאני לקיט דכבר אכל כל ימי חייו! וי"ל: דכיון דהגיע זמן, וייחד לה דוכתא בבית אביה — שוב אינה זזה משם, ולא דמיא ללקיט כהן בבית ישראל. וא"ת: ומאחר דאכלה מדאורייתא — מפני מה אסרוה למשנה אחרונה עד שתבעל, אפילו נפלה מן הנשואין, הא ליכא למיחש תו לסימפון! ויש לומר: דכיון דאסורה ארוסה בהגעת זמן למשנה אחרונה — אסרו נמי יבמה, משום דמיחלפא בה, ששתיהן זמן כניסתן לאלתר. ומיהו, הא דדרשינן לעיל (דף סו.) בת ישראל לכהן דאכלה בתרומה מ"קנין כספו" — דרשא גמורה היא. דהא לעיל (דף נז.) דרשינן מהתם פלוע דכא כהן שנשא בת גרים שמאכילה בתרומה. ואע"ג דבפ"ק דקדושין (ד' י: ושם) מייתי לה מק"ו דבן בג בג, ונשואה דריש בספרי מ"כל טהור בביתך", ואית דמפיק לה מ"אתם וביתכם" — ההיא דספרי אסמכתא הוא. וכמה דרשות יש בגמרא שדורש בתורת כהנים ובספרי מפסוקים אחרים. ומיהו, לא יתיישב הא דמייתי הך אסמכתא דהאי קנין דאחיו הוא התם בפרק "אע"פ" (כתובות דף נח. ושם*) דמייתי לה על משנה ראשונה, דקתני: היבם אין מאכיל, לפי מה שפירשנו, דהיינו דוקא היכא דלא אכלה, דמהך דרשא אפי' אכלה בחיי הבעל — לא תאכל בחיי היבם! ואמר רבינו תם: דהתם ה"פ: קנין כספו אמר רחמנא שאוכלת בתרומה, ורבנן הוא דתקון משנים עשר חדש ולהלן דאוכלת. והאי קנין דאחיו הוא, ולא תקון רבנן שתאכל מחמת היבם אלא עד שתבעל, אם לא שכבר אכלה בחיי הבעל.

אי בת כהן לישראל היא פסיל לה דהא קניה בהא הויה. מתוך הלשון משמע דמקרא דמ"כי תהיה לאיש זר" נפקא, כדפירש בקונטרס. ומיהו, לקמן מפיק ליה מ"ושבה אל בית אביה" — מכלל דמעיקרא לא אכלה, ו"כי תהיה לאיש זר" מוקמינן לנבעלה לפסול לה פסלה. והכא הך דרשא הפשוטה נקט, דאי לאו דנפקא לן מ"ושבה" הוה מוקמינן לאירוסין דפסלי. וכן דרך הגמרא בכמה מקומות*. ועוד אמר ר"י: דמשום דמהאי קרא ד"כי תהיה" דרשינן נמי דאינה חוזרת בהויה דאירוסין לחזה ושוק, להכי נקטיה נמי הכא. **קניא** ליה. לאו דוקא, אלא כלומר: זקוקה לו, דביאת בן תשע לא הוי אלא כמאמר בעלמא, ובפרק קמא דקדושין (דף יט.) ממעטין ליה דלא קניא מקרא ד"אשת איש", פרט לאשת קטן. ויש ספרים דגרסי: חזיא ליה. והכי פירושו: כיון דמדאורייתא זקוקה, וביאתו ביאה, ולא בעינן כוונה ביבמה — קס"ד דקני לה מדאורייתא, ולוכיל. קא משמע לן דלא, משום דלא קני לה.

רישא פסולי כהונה סיפא פסולי קהל. וכן גירסת ר"ת, ולא כספרים דגרסי איפכא. דהא קתני סיפא: ואם אינו ראוי לבא בישראל. וא"ת: וכיון דתנא רישא פסול כהונה, למה לי למיתני בסיפא פסול קהל? דכ"ש הוא! ויש לומר: דתנא סיפא לגלויי ארישא, שלא תאמר רישא פסולי קהל דוקא. ואם תאמר: וספק בן ט' היאך פוסל בביאתו, נוקמיה אחזקה קמייתא דהוה פחות מבן תשעה ונוקי איתתא בחזקת כשרות! ומיהו, לכהונה ניחא, דלא אזלינן בתר חזקה ליוחסין, כדקאמר רבי יהושע בפרק קמא דכתובות (דף יג.): לא מפיה אנו חיין, אלא היא בחזקת בעולה לנתין וממזר, ואפי' ברוב כשרים אצלה, כדאמר התם. ולא מוקמינן לה אחזקה. ואפילו לרבן גמליאל ורבי אליעזר דמכשרי — היינו משום דאמרה לכשר נבעלתי. אבל הכא, דלא ידעה אם הוא בן תשעה — לא. אבל לתרומה — קשיא, אמאי לא מוקמינן להו אחזקה? דאפילו לענין תרומה איירי כמו לענין *עבדים, ולתרומה מוקמינן אחזקה, דהא בכתובות בפ"ב (דף כו. ושם) גבי מוחזק לן באבוה דהאי דכהן הוא, ונפק עליה קלא דבן גרושה הוא כו', ומוקי לה בתרי ותרי. משמע דאי לאו משום זילותא דבי דינא הוה מסקי ליה לכולי עלמא. והיינו לענין תרומה, דאי לכהונה — לא מסקינן ליה בתרי ותרי, כדמוכח בקידושין ב"האומר" (דף סו.) גבי עובדא דינאי המלך! ויש לומר: דהכא כגון דהשתא דאתי קמן הוי ודאי בן תשעה, אף על פי שהיה ספק כשבא עליה — לא מוקמינן ליה אחזקה קמייתא, אלא אזלינן בתר השתא, שהוא ודאי בן תשעה, דחזקה קמייתא איתרע ליה.

[ד"ה ואפילו] | [וע' תוס' עירובין טו: ד"ה בכתובה] | נ"א עובר ויבם מהרש"א וע"ש

לימא

כח א מיי' פ"ט מהל' תרומות הלכה ט:
כט ב מיי' פ"א מהל' יבום הל' יז ופ"ה הל' יח סמג עשין נא נב טוש"ע אה"ע סימן קסז סעי' א:
ל ג מיי' פ"ח מהל' תרומות הל' יא טוי"ד סי' שלא:
לא ד מיי' פי"ח מהל' איסורי ביאה הל"ג סמג לאוין קכ טוש"ע אה"ע סי' ו סעי' ח וע"ש בטור ובב"י:
לב ה מיי' פ"ו מהל' תרומות הל' ז והל' י:
לג ו מיי' שם הלכה ה:

תוספות ישנים

ספק בן תשע. וא"ת אמאי פסל אוקמיה אחזקתיה דלא הוה בן תשע וא"ל דמעלה עשו ביוחסין דהיינו דווקא לכהונה אבל לתרומה מאי איכא למימר וי"ל כיון דסופו ליגדל אין החזקה כלום א):

א) עי' בתוס' ד"ה רישא ובקדושין ע"ע.

הגהות הב"ח

(א) גמ' וישראלית פסלוה ר' יוסי: (ב) רש"י ד"ה כותי וכו' דקסבר כותים גירי:

לד א מיי' פ"ו מהל' תרומות הלכה ט:
לה ב מיי' שם הל' ז:
לו ג מיי' שם הל' ח:

ההוא מיבעי ליה לגופיה! תרי "וכל זר" כתיבי. ואכתי מיבעי ליה לכדר' יוסי בר' חנינא. דא"ר יוסי ברבי חנינא: "וכל זר" — *זרות אמרתי לך, ולא אנינות! דרבי יוסי ברבי חנינא מן "זר" "וכל זר" נפקא, — ואכתי מיבעי ליה לכדתניא: אכשהיא חוזרת — *חוזרת לתרומה, ואינה חוזרת לחזה, ושוק ואמר רב חסדא אמר רבינא בר רב שילא: מאי קרא? דכתיב: °"ובת כהן כי תהיה לאיש (ויקרא כב) זר היא בתרומת הקדשים לא תאכל" — לא תאכל במורם *מן הקדשים. — ◦א"כ לכתוב קרא "היא בקדשים לא תאכל", מאי "בתרומת הקדשים" — בשמעת מינה תרתי. אשכחן כהנת, לויה וישראלית מנלן? *כדא"ר אבא אמר רב: "בת" "ובת", הכא נמי "בת" "ובת". — כמאן — כר"ע, *דדריש ווין! אפילו תימא רבנן, כוליה "ובת" קרא יתירא הוא. אשכחן לתרומה, לכהונה מנלן? אטו לויה וישראלית לא לכהונה מרבינן להו? דאי לתרומה — בנות מיכל תרומה נינהו? אלמה לא? משכחת לה דקאכלה בשביל בנה! בשביל בנה — ק"ו: ומה כהנת, דבקדושה דנפשה אכלה, פסיל לה, לויה וישראלית דלא אכלה אלא בשביל בנה — לא כ"ש?! והיא הנותנת: כהנת דקדיש גופה — פסיל לה, הא דלא קדיש גופה — לא פסיל לה. אלא לכהונה, ק"ו מגרושה! ומה גרושה גשמותרת בתרומה — אסורה לכהונה, זו שאסורה בתרומה — אינו דין שפסולה לכהונה? וכי מזהירין מן הדין? ◦*גלוי מילתא בעלמא הוא. ואימא: נבעלה לפסול לה — חייבי כריתות! "כי תהיה" אמר רחמנא, הנך דאית בהו הויה, חייבי כריתות — לאו בני הויה. אי הכי, גוי ועבד לא ליפסלו! הנך פסלי מדרבי ישמעאל. דא"ר יוחנן *משום רבי ישמעאל: מנין לגוי ועבד שבא על בת ישראל, ועל כהנת ולויה, שפסלוה — שנאמר °"ובת (שם) כהן כי תהיה אלמנה וגרושה וגו'". מי

רש"י

האי מיבעי ליה לגופיה. לזר גמור, אבל הך דלאו זרה היא – איצטריכא "ובת כהן" לאסרה. תרי וכל זר כתיבי. "וכל זר לא יאכל קדש" (ויקרא כב), ועוד גבי בת כהן כתיב "ושבה אל וגו' מלחם אביה תאכל וכל זר לא יאכל בו" (שם). ומהכא תיפוק לאו לבת כהן הנשאת לישראל, לאוסרה תחת בעלה לתרומה. דרבי יוסי בר' חנינא. בפרק "הערל", להתיר אונן בתרומה. ואכתי. האי ד"בת כהן כי תהיה" מיבעי ליה לליקוחין גמורים, ולאשמועינן כשהיא חוזרת לבית אביה במיתת הבעל וזרע אין לה – אינה חוזרת לחזה ושוק של שלמים לאכול כשאר חיות האוכלות, כדכתי' "אתה ובניך ובנותיך" (ויקרא י). אשכחן כהנת. דמיפסלא לתרומה בביאת פסול. כדא"ר אבא. בפ' "יש מותרות". ר' עקיבא דורש ווין. בסנהדרין בפרק "ד' מיתות" (ד' נא:): ישמעאל אחי, "בת" "ובת" אני דורש. כוליה ובת קרא יתירא הוא. דהא כתיב לעיל מיניה "וכהן כי יקנה נפש וגו' ויליד ביתו", ומצי למכתב אבתריה "וכי תהיה לאיש זר". לכהונה מנלן. שלא תנשא עוד לכהן משבא עליה פסול. אלמה לא. בתמיה, והא משכחת לה דקאכלה בשביל בנה – ואיצטריך לאשמועינן דאם תיבעל לפסול לה תיאסר. ק"ו. ולא איצטריך "ובת" לרבויה. והיא הנותנת. קושיא היא. כלומר: איצטריך לרבויה, דק"ו ההוא דקילפת מיניה איסורא – היא המדה נותנת הדין להתיר ולא לאסור. כהנת דקדיש גופה כו'. וכי מזהירים מן הדין. מדין ק"ו, לאוקמיה בלאו גמור? הא קיי"ל (מכות דף יז:) דאין מזהירין מן הדין! גלוי מילתא בעלמא הוא. ולאו מילף מיניה ילפינן לאו לכהונה מתרומה, דממילא כיון דאיפסלה לתרומה – איפסלה לכהונה, דתרומה היינו קדושת כהונה. ואימא נבעלה לפסול לה חייבי כריתות. שאם בא עליה אחיה – פסלה מתרומה דבי נשא. אבל חייבי לאוין, כיון דתפסי להו בה קידושי – לא פסלי לה. וכותי ונתין וממזר דפסלי, מנלן? הנך דאית בהו הויה. מדאפקיה להך ביאה בלשון הויה, שמע מינה בבני קידושין משתעי קרא, ואפ"ה פסלי: לאפוקי חייבי כריתות ל"ג. אי הכי. אימא קרא דווקא בני קידושין נקט, וגוי ועבד לא פסלי. וה"ה דמצי נמי למימר חייבי כריתות לא ליפסלי. אלא משום דאיירי בהו לעיל, דקתני כותי, היינו גוי. ובמתניתין (לקמן דף סט:) תנן: העבד פוסל משום ביאה: עבד כנעני לית ליה קידושין, דכתיב (בראשית כב) "עם החמור" – עם הדומה לחמור. גוי לית ליה קידושין – דאמרינן (סנהדרין דף נב:) "אשת רעהו" – פרט לאשת(א) אחרים. ובשאלתות דרב אחאי *יליף לה מדתני רב חנניה (שם מז:): בעולת בעל – יש להן, מידי אחרינא – לא. וגבי ישראל מקיש הוויות להדדי, מאן דאית ליה קידושי כסף ושטר – אית ליה בה קידושי ביאה, אבל גוי דלית ליה קידושי כסף ושטר – לית ליה קידושי ביאה, *ומשני: פסיל מדרבי יוחנן – ומהאי קרא גופיה משתמעי חייבי כריתות לפסולא. ואית דמפרשי: ואימא נבעלה לפסול לה חייבי כריתות נמי מ"ש דלא תני להו לעיל? ומשני: "כי תהיה" כתיב – מדאפקיה רחמנא לבעילה בלשון הויה – לא פסיל מתרומה אלא בר קידושי דווקא. דבני הויה לאפוקי חייבי כריתות דלאו בני הויה נינהו כו' וסבירא להו דחייבי כריתות לא פסלי. וקשיא לי בגוה טובא: חדא, (דתמיה היא, דהא חמירי חייבי כריתות מחייבי לאוין. ועוד) דתנן בפ' "ד' אחין" (לעיל דף לג:): אם היו כהנות – נפסלו מתרומה, בבעילת אשת איש. ועוד, ק"ו: חייבי לאוין פסלי – חייבי כריתות לא(ב) פסלי? ועוד: הא אמרינן ב"עשרה יוחסין" (קדושין דף עז:) דכהן הבא על אחותו עשאה זונה. וכיון דזונה היא, בעילתו פוסלתה, דתניא (לקמן דף נא.): לויה שנשבית או שנבעלה בעילת זנות נותנים לה מעשר ואוכלת. לויה – אין, אבל תרומה לכהנת – לא. ועוד: הא תנן במתניתין (לקמן דף סט:): ממזר פוסל ומאכיל, ולא משכחת לה אלא באם אמו. ואי חייבי כריתות לא פסלי בביאתם, משכחת לה דממזר פוסל ומאכיל את אמו. כיצד? בת כהן שבא עליה אחיה מאמה, והוא ישראל, וילדה לו בן – פוסל מן התרומה. ובת ישראל שבא עליה אחיה מאמה כהן, וילדה לו בן – הרי זה ממזר, ומאכילה. אלא מדלא נקט אמו – ש"מ ביאת אחיה, אפי' בלא ילדה, נמי פוסלתה. חייבי כריתות לאו בני הויה נינהו. בקדושין, בפרק "האומר לחבירו" (ד' סז:). שפסלוה. מן התרומה. מי שיש לו אלמנות וגירושין בה. אני קורא בה: "ושבה אל בית אביה, מלחם אביה תאכל", ולא מגוי ועבד. אשכחן

תוספות

לימא קרא היא בקדשים לא תאכל. פי': דאי לתרומה לחודה אתא – א"כ לימא קרא "היא בקדשים". דכולה פרשתא לתרומה קדריש. ומדכתיב ב"תרומת הקדשים" – שמע מינה דלמורם מן הקדשים נמי אתא. ואם תאמר: ואימא דכוליה להכי אתא, לומר שאין חוזרת לחזה ושוק! ואמר רבינו יצחק: דפשטא דקרא איירי בתרומה, דאיירי בה בכל הפרשה.

רבי עקיבא דדריש ווין. בסנהדרין פרק "ארבע מיתות" (דף נא.) (רבי) ישמעאל אחי, בת ובת אני דורש.

כמאן כר' עקיבא דדריש ווין. הק' הר' משה מריגנשבור"ג: דמאן תנא דפליג עליה דר' עקיבא התם גבי בת ובת בפ' "ארבע מיתות" (שם דף נא:) – רבי ישמעאל, והתם בההיא שמעתא גופא אמרינן: ור' ישמעאל האי "בת ובת" מאי דריש ביה – לרבות בת בעלי מומין, אלמא דר' ישמעאל נמי דריש ווי! ותירץ, דה"פ: כמאן כרבי עקיבא דדריש ווי דמוקי ויו ד"ובת" לרבות נשואה, ולא מצריך לרבות בת בעלי מומין. והוא הדין דמרבה הכא לויה וישראלית. אבל רבי ישמעאל דמצריך התם לרבות בת בעלי מומין, כדקאמר, לפי שמצינו שחילק הכתוב בין תמימים לבעלי מומין – יכול נחלוק בבנותיהן, ה"נ יהא צריך כאן לרבות בת בעלי מומין, ולא נוקמיה לרבות לויה וישראלית. וק"ק: בסמוך, דקאמר ר' יוחנן משום ר' ישמעאל: מנין לגוי ועבד שבאו על כהנת לויה וישראלית כו', ומרבינן *(ליה) לויה וישראלית מ"ובת". ופריך: כמאן – כרבי עקיבא, דדריש ווי, טפי הוה ליה לאקשויי דר' ישמעאל אדר' ישמעאל, דהיכי דריש מ"ובת" לויה וישראלית והא איצטריך לבת בעלי מומין, כדדריש התם! ואר"י: דלא נקט הכא ר' עקיבא לאפוקי ר' ישמעאל, דהא ר' ישמעאל נמי דריש ווי, אלא לאפוקי שאר תנאי דלא דרשי ווי בעלמא. תדע, דלא קאמר אפי' תימא רבי ישמעאל, אלא אפילו תימא רבנן. ועוד יש לומר: דר' ישמעאל לא דריש ווי, והא דקאמר בסנהדרין (שם:) ורבי ישמעאל האי "בת ובת" מאי עביד ליה – לא מסיק הכי אלא ליישב דרשא דרבי ישמעאל למאן דדריש ווי.

גוי ועבד דלאו בני הויה נינהו לא ליפסלו. פירש בקונטרס: דה"ה דה"מ למימר נמי חייבי כריתות לא ליפסלו, אלא נקט גוי ועבד משום דאיירי בהו לעיל, דקתני כותי דהיינו גוי ובמתני' (לקמן דף סט:) תנן: העבד פוסל משום ביאה. ומשני דפסלי מדר' יוחנן כו'. ומהאי קרא משתמעי נמי חייבי כריתות. וק' לר"י: דכל היכא דקתני כותי – לאו בתורת גוי נקיט ליה, אלא לפסולא בעלמא. כי ההיא דתנן (קדושין דף עד.) אלו הספקות: שתוקי ואסופי וכותי. וב"אלו נערות" (כתובות דף כט. ושם) דתנן: הבא על הממזרת והנתינה והכותית – יש להן קנס. ודייקינן בפ' "שור שנגח ד' וה'" (ב"ק דף לח: ושם) דקסבר כותים גירי אמת הן, מדיש להן קנס. ועוד: ר' יוחנן משום ר' ישמעאל דנקט גוי ועבד, אמאי לא נקט חייבי כריתות? ונראה לר"י: דפשיטא ליה להש"ס דעיקר קרא ד"לאיש זר" איירי בחייבי כריתות, כדאמר פ' "עשרה יוחסין" (קדושין דף עה:) גבי גוי ועבד: השתא ממזר הוי – מיפסל בביאתו מיבעיא? ואפילו לר' יהושע דלא הוי ממזר מחייבי כריתות, מ"מ כיון דחמירי – חשיבי "לאיש זר". ואפי' אותם חייבי כריתות דלא הוו זר אלא מעיקרא, כיון דעיקר קרא בחייבי כריתות איירי. והכי פריך: ואימא נבעלה לפסול לה חייבי כריתות דוקא, ולא חייבי לאוין! ומשני: "כי תהיה" אמר רחמנא, לרבות חייבי לאוין. ומיהו, חייבי לאוין כיון דלא חמירי בעינן דליהוי זר אלא מעיקרא, כדלקמן. ופריך: גוי ועבד דלאו בני הויה נינהו לא ליפסלו, דלא אתרבו מ"כי תהיה", וזרים נמי לא איקרו דאין בהם ממזרות, ולא חמירי דאין בהם אלא לאו בעלמא? ומשני: דפסלי מדרבי ישמעאל. אבל חייבי כריתות לא נפקי מהתם. דבני אלמנות וגירושין הוו לאחריני, אלא מ"לאיש זר", ועיקר קרא בדידהו משתעי.

גוי ועבד. וא"ת: והא איצטריך למכתב "אלמנה וגרושה" לומר שחוזרת כשנתאלמנה או נתגרשה! וי"ל: דא"כ לכתוב חד מינייהו, דלית ליה צריכותא דר' עקיבא דבסמוך. ומדכתב תרוייהו – דריש: למי שיש לו אלמנות וגירושין, יצאו כו'. ואימא

הגהות הב"ח

(א) רש"י ד"ה עבד וכו' פרט לאשת גוי ובשאלתות וכו': (ב) בא"ד חייבי כריתות לא כל שכן ועוד הא אמרי':

גליון הש"ס

גמ' א"כ לכתוב קרא היא. עיין לעיל דף ח ע"ב תד"ה ויבמה: שם גלוי מילתא בעלמא הוא. עיין בר"ש פ"ב מ"ג דטבול יום ועיין סנהדרין דף טו ע"א:

יעב"ץ מ"ז

לקמן עו. עח. | לקמן פז. | ג"ז שם כתובות כה. קדושין סט: | [לקמן סט. פז.] | [ג"ז שם סט. עב: סנהדרין כח: נה. יומא מה. סוטה כח. מנחות נה: פז:] | [סנהדרין עו.] | לעיל מה. סוטה כו: קדושין עה: | [פ' ויגלה סימן כה] | [וע' היטב רש"י לעיל מה. ד"ה חייבי] | בס"א חיוב

מי שֶׁיֵּשׁ לוֹ אַלְמְנוּת וְגֵירוּשִׁין בָּהּ, יָצְאוּ גּוֹי וְעֶבֶד שֶׁאֵין לוֹ אַלְמְנוּת וְגֵירוּשִׁין. אַשְׁכַּחַן כֹּהֶנֶת, לְוִיָּה וְיִשְׂרְאֵלִית מְנָא לָן? כִּדְאָמַר *ר' אַבָּא אָמַר רַב: "בַּת" "וּבַת" ה"נ "בַּת" "וּבַת". כְּמַאן, כְּרַבִּי עֲקִיבָא, *דְּדָרֵישׁ וָוֵי? אֲפִילּוּ תֵּימָא רַבָּנַן, כּוּלָּהּ "וּבַת" קְרָא יְתֵירָא הוּא. וְאֵימָא: מִי שֶׁיֵּשׁ לוֹ אַלְמְנוּת וְגֵירוּשִׁין בָּהּ, כִּי לֵית לֵיהּ זֶרַע – קָאָכְלָה, כִּי אִית לֵיהּ זֶרַע – לָא אָכְלָה, מִי שֶׁאֵין לוֹ אַלְמְנוּת וְגֵירוּשִׁין בָּהּ, אע"ג דְּאִית לֵיהּ זֶרַע – נַמִי תֵּיכוּל! אִם כֵּן רִבּוּיֵי לְוִיָּה וְיִשְׂרְאֵלִית לָמָּה לִי? וּלְרַבִּי עֲקִיבָא, דְּאָמַר: *אֵין קִדּוּשִׁין תּוֹפְסִין בְּחַיָּיבֵי לָאוִין, וּמַאי "כִּי תִהְיֶה לְאִישׁ זָר" כִּי תִּיבָּעֵל, "אַלְמָנָה וּגְרוּשָׁה" לָמָּה לִי? אַלְמָנָה לְהַחְמִיר עָלֶיהָ, וּגְרוּשָׁה לְהָקֵל עָלֶיהָ. וּצְרִיכָא, דְּאִי אַשְׁמְעִינַן אַלְמָנָה – אַלְמָנָה הוּא דְּכִי לֵית לָהּ זֶרַע אָכְלָה, מִשּׁוּם דַּחֲזְיָא לִכְהוּנָּה, אֲבָל גְּרוּשָׁה דְּלָא חַזְיָא לִכְהוּנָּה – אֵימָא אע"ג דְּלֵית לָהּ זֶרַע לָא אָכְלָה. וְאִי אַשְׁמְעִינַן גְּרוּשָׁה – גְּרוּשָׁה הוּא דְּכִי אִית לָהּ זֶרַע לָא אָכְלָה, מִשּׁוּם דְּלָא חַזְיָא לִכְהוּנָּה, אֲבָל אַלְמָנָה, דַּחֲזְיָא לִכְהוּנָּה, אֵימָא: אע"ג דְּאִית לָהּ זֶרַע נַמִי תֵּיכוּל – צְרִיכָא. וְאֵימָא: נִבְעֲלָה לְפָסוּל לָהּ – אַף מַחֲזִיר גְּרוּשָׁתוֹ! "לְאִישׁ זָר" אָמַר רַחֲמָנָא, מִי שֶׁזָּר אֶצְלָהּ מֵעִיקָּרָא, לְאַפּוֹקֵי הַאי דְּלָא זָר אֶצְלָהּ מֵעִיקָּרָא הוּא. אִי הָכִי, חָלָל דְּלָאו זָר הוּא(א) מֵעִיקָּרָא, לָא לִפְסוֹל! אָמַר קְרָא: °"לֹא יְחַלֵּל זַרְעוֹ בְּעַמָּיו", *מַקִּישׁ זַרְעוֹ לוֹ: מַה הוּא פּוֹסֵל [א]אַף זַרְעוֹ נַמִי פּוֹסֵל. וְאֵימָא: מִשְּׁעַת הֲוָיָה? דּוּמְיָא דְּכֹהֵן גָּדוֹל בְּאַלְמָנָה, מַה כֹּהֵן גָּדוֹל בְּאַלְמָנָה – בְּבִיאָה, אַף הַאי נַמִי – בְּבִיאָה. וְאֵימָא: עַד דְּאִיכָּא הֲוָיָה וּבִיאָה! דּוּמְיָא דְּכ"ג בְּאַלְמָנָה, [ב]מַה כֹּהֵן גָּדוֹל בְּאַלְמָנָה – בְּבִיאָה לְחוּדַהּ, אַף הַאי נַמִי בְּבִיאָה לְחוּדַהּ. "וְרַבִּי יוֹסֵי אוֹמֵר: כָּל *שֶׁזַּרְעוֹ פָּסוּל – פּוֹסֵל, וְכָל שֶׁאֵין זַרְעוֹ פָּסוּל – אֵינוֹ פּוֹסֵל". *מַאי אִיכָּא בֵּין ת"ק לְרַבִּי יוֹסֵי? אָמַר רַ' יוֹחָנָן: מִצְרִי שֵׁנִי וַאֲדוֹמִי שֵׁנִי אִיכָּא בֵּינַיְיהוּ. וּשְׁנֵיהֶם לֹא לְמָדוּהָ אֶלָּא מִכֹּהֵן גָּדוֹל בְּאַלְמָנָה. ת"ק סָבַר: מַה כ"ג בְּאַלְמָנָה, שֶׁבִּיאָתוֹ בַּעֲבֵירָה – וּפוֹסֵל, אַף הַאי נַמִי פּוֹסֵל. וְרַבִּי יוֹסֵי סָבַר: כְּכֹהֵן גָּדוֹל, מַה כֹּהֵן גָּדוֹל – שֶׁזַּרְעוֹ פָּסוּל וּפוֹסֵל, אַף כָּל שֶׁזַּרְעוֹ פָּסוּל פּוֹסֵל, לְאַפּוֹקֵי מִצְרִי שֵׁנִי [ג]דְּאֵין זַרְעוֹ פָּסוּל, דִּכְתִיב: °"בָּנִים אֲשֶׁר יִוָּלְדוּ לָהֶם דּוֹר שְׁלִישִׁי יָבֹא לָהֶם בִּקְהַל ה'". § "רשב"ג אוֹמֵר: כָּל שֶׁאַתָּה נוֹשֵׂא בִּתּוֹ אַתָּה נוֹשֵׂא אַלְמְנָתוֹ וכו'". § מַאי אִיכָּא בֵּין רַ' יוֹסֵי לְרַבָּן שִׁמְעוֹן בֶּן גַּמְלִיאֵל? אָמַר עוּלָּא: גֵּר עַמּוֹנִי וּמוֹאָבִי אִיכָּא בֵּינַיְיהוּ. וּשְׁנֵיהֶם לֹא לְמָדוּהָ אֶלָּא מִכֹּהֵן גָּדוֹל בְּאַלְמָנָה. רַבִּי יוֹסֵי סָבַר: מַה כֹּהֵן גָּדוֹל בְּאַלְמָנָה – שֶׁזַּרְעוֹ פָּסוּל וּפוֹסֵל, אַף כָּל שֶׁזַּרְעוֹ פָּסוּל – פּוֹסֵל. רשב"ג סָבַר: מַה כֹּהֵן גָּדוֹל בְּאַלְמָנָה – שֶׁכָּל זַרְעוֹ פָּסוּל וּפוֹסֵל, אַף שֶׁכָּל זַרְעוֹ פָּסוּל וּפוֹסֵל, לְאַפּוֹקֵי עַמּוֹנִי וּמוֹאָבִי דְּאֵין כָּל זַרְעוֹ פָּסוּל, דְּאָמַר מָר: *[ד]עַמּוֹנִי וְלֹא עַמּוֹנִית, מוֹאָבִי וְלֹא מוֹאָבִית. §

מתני' [ה]הָאוֹנֵס וְהַמְפַתֶּה וְהַשּׁוֹטֶה – לֹא פּוֹסְלִין וְלֹא מַאֲכִילִין, וְאִם אֵינָן רְאוּיִין לָבֹא בְּיִשְׂרָאֵל – הֲרֵי אֵלּוּ פּוֹסְלִין. כֵּיצַד?(ג) (הָיָה) יִשְׂרָאֵל שֶׁבָּא עַל בַּת כֹּהֵן – תֹּאכַל בִּתְרוּמָה. עִיבְּרָה

(ויקרא כא) (דברים כג) (ס"א ל"ג)

רש"י

אַשְׁכַּחַן כֹּהֶנֶת. דְּפָסֵיל לָהּ עֶבֶד. כּוּלָּהּ וּבַת קְרָא יְתֵירָא הוּא. דְּהָא כְּתִיב בִּקְרָא דִּלְעֵיל מִינֵּיהּ "וּבַת כֹּהֵן", וּמָצֵי לְמִכְתַּב אַבַּתְרֵיהּ "וְכִי תִהְיֶה אַלְמָנָה וּגְרוּשָׁה". אע"ג דְּאִית לָהּ זֶרַע תֵּיכוּל. וְכִבְהֵמָה בְּעָלְמָא חֲשִׁיב. אִם כֵּן. דְּהַאי קְרָא לְקוּלָּא כְּתִיב, וּלְאַשְׁמוּעִינַן דְּזֶרַע דְּגוֹי וְעֶבֶד לָא פָּסֵיל – רִבּוּיֵי לְוִיָּה וְיִשְׂרְאֵלִית דִּכְתִיב בֵּיהּ לָמָּה לִי דִּכְתַב, "וּבַת" קְרָא יְתֵירָא? הַשְׁתָּא כֹּהֶנֶת גּוּפָהּ אַשְׁמוּעִינַן דְּלָא מִיפַּסְלָא בְּזֶרַע גּוֹי וְעֶבֶד, לְוִיָּה וְיִשְׂרְאֵלִית מִיבַּעְיָא?! וְאִי מִשּׁוּם לְאַשְׁמוּעִינַן דְּמִי שֶׁיֵּשׁ לוֹ אַלְמְנוּת וְגֵירוּשִׁין, אֲפִי' הָכִי כִּי אִית לָהּ זֶרַע מִינֵּיהּ לָא תֵּיכוּל, וְאִיצְטְרִיךְ לְמֵיסַר לְוִיָּה וְיִשְׂרְאֵלִית הָאוֹכֶלֶת בִּתְרוּמָה בִּשְׁבִיל בְּנָהּ כֹּהֵן, דְּכִי תִּינָּשֵׂא לְזָר וִיהֵא לָהּ זֶרַע מִמֶּנּוּ לֹא תָּשׁוּב לִתְרוּמָה בְּמִיתַת בַּעְלָהּ – הָא פְּשִׁיטָא לָן; דְּכֵיוָן דְּכֹהֶנֶת גּוּפָהּ מִיפַּסְלָא בְּזֶרַע יִשְׂרָאֵל מִתְּרוּמָה דְּבֵי נָשָׁא, כָּל שֶׁכֵּן יִשְׂרְאֵלִית הָאוֹכֶלֶת בִּשְׁבִיל בְּנָהּ. אֶלָּא וַדַּאי, כִּי רַבֵּי קְרָא לְוִיָּה וְיִשְׂרְאֵלִית – לְהָכִי רַבְּיֵיהּ, שֶׁאִם אוֹכֶלֶת בִּשְׁבִיל בְּנָהּ, וְנִבְעֲלָה לְגוֹי וְעֶבֶד, אֲפִי' אֵין לָהּ זֶרַע – נִפְסְלָה, דְּלָא נָפְקָא לָן מִכֹּהֶנֶת, כִּדְאָמְרִינַן לְעֵיל (דף סח:): כֹּהֶנֶת הִיא דְּקָדֵישׁ גּוּפָהּ כו'. וּלְרַבִּי עֲקִיבָא דְּאָמַר אֵין קִידּוּשִׁין תּוֹפְסִין. לְאָדָם פָּסוּל, וְהַאי "כִּי תִהְיֶה לְאִישׁ זָר" דִּלְעֵיל – לָאו מִשּׁוּם הֲוָיָה נָקַט, וּלְמֵימְרָא דְּאֵין בִּיאַת פָּסוּל פּוֹסֶלֶת אֶלָּא בְּמִי שֶׁרָאוּי לְקַדֵּשׁ, דְּהָא אֵין קִידּוּשִׁין לְשׁוּם פָּסוּל. וְהַאי "כִּי תִהְיֶה" אִם בָּא לְלַמֵּד עַל בִּיאַת פְּסוּלִין – אֵינוֹ אֶלָּא לְשׁוֹן בְּעִילָה, וְכָל הַזָּרִים אֶלָּא בְּמַשְׁמַע שֶׁתְּהֵא בִּיאָתָם פּוֹסֶלֶת, אֲפִילּוּ גּוֹי וְעֶבֶד. אַלְמָנָה וּגְרוּשָׁה. לְאַשְׁמוּעִינַן גּוֹי וְעֶבֶד, לָמָּה לִי? אַלְמָנָה לְהַחְמִיר כו'. כְּלוֹמַר, לָאו לְמַעוֹטֵי מִי שֶׁיֵּשׁ לוֹ אַלְמְנוּת וְגֵירוּשִׁין. אֶלָּא לְגוּפֵיהּ אִיצְטְרִיךְ, אַלְמָנָה – כְּדֵי לְהַחְמִיר עָלֶיהָ. דְּאִי לָא כְּתִיב, ה"א אַלְמְנַת יִשְׂרָאֵל וְהִיא בַּת כֹּהֵן תֵּיכוּל, וְאע"ג דְּאִית לָהּ זֶרַע. וּגְרוּשָׁה אִיצְטְרִיךְ לִכְתְבֵיהּ רַחֲמָנָא לְהָקֵל עָלֶיהָ, וּלְמֵימַר (דְּכִי נִתְגָּרְשָׁה מִיִּשְׂרָאֵל לְהָקֵל) דְּכִי לֵית לָהּ זֶרַע מִיִּשְׂרָאֵל – תֵּיכוּל, דְּאִי לָא כְּתָבֵיהּ ה"א אע"ג דְּלֵית לָהּ זֶרַע לָא תֵּיכוּל, דְּכֵיוָן דְּאִיפַּסְלָה מִכְּהוּנָּה – מִתְּרוּמָה נַמִי מִיפַּסְלָה. וְאֵימָא נִבְעֲלָה לְפָסוּל לָהּ אַף מַחֲזִיר גְּרוּשָׁתוֹ. מִשֶּׁנִּישֵּׂאת לְאַחֵר, דְּהָא זָר הוּא אֶצְלָהּ, וְתָפְסִי לוֹ בָּהּ קִידּוּשִׁין, אַלְמָּה תַּנְיָא בְּ"הַחוֹלֵץ" (לעיל מד:) הִיא כְּשֵׁרָה וּוְלָדָהּ כָּשֵׁר, וְאוֹקִימְנָא כְּשֵׁרָה לִכְהוּנָּה – וְכ"שׁ לִתְרוּמָה! ה"ג. חָלָל דְּלָאו זָר אֶצְלָהּ הוּא לָא לִיפְסוֹל. דְּהָא חָלָל מוּתָּר אֲפִילּוּ בְּכֹהֶנֶת. מַקִּישׁ זַרְעוֹ. שֶׁל כֹּהֵן גָּדוֹל מִן הָאַלְמָנָה לוֹ, מַה הוּא פּוֹסֵל הָאַלְמָנָה בְּבִיאָתוֹ מִן הַתְּרוּמָה, כִּדְיָלֵיף בְּפֶרֶק "עֲשָׂרָה יוֹחֲסִין" (קדושין דף עז.) "וְלֹא יְחַלֵּל" – מִי שֶׁהָיָה כָּשֵׁר וְנִתְחַלֵּל, וְזוֹ הִיא הָאַלְמָנָה, אַף זַרְעוֹ הֶחָלָל פּוֹסֵל אִשָּׁה בְּבִיאָתוֹ מִן הַתְּרוּמָה. וְאֵימָא. מִדְּאַפְּקֵיהּ רַחֲמָנָא בִּלְשׁוֹן "כִּי תִהְיֶה", מִשְּׁעַת הֲוָיָה, אִי קִידֵּשׁ פָּסוּל אֶת הָאִשָּׁה – פְּסוּלָה עוֹלָמִית, וַאֲפִי' מֵת, כְּאִילּוּ בָּא עָלֶיהָ. כֹּהֵן גָּדוֹל בְּבִיאָה הוּא דְּפָסֵיל. כִּדְכְתִיב (ויקרא כא) "לֹא יְחַלֵּל זַרְעוֹ", כְּשֶׁיֵּשׁ זֶרַע חִילֵּל, וְהָכִי נַמִי תְּנַן בְּ"הַבָּא עַל יְבִמְתּוֹ" (לעיל דף נו:) נִתְאַרְמְלוּ אוֹ נִתְגָּרְשׁוּ מִן הַנִּשּׂוּאִין – פְּסוּלוֹת, מִן הָאֵירוּסִין – כְּשֵׁרוֹת. מִצְרִי שֵׁנִי. פָּסוּל, וְזַרְעוֹ כָּשֵׁר לְת"ק, כֵּיוָן דְּהוּא פָּסוּל פּוֹסְלָהּ בְּבִיאָה, לְרַבִּי יוֹסֵי – לָא פָּסֵיל: הָכִי גָּרְסִינַן: מַה כֹּהֵן גָּדוֹל בְּאַלְמָנָה בִּיאָתוֹ בַּעֲבֵירָה וּפוֹסֵל כו'. מִצְרִי וַאֲדוֹמִי שֵׁנִי. בִּיאָתָן בַּעֲבֵירָה, דִּכְתִיב (דברים כג) "שְׁלִישִׁי" וְלֹא שֵׁנִי. כָּל שֶׁאַתָּה. כֹּהֵן נוֹשֵׂא בִּתּוֹ, אַתָּה כֹּהֵן נוֹשֵׂא אַלְמְנָתוֹ. גֵּר עַמּוֹנִי. הוּא וּבְנוֹ וּבֶן בְּנוֹ עַד סוֹף הָעוֹלָם פְּסוּלִין, אֲבָל בִּתּוֹ כְּשֵׁרָה, דְּקַיְימָא לָן (לקמן דף עו:): עַמּוֹנִי וְלֹא עַמּוֹנִית. לְרַבִּי יוֹסֵי דְּתָלֵי טַעְמָא בְּכָל שֶׁזַּרְעוֹ פָּסוּל, הוֹאִיל וְיֵשׁ בְּזַרְעוֹ פָּסוּל – פּוֹסֵל, וּלְרַבִּי שִׁמְעוֹן דְּתָלֵי טַעְמָא בְּבִתּוֹ – לָא פָּסֵיל. **מתני'** וְהַשּׁוֹטֶה. אֲפִי' עַל יְדֵי חוּפָּה וְקִידּוּשִׁין – לֹא פּוֹסֵל וְלֹא מַאֲכִיל, דְּאֵין קִנְיָנוֹ קִנְיָן. הֲרֵי אֵלּוּ פּוֹסְלִין. שֶׁהֲרֵי נִתְחַלְּלָה בְּבִיאַת פָּסוּל לָהּ. הֲרֵי יִשְׂרָאֵל שֶׁבָּא עַל בַּת כֹּהֵן. בְּאוֹנֶס אוֹ בְּפִיתּוּי, שֶׁלֹּא לְשֵׁם קִידּוּשִׁין. עִיבְּרָה

תוספות

ואימא מי שיש לו אלמנות וגירושין בה כו'. תימה: דבכל דוכתא לחומרא מקשינן והכא פריך דנקיט לקולא:

אם כן רבויי לויה וישראלית. תימה: דהא איצטריך לרבויי לויה וישראלית לאשמועינן דחוזרת בשביל בנה, כדאמרינן בסוף "יש מותרות" (לקמן דף פז.)? ויש לומר: דמשמע ליה דאיצטריך לויה וישראלית לכל מילי דאיירי קרא, ולאשמועינן דכי אית לה זרע נמי מן הגוי תיכול בשביל בנה – לא איצטריך, כיון דאשמעינן בכהנת דקדיש גופה.

כי תהיה כי תבעל. ואם תאמר: לדידיה נמי איכא לאוקומי באלמנה לכהן גדול לרבי סימאי, ובבעולה לכהן גדול אפי' לרבי ישבב? ויש לומר: דכל פסולי כהונה נפקא לן דמיפסלי בתרומה מ"לא יחלל". אי נמי: לא משמע ליה לאוקמי "לאיש זר" גבי כהן. וא"ת: ולוקמא בסוטה שבא עליה בעלה בדרך, דליכא אלא עשה ד"ונטמאה"? ויש לומר: דזר אצלה מעיקרא בעינן, אפילו לרבי עקיבא, כיון דלא הוי ממזר. ומיהו, קשה: דלמה ליה למימר מאי "כי תהיה" כי תבעל – בפשיטות הוה מצי למיפרך, דלמאי איצטריך קרא לרבי עקיבא לגוי ועבד? דהשתא ממזר הוי, מיפסלא בביאתו מיבעיא?! כדאמר בפרק "עשרה יוחסין" (קדושין עה: ושם).

כהן גדול באלמנה בביאה לחודה. כדאמר בפ' "עשרה יוחסין" (שם דף עח. ושם) בעל – לוקה משום "לא יחלל". ואם תאמר: היא גופה מנלן דלא בעינן תרתי? הא כתיב "לא יקח ולא יחלל"? ויש לומר: דלגבי *כהן אין להצריך קידושין, דכ"ש בלא קידושין. וכיון שהבן נפסל – גם היא נפסלת.

ושניהם לא למדוה אלא מאלמנה לכהן גדול. עיקר טעמא הוי מ"לאיש זר", אלא דמכ"ג באלמנה ילפינן במאי מסתבר לאוקמי קרא. ואי לאו קרא ד"לאיש זר" ליכא למילף מקל וחומר דאלמנה שתתחלל, כדפירשתי לעיל (דף טו: ד"ה מה).

והמפתה והשוטה. הא דלא תנן קטן בהדייהו, דלא תקינו ליה רבנן נישואין, כדקתני בגמרא (לקמן דף לו:) שוטה וקטן שנשאו כו', – אמר רבי יצחק: דהיינו משום דבעי למיתני בסיפא וילדה, דלא מיתני ליה בקטן.

לא פוסלין ולא מאכילין. לא איצטריך לאשמועינן באונס ומפתה דאין מאכילין, ומשום לא פוסלין נקטיה, ואפילו לרבי אלעזר דאמר *פנוי הבא על הפנויה שלא לשם אישות עשאה זונה – נראה דלא מיפסלה בתרומה, דאין זה לאיש זר. ונשאת

עין משפט נר מצוה

לז א מיי' פי"ח מהל' איסורי ביאה הל' א סמג לאוין קפא טוש"ע אה"ע סימן ו סעי' ח:

לח ב מיי' פי"ז שם הל' ג סמג לאוין קכה:

לט ג מיי' פי"ב שם הל' יט סמג לאוין קיב קטז טוש"ע שם סי' ד סעי' ג:

מ ד מיי' שם הי"ח טוש"ע שם סעי' ב:

מא ה מיי' פ"ח מהל' תרומות הל' יג טוי"ד סי' שלא:

מסורת הש"ס

[לעיל סח: לקמן פז.] [לעיל סח: וש"נ] [לעיל י: וש"נ]

[שזרעו עם הכנוי חשיב ב' תיבות דלא הל"ל אלא לא יחלל זרע בעמיו שבשעת הליווי עדיין אינו זרעו שיכונה בו ומדכתיב זרעו הוא כאילו אמר זרע לו וזהו מקיש זרעו לו כ"כ בעלי סוגיות ע' של"ה דף שנג ד"ה ענין היקש]

[לקמן עו: עז. פח: קדושין סז: עה. כתובות ז: חולין סב:]

(קידושין עד:) [שם עה:] [לעיל נט:] (נ"ל בן רש"ל)

הגהות הב"ח

(א) גמ' אי הכי חלל דלאו זר הוא לא ליפסול כצ"ל ותיבת מעיקרא נמחק: (ב) שם במשנה כיצד הרי ישראל:

גליון הש"ס

תוס' ד"ה כי תהיה וכו' דליכא אלא עשה. עיין לעיל דף יא ע"ב תד"ה מאי נסתרה:

עין משפט נר מצוה

מב א מיי' פ"ח מהל' תרומות הי"ד:
מג ב מיי' פ"ו שם הל' טז טוי"ד סי' שלא:
מד ג מיי' שם הל' יג יד:
מה ד מיי' שם הל' טו:
מו ה מיי' פ"ו מהלכות יבום הל' ח סמג עשין נא נב טוש"ע אה"ע סי' קעב סעי' טז:
מז ו מיי' פ"ט מהל' תרומות הל' א סמג לאוין רכח טוי"ד סי' שלא:
מח ז ח ט מיי' שם פ"ח הל"ג טוי"ד שם:
מט י מיי' פט"ו מהל' איסורי ביאה הי"ז סמג לאוין קכה טוש"ע אה"ע סי' ד סעי' כז:

מתני'

[א]עִיבְּרָה — לֹא תֹּאכַל בִּתְרוּמָה, נֶחְתַּךְ הָעוּבָּר בְּמֵעֶיהָ — תֹּאכַל. (א) הָיָה כֹּהֵן שֶׁבָּא עַל בַּת יִשְׂרָאֵל — לֹא תֹּאכַל בִּתְרוּמָה, עִיבְּרָה — לֹא תֹּאכַל, יָלְדָה — תֹּאכַל. נִמְצָא כֹּחוֹ שֶׁל בֵּן גָּדוֹל מִשֶּׁל אָב. [ב]הָעֶבֶד פּוֹסֵל מִשּׁוּם בִּיאָה, וְאֵינוֹ פּוֹסֵל מִשּׁוּם זֶרַע. כֵּיצַד? בַּת יִשְׂרָאֵל לְכֹהֵן, בַּת כֹּהֵן לְיִשְׂרָאֵל, וְיָלְדָה הֵימֶנּוּ בֵּן, וְהָלַךְ הַבֵּן וְנִכְבַּשׁ עַל הַשִּׁפְחָה, וְיָלְדָה הֵימֶנּוּ בֵּן — הֲרֵי זֶה עֶבֶד. הָיְתָה אֵם אָבִיו בַּת יִשְׂרָאֵל לְכֹהֵן — לֹא תֹּאכַל בִּתְרוּמָה, בַּת כֹּהֵן לְיִשְׂרָאֵל — תֹּאכַל בִּתְרוּמָה. [ג]מַמְזֵר פּוֹסֵל וּמַאֲכִיל. כֵּיצַד? בַּת יִשְׂרָאֵל לְכֹהֵן, וּבַת כֹּהֵן לְיִשְׂרָאֵל, וְיָלְדָה הֵימֶנּוּ בַּת, וְהָלְכָה הַבַּת וְנִישֵּׂאת לְעֶבֶד אוֹ לְגוֹי וְיָלְדָה הֵימֶנּוּ בֵּן — הֲרֵי זֶה מַמְזֵר. הָיְתָה אֵם אִמּוֹ בַּת יִשְׂרָאֵל לְכֹהֵן — תֹּאכַל בִּתְרוּמָה. בַּת כֹּהֵן לְיִשְׂרָאֵל — לֹא תֹּאכַל בִּתְרוּמָה. [ד]כֹּהֵן גָּדוֹל, פְּעָמִים שֶׁהוּא פּוֹסֵל, כֵּיצַד? בַּת כֹּהֵן לְיִשְׂרָאֵל וְיָלְדָה הֵימֶנּוּ בַּת, וְהָלְכָה הַבַּת וְנִיסֵּת לְכֹהֵן וְיָלְדָה הֵימֶנּוּ בֵּן — ה"ז רָאוּי לִהְיוֹת כֹּהֵן גָּדוֹל עוֹמֵד וּמְשַׁמֵּשׁ עַל גַּבֵּי הַמִּזְבֵּחַ, מַאֲכִיל אֶת אִמּוֹ, וּפוֹסֵל אֵם אִמּוֹ. זֹאת אוֹמֶרֶת: לֹא כִּבְנִי כ"ג שֶׁהוּא פּוֹסְלֵנִי מִן הַתְּרוּמָה.§

גמ' תָּנֵינָא לְהָא דְּת"ר: *[ה]שׁוֹטֶה וְקָטָן שֶׁנָּשְׂאוּ נָשִׁים וָמֵתוּ — נְשׁוֹתֵיהֶן פְּטוּרוֹת מִן הַחֲלִיצָה וּמִן הַיִּבּוּם.§ כֵּיצַד? (ב) הָיָה יִשְׂרָאֵל שֶׁבָּא עַל בַּת כֹּהֵן — תֹּאכַל בִּתְרוּמָה. עִיבְּרָה — לֹא תֹּאכַל.§ כֵּיוָן דְּעִיבְּרָה לֹא תֹּאכַל — לֵיחוּשׁ שֶׁמָּא עִיבְּרָה! מִי לָא תְּנַן: *מַפְרִישִׁין אוֹתָן ג' חֳדָשִׁים שֶׁמָּא מְעוּבָּרוֹת הֵן! אָמַר רַבָּה בַּר רַב הוּנָא: לְיוּחֲסִין חָשְׁשׁוּ, לִתְרוּמָה לֹא חָשְׁשׁוּ. וְלִתְרוּמָה לֹא חָשְׁשׁוּ? וְהָתַנְיָא: *[ו]"הֲרֵי זֶה גִּיטֵּיךְ שָׁעָה אַחַת קוֹדֶם לְמִיתָתִי" — אֲסוּרָה לֶאֱכוֹל בִּתְרוּמָה מִיָּד! אֶלָּא אָמַר רַבָּה בַּר רַב הוּנָא: בְּנִישּׂוּאִין — חָשְׁשׁוּ, בִּזְנוּת — לֹא חָשְׁשׁוּ. וּבְנִישּׂוּאִין מִי חָשְׁשׁוּ? וְהָתַנְיָא: [ז]בַּת כֹּהֵן שֶׁנִּישֵּׂאת לְיִשְׂרָאֵל וָמֵת — טוֹבֶלֶת וְאוֹכֶלֶת בִּתְרוּמָה לָעֶרֶב! אָמַר רַב חִסְדָּא: [ח]טוֹבֶלֶת וְאוֹכֶלֶת עַד אַרְבָּעִים, דְּאִי לָא מִיעַבְּרָא — הָא לָא מִיעַבְּרָא, וְאִי מִיעַבְּרָא — עַד אַרְבָּעִים מַיָּא בְּעָלְמָא הִיא. אֲמַר לֵיהּ אַבַּיֵי: אִי הָכִי, אֵימָא סֵיפָא: הוּכַּר עוּבָּרָהּ בְּמֵעֶיהָ — תְּהֵא מְקוּלְקֶלֶת לְמַפְרֵעַ! מַאי [ט]מְקוּלְקֶלֶת: עַד אַרְבָּעִים. אִיתְּמַר, הַבָּא עַל אֲרוּסָתוֹ בְּבֵית חָמִיו. רַב אָמַר: הַוָּלָד מַמְזֵר, וּשְׁמוּאֵל אָמַר: הַוָּלָד שְׁתוּקִי. אָמַר רָבָא: מִסְתַּבְּרָא מִילְּתֵיהּ דְּרַב — דְּדַיְימָא מֵעָלְמָא, אֲבָל לָא דַּיְימָא מֵעָלְמָא — בַּתְרָא דִּידֵיהּ שָׁדֵינַן לֵיהּ. אֲמַר רָבָא: מְנָא אָמֵינָא לָהּ — דְּקָתָנֵי: יָלְדָה תֹּאכַל. הֵיכִי דָּמֵי? אִילֵימָא דְּדַיְימָא מֵעָלְמָא — יָלְדָה אַמַּאי תֹּאכַל? אֶלָּא לָאו — מִינֵּיהּ דַּיְימָא וְלָא דַּיְימָא מֵעָלְמָא. וּמָה הָתָם, דִּלְהַאי אִיסּוּרָא וּלְהַאי אִיסּוּרָא — בַּתְרָא דִּידֵיהּ שָׁדֵינַן לֵיהּ, הָכָא, דִּלְהַאי אִיסּוּרָא וּלְהַאי הֶיתֵּירָא — לֹא כׇּל שֶׁכֵּן?! א"ל אַבַּיֵי: לְעוֹלָם אֵימָא לָךְ: כׇּל הֵיכָא דְּדַיְימָא מִינֵּיהּ אע"ג דְּלָא דַּיְימָא מֵעָלְמָא — אָמַר רַב הַוָּלָד מַמְזֵר, מ"ט? דְּאָמְרִינַן: מִדְּאַפְקְרָא נַפְשָׁהּ לְגַבֵּי אָרוּס — אַפְקְרָא נַפְשָׁהּ לְעָלְמָא. וּמַתְנִי' — שֶׁהָיוּ שְׁנֵיהֶם חֲבוּשִׁים בְּבֵית הָאֲסוּרִין. אִיכָּא דְּאָמְרִי: *בְּבָא עָלֶיהָ — כ"ע לָא פְּלִיגִי דְּבַתְרֵיהּ דִּידֵיהּ שָׁדֵינַן לֵיהּ, וְהָכִי אִיתְּמַר: *אֲרוּסָה שֶׁעִיבְּרָה, רַב אָמַר: הַוָּלָד מַמְזֵר, וּשְׁמוּאֵל אָמַר: [י]הַוָּלָד שְׁתוּקִי. אָמַר רָבָא: *מִסְתַּבְּרָא מִילְּתֵיהּ דְּרַב — דְּלָא דַּיְימָא מִינֵּיהּ וְדַיְימָא מֵעָלְמָא, אֲבָל

רש"י

עִיבְּרָה לֹא תֹּאכַל. כִּדְיָלְפִינַן לְעֵיל (דף סז:) עוּבָּר פּוֹסֵל, דִּכְתִיב "כִּנְעוּרֶיהָ" – פְּרָט לִמְעוּבֶּרֶת. נֶחְתַּךְ הָעוּבָּר בְּמֵעֶיהָ תֹּאכַל. מִיָּד. וְה"ה נַמִּי אִם יְלָדַתּוּ וָמֵת. עִיבְּרָה לֹא תֹּאכַל. שֶׁהָעוּבָּר אֵינוֹ מַאֲכִיל אֶת אִמּוֹ יִשְׂרְאֵלִית עַד שֶׁיֵּצֵא לַאֲוִיר הָעוֹלָם, כִּדְכְתִיב (ויקרא כב) "וִילִיד בֵּיתוֹ... יֹאכְלוּ" – יָלוּד מַאֲכִיל, שֶׁאֵין יָלוּד אֵין מַאֲכִיל. גָּדוֹל מִשֶּׁל אָב. שֶׁהַבּוֹעֵל לֹא יָכוֹל לְהַאֲכִילָהּ, מִפְּנֵי שֶׁלֹּא בָּא עָלֶיהָ לְשֵׁם קִידּוּשִׁין וְלָאו קִנְיָנוֹ הוּא, וּבְנוֹ מַאֲכִילָהּ. הָעֶבֶד פּוֹסֵל מִשּׁוּם בִּיאָה. אִם בָּא עַל כֹּהֶנֶת פְּסָלָהּ מִן הַתְּרוּמָה, כִּדְאָמְרִינַן בַּגְּמָרָא לְעֵיל (דף סח:). וְאֵין פּוֹסֵל מִשּׁוּם זֶרַע. אִם יֵשׁ לָהּ זֶרַע לְבַת כֹּהֵן מִיִּשְׂרָאֵל כָּשֵׁר שֶׁהוּא עֶבֶד, וּמֵת בַּעְלָהּ יִשְׂרָאֵל וְנִשְׁאַר זֶה, לָא אָמְרִינַן הֲרֵי זֶרַע יֵשׁ לָהּ מִיִּשְׂרָאֵל, וְלֹא תָּשׁוּב לִתְרוּמַת אָבִיהָ. דְּעֶבֶד וַדַּאי לָאו זֶרַע הוּא, וּמְפָרֵשׁ וְאָזֵיל הֵיכִי מַשְׁכַּחַתְּ לָהּ שֶׁיְּהֵא בֶּן יִשְׂרָאֵל כָּשֵׁר עֶבֶד. וְנִכְבַּשׁ עַל הַשִּׁפְחָה. נִדְחַק וְנִדְבַּק עָלֶיהָ. לְשׁוֹן מַכְבֵּשׁ = פריס"א בְּלַעַ"ז, וּלְשׁוֹן גְּנַאי הוּא. הֲרֵי זֶה עֶבֶד. שֶׁוָּלָד שִׁפְחָה כָּמוֹהָ, דִּכְתִיב "הָאִשָּׁה וִילָדֶיהָ" (שמות כא). הָיְתָה אֵם אָבִיו. בַּת כֹּהֵן לְיִשְׂרָאֵל, תֹּאכַל בִּתְרוּמָה אִם מֵת אָבִיו וְהוּא קַיָּים. אע"ג דְּוָלָד וָלָד בְּעָלְמָא פָּסֵיל, כִּדְאָמְרַן (לקמן דף ע.) זֶרַע זַרְעָהּ מִנַּיִן כו' – הַאי לָא פָּסֵיל, דְּהָא לָאו בָּתַר אֲבוּהּ אָזֵיל, וְלָאו זַרְעוֹ הוּא. בַּת יִשְׂרָאֵל לְכֹהֵן, וּמֵת בְּנָהּ מִכֹּהֵן, וּבְנוֹ בֶּן בְּנָהּ קַיָּים וְהוּא עֶבֶד – לֹא תֹּאכַל בִּתְרוּמָה. דְּלָאו זֶרַע הוּא. כ"ג פְּעָמִים שֶׁהוּא פּוֹסֵל. אֶת בַּת כֹּהֵן מִן הַתְּרוּמָה, מִשּׁוּם זַרְעָהּ מִיִּשְׂרָאֵל. מַאֲכִיל אֶת אִמּוֹ. (ג) לְאַחַר מִיתַת אָבִיו. וּפוֹסֵל אֶת אֵם אִמּוֹ. אֲפִילּוּ לְאַחַר מִיתַת אִמּוֹ דְּאִי לָאו הוּא הֲוָה הָדְרָה אֵם אִמּוֹ לִתְרוּמָה דְּבֵי נָשָׂא לְאַחַר מִיתַת בִּתָּהּ, כִּדְאָמַר בְּ"יֵשׁ מוּתָּרוֹת" (לקמן ד' פז.): מֵת בְּנָהּ מִיִּשְׂרָאֵל – תֹּאכַל בִּתְרוּמָה. וְזֹאת. הָאִשָּׁה, אוֹמֶרֶת: לֹא כִּבְנִי כ"ג, כְּלוֹמַר לֹא יִרְבּוּ כְּמוֹתוֹ.

גמ' נְשׁוֹתֵיהֶן פְּטוּרוֹת. אַלְמָא: אֵין קִנְיָן לְשׁוֹטֶה. כֵּיוָן. דְּאִי פְּשִׁיטָא לָן דְּעִיבְּרָה אָמְרִינַן לָהּ לֹא תֹּאכַל – אַמַּאי קָתָנֵי מַתְנִיתִין יִשְׂרָאֵל הַבָּא עַל בַּת כֹּהֵן בְּאוֹנֶס וּפִיתּוּי תֹּאכַל? לֵיחוּשׁ שֶׁמָּא עִיבְּרָה! מִי לָא תְּנַן. בְּפֶ' "ד' אַחִין" גַּבֵּי נָשִׁים שֶׁהוּחְלְפוּ בִּשְׁעַת כְּנִיסָתָן לַחוּפָּה: מַפְרִישִׁין אוֹתָן מִבַּעֲלֵיהֶן ג' חֳדָשִׁים, שֶׁמָּא מְעוּבָּרוֹת הֵן וְהַוְּלָדוֹת מַמְזֵרִין, וּבָעֵינַן הַבְחָנָה בֵּין וָלָד כָּשֵׁר לְוָלָד פָּסוּל. אַלְמָא: לַחֲדָא בִּיאָה חָיְישִׁינַן. לְיוּחֲסִין חָשְׁשׁוּ. מַעֲלָה עָשׂוּ לְיוּחֲסִין לָחוּשׁ לְבִיאָה אַחַת וּלְסָפֵק. הֲרֵי זֶה גִּיטֵּיךְ. כֹּהֵן לְבַת יִשְׂרָאֵל. אֲסוּרָה לֶאֱכוֹל בִּתְרוּמָה מִיָּד. דְּכׇל שַׁעְתָּא אָמְרִינַן הַשְׁתָּא מָיֵית, אַלְמָא: חָסְרִי לָהּ מִסָּפֵק. אֶלָּא אָמַר רַבָּה. לָא תֵּימָא לִתְרוּמָה לֹא חָשְׁשׁוּ, דְּוַדַּאי חָיְישִׁינַן לִסְפֵיקָא, אֶלָּא תָּרֵיץ לְפִירְכָא דִּלְעֵיל הָכִי. בְּנִישּׂוּאִין. כְּגוֹן שֶׁנִּתְחַלְּפוּ בִּכְנִיסָתָן לַחוּפָּה – חָשְׁשׁוּ לְשֶׁמָּא נִתְעַבְּרוּ, דְּהָא לֹא הִפְּכוּ. אֲבָל בִּזְנוּת לֹא חָשְׁשׁוּ. כִּדְקַיְימָא לָן: *אִשָּׁה מְזַנָּה מִתְהַפֶּכֶת כְּדֵי שֶׁלֹּא תִּתְעַבֵּר, הִלְכָּךְ לֵיכָּא סָפֵק. וָמֵת. בַּעְלָהּ בּוֹ בַּיּוֹם. טוֹבֶלֶת. מִשּׁוּם בִּיאָה, דִּכְתִיב "וְאִשָּׁה אֲשֶׁר יִשְׁכַּב אִישׁ אוֹתָהּ שִׁכְבַת זֶרַע" וגו' (ויקרא טו): יְצִירַת הַוָּלָד אַרְבָּעִים יוֹם. תְּהֵא מְקוּלְקֶלֶת לְמַפְרֵעַ. לְשַׁלֵּם תְּרוּמָה שֶׁאָכְלָה קֶרֶן וָחוֹמֶשׁ, דְּאִשְׁתַּכַּח דְּזָרָה הַוְיָא וְאָכְלָה תְּרוּמָה בִּשְׁגָגָה. וְאִי כִּדְקָאָמְרַתְּ – מַאי מְקוּלְקֶלֶת? הָא וַדַּאי כׇּל מ' לָאו זָרָה הָוְיָא. עַד מ'. אִם אָכְלָה לְאַחַר מ' תְּהֵא מְקוּלְקֶלֶת לְמַפְרֵעַ עַד יוֹם אַרְבָּעִים. וּמִדִּמְתָרֵץ רַב חִסְדָּא אוֹכֶלֶת עַד אַרְבָּעִים – שְׁמַע מִינַּהּ: מֵת בַּעְלָהּ דְּקָתָנֵי בְּבָרַיְיתָא הֲוֵי דְּמֵת בּוֹ בַּיּוֹם שֶׁנְּשָׂאָהּ, דְּאִי שָׁהָה אֶצְלָהּ זְמַן מְרוּבֶּה – לְאַלְתַּר אֲסוּרָה, דִּלְמָא מְעוּבֶּרֶת הִיא, דַּהֲרֵי כְּבָר אַרְבָּעִים יוֹם. הַוָּלָד מַמְזֵר. אע"פ שֶׁשְּׁנֵיהֶם מוֹדִים שֶׁבָּא עָלֶיהָ, חָיְישִׁינַן: הוֹאִיל וּפְרוּצָה הִיא – אַחֵר נַמִּי בָּא עָלֶיהָ, וְאִיעַבְּרָה מִינֵּיהּ. שְׁתוּקִי. סָפֵק מַמְזֵר. דְּהָא מְסַפְּקָא לָן אִי מֵאָרוּס הוּא, וְכָשֵׁר, אִי מֵאִינִישׁ אַחֲרִינָא הוּא, הִלְכָּךְ מַמְזֵר סָפֵק הוּא. מִסְתַּבְּרָא מִילְּתֵיהּ דְּרַב. דְּמַשְׁוֵי לֵיהּ מַמְזֵר וַדַּאי. דְּדַיְימָא מֵעָלְמָא. שֶׁחֲשׁוּדָה מֵאֲחֵרִים, דְּלֵיכָּא לְאַכְשׁוּרֵי כְּשְׁאָר בְּנֵי דוֹמָהּ שֶׁהֵם כְּשֵׁרִים. דְּהָתָם, כֵּיוָן דִּנְשׂוּאָה הִיא, רוֹב בְּעִילוֹת הַלָּךְ אַחַר הַבַּעַל. אֲבָל הָכָא, לָאו אוֹרְחֵיהּ לְמִיבְעַל כּוּלֵּי הַאי בְּלֹא חוּפָּה. דְּקָתָנֵי בְּמַתְנִי' יָלְדָה. אֲנוּסָה וּמְפוּתָּה בַּת יִשְׂרָאֵל מִכֹּהֵן תֹּאכַל בִּתְרוּמָה מִשּׁוּם בְּנָהּ, דְּמַחְזְקִינַן לֵיהּ בְּכֹהֵן. הֵיכִי דָּמֵי אִי דְּדַיְימָא. נַמִּי מֵעָלְמָא, אַמַּאי תֹּאכַל? אֶלָּא לָאו דְּדַיְימָא מִינֵּיהּ לְחוּדֵיהּ, וְקָשָׁדֵינַן לֵיהּ אַבָּתְרֵיהּ. וְאע"ג דִּלְדִידֵיהּ אִיסּוּרָא כְּכוּלֵּי עָלְמָא, דִּגְזָרוּ עַל יִחוּד שֶׁל פְּנוּיָה, וְכׇל שֶׁכֵּן אֲרוּסָה, דִּלְגַבֵּי אָרוּס הֶיתֵּר וּלְעָלְמָא בְּאִיסּוּרָא – וַדַּאי הֵיכָא דְּדַיְימָא מִינֵּיהּ לְחוּדֵיהּ אָמְרִינַן בַּתְרֵיהּ שָׁדֵינַן לֵיהּ לַוָּלָד. בְּבָא עָלֶיהָ כּוּלֵּי עָלְמָא לָא פְּלִיגֵי. הֵיכָא דְּמוֹדֶה שֶׁבָּא עָלֶיהָ. הַוָּלָד מַמְזֵר. וַדַּאי, דְּבָתַר רוּבָּא דְּעָלְמָא שָׁדֵינַן לֵיהּ, וּמֵאִינִישׁ אַחֲרִינָא הָוֵי. הָכִי

תוספות

ונשאת לעבד. תימה: דלא קתני ונכבשה עם העבד, כדקתני ונכבש עם השפחה – דנישואין לא שייכי בה:

בזנות לא חששו. כדפי' בקונטרס, דאשה מזנה מתהפכת כדי שלא תתעבר. ושוטה נמי, אע"פ שנשאת לו – מתהפכת, ואין רוצה להתעבר ממנו, לפי שיראה שלא תוכל לסובלו, כדאמרינן בפרק "חרש" (לקמן דף קיב: ושם) דאין אדם דר עם נחש בכפיפה אחת.

רב אמר הולד ממזר כו'. בפ' "עשרה יוחסין" (קדושין דף עה.) מפרש פלוגתייהו בג' גווני.

אמר ליה אביי לעולם אימא לך אע"ג דלא דיימא מעלמא אמר רב הולד ממזר. ולהאי לישנא הא דקאמר בפ"ק דכתובות (דף יג:) ההוא ארוס וארוסתו דאתו לקמיה דרב יוסף, היא אמרה: מיניה, והוא אמר:(ד) אין, מינאי. אמר רב יוסף: למאי ניחוש להו? חדא דהא קא מודה, ועוד: האמר רב יהודה כו'. לאביי דאית ליה הכא דלרב הולד ממזר, אע"ג דלא דיימא מעלמא – לא סגי התם בטעמא קמא בלא "ועוד".

איכא דאמרי בבא עליה כ"ע לא פליגי כו'. פירוש: היכא דלא דיימא מעלמא – מודה אביי דאין הולד ממזר. אלא הכי איתמר כו', ופליגי אביי ורבא בדיימא מיניה ודיימא מעלמא. אבל

הגהות הב"ח

(א) גמ' נחתך העובר במעיה תאכל הרי כהן: (ב) שם ומן היבום כילד הרי ישראל שבא: (ג) רש"י ד"ה מאכיל את אמו אפי' לאחר מיתת אביו: (ד) תום' ד"ה אמר וכו' אמר מינאי כנ"ל ותיבת אין נמחק:

מסורת הש"ס

(תוס' ספי"א) לקמן קיב:
לעיל לג:
סוכה כג: גיטין כח. נדרים ג:
קדושין עה.
[ע' תוס' סוטה כז ד"ה רוב בעילות]
[ע' תוס' שם]
[לעיל לה.]

אבל דַּיְימָא מִנֵּיהּ, אע"ג דְּדַיְימָא מֵעָלְמָא, בַּתְרֵיהּ דִּידֵיהּ שָׁדֵינַן לֵיהּ, אֲמַר רָבָא: מְנָא אָמֵינָא לָהּ, דְּקָתָנֵי: יָלְדָה — תֹּאכַל. הֵיכִי דָּמֵי? אִילֵימָא דְּדַיְימָא מִנֵּיהּ וְלָא דַּיְימָא מֵעָלְמָא — צְרִיכָא לְמֵימַר דְּתֵיכוֹל?! אֶלָּא לָאו — דְּדַיְימָא נַמִי מֵעָלְמָא, וּמָה הָתָם, דִּלְהַאי אִיסּוּרָא וּלְהַאי אִיסּוּרָא, בַּתְרֵיהּ דִּידֵיהּ שָׁדֵינַן לֵיהּ, הָכָא דִּלְהַאי אִיסּוּרָא וּלְהַאי הֶיתֵּירָא — לֹא כָּל שֶׁכֵּן?! א"ל אַבַּיֵי: לְעוֹלָם אֵימָא לָךְ, כָּל הֵיכָא דְּדַיְימָא מֵעָלְמָא, אע"ג דְּדַיְימָא מִנֵּיהּ אֲמַר רַב הַוָּלָד מַמְזֵר, וּמתני' בִּדְלָא דַּיְימָא כְּלָל.§ "הָעֶבֶד פּוֹסֵל מִשּׁוּם בִּיאָה כו'".§ מ"ט? אָמַר קְרָא °"הָאִשָּׁה וִילָדֶיהָ תִּהְיֶה וגו'".§ "מַמְזֵר פּוֹסֵל וּמַאֲכִיל".§ ת"ר: *°"וְזֶרַע אֵין לָהּ", [א]אֵין לִי אֶלָּא *זַרְעָהּ, זֶרַע זַרְעָהּ מִנַּיִן? ת"ל "וְזֶרַע אֵין לָהּ", מִכָּל מָקוֹם, אֵין לִי אֶלָּא זֶרַע כָּשֵׁר, זֶרַע פָּסוּל מִנַּיִן? ת"ל "וְזֶרַע אֵין לָהּ" — *עַיֵּין עָלֶיהָ. וְהָא אַפֵּיקְתֵּיהּ לְזֶרַע זַרְעָהּ! זֶרַע זַרְעָהּ לָא אִיצְטְרִיךְ קְרָא, *בְּנֵי בָנִים הֲרֵי הֵן כְּבָנִים, כִּי אִיצְטְרִיךְ קְרָא — לְזֶרַע פָּסוּל. א"ל ר"ל לְרַבִּי יוֹחָנָן: כְּמַאן, כר"ע, דְּאָמַר: יֵשׁ מַמְזֵר מֵחַיָּיבֵי לָאוִין? אֲפִילּוּ תֵּימָא רַבָּנַן, בְּעוֹבֵד כּוֹכָבִים וְעֶבֶד מוֹדוּ. *דְּכִי אֲתָא רַב דִּימִי א"ר יִצְחָק בַּר אַבְדִּימִי מִשּׁוּם רַבֵּינוּ: גּוֹי וְעֶבֶד הַבָּא עַל בַּת יִשְׂרָאֵל — הַוָּלָד מַמְזֵר.§ "כ"ג פְּעָמִים שֶׁפּוֹסֵל".§ ת"ר: הֲרֵינִי כַּפָּרַת בֶּן בְּתִי כּוּזָא — שֶׁמַּאֲכִילַנִי בִּתְרוּמָה, וְאֵינִי כַּפָּרַת בֶּן בְּתִי כַּדָּא — שֶׁפּוֹסְלֵנִי מִן הַתְּרוּמָה.§

(שמות כח — ויקרא כב)

הדרן עלך אלמנה

הֶעָרֵל [ב]וְכָל הַטְּמֵאִים לֹא יֹאכְלוּ בִּתְרוּמָה, נְשֵׁיהֶן וְעַבְדֵיהֶן יֹאכְלוּ בִּתְרוּמָה. [ג]פְּצוּעַ דַּכָּא וּכְרוּת שָׁפְכָה, הֵן וְעַבְדֵיהֶן — יֹאכְלוּ, וּנְשֵׁיהֶן — לֹא יֹאכְלוּ, וְאִם לֹא *יְדָעָהּ מִשֶּׁנַּעֲשָׂה פְּצוּעַ דַּכָּא וּכְרוּת שָׁפְכָה — הֲרֵי אֵלּוּ יֹאכְלוּ. [ד]וְאֵי זֶהוּ פְּצוּעַ דַּכָּא — כָּל שֶׁנִּפְצְעוּ הַבֵּיצִים שֶׁלּוֹ, וַאֲפִילּוּ אַחַת מֵהֶן. וּכְרוּת שָׁפְכָה — כָּל שֶׁנִּכְרַת הַגִּיד. וְאִם נִשְׁתַּיֵּיר מֵעֲטָרָה אֲפִי' כְּחוּט הַשַּׂעֲרָה — כָּשֵׁר.§ **גמ'** תַּנְיָא, א"ר *אֱלִיעֶזֶר: [ה]מִנַּיִן לְעָרֵל שֶׁאֵין אוֹכֵל בִּתְרוּמָה — נֶאֱמַר °"תּוֹשָׁב וְשָׂכִיר" בְּפֶסַח, וְנֶאֱמַר °"תּוֹשָׁב וְשָׂכִיר" בִּתְרוּמָה, מַה "תּוֹשָׁב וְשָׂכִיר" הָאָמוּר בְּפֶסַח עָרֵל אָסוּר בּוֹ, אַף "תּוֹשָׁב וְשָׂכִיר" הָאָמוּר בִּתְרוּמָה עָרֵל אָסוּר בּוֹ. *רַבִּי עֲקִיבָא אוֹמֵר: אֵינוֹ צָרִיךְ, הֲרֵי הוּא אוֹמֵר °"אִישׁ אִישׁ" לְרַבּוֹת הֶעָרֵל. אָמַר מָר: ר"א אוֹמֵר נֶאֱמַר "תּוֹשָׁב וְשָׂכִיר" בְּפֶסַח וְנֶאֱמַר "תּוֹשָׁב וְשָׂכִיר" בִּתְרוּמָה, מַה "תּוֹשָׁב וְשָׂכִיר" הָאָמוּר בְּפֶסַח עָרֵל אָסוּר בּוֹ, אַף "תּוֹשָׁב וְשָׂכִיר" הָאָמוּר בִּתְרוּמָה עָרֵל אָסוּר בּוֹ. מוּפְנֶה, דְּאִי לָאו מוּפְנֶה — אִיכָּא לְמִיפְרַךְ: מַה לְּפֶסַח — שֶׁכֵּן חַיָּיבִין עָלָיו מִשּׁוּם פִּיגּוּל וְנוֹתָר וְטָמֵא. לָאֵי, אַפְנוּיֵי מוּפְנֶה. הֵי מוּפְנֶה? אִי דִּתְרוּמָה — מִצְרָךְ צְרִיכִי, דְּתַנְיָא: *[ו]"תּוֹשָׁב" זֶה קָנוּי קִנְיַן עוֹלָם, "שָׂכִיר" זֶה קָנוּי קִנְיַן שָׁנִים. וְיֹאמַר "תּוֹשָׁב" וְאַל יֹאמַר "שָׂכִיר", וַאֲנִי אוֹמַר: קָנוּי קִנְיַן עוֹלָם אֵינוֹ אוֹכֵל, קָנוּי קִנְיַן שָׁנִים — לֹא כָּל שֶׁכֵּן?! אִילּוּ כֵּן, הָיִיתִי אוֹמֵר: "תּוֹשָׁב" זֶה קָנוּי קִנְיַן שָׁנִים, אֲבָל קָנוּי קִנְיַן עוֹלָם אוֹכֵל — בָּא "שָׂכִיר" וְלִימֵּד עַל תּוֹשָׁב, שֶׁאַף עַל פִּי שֶׁקָּנוּי קִנְיַן עוֹלָם — אֵין אוֹכֵל. אֶלָּא דְּפֶסַח מוּפְנֵי. הַאי "תּוֹשָׁב וְשָׂכִיר" דִּכְתַב רַחֲמָנָא בְּפֶסַח מַאי נִיהוּ? אִי נֵימָא תּוֹשָׁב וְשָׂכִיר מַמָּשׁ — מִשּׁוּם דַּהֲוָה לֵיהּ תּוֹשָׁב וְשָׂכִיר אִיפַּטַּר לֵיהּ מִפֶּסַח?! וְהָא קַיְימָא לָן גַּבֵּי תְּרוּמָה [ז]דְּלָא אָכֵיל, אַלְמָא

(שמות יב — ויקרא כב — שם)

רש"י

הכי גרסינן: ה"ד אילימא דדיימא מניה ולא דיימא מעלמא צריכא למימר דתיכול אלא לאו דדיימא נמי מעלמא. לא כ"ש. דאי דיימא מניה ומעלמא, דבתריה דידיה שדינן ליה. ומתני' בדלא דיימא כלל. מקמי הכי, לאו מניה ולאו מעלמא. הלכך איצטריך לאשמועינן דתאכל, דאמרינן בהך ביאה נתעברה. בני בנים הרי הן כבנים. בפ' "הבא על יבמתו" (לעיל סב:). כמאן כר"ע. מתניתין דקתני גוי ועבד הבא על בת ישראל הולד ממזר. משום רבינו. רבי, ואע"ג דשמעינן דפליג אדר"ע בפ' ר"ג (לעיל נב:), דאמר: אין דברים הללו אמורים אלא לדברי ר"ע, וליה לא ס"ל, אפ"ה, בגוי ועבד מודה, כדאמר ב"החולץ" (לעיל מה.): גוי "לא תתחתן", ועבד "לא תהיה קדשה". כוזא. כלי קטן. כלומר, ממזר שהוא גרוע. כדא. כלי חשוב. כלומר, כהן גדול.

הדרן עלך אלמנה

הערל. כהן (א) שמתו אחיו מחמת מילה. נשיהם ועבדיהם יאכלו. דהא משום ערלות וטומאה לא נפקי מכלל כהנים, אלא דאינהו גופייהו מחסרי תקנתא. נשיהם. של פצוע דכא וכרות שפכה לא יאכלו דשוויה חללה בביאתן, שהרי נבעלה לפסול לה. ואם לא ידעה. לא בא עליה אחרי כן, והיתה נשואה לו קודם לכן. ואם נשתייר מעטרה. שנכרת מעטרה ואילך — כשר, דהתם בישרא בעלמא הוא ולא גיד, שאין גיד אלא מעטרה ואילך לצד הגוף עטרה (ב) שורת בשר המקפת במקום המילה בגובה, ושופע ויורד עד סופה. **גמ'** תושב ושכיר בתרומה. דכתיב "תושב כהן ושכיר לא יאכל קדש". איש איש מזרע אהרן והוא צרוע או זב לרבות ערל. בטמא אגל אכילת תרומה, דבהאי קרא תרומה כתיב, דכתיב (ויקרא כב) "ובא השמש וטהר ואחר יאכל מן הקדשים", והיינו תרומה, דסגי ליה בהערב שמש. שכן חייבין עליו. קרבן חטאת, אם אכלו פגול או נותר או בטומאת הגוף. דכולהו בכרת, דהא קדשים הוא. קנוי קנין עולם. עבד עברי הנרצע. ובא הכתוב ללמדך, שאין גופו קנוי לכהן זה שיאכילהו בתרומה ככנעני. קנין שנים. סתם עבד, שיוצא בשש שנים. אילו כן. דלא נאמר אלא תושב. הייתי אומר תושב זה קנוי קנין שנים. משום הכי אסור בתרומה, בא שכיר יתירא ולימד על כרחך דהאי קרא לנרצע אתא. וכיון דתרי כתיבי — מסתברא דתושב — זה המיושב אצלו לזמן מרובה, ושכיר — זה העומד לצאת. אלא דפסח מופני. האי שכיר ותושב דפסח, דכתיב "לא יאכלו בו". מאי נינהו אי נימא תושב ושכיר ממש. קנוי קנין שנים, או נרצע. הָכָא

תוספות

אבל דיימא מיניה אע"ג דדיימא נמי מעלמא בתר דידיה שדינן ליה. פי': דיימא מיניה — שבא עליה בודאי, ודיימא מעלמא — היינו שם רע, דאי דיימא מיניה נמי שם רע בעלמא — א"כ מאי מייתי רבא ממתני'? דהתם בא עליה ודאי, משום הכי בתר דידיה שדינן ליה.

הדרן עלך אלמנה

הערל. פי' בקונט': שמתו אחיו מחמת מילה. וכן נראה, דלא דמי לערלה שלא בזמנה דמיבעיא לן בגמ' (לקמן דף עא.) אי הויא ערלה. דהתם כיולא בו לא הוי בר מילה בשום מקום. אבל אחר ח', אע"ג דאי אפשר לו למול מפני הסכנה — הוי ערל, כיון שהגיע הזמן. תדע, דלא פשיט ליה בגמ' מטומטום שאין אוכל בתרומה אערלה שלא בזמנה, אע"ג דאין חייב לקרוע ולמול, *כדמוכח בגמרא (שם:), דקאמר: זכריו דאיתנהו בשעת אכילה וליתנהו בשעת עשיה — משכחת לה בטומטום שנקרע ביני ביני ונמצא זכר, דלא קרינן ביה בשעת עשיה "המול לו כל זכר ואז יקרב לעשותו" דלא מיחייב לקרוע ולמול. ובפ"ק דחגיגה (דף ד.) נמי אמר: "זכורך" — להוציא טומטום ואנדרוגינוס, שפטור מן הראיה, ומוקי לה כשביליו מבחוץ. ובירושלמי מייתי ראיה ממתני' אאחזתו חמה דממתינין לו למול ל' יום, דאסור בתרומה \ משמע דמתניתין איירי בערל שמתו אחיו מחמת מילה. ובהדיא מחלק בירושלמי בין ערלות שלא בזמנה ובין שהגיע זמנו למול אלא שסכנה היא לו. אלא שבזה חולק על הש"ס שלנו: דהתם פשיטא ליה דערלות שלא בזמנה לא הויא ערלות, ואכיל בתרומה, ובש"ס שלנו בעיא היא בגמ' (דף עא.) ולא איפשיטא. **מה** תושב ושכיר האמור בפסח. וא"ת: באוכל תרומה בטומאת עצמה נילף בהאי ג"ש דלילקי, ולקמן (דף עג:) אמרינן דלית בה אלא עשה "בשעריך תאכלנו" — לזה ולא לאחר! וא"ר"י: דהך ג"ש לא ניתנה אלא לענין פסול האדם האוכל, כגון ערל ואונן ויוצא בו. אבל לענין פסול גופה, כגון טומאת עצמה — לא. אבל קשה: דאכתי נילף מבכורים שילקה עליה בטומאת עצמה, דכי היכי דילפינן (שם) בכורים מתרומה משום דתרומה קרינהו רחמנא — ה"נ נילף תרומה מבכורים, דהא ב"העור והרוטב" (חולין קכ:) גמרינן תרומה מבכורים לענין דמשקין היוצאין מהן כמותן. **איש** איש לרבות הערל. מהכא אמרינן בכל דוכתי (חגיגה דף ד:) דר"ע מרבה ערל כי טמא. ומ"מ איצטריך למכתב ערל בפסח, דאי לאו דכתיב בהדיא משום מקום שהוא כטמא — לא הוה מרבינן ליה מאיש איש, אע"ג דמילת זכריו ועבדיו מעכבתו בפסח. **מה** לפסח שכן חייבין עליו משום פגול נותר וטמא. יש ספרים דל"ג טמא, דבתרומה נמי איכא איסור טומאה. ואית דגרס ליה, משום דבפסח איכא כרת לאוכל בטומאת הגוף משא"כ בתרומה. ובקונטרס נמי פי' דחייבים עליו חטאת קאמר. והוא הדין דהוי מצי למיפרך מכל פנ"ק עכ"ס.
אלמא

[עי' תוספות פסחים כח: ד"ה ערל]

[עי' תוס' לעיל כב: ד"ה בן ותוס' ב"ב קט. ד"ה כיון עוד שם קטו. ד"ה בן]

עין משפט נר מצוה

נ א מיי' פ"ו מהל' תרומות הל' יב יג סמג לאוין רל טוי"ד סי' שלא:
א ב מיי' פ"ז שם הל' י יב סמג לאוין רלה טור יו"ד שם:
ב ג מיי' שם הלכה יג:
ג ד מיי' פ"ו מהל' איסורי ביאה הלכה ג סמג לאוין קיט טוש"ע אה"ע סימן ה סעיף ב:
ד ה מיי' פ"ז מהל' תרומות הלכה י טור יו"ד סימן שלא:
ה ו ז מיי' שם פ"ז הלכה ה:

תוספות ישנים

לא כבני כ"ג פי' [לא] ירבו כמותו עוד. י"מ לא כבני בבי"ת פירוש אי אפשי בו: **זרע** פסול לאו דוקא אלא קאי אזרע זרעה דא"ל דדוקא קאמר דהא כיון דזרעה פסיל על כרחין פסולה היא וא"כ תיפוק לי דלא אכלה משום דנפסלה אלא רלה לומר זרע זרעה פסול אבל היא כשרה א"נ נוכל לומר דרולה לומר זרעה ממש ומיירי בבא עליה מלרי ואדומי דאינו פוסלה ומ"מ הזרע פסול הוא:

הדרן עלך אלמנה

פרק הערל. הערל וכל הטמאים לא יאכלו בתרומה פ"ה בכ"מ ערל שמתו אחיו מחמת מילה. ול"נ דא"כ אינה מלוה למולו פי' למול א"ע לפי שהוא אנוס והוי כמו מילה שלא בזמנה וקשה דבגמ' בעי ערל קטן מהו לסוכו שמן של תרומה ערלות שלא בזמנה מעכבה או לא מעכבה ואמאי לא פשיט ממתני' דכיון דמיירי שמתו אחיו מחמת מילה א"כ נאנס הוא וכיון שנאנס ערלות שלא בזמנה הוא לכן פר"ת דערל ר"ל משומד לערלות: **פצוע** דכא נשיהם לא יאכלו. דר"ע תימה אמאי פוסלה בביאתו הא לאו זר מעיקרא הוא ואמאי משום דהוקש לממזר דאין הפסוק רק להורות דמכוין הוא פלוע דכא וי"ל כיון דנשתנה גופו חשיב כמו זר מעיקרא:

הגהות הב"ח

(א) רש"י ד"ה הערל כהן ערל שמתו: (ב) ד"ה ואם נשתייר וכו' עטרה (שורת בשר המקפת) תא"מ ונ"ב ס"א שורש בשר המוקפת כו':

קדושין ד.
[לעיל כב: וש"נ ועמ"ש שם]
[לעיל סב:]
[לעיל מה.]
[מלשון והאדם ידע את חוה אשתו בראשית ד ועי' תוי"ט]
[נ"ל אליעזר ועי' תוס' סוטה כז. סד"ה ורבי יונתן וע"ע תוס' מנחות יז: ד"ה מאי האכל]
חגיגה ד: לקמן עב: עד.
זבחים פב. קדושין ד.